A SHAKESPEAREAN GENEALOGY

This chart reflects Shakespeare's history plays and is thus not historically accurate. Many descendants of Henry II and Edward III are omitted. On occasion, Shakespeare combined or simply invented historical figures. These deviations from fact are explained in the notes.

In the chart, the names of Kings and Queens are printed in capitals, and the dates of their reigns are printed in bold. The names of characters appearing in the plays are underlined.

Henry
d. 1183

Edward, Prince of
Wales 1330–1376

RICHARD II
1367–1400
(1377–99)

William of
Hatfield

Lionel, Duke of
Clarence 1338–1368

Philippa
m. Edmund
Mortimer, Earl
of March

RICHARD I
1157–1199
(1189–99)

Philip Faulconbridge*
(Richard Plantagenet)

John of Gaunt,
Duke of Lancaster
1340–1399
m. Blanche of
Lancaster
m. Constance of
Castile
m. Katherine
Swynford

HENRY IV
1367–1413
(1399–1413)

Thomas Beaufort,
Duke of Exeter
1377–1427

Henry Beaufort,
Bishop of Winchester
1375–1447

John Beaufort,
Earl of Somerset
1372–1409

Joan Beaufort
m. Ralph Neville,
Earl of
Westmoreland

HENRY II
1133–1189
(1154–89)
m. Eleanor
of Aquitaine
d. 1204

Geoffrey, d. 1186
m. Constance
of Brittany

Arthur
1187–1203

JOHN 1167–1216
(1199–1216)

HENRY III
1207–1272
(1216–72)

EDWARD I
1239–1307
(1272–1307)

EDWARD II
1284–1327
(1307–27)

Edmund of Langley,
Duke of York
1341–1402

Edward, Duke of
Aumerle d. 1415

Richard, Earl
of Cambridge
d. 1415 m. Anne
Mortimer (above)

EDWARD III
1312–1377
(1327–77)
m. Philippa of
Hainault

Thomas of
Woodstock, Duke of
Gloucester 1355–1397

Anne

Eleanor
m. Alfonso VIII,
King of Castile

Blanche, d. 1252
m. Louis VIII
of France

William of
Windsor

*Philip Faulconbridge, the bastard son of Richard I, had no historical existence. Such a character appears in the play *The Life and Death of King John* and is referred to in passing in Holinshed's *Chronicles*.

† In the character of Edmund Mortimer, Shakespeare combines two historical figures. The Edmund Mortimer who married Catrin, daughter of Owain Glyndŵr, was the grandson of Lionel, Duke of Clarence, and the younger brother of Roger, Earl of March. He died in 1409. Shakespeare combines him with his nephew, the Edmund Mortimer recognized by Richard II as his heir (d. 1424). This second Edmund was the brother of Anne Mortimer and the uncle of Richard Plantagenet.

‡ The character of the Duke of Somerset combines Henry Beaufort with his younger brother Edmund (d. 1471), who succeeded him as Duke.

Elizabeth Mortimer
("Kate")
m. Henry Percy
("Hotspur")
1364–1403

—Henry, Earl of
Northumberland
1394–1455

EDWARD IV
1442–1483 (1461–83)
m. Elizabeth
Woodville d. 1492

EDWARD V
1470–1483 (1483)

—Richard, Duke
of York 1472–1483

└Elizabeth of York
1465–1503
m. HENRY VII
(below)

—Edmund, Earl of
Rutland 1443–1460

—Edmund Mortimer†

—George, Duke of
Clarence 1449–1478
m. Isabel Neville
(below)

└Anne Mortimer
m. Richard, Earl of
Cambridge (below)

—Richard Plantagenet,
Duke of York
1411–1460
m. Cicely Neville
(below)

RICHARD III
1452–1485 (1483–85)
m. Anne Neville
(below)

—Edward, Prince of Wales

—HENRY V 1387–1422
(1413–22)
m. Catherine
1401–1437

—HENRY VI 1421–1471
(1422–61)
m. Margaret of Anjou
d. 1482

—Edward, Prince of
Wales 1453–1471
m. Anne Neville
(below)

—Arthur
m. Catherine of
Aragon (below)

—Thomas, Duke of
Clarence d. 1421

—Margaret
m. James IV
of Scotland

—James V
of Scotland
|
Mary, Queen of
Scots
|
JAMES I
1566–1625
(1603–25)

—John of Lancaster,
Duke of Bedford
1389–1435

└Humphrey, Duke of
Gloucester 1391–1447
m. Eleanor Cobham
d. 1454

—Margaret Beaufort
m. Edmund Tudor,
Earl of Richmond

—HENRY VII 1457–1509
(1485–1509)
m. Elizabeth of York
(above)

HENRY VIII
1491–1547
(1509–47)
m. Catherine of
Aragon

— MARY I 1516–1558
(1553–58)
m. Philip of Spain

—John Beaufort, Duke
of Somerset
1403–1444

—Henry Beaufort,
Duke of Somerset
1436–1464‡

m. Anne Boleyn

— ELIZABETH I
1533–1603
(1558–1603)

└Edmund Beaufort,
Duke of Somerset
1406–1455

m. Jane Seymour

— EDWARD VI
1537–1553
(1547–53)

—Isabel Neville
d. 1476
m. George, Duke
of Clarence
(above)

m. Anne of Cleves

m. Katherine Howard

m. Katherine Parr

—Richard Neville,
Earl of Salisbury
1400–1460

—Richard Neville,
Earl of Warwick
1428–1471

└John Neville,
Marquess of
Montague d. 1471

└Anne Neville
d. 1485
m. Edward, Prince
of Wales (above)
m. RICHARD III
(above)

└Mary
m. Charles Brandon

—Frances
|
Jane Grey
1537–1554

└Cicely Neville
m. Richard
Plantagenet,
Duke of York (above)

—Humphrey, Duke of
Buckingham
1402–1460

—Humphrey Stafford
d. 1455

—Henry, Duke of
Buckingham
1454?–1483

—Edward, Duke of
Buckingham
1478–1521

RICHARD II, 1377–99 RICHARD was the eldest son of EDWARD THE BLACK PRINCE, himself the eldest son of KING EDWARD III, who ruled England from 1327 to 1377. When the BLACK PRINCE died in battle in France in 1376, RICHARD became the legitimate heir to the throne. He ruled from EDWARD's death in 1377 until he was deposed in 1399 by HENRY BOLINGBROKE, the eldest son of JOHN OF GAUNT, DUKE OF LANCASTER. Because he was the fourth son of EDWARD III, GAUNT and his Lancastrian descendants had weaker hereditary claims to the throne than did RICHARD. When deposed, RICHARD had no children to succeed him, but he recognized EDMUND MORTIMER, FIFTH EARL OF MARCH, as his heir presumptive. This MORTIMER was descended from LIONEL, DUKE OF CLARENCE, the third son of EDWARD III, and therefore also had stronger hereditary claims to the throne than did BOLINGBROKE. SHAKESPEARE combined this MORTIMER with his uncle EDMUND MORTIMER, who married OWAIN GLYNDŴR'S DAUGHTER.

HENRY IV, 1399–1413 HENRY BOLINGBROKE, eldest son of JOHN OF GAUNT, seized the throne from RICHARD II in 1399. When HENRY died in 1413, he was succeeded by his eldest son, PRINCE HAL, who became HENRY V.

HENRY V, 1413–22 HENRY V became king in 1413 and reigned until his death in 1422. He was succeeded by his son, HENRY VI.

HENRY VI, 1422–61 HENRY VI was less than one year old when he succeeded his father, HENRY V. In the young king's minority, his uncle HUMPHREY, DUKE OF GLOUCESTER, was named Lord Protector, and the kingdom was ruled by an aristocratic council. HENRY VI assumed personal authority in 1437. He was deposed in 1461 by his third cousin, who was crowned EDWARD IV. HENRY was murdered in 1471.

EDWARD IV, 1461–83 EDWARD, the eldest son of RICHARD, DUKE OF YORK, seized the throne from HENRY VI in 1461. His Yorkist claim to the throne derived from his grandmother, ANNE MORTIMER, who was descended from LIONEL, third son of EDWARD III, and was sister to that EDMUND MORTIMER recognized by RICHARD II as his heir presumptive; EDWARD IV's grandfather, RICHARD, EARL OF CAMBRIDGE, was the son of EDMUND OF LANGLEY, fifth son of EDWARD III. EDWARD IV reigned until his death in 1483. His heir was his eldest son (EDWARD), but the throne was usurped by his brother RICHARD, DUKE OF GLOUCESTER.

RICHARD III, 1483–85 RICHARD III was the youngeer brother of EDWARD IV. After the death of EDWARD IV in 1483, RICHARD prevented the coronation of EDWARD V with a claim of illegitimacy and succeeded to the throne himself. EDWARD and his younger brother, RICHARD, DUKE OF YORK, were murdered in the Tower of London. RICHARD III was killed at the Battle of Bosworth Field in 1485, and the kingdom fell to the victor, HENRY TUDOR, EARL OF RICHMOND.

HENRY VII, 1485–1509 HENRY TUDOR seized the throne from RICHARD III in 1485. He was descended from JOHN OF GAUNT by JOHN's third marriage, with CATHERINE SWYNFORD. He married ELIZABETH, daughter of EDWARD IV, uniting the houses of Lancaster and York. He died in 1509 and was succeeded by his son, HENRY VIII.

HENRY VIII, 1509–47 HENRY was the second son of HENRY VII. His older brother, ARTHUR, died in 1502. HENRY VIII's first wife was CATHERINE OF ARAGON, who bore his daughter MARY. His second wife, ANNE BOLEYN, was the mother of ELIZABETH. His third wife, JANE SEYMOUR, bore him a son, who succeeded to the throne as EDWARD VI after HENRY VIII died in 1547.

EDWARD VI, 1547–53 EDWARD VI was nine years old when he became king. From 1547 to 1549, the realm was governed by a Lord Protector, the DUKE OF SOMERSET; power then passed to JOHN DUDLEY, DUKE OF NORTHUMBERLAND. When EDWARD VI died in 1553, NORTHUMBERLAND attempted unsuccessfully to prevent the succession of MARY TUDOR by installing as queen his daughter-in-law, LADY JANE GREY, a great-granddaughter of HENRY VII.

MARY I, 1553–58 MARY, daughter of HENRY VIII and his first wife, CATHERINE OF ARAGON, came to the throne in 1553. She married KING PHILIP OF SPAIN but died childless. She was succeeded by her half sister, ELIZABETH.

ELIZABETH I, 1558–1603 ELIZABETH, the daughter of HENRY VIII and his second wife, ANNE BOLEYN, became queen after the death of her half sister, MARY, in 1558. She ruled until her death in 1603. She was succeeded by her cousin JAMES.

JAMES I, 1603–1625 JAMES VI OF SCOTLAND became JAMES I OF ENGLAND in 1603. His claim to the throne of England derived from his great-grandmother, MARGARET TUDOR, a daughter of HENRY VII who married JAMES IV OF SCOTLAND. JAMES ruled England and Scotland until his death in 1625; he was succeeded by his son, CHARLES I.

THE NORTON
SHAKESPEARE

BASED ON THE OXFORD EDITION

Volume I
Early Plays and Poems

The original Oxford Text on which this
edition is based was prepared by

Stanley Wells
Gary Taylor
General Editors

John Jowett
William Montgomery

The Norton Shakespeare, Second Edition, is based on *William Shakespeare: The Complete Works*,
Second Edition, and is published by arrangement with Oxford University Press,
with additional material from W. W. Norton & Company, Inc.

THE NORTON SHAKESPEARE

Based on the Oxford Edition

Volume I
Early Plays and Poems

Stephen Greenblatt, *General Editor*
HARVARD UNIVERSITY

Walter Cohen
CORNELL UNIVERSITY

Jean E. Howard
COLUMBIA UNIVERSITY

Katharine Eisaman Maus
UNIVERSITY OF VIRGINIA

With an Essay on the Shakespearean stage
by Andrew Gurr

W · W · NORTON & COMPANY · NEW YORK · LONDON

W. W. Norton & Company has been independent since its founding in 1923, when William Warder Norton and Mary D. Herter Norton first published lectures delivered at the People's Institute, the adult education division of New York City's Cooper Union. The Nortons soon expanded their program beyond the Institute, publishing books by celebrated academics from America and abroad. By mid-century, the two major pillars of Norton's publishing program—trade books and college texts—were firmly established. In the 1950s, the Norton family transferred control of the company to its employees, and today—with a staff of four hundred and a comparable number of trade, college, and professional titles published each year—W. W. Norton & Company stands as the largest and oldest publishing house owned wholly by its employees.

Editor: Julia Reidhead
Manuscript editor: Carol Flechner
Electronic media editor: Eileen Connell
Editorial assistant: Rivka Genesen
Production manager: Diane O'Connor
Photo research: Rivka Genesen
Interior design: Antonina Krass
Managing editor, College: Marian Johnson

The Library of Congress has cataloged the one-volume edition as follows:

Shakespeare, William, 1564–1616.
The Norton Shakespeare / Stephen Greenblatt, general editor ; Walter Cohen, Jean E. Howard, Katharine Eisaman Maus [editors] ; with an essay on the Shakespearean stage by Andrew Gurr. — 2nd ed.
p. cm.
"Based on the Oxford edition."
Includes bibliographical references and index.
ISBN 978-0-393-92991-1
I. Greenblatt, Stephen, 1943–   II. Cohen, Walter, 1949–   III. Howard, Jean E. (Jean Elizabeth), 1948–   IV. Maus, Katharine Eisaman, 1955–   V. Gurr, Andrew. VI. Title.
PR2754.G74   2008
822.3'3—dc22
2007046599

ISBN 978-0-393-93144-0

W. W. Norton & Company, Inc., 500 Fifth Avenue, New York, NY 10110
www.wwnorton.com

W. W. Norton & Company Ltd., Castle House, 75/76 Wells Street, London W1T 3QT

2 3 4 5 6 7 8 9 0

Contents

Appendices   1837

Contents by Genre

Comedies

Histories

Tragedies

Poetry

Lost Plays

Illustrations

Preface

Shakespeare's principal medium, the drama, was thoroughly collaborative, and it involved as well continual efforts at revision and renewal. It seems appropriate, then, that this edition of his works is itself the result of sustained collaboration and revision. Two lists of editors' names on the title-page spread hint at the collaboration that has brought to fruition the *Norton Shakespeare*. But the title page does not tell the full history of this project. The text on which the *Norton Shakespeare* is based was published in both modern-spelling and original-spelling versions by Oxford University Press, in 1986. Under the general editorship of Stanley Wells and Gary Taylor, the Oxford text was a thorough rethinking of the entire body of Shakespeare's works, the most far-reaching and innovative revision of the traditional canon in centuries. When many classroom instructors who wanted to introduce their students to the works of Shakespeare through a modern text expressed a need for the pedagogical apparatus they have come to expect in an edition oriented toward students, Norton negotiated with Oxford to assemble an editorial team of its own to prepare the necessary teaching materials around the existing Oxford text. Hence ensued a collaboration of two publishers and two editorial teams.

To what extent is this the *Norton Shakespeare* and to what extent the Oxford text? Introductions (both the General Introduction and those to individual plays and poems), footnotes, glosses, bibliographies, genealogies, annals, maps, documents, and illustrations have all been the responsibility of the Norton team. Andrew Gurr's much-admired essay on the London theater in Shakespeare's time, specially commissioned for the *Norton Shakespeare*, has been moved in this second edition to the front matter.

The textual notes and variants derive for the most part from the work of the Oxford team, especially as represented in *William Shakespeare: A Textual Companion* (Oxford University Press, 1987), a remarkably comprehensive explanation of editorial decisions that is herewith strongly recommended to instructors as a valuable companion to this volume. Several of the textual notes—those to *The First Part of Henry the Sixth,* Various Poems, *The Two Noble Kinsmen, The Merry Wives of Windsor, Troilus and Cressida,* The Sonnets and "A Lover's Complaint"—have been substantially updated in the current edition, and all Textual Variants are now gathered in an appendix.

The Oxford text is widely available and already well known to scholars. A few words here may help clarify the extent of our fidelity to that text and the nature of the collaboration that has brought about this volume. The Oxford editors have profited from the massive and sustained attention accorded their edition by Shakespeare scholars across the globe, and of course they have continued to participate actively in the ongoing scholarly discussion about the nature of Shakespeare's text. In the reprintings of the Oxford volumes and in various articles over the past years, the Oxford editors have made a number of refinements of the edition they originally published. Such changes have been incorporated silently here. A small number of other changes made by the Norton team, however, were not part of the Oxford editors' design and were only accepted by them after we reached, through lengthy consultation, a mutual understanding about the nature, purpose, and intended audience of this volume. In all such changes, our main concern was for the classroom; we wished to make fully and clearly available the scholarly innovation and freshness of the Oxford text, while at the same time making certain that this was a superbly useful teaching text. It is a pleasure here to record, on behalf of the Norton team, our gratitude for the personal and professional generosity of the Oxford editors in offering advice and entertaining arguments in our common goal of providing the best student Shakespeare for our times. The Norton changes to the Oxford text are various, but in only a few instances are they major. The following brief notes are sufficient to summarize all of these changes, which are also indicated in appropriate play introductions, footnotes, or textual notes.

1. The Oxford editors, along with other scholars, have strenuously argued—in both the Oxford text and elsewhere—that the now-familiar text of *King Lear*, so nearly omnipresent in our classrooms as to seem unquestionably authoritative but in reality dating from the work of Alexander Pope (1723) and Lewis Theobald (1733), represents a wrongheaded conflation of two distinct versions of the play: Shakespeare's original creation as printed in the 1608 Quarto and his substantial revision as printed in the First Folio (1623). The Oxford text, therefore, prints both *The History of King Lear* and *The Tragedy of King Lear*. Norton follows suit, but where Oxford presents these two texts sequentially, we print them on facing pages. While each version may be read independently, and to ensure this we have provided glosses and footnotes for each, the substantial points of difference between the two are immediately apparent and available for comparison. But even many who agree with the scholarly argument for the two texts of *Lear* nevertheless favor making available a conflated text, the text on which innumerable performances of the play have been based and on which a huge body of literary criticism has been written. With the reluctant acquiescence, therefore, of the Oxford editors, we have included a conflated *Lear*, a text that has no part in the Oxford canon and that has been edited by Barbara K. Lewalski of Harvard University rather than by Gary Taylor, the editor of the Oxford *Lears*.

The *Norton Shakespeare*, then, includes three separate texts of *King Lear*. The reader can compare them, understand the role of editors in constructing the texts we now call Shakespeare's, explore in considerable detail the kinds of decisions that playwrights, editors, and printers make and remake, witness firsthand the historical transformation of what might at first glance seem fixed and unchanging. The *Norton Shakespeare* offers extraordinary access to this supremely brilliant, difficult, compelling play.

2. Among several other plays, *Hamlet* offers similar grounds for objections to the traditional conflation, but both the economics of publishing and the realities of bookbinding—not to mention our recognition of the limited time in the typical undergraduate syllabus—preclude our offering three (or even four) *Hamlets* to match three *Lears*. What we have provided in this edition is a convenient selection of parallel passages that will enable teachers to convey some of the complex, often enigmatic issues, at once stylistic and conceptual, raised by the different texts of the play.

The Oxford text of *Hamlet* was based upon the Folio text, with an appended list of Additional Passages from the Second Quarto (Q2). These additional readings total more than two hundred lines, a significant number, among which are lines that have come to seem very much part of the play as widely received, even if we may doubt that they belong with all the others in any single one of Shakespeare's *Hamlets*. The Norton team, while following the Oxford text, has moved the Q2 passages from the appendix to the body of the play. But in doing so, we have not wanted once again to produce a conflated text. We have therefore indented the Q2 passages, printed them in a different typeface, and numbered them in such a way as to make clear their provenance. Those who wish to read the Folio version of *Hamlet* can thus simply skip over the indented Q2 passages, while at the same time it is possible for readers to see clearly the place that the Q2 passages occupy. We have adopted a similar strategy with several other plays: passages printed in Oxford in appendices are generally printed here in the play texts, though clearly demarcated and not conflated. In the case of *The Taming of the Shrew* and the related quarto text, *The Taming of a Shrew*, however, we have followed Oxford's procedure and left the quarto passages in an appendix, since we believe the texts reflect two distinct plays rather than a revision of one. We have similarly reproduced Oxford's brief appendices to A *Midsummer Night's Dream* and *Henry V,* enabling readers to consider alternative revisions of certain passages.

3. For reasons understood by every Shakespearean (and rehearsed at some length in this volume), the Oxford editors chose to restore the name "Sir John Oldcastle" to the character much better known as Falstaff in *1 Henry IV*. (They made comparable changes in the names of the characters known as Bardolph and Peto.) But for reasons understood by everyone who has presented this play to undergraduates or sampled the centuries of enthusiastic criticism, the Norton editors, with the Oxford editors' gracious agreement, have for this classroom edition opted for the familiar name "Falstaff" (and those of his boon companions), properly noting the change and its significance in the play's introduction.

4. The Oxford editors chose not to differentiate between those stage directions that appeared in the early editions up to and including the Folio and those that have been added by subsequent editors. Instead, in *A Textual Companion* they include separate lists of the original stage directions. These lists are not readily available to readers of the Norton text, whose editors opted instead to bracket all stage directions that derive from editions published after the Folio. Readers can thus easily see which stage directions derive from texts that may bear at least some relation to performances in Shakespeare's time, if not to Shakespeare's own authorship. The Norton policy is more fully explained in the General Introduction.

5. The Oxford editors have newly prepared complete texts of the multiauthored *King Edward III* and *Sir Thomas More*, in which Shakespeare may have had a hand as collaborator. The texts are available online at wwnorton.com/shakespeare. In addition, the *Norton Shakespeare*, Second Edition, continues to print, with a revised introduction, notes, and glosses, passages from *Sir Thomas More* that appear in the surviving manuscript to be in Shakespeare's own handwriting, and we include for the first time an introduction and bibliography to *King Edward III*.

The collaboration with Oxford was obviously essential to the creation of the *Norton Shakespeare*. But in preparing this Second Edition and making it something fresh and engaging, the critically important collaboration has been with the thousands of people who have used the book. Many of these, teachers and students alike, have generously offered helpful suggestions along with praise. Guided by their responses, as well as by recent developments in Shakespeare scholarship, we determined to look afresh at every detail and to make a wide range of changes. The General Introduction and the individual play introductions have been substantially revised, in some cases wholly rewritten, to make them clearer and more accessible. Textual notes throughout have been updated in response to new findings, and there are hundreds of new and fine-tuned notes and glosses, designed to make this edition an even better tool for learning and pleasure. The General Bibliography has been reorganized and extensively updated, with 7 new sections and over 350 new entries. The Selected Bibliographies, too, have been updated as well as newly annotated. A new introduction provides an illuminating guide to the array of maps, three of them archival and three new, showing places important to Shakespeare's plays. The genealogies have been revised, as has been the text/contexts Timeline. New annotated film lists, including over 50 films, now follow the play introductions. Instructors who emphasize films in their courses may wish to assign *Shakespeare and Film: A Norton Guide* by Samuel Crowl, available packaged with the *Norton Shakespeare*. Finally, in response to many requests, we are making the *Norton Shakespeare* available in three different formats: the familiar one-volume clothbound edition, new two-volume chronological splits (*Early Plays and Poems* and *Later Plays*), and four genre paperbacks, each with a new introduction.

With the Second Edition of the *Norton Shakespeare,* the publisher expands its extensive online resource, Norton Literature Online (wwnorton.com/literature). Students who activate the free password in each new copy of the book gain access to an array of general resources, among them a glossary of literary terms, advice on writing about literature and using MLA documentation style, an author portrait gallery, more than 100 maps, and over 90 minutes of recorded readings and musical selections, among them 80 songs by Shakespeare. With their passwords, students also gain access to a site specifically developed to support the *Norton Shakespeare* (wwnorton.com/shakespeare). Based on content prepared by Mark Rose, University of California, Santa Barbara, this Web site invites students to explore six of the most widely taught plays—*The Merchant of Venice, 1 Henry IV, Hamlet, Othello, King Lear,* and *The Tempest*—through different contextual lenses. For each of these plays, the Web site provides materials on the elements of theater, sources, stage history, and critical receptions, as well as the complete Oxford text. Audio clips and stills from classic productions, etchings, photographs, and costume-design illustrations help students appreciate performance aspects of the plays. The student Web site also includes the redesigned "Shakespearean Chronicle, 1558–1616," an illustrated timeline that interweaves three kinds of chronologies illuminating Shakespeare's life and times. As noted above, a password-protected section of the Web site also includes the complete texts of *The Book of Sir Thomas More* and *The Reign of King Edward the Third,* prepared by the editors of the *Oxford Shakespeare.*

The creation of this edition has drawn heavily on the resources, experience, and skill of its remarkable publisher, the independent, employee-owned company W. W. Norton. Our principal guide has been our brilliant editor Julia Reidhead, whose calm intelligence, common sense, and steady focus have been essential in enabling us to reach our goal. With this Second Edition, we were blessed with the characteristically thoughtful oversight of Marian Johnson, managing editor, college department; scrupulous manuscript editing by Carol Flechner; and the assistance of an extraordinary group of Norton staffers: editorial assistant Rivka Genesen, who, among many other things, coordinated the art program; production manager Diane O'Connor; designer Antonina Krass; editor of the *Norton Shakespeare* Web site Eileen Connell; and proofreaders Paula Noonan and Ann Warren.

The *Norton Shakespeare* editors have, in addition, had the valuable—indeed, indispensable—support of a host of undergraduate and graduate research assistants, colleagues, friends, and family. Even a partial listing of those to whom we owe our heartfelt thanks is very long, but we are all fortunate enough to live in congenial and supportive environments, and the edition has been part of our lives for a long time. We owe special thanks for sustained dedication and learning to our principal assistants: Tiffany Alkan, Lianne Habinek, and Emily Peterson. Particular thanks are due to Noah Heringman for his work on the texts assembled in the documents section and for the prefatory notes and comments on those texts; to Philip Schwyzer for preparing the genealogies and the glossary and for conceiving and preparing the (now online) "Shakespearean Chronicle"; and to Holger Schott Syme for reconceiving and extensively updating the General Bibliography. In addition, we are deeply grateful to Ezra Feldman, Francesca Mari, Douglas McQueen-Thomson, Jeffrey Patterson, and Benjamin Woodring. All of these companions, and many more besides, have helped us find in this long collective enterprise what the "Dedicatorie Epistle" to the First Folio promises to its readers: delight. We make the same promise to the readers of our edition and invite them to continue the great Shakespearean collaboration.

Stephen Greenblatt
Walter Cohen
Jean E. Howard
Katharine Eisaman Maus

Acknowledgments

Among our many critics, advisers, and friends, the following were of special help in providing critiques for particular plays or of the project as a whole: Janet Adelman (University of California, Berkeley), Joel Altman (University of California, Berkeley), Rebecca Bach (University of Alabama at Birmingham), John Baxter (Dalhousie University), Edward I. Berry (University of Victoria), Timothy Billings (Middlebury College), Bruce Boehrer (Florida State University), Barbara Bono (University at Buffalo, SUNY), Gordon M. Braden (University of Virginia), Douglas Brooks (Texas A&M University), Stephen Buhler (University of Nebraska—Lincoln), Richard Burt (University of Florida), Joseph F. Ceccio (University of Akron), Julie Crawford (Columbia University), Christy Desmet (University of Georgia), Heather Dubrow (University of Wisconsin—Madison), Laurie Ellinghausen (University of Missouri—Kansas City), Chris Fitter (Rutgers, State University of New Jersey), Susan Fraiman (University of Virginia), Daniel Gil (University of Oregon), Miriam Gilbert (University of Iowa), Suzanne Gossett (Loyola University), Elizabeth Hanson (Queen's University), Jim Harner (Texas A&M University), Jonathan Gil Harris (George Washington University), Don Hedrick (Kansas State University), Roze Hentschell (Colorado State University), Clifford Huffman (Stony Brook University, SUNY), John Huntington (University of Illinois at Chicago), Sujata Iyengar (University of Georgia), Kimberly Johnson (Brigham Young University), Coppélia Kahn (Brown University), Sean Keilen (University of Pennsylvania), Theodore B. Leinwand (University of Maryland), Zachary Lesser (University of Pennsylvania), Naomi Liebler (Montclair State University), Joyce MacDonald (University of Kentucky), Leah Marcus (Vanderbilt University), Mark Matheson (University of Utah), Robert Matz (George Mason University), Kristen McDermott (Central Michigan University), Ted McGee (University of Waterloo), Scott McMillin (late of Cornell University), Gordon McMullan (King's College London), John Moore (Pennsylvania State University), Carol Neely (University of Illinois at Urbana-Champaign), Lori Newcomb (University of Illinois at Urbana-Champaign), Karen Newman (New York University), Hillary Nunn (University of Akron), Thomas G. Olsen (SUNY at New Paltz), Jim O'Rourke (Florida State University), Paul Parrish (Texas A&M University), Michael Payne (Bucknell University), Rebecca J. Perederin (University of Virginia), Curtis Perry (Arizona State University), Susan Phillips (Northwestern University), Tanya Pollard (Brooklyn College, CUNY), Kristen Poole (University of Delaware), Arnold Preussner (Truman State University), Phyllis Rackin (University of Pennsylvania), Peter L. Rudnytsky (University of Florida), Benjamin Saunders (University of Oregon), Barbara Sebek (Colorado State University), Tracey Sedinger (University of Northern Colorado), Jyotsna Singh (Michigan State University), Andrew Stott (University at Buffalo, SUNY), Garrett Sullivan (Pennsylvania State University), Ramie Targoff (Brandeis University), Henry Turner (University of Wisconsin—Madison), Martine van Elk (California State University, Long Beach), William N. West (University of Colorado at Boulder), Linda Woodbridge (Pennsylvania State University), Lingui Yang (Texas A&M University).

General Introduction
by
STEPHEN GREENBLATT

"He was not of an age, but for all time!"

The celebration of Shakespeare's genius, eloquently initiated by his friend and rival Ben Jonson, has over the centuries become an institutionalized rite of civility. The person who does not love Shakespeare has made, the rite implies, an incomplete adjustment not simply to a particular culture—English culture of the late sixteenth and early seventeenth centuries—but to "culture" as a whole, the dense network of constraints and entitlements, dreams and practices that links us to nature. Indeed, so absolute is Shakespeare's achievement that he has himself come to seem like great creating nature: the common bond of humankind, the principle of hope, the symbol of the imagination's power to transcend time-bound beliefs and assumptions, peculiar historical circumstances, and specific artistic conventions.

The near-worship that Shakespeare inspires is one of the salient facts about his art. But we must at the same time acknowledge that this art is the product of peculiar historical circumstances and specific conventions, four centuries distant from our own. The acknowledgment is important because Shakespeare the working dramatist did not typically lay claim to the transcendent, visionary truths attributed to him by his most fervent admirers; his characters more modestly say, in the words of the magician Prospero, that their project was "to please" (*The Tempest*, Epilogue, line 13). The starting point, and perhaps the ending point as well, in any encounter with Shakespeare is simply to enjoy him, to savor his imaginative richness, to take pleasure in his infinite delight in language.

"If then you do not like him," Shakespeare's first editors wrote in 1623, "surely you are in some manifest danger not to understand him." Over the years, accommodations have been devised to make liking Shakespeare easier for everyone. When the stage sank to melodrama and light opera, Shakespeare—in suitably revised texts—was there. When the populace had a craving for hippodrama, plays performed entirely on horseback, *Hamlet* was dutifully rewritten and mounted. When audiences went mad for realism, live frogs croaked in productions of *A Midsummer Night's Dream*. When the stage was stripped bare and given over to stark exhibitions of sadistic cruelty, Shakespeare was our contemporary. And when the theater itself had lost some of its cultural centrality, Shakespeare moved effortlessly to Hollywood and the soundstages of the BBC.

This virtually universal appeal is one of the most astonishing features of the Shakespeare phenomenon: plays that were performed before glittering courts thrive in junior-high-school auditoriums; enemies set on destroying one another laugh at the same jokes and weep at the same catastrophes; some of the richest and most complex English verse ever written migrates with spectacular success into German and Italian, Hindi, Swahili, and Japanese. Is there a single, stable, continuous object that underlies all of these migrations and metamorphoses? Certainly not. The global diffusion and long life of Shakespeare's works depend on their extraordinary malleability, their protean capacity to elude definition and escape secure possession. At the same time, they are not without identifiable shared features: across centuries and continents, family resemblances link many of the wildly diverse manifestations of plays such as *Romeo and Juliet*, *Hamlet*, and *Twelfth Night*. And if there is no clear limit or end point, there is a reasonably clear beginning: the

1

England of the late sixteenth and early seventeenth centuries, when the plays and poems collected in this volume made their first appearance.

An art virtually without end or limit but with an identifiable, localized, historical origin: Shakespeare's achievement defies the facile opposition between transcendent and time-bound. It is not necessary to choose between an account of Shakespeare as the scion of a particular culture and an account of him as a universal genius who created works that continually renew themselves across national and generational boundaries. On the contrary: crucial clues to understanding his art's remarkable power to soar beyond its originary time and place lie in the very soil from which that art sprang.

Shakespeare's World

Life and Death

Life expectancy at birth in early modern England was exceedingly low by our standards: under thirty years old, compared with over seventy today. Infant mortality rates were extraordinarily high, and it is estimated that in the poorer parishes of London only about half the children survived to the age of fifteen, while the children of aristocrats fared only a little better. In such circumstances, some parents must have developed a certain detachment—one of Shakespeare's contemporaries writes of losing "some three or four children"—but there are many expressions of intense grief, so that we cannot assume that the frequency of death hardened people to loss or made it routine.

Still, the spectacle of death, along with that other great threshold experience, birth, must have been far more familiar to Shakespeare and his contemporaries than to ourselves. There was no equivalent in early modern England to our hospitals, and most births and deaths occurred at home. Physical means for the alleviation of pain and suffering were extremely limited—alcohol might dull the terror, but it was hardly an effective anesthetic—and medical treatment was generally both expensive and worthless, more likely to intensify suffering than to lead to a cure. This was a world without a concept of antiseptics, with little actual understanding of disease, with few effective ways of treating earaches or venereal disease, let alone the more terrible instances of what Shakespeare calls "the thousand natural shocks that flesh is heir to."

The worst of these shocks was the bubonic plague, which repeatedly ravaged England, and particularly English towns, until the third quarter of the seventeenth century. The plague was terrifyingly sudden in its onset, rapid in its spread, and almost invariably lethal. Physicians were helpless in the face of the epidemic, though they prescribed amulets,

Bill recording plague deaths in London, 1609.

preservatives, and sweet-smelling substances (on the theory that the plague was carried by noxious vapors). In the plague-ridden year of 1564, the year of Shakespeare's birth, some 254 people died in Stratford-upon-Avon, out of a total population of 800. The year before, some 20,000 Londoners are thought to have died; in 1593, almost 15,000; in 1603, 36,000, or over a sixth of the city's inhabitants. The social effects of these horrible visitations were severe: looting, violence, and despair, along with an intensification of the age's perennial poverty, unemployment, and food shortages. The London plague regulations of 1583, reissued with modifications in later epidemics, ordered that the infected and their households be locked in their homes for a month; that the streets be kept clean; that vagrants be expelled; and that funerals and plays be restricted or banned entirely.

The plague, then, had a direct and immediate impact on Shakespeare's own profession. City officials kept records of the weekly number of plague deaths; when these surpassed a certain number, the theaters were peremptorily closed. The basic idea was not only to prevent contagion but also to avoid making an angry God still angrier with the spectacle of idleness. While restricting public assemblies may in fact have slowed the epidemic, other public policies in times of plague, such as killing the cats and dogs, may have made matters worse (since the disease, as we now know, was spread not by these animals but by the fleas that bred on the black rats that infested the poorer neighborhoods). Moreover, the playing companies, driven out of London by the closing of the theaters, may have carried plague to the provincial towns.

Even in good times, when the plague was dormant and the weather favorable for farming, the food supply in England was precarious. A few successive bad harvests, such as occurred in the mid-1590s, could cause serious hardship, even starvation. Not surprisingly, the poor bore the brunt of the burden: inflation, low wages, and rent increases left large numbers of people with very little cushion against disaster. Further, at its best, the diet of most people seems to have been seriously deficient. The lower classes then, as throughout most of history, subsisted on one or two foodstuffs, usually low in protein. The upper classes disdained green vegetables and milk and gorged themselves on meat. Illnesses that we now trace to vitamin deficiencies were rampant. Some, but not much, relief from pain was provided by the beer that Elizabethans, including children, drank almost incessantly. (Home brewing aside, enough beer was sold in England for every man, woman, and child to have consumed 40 gallons a year.)

Wealth

Despite rampant disease, the population of England in Shakespeare's lifetime was steadily growing, from approximately 3,060,000 in 1564 to 4,060,000 in 1600 and 4,510,000 in 1616. Though the death rate was more than twice what it is in England today, the birthrate was almost three times the current figure. London's population in particular soared, from 60,000 in 1520 to 120,000 in 1550, 200,000 in 1600, and 375,000 half a century later, making it the largest and fastest-growing city not only in England but in all of Europe. Every year in the first half of the seventeenth century, about 10,000 people migrated to London from other parts of England—wages in London tended to be around 50 percent higher than in the rest of the country—and it is estimated that one in eight English people lived in London at some point in their lives. The economic viability of Shakespeare's profession was closely linked to this extraordinary demographic boom: between 1567 and 1642, a theater historian has calculated, the London playhouses were paid close to 50 million visits.

As these visits to the theater indicate, in the capital city and elsewhere a substantial number of English men and women, despite hardships that were never very distant, had money to spend. After the disorder and dynastic wars of the fifteenth century, England in the sixteenth and early seventeenth centuries was for the most part a nation at peace, and with peace came a measure of enterprise and prosperity: the landowning classes busied themselves building great houses, planting orchards and hop gardens, draining marshlands, bringing untilled "wastes" under cultivation. The artisans and laborers who actually accomplished these tasks, although they were generally paid very little, often managed to accumulate something, as did the small freeholding farmers, the yeomen, who are repeatedly celebrated in the period as the backbone of English national independence and well-being. William Harrison's *Description of England* (1577) lovingly itemizes the yeoman's precious possessions: "fair garnish of pewter on his cupboard, with so much more odd vessel going about the house, three or four featherbeds, so many coverlets and carpets of tapestry, a silver salt[cellar], a bowl for wine (if not a whole nest) and a dozen of spoons." There are comparable accounts of the hard-earned acquisitions of the city dwellers—masters and apprentices in small workshops, shipbuilders, wool merchants, clothmakers, chandlers, tradesmen, shopkeepers, along with lawyers, apothecaries, schoolteachers, scriveners, and the like—whose pennies from time to time enriched the coffers of the players.

The chief source of England's wealth in the sixteenth century was its textile industry, an industry that depended on a steady supply of wool. In *The Winter's Tale*, Shakespeare provides a warm, richly comic portrayal of a rural sheepshearing festival, but the increasingly intensive production of wool had in reality its grim side. When a character in Thomas More's *Utopia* (1516) complains that "the sheep are eating the people," he is referring to the practice of enclosure: throughout the sixteenth and early seventeenth centuries, many acres of croplands once farmed in common by rural communities were enclosed with fences by wealthy landowners and turned into pasturage. The ensuing misery, displacement, and food shortages led to repeated riots, some of them violent and bloody, along with a series of government proclamations, but the process of enclosure was not reversed.

The economic stakes were high, and not only for the domestic market. In 1565, woolen cloth alone made up more than three-fourths of England's exports. (The remainder consisted mostly of other textiles and raw wool, with some trade in lead, tin, grain, and skins.) The Company of Merchant Adventurers carried cloth to distant ports on the Baltic and Mediterranean, establishing links with Russia and Morocco (each took about 2 percent of London's cloth in 1597–98). English lead and tin, as well as fabrics, were sold in Tuscany and Turkey, and merchants found a market for Newcastle coal on the island of Malta. In the latter half of the century, London, which handled more than 85 percent of all exports, regularly shipped abroad more than 100,000 woolen cloths a year at a value of at least £750,000. This figure does not include the increasingly important and profitable trade in so-called New Draperies, including textiles that went by such exotic names as bombazines, calamancoes, damazellas, damizes, mockadoes, and virgenatoes. When the Earl of Kent in *King Lear* insults Oswald as a "filthy worsted-stocking knave" (2.2.14–15) or when the aristocratic Biron in *Love's Labour's Lost* declares that he will give up "taffeta phrases, silken terms precise, / Three-piled hyperboles" and woo henceforth "in russet yeas, and honest kersey noes" (5.2.406–07, 413), Shakespeare is assuming that a substantial portion of his audience will be alert to the social significance of fabric.

There is amusing confirmation of this alertness from an unexpected source: the report of a visit made to the Fortune playhouse in London in 1614 by a foreigner, Father Orazio Busino, the chaplain of the Venetian embassy. Father Busino neglected to mention the name of the play he saw, but like many foreigners, he was powerfully struck by the presence of gorgeously dressed women in the audience. In Venice, there was a special gallery for courtesans, but socially respectable women would not have been permitted to attend plays, as they could in England. In London, not only could middle- and upper-class women go to the theater, but they could also wear masks and mingle freely with male spectators and women of ill repute. The bemused cleric was uncertain about the ambiguous social situation in which he found himself:

> These theatres are frequented by a number of respectable and handsome ladies, who come freely and seat themselves among the men without the slightest hesitation. On the evening in question his Excellency and the Secretary were pleased to play me a trick by placing me amongst a bevy of young women. Scarcely was I seated ere a very

elegant dame, but in a mask, came and placed herself beside me. . . . She asked me for my address both in French and English; and, on my turning a deaf ear, she determined to honour me by showing me some fine diamonds on her fingers, repeatedly taking off not fewer than three gloves, which were worn one over the other. . . . This lady's bodice was of yellow satin richly embroidered, her petticoat of gold tissue with stripes, her robe of red velvet with a raised pile, lined with yellow muslin with broad stripes of pure gold. She wore an apron of point lace of various patterns; her head-tire was highly perfumed, and the collar of white satin beneath the delicately-wrought ruff struck me as extremely pretty.

Father Busino may have turned a deaf ear on this "elegant dame" but not a blind eye: his description of her dress is worthy of a fashion designer and conveys something of the virtual clothes cult that prevailed in England in the late sixteenth and early seventeenth centuries, a cult whose major shrine, outside the royal court, was the theater.

Imports, Patents, and Monopolies

England produced some luxury goods, but the clothing on the backs of the most fashionable theatergoers was likely to have come from abroad. By the late sixteenth century, the English were importing substantial quantities of silks, satins, velvets, embroidery, gold and silver lace, and other costly items to satisfy the extravagant tastes of the elite and of those who aspired to dress like the elite. The government tried to put a check on the sartorial ambitions of the upwardly mobile by passing sumptuary laws—that is, laws restricting to the ranks of the aristocracy the right to wear certain of the most precious fabrics. But the very existence of these laws, in practice almost impossible to enforce, only reveals the scope and significance of the perceived problem.

Sumptuary laws were in part a conservative attempt to protect the existing social order from upstarts. Social mobility was not widely viewed as a positive virtue, and moralists repeatedly urged people to stay in their place. Conspicuous consumption that was tolerated, even admired, in the aristocratic elite was denounced as sinful and monstrous in less exalted social circles. English authorities were also deeply concerned throughout the period about the effects of a taste for luxury goods on the balance of trade. One of the principal English imports was wine: the "sherris" whose virtues Falstaff extols in 2 Henry IV came from Xeres in Spain; the malmsey in which poor Clarence is drowned in Richard III was probably made in Greece or in the Canary Islands (from whence came Sir Toby Belch's "cup of canary" in Twelfth Night); and the "flagon of rhenish" that Yorick in Hamlet had once poured on the Gravedigger's head came from the Rhine region of Germany. Other imports included canvas, linen, fish, olive oil, sugar, molasses, dates, oranges and lemons, figs, raisins, almonds, capers, indigo, ostrich feathers, and that increasingly popular drug from the New World, tobacco.

Joint-stock companies were established to import goods for the burgeoning English market. The Merchant Venturers of the city of Bristol (established in 1552) handled great shipments of Spanish sack, the light, dry wine that largely displaced the vintages of Bordeaux and Burgundy when trade with France was disrupted by war. The Muscovy Company (established in 1555) traded English cloth and manufactured goods for Russian furs, oil, and beeswax. The Venice Company and the Turkey Company—uniting in 1593 to form the wealthy Levant Company—brought silk and spices home from Aleppo and carpets from Istanbul. The East India Company (founded in 1600), with its agent at Bantam in Java, brought pepper, cloves, nutmeg, and other spices from east Asia, along with indigo, cotton textiles, sugar, and saltpeter from India. English privateers "imported" American products, especially sugar, fish, and hides, in huge quantities, along with more precious cargoes. In 1592, a privateering expedition principally funded by Sir Walter Ralegh captured a huge Portuguese carrack (sailing ship), the Madre de Dios, in the Azores and brought it back to Dartmouth. The ship, the largest that had ever entered any English port, held 536 tons of pepper, cloves, cinnamon, cochineal, mace, civet, musk, ambergris,

Cannoneer. From *Edward Webbe, . . . His Travailes* (1590).

and nutmeg, as well as jewels, gold, ebony, carpets, and silks. Before order could be established, the English seamen began to pillage this immensely rich prize, and witnesses said they could smell the spices on all the streets around the harbor. Such piratical expeditions were rarely officially sanctioned by the state, but the queen had in fact privately invested £1,800, for which she received about £80,000.

In the years of war with Spain, 1586–1604, the goods captured by the privateers annually amounted to 10 to 15 percent of the total value of England's imports. But organized theft alone could not solve England's balance-of-trade problems. Statesmen were particularly worried that the nation's natural wealth was slipping away in exchange for unnecessary things. In his *Discourse of the Commonweal* (1549), the prominent humanist Sir Thomas Smith exclaims against the importation of such trifles as mirrors, paper, laces, gloves, pins, inkhorns, tennis balls, puppets, and playing cards. And more than a century later, the same fear that England was trading its riches for trifles and wasting away in idleness was expressed by the Bristol merchant John Cary. The solution, Cary argues in "An Essay on the State of England in Relation to Its Trade" (1695), is to expand productive domestic employment. "People are or may be the Wealth of a Nation," he writes, "yet it must be where you find Employment for them, else they are a Burden to it, as the Idle Drone is maintained by the Industry of the laborious Bee, so are all those who live by their Dependence on others, as Players, Ale-House Keepers, Common Fiddlers, and such like, but more particularly Beggars, who never set themselves to work."

Stage players, all too typically associated here with vagabonds and other idle drones, could have replied in their defense that they not only labored in their vocation but also exported their skills abroad: English acting companies routinely traveled overseas and performed as far away as Bohemia. But their labor was not regarded as a productive contribution to the national wealth, and plays were in truth no solution to the trade imbalances that worried authorities.

The government attempted to stem the flow of gold overseas by establishing a patent system initially designed to encourage skilled foreigners to settle in England by granting them exclusive rights to produce particular wares by a patented method. Patents were granted for such things as the making of hard white soap (1561), ovens and furnaces (1563), window glass (1567), sailcloths (1574), drinking glasses (1574), sulphur, brimstone, and oil (1577), armor and horse harness (1587), starch (1588), white writing paper made from rags (1589), aqua vitae and vinegar (1594), playing cards (1598), and mathematical instruments (1598).

Although their ostensible purpose was to increase the wealth of England, encourage technical innovation, and provide employment for the poor, the effect of patents was often the enrichment of a few and the hounding of poor competitors by wealthy monopolists, a group that soon extended well beyond foreign-born entrepreneurs to the favorites of the monarch who vied for the huge profits to be made. "If I had a monopoly out" on folly, the Fool in *King Lear* protests, glancing at the "lords and great men" around him, "they would have part on't." The passage appears only in the quarto version of the play (*History of King Lear* 4.135–36); it may have been cut for political reasons from the Folio. For the issue of monopolies provoked bitter criticism and parliamentary debate for decades. In 1601, Elizabeth was prevailed upon to revoke a number of the most hated monopolies, including aqua vitae and vinegar, bottles, brushes, fish livers, the coarse sailcloth known as poldavis and mildernix, pots, salt, and starch. The whole system was revoked during the reign of James I by an act of Parliament.

Haves and Have-Nots

When in the 1560s Elizabeth's ambassador to France, the humanist Sir Thomas Smith, wrote a description of England, he saw the commonwealth as divided into four sorts of people: "gentlemen, citizens, yeomen artificers, and laborers." At the forefront of the class of gentlemen was the monarch, followed by a very small group of nobles—dukes, marquesses, earls, viscounts, and barons—who either inherited their exalted titles, as the eldest male heirs of their families, or were granted them by the monarch. Under Elizabeth, this aristocratic peerage numbered between 50 and 60 individuals; James's promotions increased the number to nearer 130. Strictly speaking, Smith notes, the younger sons of the nobility were only entitled to be called "esquires," but in common speech they were also called "lords."

Below this tiny cadre of aristocrats in the social hierarchy of gentry were the knights, a title of honor conferred by the monarch, and below them were the "simple gentlemen." Who was a gentleman? According to Smith, "whoever studieth the laws of the realm, who studieth in the universities, who professeth liberal sciences, and to be short, who can live idly and without manual labor, and will bear the port, charge and countenance of a gentleman, he shall be called master . . . and shall be taken for a gentleman." To "live idly and without manual labor": where in Spain, for example, the crucial mark of a gentleman was "blood," in England it was "idleness," in the sense of sufficient income to afford an education and to maintain a social position without having to work with one's hands.

For Smith, the class of gentlemen was far and away the most important in the kingdom. Below were two groups that had at least some social standing and claim to authority: the citizens, or burgesses, those who held positions of importance and responsibility in their cities, and yeomen, farmers with land and a measure of economic independence. At the bottom of the social order was what Smith calls "the fourth sort of men which do not rule." The great mass of ordinary people have, Smith writes, "no voice nor authority in our commonwealth, and no account is made of them but only to be ruled." Still, even they can bear some responsibility, he notes, since they serve on juries and are named to such positions as churchwarden and constable.

In everyday practice, as modern social historians have observed, the English tended to divide the population not into four distinct classes but into two: a very small empowered group—the "richer" or "wiser" or "better" sort—and all the rest who were without much social standing or power, the "poorer" or "ruder" or "meaner" sort. References to the "middle sort of people" remain relatively rare until after Shakespeare's lifetime; these people are absorbed into the rulers or the ruled, depending on speaker and context.

The source of wealth for most of the ruling class, and the essential measure of social status, was landownership, and changes to the social structure in the sixteenth and seventeenth centuries were largely driven by the land market. The property that passed into private hands as the Tudors and early Stuarts sold off confiscated monastic estates and then their own crown lands for ready cash amounted to nearly a quarter of all the land in England. At the same time, the buying and selling of private estates was on the rise throughout the period. Land was bought up not only by established landowners seeking to enlarge their estates but by successful merchants, manufacturers, and urban professionals; even if the taint of vulgar moneymaking lingered around such figures, their heirs would be taken for true gentlemen. The rate of turnover in landownership was great; in many counties, well over half the gentle families in 1640 had appeared since the end of the fifteenth century. The class that Smith called "simple gentlemen" was expanding rapidly: in the fifteenth century, they had held no more than a quarter of the land in the country; but by the later seventeenth century, they controlled almost half. Over the same period, the land held by the great aristocratic magnates held steady at 15 to 20 percent of the total.

Riot and Disorder

London was a violent place in the first half of Shakespeare's career. There were thirty-five riots in the city in the years 1581–1602, twelve of them in the volatile month of June 1595. These included protests against the deeply unpopular lord mayor Sir John Spencer, attempts to release prisoners, anti-alien riots, and incidents of "popular market regulation." There is an unforgettable depiction of a popular uprising in *Coriolanus*, along with many other glimpses in Shakespeare's works, including John Cade's grotesque rebellion in *The First Part of the Contention* (*2 Henry VI*), the plebeian violence in *Julius Caesar*, and Laertes' "riotous head" in *Hamlet*.

The London rioters were mostly drawn from the large mass of poor and discontented apprentices who typically chose as their scapegoats foreigners, prostitutes, and gentlemen's servingmen. Theaters were very often the site of the social confrontations that sparked disorder. For two days running in June 1584, disputes between apprentices and gentlemen triggered riots outside the Curtain Theatre involving up to a thousand participants. On one occasion, a gentleman was said to have exclaimed that "the apprentice was but a rascal, and some there were little better than rogues that took upon them the name of gentlemen, and said the prentices were but the scum of the world." These occasions culminated in attacks by the apprentices on London's law schools, the Inns of Court.

The most notorious and predictable incidents of disorder came on Shrove Tuesday (the Tuesday before the beginning of Lent), a traditional day of misrule when apprentices ran riot. Shrove Tuesday disturbances involved attacks by mobs of young men on the brothels of the South Bank, in the vicinity of the Globe and other public theaters. The city authorities took precautions to keep these disturbances from getting completely out of control but evidently did not regard them as serious threats to public order.

Of much greater concern throughout the Tudor and early Stuart years were the frequent incidents of rural rioting against the enclosure of commons and wasteland by local landlords (and, in the royal forests, by the crown). This form of popular protest was at its height during Shakespeare's career: in the years 1590–1610, the frequency of anti-enclosure rioting doubled from what it had been earlier in Elizabeth's reign.

Although they often became violent, anti-enclosure riots were usually directed not against individuals but against property. Villagers—sometimes several hundred, often

fewer than a dozen—gathered to tear down newly planted hedges. The event often took place in a carnival atmosphere, with songs and drinking, that did not prevent the participants from acting with a good deal of political canniness and forethought. Especially in the Jacobean period, it was common for participants to establish a common fund for legal defense before commencing their assault on the hedges. Women were frequently involved, and on a number of occasions wives alone participated in the destruction of the enclosure, since there was a widespread, though erroneous, belief that married women acting without the knowledge of their husbands were immune from prosecution. In fact, the powerful Court of Star Chamber consistently ruled that both the wives and their husbands should be punished.

Peddler. From Jost Amman, *The Book of Trades* (1568).

Although Stratford was never the scene of serious rioting, enclosure controversies there turned violent more than once in Shakespeare's lifetime. In January 1601, Shakespeare's friend Richard Quiney and others leveled the hedges of Sir Edward Greville, lord of Stratford manor. Quiney was elected bailiff of Stratford in September of that year but did not live to enjoy the office for long. He died from a blow to the head struck by one of Greville's men in a tavern brawl. Greville, responsible for the administration of justice, neglected to punish the murderer.

There was further violence in January 1615, when William Combe's men threw to the ground two local aldermen who were filling in a ditch by which Combe was enclosing common fields near Stratford. The task of filling in the offending ditch was completed the next day by the women and children of Stratford. Combe's enclosure scheme was eventually stopped in the courts. Although he owned land whose value would have been affected by this controversy, Shakespeare took no active role in it, since he had previously come to a private settlement with the enclosers insuring him against personal loss.

Most incidents of rural rioting were small, localized affairs, and with good reason: when confined to the village community, riot was a misdemeanor; when it spread outward to include multiple communities, it became treason, punishable by death. The greatest of the anti-enclosure riots, those in which hundreds of individuals from a large area participated, commonly took place on the eve of full-scale regional rebellions. The largest of these disturbances, Kett's Rebellion, involved some 16,000 peasants, artisans, and townspeople who rose up in 1549 under the leadership of a Norfolk tanner and landowner, Robert Kett, to protest economic exploitation. The agrarian revolts in Shakespeare's lifetime were on a much smaller scale. In the abortive Oxfordshire Rebellion of 1596, a carpenter named Bartholomew Steere attempted to organize a rising against enclosing gentlemen. The optimistic Steere promised his followers that "it was but a month's work to overrun England" and informed them "that the commons long since in Spain did rise and kill all gentlemen . . . and since that time have lived merrily there." Steere expected several hundred men to join him on Enslow Hill on November 21, 1596, for the start of the rising; no more than twenty showed up. They were captured, imprisoned, and tortured. Several were executed, but Steere apparently cheated the hangman by dying in prison.

Rebellions, most often triggered by hunger and oppression, continued into the reign of James I. The Midland Revolt of 1607, which may be reflected in *Coriolanus*, consisted of a string of agrarian risings in the counties of Northamptonshire, Warwickshire, and Leicestershire, involving assemblies of up to 5,000 rebels in various places. The best known of their leaders was John Reynolds, called "Captain Powch" because of the pouch he wore, whose magical contents were supposed to defend the rebels from harm. (According to the chronicler Edmund Howes, when Reynolds was captured and the pouch opened, it contained "only a piece of green cheese.") The rebels, who were called by themselves and others both "Levelers" and "Diggers," insisted that they had no quarrel with the king but only sought an end to injurious enclosures. But Robert Wilkinson, who preached a sermon against the leaders at their trial, credited them with the intention to "level all states as they leveled banks and ditches." Most of the rebels got off relatively lightly, but, along with other ringleaders, Captain Powch was executed.

The Legal Status of Women

Even though England was ruled for over forty years by a powerful woman, the great majority of women in the kingdom had very restricted social, economic, and legal standing. To be sure, a tiny number of influential aristocratic women, such as the formidable Countess of Shrewsbury, Bess of Hardwick, wielded considerable power. But, these rare exceptions aside, women were denied any rightful claim to institutional authority or personal autonomy. When Sir Thomas Smith thinks of how he should describe his country's social order, he declares that "we do reject women, as those whom nature hath made to keep home and to nourish their family and children, and not to meddle with matters abroad, nor to bear office in a city or commonwealth."

Then, with a kind of glance over his shoulder, he makes an exception of those few for whom "the blood is respected, not the age nor the sex": for example, the queen.

English women were not under the full range of crushing constraints that afflicted women in some countries in Europe. Foreign visitors were struck by their relative freedom, as shown, for example, by the fact that respectable women could venture unchaperoned into the streets and attend the theater. Single women, whether widowed or unmarried, could, if they were of full age, inherit and administer land, make a will, sign a contract, possess property, sue and be sued, without a male guardian or proxy. But married women had no such rights under the common law.

Early modern writings about women and the family constantly return to a political model of domination and submission, in which the father justly rules over wife and children as the monarch rules over the state. This conception of a woman's role conveniently ignores the fact that a *majority* of the adult women at any time in Shakespeare's England were not married. They were either widows or spinsters (a term that was not yet pejorative), and thus for the most part managing their own affairs. Even within marriage, women typically had more control over certain spheres than moralizing writers on the family cared to admit. For example, village wives oversaw the production of eggs, cheese, and beer, and sold these goods in the market. As seamstresses, pawnbrokers, secondhand clothing dealers, peddlers, and the like—activities not controlled by the all-male guilds—women managed to acquire some economic power of their own, and, of course, they participated as well in the unregulated, black-market economy of the age and in the underworld of thievery and prostitution.

Women were not in practice as bereft of property as, according to English common law, they should have been. Demographic studies indicate that the inheritance system called primogeniture, the orderly transmission of property from father to eldest male heir, was more often an unfulfilled wish than a reality. Some 40 percent of marriages failed to produce a son, and in such circumstances fathers often left their land to their daughters, rather than to brothers, nephews, or male cousins. In many families, the father died before his male heir was old enough to inherit property, leaving the land, at least temporarily, in the hands of the mother. And while they were less likely than their brothers to inherit land ("real property"), daughters normally inherited a substantial share of their father's personal property (cash and movables).

In fact, the legal restrictions upon women, though severe in Shakespeare's time, actually worsened in subsequent decades. The English common law, the system of law based on court decisions rather than on codified written laws, was significantly less egalitarian in its approach to wives and daughters than were alternative legal codes (manorial, civil, and ecclesiastical) still in place in the late sixteenth century. The eventual triumph of common law stripped women of many traditional rights, slowly driving them out of economically productive trades and businesses.

Limited though it was, the economic freedom of Elizabethan and Jacobean women far exceeded their political and social freedom—the opportunity to receive a grammar-school or university education, to hold office in church or state, to have a voice in public debates, or even simply to speak their mind fully and openly in ordinary conversation. Women who asserted their views too vigorously risked being perceived as shrewish and labeled "scolds." Both urban and rural communities had a horror of scolds. In the Elizabethan period, such women came to be regarded as a threat to public order, to be dealt with by the local authorities. The preferred methods of correction included public humiliation—of the sort Katherine endures in *The Taming of the Shrew*—and such physical abuse as slapping, bridling, and soaking by means of a contraption called the "cucking stool" (or "ducking stool"). This latter punishment originated in the Middle Ages, but its use spread in the sixteenth century, when it became almost exclusively a punishment for women. From 1560 onward, cucking stools were built or renovated in many English provincial towns; between 1560 and 1600, the contraptions were installed by rivers or ponds in Norwich, Bridport, Shrewsbury, Kingston-upon-Thames, Marlborough, Devizes, Clitheroe, Thornbury, and Great Yarmouth.

Such punishment was usually intensified by a procession through the town to the sound of "rough music," the banging together of pots and pans. The same cruel festivity accompanied the "carting" or "riding" of those accused of being whores. In some parts of the country, villagers also took the law into their own hands, publicly shaming women who married men much younger than themselves or who beat or otherwise domineered over their husbands. One characteristic form of these charivaris, or rituals of shaming, was known in the West Country as the Skimmington Ride. Villagers would rouse the offending couple from bed with rough music and stage a raucous pageant in which a man, holding a distaff, would ride backward on a donkey, while his "wife" (another man dressed as a woman) struck him with a ladle. In these cases, the collective ridicule and indignation was evidently directed at least as much at the henpecked husband as at his transgressive wife.

Women and Print

Books published for a female audience surged in popularity in the late sixteenth century, reflecting an increase in female literacy. (It is striking how many of Shakespeare's women are shown reading.) This increase is probably linked to a Protestant longing for direct access to the Scriptures, and the new books marketed specifically for women included devotional manuals and works of religious instruction. But there were also practical guides to such subjects as female education (for example, Giovanni Bruto's *Necessarie, Fit, and Convenient Education of a Young Gentlewoman*, 1598), midwifery (James Guillemeau's *Child-birth; or, The Happy Delivery of Women*, 1612), needlework (Federico di Vinciolo's *New and Singular Patternes and Workes of Linnen*, 1591), cooking (Thomas Dawson's *The Good Husewifes Jewell*, 1587), gardening (Pierre Erondelle's *The French Garden for English Ladyes and Gentlewomen to Walke In*, 1605), and married life (Patrick Hannay's *A Happy Husband; or, Directions for a Maide to Choose Her Mate*, 1619). As the authors' names suggest, many of these works were translations, and almost all were written by men.

Starting in the 1570s, writers and their publishers increasingly addressed works of recreational literature (romance, fiction, and poetry) partially or even exclusively to women. Some books, such as Robert Greene's *Mamillia, a Mirrour or Looking-Glasse for the Ladies of Englande* (1583), directly specified in the title their desired audience. Others, such as Sir Philip Sidney's influential and popular romance *Arcadia* (1590–93), solicited female readership in their dedicatory epistles. The ranks of Sidney's followers eventually included his own niece, Mary Wroth, whose romance *Urania* was published in 1621.

In the literature of Shakespeare's time, women readers were not only wooed but also frequently railed at, in a continuation of a popular polemical genre that had long inspired heated charges and countercharges. Both sides in the polemic generally agreed that it was the duty of women to be chaste, dutiful, shamefast, and silent; the argument was whether women fulfilled or fell short of this proper role. Ironically, then, a modern reader is more likely to find inspiring accounts of courageous women not in the books written in defense of female virtue but in attacks on those who refused to be silent and obedient.

The most famous English skirmish in this controversy took place in a rash of pamphlets at the end of Shakespeare's life. Joseph Swetnam's crude *Araignment of Lewd, Idle, Froward, and Unconstant Women* (1615) provoked three fierce responses attributed to women: Rachel Speght's *A Mouzell [Muzzle] for Melastomus*, Ester Sowernam's *Ester Hath Hang'd Haman*, and Constantia Munda's *Worming of a Mad Dogge*, all 1617. There was also an anonymous play, *Swetnam, the Woman-hater, Arraigned by Women* (1618), in which Swetnam, depicted as a braggart and a lecher, is put on trial by women and made to recant his misogynistic lies.

Prior to the Swetnam controversy, only one English woman, "Jane Anger," had published a defense of women (*Jane Anger, Her Protection for Women*, 1589). Learned women writers in the sixteenth century tended not to become involved in public debate but rather to undertake a project to which it was difficult for even obdurately chauvinistic

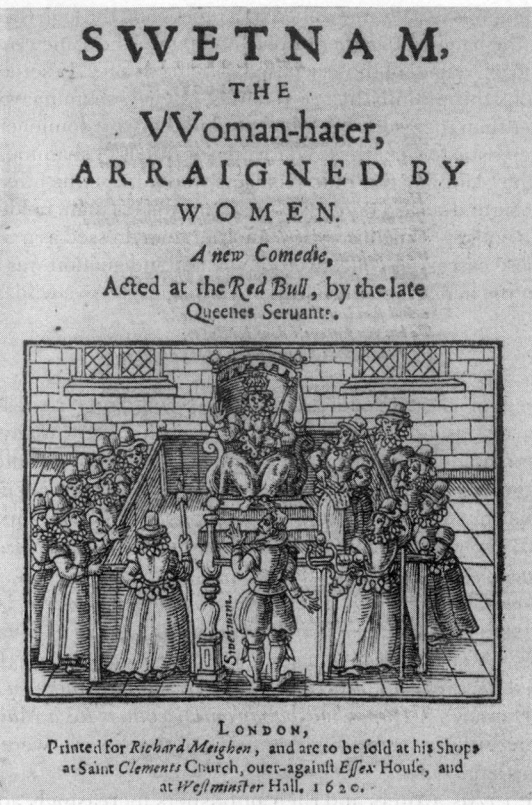

SWETNAM,

THE

WWoman-hater,

ARRAIGNED BY

WOMEN.

A new Comedie,

Acted at the *Red Bull*, by the late
Queenes Seruants.

LONDON,

Printed for *Richard Meighen*, and are to be sold at his Shops
at Saint *Clements* Church, ouer-againft *Essex* Houfe, and
at *Westminster* Hall. 1620.

Title page of *Swetnam, the Woman-hater, Arraigned by
Women* (1620), a play written in response to Joseph
Swetnam's *The Araignment of Lewd, Idle, Froward and
Unconstant Women* (1615); the woodcut depicts the
trial of Swetnam in Act 4.

males to object: the translation of devotional literature into English. Thomas More's
daughter Margaret More Roper translated Erasmus (*A Devout Treatise upon the Pater
Noster,* 1524); Francis Bacon's mother, Anne Cooke Bacon, translated Bishop John
Jewel (*An Apologie or Answere in Defence of the Churche of Englande,* 1564); Anne
Locke Prowse, a friend of John Knox, translated the *Sermons of John Calvin* in 1560;
and Mary Sidney, Countess of Pembroke, completed the metrical version of the Psalms
that her brother Sir Philip Sidney had begun. Elizabeth Tudor (the future queen) her-
self translated, at the age of eleven, Marguerite de Navarre's *Miroir de l'âme pécheresse*
(*The Glass of the Sinful Soul,* 1544). The translation was dedicated to her stepmother,
Catherine Parr, herself the author of a frequently reprinted book of prayers.

There was in the sixteenth and early seventeenth centuries a social stigma attached
to print. Far from celebrating publication, authors, and particularly female authors,
often apologized for exposing themselves to the public gaze. Nonetheless, a number of
women ventured beyond pious translations circulated in manuscript. Some, including
Elizabeth Tyrwhitt, Anne Dowriche, Isabella Whitney, Mary Sidney, and Aemilia
Lanyer, composed and published their own poems. Aemilia Lanyer's *Salve Deus Rex
Judaeorum,* published in 1611, is a poem in praise of virtuous women, from Eve and
the Virgin Mary to her noble patron, the Countess of Cumberland. "A Description of
Cookeham," appended to the poem, may be the first English-country-house poem.

The first Tudor woman to translate a play was the learned Jane Lumley, who composed an English version of Euripides' *Iphigenia at Aulis* (c. 1550). The first known original play in English by a woman was by Elizabeth Cary, Viscountess Falkland, whose *Tragedie of Mariam, the Faire Queene of Jewry* was published in 1613. This remarkable play, which was not intended to be performed, includes speeches in defense of women's equality, though the most powerful of these is spoken by the villainous Salome, who schemes to divorce her husband and marry her lover. Cary, who bore eleven children, herself had a deeply troubled marriage, which effectively came to an end in 1625, when, defying her husband's staunchly Protestant family, she openly converted to Catholicism. Her biography was written by one of her four daughters, all of whom became nuns.

Henry VIII and the English Reformation

There had long been serious ideological and institutional tensions in the religious life of England, but officially, at least, England in the early sixteenth century had a single religion, Catholicism, whose acknowledged head was the pope in Rome. In 1517, drawing upon long-standing currents of dissent, Martin Luther, an Augustinian monk and professor of theology at the University of Wittenberg, challenged the authority of the pope and attacked several key doctrines of the Catholic Church. According to Luther, the Church, with its elaborate hierarchical structure centered in Rome, its rich monasteries and convents, and its enormous political influence, had become hopelessly corrupt, a conspiracy of venal priests who manipulated popular superstitions to enrich themselves and amass worldly power. Luther began by vehemently attacking the sale of indulgences—certificates promising the remission of punishments to be suffered in the afterlife by souls sent to purgatory to expiate their sins. These indulgences were a fraud, he argued; purgatory itself had no foundation in the Bible, which in his view was the only legitimate source of religious truth. Christians would be saved not by scrupulously following the ritual practices fostered by the Catholic Church—observing fast days, reciting the ancient Latin prayers, endowing chantries to say prayers for the dead, and so on—but by faith and faith alone.

This challenge, which came to be known as the Reformation, spread and gathered force, especially in northern Europe, where major leaders like the Swiss pastor Huldrych Zwingli and the French theologian John Calvin established institutional structures and elaborated various and sometimes conflicting doctrinal principles. Calvin, whose thought came to be particularly influential in England, emphasized the obligation of governments to implement God's will in the world. He advanced too the doctrine of predestination, by which, as he put it, "God adopts some to hope of life and sentences others to eternal death." God's "secret election" of the saved made Calvin uncomfortable, but his study of the Scriptures had led him to conclude that "only a small number, out of an incalculable multitude, should obtain salvation." It might seem that such a conclusion would lead to passivity or even despair, but for Calvin predestination was a mystery bound up with faith, confidence, and an active engagement in the fashioning of a Christian community.

The Reformation had a direct and powerful impact on those territories, especially in northern Europe, where it gained control. Monasteries were sacked, their possessions seized by princes or sold off to the highest bidder; the monks and nuns, expelled from their cloisters, were encouraged to break their vows of chastity and find spouses, as Luther and his wife, a former nun, had done. In the great cathedrals and in hundreds of smaller churches and chapels, the elaborate altarpieces, bejeweled crucifixes, crystal reliquaries holding the bones of saints, and venerated statues and paintings were attacked as "idols" and often defaced or destroyed. Protestant congregations continued, for the most part, to celebrate the most sacred Christian ritual, the Eucharist, or Lord's Supper, but they did so in a profoundly different spirit from that of the Catholic Church—more as commemoration than as miracle—and they now prayed not in the ancient liturgical Latin but in the vernacular.

"The Pope as Antichrist riding the Beast of the Apocalypse." From *Fierie Tryall of God's Saints* (1611; author unknown).

The Reformation was at first vigorously resisted in England. Indeed, with the support of his ardently Catholic chancellor, Thomas More, Henry VIII personally wrote (or at least lent his name to) a vehement, often scatological attack on Luther's character and views, an attack for which the pope granted him the honorific title "Defender of the Faith." Protestant writings, including translations of the Scriptures into English, were seized by officials of the church and state and burned. Protestants who made their views known were persecuted, driven to flee the country, or arrested, put on trial, and burned at the stake. But the situation changed drastically and decisively when in 1527 Henry decided to seek a divorce from his first wife, Catherine of Aragon, in order to marry Anne Boleyn.

Catherine had given birth to six children, but since only a daughter, Mary, survived infancy, Henry did not have the son he craved. Then as now, the Catholic Church did not ordinarily grant divorce, but Henry's lawyers argued on technical grounds that the marriage was invalid (and, therefore, by extension, that Mary was illegitimate and hence unable to inherit the throne). Matters of this kind were far less doctrinal than diplomatic: Catherine, the daughter of Ferdinand of Aragon and Isabella of Castile, had powerful allies in Rome, and the pope ruled against Henry's petition for a divorce. A series of momentous events followed, as England lurched away from the Church of Rome. In 1531, Henry charged the entire clergy of England with having usurped royal authority in the administration of canon law (the ecclesiastical law that governed faith, discipline, and morals, including such matters as divorce). Under extreme pressure, including the threat of mass confiscations and imprisonment, the Convocation of the English Clergy begged for pardon, made a donation to the royal coffers of over £100,000, and admitted that the king was "supreme head of the English Church and clergy" (modified by the rider "as far as the law of Christ allows"). On May 15 of the next year, the convocation submitted to the demand that the king be the final arbiter of canon law; on the next day, Thomas More resigned his post.

In 1533, Henry's marriage to Catherine was officially declared null and void, and on June 1 Anne Boleyn was crowned queen (a coronation Shakespeare depicts in his late play *All Is True*). The king was promptly excommunicated by the pope, Clement VII. In the following year, the parliamentary Act of Succession confirmed the effects of the divorce and required an oath from all adult male subjects confirming the new dynastic settlement. Thomas More and John Fisher, Bishop of Rochester, were among the small number who refused. The Act of Supremacy, passed later in the year, formally declared the king to be "Supreme Head of the Church in England" and again required an oath to this effect. In 1535 and 1536, further acts made it treasonous to refuse the oath of royal supremacy or, as More had tried to do, to remain silent. The first victims were three Carthusian monks who rejected the oath—"How could the king, a layman," said one of them, "be Head of the Church of England?"—and in May 1535, they were duly hanged, drawn, and quartered. A few weeks later, Fisher and More were convicted and beheaded. Between 1536 and 1539, the monasteries were suppressed and their vast wealth seized by the crown.

Royal defiance of the authority of Rome was a key element in the Reformation but did not by itself constitute the establishment of Protestantism in England. On the contrary, in the same year that Fisher and More were martyred for their adherence to Roman Catholicism, twenty-five Protestants, members of a sect known as Anabaptists, were burned for heresy on a single day. Through most of his reign, Henry remained an equal-opportunity persecutor, ruthless to Catholics loyal to Rome and hostile to some of those who espoused Reformation ideas, though many of these ideas gradually established themselves on English soil.

Even when Henry was eager to do so, it proved impossible to eradicate Protestantism, as it would later prove impossible for his successors to eradicate Catholicism. In large part this tenacity arose from the passionate, often suicidal heroism of men and women who felt that their souls' salvation depended on the precise character of their Christianity. It arose, too, from a mid-fifteenth-century technological innovation that made it almost impossible to suppress unwelcome ideas: the printing press. Early Protestants quickly grasped that with a few clandestine presses they could defy the Catholic authorities and flood the country with their texts. "How many printing presses there be in the world," wrote the Protestant polemicist John Foxe, "so many block-houses there be against the high castle" of the pope in Rome, "so that either the pope must abolish knowledge and printing or printing at length will root him out." By the century's end, it was the Catholics who were using the clandestine press to propagate their beliefs in the face of Protestant persecution.

The greatest insurrection of the Tudor age was not over food, taxation, or land but over religion. On Sunday, October 1, 1536, stirred up by their vicar, the traditionalist parishioners of Louth in Lincolnshire, in the north of England, rose up in defiance of the ecclesiastical visitation sent to enforce royal supremacy. The rapidly spreading rebellion, which became known as the Pilgrimage of Grace, was led by the lawyer Robert Aske. The city of Lincoln fell to the rebels on October 6, and though it was soon retaken by royal forces, the rebels seized cities and fortifications throughout Yorkshire, Durham, Northumberland, Cumberland, Westmoreland, and northern Lancashire. Carlisle, Newcastle, and a few castles were all that were left to the king in the north. The Pilgrims soon numbered 40,000, led by some of the region's leading noblemen. The Duke of Norfolk, representing the crown, was forced to negotiate a truce, with a promise to support the rebels' demands that the king restore the monasteries, shore up the regional economy, suppress heresy, and dismiss his evil advisers.

The Pilgrims kept the peace for the rest of 1536, on the naive assumption that their demands would be met. But Henry moved suddenly early in 1537 to impose order and capture the ringleaders; 130 people, including lords, knights, heads of religious houses, and, of course, Robert Aske, were executed.

In 1549, two years after the death of Henry VIII, the west and the north of England were the sites of further unsuccessful risings for the restoration of Catholicism. The Western Rising is striking for its blend of Catholic universalism and intense regionalism among people who did not yet regard themselves as English. One of the rebels' articles, protesting against the imposition of the English Bible and religious service, declares, "We the Cornish men (whereof certain of us understand no English) utterly refuse this new English." The rebels besieged but failed to take the city of Exeter. As with almost all Tudor rebellions, the number of those executed in the aftermath of the failed rising was far greater than those killed in actual hostilities.

Henry VIII's Children: Edward, Mary, and Elizabeth

Upon Henry's death in 1547, his ten-year-old son, Edward VI, came to the throne, with his maternal uncle Edward Seymour named as Lord Protector and Duke of Somerset. Both Edward and his uncle were staunch Protestants, and reformers hastened to transform the English Church accordingly. During Edward's reign, Archbishop Thomas Cranmer formulated the forty-two articles of religion that became the core of Anglican orthodoxy and wrote the first Book of Common Prayer, which was officially adopted in 1549 as the basis of English worship services.

Somerset fell from power in 1549 and was replaced as Lord Protector by John Dudley, later Duke of Northumberland. When Edward fell seriously ill, probably of tuberculosis, Northumberland persuaded him to sign a will depriving his half sisters, Mary (the daughter of Catherine of Aragon) and Elizabeth (the daughter of Anne Boleyn), of their claim to royal succession. The Lord Protector was scheming to have his daughter-in-law, the Protestant Lady Jane Grey, a granddaughter of Henry VII, ascend to the throne. But when Edward died in 1553, Mary marshaled support, quickly secured the crown from Lady Jane (who had been titular queen for nine days), and had Lady Jane executed, along with her husband and Northumberland.

Queen Mary immediately took steps to return her kingdom to Roman Catholicism. Even though she was unable to get Parliament to agree to restore church lands seized under Henry VIII, she restored the Catholic Mass, once again affirmed the authority of the pope, and put down a rebellion that sought to depose her. Seconded by her ardently Catholic husband, Philip II, King of Spain, she initiated a series of religious persecutions that earned her (from her enemies) the name "Bloody Mary." Hundreds of Protestants took refuge abroad in cities such as Calvin's Geneva; almost three hundred less fortunate Protestants were condemned as heretics and burned at the stake.

The Family of Henry VIII: An Allegory of the Tudor Succession. By Lucas de Heere (c. 1572). Henry, in the middle, is flanked by Mary to his right, and Edward and Elizabeth to his left.

Mary died childless in 1558, and her younger half sister Elizabeth became queen. Elizabeth's succession had been by no means assured. For if Protestants regarded Henry VIII's marriage to Catherine as invalid and hence deemed Mary illegitimate, so Catholics regarded his marriage to Anne Boleyn as invalid and deemed Elizabeth illegitimate. Henry VIII himself seemed to support both views, since only three years after divorcing Catherine, he beheaded Anne Boleyn on charges of treason and adultery, and urged Parliament to invalidate the marriage. Moreover, though during her sister's reign Elizabeth outwardly complied with the official Catholic religious observance, Mary and her advisers were deeply suspicious, and the young princess's life was in grave danger. Poised and circumspect, Elizabeth warily evaded the traps that were set for her. As she ascended the throne, her actions were scrutinized for some indication of the country's future course. During her coronation procession, when a girl in an allegorical pageant presented her with a Bible in English translation—banned under Mary's reign—Elizabeth kissed the book, held it up reverently, and laid it to her breast; when the abbot and monks of Westminster Abbey came to greet her in broad daylight with candles (a symbol of Catholic devotion) in their hands, she briskly dismissed them with the telling words "Away with those torches! we can see well enough." England had returned to the Reformation.

Many English men and women, of all classes, remained loyal to the old Catholic faith, but English authorities under Elizabeth moved steadily, if cautiously, toward ensuring at least an outward conformity to the official Protestant settlement. Recusants, those who refused to attend regular Sunday services in their parish churches, were fined heavily. Anyone who wished to receive a university degree, to be ordained as a priest in the Church of England, or to be named as an officer of the state had to swear an oath to the royal supremacy. Commissioners were sent throughout the land to confirm that religious services were following the officially approved liturgy and to investigate any reported backsliding into Catholic practice or, alternatively, any attempts to introduce more radical reforms than the queen and her bishops had chosen to embrace. For the Protestant exiles who streamed back were eager not only to undo the damage Mary had done but to carry the Reformation much further. They sought to dismantle the church hierarchy, to purge the calendar of folk customs deemed pagan and the church service of ritual practices deemed superstitious, to dress the clergy in simple garb, and, at the extreme edge, to smash "idolatrous" statues, crucifixes, and altarpieces. Throughout her long reign, however, Elizabeth herself remained cautiously conservative and determined to hold in check what she regarded as the religious zealotry of Catholics, on the one side, and Puritans, on the other.

Shakespeare's plays tap into the ongoing confessional tensions: "Sometimes," Maria in *Twelfth Night* says of the sober, festivity-hating steward Malvolio, "he is a kind of puritan" (2.3.125). But they tend to avoid the risks of direct engagement: "The dev'l a puritan that he is, or anything constantly," Maria adds a moment later, "but a time-pleaser, an affectioned ass" (2.3.131–32). *The Winter's Tale* features a statue that comes to life—exactly the kind of magical image that Protestant polemicists excoriated as Catholic superstition and idolatry—but the play is set in pre-Christian world of the Delphic oracle. And as if this careful distancing might not be enough, the play's ruler goes out of his way to pronounce the wonder legitimate: "If this be magic, let it be an art / Lawful as eating" (5.3.110–11).

In the space of a single lifetime, England had gone officially from Roman Catholicism, to Catholicism under the supreme headship of the English king, to a guarded Protestantism, to a more radical Protestantism, to a renewed and aggressive Roman Catholicism, and finally to Protestantism again. Each of these shifts was accompanied by danger, persecution, and death. It was enough to make some people wary. Or skeptical. Or extremely agile.

The English Bible

Luther had undertaken a fundamental critique of the Catholic Church's sacramental system, a critique founded on the twin principles of salvation by faith alone (*sola fide*) and the absolute primacy of the Bible (*sola scriptura*). *Sola fide* contrasted faith with "works," by which was meant primarily the whole elaborate system of rituals sanctified, conducted, or directed by the priests. Protestants proposed to modify or reinterpret many of these rituals or, as with the rituals associated with purgatory, to abolish them altogether. *Sola scriptura* required direct lay access to the Bible, which meant in practice the widespread availability of vernacular translations. The Roman Catholic Church had not always and everywhere opposed such translations, but it generally preferred that the populace encounter the Scriptures through the interpretations of the priests, trained to read the Latin translation known as the Vulgate. In times of great conflict, this preference for clerical mediation hardened into outright prohibition of vernacular translation and into persecution and book burning.

Zealous Protestants set out, in the teeth of fierce opposition, to put the Bible into the hands of the laity. A remarkable translation of the New Testament, by an English Lutheran named William Tyndale, was printed on the Continent and smuggled into England in 1525; Tyndale's translation of the Pentateuch, the first five books of the Hebrew Bible, followed in 1530. Many copies of these translations were seized and burned, as was the translator himself, but the printing press made it extremely difficult for authorities to eradicate books for which there was a passionate demand. The English Bible was a force that could not be suppressed, and it became, in its various forms, the single most important book of the sixteenth century.

Tyndale's translation was completed by an associate, Miles Coverdale, whose rendering of the Psalms proved to be particularly influential. Their joint labor was the basis for the Great Bible (1539), the first authorized version of the Bible in English, a copy of which was ordered to be placed in every church in the kingdom. With the accession of Edward VI, many editions of the Bible followed, but the process was sharply reversed when Mary came to the throne in 1553. Along with people condemned as heretics, English Bibles were burned in great bonfires.

Marian persecution was indirectly responsible for what would become the most popular as well as most scholarly English Bible, the translation known as the Geneva Bible, prepared, with extensive, learned, and often fiercely polemical marginal notes, by English exiles in Calvin's Geneva and widely diffused in England after Elizabeth came to the throne. In addition, Elizabethan church authorities ordered a careful revision of the Great Bible, and this version, known as the Bishops' Bible, was the one read in the churches. The success of the Geneva Bible in particular prompted those Elizabethan Catholics who now in turn found themselves in exile to bring out a vernacular translation of their own in order to counter the Protestant readings and glosses. This Catholic translation, known as the Rheims Bible, may have been known to Shakespeare, but he seems to have been far better acquainted with the Geneva Bible, and he would also have repeatedly heard the Bishops' Bible read aloud. Scholars have identified over three hundred references to the Bible in Shakespeare's work; in one version or another, the Scriptures had a powerful impact on his imagination.

A Female Monarch in a Male World

In the last year of Mary's reign, 1558, the Scottish Calvinist minister John Knox thundered against what he called "the monstrous regiment of women." When the Protestant Elizabeth came to the throne the following year, Knox and his religious brethren were less inclined to denounce female rulers, but in England as elsewhere in Europe there remained a widespread conviction that women were unsuited to wield power over men. Many men seem to have regarded the capacity for rational thought as exclusively male; women, they assumed, were led only by their passions. While gentlemen mastered the arts of rhetoric and warfare, gentlewomen were expected to display the virtues of silence and good housekeeping. Among upper-class males, the will to dominate others was acceptable and, indeed, admired; the same will in women was condemned as a grotesque and dangerous aberration.

One of the Armada portraits (c. 1588). Note Elizabeth's hand on the globe.

Apologists for the queen countered these prejudices by appealing to historical precedent and legal theory. History offered inspiring examples of just female rulers, notably Deborah, the biblical prophetess who judged Israel. In the legal sphere, crown lawyers advanced the theory of "the king's two bodies." As England's crowned head, Elizabeth's person was mystically divided between her mortal "body natural" and the immortal "body politic." While the queen's natural body was inevitably subject to the failings of human flesh, the body politic was timeless and perfect. In political terms, therefore, Elizabeth's sex was a matter of no consequence, a thing indifferent.

Elizabeth, who had received a fine humanist education and an extended, dangerous lesson in the art of survival, made it immediately clear that she intended to rule in more than name only. She assembled a group of trustworthy advisers, foremost among them William Cecil (later named Lord Burghley, also known as Burleigh), but she insisted on making many of the crucial decisions herself. Like many Renaissance monarchs, Elizabeth was drawn to the idea of royal absolutism, the theory that ultimate power was properly concentrated in her person and, indeed, that God had appointed her to be His deputy in the kingdom. Opposition to her rule, in this view, was not only a political act but also a kind of impiety, a blasphemous grudging against the will of God. Apologists for absolutism contended that God commands obedience even to manifestly wicked rulers whom He has sent to punish the sinfulness of humankind. Such arguments were routinely made in speeches and political tracts and from the pulpits of churches, where they were incorporated into the *First* and *Second Book of Homilies,* which clergymen were required to read out to their congregations.

In reality, Elizabeth's power was not absolute. The government had a network of spies, informers, and agents provocateurs, but it lacked a standing army, a national police force, an efficient system of communication, and an extensive bureaucracy. Above all, the queen had limited financial resources and needed to turn periodically to an independent and often recalcitrant Parliament, which by long tradition had the sole right to levy taxes and to grant subsidies. Members of the House of Commons were elected from their boroughs, not appointed by the monarch, and although the queen had considerable influence over their decisions, she could by no means dictate policy. Under these constraints, Elizabeth ruled through a combination of adroit political maneuvering and imperious command, all the while enhancing her authority in the eyes of both court and country by means of an extraordinary cult of love.

"We all loved her," Elizabeth's godson Sir John Harington wrote, with just a touch of irony, a few years after the queen's death, "for she said she loved us." Ambassadors, courtiers, and parliamentarians all submitted to Elizabeth's cult of love, in which the queen's gender was transformed from a potential liability into a significant asset. Those who approached her generally did so on their knees and were expected to address her with extravagant compliments fashioned from the period's most passionate love poetry; she in turn spoke, when it suited her to do so, in the language of love poetry. The court moved in an atmosphere of romance, with music, dancing, plays, and the elaborate, fancy-dress entertainments called masques. The queen adorned herself in gorgeous clothes and rich jewels. When she went on one of her summer "progresses," ceremonial journeys through her land, she looked like an exotic, sacred image in a religious cult of love, and her noble hosts virtually bankrupted themselves to lavish upon her the costliest pleasures. England's leading artists, such as the poet Edmund Spenser and the painter Nicholas Hilliard, enlisted themselves in the celebration of Elizabeth's mystery, likening her to the goddesses and queens of mythology: Diana, Astraea, Gloriana. Her cult drew its power from cultural discourses that ranged from the secular (her courtiers could pine for her as a cruel Petrarchan mistress) to the sacred (the veneration that under Catholicism had been due to the Virgin Mary could now be directed toward England's semidivine queen).

There was a sober, even grim, aspect to these poetical fantasies: Elizabeth was brilliant at playing one dangerous faction off another, now turning her gracious smiles on one favorite, now honoring his hated rival, now suddenly looking elsewhere and raising an obscure upstart to royal favor. And when she was disobeyed or when she felt that her prerogatives had been challenged, she was capable of an anger that, as Harington put it, "left no doubtings whose daughter she was." Thus, when Sir Walter Ralegh, one of the queen's glittering favorites, married without her knowledge or consent, he found himself promptly imprisoned in the Tower of London. And when the Protestant polemicist John Stubbs ventured to publish a pamphlet stridently denouncing the queen's proposed marriage to the French Catholic Duke of Alençon, Stubbs and his publisher were arrested and had their right hands chopped off. (After receiving the blow, the now prudent Stubbs lifted his hat with his remaining hand and cried, "God save the Queen!")

The queen's marriage negotiations were a particularly fraught issue. When she came to the throne at twenty-five years old, speculation about a suitable match, already widespread, intensified and remained for decades at a fever pitch, for the stakes were high. If Elizabeth died childless, the Tudor line would come to an end. The nearest heir was her cousin Mary, Queen of Scots, a Catholic whose claim was supported by France and by the papacy, and whose penchant for sexual and political intrigue confirmed the worst fears of English Protestants. The obvious way to avert the nightmare was for Elizabeth to marry and produce an heir, and the pressure upon her to do so was intense.

More than the royal succession hinged on the question of the queen's marriage; Elizabeth's perceived eligibility was a vital factor in the complex machinations of international diplomacy. A dynastic marriage between the Queen of England and a foreign ruler would forge an alliance powerful enough to alter the balance of power in Europe. The English court hosted a steady stream of ambassadors from kings and princes eager to win the hand of the royal maiden, and Elizabeth, who prided herself on speaking fluent French and Italian (and on reading Latin and Greek), played her romantic part with exemplary skill, sighing and spinning the negotiations out for months and even years.

Most probably, she never meant to marry any of her numerous foreign (and domestic) suitors. Such a decisive act would have meant the end of her independence, as well as the end of the marriage game by which she played one power off against another. One day she would seem to be on the verge of accepting a proposal; the next, she would vow never to forsake her virginity. "She is a Princess," the French ambassador remarked, "who can act any part she pleases."

The Kingdom in Danger

Beset by Catholic and Protestant extremists, Elizabeth contrived to forge a moderate compromise that enabled her realm to avert the massacres and civil wars that poisoned France and other countries on the Continent. But menace was never far off, and there were constant fears of conspiracy, rebellion, and assassination. Many of the fears swirled around Mary, Queen of Scots, who had been driven from her own kingdom in 1568 by a powerful faction of rebellious nobles and had taken refuge in England. Her presence, under a kind of house arrest, was the source of intense anxiety and helped generate continual rumors of plots. Some of these plots were real enough, others imaginary, still others traps set in motion by the secret agents of the government's intelligence service under the direction of Sir Francis Walsingham. The situation worsened greatly after the St. Bartholomew's Day Massacre of Protestants (Huguenots) in France (August 24, 1572), after Spanish imperial armies invaded the Netherlands in order to stamp out Protestant rebels, and after the assassination there of Europe's other major Protestant leader, William of Orange (1584).

The queen's life seemed to be in even greater danger after Pope Gregory XIII's proclamation in 1580 that the assassination of the great heretic Elizabeth (who had been excommunicated a decade before) would not constitute a mortal sin. The immediate effect of the proclamation was to make existence more difficult for English Catholics, most of whom were loyal to the queen but who fell under grave suspicion. Suspicion was intensified by the clandestine presence of English Jesuits, trained at seminaries abroad and smuggled back into England to serve the Roman Catholic cause. When Elizabeth's spymaster Walsingham unearthed an assassination plot in the correspondence between the Queen of Scots and the Catholic Anthony Babington, the wretched Mary's fate was sealed. After vacillating, a very reluctant Elizabeth signed the death warrant in February 1587, and her cousin was beheaded.

The long-anticipated military confrontation with Catholic Spain was now unavoidable. Elizabeth learned that Philip II, her former brother-in-law and onetime suitor, was preparing to send an enormous fleet against her island realm. It was to sail to the Netherlands, where a Spanish army would be waiting to embark and invade England. Barring its way was England's small fleet of well-armed and highly maneuverable fighting vessels, backed up by ships from the merchant navy. The Invincible Armada reached English waters in July 1588, only to be routed in one of the most famous and decisive naval battles in European history. Then, in what many viewed as an act of God on behalf of Protestant England, the Spanish fleet was dispersed and all but destroyed by violent storms.

As England braced itself to withstand the invasion that never came, Elizabeth appeared in person to review a detachment of soldiers assembled at Tilbury. Dressed in a white gown and a silver breastplate, she declared that though some among her councillors had urged her not to appear before a large crowd of armed men, she would never fail to trust the loyalty of her faithful and loving subjects. Nor did she fear the Spanish armies. "I know I have the body of a weak and feeble woman," Elizabeth declared, "but I have the heart and stomach of a king, and of England too." In this celebrated speech, Elizabeth displayed many of her most memorable qualities: her self-consciously histrionic command of grand public occasion, her subtle blending of magniloquent rhetoric and the language of love, her strategic appropriation of traditionally masculine qualities, and her great personal courage. "We princes," she once remarked, "are set on stages in the sight and view of all the world."

The English and Otherness

Shakespeare's London had a large population of resident aliens, mainly artisans and merchants and their families, from Portugal, Italy, Spain, Germany, and, above all, France and the Netherlands. Many of these people were Protestant refugees, and they were accorded some legal and economic protection by the government. But they were not always welcome by the local populace. Throughout the sixteenth century, London was the site of repeated demonstrations and, on occasion, bloody riots against the communities of foreign artisans, who were accused of taking jobs away from Englishmen. There was widespread hostility as well toward the Welsh, the Scots, and especially the Irish, whom the English had for centuries been struggling unsuccessfully to subdue. The kings of England claimed to be rulers of Ireland, but in reality they effectively controlled only a small area known as the Pale, extending north from Dublin. The great majority of the Irish people remained stubbornly Catholic and, despite endlessly reiterated English repression, burning of villages, destruction of crops, and massacres, incorrigibly independent.

Shakespeare's *Henry V* (1598–99) seems to invite the audience to celebrate the conjoined heroism of English, Welsh, Scots, and Irish soldiers all fighting together as a "band of brothers" against the French. But such a way of imagining the national community must be set against the tensions and conflicting interests that often set these brothers at each other's throats. As Shakespeare's King Henry realizes, a feared or hated foreign enemy helps at least to mask these tensions, and, indeed, in the face of the Spanish Armada, even the bitter gulf between Catholic and Protestant Englishmen seemed to narrow significantly. But the patriotic alliance was only temporary.

Another way of partially masking the sharp differences in language, belief, and custom among the peoples of the British Isles was to group these people together in contrast to the Jews. Medieval England's Jewish population, the recurrent object of persecution, extortion, and massacre, had been officially expelled by King Edward I in 1290, but Elizabethan England harbored a tiny number of Jews or Jewish converts to Christianity who were treated with suspicion and hostility. One of these was Elizabeth's own physician, Roderigo Lopez, who was tried in 1594 for an alleged plot to poison the queen. Convicted and condemned to the hideous execution reserved for traitors, Lopez went to his death, in the words of the Elizabethan historian William Camden, "affirming that he loved the Queen as well as he loved Jesus Christ; which coming from a man of the Jewish profession moved no small laughter in the standers-by." It is difficult to gauge the meaning here of the phrase "the Jewish profession," used to describe a man who never, as far as we know, professed Judaism, just as it is difficult to gauge the meaning of the crowd's cruel laughter.

Elizabethans appear to have been fascinated by Jews and Judaism but uncertain whether the terms referred to a people, a foreign nation, a set of strange prac-

A Jewish man poisoning a well. From Pierre Boaistuau, *Certaine Secrete Wonders of Nature* (1569).

tices, a living faith, a defunct religion, a villainous conspiracy, or a messianic inheritance. Protestant Reformers brooded deeply on the Hebraic origins of Christianity; government officials ordered the arrest of those "suspected to be Jews"; villagers paid pennies to itinerant fortune-tellers who claimed to be descended from Abraham or masters of cabalistic mysteries; and London playgoers, perhaps including some who laughed at Lopez on the scaffold, enjoyed the spectacle of the downfall of the wicked Barabas in Christopher Marlowe's *Jew of Malta* (c. 1592) and the forced conversion of Shylock in Shakespeare's *Merchant of Venice* (1596–97). Few if any of Shakespeare's contemporaries would have encountered on English soil Jews who openly practiced their religion, though England probably harbored a small number of so-called Marranos, Spanish or Portuguese Jews who had officially converted to Christianity but secretly continued to observe Jewish practices. Jews were not officially permitted to resettle in England until the middle of the seventeenth century, and even then their legal status was ambiguous.

Shakespeare's England also had a small African population whose skin color was the subject of pseudoscientific speculation and theological debate. Some Elizabethans believed that Africans' blackness resulted from the climate of the regions in which they lived, where, as one traveler put it, they were "so scorched and vexed with the heat of the sun, that in many places they curse it when it riseth." Others held that blackness was a curse inherited from their forefather Chus, the son of Ham, who had, according to Genesis, wickedly exposed the nakedness of the drunken Noah. George Best, a proponent of this theory of inherited skin color, reported that "I myself have seen an Ethiopian as black as coal brought into England, who taking a fair English woman to wife, begat a son in all respects as black as the father was, although England were his native country, and an English woman his mother: whereby it seemeth this blackness proceedeth rather of some natural infection of that man."

As the word "infection" suggests, Elizabethans frequently regarded blackness as a physical defect, though the blacks who lived in England and Scotland throughout the sixteenth century were also treated as exotic curiosities. At his marriage to Anne of Denmark, James I entertained his bride and her family by commanding four naked black youths to dance before him in the snow. (The youths died of exposure shortly afterward.) In 1594, in the festivities celebrating the baptism of James's son, a "Black-Moor" entered pulling an elaborately decorated chariot that was, in the original plan, supposed to be drawn in by a lion. There was a black trumpeter in the courts of Henry VII and Henry VIII, while Elizabeth had at least two black servants, one an entertainer and the other a page. Africans became increasingly popular as servants in aristocratic and gentle households in the last decades of the sixteenth century.

Man with head beneath his shoulders. From a Spanish edition of Sir John Mandeville's *Travels*. See *Othello* 1.3.144–45: "and men whose heads / Do grow beneath their shoulders." Such men were occasionally reported by medieval travelers to the East.

An Indian dance. From Thomas Hariot, *A Briefe and True Report of the New Found Land of Virginia* (1590 ed.).

Some of these Africans were almost certainly slaves, though the legal status of slavery in England was ambiguous. In Cartwright's case (1569), the court ruled "that England was too Pure an Air for Slaves to breathe in," but there is evidence that black slaves were owned in Elizabethan and Jacobean England. Moreover, by the mid-sixteenth century, the English had become involved in the profitable trade that carried African slaves to the New World. In 1562, John Hawkins embarked on his first slaving voyage, transporting some three hundred blacks from the Guinea coast to Hispaniola, where they were sold for £10,000. Elizabeth is reported to have said of this venture that it was "detestable, and would call down the Vengeance of Heaven upon the Undertakers." Nevertheless, she invested in Hawkins's subsequent voyages and loaned him ships.

English men and women of the sixteenth century experienced an unprecedented increase in knowledge of the world beyond their island, for a number of reasons. Religious persecution compelled both Catholics and Protestants to live abroad; wealthy gentlemen (and, in at least a few cases, ladies) traveled in France and Italy to view the famous cultural monuments; merchants published accounts of distant lands such as Turkey, Morocco, and Russia; and military and trading ventures took English ships to still more distant shores. In 1496, a Venetian tradesman living in Bristol, John Cabot, was granted a license by Henry VII to sail on a voyage of exploration; with his son Sebastian, he discovered Newfoundland and Nova Scotia. Remarkable feats of seamanship and reconnaissance soon followed: on his ship the *Golden Hind,* Sir Francis Drake circumnavigated the globe in 1579 and laid claim to California on behalf of the queen; a few years later, a ship commanded by Thomas Cavendish also completed a circumnavigation. Sir Martin Frobisher explored bleak Baffin Island in search of a Northwest Passage to the Orient; Sir John Davis explored the west coast of Greenland and discovered the Falkland Islands off the coast of Argentina; Sir Walter Ralegh ventured up the Orinoco Delta, in what is now Venezuela, in search of the mythical land of El Dorado. Accounts of these and other exploits were collected by a clergyman and promoter of empire, Richard Hakluyt, and published as *The Principal Navigations* (1589; expanded edition 1599).

"To seek new worlds for gold, for praise, for glory," as Ralegh characterized such enterprises, was not for the faint of heart: Drake, Cavendish, Frobisher, and Hawkins all died at sea, as did huge numbers of those who sailed under their command. Elizabethans sensible enough to stay at home could do more than read written accounts of their fellow countrymen's far-reaching voyages. Expeditions brought back native plants (including, most famously, tobacco), animals, cultural artifacts, and, on occasion, samples of the native peoples themselves, most often seized against their will. There were exhibitions in London of a kidnapped Eskimo with his kayak and of Virginians with their canoes. Most of these miserable captives, violently uprooted and vulnerable to European diseases, quickly perished, but even in death they were evidently valuable property: when the English will not give one small coin "to relieve a lame beggar," one of the characters in *The Tempest* wryly remarks, "they will lay out ten to see a dead Indian" (2.2.30–31).

Perhaps most nations learn to define what they are by defining what they are not. This negative self-definition is, in any case, what Elizabethans seemed constantly to be doing, in travel books, sermons, political speeches, civic pageants, public exhibitions, and theatrical spectacles of otherness. The extraordinary variety of these exercises (which include public executions and urban riots, as well as more benign forms of curiosity) suggests that the boundaries of national identity were by no means clear and unequivocal. Even peoples whom English writers routinely, viciously stigmatize as irreducibly alien—Italians, Indians, Turks, and Jews—have a surprising instability in the Elizabethan imagination and may appear for brief, intense moments as powerful models to be admired and emulated before they resume their place as emblems of despised otherness.

James I and the Union of the Crowns

Though under great pressure to do so, the aging Elizabeth steadfastly refused to name her successor. It became increasingly apparent, however, that it would be James Stuart, the son of Mary, Queen of Scots, and by the time Elizabeth's health began to fail, several of her principal advisers, including her chief minister, Robert Cecil, had been for several years in secret correspondence with him in Edinburgh. Crowned King James VI of Scotland in 1567 when he was but one year old, Mary's son had been raised as a Protestant by his powerful guardians, and in 1589 he married a Protestant princess, Anne of Denmark. When Elizabeth died on March 24, 1603, English officials reported that on her deathbed the queen had named James to succeed her.

Upon his accession, James—now styled James VI of Scotland and James I of England—made plain his intention to unite his two kingdoms. As he told Parliament in 1604, "What God hath conjoined then, let no man separate. I am the husband, and all of the whole isle is my lawful wife; I am the head and it is my body; I am the shepherd and it is my flock." But the flock was less perfectly united than James optimistically envisioned: English and Scottish were sharply distinct identities, as were Welsh and Cornish and other peoples who were incorporated, with varying degrees of willingness, into the realm.

Fearing that to change the name of the kingdom would invalidate all laws and institutions established under the name of England, a fear that was partly real and partly a cover for anti-Scots prejudice, Parliament balked at James's desire to be called "King of

Funeral procession of Queen Elizabeth. From a watercolor sketch by an unknown artist (1603).

Great Britain" and resisted the unionist legislation that would have made Great Britain a legal reality. Although the English initially rejoiced at the peaceful transition from Elizabeth to her successor, there was a rising tide of resentment against James's advancement of Scots friends and his creation of new knighthoods. Lower down the social ladder, English and Scots occasionally clashed violently on the streets: in July 1603, James issued a proclamation against Scottish "insolencies," and in April 1604, he ordered the arrest of "swaggerers" waylaying Scots in London. The ensuing years did not bring the amity and docile obedience for which James hoped, and, though the navy now flew the Union Jack, combining the Scottish cross of St. Andrew and the English cross of St. George, the unification of the kingdoms remained throughout his reign an unfulfilled ambition.

Unfulfilled as well were James's lifelong dreams of ruling as an absolute monarch. Crown lawyers throughout Europe had long argued that a King, by virtue of his power to make law, must necessarily be above law. But in England, sovereignty was identified not with the King alone or with the people alone but with the "King in Parliament." Against his absolutist ambitions, James faced the crucial power to raise taxes that was vested not in the monarch but in the elected members of the Parliament. He faced as well a theory of republicanism that traced it roots back to ancient Rome and that prided itself on its steadfast and, if necessary, violent resistance to tyranny. Shakespeare's fascination with monarchy is apparent throughout his work, but in his Roman plays in particular, as well as in his long poem *The Rape of Lucrece*, he manifests an intense imaginative interest in the idea of a republic.

The Jacobean Court

With James as with Elizabeth, the royal court was the center of diplomacy, ambition, intrigue, and an intense jockeying for social position. As always in monarchies, proximity to the king's person was a central mark of favor, so that access to the royal bedchamber was one of the highest aims of the powerful, scheming lords who followed James from his sprawling London palace at Whitehall to the hunting lodges and country estates to which he loved to retreat. A coveted office, in the Jacobean as in the Tudor court, was the Groom of the Stool, the person who supervised the disposal of the king's wastes. The officeholder was close to the king at one of his most exposed and vulnerable moments, and enjoyed the further privilege of sleeping on a pallet at the foot of the royal bed and putting on the royal undershirt. Another, slightly less privileged official, the Gentleman of the Robes, dressed the king in his doublet and outer garments.

The royal lifestyle was increasingly expensive. Unlike Elizabeth, James had to maintain separate households for his queen and for the heir apparent, Prince Henry. (Upon Henry's death at the age of eighteen in 1612, his younger brother, Prince Charles, became heir, eventually succeeding his father in 1625.) James was also extremely generous to his friends, amassing his own huge debts in the course of paying off theirs. As early as 1605, he told his principal adviser that "it is a horror to me to think of the height of my place, the greatness of my debts, and the smallness of my means." This smallness notwithstanding, James continued to lavish gifts upon handsome favorites such as the Earl of Somerset, Robert Carr, and the Duke of Buckingham, George Villiers.

The attachment James formed for these favorites was highly romantic. "God so love me," the king wrote to Buckingham, "as I desire only to live in the world for your sake, and that I had rather live banished in any part of the earth with you than live a sorrowful widow's life without you." Such sentiments, not surprisingly, gave rise to widespread rumors of homosexual activities at court. The rumors are certainly plausible, even though the surviving evidence of same-sex relationships, at court or elsewhere, is extremely difficult to interpret. A statute of 1533 made "the detestable and abominable vice of buggery committed with mankind or beast" a felony punishable by death. (English law declined to recognize or criminalize lesbian acts.) The effect of the draconian laws against buggery and sodomy seems to have been to reduce actual prosecutions to the barest minimum: for the next hundred years, there are no known cases of trials resulting in a death sentence for homosexual activity alone. If the legal record is, therefore, unreliable as an index of the extent of homosexual relations, the literary record (including, most famously, the majority of Shakespeare's sonnets) is equally opaque. Any poetic avowal of male-male love may simply be a formal expression of affection based on classical models, or, alternatively, it may be an expression of passionate physical and spiritual love. The interpretive difficulty is compounded by the absence in the period of any clear reference to a homosexual "identity," even though there are many references to same-sex acts and feelings. What is clear is that male friendships at the court of James and elsewhere were suffused with a potential eroticism, at once delightful and threatening, that subsequent periods policed more anxiously.

In addition to the extravagant expenditures on his favorites, James was also the patron of ever more

James I. By John De Critz the Elder (c. 1606).

Two Young Men. By Crispin van den Broeck (c. 1590).

elaborate feasts and masques. Shakespeare's work provides a small glimpse of these in *The Tempest,* with its exotic banquet and its "majestic vision" of mythological goddesses and dancing nymphs and reapers. The actual Jacobean court masques, designed by the great architect, painter, and engineer Inigo Jones, were spectacular, fantastic, technically ingenious, and staggeringly costly celebrations of regal magnificence. With their exquisite costumes and their elegant blend of music, dancing, and poetry, the masques, generally performed by the noble lords and ladies of the court, were deliberately ephemeral exercises in conspicuous expenditure and consumption: by tradition, at the end of the performance, the private audience would rush forward and tear to pieces the gorgeous scenery. And although masques were enormously sophisticated entertainments, often on rather esoteric allegorical themes, they could on occasion collapse into grotesque excess. In a letter of 1606, Sir John Harington describes a masque in honor of the visiting Danish king in which the participants, no doubt toasting their royal majesties, had had too much to drink. A lady playing the part of the Queen of Sheba attempted to present precious gifts, "but, forgetting the steps arising to the canopy, overset her caskets into his Danish Majesty's lap. . . . His Majesty then got up and would dance with the Queen of Sheba; but he fell down and humbled himself before her, and was carried to an inner chamber and laid on a bed." Meanwhile, Harington writes, the masque continued with a pageant of Faith, Hope, and Charity, but Charity could barely keep her balance, while Hope and Faith "were both sick and spewing in the lower hall." This was, we can hope, not a typical occasion.

While the English seem initially to have welcomed James's free-spending ways as a change from the relative parsimoniousness of Queen Elizabeth, they were dismayed by its consequences. Elizabeth had died owing £400,000. In 1608, the royal debt had risen to £1,400,000 and was increasing by £140,000 a year. The money to pay off this debt, or at least to keep it under control, was raised by various means. These included customs farming (leasing the right to collect customs duties to private individuals); the highly unpopular impositions (duties on the import of nonnecessities, such as spices, silks, and currants); the sale of crown lands; the sale of baronetcies; and appeals to an increasingly grudging and recalcitrant Parliament. In 1614, Parliament demanded an end to impositions before it would relieve the king and was angrily dissolved without completing its business.

James's Religious Policy and the Persecution of Witches

Before his accession to the English throne, the king had made known his view of Puritans, the general name for a variety of Protestant sects that were agitating for a radical reform of the Church, the overthrow of its conservative hierarchy of bishops, and the rejection of a large number of traditional rituals and practices. In a book he wrote, *Basilikon Doron* (1599), James denounced "brainsick and heady preachers" who were prepared "to let King, people, law and all be trod underfoot." Yet he was not entirely unwilling to consider religious reforms. In religion, as in foreign policy, he was above all concerned to maintain peace.

On his way south to claim the throne of England in 1603, James was presented with the Millenary Petition (signed by 1,000 ministers), which urged him as "our physician" to heal the disease of lingering "popish" ceremonies. He responded by calling a conference on the ceremonies of the Church of England, which duly took place at Hampton Court Palace in January 1604. The delegates who spoke for reform were moderates, and there was little in the outcome to satisfy Puritans. Nevertheless, while the Church of England continued to cling to such remnants of the Catholic past as wedding rings, square caps, bishops, and Christmas, the conference did produce some reform in the area of ecclesiastical discipline. It also authorized a new English translation of the Bible, known as the King James Bible, which was printed in 1611, too late to have been extensively used by Shakespeare. Along with Shakespeare's works, the King James Bible has probably had the profoundest influence on the subsequent history of English literature.

Having arranged this compromise, James saw his main task as ensuring conformity. He promulgated the 1604 Canons (the first definitive code of canon law since the Reformation), which required all ministers to subscribe to three articles. The first affirmed royal supremacy; the second confirmed that there was nothing in the Book of Common Prayer "contrary to the Word of God" and required ministers to use only the authorized

The "swimming" of a suspected witch (1615).

services; the third asserted that the central tenets of the Church of England were "agreeable to the Word of God." There were strong objections to the second and third articles from those of Puritan leanings inside and outside the House of Commons. In the end, many ministers refused to conform or subscribe to the articles, but only about 90 of them, or 1 percent of the clergy, were deprived of their livings. In its theology and composition, the Church of England was little changed from what it had been under Elizabeth. In hindsight, what is most striking are the ominous signs of growing religious divisions that would by the 1640s burst forth in civil war and the execution of James's son Charles.

James seems to have taken seriously the official claims to the sacredness of kingship, and he certainly took seriously his own theories of religion and politics, which he had printed for the edification of his people. He was convinced that Satan, perpetually warring against God and His representatives on earth, was continually plotting against him. James thought, moreover, that he possessed special insight into Satan's wicked agents, the witches, and in 1597, while King of Scotland, he published his *Daemonology*, a learned exposition of their malign threat to his godly rule. Hundreds of witches, he believed, were involved in a 1590 conspiracy to kill him by raising storms at sea when he was sailing home from Denmark with his new bride.

In the 1590s, Scotland embarked on a virulent witch craze of the kind that had since the fifteenth century repeatedly afflicted France, Switzerland, and Germany, where many thousands of women (and a much smaller number of men) were caught in a nightmarish web of wild accusations. Tortured into lurid confessions of infant cannibalism, night flying, and sexual intercourse with the devil at huge, orgiastic "witches' Sabbaths," the victims had little chance to defend themselves and were routinely burned at the stake.

In England, too, there were witchcraft prosecutions, but on a much smaller scale and with significant differences in the nature of the accusations and the judicial procedures. Witch trials began in England in the 1540s; statutes against witchcraft were enacted in 1542, 1563, and 1604. English law did not allow judicial torture, stipulated lesser punishments in cases of "white magic," and mandated jury trials. Juries acquitted more than half of the defendants in witchcraft trials; in Essex, where the judicial records are particularly extensive, some 24 percent of those accused were executed, while the remainder of those convicted were pilloried and imprisoned or sentenced and reprieved. The accused were generally charged with *maleficium,* an evil deed—usually harming neighbors, causing destructive storms, or killing farm animals—but not with worshipping Satan.

After 1603, when James came to the English throne, he somewhat moderated his enthusiasm for the judicial murder of witches, for the most part defenseless, poor women resented by their neighbors. Although he did nothing to mitigate the ferocity of the ongoing witch hunts in his native Scotland, he did not try to institute Scottish-style persecutions and trials in his new realm. This relative waning of persecutorial eagerness principally reflects the differences between England and Scotland, but it may also bespeak some small, nascent skepticism on James's part about the quality of evidence brought against the accused and about the reliability of the "confessions" extracted from them. It is sobering to reflect that plays like Shakespeare's *Macbeth* (1606), Thomas Middleton's *Witch* (before 1616), and Thomas Dekker, John Ford, and William Rowley's *Witch of Edmonton* (1621) seem to be less the allies of skepticism than the exploiters of fear.

The Playing Field

Cosmic Spectacles

The first permanent, freestanding public theaters in England date only from Shakespeare's own lifetime: a London playhouse, the Red Lion, is mentioned in 1567, and James Burbage's playhouse, The Theatre, was built in 1576. (The innovative use of these new stages, crucial to a full understanding of Shakespeare's achievement, is, in this volume, the subject of a separate essay by the theater historian Andrew Gurr, pages 79–99.) But it is misleading to identify English drama exclusively with these specially constructed playhouses, for in fact there was a rich and vital theatrical tradition in England stretching back for centuries. Many towns in late medieval England were the sites of annual festivals that mounted elaborate cycles of plays depicting the great biblical stories, from the creation of the world to Christ's Passion and its miraculous aftermath. Most of these plays have been lost, but the surviving cycles, such as those from York, are magnificent and complex works of art. They are sometimes called "mystery plays," either because they were performed by the guilds of various crafts (known as "mysteries") or, more likely, because they represented the mysteries of the faith. The cycles were most often performed on the annual feast day instituted in the early fourteenth century in honor of the Corpus Christi, the sacrament of the Lord's Supper, which is perhaps the greatest of these religious mysteries.

The Feast of Corpus Christi, celebrated on the Thursday following Trinity Sunday, helped give the play cycles their extraordinary cultural resonance, but it also contributed to their downfall. For along with the specifically liturgical plays traditionally performed by religious confraternities and the "saints' plays," which depicted miraculous events in the lives of individual holy men and women, the mystery cycles were closely identified with the Catholic Church. Protestant authorities in the sixteenth century, eager to eradicate all remnants of popular Catholic piety, moved to suppress the annual procession of the Host, with its gorgeous banners, pageant carts, and cycle of visionary plays. In 1548, the Feast of Corpus Christi was abolished. Towns that continued to perform the mysteries were under increasing pressure to abandon them. It is sometimes said that the cycles were already dying out from neglect, but recent research has shown that many towns and their guilds were extremely reluctant to give them up. Desperate offers to strip away any traces of Catholic doctrine and to submit the play scripts to the authorities for their approval met with unbending opposition from the government. In 1576, the courts gave York permission to perform its cycle but only if

> in the said play no pageant be used or set forth wherein the Majesty of God the Father, God the Son, or God the Holy Ghost or the administration of either the Sacraments of baptism or of the Lord's Supper be counterfeited or represented, or anything played which tend to the maintenance of superstition and idolatry or which be contrary to the laws of God . . . or of the realm.

Such "permission" was tantamount to an outright ban. The local officials in the city of Norwich, proud of their St. George and the Dragon play, asked if they could at least parade the dragon costume through the streets, but even this modest request was refused. It is likely that as a young man Shakespeare had seen some of these plays: when Hamlet says of a noisy, strutting theatrical performance that it "out-Herods Herod," he is alluding to the famously bombastic role of Herod of Jewry in the mystery plays. But by the century's end, the cycles were no longer performed.

Early English theater was by no means restricted to these civic and religious festivals. Payments to professional and amateur performers appear in early records of towns and aristocratic households, although the terms—"ministralli," "histriones," "mimi," "lusores," and so forth—are not used with great consistency and make it difficult to distinguish among minstrels, jugglers, stage players, and other entertainers. Performers acted in town halls and the halls of guilds and aristocratic mansions, on scaffolds erected in town squares and marketplaces, on pageant wagons in the streets, and in inn yards. By the fifteenth century and probably earlier, there were organized companies of players traveling under noble patronage. Such companies earned a living providing amusement, while enhancing the prestige of the patron.

A description of a provincial performance in the late sixteenth century, written by one R. Willis, provides a glimpse of what seems to have been the usual procedure:

> In the City of Gloucester the manner is (as I think it is in other like corporations) that when the Players of Interludes come to town, they first attend the Mayor to

Panorama of London, showing two theaters, both
round and both flying flags: a flying flag indicated that
a performance was in progress. The Globe is in the
foreground, and the Beargarden or Hope is to the left.

inform him what nobleman's servant they are, and so to get licence for their public
playing; and if the Mayor like the Actors, or would show respect to their Lord and
Master, he appoints them to play their first play before himself and the Aldermen
and common Council of the City and that is called the Mayor's play, where everyone that will come in without money, the Mayor giving the players a reward as he
thinks fit to show respect unto them.

In addition to their take from this "first play," the players would almost certainly have
supplemented their income by performing in halls and inn yards, where they could pass
the hat after the performance or even on some occasions charge an admission fee. It
was no doubt a precarious existence.

The "Interludes" mentioned in Willis's description of the Gloucester performances
are likely plays that were, in effect, staged dialogues on religious, moral, and political
themes. Such works could, like the mysteries, be associated with Catholicism, but they
were also used in the sixteenth century to convey polemical Protestant messages, and
they reached outside the religious sphere to address secular concerns as well. Henry
Medwall's *Fulgens and Lucrece* (c. 1490–1501), for example, pits a wealthy but dissolute nobleman against a virtuous public servant of humble origins, while John Heywood's *Play of the Weather* (c. 1525–33) stages a debate among social rivals, including
a gentleman, a merchant, a forest ranger, and two millers. The structure of such plays
reflects the training in argumentation that students received in Tudor schools and, in
particular, the sustained practice in examining all sides of a difficult question. Some of
Shakespeare's amazing ability to look at critical issues from multiple perspectives may
be traced back to this practice and the dramatic interludes it helped to inspire.

Another major form of theater that flourished in England in the fifteenth century
and continued on into the sixteenth was the morality play. Like the mysteries, moralities addressed questions of the ultimate fate of the soul. They did so, however, not by
rehearsing scriptural stories but by dramatizing allegories of spiritual struggle. Typically,
a person named Human or Mankind or Youth is faced with a choice between a pious
life in the company of such associates as Mercy, Discretion, and Good Deeds and a dissolute life among riotous companions like Lust or Mischief. Plays like *Mankind* (c.
1465–70) and *Everyman* (c. 1495) show how powerful these unpromising-sounding
dramas could be, in part because of the extraordinary comic vitality of the evil character, or Vice, and in part because of the poignancy and terror of an individual's encounter
with death. Shakespeare clearly grasped this power. The hunchbacked Duke of
Gloucester in *Richard III* gleefully likens himself to "the formal Vice, Iniquity." And

when Othello wavers between Desdemona and Iago (himself a Vice figure), his anguished dilemma echoes the fateful choice repeatedly faced by the troubled, vulnerable protagonists of the moralities.

If such plays sound a bit like sermons, it is because they were. Clerics and actors shared some of the same rhetorical skills. It would be misleading to regard churchgoing and playgoing as comparable entertainments, but in attacking the stage, ministers often seemed to regard the professional players as dangerous rivals. The players themselves were generally too discreet to rise to the challenge; it would have been foolhardy to present the theater as the Church's direct competitor. Yet in its moral intensity and its command of impassioned language, the stage frequently emulates and outdoes the pulpit.

Music and Dance

Playacting took its place alongside other forms of public expression and entertainment as well. Perhaps the most important, from the perspective of the theater, were music and dance, since these were directly and repeatedly incorporated into plays. Many plays, comedies and tragedies alike, include occasions that call upon the characters to dance: hence Beatrice and Benedick join the other masked guests at the dance in *Much Ado About Nothing;* in *Twelfth Night,* the befuddled Sir Andrew, at the instigation of the drunken Sir Toby Belch, displays his skill, such as it is, in capering; Romeo and Juliet first see each other at the Capulet ball; the witches dance in a ring around the hideous caldron and perform an "antic round" to cheer Macbeth's spirits; and, in one of Shakespeare's strangest and most wonderful scenes, the drunken Antony in *Antony and Cleopatra* joins hands with Caesar, Enobarbus, Pompey, and others to dance "the Egyptian Bacchanals."

Moreover, virtually all plays in the period, including Shakespeare's, apparently ended with a dance. Brushing off the theatrical gore and changing their expressions from woe to pleasure, the actors in plays like *Hamlet* and *King Lear* would presumably have received the audience's applause and then bid for a second round of applause by performing a stately pavane or a lively jig. Indeed, jigs, with their comical leaping dance steps often accompanied by scurrilous ballads, became so popular that they drew not only large crowds but also official disapproval. A court order of 1612 complained about the "cutpurses and other lewd and ill-disposed persons" who flocked to the theater at the end of every play to be entertained by "lewd jigs, songs, and dances." The players were warned to suppress these disreputable entertainments on pain of imprisonment.

The displays of dancing onstage clearly reflected a widespread popular interest in dancing outside the walls of the playhouse as well. Renaissance intellectuals conjured up visions of the universe as a great cosmic dance, poets figured relations between men and women in terms of popular dance steps, stern moralists denounced dancing as an incitement to filthy lewdness, and, perhaps as significant, men of all classes evidently spent a great deal of time worrying about how shapely their legs looked in tights and how gracefully they could leap. Shakespeare assumes that his audience will be quite familiar with a variety of dances. "For hear me, Hero," Beatrice tells her friend, "wooing, wedding, and repenting is as a Scotch jig, a measure, and a cinquepace" (2.1.60–61). Her speech dwells on the comparison a bit, teasing out its implications, but it still does not make much sense if you do not already know something about the dances and perhaps occasionally venture to perform them yourself.

Closely linked to dancing and even more central to the stage was music, both instrumental and vocal. In the early sixteenth century, the Reformation had been disastrous for sacred music: many church organs were destroyed, choir schools were closed, the glorious polyphonal liturgies sung in the monasteries were suppressed. But by the latter part of the century, new perspectives were reinvigorating English music. Latin Masses were reset in English, and tunes were written for newly translated, metrical psalms. More important for the theater, styles of secular music were developed that emphasized music's link to humanist eloquence, its ability to heighten and to rival rhetorically powerful texts.

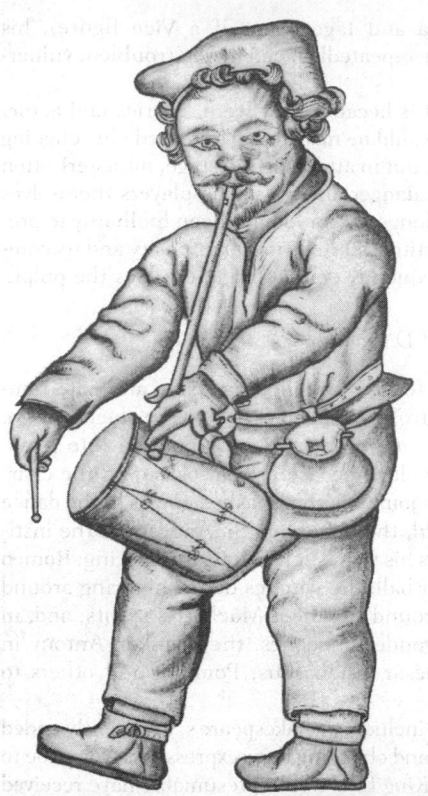

Richard Tarlton. Tarlton was the lead comedian of the Queen's Company from 1583, the year of its founding, until 1588, when he died.

This link is particularly evident in vocal music, at which Elizabethan composers excelled. Renowned composers William Byrd, Thomas Morley, John Dowland, and others wrote a rich profusion of madrigals (part songs for two to eight voices unaccompanied) and ayres (songs for solo voice, generally accompanied by the lute). These works, along with hymns, popular ballads, rounds, catches, and other forms of song, enjoyed immense popularity, not only in the royal court, where musical skill was regarded as an important accomplishment, and in aristocratic households, where professional musicians were employed as entertainers, but also in less exalted social circles. In his *Plaine and Easie Introduction to Practicall Musicke* (1597), Morley tells a story of social humiliation at a failure to perform that suggests that a well-educated Elizabethan was expected to be able to sing at sight. Even if this is an exaggeration in the interest of book sales, there is evidence of impressively widespread musical literacy, reflected in a splendid array of music for the lute, viol, recorder, harp, and virginal, as well as the marvelous vocal music.

Whether it is the aristocratic Orsino luxuriating in the dying fall of an exquisite melody or bully Bottom craving "the tongs and the bones," Shakespeare's characters frequently call for music. They also repeatedly give voice to the age's conviction that there was a deep relation between musical harmony and the harmonies of the well-ordered individual and state. "The man that hath no music in himself," warns Lorenzo in *The Merchant of Venice*, "nor is not moved with concord of sweet sounds, / Is fit for treasons, stratagems, and spoils" (5.1.82–84). This conviction, in turn, reflects a still deeper link between musical harmony and the divinely created harmony of the cosmos. When Ulysses, in *Troilus and Cressida*, wishes to convey the image of universal chaos, he speaks of the untuning of a string (1.3.109).

The playing companies must have regularly employed trained musicians, and many actors (like the actor who in playing Pandarus in *Troilus and Cressida* is supposed to accompany himself on the lute) must have possessed musical skill. Unfortunately, we possess the original settings for very few of Shakespeare's songs, possibly because many of them may have been set to popular tunes of the time that everyone knew and no one bothered to write down.

Alternative Entertainments

Plays, music, and dancing were by no means the only shows in town. There were jousts, tournaments, royal entries, religious processions, pageants in honor of newly installed civic officials or ambassadors arriving from abroad; wedding masques, court masques, and costumed entertainments known as "disguisings" or "mummings"; juggling acts, fortune-tellers, exhibitions of swordsmanship, mountebanks, folk healers, storytellers, magic shows; bearbaiting, bullbaiting, cockfighting, and other blood sports; folk festivals such as Maying, the Feast of Fools, Carnival, and Whitsun Ales. For several years, Elizabethan Londoners were delighted by a trained animal—Banks's Horse—that could, it was thought, do arithmetic and answer questions. And there was always the grim but compelling spectacle of public shaming, mutilation, and execution.

Most English towns had stocks and whipping posts. Drunks, fraudulent merchants, adulterers, and quarrelers could be placed in carts or mounted backward on asses and paraded through the streets for crowds to jeer and throw refuse at. Women accused of being scolds could be publicly muzzled by an iron device called a "brank" or tied to a cucking stool and dunked in the river. Convicted criminals could have their ears cut off, their noses slit, their foreheads branded. Public beheadings (generally reserved for the elite) and hangings were common. In the worst cases, felons were sentenced to be "hanged by the neck, and being alive cut down, and your privy members to be cut off, and your bowels to be taken out of your belly and there burned, you being alive."

Shakespeare occasionally takes note of these alternative entertainments: at the end of *Macbeth*, for example, with his enemies closing in on him, the doomed tyrant declares, "They have tied me to a stake. I cannot fly, / But bear-like I must fight the course" (5.7.1–2). The audience is reminded then that it is witnessing the human equivalent of a popular spectacle—a bear chained to a stake and attacked by fierce dogs—that they could have paid to watch at an arena near the Globe. And when, a few moments later, Macduff enters carrying Macbeth's head, the audience is seeing the theatrical equivalent of the execution of criminals and traitors that they could have also watched in the flesh, as it were, nearby. In a different key, the audiences who paid to see *A Midsummer Night's Dream* or *The Winter's Tale* got to enjoy the comic spectacle of a Maying and a Whitsun Pastoral, while the spectators of *The Tempest* could gawk at what the Folio list of characters calls a "salvage and deformed slave" and to enjoy an aristocratic magician's wedding masque in honor of his daughter.

An Elizabethan hanging.

The Enemies of the Stage

In 1624, a touring company of players arrived in Norwich and requested permission to perform. Permission was denied, but the municipal authorities, "in regard of the honorable respect which this City beareth to the right honorable the Lord Chamberlain," gave the players 20 shillings to get out of town. Throughout the sixteenth and early seventeenth centuries, there are many similar records of civic officials prohibiting performances and then, to appease a powerful patron, paying the actors to take their skills elsewhere. As early as the 1570s, there is evidence that the London authorities, while mindful of the players' influential protectors, were energetically trying to drive the theater out of the city.

Why should what we now regard as one of the undisputed glories of the age have aroused so much hostility? One answer, curiously enough, is traffic: plays drew large audiences—the public theaters could accommodate thousands—and residents objected to the crowds, the noise, and the crush of carriages. Other, more serious concerns were public health and crime. It was thought that numerous diseases, including the dreaded bubonic plague, were spread by noxious odors, and the packed playhouses were obvious breeding grounds for infection. (Patrons often tried to protect themselves by sniffing nosegays or stuffing cloves into their nostrils.) The large crowds drew pickpockets and other scoundrels. On one memorable afternoon, a pickpocket was caught in the act and tied for the duration of the play to one of the posts that held up the canopy above the stage.

The theater was, moreover, a well-known haunt of prostitutes and, it was alleged, a place where innocent maids were seduced and respectable matrons corrupted. It was darkly rumored that "chambers and secret places" adjoined the theater galleries, and in any case, taverns, disreputable inns, and whorehouses were close at hand.

There were other charges as well. Plays were performed in the afternoon and, therefore, drew people, especially the young, away from their work. They were schools of idleness, luring apprentices from their trades, law students from their studies, housewives from their kitchens, and potentially pious souls from the sober meditations to which they might otherwise devote themselves. Wasting their time and money on disreputable shows, citizens exposed themselves to sexual provocation and outright political sedition. Even when the content of plays was morally exemplary—and, of course, few plays were so gratifyingly high-minded—the theater itself, in the eyes of most mayors and aldermen, was inherently disorderly.

The attack on the stage by civic officials was echoed and intensified by many of the age's moralists and

Syphilis victim in a tub. Frontispiece to the play *Cornelianum Dolium* (1638), possibly authored by Thomas Randolph. The tub inscription translates as "I sit on the throne of love, I suffer in the tub," and the banner as "Farewell O sexual pleasures and lusts."

religious leaders, especially those associated with Puritanism. While English Protestants earlier in the sixteenth century had attempted to counter the Catholic mystery cycles and saints' plays by mounting their own doctrinally correct dramas, by the century's end a fairly widespread consensus, even among those mildly sympathetic toward the theater, held that the stage and the pulpit were in tension with one another. After 1591, a ban on Sunday performances was strictly enforced, and in 1606, Parliament passed an act imposing a fine of £10 on any person who shall "in any stage-play, interlude, show, May-game, or pageant, jestingly or profanely speak or use the holy name of God, or of Christ Jesus, or of the Holy Ghost, or of the Trinity (which are not to be spoken but with fear and reverence)." If changes in the printed texts are a reliable indication, the players seem to have complied at least to some degree with the ruling. The Folio (1623) text of *Richard III*, for example, omits the Quarto's (1597) four uses of "zounds" (for "God's wounds"), along with a mention of "Christ's dear blood shed for our grievous sins"; "God's my judge" in *The Merchant of Venice* becomes "well I know"; "By Jesu" in *Henry V* becomes a very proper "I say"; and in all the plays, "God" from time to time metamorphoses to "Jove."

But for some of the theater's more extreme critics, these modest expurgations were tiny bandages on a gaping wound. In his huge book *Histriomastix* (1633), William Prynne regurgitates half a century of frenzied attacks on the "sinful, heathenish, lewd, ungodly Spectacles." In the eyes of Prynne and his fellow antitheatricalists, stage plays were part of a demonic tangle of obscene practices proliferating like a cancer in the body of society. It is "manifest to all men's judgments," he writes, that

> effeminate mixed dancing, dicing, stage-plays, lascivious pictures, wanton fashions, face-painting, health-drinking, long hair, love-locks, periwigs, women's curling, powdering and cutting of their hair, bonfires, New-year's gifts, May-games, amorous pastorals, lascivious effeminate music, excessive laughter, luxurious disorderly Christmas-keeping, mummeries . . . [are] wicked, unchristian pastimes.

Given the anxious emphasis on effeminacy, it is not surprising that denunciations of this kind obsessively focused on the use of boy actors to play the female parts. The enemies of the stage charged that theatrical transvestism excited illicit sexual desires, both heterosexual and homosexual.

Since cross-dressing violated a biblical prohibition (Deuteronomy 22:5), religious antitheatricalists attacked it as wicked regardless of its erotic charge; indeed, they often seemed to consider any act of impersonation as inherently wicked. In their view, the theater itself was Satan's domain. Thus a Cambridge scholar, John Greene, reports the sad fate of "a Christian woman" who went to the theater to see a play: "She entered in well and sound, but she returned and came forth possessed of the devil. Whereupon certain godly brethren demanded Satan how he durst be so bold, as to enter into her a Christian. Whereto he answered, that *he found her in his own house,* and therefore took possession of her as his own" (italic in original). When the "godly brethren" came to power in the mid-seventeenth century, with the overthrow of Charles I, they saw to it that the playhouses, temporarily shut down in 1642 at the onset of the Civil War, remained closed. The theater did not resume until the restoration of the monarchy in 1660.

Faced with enemies among civic officials and religious leaders, Elizabethan and Jacobean playing companies relied on the protection of their powerful patrons. As the liveried servants of aristocrats or of the monarch, the players could refute the charge that they were mere vagabonds, and they claimed, as a convenient legal fiction, that their public performances were necessary rehearsals in anticipation of those occasions when they would be called upon to entertain their noble masters. But harassment by the mayor and aldermen continued unabated, and the players were forced to build their theaters outside the immediate jurisdiction of the city authorities, either in the suburbs or in the areas known as the "liberties." A liberty was a piece of land within the City of London itself that was not directly subject to the authority of the lord mayor. The most significant of these from the point of view of the theater was the area near St. Paul's Cathedral called "the Blackfriars," where, until the dissolution of the monasteries in 1538, there had been a

Dominican monastery. It was here that in 1608 Shakespeare's company, then called the King's Men, built the indoor playhouse in which they performed during the winter months, reserving the open-air Globe in the suburb of Southwark for their summer performances.

Censorship and Regulation

In addition to those authorities who campaigned to shut down the theater, there were others whose task was to oversee, regulate, and censor it. Given the outright hostility of the former, the latter may have seemed to the London players equivocal allies rather than enemies. After all, plays that passed the censor were at least licensed to be performed and hence conceded to have some limited legitimacy. In April 1559, at the very start of her reign, Queen Elizabeth drafted a proposal that for the first time envisaged a system for the prior review and regulation of plays throughout her kingdom:

> The Queen's Majesty doth straightly forbid all manner interludes to be played either openly or privately, except the same be notified beforehand, and licensed within any city or town corporate, by the mayor or other chief officers of the same, and within any shire, by such as shall be lieutenants for the Queen's Majesty in the same shire, or by two of the Justices of Peace inhabiting within that part of the shire where any shall be played. . . . And for instruction to every of the said officers, her Majesty doth likewise charge every of them, as they will answer: that they permit none to be played wherein either matters of religion or of the governance of the estate of the commonweal shall be handled or treated upon, but by men of authority, learning and wisdom, nor to be handled before any audience, but of grave and discreet persons.

This proposal, which may not have been formally enacted, makes an important distinction between those who are entitled to address sensitive issues of religion and politics—authors "of authority, learning and wisdom" addressing audiences "of grave and discreet persons"—and those who are forbidden to do so.

The London public theater, with its playwrights who were the sons of glovers, shoemakers, and bricklayers and its audiences in which the privileged classes mingled with rowdy apprentices, masked women, and servants, was clearly not a place to which the government wished to grant freedom of expression. In 1581, the Master of the Revels, an official in the lord chamberlain's department whose role had hitherto been to provide entertainment at court, was given an expanded commission. Sir Edmund Tilney, the functionary who held the office, was authorized

> to warn, command, and appoint in all places within this our Realm of England, as well within franchises and liberties as without, all and every player or players with their playmakers, either belonging to any nobleman or otherwise . . . to appear before him with all such plays, tragedies, comedies, or shows as they shall in readiness or mean to set forth, and them to recite before our said Servant or his sufficient deputy, whom we ordain, appoint, and authorize by these presents of all such shows, plays, players, and playmakers, together with their playing places, to order and reform, authorize and put down, as shall be thought meet or unmeet unto himself or his said deputy in that behalf.

What emerged from this commission was in effect a national system of regulation and censorship. One of its consequences was to restrict virtually all licensed theater to the handful of authorized London-based playing companies. These companies would have to submit their plays for official scrutiny, but in return they received implicit, and on occasion explicit, protection against the continued fierce opposition of the local authorities. Plays reviewed and allowed by the Master of the Revels had been deemed fit to be performed before the monarch; how could mere aldermen legitimately claim that such plays should be banned as seditious?

The key question, of course, is how carefully the Master of the Revels scrutinized the plays brought before him either to hear or, more often from the 1590s onward, to peruse. What was Tilney, who served in the office until his death in 1610, or his successor, Sir George Buc, who served from 1610 to 1621, looking for? What did they insist be cut before they would release what was known as the "allowed copy," the only version licensed for performance? Unfortunately, the office books of the Master of the Revels in Shakespeare's time have been lost; what survives is a handful of scripts on which Tilney, Buc, and their assistants jotted their instructions. These suggest that the readings were rather painstaking, with careful attention paid to possible religious, political, and diplomatic repercussions. References, directly or strongly implied, to any living Christian prince or any important English nobleman, gentleman, or government official were particularly sensitive and likely to be struck. Renaissance political life was highly personalized; people in power were exceptionally alert to insult and zealously patrolled the boundaries of their prestige and reputation.

Moreover, the censors knew that audiences and readers were quite adept at applying theatrical representations distanced in time and space to their own world. At a time of riots against resident foreigners, Tilney read *Sir Thomas More*, a play in which Shakespeare probably had a hand, and instructed the players to cut scenes that, even though they were set in 1517, might have had an uncomfortable contemporary resonance. "Leave out the insurrection wholly," Tilney's note reads, "and the cause thereof and begin with Sir Thomas More at the Mayor's sessions, with a report afterwards of his good service done being sheriff of London upon a mutiny against the Lombards only by a short report and not otherwise at your own perils. E. Tilney." Of course, as Tilney knew perfectly well, most plays succeed precisely by mirroring, if only obliquely, their own times, but this particular reflection evidently seemed to him too dangerous or provocative.

The topical significance of a play depends in large measure on the particular moment in which it is performed and on certain features of the performance—for example, a striking resemblance between one of the characters and a well-known public figure—that the script itself will not necessarily disclose to us at this great distance or even to the censor at the time. Hence the Master of the Revels noted angrily of one play performed in 1632 that "there were diverse personated so naturally, both of lords and others of the court, that I took it ill." Hence, too, a play that was deemed allowable when it was first written and performed could return, like a nightmare, to haunt a different place and time. The most famous instance of such a return involves Shakespeare, for on the day before the Earl of Essex's attempted coup against Queen Elizabeth in 1601, someone paid the Lord Chamberlain's Men (the name of Shakespeare's company at the time) 40 shillings to revive their old play about the deposition and murder of Richard II. "I am Richard II," the queen declared. "Know ye not that?" However distressed she was by this performance, the queen significantly did not take out her wrath on the players: neither the playwright nor his company was punished, nor was the Master of the Revels criticized for allowing the play in the first place. It was Essex and several of his key supporters who lost their heads.

Evidence suggests that the Master of the Revels often regarded himself not as the strict censor of the theater but as its friendly guardian, charged with averting catastrophes. He was a bureaucrat concerned less with subversive ideas per se than with potential trouble. That is, there is no record of a dramatist being called to account for his heterodox beliefs; rather, plays were censored if they risked offending influential people, including important foreign allies, or if they threatened to cause public disorder by exacerbating religious or other controversies. The distinction is not a stable one, but it helps to explain the intellectual boldness, power, and freedom of a censored theater in a society in which the perceived enemies of the state were treated mercilessly. Shakespeare could have Lear articulate a searing indictment of social injustice—

> Robes and furred gowns hide all. Plate sin with gold,
> And the strong lance of justice hurtless breaks;
> Arm it in rags, a pygmy's straw does pierce it.
>
> (4.5.155–57)

—and evidently neither the Master of the Revels nor the courtiers in their robes and furred gowns protested. But when the Spanish ambassador complained about Thomas Middleton's anti-Spanish allegory *A Game at Chess,* performed at the Globe in 1624, the whole theater was shut down, the players were arrested, and the king professed to be furious at his official for licensing the play in the first place and allowing it to be performed for nine consecutive days.

In addition to the system for the licensing of plays for performance, there was also a system for the licensing of plays for publication. At the start of Shakespeare's career, such press licensing was the responsibility of the Court of High Commission, headed by the Archbishop of Canterbury and the Bishop of London. Their deputies, a panel of junior clerics, were supposed to review the manuscripts, granting licenses to those worthy of publication and rejecting any they deemed "heretical, seditious, or unseemly for Christian ears." Without a license, the Stationers' Company, the guild of the book trade, was not supposed to register a manuscript for publication. In practice, as various complaints and attempts to close loopholes attest, some playbooks were printed without a license. In 1607, the system was significantly revised when Sir George Buc began to license plays for the press. When Buc succeeded to the post of Master of the Revels in 1610, the powers to license plays for the stage and the page were vested in one man.

Theatrical Innovations

The theater continued to flourish under this system of regulation after Shakespeare's death; by the 1630s, as many as five playhouses were operating daily in London. When the theater reemerged after the eighteen-year hiatus imposed by Puritan rule, it quickly resumed its cultural importance, but not without a number of significant changes. Major innovations in staging resulted principally from Continental influences on the English artists who accompanied the court of Charles II into exile in France, where they supplied it with masques and other theatrical entertainments.

The institutional conditions and business practices of the two companies chartered by Charles after the Restoration in 1660 also differed from those of Shakespeare's theater. In place of the more collective practice of Shakespeare's company, the Restoration theaters were controlled by celebrated actor-managers who not only assigned themselves starring roles, in both comedy and tragedy, but also assumed sole responsibility for many business decisions, including the setting of their colleagues' salaries. At the same time, the power of the actor-manager, great as it was, was limited by the new importance of outside capital. No longer was the theater, with all of its properties from script to costumes, owned by the "sharers"—that is, by those actors who held shares in the joint-stock company. Instead, entrepreneurs would raise capital for increasingly fantastic sets and stage machinery that could cost as much as £3,000, an astronomical sum, for a single production. This investment, in turn, not only influenced the kinds of new plays written for the theater but helped to transform old plays that were revived, including Shakespeare's.

In his diary entry for August 24, 1661, Samuel Pepys notes that he has been "to the Opera, and there saw Hamlet, Prince of Denmark, done with scenes very well, but above all, Betterton did the prince's part beyond imagination." This is Thomas Betterton's first review, as it were, and it is typical of the enthusiasm he would inspire throughout his fifty-year career on the London stage. Pepys's brief and scattered remarks on the plays he voraciously attended in the 1660s are precious because they are among the few records from the period of concrete and immediate responses to theatrical performances. Modern readers might miss the significance of Pepys's phrase "done with scenes": this production of *Hamlet* was only the third play to use the movable sets first introduced to England by its producer, William Davenant. The central historical fact that makes the productions of this period so exciting is that public theater had been banned altogether for eighteen years until the Restoration of Charles II.

A brief discussion of theatrical developments in the Restoration period will enable us at least to glance longingly at a vast subject that lies outside the scope of this introduction: the rich performance history that extends from Shakespeare's time to our own, involving tens of thousands of productions and adaptations for theater, opera, Broadway musicals, and, of course, films. The scale of this history is vast in space as well as time: as early as 1607, there is a record of a *Hamlet* performed on board an English ship, HMS *Dragon,* off the coast of Sierra Leone, and troupes of English actors performed in the late sixteenth and early seventeenth centuries as far afield as Poland and Bohemia.

William Davenant, who claimed to be Shakespeare's bastard son, had become an expert on stage scenery while producing masques at the court of Charles I, and when the theaters reopened, he set to work on converting an indoor tennis court into a new kind of theater. He designed a broad open platform like that of the Elizabethan stage, but he replaced the relatively shallow space for "discoveries" (tableaux set up in an opening at the center of the stage, revealed by drawing back a curtain) and the "tiring-house" (the players' dressing room) behind this space with one expanded interior, framed by a proscenium arch, in which scenes could be displayed. These elaborately painted scenes could be moved on and off, using grooves on the floor. The perspectival effect for a spectator of one central painted panel with two "wings" on either side was that of three sides of a room. This effect anticipated that of the familiar "picture frame" stage, developed fully in the nineteenth century, and began a subtle shift in theater away from the elaborate verbal descriptions that are so central to Shakespeare and toward the evocative visual poetry of the set designer's art.

Another convention of Shakespeare's stage, the use of boy actors for female roles, gave way to the more complete illusion of women playing women's parts. The king issued a decree in 1662 forcefully permitting, if not requiring, the use of actresses. The royal decree is couched in the language of social and moral reform: the introduction of actresses will require the "reformation" of scurrilous and profane passages in plays, and this, in turn, will help forestall some of the objections that shut the theaters down in 1642. In reality, male theater audiences, composed of a narrower range of courtiers and aristocrats than in Shakespeare's time, met this intended reform with the assumption that the new actresses were fair game sexually; most actresses (with the partial exception of those who married male members of their troupes) were regarded as, or actually became, whores. But despite the social stigma and the fact that their salaries were predictably lower than those of their male counterparts, the stage saw some formidable female stars by the 1680s.

The first recorded appearance of an actress was that of a Desdemona in December 1660. Betterton's Ophelia in 1661 was Mary Saunderson (c. 1637–1712), who became Mrs. Betterton a year later. The most famous Ophelia of the period was Susanna Mountfort, who appeared in that role for the first time at the age of fifteen in 1705. The performance by Mountfort that became legendary occurred in 1720, after a disappointment in love, or so it was said, had driven her mad. Hearing that *Hamlet* was being performed, Mountfort escaped from her keepers and reached the theater, where she concealed herself until the scene in which Ophelia enters in her state of insanity. At this point, Mountfort rushed onto the stage and, in the words of a contemporary, "was in truth Ophelia herself, to the amazement of the performers and the astonishment of the audience."

That the character Ophelia became increasingly and decisively identified with the mad scene owes something to this occurrence, but it is also a consequence of the text used for Restoration performances of *Hamlet.* Having received the performance rights to a good number of Shakespeare's plays, Davenant altered them for the stage in the 1660s, and many of these acting versions remained in use for generations. In the case of *Hamlet,* neither Davenant nor his successors did what they so often did with other plays by Shakespeare—that is, alter the plot radically and interpolate other material. But many of the lines were cut or "improved." The cuts included most of Ophelia's sane speeches, such as her spirited retort to Laertes' moralizing; what remained made her part almost entirely an emblem of "female love melancholy."

Thomas Betterton (1635–1710), the prototype of the actor-manager, who would be the dominant figure in Shakespeare interpretation and in the theater generally through

The Spanish Tragedie:

OR,

Hieronimo is mad againe.

Containing the lamentable end of *Don Horatio*, and
Belimperia; with the pittifull death of *Hieronimo.*

Newly corrected, amended, and enlarged with new
Additions of the *Painters* part, and others, as
it hath of late been diuers times acted.

LONDON,

Printed by W. White, for I. White and T. Langley,
and are to be sold at their Shop ouer againft the
Sarazens head without New-gate. 1615.

Title page of Thomas Kyd's *Spanish Tragedie*
(1615). The first known edition dates from 1592.

the nineteenth century, made Hamlet his premier role. A contemporary who saw his last performance in the part (at the age of seventy-four, a rather old Prince of Denmark) wrote that to *read* Shakespeare's play was to encounter "dry, incoherent, & broken sentences," but that to see Betterton was to "prove" that the play was written "correctly." Spectators especially admired his reaction to the Ghost's appearance in the Queen's bedchamber: "his Countenance . . . thro' the violent and sudden Emotions of Amazement and Horror, turn[ed] instantly on the Sight of his fathers Spirit, as pale as his Neckcloath, when every Article of his Body seem's affected with a Tremor inexpressible." A piece of stage business in this scene, Betterton's upsetting his chair on the Ghost's entrance, became so thoroughly identified with the part that later productions were censured if the actor left it out. This business could very well have been handed down from Richard Burbage, the star of Shakespeare's original production, for Davenant, who had coached Betterton in the role, had known the performances of Joseph Taylor, who had succeeded Burbage in it. It is strangely gratifying to notice that Hamlets on stage and screen still occasionally upset their chairs.

Shakespeare's Life and Art

Playwrights, even hugely successful playwrights, were not ordinarily the objects of popular curiosity in early modern England, and few personal documents survive from Shakespeare's life of the kind that usually give the biographies of artists their appeal: no diary, no letters, private or public, no accounts of his childhood, almost no contemporary gossip, no scandals. Shakespeare's exact contemporary, the great playwright Christopher Marlowe, lived a mere twenty-nine years—he was murdered in 1593—but he left behind tantalizing glimpses of himself in police documents, the memos of high-ranking government officials, and detailed denunciations by sinister double agents. Ben Jonson recorded his opinions and his reading in a remarkable published notebook, *Timber; or, Discoveries Made upon Men and Matter,* and he also shared his views of the world (including some criticisms of his fellow playwright Shakespeare) with a Scottish poet, William Drummond of Hawthornden, who had the wit to jot them down for posterity. From Shakespeare, there is nothing comparable, not even a book with his name scribbled on the cover and a few marginal notes such as we have for Jonson, let alone working notebooks.

Yet Elizabethan England was a record-keeping society, and centuries of archival labor have turned up a substantial number of traces of its greatest playwright and his family. By themselves the traces would have relatively little interest, but in the light of Shakespeare's plays and poems, they have come to seem like precious relics and manage to achieve a considerable resonance.

Shakespeare's Family

William Shakespeare's grandfather Richard farmed land by the village of Snitterfield, near the small, pleasant market town of Stratford-upon-Avon, about 96 miles northwest of London. The playwright's father, John, moved in the mid-sixteenth century to Stratford, where he became a successful glover, landowner, moneylender, and dealer in wool and other agricultural goods. In or about 1557, he married Mary Arden, the daughter of a prosperous and well-connected farmer from the same area, Robert Arden of Wilmcote.

John Shakespeare was evidently highly esteemed by his fellow townspeople, for he held a series of important posts in local government. In 1556, he was appointed ale taster, an office reserved for "able persons and discreet," in 1558 was sworn in as a constable, and in 1561 was elected as one of the town's fourteen burgesses. As burgess, John served as one of the two chamberlains, responsible for administering borough property and revenues. In 1567, he was elected bailiff, Stratford's highest elective office and the equivalent of mayor. Although John Shakespeare signed all official documents with a cross or other sign, it is likely, but not certain, that he knew how to read and write. Mary, who also signed documents only with her mark, is less likely to have been literate.

According to the parish registers, which recorded baptisms and burials, the Shakespeares had eight children, four daughters and four sons, beginning with a daughter Joan born in 1558. A second daughter, Margaret, was born in December 1562 and died a few months later. William Shakespeare ("Gulielmus, filius Johannes Shakespeare"), their first son, was baptized on April 26, 1564. Since there was usually a few days' lapse between birth and baptism, it is conventional to celebrate Shakespeare's birthday on April 23, which happens to coincide with the feast of St. George, England's patron saint, and with the day of Shakespeare's death fifty-two years later.

William Shakespeare had three younger brothers, Gilbert, Richard, and Edmund, and two younger sisters, Joan and Anne. (It was often the custom to recycle a name, so the firstborn Joan must have died before the birth in 1569 of another daughter

"Southeast Prospect of Stratford-upon-Avon, 1746." From *The Gentleman's Magazine* (December 1792).

christened Joan, the only one of the girls to survive childhood.) Gilbert, who died in his forty-fifth year in 1612, is described in legal records as a Stratford haberdasher; Edmund followed William to London and became a professional actor, but evidently of no particular repute. He was only twenty-eight when he died in 1607 and was given an expensive funeral, perhaps paid for by his successful older brother.

At the high point of his public career, John Shakespeare, the father of this substantial family, applied to the Herald's College for a coat of arms, which would have marked his (and his family's) elevation from the ranks of substantial middle-class citizenry to that of the gentry. But the application went nowhere, for soon after he initiated what would have been a costly petitioning process, John apparently fell on hard times. The decline must have begun when William was still living at home, a boy of twelve or thirteen. From 1576 onward, John Shakespeare stopped attending council meetings. He became caught up in costly lawsuits, started mortgaging his land, and incurred substantial debts. In 1586, he was finally replaced on the council; in 1592, he was one of nine Stratford men listed as absenting themselves from church out of fear of being arrested for debt.

The reason for the reversal in John Shakespeare's fortunes is unknown. Some have speculated that it may have stemmed from adherence to Catholicism, since those who remained loyal to the old faith were subject to increasingly vigorous and costly discrimination. But if John Shakespeare was a Catholic, as seems quite possible, it would not necessarily explain his decline, since other Catholics (and Puritans) in Elizabethan Stratford and elsewhere managed to hold on to their offices. In any case, his fall from prosperity and local power, whatever its cause, was not absolute. In 1601, the last year of his life, his name was included among those qualified to speak on behalf of Stratford's rights. And he was by that time entitled to bear a coat of arms, for in 1596, some twenty years after the application to the Herald's office had been initiated, it was successfully renewed. There is no record of who paid for the bureaucratic procedures that made the grant possible, but it is likely to have been John's oldest son William, by that time a highly successful London playwright.

Education

Stratford was a small provincial town, but it had long been the site of an excellent free school, originally established by the Church in the thirteenth century. The main purpose of such schools in the Middle Ages had been to train prospective clerics; since many aristocrats could neither read nor write, literacy by itself conferred no special distinction and was not routinely viewed as desirable. But the situation began to change markedly in the sixteenth century. Protestantism placed a far greater emphasis upon lay literacy: for the sake of salvation, it was crucially important to be intimately acquainted with the Holy Book, and printing made that book readily available. Schools became less strictly bound up with training for the Church and more linked to the general acquisition of "literature," in the sense both of literacy and of cultural knowledge. In keeping with this new emphasis on reading and with humanist educational reform, the school was reorganized during the reign of Edward VI (1547–53). School records from the period have not survived, but it is almost certain that William Shakespeare attended the King's New School, as it was renamed in Edward's honor.

Scholars have painstakingly reconstructed the curriculum of schools of this kind and have even turned up the names and rather impressive credentials of the schoolmasters who taught there when Shakespeare was a student. (Shakespeare's principal teacher was Thomas Jenkins, an Oxford graduate, who received £20 a year and a rent-free house.) A child's education in Elizabethan England began at age four or five with two years at what was called the "petty school," attached to the main grammar school. The little scholars carried a "hornbook," a sheet of paper or parchment framed in wood and covered, for protection, with a transparent layer of horn. On the paper was written

The Cholmondeley sisters, c. 1600–10. This striking image brings to mind Shakespeare's fascination with twinship, both identical (notably in *The Comedy of Errors*) and fraternal (in *Twelfth Night*).

the alphabet and the Lord's Prayer, which were reproduced as well in the slightly more advanced *ABC with the Catechism,* a combination primer and rudimentary religious guide.

After students demonstrated some ability to read, the boys could go on, at about age seven, to the grammar school. Shakespeare's images of the experience are not particularly cheerful. In his famous account of the Seven Ages of Man, Jaques in *As You Like It* describes

> the whining schoolboy with his satchel
> And shining morning face, creeping like snail
> Unwillingly to school.
>
> (2.7.144–46)

The schoolboy would have crept quite early: the day began at 6:00 A.M. in summer and 7:00 A.M. in winter and continued until 5:00 P.M., with very few breaks or holidays.

At the core of the curriculum was the study of Latin, the mastery of which was in effect a prolonged male puberty rite involving much discipline and pain as well as pleasure. A late sixteenth-century Dutchman (whose name fittingly was Batty) proposed that God had created the human buttocks so that they could be severely beaten without risking permanent injury. Such thoughts dominated the pedagogy of the age, so that even an able young scholar, as we might imagine Shakespeare to have been, could scarcely have escaped recurrent flogging.

Shakespeare evidently reaped some rewards for the miseries he probably endured: his works are laced with echoes of many of the great Latin texts taught in grammar schools. One of his earliest comedies, *The Comedy of Errors,* is a brilliant variation on a theme by the Roman playwright Plautus, whom Elizabethan schoolchildren often performed as well as read; and one of his earliest tragedies, *Titus Andronicus,* is heavily indebted to Seneca. These are among the most visible of the classical influences that are often more subtly and pervasively interfused in Shakespeare's works. He seems to have had a particular fondness for *Aesop's Fables,* Apuleius's *Golden Ass,* and above all Ovid's *Metamorphoses.* His learned contemporary Ben Jonson remarked that Shakespeare had "small Latin and less Greek," but from this distance what is striking is not the limits of Shakespeare's learning but rather the unpretentious ease, intelligence, and gusto with which he draws upon what he must have first encountered as laborious study.

Traces of a Life

In November 1582, William Shakespeare, at the age of eighteen, married twenty-six-year-old Anne Hathaway, who came from the village of Shottery, near Stratford. Their first daughter, Susanna, was baptized six months later. This circumstance, along with the fact that Anne was eight years Will's senior, has given rise to a mountain of speculation, all the more lurid precisely because there is no further evidence. Shakespeare depicts in several plays situations in which marriage is precipitated by a pregnancy, but he also registers, in *Measure for Measure* (1.2.125ff.), the Elizabethan belief that a "true contract" of marriage could be legitimately made and then consummated simply by the mutual vows of the couple in the presence of witnesses.

On February 2, 1585, the twins Hamnet and Judith Shakespeare were baptized in Stratford. Hamnet died at the age of eleven, when his father was already living for much of the year in London as a successful playwright. These are Shakespeare's only known children, although the playwright and impressario William Davenant in the mid-seventeenth century claimed to be his bastard son. Since people did not ordinarily advertise their illegitimacy, the claim, though impossible to verify, at least suggests the unusual strength of the Shakespeare's posthumous reputation.

William Shakespeare's father, John, died in 1601; his mother died seven years later. They would have had the satisfaction of witnessing their eldest son's prosperity, and not only from a distance, for in 1597 William purchased New Place, the second largest house in Stratford. In 1607, the playwright's daughter Susanna married a successful and well-known physician, John Hall. The next year, the Halls had a daughter, Elizabeth, Shakespeare's first grandchild. In 1616, the year of Shakespeare's death, his daughter Judith married a vintner, Thomas Quiney, with whom she had three children. Shakespeare's widow, Anne, died in 1623, at the age of sixty-seven. His first-born, Susanna, died at the age of sixty-six in 1649, the year that King Charles I was beheaded by the parliamentary army. Judith lived through Cromwell's Protectorate and on to the Restoration of the monarchy; she died in February 1662, at the age of seventy-seven. By the end of the century, the line of Shakespeare's direct heirs was extinct.

Patient digging in the archives has turned up other traces of Shakespeare's life as a family man and a man of means: assessments, small fines, real-estate deeds, minor actions in court to collect debts. In addition to his fine Stratford house and a large garden and cottage facing it, Shakespeare bought substantial parcels of land in the vicinity. When in *The Tempest* the wedding celebration conjures up a vision of "barns and garners never empty," Shakespeare could have been glancing at what the legal documents record as his own "tithes of corn, grain, blade, and hay" in the fields near Stratford. At some point after 1610, Shakespeare seems to have begun to shift his attention from the London stage to his Stratford properties, although the term "retirement" implies a more decisive and definitive break than appears to have been the case. By 1613, when the Globe Theatre burned down during a performance of *All Is True* (*Henry VIII*), Shakespeare was probably residing for the most part in Stratford, but he retained his financial interest in the rebuilt playhouse and probably continued to have some links to his theatrical colleagues. Still, by this point, his career as a playwright was substantially over. Legal documents from his last years show his main concern to be the protection of his real-estate interests in Stratford.

Half a century after Shakespeare's death, a Stratford vicar and physician, John Ward, noted in his diary that Shakespeare and his fellow poets Michael Drayton and Ben Jonson "had a merry meeting, and it seems drank too hard, for Shakespeare died of a fever there contracted." It is not inconceivable that Shakespeare's last illness was somehow linked, if only coincidentally, to the festivities on the occasion of the wedding in February 1616 of his daughter Judith (who was still alive when Ward made his diary entry). In any case, on March 25, 1616, Shakespeare revised his will, and on April 23 he died. Two days later, he was buried in the chancel of Holy Trinity Church beneath a stone bearing an epitaph he is said to have devised:

Good friend for Jesus' sake forbear,
To dig the dust enclosed here:
Blest be the man that spares these stones,
And curst be he that moves my bones.

The verses are hardly among Shakespeare's finest, but they seem to have been effective: though bones were routinely dug up to make room for others—a fate imagined with unforgettable intensity in the graveyard scene in *Hamlet*—his own remains were undisturbed. Like other vestiges of sixteenth- and early seventeenth-century Stratford, Shakespeare's grave has for centuries been the object of a tourist industry that borders on a religious cult.

Shakespeare's will has been examined with an intensity befitting this cult; every provision and formulaic phrase, no matter how minor or conventional, has borne a heavy weight of interpretation, none more so than the bequest to his wife, Anne, of only "my second-best bed." Scholars have pointed out that Anne would in any case have been provided for by custom and that the terms are not necessarily a deliberate slight, but the absence of the customary words "my loving wife" or "my well-beloved wife" is difficult to ignore.

Portrait of the Playwright as Young Provincial

The great problem with the surviving traces of Shakespeare's life is not that they are few but that they are dull. Christopher Marlowe was a double or triple agent, accused of brawling, sodomy, and atheism. Ben Jonson, who somehow clambered up from bricklayer's apprentice to classical scholar, served in the army in Flanders, killed a fellow actor in a duel, converted to Catholicism in prison in 1598, and returned to the Church of England in 1610. Provincial real-estate investments and the second-best bed cannot compete with such adventurous lives. Indeed, the relative ordinariness of Shakespeare's social background and life has contributed to a persistent current of speculation that the glover's son from Stratford-upon-Avon was not in fact the author of the plays attributed to him.

The anti-Stratfordians, as those who deny Shakespeare's authorship are sometimes called, almost always propose as the real author someone who came from a higher social class and received a more prestigious education. Francis Bacon, the Earl of Oxford, the Earl of Southampton, even Queen Elizabeth, have been advanced, among many others, as glamorous candidates for the role of clandestine playwright. Several famous people, including Mark Twain and Sigmund Freud, have espoused these theories, though very few scholars have joined them. Since Shakespeare was quite well-known in his own time as the author of the plays that bear his name, there would need to have been an extraordinary conspiracy to conceal the identity of the real master who (the theory goes) disdained to appear in the vulgarity of print or on the public stage. Like many conspiracy theories, the extreme implausibility of this one only seems to increase the fervent conviction of its advocates.

To the charge that a middle-class author from a small town could not have imagined the lives of kings and nobles, one can respond by citing the exceptional qualities that Ben Jonson praised in Shakespeare: "excellent *Phantsie*; brave notions, and gentle expressions." Even in ordinary mortals, the human imagination is a strange faculty; in Shakespeare, it seems to have been uncannily powerful, working its mysterious, transforming effects on everything it touched. His imagination was intensely engaged by what he found in books. He seems throughout his life to have been an intense, voracious reader, and it is fascinating to witness his creative encounters with Raphael Holinshed's *Chronicles of England, Scotlande, and Irelande*, Plutarch's *Lives of the Noble Grecians and Romans*, Ovid's *Metamorphoses*, Montaigne's *Essays*, and the Bible, to name only some of his favorite books. But books were clearly not the only objects of Shakespeare's attention; like most artists, he drew upon the whole range of his life experiences.

To integrate some of the probable circumstances of Shakespeare's early years with the particular shape of the theatrical imagination associated with his name, let us indulge briefly in the biographical daydreams that modern scholarship is supposed to have rendered forever obsolete. The vignettes that follow are conjectural, but they may suggest ways in which his life as we know it found its way into his art.

1. THE GOWN OF OFFICE

Shakespeare was a very young boy—not quite four years old—when the Stratford council elected his father, John, to a year's term as bailiff (the equivalent of mayor). The office, the town's highest, was attended with considerable ceremony. The bailiff and his deputy were entitled to appear in public in furred gowns, attended by leather-clad sergeants bearing maces before them. On Rogation Days (three days of prayer for the harvest, before Ascension Day), they would solemnly pace out the parish boundaries, and they would similarly walk in processions on market and fair days. On Sundays, the sergeants would accompany the bailiff to church, where he would sit with his wife in a front pew, and he would have a comparable seat of honor at sermons in the Guild Chapel.

Public deference was a matter of law as well as custom: any inhabitant who spoke disrespectfully to the bailiff or other town officer was subject to the penalty of three days and three nights in the stocks. Newcomers who sought employment—notably including traveling players who hoped to stage performances—were obliged to obtain the bailiff's permission. In the year that John Shakespeare held office, two such professional playing companies arrived in Stratford. They must have proceeded to the bailiff's house on Henley Street and presented the letters of recommendation, with wax seals, that showed that they were not vagabonds. They would have spoken with more than ordinary deference, since it was the bailiff who would decide whether they would be sent packing or—as was the case—allowed to post their bills announcing the performances. The first of these performances was usually free to all comers. The bailiff would have been expected to attend, for it was his privilege to determine the level of the reward to be paid out of the city coffers; he would, presumably, have been given one of the best seats in the guildhall, where a special stage had been erected. It is impossible to know whether John Shakespeare took his family to these plays, but his little boy would certainly have been aware of what was happening.

On a precocious child (or even, for that matter, on an ordinary child), the effect of his father's office and the elaborate rituals that attended it would be at least threefold. First, the ceremony would convey irresistibly the power of clothes (the gown of office) and of symbols (the mace) to transform identity as if by magic. Second, it would invest the father with immense power, distinction, and importance, awakening what we may call a lifelong dream of high station. And third, pulling slightly against this dream, it would provoke an odd feeling that the father's clothes do not fit, a perception that the office is not the same as the man, and an intimate, firsthand knowledge that when the robes are put off, their wearer is inevitably glimpsed in a far different, less exalted light.

2. PROGRESSES AND ELECTIONS

This second biographical fantasy, slightly less plausible than the first but still quite likely, involves a somewhat older child witnessing two characteristic forms of Elizabethan political ceremony, both of which were well known in the provinces. Queen Elizabeth was fond of going on what were known as "progresses," triumphant ceremonial journeys around her kingdom. Let us imagine that the young Shakespeare—say, in 1574, when he was ten years old—went with his kinsfolk or friends to Warwick, some 8 miles distant, to witness a progress. He would thus have participated as a spectator in an elaborate celebration of charismatic power: the courtiers in their gorgeous clothes, the nervous local officials bedecked in velvets and silks, and at the center, carried in a special litter like a painted idol, the bejeweled queen. Let us imagine further that in addition to being struck by the overwhelming force of this charisma, the boy was struck, too, by the way this force depended paradoxically on a sense that the queen was after all quite human. Elizabeth was in fact fond of calling attention to this peculiar tension between near-divinization and human ordinariness. For example, on this occasion at Warwick (and what follows really happened), after the trembling Recorder, presumably a local civil official of high standing, had made his official welcoming speech, Elizabeth offered her hand to him to be kissed: "Come hither, little Recorder," she said. "It was told me that you would be afraid to look upon me or to speak boldly; but you were not so afraid of me as I was of you; and I now thank you for putting me in mind of my duty." Of course, the charm of this royal "confession" of nervousness depends on its manifest implausibility: it is, in effect, a theatrical performance of humility by someone with immense confidence in her own histrionic power.

A royal progress was not the only form of spectacular political activity that Shakespeare might well have seen in the 1570s; it is still more likely that he would have witnessed parliamentary elections, particularly since his father was qualified to vote. In 1571, 1572, 1575, and 1578, there were shire elections conducted in nearby Warwick, elections that would certainly have attracted well over a thousand voters. These were often memorable events: large crowds came together; there was usually heavy drinking and carnivalesque festivity; and, at the same time, there was enacted, in a very different register from that of the monarchy, a ritual of empowerment. The people, those entitled to vote by virtue of meeting the property and residence requirements, chose their own representatives by giving their votes—their voices—to candidates for office. Here, legislative sovereignty was conferred not by God but by the consent of the community, a consent marked by shouts and applause.

Recent cultural historians have been so fascinated by the evident links between the spectacles of the absolutist monarchy and the theater that they have largely ignored the significance of this alternative public arena, one that generated intense excitement throughout the country. A child who was a spectator at a parliamentary election in the 1570s might well have found the occasion enormously compelling. It is striking, in any case, how often the adult Shakespeare returns to scenes of acclamation and mass consent, and striking, too, how much the theater depends on the soliciting of popular voices.

3. EXORCISMS

A third and final fantasy is even more speculative than the second and involves a controversial claim, which has long been hotly debated— that Shakespeare either was a secret Catholic or was at least raised in a Roman Catholic household in a time of official suspicion and persecution of recusancy. A late seventeenth-century Anglican clergyman, Richard Davies, jotted down in some notes on Shakespeare that "he died a papist." In a modern biographical study, E. A. J. Honigmann convincingly linked several of the schoolmasters who taught in Stratford at the time that Shakespeare would have been a pupil to a network of Catholic families in Lancashire with whom one "William Shakeshafte," possibly a young schoolmaster or player, was connected in the late 1570s or early 1580s.

Exorcism: Nicole Aubry in the cathedral at Laon, 1566.

Catholics in Elizabethan England were not free to practice their religion—any more than Protestants, in Catholic countries, were free to practice theirs—and the beleaguered faithful, beset with spies, came together only at great risk to confess and receive Communion from clandestine priests. Under the circumstances, although a substantial portion of the population may have retained a residual inward loyalty to the traditional faith, the vast majority fell away from outward Catholic practice. After all, the churches, great and small, were now the places of Protestant worship; the innumerable local saints' shrines and pilgrimage sites had been systematically destroyed; the monasteries and convents had been abolished, their property bestowed on royal favorites or sold at bargain prices to local magnates. Seeking a spectacular way to demonstrate the enduring spiritual power and authenticity of the Roman Church, the embattled Counter-Reformers turned to an ancient ritual: exorcism. Devils who possessed the souls of troubled men and women had once been exorcised in public, but now the healing rite had to be conducted in secret, in a barn in a remote village, perhaps, or in the attic of the secluded house of a Catholic loyalist. The danger for those who presided was enormous—brutal interrogation, torture, and an unspeakably horrible execution was the usual fate of the missionary priests who were caught—but the vivid demonstration of the Church's triumph over evil was sufficiently compelling to warrant the risk. For despite the lynx-eyed alertness of the Protestant authorities, Catholics staged a surprising number of clandestine exorcisms, many of which drew substantial crowds.

Accepting for the moment that William Shakespeare was raised in the recusant faith of his father and mother, let us imagine that one day in the early 1580s the young man attended an exorcism of which he had learned through the secret network of the faithful. Here, based on an eyewitness account of such an occasion recently transcribed by Gerard Kilroy, is what he is likely to have seen. At the center of a large room, emptied of other furniture in order to accommodate the many observers, stood a bed. A young woman sat on the bed, and a priest, in clerical vestments, stood over her, preaching a sermon. As he spoke, the woman began to writhe and scream. At first the screams, uttered by a deep voice that could not have been the woman's although it came from her mouth, were not intelligible. Gradually, the bystanders began to make out some of the words, blasphemous oaths—"God's wounds! God's nails!"—followed by menaces, spoken as if by a rabid Protestant: "Popish priests, popish priests, to prison with them and hang them, hang them, hang them." The exorcist held up the Eucharist over the writhing woman, and the screams intensified. "Who are you?" he demanded. "I am Modu," the voice replied. "Depart, Modu!" shouted the priest, bringing the consecrated wafer closer to the demoniac. When that did not succeed in driving the devil out, the priest advanced a chafing dish of fire and brimstone, provoking more shouting and cursing, and then displayed a painting of the Blessed Virgin. "I will not behold or see her," screamed the demonic voice.

The longer the scene continued, the more there was confirmation of the contested tenets of the Catholic faith. The devil admitted that the Virgin Mary was a particularly efficacious intercessor, that purgatory existed, that the wafer, consecrated by the priest, actually was the body and blood of Christ. The devil also revealed that all Protestants were his followers. Finally, under the irresistible force of spiritual compulsion, he agreed to depart forever from the body of the possessed. The departure was difficult: again and again the tormented young woman gaped, as if her mouth were being torn open. She screamed in pain, rose up only to be cast down violently by invisible hands, cried out that she was being drowned, and called upon Jesus and his mother to save her. Only when a sacred relic was placed directly on her flesh did the devil finally leave her.

There is no way to know if William Shakespeare actually witnessed such a scene, but if he did, he would have carried away several indelible impressions: an awareness that strange, alien voices may speak from within ordinary, familiar bodies; an intimation of the immense, cosmic forces that may impinge upon human life; a belief in the possibility of making contact with these forces and compelling them to speak. These are, after all, the foundation stones of great tragedy.

Many years later, Shakespeare brooded about demonic possession when he was writing his greatest tragedy about the presence of evil in the world, *King Lear*. "This is the foul fiend Flibbertigibbet," shouts the madman, Poor Tom; "The Prince of Darkness is a gentleman. Modo he's called, and Mahu" (3.4.103, 127–28). But Poor Tom in that play is faking it; he is actually the noble Edgar, who has disguised himself as a madman in order to escape persecution. Did Shakespeare as a teenager already think that the whole compelling event, in all of its metaphysical weirdness, was a powerful theatrical fraud, a piece of pious propaganda? Perhaps. But if so, he also clearly understood that evil exists, that persecution is real, and that illusion has an irresistible force.

These imaginary portraits of the playwright as a young provincial introduce us to several of the root conditions of the Elizabethan theater. Biographical fantasies, though entirely speculative and playful, are useful in part because some people have found it difficult to conceive how Shakespeare, with his provincial roots and his restricted range of experience, could have so rapidly and completely mastered the central imaginative themes of his times. Moreover, it is sometimes difficult to grasp how seeming abstractions such as market society, monarchical state, and theological doctrine were actually experienced directly by peculiar, distinct individuals. Shakespeare's plays were social and collective events, but they also bore the stamp of a particular artist, one endowed with a remarkable capacity to craft lifelike illusions (what Jonson called "excellent *Phantsie*"), a daring willingness to articulate an original vision ("brave notions"), and a loving command, at once precise and generous, of language ("gentle expressions"). These plays are stitched together from shared cultural experiences, inherited dramatic devices, and the pungent vernacular of the day, but we should not lose sight of the extent to which they articulate an intensely personal vision, a bold shaping of the available materials. Four centuries of feverish biographical speculation, much of it foolish, bears witness to a basic intuition: the richness of these plays, their inexhaustible openness, is the consequence not only of the auspicious collective conditions of the culture but also of someone's exceptional skill, inventiveness, and courage at taking those conditions and making of them something rich and strange.

The Theater of the Nation

What precisely are the collective conditions highlighted by these vignettes? First, the growth of Stratford-upon-Avon, the bustling market town of which John Shakespeare was bailiff, is a small version of a momentous sixteenth-century development that made Shakespeare's career possible: the making of an urban "public." That development obviously depended on adequate numbers; the period experienced a rapid and still unexplained growth in population. With it came an expansion and elaboration of market relations: markets became less periodic, more continuous, and more abstract—centered, that is, not on the familiar materiality of goods but on the liquidity of capital and goods. In practical terms, this meant that it was possible to conceive of the theater not only as festive entertainment for special events—lord mayor's pageants, visiting princes, seasonal festivals, and the like—but as a permanent, year-round business venture. The venture relied on ticket sales—it was an innovation of this period to have money advanced in the expectation of pleasure rather than offered to servants afterward as a reward—and counted on habitual playgoing with a concomitant demand for new plays from competing theater companies: "But that's all one, our play is done," sings Feste at the end of *Twelfth Night* and adds a glance toward the next afternoon's proceeds: "And we'll strive to please you every day" (5.1.394–95).

Second, the royal progress is an instance of what the anthropologist Clifford Geertz has called the Theater State, a state that manifests its power and meaning in exemplary public performances. Professional companies of players, like the one Shakespeare belonged to, understood well that they existed in relation to this Theater State and would, if they were fortunate, be called upon to serve it. Unlike Ben Jonson, Shakespeare did not, as far as we know, write royal entertainments on commission, but his plays were frequently performed before Queen Elizabeth and then before King James and Queen Anne, along with their courtiers and privileged guests. There are many fascinating glimpses of these performances, including a letter from Walter Cope to Robert Cecil, early in James's reign. "Burbage is come," Cope writes, referring to the leading actor of Shakespeare's company, "and says there is no new play that the queen hath not seen, but they have revived an old one, called *Love's Labours Lost,* which for wit and mirth he says will please her exceedingly. And this is appointed to be played tomorrow night at my Lord of Southampton's." Not only would such theatrical performances have given great pleasure—evidently, the queen had already exhausted the company's new offerings—but they conferred prestige upon those who commanded them and those in whose honor they were mounted.

Monarchical power in the period was deeply allied to spectacular manifestations of the ruler's glory and disciplinary authority. The symbology of power depended on regal magnificence, reward, punishment, and pardon, all of which were heavily theatricalized. Indeed, the conspicuous public display does not simply serve the interests of power; on many occasions in the period, power seemed to exist in order to make pageantry possible, as if the nation's identity were only fully realized in theatrical performance. It would be easy to exaggerate this perception: the subjects of Queen Elizabeth and King James were acutely aware of the distinction between shadow and substance. But they were fascinated by the political magic through which shadows could be taken for substantial realities, and the ruling elite was largely complicit in the formation and celebration of a charismatic absolutism. At the same time, the claims of the monarch who professes herself or himself to be not the representative of the nation but its embodiment were set against the counterclaims of the House of Commons. And this institution, too, as we have glimpsed, had its own theatrical rituals, centered on the crowd whose shouts of approval, in heavily stage-managed elections, chose the individuals who would stand for the polity and participate in deliberations held in a hall whose resemblance to a theater did not escape contemporary notice.

Third, illicit exorcism points both to the theatricality of much religious ritual in the late Middle Ages and the Renaissance and to the heightened possibility of secularization. English Protestant authorities banned the medieval mystery plays, along with pilgrimages and other rituals associated with holy shrines and sacred images, but playing companies could satisfy at least some of the popular longings and appropriate aspects of the social energy no longer allowed a theological outlet. That is, official attacks on certain Catholic practices made it more possible for the public theater to appropriate and exploit their allure. Hence, for example, the plays that celebrated the solemn miracle of the Catholic Mass were banned, along with the most elaborate church vestments, but in *The Winter's Tale* Dion can speak in awe of what he witnessed at Apollo's temple:

> I shall report,
> For most it caught me, the celestial habits—
> Methinks I so should term them—and the reverence
> Of the grave wearers. O, the sacrifice—
> How ceremonious, solemn, and unearthly
> It was i'th' off'ring!

(3.1.3–8)

And at the play's end, the statue of the innocent mother breathes, comes to life, and embraces her child.

The theater in Shakespeare's time, then, is intimately bound up with all three crucial cultural formations: the market society, the theater state, and the Church. But it is important to note that the institution is not *identified* with any of them. The theater may be a market phenomenon, but it is repeatedly and bitterly attacked as the enemy of diligent, sober, productive economic activity. Civic authorities generally regarded the theater as a pestilential nuisance, a parasite on the body of the commonwealth, a temptation to students, apprentices, housewives, even respectable merchants to leave their serious business and lapse into idleness and waste. That waste, it might be argued, could be partially recuperated if it went for the glorification of a guild or the entertainment of an important dignitary, but the only group regularly profiting from the theater were the players and their disreputable associates.

For his part, Shakespeare made a handsome profit from the commodification of theatrical entertainment, but he seems never to have written "city comedy"—plays set in London and more or less explicitly concerned with market relations—and his characters express deep reservations about the power of money and commerce: "That smooth-faced gentleman, tickling commodity," Philip the Bastard observes in *King John*, "wins of all, / Of kings, of beggars, old men, young men, maids" (2.1.574, 570–71). We could argue that the smooth-faced gentleman is none other than Shakespeare himself, for his drama famously mingles kings and clowns, princesses and panderers. But the mingling is set against a romantic current of social conservatism: in *Twelfth Night*, the aristocratic heiress Olivia falls in love with someone who appears far beneath her in wealth and social station, but it is revealed that he (and his sister Viola) are of noble blood; in *The Winter's Tale*, Leontes' daughter Perdita is raised as a shepherdess, but her noble nature shines through her humble upbringing, and she marries the Prince of Bohemia; the strange island maiden with whom Ferdinand, son of the King of Naples, falls madly in love in *The Tempest* turns out to be the daughter of the rightful Duke of Milan. Shakespeare pushes against this conservative logic in *All's Well That Ends Well*, but the noble young Bertram violently resists the unequal match thrust upon him by the King, and the play's mood is notoriously uneasy.

Similarly, Shakespeare's theater may have been patronized and protected by the monarchy—after 1603, his company received a royal patent and was known as the King's Men—but it was by no means identical in its interests or its ethos. To be sure, *Richard III* and *Macbeth* incorporate aspects of royal propaganda, but given the realities of censorship, Shakespeare's plays, and the period's drama as a whole, are surprisingly independent and complex in their political vision. There is, in any case, a certain inherent tension between kings and player kings: Elizabeth and James may both have likened themselves to actors onstage, but they were loath to admit their dependence on the applause and money, freely given or freely withheld, of the audience. The charismatic monarch insists that the sacredness of authority resides in the body of the ruler, not in a costume that may be worn and then discarded by an actor. Kings are not *representations* of power—or do not admit that they are—but claim to be the thing itself. The government institution that was actually based on the idea of representation, Parliament, had theatrical elements, as we have seen, but it significantly excluded any audience from its deliberations. And Shakespeare's oblique portraits of parliamentary representatives, the tribunes Sicinius Velutus and Junius Brutus in *Coriolanus*, are anything but flattering.

Finally, the theater drew significant energy from the liturgy and rituals of the late medieval Church, but as Shakespeare's contemporaries widely remarked, the playhouse and the Church were scarcely natural allies. Not only did the theater represent a potential competitor to worship services, and not only did ministers rail against prostitution and other vices associated with playgoing, but theatrical representation itself, even when ostensibly pious, seemed to many to empty out whatever it presented, turning substance into mere show. The theater could and did use the period's deep currents of religious feeling, but it had to do so carefully and with an awareness of conflicting interests.

Shakespeare Comes to London

How did Shakespeare decide to turn his prodigious talents to the stage? When did he make his way to London? How did he get his start? To these and similar questions we have a mountain of speculation but no secure answers. There is not a single surviving record of Shakespeare's existence from 1585, when his twins were baptized in Stratford church, until 1592, when a rival London playwright made an envious remark about him. In the late seventeenth century, the delightfully eccentric collector of gossip John Aubrey was informed that prior to moving to London the young Shakespeare had been a schoolteacher in the country. Aubrey also recorded a story that Shakespeare had been a rather unusual apprentice butcher: "When he killed a calf, he would do it in a high style, and make a speech."

These and other legends, including one that has Shakespeare whipped for poaching game, fill the void until the unmistakable reference in Robert Greene's *Groats-Worth of Witte, Bought with a Million of Repentance* (1592). An inspired hack writer with a university education, a penchant for self-dramatization, a taste for wild living, and a strong streak of resentment, Greene, in his early thirties, was dying in poverty when he penned his last farewell, piously urging his fellow dramatists Christopher Marlowe, Thomas Nashe, and George Peele to abandon the wicked stage before they were brought low, as he had been, by a new arrival: "For there is an upstart crow, beautified with our feathers, that with his 'Tiger's heart wrapped in player's hide' supposes he is as well able to bombast out a blank verse as the best of you, and, being an absolute *Johannes Factotum,* is in his own conceit the only Shake-scene in a country." If "Shake-scene" is not enough to identify the object of his attack, Greene parodies a line from Shakespeare's early play *Richard Duke of York* (3 *Henry VI*): "O tiger's heart wrapped in a woman's hide!" (1.4.138). Greene is accusing Shakespeare of being an upstart, a plagiarist, an egomaniacal jack-of-all-trades—and, above all perhaps, a popular success.

By 1592, then, Shakespeare had already arrived on the highly competitive London theatrical scene. He was successful enough to be attacked by Greene and, a few months later, defended by Henry Chettle, another hack writer who had seen Greene's manuscript through the press (or, some scholars speculate, had written the attack himself and passed it off as the dying Greene's). Chettle expresses his regret that he did not suppress Greene's diatribe and spare Shakespeare "because myself have seen his demeanor no less civil than he excellent in the quality he professes." Besides, Chettle adds, "divers of worship have reported his uprightness of dealing, which argues his honesty and his facetious [polished] grace in writing that approves his art." "Divers of worship": not only was Shakespeare established as an accomplished writer and actor, but he evidently had aroused the attention and the approbation of several socially prominent people. In Elizabethan England, aristocratic patronage, with the money, protection, and prestige it alone could provide, was probably a professional writer's most important asset.

This patronage, or at least Shakespeare's quest for it, is most visible in the dedications in 1593 and 1594 of his narrative poems *Venus and Adonis* and *The Rape of Lucrece* to the young nobleman Henry Wriothesley, Earl of Southampton. It may be glimpsed as well, perhaps, in the sonnets, with their extraordinary adoration of the fair youth, though the identity of that youth has never been determined. What return Shakespeare got for his exquisite offerings is likewise unknown. We do know that among wits and gallants, the narrative poems won Shakespeare a fine reputation as an immensely stylish and accomplished poet. An amateur play performed at Cambridge University at the end of the sixteenth century, *The Return from Parnassus*, makes fun of this vogue, as a foolish character effusively declares, "I'll worship sweet Mr. Shakespeare, and to honour him will lay his *Venus and Adonis* under my pillow." Many readers at the time may have done so: the poem went through sixteen editions before 1640, more than any other work by Shakespeare.

Patronage was crucially important not only for individual artists but also for the actors, playwrights, and investors who pooled their resources to form professional theater companies. The public playhouses had enemies, especially among civic and religious authorities, who wished greatly to curb performances or to ban them altogether. An act of 1572 included players among those classified as vagabonds, threatening them, therefore, with the horrible punishments meted out to those regarded as economic parasites. The players' escape route was to be nominally enrolled as the servants of high-ranking noblemen. The legal fiction was that their public performances were a kind of rehearsal for the command performances before the patron or the monarch.

When Shakespeare came to London, presumably in the late 1580s, there were more than a dozen of these companies operating under the patronage of various aristocrats.

We do not know for which of these companies, several of which had toured in Stratford, he originally worked, nor whether he began, as legend has it, as a prompter's assistant and then graduated to acting and playwriting. Shakespeare is listed among the actors in Ben Jonson's *Every Man in His Humour* (performed in 1598) and *Sejanus* (performed in 1603), but we do not know for certain what roles he played, nor are there records of any of his other performances. Tradition has it that he played Adam in *As You Like It* and the Ghost in *Hamlet*, but he was clearly not one of the leading actors of the day.

By the 1590s, the number of playing companies in London had been considerably reduced, in part through competition and in part through legislative restriction. (In 1572, knights and gentry lost the privilege of patronizing a troupe of actors; in 1598, justices of the peace lost the power to authorize performances.) By the early years of the seventeenth century, there were usually only three companies competing against one another in any season, along with two children's companies, which were often successful at drawing audiences away from the public playhouses. Shakespeare may initially have been associated with the Earl of Leicester's company or with the company of Ferdinando Stanley, Lord Strange; both groups included actors with whom Shakespeare was later linked. Or he may have belonged to the Earl of Pembroke's Men, since there is evidence that they performed *The Taming of a Shrew* and a version of *Richard Duke of York (3 Henry VI)*. At any event, by 1594, Shakespeare was a member of the Lord Chamberlain's Men, for his name, along with those of Will Kemp (or Kempe) and Richard Burbage, appears on a record of those "servants to the Lord Chamberlain" paid for performance at the royal palace at Greenwich on December 26 and 28. Shakespeare stayed with this company, which during the reign of King James received royal patronage and became the King's Men, for the rest of his career.

Many playwrights in Shakespeare's time worked freelance, moving from company to company as opportunities arose, collaborating on projects, adding scenes to old plays, scrambling from one enterprise to another. But certain playwrights, among them the most successful, wrote for a single company, often agreeing contractually to give that company exclusive rights to their theatrical works. Shakespeare seems to have followed such a pattern. For the Lord Chamberlain's Men, he wrote an average of two plays per year. His company initially performed in The Theatre, a playhouse built in 1576 by an entrepreneurial carpenter, James Burbage, the father of the actor Richard, who was to perform many of

Edward Alleyn (1566–1626). Artist unknown. Alleyn was the great tragic actor of the Lord Admiral's Men (the principal rival to Shakespeare's company). He was famous especially for playing the great Marlovian heroes.

Shakespeare's greatest roles. When in 1597 their lease on this playhouse expired, the Lord Chamberlain's Men passed through a difficult and legally perilous time, but they formed a joint-stock company, raising sufficient capital to lease a site and put up a splendid new playhouse in the suburb of Southwark, on the south bank of the Thames. This playhouse, the Globe, opened in 1599. Shakespeare is listed in the legal agreement as one of the principal investors; and when the company began to use Blackfriars as their indoor playhouse around 1609, he was a major shareholder in that theater as well. The Lord Chamberlain's Men, later the King's Men, dominated the theater scene, and the shares were quite valuable. Then as now, the theater was an extremely risky enterprise—most of those who wrote plays and performed in them made pathetically little money—but Shakespeare was a notable exception. The fine house in Stratford and the coat of arms he succeeded in acquiring were among the fruits of his multiple mastery, as actor, playwright, and investor in the London stage.

The Shakespearean Trajectory

Even though Shakespeare's England was in many ways a record-keeping society, no reliable record survives that details the performances, year by year, in the London theaters. Every play had to be licensed by a government official, the Master of the Revels, but the records kept by the relevant officials from 1579 to 1621, Sir Edmund Tilney and Sir George Buc, have not survived. A major theatrical entrepreneur, Philip Henslowe, kept a careful account of his expenditures, including what he paid for the scripts he commissioned, but unfortunately Henslowe's main business was with the Rose and the Fortune theaters and not with the playhouses at which Shakespeare's company performed. A comparable ledger must have been kept by the shareholders of the Lord Chamberlain's Men, but it has not survived. Shakespeare himself apparently did not undertake to preserve for posterity the sum of his writings, let alone to clarify the chronology of his works or specify which plays he wrote alone and which with collaborators.

The principal source for Shakespeare's works is the 1623 Folio volume of *Mr. William Shakespeares Comedies, Histories, & Tragedies*. Most scholars believe that the editors were careful to include only those plays for which they knew Shakespeare to be the main author. Their edition does not, however, include any of Shakespeare's nondramatic poems, and it omits two plays in which Shakespeare is now thought to have had a significant hand, *Pericles, Prince of Tyre* and *The Two Noble Kinsmen*, along with his probable contribution to the multiauthored *Sir Thomas More*. (A number of other plays were attributed to Shakespeare, both before and after his death, but scholars have not generally accepted any of these into the established canon.) Moreover, the Folio edition does not print the plays in chronological order, nor does it attempt to establish a chronology. We do not know how much time would normally have elapsed between the writing of a play and its first performance, nor, with

IF YOV KNOW NOT ME,
You know no body.
OR,
The troubles of Queene ELIZABETH.

LONDON.
Printed by B.A. and T.F. for *Nathanaell Butter*. 1632.

Title page of Thomas Heywood's *If You Know Not Me, You Know No Body; or, The Troubles of Queene Elizabeth* (1632 ed.).

a few exceptions, do we know with any certainty the month or even the year of the first performance of any of Shakespeare's plays. The quarto editions of those plays that were published during Shakespeare's lifetime obviously establish a date by which we know a given play had been written, but they give us little more than an end point, because there was likely to be a substantial though indeterminate gap between the first performance of a play and its publication.

With enormous patience and ingenuity, however, scholars have gradually assembled a considerable archive of evidence, both external and internal, for dating the composition of the plays. Besides actual publication, the external evidence includes explicit reference to a play, a record of its performance, or (as in the case of Greene's attack on the "upstart crow") the quoting of a line, though all of these can be maddeningly ambiguous. The most important single piece of external evidence appears in 1598 in *Palladis Tamia*, a long book of jumbled reflections by Francis Meres that includes a survey of the contemporary literary scene. Meres finds that "the sweet, witty soul of Ovid lives in mellifluous and honey-tongued Shakespeare, witness his *Venus and Adonis,* his *Lucrece,* his sugered Sonnets among his private friends, etc." Meres goes on to list Shakespeare's accomplishments as a playwright as well:

> As Plautus and Seneca are accounted the best for Comedy and Tragedy among the Latins: so Shakespeare among the English is the most excellent in both kinds for the stage; for Comedy, witness his *Gentlemen of Verona,* his *Errors,* his *Love labors lost,* his *Love labours won,* his *Midsummers night dream,* & his *Merchant of Venice:* for Tragedy his *Richard the 2, Richard the 3, Henry the 4, King John, Titus Andronicus* and his *Romeo and Juliet.*

Meres thus provides a date by which twelve of Shakespeare's plays had definitely appeared (including one, *Love's Labour's Won,* that appears to have been lost or that we know by a different title). Unfortunately, Meres provides no clues about the order of appearance of these plays, and there are no other comparable lists.

Faced with the limitations of the external evidence, scholars have turned to a bewildering array of internal evidence, ranging from datable sources and topical allusions on the one hand to evolving stylistic features (ratio of verse to prose, percentage of rhyme to blank verse, colloquialisms, use of extended similes, and the like) on the other. Thus, for example, a cluster of plays with a high percentage of rhymed verse may follow closely upon Shakespeare's writing of the rhymed poems *Venus and Adonis* and *The Rape of Lucrece* and, therefore, be datable to 1594–95. Similarly, vocabulary overlap probably indicates proximity in composition, so if four or five plays share relatively "rare" vocabulary, it is likely that they were written in roughly the same period. Again, there seems to be a pattern in Shakespeare's use of colloquialisms, with a steady increase from *As You Like It* (1599–1600) to *Coriolanus* (1608), followed in the late romances by a retreat from the colloquial.

More sophisticated computer analysis should provide further guidance in the future, even though the precise order of the plays, still very much in dispute, is never likely to be settled to universal satisfaction. Still, certain broad patterns are now widely accepted. These patterns can be readily grasped in the *Norton Shakespeare,* which presents the plays in the chronological order proposed by the Oxford editors.

Shakespeare began his career, probably in the early 1590s, by writing both comedies and history plays. The attack by Greene suggests that he made his mark with the series of theatrically vital but rather crude plays based on the foreign and domestic broils that erupted during the unhappy reign of the Lancastrian Henry VI. Modern readers and audiences are more likely to find the first sustained evidence of unusual power in *Richard III* (c. 1592), a play that combines a brilliantly conceived central character, a dazzling command of histrionic rhetoric, and an overarching moral vision of English history.

At virtually the same time that he was setting his stamp on the genre of the history play, Shakespeare was writing his first—or first surviving—comedies. Here, there are even fewer signs than in the histories of an apprenticeship: *The Comedy of Errors*, one of his early efforts in this genre, already displays a rare command of the resources of comedy: mistaken identity, madcap confusion, and the threat of disaster, giving way in the end to reconciliation, recovery, and love. Shakespeare's other comedies from the early 1590s, *The Taming of the Shrew, The Two Gentlemen of Verona*, and *Love's Labour's Lost*, are no less remarkable for their sophisticated variations on familiar comic themes, their inexhaustible rhetorical inventiveness, and their poignant intimation, in the midst of festive celebration, of loss.

Successful as are these early histories and comedies, and indicative of an extraordinary theatrical talent, Shakespeare's achievement in the later 1590s would still have been all but impossible to foresee. Starting with *A Midsummer Night's Dream* (c. 1595), Shakespeare wrote an unprecedented series of romantic comedies—*The Merchant of Venice, The Merry Wives of Windsor, Much Ado About Nothing, As You Like It*, and *Twelfth Night* (c. 1602)—whose poetic richness and emotional complexity remain unmatched. In the same period, he wrote a sequence of profoundly searching and ambitious history plays—*Richard II, 1* and *2 Henry IV*, and *Henry V*—which together explore the death throes of feudal England and the birth of the modern nation-state ruled by a charismatic monarch. Both the comedies and histories of this period are marked by their capaciousness, their ability to absorb characters who press up against the outermost boundaries of the genre: the comedy *Merchant of Venice* somehow contains the figure, at once nightmarish and poignant, of Shylock, while the *Henry IV* plays, with their somber vision of crisis in the family and the state, bring to the stage one of England's greatest comic characters, Falstaff.

If in the mid to late 1590s Shakespeare reached the summit of his art in two major genres, he also manifested a lively interest in a third. As early as 1593, he wrote the crudely violent tragedy *Titus Andronicus*, the first of several plays on themes from Roman history, and a year or two later, in *Richard II*, he created in the protagonist a figure who achieves by the play's close the stature of a tragic hero. In the same year that Shakespeare wrote the wonderfully farcical "Pyramus and Thisbe" scene in *A Midsummer Night's Dream*, he probably also wrote the deeply tragic realization of the same story in *Romeo and Juliet*. But once again, the lyric anguish of *Romeo and Juliet* and the tormented self-revelation of *Richard II*, extraordinary as they are, could not have led anyone to predict the next phase of Shakespeare's career, the great tragic dramas that poured forth in the early years of the seventeenth century: *Hamlet, Othello, King Lear, Macbeth, Antony and Cleopatra*, and *Coriolanus*. These plays, written from 1601 to 1607, seem to mark a major shift in sensibility, an existential and metaphysical darkening that many readers think must have originated in a deep personal anguish, perhaps caused by the death of Shakespeare's father, John, in 1601.

Whatever the truth of these speculations—and we have no direct, personal testimony either to support or to undermine them—there appears to have occurred in the same period a shift as well in Shakespeare's comic sensibility. The comedies written between 1601 and 1604, *Troilus and Cressida, All's Well That Ends Well*, and *Measure for Measure*, are sufficiently different from the earlier comedies—more biting in tone, more uneasy with comic conventions, more ruthlessly questioning of the values of the characters and the resolutions of the plots—to have led many twentieth-century scholars to classify them as "problem plays" or "dark comedies." This category has recently begun to fall out of favor, since Shakespeare criticism is perfectly happy to demonstrate that *all* of the plays are "problem plays." But there is another group of plays, among the last Shakespeare wrote, that continue to constitute a distinct category. *Pericles, Cymbeline, The Winter's Tale*, and *The Tempest*, written between 1608 and 1611, when the playwright had developed a remarkably fluid, dreamlike sense of plot and a poetic style that could veer, apparently effortlessly, from the tortured to the ineffably sweet, are known as the "romances." These plays share an interest in the moral and emotional life less of the adolescents who dominate the earlier comedies than of their parents. The romances are deeply concerned with patterns of loss and recovery, suffering and redemption,

despair and renewal. They have seemed to many critics to constitute a deliberate conclusion to a career that began in histories and comedies and passed through the dark
and tormented tragedies.

   One effect of the practice of printing Shakespeare's plays in a reconstructed
chronological order, as this edition does, is to produce a kind of authorial plot, a
progress from youthful exuberance and a heroic grappling with history, through psychological anguish and radical doubt, to a mature serenity built upon an understanding of loss. The ordering of Shakespeare's "complete works" in this way reconstitutes
the figure of the author as the beloved hero of his own, lived romance. There are
numerous reasons to treat this romance with considerable skepticism: the precise order
of the plays remains in dispute, the obsessions of the earliest plays crisscross with those
of the last, the drama is a collaborative art form, and the relation between authorial
consciousness and theatrical representation is murky. Yet a longing to identify Shakespeare's personal trajectory, to chart his psychic and spiritual as well as professional
progress, is all but irresistible.

The Fetishism of Dress

   Whatever the personal resonance of Shakespeare's own life, his art is deeply
enmeshed in the collective hopes, fears, and fantasies of his time. For example, throughout his plays, Shakespeare draws heavily upon his culture's investment in costume, symbols of authority, visible signs of status—the fetishism of dress he must have witnessed
from early childhood. Disguise in his drama is often assumed to be incredibly effective:
when Henry V borrows a cloak, when Portia dresses in a jurist's robes, when Viola puts
on a young man's suit, it is as if each has become unrecognizable, as if identity resided
in clothing. At the end of *Twelfth Night,* even though Viola's true identity has been disclosed, Orsino continues to call her Cesario; he will do so, he says, until she resumes
her maid's garments, for only then will she be transformed into a woman:

> Cesario, come—
> For so you shall be while you are a man;
> But when in other habits you are seen,
> Orsino's mistress, and his fancy's queen.
> (5.1.372–75)

   The pinnacle of this fetishism of costume is the royal crown, for whose identity-
conferring power men are willing to die, but the principle is everywhere from the filthy
blanket that transforms Edgar into Poor Tom to the coxcomb that is the badge of the
licensed fool. Antonio, wishing to express his utter contempt, spits on Shylocks' "Jewish gaberdine," as if the clothing were the essence of the man; Kent, pouring insults on
the loathsome Oswald, calls him a "filthy worsted-stocking knave"; and innocent Innogen, learning that her husband has ordered her murder, thinks of herself as an expensive cast-off dress, destined to be ripped at the seams:

> Poor I am stale, a garment out of fashion,
> And for I am richer than to hang by th' walls
> I must be ripped. To pieces with me!
> (*Cymbeline* 3.4.50–52)

   What can be said, thought, felt, in this culture seems deeply dependent on the
clothes one wears—clothes that one is, in effect, *permitted* or *compelled* to wear, since
there is little freedom in dress. Shakespearean drama occasionally represents something like such freedom: after all, Viola in *Twelfth Night* chooses to put off her "maiden
weeds," as does Rosalind, who declares, "We'll have a swashing and a martial outside"
(*As You Like It* 1.3.114). But these choices are characteristically made under the pressure of desperate circumstances, here shipwreck and exile. Part of the charm of Shakespeare's heroines is their ability to transform distress into an opportunity for

self-fashioning, but the plays often suggest that there is less autonomy than meets the eye. What looks like an escape from cultural determinism may be only a deeper form of constraint. We may take, as an allegorical emblem of this constraint, the transformation of the beggar Christopher Sly into a nobleman in the playful Induction to *The Taming of the Shrew*. The transformation seems to suggest that you are free to make of yourself whatever you choose to be—the play begins with the drunken Sly indignantly claiming the dignity of his pedigree ("Look in the Chronicles" [Induction 1.3–4])—but in fact he is only the subject of the mischievous lord's experiment, designed to demonstrate the interwovenness of clothing and identity. "What think you," the lord asks his huntsman,

> if he were conveyed to bed,
> Wrapped in sweet clothes, rings put upon his fingers,
> A most delicious banquet by his bed,
> And brave attendants near him when he wakes—
> Would not the beggar then forget himself?

To which the huntsman replies, in words that underscore the powerlessness of the drunken beggar, "Believe me, lord, I think he cannot choose" (Induction 1.33–38).

Petruccio's taming of Katherine is similarly constructed around an imposition of identity, an imposition closely bound up with the right to wear certain articles of clothing. When the haberdasher arrives with a fashionable lady's hat, Petruccio refuses it over his wife's vehement objections: "This doth fit the time, / And gentlewomen wear such caps as these." "When you are gentle," Petruccio replies, "you shall have one, too, / And not till then" (4.3.69–72). At the play's close, Petruccio demonstrates his authority by commanding his tamed wife to throw down her cap: "Off with that bauble, throw it underfoot" (5.2.126). Here as elsewhere in Shakespeare, acts of robing and disrobing are intensely charged, a charge that culminates in the trappings of monarchy. When Richard II, in a scene that was probably censored from the stage as well as the printed text during the reign of Elizabeth, is divested of his crown and scepter, he experiences the loss as the eradication of his name, the symbolic melting away of his identity:

> Alack the heavy day,
> That I have worn so many winters out
> And know not now what name to call myself!
> O, that I were a mockery king of snow,
> Standing before the sun of Bolingbroke
> To melt myself away in water-drops!
> (4.1.247–52)

When Lear tears off his regal "lendings" in order to reduce himself to the nakedness of the Bedlam beggar, he is expressing not only his radical loss of social identity but the breakdown of his psychic order as well, expressing, therefore, his reduction to the condition of the "poor bare forked animal" that is the primal condition of undifferentiated existence. And when Cleopatra determines to kill herself in order to escape public humiliation in Rome, she magnificently affirms her essential being by arraying herself as she had once done to encounter Antony:

> Show me, my women, like a queen. Go fetch
> My best attires. I am again for Cydnus
> To meet Mark Antony.
> (5.2.223–25)

Such scenes are a remarkable intensification of the everyday symbolic practice of Renaissance English culture, its characteristically deep and knowing commitment to illusion: "I know perfectly well that the woman in her crown and jewels and gorgeous gown is an aging, irascible, and fallible mortal—she herself virtually admits as much—yet I profess that she is the Virgin Queen, timelessly beautiful, wise, and just." Shakespeare understood how close this willed illusion was to the spirit of the theater, to the actors' ability to work on what the chorus in *Henry V* calls the "imaginary forces" of the audience. But there is throughout Shakespeare's works a counterintuition that, while it does not exactly overturn this illusion, renders it poignant, vulnerable, fraught. The "masculine usurp'd attire" that is donned by Viola, Rosalind, Portia, Jessica, and other Shakespeare heroines alters what they can say and do, reveals important aspects of their character, and changes their destiny, but it is, all the same, not theirs and not all of who they are. They have, the plays insist, natures that are neither transformed nor altogether concealed by their dress: "Pray God defend me," exclaims the frightened Viola. "A little thing would make me tell them how much I lack of a man" (*Twelfth Night* 3.4.268–69).

The Paradoxes of Identity

The gap between costume and identity is not simply a matter of what women supposedly lack; virtually all of Shakespeare's major characters, men and women, convey the sense of both a *self-division* and an *inward expansion*. The belief in a complex inward realm beyond costumes and status is a striking inversion of the clothes cult: we know perfectly well that the characters have no inner lives apart from what we see on the stage, and yet we believe that they continue to exist when we do not see them, that they exist apart from their represented words and actions, that they have hidden dimensions. How is this conviction aroused and sustained? In part, it is the effect of what the characters themselves say: "My grief lies all within," Richard II tells Bolingbroke,

> And these external manner of laments
> Are merely shadows to the unseen grief
> That swells with silence in the tortured soul.
> (4.1.285–88)

Similarly, Hamlet, dismissing the significance of his outward garments, declares, "I have that within which passeth show— / These but the trappings and the suits of woe" (1.2.85–86). And the distinction between inward and outward is reinforced throughout this play and elsewhere by an unprecedented use of the aside and the soliloquy.

The soliloquy is a continual reminder in Shakespeare that the inner life is by no means transparent to one's surrounding world. Prince Hal seems open and easy with his mates in Eastcheap, but he has a hidden reservoir of disgust:

> I know you all, and will a while uphold
> The unyoked humour of your idleness.
> Yet herein will I imitate the sun,
> Who doth permit the base contagious clouds
> To smother up his beauty from the world,
> That when he please again to be himself,
> Being wanted he may be more wondered at
> By breaking through the foul and ugly mists
> Of vapours that did seem to strangle him.
> (*1 Henry IV* 1.2.173–81)

"When he please again to be himself": the line implies that identity is a matter of free choice—you decide how much of yourself you wish to disclose—but Shakespeare employs other devices that suggest more elusive and intractable layers of inwardness. There is a peculiar, recurrent lack of fit between costume and character, in fools as in princes, that is not simply a matter of disguise and disclosure. If Hal's true identity is partially "smothered" in the tavern, it is not completely revealed either in his soldier's armor or in his royal robes, nor do his asides reach the bedrock of unimpeachable self-understanding.

Identity in Shakespeare repeatedly slips away from the characters themselves, as it does from Richard II after the deposition scene and from Lear after he has given away his land and from Macbeth after he has gained the crown. The slippage does not mean that they retreat into silence; rather, they embark on an experimental, difficult fashioning of themselves and the world, most often through role-playing. "I cannot do it," says the deposed and imprisoned Richard II. "Yet I'll hammer it out" (5.5.5). This could serve as the motto for many Shakespearean characters: Viola becomes Cesario, Rosalind calls herself Ganymede, Kent becomes Caius, Edgar presents himself as Poor Tom, Hamlet plays the madman that he has partly become, Hal pretends that he is his father and a highwayman and Hotspur and even himself. Even in comedy, these ventures into alternate identities are rarely matters of choice; in tragedy, they are always undertaken under pressure and compulsion. And often enough it is not a matter of role-playing at all, but of a drastic transformation whose extreme emblem is the harrowing madness of Lear and of Leontes.

There is a moment in *Richard II* in which the deposed King asks for a mirror and then, after musing on his reflection, throws it to the ground. The shattering of the glass serves to remind us not only of the fragility of identity in Shakespeare but of its characteristic appearance in fragmentary mirror images. The plays continually generate alternative reflections, identities that intersect with, underscore, echo, or otherwise set off that of the principal character. Hence, Desdemona and Iago are not only important figures in Othello's world, they also seem to embody partially realized aspects of himself; Falstaff and Hotspur play a comparable role in relation to Prince Hal, Fortinbras and Horatio in relation to Hamlet, Gloucester and the Fool in relation to Lear, and so forth. In many of these plays, the complementary and contrasting characters figure in subplots, subtly interwoven with the play's main plot and illuminating its concerns. The note so conspicuously sounded by Fortinbras at the close of *Hamlet*—what the hero might have been, "had he been put on"—is heard repeatedly in Shakespeare and contributes to the overwhelming intensity, poignancy, and complexity of the characters. This is a world in which outward appearance is everything and nothing, in which individuation is at once sharply etched and continually blurred, in which the victims of fate are haunted by the ghosts of the possible, in which everything is simultaneously as it must be and as it need not have been.

Are these antinomies signs of a struggle between contradictory and irreconcilable perspectives in Shakespeare? In certain plays—notably, *Measure for Measure, All's Well That Ends Well, Coriolanus,* and *Troilus and Cressida*—the tension seems both high and entirely unresolved. But Shakespearean contradictions are more often reminiscent of the capacious spirit of Montaigne, who refused any systematic order that would betray his sense of reality. Thus, individual characters are immensely important in Shakespeare—he is justly celebrated for his unmatched skill in the invention of particular dramatic identities, marked with distinct speech patterns, manifested in social status, and confirmed by costume and gesture—but the principle of individuation is not the rock on which his theatrical art is founded. After the masks are stripped away, the pretenses exposed, the claims of the ego shattered, there is a mysterious remainder; as the shamed but irrepressible Paroles declares in *All's Well That Ends Well,* "Simply the thing I am / Shall make me live" (4.3.310–11). Again and again, the audience is made to sense a deeper energy, a source of power that at once discharges itself in individual characters and seems to sweep right through them.

The Poet of Nature

In *The Birth of Tragedy,* Nietzsche called a comparable source of energy that he found in Greek tragedy "Dionysos." But the god's name, conjuring up Bacchic frenzy, does not seem appropriate to Shakespeare. In the late seventeenth and eighteenth centuries, it was more plausibly called Nature: "The world must be peopled," says the delightful Benedick in *Much Ado About Nothing* (2.3.213–14), and there are frequent invocations elsewhere of the happy, generative power that brings couples together—

> Jack shall have Jill,
> Naught shall go ill,
> the man shall have his mare again, and all shall be well.
> (*A Midsummer Night's Dream* 3.3.45–47)

—and the melancholy, destructive power that brings all living things to the grave: "Golden lads and girls all must, / As chimney-sweepers, come to dust" (*Cymbeline* 4.2.263–64).

But the celebration of Shakespeare as a poet of nature—often coupled with an inane celebration of his supposedly "natural" (that is, untutored) genius—has its distinct limitations. For Shakespearean art brilliantly interrogates the "natural," refusing to take for granted precisely what the celebrants think is most secure. His comedies are endlessly inventive in showing that love is not simply natural: the playful hint of bestiality in the line quoted above, "the man shall have his mare again" (from a play in which the Queen of the Fairies falls in love with an ass-headed laborer), lightly unsettles the boundaries between the natural and the perverse. These boundaries are called into question throughout Shakespeare's work, from the cross-dressing and erotic crosscurrents that deliciously complicate the lives of the characters in *Twelfth Night* and *As You Like It* to the terrifying violence that wells up from the heart of the family in *King Lear* or from the sweet intimacy of sexual desire in *Othello*. Even the boundary between life and death is not secure, as the ghosts in *Julius Caesar*, *Hamlet*, and *Macbeth* attest, while the principle of natural death (given its most eloquent articulation by old Hamlet's murderer, Claudius!) is repeatedly tainted and disrupted.

Disrupted, too, is the idea of order that constantly makes its claim, most insistently in the history plays. Scholars have observed the presence in Shakespeare's works of the so-called Tudor myth—the ideological justification of the ruling dynasty as a restoration of national order after a cycle of tragic violence. The violence, Tudor apologists claimed, was divine punishment unleashed after the deposition of the anointed king, Richard II, for God will not tolerate violations of the sanctified order. Traces of this propaganda certainly exist in the histories—Shakespeare may, for all we know, have personally subscribed to its premises—but a closer scrutiny of his plays has disclosed so many ironic reservations and qualifications and subversions as to call into question any straightforward adherence to a political line. The plays manifest a profound fascination with the monarchy and with the ambitions of the aristocracy, but the fascination is never simply endorsement. There is always at least the hint of a slippage between the great figures, whether admirable or monstrous, who stand at the pinnacle of authority and the vast, miscellaneous mass of soldiers, scriveners, ostlers, poets, whores, gardeners, thieves, weavers, shepherds, country gentlemen, sturdy beggars, and the like who make up the commonwealth. And the idea of order, though eloquently articulated (most memorably by Ulysses in *Troilus and Cressida*), is always shadowed by a relentless spirit of irony.

The Play of Language

If neither the individual nor nature nor order will serve, can we find a single comprehensive name for the underlying force in Shakespeare's work? Certainly not. The work is too protean and capacious. But much of the energy that surges through this astonishing body of plays and poems is closely linked to the power of language. Shakespeare was the supreme product of a rhetorical culture, a culture steeped in the arts of persuasion and verbal expressiveness. In 1512, the great Dutch humanist Erasmus published a work called *De copia verborum* that taught its readers how to cultivate "copiousness," verbal richness, in discourse. (Erasmus obligingly provides, as a sample, a list of 144 different ways of saying "Thank you for your letter.") Recommended modes of variation include putting the subject of an argument into fictional form, as well as the use of synonym, substitution, paraphrase, metaphor, metonymy, synecdoche, hyperbole, diminution, and a host of other figures of speech. To change emotional tone, he suggests trying *ironia*, *interrogatio*, *admiratio*, *dubitatio*, *abominatio*—the possibilities seem infinite.

   In Renaissance England, certain syntactic forms or patterns of words known as "figures" (also called "schemes") were shaped and repeated in order to confer beauty or heighten expressive power. Figures were usually known by their Greek and Latin names, though in an Elizabethan rhetorical manual, *The Arte of English Poesie,* George Puttenham made a valiant if short-lived attempt to give them English equivalents, such as "*Hyperbole,* or the Overreacher," "*Ironia,* or the Dry Mock," and "*Ploce,* or the Doubler." Those who received a grammar-school education throughout Europe at almost any point between the Roman Empire and the eighteenth century probably knew by heart the names of up to one hundred such figures, just as they knew by heart their multiplication tables. According to one scholar's count, Shakespeare knew and made use of about two hundred.

   As certain grotesquely inflated Renaissance texts attest, lessons from *De copia verborum* and similar rhetorical guides could encourage mere prolixity and verbal self-display. But even though he shared his culture's delight in rhetorical complexity, Shakespeare always understood how to swoop from baroque sophistication to breathtaking simplicity. Moreover, he grasped early in his career how to use figures of speech, tone, and rhythm not only to provide emphasis and elegant variety but also to articulate the inner lives of his characters. Take, for example, these lines from *Othello,* where, as scholars have noted, Shakespeare deftly combines four common rhetorical figures—*anaphora, parison, isocolon,* and *epistrophe*—to depict with painful vividness Othello's psychological torment:

> By the world,
> I think my wife be honest, and think she is not.
> I think that thou art just, and think thou art not.
> I'll have some proof.
>
> (3.3.388–91)

   Anaphora is simply the repetition of a word at the beginning of a sequence of sentences or clauses ("I/I"). *Parison* is the correspondence of word to word within adjacent sentences or clauses, either by direct repetition ("think/think") or by the matching of noun with noun, verb with verb ("wife/thou"; "be/art"). *Isocolon* gives exactly the same length to corresponding clauses ("and think she is not/and think thou art not"), and *epistrophe* is the mirror image of *anaphora* in that it is the repetition of a word at the end of a sequence of sentences or clauses ("not/not"). Do we need to know the Greek names for these figures in order to grasp the effectiveness of Othello's lines? Of course not. But Shakespeare and his contemporaries, convinced that rhetoric provided the most natural and powerful means by which feelings could be conveyed to readers and listeners, were trained in an analytical language that helped at once to promote and to account for this effectiveness. In his 1593 edition of *The Garden of Eloquence,* Henry Peacham remarks that *epistrophe* "serveth to leave a word of importance in the end of a sentence, that it may the longer hold the sound in the mind of the hearer," and in *Directions for Speech and Style* (c. 1599), John Hoskins notes that *anaphora* "beats upon one thing to cause the quicker feeling in the audience."

   Shakespeare also shared with his contemporaries a keen understanding of the ways that rhetorical devices could be used not only to express powerful feelings but to hide them: after all, the artist who created Othello also created Iago, Richard III, and Lady Macbeth. He could deftly skewer the rhetorical affectations of Polonius in *Hamlet* or the pedant Holophernes in *Love's Labour's Lost.* He could deploy stylistic variations to mark the boundaries not of different individuals but of different social realms; in *A Midsummer Night's Dream,* for example, the blank verse of Duke Theseus is played off against the rhymed couplets of the well-born young lovers, and both in turn contrast with the prose spoken by the artisans. At the same time that he thus marks boundaries between both individuals and groups, Shakespeare shows a remarkable ability to establish unifying patterns of imagery that knit together the diverse strands of his plot and suggest subtle links among characters who may be scarcely aware of how much they share with one another.

One of the hidden links in Shakespeare's own works is the frequent use he makes of a somewhat unusual rhetorical figure called *hendiadys*. An example from the Roman poet Virgil is the phrase *pateris libamus et auro*, "we drink from cups and gold" (*Georgics* 2.192). Rather than serving as an adjective or a dependent noun, as in "golden cups" or "cups of gold," the word "gold" serves as a substantive joined to another substantive, "cups," by a conjunction, "and." Shakespeare uses the figure over three hundred times in all, and since it does not appear in ancient or medieval lists of tropes and schemes and is treated only briefly by English rhetoricians, he may have come upon it directly in Virgil. *Hendiadys* literally means "one through two," though Shakespeare's versions often make us quickly, perhaps only subliminally, aware of the complexity of what ordinarily passes for straightforward perceptions. When Othello, in his suicide speech, invokes the memory of "a malignant and a turbaned Turk," the figure of speech at once associates enmity with cultural difference and keeps them slightly apart. And when Macbeth speaks of his "strange and self-abuse," the *hendiadys* seems briefly to hold both "strange" and "self" up for scrutiny. It would be foolish to make too much of any single feature in Shakespeare's varied and diverse creative achievement, and yet this curious rhetorical scheme has something of the quality of a fingerprint.

But all of his immense rhetorical gifts, though rich, beautiful, and supremely useful, do not adequately convey Shakespeare's relation to language, which is less strictly functional than a total immersion in the arts of persuasion may imply. An Erasmian admiration for copiousness cannot fully explain Shakespeare's astonishing vocabulary of some 25,000 words. (His closest rival among the great English poets of the period was John Milton, with about 12,000 words, and most major writers, let alone ordinary people, have much smaller vocabularies.) This immense word hoard, it is worth noting, was not the result of scanning a dictionary; in the late sixteenth century, there were no English dictionaries of the kind to which we are now accustomed. Shakespeare seems to have absorbed new words from virtually every discursive realm he ever encountered, and he experimented boldly and tirelessly with them. These experiments were facilitated by the very fact that dictionaries as we know them did not exist and by a flexibility in grammar, orthography, and diction that the more orderly, regularized English of the later seventeenth and eighteenth centuries suppressed.

Owing in part to the number of dialects in London, pronunciation was variable, and there were many opportunities for phonetic association between words: the words "bear," "barn," "bier," "bourne," "born," and "barne" could all sound like one another. Homonyms were given greater scope by the fact that the same word could be spelled so many different ways—Christopher Marlowe's name appears in the records as Marlowe, Marloe, Marlen, Marlyne, Merlin, Marley, Marlye, Morley, and Morle—and by the fact that a word's grammatical function could easily shift, from noun to verb, verb to adjective, and so forth. Since grammar and punctuation did not insist on relations of coordination and subordination, loose, nonsyntactic sentences were common, and etymologies were used to forge surprising or playful relations between distant words.

It would seem inherently risky for a popular playwright to employ a vocabulary so far in excess of what most mortals could possibly possess, but Shakespeare evidently counted on his audience's linguistic curiosity and adventurousness, just as he counted on its general and broad-based rhetorical competence. He was also usually careful to provide a context that in effect explained or translated his more arcane terms. For example, when Macbeth reflects with horror on his murderous hands, he shudderingly imagines that even the sea could not wash away the blood; on the contrary, his bloodstained hand, he says, "will rather / The multitudinous seas incarnadine." The meaning of the unfamiliar word "incarnadine" is explained by the next line: "Making the green one red" (2.2.59–61).

What is most striking is not the abstruseness or novelty of Shakespeare's language but its extraordinary vitality, a quality that the playwright seemed to pursue with a kind of passionate recklessness. Perhaps Samuel Johnson was looking in the right direction when he complained that the "quibble," or pun, was "the fatal Cleopatra for which

[Shakespeare] lost the world, and was content to lose it." For the power that continually discharges itself throughout the plays, at once constituting and unsettling everything it touches, is the polymorphous power of language, language that seems both costume and that which lies beneath the costume, personal identity and that which challenges the merely personal, nature and that which enables us to name nature and thereby distance ourselves from it.

Shakespeare's language has an overpowering exuberance and generosity that often resembles the experience of love. Consider, for example, Oberon's description in *A Midsummer Night's Dream* of the moment when he saw Cupid shoot his arrow at the fair vestal: "Thou rememb'rest," he asks Puck,

> Since once I sat upon a promontory
> And heard a mermaid on a dolphin's back
> Uttering such dulcet and harmonious breath
> That the rude sea grew civil at her song
> And certain stars shot madly from their spheres
> To hear the sea-maid's music?
>
> (2.1.148–54)

Here, Oberon's composition of place, lightly alluding to a classical emblem, is infused with a fantastically lush verbal brilliance. This brilliance, the result of masterful alliterative and rhythmical technique, seems gratuitous—that is, it does not advance the plot, but rather exhibits a capacity for display and self-delight that extends from the fairies to the playwright who has created them. The rich music of Oberon's words imitates the "dulcet and harmonious breath" he is intent on recalling, breath that has, in his account, an oddly contradictory effect: it is at once a principle of order, so that the rude sea is becalmed like a lower-class mob made civil by a skilled orator, and a principle of disorder, so that celestial bodies in their fixed spheres are thrown into mad confusion. And this contradictory effect, so intimately bound up with an inexplicable, supererogatory, and intensely erotic verbal magic, is a key to *A Midsummer Night's Dream,* with its exquisite blend of confusion and discipline, lunacy and hierarchical ceremony.

The fairies in this comedy seem to embody a pervasive sense found throughout Shakespeare's work that there is something uncanny about language, something that is not quite human, at least in the conventional and circumscribed sense of the human that dominates waking experience. In the comedies, this intuition is alarming but ultimately benign: Oberon and his followers trip through the great house at the play's close, blessing the bridebeds and warding off the nightmares that lurk in marriage and parenthood. But there is in Shakespeare an alternative, darker vision of the uncanniness of language, a vision also embodied in creatures that test the limits of the human—not the fairies of *A Midsummer Night's Dream* but the weird sisters of *Macbeth.* When in the tragedy's opening scene the witches chant "Fair is foul, and foul is fair" (1.1.10), they unsettle through the simplest and most radical act of linguistic equation (x is y) the fundamental antinomies through which a moral order is established. And when Macbeth appears onstage a few minutes later, his first words unconsciously echo what we have just heard from the witches' mouths: "So foul and fair a day I have not seen" (1.3.36). What is the meaning of this linguistic "unconscious"? On the face of things, Macbeth presumably means only that the day of fair victory is also a day of foul weather, but the fact that he echoes the witches (something that we hear but that he cannot know) intimates an occult link between them, even before their direct encounter. It is difficult, perhaps impossible, to specify exactly what this link signifies—generations of emboldened critics have tried without notable success—but we can at least affirm that its secret lair is in the play's language, like a half-buried pun whose full articulation will entail the murder of Duncan, the ravaging of his kingdom, and Macbeth's own destruction.

Macbeth is haunted by half-buried puns, equivocations, and ambiguous grammatical constructions known as amphibologies. They manifest themselves most obviously in the words of the witches, from the opening exchanges to the fraudulent assurances that deceive Macbeth at the close, but they are also present in his most intimate and private reflections, as in his tortured broodings about his proposed act of treason:

> If it were done when 'tis done, then 'twere well
> It were done quickly. If th'assassination
> Could trammel up the consequence, and catch
> With his surcease success: that but this blow
> Might be the be-all and the end-all, here,
> But here upon this bank and shoal of time,
> We'd jump the life to come.
>
> (1.7.1–7)

The dream is to reach a secure and decisive end, to catch as in a net (hence "trammel up") all of the slippery, unforeseen, and uncontrollable consequences of regicide, to hobble time as one might hobble a horse (another sense of "trammel up"), to stop the flow ("success") of events, to be, as Macbeth later puts it, "settled." But Macbeth's words themselves slip away from the closure he seeks; they slide into one another, trip over themselves, twist and double back and swerve into precisely the sickening uncertainties their speaker most wishes to avoid. And if we sense a barely discernible note of comedy in Macbeth's tortured language, a discordant playing with the senses of the word "done" and the hint of a childish tongue twister in the phrase "catch / With his surcease success," we are in touch with a dark pleasure to which Shakespeare was all his life addicted.

Look again at the couplet from *Cymbeline*: "Golden lads and girls all must, / As chimney-sweepers, come to dust."

The playwright who insinuated a pun into the solemn dirge is the same playwright whose tragic heroine in *Antony and Cleopatra,* pulling the bleeding body of her dying lover into the pyramid, says, "Our strength is all gone into heaviness" (4.16.34). He is the playwright whose Juliet, finding herself alone on the stage, says, "My dismal scene I needs must act alone" (*Romeo and Juliet* 4.3.19), and the playwright who can follow the long, wrenching periodic sentence that Othello speaks, just before he stabs himself, with the remark "O bloody period!" (5.2.366). The point is not merely the presence of puns in the midst of tragedy (as there are stabs of pain in the midst of Shakespearean comedy); it is rather the streak of wildness that they so deliberately disclose, the sublimely indecorous linguistic energy of which Shakespeare was at once the towering master and the most obedient, worshipful servant.

The Dream of the Master Text

Shakespeare and the Printed Book

Ben Jonson's famous tribute to Shakespeare—"He was not of an age, but for all time!"—comes in one of the dedicatory poems to the 1623 First Folio of *Mr. William Shakespeares Comedies, Histories, & Tragedies.* This large, handsome volume, the first collection of Shakespeare's plays, was not, as far as we know, the product of the playwright's own design. We do not even know if he would have approved of the Folio's division of each play into five acts or its organization of the plays into three loose generic categories. Several of the plays grouped among the histories—*Richard Duke of York* (3 *Henry VI*), *Richard II,* and *Richard III*—had been printed separately during Shakespeare's lifetime as tragedies; one of the most famous of his tragedies had appeared as *The History of King Lear.* The Folio editors evidently decided to group together as "histories" only those plays which dealt with English history after the Norman Conquest; hence, *King Lear,* set in ancient Britain, appears with the "tragedies," and so, too, despite its happy ending, does *Cymbeline, King of Britain.* One play, *Troilus and Cressida,* was printed first as a "history," then printed in a second version with a preface that describes it as a "comedy," and then printed in the Folio as a "tragedy." As a fitting

Sixteenth-century printing shop. Engraving by Jan van der Straet. From *Nova Reperta* (1580).

emblem of the confusion, *Troilus and Cressida* does not appear in the Folio title page: apparently included only at the last minute, it was placed, unpaginated, after the last of the histories and the first of the tragedies. Modern readers, who remain perplexed by its genre, may take some consolation from the fact that for Shakespeare and his contemporaries generic boundaries were not hard and fast.

Published seven years after the playwright's death, the Folio was printed by the London printers William and Isaac Jaggard, who were joined in this expensive venture by Edward Blount, John Smethwicke, and William Aspley. It was edited by two of Shakespeare's old friends and fellow actors, John Heminges and Henry Condell, who claimed to be using "True Originall Copies" in the author's own hand. (None of these copies has survived, or, more cautiously, none has to date been found.) Eighteen plays included in the First Folio had already appeared individually in print in the small-format and relatively inexpensive texts called "Quartos" (or, in one case, the still smaller format called "Octavo"); to these, Heminges and Condell added eighteen others never before published: *All's Well That Ends Well, Antony and Cleopatra, As You Like It, The Comedy of Errors, Coriolanus, Cymbeline, All Is True (Henry VIII), Julius Caesar, King John, Macbeth, Measure for Measure, The Taming of the Shrew, The Tempest, Timon of Athens, Twelfth Night, The Two Gentlemen of Verona, The Winter's Tale,* and *1 Henry VI.** None of the

---

*This sketch simplifies several complex questions such as the status of the 1594 Quarto called *The Taming of a Shrew,* sufficiently distinct from the similarly titled Folio text as to constitute for many editors a different play.

plays included in the Folio has dropped out of the generally accepted canon of Shakespeare's works, and only two plays not included in the volume (Pericles and The Two Noble Kinsmen) have been allowed to join this select company, along with the nondramatic poems. Of the latter, Venus and Adonis (1593) and The Rape of Lucrece (1594) first appeared during Shakespeare's lifetime in Quartos with dedications from the author to the Earl of Southampton. Shakespeare's Sonnets (1609) were apparently printed without his authorization, as were his poems in a collection called The Passionate Pilgrim (1599).

Over the centuries, there have been many attempts to discover and authenticate additional works partly or entirely written by Shakespeare. An interesting case has been made for sections of a history play entitled King Edward the Third and for some small traces in the eighteenth-century tragicomedy The Double Falsehood, allegedly based on a manuscript of the lost Shakespearean play Cardenio. The Norton Shakespeare includes a poem, "Shall I die?" whose original inclusion in the 1988 Oxford Shakespeare provoked vigorous debate and much skepticism. Still more skepticism greeted the attribution to Shakespeare of a long poem called "A Funeral Elegy," printed in an appendix to The Norton Shakespeare's first edition and now dropped in the wake of widespread consensus that the attribution was false. In the future, other claimants will no doubt come forward, but, with the very few additions already noted, the Folio will always remain the foundation of Shakespeare's dramatic canon.

The plays were the property of the theatrical company in which Shakespeare was a shareholder. It was not normally in the interest of such companies to have their scripts circulating in print, at least while the plays were actively in repertory: players evidently feared competition from rival companies and thought that reading might dampen playgoing. Plays were generally sold only when the theaters were temporarily closed by plague, or when the company was in need of capital (four of Shakespeare's plays were published in 1600, presumably to raise money to pay the debts incurred in building the new Globe), or when a play had grown too old to revive profitably. There is no evidence that Shakespeare himself disagreed with this professional caution, no sign that he wished to see his plays in print. Unlike Ben Jonson, who took the radical step of rewriting his own plays for publication in the 1616 folio of his Works, Shakespeare evidently was not interested in constituting his plays as a canon. If in the sonnets he imagines his verse achieving a symbolic immortality, this dream apparently did not extend to his plays, at least through the medium of print.

Moreover, there is no evidence that Shakespeare had an interest in asserting authorial rights over his scripts or that he or any other working English playwright had a public "standing," legal or otherwise, from which to do so. (Jonson was ridiculed for his presumption.) There is no indication whatever that he could, for example, veto changes in his scripts or block interpolated scenes or withdraw a play from production if a particular interpretation, addition, or revision did not please him. To be sure, in his advice to the players, Hamlet urges that those who play the clowns "speak no more than is set down for them," but—apart from the question of whether the Prince speaks for the playwright—the play within the play in Hamlet is precisely an instance of a script altered to suit a particular occasion. It seems likely that Shakespeare would have routinely accepted the possibility of such alterations. Moreover, he would of necessity have routinely accepted the possibility, and in certain cases the virtual inevitability, of cuts in order to stage his plays in the two to two and one-half hours that was the normal performing time. There is an imaginative generosity in many of Shakespeare's scripts, as if he were deliberately offering his fellow actors more than they could use on any one occasion and, hence, giving them abundant materials with which to reconceive and revivify each play again and again as they or their audiences liked it. The Elizabethan theater, like most theater in our own time, was a collaborative enterprise, and the collaboration almost certainly extended to decisions about selection, trimming, shifts of emphasis, and minor or major revision.

For many years, it was thought that Shakespeare himself did little or no revising. Some recent editors—above all the editors of the Oxford Shakespeare, whose texts the

Norton presents—have argued persuasively that there are many signs of authorial revision, even wholesale rewriting. But there is no sign that Shakespeare sought through such revision to bring each of his plays to its "perfect," "final" form. On the contrary, many of the revisions seem to indicate that the scripts remained open texts, that the playwright and his company expected to add, cut, and rewrite as the occasion demanded.

Ralph Waldo Emerson once compared Shakespeare and his contemporary Francis Bacon in terms of the relative "finish" of their work. All of Bacon's work, wrote Emerson, "lies along the ground, a vast unfinished city." Each of Shakespeare's dramas, by contrast, "is perfect, hath an immortal integrity. To make Bacon's work complete, he must live to the end of the world." Recent scholarship suggests that Shakespeare was more like Bacon than Emerson thought. Neither the Folio nor the quarto texts of Shakespeare's plays bear the seal of final authorial intention, the mark of decisive closure that has served, at least ideally, as the guarantee of textual authenticity. We want to believe, as we read the text, "This is the play as Shakespeare himself wanted it read," but there is no license for such a reassuring sentiment. To be "not of an age, but for all time" means in Shakespeare's case not that the plays have achieved a static perfection, but that they are creatively, inexhaustibly unfinished.

That we have been so eager to link certain admired scripts to a single known playwright is closely related to changes in the status of artists in the Renaissance, changes that led to a heightened interest in the hand of the individual creator. Like medieval painting, medieval drama gives us few clues as to the particular individuals who fashioned the objects we admire. We know something about the places in which these objects were made, the circumstances that enabled their creation, the spaces in which they were placed, but relatively little about the particular artists themselves. It is easy to imagine a wealthy patron or a civic authority in the late Middle Ages commissioning a play on a particular subject (appropriate, for example, to a seasonal ritual, a religious observance, or a political festivity) and specifying the date, place, and length of the performance, the number of actors, even the costumes to be used, but it is more difficult to imagine him specifying a particular playwright and still less insisting that the entire play be written by this dramatist alone. Only with the Renaissance do we find a growing insistence on the name of the maker, the signature that heightens the value and even the meaning of the work by implying that it is the emanation of a single, distinct shaping consciousness.

In the case of Renaissance painting, we know that this signature does not necessarily mean that every stroke was made by the master. Some of the work, possibly the greater part of it, may have been done by assistants, with only the faces and a few finishing touches from the hand of the illustrious artist to whom the work is confidently attributed. As the skill of individual masters became more explicitly valued, contracts began to specify how much was to come from the brush of the principal painter. Consider, for example, the Italian painter Luca Signorelli's contract of 1499 for frescoes in Orvieto Cathedral:

> The said master Luca is bound and promises to paint [1] all the figures to be done on the said vault, and [2] especially the faces and all the parts of the figures from the middle of each figure upwards, and [3] that no painting should be done on it without Luca himself being present. . . . And it is agreed [4] that all the mixing of colours should be done by the said master Luca himself.

Such a contract at once reflects a serious cash interest in the characteristic achievement of a particular artist and a conviction that this achievement is compatible with the presence of other hands, provided those hands are subordinate, in the finished work. For paintings on a smaller scale, it was more possible to commission an exclusive performance. Thus, the contract for a small altarpiece by Signorelli's great teacher, Piero della Francesca, specifies that "no painter may put his hand to the brush other than Piero himself."

There is no record of any comparable concern for exclusivity in the English theater. Unfortunately, the contracts that Shakespeare and his fellow dramatists almost certainly signed have not, with one significant exception, survived. But plays written for the professional theater are by their nature an even more explicitly collective art form than paintings; they depend for their full realization on the collaboration of others, and that collaboration may well extend to the fashioning of the script. It seems that some authors may simply have been responsible for providing plots that others then dramatized; still others were hired to "mend" old plays or to supply prologues, epilogues, or songs. A particular playwright's name came to be attached to a certain identifiable style—a characteristic set of plot devices, a marked rhetorical range, a tonality of character—but this name may refer in effect more to a certain product associated with a particular playing company than to the individual artist who may or may not have written most of the script. The one contract whose details do survive, that entered into by Richard Brome and the actors and owners of the Salisbury Court Theatre in 1635, does not stipulate that Brome's plays must be written by him alone or even that he must be responsible for a certain specifiable proportion of each script. Rather, it specifies that the playwright "should not nor would write any play or any part of a play to any other players or playhouse, but apply all his study and endeavors therein for the benefit of the said company of the said playhouse." The Salisbury Court players want rights to everything Brome writes for the stage; the issue is not that the plays associated with his name be exclusively *his* but rather that he be exclusively *theirs*.

Recent textual scholarship, then, has been moving steadily away from a conception of Shakespeare's plays as direct, unmediated emanations from the mind of the author and toward a conception of them as working scripts, composed and continually reshaped as part of a collaborative commercial enterprise in competition with other, similar enterprises. One consequence has been the progressive weakening of the idea of the solitary, inspired genius, in the sense fashioned by Romanticism and figured splendidly in the statue of Shakespeare in the public gardens in Germany's Weimar, the city of Goethe and Schiller: the poet, with his sensitive, expressive face and high domed forehead sitting alone and brooding, a skull at his feet, a long-stemmed rose in his crotch. In place of this projection of German Romanticism, we have now a playwright and sometime actor who is also (to his considerable financial advantage) a major shareholder in the company—the Lord Chamberlain's Men, later the King's Men—to which he loyally supplies for most of his career an average of two plays per year.

These developments are salutary insofar as they direct attention to the actual conditions in which the textual traces that the Folio calls Shakespeare's "Comedies, Histories, & Tragedies" came to be produced, reproduced, consumed, revised, and transmitted to future generations. They highlight elements that Shakespeare shared with his contemporaries, and they insistently remind us that we are encountering scripts written primarily for the stage and not for the study. They make us more attentive to such matters as business cycles, plague rolls, the cost of costumes, government censorship, and urban topography and less concerned with the elusive and enigmatic details of the poet's biography—his supposed youthful escapades and erotic yearnings and psychological crises.

All well and good. But the fact remains that in 1623, seven years after the playwright's death, Heminges and Condell thought they could sell copies of their expensive collection of Shakespeare's plays—"What euer you do," they urge their readers, "buy"— by insisting that their texts were "as he conceiued them." This means that potential readers in the early seventeenth century were already interested in Shakespeare's "conceits"—his "wit," his imagination, and his creative power—and were willing to assign a high value to the products of his particular, identifiable skill, one distinguishable from that of his company and of his rival playwrights. After all, Jonson's tribute praises Shakespeare not as the playwright of the incomparable King's Men but as the equal of Aeschylus, Sophocles, and Euripides. And if we now see Shakespeare's dramaturgy in the context of his contemporaries and of a collective artistic practice, readers continue to have little difficulty recognizing that most of the plays attached to his name tower over those of his rivals.

From Foul to Fair: The Making of the Printed Play

What exactly is a printed play by Shakespeare? Is it like a novel or a poem? Is it like the libretto or the score of an opera? Is it the trace of an absent event? Is it the blueprint of an imaginary structure that will never be completed? Is it a record of what transpired in the mind of a man long dead? We might say cautiously that it is a mechanically reproduced version of what Shakespeare wrote, but unfortunately, with the possible (and disputed) exception of a small fragment from a collaboratively written play called *Sir Thomas More*, virtually nothing Shakespeare actually wrote in his own hand survives. We might propose that it is a printed version of the script that an Elizabethan actor would have held in his hands during rehearsals, but here, too, no such script of a Shakespeare play survives; and besides, Elizabethan actors were evidently not given the whole play to read. To reduce the expense of copying and the risk of unauthorized reproduction, each actor received only his own part, along with the cue lines. (Shakespeare uses this fact to delicious comic effect in *A Midsummer Night's Dream* 3.1.80–88.) Nonetheless, the play certainly existed as a whole, either in the author's original manuscript or in the copy prepared for the government censor or for the company's prompter or stage manager, so we might imagine the text we hold in our hands as a printed copy of one of these manuscripts. But since no contemporary manuscript survives of any of Shakespeare's plays, we cannot verify this hypothesis. And even if we could, we would not have resolved the question of the precise relation of the printed text either to the playwright's imagination or to the theatrical performance by the company to which he belonged.

All of Shakespeare's plays must have begun their textual careers in the form of "foul papers," drafts presumably covered with revisions, crossings-out, and general "blotting." To be sure, Heminges and Condell remark that so great was the playwright's facility that they "have scarce received from him a blot in his papers." This was, however, a routine and conventional compliment in the period. The same claim, made for the playwright John Fletcher in an edition published in 1647, is clearly contradicted by the survival of Fletcher's far-from-unblotted manuscripts. It is safe to assume that, since Shakespeare was human, his manuscripts contained their share of second and third thoughts scribbled in the margins and between the lines. Once complete, this authorial draft would usually have to be written out again, either by the playwright or by a professional scribe employed by the theater company, as "fair copy."

In the hands of the theater company, the fair copy (or sometimes, it seems, the foul papers themselves) would be annotated and transformed into "the book of the play" or the "playbook" (what we would now call a "promptbook"). Shakespeare's authorial draft presumably contained a certain number of stage directions, though these may have been sketchy and inconsistent. The promptbook clarified these and added others, noted theatrical properties and sound effects, and on occasion cut the full text to meet the necessities of performance. The promptbook was presented to the Master of the Revels for licensing, and it incorporated any changes upon which the master insisted. As the editors of the *Oxford Shakespeare* put it, the difference between foul papers and promptbook is the difference between "the text in an as yet individual, private form" and "a socialized text."

But the fact remains that for Shakespeare's plays, we have neither foul papers nor fair copies nor promptbooks. We have only the earliest printed editions of these texts in numerous individual quartos and in the First Folio. (Quartos are so called because each sheet of paper was folded twice, making four leaves or eight pages front and back; folio sheets were folded once, making two leaves or four pages front and back.) From clues embedded in these "substantive" texts—substantive because (with the exception of *The Two Noble Kinsmen*) they date from Shakespeare's own lifetime or from the collected works edited by his associates using, or claiming to use, his own manuscripts—editors attempt to reconstruct each play's journey from manuscript to print. Different plays took very different journeys.

Of the thirty-six plays included in the First Folio, eighteen had previously appeared in quarto editions, some of these in more than one printing. Generations of editors have distinguished between "good Quartos," presumably prepared from the author's own draft or from a scribal transcript of the play (fair copy), and "bad Quartos." The latter category, first formulated as such by A. W. Pollard in 1909, includes, by widespread but not universal agreement, the 1594 version of *The First Part of the Contention* (*2 Henry VI*), the 1595 *Richard Duke of York* (*3 Henry VI*), the 1597 *Richard the Third*, the 1597 *Romeo and Juliet*, the 1600 *Henry the Fifth,* the 1602 *Merry Wives of Windsor,* the 1603 *Hamlet,* and *Pericles* (1609). Some editors also regard the 1591 *Troublesome Reign of King John,* the 1594 *Taming of a Shrew,* and the 1608 *King Lear* as bad Quartos, but others have strenuously argued that these are distinct rather than faulty texts, and the whole concept of the bad Quarto has come under increasingly critical scrutiny. The criteria for distinguishing between "good" and "bad" texts are imprecise, and the evaluative terms seem to raise as many questions as they answer. Nevertheless, the striking mistakes, omissions, repetitions, and anomalies in a number of the Quartos require some explanation beyond the ordinary fallibility of scribes and printers.

The explanation most often proposed for suspect Quartos is that they are the products of "memorial reconstruction." The hypothesis, first advanced in 1910 by W. W. Greg, is that a series of features found in what seem to be particularly flawed texts may be traced to the derivation of the copy from the memory of one or more of the actors. Elizabethan actors, Greg observed, often found themselves away from the London theaters—for example, on tour in the provinces during plague periods—and may not on those occasions have had access to the promptbooks they would ordinarily have used. In such circumstances, those in the company who remembered a play may have written down or dictated the text, as best they could, perhaps adapting it for provincial performance. Moreover, unscrupulous actors may have sold such texts to enterprising printers eager to turn a quick profit.

Memorially reconstructed texts tend to be much shorter than those prepared from foul papers or fair copy; they frequently paraphrase or garble lines, drop or misplace speeches and whole scenes, and on occasion fill in the gaps with scraps from other plays. In several cases, scholars think they can detect which roles the rogue actors played, since these parts (and the scenes in which they appear) are reproduced with greater accuracy than the rest of the play. Typically, these roles are minor ones, since the leading parts would be played by actors with a greater stake in the overall financial interest of the company and, hence, less inclination to violate its policy. Thus, for example, editors speculate that the bad Quarto of *Hamlet* (Q1) was provided by the actor playing Marcellus (and doubling as Lucianus). What is often impossible to determine is whether particular differences between a bad Quarto and a good Quarto or Folio text result from the actor's faulty memory or from changes introduced in performance, possibly with the playwright's own consent, or from both. Shakespearean bad Quartos ceased to appear after 1609, perhaps as a result of greater scrutiny by the Master of the Revels, who after 1606 was responsible for licensing plays for publication as well as performance.

The syndicate that prepared the Folio had access to the manuscripts of the King's Men. In addition to the previously published editions of eighteen plays, they made use of scribal transcripts (fair copies), promptbooks, and (more rarely) foul papers. The indefatigable labors of generations of bibliographers, antiquaries, and textual scholars have recovered an extraordinary fund of information about the personnel, finances, organizational structure, and material practices of Elizabethan and Jacobean printing houses, including the names and idiosyncrasies of particular compositors who calculated the page length, set the type, and printed the sheets of the Folio. This impressive scholarship has for the most part intensified respect for the seriousness with which the Folio was prepared and printed, and where the Folio is defective, it has provided plausible readings from the Quartos or proposed emendations to approximate what Shakespeare is likely to have written. But it has not succeeded, despite all its heroic efforts, in transforming the Folio, or any other text, into an unobstructed, clear window into Shakespeare's mind.

The dream of the master text is a dream of transparency. The words on the page should ideally give the reader unmediated access to the astonishing forge of imaginative power that was the mind of the dramatist. Those words welled up from the genius of the great artist, and if the world were not an imperfect place, they would have been set down exactly as he conceived them and transmitted to each of us as a precious inheritance. Such is the vision—at its core closely related to the preservation of the holy text in the great scriptural religions—that has driven many of the great editors who have for centuries produced successive editions of Shakespeare's works. The vision was not yet fully formed in the First Folio, for Heminges and Condell still felt obliged to apologize to their noble patrons for dedicating to them a collection of mere "trifles." But by the eighteenth century, there were no longer any ritual apologies for Shakespeare; instead, there was a growing recognition not only of the supreme artistic importance of his works but also of the uncertain, conflicting, and in some cases corrupt state of the surviving texts. Every conceivable step, it was thought, must be undertaken to correct mistakes, strip away corruptions, return the texts to their pure and unsullied form, and make this form perfectly accessible to readers.

Paradoxically, this feverishly renewed, demanding, and passionate editorial project has produced the very opposite of the transparency that was the dream of the master text. The careful weighing of alternative readings, the production of a textual apparatus, the writing of notes and glosses, the modernizing and regularizing of spelling and punctuation, the insertion of scene divisions, the complex calculation of the process of textual transmission from foul papers to print, the equally complex calculation of the effects that censorship, government regulation, and, above all, theatrical performance had on the surviving documents all make inescapably apparent the fact that we do not have and never will have any direct, unmediated access to Shakespeare's imagination. Every Shakespeare text, from the first that was published to the most recent, has been edited: it has come into print by means of a tangled social process and inevitably exists at some remove from the author.

Heminges and Condell, who knew the author and had access to at least some of his manuscripts, lament the fact that Shakespeare did not live "to have set forth and overseen his own writings." And even had he done so—or, alternatively, even if a cache of his manuscripts were discovered in a Warwickshire attic tomorrow—all of the editorial problems would not be solved, nor would all of the levels of mediation be swept away. Certainly, the entire textual landscape would change. But the written word has strange powers: it seems to hold on to something of the very life of the person who has written it, but it also seems to pry that life loose from the writer, exposing it to vagaries of history and chance independent of those to which the writer was personally subject. Moreover, with the passing of centuries, the language itself and the whole frame of reference within which language and symbols are understood have decisively changed. The most learned modern scholar still lives at a huge experiential remove from Shakespeare's world and, even holding a precious copy of the First Folio in hand, cannot escape having to read across a vast chasm of time what is, after all, an edited text. The rest of us cannot so much as indulge in the fantasy of direct access: our eyes inevitably wander to the glosses and the explanatory notes.

The Oxford Shakespeare

The shattering of the dream of the master text is no cause for despair, nor should it lead us to throw our hands up and declare that one text is as good as another. What it does is to encourage the reader to be actively interested in the editorial principles that underlie the particular edition that he or she is using. It is said that the great artist Brueghel once told a nosy connoisseur who had come to his studio, "Keep your nose out of my paintings; the smell of the paint will poison you." In the case of Shakespeare, it is increasingly important to bring one's nose close to the page, as it were, and sniff the ink. More precisely, it is important to understand the rationale for the choices that the editors have made.

The text of the *Norton Shakespeare* is, with very few changes, that published by the Oxford University Press in 1988 and, in a second edition, in 2005. The *Oxford Shakespeare* was the extraordinary achievement of a team of editors, Stanley Wells, Gary Taylor, John Jowett, and William Montgomery, with Wells and Taylor serving as the general editors. The Oxford editors approached their task with a clear understanding that, as we have seen, all previous texts have been mediated by agents other than Shakespeare; however, they regard this mediation not as a melancholy obstacle intervening between the reader and the "true" Shakespearean text but rather as a constitutive element of this text. The art of the playwright is thoroughly dependent on the craft of go-betweens.

Shakespeare's plays were not written to be circulated in manuscript or printed form among readers. They were written to be performed by the players and, as the preface to the Quarto *Troilus and Cressida* indelicately puts it, "clapper-clawed with the palms of the vulgar." The public was, thus, never meant to be in a direct relationship with the author but in a "triangular relationship" in which the players gave voice and gesture to the author's words. As we have seen, Shakespeare was the master of the unfinished, the perpetually open. And even if we narrow our gaze and try to find only what Shakespeare himself might have regarded as a textual resting point, a place to stop and go on to another play, we have, the Oxford editors point out, a complex task. For whatever Shakespeare wrote was meant from the start to be supplemented by an invisible "paratext" consisting of words spoken by Shakespeare to the actors and by the actors to each other concerning emphasis, stage business, tone, pacing, possible cuts, and so forth. To the extent that this paratext was ever written down, it was recorded in the promptbook. Therefore, in contrast to standard editorial practice, the Oxford editors prefer, when there is a choice, copy based on the promptbook to copy based on the author's own draft. They choose the text immersed in history—that is, in the theatrical embodiment for which it was intended by its author—over the text unstained by the messy, collaborative demands of the playhouse. The closest we can get to Shakespeare's "final" version of a play—understanding that for him as for us there is no true "finality" in a theatrical text—is the latest version of that play performed by his company during his professional life—that is, during the time in which he could still oversee and participate in any cuts and revisions.

This choice does not mean that the Oxford editors are turning away from the very idea of Shakespeare as author. On the contrary, Wells and Taylor are deeply committed to establishing a text that comes as close as possible to the plays as Shakespeare wrote them, but they are profoundly attentive to the fact that he wrote them as a member of a company of players, a company in which he was a shareholder and an actor as well as a writer. "Writing" for the theater, at least for Shakespeare, is not simply a matter of setting words to paper and letting the pages drift away; it is a social process as well as an individual act. The Oxford editors acknowledge that some aspects of this social process may have been frustrating to Shakespeare: he may, for example, have been forced on occasion to cut lines and even whole scenes to which he was attached, or his fellow players may have insisted that they could not successfully perform what he had written, compelling him to make changes he did not welcome. But compromise and collaboration are part of what it means to be in the theater, and Wells and Taylor return again and again to the recognition that Shakespeare was, supremely, a man of the theater.

Is there a tension between the Oxford editors' preference for the performed, fully socialized text and their continued commitment to recovering the text as Shakespeare himself intended it? Yes. The tension is most visible in their determination to strip away textual changes arising from circumstances, such as government censorship, over which Shakespeare had no control. ("We have, wherever possible," they write, put "profanities back in Shakespeare's mouth.") It can be glimpsed as well in the editors' belief, almost a leap of faith, that there was little revision of Shakespeare's plays in his company's revivals between the time of his death and the publication of the Folio. But the tension is mainly a creative one, for it forces them (and, therefore, us) to attend to the playwright's unique imaginative power as well as his social and historical entanglements.

The Oxford editors took a radical stance on a second major issue: the question of authorial revision. Previous editors had generally accepted the fact that Shakespeare practiced revision within individual manuscripts—that is, while he was still in the act of writing a particular play—but they generally rejected the notion that he undertook substantial revisions from one version of a play to another (and, hence, from one manuscript to another). Wells and Taylor point out that six major works (*Hamlet, Othello, 2 Henry IV, King Lear, Richard II*, and *Troilus and Cressida*) survive in two independent substantive sources, both apparently authoritative, with hundreds of significant variant readings. Previous editors have generally sought to deny authority to one edition or another ("faced with two sheep," the Oxford editors observe wryly, "it is all too easy to insist that one *must* be a goat") or have conflated the two versions into a single text in an attempt to reconstruct the ideal, definitive, complete, and perfect version that they imagine Shakespeare must have reached for each of his plays. But if one doubts that Shakespeare ever conceived of his plays as closed, finished entities, if one recalls that he wrote them for the living repertory of the commercial playing company to which he belonged, then the whole concept of the single, authoritative text of each play loses its force. In a startling departure from the editorial tradition, the *Oxford Shakespeare* printed two distinct versions of *King Lear*, quarto and Folio, and the editors glanced longingly at the impractical but alluring possibility of including two texts of *Hamlet, Othello*, and *Troilus*.

The *Oxford Shakespeare* was published in both old-spelling and modern-spelling editions. The former, the first of its kind ever published, raised some reviewers' eyebrows because the project, a critical edition rather than a facsimile, required the modern editors to invent plausible Elizabethan spellings for their emendations and to add stage directions. The modern-spelling edition, which is the basis for Norton's text, is noteworthy for taking the principles of modernization further than they had generally been taken. Gone are such words as "murther," "mushrump," "vild," and "porpentine," which confer on many modern-spelling editions a certain cozy, Olde-English quaintness; Oxford replaces them with "murder," "mushroom," "vile," and "porcupine."

The inclusion of two texts of *King Lear* aroused considerable controversy when the *Oxford Shakespeare* first appeared, although by now the arguments for doing so have received widespread, though not unanimous, scholarly support. Other features remain controversial: "Ancients" Pistol and Iago have been modernized to "Ensigns"; *Henry VIII* has reverted to its performance title *All Is True*; demonic spirits in *Macbeth* sing lyrics written by Thomas Middleton. The white-hot intensity of the debates triggered by the *Oxford Shakespeare*'s editorial choices casts an interesting light on the place of Shakespeare not only in the culture at large but in the psyches of millions of individuals: any alteration, however minor, in a deeply familiar and beloved text, even an alteration based on thoughtful and highly plausible scholarly principles, arouses genuine anxiety. The anxiety in this case was intensified not only by the boldness of certain crucial emendations but also by the fact that the editors' explanations, arguments, and justifications for all their decisions were printed in a separate, massive volume, *William Shakespeare: A Textual Companion*. This formidable, dense volume is an astonishing monument to the seriousness, scholarly rigor, and immense labor of the Oxford editors. Anyone who is interested in pursuing why Shakespeare's words appear as they do in the current edition, anyone who wishes insight into the editors' detailed reasons for making the thousands of decisions required by a project of this kind, should consult the *Textual Companion*.

The Norton Shakespeare

The primary task that the editors of the *Norton Shakespeare* set themselves was to present the modern-spelling Oxford *Complete Works* in a way that would make the text more accessible to modern readers. The *Oxford Shakespeare* prints little more than the text itself: along with one-page introductions to the individual works, it contains a short general introduction, a list of contemporary allusions to Shakespeare, and a brief glossary. But while it is possible to enjoy a Shakespeare play on stage or screen without any assistance beyond the actors' own art, many readers at least since the eighteenth century have found it far more difficult to understand and to savor the texts without some more substantial commentary.

In addition to writing introductions, textual notes, and brief bibliographies for each of the works, the Norton editors provide glosses and footnotes designed to facilitate comprehension. Such is the staggering richness of Shakespeare's language that it is tempting to gloss everything. But there is a law of diminishing returns: too much explanatory whispering at the margins makes it difficult to enjoy what the reader has come for in the first place. Our general policy is to gloss only those words that cannot be found in an ordinary dictionary or whose meanings have altered out of recognition. The glosses attempt to be simple and straightforward, giving multiple meanings for words only when the meanings are essential for making sense of the passages in which they appear. We try not to gloss the same word over and over—it becomes distracting to be told three times on a single page that "an" means "if"—but we also assume that the reader does not have a perfect memory, so after an interval we will gloss the same word again.

Marginal glosses generally refer to a single word or a short phrase. The footnotes paraphrase longer units or provide other kinds of information, such as complex plays on words, significant allusions, textual cruxes, historical and cultural contexts. Here, too, however, we have tried to check the impulse to annotate so heavily that the reader is distracted from the pleasure of the text, and we have avoided notes that provide interpretation, as distinct from information.

Following the works, the Norton editors have provided lists of textual variants. These are variants from the control text only—that is, they do not record all of the variants in all of the substantive texts, nor do they record all of the myriad shifts of meaning that may arise from modernization of spelling and repunctuation. Readers who wish to pursue these interesting, if complex, topics are encouraged to consult the *Textual Companion,* along with the old-spelling *Oxford Shakespeare,* the Norton facsimile of the First Folio, and the quarto facsimiles published by the University of California Press. The *Norton Shakespeare* does provide a convenient list for each play of the different ways the same characters are designated in the speech prefixes in the substantive texts. These variants (for example, Lady Capulet in *Romeo and Juliet* is called, variously, "Lady," "Mother," "Wife," "Old Woman," etc.) often cast an interesting light on the ways a particular character is conceived. Variants as they appear in this edition, as well as their line numbers, are printed in boldface; each is followed by the corresponding reading in the control text, and sometimes the source from which the variant is taken. Further information on readings in substantive texts is given in brackets.

Stage directions pose a complex set of problems for the editors of a one-volume Shakespeare. The printing conventions for the stage directions in sixteenth- and seventeenth-century plays were different from those of our own time. Often all of the entrances for a particular scene are grouped together at the beginning, even though some of the characters clearly do not enter until later; placement in any case seems at times haphazard or simply incorrect. There are moments when the stage directions seem to provide stunning insight into the staging of the plays in Shakespeare's time, other moments when they are absent or misleading. It is difficult to gauge how much the stage directions in the substantive editions reflect Shakespeare's own words or at least decisions. It would seem that he was often relatively careless about them, understanding perhaps that these decisions in any precise sense would be the first to be made and unmade by different productions.

The Oxford editors, like virtually all modern editors, necessarily altered and supplemented the stage directions in their control texts. They decided to mark certain of the stage directions with a special sign to indicate a dubious action or placement, but they did not distinguish between the stage directions that came from the substantive texts and those added in later texts, from the seventeenth century to the present. They referred readers instead to the *Textual Companion,* which provides lists of the exact wording of the stage directions in the substantive texts.

The editors of the *Norton Shakespeare* share a sense of the limitations of the early stage directions and share as well some skepticism about how many of these should be attributed even indirectly to Shakespeare. Hence, we do not routinely differentiate between quarto and Folio stage directions; we do so only when we think it is a significant point. But there is, it seems to us, a real interest in knowing which stage directions come from those editions of the plays published up to the 1623 Folio (and including *The Two Noble Kinsmen,* published shortly thereafter) and which were added when the editors were no longer in contact with Shakespeare's presence or his manuscripts. Therefore, we have placed brackets around all stage directions that were added after the First Folio. Unbracketed stage directions, then, all derive from editions up through the Folio.

The *Norton Shakespeare* has made several other significant departures from the Oxford text. The Oxford editors note that when *1 Henry IV* was first performed, probably in 1596, the character we know as Sir John Falstaff was called Sir John Oldcastle. But in the wake of protests from Oldcastle's descendants, one of whom, William Brooke, tenth Baron Cobham, was Elizabeth I's lord chamberlain, Shakespeare changed the name to "Falstaff" (and probably for similar reasons changed the names of Falstaff's companions, Russell and Harvey, to "Bardolph" and "Peto"). Consistent with their decision not to honor changes that Shakespeare was *compelled* to make by censorship or other forms of pressure, the Oxford editors changed the names back to their initial form. But this decision is a problem for several reasons. It draws perhaps too sharp a distinction between those things that Shakespeare did under social pressure and those he did of his own accord. More seriously, it pulls against the principle of a text that represents the latest performance version of a play during Shakespeare's lifetime: after all, even the earliest quarto title page advertises "the humorous conceits of Sir John Falstaff." And, of course, it asks the reader to ignore completely and radically centuries of response—elaboration, fascination, and love—all focused passionately on Sir John Falstaff. The response is not a modern phenomenon: it began with Shakespeare, who developed the character as Sir John Falstaff in *2 Henry IV* and *The Merry Wives of Windsor.* Norton thus restores the more familiar names.

Another major departure from the Oxford text is Norton's printing of the so-called Additional Passages, especially in *Hamlet.* Consistent with their decision not to conflate quarto and Folio texts, the Oxford editors adhere to their control text for *Hamlet,* the Folio, and print those passages that appear only in the Second Quarto in an appendix at the end of the play. As explained at length in the Textual Note to the play, the Norton editors decided not to follow this course, but instead chose a different way of demarcating the quarto and Folio texts (inserting the quarto passages, indented, in the body of the text), one that makes it easier to see how the quarto passages functioned in a version of the play that Shakespeare also authored.

The *Norton Shakespeare* follows Oxford in printing separate quarto and Folio texts of *King Lear,* to which we have added a conflated version of the play so that readers will have the opportunity to assess for themselves the effects of the traditional editorial practice. Moreover, we have departed from Oxford in printing the quarto and Folio texts of the plays on facing pages, so that their differences can be readily weighed. In the hundreds of changes, some trivial and other momentous, it is possible to glimpse, across what Prospero calls "the dark backward and abysm of time," a thrilling sight: Shakespeare at work.

The Shakespearean Stage
by
ANDREW GURR

Publication by Performance

The curt exchange between the sentries in the first six lines of *Hamlet* tells us that it is very late at night ("'Tis now struck twelve") and that "'tis bitter cold." This opening was staged originally at the Globe in London in broad daylight, at 2 o'clock probably on a hot summer's afternoon. The words required the audience, half of them standing on three sides of the stage platform and all of them as visible to one another as the players were, to imagine themselves watching a scene quite the opposite of what they could see and feel around them. The original mode of staging for a Shakespearean play was utterly different from the cinematic realism we are used to now, where the screen gives us close-ups on a simulacrum of reality, an even more privileged view of the actors' facial twitches than we get in ordinary life. Eloquence then was in words, not facial expressions.

The playgoers of Shakespeare's time knew the plays in forms at which we can only now guess. It is a severe loss. Shakespeare's own primary concept of his plays was as stories "personated" onstage, not as words on a page. He himself never bothered to get his playscripts into print, and more than half of them were not published until seven years after his death, in the First Folio of his plays published as a memorial to him in 1623. His fellow playwright Francis Beaumont called the printing of plays "a second publication"; the first was their showing onstage. Print recorded a set of scripts, written for the original players to teach them what they should speak in the ensemble of the play in production. The only technology then available to record the performances was the written word. If video recordings had existed at that time, our understanding of Shakespeare would be vastly different from what it is today.

Since the texts were composed only to be a record of the words the players were to memorize, we now have to infer how the plays were originally staged largely by guess-work. Shakespeare was himself a player and shareholder in his acting company, and he expected to be present at rehearsals. Consequently, the stage directions in his scripts are distinctly skimpy compared with some of those provided by his fellow playwrights. He was cursory even in noting entrances and exits, let alone how he expected his company to stage the more complex spectacles, such as heaving Antony up to Cleopatra on her monument. There are sometimes hints in the stage directions and more frequently in the words used to describe some of the actions, and knowing what the design of the theater was like is a help as well. Knowing more about how Shakespeare expected his plays to be staged can transform how we think about them. But gaining such knowledge is no easy matter. One of the few certainties is that Shakespeare's plays in modern performance are even more different from the originals than modern printed editions are from the first much-thumbed manuscripts.

The Shakespearean Mindset

The general mindset of the original playgoers, the patterns of thinking and expectation that Tudor culture imposed on Shakespeare's audiences, is not really difficult to identify.

It is less easy, though, to pin it down in the sort of detail that tells us what the original concept of staging the plays would have been like. We know that all the original playgoers paid for the privilege of attending the plays and committed themselves willingly to suspend their disbelief in what they were to see. They knew as we do that they were paying to be entertained by fictions. Beyond that, we need reminding today that going to open-air performances in daylight in Shakespeare's time meant being constantly aware that one was in a theater, a place designed to offer illusions. On the one hand, this consciousness of oneself and where one was meant that the players had to do more to hold attention than is needed now, when audiences have nothing but the stage to look at and armchairs to sit in. On the other hand, it made everyone more receptive to extratheatrical tricks, such as Hamlet's reference to "this distracted globe," or Polonius's claim in the same play to have taken the part of Julius Caesar at the university and been killed by Brutus. The regular playgoers at the Globe who recognized Polonius as the man who had played Caesar in Shakespeare's play of the year before, and who recognized Hamlet as the man who had played Brutus, would laugh at this theatrical in-joke. But two scenes later, when Hamlet kills Polonius, they would think of it again, in a different light.

Features of the original mindset such as these are readily identifiable. For others, though, we need to look further, into the design of the theaters and into the staging traditions that they housed and that Shakespeare exploited. Invisibility has a part to play in A Midsummer Night's Dream that we can easily underrate, for instance. Invisibility onstage is a theatrical in-joke, an obvious privileging of the audience, which is allowed to see what the characters onstage can't. The impresario Philip Henslowe's inventory of costumes used at the Rose theater in 1597, which lists "a robe for to go invisible," indicates a fictional device that openly expects the willing suspension of the audience's disbelief. In A Midsummer Night's Dream, the ostensible invisibility of all the visible fairies emphasizes the theatricality of the whole presentation while pandering to the audience's self-indulgent superiority, the feeling that it knows what is going on better than any character, whether he be Bottom or even Duke Theseus. That prepares us for the mockery of stage realism we get later, in the mechanicals' play in Act 5, and even for the doubt we as willing audience might feel over Theseus's own skepticism about the dangers of imagination that he voices in his speech at the beginning of Act 5.

More to the point, though, it throws into question our readiness to be an audience, since we have ourselves been indulging in just the games of suspending disbelief that the play staged by the mechanicals enters into so unsuccessfully. When Theseus disputes with Hippolyta about the credibility of the lovers' story, he voices the very skepticism—about the lover, the lunatic, and the poet—that any sensible realist in the audience would have been feeling for most of the previous three acts in the forest. The play starts and ends at the court in broad daylight, while the scenes of midsummer madness take place at night in a forest. At the early amphitheaters, all the plays were staged in broad daylight, between 2 and 5 o'clock in the afternoon, and without any persuasive scenery: the two stage posts served as trees onstage. So the play, moving as it does from daylight realism to nocturnal fantasy and back again, with a last challenge to credulity in the mechanicals' burlesque of how to stage a play, has already thoroughly challenged the willing suspension of the viewers' disbelief. A Midsummer Night's Dream is a play about nocturnal dreams and fictions that are accepted as truths in broad daylight. It was only a small extension of this game to have the women's parts played by boys, as well as plots in which the girls dressed as boys, to the point where in As You Like It Rosalind was played by a boy playing a girl pretending to be a boy playing a girl.

The Shakespeare plays were written for a new and unique kind of playhouse, the Elizabethan amphitheater, which had a distinctive design quite different from modern theaters. Elizabethans knew what the standard features in their theaters stood for, and Shakespeare drew on that knowledge for the staging of his plays. The physical features of the playhouses were a potent element in the ways that the plays were designed for the Elizabethan mindset. When Richard III, the archdeceiver and playactor, appears "aloft between two Bishops" to claim the crown in Richard III 3.7, his placing on the stage balcony literally above the crowd on the stage would, even without the accompanying priests, have signified his ironic claim to a social and moral superiority that ought to have matched his elevation. When Richard II comes down from the wall of Flint Castle to the "base court" in *Richard II* 3.3, Elizabethans would have seen his descent as a withdrawal from power and status. These theaters were still new when Shakespeare started to write for them, and their novelty meant that the plays were written more tightly to fit their specific design than the plays of later years, when theatergoing had become a more routine social activity and different kinds of theater were available.

London Playgoing and the Law

This heightened sense of theatricality, or "metatheater," in Shakespearean audiences was far from the only difference in their mindset from that of all modern audiences. Regular playgoing in London only started in the 1570s, and through Shakespeare's earlier years it was always a perilous and precarious activity. The Lord Mayor of London and the mayors of most of England's larger towns hated playgoing and tried to suppress it whenever and wherever it appeared. Playgoing was exciting not only because it was new but because it was dangerous. The hostility of so many authorities to plays meant that they were seen almost automatically as subversive of authority. Paradoxically, the first London companies were only able to establish themselves in London through the active support of Queen Elizabeth and her Privy Council, which tried hard, in the face of constant complaints from the Lord Mayor, to ensure that the best companies would be on hand every Christmas to entertain the Queen's leisure hours. Popular support for playgoing depended on royal protection for the leading companies.

London was by far the largest city in England. Within a few years of Shakespeare's death, it became the largest in Europe. It was generally an orderly place to live, especially in the city itself. Even in the suburbs, where the poorer people had to live, there were not many of the riots and other disorders that preachers always associated with the brothels, animal-baiting arenas, and playhouses clustering there. The reputation that the playhouses gained for promoting riots was not well justified. Any crowd of people was seen by the authorities as a potential riot, and playhouses regularly drew some of the largest crowds that London had yet seen. The city's government was not designed to control large crowds of people. There was no paid police force, and the Lord Mayor was held responsible by the Privy Council, the Queen's governing committee, for any disorders that did occur. So the city authorities found that playgoing challenged their control over their people.

The rapid growth of London did not help the situation. Officially, the city was governed by the Lord Mayor and his council. But he had authority only inside the city, and London now spread through a large suburban area in the adjacent counties of Middlesex to the north and Surrey across the river to the south. Because the court and the national government were housed in London, the Privy Council often intervened in city affairs in its own interests, as well as when orders were needed that covered broader zones than the city itself. The periodic outbreaks of bubonic plague were one clear instance of such a need, because the plague took no notice of parish or city boundaries. The intrusion of the professional companies to play in London provided another. In the early years, they were chronic travelers, and London was simply one of many stopovers. But the Queen enjoyed seeing plays at Christmas, and her council accordingly supported the best companies so that they could perform for her. It protected the playing companies against the hatred of successive Lord Mayors, except when a national emergency such as a plague epidemic erupted. The Privy Council took control then by ordering the 126 parishes in and around London to list all deaths from plague separately from ordinary deaths. Each Thursday, the parish totals were added together. When the total number of deaths from plague in these lists rose above 30 in any one week, the Privy Council closed all places of public assembly. This meant especially the playhouses, which created by far the largest gatherings. When the theaters were closed, the playing companies had to revert to their traditional practice of going on tour to play in the towns through the country, provided that the news of plague did not precede them.

Plague was not the only reason for the government to lay its controlling hand on the companies. From the time the post was inaugurated in 1578, the Master of the Revels controlled all playing. He was executive officer to the Lord Chamberlain, the Privy Council officer responsible for the annual season of royal entertainment and thus, by extension, for the professional playing companies. The Master of the Revels licensed each company and censored its plays. He was expected to cut out any references to religion or affairs of state, and he tried to prevent other offenses by banning the depiction of any living person onstage. After 1594, he issued licenses to the approved London playhouses, too. Later still, the printing of any playbook was allowed only if he gave authority for it. The companies had to accept this tight control because the government was its only protector against the hostile municipal authorities, who included not only the Lord Mayor of London but also the mayors of most of the major towns in the country.

Most mayors had the commercial interest of keeping local employees at work to justify their hostility to playgoing. But across the country, the hostility went much deeper. A large proportion of the population disliked the very idea of playacting. Their reasons, ostensibly religious, were that for actors to pretend to be characters they were unlike in life was a deception and that for boys to dress as women was contrary to what the Bible said. Somewhere beneath this was a more basic fear of pretense and deceit, of people not acting honestly. It put actors into the same category as con men, cheats, and thieves. That was probably one reason why companies of boys acting men's parts were thought rather more tolerable than men pretending to be other kinds of men. The deception involved in boys playing men was more transparent than when men played characters other than themselves. There was also a strong Puritan suspicion about shows of any kind, which looked too much like the Catholic ceremonial that the new Church of England had renounced. Playgoing found much better favor on the Catholic side of English society than on the Puritan side. Different preachers took different positions over the new phenomenon of playgoing. But few would speak in its favor, and most of them openly disapproved of it. Playgoing was an idle pastime, and the devil finds work for idle hands.

In the 1590s, when *Romeo and Juliet* and Shakespeare's histories and early comedies were exciting audiences, only two playhouses and two companies were officially approved by the Queen's Privy Council for the entertainment of London's citizens. The other main forms of paid entertainment were bear- and bullbaiting, which were much harder on the performers than was playing and so could be staged less frequently. The hostility to plays meant that the right to perform was confined to only a few of the most outstanding companies. These few companies were in competition with one another, and this led to a rapid growth in the quality of their offerings. But playacting was always a marginal activity. Paying to enter a specially built theater in order to see professional companies perform plays was still a new phenomenon, and it still met with great opposition from the London authorities. The open-air theaters like the Globe were built out in the suburbs. London as a city had no centrally located playhouses until after the civil war and the restoration of the monarchy, in 1661. And even playing in the city's suburbs, where they were free from the Lord Mayor's control, the companies had to work under the control of the Privy Council. All the great amphitheaters were built either in Middlesex or in Surrey. At the height of their success, in the years after Shakespeare's death, the Privy Council never licensed more than four or five playhouses in London.

Playgoing in London was viewed even by the playgoers as an idle occupation. The largest numbers who went to the Globe were apprentices and artisans taking time off from work, often surreptitiously, and law students from the Inns of Court doing the same. These fugitives were linked with the wealthier kind of idler, "gallants" or rich gentlemen and other men of property, along with soldiers and sailors on leave from the wars, people visiting London from the country on business or pleasure (usually both), and above all the women of London. Women were not expected to be literate, but one did not need to be able to read and write to enjoy hearing and seeing a play. A respectable woman had to make sure she was escorted by a man. He might be a husband or a friend, or her page if she was rich, or her husband's apprentice if she was a middle-class citizen. She might have a mask on, part of standard women's wear outdoors to protect the face against the weather and to assert modesty—and perhaps anonymity. Market women (applewives and fishwives) went to plays in groups. Whores were expected to be there looking for business, especially from the gallants, but they usually had male escorts, too.

The social range of playgoers at the two playhouses approved for use in 1594 was almost complete, stretching from the aristocracy to the poorest workmen and boys. Many people disapproved of plays, but at peak times up to 25,000 a week flocked to see the variety of plays being offered. Prices for playgoing remained much the same throughout the decades up to 1642, when the parliamentary government that was fighting the King closed all the theaters for eighteen years. Until then, one could get standing room at an amphitheater for 1 penny (1/240th of a modern pound, roughly 1 cent),

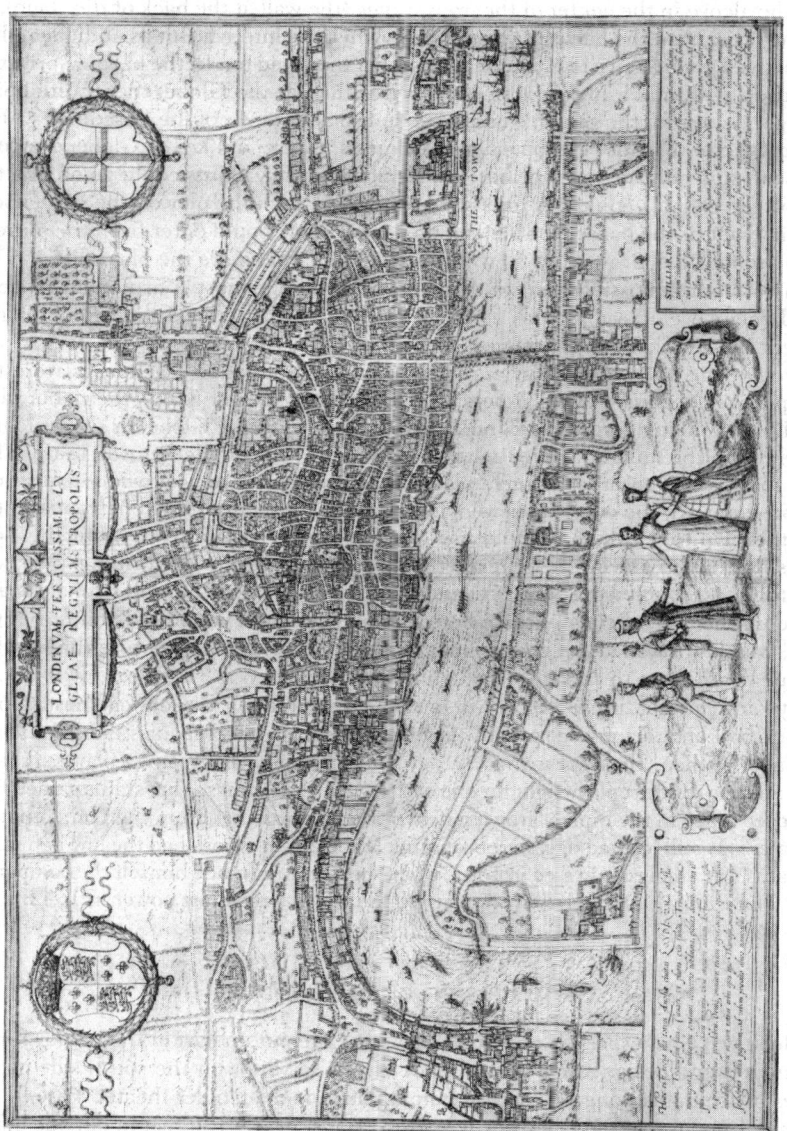

The city of London and its suburbs in 1572.

or a seat on a bench in the roofed galleries for twopence. A seat in a lord's room cost sixpence, which was not much less than a day's wage for a skilled artisan in 1600. The smaller roofed theaters that opened in 1599 were much more expensive. They were called "private" theaters to distinguish them from the "public" open-air amphitheaters, although the claim to privacy was mainly a convenient fiction to escape the controls imposed on the "public" theaters. At the Blackfriars hall theater, sixpence only gained you a seat in the topmost gallery, while a seat in the pit near the stage cost three times that amount and a seat in a box five times, or half a skilled worker's weekly wage.

It was not only the plays and players that were the sights at the playhouses. The richest lords and gallants went to be seen as much as they went to see. At the Globe, the costliest rooms were positioned alongside the balcony "above," over the stage. They were called "lords' rooms," and the playgoers who chose to sit there had a limited view of what went on beneath them. They saw no "discoveries," for instance, such as Portia's three caskets in *The Merchant of Venice,* which were uncovered underneath them inside the alcove in the center of the *frons scenae* (the wall at the back of the stage), or anything other than the backs of the players when they entered. But as audience, they were themselves highly visible, and that was what they paid for. In the hall, or "private," playhouses, with much higher admission prices than at the Globe, there were boxes flanking the stage for the gentry, which gave them a better view of the "discoveries." But at these "select" (because costlier) hall playhouses, where, unlike the Globe, everyone had a seat, some of the most colorful and exhibitionistic gallants could go one better. Up to fifteen gallants could pay for a stool to sit and watch the play on the stage itself, sitting in front of the boxes that flanked the stage. Each would enter from the players' dressing room (the "tiring-house") with his stool in hand before the play started. This gave them the best possible view of the play and easily the most conspicuous place in the audience's eye. Playgoing was a public occasion in which the visibility of audience members allowed them to play almost as large a part as the players.

Through the 1590s, the only permanent and custom-made playhouses were the large open-air theaters. Paying sixpence for a ferry across the river, as the richer playgoers did, or walking across London Bridge to the Rose or the Globe, or else trudging north through the mud of Shoreditch and Finsbury Fields or Clerkenwell to the Theatre or the Fortune in order to see a play, did not have great appeal when it was raining. Consequently, the companies were always trying to secure roofed halls nearer the city center. Up to 1594, they could use city inns, especially in winter, but the Lord Mayor's hostility to playing never made them reliable places for performing. Two constant problems troubled the players throughout these first years of professional theater in London: the city officials' chronic hatred of plays and the periodic visitations of the plague, which always led the government to close the theaters as soon as the number of plague deaths rose to dangerously high levels.

Playgoing was not firmly established in London until the Privy Council chose to protect it in 1594 and to approve specific playhouses for the two companies that it officially sanctioned. By then, Shakespeare had already made his mark. He became a player, a shareholder, and the resident playwright for one of these two companies. That status gained him a privileged place in the rapidly growing new world of playgoing. From then on, although his theater was still located only in the suburbs of the city, his work had the law behind it. That status was amply confirmed in 1603, when the new King made himself the company's patron. The King's Men held their status until the King himself lost power in 1642.

The Design of the Globe

The Globe was Shakespeare's principal playhouse. He put up part of the money for its construction and designed his best plays for it. It was built on the south side of the Thames in 1599, fashioned out of the framing timbers of an older theater. Essentially, it was a polygonal scaffold of twenty bays or sections, nearly 100 feet in outside diameter, making a circle of three levels of galleries that rose to more than 30 feet high, with wooden bench seating and cushions for those who could afford them. This surrounded an open "yard," into which the stage projected.

The yard was over 70 feet in diameter. Nearly half the audience stood on their feet to watch the play from inside this yard, closest to the stage platform. The stage extended out nearly to the middle of the yard, so the actors could stand in the center of the crowd. The uncertain privilege of having standing room in the open air around the stage platform could be bought with the minimal price for admission, 1 penny (about a cent). It had the advantage of proximity to the stage and the players; its disadvantage was keeping you on your feet for the two or three hours of the play, as well as leaving you subject to the weather. If you wanted a seat, or if it rained and you wanted shelter, you paid twice as much to sit in the three ranks of roofed galleries that circled behind the crowd standing in the yard. With some squeezing, the theater could hold over 3,000 people. It was an open-air theater because that gave it a larger capacity than a roofed hall. The drawback of its being open to the weather was more than outweighed by the gain in daylight that shone on stage and spectators alike.

The stage was a great square platform as much as 40 feet wide. It had over it a canopied roof, or "heavens," to protect the players and their expensive costumes from rain. This canopy was held up by two pillars rising through the stage. The stage platform was about 5 feet high and without any protective rails, so that the eyes of the audience in the yard were at the level of the players' feet. At the back of the stage, a wall—the *frons scenae*—stretched across the front of the players' tiring-house, the attiring or dressing room. It had a door on each flank and a wider curtained space in the center, which was used for major entrances and occasionally for set-piece scenes. Above these entry doors was a gallery or balcony, most of which was partitioned into rooms for the wealthiest spectators. A central room "above" was sometimes used in staging: for example, as Juliet's balcony, as the place for Richard II to stand between the bish-

The second Globe, from Wenceslaus Hollar's engraving of the "Long View" of London (1647). The two captions saying "The Globe" and "Beere bayting h." were accidentally transposed in the original. The Globe is the round structure in the center of the picture.

A photograph of the interior framework of the "new" Globe, on the south bank of the Thames in London, showing the general dimensions of the yard and the surrounding galleries.

ops, as the wall of Flint Castle in *Richard II,* and as the wall over the city gates of Harfleur in *Henry V.* After 1608, when Shakespeare's company acquired the Blackfriars consort of musicians, this central gallery room was turned into a curtained-off music room that could double as an "above" when required. Fewer than half of Shakespeare's plays need an "above."

The Original Staging Techniques

Shakespearean staging was emblematic. The "heavens" that covered the stage was the colorful feature from which gods descended to the earth of the stage platform. When Jupiter made his appearance in *Cymbeline,* in clouds of "sulphurous breath" provided by fireworks, he was mounted on an eagle being lowered through a trapdoor in the heavens. The other trapdoor, set in the stage platform itself, symbolized the opposite, a gateway to hell. The large stage trap was the place where the Gravedigger came to work at the beginning of Act 5 of *Hamlet.* It was the cell where Malvolio was imprisoned in *Twelfth Night.* The Shakespearean mindset accepted such conventions automatically.

Shakespeare inherited from Marlowe a tradition of using the stage trap as the dreaded hell's mouth. Barabbas plunges into it in *The Jew of Malta,* and the demons drag the screaming Faustus down it at the end of *Dr. Faustus.* Hell was not a fiction taken lightly by Elizabethans. Edward Alleyn, by far the most famous player of Faustus in the 1590s, wore a cross on his breast while he played the part, as insurance—just in case the fiction turned serious. Tracking the Elizabethan mindset about the stage trapdoor can give us a few warnings of what we might overlook when we come fresh to the plays today.

In the original staging of *Hamlet* at the Globe, the stage trap had two functions. Besides serving as Ophelia's grave, it was the distinctive entry point, not used by any other character, for the Ghost in Act 1. When he tells his son that he is "for the day confined to fast in fires," the first audiences would have already taken the point that he

The Globe as reconstructed in Southwark near the original site in London.

had come up from the underworld. His voice comes from under the stage, telling the
soldiers to swear the oath of secrecy that Hamlet lays upon them. The connection
between that original entry by the Ghost through the trap and the trap's later use for
Ophelia is one we might easily miss. At the start of Act 5, the macabre discussion
between the Gravediggers about whether she committed suicide and is, therefore, con-

The *frons scenae* of the new Globe.

A gesture using the language of hats, as shown by the man attending the brothers Browne.

signed to hell gets its sharpest edge from the association of the trap, here the grave being dug for her, with the Ghost's purgatorial fires. More to the point, though, Hamlet, as he eavesdrops on the curtailed burial ceremony, makes the same connection when he discovers that it is the body of Ophelia being so neglectfully interred. He remembers the other apparition that came up through the trap and springs forward in a grotesque parody of the Ghost, crying, "This is I, Hamlet the Dane!" It is a melodramatic claim to be acting a new role, that of his father the dead King. The first audiences would have remembered the ghost of dead King Hamlet using the stage trap at this point more readily than we do now. Hamlet's private knowledge of the Ghost and the trapdoor sets him, as so often happens in the play, at odds with his audience. Consequently, centuries of editors, like the characters onstage, have misread this claim as a declaration that young Hamlet ought to be King.

Since his own name is Hamlet, and since he alone could have made the connection between the Ghost and the trapdoor, he was all too likely to be misunderstood. In the next scene, Osric certainly shows that he understands Hamlet's graveside claim that he is his father's ghost to be a claim that he should now be King of Denmark. That explains why Osric insists on keeping his hat in his hand when he comes to invite Hamlet to duel with Laertes. With equals, an Elizabethan gentleman would doff his hat in greeting and then put it back on. Only in the presence of your master, or as a courtier in the presence of the King, did you keep it in your hand. Osric is trying tactfully to acknowledge what he thinks is Hamlet's lunatic claim to be King. He missed the private connection that Hamlet had made with the trapdoor and his father's ghost. Tudor body language, with its wordless gestures and signals that defined human relations, was an aspect of social life so widely understood that it needed no stage direction. The language of hats was a part of the Shakespearean mindset that we now have to register in footnotes.

Other signifiers are necessarily more elusive. We might take heart from the range of the comments made in *Much Ado About Nothing* 4.1 when Hero is accused and is seen to go red. Each of the viewers—Claudio, Leonato, and Friar Francis—gives a different reading (or "noting") of her blush. Different mindsets lead to visual indicators being read in different ways. Each reading tells as much about the observer as about the thing observed. We might add that since the blush is commented on so extensively, Shakespeare must have been concerned to save the boy playing Hero from the necessity of holding his breath long enough to produce the right visual effect.

Costume was a vital element in the plays, a mute and instant signifier of the scene. If a character entered carrying a candle and dressed in a gown with a nightcap on his head, he had evidently just been roused from bed. Characters who entered wearing cloaks and riding boots and possibly holding a whip had just ended a long journey. York,

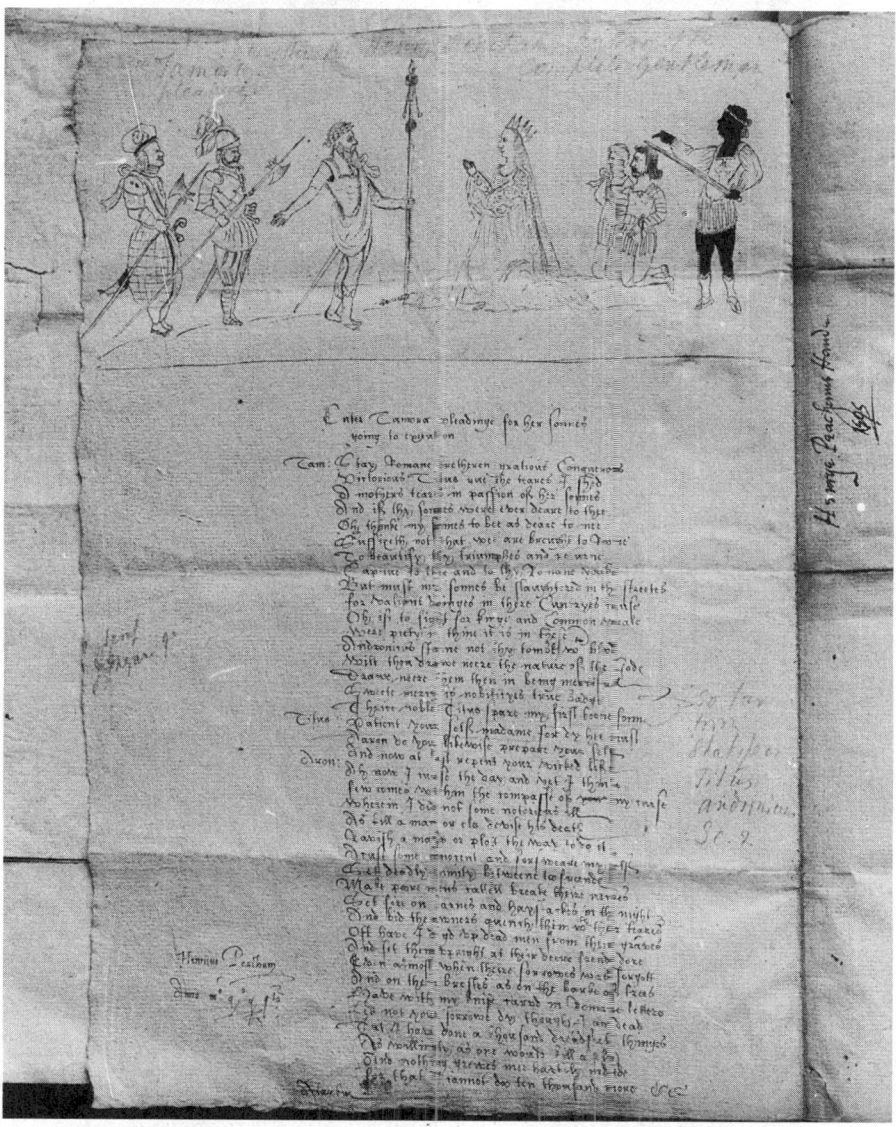

A sketch by Henry Peacham of an early staging of *Titus Andronicus* by Shakespeare's company (1595). Note the attempt at a Roman costume for Titus but not for his soldiers, who carry Tudor halberds, and note Aaron's makeup and wig.

entering in *Richard II* with a gorget (a metal neck plate, the "signs of war about his agèd neck" [2.2.74]), was preparing for battle. Even the women's wigs that the boys wore could be used to indicate the wearer's state of mind. Hair worn loose and unbound meant madness, whether in *Hamlet*'s Ophelia or *Troilus*'s Cassandra.

Comparable audience expectations could be roused by other visual features. Characters with faces blackened and wigs of curly black wool were recognized as Moors,

Johannes de Witt's drawing of the Swan Theatre in 1596, showing two boys playing women greeted by a chamberlain.

alien and dangerous non-Christians. Aaron the Moor in *Titus Andronicus* and the Prince of Morocco in *The Merchant of Venice* acquire that character as soon as they come in view. Othello, by Iago's report and by his own first appearance, takes on the same stereotype. By contrast, Iago is dressed like a simple and honest soldier. Only in the course of Act 1 does it become apparent that it is Othello who is the honest soldier, Iago the un-Christian alien. The play neatly reverses the visual stereotypes of Elizabethan staging. Twentieth-century playgoers miss most of these signals and the ways that the original players used them to show the discrepancy between outward appearance and inner person. As King Lear said, robes and furred gowns hide all.

For *The Merchant of Venice*, Shylock wore his "Jewish gabardine" and may also have put on a false nose, as Alleyn was said to have done for the title role in *The Jew of Malta*. Other national characteristics were noted by features of dress, such as the Irish "strait strossers" (tight trousers) that Macmorris would have worn in *Henry V.* The dress of the women in the plays, who were usually played by boys with unbroken voices, was always a special expense. The records kept by Philip Henslowe, owner of the Rose playhouse and impresario for the rival company to Shakespeare's, show that he paid the author less for the script of *A Woman Killed with Kindness* than he paid the costumer for the heroine's gown.

Women's clothing and the decorums and signals that women's costume contained were very different from those of men and men's clothing. Men frequently used their hats, doffing them to signal friendship and holding them in their hands while speaking to anyone in authority over them. Women's hats were fixed to their heads and were rarely if ever taken off in public. The forms and the language of women's clothes reflected the silent modesty and the quiet voices that men thought proper for women. Women had other devices to signal with, including handkerchiefs, fans, and face masks, and the boys playing the women's parts in the theaters exploited such accessories to the full. A lady out of doors commonly wore a mask to protect her complexion. When Othello is quizzing Emilia in 4.2 about his wife's behavior while she spoke to Cassio, he asks Emilia, who should have been chaperoning her mistress, whether Desdemona had not sent her away "to fetch her fan, her gloves, her mask, nor nothing?" There is little doubt that the boys would have routinely worn masks when they played gentlewomen onstage, and not just at the masked balls in *Romeo and Juliet*, *Love's Labour's Lost*, and *Much Ado About Nothing*.

Other features of the original staging stemmed from the actor–audience relationship, which differs radically in daylight, when both parties can see one another, from what we are used to in modern, darkened, theaters. An eavesdropping scene onstage, for instance, works rather on the same basis as the "invisible" fairies in *A Midsummer Night's Dream*, where the audience agrees to share the pretense. At the Globe, it also entailed adopting the eavesdropper's perspective. In *Much Ado*, the two games of eavesdropping played on Benedick and Beatrice are chiefly done around the two stage posts. In these scenes, the posts that held up the stage cover, or "heavens," near what we now think of as the front of the stage were round, like the whole auditorium, and their function was to allow things to be seen equally by all of the audience, wherever people might be standing or sitting. Members of the audience, sitting in the surrounding galleries or standing around the stage itself at the Globe or its predecessors, had the two tall painted pillars in their sight all the time, wherever they were in the playhouse. And since the audience was in a complete circle all around the stage, if the stage posts were used for concealment there was always a large proportion of the audience who could see the player trying to hide behind a post. It was a three-dimensional game in which the audience might find itself behind any of the game players, victims or eavesdroppers, complicit in either role.

The first of *Much Ado's* eavesdropping scenes, 2.3, starts as usual in Shakespeare with a verbal indication of the locality. Benedick tells his boy, "Bring it hither to me in the orchard." So we don't need stage trees to tell us where we are supposed to be. He later hides "in the arbour" to listen to what Don Pedro and the others have set for him; this means concealing himself behind a stage post, closer to the audience than the playactors who are talking about him. Don Pedro asks, "See you where Benedick hath hid himself?" a self-contradiction that confirms the game. When it is Beatrice's turn in her arbor scene, 3.1, she slips into a "bower" behind "this alley," which again signals a retreat behind the prominent stage post. These games are played with both of the eavesdroppers hiding behind the post at the stage edge, while the others do their talking at center stage between the two posts.

Such games of eavesdropping, using the same bits of the stage structure, make a strong visual contrast with all that goes on at what we two-dimensional thinkers, used to the pictorial staging of the cinema, call the "back" of the stage, or upstage—where, for instance, the Friar starts the broken-off wedding and where Claudio and Don Pedro later figure at Leonato's monument. These events are more distant from the audience, less obviously comic and intimate. The close proximity of players to audience in such activities as eavesdropping strongly influenced the audience's feeling of kinship with the different groupings of players.

A multitude of other staging differences can be identified. Quite apart from the fact that the language idioms were more familiar to the playgoers at the original Globe than they are now, all playgoers in 1600, many of them illiterate, were practiced listeners. The speed of speech, even in blank verse, was markedly higher then than the recitation of Shakespeare is today. The original performances of *Hamlet*, if the Folio version reflects what was usually acted, would have run for not much more than two and a half hours (the time quoted by Ben Jonson for a play as long as *Hamlet*), compared with the more than four hours that the full Folio or 1605 quarto text with at least one intermission would take today. Quicker speaking, quicker stage action, no intermissions, and the audience's ability to grasp the language more quickly meant that the plays galloped along. The story, not the verse, carried the thrust of the action. Occasional set speeches, like Hamlet's soliloquies or Gaunt's "sceptred isle" speech in *Richard II*, would be heard, familiar as they already were to many in the audience, like a solo aria in a modern opera. In theory if not in practice, the business of hearing, as "audience" (from the Latin *audire*, "to hear"), was more important than the business of seeing, as "spectators" (from the Latin *spectare*, "to see"). The visual aspects of acting, like scenic staging, are inherently two-dimensional and do not work well when the audience completely surrounds the actors. Most of Shakespeare's fellow writers, notably Jonson, understandably set a higher priority on the audience's hearing their verse than on their seeing what the players did with the lines. The poets wanted listeners, although the players did try to cater to the viewers. Yet for all the games with magic tricks and devils spouting fireworks that were part of the Shakespearean staging tradition, spectacle was a limited resource on the scene-free Elizabethan stage. Shakespeare in this was a poet more than a player. Even in his last and most richly staged plays—*Cymbeline, The Winter's Tale*, and *The Tempest*—he made notably less use of such "spectacles" than did his contemporaries.

One piece of internal evidence about the original staging is Hamlet's advice to the visiting players. In 3.2, before they stage the *Mousetrap* play that he has rewritten for them, he lectures them on what a noble student of the theater then considered to be good acting. He objects first to overacting and second to the clown who ad libs with his own jokes and does not keep to the script. How far this may have been Shakespeare's own view it is impossible to say. Hamlet is an amateur lecturing professionals about how they should do their job. His views are what we would expect an amateur playwright with a liking for plays that are "caviar to the general" to hold. His objections to the clown are noteworthy, because once the original performances ended, the clown would conclude the afternoon's entertainment with a comic song-and-dance jig. Thomas Platter, a young German-speaking Swiss student, went to the Globe in 1599 to see *Julius Caesar*. He reported back home that

> on 21 September after lunch I and my party crossed the river, and there in the playhouse with the thatched roof witnessed an excellent performance of the tragedy of the first emperor Julius Caesar with a cast of about fifteen people. When the play

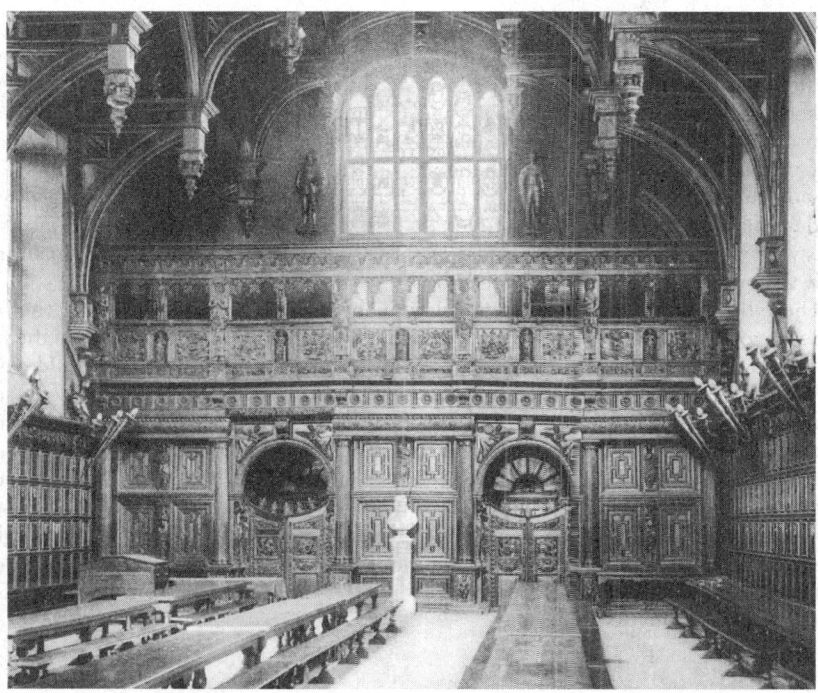

The hall screen in the Middle Temple Hall, built in 1574. Shakespeare's company staged *Twelfth Night* in this hall in February 1602.

was over they danced marvellously and gracefully together as their custom is, two dressed as men and two as women.[1]

The script for one jig survives, probably played by Will Kemp, who was the Shakespeare company clown until he left just before *Hamlet* came to the Globe. Its story is a bawdy knockabout tale of different men trying to seduce a shopkeeper's wife in rhyming couplets, hiding in a chest from her husband, and beating one another up. There is nothing to say what the audience reaction to such a jig might have been after they had seen a performance of *Julius Caesar* or *Hamlet*. It is possible that the Globe players stopped offering that kind of coda when they acquired the clown who played Feste in *Twelfth Night* in 1601. The song with which Feste ends that play might have become an alternative form of closure, replacing the traditional bawdy jig.

Vigorous and rapid staging was inevitable when the half of the audience closest to the stage had to stand throughout the performance. Shakespeare's plays were distinctive among the other plays of the time for their reliance on verbal sparkle over scenes of battle and physical movement, but even the soliloquies raced along. There was little occasion for long pauses and emoting. Dumb shows, like the players' prelude to the *Mousetrap* play in *Hamlet,* were the nearest that the players came to silent acting. There were no intermissions—apples, nuts, and drink were peddled in the auditorium throughout the performance—and the only "comfort stations" were, for the men, the nearest blank wall; for the women, whatever convenient pots or bottles they might be carrying under their long skirts.

Nor were there any pauses to change scenes. There was no static scenery apart from an emblematic candle to signify a night scene, a bed "thrust out" onto the stage, or the canopied chair of state on which the ruler or judge sat for court scenes. Usually any

1. *Thomas Platter's Travels in England* (1599), rendered into English from the German, and with introductory matter by Clare Williams (London: Cape, 1937), p. 166.

special locality would be signaled in the first words of a new scene, but unlocalized scenes were routine. Each scene ended when all the characters left the stage and another set entered. No act breaks appear in the plays before *The Tempest*. *Henry V* marked each act with a Chorus, but even he entered on the heels of the characters from the previous scene. Blue-coated stagehands were a visibly invisible presence onstage. They would draw back the central hangings on the *frons scenae* for a discovery scene, carry on the chair of state on its dais for courtroom scenes, or push out the bed with Desdemona on it for the last act of *Othello*. They served the stage like the house servants with whom the nobility peopled every room in their great houses, silent machines ready to spring into action when needed.

There has been a great deal of speculation about the tiring-house front at the rear of the stage platform: did it look more like an indoor set or an outdoor one, like the hall screen of a great house or palace or like a housefront exterior? In fact, it could easily be either. The upper level of the *frons*, the balconied "above," might equally represent a musicians' gallery, like those in the main hall of a great house, or a city wall under which the central discovery space served as the city gates, as it did for York in *Richard Duke of York* (3 *Henry VI*) 4.8, or *Henry V*'s Harfleur (3.3.78). The "above" could equally be an indoor gallery or an outdoor balcony. The appearance of the stage was everything and nothing, depending on what the play required. Players and playwrights expected the audience members to use their imagination, as they had to with the opening lines of *Hamlet*, or, as the Prologue to *Henry V* put it, to "piece out our imperfections with your thoughts."

Shakespeare's Companies and Their Playhouses

Shakespeare's plays were written for a variety of staging conditions. Until 1594, when he joined a new company under the patronage of the Lord Chamberlain, the Queen's officer responsible for licensing playing companies, poets had written their plays for any kind of playhouse. The Queen's Men, the largest and best company of the 1580s, is on record as playing at the Bell, the Bel Savage, and the Bull inns inside the city, and at the Theatre and the Curtain playhouses in the suburbs. Early in 1594, it completed this sweep of all the available London venues by playing at the Rose. But in that year, the system of playing changed. The Lord Mayor had always objected to players using the city's inns, and in May 1594 he succeeded in securing the Lord Chamberlain's agreement to a total ban. From then on, only the specially built playhouses in the suburbs were available for plays.

The Queen's Men had been set up in 1583, drawn from all the then-existing major companies with the best players. This larger and favored group at first monopolized playing in London. But it was in decline by the early 1590s, and the shortage of companies to perform for the Queen at Christmas led the Lord Chamberlain and his son-in-law, the Lord Admiral, to set up two new companies in its place as a duopoly in May 1594. Shakespeare became a "sharer," or partner, in one of these companies. As part of the same new establishment, his company, the Lord Chamberlain's Men, was allocated the Theatre to perform in, while its partner company in the duopoly, the Lord Admiral's Men, was assigned to the Rose. This was the first time any playing company secured a playhouse officially authorized for its use alone.

The Theatre, originally built in 1576 by James Burbage, father of the leading player of the Lord Chamberlain's company, was in Shoreditch, a suburb to the north of the city. The Rose, built in 1587 by Philip Henslowe, father-in-law of the Lord Admiral's leading player, Edward Alleyn, was in the suburb of Southwark, on the south bank of the Thames. Henslowe's business papers, his accounts, some lists of costumes and other resources, and his "diary," a day-by-day listing of each day's takings and the plays that brought the money in, have survived for the period from 1592 until well into the next decade. Together they provide an invaluable record of how one of the two major companies of the later 1590s, the only rival to Shakespeare's company, operated through these years.[2] Some of Shakespeare's earlier plays, written before he joined the Lord Chamberlain's Men, including *1 Henry VI* and *Titus Andronicus*, were performed at the Rose. After May 1594, the new company acquired all of his early plays; every Shakespeare play through the next three years was written for the Theatre. Its familiarity supplied one sort of resource to the playwright. But the repertory system laid heavy demands on the company.

Henslowe's papers give a remarkable record of the company repertory for these years. Each afternoon, the same team of fifteen or so players would stage a different play. With only two companies operating in London, the demand was for constant change. No play at the Rose was staged more than four or five times in any month, and it was normal to stage a different play on each of the six afternoons of each week that they performed. A new play would be introduced roughly every three weeks—after three weeks of transcribing and learning the new parts; preparing the promptbook, costumes, and properties; and rehearsing in the mornings—while each afternoon, whichever of the established plays had been advertised around town on the playbills would be put on. The leading players had to memorize on average as many as eight hundred lines for each afternoon. Richard Burbage, who played the first Hamlet in 1601, probably had to play Richard III, Orlando in *As You Like It*, and Hamlet on successive afternoons while at the same time learning the part of Duke Orsino and rehearsing the new *Twelfth Night*—and still holding at least a dozen other parts in his head for the rest of the month's program. In the evenings, he might be called on to take the company to perform a different play at court or at a nobleman's house in the Strand. The best companies made a lot of money, but not without constant effort.

The companies were formed rather like guilds, controlled by their leading "sharers." Each senior player shared the company's profits and losses equally with his fellows. Most of the plays have seven or eight major speaking parts for the men, plus two for the boys playing the women. A normal London company had eight or ten sharers, who collectively chose the repertory of plays to be performed, bought the playbooks from the poets, and put up the money for the main company resource of playbooks and costumes (not to mention the wagon and horses for touring when plague forced the London theaters to close). Shakespeare made most of his fortune from his "share," first in his company and later in its two playhouses.

As a playhouse landlord, Henslowe took half of the takings from the galleries each afternoon for his rent, while the players shared all the yard takings and the other half of the gallery money. From their takings, the sharers paid hired hands to take the walk-on parts and to work as stagehands, musicians, bookkeeper or prompter, and "gatherers" at the different entry gates. The leading players also kept the boys who played the women's parts, housing and feeding them as "apprentices" in an imitation of the London livery companies and trades, which ran apprenticeships to train boys to become skilled artisans, or "journeymen." City apprenticeships ran for seven years from the age of seventeen, but the boy players began much younger, because unbroken voices were needed. They graduated to become adult players at an age when the city apprentices were only beginning their training. Most of the "extras," apart from the playing boys, would be left in London whenever the company had to go on tour.

Because the professional companies of the kind that Shakespeare joined all started as traveling groups rather than as companies settled at a single playhouse in London, the years up to 1594 yielded plays that could be staged anywhere. The company might be summoned to play at court, at private houses, or at the halls of the Inns of Court as readily as at inns or innyards or the custom-built theaters themselves. They traveled the country with their plays, using the great halls of country houses, or town guildhalls and local inns, wherever the town they visited allowed them. Consequently, the plays could not demand elaborate resources for staging. In this highly mobile tradition of traveling

2. See *Henslowe's Diary*, ed. R. A. Foakes (Cambridge, Eng.: Cambridge University Press, 1961).

companies, they were written in the expectation of the same basic but minimal features being available at each venue. Besides the stage platform itself, the basic features appear to have been two entry doors, usually a trap in the stage floor, a pair of stage pillars, sometimes a discovery space, and very occasionally a heavens with descent machinery. Apart from these fixtures, properties such as chairs and a table, a canopied throne on a dais, and sometimes a bed were also in regular use, though in a pinch these could be as mobile as the players themselves. The only essential traveling properties were players, playbooks, and costumes.

Once the two authorized companies settled permanently at the Theatre and the Rose in 1594, they slowly lost some of this mobility. The demands of versatility and readiness to make rapid changes now had to be switched from the venues to the plays themselves. A traveling company needed very few plays, since the locations and audiences were always changing. When the venues became fixed, it was the plays that had to keep changing. The Henslowe papers record that the Lord Admiral's Men staged an amazingly varied repertory of plays at the Rose. Shakespeare's company must have been equally versatile. The practice of giving popular plays long runs did not begin until the 1630s, by which time the number of London playhouses had grown to as many as five, all offering their plays each afternoon. Shakespeare's company in London had only the one peer from 1594 until 1600; and only two from then until 1608, aside from the once-weekly plays by the two boy companies, the "little eyases" mentioned in *Hamlet*, that started with the new century.

From May 1594 to April 1597 at the Theatre, in addition to all his earlier plays that he brought to his new company, Shakespeare gave them possibly *Romeo and Juliet* and *King John*, and certainly *Richard II, A Midsummer Night's Dream, 1 Henry IV*, and *The Merchant of Venice*. But then they ran into deep trouble, because they lost the Theatre. In April 1597, its original twenty-one-year lease expired, and the landlord, who disliked plays, refused to let them renew it. Anticipating this, the company's impresario, James Burbage, had built a new theater for them, a roofed place in the Blackfriars near St. Paul's Cathedral. The Blackfriars precinct was a "liberty," free from the Lord Mayor's jurisdiction. But the plan proved a disaster. The rich residents of Blackfriars objected, and the Privy Council stopped the theater from opening. From April 1597, Shakespeare's company had to rent the Curtain, an old neighbor of their now-silent Theatre, and it was there that the next four of Shakespeare's plays—*2 Henry IV, Much Ado About Nothing, The Merry Wives of Windsor*, and probably *Henry V*—were first staged.

In December 1598, losing hope of a new lease for the old Theatre, the Burbage sons had it pulled down and quietly transported its massive framing timbers across the Thames to make the scaffold for the Globe on the river's south bank, near the Rose. Most of their capital was sunk irretrievably into the Blackfriars theater, and they could afford only half the cost of rebuilding. So they raised money as best they could. Some of the company's more popular playbooks were sold to printers, including *Romeo and Juliet, Richard III, Richard II*, and *1 Henry IV*. More to the point, the Burbage brothers raised capital for the building by cutting in five of the leading players, including Shakespeare, and asking them to put up the other half of its cost. The Globe, its skeleton taken from the old Theatre, thus became the first playhouse to be owned by its players, and, within the limits set by the old frame, the first one built to their own design.

For this theater, one-eighth of which he personally owned, Shakespeare wrote his greatest plays: *Julius Caesar, As You Like It, Hamlet, Twelfth Night, Othello, All's Well That Ends Well, Measure for Measure, King Lear, Macbeth, Pericles, Antony and Cleopatra, Coriolanus, Cymbeline, The Winter's Tale*, and most likely *Troilus and Cressida* and *Timon of Athens*. As the first playhouse to be owned by the players who expected to use it, its fittings must have satisfied all the basic needs of Shakespearean staging. At one time or another, the company staged every one of Shakespeare's plays there.

In 1600, a company consisting entirely of boys started using the Blackfriars playhouse that Richard Burbage's father had tried to open four years before. Companies of boy players had a higher social status than the adult professionals, and, playing only in halls, they commanded a more affluent clientele. The boys performed only once a week, and the relative infrequency of their crowds, plus their skills as trained singers (they were choir-school children turned to making money for their choirmasters), proved less offensive to the local residents than a noisy adult company with its drums and trumpets. Leasing the Blackfriars to the boy company made a minor profit for the Burbages, who took the rent for eight years.

In the longer run, though, this arrangement provided a different means for the Burbage–Shakespeare company to advance its career. The boys' eight years of playing in their rented hall playhouse eventually made it possible for the company of adult players to renew Burbage's old plan of 1596. Shakespeare's company had been made the King's Men when James came to the throne in 1603, and their new patron gave them a status that made it impossible for the residents of Blackfriars to prevent them from implementing the original plan. During a lengthy closure of all the theaters because of a plague epidemic in 1608, the boys' manager surrendered his lease of the hall playhouse to the Burbages. They then took possession for their own company of the playhouse that their father had built for them twelve years before. They divided the new playhouse property among the leading players as they had done in 1599 with the Globe.

A section from Wenceslaus Hollar's "Long View" of London, printed in 1644. Drawn from a standpoint on the tower of the church that is now Southwark Cathedral, Hollar's view shows the roof of the great hall in which the Blackfriars playhouse was built. It can be seen as the long angled roof with two central chimneys, below and to the east of St. Bride's Church.

They were the King's Men, the leading company in the country, and their status after ten years of playing at the Globe was matched by their wealth. By the time theaters reopened late in 1609, the company had established a new system of playing.

The King's Men now had two playhouses, a large open amphitheater and a much smaller roofed hall. Instead of selling or renting one out and using the other for themselves, they decided to use both in turn, for half of each year. It was a reversion to the old system with the city inns, where through the summer they played in the large open yards and in the winter played at inns with big indoor rooms. This time, though, the company owned both playhouses. Their affluence and their high status are signaled by the fact that they chose to keep one of their playhouses idle while they used the other, despite there now being a shortage of playhouses in London. That affluence was needed in 1613, when the Globe burned down at a performance of *All Is True (Henry VIII)* and the company chose the much more expensive option of rebuilding it instead of reverting to the Blackfriars for both winter and summer. That decision, in its way, was the ultimate gesture of affection for their original playhouse. It was a costly gesture, but it meant that the Globe continued in use by the company until all the theaters were closed down by Parliament in 1642.

In 1609, when they reopened after the closure for plague, Shakespeare's company had made several changes in their procedures. The restart was at the Blackfriars, and although they offered the same kind of plays, they began to alter their style of staging. Along with the Blackfriars playhouse, they acquired a famous consort of musicians who played on strings and woodwinds in a music room set over the stage. The new consort was a distinct enhancement of the company's musical resources, which until then had been confined to song, the occasional use of recorders or hautboys, and military drums and trumpets for the scenes with soldiery. In 1608, a central room on the Globe's stage balcony was taken over to serve as a music room like the one at the Blackfriars. From this time on, the King's Men's performances began with a lengthy overture or concert of music before the play.

With that change, the plays themselves now had music to back their singers and provide other sorts of atmospheric effects. Some of the songs and music that appear in the plays not printed until the First Folio of 1623, such as the song that Mariana hears in *Measure for Measure* 4.1, may have been added after Shakespeare's time to make use of this new resource. Shakespeare did use songs, sometimes with string accompaniment, quite regularly in the early plays, but instrumental music hardly ever appears. The last play that he wrote alone, *The Tempest,* was the only one in which he made full use of this new resource.

All the plays containing soldiers and battles used the military drums that in war conveyed signals to infantry formations, as well as the trumpets that were used for signaling to cavalry. These were usually employed for offstage noises, sound effects made from "within" (inside the dressing room or tiring-house behind the stage). Soldiers marching in procession, as in the dead march at the close of *Hamlet,* would have the time marked by an onstage drum. Shakespeare never calls for guns to be fired onstage, even though other writers did, but he did have other noises at his command. A small cannon or "chamber" might be used, fired from the gable-fronted heavens over the stage, as Claudius demands in *Hamlet* and as the Chorus to Act 3 of *Henry V* notes. It was wadding from a ceremonial cannon shot that set the gallery thatch alight at a performance of *All Is True* in July 1613 and burned the Globe to the ground. Stage battles such as Shrewsbury at the end of *1 Henry IV,* written for the Theatre, were accompanied by sword fights that were not the duels of *Hamlet*'s finale but exchanges with broadswords or "foxes" slammed against metal shields or "targets." That action guaranteed emphatic sound effects. The drums and trumpets, with clashes of swords and a great deal of to-ing and fro-ing onto and off the stage, were highlighted in between the shouted dialogue by some hard fighting between the protagonists. The leading players were practiced swordsmen, who knew they were being watched by experts. These were the scenes of "four or five most vile and ragged foils" that the fourth Chorus self-consciously derided in *Henry V* at the Curtain.

The second great reason for noise in the amphitheaters was to mark storm and tempest. Stagehands used the kind of device that Jonson mocked in the Prologue to *Every Man in His Humour,* written for its 1616 publication. His play, wrote Jonson, was free from choruses that wafted you over the seas, "nor rolled bullet heard / To say, it thunders; nor tempestuous drum / Rumbles, to tell you when the storm doth come." For centuries, lead balls rolling down a tin trough were a standard way of making thunder noises in English theaters. The tempest in Act 3 of *King Lear* is heralded several times in the text before a stage direction, "Storm and tempest" (Folio 2.2.450), tells us that it has at last arrived. In 2.2, Cornwall notes its coming twice (Folio 2.2.452, 473). Kent comments on the "Foul weather" in his first line in Act 3, prefaced by the entry stage direction for Act 3, "Storm still," which is repeated for 3.2. Such stage directions appear in both texts (Q has "Storm" for the equivalent Scenes 8, 9, and also at 11, F's 3.4, where F omits any further reference to these noises). These explicit signals indicate that the stagehands provided offstage noises, for all that Lear himself outstorms them with his violent speeches in 3.2.

The main question about the storm scenes in *King Lear* is this: with such consistent emphasis on storm in the language, what was the design behind the stage directions? In the centuries that *Lear* has been restaged, the tempest has been made to roar offstage in a wide variety of ways, often with so much effect that, in the face of complaints that the storm noises made it difficult for the audience to hear the words, some modern productions reduced the storm to solely visual effects, or even left Lear's own raging language to express it unsupported. But the two stage directions indicate that in the original performances the "storm in nature" was not left to Lear himself to convey. The two "Storm still" directions in the Folio suggest a constant rumbling, not the intermittent crashes that might allow Lear to conduct a dialogue with the occasional outbursts of storm noises, as some modern productions have done.

Shakespeare left regrettably few stage directions to indicate the special tricks or properties that he wanted. Curtained beds are called for in *Othello* 5.2 and *Cymbeline* 2.2, and there is the specification "Stocks brought out" in *King Lear* 2.2.132. Small and portable things like papers were a much more common device, from the letters in *The Two Gentlemen of Verona* 1.2.46, 1.3.44, and 2.1.95 to Lear's map at 1.1.35. Across the whole thirty-eight plays, though, there are very few such directions. Shakespeare's economy in preparing his scripts is a major impediment to the modern reader. He hardly ever bothered to note the standard physical gestures, such as kneeling or doffing a hat, and did little more to specify any special effects. Nonetheless, it is important not to imagine elaborate devices or actions where the text does not call for them. On the whole, the demands Shakespeare made of his fellows for staging his plays appear to have been remarkably modest. Since he was a company shareholder, his parsimony may have had a simple commercial motive. Stage properties cost the company money, and one had to be confident of a new play's popularity before investing much in its staging.

There may have been other reasons for avoiding extravagant staging spectacles. Shakespeare made little use of the discovery space until the last plays, for instance, for reasons that we can only guess at. The few definite discoveries in the plays include Portia's caskets in *The Merchant of Venice,* Falstaff sleeping off his sack in *1 Henry IV* 2.5.482, the body of Polonius in *Hamlet,* Hermione's statue in *The Winter's Tale* 5.3.20, and the lovers in *The Tempest* 5.1.173, who are found when discovered to be playing chess. The audience's shock when Hermione moves and comes out of the discovery space onto the main stage is rare in Shakespeare: in every other play, whether comedy or tragedy, the audience knows far more than the characters onstage about what is going on. Shakespeare matched this late innovation in *The Winter's Tale* with his last play, *The Tempest.* After the preliminary and soothing concert by the resident Blackfriars musicians, it opens with a storm at sea so realistic that it includes that peculiarly distinctive stage direction "Enter Mariners, wet" (1.1.46). That startling piece of stage realism turns out straightaway to be not real at all but a piece of stage magic.

EARLY PLAYS
AND POEMS

The Two Gentlemen of Verona

Readers and playgoers have often found both startling and disconcerting the events that conclude *The Two Gentlemen of Verona*. Proteus, a young man thwarted in his love for Silvia, who loves Proteus's friend Valentine, says that since wooing her with words has not worked, he will follow the soldier's path and "love you 'gainst the nature of love: force ye" (5.4.58). At that moment, Valentine steps out of hiding and stops the attempted rape by denouncing Proteus as a treacherous friend. Overcome with remorse for the betrayal of Valentine, though not explicitly for his attempted sexual violence, Proteus begs forgiveness. Generously, Valentine says he is content. He then announces that he will give Silvia to Proteus as a sign of the renewal of the friendship between the two men. A near rape and the blatant offer of a woman as an object of exchange between men—is this the stuff of comedy?

Apparently a number of directors, actors, and critics have thought not. In the mid-eighteenth century, it became common to cut Valentine's offer to give Silvia to his friend, a stage tradition that largely held until William Charles Macready, the famous actor and producer of Shakespeare's plays, reintroduced the lines in 1841. As late as 1952, however, Denis Carey's production at the Bristol Old Vic again deleted Valentine's offer. Some critics have been so certain Shakespeare could not have written the scene as it stands that they argued that it was altered in the playhouse. How is it that Shakespeare concluded his comedy with events that have seemed to many so distasteful and so disconcerting?

One answer might be that Shakespeare was simply a young dramatist not fully in control of his craft. *The Two Gentlemen of Verona* is, after all, one of his earliest plays, perhaps *the* earliest. It bears marks of its early date of composition. It has, for example, the smallest cast of any of the plays. Many scenes contain only two or three speakers, as if Shakespeare had not yet mastered the skill of orchestrating a full complement of stage voices and bodies. It is marked as well by a number of plot inconsistencies and confusing details. Valentine and Proteus leave Verona to go to the Emperor's court, for example, but end up attaching themselves to the Duke of Milan—an important nobleman, certainly, but not the Emperor. Likewise, the geographical placement of some scenes is vague. Verona, Milan, Mantua, and Padua are places of which characters speak, but the names often are used interchangeably and seem collectively to be Shakespeare's shorthand for "Italy" rather than distinct places.

In other ways, however, the play is both an accomplished theatrical piece and a genuine precursor of many aspects of Shakespeare's later comic techniques and structures. The contemporary film *Shakespeare in Love* takes this view, using scenes and speeches from *The Two Gentlemen of Verona* to indicate Shakespeare's youthful promise as a writer of romantic comedy and as a rival to Christopher Marlowe, the premier London dramatist of the early 1590s. The play features lovers whose fickle or thwarted passions lead them into all sorts of difficulties: treachery to friends, banishment, disguise. Strikingly, these difficulties get sorted out only after most of the drama's significant players decamp to a forest somewhere outside Milan. There, in a green world complete with a band of outlaws, the fickle Proteus reverts to his original love for Julia, Silvia's disapproving father forgoes his objections to Valentine, friendship is renewed between the two young men, the outlaws are pardoned and unworthy lovers dismissed. The utopian possibilities for social renewal in a world beyond the walls and customs of the city are celebrated in this play as they are later to be in *A Midsummer Night's Dream, As You Like It,* and other Shakespearean romantic comedies of the 1590s. *Two Gentlemen* also contains the first of Shakespeare's cross-dressed heroines, the faithful Julia, who follows her fickle lover from Verona to Milan and then, as his page, accompanies him into the woods in his pursuit of Silvia. Male disguise allows Julia a freedom of action and movement not normally granted to early modern women, but, as was often to be the case in later Shakespearean comedies, this freedom has as its ultimate goal the heroine's embrace of a mate and of marriage.

The excellence of much of the play, then, suggests that its disturbing ending may not be due to Shakespeare's relative inexperience as a playwright; rather, it may stem from the subject matter of the play itself—that is, from Shakespeare's ambitious attempt to probe the relationship between two kinds of human bonds: friendship between men and romantic love between a man and a woman. In the Renaissance, each of these was a privileged relationship, but their relative worth was a matter for debate and disagreement. In staging his exploration of the competing claims of love and friendship, Shakespeare drew on two different sources. The first was a Spanish prose romance published in 1542, Jorge de Montemayor's *Diana Enamorada*. Translated into French in 1578 and into English in the 1580s, it was published in English in 1598. Shakespeare, then, could have read the story in French or in the unpublished English version. He could also have learned of it from an anonymous court play of 1585, *The History of Felix and Philiomena*, now lost.

The Montemayor romance focuses on a man's unfaithfulness in love. Don Felix leaves Felismena for Celia; Felismena pursues him in the guise of a page; Celia falls in love with the page and conveniently dies when the page rejects her. Shakespeare retains much of this material in the Proteus-Silvia-Julia triangle but adds the Valentine plot, probably drawn from the story of two friends, Titus and Gisippus, told by Boccaccio and then recounted in Book 2, Chapter 12, of Thomas Elyot's *Book of the Governor* (1531).

Male friendship ("Steadfast is the love based on inclination"). From Richard Brathwaite, *The English Gentleman*, 2nd ed. (1633).

In this story, Titus falls in love with the woman Gisippus is to marry, and Gisippus gives the woman to his friend. Later, Gisippus takes upon himself the blame for a murder Titus is wrongly accused of committing. The story unabashedly advances the claims of heroic male friendship over other ties, including those of male-female love. Shakespeare's achievement in *The Two Gentlemen of Verona* is to join together aspects of these two stories. In his play, there are two pairs of lovers, not just a fickle Proteus figure moving between two women, and the close friendship between Valentine and Proteus is given a prominence equal to that of the male-female love stories.

In foregrounding the importance of male friendship, Shakespeare joined a long tradition of writers who celebrated such friendships, sometimes comparing them favorably with the presumably more dangerous relationships men could have with women. In *The Governor*, for example, Elyot praised male friendship in terms that would be echoed in other early modern texts: "Verily it is a blessed and stable connection of sundry wills, making of two persons one in having and suffering. And therefore a friend is properly named of philosophers the other I. For that in them is but one mind and one possession and that which more is, a man more rejoiceth at his friend's good fortune than at his own" (Book 2, Chapter 11). By contrast, Sir Francis Bacon (who also wrote an essay in praise of friendship) in his essay "Of Love" captures the fear and disdain with which passionate love between men and women was often regarded: "In life it doth much mischief, sometimes like a siren, sometimes like a fury. You may observe that amongst all the great and worthy persons (whereof the memory remaineth, either ancient or recent) there is not one that hath been transported to the mad degree of love; which shows that great spirits and great business do keep out this weak passion."

The Two Gentlemen of Verona participates both in the celebration of male friendship and to some extent in the comic deflation of male-female love. Several times male characters speak of the strange transformations of the self that passion for a woman can induce. Proteus, choosing to stay in Verona with Julia rather than follow his friend to Milan for an education in courtiership, speaks of his own choice disdainfully. Of Valentine he says:

> He after honour hunts, I after love.
> He leaves his friends to dignify them more,
> I leave myself, my friends, and all, for love.
> Thou, Julia, thou hast metamorphosed me,
> Made me neglect my studies, lose my time,
> War with good counsel, set the world at naught;
> Made wit with musing weak, heart sick with thought.
> (1.1.63–69)

The play is one of Shakespeare's first explorations of what it means to be transformed, or "metamorphosed," by love of a woman. Perhaps Shakespeare was taking his cue from the Roman poet Ovid's vastly popular book the *Metamorphoses*, which contained numerous tales of people transformed by love. In Ovid, gods sometimes assume the shapes of mortals or of animals to pursue their beloved; or women turn into trees or flowers in their flight from unwanted amorous advances. In *The Two Gentlemen of Verona*, Proteus's name echoes that of the sea god who could change shape at will and who was thus often associated with a fickle nature. It is Proteus who in the above passage first mentions being metamorphosed by love, but the play rings many changes on this idea. Sometimes the transformations wrought by love seem comic to others. Speed, for example, has excellent fun laughing at the strange transformations of his master, Valentine, who, in love with Silvia, begins to act like a perfect malcontent, "metamorphosed with a mistress" (2.1.26–27). A malcontent, here meaning someone made melancholy by love, was a stock figure in Renaissance literature and the visual arts, sometimes rendered comic by his disordered attire or his moody alienation from his fellow men.

Often, however, in this play, love is shown to have more positive consequences. It leads to heroic feats such as Julia's daring cross-dressed journey in pursuit of Proteus and to the outpouring of poetry and songs. However fickle Proteus's passion for Silvia shows him to be, it also moves him to offer her the gorgeous song "Who is Silvia? What is she, / That all our swains commend her?" (4.2.37–38). In *Shakespeare in Love*, this lyricism is what compels Viola De Lesseps, the aristocratic heroine, to fall in love with the youthful Shakespeare who wrote those verses. Valentine, under the influence of love, is prepared to scale the walls of Silvia's tower to bear her willingly away. Clearly, however, not all the metamorphoses wrought by love are either comic or admirable. Love also makes men dangerous and hurtful. Under the influence of his fickle passions, Proteus abandons one woman for another, betrays Valentine's marriage plans to Silvia's father, and threatens to rape the woman he supposedly adores. As moralists warned, the passion of man for woman can turn a man into a beast.

By contrast, friendship between men, though much compromised in this text, holds the promise of an ennobling intimacy. When Proteus and Valentine must part in the first scene, Proteus's language betrays the depth of his love for and dependence on his friend:

> Wilt thou be gone? Sweet Valentine, adieu.
> Think on thy Proteus when thou haply seest
> Some rare noteworthy object in thy travel.
> Wish me partaker in thy happiness
> When thou dost meet good hap; and in thy danger—
> If ever danger do environ thee—
> Commend thy grievance to my holy prayers;
> For I will be thy beadsman, Valentine.
>
> (1.1.11–18)

Here, the friend is imagined as "the other I," sharer of every joy, intimate of every thought. The delight with which Valentine later welcomes Proteus to the Duke's court and even his eventual offer of Silvia to his friend are signs of the potential depth of male bonds in the play.

But at what cost to women are the bonds between men to be privileged? By the way he creates the characters of Julia and Silvia, Shakespeare invites his audience to take them and their emotions seriously and makes it difficult to overlook the men's irresponsible and callous treatment of them. If Proteus can be faithful neither to his male friend nor to his female beloved, the women are models of constant affection. Each, moreover, risks a good deal for her beloved, and each is respectful of her female rival. Julia courts public scandal by dressing as a boy and following Proteus to Milan; Silvia flees her father's court to follow the banished Valentine into the forest. These are both bold and attractive women.

Julia, in particular, is a complex figure, proud and silly in the scene in which she pretends not to want to read the letter her maid has brought her from Proteus (1.2), but

The love melancholic. Isaac Oliver, *Edward, First Lord Herbert of Cherbury* (1617).

impressively dignified when, disguised as a male page, she is faced with the task of being Proteus's messenger to Silvia (4.4). Asked by Silvia to describe Julia, the disguised woman says that Julia is of her color and height. She knows this, she claims, because once she wore Julia's clothes "to play the woman's part" (4.4.152) in a holiday pageant. Moreover, the part she played

> 'twas Ariadne, passioning
> For Theseus' perjury and unjust flight;
> Which I so lively acted with my tears
> That my poor mistress. moved therewithal,
> Wept bitterly; and would I might be dead
> If I in thought felt not her very sorrow.
> (4.4.159–64)

Ariadne, of course, is an archetype of the betrayed woman. She helped her lover, Theseus, escape the man-eating Minotaur in the labyrinth on Crete, but then was abandoned by him on the island of Naxos. The abandoned Julia, so transformed by love and grief that she no longer can lay claim to her own name, finds a point of identification in Ariadne's grief and in imagining what "Julia" would have felt to see the enactment of Ariadne's story. This is a wonderfully complicated moment, a representation of a woman's grief and self-alienation and also her empathetic engagement with the story of *another* woman's grief. It at once reveals the cost, to women, of men's inconstancy and makes it difficult to accept that women should simply become the objects of exchange between male friends.

The nearly tragic consciousness here granted to Julia is countered in this play by the boisterous comic voices of Speed and Lance, two of Shakespeare's earliest and liveliest clowns. Their presence helps suggest that however complicated Shakespeare's exploration of the tension between love and friendship becomes, the outcome will not be fully tragic. Speed is a clever clown, excellent at puns and wordplay, devastatingly accurate in his parodic imitation of Valentine's lovesick behavior and clever enough to see, when his master cannot, that Silvia has induced Valentine to write a love letter to himself. Lance, who may have been added to the play in the later stages of composition, is a doltish clown whose command of the English language is remarkable mainly for its deficiencies. If Speed specializes in puns, the witty play on the double meaning of words, Lance specializes in malapropisms, the linguistic blunders by which one word is mistaken for another. He can, for example, when leaving home to follow his master to Milan, say that he has received his "proportion, like the prodigious son" (2.3.3), by which he means that he has received his portion, or inheritance, like the prodigal son in the biblical story who received his inheritance and squandered it. In Lance's fractured English, nothing is communicated straightforwardly. He blunders into meaning, his linguistic mistakes turning the language of the learned and the witty on its head. In Lance's mouth, words become unfamiliar and unpredictable, always ready to yield up an obscene innuendo or to forge unlikely connections between different domains of meaning.

Lance's larger role in the play is as comically unsettling as his language. As was to be increasingly true of many of Shakespeare's low-life characters and subplots, his behavior mirrors and comments on the behavior of his "betters," but in a deflationary and unpredictable way. Lance's great love is for his dog, Crab. When he must leave for Milan, he is in an agony of grief because his dog, like a hard-hearted mistress, sheds no tears for his departure. "I think Crab, my dog, be the sourest-natured dog that lives. My mother weeping, my father wailing, my sister crying, our maid howling, our cat wringing her hands, and all our house in a great perplexity, yet did not this cruel-hearted cur shed one tear" (2.3.4–8). So deep is Lance's affection for his dog that when Crab, who in the end does accompany his master to Milan, disgraces himself by pissing under the Duke's table at a banquet, Lance takes the blame—and the subsequent punishment—upon himself. It is "the bit with the dog" that in *Shakespeare in Love* particularly wins the approval of Queen Elizabeth.

"I'll be sworn I have sat in the stocks for puddings he hath stolen" (4.4.25–26). From Geffrey Whitney, *A Choice of Emblemes* (1586).

The highborn lovers, Proteus and Valentine, do not always show an equal devotion to their human mistresses. Lance's attachment threatens to expose both the element of absurdity lurking inside every grand passion and also the falsity of the assumption that only the well-born are capable of self-sacrifice. Moreover, when Lance contemplates marriage, he is not very romantic. As Lance and Speed read a catalog of the qualities of Lance's beloved (3.1.269–351), Lance focuses on the practical: the woman's ability to fetch and carry, to sew and to milk. And her faults, which are manifold, pale in his eyes beside her wealth. Set against the rarified courtship rituals of his masters, Lance's pragmatism underscores the mundane aspects of the institution of marriage to which courtship will lead.

Together the two clowns do much to increase the hilarity and confusion that permeate this early comedy: a play in which letters are only with great difficulty delivered to their receivers, love tokens given to one mistress are rerouted to another, and masculine affection proves remarkably fickle and unsteady. When something like order descends on this society, it does so in a locale where Lance does not go—the forest outside Milan. The initial scenes in the forest are striking in that they have the fairy-tale quality of a Robin Hood story come to life. Banished from Milan, Valentine and Speed are beset by robbers in the forest; but these outlaws are so impressed with Valentine's bearing and his skill in languages that they make him captain of their forest band (4.1.61–64). Outside the town, living apart from women, the outlaws establish an alternative community where Valentine, despite his grief at being separated from Silvia, finds a measure of contentment. Several of Shakespeare's later comedies will depend on the contrast between the flawed life of town or court and the less fettered existence of rural spaces. *The Two Gentlemen of Verona* tries out this juxtaposition, contrasting to the betrayals and confusions of urban life and male-female courtship the straightforward male camaraderie of the forest.

The arrival of women and of Proteus, Valentine's friend-turned-rival, disrupts this harmonious male community as first Silvia appears, escorted by the timid Eglamour, and then Proteus, attended by Julia, disguised as his page. Suddenly, the potential for violence escalates as the frustrated Proteus threatens Silvia with rape, and the two men both lay claim to her affections. The disguised Julia can only watch. Just moments before Proteus, Silvia, and Julia had arrived, Valentine had made a speech that obliquely suggests one way their encounter might end. Alone in the woods, Valentine describes how he can

> sit alone, unseen of any,
> And to the nightingale's complaining notes
> Tune my distresses and record my woes.
> (5.4.4–6)

By mentioning the nightingale, Valentine evokes a horrific tale of sexual violence. In a story made famous by Ovid in the *Metamorphoses*, the beautiful Philomela was raped by her brother-in-law, Tereus, and eventually transformed into a nightingale. The bird's song is so melancholy because it is a perpetual lament for Philomela's lost chastity.

As it turns out, no one undergoes Philomela's fate in *The Two Gentlemen of Verona*. Silvia escapes rape, just as Julia avoids Ariadne's fate when the fickle Proteus returns his affections to her. But the close of this early comedy, through its mythic allusions and flirtation with sexual violence, hints at the tragic endings that have narrowly been averted. In this regard, the play is not unlike *A Midsummer Night's Dream,* in which there is a properly comic ending with lover wedded to lover. However, the last act of that play includes an unintentionally comic enactment of the tragic story of Pyramus and Thisbe, lovers whose passion ended in death, not marriage. Though *Two Gentlemen* ends comically, with two couples reunited and male friendship restored, the violent and unexpected turnabouts in the play's concluding moments indicate the difficulty of joining a tale of heroic male friendship to a tale of romantic love between men and women. Especially for the women, the "happy" ending comes at a cost. The two marriages are arranged only *after* male friendship has been renewed and Valentine has offered—without consulting Silvia—to give his beloved to his friend. Moreover, once that offer has been made, Silvia never speaks again in the play. Her response to all that has happened remains cloaked in silence, while Julia's male disguise, which she never removes, continues to remind the audience of the dangers she has faced because of Proteus's fickleness. As we have seen, this is an ending that since at least the eighteenth century has bothered readers and actors, perhaps because dominant culture has come to value love between men and women over other kinds of emotional bonds. In the Renaissance, the matter was not so settled, a reminder of the different ways in which Shakespeare both is and is not our contemporary.

JEAN E. HOWARD

TEXTUAL NOTE

The Two Gentlemen of Verona was first published in the 1623 First Folio (F), though it may have been written as early as 1590–91, making it perhaps the first of Shakespeare's theatrical compositions. F includes some unusual features, such as the listing at the beginning of each scene of all the characters in the scene no matter when they come onstage. This may have been done partly to imitate classical practice. The text also lacks any other stage directions except exits. These and other features lead editors to believe the play was transcribed by Ralph Crane, a professional scribe who seems to have been employed by Shakespeare's company to prepare several of his playscripts, including *The Two Gentlemen of Verona,* for publication in F.

The Folio text contains a number of confusing plot details and frequent inconsistencies as to the exact Italian setting in which various scenes occur. This suggests that Crane may have been working from Shakespeare's unrevised working papers. On the other hand, there is unusual consistency in regard to speech prefixes for characters' names, indicating that he may have worked from a script prepared for the playhouse or that he was unusually careful in attending to such detail. It is unclear whether the act and scene divisions in the text are Crane's additions or represent playhouse practice.

SELECTED BIBLIOGRAPHY

Brooks, Harold F. "Two Clowns in a Comedy (to Say Nothing of the Dog): Speed, Launce (and Crab) in 'The Two Gentlemen of Verona.'" *Essays and Studies: Collected for the English Association.* London: John Murray, 1963. 91–100. Examines how the clowns, Lance and Speed, contribute to the play's thematic unity by paralleling events and ideas involving the main characters.

Carroll, William C. "'And love you 'gainst the nature of love': Ovid, Rape, and *The Two Gentlemen of Verona.*" *Shakespeare's Ovid: "The Metamorphoses" in the Plays and Poems.* Ed. A. B. Taylor. Cambridge: Cambridge University Press, 2000. 49–65.

Argues that this seemingly genial comedy is darkened by an Ovidian view of male desire entailing possession and control of women.

Kiefer, Frederick. "Love Letters in *The Two Gentlemen of Verona.*" *Shakespeare Studies* 18 (1986): 65–85. Explores the role of letters in the negotiation of love in *Two Gentlemen,* which contains more letters than any of Shakespeare's other comedies.

Lindenbaum, Peter. "Education in *The Two Gentlemen of Verona.*" *Studies in English Literature 1500–1800* 15 (1975): 229–44. Discusses how the play achieves unity by its focus on the education of the protagonists, especially Proteus.

Masten, Jeffrey. "*The Two Gentlemen of Verona.*" Vol. 3 of *A Companion to Shakespeare's Works: The Comedies.* Ed. Richard Dutton and Jean E. Howard. 4 vols. Oxford: Blackwells, 2003. 266–88. Argues against the idea that *Two Gentlemen* is an immature play because of its focus on male friendship rather than heterosexual love and notes the persistence of intense male friendship throughout Shakespeare's writing career.

Rivlen, Elizabeth. "Mimetic Service in *The Two Gentlemen of Verona.*" *English Literary History* 72 (2005): 105–28. Focuses on the large number of servants in *Two Gentlemen* and the capacity of servants not just to mirror but to alter elite identities.

Sargent, Ralph M. "Sir Thomas Elyot and the Integrity of *The Two Gentlemen of Verona.*" *PMLA* 65 (1950): 1166–80. Explores Jorge de Montemayor's *Diana Enamorada* and Thomas Elyot's *The Book of the Governor* as sources for Shakespeare's investigation of the conflict between heterosexual love and male friendship.

Schlueter, June, ed. *"The Two Gentlemen of Verona": Critical Essays.* New York: Garland, 1996. Gathers together eighteenth- and nineteenth-century comments on the play along with essays by twentieth-century critics and reviews of notable theater and television productions.

Slights, Camille Wells. "*The Two Gentlemen of Verona* and the Courtesy Book Tradition." *Shakespeare Studies* 16 (1983): 13–31. Argues that the play explores the fashioning of a Renaissance gentleman.

Weimann, Robert. "Laughing with the Audience: 'The Two Gentlemen of Verona' and the Popular Tradition of Comedy." *Shakespeare Survey* 22 (1969): 35–42. Discusses the use of the play's two clowns to structure the audience's comic responses.

FILMS

The Two Gentlemen of Verona. 1983. Dir. Don Taylor. UK. 137 min. This BBC-TV version, in color, employs period music and elegant Italian settings in a performance that foregrounds the heterosexual love plot.

Shakespeare in Love. 1998. Dir. John Madden. UK. 123 min. Starring Gwyneth Paltrow and Joseph Fiennes. Includes scenes and speeches from *The Two Gentlemen of Verona* as examples of Shakespeare's early success with comedy and love lyric.

The Two Gentlemen of Verona

THE PERSONS OF THE PLAY

DUKE of Milan
SILVIA, his daughter
PROTEUS, a gentleman of Verona
LANCE, his clownish servant
VALENTINE, a gentleman of Verona
SPEED, his clownish servant
THURIO, a foolish rival to Valentine
ANTONIO, father of Proteus
PANTHINO, his servant
JULIA, beloved of Proteus
LUCETTA, her waiting-woman
HOST, where Julia lodges
EGLAMOUR, agent for Silvia in her escape
OUTLAWS
Servants, musicians

1.1

[*Enter*] VALENTINE[1] *and* PROTEUS[2]

VALENTINE   Cease to persuade, my loving Proteus.
  Home-keeping youth have ever homely° wits.   *dull*
  Were't not affection° chains thy tender° days   *love / young*
  To the sweet glances of thy honoured love,
5   I rather would entreat thy company
  To see the wonders of the world abroad
  Than, living dully sluggardized° at home,   *made very lazy*
  Wear out thy youth with shapeless° idleness.   *aimless*
  But since thou lov'st, love still,° and thrive therein—   *constantly*
10   Even as I would, when I to love begin.
PROTEUS   Wilt thou be gone? Sweet Valentine, adieu.
  Think on thy Proteus when thou haply° seest   *by chance*
  Some rare noteworthy object in thy travel.
  Wish me partaker in thy happiness
15   When thou dost meet good hap;° and in thy danger—   *fortune*
  If ever danger do environ° thee—   *surround*
  Commend° thy grievance to my holy prayers;   *Entrust*
  For I will be thy beadsman,[3] Valentine.
VALENTINE   And on a love-book[4] pray for my success?

1.1 Location: Presumably Verona, though we learn this only from the title.
1. St. Valentine is the patron saint of lovers. Valentine's name may thus indicate his role as faithful lover.
2. In classical mythology, a sea god who could change shape at will. The name suggests a fickle nature. In 1.1, it is pronounced with three syllables; elsewhere in the play, often with two. In F, the names of all the characters who appear in a given scene are listed as it opens,

even if they enter at a later point. This edition marks entrances when characters actually appear onstage. In this scene, Speed enters at line 70, though in F his entrance is not marked and his name is listed with that of Proteus and Valentine at the beginning of the scene.
3. One who prays (counts the beads of a rosary) for another's spiritual welfare.
4. A book about love (instead of a prayer book). Valentine is twitting Proteus for making love his religion.

20 PROTEUS   Upon some book I love I'll pray for thee.
   VALENTINE   That's on some shallow story of deep love—
   How young Leander crossed the Hellespont.[5]
   PROTEUS   That's a deep story of a deeper love,
   For he was more than over-shoes[6] in love.
25 VALENTINE   'Tis true, for you are over-boots in love,
   And yet you never swam the Hellespont.
   PROTEUS   Over the boots? Nay, give me not the boots.°   *do not mock me*
   VALENTINE   No, I will not; for it boots° thee not.   *profits*
   PROTEUS   What?
   VALENTINE   To be in love, where scorn is bought with groans,
30   Coy looks with heart-sore sighs, one fading moment's mirth
   With twenty watchful,° weary, tedious nights.   *wakeful*
   If haply won, perhaps a hapless° gain;   *an unlucky*
   If lost, why then a grievous labour won;
   However,° but a folly bought with wit,   *Either way*
35   Or else a wit by folly vanquishèd.
   PROTEUS   So by your circumstance° you call me fool.   *lengthy discourse*
   VALENTINE   So by your circumstance° I fear you'll prove.   *situation*
   PROTEUS   'Tis love you cavil at. I am not love.
   VALENTINE   Love is your master, for he masters you,
40   And he that is so yokèd by a fool
   Methinks should not be chronicled for wise.
   PROTEUS   Yet writers say 'As in the sweetest bud
   The eating canker° dwells, so doting love   *harmful caterpillar*
   Inhabits in the finest wits of all.'
45 VALENTINE   And writers say 'As the most forward bud
   Is eaten by the canker ere it blow,°   *blossom*
   Even so by love the young and tender wit
   Is turned to folly, blasting° in the bud,   *withering*
   Losing his verdure° even in the prime,°   *greenness / spring*
50   And all the fair effects of future hopes.'
   But wherefore waste I time to counsel thee
   That art a votary[7] to fond° desire?   *foolish*
   Once more adieu. My father at the road°   *harbor*
   Expects my coming, there to see me shipped.[8]
55 PROTEUS   And thither will I bring thee, Valentine.
   VALENTINE   Sweet Proteus, no. Now let us take our leave.
   To Milan let me hear from thee by letters
   Of thy success° in love, and what news else   *fortune (good or bad)*
   Betideth° here in absence of thy friend;   *Happens*
60   And I likewise will visit thee with mine.
   PROTEUS   All happiness bechance to thee in Milan.
   VALENTINE   As much to you at home; and so farewell.   *Exit*
   PROTEUS   He after honour hunts, I after love.
   He leaves his friends to dignify° them more,   *bring honor to*
65   I leave° myself, my friends, and all, for love.   *neglect*
   Thou, Julia, thou hast metamorphosed° me,   *transformed*
   Made me neglect my studies, lose° my time,   *waste*

5. In classical mythology, Leander drowned while swimming the Hellespont to visit his love, Hero. Shakespeare probably had read in manuscript Christopher Marlowe's poem "Hero and Leander."
6. So deep as to cover the shoes (or boots); recklessly or excessively.

7. One devoted to a particular pursuit; one bound by vows to a religious life.
8. Although Verona and Milan are inland, Shakespeare writes of Verona as if it were located, like London, on a tidal river leading to the sea.

War with good counsel, set the world at naught;
Made wit with musing weak, heart sick with thought.°   *melancholy ideas*
    [*Enter* SPEED]

70 SPEED   Sir Proteus, save° you. Saw you my master?   *God save (a greeting)*

PROTEUS   But now he parted hence to embark for Milan.

SPEED   Twenty to one, then, he is shipped already,
And I have played the sheep⁹ in losing him.

PROTEUS   Indeed, a sheep doth very often stray,
75 An if° the shepherd be a while away.   *An if = If*

SPEED   You conclude that my master is a shepherd, then, and
    I a sheep?

PROTEUS   I do.

SPEED   Why then, my horns are his horns,¹ whether I wake or
    sleep.

PROTEUS   A silly answer, and fitting well a sheep.

80 SPEED   This proves me still a sheep.

PROTEUS   True, and thy master a shepherd.

SPEED   Nay, that I can deny by a circumstance.°   *argument*

PROTEUS   It shall go hard but I'll prove it by another.²

SPEED   The shepherd seeks the sheep, and not the sheep the
85 shepherd. But I seek my master, and my master seeks not me.
    Therefore I am no sheep.

PROTEUS   The sheep for fodder follow the shepherd, the shepherd
for food follows not the sheep. Thou for wages followest
thy master, thy master for wages follows not thee. Therefore
90 thou art a sheep.

SPEED   Such another proof will make me cry 'baa'.

PROTEUS   But dost thou hear: gav'st thou my letter to Julia?

SPEED   Ay, sir. I, a lost mutton,° gave your letter to her, a laced   *sheep*
mutton,° and she, a laced mutton, gave me, a lost mutton,   *prostitute (slang)*
95 nothing for my labour.

PROTEUS   Here's too small a pasture for such store° of muttons.   *abundance*

SPEED   If the ground be overcharged,° you were best stick³ her.   *overburdened*

PROTEUS   Nay, in that you are astray. 'Twere best pound° you.   *empound; beat*

SPEED   Nay sir, less than a pound shall serve me for carrying
100 your letter.

PROTEUS   You mistake. I mean the pound, a pinfold.°   *pen for stray animals*

SPEED   From a pound to a pin?⁴ Fold it° over and over   *Multiply*
'Tis threefold too little for carrying a letter to your lover.

PROTEUS   But what said she?

105 SPEED [*nods, then says*] Ay.°   *Yes*

PROTEUS   Nod-ay? Why, that's 'noddy'.°   *a fool*

SPEED   You mistook, sir. I say she did nod, and you ask me if she
did nod, and I say 'Ay'.

PROTEUS   And that set together is 'noddy'.

110 SPEED   Now you have taken the pains to set it together, take it
for your pains.

PROTEUS   No, no. You shall have it for bearing the letter.

SPEED   Well, I perceive I must be fain° to bear with you.   *willing*

PROTEUS   Why, sir, how do you bear with me?

---

9. Been foolish, with a pun on "ship." "Ship" and "sheep" were pronounced similarly.
1. As Speed's master, Valentine owns Speed's horns. Traditionally, the horns signified the cuckold and were attributed to men whose wives were unfaithful.
2. It shall fare ill with me unless I prove my claim by

using another argument.
3. Stab or slaughter the extra sheep, with a pun on "stick" as meaning "have sexual intercourse with."
4. Proverbially, pins have little value (e.g., "not worth a pin"). Speed fears he is going to be paid too little for carrying the letter to Julia.

115	SPEED Marry,[5] sir, the letter very orderly,° having nothing but the word 'noddy' for my pains.	*dutifully*
	PROTEUS Beshrew me° but you have a quick wit.	*Curse me (a mild oath)*
	SPEED And yet it cannot overtake your slow purse.	
	PROTEUS Come, come, open the matter in brief. What said she?	
120	SPEED Open your purse, that the money and the matter may be both at once delivered.	
	PROTEUS [*giving money*] Well, sir, here is for your pains. What said she?	
	SPEED Truly, sir, I think you'll hardly win her.[6]	
125	PROTEUS Why? Couldst thou perceive so much from her?	

SPEED   Sir, I could perceive[7] nothing at all from her, no, not so
   much as a ducat[8] for delivering your letter. And being so hard°   *stingy; cold*
   to me, that brought your mind,° I fear she'll prove as hard to   *wishes*
   you in telling° your mind. Give her no token but stones,[9] for   *when you tell her*
130 she's as hard as steel.

PROTEUS   What said she? Nothing?

SPEED   No, not so much as 'Take this for thy pains'. To testify°   *attest to*
   your bounty, I thank you, you have testerned me;[1] in requital
   whereof, henceforth carry your letters yourself. And so, sir, I'll
135 commend you to my master.   [*Exit*]

PROTEUS   Go, go, be gone, to save your ship from wreck,
   Which cannot perish having thee aboard,
   Being destined to a drier death on shore.[2]
   I must go send some better messenger.
140 I fear my Julia would not deign° my lines,   *graciously accept*
   Receiving them from such a worthless post.°   *Exit* *messenger; blockhead*

1.2

Enter JULIA *and* LUCETTA

JULIA   But say, Lucetta, now we are alone—
   Wouldst thou then counsel me to fall in love?

LUCETTA   Ay, madam, so you stumble not unheedfully.°   *carelessly*

JULIA   Of all the fair resort° of gentlemen   *company*
5   That every day with parle° encounter me,   *talk*
   In thy opinion which is worthiest love?

LUCETTA   Please you° repeat their names, I'll show my mind   *If you will*
   According to my shallow simple skill.

JULIA   What think'st thou of the fair Sir Eglamour?[1]

10 LUCETTA   As of a knight well spoken, neat,° and fine,   *elegant*
   But were I you, he never should be mine.

JULIA   What think'st thou of the rich Mercatio?

LUCETTA   Well of his wealth, but of himself, so-so.

JULIA   What think'st thou of the gentle Proteus?

15 LUCETTA   Lord, lord, to see what folly reigns in us!

JULIA   How now? What means this passion° at his name?   *outburst of emotion*

LUCETTA   Pardon, dear madam, 'tis a passing° shame   *great*

---

5. A mild oath suggesting surprise, from the Virgin Mary's name.
6. You'll have a hard time winning her.
7. Punning on an obsolete meaning of "perceive" as "receive."
8. A coin worth about three shillings sixpence, a generous tip.
9. Precious stones; pebbles; perhaps also, testicles. *token*: love gift.

1. Given me a testern, a coin worth much less than the ducat Speed wanted.
2. *Which . . . shore*: alluding to the proverb "He that is born to be hanged shall never be drowned."
1.2 Location: Out of doors, maybe in Julia's garden.
1. Not the same Eglamour who assists Silvia in 4.3. The name is found in medieval romances and by the 1590s seems to have acquired comic associations.

That I, unworthy body as I am,
Should censure° thus on lovely gentlemen.   *pass judgment*

20 JULIA   Why not on Proteus, as of all the rest?
LUCETTA   Then thus: of many good, I think him best.
JULIA   Your reason?
LUCETTA   I have no other but a woman's reason:
I think him so because I think him so.
25 JULIA   And wouldst thou have me cast my love on him?
LUCETTA   Ay, if you thought your love not cast away.
JULIA   Why, he of all the rest hath never moved° me   *proposed marriage to*
LUCETTA   Yet he of all the rest I think best loves ye.
JULIA   His little speaking shows his love but small.
30 LUCETTA   Fire that's closest kept° burns most of all.   *most enclosed*
JULIA   They do not love that do not show their love.
LUCETTA   O, they love least that let men know their love.
JULIA   I would I knew his mind.
LUCETTA [*giving Proteus' letter*]   Peruse this paper, madam.
35 JULIA   'To Julia'—say, from whom?
LUCETTA   That the contents will show.
JULIA   Say, say—who gave it thee?
LUCETTA   Sir Valentine's page; and sent, I think, from Proteus.
He would have given it you, but I being in the way
40 Did in your name receive it.[2] Pardon the fault, I pray.
JULIA   Now, by my modesty, a goodly broker.°   *go-between*
Dare you presume to harbour wanton lines?°   *receive love letters*
To whisper, and conspire against my youth?
Now trust me, 'tis an office of great worth,
45 And you an officer fit for the place.
There. Take the paper.
[*She gives* LUCETTA *the letter*]
See it be returned,
Or else return no more into my sight.
LUCETTA   To plead for love deserves more fee than hate.
JULIA   Will ye be gone?
LUCETTA   That you may ruminate.°   *Exit*   *meditate*
50 JULIA   And yet I would I had o'erlooked° the letter.   *examined*
It were a shame to call her back again
And pray her to° a fault for which I chid her.   *ask her to commit*
What fool is she, that knows I am a maid
And would not force the letter to my view,
55 Since maids in modesty say 'No' to that
Which they would have the profferer° construe 'Ay'.   *giver*
Fie, fie, how wayward is this foolish love
That like a testy° babe will scratch the nurse   *cranky*
And presently,° all humbled, kiss the rod.[3]   *immediately after*
60 How churlishly I chid Lucetta hence
When willingly I would have had her here.
How angerly I taught my brow to frown
When inward joy enforced my heart to smile.
My penance is to call Lucetta back
65 And ask remission for my folly past.

2. An inconsistency in the text. In 1.1, Speed said he
delivered the letter to Julia. He may have mistaken
Lucetta for Julia or may have lied to Proteus.

3. Children sometimes had to kiss the stick with which
they were beaten.

What ho! Lucetta!

[*Enter* LUCETTA]

LUCETTA   What would your ladyship?

JULIA   Is't near dinner-time?

LUCETTA   I would it were,

That you might kill° your stomach° on your meat   *expend / hunger; rage*

And not upon your maid.

[*She drops and picks up the letter*]⁴

JULIA   What is't that you

70   Took up so gingerly?°   *cautiously*

LUCETTA   Nothing.

JULIA   Why didst thou stoop then?

LUCETTA   To take a paper up that I let fall.

JULIA   And is that paper nothing?

75   LUCETTA   Nothing concerning me.

JULIA   Then let it lie for those that it concerns.

LUCETTA   Madam, it will not lie where it concerns,

Unless it have a false interpreter.

JULIA   Some love of yours hath writ to you in rhyme.

80   LUCETTA   That I might sing it, madam, to a tune,

Give me a note. Your ladyship can set.⁵

JULIA   As little by such toys° as may be possible.   *trifles*

Best sing it to the tune of 'Light o' love'.⁶

LUCETTA   It is too heavy° for so light a tune.   *serious*

85   JULIA   Heavy? Belike it hath some burden,⁷ then?

LUCETTA   Ay, and melodious were it, would you sing it.

JULIA   And why not you?

LUCETTA   I cannot reach so high.⁸

JULIA   Let's see your song.

[*She tries to take the letter*]⁹

                    How now, minion!¹

LUCETTA   Keep tune° there still. So you will sing it out.²   *in tune; in good humor*

90   And yet methinks I do not like this tune.³

JULIA   You do not?

LUCETTA   No, madam, 'tis too sharp.°   *high-pitched; bitter*

JULIA   You, minion, are too saucy.

LUCETTA   Nay, now you are too flat,°   *low-pitched; blunt*

95   And mar the concord° with too harsh a descant.°   *harmony / melody*

There wanteth but a mean to fill your song.⁴

JULIA   The mean is drowned with your unruly bass.°   *low notes; bad conduct*

LUCETTA   Indeed, I bid the base for⁵ Proteus.

JULIA   This bauble° shall not henceforth trouble me.   *trifle (the letter)*

100   Here is a coil with protestation.°   *fuss about a love vow*

[*She tears the letter and drops the pieces*]

---

4. There is no indication in F of when Lucetta drops the letter that she here picks up. Some directors and editors assume that she drops it, either advisedly or inadvertently, before leaving the stage at line 49. To have her drop and immediately retrieve the letter, as here, may suggest that Lucetta is trying once more to call her mistress's attention to this missive.
5. Set to music. Julia takes it to mean "set store by," or "give value to."
6. A popular song in Shakespeare's time.
7. Refrain; heavy load; perhaps punningly referring to the weight of a body during intercourse.
8. Sing so high a note, hope to win so high-ranking a lover.

9. Some editors and directors believe that Lucetta yields the letter at this point, but her refusal to do so seems to be what motivates Julia's anger in the ensuing lines. At some point before line 100, Julia must wrest the letter from her maid.
1. Hussy; with a possible pun on "minim," a musical term for a half note.
2. Finish singing it; come to the end of your anger.
3. Julia may have struck or threatened to strike Lucetta.
4. There lacks but a tenor to complete your song. Her implication is that Julia lacks a man to fulfill her desires.
5. I sang the bass part for; I acted in the interests of (a phrase from the game called prisoner's base).

Go, get you gone, and let the papers lie.
You would be fing'ring them to anger me.

LUCETTA [*aside*]   She makes it strange,° but she would be best   *pretends not to care*
    pleased
To be so angered with another letter.   [*Exit*]

105 JULIA   Nay, would I were so angered with the same.
O hateful hands, to tear such loving words;
Injurious wasps,[6] to feed on such sweet honey
And kill the bees that yield it with your stings.
I'll kiss each several° paper for amends.   *separate*
    [*She picks up some of the pieces of paper*]
110 Look, here is writ 'Kind Julia'—unkind Julia,
As° in revenge of thy ingratitude   *As if*
I throw thy name against the bruising stones,
Trampling contemptuously on thy disdain.
And here is writ 'Love-wounded Proteus'.
115 Poor wounded name, my bosom as a bed
Shall lodge thee till thy wound be throughly° healed;   *completely*
And thus I search° it with a sovereign° kiss.   *probe; cleanse / healing*
But twice or thrice was 'Proteus' written down.
Be calm, good wind, blow not a word away
120 Till I have found each letter in the letter
Except mine own name. That, some whirlwind bear
Unto a ragged, fearful, hanging° rock   *overhanging*
And throw it thence into the raging sea.
Lo, here in one line is his name twice writ:
125 'Poor forlorn Proteus', 'passionate Proteus',
'To the sweet Julia'—that I'll tear away.
And yet I will not, sith° so prettily   *since*
He couples it to his complaining names.
Thus will I fold them, one upon another.
130 Now kiss, embrace, contend, do what you will.
    [*Enter* LUCETTA]

LUCETTA   Madam, dinner is ready, and your father stays.°   *waits*
JULIA   Well, let us go.
LUCETTA   What, shall these papers lie like telltales here?
JULIA   If you respect° them, best to take them up.   *value*
135 LUCETTA   Nay, I was taken up° for laying them down.   *scolded*
Yet here they shall not lie, for° catching cold.   *for fear of*
JULIA   I see you have a month's mind° to them.   *strong desire*
LUCETTA   Ay, madam, you may say what sights you see.
I see things too, although you judge I wink.°   *close my eyes*
140 JULIA   Come, come, will't please you go?   *Exeunt*

1.3
    Enter ANTONIO *and* PANTHINO
ANTONIO   Tell me, Panthino, what sad° talk was that   *serious*
Wherewith my brother held you in the cloister?°   *covered walk*
PANTHINO   'Twas of his nephew Proteus, your son.
ANTONIO   Why, what of him?
PANTHINO   He wondered that your lordship
5 Would suffer him to spend his youth at home
While other men, of slender° reputation,   *insignificant*

---

6. Referring to her hurtful fingers.   1.3 Location: Antonio's house in Verona.

Put forth° their sons to seek preferment° out—   *Send / advancement*
Some to the wars, to try their fortune there,
Some to discover islands far away,

10   Some to the studious universities.
For any or for all these exercises
He said that Proteus your son was meet,°   *fit*
And did request me to importune° you   *beg*
To let him spend his time no more at home,

15   Which would be great impeachment to his age° *reproach in his old age*
In having known no travel in his youth.

ANTONIO   Nor need'st thou much importune me to that
Whereon this month I have been hammering.°   *thinking hard*
I have considered well his loss of time,

20   And how he cannot be a perfect° man,   *complete*
Not being tried and tutored in the world.
Experience is by industry achieved,
And perfected by the swift course of time.
Then tell me, whither were I best to send him?

25   PANTHINO   I think your lordship is not ignorant
How his companion, youthful Valentine,
Attends° the Emperor[1] in his royal court.   *Waits upon*

ANTONIO   I know it well.

PANTHINO   'Twere good, I think, your lordship sent him thither.

30   There shall he practise° tilts and tournaments,   *take part in*
Hear sweet discourse, converse with noblemen,
And be in eye of° every exercise   *witness*
Worthy his youth and nobleness of birth.

ANTONIO   I like thy counsel. Well hast thou advised,

35   And that thou mayst perceive how well I like it,
The execution of it shall make known.
Even with the speediest expedition°   *swiftness*
I will dispatch him to the Emperor's court.

PANTHINO   Tomorrow, may it please you, Don Alfonso,

40   With other gentlemen of good esteem,
Are journeying to salute the Emperor
And to commend their service to his will.

ANTONIO   Good company. With them shall Proteus go.
    [*Enter* PROTEUS *with a letter. He does not see* ANTONIO
    and PANTHINO]

    And in good time.° Now will we break with him.[2]   *at the right moment*

45   PROTEUS   Sweet love, sweet lines, sweet life!
Here is her hand, the agent of her heart.
Here is her oath for love, her honour's pawn.°   *pledge*
O that our fathers would applaud our loves
To seal our happiness with their consents.

50   O heavenly Julia!

ANTONIO   How now, what letter are you reading there?

PROTEUS   May't please your lordship, 'tis a word or two
Of commendations° sent from Valentine,   *greetings*
Delivered by a friend that came from him.

55   ANTONIO   Lend me the letter. Let me see what news.

PROTEUS   There is no news, my lord, but that he writes
How happily he lives, how well beloved

---

1. One of several inconsistencies in the plot. Proteus   of Milan, not at the Emperor's court.
and Valentine are later shown at the court of the Duke   2. Reveal the plan to him.

And daily gracèd° by the Emperor,   *honored*
Wishing me with him, partner of his fortune.
60 ANTONIO   And how stand you affected° to his wish?   *disposed*
PROTEUS   As one relying on your lordship's will,
And not depending on his friendly wish.
ANTONIO   My will is something sorted with° his wish.   *in agreement with*
Muse° not that I thus suddenly proceed,   *Wonder*
65 For what I will, I will, and there an end.
I am resolved that thou shalt spend some time
With Valentinus in the Emperor's court.
What maintenance° he from his friends° receives,   *money / family*
Like exhibition° thou shalt have from me.   *The same allowance*
70 Tomorrow be in readiness to go.
Excuse it not,[3] for I am peremptory.°   *resolved*
PROTEUS   My lord, I cannot be so soon provided.°   *equipped*
Please you deliberate a day or two.
ANTONIO   Look what° thou want'st shall be sent after thee.   *Whatever*
75 No more of stay. Tomorrow thou must go.
Come on, Panthino. You shall be employed
To hasten on his expedition. [*Exeunt* ANTONIO *and* PANTHINO]
PROTEUS   Thus have I shunned the fire for fear of burning
And drenched me in the sea where I am drowned.
80 I feared to show my father Julia's letter
Lest he should take exceptions° to my love,   *object*
And with the vantage of mine own excuse[4]
Hath he excepted most° against my love.   *raised most obstacles*
O, how this spring of love resembleth
85 The uncertain glory of an April day,
Which now shows all the beauty of the sun,
And by and by a cloud takes all away.
[*Enter* PANTHINO]
PANTHINO   Sir Proteus, your father calls for you.
He is in haste, therefore I pray you go.
90 PROTEUS   Why, this it is. My heart accords thereto,°   *agrees to it*
And yet a thousand times it answers 'No'.[5]   *Exeunt*

2.1

Enter VALENTINE [*and*] SPEED
SPEED [*offering* VALENTINE *a glove*]   Sir, your glove.
VALENTINE   Not mine.
My gloves are on.
SPEED   Why then, this may be yours, for this is but one.[1]
VALENTINE   Ha, let me see. Ay, give it me, it's mine—
Sweet ornament, that decks a thing divine.
5 Ah, Silvia, Silvia!
SPEED   Madam Silvia, Madam Silvia!
VALENTINE   How now, sirrah?[2]
SPEED   She is not within hearing, sir.
VALENTINE   Why, sir, who bade you call her?
10 SPEED   Your worship, sir, or else I mistook.

3. Do not offer reasons why you should be excused
from this.
4. And by taking advantage of my lie (that the letter
came from Valentine).
5. *My . . . 'No'*: Suggesting that he is divided between
desire to go and desire to stay.
2.1 Location Milan.
1. Punning on "one," which could be pronounced like
"on."
2. Fellow; a form of address to social inferiors.

VALENTINE   Well, you'll still be° too forward.   *persist in being*

SPEED   And yet I was last chidden for being too slow.

VALENTINE   Go to,[3] sir. Tell me, do you know Madam Silvia?

SPEED   She that your worship loves?

15   VALENTINE   Why, how know you that I am in love?

SPEED   Marry, by these special marks: first, you have learned,
like Sir Proteus, to wreath° your arms, like a malcontent;[4] to   *fold*
relish° a love-song, like a robin redbreast; to walk alone, like   *sing*
one that had the pestilence;° to sigh, like a schoolboy that   *plague*
20   had lost his ABC;° to weep, like a young wench that had buried   *primer; spelling book*
her grandam; to fast, like one that takes° diet; to watch,° like   *keeps to a / lie awake*
one that fears robbing; to speak puling,° like a beggar at Hal-   *whiningly*
lowmas.[5] You were wont, when you laughed, to crow like a
cock; when you walked, to walk like one of the lions. When
25   you fasted, it was presently° after dinner; when you looked   *immediately*
sadly, it was for want of money. And now you are metamor-
phosed with a mistress, that when I look on you I can hardly
think you my master.

VALENTINE   Are all these things perceived in me?

30   SPEED   They are all perceived without ye.°   *in your appearance*

VALENTINE   Without me?[6] They cannot.

SPEED   Without you? Nay, that's certain, for without° you were   *unless*
so simple, none else would.° But you are so without these fol-   *(perceive them)*
lies[7] that these follies are within you, and shine through you
35   like the water in an urinal,° that not an eye that sees you but   *glass jar for urine*
is a physician to comment on your malady.

VALENTINE   But tell me, dost thou know my lady Silvia?

SPEED   She that you gaze on so as she sits at supper?

VALENTINE   Hast thou observed that? Even she I mean.

40   SPEED   Why sir, I know[8] her not.

VALENTINE   Dost thou know her by my gazing on her, and yet
know'st her not?

SPEED   Is she not hard-favoured,° sir?   *ugly*

VALENTINE   Not so fair, boy, as well favoured.°   *gracious; esteemed*

45   SPEED   Sir, I know that well enough.

VALENTINE   What dost thou know?

SPEED   That she is not so fair as of you well favoured.°   *looked on with favor*

VALENTINE   I mean that her beauty is exquisite but her favour°   *graciousness*
infinite.

50   SPEED   That's because the one is painted° and the other out of   *wearing cosmetics*
all count.°   *unable to be counted*

VALENTINE   How painted? And how out of count?

SPEED   Marry, sir, so painted to make her fair that no man
counts° of her beauty.   *takes account; values*

55   VALENTINE   How esteem'st thou me? I account of her beauty.

SPEED   You never saw her since she was deformed.[9]

VALENTINE   How long hath she been deformed?

SPEED   Ever since you loved her.

VALENTINE   I have loved her ever since I saw her, and still I see
60   her beautiful.

---

3. Expression of impatience.
4. A person made melancholy and discontented by
love. Such people were often depicted with folded arms.
5. All Saints' Day, November 1, when it was customary
to give charity to beggars.
6. Valentine has taken Speed to mean "They are all

perceived when you are absent."
7. But you are so outwardly marked by these follies.
8. Punning on "know" as meaning "to be sexually
familiar with."
9. Altered (Speed implies that Valentine's love for Silvia distorts his view of her).

SPEED   If you love her you cannot see her.

VALENTINE   Why?

SPEED   Because love is blind. O that you had mine eyes, or your
own eyes had the lights° they were wont to have when you   *power to see clearly*
65   chid at Sir Proteus for going ungartered.[1]

VALENTINE   What should I see then?

SPEED   Your own present folly and her passing° deformity; for he   *excessive*
being in love could not see to garter his hose, and you being in
love cannot see to put on your hose.

70   VALENTINE   Belike, boy, then you are in love, for last morning you
could not see to wipe my shoes.

SPEED   True, sir. I was in love with my bed. I thank you, you
swinged° me for my love, which makes me the bolder to chide   *beat*
you for yours.

75   VALENTINE   In conclusion, I stand affected to° her.   *in love with*

SPEED   I would you were set.[2] So your affection would cease.

VALENTINE   Last night she enjoined me to write some lines to one
she loves.

SPEED   And have you?

80   VALENTINE   I have.

SPEED   Are they not lamely writ?

VALENTINE   No, boy, but as well as I can do them. Peace, here she
comes.

[*Enter* SILVIA]

SPEED [*aside*]   O excellent motion!° O exceeding puppet!° Now   *puppet show / (Silvia)*
85   will he interpret[3] to her.

VALENTINE   Madam and mistress, a thousand good-morrows.

SPEED [*aside*]   O, give° ye good e'en!° Here's a million of   *God give / evening*
manners.

SILVIA   Sir Valentine and servant,[4] to you two thousand.

90   SPEED [*aside*]   He should give her interest, and she gives it him.[5]

VALENTINE   As you enjoined me, I have writ your letter
Unto the secret, nameless friend of yours;
Which I was much unwilling to proceed in
But for my duty to your ladyship.

[*He gives her a letter*]

95   SILVIA   I thank you, gentle servant. 'Tis very clerkly° done.   *like a scholar*

VALENTINE   Now trust me, madam, it came hardly off;°   *was not done easily*
For being ignorant to whom it goes
I writ at random, very doubtfully.

SILVIA   Perchance you think too much of so much pains?

100   VALENTINE   No, madam. So it stead° you I will write—   *help*
Please you command—a thousand times as much.
And yet . . .

SILVIA   A pretty period.° Well, I guess the sequel.°   *pause / what is next*
And yet I will not name it. And yet I care not.
And yet, take this again.

[*She offers him the letter*]

105   And yet I thank you,
Meaning henceforth to trouble you no more.

---

1. Garters kept stockings from falling down. Going
"ungartered" was a traditional sign of love melancholy.
2. Seated; satisfied. Speed has interpreted "stand" as
carrying its bawdy connotation of "having an erection."
3. Provide commentary (as if in a puppet show).

4. In courtly love literature, a man devoted to a lady is
called her servant.
5. He should surpass her in compliments, but she surpasses him.

SPEED [*aside*]   And yet you will, and yet another yet.

VALENTINE   What means your ladyship? Do you not like it?

SILVIA   Yes, yes. The lines are very quaintly° writ,   *skillfully*

110   But since unwillingly, take them again.

    [*She presses the letter upon him*]

    Nay, take them.

VALENTINE   Madam, they are for you.

SILVIA   Ay, ay. You writ them, sir, at my request,

    But I will none of them. They are for you.

    I would have had them writ more movingly.

115   VALENTINE   Please you, I'll write your ladyship another.

SILVIA   And when it's writ, for my sake read it over,

    And if it please you, so. If not, why, so.

VALENTINE   If it please me, madam? What then?

SILVIA   Why, if it please you, take it for your labour.

120   And so good morrow, servant.   *Exit*

SPEED [*aside*]   O jest unseen, inscrutable, invisible

    As a nose on a man's face or a weathercock on a steeple.

    My master sues to her, and she hath taught her suitor,

    He being her pupil, to become her tutor.

125   O excellent device!° Was there ever heard a better?—   *trick*

    That my master, being scribe, to himself should write the letter.

VALENTINE   How now, sir—what, are you reasoning with your self?

SPEED   Nay, I was rhyming. 'Tis you that have the reason.

VALENTINE   To do what?

130   SPEED   To be a spokesman from Madam Silvia.

VALENTINE   To whom?

SPEED   To yourself. Why, she woos you by a figure.°   *device; indirect means*

VALENTINE   What figure?

SPEED   By a letter, I should say.

135   VALENTINE   Why, she hath not writ to me.

SPEED   What need she, when she hath made you write to yourself? Why, do you not perceive the jest?

VALENTINE   No, believe me.

SPEED   No believing you indeed, sir. But did you perceive her

140   earnest?[6]

VALENTINE   She gave me none, except an angry word.

SPEED   Why, she hath given you a letter.

VALENTINE   That's the letter I writ to her friend.

SPEED   And that letter hath she delivered, and there an end.

145   VALENTINE   I would it were no worse.

SPEED   I'll warrant you, 'tis as well.

    For often have you writ to her, and she in modesty

    Or else for want of idle time could not again reply,

    Or fearing else some messenger that might her mind discover,

150   Herself hath taught her love himself to write unto her lover.

    —All this I speak in print,° for in print I found it.[7] Why muse   *very precisely*

    you, sir? 'Tis dinner-time.

VALENTINE   I have dined.°   *(on love)*

SPEED   Ay, but hearken, sir. Though the chameleon[8] love can

---

6. To be serious. Valentine takes "perceive" to mean "receive," and takes "earnest" to mean "pledge" or "money given to seal a bargain."
7. Speed's reference to a printed speech probably shouldn't be taken literally. More likely, he is making

fun of Valentine's inability to understand Silvia's trick by stressing his own care with language.
8. A small lizard that can exist for long periods without food and was thought to feed on air.

155   feed on the air, I am one that am nourished by my victuals,
   and would fain° have meat. O, be not like your mistress—be   *be eager to*
   moved, be moved!⁹   *Exeunt*

2.2

Enter PROTEUS [*and*] JULIA

PROTEUS   Have patience, gentle Julia.

JULIA   I must where is no remedy.

PROTEUS   When possibly I can I will return.

JULIA   If you turn not,° you will return the sooner.   *are not unfaithful*
        [*She gives him a ring*]¹

5   Keep this remembrance for thy Julia's sake.

PROTEUS   Why then, we'll make exchange. Here, take you this.
        [*He gives her a ring*]

JULIA   And seal the bargain with a holy kiss.
        [*They kiss*]

PROTEUS   Here is my hand for my true constancy.
   And when that hour o'erslips° me in the day   *passes by*
10   Wherein I sigh not, Julia, for thy sake,
   The next ensuing hour some foul mischance
   Torment me for my love's forgetfulness.
   My father stays° my coming. Answer not.   *awaits*
   The tide is now. [JULIA *weeps*]   Nay, not thy tide of tears,
15   That tide will stay° me longer than I should.   *delay*
   Julia, farewell.   [*Exit* JULIA]
         What, gone without a word?
   Ay, so true love should do. It cannot speak,
   For truth hath better deeds than words to grace° it.   *adorn*
        [*Enter* PANTHINO]

PANTHINO   Sir Proteus, you are stayed for.

PROTEUS   Go, I come, I come.—
20   Alas, this parting strikes poor lovers dumb.   *Exeunt*

2.3

Enter LANCE¹ [*with his dog Crab*]²

LANCE [*to the audience*]   Nay, 'twill be this hour ere I have done
   weeping. All the kind° of the Lances have this very fault. I have   *family; kin*
   received my proportion,° like the prodigious³ son, and am   *portion*
   going with Sir Proteus to the Imperial's° court. I think Crab, my   *(for "Emperor's")*
5   dog, be the sourest-natured dog that lives. My mother weeping,
   my father wailing, my sister crying, our maid howling, our cat
   wringing her hands, and all our house in a great perplexity, yet
   did not this cruel-hearted cur shed one tear. He is a stone, a
   very pebble-stone, and has no more pity in him than a dog.
10   A Jew would have wept to have seen our parting.⁴ Why, my
   grandam, having no eyes,° look you, wept herself blind at   *being blind*
   my parting. Nay, I'll show you the manner of it.⁵ This shoe is my
   father. No, this left shoe is my father. No, no, this left shoe is

---

9. Be kind; be induced (to eat).
2.2 Location: probably Julia's house or garden.
1. The action in this scene resembles a betrothal ceremony, and thus in the Elizabethan period a legally binding agreement to marry.
2.3 Location: A street in Verona.
1. A shortened form of "Lancelot."
2. "Crab" may mean "crab apple" or a "crabbed, ill-

tempered person."
3. Lance frequently confuses one word with another. His reference here is to the biblical parable of the prodigal son, who wastes his inheritance but is welcomed home again (Luke 15:11–32).
4. Alluding to proverbs claiming that Jews and dogs lack pity.
5. Taking off his shoes for demonstration.

my mother. Nay, that cannot be so, neither. Yes, it is so, it is so,
it hath the worser sole.[6] This shoe with the hole[7] in it is my
mother, and this my father. A vengeance on't, there 'tis.[8] Now,
sir, this staff is my sister, for, look you, she is as white as a lily
and as small° as a wand.° This hat is Nan our maid. I am the   *slender / small stick*
dog. No, the dog is himself, and I am the dog. O, the dog is me,
and I am myself. Ay, so, so. Now come I to my father. 'Father,
your blessing.' Now should not the shoe speak a word for weeping. Now should I kiss my father. Well, he weeps on. Now come
I to my mother. O that she could speak now, like a moved°   *full of emotion*
woman. Well, I kiss her. Why, there 'tis. Here's my mother's
breath[9] up and down.° Now come I to my sister. Mark the moan   *exactly*
she makes.[1]—Now the dog all this while sheds not a tear nor
speaks a word. But see how I lay the dust with my tears.

     [Enter PANTHINO]

PANTHINO Lance, away, away, aboard. Thy master is shipped,
and thou art to post° after with oars.° What's the matter? Why   *hurry / in a rowboat*
weep'st thou, man? Away, ass, you'll lose° the tide if you tarry   *miss*
any longer.
LANCE It is no matter if the tied[2] were lost, for it is the unkindest tied that ever any man tied.
PANTHINO What's the unkindest tide?
LANCE Why, he that's tied here, Crab my dog.
PANTHINO Tut, man, I mean thou'lt lose the flood,° and in los-   *miss the tide*
ing the flood, lose thy voyage, and in losing thy voyage, lose
thy master, and in losing thy master, lose thy service, and in
losing thy service—

     [LANCE puts his hand over Panthino's mouth]

Why dost thou stop my mouth?
LANCE For fear thou shouldst lose thy tongue.
PANTHINO Where should I lose my tongue?
LANCE In thy tale.
PANTHINO In thy tail!°   *rear end*
LANCE Lose the tide, and the voyage, and the master, and the
service, and the tied? Why, man, if the river were dry, I am
able to fill it with my tears. If the wind were down, I could
drive the boat with my sighs.
PANTHINO Come, come away, man. I was sent to call° thee.   *summon*
LANCE Sir, call me what thou darest.
PANTHINO Wilt thou go?
LANCE Well, I will go.   *Exeunt*

2.4

     Enter VALENTINE, SILVIA, THURIO, [and] SPEED

SILVIA Servant!
VALENTINE Mistress?
SPEED *[to VALENTINE]* Master, Sir Thurio frowns on you.
VALENTINE Ay, boy, it's for love.
SPEED Not of you.

---

6. Punning on "soul" and alluding to medieval debates
about whether women had souls.
7. Punning on "hole" as "female genitalia."
8. Presumably Lance is now satisfied with his posi-
tioning of the shoes.
9. Comparing the smelly shoe to his mother's breath.

1. Perhaps Lance makes his staff "moan" by swishing
it in the air.
2. Taking "tide" for "tied," or one who is tied up, meaning Crab.
2.4 Location: The Duke's court in Milan.

	VALENTINE Of my mistress, then.	
	SPEED 'Twere good you knocked° him.	struck
	SILVIA [to VALENTINE] Servant, you are sad.	
	VALENTINE Indeed, madam, I seem so.	
10	THURIO Seem you that you are not?	
	VALENTINE Haply° I do.	Perhaps
	THURIO So do counterfeits.	
	VALENTINE So do you.	
	THURIO What seem I that I am not?	
15	VALENTINE Wise.	
	THURIO What instance° of the contrary?	evidence
	VALENTINE Your folly.	
	THURIO And how quote° you my folly?	detect; observe
	VALENTINE I quote it in your jerkin.°	short coat
20	THURIO My 'jerkin' is a doublet.°	jacket; couple or pair
	VALENTINE Well then, I'll double your folly.	
	THURIO How!	
	SILVIA What, angry, Sir Thurio? Do you change colour?	
	VALENTINE Give him leave, madam, he is a kind of chameleon.[1]	
25	THURIO That hath more mind to feed on your blood than live	
	in your air.[2]	
	VALENTINE You have said, sir.	
	THURIO Ay, sir, and done too, for this time.	
	VALENTINE I know it well, sir, you always end ere you begin.	
30	SILVIA A fine volley of words, gentlemen, and quickly shot off.	
	VALENTINE 'Tis indeed, madam, we thank the giver.	
	SILVIA Who is that, servant?	
	VALENTINE Yourself, sweet lady, for you gave the fire.° Sir Thu-	spark
	rio borrows his wit from your ladyship's looks, and spends what	
35	he borrows kindly° in your company.	properly; naturally
	THURIO Sir, if you spend word for word with me, I shall make	
	your wit bankrupt.	
	VALENTINE I know it well, sir. You have an exchequer° of words,	treasury
	and, I think, no other treasure to give your followers. For it	
40	appears by their bare liveries[3] that they live by your bare° words.	worthless
	SILVIA No more, gentlemen, no more. Here comes my father.	
	[Enter the DUKE]	
	DUKE Now, daughter Silvia, you are hard beset.°	set upon (by man)
	Sir Valentine, your father is in good health,	
	What say you to a letter from your friends	
	Of much good news?	
45	VALENTINE My lord, I will be thankful	
	To any happy messenger° from thence.	bringer of happy news
	DUKE Know ye Don Antonio, your countryman?	
	VALENTINE Ay, my good lord, I know the gentleman	
	To be of worth, and worthy estimation,	
50	And not without desert so well reputed.	
	DUKE Hath he not a son?	
	VALENTINE Ay, my good lord, a son that well deserves	
	The honour and regard of such a father.	
	DUKE You know him well?	

---

1. Chameleons can change color, perhaps suggesting that Thurio is fickle in love.
2. Chameleons were supposed to live on air (see note to 2.1.154), but Thurio would rather drink Valentine's blood.
3. By their threadbare clothing.

55	VALENTINE I knew him as myself, for from our infancy	
	We have conversed,° and spent our hours together.	*kept company*
	And though myself have been an idle truant,	
	Omitting° the sweet benefit of time	*Neglecting*
	To clothe mine age° with angel-like perfection,	*adorn my years*
60	Yet hath Sir Proteus—for that's his name—	
	Made use and fair advantage of his days:	
	His years but young, but his experience old;	
	His head unmellowed,° but his judgement ripe.	*without gray hair*
	And in a word—for far behind his worth	
65	Comes all the praises that I now bestow—	
	He is complete,° in feature° and in mind,	*perfect / appearance*
	With all good grace to grace a gentleman.	
	DUKE Beshrew me, sir, but if he make this good°	*proves this to be true*
	He is as worthy for an empress' love	
70	As meet° to be an emperor's counsellor.	*fit*
	Well, sir, this gentleman is come to me	
	With commendation from great potentates,°	*rulers; men of power*
	And here he means to spend his time awhile.	
	I think 'tis no unwelcome news to you.	
75	VALENTINE Should I have wished a thing° it had been he.	*anything*
	DUKE Welcome him then according to his worth.	
	Silvia, I speak to you, and you, Sir Thurio;	
	For Valentine, I need not cite° him to it.	*urge*
	I will send him hither to you presently. [*Exit*]	
80	VALENTINE This is the gentleman I told your ladyship	
	Had come along with me, but that his mistress	
	Did hold his eyes locked in her crystal looks.	
	SILVIA Belike that° now she hath enfranchised° them	*Perhaps / freed*
	Upon some other pawn for fealty.⁴	
85	VALENTINE Nay, sure, I think she holds them prisoners still.	
	SILVIA Nay, then he should be blind, and being blind	
	How could he see his way to seek out you?	
	VALENTINE Why, lady, love hath twenty pair of eyes.	
	THURIO They say that love hath not an eye at all.⁵	
90	VALENTINE To see such lovers, Thurio, as yourself.	
	Upon a homely object love can wink.°	*close its eyes*
	SILVIA Have done, have done. Here comes the gentleman.	
	[*Enter* PROTEUS]	
	VALENTINE Welcome, dear Proteus. Mistress, I beseech you	
	Confirm his welcome with some special favour.	
95	SILVIA His worth is warrant for his welcome hither,	
	If this be he you oft have wished to hear from.	
	VALENTINE Mistress, it is. Sweet lady, entertain him⁶	
	To be my fellow-servant to your ladyship.	
	SILVIA Too low a mistress for so high° a servant.	*tall; distinguished*
100	PROTEUS Not so, sweet lady, but too mean° a servant	*lowly*
	To have a look of° such a worthy mistress.	*from*
	VALENTINE Leave off discourse of disability.°	*unworthiness*
	Sweet lady, entertain him for your servant.	
	PROTEUS My duty will I boast of, nothing else.	
105	SILVIA And duty never yet did want his meed.°	*lack his reward*

---

4. *Upon . . . fealty:* Because of some other lover's pledge of faithful service.

5. Referring to the blindness of Cupid.

6. Take him into your service.

Servant, you are welcome to a worthless mistress.

PROTEUS I'll die on° him that says so but yourself.   *die fighting*

SILVIA That you are welcome?

PROTEUS   That you are worthless.

    [*Enter a* SERVANT][7]

SERVANT Madam, my lord your father would speak with you.

SILVIA I wait upon his pleasure.   [*Exit the* SERVANT]

110   Come, Sir Thurio,

Go with me. Once more, new servant, welcome.

I'll leave you to confer of° home affairs.   *talk about*

When you have done, we look to hear from you.

PROTEUS We'll both attend upon your ladyship.

    [*Exeunt* SILVIA *and* THURIO]

115 VALENTINE Now tell me, how do all from whence you came?

PROTEUS Your friends are well, and have them much com-

    mended.°   *sent their regards*

VALENTINE And how do yours?

PROTEUS   I left them all in health.

VALENTINE How does your lady, and how thrives your love?

PROTEUS My tales of love were wont to weary you.

120   I know you joy not in a love-discourse.

VALENTINE Ay, Proteus, but that life is altered now.

I have done penance for contemning° love,   *despising*

Whose high imperious thoughts have punished me

With bitter fasts, with penitential groans,

125 With nightly tears and daily heart-sore sighs.

For in revenge of my contempt of love

Love hath chased sleep from my enthrallèd° eyes,   *enslaved*

And made them watchers of mine own heart's sorrow.

O gentle Proteus, love's a mighty lord,

130 And hath so humbled me as° I confess   *that*

There is no woe to° his correction,°   *equal to / punishment*

Nor to his service no such joy on earth.

Now, no discourse except it be of love.

Now can I break my fast, dine, sup, and sleep

135 Upon the very naked name of love.

PROTEUS Enough. I read your fortune in your eye.

Was this the idol that you worship so?

VALENTINE Even she; and is she not a heavenly saint?

PROTEUS No, but she is an earthly paragon.

VALENTINE Call her divine.

140 PROTEUS   I will not flatter her.

VALENTINE O flatter me; for love delights in praises.

PROTEUS When I was sick you gave me bitter pills,

And I must minister the like to you.

VALENTINE Then speak the truth by° her; if not divine,   *about*

145 Yet let her be a principality,°   *angel*

Sovereign° to all the creatures on the earth.   *Superior*

PROTEUS Except my mistress.

VALENTINE   Sweet, except not any,°   *make no exceptions*

Except° thou wilt except against° my love.   *Unless / insult*

PROTEUS Have I not reason to prefer° mine own?   *advance*

---

7. Even though F does not indicate the entrance of a servant at this point and assigns the following line to Thurio, many editors have assumed that a servant must enter here to bring the message that Silvia's father would speak with her.

150   VALENTINE   And I will help thee to prefer her, too.
        She shall be dignified with this high honour,
        To bear my lady's train, lest the base earth
        Should from her vesture° chance to steal a kiss   *garments*
        And, of so great a favour growing proud,
155   Disdain to root° the summer-swelling flower,   *receive the roots of*
        And make rough winter everlastingly.
        PROTEUS   Why, Valentine, what braggartism° is this?   *excessive boasting*
        VALENTINE   Pardon me, Proteus, all I can is nothing
        To her[8] whose worth makes other worthies nothing.
        She is alone.°   *unique*
160   PROTEUS   Then let her alone.
        VALENTINE   Not for the world. Why man, she is mine own,
        And I as rich in having such a jewel
        As twenty seas, if all their sand were pearl,
        The water nectar, and the rocks pure gold.
165   Forgive me that I do not dream on thee°   *pay attention to you*
        Because thou seest me dote upon my love.
        My foolish rival, that her father likes
        Only for° his possessions are so huge,   *because*
        Is gone with her along, and I must after;
170   For love, thou know'st, is full of jealousy.
        PROTEUS   But she loves you?
        VALENTINE   Ay, and we are betrothed. Nay more, our marriage hour,
        With all the cunning manner of our flight,
        Determined of:° how I must climb her window,   *Decided upon*
175   The ladder made of cords, and all the means
        Plotted and 'greed on for my happiness.
        Good Proteus, go with me to my chamber
        In these affairs to aid me with thy counsel.
        PROTEUS   Go on before. I shall enquire you forth.°   *seek you out*
180   I must unto the road,° to disembark   *harbor*
        Some necessaries that I needs must use,
        And then I'll presently° attend you.   *at once*
        VALENTINE   Will you make haste?
        PROTEUS   I will.   *Exit* [VALENTINE]
185   Even as one heat another heat expels,[9]
        Or as one nail by strength drives out another,
        So the remembrance of my former love
        Is by° a newer object quite forgotten.   *because of*
        Is it mine eye, or Valentine's praise,
190   Her true perfection, or my false transgression
        That makes me, reasonless,° to reason thus?   *wrongly; without cause*
        She is fair, and so is Julia that I love—
        That I did love, for now my love is thawed,
        Which like a waxen image 'gainst a fire
195   Bears no impression of the thing it was.
        Methinks my zeal° to Valentine is cold,   *affection*
        And that I love him not as I was wont.
        O, but I love his lady too-too much,
        And that's the reason I love him so little.

8. *all . . . her:* all I can say is nothing in comparison   9. Referring to a popular belief that the application of
with her.   heat takes away the pain of a burn.

200 How shall I dote on her with more advice,°   *upon more deliberation*
That thus without advice begin to love her?
'Tis but her picture° I have yet beheld,   *outer appearance*
And that hath dazzled my reason's light.
But when I look on her perfections
205 There is no reason but° I shall be blind.   *doubt that*
If I can check my erring love I will,
If not, to compass° her I'll use my skill.   *Exit*   *win*

2.5

Enter SPEED *and* LANCE [*with his dog Crab*]

SPEED   Lance, by mine honesty, welcome to Milan.[1]

LANCE   Forswear° not thyself, sweet youth, for I am not wel-   *Perjure*
come. I reckon this always, that a man is never undone° till he   *ruined*
be hanged, nor never welcome to a place till some certain shot°   *tavern bill*
5   be paid and the hostess say 'Welcome'.

SPEED   Come on, you madcap. I'll to the alehouse with you
presently, where, for one shot of five pence, thou shalt have
five thousand welcomes. But sirrah, how did thy master part
with Madam Julia?

10 LANCE   Marry, after they closed[2] in earnest they parted very
fairly in jest.

SPEED   But shall she marry him?

LANCE   No.

SPEED   How then, shall he marry her?

15 LANCE   No, neither.

SPEED   What, are they broken?°   *no longer engaged*

LANCE   No, they are both as whole as a fish.[3]

SPEED   Why then, how stands the matter with them?

LANCE   Marry, thus: when it stands well with him[4] it stands well
20   with her.

SPEED   What an ass art thou! I understand thee not.

LANCE   What a block° art thou, that thou canst not! My staff[5]   *stupid person*
understands° me.   *comprehends; supports*

SPEED   What thou sayst?

25 LANCE   Ay, and what I do too. Look thee, I'll but lean, and my
staff under-stands me.

SPEED   It stands under thee indeed.

LANCE   Why, stand-under and under-stand is all one.

SPEED   But tell me true, will't be a match?

30 LANCE   Ask my dog. If he say 'Ay', it will. If he say 'No', it will.
If he shake his tail and say nothing, it will.

SPEED   The conclusion is, then, that it will.

LANCE   Thou shalt never get such a secret from me but by a
parable.°   *an indirect speech*

35 SPEED   'Tis well that I get it so. But Lance, how sayst thou[6] that
my master is become a notable lover?

LANCE   I never knew him otherwise.

SPEED   Than how?

2.5 Location: A street in Milan.
1. F reads "Padua," probably a first thought rejected but not canceled.
2. Came to an agreement; embraced.
3. Lance takes "broken" to mean "in pieces" and replies with a proverb.

4. When it goes well with him; when he has an erection.
5. A stick used when walking; also a euphemism for "penis." Lance may play with his staff during this dialogue.
6. What can you say about the fact.

40	LANCE	A notable lubber,° as thou reportest him to be.	*clumsy, stupid person*
	SPEED	Why, thou whoreson[7] ass, thou mistak'st° me.	*misunderstand*
	LANCE	Why, fool, I meant not thee, I meant thy master.[8]	
	SPEED	I tell thee my master is become a hot lover.	
	LANCE	Why, I tell thee I care not, though he burn himself in	
		love. If thou wilt, go with me to the alehouse. If not, thou art	
45		an Hebrew, a Jew, and not worth° the name of a Christian.	*worthy*
	SPEED	Why?	
	LANCE	Because thou hast not so much charity in thee as to go	
		to the ale[9] with a Christian. Wilt thou go?	
	SPEED	At thy service.	*Exeunt*

2.6

Enter PROTEUS

	PROTEUS	To leave my Julia shall I be forsworn;°	*guilty of vow-breaking*
		To love fair Silvia shall I be forsworn;	
		To wrong my friend I shall be much forsworn.	
		And e'en that power° which gave me first my oath	*(love)*
5		Provokes me to this three-fold perjury.	
		Love bade me swear, and love bids me forswear.	
		O sweet-suggesting° love, if thou hast sinned	*sweetly seductive*
		Teach me, thy tempted subject, to excuse it.	
		At first I did adore a twinkling star,	
10		But now I worship a celestial sun.	
		Unheedful° vows may heedfully° be broken,	*Careless / advisedly*
		And he wants° wit that wants resolvèd will°	*lacks / determination*
		To learn° his wit t'exchange the bad for better.	*teach*
		Fie, fie, unreverent tongue, to call her bad	
15		Whose sovereignty so oft thou hast preferred°	*recommended*
		With twenty thousand soul-confirming° oaths.	*soul-confirmed; devout*
		I cannot leave° to love, and yet I do.	*cease*
		But there I leave to love where I should love.	
		Julia I lose, and Valentine I lose.	
20		If I keep them I needs must lose myself.	
		If I lose them, thus find I by their loss	
		For Valentine, myself, for Julia, Silvia.[1]	
		I to myself am dearer than a friend,	
		For love is still° most precious in itself,	*always*
25		And Silvia—witness heaven that made her fair—	
		Shows Julia but° a swarthy Ethiope.[2]	*to be merely*
		I will forget that Julia is alive,	
		Remmb'ring that my love to her is dead,	
		And Valentine I'll hold an enemy,	
30		Aiming at Silvia as a sweeter friend.	
		I cannot now prove constant to myself	
		Without some treachery used to Valentine.	
		This night he meaneth with a corded° ladder	*rope*
		To climb celestial Silvia's chamber-window,	
35		Myself in counsel his competitor.[3]	

7. Literally, "son of a whore." A term of abuse frequently used in jest.
8. Punning on "mistake." Lance understood Speed to mean "you misjudge me" or "you confuse me with someone else."
9. Referring to a church-ale, a charitable festival at which ale was sold in aid of the church or to relieve the poor.

2.6 Location: The Duke's court in Milan.
1. Proteus claims that to hold on to his selfhood and his love (Silvia), he must give up Julia and Valentine.
2. Ethiopian, or black African. The comparison rests on a European idealization of female fairness or whiteness.
3. Myself in on the secret as his partner.

Now presently I'll give her father notice
Of their disguising and pretended° flight,   *intended*
Who, all enraged, will banish Valentine;
For Thurio he intends shall wed his daughter.
40   But Valentine being gone, I'll quickly cross°   *thwart*
By some sly trick blunt Thurio's dull proceeding.
Love, lend me wings to make my purpose swift,
As thou hast lent me wit to plot this drift.°   *Exit*   *scheme*

2.7

Enter JULIA *and* LUCETTA

JULIA   Counsel, Lucetta. Gentle girl, assist me,
And e'en in kind love I do conjure° thee,   *entreat*
Who art the table° wherein all my thoughts   *notebook; tablet*
Are visibly charactered° and engraved,   *written*
5   To lesson° me, and tell me some good mean°   *teach / way*
How with my honour I may undertake
A journey to my loving Proteus.
LUCETTA   Alas, the way is wearisome and long.
JULIA   A true-devoted pilgrim is not weary
10   To measure° kingdoms with his feeble steps.   *make his way through*
Much less shall she that hath love's wings to fly,
And when the flight is made to one so dear,
Of such divine perfection as Sir Proteus.
LUCETTA   Better forbear till Proteus make return.
15   JULIA   O, know'st thou not his looks are my soul's food?
Pity the dearth that I have pinèd in
By longing for that food so long a time.
Didst thou but know the inly° touch of love   *inward*
Thou wouldst as soon go kindle fire with snow
20   As seek to quench the fire of love with words.
LUCETTA   I do not seek to quench your love's hot fire,
But qualify° the fire's extreme rage,   *lessen*
Lest it should burn above the bounds of reason.
JULIA   The more thou damm'st it up, the more it burns.
25   The current that with gentle murmur glides,
Thou know'st, being stopped, impatiently doth rage.
But when his fair course is not hinderèd
He makes sweet music with th'enamelled° stones,   *shiny*
Giving a gentle kiss to every sedge°   *plant*
30   He overtaketh in his pilgrimage.
And so by many winding nooks he strays
With willing sport to the wild ocean.
Then let me go, and hinder not my course.
I'll be as patient as a gentle stream,
35   And make a pastime of each weary step
Till the last step have brought me to my love.
And there I'll rest as after much turmoil
A blessèd soul doth in Elysium.[1]
LUCETTA   But in what habit° will you go along?   *clothing*
40   JULIA   Not like a woman, for I would prevent°   *forestall*
The loose encounters of lascivious men.

2.7 Location: Julia's house.   1. In Greek mythology, the final abode, after death, of
blessèd souls.

Gentle Lucetta, fit° me with such weeds°   *equip / clothing*
As may beseem some well-reputed page.

LUCETTA   Why then, your ladyship must cut your hair.

45 JULIA   No, girl, I'll knit° it up in silken strings   *bind*
With twenty odd-conceited° true-love knots.[2]   *strangely devised*
To be fantastic° may become a youth   *fanciful*
Of greater time° than I shall show° to be.   *age / appear*

LUCETTA   What fashion, madam, shall I make your breeches?

50 JULIA   That fits as well as 'Tell me, good my lord,
What compass° will you wear your farthingale?'[3]   *fullness*
Why, e'en what fashion thou best likes, Lucetta.

LUCETTA   You must needs have them with a codpiece,[4] madam.

JULIA   Out, out,° Lucetta. That will be ill-favoured.°   *Not so / unbecoming*

55 LUCETTA   A round hose,[5] madam, now's not worth a pin
Unless you have a codpiece to stick pins on.

JULIA   Lucetta, as thou lov'st me let me have
What thou think'st meet and is most mannerly.°   *seemly; modest*
But tell me, wench, how will the world repute me

60 For undertaking so unstaid° a journey?   *reckless*
I fear me it will make me scandalized.°   *disgraced*

LUCETTA   If you think so, then stay at home, and go not.

JULIA   Nay, that I will not.

LUCETTA   Then never dream on infamy, but go.

65 If Proteus like your journey when you come,
No matter who's displeased when you are gone.
I fear me he will scarce be pleased withal.°   *with it*

JULIA   That is the least, Lucetta, of my fear.
A thousand oaths, an ocean of his tears,

70 And instances of infinite° of love   *an infinity*
Warrant me° welcome to my Proteus.   *Assure me I will be*

LUCETTA   All these are servants to deceitful men.

JULIA   Base men, that use them to so base effect.
But truer stars did govern Proteus' birth.[6]

75 His words are bonds, his oaths are oracles,
His love sincere, his thoughts immaculate,
His tears pure messengers sent from his heart,
His heart as far from fraud as heaven from earth.

LUCETTA   Pray heaven he prove so when you come to him.

80 JULIA   Now, as thou lov'st me, do him not that wrong
To bear a hard opinion of his truth.
Only deserve my love by loving him,
And presently° go with me to my chamber   *at once*
To take a note of what I stand in need of

85 To furnish me upon my longing° journey.   *love-prompted*
All that is mine I leave at thy dispose,°   *in your care*
My goods, my lands, my reputation;
Only in lieu thereof dispatch me hence.°   *help me hurry away*
Come, answer not, but to it presently.

90 I am impatient of my tarriance.°   *Exeunt*   *delay*

---

2. Ornamental ribbons supposed to symbolize love.
3. Hooped petticoat.
4. A pouch attached to the front of men's breeches, covering the genital area. In the Elizabethan period, codpieces could be elaborately decorated, as with pins

(line 56).
5. Breeches fitting the legs and thighs tightly and puffed out at the hips.
6. The stars' position at one's birth supposedly determined one's character.

3.1

Enter DUKE, THURIO, [*and*] PROTEUS

DUKE   Sir Thurio, give us leave,° I pray, awhile.   *leave us alone*
We have some secrets to confer about.   [*Exit* THURIO]
Now tell me, Proteus, what's your will with me?
PROTEUS   My gracious lord, that which I would discover°   *reveal*
5   The law of friendship bids me to conceal.
But when I call to mind your gracious favours
Done to me, undeserving as I am,
My duty pricks° me on to utter that   *urges*
Which else no worldly good should draw from me.
10   Know, worthy prince, Sir Valentine my friend
This night intends to steal away your daughter.
Myself am one made privy to the plot.
I know you have determined to bestow her
On Thurio, whom your gentle daughter hates,
15   And should she thus be stol'n away from you
It would be much vexation to your age.
Thus, for my duty's sake, I rather chose
To cross° my friend in his intended drift°   *thwart / plan*
Than by concealing it heap on your head
20   A pack of sorrows which would press you down,
Being unprevented,° to your timeless° grave.   *unstopped / early*
DUKE   Proteus, I thank thee for thine honest care,
Which to requite° command me[1] while I live.   *repay*
This love of theirs myself have often seen,
25   Haply,° when they have judged me fast asleep,   *Perchance*
And oftentimes have purposed to forbid
Sir Valentine her company and my court.
But fearing lest my jealous aim might err,
And so unworthily disgrace the man—
30   A rashness that I ever yet have shunned—
I gave him gentle looks, thereby to find
That which thyself hast now disclosed to me.
And that thou mayst perceive my fear of this,
Knowing that tender youth is soon suggested,°   *tempted*
35   I nightly lodge her in an upper tower,
The key whereof myself have ever kept;
And thence she cannot be conveyed away.
PROTEUS   Know, noble lord, they have devised a mean°   *plan*
How he her chamber-window will ascend,
40   And with a corded ladder fetch her down,
For which the youthful lover now is gone,
And this way comes he with it presently,
Where, if it please you, you may intercept him.
But, good my lord, do it so cunningly
45   That my discovery° be not aimèd° at;   *disclosure / guessed*
For love of you, not hate unto my friend,
Hath made me publisher of this pretence.[2]
DUKE   Upon mine honour, he shall never know
That I had any light° from thee of this.   *information*
50   PROTEUS   Adieu, my lord. Sir Valentine is coming.   [*Exit*]

3.1 Location: The Duke's court in Milan.   2. Has caused me to make this plan public.
1. Ask anything of me.

[*Enter* VALENTINE]

DUKE Sir Valentine, whither away so fast?[3]

VALENTINE Please it° your grace, there is a messenger   *If it please*
  That stays° to bear my letters to my friends,   *waits*
  And I am going to deliver them.

55 DUKE Be they of much import?

VALENTINE The tenor° of them doth but signify   *general sense*
  My health and happy being at your court.

DUKE Nay then, no matter. Stay with me awhile.
  I am to break with thee of° some affairs   *disclose to you*
60   That touch me near, wherein thou must be secret.
  'Tis not unknown to thee that I have sought
  To match my friend Sir Thurio to my daughter.

VALENTINE I know it well, my lord; and sure the match
  Were° rich and honourable. Besides, the gentleman   *Would be*
65   Is full of virtue, bounty, worth, and qualities
  Beseeming° such a wife as your fair daughter.   *Suited to*
  Cannot your grace win her to fancy him?

DUKE No, trust me. She is peevish, sullen, froward,°   *perverse*
  Proud, disobedient, stubborn, lacking duty,
70   Neither regarding° that she is my child   *taking into account*
  Nor fearing me as if I were her father.[4]
  And may I say to thee, this pride of hers
  Upon advice° hath drawn my love from her,   *After consideration*
  And where° I thought the remnant° of mine age   *whereas / remainder*
75   Should have been cherished by her child-like duty,
  I now am full resolved to take a wife,
  And turn her out to who will take her in.
  Then let her beauty be her wedding dower,
  For me and my possessions she esteems not.

80 VALENTINE What would your grace have me to do in this?

DUKE There is a lady of Verona[5] here
  Whom I affect,° but she is nice,° and coy,   *love / hard to please*
  And naught esteems° my agèd eloquence.   *does not value*
  Now therefore would I have thee to my tutor—
85   For long agone° I have forgot° to court,   *ago / forgotten how*
  Besides, the fashion of the time is changed—
  How and which way I may bestow° myself   *conduct*
  To be regarded in her sun-bright eye.

VALENTINE Win her with gifts if she respect° not words.   *heeds*
90   Dumb jewels often in their silent kind°   *nature*
  More than quick words do move a woman's mind.

DUKE But she did scorn a present that I sent her.

VALENTINE A woman sometime scorns what best contents her.
  Send her another. Never give her o'er,
95   For scorn at first makes after-love the more.
  If she do frown, 'tis not in hate of you,
  But rather to beget more love in you.
  If she do chide, 'tis not to have you gone,
  Forwhy° the fools° are mad if left alone.   *Because / (women)*
100   Take no repulse, whatever she doth say:

---

3. Valentine may be crossing the stage without noticing the Duke or starting to retreat on seeing him.
4. Nor respecting me as a father should be respected.

5. F reads "in Verona," another sign of inconsistency in regard to the play's setting.

For° 'Get you gone' she doth not mean 'Away'. By
Flatter and praise, commend, extol their graces;
Though ne'er so black,° say they have angels' faces. dark-complexioned
That man that hath a tongue I say is no man
105   If with his tongue he cannot win a woman.
DUKE   But she I mean is promised by her friends
Unto a youthful gentleman of worth,
And kept severely from resort of men,
That no man hath access by day to her.
110   VALENTINE   Why then I would resort to her by night.
DUKE   Ay, but the doors be locked and keys kept safe,
That no man hath recourse to her by night.
VALENTINE   What lets° but one may enter at her window? hinders
DUKE   Her chamber is aloft, far from the ground,
115   And built so shelving° that one cannot climb it projecting so far out
Without apparent hazard of his life.
VALENTINE   Why then, a ladder quaintly° made of cords skillfully
To cast up, with a pair of anchoring hooks,
Would serve to scale another Hero's⁶ tower,
120   So° bold Leander would adventure it. Provided
DUKE   Now as thou art a gentleman of blood,° well-born; passionate
Advise me where I may have such a ladder.
VALENTINE   When would you use it? Pray sir, tell me that.
DUKE   This very night; for love is like a child
125   That longs for everything that he can come by.
VALENTINE   By seven o'clock I'll get you such a ladder.
DUKE   But hark thee: I will go to her alone.
How shall I best convey the ladder thither?
VALENTINE   It will be light, my lord, that you may bear it
130   Under a cloak that is of any length.
DUKE   A cloak as long as thine will serve the turn?
VALENTINE   Ay, my good lord.
DUKE   Then let me see thy cloak.
I'll get me one of such another length,
VALENTINE   Why, any cloak will serve the turn, my lord.
135   DUKE   How shall I fashion me to wear° a cloak? get used to wearing
I pray thee let me feel thy cloak upon me.
[He lifts Valentine's cloak and finds a letter and a rope-ladder]
What letter is this same? What's here? 'To Silvia'?
And here an engine° fit for my proceeding. instrument (the ladder)
I'll be so bold to break the seal for once.
[Reads]
140   'My thoughts do harbour° with my Silvia nightly, dwell
And slaves they are to me, that send them flying.
O, could their master come and go as lightly,
Himself would lodge where, senseless,° they are lying. without feeling
My herald° thoughts in thy pure bosom rest them, message-bearing
145   While I, their king, that thither them importune,*
Do curse the grace° that with such grace° hath blessed them, command
good fortune / favor
Because myself do want° my servants' fortune. lack
I curse myself for° they are sent by me, because
That they should harbour where their lord should be.'
150   What's here?

6. See note to 1.1.22. Hero, Leander's beloved, lived in a tower.

'Silvia, this night I will enfranchise thee'?
'Tis so, and here's the ladder for the purpose.
Why, Phaëton,[7] for° thou art Merops' son   *since*
Wilt thou aspire to guide the heavenly car,
155 And with thy daring folly burn the world?
Wilt thou reach° stars because they shine on thee?   *grasp at*
Go, base intruder, over-weening° slave,   *presumptuous*
Bestow thy fawning smiles on equal mates,°   *mates of your own rank*
And think my patience, more than thy desert,
160 Is privilege for° thy departure hence.   *Allows*
Thank me for this more than for all the favours
Which, all too much, I have bestowed on thee.
But if thou linger in my territories
Longer than swiftest expedition°   *speed*
165 Will give thee time to leave our royal court,
By heaven, my wrath shall far exceed the love
I ever bore my daughter or thyself.
Be gone. I will not hear thy vain excuse,
But as thou lov'st thy life, make speed from hence.   *Exit*
170 VALENTINE   And why not death, rather than living torment?
To die is to be banished from myself,
And Silvia is my self. Banished from her
Is self from self, a deadly banishment.
What light is light, if Silvia be not seen?
175 What joy is joy, if Silvia be not by—
Unless it be to think that she is by,
And feed upon the shadow° of perfection.   *image; memory*
Except I be by Silvia in the night
There is no music in the nightingale.
180 Unless I look on Silvia in the day
There is no day for me to look upon.
She is my essence, and I leave° to be   *cease*
If I be not by her fair influence[8]
Fostered, illumined, cherished, kept alive.
185 I fly not death to fly his deadly doom.[9]
Tarry I here I but attend on° death,   *wait for*
But fly I hence, I fly away from life.
        [*Enter* PROTEUS *and* LANCE]
PROTEUS   Run, boy, run, run, and seek him out.
LANCE   So-ho, so-ho![1]
190 PROTEUS   What seest thou?
LANCE   Him we go to find. There's not a hair on's head but 'tis
   a Valentine.[2]
PROTEUS   Valentine?
VALENTINE   No.
195 PROTEUS   Who then—his spirit?
VALENTINE   Neither.

---

7. Famous in Greek mythology for his reckless ambition, Phaëton set the world on fire when he tried to drive the chariot of his father, Helios, the sun god. Phaëton's mother, Clymene, was married to Merops, not Helios, making Phaëton illegitimate. The rest of the line, naming Merops as Phaëton's father, may question Phaëton's status as the son of Helios (and so his ability to drive the sun god's chariot) or may be an ironic means of calling attention to his illegitimacy.

8. Alluding to the popular belief that the stars exert power, or "influence," over individuals.
9. I cannot escape death by fleeing the Duke's death sentence.
1. A cry in hare hunting and hawking.
2. Punning on "hare" and on Valentine's name. Every part, down to the "hair," of the creature he sees suggests a "valentine," or stereotypical lover.

PROTEUS What then?

VALENTINE Nothing.

LANCE Can nothing speak?

[*He threatens* VALENTINE]

200 Master, shall I strike?

PROTEUS Who wouldst thou strike?

LANCE Nothing.

PROTEUS Villain, forbear.

LANCE Why, sir, I'll strike nothing. I pray you—

205 PROTEUS Sirrah, I say forbear. Friend Valentine, a word.

VALENTINE My ears are stopped, and cannot hear good news,

So much of bad already hath possessed them.

PROTEUS Then in dumb silence will I bury mine,°   (*my news*)

For they are harsh, untuneable,° and bad.   *out of tune*

VALENTINE Is Silvia dead?

210 PROTEUS   No, Valentine.

VALENTINE No Valentine indeed, for sacred Silvia.

Hath she forsworn me?

PROTEUS   No, Valentine.

VALENTINE No Valentine, if Silvia have forsworn me.

What is your news?

215 LANCE Sir, there is a proclamation that you are vanished.°   (*for "banished"*)

PROTEUS That thou art banished. O that's the news:

From hence, from Silvia, and from me thy friend.

VALENTINE O, I have fed upon this woe already,

And now excess of it will make me surfeit.°   *sicken*

220 Doth Silvia know that I am banishèd?

PROTEUS Ay, ay; and she hath offered to the doom,°   *sentence*

Which unreversed stands in effectual force,[3]

A sea of melting pearl, which some call tears.

Those at her father's churlish feet she tendered,°   *offered*

225 With them, upon her knees, her humble self,

Wringing her hands, whose whiteness so became them

As if but now they waxèd° pale, for woe.   *turned*

But neither bended knees, pure hands held up,

Sad sighs, deep groans, nor silver-shedding tears[4]

230 Could penetrate her uncompassionate sire,

But Valentine, if he be ta'en, must die.

Besides, her intercession chafed him so

When she for thy repeal° was suppliant   *recall from exile*

That to close° prison he commanded her,   *tightly enclosed*

235 With many bitter threats of biding° there.   *staying permanently*

VALENTINE No more, unless the next word that thou speak'st

Have some malignant power upon my life.

If so I pray thee breathe it in mine ear,

As ending anthem° of my endless dolour.°   *final hymn / grief*

240 PROTEUS Cease to lament for that° thou canst not help,   *what*

And study° help for that which thou lament'st.   *devise*

Time is the nurse and breeder of all good.

Here if thou stay thou canst not see thy love.

Besides, thy staying will abridge thy life.

245 Hope is a lover's staff. Walk hence with that,

And manage it° against despairing thoughts.   *use it as a weapon*

---

3. Which, unless reversed, will be enforced.   4. Tears that flow like silver streams.

Thy letters may be here, though thou art hence,
Which, being writ to me, shall be delivered
Even in the milk-white bosom of thy love.
250 The time now serves not to expostulate.°   *complain; argue*
Come, I'll convey thee through the city gate,
And ere I part with thee confer at large°   *discuss at length*
Of all that may concern thy love affairs.
As thou lov'st Silvia, though not for thyself,
255 Regard thy danger, and along with me.
VALENTINE   I pray thee, Lance, an if° thou seest my boy   *an if=if*
Bid him make haste, and meet me at the North Gate.
PROTEUS   Go, sirrah, find him out. Come, Valentine.
VALENTINE   O my dear Silvia! Hapless Valentine.
[Exeunt PROTEUS *and* VALENTINE*]*
260 LANCE   I am but a fool, look you, and yet I have the wit to think
my master is a kind of a knave. But that's all one,° if he be but   *all right*
one knave.[5] He lives not now that knows me to be in love, yet
I am in love, but a team of horse shall not pluck that from me,
nor who 'tis I love; and yet 'tis a woman, but what woman
265 I will not tell myself; and yet 'tis a milkmaid; yet 'tis not a
maid,° for she hath had gossips;[6] yet 'tis a maid, for she is her   *virgin*
master's maid, and serves for wages. She hath more qualities°   *abilities*
than a water-spaniel,[7] which is much in a bare° Christian.   *mere*
[He takes out a paper]
Here is the catalogue of her conditions. 'Imprimis,[8] she can
270 fetch and carry'—why, a horse can do no more. Nay, a horse
cannot fetch, but only carry, therefore is she better than a
jade.° 'Item, she can milk.' Look you, a sweet virtue in a maid   *an inferior horse*
with clean hands.
[Enter SPEED*]*
SPEED   How now, Signor Lance, what news with your master-
275 ship?
LANCE   With my master's ship? Why, it is at sea.
SPEED   Well, your old vice still, mistake the word.[9] What news
then in your paper?
LANCE   The blackest news that ever thou heard'st.
280 SPEED   Why, man, how 'black'?
LANCE   Why, as black as ink.
SPEED   Let me read them.
LANCE   Fie on thee, jolt-head,° thou canst not read.   *blockhead*
SPEED   Thou liest. I can.
285 LANCE   I will try thee. Tell me this: who begot thee?
SPEED   Marry, the son of my grandfather.
LANCE   O illiterate loiterer, it was the son of thy grandmother.
This proves that thou canst not read.
SPEED   Come, fool, come. Try me in thy paper.
290 LANCE *[giving* SPEED *the paper]*   There: and Saint Nicholas[1] be
thy speed.°   *protection*
SPEED   'Imprimis, she can milk.'

5. If he is only moderately a rascal; only a knave in one
area (love).
6. Women who attended at childbirth; people who
served as sponsors at the baptism of a newborn child.
7. A dog used for hunting waterfowl.
8. The paper employs the language of official documents. "Imprimis," Latin for "in the first place," was used
to begin inventories. "Item" (line 272), meaning "also,"
was used to introduce subsequent articles in a list.
9. *your . . . word:* your customary fault of making blunders with language.
1. The patron saint of schoolchildren and scholars.

	LANCE	Ay, that she can.	
	SPEED	'*Item*, she brews good ale.'	
295	LANCE	And thereof comes the proverb 'Blessing of your heart, you brew good ale'.	
	SPEED	'*Item*, she can sew.'	
	LANCE	That's as much as to say 'Can she so?'	
	SPEED	'*Item*, she can knit.'	
300	LANCE	What need a man care for a stock° with a wench when she can knit him a stock?°	*dowry* *stocking*
	SPEED	'*Item*, she can wash and scour.'	
	LANCE	A special virtue, for then she need not be washed and scoured.[2]	
305	SPEED	'*Item*, she can spin.'	
	LANCE	Then may I set the world on wheels,° when she can spin for her living.	*take life easy*
	SPEED	'*Item*, she hath many nameless° virtues.'	*inexpressible*
	LANCE	That's as much as to say 'bastard virtues', that indeed	
310		know not their fathers, and therefore have no names.	
	SPEED	Here follows her vices.	
	LANCE	Close at the heels of her virtues.	
	SPEED	'*Item*, she is not to be broken° with fasting, in respect of° her breath.'	*tamed* *on account of*
315	LANCE	Well, that fault may be mended with a breakfast. Read on.	
	SPEED	'*Item*, she hath a sweet mouth.'[3]	
	LANCE	That makes amends for her sour breath.	
	SPEED	'*Item*, she doth talk in her sleep.'	
	LANCE	It's no matter for that, so she sleep not in her talk.	
320	SPEED	'*Item*, she is slow in words.'	
	LANCE	O villain, that set this down among her vices! To be slow in words is a woman's only virtue. I pray thee out with't, and place it for her chief virtue.	
	SPEED	'*Item*, she is proud.'°	*haughty; lascivious*
325	LANCE	Out with that, too. It was Eve's legacy,[4] and cannot be ta'en from her.	
	SPEED	'*Item*, she hath no teeth.'	
	LANCE	I care not for that, neither, because I love crusts.	
	SPEED	'*Item*, she is curst.'°	*shrewish*
330	LANCE	Well, the best is, she hath no teeth to bite.	
	SPEED	'*Item*, she will often praise° her liquor.'	*appraise (by tasting)*
	LANCE	If her liquor be good, she shall. If she will not, I will; for good things should be praised.	
	SPEED	'*Item*, she is too liberal.'°	*bold; wanton*
335	LANCE	Of her tongue she cannot, for that's writ down she is slow of. Of her purse she shall not, for that I'll keep shut. Now of another thing[5] she may, and that cannot I help. Well, proceed.	
	SPEED	'*Item*, she hath more hair than wit, and more faults than hairs, and more wealth than faults.'	
340	LANCE	Stop there. I'll have her. She was mine and not mine twice or thrice in that last article. Rehearse° that once more.	*Repeat*

2. *washed and scoured:* slang for "knocked down and beaten."
3. A sweet tooth; a wanton nature.
4. In the Garden of Eden, Satan, in the form of a serpent, tempted Eve, wife of the first man, Adam, to eat fruit from the tree of Knowledge of good and evil,

which God had forbidden humans to taste. Eve was thus guilty of the sin of pride for disobeying God and putting her will before his command. See Genesis 2:15–3:24.
5. "Purse" (line 336) and "another thing" (line 337) were colloquial terms for "female genitalia."

SPEED   '*Item*, she hath more hair than wit'—

LANCE   'More hair than wit.' It may be. I'll prove it: the cover of
the salt° hides the salt, and therefore it is more° than the salt.   *saltcellar / greater*

345   The hair that covers the wit is more than the wit, for the
greater hides the less. What's next?

SPEED   'And more faults than hairs'—

LANCE   That's monstrous. O that that were out!

SPEED   'And more wealth than faults.'

350 LANCE   Why, that word makes the faults gracious.° Well, I'll   *pleasing*
have her, and if it be a match—as nothing is impossible—

SPEED   What then?

LANCE   Why then will I tell thee that thy master stays° for thee   *waits*
at the North Gate.

355 SPEED   For me?

LANCE   For thee? Ay, who art thou? He hath stayed for a better
man than thee.

SPEED   And must I go to him?

LANCE   Thou must run to him, for thou hast stayed so long that

360   going° will scarce serve the turn.   *walking*

SPEED   Why didst not tell me sooner? Pox of⁶ your love letters!
                                               [Exit]

LANCE   Now will he be swinged° for reading my letter. An   *beaten*
unmannerly slave, that will thrust himself into secrets. I'll
after, to rejoice in the boy's correction.   *Exit*

3.2
Enter [the] DUKE [*and*] THURIO

DUKE   Sir Thurio, fear not but that she will love you
Now Valentine is banished from her sight.

THURIO   Since his exile she hath despised me most,
Forsworn my company, and railed at me,

5   That° I am desperate° of obtaining her.   *So that / hopeless*

DUKE   This weak impress° of love is as a figure   *impression*
Trenchèd° in ice, which with an hour's heat   *Cut*
Dissolves to water and doth lose his form.
A little time will melt her frozen thoughts,

10   And worthless Valentine shall be forgot.
[*Enter* PROTEUS]
How now, Sir Proteus, is your countryman,
According to our proclamation, gone?

PROTEUS   Gone, my good lord.

DUKE   My daughter takes his going grievously?

15 PROTEUS   A little time, my lord, will kill that grief.

DUKE   So I believe, but Thurio thinks not so.
Proteus, the good conceit° I hold of thee—   *opinion*
For thou hast shown some sign of good desert—
Makes me the better° to confer with thee.   *the more willing*

20 PROTEUS   Longer than I prove loyal to your grace
Let me not live to look upon your grace.

DUKE   Thou know'st how willingly I would effect
The match between Sir Thurio and my daughter?

PROTEUS   I do, my lord.

---

6. May disease take (a curse).   **3.2** Location: The Duke's court in Milan.

25 DUKE   And also, I think, thou art not ignorant
         How she opposes her° against my will?   *herself*
   PROTEUS   She did, my lord, when Valentine was here.
   DUKE   Ay, and perversely she persevers so.
         What might we do to make the girl forget
30   The love of Valentine, and love Sir Thurio?
   PROTEUS   The best way is to slander Valentine
         With falsehood, cowardice, and poor descent,
         Three things that women highly hold in hate.
   DUKE   Ay, but she'll think that it is spoke in hate.
35 PROTEUS   Ay, if his enemy deliver° it.   *report*
         Therefore it must with circumstance° be spoken   *supporting detail*
         By one whom she esteemeth as his friend.
   DUKE   Then you must undertake to slander him.
   PROTEUS   And that, my lord, I shall be loath to do.
40   'Tis an ill office for a gentleman,
         Especially against his very° friend.   *true*
   DUKE   Where your good word cannot advantage° him   *profit*
         Your slander never can endamage° him.   *harm*
         Therefore the office is indifferent,°   *neutral*
45   Being entreated to it by your friend.[1]
   PROTEUS   You have prevailed, my lord. If I can do it
         By aught that I can speak in his dispraise
         She shall not long continue love to him.
         But say this weed° her love from Valentine,   *uproot*
50   It follows not that she will love Sir Thurio.
   THURIO   Therefore, as you unwind her love from him,
         Lest it should ravel and be good to none
         You must provide to bottom it on me;[2]
         Which must be done by praising me as much
55   As you in worth dispraise Sir Valentine.
   DUKE   And Proteus, we dare trust you in this kind
         Because we know, on Valentine's report,
         You are already love's firm votary,°   *disciple*
         And cannot soon revolt, and change your mind.
60   Upon this warrant shall you have access
         Where you with Silvia may confer at large.
         For she is lumpish,° heavy, melancholy,   *low-spirited*
         And for your friend's sake will be glad of you;
         Where you may temper° her, by your persuasion,   *mold*
65   To hate young Valentine and love my friend.
   PROTEUS   As much as I can do, I will effect.
         But you, Sir Thurio, are not sharp enough.
         You must lay lime[3] to tangle° her desires   *capture*
         By wailful sonnets, whose composèd° rhymes   *well-crafted*
70   Should be full-fraught° with serviceable vows.[4]   *laden*
   DUKE   Ay, much is the force of heaven-bred poesy.
   PROTEUS   Say that upon the altar of her beauty
         You sacrifice your tears, your sighs, your heart.
         Write till your ink be dry, and with your tears
75   Moist it again; and frame some feeling line
         That may discover° such integrity;°   *reveal / sincerity*
         For Orpheus'[5] lute was strung with poets' sinews,°   *nerves*

---

1. Being asked to do it by a friend like me.
2. To wind it like a skein of thread upon me.
3. Birdlime, a sticky substance used to trap birds.
4. Promises to be of service.
5. A figure in Greek mythology famous for his entrancing music.

Whose golden touch could soften steel and stones,
Make tigers tame, and huge leviathans°   *whales*
80 Forsake unsounded deeps to dance on sands.
After your dire-lamenting elegies,°   *love poems*
Visit by night your lady's chamber-window
With some sweet consort.° To their instruments   *band of musicians*
Tune° a deploring dump.° The night's dead silence   *Sing / sad melody*
85 Will well become such sweet-complaining grievance.
This, or else nothing, will inherit° her.   *win*

DUKE   This discipline° shows thou hast been in love.   *instruction*

THURIO   And thy advice this night I'll put in practice.
Therefore, sweet Proteus, my direction-giver,
90 Let us into the city presently
To sort° some gentlemen well skilled in music.   *select*
I have a sonnet that will serve the turn
To give the onset° to thy good advice.   *start*

DUKE   About it, gentlemen.

95 PROTEUS   We'll wait upon your grace till after supper,
And afterward determine our proceedings.

DUKE   Even now about it. I will pardon you.°   *excuse you from service*
Exeunt [THURIO *and* PROTEUS *at one door, and the* DUKE *at another*]

4.1

Enter [*the*] OUTLAWS

FIRST OUTLAW   Fellows, stand fast. I see a passenger.°   *traveler*

SECOND OUTLAW   If there be ten, shrink not, but down with 'em.
[*Enter* VALENTINE *and* SPEED]

THIRD OUTLAW   Stand,° sir, and throw us that° you have about ye.   *Halt / that which*
If not, we'll make you sit, and rifle° you.   *search*

SPEED [*to* VALENTINE]   Sir, we are undone. These are the villains
5 That all the travellers do fear so much.

VALENTINE [*to the* OUTLAWS]   My friends.

FIRST OUTLAW   That's not so, sir. We are your enemies.

SECOND OUTLAW   Peace. We'll hear him.

THIRD OUTLAW   Ay, by my beard will we. For he is a proper° man.   *handsome*

10 VALENTINE   Then know that I have little wealth to lose.
A man I am, crossed with adversity.
My riches are these poor habiliments,°   *clothes*
Of which if you should here disfurnish° me   *deprive*
You take the sum and substance that I have.

15 SECOND OUTLAW   Whither travel you?

VALENTINE   To Verona.

FIRST OUTLAW   Whence came you?

VALENTINE   From Milan.

THIRD OUTLAW   Have you long sojourned there?

20 VALENTINE   Some sixteen months,[1] and longer might have stayed
If crooked° fortune had not thwarted me.   *evil*

FIRST OUTLAW   What, were you banished thence?

VALENTINE   I was.

SECOND OUTLAW   For what offence?

VALENTINE   For that which now torments me to rehearse.°   *tell*

4.1 Location: A forest between Mantua and Milan.
1. A claim not consonant with the play's overall time

scheme. Either this is a textual inconsistency or Valentine is lying.

25   I killed a man,[2] whose death I much repent,
      But yet I slew him manfully, in fight,
      Without false vantage or base treachery.°   *unfair advantage*
   FIRST OUTLAW   Why, ne'er repent it, if it were done so.
      But were you banished for so small a fault?
30   VALENTINE   I was, and held me glad of such a doom.°   *sentence*
   SECOND OUTLAW   Have you the tongues?°   *skill in languages*
   VALENTINE   My youthful travel therein made me happy,°   *fortunate; skilled*
      Or else I had been often miserable.
   THIRD OUTLAW   By the bare scalp of Robin Hood's fat friar,°   *(Friar Tuck)*
35   This fellow were a king for our wild faction.°   *band*
   FIRST OUTLAW   We'll have him. Sirs, a word.
         [*The* OUTLAWS *confer*]
   SPEED [*to* VALENTINE]   Master, be one of them.
      It's an honourable kind of thievery.
   VALENTINE   Peace, villain.
   SECOND OUTLAW   Tell us this: have you anything to take to?[3]
40   VALENTINE   Nothing but my fortune.°   *luck*
   THIRD OUTLAW   Know, then, that some of us are gentlemen
      Such as the fury of ungoverned youth
      Thrust from the company of aweful° men.   *respectable*
      Myself was from Verona banishèd
45   For practising° to steal away a lady,   *plotting*
      An heir, and near allied unto the Duke.
   SECOND OUTLAW   And I from Mantua, for a gentleman
      Who, in my mood,° I stabbed unto the heart.   *anger*
   FIRST OUTLAW   And I, for suchlike petty crimes as these.
50   But to the purpose, for we cite our faults
      That they may hold excused our lawless lives.
      And partly seeing you are beautified
      With goodly shape, and by your own report
      A linguist, and a man of such perfection
55   As we do in our quality° much want—   *profession*
   SECOND OUTLAW   Indeed because you are a banished man,
      Therefore above the rest[4] we parley° to you.   *talk*
      Are you content to be our general,
      To make a virtue of necessity
60   And live as we do in this wilderness?
   THIRD OUTLAW   What sayst thou? Wilt thou be of our consort?°   *company*
      Say 'Ay', and be the captain of us all.
      We'll do thee homage, and be ruled by thee,
      Love thee as our commander and our king.
65   FIRST OUTLAW   But if thou scorn our courtesy, thou diest.
   SECOND OUTLAW   Thou shalt not live to brag what we have
      offered.
   VALENTINE   I take your offer, and will live with you,
      Provided that you do no outrages
      On silly° women or poor passengers.   *defenseless*
70   THIRD OUTLAW   No, we detest such vile, base practices.
      Come, go with us. We'll bring thee to our crews°   *bands of men*
      And show thee all the treasure we have got,
      Which, with ourselves, all rest at thy dispose.°   *Exeunt*   *disposal*

---

2. Why Valentine lies here is much debated. He may be   3. Any way to support yourself.
protecting Silvia's reputation or trying to impress the   4. For that above all other reasons.
outlaws.

4.2

Enter PROTEUS

PROTEUS   Already have I been false to Valentine,
And now I must be as unjust to Thurio.
Under the colour° of commending him   pretext
I have access my own love to prefer.°   advance
5   But Silvia is too fair, too true, too holy
To be corrupted with my worthless gifts.
When I protest true loyalty to her
She twits me with my falsehood to my friend.
When to her beauty I commend my vows
10 She bids me think how I have been forsworn
In breaking faith with Julia, whom I loved.
And notwithstanding all her sudden quips,°   sharp rebukes
The least whereof would quell a lover's hope,
Yet, spaniel-like, the more she spurns my love,
15 The more it grows and fawneth on her still.
But here comes Thurio. Now must we to her window,
And give some evening music to her ear.

[*Enter* THURIO *with Musicians*]

THURIO   How now, Sir Proteus, are you crept before us?
PROTEUS   Ay, gentle Thurio, for you know that love
20 Will creep° in service where it cannot go.°   crawl / walk
THURIO   Ay, but I hope, sir, that you love not here.
PROTEUS   Sir, but I do, or else I would be hence.
THURIO   Who, Silvia?
PROTEUS   Ay, Silvia—for your sake.
THURIO   I thank you for your own.° Now, gentlemen,   own sake
25 Let's tune, and to it lustily awhile.

[*Enter the* HOST, *and* JULIA *dressed as a page-boy. They
talk apart*]

HOST   Now, my young guest, methinks you're allycholly.° I pray   melancholy
you, why is it?
JULIA   Marry, mine host, because I cannot be merry.
HOST   Come, we'll have you merry. I'll bring you where you
30 shall hear music, and see the gentleman that you asked for.
JULIA   But shall I hear him speak?
HOST   Ay, that you shall.
JULIA   That will be music.
HOST   Hark, hark.[1]
35 JULIA   Is he among these?
HOST   Ay. But peace, let's hear 'em.

Song[2]

Who is Silvia? What is she,
    That all our swains° commend her?   lovers
Holy, fair, and wise is she.
40   The heaven such grace did lend her
That she might admirèd be.

4.2 Location: Outside the Duke's palace under Silvia's
window by moonlight.
1. Probably music plays.

2. Not ascribed to anyone in F. Julia's later comments
suggest that Proteus sings while playing a stringed
instrument.

Is she kind as she is fair?
For beauty lives with kindness.
Love° doth to her eyes repair°   *(Cupid)* / *pay a visit*
45   To help° him of his blindness,   *cure*
And, being helped, inhabits there.

Then to Silvia let us sing
That Silvia is excelling.
She excels each mortal thing
50   Upon the dull earth dwelling.
To her let us garlands bring.

HOST   How now, are you sadder than you were before? How do
you, man? The music likes° you not.   *pleases*
JULIA   You mistake. The musician likes me not.
55   HOST   Why, my pretty youth?
JULIA   He plays false,[3] father.
HOST   How, out of tune on the strings?
JULIA   Not so, but yet so false that he grieves my very heart-strings.
HOST   You have a quick° ear.   *perceptive*
60   JULIA   Ay, I would I were deaf. It makes me have a slow° heart.   *heavy*
HOST   I perceive you delight not in music.
JULIA   Not a whit when it jars so.°   *is so discordant*
HOST   Hark what fine change° is in the music.   *modulation*
JULIA   Ay, that 'change' is the spite.
65   HOST   You would have them always play but one thing?
JULIA   I would always have one play but one thing. But host,
doth this Sir Proteus that we talk on often resort unto this
gentlewoman?
HOST   I tell you what Lance his man told me, he loved her out
70   of all nick.°   *excessively*
JULIA   Where is Lance?
HOST   Gone to seek his dog, which tomorrow, by his master's
command, he must carry for a present to his lady.
JULIA   Peace, stand aside. The company parts.
75   PROTEUS   Sir Thurio, fear not you. I will so plead
That you shall say my cunning drift° excels.   *scheme*
THURIO   Where meet we?
PROTEUS   At Saint Gregory's[4] well.
THURIO   Farewell.
                    [*Exeunt* THURIO *and the Musicians*]
                    [*Enter* SILVIA, *above*]°   *(at her window)*
PROTEUS   Madam, good even to your ladyship.
SILVIA   I thank you for your music, gentlemen.
80   Who is that that spake?
PROTEUS   One, lady, if you knew his pure heart's truth
You would quickly learn to know him by his voice.
SILVIA   Sir Proteus, as I take it.
PROTEUS   Sir Proteus, gentle lady, and your servant.
85   SILVIA   What's your will?
PROTEUS   That I may compass yours.[5]

---

3. Is unfaithful; plays out of tune.
4. Patron saint of musicians and singers.

5. *compass:* win. Punning on "will." That I may win
your good will; that I may conquer your sexual desire.

SILVIA   You have your wish. My will is even this,
  That presently you hie you home to bed.
  Thou subtle, perjured, false, disloyal man,
  Think'st thou I am so shallow, so conceitless°   *witless*
90 To be seducèd by thy flattery,
  That hast deceived so many with thy vows?
  Return, return, and make thy love amends.
  For me—by this pale queen of night° I swear—
  I am so far from granting thy request
95 That I despise thee for thy wrongful suit,
  And by and by intend to chide myself
  Even for this time I spend in talking to thee.
PROTEUS   I grant, sweet love, that I did love a lady,
  But she is dead.
JULIA [*aside*]   'Twere false if° I should speak it,   *even if*
100 For I am sure she is not burièd.
SILVIA   Say that she be, yet Valentine, thy friend,
  Survives, to whom, thyself art witness,
  I am betrothed. And art thou not ashamed
  To wrong him with thy importunacy?°   *improper requests*
105 PROTEUS   I likewise hear that Valentine is dead.
SILVIA   And so suppose am I, for in his grave,
  Assure thyself, my love is burièd.
PROTEUS   Sweet lady, let me rake it from the earth.
SILVIA   Go to thy lady's grave and call hers thence,
110 Or at the least, in hers sepulchre° thine.   *bury*
JULIA [*aside*]   He heard not that.
PROTEUS   Madam, if your heart be so obdurate,
  Vouchsafe me yet your picture for my love,
  The picture that is hanging in your chamber.
115 To that I'll speak, to that I'll sigh and weep;
  For since the substance of your perfect self
  Is else devoted,[7] I am but a shadow,°   *mere nothing*
  And to your shadow° will I make true love.   *image*
JULIA [*aside*]   If 'twere a substance, you would sure deceive it
120 And make it but a shadow, as I am.
SILVIA   I am very loath to be your idol, sir,
  But since your falsehood shall become you well°   *make you fit*
  To worship shadows and adore false shapes,
  Send to me in the morning, and I'll send it.°   *(the picture)*
  And so, good rest.   [*Exit*]
125 PROTEUS   As wretches have o'ernight,
  That wait for execution in the morn.   [*Exit*]
JULIA   Host, will you go?
HOST   By my halidom,° I was fast asleep.   *holy relic (an oath)*
JULIA   Pray you, where lies° Sir Proteus?   *lodges*
130 HOST   Marry, at my house. Trust me, I think 'tis almost day.
JULIA   Not so; but it hath been the longest night
  That e'er I watched, and the most heaviest.°   [*Exeunt*]   *saddest*

---

6. The moon, imagined as Diana, goddess of chastity.   7. Is devoted to someone else.

4.3

Enter [Sir] EGLAMOUR

EGLAMOUR   This is the hour that Madam Silvia
    Entreated me to call, and know her mind.
    There's some great matter she'd employ me in.
    Madam, madam!
        [Enter SILVIA *above]*
SILVIA   Who calls?
EGLAMOUR   Your servant, and your friend.
5   One that attends your ladyship's command.
SILVIA   Sir Eglamour, a thousand times good morrow!
EGLAMOUR   As many, worthy lady, to yourself.
    According to your ladyship's impose°   *command*
    I am thus early come, to know what service
10   It is your pleasure to command me in.
SILVIA   O Eglamour, thou art a gentleman—
    Think not I flatter, for I swear I do not—
    Valiant, wise, remorseful,° well accomplished.   *compassionate*
    Thou art not ignorant what dear good will
15   I bear unto the banished Valentine,
    Nor how my father would enforce me marry
    Vain Thurio, whom my very soul abhors.
    Thyself hast loved, and I have heard thee say
    No grief did ever come so near thy heart
20   As when thy lady and thy true love died,
    Upon whose grave thou vowed'st pure chastity.
    Sir Eglamour, I would° to Valentine,   *would go*
    To Mantua, where I hear he makes abode;
    And for° the ways are dangerous to pass   *because*
25   I do desire thy worthy company,
    Upon whose faith and honour I repose.°   *rely*
    Urge not[1] my father's anger, Eglamour,
    But think upon my grief, a lady's grief,
    And on the justice of my flying hence
30   To keep me from a most unholy match,
    Which heaven and fortune still° rewards with plagues.   *always*
    I do desire thee, even from a heart
    As full of sorrows as the sea of sands,
    To bear me company and go with me.
35   If not, to hide what I have said to thee
    That I may venture to depart alone.
EGLAMOUR   Madam, I pity much your grievances,
    Which, since I know they virtuously are placed,
    I give consent to go along with you,
40   Recking° as little what betideth° me   *Caring / happens to*
    As much I wish all good befortune° you.   *befall*
    When will you go?
SILVIA   This evening coming.
EGLAMOUR   Where shall I meet you?
SILVIA   At Friar Patrick's cell,
    Where I intend holy confession.
45   EGLAMOUR   I will not fail your ladyship.

___

4.3 Location: The same place, the next morning.   1. Do not offer as an excuse.

Good morrow, gentle lady.

SILVIA Good morrow, kind Sir Eglamour. *Exeunt*

4.4

Enter LANCE [*and his dog Crab*]

LANCE [*to the audience*] When a man's servant shall play the
cur° with him, look you, it goes hard. One that I brought up   act like a stupid dog
of° a puppy, one that I saved from drowning when three or four   from
of his blind brothers and sisters went to it.° I have taught him,   met their death
even as one would say precisely 'Thus I would teach a dog'.
I was sent to deliver him as a present to Mistress Silvia from
my master, and I came no sooner into the dining-chamber but
he steps me to[1] her trencher° and steals her capon's leg. O, 'tis   wooden plate
a foul thing when a cur cannot keep° himself in all compa-   behave
nies. I would have, as one should say, one that takes upon him
to be a dog indeed, to be, as it were, a dog at° all things. If I had adept at
not had more wit than he, to take a fault upon me that he did,
I think verily he had been hanged for't. Sure as I live, he had
suffered for't. You shall judge. He thrusts me himself into the
company of three or four gentleman-like dogs under the
Duke's table. He had not been there—bless the mark[2]—a
pissing-while[3] but all the chamber smelled him. 'Out with the
dog,' says one. 'What cur is that?' says another. 'Whip him out,'
says the third. 'Hang him up,' says the Duke. I, having been
acquainted with the smell before, knew it was Crab, and goes
me to the fellow that whips the dogs. 'Friend,' quoth I, 'you
mean to whip the dog.' 'Ay, marry do I,' quoth he. 'You do him
the more wrong,' quoth I, ''twas I did the thing you wot° of.' He   know
makes me no more ado, but whips me out of the chamber.
How many masters would do this for his servant? Nay, I'll be
sworn I have sat in the stocks[4] for puddings[5] he hath stolen,
otherwise he had been executed. I have stood on the pillory[6]
for geese he hath killed, otherwise he had suffered for't. (*To
Crab*) Thou think'st not of this now. Nay, I remember the trick
you served me when I took my leave of Madam Silvia. Did not
I bid thee still mark° me, and do as I do? When didst thou see   watch
me heave up my leg and make water against a gentlewoman's
farthingale?° Didst thou ever see me do such a trick?   hooped petticoat

[*Enter* PROTEUS, *with* JULIA *dressed as a page-boy*]

PROTEUS [*to* JULIA] Sebastian[7] is thy name? I like thee well,
And will employ thee in some service° presently.   work; sexual business

JULIA In what you please. I'll do what I can.

PROTEUS I hope thou wilt.—How now, you whoreson peasant,
Where have you been these two days loitering?

LANCE Marry, sir, I carried Mistress Silvia the dog you bade me.

PROTEUS And what says she to my little jewel?

4.4 Location: The same place, somewhat later.
1. *he steps me to:* he (the dog) steps forward to Lance's
embarrassment or to his detriment. Here and in line
14, "thrusts me," Lance is describing the dog's actions
and their negative effect on himself.
2. An apology for offensive language.
3. Slang for "a very short time." Lance here employs it
literally.
4. An instrument of punishment in which the offender

sat with feet clamped between two wooden planks into
which ankle holes had been cut.
5. Dishes made of animal intestines or stomachs
stuffed with meat and spices.
6. An instrument of punishment similar to the stocks.
One stood with head and hands clamped between
wooden planks.
7. A name sometimes associated with male homoeroticism and the arrow-pierced body of St. Sebastian.

LANCE   Marry, she says your dog was a cur, and tells you currish thanks is good enough for such a present.
PROTEUS   But she received my dog?
LANCE   No indeed did she not. Here have I brought him back
45   again.
PROTEUS   What, didst thou offer her this from me?
LANCE   Ay, sir. The other squirrel[8] was stolen from me by the   *fit for the hangman*
hangman° boys in the market place, and then I offered her
mine own, who is a dog as big as ten of yours, and therefore
50   the gift the greater.
PROTEUS   Go, get thee hence, and find my dog again,
Or ne'er return again into my sight.
Away, I say. Stay'st thou to vex me here?
        [*Exit* LANCE *with Crab*]
A slave, that still on end° turns me to shame.   *always*
55   Sebastian, I have entertainèd thee
Partly that I have need of such a youth
That can with some discretion do my business,
For 'tis no trusting to yon foolish lout,
But chiefly for thy face and thy behaviour,
60   Which, if my augury° deceive me not,   *fortune-telling skills*
Witness good bringing up, fortune, and truth.
Therefore know thou, for this I entertain thee.
Go presently, and take this ring with thee.
Deliver it to Madam Silvia.
65   She loved me well delivered° it to me.   *who gave*
JULIA   It seems you loved not her, to leave° her token.   *part with*
She is dead belike?°   *perchance*
PROTEUS   Not so. I think she lives.
JULIA   Alas.
PROTEUS   Why dost thou cry 'Alas'?
70   JULIA   I cannot choose but pity her.
PROTEUS   Wherefore shouldst thou pity her?
JULIA   Because methinks that she loved you as well
As you do love your lady Silvia.
She dreams on him that has forgot her love;
75   You dote on her that cares not for your love.
'Tis pity love should be so contrary,
And thinking on it makes me cry 'Alas'.
PROTEUS   Well, give her that ring, and therewithal°   *along with it*
This letter. [*Pointing*] That's her chamber. Tell my lady
80   I claim the promise for her heavenly picture.
Your message done, hie home unto my chamber,
Where thou shalt find me sad and solitary.   [*Exit*]
JULIA   How many women would do such a message?
Alas, poor Proteus, thou hast entertained
85   A fox to be the shepherd of thy lambs.
Alas, poor fool,[9] why do I pity him
That with his very heart despiseth me?
Because he loves her, he despiseth me.
Because I love him, I must pity him.
90   This ring I gave him when he parted from me,

8. A disparaging reference to the small dog Proteus   9. Julia is referring to herself.
intended to give Silvia.

To bind him to remember my good will.
And now am I, unhappy messenger,
To plead for that which I would not obtain;
To carry that which I would have refused;
95 To praise his faith, which I would have dispraised.
I am my master's true-confirmèd love,
But cannot be true servant to my master
Unless I prove false traitor to myself.
Yet will I woo for him, but yet so coldly
100 As, heaven it knows, I would not have him speed.°   succeed
      [Enter SILVIA]
Gentlewoman, good day. I pray you be my mean°   agent, means
To bring me where to speak with Madam Silvia.

SILVIA What would you with her, if that I be she?

JULIA If you be she, I do entreat your patience
105 To hear me speak the message I am sent on.

SILVIA From whom?

JULIA From my master, Sir Proteus, madam.

SILVIA O, he sends you for a picture?

JULIA Ay, madam.

110 SILVIA Ursula, bring my picture there.
      [An attendant brings a picture]
Go, give your master this. Tell him from me
One Julia, that his changing thoughts forget,
Would better fit his chamber than this shadow.°   portrait

JULIA Madam, please you peruse this letter.
      [She gives SILVIA a letter][1]
115 Pardon me, madam, I have unadvised°   inadvertently
Delivered you a paper that I should not.
      [She takes back the letter and gives SILVIA another letter]
This is the letter to your ladyship.

SILVIA I pray thee, let me look on that again.

JULIA It may not be. Good madam, pardon me.

120 SILVIA There, hold. I will not look upon your master's lines.
I know they are stuffed with protestations,
And full of new-found° oaths, which he will break   newly made
As easily as I do tear his paper.
      [She tears the letter]

JULIA Madam, he sends your ladyship this ring.
      [She offers SILVIA a ring]
125 SILVIA The more shame for him, that he sends it me;
For I have heard him say a thousand times
His Julia gave it him at his departure.
Though his false finger have profaned the ring,
Mine shall not do his Julia so much wrong.

130 JULIA She thanks you.

SILVIA What sayst thou?

JULIA I thank you, madam, that you tender° her.   show concern for
Poor gentlewoman, my master wrongs her much.

SILVIA Dost thou know her?

135 JULIA Almost as well as I do know myself.
To think upon her woes I do protest

---

1. Possibly the first letter is from Proteus to Julia. Whether Julia offers it to Silvia by mistake or deliberately (as she later seems deliberately to mistake two rings) is open to question.

That I have wept a hundred several times.
SILVIA Belike she thinks that Proteus hath forsook her?
JULIA I think she doth; and that's her cause of sorrow.
140 SILVIA Is she not passing° fair?   *exceedingly*
JULIA She hath been fairer, madam. than she is.
When she did think my master loved her well
She, in my judgement, was as fair as you.
But since she did neglect her looking-glass,
145 And threw her sun-expelling mask[2] away,
The air hath starved° the roses in her cheeks   *withered*
And pinched the lily tincture° of her face,   *white color*
That now she is become as black as I.
SILVIA How tall was she?
150 JULIA About my stature; for at Pentecost,[3]
When all our pageants of delight° were played,   *pleasing performances*
Our youth got me to play the woman's part,[4]
And I was trimmed° in Madam Julia's gown,   *dressed*
Which served me as fit, by all men's judgements,
155 As if the garment had been made for me;
Therefore I know she is about my height.
And at that time I made her weep agood,°   *in earnest*
For I did play a lamentable° part.   *pitiable*
Madam, 'twas Ariadne, passioning
160 For Theseus' perjury and unjust flight;[5]
Which I so lively° acted with my tears   *convincingly*
That my poor mistress, moved therewithal,
Wept bitterly; and would I might be dead
If I in thought felt not her very sorrow.
165 SILVIA She is beholden to thee, gentle youth.
Alas, poor lady, desolate and left.
I weep myself to think upon thy words.
Here, youth. There is my purse. I give thee this
For thy sweet mistress' sake, because thou lov'st her.
170 Farewell.   [*Exit*]
JULIA And she shall thank you for't, if e'er you know her.—
A virtuous gentlewoman, mild, and beautiful.
I hope my master's suit will be but cold,°   *unsuccessful*
Since she respects 'my mistress'' love so much.
175 Alas, how love can trifle with itself.
Here is her picture. Let me see, I think
If I had such a tire,° this face of mine   *headdress*
Were full as lovely as is this of hers.
And yet the painter flattered her a little,
180 Unless I flatter with myself too much.
Her hair is auburn, mine is perfect yellow.
If that be all the difference in his love,
I'll get me such a coloured periwig.
Her eyes are grey as glass, and so are mine.
185 Ay, but her forehead's low, and mine's as high.[6]

2. A mask to block the sun worn by upper-class En-
glishwomen to preserve their light complexions.
3. Religious days seven weeks after Easter, when plays
and theatrical pageants were staged in many English
towns.
4. Act the female role, as boys conventionally did in the

Elizabethan theater.
5. In Greek mythology, Ariadne hanged herself after
she was abandoned by her lover, Theseus. *passioning*:
sorrowing.
6. Mine's as high as hers is low. High foreheads were
considered a sign of beauty.

What should it be that he respects° in her   *esteems*
But I can make respective° in myself,   *worthy of esteem*
If this fond love were not a blinded god?
Come, shadow, come, and take this shadow up,[7]
For 'tis thy rival.
190   [*She picks up the portrait*]
                    O thou senseless form,
Thou shalt be worshipped, kissed, loved, and adored;
And were there sense° in his idolatry   *reason*
My substance should be statue in thy stead.[8]
I'll use thee kindly, for thy mistress' sake,
195 That used me so; or else, by Jove I vow,
I should have scratched out your unseeing eyes,
To make my master out of love with thee.   *Exit*

5.1

Enter [Sir] EGLAMOUR
EGLAMOUR   The sun begins to gild the western sky,
And now it is about the very hour
That Silvia at Friar Patrick's cell should meet me.
She will not fail; for lovers break not hours,°   *appointments*
5 Unless it be to come before their time,
So much they spur their expedition.°   *hasten their progress*
    [*Enter* SILVIA]
See where she comes. Lady, a happy evening!
SILVIA   Amen, amen. Go on, good Eglamour,
Out at the postern° by the abbey wall.   *back door or side door*
10 I fear I am attended° by some spies.   *followed*
EGLAMOUR   Fear not. The forest is not three leagues off.
If we recover° that, we are sure° enough.   *Exeunt*   *reach / safe*

5.2

Enter THURIO, PROTEUS, [*and*] JULIA [*dressed as a page-boy*]
THURIO   Sir Proteus, what says Silvia to my suit?
PROTEUS   O sir, I find her milder than she was,
And yet she takes exceptions at° your person.   *objects to*
THURIO   What? That my leg is too long?
5 PROTEUS   No, that it is too little.
THURIO   I'll wear a boot, to make it somewhat rounder.
JULIA [*aside*]   But love will not be spurred to what it loathes.[1]
THURIO   What says she to my face?
PROTEUS   She says it is a fair one.
10 THURIO   Nay, then, the wanton lies. My face is black.
PROTEUS   But pearls are fair; and the old saying is,
  'Black men are pearls in beauteous ladies' eyes'.
JULIA [*aside*]   'Tis true, such pearls[2] as put out ladies' eyes,
For I had rather wink° than look on them.   *shut my eyes*
15 THURIO   How likes she my discourse?
PROTEUS   Ill, when you talk of war.

---

7. Probably addressing herself as a "shadow," or mere nothing, Julia means "pick up Silvia's portrait" or "take up the challenge posed by this woman."
8. My person ("substance") should be an idol ("statue") to Proteus rather than Silvia's picture.
5.1 Location: An abbey in Milan.
5.2 Location: The Duke's court in Milan.

1. F assigns this line to Proteus and lines 13 and 14 to Thurio, but it makes more sense to assign them to the disguised Julia, whose covert comments on the words of Proteus and Thurio provide the scene with much of its humor.
2. Punning on the medical meaning of "pearl" as a thin film or cataract growing over the eye.

THURIO   But well when I discourse of love and peace.

JULIA [*aside*]   But better indeed when you hold your peace.

THURIO   What says she to my valour?

20 PROTEUS   O sir, she makes no doubt of that.

JULIA [*aside*]   She needs not, when she knows it cowardice.

THURIO   What says she to my birth?

PROTEUS   That you are well derived.°   descended

JULIA [*aside*]   True: from a gentleman to a fool.

25 THURIO   Considers she my possessions?

PROTEUS   O ay, and pities them.

THURIO   Wherefore?

JULIA [*aside*]   That such an ass should owe° them.   own

PROTEUS   That they are out by lease.°   rented out

JULIA   Here comes the Duke.

        [*Enter the* DUKE]

30 DUKE   How now, Sir Proteus. How now, Thurio.
    Which of you saw Eglamour of late?

THURIO   Not I.

PROTEUS   Nor I.

DUKE   Saw you my daughter?

PROTEUS   Neither.

DUKE   Why then, she's fled unto that peasant° Valentine,   rascal
    And Eglamour is in her company.

35   'Tis true, for Friar Laurence[3] met them both
    As he in penance wandered through the forest.
    Him he knew well, and guessed that it was she,
    But being masked, he was not sure of it.
    Besides, she did intend confession

40   At Patrick's cell this even, and there she was not.
    These likelihoods confirm her flight from hence;
    Therefore I pray you stand not to discourse,
    But mount you presently, and meet with me
    Upon the rising of the mountain foot

45   That leads toward Mantua, whither they are fled.
    Dispatch,° sweet gentlemen, and follow me.   [*Exit*]   Hurry

THURIO   Why, this it is to be a peevish° girl,   silly; perverse
    That flies her fortune when it follows her.
    I'll after, more to be revenged on Eglamour

50   Than for the love of reckless Silvia.   [*Exit*]

PROTEUS   And I will follow, more for Silvia's love
    Than hate of Eglamour that goes with her.   [*Exit*]

JULIA   And I will follow, more to cross that love
    Than hate for Silvia, that is gone for love.   *Exit*

5.3

    [*Enter the*] OUTLAWS [*with*] SILVIA [*captive*]

FIRST OUTLAW   Come, come, be patient. We must bring you to
   our captain.

SILVIA   A thousand more mischances than this one
    Have learned° me how to brook° this patiently.   taught / endure

5 SECOND OUTLAW   Come, bring her away.

FIRST OUTLAW   Where is the gentleman that was with her?°   (Eglamour)

3. Possibly a slip for "Friar Patrick," mentioned in the preceding scene, although there may be more than one friar in the forest.
5.3 Location: At the frontiers of the Mantua forest.

THIRD OUTLAW   Being nimble-footed he hath outrun us;
But Moses and Valerius follow him.
Go thou with her to the west end of the wood.
10   There is our captain. We'll follow him that's fled.
The thicket is beset,° he cannot scape.   surrounded
                [*Exeunt the* SECOND *and* THIRD OUTLAWS]
FIRST OUTLAW [*to* SILVIA]   Come, I must bring you to our captain's cave.
Fear not. He bears an honourable mind,
And will not use a woman lawlessly.
15   SILVIA [*aside*]   O Valentine! This I endure for thee.   *Exeunt*

                                    5.4
        Enter VALENTINE
VALENTINE   How use° doth breed a habit in a man!   *custom*
This shadowy desert,° unfrequented woods   *uninhabited spot*
I better brook° than flourishing peopled towns.   *endure*
Here can I sit alone, unseen of any,
5   And to the nightingale's¹ complaining notes
Tune my distresses and record my woes.
O thou° that dost inhabit in my breast,   *(addressing Silvia)*
Leave not the mansion² so long tenantless
Lest, growing ruinous, the building fall
10   And leave no memory of what it was.
Repair me with thy presence, Silvia.
Thou gentle nymph, cherish thy forlorn swain.
What hallooing and what stir is this today?
These are my mates, that make their wills their law,
15   Have° some unhappy passenger° in chase.   *Who have / traveler*
They love me well, yet I have much to do
To keep them from uncivil outrages.
Withdraw thee, Valentine. Who's this comes here?
        [*He stands aside.*
        Enter PROTEUS, SILVIA, *and* JULIA *dressed as a page-boy*]
PROTEUS   Madam, this service I have done for you—
20   Though you respect not aught your servant doth—
To hazard life, and rescue you from him
That would have forced your honour° and your love.   *violated your chastity*
Vouchsafe me for my meed° but one fair look.   *reward*
A smaller boon than this I cannot beg,
25   And less than this I am sure you cannot give.
VALENTINE [*aside*]   How like a dream is this I see and hear!
Love lend me patience to forbear awhile.
SILVIA   O miserable, unhappy that I am!
PROTEUS   Unhappy were you, madam, ere I came.
30   But by my coming I have made you happy.
SILVIA   By thy approach° thou mak'st me most unhappy.   *amorous advances*
JULIA [*aside*]   And me, when he approacheth to your presence.
SILVIA   Had I been seizèd by a hungry lion
I would have been a breakfast to the beast
35   Rather than have false Proteus rescue me.
O heaven be judge how I love Valentine,

5.4 Location: Another part of the forest.
1. In the classical mythology, Philomela was turned into
a nightingale after Tereus raped her; her song is a lament.
2. Referring to his body as Silvia's home.

Whose life's as tender° to me as my soul.　　　　　　　　　*precious*
And full as much, for more there cannot be,
I do detest false perjured Proteus.
40　　Therefore be gone, solicit me no more.
PROTEUS　What dangerous action, stood it next to death,
Would I not undergo for one calm° look!　　　　　　　　*gentle*
O, 'tis the curse in love, and still approved,°　　　*always confirmed*
When women cannot love where they're beloved.
45　SILVIA　When Proteus cannot love where he's beloved.
Read over Julia's heart, thy first, best love,
For whose dear sake thou didst then rend thy faith
Into a thousand oaths, and all those oaths
Descended into perjury° to love me.　　　　　　　*were forsworn*
50　Thou hast no faith left now, unless thou'dst two,³
And that's far worse than none. Better have none
Than plural faith, which is too much by one,
Thou counterfeit° to thy true friend.　　　　*deceiver; false friend*
PROTEUS　　　　　　　　　　　　In love
Who respects friend?
SILVIA　　　　　　　All men but Proteus.
55　PROTEUS　Nay, if the gentle spirit of moving words
Can no way change you to a milder form
I'll woo you like a soldier, at arm's end,°　　　　　*at swordpoint*
And love you 'gainst the nature of love: force ye.
SILVIA　O heaven!
PROTEUS [*assailing her*]　I'll force thee yield to my desire.
60　VALENTINE [*coming forward*]　Ruffian, let go that rude uncivil touch,
Thou friend of an ill fashion.
PROTEUS　　　　　　　　　Valentine!
VALENTINE　Thou common° friend, that's without faith or love,　　*superficial*
For such is a friend now. Treacherous man,
Thou hast beguiled my hopes. Naught but mine eye
65　Could have persuaded me. Now I dare not say
I have one friend alive. Thou wouldst disprove me.
Who should be trusted, when one's right hand
Is perjured to the bosom?° Proteus,　　　　　　*false to the heart*
I am sorry I must never trust thee more,
70　But count the world a stranger for thy sake.⁴
The private wound is deepest. O time most accursed,
'Mongst all foes that a friend should be the worst!
PROTEUS　My shame and guilt confounds me.
Forgive me, Valentine. If hearty sorrow
75　Be a sufficient ransom for offence,
I tender't° here. I do as truly suffer　　　　　　　　*offer it*
As e'er I did commit.
VALENTINE　　　　　Then I am paid,
And once again I do receive thee° honest.　　　*accept you as*
Who by repentance is not satisfied
80　Is nor of heaven nor earth. For these are pleased;
By penitence th' Eternal's wrath's appeased.
And that my love may appear plain and free,

---

3. You have no faithfulness left now, unless you were to
have two lovers (Julia and Silvia).

4. But cut myself off from the world (in disillusion-
ment) because of your treachery.

All that was mine in Silvia[5] I give thee.

JULIA   O me unhappy!

    [*She faints*]

PROTEUS   Look to the boy.

VALENTINE   Why, boy!

85   Why wag,° how now? What's the matter? Look up. Speak.   *sweet boy*

JULIA   O good sir, my master charged me to deliver a ring to

    Madam Silvia, which out of my neglect was never done.

PROTEUS   Where is that ring, boy?

JULIA   Here 'tis. This is it.

    [*She gives* PROTEUS *the ring*]

90   PROTEUS   How, let me see!

    Why, this is the ring I gave to Julia.

JULIA   O, cry you mercy, sir, I have mistook.

    [*She offers* PROTEUS *another ring*]

    This is the ring you sent to Silvia.

PROTEUS   But how cam'st thou by this ring? At my depart

95   I gave this unto Julia.

JULIA   And Julia herself did give it me,

    And Julia herself hath brought it hither.

PROTEUS   How? Julia?

JULIA   Behold her that gave aim to° all thy oaths   *was the object of*

100   And entertained 'em deeply in her heart.

    How oft hast thou with perjury cleft the root?°   *bottom of her heart*

    O Proteus, let this habit° make thee blush.   *disguise*

    Be thou ashamed that I have took upon me

    Such an immodest raiment, if shame live

105   In a disguise of love.[6]

    It is the lesser blot, modesty finds,

    Women to change their shapes° than men their minds.   *appearances; clothes*

PROTEUS   Than men their minds! 'Tis true. O heaven, were man

    But constant, he were perfect. That one error

110   Fills him with faults, makes him run through all th' sins;

    Inconstancy falls off ere it begins.[7]

    What is in Silvia's face but I may spy

    More fresh in Julia's, with a constant° eye?   *faithful*

VALENTINE   Come, come, a hand from either.

115   Let me be blessed to make this happy close.°   *ending; union*

    'Twere pity two such friends should be long foes.

    [JULIA *and* PROTEUS *join hands*]

PROTEUS   Bear witness, heaven, I have my wish for ever.

JULIA   And I mine.

    [*Enter the* OUTLAWS *with the* DUKE *and* THURIO *as captives*]

OUTLAWS   A prize, a prize, a prize!

VALENTINE   Forbear, forbear, I say. It is my lord the Duke.

    [*The* OUTLAWS *release the* DUKE *and* THURIO]

120   [*To the* DUKE]   Your grace is welcome to a man disgraced,

    Banishèd Valentine.

DUKE   Sir Valentine!

THURIO   Yonder is Silvia, and Silvia's mine.

---

5. All my claims to Silvia; all that was mine, in the person of Silvia; all the love I gave to Silvia.
6. *if . . . love*: if a disguise one wears for the sake of love can be considered shameful; if one who pretends to feel

love is capable of feeling shame.
7. The inconstant man begins to deceive, or "fall off," even before he swears constancy.

VALENTINE Thurio, give back,° or else embrace thy death.   *stand back*
    Come not within the measure° of my wrath.   *reach*
125   Do not name Silvia thine. If once again,
    Verona[8] shall not hold thee. Here she stands.
    Take but possession of her with a touch—
    I dare thee but to breathe upon my love.
THURIO Sir Valentine, I care not for her, I.
130   I hold him but a fool that will endanger
    His body for a girl that loves him not.
    I claim her not, and therefore she is thine.
DUKE The more degenerate and base art thou
    To make such means° for her as thou hast done,   *efforts*
135   And leave her on such slight conditions.°   *trivial reasons*
    Now by the honour of my ancestry
    I do applaud thy spirit, Valentine,
    And think thee worthy of an empress' love.
    Know then I here forget all former griefs,°   *grievances*
140   Cancel all grudge, repeal° thee home again,   *recall*
    Plead a new state in thy unrivalled merit,[9]
    To which I thus subscribe:° Sir Valentine,   *bear witness*
    Thou art a gentleman, and well derived.
    Take thou thy Silvia, for thou hast deserved her.
145 VALENTINE I thank your grace. The gift hath made me happy.
    I now beseech you, for your daughter's sake,
    To grant one boon° that I shall ask of you.   *favor*
DUKE I grant it, for thine own, whate'er it be.
VALENTINE These banished men that I have kept withal°   *lived with*
150   Are men endowed with worthy qualities.
    Forgive them what they have committed here,
    And let them be recalled from their exile.
    They are reformèd, civil, full of good,
    And fit for great employment, worthy lord.
155 DUKE Thou hast prevailed. I pardon them and thee.
    Dispose of them as thou know'st their deserts.
    Come, let us go. We will include all jars°   *end all discord*
    With triumphs,° mirth, and rare solemnity.°   *pageants / festivity*
VALENTINE And as we walk along I dare be bold
160   With our discourse to make your grace to smile.
    What think you of this page, my lord?
DUKE I think the boy hath grace in him. He blushes.
VALENTINE I warrant you, my lord, more grace than boy.[1]
DUKE What mean you by that saying?
165 VALENTINE Please you, I'll tell you as we pass along,
    That you will wonder° what hath fortunèd.°   *marvel at / happened*
    Come, Proteus, 'tis your penance but to hear
    The story of your loves discoverèd.°   *revealed*
    That done, our day of marriage shall be yours,
170   One feast, one house, one mutual happiness.   *Exeunt*

---

8. Probably another slip for "Milan."
9. Argue (that there is) a new situation created by your unparalleled merit.

1. He has more feminine charm ("grace") than male gender (that is, "he" is really a girl).

The Taming of the Shrew

One of Shakespeare's first comedies—probably written in 1592 or earlier—*The Taming of the Shrew* is also one of his most controversial, focusing as it does on the battle between the sexes and on the process by which a strong-willed woman is made to submit to the control of her husband. In actuality, the play is more complex than such a bald description indicates. An early example of Shakespeare's extraordinary theatrical craftsmanship, it consists of two interwoven plots and a frame tale. This complex structure allows for contrasts and parallels in the development of the play's main themes, complicating how the audience thinks about the drama's examination of the relationship between the sexes and the possibility that people can change their social identities either as a result of choice or of coercion. Perhaps not surprisingly, the play has elicited wildly varying reactions from generations of readers, audiences, and theater practitioners.

In the frame story, a poor tinker, Christopher Sly, is made to believe that he is a nobleman with servants, a wife, fine food, and even erotic artwork at his command. This hoax, shown in the play's first two scenes (called Inductions), is engineered by a real Lord who has found Sly drunk and asleep outside a tavern. The Lord's trick leads to many jokes at Sly's expense. While the tinker likes playing the part of a nobleman, he doesn't do it very well. His language, especially, betrays him. For example, Sly doesn't know how to address a lady, anxiously inquiring of his servants what to call his elegant spouse and settling on the absurd title "Madam wife." The hilarity of this scene is compounded by the fact that Sly's "wife" is really the Lord's page, Bartholomew, dressed up to impersonate a woman. Sly thus mistakes the sex of the person he would take to bed. He is also ignorant of the tastes and customs of the nobility asking for cheap ale when he should call for sack, the sweet wine favored by gentlemen.

While these blunders make Sly an object of humor, he is also the figure for whose viewing pleasure the main play's two central plots unroll. As a temporary lord, Sly has a troupe of actors to entertain him. At least until he falls asleep, Sly watches them enact a comedy about courtship and marriage in which the primary plot involves a strong-willed woman, Katherine Minola, who is "tamed" by a fortune-seeking suitor named Petruccio. In the other plot, Kate's seemingly demure sister, Bianca, is pursued by three adoring suitors and eventually elopes with one of them without her father's knowledge or consent. All three actions are united by themes of disguise and transformation. Snatched from the mud and given the clothes and the privileges of a lord, Sly is temporarily translated from one social class and identity to another, even though his behavior and the snickers of his "attendants" repeatedly remind the audience that he is not *really* a nobleman. In their pursuit of Bianca, several of her suitors also don disguises. One, Hortensio, poses as a teacher of music and mathematics; another, Lucentio, pretends to be Cambio, a language instructor; meanwhile, Lucentio's servant, Tranio, assumes his master's identity and in that disguise poses as yet another of Bianca's many admirers. Love makes men willing to transform themselves, although in this plot these changes are volitional and reversible. When the disguised gentlemen tire of acting as scholars-for-hire, they simply reclaim their houses, fortunes, and social positions and demote their servants.

In the main plot, more subtle questions of disguise arise. Petruccio, to teach Katherine that she must obey him, acts the part of "shrew tamer," a role in which he appears at his own wedding in outlandish and ragged clothes and, during a sojourn at his country house, turns the world on its head by denying Kate sleep, food, and any exercise of her own will. But if his servant Grumio is to be believed, this may not simply be a one-time disguise. Hearing of his master's plan to wed the rich and shrewish Katherine, Grumio says:

O' my word, an she knew him as well as I do she would think scolding would do little good upon him. She may perhaps call him half a score knaves or so. Why, that's nothing; an he begin once he'll rail in his rope-tricks. I'll tell you what, sir, an she stand him but a little he will throw a figure in her face and so disfigure her with it that she shall have no more eyes to see withal than a cat. You know him not, sir.
(1.2.104–10)

Grumio's words raise doubts about Petruccio's "real" nature. Is he temporarily adopting the role of a shrew tamer and verbal bully, or is that his customary mode of being or a role that he has previously adopted in dealing with servants and other social inferiors? And as Petruccio attempts to transform Kate from shrew to obedient spouse, new questions arise: is he forcing her to deform her nature or helping her experiment with a role that might bring out untapped aspects of her personality or lead to greater control of her social environment? Is there, in fact, anything like a "real self," or is personhood a succession of social roles adopted because of coercion, social expectations, material circumstances, or the drive for social mastery?

The multiple instances of disguise and transformation in the three plots certainly invite reflection on the sources of and possibilities for change both in people's behavior and in their social circumstances. From the play one might, for example, conclude that lords and gentlemen can play with their social roles with more success and less risk than can tinkers. Sly's transformation is thrust upon him; but his lack of wealth and education would in any case make it impossible for him to "pass" as nobility without the complicity of the Lord who found him asleep outside the tavern. His transformation is precarious, a mere dream from which he will have to awaken, no matter how much he might want to live on in his new circumstances. But for Lucentio, his role as a Latin master is nothing *but* a temporary stratagem, a part that his education allows him to play to perfection but that his social rank permits him to cast aside when he has won his bride. Similarly, the social fact of gender sets different limits on possible presentations and transformations of self. Petruccio's outrageous behavior—striking his servants and starving his wife—makes him admired by other men. Hortensio, for example, one of Bianca's suitors who eventually marries a wealthy widow, decides to model himself after Petruccio and to take lessons from him on how to tame a wife. But what is deemed to be Kate's outrageous behavior—striking a sister and defying a father and would-be husband—elicits only scorn and condemnation. Like class, gender limits one's permissible or possible range of action and the transformations of self one can effect. Unless she is willing to endure severe privation and penalties, Kate can only undergo one kind of transformation—toward greater docility and subservience to her husband. In such circumstances, it is difficult to determine—as many critics wish to do—whether Katherine finds her "real" self through her encounters with Petruccio. Like many characters in the play, she can only improvise a self in relation to the social constraints and possibilities available to her, and the constraints operating upon a tinker or a woman are very different from those affecting a university-educated gentleman or a lord.

The social hierarchies that shape the possibilities for personal transformations are, in the Sly frame tale, given a peculiarly English inflection. The Sly episodes refer repeatedly to the Warwickshire countryside that was Shakespeare's own birthplace. Sly mentions Greet, an actual village near Stratford, and Burton Heath (possibly Barton-on-the-Heath, another village close to Stratford), and the men enumerated as his tavern companions—Stephen Sly, John Naps, Peter Turf, and Henry Pimpernel—for the most part have homely English names. Moreover, the contrast between Sly and the Lord who carries him to his house mirrors the gap in sixteenth-century rural England between poor laborers, barely making a living at a succession of marginal jobs, and wealthy landowners. As arable and common land was fenced in or enclosed to increase the opportunities for grazing sheep, many landowners made huge profits, wool being one of England's most important exports. But enclosures, a number of which occurred in the Stratford region, also caused hardship for small tenant farmers forced off the enclosed land and, in some cases, driven into vagrancy.

Sly, simply called "Beggar" in the speech prefixes in the First Folio, is a poor man with a checkered employment history. He describes himself as "old Sly's son of Burton Heath, by birth a pedlar, by education a cardmaker, by transmutation a bearherd, and now by present profession a tinker" (Induction 2.17–19). A cardmaker makes the metal combs used to prepare wool for spinning; thus Sly has had some tangential involvement with the wool industry, although he seems primarily to have led an itinerant life mending pots, selling cheap goods from a pedlar's pack, and running up whatever tab he could at the local tavern. The Induction reveals the enormous gap in wealth and education separating this man from the leisured aristocrats who pick him up on the way home from hunting and use him for their evening's sport. The trick they play upon him is a fantastic one, but the details of the Lord's privilege and Sly's drunken poverty are evoked with vivid realism. For such a man as Sly, what hope is there of becoming a Lord?

By contrast, Bianca and her suitors exist in an Italian setting at many removes from Sly's English-countryside milieu. The events in this story line are drawn directly from George Gascoigne's *Supposes* (1566), itself an adaption of a work by Ariosto, *I Suppositi*, which employs the disguised identities, clever servants, and gullible fathers found in classical comedy. Wealth is also a crucial factor in this plot, for despite his speeches about the necessity for suitors to gain his daughters' love, Baptista is willing to give them to their wealthiest wooers. The suitors' money comes mostly from trade. Bianca's suitors testify to the number of ships they have at sea and to the luxury goods and property they have acquired through their ventures. In this world of prosperous urban merchants, Baptista can indulge his daughters with some training in the arts and languages, but he still expects to control their marriage choices. Kate he delivers to the frankly fortune-hunting Petruccio, but he ultimately has less luck with his supposedly compliant daughter, Bianca, whose name, meaning "white," implies her virtue and purity. Bianca not only elopes, but, in the play's final banquet scene, she refuses to come when her new husband summons her, suggesting that her earlier docility may have been a calculated pose. If her sister is gradually tamed. Bianca ultimately reveals her own considerable capacity to play the shrew, her education and social position having given her the wherewithal to manipulate the courtship process to her own advantage.

It is against this backdrop that the particular features of the main plot become apparent. The relationship between Kate and Petruccio has long been regarded as the play's most riveting story line. In fact, in the eighteenth century, the famous actor David Garrick produced a shortened version of the play simply called *Catharine and Petruchio*, which cut the Bianca plot and held the stage for nearly one hundred years. The interest in Kate and Petruccio is understandable, for Shakespeare created for them a story of taming at once enjoyable and deeply troubling. Though set in Italy, this plot line feels English, connected in subterranean ways to the world of Christopher Sly. For one thing, Petruccio is not just a creature of the city; he has a farmhouse that serves as this play's "green world," or place of transformations. Moreover, Petruccio is distinguished in many ways from the other Italian suitors. He has, for example, a sullen and quarrelsome servant, Grumio, in every respect the antithesis of the clever attendants, Tranio and Biondello, who help Lucentio win Bianca and, in fact, seem to do most of their master's thinking and plotting for him. This may be a kind of affectionate joke made at the expense of English domestic servants, who, despite their crude ways, at least aren't shown as mastering their masters. Moreover, while Hortensio, Gremio, and Lucentio woo Bianca with song and poetry, Petruccio woos Kate by contradicting her every word and taming her, like a hawk, by making her go hungry and sleepless. The language of

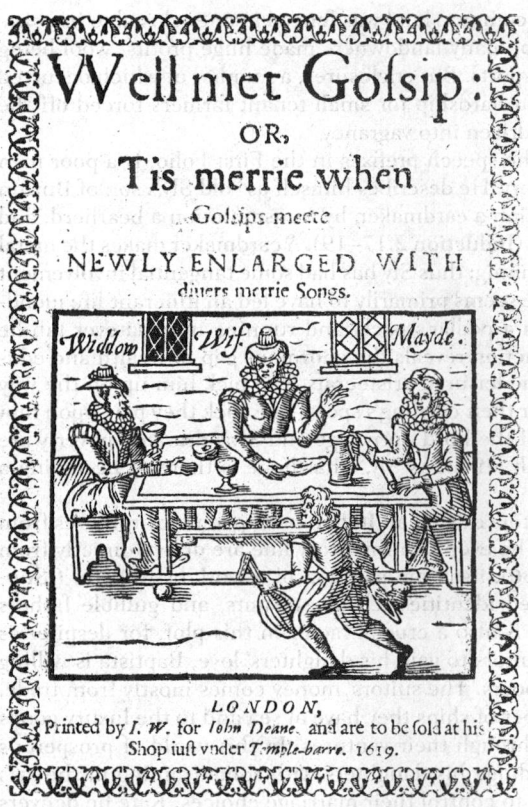

"Gadding." Title page of Samuel Rowlands, *Tis Merrie When Gossips Meete* (1619).

blood sport permeates both the Induction and the Petruccio scenes. The Lord who picks up Sly has just returned from hunting and speaks knowledgeably about the abilities of each of his hounds; Petruccio repeatedly compares the taming of a wife to the transformation of a wild hawk into a docile hunting falcon, aligning wife taming with other manly English sports.

Finally, of course, the source for the Petruccio-Kate plot is not an Italian comedy, as in the Bianca-Lucentio plot, but a folk story about taming a difficult wife, variants of which circulated throughout northern Europe in Shakespeare's day, including the vicious English ballad entitled "A Merry Jest of a Shrewd and Curst Wife Lapped in Morel's Skin for Her Good Behavior." In this ballad, a strong-willed wife is beaten bloody by her husband and then wrapped inside the salted skin of a dead horse named Morel. This mode of taming is more physically brutal than that employed by Petruccio, but both the play and the ballad assume that a husband can use extreme means to curb the will of a forward wife.

Despite his Italian name, then, Petruccio is in many ways an Englishman; and the play implicitly suggests that unlike his Italian counterpart, the true Englishman defines his manhood through the firm and, if necessary, cruel mastery of wife and servant. By contrast, the less assertive Lucentio takes direction from his servant, supplicates his betrothed on bended knee, and ends up with a wife he cannot master. Petruccio's bluff manliness constituted one of the period's privileged versions of English masculinity. In some respects he resembles the English military hero Talbot in *1 Henry VI,* a history play that Shakespeare had a hand in writing probably sometime not long after he composed *The Taming of the Shrew.* Petruccio also anticipates Shakespeare's portrait of England's great warrior king Henry V, the protagonist in a series of history plays that Shakespeare penned in the second half of the 1590s. Outspoken, commanding in battle or brawl, and adept at the blunt rhetorical and physical mastery of women, each of these male heroes in his own way helped define what distinguished a proper Englishman from what was French, Italian, or simply foreign.

This subtle Englishing of Kate and Petruccio may have heightened the original audience's interest in and even identification with them, as the play implicitly pits virile English wooing and wedding against the sophisticated ineffectiveness of Italian practices. Men and women, however, may not have been equally drawn to what they witnessed. In the wake of the modern women's movement, certainly, the very idea of "taming" a woman and curbing her tongue have seemed offensive to many readers and viewers. In *Taming of the Shrew,* language is a vehicle for domination. Sly cannot effectively play

Cucking stool, used to discipline scolds, shrews, and witches. From
T. N. Brushfield, *Chester Archaeological and Historic Society Journal*
(1855–62).

a lord because he has not mastered the language of the elite. Kate can be eloquent, but
because of her gender her verbal independence is read by her father and suitors as a
sign of shrewishness. In part, Petruccio tames Kate's tart tongue by aggressive use of
his own. A clear sign that he has succeeded occurs in 4.6, when, at her husband's
behest, Kate calls the sun the moon and an old man a budding virgin. Her words at this
point no longer express her own perceptions but her husband's blatantly willful reading of reality. In the play's last scene, she also makes a lengthy speech about a wife's
duty to obey her husband that conforms to the patriarchal ideology of the day and her
husband's wishes but is disturbingly far from her earlier expression of women's right to
independent speech and thought. Some directors have found this curbing of the female
tongue and will so intolerable that they have made production choices that downplay
the extent of Kate's submission to Petruccio or that mitigate the linguistic coercion and
physical cruelty that are part of his taming methods. For example, in many productions,
Kate delivers her last speech about wifely duty while signaling, by winks and gestures,
that she does not really believe it, or the director omits the lines in which Kate offers
to put her hand beneath her husband's foot as a token of submission. Such choices signal a desire to "save" Shakespeare from accusations that his play celebrates a crude
form of male dominance.

Even in Shakespeare's own day, it is not clear that everyone, including men, would
have found Petruccio's behavior entirely laudable. The proper relationship between husband and wife was a matter of discussion and debate. Many Protestant preachers
enjoined husbands to use no violence against their wives and to treat them as spiritual
equals and domestic helpmeets. They lauded marriage not merely as an economic
arrangement but as a union demanding mutual affection and respect from both parties.
At the same time, few disputed that in the last analysis husbands were masters of their
wives and that the household was "a little commonwealth," a realm in which the husband's supremacy over wife and children mirrored the supremacy of the monarch over
his subjects. Disorder in the domestic realm was treated as a serious matter, intimating
the possibility of a breakdown of order and hierarchy in the culture at large.

Strong-willed women were particularly apt to be labeled as disorderly in early modern towns and villages, even if their "crimes" involved nothing more than talkativeness.

Husband dominator. From a German playing card by Peter Flötner (1520).

A shrew, in fact, was commonly defined as a woman with a wagging tongue who, partly because of her garrulousness, was not properly submissive to her husband. The ideal wife, by contrast, was chaste, silent, and obedient. The talkativeness that could mark a woman as a shrew could also be interpreted as a sign of her sexual promiscuity, on the theory that one kind of looseness leads to another. Women deemed unruly were subject to various kinds of punishment. These could include being "cucked"—ducked into water on a "cucking stool"—or being fitted with a scold's bridle, a torturous harness that fitted around a woman's head with a metal bit that went into her mouth and prevented her from speaking and sometimes caused her to gag and her mouth to bleed or her teeth to be knocked loose. The husbands of disorderly and aggressive women could also be punished for failure to control their wives. Charivaris, or "rough ridings," were shaming rituals in which neighbors came to the house of a disorderly woman and made her or her husband ride backward through the town on a horse while bystanders shouted and played cacophonous music. This signaled that the world had been turned upside down and rendered inharmonious by her disorderliness and his inability to control his wife.

In *The Taming of the Shrew*, no man is submitted to a "rough riding" even though at the end of the play both Lucentio and Hortensio seem to have lost control of their wives. Instead, all the attention focuses on the taming of Kate and on the strategies employed by Petruccio to make her compliant with his will. On the eighteenth- and nineteenth-century stage, Petruccio often carried a whip, symbol of his power to control his wife and servants with physical force. Whether or not he *literally* carries a whip, Petruccio employs coercion—verbal, psychological, and physical—to control his wife, subjecting her to public humiliation and private deprivation in order to teach her proper submissiveness to the authority of her husband. In so doing, he reinforces the hierarchical principle upon which the entire Elizabethan social order was premised, warning not only unruly men but also servants and beggars that, except in jest, they cannot usurp the places of their masters. But is this account of *The Taming of the Shrew* adequate? Is the play as fiercely repressive as some critics assume? It is precisely on this point that readers, critics, and actors differ.

Some critics, for example, emphasize how Shakespeare mitigates the violence of many versions of the folktale on which the main plot is modeled. Kate is not, for example, beaten and wrapped in a salted horsehide, nor does Petruccio force her to sleep with him before their return to Padua. In his farmhouse, he keeps her awake by disordering the bed and talking at her, but only after their return to the relative safety and familiarity of her father's house does he speak of his intention to "bed" her. In short, sexual conquest does not seem to be part of his taming practices. Perhaps more importantly, many actors, audiences, and critics have seen in Kate and Petruccio's relationship an attractive mutuality and vitality they find difficult to reconcile with the idea that the play is simply a lesson in how to subordinate a woman. For example, when Petruccio first woos Kate in 2.1, the two of them engage in a verbal sparring match dazzling in its complexity and speed. Puns and insults fly back and forth, with Kate giving as good as she gets. The following exchange is typical:

> PETRUCCIO Come, come, you wasp, i faith you are too angry.
> KATHERINE If I be waspish, best beware my sting.
> PETRUCCIO My remedy is then to pluck it out.
> KATHERINE Ay, if the fool could find it where it lies.
> PETRUCCIO Who knows not where a wasp does wear his sting?
>   In his tail.
> KATHERINE In his tongue.
> PETRUCCIO   Whose tongue?
> KATHERINE Yours, if you talk of tales, and so farewell.
> PETRUCCIO What, with my tongue in your tail? Nay, come again,
>   Good Kate, I am a gentleman.
> KATHERINE   That I'll try.
>   *She strikes him*
> PETRUCCIO I swear I'll cuff you if you strike again.
>
> (2.1.207–16)

This is a beautifully orchestrated encounter, with Kate and Petruccio trading rapid-fire, one-line insults and deftly topping one another's puns. Their exchange has erotic intensity. These two are taking one another's measure, listening intently, struggling for advantage. Petruccio is not above talking dirty, and Katherine is not above making physical contact, albeit with a blow and not a caress. This is light years away from the vapid wooing of Lucentio and Bianca, hiding behind the screen of school Latin. On the stage, something vital and alive goes on between Katherine and Petruccio, and they have often been compared with Shakespeare's other witty couples, such as Benedick and Beatrice in *Much Ado About Nothing,* iconoclasts who seem more real and finally better and more equally matched than the more conventional couples with whom they are contrasted. Many critics, in fact, have argued that the real love story of the play belongs to Kate and Petruccio, and that his taming of her is merely a way of showing her the advantages of outwardly conforming to society's expectations so that she can have the husband, the home, and the social approval she surely must crave. Many argue that it is Kate's spirit that attracts Petruccio and that her spirit is never broken, just redirected, as in the final scene when Kate takes out her aggressions not against her husband but against the other wives, whom she lectures on their marriage duties.

The debate about how to interpret *The Taming of the Shrew* will surely continue. In performance, directors and actors sometimes emphasize the drama's playful and farcical elements, sometimes its dark, violent, and repressive potential. Critics and readers remain similarly divided as to what they see in this tale of woman tamed. Most agree, however, that *The Taming of the Shrew* deals with issues that deserve the thoughtful and sometimes heated critical debate the play has engendered. For example, while Kate's taming does not involve the kinds of physical brutality in the "Merry Jest" ballad, it is nonetheless true that in Petruccio's farmhouse Kate is deprived of sleep, food, and the protection of family and female companionship—techniques akin to modern methods of torture and brainwashing. As Kate says, she is "starved for meat, giddy for lack of sleep, / With oaths kept waking and with brawling fed" (4.3.9–10). This is horrifying, even if the horror is mitigated by the laughter-inducing techniques of knockabout farce. Grumio makes the audience laugh as he tantalizes Kate with one kind of food and then another, while ultimately withholding them all, but this does not erase the fact that Kate is hungry and that her hunger is used to starve her into complying with Petruccio's wishes. There is similar cruelty lurking behind the trick played on Sly in the Induction. The beggar is tantalized with the prospect of riches he can never retain. *The Taming of the Shrew* makes a joke out of the enormous gap between the poverty of a tinker and the privilege of a lord, comedy from the physical and psychic trials that lie in wait for a strong-willed woman.

It is perhaps appropriate to conclude by focusing again on the role of Sly. As he watches the play the actors perform for him, he at first makes comments on the action, but these stop after the first act, and he presumably falls asleep on stage. In another contemporary play, however, called *The Taming of a Shrew*, Sly makes interjections throughout, including a brief speech in which he vows to go home and tame his own wife, having learned from Petruccio how it is done. Scholars disagree about the relationship of *The Taming of the Shrew* and *The Taming of a Shrew*: they dispute which came first and whether Shakespeare had a hand in both (for a fuller discussion, see the Textual Note). Among the many differences between the two texts, however, is Sly's continuing stage prominence right to the end of *The Taming of a Shrew* and his final assertion that

I'll to my

Wife presently and tame her too,
An if she anger me.
(Additional Passages E.19–21)

No one knows for certain if Shakespeare wrote these lines or why they don't appear in *The Taming of the Shrew*. Like almost everything else connected to this play, they are subject to various interpretations. Perhaps because they are put in Sly's mouth they are discredited, taken as another example of the reductiveness of his responses to the pastimes of the cultural elite—in this case, to the play staged in the Lord's house by the traveling players. Maybe *only* a tinker would take this as the "message" of the play. On the other hand, perhaps Sly's response to what he has just watched indicates why this vital and attractive play seems to many readers to traffic in dangerous matters and to be easily used to justify the crudest kinds of male tyranny. It is a little disconcerting that *even* a downtrodden tinker can find comfort in the thought that while he is neither a lord nor a gentleman, he shares with them the same right to tame his wife "an if she anger me." Impoverished and ridiculed, Sly nonetheless feels entitled by virtue of his gender to dominate his spouse, perhaps thereby compensating for his powerlessness in other areas. In short, there is always something lower than a beggar—a beggar's wife. The play published in the First Folio omits Sly's speech, but in our day *The Taming of the Shrew* nonetheless remains, along with *The Merchant of Venice*, one of Shakespeare's most controversial plays: a spur to thought and to debate, a reminder of the serious matters that often lie at the heart of Shakespeare's "festive" comedies.

Jean E. Howard

TEXTUAL NOTE

The Taming of the Shrew was first printed in the 1623 First Folio (F), the control text for this edition. Certain features of the text indicate that it was set from Shakespeare's "foul papers," or perhaps a scribal copy of them, rather than from a theatrical promptbook. Stage directions, exits, and entrances are not handled with the precision customary for a text that would have been used as the basis for an actual performance.

The greatest mystery surrounding the text is its relationship to another play, *The Taming of a Shrew*, entered in the Stationers' Register on May 2, 1594, and published the same year. This play bears many resemblances to Shakespeare's, and for years scholars have debated which preceded the other or whether, in fact, they both derived from a common original, now lost. Many editors have assumed that Shakespeare's play was the source for *The Taming of a Shrew*, though the subplots, in particular, differ substantially; and an interesting argument has been advanced by Leah Marcus that *A Shrew* is earlier than *The Shrew*, that it is at least partly by Shakespeare, and that, in her view, it inscribes an older version of patriarchy than that evident in *The Shrew*. Whatever one decides about order of composition, it is significant that *A Shrew* contains a number of passages involving Christopher Sly not found in *The Shrew*, passages in which Sly continues to comment on the play he watches and finally wakes from his "dream" announcing his intention to go home and tame his own wife. No one knows why these passages appear in one play and not the other. One possibility is that they were written by Shakespeare but for some reason deleted by him or by someone else from the manuscript that served as the basis for the Folio edition of the play, or were added by him at a date later than the composition of that manuscript. For their intrinsic interest, and because of their possible Shakespearean origin, these materials concerning Sly are printed at the end of this edition of *The Shrew* as Additional Passages.

The Oxford editors believe, on balance, that *A Shrew* imitates and is later than *The Shrew*, and this assumption affects their dating of Shakespeare's play, which would have to have been written before 1594, when *A Shrew* was published and designated as belonging to Pembroke's Men, a company that went bankrupt in 1593 and so must have had the play in their repertoire before that time. In addition, a stage direction in *A Shrew* refers to "Simon," who has been plausibly identified as Simon Jewell, an actor who was buried on August 21, 1592. This circumstantial evidence, along with stylistic features that mark the play as an early example of Shakespeare's art, suggests a date of composition of 1592 or earlier.

The Folio text of *The Taming of the Shrew* bears some marks of confusion or incomplete revision in the subplot, particularly in the handling of the character of Hortensio. Shakespeare may have decided rather late to make him one of Bianca's wooers. He is, for example, not included in the "bidding" for Bianca in which Tranio (disguised as Lucentio) and Gremio engage in 2.1. Other anomalies regarding his part are mentioned in the notes to this text, but in performance these issues seldom bother audiences.

In two instances, the present edition marks new scenes where most contemporary editions do not. The first is 3.3, which follows Petruccio's arrival in disheveled dress for his wedding. During this prenuptial scene, Lucentio has no speaking part, and there is no requirement that he be onstage. Consequently, the Oxford editors mark a new scene, 3.3, after everyone exits to attend the wedding and Lucentio comes onstage speaking with Tranio about Bianca before Gremio returns at 3.3.21 to describe the offstage wedding. Another new scene is marked after 4.4—that is, after the episode in which the Pedant, posing as Lucentio's father, meets Baptista and negotiates the marriage of Bianca and Lucentio. This edition makes a separate scene of the ensuing conversation between Biondello and Lucentio in which Biondello explains how Lucentio can elope with Bianca. This change is justified both because the stage has just been cleared before Lucentio's and Biondello's entry and also because there is plausibly a time gap between the two events. In addition, 4.4 shows signs of revision on Shakespeare's part, including indecision about whether or not to include Lucentio in that scene. Making Lucentio and Biondello's conversation a separate scene clarifies the different foci of the two episodes: the first concentrating on Tranio and the Pedant's tricking of Baptista, the second on Biondello's plans for Lucentio to elope.

SELECTED BIBLIOGRAPHY

Aspinall, Dana E., ed. *The Taming of the Shrew: Critical Essays*. New York: Routledge, 2002. A broad selection of twentieth-century critical essays about the play plus reviews of notable film, television, and stage versions.

Boose, Lynda. "Scolding Brides and Bridling Scolds: Taming the Woman's Unruly Member." *Shakespeare Quarterly* 42 (1991): 179–213. Draws on the research of nineteenth-century scholars to recover the early modern punishments, including iron gags and ducking stools, used against women accused of being shrews or scolds.

Haring-Smith, Tori. *From Farce to Metadrama: A Stage History of "The Taming of the Shrew," 1594–1983*. Westport, Conn.: Greenwood Press, 1985. A comprehensive stage history of the play and of some major adaptations from the late 1590s to the early 1980s.

Huston, J. Dennis. "Enter the Hero: The Power of Play in *The Taming of the Shrew.*" *Shakespeare's Comedies of Play.* New York: Columbia University Press, 1981. 58–93. Argues that Shakespeare playfully experiments with comic form in *The Taming of the Shrew* and creates a hero, Petruccio, who teaches Kate how to play with social roles in order to gain control over her environment.

Korda, Natasha. "Household Kates: Domesticating Commodities in *The Taming of the Shrew.*" *Shakespeare's Domestic Economies: Gender and Property in Early Modern England.* Philadelphia: University of Pennsylvania Press, 2002. 52–75. Explores the play as part of an historical shift that made women managers of domestic property and suggests that in taming Kate, Petruccio educates her about the proper management and consumption of household goods.

Marcus, Leah. "The Shakespearean Editor as Shrew-Tamer." *English Literary Renaissance* 22 (1992): 177–200. Examines and queries the historical process by which *The Taming of a Shrew* came to be regarded, not as a source for Shakespeare's *The Taming of the Shrew*, but as a debased derivative of it.

Newman, Karen. "Renaissance Family Politics and Shakespeare's *Taming of the Shrew.*" *Fashioning Femininity and English Renaissance Drama.* Chicago: University of Chicago Press, 1991. 33–50. Argues that Kate's linguistic freedom constitutes her main threat to male authority and that that freedom is never completely curtailed.

Orlin, Lena Cowen. "The Performance of Things in *The Taming of the Shrew.*" *Yearbook of English Studies* 23 (1993): 167–88. Notes the abundance of objects, especially household objects, in *The Taming of the Shrew* and analyzes their functions.

Smith, Amy L. "Performing Marriage with a Difference: Wooing, Wedding, and Bedding in *The Taming of the Shrew.*" *Comparative Drama* 36 (2002): 289–320. Uses Judith Butler's theories of performativity to argue that within Kate and Petruccio's self-conscious performance of courtship and marriage lies the potential for a critical reworking of gender norms, rather than outright submission to or resistance of them.

Walker, Kim. "Wrangling Pedantry: Education in *The Taming of the Shrew.*" *Shakespeare Matters: History, Teaching, Performance.* Ed. Lloyd Davis. Newark: University of Delaware Press, 2003. 191–208. Examines the importance of women's education in the play and in several adaptations of it and suggests that humanist education plays a role in Bianca's transformation into a shrew.

FILMS

The Taming of the Shrew. 1929. Dir. Samuel Taylor. USA. 63 min. One of the first "talkies," this black-and-white film, starring Douglas Fairbanks as Petruccio and Mary Pickford as Katherine, ends with Pickford's famous "wink" at the conclusion of her speech of submission.

Kiss Me Kate. 1953. Dir. George Sidney. USA. 109 min. Film version of the Cole Porter musical starring Howard Keel and Kathryn Grayson in which a group of actors is shown performing Shakespeare's play, the events of which mirror their own circumstances. Songs include "Brush Up Your Shakespeare" and "Where Is the Life That Late I Led?"

The Taming of the Shrew. 1967. Dir. Franco Zeffirelli. Italy/USA. 122 min. Broad-comedy performance starring the real-life couple of Elizabeth Taylor and Richard Burton as Katherine and Petruccio.

The Taming of the Shrew. 1980. Dir. Jonathan Miller. UK. 127 min. Intelligent BBC-TV version starring John Cleese as Petruccio and Sarah Badel as Katherine with sets modeled on Vermeer interiors.

10 Things I Hate About You. 1999. Dir. Gil Junger. USA. 97 min. Loose adaptation of Shakespeare's plot in which Julia Stiles plays a headstrong character, Kat Stratford, who comes to an accommodation with bad boy Heath Ledger as Patrick Verona.

The Taming of the Shrew

THE PERSONS OF THE PLAY

In the Induction

CHRISTOPHER SLY, beggar and tinker
A HOSTESS
A LORD
BARTHOLOMEW, his page
HUNTSMEN
SERVANTS
PLAYERS

In the play-within-the-play

BAPTISTA Minola, a gentleman of Padua
KATHERINE, his elder daughter
BIANCA, his younger daughter
PETRUCCIO, a gentleman of Verona, suitor of Katherine
GRUMIO ⎱ his servants
CURTIS ⎰
GREMIO, a rich old man of Padua, suitor of Bianca
HORTENSIO, another suitor, who disguises himself as Licio, a
    teacher
LUCENTIO, from Pisa, who disguises himself as Cambio, a
    teacher
TRANIO ⎱ his servants
BIONDELLO ⎰
VINCENTIO, Lucentio's father
A PEDANT (schoolmaster), from Mantua
A WIDOW
A TAILOR
A HABERDASHER
An OFFICER
SERVINGMEN, including NATHANIEL, PHILIP, JOSEPH, and PETER
Other servants of Baptista and Petruccio

Induction 1

Enter CHRISTOPHER SLY *[the] beggar, and [the]*
HOSTESS

SLY I'll freeze you,° in faith.   *fix you; beat you*
HOSTESS A pair of stocks,[1] you rogue.
SLY You're a baggage.° The Slys are no rogues. Look in the   *whore*
    Chronicles[2]—we came in with Richard Conqueror,[3] therefore
5 *paucas palabras,*[4] let the world slide.° Sessa![5]   *go by*

Induction 1 Location: In front of a country tavern.
1. A threat to have him put in the stocks (an instrument of public punishment consisting of two wooden planks with semicircles carved into them; the criminal sat with his or her feet clamped between the planks).
2. Histories, especially histories of England such as

Raphael Holinshed's *Chronicles of England, Scotland, and Ireland* (2nd ed., 1587).
3. A blunder for "William the Conqueror," who took the English throne in 1066.
4. Misquoting *pocas palabras,* Spanish for "few words," a phrase from Thomas Kyd's *Spanish Tragedy* (c. 1587).
5. Probably equivalent to "Be quiet."

HOSTESS You will not pay for the glasses you have burst?

SLY No, not a denier. Go by, Saint Jeronimy![6] Go to thy cold
bed and warm thee.

HOSTESS I know my remedy, I must go fetch the headborough.°   *constable*
                                                          [*Exit*]

10 SLY Third or fourth or fifth borough, I'll answer him by law. I'll
not budge an inch, boy.[7] Let him come, and kindly.°   *and welcome! (ironic)*
                                        [*He*] *falls asleep.*
                    Wind horns.° *Enter a* LORD *from hunting, with his train*   *Horns sound*

LORD Huntsman, I charge thee, tender well° my hounds.   *care well for*
Breathe Merriman[8]—the poor cur is embossed°—   *exhausted*
And couple Clowder with the deep-mouthed brach.[9]

15 Saw'st thou not, boy, how Silver made it good
At the hedge corner, in the coldest fault?[1]
I would not lose the dog for twenty pound.

FIRST HUNTSMAN Why, Belman is as good as he, my lord.
He cried upon it at the merest loss,[2]

20 And twice today picked out the dullest scent.
Trust me, I take him for the better dog.

LORD Thou art a fool. If Echo were as fleet
I would esteem him worth a dozen such.
But sup° them well, and look unto them all.   *feed*

25 Tomorrow I intend to hunt again.

FIRST HUNTSMAN I will, my lord.

LORD [*seeing* SLY] What's here? One dead, or drunk? See, doth he breathe?

SECOND HUNTSMAN He breathes, my lord. Were he not warmed with ale
This were a bed but cold to sleep so soundly.

30 LORD O monstrous beast! How like a swine he lies.
Grim death, how foul and loathsome is thine image.[3]
Sirs, I will practise° on this drunken man.   *play a trick on*
What think you: if he were conveyed to bed,
Wrapped in sweet° clothes, rings put upon his fingers,   *scented*

35 A most delicious banquet by his bed,
And brave° attendants near him when he wakes—   *finely dressed*
Would not the beggar then forget himself?

FIRST HUNTSMAN Believe me, lord, I think he cannot choose.°   *do otherwise*

SECOND HUNTSMAN It would seem strange unto him when he waked.

40 LORD Even as a flatt'ring° dream or worthless fancy.   *pleasing*
Then take him up, and manage well the jest.
Carry him gently to my fairest chamber,
And hang it round with all my wanton pictures.°   *erotic artworks*
Balm° his foul head in warm distillèd waters,   *Anoint*

45 And burn sweet wood to make the lodging sweet.[4]

---

6. Misquoting a popular line—"Hieronimo, beware! go
by, go by!"—from Kyd's *Spanish Tragedy* and confusing
Hieronimo, Kyd's hero, with Saint Jerome. *denier*:
French coin of little value.
7. Term of abuse applicable to either sex.
8. Give Merriman time to recover his breath.
9. And put Clowder on a leash with the female hound

("brach") who bays deeply.
1. When the scent was faintest.
2. When the scent had been completely lost.
3. Your likeness (invoking the common comparison
between sleep and death).
4. Aromatic woods like juniper were often burned to
make a room smell fragrant.

Procure me music ready when he wakes
To make a dulcet° and a heavenly sound,   *melodious*
And if he chance to speak be ready straight,°   *at once*
And with a low submissive reverence°   *deep bow*
50 Say 'What is it your honour will command?'
Let one attend him with a silver basin
Full of rose-water and bestrewed with flowers;
Another bear the ewer,° the third a diaper,°   *water jug / towel*
And say 'Will't please your lordship cool your hands?'
55 Someone be ready with a costly suit,
And ask him what apparel he will wear.
Another tell him of his hounds and horse,
And that his lady mourns at his disease.
Persuade him that he hath been lunatic,
60 And when he says he is,° say that he dreams, *is indeed mad*
For he is nothing but a mighty lord.
This do, and do it kindly,° gentle sirs. *naturally; fittingly*
It will be pastime passing° excellent,   *exceedingly*
If it be husbanded with modesty.°   *prudently managed*
65 FIRST HUNTSMAN My lord, I warrant you we will play our part
As he shall think by our true diligence
He is no less than what we say he is.
 LORD Take him up gently, and to bed with him;
And each one to his office° when he wakes.   *assigned role*
      [SERVINGMEN *carry* SLY *out*]
   Trumpets sound
70 Sirrah,[5] go see what trumpet 'tis that sounds.
       [*Exit a* SERVINGMAN]
Belike° some noble gentleman that means,   *Perhaps*
Travelling some journey, to repose him here.
   Enter [*a*] SERVINGMAN
How now? Who is it?
 SERVINGMAN   An't° please your honour, players *If it*
That offer service to your lordship.
   Enter PLAYERS
75 LORD Bid them come near. Now fellows, you are welcome.
 PLAYERS We thank your honour.
 LORD Do you intend to stay with me tonight?
 A PLAYER So please your lordship to accept our duty.° *services; respect*
 LORD With all my heart. This fellow I remember
80 Since once he played a farmer's eldest son.
'Twas where you wooed the gentlewoman so well.
I have forgot your name, but sure that part
Was aptly fitted° and naturally performed. *well suited (to you)*
 ANOTHER PLAYER I think 'twas Soto[6] that your honour means.
85 LORD 'Tis very true. Thou didst it excellent.
Well, you are come to me in happy time,° *at the right time*
The rather for° I have some sport in hand *Especially since*
Wherein your cunning° can assist me much.   *skill*

---

5. A form of address to social inferiors.
6. Possibly a reference to a character of this name in John Fletcher's *Women Pleased*. Since that play was first acted around 1620, the reference must be a late addition to Shakespeare's text or else refer to a character in an earlier play, now lost.

There is a lord will hear you play tonight;
90 But I am doubtful of your modesties°   *self-control*
    Lest, over-eyeing of° his odd behaviour—   *noticing; staring at*
    For yet his honour never heard a play—
    You break into some merry passion,°   *fit of laughter*
    And so offend him; for I tell you, sirs,
95 If you should smile he grows impatient.
A PLAYER Fear not, my lord, we can contain ourselves
    Were he the veriest antic° in the world.   *most eccentric fellow*
    LORD [*to a* SERVINGMAN] Go, sirrah, take them to the buttery[7]
    And give them friendly welcome every one.
100 Let them want° nothing that my house affords.   *lack*
                        Exit one with the PLAYERS
    [*To a* SERVINGMAN] Sirrah, go you to Barthol'mew, my page,
    And see him dressed in all suits° like a lady.   *in every detail*
    That done, conduct him to the drunkard's chamber
    And call him 'madam', do him obeisance.°   *pay him respects*
105 Tell him° from me, as he will win my love,   *(Bartholomew, the page)*
    He bear himself with honourable° action   *becoming*
    Such as he hath observed in noble ladies
    Unto their lords by them accomplishèd.°   *performed*
    Such duty to the drunkard let him do
110 With soft low tongue° and lowly courtesy,   *voice*
    And say 'What is't your honour will command
    Wherein your lady and your humble wife
    May show her duty and make known her love?'
    And then with kind embracements, tempting kisses,
115 And with declining head into his bosom[8]
    Bid him shed tears, as being overjoyed
    To see her noble lord restored to health,
    Who for this seven years hath esteemèd him°   *thought himself to be*
    No better than a poor and loathsome beggar.
120 And if the boy have not a woman's gift
    To rain a shower of commanded° tears,   *produced on demand*
    An onion will do well for such a shift,°   *purpose*
    Which, in a napkin being close conveyed,°   *secretly carried*
    Shall in despite[9] enforce a watery eye.
125 See this dispatched with all the haste thou canst.
    Anon° I'll give thee more instructions.   *Soon*
                        Exit a SERVINGMAN
    I know the boy will well usurp° the grace,   *assume*
    Voice, gait, and action of a gentlewoman.
    I long to hear him call the drunkard husband,
130 And how my men will stay themselves from laughter
    When they do homage to this simple peasant.
    I'll in to counsel them. Haply° my presence   *Perhaps*
    May well abate the over-merry spleen[1]
    Which otherwise would grow into extremes.   [*Exeunt*]

---

7. Pantry, often used to store liquor as well as food.
8. And with his head bowing down into his chest.
9. In spite of an inability to cry.

1. May well lessen the impulse to laugh. Emotional outbursts, including laughter, were thought to originate in the spleen.

Induction 2

Enter aloft[1] [SLY,] the drunkard, with attendants, some
with apparel, basin, and ewer, and other appurte-
nances; and LORD

SLY   For God's sake, a pot of small ale!°   *weak, cheap ale*

FIRST SERVINGMAN   Will't please your lordship drink a cup of
sack?°   *costly imported wine*

SECOND SERVINGMAN   Will't please your honour taste of these
conserves?°   *candied fruits*

THIRD SERVINGMAN   What raiment will your honour wear today?

5   SLY   I am Christophero Sly. Call not me 'honour' nor 'lordship'.
I ne'er drank sack in my life, and if you give me any conserves,
give me conserves of beef.° Ne'er ask me what raiment I'll   *salted beef*
wear, for I have no more doublets° than backs, no more stock-   *jackets*
ings than legs, nor no more shoes than feet—nay, sometime
10   more feet than shoes, or such shoes as my toes look through
the over-leather.

LORD   Heaven cease this idle humour[2] in your honour.
O that a mighty man of such descent,
Of such possessions and so high esteem,
15   Should be infusèd with so foul a spirit.

SLY   What, would you make me mad? Am not I Christopher
Sly—old Sly's son of Burton Heath,[3] by birth a pedlar, by
education a cardmaker,[4] by transmutation a bearherd,° and   *keeper of a tame bear*
now by present profession a tinker?° Ask Marian Hacket, the   *pot mender*
20   fat alewife[5] of Wincot, if she know me not. If she say I am
not fourteen pence on the score[6] for sheer° ale, score me up   *for nothing but*
for the lying'st knave in Christendom. What, I am not
bestraught;° here's—   *crazy*

THIRD SERVINGMAN   O, this it is that makes your lady mourn.

25   SECOND SERVINGMAN   O, this is it that makes your servants droop.

LORD   Hence comes it that your kindred shuns your house,
As beaten hence by your strange lunacy.
O noble lord, bethink thee of thy birth.
Call home thy ancient° thoughts from banishment,   *former*
30   And banish hence these abject lowly dreams.
Look how thy servants do attend on thee,
Each in his office, ready at thy beck.°   *command*
Wilt thou have music?   *Music*
Hark, Apollo[7] plays,
And twenty cagèd nightingales do sing.
35   Or wilt thou sleep? We'll have thee to a couch
Softer and sweeter than the lustful bed

Induction 2 Location: A bedroom in the Lord's house.
1. Upon the gallery above the stage. Whether this long
and complex scene was in fact performed "aloft" is open
to question. At a later point (1.1.242–47), F has Sly
commenting from above on the play presented by the
traveling actors who arrive in Induction 1. If Induction 2
is played on the main stage, Sly must at some point
ascend to the gallery, or he must observe the entire play
from the side of the main stage.
2. Heaven put an end to this foolish fantasy. According
to Renaissance medical theory, humors, or bodily fluids,

determined one's disposition.
3. Possibly Barton-on-the-Heath, a village not far from
Stratford-upon-Avon.
4. Maker of metal combs used to prepare wool for
spinning.
5. Female proprietor of a tavern. Wincot is a small village near Stratford; individuals named Hacket were living there in 1591.
6. In debt. Accounts were originally kept by notching, or
"scoring," a stick, later by making marks on a wall or door.
7. Greek god of music, who played the lyre.

On purpose trimmed up for Semiramis.[8]
Say thou wilt walk, we will bestrew the ground.
Or wilt thou ride, thy horses shall be trapped,°   *fitted with adornments*
40   Their harness studded all with gold and pearl.
Dost thou love hawking? Thou hast hawks will soar
Above the morning lark. Or wilt thou hunt,
Thy hounds shall make the welkin° answer them   *sky*
And fetch shrill echoes from the hollow earth.

45 FIRST SERVINGMAN   Say thou wilt course,° thy greyhounds are as swift   *hunt hares*
  As breathèd° stags, ay, fleeter than the roe.[9]   *well-exercised*

SECOND SERVINGMAN   Dost thou love pictures?[1] We will fetch thee straight
  Adonis[2] painted by a running brook,
  And Cytherea all in sedges° hid,   *water rushes*
50   Which seem to move and wanton° with her breath   *play amorously*
  Even as the waving sedges play wi'th' wind.

LORD   We'll show thee Io[3] as she was a maid,
  And how she was beguilèd and surprised,
  As lively° painted as the deed was done.   *realistically*

55 THIRD SERVINGMAN   Or Daphne[4] roaming through a thorny wood,
  Scratching her legs that one shall swear she bleeds,
  And at that sight shall sad Apollo weep,
  So workmanly° the blood and tears are drawn.   *skillfully*

LORD   Thou art a lord, and nothing but a lord.
60   Thou hast a lady far more beautiful
  Than any woman in this waning age.[5]

FIRST SERVINGMAN   And till the tears that she hath shed for thee
  Like envious° floods o'errun her lovely face   *spiteful*
  She was the fairest creature in the world;
65   And yet° she is inferior to none.   *still*

SLY   Am I a lord, and have I such a lady?
  Or do I dream? Or have I dreamed till now?
  I do not sleep. I see, I hear, I speak.
  I smell sweet savours,° and I feel soft things.   *odors*
70   Upon my life, I am a lord indeed,
  And not a tinker, nor Christopher Sly.
  Well, bring our lady hither to our sight,
  And once again a pot o'th' smallest° ale.   *weakest*

SECOND SERVINGMAN   Will't please your mightiness to wash your hands?
75   O, how we joy to see your wit restored!
  O that once more you knew but what you are!
  These fifteen years you have been in a dream,
  Or when you waked, so waked as if you slept.

SLY   These fifteen years—by my fay,° a goodly nap.   *faith*
80   But did I never speak of° all that time?   *during*

---

8. Legendary Queen of Assyria, known for her great beauty and many sexual adventures.
9. Small deer proverbial for its swiftness.
1. Probably the "wanton pictures" referred to earlier (Induction 1.43). As described in the following lines, they are conventional erotic scenes, mostly derived from Ovid's *Metamorphoses*.
2. In classical mythology, a beautiful boy whom Aphrodite (Cytherea) loved. This scene shows Aphrodite

spying on Adonis while he bathes in the brook.
3. Raped by Zeus, who concealed himself in a cloud or thick mist, she was then turned into a cow by Hera.
4. A nymph who was turned into a laurel tree as she fled from Apollo.
5. Alluding to the popular belief that the world had steadily degenerated from the perfection of paradise or the classical Golden Age.

FIRST SERVINGMAN   O yes, my lord, but very idle words,
    For though you lay here in this goodly chamber
    Yet would you say ye were beaten out of door,
    And rail upon the hostess of the house,°   *tavern*
85   And say you would present° her at the leet°   *accuse / local court*
    Because she brought stone jugs and no sealed quarts.[6]
    Sometimes you would call out for Cicely Hacket.
SLY   Ay, the woman's maid of the house.
THIRD SERVINGMAN   Why, sir, you know no house, nor no such maid,
90   Nor no such men as you have reckoned up,
    As Stephen Sly, and old John Naps of Greet,[7]
    And Peter Turf, and Henry Pimpernel,
    And twenty more such names and men as these,
    Which never were, nor no man ever saw.
95 SLY   Now Lord be thankèd for my good amends.°   *recovery*
ALL   Amen.
SLY   I thank thee. Thou shalt not lose by it.
       Enter [BARTHOLOMEW *the Page, as*] *Lady, with attendants*
BARTHOLOMEW   How fares my noble lord?
SLY   Marry,[8] I fare° well,   *get on; feed*
    For here is cheer° enough. Where is my wife?   *food*
100 BARTHOLOMEW   Here, noble lord. What is thy will with her?
SLY   Are you my wife, and will not call me husband?
    My men should call me lord. I am your goodman.[9]
BARTHOLOMEW   My husband and my lord, my lord and husband;
    I am your wife in all obedience.
SLY   I know it well. [*To the* LORD] What must I call her?
105 LORD   Madam.
SLY   Al'ce Madam or Joan Madam?[1]
LORD   Madam, and nothing else. So lords call ladies.
SLY   Madam wife, they say that I have dreamed,
    And slept above some fifteen year or more.
110 BARTHOLOMEW   Ay, and the time seems thirty unto me,
    Being all this time abandoned° from your bed.   *banned*
SLY   'Tis much. Servants, leave me and her alone.
       [*Exeunt* LORD *and attendants*][2]
    Madam, undress you and come now to bed.
BARTHOLOMEW   Thrice-noble lord, let me entreat of you
115   To pardon me yet for a night or two,
    Or if not so, until the sun be set,
    For your physicians have expressly charged,
    In peril to incur[3] your former malady,
    That I should yet absent me from your bed.
120   I hope this reason stands for my excuse.
SLY   Ay, it stands[4] so that I may hardly tarry° so long. But I would   *delay*

6. She served from unmarked stone jugs rather than from the officially measured and stamped ("sealed") quarts.
7. Greet is a small village not far from Stratford. The names may be those of Stratford citizens.
8. Mild oath, derived from the Virgin Mary's name.
9. Husband: a term normally not used by lords.
1. Misusing the usual title for a noblewoman. "Alice"

and "Joan" are names rarely associated with the upper classes in Elizabethan texts.
2. F has no stage direction here, but those attending on Sly probably obey his command and leave the stage. It is unclear, however, whether the Lord leaves the stage with the other attendants at this point.
3. *In peril to incur*: Because of the risk of bringing on.
4. Punning on "stand" as meaning "to have an erection."

be loath to fall into my dreams again. I will therefore tarry in
despite of the flesh and the blood.

      Enter A MESSENGER

MESSENGER   Your honour's players, hearing your amendment,
125   Are come to play a pleasant comedy,
    For so your doctors hold it very meet,°   *suitable*
    Seeing too much sadness hath congealed your blood,
    And melancholy is the nurse of frenzy.[5]
    Therefore they thought it good you hear a play
130   And frame your mind to mirth and merriment,
    Which bars° a thousand harms and lengthens life.   *prevents*
SLY   Marry, I will let them play it. Is not a comonty°   *(for "comedy")*
    A Christmas gambol, or a tumbling trick?
BARTHOLOMEW   No, my good lord, it is more pleasing stuff.
SLY   What, household stuff?°   *furnishings; events*
135   BARTHOLOMEW   It is a kind of history.°   *story*
SLY   Well, we'll see't. Come, madam wife, sit by my side
    And let the world slip. We shall ne'er be younger.

      [BARTHOLOMEW sits]

1.1

    Flourish.° Enter LUCENTIO *and his man,* TRANIO   *Fanfare of trumpets*
LUCENTIO   Tranio, since for° the great desire I had   *because of*
    To see fair Padua, nursery of arts,[1]
    I am arrived fore° fruitful Lombardy,   *before*
    The pleasant garden of great Italy,
5   And by my father's love and leave am armed
    With his good will and thy good company,
    My trusty servant, well approved° in all,   *reliable*
    Here let us breathe,° and haply institute   *pause; rest*
    A course of learning and ingenious° studies.   *liberal; intellectual*
10   Pisa, renownèd for grave citizens,
    Gave me my being, and my father first°—   *before me*
    A merchant of great traffic° through the world,   *business*
    Vincentio, come of the Bentivolii.[2]
    Vincentio's son, brought up in Florence,
15   It shall become° to serve° all hopes conceived[3]   *befit / fulfill*
    To deck° his fortune with his virtuous deeds.   *adorn*
    And therefore, Tranio, for the time I study,
    Virtue and that part of philosophy
    Will I apply° that treats of happiness   *pursue; study*
20   By virtue specially to be achieved.
    Tell me thy mind, for I have Pisa left
    And am to Padua come as he that leaves
    A shallow plash° to plunge him in the deep,   *pool*
    And with satiety seeks to quench his thirst.
25   TRANIO   *Mi perdonate,*° gentle master mine.   *Pardon me*
    I am in all affected° as yourself,   *inclined*
    Glad that you thus continue your resolve

---

5. According to Renaissance humoral theory, excessive
sadness could cause thickening of the blood and thus
delirium, or "frenzy." *nurse:* nourisher.
1.1 Location: A street in Padua.
1. A center for learning ("arts"). Padua's famous univer-

sity attracted many English students in Shakespeare's
time.
2. Descended from the Bentivolii (perhaps a reference
to the famous Bentivoglio family of Bologna).
3. That is, by relatives and friends.

To suck the sweets of sweet philosophy.
Only, good master, while we do admire
30   This virtue and this moral discipline,
Let's be no stoics nor no stocks,[4] I pray,
Or so devote to Aristotle's checks[5]
As Ovid be an outcast quite abjured.[6]
Balk logic° with acquaintance that you have,   *Bandy words*
35   And practise rhetoric in your common talk.
Music and poesy use to quicken° you;   *revive; animate*
The mathematics and the metaphysics,
Fall to them as you find your stomach° serves you.   *appetite*
No profit grows where is no pleasure ta'en.
40   In brief, sir, study what you most affect.°   *like*
LUCENTIO   Gramercies,° Tranio, well dost thou advise.   *Thank you*
If, Biondello, thou wert come ashore,[7]
We could at once put us in readiness
And take a lodging fit to entertain
45   Such friends as time in Padua shall beget.
But stay a while, what company is this?
TRANIO   Master, some show to welcome us to town.

    Enter BAPTISTA *with his two daughters,* KATHERINE
    and BIANCA; GREMIO, *a pantaloon,*[8] HORTENSIO, *suitor*
    to Bianca. LUCENTIO, [*and*] TRANIO *stand by*

BAPTISTA   Gentlemen, importune me no farther,
For how I firmly am resolved you know:
50   That is, not to bestow° my youngest daughter   *give in marriage*
Before I have a husband for the elder.
If either of you both love Katherina,
Because I know you well and love you well
Leave shall you have to court her at your pleasure.
55 GREMIO   To cart her[9] rather. She's too rough for me.
There, there, Hortensio. Will you° any wife?   *Do you want*
KATHERINE [*to* BAPTISTA]   I pray you, sir, is it your will
To make a stale of me amongst these mates?[1]
HORTENSIO   'Mates', maid? How mean you that? No mates° for you   *husbands*
60   Unless you were of gentler, milder mould.°   *nature*
KATHERINE   I'faith, sir, you shall never need to fear.
Iwis it is not half-way to her heart,[2]
But if it were, doubt not her care should be
To comb your noddle° with a three-legged stool,   *hit your head*
65   And paint° your face, and use you like a fool.   *(with blood)*
HORTENSIO   From all such devils, good Lord deliver us.
GREMIO   And me too, good Lord.
TRANIO [*aside to* LUCENTIO]   Husht, master, here's some good
      pastime toward.°   *in view*

---

4. Wooden posts devoid of feeling. Punning on "stoics," the Greek philosophers who advocated both indifference to pleasure or pain and patient endurance.
5. Restraints. Aristotle defined virtue as a mean, the avoiding of excess (or deficiency).
6. *As . . . abjured:* That Ovid be renounced. Ovid was a Roman poet whose erotic writings were popular in the Renaissance. (His *Ars Amatoria* is mentioned by Lucentio at 4.2.8.)
7. Padua, an inland city, did not have a port. Shake-

speare's knowledge of Italian geography seems to have been shaky.
8. Foolish old man: a stock character from the Italian commedia del arte whose usual role was to hinder young lovers.
9. To carry her though the street in, or tied to, a cart. This was a common punishment for disorderly women.
1. To make me a laughingstock or a prostitute or a decoy (for Bianca) among these crude fellows.
2. Certainly, marriage does not even half interest her. (Kate speaks of herself in the third person here.)

That wench is stark mad or wonderful froward.°   *incredibly willful*

70 LUCENTIO [*aside to* TRANIO]   But in the other's silence do I see
    Maid's mild behaviour and sobriety.
    Peace, Tranio.

TRANIO [*aside to* LUCENTIO]   Well said, master. Mum, and gaze your fill.

BAPTISTA   Gentlemen, that I may soon make good
75   What I have said—Bianca, get you in.
    And let it not displease thee, good Bianca,
    For I will love thee ne'er the less, my girl.

KATHERINE   A pretty peat!° It is best   *pet; spoiled child*
    Put finger in the eye,° an° she knew why.   *(to weep) / if*

80 BIANCA   Sister, content you° in my discontent.   *satisfy yourself*
    [*To* BAPTISTA] Sir, to your pleasure° humbly I subscribe.°   *will / submit*
    My books and instruments shall be my company,
    On them to look and practise by myself.

LUCENTIO [*aside to* TRANIO]   Hark, Tranio, thou mayst hear
        Minerva[3] speak.

85 HORTENSIO   Signor Baptista, will you be so strange?°   *unnatural; cruel*
    Sorry am I that our good will effects°   *causes*
    Bianca's grief.

GREMIO   Why will you mew° her up,   *confine (like a falcon)*
    Signor Baptista, for° this fiend of hell,   *because of*
    And make her bear the penance° of her tongue?   *punishment*

90 BAPTISTA   Gentlemen, content ye. I am resolved.
    Go in, Bianca.   [*Exit* BIANCA]
    And for I know she taketh most delight
    In music, instruments, and poetry,
    Schoolmasters will I keep within my house
95   Fit to instruct her youth. If you, Hortensio,
    Or, Signor Gremio, you know any such,
    Prefer° them hither; for to cunning° men   *Recommend / skillful*
    I will be very kind, and liberal
    To mine own children in good bringing up.
100   And so farewell. Katherina, you may stay,
    For I have more to commune with Bianca.   *Exit*

KATHERINE   Why, and I trust I may go too, may I not? What,
    shall I be appointed hours, as though belike I knew not what
    to take and what to leave? Ha!   *Exit*

105 GREMIO   You may go to the devil's dam.[4] Your gifts are so good
    here's none will hold° you. Their love[5] is not so great, Horten-   *tolerate*
    sio, but we may blow our nails° together and fast it fairly out.[6]   *wait patiently*
    Our cake's dough on both sides.[7] Farewell. Yet for the love I
    bear my sweet Bianca, if I can by any means light on a fit man
110   to teach her that wherein she delights, I will wish° him to her   *recommend*
    father.

HORTENSIO   So will I, Signor Gremio. But a word, I pray.
    Though the nature of our quarrel yet never brooked parle,°   *permitted discussion*
    know now, upon advice,° it toucheth° us both—that we may   *reflection / concerns*
115   yet again have access to our fair mistress and be happy rivals
    in Bianca's love—to labour and effect one thing specially.

---

3. Roman goddess of wisdom.
4. The devil's mother, imagined as the stereotypical
shrew and said to be worse than the devil himself.

5. Love of them (that is, of women).
6. And abstain as best we can.
7. Proverbial expression of failure.

GREMIO   What's that, I pray?

HORTENSIO   Marry, sir, to get a husband for her sister.

GREMIO   A husband?—a devil!

120 HORTENSIO   I say a husband.

GREMIO   I say a devil. Think'st thou, Hortensio, though her
father be very rich, any man is so very° a fool to be married to   *completely*
hell?

HORTENSIO   Tush, Gremio. Though it pass° your patience and   *exceeds*

125 mine to endure her loud alarums,² why, man, there be good   *calls to arms; scoldings*
fellows in the world, an a man could light on them, would take
her with all faults, and money enough.

GREMIO   I cannot tell, but I had as lief° take her dowry with this   *would as willingly*
condition: to be whipped at the high cross⁸ every morning.

130 HORTENSIO   Faith, as you say, there's small choice in rotten
apples. But come, since this bar in law° makes us friends, it   *legal obstacle*
shall be so far forth friendly maintained⁹ till by helping Baptista's eldest daughter to a husband we set his youngest free for
a husband, and then have to't° afresh. Sweet Bianca! Happy   *begin the fight*

135 man be his dole.¹ He that runs fastest gets the ring.² How say
you, Signor Gremio?

GREMIO   I am agreed, and would I had given him the best horse
in Padua to begin his wooing that would thoroughly woo her,
wed her, and bed her, and rid the house of her. Come on.

Exeunt [HORTENSIO *and* GREMIO] *Manent*°   *Remain*
TRANIO *and* LUCENTIO

140 TRANIO   I pray, sir, tell me: is it possible
That love should of a sudden take such hold?

LUCENTIO   O Tranio, till I found it to be true
I never thought it possible or likely.
But see, while idly I stood looking on

145 I found the effect of love in idleness,³
And now in plainness do confess to thee,
That art to me as secret° and as dear   *intimate*
As Anna⁴ to the Queen of Carthage was,
Tranio, I burn, I pine, I perish, Tranio,

150 If I achieve not this young modest girl.
Counsel me, Tranio, for I know thou canst.
Assist me, Tranio, for I know thou wilt.

TRANIO   Master, it is no time to chide you now.
Affection is not rated° from the heart.   *driven out by scolding*

155 If love have touched you, naught remains but so—
*Redime te captum quam queas minimo.*⁵

LUCENTIO   Gramercies,° lad. Go forward, this contents.   *Thanks*
The rest will comfort, for thy counsel's sound.

TRANIO   Master, you looked so longly° on the maid   *persistently*

160 Perhaps you marked not what's the pith° of all.   *main point*

---

8. Cross set on a pedestal in the town center, the normal site for punishment in an English village.

9. *it . . . maintained*: we'll pursue the matter as
friends.

1. May the winner's fate be that of a happy man.

2. A proverb alluding to the ring that riders in a jousting match try to catch on their lances. Also punning on
"ring" as referring to both "wedding ring" and female
genitalia.

3. Punning on a flower known as "love-in-idleness,"

whose juice was thought to induce love. (See *A Midsummer Night's Dream* 2.1.166–68.)

4. Sister to Dido, Queen of Carthage. In both Virgil's
Aeneid and Christopher Marlowe's *Dido, Queen of
Carthage* (1594), Dido tells Anna of her secret love for
Aeneas.

5. Latin: Ransom yourself from captivity at the lowest
possible price. A phrase from Terence, quoted as it
appears in Lily's Latin grammar, a standard Elizabethan
school text.

LUCENTIO O yes, I saw sweet beauty in her face,
    Such as the daughter of Agenor[6] had,
    That made great Jove to humble him to her hand
    When with his knees he kissed the Cretan strand.
165 TRANIO Saw you no more? Marked you not how her sister
    Began to scold and raise up such a storm
    That mortal ears might hardly endure the din?
LUCENTIO Tranio, I saw her coral lips to move,
    And with her breath she did perfume the air.
170   Sacred and sweet was all I saw in her.
TRANIO [aside] Nay, then 'tis time to stir him from his trance.
    [To LUCENTIO] I pray, awake, sir. If you love the maid,
    Bend thoughts and wits to achieve her. Thus it stands:
    Her elder sister is so curst° and shrewd°   *quarrelsome / shrewish*
175   That till the father rid his hands of her,
    Master, your love must live a maid at home,
    And therefore has he closely mewed her up
    Because° she will not be annoyed with° suitors.   *So that / troubled with*
LUCENTIO Ah, Tranio, what a cruel father's he!
180   But art thou not advised° he took some care   *aware*
    To get her cunning schoolmasters to instruct her?
TRANIO Ay, marry am I, sir, and now 'tis plotted.
LUCENTIO I have it, Tranio.
TRANIO   Master, for° my hand,   *by*
    Both our inventions° meet and jump° in one.   *schemes / agree*
LUCENTIO Tell me thine first.
185 TRANIO   You will be schoolmaster
    And undertake the teaching of the maid.
    That's your device.°   *plan*
LUCENTIO   It is. May it be done?
TRANIO Not possible; for who shall bear your part,
    And be in Padua here Vincentio's son,
190   Keep house, and ply his book,° welcome his friends,   *study*
    Visit his countrymen, and banquet them?
LUCENTIO Basta,° content thee, for I have it full.°   *Enough / fully planned*
    We have not yet been seen in any house,
    Nor can we be distinguished by our faces
195   For man or master. Then it follows thus:
    Thou shalt be master, Tranio, in my stead;
    Keep house, and port,° and servants, as I should.   *social position*
    I will some other be, some Florentine,
    Some Neapolitan, or meaner° man of Pisa.   *poorer*
200   'Tis hatched, and shall be so. Tranio, at once
    Uncase° thee. Take my coloured hat and cloak.[7]   *Undress*
    When Biondello comes he waits on thee,
    But I will charm° him first to keep his tongue.   *persuade; use magic on*
TRANIO So had you need.
    [They exchange clothes][8]
205   In brief, sir, sith° it your pleasure is,   *since*

---

6. Europa. Jove transformed himself into a bull and carried her across the sea to Crete to rape her.
7. The outfit of an Elizabethan gentleman. Servants usually wore uniforms, like the "blue coats" of Petruccio's servants (4.1.74).
8. F does not indicate at what point in this exchange

Lucentio and Tranio trade clothes; perhaps they begin during Lucentio's previous speech. This exchange of clothes, emphasizing the ease with which social identity is shifted, is an important visual enactment of one of the play's main preoccupations.

And I am tied to be obedient—
For so your father charged me at our parting,
'Be serviceable° to my son,' quoth he,   *diligent in service*
Although I think 'twas in another sense—
210   I am content to be Lucentio
Because so well I love Lucentio.

LUCENTIO   Tranio, be so, because Lucentio loves,
And let me be a slave t'achieve that maid
Whose sudden sight hath thralled° my wounded⁹ eye   *enslaved*

Enter BIONDELLO

215   Here comes the rogue. Sirrah, where have you been?

BIONDELLO   Where have *I* been? Nay, how now, where are *you*?
Master, has my fellow Tranio stolen your clothes, or you
stolen his, or both? Pray, what's the news?

LUCENTIO   Sirrah, come hither. 'Tis no time to jest,
220   And therefore frame your manners to the time.
Your fellow Tranio here, to save my life
Puts my apparel and my count'nance on,
And I for my escape have put on his,
For in a quarrel since I came ashore
225   I killed a man, and fear I was descried.°   *observed*
Wait you on him, I charge you, as becomes,°   *is fitting*
While I make way from hence to save my life.
You understand me?

BIONDELLO   I sir? Ne'er a whit.°   *Not at all*

LUCENTIO   And not a jot of Tranio in your mouth.
230   Tranio is changed into Lucentio.

BIONDELLO   The better for him. Would I were so too.

TRANIO   So could I, faith, boy, to have the next wish after—
That Lucentio indeed had Baptista's youngest daughter.
But sirrah, not for my sake but your master's I advise
235   You use your manners discreetly in all kind of companies.
When I am alone, why then I am Tranio,
But in all places else your master, Lucentio.

LUCENTIO   Tranio, let's go.
One thing more rests° that thyself execute°—   *remains / must do*
240   To make one among these wooers. If thou ask me why,
Sufficeth my reasons are both good and weighty.   *Exeunt*

The presenters¹ above speak

FIRST SERVINGMAN   My lord, you nod. You do not mind° the play.   *pay attention to*

SLY   Yes, by Saint Anne² do I. A good matter, surely. Comes
there any more of it?

245   BARTHOLOMEW   My lord, 'tis but begun.

SLY   'Tis a very excellent piece of work, madam lady. Would
'twere done.

They sit and mark°   *observe*

1.2

Enter PETRUCCIO *and his man,* GRUMIO

PETRUCCIO   Verona, for a while I take my leave
To see my friends in Padua; but of all

---

9. Wounded by Cupid's arrow.
1. Figures who introduce and comment on the action
of a play for the audience.

2. A common oath. Saint Anne was the mother of
the Virgin Mary and the patron saint of married women.
1.2 Location: In front of Hortensio's house in Padua.

My best-belovèd and approvèd friend
Hortensio, and I trow° this is his house.   *believe*
5   Here, sirrah Grumio, knock, I say.
GRUMIO   Knock, sir? Whom should I knock? Is there any man
    has rebused¹ your worship?
PETRUCCIO   Villain, I say, knock me here² soundly.
GRUMIO   Knock you here, sir? Why, sir, what am I, sir, that I
10   should knock you here, sir?
PETRUCCIO   Villain, I say, knock me at this gate,
    And rap me well or I'll knock your knave's pate.
GRUMIO   My master is grown quarrelsome. I should knock you first,
    And then I know after who comes by the worst.³
15   PETRUCCIO   Will it not be?
    Faith, sirrah, an° you'll not knock, I'll ring it.⁴   *if*
    I'll try how you can sol-fa° and sing it.   *sing a scale*
        He wrings him by the ears. [GRUMIO *kneels*]⁵
GRUMIO   Help, masters, help! My master is mad.
PETRUCCIO   Now knock when I bid you, sirrah villain.
        Enter HORTENSIO
20   HORTENSIO   How now, what's the matter? My old friend Grumio
    and my good friend Petruccio? How do you all at Verona?
PETRUCCIO   Signor Hortensio, come you to part the fray?
    Con tutto il cuore ben trovato,⁶ may I say.
HORTENSIO   *Alla nostra casa ben venuto, molto onorato signor*
25   *mio Petruccio.⁷*
    Rise, Grumio, rise. We will compound° this quarrel.   *settle*
        [GRUMIO *rises*]
GRUMIO   Nay, 'tis no matter, sir, what he 'leges° in Latin. If this   *alleges*
    be not a lawful cause for me to leave his service—look you, sir:
    he bid me knock him and rap him soundly, sir. Well, was it fit
30   for a servant to use his master so, being perhaps, for aught
    I see, two-and-thirty, a pip out?⁸
    Whom would to God I had well knocked at first,
    Then had not Grumio come by the worst.
PETRUCCIO   A senseless villain. Good Hortensio,
35   I bade the rascal knock upon your gate,
    And could not get him for my heart to do it.
GRUMIO   Knock at the gate? O heavens, spake you not these
    words plain? 'Sirrah, knock me here, rap me here, knock me
    well, and knock me soundly'? And come you now with
40   knocking at the gate?
PETRUCCIO   Sirrah, be gone, or talk not, I advise you.
HORTENSIO   Petruccio, patience. I am Grumio's pledge.°   *guarantor*
    Why this' a heavy chance⁹ 'twixt him and you,

---

1. Grumio regularly blunders and puns. Here he
means "abused" or "rebuked," or perhaps both.
2. Knock here for me: a conventional usage that Grumio misunderstands or pretends to understand as
"strike me." *Villain*: low-born man (often a contemptuous term of address).
3. *I should . . . worst:* You want me to give the first
blow, but then I know I'd have the worse of it.
4. I'll ring the bell; with a pun on "wring."
5. While F gives no stage direction indicating that
Grumio kneels at this point, at line 26 Hortensio
orders him to "rise." This may mean that he has been

brought to his knees when Petruccio wrings his ears at
line 17.
6. With all my heart, welcome (Italian).
7. Welcome to our house, my most honored Signor
Petruccio.
8. Drunk; a bit crazy. Probably alluding to the card
game one-and-thirty, in which the aim is to accumulate
exactly thirty-one points. To collect thirty-two means
the player has overshot or been excessive. A "pip" is a
spot on a card; hence "a pip out" means "off by one."
9. *Why . . . chance:* This is a sad occurrence.

Your ancient,° trusty, pleasant servant Grumio.   *long-standing*
45 And tell me now, sweet friend, what happy gale
Blows you to Padua here from old Verona?

PETRUCCIO   Such wind as scatters young men through the world
To seek their fortunes farther than at home,
Where small experience grows. But in a few,°   *in short*
50 Signor Hortensio, thus it stands with me:
Antonio, my father, is deceased,
And I have thrust myself into this maze[1]
Happily to wive and thrive as best I may.
Crowns° in my purse I have, and goods at home,   *Five-shilling coins*
55 And so am come abroad to see the world.

HORTENSIO   Petruccio, shall I then come roundly° to thee   *speak plainly*
And wish thee to a shrewd, ill-favoured wife?
Thou'dst thank me but a little for my counsel,
And yet I'll promise thee she shall be rich,
60 And very rich. But thou'rt too much my friend,
And I'll not wish thee to her.

PETRUCCIO   Signor Hortensio, 'twixt such friends as we
Few words suffice; and therefore, if thou know
One rich enough to be Petruccio's wife—
65 As wealth is burden° of my wooing dance—   *refrain; chief theme*
Be she as foul° as was Florentius' love,[2]   *ugly*
As old as Sibyl,[3] and as curst and shrewd
As Socrates' Xanthippe[4] or a worse,
She moves° me not—or not° removes at least°   *annoys / nor / at all*
70 Affection's edge° in me, were she as rough   *intensity*
As are the swelling Adriatic seas.
I come to wive it wealthily in Padua;
If wealthily, then happily in Padua.

GRUMIO [*to* HORTENSIO]   Nay, look you, sir, he tells you flatly
75 what his mind is. Why, give him gold enough and marry him
to a puppet or an aglet-baby,[5] or an old trot° with ne'er a tooth   *hag*
in her head, though she have as many diseases as two-and-fifty
horses. Why, nothing comes amiss so money comes withal.°   *with it*

HORTENSIO   Petruccio, since we are stepped thus far in,
80 I will continue that° I broached in jest.   *what*
I can, Petruccio, help thee to a wife
With wealth enough, and young and beauteous,
Brought up as best becomes a gentlewoman.
Her only fault—and that is faults enough—
85 Is that she is intolerable curst,°   *shrewish*
And shrewd and froward° so beyond all measure   *willful*
That, were my state° far worser than it is,   *fortune*
I would not wed her for a mine of gold.

PETRUCCIO   Hortensio, peace. Thou know'st not gold's effect.
90 Tell me her father's name and 'tis enough,

---

1. This uncertain world; this unpredictable business of "wiving and thriving."
2. Florent, the knight in John Gower's *Confessio Amantis*, who had to marry the ugly old woman who had saved his life by answering a riddle he had been commanded to solve. On their wedding night, as a reward for his compliance, she became young and beautiful.

A version of this story also appears in Chaucer's *Wife of Bath's Tale*.
3. The Cumean Sibyl, a prophetess in classical mythology, has immortality without eternal youth.
4. The philosopher's notoriously shrewish wife.
5. Small figure used as a tag or ornament on dresses, laces, and other goods.

For I will board[6] her though she chide as loud
As thunder when the clouds in autumn crack.
HORTENSIO   Her father is Baptista Minola,
An affable and courteous gentleman.
95   Her name is Katherina Minola,
Renowned in Padua for her scolding tongue.
PETRUCCIO   I know her father, though I know not her,
And he knew my deceasèd father well.
I will not sleep, Hortensio, till I see her,
100   And therefore let me be thus bold with you   leave you
To give you over° at this first encounter,
Unless you will accompany me thither.
GRUMIO   I pray you, sir, let him go while the humour° lasts.   mood
O' my word, an she knew him as well as I do she would think
105   scolding would do little good upon him. She may perhaps call
him half a score knaves or so. Why, that's nothing; an he begin
once he'll rail in his rope-tricks.[7] I'll tell you what, sir, an she
stand° him but a little he will throw a figure[8] in her face and   withstand; arouse
so disfigure her with it that she shall have no more eyes to see
110   withal than a cat. You know him not, sir.
HORTENSIO   Tarry, Petruccio, I must go with thee,
For in Baptista's keep° my treasure is.   custody; stronghold
He hath the jewel of my life in hold,
His youngest daughter, beautiful Bianca,
115   And her withholds from me and other more,°   others besides
Suitors to her and rivals in my love,
Supposing it a thing impossible,
For those defects I have before rehearsed,
That ever Katherina will be wooed.
120   Therefore this order hath Baptista ta'en:
That none shall have access unto Bianca
Till Katherine the curst have got a husband.
GRUMIO   Katherine the curst—
A title for a maid of all titles the worst.
125   HORTENSIO   Now shall my friend Petruccio do me grace,°   a favor
And offer me disguised in sober robes
To old Baptista as a schoolmaster
Well seen° in music, to instruct Bianca,   skilled
That so I may by this device at least
130   Have leave and leisure to make love to her,
And unsuspected court her by herself.
        Enter GREMIO [*with a paper,*][9] *and* LUCENTIO *disguised*
        [*as a schoolmaster*]
GRUMIO   Here's no knavery.[1] See, to beguile the old folks, how
the young folks lay their heads together. Master, master, look
about you. Who goes there, ha?
135   HORTENSIO   Peace, Grumio, it is the rival of my love.
Petruccio, stand by a while.

---

6. Woo aggressively; go aboard, as in a sea battle; have sexual intercourse with.
7. An obscure phrase: "rope-tricks" may refer to rhetorical or sexual feats. Grumio's point seems to be that when Petruccio "rails," he will be more aggressive than Katherine.
8. A figure of speech.
9. Presumably Lucentio's list of books for Bianca's studies.
1. Spoken sarcastically; perhaps referring to the plotting of Petruccio and Hortensio rather than to that of Gremio and Lucentio, whom Grumio may not yet have seen.

GRUMIO A proper stripling,° and an amorous!   *handsome youth (ironic)*
       [PETRUCCIO, HORTENSIO, *and* GRUMIO *stand aside*]
GREMIO [*to* LUCENTIO] O, very well—I have perused the note.°   *listing of books*
    Hark you, sir, I'll have them° very fairly bound—   *(the books)*
140   All books of love, see that at any hand°—   *in any case*
    And see you read no other lectures to her.
    You understand me. Over and beside
    Signor Baptista's liberality,
    I'll mend° it with a largess.° Take your paper, too,   *increase / gift*
145   And let me have them very well perfumed,
    For she is sweeter than perfume itself
    To whom they go to. What will you read to her?
LUCENTIO Whate'er I read to her, I'll plead for you
    As for my patron, stand you so assured,
150   As firmly as yourself were still in place°—   *always present*
    Yea, and perhaps with more successful words
    Than you, unless you were a scholar, sir.
GREMIO O this learning, what a thing it is!
GRUMIO [*aside*] O this woodcock,[2] what an ass it is!
155 PETRUCCIO Peace, sirrah.
HORTENSIO Grumio, mum. [*Coming forward*] God save you, Signor Gremio.
GREMIO And you are well met, Signor Hortensio.
    Trow° you whither I am going?   *Know*
    To Baptista Minola.
160   I promised to enquire carefully
    About a schoolmaster for the fair Bianca,
    And by good fortune I have lighted well
    On this young man, for learning and behaviour
    Fit for her turn,° well read in poetry   *use*
165   And other books—good ones, I warrant ye.
HORTENSIO 'Tis well, and I have met a gentleman
    Hath promised me to help me to another,
    A fine musician, to instruct our mistress.
    So shall I no whit be behind in duty
170   To fair Bianca, so beloved of me.
GREMIO Beloved of me, and that my deeds shall prove.
GRUMIO [*aside*] And that his bags° shall prove.   *money bags*
HORTENSIO Gremio, 'tis now no time to vent° our love.   *express*
    Listen to me, and if you speak me fair°   *courteously*
175   I'll tell you news indifferent° good for either.   *equally*
    Here is a gentleman whom by chance I met,
    Upon agreement from us to his liking°   *If we accept his terms*
    Will undertake to woo curst Katherine,
    Yea, and to marry her, if her dowry please.
180 GREMIO So said, so done, is well.
    Hortensio, have you told him all her faults?
PETRUCCIO I know she is an irksome brawling scold.
    If that be all, masters, I hear no harm.
GREMIO No, sayst me so, friend? What countryman?
185 PETRUCCIO Born in Verona, old Antonio's son.
    My father dead, his fortune lives for me,°   *is mine*

2. Wild bird easily caught and so thought to be stupid.

And I do hope good days and long to see.
GREMIO   O sir, such a life with such a wife were strange.
But if you have a stomach, to't, a'° God's name.   in
190 You shall have me assisting you in all.
But will you woo this wildcat?
PETRUCCIO   Will I live!
GRUMIO   Will he woo her? Ay, or I'll hang her.
PETRUCCIO   Why came I hither but to that intent?
Think you a little din can daunt mine ears?
195 Have I not in my time heard lions roar?
Have I not heard the sea, puffed up with winds,
Rage like an angry boar chafèd with sweat?
Have I not heard great ordnance° in the field,   cannon
And heaven's artillery thunder in the skies?
200 Have I not in a pitchèd battle heard
Loud 'larums,° neighing steeds, and trumpets' clang?   calls to arms
And do you tell me of a woman's tongue,
That gives not half so great a blow° to hear   loud noise
As will a chestnut in a farmer's fire?
205 Tush, tush—fear° boys with bugs.°   frighten / bogeymen
GRUMIO   For he fears none.
GREMIO   Hortensio, hark.
This gentleman is happily° arrived,   fortunately
My mind presumes, for his own good and ours.
210 HORTENSIO   I promised we would be contributors,
And bear his charge° of wooing, whatsoe'er.   expense
GREMIO   And so we will, provided that he win her.
GRUMIO   I would I were as sure of a good dinner.

         Enter TRANIO, brave,° [as Lucentio,] and BIONDELLO   richly dressed

TRANIO   Gentlemen, God save you. If I may be bold, tell me, I
215 beseech you, which is the readiest way to the house of Signor
Baptista Minola?
BIONDELLO   He that has the two fair daughters—is't he you
mean?
TRANIO   Even he, Biondello.
220 GREMIO   Hark you, sir, you mean not her to—
TRANIO   Perhaps him and her, sir. What have you to do?[3]
PETRUCCIO   Not her that chides, sir, at any hand, I pray.
TRANIO   I love no chiders, sir. Biondello, let's away.
LUCENTIO [aside]   Well begun, Tranio.
HORTENSIO   Sir, a word ere you go.
225 Are you a suitor to the maid you talk of—yea or no?
TRANIO   And if I be, sir, is it any offence?
GREMIO   No, if without more words you will get you hence.
TRANIO   Why, sir, I pray, are not the streets as free
For me as for you?
GREMIO   But so is not she.
230 TRANIO   For what reason, I beseech you?
GREMIO   For this reason, if you'll know—
That she's the choice° love of Signor Gremio.   chosen; excellent
HORTENSIO   That she's the chosen of Signor Hortensio.
TRANIO   Softly, my masters. If you be gentlemen,

---

3. What business is it of yours?

235   Do me this right,° hear me with patience.   *justice*
         Baptista is a noble gentleman
         To whom my father is not all unknown,
         And were his daughter fairer than she is
         She may more suitors have, and me for one.
240   Fair Leda's daughter[4] had a thousand wooers;
         Then well one more may fair Bianca have,
         And so she shall. Lucentio shall make one,
         Though Paris came,[5] in hope to speed° alone.   *succeed*
     GREMIO   What, this gentleman will out-talk us all!
245   LUCENTIO   Sir, give him head, I know he'll prove a jade.°   *worn-out horse*
     PETRUCCIO   Hortensio, to what end are all these words?
     HORTENSIO   Sir, let me be so bold as ask you,
         Did you yet ever see Baptista's daughter?
     TRANIO   No, sir, but hear I do that he hath two,
250   The one as famous for a scolding tongue
         As is the other for beauteous modesty.
     PETRUCCIO   Sir, sir, the first's for me. Let her go by.
     GREMIO   Yea, leave that labour to great Hercules,
         And let it be more than Alcides' twelve.[6]
255   PETRUCCIO   Sir, understand you this of me in sooth,°   *truth*
         The youngest daughter whom you hearken° for   *lie in wait; yearn*
         Her father keeps from all access of suitors,
         And will not promise her to any man
         Until the elder sister first be wed.
260   The younger then is free, and not before.
     TRANIO   If it be so, sir, that you are the man
         Must stead° us all, and me amongst the rest,   *help*
         And if you break the ice and do this feat,
         Achieve° the elder, set the younger free   *Win*
265   For our access, whose hap shall be° to have her   *he who is lucky enough*
         Will not so graceless be to be ingrate.
     HORTENSIO   Sir, you say well, and well you do conceive°   *understand*
         And since you do profess to be a suitor
         You must, as we do, gratify° this gentleman,   *reward*
270   To whom we all rest generally beholden.
     TRANIO   Sir, I shall not be slack. In sign whereof,
         Please ye we may contrive° this afternoon,   *pass, spend (time)*
         And quaff carouses° to our mistress' health,   *toasts*
         And do as adversaries do in law—
275   Strive mightily, but eat and drink as friends.
     GRUMIO *and* BIONDELLO   O excellent motion!° Fellows, let's be gone.   *proposal*
     HORTENSIO   The motion's good indeed, and be it so.
         Petruccio, I shall be your *ben venuto*.°   *Exeunt*   *welcome (your host)*

2.1

Enter KATHERINE *and* BIANCA [*her hands bound*]
     BIANCA   Good sister, wrong me not, nor wrong yourself
         To make a bondmaid and a slave of me.

---

4. Helen of Troy. In Marlowe's *Doctor Faustus*, her face is said to have "launched a thousand ships."
5. Even if Paris (who stole Helen of Troy from her husband) were to come.
6. Hercules, the hero of classical mythology who suc-
cessfully performed twelve seemingly impossible tasks ("labours"), was also called Alcides (descendant of Alcaeus).
2.1 Location: Baptista's house in Padua.

That I disdain, but for these other goods,°   *possessions*
Unbind my hands, I'll pull them off myself,
5   Yea, all my raiment to my petticoat,
Or what you will command me will I do,
So well I know my duty to my elders.
KATHERINE   Of all thy suitors here I charge thee tell
Whom thou lov'st best. See thou dissemble not.
10   BIANCA   Believe me, sister, of all the men alive
I never yet beheld that special face
Which I could fancy more than any other.
KATHERINE   Minion,° thou liest. Is't not Hortensio?   *Hussy*
BIANCA   If you affect° him, sister, here I swear   *love*
15   I'll plead for you myself but you shall have him.
KATHERINE   O then, belike you fancy riches more.
You will have Gremio to keep you fair.
BIANCA   Is it for him you do envy me so?
Nay, then, you jest, and now I well perceive
20   You have but jested with me all this while.
I prithee, sister Kate, untie my hands.
KATHERINE   If that be jest, then all the rest was so. *Strikes her*
       Enter BAPTISTA
BAPTISTA   Why, how now, dame, whence grows this insolence?
Bianca, stand aside.— Poor girl, she weeps.—
25   Go ply thy needle, meddle not with her.
[*To* KATHERINE] For shame, thou hilding° of a devilish spirit,   *worthless creature*
Why dost thou wrong her that did ne'er wrong thee?
When did she cross thee with a bitter word?
KATHERINE   Her silence flouts° me, and I'll be revenged.   *mocks*
       [*She*] *flies after* BIANCA
30   BAPTISTA   What, in my sight? Bianca, get thee in. *Exit* [BIANCA]
KATHERINE   What, will you not suffer me?° Nay, now I see   *let me have my way*
She is your treasure, she must have a husband.
I must dance barefoot on her wedding day,[1]
And for your love to her lead apes in hell.[2]
35   Talk not to me. I will go sit and weep
Till I can find occasion of revenge.   [*Exit*]
BAPTISTA   Was ever gentleman thus grieved as I?
But who comes here?
       Enter GREMIO, LUCENTIO [*as a schoolmaster*] *in the*
       habit of a mean man,° PETRUCCIO *with* [HORTENSIO *as*   *man of low social rank*
       a musician,] TRANIO [*as Lucentio*], *with* [BIONDELLO]
       his boy bearing a lute and books
GREMIO   Good morrow, neighbour Baptista.
40   BAPTISTA   Good morrow, neighbour Gremio. God save you,
gentlemen.
PETRUCCIO   And you, good sir. Pray, have you not a daughter
Called Katherina, fair and virtuous?
BAPTISTA   I have a daughter, sir, called Katherina.
45   GREMIO   You are too blunt. Go to it orderly.°   *properly*
PETRUCCIO   You wrong me, Signor Gremio. Give me leave.
[*To* BAPTISTA] I am a gentleman of Verona, sir,

---

1. Proverbially expected of older unmarried sisters.   2. *lead apes in hell:* the proverbial destiny of unmarried
women.

That hearing of her beauty and her wit,
Her affability and bashful modesty,
50 Her wondrous qualities and mild behaviour,
Am bold to show myself a forward° guest   *eager*
Within your house to make mine eye the witness
Of that report which I so oft have heard,
And for an entrance to my entertainment[3]
55 I do present you with a man of mine [*presenting* HORTENSIO]
Cunning in music and the mathematics
To instruct her fully in those sciences,
Whereof I know she is not ignorant.
Accept of him, or else you do me wrong.
60 His name is Licio, born in Mantua.
BAPTISTA   You're welcome, sir, and he for your good sake.
But for my daughter, Katherine, this I know:
She is not for your turn,° the more my grief.   *will not suit you*
PETRUCCIO   I see you do not mean to part with her,
65 Or else you like not of my company.
BAPTISTA   Mistake me not, I speak but as I find.°   *as the facts stand*
Whence are you, sir? What may I call your name?
PETRUCCIO   Petruccio is my name, Antonio's son,
A man well known throughout all Italy.
70 BAPTISTA   I know him well.[4] You are welcome for his sake.
GREMIO   Saving° your tale, Petruccio, I pray   *With all respect to*
Let us that are poor petitioners speak too.
Baccare,° you are marvellous forward.   *Stand back (mock Latin)*
PETRUCCIO   O pardon me, Signor Gremio, I would fain be doing.[5]
75 GREMIO   I doubt it not, sir. But you will curse your wooing.
[*To* BAPTISTA] Neighbour, this is a gift[6] very grateful,° I am sure   *pleasing*
of it. To express the like kindness, myself, that have been more
kindly beholden to you than any. freely give unto you this
young scholar [*presenting* LUCENTIO] that hath been long
80 studying at Rheims,[7] as cunning in Greek, Latin, and other
languages as the other in music and mathematics. His name
is Cambio.[8] Pray accept his service.
BAPTISTA   A thousand thanks, Signor Gremio. Welcome, good
Cambio. [*To* TRANIO] But, gentle sir, methinks you walk like a
85 stranger. May I be so bold to know the cause of your coming?
TRANIO   Pardon me, sir, the boldness is mine own
That, being a stranger in this city here,
Do make myself a suitor to your daughter,
Unto Bianca, fair and virtuous.
90 Nor is your firm resolve unknown to me
In the preferment of the eldest sister.
This liberty is all that I request:
That upon knowledge of my parentage
I may have welcome 'mongst the rest that woo,
95 And free access and favour as the rest.
And toward the education of your daughters

---

3. And as an entrance fee for my reception ("entertainment") as a suitor.
4. Probably, I know him by reputation.
5. I am eager to get on with it (with a pun on "doing"
as meaning "have sexual intercourse").
6. That is, Petruccio's gift of Hortensio/Licio.
7. French city famous for its university.
8. Italian for "exchange"

       I here bestow a simple instrument,
       And this small packet of Greek and Latin books.
       If you accept them, then their worth is great.
100   BAPTISTA   Lucentio is your name⁹—of whence, I pray?
     TRANIO   Of Pisa, sir, son to Vincentio.
     BAPTISTA   A mighty man of Pisa. By report
       I know him well. You are very welcome, sir.
       [*To* HORTENSIO] Take you the lute, [*to* LUCENTIO] and you the
         set of books.
105   You shall go see your pupils presently.°   *immediately*
       Holla, within!
              Enter a Servant
                  Sirrah, lead these gentlemen
       To my daughters, and tell them both
       These are their tutors. Bid them use them well.
           [*Exit Servant with* LUCENTIO *and* HORTENSIO,
                          BIONDELLO *following*]
       [*To* PETRUCCIO] We will go walk a little in the orchard,°   *garden*
110   And then to dinner. You are passing° welcome—   *extremely*
       And so I pray you all to think yourselves.
     PETRUCCIO   Signor Baptista, my business asketh haste,
       And every day I cannot come to woo.
       You knew my father well, and in him me,
115   Left solely heir to all his lands and goods,
       Which I have bettered rather than decreased.
       Then tell me, if I get your daughter's love,
       What dowry shall I have with her to wife?
     BAPTISTA   After my death the one half of my lands,
120   And in possession° twenty thousand crowns.   *immediately*
     PETRUCCIO   And for that dowry I'll assure her of
       Her widowhood,¹ be it that she survive me,
       In all my lands and leases whatsoever.
       Let specialties° be therefore drawn between us,   *explicit contracts*
125   That covenants may be kept on either hand.
     BAPTISTA   Ay, when the special thing is well obtained—
       That is her love, for that is all in all.
     PETRUCCIO   Why, that is nothing, for I tell you, father,
       I am as peremptory as she proud-minded,
130   And where two raging fires meet together
       They do consume the thing that feeds their fury.
       Though little fire grows great with little wind,
       Yet extreme gusts will blow out fire and all.²
       So I to her, and so she yields to me,
135   For I am rough, and woo not like a babe.
     BAPTISTA   Well mayst thou woo, and happy be thy speed.°   *fortune*
       But be thou armed for some unhappy words.
     PETRUCCIO   Ay, to the proof,³ as mountains are for winds,
       That shakes not though they blow perpetually.
          Enter HORTENSIO *with his head broke*
140   BAPTISTA   How now, my friend, why dost thou look so pale?

---

9. How Baptista knows this is unclear. He may read the
name in one of the schoolbooks.
1. Widow's share of the estate.
2. Implying that those who have opposed Katherine so

far have been too weak ("little wind") and that he will
subdue her with his "extreme gusts."
3. In impenetrable armor. Proof armor was tested for
its strength.

HORTENSIO   For fear, I promise you, if I look pale.

BAPTISTA   What, will my daughter prove a good musician?

HORTENSIO   I think she'll sooner prove a soldier.
Iron may hold with° her, but never lutes.   *withstand*

145   BAPTISTA   Why then, thou canst not break° her to the lute?   *train*

HORTENSIO   Why no, for she hath broke the lute to me.
I did but tell her she mistook her frets,[4]
And bowed° her hand to teach her fingering,   *bent*
When, with a most impatient devilish spirit,

150   'Frets,[5] call you these?' quoth she, 'I'll fume° with them,'   *be in a rage*
And with that word she struck me on the head,
And through the instrument my pate made way,
And there I stood amazèd for a while,
As on a pillory,[6] looking through the lute,

155   While she did call me rascal, fiddler,
And twangling jack,° with twenty such vile terms,   *knave*
As° had she studied to misuse me so.   *As if*

PETRUCCIO   Now, by the world, it is a lusty° wench!   *lively*
I love her ten times more than e'er I did.

160   O, how I long to have some chat with her!

BAPTISTA   [*to* HORTENSIO]   Well, go with me, and be not so
discomfited.
Proceed in practice° with my younger daughter.   *Continue your lessons*
She's apt to learn, and thankful for good turns.
Signor Petruccio, will you go with us,

165   Or shall I send my daughter Kate to you?

PETRUCCIO   I pray you, do.   *Exeunt. Manet*° PETRUCCIO   *Remains*
I'll attend° her here,   *await*
And woo her with some spirit when she comes.
Say that she rail, why then I'll tell her plain
She sings as sweetly as a nightingale.

170   Say that she frown, I'll say she looks as clear
As morning roses newly washed with dew.
Say she be mute and will not speak a word,
Then I'll commend her volubility,
And say she uttereth piercing° eloquence.   *moving*

175   If she do bid me pack,° I'll give her thanks   *go away*
As though she bid me stay by her a week.
If she deny to wed, I'll crave° the day   *beg to know*
When I shall ask the banns,[7] and when be married.
But here she comes, and now, Petruccio, speak.

Enter KATHERINE

180   Good morrow, Kate, for that's your name, I hear.

KATHERINE   Well have you heard, but something° hard of hearing.   *somewhat*
They call me Katherine that do talk of me.

PETRUCCIO   You lie, in faith, for you are called plain Kate,
And bonny Kate, and sometimes Kate the curst,

185   But Kate, the prettiest Kate in Christendom,

---

4. Placed her fingers upon the wrong bars ("frets") on the lute's fingerboard.

5. Kate plays on "frets" as also meaning "annoyances" or "vexations."

6. An instrument of public punishment in which the offender's head and hands were fastened in wooden clamps.

7. Have the banns read. Banns were required announcements in church of a forthcoming wedding.

Kate of Kate Hall,[8] my super-dainty Kate—
For dainties are all cates,[9] and therefore 'Kate'—
Take this of me, Kate of my consolation:
Hearing thy mildness praised in every town,
190　Thy virtues spoke of, and thy beauty sounded[1]—
Yet not so deeply as to thee belongs—
Myself am moved to woo thee for my wife.

KATHERINE　Moved? In good time.° Let him that moved you hither　　　*Indeed*
Re-move you hence. I knew you at the first
You were a movable.[2]

195　PETRUCCIO　　　　　　　Why, what's a movable?
KATHERINE　A joint-stool.[3]
PETRUCCIO　　　　　Thou hast hit it. Come, sit on me.
KATHERINE　Asses are made to bear,° and so are you.　　　*carry loads*
PETRUCCIO　Women are made to bear,[4] and so are you.
KATHERINE　No such jade° as you, if me you mean.　　　*worn-out horse*
200　PETRUCCIO　Alas, good Kate, I will not burden[5] thee,
For knowing° thee to be but young and light.[6]　　　*Because I know*
KATHERINE　Too light° for such a swain° as you to catch,　　　*quick / bumpkin*
And yet as heavy as my weight should be.[7]
PETRUCCIO　Should be?—should buzz.[8]
KATHERINE　　　　　　　Well ta'en, and like a buzzard.[9]
205　PETRUCCIO　O slow-winged turtle,° shall a buzzard take thee?　　　*turtledove*
KATHERINE　Ay, for a turtle, as he takes a buzzard.[1]
PETRUCCIO　Come, come, you wasp, i'faith you are too angry.
KATHERINE　If I be waspish, best beware my sting.
PETRUCCIO　My remedy is then to pluck it out.
210　KATHERINE　Ay, if the fool could find it where it lies.
PETRUCCIO　Who knows not where a wasp does wear his sting?
In his tail.
KATHERINE　In his tongue.
PETRUCCIO　　　　　　Whose tongue?
KATHERINE　Yours, if you talk of tales,° and so farewell.　　　*gossip; genitals*
PETRUCCIO　What, with my tongue in your tail? Nay, come again,
Good Kate, I am a gentleman.
215　KATHERINE　　　　　　That I'll try.°　　　*test*
　　She strikes him
PETRUCCIO　I swear I'll cuff you if you strike again.
KATHERINE　So may you lose your arms.[2]
If you strike me you are no gentleman,
And if no gentleman, why then, no arms.

8. Either an obscure allusion or an ironic reference to Kate's home as a place famous because she lives there.
9. For delicacies ("dainties") are called "cates."
1. Proclaimed; tested for depth.
2. Piece of furniture; changeable person.
3. Wooden stool made by a joiner.
4. Bear children; bear the weight of a lover.
5. Lie on you in sexual intercourse; make you pregnant; make accusations against you; accompany you with a musical refrain, or "burden."
6. Not heavy; wanton; lacking a musical accompaniment.
7. She is claiming social prominence ("weight") and

refusing the implication that she is wanton ("light") or like a coin that has been clipped so that it is lighter than it should be.
8. Punning on "be" and "bee," Petruccio suggests Kate should make a buzzing sound.
9. A hawk that cannot be trained to "take," or capture, prey; a fool.
1. Obscure line probably meaning that if a fool ("buzzard") mistakes me for a faithful love ("turtledove"), he'll be making as big a mistake as the turtledove makes when it captures a buzzing insect (another meaning of "buzzard").
2. Lose your claim to a coat of arms (sign of noble status); loosen your grip on me.

220	PETRUCCIO	A herald,° Kate? O, put me in thy books [3]	*An authority on heraldry*
	KATHERINE	What is your crest[4]—a coxcomb?[5]	
	PETRUCCIO	A combless cock,[6] so Kate will be my hen.	
	KATHERINE	No cock of mine. You crow too like a craven.°	*cock that won't fight*
	PETRUCCIO	Nay, come, Kate, come. You must not look so sour.	
225	KATHERINE	It is my fashion when I see a crab.°	*crab apple; sour person*
	PETRUCCIO	Why, here's no crab, and therefore look not sour.	
	KATHERINE	There is, there is.	
	PETRUCCIO	Then show it me.	
	KATHERINE	Had I a glass° I would.	*mirror*
	PETRUCCIO	What, you mean my face?	
230	KATHERINE	Well aimed,° of such a young one.	*A good guess*
	PETRUCCIO	Now, by Saint George,° I am too young for you.	*England's patron saint*
	KATHERINE	Yet you are withered.	
	PETRUCCIO	'Tis with cares.	
	KATHERINE	I care not.	
	PETRUCCIO	Nay, hear you, Kate. In sooth, you scape° not so.	*escape*
	KATHERINE	I chafe° you if I tarry. Let me go.	*annoy; inflame*
235	PETRUCCIO	No, not a whit. I find you passing gentle.	
		'Twas told me you were rough, and coy,° and sullen,	*disdainful*
		And now I find report a very liar,	
		For thou art pleasant, gamesome,° passing° courteous,	*playful / very*
		But slow in speech, yet sweet as springtime flowers.	
240		Thou canst not frown. Thou canst not look askance,°	*scornfully*
		Nor bite the lip, as angry wenches will,	
		Nor hast thou pleasure to be cross in talk,	
		But thou with mildness entertain'st thy wooers,	
		With gentle conference,° soft, and affable.	*conversation*
245		Why does the world report that Kate doth limp?	
		O sland'rous world! Kate like the hazel twig	
		Is straight and slender, and as brown in hue	
		As hazelnuts, and sweeter than the kernels.	
		O let me see thee walk. Thou dost not halt.°	*limp*
250	KATHERINE	Go, fool, and whom thou keep'st command.[7]	
	PETRUCCIO	Did ever Dian[8] so become a grove	
		As Kate this chamber with her princely gait?	
		O, be thou Dian, and let her be Kate,	
		And then let Kate be chaste and Dian sportful.°	*playful; amorous*
255	KATHERINE	Where did you study all this goodly speech?	
	PETRUCCIO	It is extempore, from my mother-wit.°	*native intelligence*
	KATHERINE	A witty mother, witless else° her son.	*otherwise*
	PETRUCCIO	Am I not wise?	
	KATHERINE	Yes, keep you warm.[9]	
	PETRUCCIO	Marry, so I mean, sweet Katherine, in thy bed.	
260		And therefore setting all this chat aside,	
		Thus in plain terms: your father hath consented	
		That you shall be my wife, your dowry 'greed on,	

3. Heralds kept books listing gentlemen and their coats of arms.
4. Image on a coat of arms; a fleshy ridge or comb on a rooster's head.
5. Court fool's cap (resembling a cock's comb or crest).
6. A cock with its comb cut down (and thought, there-fore, to be gentle), with a pun on "cock" as "penis."
7. And command your servants (not me).
8. Goddess of the hunt and of chastity.
9. Alluding to the proverbial phrase "enough wit to keep oneself warm," implying that the person has few brains.

And will you, nill you,° I will marry you.   *if you will or not*
Now, Kate, I am a husband for your turn,°   *needs*
265   For by this light, whereby I see thy beauty—
Thy beauty that doth make me like thee well—
Thou must be married to no man but me,
        Enter BAPTISTA, GREMIO, [*and*] TRANIO [*as Lucentio*]
For I am he am born to tame you, Kate,
And bring you from a wild Kate° to a Kate   *(punning on "wildcat")*
270   Conformable° as other household Kates.   *Submissive*
Here comes your father. Never make denial.
I must and will have Katherine to my wife.
BAPTISTA   Now, Signor Petruccio, how speed you with my daughter?
PETRUCCIO   How but well, sir, how but well?
275   It were impossible I should speed amiss.
BAPTISTA   Why, how now, daughter Katherine—in your dumps?°   *dejected*
KATHERINE   Call you me daughter? Now I promise you
You have showed a tender fatherly regard,
To wish me wed to one half-lunatic,
280   A madcap ruffian and a swearing Jack,
That thinks with oaths to face the matter out.°   *get his way brazenly*
PETRUCCIO   Father, 'tis thus: yourself and all the world
That talked of her have talked amiss of her.
If she be curst, it is for policy,°   *part of a scheme*
285   For she's not froward,° but modest as the dove.   *willful*
She is not hot, but temperate as the morn.
For patience she will prove a second Grissel,[1]
And Roman Lucrece[2] for her chastity.
And to conclude, we have 'greed so well together
290   That upon Sunday is the wedding day.
KATHERINE   I'll see thee hanged on Sunday first.
GREMIO   Hark, Petruccio, she says she'll see thee hanged first.
TRANIO   Is this your speeding?° Nay then, goodnight our part.[3]   *progress*
PETRUCCIO   Be patient, gentlemen. I choose her for myself.
295   If she and I be pleased, what's that to you?
'Tis bargained 'twixt us twain, being alone,
That she shall still be curst in company.
I tell you, 'tis incredible to believe
How much she loves me. O, the kindest Kate!
300   She hung about my neck, and kiss on kiss
She vied° so fast, protesting oath on oath,   *went me one better*
That in a twink° she won me to her love.   *instant*
O, you are novices. 'Tis a world° to see   *worth a world*
How tame, when men and women are alone,
305   A meacock° wretch can make the curstest shrew.   *timid*
Give me thy hand, Kate. I will unto Venice,
To buy apparel 'gainst° the wedding day.   *in preparation for*
Provide the feast, father, and bid the guests.
I will be sure my Katherine shall be fine.°   *richly dressed*
310   BAPTISTA   I know not what to say, but give me your hands.
God send you joy, Petruccio! 'Tis a match.

1. Griselda, proverbial for "wifely patience." Chaucer's   herself after being raped by Tarquin. Shakespeare's
Clerk's Tale offers one version of her story.   *Rape of Lucrece* recounts the story.
2. In Roman legend, a married woman who killed   3. Good-bye to our chances (of gaining Bianca).

GREMIO *and* TRANIO   Amen, say we. We will be witnesses.
PETRUCCIO   Father, and wife, and gentlemen, adieu.
   I will to Venice. Sunday comes apace.
315   We will have rings, and things, and fine array;
   And kiss me, Kate. We will be married o' Sunday.
         Exeunt PETRUCCIO *and* KATHERINE [*severally*]°   *separately*
GREMIO   Was ever match clapped up° so suddenly?   *settled*
BAPTISTA   Faith, gentlemen, now I play a merchant's part,
   And venture madly on a desperate mart.°   *risky bargain*
320 TRANIO   'Twas a commodity lay fretting by you.[4]
   'Twill bring you gain, or perish on the seas.
BAPTISTA   The gain I seek is quiet in the match.
GREMIO   No doubt but he hath got a quiet catch.
   But now, Baptista, to your younger daughter.
325   Now is the day we long have looked for.
   I am your neighbour, and was suitor first.
TRANIO   And I am one that love Bianca more
   Than words can witness, or your thoughts can guess.
GREMIO   Youngling, thou canst not love so dear° as I.   *deeply; expensively*
TRANIO   Greybeard, thy love doth freeze.
330 GREMIO   But thine doth fry.
   Skipper,° stand back. 'Tis age that nourisheth.   *Irresponsible youth*
TRANIO   But youth in ladies' eyes that flourisheth.
BAPTISTA   Content you, gentlemen. I will compound° this strife.   *settle*
   'Tis deeds must win the prize, and he of both°   *whichever of you*
335   That can assure my daughter greatest dower
   Shall have my Bianca's love.
   Say, Signor Gremio, what can you assure her?
GREMIO   First, as you know, my house within the city
   Is richly furnishèd with plate and gold,
340   Basins and ewers to lave° her dainty hands;   *wash*
   My hangings all of Tyrian[5] tapestry.
   In ivory coffers I have stuffed my crowns,°   *coins*
   In cypress chests my arras counterpoints,°   *tapestry bedcovers*
   Costly apparel, tents° and canopies,   *bed curtains*
345   Fine linen, Turkey cushions bossed° with pearl,   *embossed*
   Valance° of Venice gold in needlework,   *Fringe on bed drapery*
   Pewter, and brass, and all things that belongs
   To house or housekeeping. Then at my farm
   I have a hundred milch-kine° to the pail,   *dairy cows*
350   Six score fat oxen standing in my stalls,
   And all things answerable to° this portion.   *on the same scale as*
   Myself am struck° in years, I must confess,   *advanced*
   And if I die tomorrow this is hers,
   If whilst I live she will be only mine.
355 TRANIO   That 'only' came well in. Sir, list to me.
   I am my father's heir and only son.
   If I may have your daughter to my wife
   I'll leave her houses three or four as good,
   Within rich Pisa walls, as any one
360   Old Signor Gremio has in Padua,

---

4. It (that is, Katherine) was a piece of merchandise deteriorating in value or a sexually available woman fretting with irritation while in your possession.

5. Crimson or purple. (The Mediterranean city of Tyre was famous for dye of this color.)

Besides two thousand ducats by the year
Of fruitful land,[6] all which shall be her jointure.°   *marriage settlement*
What, have I pinched° you, Signor Gremio?   *distressed*

GREMIO   Two thousand ducats by the year of land—
365   My land amounts not to so much in all.
That she shall have; besides, an argosy°   *a merchant ship*
That now is lying in Marseilles road.°   *harbor*
What, have I choked you with an argosy?

TRANIO   Gremio, 'tis known my father hath no less
370   Than three great argosies, besides two galliasses°   *large cargo ships*
And twelve tight° galleys. These I will assure her,   *watertight*
And twice as much whate'er thou off 'rest next.

GREMIO   Nay, I have offered all. I have no more,
And she can have no more than all I have.
375   If you like me, she shall have me and mine.

TRANIO   Why then, the maid is mine from all the world.
By your firm promise Gremio is out-vied.°   *outbid*

BAPTISTA   I must confess your offer is the best,
And let° your father make her the assurance,   *provided*
380   She is your own. Else, you must pardon me,
If you should die before him, where's her dower?

TRANIO   That's but a cavil. He is old, I young.

GREMIO   And may not young men die as well as old?

BAPTISTA   Well, gentlemen,
385   I am thus resolved. On Sunday next, you know,
My daughter Katherine is to be married.
[*To* TRANIO] Now, on the Sunday following shall Bianca
Be bride to you, if you make this assurance;
If not, to Signor Gremio.
390   And so I take my leave, and thank you both.

GREMIO   Adieu, good neighbour.   *Exit* [BAPTISTA]
                    Now I fear thee not.
Sirrah, young gamester, your father were a fool
To give thee all, and in his waning age
Set foot under thy table.[7] Tut, a toy!°   *nonsense*
395   An old Italian fox is not so kind, my boy.   *Exit*

TRANIO   A vengeance on your crafty withered hide!
Yet I have faced it with a card of ten.[8]
'Tis in my head to do my master good.
I see no reason° but supposed Lucentio   *possible action*
400   Must get° a father called supposed Vincentio—   *beget; obtain*
And that's a wonder; fathers commonly
Do get their children, but in this case of wooing
A child shall get a sire, if I fail not of my cunning.   *Exit*

3.1

Enter LUCENTIO [*with books, as Cambio*], HORTENSIO
[*with a lute, as Licio*], *and* BIANCA

LUCENTIO   Fiddler, forbear. You grow too forward, sir.
Have you so soon forgot the entertainment

---

6. *Besides . . . land:* As well as fertile land that brings in
an income of 2,000 ducats (Venetian gold coins) each
year.
7. Become your dependent.

8. I have bluffed and won with a card of little value (a
ten spot).
3.1 Location: Baptista's house in Padua.

Her sister Katherine welcomed you withal?°   *with*
HORTENSIO   But, wrangling pedant, this Bianca is,
5   The patroness of heavenly harmony.
Then give me leave to have prerogative,°   *precedence*
And when in music we have spent an hour
Your lecture° shall have leisure for as much.   *lesson*
LUCENTIO   Preposterous[1] ass, that never read so far
10   To know the cause why music was ordained!
Was it not to refresh the mind of man
After his studies or his usual pain?°   *labor*
Then give me leave to read philosophy,
And while I pause, serve in° your harmony.   *serve up (contemptuous)*
15   HORTENSIO   Sirrah, I will not bear these braves° of thine.   *insults*
BIANCA   Why, gentlemen, you do me double wrong
To strive for that which resteth in my choice.
I am no breeching[2] scholar in the schools.
I'll not be tied to hours nor 'pointed times,
20   But learn my lessons as I please myself;
And to cut off all strife, here sit we down.
[*To* HORTENSIO] Take you your instrument, play you the whiles.°   *in the meantime*
His lecture will be done ere you have tuned.
HORTENSIO   You'll leave his lecture when I am in tune?[3]
25   LUCENTIO   That will be never. Tune your instrument.
          [HORTENSIO *tunes his lute.* LUCENTIO *opens a book*]
BIANCA   Where left we last?
LUCENTIO   Here, madam.
      [*Reads*]   'Hic ibat Simois, hic est Sigeia tellus,
              Hic steterat Priami regia celsa senis.[4]
30   BIANCA   Construe them.°   *Translate the lines*
LUCENTIO   'Hic ibat', as I told you before—'Simois', I am
Lucentio—'hic est', son unto Vincentio of Pisa—'Sigeia tellus',
disguised thus to get your love—'hic steterat', and that Lucen-
tio that comes a-wooing—'Priami', is my man Tranio—'regia',
35   bearing my port°—'celsa senis', that we might beguile the old   *taking my social position*
pantaloon.°   *foolish old man*
HORTENSIO   Madam, my instrument's in tune.
BIANCA   Let's hear. [HORTENSIO *plays*] O fie, the treble jars.°   *is discordant*
LUCENTIO   Spit in the hole,[5] man, and tune again.
          [HORTENSIO *tunes his lute again*]
40   BIANCA   Now let me see if I can construe it. 'Hic ibat Simois',
I know you not—'hic est Sigeia tellus', I trust you not—
'hic steterat Priami', take heed he hear us not—'regia', presume
not—'celsa senis', despair not.
HORTENSIO   Madam, 'tis now in tune.
LUCENTIO   All but the bass.
45   HORTENSIO   The bass is right, 'tis the base knave that jars.
      [*Aside*] How fiery and forward our pedant is!

---

1. Literally, putting last what should come first; reversing the natural order of things.
2. Youthful (in breeches); liable to be whipped
(breeched).
3. When my lute is in the proper pitch. Lucentio
responds with a pun on "in tune" as meaning "in harmony" with Bianca.

4. Latin lines from Penelope's letter to her husband
Ulysses in Ovid's *Heroides*: "Here flowed the Simois;
here is the Sigeian land; here stood old Priam's lofty
palace."
5. Moisten the lute's peg hole (to aid tuning). Lucentio speaks contemptuously and may not be giving serious advice.

Now, for my life, the knave doth court my love.
Pedascule,° I'll watch you better yet.   *Little pedant*
BIANCA [*to* LUCENTIO]   In time I may believe; yet, I mistrust.
50 LUCENTIO   Mistrust it not, for sure Aeacides[6]
Was Ajax, called so from his grandfather.
BIANCA   I must believe my master, else, I promise you,
I should be arguing still upon that doubt.
But let it rest. Now Licio, to you.
55 Good master, take it not unkindly, pray,
That I have been thus pleasant with you both.
HORTENSIO [*to* LUCENTIO]   You may go walk and give me leave°   *allow me leisure*
    awhile.
My lessons make no music in three parts.°   *for three voices*
LUCENTIO   Are you so formal,° sir? Well, I must wait.   *precise*
60 [*Aside*] And watch withal, for but° I be deceived   *unless*
Our fine musician groweth amorous.
HORTENSIO   Madam, before you touch the instrument
To learn the order of my fingering,
I must begin with rudiments of art,
65 To teach you gamut[7] in a briefer sort,°   *quicker way*
More pleasant, pithy, and effectual
Than hath been taught by any of my trade;
And there it is in writing, fairly drawn.
        [*He gives a paper*]
BIANCA   Why, I am past my gamut long ago.
70 HORTENSIO   Yet read the gamut of Hortensio.
BIANCA [*reads*]
    'Gam-ut I am, the ground° of all accord,   *lowest note; basis*
      A—re—to plead Hortensio's passion.
    B—mi—Bianca, take him for thy lord,
      C—fa, ut—that loves with all affection.
75   D—sol, re—one clef, two notes[8] have I,
    E—la, mi—show pity, or I die.'
Call you this gamut? Tut, I like it not.
Old fashions please me best. I am not so nice°   *capricious*
To change true rules for odd inventions.
        Enter a MESSENGER
80 MESSENGER   Mistress, your father prays you leave your books
And help to dress your sister's chamber up.
You know tomorrow is the wedding day.
BIANCA   Farewell, sweet masters both. I must be gone.
LUCENTIO   Faith, mistress, then I have no cause to stay.
        [*Exeunt* BIANCA, MESSENGER, *and* LUCENTIO]
85 HORTENSIO   But I have cause to pry into this pedant.
Methinks he looks as though he were in love.
Yet if thy thoughts, Bianca, be so humble°   *low*
To cast thy wand'ring eyes on every stale,°   *bait; lure*
Seize thee that list.[9] If once I find thee ranging,°   *unfaithful*
90 Hortensio will be quit with thee by changing.[1]   *Exit*

---

6. Aeacides, or Ajax, was named after his grandfather Aeacus. Lucentio pretends to continue the lesson.
7. A musical scale, named after its lowest note, "gamma-ut."

8. Referring perhaps to his one love and two identities.
9. Let anyone who wants you take you.
1. Will get even with you or get rid of you by finding another love.

3.2

Enter BAPTISTA, GREMIO, TRANIO [AS LUCENTIO],
KATHERINE, BIANCA, AND OTHERS, ATTENDANTS[1]

BAPTISTA [*to* TRANIO] Signor Lucentio, this is the 'pointed day
That Katherine and Petruccio should be married,
And yet we hear not of our son-in-law.
What will be said, what mockery will it be,

5 To want° the bridegroom when the priest attends   *lack*
To speak the ceremonial rites of marriage?
What says Lucentio to this shame of ours?

KATHERINE No shame but mine. I must forsooth be forced
To give my hand opposed against my heart

10 Unto a mad-brain rudesby° full of spleen,[2]   *unmannerly fellow*
Who wooed in haste and means to wed at leisure.
I told you, I, he was a frantic° fool,   *mad*
Hiding his bitter jests in blunt behaviour,
And to be noted for a merry man

15 He'll woo a thousand, 'point the day of marriage,
Make friends, invite them, and proclaim the banns,
Yet never means to wed where he hath wooed.
Now must the world point at poor Katherine
And say 'Lo, there is mad Petruccio's wife,

20 If it would please him come and marry her.'

TRANIO Patience, good Katherine, and Baptista, too.
Upon my life, Petruccio means but well.
Whatever fortune stays° him from his word,   *incident keeps*
Though he be blunt, I know him passing wise;

25 Though he be merry, yet withal he's honest.[3]

KATHERINE Would Katherine had never seen him, though.
Exit weeping

BAPTISTA Go, girl. I cannot blame thee now to weep.
For such an injury would vex a very saint,
Much more a shrew of thy impatient humour.
Enter BIONDELLO

30 BIONDELLO Master, master, news—old news, and such news as
you never heard of.

BAPTISTA Is it new and old too? How may that be?

BIONDELLO Why, is it not news to hear of Petruccio's coming?

BAPTISTA Is he come?

35 BIONDELLO Why, no, sir.

BAPTISTA What then?

BIONDELLO He is coming.

BAPTISTA When will he be here?

BIONDELLO When he stands where I am and sees you there.

40 TRANIO But say, what to thine old news?

BIONDELLO Why, Petruccio is coming in a new hat and an old
jerkin,° a pair of old breeches thrice-turned,[4] a pair of boots   *jacket*

3.2 Location: In front of Baptista's house.
1. Many editors include Lucentio, disguised as Cambio, among the characters who enter at this point, though he speaks no lines in the events leading up to and including Petruccio's arrival for his wedding. The Oxford editors feel that Lucentio only comes onstage when all the characters who enter at 3.2 leave to attend Katherine and Petruccio's wedding (3.2.116–20). They then mark a new scene, 3.3, when Lucentio enters with Tranio.

2. Caprice; impulsiveness. Contemporary medical theorists claimed that high and low spirits originated in the spleen.
3. Some critics find Tranio's familiarity with Petruccio improbable. Possibly these lines were originally meant to be spoken by Hortensio.
4. Turned inside out three times (to make them last longer).

that have been candle-cases,[5] one buckled, another laced, an
old rusty sword ta'en out of the town armoury with a broken
45 hilt, and chapeless,[6] with two broken points,[7] his horse hipped,°   *lame in the hips*
with an old mothy saddle and stirrups of no kindred,° besides,   *unmatched*
possessed with the glanders[8] and like to mose in the chine,[9]
troubled with the lampass,[1] infected with the fashions,° full   *farcins (small tumors)*
of windgalls,[2] sped with spavins,[3] rayed with the yellows,°   *disfigured by jaundice*
50 past cure of the fives,[4] stark spoiled with the staggers,[5] be-
gnawn with the bots,[6] weighed in the back° and shoulder-   *swaybacked*
shotten,[7] near-legged before[8] and with a half-cheeked° bit and   *improperly attached*
a headstall[9] of sheep's leather which, being restrained° to   *tightened*
keep him from stumbling, hath been often burst and now
55 repaired with knots, one girth° six times pieced,° and a woman's   *saddle strap / mended*
crupper of velour[1] which hath two letters for her name fairly set
down in studs, and here and there pieced with packthread.°   *twine*
BAPTISTA Who comes with him?
BIONDELLO O sir, his lackey, for all the world caparisoned° like   *outfitted*
60 the horse, with a linen stock° on one leg and a kersey boot-   *stocking*
hose[2] on the other, gartered with a red and blue list;° an old   *strip of cloth*
hat, and the humour of forty fancies pricked in't for a
feather[3]—a monster, a very monster in apparel, and not like a
Christian footboy or a gentleman's lackey.
65 TRANIO 'Tis some odd humour pricks° him to this fashion;   *incites, urges*
Yet oftentimes he goes but mean-apparelled.
BAPTISTA I am glad he's come, howsoe'er he comes.
BIONDELLO Why, sir, he comes not.
BAPTISTA Didst thou not say he comes?
70 BIONDELLO Who? That Petruccio came?
BAPTISTA Ay, that Petruccio came.
BIONDELLO No, sir. I say his horse comes with him on his back.
BAPTISTA Why, that's all one.°   *the same thing*
BIONDELLO   Nay, by Saint Jamy,
75   I hold° you a penny,   *bet*
A horse and a man
Is more than one,
And yet not many.

Enter PETRUCCIO *and* GRUMIO[*fantastically dressed*]

PETRUCCIO Come, where be these gallants? Who's at home?
80 BAPTISTA You are welcome, sir.
PETRUCCIO And yet I come not well.
BAPTISTA And yet you halt° not.   *limp*

5. In other words, discarded and used to store old candle ends.
6. Without the metal tip that protects the sword's
point.
7. With two laces that don't hold up his hose; with two
points (instead of one) on his broken sword.
8. The first in a catalogue of horse diseases, most of
which are described in Gervase Markham's *Discourse of
Horsemanship* (1593). The glanders caused swellings
and nasal discharge.
9. Obscure phrase, probably meaning the horse was
apt to suffer discharge from the nostrils, indicating the
last stage of glanders.
1. A disease characterized by swellings in the mouth.
2. Soft tumors usually appearing on the fetlock, so

called because they were thought to contain air.
3. Rendered useless by swelling of the leg joints.
4. Swelling of glands below the ears.
5. A disease causing loss of balance.
6. Eaten by intestinal worms.
7. With sprained shoulders.
8. With knock-kneed forelegs.
9. The part of the bridle that fits around the horse's
head. Sheepskin would be inferior to the animal skins
normally used.
1. *crupper*: strap that passes under a horse's tail to keep
the saddle straight, *velour*: velvet.
2. A coarse wool stocking.
3. Possibly an absurdly fanciful decoration attached to
the hat instead of a feather.

TRANIO   Not so well apparelled as I wish you were.

PETRUCCIO   Were it not better I should rush in thus—

85   But where is Kate? Where is my lovely bride?
         How does my father? Gentles,[4] methinks you frown.
         And wherefore gaze this goodly company
         As if they saw some wondrous monument,
         Some comet or unusual prodigy?

90 BAPTISTA   Why, sir, you know this is your wedding day.
         First were we sad, fearing you would not come;
         Now sadder that you come so unprovided.°   *unprepared*
         Fie, doff this habit,° shame to your estate,°   *outfit / social place*
         An eyesore to our solemn festival.

95 TRANIO   And tell us what occasion of import
         Hath all so long detained you from your wife
         And sent you hither so unlike yourself?

PETRUCCIO   Tedious it were to tell, and harsh to hear
         Sufficeth I am come to keep my word,

100   Though in some part enforcèd to digress,°   *deviate from my plan*
         Which at more leisure I will so excuse
         As you shall well be satisfied withal.
         But where is Kate? I stay too long from her.
         The morning wears, 'tis time we were at church.

105 TRANIO   See not your bride in these unreverent° robes.   *disrespectful*
         Go to my chamber, put on clothes of mine.

PETRUCCIO   Not I, believe me. Thus I'll visit her.

BAPTISTA   But thus, I trust, you will not marry her.

PETRUCCIO   Good sooth,° even thus. Therefore ha' done with words.   *Yes indeed*

110   To me she's married, not unto my clothes.
         Could I repair what she will wear° in me   *wear out (in sex)*
         As I can change these poor accoutrements,
         'Twere well for Kate and better for myself.
         But what a fool am I to chat with you

115   When I should bid good morrow to my bride,
         And seal the title with a lovely° kiss!   *Exit* [*with* GRUMIO]   *loving*

TRANIO   He hath some meaning in his mad attire.
         We will persuade him, be it possible,
         To put on better ere he go to church.   [*Exit with* GREMIO]

120 BAPTISTA   I'll after him, and see the event° of this.   *Exeunt*   *outcome*

3.3

[*Enter* LUCENTIO *as Cambio, and* TRANIO *as Lucentio*]

TRANIO   But, sir, to love concerneth us to add[1]
         Her father's liking, which to bring to pass,
         As I before imparted to your worship,
         I am to get a man—whate'er he be

5   It skills° not much, we'll fit him to our turn—   *matters*
         And he shall be Vincentio of Pisa,
         And make assurance here in Padua
         Of greater sums than I have promisèd.

---

4. The polite term of address to men and women of the gentry.

3.3 Location: Scene continues.

1. To the love between Bianca and Lucentio it is necessary for us to add.

So shall you quietly enjoy your hope,°　　　　　　*what you hope for*
10　And marry sweet Bianca with consent.
　　LUCENTIO　Were it not that my fellow schoolmaster
　　　　Doth watch Bianca's steps so narrowly,
　　　　'Twere good, methinks, to steal our marriage,°　　　　*elope*
　　　　Which once performed, let all the world say no,
15　　　I'll keep mine own, despite of all the world.
　　TRANIO　That by degrees we mean to look into,
　　　　And watch our vantage° in this business.　　　　　　*opportunity*
　　　　We'll overreach the greybeard Gremio,
　　　　The narrow-prying° father Minola,　　　　　　*overly suspicious*
20　　　The quaint° musician, amorous Licio,　　　　　*skillful; crafty*
　　　　All for my master's sake, Lucentio.
　　　　　　Enter GREMIO
　　　　Signor Gremio, came you from the church?
　　GREMIO　As willingly as e'er I came from school.
　　TRANIO　And is the bride and bridegroom coming home?
25　GREMIO　A bridegroom, say you? 'Tis a groom° indeed—　　*crude, lower-class man*
　　　　A grumbling groom, and that the girl shall find.
　　TRANIO　Curster° than she? Why, 'tis impossible.　　　*More cantankerous*
　　GREMIO　Why, he's a devil, a devil, a very fiend.
　　TRANIO　Why, she's a devil, a devil, the devil's dam.°　　*mother*
30　GREMIO　Tut, she's a lamb, a dove, a fool to him.[2]
　　　　I'll tell you, Sir Lucentio: when the priest
　　　　Should ask if Katherine should be his wife,
　　　　'Ay, by Gog's woun's,'[3] quoth he, and swore so loud
　　　　That all amazed the priest let fall the book,
35　　　And as he stooped again to take it up
　　　　This mad-brained bridegroom took° him such a cuff　　*gave*
　　　　That down fell priest, and book, and book, and priest.
　　　　'Now take them up,' quoth he, 'if any list.'°　　　*choose*
　　TRANIO　What said the vicar when he rose again?
40　GREMIO　Trembled and shook, forwhy° he° stamped and swore　*because / (Petruccio)*
　　　　As if the vicar meant to cozen[4] him.
　　　　But after many ceremonies done
　　　　He calls for wine. 'A health,' quoth he, as if
　　　　He had been aboard,° carousing to his mates　　　*(a ship)*
45　　　After a storm; quaffed off the muscatel[5]
　　　　And threw the sops all in the sexton's face,
　　　　Having no other reason
　　　　But that his beard grew thin and hungerly°　　*sparsely; as if hungry*
　　　　And seemed to ask him sops as he was drinking.
50　　　This done, he took the bride about the neck
　　　　And kissed her lips with such a clamorous smack
　　　　That at the parting all the church did echo,
　　　　And I seeing this came thence for very shame,
　　　　And after me, I know, the rout° is coming.　　　　*crowd*
55　　　Such a mad marriage never was before.
　　　　　　Music plays
　　　　Hark, hark, I hear the minstrels play.

---

2. A good-natured innocent compared with him.
3. By God's (Christ's) wounds (a common oath).
4. Cheat (by not performing a legally binding ceremony).

5. Wine with small cakes, or "sops," soaked in it, traditionally drunk by the newly married couple and their
guests.

Enter PETRUCCIO, KATHERINE, BIANCA, HORTENSIO
[*as Licio*], BAPTISTA, [GRUMIO, *and others*, attendants]

PETRUCCIO   Gentlemen and friends, I thank you for your pains.
I know you think to dine with me today,
And have prepared great store of wedding cheer.°   *food and drink*
60   But so it is my haste doth call me hence,
And therefore here I mean to take my leave.
BAPTISTA   Is't possible you will away tonight?
PETRUCCIO   I must away today, before night come.
Make° it no wonder. If you knew my business,   *Consider*
65   You would entreat me rather go than stay.
And, honest° company, I thank you all   *worthy*
That have beheld me give away myself
To this most patient, sweet, and virtuous wife.
Dine with my father, drink a health to me,
70   For I must hence; and farewell to you all.
TRANIO   Let us entreat you stay till after dinner.
PETRUCCIO   It may not be.
GREMIO   Let me entreat you.
PETRUCCIO   It cannot be.
KATHERINE   Let me entreat you.
PETRUCCIO   I am content.
KATHERINE   Are you content to stay?
75   PETRUCCIO   I am content you shall entreat me stay,
But yet not stay, entreat me how you can.
KATHERINE   Now, if you love me, stay.
PETRUCCIO   Grumio, my horse.
GRUMIO   Ay, sir, they be ready. The oats have eaten the horses.[6]
KATHERINE   Nay, then, do what thou canst, I will not go today,
80   No, nor tomorrow—not till I please myself.
The door is open, sir, there lies your way.
You may be jogging whiles your boots are green.[7]
For me, I'll not be gone till I please myself.
'Tis like you'll prove a jolly,° surly groom,   *an arrogant*
85   That take it on you at the first so roundly.[8]
PETRUCCIO   O Kate, content thee. Prithee, be not angry.
KATHERINE   I will be angry. What hast thou to do?[9]
Father, be quiet. He shall stay° my leisure.   *await*
GREMIO   Ay, marry, sir. Now it begins to work.
90   KATHERINE   Gentlemen, forward to the bridal dinner.
I see a woman may be made a fool
If she had not a spirit to resist.
PETRUCCIO   They shall go forward, Kate, at thy command.
Obey the bride, you that attend on her.
95   Go to the feast, revel and domineer,°   *feast sumptuously*
Carouse full measure to her maidenhead.
Be mad and merry, or go hang yourselves.
But for my bonny Kate, she must with me.
Nay, look not big,° nor stamp, nor stare, nor fret.   *defiant*

---

6. Either Grumio gets it the wrong way around, or he
is joking about the great quantity of oats the horses
have eaten.
7. You can be off now while your boots are new

("green"). Proverbial expression for getting an early
start or getting rid of an unwelcome guest.
8. That takes charge at the outset so outspokenly.
9. What business is it of yours?

100   I will be master of what is mine own.
    She is my goods, my chattels. She is my house,
    My household-stuff, my field, my barn,
    My horse, my ox, my ass, my anything,
    And here she stands, touch her whoever dare.[1]
105   I'll bring mine action on° the proudest he   *attack; sue (in court)*
    That stops my way in Padua. Grumio,
    Draw forth thy weapon, we are beset with thieves.
    Rescue thy mistress if thou be a man.
    Fear not, sweet wench. They shall not touch thee, Kate.
110   I'll buckler° thee against a million.   *shield*
             Exeunt PETRUCCIO, KATHERINE [*and* GRUMIO]
BAPTISTA   Nay, let them go—a couple of quiet ones!
GREMIO   Went they not quickly I should die with laughing.
TRANIO   Of all mad matches never was the like.
LUCENTIO   Mistress, what's your opinion of your sister?
115 BIANCA   That being mad herself she's madly mated.
GREMIO   I warrant him, Petruccio is Kated.[2]
BAPTISTA   Neighbours and friends, though bride and bridegroom wants°   *are missing*
    For to supply° the places at the table,   *To fill*
    You know there wants no junkets° at the feast.   *sweetmeats*
120   Lucentio, you shall supply the bridegroom's place,
    And let Bianca take her sister's room.
TRANIO   Shall sweet Bianca practise how to bride it?
BAPTISTA   She shall, Lucentio. Come, gentlemen, let's go.
                     Exeunt

4.1

      Enter GRUMIO
GRUMIO   Fie, fie on all tired jades,° on all mad masters, and all   *worn-out horses*
    foul° ways. Was ever man so beaten? Was ever man so rayed?°   *muddy / dirtied*
    Was ever man so weary? I am sent before to make a fire, and
    they are coming after to warm them. Now were not I a little
5   pot and soon hot,[1] my very lips might freeze to my teeth, my
    tongue to the roof of my mouth, my heart in my belly ere
    I should come by a fire to thaw me. But I with blowing the fire
    shall warm myself, for considering the weather, a taller[2] man
    than I will take cold. Holla! Hoa, Curtis!
      Enter CURTIS
10 CURTIS   Who is that calls so coldly?
GRUMIO   A piece of ice. If thou doubt it, thou mayst slide from
    my shoulder to my heel with no greater a run but my head and
    my neck. A fire, good Curtis!
CURTIS   Is my master and his wife coming, Grumio?
15 GRUMIO   O ay, Curtis, ay, and therefore fire, fire! Cast on no
    water.[3]
CURTIS   Is she so hot a shrew as she's reported?

---

1. Petruccio warns others to leave Kate alone. In cataloguing the ways she is one of his possessions, he alludes to the Tenth Commandment, which forbids coveting a neighbor's wife or property.
2. Mated with a "Kate"; afflicted with Kate (imagined as a disease).
4.1 Location: Petruccio's country house.

1. Proverbial for a small person who quickly becomes angry.
2. Punning on "taller" as meaning "sturdier."
3. Alluding to the popular song "Scotland's Burning," in which the words "Fire, fire" are followed by "Cast on water, cast on water."

GRUMIO   She was, good Curtis, before this frost; but thou
know'st, winter tames man, woman, and beast, for it hath
20   tamed my old master, and my new mistress, and myself, fellow Curtis.

CURTIS   Away, you three-inch° fool. I am no beast.   *short*

GRUMIO   Am I but three inches? Why, thy horn⁴ is a foot, and
so long am I, at the least. But wilt thou make a fire, or shall I
25   complain on thee to our mistress, whose hand—she being
now at hand—thou shalt soon feel to thy cold comfort, for
being slow in thy hot office.°   *fire-making duties*

CURTIS   I prithee, good Grumio, tell me—how goes the world?

GRUMIO   A cold world, Curtis, in every office but thine. And
30   therefore fire, do thy duty, and have thy duty,° for my master   *take your reward*
and mistress are almost frozen to death.

CURTIS   There's fire ready, and therefore, good Grumio, the
news.

GRUMIO   Why, 'Jack boy, ho boy!',⁵ and as much news as wilt thou.

35 CURTIS   Come, you are so full of cony-catching.⁶

GRUMIO   Why, therefore fire, for I have caught extreme cold.
Where's the cook? Is supper ready, the house trimmed, rushes
strewed,⁷ cobwebs swept, the servingmen in their new fustian,°   *coarse cloth*
the white stockings, and every officer° his wedding garment   *servant*
40   on? Be the Jacks fair within, the Jills fair without,⁸ the carpets°   *table coverings*
laid, and everything in order?

CURTIS   All ready, and therefore, I pray thee, news.

GRUMIO   First, know my horse is tired, my master and mistress
fallen out.

45 CURTIS   How?

GRUMIO   Out of their saddles into the dirt, and thereby hangs a
tale.

CURTIS   Let's ha't, good Grumio.

GRUMIO   Lend thine ear.

50 CURTIS   Here.

GRUMIO   [cuffing him]   There.

CURTIS   This 'tis to feel a tale, not to hear a tale.

GRUMIO   And therefore 'tis called a sensible tale,⁹ and this cuff
was but to knock at your ear and beseech listening. Now I
55   begin. Inprimis,° we came down a foul° hill, my master riding   *First / muddy*
behind my mistress.

CURTIS   Both of° one horse?   *on*

GRUMIO   What's that to thee?

CURTIS   Why, a horse.

60 GRUMIO   Tell thou the tale. But hadst thou not crossed° me   *interrupted*
thou shouldst have heard how her horse fell and she under
her horse; thou shouldst have heard in how miry a place, how
she was bemoiled,° how he left her with the horse upon her,   *covered with mud*
how he beat me because her horse stumbled, how she waded
65   through the dirt to pluck him off me, how he swore, how she
prayed that never prayed before, how I cried, how the horses
ran away, how her bridle was burst, how I lost my crupper,

---

4. The proverbial sign of a cuckold; an erect penis. Grumio implies that he is "long" enough to cuckold Curtis.
5. A line from another popular song.
6. Trickery, with a play on the "catches," or songs of

which Grumio is fond. A cony is a rabbit.
7. Scattered on the floor.
8. Jacks and Jills were manservants and maidservants; also leather drinking vessels and metal drinking vessels.
9. Reasonable; capable of being felt.

with many things of worthy memory which now shall die in
oblivion, and thou return unexperienced° to thy grave.   *ignorant; unknowing*
70 CURTIS By this reckoning he is more shrew than she.
GRUMIO Ay, and that thou and the proudest of you all shall find
when he comes home. But what° talk I of this? Call forth   *why*
Nathaniel, Joseph, Nicholas, Philip, Walter, Sugarsop, and
the rest. Let their heads be sleekly combed, their blue coats[1]
75 brushed, and their garters of an indifferent° knit. Let them   *ordinary; a matching*
curtsy with their left legs and not presume to touch a hair of
my master's horse-tail till they kiss their hands.[2] Are they all
ready?
CURTIS They are.
80 GRUMIO Call them forth.
CURTIS [calling] Do you hear, ho? You must meet my master to
countenance[3] my mistress.
GRUMIO Why, she hath a face of her own.
CURTIS Who knows not that?
85 GRUMIO Thou, it seems, that calls for company to countenance
her.
CURTIS I call them forth to credit[4] her.
        Enter four or five servingmen
GRUMIO Why, she comes to borrow nothing of them.
NATHANIEL Welcome home, Grumio!
90 PHILIP How now, Grumio?
JOSEPH What, Grumio?
NICHOLAS Fellow Grumio!
NATHANIEL How now, old lad!
GRUMIO Welcome you, how now you, what you, fellow you, and
95 thus much for greeting. Now, my spruce° companions, is all   *smartly dressed*
ready and all things neat?
NATHANIEL All things is ready. How near is our master?
GRUMIO E'en at hand, alighted by this, and therefore be not—
Cock's° passion, silence! I hear my master.   *God's (a common oath)*
        Enter PETRUCCIO and KATHERINE
100 PETRUCCIO Where be these knaves? What, no man at door
To hold my stirrup nor to take my horse?
Where is Nathaniel, Gregory, Philip?
ALL SERVANTS Here, here sir, here sir.
PETRUCCIO Here sir, here sir, here sir, here sir!
105 You logger-headed° and unpolished grooms,   *stupid*
What! No attendance! No regard! No duty!
Where is the foolish knave I sent before?
GRUMIO Here, sir, as foolish as I was before.
PETRUCCIO You peasant swain,° you whoreson,° malthorse   *farm laborer / bastard*
drudge,[5]
110 Did I not bid thee meet me in the park[6]
And bring along these rascal knaves with thee?
GRUMIO Nathaniel's coat, sir, was not fully made,
And Gabriel's pumps° were all unpinked° i'th' heel.   *shoes / not ornamented*
There was no link[7] to colour Peter's hat,

1. The usual servant uniform.
2. A greeting signifying inordinate submissiveness.
3. Greet, pay respects to; with a pun in the next line on
"countenance" as meaning "face."
4. Honor, with pun in next line on "credit" as meaning
"offer financial assistance."

5. Stupid, menial worker. The slow, heavy malt horse
was used to grind malt by turning a treadmill.
6. A piece of ground comprising woodland and pasture
attached to a country house and used for recreation.
7. Torch, the smoke of which was used to blacken shoes.

115 And Walter's dagger was not come from sheathing.°   *having a sheath fixed*
There were none fine but Adam, Ralph, and Gregory.
The rest were ragged, old, and beggarly.
Yet as they are, here are they come to meet you.
PETRUCCIO   Go, rascals, go and fetch my supper in.
                                                      Exeunt servants
120 [*Sings*]   'Where is the life that late I led?
                        Where are those—'[8]
Sit down, Kate, and welcome. Soud, soud, soud, soud.[9]
                Enter servants with supper
Why, when, I say?—Nay, good sweet Kate, be merry.—
Off with my boots, you rogues, you villains. When?
125 [*Sings*]   'It was the friar of orders gray,
                        As he forth walkèd on his way.'[1]
Out, you rogue, you pluck my foot awry.
[*Kicking a servant*] Take that, and mend the plucking of the other.
Be merry, Kate. [*Calling*] Some water, here. What, hoa!
                Enter one with water
130 Where's my spaniel Troilus? Sirrah, get you hence,
And bid my cousin Ferdinand come hither—
One, Kate, that you must kiss and be acquainted with.
[*Calling*] Where are my slippers? Shall I have some water?
Come, Kate, and wash, and welcome heartily.
                [*A servant drops water*]
135 You whoreson villain, will you let it fall?
KATHERINE   Patience, I pray you, 'twas a fault unwilling.
PETRUCCIO   A whoreson, beetle-headed,° flap-eared knave.   *thick-headed*
Come, Kate, sit down, I know you have a stomach.°   *an appetite; temper*
Will you give thanks, sweet Kate, or else shall I?
What's this—mutton?
FIRST SERVINGMAN   Ay.
PETRUCCIO   Who brought it?
140 PETER   I.
PETRUCCIO   'Tis burnt, and so is all the meat.
What dogs are these? Where is the rascal cook?
How durst you villains bring it from the dresser°   *cook; sideboard*
And serve it thus to me that love it not?
145 There, [*throwing food*] take it to you, trenchers,° cups, and all,   *plates*
You heedless jolt-heads° and unmannered slaves.   *careless blockheads*
What, do you grumble? I'll be with you straight.
                [*He chases the servants away*]
KATHERINE   I pray you, husband, be not so disquiet.
The meat was well, if you were so contented.
150 PETRUCCIO   I tell thee, Kate, 'twas burnt and dried away,
And I expressly am forbid to touch it,
For it engenders choler,[2] planteth anger,
And better 'twere that both of us did fast,
Since of ourselves° ourselves are choleric,   *by our natures*
155 Than feed it with such overroasted flesh.

8. Probably a fragment of a ballad, now lost, lamenting
a newlywed's loss of freedom.
9. An expression of impatience.
1. Another fragment of a lost song, perhaps one of the
many songs about a friar's seduction of a nun.
2. It causes anger. An excess of the choleric humor was
believed to provoke anger.

Be patient, tomorrow't shall be mended,
And for this night we'll fast for company.°   *together*
Come, I will bring thee to thy bridal chamber.   *Exeunt*
         Enter servants severally

NATHANIEL   Peter, didst ever see the like?
160   PETER   He kills her in her own humour.[3]
         Enter CURTIS, *a servant*
GRUMIO   Where is he?
CURTIS   In her chamber,
Making a sermon of continency° to her,   *on self-control*
And rails, and swears, and rates,° that she, poor soul,   *scolds*
165   Knows not which way to stand, to look, to speak,
And sits as one new risen from a dream.
Away, away, for he is coming hither.   [*Exeunt*]
         Enter PETRUCCIO
PETRUCCIO   Thus have I politicly° begun my reign,   *cunningly*
And 'tis my hope to end successfully.
170   My falcon[4] now is sharp° and passing° empty,   *hungry / extremely*
And till she stoop[5] she must not be full-gorged,°   *fully fed*
For then she never looks upon her lure.°   *falconer's bait*
Another way I have to man my haggard,°   *tame my female hawk*
To make her come and know her keeper's call—
175   That is, to watch her° as we watch these kites°   *keep her awake / hawks*
That bate and beat,[6] and will not be obedient.
She ate no meat today, nor none shall eat.
Last night she slept not, nor tonight she shall not.
As with the meat, some undeservèd fault
180   I'll find about the making of the bed,
And here I'll fling the pillow, there the bolster,
This way the coverlet, another way the sheets,
Ay, and amid this hurly I intend°   *will pretend*
That all is done in reverent care of her,
185   And in conclusion she shall watch° all night,   *stay awake*
And if she chance to nod I'll rail and brawl
And with the clamour keep her still awake.
This is a way to kill a wife with kindness,
And thus I'll curb her mad and headstrong humour.
190   He that knows better how to tame a shrew,
Now let him speak. 'Tis charity to show.°   *Exit*   (*his methods*)

4.2
         Enter TRANIO [*as Lucentio,*] *and* HORTENSIO [*as Licio*]
TRANIO   Is't possible, friend Licio, that Mistress Bianca
Doth fancy any other but Lucentio?
I tell you, sir, she bears me fair in hand.°   *leads me on*
HORTENSIO   Sir, to satisfy you in what I have said,
5   Stand by, and mark the manner of his teaching.
         [*They stand aside.*]
         Enter BIANCA [*and* LUCENTIO *as Cambio*]
LUCENTIO   Now, mistress, profit you in what you read?
BIANCA   What, master, read you? First resolve° me that.   *answer*

---

3. He subdues her choleric humor by outdoing her in bad temper.
4. In what follows, Petruccio likens his methods of disciplining Katherine to the training of a wild hawk.
5. Fly to the bait; submit to my authority.
6. That flutter and flap their wings (instead of settling on the falconer's fist).
4.2 Location: Padua, in front of Baptista's house.

LUCENTIO   I read that I profess,° *The Art to Love.*[1]   *what I practice*
BIANCA   And may you prove, sir, master of your art.
10   LUCENTIO   While you, sweet dear, prove mistress of my heart.
     [*They stand aside*]
     HORTENSIO   Quick proceeders,[2] marry! Now tell me, I pray,
       You that durst swear that your mistress Bianca
       Loved none in the world so well as Lucentio.
     TRANIO   O despiteful° love, unconstant womankind.   *cruel*
15   I tell thee, Licio, this is wonderful.°   *astonishing*
     HORTENSIO   Mistake no more, I am not Licio,
       Nor a musician as I seem to be,
       But one that scorn to live in this disguise
       For such a one° as leaves a gentleman   *(Bianca)*
20   And makes a god of such a cullion.°   *base fellow*
       Know, sir, that I am called Hortensio.
     TRANIO   Signor Hortensio, I have often heard
       Of your entire° affection to Bianca,   *sincere*
       And since mine eyes are witness of her lightness°   *sexual infidelity*
25   I will with you, if you be so contented,
       Forswear Bianca and her love for ever.
     HORTENSIO   See how they kiss and court. Signor Lucentio,
       Here is my hand, and here I firmly vow
       Never to woo her more, but do forswear her
30   As one unworthy all the former favours
       That I have fondly° flattered her withal.   *foolishly*
     TRANIO   And here I take the like unfeignèd oath
       Never to marry with her, though she would entreat.
       Fie on her, see how beastly° she doth court him!   *lewdly*
35   HORTENSIO   Would all the world but he had quite forsworn.[3]
       For me, that I may surely keep mine oath
       I will be married to a wealthy widow
       Ere three days pass, which hath as long loved me
       As I have loved this proud disdainful haggard.°   *intractable woman; hawk*
40   And so farewell, Signor Lucentio.
       Kindness in women, not their beauteous looks,
       Shall win my love; and so I take my leave,
       In resolution as I swore before.   [*Exit*]
     TRANIO   Mistress Bianca, bless you with such grace
45   As 'longeth° to a lover's blessèd case.°   *belongs / state*
       Nay, I have ta'en you napping, gentle love,
       And have forsworn you with Hortensio.
     BIANCA   Tranio, you jest. But have you both forsworn me?
     TRANIO   Mistress, we have.
     LUCENTIO   Then we are rid of Licio.
50   TRANIO   I'faith, he'll have a lusty° widow now,   *lively; lustful*
       That shall be wooed and wedded in a day.
     BIANCA   God give him joy.
     TRANIO   Ay, and he'll tame her.
     BIANCA   He says so, Tranio.
55   TRANIO   Faith, he is gone unto the taming-school.

1. Ovid's *Ars Amatoria*, in which the poet calls himself
the "Professor of Love" and treats erotic love as a
science.
2. Taking up the allusion to a university degree implicit
in Bianca's "master of your art," Hortensio puns on

"proceeding" from a bachelor's to a master's degree.
3. I wish that everyone but Cambio had given her over
(so that she will be left an old maid as she deserves;
Hortensio apparently assumes that Bianca would never
marry a poor musician).

BIANCA   The taming-school—what, is there such a place?

TRANIO   Ay, mistress, and Petruccio is the master,
That teacheth tricks eleven-and-twenty long[4]
To tame a shrew and charm her chattering tongue.[5]

Enter BIONDELLO

60   BIONDELLO   O, master, master, I have watched so long
That I am dog-weary, but at last I spied
An ancient angel[6] coming down the hill
Will serve the turn.

TRANIO   What is he, Biondello?

BIONDELLO   Master, a marcantant[7] or a pedant,°   *schoolmaster*
65   I know not what, but formal in apparel,
In gait and countenance surely like a father.

LUCENTIO   And what of him, Tranio?

TRANIO   If he be credulous and trust my tale,
I'll make him glad to seem° Vincentio   *pretend to be*
70   And give assurance to Baptista Minola
As if he were the right Vincentio.
Take in your love, and then let me alone.

[*Exeunt* LUCENTIO *and* BIANCA]

Enter a PEDANT[8]

PEDANT   God save you, sir.

TRANIO   And you, sir. You are welcome.
Travel you farre on, or are you at the farthest?

75   PEDANT   Sir, at the farthest for a week or two,
But then up farther and as far as Rome,
And so to Tripoli,[9] if God lend me life.

TRANIO   What countryman, I pray?

PEDANT   Of Mantua.

TRANIO   Of Mantua, sir? Marry, God forbid,
80   And come to Padua careless of your life!

PEDANT   My life, sir? How, I pray? For that goes hard.°   *is difficult to deal with*

TRANIO   'Tis death for anyone in Mantua
To come to Padua. Know you not the cause?
Your ships are stayed° at Venice, and the Duke,   *detained*
85   For private quarrel 'twixt your Duke and him,
Hath published and proclaimed it openly.
'Tis marvel, but that you are but newly come,
You might have heard it else proclaimed about.[1]

PEDANT   Alas, sir, it is worse for me than so,°   *my plight is even worse*
90   For I have bills for money by exchange[2]
From Florence, and must here deliver them.

TRANIO   Well, sir, to do you courtesy
This will I do, and this I will advise you.
First tell me, have you ever been at Pisa?

95   PEDANT   Ay, sir, in Pisa have I often been,

---

4. Who teaches tricks that are exactly appropriate or of just the right number. An allusion to the card game one-and-thirty, in which the object is to accumulate exactly thirty-one points. See note to 1.2.31.
5. Tranio's apparent knowledge of Hortensio's plans is puzzling and may be an indication that some text has been lost.
6. Worthy old man. Punning on "angel" as meaning both "valuable gold coin" and "divine messenger." The coin had a picture of the archangel Michael on it.

7. Biondello's version of *mercatante*, the Italian word for "merchant."
8. Because this character is said (at line 90) to have "bills for money," some editors have designated him a "merchant" like the corresponding character in George Gascoigne's comedy *Supposes* (1566).
9. The north African trading center or the city in Syria.
1. *but that . . . about:* if you hadn't just arrived, you would have heard it announced everywhere.
2. Promissory notes that the bearer could exchange for cash.

Pisa renownèd for grave citizens.
TRANIO   Among them know you one Vincentio?
PEDANT   I know him not, but I have heard of him,
A merchant of incomparable wealth.
100   TRANIO   He is my father, sir, and sooth to say,
In count'nance somewhat doth resemble you.
BIONDELLO [aside]   As much as an apple doth an oyster, and all
one.°   but no matter
TRANIO   To save your life in this extremity
105   This favour will I do you for his sake,
And think it not the worst of all your fortunes
That you are like to Sir Vincentio.
His name and credit° shall you undertake,°   social status / assume
And in my house you shall be friendly lodged.
110   Look that you take upon you° as you should.   act your part
You understand me, sir? So shall you stay
Till you have done your business in the city.
If this be courtesy, sir, accept of it.
PEDANT   O sir, I do, and will repute° you ever   consider
115   The patron of my life and liberty.
TRANIO   Then go with me to make the matter good.
This, by the way, I let you understand—
My father is here looked for every day
To pass assurance° of a dower in marriage   convey legal guarantee
120   'Twixt me and one Baptista's daughter here.
In all these circumstances I'll instruct you.
Go with me to clothe you as becomes you.   *Exeunt*

4.3

Enter KATHERINE *and* GRUMIO

GRUMIO   No, no, forsooth. I dare not, for my life.
KATHERINE   The more my wrong, the more his spite appears.[1]
What, did he marry me to famish me?
Beggars that come unto my father's door
5   Upon entreaty have a present° alms,   immediate
If not, elsewhere they meet with charity.
But I, who never knew how to entreat,
Nor never needed that I should entreat,
Am starved for meat, giddy for lack of sleep,
10   With oaths kept waking and with brawling fed,
And that which spites° me more than all these wants,   vexes
He does it under name of perfect love,
As who should say° if I should sleep or eat   As if to say
'Twere deadly sickness, or else present° death.   instant
15   I prithee, go and get me some repast.
I care not what, so it be wholesome food.
GRUMIO   What say you to a neat's foot?°   ox foot or calf's foot
KATHERINE   'Tis passing good. I prithee, let me have it.
GRUMIO   I fear it is too choleric° a meat.   conducive to anger
20   How say you to a fat tripe finely broiled?
KATHERINE   I like it well. Good Grumio, fetch it me.
GRUMIO   I cannot tell, I fear 'tis choleric.

4.3 Location: Petruccio's country house.
1. The more injustice I suffer, the more he seems to want me to suffer.

What say you to a piece of beef, and mustard?
KATHERINE   A dish that I do love to feed upon.
25 GRUMIO   Ay, but the mustard is too hot a little.
KATHERINE   Why then, the beef, and let the mustard rest.
GRUMIO   Nay, then I will not. You shall have the mustard,
Or else you get no beef of Grumio.
KATHERINE   Then both, or one, or anything thou wilt.
30 GRUMIO   Why then, the mustard without the beef.
KATHERINE   Go, get thee gone, thou false, deluding slave,
       Beats him
That feed'st me with the very name° of meat.   *only the name*
Sorrow on thee and all the pack of you,
That triumph thus upon my misery.
35 Go, get thee gone, I say.
       Enter PETRUCCIO *and* HORTENSIO, *with meat*
PETRUCCIO   How fares my Kate? What, sweeting,° all amort?°   *sweetheart / dejected*
HORTENSIO   Mistress, what cheer?
KATHERINE   Faith, as cold as can be.
PETRUCCIO   Pluck up thy spirits, look cheerfully upon me.
Here, love, thou seest how diligent I am
40 To dress° thy meat myself and bring it thee.   *prepare*
I am sure, sweet Kate, this kindness merits thanks.
What, not a word? Nay then, thou lov'st it not,
And all my pains is sorted to no proof.°   *are to no purpose*
Here, take away this dish.
KATHERINE   I pray you, let it stand.
45 PETRUCCIO   The poorest service is repaid with thanks,
And so shall mine before you touch the meat.
KATHERINE   I thank you, sir.
HORTENSIO   Signor Petruccio, fie, you are to blame.
Come, Mistress Kate, I'll bear you company.
50 PETRUCCIO [*aside*]   Eat it up all, Hortensio, if thou lov'st me.
[*To* KATHERINE] Much good do it unto thy gentle heart.
Kate, eat apace; and now, my honey love,
Will we return unto thy father's house,
And revel it as bravely as the best,
55 With silken coats, and caps, and golden rings,
With ruffs, and cuffs, and farthingales,² and things,
With scarves, and fans, and double change of bravery,°   *finery*
With amber bracelets, beads, and all this knavery.°   *tricks of dress*
What, hast thou dined? The tailor stays thy leisure,
60 To deck thy body with his ruffling° treasure.   *ornate (with ruffles)*
       Enter TAILOR [*with a gown*]
Come, tailor, let us see these ornaments.
Lay forth the gown.
       Enter HABERDASHER [*with a cap*]
                 What news with you, sir?
HABERDASHER   Here is the cap your worship did bespeak.
PETRUCCIO   Why, this was moulded on a porringer°—   *porridge bowl*
65 A velvet dish.³ Fie, fie, 'tis lewd and filthy.
Why, 'tis a cockle° or a walnut-shell,   *mollusk shell*

---

2. *ruffs:* fashionable high collars made of starched linen or lace. *cuffs:* bands, often made of lace, sewn onto sleeves for ornament. *farthingales:* hooped petticoats.

3. It's merely a dish made of velvet. Velvet caps were often associated with prostitutes.

A knack,° a toy, a trick,° a baby's cap.   *knickknack / trifle*
Away with it! Come, let me have a bigger.
KATHERINE   I'll have no bigger. This doth fit the time,°   *suit current fashion*
70   And gentlewomen wear such caps as these.
PETRUCCIO   When you are gentle you shall have one, too,
And not till then.
HORTENSIO [*aside*]   That will not be in haste.
KATHERINE   Why, sir, I trust I may have leave to speak,
And speak I will. I am no child, no babe.
75   Your betters have endured me say my mind,
And if you cannot, best you stop your ears.
My tongue will tell the anger of my heart,
Or else my heart concealing it will break,
And rather than it shall I will be free
80   Even to the uttermost as I please in words.
PETRUCCIO   Why, thou sayst true. It is a paltry cap,
A custard-coffin,[4] a bauble, a silken pie.
I love thee well in that thou lik'st it not.
KATHERINE   Love me or love me not, I like the cap
85   And it I will have, or I will have none.   [*Exit* HABERDASHER]
PETRUCCIO   Thy gown? Why, ay. Come, tailor, let us see't.
O mercy, God, what masquing stuff[5] is here?
What's this—a sleeve? 'Tis like a demi-cannon.°   *large cannon*
What, up and down carved like an apple-tart?[6]
90   Here's snip, and nip, and cut, and slish and slash,
Like to a scissor in a barber's shop.
Why, what i'° devil's name, tailor, call'st thou this?   *in the*
HORTENSIO [*aside*]   I see she's like° to have nor cap nor gown.   *likely*
TAILOR   You bid me make it orderly and well,
95   According to the fashion and the time.
PETRUCCIO   Marry, and did,° but if you be remembered   *Indeed I did*
I did not bid you mar it to the time.
Go hop me[7] over every kennel° home,   *gutter*
For you shall hop without my custom,° sir.   *patronage; business*
100   I'll none of it. Hence, make your best of it.
KATHERINE   I never saw a better fashioned gown,
More quaint,° more pleasing, nor more commendable.   *elegant*
Belike° you mean to make a puppet of me.   *It seems*
PETRUCCIO   Why true, he means to make a puppet of thee.
105   TAILOR   She says your worship means to make a puppet of her.
PETRUCCIO   O monstrous arrogance! Thou liest, thou thread,
     thou thimble,
Thou yard, three-quarters, half-yard, quarter, nail,[8]
Thou flea, thou nit,° thou winter-cricket, thou.   *egg of a louse*
Braved° in mine own house with° a skein of thread!   *Defied; adorned / by*
110   Away, thou rag, thou quantity,° thou remnant,   *fragment*
Or I shall so bemete° thee with thy yard°   *measure; beat / ruler*
As thou shalt think on prating[9] whilst thou liv'st.
I tell thee, I, that thou hast marred her gown.

---

4. Pastry crust around a custard or open pie (perhaps with a pun on "costard," slang for "head").
5. Extravagant clothing suitable for theatrical masques.
6. With slits like the top of an apple pie. The gown's sleeves may have been designed so as to reveal fabric of another color underneath.
7. You can go hopping.
8. Measure of cloth, a sixteenth of a yard; Petruccio is literally belittling the tailor. "Yard" is slang for "penis."
9. You will think twice before you talk idly, with a pun on "prat" as slang for "beat on the buttocks."

TAILOR Your worship is deceived. The gown is made
115 Just as my master had direction.
     Grumio gave order how it should be done.
GRUMIO I gave him no order, I gave him the stuff.°   material
TAILOR But how did you desire it should be made?
GRUMIO Marry, sir, with needle and thread.
120 TAILOR But did you not request to have it cut?
GRUMIO Thou hast faced° many things.   trimmed; defied
TAILOR I have.
GRUMIO Face not me. Thou hast braved° many men. Brave°   dressed finely / Defy
     not me. I will neither be faced nor braved. I say unto thee
125 I bid thy master cut out the gown, but I did not bid him cut it
     to pieces. Ergo° thou liest.   Therefore
TAILOR [showing a paper] Why, here is the note of the fashion,
     to testify.
PETRUCCIO Read it.
130 GRUMIO The note lies in's throat if he° say I said so.   it
TAILOR [reads] 'Imprimis,° a loose-bodied gown.'[1]   First
GRUMIO Master, if ever I said loose-bodied gown, sew me in the
     skirts of it and beat me to death with a bottom° of brown   spool
     thread. I said a gown.
135 PETRUCCIO Proceed.
TAILOR [reads] 'With a small compassed° cape.'   flared
GRUMIO I confess the cape.
TAILOR [reads] 'With a trunk° sleeve.'   wide
GRUMIO I confess two sleeves.
140 TAILOR [reads] 'The sleeves curiously° cut.'   carefully; elaborately
PETRUCCIO Ay, there's the villany.
GRUMIO Error i'th' bill,° sir, error i'th' bill. I commanded the   order (for the dress)
     sleeves should be cut out and sewed up again, and that I'll
     prove upon thee though thy little finger be armed in a thimble.
145 TAILOR This is true that I say. An° I had thee in place where,°   If / in a suitable place
     thou shouldst know it.
GRUMIO I am for thee straight. Take thou the bill,[2] give me thy
     mete-yard,° and spare not me.   yardstick
HORTENSIO Godamercy, Grumio, then he shall have no odds.°   advantage
150 PETRUCCIO Well, sir, in brief, the gown is not for me.
GRUMIO You are i'th' right, sir. 'Tis for my mistress.
PETRUCCIO [to the TAILOR] Go, take it up unto° thy master's use.   take it away for
GRUMIO [to the TAILOR] Villain, not for thy life. Take up my
     mistress' gown for thy master's use!°   sexual purposes
155 PETRUCCIO Why, sir, what's your conceit° in that?   meaning
GRUMIO O, sir, the conceit is deeper than you think for. 'Take
     up my mistress' gown to his master's use'—O fie, fie, fie!
PETRUCCIO [aside] Hortensio, say thou wilt see the tailor paid.
     [To the TAILOR] Go, take it hence. Be gone, and say no more.
HORTENSIO [aside to the TAILOR] Tailor, I'll pay thee for thy
160 gown tomorrow.
     Take no unkindness of his hasty words.
     Away, I say. Commend me to thy master.   Exit TAILOR
PETRUCCIO Well, come, my Kate. We will unto your father's
     Even in these honest, mean habiliments.

1. A loose-fitting dress. In the next line, Grumio takes this   2. Grumio puns on "bill" as also meaning a "weapon" or
to mean a dress suitable for a wanton, or loose, woman.   "halberd," a staff with a blade attached.

165   Our purses shall be proud, our garments poor,
      For 'tis the mind that makes the body rich,
      And as the sun breaks through the darkest clouds,
      So honour peereth° in the meanest habit.   *can be seen*
      What, is the jay more precious than the lark
170   Because his feathers are more beautiful?
      Or is the adder better than the eel
      Because his painted skin contents the eye?
      O no, good Kate, neither art thou the worse
      For this poor furniture° and mean array.   *clothing; attire*
175   If thou account'st it shame, lay it on me,°   *blame me*
      And therefore frolic; we will hence forthwith
      To feast and sport us° at thy father's house.   *amuse ourselves*
      Go call my men, and let us straight to him,
      And bring our horses unto Long Lane end.
180   There will we mount, and thither walk on foot.
      Let's see, I think 'tis now some seven o'clock,
      And well we may come there by dinner-time.°   *about noon*
      KATHERINE   I dare assure you, sir, 'tis almost two,
      And 'twill be supper-time° ere you come there.   *about 6 P.M.*
185   PETRUCCIO   It shall be seven ere I go to horse.
      Look what I speak, or do, or think to do,
      You are still crossing° it. Sirs, let't alone.   *contradicting*
      I will not go today, and ere I do
      It shall be what o'clock I say it is.
190   HORTENSIO [*aside*]   Why, so this gallant will command the sun.
                                [*Exeunt*]

4.4

Enter TRANIO [*as Lucentio,*] *and the* PEDANT *dressed*
like Vincentio, booted and bare-headed[1]

      TRANIO   Sir, this is the house. Please it you that I call?
      PEDANT   Ay, what else. And but[2] I be deceived,
      Signor Baptista may remember me
      Near twenty years ago in Genoa—
5   TRANIO   Where we were lodgers at the Pegasus.[3]—
      'Tis well, and hold your own° in any case   *keep to your role*
      With such austerity as 'longeth° to a father.   *belongs*
          Enter BIONDELLO
      PEDANT   I warrant you. But sir, here comes your boy.
      'Twere good he were schooled.
10   TRANIO   Fear you not him. Sirrah Biondello,
      Now do your duty throughly,° I advise you.   *thoroughly*
      Imagine 'twere the right Vincentio.
      BIONDELLO   Tut, fear not me.
      TRANIO   But hast thou done thy errand to Baptista?
15   BIONDELLO   I told him that your father was at Venice
      And that you looked for him this day in Padua.

4.4 Location: Padua. In front of Baptista's house.
1. In F, the Pedant is mistakenly given a second entry at line 18, where he is described as "booted and bare-headed," indicating that he is dressed for travel but has taken off his hat, perhaps in deference to Baptista, whom he is about to meet. The present stage direction conflates F's two stage directions regarding the Pedant's entrance.
2. Unless (the Pedant is rehearsing his speech to Baptista).
3. Common name for an inn (marked by a sign of the flying horse of classical mythology).

TRANIO [*giving money*] Thou'rt a tall° fellow. Hold thee° that   *worthy / Take*
    to° drink.   *for*
  Here comes Baptista. Set your countenance, sir.
    Enter BAPTISTA, *and* LUCENTIO [*as Cambio*]
TRANIO   Signor Baptista, you are happily met.
20   [*To the* PEDANT] Sir, this is the gentleman I told you of.
  I pray you stand good father to me now.
  Give me Bianca for my patrimony.
PEDANT   Soft,° son. [*To* BAPTISTA] Sir, by your leave, having   *Just a moment*
    come to Padua
  To gather in some debts, my son Lucentio
25   Made me acquainted with a weighty cause
  Of love between your daughter and himself,
  And for the good report I hear of you,
  And for the love he beareth to your daughter,
  And she to him, to stay him° not too long   *keep him waiting*
30   I am content in a good father's care⁴
  To have him matched, and if you please to like
  No worse than I, upon some agreement
  Me shall you find ready and willing
  With one consent to have her so bestowed,
35   For curious° I cannot be with you,   *overly particular*
  Signor Baptista, of whom I hear so well.
BAPTISTA   Sir, pardon me in what I have to say.
  Your plainness and your shortness please me well.
  Right true it is your son Lucentio here
40   Doth love my daughter, and she loveth him,
  Or both dissemble deeply their affections.
  And therefore if you say no more than this,
  That like a father you will deal with him
  And pass° my daughter a sufficient dower,   *grant*
45   The match is made, and all is done.
  Your son shall have my daughter with consent.
TRANIO   I thank you, sir. Where then do you know best
  We be affied,° and such assurance ta'en   *betrothed*
  As shall with either part's agreement stand?⁵
50 BAPTISTA   Not in my house, Lucentio, for you know
  Pitchers have ears,⁶ and I have many servants.
  Besides, old Gremio is heark'ning still,°   *always listening*
  And happily° we might be interrupted.   *perhaps*
TRANIO   Then at my lodging, an it like you.°   *if it please you*
55   There doth my father lie,° and there this night   *lodge*
  We'll pass° the business privately and well.   *settle*
  Send for your daughter by your servant here.
  My boy shall fetch the scrivener° presently.   *scribe; notary*
  The worst is this, that at so slender warning
60   You are like to have a thin and slender pittance.°   *scanty meal*
BAPTISTA   It likes me well. Cambio, hie° you home   *hurry*
  And bid Bianca make her ready straight,
  And if you will, tell what hath happened—
  Lucentio's father is arrived in Padua—

---

4. Content with the care that should be shown by a good father.
5. As shall confirm the agreements of both parties.
6. Proverbial for "Someone may be eavesdropping." The handles of a pitcher are its "ears."

65   . .   And how she's like to be Lucentio's wife.   [*Exit* LUCENTIO][7]

BIONDELLO   I pray the gods she may with all my heart.

TRANIO   Dally not with the gods, but get thee gone.

Exit [BIONDELLO][8]

Signor Baptista, shall I lead the way?

Welcome. One mess° is like to be your cheer.°   *dish / entertainment*

70   Come, sir, we will better it in Pisa.

BAPTISTA   I follow you.   *Exeunt*

4.5

Enter LUCENTIO *and* BIONDELLO

BIONDELLO   Cambio.

LUCENTIO   What sayst thou, Biondello?

BIONDELLO   You saw my master wink and laugh upon you?

LUCENTIO   Biondello, what of that?

5   BIONDELLO   Faith, nothing, but he's left me here behind to expound the meaning or moral of his signs and tokens.

LUCENTIO   I pray thee, moralize° them.   *interpret*

BIONDELLO   Then thus: Baptista is safe, talking with the deceiving father of a deceitful son.

10   LUCENTIO   And what of him?

BIONDELLO   His daughter is to be brought by you to the supper.

LUCENTIO   And then?

BIONDELLO   The old priest at Saint Luke's church is at your command at all hours.

15   LUCENTIO   And what of all this?

BIONDELLO   I cannot tell, except they are busied about a counterfeit assurance.° Take you assurance[1] of her *cum privilegio*   *betrothal agreement*
ad imprimendum solum[2]—to th' church take the priest, clerk, and some sufficient honest witnesses.

20   If this be not that you look for, I have no more to say,
But bid Bianca farewell for ever and a day.

LUCENTIO   Hear'st thou, Biondello?

BIONDELLO   I cannot tarry, I knew a wench married in an afternoon as she went to the garden for parsley to stuff a rabbit,

25   and so may you, sir, and so adieu, sir. My master hath appointed me to go to Saint Luke's to bid the priest be ready t'attend against° you come with your appendix.[3]   *Exit*   *by the time*

LUCENTIO   I may and will, if she be so contented.
She will be pleased, then wherefore should I doubt?

30   Hap what hap may, I'll roundly go about her.[4]
It shall go hard° if Cambio go without her.   *Exit*[5]   *be unfortunate*

---

7. F does not mark an exit for Lucentio/Cambio here, but it makes sense that he would follow Baptista's order. If Lucentio exits here and Biondello at line 66 as in F, or at line 67 as in this text, then their reentry a few lines later can mark a new scene (see Textual Note). Some editors assume Biondello and perhaps Lucentio never leave the stage since Biondello says (at 4.5.5–6) that he has been left behind by Tranio to explain things to Lucentio. In that case, no scene break would be introduced after Baptista exits.

8. F here has a mysterious stage direction: "Enter Peter." Some editors have argued that this is the name of an actor inadvertently introduced into the stage directions. Others assume it is the name of one of Lucentio's servants, who enters to tell the disguised Tranio and Baptista that their meal is ready; this possibility is not entirely satisfactory, especially since Baptista and Tranio still have to proceed to Lucentio's house for their meal. Perhaps something has been lost or garbled in this portion of the scene.

4.5 Location: Scene continues.

1. Make yourself sure.

2. With the exclusive right to print (a Latin phrase used by printers on the title pages of their books). Biondello urges Lucentio to confirm his "exclusive right" to Bianca and may be punning on "print" as meaning "to father a child."

3. Appendage (the bride).

4. Come what may, I'll pursue her eagerly.

5. At the corresponding point in *A Shrew*, Sly, still on-stage, comments on the action. See Additional Passages B.

4.6

Enter PETRUCCIO, KATHERINE, HORTENSIO [*and servants*]

PETRUCCIO   Come on, i' God's name. Once more toward our father's.
Good Lord, how bright and goodly shines the moon!
KATHERINE   The moon?—the sun. It is not moonlight now.
PETRUCCIO   I say it is the moon that shines so bright.
5   KATHERINE   I know it is the sun that shines so bright.
PETRUCCIO   Now, by my mother's son—and that's myself—
It shall be moon, or star, or what I list°   please
Or ere° I journey to your father's house.   Before
Go on, and fetch our horses back again.
10   Evermore crossed° and crossed, nothing but crossed.   contradicted
HORTENSIO [TO KATHERINE]   Say as he says or we shall never go.
KATHERINE   Forward, I pray, since we have come so far,
And be it moon or sun or what you please,
And if you please to call it a rush-candle[1]
15   Henceforth I vow it shall be so for me.
PETRUCCIO   I say it is the moon.
KATHERINE   I know it is the moon.
PETRUCCIO   Nay then you lie, it is the blessèd sun.
KATHERINE   Then God be blessed, it is the blessèd sun,
20   But sun it is not when you say it is not,
And the moon changes even as your mind.[2]
What you will have it named, even that it is,
And so it shall be still for Katherine.
HORTENSIO   Petruccio, go thy ways.° The field is won.   do as you wish
25   PETRUCCIO   Well, forward, forward. Thus the bowl should run,
And not unluckily against the bias.[3]
But soft, company is coming here.
          Enter [*old*] VINCENTIO
[*To* VINCENTIO] Good morrow, gentle mistress, where away?
Tell me, sweet Kate, and tell me truly too,
30   Hast thou beheld a fresher gentlewoman,
Such war of white and red within her cheeks?
What stars do spangle heaven with such beauty
As those two eyes become that heavenly face?
Fair lovely maid, once more good day to thee.
35   Sweet Kate, embrace her for her beauty's sake.
HORTENSIO   A° will make the man mad to make the woman of   He
him.°   call him a woman
KATHERINE   Young budding virgin, fair, and fresh, and sweet,
Whither away, or where is thy abode?
40   Happy the parents of so fair a child,
Happier the man whom° favourable stars   to whom
Allots thee for his lovely bedfellow.
PETRUCCIO   Why, how now, Kate, I hope thou art not mad.
This is a man, old, wrinkled, faded, withered,
45   And not a maiden as thou sayst he is.
KATHERINE   Pardon, old father, my mistaking eyes

4.6 Location: A road somewhere between Petruccio's
house and Padua.
1. Candle made from rush dripped in grease, thus giving poor light.
2. Implying that Petruccio is mad as well as fickle.

Lunatics and women were imagined to be governed by
the moon.
3. A metaphor from the game of bowls in which the
ball, or bowl, was weighted so that it ran along a "bias,"
or curving path.

That have been so bedazzled with the sun
That everything I look on seemeth green.°   *youthful*
Now I perceive thou art a reverend father.
50 Pardon, I pray thee, for my mad mistaking.
PETRUCCIO   Do, good old grandsire, and withal° make known   *in addition*
Which way thou travell'st. If along with us,
We shall be joyful of thy company.
VINCENTIO   Fair sir, and you, my merry mistress,
55 That with your strange encounter° much amazed me,   *greeting*
My name is called Vincentio, my dwelling Pisa,
And bound I am to Padua, there to visit
A son of mine which long I have not seen.
PETRUCCIO   What is his name?
VINCENTIO   Lucentio, gentle sir.
60 PETRUCCIO   Happily met, the happier for thy son.
And now by law as well as reverend age
I may entitle thee my loving father.
The sister to my wife, this gentlewoman,
Thy son by this hath married.[4] Wonder not,
65 Nor be not grieved. She is of good esteem,
Her dowry wealthy, and of worthy birth,
Beside, so qualified° as may beseem   *with such qualities*
The spouse of any noble gentleman.
Let me embrace with old Vincentio,
70 And wander we to see thy honest son,
Who will of thy arrival be full joyous.
          [*He embraces* VINCENTIO]
VINCENTIO   But is this true, or is it else your pleasure
Like pleasant travellers to break a jest°   *crack a joke*
Upon the company you overtake?
75 HORTENSIO   I do assure thee, father, so it is.
PETRUCCIO   Come, go along, and see the truth hereof,
For our first merriment hath made thee jealous.°   *suspicious*
          Exeunt [*all but* HORTENSIO]
HORTENSIO   Well, Petruccio, this has put me in heart.
Have to my widow, and if she be froward,°   *difficult*
80 Then hast thou taught Hortensio to be untoward.°   *Exit*   *unmannerly*

5.1

Enter BIONDELLO, LUCENTIO, *and* BIANCA. GREMIO
is out before°   *Gremio enters first*
BIONDELLO   Softly and swiftly, sir, for the priest is ready.
LUCENTIO   I fly, Biondello; but they may chance to need thee at
home, therefore leave us.
BIONDELLO   Nay, faith, I'll see the church a' your back[1] and then
5 come back to my master's as soon as I can.
        Exeunt [LUCENTIO, BIANCA, *and* BIONDELLO][2]
GREMIO   I marvel Cambio comes not all this while.

---

4. By now has married. It is unclear how Petruccio and
Hortensio know this, especially since Hortensio has
heard "Lucentio" (Tranio) forswear Bianca (in 4.2).
The inconsistency may suggest textual alteration in the
role of Hortensio.
5.1 Location: Padua, in front of Lucentio's house.
1. At your back. Probably, I'll see the church as you

leave it after the wedding.
2. In F, Lucentio and Bianca exit first (after line 3)
and Biondello presumably follows after line 5, though
no exit is explicitly marked for him. Gremio, onstage
before this trio, apparently does not see them stealing
away to the church.

Enter PETRUCCIO, KATHERINE, VINCENTIO, GRUMIO,
with attendants

PETRUCCIO Sir, here's the door. This is Lucentio's house.
My father's bears° more toward the market-place.   lies
Thither must I, and here I leave you, sir.

10 VINCENTIO You shall not choose but drink before you go.
I think I shall command your welcome here,
And by all likelihood some cheer is toward.°   food is being prepared
[*He*] *knocks*

GREMIO They're busy within. You were best knock louder.
[VINCENTIO *knocks again. The*] PEDANT *looks out
of the window*

PEDANT What's he that knocks as he would beat down the gate?

15 VINCENTIO Is Signor Lucentio within, sir?

PEDANT He's within, sir, but not to be spoken withal.

VINCENTIO What if a man bring him a hundred pound or two
to make merry withal?

PEDANT Keep your hundred pounds to yourself. He shall need
20 none so long as I live.

PETRUCCIO [*to* VINCENTIO] Nay, I told you your son was well
beloved in Padua. [*To the* PEDANT] Do you hear, sir, to leave
frivolous circumstances,° I pray you tell Signor Lucentio that   matters
his father is come from Pisa and is here at the door to speak
25 with him.

PEDANT Thou liest. His father is come from Padua and here
looking out at the window.

VINCENTIO Art thou his father?

PEDANT Ay, sir, so his mother says, if I may believe her.

30 PETRUCCIO [*to* VINCENTIO] Why, how now, gentleman? Why,
this is flat knavery, to take upon you another man's name.

PEDANT Lay hands on the villain. I believe a° means to cozen°   he / cheat
somebody in this city under my countenance.°   name; person
Enter BIONDELLO

BIONDELLO [*aside*] I have seen them in the church together,
35 God send 'em good shipping.° But who is here? Mine old mas-   fair sailing
ter, Vincentio—now we are undone and brought to nothing.

VINCENTIO [*to* BIONDELLO] Come hither, crackhemp.³

BIONDELLO I hope I may choose, sir.

VINCENTIO Come hither, you rogue. What, have you forgot me?

40 BIONDELLO Forgot you? No, sir, I could not forget you, for
I never saw you before in all my life.

VINCENTIO What, you notorious villain, didst thou never see
thy master's father, Vincentio?

BIONDELLO What, my old worshipful old master? Yes, marry,
45 sir, see where he looks out of the window.

VINCENTIO Is't so indeed?
He beats BIONDELLO

BIONDELLO Help, help, help! Here's a madman will murder me.
[*Exit*]

PEDANT Help, son! Help, Signor Baptista!   [*Exit above*]

PETRUCCIO Prithee, Kate, let's stand aside and see the end of
50 this controversy.
[*They stand aside.*]

3. Rogue (deserving to stretch the hangman's hemp rope).

Enter PEDANT *with servants,* BAPTISTA, TRANIO [*as Lucentio*]

TRANIO [*to* VINCENTIO] Sir, what are you that offer° to beat my   *presume*
   servant?

VINCENTIO What am I, sir? Nay, what are you, sir? O immortal
   gods, O fine villain, a silken doublet, a velvet hose, a scarlet
55   cloak, and a copintank° hat—O, I am undone, I am undone!   *high-crowned*
   While I play the good husband at home, my son and my ser-
   vant spend all at the university.

TRANIO How now, what's the matter?

BAPTISTA What, is the man lunatic?

60 TRANIO Sir, you seem a sober, ancient gentleman by your habit,
   but your words show you a madman. Why sir, what 'cerns° it   *concerns*
   you if I wear pearl and gold? I thank my good father. I am able
   to maintain it.

VINCENTIO Thy father! O villain, he is a sailmaker in Bergamo.[4]

65 BAPTISTA You mistake, sir, you mistake, sir. Pray what do you
   think is his name?

VINCENTIO His name? As if I knew not his name—I have
   brought him up ever since he was three years old, and his
   name is Tranio.

70 PEDANT Away, away, mad ass. His name is Lucentio, and he is
   mine only son, and heir to the lands of me, Signor Vincentio.

VINCENTIO Lucentio? O, he hath murdered his master! Lay
   hold on him, I charge you, in the Duke's name. O my son, my
   son! Tell me, thou villain, where is my son Lucentio?

75 TRANIO Call forth an officer.

     [*Enter an* OFFICER]
   Carry this mad knave to the jail. Father Baptista, I charge you
   see that he be forthcoming.°   *available when needed*

VINCENTIO Carry me to the jail?

GREMIO Stay, officer, he shall not go to prison.

80 BAPTISTA Talk not, Signor Gremio. I say he shall go to prison.

GREMIO Take heed, Signor Baptista, lest you be cony-catched°   *duped*
   in this business. I dare swear this is the right Vincentio.

PEDANT Swear if thou dar'st.

GREMIO Nay, I dare not swear it.

85 TRANIO Then thou wert best say that I am not Lucentio.

GREMIO Yes, I know thee to be Signor Lucentio.

BAPTISTA Away with the dotard. To the jail with him.

     Enter BIONDELLO, LUCENTIO, *and* BIANCA

VINCENTIO Thus strangers may be haled° and abused. O mon-   *dragged about*
   strous villain!

90 BIONDELLO O, we are spoiled and—yonder he is. Deny him,
   forswear him, or else we are all undone.

     Exeunt BIONDELLO, TRANIO, *and* PEDANT, *as fast as may be*

LUCENTIO [*to* VINCENTIO] Pardon, sweet father.

     [*He*] *kneels*

VINCENTIO Lives my sweet son?

BIANCA [*to* BAPTISTA] Pardon, dear father.

95 BAPTISTA How hast thou offended? Where is Lucentio?

LUCENTIO Here's Lucentio, right son to the right Vincentio,
   That have by marriage made thy daughter mine,

---

4. An Italian town associated with Harlequin, the witty, resourceful servant of the Italian commedia dell'arte.

While counterfeit supposes[5] bleared thine eyne.°   *deceived your eyes*

GREMIO   Here's packing° with a witness,[6] to deceive us all.   *plotting*

100 VINCENTIO   Where is that damnèd villain Tranio,

That faced and braved° me in this matter so?   *defied*

BAPTISTA   Why, tell me, is not this my Cambio?

BIANCA   Cambio is changed into Lucentio.

LUCENTIO   Love wrought these miracles. Bianca's love

105 Made me exchange my state° with Tranio   *social position*

While he did bear my countenance in the town,

And happily I have arrived at the last

Unto the wishèd haven of my bliss.

What Tranio did, myself enforced him to.

110 Then pardon him, sweet father, for my sake.

VINCENTIO   I'll slit the villain's nose that would have sent me to
the jail.

BAPTISTA   But do you hear, sir, have you married my daughter
without asking my good will?

115 VINCENTIO   Fear not, Baptista. We will content you. Go to, but
I will in to be revenged for this villainy.   *Exit*

BAPTISTA   And I to sound the depth° of this knavery.   *Exit*   *discover the extent*

LUCENTIO   Look not pale, Bianca. Thy father will not frown.

Exeunt [LUCENTIO *and* BIANCA]

GREMIO   My cake is dough,[7] but I'll in among the rest, Out of

120 hope of all° but my share of the feast.   [*Exit*]   *With hope of nothing*

KATHERINE [*coming forward*]   Husband, let's follow to see the
end of this ado.

PETRUCCIO   First kiss me, Kate, and we will.

KATHERINE   What, in the midst of the street?

125 PETRUCCIO   What, art thou ashamed of me?

KATHERINE   No, sir, God forbid; but ashamed to kiss.

PETRUCCIO   Why then, let's home again. Come sirrah, let's away.

KATHERINE   Nay, I will give thee a kiss. Now pray thee love, stay.

[*They kiss*]

PETRUCCIO   Is not this well? Come, my sweet Kate.

130 Better once than never, for never too late.[8]   *Exeunt*

5.2

Enter BAPTISTA, VINCENTIO, GREMIO, *the* PEDANT,
LUCENTIO *and* BIANCA, [PETRUCCIO, KATHERINE,
and HORTENSIO,] TRANIO, BIONDELLO, GRUMIO, *and*
[*the*] WIDOW, *the servingmen with* TRANIO *bringing
in a banquet*[1]

LUCENTIO   At last, though long,° our jarring notes agree,   *after a long time*

And time it is when raging war is done

To smile at scapes° and perils overblown.   *escapes*

My fair Bianca, bid my father welcome,

While I with selfsame kindness welcome thine.

5 Brother Petruccio, sister Katherina,

And thou, Hortensio, with thy loving widow,

Feast with the best, and welcome to my house.

---

5. False ideas. Possibly an illusion to Gascoigne's *Supposes* (1566), which was Shakespeare's main source for
the Bianca and Lucentio plot.
6. With clear evidence; without any doubt.
7. Proverbial expression for a failed project.

8. Two proverbs combined: "Better late than never"
and "It is never too late to mend."
5.2 Location: Lucentio's house in Padua.
1. Light meal of fruit, sweetmeats, and wine following
the main meal.

My banquet is to close our stomachs up

10 After our great good cheer.° Pray you, sit down,   *feast; happiness*

For now we sit to chat as well as eat.

[*They sit*]

PETRUCCIO   Nothing but sit, and sit, and eat, and eat.

BAPTISTA   Padua affords this kindness, son Petruccio.

PETRUCCIO   Padua affords nothing but what is kind

15 HORTENSIO   For both our sakes I would that word were true.

PETRUCCIO   Now, for my life, Hortensio fears² his widow.

WIDOW   Then never trust me if I be afeard.°   *afraid*

PETRUCCIO   You are very sensible, and yet you miss my sense.

I mean Hortensio is afeard of you.

20 WIDOW   He that is giddy thinks the world turns round.³

PETRUCCIO   Roundly° replied.   *Boldly*

KATHERINE   Mistress, how mean you that?

WIDOW   Thus I conceive by him.⁴

PETRUCCIO   Conceives° by me! How likes Hortensio that?   *Becomes pregnant*

25 HORTENSIO   My widow says thus she conceives her tale.⁵

PETRUCCIO   Very well mended. Kiss him for that, good widow.

KATHERINE   'He that is giddy thinks the world turns round'—

I pray you tell me what you meant by that.

WIDOW   Your husband, being troubled with a shrew,

30 Measures my husband's sorrow by his woe.

And now you know my meaning.

KATHERINE   A very mean meaning.

WIDOW   Right, I mean you.

KATHERINE   And I am mean indeed respecting you.⁶

PETRUCCIO   To her, Kate!

35 HORTENSIO   To her, widow!

PETRUCCIO   A hundred marks⁷ my Kate does put her down.°   *defeat her*

HORTENSIO   That's my office.⁸

PETRUCCIO   Spoke like an officer!⁹ Ha' to thee,° lad.   *Here's to you*

[*He*] *drinks to* HORTENSIO

BAPTISTA   How likes Gremio these quick-witted folks?

40 GREMIO   Believe me, sir, they butt together¹ well.

BIANCA   Head and butt? An hasty-witted body

Would say your head and butt were head and horn.²

VINCENTIO   Ay, mistress bride, hath that awakened you?

BIANCA   Ay, but not frighted me, therefore I'll sleep again.

45 PETRUCCIO   Nay, that you shall not. Since you have begun,

Have at° you for a better jest or two.   *I shall come at*

BIANCA   Am I your bird? I mean to shift my bush,³

And then pursue me as you draw your bow.

You are welcome all.

Exit BIANCA [*with* KATHERINE *and the* WIDOW]

---

2. Is afraid of. The widow takes it to mean "frightens."
3. That is, people judge everything by their own experience, implying that Petruccio is afraid of his wife.
4. Thus I understand him.
5. Thus she understands or intends her remark, with a pun on "tail" as meaning "genitalia."
6. I am moderate (like the mathematical "mean") compared with you; I demean myself in dealing with you.
7. A substantial wager, since 1 mark was equivalent to 13 shillings and 4 pence, or two-thirds of a pound. An unskilled laborer might earn £6 to £8 in a year.

8. That's my job, with a pun on "put her down" as meaning "force or lay her down in sexual intercourse."
9. Like one who knows his duty.
1. They thrust their heads or horns together, with a pun on "butt" as meaning "buttocks."
2. Would say your butting head was a cuckold's horned head.
3. Alluding to the Elizabethan sport of shooting sitting birds with a bow and arrow. There may also be a bawdy pun on "bush" as meaning "pubic area" and the target of Petruccio's (phallic) arrow.

50 PETRUCCIO   She hath prevented° me here, Signor Tranio.   *stopped; anticipated*
    This bird you aimed at, though you hit her not.
    Therefore a health to all that shot and missed.
    TRANIO   O sir, Lucentio slipped° me like his greyhound,   *unleashed*
    Which runs himself and catches for his master.
55 PETRUCCIO   A good swift° simile, but something currish.°   *witty/base; doglike*
    TRANIO   'Tis well, sir, that you hunted for yourself.
    'Tis thought your deer does hold you at a bay.[4]
    BAPTISTA   O, O, Petruccio, Tranio hits you now.
    LUCENTIO   I thank thee for that gird,° good Tranio.   *taunt*
60 HORTENSIO   Confess, confess, hath he not hit you here?
    PETRUCCIO   A° has a little galled° me, I confess,   *He/wounded*
    And as the jest did glance away from me,
    'Tis ten to one it maimed you two outright.
    BAPTISTA   Now in good sadness,° son Petruccio,   *in all seriousness*
65 I think thou hast the veriest shrew of all.
    PETRUCCIO   Well, I say no.—And therefore, Sir Assurance,
    Let's each one send unto° his wife,   *summon*
    And he whose wife is most obedient
    To come at first when he doth send for her
70 Shall win the wager which we will propose.
    HORTENSIO   Content.° What's the wager?   *Agreed*
    LUCENTIO   Twenty crowns.°   *coin worth 5 shillings*
    PETRUCCIO   Twenty crowns!
    I'll venture so much of° my hawk or hound,   *on*
75 But twenty times so much upon my wife.
    LUCENTIO   A hundred, then.
    HORTENSIO   Content.
    PETRUCCIO   A match,° 'tis done.   *Agreed*
    HORTENSIO   Who shall begin?
80 LUCENTIO   That will I.
    Go, Biondello, bid your mistress come to me.
    BIONDELLO   I go.   *Exit*
    BAPTISTA   Son, I'll be your half Bianca comes.[5]
    LUCENTIO   I'll have no halves, I'll bear it all myself.
        Enter BIONDELLO
    How now, what news?
85 BIONDELLO   Sir, my mistress sends you word
    That she is busy and she cannot come.
    PETRUCCIO   How? She's busy and she cannot come?
    Is that an answer?
    GREMIO   Ay, and a kind one, too.
    Pray God, sir, your wife send you not a worse.
    PETRUCCIO   I hope, better.
90 HORTENSIO   Sirrah Biondello,
    Go and entreat my wife to come to me forthwith.
                                Exit BIONDELLO
    PETRUCCIO   O ho, 'entreat' her—nay, then she must needs come.
    HORTENSIO   I am afraid, sir, do what you can,
        Enter BIONDELLO
    Yours will not be entreated. Now, where's my wife?

4. Your deer turns on you and holds you at a distance.   of any winnings) in wagering that Bianca will come
Punning on "deer" and "dear."   first.
5. I'll put up half the stake (and therefore collect half

95 BIONDELLO She says you have some goodly jest in hand.
 She will not come. She bids you come to her.
 PETRUCCIO Worse and worse! She will not come—O vile,
 Intolerable, not to be endured!
 Sirrah Grumio, go to your mistress.
100 Say I command her come to me.   *Exit* [GRUMIO]
 HORTENSIO I know her answer.
 PETRUCCIO   What?
 HORTENSIO   She will not.
 PETRUCCIO The fouler fortune mine, and there an end.[6]
         Enter KATHERINE
 BAPTISTA Now by my halidom,° here comes Katherina.   *by all I hold sacred*
 KATHERINE [*to* PETRUCCIO] What is your will, sir, that you send
         for me?
105 PETRUCCIO Where is your sister and Hortensio's wife?
 KATHERINE They sit conferring by the parlour fire.
 PETRUCCIO Go, fetch them hither. If they deny° to come,   *refuse*
 Swinge me them soundly forth[7] unto their husbands.
 Away, I say, and bring them hither straight.   [*Exit* KATHERINE]
110 LUCENTIO Here is a wonder, if you talk of wonders.
 HORTENSIO And so it is. I wonder what it bodes.
 PETRUCCIO Marry, peace it bodes, and love, and quiet life;
 An aweful° rule and right supremacy,   *inspiring awe*
 And, to be short, what not° that's sweet and happy.   *everything*
115 BAPTISTA Now fair befall thee, good Petruccio,
 The wager thou hast won, and I will add
 Unto their losses twenty thousand crowns,
 Another dowry to another daughter,
 For she is changed as she had never been.[8]
120 PETRUCCIO Nay, I will win my wager better yet,
 And show more sign of her obedience,
 Her new-built virtue and obedience.
         Enter KATHERINE, BIANCA, *and* [*the*] WIDOW
 See where she comes, and brings your froward° wives   *willful*
 As prisoners to her womanly persuasion.
125 Katherine, that cap of yours becomes you not.
 Off with that bauble, throw it underfoot.
         [KATHERINE *throws down her cap*]
 WIDOW Lord, let me never have a cause to sigh
 Till I be brought to such a silly pass.
 BIANCA Fie, what a foolish duty call you this?
130 LUCENTIO I would your duty were as foolish, too.
 The wisdom of your duty, fair Bianca,
 Hath cost me a hundred crowns since supper-time.
 BIANCA The more fool you for laying° on my duty.   *gambling*
 PETRUCCIO Katherine, I charge thee tell these headstrong women
135 What duty they do owe their lords and husbands.
 WIDOW Come, come, you're mocking. We will have no telling.
 PETRUCCIO Come on, I say, and first begin with her.
 WIDOW She shall not.

---

6. Worse luck for me (if you're right), and that's that.   8. As if she had never existed before; as if she had never
7. Beat them soundly for me, and bring them out.   been what she was before (a shrew).

PETRUCCIO I say she shall: and first begin with her.

140 KATHERINE Fie, fie, unknit that threat'ning, unkind brow,
And dart not scornful glances from those eyes
To wound thy lord, thy king, thy governor.
It blots° thy beauty as frosts do bite the meads,°   *disfigures / meadows*
Confounds thy fame° as whirlwinds shake fair buds,   *Ruins your reputation*
145 And in no sense is meet° or amiable.   *fitting*
A woman moved° is like a fountain troubled,   *angry*
Muddy, ill-seeming,° thick, bereft of beauty,   *ugly*
And while it is so, none so dry or thirsty
Will deign to sip or touch one drop of it.
150 Thy husband is thy lord, thy life, thy keeper,
Thy head, thy sovereign, one that cares for thee,
And for thy maintenance commits his body
To painful labour both by sea and land,
To watch the night in storms, the day in cold,
155 Whilst thou liest warm at home, secure and safe,
And craves no other tribute at thy hands
But love, fair looks, and true obedience,
Too little payment for so great a debt.
Such duty as the subject owes the prince,
160 Even such a woman oweth to her husband,
And when she is froward, peevish,° sullen, sour,   *obstinate*
And not obedient to his honest will,
What is she but a foul contending rebel,
And graceless traitor to her loving lord?
165 I am ashamed that women are so simple°   *foolish*
To offer war where they should kneel for peace,
Or seek for rule, supremacy, and sway
When they are bound to serve, love, and obey.
Why are our bodies soft, and weak, and smooth,
170 Unapt to° toil and trouble in the world,   *Unfitted for*
But that our soft conditions° and our hearts   *dispositions*
Should well agree with our external parts?
Come, come, you froward and unable worms,°   *weak creatures*
My mind hath been as big° as one of yours,   *proud*
175 My heart° as great, my reason haply more,   *spirit*
To bandy word for word and frown for frown;
But now I see our lances are but straws,
Our strength as weak,° our weakness past compare,   *(as straws)*
That seeming to be most which we indeed least are.
180 Then vail your stomachs, for it is no boot,⁹
And place your hands below your husband's foot,
In token of which duty, if he please,
My hand is ready, may it do him ease.°   *give him comfort*
PETRUCCIO Why, there's a wench! Come on, and kiss me, Kate.
        [*They kiss*]
185 LUCENTIO Well, go thy ways, old lad, for thou shalt ha't.¹
VINCENTIO 'Tis a good hearing° when children are toward.²   *thing to hear*
LUCENTIO But a harsh hearing when women are froward.
PETRUCCIO Come, Kate, we'll to bed.

9. Then lower your pride, for it is of no profit.   2. Obedient (the opposite of "froward," line 187).
1. You shall have the prize.

We three are married, but you two are sped.°   *defeated*
190   'Twas I won the wager, though [*to* LUCENTIO] you hit the white,[3]
And being a winner,° God give you good night.   *since I am a winner*

Exit PETRUCCIO [*with* KATHERINE]

HORTENSIO   Now go thy ways, thou hast tamed a curst shrew.
LUCENTIO   'Tis a wonder, by your leave, she will be tamed so.

[*Exeunt*][4]

Additional Passages

The Taming of a Shrew, printed in 1594 and believed to derive from Shakespeare's play as performed, contains episodes continuing and rounding off the Christopher Sly framework that may echo passages written by Shakespeare but not printed in the Folio. They are given below.

A. The following exchange occurs at a point for which there is no exact equivalent in Shakespeare's play. It could come before 2.1. The "two fine gentlewomen" to whom Sly refers in line 8 would thus be Katherine and Bianca. The "fool" of the first line is Sander, the counterpart of Grumio. "Sim" is short for Simon, the name of the Lord with whom Sly converses.

Then SLY *speaks*

SLY   Sim, when will the fool come again?
LORD   He'll come again, my lord, anon.
SLY   Gi's° some more drink here. Zounds,[1] where's the tapster?°   *Give us / tavern keeper*
         Here, Sim, eat some of these things.
5   LORD   So I do, my lord.
SLY   Here, Sim, I drink to thee.
LORD   My lord, here comes the players again.
SLY   O brave, here's two fine gentlewomen.

B. This passage comes between 4.5 and 4.6. If it originates with Shakespeare, it implies that Grumio accompanies Petruccio at the beginning of 4.6. Ferando is the name of Petruccio's counterpart in *A Shrew*.

SLY   Sim, must they be married now?
LORD   Ay, my lord.

Enter FERANDO *and* KATE *and* SANDER

SLY   Look, Sim, the fool is come again now.

C. Sly interrupts the action of the play-within-the-play. This could be inserted at 5.1.92 of Shakespeare's play, when Biondello, Tranio, and the Pedant all run away from the angry Vincentio. In *A Shrew*, the Duke (Vincentio's counterpart) has threatened to send to prison the people (Phylotus and Valeria) who have impersonated him and his son.

PHYLOTUS *and* VALERIA *runs away*.
Then SLY *speaks*

SLY   I say we'll have no sending to prison.
LORD   My lord, this is but the play. They're but in jest.
SLY   I tell thee, Sim, we'll have no sending to prison, that's flat.°   *final*

---

3. Hit the target (with a pun on "Bianca," which means   play. See Additional Passages E.
"white" in Italian).   1. By God's wounds (a strong oath).
4. In *A Shrew*, the Christopher Sly story concludes the

Why, Sim, am not I Don Christo Vary? Therefore I say they
5   shall not go to prison.

LORD   No more they shall not, my lord. They be run away.

SLY   Are they run away, Sim? That's well. Then gi's some more
    drink, and let them play again.

LORD   Here, my lord.

        SLY   *drinks and then falls asleep*

D. Sly is carried off. This could be placed between 5.1 and 5.2 in Shakespeare's play.

                                        Exeunt omnes°   *They all exit*

        SLY *sleeps*

LORD   Who's within there? Come hither, sirs, my lord's
    Asleep again. Go take him easily° up   *gently*
    And put him in his own apparel again,
    And lay him in the place where we did find him
5   Just underneath the alehouse side below.
    But see you wake him not in any case.

BOY   It shall be done, my lord. Come help to bear him hence.
                                            Exit

E. *The Taming of a Shrew* ends with the following episode.

        Then enter two bearing of SLY *in his own apparel again*
        and leaves him where they found him and then goes out.
        Then enter the TAPSTER

TAPSTER   Now that the darksome night is overpast
    And dawning day appears in crystal sky,
    Now must I haste abroad. But soft, who's this?
    What, Sly! O wondrous, hath he lain here all night?
5   I'll wake him. I think he's starved[1] by this,°   *this time*
    But° that his belly was so stuffed with ale.   *Except*
    What ho, Sly, awake, for shame!

SLY   Sim, gi's some more wine. What, 's all the players gone?
    Am not I a lord?

10 TAPSTER   A lord with a murrain![2] Come, art thou drunken still?

SLY   Who's this? Tapster? O Lord, sirrah, I have had
    The bravest° dream tonight that ever thou   *finest*
    Heardest in all thy life.

TAPSTER   Ay, marry, but you had best get you home,
15   For your wife will course° you for dreaming here tonight.   *trounce*

SLY   Will she? I know now how to tame a shrew.
    I dreamt upon it all this night till now,
    And thou hast waked me out of the best dream
    That ever I had in my life. But I'll to my
20   Wife presently and tame her too,
    An if° she anger me.   *An if=If*

TAPSTER   Nay, Tarry, Sly, for I'll go home with thee
    And hear the rest that thou hast dreamt tonight.

                                Exeunt omnes

---

1. He'd have died from cold.
2. Pestilence or plague. "With a murrain" was often used as an oath or expression of anger. The tapster probably means "A plague on that" (Sly's dream of being a lord).

The First Part of the Contention
of the Two Famous Houses
of York and Lancaster
(The Second Part of Henry VI)

What happens to a kingdom when the sitting monarch is too weak to rule effectively? Shakespeare explores this difficult problem in *The First Part of the Contention of the Two Famous Houses of York and Lancaster,* in which Henry VI, crowned when he was nine months old, has never been able to establish control over his realm. As his assertive French wife, Margaret of Anjou, exclaims in exasperation to the Duke of Suffolk, who had wooed her for Henry:

> when in the city Tours
> Thou rann'st a-tilt in honour of my love
> And stol'st away the ladies' hearts of France,
> I thought King Henry had resembled thee
> In courage, courtship, and proportion.
> But all his mind is bent to holiness,
> To number Ave-Maries on his beads.
>
> (1.3.54–60)

Margaret thought she would be marrying a chivalric hero one adept at the arts of love and war; instead, she finds herself wed to an ineffective, pious man who elsewhere openly expresses his desire to live as a private person rather than as his country's King. Partly as a result of Henry's deficiencies, Margaret grows increasingly independent, conducting a love intrigue with Suffolk and openly defying her husband's wishes. Presented as a sexualized figure of gender disorder, Margaret is as powerful as her husband is weak. Margaret, however, represents but one of the threats to Henry's authority and the well-being of the country. Lacking the strong hand of a powerful monarch to rein them in, Henry's nobles quarrel and threaten civil war, and eventually a group of rebellious commoners storm London, killing all who oppose them. The kingdom slides into chaos.

In the early modern period, the king stood at the top of the social order and was invested with enormous responsibilities. The symbolic head and heart of the body politic, the monarch was enjoined to rule wisely, to care for the welfare of his subjects, and to take counsel from and exert control over the nobility. Some theories of kingship argued that monarchs had their authority from God; rebellion against a sitting monarch was a form of treason punishable by death. Given the centrality of the king to the health of the kingdom and its subjects, an evil or a weak king could have a disastrous impact on the realm. Tyrants—that is, kings who followed their passions, refused to take counsel, and ignored the welfare of their subjects—were anxiously discussed by the political thinkers of the period. Could they ever be overthrown? Must their tyranny be endured? In plays such as *Richard III* and *Macbeth,* Shakespeare dramatized such tyrant kings and in each case showed their deaths at the hands of

229

high-placed subjects. Henry VI poses a different kind of danger. Rather than an evil or personally ambitious monarch, he is simply ineffectual and weak, unable to control the ambition and selfish desires of his nobles or to see to the welfare of his subjects. In effect, *The First Part of the Contention* explores what happens when a kingdom is left rudderless, graphically depicting the brutality let loose when the King is unable to assert his authority, commoners are set against nobles, and nobles begin to destroy one another.

The First Part of the Contention may well be the first English history play Shakespeare wrote (for a fuller discussion of the genre of the history play and Shakespeare's work in that genre, see the introduction to *1 Henry VI*). It has been dated as early as 1591 and exists in two distinct versions: a quarto edition printed in 1594 and a longer version printed in the First Folio in 1623 (for the differences between these two texts, see the Textual Note). Historically, the protracted broils depicted in this and the following play were known as the Wars of the Roses (1455–85) because the House of York, which staked its claim to England's throne through Lionel, Duke of Clarence, third son of Edward III, took a white rose for its emblem, while the House of Lancaster, which claimed the throne through John of Gaunt, fourth son of Edward III, became identified with the red rose. While giving a war the name of a flower might suggest a trivial or symbolic struggle, Shakespeare's plays decisively refute such an idea. Collectively they explore the horror of a kingdom divided against itself.

When read, the play can seem chaotic, a series of violent acts carried out by a bewildering array of characters who rise to the forefront of attention only to disappear quickly from view. But the play is more carefully structured than may at first be apparent. For the first two acts, Henry's weakness is counterbalanced by the strength of Humphrey, Duke of Gloucester, a man who since the King's youth has served as Lord Protector of the realm and who attempts to see that the common people are fairly treated and the quarrelling nobles kept in check. The play reaches a decisive turning point in Act 3 when Gloucester is driven from office by the Queen, Suffolk, York, and the Cardinal Beaufort (who is also the Bishop of Winchester). Once Gloucester is gone, no one can protect the King or the kingdom from the ambition of Richard, Duke of York, the most powerful of the nobles who would supplant Henry. From Act 3 on, York and his minions dominate the action, countered primarily by the equally strong-willed Margaret. In the brutal struggles that follow upon Gloucester's death, one powerful figure after another suffers disgrace or death, including Cardinal Beaufort, Suffolk, and Somerset. York, however, does not fall but, like Margaret, moves with unnerving single-mindedness into the power vacuum created by the King's passivity.

Henry VI, depicted as a child, carried by the Earl of Warwick.

To register the disaster that has overtaken England, Shakespeare relentlessly focuses on the actual human bodies maimed, brutalized, and destroyed by the play's contending forces. The death of Gloucester is exemplary. In *The First Part of the Contention*, he is strangled onstage in his bed; in the Folio version of the play his death occurs offstage. But in both texts, the corpse is eventually displayed to the audience while Warwick recites a grisly description of the state of the body. In contrast to the paleness of a man who has died peacefully, the good Duke's

> face is black and full of blood;
> His eyeballs further out than when he lived,
> Staring full ghastly like a strangled man;
> His hair upreared; his nostrils stretched with struggling;
> His hands abroad displayed, as one that grasped
> And tugged for life and was by strength subdued.
> Look on the sheets. His hair, you see, is sticking;
> His well-proportioned beard made rough and rugged,
> Like to the summer's corn by tempest lodged.
> It cannot be but he was murdered here.
> The least of all these signs were probable.
>
> (3.2.168–78)

This terrible inventory of the unnatural state of Gloucester's dead body highlights the marks of his futile struggle for life—the bulging eyes, the disordered hair and beard, the outstretched hands. Warwick's point is that these are *not* the signs of a soul weighed down by sin and unprepared for death, as is true of Cardinal Beaufort, whose death occurs in the next scene; rather, Gloucester's disordered corpse testifies to the horrific and untimely circumstances in which he died.

In this extremely violent play, many other bodies suffer indignity, pain, and death. In Act 4, Suffolk, captured on his flight to France, is beheaded offstage by his captors. His body is then taken to England, where Queen Margaret, in one of the most macabre scenes in Shakespeare, carries his severed head around the court, lamenting her dead lover. Later, the rebels attacking London capture Lord Saye, a supporter of King Henry. After enumerating a catalog of his crimes, including the "crime" of literacy, the followers of Jack Cade, the chief rebel, behead Saye along with his son-in-law. Cade's followers then stick the severed heads on poles and carry them through the streets, grotesquely making them "kiss" at every corner. After five days of living in the woods without food have rendered him too famished to fight effectively, Jack Cade is himself beheaded and his head taken to the King. This is hardly an exhaustive list of the forms of violence depicted in the play. It does not, for example, take account of those slain in battle, such as Somerset, or of the shameful treatment Cade visits upon defeated enemies such as Sir Humphrey Stafford and his brother, whose armor he strips from their corpses before he drags their bodies behind his horse toward London.

Some small portion of this violence displays the monarch's sanctioned power to punish unruly or disobedient subjects. In Elizabethan England, traitors' heads were regularly displayed on London Bridge, and public executions were popular spectacles, showing the King's power over traitors and criminals. In *The First Part of the Contention*, the most spectacular scene of public correction involves Eleanor Cobham, Gloucester's wife. A proud and ambitious woman who hopes to see her husband displace Henry as King of England, Cobham dabbles in the forbidden arts of witchcraft and conjuration, soliciting prophecies about the fate of the King and two of his nobles, Suffolk and Somerset. Such prophecies were considered politically dangerous because they caused uncertainty and unrest among the common people and could be used to foment sedition. They had been specifically banned by Henry VIII, Edward VI, and Elizabeth. Like many famous prophecies, those delivered to Eleanor Cobham are ambiguous. For example, "The Duke yet lives that Henry shall depose, / But him outlive, and die a violent death" (1.4.29–30) can mean either that Henry shall depose a duke or that a duke shall depose Henry. Nor is it entirely clear who shall outlive whom and die a violent death. The ambiguity of such statements was exactly what rulers feared, since under the cover of a benign interpretation they could be used to predict and promote rebellion. For engaging in witchcraft and conjuration as well as for circulating such prophecies, Eleanor Cobham is first shamed—she must walk through London carrying a candle and wearing only a sheet, her crimes listed on a piece of paper pinned to her back—and then banished, and her confederates hanged and burned. The King here appears to be using sanctioned violence to punish dangerously seditious subjects.

Yet in much of the play, the state either fails to control violence or else uses it with questionable justice. Even Eleanor's case is more ambiguous than the above account suggests. She did undeniably dabble in witchcraft, yet she was urged on by people in the employ of Suffolk and the Cardinal, who wished through her acts to disgrace her innocent husband and dislodge him from power. Legally, Eleanor's punishment is just, yet it occurs in a context of chicanery and treachery that the King either does not or will not see until Gloucester, the chief prop of royal justice, has been removed. Between the discovery of Eleanor's witchcraft and her public shaming, the play shows the audience another troubling example of a ritual of justice. Earlier Peter Thump, an apprentice, had accused his master, Horner, of saying that the Duke of York—not Henry—was the rightful ruler of England. Thump had no proof but his own word, and Horner had no defense but denial. To resolve the issue, Gloucester orders a day of combat for the man and master: whoever wins the duel would be assumed to have spoken the truth. Such trials by combat were customary in adjudicating disputes among nobles. But the apprentice is terrified, having no experience with such contests or with the weapons commonly used in them: the sword or lance. As it is dramatized, the trial by combat becomes a parody of justice. Rather than fighting with swords, the two contestants appear with sandbags attached to poles, and Horner is roaring drunk. It is under these conditions that the apprentice kills his master, and the King, who has now taken Gloucester's staff of office from him as the result of Eleanor's treason, seems satisfied that justice has prevailed. But the ludicrous nature of the drunken encounter threatens to empty such traditional rituals of their meaning and legitimacy.

With Gloucester's death, the King's fair and effective control of the machinery of justice and of violence is further compromised. Under the pressure of an enraged commons, Henry *does* banish Suffolk for his role in Gloucester's death, but the King cannot begin to contain the escalating stage violence. In the second half of the play, his loss of control is demonstrated by the spectacular rise to power of the lower-class rebel Jack Cade, one of York's minions. As he marches toward London, Cade boasts that the laws of England are to come from his mouth, and he arrogates to himself the right to kill whom he chooses. The murder of Lord Saye, the death of the clerk of Chartham, the desecration of Stafford's body—these are a mere sampling of events in a brutal career, and the play does not shrink from showing what is cruel and arbitrary in Cade's brief reign of terror. Critics often take Shakespeare's representation of Cade as confirming Elizabethan fears about the dangers of popular rule.

Yet interpreting Cade and his actions is a complicated business. Does Shakespeare create this character simply to discredit popular rebellion, or does he use Cade to articulate the legitimate grievances of the common people and employ Cade's brutality as a disquieting mirror of the brutality of the ruling classes? It is important to remember that Cade is not synonymous with "the commons" in this play. In the opening acts, while he is still in power, Gloucester is presented as a champion of the people and promotes a commonwealth in which the king and nobles care for the needs of the commoners and are responsive to their petitions. The people, in turn, seem confident that their views will be heard by those near the King. For example, in 1.3, three commoners wait with petitions for Gloucester: Peter Thump wishes to report his master's treasonous words about the Duke of York; another man complains that Cardinal Beaufort's man has unlawfully seized his land, house, and wife; a third protests that the Duke of Suffolk has enclosed the commons of Melford. (Enclosures—fencing in land once shared by many for growing food and grazing cattle—were a main cause of rural protest in the sixteenth and seventeenth centuries.) How these commoners behave as political agents registering grievances with those in power is revealing. First, the petitioners believe that they can get redress from the Lord Protector, the figure nearest the King himself. Second, they use peaceful means to obtain their desires. Third, they act from a position of loyalty to their King and his Lord Protector. Thump, in particular, puts himself at personal risk to report an act of treason against Henry. These figures hardly constitute a mob or many-headed monster. Even when they become enraged by Gloucester's murder and demand the banishment of Suffolk, they couch their protest as a desire to protect the King rather than to seize power for themselves.

It is crucial to note, however, that in 1.3 the petitioners are largely thwarted in their appeal for justice because they mistake Suffolk for Gloucester. Suffolk and the Queen are interested in dealing with York's supposed treason because they can use that accusation to prevent York from becoming Regent of France. They ignore the other petitions, one of which details a complaint against Suffolk himself. It is the nobles and not the commoners who fail to exercise their political duties responsibly. Timid and gullible and surrounded by selfish nobles like Suffolk, the King disregards the welfare and the needs of the common people, who are presented in this scene as loyal and orderly actors in a hierarchical commonwealth.

Cade enters the picture only when the one noble—Gloucester—who cares about maintaining this paternal relationship between the commons and the King is about to be killed. At the end of 3.1, York, in soliloquy, reveals his intention to use the army levied against Ireland to further his own political ends; in addition, he will employ the Kentishman Jack Cade as his stalking horse in his move to seize the crown. Cade will pretend to be John Mortimer, a claimant to the throne through the Yorkist line, in order to test the waters for York's own bid for power. Cade is thus never an entirely independent agent of the people; rather, he is at least in part the tool of an ambitious nobleman who employs him because he is stubborn, strong, and impervious to pain. York reports that in battle against the Irish, Cade

> fought so long till that his thighs with darts
> Were almost like a sharp-quilled porcupine;
> And in the end, being rescued, I have seen
> Him caper upright like a wild Morisco,
> Shaking the bloody darts as he his bells.
>   (3.1.362–66)

Will Kemp doing his morris dance. From Kemp's *Nine Days' Wonder* (1600).

Morris dancers tied bells to their legs, and these shook and jangled as they danced. The powerful image of the wounded Cade dancing depicts a man endowed with enormous spirit and physical strength. It is worth recalling that one of the most famous clowns of the 1590s, Will Kemp, who may have played the part of Cade, was himself a noted acrobat and dancer; in 1599, he left Shakespeare's company and did a celebrated morris dance from London to Norwich. Skilled and strong, Cade and Kemp suggest both what was feared and what was admired about hardhanded men, some of whom were employed in the London theater industry and some of whom would have been in the audience. In fact, the Cade scenes must have been powerfully charged, because out of this rebel's mouth—along with arbitrary brutality and pompous self-aggrandizement—issues a critique of social and economic inequality that, endowed with a long history, also spoke to living issues in the London of the 1590s.

Historically, Cade's rebellion occurred in 1450, but in portraying it, Shakespeare draws on accounts of many instances of popular social protest. For example, he takes from Raphael Holinshed's *Chronicles of England, Scotland, and Ireland* (1587) details from the Peasants' Revolt of 1381, in which rebels such as Wat Tyler burned London Bridge and attacked the Savoy (John of Gaunt's house) and the Inns of Court, both places of privilege that became a focus for lower-class anger. Other popular uprisings occurred in 1517, when apprentices on Ill May Day attacked foreign workers in the City of London; in 1549 (Kett's Rebellion); and in London itself throughout the decade of the 1590s. Between 1581 and 1602, there were numerous outbreaks of disorder in London directed against various forms of economic hardship, some of which stemmed from disruptions and changes in the English cloth trade that disadvantaged English weavers. Protests also occurred against the high price of commodities such as butter and fish and against the granting of monopolies that put the sale of key goods, such as starch, in the hands of a small group. Apprentices were often involved in and blamed for these riots. Many of Cade's followers in *The First Part of the Contention* are artisans: weavers and butchers. Through Cade, their economic grievances find expression, along with the articulation of an alternative model of social and economic organization much more radically utopian than that implied in Gloucester's hierarchical paternalism.

This tradition of popular radicalism, whose roots went back at least to the fourteenth century, stressed that all men had been equally redeemed by Christ's blood and that there was as much nobility in the labor of an honest man as in the fine silks and the educated speech of a gentleman. A riddle common throughout Europe from the fourteenth century on—"When Adam delved and Eve span, who then was the gentleman?"—suggests the egalitarian purposes for which the Bible could be appropriated. The first man and woman, digging in the earth and spinning cloth, knew no distinctions of rank, simply the dignity of labor. Often, popular protest stressed the value of manual labor, as opposed to the idleness of the rich, and claimed the clouted shoe or hobnailed boot of the rural peasant and the leather apron of the urban laborer as valued emblems of their working lives.

The Cade scenes are filled with references to this egalitarian tradition. In 4.2, when the rebels first describe how Cade means to reform the commonwealth, they make clear that in their view working men, and only working men, should be magistrates and rulers. Referring to Scripture, the second rebel says: "Yet it is said 'Labour in thy vocation'; which is as much to say as 'Let the magistrates be labouring men'; and therefore should we be magistrates" (4.2.14–16). By contrast, the present nobility "scorn to go in leather aprons" (4.2.10–11) and have no respect for handicraftsmen. Part of Cade's success is that he is able to mobilize such artisan anger against the privileges of gentlemen, whether those be conferred by literacy or by inherited wealth. Much of Cade's violence is directed against those who can read and write, like the clerk of Chartham or Lord Saye. Literacy, whether defined as the ability to read or to read and write, was not nearly so widespread as it has since become. These skills were acquired by only a small part of the population, who thereby had certain advantages wherever the reading or writing of documents had importance, such as in courts of law. Cade would not only kill all the lawyers, but he would also punish all those who wrote on parchment, that is, those in control of written documents. He also promises that when he is in charge, bread will be cheap, beer of the highest quality, all material goods enjoyed in common, and all men dressed in a common livery.

It is hardly necessary to point out how often Cade contradicts himself in articulating his vision of a commonwealth of equals and how he undermines the utopian aspirations of the tradition of popular radicalism to which his words repeatedly refer. In his egalitarian commonwealth, Cade, of course, would be King and from his mouth would come all the laws by which others would live. Women would have no rights in his commonwealth but would be fair game for rape. When a Sergeant complains to Cade that his wife has been ravished by one of Cade's men, Cade authorizes his man to cut out the Sergeant's tongue, cripple him, and then knock out his brains. Cade then invites his followers to enter London, where they will "lustily stand to it" and "take up these commodities following—item, a gown, a kirtle, a petticoat, and a smock" (4.7.134–36). The violence and arbitrary cruelty repeatedly displayed make Cade a frightening figure and one whom even his followers often recognize as a charlatan and a hypocrite.

Yet Cade's personal viciousness does not simply wipe away the power of the social critique to which he intermittently gives voice and which had a history extending far beyond this play. When Cade learns that Lord Saye has his horse covered with an elaborate cloth, he bluntly states a point of view that must have resonated with some in Shakespeare's audience: "Marry, thou ought'st not to let thy horse wear a cloak when honester men than thou go in their hose and doublets" (4.7.42–43). Moreover, Shakespeare gives plenty of evidence in the play that if many commoners feel anger and resentment toward the nobility, many nobility are in their turn full of contempt for the lower classes. Act 4, which is dominated by Cade, opens with the scene in which Suffolk is captured and questioned by the Captain of a ship. Furious that when he reveals himself as the Duke of Suffolk his captors do not free him immediately, Suffolk contemptuously attacks the Captain:

> Obscure and lousy swain, King Henry's blood,
> The honourable blood of Lancaster,
> Must not be shed by such a jady groom.
> (4.1.51–53)

The speech goes on in a similar vein for twelve more lines, making clear the truth of the second rebel's claim that the gentlemen of England do not have much respect for hardhanded men. Nor, after the grisly murder of Gloucester, can it be thought that only the common people have the capacity for lawless violence. In short, the play dramatizes many instances of class-based antagonisms rooted in the unequal distribution of wealth and cultural capital.

This complicated political drama seems unequivocally to confirm only one principle: the absence of a strong and just king leaves the commonwealth at risk, but at risk not solely from its most disenfranchised members. Cade, who offers the most radical critique of social inequality, is personally vilified and discredited within the play; but it is arguable that the larger context for his grim saturnalia of violence is the unspeakable selfishness of the English nobles. Many of them—York, Suffolk, Winchester—are everything Cade accuses the nobility of being. Moreover, though Cade is killed in this play, civil war does not vanish with his death, because the ambition and selfishness of these English nobles have not been contained. York still lives, and it will take Shakespeare another two plays to trace the destructive legacy of his ambition.

Some critics have suggested that given the venality of many of the nobles and the cruelty and hypocrisy of Cade, the play privileges the point of view of Alexander Iden, the landowning gentleman who kills Cade. Iden is well worth scrutiny. A property holder, a man who has built a brick wall around his garden, Iden also has charitable impulses. He "sends the poor well pleasèd from [his] gate" and at first does not want to fight with Cade, a "poor famished man" (4.9.21, 41). Does Iden's garden represent an

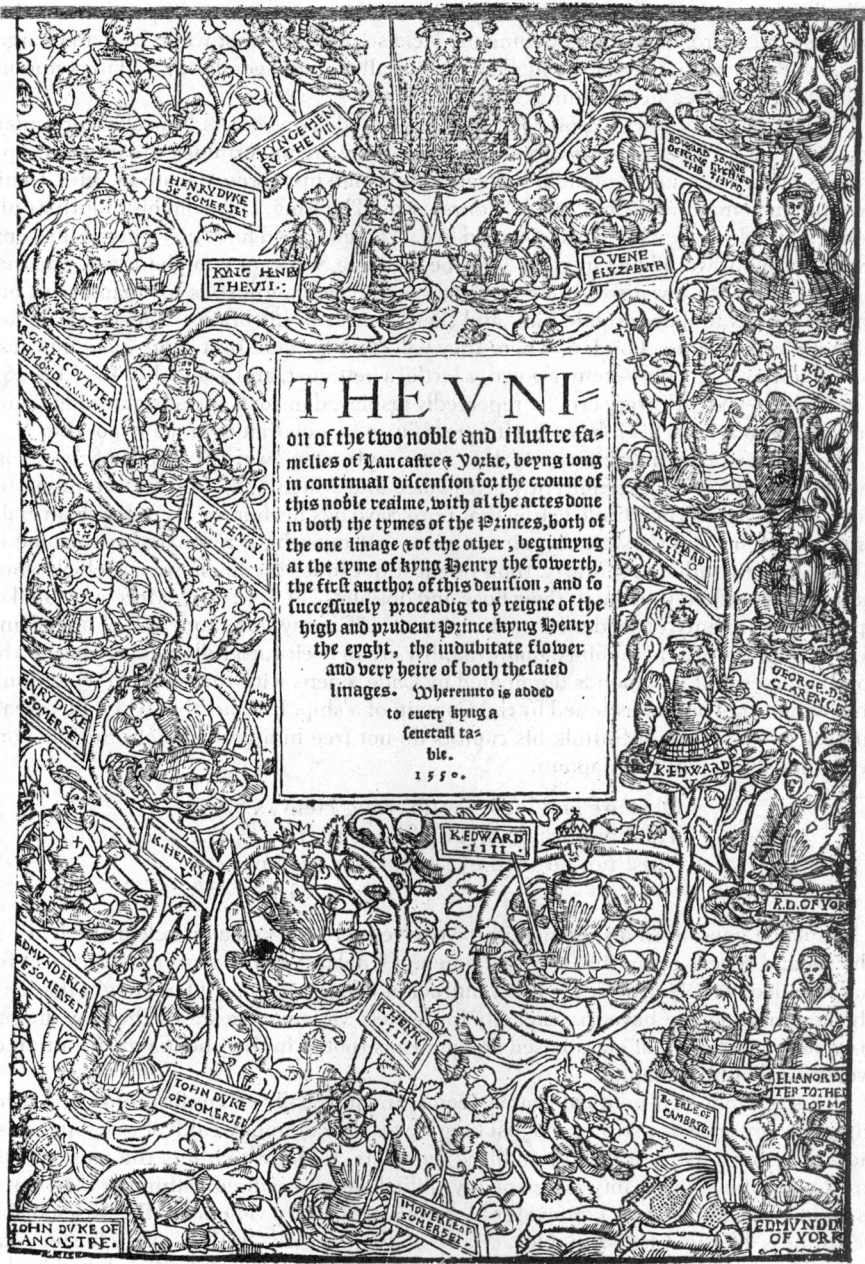

The houses of York and Lancaster depicted as two parts of a rosebush conjoined,
by the marriage of Henry VII and Elizabeth of York, to form the Tudor dynasty.
Title page to Edward Halle's (or Hall's) *Union of the Two Noble and Illustre Famelies
of Lancastre & Yorke* (1550 ed.).

English Eden? Shakespeare sounds several evocative notes through the creation of
this figure. Iden conjures up the virtues of rural England as opposed to the values of
the corrupt court or the rampaging urban artisans. And he anticipates the emergence
of the bourgeois property holder as the backbone of the nation. But Iden is not the

dominant force in the political landscape of the play, nor, despite his seeming independence, are his loyalties in doubt. When he learns who the poor famished man really is, Iden is glad to have killed Cade; and when he delivers the rebel's head to King Henry, he receives a knighthood in return. The independent property holder is certainly the King's man and no friend to those who would level the social order and make property common. How deeply Shakespeare—the man from rural Stratford who eventually became a major property holder in that town—idealized Iden, or replicated his political stance, is a matter for debate.

JEAN E. HOWARD

TEXTUAL NOTE

The play commonly known as *2 Henry VI* existed in two versions in the early modern period. In 1594, a quarto version (Q) entitled *The First Part of the Contention of the Two Famous Houses of York and Lancaster* was published; it was followed in 1600 and 1619 by two other quartos based on the first. In 1623, a version of the play about a third longer than Q was included in the First Folio (F), where it was entitled *The Second Part of Henry VI*. The relationship between these two texts is one of the vexed issues in Shakespearean scholarship. In the 1920s, several scholars proposed that Q had been prepared by several actors who had performed in a London production of the play and had reconstructed as much of the script as they could remember. The stage directions in Q are unusually full, indicating the quarto's probable theatrical origins. It may derive, indirectly, from the promptbook prepared for either a London performance or a provincial tour.

Recently, some scholars have questioned whether memorial reconstruction (actors piecing together scripts from memory) provides an adequate explanation for the differences so often found among variant texts that survive for many early modern plays. In particular, Steven Urkowitz has argued that the 1594 Quarto of this play is not a product of memorial reconstruction but is Shakespeare's early version, which he later revised. Urkowitz maintains that both the 1594 and the 1623 texts were prepared by Shakespeare, even though they differ from one another in important ways. He argues, for example, that Queen Margaret is a fiercer and more assertive figure in F than in Q. Urkowitz urges that each version of the play be studied on its own. Other textual editors argue that many people—actors, compositors, censors, scribes—may have had a hand in altering a play as it moved onto the stage or into print. Shakespeare may not himself have been responsible for all the differences we now perceive between quarto and Folio texts; nonetheless, the existing texts are distinct entities and should be examined separately rather than conflated into one amalgamated version.

The Oxford edition of the play adheres to the view, dominant since the 1920s, that the quarto is, indeed, a memorial reconstruction of some version of the Folio text, probably a version that had been abridged and otherwise revised on its way from the authorial "foul papers" on which F is based to the promptbook that lies behind Q. Therefore, while F serves as the primary control text, the Oxford edition, like most others, uses many of Q's stage directions to clarify playhouse practice. More controversially, the Oxford edition also assumes that in preparing the Folio text, the compositors who set type drew on the printed quarto versions in some places, probably because the manuscript serving as the basis of F was occasionally illegible or hard to use. At five points (indicated in the Textual Variants), the Oxford editors use Q rather than F as control text. At other points, they follow the quarto placement of particular events, interpolate material found only in Q, or replace Folio material with quarto material when they believe that the changes represent authorial revisions to the version of the Folio text on which Q was based. The Oxford editors also retain the title used for the 1594 Quarto on the grounds that it is more descriptive of the play's content than the blander

Second Part of Henry VI, and because it is the title by which the play was probably known during Shakespeare's own lifetime.

The Oxford text differs, then, in many ways from modern texts based more exclusively on F. One striking change occurs at the beginning of 3.2: the Oxford edition follows Q in showing the actual murder of Gloucester onstage; F only shows the murderers running from the scene of the crime. The Oxford text also incorporates some quarto material about the Cade rebellion not found in F. These additions, lines 116–31 and 134–36 of 4.7, report the burning of London Bridge, the rape of a Sergeant's wife by one of Cade's men, and Cade's own boast that he will lead his men in sexual assaults upon the women of the city. Together, they darken further F's depiction of Cade's lawlessness. Another substantive change involves the Oxford editors' choice to print the quarto version of the final fight between York and Clifford (5.3.20–30) rather than the Folio version. The two differ markedly in tone; Q stresses the enmity of York and Clifford, F their mutual respect and chivalric honor. This edition prints both, providing the Folio version as an inset passage, and this juxtaposition affords an excellent opportunity to examine one of the important places where F and Q diverge.

The Oxford text in two places follows Q's ordering of particular incidents. In 1.4, a scene involving conjuration, F has a spirit deliver prophecies concerning the fate of several characters—the King, Suffolk, Somerset. York then breaks in upon the scene, seizes the written transcription of the prophecies, and reads them out a second time. The Oxford editors, however, follow Q: when York breaks into the scene of conjuration, he does *not* read the prophecies aloud, an act that seems theatrically redundant. Rather, they are read aloud by King Henry in the next scene (2.1.177–87), when the conjuring episode is reported to him. Similarly, in Act 5, the Oxford edition follows Q in having the final fight between Richard and Somerset occur as 5.2, right before Clifford's battle with York, rather than placing Somerset's death later as young Clifford is bearing off the body of his dead father. The quarto arrangement thus puts maximum emphasis on York's triumph over old Clifford, King Henry's champion.

The Oxford edition differs from most modern texts in one other interesting way. At the beginning of 4.2 in F, two minor characters are listed as Bevis and John Holland. Most editors assume that these are the names of actual players, George Bevis and John Holland, who at some time acted in the play, rather than of fictional characters, yet they use these names as speech prefixes. In the Oxford text, Bevis and Holland are designated, as in Q, simply as "rebels."

Scene numbers follow most modern editions, except that the Oxford edition makes one continuous scene of what are traditionally Scenes 7 and 8 of Act 4, Cade's attack on London and his encounter with Buckingham and Clifford. Oxford also divides Act 5 into five scenes rather than the usual three. Placing the fight between Richard and Somerset after Scene 1 requires setting that fight off as 5.2. In addition, the Oxford editors believe that the stage is cleared after the encounter in which York kills old Clifford, whose body is carried off by his son. Henry and Margaret's ensuing flight from the battlefield is thus set off as a separate scene, 5.4.

SELECTED BIBLIOGRAPHY

Carroll, William. "Theories of Kingship in Shakespeare's England." *A Companion to Shakespeare's Works.* Vol. II: *The Histories.* Ed. Richard Dutton and Jean E. Howard. Malden, Mass.: Blackwell, 2003. 125–45. Lays out the main ideas circulating in early modern England and Scotland about the powers and duties of the king as well as limits to his power.

Cartelli, Thomas. "Jack Cade in the Garden: Class Consciousness and Class Conflict in *2 Henry VI.*" *Enclosure Acts: Sexuality, Property, and Culture in Early Modern England.* Ed. Richard Burt and John Michael Archer. Ithaca, N.Y.: Cornell University Press, 1994. 48–64. Explores the class-based antagonism between Jack Cade and members of the propertied elite, including Alexander Iden, into whose garden the starving Cade intrudes.

Fitter, Chris. "Emergent Shakespeare and the Politics of Protest: 2 Henry VI in Historical Contexts." *English Literary History* 72 (2005): 129–58. Discusses the connections between the play and political events in Shakespeare's own lifetime and argues for Shakespeare's radical political leanings.

Greenblatt, Stephen. "Murdering Peasants: Status, Genre, and the Representation of Rebellion." *Representations* no. 1 (1983): 1–29. Explores the difficulties of representing early modern popular insurrection and the ideological instability of such representations.

Helgerson, Richard. "Staging Exclusion." *Forms of Nationhood: The Elizabethan Writing of England*. Chicago: University of Chicago Press, 1992. 195–245. Argues that through a predominantly negative representation of Cade and through a focus on the consolidation of monarchical rule, Shakespeare was instrumental in disrupting the traditional link between the theater and popular revolt.

Howard, Jean E., and Phyllis Rackin. "Henry VI, Part II." *Engendering a Nation: A Feminist Account of Shakespeare's English Histories*. London: Routledge, 1997. 65–82. Examines the relationship between political disorder and gender disorder with special attention paid to Queen Margaret, King Henry, Eleanor Cobham, and Jack Cade.

Knowles, Ronald. "The Farce of History: Miracle, Combat, and Rebellion in 2 Henry VI." *The Yearbook of English Studies* 21 (1991): 168–86. Examines the dramatic techniques of ironic juxtaposition, mirroring, and parody through which Shakespeare staged historical events and processes.

Manley, Lawrence. "From Strange's Men to Pembroke's Men: 2 Henry VI and The First Part of the Contention." *Shakespeare Quarterly* 54 (2003): 253–87. Argues that the Quarto is a revision of some version of the longer Folio text and that this revision, which includes a harsher treatment of Eleanor Cobham, sprang from the play's transfer from Lord Strange's Men to Pembroke's Men.

Patterson, Annabel. "The Peasant's Toe: Popular Culture and Popular Pressure." *Shakespeare and the Popular Voice*. Cambridge, Mass.: Blackwell, 1989. 32–51. Argues that there was a cultural tradition of popular protest in Shakespeare's England to which his representation of Jack Cade is indebted.

Urkowitz, Steven. "'If I Mistake in These Foundations Which I Build Upon': Peter Alexander's Textual Analysis of Henry VI Parts 2 and 3." *English Literary Renaissance* 18 (1988): 230–56. Refutes the idea of memorial reconstruction—that is, that the Quarto is a text derived from actors' memories of performance—and, instead, sees the Folio text as Shakespeare's purposeful revision of the Quarto.

FILM

Henry VI, Part Two. 1983. Dir. Jane Howell. UK/USA. Sumptuously costumed but tepid BBC-TV production with Julia Foster as Margaret, David Burke as Gloucester, Peter Benson as Henry VI, and Trevor Peacock as Cade.

The First Part of the Contention
of the Two Famous Houses
# of York and Lancaster
(The Second Part of Henry VI)

THE PERSONS OF THE PLAY

Of the King's Party

KING HENRY VI
QUEEN MARGARET
William de la Pole, Marquis, later Duke, of SUFFOLK, the Queen's lover
Duke Humphrey of GLOUCESTER, the Lord Protector, the King's uncle
Dame Eleanor Cobham, the DUCHESS of Gloucester
CARDINAL BEAUFORT, Bishop of Winchester, Gloucester's uncle
   and the King's great-uncle
Duke of BUCKINGHAM
Duke of SOMERSET
Old Lord CLIFFORD
YOUNG CLIFFORD, his son

Of the Duke of York's Party

Duke of YORK
EDWARD, Earl of March }
Crookback RICHARD } his sons
Earl of SALISBURY
Earl of WARWICK, his son

The petitions and the combat

Two or three PETITIONERS
Thomas HORNER, an armourer
PETER Thump, his man
Three NEIGHBOURS, who drink to Horner
Three PRENTICES, who drink to Peter

The conjuration

Sir John HUME }
John SOUTHWELL } priests
Margery Jordan, a WITCH
Roger BOLINGBROKE, a conjurer
ASNATH, a spirit

The false miracle

Simon SIMPCOX
SIMPCOX'S WIFE
The MAYOR of Saint Albans
Aldermen of Saint Albans
A BEADLE of Saint Albans
Townsmen of Saint Albans

Eleanor's penance
Gloucester's SERVANTS
Two SHERIFFS of London
Sir John STANLEY
HERALD

The murder of Gloucester
TWO MURDERERS
COMMONS

The murder of Suffolk
CAPTAIN of a ship
MASTER of that ship
The Master's MATE
Walter WHITMORE
TWO GENTLEMEN

The Cade Rebellion
Jack CADE, a Kentishman suborned by the Duke of York
Dick the BUTCHER ⎫
Smith the WEAVER ⎪
A Sawyer   } Cade's followers
JOHN ⎪
REBELS ⎭
Emmanuel, the CLERK of Chatham ⎤
Sir Humphrey STAFFORD ⎪
STAFFORD'S BROTHER ⎪
Lord SAYE   } those who die at the rebels' hands
Lord SCALES ⎪
Matthew Gough ⎪
A SERGEANT ⎦
Three or four CITIZENS of London
Alexander IDEN, an esquire of Kent, who kills Cade

Others
VAUX, a messenger
A POST
MESSENGERS
A SOLDIER
Attendants, guards, servants, soldiers, falconers

1.1

Flourish° of trumpets, then hautboys.° Enter, at one   *Fanfare / oboes*
door, KING HENRY *and Humphrey Duke of* GLOUCESTER,
the Duke of SOMERSET, *the Duke of* BUCKINGHAM, CAR-
DINAL BEAUFORT, *and others. Enter, at the other door,*
the Duke of YORK, *and the Marquis of* SUFFOLK, *and*
QUEEN MARGARET, *and the Earl[s] of* SALISBURY *and*
WARWICK[1]

1.1 Location: The palace, London.
1. This stage direction, like many others, is modeled primarily upon that in Q. Many editors believe Q is based
indirectly on a promptbook and closely reflects playhouse practice. In F, Salisbury, Warwick, Gloucester, and
Beaufort enter with the King, while Somerset and Buckingham enter with the Queen, Suffolk, and York.

SUFFOLK [*kneeling before* KING HENRY] As by your high imperial majesty
    I had in charge° at my depart° for France,   *was charged / departure*
    As Procurator° to your excellence,   *deputy*
    To marry Princess Margaret for your grace,°   *on your behalf*
5   So, in the famous ancient city Tours,
    In presence of the Kings of France and Sicil,²
    The Dukes of Orléans, Calaber,° Bretagne, and Alençon,   *Calabria*
    Seven earls, twelve barons, and twenty reverend bishops,
    I have performed my task and was espoused,
10   And humbly now upon my bended knee,
    In sight of England and her lordly peers,
    Deliver up my title in the Queen
    To your most gracious hands, that are the substance
    Of that great shadow° I did represent—   *image (of royalty)*
15   The happiest° gift that ever marquis³ gave,   *most fortunate; best*
    The fairest queen that ever king received.
KING HENRY   Suffolk, arise. Welcome, Queen Margaret.
    I can express no kinder° sign of love   *more natural*
    Than this kind° kiss.   *affectionate*
    [*He kisses her*]
                  O Lord that lends me life,
20   Lend me a heart replete with thankfulness!
    For thou hast given me in this beauteous face
    A world of earthly blessings to my soul,
    If sympathy° of love unite our thoughts.   *mutual feeling*
QUEEN MARGARET   Th'excess of love I bear unto your grace
25   Forbids me to be lavish of my tongue
    Lest I should speak more than beseems a woman.
    Let this suffice: my bliss is in your liking,°   *your affection for me*
    And naught can make poor Margaret miserable
    Unless the frown of mighty England's King.⁴
29.1   QUEEN MARGARET   *Great King of England, and my gracious lord,*
       The mutual conference° that my mind hath had—   *intimate talk*
       By day, by night; waking, and in my dreams;
       In courtly company, or at my beads°—   *while praying*
29.5   *With you, mine alder liefest° sovereign,*   *entirely most precious*
       Makes me the bolder to salute my king
       With ruder terms, such as my wit affords
       And overjoy of heart doth minister.°   *suggest*
30 KING HENRY   Her sight did ravish, but her grace in speech,
    Her words yclad° with wisdom's majesty,   *clad*
    Makes me from wond'ring° fall to weeping joys,   *admiring*
    Such is the fullness of my heart's content.
    Lords, with one cheerful voice, welcome my love.

---

2. Sicily. Queen Margaret's father, René, the Duke of Anjou, was Sicily's king in name only.
3. A nobleman ranking below a duke and above an earl. In *1 Henry VI*, Suffolk holds the rank of earl; here he appears as a marquis; later in this scene, Henry will make him a duke for his service as royal marriage broker.
4. Oxford adopts the 1594 Quarto version of the Queen's initial speech, lines 24–29; the Folio version, which follows as an indented passage (lines 29.1–29.8), may be the author's original draft.

35 LORDS *kneel[ing]*   Long live Queen Margaret, England's happiness.
QUEEN MARGARET   We thank you all.
          Flourish. [They all rise]
SUFFOLK [*to* GLOUCESTER]   My Lord Protector, so it please your grace,
     Here are the articles of contracted peace
     Between our sovereign and the French King Charles,
40   For eighteen months concluded by consent.
GLOUCESTER (*reads*)   Imprimis:° it is agreed between the French   *First*
     King Charles and William de la Pole, Marquis of Suffolk,
     ambassador for Henry, King of England, that the said Henry
     shall espouse the Lady Margaret, daughter unto René, King
45   of Naples, Sicilia, and Jerusalem, and crown her Queen of
     England, ere the thirtieth of May next ensuing.
          Item:° it is further agreed between them that the duchy of   *Likewise*
     Anjou and the county of Maine shall be released and delivered
     to the King her fa—
          *Duke Humphrey [*GLOUCESTER*] lets [the paper] fall*[5]
KING HENRY   Uncle, how now?
50 GLOUCESTER   Pardon me, gracious lord.
     Some sudden qualm° hath struck me at the heart   *illness; fear*
     And dimmed mine eyes that I can read no further.
KING HENRY [*to* CARDINAL BEAUFORT]   Uncle of Winchester,
          I pray read on.
CARDINAL BEAUFORT [*reads*]   Item: it is further agreed between
55   them that the duchy of Anjou and the county of Maine shall
     be released and delivered to the King her father, and she sent
     over of° the King of England's own proper° cost and charges,   *at / personal*
     without dowry.
KING HENRY   They please us well. [*To* SUFFOLK] Lord Marquis,
          kneel down.
          [SUFFOLK *kneels*]
60   We here create thee first Duke of Suffolk,
     And gird thee with the sword.
          [SUFFOLK *rises*]
                         Cousin[6] of York,
     We here discharge your grace from being regent
     I'th' parts° of France till term of eighteen months   *(English) regions*
     Be full° expired. Thanks uncle Winchester,   *fully*
65   Gloucester, York, and Buckingham, Somerset,
     Salisbury, and Warwick.
     We thank you all for this great favour done
     In entertainment° to my princely Queen.   *welcome*
     Come, let us in, and with all speed provide
70   To see her coronation be performed.
          Exeunt KING [HENRY], QUEEN [MARGARET],
          and Suffolk. GLOUCESTER *stays all the rest*
GLOUCESTER   Brave peers of England, pillars of the state,
     To you Duke Humphrey must unload his grief,

---

5. In subsequent stage directions, "Humphrey" will often be silently changed to "Gloucester." As with many directions, this one appears only in Q, not in F.

6. A form of address customarily used by English monarchs to nobles.

Your grief, the common grief of all the land.
What—did my brother Henry° spend his youth,   Henry V
His valour, coin, and people in the wars?
Did he so often lodge in open field
In winter's cold and summer's parching heat
To conquer France, his true inheritance?[7]
And did my brother Bedford toil his wits
To keep by policy° what Henry got?   political skill
Have you yourselves, Somerset, Buckingham,
Brave York, Salisbury, and victorious Warwick,
Received deep scars in France and Normandy?
Or hath mine uncle Beaufort and myself,
With all the learnèd Council of the realm,
Studied so long, sat in the Council House
Early and late, debating to and fro,
How France and Frenchmen might be kept in awe,°   obedience
And had his highness in his infancy
Crownèd in Paris in despite of foes?
And shall these labours and these honours die?
Shall Henry's conquest, Bedford's vigilance,
Your deeds of war, and all our counsel die?
O peers of England, shameful is this league,
Fatal this marriage, cancelling your fame,
Blotting your names from books of memory,
Razing the characters° of your renown,   Erasing the records
Defacing monuments of conquered France,
Undoing all, as° all had never been!   as though
CARDINAL BEAUFORT Nephew, what means this passionate discourse,
This peroration° with such circumstance?[8]   rhetorical speech
For France, 'tis ours; and we will keep it still.°   always
GLOUCESTER Ay, uncle, we will keep it if we can—
But now it is impossible we should.
Suffolk, the new-made duke that rules the roast,°   roost
Hath given the duchy of Anjou and Maine
Unto the poor King René, whose large style°   exalted title
Agrees not with the leanness of his purse.
SALISBURY Now by the death of Him that died for all,[9]
These counties were the keys of Normandy—
But wherefore weeps Warwick, my valiant son?
WARWICK For grief that they are past recovery.
For were there hope to conquer them again
My sword should shed hot blood, mine eyes no tears.
Anjou and Maine? Myself did win them both!
Those provinces these arms of mine did conquer—
And are the cities that I got with wounds
Delivered up again with peaceful words?
Mort Dieu![1]
YORK For Suffolk's duke, may he be suffocate,°   choked (a pun)
That dims the honour of this warlike isle!

---

7. England laid claim to France throughout the four-   8. Such long-winded formality; so many details.
teenth century, and Henry V won the title "heir of   9. An oath equivalent to "by Christ's death."
France" with the Treaty of Troyes in 1420. See Henry V   1. God's death (French oath).
1.1.85–90.

France should have torn and rent my very heart
Before I would have yielded to this league.
I never read but° England's kings have had   *I have always read that*
125 Large sums of gold and dowries with their wives—
And our King Henry gives away his own,
To match with° her that brings no vantages.°   *wed / profits (dowry)*
GLOUCESTER   A proper jest, and never heard before
That Suffolk should demand a whole fifteenth[2]
130 For costs and charges in transporting her!
She should have stayed in France and starved in France
Before—
CARDINAL BEAUFORT   My lord of Gloucester, now ye grow too hot!
It was the pleasure of my lord the King.
135 GLOUCESTER   My lord of Winchester, I know your mind.
'Tis not my speeches that you do mislike,
But 'tis my presence that doth trouble ye.
Rancour will out. Proud prelate, in thy face
I see thy fury. If I longer stay
140 We shall begin our ancient bickerings—
But I'll be gone, and give thee leave to speak.
Lordings,° farewell, and say when I am gone,   *My lords*
I prophesied France will be lost ere long.   *Exit*
CARDINAL BEAUFORT   So, there goes our Protector in a rage.
145 'Tis known to you he is mine enemy;
Nay more, an enemy unto you all,
And no great friend, I fear me, to the King.
Consider, lords, he is the next of blood[3]
And heir apparent to the English crown.
150 Had Henry got an empire by his marriage,
And all the wealthy kingdoms of the west,[4]
There's reason he° should be displeased at it.   *(Gloucester)*
Look to it, lords—let not his smoothing° words   *flattering*
Bewitch your hearts. Be wise and circumspect.
155 What though the common people favour him,
Calling him 'Humphrey, the good Duke of Gloucester',
Clapping their hands and crying with loud voice
'Jesu maintain your royal excellence!'
With 'God preserve the good Duke Humphrey!'
160 I fear me, lords, for all this flattering gloss,°   *fair appearance*
He will be found a dangerous Protector.
BUCKINGHAM   Why should he then protect our sovereign,
He being of age[5] to govern of himself?
Cousin of Somerset, join you with me,
165 And all together, with the Duke of Suffolk,
We'll quickly hoist° Duke Humphrey from his seat.   *remove*
CARDINAL BEAUFORT   This weighty business will not brook° delay—   *permit*
I'll to the Duke of Suffolk presently.°   *Exit*   *immediately*

---

2. A tax of one-fifteenth of the value of personal property.
3. Because Henry VI did not yet have children, the heir to the throne was Gloucester, his father's brother.
4. An anachronistic reference to the European conquest of the Americas.

5. Henry VI being old enough. At the time represented in this scene, the historical King was twenty-four and Gloucester was no longer Protector. Shakespeare here as elsewhere alters his sources.

SOMERSET   Cousin of Buckingham, though Humphrey's pride
170   And greatness of his place be grief to us,
     Yet let us watch the haughty Cardinal;
     His insolence is more intolerable
     Than all the princes in the land beside.
     If Gloucester be displaced, he'll be Protector.
175 BUCKINGHAM   Or° thou or I, Somerset, will be Protector,   *Either*
     Despite Duke Humphrey or the Cardinal.

Exeunt BUCKINGHAM *and* SOMERSET

SALISBURY   Pride went before, ambition follows him.[6]
     While these do labour for their own preferment,°   *advancement*
     Behoves it us to labour for the realm.
180   I never saw but Humphrey Duke of Gloucester
     Did bear him like a noble gentleman.
     Oft have I seen the haughty Cardinal,
     More like a soldier than a man o'th' church,
     As stout° and proud as° he were lord of all,   *arrogant / as if*
185   Swear like a ruffian, and demean° himself   *conduct*
     Unlike the ruler of a commonweal.
     Warwick, my son, the comfort of my age,
     Thy deeds, thy plainness,° and thy housekeeping°   *honesty / hospitality*
     Hath won thee greatest favour of the commons,
190   Excepting none but good Duke Humphrey.
     And, brother York,[7] thy acts in Ireland,
     In bringing them to civil discipline,°   *civilized order*
     Thy late exploits done in the heart of France,
     When thou wert Regent for our sovereign,
195   Have made thee feared and honoured of the people.
     The reverence of° mine age and Neville's name[8]   *respect for*
     Is of no little force if I command.
     Join we together for the public good,
     In what we can to bridle° and suppress   *restrain*
200   The pride of Suffolk and the Cardinal
     With Somerset's and Buckingham's ambition;
     And, as we may, cherish° Duke Humphrey's deeds   *encourage*
     While they do tend° the profit of the land.   *promote*
WARWICK   So God help Warwick, as he loves the land,
205   And common profit of his country!
YORK   And so says York, [*aside*] for he hath greatest cause.
SALISBURY   Then let's away, and look unto the main.[9]
WARWICK   Unto the main? O, father, Maine is lost!
     That Maine which by main° force Warwick did win,   *overwhelming*
210   And would have kept so long as breath did last!
     Main chance, father, you meant—but I meant Maine,
     Which I will win from France or else be slain.

Exeunt WARWICK *and* SALISBURY. Manet° YORK   *Remains*

YORK   Anjou and Maine are given to the French,
     Paris is lost, the state of Normandy
215   Stands on a tickle° point now they are gone;   *an unstable*
     Suffolk concluded on the articles,

---

6. A variation on the proverb "Pride goes before and shame comes after." Salisbury seems to refer to the Cardinal, who exited first, as "pride" and to Buckingham and Somerset as "ambition."
7. York was actually Salisbury's brother-in-law, having married Salisbury's sister Cicely.

8. Neville was the family name of the Earl of Salisbury and of his son, Warwick.
9. And consider the principal matter at stake. A gambling term, with subsequent puns on the several meanings of "main," including wordplay on "Maine," a French province lost in Suffolk's treaty.

    The peers agreed, and Henry was well pleased
    To change two dukedoms for a duke's fair daughter.
    I cannot blame them all—what is't to them?
220   'Tis thine[1] they give away and not their own!
    Pirates may make cheap pennyworths of° their pillage,   *sell at a low price*
    And purchase friends, and give to courtesans,
    Still° revelling like lords till all be gone,   *Continually*
    Whileas the seely° owner of the goods   *While the helpless*
225   Weeps over them, and wrings his hapless° hands,   *unlucky*
    And shakes his head, and, trembling, stands aloof
    While all is shared and all is borne away,
    Ready to starve and dare not touch his own.
    So York must sit and fret and bite his tongue,
230   While his own lands are bargained for and sold.
    Methinks the realms of England, France, and Ireland
    Bear that proportion° to my flesh and blood   *relation*
    As did the fatal brand Althaea burnt
    Unto the prince's heart of Calydon.[2]
235   Anjou and Maine both given unto the French!
    Cold° news for me—for I had hope of France,   *Unwelcome*
    Even as I have of fertile England's soil.
    A day will come when York shall claim his own,
    And therefore I will take the Nevilles' parts,[3]
240   And make a show of love to proud Duke Humphrey,
    And, when I spy advantage,° claim the crown,   *opportunity*
    For that's the golden mark° I seek to hit.   *target*
    Nor shall proud Lancaster[4] usurp my right,
    Nor hold the sceptre in his childish fist,
245   Nor wear the diadem upon his head
    Whose church-like humours° fits not for a crown.   *pious temperament*
    Then, York, be still a while till time do serve.
    Watch° thou, and wake when others be asleep,   *Stay awake*
    To pry into the secrets of the state—
250   Till Henry, surfeit° in the joys of love   *sickened from excess*
    With his new bride and England's dear-bought queen,
    And Humphrey with the peers be fall'n at jars.°   *into contention*
    Then will I raise aloft the milk-white rose,[5]
    With whose sweet smell the air shall be perfumed,
255   And in my standard° bear the arms of York,   *military flag*
    To grapple with the house of Lancaster;
    And force perforce° I'll make him yield the crown,   *by violent coercion*
    Whose bookish rule hath pulled fair England down.   *Exit*

1.2

Enter Duke Humphrey [of GLOUCESTER] *and his wife*
    Eleanor [the DUCHESS]
DUCHESS   Why droops my lord, like over-ripened corn°   *grain*
    Hanging the head at Ceres' plenteous load?[1]

---

1. It is your own (York is addressing himself and referring to his claim to the throne).
2. Althaea, mother of Meleager, Prince of Calydon, was told by the Fates that her son would live only as long as a log burning in the fire at his birth. She snatched the log from the flames, but later, when Meleager killed her brothers, Althaea returned the log to the fire and Meleager's heart stopped beating. See Ovid, *Metamorphoses* 8.

3. And therefore will I ally myself with Salisbury and Warwick.
4. Henry VI was also Duke of Lancaster.
5. The emblem of the Yorkists; the red rose was the Lancastrian emblem.
1.2 Location: The Duke of Gloucester's house, London.
1. At the rich harvest of Ceres (the Roman goddess of agriculture and the harvest).

Why doth the great Duke Humphrey knit his brows,
As frowning at the favours of the world?
5   Why are thine eyes fixed to the sullen earth,
Gazing on that which seems to dim thy sight?
What seest thou there? King Henry's diadem,
Enchased° with all the honours of the world?   Adorned
If so, gaze on, and grovel on thy face[2]
10   Until thy head be circled with the same.
Put forth thy hand, reach at the glorious gold.
What, is't too short? I'll lengthen it with mine;
And having both together heaved° it up,   raised
We'll both together lift our heads to heaven
15   And never more abase our sight so low
As to vouchsafe one glance unto the ground.
GLOUCESTER   O Nell, sweet Nell, if thou dost love thy lord,
Banish the canker° of ambitious thoughts!   ulcer
And may that hour when I imagine ill
20   Against my king and nephew, virtuous Henry,
Be my last breathing in this mortal world!
My troublous dream this night° doth make me sad.   this past night
DUCHESS   What dreamed my lord? Tell me and I'll requite it
With sweet rehearsal° of my morning's dream.[3]   recital
25   GLOUCESTER   Methought this staff, mine office-badge° in court,   symbol of my position
Was broke in twain—by whom I have forgot,
But, as I think, it was by th' Cardinal—
And on the pieces of the broken wand
Were placed the heads of Edmund, Duke of Somerset,
30   And William de la Pole, first Duke of Suffolk.
This was my dream—what it doth bode, God knows.
DUCHESS   Tut, this was nothing but an argument°   a proof
That he that breaks a stick of Gloucester's grove
Shall lose his head for his presumption.
35   But list° to me, my Humphrey, my sweet duke: listen
Methought I sat in seat of majesty
In the cathedral church of Westminster,
And in that chair° where kings and queens are crowned,   throne
Where Henry and Dame Margaret kneeled to me,
40   And on my head did set the diadem.
GLOUCESTER   Nay, Eleanor, then must I chide outright.
Presumptuous dame! Ill-nurtured° Eleanor!   Ill-bred
Art thou not second woman in the realm,
And the Protector's wife beloved of him?
45   Hast thou not worldly pleasure at command
Above the reach or compass of thy thought?
And wilt thou still be hammering° treachery   devising
To tumble down thy husband and thyself
From top of honour to disgrace's feet?
50   Away from me, and let me hear no more!
DUCHESS   What, what, my lord? Are you so choleric°   hot-tempered
With Eleanor for telling but her dream?
Next time I'll keep my dreams unto myself
And not be checked.°   rebuked

2. Crawl on the ground (perhaps to seek supernatural   3. Morning dreams were popularly believed to be true.
aid).

55 GLOUCESTER Nay, be not angry; I am pleased again.

Enter a MESSENGER

MESSENGER My Lord Protector, 'tis his highness' pleasure
You do prepare to ride unto Saint Albans,
Whereas° the King and Queen do mean to hawk.   *Where*

GLOUCESTER I go. Come, Nell, thou wilt ride with us?

60 DUCHESS Yes, my good lord, I'll follow presently.°   *immediately*

Exeunt GLOUCESTER [*and the* MESSENGER]

Follow I must; I cannot go before
While Gloucester bears this base° and humble mind.   *servile*
Were I a man, a duke, and next of blood,
I would remove these tedious stumbling blocks
65 And smooth my way upon their headless necks.
And, being a woman, I will not be slack
To play my part in fortune's pageant.[4]
[*Calling within*] Where are you there? Sir John![5] Nay, fear not man.
We are alone. Here's none but thee and I.

Enter Sir John HUME

70 HUME Jesus preserve your royal majesty.

DUCHESS What sayst thou? 'Majesty'? I am but 'grace'.[6]

HUME But by the grace of God and Hume's advice
Your grace's title shall be multiplied.

DUCHESS What sayst thou, man? Hast thou as yet conferred
75 With Margery Jordan, the cunning witch[7] of Eye,
With Roger Bolingbroke, the conjuror?
And will they undertake to do me good?

HUME This they have promisèd: to show your highness
A spirit raised from depth of underground
80 That shall make answer to such questions
As by your Grace shall be propounded him.

DUCHESS It is enough. I'll think upon the questions.
When from Saint Albans we do make return,
We'll see these things effected to the full.
85 Here, Hume [*giving him money*], take this reward. Make merry, man,
With thy confederates in this weighty cause.   *Exit*

HUME Hume must make merry with the Duchess' gold;
Marry,[8] and shall. But how now, Sir John Hume?
Seal up your lips, and give no words but mum;
90 The business asketh silent secrecy.
Dame Eleanor gives gold to bring the witch.
Gold cannot come amiss were she a devil.
Yet have I gold flies from another coast[9]—
I dare not say from the rich Cardinal
95 And from the great and new-made Duke of Suffolk,
Yet I do find it so; for, to be plain,
They, knowing Dame Eleanor's aspiring humour,°   *ambitious nature*
Have hired me to undermine the Duchess,

---

4. In Roman mythology, the goddess Fortune symbolized the element of chance in human life and was often depicted with a rudder (as the pilot of destiny), wings, or a wheel. Here Fortune is imagined as directing a medieval play ("pageant") or leading a ceremonial procession.
5. Priests were commonly addressed as "sir."
6. The appropriate title for a duchess.
7. Cunning women, sometimes prosecuted for witchcraft, were familiar village figures who made a living by telling fortunes, healing sicknesses, making love potions, and finding lost objects.
8. By the Virgin Mary (a mild oath).
9. I have gold that comes from another quarter.

And buzz° these conjurations in her brain.   *whisper*
100   They say 'A crafty knave does need no broker',°   *middleman; agent*
  Yet am I Suffolk and the Cardinal's broker.
  Hume, if you take not heed you shall go near
  To call them both a pair of crafty knaves.
  Well, so it stands; and thus, I fear, at last
105   Hume's knavery will be the Duchess' wrack,°   *ruin*
  And her attainture° will be Humphrey's fall.   *conviction*
  Sort° how it will, I shall have gold for all.   *Exit*   *Turn out*

1.3

Enter PETER, *the armourer's man,*° [*with*] *two or three*   *apprentice*
[*other*] PETITIONERS

FIRST PETITIONER   My masters, let's stand close. My Lord Protector will come this way by and by and then we may deliver
our supplications in the quill.°   *as a group*
SECOND PETITIONER   Marry, the Lord protect him, for he's a
5   good man, Jesu bless him.

Enter the Duke of SUFFOLK *and* QUEEN [MARGARET]

FIRST PETITIONER   Here a° comes, methinks, and the Queen   *he*
with him. I'll be the first, sure.[1]

[*He goes to meet* SUFFOLK *and the* QUEEN]

SECOND PETITIONER   Come back, fool—this is the Duke of Suffolk and not my Lord Protector.
10 SUFFOLK [*to the* FIRST PETITIONER]   How now, fellow[2]—wouldst
anything with me?
FIRST PETITIONER   I pray, my lord, pardon me—I took ye for my
Lord Protector.
QUEEN MARGARET [*seeing his supplication, she reads*]   'To my
15   Lord Protector'—are your supplications to his lordship? Let
me see them.

[*She takes First Petitioner's supplication*]

What is thine?
FIRST PETITIONER   Mine is, an't° please your grace, against   *if it*
John Goodman, my lord Cardinal's man, for keeping my
20   house and lands and wife and all from me.
SUFFOLK   Thy wife too? That's some wrong indeed. [*To the* SEC-
OND PETITIONER] What's yours?

[*He takes the supplication*]

What's here? [*Reads*] 'Against the Duke of Suffolk for enclosing the commons[3] of Melford'! [*To the* SECOND PETITIONER]
25   How now, Sir Knave?
SECOND PETITIONER   Alas, sir, I am but a poor petitioner of our
whole township.
PETER [*offering his petition*]   Against my master, Thomas
Horner, for saying that the Duke of York was rightful heir to
30   the crown.

1.3 Location: The palace, London.
1. In F, these lines are assigned to Peter, but lines
12–13 suggest they are spoken by the First Petitioner,
who here pushes himself forward to get the attention of
the Queen and Suffolk (whom he believes to be
Gloucester).

2. A common form of address to a social inferior.
3. Fencing in for private use land once used by the entire
community. The practice of enclosure, which benefited
landowners while forcing into poverty the lower classes
who had farmed the land, was a chronic source of unrest
in many regions in early modern England.

QUEEN MARGARET   What sayst thou? Did the Duke of York say
    he was rightful heir to the crown?
PETER   That my master was? No, forsooth, my master said that
    he was and that the King was an usurer.
35 QUEEN MARGARET   An usurper thou wouldst say.
PETER   Ay, forsooth—an usurper.
SUFFOLK [calling within]   Who is there?
                 Enter [a] servant
    Take this fellow in and send for his master with a pursuivant°   an officer
    presently. [To PETER] We'll hear more of your matter before
40 the King.   Exit [the servant] with [PETER] the armourer's man
QUEEN MARGARET [to the PETITIONERS]   And as for you that love to be protected
    Under the wings of our Protector's grace,
    Begin your suits anew and sue to him.
        [She] tears the supplication[4]
    Away, base cullions![5] Suffolk, let them go.
45 ALL PETITIONERS   Come, let's be gone.   Exeunt PETITIONERS
QUEEN MARGARET   My lord of Suffolk, say, is this the guise?°   custom
    Is this the fashions in the court of England?
    Is this the government of Britain's isle,
    And this the royalty of Albion's° king?   England's
50 What, shall King Henry be a pupil still
    Under the surly Gloucester's governance?
    Am I a queen in title and in style,°   form of address
    And must be made a subject to a duke?
    I tell thee, Pole, when in the city Tours
55 Thou rann'st a-tilt[6] in honour of my love
    And stol'st away the ladies' hearts of France,
    I thought King Henry had resembled thee
    In courage, courtship,° and proportion.[7]   courtly manners
    But all his mind is bent to holiness,
60 To number Ave-Maries on his beads.[8]
    His champions are the prophets and apostles,[9]
    His weapons holy saws° of sacred writ,   sayings
    His study is his tilt-yard,° and his loves   jousting arena
    Are brazen images of canonizèd saints.
65 I would the college of the cardinals
    Would choose him Pope, and carry him to Rome,
    And set the triple crown° upon his head—   papal crown
    That were a state fit for his holiness.
SUFFOLK   Madam, be patient—as I was cause
70 Your highness came to England, so will I
    In England work your grace's full content.
QUEEN MARGARET   Beside the haught° Protector have we Beaufort   arrogant
    The imperious churchman, Somerset, Buckingham,
    And grumbling York; and not the least of these
75 But can do more in England than the King.

---

4. In Q, Suffolk is the one who "tears the papers." This
is one of the places where F gives more initiative to
Margaret than does Q.
5. Lowborn rascals. "Cullion" comes from the Italian
word *coglioni,* meaning "testicles."
6. You took part in a jousting tournament.
7. Physical grace; physique.

8. Referring to a Roman Catholic devotion in which a
string of beads (a rosary) is used to keep track of prayers
said in a particular sequence. Among the prayers are "Ave
Maria," or "Hail Mary," addressed to the Virgin Mary.
9. A champion stood in for the King at jousts and tournaments. Margaret scornfully suggests that Henry VI
makes holy men rather than real warriors his champions.

SUFFOLK   And he of these that can do most of all
　　Cannot do more in England than the Nevilles:
　　Salisbury and Warwick are no simple peers.
QUEEN MARGARET   Not all these lords do vex me half so much
80　As that proud dame, the Lord Protector's wife.
　　She sweeps it through the court with troops of ladies
　　More like an empress than Duke Humphrey's wife.
　　Strangers in court do take her for the queen.
　　She bears a duke's revenues on her back,°　　　　　*wears costly clothing*
85　And in her heart she scorns our poverty.
　　Shall I not live to be avenged on her?
　　Contemptuous° base-born callet° as she is,　　　*Despicable / whore*
　　She vaunted 'mongst her minions° t'other day　　　*followers*
　　The very train of her worst-wearing° gown　　　*poorest*
90　Was better worth° than all my father's lands,　　　*worth more*
　　Till Suffolk gave two dukedoms° for his daughter.　　*(Maine and Anjou)*
SUFFOLK   Madam, myself have limed a bush[1] for her,
　　And placed a choir of such enticing birds
　　That she will light° to listen to their lays,°　　　*perch / songs*
95　And never mount to trouble you again.
　　So let her rest; and, madam, list to me,
　　For I am bold to counsel you in this:
　　Although we fancy not the Cardinal,
　　Yet must we join with him and with the lords
100　Till we have brought Duke Humphrey in disgrace.
　　As for the Duke of York, this late complaint[2]
　　Will make but little for his benefit.
　　So one by one we'll weed them all at last,
　　And you yourself shall steer the happy helm.
　　　　Sound a sennet.° Enter KING HENRY, [*with*] *the Duke*　　*trumpet call*
　　　　of YORK *and the Duke of* SOMERSET *on both sides,*
　　　　whispering with him. [*Also*] *enter Duke Humphrey*
　　　　[*of* GLOUCESTER], *Dame Eleanor the* DUCHESS
　　　　[*of Gloucester*], *the Duke of* BUCKINGHAM,
　　　　the Earl[*s*] *of* SALISBURY *and* WARWICK, *and* CARDINAL
　　　　[BEAUFORT *Bishop*] *of Winchester*
105　KING HENRY   For my part, noble lords, I care not which:
　　Or° Somerset or York, all's one to me.　　　　*Either*
YORK   If York have ill demeaned° himself in France　　*conducted*
　　Then let him be denied the regentship.
SOMERSET   If Somerset be unworthy of the place,
110　Let York be regent—I will yield to him.
WARWICK   Whether your grace be worthy, yea or no,
　　Dispute not that: York is the worthier.
CARDINAL BEAUFORT   Ambitious Warwick, let thy betters speak.
WARWICK   The Cardinal's not my better in the field.°　　*in battle*
115　BUCKINGHAM   All in this presence are thy betters, Warwick.
WARWICK   Warwick may live to be the best of all.
SALISBURY   Peace, son; [*to* BUCKINGHAM] and show some reason,
　　　　Buckingham,
　　Why Somerset should be preferred in this.

---

1. Have set a trap. Elizabethans caught birds by smearing bushes and twigs with a sticky substance known as
birdlime.

2. This recent complaint. Suffolk means that Peter's
claim against his master casts doubt on York's loyalty to
the King.

QUEEN MARGARET   Because the King, forsooth, will have it so.

120 GLOUCESTER   Madam, the King is old enough himself
To give his censure.° These are no women's matters.   *judgment*

QUEEN MARGARET   If he be old enough, what needs your grace
To be Protector of his excellence?

GLOUCESTER   Madam, I am Protector of the realm,

125 And at his pleasure will resign my place.

SUFFOLK   Resign it then, and leave thine insolence.
Since thou wert king—as who is king but thou?—
The commonwealth hath daily run to wrack,
The Dauphin³ hath prevailed beyond the seas,

130 And all the peers and nobles of the realm
Have been as bondmen to thy sovereignty.

CARDINAL BEAUFORT [*to* GLOUCESTER]   The commons hast thou
racked,° the clergy's bags   *overtaxed*
Are lank and lean with thy extortions.

SOMERSET [*to* GLOUCESTER]   Thy sumptuous buildings⁴ and thy wife's attire

135 Have cost a mass of public treasury.

BUCKINGHAM [*to* GLOUCESTER]   Thy cruelty in execution
Upon offenders hath exceeded law
And left thee to the mercy of the law.

QUEEN MARGARET [*to* GLOUCESTER]   Thy sale of offices and
towns in France—

140 If they were known, as the suspectᶜ is great—   *suspicion*
Would make thee quickly hop without thy head.⁵

Exit GLOUCESTER

QUEEN [MARGARET] *lets fall her fan*⁶
[*To the* DUCHESS] Give me my fan—what, minion,° can ye not?   *hussy*
She gives the DUCHESS *a box on the ear*
I cry you mercy,° madam! Was it you?   *beg your pardon*

DUCHESS   Was't I? Yea, I it was, proud Frenchwoman!

145 Could I come near your beauty with my nails,
I'd set my ten commandments° in your face.   *(ten fingers)*

KING HENRY   Sweet aunt, be quiet—'twas against her will.°   *unintentional*

DUCHESS   Against her will? Good King, look to't in time!
She'll pamper thee and dandle thee like a baby.

150 Though in this place most master⁷ wear no breeches
She shall not strike Dame Eleanor unrevenged!   *Exit*

BUCKINGHAM [*aside to* CARDINAL BEAUFORT]   Lord Cardinal, I
will follow Eleanor
And listen after Humphrey how he proceeds.
She's tickled° now, her fury needs no spurs—   *vexed*

155 She'll gallop far enough to her destruction.   *Exit*

Enter Duke Humphrey [*of* GLOUCESTER]

GLOUCESTER   Now, lords, my choler being overblown°   *dispelled*
With walking once about the quadrangle,
I come to talk of commonwealth affairs.
As for your spiteful false objections,

---

3. "Dauphin" was the title of the oldest son of the
French King, but here it refers to the French King
himself, Charles VII, and bears witness to the fact that
England did not acknowledge Charles's right to the
throne.

4. Probably a reference to Greenwich Palace. In 1437,

Gloucester obtained a grant to expand the old manor,
which he lent to Henry VI and Margaret for their
honeymoon.

5. Proverbial expression meaning to be beheaded.

6. In Q, the Queen lets fall a glove, not a fan.

7. The one most in control (the Queen).

160   Prove them, and I lie open to the law.
         But God in mercy so deal with my soul
         As I in duty love my King and country.
         But to the matter that we have in hand—
         I say, my sovereign, York is meetest° man   *the most suitable*
165   To be your regent in the realm of France.
       SUFFOLK   Before we make election,° give me leave   *a choice*
         To show some reason of no little force
         That York is most unmeet of any man.
       YORK   I'll tell thee, Suffolk, why I am unmeet:
170   First, for° I cannot flatter thee in pride;   *because*
         Next, if I be appointed for the place,
         My lord of Somerset will keep me here
         Without discharge,° money, or furniture,°   *payment / equipment*
         Till France be won into the Dauphin's hands.
175   Last time I danced attendance on his will[8]
         Till Paris was besieged, famished, and lost.
       WARWICK   That can I witness, and a fouler fact°   *deed*
         Did never traitor in the land commit.
       SUFFOLK   Peace, headstrong Warwick.
180   WARWICK   Image of pride, why should I hold my peace?
            Enter [guarded, HORNER *the] armourer and [*PETER*] his*
            man
       SUFFOLK   Because here is a man accused of treason—
         Pray God the Duke of York excuse himself!
       YORK   Doth anyone accuse York for a traitor?
       KING HENRY   What mean'st thou, Suffolk? Tell me, what are these?
185   SUFFOLK   Please it your majesty, this is the man
            [He indicates PETER*]*
         That doth accuse his master [*indicating* HORNER] of high treason.
         His words were these: that Richard Duke of York
         Was rightful heir unto the English crown,
         And that your majesty was an usurper.
190   KING HENRY [*to* HORNER]   Say, man, were these thy words?
       HORNER   An't shall please your majesty, I never said nor
         thought any such matter. God is my witness, I am falsely
         accused by the villain.
       PETER [*raising his hands*]   By these ten bones,° my lords, he did   *(ten fingers)*
195   speak them to me in the garret one night as we were scouring
         my lord of York's armour.
       YORK   Base dunghill villain and mechanical,°   *manual laborer*
         I'll have thy head for this thy traitor's speech!
         [*To* KING HENRY] I do beseech your royal majesty,
200   Let him have all the rigour of the law.
       HORNER   Alas, my lord, hang me if ever I spake the words. My
         accuser is my prentice, and when I did correct him for his
         fault the other day, he did vow upon his knees he would be
         even with me. I have good witness of this, therefore, I beseech
205   your majesty, do not cast away° an honest man for a villain's   *destroy*
         accusation.

---

8. I did as he wished. York refers to events depicted in *1 Henry VI*, specifically to Somerset's failure to supply him with reinforcements during the wars in France. See *1 Henry VI* 4.3.9–11.

KING HENRY [*to* GLOUCESTER]   Uncle, what shall we say to this in law?

GLOUCESTER   This doom,° my lord, if I may judge by case: *judgment*
Let Somerset be regent o'er the French,

210   Because in York this breeds suspicion.[9]
[*Indicating* HORNER *and* PETER] And let these have a day
    appointed them
For single combat in convenient place,
For he [*indicating* HORNER] hath witness of his servant's malice.
This is the law, and this Duke Humphrey's doom.

215   KING HENRY   Then be it so. [*To* SOMERSET] My lord of Somerset,
We make you regent o'er the realm of France
There to defend our rights 'gainst foreign foes.

SOMERSET   I humbly thank your royal majesty.

HORNER   And I accept the combat willingly.

220   PETER [*to* GLOUCESTER]   Alas, my lord, I cannot fight; for God's
sake, pity my case! The spite of man prevaileth against me.
O Lord, have mercy upon me—I shall never be able to fight a
blow! O Lord, my heart!

GLOUCESTER   Sirrah,[1] or° you must fight or else be hanged.   *either*

225   KING HENRY   Away with them to prison, and the day
Of combat be the last of the next month.
Come, Somerset, we'll see thee sent away.   *Flourish. Exeunt*

1.4

Enter Margery Jordan, a WITCH; *Sir John* HUME
[*and John* SOUTHWELL, *two priests*]; *and Roger*
BOLINGBROKE, *a conjuror*[1]

HUME   Come, my masters, the Duchess, I tell you, expects performance of your promises.

BOLINGBROKE   Master Hume, we are therefore° provided. Will   *for that purpose*
her ladyship behold and hear our exorcisms?°   *conjuring of spirits*

5   HUME   Ay, what else? Fear you not her courage.

BOLINGBROKE   I have heard her reported to be a woman of an
invincible spirit. But it shall be convenient, Master Hume,
that you be by her, aloft, while we be busy below. And so, I
pray you, go in God's name and leave us.   *Exit* HUME

10   Mother Jordan, be you prostrate and grovel on the earth.
She lies down upon her face.
Enter Eleanor [*the* DUCHESS *of Gloucester*] *aloft*
John Southwell, read you and let us to our work.

DUCHESS   Well said, my masters, and welcome all. To this gear°   *business*
the sooner the better.
[*Enter* HUME *aloft*]

BOLINGBROKE   Patience, good lady—wizards know their times.

15   Deep night, dark night, the silent of the night,
The time of night when Troy was set on fire,[2]
The time when screech-owls cry and bandogs° howl,   *chained watchdogs*

---

9. Because this matter casts doubt on York's loyalty.
1. A common form of address to a social inferior.
1.4 Location: Gloucester's garden, London.
1. Neither Q nor F names John Southwell as one of the
two priests in this scene, but he is named in dialogue at
line 11. Q has Eleanor enter at the beginning of the
scene; F, as here, has her enter aloft a few lines into the
scene. After Hume's exit at line 9, he must reenter aloft

at some point to attend Eleanor. This entry is not
marked, but having Hume reenter after line 13 leaves
enough time for him to exit the stage at line 9 and make
an entrance above.
2. Virgil's *Aeneid*, Book 2, describes how the Greeks,
having entered Troy through treachery, set fire to the
ancient city.

And spirits walk, and ghosts break up° their graves—   *burst open*
That time best fits the work we have in hand.
20   Madam, sit you, and fear not. Whom we raise
We will make fast within a hallowed verge.°   *magic circle*
        Here do the ceremonies belonging,[3] *and make the*
        circle. SOUTHWELL *reads 'Coniuro te',*[4] *&c. It thunders*
        and lightens terribly, then the spirit [ASNATH][5] *riseth*
ASNATH   Adsum.°   *I am here*
WITCH   Asnath,
By the eternal God whose name and power
25   Thou tremblest at, answer that° I shall ask,   *what*
For till thou speak, thou shalt not pass from hence.
ASNATH   Ask what thou wilt, that° I had said and done.   *would that*
BOLINGBROKE [*reads*] 'First, of the King: what shall of him
        become?'
ASNATH   The Duke yet lives that Henry shall depose,
30   But him outlive, and die a violent death.[6]
        [*As the spirit speaks,* SOUTHWELL *writes the answer*]
BOLINGBROKE [*reads*] 'Tell me what fate awaits the Duke of Suffolk.'
ASNATH   By water shall he die, and take his end.
BOLINGBROKE [*reads*] 'What shall betide the Duke of Somerset?'
ASNATH   Let him shun castles. Safer shall he be
35   Upon the sandy plains than where castles mounted° stand.   *on mountains*
Have done—for more I hardly can endure.
BOLINGBROKE   Descend to darkness and the burning lake!
        False° fiend, avoid!°   *Treacherous / be gone*
            Thunder and lightning. [*The spirit*] *sinks down again*[7]
38.1   BOLINGBROKE   *Then down, I say, unto the damnèd pool*
            Where Pluto[8] *in his fiery wagon° sits*   *chariot*
            Riding, amidst the singed and parchèd smokes,
            The roads of Ditis by the River Styx.[9]
38.5   *There howl and burn for ever in those flames.*
            Rise, Jordan, rise and stay° thy charming spells—   *halt*
            Zounds,° we are betrayed!   *By God's wounds (oath)*
        Enter the Duke[s] *of* YORK *and* BUCKINGHAM *with their guard,* [*among them*
        Sir Humphrey STAFFORD] *and break in*
YORK   Lay hands upon these traitors and their trash.
            [BOLINGBROKE, SOUTHWELL, *and Jordan are taken pris-*
            oner. BUCKINGHAM *takes the writings from*
            BOLINGBROKE *and* SOUTHWELL]
40   [*To Jordan*] Beldam,° I think we watched you at an inch.°   *Witch / closely*
        [*To the* DUCHESS] What, madam, are you there? The King
            and common weal
Are deep indebted for this piece of pains.°   *your trouble*

---

3. The rituals necessary (for conjuring spirits).
4. I conjure you (Latin), the beginning of a spell.
5. An anagram of "Sathan," a variant form of "Satan."
Demons were supposed to be invoked by anagrams.
6. *The . . . death:* Like many prophecies, this one is
ambiguous. The syntax of the first line can mean that
there lives a duke whom Henry shall depose or who
shall depose Henry. The duke is probably York, who in
Richard Duke of York (3 Henry VI) forces Henry to
entail the crown to York rather than to Henry's own son,
thus symbolically deposing him. York, however, dies a
violent death after the Battle of Wakefield, and Henry
outlives him. But Henry also dies a violent death, murdered in the Tower of London by the Duke of York's son,
Richard, Duke of Gloucester, who eventually becomes
King Richard III.
7. For lines 37–38, Q substitutes the following
indented passage (lines 38.1–38.7); it may record a
revision made in rehearsal to cover the spirit's descent.
8. In classical mythology, the god of the infernal regions.
9. The river of Hades over which Charon ferried the
dead.

My lord Protector will, I doubt it not,
See you well guerdoned° for these good deserts.   *rewarded*
DUCHESS   Not half so bad as thine to England's king,
45   Injurious° Duke, that threatest where's no cause.   *Abusive*
BUCKINGHAM   True, madam, none at all—
[*He raises the writings*]
what call you this?
[*To his men*] Away with them. Let them be clapped up close°   *imprisoned securely*
And kept asunder. [*To the* DUCHESS] You, madam, shall with us.
50   Stafford, take her to thee.
[*Exeunt* STAFFORD *and others to the* DUCHESS
and HUME *above*]
We'll see your trinkets here all forthcoming.[1]
All away!
Exeunt [below, Jordan, SOUTHWELL, *and*
BOLINGBROKE, *guarded, and, above,* HUME *and*
the DUCHESS *guarded by* STAFFORD *and others.*
YORK *and* BUCKINGHAM *remain*]
YORK   Lord Buckingham, methinks you watched her well.
A pretty plot,° well chosen to build upon.   *trick; plot of ground*
55   Now pray, my lord, let's see the devil's writ.
[BUCKINGHAM *gives him the writings*]
What have we here?
[*He*] *reads* [*the writings*]
Why, this is just°   *precisely*
Aio Aeacidam, Romanos vincere posse.[2]
These oracles are hardily° attained   *with difficulty*
And hardly understood. Come, come, my lord,
60   The King is now in progress towards Saint Albans;
With him the husband of this lovely lady.
Thither goes these news as fast as horse can carry them—
A sorry breakfast for my lord Protector.
BUCKINGHAM   Your grace shall give me leave, my lord of York,
65   To be the post° in hope of his reward.   *messenger*
YORK [*returning the writings to* BUCKINGHAM]   At your pleasure,
my good lord.   *Exit* BUCKINGHAM
[*Calling within*] Who's within there, ho!
Enter a SERVINGMAN
Invite my lords of Salisbury and Warwick
To sup with me tomorrow night. Away.   *Exeunt [severally]°*   *separately*

2.1

Enter KING [HENRY], QUEEN [MARGARET] *with her hawk*
on her fist, Duke Humphrey [of GLOUCESTER],
CARDINAL [BEAUFORT], *and* [*the Duke of*] SUFFOLK, *with*
falconers hollering
QUEEN MARGARET   Believe me, lords, for flying at the brook°   *hawking for waterfowl*
I saw not better sport these seven years' day;
Yet, by your leave, the wind was very high,
And, ten to one, old Joan had not gone out.[1]

---

1. We'll see that your worthless goods (the conjuring paraphernalia) are produced as evidence against you.
2. I say that you, descendant of Aeacus, the Romans can conquer. A famously ambiguous response by an oracle to King Pyrrhus's question about whether he would conquer Rome.
2.1 Location: St. Albans.
1. The hawk named "Old Joan" would probably not have flown because of the high wind.

KING HENRY [*to* GLOUCESTER]   But what a point,[2] my lord, your falcon made,
5   And what a pitch° she flew above the rest!   height
To see how God in all his creatures works!
Yea, man and birds are fain° of climbing high.   fond
SUFFOLK   No marvel, an it like° your majesty,   if it please
My Lord Protector's hawks do tower so well;
10   They know their master loves to be aloft,°   to rule over others
And bears his thoughts above his falcon's pitch.[3]
GLOUCESTER   My lord, 'tis but a base ignoble mind
That mounts no higher than a bird can soar.
CARDINAL BEAUFORT   I thought as much; he would be above the clouds.
15   GLOUCESTER   Ay, my lord Cardinal, how think you by that?
Were it not good your grace could fly to heaven?
KING HENRY   The treasury of everlasting joy.
CARDINAL BEAUFORT [*to* GLOUCESTER]   Thy heaven is on earth;
      thine eyes and thoughts
20   Beat on° a crown, the treasure of thy heart,   Think obsessively about
Pernicious Protector, dangerous peer,
That smooth'st it so with° King and common weal!   Who so flatters
GLOUCESTER   What, Cardinal? Is your priesthood grown peremptory?
Tantaene animis caelestibus irae?[4]
25   Churchmen so hot? Good uncle, hide such malice
With some holiness—can you do it?
SUFFOLK   No malice, sir, no more than well becomes°   is appropriate to
So good° a quarrel and so bad a peer.   just
GLOUCESTER   As who, my lord?
SUFFOLK   Why, as you, my lord—
30   An't like your lordly Lord's Protectorship.
GLOUCESTER   Why, Suffolk, England knows thine insolence.
QUEEN MARGARET   And thy ambition, Gloucester.
KING HENRY   I prithee peace,
Good Queen, and whet not on° these furious peers—   do not encourage
For blessèd are the peacemakers on earth.[5]
35   CARDINAL BEAUFORT   Let me be blessèd for the peace I make
Against this proud Protector with my sword.
            [GLOUCESTER *and* CARDINAL BEAUFORT *speak privately to*
                  one another]
GLOUCESTER   Faith, holy uncle, would't were come to that.
CARDINAL BEAUFORT   Marry, when thou dar'st.
GLOUCESTER   Dare? I tell thee, priest,
Plantagenets[6] could never brook° the dare!   tolerate
40   CARDINAL BEAUFORT   I am Plantagenet as well as thou,
And son to John of Gaunt.

---

2. High position to which hawks fly to await prey.
3. Alluding to Gloucester's heraldic crest, which consisted of a falcon with a maiden's head. Suffolk is accusing Gloucester of overweening ambition.
4. Quoting Virgil's *Aeneid* 1.11, "Can there be such anger in heavenly minds?"
5. Quoting Jesus' Sermon on the Mount (Matthew 5:9).
6. "Plantagenet" was a name given the kings descended from Geoffrey, Count of Anjou, and Matilda, daughter of Henry I, thought to derive from the Latin words for

"a sprig of broom," which Geoffrey wore in his cap. Gloucester, a grandson of John of Gaunt, was a Plantagenet. John of Gaunt was Beaufort's father, but Beaufort's mother, Catherine Swynford, gave birth to him and his brothers before she married Gaunt; this explains why Gloucester calls Beaufort a bastard (line 42). Historically, the Beauforts, though eventually legitimated, were barred from any claim to the throne. The lines referring to Beaufort's bastardy, 38–43, appear only in Q and not in F.

GLOUCESTER   In bastardy.

CARDINAL BEAUFORT   I scorn thy words.

GLOUCESTER   Make up no factious numbers for the matter,[7]

45   In thine own person answer thy abuse.°   insult; offense

CARDINAL BEAUFORT   Ay, where thou dar'st not peep; an if° thou dar'st,   an if = if
     This evening on the east side of the grove.

KING HENRY   How now, my lords?

CARDINAL BEAUFORT [aloud]   Believe me, cousin Gloucester,
     Had not your man put up° the fowl so suddenly,   raised; startled
     We had had more sport. [Aside to GLOUCESTER] Come with thy
50   two-hand sword.

GLOUCESTER [aloud]   True, uncle.
     [Aside to CARDINAL BEAUFORT] Are ye advised?° The east side   agreed
         of the grove.

CARDINAL BEAUFORT [aside to GLOUCESTER]
     I am with you.

KING HENRY   Why, how now, uncle Gloucester?

GLOUCESTER   Talking of hawking, nothing else, my lord.
     [Aside to the CARDINAL] Now, by God's mother, priest, I'll shave
55   your crown[8] for this,
     Or all my fence° shall fail.   skill in fencing

CARDINAL BEAUFORT [aside to GLOUCESTER]
                   Medice, teipsum[9]—
     Protector, see to't well; protect yourself.

KING HENRY   The winds grow high; so do your stomachs,° lords.   tempers
     How irksome is this music to my heart!
60   When such strings jar,[1] what hope of harmony?
     I pray, my lords, let me compound° this strife.   settle
           Enter one crying 'a miracle'

GLOUCESTER   What means this noise?
     Fellow, what miracle dost thou proclaim?

ONE   A miracle, a miracle!

65   SUFFOLK   Come to the King—tell him what miracle.

ONE [to KING HENRY]   Forsooth, a blind man at Saint Alban's shrine[2]
     Within this half-hour hath received his sight—
     A man that ne'er saw in his life before.

KING HENRY   Now God be praised, that to believing souls
70   Gives light in darkness, comfort in despair!
           Enter the MAYOR of Saint Albans and his brethren
           [aldermen] with music, bearing the man [SIMPCOX]
           between two in a chair. [Enter SIMPCOX'S WIFE
           and other townsmen with them]

CARDINAL BEAUFORT   Here comes the townsmen on° procession   in
     To present your highness with the man.
           [The townsmen kneel]

KING HENRY   Great is his comfort in this earthly vale,
     Although by sight his sin be multiplied.[3]

GLOUCESTER [to the townsmen]   Stand by, my masters; bring
75   him near the King.

---

7. Call in no supporters for this quarrel.
8. Alluding to a tonsure, or a shaved circular patch,
often seen on the heads of religious men.
9. Physician, (heal) thyself (see Luke 4:23).

1. When instruments such as these grow discordant.
2. A shrine to the first British martyr, who was beheaded
by the Romans for giving sanctuary to Christians.
3. Although his sight will lead him into more temptation.

His highness' pleasure is to talk with him.
            [*They rise and bear* SIMPCOX *before the* KING]
KING HENRY [*to* SIMPCOX]   Good fellow, tell us here the circumstance,
    That we for thee may glorify the Lord.
    What, hast thou been long blind and now restored?
SIMPCOX   Born blind, an't please your grace.
80 SIMPCOX'S WIFE   Ay, indeed, was he.
SUFFOLK   What woman is this?
SIMPCOX'S WIFE   His wife, an't like your worship.
GLOUCESTER   Hadst thou been his mother
    Thou couldst have better told.
KING HENRY [*to* SIMPCOX]   Where wert thou born?
85 SIMPCOX   At Berwick,⁴ in the north, an't like your grace.
KING HENRY   Poor soul, God's goodness hath been great to thee.
    Let never day nor night unhallowed° pass,   *unblessed*
    But still° remember what the Lord hath done.   *continually*
QUEEN MARGARET [*to* SIMPCOX]   Tell me, good fellow, cam'st
            thou here by chance,
90   Or of devotion to this holy shrine?
SIMPCOX   God knows, of pure devotion, being called
    A hundred times and oftener, in my sleep,
    By good Saint Alban, who said, 'Simon, come;
    Come offer° at my shrine and I will help thee.'   *make an offering*
95 SIMPCOX'S WIFE   Most true, forsooth, and many time and oft
    Myself have heard a voice to call him so.
CARDINAL BEAUFORT [*to* SIMPCOX]
    What, art thou lame?
SIMPCOX   Ay, God almighty help me.
SUFFOLK   How cam'st thou so?
SIMPCOX   A fall off of a tree.
SIMPCOX'S WIFE [*to* SUFFOLK]
    A plum tree,⁵ master.
GLOUCESTER   How long hast thou been blind?
SIMPCOX   O, born so, master.
100 GLOUCESTER   What, and wouldst climb a tree?
SIMPCOX   But that° in all my life, when I was a youth.   *Only that once*
SIMPCOX'S WIFE [*to* GLOUCESTER]   Too true—and bought his
            climbing very dear.
GLOUCESTER [*to* SIMPCOX]   Mass,° thou loved'st plums well   *By the Mass (an oath)*
            that wouldst venture so.
SIMPCOX   Alas, good master, my wife desired some damsons,°   *tiny plums; testicles*
105   And made me climb with danger of my life.
GLOUCESTER [*aside*]   A subtle knave, but yet it shall not serve.
    [*To* SIMPCOX] Let me see thine eyes: wink° now, now open   *close your eyes*
    them. In my opinion yet thou seest not well.
SIMPCOX   Yes, master, clear as day, I thank God and Saint Alban.
110 GLOUCESTER   Sayst thou me so? [*Pointing*] What colour is this cloak of?
SIMPCOX   Red, master; red as blood.
GLOUCESTER   Why, that's well said.
    [*Pointing*] And his cloak?
SIMPCOX   Why, that's green.

---

4. Town on the Scottish border, far from St. Albans.   5. Slang for "female thighs and genitals."

GLOUCESTER [*pointing*]   And what colour's
    His hose?
SIMPCOX   Yellow, master; yellow as gold.
GLOUCESTER   And what colour's my gown?
SIMPCOX   Black, sir; coal-black, as jet.°   *glossy black stone*
115 KING HENRY   Why, then, thou know'st what colour jet is of?
SUFFOLK   And yet I think jet did he never see.
GLOUCESTER   But cloaks and gowns before this day a many.°   *a multitude*
SIMPCOX'S WIFE   Never before this day in all his life
GLOUCESTER   Tell me, sirrah, what's my name?
120 SIMPCOX   Alas, master, I know not.
GLOUCESTER [*pointing*]   What's his name?
SIMPCOX   I know not.
GLOUCESTER [*pointing*]   Nor his?
SIMPCOX   No, truly, sir.
125 GLOUCESTER [*pointing*]   Nor his name?
SIMPCOX   No indeed, master.
GLOUCESTER   What's thine own name?
SIMPCOX   Simon[6] Simpcox, an it please you, master.
GLOUCESTER   Then, Simon, sit thou there the lying'st knave
130   In Christendom. If thou hadst been born blind
    Thou mightst as well have known our names as thus
    To name the several colours we do wear.
    Sight may distinguish colours, but suddenly
    To nominate° them all—it is impossible.   *name*
135   Saint Alban here hath done a miracle.
    Would you not think his cunning° to be great   *skill*
    That could restore this cripple to his legs again?
SIMPCOX   O master, that you could!
GLOUCESTER [*to the* MAYOR *and aldermen*]   My masters of Saint
    Albans, have you not
140   Beadles[7] in your town, and things called whips?
MAYOR   We have, my lord, an if it please your grace.
GLOUCESTER   Then send for one presently.°   *immediately*
MAYOR [*to a townsman*]   Sirrah, go fetch the beadle hither
    straight.   *Exit one*
GLOUCESTER   Bring me a stool.
        [*A stool is brought*]
    [*To* SIMPCOX]   Now, sirrah, if you mean
145   To save yourself from whipping, leap me° o'er   *for me*
    This stool and run away.
SIMPCOX   Alas, master,
    I am not able even to stand alone.
    You go about to torture me in vain.
        Enter a BEADLE *with whips*
GLOUCESTER   Well, sirrah, we must have you find your legs.
150   [*To the* BEADLE] Whip him till he leap over that same stool.
BEADLE   I will, my lord.
        [*To* SIMPCOX] Come on, sirrah, off with your doublet quickly.

---

6. Q and F both call the character "Sander Simpcox" at this point. At line 93 of F, however, Simpcox refers to himself as "Simon." It has been proposed that "Sander" was the name of an actor who played the part of Simpcox, that his name entered Q at this point, and that this portion of F derives from Q.

7. Minor parish officials who administered punishment to vagabonds and those guilty of petty offenses.

SIMPCOX   Alas, master, what shall I do? I am not able to stand.
    After the BEADLE *hath hit him once, he leaps over the*
    stool and runs away. [Some of the townsmen] follow
    and cry, 'A miracle! A miracle!'
KING HENRY   O God, seest thou this and bear'st so long?
155 QUEEN MARGARET   It made me laugh to see the villain run!
GLOUCESTER [*to the* BEADLE]   Follow the knave, and take this
    drab° away.   *slut*
SIMPCOX'S WIFE   Alas, sir, we did it for pure need.°   *out of utter poverty*
    [*Exit the* BEADLE *with the* WIFE]
GLOUCESTER [*to the* MAYOR]   Let them be whipped through
    every market-town
  Till they come to Berwick, from whence they came.
    Exeunt [the] MAYOR [*and any remaining townsmen*]
160 CARDINAL BEAUFORT   Duke Humphrey has done a miracle today.
SUFFOLK   True: made the lame to leap and fly away.
GLOUCESTER   But you have done more miracles than I—
  You made, in a day, my lord, whole towns to fly.[8]
    Enter the Duke of BUCKINGHAM
KING HENRY   What tidings with our cousin Buckingham?
165 BUCKINGHAM   Such as my heart doth tremble to unfold.
  A sort of naughty persons, lewdly bent,[9]
  Under the countenance and confederacy°   *protection and complicity*
  Of Lady Eleanor, the Protector's wife,
  The ringleader and head of all this rout,
170 Have practised° dangerously against your state,   *plotted*
  Dealing with witches and with conjurors,
  Whom we have apprehended in the fact,°   *in the very act*
  Raising up wicked spirits from under ground,
  Demanding of King Henry's life and death
175 And other° of your highness' Privy Council.   *other members*
  And here's the answer the devil did make to them.
    [BUCKINGHAM *gives* KING HENRY *the writings*][1]
KING HENRY [*reads*]   'First of the King: what shall of him become?
  The Duke yet lives that Henry shall depose,
  But him outlive and die a violent death.'
180 God's will be done in all. Well, to the rest.
  [*Reads*] 'Tell me what fate awaits the Duke of Suffolk?
  By water shall he die, and take his end.'
SUFFOLK [*aside*]   By water must the Duke of Suffolk die?
  It must be so, or else the devil doth lie.
185 KING HENRY [*reads*]   'What shall betide the Duke of Somerset?
  Let him shun castles. Safer shall he be
  Upon the sandy plains than where castles mounted stand.'
CARDINAL BEAUFORT [*to* GLOUCESTER]   And so, my Lord
    Protector, by this means
  Your lady is forthcoming° yet at London.   *in custody*
190 [*Aside to* GLOUCESTER] This news, I think, hath turned your
    weapon's edge.°   *blunted your sword*

---

8. Referring to the French towns Suffolk gave away
when he arranged Henry's marriage to Margaret.
9. A gang of evil people, wickedly inclined.
1. Neither Q nor F directs Buckingham to hand Henry
the prophecies, but he clearly must do so if, as in Q,

Henry is to read them out at this point. Lines 177–87
follow the substance of York's reading of the prophecies
in F's 1.4, but they have been reconstructed by the
Oxford editors to fit their quarto placement here. For
details, see the Textual Variants.

'Tis like, my lord, you will not keep your hour.[2]

GLOUCESTER Ambitious churchman, leave° to afflict my heart.　　　　cease
Sorrow and grief have vanquished all my powers,
And, vanquished as I am, I yield to thee
195　Or to the meanest groom.°　　　　poorest servant

KING HENRY O God, what mischiefs work the wicked ones,
Heaping confusion on their own heads thereby!

QUEEN MARGARET Gloucester, see here the tainture° of thy nest,　　　　defilement
And look thyself be faultless, thou wert best.

200　GLOUCESTER Madam, for myself, to heaven I do appeal,
How I have loved my King and common weal;
And for my wife, I know not how it stands.
Sorry I am to hear what I have heard.
Noble she is, but if she have forgot
205　Honour and virtue and conversed° with such　　　　consulted
As, like to pitch, defile nobility,
I banish her my bed and company,[3]
And give her as a prey to law and shame
That hath dishonoured Gloucester's honest name.

210　KING HENRY Well, for this night we will repose us here;
Tomorrow toward London back again,
To look into this business thoroughly,
And call these foul offenders to their answers,
And poise° the cause in justice' equal scales,　　　　weigh
215　Whose beam stands sure,[4] whose rightful cause prevails.

Flourish. Exeunt

2.2

Enter the Duke of YORK and the Earls of SALISBURY
and WARWICK

YORK Now, my good lords of Salisbury and Warwick,
Our simple supper ended, give me leave
In this close walk° to satisfy myself　　　　secluded path
In craving your opinion of my title,
5　Which is infallible, to England's crown.

SALISBURY My lord, I long to hear it out at full.

WARWICK Sweet York, begin, and if thy claim be good,
The Nevilles are thy subjects to command.

YORK Then thus:
10　Edward the Third, my lords, had seven sons:
The first, Edward the Black Prince, Prince of Wales;
The second, William of Hatfield; and the third,
Lionel Duke of Clarence; next to whom
Was John of Gaunt, the Duke of Lancaster;
15　The fifth was Edmund Langley, Duke of York;
The sixth was Thomas of Woodstock, Duke of Gloucester;
William of Windsor was the seventh and last.
Edward the Black Prince died before his father
And left behind him Richard, his only son,

---

2. Appointment (for the duel previously arranged between Gloucester and Cardinal Beaufort).
3. Echoing the language of church law, which permitted marital separation "from bed and board" in cases of adultery, heresy, and cruelty.

4. Whose bar (from which the two scales are suspended) is perfectly balanced and therefore allows accurate measurements.
2.2 Location: The Duke of York's garden, London.

20   Who, after Edward the Third's death, reigned as king
     Till Henry Bolingbroke, Duke of Lancaster,
     The eldest son and heir of John of Gaunt,
     Crowned by the name of Henry the Fourth,
     Seized on the realm, deposed the rightful king,
25   Sent his poor queen to France from whence she came,
     And him to Pomfret; where, as well you know,
     Harmless Richard was murdered traitorously.
     WARWICK [*to* SALISBURY]   Father, the Duke of York hath told the truth;
     Thus got the house of Lancaster the crown.
30   YORK   Which now they hold by force and not by right;
     For Richard, the first son's heir, being dead,
     The issue of the next son should have reigned.
     SALISBURY   But William of Hatfield died without an heir.
     YORK   The third son, Duke of Clarence, from whose line
35   I claim the crown, had issue Phillipe, a daughter,
     Who married Edmund Mortimer, Earl of March;[1]
     Edmund had issue, Roger, Earl of March;
     Roger had issue, Edmund, Anne and Eleanor.
     SALISBURY   This Edmund, in the reign of Bolingbroke,
40   As I have read, laid claim unto the crown,
     And, but for Owain Glyndŵr, had been king,
     Who kept him in captivity till he died.
     But to the rest.
     YORK   His eldest sister, Anne,
     My mother, being heir unto the crown,
45   Married Richard, Earl of Cambridge, who was son
     To Edmund Langley, Edward the Third's fifth son.
     By her I claim the kingdom: she was heir
     To Roger, Earl of March, who was the son
     Of Edmund Mortimer, who married Phillipe,
50   Sole daughter unto Lionel, Duke of Clarence.
     So if the issue of the elder son
     Succeed before the younger, I am king.
     WARWICK   What plain proceedings is more plain than this?
     Henry doth claim the crown from John of Gaunt,
55   The fourth son; York claims it from the third:
     Till Lionel's issue fails, John's should not reign.
     It fails not yet, but flourishes in thee
     And in thy sons, fair slips of such a stock.[2]
     Then, father Salisbury, kneel we together,
60   And in this private plot° be we the first   *plot of ground*
     That shall salute our rightful sovereign
     With honour of his birthright to the crown.
     SALISBURY *and* WARWICK [*kneeling*]   Long live our sovereign
          Richard, England's king!
     YORK   We thank you, lords;

---

1. Like Raphael Holinshed and Edward Hall, whose chronicles Shakespeare used as sources for this play, Shakespeare conflates Edmund Mortimer, the fifth Earl of March, who was named heir to the throne by Richard II, with his uncle of the same name who was captured by Glyndŵr, a Welsh lord Shakespeare was later to depict in 1 *Henry IV* as a rebel against the King. Although Shakespeare here says Glyndŵr kept Mortimer imprisoned until he died, in 1 *Henry IV* he follows the chronicles in having Mortimer eventually marry Glyndŵr's daughter.
2. Fair cuttings of such a tree.

[SALISBURY *and* WARWICK *rise*]
                    but I am not your king
65 Till I be crowned, and that° my sword be stained   *until*
   With heart-blood of the house of Lancaster—
   And that's not suddenly to be performed,
   But with advice° and silent secrecy.   *deliberation*
   Do you, as I do, in these dangerous days,
70 Wink at° the Duke of Suffolk's insolence,   *Ignore*
   At Beaufort's pride, at Somerset's ambition,
   At Buckingham, and all the crew of them,
   Till they have snared the shepherd of the flock,
   That virtuous prince, the good Duke Humphrey.
75 'Tis that they seek, and they, in seeking that,
   Shall find their deaths, if York can prophesy.
SALISBURY   My lord, break off—we know your mind at full.
WARWICK   My heart assures me that the Earl of Warwick
   Shall one day make the Duke of York a king.
80 YORK   And Neville, this I do assure myself—
   Richard shall live to make the Earl of Warwick
   The greatest man in England but the King.   *Exeunt*

2.3

Sound trumpets. Enter KING HENRY *and state,*° *with*   *persons of rank*
guard, to banish the DUCHESS: KING HENRY *and* QUEEN
[MARGARET], *Duke Humphrey* [*of* GLOUCESTER], *the*
Duke of SUFFOLK *and the Duke of* BUCKINGHAM,
CARDINAL [BEAUFORT], *and, led with officers, Dame*
Eleanor Cobham [*the* DUCHESS, *Margery Jordan the*
WITCH, *John* SOUTHWELL *and Sir John* HUME *the two*
priests, and Roger BOLINGBROKE *the conjuror*]*; then*
enter to them the Duke of YORK *and the Earls of*
SALISBURY *and* WARWICK[1]
KING HENRY [*to the* DUCHESS]   Stand forth, Dame Eleanor
   Cobham, Gloucester's wife.
   [*She comes forward*]
   In sight of God and us your guilt is great;
   Receive the sentence of the law for sins
   Such as by God's book are adjudged to death.[2]
   [*To the* WITCH, SOUTHWELL, HUME, *and* BOLINGBROKE] You
5   four, from hence to prison back again;
   From thence, unto the place of execution.
   The witch in Smithfield[3] shall be burned to ashes,
   And you three shall be strangled° on the gallows.   *hanged*
             [*Exeunt* WITCH, SOUTHWELL, HUME, *and*
                        BOLINGBROKE, *guarded*]
   [*To the* DUCHESS] You, madam, for° you are more nobly born,   *because*
10 Despoilèd° of your honour in your life   *Deprived*
   Shall, after three days' open penance done,
   Live in your country here in banishment

2.3 Location: A London hall of justice.
1. F's stage direction simply reads "Sound Trumpets.
Enter the King and State, with Guard to banish the
Duchess." Q does not mention Jordan, the two priests,
or Bolingbroke, but F clearly requires them.
2. *Receive . . . death*: alluding to Exodus 22:18: "Thou

shalt not suffer a witch to live." At times throughout
Elizabeth's reign, witch hunts were conducted and laws
against witchcraft strictly enforced.
3. Famous as the site in London where heretics were
burned.

With Sir John Stanley in the Isle of Man.[4]

DUCHESS   Welcome is banishment; welcome were my death.

15   GLOUCESTER   Eleanor, the law, thou seest, hath judgèd thee;
I cannot justify° whom the law condemns.   *excuse*

Exit [the DUCHESS, guarded]

Mine eyes are full of tears, my heart of grief.
Ah, Humphrey, this dishonour in thine age
Will bring thy head with sorrow to the grave.
20   [*To* KING HENRY] I beseech your majesty, give me leave to go.
Sorrow would° solace, and mine age would ease.   *desires*

KING HENRY   Stay, Humphrey Duke of Gloucester. Ere thou go,
Give up thy staff.[5] Henry will to himself
Protector be; and God shall be my hope,
25   My stay, my guide, and lantern to my feet.
And go in peace, Humphrey, no less beloved
Than when thou wert Protector to thy King.

QUEEN MARGARET   I see no reason why a king of years°   *who is of age*
Should be to be° protected like a child.   *need to be*
30   God and King Henry govern England's helm!
Give up your staff, sir, and the King his° realm.   *the king's*

GLOUCESTER   My staff? Here, noble Henry, is my staff.
As willingly do I the same resign
As erst° thy father Henry made it mine;   *formerly*
35   And even as willing at thy feet I leave it
As others would ambitiously receive it.

[*He lays the staff at King Henry's feet*]

Farewell, good King. When I am dead and gone,
May honourable peace attend thy throne.   *Exit*

QUEEN MARGARET   Why, now is Henry King and Margaret Queen,
40   And Humphrey Duke of Gloucester scarce himself,
That bears so shrewd a maim;[6] two pulls° at once—   *pluckings; tugs*
His lady banished and a limb° lopped off.   *(his staff)*

[*She picks up the staff*]

This staff of honour raught,° there let it stand   *seized*
Where it best fits to be, in Henry's hand.

[*She gives the staff to KING HENRY*]

45   SUFFOLK   Thus droops this lofty pine and hangs his sprays;°   *branches*
Thus Eleanor's pride dies in her youngest days.°   *in its youth*

YORK   Lords, let him go. Please it your majesty,
This is the day appointed for the combat,
And ready are the appellant° and defendant—   *challenger*
50   The armourer and his man—to enter the lists,°   *dueling area*
So please your highness to behold the fight.

QUEEN MARGARET   Ay, good my lord, for purposely therefor
Left I the court to see this quarrel tried.

KING HENRY   A° God's name, see the lists and all things fit;   *In*
55   Here let them end it, and God defend the right.

YORK   I never saw a fellow worse bestead,°   *prepared*
Or more afraid to fight, than is the appellant,
The servant of this armourer, my lords.

---

4. An island off England's northwest coast.   6. Who endures so painful a mutilation.
5. Emblem of his office as Protector.

Enter at one door [HORNER] *the armourer and his*
NEIGHBOURS, *drinking to him so much that he is*
drunken; and he enters with a drum[mer] before him
and [carrying] his staff with a sandbag fastened to it.
[Enter] at the other door [PETER] *his man, [also] with*
a drum[mer] and [a staff with] sandbag, and PRENTICES
drinking to him

FIRST NEIGHBOUR [*offering drink to* HORNER] Here, neighbour
60 Horner, I drink to you in a cup of sack,° and fear not, neigh-   *sherry*
bour, you shall do well enough.
SECOND NEIGHBOUR [*offering drink to* HORNER] And here,
neighbour, here's a cup of charneco.°   *port*
THIRD NEIGHBOUR [*offering drink to* HORNER] Here's a pot of
65 good double° beer, neighbour, drink and be merry, and fear   *extra-strong*
not your man.
HORNER [*accepting the offers of drink*] Let it come,° i'faith I'll   *Pass it around*
pledge you all, and a fig[7] for Peter.
FIRST PRENTICE [*offering drink to* PETER] Here, Peter, I drink to
70 thee, and be not afeard.
SECOND PRENTICE [*offering drink to* PETER] Here, Peter, here's
a pint of claret wine for thee.
THIRD PRENTICE [*offering drink to* PETER] And here's a quart for
me, and be merry, Peter, and fear not thy master. Fight for
75 credit° of the prentices!   *the honor*
PETER [*refusing the offers of drink*] I thank you all. Drink and
pray for me, I pray you, for I think I have taken my last
draught in this world. Here, Robin, an if° I die, I give thee my   *an if = if*
apron; and, Will, thou shalt have my hammer; and here, Tom,
80 take all the money that I have. O Lord bless me, I pray God,
for I am never able to deal with my master, he hath learned so
much fence° already.   *fencing skill*
SALISBURY Come, leave your drinking and fall to blows.
[*To* PETER] Sirrah, what's thy name?
85 PETER Peter, forsooth.
SALISBURY Peter? What more?
PETER Thump.
SALISBURY Thump! Then see that thou thump thy master well.
HORNER Masters, I am come hither, as it were, upon my man's
90 instigation, to prove him a knave and myself an honest man;
and touching the Duke of York, I will take my death° I never   *stake my life on it*
meant him any ill, nor the King, nor the Queen; and therefore,
Peter, have at thee° with a downright° blow.   *I come at thee / vertical*
YORK Dispatch; this knave's tongue begins to double.°   *to slur his words*
Sound trumpets [an] alarum to the combatants.[8]
They fight and PETER *hits* [HORNER] *on the head and*
strikes him down
95 HORNER Hold, Peter, hold—I confess, I confess treason.
He dies
YORK [*to an attendant, pointing to* HORNER] Take away his
weapon. [*To* PETER] Fellow, thank God and the good wine in
thy master's wame.°   *belly*

---

7. Slang for "vulva"; hence, an obscene insult. It was typically accompanied by a gesture in which the thumb was thrust between two closed fingers or into the mouth.
8. In F, the line "Sound Trumpets, Alarum to the Combatants" is spoken by York as part of his prior speech.

PETER *He kneels down*[9]   O God, have I overcome mine enemy
100   in this presence? O, Peter, thou hast prevailed in right.
KING HENRY [*to attendants, pointing to* HORNER] Go, take hence
      that traitor from our sight,
   For by his death we do perceive his guilt.
   And God in justice hath revealed to us
   The truth and innocence of this poor fellow,
105   Which he° had thought to have murdered wrongfully.   *Whom he (Horner)*
   [*To* PETER] Come, fellow, follow us for thy reward.
      Sound a flourish. Exeunt [some carrying HORNER'*s body]*

                                  2.4
         Enter Duke Humphrey [of GLOUCESTER] *and his men*
         in mourning cloaks[1]
GLOUCESTER   Thus sometimes hath the brightest day a cloud;
   And after summer evermore succeeds°   *follows*
   Barren winter, with his wrathful nipping° cold;   *biting*
   So cares and joys abound as seasons fleet.°   *fly by*
5   Sirs, what's o'clock?
SERVANT   Ten, my lord.
GLOUCESTER   Ten is the hour that was appointed me
   To watch the coming of my punished Duchess;
   Uneath° may she endure the flinty streets,   *Scarcely*
10   To tread them with her tender-feeling feet.
   Sweet Nell, ill can thy noble mind abrook°   *endure*
   The abject° people gazing on thy face   *lowly born*
   With envious° looks, laughing at thy shame,   *spiteful*
   That erst did follow thy proud chariot wheels
15   When thou didst ride in triumph through the streets.
   But soft, I think she comes; and I'll prepare
   My tear-stained eyes to see her miseries.
         Enter the DUCHESS, *Dame Eleanor Cobham, barefoot,*
         [*with*] *a white sheet about her, written verses pinned*
         on her back[2] [*and carrying a*] *wax candle in her hand;*
         [*she is*] *accompanied with the [two]* SHERIFFS
         of London, and Sir John STANLEY, *and officers with*
         bills and halberds[3]
SERVANT [*to* GLOUCESTER]   So please your grace, we'll take her°   *rescue her by force*
   from the sheriffs.
GLOUCESTER   No, stir not for your lives, let her pass by.
20   DUCHESS   Come you, my lord, to see my open shame?
   Now thou dost penance too. Look how they gaze,
   See how the giddy multitude do point
   And nod their heads, and throw their eyes on thee.
   Ah, Gloucester, hide thee from their hateful° looks,   *full of hate*
25   And, in thy closet° pent up, rue my shame,   *private chamber*
   And ban° thine enemies—both mine and thine.   *curse*
GLOUCESTER   Be patient, gentle Nell; forget this grief.
DUCHESS   Ah, Gloucester, teach me to forget myself;
   For whilst I think I am thy married wife,

---

9. Only Q records, "He [Peter] kneels down," just as Q, and not F, indicates, "He [Horner] dies" (line 95).
2.4 Location: A London street.
1. Hooded black garments worn to funerals to express sorrow.

2. Eleanor's offenses were presumably detailed in these verses.
3. Both bills and halberds were long-handled weapons. Bills had a curved blade, halberds an axlike blade with a spike at the back.

30 And thou a prince, Protector of this land,
Methinks I should not thus be led along,
Mailed up⁴ in shame, with papers on my back,
And followed with a rabble that rejoice
To see my tears and hear my deep-fet groans.⁵
35 The ruthless flint doth cut my tender feet,
And when I start,° the envious people laugh,   *flinch*
And bid me be advisèd how I tread.
Ah, Humphrey, can I bear this shameful yoke?
Trowest° thou that e'er I'll look upon the world,   *Believeth*
40 Or count them happy that° enjoys the sun?   *who*
No, dark shall be my light, and night my day;
To think upon my pomp shall be my hell.
Sometime I'll say I am Duke Humphrey's wife,
And he a prince and ruler of the land;
45 Yet so he ruled, and such a prince he was,
As he stood by whilst I, his forlorn Duchess,
Was made a wonder and a pointing stock°   *an object of scorn*
To every idle rascal° follower.   *lowborn*
But be thou mild and blush not at my shame,
50 Nor stir at nothing till the axe of death
Hang over thee, as sure it shortly will.
For Suffolk, he that can do all in all
With her° that hateth thee and hates us all,   *(Margaret)*
And York, and impious Beaufort that false priest,
55 Have all limed bushes⁶ to betray thy wings,
And fly thou how thou canst, they'll tangle thee.
But fear not thou until thy foot be snared,
Nor never seek prevention of° thy foes.   *safeguards against*
GLOUCESTER   Ah, Nell, forbear; thou aimest all awry.
60 I must offend before I be attainted,°   *condemned for treason*
And had I twenty times so many foes,
And each of them had twenty times their power,
All these could not procure me any scathe°   *harm*
So long as I am loyal, true, and crimeless.
65 Wouldst have me rescue thee from this reproach?
Why, yet thy scandal were not wiped away,
But I in danger for the breach of law.
Thy greatest help is quiet, gentle Nell.
I pray thee sort° thy heart to patience.   *adapt*
70 These few days' wonder will be quickly worn.⁷
     Enter a HERALD
HERALD   I summon your grace to his majesty's parliament
holden° at Bury⁸ the first of this next month.   *to be held*
GLOUCESTER   And my consent ne'er asked herein before?
This is close° dealing. Well, I will be there. *Exit* HERALD   *secret*
75 My Nell, I take my leave; and, Master Sheriff,
Let not her penance exceed the King's commission.
FIRST SHERIFF   An't please your grace, here my commission stays,°   *ends*

---

4. Enveloped: a term from falconry that describes the condition of a hawk wrapped in cloth so as to prevent its flying away.
5. Moans fetched from deep within me.

6. Coated bushes with birdlime (see note to 1.3.92).
7. What was marveled at for a few days will soon be forgotten.
8. Bury St. Edmunds, a town in Suffolk.

And Sir John Stanley is appointed now
To take her with him to the Isle of Man.

80 GLOUCESTER   Must you, Sir John, protect° my lady here?   *keep in custody*
STANLEY   So am I given in charge, may't please your grace.
GLOUCESTER   Entreat° her not the worse in that° I pray   *Treat / just because*
You use her well. The world may laugh again,
And I may live to do you kindness if
85 You do it her. And so, Sir John, farewell.
            [GLOUCESTER *begins to leave*]
DUCHESS   What, gone, my lord, and bid me not farewell?
GLOUCESTER   Witness my tears—I cannot stay to speak.
                  Exeunt GLOUCESTER *and his men*
DUCHESS   Art thou gone too? All comfort go with thee,
For none abides with me. My joy is death—
90 Death, at whose name I oft have been afeard,
Because I wished this world's eternity.°   *immortality on earth*
Stanley, I prithee go and take me hence.
I care not whither, for I beg no favour,
Only convey me where thou art commanded.
95 STANLEY   Why, madam, that is to the Isle of Man,
There to be used according to your state.°   *rank; condition*
DUCHESS   That's bad enough, for I am but reproach;°   *in a state of shame*
And shall I then be used reproachfully?
STANLEY   Like to a duchess and Duke Humphrey's lady,
100 According to that state you shall be used.
DUCHESS   Sheriff, farewell, and better than I fare,
Although thou hast been conduct° of my shame.   *conductor*
FIRST SHERIFF   It is my office, and, madam, pardon me.
DUCHESS   Ay, ay, farewell—thy office is discharged.
                                    [*Exeunt* SHERIFFS]
105 Come, Stanley, shall we go?
STANLEY   Madam, your penance done, throw off this sheet,
And go we to attire you for our journey.
DUCHESS   My shame will not be shifted⁹ with my sheet—
No, it will hang upon my richest robes
110 And show itself, attire me how I can.
Go, lead the way, I long to see my prison.   *Exeunt*

3.1

*Sound a sennet. Enter to the parliament: enter two
heralds before, then the Duke[s] of* BUCKINGHAM *and*
SUFFOLK, *and then the Duke of* YORK *and* CARDINAL
[BEAUFORT], *and then* KING [HENRY] *and* QUEEN [MAR-
GARET,] *and then the Earl[s]* OF SALISBURY *and* WAR-
WICK [*with attendants*]

KING HENRY   I muse° my lord of Gloucester is not come   *am surprised*
'Tis not his wont° to be the hindmost man,   *habit*
Whate'er occasion keeps him from us now.
QUEEN MARGARET   Can you not see, or will ye not observe,
5 The strangeness of his altered countenance?
With what a majesty he bears himself?

---

9. Changed, with a pun on "shifted" as meaning "put   3.1 Location: A great hall, Bury St. Edmunds.
on new undergarments."

How insolent of late he is become?
How proud, how peremptory, and unlike himself?
We know the time since° he was mild and affable,   *We remember when*
10 And if we did but glance a far-off look,
Immediately he was upon his knee,
That all the court admired him for° submission.   *was amazed at his*
But meet him now, and be it in the morn
When everyone will give the time of day,°   *say good morning*
15 He knits his brow, and shows an angry eye,
And passeth by with stiff unbowèd knee,
Disdaining° duty that to us belongs.   *Not paying*
Small curs are not regarded when they grin,°   *snarl; show the teeth*
But great men tremble when the lion roars—
20 And Humphrey is no little man in England.
First, note that he is near you in descent,
And, should you fall, he is the next will mount.°   *mount the throne*
Meseemeth then it is no policy,°   *not prudent*
Respecting° what a rancorous mind he bears   *Considering*
25 And his advantage following your decease,
That he should come about your royal person,
Or be admitted to your highness' Council.
By flattery hath he won the commons' hearts,
And when he please to make commotion,°   *incite rebellion*
30 'Tis to be feared they all will follow him.
Now 'tis the spring, and weeds are shallow-rooted;
Suffer° them now, and they'll o'ergrow the garden,   *Tolerate*
And choke the herbs for want of husbandry.
The reverent care I bear unto my lord
35 Made me collect° these dangers in the Duke.   *deduce*
If it be fond,° call it a woman's fear;   *foolish*
Which fear, if better reasons can supplant,
I will subscribe° and say I wronged the Duke.   *concur*
My lord of Suffolk, Buckingham, and York,
40 Reprove° my allegation if you can,   *Refute*
Or else conclude my words effectual.°   *decisive*
SUFFOLK   Well hath your highness seen into this Duke,
And had I first been put to speak my mind,
I think I should have told your grace's tale.
45 The Duchess by his subornation,°   *instigation*
Upon my life, began her devilish practices;
Or if he were not privy to those faults,°   *crimes*
Yet by reputing° of his high descent,   *boasting*
As next the King he was successive heir,
50 And such high vaunts° of his nobility,   *boasts*
Did instigate the bedlam[1] brainsick Duchess
By wicked means to frame° our sovereign's fall.   *devise*
Smooth runs the water where the brook is deep,
And in his simple show° he harbours treason.   *outward appearance*
55 The fox barks not when he would steal the lamb.
[*To* KING HENRY] No, no, my sovereign, Gloucester is a man
Unsounded° yet, and full of deep deceit.   *Unfathomed*

---

1. Insane (a shortened form of "Bethlehem Hospital," a notorious asylum maintained by the City of London).

CARDINAL BEAUFORT [*to* KING HENRY]   Did he not, contrary to
    form of law,
  Devise strange° deaths for small offences done?   *cruel; illegal*
60   YORK [*to* KING HENRY]   And did he not, in his Protectorship,
  Levy great sums of money through the realm
  For soldiers' pay in France, and never sent it,
  By means whereof the towns each day revolted?
  BUCKINGHAM [*to* KING HENRY]   Tut, these are petty faults to°   *compared to*
    faults unknown,
65   Which time will bring to light in smooth Duke Humphrey.
  KING HENRY   My lords, at once:° the care you have of us   *once and for all*
  To mow down thorns that would annoy our foot
  Is worthy praise, but shall I speak my conscience?
  Our kinsman Gloucester is as innocent
70   From meaning treason to our royal person
  As is the sucking lamb or harmless dove.
  The Duke is virtuous, mild, and too well given
  To dream on evil or to work my downfall.
  QUEEN MARGARET   Ah, what's more dangerous than this fond
    affiance?°   *foolish confidence*
75   Seems he a dove? His feathers are but borrowed,
  For he's disposèd as the hateful raven.
  Is he a lamb? His skin is surely lent him,
  For he's inclined as is the ravenous wolf.[2]
  Who cannot steal a shape that means deceit?[3]
80   Take heed, my lord, the welfare of us all
  Hangs on the cutting short that fraudful° man.   *treacherous*
      Enter the Duke of SOMERSET
  SOMERSET [*kneeling before* KING HENRY]   All health unto my
    gracious sovereign.
  KING HENRY   Welcome, Lord Somerset. What news from France?
  SOMERSET   That all your interest in those territories
85   Is utterly bereft you—all is lost.
  KING HENRY   Cold news, Lord Somerset; but God's will be done.
      [SOMERSET *rises*]
  YORK [*aside*]   Cold news for me, for I had hope of France,
  As firmly as I hope for fertile England.
  Thus are my blossoms blasted° in the bud,   *withered*
90   And caterpillars eat my leaves away.
  But I will remedy this gear° ere long,   *business*
  Or sell my title for a glorious grave.
      Enter Duke Humphrey [of] GLOUCESTER
  GLOUCESTER [*kneeling before* KING HENRY]   All happiness unto
    my lord the King.
  Pardon, my liege, that I have stayed° so long.   *delayed*
95   SUFFOLK   Nay, Gloucester, know that thou art come too soon
  Unless thou wert more loyal than thou art.
  I do arrest thee of high treason here.
  GLOUCESTER [*rising*]   Well, Suffolk's Duke, thou shalt not see me blush,
  Nor change my countenance for this arrest.

---

2. *Is he . . . wolf*: alluding to the Sermon on the Mount,
which warns of "false prophets, which come to you in
sheep's clothing, but inwardly they are ravening wolves"
(Matthew 7:15).
3. Who that intends to deceive cannot assume an
appropriate disguise?

100   A heart unspotted is not easily daunted.
         The purest spring is not so free from mud
         As I am clear from treason to my sovereign.
         Who can accuse me? Wherein am I guilty?
         YORK   'Tis thought, my lord, that you took bribes of France,
105   And, being Protector, stayed° the soldiers' pay,   *withheld*
         By means whereof his highness hath lost France
         GLOUCESTER   Is it but thought so? What are they that think it?
         I never robbed the soldiers of their pay,
         Nor ever had one penny bribe from France.
110   So help me God, as I have watched the night,°   *stayed up all night*
         Ay, night by night, in studying good for England,
         That doit° that e'er I wrested from the King,   *a coin of little value*
         Or any groat° I hoarded to my use,   *a coin worth 4 pence*
         Be brought against me at my trial day!
115   No: many a pound of mine own proper store,°   *personal fortune*
         Because I would not tax the needy commons,
         Have I dispursèd° to the garrisons,   *paid*
         And never asked for restitution.
         CARDINAL BEAUFORT   It serves you well, my lord, to say so much.
120   GLOUCESTER   I say no more than truth, so help me God.
         YORK   In your Protectorship you did devise
         Strange tortures for offenders, never heard of,
         That° England was defamed by° tyranny.   *So that / was infamous for*
         GLOUCESTER   Why, 'tis well known that whiles I was Protector
125   Pity was all the fault that was in me,
         For I should° melt at an offender's tears,   *would*
         And lowly words were ransom for their fault.
         Unless it were a bloody murderer,
         Or foul felonious thief that fleeced poor passengers,°   *travelers*
130   I never gave them condign° punishment.   *well-deserved*
         Murder, indeed—that bloody sin—I tortured
         Above the felon or what trespass else.[4]
         SUFFOLK   My lord, these faults are easy,° quickly answerèd,   *slight*
         But mightier crimes are laid unto your charge
135   Whereof you cannot easily purge yourself.
         I do arrest you in his highness' name,
         And here commit you to my good lord Cardinal
         To keep until your further time of trial.
         KING HENRY   My lord of Gloucester, 'tis my special hope
140   That you will clear yourself from all suspense.°   *suspicion*
         My conscience tells me you are innocent.
         GLOUCESTER   Ah, gracious lord, these days are dangerous.
         Virtue is choked with foul ambition,
         And charity chased hence by rancour's hand.
145   Foul subornation[5] is predominant,
         And equity exiled° your highness' land.   *exiled from*
         I know their complot° is to have my life,   *plot*
         And if my death might make this island happy
         And prove the period° of their tyranny,   *mark the end*
150   I would expend it with all willingness.
         But mine is made the prologue to their play,

4. More than any other kind of crime.   5. Instigating others to commit crimes, including perjury.

For thousands more that yet suspect no peril
Will not conclude their plotted tragedy.
Beaufort's red sparkling eyes blab his heart's malice,
155 And Suffolk's cloudy brow his stormy hate;
Sharp Buckingham unburdens with his tongue
The envious load that lies upon his heart;
And doggèd° York that reaches at the moon,   *currish; determined*
Whose overweening arm I have plucked back,
160 By false accuse° doth level° at my life.   *accusation / aim*
[*To* QUEEN MARGARET] And you, my sovereign lady, with the rest,
Causeless have laid disgraces on my head,
And with your best endeavour have stirred up
My liefest liege° to be mine enemy.   *dearest sovereign*
165 Ay, all of you have laid your heads together—
Myself had notice of your conventicles°—   *secret meetings*
And all to make away my guiltless life.
I shall not want° false witness to condemn me,   *lack*
Nor store of treasons to augment my guilt.
170 The ancient proverb will be well effected:
'A staff is quickly found to beat a dog'.
CARDINAL BEAUFORT [*to* KING HENRY]   My liege, his railing is intolerable.
If those that care to keep your royal person
From treason's secret knife and traitor's rage
175 Be thus upbraided, chid, and rated at,°   *berated; scolded*
And the offender granted scope of speech,
'Twill make them cool in zeal unto your grace.
SUFFOLK [*to* KING HENRY]   Hath he not twit° our sovereign lady here   *upbraided*
With ignominious words, though clerkly couched,°   *cleverly phrased*
180 As if she had subornèd some to swear
False allegations to o'erthrow his state?°   *high position*
QUEEN MARGARET   But I can give the loser leave to chide.
GLOUCESTER   Far truer spoke than meant. I lose indeed;
Beshrew° the winners, for they played me false!   *Curse*
185 And well such losers may have leave to speak.
BUCKINGHAM [*to* KING HENRY]   He'll wrest the sense,° and hold   *distort the meaning*
us here all day.
Lord Cardinal, he is your prisoner.
CARDINAL BEAUFORT [*to some of his attendants*]   Sirs, take
away the Duke and guard him sure.
GLOUCESTER   Ah, thus King Henry throws away his crutch
190 Before his legs be firm to bear his body.
Thus is the shepherd beaten from thy side,
And wolves are gnarling° who shall gnaw thee first.   *snarling*
Ah, that my fear were false; ah, that it were!
For, good King Henry, thy decay° I fear.   *ruin*
Exit GLOUCESTER, [*guarded by*] *the Cardinal's men*
195 KING HENRY   My lords, what to your wisdoms seemeth best
Do or undo, as if ourself were here.
QUEEN MARGARET   What, will your highness leave the Parliament?
KING HENRY   Ay, Margaret, my heart is drowned with grief,
Whose flood begins to flow within mine eyes,
200 My body round engirt with misery;
For what's more miserable than discontent?
Ah, uncle Humphrey, in thy face I see

The map of honour, truth, and loyalty;
And yet, good Humphrey, is the hour to come
205 That e'er I proved thee false, or feared thy faith.°   *doubted your loyalty*
What louring° star now envies thy estate,   *gloomy*
That these great lords and Margaret our Queen
Do seek subversion of thy harmless life?
Thou never didst them wrong, nor no man wrong.
210 And as the butcher takes away the calf,
And binds the wretch, and beats it when it strains,
Bearing it to the bloody slaughterhouse,
Even so remorseless have they borne him hence;
And as the dam° runs lowing up and down,   *mother*
215 Looking the way her harmless young one went,
And can do naught but wail her darling's loss;
Even so myself bewails good Gloucester's case
With sad unhelpful tears, and with dimmed eyes
Look after him, and cannot do him good,°   *give him help*
220 So mighty are his vowèd enemies.
His fortunes I will weep, and 'twixt each groan,
Say 'Who's a traitor? Gloucester, he is none'.
Exeunt KING, SALISBURY, *and* WARWICK
QUEEN MARGARET Free° lords, cold snow melts with the sun's hot beams.   *Noble*
Henry my lord is cold in great affairs,
225 Too full of foolish pity; and Gloucester's show
Beguiles him as the mournful crocodile
With sorrow snares relenting passengers,[6]
Or as the snake rolled in a flow'ring bank
With shining chequered slough° doth sting a child   *skin*
230 That for the beauty thinks it excellent.
Believe me, lords, were none more wise than I—
And yet herein I judge mine own wit good—
This Gloucester should be quickly rid the world
To rid us from the fear we have of him.
235 CARDINAL BEAUFORT That he should die is worthy policy;
But yet we want a colour° for his death.   *pretext*
'Tis meet he be condemned by course of law.
SUFFOLK But, in my mind, that were no policy.
The King will labour still° to save his life,   *continually*
240 The commons haply° rise to save his life;   *perhaps*
And yet we have but trivial argument°   *evidence*
More than mistrust° that shows him worthy death.   *Other than suspicion*
YORK So that, by this, you would not have him die?
SUFFOLK Ah, York, no man alive so fain as I.
245 YORK [*aside*] 'Tis York that hath more reason for his death.
[*Aloud*] But my lord Cardinal, and you my lord of Suffolk,
Say as you think, and speak it from your souls.
Were't not all one an empty° eagle were set   *a hungry*
To guard the chicken from a hungry kite,°   *bird of prey*
250 As place Duke Humphrey for the King's Protector?

6. Compassionate travelers. Sixteenth-century natural historians claimed that crocodiles moaned and wept in order to lure sympathetic humans to their death.

QUEEN MARGARET   So the poor chicken should be sure of death.

SUFFOLK   Madam, 'tis true; and were't not madness then

To make the fox surveyor° of the fold,   *guardian*

Who being accused a crafty murderer,

His guilt should be but idly posted over°   *foolishly ignored*

Because his purpose is not executed?

No—let him die in that he is a fox,

By nature proved an enemy to the flock,

Before his chaps° be stained with crimson blood,   *jaws*

As Humphrey, proved by reasons, to my liege.[7]

And do not stand on quillets° how to slay him;   *subtle distinctions*

Be it by gins,° by snares, by subtlety,   *traps*

Sleeping or waking, 'tis no matter how,

So he be dead; for that is good conceit°   *a good idea*

Which mates° him first that first intends deceit.   *checkmates; kills*

QUEEN MARGARET   Thrice-noble Suffolk, 'tis resolutely spoke.

SUFFOLK   Not resolute, except° so much were done;   *unless*

For things are often spoke and seldom meant;

But that° my heart accordeth with my tongue,   *to show that*

Seeing the deed is meritorious,

And to preserve my sovereign from his foe,

Say but the word and I will be his priest.[8]

CARDINAL BEAUFORT   But I would have him dead, my lord of Suffolk,

Ere you can take due orders for a priest.[9]

Say you consent and censure° well the deed,   *approve*

And I'll provide his executioner;

I tender so the safety of my liege.

SUFFOLK   Here is my hand; the deed is worthy doing.

QUEEN MARGARET   And so say I.

YORK   And I. And now we three have spoke it,

It skills not greatly who impugns our doom.[1]

Enter a POST

POST   Great lord, from Ireland am I come amain°   *in haste*

To signify that rebels there are up°   *up in arms*

And put the Englishmen unto the sword.

Send succours, lords, and stop the rage betime,°   *promptly*

Before the wound do grow uncurable;

For, being green,° there is great hope of help.   [*Exit*]   *fresh*

CARDINAL BEAUFORT   A breach that craves a quick expedient stop!

What counsel give you in this weighty cause?

YORK   That Somerset be sent as regent thither.

'Tis meet° that lucky ruler be employed—   *fit (said scornfully)*

Witness the fortune he hath had in France.

SOMERSET   If York, with all his far-fet° policy,   *cunning*

Had been the regent there instead of me,

He never would have stayed in France so long.

YORK   No, not to lose it all as thou hast done.

I rather would have lost my life betimes

---

7. Just as Humphrey proved (to be a fox or enemy) to Henry.
8. I will kill him. Suffolk alludes to the priest's role in administering the sacrament of last rites to dying Christians.
9. Can become a priest; can arrange to have a priest there.
1. It doesn't matter who questions our decision.

Than bring a burden of dishonour home
By staying there so long till all were lost.
300 Show me one scar charactered° on thy skin.   *inscribed*
Men's flesh preserved so whole do seldom win.
QUEEN MARGARET   Nay, then, this spark will prove a raging fire
If wind and fuel be brought to feed it with.
No more, good York; sweet Somerset, be still.
305 Thy fortune, York, hadst thou been regent there,
Might happily° have proved far worse than his.   *perhaps*
YORK   What, worse than naught? Nay, then a shame take all!
SOMERSET   And, in the number,° thee that wishest shame.   *among them*
CARDINAL BEAUFORT   My lord of York, try what your fortune is.
310 Th'uncivil kerns of Ireland[2] are in arms
And temper clay° with blood of Englishmen.   *moisten the earth*
To Ireland will you lead a band of men
Collected choicely, from each county some,
And try your hap° against the Irishmen?   *luck*
315 YORK   I will, my lord, so please his majesty.
SUFFOLK   Why, our authority is his consent,
And what we do establish he confirms.
Then, noble York, take thou this task in hand.
YORK   I am content. Provide me soldiers, lords,
320 Whiles I take order° for mine own affairs.   *arrange*
SUFFOLK   A charge, Lord York, that I will see performed.
But now return we to the false Duke Humphrey.
CARDINAL BEAUFORT   No more of him—for I will deal with him
That henceforth he shall trouble us no more.
325 And so, break off; the day is almost spent.
Lord Suffolk, you and I must talk of that event.
YORK   My lord of Suffolk, within fourteen days
At Bristol I expect my soldiers;
For there I'll ship them all for Ireland.
330 SUFFOLK   I'll see it truly done, my lord of York.
Exeunt. Manet YORK[3]
330.1   YORK   *Let me have some bands of chosen soldiers,*
And York shall try his fortune 'gainst those kerns.
QUEEN MARGARET   *York, thou shalt. My lord of Buckingham,*
Let it be your charge to muster up such soldiers
330.5 *As shall suffice him in these needful wars.*
BUCKINGHAM   *Madam, I will, and levy such a band*
As soon shall overcome those Irish rebels.
But, York, where shall those soldiers stay° for thee   *wait*
YORK   *At Bristol I will expect them ten days hence.*
330.10 BUCKINGHAM   *Then thither shall they come, and*
    so farewell.   *Exit*
YORK   *Adieu, my lord of Buckingham.*
QUEEN MARGARET   *Suffolk, remember what you have to do—*
And you, Lord Cardinal—concerning Duke Humphrey.

---

2. Barbaric Irish foot soldiers or rebels. Kerns were the most numerous, poorest, and most lightly armed of the Irish soldiers who fought against the English during Elizabeth's reign. Many Elizabethan writers described the Irish as an inferior, uncivilized "race" and used the term "kern" to signify all Irish opponents of England.

3. The entire debate on Duke Humphrey's death in 3.1 is handled differently by Q and F. Oxford retains F's version of the debate, but Q may represent authorial revision. The following indented Q lines (330.1–330.15), roughly corresponding to lines 310–30, are of particular interest because they supply Buckingham with speeches for this latter part of the scene.

'Twere good that you did see to it in time.
330.15 *Come, let us go, that it may be performed.*
Exeunt all. Manet YORK

YORK Now, York, or never, steel thy fearful thoughts,
And change misdoubt° to resolution.   fear
Be that thou hop'st to be, or what thou art
Resign to death; it is not worth th'enjoying.
335 Let pale-faced fear keep° with the mean-born° man   dwell / lowborn
And find no harbour in a royal heart.
Faster than springtime showers comes thought on thought,
And not a thought but thinks on dignity.°   high estate (kingship)
My brain, more busy than the labouring spider,
340 Weaves tedious° snares to trap mine enemies.   laborious
Well, nobles, well: 'tis politicly done
To send me packing with an host of men.
I fear me° you but warm the starvèd° snake,   I am afraid / frozen
Who, cherished in your breasts, will sting your hearts.
345 'Twas men I lacked, and you will give them me.
I take it kindly. Yet be well assured
You put sharp weapons in a madman's hands.
Whiles I in Ireland nurse a mighty band,
I will stir up in England some black storm
350 Shall blow ten thousand souls to heaven or hell,
And this fell° tempest shall not cease to rage   ferocious
Until the golden circuit° on my head   crown
Like to the glorious sun's transparent beams
Do calm the fury of this mad-bred flaw.[4]
355 And for a minister° of my intent,   an agent
I have seduced a headstrong Kentishman,
John Cade of Ashford,
To make commotion,° as full well he can,   rebellion
Under the title of John Mortimer.[5]
360 In Ireland have I seen this stubborn Cade
Oppose himself against a troop of kerns,
And fought so long till that his thighs with darts[6]
Were almost like a sharp-quilled porcupine;
And in the end, being rescued, I have seen
365 Him caper° upright like a wild Morisco,[7]   leap
Shaking the bloody darts as he° his bells.   as would the dancer
Full often like a shag-haired[8] crafty kern
Hath he conversèd with the enemy
And, undiscovered, come to me again
370 And given me notice of their villainies.
This devil here shall be my substitute,
For that° John Mortimer, which now is dead,   Because
In face, in gait, in speech, he doth resemble.
By this I shall perceive the commons' mind,

4. This storm ("flaw") created by madness.
5. The Mortimers are the family line by which York claims the crown. See York's account of his claim in 2.2.10–52.
6. Light spears or arrows, the weapons for which kerns were known.
7. A Moor who converted to Christianity; a morris dancer. Deriving from the Spanish word for "Moor," the morris dance was originally a Spanish dance that

reenacted Christian battles with Moors. From the fifteenth century, it was associated with English popular festivals and was usually performed by men with bells attached to their legs who carried sticks and wore costumes from English folklore.
8. Alluding to the popular notion that the Irish grew "glibs," or long, thick bangs, in order to disguise themselves and escape punishment for their crimes.

375 How they affect° the house and claim of York.   *like*
Say he be taken, racked,⁹ and torturèd—
I know no pain they can inflict upon him
Will make him say I moved him to those arms.
Say that he thrive, as 'tis great like° he will—   *very likely*
380 Why then from Ireland come I with my strength
And reap the harvest which that coistrel° sowed.   *base fellow*
For Humphrey being dead, as he shall be,
And Henry put apart, the next for me.   *Exit*

3.2

The curtains [are] drawn [apart, revealing] Duke
Humphrey [of GLOUCESTER*] in his bed [with] two men*
*lying on his breast, smothering him in his bed*¹

FIRST MURDERER [*to the* SECOND MURDERER]   Run to my lord
  of Suffolk—let him know
We have dispatched the Duke as he commanded.
SECOND MURDERER   O that it were to do!² What have we done?
Didst ever hear a man so penitent?
  Enter the Duke of SUFFOLK
5 FIRST MURDERER   Here comes my lord.
SUFFOLK   Now, sirs, have you dispatched this thing?
FIRST MURDERER   Ay, my good lord, he's dead.
SUFFOLK   Why, that's well said. Go, get you to my house.
  I will reward you for this venturous° deed.   *dangerous*
10 The King and all the peers are here at hand.
Have you laid fair° the bed? Is all things well,   *rearranged*
According as I gave directions?
FIRST MURDERER   'Tis, my good lord.
SUFFOLK   Then draw the curtains close; away, be gone!
  Exeunt [the] MURDERERS [*drawing the curtains as they leave*]
  Sound trumpets, then enter KING [HENRY] *and* QUEEN
  [MARGARET], CARDINAL [BEAUFORT], *the Duke of* SOM-
  ERSET, [*and*] *attendants*
15 KING HENRY [*to* SUFFOLK]   Go call our uncle to our presence straight.°   *immediately*
Say we intend to try his grace today
If° he be guilty, as 'tis publishèd.   *To find whether*
SUFFOLK   I'll call him presently,° my noble lord.   *Exit*   *at once*
KING HENRY   Lords, take your places; and, I pray you all,
20 Proceed no straiter° 'gainst our uncle Gloucester   *more severely*
Than from true evidence, of good esteem,°   *worthy of belief*
He be approved in practice culpable.°   *determined guilty*
QUEEN MARGARET   God forbid any malice should prevail
That faultless may condemn a noble man!³
25 Pray God he may acquit him° of suspicion!   *himself*
KING HENRY   I thank thee, Meg. These words content me much.
  Enter SUFFOLK
How now? Why look'st thou pale? Why tremblest thou?
Where is our uncle? What's the matter, Suffolk?

---

9. Tortured by having one's limbs fastened to a frame that stretched the body.
3.2 Location: Gloucester's bedchamber and an adjoining room of state, Bury St. Edmunds.
1. F's stage direction reads, "Enter two or three running over the Stage, from the Murder of Duke

Humfrey." Q, by contrast, indicates that the actual smothering of Gloucester is shown onstage.
2. Would that it were still to be done (so that it could remain undone).
3. That may condemn a noble man who is blameless.

SUFFOLK   Dead in his bed, my lord—Gloucester is dead.

30   QUEEN MARGARET   Marry, God forfend!°   *forbid*

CARDINAL BEAUFORT   God's secret judgement. I did dream tonight°   *last night*
     The Duke was dumb and could not speak a word.

          KING HENRY *falls [to the ground]*[4]

QUEEN MARGARET   How fares my lord? Help, lords—the King is
     dead!

SOMERSET   Rear° up his body; wring him by the nose.[5]   *Raise*

35   QUEEN MARGARET   Run, go, help, help! O Henry, ope thine eyes!

SUFFOLK   He doth revive again. Madam, be patient.

KING HENRY   O heavenly God!

QUEEN MARGARET   How fares my gracious lord?

SUFFOLK   Comfort, my sovereign; gracious Henry, comfort.

KING HENRY   What, doth my lord of Suffolk comfort me?

40   Came he right now° to sing a raven's note[6]   *a moment ago*
     Whose dismal tune bereft° my vital powers;   *robbed me of*
     And thinks he that the chirping of a wren,
     By crying comfort from a hollow° breast   *an insincere*
     Can chase away the first-conceivèd° sound?   *previously perceived*
45   Hide not thy poison with such sugared words.

          [*He begins to rise.* SUFFOLK *offers to assist him*]

     Lay not thy hands on me—forbear, I say!
     Their touch affrights me as a serpent's sting.
     Thou baleful messenger, out of my sight!
     Upon thy eyeballs murderous tyranny
50   Sits in grim majesty to fright the world.
     Look not upon me, for thine eyes are wounding—
     Yet do not go away. Come, basilisk,[7]
     And kill the innocent gazer with thy sight.
     For in the shade° of death I shall find joy;   *shadow*
55   In life, but double death, now Gloucester's dead.

QUEEN MARGARET   Why do you rate° my lord of Suffolk thus?   *chide*
     Although the Duke was enemy to him,
     Yet he most Christian-like laments his death.
     And for myself, foe as he was to me,
60   Might liquid tears, or heart-offending° groans,   *heart-wounding*
     Or blood-consuming[8] sighs recall his life,
     I would be blind with weeping, sick with groans,
     Look pale as primrose with blood-drinking sighs,
     And all to have the noble Duke alive.
65   What know I how the world may deem° of me?   *judge*
     For it is known we were but hollow friends,
     It may be judged I made the Duke away.
     So shall my name with slander's tongue be wounded
     And princes' courts be filled with my reproach.
70   This get I by his death. Ay me, unhappy,
     To be a queen, and crowned with infamy.

KING HENRY   Ah, woe is me for Gloucester, wretched man!

---

4. In Q, the stage direction reads, "The King falls in a sound" (swoon). F reads, "King sounds."
5. This was thought to revive circulation and restore consciousness.
6. According to popular superstition, an omen of death.

7. A mythical reptile, hatched from a cock's egg, whose look was supposed to be fatal.
8. It was popularly believed that each sigh or groan drew a drop of blood from the heart.

QUEEN MARGARET   Be woe° for me, more wretched than he is.   *woeful; sorry*
      What, dost thou turn away and hide thy face?
75   I am no loathsome leper—look on me!
      What, art thou, like the adder, waxen deaf?⁹
      Be poisonous too and kill thy forlorn queen.
      Is all thy comfort shut in Gloucester's tomb?
      Why, then Queen Margaret was ne'er thy joy.
80   Erect his statuë and worship it,
      And make my image but an alehouse sign.¹
      Was I for this nigh wrecked upon the sea,
      And twice by awkward° winds from England's bark°   *unfavorable / shore*
      Drove back again unto my native clime?
85   What boded this, but° well forewarning winds   *but that*
      Did seem to say, 'Seek not a scorpion's nest,
      Nor set no footing on this unkind shore'.
      What did I then, but cursed the gentle gusts
      And he that loosed them forth their brazen caves,²
90   And bid them blow towards England's blessèd shore,
      Or turn our stern upon a dreadful rock.
      Yet Aeolus would not be a murderer,
      But left that hateful office unto thee.
      The pretty vaulting° sea refused to drown me,   *bounding*
95   Knowing that thou wouldst have me drowned on shore
      With tears as salt as sea through thy unkindness.
      The splitting rocks cow'red in the sinking sands,³
      And would not dash me with their ragged sides,
      Because thy flinty heart, more hard than they,
100 Might in thy palace perish° Margaret.   *destroy*
      As far as I could ken° thy chalky cliffs,   *see*
      When from thy shore the tempest beat us back,
      I stood upon the hatches° in the storm,   *deck*
      And when the dusky sky began to rob
105 My earnest-gaping° sight of thy land's view,   *earnestly peering*
      I took a costly jewel from my neck—
      A heart it was, bound in with diamonds—
      And threw it towards thy land. The sea received it,
      And so I wished thy body might my heart.
110 And even with this I lost fair England's view,
      And bid mine eyes be packing° with my heart,   *be gone*
      And called them blind and dusky spectacles°   *instruments of sight*
      For losing ken of Albion's° wishèd coast.   *England's*
      How often have I tempted Suffolk's tongue—
115 The agent of thy foul inconstancy—
      To sit and witch° me, as Ascanius⁴ did,   *bewitch*
      When he to madding° Dido would unfold   *going mad (with love)*
      His father's acts, commenced in burning Troy!
      Am I not witched like her? Or thou not false like him?
120 Ay me, I can no more.° Die, Margaret,   *my strength fails*

9. Alluding to the belief that adders stopped up their ears to resist attempts to charm them.
1. Inns and shops in Elizabethan London were usually distinguished by signs bearing images rather than words.
2. Referring to Aeolus, whom Zeus appointed ruler of the winds, which he kept in caves. *brazen*: strong (as brass).

3. Rocks that ordinarily break ships into pieces crouched down fearfully in the sands where ships usually sink.
4. In Book 1 of the *Aeneid*, Venus sends Cupid in the form of Ascanius, son of Aeneas, to bewitch Dido, Queen of Carthage, and inflame her with love for Aeneas.

For Henry weeps that thou dost live so long.
    Noise within. Enter the Earls of WARWICK *and*
      SALISBURY, [*with*] *many* COMMONS
  WARWICK [*to* KING HENRY]   It is reported, mighty sovereign,
  That good Duke Humphrey traitorously is murdered
  By Suffolk and the Cardinal Beaufort's means.
125 The commons, like an angry hive of bees
  That want° their leader, scatter up and down   *lack*
  And care not who they sting in his revenge.
  Myself have calmed their spleenful° mutiny,   *angry*
  Until they hear the order° of his death.   *manner*
130 KING HENRY   That he is dead, good Warwick, 'tis too true.
  But how he died God knows, not Henry.
  Enter his chamber, view his breathless corpse,
  And comment then upon° his sudden death.   *And then explain*
  WARWICK   That shall I do, my liege.—Stay, Salisbury,
135 With the rude multitude till I return.
      Exeunt [WARWICK *at one door,*] SALISBURY [*and*
           COMMONS *at another*][5]
  KING HENRY   O thou that judgest all things, stay° my thoughts,   *restrain*
  My thoughts that labour to persuade my soul
  Some violent hands were laid on Humphrey's life.
  If my suspect° be false, forgive me God,   *suspicion*
140 For judgement only doth belong to thee.
  Fain would I go to chafe his paly° lips   *pale*
  With twenty thousand kisses, and to drain°   *rain; let fall*
  Upon his face an ocean of salt tears,
  To tell my love unto his dumb, deaf trunk,°   *body*
145 And with my fingers feel his hand unfeeling.° *which lacks feeling*
  But all in vain are these mean obsequies,°   *funeral rites*
      [*Enter*] WARWICK [*who*] *draws* [*apart*] *the curtains and*
      shows GLOUCESTER [*dead*] *in his bed. Bed put forth*
  And to survey his dead and earthy image,
  What were it but to make my sorrow greater?
  WARWICK   Come hither, gracious sovereign, view this body.
150 KING HENRY   That is to see how deep my grave is made:
  For with his soul fled all my worldly solace,
  For seeing him I see my life° in death.   *that my life will end*
  WARWICK   As surely as my soul intends to live
  With that dread King° that took our state° upon Him *(Christ)/condition*
155 To free us from his Father's wrathful curse,
  I do believe that violent hands were laid
  Upon the life of this thrice-famèd° Duke.   *very famous*
  SUFFOLK   A dreadful oath, sworn with a solemn tongue!
  What instance° gives Lord Warwick for his vow?   *evidence*
160 WARWICK   See how the blood is settled in his face.
  Oft have I seen a timely-parted ghost[6]
  Of ashy semblance, meagre, pale, and bloodless,

---

5. Q has Salisbury exit at this point, while the dialogue
in F and Q indicates that Warwick also leaves the stage.
He must return to reveal Gloucester's corpse at line
146. Some editors have suggested that Salisbury stays

onstage with the Commons here, but at line 243 he is
directed to enter, and it appears that the Commons are
also then offstage. Both must have exited at some point.
6. The corpse of someone who died a natural death.

Being all descended to the labouring heart;[7]
Who, in the conflict that it holds with death,
165 Attracts the same° for aidance° 'gainst the enemy;   *(the blood)/aid*
Which, with the heart, there cools, and ne'er returneth
To blush and beautify the cheek again.
But see, his face is black and full of blood;
His eyeballs further out than when he lived,
170 Staring full ghastly like a strangled man;
His hair upreared; his nostrils stretched with struggling;
His hands abroad displayed,° as one that grasped   *spread wide*
And tugged for life and was by strength subdued.
Look on the sheets. His hair, you see, is sticking;
175 His well-proportioned beard made rough and rugged,
Like to the summer's corn by tempest lodged.°   *beaten down*
It cannot be but he was murdered here.
The least of all these signs were probable.°   *sufficient proof*
SUFFOLK   Why, Warwick, who should do the Duke to death?
180 Myself and Beaufort had him in protection,
And we, I hope, sir, are no murderers.
WARWICK   But both of you were vowed Duke Humphrey's foes,
[*To* CARDINAL BEAUFORT] And you, forsooth, had the good
Duke to keep.°   *guard*
'Tis like you would not feast him like a friend;
185 And 'tis well seen he found an enemy.
QUEEN MARGARET   Then you, belike.° suspect these noblemen   *perchance*
As guilty of Duke Humphrey's timeless° death?   *untimely*
WARWICK   Who finds the heifer dead and bleeding fresh,
And sees fast° by a butcher with an axe,   *near*
190 But will suspect 'twas he that made the slaughter?
Who finds the partridge in the puttock's° nest   *kite's (bird of prey)*
But may imagine how the bird was dead,°   *killed*
Although the kite soar with unbloodied beak?
Even so suspicious is this tragedy.
195 QUEEN MARGARET   Are you the butcher, Suffolk? Where's your knife?
Is Beaufort termed a kite? Where are his talons?
SUFFOLK   I wear no knife to slaughter sleeping men.
But here's a vengeful sword, rusted with ease,°   *lack of use*
That shall be scoured in his rancorous heart
200 That° slanders me with murder's crimson badge.   *Who*
Say, if thou dar'st, proud Lord of Warwickshire,
That I am faulty in Duke Humphrey's death.
              Exit CARDINAL [BEAUFORT *assisted by* SOMERSET]
WARWICK   What dares not Warwick, if false Suffolk dare him?
QUEEN MARGARET   He dares not calm his contumelious° spirit,   *insolent*
205 Nor cease to be an arrogant controller,°   *critic; slanderer*
Though Suffolk dare him twenty thousand times.
WARWICK   Madam, be still, with reverence may I say,
For every word you speak in his behalf
Is slander to your royal dignity.
210 SUFFOLK   Blunt-witted lord, ignoble in demeanour!
If ever lady wronged her lord so much,
Thy mother took into her blameful bed
Some stern° untutored churl, and noble stock   *rough*

7. The blood having all drained into the palpitating heart.

Was graffed with crabtree slip, whose fruit thou art,⁸

215 And never of the Nevilles' noble race.

WARWICK But that the guilt of murder bucklers° thee   *shields*

And I should rob the deathsman° of his fee,   *executioner*

Quitting° thee thereby of ten thousand shames,   *Freeing*

And that my sovereign's presence makes me mild,⁹

220 I would, false murd'rous coward, on thy knee

Make thee beg pardon for thy passèd° speech,   *just uttered*

And say it was thy mother that thou meant'st—

That thou thyself wast born in bastardy!

And after all this fearful homage° done,   *cowardly submission*

225 Give thee thy hire° and send thy soul to hell,   *reward*

Pernicious blood-sucker of sleeping men!

SUFFOLK Thou shalt be waking while I shed thy blood,

If from this presence° thou dar'st go with me.   *the King's presence*

WARWICK Away, even now, or I will drag thee hence.

230 Unworthy though thou art, I'll cope° with thee,   *fight*

And do some service to Duke Humphrey's ghost.

Exeunt SUFFOLK *and* WARWICK

KING HENRY What stronger breastplate than a heart untainted?

Thrice is he armed that hath his quarrel just;

And he but naked, though locked up in steel,°   *armored*

235 Whose conscience with injustice is corrupted.

COMMONS (*within*) Down with Suffolk! Down with Suffolk!¹

QUEEN MARGARET What noise is this?

Enter SUFFOLK *and* WARWICK *with their weapons drawn*

KING HENRY Why, how now, lords? Your wrathful weapons drawn

Here in our presence? Dare you be so bold?

240 Why, what tumultuous clamour have we here?

SUFFOLK The trait'rous Warwick with the men of Bury

Set all upon me, mighty sovereign!

COMMONS [*within*] Down with Suffolk! Down with Suffolk!

Enter from [*the* COMMONS] *the Earl of* SALISBURY

SALISBURY [*to the* COMMONS, *within*] Sirs, stand apart. The

King shall know your mind.

[*To* KING HENRY] Dread lord, the commons send you word

245 by me

Unless Lord Suffolk straight be done to death,

Or banishèd° fair England's territories,   *banished from*

They will by violence tear him from your palace

And torture him with grievous ling'ring death.

250 They say, by him the good Duke Humphrey died;

They say, in him they fear your highness' death;

And mere° instinct of love and loyalty,   *pure*

Free from a stubborn opposite° intent,   *antagonistic*

As being thought to contradict your liking,²

255 Makes them thus forward in° his banishment.   *insistent upon*

---

8. *noble . . . art*: into the trunk of a great tree was inserted a cutting, or "slip," from an inferior, wild one, and you are the result. The analogy puns on "stock" as meaning "an aristocratic line of descent" and implies that the pedigree has been tainted. "Noble stock" may also refer to the trunk of a noblewoman's body into which a worthless "slip," such as the penis of a lowborn man, has been inserted.

9. It was illegal to draw weapons in the King's presence. 1. In Q, this line is printed inside a longer stage direction: "Exit Warwick and Suffolk, and then all the Commons within, cries, down with Suffolk, down with Suffolk. And then enter again, the Duke of Suffolk and Warwick, with their weapons drawn."
2. That might be thought to contradict your wishes.

They say, in care of your most royal person,
That if your highness should intend to sleep,
And charge that no man should disturb your rest
In pain of your dislike, or pain of death,
260 Yet, notwithstanding such a strait° edict,   *strict*
Were there a serpent seen with forkèd tongue,
That slily glided towards your majesty,
It were but necessary you were waked,
Lest, being suffered° in that harmful slumber,   *permitted to remain*
265 The mortal worm° might make the sleep eternal.   *deadly serpent*
And therefore do they cry, though you forbid,
That they will guard you, whe'er° you will or no,   *whether*
From such fell° serpents as false Suffolk is,   *cruel*
With whose envenomèd and fatal sting
270 Your loving uncle, twenty times his worth,
They say, is shamefully bereft of life.
COMMONS (*within*)   An answer from the King, my lord of Salisbury!
SUFFOLK   'Tis like° the commons, rude unpolished hinds,°   *probable / boors*
Could send such message to their sovereign.
275 But you, my lord, were glad to be employed,
To show how quaint° an orator you are.   *skilled*
But all the honour Salisbury hath won
Is that he was the Lord Ambassador
Sent from a sort° of tinkers[3] to the King.   *gang*
280 COMMONS (*within*)   An answer from the King, or we will all break in!
KING HENRY   Go, Salisbury, and tell them all from me
I thank them for their tender loving care,
And had I not been 'cited° so by them,   *urged*
Yet did I purpose as they do entreat;
285 For sure my thoughts do hourly prophesy
Mischance unto my state by Suffolk's means.
And therefore by His° majesty I swear,   *(God's)*
Whose far unworthy deputy I am,
He shall not breathe° infection in this air   *breathe out; spread*
290 But three days longer, on the pain of death.   *Exit* SALISBURY
QUEEN MARGARET [*kneeling*]   O Henry, let me plead for gentle°   *noble*
    Suffolk.
KING HENRY   Ungentle Queen, to call him gentle Suffolk.
No more, I say! If thou dost plead for him
Thou wilt but add increase unto my wrath.
295 Had I but said, I would have kept my word;
But when I swear, it is irrevocable.
[*To* SUFFOLK] If after three days' space thou here beest found
On any ground that I am ruler of,
The world shall not be ransom for thy life.
300 Come, Warwick; come, good Warwick, go with me.
I have great matters to impart to thee.
        Exeunt KING [HENRY] *and* WARWICK [*with attendants*
        who draw the curtains as they leave]. *Manent*°   *Remain*
        QUEEN [MARGARET] *and* SUFFOLK

---

3. Tinkers were usually itinerant pot menders and were synonymous with vagrants and gypsies.

QUEEN MARGARET [*rising*] Mischance and sorrow go along with you!
Heart's discontent and sour affliction
Be playfellows to keep you company!
305 There's two of you, the devil make a third,
And threefold vengeance tend upon your steps!
SUFFOLK Cease, gentle Queen, these execrations,
And let thy Suffolk take his heavy° leave.   *sorrowful*
QUEEN MARGARET Fie, coward woman[4] and soft-hearted wretch!
310 Hast thou not spirit to curse thine enemies?
SUFFOLK A plague upon them! Wherefore° should I curse them?   *Why*
Could curses kill, as doth the mandrake's groan,[5]
I would invent as bitter searching° terms,   *piercing*
As curst, as harsh, and horrible to hear,
315 Delivered strongly through my fixèd° teeth,   *clenched*
With full as many signs of deadly hate,
As lean-faced envy[6] in her loathsome cave.
My tongue should stumble in mine earnest words;
Mine eyes should sparkle like the beaten flint;
320 My hair be fixed on end, as one distraught;
Ay, every joint should seem to curse and ban.°   *curse*
And, even now, my burdened heart would break
Should I not curse them. Poison be their drink!
Gall,° worse than gall, the daintiest that they taste!   *Bile (a bitter fluid)*
325 Their sweetest shade a grove of cypress trees![7]
Their chiefest prospect° murd'ring basilisks![8]   *view*
Their softest touch as smart° as lizards' stings!   *sharp*
Their music frightful as the serpent's hiss,
And boding screech-owls[9] make the consort° full!   *group of musicians*
330 All the foul terrors in dark-seated hell—
QUEEN MARGARET Enough, sweet Suffolk, thou torment'st thyself,
And these dread curses, like the sun 'gainst glass,
Or like an overchargèd gun, recoil
And turn the force of them upon thyself.
335 SUFFOLK You bade me ban, and will you bid me leave?°   *stop*
Now by this ground that I am banished from,
Well could I curse away a winter's night,
Though standing naked on a mountain top,
Where biting cold would never let grass grow,
340 And think it but a minute spent in sport.
QUEEN MARGARET O let me entreat thee cease. Give me thy hand,
That I may dew it with my mournful tears;
Nor let the rain of heaven wet this place
To wash away my woeful monuments.°   *signs of grief (tears)*
[*She kisses his palm*]
345 O, could this kiss be printed in thy hand
That thou mightst think upon these lips by the seal,°   *imprint*

---

4. In calling Suffolk a woman, Margaret questions his manhood. The pun in the next line on "spirit" as meaning "semen" as well as "courage" continues Margaret's assault on Suffolk's masculinity.
5. It was popularly believed that the mandrake—an herb whose root was thought to resemble a man and to grow wherever the semen of a man executed for murder had fallen—killed humans with its dreadful scream when it was uprooted.
6. Envy was traditionally described as an emaciated woman. See Ovid, *Metamorphoses* 2.949ff.
7. From ancient times, trees associated with death. Frequently planted in graveyards, their wood was used for coffins.
8. See note to line 52 above.
9. Thought to be harbingers of death.

Through whom° a thousand sighs are breathed for thee!   *which (her lips)*
So get thee gone, that I may know my grief.
'Tis but surmised whiles thou art standing by,
350   As one that surfeits° thinking on a want.°   *gorges / famine*
I will repeal thee,° or, be well assured,   *win your recall*
Adventure to be banishèd° myself.   *Risk banishment*
And banishèd I am, if but from thee.
Go, speak not to me; even now be gone!
355   O, go not yet. Even thus two friends condemned
Embrace, and kiss, and take ten thousand leaves,
Loather a hundred times to part than die.
Yet now farewell, and farewell life with thee.
SUFFOLK   Thus is poor Suffolk ten times banishèd—
360   Once by the King, and three times thrice by thee.
'Tis not the land I care for, wert thou thence,
A wilderness is populous enough,
So Suffolk had thy heavenly company.
For where thou art, there is the world itself,
365   With every several° pleasure in the world;   *distinct*
And where thou art not, desolation.
I can no more. Live thou to joy° thy life;   *enjoy*
Myself no joy in naught but that thou liv'st.
        Enter VAUX
QUEEN MARGARET   Whither goes Vaux so fast? What news, I prithee?
370   VAUX   To signify unto his majesty
That Cardinal Beaufort is at point of death.
For suddenly a grievous sickness took him
That makes him gasp, and stare, and catch the air,
Blaspheming God and cursing men on earth.
375   Sometime he talks as if Duke Humphrey's ghost
Were by his side; sometime he calls the King,
And whispers to his pillow as to him
The secrets of his over-chargèd° soul;   *overburdened*
And I am sent to tell his majesty
380   That even now he cries aloud for him.
QUEEN MARGARET   Go tell this heavy message to the King.
                                                    Exit VAUX
Ay me! What is this world? What news are these?
But wherefore grieve I at an hour's poor loss[1]
Omitting° Suffolk's exile, my soul's treasure?   *Ignoring*
385   Why only, Suffolk, mourn I not for thee,
And with the southern clouds[2] contend in tears—
Theirs for the earth's increase, mine for my sorrow's?
Now get thee hence. The King, thou know'st, is coming.
If thou be found by° me, thou art but dead.   *near*
390   SUFFOLK   If I depart from thee, I cannot live.
And in thy sight to die, what were it else
But like a pleasant slumber in thy lap?[3]
Here could I breathe my soul into the air,

---

1. Alluding to the Cardinal's old age and suggesting that   south.
he has in any case but a short time (an hour) to live.   3. Punning on "die in thy lap" as meaning "have an
2. It was generally thought that rain came from the   orgasm while in your embrace."

As mild and gentle as the cradle babe
395   Dying with mother's dug° between his lips;   *nipple*
Where, from° thy sight, I should be raging mad,   *out of*
And cry out for thee to close up mine eyes,
To have thee with thy lips to stop my mouth,
So shouldst thou either turn° my flying soul   *return to me*
400   Or I should breathe it, so, into thy body—
            [*He kisseth her*]
And then it lived in sweet Elysium.[4]
By thee to die were but to die in jest;[5]
From thee to die were torture more than death.
O, let me stay, befall what may befall!
405   QUEEN MARGARET   Away. Though parting be a fretful corrosive,°   *painful remedy*
It is applièd to a deathful° wound.   *deadly*
To France, sweet Suffolk. Let me hear from thee.
For wheresoe'er thou art in this world's Globe
I'll have an Iris[6] that shall find thee out.
410   SUFFOLK   I go.
QUEEN MARGARET   And take my heart with thee.
            She kisseth him
SUFFOLK   A jewel, locked into the woefull'st cask°   *casket*
That ever did contain a thing of worth.
Even as a splitted barque,° so sunder° we—   *boat / part*
This way fall I to death.
415   QUEEN MARGARET   This way for me.   *Exeunt [severally]*

3.3

Enter KING [HENRY *and the Earls of*] SALISBURY
and WARWICK. *Then the curtains be drawn [revealing]*
CARDINAL [BEAUFORT] *in his bed raving and staring as*
if he were mad

KING HENRY [*to* CARDINAL BEAUFORT]   How fares my lord? Speak, Beaufort,
to thy sovereign.
CARDINAL BEAUFORT   If thou beest death, I'll give thee England's treasure
Enough to purchase such another island,
So° thou wilt let me live and feel no pain.   *If*
5   KING HENRY   Ah, what a sign it is of evil life
Where death's approach is seen so terrible.
WARWICK   Beaufort, it is thy sovereign speaks to thee.
CARDINAL BEAUFORT   Bring me unto my trial when you will.
Died he° not in his bed? Where should he die?   *(Gloucester)*
10   Can I make men live whe'er° they will or no?   *whether*
O, torture me no more—I will confess.
Alive again? Then show me where he is.
I'll give a thousand pound to look upon him.
He hath no eyes! The dust hath blinded them.
15   Comb down his hair—look, look: it stands upright,
Like lime twigs[1] set to catch my wingèd soul.

---

4. In classical mythology, the paradise where blessed
souls dwelled.
5. To die near you or by means of you is not really to die
(with a continuing pun on "die" as meaning "attain
orgasm").

6. In Greek mythology, Iris was a messenger of the
gods, particularly of Hera.
3.3 Location: The Cardinal's bedchamber, London.
1. Twigs smeared with birdlime. See note to 1.3.92.

Give me some drink, and bid the apothecary
Bring the strong poison that I bought of him.
KING HENRY   O Thou eternal mover of the heavens,°   (God)
20   Look with a gentle eye upon this wretch.
O, beat away the busy meddling fiend
That lays strong siege unto this wretch's soul,
And from his bosom purge this black despair.
WARWICK   See how the pangs of death do make him grin.°   bare his teeth
25   SALISBURY   Disturb him not; let him pass peaceably.
KING HENRY   Peace to his soul, if God's good pleasure be.
Lord Card'nal, if thou think'st on heaven's bliss,
Hold up thy hand, make signal of thy hope.
          CARDINAL [BEAUFORT] dies
He dies and makes no sign. O God, forgive him.
30   WARWICK   So bad a death argues a monstrous life.
KING HENRY   Forbear to judge, for we are sinners all.
Close up his eyes and draw the curtain close,
And let us all to meditation.°   prayer
          Exeunt [drawing the curtains. The bed is removed]

4.1

Alarums within, and the chambers° be discharged like as   small cannon
it were a fight at sea. And then enter the CAPTAIN of the
ship, the MASTER, the Master's mate, Walter WHITMORE[1]
and others. [With them, as their prisoners,] the Duke of
SUFFOLK, disguised [and two GENTLEMEN]
CAPTAIN   The gaudy, blabbing, and remorseful day[2]
Is crept into the bosom of the sea;
And now loud-howling wolves arouse the jades[3]
That drag the tragic melancholy night;
Who, with their drowsy, slow, and flagging wings
5   Clip° dead men's graves, and from their misty jaws   Embrace
Breathe foul contagious darkness in the air.
Therefore bring forth the soldiers of our prize,°   captured ship
For whilst our pinnace° anchors in the downs,°   small ship / anchorage
Here shall they make their ransom on the sand,
10   Or with their blood stain this discoloured shore.[4]
Master, [pointing to the FIRST GENTLEMAN] this prisoner freely give I thee,
[To the MATE] And thou, that art his mate, make boot of this.[5]
          [He points to the SECOND GENTLEMAN]
[To Walter WHITMORE] The other [pointing to SUFFOLK],
          Walter Whitmore, is thy share.
FIRST GENTLEMAN [to the MASTER]   What is my ransom Master,
15   let me know.
MASTER   A thousand crowns, or else lay down your head.
MATE [to the SECOND GENTLEMAN] And so much shall you give,
          or off goes yours.

4.1 Location: At sea off the Kentish coast.
1. Q's stage direction reads, "Water Whickmore,"
anticipating the later play on "Walter" and "Water."
2. The garish, telltale (revealing secrets of the dark),
and guilty day.
3. Usually worn-out cart horses, here an allusion to the

dragons of Hecate that, according to classical mythology, drew Night's chariot.
4. Or discolor this shore with their blood.
5. Make a profit from (the ransom of) this second
prisoner.

CAPTAIN [*to both the* GENTLEMEN]   What, think you much to
　　　pay two thousand crowns,
　　And bear the name and port° of gentlemen?　　　　　　　　　*demeanor*
20   WHITMORE   Cut both the villains' throats! [*To* SUFFOLK] For die you shall.
　　The lives of those which we have lost in fight
　　[　　　　　　　　　　　　　　　　　　]⁶
　　Be counterpoised° with such a petty sum.　　　　　　*Be compensated*
FIRST GENTLEMAN [*to the* MASTER]   I'll give it, sir, and therefore
　　　spare my life.
SECOND GENTLEMAN [*to the* MATE]   And so will I, and write
25   　　home for it straight.
WHITMORE [*to* SUFFOLK]   I lost mine eye in laying the prize aboard,°　*boarding the ship*
　　And therefore to revenge it, shalt thou die—
　　And so should these, if I might have my will.
CAPTAIN   Be not so rash; take ransom; let him live.
30   SUFFOLK   Look on my George⁷—I am a gentleman.
　　Rate° me at what thou wilt, thou shalt be paid.　　　　　　*Value*
WHITMORE   And so am I; my name is Walter⁸ Whitmore.
　　　　[SUFFOLK] *starteth*
　　How now—why starts thou? What doth thee affright?
SUFFOLK   Thy name affrights me, in whose sound is death.
35   　A cunning man did calculate my birth,⁹
　　And told me that by 'water' I should die.
　　Yet let not this make thee be bloody-minded;
　　Thy name is Gualtier,¹ being rightly sounded.
WHITMORE   Gualtier or Walter—which it is I care not.
40   Never yet did base dishonour blur our name
　　But with our sword we wiped away the blot.
　　Therefore, when merchant-like I sell revenge,
　　Broke be my sword, my arms° torn and defaced,　　　　　*coat of arms*
　　And I proclaimed a coward through the world.
45   SUFFOLK   Stay, Whitmore; for thy prisoner is a prince,
　　The Duke of Suffolk, William de la Pole.
WHITMORE   The Duke of Suffolk muffled up in rags?
SUFFOLK   Ay, but these rags are no part of the Duke.
　　Jove sometime went disguised, and why not I?
50   CAPTAIN   But Jove was never slain as thou shalt be.
SUFFOLK   Obscure and lousy° swain, King Henry's blood,²　　*lice-infested*
　　The honourable blood of Lancaster,
　　Must not be shed by such a jady groom.³
　　Hast thou not kissed thy hand° and held my stirrup?　　*(a gesture of servility)*
55   Bare-headed plodded by my foot-cloth mule⁴
　　And thought thee happy when I shook° my head?　　　　　*nodded*
　　How often hast thou waited at my cup,
　　Fed from my trencher,° kneeled down at the board°　　*platter / table*
　　When I have feasted with Queen Margaret?

6. A line appears to be missing from F at this point, probably one indicating that the ransom demanded can never compensate for the lives lost in battle.
7. Alluding to the image of St. George and the dragon on the insignia of the Order of the Garter, the highest order of English knighthood.
8. "Walter" was usually pronounced "water." The spirit Asnath, conjured by Roger Bolingbroke, had predicted that Suffolk should die by "water" (see 1.4.32).
9. An astrologer cast my horoscope.
1. French for "Walter."
2. A dubious claim: Suffolk's mother was a distant cousin to Henry VI.
3. Servant in charge of horses; contemptible fellow.
4. The animal used to bear the large, richly ornamented cloth displayed in royal processions.

60	Remember it, and let it make thee crestfall'n,[5]	
	Ay, and allay this thy abortive° pride,	*monstrous*
	How in our voiding lobby° hast thou stood	*antechamber*
	And duly waited for my coming forth?	
	This hand of mine hath writ° in thy behalf,	*written testimonials*
65	And therefore shall it charm° thy riotous tongue.	*silence*
	WHITMORE Speak, Captain—shall I stab the forlorn swain?°	*wretched peasant*
	CAPTAIN First let my words stab him as he hath me.	
	SUFFOLK Base slave, thy words are blunt° and so art thou.	*harmless*
	CAPTAIN Convey him hence and, on our longboat's side,	
	Strike off his head.	
70	SUFFOLK Thou dar'st not for thy own.	
	CAPTAIN Pole—	
	SUFFOLK Pole?[6]	
	CAPTAIN Ay, kennel,° puddle, sink,° whose filth	*open gutter / cesspool*
	and dirt	
	Troubles the silver spring where England drinks,	
	Now will I dam up this thy yawning mouth	
	For swallowing the treasure of the realm.	
75	Thy lips that kissed the Queen shall sweep the ground,	
	And thou that smiledst at good Duke Humphrey's death	
	Against the senseless° winds shalt grin in vain,	*unfeeling*
	Who in contempt shall hiss at thee again.	
	And wedded be thou to the hags of hell,	
80	For daring to affy° a mighty lord	*betroth*
	Unto the daughter of a worthless king,	
	Having neither subject, wealth, nor diadem.	
	By devilish policy art thou grown great,	
	And like ambitious Sylla,[7] overgorged	
85	With gobbets° of thy mother's° bleeding heart.	*chunks / (England's)*
	By thee Anjou and Maine were sold to France,	
	The false revolting° Normans, thorough° thee,	*rebellious / because of*
	Disdain to call us lord, and Picardy	
	Hath slain their governors, surprised our forts,	
90	And sent the ragged soldiers, wounded, home.	
	The princely Warwick, and the Nevilles all,	
	Whose dreadful swords were never drawn in vain,	
	As hating thee, are rising up in arms;	
	And now the house of York, thrust from the crown,	
95	By shameful murder of a guiltless king[8]	
	And lofty, proud, encroaching tyranny,	
	Burns with revenging fire, whose hopeful colours	
	Advance° our half-faced sun,[9] striving to shine,	*Display*
	Under the which is writ, '*Invitis nubibus*'.°	*In spite of clouds*
100	The commons here in Kent are up in arms,	
	And, to conclude, reproach and beggary	
	Is crept into the palace of our King,	

---

5. Humble; deprived of a "crest" (coat of arms).
6. The fact that Suffolk's family name could be pronounced "pool" leads to the punning insults that follow. Lines 71–72 are garbled in F (see Textual Variants). Oxford's reconstruction assumes that abbreviations for "Suffolk" and "Lieutenant" were misread as "Sir" and "Lord" by those who set type from the Folio manuscript.
7. The Roman dictator Lucius Cornelius Sulla (138–78

b.c.e.), notorious for drawing up lists of enemies whom he executed or banished.
8. Alluding to the deposition and murder of Richard II, which allowed the Lancastrian branch of the royal family to seize the throne. Shakespeare dramatizes these events in *Richard II*.
9. A sun emerging above clouds was the badge of Edward III and his successor, Richard II.

And all by thee. [*To* WHITMORE] Away, convey him hence.

SUFFOLK   O that I were a god, to shoot forth thunder
105   Upon these paltry, servile, abject drudges.
Small things make base men proud. This villain here,
Being captain of a pinnace, threatens more
Than Bargulus, the strong Illyrian pirate.[1]
Drones° suck not eagles' blood, but rob beehives.   *Beetles; parasites*
110   It is impossible that I should die
By such a lowly vassal as thyself.
Thy words move rage, and not remorse in me.

CAPTAIN   But my deeds, Suffolk, soon shall stay thy rage.

SUFFOLK   I go of message° from the Queen to France—   *as messenger*
115   I charge thee, waft° me safely cross the Channel!   *convey*

CAPTAIN   Walter—

WHITMORE   Come, Suffolk, I must waft thee to thy death.

SUFFOLK   *Paene gelidus timor occupat artus*[2]—
It is thee I fear.

120 WHITMORE   Thou shalt have cause to fear before I leave thee.
What, are ye daunted now? Now will ye stoop?

FIRST GENTLEMAN [*to* SUFFOLK]   My gracious lord, entreat
him—speak him fair.

SUFFOLK   Suffolk's imperial tongue is stern and rough,
Used to command, untaught to plead for favour.
125   Far be it we should honour such as these
With humble suit. No, rather let my head
Stoop to the block than these knees bow to any
Save to the God of heaven and to my king;
And sooner dance upon a bloody pole[3]
130   Than stand uncovered to the vulgar groom.
True nobility is exempt from fear;
More can I bear than you dare execute.

CAPTAIN   Hale° him away, and let him talk no more.   *Drag*

SUFFOLK   Come, 'soldiers', show what cruelty ye can,
135   That this my death may never be forgot.
Great men oft die by vile Besonians;[4]
A Roman sworder and banditto° slave   *cutthroat and lawless*
Murdered sweet Tully; Brutus' bastard hand[5]
Stabbed Julius Caesar; savage islanders
140   Pompey the Great;[6] and Suffolk dies by pirates.

Exit WHITMORE *with* SUFFOLK

CAPTAIN   And as for these whose ransom we have set,
It is our pleasure one of them depart.
[*To the* SECOND GENTLEMAN] Therefore, come you with us and
[*to his men, pointing to the* FIRST GENTLEMAN] let him go.

Exeunt. Manet the FIRST GENTLEMAN

---

1. An ancient pirate alluded to in Ciero's *De Officiis* (*On Public Duties*), a text much used in Elizabethan schools.
2. Cold fear seizes my limbs almost entirely (perhaps alluding to Virgil, *Aeneid* 7.446; Lucan, *Pharsalia* 1.246; or both).
3. Punning on his name ("Pole") and on Elizabethan slang for "head" ("poll"), Suffolk alludes to the fact that heads of executed criminals were set upon poles in public places. Londoners would often pass by such poles as they crossed the bridge on their way to the theaters in Southwark.
4. Base fellows. From the Spanish word *bisoño*, meaning "recruit": foot soldiers were usually poor commoners.
5. Brutus, who helped murder Caesar, was rumored to have been his illegitimate son. *Tully*: the Roman orator Cicero, who was in fact murdered by Roman soldiers.
6. Alluding either to Plutarch's claim that the Egyptians who murdered this Roman general were led by one born on the island of Chios or to the tradition that Pompey was murdered on the island of Lesbos.

Enter WHITMORE *with [Suffolk's head and] body*

WHITMORE There let his head and lifeless body lie,

145 Until the Queen his mistress bury it.   *Exit*

FIRST GENTLEMAN O barbarous and bloody spectacle!

His body will I bear unto the King.

If he revenge it not, yet will his friends;

So will the Queen, that living held him dear.

[*Exit with Suffolk's head and body*]

4.2

Enter two REBELS *with long staves*[1]

FIRST REBEL Come and get thee a sword, though made of a
lath;[2] they have been up° these two days.   *in revolt*

SECOND REBEL They have the more need to sleep now then.

FIRST REBEL I tell thee, Jack Cade the clothier[3] means to dress
5 the commonwealth, and turn it,[4] and set a new nap upon it.[5]

SECOND REBEL So he had need, for 'tis threadbare. Well, I say it
was never merry world in England since gentlemen came up.°   *came into fashion*

FIRST REBEL O, miserable age! Virtue is not regarded in handicraftsmen.°   *artisans*

10 SECOND REBEL The nobility think scorn to go in leather
aprons.°   *(workers' attire)*

FIRST REBEL Nay more, the King's Council are no good
workmen.

SECOND REBEL True; and yet it is said 'Labour in thy vocation';
15 which is as much to say as 'Let the magistrates be labouring
men'; and therefore should we be magistrates.

FIRST REBEL Thou hast hit it; for there's no better sign of a
brave° mind than a hard° hand.   *fine / calloused*

SECOND REBEL I see them! I see them! There's Best's son, the
20 tanner of Wingham—

FIRST REBEL He shall have the skins of our enemies to make
dog's leather[6] of.

SECOND REBEL And Dick the butcher—

FIRST REBEL Then is sin struck down like an ox, and iniquity's
25 throat cut like a calf.

SECOND REBEL And Smith the weaver—

FIRST REBEL Argo,[7] their thread of life is spun.

SECOND REBEL Come, come, let's fall in with them.

Enter Jack CADE, *Dick [the]* BUTCHER, *Smith the*
WEAVER, *a sawyer, [and a drummer,] with infinite num-*
bers, [all] with long staves

CADE We, John Cade, so termed of° our supposed father—   *named for*

30 BUTCHER [*to his fellows*] Or rather of stealing a cade° of   *barrel*
herrings.

CADE For our enemies shall fall before us,[8] inspired with the
spirit of putting down kings and princes—command silence!

4.2 Location: Blackheath, Kent.
1. Staves are mentioned only in the Q stage directions
and dialogue, and may reflect performance.
2. A strip of wood commonly used as a sword or dagger
by the Vice figure in English morality plays.
3. Clothiers, or textile workers, were involved in
a number of uprisings throughout the sixteenth
century.

4. Turn it inside out (as a way of renewing old cloth),
with a secondary sense of inverting the social hierarchy.
5. Improve its surface texture, probably by brushing
the outer fibers ("nap") of the cloth; reform it.
6. Inferior leather used in glove making.
7. A variant of *ergo*, Latin for "therefore."
8. Borrowing biblical language and punning on the
Latin *cadere*, meaning "fall."

BUTCHER Silence!

35 CADE My father was a Mortimer—

BUTCHER [to his fellows] He was an honest man and a good bricklayer.[9]

CADE My mother a Plantagenet—

BUTCHER [to his fellows] I knew her well, she was a midwife.

40 CADE My wife descended of the Lacys[1]—

BUTCHER [to his fellows] She was indeed a pedlar's daughter and sold many laces.

WEAVER [to his fellows] But now of late, not able to travel with her furred pack,[2] she washes bucks[3] here at home.

45 CADE Therefore am I of an honourable house.

BUTCHER [to his fellows] Ay, by my faith, the field is honourable, and there was he born, under a hedge; for his father had never a house but the cage.° prison

CADE Valiant I am—

50 WEAVER [to his fellows] A° must needs, for beggary is valiant.[4] He

CADE I am able to endure much—

BUTCHER [to his fellows] No question of that, for I have seen him whipped[5] three market days together.

CADE I fear neither sword nor fire.

55 WEAVER [to his fellows] He need not fear the sword, for his coat is of proof.[6]

BUTCHER [to his fellows] But methinks he should stand in fear of fire, being burned i'th' hand for stealing of sheep.[7]

CADE Be brave, then, for your captain is brave and vows refor-

60 mation. There shall be in England seven halfpenny loaves sold for a penny, the three-hooped pot shall have ten hoops,[8] and I will make it felony to drink small° beer. All the realm shall weak
be in° common, and in Cheapside[9] shall my palfrey° go to held in / saddle horse
grass. And when I am king, as king I will be—

65 ALL CADE'S FOLLOWERS God save your majesty!

CADE I thank you good people!—there shall be no money. All shall eat and drink on my score,° and I will apparel them all at my expense
in one livery that they may agree like brothers, and worship me their lord.

70 BUTCHER The first thing we do let's kill all the lawyers.

CADE Nay, that I mean to do. Is not this a lamentable thing that of the skin of an innocent lamb should be made parchment? That parchment, being scribbled o'er, should undo a man? Some say the bee stings, but I say 'tis the bee's wax.° For sealing wax

75 I did but seal[1] once to a thing, and I was never mine own man since. How now? Who's there?

Enter [some bringing forth] the CLERK *of Chatham*

WEAVER The Clerk of Chatham—he can write and read and cast account.° do arithmetic

9. Punning on "Mortimer" and "mortarer" (meaning "builder").
1. The family name of the earls of Lincoln.
2. Not able to travel with her peddler's pack made of skins with the hair turned outward; not able to make a living ("travail") with her sexual organs.
3. She washes laundry; she absolves ("washes") cuckolds (husbands with horns, like bucks) of their shame by helping them get even with their unfaithful wives.
4. Worthy of praise; sturdy. The Weaver is referring ironically to the fact that Elizabethan poor laws made it

illegal to give alms to able-bodied, or "valiant," beggars.
5. The usual punishment for vagabonds.
6. Impenetrable (from dirt?); well worn.
7. Thieves were branded on one hand with a "T" for "thief."
8. "Hoops," or regularly spaced bands on pots, were used for measuring. Cade means that for the price of a three-hooped pot (about a quart), one will receive over three times that amount.
9. Elizabethan London's chief commercial district.
1. Sign and seal (a legal document).

CADE O, monstrous!

80 WEAVER We took him setting of boys' copies.[2]

CADE Here's a villain.

WEAVER He's a book in his pocket with red letters[3] in't.

CADE Nay, then he is a conjuror!

BUTCHER Nay, he can make obligations° and write court hand.[4]   *bonds*

85 CADE I am sorry for't. The man is a proper° man, of mine   *handsome*
    honour. Unless I find him guilty, he shall not die. Come
    hither, sirrah, I must examine thee. What is thy name?

CLERK Emmanuel.

BUTCHER They use to write that on the top of letters[5]—'twill go
90   hard with you.

CADE Let me alone. [*To the* CLERK] Dost thou use to write thy
    name? Or hast thou a mark[6] to thyself like an honest plain-
    dealing man?

CLERK Sir, I thank God I have been so well brought up that I
95   can write my name.

ALL CADE'S FOLLOWERS He hath confessed—away with him!
    He's a villain and a traitor.

CADE Away with him, I say, hang him with his pen and inkhorn
    about his neck.   *Exit one with the* CLERK
    Enter [a MESSENGER]*[7]*

100 MESSENGER Where's our general?

CADE Here I am, thou particular[8] fellow.

MESSENGER Fly, fly, fly! Sir Humphrey Stafford and his brother
    are hard by with the King's forces.

CADE Stand, villain, stand—or I'll fell thee down. He shall be
105   encountered with a man as good as himself. He is but a
    knight, is a?

MESSENGER No.[9]

CADE To equal him I will make myself a knight presently.
    [*He kneels and knights himself*]
    Rise up, Sir John Mortimer.
    [*He rises*]
110   Now have at him!
    Enter Sir Humphrey STAFFORD *and his brother,*
    with [a] drum[mer] and soldiers

STAFFORD [*to Cade's followers*] Rebellious hinds,° the filth and   *peasants*
    scum of Kent,
    Marked for the gallows, lay your weapons down;
    Home to your cottages, forsake this groom.
    The King is merciful, if you revolt.°   *turn against Cade*

STAFFORD'S BROTHER [*to Cade's followers*] But angry, wrathful,
115   and inclined to blood,
    If you go forward. Therefore, yield or die.

CADE [*to his followers*] As for these silken-coated slaves, I pass° not.   *care*
    It is to you, good people, that I speak,

---

2. Preparing writing exercises for schoolboys. Village clerks often doubled as schoolmasters.

3. Alluding to the red printing in almanacs and primers.

4. The script used for legal documents.

5. The name, which means "God is with us," commonly appeared on legal documents.

6. Those who were illiterate often "signed" documents by using distinctive marks.

7. Q calls this figure 'Tom,' F "Michael."

8. Private (as opposed to "general" in the previous line).

9. No, nothing but a knight. The Messenger is replying to the negative implied in the prior sentence: "He is nothing but a knight, is he?"

Over whom, in time to come, I hope to reign—
120   For I am rightful heir unto the crown.
STAFFORD   Villain, thy father was a plasterer
    And thou thyself a shearman,[1] art thou not?
CADE   And Adam was a gardener.
STAFFORD'S BROTHER   And what of that?
CADE   Marry, this: Edmund Mortimer, Earl of March,
125   Married the Duke of Clarence' daughter, did he not?
STAFFORD   Ay, sir.
CADE   By her he had two children at one birth.
STAFFORD'S BROTHER   That's false.
CADE   Ay, there's the question—but I say 'tis true.
130   The elder of them, being put to nurse,
    Was by a beggar-woman stol'n away,
    And, ignorant of his birth and parentage,
    Became a bricklayer when he came to age.
    His son am I—deny it an° you can.   *if*
135 BUTCHER   Nay, 'tis too true—therefore he shall be king.
WEAVER   Sir, he made a chimney in my father's house, and the
    bricks are alive at this day to testify. Therefore deny it not.
STAFFORD [*to Cade's followers*]   And will you credit this base drudge's words
    That speaks he knows not what?
140 ALL CADE'S FOLLOWERS   Ay, marry, will we—therefore get ye gone.
STAFFORD'S BROTHER   Jack Cade, the Duke of York hath taught you this.
CADE [*aside*]   He lies, for I invented it myself.
    [*Aloud*] Go to, sirrah[2]—tell the King from me that for his
    father's sake, Henry the Fifth, in whose time boys went to
145   span-counter° for French crowns,[3] I am content he shall   *played a game of toss*
    reign; but I'll be Protector over him.
BUTCHER   And, furthermore, we'll have the Lord Saye's[4] head
    for selling the dukedom of Maine.
CADE   And good reason, for thereby is England maimed, and
150   fain to go with a staff, but that my puissance° holds it up.   *power*
    Fellow-kings, I tell you that that Lord Saye hath gelded the
    commonwealth, and made it an eunuch, and, more than that,
    he can speak French, and therefore he is a traitor!
STAFFORD   O gross and miserable ignorance!
155 CADE   Nay, answer if you can: the Frenchmen are our enemies;
    go to, then, I ask but this—can he that speaks with the tongue
    of an enemy be a good counsellor or no?
ALL CADE'S FOLLOWERS   No, no—and therefore we'll have his
    head!
STAFFORD'S BROTHER [*to* STAFFORD]   Well, seeing gentle words
160   will not prevail,
    Assail them with the army of the King.
STAFFORD   Herald, away, and throughout every town
    Proclaim them traitors that are up with Cade;

---

1. One who cuts the nap from cloth during its manufacture.
2. Term used to address inferiors.
3. Alluding to Henry V's conquest of France. "French crowns" might refer to French coins, kings, kingdoms,

or the bald heads that were symptomatic of the venereal diseases blamed on the French.
4. *Lord Saye:* James Fiennes, Treasurer of England, was associated with Suffolk in the loss of Anjou and Maine.

That those which fly before the battle ends
165 May, even in their wives' and children's sight,
Be hanged up for° example at their doors.   *to make an*
And you that be the King's friends, follow me!
          Exeunt [*the*] STAFFORD[*s*] *and his men* [*their soldiers*]
CADE   And you that love the commons, follow me!
Now show yourselves men—'tis for liberty.
170 We will not leave one lord, one gentleman—
Spare none but such as go in clouted shoon,°   *hobnailed shoes*
For they are thrifty honest men, and such
As would, but that they dare not, take our parts.
BUTCHER   They are all in order, and march toward us.
175 CADE   But then are we in order when we are
Most out of order.° Come, march forward!   *rebellious*
                                        Exeunt

                            4.3

Alarums to the fight; [*excursions,*]° *wherein both the*   *skirmishes*
STAFFORDS *are slain. Enter Jack* CADE, [*Dick the*
BUTCHER,] *and the rest*
CADE   Where's Dick, the butcher of Ashford?
BUTCHER   Here, sir.
CADE   They fell before thee like sheep and oxen, and thou
behaved'st thyself as if thou hadst been in thine own slaughter-
5 house. Therefore, thus will I reward thee—the Lent shall be
as long again as it is. Thou shalt have licence to kill for a hundred, lacking one.[1]
BUTCHER   I desire no more.
CADE   And to speak truth, thou deserv'st no less.
          [*He apparels himself in the Staffords' armour*]
10 This monument of the victory will I bear, and the bodies shall
be dragged at my horse heels till I do come to London, where
we will have the Mayor's sword borne before us.
BUTCHER   If we mean to thrive and do good, break open the
jails and let out the prisoners.
15 CADE   Fear not° that, I warrant thee. Come, let's march towards   *Don't worry about*
London.   *Exeunt* [*dragging the Staffords' bodies*]

                            4.4

Enter KING [HENRY] *reading a supplication,* QUEEN
[MARGARET] *with Suffolk's head, the Duke of*
BUCKINGHAM, *and the Lord* SAYE, *with others*
QUEEN MARGARET [*aside*]   Oft have I heard that grief softens the mind,
And makes it fearful and degenerate;
Think, therefore, on revenge, and cease to weep.
But who can cease to weep and look on this?
5 Here may his head lie on my throbbing breast,
But where's the body that I should embrace?

4.3 Location: Scene continues.
1. Butchers were not permitted to slaughter meat during Lent (the forty-day period before Easter during
which Christians were to avoid eating flesh) except by
special license to provide food for the ill. Cade promises
the Butcher that he will have such a license and that
Lent will be twice as long as it is now. *Thou . . . one:*
You can kill ninety-nine animals, or serve ninety-nine
customers.
4.4 Location: The palace, London.

BUCKINGHAM [*to* KING HENRY]   What answer makes your grace
    to the rebels' supplication?
KING HENRY   I'll send some holy bishop to entreat,
    For God forbid so many simple souls
10   Should perish by the sword. And I myself,
    Rather than bloody war shall cut them short,
    Will parley° with Jack Cade their general.   *speak*
    But stay, I'll read it over once again.
        [*He*] *read*[s]
QUEEN MARGARET [*to* Suffolk's head]   Ah, barbarous villains!
    Hath this lovely face
15   Ruled like a wandering planet over me,[1]
    And could it not enforce them to relent,
    That were unworthy to behold the same?
KING HENRY   Lord Saye, Jack Cade hath sworn to have thy head.
SAYE   Ay, but I hope your highness shall have his.
KING HENRY [*to* QUEEN MARGARET]   How now, madam? Still
20   lamenting and mourning
    Suffolk's death?
    I fear me, love, if that I had been dead,
    Thou wouldest not have mourned so much for me.
QUEEN MARGARET   No, my love, I should not mourn, but die for thee.
        Enter a MESSENGER [*in haste*]
25 KING HENRY   How now? What news? Why com'st thou in such haste?
MESSENGER   The rebels are in Southwark[2]—fly, my lord!
    Jack Cade proclaims himself Lord Mortimer,
    Descended from the Duke of Clarence' house,
    And calls your grace usurper, openly,
30   And vows to crown himself in Westminster.
    His army is a ragged multitude
    Of hinds and peasants, rude and merciless.
    Sir Humphrey Stafford and his brother's death
    Hath given them heart and courage to proceed.
35   All scholars, lawyers, courtiers, gentlemen,
    They call false caterpillars° and intend their death.   *treacherous parasites*
KING HENRY   O, graceless° men; they know not what they do.[3]   *sinful*
BUCKINGHAM   My gracious lord, retire to Kenilworth°   *(a royal castle)*
    Until a power be raised to put them down.
40 QUEEN MARGARET   Ah, were the Duke of Suffolk now alive
    These Kentish rebels would be soon appeased!°   *made peaceful*
KING HENRY   Lord Saye, the trait'rous rabble hateth thee—
    Therefore away with us to Kenilworth.
SAYE   So might your grace's person be in danger.
45   The sight of me is odious in their eyes,
    And therefore in this city will I stay
    And live alone as secret as I may.
        Enter another MESSENGER
SECOND MESSENGER [*to* KING HENRY]   Jack Cade hath almost gotten
    London Bridge;

---

1. It was popularly believed that influences from the stars ("wandering planets") determined the fate of those born under them.
2. A suburb of London (in Shakespeare's time, the site of brothels and theaters).
3. An echo of Jesus' words on the cross to those who crucified and mocked him. See Luke 23:34.

The citizens fly and forsake their houses;	
50 The rascal people, thirsting after prey,	
Join with the traitor; and they jointly swear	
To spoil° the city and your royal court.	*plunder*

BUCKINGHAM [*to* KING HENRY]   Then linger not, my lord; away,
take horse!

KING HENRY   Come, Margaret. God, our hope, will succour us.

QUEEN MARGARET [*aside*]   My hope is gone, now Suffolk is
55   deceased.

KING HENRY [*to* SAYE]   Farewell, my lord. Trust not the Kentish
rebels.

BUCKINGHAM [*to* SAYE]   Trust nobody, for fear you be betrayed.

SAYE   The trust I have is in mine innocence,
And therefore am I bold and resolute.

Exeunt [SAYE *at one door, the rest at another*]

4.5

Enter the Lord SCALES *upon the Tower, walking.*
Enter three or four CITIZENS *below*

SCALES   How now? Is Jack Cade slain?

FIRST CITIZEN   No, my lord Scales,[1] nor likely to be slain, for he
and his men have won the bridge, killing all those that did
withstand them. The Lord Mayor craveth aid of your honour
5   from the Tower to defend the city from the rebels.

SCALES Such aid as I can spare you shall command,	
But I am troubled here with them myself.	
The rebels have essayed° to win the Tower.	*attempted*
Get you to Smithfield,[2] there to gather head,°	*raise forces*
10 And thither will I send you Matthew Gough.	
Fight for your king, your country, and your lives!	
And so, farewell, for I must hence again.	

Exeunt [SCALES *above, the* CITIZENS *below*]

4.6

Enter Jack Cade, [*the* WEAVER, *the* BUTCHER,] *and the*
rest. [CADE] *strikes his sword on London Stone*

CADE   Now is Mortimer lord of this city. And, here sitting upon
London Stone, I charge and command that, of the city's cost,
the Pissing Conduit[2] run nothing but claret wine this first
year of our reign. And now henceforward it shall be treason
5   for any that calls me otherwise than Lord Mortimer.

Enter a SOLDIER, *running*

SOLDIER   Jack Cade, Jack Cade!

CADE Zounds,° knock him down there!	*God's wounds (an oath)*

They kill him

BUTCHER   If this fellow be wise, he'll never call ye Jack Cade
more; I think he hath a very fair warning.

[*He takes a paper from the soldier's body and reads it*]
10   My lord, there's an army gathered together in Smithfield.

4.5 Location: The Tower, London.
1. Thomas de Scales fought with Talbot in France and
was charged by the King with the defense of the Tower.
2. Area just outside London's walls and to the northwest.
4.6 Location: Cannon Street, London.

1. An ancient stone found in Cannon Street and
famous as a London landmark.
2. The nickname for Little Conduit, a fountain used by
lower-class Londoners as a water supply.

CADE   Come then, let's go fight with them—but first, go on and
set London Bridge afire, and, if you can, burn down the Tower
too. Come, let's away.   *Exeunt*

4.7

Alarums. [Excursions, wherein] Matthew GOUGH *is*
slain, and all the rest [of his men] with him. Then enter
Jack CADE *with his company [among them the* BUTCHER,
the WEAVER, *and* JOHN, *a rebel]*

CADE   So, sirs, now go some and pull down the Savoy;[1] others
to th' Inns of Court[2]—down with them all.
BUTCHER   I have a suit unto your lordship.
CADE   Be it a lordship, thou shalt have it for that word.
5   BUTCHER   Only that the laws of England may come out of your
mouth.
JOHN [*aside to his fellows*]   Mass, 'twill be sore° law then, for he   harsh
was thrust in the mouth with a spear, and 'tis not whole yet.
WEAVER [*aside to* JOHN]   Nay, John, it will be stinking law, for his
10   breath stinks with eating toasted cheese.
CADE   I have thought upon it—it shall be so. Away! Burn all
the records of the realm. My mouth shall be the Parliament
of England.
JOHN [*aside to his fellows*]   Then we are like to have biting°   severe
15   statutes unless his teeth be pulled out.
CADE   And henceforward all things shall be in common.
            Enter a MESSENGER
MESSENGER   My lord, a prize, a prize! Here's the Lord Saye
which sold the towns in France. He that made us pay one-and-
twenty fifteens and one shilling to the pound the last subsidy.[3]
            Enter a rebel with the Lord SAYE[4]
20   CADE   Well, he shall be beheaded for it ten times. [*To* SAYE] Ah,
thou say, thou serge—nay, thou buckram lord![5] Now art thou
within point-blank° of our jurisdiction regal. What canst thou   within reach
answer to my majesty for giving up of Normandy unto Moun-
sieur Basimecu,[6] the Dauphin of France? Be it known unto
25   thee by these presence,[7] even the presence of Lord Mortimer,
that I am the besom° that must sweep the court clean of such   broom
filth as thou art. Thou hast most traitorously corrupted the
youth of the realm in erecting a grammar school; and,
whereas before, our forefathers had no other books but the
30   score and the tally,[8] thou hast caused printing to be used and,
contrary to the King his° crown and dignity, thou hast built a   the King's
paper-mill.[9] It will be proved to thy face that thou hast men

---

4.7 Location: Smithfield; London.
1. An anachronistic reference to the London residence
of the Duke of Lancaster, which was burned down during a 1381 uprising and not rebuilt until 1505.
2. The buildings where London's lawyers were trained
and lived.
3. He who made us pay very high personal property taxes
in the last tax assessment. A "fifteen" was a levy of one-
fifteenth of the property value; "twenty-one fifteens"
would be a tax in excess of the value of the property itself.
4. F and Q both read, "Enter George." As elsewhere,
the Oxford editors change what is assumed to be an
actor's name to the generic "a rebel."
5. Say was an expensive silk fabric, serge a durable

woolen fabric often worn by the lower classes, and
buckram a coarse linen also worn by the poor.
6. Punning on *baise mon cul*, French for "kiss my ass."
7. "These presents" was a legal term meaning "the
present document," a phrase that begins many legal
writings of the period. Cade, however, means "in the
presence of the King, who declares the law."
8. A rudimentary device for keeping track of financial
transactions. Sticks were marked, or "scored," split into
two pieces, and then divided between the debtor and
creditor. Each half was called a "tally."
9. Printing presses and paper mills were not in fact established in England until late in the fifteenth century.
Under Elizabeth, they were subject to strict regulation.

about thee that usually talk of a noun and a verb and such
abominable words as no Christian ear can endure to hear.
35 Thou hast appointed justices of peace to call poor men before
them about matters they were not able to answer. Moreover,
thou hast put them in prison, and, because they could not
read,[1] thou hast hanged them when indeed only for that
cause° they have been most worthy to live. Thou dost ride on   *for that reason alone*
40 a foot-cloth,[2] dost thou not?
SAYE   What of that?
CADE   Marry, thou ought'st not to let thy horse wear a cloak
when honester men than thou go in° their hose and doublets.   *wear only*
BUTCHER   And work in their shirts, too; as myself, for example,
45 that am a butcher.
SAYE   You men of Kent.
BUTCHER   What say you of Kent?
SAYE   Nothing but this—'tis *bona terra, mala gens.*[3]
CADE   *Bonum terrum*—zounds, what's that?
50 BUTCHER   He speaks French.
FIRST REBEL   No, 'tis Dutch.
SECOND REBEL   No, 'tis Out-talian, I know it well enough.
SAYE   Hear me but speak, and bear me where you will.
Kent, in the commentaries Caesar writ,
55 Is termed the civil'st° place of all this isle;   *most civilized*
Sweet is the country, because full of riches;
The people liberal,° valiant, active, wealthy;   *generous*
Which makes me hope you are not void of pity.
I sold not Maine, I lost not Normandy;
60 Yet to recover them would lose my life.
Justice with favour° have I always done,   *leniency*
Prayers and tears have moved me—gifts could never.
When have I aught° exacted at your hands,   *anything*
But to maintain the King, the realm, and you?
65 Large gifts have I bestowed on learnèd clerks°   *scholars*
Because my book preferred me to[4] the King,
And seeing ignorance is the curse of God,
Knowledge the wing wherewith we fly to heaven.
Unless you be possessed with devilish spirits,
70 You cannot but forbear to murder me.
This tongue hath parleyed unto° foreign kings   *negotiated with*
For your behoof°—   *behalf*
CADE   Tut, when struck'st thou one blow in the field?°   *battlefield*
SAYE   Great men have reaching hands.[5] Oft have I struck
75 Those that I never saw, and struck them dead.
REBEL   O monstrous coward! What, to come behind folks?
SAYE   These cheeks are pale for watching for your good—
CADE   Give him a box o'th' ear, and that will make 'em red again.
    [*One of the rebels strikes* SAYE]
SAYE   Long sitting° to determine poor men's causes   *(as a judge)*
80 Hath made me full of sickness and diseases.

---

1. Read Latin. By demonstrating reading knowledge of
Latin, a person charged with a crime in early modern
England could plead "benefit of clergy" and thereby be
excused from hanging.
2. An ornamented cloth hung over the back of a horse
and reaching to the ground on each side.
3. A good land, a bad people.

4. Because my own education brought me to the attention of the King (and improved my social position).
5. A variation on the classical proverb "Kings have long
hands," suggesting that monarchs and influential
people such as lord Saye have influence that causes
much to happen even when they are not present.

CADE   Ye shall have a hempen caudle,[6] then, and the health   *executioner's ax*
o'th' hatchet.°
BUTCHER [*to* SAYE]   Why dost thou quiver, man?
SAYE   The palsy, and not fear, provokes me.
85   CADE   Nay, he nods at us as who should say 'I'll be even with
you'. I'll see if his head will stand steadier on a pole or no.
Take him away, and behead him.
SAYE   Tell me wherein have I offended most?
Have I affected wealth or honour? Speak.
90   Are my chests filled up with extorted gold?
Is my apparel sumptuous to behold?
Whom have I injured, that ye seek my death?
These hands are free from guiltless bloodshedding,
This breast from harbouring foul deceitful thoughts.
95   O let me live!
CADE [*aside*]   I feel remorse in myself with his words, but I'll bri-
dle it. He shall die an it be but for pleading so well for his life.
[*Aloud*] Away with him—he has a familiar° under his tongue;   *demon*
he speaks not a God's name. Go, take him away, I say, to the
100   Standard[7] in Cheapside, and strike off his head presently;° and   *immediately*
then go to Mile End Green—break into his son-in-law's house,
Sir James Cromer, and strike off his head, and bring them both
upon two poles hither.
ALL CADE'S FOLLOWERS   It shall be done!
105   SAYE   Ah, countrymen, if, when you make your prayers,
God should be so obdurate as yourselves,
How would it fare with your departed souls?
And therefore yet relent and save my life!
CADE   Away with him, and do as I command ye!
            Exeunt [the BUTCHER *and] one or two*
                        with the Lord SAYE
110   The proudest peer in the realm shall not wear a head on his
shoulders unless he pay me tribute. There shall not a maid be
married but she shall pay to me her maidenhead,[8] ere they
have it. Married men shall hold of me *in capite*.[9] And we
charge and command that their wives be as free° as heart can   *sexually available*
115   wish or tongue can tell.
            Enter a REBEL
REBEL   O captain, London Bridge is afire!
CADE   Run to Billingsgate and fetch pitch and flax and
quench it.
            Enter the BUTCHER *and a* SERGEANT
SERGEANT   Justice, justice, I pray you, sir, let me have justice of
120   this fellow here.
CADE   Why, what has he done?
SERGEANT   Alas, sir, he has ravished° my wife.   *raped*
BUTCHER [*to* CADE]   Why, my lord, he would have 'rested° me   *arrested*
and I went and entered my action in his wife's proper house.[1]

---

6. Caudel was a warm gruel, but "a hempen caudel"
was a slang term for "hangman's noose."
7. A water conduit in Cheapside often used as a place
of execution.
8. Alluding to a supposed feudal practice by which a
lord had the right to sleep with the bride of any of his

vassals on the night of her wedding.
9. A Latin phrase indicating property held by grant
directly from the king, with a pun on *caput* (Latin for
"head") as slang for "maidenhead."
1. Stated my case in his wife's own house; had sex in
his wife's own body.

125   CADE   Dick, follow thy suit in her common place.² [*To the*
       SERGEANT] You whoreson° villain, you are a sergeant—you'll   *bastard*
       take any man by the throat for twelve pence, and 'rest a man
       when he's at dinner, and have him to prison ere the meat be
       out of his mouth. [*To the* BUTCHER] Go, Dick, take him hence:
130   cut out his tongue for cogging,° hough° him for running, and,   *deception / cripple*
       to conclude, brain him with his own mace.°   *staff of office*
                       Exit [*the* BUTCHER] *with the* SERGEANT

       REBEL   My lord, when shall we go to Cheapside and take up
       commodities upon our bills?³
       CADE   Marry, presently. He that will lustily stand to it⁴ shall go
135   with me and take up these commodities following—item, a
       gown, a kirtle, a petticoat, and a smock.⁵
       ALL CADE'S FOLLOWERS   O brave!
            Enter two with the Lord Saye's head and Sir James
            Cromer's upon two poles
       CADE   But is not this braver? Let them kiss one another, for they
       loved well when they were alive.
            [*The two heads are made to kiss*]
140   Now part them again, lest they consult about the giving up
       of some more towns in France. Soldiers, defer the spoil°   *destruction; plunder*
       of the city until night. For with these borne before us
       instead of maces will we ride through the streets, and at
       every corner have them kiss. Away!
            Exeunt [*two with the heads. The others begin to follow*]
145   Up Fish Street! Down Saint Magnus' Corner!⁶ Kill and
       knock down! Throw them into Thames!
            Sound a parley
       What noise is this? Dare any be so bold to sound retreat or
       parley when I command them kill?
            Enter the Duke of BUCKINGHAM *and old Lord* CLIFFORD
       BUCKINGHAM   Ay, here they be that dare and will disturb thee!
150   Know, Cade, we come ambassadors from the King
       Unto the commons, whom thou hast misled,
       And here pronounce free pardon to them all
       That will forsake thee and go home in peace.
       CLIFFORD   What say ye, countrymen, will ye relent
155   And yield to mercy whilst 'tis offered you,
       Or let a rebel lead you to your deaths?
       Who loves the King and will embrace his pardon,
       Fling up his cap and say 'God save his majesty'.
       Who hateth him and honours not his father,
160   Henry the Fifth, that made all France to quake,
       Shake he his weapon at us,° and pass by.   *Defy us*
            They [*fling up their caps and*] *forsake* CADE
       ALL CADE'S FOLLOWERS   God save the King! God save the King!
       CADE   What, Buckingham and Clifford, are ye so brave?° [*To*   *arrogant*
       the rabble] And you, base peasants, do ye believe him? Will
165   you needs be hanged with your pardons about your necks?

---

2. Pursue your sexual desire in her vagina; pursue your legal suit in her meetinghouse.
3. And acquire goods on credit or by means of our weapons ("bills"); and rape women, punning on "commodity" as meaning "female sexual organs" and "bills"
as meaning "penises."
4. Apply himself manfully; have an erection.
5. Slang terms for "female sexual organs."
6. Place at the north end of London Bridge opposite Southwark.

Hath my sword, therefore, broke through London gates that
you should leave me at the White Hart[7] in Southwark?
I thought ye would never have given out° these arms till you   *abandoned*
had recovered your ancient freedom. But you are all recreants
170 and dastards,° and delight to live in slavery to the nobility. Let   *traitors and cowards*
them break your backs with burdens, take your houses over
your heads, ravish your wives and daughters before your
faces. For me, I will make shift for one,° and so God's curse   *take care of myself*
light upon you all.
175 ALL CADE'S FOLLOWERS   We'll follow Cade! We'll follow Cade!
          They run to CADE *again*
CLIFFORD   Is Cade the son of Henry the Fifth
That thus you do exclaim you'll go with him?
Will he conduct you through the heart of France
And make the meanest° of you earls and dukes?   *lowest born*
180 Alas, he hath no home, no place to fly to,
Nor knows he how to live but by the spoil—
Unless by robbing of your friends and us.
Were't not a shame that whilst you live at jar°   *at odds*
The fearful° French, whom you late vanquishèd,   *timid*
185 Should make a start° o'er seas and vanquish you?   *rouse themselves*
Methinks already in this civil broil
I see them lording it in London streets,
Crying 'Villiago!'[8] unto all they meet.
Better ten thousand base-born Cades miscarry°   *meet disaster*
190 Than you should stoop unto a Frenchman's mercy.
To France! To France! And get what you have lost!
Spare England, for it is your native coast.
Henry hath money; you are strong and manly;
God on our side, doubt not of victory.
195 ALL CADE'S FOLLOWERS   A Clifford!° A Clifford! We'll follow   *To Clifford*
the King and Clifford!
          [They forsake CADE*]*
CADE *[aside]*   Was ever feather so lightly blown to and fro as this
multitude? The name of Henry the Fifth hales° them to   *draws*
an hundred mischiefs, and makes them leave me desolate.
200 I see them lay their heads together to surprise° me. My sword   *capture*
make way for me, for here is no staying. *[Aloud]* In despite of
the devils and hell, have through° the very middest of you!   *here I come through*
And heavens and honour be witness that no want of resolu-
tion in me, but only my followers' base and ignominious trea-
205 sons, makes me betake me to my heels.
       He runs through them with his staff, and flies away
BUCKINGHAM   What, is he fled? Go, some, and follow him,
And he that brings his head unto the King
Shall have a thousand crowns for his reward.
       Exeunt some of them [after CADE*]*
[To the remaining rebels] Follow me, soldiers, we'll devise a mean°   *way*
210 To reconcile you all unto the King.   *Exeunt*

---

7. An inn, with a pun on the coward's "white heart"   8. A variation on the Italian word for "coward."
(because drained of its blood or spirit).

4.8

Sound trumpets. Enter KING HENRY, QUEEN
[MARGARET], *and* [*the Duke of*] SOMERSET
on the terrace

KING HENRY   Was ever King that joyed° an earthly throne   *enjoyed*
And could command no more content than I?
No sooner was I crept out of my cradle
But I was made a king at nine months old.
5   Was never subject longed to be a king
As I do long and wish to be a subject.

Enter the Duke of BUCKINGHAM *and* [*Lord*] CLIFFORD
[*on the terrace*]

BUCKINGHAM [*to* KING HENRY]   Health and glad tidings to your majesty.
KING HENRY   Why, Buckingham, is the traitor Cade surprised?
Or is he but retired to make him strong?

Enter [*below*] *multitudes with halters*[1] *about their
necks*

10   CLIFFORD   He is fled, my lord, and all his powers do yield,
And humbly thus with halters on their necks
Expect° your highness' doom° of life or death.   *Await / sentence*
KING HENRY   Then, heaven, set ope° thy everlasting gates   *open*
To entertain my vows of thanks and praise.
15   [*To the multitudes below*] Soldiers, this day have you redeemed your lives,
And showed how well you love your prince and country.
Continue still° in this so good a mind,   *always*
And Henry, though he be infortunate,°   *unlucky*
Assure yourselves will never be unkind.
20   And so, with thanks and pardon to you all,
I do dismiss you to your several countries.°   *different regions*
ALL CADE'S FORMER FOLLOWERS   God save the King! God save
the King!   [*Exeunt multitudes below*]

Enter a MESSENGER [*on the terrace*]

MESSENGER [*to* KING HENRY]   Please it your grace to be advertisèd°   *informed*
25   The Duke of York is newly come from Ireland,
And with a puissant and a mighty power
Of galloglasses and stout Irish kerns[2]
Is marching hitherward in proud array,
And still proclaimeth, as he comes along,
30   His arms are only to remove from thee
The Duke of Somerset, whom he terms a traitor.
KING HENRY   Thus stands my state,° 'twixt Cade and York distressed,   *condition*
Like to a ship that, having scaped a tempest,
Is straightway calmed° and boarded with a pirate.   *becalmed*
35   But now is Cade driven back, his men dispersed,
And now is York in arms to second° him.   *support*
I pray thee, Buckingham, go and meet him,
And ask him what's the reason of these arms.

4.8 Location: Kenilworth Castle.
1. Cade's followers wore nooses as a sign of their
submission.

2. See note to 3.1.310. *galloglasses*: professional Irish
mercenary soldiers who were usually armed with axes
and rode on horseback.

Tell him I'll send Duke Edmund° to the Tower;   *Somerset*
40   And, Somerset, we will commit thee thither,
     Until his army be dismissed from him.
SOMERSET   My lord, I'll yield myself to prison willingly,
     Or unto death, to do my country good.
KING HENRY [*to* BUCKINGHAM]   In any case, be not too rough in terms,°   *language*
45   For he is fierce and cannot brook° hard language.   *endure*
BUCKINGHAM   I will, my lord, and doubt not so to deal
     As all things shall redound unto your good.
KING HENRY   Come, wife, let's in and learn to govern better;
     For yet° may England curse my wretched reign.   *up until now*

Flourish. Exeunt

4.9

          Enter Jack CADE[1]
CADE   Fie on ambitions; fie on myself that have a sword and yet
     am ready to famish. These five days have I hid me in these
     woods and durst not peep out, for all the country is laid° for   *set with traps*
     me. But now am I so hungry that if I might have a lease of my
5   life for a thousand years, I could stay° no longer. Wherefore   *delay*
     o'er a brick wall have I climbed into this garden to see if I can
     eat grass or pick a sallet° another while, which is not amiss to   *salad*
     cool a man's stomach° this hot weather. And I think this word   *hunger; anger*
     'sallet' was born to do me good; for many a time, but for a
10   sallet,° my brain-pan had been cleft with a brown bill;[2] and   *helmet*
     many a time, when I have been dry, and bravely marching, it
     hath served me instead of a quart pot to drink in; and now the
     word 'sallet' must serve me to feed on.
          [*He*] *lies down picking of herbs and eating them.*
          Enter [*Sir*] *Alexander* IDEN *and* [*five of*] *his men*
IDEN   Lord, who would live turmoilèd° in the court   *harried*
15   And may enjoy such quiet walks as these?
     This small inheritance my father left me
     Contenteth me, and worth a monarchy.
     I seek not to wax great by others' waning,
     Or gather wealth I care not with what envy;
20   Sufficeth that° I have maintains my state,   *that what*
     And sends the poor well pleasèd° from my gate.   *(with their alms)*
          [CADE *rises to his knees*]
CADE [*aside*]   Zounds, here's the lord of the soil come to seize
     me for a stray° for entering his fee-simple[3] without leave. [*To*   *trespasser*
     IDEN] A villain, thou wilt betray me and get a thousand crowns
25   of the king by carrying my head to him; but I'll make thee eat
     iron like an ostrich[4] and swallow my sword like a great pin, ere
     thou and I part.

4.9 Location: Alexander Iden's garden, in Kent.
1. Q's stage direction indicates that Jack Cade enters at
one door and Alexander Iden and his men at another.
Q's version of this scene is shorter than F's and makes
clear what F only implies: that Iden is accompanied by
attendants. The presence of these figures makes Cade's
offer to fight Iden seem the more courageous. In Q,
Iden enters unarmed, orders one of his men to fetch his

sword, and chivalrously orders them to stand aside
while he fights Cade. In F, Iden presumably enters
armed.
2. A long-handled weapon with an axlike blade. The
brown color is from blood or varnish.
3. Property that belonged forever to its owner and his
or her heirs; on it, stray animals could legally be seized.
4. It was popularly believed that ostriches ate iron.

IDEN   Why, rude companion,° whatsoe'er thou be,   *lowborn fellow*
          I know thee not. Why then should I betray thee?
30   Is't not enough to break into my garden,
          And, like a thief, to come to rob my grounds,
          Climbing my walls in spite of me the owner,
          But thou wilt brave° me with these saucy terms?   *taunt*
CADE   Brave thee? Ay, by the best blood that ever was
35   broached°—and beard° thee too! Look on me well—I have eat   *shed / defy*
          no meat these five days, yet come thou and thy five men, an
          if I do not leave you all as dead as a doornail I pray God I may
          never eat grass more.
IDEN   Nay, it shall ne'er be said while England stands
40   That Alexander Iden, an esquire of Kent,
          Took odds° to combat a poor famished man.   *advantage*
          Oppose thy steadfast gazing eyes to mine—
          See if thou canst outface me with thy looks.
          Set limb to limb, and thou art far the lesser—
45   Thy hand is but a finger to my fist.
          Thy leg a stick comparèd with this truncheon.°   *thick staff (his leg)*
          My foot shall fight with all the strength thou hast,
          And if mine arm be heavèd in the air,
          Thy grave is digged already in the earth.
50   As for words, whose greatness answers words,[5]
          Let this my sword report what speech forbears.
          [*To his men*] Stand you all aside.
CADE   By my valour, the most complete° champion that ever I   *accomplished*
          heard. [*To his sword*] Steel, if thou turn the edge° or cut not   *fail to cut*
55   out the burly-boned clown in chines° of beef ere thou sleep in   *roasts*
          thy sheath, I beseech God on my knees thou mayst be turned
          to hobnails.
             [CADE *stands.*] *Here they fight, and* CADE *falls down*
          O, I am slain! Famine and no other hath slain me! Let ten
          thousand devils come against me, and give me but the ten
60   meals I have lost, and I'd defy them all. Wither, garden, and
          be henceforth a burying place to all that do dwell in this
          house, because the unconquered soul of Cade is fled.
IDEN   Is't Cade that I have slain, that monstrous traitor?
          Sword, I will hallow thee for this thy deed
65   And hang thee o'er my tomb when I am dead.
          Ne'er shall this blood be wipèd from thy point
          But thou shalt wear it as a herald's coat
          To emblaze the honour that thy master got.[6]
CADE   Iden, farewell, and be proud of thy victory. Tell Kent
70   from me she hath lost her best man, and exhort all the world
          to be cowards. For I, that never feared any, am vanquished by
          famine, not by valour.   *He dies*
IDEN   How much thou wrong'st me, heaven be my judge.
          Die, damnèd wretch, the curse of her that bore thee!
75   And [*stabbing him again*] as I thrust thy body in with my sword,[7]
          So wish I I might thrust thy soul to hell.

---

5. This line may be corrupt. It may mean "As for words, I whose might more than matches your words."
6. *But . . . got:* Just as a device on a herald's coat proclaims his lord's identity and status, so the blood on Iden's sword proclaims the fame he has won for killing Cade.
7. As I thrust my sword into your body.

Hence will I drag thee headlong° by the heels   *head downward*
Unto a dunghill, which shall be thy grave,
And there cut off thy most ungracious head,
80   Which I will bear in triumph to the King,
Leaving thy trunk for crows to feed upon.
                                    Exeunt [with the body]

5.1

Enter the Duke of YORK *and his army of Irish*
with [a] drum[mer] and soldiers [bearing] colours

YORK   From Ireland thus comes York to claim his right,
And pluck the crown from feeble Henry's head.
Ring, bells, aloud; burn, bonfires, clear and bright,
To entertain° great England's lawful king.   *welcome*
5   Ah, *sancta maiestas!*° Who would not buy thee dear?   *sacred majesty*
Let them obey that knows not how to rule;
This hand was made to handle naught but gold.
I cannot give due action to my words,
Except° a sword or sceptre balance it.   *Unless*
10   A sceptre shall it have, have I° a sword,   *as sure as I have*
On which I'll toss the fleur-de-lis of France.[1]
                    Enter the Duke of BUCKINGHAM
[*Aside*] Whom have we here? Buckingham to disturb me?
The King hath sent him sure—I must dissemble.
BUCKINGHAM   York, if thou meanest well, I greet thee well.
15   YORK   Humphrey of Buckingham, I accept thy greeting.
Art thou a messenger, or come of pleasure?
BUCKINGHAM   A messenger from Henry, our dread liege,
To know the reason of these arms° in peace;   *armed men*
Or why thou, being a subject as I am,
20   Against thy oath and true allegiance sworn,
Should raise so great a power without his leave,
Or dare to bring thy force so near the court?
YORK [*aside*]   Scarce can I speak, my choler is so great.
O, I could hew up rocks and fight with flint,
25   I am so angry at these abject terms;°   *insulting words*
And now, like Ajax Telamonius,[2]
On sheep or oxen could I spend my fury.
I am far better born than is the King,
More like a king, more kingly in my thoughts;
30   But I must make fair weather° yet a while,   *pretend to be mild*
Till Henry be more weak and I more strong.
[*Aloud*] Buckingham, I prithee pardon me,
That I have given no answer all this while;
My mind was troubled with deep melancholy.
35   The cause why I have brought this army hither
Is to remove proud Somerset from the King,
Seditious to his grace and to the state.
BUCKINGHAM   That is too much presumption on thy part;
But if thy arms be to no other end,

5.1 Location: The remainder of the play takes place in
an open field between St. Albans and London.
1. On which I'll impale the national emblem of France,
the lily flower.

2. A Greek hero of the Trojan War who went mad and
slaughtered a flock of sheep, taking them to be his
Greek enemies.

40   The King hath yielded unto thy demand:
      The Duke of Somerset is in the Tower.
YORK   Upon thine honour, is he prisoner?
BUCKINGHAM   Upon mine honour, he is prisoner.
YORK   Then, Buckingham, I do dismiss my powers.
45   Soldiers, I thank you all; disperse yourselves;
      Meet me tomorrow in Saint George's field³
      You shall have pay and everything you wish.   *Exeunt soldiers*
      [*To* BUCKINGHAM] And let my sovereign, virtuous Henry,
      Command° my eldest son—nay, all my sons—   *Demand*
50   As pledges of my fealty and love.
      I'll send them all as willing as I live.
      Lands, goods, horse, armour, anything I have
      Is his to use, so° Somerset may die.   *provided that*
BUCKINGHAM   York, I commend this kind° submission.   *natural; proper*
55   We twain will go into his highness' tent.
            Enter KING HENRY *and attendants*
KING HENRY   Buckingham, doth York intend no harm to us,
      That thus he marcheth with thee arm in arm?
YORK   In all submission and humility
      York doth present himself unto your highness.
60   KING HENRY   Then what intends these forces thou dost bring?
YORK   To heave the traitor Somerset from hence,
      And fight against that monstrous rebel Cade,
      Who since I heard to be discomfited.°   *defeated*
            Enter IDEN *with Cade's head*
IDEN   If one so rude° and of so mean condition°   *uncultivated / low rank*
65   May pass into the presence of a king,
      [*Kneeling*] Lo, I present your grace a traitor's head,
      The head of Cade, whom I in combat slew.
KING HENRY   The head of Cade? Great God, how just art thou!
      O let me view his visage, being dead,
70   That living wrought me such exceeding trouble.
      Tell me, my friend, art thou the man that slew him?
IDEN [*rising*]   Iwis,° an't like° your majesty.   *Truly / if it please*
KING HENRY   How art thou called? And what is thy degree?°   *rank*
IDEN   Alexander Iden, that's my name;
75   A poor esquire⁴ of Kent that loves his king.
BUCKINGHAM [*to* KING HENRY]   So please it you, my lord, 'twere not amiss
      He were created knight for his good service.
KING HENRY   Iden, kneel down.
            [IDEN *kneels and* KING HENRY *knights him*]
                              Rise up a knight.
            [IDEN *rises*]
      We give thee for reward a thousand marks,
80   And will° that thou henceforth attend on us.   *command*
IDEN   May Iden live to merit such a bounty,
      And never live but true unto his liege.   *Exit*
            Enter Queen [MARGARET] *and the Duke of* SOMERSET
KING HENRY   See, Buckingham, Somerset comes wi'th' Queen.
      Go bid her hide him quickly from the Duke.

---

3. One of the main drill grounds for Elizabethan militia, located south of the Thames.

4. A member of the gentry ranking just below a
knight.

85 QUEEN MARGARET   For thousand Yorks he shall not hide his head,
But boldly stand and front° him to his face.   *confront*
YORK   How now? Is Somerset at liberty?
Then, York, unloose thy long imprisoned thoughts,
And let thy tongue be equal with thy heart.
90 Shall I endure the sight of Somerset?
False King, why hast thou broken faith with me,
Knowing how hardly I can brook abuse?[5]
'King' did I call thee? No, thou art not king;
Not fit to govern and rule multitudes,
95 Which dar'st not—no, nor canst not—rule a traitor.
That head of thine doth not become a crown;
Thy hand is made to grasp a palmer's° staff,   *pilgrim's*
And not to grace an aweful° princely sceptre.   *awe-inspiring*
That gold must round engird these brows of mine,
100 Whose smile and frown, like to Achilles' spear,
Is able with the change to kill and cure.[6]
Here is a hand to hold a sceptre up,
And with the same to act° controlling laws.   *enact*
Give place! By heaven, thou shalt rule no more
105 O'er him whom heaven created for thy ruler.
SOMERSET   O monstrous traitor! I arrest thee, York,
Of capital treason 'gainst the King and crown.
Obey, audacious traitor; kneel for grace.
YORK [*to an attendant*]   Sirrah, call in my sons to be my bail.
                                                                [*Exit attendant*]
110 I know, ere they will have me go to ward,°   *into custody*
They'll pawn° their swords for my enfranchisement.°   *pledge / freedom*
QUEEN MARGARET [*to* BUCKINGHAM]   Call hither Clifford; bid
him come amain,°   *at once*
To say if that the bastard boys of York
Shall be the surety for their traitor father.   [*Exit* BUCKINGHAM]
115 YORK   O blood-bespotted Neapolitan,[7]
Outcast of Naples, England's bloody scourge!
The sons of York, thy betters in their birth,
Shall be their father's bail, and bane° to those   *destruction*
That for my surety will refuse the boys.
        Enter at one door York's sons EDWARD *and crookback*
        RICHARD *with* [*a*] *drum*[*mer*] *and soldiers*[8]
120 See where they come. I'll warrant they'll make it good.
        Enter at the other door CLIFFORD *and his son, with* [*a*]
        drum[*mer*] *and soldiers*
QUEEN MARGARET   And here comes Clifford to deny their bail.
CLIFFORD [*kneeling before* KING HENRY]   Health and all happi-
ness to my lord the King.
        [*He rises*]
YORK   I thank thee, Clifford. Say, what news with thee?
Nay, do not fright us with an angry look—

5. Knowing with what difficulty I can tolerate deception.
6. Telephus, wounded by Achilles' spear, was cured by rust from that same spear.
7. Margaret's father claimed the throne of Naples. Elizabethan writers typically associated Italy with sexual vice, criminality, and the evils of Roman Catholicism.

8. This spectacular double entry of York's sons, followed by Clifford and his son, each accompanied by drummer and soldiers, is indicated only in Q. F's stage directions read, "Enter Edward and Richard" and "Enter Clifford."

125   We are thy sovereign, Clifford; kneel again.
For thy mistaking so, we pardon thee.
     CLIFFORD   This is my king, York; I do not mistake.
But thou mistakes me much to think I do.
[*To* KING HENRY] To Bedlam⁹ with him! Is the man grown mad?

130   KING HENRY   Ay, Clifford, a bedlam² and ambitious humour°   *mad / disposition*
Makes him oppose himself against his king.
     CLIFFORD   He is a traitor; let him to the Tower,
And chop away that factious pate° of his.   *rebellious head*
     QUEEN MARGARET   He is arrested, but will not obey.

135   His sons, he says, shall give their words for him.
     YORK [*to* EDWARD *and* RICHARD]   Will you not, sons?
     EDWARD   Ay, noble father, if our words will serve.
     RICHARD   And if words will not, then our weapons shall.
     CLIFFORD   Why, what a brood of traitors have we here!

140   YORK   Look in a glass,° and call thy image so.   *mirror*
I am thy king, and thou a false-heart traitor.
Call hither to the stake my two brave bears,
That with the very shaking of their chains,
They may astonish these fell-lurking° curs.¹   *savagely waiting*

145   [*To an attendant*] Bid Salisbury and Warwick come to me.
                                         [*Exit attendant*]
        Enter the Earls of WARWICK *and* SALISBURY *with* [*a*]
        drum[*mer*] *and soldiers*
     CLIFFORD   Are these thy bears? We'll bait thy bears to death,
And manacle the bearherd° in their chains,   *bear keeper (York)*
If thou dar'st bring them to the baiting place.°   *bear pit*
     RICHARD   Oft have I seen a hot o'erweening° cur   *overconfident*

150   Run back and bite,° because he was withheld;   *(his keeper)*
Who, being suffered with° the bear's fell° paw,   *injured by / savage*
Hath clapped his tail between his legs and cried;
And such a piece of service will you do,
If you oppose yourselves° to match Lord Warwick.   *undertake*

155   CLIFFORD   Hence, heap of wrath, foul indigested lump,
As crooked in thy manners as thy shape!²
     YORK   Nay, we shall heat you thoroughly anon.°   *soon*
     CLIFFORD   Take heed, lest by your heat you burn yourselves.
     KING HENRY   Why, Warwick, hath thy knee forgot to bow?

160   Old Salisbury, shame to thy silver hair,
Thou mad misleader of thy brainsick son!
What, wilt thou on thy deathbed play the ruffian,
And seek for sorrow with thy spectacles?°   *eyes; eyeglasses*
O, where is faith? O, where is loyalty?

165   If it be banished from the frosty head,
Where shall it find a harbour in the earth?
Wilt thou go dig a grave to find out° war,   *in seeking out*
And shame thine honourable age with blood?

---

9. The shortened name of a London lunatic asylum. See note to 3.1.51.
1. York refers to the Elizabethan sport of bearbaiting in which a tame bear was chained to a stake and set upon with dogs. Warwick's family crest depicted a bear chained to a staff. See below, lines 200–1.

2. *foul . . . shape:* alluding to the fact that Richard of Gloucester was deformed from birth (he was a hunchback) and to the notion that bears are born as formless lumps and licked into shape by their mothers. *indigested:* ill-formed.

Why, art thou old and want'st° experience?   *lack*
170   Or wherefore dost abuse it if thou hast it?
For shame in duty bend thy knee to me,
That bows unto the grave with mickle° age.   *much*
SALISBURY   My lord, I have considered with myself
The title of this most renownèd Duke,
175   And in my conscience do repute his grace
The rightful heir to England's royal seat.
KING HENRY   Hast thou not sworn allegiance unto me?
SALISBURY   I have.
KING HENRY   Canst thou dispense with heaven for³ such an oath?
180 SALISBURY   It is great sin to swear unto a sin,
But greater sin to keep a sinful oath.
Who can be bound by any solemn vow
To do a murd'rous deed, to rob a man,
To force a spotless virgin's chastity,
185   To reave° the orphan of his patrimony,   *bereave*
To wring the widow from her customed right,⁴
And have no other reason for this wrong
But that he was bound by a solemn oath?
QUEEN MARGARET   A subtle traitor needs no sophister.°   *expert in false reasoning*
KING HENRY [*to an attendant*]   Call Buckingham, and bid him
190   arm himself.   [*Exit attendant*]
YORK [*to* KING HENRY]   Call Buckingham and all the friends thou hast,
I am resolved for death or dignity.°   *(the crown)*
CLIFFORD   The first, I warrant thee, if dreams prove true.
WARWICK   You were best to go to bed and dream again,
195   To keep you from the tempest of the field.
CLIFFORD   I am resolved to bear a greater storm
Than any thou canst conjure up today—
And that I'll write upon thy burgonet°   *helmet*
Might I but know thee by thy household badge.°   *family crest*
200 WARWICK   Now by my father's badge, old Neville's crest,⁵
The rampant bear chained to the ragged° staff,   *jagged*
This day I'll wear aloft° my burgonet,   *on top of*
As on a mountain top the cedar shows
That keeps his leaves in spite of any storm,
205   Even to affright thee with the view thereof.
CLIFFORD   And from thy burgonet I'll rend thy bear,
And tread it under foot with all contempt,
Despite the bearherd that protects the bear.
YOUNG CLIFFORD   And so to arms, victorious father,
210   To quell the rebels and their complices.°   *accomplices*
RICHARD   Fie, charity, for shame! Speak not in spite—
For you shall sup with Jesu Christ tonight.
YOUNG CLIFFORD   Foul stigmatic,⁶ that's more than thou canst tell.
RICHARD   If not in heaven, you'll surely sup in hell.

Exeunt [*severally*]

---

3. Can you win dispensation from heaven for breaking.   inherited the badge of a bear from his father-in-law,
4. Her traditional right to a portion of her husband's   Richard Beauchamp.
estate.   6. One branded with the mark of crime, as Richard is
5. The Neville badge was actually a bull. Warwick   "branded" with deformity.

5.2

[An alehouse sign: a castle.] Alarums to the battle. Then
enter the Duke of SOMERSET *and* RICHARD *fighting.*
RICHARD *kills* [SOMERSET] *under the sign*

RICHARD   So lie thou there—
  For underneath an alehouse' paltry sign,
  The Castle in Saint Albans, Somerset
  Hath made the wizard famous in his death.[1]
5 Sword, hold thy temper;[2] heart, be wrathfull still—
  Priests pray for enemies, but princes kill.
                    Exit [with Somerset's body. The sign is removed]

5.3

Alarum again. Enter the Earl of WARWICK
WARWICK   Clifford of Cumberland, 'tis Warwick calls!
  An if thou dost not hide thee from the bear,
  Now, when the angry trumpet sounds alarum,
  And dead° men's cries do fill the empty air,   dying
5 Clifford I say, come forth and fight with me!
  Proud northern lord, Clifford of Cumberland,
  Warwick is hoarse with calling thee to arms!
CLIFFORD *[within]*   Warwick, stand still; and stir not till I come.
                    Enter [the Duke of] YORK
WARWICK   How now, my noble lord? What, all afoot?°   not on horseback
10 YORK   The deadly-handed Clifford slew my steed.
  But match to match I have encountered him,
  And made a prey for carrion kites and crows
  Even of the bonny beast he loved so well.
                    Enter [Lord] CLIFFORD
WARWICK *[to* CLIFFORD*]*   Of one or both of us the time is come.
15 YORK   Hold, Warwick—seek thee out some other chase,°   game
  For I myself must hunt this deer to death.
WARWICK   Then nobly, York; 'tis for a crown thou fight'st.
  [To CLIFFORD*]* As I intend, Clifford, to thrive today,
  It grieves my soul to leave thee unassailed.   *Exit*
20 YORK   Clifford, since we are singled here alone,
  Be this the day of doom to one of us.
  For know my heart hath sworn immortal hate
  To thee and all the house of Lancaster.
CLIFFORD   And here I stand and pitch my foot to thine,
25 Vowing not to stir till thou or I be slain.
  For never shall my heart be safe at rest
  Till I have spoiled° the hateful house of York.   stripped of honor
                    Alarums. They fight. YORK *kills* CLIFFORD
YORK   Now, Lancaster, sit sure—thy sinews shrink.°   powers fail
  Come, fearful° Henry, grovelling on thy face—   timid
30 Yield up thy crown unto the prince of York.[1]   *Exit*
30.1   CLIFFORD   *What seest thou in me, York? Why dost thou pause?*
    YORK   *With thy brave bearing° should I be in love,*   fine appearance

---

5.2 Location: Scene continues.
1. Somerset's death under the sign of the Castle Inn
confirms the spirit's warning that he shun castles (see
1.4.34–36). *in his:* by his (Somerset's).
2. Retain the resiliency of steel.

5.3 Location: Scene continues.
1. Oxford adopts Q's version of the confrontation
between Clifford and York at lines 20–30; the F version,
an edited text of which follows in the indented passage
(lines 30.1–30.12), may be the author's original draft.

But that thou art so fast mine enemy.

CLIFFORD   *Nor should thy prowess want° praise and esteem,*   lack

30.5   *But that 'tis shown ignobly and in treason.*

YORK   *So let it help me now against thy sword,*

As I in justice and true right express it.

CLIFFORD   *My soul and body on the action both.²*

YORK   *A dreadful lay.° Address° thee instantly.*   wager / Prepare

30.10   CLIFFORD   *La fin couronne les oeuvres.³*

Alarums. They fight. YORK *kills* CLIFFORD

YORK   *Thus war hath given thee peace, for thou art still.*

Peace with his soul, heaven, if it be thy will.   Exit

Alarums, then enter YOUNG CLIFFORD

YOUNG CLIFFORD   *Shame and confusion, all is on the rout!°*   in disorderly retreat

Fear frames° disorder, and disorder wounds   gives rise to

Where it should guard. O, war, thou son of hell,

Whom angry heavens do make their minister,

35   *Throw in the frozen° bosoms of our part°*   cowardly / faction

Hot coals of vengeance! Let no soldier fly!

He that is truly dedicate° to war   dedicated

Hath no self-love; nor he that loves himself

Hath not essentially, but by circumstance,°   merely by accident

The name of valour.

[He sees his father's body]

40   *O, let the vile world end,*

And the premisèd° flames of the last day   foreordained

Knit earth and heaven together.

Now let the general trumpet blow his blast,⁴

Particularities° and petty sounds   Individual affairs

45   *To cease! Wast thou ordainèd, dear father,*

To lose thy youth in peace, and to achieve

The silver livery of advisèd° age,   wise

And in thy reverence and thy chair-days,° thus   old age

To die in ruffian battle? Even at this sight

50   *My heart is turned to stone, and while 'tis mine*

It shall be stony. York not our old men spares;

No more will I their babes. Tears virginal

Shall be to me even as the dew to fire,⁵

And beauty that the tyrant oft reclaims°   calms the tyrant

55   *Shall to my flaming wrath be oil and flax.*

Henceforth I will not have to do with pity.

Meet I an infant of the house of York,

Into as many gobbets° will I cut it   lumps of flesh

As wild Medea young Absyrtus did.⁶

60   *In cruelty will I seek out my fame.*

Come, thou new ruin of old Clifford's house,

He takes [his father's body] up on his back

As did Aeneas old Anchises bear,⁷

2. I wager both my soul and body on the outcome of this fight (action).

3. The end crowns the works (French).

4. Young Clifford is evoking doomsday, when a trumpet will summon everyone to judgment (see 1 Corinthians 15:52).

5. Dew was popularly believed to make fire burn more fiercely.

6. According to classical mythology, as Medea fled over the sea with her lover, Jason, she murdered her brother Absyrtus and scattered bits of his body on the waves so that her father would stop to collect the fragments and be delayed in his pursuit of her.

7. In Virgil's *Aeneid* 2.707–29, Aeneas carries his aged father, Anchises, on his back in their escape from the burning city of Troy.

So bear I thee upon my manly shoulders.
But then Aeneas bare a living load,
65 Nothing so heavy as these woes of mine.   [*Exit with the body*]

5.4

Alarums again. Then enter three or four bearing the
Duke of BUCKINGHAM *wounded to his tent. Alarums*
still. Enter KING [HENRY], QUEEN [MARGARET], *and*
others

QUEEN MARGARET Away, my lord! You are slow. For shame, away!
KING HENRY Can we outrun the heavens?° Good Margaret, stay.   *escape our fate*
QUEEN MARGARET What are you made of? You'll nor° fight nor fly.   *neither*
Now is it manhood, wisdom, and defence,
5 To give the enemy way, and to secure us°   *save ourselves*
By what° we can, which° can no more but fly.   *whatever means / who*
        Alarum afar off
If you be ta'en, we then should see the bottom
Of all our fortunes; but if we haply scape°—   *by chance escape*
As well we may if not° through your neglect—   *if we don't fail*
10 We shall to London get where you are loved,
And where this breach now in our fortunes made
May readily be stopped.
        Enter [YOUNG] CLIFFORD
YOUNG CLIFFORD [*to* KING HENRY] But that my heart's on future
        mischief set,
I would speak blasphemy ere° bid you fly;   *before I would*
15 But fly you must; uncurable discomfit°   *irreversible defeat*
Reigns in the hearts of all our present parts.°   *remaining forces*
Away for your relief, and we will live
To see their day and them our fortune give.[1]
Away, my lord, away!   *Exeunt*

5.5

Alarum. Retreat. Enter the Duke of YORK, [*his sons*
EDWARD *and*] RICHARD, *and soldiers, [including c]*
drum[mer] and [some bearing] colours

YORK [*to* EDWARD *and* RICHARD] How now, boys! Fortunate this
        fight hath been,
I hope, to us and ours for England's good
And our great honour, that so long we lost
Whilst faint-heart Henry did usurp our rights.
5 Of Salisbury, who can report of him?
That winter° lion who in rage forgets   *aged*
Agèd contusions and all brush of time,[1]
And, like a gallant in the brow° of youth,   *prime*
Repairs° him with occasion.° This happy day   *Revives / action*
10 Is not itself, nor have we won one foot
If Salisbury be lost.
RICHARD   My noble father,

5.4 Location: Scene continues.
1. *we . . . give:* we will survive to see a day of victory like
theirs and to make them suffer misfortunes like ours.

5.5 Location: Scene continues.
1. Bruises of old age and all assaults of time.

Three times today I holp° him to his horse;   *helped*
Three times bestrid him;[2] thrice I led him off,
Persuaded him from any further act;
15   But still° where danger was, still there I met him,   *always*
And like rich hangings in a homely° house,   *humble*
So was his will in his old feeble body.
              Enter [the Earls of] SALISBURY *and* [WARWICK]
EDWARD [*to* YORK]   See, noble father, where they both do come—
The only props unto the house of York!
20   SALISBURY   Now, by my sword, well hast thou fought today;
By th' mass, so did we all. I thank you, Richard.
God knows how long it is I have to live,
And it hath pleased him that three times today
You have defended me from imminent death.
25   Well, lords, we have not got that which we have[3]—
'Tis not enough our foes are this time fled,
Being opposites of such repairing nature.[4]
YORK   I know our safety is to follow them,
For, as I hear, the King is fled to London,
30   To call a present court of Parliament.
Let us pursue him ere the writs° go forth.   *summons to Parliament*
What says Lord Warwick, shall we after them?
WARWICK   After them? Nay, before them if we can!
Now by my hand, lords, 'twas a glorious day!
35   Saint Albans battle won by famous York
Shall be eternized° in all age to come.   *immortalized*
Sound drums and trumpets, and to London all,
And more such days as these to us befall! [*Flourish.*] *Exeunt*

---

2. Stood over the fallen Salisbury to protect him.   4. Since they are enemies who can quickly recover
3. We have not secured what we have won.   what they have lost.

Richard Duke of York
(3 Henry VI)

There are two Richards in the play known in its octavo version as *The True Tragedy of Richard Duke of York and the Good King Henry the Sixth* (3 *Henry VI*). As the play begins, the title character, Richard of York, is leading an attempt to seize the English throne from Henry VI, the Lancastrian King. This Richard is killed at the end of the first act, and it is his tragic death to which the play's title refers. He, however, has four sons: Edward, Edmund (known as the Earl of Rutland), George, and Richard. This second Richard, who eventually acquires the title Duke of Gloucester, is a hunchback; and much of the play chronicles his attempts to continue his father's efforts to seize the English throne. Near the end of the play, this second Richard meditates on his condition:

> Then, since the heavens have shaped my body so,
> Let hell make crooked my mind to answer it.
> I had no father, I am like no father;
> I have no brother, I am like no brother;
> And this word, 'love', which greybeards call divine,
> Be resident in other men like one another
> And not in me—I am myself alone.
> (5.6.78–84)

This chilling pronouncement places Richard outside kinship networks, even though his two older brothers, Edward and George, are very much alive; and it exempts him from ordinary bonds of human affection.

Claiming to know nothing of love, Richard blames his isolation on his deformity. He is not "like" other men, not like his brothers, because heaven has shaped his body crookedly. This is a convenient explanation for villainy and alienation. But the play's exploration of deformity and its relationship to the breakdown of social order and emotional bonds is more complex than Richard here allows. Is Richard's hunchback the cause of his villainy or merely its outward sign? Are his villainy and deformity unique or simply the most tangible manifestation of a social deformity that reaches far beyond this single character? Richard's hump invites such questions, but the answers must be sought by broadly surveying the dramatic world in which Richard is placed.

Richard Duke of York is one of the most ambitious of Shakespeare's history plays simply in terms of the historical matter it covers. It is in part a continuation of *The First Part of the Contention of the Two Famous Houses of York and Lancaster* (2 *Henry VI*), the play in which Shakespeare began to dramatize the Wars of the Roses between the Lancastrian descendants of Edward III, who took the red rose for their symbol, and his Yorkist descendants, who claimed the white. In the struggles between these two branches of the family, the Yorkists asserted that Henry VI's grandfather, Henry IV, had illegitimately usurped the throne from Richard II, the son of Edward III's oldest male offspring, Edward, the Black Prince. Even though the Lancastrians could claim the throne through John of Gaunt, Edward III's fourth son, the Yorkists felt that they had a superior claim as descendants of the third son, Lionel, Duke of Clarence, and his daughter Philippa. In *Richard Duke of York*, Shakespeare depicts many of the most significant military encounters stemming from the struggle between the two branches of the family, stretching from the Battle of Wakefield (1460), in which the Duke of York was captured and killed by the Lancastrian forces of Henry VI, to the Battle of Tewkes-bury in 1471, in which Edward, the eldest son of Richard Duke of York, decisively defeated the Lancastrian army. It is after the latter battle, and Richard Duke of Gloucester's subsequent murder of Henry VI in the Tower of London, that the hunch-backed Richard speaks his chilling lines about having no father and no brother.

As with all his history plays, Shakespeare's *Richard Duke of York* takes many liberties with its historical sources, in this case Raphael Holinshed's *Chronicles of England, Scot-land, and Ireland* (1587 edition) and Edward Hall's *Union of the Two Noble and Illustre [Illustrious] Famelies of Lancastre & Yorke* (1548). Many historical events are simply omit-ted or conflated with other events, and aspects of the historical record are altered for dra-matic or thematic purposes. For example, at the time of the Battle of Wakefield, at which Richard Duke of York was killed, his son Richard was only seven years old. But in Shake-speare's play, he is a grown man who himself participates in the battle and after it vows revenge for his father's death. Moreover, that death is handled with grim originality. In

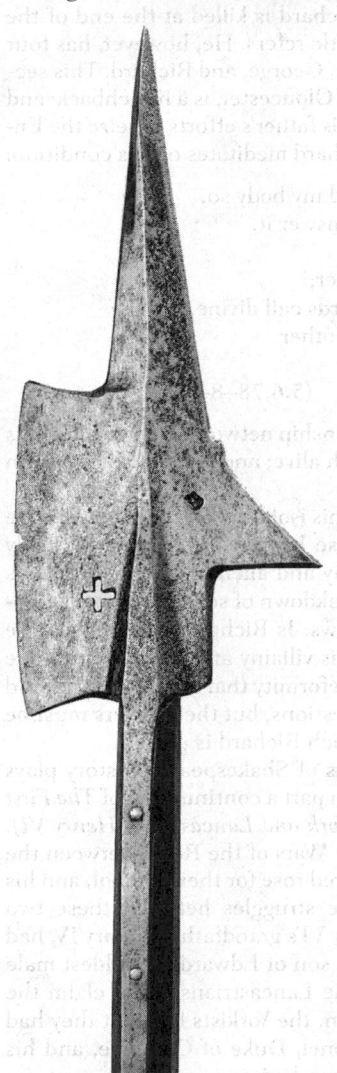

Seventeenth-century ornamental halberd from southern Germany.

Hall, Clifford decapitates York, then puts a paper crown on his severed head and presents it on a pole to Margaret, Henry VI's warlike queen. In Holinshed, Clifford verbally torments York before beheading him. But in none of the sources does Margaret dominate the scene as she does in Shake-speare's play. In *Richard Duke of York,* she taunts York ferociously and—a detail found in none of the sources—to wipe his tears gives him a handkerchief that has been dipped in the blood of Rutland, York's twelve-year-old son, who had been butchered by Clifford earlier in the same battle. Eventually both Margaret and Clifford stab York, and Margaret orders his head displayed on the gates of the city of York. This act is typical of Margaret's audacity throughout the play. The only character to appear in all four of Shakespeare's first histories (*The First Part of the Contention* [*2 Henry VI*], *Richard Duke of York* [*3 Henry VI*], *1 Henry VI,* and *Richard III*), Margaret dominates much of the action of this one. Fiercely protective of her son's rights and skilled as both general and diplomat, she is unmatched as a publicly powerful figure by any of the female char-acters in Shakespeare's later histories.

The scene in which Margaret tortures York and he excoriates her as an Amazonian whore must have been riveting theater. In September of 1592, Robert Greene, a rival playwright, published *Greene's Groats-worth of Wit,* in which he makes fun of Shakespeare by parodying a line from this scene. Richard at one point exclaims of Margaret, "O tiger's heart wrapped in a woman's hide!" (1.4.138). Greene writes of Shakespeare that "there is an upstart Crow, beautified with our feathers, that with his *Tiger's heart wrapt in a Player's hide,* supposes he is as well able to bombast out a blank verse as the best of you: and being an absolute *Johannes fac totum* [jack-of-all-trades], is in his own conceit the onely Shakes-scene in a country." Greene, who had a university education, clearly resented Shakespeare, who did not but who was nonetheless having considerable theatrical success. Greene accuses Shakespeare either of appropriating his work or of acting in his dramas ("beautified with our feathers") and of thinking too well of himself and his many theatrical skills. Particularly striking is Greene's own appropriation of Richard's line about Margaret to apply to Shakespeare. Implicitly, Greene suggests that there is something as unnatural and presumptuous in Shakespeare's theatrical ambition as in the cruelty and ambition of Henry's manlike Queen. At the same time, this appropriative gesture pays tribute, however grudging, to Shakespeare's skill as a writer of memorable dialogue. Affronted by Shakespeare's success, Greene nonetheless grants his rival the homage of parody. The lines have another value as well. Although *Richard Duke of York* was first printed in a shortened octavo version in 1595, Greene's comments suggest that some version of the play had been staged or was circulating in manuscript by late summer of 1592 (see Textual Note).

This early play, then, may have brought Shakespeare contemporary notoriety. It certainly shows his boldness in adopting chronicle history to fit the requirements of the theater. And while some critics have seen *Richard Duke of York* as flawed, evidencing Shakespeare's weariness with his dramatization of the Wars of the Roses or his inability to shape so much matter into coherent form, theatrical productions of this play attest to its viability on the stage. The vicious energies of hate and ambition that propel the play make its enactment an intense and exhausting experience. The vigorous stage battles, the soaring rhetorical duels between the contending factions, the centrality of the ruthless Margaret, the emergence of the alienated Richard, Duke of Gloucester as the brooding antihero—these are elements that, particularly in the post–World War II period, have led to many memorable productions, productions that emphasize a once-civil world spiraling vertiginously toward chaos.

But the play is also more than the sum of its memorable parts. When Richard asserts, "I am myself alone," his chosen isolation follows from the play's carefully orchestrated dramatization of the breakdown of social order, particularly as epitomized in the breakdown of family ties. From its inception, the Wars of the Roses, a continuing civil war, was also a family feud in that it pitted the Lancastrian and Yorkist descendants of Edward III against one another. But in the prior play, *The First Part of the Contention*, members of each family line and their followers typically remained loyal to their faction. Family lineage was a source of pride and identity. One sees this also in *1 Henry VI* in the idealized relationship between the English hero Lord Talbot and his son John. John aspires in all respects to emulate his father, and the two of them die together in battle defending England and the honor of their family name. In *Richard Duke of York*, by contrast, family bonds are hideously fragile; and when they break, chaos ensues. Unflinching in its depiction of emotional and physical violence, the play examines the forms of monstrous individualism that emerge when the social identities provided by networks of kinship and feudal loyalty no longer exert their hold. In effect, *Richard Duke of York* depicts the radical separation of self from defining social networks as a species of monstrosity.

The signal event in the play's treatment of the sundering of family bonds is King Henry's startling offer, at the beginning of Act 1, to entail the crown to Richard, Duke of York in exchange for Henry's right to hold the throne during his lifetime. Henry has a son, Prince Edward, and his act negates his son's right to the throne. It also transforms the crown of England from a symbol of lineal succession into an alienable property. The immediate consequence is that Henry's supporters turn from him in disgust and his wife, Queen Margaret, proclaims:

> I here divorce myself
> Both from thy table, Henry, and thy bed,
> Until that act of Parliament be repealed
> Whereby my son is disinherited.
> (1.1.248–51)

Suddenly, Edward is *her* son, not Henry's; and soon thereafter she is raising an army to lead against the Yorkists. Many in the play describe Margaret's acts as unnatural, yet they

Edward IV (1442–1483). Probably painted
during his reign; artist unknown.

follow from Henry's feckless negation of his role as guarantor of his
son's succession. It was a truism of
the early modern gender system that
unmanly men, unnatural in their
weakness, opened the door to a corresponding anomaly, the manlike
woman. Margaret is represented as
such a figure, taking Henry's place
both at the head of his army and also
as champion of young Edward's lineal rights. In both roles, the Queen
is highly effective for much of the
play. Though demonized, Margaret
embodies strengths that contradict
the patriarchal view that women are
inherently weaker than men and
therefore less suited to have dominion either in the state or in the
household.

Occasionally, especially in his
early plays, Shakespeare wrote what
Hereward T. Price called "mirror
scenes," that is, scenes that are separate from the main line of plot
development but that symbolically
encapsulate, or mirror, some of the
play's chief thematic concerns. In
Richard Duke of York, 2.5 is such a
scene. Having given command of his army to Clifford and Margaret, Henry sits con-
templatively upon a molehill while the Battle of Towton proceeds without him. Voicing
his longing for the simplicity of a pastoral life, Henry suddenly sees a soldier carry
onstage a man he has killed. It turns out to be the soldier's father, who was forced to
serve with the Yorkist forces, while the son had been impressed into King Henry's service. The King then observes a second soldier carry onstage a man *he* has killed. It turns
out to be the soldier's son. The scene schematically underscores one of the play's primary emblems of social disintegration: namely, the severing of bonds between father
and son, son and father, leaving nothing to replace these bonds but individual rapa-
ciousness. In both instances, the killers of the dead men have brought the bodies
onstage to search them for money—"some store of crowns" (2.5.57) and "gold" (80).
The ironic power of the scene is heightened, of course, because its central events
are witnessed and lamented by King Henry, who has already disinherited his own son
and as King is the symbolic fountainhead from which the familial disorder before him
flows.

But the most interesting variation on the theme of dissevered families is embodied
in the persons of Richard, Duke of York and his four sons: Edward, George, Richard,
and Rutland. At the beginning of the play, the Yorks constitute an unusually integrated
unit. Richard's sons support their father and urge him to seize the crown. Before he is
captured at the Battle of Wakefield, Richard praises his offspring, assuming that in the
battle "they have demeaned themselves / Like men born to renown by life or death"
(1.4.7–8). At Wakefield, one of Richard's sons, the young Rutland, is killed. Just before
the remaining three sons learn that their father has also died as a consequence of that
battle, they praise him, as he has praised them. No one is more gracious than young
Richard, who says, "Methinks 'tis prize enough to be his son" (2.1.20). At that moment,
three suns appear in the heavens, each distinct, and then these suns join together.

The pun on "suns/sons" seems to lead Edward to interpret this odd spectacle to mean that the three sons of Richard,

> Each one already blazing by our meeds,
> Should notwithstanding join our lights together
> And over-shine the earth as this the world.
>
> (2.1.36–38)

He then pledges to have three suns emblazoned on his shield.

Like all portents, the exact significance of this one is unclear. To Edward, it seems to imply the unwavering unity of the three sons of York. Yet Richard, who is to be as devastated as any of them by the news of their father's death, treats Edward's assertion that he will wear three suns on his shields as the occasion for a joke that distances him from his brother. "Nay, bear three daughters— by your leave I speak it— / You love the breeder better than the male" (2.1.41–42). With the death of the powerful patriarch, Richard, Duke of York, fraternal rivalry quickly replaces fraternal unity, and broken allegiances multiply. When Edward insists on marrying a commoner, the widow Lady Elizabeth Gray, War-

"My ashes, as the phoenix, may bring forth / A bird that will revenge upon you all" (1.4.36–37). From Geffrey Whitney, *A Choice of Emblemes* (1586).

wick, who is Edward's strongest supporter and who has been sent to France to secure a French bride for Edward, turns against him in disgust. George temporarily abandons his brother, marries Warwick's daughter, and joins the Lancastrian cause. Richard, always outwardly loyal, privately vows to hack his way to the throne and displace both of his brothers in the process.

With ties of kinship and loyalty broken, nothing remains but the sheer exertion of individual will. Richard emerges as both the most fascinating and the most horrific character in the second half of the play because his will is indomitable and his desires unchecked by any moral constraints. The audience probably registers this fact most decisively during the bravura soliloquy that Richard speaks after he and George have watched—and obscenely commented upon—Edward's wooing of Lady Gray. Soliloquies, in which a character speaks to himself but is overheard by the theater audience, help create the illusion of interiority and inner subjectivity. Perhaps goaded by jealousy at the sight of Edward's successful wooing of Lady Gray, Richard in his soliloquy both reveals his frustrations and desires and hardheadedly maps a future course. In quick succession, he contemplates the number of people who before him have claims on the throne; resigns himself to seek instead the pleasures of courtship and love; despairs, since his deformed body prevents him from being loved; resolves therefore to seek the crown at any cost; and vows to change himself into any imaginable persona necessary to achieve his end. The soliloquy is long (3.2.124–95) and relentless. Richard tracks his argument like a bloodhound, registering his predicament with memorably vivid language.

> And yet I know not how to get the crown,
> For many lives stand between me and home.
> And I—like one lost in a thorny wood,

> That rends the thorns and is rent with the thorns,
> Seeking a way and straying from the way,
> Not knowing how to find the open air,
> But toiling desperately to find it out—
> Torment myself to catch the English crown.
>
> (3.2.172–79)

Struggle and frustration are evident in the repetitions of this passage. Seeking, straying, toiling, Richard is in constant motion, throwing himself against impossible barriers. The crown eludes him, yet he goes on. He is by turns attractive and frightening.

Many prototypes are drawn upon to create this distinctive character. His "individuality" does not emerge from nowhere but depends on Shakespeare's skillful appropriation of prior dramatic resources. Richard's characterization owes much, for example, to the striving, overreaching stage heroes created by Shakespeare's early rival Christopher Marlowe. Like Marlowe's Tamburlaine, Richard makes his heaven "to dream upon the crown" (3.2.168) and stops at nothing to achieve that goal. In part, he is also fashioned after the Vice figure from the medieval religious drama. The Vice was the character—often witty and quite disconcertingly entertaining—who embodied the principle of evil and tried to compel others to sin. Richard's witty asides, as much as his aggression and lack of scruple, reveal his kinship to the Vice. Perhaps this character's strongest association, however, is with the figure of the stage Machiavel, whom Richard himself evokes at the end of his soliloquy. The historical Niccolò Machiavelli was an Italian political philosopher whose influential book *The Prince* pragmatically rather than moralistically detailed the tactics and principles that made for successful government in the modern world. In the popular imagination, he came to stand for the hypocrisy and political cunning associated with Protestant England's symbolic enemy, Catholic Italy.

Sharing affinities with each of these figures but not fully modeled on any of them, Richard functions in Shakespeare's play to suggest what emerges when one no longer acknowledges the primacy of the identities constructed by the words "son" and "brother." In a society that defined people in terms of their place within family structures and social hierarchies, to separate oneself from those structures and hierarchies risked being read as monstrous and unnatural. Richard is riveting precisely because he seems so autonomous and so indifferent to the bonds and loyalties—to family and to king—that supposedly hold his society together and constrain the actions of its members. Though not the only one in the play whose ambition corrodes ties of blood and allegiance, Richard most fully epitomizes ambition's deforming effects. One way to read Richard's crooked back is as a physical sign of his unnatural inner being. Yet it is also true that to Richard his crooked body is the cause of (or at least the excuse for) his behavior. In modern psychological terms, he is compensating for a handicap in the only way he can. But it is a measure of Shakespeare's distance from us that such a reading of Richard's deformity is countered by another that emphasizes the moral significance of physical signs and is deeply ambivalent about the very idea of the socially autonomous individual.

Marriage is one way to incorporate individuals into social structures, but in *Richard Duke of York* the breakdown of social bonds is both caused and symbolized by its disorderly marriages. In the feudal world depicted in most of Shakespeare's early history plays, marriages in noble or monarchical families were primarily premised not on love but on dynastic convenience. Wives were to be chosen for the dowry or the territory or the alliances they brought with them. To marry for love was viewed as dangerous because it introduced irrational passion into what was supposed to be a rational choice and threatened the husband's control of himself and of his spouse. In marrying the widow Lady Gray, Edward makes such a passion-driven marriage and thereby nearly loses control of the kingdom. By his actions, he forfeits Warwick's loyalty and temporarily that of his brother George. King Henry had also made an irrational match in marrying the dowerless Margaret (see *The First Part of the Contention* 1.1). In *Richard Duke of York,* this initial lack of control finds its consequence in Henry's inability to govern Margaret and in the increasingly topsy-turvy nature of their marriage.

The end of the play, however, refocuses on the marriage of Edward and Lady Gray to bring a tenuous and highly ironized sense of resolution to the play's action. In the final scene, King Edward admires the son to which his wife, now Queen Elizabeth, has given birth and invites his brothers Richard and Clarence to do the same. The ambience is domestic in a modern way. This is a marriage of affection more than utility. Edward calls the babe "Ned" (5.7.16) and his wife "Bess" (15), the nicknames suggesting intimacy. But if Edward thinks this cozy domesticity, so pleasing to him but so politically ill advised, can reestablish the Yorkist dynasty and center it on him and his descendants, the presence of Richard signals otherwise. Leaning down to kiss the babe, Richard says, "And that I love the tree from whence thou sprang'st, / Witness the loving kiss I give the fruit" (31–32). The tree he refers to is, of course, the family of York, the family tree from which he himself springs. But then, in an aside, he adds: "To say the truth, so Judas kissed his master, / And cried 'All hail!' whenas he meant all harm" (33–34). For Richard to cast himself as the betrayer of Christ bodes badly for the happy family: Edward, Ned, and Bess. To late twentieth-century audiences and theatergoers, the King's doting attention to his wife and son may make him seem quite modern and quite human. Yet viewed historically and in its dramatic context, the King's behavior also signals his weakness, his propensity to let his affections overrule his reason. Fixated on his Ned and his Bess, he seems oblivious to the threat posed by his alienated, thoroughly undomestic brother.

Richard Duke of York ends, then, with a scene that underscores the tenuousness of Edward's purchase on power and threatens a renewal of civil war and family strife. The play's imaginative landscape is dominated by those willful, monstrous individuals such as Richard and Margaret who thrive amid the chaos of a disintegrating society. Few can oppose them, most especially not "the good King Henry," a man disastrously unsuited to play a monarch's part. Hovering on the periphery of this play's action and killed before its final scene, Henry is gradually transformed into a mere observer of the public world around him. Saintly and detached, he comes to represent the antithesis of Richard's surging, self-centered ambition, finally serving almost as choric commentator and as prophet. He predicts, for example, that Henry, Earl of Richmond (later Henry VII) will be England's savior (4.7.68–76), and he predicts (5.6.37–43) that many will come to curse the hunchbacked Richard (later Richard III). But hope for release from Richard's evil lies far in the future, and Henry's increasing saintliness neither erases his responsibility for civil war nor solves the immediate problem of secular rule. Neither saints nor monsters are particularly suited to govern other men. Edward is neither and so seems more fit to rule; yet he is unable to control, or even to recognize, his brother's villainy. *Richard Duke of York* feels so grim because its compelling depiction of the unraveling of England's social fabric suggests little about how that fabric can once again be rewoven.

JEAN E. HOWARD

TEXTUAL NOTE

In 1595, *The True Tragedy of Richard Duke of York and the Good King Henry the Sixth* was published in an octavo volume, and the same text appeared in quarto format in 1600. In 1602, control of the play fell to Thomas Pavier, who in 1619 issued another, edited, quarto version. Both of these quartos are based on the Octavo of 1595 (O) and have no independent textual authority. In 1623, a play approximately one thousand lines longer than any of these early texts appeared in Shakespeare's First Folio (F) under the title *The third part of Henry the Sixt.* While some scholars believe that the 1595 Octavo text is an early draft of the play included in the First Folio, the Oxford editors follow the majority of editors since the 1920s in assuming that the Octavo is a memorial reconstruction of an abridged and revised version of the Folio text. (For a discussion of theories of memorial reconstruction, see the Textual Note to *The First Part of the Contention [2 Henry VI].*) Consequently, the control text for *Richard Duke of York* is F, though the Oxford editors have retained the title used in the Octavo text on the theory that that was the title by which the play was probably known during Shakespeare's lifetime. They assume that the manuscript used for setting the Folio copy was the author's "foul papers," which had not been marked up for theatrical performance, because F contains a number of vague and unspecific stage directions as well as a high proportion of musical cues. Interestingly, several speeches bear actor's names (Gabriel, Sinklo, Humfrey) rather than characters' (Messenger [1.2.49] and First Gamekeeper and Second Gamekeeper [3.1]). The Octavo text, however, is believed to have been based on the promptbook for a theatrical production and contains important stage directions and perhaps some authorial revisions that occurred between the play's foul-papers stage and the promptbook. In some cases, when Octavo staging seems preferable to that suggested in F, this edition has rearranged dialogue or speech assignments to accord with such staging. These changes are marked in the notes and Textual Variants.

The Oxford text employs the standard act and scene divisions into which the play was divided in the eighteenth century, with two exceptions. A new scene is marked at 4.3.27, indicating that the stage is cleared between the time Edward's guards fly from his tent and Edward is subsequently brought onstage as a captive. And at the very end of Act 4, Scene 10 is introduced to separate Henry's conversation with Warwick about Edward's return from the Low Countries from his subsequent conversation with Exeter before he is surprised and seized by Edward and Richard, Duke of Gloucester.

SELECTED BIBLIOGRAPHY

Bergeron, David. "The Play-Within-the-Play in 3 *Henry VI.*" *Tennessee Studies in Literature* 22 (1977): 37–47. Examines four instances of Shakespeare's early use of the play within the play in 3 *Henry VI.*

Berman, Ronald. "Fathers and Sons in the *Henry VI* Plays." *Shakespeare Quarterly* 13 (1962): 487–97. Explores the disruption of relations between fathers and sons, kings and subjects under conditions of war and unstable monarchy.

Carroll, D. Allen. "Greene's 'Upstart Crow' Passage: A Survey of Commentary." *Research Opportunities in Renaissance Drama* 28 (1985): 111–27. Explores the possible meanings of Robert Greene's attack on Shakespeare as an "upstart Crow," a phrase used in Shakespeare's play to describe Queen Margaret.

Champion, Larry. "Developmental Structure in Shakespeare's Early Histories: The Perspective of 3 *Henry VI.*" *Studies in Philology* 76 (1979): 218–38. Argues that the play reveals Shakespeare's increasing technical sophistication and mastery of dramatic structure.

Hunt, Maurice. "Unnaturalness in Shakespeare's 3 *Henry VI.*" *English Studies: A Journal of English Language and Literature* 80 (1999): 146–67. Links Shakespeare's play to Thomas Sackville and Thomas Norton's earlier tragedy, *Gorboduc,* as each explores the motif of unnatural behavior and its political consequences.

Kahn, Coppélia. "'The Shadow of the Male': Masculine Identity in the History Plays." *Man's Estate: Masculine Identity in Shakespeare.* Berkeley: University of California Press, 1981. 47–81. Argues that in the early history plays masculine identity emerges primarily from emulation of or rivalry with the father.

Leggatt, Alexander. "Henry VI." *Shakespeare's Political Drama: The History Plays and the Roman Plays.* London: Routledge, 1988. 1–31. Explores the undermining of heroism and the breakdown of social order in the three plays featuring Henry VI.

Levine, Nina S. "Ruling Women and the Politics of Gender in 2 and 3 *Henry VI.*" *Women's Matters: Politics, Gender, and Nation in Shakespeare's Early History Plays.* Newark: University of Delaware Press, 1998. 68–96. Argues that in 3 *Henry VI* the misogyny surrounding Margaret's representation is tempered by her role in fighting for her son's succession to the throne and her defense of the English national interest.

Loehlin, James N. "Brecht and the Rediscovery of 1 *Henry VI.*" *Shakespeare's History Plays: Performance, Translation and Adaptation in Britain and Abroad.* Ed. Ton Hoenselaars. Cambridge: Cambridge University Press, 2004. 133–50. Examines the role of Bertolt Brecht's dramatic theory on the resurgence of interest in performing the Henry VI plays after 1960.

Williamson, Marilyn L. "'When Men Are Rul'd by Women': Shakespeare's First Tetralogy." *Shakespeare Studies* 19 (1987): 41–59. Explores how strong female characters such as Margaret become scapegoats for the chaos of civil war.

FILM

The Tragedy of Richard the Third. 1983. Dir. Jane Howell. UK/USA. 112 min. A BBC-TV production with Julia Foster as Margaret and Peter Benson as a bookish and ineffectual Henry VI. (Released as *Richard III* in the United Kingdom.)

The True Tragedy of Richard Duke of York and the Good King Henry the Sixth

THE PERSONS OF THE PLAY

Of the King's Party

KING HENRY VI
QUEEN MARGARET
PRINCE EDWARD, their son
Duke of SOMERSET
Duke of EXETER
Earl of NORTHUMBERLAND
Earl of WESTMORLAND
Lord CLIFFORD
Lord Stafford
SOMERVILLE
Henry, young Earl of Richmond
A SOLDIER who has killed his father
A HUNTSMAN who guards King Edward

The Divided House of Neville

Earl of WARWICK, first of York's party, later of Lancaster's
Marquis of MONTAGUE, his brother, of York's party
Earl of OXFORD, their brother-in-law, of Lancaster's party
Lord HASTINGS, their brother-in-law, of York's party

Of the Duke of York's Party

Richard Plantagenet, Duke of YORK
EDWARD, Earl of March, his son, later Duke of York and KING EDWARD IV
LADY GRAY, a widow, later Edward's wife and queen
Earl RIVERS, her brother
GEORGE, Edward's brother, later Duke OF CLARENCE
RICHARD, Edward's brother, later Duke OF GLOUCESTER
Earl of RUTLAND, Edward's brother
Rutland's TUTOR, a chaplain
SIR JOHN Mortimer, York's uncle
Sir Hugh Mortimer, his brother
Duke of NORFOLK
Sir William Stanley
Earl of Pembroke
Sir John MONTGOMERY
A NOBLEMAN
Two GAMEKEEPERS
Three WATCHMEN, who guard King Edward's tent
LIEUTENANT of the Tower

The French

KING LOUIS
LADY BONA, his sister-in-law
Lord Bourbon, the French High Admiral

Others

A SOLDIER who has killed his son
A SECOND SOLDIER who has killed his father
Mayor of Coventry
MAYOR of York
Aldermen of York
Soldiers, messengers, and attendants

1.1

[A chair of state.]¹ Alarum.° Enter Richard Plantagenet,   Call to arms
Duke of YORK, *[his two sons]* EDWARD, *Earl of March,*
[and] Crookback° RICHARD, the Duke of NORFOLK,   hunchback
[the] Marquis [of] MONTAGUE, *[and] the Earl of*
WARWICK, *with drum[mers] and soldiers. They all*
wear] white roses² in their hats

WARWICK   I wonder how the King escaped our hands?
YORK   While we pursued the horsemen of the north,
   He slyly stole away and left his men;
   Whereat the great lord of Northumberland,
5   Whose warlike ears could never brook retreat,³
   Cheered up the drooping army; and himself,
   Lord Clifford, and Lord Stafford, all abreast,
   Charged our main battle's° front, and, breaking in,   army's
   Were by the swords of common soldiers slain.⁴
10 EDWARD   Lord Stafford's father, Duke of Buckingham,
   Is either slain or wounded dangerous.°   dangerously
   I cleft his beaver° with a downright° blow.   helmet visor / vertical
   That this is true, father, behold his blood.
   [He shows a bloody sword]
MONTAGUE *[to* YORK*]*   And, brother,⁵ here's the Earl of Wiltshire's blood,
   [He shows a bloody sword]
15   Whom I encountered as the battles joined.
RICHARD *[to Somerset's head, which he shows]*
   Speak thou for me, and tell them what I did.
YORK   Richard hath best deserved of all my sons.
   [To the head] But is your grace dead, my lord of Somerset?

1.1 Location: The Parliament House, London.
1. Although neither O nor F indicates a chair or a
raised platform ("a state"), Warwick's lines at 22–27,
King Henry's at 50–51, and the stage direction at 32
("They go up") all suggest that both stage properties are
required here. Since the play focuses on the struggle for
the English throne, it is fitting that it open with a vacant
chair of state.
2. Emblem of the Yorkists. This play depicts part of
what is called the Wars of the Roses between the Yorkists, who wore the white rose, and the Lancastrians, who
wore the red rose. For Shakespeare's dramatization of
the origin of this convention, see *1 Henry VI* 2.4. In O,
when the Lancastrian faction enters at line 49, below,

they wear red roses. Both here and at line 49, F's stage
directions make no mention of roses. O concludes this
direction "with Drum and Soldiers, with white Roses in
their hats," leaving ambiguous whether the roses are
worn by the soldiers alone or by the entire party.
3. Could never endure hearing the trumpet call signaling retreat.
4. Shakespeare names York (rather than a common soldier) as the person who killed Clifford at several points
later in the play. *The First Part of the Contention*
(*2 Henry VI*) dramatizes this death in 5.3.
5. The historical Montague was York's nephew. He was
also, as Shakespeare suggests elsewhere in this play,
Warwick's brother.

NORFOLK   Such hap have all the line of John of Gaunt.[6]
20   RICHARD   Thus do I hope to shake King Henry's head.
     [*He holds aloft the head, then throws it down*]
WARWICK   And so do I, victorious prince of York.
    Before I see thee seated in that throne
    Which now the house of Lancaster usurps,
    I vow by heaven these eyes shall never close.
25   This is the palace of the fearful° King,   *frightened*
    And this [*pointing to the chair of state*], the regal seat—possess it, York,
    For this is thine, and not King Henry's heirs'.
YORK   Assist me then, sweet Warwick, and I will,
    For hither we have broken in by force.
30   NORFOLK   We'll all assist you—he that flies shall die.
YORK   Thanks, gentle° Norfolk. Stay by me, my lords   *noble*
    And soldiers—stay, and lodge by me this night.
      They go up [*upon the state*]
WARWICK   And when the King comes, offer him no violence
    Unless he seek to thrust you out perforce.°   *by force*
     [*The soldiers withdraw*][7]
35   YORK   The Queen this day here holds her Parliament,
    But little thinks we shall be of her council;
    By words or blows here let us win our right.
RICHARD   Armed as we are, let's stay within this house.
WARWICK   'The Bloody Parliament' shall this be called,
40   Unless Plantagenet, Duke of York, be king,
    And bashful Henry deposed, whose cowardice
    Hath made us bywords° to our enemies.   *objects of scorn*
YORK   Then leave me not, my lords. Be resolute—
    I mean to take possession of my right.
45   WARWICK   Neither the King nor he that loves him best—
    The proudest he that holds up° Lancaster—   *supports*
    Dares stir a wing if Warwick shake his bells.[8]
    I'll plant Plantagenet,[9] root him up who dares.
    Resolve thee, Richard—claim the English crown.
      [YORK *sits in the chair.*]
     Flourish.° *Enter* KING HENRY, [*Lord*] CLIFFORD,   *Trumpet fanfare*
     the Earl of NORTHUMBERLAND, *the Earl of*
     WESTMORLAND, *the Duke of* EXETER, *and the rest.*
     [*They all wear*] *red roses in their hats*
50   KING HENRY   My lords, look where the sturdy° rebel sits—   *stubborn*
    Even in the chair of state! Belike he means,
    Backed by the power of Warwick, that false peer,
    To aspire unto the crown and reign as king.
    Earl of Northumberland, he slew thy father—

---

6. May all the descendants of John of Gaunt have the same fate. John of Gaunt held the title Duke of Lancaster; Somerset was his grandson, and Henry VI his great-grandson. The Yorkists contended that John of Gaunt's son Henry IV had usurped Richard II's crown.
7. Neither F nor O indicates when the soldiers leave the stage, but we can assume that they do leave since they are given a reentrance at line 170.

8. If Warwick makes a move. Elizabethans attached bells to the legs of falcons in order to further frighten the falcon's prey; Warwick is comparing himself to such a threatening bird.
9. Richard, Duke of York was also called Richard Plantagenet. The Plantagenets were the medieval dynasty that began to rule England in 1154, when Henry II assumed the throne. The Yorkist and Lancastrian families were both descended from this dynasty.

55 And thine, Lord Clifford—and you both have vowed revenge
    On him, his sons, his favourites, and his friends.
  NORTHUMBERLAND   If I be not, heavens be revenged on me.
  CLIFFORD   The hope thereof makes Clifford mourn in steel.[1]
  WESTMORLAND   What, shall we suffer this? Let's pluck him down.
60 My heart for anger burns—I cannot brook it.
  KING HENRY   Be patient, gentle Earl of Westmorland.
  CLIFFORD   Patience is for poltroons,° such as he [*indicating* YORK].   cowards
    He durst not sit there had your father lived.
    My gracious lord, here in the Parliament
65 Let us assail the family of York.
  NORTHUMBERLAND   Well hast thou spoken, cousin,° be it so.   kinsman
  KING HENRY   Ah, know you not the city° favours them   (London)
    And they have troops of soldiers at their beck?°   absolute command
  EXETER   But when the Duke is slain, they'll quickly fly.
70 KING HENRY   Far be the thought of this from Henry's heart,
    To make a shambles° of the Parliament House.   slaughterhouse
    Cousin of Exeter, frowns, words, and threats
    Shall be the war that Henry means to use.
    [*To* YORK] Thou factious° Duke of York, descend my throne   rebellious
75 And kneel for grace and mercy at my feet.
    I am thy sovereign.
  YORK   I am thine.
  EXETER   For shame, come down—he made thee Duke of York.
  YORK   It was mine inheritance, as the earldom[2] was.
  EXETER   Thy father was a traitor to the crown.[3]
80 WARWICK   Exeter, thou art a traitor to the crown
    In following this usurping Henry.
  CLIFFORD   Whom should he follow but his natural king?
  WARWICK   True, Clifford, and that's Richard Duke of York.
  KING HENRY [*to* YORK]   And shall I stand and thou sit in my throne?
85 YORK   It must and shall be so—content thyself.
  WARWICK [*to* KING HENRY]   Be Duke of Lancaster, let him be king.
  WESTMORLAND   He is both king and Duke of Lancaster—
    And that, the Lord of Westmorland shall maintain.
  WARWICK   And Warwick shall disprove it. You forget
90 That we are those which chased you from the field,
    And slew your fathers, and, with colours° spread,   flags
    Marched through the city to the palace gates.
  NORTHUMBERLAND   Yes, Warwick, I remember it to my grief,
    And, by his soul, thou and thy house shall rue it.
95 WESTMORLAND [*to* YORK]   Plantagenet, of thee, and these thy sons,
    Thy kinsmen, and thy friends, I'll have more lives
    Than drops of blood were in my father's veins.
  CLIFFORD [*to* WARWICK]   Urge it no more, lest that, instead of words,
    I send thee, Warwick, such a messenger
100 As shall revenge his death before I stir.

---

1. In armor (rather than the black cloaks that were
conventionally worn by mourners).
2. The earldom of March, which York inherited from

his mother and through which he claimed the throne.
3. York's father, the Earl of Cambridge, was executed
for treason (see *Henry V* 2.2).

WARWICK [*to* YORK]   Poor Clifford, how I scorn his worthless threats.

YORK [*to* KING HENRY]   Will you we° show our title to the crown?   *Do you wish us to*
   If not, our swords shall plead it in the field.

KING HENRY   What title hast thou, traitor, to the crown?

105   Thy father was, as thou art, Duke of York;[4]
   Thy grandfather, Roger Mortimer, Earl of March.
   I am the son of Henry the Fifth,
   Who made the Dauphin[5] and the French to stoop
   And seized upon their towns and provinces.

110 WARWICK   Talk not of France, sith° thou hast lost it all.   *since*

KING HENRY   The Lord Protector[6] lost it, and not I.
   When I was crowned, I was but nine months old.

RICHARD   You are old enough now, and yet,° methinks, you lose.   *and even now*
   [*To* YORK] Father, tear the crown from the usurper's head.

115 EDWARD [*to* YORK]   Sweet father, do so—set it on your head.

MONTAGUE [*to* YORK]   Good brother, as thou lov'st and honour'st arms,
   Let's fight it out and not stand cavilling thus.

RICHARD   Sound drums and trumpets, and the King will fly.

YORK   Sons, peace!

NORTHUMBERLAND[7]   Peace, thou—and give King Henry leave°   *permission*
120   to speak.

KING HENRY   Ah, York, why seekest thou to depose me?
   Are we not both Plantagenets by birth,
   And from two brothers lineally descent?
   Suppose by right and equity thou be king—

      KING HENRY   Peace, thou—and give King Henry leave to
124.1   *speak.*

      WARWICK   Plantagenet shall speak first—hear him, lords,
        And be you silent and attentive too,
        For he that interrrupts him shall not live.

      KING HENRY [to YORK]   Think'st thou that I will leave my
124.5   *kingly throne,*

125   Think'st thou that I will leave my Kingly throne,
   Wherein my grandsire and my father sat?
   No—first shall war unpeople this my realm;
   Ay, and their colours, often borne in France,
   And now in England to our heart's great sorrow,
130   Shall be my winding-sheet.° Why faint you,[8] lords?   *burial shroud*
   My title's good, and better far than his.

WARWICK   Prove it, Henry, and thou shalt be king.

KING HENRY   Henry the Fourth by conquest got the crown.

YORK   'Twas by rebellion against his king.°   *(Richard II)*

135 KING HENRY [*aside*]   I know not what to say—my title's weak.

---

4. In fact, the historical York's father was not the Duke of York. York inherited that title from his uncle (Edward).

5. Title of the oldest son of the French King.

6. Humphrey, Duke of Gloucester, was Lord Protector during Henry VI's youth and, as such, had oversight of the King and kingdom. His downfall is dramatized in *The First Part of the Contention* (2 *Henry VI*).

7. For lines 120–25, Oxford follows O. F. assigns line 120 to King Henry, then gives three lines to Warwick and has Henry begin again at 125, omitting the Octavo passage here printed as 121–24. For the F version, see the inset passage that follows (lines 124.1–124.5). Critics such as Steven Urkowitz have argued that the difference here between O and F indicates two different views of Henry's character, and they treat O and F as completely separate texts, with O composed first. Here as elsewhere, Oxford takes these Octavo lines as an authorial revision that occurred sometime between the play's foul-paper stage and the subsequent prompt-book.

8. Why do you lose heart?

[*To* YORK] Tell me, may not a king adopt an heir?

YORK What then?

KING HENRY An if° he may, then am I lawful king—   *An if=If*
  For Richard, in the view of many lords,

140 Resigned the crown to Henry the Fourth,
  Whose heir my father was, and I am his.

YORK He rose against him,° being° his sovereign,   *(Richard) / who was*
  And made him to resign his crown perforce.

WARWICK Suppose, my lords, he did it unconstrained—

145 Think you 'twere prejudicial to his crown?°   *his claim to the throne*

EXETER No, for he could not so resign his crown
  But° that the next heir should succeed and reign.   *Without ensuring*

KING HENRY Art thou against us, Duke of Exeter?

EXETER His° is the right, and therefore pardon me.   *(York's)*

150 YORK Why whisper you, my lords, and answer not?

EXETER [*to* KING HENRY] My conscience tells me he is lawful king.

KING HENRY [*aside*] All will revolt from me and turn to him

NORTHUMBERLAND [*to* YORK] Plantagenet, for all the claim thou lay'st,
  Think not that Henry shall be so deposed.

155 WARWICK Deposed he shall be, in despite° of all.   *spite*

NORTHUMBERLAND Thou art deceived— 'tis not thy southern power
  Of Essex, Norfolk, Suffolk, nor of Kent,
  Which makes thee thus presumptuous and proud,
  Can set the Duke up° in despite of me.   *(on the throne)*

160 CLIFFORD King Henry, be thy title right or wrong,
  Lord Clifford vows to fight in thy defence.
  May that ground gape and swallow me alive
  Where I shall kneel to him that slew my father.

KING HENRY O, Clifford, how thy words revive my heart!

165 YORK Henry of Lancaster, resign thy crown.
  What mutter you, or what conspire you, lords?

WARWICK Do right unto this princely Duke of York,
  Or I will fill the house with armèd men
  And over the chair of state, where now he sits,

170 Write up his title with usurping blood.⁹
    He stamps with his foot and the soldiers
    show themselves

KING HENRY My lord of Warwick, hear me but one word—
  Let me for this my lifetime reign as king.

YORK Confirm the crown to me and to mine heirs,
  And thou shalt reign in quiet while thou liv'st.

175 KING HENRY I am content. Richard Plantagenet,
  Enjoy the kingdom after my decease.

CLIFFORD What wrong is this unto the prince your son?

WARWICK What good is this to England and himself?

WESTMORLAND Base, fearful, and despairing Henry.

180 CLIFFORD How hast thou injured both thyself and us?

WESTMORLAND I cannot stay to hear these articles.°   *terms of agreement*

NORTHUMBERLAND Nor I.

CLIFFORD Come, cousin, let us tell the Queen these news.

---

9. With the blood of Henry, whom Warwick considers a usurper.

WESTMORLAND [*to* KING HENRY]   Farewell, faint-hearted and
    degenerate king,
185   In whose cold blood no spark of honour bides.°   *lives*
                    Exit [*with his soldiers*][1]

NORTHUMBERLAND [*to* KING HENRY]   Be thou a prey unto the
    house of York,
    And die in bands° for this unmanly deed.   *fetters*
                    Exit [*with his soldiers*]

CLIFFORD [*to* KING HENRY]   In dreadful war mayst thou be overcome,
    Or live in peace, abandoned and despised.
                    Exit [*with his soldiers*]

190   WARWICK [*to* KING HENRY]   Turn this way, Henry, and regard them not.
    EXETER [*to* KING HENRY]   They seek revenge and therefore will not yield.
    KING HENRY   Ah, Exeter.
    WARWICK   Why should you sigh, my lord?
    KING HENRY   Not for myself, Lord Warwick, but my son,
    Whom I unnaturally shall disinherit.
195   But be it as it may. [*To* YORK] I here entail°   *bequeath*
    The crown to thee and to thine heirs for ever,
    Conditionally, that here thou take thine oath
    To cease this civil war, and whilst I live
    To honour me as thy king and sovereign,
200   And nor by treason nor hostility
    To seek to put me down and reign thyself.
    YORK   This oath I willingly take and will perform.
    WARWICK   Long live King Henry. [*To* YORK] Plantagenet, embrace him.
          [YORK *descends.* HENRY *and* YORK *embrace*]
    KING HENRY [*to* YORK]   And long live thou, and these thy forward° sons.   *precocious*
205   YORK   Now York and Lancaster are reconciled.
    EXETER   Accursed be he that seeks to make them foes.
          Sennet.[2] *Here* [York's train] *comes down* [*from the state*][3]
    YORK [*to* KING HENRY]   Farewell, my gracious lord, I'll to my castle.[4]
          Exeunt YORK *and his sons* [EDWARD *and*
                    RICHARD, *with soldiers*]
    WARWICK   And I'll keep London with my soldiers.
                    Exit [*with soldiers*]
    NORFOLK   And I to Norfolk with my followers.
                    Exit [*with soldiers*]
210   MONTAGUE   And I unto the sea from whence I came.
                    Exit [*with soldiers*]
    KING HENRY   And I with grief and sorrow to the court.
    [KING HENRY *and* EXETER *turn to leave.*]
    Enter QUEEN [MARGARET] *and* PRINCE [EDWARD]
    EXETER   Here comes the Queen, whose looks bewray° her anger.   *reveal*
    I'll steal away.

---

1. F gives no exit for Westmorland, Northumberland, or Clifford; O marks a separate exit for each, as here. Each man is probably followed out by his soldiers.
2. Trumpet notes signaling a procession.

3. F's "Here they come down" again indicates that a state is required for the scene.
4. Sandal, located near Wakefield in Yorkshire.

KING HENRY   Exeter, so will I.

QUEEN MARGARET   Nay, go not from me—I will follow thee.

215   KING HENRY   Be patient, gentle Queen, and I will stay.

QUEEN MARGARET   Who can be patient in such extremes?
       Ah, wretched man, would I had died a maid
       And never seen thee, never borne thee son,
       Seeing thou hast proved so unnatural a father.
220   Hath he deserved to lose his birthright thus?
       Hadst thou but loved him half so well as I,
       Or felt that pain° which I did for him once,   (labor pains)
       Or nourished him as I did with my blood,
       Thou wouldst have left thy dearest heart-blood there
225   Rather than have made that savage Duke thine heir
       And disinherited thine only son.

PRINCE EDWARD   Father, you cannot disinherit me.
       If you be king, why should not I succeed?

KING HENRY   Pardon me, Margaret; pardon me, sweet son—
230   The Earl of Warwick and the Duke enforced me.

QUEEN MARGARET   Enforced thee? Art thou king, and wilt be forced?
       I shame° to hear thee speak! Ah, timorous wretch,   (am ashamed)
       Thou hast undone thyself, thy son, and me,
       And giv'n unto the house of York such head[5]
235   As thou shalt reign but by their sufferance.
       To entail him and his heirs unto the crown—
       What is it, but to make thy sepulchre
       And creep into it far before thy time?
       Warwick is Chancellor and the Lord of Calais;
240   Stern Falconbridge commands the narrow seas;°   (Straits of Dover)
       The Duke° is made Protector of the Realm;   (York)
       And yet shalt thou be safe? Such safety finds
       The trembling lamb environèd° with wolves.   surrounded
       Had I been there, which am a seely° woman,   helpless
245   The soldiers should have tossed me on their pikes°   axlike weapons
       Before I would have granted° to that act.   assented
       But thou preferr'st thy life before thine honour.
       And seeing thou dost, I here divorce myself
       Both from thy table, Henry, and thy bed,[6]
250   Until that act of Parliament be repealed
       Whereby my son is disinherited.
       The northern lords that have forsworn thy colours
       Will follow mine, if once they see them spread—
       And spread they shall be, to thy foul disgrace
255   And the utter ruin of the house of York.
       Thus do I leave thee. [To PRINCE EDWARD] Come, son, let's away.
       Our army is ready—come, we'll after them.

KING HENRY   Stay, gentle Margaret, and hear me speak.

QUEEN MARGARET   Thou hast spoke too much already.

[To PRINCE EDWARD]   Get thee gone.

---

5. Such freedom to act. To give a horse its head means to loosen its reins and let it go where it will.
6. *I here . . . bed*: echoing the language of church law, which permitted marital separation "from bed and board' in cases of adultery, heresy, and cruelty.

260 KING HENRY   Gentle son Edward, thou wilt stay with me?
QUEEN MARGARET   Ay, to be murdered by his enemies.
PRINCE EDWARD [*to* KING HENRY]   When I return with victory
    from the field,
I'll see your grace. Till then, I'll follow her.
QUEEN MARGARET   Come, son, away—we may not linger thus.
                                    [*Exit with* PRINCE EDWARD][7]
265 KING HENRY   Poor Queen, how love to me and to her son
Hath made her break out into terms of rage.
Revenged may she be on that hateful Duke,
Whose haughty spirit, wingèd with desire,
Will coast° my crown, and, like an empty° eagle,   *attack / a hungry*
270 Tire° on the flesh of me and of my son.   *Feed ravenously*
The loss of those three lords torments my heart.
I'll write unto them and entreat them fair.°   *courteously*
Come, cousin, you shall be the messenger.
EXETER   And I, I hope, shall reconcile them all.

                                    Flourish. Exeunt[8]

                                    1.2
                    Enter RICHARD, EDWARD [*Earl of March*],
                    and [*the Marquis of*] MONTAGUE
RICHARD   Brother, though I be youngest give me leave.°   *allow me (to speak)*
EDWARD   No, I can better play the orator.
MONTAGUE   But I have reasons strong and forcible.
                    Enter the Duke of YORK
YORK   Why, how now, sons and brother—at a strife?
5   What is your quarrel? How began it first?
EDWARD   No quarrel, but a slight contention.
YORK   About what?
RICHARD   About that which concerns your grace and us—
The crown of England, father, which is yours.
10 YORK   Mine, boy? Not till King Henry be dead.
RICHARD   Your right depends not on his life or death.
EDWARD   Now you are heir—therefore enjoy it now.
By giving the house of Lancaster leave to breathe,°   *permission to rest*
It will outrun you, father, in the end.
15 YORK   I took an oath that he should quietly reign.
EDWARD   But for a kingdom any oath may be broken.
I would break a thousand oaths to reign one year.
RICHARD [*to* YORK]   No—God forbid your grace should be forsworn.
YORK   I shall be if I claim by open war.
20 RICHARD   I'll prove the contrary, if you'll hear me speak.
YORK   Thou canst not, son—it is impossible.
RICHARD   An oath is of no moment° being not took   *consequence*
Before a true and lawful magistrate
That hath authority over him that swears.
25 Henry had none, but did usurp the place.
Then, seeing 'twas he that made you to depose,°   *swear an oath*

7. O omits the Queen's last line and has her exit at line
261, Prince Edward at 263.
8. F marks a single exit for Exeter here and places the

"Flourish" before Richard's entrance in the next line.
1.2 Location: York's castle, Sandal (in Yorkshire).

Your oath, my lord, is vain and frivolous.
Therefore to arms—and, father, do but think
How sweet a thing it is to wear a crown,
30   Within whose circuit° is Elysium[1]   circumference
And all that poets feign° of bliss and joy.   imagine
Why do we linger thus? I cannot rest
Until the white rose that I wear be dyed
Even in the luke-warm blood of Henry's heart.
35 YORK   Richard, enough! I will be king or die.
[To MONTAGUE] Brother, thou shalt to London presently°   at once
And whet on Warwick to this enterprise.
Thou, Richard, shalt to the Duke of Norfolk
And tell him privily° of our intent.   secretly
40   You, Edward, shall to Edmund Brook, Lord Cobham,
With whom the Kentishmen will willingly rise.°   rebel; take arms
In them I trust, for they are soldiers
Witty, courteous, liberal, full of spirit.
While you are thus employed, what resteth more°   what else remains
45   But that I seek occasion how to rise,
And yet the King not privy to my drift,°   aware of my intent
Nor any of the house of Lancaster.
            Enter a MESSENGER
But stay, what news? Why com'st thou in such post?°   haste
     MESSENGER   The Queen, with all the northern earls and lords,
50   Intend here to besiege you in your castle.
She is hard by with twenty thousand men,
And therefore fortify your hold,° my lord.   castle
     YORK   Ay, with my sword. What—think'st thou that we fear them?
Edward and Richard, you shall stay with me;
55   My brother Montague shall post to London.
Let noble Warwick, Cobham, and the rest,
Whom we have left protectors of the King,
With powerful policy° strengthen themselves,   cunning
And trust not simple Henry nor his oaths.
60 MONTAGUE   Brother, I go—I'll win them, fear it not.
And thus most humbly I do take my leave.   Exit
            Enter SIR JOHN Mortimer and his brother Sir Hugh
     YORK   Sir John and Sir Hugh Mortimer, mine uncles,
You are come to Sandal in a happy° hour.   fortunate
The army of the Queen mean to besiege us.
65 SIR JOHN   She shall not need, we'll meet her in the field.
     YORK   What, with five thousand men?
     RICHARD   Ay, with five hundred, father, for a need.°   if necessary
A woman's general—what should we fear?
            A march [sounds] afar off
     EDWARD   I hear their drums. Let's set our men in order,
70   And issue forth and bid them battle straight.°   at once
     YORK [to SIR JOHN and Sir Hugh]   Five men to twenty—though
            the odds be great,
I doubt not, uncles, of our victory.
Many a battle have I won in France

1. In classical mythology, the paradise where blessed souls dwelled.

Whenas° the enemy hath been ten to one—   *When*
75   Why should I not now have the like success?   *Exeunt*

1.3

Alarums, and then enter the young Earl of RUTLAND
and his TUTOR [*a chaplain*]

RUTLAND   Ah, whither shall I fly to scape° their hands?   *escape*
Enter [*Lord*] CLIFFORD [*with soldiers*]
Ah, tutor, look where bloody Clifford comes.
CLIFFORD [*to the* TUTOR]   Chaplain, away—thy priesthood saves thy life.
As for the brat of this accursèd duke,
5   Whose father slew my father—he shall die.
TUTOR   And I, my lord, will bear him company.
CLIFFORD   Soldiers, away with him.
TUTOR   Ah, Clifford, murder not this innocent child
Lest thou be hated both of° God and man.   *Exit* [*guarded*]   *by*
[RUTLAND *falls to the ground*]
10   CLIFFORD   How now—is he dead already?
Or is it fear that makes him close his eyes?
I'll open them.
RUTLAND [*reviving*]   So looks the pent-up° lion o'er the wretch   *caged*
That trembles under his devouring paws,
15   And so he walks, insulting° o'er his prey,   *scornfully triumphing*
And so he comes to rend his limbs asunder.
Ah, gentle Clifford, kill me with thy sword
And not with such a cruel threat'ning look.
Sweet Clifford, hear me speak before I die.
20   I am too mean° a subject for thy wrath.   *lowly*
Be thou revenged on men, and let me live.
CLIFFORD   In vain thou speak'st, poor boy. My father's blood
Hath stopped the passage where thy words should enter.
RUTLAND   Then let my father's blood open it again.
25   He is a man, and, Clifford, cope° with him.   *fight*
CLIFFORD   Had I thy brethren here, their lives and thine
Were not revenge sufficient for me.
No—if I digged up thy forefathers' graves,
And hung their rotten coffins up in chains,
30   It could not slake° mine ire nor ease my heart.   *lessen*
The sight of any of the house of York
Is as a fury to torment my soul.
And till I root out their accursèd line,
And leave not one alive, I live in hell.
35   Therefore—
RUTLAND   O, let me pray before I take my death.
[*Kneeling*] To thee I pray: sweet Clifford, pity me.
CLIFFORD   Such pity as my rapier's point affords.
RUTLAND   I never did thee harm—why wilt thou slay me?
CLIFFORD   Thy father hath.
40   RUTLAND   But 'twas ere I was born.
Thou hast one son—for his sake pity me,
Lest in revenge thereof, sith° God is just,   *since*

1.3   Location: A battlefield between Sandal and Wakefield.

He be as miserably slain as I.
Ah, let me live in prison all my days,
45 And when I give occasion of offence,
Then let me die, for now thou hast no cause.
CLIFFORD   No cause? Thy father slew my father, therefore die.
      [*He stabs him*]
RUTLAND   *Dii faciant laudis summa sit ista tuae.*   [*He dies*]
CLIFFORD   Plantagenet—I come, Plantagenet!
50 And this thy son's blood cleaving to my blade
Shall rust upon my weapon till thy blood,
Congealed with this, do make me wipe off both.
      Exit [*with Rutland's body and soldiers*][2]

1.4

Alarum. Enter Richard Duke of YORK

YORK   The army of the Queen hath got° the field;   *won*
My uncles[1] both are slain in rescuing me;
And all my followers to the eager foe
Turn back,° and fly like ships before the wind,   *Turn their backs*
5 Or lambs pursued by hunger-starvèd wolves.
My sons—God knows what hath bechancèd° them.   *happened to*
But this I know—they have demeaned° themselves   *conducted*
Like men born to renown by life or death.
Three times did Richard make a lane to me,
10 And thrice cried, 'Courage, father, fight it out!'
And full as oft came Edward to my side,
With purple falchion° painted to the hilt   *curved sword*
In blood of those that had encountered him.
And when the hardiest warriors did retire,
15 Richard cried, 'Charge and give no foot of ground!'
[   ][2]
And cried 'A crown or else a glorious tomb!
A sceptre or an earthly sepulchre!'
With this, we charged again—but out, alas—
20 We bodged° again, as I have seen a swan   *gave way*
With bootless° labour swim against the tide   *fruitless*
And spend her strength with over-matching° waves.   *against too powerful*
      A short alarum within
Ah, hark—the fatal followers do pursue,
And I am faint and cannot fly their fury;
25 And were I strong, I would not shun their fury.
The sands° are numbered that makes up my life.   *(of the hourglass)*
Here must I stay, and here my life must end.
      Enter QUEEN [MARGARET, *Lord*] CLIFFORD, [*the Earl of*]
      NORTHUMBERLAND, [*and*] *the young* PRINCE [EDWARD,
      with] *soldiers*
Come bloody Clifford, rough Northumberland—
I dare your quenchless fury to more rage!

1. "The gods grant that this may be the height of your glory" (Ovid, *Heroides* 2.66).
2. Although no Folio or Octavo stage direction indicates whether any soldiers are present during this scene, Clifford's command at line 7 makes it clear that some, at least, escort the tutor offstage. Some may remain to exit here. Oxford notes that "the question, unresolvable, is an important one, for it asks, essentially, whether Clifford's murder of Rutland is witnessed by anyone."
1.4 Location: Scene continues.
1. Sir John and Sir Hugh Mortimer.
2. It has been conjectured that this missing line referred to Edward, who, like his brother Richard, may have cried out encouragement to York's forces.

30   I am your butt,° and I abide your shot.   *target (in archery)*
      NORTHUMBERLAND   Yield to our mercy, proud Plantagenet.
      CLIFFORD   Ay, to such mercy as his ruthless arm,
      With downright payment,³ showed unto my father.
      Now Phaëton hath tumbled from his car,⁴
35   And made an evening at the noontide prick.⁵
      YORK   My ashes, as the phoenix,⁶ may bring forth
      A bird° that will revenge upon you all,   *child*
      And in that hope I throw mine eyes to heaven,
      Scorning whate'er you can afflict me with.
40   Why come you not? What—multitudes, and fear?
      CLIFFORD   So cowards fight when they can fly no further;
      So doves do peck the falcon's piercing talons;
      So desperate thieves, all hopeless of their lives,
      Breathe out invectives 'gainst the officers.
45   YORK   O, Clifford, but bethink thee once again,
      And in thy thought o'errun° my former time,   *review*
      And, if thou canst for blushing, view this face
      And bite thy tongue, that slanders him with cowardice
      Whose frown hath made thee faint and fly ere this.
50   CLIFFORD   I will not bandy with thee word for word,
      But buckle° with thee blows twice two for one.   *join in close combat*
           [*He draws his sword*]
      QUEEN MARGARET   Hold, valiant Clifford: for a thousand causes
      I would prolong a while the traitor's life.
      Wrath makes him deaf—speak thou, Northumberland.
55   NORTHUMBERLAND   Hold, Clifford—do not honour him so much
      To prick thy finger though to wound his heart.
      What valour were it when a cur doth grin°   *show its teeth*
      For one to thrust his hand between his teeth
      When he might spurn° him with his foot away?   *kick*
60   It is war's prize to take all vantages,°   *opportunities*
      And ten to one is no impeach of valour.⁷
           [*They*] *fight and take* [YORK]
      CLIFFORD   Ay, ay, so strives the woodcock with the gin.⁸
      NORTHUMBERLAND   So doth the cony° struggle in the net.   *rabbit*
      YORK   So triumph thieves upon their conquered booty,
65   So true° men yield, with robbers so o'ermatched.   *honest*
      NORTHUMBERLAND [*to the* QUEEN]   What would your grace have
           done unto him now?
      QUEEN MARGARET   Brave warriors, Clifford and Northumberland,
      Come make him stand upon this molehill here,
      That wrought° at mountains with outstretchèd arms   *reached*
70   Yet parted but° the shadow with his hand.   *only*
      [*To* YORK] What—was it you that would be England's king?
      Was't you that revelled in our Parliament,

---

3. Alluding to the "downright," or vertical, sword stroke that York used to kill Clifford's father in *The First Part of the Contention.*
4. Phaeton, in classical mythology, was the son of Phoebus (the sun god) and nearly set the world on fire when he attempted to drive his father's chariot ("car," the sun). Zeus hurled a thunderbolt, and Phaeton fell blazing to his death. This is one of the play's many allusions to the fact that the sun was an emblem of the

house of York. See note to 2.1.40.
5. The noon mark on a sundial.
6. A mythological bird that periodically built an elaborate funeral pyre, set itself on fire, and was reborn from its own ashes.
7. And for ten to fight with one does not call our bravery into question.
8. Trap. *woodcock:* a bird reputed to lack brains and thus easily caught in traps.

And made a preachment° of your high descent?   sermon
Where are your mess of° sons to back you now?   group of four
75   The wanton Edward and the lusty George?
And where's that valiant crookback prodigy,°   marvel; monster
Dickie, your boy, that with his grumbling voice
Was wont to cheer his dad in mutinies?
Or with the rest where is your darling Rutland?
80   Look, York, I stained this napkin° with the blood   handkerchief
That valiant Clifford with his rapier's point
Made issue from the bosom of thy boy.
And if thine eyes can water for his death,
I give thee this to dry thy cheeks withal.°   with
85   Alas, poor York, but that I hate thee deadly
I should lament thy miserable state.
I prithee, grieve, to make me merry, York.
What—hath thy fiery heart so parched thine entrails°   inner organs
That not a tear can fall for Rutland's death?
90   Why art thou patient, man? Thou shouldst be mad,
And I, to make thee mad, do mock thee thus.
Stamp, rave, and fret, that I may sing and dance.
Thou wouldst be fee'd,° I see, to make me sport.   paid
York cannot speak unless he wear a crown.
95   [To her men] A crown for York, and, lords, bow low to him.
Hold you his hands whilst I do set it on.
          [She puts a paper crown on York's head]
Ay, marry, sir, now looks he like a king,
Ay, this is he that took King Henry's chair,
And this is he was his adopted heir.
100   But how is it that great Plantagenet
Is crowned so soon and broke his solemn oath?
As I bethink me, you should not be king
Till our King Henry had shook hands with death.
And will you pale° your head in Henry's glory,   enclose
105   And rob his temples of the diadem
Now, in his life, against your holy oath?
O 'tis a fault too, too, unpardonable.
Off with the crown,
          [She knocks it from his head]
                              and with the crown his head,
And whilst we breathe,° take time to do him dead.°   rest / kill him
110   CLIFFORD   That is my office for my father's sake.
QUEEN MARGARET   Nay, stay—let's hear the orisons° he makes.   prayers
YORK   She-wolf of France, but worse than wolves of France,
Whose tongue more poisons than the adder's tooth—
How ill-beseeming° is it in thy sex   unbecoming
115   To triumph like an Amazonian trull⁹
Upon their woes whom fortune captivates!°   subdues
But that° thy face is visor-like,¹ unchanging,   Were it not that
Made impudent with use of evil deeds,
I would essay,° proud Queen, to make thee blush.   attempt

---

9. In the manner of an Amazonian whore. Amazons were a tribe of mythical warrior women who governed themselves and lived separate from men. Sometimes they were accused of sexual impropriety because to beget offspring they would mate with men they had conquered but did not marry.

1. Masklike; fixed in expression like the frontpiece of a helmet. Perhaps alluding to the practice of prostitutes who wore masks.

120   To tell thee whence thou cam'st, of whom derived,
       Were shame enough to shame thee— wert thou not shameless.
       Thy father bears the type° of King of Naples,   *title*
       Of both the Sicils,[2] and Jerusalem—
       Yet not so wealthy as an English yeoman.[3]
125   Hath that poor monarch taught thee to insult?
       It needs not, nor it boots° thee not, proud Queen,   *profits*
       Unless the adage must be verified
       That beggars mounted run their horse to death.
       'Tis beauty that doth oft make women proud—
130   But, God he knows, thy share thereof is small;
       'Tis virtue that doth make them most admired—
       The contrary doth make thee wondered at;
       'Tis government° that makes them seem divine—   *self-control*
       The want thereof makes thee abominable.
135   Thou art as opposite to every good
       As the antipodes[4] are unto us,
       Or as the south to the septentrion.[5]
       O tiger's heart wrapped in a woman's hide!
       How couldst thou drain the life-blood of the child
140   To bid the father wipe his eyes withal,
       And yet be seen to bear a woman's face?
       Women are soft, mild, pitiful,° and flexible—   *full of pity*
       Thou stern, obdurate, flinty, rough, remorseless.
       Bidd'st thou me rage? Why, now thou hast thy wish.
145   Wouldst have me weep? Why, now thou hast thy will.
       For raging wind blows up incessant showers,
       And when the rage allays° the rain begins.   *abates*
       These tears are my sweet Rutland's obsequies,
       And every drop cries vengeance for his death
150   'Gainst thee, fell° Clifford, and thee, false Frenchwoman.   *cruel*
NORTHUMBERLAND   Beshrew° me, but his passions move me so   *Curse*
       That hardly can I check my eyes from tears.
YORK   That face of his the hungry cannibals
       Would not have touched, would not have stained with blood—
155   But you are more inhuman, more inexorable,
       O, ten times more than tigers of Hyrcania.[6]
       See, ruthless Queen, a hapless° father's tears.   *an unlucky*
       This cloth thou dipped'st in blood of my sweet boy,
       And I with tears do wash the blood away.
160   Keep thou the napkin and go boast of this,
       And if thou tell'st the heavy° story right,   *sorrowful*
       Upon my soul the hearers will shed tears,
       Yea, even my foes will shed fast-falling tears
       And say, 'Alas, it was a piteous deed'.
165   There, take the crown—and with the crown, my curse:
       And in thy need such comfort come to thee
       As now I reap at thy too cruel hand.
       Hard-hearted Clifford, take me from the world.
       My soul to heaven, my blood upon your heads.

2. Naples and Sicily (known as the Kingdom of the   5. North. The word refers to the seven stars that make
Two Sicilies).   up the Great Bear constellation.
3. Landowner below the rank of gentleman.   6. Region in ancient Persia known for the cruelty of its
4. People living on the opposite side of the world.   tigers (see *Aeneid* 4.366–67).

170 NORTHUMBERLAND Had he been slaughter-man to all my kin,
     I should not, for my life, but weep with him,
     To see how inly° sorrow gripes his soul.   *inward*
     QUEEN MARGARET What—weeping-ripe,° my lord Northumberland?   *ready to weep*
     Think but upon the wrong he did us all,
175 And that will quickly dry thy melting tears.
     CLIFFORD Here's for my oath, here's for my father's death.
          [*He stabs* YORK]
     QUEEN MARGARET And here's to right our gentle-hearted King.
          [*She stabs* YORK]
     YORK Open thy gate of mercy, gracious God—
     My soul flies through these wounds to seek out thee.
                                                                                        [*He dies*]
180 QUEEN MARGARET Off with his head and set it on York gates,
     So York may overlook the town of York.
                                        Flourish. Exeunt [*with York's body*]

2.1

          [A] *march. Enter* EDWARD [*Earl of March*]
          and RICHARD, *with* [*a*] *drum*[*mer*] *and soldiers*
     EDWARD I wonder how our princely father scaped,
     Or whether he be scaped away or no
     From Clifford's and Northumberland's pursuit.
     Had he been ta'en we should have heard the news;
5   Had he been slain we should have heard the news;
     Or had he scaped, methinks we should have heard
     The happy tidings of his good escape.
     How fares my brother? Why is he so sad?
     RICHARD I cannot joy until I be resolved
10   Where our right valiant father is become.°   *has betaken himself*
     I saw him in the battle range about,
     And watched him how he singled Clifford forth.
     Methought he bore him in the thickest troop,
     As doth a lion in a herd of neat;°   *cattle*
15   Or as a bear encompassed round with dogs,
     Who having pinched° a few and made them cry,   *bitten*
     The rest stand all aloof and bark at him.
     So fared our father with his enemies;
     So fled his enemies my warlike father.
20   Methinks 'tis prize enough to be his son.
               Three suns appear in the air[1]
     See how the morning opes her golden gates
     And takes her farewell of the glorious sun.
     How well resembles it the prime of youth,
     Trimmed° like a younker° prancing to his love!   *Dressed up / young man*
25   EDWARD Dazzle mine eyes, or do I see three suns?
     RICHARD Three glorious suns, each one a perfect sun;
     Not separated with the racking° clouds,   *drifting*
     But severed in a pale clear-shining sky.
          [*The three suns begin to join*]

2.1. Location: Fields near the border, or marches, between Wales and England.
1. This stage direction appears in O, which may have been based on a theatrical promptbook (see Textual Note). I suggests that the acting company who performed the play had some kind of artificial "suns" they used as properties for this scene.

See, see—they join, embrace, and seem to kiss,
30   As if they vowed some league inviolable.
Now are they but one lamp, one light, one sun.
In this the heaven figures° some event.   *prefigures*
EDWARD   'Tis wondrous strange, the like yet never heard of.
I think it cites° us, brother, to the field,   *urges*
35   That we, the sons of brave Plantagenet,
Each one already blazing by our meeds,°   *merits*
Should notwithstanding join our lights together
And over-shine the earth as this° the world.   *this phenomenon*
Whate'er it bodes, henceforward will I bear
40   Upon my target three fair-shining suns.[2]
RICHARD   Nay, bear three daughters—by your leave I speak it—
You love the breeder° better than the male.   *childbearer; woman*
        Enter one blowing[3]
But what art thou whose heavy looks foretell
Some dreadful story hanging on thy tongue?
45   MESSENGER   Ah, one that was a woeful looker-on
Whenas° the noble Duke of York was slain—   *When*
Your princely father and my loving lord.
EDWARD   O, speak no more, for I have heard too much.
RICHARD   Say how he died, for I will hear it all.
50   MESSENGER   Environèd° he was with many foes,   *Surrounded*
And stood against them as the hope of Troy[4]
Against the Greeks that would have entered Troy.
But Hercules[5] himself must yield to odds;
And many strokes, though with a little axe,
55   Hews down and fells the hardest-timbered oak.
By many hands your father was subdued,
But only slaughtered by the ireful arm
Of unrelenting Clifford and the Queen,
Who crowned the gracious Duke in high despite,°   *in great contempt*
60   Laughed in his face, and when with grief he wept,
The ruthless Queen gave him to dry his cheeks
A napkin steepèd in the harmless blood
Of sweet young Rutland, by rough Clifford slain;
And after many scorns, many foul taunts,
65   They took his head, and on the gates of York
They set the same; and there it doth remain,
The saddest spectacle that e'er I viewed.
EDWARD   Sweet Duke of York, our prop to lean upon,
Now thou art gone, we have no staff, no stay.°   *support*
70   O Clifford, boist'rous° Clifford—thou hast slain   *savage*
The flower of Europe for his chivalry,
And treacherously hast thou vanquished him—
For hand to hand he would have vanquished thee.
Now my soul's palace° is become a prison.   *(my body)*
75   Ah, would she° break from hence that this my body   *(my soul)*
Might in the ground be closèd up in rest.

2. As elsewhere, Shakespeare here slightly changes his sources. In Holinshed's *Chronicles,* Edward chose the sun as his badge because he had seen three suns join in one before the Battle of Mortimer's Cross, which he won. *target:* shield.
3. Blowing a horn as messengers did to announce themselves.
4. *hope of Troy:* Hector, a mighty warrior in Homer's *Iliad,* who defended the city of Troy against Greek invaders.
5. A mythic hero of enormous physical strength and courage.

For never henceforth shall I joy again—
Never, O never, shall I see more joy.
RICHARD   I cannot weep, for all my body's moisture
80   Scarce serves to quench my furnace-burning heart;
Nor can my tongue unload my heart's great burden,
For selfsame wind° that I should speak withal   *breath*
Is kindling coals that fires all my breast,
And burns me up with flames that tears would quench.
85   To weep is to make less the depth of grief;
Tears, then, for babes—blows and revenge for me!
Richard, I bear thy name; I'll venge° thy death   *revenge*
Or die renownèd by attempting it.
EDWARD   His name that valiant Duke hath left with thee,
90   His dukedom and his chair[6] with me is left.
RICHARD   Nay, if thou be that princely eagle's bird,
Show thy descent by gazing 'gainst the sun:[7]
For 'chair and dukedom', 'throne and kingdom' say—
Either that is thine or else thou wert not his.
          March. Enter the Earl of WARWICK *[and the] Marquis*
          [of] MONTAGUE, *with drum[mers], [an] ensign,*
          and soldiers
95   WARWICK   How now, fair lords? What fare?° What news abroad?   *success*
RICHARD   Great lord of Warwick, if we should recount
Our baleful° news, and at each word's deliverance   *deadly*
Stab poniards° in our flesh till all were told,   *daggers*
The words would add more anguish than the wounds.
100 O valiant lord, the Duke of York is slain.
EDWARD   O Warwick, Warwick! That Plantagenet,
Which held thee dearly as his soul's redemption,
Is by the stern Lord Clifford done to death.
WARWICK   Ten days ago I drowned these news in tears.
105 And now, to add more measure to your woes,
I come to tell you things sith° then befall'n.   *since*
After the bloody fray at Wakefield fought,
Where your brave father breathed his latest° gasp,   *last*
Tidings, as swiftly as the posts° could run,   *messengers*
110 Were brought me of your loss and his depart.°   *death*
I then in London, keeper of the King,
Mustered my soldiers, gathered flocks of friends,
And, very well appointed° as I thought,   *equipped*
Marched toward Saint Albans to intercept the Queen,
115 Bearing the King in my behalf along—
For by my scouts I was advertisèd°   *informed*
That she was coming with a full intent
To dash our late° decree in Parliament   *recent*
Touching King Henry's oath and your succession.
120 Short tale to make, we at Saint Albans met,
Our battles° joined, and both sides fiercely fought;   *armies*
But whether 'twas the coldness of the King,
Who looked full gently on his warlike queen,
That robbed my soldiers of their heated spleen,°   *fiery passion*
125 Or whether 'twas report of her success,

---

6. Seat of his authority as Duke.
7. Eagles, described by Elizabethans as the king of

birds, were supposed to be able to gaze unblinkingly at
the sun.

Or more than common fear of Clifford's rigour—
Who thunders to his captains blood and death—
I cannot judge; but, to conclude with truth,
Their weapons like to lightning came and went;
130   Our soldiers', like the night-owl's lazy flight,
Or like an idle thresher with a flail,[8]
Fell gently down, as if they struck their friends.
I cheered them up with justice of our cause,
With promise of high pay, and great rewards.
135   But all in vain. They had no heart to fight,
And we in them no hope to win the day.
So that we fled—the King unto the Queen,
Lord George your brother, Norfolk, and myself
In haste, post-haste, are come to join with you.
140   For in the Marches° here we heard you were,   *Welsh borders*
Making another head° to fight again.   *Raising another army*
EDWARD   Where is the Duke of Norfolk, gentle Warwick?
And when came George from Burgundy to England?
WARWICK   Some six miles off the Duke is with his soldiers;
145   And for your brother—he was lately sent
From your kind aunt, Duchess of Burgundy,[9]
With aid of soldiers to this needful war.
RICHARD   'Twas odd belike[1] when valiant Warwick fled.
Oft have I heard his praises in pursuit,°   *(of enemies)*
150   But ne'er till now his scandal of retire.[2]
WARWICK   Nor now my scandal, Richard, dost thou hear—
For thou shalt know this strong right hand of mine
Can pluck the diadem from faint° Henry's head   *weak*
And wring the aweful° sceptre from his fist,   *awe-inspiring*
155   Were he as famous and as bold in war
As he is famed for mildness, peace, and prayer.
RICHARD   I know it well, Lord Warwick—blame me not.
'Tis love I bear thy glories make me speak.
But in this troublous time what's to be done?
160   Shall we go throw away our coats of steel,
And wrap our bodies in black mourning gowns,
Numb'ring our Ave-Maries with our beads?[3]
Or shall we on the helmets of our foes
Tell our devotion[4] with revengeful arms?
165   If for the last, say 'ay', and to it, lords.
WARWICK   Why, therefore Warwick came to seek you out,
And therefore comes my brother Montague.
Attend me, lords. The proud insulting Queen,
With Clifford and the haught° Northumberland,   *haughty*
170   And of their feather many more proud birds,
Have wrought° the easy-melting King like wax.   *worked on*
[*To* EDWARD] He swore consent to your succession,

8. Threshers beat grain from wheat with specially
designed sticks, or "flails."
9. According to the chronicles, both George and Richard
were sent for safety to the court of Philip of Burgundy;
his wife, the Duchess of Burgundy, whom Warwick mentions, was a granddaughter of John of Gaunt.
1. The odds must have been much against him.
2. Defamation or condemnation of him for retreating

(from his enemies).
3. Rosary beads are used in Roman Catholic devotion
for keeping track of the prayers one has said, including
"Ave Marias" ("Hail Marys"), prayers addressed to the
Virgin Mary.
4. Proclaim the object of our devotion (York), with a
pun on "telling" as meaning "counting," which is what
one does when saying the rosary.

His oath enrollèd° in the Parliament.   *officially recorded*
And now to London all the crew are gone,
175   To frustrate both his oath and what beside
May make against° the house of Lancaster.   *be unfavorable to*
Their power, I think, is thirty thousand strong.
Now, if the help of Norfolk and myself,
With all the friends that thou, brave Earl of March,⁵
180   Amongst the loving Welshmen canst procure,
Will but amount to five-and-twenty thousand,
Why, via,° to London will we march,   *onward*
And once again bestride our foaming steeds,
And once again cry 'Charge!' upon our foes—
185   But never once again turn back and fly.

RICHARD   Ay, now methinks I hear great Warwick speak.
Ne'er may he live to see a sunshine day
That cries 'Retire!' if Warwick bid him stay.

EDWARD   Lord Warwick, on thy shoulder will I lean,
190   And when thou fail'st—as God forbid the hour—
Must Edward fall, which peril heaven forfend!°   *forbid*

WARWICK   No longer Earl of March, but Duke of York;
The next degree° is England's royal throne—   *step*
For King of England shalt thou be proclaimed
195   In every borough as we pass along,
And he that throws not up his cap for joy,
Shall for the fault make forfeit of his head.
King Edward, valiant Richard, Montague—
Stay we no longer dreaming of renown,
200   But sound the trumpets and about our task.

RICHARD   Then, Clifford, were thy heart as hard as steel,
As thou hast shown it flinty by thy deeds,
I come to pierce it or to give thee mine.

EDWARD   Then strike up drums—God and Saint George°   *patron saint of England*
for us!

Enter a MESSENGER

205   WARWICK   How now? What news?

MESSENGER   The Duke of Norfolk sends you word by me
The Queen is coming with a puissant° host,   *powerful*
And craves your company for speedy counsel.

WARWICK   Why then it sorts.° Brave warriors, let's away.   *is fitting*

[March.] Exeunt

2.2

*[York's head is thrust out, above.]*¹
Flourish. Enter KING *[*HENRY*],* QUEEN *[*MARGARET*],*
[Lord] CLIFFORD, *[the Earl of]* NORTHUMBERLAND,
and young PRINCE EDWARD, *with [a] drum[mer]*
and trumpet[er]s

QUEEN MARGARET   Welcome, my lord, to this brave town of York.
Yonder's the head of that arch-enemy
That sought to be encompassed with your crown.

---

5. The title by which Edward and his father before him laid claim to the throne of England. See line 192 and note to 1.1.78.
2.2. Location: Before the walls of York.
1. Neither F nor O indicates in stage directions that York's head is displayed above the stage, but Queen Margaret's words in lines 2–4 and King Henry's response suggest that it remains visible, perhaps (as Oxford proposes) until 2.6.110.

Doth not the object cheer your heart, my lord?
5   KING HENRY   Ay, as the rocks cheer them that fear their wreck.
To see this sight, it irks my very soul.
Withhold revenge, dear God—'tis not my fault,
Nor wittingly have I infringed my vow.
CLIFFORD   My gracious liege,° this too much lenity   sovereign
10   And harmful pity must be laid aside.
To whom do lions cast their gentle looks?
Not to the beast that would usurp their den.
Whose hand is that the forest bear doth lick?
Not his that spoils° her young before her face.   takes as prey
15   Who scapes the lurking serpent's mortal sting?
Not he that sets his foot upon her back.
The smallest worm will turn, being trodden on,
And doves will peck in safeguard of their brood.
Ambitious York did level° at thy crown,   aim
20   Thou smiling while he knit his angry brows.
He, but a duke, would have his son a king,
And raise° his issue° like a loving sire;   raise in rank / offspring
Thou, being a king, blest with a goodly son,
Didst yield consent to disinherit him,
25   Which argued thee a most unloving father.
Unreasonable creatures° feed their young,   Animals
And though man's face be fearful to their eyes,
Yet, in protection of their tender ones,
Who hath not seen them, even with those wings
30   Which sometime they have used with fearful flight,
Make war with him that climbed unto their nest,
Offering their own lives in their young's defence?
For shame, my liege, make them your precedent!
Were it not pity that this goodly boy
35   Should lose his birthright by his father's fault,
And long hereafter say unto his child
'What my great-grandfather and grandsire got
My careless father fondly° gave away'?   foolishly
Ah, what a shame were this! Look on the boy,
40   And let his manly face, which promiseth
Successful fortune, steel thy melting heart
To hold thine own and leave thine own with him.
KING HENRY   Full well hath Clifford played the orator,
Inferring° arguments of mighty force.   Offering
45   But, Clifford, tell me—didst thou never hear
That things ill got had ever bad success?°   outcome
And happy always was it for that son
Whose father for his hoarding went to hell?
I'll leave my son my virtuous deeds behind,
50   And would my father had left me no more.
For all the rest is held at such a rate°   cost
As brings a thousandfold more care to keep
Than in possession any jot of pleasure.
Ah, cousin York, would thy best friends did know
55   How it doth grieve me that thy head is here.
QUEEN MARGARET   My lord, cheer up your spirits—our foes are nigh,
And this soft courage makes your followers faint.°   lose heart
You promised knighthood to our forward° son.   precocious

Unsheathe your sword and dub[2] him presently.°   *at once*
60   Edward, kneel down.
       [PRINCE EDWARD *kneels*]
   KING HENRY   Edward Plantagenet, arise a knight—
   And learn this lesson: draw thy sword in right.
   PRINCE EDWARD [*rising*]   My gracious father, by your kingly leave,
   I'll draw it as apparent° to the crown,   *heir*
65   And in that quarrel° use it to the death.   *cause*
   CLIFFORD   Why, that is spoken like a toward° prince.   *bold*
       Enter a MESSENGER
   MESSENGER   Royal commanders, be in readiness—
   For with a band of thirty thousand men
   Comes Warwick backing of° the Duke of York;[3]   *supporting*
70   And in the towns, as they do march along,
   Proclaims him king, and many fly to him.
   Darraign your battle,° for they are at hand.   *Deploy your troops*
   CLIFFORD [*to* KING HENRY]   I would your highness would depart
      the field—
   The Queen hath best success when you are absent.
   QUEEN MARGARET [*to* KING HENRY]   Ay, good my lord, and leave
75   us to our fortune.
   KING HENRY   Why, that's my fortune too—therefore I'll stay.
   NORTHUMBERLAND   Be it with resolution then to fight.
   PRINCE EDWARD [*to* KING HENRY]   My royal father, cheer these
      noble lords
   And hearten those that fight in your defence.
80   Unsheathe your sword, good father; cry 'Saint George!'°   *England's patron saint*
       March. Enter EDWARD [*Duke of York, the Earl of*] WAR-
       WICK, RICHARD, [GEORGE,[4] *the Duke of*]
       NORFOLK, [*the Marquis of*] MONTAGUE, *and soldiers*
   EDWARD   Now, perjured Henry, wilt thou kneel for grace,
   And set thy diadem upon my head—
   Or bide° the mortal° fortune of the field?   *wait for / fatal*
   QUEEN MARGARET   Go rate° thy minions,° proud insulting boy!   *chide / favorites*
85   Becomes it thee to be thus bold in terms
   Before thy sovereign and thy lawful king?
   EDWARD   I am his king, and he should bow his knee.
   I was adopted heir by his consent.
   GEORGE [*to* QUEEN MARGARET]   Since when his oath is broke—
      for, as I hear,
90   You that are king, though he do wear the crown,
   Have caused him by new act of Parliament
   To blot our brother out, and put his own son in.
   CLIFFORD   And reason too—
   Who should succeed the father but the son?
95   RICHARD   Are you there, butcher? O, I cannot speak!
   CLIFFORD   Ay, crookback, here I stand to answer thee,
   Or any he the proudest of thy sort.°   *gang*
   RICHARD   'Twas you that killed young Rutland, was it not?
   CLIFFORD   Ay, and old York, and yet not satisfied.

---

2. Confer the rank of knight by the ceremony of striking the shoulder with a sword.
3. Edward has now assumed the title Duke of York
after the death of his father at Margaret's hands.

4. Here and elsewhere, F's stage directions read
"Clarence" rather than "George." The Duke of Clarence
is the title he eventually assumes.

100 RICHARD   For God's sake, lords, give signal to the fight.
WARWICK   What sayst thou, Henry, wilt thou yield the crown?
QUEEN MARGARET   Why, how now, long-tongued Warwick, dare
       you speak?
    When you and I met at Saint Albans last,
    Your legs did better service than your hands.
105 WARWICK   Then 'twas my turn to fly—and now 'tis thine.
CLIFFORD   You said so much before, and yet you fled.
WARWICK   'Twas not your valour, Clifford, drove me thence.
NORTHUMBERLAND   No, nor your manhood that durst make you stay.
RICHARD   Northumberland, I hold thee reverently.°   in respect
110   Break off the parley, for scarce I can refrain
    The execution of my big-swoll'n heart⁵
    Upon that Clifford, that cruel child-killer.
CLIFFORD   I slew thy father—call'st thou him a child?
RICHARD   Ay, like a dastard° and a treacherous coward,   base coward
115   As thou didst kill our tender brother Rutland.
    But ere sun set I'll make thee curse the deed.
KING HENRY   Have done with words, my lords, and hear me speak.
QUEEN MARGARET   Defy them, then, or else hold close thy lips.
KING HENRY   I prithee give no limits to my tongue—
120   I am a king, and privileged to speak.
CLIFFORD   My liege, the wound that bred this meeting here
    Cannot be cured by words—therefore be still.
RICHARD   Then, executioner, unsheathe thy sword.
    By him that made us all, I am resolved
125   That Clifford's manhood lies upon his tongue.°   exists only in words
EDWARD   Say, Henry, shall I have my right or no?
    A thousand men have broke their fasts today
    That ne'er shall dine unless thou yield the crown.
WARWICK [to KING HENRY]   If thou deny,° their blood upon thy head;   refuse
130   For York in justice puts his armour on.
PRINCE EDWARD   If that be right which Warwick says is right,
    There is no wrong, but everything is right.
RICHARD   Whoever got° thee, there thy mother stands—   sired
    For, well I wot,° thou hast thy mother's tongue.   know
135 QUEEN MARGARET   But thou art neither like thy sire nor dam,
    But like a foul misshapen stigmatic,⁶
    Marked by the destinies⁷ to be avoided,
    As venom° toads or lizards' dreadful stings.   poisonous
RICHARD   Iron of Naples, hid with English gilt,⁸
140   Whose father bears the title of a king—
    As if a channel° should be called the sea—   gutter
    Sham'st thou not, knowing whence thou art extraught,°   descended
    To let thy tongue detect° thy base-born heart?   reveal

---

5. From acting passionately. Passions were supposed to cause the heart to swell.
6. A deformed person; a criminal marked by means of an iron brand for his or her crime.
7. The Fates, three goddesses in classical mythology thought to determine the course of a person's life.

8. You cheap product of Naples, hiding under the gold veneer of an English marriage. Since Naples is synonymous in many Elizabethan texts with prostitution and venereal disease, "iron" may also refer to the metal noses allegedly worn by wealthy people to disguise the disfiguring effects of syphilis.

EDWARD   A wisp of straw[9] were° worth a thousand crowns   *would be*
145   To make this shameless callet° know herself.   *whore*
       Helen of Greece was fairer far than thou,
       Although thy husband may be Menelaus;[1]
       And ne'er was Agamemnon's brother° wronged   *(Menelaus)*
       By that false woman, as this king by thee.
150   His father° revelled in the heart of France,   *(Henry V)*
       And tamed the King, and made the Dauphin[2] stoop;
       And had he matched° according to his state,°   *(Henry VI) wed / rank*
       He might have kept that glory to this day.
       But when he took a beggar to his bed,
155   And graced thy poor sire with his bridal day,[3]
       Even then that sunshine brewed a shower for him
       That washed his father's fortunes forth of° France,   *out of*
       And heaped sedition on his crown at home.
       For what hath broached this tumult but thy pride?
160   Hadst thou been meek, our title° still had slept,   *claim to the throne*
       And we, in pity of the gentle King,
       Had slipped° our claim until another age.   *postponed*
       GEORGE [*to* QUEEN MARGARET]   But when we saw our sunshine
              made thy spring,
       And that thy summer bred us no increase,°   *harvest*
165   We set the axe to thy usurping root.
       And though the edge hath something° hit ourselves,   *to some extent*
       Yet know thou, since we have begun to strike,
       We'll never leave till we have hewn thee down,
       Or bathed thy growing with our heated bloods.
170   EDWARD [*to* QUEEN MARGARET]   And in this resolution I defy thee,
       Not willing any longer conference
       Since thou deniest the gentle King to speak.
       Sound trumpets—let our bloody colours wave!
       And either victory, or else a grave!
175   QUEEN MARGARET   Stay, Edward.
       EDWARD   No, wrangling woman, we'll no longer stay—
       These words will cost ten thousand lives this day.
              [*Flourish. March.*] *Exeunt* [EDWARD *and his men*
                    at one door and QUEEN MARGARET *and her men*
                                        at another door][4]

2.3

              Alarum. Excursions.° *Enter* [*the Earl of*] WARWICK[1]   *Skirmishes*
WARWICK   Forespent° with toil, as runners with a race   *Exhausted*
       I lay me down a little while to breathe;°   *rest*
       For strokes received, and many blows repaid,

---

9. Being made to wear or hold straw was a practice by which women were marked as scolds in public shaming rituals.
1. The Trojan War was said to have begun because the Greek Helen, the most beautiful woman in the world, betrayed her husband, Menelaus, and eloped with the Trojan warrior Paris.
2. The French King's oldest son, later Charles VII of France.
3. And brought honor to your impoverished father by marrying you.

4. Oxford proposes that Edward and Margaret and their men exit at separate stage doors to indicate symbolically their enmity. F and O read simply "Exeunt omnes."
2.3 Location: The remaining scenes in Act 2 take place in the fields near York.
1. While Shakespeare does not specify the locale, the events in this and the following three scenes resemble those associated with a battle waged at Towton in Yorkshire in 1461.

Have robbed my strong-knit° sinews of their strength,   *powerful*

5   And, spite of spite,° needs must I rest a while.   *come what may*

              Enter EDWARD [*the Duke of York*] *running*

EDWARD   Smile, gentle heaven, or strike, ungentle° death!   *ignoble*

For this world frowns, and Edward's sun² is clouded.

WARWICK   How now, my lord, what hap?° What hope of good?   *fortune*

              Enter GEORGE [*running*]

GEORGE   Our hap is loss, our hope but sad despair;

10   Our ranks are broke, and ruin follows us.

What counsel give you? Whither shall we fly?

EDWARD   Bootless° is flight—they follow us with wings,   *Useless*

And weak we are, and cannot shun pursuit.

              Enter RICHARD, *running*

RICHARD   Ah, Warwick, why hast thou withdrawn thyself?

15   Thy brother's³ blood the thirsty earth hath drunk,

Broached° with the steely point of Clifford's lance.   *Set flowing*

And in the very pangs of death he cried,

Like to a dismal clangour heard from far,

'Warwick, revenge—brother, revenge my death!'

20   So, underneath the belly of their steeds

That stained their fetlocks in his smoking° blood,   *steaming*

The noble gentleman gave up the ghost.

WARWICK   Then let the earth be drunken with our blood.

I'll kill my horse, because I will not fly.

25   Why stand we like soft-hearted women here,

Wailing our losses, whiles the foe doth rage;

And look upon,° as if the tragedy   *on*

Were played in jest by counterfeiting actors?

[*Kneeling*]   Here, on my knee, I vow to God above

30   I'll never pause again, never stand still,

Till either death hath closed these eyes of mine

Or fortune given me measure of revenge.

EDWARD [*kneeling*]   O, Warwick, I do bend my knee with thine,

And in this vow do chain my soul to thine.

35   And, ere my knee rise from the earth's cold face,

I throw my hands, mine eyes, my heart to Thee,°   *(God)*

Thou setter up and plucker down of kings,⁴

Beseeching Thee, if with Thy will it stands°   *agrees*

That to my foes this body must be prey,

40   Yet that Thy brazen gates of heaven may ope

And give sweet passage to my sinful soul.

          [*They rise*]

Now, lords, take leave until we meet again,

Where'er it be, in heaven or in earth.

RICHARD   Brother, give me thy hand; and, gentle° Warwick,   *noble*

45   Let me embrace thee in my weary arms.

I, that did never weep, now melt with woe

That winter should cut off our springtime so.

WARWICK   Away, away! Once more, sweet lords, farewell.

GEORGE   Yet let us all together to our troops,

50   And give them leave° to fly that will not stay;   *permission*

---

2. Good fortune, alluding to the sun as Edward's emblem.

3. Warwick's half brother, the Bastard of Salisbury.

4. Echoing a biblical description of God in Daniel 2:21 See also 3.3.157, where Margaret calls Warwick the "setter-up and puller-down of kings."

And call them pillars that will stand to° us;   *by*
And, if we thrive, promise them such rewards
As victors wear at the Olympian games.[5]
This may plant courage in their quailing breasts,
55   For yet is hope of life and victory.
Forslow° no longer—make we hence amain.°   *Exeunt*   *Delay / speedily*

2.4

Alarums. Excursions. Enter RICHARD *at one door*
and [Lord] CLIFFORD *at the other*

RICHARD   Now, Clifford, I have singled thee alone[1]
Suppose this arm is for the Duke of York,
And this for Rutland, both bound to revenge,
Wert thou environed° with a brazen wall.   *surrounded*
5   CLIFFORD   Now, Richard, I am with thee here alone.
This is the hand that stabbed thy father York,
And this the hand that slew thy brother Rutland,
And here's the heart that triumphs in their death
And cheers these hands that slew thy sire and brother
10   To execute the like upon thyself—
And so, have at thee!
        They fight. [The Earl of] WARWICK *comes and rescues*
        RICHARD. *[Lord]* CLIFFORD *flies*
RICHARD   Nay, Warwick, single out some other chase°—   *prey*
For I myself will hunt this wolf to death.   *Exeunt*

2.5

Alarum. Enter KING HENRY

KING HENRY   This battle fares like to the morning's war,[1]
When dying clouds contend with growing light.
What time° the shepherd, blowing of° his nails,   *When / on*
Can neither call it perfect day nor night.
5   Now sways it this way like a mighty sea
Forced by the tide to combat with the wind,
Now sways it that way like the selfsame sea
Forced to retire by fury of the wind.
Sometime the flood prevails, and then the wind;
10   Now one the better, then another best—
Both tugging to be victors, breast to breast,
Yet neither conqueror nor conquerèd.
So is the equal poise° of this fell° war.   *balance / deadly*
Here on this molehill[2] will I sit me down.
15   To whom God will, there be the victory.
For Margaret my queen, and Clifford, too,
Have chid me from the battle, swearing both
They prosper best of all when I am thence.
Would I were dead, if God's good will were so—
20   For what is in this world but grief and woe?

---

5. The Olympian Games in ancient Greece were festivals that included athletic contests. Victors were presented with garlands of olive leaves.
2.4
1. I have isolated you from the herd (a hunting
term).

2.5
1. In O, King Henry's ensuing fifty-four-line soliloquy
as found in F is reduced to thirteen lines, perhaps
shortened for performance.
2. See 1.4.68, where Richard, Duke of York is made to
stand on a molehill before his death.

O God! Methinks it were a happy life
To be no better than a homely swain.°   *simple shepherd*
To sit upon a hill, as I do now;
To carve out dials quaintly,° point by point,   *sundials artfully*
25   Thereby to see the minutes how they run:
How many makes the hour full complete,
How many hours brings about° the day,   *completes*
How many days will finish up the year,
How many years a mortal man may live.
30   When this is known, then to divide the times:
So many hours must I tend my flock,
So many hours must I take my rest,
So many hours must I contemplate,
So many hours must I sport myself,
35   So many days my ewes have been with young,
So many weeks ere the poor fools will ean,°   *give birth*
So many years ere I shall shear the fleece.
So minutes, hours, days, weeks, months, and years,
Passed over to the end they° were created,   *for which they*
40   Would bring white hairs unto a quiet grave.
Ah, what a life were this! How sweet! How lovely!
Gives not the hawthorn bush a sweeter shade
To shepherds looking on their seely° sheep   *innocent*
Than doth a rich embroidered canopy
45   To kings that fear their subjects' treachery?
O yes, it doth—a thousandfold it doth.
And to conclude, the shepherd's homely curds,
His cold thin drink out of his leather bottle,
His wonted° sleep under a fresh tree's shade,   *customary*
50   All which secure and sweetly he enjoys,
Is far beyond a prince's delicates,°   *delicacies*
His viands° sparkling in a golden cup,   *food*
His body couchèd in a curious° bed,   *an ornate*
When care, mistrust, and treason waits on him.
      Alarum. Enter at one door a SOLDIER *with a dead man*
      in his arms. [KING HENRY *stands apart*]³
55   SOLDIER   Ill blows the wind that profits nobody.
This man, whom hand to hand I slew in fight,
May be possessèd with some store of crowns;°   *coins*
And I, that haply° take them from him now,   *by chance*
May yet ere night yield both my life and them
60   To some man else, as this dead man doth me.
      [*He removes the dead man's helmet*]
Who's this? O God! It is my father's face
Whom in this conflict I, unwares, have killed.
O, heavy times, begetting such events!
From London by the King was I pressed forth;⁴
65   My father, being the Earl of Warwick's man,°   *servant*

3. Here Oxford adopts a combination of Folio and Octavo staging. F indicates a simultaneous entrance, at two different doors, of a "Son that hath kill'd his Father" and a "Father that hath kill'd his Son." O, as here, designates both figures as simply "a soldier with a dead man in his arms" and "another soldier with a dead man," and gives them entrances at lines 54 and 78,

respectively, but without mention of two doors. In O, the relationship between the living and the dead is revealed through the dialogue only.
4. Forcibly enlisted. Because England had no standing army until the latter half of the seventeenth century, many soldiers in Elizabethan England were conscripts.

Came on the part° of York, pressed by his master;   *side*
And I, who at his hands received my life,
Have by my hands of life bereavèd him.
Pardon me, God, I knew not what I did;
70   And pardon, father, for I knew not thee.
My tears shall wipe away these bloody marks,
And no more words till they have flowed their fill.
      [*He weeps*]
KING HENRY   O piteous spectacle! O bloody times!
Whiles lions war and battle for their dens,
75   Poor harmless lambs abide their enmity.
Weep, wretched man, I'll aid thee tear for tear;
And let our hearts and eyes, like civil war,
Be blind with tears, and break, o'ercharged° with grief.   *overburdened*
      Enter at another door another SOLDIER *with a dead*
      man [*in his arms*]
SECOND SOLDIER   Thou that so stoutly hath resisted me,
80   Give me thy gold, if thou hast any gold—
For I have bought it with an hundred blows.
      [*He removes the dead man's helmet*]
But let me see: is this our foeman's° face?   *enemy's*
Ah, no, no, no—it is mine only son!
Ah, boy, if any life be left in thee,
85   Throw up thine eye! [*Weeping*] See, see, what showers arise,
Blown with the windy tempest of my heart,
Upon thy wounds, that kills mine eye and heart!
O, pity, God, this miserable age!
What stratagems,° how fell,° how butcherly,   *violent acts / cruel*
90   Erroneous,° mutinous, and unnatural,   *Criminal*
This deadly quarrel daily doth beget!
O boy, thy father gave thee life too soon,
And hath bereft thee of thy life too late!°   *recently*
KING HENRY   Woe above woe! Grief more than common grief!
95   O that my death would stay° these ruthful° deeds!   *stop / pitiful*
O, pity, pity, gentle heaven, pity!
The red rose and the white are on his face,
The fatal colours of our striving houses;
The one his purple blood right well resembles,
100 The other his pale cheeks, methinks, presenteth.
Wither one rose, and let the other flourish—
If you contend, a thousand lives must wither.
FIRST SOLDIER   How will my mother for a father's death
Take on with° me, and ne'er be satisfied!   *Rage against*
105 SECOND SOLDIER   How will my wife for slaughter of my son
Shed seas of tears, and ne'er be satisfied!
KING HENRY   How will the country for these woeful chances°   *events*
Misthink° the King, and not be satisfied!   *Think ill of*
FIRST SOLDIER   Was ever son so rued a father's death?
110 SECOND SOLDIER   Was ever father so bemoaned his son?
KING HENRY   Was ever king so grieved for subjects' woe?
Much is your sorrow, mine ten times so much.
FIRST SOLDIER [*to his father's body*]   I'll bear thee hence where
I may weep my fill.
      Exit [*at one door*] *with* [*the body of*] *his father*

SECOND SOLDIER [*to his son's body*]   These arms of mine shall be
         thy winding sheet;°   *shroud*
115   My heart, sweet boy, shall be thy sepulchre,
      For from my heart thine image ne'er shall go.
      My sighing breast shall be thy funeral bell,
      And so obsequious° will thy father be,   *dutiful in mourning*
      E'en for the loss of thee, having no more,
120   As Priam⁵ was for all his valiant sons.
      I'll bear thee hence, and let them fight that will—
      For I have murdered where I should not kill.
              Exit [*at another door*] *with* [*the body of*] *his son*
KING HENRY   Sad-hearted men, much overgone° with care,   *overcome*
      Here sits a king more woeful than you are.
              Alarums. Excursions. Enter PRINCE EDWARD⁶
125   PRINCE EDWARD   Fly, father, fly—for all your friends are fled,
      And Warwick rages like a chafèd° bull!   *an angered*
      Away—for death doth hold us in pursuit!
              Enter QUEEN [MARGARET]
QUEEN MARGARET   Mount you, my lord—towards Berwick⁷ post
         amain.°   *ride speedily*
      Edward and Richard, like a brace° of greyhounds   *pair*
130   Having the fearful flying hare in sight,
      With fiery eyes sparkling for very wrath,
      And bloody steel grasped in their ireful hands,
      Are at our backs—and therefore hence amain.°   *at full speed*
              Enter EXETER
EXETER   Away—for vengeance comes along with them!
135   Nay—stay not to expostulate°—make speed—   *argue*
      Or else come after. I'll away before.
KING HENRY   Nay, take me with thee, good sweet Exeter.
      Not that I fear to stay, but love to go
      Whither the Queen intends. Forward, away.   *Exeunt*

2.6

              A loud alarum. Enter [*Lord*] CLIFFORD, *wounded with*
              an arrow in his neck
CLIFFORD   Here burns my candle out—ay, here it dies,
      Which, whiles it lasted, gave King Henry light.
      O Lancaster, I fear thy overthrow
      More than my body's parting with my soul!
5   My love and fear° glued many friends to thee—   *Love and fear of me*
      And, now I fall, thy tough commixture¹ melts,
      Impairing Henry, strength'ning misproud° York.   *arrogant*
      The common people swarm like summer flies,
      And whither fly the gnats but to the sun?²
10   And who shines now but Henry's enemies?
      O Phoebus, hadst thou never given consent
      That Phaëton³ should check° thy fiery steeds,   *manage*

5. King of Troy during the Trojan War. His fifty sons,
of whom Hector was one, were killed defending the city.
6. F indicates a single entrance for "the Queen, the
Prince, and Exeter" at line 124, and they speak in the
order Prince-Queen-Exeter; O has Margaret enter first,
then Prince Edward, and finally Exeter. Oxford follows
O and divides the entrances, but places them in F's
order of speech.

7. Berwick-upon-Tweed, a village near Scotland in
Northumberland.
2.6
1. The compound of love and fear that I commanded.
2. Alluding to the sun as Edward's emblem. See note
to 2.1.40.
3. The son of Phoebus, god of the sun. See note
to 1.4.34.

Thy burning car° never had scorched the earth!   *chariot*
And, Henry, hadst thou swayed° as kings should do,   *ruled*
15 Or as thy father and his father did,
Giving no ground unto the house of York,
They never then had sprung like summer flies;
I and ten thousand in this luckless realm
Had left no mourning widows for our death;
20 And thou this day hadst kept thy chair° in peace.   *throne*
For what doth cherish° weeds, but gentle air?   *nurture*
And what makes robbers bold, but too much lenity?
Bootless are plaints,° and cureless are my wounds;   *Useless are pleas*
No way to fly, nor strength to hold out flight;
25 The foe is merciless and will not pity,
For at their hands I have deserved no pity.
The air hath got into my deadly wounds,
And much effuse° of blood doth make me faint.   *effusion*
Come York and Richard, Warwick and the rest—
30 I stabbed your fathers' bosoms; split my breast.
      [*He faints.*]
      Alarum and retreat. Enter EDWARD [*Duke of York, his*
      brothers] GEORGE *and* RICHARD, [*the Earl of*] WARWICK,
      [*the Marquis of*] MONTAGUE, *and soldiers*[4]
EDWARD   Now breathe we, lords—good fortune bids us pause,
And smooth the frowns of war with peaceful looks.
Some troops pursue the bloody-minded Queen,
That led calm Henry, though he were a king,
35 As doth a sail filled with a fretting° gust   *blowing fitfully*
Command an argosy° to stem° the waves.   *a merchant ship / resist*
But think you, lords, that Clifford fled with them?
WARWICK   No—'tis impossible he should escape;
For, though before his face I speak the words,
40 Your brother Richard marked him for the grave.
And whereso'er he is, he's surely dead.
      CLIFFORD *groans*
EDWARD   Whose soul is that which takes her heavy leave?[5]
RICHARD   A deadly groan, like life and death's departing.
EDWARD [*to* RICHARD]   See who it is.
      [RICHARD *goes to* CLIFFORD]
                    And now the battle's ended,
45 If friend or foe, let him be gently used.
RICHARD   Revoke that doom° of mercy, for 'tis Clifford;   *sentence*
Who not contented that he lopped the branch
In hewing Rutland when his leaves put forth,
But set his murd'ring knife unto the root
50 From whence that tender spray° did sweetly spring—   *shoot*
I mean our princely father, Duke of York.
WARWICK   From off the gates of York fetch down the head,
Your father's head, which Clifford placèd there.
Instead whereof let this supply the room[6]—

---

4. In F, the order of names in the stage direction ends with "Montague and Clarence" (George) placed after "Soldiers." The peculiarity of listing these noble figures last may suggest that they were added as an afterthought. Montague does not speak during the scene. Neither he nor George is indicated in O's stage directions, in which George speaks the same lines as in F.
5. In F, lines 42 and 43 and half of line 44 are assigned to Richard. O divides them as here. Oxford, as elsewhere, argues that this is an instance of authorial revision between foul papers and promptbook.
6. Let Clifford's head take its place.

55   Measure for measure⁷ must be answerèd.°   *given in return*

    EDWARD   Bring forth that fatal screech-owl to our house,⁸

        That nothing sung but death to us and ours.

        [CLIFFORD *is dragged forward*]

        Now death shall stop his dismal threat'ning sound

        And his ill-boding° tongue no more shall speak.   *doom-promising*

60   WARWICK   I think his understanding is bereft.°   *destroyed*

        Speak, Clifford, dost thou know who speaks to thee?

        Dark cloudy death o'ershades his beams of life,

        And he nor° sees nor hears us what we say.   *neither*

    RICHARD   O, would he did—and so perhaps he doth.

65   'Tis but his policy to counterfeit,

        Because he would avoid such bitter taunts

        Which in the time of death he gave our father.

    GEORGE   If so thou think'st, vex him with eager° words.   *bitter*

    RICHARD   Clifford, ask mercy and obtain no grace.

70   EDWARD   Clifford, repent in bootless penitence.

    WARWICK   Clifford, devise excuses for thy faults.

    GEORGE   While we devise fell° tortures for thy faults.   *cruel*

    RICHARD   Thou didst love York, and I am son to York.

    EDWARD   Thou pitied'st Rutland—I will pity thee.

75   GEORGE   Where's Captain Margaret to fence° you now?   *protect*

    WARWICK   They mock thee, Clifford—swear as thou wast wont.

    RICHARD   What, not an oath? Nay, then, the world goes hard

        When Clifford cannot spare his friends an oath.

        I know by that he's dead—and, by my soul,

80   If this right hand would buy but two hours' life

        That I, in all despite, might rail at him,

        This hand° should chop it off, and with the issuing blood   *(his left hand)*

        Stifle° the villain whose unstanchèd° thirst   *Choke / insatiable*

        York and young Rutland could not satisfy.

85   WARWICK   Ay, but he's dead. Off with the traitor's head,

        And rear it in the place your father's stands.

        And now to London with triumphant march,

        There to be crownèd England's royal king;

        From whence shall Warwick cut the sea to France,

90   And ask the Lady Bona⁹ for thy queen.

        So shalt thou sinew° both these lands together.   *tie firmly*

        And, having France thy friend, thou shalt not dread

        The scattered foe that hopes to rise again,

        For though they cannot greatly sting to hurt,

95   Yet look to have them buzz to offend thine ears.

        First will I see the coronation,

        And then to Brittany I'll cross the sea

        To effect this marriage, so it please my lord.

    EDWARD   Even as thou wilt, sweet Warwick, let it be.

100   For in thy shoulder° do I build my seat,   *with your support*

        And never will I undertake the thing

        Wherein thy counsel and consent is wanting.

        Richard, I will create thee Duke of Gloucester,

---

7. Alluding to the strict rule of justice described in Mark 4:24: "With what measure ye mete, it shall be measured unto you."

8. Bring forth that creature ominous to our house.

Screech owls were traditionally thought to be harbingers of death.

9. The sister-in-law of King Louis XI of France and daughter of Louis, Duke of Savoy.

And George, of Clarence; Warwick, as ourself,
105   Shall do and undo as him pleaseth best.
RICHARD   Let me be Duke of Clarence. George of Gloucester—
    For Gloucester's dukedom is too ominous.[1]
WARWICK   Tut, that's a foolish observation—
    Richard, be Duke of Gloucester. Now to London
110   To see these honours in possession.
                     Exeunt. [York's head is removed]

3.1

Enter two [GAME]KEEPERS, *with crossbows in their hands*

FIRST GAMEKEEPER   Under this thick-grown brake° we'll shroud   *thicket*
    ourselves,
    For through this laund° anon the deer will come,   *clearing*
    And in this covert will we make our stand,
    Culling the principal° of all the deer.   *Selecting the best*
5 SECOND GAMEKEEPER   I'll stay above the hill, so both may shoot.
FIRST GAMEKEEPER   That cannot be—the noise of thy crossbow
    Will scare the herd, and so my shoot is lost.
    Here stand we both, and aim we at the best.°   *as well as we can*
    And, for° the time shall not seem tedious,   *so that*
10   I'll tell thee what befell me on a day
    In this self place where now we mean to stand.
FIRST GAMEKEEPER   Here comes a man—let's stay till he be past.
    [*They stand apart.*]
    Enter KING HENRY, *disguised, with a prayer-book*
KING HENRY   From Scotland am I stolen, even of° pure love,   *out of*
    To greet mine own land with my wishful° sight.   *longing*
15   No, Harry, Harry—'tis no land of thine.
    Thy place is filled, thy sceptre wrung from thee,
    Thy balm washed off wherewith thou wast anointed.
    No bending knee will call thee Caesar° now,   *emperor*
    No humble suitors press to speak for right,°   *beg for justice*
20   No, not a man comes for redress of° thee—   *from*
    For how can I help them and not myself?
FIRST GAMEKEEPER [*to the* SECOND GAMEKEEPER]   Ay, here's a
    deer whose skin's a keeper's fee:[1]
    This is the quondam° king—let's seize upon him.   *former*
KING HENRY   Let me embrace thee, sour adversity,
25   For wise men say it is the wisest course.
SECOND GAMEKEEPER [*to the* FIRST GAMEKEEPER]   Why linger
    we? Let us lay hands upon him
FIRST GAMEKEEPER [*to the* SECOND GAMEKEEPER]   Forbear
    awhile—we'll hear a little more.
KING HENRY   My queen and son are gone to France for aid,
    And, as I hear, the great commanding Warwick
30   Is thither gone to crave the French King's sister
    To wife for Edward. If this news be true,
    Poor Queen and son, your labour is but lost—
    For Warwick is a subtle orator,
    And Louis a prince soon won with moving words.

---

1. Referring to the fact that three previous Dukes of Gloucester had suffered violent deaths.
3.1 Location: A forest in northern England near the Scottish border.
1. Traditionally, hunters presented the horns and skin of a captured deer to the park's gamekeeper.

35	By this account, then, Margaret may win him—
	For she's a woman to be pitied much.
	Her sighs will make a batt'ry° in his breast,	*a breach*
	Her tears will pierce into a marble heart,
	The tiger will be mild whiles she doth mourn,
40	And Nero² will be tainted° with remorse	*touched*
	To hear and see her plaints,° her brinish° tears.	*pleas / salty*
	Ay, but she's come to beg; Warwick to give.
	She on his left side, craving aid for Henry;
	He on his right, asking a wife for Edward.
45	She weeps and says her Henry is deposed,
	He smiles and says his Edward is installed;
	That she, poor wretch, for grief can speak no more,
	Whiles Warwick tells his title,³ smooths the wrong,
	Inferreth° arguments of mighty strength,	*Presents*
50	And in conclusion wins the King from her
	With promise of his sister and what else
	To strengthen and support King Edward's place.
	O, Margaret, thus 'twill be; and thou, poor soul,
	Art then forsaken, as thou went'st forlorn.
	SECOND GAMEKEEPER [*coming forward*] Say, what art thou that
55	talk'st of kings and queens?
	KING HENRY More than I seem, and less than I was born to:
	A man at least, for less I should not be;
	And men may talk of kings, and why not I?
	SECOND GAMEKEEPER Ay, but thou talk'st as if thou wert a king.
60	KING HENRY Why, so I am, in mind—and that's enough.
	SECOND GAMEKEEPER But if thou be a king, where is thy crown?
	KING HENRY My crown is in my heart, not on my head;
	Not decked with diamonds and Indian stones,°	*pearls*
	Nor to be seen. My crown is called content—
65	A crown it is that seldom kings enjoy.
	SECOND GAMEKEEPER Well, if you be a king crowned with content,
	Your crown content and you must be contented
	To go along with us—for, as we think,
	You are the king King Edward hath deposed,
70	And we his subjects sworn in all allegiance
	Will apprehend you as his enemy.
	KING HENRY But did you never swear and break an oath?
	SECOND GAMEKEEPER No—never such an oath, nor will not now.
	KING HENRY Where did you dwell when I was King of England?
75	SECOND GAMEKEEPER Here in this country, where we now remain.
	KING HENRY I was anointed king at nine months old,
	My father and my grandfather were kings,
	And you were sworn true subjects unto me—
	And tell me, then, have you not broke your oaths?
80	FIRST GAMEKEEPER No, for we were subjects but° while you were king.	*only*
	KING HENRY Why, am I dead? Do I not breathe a man?
	Ah, simple men, you know not what you swear.
	Look as I blow this feather from my face,

---

2. A notoriously cruel Roman Emperor.   3. While Warwick asserts Edward's claim to the throne.

And as the air blows it to me again.
85 Obeying with° my wind when I do blow,   *Submitting to*
And yielding to another when it blows,
Commanded always by the greater gust—
Such is the lightness° of you common men.   *fickleness*
But do not break your oaths, for of that sin
90 My mild entreaty shall not make you guilty.
Go where you will, the King shall be commanded;
And be you kings, command, and I'll obey.

FIRST GAMEKEEPER   We are true subjects to the King, King Edward.

KING HENRY   So would you be again to Henry,
95 If he were seated as King Edward is.

FIRST GAMEKEEPER   We charge you, in God's name and in the King's,
To go with us unto the officers.

KING HENRY   In God's name, lead; your king's name be obeyed;
And what God will, that let your king perform;
100 And what he will I humbly yield unto.   *Exeunt*

3.2

Enter KING EDWARD, [RICHARD *Duke* OF] GLOUCESTER,
[GEORGE *Duke* OF] CLARENCE, *and the* LADY GRAY

KING EDWARD   Brother of Gloucester, at Saint Albans field
This lady's husband, Sir Richard Gray, was slain,
His lands then seized on by the conqueror.
Her suit is now to repossess those lands,
5 Which we in justice cannot well deny,
Because in quarrel of the house of York
The worthy gentleman did lose his life.

RICHARD OF GLOUCESTER   Your highness shall do well to grant her suit—
It were dishonour to deny it her.

10 KING EDWARD   It were no less; but yet I'll make a pause.

RICHARD OF GLOUCESTER [*aside to* GEORGE]   Yea, is it so?
I see the lady hath a thing° to grant   *(sexual) favor*
Before the King will grant her humble suit.

GEORGE OF CLARENCE [*aside to* RICHARD]   He knows the game;
how true he keeps the wind![1]

15 RICHARD OF GLOUCESTER [*aside to* GEORGE]   Silence.

KING EDWARD [*to* LADY GRAY]   Widow, we will consider of your suit;
And come some other time to know our mind.

LADY GRAY   Right gracious lord, I cannot brook° delay.   *tolerate*
May it please your highness to resolve me now,
20 And what your pleasure° is shall satisfy me.   *will; sexual desire*

RICHARD OF GLOUCESTER [*aside to* GEORGE]   Ay, widow? Then
I'll warrant° you all your lands   *guarantee*
An if° what pleases him shall pleasure you.   *An if = If*

3.2 Location: The palace, London.
1. "The game" suggests the "sport" of hunting animals
or of pursuing sex partners, as well as the objects of
both pursuits. Hounds "keep the wind" by keeping the
prey against the wind so that it does not catch the scent
of the hunter and run away. Clarence implies that
Edward pursues Lady Gray with similar skill. The following lines are full of sexual wordplay that Clarence
and Richard clearly intend, but that Lady Gray probably does not.

Fight closer, or, good faith, you'll catch a blow.[2]

GEORGE OF CLARENCE [*aside to* RICHARD]   I fear° her not unless   *fear for*
   she chance to fall.[3]

RICHARD OF GLOUCESTER [*aside to* GEORGE]   God forbid that!
25   For he'll take vantages.°   *opportunities*

KING EDWARD [*to* LADY GRAY]   How many children hast thou,
   widow? Tell me.

GEORGE OF CLARENCE [*aside to* RICHARD]   I think he means to
   beg a child of her.[4]

RICHARD OF GLOUCESTER [*aside to* GEORGE]   Nay, whip me
   then—he'll rather give her two.

LADY GRAY [*to* KING EDWARD]   Three, my most gracious lord.

RICHARD OF GLOUCESTER [*aside*]   You shall have four, an° you'll   *if*
30   be ruled by him.

KING EDWARD [*to* LADY GRAY]   'Twere pity they should lose their
   father's lands.

LADY GRAY   Be pitiful, dread lord, and grant it them.

KING EDWARD [*to* RICHARD *and* GEORGE]   Lords, give us leave°—   *leave us alone*
   I'll try this widow's wit.

RICHARD OF GLOUCESTER [*aside to* GEORGE]   Ay, good leave
   have you; for you will have leave,
35   Till youth take leave and leave you to the crutch.[5]
     [RICHARD *and* GEORGE *stand apart*]

KING EDWARD [*to* LADY GRAY]   Now tell me, madam, do you love
   your children?

LADY GRAY   Ay, full as dearly as I love myself.

KING EDWARD   And would you not do much to do them good?

LADY GRAY   To do them good I would sustain some harm.

40 KING EDWARD   Then get your husband's lands, to do them good.

LADY GRAY   Therefore I came unto your majesty.

KING EDWARD   I'll tell you how these lands are to be got.

LADY GRAY   So shall you bind me to your highness' service.

KING EDWARD   What service wilt thou do me, if I give them?

45 LADY GRAY   What you command, that rests in me to do.

KING EDWARD   But you will take exceptions to my boon.°   *request*

LADY GRAY   No, gracious lord, except° I cannot do it.   *unless*

KING EDWARD   Ay, but thou canst do what I mean to ask.

LADY GRAY   Why, then, I will do what your grace commands.

RICHARD OF GLOUCESTER [*to* GEORGE]   He plies her hard, and
50   much rain wears the marble.

GEORGE OF CLARENCE   As red as fire! Nay, then her wax must
   melt.

LADY GRAY [*to* KING EDWARD]   Why stops my lord? Shall I not
   hear my task?

KING EDWARD   An easy task—'tis but to love a king.

LADY GRAY   That's soon performed, because I am a subject.

---

2. Fight nearer to avoid his thrusts. Conflating sexual slang and the language of dueling, Richard puns on "blow" as meaning both "hit" and "sexual thrust."
3. Stumble; submit to sex.
4. To ask her to bear him a child; to petition for guardianship of one of her children. English monarchs generated income by gaining control of wealthy orphans from the Court of Wards and Liveries and arranging their marriages in ways profitable to the monarch.
5. *Ay . . . crutch:* Yes, we will leave you alone, for you will take liberties (with Lady Gray) until your youth departs and leaves you walking on crutches (too old for love). The multiple puns in these lines include "crutch" as a play on "crotch."

55   KING EDWARD   Why, then, thy husband's lands I freely give thee.

LADY GRAY [*curtsies*]   I take my leave, with many thousand thanks.

RICHARD OF GLOUCESTER [*to* GEORGE]   The match is made—she
    seals it with a curtsy.

KING EDWARD [*to* LADY GRAY]   But stay thee—'tis the fruits of
    love I mean.

LADY GRAY   The fruits of love *I* mean, my loving liege.

60   KING EDWARD   Ay, but I fear me in another sense.
    What love think'st thou I sue so much to get?

LADY GRAY   My love till death, my humble thanks, my prayers—
    That love which virtue begs and virtue grants.

KING EDWARD   No, by my troth, I did not mean such love.

65   LADY GRAY   Why, then, you mean not as I thought you did.

KING EDWARD   But now you partly may perceive my mind.

LADY GRAY   My mind will never grant what I perceive
    Your highness aims at, if I aim aright.°   *guess correctly*

KING EDWARD   To tell thee plain, I aim to lie with thee.

70   LADY GRAY   To tell *you* plain, I had rather lie in prison.

KING EDWARD   Why, then, thou shalt not have thy husband's
    lands.

LADY GRAY   Why, then, mine honesty° shall be my dower;   *chastity*
    For by that loss I will not purchase them.

KING EDWARD   Therein thou wrong'st thy children mightily.

75   LADY GRAY   Herein your highness wrongs both them and me.
    But, mighty lord, this merry inclination
    Accords not with the sadness° of my suit.   *seriousness*
    Please you dismiss me either with ay or no.

KING EDWARD   Ay, if thou wilt say 'ay' to my request;

80   No, if thou dost say 'no' to my demand.

LADY GRAY   Then, no, my lord—my suit is at an end.

RICHARD OF GLOUCESTER [*to* GEORGE]   The widow likes him
    not—she knits her brows.

GEORGE OF CLARENCE   He is the bluntest wooer in Christendom.

KING EDWARD [*aside*]   Her looks doth argue° her replete with modesty;   *prove*

85   Her words doth show her wit incomparable;
    All her perfections challenge° sovereignty.   *lay claim to*
    One way or other, she is for a king;
    And she shall be my love or else my queen.
    [*To* LADY GRAY] Say that King Edward take thee for his queen?

90   LADY GRAY   'Tis better said than done, my gracious lord.
    I am a subject fit to jest withal,
    But far unfit to be a sovereign.

KING EDWARD   Sweet widow, by my state° I swear to thee   *kingship*
    I speak no more than what my soul intends,

95   And that is to enjoy thee for my love.

LADY GRAY   And that is more than I will yield unto.
    I know I am too mean to be your queen,
    And yet too good to be your concubine.

KING EDWARD   You cavil,° widow—I did mean my queen.   *object frivolously*

100   LADY GRAY   'Twill grieve your grace my sons should call you father.

KING EDWARD   No more than when my daughters call thee mother.
    Thou art a widow and thou hast some children;
    And, by God's mother, I, being but a bachelor,
    Have other some.° Why, 'tis a happy thing   *some others*

105   To be the father unto many sons.
    Answer no more, for thou shalt be my queen.
    RICHARD OF GLOUCESTER [*to* GEORGE]   The ghostly father°   *priest*
    now hath done his shrift.[6]
    GEORGE OF CLARENCE   When he was made a shriver, 'twas for
    shift.[7]
    KING EDWARD [*to* RICHARD *and* GEORGE]   Brothers, you muse°   *wonder*
    what chat we two have had.
    [RICHARD *and* GEORGE *come forward*]
    RICHARD OF GLOUCESTER   The widow likes it not, for she looks
110   very sad.
    KING EDWARD   You'd think it strange if I should marry her.
    GEORGE OF CLARENCE   To who, my lord?
    KING EDWARD   Why, Clarence, to myself.
    RICHARD OF GLOUCESTER   That would be ten days' wonder at
    the least.
    GEORGE OF CLARENCE   That's a day longer than a wonder lasts.[8]
115   RICHARD OF GLOUCESTER   By so much is the wonder in extremes.°   *exceedingly great*
    KING EDWARD   Well, jest on, brothers—I can tell you both
    Her suit is granted for her husband's lands.
          Enter a NOBLEMAN
    NOBLEMAN   My gracious lord, Henry your foe is taken
    And brought as prisoner to your palace gate.
120   KING EDWARD   See that he be conveyed unto the Tower—
    [*To* RICHARD *and* GEORGE] And go we, brothers, to the man
    that took him,
    To question of his apprehension.
    [*To* LADY GRAY] Widow, go you along. [*To* RICHARD *and* GEORGE]
    Lords, use her honourably.
             Exeunt. Manet° RICHARD   *Remains*
    RICHARD OF GLOUCESTER   Ay, Edward will use women honourably.
125   Would he were wasted, marrow, bones, and all,[9]
    That from his loins no hopeful branch may spring
    To cross° me from the golden time I look for.   *keep*
    And yet, between my soul's desire and me—
    The lustful Edward's title burièd°—   *eliminated*
130   Is Clarence, Henry, and his son young Edward,
    And all the unlooked-for° issue of their bodies,   *unforeseen*
    To take their rooms° ere I can place myself.   *places*
    A cold premeditation° for my purpose.   *A discouraging prospect*
    Why, then, I do but dream on sovereignty
135   Like one that stands upon a promontory
    And spies a far-off shore where he would tread,
    Wishing his foot were equal with his eye,[1]
    And chides the sea that sunders him from thence,
    Saying he'll lade° it dry to have his way—   *empty*
140   So do I wish° the crown being so far off,   *wish for*
    And so I chide the means that keeps me from it,

---

6. Has heard her confession and given absolution.
7. It was for a purpose; it was in order to gain access to her undergarments ("shift").
8. Referring to the proverbial expression "nine day's wonder," something that for a short while causes a sensation.
9. Would he were destroyed by disease. Elizabethan medical theory held that syphilis attacked the bones, affected male "mettle," or semen, and caused sterility.
1. Wishing he were able to attain what his eye sees.

And so I say I'll cut the causes off,
Flattering me with impossibilities.
My eye's too quick, my heart o'erweens° too much,   *presumes*
145   Unless my hand and strength could equal them.
Well, say there is no kingdom then for Richard—
What other pleasure can the world afford?
I'll make my heaven in a lady's lap,
And deck my body in gay ornaments,
150   And 'witch° sweet ladies with my words and looks.   *bewitch*
O, miserable thought! And more unlikely
Than to accomplish° twenty golden crowns.   *obtain*
Why, love forswore° me in my mother's womb,   *abandoned*
And, for° I should not deal in her soft laws,   *so that*
155   She did corrupt frail nature with some bribe
To shrink mine arm up like a withered shrub,
To make an envious° mountain on my back—   *a detested*
Where sits deformity to mock my body—
To shape my legs of an unequal size,
160   To disproportion me in every part,
Like to a chaos,° or an unlicked bear whelp[2]   *formless mass*
That carries no impression like the dam.[3]
And am I then a man to be beloved?
O, monstrous fault, to harbour such a thought!
165   Then, since this earth affords no joy to me
But to command, to check,° to o'erbear° such   *rebuke / dominate*
As are of better person° than myself,   *appearance*
I'll make my heaven to dream upon the crown,
And whiles I live, t'account this world but hell,
170   Until my misshaped trunk that bears this head
Be round impalèd° with a glorious crown.   *enclosed*
And yet I know not how to get the crown,
For many lives stand between me and home.°   *(my goal)*
And I—like one lost in a thorny wood,
175   That rends the thorns and is rent with the thorns,
Seeking a way and straying from the way,
Not knowing how to find the open air,
But toiling desperately to find it out—
Torment myself to catch the English crown.
180   And from that torment I will free myself,
Or hew my way out with a bloody axe.
Why, I can smile, and murder whiles I smile,
And cry 'Content!' to that which grieves my heart,
And wet my cheeks with artificial tears,
185   And frame my face to all occasions.
I'll drown more sailors than the mermaid[4] shall;
I'll slay more gazers than the basilisk;[5]
I'll play the orator as well as Nestor,[6]
Deceive more slyly than Ulysses[7] could,

---

2. Alluding to the popular belief that bears were born as formless lumps and licked into shape by their mothers.
3. That does not resemble its mother.
4. A fabulous marine monster, resembling a woman, who sang sweet songs to lure sailors onto the rocks and to their death.

5. A mythical reptile, hatched from a cock's egg, whose look was supposed to be fatal.
6. The Greek King and aged counselor present at the siege of Troy, famous for his skill in speech.
7. The Greek warrior famous for his cunning, hero of Homer's *Odyssey*.

190   And, like a Sinon,[8] take another Troy.
        I can add colours to the chameleon,[9]
        Change shapes with Proteus[1] for advantages,
        And set the murderous Machiavel[2] to school.
        Can I do this, and cannot get a crown?
195   Tut, were it farther off, I'll pluck it down.   *Exit*

3.3

[Two chairs of state.][1] Flourish. Enter KING LOUIS
[of France], his sister the LADY BONA, *[Lord] Bourbon*
his admiral, PRINCE EDWARD, QUEEN MARGARET,
and the Earl of OXFORD. LOUIS *[goes up upon the*
state,] sits, and riseth up again

    KING LOUIS   Fair Queen of England, worthy Margaret,
        Sit down with us. It ill befits thy state
        And birth that thou shouldst stand while Louis doth sit.
    QUEEN MARGARET   No, mighty King of France, now Margaret
5   Must strike her sail° and learn a while to serve   *humble herself*
        Where kings command. I was, I must confess,
        Great Albion's° queen in former golden days,   *England's*
        But now mischance hath trod my title down,
        And with dishonour laid me on the ground,
10   Where I must take like seat unto my fortune[2]
        And to my humble state conform myself.
    KING LOUIS   Why, say, fair Queen, whence springs this deep despair?
    QUEEN MARGARET   From such a cause as fills mine eyes with tears
        And stops my tongue, while heart is drowned in cares.
15   KING LOUIS   Whate'er it be, be thou still like thyself,
        And sit thee by our side.
        Seats her by him
                          Yield not thy neck
        To fortune's yoke, but let thy dauntless mind
        Still ride in triumph over all mischance.
        Be plain, Queen Margaret, and tell thy grief.
20   It shall be eased if France° can yield relief.   *the King of France*
    QUEEN MARGARET   Those gracious words revive my drooping
            thoughts,
        And give my tongue-tied sorrows leave to speak.
        Now, therefore, be it known to noble Louis
        That Henry, sole possessor of my love,
25   Is of° a king become a banished man,   *Instead of*

8. Like a treacherous man. According to Virgil, Sinon's lies convinced the Trojans to accept as a gift the wooden horse in which the Greek soldiers who later sacked Troy were concealed.
9. A reptile able to change the color of its skin in order to blend into its surroundings.
1. A Greek sea god who was able to assume different shapes at will.
2. Niccolò Machiavelli (1469–1527), an Italian political

philosopher popularly known in England as a depraved advocate of political cunning and ruthlessness.
3.3 Location: The King's palace, France.
1. Louis's request for Margaret to "sit down with us" at line 2 suggests that at least two chairs of state are required, possibly three (including one for Lady Bona).
2. Where I must take a position in keeping with my fortune.

And forced to live in Scotland a forlorn,°   *an outcast*
While proud ambitious Edward, Duke of York,
Usurps the regal title and the seat
Of England's true-anointed lawful King.
30   This is the cause that I, poor Margaret,
With this my son, Prince Edward, Henry's heir,
Am come to crave thy just and lawful aid.
An if thou fail us all our hope is done.
Scotland hath will to help, but cannot help;
35   Our people and our peers are both misled,
Our treasure seized, our soldiers put to flight,
And, as thou seest, ourselves in heavy plight.
KING LOUIS   Renownèd Queen, with patience calm the storm,
While we bethink a means to break it off.
40 QUEEN MARGARET   The more we stay,° the stronger grows our foe.   *delay*
KING LOUIS   The more I stay, the more I'll succour thee.
QUEEN MARGARET   O, but impatience waiteth on° true sorrow.   *attends*
        Enter [the Earl of] WARWICK
And see where comes the breeder of my sorrow.
KING LOUIS   What's he approacheth boldly to our presence?
45 QUEEN MARGARET   Our Earl of Warwick, Edward's greatest friend.
KING LOUIS   Welcome, brave Warwick. What brings thee to France?
        He descends. She ariseth
QUEEN MARGARET [*aside*]   Ay, now begins a second storm to rise,
For this is he that moves both wind and tide.
WARWICK [*to* KING LOUIS]   From worthy Edward, King of Albion,
50   My lord and sovereign, and thy vowèd friend,
I come in kindness and unfeignèd love,
First, to do greetings to thy royal person,
And then, to crave a league of amity,°   *friendship*
And lastly, to confirm that amity
55   With nuptial knot, if thou vouchsafe to grant
That virtuous Lady Bona, thy fair sister,
To England's King in lawful marriage.
QUEEN MARGARET [*aside*]   If that go forward, Henry's hope is done.
WARWICK (*to* [LADY] BONA)   And, gracious madam, in our King's behalf
60   I am commanded, with your leave and favour,
Humbly to kiss your hand, and with my tongue
To tell the passion of my sovereign's heart,
Where fame, late ent'ring at his heedful ears,
Hath placed thy beauty's image and thy virtue.
65 QUEEN MARGARET   King Louis and Lady Bona, hear me speak
Before you answer Warwick. His demand
Springs not from Edward's well-meant honest love,
But from deceit, bred by necessity.
For how can tyrants safely govern home
70   Unless abroad they purchase° great alliance?   *obtain*
To prove him tyrant this reason may suffice—
That Henry liveth still; but were he dead,
Yet here Prince Edward stands, King Henry's son.
Look, therefore, Louis, that by this league and marriage
75   Thou draw not on thy danger and dishonour,
For though usurpers sway the rule° a while,   *wield power*
Yet heav'ns are just and time suppresseth wrongs.

WARWICK	Injurious° Margaret.	*Insulting*
PRINCE EDWARD	And why not 'Queen'?	

WARWICK   Because thy father Henry did usurp,
80 And thou no more art prince than she is queen.

OXFORD   Then Warwick disannuls° great John of Gaunt,   *cancels*
Which did subdue the greatest part of Spain;
And, after John of Gaunt, Henry the Fourth,
Whose wisdom was a mirror to the wisest;
85 And, after that wise prince, Henry the Fifth,
Who by his prowess conquerèd all France.
From these our Henry lineally descends.

WARWICK   Oxford, how haps it in this smooth discourse
You told not how Henry the Sixth hath lost
90 All that which Henry the Fifth had gotten?
Methinks these peers of France should smile at that.
But for the rest, you tell a pedigree
Of threescore and two years³—a silly° time   *trifling*
To make prescription for a kingdom's worth.⁴
95 OXFORD   Why, Warwick, canst thou speak against thy liege,
Whom thou obeyedest thirty and six years,
And not bewray° thy treason with a blush?   *reveal*

WARWICK   Can Oxford, that did ever fence the right,°   *defend justice*
Now buckler° falsehood with a pedigree?   *shield*
100 For shame—leave Henry, and call Edward king.

OXFORD   Call him my king by whose injurious doom°   *insulting judgment*
My elder brother, the Lord Aubrey Vere,⁵
Was done to death? And more than so, my father,
Even in the downfall° of his mellowed years,   *decline*
105 When nature brought him to the door of death?
No, Warwick, no—while life upholds this arm,
This arm upholds the house of Lancaster.

WARWICK   And I the house of York.

KING LOUIS   Queen Margaret, Prince Edward, and Oxford,
110 Vouchsafe, at our request, to stand aside
While I use further conference° with Warwick.   *talk further*
[QUEEN MARGARET *comes down from the state and,*
with PRINCE EDWARD *and* OXFORD, *stands apart*]⁶

QUEEN MARGARET   Heavens grant that Warwick's words bewitch him not.

KING LOUIS   Now, Warwick, tell me even upon thy conscience,
Is Edward your true king? For I were loath
115 To link with him that were not lawful chosen.

WARWICK   Thereon I pawn my credit and mine honour.

KING LOUIS   But is he gracious in the people's eye?

WARWICK   The more that⁷ Henry was unfortunate.

KING LOUIS   Then further, all dissembling set aside,
120 Tell me for truth the measure of his love
Unto our sister Bona.

---

3. Meaning the sixty-two years between 1399, when Henry IV deposed Richard II, and 1461, when Henry VI was deposed by Edward.
4. To make a claim based on custom for something as valuable as a kingdom.

5. Eldest son of the twelfth Earl of Oxford, John de Vere. Both were executed for treason by the Yorkists in 1462.
6. F's stage direction reads "They stand aloof."
7. The more (gracious) because.

WARWICK   Such it seems
          As may beseem° a monarch like himself.   *befit*
          Myself have often heard him say and swear
          That this his love was an eternal plant,
125   Whereof the root was fixed in virtue's ground,
          The leaves and fruit maintained with beauty's sun,
          Exempt from envy, but not from disdain,[8]
          Unless the Lady Bona quit° his pain.°   *end / (by loving him)*
          KING LOUIS [*to* LADY BONA]   Now, sister, let us hear your firm resolve.
130   LADY BONA   Your grant, or your denial, shall be mine.
          (*To* WARWICK) Yet I confess that often ere this day,
          When I have heard your king's desert° recounted,   *merit*
          Mine ear hath tempted judgement to desire.
          KING LOUIS [*to* WARWICK]   Then, Warwick, thus—our sister
               shall be Edward's.
135   And now, forthwith, shall articles be drawn
          Touching the jointure° that your king must make,   *marriage settlement*
          Which with her dowry shall be counterpoised.°   *equally balanced*
          [*To* QUEEN MARGARET] Draw near, Queen Margaret, and be a
               witness
          That Bona shall be wife to the English king.
               [QUEEN MARGARET, PRINCE EDWARD, *and* OXFORD *come*
               forward]
140   PRINCE EDWARD   To Edward, but not to the English king.
          QUEEN MARGARET   Deceitful Warwick—it was thy device
          By this alliance to make void my suit!
          Before thy coming Louis was Henry's friend.
          KING LOUIS   And still is friend to him and Margaret.
145   But if your title to the crown be weak,
          As may appear by Edward's good success,
          Then 'tis but reason that I be released
          From giving aid which late° I promised.   *recently*
          Yet shall you have all kindness at my hand
150   That your estate requires and mine can yield.
          WARWICK [*to* QUEEN MARGARET]   Henry now lives in Scotland at his ease,
          Where having nothing, nothing can he lose.
          And as for you yourself, our quondam° queen,   *former*
          You have a father able to maintain you,
155   And better 'twere you troubled him than France.
          QUEEN MARGARET   Peace, impudent and shameless Warwick, peace!
          Proud setter-up and puller-down of kings!
          I will not hence till, with my talk and tears,
          Both full of truth, I make King Louis behold
160   Thy sly conveyance° and thy lord's false love,   *deceit*
               POST° *blowing a horn within*   *Messenger*
          For both of you are birds of selfsame feather.
          KING LOUIS   Warwick, this is some post to us or thee.
               Enter the POST
          POST (*to* WARWICK)   My lord ambassador, these letters are for you,

---

8. Exempt from malice, but not exempt from (being hurt by) her disdain for him.

Sent from your brother Marquis Montague;
165   (*To* LOUIS) These from our King unto your majesty;
    (*To* [QUEEN] MARGARET) And, madam, these for you, from
        whom I know not.
          They all read their letters
  OXFORD [*to* PRINCE EDWARD]   I like it well that our fair Queen and mistress
  Smiles at her news, while Warwick frowns at his.
  PRINCE EDWARD   Nay, mark how Louis stamps° as he were   *(his foot)*
    nettled.°   *angry*
170   I hope all's for the best.
  KING LOUIS   Warwick, what are thy news? And yours, fair Queen?
  QUEEN MARGARET   Mine, such as fill my heart with unhoped joys.
  WARWICK   Mine, full of sorrow and heart's discontent.
  KING LOUIS   What! Has your king married the Lady Gray?
175   And now to soothe° your forgery° and his,   *smooth over / deceit*
  Sends me a paper to persuade me patience?
  Is this th'alliance that he seeks with France?
  Dare he presume to scorn us in this manner?
  QUEEN MARGARET   I told your majesty as much before—
180   This proveth Edward's love and Warwick's honesty.
  WARWICK   King Louis, I here protest in sight of heaven
  And by the hope I have of heavenly bliss,
  That I am clear from this misdeed of Edward's,
  No more my king, for he dishonours me,
185   But most himself, if he could see his shame.
  Did I forget that by the house of York
  My father came untimely to his death?°
  Did I let pass th'abuse done to my niece?¹
  Did I impale him° with the regal crown?   *encircle his head*
190   Did I put Henry from his native right?
  And am I guerdoned° at the last with shame?   *rewarded*
  Shame on himself, for my desert is honour.
  And to repair my honour, lost for him,
  I here renounce him and return to Henry.
195   [*To* QUEEN MARGARET] My noble Queen, let former grudges pass,
  And henceforth I am thy true servitor.°   *servant*
  I will revenge his wrong to Lady Bona
  And replant Henry in his former state.
  QUEEN MARGARET   Warwick, these words have turned my hate to love,
200   And I forgive and quite forget old faults,
  And joy that thou becom'st King Henry's friend.
  WARWICK   So much his friend, ay, his unfeignèd friend,
  That if King Louis vouchsafe to furnish us
  With some few bands of chosen soldiers,
205   I'll undertake to land them on our coast
  And force the tyrant from his seat by war.

---

9. Actually, Warwick's father, the Earl of Salisbury of *The First Part of the Contention*, was executed by the Lancastrians. Perhaps Warwick means that his father would not have died in the Yorkist cause had the Yorkists never tried to seize the throne.

1. Holinshed's *Chronicles* reports that while visiting Warwick's house, Edward attempted to sexually assault his host's daughter or niece.

'Tis not his new-made bride shall succour him.
And as for Clarence, as my letters tell me,
He's very likely now to fall from° him   *desert*
210 For matching° more for wanton lust than honour,   *marrying*
Or than for strength and safety of our country.
LADY BONA [*to* KING LOUIS]   Dear brother, how shall Bona be revenged,
But by thy help to this distressèd Queen?
QUEEN MARGARET [*to* KING LOUIS]   Renownèd Prince, how shall
poor Henry live
215 Unless thou rescue him from foul despair?
LADY BONA [*to* KING LOUIS]   My quarrel and this English
Queen's are one.
WARWICK   And mine, fair Lady Bona, joins with yours.
KING LOUIS   And mine with hers, and thine, and Margaret's.
Therefore at last I firmly am resolved:
220 You shall have aid.
QUEEN MARGARET   Let me give humble thanks for all at once.
KING LOUIS [*to the* POST]   Then, England's messenger, return in post°   *haste*
And tell false Edward, thy supposèd king,
That Louis of France is sending over masquers²
225 To revel it with him and his new bride.
Thou seest what's passed, go fear° thy king withal.°   *frighten / with it*
LADY BONA [*to the* POST]   Tell him, in hope he'll prove a widower shortly,
I'll wear the willow garland³ for his sake.
QUEEN MARGARET [*to the* POST]   Tell him my mourning weeds°   *apparel*
are laid aside,
230 And I am ready to put armour on.
WARWICK [*to the* POST]   Tell him from me that he hath done me wrong,
And therefore I'll uncrown him ere't be long.
[*Giving money*] There's thy reward—be gone.   *Exit* POST
KING LOUIS   But, Warwick, thou and Oxford, with five thousand men,
235 Shall cross the seas and bid false Edward battle;
And, as occasion serves, this noble Queen
And Prince shall follow with a fresh supply.
Yet, ere thou go, but answer me one doubt:
What pledge have we of thy firm loyalty?
240 WARWICK   This shall assure my constant loyalty:
That if our Queen and this young Prince agree,
I'll join mine eldest daughter⁴ and my joy
To him forthwith in holy wedlock bands.
QUEEN MARGARET   Yes, I agree, and thank you for your motion.°   *proposal*
245 [*To* PRINCE EDWARD] Son Edward, she is fair and virtuous,
Therefore delay not. Give thy hand to Warwick,
And with thy hand thy faith irrevocable
That only Warwick's daughter shall be thine.
PRINCE EDWARD   Yes, I accept her, for she well deserves it,

---

2. The actors in courtly revels and entertainments that
were often staged to celebrate the marriages of members
of the Elizabethan aristocracy.
3. Token of a forsaken lover.
4. The historical Edward was betrothed (but never

married) to Warwick's second daughter, Anne. She
eventually married Richard Duke of York (later Richard
III). Warwick's eldest daughter married George of
Clarence.

250   And here to pledge my vow I give my hand.
        He gives his hand to WARWICK
    KING LOUIS   Why stay we now? These soldiers shall be levied,
    And thou, Lord Bourbon, our high admiral,
    Shall waft° them over with our royal fleet.   *convey by water*
    I long till Edward fall by war's mischance
255   For mocking marriage with a dame of France.
                             Exeunt. Manet WARWICK
    WARWICK   I came from Edward as ambassador,
    But I return his sworn and mortal foe.
    Matter of marriage was the charge he gave me,
    But dreadful war shall answer his demand.
260   Had he none else to make a stale° but me?   *laughingstock*
    Then none but I shall turn his jest to sorrow.
    I was the chief that raised him to the crown,
    And I'll be chief to bring him down again.
    Not that I pity Henry's misery,
265   But seek revenge on Edward's mockery.   *Exit*

4.1

    Enter RICHARD [*Duke of* GLOUCESTER, GEORGE
    Duke of] CLARENCE, [*the Duke of*] SOMERSET, *and*
    [*the Marquis of*] MONTAGUE
    RICHARD OF GLOUCESTER   Now tell me, brother Clarence, what think you
    Of this new marriage with the Lady Gray?
    Hath not our brother made a worthy choice?
    GEORGE OF CLARENCE   Alas, you know 'tis far from hence to France;
5   How could he stay° till Warwick made return?   *wait*
    SOMERSET   My lords, forbear this talk—here comes the King.
        Flourish. Enter KING EDWARD, *the* LADY GRAY [*his*]
        Queen, [*the Earl of*] *Pembroke,* [*and the Lords*]
        Stafford [*and*] HASTINGS. *Four stand on one side* [*of*
        the King], *and four on the other*
    RICHARD OF GLOUCESTER   And his well-chosen bride.
    GEORGE OF CLARENCE   I mind° to tell him plainly what I think.   *intend*
    KING EDWARD   Now, brother of Clarence, how like you our choice,
10   That you stand pensive, as half-malcontent?°   *partly discontented*
    GEORGE OF CLARENCE   As well as Louis of France, or the Earl
        of Warwick,
    Which° are so weak of courage and in judgement   *Who*
    That they'll take no offence at our abuse.°   *insult*
    KING EDWARD   Suppose they take offence without a cause—
15   They are but Louis and Warwick; I am Edward,
    Your king and Warwick's, and must have my will.°   *way; sexual desire*
    RICHARD OF GLOUCESTER   And you shall have your will,
        because our king.
    Yet hasty marriage seldom proveth well.
    KING EDWARD   Yea, brother Richard, are you offended too?
    RICHARD OF GLOUCESTER   Not I, no—God forbid that I should
20   wish them severed

4.1 Location: The palace, London.

Whom God hath joined together. Ay, and 'twere pity
To sunder them that yoke° so well together.   *who are coupled*
KING EDWARD Setting your scorns and your mislike° aside, *displeasure*
Tell me some reason why the Lady Gray
25 Should not become my wife and England's queen.
And you too, Somerset and Montague,
Speak freely what you think.
GEORGE OF CLARENCE Then this is my opinion: that King Louis
Becomes your enemy for mocking him
30 About the marriage of the Lady Bona.
RICHARD OF GLOUCESTER And Warwick, doing what you gave in charge,
Is now dishonourèd by this new marriage.
KING EDWARD What if both Louis and Warwick be appeased
By such invention° as I can devise?   *scheme*
35 MONTAGUE Yet, to have joined with France in such alliance
Would more have strengthened this our commonwealth
'Gainst foreign storms than any home-bred marriage.
HASTINGS Why, knows not Montague that of itself
England is safe, if true within itself?
40 MONTAGUE But the safer when 'tis backed with France.
HASTINGS 'Tis better using France than trusting France.
Let us be backed with God and with the seas
Which he hath giv'n for fence impregnable,
And with their helps only° defend ourselves.   *alone*
45 In them and in ourselves our safety lies.
GEORGE OF CLARENCE For this one speech Lord Hastings well deserves
To have the heir of the Lord Hungerford.[1]
KING EDWARD Ay, what of that? It was my will and grant—
And for this once my will shall stand for law.
RICHARD OF GLOUCESTER And yet, methinks, your grace hath
50 not done well
To give the heir and daughter of Lord Scales
Unto the brother[2] of your loving bride.
She better would have fitted me or Clarence,
But in° your bride you bury° brotherhood. *because of / forget*
GEORGE OF CLARENCE Or else you would not have bestowed
55 the heir
Of the Lord Bonville on your new wife's son,° *(Sir Thomas Gray)*
And leave your brothers to go speed elsewhere.
KING EDWARD Alas, poor Clarence, is it for a wife
That thou art malcontent? I will provide thee.
GEORGE OF CLARENCE In choosing for yourself you showed
60 your judgement,
Which being shallow, you shall give me leave
To play the broker° in mine own behalf, *marriage broker*
And to that end I shortly mind to leave you.
KING EDWARD Leave me, or tarry. Edward will be king,
65 And not be tied unto his brother's will.

---

1. To marry a rich heiress. Clarence is objecting to the wealthy marriage partners.
Queen's upstart relatives, such as Hastings, being given 2. That is, Anthony Woodville, second Earl Rivers.

LADY GRAY   My lords, before it pleased his majesty
To raise my state to title of a queen,
Do me but right, and you must all confess
That I was not ignoble of descent—
70   And meaner° than myself have had like fortune.[3]   *people of lower rank*
But as this title honours me and mine,
So your dislikes, to whom I would be pleasing,
Doth cloud my joys with danger° and with sorrow.   *apprehension*
KING EDWARD   My love, forbear to fawn upon° their frowns.   *be abject before*
75   What danger or what sorrow can befall thee
So long as Edward is thy constant friend,
And their true sovereign, whom they must obey?
Nay, whom they shall obey, and love thee too—
Unless they seek for hatred at my hands,
80   Which if they do, yet will I keep thee safe,
And they shall feel the vengeance of my wrath.
RICHARD OF GLOUCESTER [*aside*]   I hear, yet say not much, but
       think the more.
            Enter [the] POST [*from France*]
KING EDWARD   Now, messenger, what letters or what news from France?
POST   My sovereign liege, no letters and few words,
85   But such as I, without your special pardon,
Dare not relate.
KING EDWARD   Go to, we pardon thee. Therefore, in brief,
Tell me their words as near as thou canst guess° them.   *approximate*
What answer makes King Louis unto our letters?
90   POST   At my depart these were his very words:
'Go tell false Edward, thy supposèd king,
That Louis of France is sending over masquers
To revel it with him and his new bride.'
KING EDWARD   Is Louis so brave? Belike° he thinks me Henry.   *Perhaps*
95   But what said Lady Bona to my marriage?
POST   These were her words, uttered with mild disdain:
'Tell him in hope he'll prove a widower shortly,
I'll wear the willow garland for his sake.'
KING EDWARD   I blame not her, she could say little less;
100   She had the wrong. But what said Henry's queen?
For I have heard that she was there in place.
POST   'Tell him', quoth she, 'my mourning weeds are done,
And I am ready to put armour on.'
KING EDWARD   Belike she minds to play the Amazon.[4]
105   But what said Warwick to these injuries?
POST   He, more incensed against your majesty
Than all the rest, discharged me with these words:
'Tell him from me that he hath done me wrong,
And therefore I'll uncrown him ere't be long.'
110   KING EDWARD   Ha! Durst the traitor breathe out so proud words?
Well, I will arm me, being thus forewarned.
They shall have wars and pay for their presumption.
But say, is Warwick friends with Margaret?

---

3. In fact, the historical Lady Gray was the first com-   4. Legendary warrior woman. See note to 1.4.115.
moner to become Queen of England.

POST   Ay, gracious sovereign, they are so linked in friendship

115   That young Prince Edward marries Warwick's daughter.

GEORGE OF CLARENCE   Belike the elder; Clarence will have the younger.

    Now, brother King, farewell, and sit you fast,

    For I will hence to Warwick's other daughter,

    That, though I want° a kingdom, yet in marriage   *lack*

120   I may not prove inferior to yourself.

    You that love me and Warwick, follow me.

                  Exit CLARENCE, *and* SOMERSET *follows*

RICHARD OF GLOUCESTER   Not I—[*aside*] my thoughts aim at a

      further matter.

    I stay not for the love of Edward, but the crown.

KING EDWARD   Clarence and Somerset both gone to Warwick?

125   Yet am I armed against the worst can happen,

    And haste is needful in this desp'rate case.

    Pembroke and Stafford, you in our behalf

    Go levy men and make prepare° for war.   *preparation*

    They are already, or quickly will be, landed.

130   Myself in person will straight follow you.

                  Exeunt Pembroke and Stafford

    But ere I go, Hastings and Montague,

    Resolve my doubt. You twain, of all the rest,

    Are near'st to Warwick by blood and by alliance.

    Tell me if you love Warwick more than me.

135   If it be so, then both depart to him—

    I rather wish you foes than hollow° friends.   *false*

    But if you mind to hold your true obedience,

    Give me assurance with some friendly vow

    That I may never have you in suspect.°   *under suspicion*

140 MONTAGUE   So God help Montague as he proves true.

HASTINGS   And Hastings as he favours Edward's cause.

KING EDWARD   Now, brother Richard, will you stand by us?

RICHARD OF GLOUCESTER   Ay, in despite of all that shall withstand you.

KING EDWARD   Why, so. Then am I sure of victory.

145   Now, therefore, let us hence and lose no hour

    Till we meet Warwick with his foreign power.°   *Exeunt*   *army*

4.2

    Enter [the Earls of] WARWICK *and* OXFORD *in England,*

    with French soldiers

WARWICK   Trust me, my lord, all hitherto° goes well.   *thus far*

    The common sort by numbers swarm to us.

            Enter [the Dukes of] CLARENCE *and* SOMERSET

    But see where Somerset and Clarence comes.

    Speak suddenly, my lords, are we all friends?

5 GEORGE OF CLARENCE   Fear not that, my lord.

WARWICK   Then, gentle Clarence, welcome unto Warwick—

    And welcome, Somerset. I hold it cowardice

    To rest mistrustful where a noble heart

    Hath pawned° an open hand in sign of love,   *pledged*

10   Else might I think that Clarence, Edward's brother,
        Were but a feignèd friend to our proceedings.
        But come, sweet Clarence, my daughter shall be thine.
        And now what rests° but, in night's coverture,°   *remains / shadow*
        Thy brother being carelessly encamped,
15   His soldiers lurking° in the towns about,   *idling*
        And but attended by a simple guard,
        We may surprise and take him at our pleasure?
        Our scouts have found the adventure very easy;
        That, as Ulysses and stout Diomed
20   With sleight° and manhood° stole to Rhesus' tents   *stealth / bravery*
        And brought from thence the Thracian fatal steeds,[1]
        So we, well covered with the night's black mantle,
        At unawares° may beat down Edward's guard   *Suddenly*
        And seize himself—I say not 'slaughter him',
25   For I intend but only to surprise° him.   *capture*
        You that will follow me to this attempt,
        Applaud the name of Henry with your leader.
            They all cry 'Henry'
        Why, then, let's on our way in silent sort,°   *manner*
        For Warwick and his friends, God and Saint George!°   *patron saint of England*
                                    Exeunt

                        4.3
        Enter three WATCHMEN, *to guard the King's*
        [Edward's] *tent*
FIRST WATCHMAN   Come on, my masters, each man take his stand.°   *post*
        The King by this is set him down° to sleep.   *settled (in a chair)*
SECOND WATCHMAN   What, will he not to bed?
FIRST WATCHMAN   Why, no—for he hath made a solemn vow
5   Never to lie and take his natural rest
        Till Warwick or himself be quite suppressed.°   *vanquished*
SECOND WATCHMAN   Tomorrow then belike shall be the day,
        If Warwick be so near as men report.
THIRD WATCHMAN   But say, I pray, what nobleman is that
10   That with the King here resteth in his tent?
FIRST WATCHMAN   'Tis the Lord Hastings, the King's chiefest friend.
THIRD WATCHMAN   O, is it so? But why commands the King
        That his chief followers lodge in towns about him,
        While he himself keeps° in the cold field?   *lodges*
15 SECOND WATCHMAN   'Tis the more honour, because more dangerous.
THIRD WATCHMAN   Ay, but give me worship° and quietness—   *dignity*
        I like it better than a dangerous honour.
        If Warwick knew in what estate° he° stands,   *condition / (Edward)*
        'Tis to be doubted° he would waken him.   *feared*
20 FIRST WATCHMAN   Unless our halberds[1] did shut up° his passage.   *bar*
SECOND WATCHMAN   Ay, wherefore else guard we his royal tent

---

1. The Greek warriors Ulysses and Diomedes captured the horses of the Thracian prince Rhesus in a night raid, after an oracle predicted that Troy would not fall to the Greeks as long as the horses of Rhesus grazed on the plains of Troy (see *The Iliad*, Book 10). *fatal:* fateful.
4.3 Location: King Edward's camp near Warwick.
1. Long-handled weapons with axlike blades.

But to defend his person from night-foes?
    Enter [the Earl of] WARWICK, [GEORGE *Duke of*]
    CLARENCE, [*the Earl of*] OXFORD, [*and the Duke of*]
    SOMERSET, *and French soldiers. Silent all*

WARWICK   This is his tent—and see where stand his guard.
    Courage, my masters—honour now or never!
25   But follow me, and Edward shall be ours.
FIRST WATCHMAN   Who goes there?
SECOND WATCHMAN   Stay or thou diest.
    WARWICK *and the rest all cry* Warwick, Warwick!
    and set upon the guard, who fly, crying 'Arm, arm!' WAR-
    WICK *and the rest follow them*

4.4

    [*With*] *the drum[mer] playing and trumpet[er] sound-
    ing, enter* [*the Earl of*] WARWICK, [*the Duke of*]
    SOMERSET, *and the rest bringing the* KING [EDWARD]
    out in his gown, sitting in a chair.* RICHARD [*Duke of*
    GLOUCESTER] *and* [*Lord*] HASTINGS *flies over the stage*

SOMERSET   What are they that fly there?
WARWICK   Richard and Hastings—let them go. Here is the Duke.
KING EDWARD   'The Duke'! Why, Warwick, when we parted,
    Thou calledst me king.
WARWICK   Ay, but the case is altered.[1]
5   When you disgraced me in my embassade,°   *diplomatic mission*
    Then I degraded you from being king,
    And come now to create you Duke of York.
    Alas, how should you govern any kingdom
    That know not how to use ambassadors,
10   Nor how to be contented with one wife,
    Nor how to use your brothers brotherly,
    Nor how to study for the people's welfare,
    Nor how to shroud° yourself from enemies?   *conceal*
KING EDWARD [*seeing* GEORGE]   Yea, brother of Clarence, art
    thou here too?
15   Nay, then, I see that Edward needs must down.°   *must fall*
    Yet, Warwick, in despite of all mischance,
    Of thee thyself and all thy complices,
    Edward will always bear himself as king.
    Though fortune's malice overthrow my state,°   *sovereignty*
20   My mind exceeds the compass of her wheel.[2]
WARWICK   Then, for his° mind, be Edward England's king.   *in his (Edward's)*
    [WARWICK] *takes off* [*Edward's*] *crown*
    But Henry now shall wear the English crown,
    And be true king indeed, thou but the shadow.
    My lord of Somerset, at my request,
25   See that, forthwith, Duke Edward be conveyed
    Unto my brother, Archbishop of York.
    When I have fought with Pembroke and his fellows,
    I'll follow you, and tell what answer
    Louis and the Lady Bona send to him.

4.4 Location: Scene continues.
1. Proverbial for "things have changed."
2. My thoughts escape the control of fortune. The
goddess Fortune was often depicted turning a wheel on
which human destinies both rose and fell, sometimes
coming full circle.

30   Now for a while farewell, good Duke of York.
                They [begin to] lead [Edward] out forcibly
        King Edward   What fates impose, that men must needs abide.°   *endure*
        It boots not to resist both wind and tide.³
                                Exeunt some with Edward
        Oxford   What now remains, my lords, for us to do
        But march to London with our soldiers?
35   Warwick   Ay, that's the first thing that we have to do—
        To free King Henry from imprisonment
        And see him seated in the regal throne.   *Exeunt*

                                4.5
                Enter [Earl] Rivers and [his sister,] Lady Gray
                [Edward's queen]
        Rivers   Madam, what makes you in this sudden change?¹
        Lady Gray   Why, brother Rivers, are you yet to learn
        What late misfortune is befall'n King Edward?
        Rivers   What? Loss of some pitched battle against Warwick?
5   Lady Gray   No, but the loss of his own royal person.
        Rivers   Then is my sovereign slain?
        Lady Gray   Ay, almost slain—for he is taken prisoner,
        Either betrayed by falsehood of his guard
        Or by his foe surprised at unawares,
10   And, as I further have to understand,
        Is new committed to the Bishop of York,
        Fell° Warwick's brother, and by that° our foe.   *Cruel / therefore*
        Rivers   These news, I must confess, are full of grief.
        Yet, gracious madam, bear it as you may.
15   Warwick may lose, that now hath won the day.
        Lady Gray   Till then fair hope must hinder life's decay,
        And I the rather° wean me from despair   *I am the more obliged to*
        For love of Edward's offspring in my womb.
        This is it that makes me bridle° passion   *control*
20   And bear with mildness my misfortune's cross.
        Ay, ay, for this I draw in many a tear
        And stop the rising of blood-sucking² sighs,
        Lest with my sighs or tears I blast° or drown   *blight*
        King Edward's fruit, true heir to th'English crown.
25   Rivers   But, madam, where is Warwick then become?°   *gone*
        Lady Gray   I am informèd that he comes towards London
        To set the crown once more on Henry's head.
        Guess thou the rest—King Edward's friends must down.
        But to prevent the tyrant's violence—
30   For trust not him that hath once broken faith—
        I'll hence forthwith unto the sanctuary,³
        To save at least the heir of Edward's right.
        There shall I rest secure from force and fraud.
        Come, therefore, let us fly while we may fly.
35   If Warwick take us, we are sure to die.   *Exeunt*

3. Compare with 3.3.48, where Margaret says that Warwick "moves both wind and tide." *boots*: profits.
4.5 Location: The palace, London.
1. What is the reason for this sudden change of mind?

2. It was popularly believed that each sigh consumed a drop of blood from the heart.
3. Place that by law conferred immunity from arrest.

4.6

Enter RICHARD [*Duke of* GLOUCESTER], *Lord*
HASTINGS, *and Sir William Stanley* [*with soldiers*]

RICHARD OF GLOUCESTER Now my lord Hastings and Sir
William Stanley,
  Leave off to wonder why I drew you hither
  Into this chiefest thicket of the park.°   *hunting grounds*
  Thus stands the case: you know our King, my brother,
5 Is prisoner to the Bishop here, at whose hands
  He hath good usage and great liberty,
  And, often but attended with weak guard,
  Comes hunting this way to disport° himself.   *amuse*
  I have advertised° him by secret means   *informed*
10 That if about this hour he make this way
  Under the colour° of his usual game,°   *pretext / hunting*
  He shall here find his friends with horse and men
  To set him free from his captivity.

Enter KING EDWARD *and a* HUNTSMAN *with him*

HUNTSMAN This way, my lord—for this way lies the game.
15 KING EDWARD Nay, this way, man—see where the huntsmen stand.
  Now, brother of Gloucester, Lord Hastings, and the rest,
  Stand you thus close° to steal the Bishop's deer?   *concealed*
RICHARD OF GLOUCESTER Brother, the time and case requireth haste.
  Your horse stands ready at the park corner.
20 KING EDWARD But whither shall we then?
HASTINGS To Lynn,[1] my lord,
  And shipped from thence to Flanders.
RICHARD OF GLOUCESTER [*aside*] Well guessed, believe me—for
  that was my meaning.
KING EDWARD Stanley, I will requite thy forwardness.°   *reward your zeal*
RICHARD OF GLOUCESTER But wherefore stay we? 'Tis no time
25 to talk.
KING EDWARD Huntsman, what sayst thou? Wilt thou go along?
HUNTSMAN Better do so than tarry and be hanged.
RICHARD OF GLOUCESTER Come then, away—let's have no more ado.
KING EDWARD Bishop, farewell—shield thee from Warwick's frown,
30 And pray that I may repossess the crown.   *Exeunt*

4.7

Flourish. Enter [*the Earl of*] WARWICK *and* [GEORGE
Duke of] CLARENCE *with the crown. Then* [*enter*] KING
HENRY, [*the Earl of*] OXFORD, [*the Duke of*] SOMERSET,
[*with*] *young Henry Earl of Richmond,* [*the Marquis of*]
MONTAGUE, *and* [*the*] LIEUTENANT [*of the Tower*]

KING HENRY Master Lieutenant, now that God and friends
  Have shaken Edward from the regal seat
  And turned my captive state to liberty,

4.6 Location; The Archbishop of York's park or hunting ground, Yorkshire.

1. King's Lynn, a town on the Norfolk coast.
4.7 Location: The Tower, London.

My fear to hope, my sorrows unto joys,
5 At our enlargement° what are thy due fees?[1]   *release*
LIEUTENANT Subjects may challenge° nothing of their sovereigns—   *demand*
But if an humble prayer may prevail,
I then crave pardon of your majesty.
KING HENRY For what, Lieutenant? For well using me?
10 Nay, be thou sure I'll well requite thy kindness,
For that it made my prisonment a pleasure—
Ay, such a pleasure as encagèd birds
Conceive when, after many moody thoughts,
At last by notes of household harmony
15 They quite forget their loss of liberty.
But, Warwick, after God, thou sett'st me free,
And chiefly therefore I thank God and thee.
He was the author, thou the instrument.
Therefore, that I may conquer fortune's spite
20 By living low,° where fortune cannot hurt me,   *humbly*
And that the people of this blessèd land
May not be punished with my thwarting stars,[2]
Warwick, although my head still wear the crown,
I here resign my government to thee,
25 For thou art fortunate in all thy deeds.
WARWICK Your grace hath still° been famed for virtuous,   *always*
And now may seem as wise as virtuous
By spying and avoiding fortune's malice,
For few men rightly temper with the stars.[3]
30 Yet in this one thing let me blame your grace:
For choosing me when Clarence is in place.
GEORGE OF CLARENCE No, Warwick, thou art worthy of the sway,°   *rule*
To whom the heav'ns in thy nativity[4]
Adjudged an olive branch and laurel crown,[5]
35 As likely to be blest in peace and war.
And therefore I yield thee my free consent.
WARWICK And I choose Clarence only° for Protector.[6]   *alone*
KING HENRY Warwick and Clarence, give me both your hands.
Now join your hands, and with your hands your hearts,
40 That no dissension hinder government.
I make you both Protectors of this land,
While I myself will lead a private life
And in devotion spend my latter days,
To sin's rebuke and my creator's praise.
45 WARWICK What answers Clarence to his sovereign's will?
GEORGE OF CLARENCE That he consents, if Warwick yield consent,
For on thy fortune I repose myself.
WARWICK Why, then, though loath, yet must I be content.

1. Wealthy prisoners paid fees for special food and services.
2. My bad luck. Stars were believed to emit influences that might either favor or thwart the actions of individuals.
3. Because not many men correctly conform to or come to terms with their fate.

4. The precise position of the stars at one's birth was held to determine the course of one's life.
5. Symbols of peace and victory, respectively.
6. The title of an individual given charge of the kingdom while the monarch is absent, incapacitated, or a youth.

We'll yoke together, like a double shadow
50 To Henry's body, and supply° his place—   *take*
I mean in bearing weight of government—
While he enjoys the honour and his ease.
And, Clarence, now then it is more than needful
Forthwith that Edward be pronounced a traitor,
55 And all his lands and goods be confiscate.
GEORGE OF CLARENCE   What else? And that succession be
          determined.
WARWICK   Ay, therein Clarence shall not want his part.[7]
KING HENRY   But with the first of all your chief affairs,
          Let me entreat—for I command no more—
60 That Margaret your queen and my son Edward
Be sent for, to return from France with speed.
For, till I see them here, by doubtful fear
My joy of liberty is half eclipsed.
GEORGE OF CLARENCE   It shall be done, my sovereign, with all speed.
65 KING HENRY   My lord of Somerset, what youth is that
Of whom you seem to have so tender care?
SOMERSET   My liege, it is young Henry, Earl of Richmond.[8]
KING HENRY   Come hither, England's hope.
          [KING HENRY] *lays his hand on* [Richmond's] *head*
                                        If secret powers
Suggest but truth to my divining° thoughts,   *prophesying*
70 This pretty lad will prove our country's bliss.
His looks are full of peaceful majesty,
His head by nature framed to wear a crown,
His hand to wield a sceptre, and himself
Likely in time to bless a regal throne.
75 Make much of him, my lords, for this is he
Must help you more than you are hurt by me.
          Enter a POST
WARWICK   What news, my friend?
POST   That Edward is escapèd from your brother°   (*the Archbishop of York*)
And fled, as he hears since, to Burgundy.
80 WARWICK   Unsavoury news—but how made he escape?
POST   He was conveyed by Richard Duke of Gloucester
And the Lord Hastings, who attended him
In secret ambush on the forest side
And from the Bishop's huntsmen rescued him—
85 For hunting was his daily exercise.
WARWICK   My brother was too careless of his charge.
          [*To* KING HENRY]   But let us hence, my sovereign, to provide
A salve for any sore that may betide.°   *occur*
          Exeunt. Manent° SOMERSET, RICHMOND, *and* OXFORD   *Remain*
SOMERSET [*to* OXFORD]   My lord, I like not of this flight of Edward's,

---

7. George of Clarence would be next in line to the throne if the Lancastrian claim were dismissed and Edward pronounced a traitor. *want*: lack.
8. Somerset's nephew was the future Henry VII, the founder of the Tudor dynasty. The Wars of the Roses, represented in this play and in *The First Part of the Contention*, ended upon his accession to the throne, depicted at the end of *Richard III*.

90   For doubtless Burgundy will yield him help,
      And we shall have more wars before't be long.
      As Henry's late presaging prophecy
      Did glad my heart with hope of this young Richmond,
      So doth my heart misgive me, in these conflicts,
95   What may befall him, to his harm and ours.
      Therefore, Lord Oxford, to prevent the worst,
      Forthwith we'll send him hence to Brittany,
      Till storms be past of civil enmity.
OXFORD   Ay, for if Edward repossess the crown,
100   'Tis like that Richmond with the rest shall down.°   fall
SOMERSET   It shall be so—he shall to Brittany.
      Come, therefore, let's about it speedily.   *Exeunt*

                            4.8
            Flourish. Enter [KING] EDWARD, RICHARD [*Duke* OF
            GLOUCESTER], *and* [*Lord*] HASTINGS, *with a troop of
            Hollanders*
KING EDWARD   Now, brother Richard, Lord Hastings, and the rest,
      Yet thus far fortune maketh us amends,
      And says that once more I shall interchange
      My wanèd° state for Henry's regal crown.   diminished
5   Well have we passed and now repassed the seas
      And brought desirèd help from Burgundy.
      What then remains, we being thus arrived
      From Ravenspurgh[1] haven before the gates of York,
      But that we enter, as into our dukedom?
            [HASTINGS *knocks at the gates of York*]
10   RICHARD OF GLOUCESTER   The gates made fast? Brother, I like not this.
      For many men that stumble at the threshold
      Are well foretold that danger lurks within.
KING EDWARD   Tush, man, abodements° must not now affright us.   omens
      By fair or foul means we must enter in,
15   For hither will our friends repair to us.
HASTINGS   My liege, I'll knock once more to summon them.
            [*He knocks.*]
            Enter, on the walls, the MAYOR *of York, and his Brethren*
            [*aldermen*]
MAYOR   My lords, we were forewarnèd of your coming,
      And shut the gates for safety of ourselves—
      For now we owe allegiance unto Henry.
20   KING EDWARD   But, Master Mayor, if Henry be your king,
      Yet Edward at the least is Duke of York.
MAYOR   True, my good lord, I know you for no less.
KING EDWARD   Why, and I challenge nothing but my dukedom,
      As being well content with that alone.
RICHARD OF GLOUCESTER [*aside*]   But when the fox hath once
25   got in his nose,

4.8 Location: Outside the walls of York.   1. Town on the coast of Yorkshire.

He'll soon find means to make the body follow.

HASTINGS   Why, Master Mayor, why stand you in a doubt?
Open the gates—we are King Henry's friends.

MAYOR   Ay, say you so? The gates shall then be opened.
[They] descend[2]

RICHARD OF GLOUCESTER   A wise stout° captain, and soon   valiant
30   persuaded.

HASTINGS   The good old man would fain° that all were well,   wish
So 'twere not long of him;[3] but being entered,
I doubt not, I, but we shall soon persuade
Both him and all his brothers unto reason.
Enter [below] the MAYOR and two aldermen

35   KING EDWARD   So, Master Mayor, these gates must not be shut
But in the night or in the time of war.
What—fear not, man, but yield me up the keys,
[KING EDWARD] takes [some] keys [from the MAYOR]
For Edward will defend the town and thee,
And all those friends that deign° to follow me.   are willing
*March. Enter Sir John MONTGOMERY with [a]
drum[mer] and soldiers*

40   RICHARD OF GLOUCESTER   Brother, this is Sir John Montgomery,
Our trusty friend, unless I be deceived.

KING EDWARD   Welcome, Sir John—but why come you in arms?

MONTGOMERY   To help King Edward in his time of storm,
As every loyal subject ought to do.

45   KING EDWARD   Thanks, good Montgomery, but we now forget
Our title to the crown, and only claim
Our dukedom till God please to send the rest.

MONTGOMERY   Then fare you well, for I will hence again.
I came to serve a king and not a duke.

50   Drummer, strike up, and let us march away.
The drum[mer] begins to [sound a] march

KING EDWARD   Nay, stay, Sir John, a while, and we'll debate
By what safe means the crown may be recovered.

MONTGOMERY   What talk you of debating? In few words,
If you'll not here proclaim yourself our king

55   I'll leave you to your fortune and be gone
To keep them back that come to succour you.
Why shall we fight, if you pretend° no title?   claim

RICHARD OF GLOUCESTER   *[to KING EDWARD]*   Why, brother,
wherefore stand you on nice points?[4]

KING EDWARD   When we grow stronger, then we'll make our claim.

60   Till then 'tis wisdom to conceal our meaning.

HASTINGS   Away with scrupulous wit![5] Now arms must rule.   reasoning

RICHARD OF GLOUCESTER   And fearless minds climb soonest unto crowns.
Brother, we will proclaim you out of hand,
The bruit° thereof will bring you many friends.   news

65   KING EDWARD   Then be it as you will, for 'tis my right,

---

2. F's stage direction reads "He descends," as if only
the Mayor comes down from the walls.

3. So long as he is not held responsible.
4. Why do you dwell on such overly precise distinctions?

And Henry but usurps the diadem.

MONTGOMERY   Ay, now my sovereign speaketh like himself,
And now will I be Edward's champion.

HASTINGS   Sound trumpet, Edward shall be here proclaimed.
[*To* MONTGOMERY]⁵

70   Come, fellow soldier, make thou proclamation.
Flourish

MONTGOMERY   Edward the Fourth, by the grace of God King of
England and France, and Lord of Ireland—
And whosoe'er gainsays° King Edward's right,   denies
By this I challenge him to single fight.
[*He*] *throws down his gauntlet*⁶

75   ALL   Long live Edward the Fourth!

KING EDWARD   Thanks, brave Montgomery, and thanks unto you all.
If fortune serve me I'll requite° this kindness.   repay
Now, for this night, let's harbour here in York;
And when the morning sun shall raise his car°   chariot

80   Above the border of this horizon,
We'll forward towards Warwick and his mates.
For well I wot° that Henry is no soldier.   know
Ah, froward° Clarence, how evil it beseems thee   perverse
To flatter Henry and forsake thy brother!

85   Yet, as we may, we'll meet both thee and Warwick.
Come on, brave soldiers—doubt not of the day
And, that once gotten, doubt not of large pay.   *Exeunt*

4.9

Flourish. Enter KING [HENRY, *the Earl of*] WARWICK,
[*the Marquis of*] MONTAGUE, [GEORGE *Duke of*]
CLARENCE, *and* [*the Earl of*] OXFORD¹

WARWICK   What counsel, lords? Edward from Belgia,°   *the Low Countries*
With hasty° Germans and blunt° Hollanders,   *rash / merciless*
Hath passed in safety through the narrow seas,
And with his troops doth march amain° to London,   *at full speed*

5   And many giddy people flock to him.

KING HENRY   Let's levy men and beat him back again.

GEORGE OF CLARENCE   A little fire is quickly trodden out,
Which, being suffered, rivers cannot quench.

WARWICK   In Warwickshire I have true-hearted friends,

10   Not mutinous in peace, yet bold in war.
Those will I muster up. And thou, son° Clarence,   *son-in-law*
Shalt stir in Suffolk, Norfolk, and in Kent,
The knights and gentlemen to come with thee.
Thou, brother Montague, in Buckingham,

15   Northampton, and in Leicestershire shalt find
Men well inclined to hear what thou command'st.
And thou, brave Oxford, wondrous well beloved

---

5. F assigns lines 71–72 to a "Soul⟨dier⟩" and 73–74 to
Montgomery; O omits line 70 and the following stage
direction and assigns all the lines to Montgomery.
6. Throwing down a gauntlet, or glove, was a medieval
rite of chivalry. To pick it up was to accept a challenge
to duel.

4.9 Location: The Bishop of London's palace.
1. F includes Somerset at this entrance and does not
mark a scene division here or at line 32. Somerset has
no lines in this scene. Oxford omits him until the stage
direction at 5.1.71, begins a new scene (4.10) after
4.9.32, and places Exeter's entrance there.

In Oxfordshire, shalt muster up thy friends.
My sovereign, with the loving citizens,
20   Like to his island girt in with the ocean,
Or modest Dian² circled with her nymphs,
Shall rest in London till we come to him.
Fair lords, take leave and stand not to reply.
Farewell, my sovereign.
25   KING HENRY   Farewell, my Hector,³ and my Troy's true hope.
GEORGE OF CLARENCE   In sign of truth, I kiss your highness'
        hand.
        [*He kisses King Henry's hand*]
KING HENRY   Well-minded Clarence, be thou fortunate.
MONTAGUE   Comfort, my lord, and so I take my leave.
        [*He kisses King Henry's hand*]
OXFORD   And thus I seal my truth° and bid adieu.   affirm my loyalty
        [*He kisses King Henry's hand*]
30   KING HENRY   Sweet Oxford, and my loving Montague,
And all at once,° once more a happy farewell.   [*Exit*]   together
WARWICK   Farewell, sweet lords—let's meet at Coventry.
                            Exeunt [*severally*]°   separately

4.10
[*Enter* KING HENRY *and the Duke of* EXETER]
KING HENRY   Here at the palace will I rest a while.
Cousin of Exeter, what thinks your lordship?
Methinks the power that Edward hath in field
Should not be able to encounter mine.
5   EXETER   The doubt° is that he will seduce the rest.   fear
KING HENRY   That's not my fear. My meed° hath got° me fame.   merit / won
I have not stopped mine ears to their demands,
Nor posted off° their suits with slow delays.   postponed
My pity hath been balm to heal their wounds,
10   My mildness hath allayed their swelling griefs,
My mercy dried their water-flowing tears.
I have not been desirous of their wealth,
Nor much oppressed them with great subsidies,°   taxes
Nor forward of° revenge, though they much erred.   eager for
15   Then why should they love Edward more than me?
No, Exeter, these graces challenge grace;°   claim favor
And when the lion fawns upon the lamb,
The lamb will never cease to follow him.
        Shout within 'A Lancaster'[*, 'A York'*]¹
EXETER   Hark, hark, my lord—what shouts are these?
        Enter [KING] EDWARD *and* [RICHARD *Duke* OF
        GLOUCESTER, *with*] soldiers
20   KING EDWARD   Seize on the shame-faced° Henry—bear him hence,   timid
And once again proclaim us King of England.

---

2. The goddess of the moon, of hunting, and of chastity, often depicted presiding over a circle of virginal nymphs in the forest. Queen Elizabeth was sometimes represented as Diana.
3. The greatest warrior of Troy, killed when the Greeks conquered the city (see note to 2.1.51). By one legendary account, London was founded as a second Troy by

Brutus (or Brute), a Trojan who conquered Albion and renamed it Britain.
4.10 Location Scene continues.
1. F indicates "A Lancaster, A Lancaster"; Oxford's emendation suggests offstage conflict between the two armies.

You are the fount that makes small brooks to flow.
Now stops thy spring—my sea shall suck them dry,
And swell so much the higher by their ebb.
25   Hence with him to the Tower—let him not speak.
          Exeunt [some] with KING HENRY *[and* EXETER*]*
      And lords, towards Coventry bend we our course,
      Where peremptory° Warwick now remains.   *overbearing*
      The sun shines hot, and, if we use delay,
      Cold biting winter mars our hoped-for hay.°   *expected harvest*
30   RICHARD OF GLOUCESTER Away betimes,° before his forces join,   *quickly*
      And take the great-grown traitor unawares.
      Brave warriors, march amain towards Coventry.   *Exeunt*

                              5.1
          Enter [the Earl of] WARWICK, *the Mayor of Coventry,*
             two MESSENGERS, *and others upon the walls*[1]
      WARWICK Where is the post that came from valiant Oxford?
          [The FIRST MESSENGER *steps forward]*
      How far hence is thy lord, mine honest fellow?
      FIRST MESSENGER By this° at Dunsmore,[2] marching hitherward.   *By now*
      WARWICK How far off is our brother Montague?
5   Where is the post that came from Montague?
          [The SECOND MESSENGER *steps forward]*
      SECOND MESSENGER By this at Da'ntry,[3] with a puissant° troop.   *powerful*
          Enter SOMERVILLE *[to them, above]*
      WARWICK Say, Somerville—what says my loving son?
      And, by thy guess, how nigh is Clarence now?
      SOMERVILLE At Southam[4] I did leave him with his forces,
10   And do expect him here some two hours hence.
          [A march afar off]
      WARWICK Then Clarence is at hand—I hear his drum.
      SOMERVILLE It is not his, my lord. Here Southam lies.[5]
      The drum your honour hears marcheth from Warwick.
      WARWICK Who should that be? Belike,° unlooked-for friends.   *Perhaps*
15   SOMERVILLE They are at hand, and you shall quickly know.
          Flourish. Enter [below KING*]* EDWARD, *[and]* RICHARD
             [Duke OF GLOUCESTER, *with] soldiers*
      KING EDWARD Go, trumpet, to the walls, and sound a parley.[6]
          [Sound a parley]
      RICHARD OF GLOUCESTER See how the surly Warwick mans the wall.
      WARWICK O, unbid° spite—is sportful° Edward come?   *unwelcome / lecherous*
      Where slept our scouts, or how are they seduced,
20   That we could hear no news of his repair?°   *approach*

5.1 Location: Before the walls of Coventry.
1. This entire scene was probably played with Warwick's party in the gallery above the main stage and
King Edward and Richard of Gloucester below, looking
upward in lines 16–17 and throughout. In stage directions following lines 59, 67, and 72, first Oxford, then
the Marquis of Montague, and then the Duke of Somerset enter. They may enter above to Warwick or, more
probably, enter below, cross the stage, and then exit
through a stage door as if "into the city" and thus out of

view. F gives each an entrance but no exit; O marks
both an entrance and an exit for each.
2. Dunsmore Heath, between Coventry and Daventry.
3. Daventry, a Northamptonshire town about 20 miles
southeast of Coventry.
4. A town about 10 miles southeast of Coventry.
5. Southam is in this direction.
6. A trumpet signal requesting a conference between
warring troops.

KING EDWARD Now, Warwick, wilt thou ope the city gates.
  Speak gentle words, and humbly bend thy knee,
  Call Edward king, and at his hands beg mercy?
  And he shall pardon thee these outrages.
25 WARWICK Nay, rather, wilt thou draw thy forces hence,
  Confess who set thee up and plucked thee down,
  Call Warwick patron, and be penitent?
  And thou shalt still remain the Duke of York.
RICHARD OF GLOUCESTER I thought at least he would have said 'the King'.
30   Or did he make the jest against his will?
WARWICK Is not a dukedom, sir, a goodly gift?
RICHARD OF GLOUCESTER Ay, by my faith, for a poor earl[7] to give.
  I'll do thee service for so good a gift.
WARWICK 'Twas I that gave the kingdom to thy brother.
35 KING EDWARD Why then, 'tis mine, if but by Warwick's gift.
WARWICK Thou art no Atlas[8] for so great a weight;
  And, weakling, Warwick takes his gift again;
  And Henry is my king, Warwick his subject.
KING EDWARD But Warwick's king is Edward's prisoner,
40   And, gallant Warwick, do but answer this:
  What is the body when the head is off?
RICHARD OF GLOUCESTER Alas, that Warwick had no more forecast,°   *anticipated*
  But whiles he thought to steal the single ten,[9]
  The king was slyly fingered° from the deck.   *stolen*
45   [*To* WARWICK] You left poor Henry at the Bishop's palace,
  And ten to one you'll meet him in the Tower.
KING EDWARD 'Tis even so—[*to* WARWICK] yet you are Warwick still.
RICHARD OF GLOUCESTER Come, Warwick, take the time°—   *seize the moment*
  kneel down, kneel down.
  Nay, when? Strike now, or else the iron cools.[1]
50 WARWICK I had rather chop this hand off at a blow,
  And with the other fling it at thy face,
  Than bear so low a sail° to strike to thee.   *be so humble as*
KING EDWARD Sail how thou canst, have wind and tide thy friend,
  This hand, fast wound about thy coal-black hair,
55   Shall, whiles thy head is warm and new cut off,
  Write in the dust this sentence with thy blood:
  'Wind-changing° Warwick now can change no more.   *Fickle*
    Enter [*the Earl of*] OXFORD, *with* [*a*] *drum*[*me-*]
    and soldiers [*bearing*] *colours*°   *flags*
WARWICK O cheerful colours! See where Oxford comes.
OXFORD Oxford, Oxford, for Lancaster!
    [OXFORD *and his men pass over the stage and*
               exeunt into the city]
RICHARD OF GLOUCESTER [*to* KING EDWARD] The gates are
60   open—let us enter too.
KING EDWARD So other foes may set upon our backs?
  Stand we in good array, for they no doubt

---

7. Dukes are higher in rank than earls.
8. In Greek mythology, a giant who bore the weight of the heavens on his shoulders.
9. Alluding to the conventions of card games in which

the ten is valuable, but less so than the king. *single*: mere.
1. Referring to the proverb "Strike while the iron is hot," with a pun on "strike" as meaning "to lower a sail" or "to yield."

Will issue out again and bid us battle.
If not, the city being but of small defence,
65 We'll quickly rouse² the traitors in the same.
WARWICK [to OXFORD, within]   O, welcome, Oxford—for we want° thy help.   need
        Enter [the Marquis of] MONTAGUE with [a]
        drum[mer] and soldiers [bearing] colours
MONTAGUE   Montague, Montague, for Lancaster!
        [MONTAGUE *and his men pass over the stage and*
                                exeunt into the city]
RICHARD OF GLOUCESTER   Thou and thy brother both shall
        bye° this treason   atone for
Even with the dearest blood your bodies bear.
70 KING EDWARD   The harder matched, the greater victory.
My mind presageth happy gain and conquest.
        Enter [the Duke of] SOMERSET with [a] drum[mer]
        and soldiers [bearing] colours
SOMERSET   Somerset, Somerset, for Lancaster!
        [SOMERSET *and his men pass over the stage*
                and exeunt into the city]
RICHARD OF GLOUCESTER   Two of thy name, both dukes of Somerset,
Have sold their lives unto the house of York—
75 And thou shalt be the third, an° this sword hold.³   if
        Enter [GEORGE Duke of] CLARENCE with [a]
        drum[mer] and soldiers [bearing] colours
WARWICK   And lo, where George of Clarence sweeps along,
Of force enough to bid his brother battle;
With whom an upright zeal to right° prevails   for justice
More than the nature of a brother's love.
80 GEORGE OF CLARENCE   Clarence, Clarence, for Lancaster!
KING EDWARD   *Et tu, Brute*⁴—wilt thou stab Caesar too?
        [To a trumpeter] A parley, sirra,⁵ to George of Clarence.
        Sound a parley. RICHARD [OF GLOUCESTER] *and*
        [GEORGE OF] CLARENCE *whisper together*
WARWICK   Come, Clarence, come—thou wilt if Warwick call.
GEORGE OF CLARENCE   Father of Warwick, know you what this means?
        [He] *takes his red rose out of his hat and throws*
        it at WARWICK
85 Look—here I throw my infamy at thee!
I will not ruinate my father's house,
Who gave his blood to lime° the stones together,   cement
And set up Lancaster. Why, trowest thou,° Warwick,   do you believe
That Clarence is so harsh, so blunt,° unnatural,   uncivilized
90 To bend the fatal instruments of war
Against his brother and his lawful king?
Perhaps thou wilt object° my holy oath.   invoke

---

2. A hunting term meaning "to surprise creatures in their lair."
3. Richard addresses Edmund, the fourth Duke of Somerset. The defection of his older brother Henry, the third Duke, from Edward's cause is described in 4.1 and 4.2. Richard threw the head of their father, the sec-

ond Duke, across the stage in the play's first scene.
4. "You, too, Brutus": Julius Caesar's exclamation when he realized that his friend was one of the conspirators to his murder.
5. Fellow: a customary form of address to a social inferior.

To keep that oath were more impiety
Than Jephthah, when he sacrificed his daughter.[6]
95 I am so sorry for my trespass made
That, to deserve well at my brothers' hands,
I here proclaim myself thy mortal foe,
With resolution, wheresoe'er I meet thee—
As I will meet thee, if thou stir abroad°—   *(outside Coventry)*
100 To plague thee for thy foul misleading me.
And so, proud-hearted Warwick, I defy thee,
And to my brothers turn my blushing cheeks.
[*To* KING EDWARD] Pardon me, Edward—I will make amends.
[*To* RICHARD] And, Richard, do not frown upon my faults,
105 For I will henceforth be no more unconstant.
KING EDWARD Now welcome more, and ten times more beloved,
Than if thou never hadst deserved our hate.
RICHARD OF GLOUCESTER [*to* GEORGE] Welcome, good
Clarence—this is brother-like.
WARWICK [*to* GEORGE] O, passing° traitor—perjured and unjust!   *unsurpassed*
110 KING EDWARD What, Warwick, wilt thou leave the town and fight?
Or shall we beat the stones about thine ears?
WARWICK [*aside*] Alas, I am not cooped° here for defence.   *shut up*
[*To* KING EDWARD] I will away towards Barnet[7] presently,
And bid thee battle, Edward, if thou dar'st.
115 KING EDWARD Yes, Warwick—Edward dares, and leads the way.
Lords, to the field—Saint George and victory!
Exeunt [below KING EDWARD *and his company].*
March. [The Earl of] WARWICK *and his company*
[descend and] follow

5.2

*Alarum and excursions. Enter [*KING*] EDWARD*
bringing forth [the Earl of] WARWICK, *wounded*
KING EDWARD So lie thou there. Die thou, and die our fear—
For Warwick was a bug° that feared° us all.   *goblin / frightened*
Now, Montague, sit fast°—I seek for thee   *be on guard*
That Warwick's bones may keep thine company.   *Exit*
5 WARWICK Ah, who is nigh? Come to me, friend or foe,
And tell me who is victor, York or Warwick?
Why ask I that? My mangled body shows,
My blood, my want of strength, my sick heart shows,
That I must yield my body to the earth
10 And by my fall the conquest to my foe.
Thus yields the cedar[1] to the axe's edge,
Whose arms gave shelter to the princely eagle,[2]
Under whose shade the ramping lion[3] slept,

6. Alluding to the biblical story in which Jephthah, an Israelite leader, kills his daughter in fulfillment of a vow. He swore that if he were victorious in battle, he would sacrifice to God whoever first met him from his house when he returned from the battlefield (see Judges 11).
7. Shakespeare treats this town, which is about 10 miles north of London and 75 miles southeast of Coventry, as though it were near Coventry.
5.2 Location: Near Barnet.
1. Often regarded as the king of evergreens and thus a

symbol of sovereignty.
2. Probably referring to Richard, Duke of York. In 2.1.91, his son Richard refers to the Duke of York as a "princely eagle." The eagle was often described as the king of birds.
3. Under whose protection Henry VI rested. A reference both to the lion as king of the animal world and to the Lancastrian coat of arms, which showed three lions rampant or reared on their hind legs.

Whose top-branch over-peered° Jove's spreading tree[4]   *rose above*
15 And kept low shrubs from winter's powerful wind.
These eyes, that now are dimmed with death's black veil,
Have been as piercing as the midday sun
To search the secret treasons of the world.
The wrinkles in my brows, now filled with blood,
20 Were likened oft to kingly sepulchres—
For who lived king, but I could dig his grave?
And who durst smile when Warwick bent his brow?
Lo now my glory smeared in dust and blood.
My parks,° my walks, my manors that I had,   *hunting grounds*
25 Even now forsake me, and of all my lands
Is nothing left me but my body's length.
Why, what is pomp, rule, reign, but earth and dust?
And, live we how we can, yet die we must.
        Enter [the Earl of] OXFORD *and [the Duke of]* SOMERSET
SOMERSET   Ah, Warwick, Warwick—wert thou as we are,
30 We might recover all our loss again.
The Queen from France hath brought a puissant power.°   *powerful army*
Even now we heard the news. Ah, couldst thou fly!
WARWICK   Why, then I would not fly. Ah, Montague,
If thou be there, sweet brother, take my hand,
35 And with thy lips keep in my soul a while.[5]
Thou lov'st me not—for, brother, if thou didst,
Thy tears would wash this cold congealèd blood
That glues my lips and will not let me speak.
Come quickly, Montague, or I am dead.
40 SOMERSET   Ah, Warwick—Montague hath breathed his last,
And to the latest gasp cried out for Warwick,
And said 'Commend me to my valiant brother.'
And more he would have said, and more he spoke,
Which sounded like a canon in a vault,
45 That mote° not be distinguished; but at last   *might*
I well might hear, delivered with a groan,
'O, farewell, Warwick.'
WARWICK   Sweet rest his soul. Fly, lords, and save yourselves—
For Warwick bids you all farewell, to meet in heaven. *He dies*
50 OXFORD   Away, away—to meet the Queen's great power!
        Here they bear away [Warwick's] body. Exeunt

5.3

        Flourish. Enter KING EDWARD *in triumph, with*
        RICHARD [*Duke of* GLOUCESTER, GEORGE *Duke of*]
        CLARENCE, *and soldiers*
KING EDWARD   Thus far our fortune keeps an upward course,
And we are graced with wreaths of victory.
But in the midst of this bright-shining day
I spy a black suspicious threatening cloud
5 That will encounter with our glorious sun
Ere he attain his easeful western bed.
I mean, my lords, those powers that the Queen

---

4. Jove's tree, according to Virgil, was the oak, the king of deciduous trees.
5. Kiss me. Many Elizabethans believed the soul escaped through the mouth at death.
5.3 Location: Scene continues.

Hath raised in Gallia° have arrived cur coast,   *France*
And, as we hear, march on to fight with us.
10 GEORGE OF CLARENCE   A little gale will soon disperse that cloud,
And blow it to the source from whence it came.
Thy very beams will dry those vapours up,
For every cloud engenders not a storm.
RICHARD OF GLOUCESTER   The Queen is valued° thirty thousand   *estimated to be*
    strong,
15 And Somerset, with Oxford, fled to her.
If she have time to breathe,° be well assured,   *gather her strength*
Her faction will be full as strong as ours.
KING EDWARD   We are advertised° by our loving friends   *informed*
That they do hold their course toward Tewkesbury.[1]
20 We, having now the best at Barnet field,
Will thither straight, for willingness rids way[2]—
And, as we march, our strength will be augmented
In every county as we go along.
Strike up the drum, cry 'Courage!'; and away.
                                    [*Flourish. March.*] *Exeunt*

5.4

Flourish. March. Enter QUEEN [MARGARET], PRINCE
EDWARD, [*the Duke of*] SOMERSET, [*the Earl of*]
OXFORD, *and soldiers*

QUEEN MARGARET   Great lords, wise men ne'er sit and wail their loss,
But cheerly° seek how to redress their harms.   *cheerfully*
What though the mast be now blown overboard,
The cable broke, the holding-anchor[1] lost,
5   And half our sailors swallowed in the flood?
Yet lives our pilot° still. Is't meet that he   *(Henry)*
Should leave the helm and, like a fearful lad,
With tearful eyes add water to the sea,
And give more strength to that which hath too much,
10 Whiles, in his moan,° the ship splits on the rock   *state of grief*
Which industry and courage might have saved?
Ah, what a shame; ah, what a fault were this.
Say Warwick was our anchor—what of that?
And Montague our top-mast—what of him?
15 Our slaughtered friends the tackles[2]—what of these?
Why, is not Oxford here another anchor?
And Somerset another goodly mast?
The friends of France our shrouds[3] and tacklings?
And, though unskilful, why not Ned° and I   *(her son Edward)*
20 For once allowed the skilful pilot's charge?°   *responsibility*
We will not from the helm to sit and weep,
But keep our course, though the rough wind say no,
From shelves° and rocks that threaten us with wreck.   *sandbanks*
As good to chide the waves as speak them fair.

---

1. A town in Gloucestershire.   hold of the sea bottom.
2. For eagerness to travel makes the journey seem   2. Ropes and pulleys used for raising and lowering
shorter.   sails.
5.4 Location: Fields near Tewkesbury.   3. Ropes that brace and support the mast.
1. The anchor meant to stabilize the ship by taking

25 And what is Edward but a ruthless sea?
What Clarence but a quicksand of deceit?
And Richard but a raggèd° fatal rock?　　　　　　　　　*jagged*
All these the enemies to our poor barque.°　　　　　　*ship*
Say you can swim—alas, 'tis but a while;
30 Tread on the sand—why, there you quickly sink;
Bestride the rock—the tide will wash you off,
Or else you famish. That's a threefold death.
This speak I, lords, to let you understand,
If° case some one of you would fly from us,　　　　　　*In*
35 That there's no hoped-for mercy with the brothers York
More than with ruthless waves, with sands, and rocks.
Why, courage then—what cannot be avoided
'Twere childish weakness to lament or fear.

PRINCE EDWARD　Methinks a woman of this valiant spirit
40 Should, if a coward heard her speak these words,
Infuse his breast with magnanimity°　　　　　　　*great courage*
And make him, naked,° foil° a man at arms.　　*unarmed / defeat*
I speak not this as doubting any here—
For did I but suspect a fearful man,
45 He should have leave to go away betimes,°　　　　　*at once*
Lest in our need he might infect another
And make him of like spirit to himself.
If any such be here—as God forbid—
Let him depart before we need his help.

50 OXFORD　Women and children of so high a courage,
And warriors faint°—why, 'twere perpetual shame!　*fainthearted*
O brave young Prince, thy famous grandfather°　　*(Henry V)*
Doth live again in thee! Long mayst thou live
To bear his image and renew his glories!

55 SOMERSET　And he that will not fight for such a hope,
Go home to bed, and like the owl by day,
If he arise, be mocked and wondered at.

QUEEN MARGARET　Thanks, gentle Somerset; sweet Oxford, thanks.

PRINCE EDWARD　And take his thanks that yet° hath nothing else.　*who as yet*

Enter a MESSENGER

60 MESSENGER　Prepare you, lords, for Edward is at hand
Ready to fight—therefore be resolute.

OXFORD　I thought no less. It is his policy
To haste thus fast to find us unprovided.°　　　　*unprepared*

SOMERSET　But he's deceived; we are in readiness.

65 QUEEN MARGARET　This cheers my heart, to see your forwardness.

OXFORD　Here pitch our battle°—hence we will not budge.　*deploy our army*

Flourish and march. Enter KING EDWARD, RICHARD
[*Duke* OF GLOUCESTER], *and* [GEORGE *Duke* OF]
CLARENCE, [*with*] *soldiers*

KING EDWARD [*to his followers*]　Brave followers, yonder stands
the thorny wood
Which, by the heavens' assistance and your strength,
Must by the roots be hewn up yet ere night.
70 I need not add more fuel to your fire,
For well I wot° ye blaze to burn them out.　　　　　*know*
Give signal to the fight, and to it, lords.

QUEEN MARGARET [to her followers]   Lords, knights, and
    gentlemen—what I should say
    My tears gainsay;° for every word I speak   hinder
75   Ye see I drink the water of my eye.
    Therefore, no more but this: Henry your sovereign
    Is prisoner to the foe, his state usurped,
    His realm a slaughter-house, his subjects slain,
    His statutes cancelled, and his treasure spent—
80   And yonder is the wolf that makes this spoil.
    You fight in justice; then in God's name, lords,
    Be valiant, and give signal to the fight.
        Alarum, retreat, excursions. Exeunt

5.5

Flourish. Enter [KING] EDWARD, RICHARD [DUKE OF]
GLOUCESTER, *and* GEORGE *Duke* OF] CLARENCE, [*with*]
QUEEN [MARGARET, *the Earl of*] OXFORD, [*and the Duke
of*] SOMERSET [*guarded*]

KING EDWARD   Now here a period of° tumultuous broils.   *an end to*
    Away with Oxford to Hames Castle straight;
    For Somerset, off with his guilty head.
    Go bear them hence—I will not hear them speak.
5 OXFORD   For my part, I'll not trouble thee with words.
                               Exit [*guarded*]
SOMERSET   Nor I, but stoop with patience to my fortune.
                               Exit [*guarded*]
QUEEN MARGARET   So part we sadly in this troublous world
    To meet with joy in sweet Jerusalem.²
KING EDWARD   Is proclamation made that who finds Edward
10   Shall have a high reward and he his life?
RICHARD OF GLOUCESTER   It is, and lo where youthful Edward
    comes.
        Enter PRINCE [EDWARD, *guarded*]
KING EDWARD   Bring forth the gallant—let us hear him speak.
    What, can so young a thorn begin to prick?
    Edward, what satisfaction° canst thou make   *amends*
15   For bearing arms, for stirring up my subjects,
    And all the trouble thou hast turned me to?
PRINCE EDWARD   Speak like a subject, proud ambitious York.³
17.1   ALL THE LANCASTER PARTY   *Saint George for Lancaster!*
    Alarums to the battle. [*The house of*] *York flies, then
    the chambers°* [*are*] *discharged. Then enter* KING   *small cannon*
    [EDWARD, GEORGE OF] CLARENCE, *and* [RICHARD OF]
    GLOUCESTER, *and* [*their followers; they*] *make a great
    shout, and cry 'For York! For York!' Then* QUEEN [MAR-
    GARET], PRINCE [EDWARD], OXFORD *and* SOMERSET
    [*are all*] *taken* [*prisoner. Flourish,*] *and enter all
    again*

5.5 Location: Scene continues.
1. Hammes Castle, near Calais.
2. Referring to heaven, which is described as the new
Jerusalem in Revelation 21:2.

3. O abridges 5.4.82–5.5.17 and may reflect authorial
revision. An edited text of the abridged passage is given
as the inset passage that follows (lines 17.1–17.10).

KING EDWARD   *Now here a period of° tumultuous broils*   *an end to*
    Away with Oxford to Hames Castle straight;
    For Somerset, off with his guilty head.
17.5   *Go, bear them hence—I will not hear them speak.*
OXFORD   *For my part, I'll not trouble thee with words.*
                                Exit [guarded]
SOMERSET   *Nor I, but stoop with patience to my death.*
                                Exit [guarded]
KING EDWARD *[to PRINCE EDWARD]   Edward, what*
    satisfaction° canst thou make   *amends*
    For stirring up my subjects to rebellion?
17.10   PRINCE EDWARD   *Speak like a subject, proud ambitious York.*
    Suppose that I am now my father's mouth—
    Resign thy chair, and where I stand, kneel thou,
20   Whilst I propose the self-same words to thee,
    Which, traitor, thou wouldst have me answer to.
QUEEN MARGARET   Ah, that thy father had been so resolved.
RICHARD OF GLOUCESTER   That you might still have worn the petticoat
    And ne'er have stolen the breech° from Lancaster.   *trousers*
25   PRINCE EDWARD   Let Aesop[4] fable in a winter's night—
    His currish riddles sorts not with this place.[5]
RICHARD OF GLOUCESTER   By heaven, brat, I'll plague ye for that word.
QUEEN MARGARET   Ay, thou wast born to be a plague to men.
RICHARD OF GLOUCESTER   For God's sake take away this captive scold.
30   PRINCE EDWARD   Nay, take away this scolding crookback° rather.   *hunchback*
KING EDWARD   Peace, wilful boy, or I will charm° your tongue.   *silence with a spell*
GEORGE OF CLARENCE *[to PRINCE EDWARD]   Untutored lad,*
      thou art too malapert.°   *saucy*
PRINCE EDWARD   I know my duty—you are all undutiful.
    Lascivious Edward, and thou, perjured George,
35   And thou, misshapen Dick—I tell ye all
    I am your better, traitors as ye are,
    And thou usurp'st my father's right and mine.
KING EDWARD   Take that, the likeness of this railer° here.   *scold (Margaret)*
    [KING EDWARD] stabs [PRINCE EDWARD]
RICHARD OF GLOUCESTER   Sprawl'st thou?[6] Take that, to end thy agony.
    RICHARD stabs [PRINCE EDWARD]
40   GEORGE OF CLARENCE   And there's for twitting me with perjury.
    [GEORGE] stabs [PRINCE EDWARD, who dies]
QUEEN MARGARET   O, kill me too!
RICHARD OF GLOUCESTER   Marry,[7] and shall.
    [He] offers to kill her
KING EDWARD   Hold, Richard, hold—for we have done too much.
RICHARD OF GLOUCESTER   Why should she live to fill the world
    with words?
    [QUEEN MARGARET faints]

---

4. An ancient storyteller famous for his fables about
animals. Like Richard, he reputedly was physically
deformed. *fable:* tell tales.
5. His mean and cynical comments are not welcome
here.
6. Do you convulse in the agonies of death?
7. A mild oath invoking the name of the Virgin Mary.

KING EDWARD   What—doth she swoon? Use means for her recovery.
RICHARD OF GLOUCESTER [*aside to* GEORGE]   Clarence, excuse
45   me to the King my brother.
I'll hence to London on a serious matter.
Ere ye come there, be sure° to hear some news.   *expect*
GEORGE OF CLARENCE [*aside to* RICHARD]   What? What?
50   RICHARD OF GLOUCESTER [*aside to* GEORGE]   The Tower, the Tower.
                                                          Exit
QUEEN MARGARET   O Ned, sweet Ned—speak to thy mother, boy.
Canst thou not speak? O traitors, murderers!
They that stabbed Caesar shed no blood at all,
Did not offend, nor were not worthy blame,
55   If this foul deed were by to equal it.°   *to compare with it*
He was a man—this, in respect,° a child;   *in comparison*
And men ne'er spend their fury on a child.
What's worse than murderer that I may name it?
No, no, my heart will burst an if I speak;
60   And I will speak that so my heart may burst.
Butchers and villains! Bloody cannibals!
How sweet a plant have you untimely cropped!
You have no children, butchers; if you had,
The thought of them would have stirred up remorse.
65   But if you ever chance to have a child,
Look in his youth to have him so cut off
As, deathsmen, you have rid° this sweet young Prince!   *killed*
KING EDWARD   Away with her—go, bear her hence perforce.
QUEEN MARGARET   Nay, never bear me hence—dispatch° me here.   *kill*
70   Here sheathe thy sword—I'll pardon thee my death.
What? Wilt thou not? Then, Clarence, do it thou.
GEORGE OF CLARENCE   By heaven, I will not do thee so much ease.
QUEEN MARGARET   Good Clarence, do; sweet Clarence, do thou do it.
GEORGE OF CLARENCE   Didst thou not hear me swear I would not do it?
75   QUEEN MARGARET   Ay, but thou usest° to forswear thyself.   *are accustomed*
'Twas sin before, but now 'tis charity.
What, wilt thou not? Where is that devil's butcher,
Hard-favoured° Richard? Richard, where art thou?   *Ugly*
Thou art not here. Murder is thy alms-deed°—   *act of charity*
80   Petitioners for blood thou ne'er putt'st back.°   *you never turn away*
KING EDWARD   Away, I say—I charge ye, bear her hence.
QUEEN MARGARET   So come to you and yours as to this Prince!
                                            Exit [*guarded*]
KING EDWARD   Where's Richard gone?
GEORGE OF CLARENCE   To London all in post° [—*aside*] and as I guess,   *haste*
85   To make a bloody supper in the Tower.
KING EDWARD   He's sudden if a thing comes in his head.
Now march we hence. Discharge the common sort°   *ordinary soldiers*
With pay and thanks, and let's away to London,
And see our gentle Queen how well she fares.
90   By this° I hope she hath a son for me.   *Exeunt*   *By now*

5.6

Enter on the walls [KING] HENRY VI, [reading a book,]
RICHARD [*Duke* OF GLOUCESTER, *and*] *the* LIEUTENANT
[*of the Tower*][1]

RICHARD OF GLOUCESTER   Good day, my lord. What, at your
  book so hard?

KING HENRY   Ay, my good lord—'my lord', I should say, rather.
  'Tis sin to flatter; 'good' was little better.°   (*than flattery*)
  'Good Gloucester' and 'good devil' were alike,

5 And both preposterous°—therefore not 'good lord'.   *unnatural*

RICHARD OF GLOUCESTER [*to the* LIEUTENANT]   Sirrah,° leave us   *Fellow*
  to ourselves. We must confer.   [*Exit* LIEUTENANT]

KING HENRY   So flies the reckless° shepherd from the wolf;   *careless*
  So first the harmless sheep doth yield his fleece,
  And next his throat unto the butcher's knife.

10 What scene of death hath Roscius[2] now to act?

RICHARD OF GLOUCESTER   Suspicion always haunts the guilty mind;
  The thief doth fear each bush an officer.

KING HENRY   The bird that hath been limèd[3] in a bush
  With trembling wings misdoubteth° every bush.   *fears*

15 And I, the hapless male° to one sweet bird,°   *father / child*
  Have now the fatal object in my eye
  Where my poor young was limed, was caught and killed.

RICHARD OF GLOUCESTER   Why, what a peevish° fool was that of Crete,   *silly*
  That taught his son the office of a fowl![4]

20 And yet, for all his wings, the fool was drowned.

KING HENRY   I, Daedalus; my poor boy, Icarus;
  Thy father, Minos,[5] that denied our course;
  The sun that seared the wings of my sweet boy,
  Thy brother Edward;[6] and thyself, the sea,

25 Whose envious gulf did swallow up his life.
  Ah, kill me with thy weapon, not with words!
  My breast can better brook° thy dagger's point   *tolerate*
  Than can my ears that tragic history.
  But wherefore dost thou come? Is't for my life?

30 RICHARD OF GLOUCESTER   Think'st thou I am an executioner?

KING HENRY   A persecutor I am sure thou art;
  If murdering innocents be executing,
  Why, then thou art an executioner.

RICHARD OF GLOUCESTER   Thy son I killed for his presumption.

35 KING HENRY   Hadst thou been killed when first thou didst presume,
  Thou hadst not lived to kill a son of mine.

5.6 Location: The Tower, London.
1. The precise setting is ambiguous. F's stage directions
indicate that the scene takes place "on the Walls," O's
that it occurs "in the Tower." Richard's first line makes
clear that Henry is reading, which may mean he is in an
inner chamber. His murder could be staged in a small
alcove at the back of the main stage, on the walls (up in
the gallery), or in full view on the main stage.
2. An ancient Roman actor (actually best known as a
comedian) whom many Elizabethans cited as the
archetype of a great tragedian.

3. Caught with birdlime, a sticky substance smeared
on twigs.
4. Alluding to the myth of Daedalus, who, in order to
escape imprisonment in Crete, designed wings made of
wax and feathers for himself and his son Icarus. When
Icarus flew too near the sun, the wax melted, and he fell
to his death in the sea.
5. The King of Crete who imprisoned Daedalus and
Icarus.
6. Referring to the sun insignia associated with
Edward.

And thus I prophesy: that many a thousand
Which now mistrust no parcel of my fear,[7]
And many an old man's sigh, and many a widow's,
40 And many an orphan's water-standing° eye—   *flooded with tears*
Men for their sons', wives for their husbands',
Orphans for their parents' timeless° death—   *untimely*
Shall rue the hour that ever thou wast born.
The owl shrieked at thy birth—an evil sign;
45 The night-crow[8] cried, aboding° luckless time;   *foretelling*
Dogs howled, and hideous tempests shook down trees;
The raven rooked her° on the chimney's top;   *crouched*
And chatt'ring pies° in dismal discords sung.   *magpies*
Thy mother felt more than a mother's pain,
50 And yet brought forth less than a mother's hope—
To wit, an indigested° and deformèd lump,   *a shapeless*
Not like the fruit of such a goodly tree.
Teeth hadst thou in thy head when thou wast born,[9]
To signify thou cam'st to bite the world;
55 And if the rest be true which I have heard
Thou cam'st—
RICHARD   I'll hear no more. Die, prophet, in thy speech,
    He stabs him
For this, amongst the rest, was I ordained.
KING HENRY   Ay, and for much more slaughter after this.
60 O, God forgive my sins, and pardon thee.   *He dies*
RICHARD OF GLOUCESTER   What—will the aspiring blood of
        Lancaster
Sink in the ground? I thought it would have mounted.
See how my sword weeps for the poor King's death.
O, may such purple° tears be alway shed   *blood-red*
65 From those that wish the downfall of our house!
If any spark of life be yet remaining,
Down, down to hell, and say I sent thee thither—
    [He] stabs him again
I that have neither pity, love, nor fear.
Indeed, 'tis true that Henry told me of,
70 For I have often heard my mother say
I came into the world with my legs forward.
Had I not reason, think ye, to make haste,
And seek their ruin that usurped our right?
The midwife wondered and the women cried
75 'O, Jesus bless us, he is born with teeth!'—
And so I was, which plainly signified
That I should snarl and bite and play the dog.
Then, since the heavens have shaped my body so,
Let hell make crooked my mind to answer° it.   *match*
80 I had no father, I am like no father;
I have no brother, I am like no brother;
And this word, 'love', which greybeards call divine,
Be resident in men like one another
And not in me—I am myself alone.

7. Who do not share any of my fears.
8. A mythical bird supposed to be an evil omen.

9. Richard III was popularly believed to have been born
with teeth, a physical sign of his monstrous character.

85   Clarence, beware; thou kept'st me from the light—
      But I will sort° a pitchy° day for thee.   *arrange / dark*
      For I will buzz° abroad such prophecies   *whisper*
      That Edward shall be fearful of his life,
      And then, to purge his fear, I'll be thy death.
90   Henry and his son are gone; thou, Clarence, art next;
      And by one and one I will dispatch the rest,
      Counting myself but bad till I be best.
      I'll throw thy body in another room
      And triumph, Henry, in thy day of doom. *Exit [with the body]*

                              5.7
            [*A chair of state.*] *Flourish. Enter* KING EDWARD, [LADY
            GRAY *his*] *Queen,* [GEORGE *Duke of*] CLARENCE, RICH-
            ARD [*Duke of* GLOUCESTER, *the Lord*] HASTINGS, *a*
            nurse, [*carrying the infant*] *Prince* [*Edward*], *and*
            attendants
      KING EDWARD   Once more we sit in England's royal throne,
      Repurchased with the blood of enemies.
      What valiant foemen, like to autumn's corn,
      Have we mowed down in tops° of all their pride!   *at the peak*
5   Three dukes of Somerset, threefold renowned
      For hardy and undoubted° champions;   *fearless*
      Two Cliffords, as the father and the son;
      And two Northumberlands—two braver men
      Ne'er spurred their coursers° at the trumpet's sound.   *warhorses*
10   With them, the two brave bears, Warwick and Montague,[1]
      That in their chains fettered the kingly lion
      And made the forest tremble when they roared.
      Thus have we swept suspicion° from our seat°   *worry / throne*
      And made our footstool of security.
15   [*To* LADY GRAY] Come hither, Bess, and let me kiss my boy.
            [*The nurse brings forth the infant prince.* KING
            EDWARD *kisses him*]
      Young Ned, for thee, thine uncles and myself
      Have in our armours watched° the winter's night,   *stayed awake during*
      Went all afoot in summer's scalding heat,
      That thou mightst repossess the crown in peace;
20   And of our labours thou shalt reap the gain.
      RICHARD OF GLOUCESTER [*aside*]   I'll blast° his harvest, an your   *wither*
            head were laid;[2]
      For yet I am not looked on° in the world.   *noticed*
      This shoulder was ordained so thick to heave;
      And heave it shall some weight or break my back.
25   Work thou the way, and thou shalt execute.[3]
      KING EDWARD   Clarence and Gloucester, love my lovely queen;
      And kiss your princely nephew, brothers, both.
      GEORGE OF CLARENCE   The duty that I owe unto your majesty
      I seal upon the lips of this sweet babe.
            [*He kisses the infant prince*]
30   LADY GRAY   Thanks, noble Clarence—worthy brother, thanks.

5.7 Location: The Palace, London.   2. Once your head is laid in the grave.
1. The coat of arms of these brothers included the   3. Devise a way, (my head), and you, (shoulder and
image of a bear chained to a staff.   hand), shall carry it out.

RICHARD OF GLOUCESTER   And that I love the tree° from whence   *(family of York)*
    thou sprang'st,
Witness the loving kiss I give the fruit.
    [*He kisses the infant prince*]
[*Aside*] To say the truth, so Judas kissed his master,
And cried 'All hail!' whenas he meant all harm.[4]
35   KING EDWARD   Now am I seated as my soul delights,
Having my country's peace and brothers' loves.
GEORGE OF CLARENCE   What will your grace have done with
    Margaret?
René her father, to the King of France
Hath pawned the Sicils° and Jerusalem,   *Naples and Sicily*
40   And hither have they sent it° for her ransom.   *(the money raised)*
KING EDWARD   Away with her, and waft her° hence to France.   *convey her by water*
And now what rests° but that we spend the time   *remains*
With stately triumphs,° mirthful comic shows,   *festivals*
Such as befits the pleasure of the court?
45   Sound drums and trumpets—farewell, sour annoy!°   *bitter troubles*
For here, I hope, begins our lasting joy.   [*Flourish.*] *Exeunt*

---

4. Judas, identifying Jesus to the officers eager to arrest him, greeted him with a kiss and the salutation "All hail."
whenas: when.

Titus Andronicus

Human sacrifice. Gang rape. Mutilation. Ritual butchery. Mother-son cannibalism. *Titus Andronicus* delighted audiences of the 1590s, and the memory of its enormous popular success was still alive more than twenty years later, when Shakespeare's contemporary, Ben Jonson, referred to it as a famous old crowd-pleaser in his comedy *Bartholomew Fair*. Several centuries of critics since then, however, have deplored the play's gratuitous violence. The late-seventeenth-century playwright Edward Ravenscroft considered *Titus Andronicus* "a heap of rubbish"; the twentieth-century poet and critic T. S. Eliot called it "one of the stupidest and most uninspired plays ever written." Some have even claimed that Shakespeare could not have written *Titus Andronicus*, even though contemporaries testify to his authorship and it inaugurates themes that will interest him again: he returns to the Machiavellian villain in *Richard III*, to the urgency of revenge in *Hamlet*, to the old man unwisely relinquishing power in *Lear*, to questions of race and intermarriage in *Othello* and *The Tempest*, to important moments in Roman history in *The Rape of Lucrece, Julius Caesar, Coriolanus*, and *Antony and Cleopatra*.

Of course, Shakespeare himself, writing his first tragedy in 1592 (with, some scholars argue, the help of George Peele), could not have anticipated the reasons for which he would eventually be canonized. Moreover, the distinction between "high art" and "low entertainment" that often underlies complaints about *Titus Andronicus* would have been unfamiliar to Shakespeare and to his audience: the contrast between popular and elite culture was drawn differently in early modern England than it has been in later centuries. Even by the standards of Shakespeare's contemporaries, however, *Titus Andronicus* is an extravagantly bloody play, often deliberately shocking or grotesque. It seems worth asking how it fits into an oeuvre in which many have been reluctant to grant it a place.

Generically speaking, *Titus Andronicus* is a tragedy of revenge, a very old form that originated in ancient Greece, flourished in ancient Rome, and was revived in the 1580s in England by Shakespeare's predecessor Thomas Kyd. English Renaissance revenge tragedies typically feature a man whose family members have been raped or murdered by a king, duke, or emperor. Because the administration of justice rests in the hands of the very person who has committed the outrage, no redress is obtainable through established institutions. As a result, the hero takes matters into his own hands. Ironically, as he struggles to impose a just order upon his world, he loses his own moral bearings and even his sanity: the commonsensical standards of "justice" upon which he has initially relied often come to seem either flawed or unreachable. In the final scenes, the revenger wreaks some appalling vengeance upon his enemies and then is killed or commits suicide himself. By staging the spectacle of a subject exterminating his "betters," Renaissance revenge tragedy taps into frustrations and ambivalences that must have accumulated in the hierarchical, deliberately inequitable social arrangements of early modern England. Spectators could experience a vicarious thrill of sympathy with the revenger and relish the atrocities represented onstage, even while, at the end of the play, acknowledging the moral unacceptability of revenge and the necessity for the revenger's death.

Titus Andronicus differs from roughly contemporary revenge tragedies in degree rather than in kind. Revengers typically begin as conscientious, law-abiding types: otherwise their eventual descent into illegality would furnish little dramatic interest. In Titus's case, these traits are highly exaggerated: when offered the imperial diadem, his sense of propriety induces him to defer to Saturninus, the eldest son of the last emperor, even though in Rome the office of emperor was not necessarily an inherited one. Of course, the obligation that Saturninus thus incurs makes Titus's later suffering at the hands of the imperial family seem all the more galling. At the same time, Shakespeare complicates the action by giving Saturninus's wife, Tamora, an excellent reason for hating Titus: in the first scene, he has ignored her desperate pleas and sacrificed her eldest son. So, in fact, Titus's revenge is a response to Tamora's own vengeance. The doubling of reprisals in *Titus Andronicus* gives some pretext for the play's relentless bloodiness; but it is worth remembering too that bloodiness is an earmark of revenge tragedy then and now. One modern corollary to a play like *Titus Andronicus* is the movie thriller in which a rogue cop or ex-military officer brutally retaliates against those who have murdered his partners or loved ones: the kind of film, in other words, that is likely to attract a vast audience even while provoking condemnation of "media violence." *Titus* seems considerably less grotesque when it is compared with other plays of its kind rather than, say, with *Romeo and Juliet*.

In its elaborately detailed antique setting, however, *Titus Andronicus* differs strikingly from most Renaissance revenge tragedies. The play is an early manifestation of Shakespeare's enduring interest in classical culture, a "Roman" play akin to *Julius Caesar, Coriolanus,* and *Antony and Cleopatra*. But in contrast to the later Roman plays, which are based on history and biography, the plot of *Titus Andronicus* is pure fiction. Unfettered by fact, Shakespeare is free to fabricate an extravagant nightmare universe that presses against the frontiers of plausibility. At the same time, he puts a great deal of emphasis on the play's "Roman-ness," making constant reference to classical myths, to legendary and historical figures, to imperial institutions, to the places and customs of ancient Rome.

Shakespeare creates what might be called a "Rome effect" by an eclectic process of extracting and combining motifs from a wide variety of classical stories. Titus as he appears in the opening scene, for instance—in his austere patriotism, his intolerance of dissent, his acute sense of personal and family honor, his traditional piety, and his ferocious commitment to patriarchal hierarchy—is a recurrent Roman personality type. Shakespeare could have found precedents for these traits in numerous figures from Roman history. After a victory in battle, Horatius killed his sister for lamenting her betrothed, a man of the enemy nation whom he himself had slain in combat; Gaius Mucius Scaevola deliberately burned off his right hand in the presence of an enemy king to demonstrate the resolution of the Romans; Titus Manlius Torquatus was a general so severe that he had his own son executed for eagerly anticipating an order to engage the enemy; Marcus Portius Cato's contempt for "softness" made him both an extraordinary military leader and an eloquent misogynist; Appius Claudius killed his daughter after her sexual honor was compromised. Most likely, Shakespeare had all these exemplary figures in mind, and probably more. Likewise the career of Titus's son Lucius, a soldier who defends Rome bravely against external enemies but who finds himself persecuted by his own countrymen, recalls the experience of several historic figures: the brothers Publius Scipio Africanus and Lucius Scipio Asiaticus, who subdued much of North Africa and Asia only to be falsely accused of embezzlement; or Caius Marcius Coriolanus, who after his exile joined Rome's enemies and marched on his native city.

Similarly, Titus's daughter Lavinia has a number of classical precursors. The story of her rape and mutilation is loosely based on a story that, as retold in Ovid's *Metamorphoses,* was commonly assigned to Elizabethan boys in school. In this ancient legend, King Tereus rapes his sister-in-law Philomela and cuts out her tongue in order to prevent her from revealing his identity. Philomela, however, imparts the truth to her sister Progne (or Procne), Tereus's wife, by weaving a tapestry that illustrates the crime. In revenge, Progne butchers her own son by Tereus and serves him to her husband as part of a feast. The similarities between Lavinia's plight and Philomela's are often noted in *Titus Andronicus,* and Lavinia herself reveals the truth about the crime when she gets her stumps on a copy of the *Metamorphoses*.

Progne serving Itys to Tereus. From Antonio Tempesta, *Ovid's "Metamorphoses"* (1606).

But Philomela is not the only model for Lavinia. Shakespeare draws upon the story of the rape of Lucretia, an ancient Roman matron violated by Tarquin, the king's son; she committed suicide after revealing the crime to her male relatives. She was revenged by a group of men who, like Lucius in *Titus Andronicus,* used the outrage as a pretext for overthrowing tyrannical power and setting up a new government. Shakespeare also incorporates into *Titus Andronicus* some features of the story of Appius and Virginia. Virginia was a young Roman woman who was sexually threatened by a powerful judge and killed by her father to prevent her rape; like Lucretia, she became the pretext for a revolutionary uprising. Lavinia's story, then, is an amalgam of classical rape narratives. Her terribly mutilated body condenses a long history of sporadic violence against women into a single, intensely imagined brutalization. Like Titus Lavinia seems to sum up a whole tradition, one highly prestigious in an age that venerated the classics, and at the same time deeply disturbing.

This particular way of imagining "Rome," as an anthology of stories, reflects Shakespeare's education in Renaissance England. England had, of course, been a Roman territory, and marks of the Roman occupation persisted. Romans had built the road system still in use in Shakespeare's time; the remains of their fortifications were (and are) still visible in many locations. But England had been a remote outpost of the empire, not a place where the treasures of antiquity were commonly to be found. While Renaissance Italians could ground their knowledge of antiquity upon great architecture and statuary all around them, the English, few of whom traveled to Italy in the sixteenth century, imbibed the classical past through books, through a grammar-school curriculum that emphasized a firm grounding in Latin literature and history. For Shakespeare and his compatriots, in other words, the Roman past had less to do with places or artifacts than with texts.

The influence of these texts echoes through *Titus Andronicus*: Ovid's *Metamorphoses,* a fantastic compilation of pagan myths; Virgil's *Aeneid,* which recounts the epic voyage of the Trojan prince Aeneas to Carthage and then Italy; the gory legends of vengeance dramatized by the tragedian Seneca; the histories of the Roman Republic and Empire, written by Livy, Plutarch, Tacitus, Sallust, and Suetonius. In *Titus Andronicus,* the sign of Rome's dominion often seems less a moral or political superiority than a kind of narrative ascendancy. Shakespeare's Goths and Africans apparently have no history, no myths, of their own: instead, they invoke and mimic examples provided by their conquerors, just as Renaissance Europeans revived the classical literary inheritance, testifying to its importance in the very acts of reading and imitating it.

In *Titus Andronicus,* all the characters in the play are acutely conscious of the glorious Roman past as it is enshrined in narrative. Their dependence on old stories means that their lives have a curiously derivative quality. The characters not only model their behavior on these stories, but they consistently exceed the prototype. Whereas in the *Metamorphoses* one man rapes Philomela and cuts out her tongue afterward, in *Titus Andronicus* two men rape Lavinia, and they cut off her hands as well. Whereas Progne cooks one child, Titus bakes two. "For worse than Philomel you used my daughter," Titus declares, "And worse than Progne I will be revenged" (5.2.193–94). He both invokes and goes beyond his original example, intensifying the original crime in a way characteristic of revengers ancient and modern: "An act is not revenged," writes the ancient tragedian Seneca, "unless it is surpassed." Thus there is an interesting corollary between the spiraling ferocity typical of the revenge plot and the competitive way in which the characters in Shakespeare's revenge play fit themselves into a Roman tradition by exceeding its paradigms, enacting its stories "with a vengeance," as one says.

Triumphal arch and its collapse. From Jan van der Noot, *A Theatre for Worldlings* (1569).

Of course, the oppressive weight of the past is a problem not merely for the characters of *Titus Andronicus* but also for its playwright. Like his characters, Shakespeare recycles the old stories with a difference, "surpassing" them just as the revenger surpasses the original crime. From our point of view, Shakespeare seems the world's preeminent dramatist, secure in the greatness that was already beginning to be accorded him at the time of his death. But in the early years of his career, Shakespeare might well have wondered whether and how it was possible to use, even while surpassing, the examples earlier writers had set for him. The notorious excesses of *Titus Andronicus* are one way of employing, even while going beyond, the examples he inherited.

If, in fact, Shakespeare worried about how he would measure up against his predecessors, and about whether the present and future would be able to compete with the past, it is interesting that he sets *Titus Andronicus* in the late fourth century C.E. At this point in history, Rome had dominated Europe, North Africa, and the Middle East for almost five hundred years: in both extent and duration, its empire was historically unprecedented and has never been achieved again. The Roman ritual that embodies and celebrates that rule is the "triumph" with which *Titus Andronicus* begins: a victory procession accorded, from time immemorial, to conquering Roman generals when they returned from the perimeters of the empire with barbarian chieftains in tow. By the fourth century, however, the long Roman dominion was drawing to a close. Shakespeare's sixteenth-century audience knows that although Titus may still be winning battles against the Goths, the time is near when the boundaries of the empire will crumble and invaders will sweep down from the north, annihilating Rome's power and bringing the era of classical civilization to an end.

In *Titus Andronicus*, then, Shakespeare portrays a society teetering on the verge of obsolescence: it has a long, long history but not much of a future. The signs of decadence, corruption, and loss of cultural confidence are everywhere. For instance, the difference between Roman and barbarian initially seems clearly, even absolutely, marked: Tamora and her sons are in chains, Titus and his sons conquering heroes. "Thou art a Roman, be not barbarous," Marcus advises Titus, as if the two terms were necessarily incompatible. Even in the first scene, however, the Roman sense of superiority seems unwarranted. The quarrel over the imperial throne precedes Titus's victory celebration, suggesting the institutional instability that will ultimately subvert Rome from within even as uncouth armies threaten to overwhelm it from without. Moreover, the climax of Titus's victory celebration is his insistence on sacrificing Alarbus despite Tamora's maternal pleas: a case in which the traditional forms of piety that underlie Roman civilization seem to require the barbaric practice of human sacrifice. If Rome's conviction of racial and cultural supremacy—of *deserving* to rule the world—was once a workable notion, it is so no longer. The obsession with the past that pervades *Titus Andronicus* thus seems oddly empty. Even as inherited stories provide the only paradigms for action, they fail to nourish a fertile sense of tradition that might help Rome renew itself.

As traditional distinctions lose their prestige and their plausibility, the social procedures that depend on such distinctions likewise begin to collapse. The play's first scene neatly exemplifies the problem. The brothers Saturninus and Bassianus quarrel first over the possession of the imperial throne and then over the possession of Lavinia, whom both wish to marry. In Shakespeare's England, the first dispute would have been settled according to the principle of "primogeniture," which gave priority in inheritance to the elder brother; the second would have been settled in favor of the younger brother, on the grounds of his preexisting betrothal to Lavinia. In Rome, however, it seems impossible to settle competing claims in an orderly way. In fact, Saturninus does eventually get the throne and Bassianus the woman, but not without a good deal of confusion and some lethal violence. The suggestion is that established methods of allocating property or privilege to one or another person may be quite arbitrary, but that the alternative to such methods is chaos.

In case the point is not sufficiently clear, Shakespeare immediately follows the quarrel between the two Roman brothers with another scene of sibling rivalry, this time between Tamora's sons, once again over sexual access to Lavinia. Unlike their Roman counterparts, these men are seeking not marriage but an adulterous relationship, and their villainous confidant Aaron has little difficulty massaging their illicit ambitions into plans for a rape. Adultery and rape seem the "opposites" of the marriage desired by the Roman men; and certainly the ferocity of the Gothic brothers' attack on Lavinia makes abundantly clear why such behavior is intolerable. At the same time, Shakespeare's juxtaposition of scenes suggests, subversively, the *similarities* between Roman marriage and rape. In neither case is Lavinia's consent at issue: she becomes the property of whoever happens to carry her off by force. Once again the distinction between legitimate and illegitimate behavior seems indispensable and at the same time remarkably indistinct.

The characters apparently best equipped to function in this world of collapsing distinctions are Aaron and Tamora, whose interracial adultery is perceived as particularly scandalous by both Romans and Goths. Their relationship is perhaps the most obvious example of the play's tendency to juxtapose opposites that turn out to have a great deal in common. Both Tamora and Aaron are outsiders who recognize from the outset the artificiality of the precepts by which Rome pretends to govern itself and the world. Neither character has much to gain by endorsing Rome's view of itself, which has relegated them to positions of servitude and powerlessness. In a world in which women are treated as the sexual property of their male relatives, "good" women like Lavinia seem destined for passivity and victimization. One acquires power in such circumstances by refusing to play by the rules. In a few lines, Tamora—manipulative, ruthless, and cunning—transfers herself from the extreme of subjugation, as Titus's captive, to the apex of power as empress of Rome.

Aaron is Tamora's natural counterpart. He is a stage descendant of the "black men" of the medieval morality plays, which conflated traditional depictions of the devil with racist conceptions of "Moors" and "Africans." But at the same time that Shakespeare exploits to the full Aaron's capacity for gleeful villainy, he makes Aaron's point of view comprehensible, even at some points attractive, to the audience. Roman hierarchies would consign Aaron permanently to a subordinate position, for racial rather than sexual reasons; and like Tamora, he sees no reason to accept the validity of that assignment. Why should he collaborate in his own oppression? It is no coincidence that Shakespeare's verse seems at its best in this play when Aaron is delivering a soliloquy. His view of the world is very close to what the play as a whole seems to endorse: that the assumptions upon which ethical behavior and social institutions depend represent fictions rather than facts.

For the dramatic technique of *Titus Andronicus,* like its villains, seems to insist that the "normal" or the "proper" is a mere construct, that apparently vivid distinctions are not as clear-cut as they seem, that moral opposites have a way of turning into one another. We have already seen Shakespeare setting the behavior of Bassianus and Saturninus beside the behavior of Chiron and Demetrius, as well as associating his white empress with his black slave. Such juxtapositions seem to be designed to induce a sort of evaluative vertigo, an effect that becomes most intense, perhaps, in the figure of the unnamed infant who results from Tamora's adultery with Aaron. In the view of most of the play's characters, this child physically embodies, and thus serves as both proof and symbol of, its parents' utter depravity. At the same time, Aaron's unexpectedly fierce solicitude for the child—which contrasts attractively with Titus's casual willingness to slaughter his own son—prevents the audience from taking at face value the rhetoric of disgust and fear discharged upon the little unfortunate from everyone else in the play. This is, after all, a baby. Every time it is brought onstage, the function it seems designed to serve in the play's symbolic economy powerfully conflicts with its intrinsic infant appeal.

In other cases, Shakespeare produces jarringly appropriate incongruities not by juxtaposing characters but by evoking apparently inappropriate dramatic genres.

Ethiopian soldier. From Cesare Vecellio, *De gli habiti antichi et moderni* (1590).

For instance, when Quintus and Martius find Bassianus's body, the audience knows they are being framed for murder, and one might expect a playwright to exploit the pathos of the situation, encouraging the audience to pity and sympathize with the innocent characters. Instead, the scene is played for laughs, as Titus's sons struggle farcically to pull one another out of a hole. Another jarring technique in *Titus Andronicus* is the deliberately awful play on words: "Mark, Marcus, mark" (3.1.143), cries Titus as they behold the ravished and mutilated Lavinia. In such cases, Shakespeare's humor shatters the norms of dramatic and moral suitability, implying the artificiality of what is conventionally considered "normal" or "proper."

If the moral and social problem of *Titus* is that eventually nothing is taboo, the aesthetic problem of the play is that literary convention too comes to seem entirely artificial. Shakespeare's deliberate rule breaking in *Titus Andronicus* risks looking like, or simply being the equivalent of, tasteless incompetence. This is especially true when terrible suffering is at stake. Marcus's long, garishly metaphorical speech at the sight of his niece's bleeding body, for instance, seems grossly beside the point. Is Shakespeare merely being inept here—is he as out of control as Marcus seems to be? Or is he deliberately exploring the limits of his medium by unexpectedly violating its usual rules, in the manner of modern surrealists, absurdists, or postmodernists? The critical debate about *Titus Andronicus* has largely involved quarrels between those who would claim the former and those who would claim the latter.

Even if Shakespeare sometimes seems to share the heartlessness of Aaron and Tamora, he does not represent the Goth and the African as admirable characters. Rebelling against the principles of "civilization" puts them outside any moral community. At the end of the play, Lucius orders Aaron starved to death and Tamora's body thrown over the city walls, as if it were mere garbage. Their treatment indicates his conviction that their behavior has put themselves outside the classification of the human, so that when they are starving, no one has an obligation to relieve them, and when they are dead, no one need respect their remains. The final scene reasserts the difference between human society and what Titus calls "a wilderness of tigers," a difference that the revenge plot has come close to erasing. And despite the abundant evidence that Roman social organization is fundamentally flawed and soon to be toppled, it is not surprising that both Goths and Romans should greet Lucius's restoration of order at the end of the play with profound relief.

Titus Andronicus, then, suggests that the principles of Roman order are patently false and often arbitrarily oppressive; but it also suggests that acknowledging this arbitrariness or rebelling against this falsity and oppression will have disastrous consequences. What produces Roman "virtue" seems to be a delusion, but being undeluded, as Tamora and Aaron are and Titus becomes, is even more terrible. In Shakespeare's later tragedies, the alternative to normality is often a visionary possibility that seems, if only it could be lived out, to improve upon the status quo: the loves of Romeo and Juliet, Antony and Cleopatra, Othello and Desdemona are examples of such "constructive rule breaking." In *Titus Andronicus,* however, traditional taboos, however cruel, brittle, or despotic they seem, are the sole guarantors of order. Once they are shattered, nothing can take their place, and sheer chaos ensues.

The pessimism, even nihilism, of this vision, combined with Shakespeare's almost playful emphasis on what most writers prefer to skirt or play down, is doubtless what has made *Titus* seem merely bad to so many readers since the late seventeenth century. From another point of view, however, *Titus Andronicus* is a daring experiment, one that Shakespeare did not repeat but that nonetheless provides fascinating insight into his development as a dramatist.

KATHARINE EISAMAN MAUS

TEXTUAL NOTE

There are three extant quarto editions of *Titus Andronicus.* The First Quarto (Q1) was printed in 1594 and seems to derive directly from Shakespeare's manuscript. Only one copy of Q1 now survives. Q2, published in 1600, was prepared from a copy of Q1 whose last few pages had been damaged; the printer invented several lines to fill in text missing from the final scene of the play. In most cases, Q2's deviations from Q1 have no authority, but in several instances, it seems to have preserved corrected readings not found in the single copy of Q1 now extant. (Since proofreading in Elizabethan times was done while the text was in the process of being printed instead of beforehand, it is often the case that copies printed late in a press run will rectify errors present in earlier copies.) The most notable of Q2's corrections is the omission of three and a half lines from 1.1. These lines seem inappropriate to their context: they suggest that Alarbus has already been sacrificed, an act portrayed later in the scene. Q3 reprints Q2 with some minor corrections and corruptions.

The First Folio of 1623 (F) was prepared from Q3, apparently a copy annotated by comparison with the playhouse promptbook. It includes one entire scene missing from the quartos, the "fly-killing scene" at the end of Act 3, probably written by Shakespeare for a revival of the play in 1594. It also includes more stage directions than the quarto texts, as well as one complete and one fragmentary line that are probably authentic.

In general, Q1 is the most authoritative text, but the Oxford editors accept eight substantive readings from Q2 and resort to F for the fly-killing scene and some stage directions. The three and a half lines omitted from 1.1 and two other passages from Q1 probably intended for deletion are to be found, indented, after 1.1.35, 1.1.283, and 4.3.91, respectively.

SELECTED BIBLIOGRAPHY

Barker, Francis. "A Wilderness of Tigers: *Titus Andronicus,* Anthropology, and the Occlusion of Violence." *The Culture of Violence: Tragedy and History.* Chicago: University of Chicago Press, 1993. 143–206. Cultural anthropology and the history of criminal prosecution in early modern England illuminate *Titus Andronicus,* particularly the "Clown scene."

Bartels, Emily. "Making More of the Moor: Aaron, Othello, and Renaissance Refashionings of Race." *Shakespeare Quarterly* 41 (1990): 433–54. Aaron in the context of other sixteenth-century English depictions of black Africans.

James, Heather. "Cultural Disintegration in *Titus Andronicus:* Mutilating Titus, Virgil, and Rome." *Violence in Drama.* Ed. James Redmond. New York: Cambridge University Press, 1991. 123–40. Shakespeare's debt to Virgil's *Aeneid.*

Kahn, Coppélia. "The Daughter's Seduction in *Titus Andronicus*; or, Writing Is the Best Revenge." *The Roman Shakespeare: Warriors, Wounds, and Women*. New York: Routledge, 1997. 46–76. Discussion of the play, focusing primarily on Lavinia.

Loomba, Ania. "Wilderness and Civilization in *Titus Andronicus*." *Shakespeare, Race, and Colonialism*. New York: Oxford University Press, 2002. 75–90. Focuses on the alliance between Aaron and Tamora.

Palmer, D. J. "The Unspeakable in Pursuit of the Uneatable: Language and Action in *Titus Andronicus*." *Critical Quarterly* 14 (1972): 320–39. The representation of suffering.

Vickers, Brian. "*Titus Andronicus* with George Peele." *Shakespeare, Co-Author: A Historical Study of Five Collaborative Plays*. New York: Oxford University Press, 2002. 148–243. Discusses the likelihood that Shakespeare and George Peele collaborated on *Titus Andronicus*.

Waith, Eugene. "The Metamorphosis of Violence in *Titus Andronicus*." *Shakespeare Survey* 10 (1957): 39–59. Shakespeare's debt to Ovid's *Metamorphoses*.

FILMS

Titus Andronicus. 1985. Dir. Jane Howell. UK. 120 min. This production, stylized and self-consciously theatrical, is often considered one of the best of the BBC series and a major influence on Taymor's bigger-budget film (1999).

Titus. 1999. Dir. Julie Taymor. USA. 162 min. A visually stunning adaptation of Shakespeare's play, emphasizing its stomach-churning violence. The fine cast includes Anthony Hopkins as Titus and Jessica Lange as Tamora.

Titus Andronicus

THE PERSONS OF THE PLAY

SATURNINUS, eldest son of the late Emperor of Rome; later
    Emperor
BASSIANUS, his brother
TITUS ANDRONICUS, a Roman nobleman, general against the
    Goths
LUCIUS ⎫
QUINTUS ⎪
MARTIUS ⎬ sons of Titus
MUTIUS ⎭
LAVINIA, daughter of Titus
YOUNG LUCIUS, a boy, son of Lucius
MARCUS ANDRONICUS, a tribune of the people, Titus' brother
PUBLIUS, his son
SEMPRONIUS ⎫
CAIUS ⎬ kinsmen of Titus
VALENTINE ⎭
A CAPTAIN
AEMILIUS
TAMORA, Queen of the Goths, later wife of Saturninus
ALARBUS ⎫
DEMETRIUS ⎬ her sons
CHIRON ⎭
AARON, a Moor, her lover
A NURSE
A CLOWN
Senators, tribunes, Romans, Goths, soldiers, and attendants

1.1

*Flourish. Enter the Tribunes and Senators¹ aloft, and
then enter [below]* SATURNINUS *and his followers at one
door and* BASSIANUS *and his followers at the other, with
drum° and colours°*   *drummer / standard-bearer*
SATURNINUS   Noble patricians, patrons° of my right,   *supporters*
  Defend the justice of my cause with arms.
  And countrymen, my loving followers,
  Plead my successive title° with your swords.   *right to succeed*
5   I am his first-born son that was the last
  That ware° the imperial diadem of Rome.   *wore*
  Then let my father's honours live in me,
  Nor wrong mine age° with this indignity.   *seniority*
BASSIANUS   Romans, friends, followers, favourers of my right,

---

1.1 Location: Before the Roman Capitol, represented
by the upper stage ("aloft"). The tomb of the Andronicus family, a stage structure or a trapdoor, is accessible
onstage.

1. Respectively the representatives of the common
people (plebeians) and the upper classes (patricians).

10 If ever Bassianus, Caesar's[2] son,
   Were gracious° in the eyes of royal Rome,   *Found favor*
   Keep° then this passage° to the Capitol,   *Defend / path*
   And suffer not dishonour to approach
   The imperial seat, to virtue consecrate,°   *consecrated*
15 To justice, continence, and nobility;
   But let desert[3] in pure election[4] shine,
   And, Romans, fight for freedom in your choice.
            Enter MARCUS ANDRONICUS *aloft with the crown*
   MARCUS   Princes that strive by factions and by friends
   Ambitiously for rule and empery,°   *imperial rule*
20 Know that the people of Rome, for whom we stand
   A special party,[5] have by common voice
   In election for the Roman empery
   Chosen Andronicus, surnamèd *Pius*[5]
   For many good and great deserts to Rome.
25 A nobler man, a braver warrior,
   Lives not this day within the city walls.
   He by the Senate is accited° home   *summoned*
   From weary wars against the barbarous Goths,
   That with his sons, a terror to our foes,
30 Hath yoked° a nation strong, trained up in arms.   *subdued*
   Ten years are spent since first he undertook
   This cause of Rome, and chastisèd with arms
   Our enemies' pride. Five times he hath returned
   Bleeding to Rome, bearing his valiant sons
35 In coffins from the field;[7]
35.1   *and at this day*
            To the monument of the Andronici
            Done sacrifice of expiation,
            And slain the noblest prisoner of the Goths.
   And now at last, laden with honour's spoils,
   Returns the good Andronicus to Rome,
   Renownèd Titus, flourishing in arms.
   Let us entreat by honour of his° name   *(the late Emperor's)*
40 Whom worthily you would have now succeeded,[8]
   And in the Capitol and Senate's right,[9]
   Whom you pretend° to honour and adore,   *claim*
   That you withdraw you and abate your strength,
   Dismiss your followers, and, as suitors should,
45 Plead your deserts in peace and humbleness.
   SATURNINUS   How fair the Tribune speaks to calm my thoughts.
   BASSIANUS   Marcus Andronicus, so I do affy°   *trust*
   In thy uprightness and integrity,
   And so I love and honour thee and thine,
50 Thy noble brother Titus and his sons,
   And her to whom my thoughts are humbled all,

---

2. The previous Emperor (Bassianus is Saturninus's younger brother).
3. Merit (as opposed to birth order).
4. Free choice of the citizens.
5. A representative elected for a particular purpose.
6. He has been given the honorary title of "Dutiful."
7. The following indented passage (lines 35.1–35.4),

found in Q1 following a comma after "field" but not included in Q2 or Q3 or F, conflicts with the subsequent action and presumably should have been deleted. (In the second line, Q1 reads "of that" for "of the.")
8. Whose place you want a worthy candidate to fill.
9. To choose a new emperor, traditionally an elected and not an inherited office.

Gracious Lavinia, Rome's rich ornament,
That I will here dismiss my loving friends
And to my fortunes and the people's favour
55 Commit my cause in balance to be weighed.
                                Exeunt [his] soldiers [and followers]
SATURNINUS   Friends that have been thus forward in my right,
I thank you all, and here dismiss you all,
And to the love and favour of my country
Commit myself, my person, and the cause.
                    [Exeunt his soldiers and followers]
          [To the Tribunes and Senators]
60 Rome, be as just and gracious unto me
As I am confident° and kind to thee.   *trusting*
Open the gates and let me in.
BASSIANUS   Tribunes, and me, a poor competitor.°   *co-petitioner*
          Flourish.° They go up into the Senate House.   *Trumpet fanfare*
          Enter a CAPTAIN
CAPTAIN   Romans, make way. The good Andronicus,
65 Patron° of virtue, Rome's best champion,   *Representative; pattern*
Successful in the battles that he fights,
With honour and with fortune is returned
From where he circumscribèd° with his sword   *restrained*
And brought to yoke the enemies of Rome.
          *Sound drums and trumpets, and then enter [*MARTIUS
          and MUTIUS,] *two of Titus' sons, and then men bearing*
          *coffin[s] covered with black, then [*LUCIUS *and* QUINTUS,]
          two other sons; then TITUS ANDRONICUS *[in his chariot],*
          and then TAMORA *the Queen of Goths and her sons*
          *[*ALARBUS,] CHIRON, *and* DEMETRIUS, *with* AARON *the*
          Moor[1] *and others as many as can be. Then set down the*
          coffin[s], and TITUS *speaks*
70 TITUS   Hail, Rome, victorious in thy mourning weeds!°   *garments*
Lo, as the bark° that hath discharged his° freight   *ship / its*
Returns with precious lading° to the bay   *cargo*
From whence at first she weighed her anchorage,°   *anchor*
Cometh Andronicus, bound with laurel bows,[2]
75 To re-salute his country with his tears,
Tears of true joy for his return to Rome.
Thou great defender[3] of this Capitol,
Stand gracious to the rites that we intend.
Romans, of five-and-twenty valiant sons,
80 Half of the number that King Priam[4] had,
Behold the poor remains, alive and dead.
These that survive let Rome reward with love;
These that I bring unto their latest° home,   *last*
With burial amongst their ancestors.
85 Here Goths have given me leave[5] to sheathe my sword.
Titus unkind,[6] and careless of thine own,

---

1. "Moor" in classical times referred to an inhabitant of Mauretania, in northwest Africa; the term was later applied to Islamic Africans of Arab descent who conquered Spain in the Middle Ages. In Renaissance England, the word often was used of any black-skinned African.
2. Laurel wreath, symbol of victory.

3. Jupiter Capitolinus, king of the Roman gods, to whose shrine on the Capitol victorious generals brought their spoils.
4. King of Troy during the Trojan War.
5. Allowed me (ironic, since the Goths were defeated in battle).
6. Devoid of natural feeling; undutiful.

Why suffer'st thou thy sons unburied yet
To hover on the dreadful shore of Styx?[7]
Make way to lay them by their brethren.
    They open the tomb
90   There greet in silence as the dead are wont,
And sleep in peace, slain in your country's wars.
O sacred receptacle of my joys,
Sweet cell of virtue and nobility.
How many sons hast thou of mine in store
95   That thou wilt never render° to me more!°   *return / again*
LUCIUS   Give us the proudest prisoner of the Goths,
That we may hew his limbs and on a pile
Ad manes fratrum° sacrifice his flesh   *To our brothers' shades*
Before this earthy prison of their bones,
100   That so the shadows° be not unappeased,   *spirits*
Nor we disturbed with prodigies° on earth.   *evil happenings*
TITUS   I give him you, the noblest that survives,
The eldest son of this distressèd Queen.
TAMORA [*kneeling*]   Stay, Roman brethren! Gracious conqueror,
105   Victorious Titus, rue° the tears I shed—   *pity*
A mother's tears in passion° for her son—   *grief*
And if thy sons were ever dear to thee,
O, think my son to be as dear to me!
Sufficeth not that we are brought to Rome
110   To beautify thy triumphs,° and return   *triumphal processions*
Captive to thee and to thy Roman yoke;
But must my sons be slaughtered in the streets
For valiant doings in their country's cause?
O, if to fight for king and commonweal
115   Were piety in thine,° it is in these.°   *(your sons) / (my sons)*
Andronicus, stain not thy tomb with blood.
Wilt thou draw near the nature of the gods?
Draw near them then in being merciful.
Sweet mercy is nobility's true badge.
120   Thrice-noble Titus, spare my first-born son.
TITUS   Patient° yourself, madam, and pardon me.   *Calm*
These are their brethren whom your Goths beheld
Alive and dead, and for their brethren slain
Religiously° they ask a sacrifice.   *On religious grounds*
125   To this your son is marked, and die he must
T'appease their groaning shadows that are gone.
LUCIUS   Away with him, and make a fire straight,°   *immediately*
And with our swords upon a pile of wood
Let's hew his limbs till they be clean consumed.
    Exeunt Titus' sons with ALARBUS
130   TAMORA [*rising*]   O cruel irreligious piety!
CHIRON   Was never Scythia[8] half so barbarous.
DEMETRIUS   Oppose not Scythia to ambitious Rome.
Alarbus goes to rest, and we survive
To tremble under Titus' threat'ning look.
135   Then, madam, stand resolved; but hope withal

---

7. River surrounding the underworld; the dead could   8. Uncivilized region north of the Black Sea.
not cross it until they had been properly buried.

The selfsame gods that armed the Queen of Troy[9]
With opportunity of sharp revenge
Upon the Thracian tyrant in his tent
May favour Tamora, the Queen of Goths—
140 When Goths were Goths and Tamora was queen—
To quit° her bloody wrongs upon her foes.   *revenge*
      Enter [QUINTUS, MARCUS, MUTIUS, *and* LUCIUS,] *the sons*
      of Andronicus, again, with bloody swords
LUCIUS See, lord and father, how we have performed
Our Roman rites. Alarbus' limbs are lopped
And entrails feed the sacrificing fire,
145 Whose smoke like incense doth perfume the sky.
Remaineth naught but to inter our brethren
And with loud 'larums° welcome them to Rome.   *trumpet calls*
TITUS Let it be so, and let Andronicus
Make this his latest° farewell to their souls.   *last*
      Flourish. Then sound trumpets and lay the coffins in
      the tomb
150 In peace and honour rest you here, my sons;
Rome's readiest champions, repose you here in rest,
Secure from worldly chances and mishaps.
Here lurks no treason, here no envy° swells,   *malice*
Here grow no damnèd drugs,° here are no storms,   *poisons*
155 No noise, but silence and eternal sleep.
In peace and honour rest you here, my sons.
      Enter LAVINIA
LAVINIA In peace and honour live Lord Titus long,
My noble lord and father, live in fame.
Lo, at this tomb my tributary° tears   *tribute-bearing*
160 I render for my brethren's obsequies,°   *funeral rites*
[*Kneeling*] And at thy feet I kneel with tears of joy
Shed on this earth for thy return to Rome.
O, bless me here with thy victorious hand,
Whose fortunes Rome's best citizens applaud.
165 TITUS Kind Rome, that hast thus lovingly reserved
The cordial° of mine age to glad my heart!   *comfort*
Lavinia, live; outlive thy father's days
And fame's eternal date, for virtue's praise.[1]
      [LAVINIA *rises*]
MARCUS [*aloft*] Long live Lord Titus, my belovèd brother,
170 Gracious triumpher in the eyes of Rome!
TITUS Thanks, gentle Tribune, noble brother Marcus.
MARCUS And welcome, nephews, from successful wars,
You that survive and you that sleep in fame.
Fair lords, your fortunes are alike in all,
175 That in your country's service drew your swords,
But safer triumph is this funeral pomp
That hath aspired to Solon's happiness[2]
And triumphs over chance in honour's bed.
Titus Andronicus, the people of Rome,

9. In Ovid's *Metamorphoses* 13, Queen Hecuba, enslaved by the Greeks after the defeat of Troy, avenged her son Polydorus by killing the sons of his murderer, Polymnestor, tyrant of Thrace.

1. And may the praise of your virtue outlive eternity.
2. Solon, a Greek statesman, said, "Call no man happy until he is dead."

180   Whose friend in justice thou hast ever been,
         Send thee by me, their tribune and their trust,
         This palliament[3] of white and spotless hue,
         And name thee in election for the empire
         With these our late-deceasèd emperor's sons.
185   Be *candidatus*[4] then, and put it on,
         And help to set a head on headless Rome.
         TITUS   A better head her glorious body fits
         Than his that shakes for age and feebleness.
         What should I don this robe and trouble you?—
190   Be chosen with proclamations today,
         Tomorrow yield up rule, resign my life,
         And set abroad new business for you all.°   *make you busy once again*
         Rome, I have been thy soldier forty years,
         And led my country's strength successfully,
195   And buried one-and-twenty valiant sons
         Knighted in field, slain manfully in arms
         In right° and service of their noble country.   *the just cause*
         Give me a staff of honour for mine age,
         But not a sceptre to control the world.
200   Upright he held it, lords, that held it last.
         MARCUS   Titus, thou shalt obtain and ask° the empery.   *simply by asking*
         SATURNINUS   Proud and ambitious Tribune, canst thou tell?°   *how do you know*
         TITUS   Patience, Prince Saturninus.
         SATURNINUS   Romans, do me right.
         Patricians, draw your swords, and sheathe them not
205   Till Saturninus be Rome's emperor.
         Andronicus, would thou were shipped to hell
         Rather than rob me of the people's hearts!
         LUCIUS   Proud Saturnine, interrupter of the good
         That noble-minded Titus means to thee.
210   TITUS   Content thee, Prince. I will restore to thee
         The people's hearts, and wean them from themselves.
         BASSIANUS   Andronicus, I do not flatter thee
         But honour thee, and will do till I die.
         My faction if thou strengthen with thy friends
215   I will most thankful be; and thanks to men
         Of noble minds is honourable meed.°   *reward*
         TITUS   People of Rome, and people's tribunes here,
         I ask your voices and your suffrages.°   *votes*
         Will ye bestow them friendly on Andronicus?
220   TRIBUNES   To gratify the good Andronicus
         And gratulate° his safe return to Rome   *salute*
         The people will accept whom he admits.°   *allows into office*
         TITUS   Tribunes, I thank you, and this suit I make:
         That you create° our emperor's eldest son   *elect*
225   Lord Saturnine, whose virtues will, I hope,
         Reflect on Rome as Titan's° rays on earth,   *the sun god*
         And ripen justice in this commonweal.°   *community*
         Then if you will elect by my advice,
         Crown him and say, 'Long live our Emperor!'

---

3. Ceremonial garment worn by aspirants to public office.   4. Candidate (literally, "one wearing the white toga").

230 MARCUS   With voices and applause of every sort,
    Patricians and plebeians, we create
    Lord Saturninus Rome's great emperor,
    And say, 'Long live our Emperor Saturnine!'
        A long flourish [while MARCUS *and the other Tribunes,*
        with SATURNINUS *and* BASSIANUS]*, come down*
        [MARCUS *invests°* SATURNINUS *in the white palliament*
        and hands him a sceptre]   *dresses*
SATURNINUS   Titus Andronicus, for thy favours done
235   To us in our election this day
    I give thee thanks in part of thy deserts,[5]
    And will with deeds requite thy gentleness.°   *pay back your kindness*
    And for an onset, Titus, to advance
    Thy name and honourable family,
240   Lavinia will I make my empress,
    Rome's royal mistress, mistress of my heart,
    And in the sacred Pantheon[6] her espouse.
    Tell me, Andronicus, doth this motion please thee?
TITUS   It doth, my worthy lord, and in this match
245   I hold me highly honoured of your grace,
    And here in sight of Rome to Saturnine,
    King and commander of our commonweal,
    The wide world's emperor, do I consecrate
    My sword, my chariot, and my prisoners—
250   Presents well worthy Rome's imperious° lord.   *imperial*
    Receive them, then, the tribute that I owe,
    Mine honour's ensigns° humbled at thy feet.   *symbols*
SATURNINUS   Thanks, noble Titus, father of my life.
    How proud I am of thee and of thy gifts
255   Rome shall record; and when I do forget
    The least of these unspeakable° deserts,   *inexpressible*
    Romans, forget your fealty° to me.   *duty*
TITUS [*to* TAMORA]   Now, madam, are you prisoner to an emperor,
    To him that for your honour and your state°   *royal dignity*
260   Will use you nobly, and your followers.
SATURNINUS   A goodly lady, trust me, of the hue°   *appearance; color*
    That I would choose were I to choose anew.[7]
    Clear up, fair queen, that cloudy countenance.
    Though chance of war hath wrought this change of cheer,°   *expression*
265   Thou com'st not to be made a scorn in Rome.
    Princely shall be thy usage every way.
    Rest° on my word, and let not discontent   *Rely*
    Daunt all your hopes. Madam, he comforts you
    Can° make you greater than the Queen of Goths.   *Who can*
270   Lavinia, you are not displeased with this?
LAVINIA   Not I, my lord, sith° true nobility   *since*
    Warrants° these words in princely courtesy.   *Justifies*
SATURNINUS   Thanks, sweet Lavinia. Romans, let us go.
    Ransomless here we set our prisoners free.
275   Proclaim our honours, lords, with trump° and drum.   *trumpet*
        [*Flourish. Exeunt* SATURNINUS, TAMORA,
        DEMETRIUS, CHIRON, *and* AARON *the Moor*]

5. *in . . . deserts:* as part of what you deserve.   7. *A goodly . . . anew:* these two lines may be spoken as
6. Roman temple dedicated to all the gods.   an aside.

BASSIANUS   Lord Titus, by your leave, this maid° is mine.   (*Lavinia*)
TITUS   How, sir, are you in earnest then, my lord?
BASSIANUS   Ay, noble Titus, and resolved withal
   To do myself this reason and this right.
280 MARCUS   *Suum cuique*° is our Roman justice.   *To each his own*
   This prince in justice seizeth but his own.
LUCIUS   And that he will and shall, if Lucius live.
TITUS   Traitors, avaunt!° Where is the Emperor's guard?[8]   *be off*
283.1   TITUS   *Treason, my lord! Lavinia is surprised.*
    SATURNINUS   *Surprised, by whom?*
    BASSIANUS   *By him that justly may*
    Bear his betrothed from all the world away.
MUTIUS   Brothers, help to convey her hence away,
285 And with my sword I'll keep this door safe.
          [*Exeunt* BASSIANUS, MARCUS, QUINTUS, *and*
                   MARTIUS, *with* LAVINIA]
   [*To* TITUS] My lord, you pass not here.
TITUS   What, villain boy,
   Barr'st me my way in Rome?
       [*He attacks* MUTIUS]
MUTIUS   Help, Lucius, help!
   [TITUS] *kills him*
LUCIUS [to TITUS]   My lord, you are unjust; and more than so,
   In wrongful quarrel you have slain your son.
290 TITUS   Nor thou nor he are any sons of mine.
   My sons would never so dishonour me.
   Traitor, restore Lavinia to the Emperor.
LUCIUS   Dead, if you will, but not to be his wife
   That is another's lawful promised love.
              [*Exit with Mutius' body*]
   Enter aloft [SATURNINUS] *the Emperor with* TAMORA
   and [CHIRON *and* DEMETRIUS,] *her two sons, and*
   AARON *the Moor*
295 TITUS   Follow, my lord, and I'll soon bring her back.
SATURNINUS   No, Titus, no. The Emperor needs her not,
   Nor° her, nor thee, nor any of thy stock.   *Neither*
   I'll trust by leisure° him that mocks me once,   *I'm in no hurry to trust*
   Thee never, nor thy traitorous haughty sons,
300   Confederates all thus to dishonour me.
   Was none in Rome to make a stale°   *laughingstock*
   But Saturnine? Full well, Andronicus,
   Agree these deeds with that proud brag of thine
   That saidst I begged the empire at thy hands.
305 TITUS   O monstrous, what reproachful words are these?
SATURNINUS   But go thy ways, go give that changing piece°   *fickle wench*
   To him that flourished for her with his sword.[9]
   A valiant son-in-law thou shalt enjoy,
   One fit to bandy° with thy lawless sons,   *brawl*
310   To ruffle° in the commonwealth of Rome.   *swagger*

---

8. The following indented passage (lines 283.1–283.3), found in the quartos and F, is difficult to reconcile with the apparent need for Saturninus and his party to leave the stage at line 275 stage direction before entering "aloft" at line 294 stage direction. The Oxford editors believe that Shakespeare intended it to be deleted after adding the episode of Mutius's killing to his original draft, and that the printers of Q1 included it by accident.
9. To him who brandished his sword to win her.

TITUS   These words are razors to my wounded heart.

SATURNINUS   And therefore, lovely Tamora, Queen of Goths,
   That like the stately Phoebe° 'mongst her nymphs   *Diana (the moon)*
   Dost overshine the gallant'st dames of Rome,
315   If thou be pleased with this my sudden choice,
   Behold, I choose thee, Tamora, for my bride,
   And will create thee Empress of Rome.
   Speak, Queen of Goths, dost thou applaud my choice?
   And here I swear by all the Roman gods,
320   Sith priest and holy water are so near,
   And tapers burn so bright, and everything
   In readiness for Hymenaeus° stand,   *god of marriage*
   I will not re-salute the streets of Rome,
   Or climb° my palace, till from forth this place   *ascend to*
325   I lead espoused my bride along with me.

TAMORA   And here, in sight of heaven, to Rome I swear
   If Saturnine advance the Queen of Goths
   She will a handmaid be to his desires,
   A loving nurse, a mother to his youth.°   *youthfulness*

330 SATURNINUS   Ascend, fair Queen, Pantheon. Lords, accompany
   Your noble emperor and his lovely bride,
   Sent by the heavens for Prince Saturnine,
   Whose wisdom[1] hath her fortune conquerèd.
   There shall we consummate our spousal rites.

                                Exeunt [all but TITUS]

335 TITUS   I am not bid° to wait upon this bride.   *invited*
   Titus, when wert thou wont to walk alone,
   Dishonoured thus and challengèd° of wrongs?   *accused*

      Enter MARCUS *and Titus' sons* [LUCIUS, QUINTUS, *and*
      MARTIUS, *carrying Mutius' body*]

MARCUS   O Titus, see, O see what thou hast done—
   In a bad quarrel slain a virtuous son.

340 TITUS   No, foolish Tribune, no; no son of mine,
   Nor thou, nor these, confederates in the deed
   That hath dishonoured all our family;
   Unworthy brother and unworthy sons!

LUCIUS   But let us give him burial as becomes,°   *as is proper*
345   Give Mutius burial with our brethren.

TITUS   Traitors, away, he rests not in this tomb.
   This monument five hundred years hath stood,
   Which I have sumptuously re-edified.°   *rebuilt*
   Here none but soldiers and Rome's servitors°   *defenders*
350   Repose in fame, none basely slain in brawls.
   Bury him where you can; he comes not here.

MARCUS   My lord, this is impiety in you.
   My nephew Mutius' deeds do plead for him.
   He must be buried with his brethren.

355 QUINTUS *and* MARTIUS   And shall, or him we will accompany.

TITUS   'And shall'? What villain was it spake that word?

QUINTUS   He that would vouch it° in any place but here.   *back it up*

TITUS   What, would you bury him in my despite?°   *in defiance of me*

MARCUS   No, noble Titus, but entreat of thee

---

1. Wise consent to my proposal

360   To pardon Mutius and to bury him.

    TITUS   Marcus, even thou hast struck upon my crest,
      And with these boys mine honour thou hast wounded.
      My foes I do repute° you every one,   *consider*
      So trouble me no more, but get you gone.

365   MARTIUS   He is not with° himself, let us withdraw.   *is beside*

    QUINTUS   Not I, till Mutius' bones be buried.

             [MARCUS, LUCIUS, QUINTUS, *and* MARTIUS] *kneel*

    MARCUS   Brother, for in that name doth nature plead—

    QUINTUS   Father, and in that name doth nature speak—

    TITUS   Speak thou no more, if all the rest will speed.²

370   MARCUS   Renownèd Titus, more than half my soul—

    LUCIUS   Dear father, soul and substance of us all—

    MARCUS   Suffer thy brother Marcus to inter
      His noble nephew here in virtue's nest,
      That died in honour and Lavinia's cause.

375   Thou art a Roman; be not barbarous.
      The Greeks upon advice° did bury Ajax,³   *deliberation*
      That slew himself; and wise Laertes' son
      Did graciously plead for his funerals.
      Let not young Mutius then, that was thy joy,
      Be barred his entrance here.

380   TITUS   Rise, Marcus, rise.
      The dismall'st day is this that e'er I saw,
      To be dishonoured by my sons in Rome.
      Well, bury him, and bury me the next.

             They put [MUTIUS] *in the tomb*

    LUCIUS   There lie thy bones, sweet Mutius, with thy friends',

385   Till we with trophies° do adorn thy tomb.   *memorial tributes*

    ALL BUT TITUS [*kneeling*]   No man shed tears for noble Mutius;
      He lives in fame, that died in virtue's cause.

             Exeunt [*all but* MARCUS *and* TITUS]

    MARCUS   My lord—to step out of these dreary dumps°—   *melancholy*
      How comes it that the subtle° Queen of Goths   *cunning*

390   Is of a sudden thus advanced in Rome?

    TITUS   I know not, Marcus, but I know it is—
      Whether by device° or no, the heavens can tell.   *scheming*
      Is she not then beholden to the man
      That brought her for this high good turn⁴ so far?

395   MARCUS   Yes, and will nobly him remunerate.

          Flourish. Enter the Emperor [SATURNINUS], TAMORA,
          and her two sons [CHIRON *and* DEMETRIUS], *with*
          [AARON] *the Moor at one door.*
          Enter at the other door BASSIANUS *and* LAVINIA *with*
          [LUCIUS, QUINTUS, *and* MARTIUS]

    SATURNINUS   So, Bassianus, you have played your prize.°   *won your bout*
      God give you joy, sir, of your gallant bride.

    BASSIANUS   And you of yours, my lord. I say no more,
      Nor wish no less; and so I take my leave.

---

2. If the rest of you wish to meet with good fortune
(that is, escape my anger).
3. In the Trojan War, after the Greek hero Ajax committed suicide, Odysseus ("wise Laertes' son") convinced Agamemnon, leader of the Greeks, to grant him

honorable burial.
4. Recompense. "turn" was also slang for the sexual act. "Remunerate" (line 395) continues the sexual innuendo.

400 SATURNINUS   Traitor, if Rome have law or we have power,
    Thou and thy faction shall repent this rape.°   *abduction*
  BASSIANUS   'Rape' call you it, my lord, to seize my own—
    My true betrothèd love, and now my wife?
    But let the laws of Rome determine all;
405   Meanwhile am I possessed of that° is mine.   *what*
  SATURNINUS   'Tis good, sir; you are very short with us.
    But if we live we'll be as sharp with you.
  BASSIANUS   My lord, what I have done, as best I may
    Answer I must, and shall do with my life.
410   Only thus much I give your grace to know:
    By all the duties that I owe to Rome,
    This noble gentleman, Lord Titus here,
    Is in opinion° and in honour wronged,   *reputation*
    That, in the rescue of Lavinia,
415   With his own hand did slay his youngest son
    In zeal to you, and highly moved to wrath
    To be controlled° in that he frankly gave.[5]   *opposed*
    Receive him then to favour, Saturnine,
    That hath expressed himself in all his deeds
420   A father and a friend to thee and Rome.
  TITUS   Prince Bassianus, leave to plead° my deeds.   *stop defending*
    'Tis thou and those that have dishonoured me.
      [*He kneels*]
    Rome and the righteous heavens be my judge
    How I have loved and honoured Saturnine!
425 TAMORA [*to* SATURNINUS]   My worthy lord, if ever Tamora
    Were gracious in those princely eyes of thine,
    Then hear me speak indifferently° for all;   *impartially*
    And at my suit, sweet, pardon what is past.
  SATURNINUS   What, madam—be dishonoured openly
430   And basely put it up° without revenge?   *ignobly submit*
  TAMORA   Not so, my lord. The gods of Rome forfend°   *forbid*
    I should be author to dishonour[6] you.
    But on mine honour dare I undertake°   *vouch*
    For good lord Titus' innocence in all,
435   Whose fury not dissembled speaks his griefs.
    Then at my suit look graciously on him.
    Lose not so noble a friend on vain suppose,°   *idle conjecture*
    Nor with sour looks afflict his gentle heart.
    [*Aside to* SATURNINUS] My lord, be ruled by me, be won at last,
440   Dissemble all your griefs and discontents.
    You are but newly planted in your throne;
    Lest then the people, and patricians too,
    Upon a just survey° take Titus' part,   *examination*
    And so supplant you for ingratitude,
445   Which Rome reputes to be a heinous sin,
    Yield at entreats;° and then let me alone: *to entreaty*
    I'll find a day to massacre them all,
    And raze their faction and their family,
    The cruel father and his traitorous sons
450   To whom I suèd for my dear son's life,

---

5. Freely bestowed (Lavinia upon Saturninus).   6. I should be responsible for dishonoring.

And make them know what 'tis to let a queen
Kneel in the streets and beg for grace in vain.
[*Aloud*] Come, come, sweet Emperor; come, Andronicus,°   (*Marcus*)
Take up° this good old man, and cheer the heart   *Raise to his feet*
455   That dies in tempest of thy angry frown.
SATURNINUS   Rise, Titus, rise; my empress hath prevailed.
TITUS [*rising*]   I thank your majesty and her, my lord.
These words, these looks, infuse new life in me.
TAMORA   Titus, I am incorporate in° Rome,   *made a part of*
460   A Roman now adopted happily,
And must advise the Emperor for his good.
This day all quarrels die, Andronicus;
And let it be mine honour, good my lord,
That I have reconciled your friends and you.
465   For you, Prince Bassianus, I have passed
My word and promise to the Emperor
That you will be more mild and tractable.
And fear not, lords, and you, Lavinia;
By my advice, all humbled on your knees,
470   You shall ask pardon of his majesty.
        [BASSIANUS, LAVINIA, LUCIUS, QUINTUS, *and* MARTIUS
        kneel]
LUCIUS   We do, and vow to heaven and to his highness
That what we did was mildly as we might,°   *possible*
Tend'ring° our sister's honour and our own.   *Having regard for*
MARCUS [*kneeling*]   That on mine honour here do I protest.°   *solemnly declare*
475 SATURNINUS   Away, and talk not, trouble us no more.
TAMORA   Nay, nay, sweet Emperor, we must all be friends.
The Tribune and his nephews kneel for grace.
I will not be denied; sweetheart, look back.
SATURNINUS   Marcus, for thy sake and thy brother's here
480   And at my lovely Tamora's entreats,
I do remit° these young men's heinous faults.   *forgive*
Stand up!
        [MARCUS, BASSIANUS, LAVINIA, *and Titus' sons stand*]
        Lavinia, though you left me like a churl,°   *boorishly*
I found a friend, and sure as death I swore
I would not part° a bachelor from the priest.   *depart*
485   Come, if the Emperor's court can feast two brides
You are my guest, Lavinia, and your friends.
This day shall be a love-day,[7] Tamora.
TITUS   Tomorrow an° it please your majesty   *if*
To hunt the panther and the hart with me,
490   With horn and hound we'll give your grace *bonjour.*°   *good day*
SATURNINUS   Be it so, Titus, and gramercy,° too.   *thank you*
              Exeunt. Flourish

2.1

    [*Enter* AARON *alone*]
AARON   Now climbeth Tamora Olympus' top,[1]
Safe out of fortune's shot,° and sits aloft,   *range*
Secure of° thunder's crack or lightning flash,   *from*

---

7. Day for love; day appointed to settle disputes amica-
bly.

2.1 Scene continues, but the tomb is no longer needed.
1. Mountain home of the Greek gods.

Advanced above pale envy's° threat'ning reach.   *malice's*
5   As when the golden sun salutes the morn
And, having gilt the ocean with his beams,
Gallops° the zodiac in his glistering coach   *Gallops through*
And overlooks the highest-peering hills,
So Tamora.
10   Upon her wit° doth earthly honour wait,°   *intelligence / attend*
And virtue stoops and trembles at her frown.
Then, Aaron, arm thy heart and fit thy thoughts
To mount aloft with thy imperial mistress,
And mount her pitch² whom thou in triumph long
15   Hast prisoner held fettered in amorous chains,
And faster bound to Aaron's charming eyes
Than is Prometheus tied to Caucasus.³
Away with slavish weeds° and servile thoughts!   *clothes*
I will be bright, and shine in pearl and gold
20   To wait upon this new-made empress.
To wait, said I?—to wanton° with this queen,   *play amorously*
This goddess, this Semiramis,⁴ this nymph,
This siren⁵ that will charm Rome's Saturnine
And see his shipwreck and his commonweal's.
25   Hollo, what storm is this?
        Enter CHIRON *and* DEMETRIUS, *braving*°   *defying each other*
DEMETRIUS   Chiron, thy years wants° wit, thy wits wants edge°   *lack / sharpness*
And manners to intrude where I am graced°   *favored*
And may, for aught thou knowest, affected° be.   *loved*
CHIRON   Demetrius, thou dost overween° in all,   *behave presumptuously*
30   And so in this, to bear me down with braves.°   *threats*
'Tis not the difference of a year or two
Makes me less gracious, or thee more fortunate.
I am as able and as fit as thou
To serve, and to deserve my mistress' grace,
35   And that my sword upon thee shall approve,°   *prove*
And plead my passions for Lavinia's love.
AARON [*aside*]   Clubs, clubs!⁶ These lovers will not keep the peace.
DEMETRIUS   Why, boy, although our mother, unadvised,°   *rashly*
Gave you a dancing-rapier° by your side,   *an ornamental sword*
40   Are you so desperate grown to threat° your friends?   *threaten*
Go to, have your lath⁷ glued within your sheath
Till you know better how to handle it.
CHIRON   Meanwhile, sir, with the little skill I have
Full well shalt thou perceive how much I dare.
DEMETRIUS   Ay, boy, grow ye so brave?
        They draw
45   AARON   Why, how now, lords?
So near the Emperor's palace dare ye draw
And maintain such a quarrel openly?⁸

2. Rise to her height, a hawking term (sexually suggestive).
3. In Greek mythology, Zeus punished Prometheus by
chaining him to a rock in the Caucasus Mountains; a
vulture fed on his liver daily.
4. In Mesopotamian mythology, the Assyrian Queen
who founded and ruled Babylon, and who also had
attributes of Ishtar, goddess associated with sexual lust.

5. In Greek mythology, sirens were female creatures
that lured sailors to destruction.
6. Here's a brawl (a cry among London apprentices to
join or quell a fight).
7. Wooden sword used in theatrical productions.
8. In the Renaissance, it was illegal to draw a sword in
the presence of the sovereign or at court.

Full well I wot° the ground of all this grudge.°   *know / quarrel*
I would not for a million of gold
50   The cause were known to them it most concerns,
Nor would your noble mother for much more
Be so dishonoured in the court of Rome.
For shame, put up.°   *sheathe your swords*
DEMETRIUS   Not I, till I have sheathed
My rapier in his bosom, and withal
55   Thrust those reproachful speeches down his throat
That he hath breathed in my dishonour here.
CHIRON   For that I am prepared and full resolved,
Foul-spoken coward, that thund'rest with thy tongue,
And with thy weapon nothing dar'st perform.
60 AARON   Away, I say.
Now, by the gods that warlike Goths adore,
This petty brabble° will undo us all.   *quarrel*
Why, lords, and think you not how dangerous
It is to jet° upon a prince's right?   *encroach*
65   What, is Lavinia then become so loose,
Or Bassianus so degenerate,
That for her love such quarrels may be broached°   *begun*
Without controlment,° justice, or revenge?   *restraint*
Young lords, beware; and should the Empress know
70   This discord's ground,[9] the music would not please.
CHIRON   I care not, I, knew she° and all the world,   *if she knew*
I love Lavinia more than all the world.
DEMETRIUS   Youngling, learn thou to make some meaner°   *lesser*
    choice.
Lavinia is thine elder brother's hope.
75 AARON   Why, are ye mad? Or know ye not in Rome
How furious and impatient they be,
And cannot brook° competitors in love?   *endure*
I tell you, lords, you do but plot your deaths
By this device.
CHIRON   Aaron, a thousand deaths
80   Would I propose° to achieve her whom I love.   *face*
AARON   To achieve her how?
DEMETRIUS   Why makes thou it so strange?
She is a woman, therefore may be wooed;
She is a woman, therefore may be won;
She is Lavinia, therefore must be loved.
85   What, man, more water glideth by the mill
Than wots the miller of, and easy it is
Of a cut loaf to steal a shive,° we know.   *slice*
Though Bassianus be the Emperor's brother,
Better than he have worn Vulcan's badge.[1]
90 AARON [*aside*]   Ay, and as good as Saturninus may.
DEMETRIUS   Then why should he despair that knows to court it°   *carry on a courtship*
With words, fair looks, and liberality?°   *generosity*
What, hast not thou full often struck° a doe   *struck dead*

---

9. Basis; in music, the bass line.
1. *worn Vulcan's badge*: been cuckolded, as the god Vulcan was by Venus, the goddess of love.

And borne her cleanly° by the keeper's nose?   *deftly and unnoticed*

95   AARON   Why then, it seems some certain snatch[2] or so
      Would serve your turns.

      CHIRON   Ay, so the turn were served.°   *(with sexual innuendo)*

      DEMETRIUS   Aaron, thou hast hit it.

      AARON   Would you had hit it[3] too,
      Then should not we be tired with this ado.
      Why, hark ye, hark ye, and are you such fools

100   To square° for this? Would it offend you then   *quarrel*
      That both should speed?°   *succeed*

      CHIRON   Faith, not me.

      DEMETRIUS   Nor me, so° I were one.   *provided that*

      AARON   For shame, be friends, and join for that you jar.[4]

105   'Tis policy° and stratagem must do   *cunning*
      That° you affect,° and so must you resolve   *What / desire*
      That what you cannot as you would achieve,
      You must perforce accomplish as you may.
      Take this of me: Lucrece[5] was not more chaste

110   Than this Lavinia, Bassianus' love.
      A speedier course than ling'ring languishment°   *lovesickness*
      Must we pursue, and I have found the path.
      My lords, a solemn° hunting is in hand;   *ceremonial*
      There will the lovely Roman ladies troop.°   *walk together*

115   The forest walks are wide and spacious,
      And many unfrequented plots° there are,   *places*
      Fitted by kind° for rape and villainy.   *nature*
      Single° you thither then this dainty doe,   *Isolate*
      And strike her home by force, if not by words,

120   This way or not at all stand you in hope.
      Come, come; our Empress, with her sacred wit
      To villainy and vengeance consecrate,
      Will we acquaint with all what we intend,
      And she shall file our engines° with advice   *sharpen our wits*

125   That will not suffer you to square yourselves,°   *be at odds*
      But to your wishes' height advance you both.
      The Emperor's court is like the house of Fame,[6]
      The palace full of tongues, of eyes and ears,
      The woods are ruthless, dreadful, deaf, and dull.°   *insensible*

130   There speak and strike, brave boys, and take your turns.
      There serve your lust, shadowed from heaven's eye,
      And revel in Lavinia's treasury.

      CHIRON   Thy counsel, lad, smells of no cowardice.

      DEMETRIUS   *Sit fas aut nefas,*° till I find the stream   *Be it right or wrong*

135   To cool this heat, a charm to calm these fits,
      Per Styga, per manes vehor.[7]   *Exeunt*

---

2. Bite (with sexual innuendo).
3. Hit the nail on the head; "scored" sexually.
4. And join to get what you fight over.
5. Virtuous Roman matron raped by Tarquin, a member of the Roman royal family; after her suicide, her kin avenged her by overthrowing the King and establishing the Roman Republic. Shakespeare retells the story in

The Rape of Lucrece.
6. Rumor; the House of Fame is described by Ovid in *Metamorphoses* 12 and by Chaucer in *The House of Fame.*
7. I am carried through the underworld, through the spirits (that is, I am in hell). Adapted from Seneca's *Hippolytus.*

2.2

Enter TITUS ANDRONICUS *and his three sons [*QUINTUS,
LUCIUS, *and* MARTIUS], *and* MARCUS, *making a noise
with hounds and horns*

TITUS   The hunt is up, the morn is bright and grey,°   *(used of dawn light)*
The fields are fragrant and the woods are green.
Uncouple¹ here, and let us make a bay°   *deep barking*
And wake the Emperor and his lovely bride,
5   And rouse the Prince, and ring° a hunter's peal,   *sound*
That all the court may echo with the noise.
Sons, let it be your charge, as it is ours,
To attend the Emperor's person carefully.
I have been troubled in my sleep this night,
10   But dawning day new comfort hath inspired.

Here a cry of hounds, and wind° horns in a peal; then   *blow*
enter SATURNINUS, TAMORA, BASSIANUS, LAVINIA,
CHIRON, DEMETRIUS, *and their attendants*

Many good-morrows to your majesty.
Madam, to you as many, and as good.
I promisèd your grace a hunter's peal.
SATURNINUS   And you have rung it lustily,° my lords,   *heartily*
15   Somewhat too early for new-married ladies.
BASSIANUS   Lavinia, how say you?
LAVINIA   I say no.
I have been broad awake two hours and more.
SATURNINUS   Come on then, horse and chariots let us have,
And to our sport. [*To* TAMORA] Madam, now shall ye see
Our Roman hunting.
20   MARCUS   I have dogs, my lord,
Will rouse the proudest panther in the chase,°   *hunting ground*
And climb the highest promontory top.
TITUS   And I have horse will follow where the game
Makes way, and run like swallows o'er the plain.
25   DEMETRIUS [*aside*]   Chiron, we hunt not, we, with horse nor hound,
But hope to pluck a dainty doe to ground.   *Exeunt*

2.3

Enter AARON *alone [with gold]*

AARON   He that had wit would think that I had none,
To bury so much gold under a tree
And never after to inherit° it.   *possess*
Let him that thinks of me so abjectly
5   Know that this gold must coin a stratagem
Which, cunningly effected, will beget
A very excellent piece of villainy.
And so repose, sweet gold, for their unrest
That have their alms out of the Empress' chest.¹

[*He hides the gold*]
Enter TAMORA *alone to the Moor*

10   TAMORA   My lovely Aaron, wherefore look'st thou sad

2.2 Location: A forest near the Emperor's palace.   1. *That . . . chest*: Who get this gold, which comes from
1. Unleash the hounds.   the Empress's treasury.
2.3 Location: The forest.

When everything doth make a gleeful boast?°   *display*
The birds chant melody on every bush,
The snakes lies rollèd in the cheerful sun,
The green leaves quiver with the cooling wind
15   And make a chequered shadow on the ground.
Under their sweet shade, Aaron, let us sit,
And whilst the babbling echo mocks the hounds,
Replying shrilly to the well-tuned horns,
As if a double hunt were heard at once,
20   Let us sit down and mark their yellowing° noise,   *bellowing*
And after conflict such as was supposed
The wand'ring prince and Dido once enjoyed²
When with a happy storm they were surprised,
And curtained with a counsel-keeping° cave,   *secret-keeping*
25   We may, each wreathèd in the other's arms,
Our pastimes done, possess a golden slumber
Whiles hounds and horns and sweet melodious birds
Be unto us as is a nurse's song
Of lullaby to bring her babe asleep.
30   AARON   Madam, though Venus govern your desires,
Saturn is dominator over mine.³
What signifies my deadly-standing° eye,   *murderously glaring*
My silence, and my cloudy° melancholy,   *gloomy*
My fleece of woolly hair that now uncurls
35   Even as an adder when she doth unroll
To do some fatal execution?
No, madam, these are no venereal⁴ signs.
Vengeance is in my heart, death in my hand,
Blood and revenge are hammering in my head.
40   Hark, Tamora, the empress of my soul,
Which never hopes more heaven than rests in thee,
This is the day of doom for Bassianus.
His Philomel⁵ must lose her tongue today,
Thy sons make pillage of her chastity
45   And wash their hands in Bassianus' blood.
Seest thou this letter? [*Giving a letter*] Take it up, I pray thee,
And give the King this fatal-plotted scroll.
Now question me no more. We are espied.
Here comes a parcel° of our hopeful° booty,   *part / hoped-for*
50   Which dreads not yet their lives' destruction.
          Enter BASSIANUS *and* LAVINIA
TAMORA [*aside to* AARON]   Ah, my sweet Moor, sweeter to me than life!
AARON [*aside to* TAMORA]   No more, great Empress; Bassianus comes.
Be cross with him, and I'll go fetch thy sons
To back thy quarrels, whatsoe'er they be.   *Exit*
55   BASSIANUS   Who have we here? Rome's royal empress
Unfurnished of her well-beseeming troop?⁶

---

2. In Virgil's *Aeneid* 4, the Carthaginian Queen Dido and Aeneas, later founder of Rome, make love in a cave where they have taken refuge.
3. Those born when the planet Venus was ascendant were supposed to be amorous; Saturn produced a colder, gloomier temperament.
4. Sexual; derived from Venus.

5. In Greek mythology, an Athenian princess raped by her brother-in-law Tereus; he cut out her tongue, but she wove a tapestry incriminating him (see Introduction and Ovid, *Metamorphoses* 6).
6. *Unfurnished . . . troop:* Not accompanied by an appropriate escort.

Or is it Dian,[7] habited° like her   *dressed*
Who hath abandonèd her holy groves
To see the general hunting in this forest?
60   TAMORA   Saucy controller° of my private steps,   *Insolent observer*
Had I the power that some say Dian had,
Thy temples should be planted presently°   *immediately*
With horns, as was Actaeon's, and the hounds
Should drive° upon thy new-transformèd limbs,   *rush*
65   Unmannerly intruder as thou art![8]
LAVINIA   Under your patience, gentle Empress,
'Tis thought you have a goodly gift in horning.[9]
And to be doubted° that your Moor and you   *suspected*
Are singled forth° to try experiments.   *drawn apart*
70   Jove shield your husband from his hounds today—
'Tis pity they should take him for a stag.
BASSIANUS   Believe me, Queen, your swart° Cimmerian[1]   *swarthy*
Doth make your honour of his body's hue,
Spotted, detested, and abominable.
75   Why are you sequestered from all your train,
Dismounted from your snow-white goodly steed,
And wandered hither to an obscure plot,
Accompanied but with a barbarous Moor,
If foul desire had not conducted you?
80   LAVINIA   And being intercepted in your sport,
Great reason that my noble lord be rated°   *scolded*
For sauciness. [*To* BASSIANUS] I pray you, let us hence,
And let her joy° her raven-coloured love.   *enjoy*
This valley fits the purpose passing well.
85   BASSIANUS   The King my brother shall have note of this.
LAVINIA   Ay, for these slips have made him noted° long.   *notorious*
Good King, to be so mightily abused!°   *deceived*
TAMORA   Why have I patience to endure all this?
Enter CHIRON *and* DEMETRIUS
DEMETRIUS   How now, dear sovereign and our gracious mother,
90   Why doth your highness look so pale and wan?
TAMORA   Have I not reason, think you, to look pale?
These two have 'ticed° me hither to this place.   *enticed*
A barren detested vale you see it is
The trees, though summer, yet forlorn and lean,
95   Overcome° with moss and baleful[2] mistletoe.   *Overgrown*
Here never shines the sun, here nothing breeds
Unless the nightly owl or fatal° raven,   *ominous*
And when they showed me this abhorrèd pit
They told me here at dead time of the night
100   A thousand fiends, a thousand hissing snakes,
Ten thousand swelling toads, as many urchins°   *goblins*
Would make such fearful and confusèd cries
As any mortal body hearing it

---

7. Diana, chaste goddess of the hunt (sarcastic).
8. In Greek mythology, the hunter Actaeon came upon
Diana naked; she turned him into a stag, and his own
hounds tore him apart (see Ovid, *Metamorphoses* 3).
9. The husbands of unfaithful women were supposed

to grow staglike horns.
1. The Cimmerians were a legendary people upon
whom the sun never shone.
2. Harmful (mistletoe is parasitic).

Should straight fall mad or else die suddenly.
105 No sooner had they told this hellish tale
But straight they told me they would bind me here
Unto the body of a dismal yew[3]
And leave me to this miserable death.
And then they called me foul adulteress,
110 Lascivious Goth,[4] and all the bitterest terms
That ever ear did hear to such effect.
And had you not by wondrous fortune come,
This vengeance on me had they executed.
Revenge it as you love your mother's life,
115 Or be ye not henceforward called my children.

DEMETRIUS   This is a witness that I am thy son.
          [He] stab[s BASSIANUS]
CHIRON   And this for me, struck home to show my strength.
          [He stabs BASSIANUS, who dies.
          TAMORA turns to LAVINIA]
LAVINIA   Ay, come, Semiramis[5]—nay, barbarous Tamora,
For no name fits thy nature but thy own.
120 TAMORA [to CHIRON]   Give me the poniard. You shall know, my boys,
Your mother's hand shall right your mother's wrong.
DEMETRIUS   Stay, madam, here is more belongs to her.
First thresh the corn, then after burn the straw.
This minion stood° upon her chastity,   hussy prided herself
125 Upon her nuptial vow, her loyalty,
And with that quaint° hope braves° your mightiness.   fine / defies
And shall she carry this unto her grave?
CHIRON   An if° she do I would I were an eunuch.   An if = If
Drag hence her husband to some secret hole,
130 And make his dead trunk pillow to our lust.
TAMORA   But when ye have the honey ye desire
Let not this wasp outlive, us both to sting.
CHIRON   I warrant you, madam, we will make that sure.
Come, mistress, now perforce we will enjoy
135 That nice-preservèd honesty[6] of yours.
LAVINIA   O Tamora, thou bearest a woman's face—
TAMORA   I will not hear her speak. Away with her!
LAVINIA   Sweet lords, entreat her hear me but a word.
DEMETRIUS [to TAMORA]   Listen, fair madam, let it be your glory
140 To see her tears, but be your heart to them
As unrelenting flint to drops of rain.
LAVINIA   When did the tiger's young ones teach the dam?°   mother
O, do not learn her wrath! She taught it thee.
The milk thou sucked'st from her did turn to marble,
145 Even at thy teat thou hadst° thy tyranny.   took in
Yet every mother breeds not sons alike.
          [To CHIRON] Do thou entreat her show a woman's pity.
CHIRON   What, wouldst thou have me prove myself a bastard?
LAVINIA   'Tis true, the raven doth not hatch a lark.
150 Yet have I heard—O, could I find it now!—

---

3. The yew tree is associated with sadness.
4. Punning on "goat," a proverbially lustful animal.
5. See note to 2.1.22.
6. Fastidiously guarded chastity.

The lion, moved with pity, did endure
To have his princely paws° pared all away.   *claws*
Some say that ravens foster forlorn children°   *abandoned baby birds*
The whilst their own birds famish in their nests.
155 O, be to me, though thy hard heart say no,
Nothing so kind, but something pitiful.[7]

TAMORA   I know not what it means. Away with her!

LAVINIA   O, let me teach thee for my father's sake,
That gave thee life when well he might have slain thee.
160 Be not obdurate, open thy deaf ears.

TAMORA   Hadst thou in person ne'er offended me
Even for his sake am I pitiless.
Remember, boys, I poured forth tears in vain
To save your brother from the sacrifice,
165 But fierce Andronicus would not relent.
Therefore away with her, and use her as you will—
The worse to her, the better loved of me.

LAVINIA   O Tamora, be called a gentle queen,
And with thine own hands kill me in this place;
170 For 'tis not life that I have begged so long;
Poor I was slain when Bassianus died.

TAMORA   What begg'st thou then, fond° woman? Let me go.   *foolish*

LAVINIA   'Tis present° death I beg, and one thing more   *immediate*
That womanhood denies° my tongue to tell.   *forbids*
175 O, keep me from their worse-than-killing lust,
And tumble me into some loathsome pit
Where never man's eye may behold my body.
Do this, and be a charitable murderer.

TAMORA   So should I rob my sweet sons of their fee.
180 No, let them satisfy their lust on thee.

DEMETRIUS [*to* LAVINIA]   Away, for thou hast stayed us here
too long.

LAVINIA   No grace, no womanhood—ah, beastly creature,
The blot and enemy to our general name,°   *the reputation of women*
Confusion° fall—   *Destruction*

CHIRON   Nay then, I'll stop your mouth. [*To* DEMETRIUS]
185 Bring thou her husband.
This is the hole where Aaron bid us hide him.
    [DEMETRIUS *and* CHIRON *cast Bassianus' body into the pit*
    and cover the mouth of it with branches, then exeunt
    dragging LAVINIA]

TAMORA   Farewell, my sons. See that you make her sure.[8]
Ne'er let my heart know merry cheer indeed
Till all the Andronici[9] be made away.°   *murdered*
190 Now will I hence to seek my lovely Moor,
And let my spleenful° sons this trull° deflower.   *Exit*   *lustful / whore*
    Enter AARON *with* [QUINTUS *and* MARTIUS,] *two of*
    Titus' sons

AARON   Come on, my lords, the better foot before.
Straight will I bring you to the loathsome pit
Where I espied the panther fast asleep.

---

7. Not so kind as the raven, but showing some pity.   9. Family of Andronicus.
8. Make sure of her, keep her from doing harm; kill her.

195 QUINTUS   My sight is very dull, whate'er it bodes.[1]
     MARTIUS   And mine, I promise you. Were it not for shame,
     Well could I leave our sport to sleep awhile.
                    [*He falls into the pit*]
     QUINTUS   What, art thou fallen? What subtle° hole is this,   *treacherous*
     Whose mouth is covered with rude-growing briers
200 Upon whose leaves are drops of new-shed blood
     As fresh as morning dew distilled on flowers?
     A very fatal° place it seems to me.   *ill-omened*
     Speak, brother. Hast thou hurt thee with the fall?
     MARTIUS   O brother, with the dismall'st object hurt
205 That ever eye with sight made heart lament.
     AARON [*aside*]   Now will I fetch the King to find them here,
     That he thereby may have a likely guess
     How these were they that made away his brother.   *Exit*
     MARTIUS   Why dost not comfort me and help me out
210 From this unhallowed and bloodstained hole?
     QUINTUS   I am surprisèd with an uncouth° fear.   *uncanny*
     A chilling sweat o'erruns my trembling joints;
     My heart suspects more than mine eye can see.
     MARTIUS   To prove thou hast a true-divining heart,
215 Aaron and thou look down into this den,
     And see a fearful sight of blood and death.
     QUINTUS   Aaron is gone, and my compassionate heart
     Will not permit mine eyes once to behold
     The thing whereat it trembles by surmise.°   *merely by imagining it*
220 O, tell me who it is, for ne'er till now
     Was I a child to fear I know not what.
     MARTIUS   Lord Bassianus lies berayed° in blood   *defiled*
     All on a heap, like to a slaughtered lamb,
     In this detested, dark, blood-drinking pit.
225 QUINTUS   If it be dark how dost thou know 'tis he?
     MARTIUS   Upon his bloody finger he doth wear
     A precious ring[2] that lightens all this hole,
     Which like a taper° in some monument   *candle*
     Doth shine upon the dead man's earthy° cheeks   *clay-colored*
230 And shows the ragged entrails° of this pit.   *rough interior*
     So pale did shine the moon on Pyramus[3]
     When he by night lay bathed in maiden° blood.   *innocent*
     O brother, help me with thy fainting hand—
     If fear hath made thee faint, as me it hath—
235 Out of this fell° devouring receptacle,   *dreadful*
     As hateful as Cocytus'° misty mouth.   *a river of hell*
     QUINTUS   Reach me thy hand, that I may help thee out,
     Or, wanting° strength to do thee so much good,   *lacking*
     I may be plucked into the swallowing womb
240 Of this deep pit, poor Bassianus' grave.
     I have no strength to pluck thee to the brink,
     MARTIUS   Nor I no strength to climb without thy help.
     QUINTUS   Thy hand once more, I will not loose again
     Till thou art here aloft or I below.

1. Sleepiness was a bad omen.
2. Perhaps a carbuncle, thought to emit light.
3. In Ovid's version of a classical legend (*Metamor-*
phoses 4), Pyramus thinks his beloved Thisbe dead and
kills himself; this is the subject of the mechanicals' play
in *A Midsummer Night's Dream*.

245 Thou canst not come to me; I come to thee.
   [He] fall[s into the pit]
   Enter [SATURNINUS] *the Emperor [with attendants],*
   and AARON *the Moor*

SATURNINUS Along with me! I'll see what hole is here,
 And what he is that now is leapt into it.
   [He speaks into the pit]
 Say, who art thou that lately didst descend
 Into this gaping hollow of the earth?

250 MARTIUS The unhappy sons of old Andronicus,
 Brought hither in a most unlucky hour
 To find thy brother Bassianus dead.

SATURNINUS My brother dead! I know thou dost but jest.
 He and his lady both are at the lodge

255 Upon the north side of this pleasant chase.°   *hunting ground*
 'Tis not an hour since I left them there.

MARTIUS We know not where you left them all alive,
 But, out° alas, here have we found him dead!   *(emphatic)*
   Enter TAMORA, TITUS ANDRONICUS, *and* LUCIUS

TAMORA Where is my lord the King?

260 SATURNINUS Here, Tamora, though gripped with killing grief.

TAMORA Where is thy brother Bassianus?

SATURNINUS Now to the bottom dost thou search° my wound.   *probe*
 Poor Bassianus here lies murderèd.

TAMORA Then all too late I bring this fatal writ,°   *document*
265 The complot° of this timeless° tragedy,   *plot / untimely*
 And wonder greatly that man's face can fold
 In pleasing smiles such murderous tyranny.
   She giveth SATURNINE *a letter*

SATURNINUS [*reads*] 'An if we miss to meet him handsomely,°   *conveniently*
 Sweet huntsman—Bassianus 'tis we mean—
270 Do thou so much as dig the grave for him.
 Thou know'st our meaning. Look for thy reward
 Among the nettles at the elder tree
 Which overshades the mouth of that same pit
 Where we decreed to bury Bassianus.
275 Do this, and purchase us thy lasting friends.'
 O Tamora, was ever heard the like!
 This is the pit, and this the elder tree.
 Look, sirs, if you can find the huntsman out
 That should° have murdered Bassianus here.   *was to*

280 AARON My gracious lord, here is the bag of gold.

SATURNINUS [*to* TITUS] Two of thy whelps,° fell curs of bloody *puppies; literally, sons*
  kind,°   *nature; breed*
 Have here bereft my brother of his life.
 Sirs, drag them from the pit unto the prison.
 There let them bide until we have devised
285 Some never-heard-of torturing pain for them.

TAMORA What, are they in this pit? O wondrous thing!
 How easily murder is discoverèd!°   *revealed*
   [Attendants drag QUINTUS, MARTIUS, *and Bassianus'*
   body from the pit]

TITUS [*kneeling*] High Emperor, upon my feeble knee
 I beg this boon with tears not lightly shed:
290 That this fell fault of my accursèd sons—

Accursèd if the fault be proved in them—

SATURNINUS   If it be proved? You see it is apparent.°   *obvious*
Who found this letter? Tamora, was it you?

TAMORA   Andronicus himself did take it up.

295   TITUS   I did, my lord, yet let me be their bail,
For by my father's reverend tomb I vow
They shall be ready at your highness' will
To answer their suspicion⁴ with their lives.

SATURNINUS   Thou shalt not bail them. See thou follow me.

300   Some bring the murdered body, some the murderers.
Let them not speak a word—the guilt is plain;
For by my soul, were there worse end than death
That end upon them should be executed.   [*Exit*]

TAMORA   Andronicus, I will entreat the King.

305   Fear not° thy sons, they shall do well enough.   *Fear not for*

TITUS [*rising*]   Come, Lucius, come, stay not to talk with
them.°   *Exeunt*   (*Quintus and Marcus*)

2.4

*Enter the Empress' sons, [*CHIRON *and* DEMETRIUS,] *with*
LAVINIA, *her hands cut off and her tongue cut out, and
ravished*

DEMETRIUS   So, now go tell, an if thy tongue can speak,
Who 'twas that cut thy tongue and ravished thee.

CHIRON   Write down thy mind, bewray° thy meaning so,   *reveal*
An if thy stumps will let thee play the scribe.

5   DEMETRIUS   See how with signs and tokens she can scrawl.

CHIRON [*to* LAVINIA]   Go home, call for sweet° water, wash thy   *perfumed*
hands.

DEMETRIUS   She hath no tongue to call nor hands to wash,
And so let's leave her to her silent walks.

CHIRON   An 'twere my cause¹ I should go hang myself.

10   DEMETRIUS   If thou hadst hands to help thee knit° the cord.   *knot*
Exeunt [CHIRON *and* DEMETRIUS]
Wind° horns. Enter MARCUS *from hunting to* LAVINIA   *Blow*

MARCUS   Who is this—my niece that flies away so fast?
Cousin,° a word. Where is your husband?   *Kinswoman*
If I do dream, would all my wealth would wake me.²
If I do wake, some planet strike me down

15   That I may slumber an eternal sleep.
Speak, gentle niece, what stern ungentle hands
Hath lopped and hewed and made thy body bare
Of her two branches, those sweet ornaments
Whose circling shadows kings have sought to sleep in,

20   And might not gain so great a happiness
As half thy love. Why dost not speak to me?
Alas, a crimson river of warm blood,
Like to a bubbling fountain stirred with wind,
Doth rise and fall between thy rosèd lips,

25   Coming and going with thy honey breath.
But sure some Tereus³ hath deflowered thee

---

4. The suspicion they are under.   2. *would all . . . me*: I would give all I had to wake up.
2.4 Location: Scene continues.   3. See note to 2.3.43.
1. If I were in her position.

And, lest thou shouldst detect° him, cut thy tongue. *expose*
Ah, now thou turn'st away thy face for shame,
And notwithstanding all this loss of blood,
30 As from a conduit with three issuing spouts,
Yet do thy cheeks look red as Titan's face° *(the sun)*
Blushing to be encountered with a cloud.
Shall I speak for thee? Shall I say 'tis so?
O that I knew thy heart,° and knew the beast, *what is in thy heart*
35 That I might rail at him to ease my mind!
Sorrow concealèd, like an oven stopped,° *stopped up*
Doth burn the heart to cinders where it is.
Fair Philomel, why she but lost her tongue
And in a tedious sampler° sewed her mind. *laborious tapestry*
40 But, lovely niece, that mean° is cut from thee. *method*
A craftier Tereus, cousin, hast thou met,
And he hath cut those pretty fingers off
That could have better sewed than Philomel.
O, had the monster seen those lily hands
45 Tremble like aspen leaves upon a lute
And make the silken strings delight to kiss them,
He would not then have touched them for his life.
Or had he heard the heavenly harmony
Which that sweet tongue hath made,
50 He would have dropped his knife and fell asleep,
As Cerberus at the Thracian poet's feet.[4]
Come, let us go and make thy father blind,
For such a sight will blind a father's eye.
One hour's storm will drown the fragrant meads:° *meadows*
55 What will whole months of tears thy father's eyes?
Do not draw back, for we will mourn with thee.
O, could our mourning ease thy misery! *Exeunt*

3.1

*Enter the Judges, [Tribunes,][1] and Senators with Titus'
two sons, [MARTIUS and QUINTUS,] bound, passing [over]
the stage to the place of execution, and TITUS going
before, pleading*

TITUS Hear me, grave fathers; noble Tribunes, stay.
For pity of mine age, whose youth was spent
In dangerous wars whilst you securely slept;
For all my blood in Rome's great quarrel shed;
5 For all the frosty nights that I have watched,
And for these bitter tears which now you see
Filling the agèd wrinkles in my cheeks,
Be pitiful to my condemnèd sons,
Whose souls is not corrupted as 'tis thought.
10 For two-and-twenty sons I never wept,
Because they died in honour's lofty bed.
        ANDRONICUS *lieth down, and the Judges pass by him*
For these two, Tribunes, in the dust I write

---

4. The Thracian poet Orpheus, attempting to rescue
his dead wife, Eurydice, used his music to lull to sleep
Cerberus, the watchdog of the underworld.

3.1 Location: A Roman street.
1. Not including Marcus, who enters at line 58.

My heart's deep languor° and my soul's sad tears.   *grief*
Let my tears stanch° the earth's dry appetite;   *satisfy*
15 My sons' sweet blood will make it shame° and blush.   *feel shame*

Exeunt [all but TITUS]

O earth, I will befriend thee more with rain
That shall distil from these two ancient ruins°   *(his eyes)*
Than youthful April shall with all his showers.
20 In summer's drought I'll drop upon thee still.
In winter with warm tears I'll melt the snow
And keep eternal springtime on thy face,
So° thou refuse to drink my dear sons' blood.   *Provided that*

Enter LUCIUS *with his weapon drawn*

O reverend Tribunes, O gentle, agèd men,
Unbind my sons, reverse the doom of death,
25 And let me say, that never wept before,
My tears are now prevailing° orators!   *persuasive*
LUCIUS   O noble father, you lament in vain.
The Tribunes hear you not. No man is by,
And you recount your sorrows to a stone.
30 TITUS   Ah Lucius, for thy brothers let me plead.
Grave Tribunes, once more I entreat of you—
LUCIUS   My gracious lord, no tribune hears you speak.
TITUS   Why, 'tis no matter, man. If they did hear,
They would not mark° me; if they did mark,   *attend to*
35 They would not pity me; yet plead I must.
Therefore I tell my sorrows to the stones,
Who, though they cannot answer my distress,
Yet in some sort they are better than the Tribunes
For that they will not intercept° my tale.   *interrupt*
40 When I do weep they humbly at my feet
Receive my tears and seem to weep with me,
And were they but attirèd in grave weeds°   *sober garments*
Rome could afford° no tribunes like to these.   *provide*
A stone is soft as wax, tribunes more hard than stones.
45 A stone is silent and offendeth not,
And tribunes with their tongues doom men to death.
But wherefore stand'st thou with thy weapon drawn?
LUCIUS   To rescue my two brothers from their death,
For which attempt the Judges have pronounced
50 My everlasting doom of banishment.
TITUS [*rising*]   O happy man, they have befriended thee!
Why, foolish Lucius, dost thou not perceive
That Rome is but a wilderness of tigers?
Tigers must prey, and Rome affords no prey
55 But me and mine. How happy art thou then
From these devourers to be banishèd!
But who comes with our brother Marcus here?

Enter MARCUS *with* LAVINIA

MARCUS   Titus, prepare thy agèd eyes to weep,
Or if not so, thy noble heart to break.
60 I bring consuming sorrow to thine age.
TITUS   Will it consume me? Let me see it then.
MARCUS   This was thy daughter.
TITUS   Why, Marcus, so she is.
LUCIUS [*falling on his knees*]   Ay me, this object° kills me.   *spectacle*

<table>
<tbody>
<tr><td>65</td><td>TITUS Faint-hearted boy, arise and look upon her.</td><td></td></tr>
<tr><td></td><td>[LUCIUS rises]</td><td></td></tr>
<tr><td></td><td>Speak, Lavinia, what accursèd hand</td><td></td></tr>
<tr><td></td><td>Hath made thee handless in thy father's sight?</td><td></td></tr>
<tr><td></td><td>What fool hath added water to the sea,</td><td></td></tr>
<tr><td></td><td>Or brought a faggot° to bright-burning Troy?[2]</td><td>piece of firewood</td></tr>
<tr><td>70</td><td>My grief was at the height before thou cam'st,</td><td></td></tr>
<tr><td></td><td>And now like Nilus it disdaineth bounds.[3]</td><td></td></tr>
<tr><td></td><td>Give me a sword, I'll chop off my hands too,</td><td></td></tr>
<tr><td></td><td>For they have fought for Rome, and all in vain;</td><td></td></tr>
<tr><td></td><td>And they have nursed this woe in feeding life;[4]</td><td></td></tr>
<tr><td>75</td><td>In bootless° prayer have they been held up,</td><td>useless</td></tr>
<tr><td></td><td>And they have served me to effectless° use.</td><td>fruitless</td></tr>
<tr><td></td><td>Now all the service I require of them</td><td></td></tr>
<tr><td></td><td>Is that the one will help to cut the other.</td><td></td></tr>
<tr><td></td><td>'Tis well, Lavinia, that thou hast no hands,</td><td></td></tr>
<tr><td>80</td><td>For hands to do Rome service is but vain.</td><td></td></tr>
<tr><td></td><td>LUCIUS Speak, gentle sister, who hath martyred° thee.</td><td>mutilated</td></tr>
<tr><td></td><td>MARCUS O, that delightful engine° of her thoughts,</td><td>instrument</td></tr>
<tr><td></td><td>That blabbed° them with such pleasing eloquence,</td><td>uttered</td></tr>
<tr><td></td><td>Is torn from forth that pretty hollow cage</td><td></td></tr>
<tr><td>85</td><td>Where, like a sweet melodious bird, it sung</td><td></td></tr>
<tr><td></td><td>Sweet varied notes, enchanting every ear.</td><td></td></tr>
<tr><td></td><td>LUCIUS O, say thou for her, who hath done this deed?</td><td></td></tr>
<tr><td></td><td>MARCUS O, thus I found her, straying in the park,</td><td></td></tr>
<tr><td></td><td>Seeking to hide herself, as doth the deer</td><td></td></tr>
<tr><td>90</td><td>That hath received some unrecuring° wound.</td><td>incurable</td></tr>
<tr><td></td><td>TITUS It was my dear, and he that wounded her</td><td></td></tr>
<tr><td></td><td>Hath hurt me more than had he killed me dead;</td><td></td></tr>
<tr><td></td><td>For now I stand as one upon a rock</td><td></td></tr>
<tr><td></td><td>Environed° with a wilderness of sea,</td><td>Surrounded</td></tr>
<tr><td>95</td><td>Who marks the waxing tide grow wave by wave,</td><td></td></tr>
<tr><td></td><td>Expecting° ever when some envious° surge</td><td>Awaiting / malignant</td></tr>
<tr><td></td><td>Will in his° brinish bowels swallow him.</td><td>its</td></tr>
<tr><td></td><td>This way to death my wretched sons are gone.</td><td></td></tr>
<tr><td></td><td>Here stands my other son, a banished man,</td><td></td></tr>
<tr><td>100</td><td>And here my brother, weeping at my woes.</td><td></td></tr>
<tr><td></td><td>But that which gives my soul the greatest spurn°</td><td>contemptuous blow</td></tr>
<tr><td></td><td>Is dear Lavinia, dearer than my soul.</td><td></td></tr>
<tr><td></td><td>Had I but seen thy picture in this plight</td><td></td></tr>
<tr><td></td><td>It would have madded me.° What shall I do</td><td>made me insane</td></tr>
<tr><td>105</td><td>Now I behold thy lively° body so?</td><td>living</td></tr>
<tr><td></td><td>Thou hast no hands to wipe away thy tears,</td><td></td></tr>
<tr><td></td><td>Nor tongue to tell me who hath martyred thee.</td><td></td></tr>
<tr><td></td><td>Thy husband he is dead, and for his death</td><td></td></tr>
<tr><td></td><td>Thy brothers are condemned and dead by this.°</td><td>this time</td></tr>
<tr><td>110</td><td>Look, Marcus, ah, son Lucius, look on her!</td><td></td></tr>
<tr><td></td><td>When I did name her brothers, then fresh tears</td><td></td></tr>
<tr><td></td><td>Stood on her cheeks, as doth the honey-dew</td><td></td></tr>
<tr><td></td><td>Upon a gathered lily almost witherèd.</td><td></td></tr>
</tbody>
</table>

2. Troy was torched by the Greeks after their victory.
3. Before it was dammed, the river Nile flooded annually.
4. And by defending Rome, they have induced this misery.

MARCUS   Perchance she weeps because they killed her husband;
115   Perchance because she knows them innocent.
TITUS   If they did kill thy husband, then be joyful,
    Because the law hath ta'en revenge on them.
    No, no, they would not do so foul a deed;
    Witness the sorrow that their sister makes.
120   Gentle Lavinia, let me kiss thy lips;
    Or make some sign how I may do thee ease.
    Shall thy good uncle, and thy brother Lucius,
    And thou, and I, sit round about some fountain,
    Looking all downwards to behold our cheeks
125   How they are stained, like meadows yet not dry
    With miry slime left on them by a flood?
    And in the fountain shall we gaze so long
    Till the fresh taste be taken from that clearness,
    And made a brine pit with our bitter tears?
130   Or shall we cut away our hands like thine?
    Or shall we bite our tongues, and in dumb shows
    Pass the remainder of our hateful days?
    What shall we do? Let us that have our tongues
    Plot some device° of further misery,   *contrivance*
135   To make us wondered at in time to come.
LUCIUS   Sweet father, cease your tears, for at your grief
    See how my wretched sister sobs and weeps.
MARCUS   Patience, dear niece. Good Titus, dry thine eyes.
TITUS   Ah, Marcus, Marcus, brother, well I wot°   *know*
140   Thy napkin° cannot drink a tear of mine,   *handkerchief*
    For thou, poor man, hast drowned it with thine own.
LUCIUS   Ah, my Lavinia, I will wipe thy cheeks.
TITUS   Mark, Marcus, mark. I understand her signs.
    Had she a tongue to speak, now would she say
145   That to her brother which I said to thee.
    His napkin with his true tears all bewet
    Can do no service on her sorrowful cheeks.
    O, what a sympathy° of woe is this—   *consensus*
    As far from help as limbo⁵ is from bliss.
            Enter AARON *the Moor, alone*
150   AARON   Titus Andronicus, my lord the Emperor
    Sends thee this word: that, if thou love thy sons,
    Let Marcus, Lucius or thyself, old Titus,
    Or any one of you, chop off your hand
    And send it to the King. He for the same
155   Will send thee hither both thy sons alive,
    And that shall be the ransom for their fault.
TITUS   O gracious Emperor! O gentle Aaron,
    Did ever raven sing so like a lark
    That gives sweet tidings of the sun's uprise?
160   With all my heart I'll send the Emperor my hand.
    Good Aaron, wilt thou help to chop it off?
LUCIUS   Stay, father, for that noble hand of thine,
    That hath thrown down so many enemies,

5. Region in hell dedicated to those denied entrance to heaven ("bliss") through no fault of their own: for instance, unbaptized infants, or virtuous people who lived before the advent of Christianity.

Shall not be sent. My hand will serve the turn.
165 My youth can better spare my blood than you,
And therefore mine shall save my brothers' lives.
MARCUS Which of your hands hath not defended Rome
And reared aloft the bloody battleaxe,
Writing destruction on the enemy's castle?
170 O, none of both but are of high desert.
My hand hath been but idle; let it serve
To ransom my two nephews from their death,
Then have I kept it to a worthy end.
AARON Nay, come, agree whose hand shall go along
175 For fear they die before their pardon come.
MARCUS My hand shall go.
LUCIUS   By heaven it shall not go.
TITUS Sirs, strive no more. Such withered herbs as these
Are meet° for plucking up, and therefore mine.   *proper*
LUCIUS Sweet father, if I shall be thought thy son,
180 Let me redeem my brothers both from death.
MARCUS And for our father's sake and mother's care,
Now let me show a brother's love to thee.
TITUS Agree between you. I will spare my hand.
LUCIUS Then I'll go fetch an axe.
MARCUS   But I will use the axe.
                    Exeunt [LUCIUS *and* MARCUS]
185 TITUS Come hither, Aaron. I'll deceive them both.
Lend me thy hand, and I will give thee mine.
AARON [*aside*] If that be called deceit, I will be honest
And never whilst I live deceive men so.
But I'll deceive you in another sort,°   *way*
190 And that you'll say ere half an hour pass.
                    He cuts off Titus' hand.
                    Enter LUCIUS *and* MARCUS *again*
TITUS Now stay your strife. What shall be is dispatched.
Good Aaron, give his majesty my hand.
Tell him it was a hand that warded° him   *defended*
From thousand dangers; bid him bury it.
195 More hath it merited; that° let it have.   *(burial)*
As for my sons, say I account of them
As jewels purchased at an easy price,
And yet dear too, because I bought mine own.
AARON I go, Andronicus; and for thy hand
200 Look by and by to have thy sons with thee.
[*Aside*] Their heads, I mean. O, how this villainy
Doth fat° me with the very thoughts of it!   *feast*
Let fools do good, and fair men call for grace:
Aaron will have his soul black like his face.   *Exit*
205 TITUS O, here I lift this one hand up to heaven
And bow this feeble ruin to the earth.
          [*He kneels*]
If any power pities wretched tears,
To that I call. [*To* LAVINIA, *who kneels*] What, wouldst thou
          kneel with me?
Do then, dear heart; for heaven shall hear our prayers,
210 Or with our sighs we'll breathe the welkin dim°   *make the heavens misty*
And stain the sun with fog, as sometime° clouds   *sometimes do*

When they do hug him in their melting° bosoms.   *(with rain)*

MARCUS   O brother, speak with possibility,°   *what is possible*

And do not break into these deep extremes.

215   TITUS   Is not my sorrows deep, having no bottom?

Then be my passions° bottomless with them.   *expression of suffering*

MARCUS   But yet let reason govern thy lament.

TITUS   If there were reason for these miseries,

Then into limits could I bind my woes.

220   When heaven doth weep, doth not the earth o'erflow?

If the winds rage, doth not the sea wax mad,

Threat'ning the welkin with his big-swoll'n face?

And wilt thou have a reason for this coil?°   *turmoil*

I am the sea. Hark how her sighs doth blow.

225   She is the weeping welkin, I the earth.

Then must my sea be movèd with° her sighs,   *by*

Then must my earth with her continual tears

Become a deluge overflowed and drowned,

Forwhy° my bowels[6] cannot hide her woes,   *Because*

230   But like a drunkard must I vomit them.

Then give me leave, for losers will have leave

To ease their stomachs[7] with their bitter tongues.

       Enter a MESSENGER *with two heads and a hand*

MESSENGER   Worthy Andronicus, ill art thou repaid

For that good hand thou sent'st the Emperor.

235   Here are the heads of thy two noble sons,

And here's thy hand in scorn to thee sent back—

Thy grief their sports, thy resolution mocked,

That° woe is me to think upon thy woes   *So that*

More than remembrance of my father's death.

       [*He sets down the heads and hand*]   *Exit*

240   MARCUS   Now let hot Etna° cool in Sicily,   *volcano in Sicily*

And be my heart an ever-burning hell.

These miseries are more than may be borne.

To weep with them that weep doth ease some deal,°   *somewhat*

But sorrow flouted° at is double death.   *mocked*

245   LUCIUS   Ah, that this sight should make so deep a wound

And yet detested life not shrink thereat—

That ever death should let life bear his name°   *be called life*

Where life hath no more interest but to breathe![8]

       [LAVINIA *kisses* TITUS]

MARCUS   Alas, poor heart, that kiss is comfortless

250   As frozen water to a starvèd° snake.   *numb with cold*

TITUS   When will this fearful slumber° have an end?   *nightmare*

MARCUS   Now farewell, flatt'ry;° die, Andronicus.   *pleasing delusion*

Thou dost not slumber. See thy two sons' heads,

Thy warlike hand, thy mangled daughter here,

255   Thy other banished son with this dear sight

Struck pale and bloodless, and thy brother, I,

Even like a stony image, cold and numb.

Ah, now no more will I control° thy griefs.   *try to restrain*

Rend off thy silver hair, thy other hand

---

6. The bowels were thought to be the seat of compassion.

7. Resentments (with play on "vomit").

8. Where nothing is left of life but breathing.

260   Gnawing with thy teeth, and be this dismal sight
          The closing up° of our most wretched eyes.   *(in death)*
          Now is a time to storm. Why art thou still?
       TITUS   Ha, ha, ha!
       MARCUS   Why dost thou laugh? It fits not with this hour.
265   TITUS   Why, I have not another tear to shed.
          Besides, this sorrow is an enemy,
          And would usurp upon my wat'ry eyes
          And make them blind with tributary[9] tears.
          Then which way shall I find Revenge's cave?—
270   For these two heads do seem to speak to me
          And threat me I shall never come to bliss
          Till all these mischiefs° be returned° again   *calamities / turned back*
          Even in their throats that hath committed them.
          Come, let me see what task I have to do.
          [*He and* LAVINIA *rise*]
275   You heavy° people, circle me about,   *sad*
          That I may turn me to each one of you
          And swear unto my soul to right your wrongs.
          [MARCUS, LUCIUS, *and* LAVINIA *circle* TITUS. *He pledges them*]
          The vow is made. Come, brother, take a head,
          And in this hand the other will I bear.
280   And Lavinia, thou shalt be employed.
          Bear thou my hand, sweet wench, between thine arms.
          As for thee, boy, go get thee from my sight.
          Thou art an exile and thou must not stay.
          Hie° to the Goths, and raise an army there,   *Hurry*
285   And if ye love me, as I think you do,
          Let's kiss and part, for we have much to do.
          [*They kiss.*] *Exeunt* [*all but* LUCIUS]
       LUCIUS   Farewell, Andronicus, my noble father,
          The woefull'st man that ever lived in Rome.
          Farewell, proud Rome, till Lucius come again;
290   He loves his pledges[1] dearer than his life.
          Farewell, Lavinia, my noble sister:
          O, would thou wert as thou tofore° hast been!   *formerly*
          But now nor° Lucius nor Lavinia lives   *neither*
          But in oblivion and hateful griefs.
295   If Lucius live he will requite your wrongs
          And make proud Saturnine and his empress
          Beg at the gates like Tarquin and his queen.[2]
          Now will I to the Goths and raise a power,°   *an army*
          To be revenged on Rome and Saturnine.   *Exit*

3.2

          A banquet.° Enter ANDRONICUS, MARCUS, LAVINIA, *and*   *light meal*
          the boy [YOUNG LUCIUS]
       TITUS   So, so, now sit, and look you eat no more
          Than will preserve just so much strength in us
          As will revenge these bitter woes of ours.
          [*They sit*]

---

9. Paying tribute (to sorrow, the enemy).
1. Vows; hostages (family members left behind in Rome).

2. Tarquin and his family were banished from Rome after the rape of Lucrece; see note to 2.1.109.
3.2 Location: In Titus's house.

Marcus, unknit° that sorrow-wreathen knot.   *unfold (your arms)*

5   Thy niece and I, poor creatures, want° our hands,   *lack*

And cannot passionate° our tenfold grief   *feelingly express*

With folded arms. This poor right hand of mine

Is left to tyrannize° upon my breast,   *(by beating)*

Who,° when my heart, all mad with misery,   *Which*

10   Beats in this hollow prison of my flesh,

Then thus I thump it down.

        [*He beats his breast*]

[*To* LAVINIA] Thou map° of woe, that thus dost talk in signs,   *image*

When thy poor heart beats with outrageous beating

Thou canst not strike it thus to make it still!

15   Wound it with sighing,[1] girl; kill it with groans,

Or get some little knife between thy teeth

And just against° thy heart make thou a hole,   *next to*

That all the tears that thy poor eyes let fall

May run into that sink° and, soaking in,   *receptacle*

20   Drown the lamenting fool[2] in sea-salt tears.

MARCUS   Fie, brother, fie! Teach her not thus to lay

Such violent hands upon her tender life.

TITUS   How now! Has sorrow made thee dote° already?   *insane*

Why, Marcus, no man should be mad but I.

25   What violent hands can she lay on her life?

Ah, wherefore dost thou urge the name of hands

To bid Aeneas tell the tale twice o'er

How Troy was burnt and he made miserable?[3]

O, handle not the theme, to talk of hands,

30   Lest we remember still that we have none.

Fie, fie, how franticly I square° my talk,   *regulate*

As if we should forget we had no hands

If Marcus did not name the word of hands!

Come, let's fall to; and, gentle girl, eat this.

35   Here is no drink! Hark, Marcus, what she says.

I can interpret all her martyred signs.

She says she drinks no other drink but tears,

Brewed with her sorrow, mashed[4] upon her cheeks.

Speechless complainer, I will learn thy thought.

40   In thy dumb action° will I be as perfect°   *gesture / expert*

As begging hermits in their holy prayers.

Thou shalt not sigh, nor hold thy stumps to heaven,

Nor wink, nor nod, nor kneel, nor make a sign,

But I of these will wrest an alphabet,

45   And by still° practice learn to know thy meaning.   *continual*

YOUNG LUCIUS   Good grandsire, leave these bitter deep laments.

Make my aunt merry with some pleasing tale.

MARCUS   Alas, the tender boy in passion° moved   *sorrow*

Doth weep to see his grandsire's heaviness.

50   TITUS   Peace, tender sapling, thou art made of tears,°   *(i.e., still soft)*

And tears will quickly melt thy life away.

        MARCUS *strikes the dish with a knife*

---

1. Sighs were thought to draw blood from the heart.   Troy's fall.
2. Often a term of endearment.   4. Mixed with water, like beer for brewing.
3. In Virgil's *Aeneid* 2, Aeneas tells Dido the story of

What dost thou strike at, Marcus, with thy knife?

MARCUS At that that I have killed, my lord—a fly.

TITUS Out on thee, murderer! Thou kill'st my heart.
55 Mine eyes are cloyed with view of tyranny.
A deed of death done on the innocent
Becomes not Titus' brother. Get thee gone.
I see thou art not for my company.

MARCUS Alas, my lord, I have but killed a fly.
60 TITUS 'But'? How if that fly had a father, brother?
How would he° hang his slender gilded wings   (the father)
And buzz lamenting dirges in the air!
Poor harmless fly,
That with his pretty buzzing melody
65 Came here to make us merry—and thou hast killed him!

MARCUS Pardon me, sir, it was a black ill-favoured° fly,   ugly
Like to the Empress' Moor. Therefore I killed him.

TITUS O, O, O!
Then pardon me for reprehending thee,
70 For thou hast done a charitable deed.
Give me thy knife. I will insult on° him,   triumph over
Flattering myself as if⁵ it were the Moor
Come hither purposely to poison me.
     [He takes a knife, and strikes]
There's for thyself, and that's for Tamora. Ah, sirrah!
75 Yet I think we are not brought so low
But that between us we can kill a fly
That comes in likeness of a coal-black Moor.

MARCUS Alas, poor man! Grief has so wrought on him
He takes false shadows for true substances.
80 TITUS Come, take away.° Lavinia, go with me.   (the meal)
I'll to thy closet° and go read with thee   private room
Sad stories chancèd° in the times of old.   that happened
Come, boy, and go with me. Thy sight is young,
And thou shalt read when mine begin to dazzle.°   Exeunt   my eyes grow dim

4.1

Enter Lucius' son and LAVINIA *running after him, and
the boy flies from her with his books under his arm.
Enter* TITUS *and* MARCUS

YOUNG LUCIUS Help, grandsire, help! My aunt Lavinia
Follows me everywhere, I know not why.
Good uncle Marcus, see how swift she comes.
Alas, sweet aunt, I know not what you mean.
     [He drops his books]
5 MARCUS Stand by me, Lucius. Do not fear thine aunt.

TITUS She loves thee, boy, too well to do thee harm.

YOUNG LUCIUS Ay, when my father was in Rome¹ she did.

MARCUS What means my niece Lavinia by these signs?

TITUS Fear her not, Lucius; somewhat° doth she mean.   something
10 MARCUS See, Lucius, see how much she makes of thee.
Somewhither° would she have thee go with her.   Somewhere

---

5. Pleasing myself with the thought that.   1. That is, here to protect me.
4.1 Location: Titus's garden.

Ah, boy, Cornelia[2] never with more care
Read to her sons than she hath read to thee
Sweet poetry and Tully's[3] *Orator*.
15 Canst thou not guess wherefore she plies° thee thus?   *importunes*
YOUNG LUCIUS   My lord, I know not, I, nor can I guess,
Unless some fit or frenzy do possess her;
For I have heard my grandsire say full oft
Extremity of griefs would make men mad,
20 And I have read that Hecuba of Troy[4]
Ran mad for sorrow. That made me to fear,
Although, my lord, I know my noble aunt
Loves me as dear as e'er my mother did,
And would not but in fury° fright my youth,   *except in madness*
25 Which made me down to throw my books and fly,
Causeless, perhaps. But pardon me, sweet aunt;
And, madam, if my uncle Marcus go°   *go with us*
I will most willingly attend your ladyship.
MARCUS   Lucius, I will
      [LAVINIA *turns the books over with her stumps*]
30 TITUS   How now, Lavinia? Marcus, what means this?
Some book there is that she desires to see.
Which is it, girl, of these?—Open them, boy.
[*To* LAVINIA] But thou art deeper read and better skilled.[5]
Come and take choice of all my library,
35 And so beguile thy sorrow till the heavens
Reveal the damned contriver of this deed.—
Why lifts she up her arms in sequence° thus?   *one after the other*
MARCUS   I think she means that there were more than one
Confederate in the fact.° Ay, more there was,   *crime*
40 Or else to heaven she heaves them for revenge.
TITUS   Lucius, what book is that she tosseth[6] so?
YOUNG LUCIUS   Grandsire, 'tis Ovid's *Metamorphoses*.
My mother gave it me.
MARCUS   For love of her that's gone,
Perhaps, she culled° it from among the rest.   *picked*
45 TITUS   Soft, so busily she turns the leaves.
Help her. What would she find? Lavinia, shall I read?
This is the tragic tale of Philomel,
And treats of Tereus' treason and his rape,[7]
And rape, I fear, was root of thy annoy.°   *injury*
50 MARCUS   See, brother, see. Note how she quotes° the leaves.   *examines*
TITUS   Lavinia, wert *thou* thus surprised, sweet girl,
Ravished and wronged as Philomela was,
Forced in the ruthless, vast, and gloomy woods?
See, see. Ay, such a place there is where we did hunt—
55 O, had we never, never hunted there!—
Patterned by° that the poet here describes,   *On the pattern of*
By nature made for murders and for rapes.
MARCUS   O, why should nature build so foul a den,
Unless the gods delight in tragedies?

---

2. Mother of the two Gracchi, famous tribunes; Cornelia was viewed as the ideal Roman mother because of
her devotion to their education.
3. Cicero's; his *Orator* and *De Oratore*, treatises on
rhetoric written c. 50 B.C.E., were both standard texts in

Renaissance grammar schools.
4. See 1.1.136 and note.
5. Than to read schoolbooks.
6. Clumsily turns the pages.
7. See note to 2.3.43.

60 TITUS   Give signs, sweet girl, for here are none but friends,
         What Roman lord it was durst do the deed.
         Or slunk not Saturnine,[8] as Tarquin erst,°   *once*
         That left the camp to sin in Lucrece' bed?[9]

   MARCUS   Sit down, sweet niece. Brother, sit down by me.
         [*They sit*]

65   Apollo, Pallas, Jove, or Mercury[1]
         Inspire me, that I may this treason find.°   *discover the truth of*
         My lord, look here. Look here, Lavinia.
         This sandy plot is plain.° Guide if thou canst   *flat*
         This after me.
                 He writes his name with his staff, and guides it with feet
                 and mouth
                       I here have writ my name
70   Without the help of any hand at all.
         Cursed be that heart that forced us to this shift!°   *contrivance*
         Write thou, good niece, and here display at last
         What God will have discovered° for revenge.   *revealed*
         Heaven guide thy pen to print thy sorrows plain,
75   That we may know the traitors and the truth.
                 She takes the staff in her mouth, and guides it with her
                 stumps, and writes[2]
         O, do ye read, my lord, what she hath writ?
   TITUS   'Stuprum°—Chiron—Demetrius.'   *Defilement*
   MARCUS   What, what!—The lustful sons of Tamora
         Performers of this heinous bloody deed?
80 TITUS   *Magni dominator poli,*
         Tam lentus audis scelera, tam lentus vides?[3]
   MARCUS   O, calm thee, gentle lord, although I know
         There is enough written upon this earth
         To stir a mutiny in the mildest thoughts,
85   And arm the minds of infants to exclaims.°   *exclamations*
         My lord, kneel down with me; Lavinia, kneel;
         And kneel, sweet boy, the Roman Hector's[4] hope,
                 [*All kneel*]
         And swear with me—as, with the woeful fere°   *husband*
         And father of that chaste dishonoured dame
90   Lord Junius Brutus[5] sware for Lucrece' rape—
         That we will prosecute by good advice°   *after careful planning*
         Mortal revenge upon these traitorous Goths,
         And see their blood, or die with this reproach.°   *dishonor*
                 [*They rise*]
   TITUS   'Tis sure enough an° you knew how,   *if*
95   But if you hunt these bear-whelps, then beware.
         The dam° will wake, and if she wind° ye once   *mother / scent*
         She's with the lion deeply still in league,

8. Was it Saturninus who slunk.
9. See note to 2.1.109.
1. Roman gods: Apollo was the god of prophecy Pallas (Minerva) of wisdom, Mercury of hidden knowledge. Jove (Jupiter), the king of the gods, was often imagined as all-knowing.
2. This action recalls Io in Ovid's *Metamorphoses* 1, who after her rape by Jove was turned into a heifer by

Jove's jealous wife, Juno; she revealed her identity to her family by writing her story in the dust with her hoof.
3. Ruler of the great heavens, are you so slow to hear and see crimes? (adapted from Seneca's *Hippolytus*).
4. Lucius the elder, champion of Rome as Hector was of Troy.
5. Leader of those who drove the Tarquins from Rome.

And lulls him whilst she playeth on her back,
And when he sleeps will she do what she list.°   pleases
100   You are a young huntsman, Marcus. Let alone,
And come, I will go get a leaf° of brass   sheet
And with a gad° of steel will write these words,   spike
And lay it by. The angry northern wind
Will blow these sands like Sibyl's leaves abroad,[6]
105   And where's our lesson then? Boy, what say you?
YOUNG LUCIUS   I say, my lord, that if I were a man
Their mother's bedchamber should not be safe
For these base bondmen to the yoke of Rome.
MARCUS   Ay, that's my boy! Thy father hath full oft
110   For his ungrateful country done the like.[7]
YOUNG LUCIUS   And, uncle, so will I, an if I live.
TITUS   Come go with me into mine armoury.
Lucius, I'll fit° thee; and withal,° my boy   equip / in addition
Shall carry from me to the Empress' sons
115   Presents that I intend to send them both.
Come, come, thou'lt do my message, wilt thou not?
YOUNG LUCIUS   Ay, with my dagger in their bosoms, grandsire.
TITUS   No, boy, not so. I'll teach thee another course.
Lavinia, come. Marcus, look to my house.
120   Lucius and I'll go brave it° at the court.   cut a fine figure
Ay, marry, will we, sir, and we'll be waited on.
                                 Exeunt [all but MARCUS]
MARCUS   O heavens, can you hear a good man groan
And not relent, or not compassion° him?   pity
Marcus, attend him in his ecstasy,°   madness
125   That hath more scars of sorrow in his heart
Than foemen's marks upon his battered shield,
But yet so just that he will not revenge.
Revenge the heavens[8] for old Andronicus!   *Exit*

4.2

Enter AARON, CHIRON, *and* DEMETRIUS *at one door, and
at the other door young* LUCIUS *and another with a
bundle of weapons, and verses writ upon them*
CHIRON   Demetrius, here's the son of Lucius.
He hath some message to deliver us.
AARON   Ay, some mad message from his mad grandfather.
YOUNG LUCIUS   My lords, with all the humbleness I may
5   I greet your honours from Andronicus.
[*Aside*] And pray the Roman gods confound° you both.   destroy
DEMETRIUS   Gramercy,° lovely Lucius. What's the news?   Thank you
YOUNG LUCIUS [*aside*]   That you are both deciphered,° that's the   detected
     news,
For villains marked with rape. [*Aloud*] May it please you,
10   My grandsire, well advised, hath sent by me
The goodliest weapons of his armoury
To gratify° your honourable youth,   grace

6. The Sybil of Cumae (in Italy) wrote prophecies on leaves and placed them outside her cave; they sometimes blew away before they could be read.

7. That is, fought against the Goths.
8. May the heavens take revenge.
4.2 Location: The imperial palace.

The hope of Rome, for so he bid me say;
   [*His attendant gives the weapons*]
And so I do, and with his gifts present

15 Your lordships that, whenever you have need,
You may be armèd and appointed° well;   *equipped*
And so I leave you both [*aside*] like bloody villains.

                                Exit [*with attendant*]

DEMETRIUS   What's here—a scroll, and written round about?
Let's see.

20 'Integer vitae, scelerisque purus,
Non eget Mauri iaculis, nec arcu.'[1]

CHIRON   O, 'tis a verse in Horace, I know it well.
I read it in the grammar long ago.

AARON   Ay, just,° a verse in Horace; right, you have it.   *exactly*

25 [*Aside*] Now what a thing it is to be an ass!
Here's no sound° jest. The old man hath found their guilt,   *wholesome*
And sends them weapons wrapped about with lines
That wound beyond their feeling to the quick.[2]
But were our witty° Empress well afoot°   *clever / up and about*

30 She would applaud Andronicus' conceit.°   *device*
But let her rest in her unrest[3] a while.
[*To* CHIRON *and* DEMETRIUS] And now, young lords, was't not a
      happy star
Led us to Rome, strangers and, more than so,
Captives, to be advancèd to this height?

35 It did me good before the palace gate
To brave[4] the Tribune in his brother's hearing.

DEMETRIUS   But me more good to see so great a lord
Basely insinuate° and send us gifts.   *curry favor*

AARON   Had he not reason, Lord Demetrius?

40 Did you not use his daughter very friendly?

DEMETRIUS   I would we had a thousand Roman dames
At such a bay,° by turn to serve our lust.   *Cornered like that*

CHIRON   A charitable wish, and full of love.

AARON   Here lacks but your mother for to say amen.

45 CHIRON   And that would she, for twenty thousand more.

DEMETRIUS   Come, let us go and pray to all the gods
For our belovèd mother in her pains.°   *(labor pains)*

AARON   Pray to the devils; the gods have given us over.
     Trumpets sound

DEMETRIUS   Why do the Emperor's trumpets flourish thus?

50 CHIRON   Belike° for joy the Emperor hath a son.   *Probably*

DEMETRIUS   Soft, who comes here?
     Enter NURSE *with a blackamoor child*

NURSE   Good morrow, lords.
O tell me, did you see Aaron the Moor?

AARON   Well, more° or less, or ne'er a whit at all,   *(punning on "Moor")*
Here Aaron is; and what with Aaron now?

55 NURSE   O gentle Aaron, we are all undone.

---

1. "The man upright in life and free from crime needs neither the Moorish javelin nor the bow" (Horace, *Odes* 1.22.1–2); quoted in William Lily's Latin grammar, standard in Elizabethan schools.
2. That pierce them deeply though they are too dull to feel it.
3. Remain in her distress (Tamora is in childbirth).
4. To defy (not shown in the play).

Now help, or woe betide thee evermore!

AARON   Why, what a caterwauling dost thou keep!

What dost thou wrap and fumble° in thy arms?   *bundle up*

NURSE   O, that which I would hide from heaven's eye,

60   Our Empress' shame and stately Rome's disgrace.

She is delivered, lords, she is delivered.

AARON   To whom?

NURSE   I mean she is brought abed.°   *delivered of a child*

AARON   Well, God give her good rest. What hath he sent her?

NURSE   A devil.[5]

AARON   Why then, she is the devil's dam.

65   A joyful issue!°   *outcome; child*

NURSE   A joyless, dismal, black, and sorrowful issue.

Here is the babe, as loathsome as a toad

Amongst the fair-faced breeders of our clime.

The Empress sends it thee, thy stamp, thy seal,[6]

70   And bids thee christen it with thy dagger's point.

AARON   Zounds,° ye whore, is black so base a hue?   *God's wounds*

Sweet blowze,° you are a beauteous blossom, sure.   *red-cheeked wench*

DEMETRIUS   Villain, what hast thou done?

AARON   That which thou canst not undo.

75   CHIRON   Thou hast undone our mother.

AARON   Villain, I have done° thy mother.   *used sexually*

DEMETRIUS   And therein, hellish dog, thou hast undone her.

Woe to her chance, and damned her loathèd choice,

Accursed the offspring of so foul a fiend.

CHIRON   It shall not live.

80   AARON   It shall not die.

NURSE   Aaron, it must; the mother wills it so.

AARON   What, must it, nurse? Then let no man but I

Do execution on my flesh and blood.

DEMETRIUS   I'll broach° the tadpole on my rapier's point.   *impale*

85   Nurse, give it me. My sword shall soon dispatch it.

AARON   Sooner this sword shall plough thy bowels up.

[*He takes the child and draws his sword*]

Stay, murderous villains, will you kill your brother?

Now, by the burning tapers of the sky

That shone so brightly when this boy was got,°   *conceived*

90   He dies upon my scimitar's sharp point

That touches this, my first-born son and heir.

I tell you, younglings, not Enceladus[7]

With all his threat'ning band of Typhon's° brood,   *father of the Titans*

Nor great Alcides,[8] nor the god of war

95   Shall seize this prey out of his father's hands.

What, what, ye sanguine,[9] shallow-hearted boys,

Ye whitelimed° walls, ye alehouse painted signs,[1]   *whitewashed*

Coal-black is better than another hue

In that it scorns to bear another hue;

100   For all the water in the ocean

Can never turn the swan's black legs to white,

---

5. The devil was often imagined as black, and Africans as devils.

6. *thy stamp, thy seal:* bearing your imprint.

7. In Greek mythology, a Titan who warred against the gods.

8. Hercules (literally, descendant of Alcaeus).

9. Ruddy (as opposed to black).

1. Cheap, garish images of men.

Although she lave° them hourly in the flood.[2]   *bathe*
Tell the Empress from me I am of age
To keep mine own, excuse it how she can.

105 DEMETRIUS Wilt thou betray thy noble mistress thus?

AARON My mistress is my mistress, this myself,
The figure° and the picture of my youth.   *image*
This before all the world do I prefer;
This maugre° all the world will I keep safe,   *in spite of*
110 Or some of you shall smoke° for it in Rome.   *suffer*

DEMETRIUS By this our mother is for ever shamed.

CHIRON Rome will despise her for this foul escape.°   *escapade*

NURSE The Emperor in his rage will doom° her death.   *decree*

CHIRON I blush to think upon this ignomy.°   *ignominy*

115 AARON Why, there's the privilege your beauty bears.
Fie, treacherous hue, that will betray with blushing
The close enacts° and counsels of thy heart.   *secret purposes*
Here's a young lad framed of another leer.°   *complexion*
Look how the black slave smiles upon the father,
120 As who should say 'Old lad, I am thine own.'
He is your brother, lords, sensibly° fed   *manifestly*
Of that self° blood that first gave life to you,   *same*
And from that womb where you imprisoned were
He is enfranchisèd° and come to light.   *freed*
125 Nay, he is your brother by the surer side,°   *(the mother's)*
Although my seal be stampèd in his face.

NURSE Aaron, what shall I say unto the Empress?

DEMETRIUS Advise thee,° Aaron, what is to be done,   *Consider*
And we will all subscribe to° thy advice.   *follow*
130 Save thou the child, so° we may all be safe.   *provided that*

AARON Then sit we down, and let us all consult.
My son and I will have the wind of you.[3]
Keep there; now talk at pleasure of your safety.
      [*They sit*]

DEMETRIUS [*to the* NURSE] How many women saw this child of his?

135 AARON Why, so, brave lords, when we do join in league
I am a lamb; but if you brave the Moor,
The chafèd° boar, the mountain lioness,   *enraged*
The ocean swells not so as Aaron storms.
      [*To the* NURSE] But say again, how many saw the child?

140 NURSE Cornelia the midwife, and myself,
And no one else but the delivered Empress.

AARON The Empress, the midwife, and yourself.
Two may keep counsel when the third's away.
Go to the Empress, tell her this I said.
      He kills her
145 'Wheak, wheak'[4]—so cries a pig preparèd to the spit.

DEMETRIUS What mean'st thou, Aaron? Wherefore didst thou this?

AARON O Lord, sir, 'tis a deed of policy.°   *prudence*
Shall she live to betray this guilt of ours—
A long-tongued, babbling gossip? No, lords, no.

---

2. Stream; alluding to the proverb "One cannot wash stalking game).
an Ethiop white."   4. Aaron imitates her death cry.
3. Will keep downwind (as a wary hunter does when

150 And now be it known to you my full intent.
Not far, one Muliteus my countryman
His wife⁵ but yesternight was brought to bed.
His child is like to° her, fair as you are.   resembles
Go pack° with him, and give the mother gold,   conspire
155 And tell them both the circumstance of all,°   the full details
And how by this their child shall be advanced
And be receivèd for the Emperor's heir,
And substituted in the place of mine,
To calm this tempest whirling in the court;
160 And let the Emperor dandle him for his own.
Hark ye, lords, you see I have given her physic,°   medicine
And you must needs bestow her funeral.
The fields are near, and you are gallant grooms.°   fellows
This done, see that you take no longer days,°   waste no time
165 But send the midwife presently to me.
The midwife and the nurse well made away,
Then let the ladies tattle what they please.

CHIRON   Aaron, I see thou wilt not trust the air
With secrets.

DEMETRIUS   For this care of Tamora,
170 Herself and hers are highly bound to thee.
          Exeunt [CHIRON *and* DEMETRIUS *with the Nurse's body*]

AARON   Now to the Goths, as swift as swallow flies,
There to dispose° this treasure in mine arms   bestow
And secretly to greet the Empress' friends.
Come on, you thick-lipped slave, I'll bear you hence,
175 For it is you that puts us to our shifts.°   force us to scheme
I'll make you feed on berries and on roots,
And fat on curds and whey, and suck the goat,
And cabin in a cave, and bring you up
To be a warrior and command a camp.°   *Exit* [*with the child*]   an army

4.3

Enter TITUS, *old* MARCUS, [*his son* PUBLIUS,] YOUNG
LUCIUS, *and other gentlemen* [SEMPRONIUS, CAIUS] *with
bows; and* TITUS *bears the arrows with letters on the
ends of them*

TITUS   Come, Marcus, come; kinsmen, this is the way.
Sir boy, let me see your archery.
Look ye draw home° enough, and 'tis there straight.°   fully / immediately
*Terras Astraea reliquit.*¹
5 Be you remembered,° Marcus: she's gone, she's fled.   Remember
Sirs, take you to your tools. You, cousins, shall
Go sound the ocean and cast your nets.
Happily° you may catch her in the sea;   Perhaps
Yet there's as little justice as at land.
10 No, Publius and Sempronius, you must do it.
'Tis you must dig with mattock and with spade
And pierce the inmost centre of the earth.

---

5. *one . . . wife*: the wife of a certain Muliteus, my
countryman.
4.3 Location: Outside the Emperor's palace.

1. "Astraea [goddess of justice] has abandoned the
earth" (Ovid, *Metamorphoses* 1.150).

Then, when you come to Pluto's region,[2]
I pray you deliver him this petition.
15 Tell him it is for justice and for aid,
And that it comes from old Andronicus,
Shaken with sorrows in ungrateful Rome.
Ah, Rome! Well, well, I made thee miserable
What time° I threw the people's suffrages°   *When / votes*
20 On him that thus doth tyrannize o'er me.
Go, get you gone, and pray be careful all,
And leave you not a man-of-war unsearched.
This wicked Emperor may have shipped her[3] hence,
And, kinsmen, then we may go pipe[4] for justice.
25 MARCUS   O, Publius, is not this a heavy case,°   *sad situation*
To see thy noble uncle thus distraught?
PUBLIUS   Therefore, my lords, it highly us concerns
By day and night t'attend him carefully
And feed his humour° kindly as we may,   *humor him*
30 Till time beget some careful° remedy.   *solicitous; laborious*
MARCUS   Kinsmen, his sorrows are past remedy,
But [   ][5]
Join with the Goths, and with revengeful war
Take wreak on Rome for this ingratitude,
35 And vengeance on the traitor Saturnine.
TITUS   Publius, how now? How now, my masters?
What, have you met with her?
PUBLIUS   No, my good lord, but Pluto sends you word
If you will have Revenge from hell, you shall.
40 Marry, for° Justice, she is now employed,   *as for*
He thinks, with Jove, in heaven or somewhere else,
So that perforce you must needs stay a time.[6]
TITUS   He doth me wrong to feed me with delays.
I'll dive into the burning lake[7] below
45 And pull her out of Acheron° by the heels.   *river of the underworld*
Marcus, we are but shrubs, no cedars we,
No big-boned men framed of the Cyclops'[8] size,
But metal, Marcus, steel to the very back,
Yet wrung with wrongs more than our backs can bear,
50 And sith° there's no justice in earth nor hell,   *since*
We will solicit heaven and move the gods
To send down Justice for to wreak° our wrongs.   *revenge*
Come, to this gear.° You are a good archer, Marcus.   *business*
      He gives them the arrows
'Ad Iovem', that's for you. Here, 'ad Apollinem'.
55 'Ad Martem',[9] that's for myself.
Here, boy, 'to Pallas'.° Here 'to Mercury'.   *Minerva*
'To Saturn',° Caius—not 'to Saturnine'!   *father of Jove*
You were as good to° shoot against the wind.   *might as well*
To it, boy! Marcus, loose° when I bid.   *(the arrows)*

2. The underworld, ruled by Pluto.
3. Astraea, whom the mad Titus imagines being smuggled out of Rome in a war boat.
4. Whistle (that is, seek in vain).
5. A line may be missing here; see Textual Variants.
6. So that by necessity ("preface") you must wait a while.
7. Phlegethon, river of fire of the underworld.
8. One-eyed giants of Greek legend.
9. "To Jove," "to Apollo," "to Mars"; Mars was the god of war.

60   Of° my word, I have written to effect.   *On*
           There's not a god left unsolicited.
       MARCUS   Kinsmen, shoot all your shafts into the court.
       We will afflict the Emperor in his pride.
       TITUS   Now, masters, draw.
           [They shoot]
                            O, well said,° Lucius!   *done*
65   Good boy, in Virgo's[1] lap! Give it Pallas.
       MARCUS   My lord, I aim a mile beyond the moon.[2]
       Your letter is with Jupiter by this.
       TITUS   Ha, ha! Publius, Publius, what hast thou done?
       See, see, thou hast shot off one of Taurus'[3] horns.
70   MARCUS   This was the sport, my lord. When Publius shot,
       The Bull, being galled,° gave Aries[4] such a knock   *angered*
       That down fell both the Ram's horns in the court,
       And who should find them but the Empress' villain!°   *servant; scoundrel*
       She laughed, and told the Moor he should not choose
75   But give them[5] to his master for a present.
       TITUS   Why, there it goes. God give his lordship joy.
           Enter the CLOWN° *with a basket and two pigeons in it*   *rustic*
       News, news from heaven; Marcus, the post is come.
       Sirrah, what tidings? Have you any letters?
       Shall I have justice? What says Jupiter?
80   CLOWN   Ho, the gibbet-maker?[6] He says that he hath taken them
       down again, for the man must not be hanged till the next week.
       TITUS   But what says Jupiter, I ask thee?
       CLOWN   Alas, sir, I know not 'Jupiter'. I never drank with him in
       all my life.
       TITUS   Why, villain, art not thou the carrier?
85   CLOWN   Ay, of my pigeons, sir; nothing else.
       TITUS   Why, didst thou not come from heaven?
       CLOWN   From heaven? Alas, sir, I never came there. God forbid
       I should be so bold to press to heaven in my young days. Why,
       I am going with my pigeons to the tribunal plebs[7] to take up
90   a matter of brawl betwixt my uncle and one of the Emperal's°   *(for "Emperor")*
       men.[8]
91.1   MARCUS *[to* TITUS*]   Why, sir, that is as fit as can be to serve*
            for your oration, and let him deliver the pigeons to the
            Emperor from you.
          TITUS *[to the* CLOWN*]   Tell me, can you deliver an oration to*
            the Emperor with a grace?
91.6   CLOWN   *Nay, truly, sir, I could never say grace in all my life.*
       TITUS   Sirrah, come hither. Make no more ado,
       But give your pigeons to the Emperor.
       By me thou shalt have justice at his hands.
95   Hold, hold—*[giving money]* meanwhile, here's money for thy
       charges.

---

1. Constellation identified with Astraea after her flight from earth.
2. Marcus, humoring Titus, expects him to take the words literally; but they also mean "talk wildly, make extravagant claims."
3. Constellation of the bull.
4. Constellation of the ram.

5. The horns, as the sign of the cuckold.
6. The Clown hears "gibbetter" for "Jupiter."
7. *Tribunus plebis*, tribune of the common people.
8. The following indented passage (lines 91.1–91.6), found in the early texts, appear to be a draft of the subsequent six lines.

Give me pen and ink. Sirrah, can you with a grace
Deliver up a supplication?

CLOWN Ay, sir.

100 TITUS [*writing and giving the* CLOWN *a paper*] Then here is a
supplication for you, and when you come to him, at the first
approach you must kneel, then kiss his foot, then deliver up
your pigeons, and then look for your reward. I'll be at hand,
sir; see you do it bravely.°   handsomely

105 CLOWN I warrant you, sir. Let me alone.°   Leave it to me

TITUS Sirrah, hast thou a knife? Come, let me see it.
Here, Marcus, fold it in the oration,
For thou hast made it like an humble suppliant.
And when thou hast given it to the Emperor,

110 Knock at my door and tell me what he says.

CLOWN God be with you, sir. I will.   *Exit*

TITUS Come, Marcus, let us go. Publius, follow me.   *Exeunt*

4.4

*Enter [*SATURNINUS,*] the Emperor, and [*TAMORA,*] the*
*Empress, and [*CHIRON and DEMETRIUS,*] her two sons,*
and others. The Emperor brings the arrows in his hand
that TITUS *shot at him*

SATURNINUS Why, lords, what wrongs are these! Was ever seen
An emperor in Rome thus overborne,°   insolently treated
Troubled, confronted thus, and for the extent
Of egall justice[1] used in such contempt?

5 My lords, you know, as know the mightful gods,
However these disturbers of our peace
Buzz in the people's ears, there naught hath passed
But even with° law against the wilful sons   according to
Of old Andronicus. And what an if

10 His sorrows have so overwhelmed his wits?
Shall we be thus afflicted in his wreaks,°   vindictive deeds
His fits, his frenzy, and his bitterness?
And now he writes to heaven for his redress.
See, here's 'to Jove' and this 'to Mercury',

15 This 'to Apollo', this 'to the god of war'—
Sweet scrolls to fly about the streets of Rome!
What's this but libelling against the Senate
And blazoning° our unjustice everywhere?   proclaiming
A goodly humour,° is it not, my lords?—   whim

20 As who would° say, in Rome no justice were.   As if one were to
But, if I live, his feignèd ecstasies°   pretended insanity
Shall be no shelter to these outrages,
But he and his shall know that justice lives
In Saturninus' health, whom if he sleep

25 He'll so awake[2] as he in fury shall
Cut off the proud'st conspirator that lives.

TAMORA My gracious lord, my lovely Saturnine,

4.4 Location: The Emperor's Palace.
1. *for . . . justice:* in return for exercising impartial justice.
2. *whom . . . awake:* A confusing passage. If the first
"he" (in line 24) refers to Titus, then the meaning is "If
Titus impairs Saturninus's health (tries to 'put him to

sleep'), then Saturninus will rouse himself angrily." If
the first "he" refers to Saturninus, then "Althouth Saturninus seems not to respond now, he will awaken."
Some editors change the first and third (line 25) "he"s
to "she"s, making the phrase refer to justice.

Lord of my life, commander of my thoughts,
Calm thee, and bear the faults of Titus' age,
30 Th'effects of sorrow for his valiant sons
Whose loss hath pierced him deep and scarred his heart;
And rather comfort his distressèd plight
Than prosecute the meanest or the best³
For these contempts. *(Aside)* Why, thus it shall become
35 High-witted° Tamora to gloze° with all.   *Intelligent / delude*
But, Titus, I have touched thee to the quick.
Thy life blood out if Aaron now be wise,
Then is all safe, the anchor in the port.
          Enter CLOWN
How now, good fellow, wouldst thou speak with us?
40 CLOWN   Yea, forsooth, an° your mistress-ship be Emperial.   *if*
TAMORA   Empress I am, but yonder sits the Emperor.
CLOWN   'Tis he. God and Saint Stephen give you good-e'en.°   *good evening*
I have brought you a letter and a couple of pigeons here.
          [SATURNINUS] *reads the letter*
SATURNINUS [*to an attendant*]   Go, take him away, and hang
          him presently.°   *instantly*
45 CLOWN   How much money must I° have?   *am I to*
TAMORA   Come, sirrah, you must be hanged.
CLOWN   Hanged, by' Lady?⁴ Then I have brought up a neck to a
          fair end.   *Exit* [*with attendant*]
SATURNINUS   Despiteful and intolerable wrongs!
50 Shall I endure this monstrous villainy?
I know from whence this same device proceeds.
May this be borne?—As if his traitorous sons,
That died by law for murder of our brother,
Have by my means been butchered wrongfully!
55 Go, drag the villain hither by the hair.
Nor° age nor honour shall shape privilege.°   *Neither / afford immunity*
For this proud mock I'll be thy slaughterman,
Sly frantic wretch, that holp'st° to make me great   *helped*
In hope thyself should govern Rome and me.
          Enter AEMILIUS [*a messenger*]
60 SATURNINUS   What news with thee, Aemilius?
AEMILIUS   Arm, my lords! Rome never had more cause.
The Goths have gathered head,° and with a power   *an army*
Of high-resolvèd men bent to the spoil°   *eager to plunder*
They hither march amain° under conduct°   *swiftly / command*
65 Of Lucius, son to old Andronicus,
Who threats in course of this revenge to do
As much as ever Coriolanus⁵ did.
SATURNINUS   Is warlike Lucius general of the Goths?
These tidings nip me, and I hang the head,
70 As flowers with frost, or grass beat down with storms.
Ay, now begins our sorrows to approach.
'Tis he the common people love so much.
Myself hath often heard them say,

---

3. Lowest or highest ranking.
4. By our Lady (the Virgin Mary).
5. Early Roman warrior who, after he was banished,

joined his former enemies and led an army against
Rome; the subject of Shakespeare's *Coriolanus*.

When I have walkèd like a private man,[6]
75 That Lucius' banishment was wrongfully,°   *wrongfully imposed*
And they have wished that Lucius were their emperor.
TAMORA Why should you fear? Is not your city strong?
SATURNINUS Ay, but the citizens favour Lucius,
And will revolt from me to succour him.
80 TAMORA King, be thy thoughts imperious like thy name.
Is the sun dimmed, that° gnats do fly in it?   *because*
The eagle suffers little birds to sing,
And is not careful° what they mean thereby,   *troubled*
Knowing that with the shadow of his wings
85 He can at pleasure stint° their melody.   *stop*
Even so mayst thou the giddy° men of Rome.   *fickle*
Then cheer thy spirit; for know thou, Emperor,
I will enchant the old Andronicus
With words more sweet and yet more dangerous
90 Than baits to fish or honey-stalks[7] to sheep
Whenas° the one is wounded with the bait,   *When*
The other rotted[8] with delicious feed.
SATURNINUS But he will not entreat his son for us.
TAMORA If Tamora entreat him, then he will,
95 For I can smooth° and fill his agèd ears   *flatter*
With golden promises that, were his heart
Almost impregnable, his old ears deaf,
Yet should both ear and heart obey my tongue.
[*To* AEMILIUS] Go thou before to be our ambassador.
100 Say that the Emperor requests a parley
Of warlike Lucius, and appoint the meeting
Even at his father's house, the old Andronicus.
SATURNINUS Aemilius, do this message honourably.
And if he stand on hostage[9] for his safety,
105 Bid him demand what pledge will please him best.
AEMILIUS Your bidding shall I do effectually.   *Exit*
TAMORA Now will I to that old Andronicus,
And temper° him with all the art I have   *work on*
To pluck proud Lucius from the warlike Goths.
110 And now, sweet Emperor, be blithe again,
And bury all thy fear in my devices.
SATURNINUS Then go incessantly,° and plead to him.   *immediately*
                              Exeunt [*severally*]°   *separately*

5.1

Flourish. Enter LUCIUS *with an army of Goths with*
drums° and soldiers   *drummers*
LUCIUS Approvèd° warriors and my faithful friends,   *Proven*
I have receivèd letters from great Rome
Which signifies what hate they bear their emperor
And how desirous of our sight they are.
5 Therefore, great lords, be as your titles witness,
Imperious, and impatient of your wrongs,
And wherein Rome hath done you any scath°   *harm*

---

6. Disguised as an ordinary man.
7. Clover (large quantities make sheep ill).
8. Afflicted by the rot, a liver disease in sheep.

9. If he demand a hostage (to be killed if Titus is threatened).
5.1 Location: Outside Rome.

Let him make treble satisfaction.

A GOTH   Brave slip° sprung from the great Andronicus,   *offspring*
10   Whose name was once our terror, now our comfort,
Whose high exploits and honourable deeds
Ingrateful Rome requites with foul contempt,
Be bold° in us. We'll follow where thou lead'st,   *confident*
Like stinging bees in hottest summer's day
15   Led by their master¹ to the flowered fields,
And be avengèd on cursèd Tamora.

GOTHS   And as he saith, so say we all with him.

LUCIUS   I humbly thank him, and I thank you all.
But who comes here, led by a lusty Goth?

    Enter a GOTH, *leading of* AARON *with his child in his arms*

20   GOTH   Renownèd Lucius, from our troops I strayed
To gaze upon a ruinous monastery,
And as I earnestly did fix mine eye
Upon the wasted° building, suddenly   *ruined*
I heard a child cry underneath a wall.
25   I made unto the noise, when soon I heard
The crying babe controlled° with this discourse: *calmed*
'Peace, tawny slave,² half me and half thy dam!
Did not thy hue bewray° whose brat thou art,   *show*
Had nature lent thee but thy mother's look,
30   Villain, thou mightst have been an emperor.
But where the bull and cow are both milk-white
They never do beget a coal-black calf.
Peace, villain, peace!'—even thus he rates° the babe—   *scolds*
'For I must bear thee to a trusty Goth
35   Who, when he knows thou art the Empress' babe,
Will hold thee dearly for thy mother's sake.'
With this, my weapon drawn, I rushed upon him,
Surprised him suddenly, and brought him hither
To use as you think needful of° the man.   *appropriate to*

40   LUCIUS   O worthy Goth, this is the incarnate devil
That robbed Andronicus of his good hand.
This is the pearl that pleased your Empress' eye,
And here's the base fruit of her burning lust.
[*To* AARON] Say, wall-eyed slave, whither wouldst thou convey
45   This growing image of thy fiendlike face?
Why dost not speak? What, deaf? What, not a word?
A halter, soldiers! Hang him on this tree,
And by his side his fruit of bastardy.

AARON   Touch not the boy; he is of royal blood.

50   LUCIUS   Too like the sire for ever being° good.   *ever to be*
First hang the child, that he may see it sprawl°—   *twitch convulsively*
A sight to vex the father's soul withal.
Get me a ladder.

    [*A* GOTH *brings a ladder, which* AARON *climbs*]

AARON   Lucius, save the child,
And bear it from me to the Empress.
55   If thou do this, I'll show thee wondrous things
That highly may advantage thee to hear.

---

1. The queen bee was thought to be male.   2. Used affectionately, like "brat," and "villain," below.

If thou wilt not, befall what may befall,
I'll speak no more but 'Vengeance rot you all!'
LUCIUS   Say on, and if it please me which thou speak'st
60   Thy child shall live, and I will see it nourished.
AARON   And if it please thee? Why, assure thee, Lucius,
'Twill vex thy soul to hear what I shall speak;
For I must talk of murders, rapes, and massacres,
Acts of black night, abominable deeds,
65   Complots° of mischief, treason, villainies   Conspiracies
Ruthful° to hear yet piteously[3] performed,   Lamentable
And this shall all be buried in my death
Unless thou swear to me my child shall live.
LUCIUS   Tell on thy mind. I say thy child shall live.
70   AARON   Swear that he shall, and then I will begin.
LUCIUS   Who should I swear by? Thou believest no god.
That granted, how canst thou believe an oath?
AARON   What if I do not?—as indeed I do not—
Yet for I know thou art religious
75   And hast a thing within thee callèd conscience,
With twenty popish tricks and ceremonies
Which I have seen thee careful to observe,
Therefore I urge° thy oath; for that I know   insist on
An idiot holds his bauble° for a god,   jester's stick
80   And keeps the oath which by that god he swears,
To that I'll urge him, therefore thou shalt vow
By that same god, what god soe'er it be,
That thou adorest and hast in reverence,
To save my boy, to nurse and bring him up,
85   Or else I will discover naught to thee.
LUCIUS   Even by my god I swear to thee I will.
AARON   First know thou I begot him on the Empress.
LUCIUS   O most insatiate and luxurious° woman!   lascivious
AARON   Tut, Lucius, this was but a deed of charity
90   To° that which thou shalt hear of me anon.   Compared to
'Twas her two sons that murdered Bassianus.
They cut thy sister's tongue, and ravished her,
And cut her hands, and trimmed her as thou sawest.
LUCIUS   O detestable villain! Call'st thou that trimming?
95   AARON   Why, she was washed and cut and trimmed, and 'twas
Trim° sport for them which had the doing of it.   Fine
LUCIUS   O barbarous beastly villains, like thyself!
AARON   Indeed, I was their tutor to instruct them.
That codding° spirit had they from their mother,   lustful
100   As sure a card as ever won the set,   game
That bloody mind I think they learned of me,
As true a dog as ever fought at head.[4]
Well, let my deeds be witness of my worth.
I trained° thy brethren to that guileful hole   lured
105   Where the dead corpse of Bassianus lay.
I wrote the letter that thy father found,
And hid the gold within that letter mentioned,

3. In a way that would excite pity.
4. As ever went for the bull's head (in the sport of bullbaiting).

Confederate with the Queen and her two sons;
And what not done that thou hast cause to rue
110 Wherein I had no stroke of mischief in it?
I played the cheater[5] for thy father's hand,
And when I had it drew myself apart,°   *went off alone*
And almost broke my heart° with extreme laughter.   *died*
I pried me° through the crevice of a wall   *I peered*
115 When for his hand he had his two sons' heads,
Beheld his tears, and laughed so heartily
That both mine eyes were rainy like to his;
And when I told the Empress of this sport
She swoonèd almost at my pleasing tale,
120 And for my tidings gave me twenty kisses.
    A GOTH   What, canst thou say all this and never blush?
    AARON   Ay, like a black dog, as the saying is.
    LUCIUS   Art thou not sorry for these heinous deeds?
    AARON   Ay, that I had not done a thousand more.
125 Even now I curse the day—and yet I think
Few come within the compass of my curse—
Wherein I did not some notorious ill,
As kill a man, or else devise his death;
Ravish a maid, or plot the way to do it;
130 Accuse some innocent and forswear myself;
Set deadly enmity between two friends;
Make poor men's cattle break their necks;
Set fire on barns and haystacks in the night,
And bid the owners quench them with their tears.
135 Oft have I digged up dead men from their graves
And set them upright at their dear friends' door,
Even when their sorrows almost was forgot,
And on their skins, as on the bark of trees,
Have with my knife carvèd in Roman letters
140 'Let not your sorrow die though I am dead.'
But I have done a thousand dreadful things
As willingly as one would kill a fly,
And nothing grieves me heartily indeed
But that I cannot do ten thousand more.
145   LUCIUS   Bring down the devil, for he must not die
So sweet a death as hanging presently.°   *immediately*
      [*Goths bring* AARON *down the ladder*]
    AARON   If there be devils, would I were a devil,
To live and burn in everlasting fire,
So I might have your company in hell
150 But to torment you with my bitter tongue.
    LUCIUS   Sirs, stop his mouth, and let him speak no more.
      [*Goths gag* AARON]
      Enter AEMILIUS
    A GOTH   My lord, there is a messenger from Rome
Desires to be admitted to your presence.
    LUCIUS   Let him come near.
155 Welcome, Aemilius. What's the news from Rome?
    AEMILIUS   Lord Lucius, and you princes of the Goths,

---

5. Swindler; escheator, an officer appointed to look after property forfeited to the crown.

The Roman Emperor greets you all by me,
And for he understands you are in arms,
He craves a parley at your father's house,
160　Willing you to demand your hostages,
And they shall be immediately delivered.
A GOTH　What says our general?
LUCIUS　Aemilius, let the Emperor give his pledges
Unto my father and my uncle Marcus,
165　And we will come. Away!　　*Flourish. Exeunt marching*]

5.2

Enter TAMORA *and* [CHIRON *and* DEMETRIUS, *her two
sons, disguised*

TAMORA　Thus, in this strange and sad habiliment,°　　　　*somber costume*
I will encounter with Andronicus
And say I am Revenge, sent from below
To join with him and right his heinous wrongs.
5　Knock at his study, where they say he keeps°　　　　　*stays*
To ruminate strange plots of dire revenge.
Tell him Revenge is come to join with him
And work confusion on his enemies.
　　　They knock, and TITUS [*aloft*] *opens his study door*
TITUS　Who doth molest my contemplation?
10　Is it your trick to make me ope the door,
That so my sad decrees° may fly away　　　　　*solemn resolutions*
And all my study be to no effect?
You are deceived; for what I mean to do,
See here, in bloody lines I have set down,
15　And what is written shall be executed.
TAMORA　Titus, I am come to talk with thee.
TITUS　No, not a word. How can I grace my talk,
Wanting° a hand to give it action?　　　　　*Lacking / gesture*
Thou hast the odds° of me, therefore no more.　　　　*advantage*
20　TAMORA　If thou didst know me thou wouldst talk with me.
TITUS　I am not mad, I know thee well enough;
Witness this wretched stump, witness these crimson lines,
Witness these trenches° made by grief and care,　　　　*wrinkles*
Witness the tiring day and heavy night,
25　Witness all sorrow that I know thee well
For our proud empress, mighty Tamora.
Is not thy coming for my other hand?
TAMORA　Know, thou sad man, I am not Tamora.
She is thy enemy, and I thy friend.
30　I am Revenge, sent from th'infernal kingdom
To ease the gnawing vulture[1] of thy mind
By working wreakful° vengeance on thy foes.　　　　*vindictive*
Come down, and welcome me to this world's light.
Confer with me of murder and of death.
35　There's not a hollow cave or lurking-place,
No vast obscurity° or misty vale　　　　　*dark wasteland*
Where bloody murder or detested rape

5.2 Location: Titus's courtyard.
1. Alluding to the story of Prometheus; see note to 2.1.17.

Can couch° for fear, but I will find them out,   *hide*
And in their ears tell them my dreadful name,

40   Revenge, which makes the foul offender quake.
TITUS   Art thou Revenge, and art thou sent to me
     To be a torment to mine enemies?
TAMORA   I am; therefore come down, and welcome me.
TITUS   Do me some service ere I come to thee.

45   Lo by thy side where Rape and Murder stands.
     Now give some surance° that thou art Revenge,   *proof*
     Stab them, or tear them on thy chariot wheels,
     And then I'll come and be thy wagoner,
     And whirl along with thee about the globe,

50   Provide two proper palfreys,° black as jet,   *handsome horses*
     To hale° thy vengeful wagon swift away   *draw*
     And find out murderers in their guilty caves.
     And when thy car is loaden with their heads
     I will dismount, and by thy wagon wheel

55   Trot like a servile footman all day long,
     Even from Hyperion's° rising in the east   *the sun god*
     Until his very downfall in the sea;
     And day by day I'll do this heavy task,
     So° thou destroy Rapine and Murder there.   *Provided that*

60 TAMORA   These are my ministers, and come with me.
TITUS   Are they thy ministers? What are they called?
TAMORA   Rape and Murder, therefore callèd so
     'Cause they take vengeance of such kind of men.
TITUS   Good Lord, how like the Empress' sons they are,

65   And you the Empress! But we worldly° men   *mortal*
     Have miserable, mad, mistaking eyes.
     O sweet Revenge, now do I come to thee,
     And if one arm's embracement will content thee,
     I will embrace thee in it by and by.   *[Exit aloft]*

70 TAMORA   This closing° with him fits his lunacy.   *agreeing*
     Whate'er I forge° to feed his brainsick humours   *invent*
     Do you uphold and maintain in your speeches,
     For now he firmly takes me for Revenge,
     And being credulous in this mad thought

75   I'll make him send for Lucius his son,
     And whilst I at a banquet hold him sure
     I'll find some cunning practice out of hand[2]
     To scatter and disperse the giddy Goths,
     Or at the least make them his enemies.

80   See, here he comes, and I must ply my theme.°   *keep up the act*
     [Enter TITUS, *below]*
TITUS   Long have I been forlorn, and all for thee.
     Welcome, dread Fury, to my woeful house.
     Rapine and Murder, you are welcome, too.
     How like the Empress and her sons you are!

85   Well are you fitted, had you but a Moor.
     Could not all hell afford you such a devil?—
     For well I wot° the Empress never wags°   *know / stirs*
     But in her company there is a Moor,
     And would you represent our Queen aright

2. I'll find some scheme on the spur of the moment.

90   It were convenient° you had such a devil.   *fitting*
        But welcome as you are. What shall we do?
        TAMORA   What wouldst thou have us do, Andronicus?
        DEMETRIUS   Show me a murderer, I'll deal with him
        CHIRON   Show me a villain that hath done a rape,
95   And I am sent to be revenged on him.
        TAMORA   Show me a thousand that hath done thee wrong,
        And I will be revengèd on them all.
        TITUS [to DEMETRIUS]   Look round about the wicked streets of Rome,
        And when thou find'st a man that's like thyself,
100   Good Murder, stab him; he's a murderer.
        [To CHIRON] Go thou with him, and when it is thy hap°   *chance*
        To find another that is like to thee,
        Good Rapine, stab him; he is a ravisher.
        [To TAMORA] Go thou with them, and in the Emperor's court
105   There is a queen attended by a Moor.
        Well shalt thou know her by thine own proportion,
        For up and down° she doth resemble thee.   *top to toe*
        I pray thee, do on them some violent death;
        They have been violent to me and mine.
110   TAMORA   Well hast thou lessoned us. This shall we do;
        But would it please thee, good Andronicus,
        To send for Lucius, thy thrice-valiant son,
        Who leads towards Rome a band of warlike Goths,
        And bid him come and banquet at thy house—
115   When he is here, even at thy solemn° feast,   *ceremonious*
        I will bring in the Empress and her sons,
        The Emperor himself, and all thy foes,
        And at thy mercy shall they stoop and kneel,
        And on them shalt thou ease thy angry heart.
120   What says Andronicus to this device?
        TITUS   Marcus, my brother! 'Tis sad Titus calls.
                 Enter MARCUS
        Go, gentle Marcus, to thy nephew Lucius.
        Thou shalt enquire him out among the Goths.
        Bid him repair° to me, and bring with him   *come*
125   Some of the chiefest princes of the Goths.
        Bid him encamp his soldiers where they are.
        Tell him the Emperor and the Empress too
        Feast at my house, and he shall feast with them.
        This do thou for my love, and so let him,
130   As he regards his agèd father's life.
        MARCUS   This will I do, and soon return again   [*Exit*]
        TAMORA   Now will I hence about thy business,
        And take my ministers along with me.
        TITUS   Nay, nay, let Rape and Murder stay with me,
135   Or else I'll call my brother back again,
        And cleave to no revenge but Lucius.³
        TAMORA [*aside to her sons*]   What say you, boys, will you abide
                 with him
        Whiles I go tell my lord the Emperor

---

3. That is, depend on Lucius's invading army for revenge.

How I have governed our determined jest?[4]

140 Yield to his humour, smooth and speak him fair,° *flatter and humor him*
And tarry with him till I turn° again. *return*

TITUS [*aside*] I knew them all, though they supposed me mad,
And will o'erreach them in their own devices—
A pair of cursèd hell-hounds and their dam.

145 DEMETRIUS   Madam, depart at pleasure. Leave us here.

TAMORA   Farewell, Andronicus. Revenge now goes
To lay a complot to betray thy foes.

TITUS   I know thou dost, and sweet Revenge, farewell.

[*Exit* TAMORA]

CHIRON   Tell us, old man, how shall we be employed?

150 TITUS   Tut, I have work enough for you to do.
Publius, come hither; Caius and Valentine.

[*Enter* PUBLIUS, CAIUS, *and* VALENTINE]

PUBLIUS   What is your will?

TITUS   Know you these two?

PUBLIUS   The Empress' sons I take them°—Chiron, Demetrius. *take them to be*

TITUS   Fie, Publius, fie! Thou art too much deceived.

155 The one is Murder, and Rape is the other's name.
And therefore bind them, gentle Publius;
Caius and Valentine, lay hands on them.
Oft have you heard me wish for such an hour,
And now I find it. Therefore bind them sure,

160 And stop their mouths if they begin to cry. [*Exit*]

CHIRON   Villains, forbear! We are the Empress' sons.

PUBLIUS   And therefore do we what we are commanded.

[PUBLIUS, CAIUS, *and* VALENTINE *bind and gag* CHIRON
and DEMETRIUS]

Stop close their mouths. Let them not speak a word.
Is he sure° bound? Look that you bind them fast. *securely*

Enter TITUS ANDRONICUS *with a knife, and* LAVINIA
with a basin

165 TITUS   Come, come, Lavinia. Look, thy foes are bound.
Sirs, stop their mouths. Let them not speak to me,
But let them hear what fearful words I utter.
O villains, Chiron and Demetrius!
Here stands the spring whom you have stained with mud,

170 This goodly summer with your winter mixed.
You killed her husband, and for that vile fault
Two of her brothers were condemned to death,
My hand cut off and made a merry jest,
Both her sweet hands, her tongue, and that more dear

175 Than hands or tongue, her spotless chastity,
Inhuman traitors, you constrained and forced.
What would you say if I should let you speak?
Villains, for shame. You could not beg for grace.° *mercy*
Hark, wretches, how I mean to martyr you.

180 This one hand yet is left to cut your throats,
Whiles that Lavinia 'tween her stumps doth hold
The basin that receives your guilty blood.

4. How have I managed the jest we planned?

You know your mother means to feast with me,
And calls herself Revenge, and thinks me mad.
185 Hark, villains, I will grind your bones to dust,
And with your blood and it I'll make a paste,°   *dough*
And of the paste a coffin° I will rear,   *piecrust (with wordplay)*
And make two pasties of your shameful heads,
And bid that strumpet, your unhallowed dam,
190 Like to the earth swallow her own increase.°   *progeny*
This is the feast that I have bid her to,
And this the banquet she shall surfeit on;
For worse than Philomel you used my daughter,
And worse than Progne I will be revenged.[5]
195 And now, prepare your throats. Lavinia, come.
Receive the blood, and when that they are dead
Let me go grind their bones to powder small,
And with this hateful liquor temper° it,   *mix*
And in that paste let their vile heads be baked.
200 Come, come, be everyone officious°   *busy*
To make this banquet, which I wish may prove
More stern and bloody than the Centaurs' feast.[6]
    He cuts their throats
So, now bring them in, for I'll play the cook
And see them ready against° their mother comes.   *by the time*
    Exeunt [carrying the bodies]

5.3

    Enter LUCIUS, MARCUS, *and the Goths [with* AARON, *prisoner, and an attendant with his child]*
LUCIUS   Uncle Marcus, since 'tis my father's mind
    That I repair to Rome, I am content.
A GOTH   And ours with thine,[1] befall what fortune will.
LUCIUS   Good uncle, take you in this barbarous Moor,
5   This ravenous tiger, this accursèd devil.
    Let him receive no sust'nance, fetter him
    Till he be brought unto the Empress' face
    For testimony of her foul proceedings,
    And see the ambush° of our friends be strong.   *troops lying in wait*
10   I fear the Emperor means no good to us.
AARON   Some devil whisper curses in my ear
    And prompt me, that my tongue may utter forth
    The venomous malice of my swelling heart.
LUCIUS   Away, inhuman dog, unhallowed slave!
15   Sirs, help our uncle to convey him in.
          [Exeunt Goths with AARON *and his child]*
    Flourish
    The trumpets show the Emperor is at hand.
    *Enter [*SATURNINUS*] the Emperor, and [*TAMORA*] the
    Empress, with [*AEMILIUS,*] Tribunes, [*Senators,*] and
    others*

---

5. Philomela's sister, Progne, revenged herself on her rapist husband, Tereus, by killing their son Itys and serving his flesh in a meal (see Introduction).
6. In Greek legend, the wedding feast of Hippodamia ended in a bloody battle when the Centaurs tried to carry off the bride and other women (see Ovid, *Metamorphoses* 12).
5.3 Location: Titus's courtyard.
1. Our minds accord with yours.

SATURNINUS   What, hath the firmament more suns than one?

LUCIUS   What boots° it thee to call thyself a sun?   *avails*

MARCUS   Rome's emperor and nephew, break the parle.°   *stop the dispute*

20   These quarrels must be quietly debated.

The feast is ready which the careful° Titus   *assiduous; troubled*

Hath ordained to an honourable end,

For peace, for love, for league, and good to Rome.

Please you therefore draw nigh, and take your places.

25   SATURNINUS   Marcus, we will.

>   *Hautboys.[2] A table brought in. [They sit.]*

>   *Enter* TITUS *like a cook, placing the dishes, and* LAVINIA

>   *with a veil over her face;* [YOUNG LUCIUS, *and others*]

TITUS   Welcome, my gracious lord; welcome, dread Queen;

Welcome, ye warlike Goths; welcome, Lucius;

And welcome, all. Although the cheer° be poor,   *refreshments*

'Twill fill your stomachs. Please you, eat of it.

30   SATURNINUS   Why art thou thus attired, Andronicus?

TITUS   Because I would be sure to have all well

To entertain your highness and your Empress.

TAMORA   We are beholden to you, good Andronicus.

TITUS   An if your highness knew my heart, you were.

35   My lord the Emperor, resolve me this:

Was it well done of rash Virginius[3]

To slay his daughter with his own right hand

Because she was enforced, stained, and deflowered?

SATURNINUS   It was, Andronicus.

TITUS   Your reason, mighty lord?

40   SATURNINUS   Because the girl should not survive her shame,

And by her presence still renew his sorrows.

TITUS   A reason mighty, strong, effectual;

A pattern, precedent, and lively warrant

For me, most wretched, to perform the like.

45   Die, die, Lavinia, and thy shame with thee,

And with thy shame thy father's sorrow die.

>   *He kills her*

SATURNINUS   What hast thou done, unnatural and unkind?

TITUS   Killed her for whom my tears have made me blind.

I am as woeful as Virginius was,

50   And have a thousand times more cause than he

To do this outrage, and it now is done.

SATURNINUS   What, was she ravished? Tell who did the deed.

TITUS   Will't please you eat? Will't please your highness feed?

TAMORA   Why hast thou slain thine only daughter thus?

55   TITUS   Not I, 'twas Chiron and Demetrius.

They ravished her, and cut away her tongue,

And they, 'twas they, that did her all this wrong.

SATURNINUS   Go, fetch them hither to us presently.°   *at once*

TITUS [*revealing the heads*]   Why, there they are, both bakèd in

>   this pie,

60   Whereof their mother daintily hath fed,

---

2. Oboes, used to provide music for ceremonial occasions.
3. A Roman centurion who in some versions of the
story killed his daughter to prevent her rape; in other
versions, he acted as Titus describes.

Eating the flesh that she herself hath bred.
'Tis true, 'tis true, witness my knife's sharp point.°   *(with pun on "period")*
    He stabs the Empress
SATURNINUS   Die, frantic° wretch, for this accursèd deec.   *deranged*
    [*He kills* TITUS]
LUCIUS   Can the son's eye behold his father bleed?
65   There's meed for meed,° death for a deadly deed.   *measure for measure*
    [*He kills* SATURNINUS. *Confusion follows.*
    Enter Goths. LUCIUS, MARCUS, *and others go aloft*]
MARCUS   You sad-faced men, people and sons of Rome,
    By uproars severed, as a flight of fowl
    Scattered by winds and high tempestuous gusts,
    O, let me teach you how to knit again
70   This scattered corn° into one mutual° sheaf,   *grain / unified*
    These broken limbs again into one body.
A ROMAN LORD   Let Rome herself be bane° unto herself,   *destroyer*
    And she whom mighty kingdoms curtsy to,
    Like a forlorn and desperate castaway,
75   Do shameful execution on herself
    But if my frosty signs and chaps° of age,   *white hair and wrinkles*
    Grave witnesses of true experience,
    Cannot induce you to attend my words.
    [*To* LUCIUS] Speak, Rome's dear friend, as erst° our ancestor[4]   *once*
80   When with his solemn tongue he did discourse
    To lovesick Dido's sad-attending° ear   *seriously listening*
    The story of that baleful-burning night
    When subtle Greeks surprised King Priam's Troy.
    Tell us what Sinon[5] hath bewitched our ears,
85   Or who hath brought the fatal engine[6] in
    That gives our Troy, our Rome, the civil° wound.   *incurred in civil war*
    My heart is not compact° of flint nor steel,   *composed*
    Nor can I utter all our bitter grief,
    But floods of tears will drown my oratory
90   And break° my utt'rance even in the time   *interrupt*
    When it should move ye to attend me most,
    And force you to commiseration.
    Here's Rome's young captain. Let him tell the tale,
    While I stand by and weep to hear him speak.
95 LUCIUS   Then, gracious auditory,° be it known to you   *audience*
    That Chiron and the damned Demetrius
    Were they that murderèd our Emperor's brother,
    And they it were that ravishèd our sister.
    For their fell° faults our brothers were beheaded,   *cruel*
100   Our father's tears despised, and basely cozened°   *cheated*
    Of that true hand that fought Rome's quarrel out°   *to the finish*
    And sent her enemies unto the grave.
    Lastly myself, unkindly° banishèd,   *unnaturally*
    The gates shut on me, and turned weeping out
105   To beg relief among Rome's enemies,
    Who drowned their enmity in my true tears
    And oped their arms to embrace me as a friend.

4. Aeneas, Trojan ancestor of the Roman people.   wooden horse full of soldiers.
5. The Greek who persuaded the Trojans to admit the   6. Instrument (the wooden horse).

I am the turned-forth, be it known to you,
That have preserved her° welfare in my blood,   (Rome's)
110 And from her bosom took the enemy's point,
Sheathing the steel in my advent'rous body.
Alas, you know I am no vaunter,° I.   boaster
My scars can witness, dumb although they are,
That my report is just and full of truth.
115 But soft, methinks I do digress too much,
Citing my worthless praise. O, pardon me,
For when no friends are by, men praise themselves.
MARCUS   Now is my turn to speak. Behold the child.
Of this was Tamora deliverèd,
120 The issue of an irreligious Moor,
Chief architect and plotter of these woes.
The villain is alive in Titus' house,
And as he is to witness, this is true.
Now judge what cause had Titus to revenge
125 These wrongs unspeakable, past patience,°   endurance
Or more than any living man could bear.
Now have you heard the truth. What say you, Romans?
Have we° done aught amiss, show us wherein,   If we have
And from the place where you behold us pleading
130 The poor remainder of Andronici
Will hand in hand all headlong hurl ourselves⁷
And on the ragged stones beat forth our souls
And make a mutual closure° of our house.°   end / family
Speak, Romans, speak, and if you say we shall,
135 Lo, hand in hand Lucius and I will fall.
AEMILIUS   Come, come, thou reverend man of Rome,
And bring our emperor gently in thy hand,
Lucius, our emperor—for well I know
The common voice do cry it shall be so.
140 ROMANS   Lucius, all hail, Rome's royal emperor!
MARCUS [to attendants]   Go, go into old Titus' sorrowful house
And hither hale that misbelieving Moor
To be adjudged some direful slaught'ring death
As punishment for his most wicked life.   [Exeunt some]
                    [LUCIUS, MARCUS, and the others come down]
145 ROMANS   Lucius, all hail, Rome's gracious governor!
LUCIUS   Thanks, gentle Romans. May I govern so
To heal Rome's harms and wipe away her woe.
But, gentle people, give me aim° awhile,   encourage me
For nature puts me to° a heavy task.   sets me
150 Stand all aloof, but, uncle, draw you near
To shed obsequious° tears upon this trunk.   mournful
[Kissing TITUS] O, take this warm kiss on thy pale cold lips,
These sorrowful drops upon thy bloodstained face,
The last true duties of thy noble son.
155 MARCUS [kissing TITUS]   Tear for tear, and loving kiss for kiss,
Thy brother Marcus tenders on thy lips.
O, were the sum of these that I should pay
Countless and infinite, yet would I pay them.

---

7. Traditionally, traitors were thrown from the Tarpeian Rock on the Capitoline Hill.

LUCIUS [*to* YOUNG LUCIUS]   Come hither, boy, come, come, and
    learn of us
160   To melt in showers. Thy grandsire loved thee well.
    Many a time he danced thee on his knee,
    Sung thee asleep, his loving breast thy pillow.
    Many a story hath he told to thee,
    And bid thee bear his pretty tales in mind,
165   And talk of them when he was dead and gone.
MARCUS   How many thousand times hath these poor lips,
    When they were living, warmed themselves on thine!
    O now, sweet boy, give them their latest° kiss.   *last*
    Bid him farewell. Commit him to the grave.
170   Do them° that kindness, and take leave of them.   *(his lips)*
YOUNG LUCIUS [*kissing* TITUS]   O grandsire, grandsire, ev'n with
    all my heart
    Would I were dead, so° you did live again.   *provided that*
    O Lord, I cannot speak to him for weeping.
    My tears will choke me if I ope my mouth.
        [*Enter some with* AARON]
175 A ROMAN   You sad Andronici, have done with woes.
    Give sentence on this execrable wretch
    That hath been breeder of these dire events.
LUCIUS   Set him breast-deep in earth and famish him.
    There let him stand, and rave, and cry for food.
180   If anyone relieves or pities him,
    For the offence he dies. This is our doom.°   *judgment*
    Some stay to see him fastened in the earth.
AARON   Ah, why should wrath be mute and fury dumb?
    I am no baby, I, that with base prayers
185   I should repent the evils I have done.
    Ten thousand worse than ever yet I did
    Would I perform if I might have my will.
    If one good deed in all my life I did
    I do repent it from my very soul.
190 LUCIUS   Some loving friends convey the Emperor hence
    And give him burial in his father's grave.°   *ancestral tomb*
    My father and Lavinia shall forthwith
    Be closèd in our household's monument.
    As for that ravenous tiger, Tamora,
195   No funeral rite nor man in mourning weed,°   *garments*
    No mournful bell shall ring her burial;
    But throw her forth to beasts and birds to prey.°   *prey upon*
    Her life was beastly and devoid of pity,
    And being dead, let birds on her take pity.
        Exeunt [*with the bodies*]

The First Part of Henry the Sixth

Battles dominate *1 Henry VI*. Set in the fifteenth century, the play depicts England's attempts to retain a military and political foothold in France. Orléans, Rouen, Angiers (modern Angers), Bordeaux—the English and French clash at each place, spilling vast amounts of blood to assert control over the territories to which each laid claim. The English claimed parts of France both by treaty and by inheritance. In 1360, the English King, Edward III, was granted sovereignty over Calais and Bordeaux by the Treaty of Bretigny, which concluded part of what came to be known as the Hundred Years' War. This same Edward, from whom Henry VI was descended also claimed the French Crown itself through his mother, Isabella, the daughter of Philip IV of France. Philip's three sons died without producing male heirs, but Isabella, married to Edward II of England, gave birth to Edward III, who vigorously pursued both the Crown and the territory of France. In the fifteenth century, his great-grandson, Henry V, renewed these efforts and achieved remarkable military successes at Harfleur and Agincourt (see Shakespeare's *Henry V* for an account of his reign). His son, Henry VI, struggled to retain what his father had won.

In this struggle, depicted in the present play, England has one incomparable hero, the valiant Lord Talbot, who fights with such ferocity that the French flee at the very sound of his name. In 1592, probably just a few months after the play was first performed, Thomas Nashe, Shakespeare's contemporary (and himself a playwright who may have had a hand in the composition of the play—see Textual Note), wrote: "How would it have joyed brave Talbot (the terror of the French) to think that after he had lain two hundred yeares in his tomb, he should triumph again on the stage, and have his bones new embalmed with the tears of ten thousand spectators at least (at several times), who, in the Tragedian that represents his person, imagine they behold him fresh bleeding?" This comment—which imagines the long-dead Talbot cheered by the thought of having his mighty victories and lamentable death played again and again— forms part of Nashe's extended defense of stage plays. While many Elizabethan writers attacked the theater as a place of idleness where lies and lewd stories were circulated, Nashe used plays like *1 Henry VI* to argue for the value of the stage, partly because of its role in preserving the memory of England's glorious heroes. As Nashe says, "For the subject of them (for the most part) it is borrowed out of our English Chronicles, wherein our forefathers' valiant acts (that have lain long buried in rusty brass and worm-eaten books) are revived, and they themselves raised from the grave of oblivion, and brought to plead their aged honors in open presence." For Nashe, Talbot is one of those worthy forefathers, pleased to be resurrected in the person of an English actor.

Shakespeare was instrumental in creating the vogue in the 1590s for stage plays based on events from the reigns of England's former monarchs. The division of the 1623 First Folio into histories, comedies, and tragedies indicates that the plays dealing with English history were perceived as a distinct and important group of works. From the beginning of his career until 1599, when *Henry V* was first acted, Shakespeare contributed to the writing of at least eight plays based loosely on the reigns of English Kings from Richard II, who was deposed in 1399, to Henry VII, who assumed the English throne in 1485 after the Battle of Bosworth Field; in addition, there was one play on the reign of King John (1199–1216). Some of these plays chronicle the English wars in France. And some depict the lengthy struggle, known as the Wars of the Roses, between two branches of England's royal family for possession of the English throne:

on one side of this struggle were the Lancastrians, who wore the red rose as their badge; on the other side were the Yorkists, who wore the white. Both groups claimed descent from King Edward III. (For charts showing the genealogies of the Lancastrians and the Yorkists, see the endpapers at back.) The Battle of Bosworth Field ended this civil strife when Henry Tudor, a descendant of John of Gaunt, Duke of Lancaster, defeated Richard III, the last of the Yorkist Kings, and then married Elizabeth of York, the daughter of an earlier Yorkist King, Edward IV. Henry Tudor thus united the red rose and the white, and the Tudors ruled England until 1603, when Elizabeth I, granddaughter of Henry VII, died without issue. It was during the final years of Elizabeth's reign that Shakespeare wrote his history plays.

Many have speculated about why these plays about England's past became so popular. Nashe gives us a clue when he emphasizes their role in celebrating martial heroes and in creating for the common people a collective memory of their national past. In the sixteenth century, many chronicle histories of England were written, such as Edward Hall's *Union of the Two Noble and Illustre Famelies of Lancastre & Yorke* (1548) and Raphael Holinshed's *Chronicles of England, Scotland, and Ireland*; the second edition of Holinshed, published in 1587, was used extensively by Shakespeare in composing his history plays. These prose chronicles, in fact, may have been some of the "worm-eaten" books from which Nashe imagined Talbot being revived for a more pleasurable life on the stage. The theater, unlike obscure and musty texts, made a version of English history accessible even to those who could not read. For a penny, a common person could go to the theater, stand in the pit, and thrill to the exploits of Talbot, the embodiment of English martial valor. Dramatized history thus contributed to an emerging sense of national identity that depended not only on allegiance to a monarch, but also on pride in a shared English culture, language, and identity. The theater played a role in constructing this shared identity, providing ordinary people with riveting representations of a common national past.

In the early 1590s, there were good reasons why arousing patriotic sentiment for an English military hero like Talbot might have been popular. In 1588, England had, with the help of bad weather, repulsed an attack by the Spanish Armada, an invasion fleet sent by Europe's most powerful Catholic power, Spain. This victory had encouraged many English people to feel that their country should play a more active role in supporting the Protestant powers of Europe against their Catholic enemies. In 1591–92, Elizabeth had with some reluctance sent her charismatic nobleman the Earl of Essex into France to aid Henry IV of Navarre and the French Protestant faction. In this campaign, Essex participated in a struggle for control of the city of Rouen. We can date *1 Henry VI* to sometime in 1592 both because Nashe's comments on Talbot were published that year and because the play seems to refer to this French campaign. It depicts fifteenth-century Englishmen invading French soil—and attacking Rouen—at the very moment an English army was once again before the city's walls. Many in England might thus have seen in Talbot an image of their contemporary champion, the dashing Earl of Essex.

Shakespeare was involved in writing two more plays on the reign of Henry VI; in the First Folio, these were entitled, respectively, *The Second Part of Henry the Sixth* and *The Third Part of Henry the Sixth*. These two plays, however, were also published in earlier Octavo or quarto versions, where they bore the titles *The First Part of the Contention of the Two Famous Houses of York and Lancaster* and *The True Tragedy of Richard Duke of York and the Good King Henry the Sixth*. No one is certain whether these plays were written before or after *1 Henry VI*, although the Oxford editors believe they precede *Part 1*. Whatever the exact order of composition, these three plays represent Shakespeare's earliest efforts in the history genre. They were quickly followed by *Richard III*, about the Yorkist monarchs Edward IV and Richard III, who pushed their way to the throne after Henry VI and his son had been killed. This completed Shakespeare's treatment of the reign of Henry VI and of the bloody civil war that erupted during it. Only later in the decade did Shakespeare dramatize the events leading up to Henry VI's kingship. These

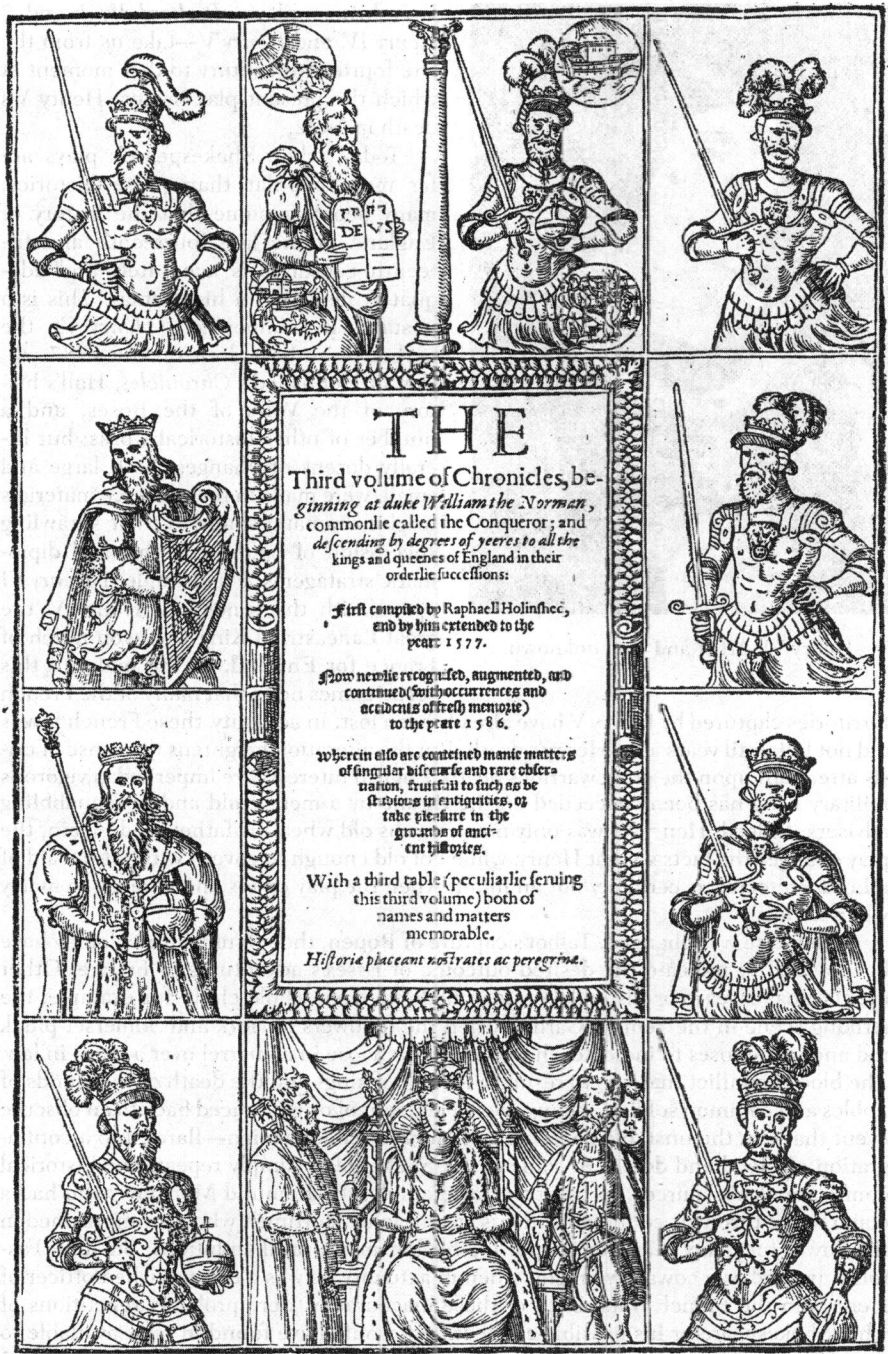

The title page of the third volume of Raphael Holinshed's *Chronicles* (1587 ed.).

King Henry VI. Artist and date unknown.

later history plays—*Richard II, 1* and *2 Henry IV,* and *Henry V*—take us from the late fourteenth century to that moment at which the present play begins: Henry V's death in 1422.

Today, when Shakespeare's plays are far more popular than prose histories, many people assume that the history of England in the late fourteenth and fifteenth centuries is accurately and adequately depicted in his dramas. This is a mistake. In composing *1 Henry VI,* the author or authors drew on the 1587 edition of Holinshed's *Chronicles,* Hall's history of the Wars of the Roses, and a number of other historical works; but literally dozens of changes, both large and small, were made in these source materials to give dramatic shape to their sprawling succession of battles, deaths, and diplomatic stratagems. For example, *1 Henry VI* opens with the funeral of Henry V, the great Lancastrian King who won much of France for England. In the midst of this scene comes news that many of the French territories captured by Henry V have already been lost. In actuality, these French towns did not fall until years after Henry's death. But the alteration heightens the sense of crisis attendant upon the great warrior's death. English interests are imperiled; a vigorous military King has been succeeded on the throne by a mere child and his squabbling advisers. Indeed, Henry VI was only nine months old when his father died. Again, the play changes the facts so that Henry, while not old enough to govern without the aid of a Lord Protector, is certainly not an infant when the play opens and is ready to marry when it ends.

Much else was changed. Talbot's capture of Rouen, though unhistorical, may have been added to indicate the desired outcome of Essex's adventures in France. Other events Shakespeare or his collaborators made up from whole cloth: for example, the striking scene in the Temple Garden when the followers of York and Somerset pluck red and white roses to indicate whose side they choose in a quarrel over a point in law. The bloody conflict that was to result in the fall of kings and the death of thousands of nobles and common soldiers is thus given a moment of origin, traced back to an obscure event that—in the unstable conditions of Henry's tenuous reign—flares into a conflagration of blood and death. In some cases, Shakespeare simply repeats the historical confusion of his sources. In this play, for example, the Edmund Mortimer who had a claim to the throne is conflated with his cousin John Mortimer, who was imprisoned in the Tower for many years for supporting his kinsman's royal ambitions. Sir John Fastolf is treated as a cowardly knight, when in actuality he was a distinguished officer of Henry's in the French wars. Both of these inaccuracies were probably repetitions of what Shakespeare or his possible collaborators would have found in texts available to them. (Later, a cowardly character named Falstaff appears in Shakespeare's *1* and *2 Henry IV* and in *The Merry Wives of Windsor.*)

Indisputably, the play depicts events neither exactly as they were presented in the chronicles nor as a modern historian might present them. In turning historical materials into effective drama, Shakespeare or his collaborators gave one of many possible shapes to the welter of events recorded in the various sources. Many have tried to discern what Shakespeare's "philosophy of history" could have been. Did he, for example, subscribe to the view expressed in Edward Hall's history that the turmoil of the fifteenth century was God's punishment for Henry IV's crime in deposing a rightful King, Richard II—a crime for which England paid in blood for over a hundred years? Or did he take a more secular view of history, in which events unfold as they do because of human choices and actions rather than because of God's intervention? One must read the plays to decide about these questions, and the answers may differ from play to play. An early and possibly a collaborative work, *1 Henry VI* does not necessarily adopt a single point of view toward why historical events unfold as they do. Unlike some of Shakespeare's other history plays, such as *Richard III*, this one contains very little language suggesting that an angry God is punishing England for Henry IV's earlier deposition of Richard II. Rather, events seem to unfold as a direct consequence of human decisions and human rivalries. That demons actually appear to Joan of Arc in Act V, however, complicates matters. Their presence suggests the existence of a supernatural realm that has some influence, however ambiguous, on the course of human affairs.

In dramatic terms, *1 Henry VI* is structured by juxtaposing two conflicts. In the foreground is the struggle between the French and English forces in France. The English, led by Talbot, clash repeatedly with the army of Charles, the French Dauphin. He, in turn, is given aid throughout much of the play by a remarkable figure: the martial maid, Joan of Arc. But a counterpoint to the struggle between French and English emerges by way of the feuding the play depicts among the English nobility. These two lines of action impinge on one another, as the internal squabbling among the English leaders keeps them from giving proper support to their soldiers in the field, eventually allowing Joan and Charles to kill Talbot before the walls of Bordeaux.

If the play has a message to deliver to the English, it would seem to be that petty rivalries and divisions among the English nobility can destroy England from within. As the boy King says to his quarreling nobles, Gloucester and Winchester,

> Believe me, lords, my tender years can tell
> Civil dissension is a viperous worm
> That gnaws the bowels of the commonwealth.
> (3.1.72–74)

The play seldom lets the audience forget about this worm. As early as the first scene, Winchester, whose status as bishop and then later as cardinal connects him to the Church of Rome, quarrels with Gloucester, who has been appointed the Protector of the Realm—that is, the one who effectively holds royal power while the King is still a child. Secular and religious authority clash, and the rent that this causes in the fabric of the commonwealth finds visual embodiment in the several arguments and stage fights that break out between Winchester's tawny-clothed followers and Gloucester's blue-coated serving men. This striking visual juxtaposition of the two factions vividly reveals the cankerworm of civil dissension at work. The red and white roses worn by the followers, respectively, of Somerset and York serve the same purpose, splitting England into two parties just when a united front is needed to sustain the French wars. Young Henry, although aware of the danger of civil dissension, can do little to stop it. On the one hand, he empowers Richard of York by returning to him the lands and titles taken from his father, the Earl of Cambridge, who had been accused of treason; and on the other hand, he decides to wear the red rose of the House of Lancaster. Striving, perhaps, for even-handedness, he inadvertently encourages the dissension he would suppress.

Yet to modern readers, perhaps the most interesting part of the play is not its demonstration of the dangers of civil dissension but its handling of the opposition between Talbot, terror of the French, and Joan, scourge of the English. In contrast to the rivalrous and selfish nobles who surround the young Henry, Talbot is the epitome of the unselfish heroism that Nashe found so compelling. Like a good feudal lord, he lives to serve his King in battle, an arena in which he repeatedly confirms his noble lineage and demonstrates his masculinity. Captured by the French when stabbed in the back by "a base Walloon" (an inhabitant of a French-speaking province now in Belgium), he nonetheless so terrifies his captors that they keep a guard of armed bowmen around him even when he sleeps. Talbot embodies the play's nostalgia for an idealized feudal world in which the values of valor and loyalty are shared by a community of men and passed on by them to their sons. In this regard, the play quite possibly spoke to a longing on the part of some of Elizabeth's subjects to be ruled once more by a king, not by an aging female monarch. When *1 Henry VI* was written, Elizabeth, no longer young and with no heir, was entering the fourth decade of her long reign. The play seems to tap into a yearning for a return to masculine rule and martial values.

In France, Talbot is surrounded by other great English warriors: most notably Salisbury, who dies at the siege of Orléans, and Bedford, who, though sick and dying, insists on being carried in a chair to the battlefield at Rouen in order to give courage to his men. Perhaps most touchingly, at Bordeaux, where the warring English nobles refuse to send him aid, Talbot is joined on the battlefield by his son John, a fledgling warrior come to learn from his father the skills and the values of the warrior class he aspires to join. Urged to flee, he refuses, certain that flight would prove him both effeminate and baseborn. Instead, he is initiated into the rites of manhood by shedding blood and sustaining wounds in what can only be described as an erotics of battle. Having rescued him from the Bastard of Orléans, his father says:

> When from the Dauphin's crest thy sword struck fire
> It warmed thy father's heart with proud desire
> Of bold-faced victory. Then leaden age,
> Quickened with youthful spleen and warlike rage,
> Beat down Alençon, Orléans, Burgundy,
> And from the pride of Gallia rescued thee.
> The ireful Bastard Orléans, that drew blood
> From thee, my boy, and had the maidenhood
> Of thy first fight, I soon encounterèd,
> And interchanging blows, I quickly shed
> Some of his bastard blood. . . .
>
> (4.6.10–20)

Young Talbot, shedding blood in his first battle, is compared to a young girl who bleeds during her first experience of intercourse. The cut and thrust of battle is thus imaged as a sexual encounter in which the goal is to penetrate the body and shed the blood of one's enemy. Young Talbot's willingness to participate in such struggles, no matter how inevitable his ultimate defeat, signifies the purity of his lineage and blood. Bound together by a code of chivalric values and by the rites of blood, Talbot, his son, and Bedford, Salisbury, and those who fight with them upon the fields of France embody the heroism Nashe suggested would stir the hearts of English theatergoers. By play's end, however, all these warriors are dead. With young Talbot's premature slaughter on the plains of Bordeaux, the bright flame of English chivalry flickers out. England passes into the hands of mere politicians and rivalrous churchmen who, if they fight, fight not for king and country but for their own particular interests.

The English in this play are defeated in part because of their failure to live up to and support their own best ideals as embodied in the figure of Talbot. Their defeat, however, also owes much to Talbot's chief antagonist, Joan of Arc, in Shakespeare's play a magnetic and complicated figure. Depending on the vantage point from which she is viewed, Joan is a holy maid sent by God to aid her country, a servant of the devil, or a deceitful whore. When the Bastard of Orléans first introduces her to the Dauphin, he calls Joan a holy maid and a prophet, and after she both sees through the Dauphin's trick to substitute René for himself and defeats the Dauphin in single combat, he proclaims her an Amazon (one of the legendary race of women warriors) and a Deborah (an Old Testament prophet and judge who accompanied an Israelite army against their Canaanite oppressors). These comparisons suggest how highly the French at first value their female champion. For a time, Joan seems possessed of uncanny powers. Not only does she recognize the Dauphin without ever having seen him before, but, perhaps more remarkably, she seems to suck away the great Talbot's strength, leaving him confused and ashamed before the walls of Orléans.

The English respond to this powerful but disarmingly down-to-earth peasant girl by calling her a witch and a whore. Much of their language concerning Joan is filled with bawdy double meanings, beginning with their play on the word *pucelle,* meaning "maid" or "virgin" in French, but sounding like "puzzel," English slang for "whore." From the first time he meets her in battle, Talbot assumes that Joan's powers can come only from witchcraft, rather than from a heavenly or merely human source. Joan's circumstances invite this kind of denigration. She is an unmarried woman who has turned

Fifteenth-century Franco-Flemish portrait of Joan of Arc.

soldier and assumed the garments of a man. In the early modern period, to dress like a man was often read as a violation of woman's assigned place in the gender hierarchy and an indication of the cross-dresser's uncontrolled will and appetites. Such women were easily assumed to be sexually transgressive, as well as vulnerable to the temptations of the devil.

Even Elizabeth, the unmarried Queen, was subject to endless rumors concerning her sexuality. Some whispered that she had had bastard children with the Earl of Leicester, some that her hymen was so thick that no man could penetrate her. The virgin and the whore, the heaven-sent exception and the unnatural monster—the one could easily be turned into the other. While it seems implausible that Joan was constructed explicitly to remind spectators of the English Queen, nonetheless the shepherd girl serves as a lightning rod to capture some of the ambivalent emotions attached to the Queen and to the idea of powerful public women more generally. Occasionally Joan is portrayed in language echoing that used of Elizabeth. Charles, for example, calls her Astraea's daughter—that is, daughter of the goddess of justice—a title often applied to Elizabeth. Several critics have argued that Joan's battlefield exploits recall the stories circulated about Elizabeth in 1588, when she was said to have appeared in armor before her troops at Tilbury as they prepared to go into battle against the Spanish. Having the body of a woman but the role and the clothing of a man, each of these women could incite reverence but also demonization. Anomalies, they could be read as criminals or fiends rather than as miraculous exceptions to their cultures' expectations concerning virtuous women.

Shakespeare's Joan is built of contradictions. At first, she seems a miracle worker who speaks confidently of her role as servant of "God's mother" (1.3.57) and savior of France. At times, she demonstrates Amazonian strength and shrewd military leadership. At other times, she speaks with the sharp tongue and pragmatic realism of a shepherd girl. When, for example, the English herald delivers an extended eulogy over the body of Talbot on the plains of Bordeaux, Joan interrupts him: "Him that thou magnifi'st with all these titles / Stinking and flyblown lies here at our feet" (4.7.75–76). Elsewhere, having persuaded Burgundy to leave his alliance with Talbot and rejoin the French side, she remarks with irony: "Done like a Frenchman—[*aside*] turn and turn again" (3.7.85).

The greatest shift in the presentation of Joan, however, occurs in Act 5, when she unexpectedly dwindles into a frightened and ineffectual practitioner of witchcraft. Summoning demons, she offers to let them suck her blood in return for doing her bidding. They refuse, leaving her vainly attempting to save herself from burning by pleading pregnancy. This diminished Joan of the last act—who, when directly depicted as a witch, is presented as an impotent one—seems deployed in part to bring the play to a closure acceptable to English pride. Talbot may have been defeated, but Joan is not allowed to win the war or even to live. This ending also echoes historical fact. The English handed the actual Joan of Arc over to the Inquisition, and, found guilty of heresy and witchcraft, she was burned in May 1431.

Joan's connection with witchcraft also capitalizes on the widespread interest in the phenomenon in the early 1590s. In 1591, accounts had reached England of the Scottish King James's prosecution of witches; and some had dared to hint that Elizabeth herself had used witchcraft to defeat the Spanish Armada. Several English treatises had been published in the 1580s debating whether witches were indeed the servants of the devil or were simply people, usually old women, scapegoated by their communities or deluded into thinking they had powers they actually lacked. The play, of course, doesn't settle the matter, giving us a Joan whose success against the English could have either a supernatural cause or a more mundane origin in her own strength, cleverness, and ability to inspire others. And while she does summon demons in the last act, they fail to aid her.

But Joan is not the only woman in 1 Henry VI. There are two others: the Countess of Auvergne and Margaret of Anjou, both French and both allied to Joan in the threat they pose to English manhood. While the play certainly highlights the political and military damage done to England by dissension among the English nobility, it also constructs women, especially French women, as a source of danger to England and her male leaders. While no English women appear in 1 Henry VI, three French women play important roles, and all threaten English interests. Joan almost ousts the English from France. The Countess of Auvergne attempts to imprison Talbot in her castle. Margaret conquers men's hearts by her great beauty, causing Henry VI to accept the dowerless Margaret as his bride, despite his promise to marry another woman. Suffolk, the King's retainer, has already fallen prey to her charms, setting up the possibility that, Joan gone, yet another French woman will cause rivalries and dissension in England.

In the warrior culture idealized in the person of Talbot, women would not seem to figure very importantly, except perhaps as mothers who give birth to sons who will continue the lineage and the values of the fathers. But 1 Henry VI depicts a more complicated reality. It shows, for example, how a potential wife, like Margaret, can incite uncontrollable desires in men and so become much more than a vehicle for reproduction or a pawn in a dynastic settlement. It also shows that some men, like the French of this play, seem unable to be martial heroes without the extraordinary and exceptional help of a woman. And it acknowledges that sometimes fathers don't beget sons worthy of the paternal name, as seems to be the case with Henry VI. Sometimes women must fill the void left by masculine failings; occasionally, as with Elizabeth I, a woman must even become King. 1 Henry VI puts all of these complex and contradictory knowledges in play. While it creates heroes for men weary of feminine rule, in the process it also acknowledges the potential weaknesses of men, the occasional failures of the patriarchal gender system to function as it should, and the sometimes surprising and terrifying powers of women. As it turns out, Nashe painted too simple a picture of the history plays. They are not only about the valiant acts of "our forefathers" but also about the failings of less admirable Englishmen and indeed about the actions of women, some of whom, though foreign, seem to have spoken to anxieties generated very close to home.

Jean E. Howard

TEXTUAL NOTE

The only text of *1 Henry VI* is found in the First Folio (F) of 1623. Using several types of stylistic and metrical evidence, the Oxford editors have returned to an existing editorial tradition of assigning authorship to several dramatists. Much of Act 1, they believe, was written by Thomas Nashe; Shakespeare is assigned only 2.4, the scene in the Temple Garden in which the followers of York and Somerset pluck the white roses and the red, and 4.2 through 4.7.32, the battle scenes at Bordeaux in which Talbot and his son meet their deaths after being denied aid by the quarreling English nobles. While the identities of other collaborators are suggested with less certainty, Robert Greene and George Peele are possibilities. Other contemporary textual critics, who attribute the entire play to Shakespeare, feel that the kinds of textual evidence used to adduce multiple authorship are unreliable for work produced so early in Shakespeare's career and discern no marked differences between the quality of this and other plays attributed to him in the early 1590s.

Act and scene divisions are incomplete in the Folio text and may not be theatrical in origin. The Oxford editors have divided the text in Acts 1, 3, and 5 into more scenes than are found in most modern editions. Generally, additional scenes are marked at points during a battle when the stage appears momentarily to be clear of all characters, the traditional indication in the Renaissance theater that one scene has ended and another begun. Thus, during the battle for Orléans, what are traditionally designated as 1.2 and 1.4 are each divided into two shorter scenes (1.2–1.3 and 1.5–1.6); during the struggle for Rouen, the scene traditionally designated as 3.2 is divided into five parts (3.2–3.6); and during the battle for Angiers, 5.3 is divided in this text into three scenes (5.3–5.5).

In addition, the Oxford editors have disposed of what has long been a confusion in F concerning whether Winchester is a cardinal for the whole duration of the play or is elevated to cardinal in Act 5. In Act 1, he is referred to both as a bishop and as a cardinal. The Oxford editors have taken the liberty of deleting or altering all Act 1 references to Winchester as a cardinal. Thus, for example, at 1.4.41, the Oxford text refers to Winchester's "purple robes," while F refers to his "scarlet robes," the color traditionally worn by cardinals.

SELECTED BIBLIOGRAPHY

Hodgdon, Barbara. "Enclosing Contention: 1, 2, and 3 *Henry VI*." *The End Crowns All: Closure and Contradiction in Shakespeare's History*. Princeton: Princeton University Press, 1991. 44–99. Analyzes techniques for creating or disrupting dramatic closure in Shakespeare's early histories.

Jackson, Gabriele Bernhard. "Topical Ideology: Witches, Amazons, and Shakespeare's Joan of Arc." *English Literary Renaissance* 18 (1988): 40–65. Examines the contradictory aspects of the characterization of Joan of Arc, arguing that she is represented both as a positive force and analogue of Queen Elizabeth and also as a witch and strumpet.

Knowles. Ric. "The First Tetralogy in Performance." *A Companion to Shakespeare's Works*. Vol. II: *The Histories*. Ed. Richard Dutton and Jean E. Howard. Malden, Mass.: Blackwell, 2003. 263–86. Discusses key theatrical performances of Shakespeare's earliest history plays, including *1 Henry VI*.

Lee, Patricia-Ann. "Reflections of Power: Margaret of Anjou and the Dark Side of Queenship." *Renaissance Quarterly* 39 (1986): 183–217. Analyzes how the historical Margaret was represented not only in Shakespeare's plays but in the historical chronicles of the fifteenth and sixteenth centuries.

Rackin, Phyllis. *Stages of History: Shakespeare's English Chronicles*. Ithaca, N.Y.: Cornell University Press, 1990. 146–200. Discusses how women in Shakespeare's English history plays subvert and challenge the masculine writing of history.

Riggs, David. *Shakespeare's Heroical Histories: Henry VI and Its Literary Tradition*. Cambridge, Mass.: Harvard University Press, 1971. 93–139. Explores the deterioration of heroic ideals in Shakespeare's early English histories with special attention paid to the opposition of Talbot, the English hero, and Joan of Arc, his French antithesis.

Saccio, Peter. *Shakespeare's English Kings: History, Chronicle, and Drama*. 2nd ed. New York: Oxford University Press, 2000. 90–113. Discusses the differences between the historical events of Henry VI's reign and Shakespeare's representation of them.

Taylor, Gary. "Shakespeare and Others: The Authorship of *Henry the Sixth, Part I*." *Medieval and Renaissance Drama in England* 7 (1995) : 145–205. Lays out evidence for his view that *1 Henry VI* was collaboratively written.

Tricomi, Albert. "Joan la Pucelle and the Inverted Saints Play in *1 Henry VI*." *Renaissance and Reformation* 25 (2001): 5–31. Reads *1 Henry VI* as a Reformation critique of Joan of Arc as a false prophet who incites men to idolatry and of *1 Henry VI* as an inversion of a Catholic saint's play.

Walsh, Brian. "'Unkind Division': The Double Absence of Performing History in *1 Henry VI*." *Shakespeare Quarterly* 55 (2004): 119–47. Discusses the role of performance in evoking, but never fully capturing, the historical past to which *1 Henry VI* refers.

FILM

Henry VI, Part One. 1983. Dir. Jane Howell. UK/USA. 112 min. A BBC-TV production featuring Trevor Peacock as Talbot, Peter Benson as Henry VI, and Brenda Blethyn as Joan. Lavish costumes and some strong performances in a textually faithful version of the play.

The First Part of Henry the Sixth

THE PERSONS OF THE PLAY

The English

KING HENRY VI
Duke of GLOUCESTER, Lord Protector, uncle of King Henry
Duke of BEDFORD, Regent of France
Duke of EXETER
Bishop of WINCHESTER (later Cardinal), uncle of King Henry
Duke of SOMERSET
RICHARD PLANTAGENET, later DUKE OF YORK, and Regent of France
Earl of WARWICK
Earl of SALISBURY
Earl of SUFFOLK
Lord TALBOT
JOHN Talbot
Edmund MORTIMER
Sir William GLASDALE
Sir Thomas GARGRAVE
Sir John FASTOLF
Sir William LUCY
WOODVILLE, Lieutenant of the Tower of London
MAYOR of London
VERNON
BASSET
A LAWYER
A LEGATE and ambassadors
Messengers, warders and keepers of the Tower of London, servingmen, officers, captains, soldiers, heralds, watch

The French

CHARLES, Dauphin of France
RENÉ, Duke of Anjou, King of Naples
MARGARET, his daughter
Duke of ALENÇON
BASTARD of Orléans
Duke of BURGUNDY, uncle of King Henry
GENERAL of the French garrison at Bordeaux
COUNTESS of Auvergne
MASTER GUNNER of Orléans
A BOY, his son
JOAN la Pucelle
A SHEPHERD, father of Joan
Porter, French sergeant, French sentinels, French scout, French herald, the Governor of Paris, fiends, and soldiers

475

1.1

Dead march.° Enter the funeral of King Henry the   *Funeral march*
Fifth, attended on by the Duke of BEDFORD *(Regent of*
France), the Duke of GLOUCESTER *(Protector), the Duke*
of EXETER, [*the Earl of*] WARWICK, *the Bishop of* WIN-
CHESTER, *and the Duke of* SOMERSET

BEDFORD   Hung be the heavens with black![1] Yield, day, to night!
     Comets, importing° change of times and states,   *foretelling*
     Brandish your crystal tresses[2] in the sky,
     And with them scourge the bad revolting° stars   *rebellious*
5   That have consented unto Henry's death—
     King Henry the Fifth, too famous to live long.[3]
     England ne'er lost a king of so much worth.
GLOUCESTER   England ne'er had a king until his time.
     Virtue° he had, deserving to command.   *Merit; power*
10   His brandished sword did blind men with his° beams.   *its*
     His arms spread wider than a dragon's wings.
     His sparkling eyes, replete with wrathful fire,
     More dazzled and drove back his enemies
     Than midday sun, fierce bent against their faces.
15   What should I say? His deeds exceed all speech.
     He ne'er lift up his hand but conquerèd.[4]
EXETER   We mourn in black; why mourn we not in blood?°   *by shedding blood*
     Henry is dead, and never shall revive.
     Upon a wooden coffin we attend,
20   And death's dishonourable victory
     We with our stately presence glorify,
     Like captives bound to a triumphant car.°   *chariot*
     What, shall we curse the planets of mishap,
     That plotted thus our glory's overthrow?
25   Or shall we think the subtle-witted French
     Conjurers and sorcerers, that, afraid of him,
     By magic verses have contrived his end?
WINCHESTER   He was a king blest of the King of Kings.[5]
     Unto the French, the dreadful judgement day
30   So dreadful will not be as was his sight.
     The battles of the Lord of Hosts[6] he fought.
     The Church's prayers made him so prosperous.°   *successful*
GLOUCESTER   The Church? Where is it? Had not churchmen prayed,[7]
     His thread of life had not so soon decayed.°   *grown weak*
35   None do you like but an effeminate prince,
     Whom like a schoolboy you may overawe.
WINCHESTER   Gloucester, whate'er we like, thou art Protector,[8]
     And lookest to command the Prince and realm.

1.1 Location: Westminster Abbey, England.
1. Alluding to the theatrical practice, when a tragedy
was to be performed, of hanging black draperies from
the "heavens," or roof projecting over the stage.
2. Flash your bright hair (the tails of the comets).
3. Henry V, the English conqueror of France who is the
subject of a later play by Shakespeare, lived from 1387
until 1422. The assertion that he was too famous to live
long may refer to the popular belief that jealous fate
(the stars of line 4) prematurely cut down those whose
fame became too great.

4. He never lifted up his hand (in battle) without
conquering.
5. The name for God in biblical descriptions of the
Last Judgment (see Revelation 19:16).
6. Another biblical name for God (see Psalms 24:10,
Isaiah 13:13).
7. Punning on "preyed" and implying that Winchester
conspired against the King.
8. Ruler of the kingdom during the King's youth.
(Henry VI was an infant when his father died.)

	Thy wife[9] is proud: she holdeth thee in awe,°	*overawes or rules you*
40	More than God or religious churchmen may.	
	GLOUCESTER Name not religion, for thou lov'st the flesh,	
	And ne'er throughout the year to church thou go'st,	
	Except it be to pray against thy foes.	
	BEDFORD Cease, cease these jars,° and rest your minds in peace.	*discords*
45	Let's to the altar. Heralds, wait on us.°	*attend us*
	[*Exeunt* WARWICK, SOMERSET, *and heralds with coffin*][1]	
	Instead of gold, we'll offer up our arms—	
	Since arms avail not, now that Henry's dead.	
	Posterity, await for° wretched years,	*expect*
	When, at their mothers' moistened eyes, babes shall suck,[2]	
50	Our isle be made a marish° of salt tears,	*marsh*
	And none but women left to wail the dead.	
	Henry the Fifth, thy ghost I invocate:	
	Prosper this realm; keep it from civil broils;°	*wars*
	Combat with adverse planets in the heavens.	
55	A far more glorious star thy soul will make	
	Than Julius Caesar[3] or bright—	
	Enter a MESSENGER	
	MESSENGER My honourable lords, health to you all.	
	Sad tidings bring I to you out of France,	
	Of loss, of slaughter, and discomfiture.	
60	Guyenne, Compiègne, Rouen, Rheims, Orléans,	
	Paris, Gisors, Poitiers are all quite lost.	
	BEDFORD What sayst thou, man, before dead Henry's corpse?	
	Speak softly, or the loss of those great towns	
	Will make him burst his lead° and rise from death.	*lead lining of coffin*
65	GLOUCESTER [*to the* MESSENGER] Is Paris lost? Is Rouen yielded up?	
	If Henry were recalled to life again,	
	These news would cause him once more yield the ghost.°	*to die*
	EXETER [*to the* MESSENGER] How were they lost? What	
	treachery was used?	
	MESSENGER No treachery, but want° of men and money.	*lack*
70	Amongst the soldiers this is mutterèd:	
	That here you maintain several factions,	
	And whilst a field° should be dispatched and fought,	*an army; battle*
	You are disputing of° your generals.	*about*
	One would have ling'ring wars, with little cost;	
75	Another would fly swift, but wanteth wings;	
	A third thinks, without expense at all,	
	By guileful fair words peace may be obtained.	
	Awake, awake, English nobility!	
	Let not sloth dim your honours new-begot.	
80	Cropped° are the flower-de-luces[4] in your arms;	*Plucked*

---

9. Eleana Cobham. Accused of pride and overweening ambition, she is found guilty of witchcraft in *The First Part of the Contention*.

1. F does not indicate when the funeral procession exits. If it exits now rather than at the end of the scene, then Henry's coffin is not onstage when the messengers from France arrive; but the actors carrying the coffin would have more time to prepare for their parts in the battle scene in 1.2.

2. When babies are fed only with their mother's tears.

3. According to Roman tradition, Caesar's soul was turned into a shining star (Ovid's *Metamorphoses*) or comet (Suetonius) after his murder.

4. English name for the French national emblem, the fleur-de-lis (lily flower), which appeared in the English coat of arms and signified the English claim to the French throne. By the Treaty of Troyes (1420), Henry V was named heir to the French King Charles VI, but Henry died shortly before Charles; at Charles's death, the French throne passed to his son, the Dauphin, leading to the renewed struggles between the French and English depicted here.

Of England's coat,° one half is cut away.   [*Exit*]   *coat of arms*
EXETER   Were our tears wanting to this funeral,
These tidings would call forth her° flowing tides.   *(England's)*
BEDFORD   Me they concern; Regent⁵ I am of France.
85   Give me my steelèd coat. I'll fight for France.
Away with these disgraceful wailing robes!
     [*He removes his mourning robe*]
Wounds will I lend the French, instead of eyes,
To weep⁶ their intermissive° miseries.   *temporarily interrupted*
     Enter to them another MESSENGER [*with letters*]
SECOND MESSENGER   Lords, view these letters, full of bad mischance.
90   France is revolted from the English quite,
Except some petty towns of no import.
The Dauphin⁷ Charles is crownèd king in Rheims;
The Bastard of Orléans⁸ with him is joined;
René, Duke of Anjou, doth take his part;
95   The Duke of Alençon flyeth to his side.   *Exit*
EXETER   The Dauphin crownèd King? All fly to him?
O whither shall *we* fly from this reproach?
GLOUCESTER   We will not fly, but to our enemies' throats.
Bedford, if thou be slack, I'll fight it out.
100   BEDFORD   Gloucester, why doubt'st thou of my forwardness?
An army have I mustered in my thoughts,
Wherewith already France is overrun.
     Enter another MESSENGER
THIRD MESSENGER   My gracious lords, to add to your laments,
Wherewith you now bedew King Henry's hearse,
105   I must inform you of a dismal° fight   *disastrous*
Betwixt the stout° Lord Talbot⁹ and the French.   *brave*
WINCHESTER   What, wherein Talbot overcame—is't so?
THIRD MESSENGER   O no, wherein Lord Talbot was o'erthrown.
The circumstance I'll tell you more at large.°   *in greater detail*
110   The tenth of August last, this dreadful° lord,   *fear-inspiring*
Retiring from the siege of Orléans,
Having full scarce° six thousand in his troop,   *barely*
By three-and-twenty thousand of the French
Was round encompassèd and set upon.
115   No leisure had he to enrank° his men.   *to set in battle lines*
He wanted pikes¹ to set before his archers—
Instead whereof, sharp stakes plucked out of hedges
They pitchèd in the ground confusèdly,
To keep the horsemen off from breaking in.
120   More than three hours the fight continuèd,

---

5. Ruler in the King's absence.
6. *Wounds . . . weep*: I will give the French wounds, so that they will weep blood (from the wounds, instead of tears from the eyes).
7. Charles VII (1403–1461) held the title of Dauphin (heir to the French throne) until he became King in 1422. Historically, his coronation at Reims did not occur until 1429.
8. Jean, Count of Dunois (1403–1468), illegitimate

son of the Duke of Orléans and nephew of King Charles VI.
9. John Talbot, first Earl of Shrewsbury (1388–1453) and perhaps the most celebrated English military hero of his day, was captured by the French at the Battle of Patay, the "dismal fight" described here.
1. He lacked ironbound stakes (normally set in the ground in front of archers to protect against attacking cavalry).

Where valiant Talbot above human thought
Enacted wonders with his sword and lance.
Hundreds he sent to hell, and none durst stand° him;   face
Here, there, and everywhere, enraged he slew.
125 The French exclaimed the devil was in arms:
All the whole army stood agazed on° him.   astonished at
His soldiers, spying his undaunted spirit,
'A° Talbot! A Talbot!' cried out amain,°   To / strongly
And rushed into the bowels of the battle.
130 Here had the conquest fully been sealed up,
If Sir John Fastolf[2] had not played the coward.
He, being in the vanguard placed behind,[3]
With purpose to relieve and follow them,
Cowardly fled, not having struck one stroke.
135 Hence grew the general wrack° and massacre.   destruction
Enclosèd were they with° their enemies.   by
A base Walloon,[4] to win the Dauphin's grace,
Thrust Talbot with a spear into the back—
Whom all France, with their chief assembled strength,
140 Durst not presume to look once in the face.
BEDFORD   Is Talbot slain then? I will slay myself,
For living idly here in pomp and ease
Whilst such a worthy leader, wanting aid,
Unto his dastard foemen° is betrayed.   enemies
145 THIRD MESSENGER   O no, he lives, but is took prisoner,
And Lord Scales with him, and Lord Hungerford;
Most of the rest slaughtered, or took likewise.
BEDFORD   His ransom there is none but I shall pay.
I'll hale the Dauphin headlong from his throne;
150 His crown shall be the ransom of my friend.
Four of their lords I'll change° for one of ours.   exchange (kill)
Farewell, my masters; to my task will I.
Bonfires in France forthwith I am to make,
To keep our great Saint George's feast[5] withal.
155 Ten thousand soldiers with me I will take,
Whose bloody deeds shall make all Europe quake.
THIRD MESSENGER   So you had need. Fore Orléans, besieged,
The English army is grown weak and faint.
The Earl of Salisbury craveth supply,°   reinforcements
160 And hardly keeps his men from mutiny,
Since they, so few, watch such a multitude.   [Exit]
EXETER   Remember, lords, your oaths to Henry sworn:
Either to quell the Dauphin utterly,
Or bring him in obedience to your yoke.
165 BEDFORD   I do remember it, and here take my leave
To go about my preparation.   Exit

---

2. Shakespeare follows a doubtful historical tradition here. Even though in some chronicles depicted as a coward, Sir John Fastolf (1378?–1459) was actually a distinguished soldier and officer of Henry V in the French wars. For this character's relationship with the cowardly knight Falstaff in (1 and 2) Henry IV, see the Introduction to 1 Henry IV.

3. He being stationed in the rear of the vanguard.
4. Inhabitant of a French-speaking province in what is now southern Belgium.
5. The feast day of St. George, England's patron saint, April 23, was traditionally celebrated with bonfires. Bedford suggests that he will celebrate it every day with military victories over the French.

GLOUCESTER I'll to the Tower[6] with all the haste I can,
    To view th'artillery and munition,
    And then I will proclaim young Henry king.   *Exit*

170 EXETER To Eltham[7] will I, where the young King is,
    Being ordained his special governor,
    And for his safety there I'll best devise.   *Exit*

WINCHESTER Each hath his place and function to attend;
    I am left out; for me, nothing remains.
175 But long I will not be Jack-out-of-office.[8]
    The King from Eltham I intend to steal,
    And sit at chiefest stern° of public weal.   *Exit*   *(as steersman)*

1.2

Sound a flourish.° Enter CHARLES [*the Dauphin, the*   *fanfare of trumpets*
Duke of] ALENÇON, *and* RENÉ [*Duke of Anjou*], *march-*
ing with drum[mer] and soldiers

CHARLES Mars his true moving—even as in the heavens,
    So in the earth—to this day is not known.[1]
    Late° did he shine upon the English side;   *Recently*
    Now we are victors: upon us he smiles.
5 What towns of any moment° but we have?   *importance*
    At pleasure here we lie near Orléans
    Otherwhiles° the famished English, like pale ghosts,   *Occasionally*
    Faintly besiege us one hour in a month.

ALENÇON They want their porrage° and their fat bull beeves.   *porridge; stew*
10 Either they must be dieted° like mules,   *fed*
    And have their provender tied to their mouths,
    Or piteous they will look, like drownèd mice.

RENÉ Let's raise the siege. Why live we idly here?
    Talbot is taken, whom we wont° to fear.   *were accustomed*
15 Remaineth none but mad-brained Salisbury,
    And he may well in fretting spend his gall:°   *exhaust his anger*
    Nor° men nor money hath he to make war.   *Neither*

CHARLES Sound, sound, alarum!° We will rush on them.   *(the call to arms)*
    Now for the honour of the forlorn[2] French,
20 Him I forgive my death that killeth me
    When he sees me go back one foot or flee.   *Exeunt*

1.3

Here alarum. They [the French] are beaten back by the
English with great loss. Enter CHARLES [*the Dauphin,*
the Duke of] ALENÇON, *and* RENÉ [*Duke of Anjou*]

CHARLES Who ever saw the like? What men have I?
    Dogs, cowards, dastards! I would ne'er have fled,
    But that they left me 'midst my enemies.

RENÉ Salisbury is a desperate homicide.
5 He fighteth as one weary of his life.
    The other lords, like lions wanting food,
    Do rush upon us as their hungry prey.°   *prey to their hunger*

---

6. The Tower of London, which served as both a royal
residence and an arsenal.
7. Another royal residence, located south of London.
8. Proverbial for someone who had been dismissed
from a job.
1.2 Location: Near Orléans, France.

1. The precise nature of the planet Mars's orbit was a
subject of debate until Johannes Kepler described it in
1609. Mars, the god of war, was known for his unpre-
dictability.
2. Performing their duty at the risk of death.
1.3 Location: Near Orléans.

ALENÇON Froissart,[1] a countryman of ours, records
England all Olivers and Rolands[2] bred
10 During the time Edward the Third did reign.
More truly now may this be verified,
For none but Samsons and Goliases[3]
It sendeth forth to skirmish. One to ten?
Lean raw-boned rascals,° who would e'er suppose   *thin, inferior deer*
15 They had such courage and audacity?
CHARLES Let's leave this town, for they are hare-brained slaves,
And hunger will enforce them to be more eager.°   *fierce*
Of old I know them: rather with their teeth
The walls they'll tear down, than forsake the siege.
20 RENÉ I think by some odd gimmers[4] or device
Their arms are set, like clocks, still to strike on,
Else ne'er could they hold out so as they do.
By my consent we'll even let them alone.
ALENÇON Be it so.
     Enter the BASTARD *of Orléans*
25 BASTARD Where's the Prince Dauphin? I have news for him.
CHARLES Bastard of Orléans, thrice welcome to us.
BASTARD Methinks your looks are sad, your cheer appalled.°   *countenance made pale*
Hath the late overthrow wrought this offence?
Be not dismayed, for succour is at hand.
30 A holy maid hither with me I bring,
Which, by a vision sent to her from heaven,
Ordainèd is to raise this tedious siege
And drive the English forth° the bounds of France.   *out of*
The spirit of deep prophecy she hath,
35 Exceeding the nine sibyls of old Rome.[5]
What's past and what's to come she can descry.
Speak: shall I call her in? Believe my words,
For they are certain and unfallible.
CHARLES Go call her in.   *[Exit* BASTARD*]*[6]
But first, to try her skill,
40 René stand thou as Dauphin in my place.
Question her proudly; let thy looks be stern.
By this means shall we sound° what skill she hath.   *test*
     Enter [the BASTARD *of Orléans with]* JOAN *[la]*
     Pucelle[7] [armed]
RENÉ *[as Charles]* Fair maid, is't thou wilt do these wondrous feats?
JOAN René, is't thou that thinkest to beguile me?
45 Where is the Dauphin? *[To* CHARLES*]* Come, come from behind.
I know thee well, though never seen before.
Be not amazed. There's nothing hid from me.
In private will I talk with thee apart.

---

1. Jean Froissart, author of a history of medieval France and England.
2. The most famous of Charlemagne's knights.
3. The biblical warriors Samson and Goliath were noted for their exceptional strength.
4. Gimmals, mechanical parts for transmitting motion (as in clockwork).
5. Sibyls were women in antiquity possessing the power of prophecy, perhaps "nine" here because of confusion with the nine prophetic books offered to Tarquin, the ruler of Rome, by the Cumaean Sibyl.
6. F does not indicate who brings in Joan, but it seems likely that it is the Bastard himself rather than a servant.
7. French for "the maid" or "the virgin." Joan of Arc (1412–1431) was celebrated by the French as the "Maid of Orléans" after she fought in the battle depicted here. A formidable warrior, she eventually became a prisoner of the English and was burned alive for heresy.

Stand back you lords, and give us leave awhile.
              [RENÉ, ALENÇON *and* BASTARD *stand apart*]
          RENÉ [*to* ALENÇON *and* BASTARD] She takes upon her bravely, at
50   first dash.[8]
          JOAN   Dauphin, I am by birth a shepherd's daughter,
          My wit untrained in any kind of art.
          Heaven and our Lady gracious° hath it pleased   (*the Virgin Mary*)
          To shine on my contemptible estate.
55   Lo, whilst I waited on my tender lambs,
          And to sun's parching heat displayed my cheeks,
          God's mother deignèd to appear to me,
          And in a vision, full of majesty,
          Willed me to leave my base vocation
60   And free my country from calamity.
          Her aid she promised, and assured success.
          In complete glory she revealed herself—
          And whereas I was black[9] and swart° before,   *dark; swarthy*
          With those clear rays which she infused° on me   *shed*
65   That beauty am I blest with, which you may see.
          Ask me what question thou canst possible,
          And I will answer unpremeditated.
          My courage try by combat, if thou dar'st,
          And thou shalt find that I exceed my sex.
70   Resolve on° this: thou shalt be fortunate,   *Be sure of*
          If thou receive me for thy warlike mate.°   *co-worker; lover*
          CHARLES   Thou hast astonished me with thy high terms.°   *lofty phrases*
          Only this proof ° I'll of thy valour make: *test*
          In single combat thou shalt buckle° with me.   *contend; make love*
75   An if° thou vanquishest, thy words are true;   *An if=If*
          Otherwise, I renounce all confidence.
          JOAN   I am prepared. Here is my keen-edged sword,
          Decked with five flower-de-luces on each side—
          The which at Touraine, in Saint Katherine's[1] churchyard,
80   Out of a great deal of old iron I chose forth.
          CHARLES   Then come a° God's name. I fear no woman.   *in*
          JOAN   And while I live, I'll ne'er fly from a man.
                  Here they fight and JOAN [*la*] *Pucelle overcomes*
          CHARLES   Stay, stay thy hands! Thou art an Amazon,[2]
          And fightest with the sword of Deborah.[3]
85   JOAN   Christ's mother helps me, else I were too weak.
          CHARLES   Whoe'er helps thee, 'tis thou that must help me.
          Impatiently I burn with thy desire.°   *with desire for you*
          My heart and hands thou hast at once subdued.
          Excellent Pucelle if thy name be so,
90   Let me thy servant,° and not sovereign be.   *lover*
          'Tis the French Dauphin sueth to thee thus.
          JOAN   I must not yield to any rites of love,
          For my profession's sacred from above.
          When I have chasèd all thy foes from hence,
95   Then will I think upon a recompense.

---

8. She plays her part well from the start.
9. Dark-skinned (probably from the sun).
1. Patroness of young maidens and female students;
reputed to be the holiest of Christ's virgins.
2. One of the tribe of legendary female warriors

claimed by Herodotus to live in Scythia.
3. An Old Testament prophet and judge who accompanied Barak as he led a victorious Israelite army against the Canaanites (see Judges 4–5).

CHARLES   Meantime, look gracious on thy prostrate thrall.

RENÉ [*to the other lords apart*]   My lord, methinks, is very long
    in talk.

ALENÇON   Doubtless he shrives this woman to her smock,[4]
    Else ne'er could he so long protract his speech.

100 RENÉ   Shall we disturb him, since he keeps no mean?°   *moderation*

ALENÇON   He may mean more than we poor men do know.
    These women are shrewd tempters with their tongues.

RENÉ [*to* CHARLES]   My lord, where are you? What devise° you on?   *decide*
    Shall we give o'er Orléans, or no?

105 JOAN   Why, no, I say. Distrustful recreants,°   *cowards*
    Fight till the last gasp; I'll be your guard.

CHARLES   What she says, I'll confirm. We'll fight it out.

JOAN   Assigned am I to be the English scourge.[5]
    This night the siege assuredly I'll raise.

110 Expect Saint Martin's summer, halcyon's days,[6]
    Since I have entered into these wars.
    Glory is like a circle in the water,
    Which never ceaseth to enlarge itself
    Till, by broad spreading, it disperse to naught.

115 With Henry's death, the English circle ends.
    Dispersèd are the glories it included.
    Now am I like that proud insulting° ship   *exultant*
    Which Caesar and his fortune bore at once.[7]

CHARLES   Was Mohammed inspirèd with a dove?[8]

120 Thou with an eagle[9] art inspirèd then.
    Helen,[1] the mother of great Constantine,
    Nor yet Saint Philip's daughters[2] were like thee.
    Bright star of Venus,° fall'n down on the earth,   *Roman goddess of love*
    How may I reverently worship thee enough?

125 ALENÇON   Leave off delays, and let us raise the siege.

RENÉ   Woman, do what thou canst to save our honours.
    Drive them from Orléans, and be immortalized.

CHARLES   Presently° we'll try. Come, let's away about it.   *Immediately*
    No prophet will I trust, if she prove false.   *Exeunt*

1.4

Enter [*the Duke of*] GLOUCESTER, *with his* SERVINGMEN
[*in blue coats*][1]

GLOUCESTER   I am come to survey the Tower this day.
    Since Henry's death, I fear there is conveyance.°   *dishonesty*
    Where be these warders,° that they wait not here?   *guards*
    [A SERVINGMAN *knocketh on the gates*]

---

4. Hears her confession completely; examines her intimately (to her "smock," or undergarments).

5. An individual sent by God to punish sin.

6. A period of unseasonable calm (the sea was thought to grow calm in December so that halcyons, or kingfishers, could build their nests upon it). *Saint Martin's summer:* Indian summer (St. Martin's Day falls on November 11).

7. According to Plutarch, an anxious sea captain was calmed when Caesar told him that his ship contained both Caesar and Caesar's natural good fortune.

8. Mohammed was the prophet and founder of Islam. Some Elizabethans claimed he was a fraud who fooled followers into thinking he was divinely inspired by

training a dove to take seeds from his ear. Christians saw the dove as an incarnation of the Holy Spirit.

9. Attribute of the apostle St. John and hence a symbol of divine inspiration; also an aggressive enemy of the dove.

1. St. Helena, the mother of the emperor who made Christianity the official religion of the Roman Empire, was said to have been led by a vision to discover Jesus' cross and sepulcher.

2. Four virgins noted in the New Testament (Acts 21:9) for their powers of prophecy.

1.4 Location: The Tower of London.

1. The typical attire of Elizabethan servants.

Open the gates: 'tis Gloucester that calls.

FIRST WARDER [*within the Tower*]   Who's there that knocketh so
5   imperiously?

GLOUCESTER'S FIRST MAN   It is the noble Duke of Gloucester.

SECOND WARDER [*within the Tower*]   Whoe'er he be, you may
          not be let in.

GLOUCESTER'S FIRST MAN   Villains,° answer you so the Lord   *Scoundrels; peasants*
          Protector?

FIRST WARDER [*within the Tower*]   The Lord protect him, so we
          answer him.
10   We do no otherwise than we are willed.°   *commanded*

GLOUCESTER   Who willèd you? Or whose will stands, but mine?
          There's none Protector of the realm but I.
          [*To* SERVINGMEN] Break up the gates. I'll be your warrantize.°   *surety; authorization*
          Shall I be flouted thus by dunghill grooms?
          Gloucester's men rush at the Tower gates

WOODVILLE[2] [*within the Tower*][3]   What noise is this? What
15   traitors have we here?

GLOUCESTER   Lieutenant, is it you whose voice I hear?
          Open the gates! Here's Gloucester, that would enter.

WOODVILLE [*within the Tower*]   Have patience, noble duke:
          I may not open.
          My lord of Winchester forbids.
20   From him I have express commandèment
          That thou, nor none of thine, shall be let in.

GLOUCESTER   Faint-hearted Woodville! Prizest him fore me?—
          Arrogant Winchester, that haughty prelate,
          Whom Henry, our late sovereign, ne'er could brook?°   *tolerate*
25   Thou art no friend to God or to the King.
          Open the gates, or I'll shut thee out shortly.

SERVINGMEN   Open the gates unto the Lord Protector,
          Or we'll burst them open, if that you come not quickly.
          Enter, to the [Lord] Protector at the Tower gates, [the
          Bishop of] WINCHESTER *and his men in tawny coats*[4]

WINCHESTER   How now, ambitious vizier![5] What means this?

GLOUCESTER   Peeled° priest, dost thou command me to be   *Shaven; tonsured*
30   shut out?

WINCHESTER   I do, thou most usurping proditor,°   *traitor*
          And not 'Protector', of the King or realm.

GLOUCESTER   Stand back, thou manifest conspirator.
          Thou that contrived'st to murder our dead lord,
35   Thou that giv'st whores indulgences to sin,[6]
          If thou proceed in this thy insolence—

WINCHESTER   Nay, stand thou back! I will not budge a foot.

---

2. Richard Woodville (died c. 1441) was a loyal follower of the Lancastrian King Henry VI. His granddaughter Elizabeth married the Yorkist King Edward IV
in 1464, a marriage Shakespeare depicts in *Richard III*.
3. The original stage direction at 1.4.14 reads:
"Gloucester's men rush at the Tower gates, and
Woodville the Lieutenant speaks within." The First and
Second Warders most likely also speak here from within
the Tower, but it is unclear whether they speak from the
upper stage or from behind some stage device suggesting a grate or window.

4. Typically worn by attendants of important churchmen.
5. A high state official in the Turkish Empire, which
Elizabethans frequently denounced as barbaric.
6. In 1426, Gloucester charged Winchester with
attempting to have King Henry V ("our dead lord")
killed. He here also accuses Winchester of encouraging
prostitution, referring to the revenues that the Bishop
of Winchester collected from the brothels on the south
bank of the Thames (where, in Shakespeare's time,
many theaters were also located).

This be Damascus,[7] be thou cursèd Cain,
To slay thy brother Abel, if thou wilt.
40 GLOUCESTER   I will not slay thee, but I'll drive thee back.
Thy purple robes, as a child's bearing-cloth,°   *christening gown*
I'll use to carry thee out of this place.
WINCHESTER   Do what thou dar'st, I beard° thee to thy face.   *defy*
GLOUCESTER   What, am I dared and bearded to my face?
45 Draw, men, for all this privilegèd place.[8]
        [*All draw their swords*]
Blue coats to tawny coats!—Priest, beware your beard.
I mean to tug it, and to cuff you soundly.
Under my feet I'll stamp thy bishop's mitre.
In spite of Pope, or dignities of church,
50 Here by the cheeks I'll drag thee up and down.
WINCHESTER   Gloucester, thou wilt answer this before the Pope.
GLOUCESTER   Winchester goose! I cry, 'A rope, a rope!'[9]
[*To his* SERVINGMEN] Now beat them hence. Why do you let them stay?
[*To* WINCHESTER] Thee I'll chase hence, thou wolf in sheep's array.
55 Out, tawny coats! Out, cloakèd hypocrite!
        Here Gloucester's men beat out the Bishop's men.[1] *Enter*
        in the hurly-burly the MAYOR *of London and his Officers*
MAYOR   Fie, lords!—that you, being supreme magistrates
Thus contumeliously° should break the peace.   *contemptuously*
GLOUCESTER   Peace, mayor, thou know'st little of my wrongs.
Here's Beaufort—that regards nor° God nor king—   *neither*
60 Hath here distrained° the Tower to his use.   *seized*
WINCHESTER [*to* MAYOR]   Here's Gloucester—a foe to citizens,
One that still motions° war, and never peace,   *who always advocates*
O'ercharging your free purses[2] with large fines°—   *taxes*
That seeks to overthrow religion,
65 Because he is Protector of the realm,
And would have armour here out of the Tower
To crown himself king and suppress the Prince.
GLOUCESTER   I will not answer thee with words but blows.
        Here they [*the factions*] *skirmish again*
MAYOR   Naught rests° for me, in this tumultuous strife,   *is left*
70 But to make open proclamation.
Come, officer, as loud as e'er thou canst, cry.
OFFICER   All manner of men, assembled here in arms this day
against God's peace and the King's, we charge and command
you in his highness' name to repair to your several dwelling
75 places, and not to wear, handle, or use any sword, weapon, or
dagger henceforward, upon pain of death.
        [*The skirmishes cease*]
GLOUCESTER   Bishop, I'll be no breaker of the law.
But we shall meet and break our minds° at large.   *express our views*

---

7. Damascus, in Syria, was believed to have been built on the spot where Adam and Eve's son Cain murdered his brother Abel (see Genesis 4).
8. It was illegal to draw swords near "privileged" sites, including royal residences. *for all this:* though this is a.
9. A call for a hangman's noose. *Winchester goose:* slang expression for a swelling in the groin caused by venereal disease; a prostitute or a victim of venereal disease.
1. F's stage direction reads: "Cardinal's men." Here, as elsewhere, the Oxford editors have removed the confusion about when Winchester is made a cardinal by assuming him to be a bishop until Act 5.
2. Overburdening your generous purses.

WINCHESTER   Gloucester, we'll meet to thy cost, be sure.

80   Thy heart-blood I will have for this day's work.

MAYOR   I'll call for clubs,³ if you will not away.

[*Aside*] This bishop is more haughty than the devil.

GLOUCESTER   Mayor, farewell. Thou dost but what thou mayst.

WINCHESTER   Abominable Gloucester, guard thy head,

85   For I intend to have it ere long.

       Exeunt [*both factions severally*]°   *separately*

MAYOR [*to* OFFICERS]   See the coast cleared, and then we will depart.—

Good God, these nobles should such stomachs° bear! *angry tempers*

I myself fight not once in forty year.   *Exeunt*

1.5

Enter the MASTER GUNNER *of Orléans and his* BOY

MASTER GUNNER   Sirrah,¹ thou know'st how Orléans is besieged,

And how the English have the suburbs won.

BOY   Father, I know, and oft have shot at them;

Howe'er, unfortunate, I missed my aim.

5   MASTER GUNNER   But now thou shalt not. Be thou ruled by me.

Chief Master Gunner am I of this town;

Something I must do to procure me grace.°   *honor*

The Prince's spials° have informèd me   *spies*

How the English, in the suburbs close entrenched,

10   Wont,° through a secret grate of iron bars *Are accustomed*

In yonder tower, to overpeer the city,

And thence discover how with most advantage

They may vex us with shot or with assault.

To intercept this inconvenience,°   *harm*

15   A piece of ordnance 'gainst° it I have placed, *directed toward*

And even these three days have I watched, if I could see them.

Now do thou watch, for I can stay no longer.

If thou spy'st any, run and bring me word,

And thou shalt find me at the governor's.

20   BOY   Father, I warrant you, take you no care°— *don't worry*

      Exit [MASTER GUNNER *at one door*]

I'll never trouble you, if I may spy them.

       Exit [*at the other door*]

1.6

Enter [*the Earl of*] SALISBURY *and* [*Lord*] TALBOT

[*above*] *on the turrets with others* [*among them*

Sir Thomas GARGRAVE *and Sir William* GLASDALE]

SALISBURY   Talbot, my life, my joy, again returned?

How wert thou handled, being prisoner?

Or by what means got'st thou to be released?

Discourse, I prithee, on this turret's top.

5   TALBOT   The Duke of Bedford had a prisoner,

Called the brave Lord Ponton de Santrailles;

For him was I exchanged and ransomèd.

---

3. I'll shout for London apprentices to bring their clubs and quell this riot. "Prentices and clubs" was a common rallying cry.
1.5 Location: Orléans.

1. Normally used to address social inferiors, but here used to address the Master Gunner's young son.
1.6 Location: Tower before the walls of Orléans.

But with a baser man-of-arms° by far   *soldier of lower rank*
Once in contempt they would have bartered me—
10 Which I, disdaining, scorned, and cravèd death
Rather than I would be so pilled esteemed.°   *so cheaply valued*
In fine,° redeemed I was, as I desired.   *In short*
But O, the treacherous Fastolf wounds my heart,
Whom with my bare fists I would execute
15 If I now had him brought into my power.
SALISBURY   Yet tell'st thou not how thou wert entertained.°   *treated*
TALBOT   With scoffs and scorns and contumelious taunts.
In open market place produced they me,
To be a public spectacle to all.
20 'Here', said they, 'is the terror of the French,
The scarecrow that affrights our children so.'
Then broke I from the officers that led me
And with my nails digged stones out of the ground
To hurl at the beholders of my shame.
25 My grisly countenance made others fly.
None durst come near, for fear of sudden death.
In iron walls they deemed me not secure:
So great fear of my name 'mongst them were spread
That they supposed I could rend bars of steel
30 And spurn° in pieces posts of adamant.[1]   *kick*
Wherefore a guard of chosen shot° I had   *selected marksmen*
That walked about me every minute while;°   *constantly*
And if I did but stir out of my bed,
Ready they were to shoot me to the heart.
The BOY [*passes over the stage*] *with a linstock*[2]
35 SALISBURY   I grieve to hear what torments you endured.
But we will be revenged sufficiently.
Now it is supper time in Orléans.
Here, through this grate, I count each one,
And view the Frenchmen how they fortify.
40 Let us look in: the sight will much delight thee.—
Sir Thomas Gargrave and Sir William Glasdale,
Let me have your express° opinions   *precise*
Where is best place to make our batt'ry next.
[*They look through the grate*]
GARGRAVE   I think at the north gate, for there stands Lou.°   *fortress of St. Lou*
45 GLASDALE   And I here, at the bulwark of the Bridge.
TALBOT   For aught I see, this city must be famished°   *starved out*
Or with light skirmishes enfeebled.
Here they° *shoot* [*off chambers within*] *and* SALISBURY   (*the French*)
[*and* GARGRAVE] *fall down*
SALISBURY   O Lord have mercy on us, wretched sinners!
GARGRAVE   O Lord have mercy on me, woeful man!
50 TALBOT   What chance is this that suddenly hath crossed us?
Speak, Salisbury—at least, if thou canst, speak.
How far'st thou, mirror° of all martial men?   *best example*
One of thy eyes and thy cheek's side struck off?

1. A legendary stony substance said to be impregnable.
2. F's stage direction reads: "Enter the Boy with a linstock." He probably does not stay onstage, however, but
passes from one side to the other on his way to light the
    charge that will strike down Salisbury and Gargrave.
linstock: a stick used to hold a lighted match or torch
for firing cannon.

Accursèd tower! Accursèd fatal hand
55 That hath contrived this woeful tragedy!
In thirteen battles Salisbury o'ercame;
Henry the Fifth he first trained to the wars;
Whilst any trump did sound or drum struck up
His sword did ne'er leave striking in the field.
60 Yet liv'st thou, Salisbury? Though thy speech doth fail,
One eye thou hast to look to heaven for grace.
The sun with one eye vieweth all the world.
Heaven, be thou gracious to none alive
If Salisbury wants° mercy at thy hands.—   lacks
65 Sir Thomas Gargrave, hast thou any life?
Speak unto Talbot. Nay, look up to him.—
Bear hence his body; I will help to bury it.
                    [*Exit one with Gargrave's body*]
Salisbury, cheer thy spirit with this comfort:
Thou shalt not die whiles°—   until
70 He beckons with his hand, and smiles on me,
As who should say, 'When I am dead and gone,
Remember to avenge me on the French.'
Plantagenet, I will—and like thee, Nero,³
Play on the lute, beholding the towns burn.
75 Wretched shall France be only in° my name.   at the mere sound of
              Here an alarum, and it thunders and lightens
What stir is this? What tumult's in the heavens?
Whence cometh this alarum and the noise?
                    Enter a MESSENGER
MESSENGER My lord, my lord, the French have gathered head.°   assembled an army
The Dauphin, with one Joan la Pucelle joined,
80 A holy prophetess new risen up,
Is come with a great power° to raise the siege.   army
              Here SALISBURY *lifteth himself up and groans*
TALBOT Hear, hear, how dying Salisbury doth groan!
It irks his heart he cannot be revenged.
Frenchmen, I'll be a Salisbury to you.
85 *Pucelle* or pucelle,⁴ Dauphin or dog-fish,⁵
Your hearts I'll stamp out with my horse's heels
And make a quagmire of your mingled brains.—
Convey me° Salisbury into his tent,   for me
And then we'll try what these dastard Frenchmen dare.
              Alarum. Exeunt [carrying SALISBURY]

1.7

              Here an alarum again, and [Lord] TALBOT *pursueth the*
              Dauphin and driveth him. Then enter JOAN *[la] Pucelle*
              driving Englishmen before her [and exeunt]. Then enter
              [Lord] TALBOT
TALBOT Where is my strength, my valour, and my force?
Our English troops retire; I cannot stay them.
A woman clad in armour chaseth men.

---

3. Talbot here compares himself with Nero, the emperor who played music while he watched Rome burn. Salisbury was a descendant of the Plantagenet dynasty, which ruled England from 1154 to 1485.
4. Talbot puns on the French word for "virgin" (*pucelle*), which sounds like the English slang for "slut" ("puzzel").
5. Punning on the Elizabethan spelling of "dauphin" as "dolphin": hence the taunt that the Dauphin is a "dog-fish."
1.7 Location: In and before Orléans.

Enter [JOAN *la*] *Pucelle*
Here, here she comes. [*To* JOAN] I'll have a bout[1] with thee.
5   Devil or devil's dam,° I'll conjure thee.   *mother*
Blood will I draw on thee—thou art a witch[2]—
And straightway give thy soul to him thou serv'st.
JOAN   Come, come, 'tis only I that must disgrace thee.
      Here they fight
TALBOT   Heavens, can you suffer hell so to prevail?
10 My breast I'll burst with straining of my courage°   *vital energy*
And from my shoulders crack my arms asunder
But I will° chastise this high-minded° strumpet.   *If I do not / arrogant*
      They fight again
JOAN   Talbot, farewell. Thy hour is not yet come.
I must go victual° Orléans forthwith.   *supply with provisions*
      A short alarum, then [*the French pass over the stage*
      and] *enter the town with soldiers*
15 O'ertake me if thou canst. I scorn thy strength.
Go, go, cheer up thy hungry-starvèd° men.   *starving to death*
Help Salisbury to make his testament.
This day is ours, as many more shall be.   *Exit* [*into the town*]
TALBOT   My thoughts are whirlèd like a potter's wheel.
20 I know not where I am nor what I do.
A witch by fear, not force, like Hannibal[3]
Drives back our troops and conquers as she lists.
So bees with smoke and doves with noisome° stench   *noxious*
Are from their hives and houses driven away.
25 They called us, for our fierceness, English dogs;
Now, like to whelps, we crying run away.
      A short alarum. [*Enter English soldiers*]
Hark, countrymen: either renew the fight
Or tear the lions out of England's coat.°   *coat of arms*
Renounce your style;° give sheep in lions' stead.[4]   *distinguishing mark*
30 Sheep run not half so treacherous° from the wolf,   *cowardly*
Or horse or oxen from the leopard,
As you fly from your oft-subduèd slaves.
      Alarum. Here another skirmish
It will not be. Retire into your trenches.
You all consented unto Salisbury's death,
35 For none would strike a stroke in his revenge.°   *in revenge of his death*
Pucelle is entered into Orléans
In spite of us or aught that we could do.   [*Exeunt Soldiers*]
O would I were to die with Salisbury!
The shame hereof will make me hide my head.
                              Exit. Alarum. Retreat[5]

1.8

Flourish. Enter on the walls [JOAN *la*] *Pucelle,* [CHARLES
the] *Dauphin,* RENÉ [*Duke of Anjou, the Duke of*]
ALENÇON *and* [*French*] *Soldiers* [*with colours*]
JOAN   Advance° our waving colours on the walls;   *Raise*
Rescued is Orléans from the English.

1. Fight; sexual encounter. Much of the speech to and
about Joan has sexual overtones.
2. Whoever drew blood from a witch was supposed to
be protected from her magic.
3. The Carthaginian military leader who once put to

flight his Roman enemies by tying firebrands to the
horns of two thousand oxen.
4. Display (on your coat of arms) sheep instead of lions.
5. A trumpet call to signal a retreat.
1.8 Location: Scene continues.

Thus Joan la Pucelle hath performed her word.

CHARLES   Divinest creature, Astraea's[1] daughter,
5   How shall I honour thee for this success?
Thy promises are like Adonis' garden,[2]
That one day bloomed and fruitful were the next.
France, triumph in thy glorious prophetess!
Recovered is the town of Orléans.
10   More blessèd hap° did ne'er befall our state.   °event
RENÉ   Why ring not out the bells aloud throughout the town?
Dauphin, command the citizens make bonfires
And feast and banquet in the open streets
To celebrate the joy that God hath given us.
15   ALENÇON   All France will be replete with mirth and joy
When they shall hear how we have played the men.°   °acted like men
CHARLES   'Tis Joan, not we, by whom the day is won—
For which I will divide my crown with her,
And all the priests and friars in my realm
20   Shall in procession sing her endless praise.
A statelier pyramid to her I'll rear
Than Rhodope's[3] of Memphis ever was.
In memory of her, when she is dead
Her ashes, in an urn more precious
25   Than the rich-jewelled coffer of Darius,[4]
Transported shall be at high festivals
Before the kings and queens of France.
No longer on Saint Denis° will we cry,   °patron saint of France
But Joan la Pucelle shall be France's saint.
30   Come in, and let us banquet royally
After this golden day of victory.

                                                      Flourish. Exeunt

2.1

Enter [on the walls] a [French] SERGEANT *of a band,*
    with two SENTINELS

SERGEANT   Sirs, take your places and be vigilant.
If any noise or soldier you perceive
Near to the walls, by some apparent° sign   °obvious
Let us have knowledge at the court of guard.°   °guardroom
A SENTINEL   Sergeant, you shall.   [*Exit* SERGEANT]
5   Thus are poor servitors,
When others sleep upon their quiet beds,
Constrained to watch in darkness, rain, and cold.

Enter [Lord] TALBOT, *[the Dukes of]* BEDFORD *and* BUR-
GUNDY *[and soldiers], with scaling ladders, their drums*
beating a dead march[1]

TALBOT   Lord regent, and redoubted° Burgundy—   °distinguished
By whose approach the regions of Artois,
10   Wallon, and Picardy are friends to us[2]—

1. Greek goddess of justice; she lived on earth during the Golden Age but fled to the heavens during the corruption of the Iron Age. Queen Elizabeth I was often compared to Astraea.
2. A mythical garden noted for its fertility and described by Spenser in *The Faerie Queene*.
3. A Greek courtesan who married the King of Memphis (city in Egypt) and reputedly built the third pyramid.
4. A jeweled treasure chest that Alexander allegedly won from the Persian King Darius III and used to store the works of Homer.
2.1 Location: In and before Orléans.
1. Either a funeral march for Salisbury or the muffled march that signifies a secret attack.
2. *By . . . us:* during Henry V's reign, the Duke of Burgundy became an English ally and won support for the English from the French and Netherlandish regions to which Talbot refers.

This happy night the Frenchmen are secure,°   *overconfident*
Having all day caroused and banqueted.
Embrace we then this opportunity,
As fitting best to quittance° their deceit,   *repay*
15   Contrived by art° and baleful sorcery.   *craftiness*
BEDFORD   Coward of France!³ How much he wrongs his fame,°   *reputation*
Despairing of his own arms' fortitude,
To join with witches and the help of hell.
BURGUNDY   Traitors have never other company.
20   But what's that 'Pucelle' whom they term so pure?
TALBOT   A maid, they say.
BEDFORD   A maid? And be so martial?⁴
BURGUNDY   Pray God she prove not masculine ere long,⁴
If underneath the standard of the French⁵
She carry armour⁶ as she hath begun—
25   TALBOT   Well, let them practise and converse⁷ with spirits.
God is our fortress, in whose conquering name
Let us resolve to scale their flinty bulwarks.
BEDFORD   Ascend, brave Talbot. We will follow thee.
TALBOT   Not all together. Better far, I guess,
30   That we do make our entrance several ways—
That, if it chance the one of us do fail,
The other yet may rise against their force.⁸
BEDFORD   Agreed. I'll to yon corner.
BURGUNDY   And I to this.

          [Exeunt severally BEDFORD *and* BURGUNDY
                       *with some soldiers]*⁹

TALBOT   And here will Talbot mount, or make his grave.
35   Now, Salisbury, for thee, and for the right
Of English Henry, shall this night appear
How much in duty I am bound to both.

          *[*TALBOT *and his soldiers scale the walls]*
SENTINELS   Arm! Arm! The enemy doth make assault
ENGLISH SOLDIERS   Saint George! A Talbot!¹   *[Exeunt above.]*
        [Alarum.] The French [soldiers] leap o'er the walls in
        their shirts [and exeunt]. Enter several ways [the]
        BASTARD *[of Orléans, the Duke of]* ALENÇON, *[and]* RENÉ
        *[Duke of Anjou], half ready and half unready*²
40   ALENÇON   How now, my lords? What, all unready so?
BASTARD   Unready? Ay, and glad we scaped so well.
RENÉ   'Twas time, I trow,° to wake and leave our beds,   *believe*
Hearing alarums at our chamber doors.
ALENÇON   Of all exploits since first I followed arms
45   Ne'er heard I of a warlike enterprise
More venturous or desperate than this.

---

3. The Dauphin.
4. She does not turn out to be a man; she does not turn out to be carrying a male child. The following lines are full of sexual innuendoes.
5. French ensign; French penis.
6. Wear armor; bear the weight of an armed man (in intercourse).
7. Scheme and talk; have sex and be intimate.
8. May scale the walls despite French resistance.
9. The staging of this scene is complex. Bedford and Burgundy may stay onstage and attack different parts of the tiring-house wall, or, as here, they may exit in

several directions and fight offstage.
1. To Talbot. This cry is included in the actual stage directions in F, but here it is assigned to nameless "English soldiers" (see also line 79).
2. In this complicated piece of stage business, Talbot's men ascend ladders to the upper stage, which represents the walls of Orléans. They there surprise French soldiers, some of whom leap down from the upper to the lower stage as if fleeing from Orléans. On the lower stage, the fleeing and defeated French nobles debate their plight. *half ready and half unready*: half dressed and half undressed.

BASTARD   I think this Talbot be a fiend of hell.

RENÉ   If not of hell, the heavens sure favour him.

ALENÇON   Here cometh Charles. I marvel how he sped.°   fared

    Enter CHARLES [*the Dauphin*] *and* JOAN [*la Pucelle*]

50   BASTARD   Tut, holy Joan³ was his defensive guard.

CHARLES [*to* JOAN]   Is this thy cunning,° thou deceitful dame?   skill; sorcery

    Didst thou at first, to flatter us withal,

    Make us partakers of a little gain

    That now our loss might be ten times so much?

55   JOAN   Wherefore is Charles impatient with his friend?

    At all times will you have my power alike?

    Sleeping or waking must I still prevail,

    Or will you blame and lay the fault on me?—

    Improvident° soldiers, had your watch been good,   Negligent

60   This sudden mischief never could have fall'n.

CHARLES   Duke of Alençon, this was your default,

    That, being captain of the watch tonight,

    Did look no better to that weighty charge.

ALENÇON   Had all your quarters been as safely kept

65   As that whereof I had the government,

    We had not been thus shamefully surprised.

BASTARD   Mine was secure.

RENÉ   And so was mine, my lord.

CHARLES   And for myself, most part of all this night

    Within her° quarter and mine own precinct   (Joan's)

70   I was employed in passing to and fro

    About relieving of the sentinels.

    Then how or which way should they first break in?

JOAN   Question, my lords, no further of the case,

    How or which way. 'Tis sure they found some place

75   But weakly guarded, where the breach was made.

    And now there rests° no other shift° but this—   remains / device

    To gather our soldiers, scattered and dispersed,

    And lay new platforms° to endamage them.   plots; schemes

    Alarum. Enter [*an* ENGLISH] SOLDIER

ENGLISH SOLDIER   A Talbot! A Talbot!

    They [*the French*] *fly, leaving their clothes behind*

80   ENGLISH SOLDIER   I'll be so bold to take what they have left.

    The cry of 'Talbot' serves me for a sword,

    For I have loaden me with many spoils,

    Using no other weapon but his name.   *Exit* [*with spoils*]

2.2

    Enter [*Lord*] TALBOT, [*the Dukes of*] BEDFORD [*and*]

    BURGUNDY [*a* CAPTAIN, *and soldiers*]

BEDFORD   The day begins to break and night is fled,

    Whose pitchy mantle overveiled the earth.

    Here sound retreat and cease our hot pursuit.

    Retreat [*is sounded*]

TALBOT   Bring forth the body of old Salisbury

5   And here advance it° in the market place,   raise it up (on a bier)

3. A reference to her sexual availability; "hole" was   2.2 Location: Within Orléans.
slang for "vagina."

The middle centre of this cursèd town.   [*Exit one or more*]
Now have I paid my vow unto his soul:
For every drop of blood was° drawn from him   *that was*
There hath at least five Frenchmen died tonight.
10 And that hereafter ages may behold
What ruin happened in revenge of him,
Within their chiefest temple I'll erect
A tomb, wherein his corpse shall be interred—
Upon the which, that everyone may read,
15 Shall be engraved the sack of Orléans,
The treacherous manner of his mournful death,
And what a terror he had been to France.
But, lords, in all our bloody massacre
I muse° we met not with the Dauphin's grace,   *wonder*
20 His new-come champion, virtuous[1] Joan of Arc,
Nor any of his false confederates.
BEDFORD 'Tis thought, Lord Talbot, when the fight began,
Roused on the sudden from their drowsy beds,
They did amongst the troops of armèd men
25 Leap o'er the walls for refuge in the field.
BURGUNDY Myself, as far as I could well discern
For smoke and dusky vapours of the night,
Am sure I scared the Dauphin and his trull,°   *whore*
When arm-in-arm they both came swiftly running,
30 Like to a pair of loving turtle-doves
That could not live asunder day or night.
After that things are set in order here,
We'll follow them with all the power we have.
       Enter a MESSENGER
MESSENGER All hail, my lords! Which of this princely train
35 Call ye the warlike Talbot, for his acts
So much applauded through the realm of France?
TALBOT Here is the Talbot. Who would speak with him?
MESSENGER The virtuous lady, Countess of Auvergne,
With modesty admiring thy renown,
40 By me entreats, great lord, thou wouldst vouchsafe
To visit her poor castle where she lies,°   *dwells*
That she may boast she hath beheld the man
Whose glory fills the world with loud report.°   *acclaim; din of war*
BURGUNDY Is it even so? Nay, then I see our wars
45 Will turn unto a peaceful comic sport,
When ladies crave to be encountered with.
You may not, my lord, despise her gentle suit.°   *well-bred request*
TALBOT Ne'er trust me then, for when a world of men
Could not prevail with all their oratory,
50 Yet hath a woman's kindness overruled.—
And therefore tell her I return great thanks,
And in submission will attend on her.—
Will not your honours bear me company?
BEDFORD No, truly, 'tis more than manners will.°   *etiquette allows*
55 And I have heard it said, 'Unbidden guests

1. Full of virtue or manly courage; chaste (said ironically).

Are often welcomest when they are gone'.
TALBOT   Well then, alone—since there's no remedy—
    I mean to prove° this lady's courtesy.   *test*
    Come hither, captain.
        [*He*] *whispers*
                            You perceive my mind?
60 CAPTAIN   I do, my lord, and mean° accordingly.   *intend to act*
                            Exeunt [*severally*]

2.3

Enter [*the*] COUNTESS [*of Auvergne and her* PORTER]
COUNTESS   Porter, remember what I gave in charge,°   *I commanded*
    And when you have done so, bring the keys to me.
PORTER   Madam, I will.   *Exit*
COUNTESS   The plot is laid. If all things fall out right,
5   I shall as famous be by this exploit
    As Scythian Tomyris[1] by Cyrus' death.
    Great is the rumour° of this dreadful° knight,   *fame / fear-inspiring*
    And his achievements of no less account.
    Fain° would mine eyes be witness with mine ears,   *Gladly*
10   To give their censure° of these rare° reports.   *opinion / remarkable*
        Enter MESSENGER *and* [*Lord*] TALBOT
MESSENGER   Madam, according as your ladyship desired,
    By message craved, so is Lord Talbot come.
COUNTESS   And he is welcome. What, is this the man?
MESSENGER   Madam, it is.
COUNTESS   Is this the scourge[2] of France?
15 Is this the Talbot, so much feared abroad
    That with his name the mothers still their babes?
    I see report is fabulous and false.
    I thought I should have seen some Hercules,[3]
    A second Hector,[4] for his grim aspect°   *appearance*
20 And large proportion of his strong-knit limbs.
    Alas, this is a child, a seely° dwarf.   *feeble*
    It cannot be this weak and writhled° shrimp   *wrinkled*
    Should strike such terror to his enemies.
TALBOT   Madam, I have been bold to trouble you.
25 But since your ladyship is not at leisure,
    I'll sort some other time to visit you.
        [*He is going*]
COUNTESS [*to* MESSENGER]   What means he now? Go ask him
        whither he goes.
MESSENGER   Stay, my Lord Talbot, for my lady craves
    To know the cause of your abrupt departure.
30 TALBOT   Marry,[5] for that° she's in a wrong belief,   *because*
    I go to certify her Talbot's here.
        Enter PORTER *with keys*
COUNTESS   If thou be he, then art thou prisoner.
TALBOT   Prisoner? To whom?

2.3 Location: The Countess's castle, Auvergne.
1. Asian queen who, in revenge for her son's death,
killed the Persian King Cyrus and kept his head in a
wineskin filled with human blood.
2. Individual sent by God to punish sin. Joan describes

herself as "the English scourge" at 1.3.108.
3. Mythical hero famous for his immense strength.
4. Greatest of the Trojan warriors, celebrated in Homer's
Iliad.
5. By the Virgin Mary, a mild oath.

	COUNTESS	To me, bloodthirsty lord;	

COUNTESS   To me, bloodthirsty lord;
And for that cause I trained° thee to my house.   *enticed*
35   Long time thy shadow° hath been thrall° to me,   *image / slave*
For in my gallery thy picture hangs;
But now the substance shall endure the like,
And I will chain these legs and arms of thine
That hast by tyranny these many years
40   Wasted our country, slain our citizens,
And sent our sons and husbands captivate°—   *into captivity*
TALBOT   Ha, ha, ha!
COUNTESS   Laughest thou, wretch? Thy mirth shall turn to moan.
TALBOT   I laugh to see your ladyship so fond°   *foolish*
45   To think that you have aught but Talbot's shadow
Whereon to practise your severity.
COUNTESS   Why? Art not thou the man?
TALBOT   I am indeed.
COUNTESS   Then have I substance too.
50   TALBOT   No, no, I am but shadow of myself.
You are deceived; my substance is not here.
For what you see is but the smallest part
And least proportion of humanity.[6]
I tell you, madam, were the whole frame[7] here,
55   It is of such a spacious lofty pitch°   *height*
Your roof were not sufficient to contain't.
COUNTESS   This is a riddling merchant for the nonce.[8]
He will be here, and yet he is not here.
How can these contrarieties agree?
60   TALBOT   That will I show you presently.°   *immediately*
[*He*] *winds*° *his horn.* [*Within,*] *drums strike up; a peal*   *blows*
of ordnance. Enter [*English*] *soldiers*
How say you, madam? Are you now persuaded
That Talbot is but shadow of himself?
These are his substance, sinews, arms, and strength,
With which he yoketh your rebellious necks,
65   Razeth your cities and subverts° your towns,   *overthrows*
And in a moment makes them desolate.
COUNTESS   Victorious Talbot, pardon my abuse.°   *error; deception*
I find thou art no less than fame hath bruited,°   *proclaimed*
And more than may be gathered by thy shape.
70   Let my presumption not provoke thy wrath,
For I am sorry that with reverence
I did not entertain° thee as thou art.   *receive*
TALBOT   Be not dismayed, fair lady, nor misconster°   *misconstrue*
The mind of Talbot, as you did mistake
75   The outward composition of his body.
What you have done hath not offended me;
Nor other satisfaction do I crave
But only, with your patience,° that we may   *permission*
Taste of your wine and see what cates° you have: *delicacies*
80   For soldiers' stomachs always serve them well.

6. Smallest part of the whole man (and, by implication, of the whole army that constitutes Talbot's military presence).

7. The entire structure of my body (and of my army).
8. This is a dealer in riddles as occasion requires.

COUNTESS   With all my heart; and think me honourèd
To feast so great a warrior in my house.   *Exeunt*

2.4

[*A rose brier.*] Enter RICHARD PLANTAGENET, [*the Earl
of*] WARWICK, [*the Duke of*] SOMERSET, [*William de la*]
Pole [*the Earl of* SUFFOLK], *and others* [VERNON, *and a*
LAWYER]

RICHARD PLANTAGENET   Great lords and gentlemen, what
   means this silence?
Dare no man answer in a case of truth?
SUFFOLK   Within the Temple hall we were° too loud.   *would have been*
The garden here is more convenient.
5 RICHARD PLANTAGENET   Then say at once if I maintained the truth;
Or else was wrangling Somerset in th'error?
SUFFOLK   Faith, I have been a truant° in the law,   *neglectful of study*
And never yet could frame° my will to it,   *adapt*
And therefore frame the law unto my will.
10 SOMERSET   Judge you, my lord of Warwick, then between us.
WARWICK   Between two hawks, which flies the higher pitch,°   *height*
Between two dogs, which hath the deeper mouth,°   *voice*
Between two blades, which bears the better temper,[1]
Between two horses, which doth bear him best,
15 Between two girls, which hath the merriest eye,
I have perhaps some shallow spirit of judgement;
But in these nice° sharp quillets° of the law,   *precise / distinctions*
Good faith, I am no wiser than a daw.[2]
RICHARD PLANTAGENET   Tut, tut, here is a mannerly forbearance.
20 The truth appears so naked on my side
That any purblind° eye may find it out.   *half-blind*
SOMERSET   And on my side it is so well apparelled,
So clear, so shining, and so evident,
That it will glimmer through a blind man's eye.
25 RICHARD PLANTAGENET   Since you are tongue-tied and so loath to speak,
In dumb significants° proclaim your thoughts.   *silent gestures*
Let him that is a true-born gentleman
And stands upon the honour of his birth,
If he suppose that I have pleaded truth,[3]
30 From off this briar pluck a white rose[4] with me.
   [*He plucks a white rose*]
SOMERSET   Let him that is no coward nor no flatterer,
But dare maintain the party° of the truth,   *side*
Pluck a red rose[5] from off this thorn with me.
   [*He plucks a red rose*]

2.4 Location: The Temple Garden, near the Middle and Inner Temple, two buildings that housed the London law schools known as the Inns of Court.
1. *the better temper:* this refers to the degree of hardness attained by a steel sword blade when it is tempered (that is, heated to a required temperature and then plunged into cold liquid).
2. Jackdaw (a proverbially stupid bird).
3. Presented the case for truth according to proper procedures. (This scene contains many legal terms.)

4. Badge of the House of York. In the mid-fifteenth century, two branches of the Plantagenet dynasty, the Yorkists and the Lancastrians, fought what was termed the Wars of the Roses over who would hold the English throne. Shakespeare invented this scene to provide a point of origin for the quarrel that grew into the civil wars he depicted in his plays on the reigns of Henry VI, Edward IV, and Richard III.
5. Badge of the House of Lancaster.

WARWICK   I love no colours,° and without all colour   *hues; pretenses*
35   Of base insinuating flattery
          I pluck this white rose with Plantagenet.
SUFFOLK   I pluck this red rose with young Somerset,
          And say withal° I think he held the right.   *besides*
VERNON   Stay, lords and gentlemen, and pluck no more
40   Till you conclude that he upon whose side
          The fewest roses from the tree are cropped
          Shall yield° the other in the right opinion.   *concede*
SOMERSET   Good Master Vernon, it is well objected.°   *urged*
          If I have fewest, I subscribe° in silence.   *submit*
45 RICHARD PLANTAGENET   And I.
VERNON   Then for the truth and plainness of the case
          I pluck this pale and maiden blossom here,
          Giving my verdict on the white rose' side.
SOMERSET   Prick not your finger as you pluck it off,
50   Lest, bleeding, you do paint the white rose red,
          And fall on my side so against your will.
VERNON   If I, my lord, for my opinion° bleed,   *conviction*
          Opinion° shall be surgeon to my hurt   *Reputation*
          And keep me on the side where still I am.
55 SOMERSET   Well, well, come on! Who else?
LAWYER   Unless my study and my books be false,
          The argument you held was wrong in law;
          In sign whereof I pluck a white rose too.
RICHARD PLANTAGENET   Now Somerset, where is your argument?
60 SOMERSET   Here in my scabbard, meditating that°   *thinking of what*
          Shall dye your white rose in a bloody red.
RICHARD PLANTAGENET   Meantime your cheeks do counterfeit° our roses,   *imitate*
          For pale they look with fear, as witnessing
          The truth on our side.
SOMERSET   No, Plantagenet,
65   'Tis not for fear, but anger, that thy cheeks
          Blush for pure shame to counterfeit our roses,
          And yet thy tongue will not confess thy error.
RICHARD PLANTAGENET   Hath not thy rose a canker,° Somerset?   *cankerworm; grub*
SOMERSET   Hath not thy rose a thorn, Plantagenet?
70 RICHARD PLANTAGENET   Ay, sharp and piercing, to maintain his° truth,   *its*
          Whiles thy consuming canker eats his falsehood.
SOMERSET   Well, I'll find friends to wear my bleeding roses,
          That shall maintain what I have said is true,
          Where false Plantagenet dare not be seen.
75 RICHARD PLANTAGENET   Now, by this maiden blossom in my hand,
          I scorn thee and thy fashion,° peevish boy.   *sort*
SUFFOLK   Turn not thy scorns this way, Plantagenet.
RICHARD PLANTAGENET   Proud Pole.⁶ I will, and scorn both him
              and thee.
SUFFOLK   I'll turn my part thereof into thy throat.⁷
80 SOMERSET   Away, away, good William de la Pole.

---

6. The Duke of Suffolk's family name.   7. I'll throw the slanders back into your throat.

We grace° the yeoman[8] by conversing with him.   *do honor to*
WARWICK   Now, by God's will, thou wrong'st him, Somerset.
 His grandfather was Lionel Duke of Clarence,
 Third son to the third Edward, King of England.[9]
85 Spring crestless° yeomen from so deep a root?   *without a coat of arms*
RICHARD PLANTAGENET   He bears him on the place's privilege,[1]
 Or durst not for his craven° heart say thus.   *cowardly*
SOMERSET   By him that made me, I'll maintain my words
 On any plot of ground in Christendom.
90 Was not thy father, Richard Earl of Cambridge,
 For treason executed in our late king's days?
 And by his treason stand'st not thou attainted,[2]
 Corrupted, and exempt° from ancient gentry?   *excluded*
 His trespass yet lives guilty in thy blood,
95 And till thou be restored[3] thou art a yeoman.
RICHARD PLANTAGENET   My father was attachèd, not attainted;[4]
 Condemned to die for treason, but no traitor—
 And that I'll prove on better men than Somerset,
 Were growing time once ripened to my will.[5]
100 For your partaker° Pole, and you yourself,   *As for your ally*
 I'll note you in my book of memory,
 To scourge you for this apprehension.°   *opinion*
 Look to it well, and say you are well warned.
SOMERSET   Ah, thou shalt find us ready for thee still,
105 And know us by these colours for thy foes,
 For these my friends, in spite of° thee, shall wear.   *in contempt of*
RICHARD PLANTAGENET   And, by my soul, this pale and angry rose,
 As cognizance° of my blood-drinking hate,   *an emblem*
 Will I forever, and my faction, wear
110 Until it wither with me to my grave,
 Or flourish to the height of my degree.°   *noble rank*
SUFFOLK   Go forward, and be choked with thy ambition.
 And so farewell until I meet thee next.   *Exit*
SOMERSET   Have with thee,° Pole.—Farewell, ambitious Richard.   *Let us go*
               Exit
115   RICHARD PLANTAGENET   How I am braved,° and must perforce endure it!   *insulted*
WARWICK   This blot that they object° against your house   *allege*
 Shall be wiped out in the next parliament,
 Called for the truce of° Winchester and Gloucester.   *to make peace between*
 An if° thou be not then created York,   *An if=If*
120 I will not live to be accounted Warwick.
 Meantime, in signal of my love to thee,

---

8. A man, below the rank of gentleman, holding a small estate. (Richard Plantagenet lost his lands and titles when Henry V executed his father, Richard, Earl of Cambridge, for treason.)
9. Clarence was actually Richard's great-great-grandfather on his mother's side. Edmund, Duke of York, fifth son of Edward III, was his paternal grandfather; thus Richard could trace his descent from Edward III through both his mother and his father.
1. He takes advantage of the safety provided by a privileged place. Quarreling with drawn weapons was prohibited in some precincts, but the Temple, though

originally founded as a religious house, was not one of them.
2. Condemned for treason. One so convicted lost his estate and property. His blood was declared "corrupted" (see line 93), so he could neither inherit nor transmit property and titles.
3. Are given back your lands and titles.
4. Was arrested, not convicted. Plantagenet implies that his father's execution was illegal because there was no parliamentary bill of attainder.
5. If the unfolding of time brings me my desire.

Against proud Somerset and William Pole,
Will I upon thy party wear this rose.
And here I prophesy: this brawl today,
125 Grown to this faction° in the Temple garden,   *conflict*
Shall send, between the red rose and the white,
A thousand souls to death and deadly night.
RICHARD PLANTAGENET   Good Master Vernon, I am bound to you,
That you on my behalf would pluck a flower.
130 VERNON   In your behalf still will I wear the same.
LAWYER   And so will I.
RICHARD PLANTAGENET   Thanks, gentles.
Come, let us four to dinner. I dare say
This quarrel will drink blood another day.
                Exeunt. [The rose brier is removed]

2.5

Enter [Edmund] MORTIMER, *brought in a chair*
[by his KEEPERS]*[1]*
MORTIMER   Kind keepers of my weak decaying age,
Let dying Mortimer here rest himself.
Even like a man new-halèd° from the rack,[2]   *newly dragged*
So fare my limbs with long imprisonment;
5 And these grey locks, the pursuivants° of death,   *heralds*
Argue the end of Edmund Mortimer,[3]
Nestor-like[4] agèd in an age of care.
These eyes, like lamps whose wasting oil is spent,
Wax dim, as drawing to their exigent;°   *end*
10 Weak shoulders, overborne with burdening grief,
And pithless° arms, like to a withered vine   *strengthless*
That droops his° sapless branches to the ground.   *its*
Yet are these feet—whose strengthless stay° is numb,   *support*
Unable to support this lump of clay—
15 Swift-wingèd with desire to get a grave,
As witting° I no other comfort have.   *knowing*
But tell me, keeper, will my nephew come?
KEEPER   Richard Plantagenet, my lord, will come.
We sent unto the Temple, unto his chamber,
20 And answer was returned that he will come.
MORTIMER   Enough. My soul shall then be satisfied.
Poor gentleman, his wrong° doth equal mine.   *(wrong done to him)*
Since Henry Monmouth° first began to reign—   *(Henry V)*
Before whose glory I was great in arms—
25 This loathsome sequestration° have I had;   *imprisonment*

2.5 Location: A cell in the Tower of London.
1. F's stage direction reads: "Enter Mortimer, brought in in a Chair and Jailors."
2. Instrument of torture on which the victim's body was stretched.
3. As in the sources that Shakespeare probably used, several historical Mortimers are conflated here. In 1385, Richard II declared Roger Mortimer, fourth Earl of March, his heir. When Roger died in battle in

1398, his claim passed to Edmund Mortimer, fifth Earl of March and uncle of Richard Plantagenet, who in turn inherited the Mortimer claim to the throne. It was Edmund's cousin Sir John Mortimer, however, who lay imprisoned in the Tower until 1424, when he was executed for advocating Edmund's claim to the throne.
4. Like Nestor, the agèd Homeric hero and adviser famous for his wisdom.

And even since then hath Richard been obscured,
Deprived of honour and inheritance.
But now the arbitrator of despairs,
Just Death, kind umpire of men's miseries,
30   With sweet enlargement° doth dismiss me hence.   *release*
I would his° troubles likewise were expired,   *(Richard's)*
That so he might recover what was lost.
            Enter RICHARD [PLANTAGENET]
    KEEPER   My lord, your loving nephew now is come.
    MORTIMER   Richard Plantagenet, my friend, is he come?
35   RICHARD PLANTAGENET   Ay, noble uncle, thus ignobly used:
        Your nephew, late° despisèd Richard, comes.   *recently*
    MORTIMER [*to* KEEPERS]   Direct mine arms I may embrace his neck
        And in his bosom spend my latter° gasp.   *final*
        O tell me when my lips do touch his cheeks,
40   That I may kindly give one fainting kiss.
            [*He embraces* RICHARD]
        And now declare, sweet stem from York's great stock,°   *trunk*
        Why didst thou say of late thou wert despised?
    RICHARD PLANTAGENET   First lean thine agèd back against mine arm,
        And in that ease I'll tell thee my dis-ease.°   *trouble*
45   This day in argument upon a case
        Some words there grew 'twixt Somerset and me;
        Among which terms he used his lavish tongue
        And did upbraid me with my father's death;
        Which obloquy° set bars before my tongue,   *disgrace*
50   Else with the like I had requited him.
        Therefore, good uncle, for my father's sake,
        In honour of a true Plantagenet,
        And for alliance'° sake, declare the cause   *kinship's*
        My father, Earl of Cambridge, lost his head.
55   MORTIMER   That cause, fair nephew, that imprisoned me,
        And hath detained me all my flow'ring youth
        Within a loathsome dungeon, there to pine,
        Was cursèd instrument of his decease.
    RICHARD PLANTAGENET   Discover° more at large what cause that was, *Explain*
60   For I am ignorant and cannot guess.
    MORTIMER   I will, if that my fading breath permit
        And death approach not ere my tale be done.
        Henry the Fourth, grandfather to this King,
        Deposed his nephew° Richard, Edward's son,   *kinsman (here, cousin)*
65   The first begotten and the lawful heir
        Of Edward king, the third of that descent;
        During whose° reign the Percies of the north,   *(Henry IV's)*
        Finding his usurpation most unjust,
        Endeavoured my advancement to the throne.
70   The reason moved° these warlike lords to this   *that moved*
        Was for that°—young King Richard thus removed,   *Was because*
        Leaving no heir begotten of his body—
        I was the next° by birth and parentage,   *(in line for the throne)*
        For by my mother I derivèd° am   *descended*
75   From Lionel Duke of Clarence, the third son
        To King Edward the Third—whereas the King
        From John of Gaunt doth bring his pedigree,

Being but fourth of that heroic line.
But mark: as in this haughty° great attempt   *lofty*
80   They laboured to plant the rightful heir,
I lost my liberty, and they their lives.
Long after this, when Henry the Fifth,
Succeeding his father Bolingbroke, did reign,
Thy father, Earl of Cambridge then, derived
85   From famous Edmund Langley, Duke of York,
Marrying my sister that thy mother was,
Again, in pity of my hard distress,
Levied an army, weening° to redeem   *intending*
And have installed me in the diadem;°   *crown*
90   But, as the rest, so fell that noble earl,
And was beheaded. Thus the Mortimers,
In whom the title rested, were suppressed.
RICHARD PLANTAGENET   Of which, my lord, your honour is the last.
MORTIMER   True, and thou seest that I no issue have,
95   And that my fainting words do warrant° death.   *promise*
Thou art my heir. The rest I wish thee gather°—   *infer*
But yet be wary in thy studious° care.   *diligent*
RICHARD PLANTAGENET   Thy grave admonishments prevail with me.
But yet methinks my father's execution
100   Was nothing less than bloody tyranny.
MORTIMER   With silence, nephew, be thou politic.°   *prudent*
Strong-fixèd is the house of Lancaster,
And like a mountain, not to be removed.
But now thy uncle is removing° hence,   *departing*
105   As princes do their courts, when they are cloyed°   *sickened*
With long continuance in a settled place.
RICHARD PLANTAGENET   O uncle, would some part of my young years
Might but redeem the passage of your age.
MORTIMER   Thou dost then wrong me, as that slaughterer doth
110   Which giveth many wounds when one will kill.
Mourn not, except° thou sorrow for my good.   *unless*
Only give order for my funeral.
And so farewell, and fair be all thy hopes,
And prosperous be thy life in peace and war. *Dies*
115   RICHARD PLANTAGENET   And peace, no war, befall thy parting soul.
In prison hast thou spent a pilgrimage,
And like a hermit overpassed° thy days.   *spent*
Well, I will lock his counsel in my breast,
And what I do imagine, let that rest.
120   Keepers, convey him hence, and I myself
Will see his burial better than his life.[5]
              Exeunt [KEEPERS *with Mortimer's body*]
Here dies the dusky torch of Mortimer,
Choked with° ambition of the meaner sort.[6]   *by*
And for° those wrongs, those bitter injuries,   *And as for*

---

5. *better than his life*: more sumptuous than the life he led (in prison).

6. *meaner sort*: people of lower rank (referring to Bolingbroke and his line).

₁₂₅ Which Somerset hath offered to my house,
I doubt not but with honour to redress.
And therefore haste I to the Parliament,
Either to be restorèd to my blood,°   *inherited rights*
Or make mine ill th'advantage of my good.[7]   *Exit*

3.1

Flourish. Enter [young] KING [HENRY],[1] *[the Dukes of]*
EXETER, *[and]* GLOUCESTER, *[the Bishop of]*
WINCHESTER, *[the Duke of]* SOMERSET, *[and the Earl*
of] SUFFOLK, *[with red roses, the Earl of]* WARWICK,
[and] RICHARD PLANTAGENET *[with white roses].*[2]
GLOUCESTER *offers to put up a bill;*° WINCHESTER   *written statement*
snatches it, tears it

WINCHESTER   Com'st thou with deep premeditated lines?
With written pamphlets studiously devised?
Humphrey of Gloucester, if thou canst accuse,
Or aught intend'st to lay unto my charge,
₅ Do it without invention,° suddenly,   *premeditated design*
As I with sudden and extemporal speech
Purpose to answer what thou canst object.°   *lay to my charge*
GLOUCESTER   Presumptuous priest, this place° commands my patience,   *(Parliament)*
Or thou shouldst find thou hast dishonoured me.
₁₀ Think not, although in writing I preferred°   *set out*
The manner of thy vile outrageous crimes,
That therefore I have forged, or am not able
Verbatim° to rehearse the method of my pen.[3]   *Orally*
No, prelate, such is thy audacious wickedness,
₁₅ Thy lewd,° pestiferous,° and dissentious pranks,   *base / deadly*
As very° infants prattle of thy pride.   *That even*
Thou art a most pernicious usurer,[4]
Froward° by nature, enemy to peace,   *Perverse*
Lascivious, wanton, more than well beseems
₂₀ A man of thy profession and degree.°   *rank*
And for° thy treachery, what's more manifest?—   *And as for*
In that thou laid'st a trap to take my life,
As well at London Bridge as at the Tower.
Beside, I fear me, if thy thoughts were sifted,°   *closely examined*
₂₅ The King thy sovereign is not quite exempt
From envious malice of thy swelling heart.
WINCHESTER   Gloucester, I do defy thee.—Lords, vouchsafe
To give me hearing what I shall reply.
If I were covetous, ambitious, or perverse,
₃₀ As he will have me, how am I so poor?
Or how haps it I seek not to advance
Or raise myself, but keep my wonted° calling?   *customary*

---

7. Or turn the injuries I have suffered to my advantage.
3.1 Location: The Parliament House, London.
1. The historical Henry VI was five years old at the time of this Parliament in 1327. In this scene, Shakespeare refers to the King's "tender years" but does not specify his age.
2. F does not mention that roses are worn in this scene, but in 2.4 the rival factions promised to wear them forever. This edition indicates their presence throughout

the ensuing action.
3. To recount the order of the argument I wrote.
4. Alluding to the fact that Winchester's wealth was partly derived from his use of a papal bull and partly from the Southwark brothels (see 1.4.35 and note). In *Measure for Measure*, Shakespeare refers to prostitution as one of the "two usuries" (3.1.263). Moneylending bred interest; prostitution bred both illicit offspring and financial profit.

And for dissension, who preferreth peace
More than I do?—except I be provoked.
35 No, my good lords, it is not that offends;
It is not that that hath incensed the Duke.
It is because no one should sway° but he,   *rule*
No one but he should be about the King—
And that engenders thunder in his breast
40 And makes him roar these accusations forth.
But he shall know I am as good—
GLOUCESTER As good?—
Thou bastard of my grandfather.[5]
WINCHESTER Ay, lordly sir; for what are you, I pray,
45 But one imperious° in another's throne?   *ruling*
GLOUCESTER Am I not Protector, saucy priest?
WINCHESTER And am not I a prelate of the Church?
GLOUCESTER Yes—as an outlaw in a castle keeps°   *dwells*
And useth it to patronage° his theft.   *protect*
WINCHESTER Unreverent Gloucester.
50 GLOUCESTER   Thou art reverend
Touching° thy spiritual function, not thy life.   *With regard to*
WINCHESTER Rome shall remedy this.
GLOUCESTER[6]   Roam thither then.
WARWICK [to WINCHESTER] My lord, it were your duty to forbear.
SOMERSET Ay, so° the bishop be not overborne:°   *as long as / overruled*
55 Methinks my lord° should be religious,°   *(Gloucester) / pious*
And know the office° that belongs to such.°   *duty / (prelates)*
WARWICK Methinks his lordship° should be humbler.   *(Winchester)*
It fitteth not a prelate so to plead.   *wrangle*
SOMERSET Yes, when his holy state is touched so near.° *affected so directly*
60 WARWICK State holy or unhallowed, what of that?
Is not his grace Protector to the King?
RICHARD PLANTAGENET [aside] Plantagenet, I see, must hold his tongue,
Lest it be said, 'Speak, sirrah,[7] when you should;
Must your bold verdict intertalk° with lords?'   *hold opinion; converse*
65 Else would I have a fling at Winchester.
KING HENRY Uncles of Gloucester and of Winchester,
The special watchmen of our English weal,°   *well-being; state*
I would prevail, if prayers might prevail,
To join your hearts in love and amity.
70 O what a scandal is it to our crown
That two such noble peers as ye should jar!°   *quarrel*
Believe me, lords, my tender years can tell
Civil dissension is a viperous worm
That gnaws the bowels of the commonwealth.
    A noise within
75 SERVINGMEN [within] Down with the tawny coats![8]
KING HENRY What tumult's this?
WARWICK   An uproar, I dare warrant,

---

5. Winchester was born an illegitimate son of Gloucester's grandfather, John of Gaunt, though later he was
made legitimate by an act of Parliament.
6. F assigns this line to Warwick, but giving it to
Gloucester further heightens the antipathy between
Winchester and the Lord Protector.

7. Term used to address social inferiors.
8. Again, this line is included as part of the stage directions in F and is here plausibly assigned to "Servingmen." The same is true at line 78, where F's stage
direction reads: "A noise again, Stones, Stones."

Begun through malice of the Bishop's men.
    A noise again
SERVINGMEN [*within*]   Stones, stones!
    Enter [the] MAYOR [*of London*]
  MAYOR   O my good lords, and virtuous Henry,
80   Pity the city of London, pity us!
    The Bishop and the Duke of Gloucester's men,
    Forbidden late° to carry any weapon,   *lately*
    Have filled their pockets full of pebble stones
    And, banding themselves in contrary parts,°   *opposing parties*
85   Do pelt so fast at one another's pate
    That many have their giddy brains knocked out.
    Our windows are broke down in every street,
    And we for fear compelled to shut our shops.
    Enter in skirmish, with bloody pates[, Winchester's
    SERVINGMEN *in tawny coats and Gloucester's in blue*
    coats]
  KING HENRY   We charge you, on allegiance to ourself,
90   To hold your slaught'ring hands and keep the peace.
    [*The skirmish ceases*]
    Pray, Uncle Gloucester, mitigate this strife.
  FIRST SERVINGMAN   Nay, if we be forbidden stones, we'll fall to
    it with our teeth.
  SECOND SERVINGMAN   Do what ye dare, we are as resolute.
    Skirmish again
95 GLOUCESTER   You of my household, leave this peevish broil,°   *this foolish fight*
    And set this unaccustomed° fight aside.   *unusual; disorderly*
  THIRD SERVINGMAN   My lord, we know your grace to be a man
    Just and upright and, for your royal birth,
    Inferior to none but to his majesty;
100   And ere that° we will suffer such a prince,   *And before*
    So kind a father of the commonweal,
    To be disgracèd° by an inkhorn mate,°   *insulted / scribbler*
    We and our wives and children all will fight
    And have our bodies slaughtered by thy foes.
105 FIRST SERVINGMAN   Ay, and the very parings of our nails
    Shall pitch a field[9] when we are dead.
    [*They*] *begin* [*to skirmish*] *again*
  GLOUCESTER   Stay, stay, I say!
    An if you love me as you say you do,
    Let me persuade you to forbear a while.
  KING HENRY   O how this discord doth afflict my soul!
110   Can you, my lord of Winchester, behold
    My sighs and tears, and will not once relent?
    Who should be pitiful° if you be not?   *merciful*
    Or who should study to prefer° a peace,   *propose*
    If holy churchmen take delight in broils?
115 WARWICK   Yield, my lord Protector; yield, Winchester—
    Except you mean with obstinate repulse°   *refusal*
    To slay your sovereign and destroy the realm.
    You see what mischief—and what murder, too—
    Hath been enacted through your enmity.
120   Then be at peace, except° ye thirst for blood.   *unless*

9. Shall fortify a battlefield (usually with defensive wood or iron stakes).

WINCHESTER He shall submit, or I will never yield.

GLOUCESTER Compassion on the King commands me stoop,
  Or I would see his heart out ere the priest
  Should ever get that privilege of° me.   *advantage over*

125 WARWICK Behold, my lord of Winchester, the Duke
  Hath banished moody° discontented fury,   *sullen*
  As by his smoothèd brows it doth appear.
  Why look you still so stern and tragical?

GLOUCESTER Here, Winchester, I offer thee my hand.

130 KING HENRY [*to* WINCHESTER] Fie, Uncle Beaufort! I have heard you preach
  That malice was a great and grievous sin;
  And will not you maintain the thing you teach,
  But prove a chief offender in the same?

WARWICK Sweet King! The Bishop hath a kindly gird.°   *a gentle rebuke*
135   For shame, my lord of Winchester, relent.
  What, shall a child instruct you what to do?

WINCHESTER Well, Duke of Gloucester, I will yield to thee
  Love for thy love, and hand for hand I give.

GLOUCESTER [*aside*] Ay, but I fear me with a hollow° heart.   *an insincere*
140   [*To the others*] See here, my friends and loving countrymen,
  This token serveth for a flag of truce
  Betwixt ourselves and all our followers.
  So help me God, as I dissemble not.

WINCHESTER So help me God [*aside*] as I intend it not.

145 KING HENRY O loving uncle, kind Duke of Gloucester,
  How joyful am I made by this contract!
  [*To* SERVINGMEN] Away, my masters, trouble us no more,
  But join in friendship as your lords have done.

FIRST SERVINGMAN Content. I'll to the surgeon's.

150 SECOND SERVINGMAN And so will I.

THIRD SERVINGMAN And I will see what physic° the tavern   *medicine*
  affords.

Exeunt [*the* MAYOR *and* SERVINGMEN]

WARWICK Accept this scroll, most gracious sovereign,
  Which in the right of Richard Plantagenet
155   We do exhibit to your majesty.

GLOUCESTER Well urged, my lord of Warwick—for, sweet prince,
  An if your grace mark every circumstance,
  You have great reason to do Richard right,
  Especially for those occasions°   *reasons*
160   At Eltham Place I told your majesty.

KING HENRY And those occasions, uncle, were of force.—
  Therefore, my loving lords, our pleasure is
  That Richard be restorèd to his blood.

WARWICK Let Richard be restorèd to his blood.
165   So shall his father's wrongs be recompensed.

WINCHESTER As will the rest, so willeth Winchester.

KING HENRY If Richard will be true,° not that alone   *loyal*
  But all the whole inheritance I give
  That doth belong unto the house of York,
170   From whence you spring by lineal descent.[1]

---

1. *But . . . descent*: The King restores Richard not only to the earldom of Cambridge (inherited from his father) but also to the dukedom of York (inherited from his uncle).

RICHARD PLANTAGENET   Thy humble servant vows obedience
  And humble service till the point of death.
KING HENRY   Stoop then, and set your knee against my foot.
    [RICHARD *kneels*]
  And in reguerdon° of that duty done,   *reward*
175 I gird thee with the valiant sword of York.
  Rise, Richard, like a true Plantagenet,
  And rise created princely Duke of York.
RICHARD DUKE OF YORK [*rising*]   And so thrive Richard, as thy
    foes may fall;
  And as my duty springs, so perish they
180 That grudge one thought° against your majesty.   *hold any grudges*
ALL BUT RICHARD AND SOMERSET   Welcome, high prince, the
    mighty Duke of York!
SOMERSET [*aside*]   Perish, base prince, ignoble Duke of York!
GLOUCESTER   Now will it best avail your majesty
  To cross the seas and to be crowned in France.
185 The presence of a king engenders love
  Amongst his subjects and his loyal friends,
  As it disanimates° his enemies.   *discourages*
KING HENRY   When Gloucester says the word, King Henry goes,
  For friendly counsel cuts off many foes.
190 GLOUCESTER   Your ships already are in readiness.
                Sennet.[2] *Exeunt. Manet°* EXETER   *Remains*
EXETER   Ay, we may march in England or in France,
  Not seeing what is likely to ensue.
  This late° dissension grown betwixt the peers   *recent*
  Burns under feignèd ashes of forged love,
195 And will at last break out into a flame.
  As festered members° rot but by degree   *parts of the body*
  Till bones and flesh and sinews fall away,
  So will this base and envious discord breed.
  And now I fear that fatal prophecy
200 Which, in the time of Henry named the Fifth,
  Was in the mouth of every sucking babe:
  That 'Henry born at Monmouth° should win all,   *(Henry V)*
  And Henry born at Windsor° should lose all'—   *(Henry VI)*
  Which is so plain that Exeter doth wish
205 His days may finish, ere that hapless time.   *Exit*

3.2

Enter [JOAN *la*] *Pucelle, disguised, with four* [*French*]
SOLDIERS *with sacks upon their backs*
JOAN   These are the city gates, the gates of Rouen,
  Through which our policy° must make a breach.   *trickery*
  Take heed. Be wary how you place your words.
  Talk like the vulgar° sort of market men   *common*
5 That come to gather money for their corn.°   *grain*
  If we have entrance, as I hope we shall,
  And that° we find the slothful watch but weak,   *if*

---

2. Trumpet notes that accompany a procession.   **3.2.** Location: In and around Rouen, France.

I'll by a sign give notice to our friends,
That Charles the Dauphin may encounter them.
10 A SOLDIER   Our sacks shall be a mean° to sack the city,   *means*
And we be lords and rulers over Rouen.
Therefore we'll knock.
        [*They*] *knock*
WATCH [*within*]   *Qui là?*°   *Who is there*
JOAN   *Paysans, la pauvre gens de France:*[1]
Poor market folks that come to sell their corn.
15 WATCH [*opening the gates*]   Enter, go in. The market bell is rung.
JOAN [*aside*]   Now, Rouen, I'll shake thy bulwarks to the ground.
                                                        Exeunt

                    3.3
        Enter CHARLES [*the Dauphin, the*] BASTARD
        [*of Orléans, the Duke of*] ALENÇON[, RENÉ *Duke of*
        Anjou, and French soldiers]
CHARLES   Saint Denis bless this happy stratagem,
And once again we'll sleep secure in Rouen.
BASTARD   Here entered Pucelle and her practisants.°   *conspirators*
Now she is there, how will she specify
5 'Here is the best and safest passage in'?
RENÉ   By thrusting out a torch from yonder tower—
Which, once discerned, shows that her meaning is:
No way to that, for weakness, which she entered.[1]
        Enter [JOAN *la*] *Pucelle on the top, thrusting out a torch*
        burning
JOAN   Behold, this is the happy wedding torch
10 That joineth Rouen unto her countrymen,
But burning fatal to the Talbonites.°   *followers of Talbot*
BASTARD   See, noble Charles, the beacon of our friend.
The burning torch in yonder turret stands.
CHARLES   Now shine it° like a comet of revenge,   *may it shine*
15 A prophet to the fall of all our foes!
RENÉ   Defer no time; delays have dangerous ends.
Enter and cry, 'The Dauphin!', presently,°   *at once*
And then do execution on the watch.°   *Alarum* [*Exeunt*]   *then kill the guards*

                    3.4
        An alarum. [*Enter Lord*] TALBOT *in an excursion*°   *a skirmish*
TALBOT   France, thou shalt rue this treason with thy tears,
If Talbot but survive thy treachery.
Pucelle, that witch, that damnèd sorceress,
Hath wrought this hellish mischief unawares,°   *unexpectedly*
5 That hardly we escaped the pride of France.[1]   *Exit*

---

1. Peasants, the poor folk of France.
3.3 Location: Scene continues.
1. No entrance is as weakly guarded as the one she
entered.

3.4 Location: Scene continues.
1. That only with difficulty we escaped the princely
power of France.

3.5

An alarum. Excursions. [The Duke of] BEDFORD
brought in sick, in a chair. Enter [Lord] TALBOT and
[the Duke of] BURGUNDY, without; within,[1] [JOAN la]
Pucelle, CHARLES [the Dauphin, the] BASTARD
[of Orléans, the Duke of ALENÇON], and RENÉ [Duke
of Anjou] on the walls

JOAN   Good morrow gallants. Want ye corn for bread?
    I think the Duke of Burgundy will fast
    Before he'll buy again at such a rate.
    'Twas full of darnel.° Do you like the taste?   *weeds*
5 BURGUNDY   Scoff on, vile fiend and shameless courtesan.
    I trust ere long to choke thee with thine own,°   *your own bread*
    And make thee curse the harvest of that corn.
  CHARLES   Your grace may starve, perhaps, before that time.
  BEDFORD   O let no words, but deeds, revenge this treason.
10 JOAN   What will you do, good graybeard? Break a lance
    And run a-tilt at° death within a chair?   *joust with*
  TALBOT   Foul fiend of France, and hag of all despite,°   *most despicable*
    Encompassed with thy lustful paramours,
    Becomes it thee to taunt his valiant age
15   And twit with cowardice a man half dead?
    Damsel, I'll have a bout° with you again,   *fight; sexual struggle*
    Or else let Talbot perish with this shame.
  JOAN   Are ye so hot,° sir?—Yet, Pucelle, hold thy peace.   *angry; lustful*
    If Talbot do but thunder, rain will follow.
    They [the English] whisper together in counsel
20   God speed the parliament; who shall be the Speaker?
  TALBOT   Dare ye come forth and meet us in the field?
  JOAN   Belike your lordship takes us then for fools,
    To try if that our own be ours or no.
  TALBOT   I speak not to that railing Hecate[2]
25   But unto thee, Alençon, and the rest.
    Will ye, like soldiers, come and fight it out?
  ALENÇON   Seignieur, no.
  TALBOT   Seignieur, hang! Base muleteers° of   *Lowborn mule drivers*
    France,
    Like peasant footboys do they keep° the walls   *stay near*
    And dare not take up arms like gentlemen.
30 JOAN   Away, captains, let's get us from the walls,
    For Talbot means no goodness by his looks.
    Goodbye, my lord. We came but to tell you
    That we are here.   *Exeunt [French] from the walls*
  TALBOT   And there will we be, too, ere it be long,
35   Or else reproach be Talbot's greatest fame.
    Vow Burgundy, by honour of thy house,
    Pricked on° by public wrongs sustained in France,   *Urged on*
    Either to get the town again or die.
    And I—as sure as English Henry lives,
40   And as his father here was conqueror;[3]

3.5 Location: Scene continues.
1. The stage directions suggest that Talbot's party is on the main stage; Joan's party may appear on the upper stage gallery.

2. In classical mythology, the goddess of night and the underworld and the patron of witchcraft.
3. Henry V had captured Rouen in 1419.

As sure as in this late° betrayèd town   recently
Great Cœur-de-lion's heart was buried[4]—
So sure I swear to get the town or die.

BURGUNDY   My vows are equal partners with thy vows.

45 TALBOT   But ere we go, regard this dying prince,
The valiant Duke of Bedford. [To BEDFORD] Come, my lord,
We will bestow you in some better place,
Fitter for sickness and for crazy° age.   feeble

BEDFORD   Lord Talbot, do not so dishonour me.

50 Here will I sit before the walls of Rouen,
And will be partner of your weal° or woe.   happiness

BURGUNDY   Courageous Bedford, let us now persuade you.

BEDFORD   Not to be gone from hence; for once I read
That stout Pendragon,[5] in his litter sick,

55 Came to the field and vanquishèd his foes.
Methinks I should revive the soldiers' hearts,
Because I ever found them as myself.

TALBOT   Undaunted spirit in a dying breast!
Then be it so; heavens keep old Bedford safe.

60 And now no more ado, brave Burgundy,
But gather we our forces out of hand,°   at once
And set upon our boasting enemy.   *Exit [with* BURGUNDY]
        An alarum. Excursions. Enter Sir John FASTOLF
        and a CAPTAIN

CAPTAIN   Whither away, Sir John Fastolf, in such haste?

FASTOLF   Whither away? To save myself by flight.

65 We are like to have the overthrow° again.   to be defeated

CAPTAIN   What, will you fly, and leave Lord Talbot?

FASTOLF   Ay, all the Talbots in the world, to save my life.   *Exit*

CAPTAIN   Cowardly knight, ill fortune follow thee!   *Exit*
        Retreat. Excursions. [JOAN la] *Pucelle,* ALENÇON,
        and CHARLES *fly*

BEDFORD   Now, quiet soul, depart when heaven please,

70 For I have seen our enemies' overthrow.
What is the trust or strength of foolish man?
They that of late were daring with their scoffs
Are glad and fain° by flight to save themselves.   eager
        BEDFORD *dies, and is carried in by two in his chair*

3.6

        An alarum. Enter [Lord] TALBOT, [*the Duke of*]
        BURGUNDY, *and the rest [of the English soldiers]*

TALBOT   Lost and recovered in a day again!
This is a double honour, Burgundy
Yet heavens have glory for this victory!

BURGUNDY   Warlike and martial Talbot, Burgundy

5 Enshrines thee in his heart, and there erects
Thy noble deeds as valour's monuments.

TALBOT   Thanks, gentle° Duke. But where is Pucelle now?   noble
I think her old familiar° is asleep.   attendant demon

4. According to Holinshed's *Chronicles*, Richard
Cœur-de-Lion (the Lion-Hearted), who ruled England
from 1189 to 1199, willed that his heart be buried in
Rouen as a sign of his love for the city.

5. Uther Pendragon, the father of King Arthur. This
story is told in Geoffrey of Monmouth's history of
Britain (*Historia Regum Britanniae*). *stout:* brave.
3.6 Location: Scene continues.

Now where's the Bastard's braves,° and Charles his gleeks?°   *boasts / Charles's jests*
10   What, all amort?° Rouen hangs her head for grief   *dispirited*
    That such a valiant company are fled.
    Now will we take some order° in the town,   *establish order*
    Placing therein some expert officers,
    And then depart to Paris, to the King,
15   For there young Henry with his nobles lie.°   *lives*
BURGUNDY   What wills Lord Talbot pleaseth Burgundy.
TALBOT   But yet, before we go, let's not forget
    The noble Duke of Bedford late deceased,
    But see his exequies° fulfilled in Rouen.   *funeral rites*
20   A braver soldier never couchèd° lance;   *leveled (for attack)*
    A gentler heart did never sway in court.
    But kings and mightiest potentates must die,
    For that's the end of human misery.   *Exeunt*

3.7

Enter CHARLES [*the Dauphin, the*] BASTARD [*of Orléans,*
the Duke of] ALENÇON, [JOAN *la*] *Pucelle* [*and French*
soldiers]

JOAN   Dismay not, princes, at this accident,
    Nor grieve that Rouen is so recoverèd.
    Care° is no cure, but rather corrosive,°   *Sorrow / destructive*
    For things that are not to be remedied.
5   Let frantic° Talbot triumph for a while,   *mad*
    And like a peacock sweep along his tail;
    We'll pull his plumes and take away his train,°   *peacock's tail; army*
    If Dauphin and the rest will be but ruled.
CHARLES   We have been guided by thee hitherto,
10   And of thy cunning had no diffidence.°   *doubt*
    One sudden foil° shall never breed distrust.   *defeat*
BASTARD [*to* JOAN]   Search out thy wit for secret policies,°   *stratagems*
    And we will make thee famous through the world.
ALENÇON [*to* JOAN]   We'll set thy statue in some holy place
15   And have thee reverenced like a blessèd saint.
    Employ thee then, sweet virgin, for our good.
JOAN   Then thus it must be; this doth Joan devise:
    By fair persuasions mixed with sugared words
    We will entice the Duke of Burgundy
20   To leave the Talbot and to follow us.
CHARLES   Ay, marry, sweeting,° if we could do that   *(a lover's nickname)*
    France were no place for Henry's warriors,
    Nor should that nation boast it so with us,
    But be extirpèd° from our provinces.   *rooted out*
25   ALENÇON   For ever should they be expulsed from France
    And not have title of an earldom here.
JOAN   Your honours shall perceive how I will work
    To bring this matter to the wishèd end.
    Drum sounds afar off
    Hark, by the sound of drum you may perceive
30   Their powers are marching unto Paris-ward.°   *toward Paris*
    Here sound an English march

3.7 Location: Plains near Rouen.

There goes the Talbot, with his colours spread,°   *flags unfurled*
And all the troops of English after him.
    [*Here sound a*] *French march*
Now in the rearward comes the Duke and his.
Fortune in favour° makes him lag behind.   *as a favor to us*
35   Summon a parley.[1] We will talk with him.
    Trumpets sound a parley
CHARLES [*calling*]   A parley with the Duke of Burgundy.
    [*Enter the Duke of* BURGUNDY]
BURGUNDY   Who craves a parley with the Burgundy?
JOAN   The princely Charles of France, thy countryman.
BURGUNDY   What sayst thou, Charles?—for I am marching hence.
40   CHARLES   Speak, Pucelle, and enchant him with thy words.
JOAN   Brave Burgundy, undoubted° hope of France,   *certain*
Stay. Let thy humble handmaid speak to thee.
BURGUNDY   Speak on, but be not over-tedious.
JOAN   Look on thy country, look on fertile France,
45   And see the cities and the towns defaced
By wasting ruin of the cruel foe.
As looks the mother on her lowly babe
When death doth close his tender-dying° eyes,   *young-dying*
See, see the pining malady of France;
50   Behold the wounds, the most unnatural wounds,
Which thou thyself hast given her woeful breast.
O turn thy edgèd sword another way,
Strike those that hurt, and hurt not those that help.
One drop of blood drawn from thy country's bosom
55   Should grieve thee more than streams of foreign gore.
Return thee, therefore, with a flood of tears,
And wash away thy country's stainèd spots.[2]
BURGUNDY [*aside*]   Either she hath bewitched me with her words,
Or nature makes me suddenly relent.
60   JOAN   Besides, all French and France exclaims on° thee,   *denounces*
Doubting thy birth and lawful progeny.°   *ancestry*
Who join'st thou with but with a lordly nation
That will not trust thee but for profit's sake?
When Talbot hath set footing once in France
65   And fashioned thee that instrument of ill,
Who then but English Henry will be lord,
And thou be thrust out like a fugitive?
Call we to mind, and mark but this for proof:
Was not the Duke of Orléans thy foe?
70   And was he not in England prisoner?
But when they heard he was thine enemy
They set him free, without his ransom paid,
In spite of Burgundy and all his friends.[3]
See, then, thou fight'st against thy countrymen,
75   And join'st with them will be thy slaughtermen.
Come, come, return; return, thou wandering lord,

---

1. Sound a trumpet to request a conference.
2. And wash away the spots of blood that defile your country.
3. The historical Orléans was not released by the English until five years after Burgundy abandoned the English alliance.

Charles and the rest will take thee in their arms.

BURGUNDY [*aside*]   I am vanquishèd.[4] These haughty° words of hers   *lofty*
Have battered me like roaring cannon-shot

80   And made me almost yield upon my knees.
[*To the others*] Forgive me, country, and sweet countrymen;
And lords, accept this hearty kind embrace.
My forces and my power of men are yours.
So farewell, Talbot. I'll no longer trust thee.

85   JOAN   Done like a Frenchman—[*aside*] turn and turn again.

CHARLES   Welcome, brave Duke. Thy friendship makes us fresh.

BASTARD   And doth beget new courage in our breasts.

ALENÇON   Pucelle hath bravely played her part in this,
And doth deserve a coronet of gold.

90   CHARLES   Now let us on, my lords, and join our powers,
And seek how we may prejudice° the foe.   *Exeunt*   *hurt*

3.8

[*Flourish.*] *Enter* KING [HENRY, *the Duke of*] GLOUCES-
TER, [*the Bishop of*] WINCHESTER, [*the Duke of*] EXE-
TER; [RICHARD DUKE OF] YORK, [*the Earl of*] WARWICK,
[*and* VERNON *with white roses; the Earl of*] SUFFOLK,
[*the Duke of*] SOMERSET [*and* BASSET *with red roses*]. *To
them, with his soldiers,* [*enter Lord*] TALBOT

TALBOT   My gracious prince and honourable peers,
Hearing of your arrival in this realm
I have a while given truce unto my wars
To do my duty° to my sovereign;   *give homage*

5   In sign whereof, this arm that hath reclaimed
To your obedience fifty fortresses,
Twelve cities, and seven walled towns of strength,
Beside five hundred prisoners of esteem,°   *noble rank*
Lets fall his sword before your highness' feet,

10   And with submissive loyalty of heart
Ascribes the glory of his conquest got
First to my God, and next unto your grace.
[*He kneels*][1]

KING HENRY   Is this the Lord Talbot, uncle Gloucester,
That hath so long been resident in France?

15   GLOUCESTER   Yes, if it please your majesty, my liege.

KING HENRY [*to* TALBOT]   Welcome, brave captain and victorious lord.
When I was young—as yet I am not old—
I do remember how my father said
A stouter champion never handled sword.

20   Long since we were resolvèd° of your truth,°   *convinced / loyalty*
Your faithful service and your toil in war,
Yet never have you tasted our reward,
Or been reguerdoned° with so much as thanks,   *rewarded*
Because till now we never saw your face.

---

4. The historical Burgundy did not return to the
French side until four years after Joan's death.
3.8 Location: The palace, Paris.

1. F does not indicate when Talbot kneels, but he must
do so: at line 25, he is urged to "stand up."

Therefore stand up,
　　　　　[TALBOT *rises*]
25　　　　　　　　　　　　and for these good deserts
We here create you Earl of Shrewsbury;
And in our coronation take your place.[2]
　　　　　Sennet. Exeunt. Manent° VERNON *and* BASSET　　　　*Remain*
VERNON　Now sir, to you that were so hot° at sea,　　　　*angry*
Disgracing of these colours° that I wear　　　　*this badge (the rose)*
30　In honour of my noble lord of York
Dar'st thou maintain the former words thou spak'st?
BASSET　Yes, sir, as well as you dare patronage°　　　　*defend*
The envious barking of your saucy tongue
Against my lord the Duke of Somerset.
35　VERNON　Sirrah, thy lord I honour as he is.
BASSET　Why, what is he?—as good a man as York.
VERNON　Hark ye, not so. In witness, take ye that.
　　　　　[VERNON] *strikes him*
BASSET　Villain, thou know'st the law of arms[3] is such
That whoso draws a sword 'tis present° death,　　　　*immediate*
40　Or else this blow should broach° thy dearest blood.　　　　*tap (as a wine vat)*
But I'll unto his majesty and crave
I may have liberty° to venge this wrong,　　　　*permission*
When thou shalt see I'll meet thee to thy cost.
VERNON　Well, miscreant,° I'll be there as soon as you,　　　　*villain*
45　And after meet you sooner than you would.°　　　　*Exeunt*　　　*would wish*

4.1

[*Flourish.*] *Enter* KING [HENRY, *the Duke of*]
GLOUCESTER, [*the Bishop of*] WINCHESTER, [*the Duke*
of] EXETER, [RICHARD DUKE OF] YORK, [*and the Earl of*]
WARWICK, [*with white roses; the Earl of*] SUFFOLK, [*and*
the Duke of] SOMERSET, [*with red roses; Lord* TALBOT,
and [*the*] Governor [*of Paris*]
GLOUCESTER　Lord Bishop, set the crown upon his head.
WINCHESTER　God save King Henry, of that name the sixth!
　　　　　[WINCHESTER *crowns the* KING]
GLOUCESTER　Now, Governor of Paris, take your oath
That you elect° no other king but him;　　　　*acknowledge*
5　Esteem none friends but such as are his friends,
And none your foes but such as shall pretend°　　　　*propose*
Malicious practices against his state.
This shall ye do, so help you righteous God.
　　　　　Enter [*Sir John*] FASTOLF [*with a letter*]
FASTOLF　My gracious sovereign, as I rode from Calais
10　To haste unto your coronation
A letter was delivered to my hands,
　　　　　[*He presents the letter*]
Writ to your grace from th' Duke of Burgundy.
TALBOT　Shame to the Duke of Burgundy and thee!
I vowed, base knight, when I did meet thee next,

---

2. The historical Talbot was created Earl of Shrewsbury in 1442, more than ten years after Henry's
coronation.

3. The law that forbade fighting near a royal residence
(see also 1.4.45 and 2.4.86).
4.1 Location: The palace, Paris.

15   To tear the Garter¹ from thy craven's° leg,   *coward's*
        [*He tears it off*]
    Which I have done because unworthily
    Thou wast installèd in that high degree.—
    Pardon me, princely Henry and the rest.
    This dastard° at the battle of Patay   *coward*
20   When but in all° I was six thousand strong,   *When all told*
    And that the French were almost ten to one,
    Before we met, or that a stroke was given,
    Like to a trusty° squire did run away;   *faithful (here ironic)*
    In which assault we lost twelve hundred men.
25   Myself and divers gentlemen beside
    Were there surprised and taken prisoners.
    Then judge, great lords, if I have done amiss,
    Or whether that such cowards ought to wear
    This ornament of knighthood: yea or no?
30 GLOUCESTER   To say the truth, this fact° was infamous   *deed*
    And ill beseeming any common man,
    Much more a knight, a captain and a leader.
  TALBOT   When first this order was ordained, my lords,
    Knights of the Garter were of noble birth,
35   Valiant and virtuous, full of haughty° courage,   *lofty*
    Such as were grown to credit° by the wars;   *fame*
    Not fearing death nor shrinking for distress,
    But always resolute in most extremes.°   *in greatest extremities*
    He then that is not furnished in this sort°   *not endowed like this*
40   Doth but usurp the sacred name of knight,
    Profaning this most honourable order,
    And should—if I were worthy to be judge—
    Be quite degraded,° like a hedge-born swain²   *reduced in rank*
    That doth presume to boast of gentle° blood.   *noble*
  KING HENRY [*to* FASTOLF]   Stain to thy countrymen, thou hear'st
45   thy doom.°   *sentence*
    Be packing, therefore, thou that wast a knight.
    Henceforth we banish thee on pain of death.   [*Exit* FASTOLF]
    And now, my Lord Protector, view the letter
    Sent from our uncle, Duke of Burgundy.³
  GLOUCESTER   What means his grace that he hath changed his
50   style?°   *form of address*
    No more but plain and bluntly 'To the King'?
    Hath he forgot he is his sovereign?
    Or doth this churlish superscription°   *rude address*
    Pretend° some alteration in good will?   *Indicate*
55   What's here? 'I have upon especial cause,
    Moved with compassion of my country's wrack°   *destruction*
    Together with the pitiful complaints
    Of such as your oppression feeds upon,
    Forsaken your pernicious faction
60   And joined with Charles, the rightful King of France.'
    O monstrous treachery! Can this be so?

---

1. A ribbon, worn below the left knee, signifying membership in the Order of the Garter, the highest rank of English knighthood.

2. A lowly or illegitimate country person.
3. Henry VI's uncle, the Duke of Bedford, married Burgundy's sister Anne.

That in alliance, amity, and oaths
There should be found such false dissembling guile?

KING HENRY   What? Doth my uncle Burgundy revolt?

65   GLOUCESTER   He doth, my lord, and is become your foe.

KING HENRY   Is that the worst this letter doth contain?

GLOUCESTER   It is the worst, and all, my lord, he writes.

KING HENRY   Why then, Lord Talbot there shall talk with him
And give him chastisement for this abuse.

70   [*To* TALBOT] How say you, my lord? Are you not content?

TALBOT   Content, my liege? Yes. But that I am prevented,°   anticipated
I should have begged I might have been employed.

KING HENRY   Then gather strength and march unto him straight.°   at once
Let him perceive how ill we brook° his treason,   tolerate

75   And what offence it is to flout his friends.

TALBOT   I go, my lord, in heart desiring still°   always
You may behold confusion of your foes.   [*Exit*]

Enter VERNON [*wearing a white rose,*] *and* BASSET [*wear-*
ing a red rose]

VERNON [*to* KING HENRY]   Grant me the combat,° gracious   permission to duel
sovereign.

BASSET [*to* KING HENRY]   And me, my lord; grant me the combat, too.

RICHARD DUKE OF YORK [*to* KING HENRY, *pointing to* VERNON]

80   This is my servant;° hear him, noble Prince.   follower

SOMERSET [*to* KING HENRY, *pointing to* BASSET]   And this is mine,
sweet Henry; favour him.

KING HENRY   Be patient, lords, and give them leave to speak.
Say, gentlemen, what makes you thus exclaim,
And wherefore crave you combat, or with whom?

85   VERNON   With him, my lord; for he hath done me wrong.

BASSET   And I with him; for he hath done me wrong.

KING HENRY   What is that wrong whereof you both complain?
First let me know, and then I'll answer you.

BASSET   Crossing the sea from England into France,

90   This fellow here with envious carping tongue
Upbraided me about the rose I wear,
Saying the sanguine° colour of the leaves°   blood-red / petals
Did represent my master's blushing cheeks
When stubbornly he did repugn° the truth   reject

95   About a certain question[4] in the law
Argued betwixt the Duke of York and him,
With other vile and ignominious terms;
In confutation of which rude reproach,
And in defence of my lord's worthiness,

100   I crave the benefit of law of arms.[5]

VERNON   And that is my petition, noble lord;
For though he seem with forgèd quaint conceit°   false cunning words
To set a gloss° upon his bold intent,   good appearance
Yet know, my lord, I was provoked by him,

105   And he first took exceptions at this badge,
Pronouncing that the paleness of this flower
Bewrayed° the faintness of my master's heart.   Revealed

---

4. The "certain question" apparently concerns the
question of York's succession to the throne and the

attainder of his father. See 2.4 and 2.5.45–129.
5. The right to decide the matter in a duel.

RICHARD DUKE OF YORK   Will not this malice, Somerset, be left?°   put aside
SOMERSET   Your private grudge, my lord of York, will out,
110   Though ne'er so cunningly you smother it.
KING HENRY   Good Lord, what madness rules in brainsick men
    When for so slight and frivolous a cause
    Such factious emulations° shall arise?   divisive jealousies
    Good cousins both of York and Somerset,
115   Quiet yourselves, I pray, and be at peace.
RICHARD DUKE OF YORK   Let this dissension first be tried by fight,
    And then your highness shall command a peace.
SOMERSET   The quarrel toucheth none but us alone;
    Betwixt ourselves let us decide it then.
120   RICHARD DUKE OF YORK   There is my pledge.⁶ Accept it, Somerset.
VERNON [to KING HENRY]   Nay, let it rest where it began at first.⁷
BASSET [to KING HENRY]   Confirm it so, mine honourable lord.
GLOUCESTER   Confirm it so? Confounded be your strife,
    And perish ye with your audacious prate!°   prattling
125   Presumptuous vassals, are you not ashamed
    With this immodest clamorous outrage
    To trouble and disturb the King and us?
    And you, my lords, methinks you do not well
    To bear with their perverse objections,°   accusations
130   Much less to take occasion° from their mouths   the opportunity
    To raise a mutiny betwixt yourselves.
    Let me persuade you take a better course.
EXETER   It grieves his highness. Good my lords, be friends.
KING HENRY   Come hither, you that would be combatants.
135   Henceforth I charge you, as you love our favour,
    Quite to forget this quarrel and the cause.
    And you, my lords, remember where we are—
    In France, amongst a fickle wavering nation.
    If they perceive dissension in our looks,
140   And that within ourselves we disagree,
    How will their grudging stomachs° be provoked   resentful tempers
    To wilful disobedience, and rebel!
    Beside, what infamy will there arise
    When foreign princes shall be certified°   informed
145   That for a toy,° a thing of no regard,   trifle
    King Henry's peers and chief nobility
    Destroyed themselves and lost the realm of France!
    O, think upon the conquest of my father,
    My tender years, and let us not forgo
150   That for a trifle that was bought with blood.⁸
    Let me be umpire in this doubtful° strife.   uncertain
    I see no reason, if I wear this rose,
        [He takes a red rose]
    That anyone should therefore be suspicious
    I more incline to Somerset than York.
155   Both are my kinsmen, and I love them both.

6. A glove or gauntlet thrown down in a duel.   8. let . . . blood: let us not lose for a trifle what was
7. Let the quarrel remain with me and Basset, who   bought with blood (that is, let us not lose France).
began it.

As well they may upbraid me with my crown
Because, forsooth, the King of Scots is crowned.
But your discretions better can persuade
Than I am able to instruct or teach,
160 And therefore, as we hither came in peace,
So let us still continue peace and love.
Cousin of York, we institute° your grace   appoint
To be our regent in these parts of France;
And good my lord of Somerset, unite
165 Your troops of horsemen with his bands of foot,°   infantry
And like true subjects, sons of your progenitors,
Go cheerfully together and digest°   dissipate
Your angry choler on your enemies.
Ourself, my Lord Protector, and the rest,
170 After some respite, will return to Calais,
From thence to England, where I hope ere long
To be presented by your victories
With Charles, Alençon, and that traitorous rout.°   rabble
          [Flourish.] Exeunt. Manent YORK, WARWICK,
                              VERNON, [and] EXETER
WARWICK   My lord of York, I promise you, the King
175 Prettily, methought, did play the orator.
RICHARD DUKE OF YORK   And so he did; but yet I like it not
In that he wears the badge of Somerset.
WARWICK   Tush, that was but his fancy; blame him not.
I dare presume, sweet Prince, he thought no harm.
180 RICHARD DUKE OF YORK   An if I wist° he did—but let it rest.   If I knew for certain
Other affairs must now be managed. Exeunt. Manet EXETER
EXETER   Well didst thou, Richard, to suppress thy voice;
For had the passions of thy heart burst out
I fear we should have seen deciphered° there   revealed
185 More rancorous spite, more furious raging broils,
Than yet can be imagined or supposed.
But howsoe'er, no simple man that sees
This jarring discord of nobility,
This shouldering of each other in the court,
190 This factious bandying° of their favourites,°   quarreling / followers
But that° it doth presage some ill event.°   But sees that / outcome
'Tis much when sceptres are in children's hands,
But more when envy breeds unkind° division: unnatural
There comes the ruin, there begins confusion.   Exit

4.2
          Enter [Lord] TALBOT WITH [a] trump[eter] and
          drum[mer and soldiers] before Bordeaux
TALBOT   Go to the gates of Bordeaux, trumpeter.
Summon their general unto the wall.
          [The trumpeter] sounds [a parley]. Enter [French]
          GENERAL, aloft
English John Talbot, captain, calls you forth,
Servant in arms to Harry King of England;
5 And thus he would:° open your city gates,   desires
Be humble to us, call my sovereign yours

4.2 Location: Before Bordeaux.

And do him homage as obedient subjects,
And I'll withdraw me and my bloody power.
But if you frown upon this proffered peace,
10   You tempt the fury of my three attendants—
Lean famine, quartering° steel, and climbing fire—   *dismembering*
Who in a moment even° with the earth   *level*
Shall lay your stately and air-braving° towers   *air-defying; lofty*
If you forsake the offer of their love.
15   GENERAL   Thou ominous and fearful owl[1] of death,
Our nation's terror and their bloody scourge,
The period° of thy tyranny approacheth.   *end*
On us thou canst not enter but by death,
For I protest we are well fortified
20   And strong enough to issue out and fight.
If thou retire, the Dauphin well appointed°   *equipped*
Stands with the snares of war to tangle thee.
On either hand thee° there are squadrons pitched[2]   *On both sides of you*
To wall thee from the liberty of flight,
25   And no way canst thou turn thee for redress
But death doth front thee with apparent spoil,[3]
And pale destruction meets thee in the face.
Ten thousand French have ta'en the sacrament[4]
To fire their dangerous artillery
30   Upon no Christian soul but English Talbot.
Lo, there thou stand'st, a breathing valiant man
Of an invincible unconquered spirit.
This is the latest° glory of thy praise,   *final*
That I thy enemy due° thee withal,   *endow*
35   For ere the glass° that now begins to run   *hourglass*
Finish the process of his° sandy hour,   *progress of its*
These eyes that see thee now well colourèd°   *in good health*
Shall see thee withered, bloody, pale, and dead.
      Drum afar off
Hark, hark, the Dauphin's drum, a warning bell,
40   Sings heavy music to thy timorous soul,
And mine shall ring thy dire departure out.[5]   *Exit*
TALBOT   He fables not. I hear the enemy.
Out, some light horsemen, and peruse their wings.°   *survey their flanks*
      [*Exit one or more*]
O negligent and heedless° discipline,   *careless*
45   How are we parked° and bounded in a pale!°—   *enclosed / fenced area*
A little herd of England's timorous deer
Mazed with[6] a yelping kennel of French curs.
If we be English deer, be then in blood,°   *vigorous*
Not rascal-like[7] to fall down with a pinch,°   *nip (from hounds)*
50   But rather, moody-mad° and desperate stags,   *enraged*
Turn on the bloody hounds with heads of steel
And make the cowards stand aloof at bay.
Sell every man his life as dear as mine

---

1. The owl's cry was thought to portend evil or death
(see Ovid's *Metamorphoses* 10.521–52 and *Macbeth*
2.2.3).
2. Arranged on the field for battle.
3. But death confronts you with obvious destruction.
4. Have received the Christian sacrament of Holy

Communion (as a way of confirming their oaths).
5. And my drum—the alarm signal given when the general's army is to "issue out and fight" (line 20) against
Talbot—shall signal your death.
6. Bewildered by; trapped in maze with.
7. Not like lean, worthless deer.

And they shall find dear° deer of us, my friends.   *costly*
55   God and Saint George,° Talbot and England's right,   *England's patron saint*
Prosper our colours in this dangerous fight!   [*Exeunt*]

4.3

Enter a MESSENGER *that meets* [*the* DUKE OF] YORK.
Enter [RICHARD DUKE OF] YORK *with* [*a*] *trumpet*[*er*] *and
many soldiers*

RICHARD DUKE OF YORK   Are not the speedy scouts returned again
That dogged° the mighty army of the Dauphin?   *tracked*
MESSENGER   They are returned, my lord, and give it out
That he is marched to Bordeaux with his power
5   To fight with Talbot. As he marched along,
By your espials° were discoverèd   *spies*
Two mightier troops than that the Dauphin led,
Which joined with him and made their march for Bordeaux.
RICHARD DUKE OF YORK   A plague upon that villain Somerset
10   That thus delays my promisèd supply
Of horsemen that were levied for this siege!
Renownèd Talbot doth expect my aid,
And I am louted° by a traitor villain   *made a fool of*
And cannot help the noble chevalier.
15   God comfort him in this necessity
If he miscarry,° farewell wars in France!   *come to harm*
Enter another messenger [Sir William LUCY]
LUCY[1]   Thou princely leader of our English strength,
Never so needful on the earth of France,
Spur to the rescue of the noble Talbot,
20   Who now is girdled with a waste° of iron   *vast expanse; belt*
And hemmed about with grim destruction.
To Bordeaux, warlike Duke; to Bordeaux, York,
Else farewell Talbot, France, and England's honour.
RICHARD DUKE OF YORK   O God, that Somerset, who in proud heart
25   Doth stop my cornets,° were in Talbot's place!   *troops of cavalry*
So should we save a valiant gentleman
By forfeiting a traitor and a coward.
Mad ire and wrathful fury makes me weep,
That thus we die while remiss° traitors sleep.   *idle; negligent*
30 LUCY   O, send some succour to the distressed lord.
RICHARD DUKE OF YORK   He dies, we lose; I break my warlike word;
We mourn, France smiles; we lose they daily get,
All 'long° of this vile traitor Somerset.   *because*
LUCY   Then God take mercy on brave Talbot's soul,
35   And on his son young John, who two hours since
I met in travel toward his warlike father.
This seven years did not Talbot see his son,
And now they meet where both their lives are done.
RICHARD DUKE OF YORK   Alas, what joy shall noble Talbot have
40   To bid his young son welcome to his grave?

4.3 Location: An unspecified field in France.
1. In F, this and the subsequent three speeches
assigned to Lucy are spoken by "Second Messenger"
and "Messenger." However, at line 43, York addresses
the speaker as "Lucy."

Away—vexation almost stops my breath
That sundered friends greet in the hour of death.
Lucy, farewell. No more my fortune can°   can do
But curse the cause I cannot aid the man.
45   Maine, Blois, Poitiers, and Tours are won away
'Long all° of Somerset and his delay.   *Exeunt* [*all but* LUCY]   All because
LUCY   Thus while the vulture of sedition
Feeds in the bosom of such great commanders,
Sleeping neglection° doth betray to loss   Careless disregard
50   The conquest of our scarce-cold conqueror,[2]
That ever-living man of memory[3]
Henry the Fifth. Whiles they each other cross,
Lives, honours, lands, and all hurry to loss.   [*Exit*][4]

4.4
Enter [*the Duke of*] SOMERSET *with his army*

SOMERSET [*to a* CAPTAIN]   It is too late, I cannot send them now.
This expedition was by York and Talbot
Too rashly plotted. All our general force
Might with a sally of the very town
5   Be buckled with.[1] The over-daring Talbot
Hath sullied all his gloss of former honour
By this unheedful, desperate, wild adventure.
York set him on to fight and die in shame
That, Talbot dead, great York might bear the name.°   claim preeminence
[*Enter* LUCY]
10   CAPTAIN   Here is Sir William Lucy, who with me
Set from our o'ermatchèd forces forth for aid.
SOMERSET   How now, Sir William, whither were you sent?
LUCY   Whither, my lord? From bought and sold[2] Lord Talbot,
Who, ringed about with bold adversity,
15   Cries out for noble York and Somerset
To beat assailing death from his weak legions;
And whiles the honourable captain there
Drops bloody sweat from his war-wearied limbs
And, unadvantaged,° ling'ring looks for rescue,   disadvantaged
20   You his false hopes, the trust of England's honour,
Keep off aloof with worthless emulation.°   rivalry
Let not your private discord keep away
The levied succours° that should lend him aid,   reinforcements
While he, renownèd noble gentleman,
25   Yield up his life unto a world of ° odds.   immense
Orléans the Bastard, Charles, and Burgundy,
Alençon, René, compass him about,
And Talbot perisheth by your default.
SOMERSET   York set him on; York should have sent him aid.

---

2. The conquest made by our recently dead conqueror.
(The events of this scene actually took place thirty-one
years after the death of the historical Henry V.)
3. *That man who will live forever in memory.*
4. F does not mark Lucy's exit at this point. Conceivably, he stays onstage as Somerset enters to him.
4.4 Location: Scene continues.
1. *All . . . with:* Our entire army might be engaged by

an attack simply from the French garrison in the town
(without taking into account the other French forces
coming as reinforcements).
2. *bought and sold:* a proverbial expression meaning
"betrayed," perhaps alluding to the biblical account of
Christ's betrayal by his disciple Judas for forty pieces of
silver.

30 LUCY   And York as fast upon your grace exclaims,
Swearing that you withhold his levied horse
Collected for this expedition.
SOMERSET   York lies. He might have sent° and had the horse.   *sent for*
I owe him little duty and less love,
35 And take foul scorn° to fawn on him by sending.   *find it disgraceful*
LUCY   The fraud of England, not the force of France,
Hath now entrapped the noble-minded Talbot.
Never to England shall he bear his life,
But dies betrayed to fortune by your strife.
40 SOMERSET   Come, go. I will dispatch the horsemen straight.°   *immediately*
Within six hours they will be at his aid.
LUCY   Too late comes rescue. He is ta'en or slain,
For fly he could not if he would have fled,
And fly would Talbot never, though he might.
45 SOMERSET   If he be dead, brave Talbot, then adieu.
LUCY   His fame lives in the world, his shame in you.
Exeunt [severally]

4.5
Enter [Lord] TALBOT *and his son [*JOHN*]*

TALBOT   O young John Talbot, I did send for thee
To tutor thee in stratagems of war,
That Talbot's name might be in thee revived
When sapless° age and weak unable limbs   *withered*
5 Should bring thy father to his drooping chair.¹
But O—malignant and ill-boding stars!—
Now thou art come unto a feast of death,
A terrible and unavoided° danger.   *unavoidable*
Therefore, dear boy, mount on my swiftest horse,
10 And I'll direct thee how thou shalt escape
By sudden flight. Come, dally not, be gone.
JOHN   Is my name Talbot, and am I your son,
And shall I fly? O, if you love my mother,
Dishonour not her honourable name
15 To make a bastard and a slave of me.
The world will say he is not Talbot's blood
That basely fled when noble Talbot stood.
TALBOT   Fly to revenge my death if I be slain.
JOHN   He that flies so will ne'er return again.
20 TALBOT   If we both stay, we both are sure to die.
JOHN   Then let me stay and, father, do you fly.
Your loss is great; so your regard° should be.   *concern for yourself*
My worth unknown, no loss is known in me.
Upon my death the French can little boast;
25 In yours they will: in you all hopes are lost.
Flight cannot stain the honour you have won,
But mine it will, that no exploit have done.
You fled for vantage,° everyone will swear,   *military advantage*
But if I bow, they'll say it was for fear.
30 There is no hope that ever I will stay
If the first hour I shrink and run away.

4.5 Location: Battlefield near Bordeaux.
1. Chair where he sits wearily, as his strength and life decline.

Here on my knee I beg mortality°   death
Rather than life preserved with infamy.
TALBOT   Shall all thy mother's hopes lie in one tomb?
35   JOHN   Ay, rather than I'll shame my mother's womb.
TALBOT   Upon my blessing I command thee go.
JOHN   To fight I will, but not to fly the foe.
TALBOT   Part of thy father may be saved in thee.
JOHN   No part of him but will be shamed in me.
40   TALBOT   Thou never hadst renown, nor canst not lose it.
JOHN   Yes, your renownèd name—shall flight abuse it?
TALBOT   Thy father's charge° shall clear thee from that stain.   order
JOHN   You cannot witness for me, being slain.°   if you are slain
If death be so apparent,° then both fly.   appear so likely
45   TALBOT   And leave my followers here to fight and die?
My age° was never tainted with such shame.   life
JOHN   And shall my youth be guilty of such blame?
No more can I be severed from your side
Than can yourself your self in twain divide.
50   Stay, go, do what you will: the like do I,
For live I will not if my father die.
TALBOT   Then here I take my leave of thee, fair son,
Born to eclipse° thy life this afternoon.   extinguish
Come, side by side together live and die,
55   And soul with soul from France to heaven fly.   *Exeunt*

4.6

Alarum. Excursions, wherein [Lord] Talbot's son [JOHN]
is hemmed about [by French soldiers] and TALBOT
rescues him. [The English drive off the French]
TALBOT   Saint George° and victory! Fight, soldiers, fight!   patron saint of England
The Regent[1] hath with Talbot broke his word,
And left us to the rage of France his° sword.   (France's)
Where is John Talbot? [*To* JOHN] Pause and take thy breath.
5   I gave thee life, and rescued thee from death.
JOHN   O twice my father, twice am I thy son:
The life thou gav'st me first was lost and done
Till with thy warlike sword, despite of fate,
To my determined° time thou gav'st new date.°   exactly defined / limit
10   TALBOT   When from the Dauphin's crest thy sword struck fire
It warmed thy father's heart with proud desire
Of bold-faced victory. Then leaden age,
Quickened with youthful spleen° and warlike rage,   courage
Beat down Alençon, Orléans, Burgundy,
15   And from the pride of Gallia° rescued thee.   France
The ireful Bastard Orléans, that drew blood
From thee, my boy, and had the maidenhood
Of thy first fight,[2] I soon encounterèd,
And interchanging blows, I quickly shed
20   Some of his bastard blood, and in disgrace°   disdain
Bespoke him thus: 'Contaminated, base,
And misbegotten blood I spill of thine,

4.6 Location: Scene continues.
1. York, who was appointed regent at 4.1.162–63.
2. *that drew . . . fight:* an allusion to the notion that a
woman bleeds during her first experience of heterosexual intercourse. So young Talbot has bled during his
first battle.

Mean° and right poor, for that pure blood of mine   *Base*
Which thou didst force from Talbot, my brave boy.
25 Here, purposing° the Bastard to destroy,   *as I was intending*
Came in strong rescue. Speak thy father's care:
Art thou not weary, John? How dost thou fare?
Wilt thou yet leave the battle, boy, and fly,
Now thou art sealed° the son of chivalry?   *confirmed*
30 Fly to revenge my death when I am dead;
The help of one stands me in little stead.°   *does me little good*
O, too much folly is it, well I wot,°   *knew*
To hazard all our lives in one small boat.
If I today die not with Frenchmen's rage,
35 Tomorrow I shall die with mickle° age.   *great*
By me they nothing gain, and if I stay
'Tis but the short'ning of my life one day.
In thee thy mother dies, our household's name,
My death's revenge, thy youth, and England's fame.
40 All these and more we hazard by thy stay;
All these are saved if thou wilt fly away.
JOHN   The sword of Orléans hath not made me smart;°   *suffer*
These words of yours draw life-blood from my heart.
On that advantage,[3] bought with such a shame,
45 To save a paltry life and slay bright fame,
Before young Talbot from old Talbot fly
The coward horse that bears me fall° and die;   *may it fall*
And like me° to the peasant boys of France,   *compare me*
To be shame's scorn and subject of mischance![4]
50 Surely, by all the glory you have won,
An if I fly I am not Talbot's son.
Then talk no more of flight; it is no boot.°   *use; profit*
If son to Talbot, die at Talbot's foot.
TALBOT   Then follow thou thy desp'rate sire of Crete,
55 Thou Icarus;[5] thy life to me is sweet.
If thou wilt fight, fight by thy father's side,
And commendable proved, let's die in pride.   *Exeunt*

4.7

Alarum. Excursions. Enter old [Lord] TALBOT led
[by a SERVANT]

TALBOT   Where is my other life? Mine own is gone.
O where's young Talbot, where is valiant John?
Triumphant death smeared with captivity,°   *the blood of captives*
Young Talbot's valour makes me smile at thee.
5 When he perceived me shrink° and on my knee,   *weaken*
His bloody sword he brandished over me,
And like a hungry lion did commence
Rough deeds of rage and stern impatience.
But when my angry guardant° stood alone,   *protector*
10 Tend'ring° my ruin and assailed of none,   *Concerned for*

---

3. For the sake of that advantage (of safety).
4. To be an ashamed object of scorn and a victim of misfortune.
5. According to classical mythology, Icarus and his father, Daedalus, tried to escape imprisonment in Crete

using artificial wings of feathers and wax. Daedalus succeeded, but Icarus flew too close to the sun and died.
4.7 Location: Scene continues.

Dizzy-eyed fury and great rage of heart
Suddenly made him from my side to start
Into the clust'ring battle° of the French,   *crowded ranks*
And in that sea of blood my boy did drench°   *drown*
15   His over-mounting spirit; and there died
My Icarus, my blossom, in his pride.
        Enter [English soldiers] with John Talbot['s body], borne
SERVANT   O my dear lord, lo where your son is borne.
TALBOT   Thou antic° death, which laugh'st us here to scorn,   *grotesquely grinning*
Anon° from thy insulting tyranny,   *Soon*
20   Coupled in bonds of perpetuity,
Two Talbots wingèd through the lither° sky   *yielding*
In thy despite shall scape mortality.
        [*To* JOHN] O thou whose wounds become hard-favoured death,[1]
Speak to thy father ere thou yield thy breath.
25   Brave° death by speaking, whether he will or no;   *Defy*
Imagine him a Frenchman and thy foe.—
Poor boy, he smiles, methinks, as who° should say   *as one who*
'Had death been French, then death had died today'.
Come, come, and lay him in his father's arms.
        [*Soldiers lay* JOHN *in Talbot's arms*]
30   My spirit can no longer bear these harms.
Soldiers, adieu. I have what I would have,
Now my old arms are young John Talbot's grave.
        [*He*] *dies.* [*Alarum. Exeunt soldiers leaving the bodies*]
        Enter CHARLES [*the Dauphin, the dukes of*] ALENÇON
        [*and*] BURGUNDY, [*the*] BASTARD [*of Orléans*], *and* [JOAN
        la] Pucelle
CHARLES   Had York and Somerset brought rescue in,
We should have found a bloody day of this.
35   BASTARD   How the young whelp of Talbot's,[2] raging wood,° *mad*
Did flesh his puny sword[3] in Frenchmen's blood!
JOAN   Once I encountered[4] him, and thus I said:
'Thou maiden[5] youth, be vanquished by a maid.'
But with a proud, majestical high scorn
40   He answered thus: 'Young Talbot was not born
To be the pillage of a giglot° wench.'   *plunder of a wanton*
So rushing in the bowels° of the French,   *center*
He left me proudly, as unworthy fight.
BURGUNDY   Doubtless he would have made a noble knight.
45   See where he lies inhearsèd° in the arms   *(as in a coffin)*
Of the most bloody nurser of his harms.[6]
BASTARD   Hew them to pieces, hack their bones asunder,
Whose life was England's glory, Gallia's° wonder.   *France's*
CHARLES   O no, forbear; for that which we have fled
50   During the life, let us not wrong it dead.
        Enter [Sir William] LUCY [*with a French herald*]
LUCY   Herald, conduct me to the Dauphin's tent

---

1. Whose wounds make ugly death attractive.
2. The young puppy of Talbot's (John Talbot). The Bastard is punning on "talbot" as the name for a kind of hunting dog.
3. Plunged in his inexperienced sword for the first time, with a sexual wordplay: plunged in his inexperienced or diminutive penis for the first time.
4. Another bawdy pun: "encounter" may mean "to meet sexually."
5. Virginal; inexperienced in battle.
6. Person who taught him to harm his enemies; person who caused his injuries.

To know who hath obtained the glory of the day.
CHARLES   On what submissive message art thou sent?
LUCY   Submission, Dauphin? 'Tis a mere° French word.   *pure*
55   We English warriors wot° not what it means.   *know*
I come to know what prisoners thou hast ta'en,
And to survey the bodies of the dead.
CHARLES   For prisoners ask'st thou? Hell our prison is.[7]
But tell me whom thou seek'st.
60   LUCY   But where's the great Alcides[8] of the field,
Valiant Lord Talbot, Earl of Shrewsbury,
Created for his rare success in arms
Great Earl of Wexford, Waterford, and Valence,
Lord Talbot of Goodrich and Urchinfield,
65   Lord Strange of Blackmere, Lord Verdun of Alton,
Lord Cromwell of Wingfield, Lord Furnival of Sheffield,
The thrice victorious lord of Falconbridge,
Knight of the noble order of Saint George,
Worthy[9] Saint Michael and the Golden Fleece,
70   Great *Maréhal*° to Henry the Sixth   *commander in chief*
Of all his wars within the realm of France?
JOAN   Here's a silly, stately style° indeed.   *list of titles*
The Turk,° that two-and-fifty kingdoms hath,   *Sultan of Turkey*
Writes not so tedious a style as this.
75   Him that thou magnifi'st with all these titles
Stinking and flyblown° lies here at our feet.   *putrified*
LUCY   Is Talbot slain, the Frenchmen's only scourge,
Your kingdom's terror and black Nemesis?[1]
O, were mine eye-balls into bullets turned,
80   That I in rage might shoot them at your faces!
O, that I could but call these dead to life!—
It were enough to fright the realm of France.
Were but his picture left amongst you here
It would amaze° the proudest of you all.   *terrify*
85   Give me their bodies, that I may bear them hence
And give them burial as beseems° their worth.   *as is appropriate to*
JOAN [*to* CHARLES]   I think this upstart is old Talbot's ghost,
He speaks with such a proud commanding spirit.
For God's sake let him have them. To keep them here
90   They would but stink and putrefy the air.
CHARLES   Go, take their bodies hence.
LUCY   I'll bear them hence, but from their ashes shall be reared
A phoenix[2] that shall make all France afeard.
CHARLES   So we be rid of them, do with them what thou wilt.
                [*Exeunt* LUCY *and herald with the bodies*]
95   And now to Paris in this conquering vein.
All will be ours, now bloody Talbot's slain.   *Exeunt*

---

7. Charles implies that the French have killed their enemies (sent them to hell) rather than taking prisoners.
8. Hercules (a descendant of Alcaeus), the hero of
classical mythology, famous for performing difficult
feats of strength and bravery.
9. Worthy of; equal in value to. The Order of St.
Michael was a French chivalric order established in
1469, after the events of the play occurred. The Order
of the Golden Fleece was formed in Burgundy in 1430.
1. The Greek goddess of avenging justice.
2. A legendary bird that was said to live five hundred
years, burn itself to ashes, and then be reborn from the
ashes.

5.1

Sennet. Enter KING [HENRY, *the Dukes of*]
GLOUCESTER, *and* EXETER [*and others*]

KING HENRY [*to* GLOUCESTER]   Have you perused the letters from the Pope,
    The Emperor, and the Earl of Armagnac?
GLOUCESTER   I have, my lord, and their intent is this:
    They humbly sue unto your excellence
5   To have a godly peace concluded of
    Between the realms of England and of France.
KING HENRY   How doth your grace affect their motion?°   *like their proposal*
GLOUCESTER   Well, my good lord, and as the only means
    To stop effusion° of our Christian blood   *spilling*
10   And 'stablish quietness on every side.
KING HENRY   Ay, marry, uncle; for I always thought
    It was both impious and unnatural
    That such immanity° and bloody strife   *barbarity*
    Should reign among professors of one faith.
15 GLOUCESTER   Beside, my lord, the sooner to effect
    And surer bind this knot of amity,
    The Earl of Armagnac, near knit° to Charles—   *closely related*
    A man of great authority in France—
    Proffers his only daughter to your grace
20   In marriage, with a large and sumptuous dowry.
KING HENRY   Marriage, uncle? Alas, my years are young,
    And fitter is my study and my books
    Than wanton dalliance with a paramour.
    Yet call th'ambassadors,   [*Exit one or more*]
             and as you please,
25   So let them have their answers every one.
    I shall be well content with any choice
    Tends° to God's glory and my country's weal.°   *That tends / welfare*
    Enter [*the Bishop of*] WINCHESTER, [*now in cardinal's*
    habit,] *and three ambassadors* [*one a Papal* LEGATE]
EXETER [*aside*]   What, is my lord of Winchester installed
    And called unto a cardinal's degree?
30   Then I perceive that will be verified
    Henry the Fifth did sometime° prophesy: *at one time*
    'If once he come to be a cardinal,
    He'll make his cap° co-equal with the crown.'   *(a cardinal's red hat)*
KING HENRY   My lords ambassadors, your several suits
35   Have been considered and debated on.
    Your purpose is both good and reasonable,
    And therefore are we certainly resolved
    To draw° conditions of a friendly peace,   *draft*
    Which by my lord of Winchester we mean
40   Shall be transported presently to France.
GLOUCESTER [*to ambassadors*]   And for the proffer of my lord your master,
    I have informed his highness so at large°   *in full*
    As,° liking of the lady's virtuous gifts,   *That*
    Her beauty, and the value of her dower,
45   He doth intend she shall be England's queen.

5.1 Location: The palace, London.

KING HENRY [*to ambassadors*] In argument° and proof of which   *As evidence*
    contract
  Bear her this jewel, pledge of my affection.
  [*To* GLOUCESTER] And so, my lord Protector, see them guarded
  And safely brought to Dover, wherein shipped,°   *where once embarked*
50 Commit them to the fortune of the sea.
             Exeunt [*severally all but* WINCHESTER *and* LEGATE]
WINCHESTER Stay, my lord legate; you shall first receive
  The sum of money which I promisèd
  Should be delivered to his holiness
  For clothing me in these grave ornaments.°   *solemn robes of office*
55 LEGATE I will attend upon your lordship's leisure.   [*Exit*][1]
WINCHESTER Now Winchester will not submit, I trow,°   *trust*
  Or be inferior to the proudest peer.
  Humphrey of Gloucester, thou shalt well perceive
  That nor° in birth or for authority   *neither*
60 The Bishop will be overborne° by thee.   *overruled*
  I'll either make thee stoop and bend thy knee,
  Or sack this country with a mutiny.°   *Exit*   *an open revolt*

5.2

Enter CHARLES [*the Dauphin reading a letter,*
the Dukes of] BURGUNDY [*and*] ALENÇON, [*the*]
BASTARD [*of Orléans*], RENÉ [*Duke of Anjou*], *and* JOAN
[*la Pucelle*]

CHARLES These news, my lords, may cheer our drooping spirits.
  'Tis said the stout° Parisians do revolt   *valiant*
  And turn again unto the warlike French.
ALENÇON Then march to Paris, royal Charles of France,
5 And keep not back your powers in dalliance.°   *idleness*
JOAN Peace be amongst them if they turn to us;
  Else, ruin combat with their palaces![1]
             Enter [*a*] SCOUT
SCOUT Success unto our valiant general,
  And happiness to his accomplices.°   *allies*
10 CHARLES What tidings send our scouts? I prithee speak.
SCOUT The English army, that divided was
  Into two parties, is now conjoined in one,[2]
  And means to give you battle presently.°   *immediately*
CHARLES Somewhat too sudden, sirs, the warning is;
15 But we will presently provide for them.
BURGUNDY I trust the ghost of Talbot is not there.
JOAN Now he is gone, my lord, you need not fear.[3]
  Of all base passions, fear is most accursed.
  Command the conquest, Charles, it shall be thine
20 Let Henry fret and all the world repine.°   *complain*
CHARLES Then on, my lords; and France be fortunate! *Exeunt*

---

1. The legate may leave at this point, but there is no
exit marked in F. He may simply step to the side while
Winchester makes his final speech and then exit with
the prelate.

5.2 Location: Plains in Anjou, France.
1. Otherwise, let ruin destroy their palaces.
2. In other words, York and Suffolk have joined forces.
3. F assigns this line to Burgundy.

5.3

Alarum. Excursions. Enter JOAN *[la] Pucelle*

JOAN   The Regent° conquers, and the Frenchmen fly.   *(Richard Duke of York)*

Now help, ye charming° spells and periapts,°   *magic / amulets*

And ye choice spirits that admonish° me   *forewarn*

And give me signs of future accidents.°   *events*

     Thunder

5   You speedy helpers, that are substitutes°   *deputies*

Under the lordly monarch of the north,[1]

Appear, and aid me in this enterprise.

     Enter Fiends

This speed and quick appearance argues° proof   *offers*

Of your accustomed° diligence to me.   *customary*

10   Now, ye familiar spirits[2] that are culled

Out of the powerful regions under earth,

Help me this once, that France may get the field.°   *win the battle*

     They walk and speak not

O, hold me not with silence overlong!

Where I was wont to feed you with my blood,[3]

15   I'll lop a member° off and give it you   *limb*

In earnest° of a further benefit,   *As an advance payment*

So you do condescend to help me now.

     They hang their heads

No hope to have redress? My body shall

Pay recompense if you will grant my suit.

     They shake their heads

20   Cannot my body nor blood-sacrifice

Entreat you to your wonted furtherance?°   *usual assistance*

Then take my soul—my body, soul, and all—

Before that England give the French the foil.°   *defeat*

     They depart

See, they forsake me. Now the time is come

25   That France must vail her lofty-plumèd crest[4]

And let her head fall into England's lap.

My ancient° incantations are too weak,   *former*

And hell too strong for me to buckle° with.   *fight; do combat*

Now, France, thy glory droopeth to the dust.   *Exit*

5.4

Excursions. [The Dukes of] BURGUNDY *and* YORK *fight
hand to hand. [The] French fly. [*JOAN *la Pucelle
is taken]*

RICHARD DUKE OF YORK   Damsel of France, I think I have you fast.

Unchain your spirits now with spelling° charms,   *conjuring*

And try if they can gain your liberty.

A goodly prize, fit for the devil's grace![1]

5   [*To his soldiers*] See how the ugly witch doth bend her brows,°   *scowls*

As if with Circe[2] she would change my shape.

5.3 Location: Before Angiers (i.e., Angers), France.
1. The devil and his demons were frequently associated with the north.
2. Attendant spirits that could be summoned by a witch; often they inhabited the bodies of animals.
3. Witches were thought to have extra nipples with which they fed their familiars, or attendant spirits.

4. Must lower her high-feathered helmet.
5.4 Location: Scene continues.
1. Fit for his grace, the devil (said sarcastically).
2. According to Greek mythology, a witch who seduced Odysseus and turned his men into swine (see Homer, *Odyssey* 10).

JOAN   Changed to a worser shape thou canst not be.

RICHARD DUKE OF YORK   O, Charles the Dauphin is a proper° man. *handsome*
No shape but his can please your dainty° eye. *fastidious*

10 JOAN   A plaguing mischief light on Charles and thee,
And may ye both be suddenly surprised
By bloody hands in° sleeping on your beds! *while*

RICHARD DUKE OF YORK   Fell banning° hag, enchantress, hold *Fierce cursing*
thy tongue.

JOAN   I prithee give me leave to curse awhile.

RICHARD DUKE OF YORK   Curse, miscreant,° when thou comest *heretic*
15 to the stake. *Exeunt*

5.5

Alarum. Enter [the Earl of] SUFFOLK *with* MARGARET
in his hand° *led by the hand*

SUFFOLK   Be what thou wilt, thou art my prisoner.
[*He*] *gazes on her*
O fairest beauty, do not fear nor fly,
For I will touch thee but with reverent hands,
And lay them gently on thy tender side.
5 I kiss these fingers for eternal peace.
Who art thou? Say, that I may honour thee.

MARGARET   Margaret my name, and daughter to a king,
The King of Naples,[1] whosoe'er thou art.

SUFFOLK   An earl I am, and Suffolk am I called.
10 Be not offended, nature's miracle,
Thou art allotted° to be ta'en by me. *destined*
So doth the swan his downy cygnets save,° *young swans protect*
Keeping them prisoner underneath his wings.
Yet if this servile usage° once offend, *treatment as a slave*
15 Go, and be free again, as Suffolk's friend.
She is going
O stay! [*Aside*] I have no power to let her pass.
My hand would free her, but my heart says no.
As plays the sun upon the glassy stream,
Twinkling another counterfeited° beam, *reflected*
20 So seems this gorgeous beauty to mine eyes.
Fain would I woo her, yet I dare not speak.
I'll call for pen and ink, and write my mind.
Fie, de la Pole,[2] disable° not thyself! *disparage*
Hast not a tongue? Is she not here to hear?
25 Wilt thou be daunted at a woman's sight?[3]
Ay, beauty's princely majesty is such
Confounds° the tongue, and makes the senses rough.° *That it confuses / dull*

MARGARET   Say, Earl of Suffolk—if thy name be so—
What ransom must I pay before I pass?
30 For I perceive I am thy prisoner.

SUFFOLK [*aside*]   How canst thou tell she will deny° thy suit *refuse*

5.5 Location: Scene continues.
1. That is, the René of earlier scenes, Duke of Anjou
and also titular King of Naples and Sicily.

2. Suffolk's family name.
3. At the sight of a woman; at a woman's gaze.

Before thou make a trial of her love?

MARGARET   Why speak'st thou not? What ransom must I pay?

SUFFOLK [*aside*]   She's beautiful, and therefore to be wooed;

35   She is a woman, therefore to be won.

MARGARET   Wilt thou accept of ransom, yea or no?

SUFFOLK [*aside*]   Fond° man, remember that thou hast a wife;   *Foolish*

Then how can Margaret be thy paramour?°   *mistress*

MARGARET [*aside*]   I were best to leave him, for he will not hear.

40 SUFFOLK [*aside*]   There° all is marred; there lies a cooling card.[4]   *By that fact*

MARGARET [*aside*]   He talks at random; sure the man is mad.

SUFFOLK [*aside*]   And yet a dispensation[5] may be had.

MARGARET   And yet I would that you would answer me.

SUFFOLK [*aside*]   I'll win this Lady Margaret. For whom?

45   Why, for my king—tush, that's a wooden[6] thing.

MARGARET [*aside*]   He talks of wood. It is some carpenter.

SUFFOLK [*aside*]   Yet so my fancy° may be satisfied,   *love*

And peace establishèd between these realms.

But there remains a scruple° in that too,   *an objection*

50   For though her father be the King of Naples,

Duke of Anjou and Maine, yet is he poor,

And our nobility will scorn the match.

MARGARET   Hear ye, captain? Are you not at leisure?

SUFFOLK [*aside*]   It shall be so, disdain they ne'er so much.

55   Henry is youthful, and will quickly yield.

[*To* MARGARET] Madam, I have a secret to reveal.

MARGARET [*aside*]   What though I be enthralled,° he seems a knight   *taken captive*

And will not any way dishonour me.

SUFFOLK   Lady, vouchsafe to listen° what I say.   *listen to*

60 MARGARET [*aside*]   Perhaps I shall be rescued by the French,

And then I need not crave his courtesy.

SUFFOLK   Sweet madam, give me hearing in a cause.

MARGARET [*aside*]   Tush, women have been captivate[7] ere now.

SUFFOLK   Lady, wherefore talk you so?

65 MARGARET   I cry you mercy, 'tis but *quid* for *quo*.°   *tit for tat*

SUFFOLK   Say, gentle Princess, would you not suppose

Your bondage happy to be° made a queen?   *if you were to be*

MARGARET   To be a queen in bondage is more vile

Than is a slave in base servility,°   *slavery*

For princes should be free.

70 SUFFOLK   And so shall you,

If happy England's royal king be free.

MARGARET   Why, what concerns his freedom unto me?

SUFFOLK   I'll undertake to make thee Henry's queen,

To put a golden sceptre in thy hand,

75   And set a precious crown upon thy head,

If thou wilt condescend° to be my—   *agree*

MARGARET   What?

SUFFOLK   His love.

MARGARET   I am unworthy to be Henry's wife.

---

4. An obstacle; literally, a card that, when played, dashes the hopes of one's opponent.
5. Special permission from the Pope to dissolve a marriage.
6. Stupid (referring either to King Henry or to his own scheme to woo Margaret).
7. Have been taken prisoner; have fallen in love against their will.

SUFFOLK   No, gentle madam, I unworthy am
80   To woo so fair a dame to be his wife
        [*Aside*] And have no portion° in the choice myself.—   *share*
        How say you, madam; are ye so content?
MARGARET   An if my father please, I am content.
SUFFOLK   Then call our captains and our colours forth,
            [*Enter captains, colours, and trumpeters*]
85   And, madam, at your father's castle walls
        We'll crave a parley to confer with him.
            Sound [*a parley*]. *Enter* RENÉ [*Duke of Anjou*]
            on the walls
        See, René, see thy daughter prisoner.
RENÉ   To whom?
SUFFOLK   To me.
RENÉ   Suffolk, what remedy?
        I am a soldier, and unapt° to weep   *unsuited*
90   Or to exclaim on° fortune's fickleness.   *complain of*
SUFFOLK   Yes, there is remedy enough, my lord.
        Assent, and for thy honour give consent
        Thy daughter shall be wedded to my king,
        Whom I with pain have wooed and won thereto;
95   And this her easy-held° imprisonment   *easily endured*
        Hath gained thy daughter princely liberty.
RENÉ   Speaks Suffolk as he thinks?
SUFFOLK   Fair Margaret knows
        That Suffolk doth not flatter, face° or feign.   *deceive*
RENÉ   Upon thy princely warrant° I descend   *guarantee*
100   To give thee answer of thy just demand.
SUFFOLK   And here I will expect° thy coming.   *await*
                              [*Exit* RENÉ *above*]
            Trumpets sound. Enter RENÉ
RENÉ   Welcome, brave Earl, into our territories.
        Command in Anjou what your honour pleases.
SUFFOLK   Thanks, René, happy for° so sweet a child,   *fortunate in having*
105   Fit to be made companion with a king.
        What answer makes your grace unto my suit?
RENÉ   Since thou dost deign to woo her little worth
        To be the princely bride of such a lord,
        Upon condition I may quietly
110   Enjoy mine own, the countries Maine and Anjou,
        Free from oppression or the stroke of war,
        My daughter shall be Henry's, if he please.
SUFFOLK   That is her ransom. I deliver her,
        And those two counties° I will undertake   *domains of a count*
115   Your grace shall well and quietly enjoy.
RENÉ   And I again° in Henry's royal name,   *in return*
        As deputy unto that gracious king,
        Give thee her hand for sign of plighted faith.°   *a marriage pledge*
SUFFOLK   René of France, I give thee kingly thanks,
120   Because this is in traffic° of a king.   *business*
        [*Aside*] And yet methinks I could be well content
        To be mine own attorney in this case.[8]
        [*To* RENÉ] I'll over then to England with this news,

8. To act on my own behalf in this instance, with a pun on "case" as slang for "vagina."

And make this marriage to be solemnized.
125   So farewell, René; set this diamond safe
In golden palaces, as it becomes.°   *as befits it*
RENÉ   I do embrace thee as I would embrace
The Christian prince King Henry, were he here.
MARGARET [*to* SUFFOLK]   Farewell, my lord. Good wishes, praise, and prayers
130   Shall Suffolk ever have of Margaret.
            She is going
SUFFOLK   Farewell, sweet madam; but hark you, Margaret—
No princely commendations° to my king?   *greetings*
MARGARET   Such commendations as becomes a maid,
A virgin, and his servant, say to him.
135   SUFFOLK   Words sweetly placed, and modestly directed.
            [*She is going*]
But madam, I must trouble you again—
No loving token to his majesty?
MARGARET   Yes, my good lord: a pure unspotted heart,
Never yet taint° with love, I send the King.   *tinged*
140   SUFFOLK   And this withal.°   *in addition*
            [*He*] kiss[*es*] *her*
MARGARET   That for thyself; I will not so presume
To send such peevish° tokens to a king.   *trifling*
            [*Exeunt* RENÉ *and* MARGARET]
SUFFOLK [*aside*]   O, wert thou for myself!—but Suffolk, stay.
Thou mayst not wander in that labyrinth.[9]
145   There Minotaurs and ugly treasons lurk.
Solicit° Henry with her wondrous praise.   *Entice*
Bethink thee on her virtues that surmount,
Mad° natural graces that extinguish° art.   *Extravagant / eclipse*
Repeat their semblance[1] often on the seas,
150   That when thou com'st to kneel at Henry's feet
Thou mayst bereave° him of his wits with wonder.   *Exeunt*   *dispossess*

5.6

            Enter [RICHARD DUKE OF] YORK, [*the Earl of*]
            WARWICK, [*and a*] SHEPHERD
RICHARD DUKE OF YORK   Bring forth that sorceress condemned
    to burn.
            [*Enter* JOAN la Pucelle *guarded*][1]
SHEPHERD   Ah, Joan, this kills thy father's heart outright.
Have I sought° every country far and near,   *searched*
And now it is my chance to find thee out°   *discover you*
5   Must I behold thy timeless° cruel death?   *untimely*
Ah Joan, sweet daughter Joan, I'll die with thee.
JOAN   Decrepit miser,° base ignoble wretch,   *miserable person*
I am descended of a gentler° blood.   *more aristocratic*
Thou art no father nor no friend° of mine.   *kinsman*
10   SHEPHERD   Out, out!—My lords, an't please you, 'tis not so.

---

9. A maze built by Daedalus for King Minos of Crete, who kept in it the Minotaur (a monster born from Queen Pasiphaë's sexual encounter with a bull).
1. Recall the image or description of her virtues.
5.6 Location: Camp of the Duke of York, France.

1. In F, Joan is included in the list of those who enter at the beginning of this scene, but it makes sense to have her enter after York commands that she be brought forth.

I did beget her, all the parish knows.
Her mother liveth yet, can testify
She was the first fruit of my bach'lorship.[2]

WARWICK [*to* JOAN]   Graceless,° wilt thou deny thy parentage?   *Depraved person*

RICHARD DUKE OF YORK   This argues° what her kind of life hath   *testifies to*
been—
Wicked and vile; and so her death concludes.°   *confirms; ends*

SHEPHERD   Fie, Joan, that thou wilt be so obstacle.[3]
God knows thou art a collop° of my flesh,   *slice*
And for thy sake have I shed many a tear.
Deny me not, I prithee, gentle Joan.

JOAN   Peasant, avaunt! [*To the English*] You have suborned[4] this man
Of purpose to obscure my noble birth.

SHEPHERD [*to the English*]   'Tis true I gave a noble[5] to the priest
The morn that I was wedded to her mother.
[*To* JOAN] Kneel down, and take my blessing, good my girl.
Wilt thou not stoop? Now cursèd be the time
Of thy nativity. I would the milk
Thy mother gave thee when thou sucked'st her breast
Had been a little ratsbane° for thy sake.   *rat poison*
Or else, when thou didst keep° my lambs afield,   *tend*
I wish some ravenous wolf had eaten thee.
Dost thou deny thy father, cursèd drab?°   *whore*
[*To the English*] O burn her, burn her! Hanging is too good.

Exit

RICHARD DUKE OF YORK [*to guards*]   Take her away, for she hath
lived too long,
To fill the world with vicious qualities.

JOAN   First let me tell you whom you have condemned:
Not one begotten of a shepherd swain,
But issued from the progeny of kings;
Virtuous and holy, chosen from above
By inspiration of celestial grace
To work exceeding° miracles on earth.   *exceptional*
I never had to do with wicked spirits;
But you that are polluted with your lusts,
Stained with the guiltless blood of innocents,
Corrupt and tainted with a thousand vices—
Because you want° the grace that others have,   *lack*
You judge it straight° a thing impossible   *immediately*
To compass° wonders but by help of devils.   *accomplish*
No, misconceivèd[6] Joan of Arc hath been
A virgin from her tender infancy,
Chaste and immaculate in very thought,
Whose maiden-blood thus rigorously effused°   *cruelly shed*
Will cry for vengeance at the gates of heaven.

RICHARD DUKE OF YORK   Ay, ay, [*to guards*] away with her to execution.

WARWICK [*to guards*]   And hark ye, sirs: because she is a maid,
Spare for no faggots. Let there be enough.

---

2. The first child I had as an unmarried man.
3. Obstinate. This use of "obstacle" suggests the
shepherd's country dialect.
4. Hired to give false evidence.

5. English gold coin worth about one-third of a
pound.
6. Misunderstood, with a pun on "misconceived" as
"miscreated in the womb."

Place barrels of pitch upon the fatal stake,
That so her torture may be shortenèd.[7]

JOAN Will nothing turn° your unrelenting hearts?   *change*
60   Then Joan, discover° thine infirmity,   *reveal*
        That warranteth by law to be thy privilege:[8]
        I am with child, ye bloody homicides.
        Murder not then the fruit within my womb,
        Although ye hale° me to a violent death.   *drag*
RICHARD DUKE OF YORK Now heaven forfend—the holy maid
65   with child?
WARWICK [*to* JOAN] The greatest miracle that e'er ye wrought.
        Is all your strict preciseness° come to this?   *propriety*
RICHARD DUKE OF YORK She and the Dauphin have been
            ingling.°   *having sex; dallying*
        I did imagine° what would be her refuge.°   *wonder / last defense*
70 WARWICK Well, go to, we will have no bastards live,
        Especially since Charles must father it.
JOAN You are deceived. My child is none of his.
        It was Alençon[9] that enjoyed my love.
RICHARD DUKE OF YORK Alençon, that notorious Machiavel?[1]
75   It dies an if it had a thousand lives.
JOAN O give me leave, I have deluded you.
        'Twas neither Charles nor yet the Duke I named,
        But René King of Naples that prevailed.
WARWICK A married man?—That's most intolerable.
80 RICHARD DUKE OF YORK Why, here's a girl; I think she knows not well—
        There were so many—whom she may accuse.
WARWICK It's sign she hath been liberal° and free.   *generous; promiscuous*
RICHARD DUKE OF YORK And yet forsooth she is a virgin pure!
        [*To* JOAN] Strumpet, thy words condemn thy brat and thee.
85   Use no entreaty, for it is in vain.
JOAN Then lead me hence; with whom I leave my curse.
        May never glorious sun reflex° his beams   *throw*
        Upon the country where you make abode,
        But darkness and the gloomy shade of death
90   Environ you till mischief° and despair   *misfortune*
        Drive you to break your necks or hang yourselves.
            Enter [*the Bishop of* WINCHESTER, *now*] *Cardinal*
RICHARD DUKE OF YORK [*to* JOAN] Break thou in pieces, and
            consume° to ashes,   *burn away*
        Thou foul accursèd minister of hell.   [*Exit* JOAN, *guarded*]
WINCHESTER Lord Regent, I do greet your excellence
95   With letters of commission from the King.
        For know, my lords, the states of Christendom,
        Moved with remorse of° these outrageous broils,   *pity for*
        Have earnestly implored a general peace
        Betwixt our nation and the aspiring French,

---

7. The orders for wood and pitch are meant to ensure either that Joan will die quickly as a result of asphyxiation from the smoke, rather than from the flames themselves, or that she will die swiftly from the intensity of the fire.
8. The legal right of a pregnant woman to postpone her

execution until after she has given birth.
9. Jean, second Duke of Alençon, was cousin to Charles, the Dauphin.
1. Scheming politician. Niccolò Machiavelli (1469–1527), author of *The Prince*, became associated with principles of cunning statecraft.

100   And here at hand the Dauphin and his train
    Approacheth to confer about some matter.
  RICHARD DUKE OF YORK   Is all our travail° turned to this effect?   *labor*
    After the slaughter of so many peers,
    So many captains, gentlemen, and soldiers
105   That in this quarrel have been overthrown
    And sold their bodies for their country's benefit,
    Shall we at last conclude effeminate peace?
    Have we not lost most part of all the towns
    By treason, falsehood, and by treachery,
110   Our great progenitors had conquerèd?
    O Warwick, Warwick, I foresee with grief
    The utter loss of all the realm of France!
  WARWICK   Be patient, York. If we conclude a peace
    It shall be with such strict and severe covenants
115   As° little shall the Frenchmen gain thereby.   *That*
      Enter CHARLES [*the Dauphin, the Duke of*] ALENÇON,
      [*the*] BASTARD [*of Orléans, and*] RENÉ [*Duke of Anjou*]
  CHARLES   Since, lords of England, it is thus agreed
    That peaceful truce shall be proclaimed in France
    We come to be informèd by yourselves
    What the conditions of that league° must be.   *treaty*
120   RICHARD DUKE OF YORK   Speak, Winchester; for boiling choler° chokes   *anger*
    The hollow passage of my poisoned voice
    By sight of these our baleful° enemies.   *deadly*
  WINCHESTER   Charles and the rest, it is enacted thus:
    That, in regard° King Henry gives consent,   *since*
125   Of mere° compassion and of lenity,°   *Out of pure / mildness*
    To ease your country of distressful war
    And suffer° you to breathe in fruitful peace,   *allow*
    You shall become true liegemen[2] to his crown.
    And, Charles, upon condition thou wilt swear
130   To pay him tribute and submit thyself,
    Thou shalt be placed as viceroy under him,
    And still enjoy thy regal dignity.
  ALENÇON   Must he be then as shadow of himself?—
    Adorn his temples with a coronet,[3]
135   And yet in substance and authority
    Retain but privilege of a private man?
    This proffer is absurd and reasonless.
  CHARLES   'Tis known already that I am possessed
    With more than half the Gallian° territories,   *French*
140   And therein reverenced for their lawful king.
    Shall I, for lucre° of the rest° unvanquished,   *gain / rest that are*
    Detract so much from that prerogative
    As to be called but° viceroy of the whole?   *merely*
    No, lord ambassador, I'll rather keep
145   That which I have than, coveting for more,
    Be cast° from possibility of all.   *excluded*
  RICHARD DUKE OF YORK   Insulting Charles, hast thou by secret means
    Used intercession to obtain a league

---

2. Those bound to serve a feudal lord; faithful subjects.   3. Small crown worn by nobles.

	And, now the matter grows to compromise,°	*toward resolution*
150	Stand'st thou aloof upon comparison?[4]	
	Either accept the title thou usurp'st,	
	Of benefit° proceeding from our king	*As a benefaction*
	And not of any challenge of desert,[5]	
	Or we will plague thee with incessant wars.	
155	RENÉ [*aside to* CHARLES] My lord, you do not well in obstinacy	
	To cavil[6] in the course of this contract.	
	If once it be neglected,° ten to one	*disregarded*
	We shall not find like opportunity.	
	ALENÇON [*aside to* CHARLES] To say the truth, it is your policy°	*astute course*
160	To save your subjects from such massacre	
	And ruthless slaughters as are daily seen	
	By our proceeding in hostility;	
	And therefore take this compact of a truce,	
	Although you break it when your pleasure serves.	
165	WARWICK How sayst thou, Charles? Shall our condition stand?	
	CHARLES It shall,	
	Only reserved° you claim no interest	*With the reservation*
	In any of our towns of garrison.°	*fortified towns*
	RICHARD DUKE OF YORK Then swear allegiance to his majesty,	
170	As thou art knight, never to disobey	
	Nor be rebellious to the crown of England,	
	Thou nor thy nobles, to the crown of England.	
	[*They swear*]	
	So, now dismiss your army when ye please.	
	Hang up your ensigns, let your drums be still;	
175	For here we entertain a solemn peace. *Exeunt*	

5.7

Enter [the Earl of] SUFFOLK, *in conference with* KING
[HENRY, *and the Dukes of*] GLOUCESTER *and* EXETER

	KING HENRY [*to* SUFFOLK] Your wondrous rare description, noble Earl,	
	Of beauteous Margaret hath astonished me.	
	Her virtues gracèd with external gifts	
	Do breed love's settled° passions in my heart,	*unchanging*
5	And like as rigour° of tempestuous gusts	*violent force*
	Provokes° the mightiest hulk° against the tide,	*Drives / ship*
	So am I driven by breath of her renown°	*word of her fame*
	Either to suffer shipwreck or arrive	
	Where I may have fruition of her love.	
10	SUFFOLK Tush, my good lord, this superficial tale	
	Is but a preface of her worthy praise.°	*the praise she deserves*
	The chief perfections of that lovely dame,	
	Had I sufficient skill to utter them,	
	Would make a volume of enticing lines	
15	Able to ravish any dull conceit;°	*imagination*
	And, which is more, she is not so divine,	
	So full° replete with choice of all delights,	*fully*
	But with as humble lowliness of mind	
	She is content to be at your command—	

---

4. Do you hold off in order to quibble about the terms?   6. To raise frivolous objections.
5. And not by any claim of inherent right.   **5.7** Location: The palace, London.

20   Command, I mean, of virtuous chaste intents,
    To love and honour Henry as her lord.
  KING HENRY   And otherwise will Henry ne'er presume.
    [*To* GLOUCESTER] Therefore, my lord Protector, give consent
    That Marg'ret may be England's royal queen.
25   GLOUCESTER   So should I give consent to flatter sin.
    You know, my lord, your highness is betrothed
    Unto another lady of esteem.[1]
    How shall we then dispense with that contract
    And not deface your honour with reproach?
30   SUFFOLK   As doth a ruler with unlawful oaths,
    Or one that, at a triumph[2] having vowed
    To try his strength, forsaketh yet the lists[3]
    By reason of his adversary's odds.
    A poor earl's daughter is unequal odds,
35   And therefore may be broke[4] without offence.
  GLOUCESTER   Why, what, I pray, is Margaret more than that?
    Her father is no better than an earl,
    Although in glorious titles he excel.
  SUFFOLK   Yes, my lord; her father is a king,
40   The King of Naples and Jerusalem,
    And of such great authority in France
    As his alliance will confirm our peace
    And keep the Frenchmen in allegiance.
  GLOUCESTER   And so the Earl of Armagnac may do,
45   Because he is near kinsman unto Charles.
  EXETER   Beside, his wealth doth warrant° a liberal dower,   *guarantee*
    Where René sooner will receive than give.
  SUFFOLK   A dower, my lords? Disgrace not so your King
    That he should be so abject, base, and poor
50   To choose for wealth and not for perfect love.
    Henry is able to enrich his queen,
    And not to seek a queen to make him rich.
    So worthless peasants bargain for their wives,
    As market men for oxen, sheep, or horse.
55   Marriage is a matter of more worth
    Than to be dealt in by attorneyship.°   *proxy*
    Not whom *we* will but whom his grace affects°   *desires*
    Must be companion of his nuptial bed.
    And therefore, lords, since he affects her most,
60   That most of all these reasons bindeth us:
    In our opinions she should be preferred.
    For what is wedlock forcèd° but a hell,   *enforced marriage*
    An age of discord and continual strife,
    Whereas the contrary bringeth bliss,
65   And is a pattern° of celestial peace.   *an example*
    Whom should we match with Henry, being a king,
    But Margaret, that is daughter to a king?
    Her peerless feature° joinèd with her birth°   *form / high rank*
    Approves her° fit for none but for a king.   *Confirms that she is*
70   Her valiant courage and undaunted spirit,

---

1. The daughter of the Earl of Armagnac (see 5.1.15–20).
2. Tournament or combat between two opponents on horseback and armed with lances.
3. *forsaketh yet the lists:* nevertheless leaves the tournament grounds
4. That is, the marriage pledge may be broken.

More than in women commonly is seen,
Will answer our hope in issue of a king.[5]
For Henry, son unto a conqueror,
Is likely to beget more conquerors
75 If with a lady of so high resolve°   *determination*
As is fair Margaret he be linked in love.
Then yield, my lords, and here conclude with me:
That Margaret shall be queen, and none but she.
KING HENRY   Whether it be through force of your report,
80 My noble lord of Suffolk, or for that°   *or because*
My tender youth was never yet attaint°   *infected*
With any passion of inflaming love,
I cannot tell; but this I am assured:
I feel such sharp dissension in my breast,
85 Such fierce alarums° both of hope and fear,   *alarms*
As I am sick with working of my thoughts.
Take therefore shipping; post,° my lord, to France;   *hasten*
Agree to any covenants, and procure
That Lady Margaret do vouchsafe° to come   *promise*
90 To cross the seas to England and be crowned
King Henry's faithful and anointed queen.
For your expenses and sufficient charge,°   *money to spend*
Among the people gather up a tenth.[6]
Be gone, I say; for till you do return
95 I rest perplexèd° with a thousand cares.   *I remain troubled*
[*To* GLOUCESTER] And you, good uncle, banish all offence.°   *hostility*
If you do censure me by what you were,[7]
Not what you are, I know it will excuse
This sudden execution of my will.
100 And so conduct me where from° company   *away from*
I may revolve and ruminate my grief.[8]   *Exit* [*with* EXETER]
GLOUCESTER   Ay, grief, I fear me, both at first and last.   *Exit*
SUFFOLK   Thus Suffolk hath prevailed, and thus he goes
As did the youthful Paris[9] once to Greece,
105 With hope to find the like event° in love,   *the same outcome*
But prosper better than the Trojan did.
Margaret shall now be queen and rule the King;
But I will rule both her, the King, and realm.   *Exit*

---

5. Will satisfy our hopes by bringing forth a king.
6. A tax of 10 percent on income or property.
7. If you judge me by how you behaved when you were young.
8. I may return again and again in my mind to my grief.

9. According to Greek mythology, Paris went to Greece from Troy and abducted Helen, the wife of Menelaus. This act was said to have brought about the Trojan War, in which Paris was killed.

Richard III

Among the very few anecdotes about Shakespeare that date from his own lifetime is a ribald story recorded in 1602 in the diary of a London law student, John Manningham:

> Upon a time when Burbage played Richard III there was a citizen grew so far in liking with him, that before she went from the play she appointed him to come that night unto her by the name of Richard III. Shakespeare, overhearing their conclusion, went before, was entertained and at his game ere Burbage came. The message being brought that Richard III was at the door, Shakespeare caused return to be made that William the Conqueror was before Richard III.

Like most stories about celebrities, this one probably says more about those who circulated it than about those it describes. But it does at least suggest that Richard Burbage, the famous actor who first played Richard III (as well as such parts as Romeo and Hamlet), had not by virtue of his villainous role lost all of his glamour. Indeed, it is striking that Richard—the "elvish-marked, abortive, rooting hog" (1.3.225), the "poisonous bunch-backed toad" (1.3.244), the heartless cur sent, as he himself puts it, "deformed" and "unfinished" (1.1.20) into the world—has seemed weirdly and compellingly attractive to generations of playgoers. From the start, the play seems to have aroused intense interest: first performed in 1592 or 1593, *Richard III* was published in quarto no fewer than five times during Shakespeare's lifetime.

What can account for this attraction? It is not an obvious feature in the chronicle histories upon which Shakespeare relied, nor does Richard seem to have a comparable allure in another play of unknown authorship that dates from the same period, *The True Tragedy of Richard III*. In these works, Richard figures as the pitiless, treacherous villain of what has been called the "Tudor Myth"—that is, the officially sanctioned account of the origin and legitimacy of the Tudor dynasty. That dynasty was founded by Henry, Earl of Richmond, who defeated Richard III at the Battle of Bosworth Field (1485), reigned until his death in 1509 as Henry VII, and was the grandfather of Queen Elizabeth (1533–1603). It is hardly surprising that the new regime, whose claim to the throne was somewhat shaky, would wish to discredit the old. Modern historians emphasize Richard's solid administrative skills; Tudor apologists depict Richard not merely as venal or unscrupulous but as a monster of evil, a creature whose moral viciousness was vividly stamped on his twisted body.

The principal literary source for this spectacularly partisan depiction was not a piece of simple propaganda but an unusually subtle and complex *History of King Richard the Third* (c. 1513) by the great humanist Thomas More. Later sixteenth-century historians, notably Edward Halle in *The Union of the Two Noble and Illustre Famelies of Lancastre & Yorke* (1548) and Raphael Holinshed in *The Chronicles of England, Scotland, and Ireland* (1577, revised in 1587), followed closely in More's wake, repeating many of the details that Shakespeare in turn borrowed: Richard's habit of gnawing his lip, for example, or his restlessness, or the rumor that he was born with teeth. More and his followers deftly interwove three distinct explanatory accounts of Richard's behavior: political, psychological, and metaphysical. As a politician (a word with nasty connotations in the Renaissance), More's Richard is a particularly cunning player in a corrupt world, a schemer plotting to seize power and destroy all real or potential rivals. Psychologically, he is a strange blend of courage, wit, skillful dissembling, and fathomless malice. And on the metaphysical plane, he is a horrible instrument of God's wrath, a virtual devil incarnate.

Most sixteenth-century historians and chroniclers were, by our standards, far more interested in conveying moral meanings than in impartially recounting facts. Shakespeare allowed himself an even greater latitude, freely reshaping and condensing his historical materials in order to heighten dramatic effect and to intensify the political, psychological, and metaphysical dimensions of his villainous antihero. The play compresses events that in reality occurred over a long period of time, so that, for example, Richard's murderous plot against his brother George, Duke of Clarence (1478), is cleverly twined around his cynical courtship of Lady Anne (1472), which is in turn depicted as occurring during the funeral procession of King Henry (1471). The historical Lady Anne had only been betrothed to King Henry's son Edward, but Shakespeare writes as if she had actually been married to him; likewise, he folds Richmond's unsuccessful attempt to invade England in 1483 into his successful invasion of 1485, and he has old Queen Margaret, who was not even in England during most of the events that the play depicts, haunting the royal court like a bitter, half-crazed Greek tragic chorus.

Manipulating the insecurities, factional rivalries, and ambitions of everyone around him, Shakespeare's Richard is a consummate portrait of what sixteenth-century Englishmen termed a "machiavel"—that is, a person who acts on the immoral advice allegedly offered by the Florentine humanist Niccolò Machiavelli in *The Prince* (written in 1513, first printed in 1532). According to the period's lurid and grossly distorted account of this advice, Machiavelli had counseled princes to lie, cheat, and murder under the cover of hypocritical professions of virtue and piety. "I count Religion but a childish Toy," declares the character called Machevil, who speaks the prologue to Marlowe's *Jew of Malta* (c. 1590). Shakespeare's Richard, at first terrified by the apparition of the ghosts in Act 5, rallies to express comparable sentiments: "Conscience is but a word that cowards use, / Devised at first to keep the strong in awe" (5.6.39–40). These are sentiments that, for the most part, Richard keeps to himself—or, rather, shares only with the audience in a succession of gleeful asides—for he is highly skilled at assuming the pose of religious faith. Aided by his fellow hypocrite Buckingham, Richard appears in a memorable scene, prayer book in hand, miming "devotion and right Christian zeal" (3.7.103) while cynically stage-managing the supposedly popular call for his coronation.

Richard III. Portrait by unknown artist (c. 1590).

Shakespeare's vision of Richard as a consummate role-player goes back to a brilliant sketch of the same character in one of the three earlier plays he had written on fifteenth-century English history. Taken together, these plays—*The First Part of Henry the Sixth*, *The First Part of the Contention of the Two Famous Houses of York and Lancaster* (*2 Henry VI*), and *The True Tragedy of Richard Duke of York and the Good King Henry the Sixth* (*3 Henry VI*)—depict the chaotic, violent struggle known as the Wars of the Roses, between two noble houses, the Lancastrians and the Yorkists. At the close of *Richard Duke of York* (*3 Henry VI*), the Yorkist faction, led by the Duke of York's three surviving sons (Edward, George, and Richard), has triumphed. The last Lancastrian king, Henry VI, has been killed, and Richard's eldest brother has been crowned King Edward IV. But a shadow is cast across this decisive Yorkist victory by the ruthless and unsatisfied ambition of Richard.

Even though it can stand (and be performed) entirely on its own, *Richard III* may be regarded as the fourth part of a tetralogy, for it picks up directly from the turbulent events depicted in *Richard Duke of York* and, more particularly, from the project Richard announces in a long soliloquy. He declares that since nature has seen fit to deform his body and so exclude him from sensual pleasures, he will instead pursue the crown. "I can add colours to the chameleon," he boasts, "change shapes with Proteus for advantages, / And set the murderous Machiavel to school" (*Richard Duke of York* 3.2.191–93). Here Shakespeare is beginning to psychologize the machiavel, to provide inner motives for his violent ambition and his compulsive shape changing. *Richard III* continues and intensifies this process: as his opening soliloquy suggests, Richard feels that from birth he has been cruelly cheated by dissembling nature. Deprived of the normal satisfactions of nurturing and kindness—it is as if his mother's womb itself had rejected him—he tries to find compensatory satisfaction in cruelty and dissembling of his own. He seeks not only vengeance against an unloving world but also the pleasure of cherishing himself. Yet at the end, in a vigorous if crude moment of self-analysis, he discovers that even self-love eludes him: "I love myself. Wherefore? . . . O no, alas, I rather hate myself" (5.5.141–43).

Richard's self-hatred is psychologically revealing—evidently, he has internalized the loathing that he inspires in virtually everyone around him—but it is not simply generated from within: there is, the play's characters continually imply, a divinely sanctioned, objective moral order independent of both individuals and society, and by the fixed norms of this order Richard *is* hateful. It is possible for villains like Richard or the murderers of Clarence to close their ears to the admonitions of conscience, but all human actions are part of a larger design and will ultimately be judged by a heavenly power. From this higher perspective, Richard's deformity is less the *cause* of his evil nature than its *sign*. Similarly, the ghosts in Act 5 are not merely psychological projections but metaphysical emissaries. The dead do not simply rot and disappear, nor do they survive only in the memories and dreams of the living: they are an ineradicable presence, a part of the structure of reality, an uncanny age group capable of blessing and cursing. Richard tries to shake off their condemnation, as earlier he had jauntily deflected Margaret's elaborate curse, but their words bring beads of sweat to his trembling flesh. For while he may tell himself that his victims' words are merely the impotent weapons of the powerless, he cannot escape the play's pervasive sense that there is something eerie and disturbing about curses, as if through incantatory verbal ritual they magically touch the hidden order of things.

Despite Richard's disruptive mockery and unceremonious violence, an atmosphere of ritual lingers over much of *Richard III,* tingeing the rhetorically elaborate expressions of grief and

Henry VII. Portrait by Michael Sittow (1505).

"For they account his head upon the bridge"
(3.2.67). London Bridge adorned with the heads
of traitors. From Claes Jansz. Visscher, *Lon-
dinum florentissima Britanniae urbs* (1625).

anger, solemnizing formal ceremonies, and shaping the perceptions
of the guilt-ridden characters.
Although the play gives us historical
figures with psychological motiva-
tions and political stratagems, often
we seem less in the secular world of
disenchanted politics than in the
world of classical tragedy or medieval
rite. Thus, for example, Clarence's
terrible nightmare just before his
murder recalls the hell of the
Roman playwright Seneca and, still
more, the hell of fourteenth-century
Christian painting, with its howling
fiends and damned souls. Clarence
is haunted by the sense of an unap-
peasable God preparing to punish
him for his crimes, and his dream
discloses what he does not yet consciously know: that the agent of
divine retribution is his own brother,
Richard.

This ritual process—the inexorable working out, through the
agency of Richard, of retributive justice or (as ancient tragedians per-
sonified it) Nemesis—is best conveyed perhaps by the chorus of grief-crazed women,
above all by old Queen Margaret, who identifies Richard as "hell's black intelligencer"
(4.4.71), or secret agent. In a series of stiff antiphonal laments (4.4.35ff.), Margaret
(the widow of the slain Henry VI), Queen Elizabeth (the widow of Edward IV), and the
Duchess of York (the widowed mother of Edward and his brothers, including Richard)
tease out the strict eye-for-an-eye logic of the action. And at one startling moment,
Richard himself comes close to acknowledging his role within this scheme: he likens
himself to "the formal Vice, Iniquity" (3.1.82).

The character called the Vice is an inheritance of the medieval morality play: the
busy enemy of mankind, the Vice was at once the agent of hell and the tool of divine
providence, a master plotter and a puppet in a play that is not of his own making. Yet
this fixed place in the divine plan did not preclude his acquiring an extraordinary theatrical power and resourcefulness, qualities that Shakespeare would later exploit in
characters as different (and as magnificent) as Falstaff and Iago. Shakespeare constructs Richard out of many elements in the Vice tradition: a jaunty use of asides, a
delight in sharing his schemes with the audience, a grotesque appearance, a penchant
for disguise, a manic energy and humor, and a wickedly engaging ability to defer though
not finally to escape well-deserved punishment. Richard's own allusion to the Vice calls
attention to yet another element, a skill in playing with the doubleness of words and
exploiting the slipperiness of language: "Thus like the formal Vice, Iniquity, / I moralize two meanings in one word" (3.1.82–83). *Richard III* puts the demonic master of this
vicious skill on display and, in the end, stages his destruction: in a sense, the ritual that
lingers over the play is an exorcism.

But, of course, *Richard III* is not in fact a ritual, and Shakespeare's subtle blending
of psychological, metaphysical, and political perspectives carefully suspends any determination of their relative significance in the events he dramatizes. The psychological
development of Richard is arrested by the intimation that psychology is itself the tool
of a supernatural scheme; the supernatural is subverted (at least until the ghost scene)

by the Machiavellian subordination of religion to power politics; but power politics is itself undermined by the suggestion that individuals act in the grip not of rational calculation but of psychological pressures and passions over which they have little or no control. The complex interplay of forces is reflected perhaps in an ambiguity about the play's genre: first appearing in print as *The Tragedy of King Richard the Third*, it was rechristened in the First Folio as one of Shakespeare's history plays, *The Life & Death of Richard the Third*.

That these multiple perspectives do not simply cancel each other out is the result of the extraordinary theatrical force of Richard himself. Only *Hamlet*, of all Shakespeare's plays, is comparably dominated by a single character, and only *Macbeth* is comparably structured around an evil hero. (The villains Richard most anticipates—Philip the Bastard in *King John*, Don John in *Much Ado About Nothing*, Iago in *Othello*, and Edmund in *King Lear*—are all at varying degrees of distance from the main protagonist.) Without for a moment concealing from the audience Richard's appalling, monstrous evil, Shakespeare makes his villain immensely captivating. In large part, his allure derives from what Keats called the "gusto," the overwhelming liveliness, of Shakespeare's characters: "Your eyes drop millstones when fools' eyes fall tears," says Richard to the murderers; "I like you, lads" (1.3.351–52). The startling frankness of this villainy has a comic charge, a charge renewed in the open wickedness of his plans for unsuspecting Hastings—"Chop off his head" (3.1.190)—or for the innocent young princes: "I wish the bastards dead" (4.2.19). There is gusto in Richard's slyness as well as in his frankness, a slyness that also is often comic: "So wise so young, they say, do never live long" (3.1.79).

The allure of such moments seems to be bound up with the allure of the theater itself, with its capacity for emotional intensification, surprise, deception, and heightened energy. The religious enemies of the theater in Shakespeare's age charged that this energy was essentially erotic—the playhouse, they complained, aroused sexual desire—and before dismissing their charges as preposterous, we might recall the comic anecdote from John Manningham's diary with which this introduction began. Shakespeare himself in *Richard III* seems to play with the seductive power of theatrical performance in the bizarre scene in which Richard successfully courts Lady Anne over the body of her father-in-law, the King, whom he has murdered: "Was ever woman in this humour wooed?" Richard exults; "Was ever woman in this humour won?" (1.2.215–16). Richard's wooing has nothing to do with tenderness, affection, sympathy, or even physical attraction; we witness an aggressive male assault upon Lady Anne's rooted, eloquently expressed, and eminently justified fear and loathing. Here, as elsewhere, Richard gets what he wants because he possesses greater power to control the scenario: more than Anne, more than anyone, he knows how to initiate action, conceal motives, threaten, intimidate, and hurt. He has killed Anne's husband as well as her father-in-law; he will, when she has served his purpose, kill Anne too. Anne knows this well enough—"Ill rest betide the chamber where thou liest" (1.2.112)—but she virtually invents uncertainties to mask the calculating murderousness she herself has perceived with cold clarity: "I would I knew thy heart," she muses, seconds after she has thoroughly inventoried Richard's villainous heart (1.2.180).

Anne is shallow, corruptible, naively ambitious, and, above all, frightened—all qualities that help to account for her spectacular surrender—but the scene's theatrical power rests less upon a depiction of her character than upon the spectacle of Richard's restless aggression transformed during the rapid-fire exchange of one-liners (called in rhetoric *stichomythia*) into a perverse form of sexual provocation and of Anne's verbal violence transformed, in spite of itself, into an erotic response. In light of this transformation, the misshapen Richard's celebration of his sexual attractiveness—

> I do mistake my person all this while.
> Upon my life she finds, although I cannot,
> Myself to be a marv'lous proper man—

is not wholly ironic, even if he himself thinks it is (1.2.239–50).

Eros has not been excluded from Richard's career; it has found a new and compelling form in his energetic, witty, and murderous chafing against the obstacles in his path. These obstacles are not simply set in opposition to his desire; rather they virtually constitute it, for it is the extent of his distance from power that generates Richard's craving for it. His politics, and hence the sexuality implied by that politics, is transgressive; it thrives on the violation of social and natural bonds. His is the psychology of the rapist, and the character in Shakespeare closest to Richard III is the rapist Tarquin (in *The Rape of Lucrece*), whose lust is excited precisely by the barriers he is forced to overcome. This chafing structure is why the violent verbal assaults upon Richard, most intense from the women in the play, seem only to intensify his aggressive energies. It is perhaps also why Richard seems to lose much of his erotic power as soon as he has established himself on the throne. When the obstacles in his path to the crown have been removed, when there is no legitimate authority to transgress, the erotic quality of his ambition immediately begins to wane.

The play has allowed Richard to be a perverse erotic champion—a role probably possible only in this highly theatrical vision of history—but the desire he embodies cannot be integrated into any viable social or natural order; nor does it constitute a coherent, stable inner life. By the play's end, he seems a hollow man, a set of theatrical masks that project grotesque shadows upon the world. Fittingly, when "shadows," in the form of those he has murdered, return to terrify him, he can only express his fear in histrionic terms, staging a miniature dialogue with himself and then imagining his conscience as the audience, with its thousand tongues condemning him for a villain.

Richard's manifest theatricality is only the extreme form of a theatricality diffused throughout the play. Virtually all of the speeches—lamentation, cursing, debate, persuasion—are cast as self-conscious performances: "What means this scene of rude impatience?" asks the Duchess of York; Queen Elizabeth replies, "To mark an act of tragic violence" (2.2.38–39). Moreover, there is a pervasive sense that the characters exist as figures in someone else's play: through most of the performance, they are figures, without knowing it, in Richard's play, but Richard himself is a figure in another play, larger than himself. That larger play is at once the drama of history, scripted (as Tudor ideology claimed) by God, and the historical drama or tragedy, scripted by Shakespeare. If the script obliges all of the characters to display the power of divine providence, it obliges them at the same time to display the power of the theater. For if the stage pays homage to the state, it also makes the state into a histrionic spectacle on the public stage. *Richard III* manages to imply that the whole vast enterprise of Tudor power exists to make this play, and the theater in which it is performed, possible.

STEPHEN GREENBLATT

TEXTUAL NOTE

Richard III first appeared in quarto (Q1) in 1597, without the playwright's name but with a very full title page:

> THE TRAGEDY OF King Richard the third. Containing, His treacherous Plots against his brother Clarence: the pittiefull murther of his iunocent nephewes: his tyrannicall vsurpation: with the whole course of his detested life, and most deserued death. As it hath beene lately Acted by the Right honourable the Lord Chamberlaine his seruants AT LONDON Printed by Valentine Sims, for Andrew Wise, dwelling in Paules Chu[r]chyard, at the Signe of the Angell. 1597.

The play proved to be a popular one: so much so that five more quarto versions came out before the appearance of the First Folio (F) in 1623. These quarto editions (Q2–Q6) can claim no textual authority, because of their means of composition; each was based on the text of the one immediately preceding it. Each not only carried forward, therefore, the accumulated errors of its predecessors but added some of its own. The main editorial questions revolve, then, about the authority of, and the relationship between, Q1 and F.

Certainly the quarto text influenced F. But the hundreds of differences between the two suggest that a further source, an independent manuscript, was also used in the construction of F. The Oxford editor Gary Taylor believes that this manuscript was probably a transcript, presumably done by a scribe, of Shakespeare's "foul papers," that is, a version of the play in Shakespeare's own hand, with whatever additions, corrections, and revisions he may have inserted in the course of its composition.

It appears that neither Q nor F derives directly from Shakespeare's own manuscript. It has, however, been proposed that Q, the shorter text, might represent a first draft of the play. Gary Taylor rejects this hypothesis. In his view, Q is a "bad" Quarto—that is, one reconstructed from memory of the play as performed. If so, it is a surprisingly thorough reconstruction, carried out, probably, not by one or two renegade players of minor roles but by Shakespeare's company itself, or rather by those members to hand when the reconstructed text was being written down. Some part of the company on tour in the provinces, for example, could have found itself without a prompt copy of *Richard III.* A text hurriedly assembled in such circumstances might be substantially complete, except for gaps in the minor roles, which would have been played by hired men. Such gaps, showing up as omissions and textual variants, do in fact occur in the quarto version of the play and therefore lend support to Taylor's theory. Given that the passages Q omits tend to slow down the dramatic action and that its only substantial additional passage is a particularly impressive one (the "clock" dialogue, 4.2.101–20), it seems to follow that Q is a later text—one more theatrically attuned, one trimmed of some superfluous bulk. Hence, Oxford adopts a substantial number of the quarto variants.

Other omissions appear to show the effects of censorship. The exclamation "Zounds" ("by His wounds") appears four times in Q but not in F, as does a reference to "Christ's dear blood shed for our grievous sins." The name "God," however, appears frequently in both texts. Political rather than purely religious concerns seem to have caused a further omission. Hastings's lines at the conclusion of 3.4, in which he prophesies "the fearful'st time" in a coming "miserable England," could well be seen as unsettling to an audience that laid great store by prophecy. These lines do not appear in F. But what of the inclusion only in Q of the "clock" dialogue mentioned above? In fact, this seeming anomaly (it is the only major passage not in F) adds weight to the early F hypothesis. The very singular nature of this passage leads Oxford to see it as "an inspired afterthought." No political considerations—far less theatrical ones—could justify its deletion. We might also note that in what was an already very long play, Shakespeare might have been more inclined to deletion than to addition.

F, we can see, is closer to its sources, Halle and Holinshed, and is manifestly the superior text. Many passages are better crafted in meter and meaning than their quarto counterparts. F, then, is the control text for substantive readings. Recalling, however, that the quarto reconstruction would have taken place at a time when Shakespeare himself was active in the company and may have had a hand in revision for the stage, an unusually large number of departures from the control text have been retained. The reader is thus presented, we hope, with the play in its most fully realized theatrical form.

In this edition, Folio passages that were omitted from Q and relegated in the *Oxford Shakespeare* to an appendix are printed inset and in italics.

SELECTED BIBLIOGRAPHY

Burnett, Mark Thornton. "'Monsters' and 'Molas': Body Politics in *Richard III.*" *Constructing "Monsters" in Shakespearean Drama and Early Modern Culture.* New York: Palgrave Macmillan, 2002. 65–94. Fluctuating between images of monsters shaped and unfinished, Richard represents the anxieties of a barren Tudor line seeking new political form.

Carroll, William. " 'The Form of Law': Ritual and Succession in *Richard III*." *True Rites and Maimed Rites: Ritual and Anti-Ritual in Shakespeare and His Age.* Ed. Linda Woodbridge and Edward Berry. Urbana: University of Illinois Press, 1992. 203–19.

Howard, Jean E., and Phyllis Rackin. "Weak Kings, Warrior Women, and the Assault on Dynastic Authority." *Engendering a Nation: A Feminist Account of Shakespeare's English Histories.* London: Routledge, 1997. 100–18. Shifting from history to tragedy, *Richard III* ennobles and disempowers women as passive emblems of pity, while Richard appropriates their seductive theatrical energy.

Hunter, Robert G. *Shakespeare and the Mystery of God's Judgments.* Athens: University of Georgia Press, 1976. Poised between Augustinian and Calvinist conceptions of God's will, Richard's seemingly contradictory status as a tragic figures acting in a providential frame generates the complexity of Shakespeare's art.

Marche, Stephen. "Mocking Dead Bones: Historical Memory and the Theater of the Dead in *Richard III*." *Comparative Drama* 37.1 (2003): 37–57. The play's ambivalent generic status—between tragedy and history—is reflected in Richard's tragic inability to overcome history by silencing the dead who challenge his shaping narrative.

Moulton, Ian Frederick. " 'A Monster Great Deformed': The Unruly Masculinities of *Richard III*." *Shakespeare Quarterly* 47.3 (1996): 251–68. Shakespeare both critiques and celebrates masculine aggression, revealing the incoherence of masculinity as an early modern cultural concept.

Rossiter, A. P. *Angel with Horns, and Other Shakespeare Lectures.* Ed. Graham Storey. New York: Theatre Arts Books, 1961. Richard's demonic appeal as God's avenging angel makes the play less moral history than comic history built on paradoxical irony and inversion.

Targoff, Ramie. " 'Dirty' Amens: Devotion, Applause, and Consent in *Richard III*." *Renaissance Drama* 31 (2002): 61–84. The question of what constitutes true consent on the part of the English toward their King can be tracked through the play's odd use of the liturgical term "Amen," which both Richard and Richmond solicit in different ways from their audiences in order to legitimate their rule.

Torey, Michael. " 'The Plain Devil and Dissembling Looks': Ambivalent Physiognomy and Shakespeare's *Richard III*." *English Literary Renaissance* 30.2 (2000): 123–53. Richard's ability to deceive his victims and manipulate his corporal image complicates the seeming intelligibility of his deformity.

Wheeler, Richard P. "History, Character, and Conscience in *Richard III*." *Comparative Drama* 5 (1971–72): 301–21. The play dramatizes the struggle between divine and profane views of history, between conscience and egoism, that troubled the late Elizabethan era.

FILMS

Richard III. 1912. Dir. André Calmettes and James Keane. USA. 55 min. The silent film version, with Robert Gemp as Edward IV and Frederick Warde as Richard.

Richard III. 1955. Dir. Laurence Olivier. UK. 161 min. A deformed and morally twisted yet seductively charismatic Richard, played by Olivier, with John Gielgud as Clarence.

Richard III. 1995. Dir. Richard Loncraine. UK/USA. 104 min. Richard as a sly and ruthless fascist dictator in a stylishly corrupt 1930s Britain. Ian McKellan is Richard, Robert Downey, Jr. is Lord Rivers.

Looking for Richard. 1996. Dir. Al Pacino. USA. 111 min. Part adaptation, part behind-the-scenes documentary about bringing the Shakespeare play to modern audiences. With Pacino playing Richard and Kevin Spacey playing Buckingham.

The Tragedy of King Richard the Third

THE PERSONS OF THE PLAY

KING EDWARD IV
DUCHESS OF YORK, his mother
PRINCE EDWARD
Richard, the young Duke of YORK } his sons
George, Duke of CLARENCE
RICHARD, Duke of GLOUCESTER, later KING RICHARD III } his brothers
Clarence's SON
Clarence's DAUGHTER
QUEEN ELIZABETH, King Edward's wife
Anthony Woodeville, Earl RIVERS, her brother
Marquis of DORSET }
Lord GRAY } her sons
Sir Thomas VAUGHAN
GHOST OF KING HENRY VI
QUEEN MARGARET, his widow
GHOST OF PRINCE EDWARD, his son
LADY ANNE, Prince Edward's widow
William, LORD HASTINGS, Lord Chamberlain
Lord STANLEY, Earl of Derby, his friend
HENRY EARL OF RICHMOND, later KING HENRY VII, Stanley's son-in-law
Earl of OXFORD }
Sir James BLUNT } Richmond's followers
Sir Walter HERBERT }
Duke of BUCKINGHAM }
Duke of NORFOLK }
Sir Richard RATCLIFFE }
Sir William CATESBY } Richard Gloucester's followers
Sir James TYRRELL }
Two MURDERERS }
A PAGE }
CARDINAL
BISHOP OF ELY
John, a PRIEST
SIR CHRISTOPHER, a Priest
Sir Robert BRACKENBURY, Lieutenant of the Tower of London
Lord MAYOR of London
A SCRIVENER
Hastings, a PURSUIVANT
SHERIFF
Aldermen and Citizens
Attendants, two bishops, messengers, soldiers

1.1

Enter RICHARD *Duke of* GLOUCESTER[1]

RICHARD GLOUCESTER   Now is the winter of our discontent
Made glorious summer by this son of York;[2]
And all the clouds that loured° upon our house°   glowered / family
In the deep bosom of the ocean buried.
5   Now are our brows bound with victorious wreaths,
Our bruisèd arms° hung up for monuments,°   armor / memorials
Our stern alarums° changed to merry meetings,   call to arms
Our dreadful marches to delightful measures.°   dances
Grim-visaged war hath smoothed his wrinkled front,°   forehead
10   And now—instead of mounting barbèd° steeds   armored
To fright the souls of fearful adversaries—
He capers[3] nimbly in a lady's chamber
To the lascivious pleasing of a lute.
But I, that am not shaped for sportive° tricks   amorous
15   Nor made to court an amorous looking-glass,
I that am rudely stamped[4] and want° love's majesty   lack
To strut before a wanton ambling nymph,
I that am curtailed of this fair proportion,°   shape
Cheated of feature° by dissembling nature,   good appearance
20   Deformed, unfinished, sent before my time premature
Into this breathing world scarce half made up—
And that so lamely and unfashionable°   badly formed
That dogs bark at me as I halt° by them—   limp
Why, I in this weak piping[5] time of peace
25   Have no delight to pass away the time,
Unless to spy my shadow in the sun
And descant on° mine own deformity.   remark upon
And therefore since I cannot prove° a lover   prove to be
To entertain these fair well-spoken days,
30   I am determinèd° to prove a villain   resolved; fated
And hate the idle pleasures of these days.
Plots have I laid, inductions[6] dangerous,
By drunken prophecies, libels and dreams
To set my brother Clarence[7] and the King
35   In deadly hate the one against the other.
And if King Edward be as true and just
As I am subtle false and treacherous,
This day should Clarence closely be mewed up°   caged (like a hawk)
About a prophecy which says that 'G'[8]
40   Of Edward's heirs the murderer shall be.

Enter [George Duke of] CLARENCE, *guarded, and [Sir
Robert]* BRACKENBURY

Dive, thoughts, down to my soul: here Clarence comes.
Brother, good day. What means this armèd guard
That waits upon your grace?

1.1 Location: A street in London.
1. Pronounced "Gloster."
2. *son of York*: Edward IV, son of Richard, Duke of York;
with wordplay on Edward's emblem, a sun in splendor.
3. In court dances, men often made "capers," or showy
leaps; also suggests a sexual escapade.
4 Roughly, imperfectly shaped (alluding to the stamp-
ing of a coin with an image).
5. Characterized by the music of a peaceful shepherd's

flute: shrill-voiced, like women or children.
6. Initial moves, prologues.
7. George, Duke of Clarence, Richard, Duke of
Gloucester, and King Edward IV were brothers;
Clarence, being older than Richard, would become
King if Edward and his heirs died.
8. Which Edward interprets as "George," but which
could—and does—mean "Gloucester."

CLARENCE His majesty,
  Tend'ring° my person's safety, hath appointed   *Caring about*
45 This conduct° to convey me to the Tower.[9]   *escort*
RICHARD GLOUCESTER   Upon what cause?
CLARENCE   Because my name is George.
RICHARD GLOUCESTER   Alack, my lord, that fault is none of yours.
  He should for that commit your godfathers.[1]
  Belike° his majesty hath some intent   *Probably*
50 That you should be new-christened in the Tower.
  But what's the matter, Clarence? May I know?
CLARENCE   Yea, Richard, when I know—for I protest
  As yet I do not. But as I can learn
  He hearkens after prophecies and dreams,
55 And from the cross-row° plucks the letter 'G'   *alphabet*
  And says a wizard told him that by 'G'
  His issue° disinherited should be.   *children*
  And for my name of George begins with 'G',
  It follows in his thought that I am he.
60 These, as I learn, and suchlike toys° as these,   *trifles*
  Hath moved his highness to commit° me now.   *arrest*
RICHARD GLOUCESTER   Why, this it is when men are ruled by women.
  'Tis not the King that sends you to the Tower:
  My Lady Gray,[2] his wife—Clarence, 'tis she
65 That tempts him to this harsh extremity.
  Was it not she, and that good man of worship[3]
  Anthony Woodeville her brother there,
  That made him send Lord Hastings to the Tower,
  From whence this present day he is delivered?
70 We are not safe, Clarence; we are not safe.
CLARENCE   By heaven, I think there is no man secure
  But the Queen's kindred, and night-walking heralds°   *secret go-betweens*
  That trudge betwixt the King and Mrs Shore.[4]
  Heard ye not what an humble suppliant
75 Lord Hastings was for his delivery?
RICHARD GLOUCESTER   Humbly complaining to her deity[5]
  Got my Lord Chamberlain[6] his liberty.
  I'll tell you what: I think it is our way,°   *strategy*
  If we will keep in favour with the King,
80 To be her men and wear her livery.[7]
  The jealous, o'erworn widow[8] and herself,°   *(Jane Shore)*
  Since that our brother dubbed them[9] gentlewomen,
  Are mighty gossips° in our monarchy.   *busybodies*
BRACKENBURY   I beseech your graces both to pardon me.
85 His majesty hath straitly given in charge°   *has strictly ordered*

---

9. Tower of London, used to house noble prisoners as well as (in Elizabethan England) traitors and political agitators.
1. The godfather was responsible for the naming of a newborn child.
2. A sarcastic reference to the Queen, widow of Sir John Gray before her marriage to the King. Her maiden name was Elizabeth Woodeville (also Woodville).
3. Honor (here, a sarcastic phrase, more appropriate to a solid, middle-class citizen than to the Queen's brother, Anthony Woodeville, who succeeded his father as Earl Rivers).
4. Jane Shore, wife of a London goldsmith. Her liaison

with Edward was notorious. *Mrs:* Mistress (here in both the polite and the abusive sense).
5. Jane Shore (ironically, by analogy with "her majesty").
6. Hastings's title According to Shakespeare's sources, Jane Shore became his mistress when her affair with the King ended.
7. Servants ("men") in noble households wore the colors ("livery") of the family.
8. The Queen, a widow before she married Edward IV. *o'erworn:* faded.
9. Invested them with the status of (usually used of knights). Richard grossly exaggerates the lowly status of the Queen's family before her marriage.

That no man shall have private conference,
Of what degree soever,[1] with your brother.

RICHARD GLOUCESTER   Even so. An't° please your worship, Brackenbury,   *If it*
You may partake of anything we say.
90 We speak no treason, man. We say the King
Is wise and virtuous, and his noble Queen
Well struck° in years, fair, and not jealous.   *advanced*
We say that Shore's wife hath a pretty foot,
A cherry lip,
95 A bonny eye, a passing° pleasing tongue,   *an exceedingly*
And that the Queen's kin are made gentlefolks.
How say you, sir? Can you deny all this?

BRACKENBURY   With this, my lord, myself have naught° to do.   *nothing*

RICHARD GLOUCESTER   Naught[2] to do with Mrs Shore? I tell thee, fellow:
100 He that doth naught with her—excepting one—
Were best to do it secretly alone.

BRACKENBURY   What one, my lord?

RICHARD GLOUCESTER   Her husband, knave. Wouldst thou betray me?

BRACKENBURY   I beseech your grace to pardon me, and do withal°   *moreover*
105 Forbear your conference with the noble Duke.

CLARENCE   We know thy charge, Brackenbury, and will obey.

RICHARD GLOUCESTER   We are the Queen's abjects,° and must obey.   *base subjects*
Brother, farewell. I will unto the King,
And whatsoe'er you will employ me in—
110 Were it to call King Edward's widow° 'sister'—   *(Queen Elizabeth)*
I will perform it to enfranchise° you.   *free*
Meantime, this deep disgrace in brotherhood
Touches me dearer[3] than you can imagine.

CLARENCE   I know it pleaseth neither of us well.

115 RICHARD GLOUCESTER   Well, your imprisonment shall not be long.
I will deliver you or lie for you.[4]
Meantime, have patience.

CLARENCE   I must perforce.° Farewell.   *of necessity*
    Exeunt CLARENCE[, BRACKENBURY, *and guard, to the* Tower]

RICHARD GLOUCESTER   Go tread the path that thou shalt ne'er return.
Simple plain Clarence, I do love thee so
120 That I will shortly send thy soul to heaven,
If heaven will take the present at° our hands.   *from*
But who comes here? The new-delivered° Hastings?   *newly released*
    Enter LORD HASTINGS [*from the Tower*]

LORD HASTINGS   Good time of day unto my gracious lord.

RICHARD GLOUCESTER   As much unto my good Lord Chamberlain.
125 Well are you welcome to the open air.
How hath your lordship brooked° imprisonment?   *tolerated*

LORD HASTINGS   With patience, noble lord, as prisoners must.
But I shall live, my lord, to give them thanks
That were the cause of my imprisonment.

130 RICHARD GLOUCESTER   No doubt, no doubt—and so shall Clarence too,
For they that were your enemies are his,
And have prevailed as much on him as you.

---

1. *no . . . soever*: that is, despite Richard's high rank
("degree"), he must not speak with the prisoner.
2. Wickedness; here, specifically sexual intercourse.
3. Wounds me more, but also (as a hidden meaning),

implicates me more.
4. In prison, in place of Clarence (with a pun on "lie"
as "tell falsehoods about"). "Deliver" and "lie for" rhyme.

LORD HASTINGS More pity that the eagles should be mewed

While kites° and buzzards prey at liberty.　　　　*scavenger birds*

135　RICHARD GLOUCESTER What news abroad?°　　　　*circulating*

LORD HASTINGS No news so bad abroad as this at home:

The King is sickly, weak, and melancholy,

And his physicians fear° him mightily.　　　　*fear for*

RICHARD GLOUCESTER Now by Saint Paul, that news is bad indeed.

140　O he hath kept an evil diet° long,　　　　*way of life*

And overmuch consumed his royal person.[5]

'Tis very grievous to be thought upon.

Where is he? In his bed?

LORD HASTINGS　　　　He is.

RICHARD GLOUCESTER Go you before and I will follow you.

　　　　　　　　　　　Exit HASTINGS

145　He cannot live, I hope, and must not die

Till George be packed with post-haste° up to heaven.　　　　*by express*

I'll in to urge his hatred more to Clarence,

With lies well steeled° with weighty arguments.　　　　*made strong*

And if I fail not in my deep intent,

150　Clarence hath not another day to live—

Which done, God take King Edward to his mercy

And leave the world for me to bustle in.

For then I'll marry Warwick's youngest daughter.[6]

What though I killed her husband and her father?[7]

155　The readiest way to make the wench amends

Is to become her husband and her father,

The which will I: not all so much for love,

As for another secret close intent,°　　　　*private purpose*

By marrying her, which I must reach unto.

160　But yet I run before my horse to market.

Clarence still breathes, Edward still lives and reigns;

When they are gone, then must I count my gains.　　　　*Exit*

1.2

Enter [gentlemen, bearing] the corpse of [King] Henry VI
[in an open coffin], with halberdiers[1] to guard it,
LADY ANNE being the mourner

LADY ANNE Set down, set down your honourable load,

If honour may be shrouded in a hearse,°　　　　*an open coffin*

Whilst I a while obsequiously° lament　　　　*mournfully*

Th'untimely fall of virtuous Lancaster.[2]

　　　　[They set the coffin down]

5　Poor key-cold[3] figure of a holy king,

Pale ashes of the house of Lancaster,

Thou bloodless remnant of that royal blood:

Be it lawful that I invocate thy ghost[4]

To hear the lamentations of poor Anne,

10　Wife to thy Edward, to thy slaughtered son,

---

5. And has been weakened by extravagant living.
6. Lady Anne Neville, who had been betrothed (but not married) to Edward, Prince of Wales, the son of King Henry VI. Shakespeare, however, writes of Anne as Edward's widow.
7. *her father:* Henry VI (father-in-law).
1.2 Location: A street in London.
1. Men carrying halberds (a spearlike weapon with a

blade as well as a point).
2. Henry VI, of the house of Lancaster, was deposed and murdered by the Yorkists. The dynastic quarrel dates from the deposition of Richard II and is dramatized in Shakespeare's three *Henry VI* plays.
3. Proverbial for "cold as death."
4. Conjuring of spirits was generally condemned. *invocate:* invoke.

Stabbed by the selfsame hand that made these wounds.
Lo, in these windows⁵ that let forth thy life,
I pour the helpless° balm of my poor eyes.   useless
O cursèd be the hand that made these holes,
15 Cursèd the blood that let this blood from hence,
Cursèd the heart that had the heart to do it.
More direful hap betide° that hated wretch   fate befall
That makes us wretched by the death of thee
Than I can wish to wolves, to spiders, toads,
20 Or any creeping venomed thing that lives.
If ever he have child, abortive° be it,   incompletely formed
Prodigious,° and untimely brought to light,   Monstrous
Whose ugly and unnatural aspect°   appearance
May fright the hopeful mother at the view,
25 And that be heir to his unhappiness.⁶
If ever he have wife, let her be made
More miserable by the death of him
Than I am made by my young lord and thee.⁷—
Come now towards Chertsey° with your holy load,   monastery near London
30 Taken from Paul's⁸ to be interrèd there,
       [*The gentlemen lift the coffin*]
And still as° you are weary of this weight   Whenever
Rest you, whiles I lament King Henry's corpse.
       Enter RICHARD *Duke of* GLOUCESTER
RICHARD GLOUCESTER [*to the gentlemen*] Stay, you that bear
     the corpse, and set it down.
LADY ANNE   What black magician conjures up this fiend
35 To stop devoted charitable deeds?
RICHARD GLOUCESTER [*to the gentlemen*] Villains,° set down   Scoundrels; peasants
     the corpse, or by Saint Paul
I'll make a corpse of him that disobeys.
HALBERDIER   My lord, stand back and let the coffin pass.
RICHARD GLOUCESTER   Unmannered dog, stand thou when I command.
40 Advance⁹ thy halberd higher than my breast,
Or by Saint Paul I'll strike thee to my foot
And spurn° upon thee, beggar, for thy boldness.   kick
       [*They set the coffin down*]
LADY ANNE [*to gentlemen and halberdiers*] What, do you tremble?
     Are you all afraid?
Alas, I blame you not, for you are mortal,
45 And mortal eyes cannot endure the devil.—
Avaunt,° thou dreadful minister of hell.   Be gone
Thou hadst but power over his mortal body;
His soul thou canst not have; therefore be gone.
RICHARD GLOUCESTER   Sweet saint, for charity be not so cursed.° bad-tempered
50 LADY ANNE   Foul devil, for God's sake hence and trouble us not,
For thou hast made the happy earth thy hell,
Filled it with cursing cries and deep exclaims.
If thou delight to view thy heinous deeds,
Behold this pattern° of thy butcheries.—   example
55 O gentlemen, see, see! Dead Henry's wounds

---

5. Stab wounds (possibly referring to the custom of
opening the windows to let a dying soul pass).
6. Evil nature; ill fortune.

7. By the deaths of Prince Edward and King Henry VI.
8. St. Paul's, cathedral of the City of London.
9. Raise upright (rather than hold it pointing at Richard).

Ope their congealèd mouths and bleed afresh.[1]—
Blush, blush, thou lump of foul deformity,
For 'tis thy presence that ex-hales° this blood   *calls forth*
From cold and empty veins where no blood dwells.
60   Thy deed, inhuman and unnatural,
Provokes this deluge supernatural[2]
O God, which this blood mad'st, revenge his death.
O earth, which this blood drink'st, revenge his death.
Either heav'n with lightning strike the murd'rer dead,
65   Or earth gape open wide and eat him quick°   *alive*
As thou dost swallow up this good king's blood,
Which his hell-governed arm hath butcherèd.
RICHARD GLOUCESTER   Lady, you know no rules of charity,
Which renders good for bad, blessings for curses.
70   LADY ANNE   Villain, thou know'st no law of God nor man.
No beast so fierce but knows some touch of pity.
RICHARD GLOUCESTER   But I know none, and therefore am no beast.
LADY ANNE   O wonderful, when devils tell the truth![3]
RICHARD GLOUCESTER   More wonderful, when angels are so angry.
75   Vouchsafe,° divine perfection of a woman,   *Grant*
Of these supposèd crimes to give me leave
By circumstance° but to acquit myself.   *detailed argument*
LADY ANNE   Vouchsafe, diffused[4] infection of a man,
Of these known evils but to give me leave
80   By circumstance t'accuse thy cursèd self.
RICHARD GLOUCESTER   Fairer than tongue can name thee, let me have
Some patient leisure to excuse myself.
LADY ANNE   Fouler than heart can think thee, thou canst make
No excuse current° but to hang thyself.   *valid*
85   RICHARD GLOUCESTER   By such despair I should accuse myself.
LADY ANNE   And by despairing shalt thou stand excused
For doing worthy vengeance on thyself
That didst unworthy slaughter upon others.
RICHARD GLOUCESTER   Say that I slew them not.
LADY ANNE   Then say they were not slain.
90   But dead they are—and, devilish slave, by thee.
RICHARD GLOUCESTER   I did not kill your husband.
LADY ANNE   Why, then he is alive.
RICHARD GLOUCESTER   Nay, he is dead, and slain by Edward's hand.
LADY ANNE   In thy foul throat thou liest. Queen Margaret saw
Thy murd'rous falchion° smoking in his blood,[5]   *curved sword*
95   The which thou once didst bend against° her breast,   *turn toward*
But that thy brothers beat aside the point.
RICHARD GLOUCESTER   I was provokèd by her sland'rous tongue,
That laid their guilt upon my guiltless shoulders.
LADY ANNE   Thou wast provokèd by thy bloody mind,
100   That never dream'st on aught° but butcheries.   *anything*
Didst thou not kill this king?
RICHARD GLOUCESTER   I grant ye.

---

1. A murdered victim's wounds were supposed to bleed
again in the presence of the murderer.
2. Q, F: most unnatural. The emendation underscores
Anne's call (in the next line) for divine intervention.
3. That is, Richard is a devil, not man or beast.

4. Misshapen, but also an infection whose harmful
effects are dispersed widely.
5. In *Richard Duke of York* (3 *Henry VI*) 5.5, King
Edward stabbed the Prince first, and Richard followed.

LADY ANNE   Dost grant me, hedgehog?[6] Then God grant me, too,
    Thou mayst be damnèd for that wicked deed.
    O he was gentle, mild, and virtuous.
105 RICHARD GLOUCESTER   The better for the King of Heaven that hath him.
    LADY ANNE   He *is* in heaven, where thou shalt never come.
    RICHARD GLOUCESTER   Let him thank me that holp° that sent him thither,   helped
    For he was fitter for that place than earth.
    LADY ANNE   And thou unfit for any place but hell.
110 RICHARD GLOUCESTER   Yes, one place else, if you will hear me name it.
    LADY ANNE   Some dungeon.
    RICHARD GLOUCESTER   Your bedchamber.
    LADY ANNE   Ill rest betide° the chamber where thou liest.   befall
    RICHARD GLOUCESTER   So will it, madam, till I lie with you.
    LADY ANNE   I hope so.
    RICHARD GLOUCESTER   I know so. But gentle Lady Anne,
115 To leave this keen encounter of our wits
    And fall something into a slower method,[7]
    Is not the causer of the timeless° deaths   untimely
    Of these Plantagenets,[8] Henry and Edward,
    As blameful as the executioner?
120 LADY ANNE   Thou wast the cause of that accursèd effect.
    RICHARD GLOUCESTER   Your beauty was the cause of that effect—
    Your beauty that did haunt me in my sleep
    To undertake the death of all the world
    So I might live one hour in your sweet bosom.
125 LADY ANNE   If I thought that, I tell thee, homicide,°   murderer
    These nails should rend that beauty from my cheeks.
    RICHARD GLOUCESTER   These eyes could not endure sweet beauty's wreck.
    You should not blemish it if I stood by.
    As all the world is cheerèd by the sun,
130 So I by that: it is my day, my life.
    LADY ANNE   Black night o'ershade thy day, and death thy life.
    RICHARD GLOUCESTER   Curse not thyself, fair creature: thou art both.
    LADY ANNE   I would I were, to be revenged on thee.[9]
    RICHARD GLOUCESTER   It is a quarrel most unnatural,
135 To be revenged on him that loveth you.
    LADY ANNE   It is a quarrel just and reasonable,
    To be revenged on him that killed my husband.
    RICHARD GLOUCESTER   He that bereft thee, lady, of thy husband,
    Did it to help thee to a better husband.
140 LADY ANNE   His better doth not breathe upon the earth.
    RICHARD GLOUCESTER   He lives that loves thee better than he° could.   (Edward)
    LADY ANNE   Name him.
    RICHARD GLOUCESTER   Plantagenet.
    LADY ANNE   Why, that was he.
    RICHARD GLOUCESTER   The selfsame name, but one of better nature.
    LADY ANNE   Where is he?
    RICHARD GLOUCESTER   Here.
        She spits at him
                Why dost thou spit at me?
145 LADY ANNE   Would it were mortal poison for thy sake.

6. Term of abuse applied to someone who pays no attention to others' feelings; alluding to Richard's humped back and his heraldic badge, the boar.
7. And argue somewhat less hastily.
8. The royal house from which both Lancastrians,

including Henry and his son Edward, and Yorkists, including Richard himself, descended.
9. That is, if Anne were Richard's day and his life, she could end both and thus be revenged on him.

RICHARD GLOUCESTER   Never came poison from so sweet a place.

LADY ANNE   Never hung poison on a fouler toad.[1]
    Out of my sight! Thou dost infect mine eyes.

RICHARD GLOUCESTER   Thine eyes, sweet lady, have infected mine.

150   LADY ANNE   Would° they were basilisks[2] to strike thee dead.   *I wish that*

RICHARD GLOUCESTER   I would they were, that I might die at once,°   *once and for all*
    For now they kill me with a living death.
    Those eyes of thine from mine have drawn salt tears,
    Shamed their aspects° with store of childish drops.[3]   *appearance*

154.1   *These eyes, which never shed remorseful tear—*
    No, when my father York and Edward[4] wept
    To hear the piteous moan that Rutland[5] made
    When black-faced° Clifford shook his sword at him;   *threatening*

154.5   *Nor when thy warlike father° like a child*   *(Warwick)*
    Told the sad story of my father's death
    And twenty times made pause to sob and weep,
    That all the standers-by had wet their cheeks
    Like trees bedashed with rain. In that sad time

154.10   *My manly eyes did scorn an humble tear,*
    And what these sorrows could not thence exhale^c   *draw out*
    Thy beauty hath, and made them blind with weeping.

155   I never sued° to friend nor enemy;   *petitioned*
    My tongue could never learn sweet smoothing° word;   *flattering*
    But now thy beauty is proposed my fee,°   *recompense*
    My proud heart sues and prompts my tongue to speak.
    She looks scornfully at him
    Teach not thy lip such scorn, for it was made

160   For kissing, lady, not for such contempt.
    If thy revengeful heart cannot forgive,
    [He kneels and offers her his sword]
    Lo, here I lend thee this sharp-pointed sword,
    Which if thou please to hide in this true breast
    And let the soul forth that adoreth thee,

165   I lay it naked to the deadly stroke
    And humbly beg the death upon my knee.
    He lays his breast open;° she offers° at [it] *with his sword*   *bare / thrusts*
    Nay, do not pause, for I did kill King Henry;
    But 'twas thy beauty that provokèd me.
    Nay, now dispatch: 'twas I that stabbed young Edward;

170   But 'twas thy heavenly face that set me on.
    She lets fall the sword
    Take up the sword again, or take up me.

LADY ANNE   Arise, dissembler.
    [He rises]
                    Though I wish thy death,
    I will not be thy executioner.

RICHARD GLOUCESTER   Then bid me kill myself, and I will do it.

LADY ANNE   I have already.

175   RICHARD GLOUCESTER   That was in thy rage.
    Speak it again, and even with the word

---

1. Toads were popularly regarded as "ugly and venomous" (*As You Like It* 2.1.13).
2. Legendary monsters, supposed to kill with a glance.
3. The indented passage that follows, 154.1–154.12, appears only in F.

4. His brother, now the King.
5. Historically, Rutland was Richard's older brother. Shakespeare unhistorically makes him a child. His death is dramatized in *Richard Duke of York* 1.3–2.1.

This hand—which for thy love did kill thy love—
Shall, for thy love, kill a far truer love.
To both their deaths shalt thou be accessary.
180 LADY ANNE I would I knew thy heart.
RICHARD GLOUCESTER 'Tis figured in my tongue.
LADY ANNE I fear me both are false.
RICHARD GLOUCESTER Then never man was true.
LADY ANNE Well, well, put up your sword.
185 RICHARD GLOUCESTER Say then my peace is made.
LADY ANNE That shalt thou know hereafter.
RICHARD GLOUCESTER But shall I live in hope?
LADY ANNE All men, I hope, live so.
RICHARD GLOUCESTER Vouchsafe° to wear this ring.   Consent
190 LADY ANNE To take is not to give.⁶
RICHARD GLOUCESTER Look how my ring encompasseth° thy finger;   encircles
Even so thy breast encloseth my poor heart.
Wear both of them, for both of them are thine.
And if thy poor devoted servant° may   lover
195 But beg one favour at thy gracious hand,
Thou dost confirm his happiness for ever.
LADY ANNE What is it?
RICHARD GLOUCESTER That it may please you leave these sad designs°   affairs
To him that hath most cause to be a mourner,
200 And presently° repair to Crosby House,⁷   at once
Where—after I have solemnly interred
At Chertsey monast'ry this noble king,
And wet his grave with my repentant tears—
I will with all expedient° duty see you.   prompt
205 For divers unknown° reasons, I beseech you   various secret
Grant me this boon.°   favor
LADY ANNE With all my heart—and much it joys me, too,
To see you are become so penitent.
Tressell and Berkeley, go along with me.
RICHARD GLOUCESTER Bid me farewell.
210 LADY ANNE   'Tis more than you deserve.⁸
But since you teach me how to flatter you,
Imagine I have said farewell already.   *Exeunt two with* ANNE
RICHARD GLOUCESTER Sirs, take up the corpse.
GENTLEMAN   Towards Chertsey, noble lord?
RICHARD GLOUCESTER No, to Blackfriars; there attend° my coming.   await
        Exeunt [with] corpse. Manet° GLOUCESTER   Remains
215 Was ever woman in this humour° wooed?   mood; manner
Was ever woman in this humour won?
I'll have her, but I will not keep her long.
What, I that killed her husband and his father,
To take her in her heart's extremest hate,
220 With curses in her mouth, tears in her eyes,
The bleeding witness of my hatred by,
Having God, her conscience, and these bars° against me,   obstacles
And I no friends to back my suit withal
But the plain devil and dissembling looks—
225 And yet to win her, all the world to nothing?° Ha!   against such odds

6. To take your ring is not to give myself.   8. That is, to fare well is more than you deserve.
7. One of Richard's London residences.

Hath she forgot already that brave prince,
Edward her lord, whom I some three months since
Stabbed in my angry mood at Tewkesbury?
A sweeter and a lovelier gentleman,
230 Framed in the prodigality of nature⁹
Young, valiant, wise, and no doubt right royal,
The spacious world cannot again afford°—   *provide*
And will she yet abase° her eyes on me,   *lower; humble*
That cropped the golden prime¹ of this sweet prince
235 And made her widow to a woeful bed?
On me, whose all not equals Edward's moiety?°   *half*
On me, that halts° and am misshapen thus?   *limp*
My dukedom to a beggarly *denier*,²
I do mistake my person all this while.
240 Upon my life she finds, although I cannot,
Myself to be a marv'lous proper° man.   *handsome*
I'll be at charges for° a looking-glass   *I'll buy*
And entertain° a score or two of tailors   *hire*
To study fashions to adorn my body.
245 Since I am crept in° favour with myself,   *into*
I will maintain it with some little cost.
But first I'll turn yon fellow in his grave,
And then return lamenting to my love.
Shine out, fair sun, till I have bought a glass,
250 That I may see my shadow as I pass.   *Exit*

1.3

Enter QUEEN [ELIZABETH], *Lord* RIVERS, [*Marquis* DORSET],
and Lord GRAY

RIVERS [*to* ELIZABETH]   Have patience, madam. There's no doubt his majesty
Will soon recover his accustomed health.
GRAY [*to* ELIZABETH]   In that you brook it ill,° it makes him worse.   *take it badly*
Therefore, for God's sake entertain good comfort,
5   And cheer his grace with quick° and merry eyes.   *lively*
QUEEN ELIZABETH   If he were dead, what would betide on° me?   *befall*
RIVERS¹   No other harm but loss of such a lord.
QUEEN ELIZABETH   The loss of such a lord includes all harms.
GRAY   The heavens have blessed you with a goodly son
10   To be your comforter when he is gone.
QUEEN ELIZABETH   Ah, he is young, and his minority
Is put unto the trust of Richard Gloucester,
A man that loves not me—nor none of you.
RIVERS   Is it concluded° he shall be Protector?   *officially decreed*
15 QUEEN ELIZABETH   It is determined,° not concluded yet;   *decided*
But so it must be, if the King miscarry.°   *die*

Enter [*the Duke of*] BUCKINGHAM *and* [*Lord* STANLEY
Earl of] Derby

GRAY   Here come the Lords of Buckingham and Derby.
BUCKINGHAM   [*to* ELIZABETH]   Good time of day unto your royal grace.
STANLEY   [*to* ELIZABETH]   God make your majesty joyful, as you have been.

---

9. Made when nature in its gift giving was being lavish.   *to:* against (as in betting).
1. Springtime (Richard "cropped," or harvested,   1.3 Location: The royal palace of Westminster.
Edward's life prematurely).   1. F: Gray. Rivers's role in the conversation is far fuller
2. French coin, one-twelfth of a sou (extremely little).   in Q than in F (see lines 30, 54).

20   QUEEN ELIZABETH   The Countess Richmond,[2] good my lord of Derby,
      To your good prayer will scarcely say 'Amen'.
      Yet, Derby—notwithstanding she's your wife,
      And loves not me—be you, good lord, assured
      I hate not you for her proud arrogance.
25   STANLEY   I do beseech you, either not believe
      The envious° slanders of her false accusers   *malicious*
      Or, if she be accused on true report,
      Bear with her weakness, which I think proceeds
      From wayward° sickness, and no grounded malice.   *not easily treated*
30   RIVERS   Saw you the King today, my lord of Derby?
      STANLEY   But° now the Duke of Buckingham and I   *Just*
      Are come from visiting his majesty.
      QUEEN ELIZABETH   With likelihood of his amendment,° lords?   *recovery*
      BUCKINGHAM   Madam, good hope: his grace speaks cheerfully.
35   QUEEN ELIZABETH   God grant him health. Did you confer with him?
      BUCKINGHAM   Ay, madam. He desires to make atonement°   *reconciliation*
      Between the Duke of Gloucester and your brothers,
      And between them and my Lord Chamberlain,°   *(Hastings)*
      And sent to warn° them to his royal presence.   *summon*
40   QUEEN ELIZABETH   Would all were well! But that will never be.
      I fear our happiness is at the height.[3]
         Enter RICHARD [*Duke of*] GLOUCESTER [*and* LORD
         HASTINGS]
      RICHARD GLOUCESTER   They do me wrong, and I will not endure it.
      Who are they that complain unto the King
      That I forsooth am stern and love them not?
45   By holy Paul, they love his grace but lightly
      That fill his ears with such dissentious rumours.
      Because I cannot flatter and look fair,
      Smile in men's faces, smooth,° deceive, and cog,°   *flatter / cheat*
      Duck with French nods[4] and apish° courtesy,   *imitative; clumsy*
50   I must be held a rancorous enemy.
      Cannot a plain man live and think no harm,
      But thus his simple truth must be abused
      With° silken, sly, insinuating jacks?°   *By / nobodies*
      RIVERS   To whom in all this presence° speaks your grace?   *present company*
55   RICHARD GLOUCESTER   To thee, that hast nor honesty nor grace.
      When have I injured thee? When done thee wrong?
      Or thee? Or thee? Or any of your faction?
      A plague upon you all! His royal grace—
      Whom God preserve better than you would wish—
60   Cannot be quiet scarce a breathing while[5]
      But you must trouble him with lewd° complaints.   *ignorant*
      QUEEN ELIZABETH   Brother of Gloucester, you mistake the matter.
      The King—on his own royal disposition,°   *inclination*
      And not provoked by any suitor else—
65   Aiming belike° at your interior hatred,   *Guessing probably*
      That in your outward action shows itself
      Against my children, brothers, and myself,

2. Lady Margaret Beaufort, Lord Stanley's wife, was (by an earlier marriage) the mother of Henry Tudor, Earl of Richmond, who at play's end succeeds Richard and becomes Henry VII. As a descendant of the house of Lancaster, she was unlikely to have friendly feelings toward the Yorkist King Edward IV or his family.
3. At its highest point on Fortune's proverbial wheel, and thus about to decline.
4. *French nods*: elaborate bows.
5. Long enough to catch his breath.

Makes[6] him to send, that he may learn the ground
Of your ill will, and thereby to remove it.

70 RICHARD GLOUCESTER I cannot tell. The world is grown so bad
That wrens make prey where eagles dare not perch.
Since every jack became a gentleman,
There's many a gentle person made a jack.

QUEEN ELIZABETH Come, come, we know your meaning, brother Gloucester.
75 You envy my advancement, and my friends'.
God grant we never may have need of you.

RICHARD GLOUCESTER Meantime, God grants that I have need of you.
Our brother° is imprisoned by your means,   (Clarence)
Myself disgraced, and the nobility
80 Held in contempt, while great promotions
Are daily given to ennoble those
That scarce some two days since were worth a noble.[7]

QUEEN ELIZABETH By him° that raised me to this care-full height   (God)
From that contented hap° which I enjoyed,   fortune; lot
85 I never did incense his majesty
Against the Duke of Clarence, but have been
An earnest advocate to plead for him.
My lord, you do me shameful injury
Falsely to draw me in these vile suspects.°   suspicions

90 RICHARD GLOUCESTER You may deny that you were not the mean°   instigation
Of my Lord Hastings' late imprisonment.

RIVERS She may, my lord, for—

RICHARD GLOUCESTER She may, Lord Rivers; why, who knows not so?
She may do more, sir, than denying that.
95 She may help you to many fair preferments,°   lucrative positions
And then deny her aiding hand therein,
And lay those honours on[8] your high desert.
What may she not? She may—ay, marry,[9] may she.

RIVERS What 'marry, may she'?

100 RICHARD GLOUCESTER What marry, may she? Marry with a king:
A bachelor, and a handsome stripling,° too.   young man
Iwis your grandam had a worser match.[1]

QUEEN ELIZABETH My lord of Gloucester, I have too long borne
Your blunt upbraidings and your bitter scoffs.
105 By heaven, I will acquaint his majesty
Of those gross taunts that oft I have endured.
I had rather be a country servant-maid
Than a great queen, with this condition:
To be so baited,° scorned, and stormèd at.   provoked
    Enter old QUEEN MARGARET[2] *[unseen behind them]*
110 Small joy have I in being England's queen.

QUEEN MARGARET *[aside]* And lessened be that small, God I beseech him.
Thy honour, state,° and seat° is due to me.   rank / throne

RICHARD GLOUCESTER *[to* ELIZABETH] What? Threat you me
    with telling of the King?
Tell him, and spare not. Look what° I have said,   Whatever

---

6. The grammatical subject is still "the King."
7. Gold coin, worth one-third of a pound sterling.
8. And attribute those honors to.
9. Indeed (originally, an oath on the Virgin Mary), with pun in nest line on "wed."
1. Your mother (and the Queen's) was born of a less

distinguished union. Iwis: Assuredly (already archaic).
2. Historically, Margaret—widow of the Lancastrian King Henry VI—was held prisoner in England for five years after her husband's defeat at the Battle of Tewkesbury and then exiled to France.

115   I will avouch't in presence of the King.

I dare adventure to be° sent to th' Tower.   *I risk being*

'Tis time to speak; my pains³ are quite forgot.

QUEEN MARGARET [*aside*] Out, devil! I remember them too well.

Thou killed'st my husband Henry in the Tower,

120   And Edward, my poor son, at Tewkesbury.

RICHARD GLOUCESTER [*to* ELIZABETH] Ere you were queen—

ay, or your husband king—

I was a packhorse° in his great affairs,   *beast of burden*

A weeder-out of his proud adversaries,

A liberal rewarder of his friends.

125   To royalize his blood, I spent mine own.

QUEEN MARGARET [*aside*] Ay, and much better blood than his or thine.

RICHARD GLOUCESTER [*to* ELIZABETH] In all which time you

and your husband Gray

Were factious° for the house of Lancaster;   *partisan*

And Rivers, so were you.—Was not your husband

130   In Margaret's battle° at Saint Albans slain?⁴   *army*

Let me put in your minds, if you forget,

What you have been ere this, and what you are;

Withal,° what I have been, and what I am.   *In addition; also*

QUEEN MARGARET [*aside*] A murd'rous villain, and so still thou art.

135   RICHARD GLOUCESTER Poor Clarence did forsake his father⁵ Warwick—

Ay, and forswore himself, which Jesu pardon—

QUEEN MARGARET [*aside*] Which God revenge!

RICHARD GLOUCESTER To fight on Edward's party° for the crown,   *side*

And for his meed,° poor lord, he is mewed up.   *reward*

140   I would to God my heart were flint like Edward's,

Or Edward's soft and pitiful like mine.

I am too childish-foolish for this world.

QUEEN MARGARET [*aside*] Hie° thee to hell for shame, and leave this world,   *Hurry*

Thou cacodemon;° there thy kingdom is.   *evil spirit*

145   RIVERS My lord of Gloucester, in those busy days

Which here you urge° to prove us enemies,   *recall*

We followed then our lord, our sovereign king.

So should we you, if you should be our king.

RICHARD GLOUCESTER If I should be? I had rather be a pedlar.

150   Far be it from my heart, the thought thereof.

QUEEN ELIZABETH As little joy, my lord, as you suppose

You should enjoy, were you this country's king,

As little joy may you suppose in me,

That I enjoy being the queen thereof.

155   QUEEN MARGARET [*aside*] Ah, little joy enjoys the queen thereof,

For I am she, and altogether joyless.

I can no longer hold me patient.

[*She comes forward*]

Hear me, you wrangling pirates, that fall out

In sharing that which you have pilled° from me.   *pillaged*

160   Which of you trembles not that looks on me?

If not that I am Queen, you bow like subjects;

---

3. Efforts, trouble (on the King's behalf).
4. Queen Elizabeth's first husband, Sir John Gray, died fighting for the Lancastrian faction.
5. Father-in-law. Clarence married Warwick's daughter Isabella, sister of this play's Lady Anne, and for a time defied his brothers by supporting the Lancastrian faction. He "forswore himself" (line 136) by returning to fight for the Yorkish faction.

Yet that by you deposed, you quake like rebels.[6]
[*To* RICHARD] Ah, gentle villain,[7] do not turn away.

RICHARD GLOUCESTER   Foul wrinkled witch, what mak'st thou°   *what are you doing*
    in my sight?

165 QUEEN MARGARET   But repetition° of what thou hast marred: *recounting*
    That will I make before I let thee go.[8]

166.1   RICHARD GLOUCESTER   *Wert thou not banishèd on pain of death?*
    QUEEN MARGARET   *I was, but I do find more pain in banishment*
        Than death can yield me here by my abode.
    A husband and a son thou ow'st to me,
    [*To* ELIZABETH] And thou a kingdom; [*to the rest*] all of you allegiance.
    This sorrow that I have by right is yours,
170   And all the pleasures you usurp are mine.

RICHARD GLOUCESTER   The curse my noble father laid on thee—
    When thou didst crown his warlike brows with paper,
    And with thy scorns° drew'st rivers from his eyes,   *mocking speeches*
    And then, to dry them, gav'st the duke a clout°   *rag; handkerchief*
175   Steeped in the faultless° blood of pretty Rutland[9]—   *innocent*
    His curses then, from bitterness of soul
    Denounced against thee, are all fall'n upon thee,
    And God, not we, hath plagued thy bloody deed.

QUEEN ELIZABETH [*to* MARGARET]   So just is God to right the innocent.
LORD HASTINGS [*to* MARGARET]   O 'twas the foulest deed to slay
180   that babe,°   *(Rutland)*
    And the most merciless that e'er was heard of.

RIVERS [*to* MARGARET]   Tyrants themselves wept when it was reported.
DORSET [*to* MARGARET]   No man but prophesied revenge for it.
BUCKINGHAM [*to* MARGARET]   Northumberland, then present, wept to see it.

185 QUEEN MARGARET   What? Were you snarling all before I came,
    Ready to catch each other by the throat,
    And turn you all your hatred now on me?
    Did York's dread curse prevail so much with heaven
    That Henry's death, my lovely Edward's death,
190   Their kingdom's loss, my woeful banishment,
    Should all but answer for° that peevish brat?   *Should merely equal*
    Can curses pierce the clouds and enter heaven?
    Why then, give way, dull clouds, to my quick° curses!   *lively*
    Though not by war, by surfeit° die your king,   *high living*
195   As ours by murder to make him a king.
    [*to* ELIZABETH] Edward thy son, that now is Prince of Wales,
    For Edward my son, that was Prince of Wales,
    Die in his youth by like° untimely violence.   *similarly*
    Thyself, a queen, for me that was a queen,
200   Outlive thy glory like my wretched self.
    Long mayst thou live—to wail thy children's death,
    And see another, as I see thee now,
    Decked° in thy rights, as thou art 'stalled° in mine.   *Dressed / installed*
    Long die thy happy days before thy death,
205   And after many lengthened hours of grief
    Die, neither mother, wife, nor England's queen.—

6. *If . . . rebels*: Even if you do not bow because I am Queen, at least you tremble like rebels because you deposed me.
7. Well-born peasant; kindly scoundrel.
8. The indented passage that follows, 166.1–166.3,

appears only in F
9. This is dramatized in *Richard Duke of York* 1.4.80–96, in which Margaret crowns the Duke of York with a paper crown and waves a handkerchief dipped in his son Rutland's blood in front of his eyes.

Rivers and Dorset, you were standers-by,
And so wast thou, Lord Hastings,[1] when my son
Was stabbed with bloody daggers. God I pray him,
210   That none of you may live his natural age,
But by some unlooked° accident cut off.   unlooked-for
RICHARD GLOUCESTER   Have done thy charm,° thou hateful,   spell; curse
withered hag.
QUEEN MARGARET   And leave out thee? Stay, dog, for thou shalt hear me.
If heaven have any grievous plague in store
215   Exceeding those that I can wish upon thee,
O let them keep it till thy sins be ripe,
And then hurl down their indignation
On thee, the troubler of the poor world's peace.
The worm of conscience still begnaw thy soul.
220   Thy friends suspect for° traitors while thou liv'st,   to be
And take deep traitors for thy dearest friends.
No sleep close up that deadly eye of thine,
Unless it be while some tormenting dream
Affrights thee with a hell of ugly devils.
225   Thou elvish-marked, abortive, rooting hog,[2]
Thou that wast sealed° in thy nativity   stamped
The slave of nature[3] and the son of hell,
Thou slander of thy heavy° mother's womb,   sorrowful
Thou loathèd issue of thy father's loins,
230   Thou rag of honour, thou detested—
RICHARD GLOUCESTER   Margaret.
QUEEN MARGARET   Richard.
RICHARD GLOUCESTER   Ha?
QUEEN MARGARET   I call thee not.
RICHARD GLOUCESTER   I cry thee mercy° then, for I did think   I beg your pardon
That thou hadst called me all these bitter names.
235   QUEEN MARGARET   Why so I did, but looked for no reply.
O let me make the period° to my curse.   full stop; finish
RICHARD GLOUCESTER   'Tis done by me, and ends in 'Margaret'.
QUEEN ELIZABETH [to MARGARET]   Thus have you breathed your
curse against yourself.
QUEEN MARGARET   Poor painted Queen, vain flourish[4] of my fortune,
240   Why strew'st thou sugar on that bottled° spider   bottle-shaped; swollen
Whose deadly web ensnareth thee about?
Fool, fool, thou whet'st a knife to kill thyself.
The day will come that thou shalt wish for me
To help thee curse this poisonous bunch-backed° toad.   hunchbacked
245   LORD HASTINGS   False-boding° woman, end thy frantic curse,   Falsely prophesying
Lest to thy harm thou move our patience.
QUEEN MARGARET   Foul shame upon you, you have all moved mine.
RIVERS   Were you well served, you would be taught your duty.
QUEEN MARGARET   To serve me well you all should do me duty.°   show me deference
250   Teach me to be your queen, and you my subjects:
O serve me well, and teach yourselves that duty.
DORSET   Dispute not with her: she is lunatic.

---

1. Rivers, Dorset, and Hastings were not present at
Prince Edward's murder at Tewkesbury as dramatized in
Richard Duke of York 5.5, but they are in the chronicles
that served as Shakespeare's sources. The Prince, in fact,
was slain by unknown combatants during the battle.

2. Richard's emblem was the white boar. *elvish-
marked:* deformed by evil fairies. *abortive:* misshapen.
3. Because he was deformed from birth.
4. *painted:* counterfeit, with play on "use of cosmetics." *vain flourish:* empty, meaningless decoration.

QUEEN MARGARET   Peace, master Marquis, you are malapert.°   *impertinent*
Your fire-new stamp of honour is scarce current.[5]
255   O that your young nobility could judge
What 'twere to lose it and be miserable.
They that stand high have many blasts to shake them,
And if they fall they dash themselves to pieces.
RICHARD GLOUCESTER   Good counsel, marry!—Learn it, learn it, Marquis.
260   DORSET   It touches you, my lord, as much as me.
RICHARD GLOUCESTER   Ay, and much more; but I was born so high.
Our eyrie[6] buildeth in the cedar's top,
And dallies with the wind, and scorns the sun.
QUEEN MARGARET   And turns the sun to shade. Alas, alas!
265   Witness my son, now in the shade of death,
Whose bright outshining beams thy cloudy wrath
Hath in eternal darkness folded up.
Your eyrie buildeth in our eyrie's nest.—
O God that seest it, do not suffer it;
270   As it was won with blood, lost be it so.
RICHARD GLOUCESTER   Peace, peace! For shame, if not for charity.
QUEEN MARGARET   Urge neither charity nor shame to me.
Uncharitably with me have you dealt,
And shamefully my hopes by you are butchered.
275   My charity is outrage; life, my shame;°   *my life is one of shame*
And in that shame still live my sorrow's rage.
BUCKINGHAM   Have done, have done.
QUEEN MARGARET   O princely Buckingham, I'll kiss thy hand
In sign of league and amity with thee.
280   Now fair befall° thee and thy noble house!   *good fortune to*
Thy garments are not spotted with our blood,
Nor thou within the compass° of my curse.   *scope*
BUCKINGHAM   Nor no one here, for curses never pass
The lips of those that breathe them in the air.[7]
285   QUEEN MARGARET   I will not think but they ascend the sky
And there awake God's gentle sleeping peace.
O Buckingham, take heed of yonder dog.
      [*She points at* RICHARD]
Look when he fawns, he bites; and when he bites,
His venom tooth will rankle[8] to the death.
290   Have naught to do with him; beware of him;
Sin, death, and hell have set their marks on him,
And all their ministers attend on him.
RICHARD GLOUCESTER   What doth she say, my lord of Buckingham?
BUCKINGHAM   Nothing that I respect, my gracious lord.
295   QUEEN MARGARET   What, dost thou scorn me for my gentle counsel,
And soothe the devil that I warn thee from?
O but remember this another day,
When he shall split thy very heart with sorrow,
And say, 'Poor Margaret was a prophetess'.—
300   Live each of you the subjects to his hate,
And he to yours, and all of you to God's.   *Exit*
HASTINGS   My hair doth stand on end to hear her curses.

5. Your recently acquired title is not yet secure (as newly minted coins that have not yet achieved common currency).
6. Eagle's brood (the sons of York).

7. *curses . . . air:* it is as if curses were never spoken or afflict only the curser.
8. Will cause a wound that will fester.

RIVERS   And so doth mine. I muse why she's at liberty.

RICHARD GLOUCESTER   I cannot blame her, by God's holy mother.

305   She hath had too much wrong, and I repent
My part thereof that I have done to her.

QUEEN ELIZABETH   I never did her any, to my knowledge.

RICHARD GLOUCESTER   Yet you have all the vantage of her wrong.⁹
I was too hot° to do somebody good,   *eager*

310   That° is too cold° in thinking of it now.   *Who / ungrateful*
Marry, as for Clarence, he is well repaid:
He is franked up to fatting¹ for his pains.
God pardon them that are the cause thereof.

RIVERS   A virtuous and a Christian-like conclusion,

315   To pray for them that have done scathe° to us.   *harm*

RICHARD GLOUCESTER   So do I ever—(*speaks to himself*) being well advised:
For had I cursed now, I had cursed myself.

       Enter [Sir William] CATESBY

CATESBY   Madam, his majesty doth call for you,
And for your grace, and you my gracious lords.

320 QUEEN ELIZABETH   Catesby, I come.—Lords, will you go with me?

RIVERS   We wait upon your grace.   *Exeunt. Manet* RICHARD

RICHARD GLOUCESTER   I do the wrong, and first begin to brawl.°   *complain; protest*
The secret mischiefs that I set abroach°   *set in motion*
I lay unto the grievous charge of² others.

325   Clarence, whom I indeed have cast in darkness,
I do beweep to many simple gulls°—   *credulous fools*
Namely to Derby, Hastings, Buckingham—
And tell them, ' 'Tis the Queen and her allies
That stir the King against the Duke my brother'.

330   Now they believe it, and withal whet me
To be revenged on Rivers, Dorset, Gray;
But then I sigh, and with a piece of scripture
Tell them that God bids us do good for evil;
And thus I clothe my naked villainy

335   With odd old ends,° stol'n forth of Holy Writ,   *old bits and pieces*
And seem a saint when most I play the devil.

       Enter two MURDERERS

But soft, here come my executioners.—
How now, my hardy, stout, resolvèd° mates!   *resolute*
Are you now going to dispatch this thing?

340 A MURDERER   We are, my lord, and come to have the warrant,
That we may be admitted where he is.

RICHARD GLOUCESTER   Well thought upon; I have it here about me.

       [*He gives them the warrant*]

When you have done, repair° to Crosby Place.   *return*
But sirs, be sudden° in the execution,   *swift*

345   Withal obdurate; do not hear him plead,
For Clarence is well spoken, and perhaps
May move your hearts to pity, if you mark° him.   *listen to*

A MURDERER   Tut, tut, my lord, we will not stand to prate.
Talkers are no good doers. Be assured,

350   We go to use our hands, and not our tongues.

---

9. All the benefits acquired as a result of the wrong she   2. I make into a serious accusation against.
has suffered.
1. He is penned up to fatten (for slaughter, like a pig).

RICHARD GLOUCESTER   Your eyes drop millstones when fools'
      eyes fall° tears.   *let fall*
  I like you, lads. About your business straight.°   *straightaway*
  Go, go, dispatch.
MURDERERS   We will, my noble lord.
      Exeunt [RICHARD at one door, the MURDERERS at another]

1.4

Enter [George Duke of] CLARENCE [and Sir Robert
    BRACKENBURY[1]]

BRACKENBURY Why looks your grace so heavily° today?   *melancholy*
CLARENCE O I have passed a miserable night,
  So full of fearful dreams, of ugly sights,
  That as I am a Christian faithful man,
5 I would not spend another such a night
  Though 'twere to buy a world of happy days,
  So full of dismal terror was the time.
BRACKENBURY What was your dream, my lord? I pray you, tell me.
CLARENCE Methoughts that I had broken from the Tower,
10 And was embarked to cross to Burgundy,
  And in my company my brother Gloucester,
  Who from my cabin tempted me to walk
  Upon the hatches;[2] there we looked toward England,
  And cited up° a thousand heavy times   *recalled*
15 During the wars of York and Lancaster
  That had befall'n us. As we paced along
  Upon the giddy footing of the hatches,
  Methought that Gloucester stumbled, and in falling
  Struck me—that sought to stay° him—overboard   *steady*
20 Into the tumbling billows of the main.
  O Lord! Methought what pain it was to drown,
  What dreadful noise of waters in my ears,
  What sights of ugly death within my eyes.
  Methoughts I saw a thousand fearful wrecks,
25 Ten thousand men that fishes gnawed upon,
  Wedges of gold, great ouches,[3] heaps of pearl,
  Inestimable° stones, unvalued° jewels,   *Countless / invaluable*
  All scattered in the bottom of the sea.
  Some lay in dead men's skulls; and in those holes
30 Where eyes did once inhabit, there were crept—
  As 'twere in scorn of eyes—reflecting gems,
  Which wooed the slimy bottom of the deep
  And mocked the dead bones that lay scattered by.
BRACKENBURY Had you such leisure in the time of death,
35 To gaze upon these secrets of the deep?
CLARENCE Methought I had, and often did I strive
  To yield the ghost,° but still° the envious° flood   *To die / always / malicious*
  Stopped-in° my soul and would not let it forth   *Stopped up*
  To find the empty, vast, and wand'ring air,
40 But smothered it within my panting bulk,°   *body*
  Who° almost burst to belch it in the sea.   *Which*

1.4 Location: In the Tower of London.
1. F gives this part to an anonymous keeper, Brackenbury not entering until line 72.

2. Planks laid across the hold of a ship, forming a temporary deck.
3. Gold or silver brooches set with jewels. Q, F: anchors.

BRACKENBURY   Awaked you not in this sore agony?
CLARENCE   No, no, my dream was lengthened after life.[4]
O then began the tempest to my soul!
45   I passed, methought, the melancholy flood,[5]
With that sour ferryman which poets write of,
Unto the kingdom of perpetual night.
The first that there did greet my stranger soul
Was my great father-in-law, renownèd Warwick,
50   Who cried aloud, 'What scourge° for perjury   *punishment*
Can this dark monarchy afford false Clarence?'
And so he vanished. Then came wand'ring by
A shadow[6] like an angel, with bright hair,
Dabbled in blood, and he shrieked out aloud,
55   'Clarence is come: false, fleeting,° perjured Clarence,   *fickle*
That stabbed me in the field by Tewkesbury.
Seize on him, furies![7] Take him unto torment!'
With that, methoughts a legion of foul fiends
Environed° me, and howlèd in mine ears   *Surrounded*
60   Such hideous cries that with the very noise
I trembling waked, and for a season after
Could not believe but that I was in hell,
Such terrible impression made my dream.
BRACKENBURY   No marvel, lord, though° it affrighted you;   *that*
65   I am afraid, methinks, to hear you tell it.
CLARENCE   Ah, Brackenbury, I have done these things,
That now give evidence against my soul,
For Edward's sake; and see how he requites me.[8]
68.1   *O God! If my deep prayers cannot appease thee*
But thou wilt be avenged on my misdeeds,
Yet execute thy wrath in me alone.
O spare my guiltless wife and my poor children.
Keeper, I pray thee, sit by me awhile.
70   My soul is heavy, and I fain would° sleep.   *I desire to*
BRACKENBURY   I will, my lord. God give your grace good rest.
[CLARENCE *sleeps*]
Sorrow breaks seasons and reposing hours,[9]
Makes the night morning and the noontide night.
Princes have but their titles for their glories,
75   An outward honour for an inward toil,
And for unfelt imaginations[1]
They often feel a world of restless cares;
So that, between their titles and low name,
There's nothing differs but the outward fame.
Enter two MURDERERS
80   FIRST MURDERER   Ho, who's here?
BRACKENBURY   What wouldst thou, fellow? And how cam'st thou hither?
SECOND MURDERER   I would speak with Clarence, and I came
hither on my legs.

---

4. My dream also depicted my fate after death.
5. The river Styx, across which Charon (the "sour ferryman" of the next line) ferried souls to Hades, the classical hell.
6. Shade, ghost (Edward, Prince of Wales—son of
Henry VI, and Clarence's brother-in-law—whom
Clarence helped to murder; see *Richard Duke of York*
5.5.40).

7. In Greek mythology, female spirits who enacted
vengeance for blood crimes against relatives.
8. The indented passage that follows, 68.1–68.4,
appears only in F. *requites*: repays.
9. Sorrow disrupts life's normal rhythms and disregards the hours appropriate to sleep.
1. *for unfelt imaginations*: "for the sake of imaginary
and unreal gratifications" (Dr. Johnson).

BRACKENBURY What, so brief?

85 FIRST MURDERER 'Tis better, sir, than to be tedious. [*To* SECOND
MURDERER] Let him see our commission,° and talk no more.   *authorization*
[BRACKENBURY] *reads*

BRACKENBURY I am in this commanded to deliver
The noble Duke of Clarence to your hands.
I will not reason what is meant hereby,
90 Because I will be° guiltless of the meaning.   *wish to be*
There lies the Duke asleep, and there the keys.
[*He throws down the keys*]
I'll to the King and signify to him
That thus I have resigned to you my charge.°   *responsibility*

FIRST MURDERER You may, sir; 'tis a point of wisdom. Fare you
95 well.   *Exit* [BRACKENBURY]

SECOND MURDERER What, shall I stab him as he sleeps?

FIRST MURDERER No. He'll say 'twas done cowardly, when he
wakes.

SECOND MURDERER Why, he shall never wake until the great
100 judgement day.

FIRST MURDERER Why, then he'll say we stabbed him sleeping.

SECOND MURDERER The urging of that word 'judgement' hath
bred a kind of remorse in me.

FIRST MURDERER What, art thou afraid?

105 SECOND MURDERER Not to kill him, having a warrant, but to
be damned for killing him, from the which no warrant can
defend me.

FIRST MURDERER I thought thou hadst been resolute.

SECOND MURDERER So I am—to let him live.

110 FIRST MURDERER I'll back to the Duke of Gloucester and tell
him so.

SECOND MURDERER Nay, I pray thee. Stay a little. I hope this
passionate humour° of mine will change. It was wont to hold   *compassionate mood*
me but while one tells° twenty.   *counts*
[*He counts to twenty*]

115 FIRST MURDERER How dost thou feel thyself now?

SECOND MURDERER Some certain dregs of conscience are yet
within me.

FIRST MURDERER Remember our reward, when the deed's done.

SECOND MURDERER 'Swounds,° he dies. I had forgot the reward.   *By God's wounds*

120 FIRST MURDERER Where's thy conscience now?

SECOND MURDERER O, in the Duke of Gloucester's purse.

FIRST MURDERER When he opens his purse to give us our
reward, thy conscience flies out.

SECOND MURDERER 'Tis no matter. Let it go. There's few or
125 none will entertain° it.   *host; employ*

FIRST MURDERER What if it come to thee again?

SECOND MURDERER I'll not meddle with it. It makes a man a coward. A man cannot steal but it accuseth him. A man cannot
swear but it checks him. A man cannot lie with his neighbour's
130 wife but it detects him. 'Tis a blushing, shamefaced spirit, that
mutinies in a man's bosom. It fills a man full of obstacles. It
made me once restore a purse of gold that by chance I found.
It beggars any man that keeps it. It is turned out of towns and
cities for a dangerous thing, and every man that means to live
135 well endeavours to trust to himself and live without it.

FIRST MURDERER   'Swounds, 'tis even now at my elbow, persuading me not to kill the Duke.

SECOND MURDERER   Take the devil in thy mind, and believe him°   (conscience)
not: he would insinuate with thee but to make thee sigh.[2]

140 FIRST MURDERER   I am strong framed; he cannot prevail with
me.

SECOND MURDERER   Spoke like a tall° man that respects thy rep-
utation. Come, shall we fall to work?   valiant

FIRST MURDERER   Take him on the costard with the hilts of thy
145 sword, and then throw him into the malmsey butt[3] in the next
room.

SECOND MURDERER   O excellent device!—and make a sop[4] of
him.

FIRST MURDERER   Soft,° he wakes.   Hush

150 SECOND MURDERER   Strike!

FIRST MURDERER   No, we'll reason with him.

CLARENCE   Where art thou, keeper? Give me a cup of wine.

SECOND MURDERER   You shall have wine enough, my lord, anon.

CLARENCE   In God's name, what art thou?

FIRST MURDERER   A man, as you are.

155 CLARENCE   But not as I am, royal.

FIRST MURDERER   Nor you as we are, loyal.

CLARENCE   Thy voice is thunder, but thy looks are humble.

FIRST MURDERER   My voice is now the King's;[5] my looks, mine own.

CLARENCE   How darkly and how deadly dost thou speak.
160 Your eyes do menace me. Why look you pale?
Who sent you hither? Wherefore do you come?

SECOND MURDERER   To, to, to—

CLARENCE   To murder me.

BOTH MURDERERS   Ay, ay.

CLARENCE   You scarcely have the hearts to tell me so,
And therefore cannot have the hearts to do it.
165 Wherein, my friends, have I offended you?

FIRST MURDERER   Offended us you have not, but the King.

CLARENCE   I shall be reconciled to him again.

SECOND MURDERER   Never, my lord; therefore prepare to die.

CLARENCE   Are you drawn forth° among a world of men   selected from
170 To slay the innocent? What is my offence?
Where is the evidence that doth accuse me?
What lawful quest° have given their verdict up   jury
Unto the frowning judge, or who pronounced
The bitter sentence of poor Clarence' death?
175 Before I be convict by course of law,
To threaten me with death is most unlawful.
I charge you, as you hope to have redemption
By Christ's dear blood, shed for our grievous sins,
That you depart and lay no hands on me.
180 The deed you undertake is damnable.

FIRST MURDERER   What we will do, we do upon command.

SECOND MURDERER   And he that hath commanded is our king.

CLARENCE   Erroneous vassals,° the great King of Kings   Misguided subjects

---

2. *he . . . sight:* he (conscience) would ingratiate him-   *costard:* head (literally, a large apple).
self with you simply to cause you grief.   4. Piece of bread or wafer soaked in wine.
3. Wine barrel (malmsey is a strong, sweet wine).   5. I am now acting on the King's command.

Hath in the table of his law° commanded   *the Ten Commandments*
185   That thou shalt do no murder. Will you then
      Spurn at his edict, and fulfil a man's?
      Take heed, for he holds vengeance in his hand
      To hurl upon their heads that break his law.
    SECOND MURDERER   And that same vengeance doth he hurl on thee,
190   For false forswearing, and for murder too.
      Thou didst receive the sacrament⁶ to fight
      In quarrel of° the house of Lancaster.   *On the side of*
    FIRST MURDERER   And, like a traitor to the name of God
      Didst break that vow, and with thy treacherous blade
195   Unripped'st the bowels of thy sov'reign's son.⁷
    SECOND MURDERER   Whom thou wast sworn to cherish and defend.
    FIRST MURDERER   How canst thou urge God's dreadful law to us,
      When thou hast broke it in such dear degree?
    CLARENCE   Alas, for whose sake did I that ill deed?
200   For Edward, for my brother, for his sake.
      He sends ye not to murder me for this,
      For in that sin he is as deep as I.
      If God will be avengèd for the deed,
      O know you yet, he doth it publicly.
205   Take not the quarrel from his pow'rful arm;
      He needs no indirect or lawless course
      To cut off those that have offended him.
    FIRST MURDERER   Who made thee then a bloody minister°   *agent*
      When gallant springing° brave Plantagenet,°   *sprightly / (Edward)*
210   That princely novice,° was struck dead by thee?   *youth*
    CLARENCE   My brother's love,° the devil, and my rage.   *My love for my brother*
    FIRST MURDERER   Thy brother's love, our duty, and thy faults
      Provoke us hither now to slaughter thee.
    CLARENCE   If you do love my brother, hate not me.
215   I am his brother, and I love him well.
      If you are hired for meed,° go back again,   *reward*
      And I will send you to my brother Gloucester,
      Who shall reward you better for my life
      Than Edward will for tidings of my death.
220   SECOND MURDERER   You are deceived. Your brother Gloucester hates you.
    CLARENCE   O no, he loves me, and he holds me dear.
      Go you to him from me.
    FIRST MURDERER   Ay, so we will.
    CLARENCE   Tell him, when that our princely father York
      Blessed his three sons with his victorious arm,
225   And charged us from his soul to love each other,
      He little thought of this divided friendship.
      Bid Gloucester think of this, and he will weep.
    FIRST MURDERER   Ay, millstones, as he lessoned° us to weep.   *taught*
    CLARENCE   O do not slander him, for he is kind.⁸
230   FIRST MURDERER   As snow in harvest. Come, you deceive yourself.
      'Tis he that sends us to destroy you here.
    CLARENCE   It cannot be, for he bewept my fortune,

---

6. Take communion and in doing so swear by the body
of God.
7. That is, Prince Edward, son of the then sovereign,

Henry VI.
8. He is full of natural feelings (and hence a loving
brother).

And hugged me in his arms, and swore with sobs
That he would labour° my delivery.   *work for*
235   FIRST MURDERER   Why, so he doth, when he delivers you
From this earth's thraldom to the joys of heaven.
  SECOND MURDERER   Make peace with God, for you must die, my lord.
  CLARENCE   Have you that holy feeling in your souls
To counsel me to make my peace with God,
240 And are you yet to your own souls so blind
That you will war with God by murd'ring me?
O sirs, consider: they that set you on
To do this deed will hate you for the deed.
  SECOND MURDERER [*to* FIRST]   What shall we do?
  CLARENCE   Relent? and save your souls.
245   FIRST MURDERER   Relent? No. 'Tis cowardly and womanish.
  CLARENCE   Not to relent is beastly, savage, devilish.—
My friend, I spy some pity in thy looks.
O if thine eye be not a flatterer,°   *deceiver (of Clarence)*
Come thou on my side, and entreat for me.
250 A begging prince, what beggar pities not?
Which of you, if you were a prince's son,
Being pent° from liberty as I am now,   *restrained*
If two such murderers as yourselves came to you,
Would not entreat for life? As you would beg
255 Were you in my distress—
  SECOND MURDERER   Look behind you, my lord!
  FIRST MURDERER (*He stabs* [CLARENCE]) Take that, and that! If
all this will not serve,
I'll drown you in the malmsey butt within.
                        Exit [*with Clarence's body*]
  SECOND MURDERER   A bloody deed, and desperately dispatched!
260 How fain,° like Pilate, would I wash my hands   *gladly*
Of this most grievous, guilty murder done.
    Enter FIRST MURDERER
  FIRST MURDERER   How now? What mean'st thou, that thou help'st me not?
By heaven, the Duke shall know how slack you have been.
  SECOND MURDERER   I would he knew that I had saved his brother.
265 Take thou the fee, and tell him what I say,
For I repent me that the Duke is slain.   *Exit*
  FIRST MURDERER   So do not I. Go, coward as thou art.—
Well, I'll go hide the body in some hole
Till that the Duke give order for his burial.
270 And, when I have my meed, I will away,
For this will out,⁹ and then I must not stay.   *Exit*

2.1

    Flourish.° *Enter* KING [EDWARD], *sick,* QUEEN [ELIZA-   *Trumpet call*
    BETH], *Lord Marquis* DORSET, [*Lord*] RIVERS, [LORD]
    HASTINGS, [*Sir William*] CATESBY, [*the Duke of*] BUCK-
    INGHAM [*and Lord Gray*]
  KING EDWARD   Why, so! Now have I done a good day's work.
You peers, continue this united league.
I every day expect an embassage
From my redeemer to redeem me hence,

---

9. "Murder will out" was proverbial.   **2.1** Location: The palace, London.

5   And more in peace my soul shall part to heaven
    Since I have made my friends at peace on earth.
    Hastings and Rivers, take each other's hand.
    Dissemble not¹ your hatred; swear your love.
    RIVERS By heaven, my soul is purged from grudging hate,
10 And with my hand I seal my true heart's love.
        [*He takes Hastings' hand*]
    LORD HASTINGS So thrive I,° as I truly swear the like.   *May I prosper*
    KING EDWARD Take heed you dally° not before your king,   *trifle*
    Lest he that is the supreme King of Kings
    Confound° your hidden falsehood, and award°   *Defeat / cause*
15 Either of you to be the other's end.²
    LORD HASTINGS So prosper I, as I swear perfect love.
    RIVERS And I, as I love Hastings with my heart.
    KING EDWARD [*to* ELIZABETH] Madam, yourself is not exempt from this,
    Nor your son Dorset;—Buckingham, nor you.
20 You have been factious one against the other.
    Wife, love Lord Hastings, let him kiss your hand—
    And what you do, do it unfeignedly.
    QUEEN ELIZABETH [*giving* HASTINGS *her hand to kiss*] There,
        Hastings. I will never more remember
    Our former hatred: so thrive I, and mine.°   *my family*
25 KING EDWARD Dorset, embrace him. Hastings, love Lord Marquis.
    DORSET This interchange of love, I here protest,°   *affirm*
    Upon my part shall be inviolable.
    LORD HASTINGS And so swear I.
        [*They embrace*]
    KING EDWARD Now, princely Buckingham, seal thou this league
30 With thy embracements to my wife's allies,
    And make me happy in your unity.
    BUCKINGHAM [*to* ELIZABETH] Whenever Buckingham doth turn his hate
    Upon your grace, but° with all duteous love   *nor*
    Doth cherish you and yours, God punish me
35 With hate in those where I expect most love.
    When I have most need to employ a friend,
    And most assurèd that he is a friend,
    Deep,° hollow, treacherous, and full of guile   *Crafty*
    Be he unto me. This do I beg of heaven,
40 When I am cold in love to you or yours.
        [*They*] embrace
    KING EDWARD A pleasing cordial,° princely Buckingham,   *health-giving drink*
    Is this thy vow unto my sickly heart.
    There wanteth now our brother Gloucester here,
    To make the blessèd period° of this peace.   *conclusion*
        Enter [*Sir Richard*] RATCLIFFE *and* [RICHARD *Duke of*]
        GLOUCESTER
45 BUCKINGHAM And in good time,
    Here comes Sir Richard Ratcliffe and the Duke.
    RICHARD GLOUCESTER Good morrow to my sovereign King and Queen.—
    And princely peers, a happy time of day.
    KING EDWARD Happy indeed, as we have spent the day.
50 Brother, we have done deeds of charity,
    Made peace of enmity, fair love of hate,

---

1. Do not merely disguise.   2. Each of you to cause the death of the other.

Between these swelling wrong-incensèd[3] peers.

RICHARD GLOUCESTER   A blessèd labour, my most sovereign lord.

Among this princely heap° if any here,   *company*
55 By false intelligence° or wrong surmise,   *information*
    Hold me a foe,
    If I unwittingly or in my rage
    Have aught committed that is hardly borne°   *is deeply resented*
    By any in this presence, I desire
60 To reconcile me to his friendly peace.
    'Tis death to me to be at enmity.
    I hate it, and desire all good men's love.—
    First, madam, I entreat true peace of you,
    Which I will purchase with my duteous service.—
65 Of you, my noble cousin Buckingham,
    If ever any grudge were lodged between us.—
    Of you, Lord Rivers, and Lord Gray of you,
    That all without desert° have frowned on me.—   *entirely without cause*
    Dukes, earls, lords, gentlemen, indeed of all!
70 I do not know that Englishman alive
    With whom my soul is any jot at odds
    More than the infant that is born tonight.
    I thank my God for my humility.

QUEEN ELIZABETH   A holy day shall this be kept hereafter.
75 I would to God all strifes were well compounded.°—   *resolved*
    My sovereign lord, I do beseech your highness
    To take our brother Clarence to your grace.

RICHARD GLOUCESTER   Why, madam, have I offered love for this,
    To be so flouted° in this royal presence?   *mocked*
80 Who knows not that the gentle Duke is dead?
            They all start
    You do him injury to scorn his corpse.[4]

RIVERS[5]   Who knows not he is dead? Who knows he is?

QUEEN ELIZABETH   All-seeing heaven, what a world is this?

BUCKINGHAM   Look I so pale, Lord Dorset, as the rest?

85 DORSET   Ay, my good lord, and no one in the presence°   *(of the King)*
    But his red colour hath forsook his cheeks.

KING EDWARD   Is Clarence dead? The order was reversed.

RICHARD GLOUCESTER   But he, poor man, by your first order died,
    And that a wingèd Mercury[6] did bear;
90 Some tardy cripple bore the countermand,
    That came too lag° to see him buried.   *late*
    God grant that some, less noble and less loyal,
    Nearer in bloody thoughts, but not in blood,[7]
    Deserve not worse than wretched Clarence did,
95 And yet go current from suspicion.[8]
            Enter [Lord STANLEY] Earl of Derby

STANLEY [*kneeling*]   A boon,° my sovereign, for my service done.   *favor*

KING EDWARD   I pray thee, peace! My soul is full of sorrow.

STANLEY   I will not rise, unless your highness hear me.

---

3. *swelling:* inflated with anger and pride. *wrong-incensèd:* mistakenly provoked; provoked by wrongs, injuries.
4. *to scorn his corpse:* by (supposedly) speaking ironically of him.
5. F assigns this line to King Edward.

6. The speedy messenger of the gods in classical mythology.
7. That is, nearer to bloody plots than was the innocent Clarence, but not so near the King in blood (another dig at the Queen's upstart relatives).
8. And yet are accepted at face value without suspicion.

KING EDWARD   Then say at once, what is it thou requests?
100 STANLEY   The forfeit, sovereign, of my servant's life,⁹
Who slew today a riotous gentleman,
Lately attendant on the Duke of Norfolk.
KING EDWARD   Have I a tongue to doom° my brother's death,   order
And shall that tongue give pardon to a slave?
105 My brother slew no man; his fault was thought;
And yet his punishment was bitter death.
Who sued to me for him? Who in my wrath
Kneeled at my feet, and bid me be advised?°   consider carefully
Who spoke of brotherhood? Who spoke of love?
110 Who told me how the poor soul did forsake
The mighty Warwick and did fight for me?
Who told me, in the field at Tewkesbury,
When Oxford had me down, he rescued me,
And said, 'Dear brother, live, and be a king'?
115 Who told me, when we both lay in the field,
Frozen almost to death, how he did lap° me   wrap
Even in his garments, and did give himself
All thin° and naked to the numb-cold night?   thinly clad
All this from my remembrance brutish wrath
120 Sinfully plucked, and not a man of you
Had so much grace to put it in my mind.
But when your carters° or your waiting vassals   cart drivers
Have done a drunken slaughter, and defaced
The precious image¹ of our dear redeemer,
125 You straight° are on your knees for 'Pardon, pardon!'—   straightaway
And I, unjustly too, must grant it you.
But, for my brother, not a man would speak,
Nor I, ungracious, speak unto myself
For him, poor soul. The proudest of you all
130 Have been beholden to him in his life,
Yet none of you would once beg for his life.
O God, I fear thy justice will take hold
On me—and you, and mine, and yours, for this.—
Come, Hastings, help me to my closet.°   private (bed)room
135 Ah, poor Clarence!   *Exeunt some with* KING *and* QUEEN
RICHARD GLOUCESTER   This is the fruits of rashness. Marked you not
How that the guilty kindred of the Queen
Looked pale, when they did hear of Clarence' death?
O, they did urge it still unto the King.
140 God will revenge it. Come, lords, will you go
To comfort Edward with our company?
BUCKINGHAM   We wait upon your grace.   *Exeunt*

2.2

Enter the old DUCHESS OF YORK *with the two children of*
*Clarence*¹
BOY   Good grannam, tell us, is our father dead?
DUCHESS OF YORK   No, boy.
GIRL   Why do you weep so oft, and beat your breast,

9. That is, the release of his servant from a sentence of   2.2 Location: The palace, London.
death.   1. Edward and Margaret Plantagenet (not to be confused
1. A man, thought to be created in God's image.   with King Edward, Prince Edward, or Queen Margaret).

And cry, 'O Clarence, my unhappy son'?
5 BOY   Why do you look on us and shake your head,
And call us orphans, wretches, castaways,
If that our noble father were alive?
DUCHESS OF YORK   My pretty cousins,° you mistake me both.   *kinsmen*
I do lament the sickness of the King,
10 As loath to lose him, not your father's death.
It were lost sorrow to wail one that's lost.
BOY   Then you conclude, my grannam, he is dead.
The King mine uncle is to blame for this.
God will revenge it—whom I will importune°   *beg*
15 With earnest prayers, all to that effect.
GIRL   And so will I.
DUCHESS OF YORK   Peace, children, peace! The King doth love you well.
Incapable° and shallow innocents,   *Uncomprehending*
You cannot guess who caused your father's death.
20 BOY   Grannam, we can. For my good uncle Gloucester
Told me the King, provoked to it by the Queen,
Devised impeachments° to imprison him,   *charges*
And when my uncle told me so he wept,
And pitied me, and kindly kissed my cheek,
25 Bade me rely on him as on my father,
And he would love me dearly as his child.
DUCHESS OF YORK   Ah, that deceit should steal such gentle shapes,°   *appearances*
And with a virtuous visor° hide deep vice!   *mask*
He is my son, ay, and therein my shame;
30 Yet from my dugs° he drew not this deceit.   *breasts*
BOY   Think you my uncle did dissemble, grannam?
DUCHESS OF YORK   Ay, boy.
BOY   I cannot think it. Hark, what noise is this?
Enter QUEEN [ELIZABETH] *with her hair about her ears*[2]
QUEEN ELIZABETH   Ah, who shall hinder me to wail and weep?
35 To chide my fortune, and torment myself?
I'll join with black despair against my soul,
And to myself become an enemy.
DUCHESS OF YORK   What means this scene of rude° impatience?   *violent*
QUEEN ELIZABETH   To mark an act of tragic violence.
40 Edward, my lord, thy son, our king, is dead.[3]
Why grow the branches when the root is gone?
Why wither not the leaves that want° their sap?   *lack*
If you will live, lament; if die, be brief,
That our swift-wingèd souls may catch the King's,
45 Or like obedient subjects follow him
To his new kingdom of ne'er-changing night.
DUCHESS OF YORK   Ah, so much interest° have I in thy sorrow   *right to share*
As I had title[4] in thy noble husband.
I have bewept a worthy husband's[5] death,
50 And lived with looking on his images.°   *likenesses (his sons)*
But now two mirrors[6] of his princely semblance

---

2. Disheveled hair was a conventional expression of grief on the Elizabethan stage. F adds "Rivers and Dorset after her" and gives them lines to speak later in the scene.
3. Shakespeare is telescoping events. Edward actually died some five years after Clarence.
4. Legal right (as Edward's mother, the Duchess of York has a right to mourn).
5. The Duke of York (whose death is dramatized in *Richard Duke of York*).
6. Clarence and King Edward.

Are cracked in pieces by malignant death,
And I for comfort have but one false glass,°   *(Richard)*
That grieves me when I see my shame in him.
55   Thou art a widow, yet thou art a mother,
And hast the comfort of thy children left.
But death hath snatched my husband from mine arms
And plucked two crutches from my feeble hands,
Clarence and Edward. O what cause have I,
60   Thine being but a moiety° of my moan,   *half*
To overgo° thy woes, and drown thy cries?   *exceed*
    BOY [*to* ELIZABETH]   Ah, aunt, you wept not for our father's death.
How can we aid you with our kindred tears?°   *tears of relatives*
    DAUGHTER [*to* ELIZABETH]   Our fatherless distress was left unmoaned;
65   Your widow-dolour° likewise be unwept.   *widow's grief*
    QUEEN ELIZABETH   Give me no help in lamentation.
I am not barren to bring forth complaints.[7]
All springs reduce[8] their currents to mine eyes,
That I, being governed by the wat'ry moon,
70   May send forth plenteous tears to drown the world.
Ah, for my husband, for my dear Lord Edward!
    CHILDREN   Ah, for our father, for our dear Lord Clarence!
    DUCHESS OF YORK   Alas, for both, both mine, Edward and Clarence!
    QUEEN ELIZABETH   What stay° had I but Edward, and he's gone?   *support*
75   CHILDREN   What stay had we but Clarence, and he's gone?
    DUCHESS OF YORK   What stays had I but they, and they are gone?
    QUEEN ELIZABETH   Was never widow had so dear° a loss!   *grievous*
    CHILDREN   Were never orphans had so dear a loss!
    DUCHESS OF YORK   Was never mother had so dear a loss!
80   Alas, I am the mother of these griefs.
Their woes are parcelled;° mine is general.   *inclusive*
She for an Edward weeps, and so do I;
I for a Clarence weep, so doth not she.
These babes for Clarence weep, and so do I;
85   I for an Edward weep, so do not they.
Alas, you three on me, threefold distressed,
Pour all your tears. I am your sorrow's nurse,
And I will pamper° it with lamentation.[9]   *(over)feed*
88.1   *DORSET*   *Comfort, dear mother. God is much displeased*
           That you take with unthankfulness his doing.
           In common worldly things 'tis called ungrateful
           With dull unwillingness to pay a debt
88.5   *Which with a bounteous hand was kindly lent;*
           Much more to be thus opposite with° heaven   *in opposition to*
           For it requires° the royal debt it lent you.   *calls back*
       RIVERS   *Madam, bethink you like a careful mother*
           Of the young Prince your son. Send straight for him;
88.10   *Let him be crowned. In him your comfort lives.*
           Drown desperate sorrow in dead Edward's grave
           And plant your joys in living Edward's throne.

---

7. I can deliver my own lamentations.
8. Lead back (as to the sea, which is governed by the moon).

9. The indented passage that follows, 88.1–88.12, appears only in F.

Enter RICHARD [*Duke of*] GLOUCESTER, *the* [*Duke of*]
BUCKINGHAM, [*Lord* STANLEY *Earl of*] *Derby,* [LORD]
HASTINGS, *and* [*Sir Richard*] RATCLIFFE

RICHARD GLOUCESTER [*to* ELIZABETH]   Sister, have comfort. All of us have cause

90   To wail the dimming of our shining star,
But none can help our harms by wailing them.—
Madam, my mother, I do cry you mercy.°   *I beg your pardon*
I did not see your grace. Humbly on my knee
I crave your blessing.

95   DUCHESS OF YORK   God bless thee, and put meekness in thy breast,
Love, charity, obedience, and true duty.

RICHARD GLOUCESTER   Amen. [*Aside*] 'And make me die a good old man.'
That is the butt-end° of a mother's blessing;   *conclusion*
I marvel that her grace did leave it out.

100   BUCKINGHAM   You cloudy° princes and heart-sorrowing peers   *sad; raining (tears)*
That bear this heavy mutual load of moan,°   *lamentation*
Now cheer each other in each other's love.
Though we have spent our harvest of this king,
We are to reap the harvest of his son.

105   The broken rancour¹ of your high-swoll'n hearts
But lately° splinted, knit, and joined together,   *Only recently*
Must gently be preserved, cherished, and kept.
Meseemeth° good that, with some little train,°   *I think it / entourage*
Forthwith from Ludlow² the young Prince be fet°   *fetched*

110   Hither to London to be crowned our king.³

110.1   RIVERS   *Why with some little train, my lord of Buckingham?*
BUCKINGHAM   *Marry, my lord, lest by a multitude*°   *large entourage*
The new-healed wound of malice should break out,
Which would be so much the more dangerous

110.5   *By how much the estate is green and yet ungoverned.*⁴
*Where every horse bears his commanding rein*⁵
And may direct his course as please himself°   *as he pleases*
As well the fear of harm as harm apparent°   *as actual harm*
In my opinion ought to be prevented.

110.10   RICHARD GLOUCESTER   *I hope the King made peace with all of us,*
And the compact is firm and true in me.
RIVERS   *And so in me, and so I think in all.*
Yet since it is but green, it should be put
To no apparent likelihood of breach,

110.15   *Which haply*° *by much company might be urged.*   *perhaps*
Therefore I say, with noble Buckingham,
That it is meet° *so few should fetch the Prince.*   *fitting*
HASTINGS   *And so say I.*

RICHARD GLOUCESTER   Then be it so, and go we to determine
Who they shall be that straight shall post° to Ludlow.—   *ride speedily*
Madam, and you my sister, will you go
To give your censures° in this weighty business?   *opinions*

115   QUEEN ELIZABETH *and* DUCHESS OF YORK   With all our hearts.
Exeunt. Manent RICHARD *and* BUCKINGHAM

1. Bitterness that caused you to be divided (unnaturally, like a broken limb).
2. Royal castle in Shropshire, near the Welsh border,
where Prince Edward, as Prince of Wales, was staying.
3. The indented passage that follows, 110.1–110.18,

appears only in F.
4. *By . . . ungoverned:* Considering that the government is newly established and not yet in full control.
5. *bears . . . rein:* takes charge of the rein that should
restrain him.

BUCKINGHAM My lord, whoever journeys to the Prince,
For God's sake let not us two stay at home,
For by the way I'll sort° occasion,   *find*
As index° to the story we late° talked of,   *prologue / lately*
120 To part the Queen's proud kindred from the Prince.
RICHARD GLOUCESTER My other self, my counsel's consistory,°   *council chamber*
My oracle, my prophet, my dear cousin!
I, as a child, will go by thy direction.
Towards Ludlow then, for we'll not stay behind.   *Exeunt*

2.3

Enter one CITIZEN *at one door and another at the other*
FIRST CITIZEN Good morrow, neighbour. Whither away so fast?
SECOND CITIZEN I promise° you, I scarcely know myself.   *assure*
Hear you the news abroad?
FIRST CITIZEN   Yes, that the King is dead.
SECOND CITIZEN Ill news, by'r Lady,° seldom comes the better.[1]   *by the Virgin Mary*
5   I fear, I fear, 'twill prove a giddy° world.   *mad*
Enter another CITIZEN
THIRD CITIZEN Neighbours, God speed.
FIRST CITIZEN   Give you good morrow, sir.
THIRD CITIZEN Doth the news hold of good King Edward's death?
SECOND CITIZEN Ay, sir, it is too true. God help the while.
THIRD CITIZEN Then, masters,° look to see a troublous world.   *sirs*
10   FIRST CITIZEN No, no, by God's good grace his son shall reign.
THIRD CITIZEN Woe to that land that's governed by a child.
SECOND CITIZEN In him there is a hope of government,[2]
Which in his nonage council under him,
And in his full and ripened years himself,
15   No doubt shall then, and till then, govern well.
FIRST CITIZEN So stood the state when Henry the Sixth
Was crowned in Paris but at nine months old.
THIRD CITIZEN Stood the state so? No, no, good friends, God wot.°   *knows*
For then this land was famously enriched
20   With politic,° grave counsel;° then the King   *astute / advisers*
Had virtuous uncles to protect his grace.
FIRST CITIZEN Why, so hath this, both by his father and mother.
THIRD CITIZEN Better it were they all came by his father,
Or by his father there were none at all.
25   For emulation° who shall now be near'st[3]   *competition*
Will touch us all too near, if God prevent not.
O full of danger is the Duke of Gloucester,
And the Queen's sons and brothers haught° and proud.   *haughty*
And were they° to be ruled, and not to rule,   *(both factions)*
30   This sickly land might solace° as before.   *prosper*
FIRST CITIZEN Come, come, we fear the worst. All will be well.
THIRD CITIZEN When clouds are seen, wise men put on their cloaks;
When great leaves fall, then winter is at hand;
When the sun sets, who doth not look for night?
35   Untimely storms make men expect a dearth.

2.3 Location: A street in London.
1. Things rarely change for the better (proverbial).
2. The Privy Council governing in his name during the

years of his minority.
3. Most influential with the King.

All may be well, but if God sort° it so   *ordain*
'Tis more than we deserve, or I expect.
SECOND CITIZEN   Truly the hearts of men are full of fear.
You cannot reason° almost with a man   *converse*
40   That looks not heavily and full of dread.
THIRD CITIZEN   Before the days of change still is it so.
By a divine instinct men's minds mistrust°   *suspect*
Ensuing danger, as by proof° we see   *experience*
The water swell before a boist'rous storm.
45   But leave it all to God. Whither away?
SECOND CITIZEN   Marry, we were sent for to the justices.
THIRD CITIZEN   And so was I. I'll bear you company.   *Exeunt*

2.4

Enter [Lord] CARDINAL, *young [Duke of]* YORK, QUEEN
*[*ELIZABETH*], and the [old]* DUCHESS OF YORK
CARDINAL   Last night, I hear, they lay them at Northampton.
At Stony Stratford[1] they do rest tonight.
Tomorrow, or next day, they will be here.
DUCHESS OF YORK   I long with all my heart to see the Prince.
5   I hope he is much grown since last I saw him.
QUEEN ELIZABETH   But I hear, no. They say my son of York
Has almost overta'en him in his growth.
YORK   Ay, mother, but I would not have it so.
DUCHESS OF YORK   Why, my young cousin, it is good to grow.
10   YORK   Grandam, one night as we did sit at supper,
My uncle Rivers talked how I did grow
More than my brother. 'Ay', quoth my nuncle° Gloucester,   *uncle (colloquial)*
'Small herbs have grace; gross weeds do grow apace'.°   *rapidly*
And since, methinks I would not grow so fast,
15   Because sweet flow'rs are slow, and weeds make haste.
DUCHESS OF YORK   Good faith, good faith, the saying did not hold°   *hold true*
In him that did object° the same to thee.   *argue*
He was the wretched'st thing when he was young,
So long a-growing, and so leisurely,
20   That if his rule were true he should be gracious.
CARDINAL   Why, so no doubt he is, my gracious madam.
DUCHESS OF YORK   I hope he is, but yet let mothers doubt.
YORK   Now, by my troth, if I had been remembered,
I could have given my uncle's grace a flout[2]
25   To touch his growth, nearer than he touched° mine.   *hit*
DUCHESS OF YORK   How, my young York? I pray thee, let me hear it.
YORK   Marry, they say my uncle grew so fast
That he could gnaw a crust at two hours old.
'Twas full two years ere I could get a tooth.
30   Grannam, this would have been a biting jest.
DUCHESS OF YORK   I pray thee, pretty York, who told thee this?
YORK   Grannam, his nurse.
DUCHESS OF YORK   His nurse? Why, she was dead ere thou wast born.
YORK   If 'twere not she, I cannot tell who told me.

2.4 Location: The palace, London.   2. *if . . . flout:* if I had been told this, I could have
1. Town in Buckinghamshire (south of Northampton).   taunted my noble uncle.
F reverses the order of the towns.

35 QUEEN ELIZABETH A parlous° boy! Go to,³ you are too shrewd.°   *mischievous / sharp*
    CARDINAL Good madam, be not angry with the child.
    QUEEN ELIZABETH Pitchers have ears.⁴
         Enter [Marquis] DORSET
    CARDINAL   Here comes your son, Lord Dorset.
    What news, Lord Marquis?
    DORSET   Such news, my lord,
    As grieves me to report.
    QUEEN ELIZABETH   How doth the Prince?
    DORSET Well, madam, and in health.
40 DUCHESS OF YORK   What is thy news then?
    DORSET Lord Rivers and Lord Gray are sent to Pomfret,⁵
    And with them Thomas Vaughan, prisoners.
    DUCHESS OF YORK Who hath committed them?
    DORSET   The mighty dukes,
    Gloucester and Buckingham.
    CARDINAL   For what offence?
45 DORSET The sum of all I can,° I have disclosed.   *know*
    Why or for what the nobles were committed
    Is all unknown to me, my gracious lord.
    QUEEN ELIZABETH Ay me! I see the ruin of our house.
    The tiger now hath seized the gentle hind.°   *doe*
50 Insulting tyranny begins to jet°   *encroach; strut*
    Upon the innocent and aweless⁶ throne.
    Welcome destruction, blood, and massacre!
    I see, as in a map, the end of all.
    DUCHESS OF YORK Accursèd and unquiet wrangling days,
55 How many of you have mine eyes beheld?
    My husband lost his life to get the crown,
    And often up and down my sons were tossed,
    For me to joy and weep their gain and loss.
    And being seated,° and domestic broils°   *enthroned / disorders*
60 Clean overblown,° themselves the conquerors   *Completely ended*
    Make war upon themselves, brother to brother,
    Blood to blood, self against self. O preposterous
    And frantic outrage, end thy damnèd spleen,°   *malice*
    Or let me die, to look on death no more.
65 QUEEN ELIZABETH [*to* YORK] Come, come, my boy, we will to sanctuary.⁷—
    Madam, farewell.
    DUCHESS OF YORK Stay, I will go with you.
    QUEEN ELIZABETH You have no cause.
    CARDINAL [*to* ELIZABETH]   My gracious lady, go,
    And thither bear your treasure and your goods.
    For my part, I'll resign° unto your grace   *hand over*
70 The seal⁸ I keep, and so betide° to me   *and so may it happen*
    As well I tender° you and all of yours.   *care for*
    Go, I'll conduct you to the sanctuary.   *Exeunt*

---

3. Expression of disapproval.
4. Proverbially said of children who overhear remarks made by adults: "Little pitchers have big ears."
5. Modern Pontefract, in west Yorkshire, site of the castle where Richard II was murdered.
6. Not able to command respect (because the King is so young).

7. Anyone, including criminals, could claim the protection of the church ("sanctuary") and thus immunity from civil law, initially for forty days. The Queen sought sanctuary at Westminster Abbey.
8. An engraved stamp, signifying the authority of the bearer, used to authenticate legal documents; here, the Great Seal of England.

3.1[1]

The Trumpets sound. Enter young PRINCE [EDWARD],
the Dukes of GLOUCESTER *and* BUCKINGHAM, *Lord* CAR-
DINAL, *with others* [*including Lord* STANLEY *Earl of*
Derby and Sir William CATESBY]

BUCKINGHAM   Welcome, sweet Prince, to London, to your chamber.[2]

RICHARD GLOUCESTER [*to* PRINCE EDWARD]   Welcome, dear
    cousin, my thoughts' sovereign.°   *ruler of my thoughts*
The weary way hath made you melancholy.

PRINCE EDWARD   No, uncle, but our crosses[3] on the way
5   Have made it tedious, wearisome, and heavy.
I want° more uncles here to welcome me.   *lack; desire*

RICHARD GLOUCESTER   Sweet Prince, the untainted virtue of your years
Hath not yet dived into the world's deceit,
Nor more can you distinguish of a man
10 Than of his outward show, which God he knows
Seldom or never jumpeth° with the heart.   *coincides*
Those uncles[4] which you want were dangerous.
Your grace attended to their sugared words,
But looked not on the poison of their hearts.
15 God keep you from them, and from such false friends.

PRINCE EDWARD   God keep me from false friends; but they were none.

Enter Lord MAYOR [*and his train*]

RICHARD GLOUCESTER   My lord, the Mayor of London comes to greet you.

MAYOR [*kneeling to* PRINCE EDWARD]   God bless your grace with
    health and happy days.

PRINCE EDWARD   I thank you, good my lord, and thank you all.—
20 I thought my mother and my brother York
Would long ere this have met us on the way.
Fie, what a slug° is Hastings, that he hastes not   *sluggard*
To tell us whether they will come or no.

Enter LORD HASTINGS

BUCKINGHAM   In happy time here comes the sweating lord.
25 PRINCE EDWARD [*to* HASTINGS]   Welcome, my lord. What, will
    our mother come?

LORD HASTINGS   On what occasion° God he knows, not I,   *For what reason*
The Queen your mother, and your brother York,
Have taken sanctuary. The tender° Prince   *young; affectionate*
Would fain have° come with me to meet your grace,   *Would have liked to*
30 But by his mother was perforce° withheld.   *forcibly*

BUCKINGHAM   Fie, what an indirect and peevish° course   *perverse*
Is this of hers!—Lord Cardinal, will your grace
Persuade the Queen to send the Duke of York
Unto his princely brother presently?°—   *immediately*
35 If she deny, Lord Hastings, go with him,
And from her jealous° arms pluck him perforce. *suspicious; mistrustful*

CARDINAL   My lord of Buckingham, if my weak oratory
Can from his mother win the Duke of York,

3.1 Location: A street in London.
1. Either because of defects in the original manuscript or because of blunders in the printing house, the text of this scene, up to line 148, is exceptionally corrupt and has been editorially reconstructed.
2. Capital (London was known as *camera regis*, "the King's chamber").

3. Referring to the arrests of his uncle and half-brothers on the journey.
4. Of the two arrested, only Rivers, being Elizabeth's brother, was Prince Edward's real uncle; Gray, a son by Elizabeth's previous marriage, was therefore actually half brother to the Prince.

40	Anon° expect him. But if she be obdurate	*Very soon*
	To mild entreaties, God in heaven forbid	
	We should infringe the sacred privilege	
	Of blessèd sanctuary. Not for all this land	
	Would I be guilty of so deep a sin.	

BUCKINGHAM You are too senseless-obstinate, my lord,
45 Too ceremonious° and traditional. *rule-bound*
Weigh it not with the grossness° of this age. *coarseness*
You break not sanctuary in seizing him.
The benefit thereof is always granted
To those whose dealings have deserved the place,
50 And those who have the wit to claim the place.
This prince hath neither claimed it nor deserved it,
And therefore, in my mind, he cannot have it.
Then taking him from thence that 'longs not there,[5]
You break thereby no privilege nor charter.
55 Oft have I heard of 'sanctuary men',[6]
But 'sanctuary children' ne'er till now.
CARDINAL My lord, you shall o'errule my mind for once.—
Come on, Lord Hastings, will you go with me?
LORD HASTINGS I come, my lord.
60 PRINCE EDWARD Good lords, make all the speedy haste you may.—

Exeunt CARDINAL *and* HASTINGS

Say, uncle Gloucester, if our brother come,
Where shall we sojourn° till our coronation? *stay*
RICHARD GLOUCESTER Where it seems best unto your royal self.
If I may counsel you, some day or two
65 Your highness shall repose you at the Tower,[7]
Then where you please and shall be thought most fit
For your best health and recreation.
PRINCE EDWARD I do not like the Tower of any place.°— *of all places*
Did Julius Caesar build that place, my lord?
70 BUCKINGHAM He did, my gracious lord, begin that place,
Which since succeeding ages have re-edified.° *built further*
PRINCE EDWARD Is it upon record, or else reported[8]
Successively from age to age, he built it?
BUCKINGHAM Upon record, my gracious liege.
75 PRINCE EDWARD But say, my lord, it were not registered,° *documented*
Methinks the truth should live from age to age,
As 'twere retailed° to all posterity *related orally*
Even to the general all-ending day.° *Day of Judgment*
RICHARD GLOUCESTER [*aside*] So wise so young, they say, do
    never live long.
80 PRINCE EDWARD What say you, uncle?
RICHARD GLOUCESTER I say, 'Without characters° fame lives long'. *writing*
[*Aside*] Thus like the formal Vice, Iniquity,[9]
I moralize two meanings in one word.[1]
PRINCE EDWARD That Julius Caesar was a famous man:

---

5. Taking the Prince from a place he has not claimed as sanctuary.
6. Criminals seeking to avoid prosecution.
7. It was customary for Kings of England (before James II) to spend the night before their coronation in the Tower, it being a royal palace and one of the strongest fortresses in the country. But Edward fears its other aspect, as a prison.
8. Is it on written record or otherwise told orally.
9. The conventional Vice figure, called Iniquity, who in sixteenth-century morality plays symbolized all of the vices.
1. As the Vice often did, Richard makes the same phrase have a double meaning.

85 With what his valour did t'enrich his wit,
    His wit set down to make his valour live.[2]
    Death made no conquest of this conqueror,
    For yet he lives in fame though not in life.
    I'll tell you what, my cousin Buckingham.

90 BUCKINGHAM What, my good lord?
    PRINCE EDWARD <u>An if° I live until I be a man,</u>   *An if = If*
    <u>I'll win our ancient right[3] in France again,</u>
    <u>Or die a soldier, as I lived a king.</u>
    RICHARD GLOUCESTER *[aside]* Short summers lightly have a
        forward spring.[4]
            Enter young [Duke of] YORK, [LORD] HASTINGS, *and*
                [*Lord*] CARDINAL
95 BUCKINGHAM Now in good time, here comes the Duke of York.
    PRINCE EDWARD Richard of York, how fares our loving brother?
    YORK Well, my dread[5] lord—so must I call you now.
    PRINCE EDWARD Ay, brother, to our grief, as it is yours.
    Too late° he died that might have kept that title,   *recently*
100 Which by his death hath lost much majesty.
    RICHARD GLOUCESTER How fares our noble cousin, Lord of York?
    YORK I thank you, gentle uncle, well. O, my lord,
    You said that idle° weeds are fast in growth;   *useless*
    The Prince, my brother, hath outgrown me far.
105 RICHARD GLOUCESTER He hath, my lord.
    YORK   And therefore is he idle?
    RICHARD GLOUCESTER O my fair cousin, I must not say so.
    YORK He is more beholden to you then than I.
    RICHARD GLOUCESTER He may command me as my sovereign,
    But you have power in me as a kinsman.
110 YORK I pray you, uncle, render me this dagger.
    RICHARD GLOUCESTER My dagger, little cousin? With all my heart.
    PRINCE EDWARD A beggar, brother?
    YORK Of my kind uncle that I know will give,
    It being but a toy° which is no grief to give.   *trifle*
115 RICHARD GLOUCESTER A greater gift than that I'll give my cousin.
    YORK A greater gift? O, that's the sword to it.[6]
    RICHARD GLOUCESTER Ay, gentle cousin, were it light enough.
    YORK O, then I see you will part but° with light° gifts.   *only / trivial*
    In weightier things you'll say a beggar nay.
120 RICHARD GLOUCESTER It is too heavy for your grace to wear.
    YORK I'd weigh it lightly, were it heavier.[7]
    RICHARD GLOUCESTER What, would you have my weapon, little lord?
    YORK I would, that I might thank you as you call me.
    RICHARD GLOUCESTER How?
125 YORK Little.
    PRINCE EDWARD My lord of York will still be cross° in talk.— *perverse; quarrelsome*
    Uncle, your grace knows how to bear with him.
    YORK You mean to bear me, not to bear with me.—
    Uncle, my brother mocks both you and me.

---

2. *With . . . live:* The same valorous deeds that enlivened Caesar's writing were themselves made immortal by his retelling of them.
3. Right to the throne (claimed by Henry V and his son Henry VI).
4. Proverbial: Those who die young ("forward") are often ("lightly") precocious.
5. Held in awe (a common formula for addressing a king).
6. *to it:* that is, to the dagger (the sword is to the dagger as the greater gift is to the lesser).
7. I'd consider it of little value, even if it were heavier.

130   <u>Because that I am little like an ape,</u>
    <u>He thinks that you should bear me on your shoulders.</u>⁸

BUCKINGHAM   With what a sharp, prodigal wit⁹ he reasons.
    To mitigate the scorn he gives his uncle,
    He prettily and aptly taunts himself.
135   So cunning and so young is wonderful.°   *a cause of wonder*

RICHARD GLOUCESTER [*to* PRINCE EDWARD] My lord, will't
    please you pass along?
    Myself and my good cousin Buckingham
    Will° to your mother to entreat of her   *Will go*
    To meet you at the Tower and welcome you.
140 YORK [*to* PRINCE EDWARD]   What, will you go unto the Tower, my lord?

PRINCE EDWARD   My Lord Protector needs will have it so.

YORK   I shall not sleep in quiet at the Tower.

RICHARD GLOUCESTER   Why, what should you fear there?

YORK   Marry, my uncle Clarence' angry ghost.
145   My grannam told me he was murdered there.

PRINCE EDWARD   I fear no uncles dead.

RICHARD GLOUCESTER   Nor none that live, I hope.

PRINCE EDWARD   An if they¹ live, I hope I need not fear.
    [*To* YORK] But come, my lord, and with a heavy heart,
    Thinking on them, go we unto the Tower.
    *A sennet.*²

           Exeunt. Manent RICHARD, BUCKINGHAM, *and* CATESBY

BUCKINGHAM [*to* RICHARD]   Think you, my lord, this little prating°   *chattering*
150   York
    Was not incensèd° by his subtle mother   *incited*
    To taunt and scorn you thus opprobriously?

RICHARD GLOUCESTER   No doubt, no doubt. O, 'tis a parlous° boy,   *shrewd*
    Bold, quick, ingenious, forward, capable.
155   He is all the mother's, from the top to toe.

BUCKINGHAM   Well, let them rest.—Come hither, Catesby. Thou art sworn
    As deeply° to effect what we intend   *cunningly*
    As closely° to conceal what we impart.   *secretly*
    Thou know'st our reasons, urged upon the way.³
160   What think'st thou? Is it not an easy matter
    To make Lord William Hastings of our mind,⁴
    For the instalment° of this noble duke   *enthroning*
    In the seat royal of this famous isle?

CATESBY   He for his father's sake so loves the Prince⁵
165   That he will not be won to aught against him.

BUCKINGHAM   What think'st thou then of Stanley?° Will not he?   *(Earl of Derby)*

CATESBY   He will do all-in-all as Hastings doth.

BUCKINGHAM   Well then, no more but this. Go, gentle Catesby,
    And, as it were far off, sound thou Lord Hastings
170   How he doth stand affected to our purpose.⁶
170.1   *And summon him tomorrow to the Tower*
        To sit about° the coronation.   *To discuss in council*
    If thou dost find him tractable° to us,   *compliant*

---

8. Alluding to Richard's hunched back, which is compared to the saddle worn by jesters who carried monkeys about at carnivals and fairs.
9. A nimble wit (intelligence); a wit both sharp and prodigal (abundant or excessive).
1. Richard meant himself; Edward refers to Rivers and Gray.

2. Trumpet notes to signal a procession.
3. On the journey from London to Ludlow.
4. To have Hastings share in our opinion.
5. Hastings loves the Prince as the son of the beloved King Edward
6. The following indented passage, 170.1–170.2, appears only in F. *stand affected to*: regard, like.

Encourage him, and tell him all our reasons.
If he be leaden, icy, cold, unwilling,
Be thou so too, and so break off your talk,
175 And give us notice of his inclination,
For we tomorrow hold divided counsels,[7]
Wherein thyself shalt highly° be employed.   *importantly*
RICHARD GLOUCESTER   Commend me to Lord William.° Tell   *(Hastings)*
him, Catesby,
His ancient knot[8] of dangerous adversaries
180 Tomorrow are let blood° at Pomfret Castle,   *are executed*
And bid my lord, for joy of this good news,
Give Mrs Shore[9] one gentle kiss the more.
BUCKINGHAM   Good Catesby, go effect this business soundly.° *thoroughly; well*
CATESBY   My good lords both, with all the heed I can.
185 RICHARD GLOUCESTER   Shall we hear from you, Catesby, ere we sleep?
CATESBY   You shall, my lord.
RICHARD GLOUCESTER   At Crosby House,° there shall you find   *(Richard's residence)*
us both.   *Exit* CATESBY
BUCKINGHAM   My lord, what shall we do if we perceive
Lord Hastings will not yield to our complots?°   *plots*
190 RICHARD GLOUCESTER   Chop off his head. Something we will determine.
And look when° I am king, claim thou of me   *And as soon as*
The earldom of Hereford, and all the movables[1]
Whereof the King my brother was possessed.
BUCKINGHAM   I'll claim that promise at your grace's hand.
195 RICHARD GLOUCESTER   And look° to have it yielded with all kindness.   *And expect*
Come, let us sup betimes,° that afterwards   *early*
We may digest our complots in some form.[2]   *Exeunt*

3.2

Enter a MESSENGER *to the door of* LORD HASTINGS
MESSENGER [*knocking*]   My lord, my lord!
LORD HASTINGS [*within*]   Who knocks?
MESSENGER   One from Lord Stanley.
Enter LORD HASTINGS
LORD HASTINGS   What is't o'clock?
MESSENGER   Upon the stroke of four.
LORD HASTINGS   Cannot my Lord Stanley sleep these tedious nights?
MESSENGER   So it appears by that I have to say.
5 First he commends him to your noble self.
LORD HASTINGS   What then?
MESSENGER   Then certifies° your lordship that this night   *assures*
He dreamt the boar had razèd off his helm.[1]
Besides, he says there are two councils kept,
10 And that may be determined at the one
Which may make you and him to rue at° th'other.   *regret*
Therefore he sends to know your lordship's pleasure,
If you will presently° take horse with him,   *immediately*

7. There will be two separate council meetings, one public to plan the Prince's coronation, the other private to plot Richard's seizing of the crown.
8. Conspiracy, with additional meaning of "tumor," picked up in the next line in the image of bloodletting as medical treatment.
9. After Edward's death, Jane Shore (see 1.1.71–77) became Hastings's mistress.
1. Personal as opposed to real property: furnishings, rather than land.
2. We may break plans down into an orderly system (with pun on "digest").
3.2 Location: Outside Lord Hastings's house, in London.
1. He dreamed the boar (Richard's emblem) had sheared off his helmet (figuratively, cut off his head).

And with all speed post with him toward the north
15 To shun the danger that his soul divines.°   *prophesies*
LORD HASTINGS   Go, fellow, go, return unto thy lord.
Bid him not fear the separated councils.
His honour and myself are at the one,
And at the other is my good friend Catesby,
20 Where nothing can proceed that toucheth° us   *concerns; harms*
Whereof I shall not have intelligence.°   *secret information*
Tell him his fears are shallow, without instance.°   *evidence*
And for his dreams, I wonder he's so simple,°   *childish*
To trust the mock'ry of unquiet slumbers.
25 To fly the boar before the boar pursues
Were to incense the boar to follow us,
And make pursuit where he did mean° no chase.   *intend*
Go, bid thy master rise, and come to me,
And we will both together to the Tower,
30 Where he shall see the boar will use us kindly.[2]
MESSENGER   I'll go, my lord, and tell him what you say.   *Exit*
          Enter CATESBY
CATESBY   Many good morrows to my noble lord.
LORD HASTINGS   Good morrow, Catesby. You are early stirring.
What news, what news, in this our tott'ring state?
35 CATESBY   It is a reeling° world indeed, my lord,   *an unstable*
And I believe will never stand upright
Till Richard wear the garland of the realm.
LORD HASTINGS   How? 'Wear the garland'? Dost thou mean the crown?
CATESBY   Ay, my good lord.
40 LORD HASTINGS   I'll have this crown° of mine cut from my shoulders   *head*
Before I'll see the crown so foul misplaced.
But canst thou guess that he doth aim at it?
CATESBY   Ay, on my life, and hopes to find you forward°   *a strong supporter*
Upon his party° for the gain thereof—   *On his side*
45 And thereupon he sends you this good news:
That this same very day your enemies,
The kindred of the Queen, must die at Pomfret.
LORD HASTINGS   Indeed I am no mourner for that news,
Because they have been still my adversaries.
50 But that I'll give my voice on Richard's side
To bar my master's heirs in true descent,
God knows I will not do it, to the death.[3]
CATESBY   God keep your lordship in that gracious mind!
LORD HASTINGS   But I shall laugh at this a twelvemonth hence:
55 That they which brought me in my master's hate,[4]
I live to look upon their tragedy.
Well, Catesby, ere a fortnight make me older,
I'll send some packing that yet think not on't.
CATESBY   'Tis a vile thing to die, my gracious lord,
60 When men are unprepared, and look not for it.
LORD HASTINGS   O monstrous, monstrous! And so falls it out
With Rivers, Vaughan, Gray—and so 'twill do
With some men else, that think themselves as safe

2. Gently (but also, with unintended irony, characteristically).
3. Even at the risk of death.

4. That those (Rivers, Vaughan, and Gray) who turned
King Edward against me.

As thou and I, who as thou know'st are dear
65   To princely Richard and to Buckingham.
CATESBY   The Princes both make high account of° you—   *highly esteem*
  [*Aside*] For they account° his head upon the bridge.⁵   *expect*
LORD HASTINGS   I know they do, and I have well deserved it.
    Enter Lord STANLEY
  Come on, come on, where is your boar-spear,⁶ man?
70   Fear you the boar, and go so unprovided?⁷
STANLEY   My lord, good morrow.—Good morrow, Catesby.—
  You may jest on, but by the Holy Rood°   *Cross*
  I do not like these several° councils, I.   *separate*
LORD HASTINGS   My lord, I hold my life as dear as you do yours,
75   And never in my days, I do protest,
  Was it so precious to me as 'tis now.
  Think you, but° that I know our state secure,   *if it were not*
  I would be so triumphant as I am?
STANLEY   The lords at Pomfret, when they rode from London,
80   Were jocund,° and supposed their states were sure,°   *merry / secure*
  And they indeed had no cause to mistrust;
  But yet you see how soon the day o'ercast.°   *became overcast*
  This sudden stab of rancour I misdoubt.⁸
  Pray God, I say, I prove a needless coward.
85   What, shall we toward the Tower? The day is spent.⁹
LORD HASTINGS   Come, come, have with you!° Wot° you what,
    my lord?   *I'll go with you / Know*
  Today the lords you talked of are beheaded.
STANLEY   They for their truth° might better wear their heads   *honesty*
  Than some that have accused them wear their hats.°   *retain their offices*
90   But come, my lord, let us away.
    Enter a PURSUIVANT [*named*] *Hastings*¹
LORD HASTINGS   Go on before; I'll follow presently.
    Exeunt STANLEY *and* CATESBY
  Well met, Hastings. How goes the world with thee?
PURSUIVANT   The better that your lordship please° to ask.   *is pleased*
LORD HASTINGS   I tell thee, man, 'tis better with me now
95   Than when I met thee last, where now we meet.
  Then was I going prisoner to the Tower,
  By the suggestion° of the Queen's allies;   *incitement*
  But now, I tell thee—keep it to thyself—
  This day those enemies are put to death,
100   And I in better state than e'er I was.
PURSUIVANT   God hold it² to your honour's good content.
LORD HASTINGS   Gramercy,° Hastings. There, drink that for me.   *Many thanks*
    He throws him his purse
PURSUIVANT   God save your lordship.   *Exit*
    Enter a PRIEST

---

5. London Bridge (where the heads of traitors were displayed high on poles).
6. Specialized hunting spear with a crossbar to prevent the impaled boar's tusks from wounding the hunter.
7. Do you fear the boar, and (yet) go unprepared?
8. I mistrust such sudden attacks (as those that befell Rivers, Vaughan, and Gray).
9. It's getting late (in the morning). The scene had opened at 4:00 A.M.
1. F omits his name (taken from Holinshed's *Chroni-*

cles), here and in the dialogue. The name may be important in calling attention to the significance of Lord Hastings's own name: the word means either "someone who hurries" (here, to his destruction) or "a fruit that ripens early or before its time." *pursuivant:* state messenger with authority to execute warrants (particularly of treason). Figuratively, a pursuivant was any summoner or messenger.
2. May God maintain your prosperity.

PRIEST   Well met, my lord. I am glad to see your honour
105   LORD HASTINGS   I thank thee, good Sir³ John, with all my heart.
I am in your debt for your last exercise.°   *sermon*
Come the next sabbath, and I will content you.⁴
          He whispers in his ear.
          Enter BUCKINGHAM
BUCKINGHAM   What, talking with a priest, Lord Chamberlain?
Your friends at Pomfret, they do need the priest:
110   Your honour hath no shriving work⁵ in hand.
LORD HASTINGS   Good faith, and when I met this holy man
The men you talk of came into my mind.
What, go you toward the Tower?
BUCKINGHAM   I do, my lord, but long I cannot stay there;
115   I shall return before your lordship thence.
LORD HASTINGS   Nay, like enough, for I stay dinner⁶ there.
BUCKINGHAM [*aside*]   And supper° too, although thou⁷ know'st it not.   *evening meal*
Come, will you go?
LORD HASTINGS   I'll wait upon° your lordship.   *Exeunt*   *attend; go with*

3.3

Enter Sir Richard RATCLIFFE *with halberdiers carrying*
Lords RIVERS, GRAY, *and [Sir Thomas]* VAUGHAN *to*
*death at Pomfret*¹
RIVERS   Sir Richard Ratcliffe, let me tell thee this:
Today shalt thou behold a subject die
For truth, for duty, and for loyalty.
GRAY [*to* RATCLIFFE]   God bless the Prince from all the pack of you!
5   A knot° you are of damnèd bloodsuckers.   *group*
VAUGHAN [*to* RATCLIFFE]   You live, that shall cry woe for° this   *shall regret*
          hereafter.
RATCLIFFE   Dispatch.° The limit of your lives is out.   *Be quick*
RIVERS   O Pomfret, Pomfret! O thou bloody prison,
Fatal and ominous to noble peers!
10   Within the guilty closure° of thy walls,   *enclosure*
Richard the Second here was hacked to death,
And, for more slander to thy dismal seat,²
We give to thee our guiltless blood to drink.
GRAY   Now Margaret's curse is fall'n upon our heads,
15   For standing by when Richard stabbed her son.
RIVERS   Then cursed she Hastings; then cursed she Buckingham;
Then cursed she Richard. O remember, God,
To hear her prayer for them as now for us.
And for° my sister and her princely sons,   *as for*
20   Be satisfied, dear God, with our true blood,
Which, as thou know'st, unjustly must be spilt.
RATCLIFFE   Make haste: the hour of death is expiate.°   *fully come*
RIVERS   Come, Gray; come, Vaughan; let us here embrace.
Farewell, until we meet again in heaven.   *Exeunt*

---

3. Courteous title of respect for clergymen.
4. I will pay your "debt" with a donation.
5. Confession and absolution (here, before execution).
6. I stay for dinner (eaten at about 11:00 A.M.).
7. Here, used contemptuously, as opposed to the formal "you" in line 118.

3.3 Location: Pontefract Castle.
1. Q has an extra opening line for this scene: RATCLIFFE Come, bring forth the prisoners.
2. And, in order to increase the notoriety of this gloomy place.

3.4

Enter [the Duke of] BUCKINGHAM, *[Lord* STANLEY *Earl of] Derby, [*LORD] HASTINGS, BISHOP OF ELY, *[the Duke of]* NORFOLK, *[Sir William* CATESBY,]¹ *with others at a table*

LORD HASTINGS   Now, noble peers, the cause why we are met
Is to determine of° the coronation.   *decide upon*
In God's name, speak: when is the royal day?
BUCKINGHAM   Is all things ready for that solemn time?
5   STANLEY   It is, and wants but nomination.°   *naming the day*
BISHOP OF ELY   Tomorrow, then, I judge a happy° day.   *suitable*
BUCKINGHAM   Who knows the Lord Protector's mind herein?
Who is most inward° with the noble Duke?   *intimate*
BISHOP OF ELY   Your grace, methinks, should soonest know his mind.
10   BUCKINGHAM   We know each other's faces. For° our hearts,   *As for*
He knows no more of mine than I of yours,
Or I of his, my lord, than you of mine.—
Lord Hastings, you and he are near in love.
LORD HASTINGS   I thank his grace; I know he loves me well.
15   But for his purpose in the coronation,
I have not sounded him,° nor he delivered   *sounded him out*
His gracious pleasure any way therein.
But you, my honourable lords, may name the time,
And in the Duke's behalf I'll give my voice,°   *vote*
20   Which I presume he'll take in gentle part.°   *he'll graciously approve*
*Enter [*RICHARD *Duke of]* GLOUCESTER
BISHOP OF ELY   In happy time, here comes the Duke himself.
RICHARD GLOUCESTER   My noble lords, and cousins all, good morrow.
I have been long a sleeper, but I trust
My absence doth neglect no great design²
25   Which by my presence might have been concluded.
BUCKINGHAM   Had not you come upon your cue, my lord,
William Lord Hastings had pronounced your part—
I mean, your voice, for crowning of the King.
RICHARD GLOUCESTER   Than my Lord Hastings no man might be bolder.³
30   His lordship knows me well, and loves me well.—
My lord of Ely, when I was last in Holborn⁴
I saw good strawberries in your garden there.
I do beseech you send for some of them.
BISHOP OF ELY   Marry, and will, my lord, with all my heart.   *Exit*
35   RICHARD GLOUCESTER   Cousin of Buckingham, a word with you.
[Aside] Catesby hath sounded Hastings in° our business,   *in respect to*
And finds the testy gentleman so hot
That he will lose his head ere give consent
His 'master's child'—as worshipful° he terms it—   *reverentially*
40   Shall lose the royalty° of England's throne.   *sovereignty*
BUCKINGHAM   Withdraw yourself a while; I'll go with you.
*Exeunt [*RICHARD *and* BUCKINGHAM]⁵
STANLEY   We have not yet set down this day of triumph.

3.4 Location: The Tower of London.
1. F has Ratcliffe and Lovell (Sir Thomas Lovell; see 4.4.449) instead of Catesby.
2. My absence delays no important project.
3. No one could more confidently speak for me than

Lord Hastings; but also, no one could be more presumptuous.
4. The Bishop of Ely's official London residence.
5. Q keeps Buckingham on, and changes "I'll go with you" to "I'll follow you."

Tomorrow, in my judgement, is too sudden,
For I myself am not so well provided°   well equipped
45   As else I would be, were the day prolonged.°   further off
         Enter BISHOP OF ELY
BISHOP OF ELY   Where is my lord, the Duke of Gloucester?
I have sent for these strawberries.
LORD HASTINGS   His grace looks cheerfully and smooth° this morning.   untroubled
There's some conceit° or other likes° him well,   thought / pleases
50   When that he bids good morrow with such spirit.
I think there's never a man in Christendom
Can lesser hide his love or hate than he,
For by his face straight° shall you know his heart.   immediately
STANLEY   What of his heart perceive you in his face
55   By any likelihood° he showed today?   appearance
LORD HASTINGS   Marry, that with no man here he is offended—
For were he, he had shown it in his looks.
STANLEY   I pray God he be not.
         Enter RICHARD[6] *and* BUCKINGHAM
RICHARD GLOUCESTER   I pray you all tell me what they deserve
60   That do conspire my death with devilish plots
Of damnèd witchcraft, and that have prevailed
Upon my body with their hellish charms?
LORD HASTINGS   The tender love I bear your grace, my lord,
Makes me most forward in this princely presence
65   To doom th'offenders, whatsoe'er they be.
I say, my lord, they have deservèd death.
RICHARD GLOUCESTER   Then be your eyes the witness of their evil:
See how I am bewitched. Behold, mine arm
Is like a blasted sapling withered up.
70   And this is° Edward's wife, that monstrous witch,   this is the work of
Consorted° with that harlot, strumpet Shore,   In league with
That by their witchcraft thus have markèd me.
LORD HASTINGS   If they have done this deed, my noble lord—
RICHARD GLOUCESTER   'If'? Thou protector of this damnèd strumpet,
75   Talk'st thou to me of 'ifs'? Thou art a traitor.—
Off with his head. Now, by Saint Paul I swear,
I will not dine until I see the same.
Some see it done.
The rest that love me, rise and follow me.
         Exeunt. Manent CATESBY[7] *with* HASTINGS
80   LORD HASTINGS   Woe, woe for England! Not a whit for me,
For I, too fond,° might have prevented this.   foolish
Stanley did dream the boar did raze our helms,
But I did scorn it and disdain to fly.
Three times today my footcloth horse[8] did stumble,
85   And started when he looked upon the Tower,
As° loath to bear me to the slaughterhouse.   As though
O now I need the priest that spake to me.
I now repent I told the pursuivant,
As too triumphing,° how mine enemies   exulting

6. According to Holinshed, "He returned into the
chamber . . . with a wonderful sour, angry countenance,
knitting the brows, frowning and fretting, and gnawing
on his lips."

7. F calls for Ratcliffe and Lovell.
8. Horse draped with a richly ornamented covering
reaching almost to the ground.

90   Today at Pomfret bloodily were butchered,
      And I myself secure in grace and favour.
      O Margaret, Margaret! Now thy heavy curse
      Is lighted on poor Hastings' wretched head.
CATESBY   Come, come, dispatch: the Duke would be at dinner.
95   Make a short shrift;° he longs to see your head.   *confession (to a priest)*
LORD HASTINGS   O momentary grace of mortal men,
      Which we more hunt for than the grace of God.
      Who builds his hope in th'air of your good looks⁹
      Lives like a drunken sailor on a mast,
100   Ready with every nod¹ to tumble down
      Into the fatal bowels of the deep.²
CATESBY   Come, come, dispatch. 'Tis bootless to exclaim.°   *pointless to protest*
LORD HASTINGS   O bloody Richard! Miserable England!
      I prophesy the fearful'st time to thee
105   That ever wretched age hath looked upon.—
      Come lead me to the block; bear him my head.
      They smile at me, who shortly shall be dead.   *Exeunt*

3.5

      Enter RICHARD *Duke of* GLOUCESTER *and* [*the Duke of*]
      BUCKINGHAM *in rotten*° *armour, marvellous ill-favoured*°   *rusty / ugly*
RICHARD GLOUCESTER   Come, cousin, canst thou quake and change thy
      colour?
      Murder thy breath in middle of a word?
      And then again begin, and stop again,
      As if thou wert distraught and mad with terror?
5   BUCKINGHAM   Tut, I can counterfeit the deep tragedian,
      Tremble and start at wagging of a straw,¹
      Speak, and look back, and pry° on every side,   *peer*
      Intending° deep suspicion; ghastly looks   *Suggesting*
      Are at my service, like enforcèd smiles,
10   And both are ready in their offices²
      At any time to grace my stratagems.
            Enter the [Lord] MAYOR
RICHARD GLOUCESTER [*aside to* BUCKINGHAM]   Here comes the Mayor.
BUCKINGHAM [*aside to* RICHARD]   Let me alone to entertain him.—Lord Mayor—
RICHARD GLOUCESTER [*calling as to one within*]   Look to the drawbridge there!
15 BUCKINGHAM   Hark, a drum!
RICHARD GLOUCESTER [*calling as to one within*]   Catesby, o'erlook°   *look (out) over*
      the walls!
BUCKINGHAM   Lord Mayor, the reason we have sent—
RICHARD GLOUCESTER   Look back, defend thee! Here are enemies.
BUCKINGHAM   God and our innocence defend and guard us.
            Enter [Sir William] CATESBY³ *with Hastings' head*
20 RICHARD GLOUCESTER   O, O, be quiet! It is Catesby.
CATESBY   Here is the head of that ignoble traitor,
      The dangerous and unsuspected Hastings.
RICHARD GLOUCESTER   So dear I loved the man that I must weep.

---

9. *Who . . . looks:* Anyone who puts his faith in your
seemingly favorable glances.
1. Complex play on words: Ready as he dozes off; as the
ship rolls; as the monarch, whose "good looks" upheld
him, condemns him with a silent nod.
2. Lines 102–7 appear only in F. Censorship or the fear
of censorship may well be why Hastings's ominous pre-

diction was omitted from Q.
3.5 Location: The Tower of London.
1. Act startled by the least movement or gesture.
2. Both are eager to perform their functions.
3. F calls for Ratcliffe and Lovell, and brings on
Catesby earlier, with the Mayor.

I took him for the plainest° harmless creature   *most manifestly*
25   That breathed upon the earth, a Christian,
Made him my book° wherein my soul recorded   *diary*
The history of all her secret thoughts.
So smooth he daubed his vice with show of virtue
That, his apparent open guilt omitted—
30   I mean, his conversation[4] with Shore's wife—
He lived from all attainture of suspect.[5]

BUCKINGHAM   The covert'st sheltered° traitor that ever lived.   *The most hidden*
[*To the* MAYOR] Would you imagine, or almost believe—
Were't not that, by great preservation,[6]
35   We live to tell it—that the subtle traitor
This day had plotted in the Council house
To murder me and my good lord of Gloucester?

MAYOR   Had he done so?

RICHARD GLOUCESTER   What, think you we are Turks or infidels,
40   Or that we would against the form of law
Proceed thus rashly in the villain's death
But that the extreme peril of the case,
The peace of England, and our persons' safety,
Enforced us to this execution?

45   MAYOR   Now fair befall you, he deserved his death,
And your good graces both have well proceeded,°   *acted*
To warn false traitors from the like° attempts.   *similar*
I never looked for better at his hands
After he once fell in with Mrs Shore.

50   RICHARD GLOUCESTER[7]   Yet had not we determined he should die,
Until your lordship came to see his end,
Which now the loving haste of these our friends°—   *(Catesby and Buckingham)*
Something against our meanings°—have prevented;   *intentions*
Because, my lord, we would have had you hear
55   The traitor speak, and timorously confess
The manner and the purpose of his treason,
That you might well have signified the same
Unto the citizens, who haply° may   *perhaps*
Misconster us in him,[8] and wail his death.

60   MAYOR   But, my good lord, your graces' word shall serve
As well as° I had seen and heard him speak.   *As well as = As if*
And do not doubt, right noble princes both,
But° I'll acquaint our duteous citizens   *That*
With all your just proceedings in this cause.°   *action*

65   RICHARD GLOUCESTER   And to that end we wished your lordship here,
T'avoid the censures of the carping° world.   *overcritical*

BUCKINGHAM   Which, since you come too late of our intent,°   *for what we intended*
Yet witness° what you hear we did intend,   *bear witness to*
And so, my good Lord Mayor, we bid farewell.   *Exit* MAYOR

70   RICHARD GLOUCESTER   Go after; after, cousin Buckingham!
The Mayor towards Guildhall[9] hies him in all post;°   *haste*
There, at your meetest vantage of the time,[1]
Infer° the bastardy of Edward's children.   *Allege*
Tell them how Edward put to death a citizen

4. Intercourse (in both senses).
5. He lived free from all taint of suspicion.
6. By the most fortunate preservation (of our lives).
7. F assigns this speech and the two preceding lines to Buckingham.
8. Misunderstand our treatment of him.
9. Center of municipal government in London.
1. At your most appropriate and advantageous moment.

75 Only for saying he would make his son
'Heir to the Crown'—meaning indeed, his house,° *tavern*
Which by the sign thereof was termèd so.
Moreover, urge his hateful luxury° *lasciviousness*
And bestial appetite in change of lust,[2]
80 Which stretched unto their servants, daughters, wives,
Even where° his raging eye, or savage heart, *Wherever*
Without control, listed° to make a prey. *desired*
Nay, for a need, thus far come near my person:[3]
Tell them, when that my mother went with child
85 Of that insatiate Edward,[4] noble York,
My princely father, then had wars in France,
And by true computation of the time
Found that the issue° was not his begot— *offspring*
Which well appearèd in his lineaments,° *features*
90 Being nothing like the noble Duke my father.
Yet touch this sparingly, as 'twere far off,
Because, my lord, you know my mother lives.
BUCKINGHAM Doubt not, my lord, I'll play the orator
As if the golden fee[5] for which I plead
95 Were for myself. And so, my lord, adieu. [*He starts to go*]
RICHARD GLOUCESTER If you thrive well, bring them to Baynard's Castle,[6]
Where you shall find me well accompanied
With reverend fathers and well-learnèd bishops.
BUCKINGHAM I go, and towards three or four o'clock
100 Look for the news that the Guildhall affords.[7] *Exit*
100.1 *KING RICHARD Go, Lovell, with all speed to Doctor Shaw;*
[To RATCLIFFE] Go thou to Friar Penker.[8] Bid them both
Meet me within this hour at Baynard's Castle.
[*Exeunt* LOVELL *and* RATCLIFFE]
RICHARD GLOUCESTER Now will I in, to take some privy order[9]
To draw the brats of Clarence[1] out of sight,
And to give notice that no manner[2] person
Have any° time recourse unto the Princes. *Exeunt* *at any*

3.6

Enter a SCRIVENER° *with a paper in his hand* *scribe*
SCRIVENER Here is the indictment of the good Lord Hastings,
Which in a set hand fairly is engrossed,[1]
That it may be today read o'er in Paul's[2]—
And mark how well the sequel° hangs together: *sequence of events*
5 Eleven hours I have spent to write it over,
For yesternight by Catesby was it sent me;
The precedent° was full as long a-doing; *rough draft*
And yet, within these five hours, Hastings lived,

2. In continually shifting the object of his lust.
3. *for . . . person:* if necessary, impugn even to this extent my own honor (by implying that his mother was unfaithful).
4. *went . . . Edward:* was pregnant with dissolute Edward. *insatiate:* impossible to satisfy.
5. The crown (punning on "lawyer's fee").
6. Richard's stronghold, between Blackfriars and London Bridge.
7. The indented passage that follows, 100.1–100.3, appears only in F.
8. Dr. Shaw, brother to the Lord Mayor, and Friar

Perkins, provincial of the Augustinian Order, were prominent clerics who made public speeches supporting Richard's claim to the throne.
9. To make some secret arrangements.
1. The two children seen in 2.2.
2. No kind of (in other words, of whatever status or importance).
3.6 Location: Somewhere in London.
1. Which is written in official script (as opposed to a draft copy) and in the format of a legal document.
2. St. Paul's Cathedral, which served as a secular as well as sacred gathering place.

Untainted,° unexamined, free, at liberty.   *Unaccused*
10   Here's a good world the while! Who is so gross°   *stupid*
That cannot see this palpable device?°   *obvious stratagem*
Yet who so bold but says he sees it not?
Bad is the world, and all will come to naught,°   *wickedness; nothing*
When such ill dealing must be seen in thought.[3]   *Exit*

3.7

Enter RICHARD [*Duke of*] GLOUCESTER *at one door and*
[*the Duke of*] BUCKINGHAM *at another*

RICHARD GLOUCESTER   How now, how now! What say the citizens?
BUCKINGHAM   Now, by the holy mother of our Lord,
The citizens are mum, say not a word.
RICHARD GLOUCESTER   Touched you° the bastardy of Edward's   *Did you touch on*
children?
5   BUCKINGHAM   I did, with his contract with Lady Lucy,[1]
And his contract by deputy[2] in France,
Th'insatiate greediness of his desire,
And his enforcement° of the city wives,   *violation*
His tyranny for trifles, his own bastardy—
10   As being got° your father then in France,   *conceived*
And his resemblance,° being not like the Duke.   *appearance*
Withal, I did infer your lineaments°—   *lineage*
Being the right idea° of your father   *true image*
Both in your face[3] and nobleness of mind;
15   Laid open all your victories in Scotland,[4]
Your discipline in war, wisdom in peace,
Your bounty, virtue, fair humility—
Indeed, left nothing fitting for your purpose
Untouched or slightly handled° in discourse.   *lightly mentioned*
20   And when mine oratory grew toward end,
I bid them that did love their country's good
Cry 'God save Richard, England's royal king!'
RICHARD GLOUCESTER   And did they so?
BUCKINGHAM   No, so God help me. They spake not a word,
25   But, like dumb statues or breathing stones,
Stared each on other and looked deadly pale—
Which, when I saw, I reprehended them,
And asked the Mayor, what meant this wilful silence?
His answer was, the people were not used
30   To be spoke to but by the Recorder.°   *(a city official)*
Then he was urged to tell my tale again:
'Thus saith the Duke . . . thus hath the Duke inferred'°—   *asserted*
But nothing spoke in warrant from himself.°   *on his own authority*
When he had done, some followers of mine own,
35   At lower end of the Hall, hurled up their caps.

3. Must be perceived but not spoken of.
3.7 Location: Baynard's Castle.
1. Lady Elizabeth Lucy bore Edward a child. If, as
Buckingham alleges, there had been a formal engagement between them, Edward's subsequent marriage to
Elizabeth Gray would have been ruled invalid. His children by that marriage would have been bastards and
hence ineligible to inherit the throne.
2. The Earl of Warwick, as deputy, had contracted with
Louis XI of France for the marriage of Edward to Bona

of Savoy, the French queen's sister (see *Richard Duke
of York* 3.3).
3. Q, F: forme. The Oxford editors observe that since
Richard is prominently deformed, "form" is inappropriate; in the chronicles, it is Richard's *face* that is compared with his father's.
4. In 1482, as leader of an English expeditionary force
against the Scots, Richard had advanced all the way to
Edinburgh.

And some ten voices cried 'God save King Richard!'
And thus I took the vantage of° those few: *opportunity presented by*
'Thanks, gentle citizens and friends', quoth I;
'This general applause and cheerful shout
40   Argues your wisdoms and your love to Richard'—
And even here brake off and came away.
RICHARD GLOUCESTER   What tongueless blocks were they!
    Would they not speak?
BUCKINGHAM[5]   No, by my troth, my lord.
RICHARD GLOUCESTER   Will not the Mayor then, and his brethren, come?
45   BUCKINGHAM   The Mayor is here at hand. Intend° some fear;   *Pretend*
Be not you spoke with, but by mighty suit;[6]
And look you get a prayer book in your hand,
And stand between two churchmen, good my lord,
For on that ground I'll build a holy descant.[7]
50   And be not easily won to our request.
Play the maid's part:[8] still answer 'nay'—and take it.
RICHARD GLOUCESTER   I go. An if you plead as well for them
As I can say nay to thee for myself,
No doubt we'll bring it to a happy issue.
    [*One knocks within*]
55   BUCKINGHAM   Go, go, up to the leads![9] The Lord Mayor knocks.—
            Exit [RICHARD]
    Enter the [*Lord*] MAYOR, [*aldermen,*] *and citizens*
Welcome, my lord. I dance attendance° here.   *am kept waiting*
I think the Duke will not be spoke withal.
    Enter CATESBY
Now Catesby, what says your lord to my request?
CATESBY   He doth entreat your grace, my noble lord,
60   To visit him tomorrow, or next day.
He is within with two right reverend fathers,
Divinely bent to meditation,
And in no worldly suits would he be moved,
To draw him from his holy exercise.
65   BUCKINGHAM   Return, good Catesby, to the gracious Duke.
Tell him myself, the Mayor, and aldermen,
In deep designs, in matter of great moment,
No less importing than[1] our general good,
Are come to have some conference with his grace.
70   CATESBY   I'll signify so much unto him straight.   *Exit*
BUCKINGHAM   Ah ha! My lord, this prince is not an Edward.
He is not lolling on a lewd day-bed,
But on his knees at meditation;
Not dallying with a brace° of courtesans,   *pair*
75   But meditating with two deep° divines;   *profoundly learned*
Not sleeping to engross° his idle body,   *fatten*
But praying to enrich his watchful° soul.   *vigilant*
Happy were England would this virtuous prince
Take on his grace the sovereignty thereof.
80   But, sure I fear, we shall not win him to it.

5. F omits this line.
6. Do not let them speak with you unless they beg you.
7. Comment; improvised musical variation, usually the highest part. *ground*: basis; musical theme or air, often the bass line.
8. Keep refusing, but at the same time take whatever is offered (proverbial, with sexual innuendo).
9. Flat roof covered with lead.
1. Of no less significance than.

MAYOR   Marry, God defend° his grace should say us nay.   *forbid*
BUCKINGHAM   I fear he will. Here Catesby comes again.
      Enter CATESBY
      Now Catesby, what says his grace?
CATESBY   He wonders to what end you have assembled
85   Such troops of citizens to come to him,
      His grace not being warned thereof before.
      He fears, my lord, you mean no good to him.
BUCKINGHAM   Sorry I am my noble cousin should
      Suspect me that I mean no good to him.
90   By heaven, we come to him in perfect love,
      And so once more return and tell his grace.   *Exit* CATESBY
      When holy and devout religious men
      Are at their beads,° 'tis much to draw them thence.   *prayers*
      So sweet is zealous contemplation.
      Enter RICHARD *aloft, between two bishops.* [*Enter*
      CATESBY *below*]
95 MAYOR   See where his grace stands 'tween two clergymen.
BUCKINGHAM   Two props of virtue for a Christian prince,
      To stay him from the fall of vanity;
      And see, a book of prayer in his hand—
      True ornaments to know[3] a holy man.—
100   Famous Plantagenet, most gracious prince,
      Lend favourable ear to our request
      And pardon us the interruption
      Of thy devotion and right Christian zeal.
RICHARD GLOUCESTER   My lord, there needs no such apology.
105   I do beseech your grace to pardon me,
      Who, earnest in the service of my God,
      Deferred the visitation of my friends.
      But leaving this, what is your grace's pleasure?
BUCKINGHAM   Even that, I hope, which pleaseth God above,
110   And all good men of this ungoverned isle.
RICHARD GLOUCESTER   I do suspect I have done some offence
      That seems disgracious° in the city's eye,   *displeasing*
      And that you come to reprehend my ignorance.
BUCKINGHAM   You have, my lord. Would it might please your grace
115   On our entreaties to amend your fault.
RICHARD GLOUCESTER   Else wherefore breathe I in a Christian land?[4]
BUCKINGHAM   Know then, it is your fault that you resign
      The supreme seat, the throne majestical,
      The sceptred office of your ancestors,
120   Your state of fortune[5] and your due of birth,
      The lineal glory of your royal house,
      To the corruption of a blemished stock,[6]
      Whiles in the mildness of your sleepy° thoughts—   *contemplative*
      Which here we waken to our country's good—
125   The noble isle doth want her proper° limbs: *lack her own*
      Her face defaced with scars of infamy,
      Her royal stock graft with ignoble plants
      And almost shouldered in° the swallowing gulf   *shoved into*

2. To prevent him from falling into the sin of vanity.
3. *True . . . know:* Prayer books (and also, perhaps, the clergymen) by which to recognize.
4. Why else do I lead a Christian life?
5. The position that fortune has given you.
6. Edward's "family tree" is degraded by bastardy and immorality.

Of dark forgetfulness and deep oblivion,
130   Which to recure° we heartily solicit   restore
Your gracious self to take on you the charge
And kingly government of this your land—
Not as Protector, steward, substitute,
Or lowly factor° for another's gain,   agent
135   But as successively,° from blood to blood,   in order of succession
Your right of birth, your empery,° your own.   absolute dominion
For this, consorted° with the citizens,   together
Your very worshipful° and loving friends,   respectful
And by their vehement instigation,
140   In this just cause come I to move your grace.
RICHARD GLOUCESTER   I cannot tell if to depart in silence
Or bitterly to speak in your reproof
Best fitteth my degree° or your condition.[7]   rank
143.1   *If not to answer, you might haply° think*   *perhaps*
           Tongue-tied ambition, not replying, yielded°   *agreed*
           To bear the golden yoke of sovereignty,
           Which fondly° you would here impose on me.   *foolishly*
143.5   *If to reprove you for this suit of yours,*
           So seasoned° with your faithful love to me,   *made palatable*
           Then on the other side I checked° my friends.   *rebuked*
           Therefore to speak, and to avoid the first,
           And then in speaking not to incur the last,
143.10   *Definitively thus I answer you.*
Your love deserves my thanks; but my desert,
145   Unmeritable,° shuns your high request.   Undeserving
First, if all obstacles were cut away
And that my path were even° to the crown,   smooth
As the ripe revenue and due of birth,
Yet so much is my poverty of spirit,
150   So mighty and so many my defects,
That I would rather hide me from my greatness—
Being a barque to brook° no mighty sea—   a boat to endure
Than in my greatness covet to be hid,[8]
And in the vapour of my glory smothered.
155   But God be thanked, there is no need of me,
And much I need° to help you, were there need.   lack (ability)
The royal tree hath left us royal fruit,
Which, mellowed by the stealing hours of time,
Will well become the seat of majesty
160   And make, no doubt, us happy by his reign.
On him I lay that° you would lay on me,   what
The right and fortune of his happy° stars,   auspicious
Which God defend that I should wring from him.
BUCKINGHAM   My lord, this argues conscience in your grace,
165   But the respects thereof are nice and trivial,[9]
All circumstances well considerèd.
You say that Edward is your brother's son;
So say we, too—but not by Edward's wife.
For first was he contract° to Lady Lucy—   betrothed

7. Social rank. The indented passage that follows,   9. But the reasons you advance are nit-picking (thus,
143.1–143.10, appears only in F.   overscrupulous).
8. Than desire to be enveloped by my greatness.

170　Your mother lives a witness to his vow[1]—
　　　And afterward, by substitute,° betrothed　　　　　　　　　　　*proxy*
　　　To Bona, sister to the King of France.
　　　These both put off, a poor petitioner,
　　　A care-crazed mother to a many sons,
175　A beauty-waning and distressèd widow
　　　Even in the afternoon of her best days,
　　　Made prize and purchase° of his wanton eye,　　　　　　　*booty*
　　　Seduced the pitch and height of his degree[2]
　　　To base declension° and loathèd bigamy.　　　　　　　　*degradation*
180　By her in his unlawful bed he got
　　　This Edward, whom our manners° call the Prince.　　*we in politeness*
　　　More bitterly could I expostulate,
　　　Save that for reverence to some alive[3]
　　　I give a sparing limit to my tongue.
185　Then, good my lord, take to your royal self
　　　This proffered benefit° of dignity—　　　　　　　　　　*bestowal*
　　　If not to bless us and the land withal,
　　　Yet to draw forth° your noble ancestry　　　　　　　　　*to rescue*
　　　From the corruption of abusing times,
190　Unto a lineal, true-derivèd course.
　　　MAYOR [*to* RICHARD]　Do, good my lord; your citizens entreat you.
　　　BUCKINGHAM [*to* RICHARD]　Refuse not, mighty lord, this proffered love.
　　　CATESBY [*to* RICHARD]　O make them joyful: grant their lawful suit.
　　　RICHARD GLOUCESTER　Alas, why would you heap this care on me?
195　I am unfit for state and majesty.
　　　I do beseech you, take it not amiss.
　　　I cannot, nor I will not, yield to you.
　　　BUCKINGHAM　If you refuse it—as, in love and zeal,
　　　Loath to depose the child, your brother's son,
200　As well we know your tenderness of heart
　　　And gentle, kind, effeminate remorse,[4]
　　　Which we have noted in you to your kindred,
　　　And equally indeed to all estates°—　　　　　　　　　*social classes*
　　　Yet know, whe'er° you accept our suit or no,　　　　　　*whether*
205　Your brother's son shall never reign our king,
　　　But we will plant some other in the throne,
　　　To the disgrace and downfall of your house.
　　　And in this resolution here we leave you.—
　　　Come, citizens. 'Swounds,° I'll entreat no more.　　　*By God's wounds*
210　RICHARD GLOUCESTER　O do not swear, my lord of Buckingham.
　　　　　　　　Exeunt [BUCKINGHAM *and some others*]
　　　CATESBY　Call him again, sweet prince. Accept their suit.
　　　ANOTHER[5]　If you deny them, all the land will rue° it.　　*suffer for*
　　　RICHARD GLOUCESTER　Will you enforce° me to a world of cares?　　*condemn*
　　　Call them again.　　　　　　　　　　　　[*Exit one or more*]
　　　I am not made of stone,
215　But penetrable to your kind entreats,°　　　　　　　　　*entreaties*
　　　Albeit against my conscience and my soul.

1. Buckingham draws attention to the Duchess of York's objection to her son Edward's marriage to Elizabeth Gray; Edward's supposed betrothals (see notes to lines 5–6), along with the fact of Elizabeth's widowhood, are put forward as evidence that the marriage should be considered bigamous and hence the offspring illegitimate.
2. Drew him down from the eminence appropriate to his noble rank.
3. Richard's own mother, the Duchess of York.
4. And natural, tender pity (feelings thought of at that time as primarily feminine).
5. One of the remaining citizens, city officials, or bishops. In F, Catesby speaks this line.

Enter BUCKINGHAM *and the rest*

Cousin of Buckingham, and sage, grave men,
Since you will buckle fortune on my back,
To° bear her burden, whe'er I will or no,   *To make me*
220   I must have patience to endure the load.
But if black scandal or foul-faced reproach
Attend the sequel of your imposition,°   *what you impose on me*
Your mere° enforcement shall acquittance° me   *outright / acquit*
From all the impure blots and stains thereof;
225   For God doth know, and you may partly see,
How far I am from the desire of this.

MAYOR   God bless your grace! We see it, and will say it.

RICHARD GLOUCESTER   In saying so, you shall but say the truth.

BUCKINGHAM   Then I salute you with this royal title:
230   Long live kind Richard, England's worthy king!

ALL BUT RICHARD[6]   Amen.

BUCKINGHAM   Tomorrow may it please you to be crowned?

RICHARD GLOUCESTER   Even when you please, for you will have it so.

BUCKINGHAM   Tomorrow then, we will attend your grace.
235   And so, most joyfully, we take our leave.

RICHARD GLOUCESTER [*to the bishops*]   Come, let us to our holy work again.—
Farewell, my cousin. Farewell, gentle friends.

Exeunt [RICHARD *and bishops above, the rest below*]

4.1

Enter QUEEN [ELIZABETH], *the* [*old*] DUCHESS OF YORK,
and Marquis DORSET *at one door;* [LADY] ANNE *Duchess
of Gloucester* [*with Clarence's daughter*] *at another door*

DUCHESS OF YORK   Who meets us here? My niece° Plantagenet,   *granddaughter*
Led in° the hand of her kind aunt of Gloucester?   *by*
Now for° my life, she's wand'ring to the Tower,   *upon*
On pure heart's love, to greet the tender° Prince.—   *young*
Daughter,° well met.   *Daughter-in-law*

5   LADY ANNE   God give your graces both
A happy and a joyful time of day.

QUEEN ELIZABETH   As much to you, good sister.° Whither away?   *sister-in-law*

LADY ANNE   No farther than the Tower, and—as I guess—
Upon the like devotion° as yourselves: *devout duty*
10   To gratulate° the gentle princes there.   *greet*

QUEEN ELIZABETH   Kind sister, thanks. We'll enter all together—

Enter [*from the Tower* BRACKENBURY] *the Lieutenant*

And in good time, here the Lieutenant comes.
Master Lieutenant, pray you by your leave,
How doth the Prince, and my young son of York?

15   BRACKENBURY   Right well, dear madam. By your patience,
I may not suffer° you to visit them.   *permit*
The King hath strictly charged the contrary.

QUEEN ELIZABETH   The King? Who's that?

BRACKENBURY   I mean, the Lord Protector.

QUEEN ELIZABETH   The Lord protect him from that kingly title.[1]
20   Hath he set bounds° between their love and me?   *barriers*

---

6. Q assigns this word to the Mayor only.
4.1 Location: Before the Tower.

1. May God prevent Richard from acquiring the title of King.

I am their mother; who shall bar me from them?

DUCHESS OF YORK   I am their father's mother; I will see them.

LADY ANNE   Their aunt I am in law, in love their mother;
    Then bring me to their sights. I'll bear thy blame,
25   And take thy office from thee on my peril.²

BRACKENBURY   No, madam, no; I may not leave it° so.   *give up my office*
    I am bound by oath, and therefore pardon me.   *Exit*
        Enter Lord STANLEY [*Earl of Derby*]

STANLEY   Let me but meet you ladies one hour hence,
    And I'll salute your grace of York as mother
30   And reverend looker-on° of two fair queens.³   *beholder*
    [*To* ANNE] Come, madam, you must straight to Westminster,⁴
    There to be crownèd Richard's royal queen.

QUEEN ELIZABETH   Ah, cut my lace asunder,⁵ that my pent heart
    May have some scope to beat, or else I swoon
35   With this dead-killing news.

LADY ANNE   Despiteful tidings! O unpleasing news!

DORSET [*to* ANNE]   Be of good cheer.—Mother, how fares your grace?

QUEEN ELIZABETH   O Dorset, speak not to me. Get thee gone.
    Death and destruction dogs thee at thy heels.
40   Thy mother's name is ominous to children.⁶
    If thou wilt outstrip death, go cross the seas,
    And live with Richmond from⁷ the reach of hell.
    Go, hie thee! Hie thee from this slaughterhouse,
    Lest thou increase the number of the dead,
45   And make me die the thrall° of Margaret's curses: *slave*
    'Nor mother, wife, nor counted° England's Queen'.   *regarded as*

STANLEY   Full of wise care is this your counsel, madam.
    [*To* DORSET] Take all the swift advantage of the hours.
    You shall have letters from me to my son°   *stepson (Richmond)*
50   In your behalf, to meet you on the way.
    Be not ta'en tardy by unwise delay.

DUCHESS OF YORK   O ill-dispersing° wind of misery!   *misfortune-scattering*
    O my accursèd womb, the bed° of death!   *birthplace*
    A cockatrice⁸ hast thou hatched to the world,
55   Whose unavoided eye is murderous.

STANLEY [*to* ANNE]   Come, madam, come. I in all haste was sent.

LADY ANNE   And I in all unwillingness will go.
    O would to God that the inclusive verge°   *enclosing rim*
    Of golden metal that must round° my brow   *encircle*
60   Were red-hot steel, to sear me to the brains.
    Anointed let me be with deadly venom,⁹
    And die ere men can say 'God save the Queen'.

QUEEN ELIZABETH   Go, go, poor soul. I envy not thy glory.
    To feed my humour,° wish thyself no harm.   *To humor me*
65   LADY ANNE   No? Why? When he that is my husband now
    Came to me as I followed Henry's corpse,
    When scarce the blood was well washed from his hands,

---

2. And take on the responsibilities of your position at my own risk.
3. Elizabeth, widow of Edward IV, and Anne, wife of Richard III.
4. To Westminster Abbey, where English monarchs are traditionally crowned.
5. Elizabethan women wore tightly laced bodices.

6. The fact that you are my son places you in danger.
7. Away from. Henry Tudor, Earl of Richmond, had fled to Brittany in 1472, when Edward IV secured his grasp on the throne.
8. Basilisk (see note to 1.2.150).
9. Instead of the holy oil used in the ceremony of coronation.

Which issued from my other angel husband
And that dear saint which then I weeping followed—
70 O when, I say, I looked on Richard's face,
This was my wish: 'Be thou', quoth I, 'accursed
For making me, so young, so old a widow,[1]
And when thou wedd'st, let sorrow haunt thy bed;
And be thy wife—if any be so mad—
75 More miserable made by the life of thee
Than thou hast made me by my dear lord's death.'
Lo, ere I can repeat this curse again,
Within so small a time, my woman's heart
Grossly° grew captive to his honey words   *Stupidly*
80 And proved the subject of mine own soul's curse,
Which hitherto hath held mine eyes from rest—
For never yet one hour in his bed
Did I enjoy the golden dew of sleep,
But with his timorous° dreams was still° awaked.   *fearful / continually*
85 Besides, he hates me for° my father Warwick,   *because of*
And will, no doubt, shortly be rid of me.
QUEEN ELIZABETH   Poor heart, adieu. I pity thy complaining.°   *lamenting*
LADY ANNE   No more than with my soul I mourn for yours.
DORSET   Farewell, thou woeful welcomer of glory.
90 LADY ANNE   Adieu, poor soul, that tak'st thy leave of it.
DUCHESS OF YORK [*to* DORSET] Go thou to Richmond, and good fortune guide thee.
   [*To* ANNE, STANLEY, *and Clarence's daughter*] Go thou to Richard, and good angels
      tend thee.
   [*To* ELIZABETH] Go thou to sanctuary, and good thoughts possess thee.
   I to my grave, where peace and rest lie with me.
95 Eighty odd years of sorrow have I seen,
   And each hour's joy racked with a week of teen.[2]   [*Exit*]
96.1   QUEEN ELIZABETH   *Stay: yet look back with me unto the Tower.—*
           Pity, you ancient stones, those tender babes,
           Whom envy° hath immured within your walls.   *malice; jealousy*
           Rough cradle for such little pretty ones,
96.5   *Rude ragged nurse, old sullen playfellow*
           For tender princes: use my babies well.
           So foolish sorrow bids your stones farewell.   *Exeunt*

4.2

Sound a sennet. Enter [KING] RICHARD *in pomp,* [*the*
Duke of] BUCKINGHAM, [*Sir William*] CATESBY, *other*
nobles[1] [*and a* PAGE]
KING RICHARD   Stand all apart.°—Cousin of Buckingham.   *aside*
BUCKINGHAM   My gracious sovereign?
KING RICHARD   Give me thy hand.
      Sound [*a sennet*]. *Here he ascendeth the throne*
   Thus high by thy advice.
5   And thy assistance is King Richard seated.
   But shall we wear these glories for a day?
   Or shall they last, and we rejoice in them?
BUCKINGHAM   Still° live they, and for ever let them last.   *Perpetually*

---

1. Doomed to a long life of widowhood.
2. Grief. The indented passage that follows, 96.1–96.7, appears only in F; the other characters remain onstage.
4.2 Location: The palace, London.
1. In F, specifically Ratcliffe and Lovell.

	KING RICHARD Ah, Buckingham, now do I play the touch,[2]	
10	To try if thou be current° gold indeed.	*real, genuine*
	Young Edward lives. Think now what I would speak.	
	BUCKINGHAM Say on, my loving lord.	
	KING RICHARD Why, Buckingham, I say I would be king.	
	BUCKINGHAM Why, so you are, my thrice-renownèd liege.	
15	KING RICHARD Ha? Am I king? 'Tis so. But Edward lives.	
	BUCKINGHAM True, noble prince.	
	KING RICHARD O bitter consequence,°	*conclusion; retort*
	That Edward still should live 'true noble prince'.	
	Cousin, thou wast not wont° to be so dull.	*accustomed*
	Shall I be plain? I wish the bastards dead,	
20	And I would have it immediately performed.	
	What sayst thou now? Speak suddenly,° be brief.	*at once*
	BUCKINGHAM Your grace may do your pleasure.	
	KING RICHARD Tut, tut, thou art all ice. Thy kindness freezes.	
	Say, have I thy consent that they shall die?	
25	BUCKINGHAM Give me some little breath, some pause, dear lord,	
	Before I positively speak in this.	
	I will resolve° you herein presently.° *Exit*	*answer / shortly*
	CATESBY [*to another, aside*] The King is angry. See, he gnaws his lip.	
	KING RICHARD [*aside*] I will converse with iron-witted fools	
30	And unrespective° boys. None are for me	*unobservant*
	That look into me with considerate° eyes.	*critical*
	High-reaching° Buckingham grows circumspect.—	*Ambitious*
	Boy.	
	PAGE My lord?	
35	KING RICHARD Know'st thou not any whom corrupting gold	
	Will tempt unto a close° exploit of death?	*secret*
	PAGE I know a discontented gentleman	
	Whose humble means match not his haughty spirit.	
	Gold were as good as twenty orators.	
40	And will no doubt tempt him to anything.	
	KING RICHARD What is his name?	
	PAGE His name, my lord, is Tyrrell.	
	KING RICHARD I partly know the man. Go call him hither, boy.	
	Exit [PAGE]	
	[*Aside*] The deep-revolving,° witty° Buckingham	*deeply scheming / clever*
	No more shall be the neighbour to my counsels.	
45	Hath he so long held out° with me untired,	*kept up*
	And stops he now for breath? Well, be it so.	
	Enter [*Lord*] STANLEY [*Earl of*] *Derby*	
	How now, Lord Stanley? What's the news?	
	STANLEY Know, my loving lord,	
	The Marquis Dorset, as I hear, is fled	
50	To Richmond, in those parts beyond the seas	
	Where he abides.	
	KING RICHARD Come hither, Catesby. [*Aside to* CATESBY] Rumour it abroad	
	That Anne, my wife, is very grievous sick.	
	I will take order for her keeping close.[3]	
55	Enquire me out some mean-born gentleman,	
	Whom I will marry straight to Clarence' daughter.	

2. Touchstone: a means of testing gold.   3. I will arrange to have her kept out of sight.

The boy⁴ is foolish,° and I fear not him.   *simpleminded*
Look how thou dream'st. I say again, give out
That Anne, my queen, is sick, and like to die.
60   About it, for it stands me much upon°   *is very important to me*
To stop all hopes whose growth may damage me.

                                                  [*Exit* CATESBY]

[*Aside*] I must be married to my brother's daughter,⁵
Or else my kingdom stands on brittle glass.
Murder her brothers, and then marry her?
65   Uncertain way of gain, but I am in
So far in blood that sin will pluck on° sin.   *incite*
Tear-falling pity dwells not in this eye.—

               Enter [*Sir James*] TYRRELL; [*he kneels*]

Is thy name Tyrrell?
TYRRELL   James Tyrrell, and your most obedient subject.
KING RICHARD   Art thou indeed?
70   TYRRELL   Prove° me, my gracious lord.   *Test*
KING RICHARD   Dar'st thou resolve to kill a friend of mine?
TYRRELL   Please you,° but I had rather kill two enemies.   *If you wish*
KING RICHARD   Why there thou hast it: two deep enemies,
Foes to my rest, and my sweet sleep's disturbers,
75   Are they that I would have thee deal upon.°   *set to work upon*
Tyrrell, I mean those bastards in the Tower.
TYRRELL   Let me have open means to come⁶ to them,
And soon I'll rid you from the fear of them.
KING RICHARD   Thou sing'st sweet music. Hark, come hither, Tyrrell.
80   Go, by this token. Rise, and lend thine ear.

               [RICHARD] *whispers in his ear*

'Tis no more but so.° Say it is done,   *That's all*
And I will love thee, and prefer° thee for it.   *promote*
TYRRELL   I will dispatch it straight.
KING RICHARD   Shall we hear from thee, Tyrrell, ere we sleep?⁷

               Enter BUCKINGHAM

85   TYRRELL   Ye shall, my lord.   *Exit*
BUCKINGHAM   My lord, I have considered in my mind
The late request that you did sound me in.
KING RICHARD   Well, let that rest. Dorset is fled to Richmond.
BUCKINGHAM   I hear the news, my lord.
90   KING RICHARD   Stanley, he° is your wife's son. Well, look to it.   *(Richmond)*
BUCKINGHAM   My lord, I claim the gift, my due by promise,
For which your honour and your faith is pawned:
Th'earldom of Hereford, and the movables
Which you have promisèd I shall possess.
95   KING RICHARD   Stanley, look to your wife. If she convey
Letters to Richmond, you shall answer it.°   *for it*
BUCKINGHAM   What says your highness to my just request?
KING RICHARD   I do remember me, Henry the Sixth
Did prophesy that Richmond should be king,
100   When Richmond was a little peevish boy.
A king . . . perhaps . . . perhaps.⁸
BUCKINGHAM   My lord?

---

4. Clarence's eldest son, Edward, Earl of Warwick.
5. To Edward's daughter, Elizabeth of York, who was later to unite the two houses by becoming queen to the Lancastrian Henry VII, formerly the Earl of Richmond.
6. Let me have free access.
7. F omits this and the following line.
8. The passage that follows, lines 101–119, appears only in Q.

KING RICHARD How chance the prophet could not at that time
Have told me, I being by, that I should kill him?
BUCKINGHAM My lord, your promise for the earldom.
105 KING RICHARD Richmond? When last I was at Exeter,
The Mayor in courtesy showed me the castle,
And called it 'Ruge-mount'⁹—at which name I started,
Because a bard of Ireland¹ told me once
I should not live long after I saw 'Richmond'.
110 BUCKINGHAM My lord?
KING RICHARD Ay? What's o'clock?
BUCKINGHAM I am thus bold to put your grace in mind
Of what you promised me.
KING RICHARD   But what's o'clock?
BUCKINGHAM Upon the stroke of ten.
115 KING RICHARD Well, let it strike!
BUCKINGHAM Why 'let it strike'?
KING RICHARD Because that, like a jack,² thou keep'st the stroke
Betwixt thy begging and my meditation.
I am not in the giving vein today.
120 BUCKINGHAM Why then resolve me,° whe'er you will or no?   °answer me resolutely
KING RICHARD Thou troublest me. I am not in the vein.°   °mood
            Exit [RICHARD, *followed by all but* BUCKINGHAM]
BUCKINGHAM And is it thus? Repays he my deep° service   °i.e., rendered at great risk
With such contempt? Made I him king for this?
O let me think on Hastings, and be gone
125 To Brecon,° while my fearful head is on.   °manor house in Wales
                    Exit [*at another door*]

<h2 style="text-align:center">4.3</h2>

Enter Sir [*James*] TYRRELL

TYRRELL The tyrannous and bloody act is done—
The most arch° deed of piteous massacre   °preeminent
That ever yet this land was guilty of.
Dighton and Forrest,¹ whom I did suborn°   °induce
5 To do this piece of ruthless butchery,
Albeit they were fleshed² villains, bloody dogs,
Melted with tenderness and mild compassion,
Wept like two children in their deaths' sad story.³
'O thus', quoth Dighton, 'lay the gentle babes';
10 'Thus, thus', quoth Forrest, 'girdling° one another   °embracing
Within their alabaster° innocent arms.   °marble-white
Their lips were four red roses on a stalk,
And in their summer beauty kissed each other.
A book of prayers on their pillow lay,
15 'Which once', quoth Forrest, 'almost changed my mind.
But O, the devil'—there the villain stopped,
When° Dighton thus told on, 'We smotherèd   °At which point
The most replenishéd° sweet work of nature,   °complete

9. Redhill (but punning on "Richmond").
1. Celtic bards, or poets, were also considered prophets.
2. A Jack was the mechanical figure who appeared to strike the hours in early clocks. By clockwork reiterations of his suit, Richard suggests, Buckingham is behaving like an annoying beggar and interfering with Richard's "meditation."
4.3 Location: The palace, London.

1. For the murder of the princes, Tyrrell recruited his servant, John Dighton, along with Myles Forrest and two others.
2. Experienced in killing; applied to hounds that had been fed part of their first kill in order to give them a taste for blood.
3. Wept in telling the sad story of the Princes' deaths.

That from the prime° creation e'er she framed.'   *first*
20   Hence both are gone,° with conscience and remorse.   *overcome*
They could not speak, and so I left them both,
To bear this tidings to the bloody king.
          Enter KING RICHARD
And here he comes.—All health, my sovereign lord.
          KING RICHARD   Kind Tyrrell, am I happy in thy news?
25   TYRRELL   If to have done the thing you gave in charge
Beget your happiness,[4] be happy then,
For it is done.
          KING RICHARD   But didst thou see them dead?
          TYRRELL   I did, my lord.
          KING RICHARD   And buried, gentle Tyrrell?
          TYRRELL   The chaplain of the Tower hath buried them;
30   But where, to say the truth, I do not know.
          KING RICHARD   Come to me, Tyrrell, soon, at after-supper,°   *dessert*
When thou shalt tell the process° of their death.   *story*
Meantime, but think how I may do thee good,
And be inheritor of thy desire.[5]
Farewell till then.
35   TYRRELL   I humbly take my leave.   *Exit*
          KING RICHARD   The son of Clarence have I pent° up close.   *locked*
His daughter meanly have I matched in marriage.[6]
The sons of Edward sleep in Abraham's bosom,[7]
And Anne, my wife, hath bid this world goodnight.
40   Now, for° I know the Breton[8] Richmond aims   *because*
At young Elizabeth, my brother's daughter,
And by that knot° looks proudly o'er the crown,   *marriage; alliance*
To her go I, a jolly thriving wooer[9]—
          Enter [Sir Richard] RATCLIFFE[1] *[running]*
          RATCLIFFE   My lord.
45   KING RICHARD   Good news or bad, that thou com'st in so bluntly?
          RATCLIFFE   Bad news, my lord. Ely° is fled to Richmond,   *(Bishop of Ely)*
And Buckingham, backed with the hardy Welshmen,
Is in the field, and still his power increaseth.
          KING RICHARD   Ely with Richmond troubles me more near°   *deeply*
50   Than Buckingham and his rash-levied strength.°   *hastily raised army*
Come, I have learned that fearful commenting
Is leaden servitor[2] to dull delay.
Delay leads impotent and snail-paced beggary.°   *ruin*
Then fiery expedition° be my wing: *speed*
55   Jove's Mercury,[3] an herald for a king.
Go, muster men. My counsel is my shield.[4]
We must be brief, when traitors brave the field.[5]   *Exeunt*

---

4. *If . . . happiness:* If it pleases you to have accomplished what you ordered done.
5. *but . . . desire:* you have only to think what you want of me, and you will possess it.
6. I have married off to a poor man.
7. In heaven (see Luke 16:22–23).
8. Person from Brittany; Richmond spent fourteen years in exile there before returning to England to face Richard III in 1485.
9. It was widely rumored that Anne was poisoned in order to facilitate a plan by Richard to marry Elizabeth,

sister to the missing princes; modern historians believe that these allegations are probably untrue. Richard's alleged actions regarding Clarence's son and daughter (lines 36–37) are certainly untrue.
1. Q calls for Catesby.
2. *fearful . . . servitor:* frightened talk is the sluggish attendant.
3. The swift messenger of the gods.
4. *My . . . shield:* I do not talk, but arm myself to fight. *counsel:* adviser.
5. When traitors defy (us on) the battlefield.

)

4.4

Enter old QUEEN MARGARET

QUEEN MARGARET   So now prosperity begins to mellow°   ripen
And drop into the rotten mouth of death.
Here in these confines slyly have I lurked
To watch the waning of mine enemies.
5   A dire induction° am I witness to,   prologue (as to a play)
And will to France, hoping the consequence°   conclusion (as of a play)
Will prove as bitter, black, and tragical.

Enter the [old] DUCHESS OF YORK *and* QUEEN [ELIZABETH]

Withdraw thee, wretched Margaret. Who comes here?
QUEEN ELIZABETH   Ah, my poor princes! Ah, my tender babes!
10   My unblown° flowers, new-appearing sweets!°   unopened / blooms
If yet your gentle souls fly in the air,
And be not fixed in doom perpetual,[1]
Hover about me with your airy wings
And hear your mother's lamentation.
15   QUEEN MARGARET *[aside]*   Hover about her, say that right for right
Hath dimmed your infant morn to agèd night.[2]
DUCHESS OF YORK[3]   So many miseries have crazed° my voice   cracked
That my woe-wearied tongue is still and mute.
Edward Plantagenet, why art thou dead?
20   QUEEN MARGARET *[aside]*   Plantagenet doth quit° Plantagenet;   pay for (the deeds of)
Edward for Edward pays a dying debt.[4]
QUEEN ELIZABETH   Wilt thou, O God, fly from such gentle lambs
And throw them in the entrails of the wolf?
When° didst thou sleep, when such a deed was done?   Whenever (up until now)
25   QUEEN MARGARET *[aside]*   When holy Harry[5] died, and my sweet son.
DUCHESS OF YORK   Dead life, blind sight, poor mortal living ghost,[6]
Woe's scene, world's shame, grave's due by life usurped,[7]
Brief abstract° and record of tedious days,   epitome; summary
Rest thy unrest on England's lawful earth,
30   Unlawfully made drunk with innocents' blood.
    [They sit]
QUEEN ELIZABETH   Ah that thou[8] wouldst as soon afford a grave
As thou canst yield a melancholy seat.
Then would I hide my bones, not rest them here.
Ah, who hath any cause to mourn but we?
35   QUEEN MARGARET *[coming forward]*   If ancient sorrow be most reverend,
Give mine the benefit of seniory,[9]
And let my griefs frown on the upper hand.[1]
If sorrow can admit society,
Tell o'er° your woes again by viewing mine.   Count; narrate
40   I had an Edward, till a Richard killed him;
I had a husband, till a Richard killed him.

4.4 Location: Before the palace.
1. *fixed in doom perpetual:* assigned by an irrevocable sentence to your final place of punishment or reward.
2. *right for . . . night:* evenhanded justice has destroyed the bright hopes of your young lives.
3. Q places this after line 34 (making it the last speech before Margaret's intervention) and omits lines 20–21.
4. A debt for which payment is death. *Edward for Edward:* Prince Edward (Elizabeth's son) for Prince Edward (Margaret's son, whose murder is dramatized in *Richard Duke of York*).

5. Henry VI (Margaret's husband).
6. *mortal living ghost:* a dead person doomed to exist among the living.
7. *graves . . . usurped:* person who ought to be dead, unlawfully alive.
8. Here, Elizabeth is addressing the earth directly.
9. Seniority; Q1–5 have "signorie," F "signeurie," which suggests that Margaret may mean "sovereignty" or "lordship" ("seigniory").
1. *frown . . . hand:* have precedence in mourning.

[*To* ELIZABETH] Thou hadst an Edward, till a Richard killed him;
Thou hadst a Richard,[2] till a Richard killed him.

DUCHESS OF YORK [*rising*] I had a Richard too, and thou didst kill him;
45   I had a Rutland too,[3] thou holpst to kill him.

QUEEN MARGARET   Thou hadst a Clarence too, and Richard killed him.
From forth the kennel of thy womb hath crept
A hell-hound that doth hunt us all to death:
That dog that had his teeth before his eyes,[4]
50   To worry° lambs and lap their gentle blood;   *tear apart*
That foul defacer of God's handiwork,
That reigns in gallèd° eyes of weeping souls;   *sore (from crying)*
That excellent grand tyrant of the earth
Thy womb let loose to chase us to our graves.
55   O upright, just, and true-disposing God,
How do I thank thee that this charnel[5] cur
Preys on the issue° of his mother's body,   *offspring*
And makes her pewfellow° with others' moan.   *companion at church*

DUCHESS OF YORK   O Harry's wife, triumph not in my woes.
60   God witness with me, I have wept for thine.

QUEEN MARGARET   Bear with me. I am hungry for revenge,
And now I cloy me° with beholding it.   *gorge myself*
Thy Edward, he is dead, that killed my Edward;
Thy other Edward dead, to quite° my Edward;   *requite*
65   Young York, he is but boot,[6] because both they
Matched not the high perfection of my loss;
Thy Clarence, he is dead, that stabbed my Edward,
And the beholders of this frantic° play—   *insane*
Th'adulterate° Hastings, Rivers, Vaughan, Gray—   *adulterous*
70   Untimely smothered° in their dusky graves.   *buried*
Richard yet lives, hell's black intelligencer,°   *spy*
Only reserved their factor[7] to buy souls
And send them thither; but at hand, at hand
Ensues his piteous and unpitied end.
75   Earth gapes, hell burns, fiends roar, saints pray, *spondaic*
To have him suddenly conveyed from hence.   *tetrameter*
Cancel his bond of life, dear God, I plead,
That I may live and say, 'The dog is dead'. *Iambic pentameter*

QUEEN ELIZABETH   O thou didst prophesy the time would come
80   That I should wish for thee to help me curse
That bottled spider, that foul bunch-backed toad.

QUEEN MARGARET   I called thee then 'vain flourish of my fortune';
I called thee then, poor shadow,° 'painted queen'[8]—   *semblance*
The presentation° of but what I was,   *copy*
85   The flattering index° of a direful pageant,°   *prologue / play*
One heaved a-high to be hurled down below,
A mother only mocked with two fair babes,
A dream of what thou wast, a garish flag

---

2. Edward and Richard were Queen Elizabeth's two sons (smothered in the Tower).
3. Her husband (Richard, Duke of York) and youngest son; both deaths are dramatized in Act 1 of *Richard Duke of York*.
4. His enemies rumored that the savage Richard was born with teeth.

5. Of the charnel house or tomb. Q, F print "carnal."
6. He is thrown in simply to make the bargain even.
7. *Only . . . factor*: Retained (or preserved from death) only in order to serve as hell's agent. *their*: the demonic inhabitants of hell.
8. See 1.3.239.

To be the aim of every dangerous shot,⁹
90   A sign° of dignity, a breath, a bubble,   *mere symbol*
     A queen in jest, only to fill the scene.
     Where is thy husband now? Where be thy brothers?
     Where are thy two sons? Wherein dost thou joy?
     Who sues, and kneels, and says 'God save the Queen'?
95   Where be the bending° peers that flattered thee?   *bowing; yielding*
     Where be the thronging troops that followed thee?
     Decline¹ all this, and see what now thou art:
     For happy wife, a most distressèd widow;
     For joyful mother, one that wails the name;
100 For queen, a very caitiff,° crowned with care;   *wretch*
     For one being sued to, one that humbly sues;
     For she that scorned at me, now scorned of° me;   *by*
     For she being feared of all, now fearing one;
     For she commanding all, obeyed of none.
105 Thus hath the course of justice whirled about,
     And left thee but a very prey to time,
     Having no more but thought of what thou wert
     To torture thee the more, being what thou art.
     Thou didst usurp my place, and dost thou not
110 Usurp the just proportion of my sorrow?
     Now thy proud neck bears half my burdened° yoke—   *burdensome*
     From which, even here, I slip my weary head,
     And leave the burden of it all on thee.
     Farewell, York's wife, and queen of sad mischance.
115 These English woes shall make me smile in France.
QUEEN ELIZABETH [*rising*] O thou, well skilled in curses, stay a while,
     And teach me how to curse mine enemies.
QUEEN MARGARET Forbear to sleep the nights, and fast the days;
     Compare dead happiness with living woe;
120 Think that thy babes were sweeter than they were,
     And he that slew them fouler than he is.
     Bett'ring° thy loss makes the bad causer worse.   *Magnifying*
     Revolving° this will teach thee how to curse.   *Musing on*
QUEEN ELIZABETH My words are dull. O quicken° them with   *enliven; sharpen*
     thine!
QUEEN MARGARET Thy woes will make them sharp and fierce
125 like mine.   *Exit*
DUCHESS OF YORK Why should calamity be full of words?
QUEEN ELIZABETH Windy attorneys to their client woes,²
     Airy recorders of intestate joys,³
     Poor breathing° orators of miseries.   *speaking*
130 Let them have scope. Though what they will impart
     Help nothing else, yet do they ease the heart.
DUCHESS OF YORK If so, then be not tongue-tied; go with me,
     And in the breath of bitter words let's smother
     My damnèd son, that thy two sweet sons smothered.
          [*A march within*]
135 The trumpet sounds. Be copious in exclaims.°   *exclamation*

---

9. *garish . . . shot*: bearer of a brightly colored standard who draws the enemy fire.
1. Recite in order with the proper endings (as a noun in Latin grammar).
2. Words are long-winded pleaders for the sufferings that have hired them.
3. Words record joys that have died without bequeathing anything.

Enter KING RICHARD *and his train marching with*
drummers and trumpeters

KING RICHARD Who intercepts me in my expedition?°   *haste; march*

DUCHESS OF YORK O, she that might have intercepted thee,
By strangling thee in her accursèd womb,
From all the slaughters, wretch, that thou hast done.

140 QUEEN ELIZABETH Hid'st thou that forehead with a golden crown,
Where should be branded—if that right were right—
The slaughter of the prince that owed° that crown,   *rightfully owned*
And the dire death of my poor sons and brothers?
Tell me, thou villain-slave, where are my children?

145 DUCHESS OF YORK Thou toad, thou toad, where is thy brother Clarence?
And little Ned Plantagenet his son?

QUEEN ELIZABETH Where is the gentle Rivers, Vaughan, Gray?

DUCHESS OF YORK Where is kind Hastings?

KING RICHARD [*to his train*] A flourish, trumpets! Strike
       alarum,° drums!   *Call to arms*

150 Let not the heavens hear these tell-tale women
Rail on the Lord's anointed. Strike, I say!
      Flourish. Alarums
[*To the women*] Either be patient and entreat me fair,°   *treat me courteously*
Or with the clamorous report° of war   *noise*
Thus will I drown your exclamations.

155 DUCHESS OF YORK Art thou my son?

KING RICHARD Ay, I thank God, my father, and yourself.

DUCHESS OF YORK Then patiently hear my impatience.

KING RICHARD Madam, I have a touch of your condition,°   *temperament*
That cannot brook the accent° of reproof.   *abide the language*

DUCHESS OF YORK O let me speak!

160 KING RICHARD   Do, then; but I'll not hear.

DUCHESS OF YORK I will be mild and gentle in my words.

KING RICHARD And brief, good mother, for I am in haste.

DUCHESS OF YORK Art thou so hasty? I have stayed° for thee,   *waited*
God knows, in torment and in agony—

165 KING RICHARD And came I not at last to comfort you?

DUCHESS OF YORK No, by the Holy Rood,° thou know'st it well.   *Cross*
Thou cam'st on earth to make the earth my hell.
A grievous burden was thy birth to me;
Tetchy° and wayward was thy infancy;   *Irritable*

170 Thy schooldays frightful,° desp'rate, wild, and furious;   *frightening*
Thy prime° of manhood daring, bold, and venturous;   *beginning*
Thy age confirmed,° proud, subtle, sly, and bloody;   *settled maturity*
More mild, but yet more harmful; kind in hatred.[4]
What comfortable hour canst thou name

175 That ever graced me[5] in thy company?

KING RICHARD Faith, none but Humphrey Hewer,[6] that called your grace
To breakfast once, forth° of my company.   *out*
If I be so disgracious° in your eye,   *unpleasing*
Let me march on, and not offend you, madam.—
Strike up the drum.

180 DUCHESS OF YORK   I pray thee, hear me speak.

---

4. Concealing hatred under cover of kindness.
5. Gave me pleasure; but Richard interprets as "called
me by the title 'your grace.'"
6. A proper name, based on "ewer" (a servant who waits
at table), but also suggesting "huer" (someone who
makes a hue or cry) and playing on "hour" (line 174).
Proverbially, "to dine with Duke Humphrey" was not to
dine at all.

KING RICHARD   You speak too bitterly.

DUCHESS OF YORK   Hear me a word,
  For I shall never speak to thee again.

KING RICHARD   So.

DUCHESS OF YORK   Either thou wilt die by God's just ordinance

185 Ere from this war thou turn° a conqueror,   return
  Or I with grief and extreme age shall perish,
  And never more behold thy face again.
  Therefore take with thee my most heavy curse,
  Which in the day of battle tire thee more
190 Than all the complete armour that thou wear'st.
  My prayers on the adverse party° fight,   opposite side
  And there the little souls of Edward's children
  Whisper° the spirits of thine enemies,   Whisper to
  And promise them success and victory.
195 Bloody thou art, bloody will be thy end;
  Shame serves° thy life, and doth thy death attend.   Exit   accompanies

QUEEN ELIZABETH   Though far more cause, yet much less spirit to curse
  Abides in me; I say 'Amen' to all.

KING RICHARD   Stay, madam. I must talk a word with you.

200 QUEEN ELIZABETH   I have no more sons of the royal blood
  For thee to slaughter. For my daughters, Richard,
  They shall be praying nuns, not weeping queens,
  And therefore level not to hit their lives.[7]

KING RICHARD   You have a daughter called Elizabeth,
205 Virtuous and fair, royal and gracious.

QUEEN ELIZABETH   And must she die for this? O let her live,
  And I'll corrupt her manners,° stain her beauty.   morals
  Slander myself as false to Edward's bed,
  Throw over her the veil of infamy.
210 So° she may live unscarred of bleeding slaughter,   Provided that
  I will confess she was not Edward's daughter.

KING RICHARD   Wrong not her birth. She is a royal princess.

QUEEN ELIZABETH   To save her life I'll say she is not so.

KING RICHARD   Her life is safest only in her birth.[8]

215 QUEEN ELIZABETH   And only in that safety died her brothers.

KING RICHARD   Lo, at their births good stars were opposite.°   adverse

QUEEN ELIZABETH   No, to their lives ill friends were contrary.° opposed

KING RICHARD   All unavoided° is the doom° of destiny—   unavoidable / sentence

QUEEN ELIZABETH   True, when avoided grace° makes destiny.
220 My babes were destined to a fairer death,
  If grace had blessed thee with a fairer life.[1]

221.1   KING RICHARD   You speak as if that I had slain my cousins.

  QUEEN ELIZABETH   Cousins indeed, and by their uncle cozened°   cheated
    Of comfort, kingdom, kindred, freedom, life.
    Whose hand soever lanced their tender hearts,
221.5   Thy head all indirectly gave direction.[2]
    No doubt the murd'rous knife was dull and blunt
    Till it was whetted on thy stone-hard heart
    To revel in the entrails of my lambs.
    But that still° use of grief makes wild grief tame,   Except that continual

---

7. And therefore do not take aim to kill them.
8. Her life is safe only because of her high birth.
9. When a man who has rejected God's grace (that is, Richard).

1. The indented passage that follows, 221.1–221.14, appears only in F.
2. Whose . . . direction: No matter who killed them, it was you, though indirectly, who caused it.

221.10 *My tongue should to thy ears not name my boys*
Till that my nails were anchored in thine eyes—
And I in such a desp'rate bay³ of death,
Like a poor barque° of sails and tackling reft,° boat / deprived
Rush all to pieces on thy rocky bosom.

KING RICHARD   Madam, so thrive I in my enterprise
And dangerous success of bloody wars,
As I intend more good to you and yours
225   Than ever you or yours by me were harmed.⁴
QUEEN ELIZABETH   What good is covered with the face of heaven,⁵
To be discovered, that can do me good?
KING RICHARD   Th'advancement of your children, gentle lady.
QUEEN ELIZABETH   Up to some scaffold, there to lose their heads.
230   KING RICHARD   Unto the dignity and height of fortune,
The high imperial type° of this earth's glory. symbol
QUEEN ELIZABETH   Flatter my sorrow with report of it.
Tell me what state, what dignity, what honour,
Canst thou demise° to any child of mine? transmit
235   KING RICHARD   Even all I have—ay, and myself and all,
Will I withal endow a child of thine,
So° in the Lethe⁶ of thy angry soul If
Thou drown the sad remembrance of those wrongs,
Which thou supposest I have done to thee.
240   QUEEN ELIZABETH   Be brief, lest that the process° of thy kindness story
Last longer telling° than thy kindness' date.° in the telling / duration
KING RICHARD   Then know that, from my soul,⁷ I love thy daughter.
QUEEN ELIZABETH   My daughter's mother thinks that with her soul.
KING RICHARD   What do you think?
245   QUEEN ELIZABETH   That thou dost love my daughter *from* thy soul;
So *from* thy soul's love didst thou love her brothers,
And *from* my heart's love I do thank thee for it.
KING RICHARD   Be not so hasty to confound° my meaning. deliberately misconstrue
I mean, that *with* my soul I love thy daughter,
250   And do intend to make her queen of England.
QUEEN ELIZABETH   Well then, who dost thou mean shall be her king?
KING RICHARD   Even he that makes her queen. Who else should be?
QUEEN ELIZABETH   What, thou?
KING RICHARD   Even so. How think you of it?
QUEEN ELIZABETH   How canst thou woo her?
KING RICHARD   That would I learn of you,
255   As one being best acquainted with her humour.° temperament
QUEEN ELIZABETH   And wilt thou learn of me?
KING RICHARD   Madam, with all my heart.
QUEEN ELIZABETH   Send to her, by the man that slew her brothers,
A pair of bleeding hearts; thereon engrave
'Edward' and 'York'; then haply° will she weep. perhaps
260   Therefore present to her—as sometimes° Margaret once
Did to thy father, steeped in Rutland's blood⁸—
A handkerchief which, say to her, did drain

3. Inlet; the situation of a cornered animal when it turns to face its hunters.
4. *Madam . . . harmed:* (I pray) that the success of my upcoming battles be as certain as is my intention to do to you more good in the future than I have done you harm in the past. *success:* consequence.
5. What good is there on earth.
6. A river in the underworld whose waters induced forgetfulness.
7. With all my soul (but Queen Elizabeth takes it as "separated from," "at variance with").
8. Dramatized in *Richard Duke of York* 1.4.

The purple sap° from her sweet brother's body.   blood
And bid her wipe her weeping eyes withal.°   with it
265   If this inducement move her not to love,
Send her a letter of thy noble deeds.
Tell her thou mad'st away her uncle Clarence,
Her uncle Rivers—ay, and for her sake
Mad'st quick conveyance with° her good aunt Anne.   Got rid of
270   KING RICHARD   You mock me, madam. This is not the way
To win your daughter.
QUEEN ELIZABETH   There is no other way,
Unless thou couldst put on some other shape,
And not be Richard, that hath done all this.⁹

273.1   *KING RICHARD   Say that I did all this for love of her.*
QUEEN ELIZABETH   Nay, then indeed she cannot choose but hate thee,
Having bought love with such a bloody spoil.°   slaughter
KING RICHARD   Look what° is done cannot be now amended.   Whatever
273.5   *Men shall deal° unadvisedly sometimes,*   act
Which after-hours gives leisure to repent.
If I did take the kingdom from your sons,
To make amends I'll give it to your daughter.
If I have killed the issue of your womb,
273.10   *To quicken your increase¹ I will beget*
Mine issue of your blood upon your daughter.
A grandam's name is little less in love
Than is the doting title of a mother.
They are as children but one step below,
273.15   *Even of your mettall,° of your very blood:*   spirit
Of all one pain, save for a night of groans
Endured of her for whom you bid like sorrow.²
Your children were vexation to your youth,
But mine shall be a comfort to your age.
273.20   *The loss you have is but a son being king,*
And by that loss your daughter is made queen.
I cannot make you what amends I would,
Therefore accept such kindness as I can.°   can give
Dorset your son, that with a fearful soul
273.25   *Leads discontented steps in foreign soil,*
This fair alliance quickly shall call home
To high promotions and great dignity.
The king that calls your beauteous daughter wife,
Familiarly shall call thy Dorset brother.
273.30   *Again shall you be mother to a king,*
And all the ruins of distressful times
Repaired with double riches of content.
What? We have many goodly days to see.
The liquid drops of tears that you have shed
273.35   *Shall come again, transformed to orient° pearl,*   shining
Advantaging° their loan with interest   Augmenting
Of ten times double gain of happiness.
Go then, my mother, to thy daughter go.
Make bold her bashful years with your experience.

9. The indented passage that follows, 273.1–273.55, appears only in F.
1. To give (new) life to your offspring.
2. Of all . . . sorrow: Originating from a single bout of labor (Elizabeth's), with the addition of just one more night of pain by the daughter you bore.

273.40   Prepare her ears to hear a wooer's tale.
    Put in her tender heart th'aspiring flame
    Of golden sovereignty. Acquaint the Princess
    With the sweet silent hours of marriage joys.
    And when this arm of mine hath chastisèd
273.45   The petty rebel, dull-brained Buckingham,
    Bound with triumphant garlands will I come
    And lead thy daughter to a conqueror's bed—
    To whom I will retail° my conquest won,   *relate*
    And she shall be sole victoress: Caesar's Caesar.
273.50 QUEEN ELIZABETH   What were I best to say? Her father's brother
    Would° be her lord?° Or shall I say her uncle?   *Wishes to / husband*
    Or he that slew her brothers and her uncles?
    Under what title shall I woo for thee,
    That God, the law, my honour, and her love
273.55   Can make seem pleasing to her tender years?
    KING RICHARD   Infer° fair England's peace by this alliance.   *Give as a reason*
275   QUEEN ELIZABETH   Which she shall purchase with still-lasting° war.   *perpetual*
    KING RICHARD   Tell her the King, that may command, entreats.
    QUEEN ELIZABETH   That at her hands which the King's King° forbids.   *(God)*
    KING RICHARD   Say she shall be a high and mighty queen.
    QUEEN ELIZABETH   To vail° the title,° as her mother doth.   *yield / (of Queen)*
280   KING RICHARD   Say I will love her everlastingly.
    QUEEN ELIZABETH   But how long shall that title 'ever' last?
    KING RICHARD   Sweetly in force unto her fair life's end.
    QUEEN ELIZABETH   But how long fairly° shall her sweet life last?   *without foul play*
    KING RICHARD   As long as heaven and nature lengthens it.
285   QUEEN ELIZABETH   As long as hell and Richard likes of it.
    KING RICHARD   Say I, her sovereign, am her subject love.
    QUEEN ELIZABETH   But she, your subject, loathes such sovereignty.
    KING RICHARD   Be eloquent in my behalf to her.
    QUEEN ELIZABETH   An honest tale speeds° best being plainly told.   *succeeds*
290   KING RICHARD   Then plainly to her tell my loving tale.
    QUEEN ELIZABETH   Plain and not honest is too harsh a style.[3]
    KING RICHARD   Your reasons are too shallow and too quick.[4]
    QUEEN ELIZABETH   O no, my reasons are too deep and dead—
    Too deep and dead, poor infants, in their graves.
295   KING RICHARD   Harp not on that string, madam. That is past.
    QUEEN ELIZABETH   Harp on it still shall I, till heart-strings break.
    KING RICHARD   Now by my George, my garter,[5] and my crown—
    QUEEN ELIZABETH   Profaned, dishonoured, and the third usurped.
    KING RICHARD   I swear—
    QUEEN ELIZABETH   By nothing, for this is no oath.
300   Thy George, profaned, hath lost his° holy honour;   *its*
    Thy garter, blemished, pawned his lordly virtue;
    Thy crown, usurped, disgraced his kingly glory.
    If something thou wouldst swear to be believed,
    Swear then by something that thou hast not wronged.
    KING RICHARD   Then by myself—
305   QUEEN ELIZABETH   Thy self is self-misused.
    KING RICHARD   Now by the world—

---

3. The plain style (as in the proverb "Truth is plain"), unless it is truth telling, will be too harsh; lies need elaborate decoration.
4. Rash, ill considered; but Elizabeth's response plays on "quick" as "alive."
5. A garter and a jeweled pendant with the figure of St. George were parts of the insignia of the Order of the Garter, the highest order of knighthood.

QUEEN ELIZABETH   'Tis full of thy foul wrongs.
KING RICHARD   My father's death—
QUEEN ELIZABETH   Thy life hath that dishonoured.
KING RICHARD   Why then, by God—
QUEEN ELIZABETH   God's wrong is most of all.
    If thou didst fear to break an oath with him,
310   The unity the King my husband made[6]
    Thou hadst not broken, nor my brothers died.
    If thou hadst feared to break an oath by him,
    Th'imperial metal circling now thy head
    Had graced the tender temples of my child,
315   And both the princes had been breathing here,
    Which now—two tender bedfellows for dust—
    Thy broken faith hath made the prey for worms.
    What canst thou swear by now?
KING RICHARD   The time to come.
QUEEN ELIZABETH   That thou hast wrongèd in the time o'erpast,
320   For I myself have many tears to wash
    Hereafter time,° for time past wronged by thee.   *The future*
    The children live, whose fathers thou hast slaughtered—
    Ungoverned youth,[7] to wail it in their age.°   *when they grow older*
    The parents live, whose children thou hast butchered—
325   Old barren plants, to wail it with° their age.   *along with*
    Swear not by time to come, for that thou hast
    Misused ere used, by times ill-used o'erpast.[8]
KING RICHARD   As I intend[9] to prosper and repent,
    So thrive I in my dangerous affairs
330   Of hostile arms—myself myself confound,°   *may I ruin myself*
    Heaven and fortune bar me happy hours,
    Day yield me not thy light nor night thy rest;
    Be opposite, all planets of good luck,
    To my proceeding—if, with dear heart's love,
335   Immaculate devotion, holy thoughts,
    I tender° not thy beauteous, princely daughter.   *love*
    In her consists my happiness and thine.
    Without her follows—to myself and thee,
    Herself, the land, and many a Christian soul—
340   Death, desolation, ruin, and decay.
    It cannot be avoided but by this;
    It will not be avoided but by this.
    Therefore, good-mother°—I must call you so—   *mother-in-law*
    Be the attorney of my love to her.
345   Plead what I will be, not what I have been;
    Not my deserts, but what I will deserve.
    Urge the necessity and state of times,°   *state of affairs*
    And be not peevish-fond° in great designs.   *foolishly obstinate*
QUEEN ELIZABETH   Shall I be tempted of the devil thus?
350 KING RICHARD   Ay, if the devil tempt you to do good.
QUEEN ELIZABETH   Shall I forget myself to be myself?[1]
KING RICHARD   Ay, if yourself 's remembrance wrong yourself.

---

6. The "reconciliation" staged in 2.1 between Queen
Elizabeth and her enemies.
7. Youth without a father's guidance.
8. *thou . . . o'erpast:* you have, by the continuing effects
of your past crimes, misused the future even before it

comes to pass.
9. *As I intend:* the formulation has the force of "I swear
that as I intend."
1. Am I to overlook all wrongs done me in order to
become Queen Mother (as I already have been)?

QUEEN ELIZABETH   Yet thou didst kill my children.

KING RICHARD   But in your daughter's womb I bury them,

355   Where, in that nest of spicery,² they will breed

Selves of themselves, to your recomfiture.°   *consolation*

QUEEN ELIZABETH   Shall I go win my daughter to thy will?

KING RICHARD   And be a happy mother by the deed.

QUEEN ELIZABETH   I go. Write to me very shortly,

360   And you shall understand from me her mind.

KING RICHARD   Bear her my true love's kiss,

[*He kisses her*]   and so farewell—

Exit [ELIZABETH]

Relenting fool, and shallow, changing woman.

Enter [*Sir Richard*] RATCLIFFE

How now, what news?

RATCLIFFE   Most mighty sovereign, on the western coast

365   Rideth a puissant° navy. To our shores   *mighty*

Throng many doubtful, hollow-hearted friends,

Unarmed and unresolved, to beat them back.

'Tis thought that Richmond is their° admiral,   *(the navy's)*

And there they hull,° expecting but the aid   *drift; wait*

370   Of Buckingham to welcome them ashore.

KING RICHARD   Some light-foot° friend post° to the Duke of   *swift-footed / hasten*

Norfolk.

Ratcliffe thyself, or Catesby—where is he?³

CATESBY   Here, my good lord.

KING RICHARD   Catesby, fly to the Duke.

CATESBY   I will, my lord, with all convenient° haste.   *due*

375   KING RICHARD   Ratcliffe, come hither. Post to Salisbury;

When thou com'st thither—[*to* CATESBY] dull, unmindful villain,

Why stay'st thou here, and goest not to the Duke?

CATESBY   First, mighty liege, tell me your highness' pleasure:

What from your grace I shall deliver to him?

380   KING RICHARD   O true, good Catesby. Bid him levy straight

The greatest strength and power that he can make,°   *raise*

And meet me suddenly° at Salisbury.   *without delay*

CATESBY   I go.   *Exit*

RATCLIFFE   What, may it please you, shall I do at Salisbury?

385   KING RICHARD   Why, what wouldst thou do there before I go?

RATCLIFFE   Your highness told me I should post before.

KING RICHARD   My mind is changed.

Enter Lord STANLEY

Stanley, what news with you?

STANLEY   None, good my liege, to please you with the hearing,

Nor none so bad but well may be reported.

390   KING RICHARD   Hoyday,° a riddle! Neither good nor bad.   *(an exclamation)*

Why need'st thou run so many mile about

When thou mayst tell thy tale the nearest° way?   *most direct*

Once more, what news?

STANLEY   Richmond is on the seas.

KING RICHARD   There let him sink, and be the seas on him.

395   White-livered° renegade, what doth he there?   *Cowardly*

---

2. Fragrant spices—in contrast to the stench of other burial places; the spices on the phoenix's pyre. *nest:* place where eggs are hatched, but also specifically the nest or pyre on which the legendary phoenix burned itself and then rose from its own ashes.
3. Parts of lines 373–74 appear only in F.

STANLEY I know not, mighty sovereign, but by guess.

KING RICHARD Well, as you guess?

STANLEY Stirred up by Dorset, Buckingham, and Ely,
He makes for England, here to claim the crown.

400 KING RICHARD Is the chair° empty? Is the sword unswayed?   throne
Is the King dead? The empire° unpossessed?   state
What heir of York is there alive but we?
And who is England's king but great York's heir?
Then tell me, what makes he° upon the seas?   what is he doing

405 STANLEY Unless for that, my liege, I cannot guess.

KING RICHARD Unless for that° he comes to be your liege,   because
You cannot guess wherefore the Welshman⁴ comes.
Thou wilt revolt and fly to him, I fear.

STANLEY No, my good lord, therefore mistrust me not.

410 KING RICHARD Where is thy power then? To beat him back,
Where be thy tenants and thy followers?
Are they not now upon the western shore,
Safe-conducting the rebels from their ships?

STANLEY No, my good lord, my friends are in the north.

415 KING RICHARD Cold friends to me. What do they in the north,
When they should serve their sovereign in the west?

STANLEY They have not been commanded, mighty King.
Pleaseth° your majesty to give me leave,   If it please
I'll muster up my friends and meet your grace

420 Where and what time your majesty shall please.

KING RICHARD Ay, ay, thou wouldst be gone to join with Richmond.
But I'll not trust thee.

STANLEY   Most mighty sovereign,
You have no cause to hold my friendship doubtful.
I never was, nor never will be, false.

425 KING RICHARD Go then and muster men—but leave behind
Your son George Stanley. Look your heart be firm,
Or else his head's assurance is but frail.

STANLEY So deal with him as I prove true to you.   *Exit*
        Enter a MESSENGER

MESSENGER My gracious sovereign, now in Devonshire,

430 As I by friends am well advisèd,°   well informed
Sir Edward Courtenay and the haughty prelate,
Bishop of Exeter, his elder brother,
With many more confederates are in arms.
        Enter another MESSENGER

SECOND MESSENGER In Kent, my liege, the Guildfords are in arms,

435 And every hour more competitors°   associates
Flock to the rebels, and their power grows strong.
        Enter another MESSENGER

THIRD MESSENGER My lord, the army of great Buckingham—

KING RICHARD Out on ye, owls!⁵ Nothing but songs of death?
        He striketh him
There, take thou that, till thou bring better news.

440 THIRD MESSENGER The news I have to tell your majesty
Is that, by sudden flood and fall of water,°   rain
Buckingham's army is dispersed and scattered,
And he himself wandered away alone,

---

4. Richmond's grandfather, Owen Tudor, was Welsh.   5. The cry of the owl was thought to portend evil.

No man knows whither.

KING RICHARD   I cry thee mercy.°—   *I beg your pardon*
445 Ratcliffe, reward him for the blow I gave him.—
Hath any well-advisèd° friend proclaimed   *foresighted*
Reward to him that brings the traitor in?

THIRD MESSENGER   Such proclamation hath been made, my lord.

Enter another MESSENGER

FOURTH MESSENGER   Sir Thomas Lovell and Lord Marquis Dorset—
450 'Tis said, my liege—in Yorkshire are in arms.
But this good comfort bring I to your highness:
The Breton navy is dispersed by tempest.
Richmond in Dorsetshire sent out a boat
Unto the shore, to ask those on the banks
455 If they were his assistants,° yea or no?   *allies*
Who answered him they came from Buckingham
Upon his party.° He, mistrusting them,   *faction*
Hoist sail and made his course again for Bretagne.°   *Brittany*

KING RICHARD   March on, march on, since we are up in arms,
460 If not to fight with foreign enemies,
Yet to beat down these rebels here at home.

Enter CATESBY

CATESBY   My liege, the Duke of Buckingham is taken.
That is the best news. That the Earl of Richmond
Is with a mighty power landed at Milford⁶
465 Is colder tidings, yet they must be told.

KING RICHARD   Away, towards Salisbury! While we reason° here,   *talk*
A royal battle might be won and lost.
Someone take order Buckingham be brought
To Salisbury. The rest march on with me.   *Flourish. Exeunt*

4.5

Enter [Lord STANLEY *Earl of] Derby and* SIR CHRISTO-
PHER *[a priest]*

STANLEY   Sir Christopher, tell Richmond this from me:
That in the sty of this most deadly boar
My son George Stanley is franked up in hold.¹
If I revolt, off goes young George's head.
5   The fear of that holds off my present aid.
But tell me, where is princely Richmond now?

SIR CHRISTOPHER   At Pembroke, or at Ha'rfordwest² in Wales.

STANLEY   What men of name° resort to him?   *rank*

SIR CHRISTOPHER   Sir Walter Herbert, a renownèd soldier,
10   Sir Gilbert Talbot, Sir William Stanley,³
Oxford, redoubted° Pembroke,⁴ Sir James Blunt,   *dreaded*
And Rhys-ap-Thomas with a valiant crew,
And many other of great name and worth—
And towards London do they bend their power,°   *lead their troops*

6. Milford Haven, a large, deep natural harbor on the Welsh coast, far enough from centers of population to be ideal for an invading army. The events of Richmond's successful invasion at Milford in 1485 are telescoped, in the mouths of the four messengers, with those of his unsuccessful rebellion against Richard two years earlier.

4.5 Location: A private place, perhaps Derby's house.
1. Is shut up (in a sty) in custody.
2. Haverford West, town at the northern end of Milford Haven. Pembroke was the county town of Pembrokeshire, situated on Milford Haven.
3. Lord Stanley, the Earl of Derby's brother.
4. Jasper Tudor, Richmond's uncle.

15   If by the way they be not fought withal.
      STANLEY   Well, hie° thee to thy lord. Commend me to him.   *hasten*
          Tell him the Queen hath heartily consented
          He should espouse Elizabeth her daughter.
          My letter will resolve him of my mind.⁵
20   Farewell.   *Exeunt [severally]*

5.1

Enter [the Duke of] BUCKINGHAM *with halberdiers, led*
[by a SHERIFF*] to execution*
      BUCKINGHAM   Will not King Richard let me speak with him?
      SHERIFF   No, my good lord, therefore be patient.
      BUCKINGHAM   Hastings, and Edward's children, Gray and Rivers,
          Holy King Henry and thy fair son Edward,
5   Vaughan, and all that have miscarrièd°   *died*
          By underhand, corrupted, foul injustice:
          If that your moody, discontented souls¹
          Do through the clouds behold this present hour,
          Even for revenge mock my destruction.
10   This is All-Souls' day,² fellow, is it not?
      SHERIFF   It is.
      BUCKINGHAM   Why then All-Souls' day is my body's doomsday.
          This is the day which, in King Edward's time,
          I wished might fall on me,³ when I was found
15   False to his children and his wife's allies.°   *kinsmen*
          This is the day wherein I wished to fall
          By the false faith of him whom most I trusted.
          This, this All-Souls' day to my fearful soul
          Is the determined respite of my wrongs.⁴
20   That high all-seer which I dallied with
          Hath turned my feignèd prayer on my head,
          And given in earnest what I begged in jest.
          Thus doth he force the swords of wicked men
          To turn their own points in their masters' bosoms.
25   Thus Margaret's curse falls heavy on my neck.
          'When he', quoth she, 'shall split thy heart with sorrow
          Remember Margaret was a prophetess.'⁵
          Come lead me, officers, to the block of shame.
          Wrong hath but wrong, and blame the due of blame.   *Exeunt*

5.2

*Enter [*HENRY EARL OF*]* RICHMOND *[with a letter, the*
Earl of] OXFORD, *[Sir James]* BLUNT, *[Sir Walter]* HER-
BERT, *and others, with drum and colours*
      HENRY EARL OF RICHMOND   Fellows in arms, and my most loving friends,
          Bruised underneath the yoke of tyranny,
          Thus far into the bowels° of the land   *center*

5. Will make my intentions clear to him.
5.1 Location: Salisbury.
1. Because they are unable to rest in peace until their violent deaths have been avenged. *moody:* angry.
2. November 2, the day on which the Roman Catholic Church intercedes for all Christian souls and on which spirits were supposed to walk (as in the following scenes at Shrewsbury).

3. See Buckingham's prophetic speech in 2.1.32–40.
4. Is the preordained ending of my wrongdoing (but alluding to the more usual significance of All Souls' Day, "preordained final rest from suffering"). *respite:* day to which something is postponed.
5. See 1.3.298–99.
5.2 Location: Near Tamworth in Staffordshire.

Have we marched on without impediment,
5 And here receive we from our father[1] Stanley
Lines of fair comfort and encouragement.
The wretched, bloody, and usurping boar,
That spoils your summer fields and fruitful vines,
Swills your warm blood like wash,° and makes his trough   *pig fodder*
10 In your inbowelled° bosoms, this foul swine   *disemboweled*
Lies now even in the centry° of this isle,   *center; sentry post*
Near to the town of Leicester, as we learn.
From Tamworth thither is but one day's march.
In God's name, cheerly° on, courageous friends,   *cheerfully*
15 To reap the harvest of perpetual peace
By this one bloody trial of sharp war.
OXFORD   Every man's conscience is a thousand swords
To fight against this guilty homicide.°   *murderer*
HERBERT   I doubt not but his friends will turn to us.
20 BLUNT   He hath no friends but what are friends for fear,
Which in his dearest° need will fly from him.   *most extreme*
HENRY EARL OF RICHMOND   All for our vantage.° Then, in God's   *advantage*
    name, march.
True hope is swift, and flies with swallows' wings;
Kings it makes gods, and meaner° creatures kings.   *baser*
                                    Exeunt [marching]

5.3

Enter KING RICHARD *in arms, with [the Duke of]* NOR-
FOLK, *[Sir Richard]* RATCLIFFE, *Sir William [*CATESBY,
and others][1]
KING RICHARD   Here pitch our tent, even here in Bosworth field.
    [*Soldiers begin to pitch a tent*]
Why, how now, Catesby? Why look you so sad?
CATESBY   My heart is ten times lighter than my looks.
KING RICHARD   My lord of Norfolk.
NORFOLK   Here, most gracious liege.
5 KING RICHARD   Norfolk, we must have knocks.° Ha, must we not?   *blows*
NORFOLK   We must both give and take, my loving lord.
KING RICHARD   Up with my tent! Here will I lie tonight.
But where tomorrow? Well, all's one for that.°   *it makes no difference*
Who hath descried° the number of the traitors?   *discerned*
10 NORFOLK   Six or seven thousand is their utmost power.
KING RICHARD   Why, our battalia° trebles that account.°   *army / number*
Besides, the King's name is a tower of strength,
Which they upon the adverse faction want.°   *lack*
Up with the tent! Come, noble gentlemen,
15 Let us survey the vantage of the ground.[2]
Call for some men of sound direction.°   *military judgment*
Let's lack no discipline, make no delay—
For, lords, tomorrow is a busy day.   *Exeunt [at one door]*

---

1. Stepfather (Richmond was the son of Edmund Tudor
and Margaret Beaufort; Lord Stanley, Earl of Derby, was
his mother's third husband). *our:* royal plural.
5.3 Location: The rest of the play takes place on
Bosworth Field.

1. Instead of Catesby, the stage direction in F has the
Earl of Surrey, who speaks with Richard at line 3.
2. *vantage of the ground:* military advantages offered by
the spot chosen for battle.

5.4

Enter [at another door HENRY EARL OF] RICHMOND,
[Sir James BLUNT,] *Sir William Brandon, [the Earl of]*
OXFORD, *[Marquis]* DORSET *[and others]*[1]

HENRY EARL OF RICHMOND The weary sun hath made a golden set,
And by the bright track of his fiery car[2]
Gives token of a goodly day tomorrow.
Sir William Brandon, you shall bear my standard.
5 The Earl of Pembroke keeps° his regiment;   *stays with*
Good Captain Blunt, bear my good night to him,
And by the second hour in the morning
Desire the Earl to see me in my tent.
Yet one thing more, good Captain, do for me:
10 Where is Lord Stanley quartered, do you know?
BLUNT Unless I have mista'en his colours much,
Which well I am assured I have not done,
His regiment lies half a mile, at least,
South from the mighty power of the King.
15 HENRY EARL OF RICHMOND If without peril it be possible,
Sweet Blunt, make some good means to speak with him,
And give him from me this most needful note.
BLUNT Upon my life, my lord, I'll undertake it.
And so God give you quiet rest tonight.
HENRY EARL OF RICHMOND Good night, good Captain Blunt.
                                                               [*Exit* BLUNT]
20   Come, gentlemen.
Give me some ink and paper in my tent.
I'll draw the form and model° of our battle,   *plan*
Limit° each leader to his several charge,°   *Appoint / separate duty*
And part° in just proportion our small power.   *divide*
25 Let us consult upon tomorrow's business.
Into my tent: the dew is raw and cold.
                                        They withdraw into the tent

5.5

[A table brought in.] Enter KING RICHARD, [*Sir
Richard*] RATCLIFFE, [*the Duke of*] NORFOLK, *Sir
William*] CATESBY [*and others*]

KING RICHARD What is't o'clock?
CATESBY It's supper-time, my lord. It's nine o'clock.
KING RICHARD I will not sup tonight. Give me some ink and paper.
What, is my beaver easier° than it was?   *my helmet visor looser*
5 And all my armour laid into my tent?
CATESBY It is, my liege, and all things are in readiness.
KING RICHARD Good Norfolk, hie thee° to thy charge.   *hasten*
Use careful watch; choose trusty sentinels.
NORFOLK I go, my lord.
10 KING RICHARD Stir with the lark tomorrow, gentle Norfolk.
NORFOLK I warrant° you, my lord.   *Exit*   *assure; guarantee*
KING RICHARD   Catesby.
CATESBY   My lord?

5.4
1. Although Q and F are silent on the question of how
many tents are onstage at the end of this scene, most
editors direct these attendants to pitch another for Richmond during the following dialogue. Oxford and Dorset

are specified in F but not in Q, which calls only for "the
lords."
2. Chariot (of the sun god Phoebus).
5.5

KING RICHARD   Send out a pursuivant-at-arms°   *one who attends a herald*
    To Stanley's regiment. Bid him bring his power°   *forces*
    Before sun-rising, lest his son George fall
15 Into the blind cave of eternal night.   [*Exit* CATESBY]
    Fill me a bowl of wine. Give me a watch.[1]
    Saddle white Surrey[2] for the field tomorrow.
    Look that my staves° be sound, and not too heavy.   *lance shafts*
    Ratcliffe.
20 RATCLIFFE   My lord?
    KING RICHARD   Saw'st thou the melancholy Lord Northumberland?
    RATCLIFFE   Thomas the Earl of Surrey and himself,
        Much about cockshut° time, from troop to troop   *twilight*
        Went through the army, cheering up the soldiers.
25 KING RICHARD   So, I am satisfied. Give me some wine.
    I have not that alacrity of spirit,
    Nor cheer of mind, that I was wont to have.
        [*The wine is brought*]
        Set it down. Is ink and paper ready?
    RATCLIFFE   It is, my lord.
    KING RICHARD   Leave me. Bid my guard watch.
30 About the mid of night come to my tent,
    Ratcliffe, and help to arm me. Leave me, I say.
        Exit RATCLIFFE [*with others.* RICHARD *writes, and later sleeps*]
        Enter [*Lord* STANLEY *Earl of*] *Derby to* HENRY EARL
        OF] RICHMOND [*and the lords*] *in his tent*
    STANLEY   Fortune and victory sit on thy helm!°   *helmet*
    HENRY EARL OF RICHMOND   All comfort that the dark night can afford
        Be to thy person, noble father-in-law.°   *stepfather*
35 Tell me, how fares our loving mother?
    STANLEY   I, by attorney,° bless thee from thy mother,   *by proxy*
    Who prays continually for Richmond's good.
    So much for that. The silent hours steal on,
    And flaky° darkness breaks within the east.   *streaked with light*
40 In brief—for so the season° bids us be—   *time of day*
    Prepare thy battle early in the morning,
    And put thy fortune to th'arbitrement°   *determination; verdict*
    Of bloody strokes and mortal-sharing[3] war.
    I, as I may—that which I would, I cannot—
45 With best advantage will deceive the time,[4]
    And aid thee in this doubtful shock° of arms.   *this uncertain clash*
    But on thy side I may not be too forward—
    Lest, being seen, thy brother,° tender° George,   *stepbrother / young*
    Be executed in his father's sight.
50 Farewell. The leisure° and the fearful time   *time available*
    Cuts off the ceremonious vows of love
    And ample interchange of sweet discourse,
    Which so long sundered friends should dwell upon.
    God give us leisure for these rights of love.
55 Once more, adieu. Be valiant, and speed well.

---

1. Probably a watch light (a slow-burning candle, to write by); possibly a special guard (see line 29).
2. The chroniclers report that Richard was mounted on a "great white course," but the name is Shakespeare's.
3. Apportioning to mortals their lot; shearing or cutting down mortals. Q has "mortal staring," giving the commonplace image of war as both evil-looking and able to cause damage with its glance (like a basilisk).
4. *as . . . time:* as best I can—for I cannot fight openly on your side—I will mislead Richard.

HENRY EARL OF RICHMOND   Good lords, conduct him to his regiment.
    I'll strive with° troubled thoughts to take a nap,   *despite*
    Lest leaden slumber peise° me down tomorrow,   *weigh*
    When I should mount with wings of victory.
60   Once more, good night, kind lords and gentlemen.
        Exeunt [STANLEY *and the lords*]. *Manet* RICHMOND
        [RICHMOND *kneels*]
    O thou, whose captain I account myself,   *prayer*
    Look on my forces with a gracious eye,
    Put in their hands thy bruising irons° of wrath,   *swords*
    That they may crush down with a heavy fall
65   Th'usurping helmets of our adversaries.
    Make us thy ministers of chastisement,
    That we may praise thee in the victory.
    To thee I do commend my watchful° soul,   *alert*
    Ere I let fall the windows° of mine eyes.   *eyelids*
70   Sleeping and waking, O defend me still!   [*He*] *sleeps*
        Enter the GHOST OF *young* PRINCE EDWARD [*above*][5]
GHOST OF PRINCE EDWARD [(*to* RICHARD)]   Let me sit heavy on
      thy soul tomorrow,
    Prince Edward, son to Henry the Sixth.[6]
    Think how thou stabbedst me in my prime of youth
    At Tewkesbury. Despair, therefore, and die.
75   [*To* RICHMOND] Be cheerful, Richmond, for the wrongèd souls
    Of butchered princes fight in thy behalf.
    King Henry's issue,° Richmond, comforts thee.   [*Exit*][7]   *offspring*
        Enter [*above*] *the* GHOST OF [KING] HENRY VI
GHOST OF KING HENRY (*to* RICHARD)   When I was mortal, my
      anointed° body   (*with sacred oil*)
    By thee was punchèd full of deadly holes.
80   Think on the Tower[8] and me. Despair and die.
    Harry the Sixth bids thee despair and die.
    [*To* RICHMOND] Virtuous and holy, be thou conqueror.
    Harry that prophesied[9] thou shouldst be king
    Comforts thee in thy sleep. Live and flourish!   [*Exit*]
        Enter [*above*] *the* GHOST OF [*George Duke of*] CLARENCE
85 GHOST OF CLARENCE [(*to* RICHARD)]   Let me sit heavy on thy soul tomorrow,
    I that was washed to death with fulsome° wine,   *sickening*
    Poor Clarence, by thy guile betrayed to death.
    Tomorrow in the battle think on me,
    And fall° thy edgeless sword. Despair and die.   *drop*
90   [*To* RICHMOND] Thou offspring of the house of Lancaster,
    The wrongèd heirs of York do pray for thee.
    Good angels guard thy battle.° Live and flourish!   [*Exit*]   *army*
        Enter [*above*] *the* GHOSTS OF [*Lords*] RIVERS, GRAY, *and*
        [*Sir Thomas*] VAUGHAN
GHOST OF RIVERS [*to* RICHARD]   Let me sit heavy on thy soul tomorrow,
    Rivers that died at Pomfret. Despair and die.
95 GHOST OF GRAY [*to* RICHARD]   Think upon Gray, and let thy soul despair.

---

5. Q, F do not specify how or where the ghosts enter.
6. Line not present in Q, F; it is added here because Edward is the one character not seen previously, and it is possible that information originally intended as dialogue ended up as the stage direction when the text was printed.
7. Exits not given in Q, F. The ghosts could exeunt together at the end.

8. Where Henry VI was supposedly murdered.
9. See *Richard Duke of York* 4.7, in which King Henry (sometimes "Harry"), declaring the young Richmond "England's hope," foresees Richmond's accession to the throne and the beginning of what was to become the Tudor dynasty.

GHOST OF VAUGHAN [*to* RICHARD]   Think upon Vaughan, and with guilty fear
    Let fall thy pointless lance. Despair and die.
ALL THREE (*to* RICHMOND)   Awake, and think our wrongs in Richard's bosom
    Will conquer him. Awake, and win the day!   [*Exeunt* GHOSTS]
        Enter [above] the GHOSTS OF THE *two young* PRINCES
GHOSTS OF THE PRINCES (*to* RICHARD)   Dream on thy cousins,[1]
100   smothered in the Tower.
    Let us be lead within thy bosom, Richard,
    And weigh thee down to ruin, shame, and death.
    Thy nephews' souls bid thee despair and die.
    (*To* RICHMOND) Sleep, Richmond, sleep in peace and wake in joy.
105   Good angels guard thee from the boar's annoy.
    Live, and beget a happy race of kings!
    Edward's unhappy sons do bid thee flourish. [*Exeunt* GHOSTS]
        Enter [above] the GHOST OF *Lord* HASTINGS[2]
GHOST OF HASTINGS [*to* RICHARD]   Bloody and guilty, guiltily awake,
    And in a bloody battle end thy days.
110   Think on Lord Hastings, then despair and die.
    (*To* RICHMOND) Quiet, untroubled soul, awake, awake!
    Arm, fight, and conquer for fair England's sake.   [*Exit*]
        Enter [above] the GHOST OF LADY ANNE
GHOST OF LADY ANNE (*to* RICHARD)   Richard, thy wife, that wretched Anne thy wife,
    That never slept a quiet hour with thee,
115   Now fills thy sleep with perturbations.
    Tomorrow in the battle think on me,
    And fall thy edgeless sword. Despair and die.
    (*To* RICHMOND) Thou quiet soul, sleep thou a quiet sleep.
    Dream of success and happy victory.
120   Thy adversary's wife doth pray for thee.   [*Exit*]
        Enter [above] the GHOST [OF *the Duke*] *of* BUCKINGHAM
GHOST OF BUCKINGHAM (*to* RICHARD)   The first was I that helped thee to the crown;
    The last was I that felt thy tyranny.
    O in the battle think on Buckingham,
    And die in terror of thy guiltiness!
125   Dream on, dream on, of bloody deeds and death;
    Fainting,° despair; despairing, yield thy breath.   *Losing heart*
    (*To* RICHMOND) I died for hope[3] ere I could lend thee aid.
    But cheer thy heart, and be thou not dismayed.
    God and good angels fight on Richmond's side,
130   And Richard falls in height of all his pride.   [*Exit*]
        RICHARD *starteth up out of a dream*
KING RICHARD   Give me another horse! Bind up my wounds!
    Have mercy, Jesu!—Soft, I did but dream.
    O coward conscience, how dost thou afflict me?
    The lights burn blue.[4] It is now dead midnight.
135   Cold fearful drops stand on my trembling flesh.
    What do I fear? Myself? There's none else by.
    Richard loves Richard; that is, I am I.
    Is there a murderer here? No. Yes, I am.
    Then fly! What, from myself? Great reason. Why?

---

1. Nephews ("cousins" was a term used for any kins-   3. I died hoping I could aid you.
men).   4. Thought to indicate the presence of ghosts.
2. Q has him enter before the princes, as he had died
before them.

140   Lest I revenge. Myself upon myself?
    Alack, I love myself. Wherefore?° For any good   *Why*
    That I myself have done unto myself?
    O no, alas, I rather hate myself
    For hateful deeds committed by myself.
145   I am a villain. Yet I lie: I am not.
    Fool, of thyself speak well.—Fool, do not flatter.
    My conscience hath a thousand several° tongues,   *separate*
    And every tongue brings in a several tale,
    And every tale condemns me for a villain.
150   Perjury, perjury, in the high'st degree!⁵
    Murder, stern murder, in the dir'st degree!
    All several sins, all used in each degree,
    Throng to the bar,° crying all, 'Guilty, guilty!'   *(of the court)*
    I shall despair.⁶ There is no creature loves me,
155   And if I die no soul will pity me.
    Nay, wherefore should they?—Since that I myself
    Find in myself no pity to myself.
    Methought the souls of all that I had murdered
    Came to my tent, and every one did threat
160   Tomorrow's vengeance on the head of Richard.
        Enter RATCLIFFE
    RATCLIFFE   My lord?
    KING RICHARD   'Swounds, who is there?
    RATCLIFFE   My lord, 'tis I. The early village cock
    Hath twice done salutation to the morn.
165   Your friends are up, and buckle on their armour.
    KING RICHARD   O Ratcliffe, I have dreamed a fearful dream.
    What thinkest thou, will all our friends prove true?
    RATCLIFFE   No doubt, my lord.
    KING RICHARD   Ratcliffe, I fear, I fear.
    RATCLIFFE   Nay, good my lord, be not afraid of shadows.°   *illusions; ghosts*
170   KING RICHARD   By the Apostle Paul, shadows tonight
    Have struck more terror to the soul of Richard
    Than can the substance of ten thousand soldiers
    Armèd in proof° and led by shallow Richmond.   *impenetrable armor*
    'Tis not yet near day. Come, go with me.
175   Under our tents I'll play the eavesdropper,
    To see if any mean to shrink from me.
        Exeunt RICHARD *and* RATCLIFFE
        Enter the lords to [HENRY EARL OF] RICHMOND, *sitting*
        in his tent
    LORDS   Good morrow, Richmond.
    HENRY EARL OF RICHMOND   Cry mercy,° lords and watchful   *Beg your pardon*
        gentlemen,
    That you have ta'en a tardy sluggard here.
180   A LORD   How have you slept, my lord?
    HENRY EARL OF RICHMOND   The sweetest sleep and fairest
        boding° dreams   *most propitious*
    That ever entered in a drowsy head
    Have I since your departure had, my lords.

5. Every kind of sin, from least to most wicked.
6. Despair was considered the only unforgivable sin; see 1.2.85–88.

Methought their souls whose bodies Richard murdered
185 Came to my tent and cried on[7] victory.
I promise you, my soul is very jocund°   *joyful*
In the remembrance of so fair a dream.
How far into the morning is it, lords?
A LORD Upon the stroke of four.
190 HENRY EARL OF RICHMOND Why then, 'tis time to arm, and give direction.
His oration to his soldiers
Much that I could say, loving countrymen,
The leisure° and enforcement of the time   *time available*
Forbids to dwell on. Yet remember this:
God and our good cause fight upon our side.
195 The prayers of holy saints and wrongèd souls,
Like high-reared bulwarks, stand before our forces.
Richard except,° those whom we fight against   *excepted*
Had rather have us win than him they follow.
For what is he they follow? Truly, friends,
200 A bloody tyrant and a homicide;
One raised in blood, and one in blood established;[8]
One that made means° to come by what he hath,   *that contrived*
And slaughtered those that were the means to help him;
A base, foul stone, made precious by the foil[9]
205 Of England's chair, where he is falsely set;[1]
One that hath ever been God's enemy.
Then if you fight against God's enemy,
God will, in justice, ward° you as his soldiers.   *guard*
If you do sweat to put a tyrant down,
210 You sleep in peace, the tyrant being slain.
If you do fight against your country's foes,
Your country's foison° pays your pains the hire.   *abundance*
If you do fight in safeguard of your wives,
Your wives shall welcome home the conquerors.
215 If you do free your children from the sword,
Your children's children quites° it in your age.   *requites*
Then, in the name of God and all these rights,
Advance° your standards! Draw your willing swords!   *Raise*
For me, the ransom of this bold attempt
220 Shall be my cold corpse on the earth's cold face;[2]
But if I thrive,° to gain of my attempt,   *succeed*
The least of you shall share his part thereof.
Sound, drums and trumpets, bold and cheerfully!
God and Saint George!° Richmond and victory!   *patron saint of England*
[*Exeunt to the sound of drums and trumpets*]

5.6

Enter KING RICHARD, [*Sir Richard*] RATCLIFFE, [*Sir
William*] CATESBY [*and others*]

KING RICHARD What said Northumberland, as touching° Richmond?   *regarding*
RATCLIFFE That he was never trainèd up in arms.

7. And called out (a hunting term); here, urged me on to.
8. *One raised . . . established:* One who has come to the throne by bloodshed and has held it through further bloodshed.
9. Metal leaf was often placed under a jewel as a part

of its setting, in order to increase its radiance.
1. Of the throne of England, on which he is wrongly placed; with a pun on "being set like a jewel."
2. *the ransom . . . face:* the only ransom I will give them is my dead body.
5.6

KING RICHARD He said the truth. And what said Surrey then?

RATCLIFFE He smiled and said, 'The better for our purpose.'

5 KING RICHARD He was in the right, and so indeed it is.

    Clock strikes

Tell the clock there.¹ Give me a calendar.°   *an almanac*

Who saw the sun today?

    [A book is brought]

RATCLIFFE   Not I, my lord.

KING RICHARD Then he disdains to shine, for by the book°   *(the almanac)*

He should have braved° the east an hour ago.   *made resplendent*

10 A black day will it be to somebody.

Ratcliffe.

RATCLIFFE My lord?

KING RICHARD   The sun will not be seen today.

The sky doth frown and lour° upon our army.   *glower*

I would these dewy tears were from° the ground.   *gone from*

15 Not shine today—why, what is that to me

More than to Richmond? For the selfsame heaven

That frowns on me looks sadly upon him.

    Enter [the Duke of] NORFOLK

NORFOLK Arm, arm, my lord! The foe vaunts° in the field.   *flaunts his strength*

KING RICHARD Come, bustle, bustle! Caparison° my horse.   *Put the trappings on*

    [RICHARD arms]

20 Call up Lord Stanley, bid him bring his power.°   *[Exit one]*   *forces*

I will lead forth my soldiers to the plain,

And thus my battle° shall be orderèd.   *army*

My forward° shall be drawn out all in length,   *front rank*

Consisting equally of horse and foot,

25 Our archers placèd strongly in the midst.

John Duke of Norfolk, Thomas Earl of Surrey,

Shall have the leading of this multitude.

They thus directed,° we ourself will follow   *positioned*

In the main battle, whose puissance° on both sides   *power*

30 Shall be well wingèd° with our chiefest horse.°   *flanked / best cavalry*

This, and Saint George to boot!² What think'st thou, Norfolk?

NORFOLK A good direction, warlike sovereign.

    He showeth him a paper

This paper found I on my tent this morning.

    [He reads]

    'Jackie of Norfolk be not too bold,

35   For Dickon thy master is bought and sold.³

KING RICHARD A thing devisèd by the enemy.—

Go, gentlemen, each man unto his charge.

Let not our babbling dreams affright our souls.

Conscience is but a word that cowards use,

40 Devised at first to keep the strong in awe.

Our strong arms be our conscience; swords, our law.

March on, join° bravely! Let us to't, pell mell—   *join battle*

If not to heaven, then hand in hand to hell.

    His oration to his army

What shall I say, more than I have inferred?°   *put forward*

45 Remember whom you are to cope withal:°   *with*

---

1. Count the clock's strokes.
2. *and . . . boot*: with the aid of our patron saint as a bonus.

3. Is betrayed *Jackie of Norfolk*: John, Duke of Norfolk. *Dickon*: Dick (that is, Richard).

A sort° of vagabonds, rascals and runaways,　　　　　　　　　　*gang*
A scum of Bretons and base lackey° peasants,　　　　　　　　*lowly*
Whom their o'ercloyèd° country vomits forth　　　　*nauseously overfull*
To desperate ventures and assured destruction.
50　You sleeping safe, they bring to you unrest;
You having lands and blessed with beauteous wives,
They would distrain° the one, distain° the other.　　　*confiscate / dishonor*
And who doth lead them, but a paltry fellow?
Long kept in Bretagne at our mother's[4] cost;
55　A milksop; one that never in his life
Felt so much cold as over shoes in snow.[5]
Let's whip[6] these stragglers o'er the seas again,
Lash hence these overweening rags of France,
These famished beggars, weary of their lives,
60　Who—but for° dreaming on this fond° exploit—　　*were it not for / foolish*
For want of means,° poor rats, had hanged themselves.　　　*livelihood*
If we be conquered, let *men* conquer us,
And not these bastard Bretons, whom our fathers
Have in their own land beaten, bobbed,° and thumped,　　　*pounded*
65　And in record left them the heirs of shame.[7]
Shall these enjoy our lands? Lie with our wives?
Ravish our daughters?
　　　　Drum afar off
　　　　　　　　　　Hark, I hear their drum.
Fight, gentlemen of England! Fight, bold yeomen!
Draw, archers, draw your arrows to the head!
70　Spur your proud horses hard, and ride in blood!
Amaze the welkin° with your broken staves!　　　　　　　　*sky*
　　　　Enter a MESSENGER
What says Lord Stanley? Will he bring his power?
MESSENGER　My lord, he doth deny° to come.　　　　　　　*refuse*
KING RICHARD　Off with young George's head!
75　NORFOLK　My lord, the enemy is past the marsh.
After the battle let George Stanley die.
KING RICHARD　A thousand hearts are great within my bosom.
Advance our standards! Set upon our foes!
Our ancient word° of courage, fair Saint George,　　　　*battle cry*
80　Inspire us with the spleen° of fiery dragons.　　　　　　*anger*
Upon them! Victory sits on our helms!°　　　　*Exeunt*　　*helmets*

5.7

　　　Alarum. Excursions.° Enter [Sir William] CATESBY　　*Military sallies*
CATESBY *[calling]*[1]　Rescue, my lord of Norfolk! Rescue, rescue!
[To a soldier] The King enacts more wonders than a man,[2]
Daring an opposite° to every danger.　　　　　　　*to oppose himself*
His horse is slain, and all on foot he fights,
5　Seeking for Richmond in the throat of death.
[Calling] Rescue, fair lord, or else the day is lost!

4. Apparently from a misprint in Holinshed, which should have read "brother's" (that is, Richard's brother-in-law, Charles, Duke of Burgundy, who supported Richmond in exile). Possibly: to the detriment of England, the mother country.
5. *as . . . snow*: as one does who walks in snow that covers the tops of his shoes.
6. English vagabonds were whipped out of the parish by a local official.
7. And gave them a shameful record in history.
5.7
1. Some editors bring Norfolk onstage, although the stage directions do not call for him in either Q or F.
2. More wonders than seems possible for a man.

Alarums. Enter [KING] RICHARD

KING RICHARD   A horse! A horse! My kingdom for a horse!

CATESBY   Withdraw, my lord. I'll help you to a horse.

KING RICHARD   Slave, I have set my life upon a cast,[3]

10 And I will stand the hazard of the die.

I think there be six Richmonds[4] in the field.

Five have I slain today, instead of him.

A horse! A horse! My kingdom for a horse!   [*Exeunt*]

Henry IV Battle line

5.8

Alarum. Enter [KING] RICHARD [*at one door*] *and*
[HENRY EARL OF] RICHMOND [*at another*]. *They fight.*
RICHARD *is slain.* [*Exit* RICHMOND.] *Retreat*[1] *and flour-*
ish. Enter [HENRY EARL OF] RICHMOND *and* [*Lord* STAN-
LEY *Earl of*] *Derby, with divers other lords* [*and soldiers*]

HENRY EARL OF RICHMOND   God and your arms be praised, victorious friends!

The day is ours. The bloody dog is dead.

STANLEY [*bearing the crown*]   Courageous Richmond, well hast
    thou acquit° thee.   acquitted; conducted

Lo, here this long usurpèd royalty

5 From the dead temples of this bloody wretch

Have I plucked off, to grace thy brows withal.°   with

Wear it, enjoy it, and make much of it.

    [*He sets the crown on Henry's head*]

KING HENRY VII   Great God of heaven, say 'Amen' to all.

But tell me—young George Stanley, is he living?

10 STANLEY   He is, my lord, and safe in Leicester town,

Whither, if it please you, we may now withdraw us.

KING HENRY VII   What men of name are slain on either side?

STANLEY [*reads*]   John Duke of Norfolk, Robert Brackenbury,

Walter Lord Ferrers, and Sir William Brandon.

15 KING HENRY VII   Inter their bodies as becomes their births.°   befits their rank

Proclaim a pardon to the soldiers fled

That in submission will return to us,

And then—as we have ta'en the sacrament[3]—

We will unite the white rose and the red.[4]

20 Smile, heaven, upon this fair conjunction,°   union

That long have frowned upon their enmity.

What traitor hears me and says not 'Amen'?

England hath long been mad, and scarred herself;

The brother blindly shed the brother's blood;

25 The father rashly slaughtered his own son;

The son, compelled, been butcher to the sire;

All that divided York and Lancaster,

United in their dire division.[5]

O now let Richmond and Elizabeth,

30 The true succeeders of each royal house,

By God's fair ordinance° conjoin together,   decree

3. A throw of the die (one of a pair of dice) in line 10.
4. In addition to Richmond, five other men dressed and armed to resemble him (a common safety measure).
5.8
1. A trumpet signal for (Richard's) men to retire.
2. Emblem of sovereignty; here, the crown.
3. Referring to the oath, taken by Richmond in the cathedral at Rheims, that he would marry Princess

Elizabeth as soon as he was crowned.
4. The badges of the Yorkist (white) and Lancastrian (red) factions. The marriage of Richmond (Lancastrian) and Princess Elizabeth (Yorkist) brought to an end the so-called Wars of the Roses, dramatized in the three *Henry VI* plays.
5. Joined by hatred, having nothing in common but mutual antagonism.

And let their heirs—God, if his will be so—
Enrich the time to come with smooth-faced peace,
With smiling plenty, and fair prosperous days.
35 Abate° the edge of traitors, gracious Lord,   *Blunt*
That would reduce° these bloody days again   *bring back*
And make poor England weep forth streams of blood.
Let them not live to taste this land's increase,°   *prosperity*
That would with treason wound this fair land's peace.
40 Now civil wounds are stopped; peace lives again.
That she may long live here, God say 'Amen'.
                                            [*Flourish.*] *Exeunt*

Venus and Adonis

When Shakespeare wrote the narrative poem *Venus and Adonis*, he was already an up-and-coming playwright; but he called his poem "the first heir of my invention" because, in 1593, it was his earliest work to see print. While plays were considered the property of the theater company and found their way to the printing house erratically if at all, an author could publish nondramatic works like *Venus and Adonis* and *The Rape of Lucrece* without impediment. It was customary to dedicate such published poems to aristocrats who might provide financial support or other form of patronage. Shakespeare dedicated *Venus and Adonis* to Henry Wriothesley, Earl of Southampton, a handsome nineteen-year-old aristocrat with sophisticated literary tastes, who was soon to come into a substantial fortune. But despite the conventionally flattering language of the dedication, Shakespeare intended to appeal to a larger audience than merely the patron to whom the poem was nominally addressed. Indeed, *Venus and Adonis* was exceedingly popular in Shakespeare's lifetime: it went through nine editions, and his contemporaries quote passages from it more often than they quote from any other Shakespearean play or poem.

Part of the attraction of the poem for Shakespeare's contemporaries was its extended and apparently effortless deployment of an elaborate poetic form. The poem's *ababcc* stanza, a quatrain followed by a couplet, was popular among many Elizabethan poets—George Gascoigne, Thomas Lodge, Edmund Spenser, and Philip Sidney, among others—but Shakespeare's virtuosity was so widely recognized that it has henceforth been known in English not by its Italian name, *sesta rima*, but as the "Venus and Adonis stanza." A sort of abbreviated sonnet, this stanza, in Shakespeare's hands, tends often to proffer a snatch of narrative in the quatrain, followed by a summarizing or reflective couplet, thus alternating between advancing the plot and commenting, pithily and wittily, upon the action.

Shakespeare found the story of Venus and Adonis in Ovid's *Metamorphoses,* a poem in fifteen books that retells, in beautiful Latin, more than two hundred pagan myths of transformation. Since Elizabethan schoolboys were required to memorize long passages from the *Metamorphoses,* many of Shakespeare's readers knew Ovid in the original; others read him in a popular 1567 English translation by Arthur Golding. Shakespeare would have been aware that the cult of Adonis was widespread in antiquity, a cult that involved rites of fertility and seasonal renewal and was associated with the adoration of a mother goddess variously identified as Venus, Aphrodite, Astoreth, Isis, or Cybele. In the Old Testament, the Israelites are periodically chastised for abandoning their male divinity for the worship of this heathen goddess; her cult thus seems, at least for the Jews of antiquity, to have constituted an alluring alternative to patriarchal monotheism. For Christian interpreters, the myth of the mutilated, transformed Adonis resembles the story of Christ closely enough to be read, on the one hand, as a pagan analogue to Christ's death and resurrection and, on the other hand, as a demonstration of the superior power of the Judeo-Christian God, who, unlike Venus, can confer true immortality.

Shakespeare was not the only Elizabethan writer to adapt Ovid's stories to an English idiom. *Venus and Adonis* is an erotic narrative poem of a type that had become popular in the 1580s and grew even more so in the 1590s, partly because of the success of Shakespeare's poem and of Christopher Marlowe's roughly contemporaneous *Hero and Leander.* The writers of such poems acquired their plots from classical sources, but they got their idea of how to treat those plots from a medieval and Renaissance tradition of erotic

Two horses mating. From Antonio Tempesta, *Horses of Different Lands.*

poetry, deriving from the Italian poet Petrarch and developed in English by such poets as Thomas Wyatt, Philip Sidney, and Edmund Spenser. In *Venus and Adonis,* Shakespeare reconceives his mythological protagonists so that his poem might in some respects more closely approximate a Petrarchan norm. When Ovid's Venus is dazzled by Adonis, she resolves to appeal to him by feigning an interest in his favorite sport. By donning hunting gear and resolutely chasing rabbits, she successfully captures the gorgeous huntsman, her true quarry. Shakespeare's Venus declares herself in a much more forthright fashion, but his Adonis, unlike Ovid's, remains unresponsive to her charms. Thus *Venus and Adonis* reproduces a dynamic that Petrarch and his followers had made familiar by the late sixteenth century, in which a yearning lover pleads endlessly with a chilly love object.

The enduring fascination of this scenario for Renaissance poets lay in their recognition that the absence of sexual gratification can enhance erotic desire: "An oven that is stopped, or river stayed, / Burneth more hotly, swelleth with more rage" (lines 331–32). In Petrarchan poetry, little of consequence seems to happen, but the apparent lack of momentum is actually a prime stimulus to creativity. Frustration hones techniques of erotic persuasion; it energizes lament; it interestingly complicates the poet-lover's state of mind. The sophisticated pleasure of intense self-awareness replaces the straightforward, even mindless pleasure of the sex act itself. In *Venus and Adonis,* Shakespeare's concentration on psychological detail produces an extraordinary slowing-down and drawing-out of the action. Ovid spends about eighty-five lines on Adonis, beginning with a brisk description of his birth and ending with an equally succinct account of his metamorphosis into an anemone flower. Shakespeare manages to devote almost twelve hundred lines to the last twenty-four hours of Adonis's life.

In some important respects, however, Shakespeare departs from his Petrarchan precedents. The Ovidian retelling of the story of Venus and Adonis appears in *Metamor-*

phoses 10, a book that, as Ovid's translator Arthur Golding writes, "chiefly doth contain one kind of argument / Reproving most prodigious lusts." Taken together, the stories of Book 10 treat necrophilia, homosexuality, bestiality, fetishism, and incest; in this context, the story of Venus and Adonis seems relatively tame. But the "prodigiousness" of the Venus and Adonis story becomes clear when it is compared with similar Ovidian tales, which usually involve gods—Jove, Neptune, Apollo, or Pluto—who rape or attempt to rape beautiful young women. The story of Venus and Adonis reverses the "normal" gender of eager divinity and reluctant mortal.

Shakespeare's revisions of the story exaggerate the effects of this transposition. He attributes some conventionally "masculine" traits to his heroine and some conventionally "feminine" ones to his hero. His Venus is experienced, immensely strong, and apparently quite a bit larger than the Adonis whom she effortlessly tucks under one arm. Shakespeare's Adonis is dimpled, tender, coy, and virginal. At the same time, a female, even one as formidable as Venus, is imagined to be incapable of rape, so Venus cannot simply overpower her beloved as Apollo or Jove might do. Anatomical constraints force her to play a quite different but also conventionally masculine part: the pleading, unsatisfied role conventionally assigned to the male lover in Petrarchan poetry.

Since in Renaissance erotic poetry the positions of actively desiring, rhetorically fluent male and passive, unwilling female are ordinarily strictly demarcated, the sexual transpositions in the Venus and Adonis story have immediate consequences for Shakespeare's use of poetic conventions. Obviously they give those conventions a fresh twist. In Shakespeare's hands, such novelty is often comic: the aggressive, rhetorically hyperbolic Venus and the fastidious Adonis are funny, because now as then they violate conventional notions of appropriate gender-specific behavior. Some of these reversals are obvious to a modern reader, since our courtship rituals retain vestiges of the assumption that males are naturally dominant and inclined to take the sexual initiative. Other reversals are more specific to the poetic tradition in which Shakespeare wrote. In traditional love poetry, for instance, the enamored man "blazons," or elaborately describes, the features of the woman he desires, dwelling on the incomparable beauty of her eyes, hair, lips, hands, voice, gestures, and so forth. But in *Venus and Adonis,* Venus is compelled to blazon her own charms, because Adonis will not do it for her.

> Mine eyes are grey, and bright, and quick in turning.
> My beauty as the spring doth yearly grow.
> My flesh is soft and plump, my marrow burning.
> . . . .
> Bid me discourse, I will enchant thine ear;
> Or like a fairy, trip upon the green;
> Or like a nymph, with long, dishevelled hair,
> Dance on the sands, and yet no footing seen.
>
> (lines 140–48)

While in the conventional love situation the blazon is a man's cry of yearning for an exquisite object, here it becomes a woman's calculated, but unsuccessful, advertising campaign.

Shakespeare also dwells on the comic quality of Venus's divine attributes, such as the miraculous weightlessness of her robust body. At one point, Venus describes herself as a kind of giant balloon: "Witness this primrose bank whereon I lie: / These forceless flowers like sturdy trees support me" (lines 151–52). Her physical strength contrasts vividly with her quintessentially feminine body: when Venus "locks her lily fingers one in one" (line 228), she turns out to have a grip of steel. Shakespeare's interest in such apparent incongruities foreshadowed his much more elaborate exploration of the effects of transvestism and sexual reversal in such plays as *As You Like It, Twelfth Night, All's Well That Ends Well, Macbeth,* and *Antony and Cleopatra.* The humor of *Venus and Adonis* is two-edged, however, for it implicitly mocks not merely the aberrant protagonists but the standards from which they deviate. In what sense are particular

Cupid taking aim. From George Wither, *A Collection of Emblemes* (1635). The motto reads: "Be wary, whosoe're thou be, / For from Love's arrows, none are free."

traits or behaviors "naturally" masculine or feminine if actual males and females do not possess them?

The upending of gender stereotypes in *Venus and Adonis* is only one of the strategies of reversal that structure the imagery of the poem. Again and again, its metaphors and similes insist on the similarity of what seems different, the difference in what seems the same. Hunting is and is not like sexual pursuit; killing is and is not like loving; female sexual desire is and is not like maternal nurture; the boar, savagely rooting in Adonis's groin, is and is not like Venus; Adonis is and is not like the sun god or the flower into which he eventually transforms. Many of these comparisons or implied comparisons are traditional ones; Shakespeare's virtuosity is evident not as much in the originality of his individual conceits as in their extraordinary profusion and in the surprising way in which apparently incompatible images are tellingly juxtaposed.

The handling of imagery corresponds with the poem's abrupt reversals of mood and with the unpredictable, accidental quality of the story. The frank comedy of the beginning swerves into tragedy, or at least pathos, at the close, as the immortal goddess confronts the death of her reluctant beloved. Over the course of the poem, our estimation of both characters undergoes dizzying shifts. Venus—goddess, whore, cradle robber, and queen—is funny, scary, eloquent, and pitiable by turns. Adonis's sexual diffidence at first seems as ridiculous to the readers as it does to Venus; but he suddenly seems less absurd when he replies, gravely even if rather too sanctimoniously, to Venus's importunities.

Venus's frank joy in the pleasures of sex suggests an uninhibited pagan universe, in which gods, animals, and human beings all are ruled by the same laws of generation and sensual enjoyment. Shakespeare's lavish attention to the forest setting in which the poem takes place suggests his keen appreciation of the sensuous possibilities of a purely natural world. The bodies of animals—Adonis's splendid courser, inflamed by lust; the ferocious boar, bursting through the thorniest thickets; the zigzagging hunted hare—all are accorded blazons of their own, as if they, not merely the human lovers, were full participants in the story of love and death. At such moments, the poem seems enthusiastically to endorse the original religious significance of the Venus and Adonis story, which linked human lives with the rhythms of a natural environment.

But Shakespeare's poem hardly evokes a sexual utopia. Even though the pagan setting of the poem presumably frees the characters from the sexually abstemious culture of Christianity, the heroine and hero still disagree vehemently about the value of sexual indulgence. Chastity has its attractions even apart from whatever supernatural reinforcement Christian faith might lend to it—especially, as Adonis notes, for those who are not yet fully adult. The

The boar attacking Adonis. From Henry Peacham, *Minerva Britanna* (1612).

immortal Venus thinks of experience as an endless series of pleasurable present-tense moments; the mortal Adonis wants to conceive of his life in terms of narrative development, building slowly and coherently to a future maturity. His untimely death suggests the risks of thinking of one's life in this fashion; he seems unwisely to have forgone present satisfaction in the hope of a reward that will never materialize.

On the other hand, why should Adonis, the victim of a sexual attack, enjoy caresses he has neither invited nor encouraged? Just as Shakespeare's reversal of gender stereotypes calls into question the adequacy of those stereotypes, so Adonis's recoil from Venus calls into question the naturalness of reproductive sexuality. Venus, the goddess of love, is supposed to be the apex of heterosexual desirability, both source and goal of every man's desire. Adonis, however, does not desire her even when she presses herself upon him. The congress of male and female thus seems simultaneously natural—what Adonis's palfrey and a passing mare know without tutelage—and optional, a possibility that some males, at any rate, may be willing to do without.

Shakespeare writes almost entirely from Venus's perspective: the boy, not the woman, is the sex object of *Venus and Adonis*. In an age lacking our comparatively rigid conception of sexual orientation, lovely androgynous boys were assumed to be attractive to adult men and women alike. Shakespeare returned to the subject of the adolescent boy's ambiguous, half-conscious sexiness in his transvestite comedies, and to the adult man's reluctance to commit himself to exclusively heterosexual alliances in those plays as well as in *The Merchant of Venice Venus and Adonis* can thus be read both as a narrative of frustrated heterosexual desire and, perhaps, as a parable of desire for a beautiful, aloof boy by a male poet—a scenario also sketched in many of Shakespeare's sonnets.

What is the meaning of sexuality? *Venus and Adonis* suggests a wide variety of possibilities: it is both a joke and a cosmic principle, a function of stern reproductive necessity and of sheer animal exuberance, a link with the animal world and an escape from it, a necessity and an option, a reminder of mortality and an intimation of immortality, a celebration of personal uniqueness and a threat to the formation of an individual identity. The shifting perspectives of the poem exploit the ambivalence with which Shakespeare's culture, as well as our own, treats sexual matters as simultaneously comical and deeply serious. The language of *Venus and Adonis* is especially good at capturing the confusing, contradictory array of sensations produced by another person's unfamiliar body close to one's own, a sensation at once grand, comic, oppressive, arousing, and repellant. The sweating, reeking, melting, and liquefying that at first seem specific to Venus's courtship of Adonis appear, by the end of the poem, to represent a principle of mortal existence and moral evaluation, as one thing merges unsteadily, unexpectedly, into another.

Biographical critics have found in *Venus and Adonis* ample grounds for speculation. Does the sexual dynamic of this poem reflect Shakespeare's experience with the older

Anne Hathaway, hauling him into some bosky nook outside Stratford, or alternatively an infatuation with Henry Wriothesley, the gorgeous youth to whom, some speculate, the early sonnets are devoted in both senses of the word? Given the scanty biographical data that have come down to us, it is impossible to know. What is clear is that *Venus and Adonis* inaugurates many of the distinctive features of Shakespeare's later work: a fascination, and capacity to sympathize, with sexually assertive women and self-contained, immature young men; an erotic energy that is both exuberant and hard to pin down; a complex moral sensibility capable of apprehending contradictory ethical imperatives at the same time; and an uncanny ability to combine comic, tragic, pathetic, and sensuous effects in a single work, even in a single poetic moment.

KATHARINE EISAMAN MAUS

TEXTUAL NOTE

The textual history of *Venus and Adonis* is much less tangled than that of most of the plays. Critics have theorized that Shakespeare wrote the narrative poems in 1592 and 1593, when an epidemic of bubonic plague forced the London theaters to close. At the time, it was unclear whether the playhouses would be allowed to reopen, so Shakespeare may have had not merely plenty of time on his hands but an urgent practical motive for establishing his credentials as a nondramatic writer. *Venus and Adonis* was first published in quarto in 1593 by the printer Richard Field, who was, like Shakespeare, a native of Stratford-upon-Avon. Only one copy of this edition survives. It contains very few obvious misprints and was presumably prepared from Shakespeare's manuscript, perhaps under his direct supervision. *Venus and Adonis* was frequently reprinted during Shakespeare's lifetime, but there is little substantive variation from one printing to another.

SELECTED BIBLIOGRAPHY

Bate, Jonathan. "Sexual Poetry." *Shakespeare and Ovid.* Oxford: Clarendon, 1993. 48–65. Shakespeare's adaptation of Ovid's story of transgressive desire.

Hughes, Ted. "Conception and Gestation of the Equation's Tragic Myth." *Shakespeare and the Goddess of Complete Being.* London: Faber and Faber, 1992. 49–92. *Venus and Adonis* as Shakespeare's version of an ancient myth, filtered through Roman Catholicism, of goddess and sacrificed consort.

Hulse, Clark. *Metamorphic Verse: The Elizabethan Minor Epic.* Princeton: Princeton University Press, 1981. 141–75. *Venus and Adonis* in relation to its sources and immediate predecessors.

Kahn, Coppélia. "Self as Eros in *Venus and Adonis.*" *Man's Estate: Masculine Identity in Shakespeare.* Berkeley: University of California Press, 1981. 21–46. Adonis as narcissist.

Keach, William. "Venus and Adonis." *Elizabethan Erotic Narratives: Irony and Pathos in the Ovidian Poetry of Shakespeare, Marlowe, and Their Contemporaries.* New Brunswick, N.J.: Rutgers University Press, 1977. 52–84. The poem considered among others of its genre.

Kolin, Philip C. *Venus and Adonis: Critical Essays.* New York: Garland, 1997. A collection of articles.

Rambuss, Richard. "What It Feels Like for a Boy: Shakespeare's *Venus and Adonis.*" *A Companion to Shakespeare's Works,* vol. IV: *Poems, Problem Comedies, Late Plays.* Ed. Richard Dutton and Jean Howard. Malden, Mass.: Blackwell, 2003. *Venus and Adonis* as a "proto-gay" poem.

Venus and Adonis

Vilia miretur vulgus; mihi flavus Apollo
Pocula Castalia plena ministret aqua.[1]

TO THE RIGHT HONOURABLE
HENRY WRIOTHESLEY,
EARL OF SOUTHAMPTON, AND
BARON OF TITCHFIELD[2]

Right Honourable, I know not how I shall offend in dedicating
my unpolished lines to your lordship, nor how the world will
censure° me for choosing so strong a prop to support so weak a   *judge*
burden. Only, if your honour seem but pleased, I account myself
highly praised, and vow to take advantage of all idle hours till I
have honoured you with some graver labour. But if the first heir[3]
of my invention prove deformed, I shall be sorry it had so noble
a godfather, and never after ear° so barren a land for fear it yield   *cultivate*
me still° so bad a harvest. I leave it to your honourable survey,   *always*
and your honour to your heart's content, which I wish may always
answer your own wish and the world's hopeful expectation.

YOUR HONOUR'S IN ALL DUTY,
WILLIAM SHAKESPEARE

Even as the sun with purple-coloured face
Had ta'en his last leave of the weeping morn,[1]
Rose-cheeked Adonis hied him° to the chase.   *hurried*
Hunting he loved, but love he laughed to scorn.
5   Sick-thoughted° Venus makes amain° unto him,   *Lovesick / speedily*
   And like a bold-faced suitor 'gins to woo him.

'Thrice fairer than myself,' thus she began,
'The fields' chief flower, sweet above compare,
Stain to all nymphs,° more lovely than a man,   *Eclipsing all women*
10   More white and red than doves or roses are—
   Nature that made thee with herself at strife
   Saith that the world hath ending with thy life.[2]

'Vouchsafe, thou wonder, to alight thy steed
And rein his proud head to the saddle-bow;

Dedication
1. "Let vile people admire vile things; may fair-haired
Apollo serve me goblets filled with Castalian water"
(Ovid, *Amores* 1.15.35–36). Apollo is the god of poetry;
the Castalian spring is sacred to the Muses.
2. Prominent courtier, nineteen years old at the time of
Venus and Adonis's publication. Shakespeare also dedicated *The Rape of Lucrece* to him.

3. *Venus and Adonis* was Shakespeare's first published
work.
Poem
1. Aurora, goddess of the dawn, weeps tears of dew
when forsaken each morning by her lover, the sun.
2. *Nature . . . life*: Nature, who strove to surpass herself in making you says that if you die, the world will
end.

15 If thou wilt deign this favour, for thy meed°   *reward*
    A thousand honey secrets shalt thou know.
        Here come and sit where never serpent hisses;
        And, being sat, I'll smother thee with kisses,

    'And yet not cloy thy lips with loathed satiety,
20 But rather famish them amid their plenty,
    Making them red, and pale, with fresh variety;
    Ten kisses short as one, one long as twenty.
        A summer's day will seem an hour but short,
        Being wasted° in such time-beguiling sport.'   *spent*

25 With this, she seizeth on his sweating palm,
    The precedent of pith and livelihood,[3]
    And, trembling in her passion, calls it balm—
    Earth's sovereign° salve to do a goddess good.   *potent*
        Being so enraged, desire doth lend her force
30   Courageously to pluck him from his horse.

    Over one arm, the lusty courser's rein;
    Under her other was the tender boy,
    Who blushed and pouted in a dull disdain
    With leaden appetite, unapt to toy.[4]
35   She red and hot as coals of glowing fire;
        He red for shame, but frosty in desire.

    The studded bridle on a ragged bough
    Nimbly she fastens—O, how quick is love!
    The steed is stallèd° up, and even now   *fastened*
40 To tie the rider she begins to prove.°   *try*
        Backward she pushed him, as she would be thrust,
        And governed him in strength, though not in lust.

    So soon was she along° as he was down,   *alongside him*
    Each leaning on their elbows and their hips.
45 Now doth she stroke his cheek, now doth he frown
    And 'gins to chide, but soon she stops his lips,
        And, kissing, speaks, with lustful language broken:°   *interrupted*
        'If thou wilt chide, thy lips shall never open.'

    He burns with bashful shame; she with her tears
50 Doth quench the maiden burning of his cheeks.
    Then, with her windy sighs and golden hairs,
    To fan and blow them dry again she seeks.
        He saith she is immodest, blames her miss;°   *misbehavior*
        What follows more she murders with a kiss.

55 Even as an empty eagle, sharp by fast,°   *hungry from fasting*
    Tires° with her beak on feathers, flesh, and bone,   *Tears*
    Shaking her wings, devouring all in haste
    Till either gorge° be stuffed or prey be gone,   *stomach*
        Even so she kissed his brow, his cheek, his chin,
60   And where she ends she doth anew begin.

3. The evidence of strength and liveliness.   4. Uninterested in sex play.

Forced to content,° but never to obey,°   *acquiesce / respond*
Panting he lies and breatheth in her face.
She feedeth on the steam as on a prey
And calls it heavenly moisture, air of grace,
65   Wishing her cheeks were gardens full of flowers,
    So they were dewed with such distilling° showers.   *gently dropping*

Look how a bird lies tangled in a net,
So fastened in her arms Adonis lies.
Pure shame and awed° resistance made him fret,   *overpowered*
70 Which bred more beauty in his angry eyes.
    Rain added to a river that is rank°   *full*
    Perforce will force it overflow the bank.

Still she entreats, and prettily entreats,
For to a pretty ear she tunes her tale.
75 Still is he sullen, still he lours° and frets   *frowns*
'Twixt crimson shame and anger ashy-pale.
    Being red, she loves him best; and being white,
    Her best is bettered with a more delight.

Look how he can, she cannot choose but love;
80 And by her fair immortal hand she swears
From his soft bosom never to remove
Till he take truce° with her contending tears,   *come to terms*
    Which long have rained, making her cheeks all wet;
    And one sweet kiss shall pay this countless debt.

85 Upon this promise did he raise his chin,
Like a divedapper⁵ peering through a wave
Who, being looked on, ducks as quickly in—
So offers he to give what she did crave.
    But when her lips were ready for his pay,
90   He winks,° and turns his lips another way.   *shuts his eyes*

Never did passenger° in summer's heat   *traveler*
More thirst for drink than she for this good turn.
Her help she sees, but help she cannot get.
She bathes in water, yet her fire must burn.
95   'O pity,' gan she cry, 'flint-hearted boy!
    'Tis but a kiss I beg—why art thou coy?

'I have been wooed as I entreat thee now
Even by the stern and direful god of war,°   *Mars*
Whose sinewy neck in battle ne'er did bow,
100 Who conquers where he comes in every jar.°   *conflict*
    Yet hath he been my captive and my slave,
    And begged for that which thou unasked shalt have.

'Over my altars hath he hung his lance,
His battered shield, his uncontrollèd° crest,   *unvanquished*
105 And for my sake hath learned to sport and dance,

5. Grebe (small English waterbird).

To toy, to wanton, dally, smile, and jest,
  Scorning his churlish drum and ensign red,
  Making my arms° his field, his tent my bed.   *(a pun)*

'Thus he that over-ruled I overswayed,
110 Leading him prisoner in a red-rose chain.
  Strong-tempered steel his stronger strength obeyed,
  Yet was he servile to my coy disdain.
    O, be not proud, nor brag not of thy might,
    For mast'ring her that foiled° the god of fight.   *conquered*

115 'Touch but my lips with those fair lips of thine—
  Though mine be not so fair, yet are they red—
  The kiss shall be thine own as well as mine.
  What seest thou in the ground? Hold up thy head.
    Look in mine eyeballs: there thy beauty lies.°   *lies reflected*
120   Then why not lips on lips, since eyes in eyes?

'Art thou ashamed to kiss? Then wink again,
  And I will wink. So shall the day seem night.
  Love keeps his revels where there are but twain.
  Be bold to play—our sport is not in sight.°   *unobserved*
125   These blue-veined violets whereon we lean
    Never can blab, nor know not⁶ what we mean.

'The tender spring° upon thy tempting lip   *growth of new beard*
  Shows thee unripe; yet mayst thou well be tasted.
  Make use of time; let not advantage slip.
130 Beauty within itself should not be wasted.
    Fair flowers that are not gathered in their prime
    Rot, and consume themselves in little time.

'Were I hard-favoured,° foul, or wrinkled-old,   *ugly*
  Ill-nurtured, crooked, churlish, harsh in voice,
135 O'er-worn,° despisèd, rheumatic, and cold,   *Worn out*
  Thick-sighted,° barren, lean, and lacking juice,   *Partly blind*
    Then mightst thou pause, for then I were not for thee.
    But having no defects, why dost abhor me?

'Thou canst not see one wrinkle in my brow.
140 Mine eyes are grey,⁷ and bright, and quick in turning.
  My beauty as the spring doth yearly grow.°   *rejuvenate*
  My flesh is soft and plump, my marrow° burning.   *vital spirits*
    My smooth moist hand, were it with thy hand felt,
    Would in thy palm dissolve, or seem to melt.

145 'Bid me discourse, I will enchant thine ear;
  Or like a fairy, trip upon the green;
  Or like a nymph, with long, dishevelled hair,
  Dance on the sands, and yet no footing° seen.   *footprint*
    Love is a spirit all compact° of fire,   *made up*
150   Not gross° to sink, but light, and will aspire.°   *heavy / rise*

---

6. The double negative ("nor . . . not") was acceptable in Elizabethan English.

7. Considered the best eye color by medieval and Renaissance love poets.

'Witness this primrose bank whereon I lie:
These forceless flowers like sturdy trees support me.
Two strengthless doves[8] will draw me through the sky
From morn till night, even where I list° to sport me.   *wherever I wish*
155   Is love so light, sweet boy, and may it be
        That thou should think it heavy unto thee?

'Is thine own heart to thine own face affected?°   *attracted*
Can thy right hand seize love upon thy left?°   *by clasping the left*
Then woo thyself, be of thyself rejected;
160   Steal thine own freedom,° and complain on theft.   *Capture your affections*
        Narcissus[9] so himself himself forsook,
        And died to kiss his shadow in the brook.

'Torches are made to light, jewels to wear,
Dainties to taste, fresh beauty for the use,
165   Herbs for their smell, and sappy plants to bear.
Things growing to themselves° are growth's abuse.   *only for themselves*
        Seeds spring from seeds, and beauty breedeth beauty:
        Thou wast begot; to get° it is thy duty.   *beget*

'Upon the earth's increase why shouldst thou feed
170   Unless the earth with thy increase be fed?
By law of nature thou art bound to breed,
That thine° may live when thou thyself art dead;   *(your children)*
        And so in spite of death thou dost survive,
        In that thy likeness still is left alive.'

175   By this,° the lovesick queen began to sweat,   *By this time*
For where they lay the shadow had forsook them,
And Titan,° tired in the midday heat,   *the sun god*
With burning eye did hotly overlook them,
        Wishing Adonis had his team° to guide   *(of sun horses)*
180   So he° were like him,° and by Venus' side.   *(Titan) / (Adonis)*

And now Adonis, with a lazy sprite°   *dull spirit*
And with a heavy, dark, disliking eye,
His louring brows o'erwhelming° his fair sight,   *overhanging*
Like misty vapours when they blot the sky,
185   Souring his cheeks,° cries, 'Fie, no more of love!   *Frowning*
        The sun doth burn my face; I must remove.'°   *leave*

'Ay me,' quoth Venus, 'young, and so unkind?°   *unnatural*
What bare° excuses mak'st thou to be gone?   *poor*
I'll sigh celestial breath, whose gentle wind
190   Shall cool the heat of this descending sun.
        I'll make a shadow for thee of my hairs;
        If they burn too, I'll quench them with my tears.

'The sun that shines from heaven shines but warm,°   *merely warms me*
And lo, I lie between that sun and thee.

8. Traditionally, Venus's chariot was drawn by swans or doves; see lines 1190–92.
9. In classical mythology, a young man who fell in love with his own image reflected in the water; after he pined to death he was turned into a flower.

195 The heat I have from thence doth little harm;
Thine eye darts forth the fire that burneth me,
 And were I not immortal, life were done°   *destroyed*
 Between this heavenly and earthly sun.

'Art thou obdurate, flinty, hard as steel?
200 Nay, more than flint, for stone at rain relenteth.°   *wears away*
Art thou a woman's son, and canst not feel
What 'tis to love, how want of love° tormenteth? *being denied love*
 O, had thy mother borne so hard a mind,
 She had not brought forth thee, but died unkind.

205 'What am I, that thou shouldst contemn° me this?   *deny; scorn*
Or what great danger dwells upon my suit?
What were thy lips the worse for one poor kiss?
Speak, fair; but speak fair words, or else be mute.
 Give me one kiss, I'll give it thee again,
210 And one for int'rest, if thou wilt have twain.

'Fie, lifeless picture, cold and senseless° stone,   *insensible*
Well painted idol, image dull and dead,
Statue contenting but the eye alone,
Thing like a man, but of no woman bred:
215 Thou art no man, though of a man's complexion,° *appearance*
 For men will kiss even by their own direction.'°   *inclination*

This said, impatience chokes her pleading tongue,
And swelling passion doth provoke a pause.
Red cheeks and fiery eyes blaze forth° her wrong. *display; flame out*
220 Being judge in love, she cannot right her cause;[1]
 And now she weeps, and now she fain° would speak, *gladly*
 And now her sobs do her intendments° break. *intended words*

Sometime she shakes her head, and then his hand;
Now gazeth she on him, now on the ground.
225 Sometime her arms enfold him like a band;°   *fetter*
She would, he will not in her arms be bound.
 And when from thence he struggles to be gone,
 She locks her lily fingers one in one.

'Fondling,'° she saith, 'since I have hemmed thee here *Foolish one; beloved*
230 Within the circuit of this ivory pale,°   *fence*
I'll be a park, and thou shalt be my deer.
Feed where thou wilt, on mountain or in dale;
 Graze on my lips, and if those hills be dry,
 Stray lower, where the pleasant fountains lie.

235 'Within this limit is relief[2] enough,
Sweet bottom-grass,[3] and high delightful plain,
Round rising hillocks, brakes obscure and rough,° *dark, shaggy thickets*
To shelter thee from tempest and from rain.

---

1. Although (or because) she is love's arbiter, she cannot win her own case.
2. Pasture; variety of landscape; sexual gratification.

3. Valley grass (pubic hair); Venus's body-landscape is
intentionally suggestive throughout.

Then be my deer, since I am such a park;
240 No dog shall rouse thee,° though a thousand bark.¹　　　*drive you from cover*

At this Adonis smiles as in disdain,
That in each cheek appears a pretty dimple.
Love made those hollows, if° himself were slain,　　　*so that if*
He might be buried in a tomb so simple,
245 　Foreknowing well, if there he came to lie,
　Why, there love lived, and there he could not die.

These lovely caves, these round enchanting pits,
Opened their mouths to swallow Venus' liking.°　　　*to engulf her desire*
Being mad before, how doth she now for wits?⁴
250 Struck dead at first, what needs a second striking?
　Poor queen of love, in thine own law forlorn,°　　　*condemned to suffer*
　To love a cheek that smiles at thee in scorn!

Now which way shall she turn? What shall she say?
Her words are done, her woes the more increasing.
255 The time is spent; her object will away,
And from her twining arms doth urge releasing.
　'Pity,' she cries; 'some favour, some remorse!'°　　　*compassion*
　Away he springs, and hasteth to his horse.

But lo, from forth a copse° that neighbours by　　　*thicket*
260 A breeding jennet,° lusty, young, and proud,　　　*mare in heat*
Adonis' trampling courser doth espy,
And forth she rushes, snorts, and neighs aloud.
　The strong-necked steed, being tied unto a tree,
　Breaketh his rein, and to her straight goes he.

265 Imperiously he leaps, he neighs, he bounds,
And now his woven girths he breaks asunder.
The bearing⁵ earth with his hard hoof he wounds,
Whose hollow womb resounds like heaven's thunder.
　The iron bit he crusheth 'tween his teeth,
270 　Controlling what he was controllèd with.

His ears up-pricked, his braided hanging mane
Upon his compassed crest° now stand on end;　　　*arched neck*
His nostrils drink the air, and forth again,
As from a furnace, vapours doth he send.
275 　His eye, which scornfully glisters like fire,
　Shows his hot courage° and his high desire.　　　*lust*

Sometime he trots, as if he told° the steps,　　　*counted*
With gentle majesty and modest pride.
Anon he rears upright, curvets,⁶ and leaps,
280 As who° should say, 'Lo, thus my strength is tried.°　　　*one who / tested*
　And this I do to captivate the eye
　Of the fair breeder that is standing by.'

4. How does she keep her sanity now?　　　6. Bounds on his hind legs with raised forelegs.
5. Supporting; suffering; generative.

What recketh he° his rider's angry stir,°   *cares he about / noise*
His flattering° 'Holla', or his 'Stand, I say!'?   *cajoling*
285   What cares he now for curb° or pricking spur,   *bit*
For rich caparisons or trappings gay?
    He sees his love, and nothing else he sees,
    For nothing else with his proud sight agrees.

Look when° a painter would surpass the life   *Just as*
290   In limning out° a well proportioned steed,   *depicting*
His art with nature's workmanship at strife,
As if the dead the living should exceed:
    So did this horse excel a common one
    In shape, in courage, colour, pace, and bone.°   *frame*

295   Round-hoofed, short-jointed, fetlocks shag and long,[7]
Broad breast, full eye, small head, and nostril wide,
High crest, short ears, straight legs, and passing° strong;   *extremely*
Thin mane, thick tail, broad buttock, tender hide—
    Look what° a horse should have he did not lack,   *Whatever*
300   Save a proud rider on so proud a back.

Sometime he scuds far off, and there he stares;
Anon he starts at stirring of a feather.
To bid the wind a base[8] he now prepares,
And whe'er° he run or fly they know not whether;°   *whether / which*
305   For through his mane and tail the high wind sings,
    Fanning the hairs, who wave like feathered wings.

He looks upon his love, and neighs unto her;
She answers him as if she knew his mind.
Being proud, as females are, to see him woo her,
310   She puts on outward strangeness,° seems unkind,   *reserve*
    Spurns at° his love, and scorns the heat he feels,   *Repels; kicks*
    Beating his kind° embracements with her heels.   *amorous; natural*

Then, like a melancholy malcontent,
He vails° his tail that, like a falling plume,   *lowers*
315   Cool shadow to his melting buttock lent.
He stamps, and bites the poor flies in his fume.°   *anger*
    His love, perceiving how he was enraged,
    Grew kinder, and his fury was assuaged.

His testy° master goeth about° to take him,   *angry / tries*
320   When lo, the unbacked breeder,[9] full of fear,
Jealous of catching,° swiftly doth forsake him,   *Fearful of being caught*
With her the horse, and left Adonis there.
    As they were mad unto the wood they hie them,
    Outstripping crows that strive to overfly them.

325   All swoll'n with chafing,° down Adonis sits,   *anger*
Banning° his boist'rous and unruly beast;   *Cursing*

---

7. *short-jointed . . . long:* with short pasterns (the bone just above the horse's hoof) and shaggy joints above the hooves.

8. To dare the wind to run (from a children's game, prisoner's base).
9. Mare without mount (rider or stallion).

And now the happy season once more fits°   *is suited*
That lovesick love by pleading may be blessed;
   For lovers say the heart hath treble wrong
330   When it is barred the aidance of the tongue.

An oven that is stopped, or river stayed,°   *dammed*
Burneth more hotly, swelleth with more rage.
So of concealèd sorrow may be said
Free vent of words love's fire doth assuage.
335   But when the heart's attorney° once is mute,   *pleader (the tongue)*
   The client breaks,[1] as desperate in his suit.

He sees her coming, and begins to glow,
Even as a dying coal revives with wind,
And with his bonnet° hides his angry brow,   *hat*
340 Looks on the dull earth with disturbèd mind,
   Taking no notice that she is so nigh,
   For all askance he holds her in his eye.

O, what a sight it was wistly° to view   *intently*
How she came stealing to the wayward boy,
345 To note the fighting conflict of her hue,
   How white and red each other did destroy!
   But now her cheek was pale; and by and by
   It flashed forth fire, as lightning from the sky.

Now was she just before him as he sat,
350 And like a lowly lover down she kneels;
With one fair hand she heaveth up his hat;
Her other tender hand his fair cheek feels.
   His tend'rer cheek receives her soft hand's print
   As apt as new-fall'n snow takes any dint.°   *dent*

355 O, what a war of looks was then between them,
Her eyes petitioners to his eyes suing!
His eyes saw her eyes as they had not seen them;
Her eyes wooed still; his eyes disdained the wooing;
   And all this dumb play had his° acts made plain   *its*
360   With tears which, chorus-like, her eyes did rain.[2]

Full gently now she takes him by the hand,
A lily prisoned in a jail of snow,
Or ivory in an alabaster band;
So white a friend engirds so white a foe.
365   This beauteous combat, wilful and unwilling,
   Showed° like two silver doves that sit a-billing.   *Looked*

Once more the engine of her thoughts began:
'O fairest mover on this mortal round,°   *earth*
Would thou wert as I am, and I a man,
370 My heart all whole as thine, thy heart my wound;°   *suffering my wound*

---

1. Breaks apart; goes bankrupt.
2. Venus's tears interpret her mute gestures as the chorus in a play explains a dumb show.

For one sweet look thy help I would assure thee,
Though nothing but my body's bane° would cure thee.'   *destruction*

'Give me my hand,' saith he. 'Why dost thou feel it?'
'Give me my heart,' saith she, 'and thou shalt have it.
375 O, give it me, lest thy hard heart do steel it,[3]
And, being steeled, soft sighs can never grave° it;   *engrave*
    Then love's deep groans I never shall regard,
    Because Adonis' heart hath made mine hard.'

'For shame,' he cries, 'let go, and let me go!
380 My day's delight is past; my horse is gone,
And 'tis your fault I am bereft him so.
I pray you hence, and leave me here alone;
    For all my mind, my thought, my busy care
    Is how to get my palfrey° from the mare.'   *riding horse*

385 Thus she replies: 'Thy palfrey, as he should,
Welcomes the warm approach of sweet desire.
Affection° is a coal that must be cooled,   *Passion*
Else, suffered,° it will set the heart on fire.   *allowed to persist*
    The sea hath bounds, but deep desire hath none;
390   Therefore no marvel though thy horse be gone.

'How like a jade° he stood tied to the tree,   *nag*
Servilely mastered with a leathern rein!
But when he saw his love, his youth's fair fee,°   *reward*
He held such petty bondage in disdain,
395   Throwing the base thong from his bending crest,
    Enfranchising his mouth, his back, his breast.

'Who sees his true-love in her naked bed,
Teaching the sheets a whiter hue than white,
But when his glutton eye so full hath fed
400 His other agents° aim at like delight?   *faculties*
    Who is so faint that dares not be so bold
    To touch the fire, the weather being cold?

'Let me excuse thy courser, gentle boy;
And learn of him, I heartily beseech thee,
405 To take advantage on° presented joy.   *of*
Though I were dumb, yet his proceedings teach thee.
    O, learn to love! The lesson is but plain,
    And, once made perfect,° never lost again.'   *learned by heart*

'I know not love,' quoth he, 'nor will not know it,
410 Unless it be a boar, and then I chase it.
'Tis much to borrow, and I will not owe it.
My love to love is love but to disgrace it;[4]
    For I have heard it is a life in death,
    That laughs and weeps, and all but with a breath.

---

3. Turn my heart to steel; steal my heart.   4. My only interest in love is in discrediting it.

415 'Who wears a garment shapeless and unfinished?
   Who plucks the bud before one leaf put forth?
   If springing° things be any jot diminished,   *immature*
   They wither in their prime, prove nothing worth.
      The colt that's backed° and burdened being young,   *ridden*
420   Loseth his pride, and never waxeth strong.

   'You hurt my hand with wringing. Let us part,
   And leave this idle° theme, this bootless° chat.   *useless / pointless*
   Remove your siege from my unyielding heart;
   To love's alarms° it will not ope the gate.   *assaults*
425   Dismiss your vows, your feignèd tears, your flatt'ry;
       For where a heart is hard they make no batt'ry.'°   *breach*

   'What, canst thou talk?' quoth she. 'Hast thou a tongue?
   O, would thou hadst not, or I had no hearing!
   Thy mermaid's voice⁵ hath done me double wrong.
430 I had my load before, now pressed° with bearing: *oppressed*
       Melodious discord, heavenly tune harsh sounding,
       Ears' deep-sweet music, and heart's deep-sore wounding.

   'Had I no eyes but ears, my ears would love
   That inward beauty and invisible;
435 Or were I deaf, thy outward parts would move
   Each part in me that were but sensible.°   *perceiving*
       Though neither eyes nor ears to hear nor see,
       Yet should I be in love by touching thee.

   'Say that the sense of feeling were bereft me,
440 And that I could not see, nor hear, nor touch,
   And nothing but the very smell were left me,
   Yet would my love to thee be still as much;
       For from the stillitory⁶ of thy face excelling°   *incomparable*
       Comes breath perfumed, that breedeth love by smelling.

445 'But O, what banquet wert thou to the taste,
   Being nurse and feeder of the other four!
   Would they not wish the feast might ever last
   And bid suspicion° double-lock the door   *wariness*
       Lest jealousy, that sour unwelcome guest,
450   Should by his stealing-in disturb the feast?'

   Once more the ruby-coloured portal° opened   *threshold (mouth)*
   Which to his speech did honey passage yield,
   Like a red morn that ever yet betokened
   Wrack° to the seaman, tempest to the field,   *Shipwreck*
455   Sorrow to shepherds, woe unto the birds,
       Gusts and foul flaws° to herdmen and to herds.   *winds*

   This ill presage advisedly she marketh.⁷
   Even as the wind is hushed before it raineth,
   Or as the wolf doth grin° before he barketh,   *show his teeth*

---

5. Which, irresistible in song, was supposed to lure sailors onto rocks.

6. Apparatus used to distill perfume.
7. She notices this bad omen carefully.

460 Or as the berry breaks before it staineth,
   Or like the deadly bullet of a gun,
   His meaning struck her ere his words begun,

And at his look she flatly falleth down,
For looks kill love, and love by looks reviveth;
465 A smile recures° the wounding of a frown,   *cures*
But blessèd bankrupt that by loss so thriveth!
   The silly° boy, believing she is dead,   *naive*
   Claps her pale cheek till clapping makes it red,

And, all amazed,° brake° off his late intent,   *perplexed / broke*
470 For sharply he did think to reprehend her,
   Which cunning love did wittily prevent.
   Fair fall[8] the wit that can so well defend her!
    For on the grass she lies as she were slain,
    Till his breath breatheth life in her again.

475 He wrings her nose, he strikes her on the cheeks,
   He bends her fingers, holds her pulses hard;°   *takes her pulse*
   He chafes her lips; a thousand ways he seeks
   To mend the hurt that his unkindness marred.°   *caused to injure her*
    He kisses her; and she, by her good will,°   *consent*
480   Will never rise, so he will kiss her still.°   *keep kissing her*

The night of sorrow now is turned to day.
Her two blue windows° faintly she upheaveth,   *(her eyes)*
Like the fair sun when, in his fresh array,
He cheers the morn, and all the earth relieveth;
485   And as the bright sun glorifies the sky,
    So is her face illumined with her eye,

Whose beams upon his hairless face are fixed,
As if from thence they borrowed all their shine.
Were never four such lamps together mixed,
490 Had not his clouded with his brow's repine.°   *discontent*
    But hers, which through the crystal tears gave light,
    Shone like the moon in water seen by night.

'O, where am I?' quoth she; 'in earth or heaven,
Or in the ocean drenched,° or in the fire?   *submerged*
495 What hour is this: or° morn or weary even?°   *either / evening*
Do I delight to die, or life desire?
    But now I lived, and life was death's annoy;°   *deathly pain*
    But now I died, and death was lively° joy.   *living*

'O, thou didst kill me; kill me once again!
500 Thy eyes' shrewd° tutor, that hard heart of thine,   *stern*
Hath taught them scornful tricks, and such disdain
That they have murdered this poor heart of mine,
    And these mine eyes, true leaders° to their queen,   *guides*
    But for thy piteous° lips no more had seen.   *pitying*

8. Good luck befall (with wordplay on "fall down").

505 'Long may they kiss each other, for this cure!
O, never let their crimson liveries wear,°   *wear out*
And as they last, their verdure⁹ still endure
To drive infection from the dangerous year,
    That the star-gazers, having writ on death,°   *predicted plague*
510   May say the plague is banished by thy breath!

'Pure lips, sweet seals in my soft lips imprinted,
What bargains may I make still to be sealing?°   *kissing; making deals*
To sell myself I can be well contented,
So° thou wilt buy, and pay, and use good dealing;   *If*
515   Which purchase if thou make, for fear of slips°   *fraud*
    Set thy seal manual° on my wax-red lips.   *identifying stamp*

'A thousand kisses buys my heart from me;
And pay them at thy leisure, one by one.
What is ten hundred touches° unto thee?   *(of the lips)*
520 Are they not quickly told,° and quickly gone?   *counted*
    Say for non-payment that the debt should double,
    Is twenty hundred kisses such a trouble?'

'Fair queen,' quoth he, 'if any love you owe me,
Measure my strangeness° with my unripe years.   *Explain my coldness*
525 Before I know myself, seek not to know me.
No fisher but the ungrown fry forbears.¹
    The mellow plum doth fall, the green sticks fast,
    Or, being early plucked, is sour to taste.

'Look, the world's comforter° with weary gait   *(the sun)*
530 His day's hot task hath ended in the west.
The owl, night's herald, shrieks 'tis very late;
The sheep are gone to fold, birds to their nest,
    And coal-black clouds, that shadow heaven's light,
    Do summon us to part and bid good night.

535 'Now let me say good night, and so say you.
If you will say so, you shall have a kiss.'
'Good night,' quoth she; and ere he says adieu
The honey° fee of parting tendered° is.   *sweet / given*
    Her arms do lend his neck a sweet embrace.
540   Incorporate° then they seem; face grows to face,   *United in one body*

Till breathless he disjoined, and backward drew
The heavenly moisture, that sweet coral mouth,
Whose precious taste her thirsty lips well knew,
Whereon they surfeit, yet complain on drought.
545   He with her plenty pressed, she faint with dearth,
    Their lips together glued, fall to the earth.

Now quick desire hath caught the yielding prey,
And glutton-like she feeds, yet never filleth.
Her lips are conquerors, his lips obey,

---

9. Literally, greenness; here, freshness. The lips ward off disease as fresh parsley was believed to do.

1. Every fisherman spares the young fish.

550   Paying what ransom the insulter° willeth,   *conqueror*
        Whose vulture° thought doth pitch the price so high   *ravenous*
        That she will draw his lips' rich treasure dry,

        And, having felt the sweetness of the spoil,
        With blindfold fury she begins to forage.
555   Her face doth reek° and smoke, her blood doth boil,   *steam*
        And careless° lust stirs up a desperate courage,   *reckless*
           Planting° oblivion, beating reason back,   *Implanting*
           Forgetting shame's pure blush and honour's wrack.°   *ruin*

        Hot, faint, and weary with her hard embracing,
560   Like a wild bird being tamed with too much handling,
        Or as the fleet-foot roe that's tired with chasing,
        Or like the froward° infant stilled with dandling,   *fretful*
           He now obeys, and now no more resisteth,
           While she takes all she can, not all she listeth.°   *desires*

565   What wax so frozen but dissolves with temp'ring°   *fingering*
        And yields at last to every light impression?
        Things out of° hope are compassed° oft with vent'ring,   *beyond / accomplished*
        Chiefly in love, whose leave° exceeds commission.°   *liberty / warrant*
           Affection faints° not, like a pale-faced coward,   *Passion relents*
570   But then woos best when most his choice is froward.

        When he did frown, O, had she then gave over,
        Such nectar from his lips she had not sucked.
        Foul° words and frowns must not repel a lover.   *Harsh*
        What though the rose have prickles, yet 'tis plucked!
575   Were beauty under twenty locks kept fast,
           Yet love breaks through, and picks them all at last.

        For pity now she can no more detain him.
        The poor fool° prays her that he may depart.   *(term of affection)*
        She is resolved no longer to restrain him,
580   Bids him farewell, and look well to° her heart,   *take good care of*
           The which, by Cupid's bow she doth protest,
           He carries thence encagèd in his breast.

        'Sweet boy,' she says, 'this night I'll waste in sorrow,
        For my sick heart commands mine eyes to watch.
585   Tell me, love's master, shall we meet tomorrow?
        Say, shall we, shall we? Wilt thou make the match?'
           He tells her no, tomorrow he intends
           To hunt the boar with certain of his friends.

        'The boar!' quoth she; whereat a sudden pale,
590   Like lawn° being spread upon the blushing rose,   *fine linen*
        Usurps her cheek. She trembles at his tale,
        And on his neck her yoking arms she throws.
           She sinketh down, still hanging by his neck.
           He on her belly falls, she on her back.

595 Now is she in the very lists² of love,
Her champion mounted for the hot encounter.
All is imaginary she doth prove.³
He will not manage her,° although he mount her,   *ride her (like a horse)*
    That worse than Tantalus' is her annoy,⁴
600 To clip Elysium,⁵ and to lack her joy.

Even so poor birds, deceived with painted grapes,
Do surfeit by the eye, and pine the maw;⁶
Even so she languisheth in her mishaps
As° those poor birds that helpless° berries saw.   *Like / unusable*
605   The warm effects° which she in him finds missing   *outward signs*
    She seeks to kindle with continual kissing.

But all in vain, good queen! It will not be.
She hath assayed° as much as may be proved;°   *attempted / tried*
Her pleading hath deserved a greater fee:⁷
610 She's Love; she loves; and yet she is not loved.
    'Fie, fie,' he says, 'you crush me. Let me go.
    You have no reason to withhold me so.'

'Thou hadst been gone,' quoth she, 'sweet boy, ere this,
But that thou told'st me thou wouldst hunt the boar.
615 O, be advised; thou know'st not what it is
With javelin's point a churlish swine to gore,
    Whose tushes,° never sheathed, he whetteth still,°   *tusks / continually*
    Like to a mortal° butcher, bent° to kill.   *deadly / intending*

'On his bow-back° he hath a battle⁸ set   *arched back*
620 Of bristly pikes that ever threat his foes.
His eyes like glow-worms shine; when he doth fret
His snout digs sepulchres where'er he goes.
    Being moved,° he strikes, whate'er is in his way,   *angered*
    And whom he strikes his crooked tushes slay.

625 'His brawny sides with hairy bristles armed
Are better proof° than thy spear's point can enter.   *armor*
His short thick neck cannot be easily harmed.
Being ireful,° on the lion he will venture.   *angry*
    The thorny brambles and embracing bushes,
630   As° fearful of him, part; through whom° he rushes.   *As if / which*

'Alas, he naught esteems that face of thine,
To which love's eyes pays tributary gazes,
Nor thy soft hands, sweet lips, and crystal eyne,°   *eyes (archaic)*
Whose full perfection all the world amazes;
635   But having thee at vantage°—wondrous dread!—   *his mercy*
    Would root° these beauties as he roots the mead.°   *root up / meadow*

---

2. Enclosed tournament arena.
3. The hot encounter is only imaginary, she finds.
4. Torment. In classical mythology, Tantalus was punished by eternal hunger and thirst; food and water were always visible but receded at his approach.
5. In classical mythology, the abode of the blessed dead. *clip:* embrace.
6. Starve the stomach. The ancient Greek artist Zeuxis painted grapes so realistic that birds pecked at them.
7. A legal metaphor: Venus, acting as an attorney, deserves a better payment.
8. Row of armed soldiers.

'O, let him keep° his loathsome cabin° still.   *stay in / lair*
Beauty hath naught to do with such foul fiends.
Come not within his danger by thy will.
640 They that thrive well take counsel of their friends.
  When thou didst name the boar, not to dissemble,[9]
  I feared thy fortune, and my joints did tremble.

'Didst thou not mark my face? Was it not white?
Saw'st thou not signs of fear lurk in mine eye?
645 Grew I not faint, and fell I not downright?
Within my bosom, whereon thou dost lie,
  My boding heart pants, beats, and takes no rest,
  But like an earthquake shakes thee on my breast.

'For where love reigns, disturbing jealousy°   *apprehension*
650 Doth call himself affection's sentinel,
Gives false alarms, suggesteth mutiny,°   *incites rebellion*
And in a peaceful hour doth cry, "Kill, kill!",° *(a battle cry)*
  Distemp'ring° gentle love in his desire,   *Quenching*
  As air and water do abate the fire.

655 'This sour informer, this bate-breeding° spy, *conflict-breeding*
This canker° that eats up love's tender spring,° *cankerworm / sprout*
This carry-tale, dissentious jealousy,
That sometime true news, sometime false doth bring,
  Knocks at my heart, and whispers in mine ear
660   That if I love thee, I thy death should fear;

'And, more than so, presenteth to mine eye
The picture of an angry chafing boar,
Under whose sharp fangs on his back doth lie
An image like thyself, all stained with gore,
665   Whose blood upon the fresh flowers being shed
  Doth make them droop with grief, and hang the head.

'What should I do, seeing thee so indeed,
That tremble at th'imagination?
The thought of it doth make my faint heart bleed,
670 And fear doth teach it divination.
  I prophesy thy death, my living sorrow,
  If thou encounter with the boar tomorrow.

'But if thou needs wilt hunt, be ruled by me:
Uncouple° at the timorous flying° hare, *Unleash the dogs / fleeing*
675 Or at the fox which lives by subtlety,
Or at the roe which no encounter dare.
  Pursue these fearful° creatures o'er the downs, *timid*
  And on thy well-breathed horse keep with thy hounds.

'And when thou hast on foot the purblind° hare, *dim-sighted*
680 Mark the poor wretch, to overshoot° his troubles, *run past*
How he outruns the wind, and with what care
He cranks and crosses° with a thousand doubles. *twists and turns*

9. *not to dissemble*: to tell the truth.

The many musits° through the which he goes   *hedge gaps*
Are like a labyrinth to amaze° his foes.   *confuse*

685 'Sometime he runs among a flock of sheep
To make the cunning hounds mistake their smell,
And sometime where earth-delving conies° keep,   *rabbits*
To stop the loud pursuers in their yell;
And sometime sorteth° with a herd of deer.   *consorts*
690 Danger deviseth shifts;° wit waits on fear.   *tricks*

'For there his smell with others being mingled,
The hot scent-snuffing hounds are driven to doubt,
Ceasing their clamorous cry till they have singled,
With much ado, the cold fault° cleanly out.   *lost scent*
695 Then do they spend their mouths.° Echo replies,   *give tongue*
As if another chase were in the skies.

'By this, poor Wat,° far off upon a hill,   *(name for a hare)*
Stands on his hinder legs with list'ning ear,
To hearken if his foes pursue him still.
700 Anon their loud alarums he doth hear,
And now his grief may be comparèd well
To one sore sick that hears the passing-bell.[1]

'Then shalt thou see the dew-bedabbled wretch
Turn, and return, indenting° with the way.   *zigzagging*
705 Each envious° brier his weary legs do scratch;   *malicious*
Each shadow makes him stop, each murmur stay;
For misery is trodden on by many,
And, being low, never relieved by any.

'Lie quietly, and hear a little more;
710 Nay, do not struggle, for thou shalt not rise.
To make thee hate the hunting of the boar
Unlike myself thou hear'st me moralize,[2]
Applying° this to that, and so to so,   *Showing the pertinence of*
For love can comment upon every woe.

715 'Where did I leave?'° 'No matter where,' quoth he;   *leave off*
'Leave me, and then the story aptly ends.
The night is spent.' 'Why what of that?' quoth she.
'I am,' quoth he, 'expected of° my friends,   *by*
And now 'tis dark, and going I shall fall.'
720 'In night,' quoth she, 'desire sees best of all.

'But if thou fall, O, then imagine this:
The earth, in love with thee, thy footing trips,
And all is but to rob thee of a kiss.
Rich preys° make true° men thieves; so do thy lips   *spoils / honest*
725 Make modest Dian[3] cloudy and forlorn
Lest she should steal a kiss, and die forsworn.[4]

---

1. Bell tolled for one who has just died.
2. Although I (the goddess of love) do not usually make moral points, I do so now.
3. Goddess of the moon, hunting, and virginity, also called "Cynthia" (line 728); "cloudy" because covered with clouds and because made sorrowful by her love of Adonis.
4. Die having violated her oath of chastity.

'Now of this dark night I perceive the reason.
Cynthia, for shame, obscures her silver shine
Till forging° nature be condemned of treason   counterfeiting
730   For stealing moulds from heaven, that were divine,
    Wherein she framed thee, in high heaven's despite,°   defiance
    To shame the sun by day and her by night.

'And therefore hath she bribed the destinies
To cross the curious° workmanship of nature,   elaborate
735   To mingle beauty with infirmities,
And pure perfection with impure defeature,°   disfigurement
    Making it subject to the tyranny
    Of mad mischances and much misery;

'As burning fevers, agues pale and faint,
740   Life-poisoning pestilence, and frenzies wood,°   insane fits
The marrow-eating sickness⁵ whose attaint°   infection
Disorder breeds by heating of the blood;
    Surfeits, impostumes,° grief, and damned despair   abscesses
    Swear nature's death for framing° thee so fair.   making

745   'And not the least of all these maladies
But in one minute's fight brings beauty under.
Both favour, savour,° hue, and qualities,   beauty; smell
Whereat th'impartial gazer late did wonder,
    Are on the sudden wasted,° thawed, and done,   wasted away
750   As mountain snow melts with the midday sun.

'Therefore, despite of fruitless° chastity,   defying barren
Love-lacking vestals and self-loving nuns,
That on the earth would breed a scarcity
And barren dearth of daughters and of sons,
755   Be prodigal. The lamp that burns by night
    Dries up his oil to lend the world his light.

'What is thy body but a swallowing grave,
Seeming to bury that posterity
Which, by the rights of time, thou needs must have
760   If thou destroy them not in dark obscurity?
    If so, the world will hold thee in disdain,
    Sith° in thy pride so fair a hope is slain.   Since

'So in thyself thyself art made away,°   destroyed
A mischief° worse than civil, home-bred strife,   An evil
765   Or theirs whose desperate hands themselves do slay,
Or butcher sire that reaves° his son of life.   robs
    Foul cank'ring rust the hidden treasure frets,°   eats away
    But gold that's put to use more gold begets.'

'Nay, then,' quoth Adon, 'You will fall again
770   Into your idle,° over-handled theme.   unprofitable
The kiss I gave you is bestowed in vain,
And all in vain you strive against the stream;

5. Syphilis, which attacks the bones.

For, by this black-faced night, desire's foul nurse,
Your treatise° makes me like you worse and worse.   *discussion; plea*

775 'If love have lent you twenty thousand tongues,
And every tongue more moving than your own,
Bewitching like the wanton mermaid's songs,
Yet from mine ear the tempting tune is blown;
    For know, my heart stands armèd in mine ear,
780   And will not let a false sound enter there,

'Lest the deceiving harmony should run
Into the quiet closure° of my breast,   *enclosure*
And then my little heart were quite undone,
In his bedchamber to be barred of rest.
785   No, lady, no. My heart longs not to groan,
    But soundly sleeps, while now it sleeps alone.

'What have you urged that I cannot reprove?
The path is smooth that leadeth on to danger.
I hate not love, but your device° in love,   *tactics*
790 That lends embracements unto every stranger.
    You do it for increase—O strange excuse,
    When reason is the bawd to lust's abuse!

'Call it not love, for love to heaven is fled
Since sweating lust on earth usurped his name,
795 Under whose simple° semblance he hath fed   *innocent*
Upon fresh beauty, blotting it with blame;
    Which the hot tyrant stains, and soon bereaves,
    As caterpillars do the tender leaves.

'Love comforteth, like sunshine after rain,
800 But lust's effect is tempest after sun.
Love's gentle spring doth always fresh remain;
Lust's winter comes ere summer half be done.
    Love surfeits not; lust like a glutton dies.
    Love is all truth, lust full of forgèd lies.

805 'More I could tell, but more I dare not say;
The text is old, the orator too green.
Therefore in sadness° now I will away;   *truly*
My face is full of shame, my heart of teen.°   *grief*
    Mine ears that to your wanton talk attended
810   Do burn themselves for having so offended.'

With this he breaketh from the sweet embrace
Of those fair arms which bound him to her breast,
And homeward through the dark laund° runs apace,   *glade*
Leaves love upon her back, deeply distressed.
815   Look how a bright star shooteth from the sky,
    So glides he in the night from Venus' eye,

Which after him she darts, as one on shore
Gazing upon a late-embarkèd friend
Till the wild waves will have him seen no more,

820 Whose ridges with the meeting clouds contend.
    So did the merciless and pitchy night
    Fold in the object that did feed her sight.

    Whereat amazed,° as one that unaware   *shocked*
    Hath dropped a precious jewel in the flood,
825 Or stonished,° as night wand'rers often are,   *confused*
    Their light blown out in some mistrustful° wood: *anxiety-producing*
    Even so, confounded in the dark she lay,
    Having lost the fair discovery of her way.⁶

    And now she beats her heart, whereat it groans,
830 That all the neighbour caves, as seeming troubled,
    Make verbal repetition of her moans;
    Passion° on passion deeply is redoubled.   *Lamentation*
    'Ay me,' she cries, and twenty times 'Woe, woe!'
    And twenty echoes twenty times cry so.

835 She, marking them, begins a wailing note,
    And sings extemporally a woeful ditty,
    How love makes young men thrall,° and old men dote,   *enslaved*
    How love is wise in folly, foolish-witty.
    Her heavy° anthem still concludes in woe,   *sorrowful*
840 And still the choir of echoes answer so.

    Her song was tedious, and outwore the night;
    For lovers' hours are long, though seeming short.
    If pleased themselves, others, they think, delight
    In such-like circumstance, with such-like sport.
845   Their copious stories oftentimes begun
       End without audience, and are never done.

    For who hath she to spend the night withal°   *with*
    But idle sounds resembling parasites,°   *flattering hangers-on*
    Like shrill-tongued tapsters° answering every call,   *tavern keepers*
850 Soothing the humour of fantastic wits?⁷
       She says ''Tis so'; they answer all ''Tis so',
       And would say after her, if she said 'No'.

    Lo, here the gentle lark, weary of rest,
    From his moist cabinet° mounts up on high   *nest*
855 And wakes the morning,° from whose silver breast   *(Aurora)*
    The sun ariseth in his majesty,
       Who doth the world so gloriously behold
       That cedar tops and hills seem burnished gold.

    Venus salutes him with this fair good-morrow:
860 'O thou clear° god, and patron of all light,   *bright*
    From whom each lamp and shining star doth borrow
    The beauteous influence⁸ that makes him bright:

---

6. *the fair . . . way:* a clear view of her path; a beautiful
guide.
7. Catering to the moods of erratic people.

8. The ethereal stream that in Renaissance astrology
was supposed to flow from stars and planets.

There lives a son° that sucked an earthly mother   *(Adonis)*
May° lend thee light, as thou dost lend to other.'   *Who may*

865 This said, she hasteth to a myrtle grove,
Musing° the morning is so much o'erworn°   *Wondering / spent*
And yet she hears no tidings of her love.
She hearkens for his hounds, and for his horn.
    Anon she hears them chant it lustily,°   *sing out heartily*
870   And all in haste she coasteth° to the cry.   *rushes*

And as she runs, the bushes in the way
Some catch her by the neck, some kiss her face,
Some twine about her thigh to make her stay.
She wildly breaketh from their strict° embrace,   *restricting*
875   Like a milch° doe whose swelling dugs° do ache,   *milk / udders*
    Hasting to feed her fawn hid in some brake.°   *thicket*

By this° she hears the hounds are at a bay,[9]   *By now*
Whereat she starts, like one that spies an adder
Wreathed up in fatal folds just in his way,
880 The fear whereof doth make him shake and shudder;
    Even so the timorous yelping of the hounds
    Appals her senses, and her spirit confounds.

For now she knows it is no gentle chase,
But the blunt° boar, rough bear, or lion proud,   *rude*
885 Because the cry remaineth in one place,
Where fearfully the dogs exclaim aloud.
    Finding their enemy to be so curst.°   *vicious*
    They all strain court'sy[1] who shall cope° him first.   *contend with*

This dismal cry rings sadly in her ear,
890 Through which it enters to surprise° her heart,   *assault*
Who, overcome by doubt and bloodless fear,
With cold-pale weakness numbs each feeling part;°   *sense organ*
    Like soldiers when their captain once doth yield,
    They basely fly, and dare not stay° the field.   *remain in*

895 Thus stands she in a trembling ecstasy,°   *stupor*
Till, cheering up her senses all dismayed,
She tells them 'tis a causeless fantasy
And childish error that they are afraid;
    Bids them leave quaking, bids them fear no more;
900   And with that word she spied the hunted boar,

Whose frothy mouth, bepainted all with red,
Like milk and blood being mingled both together,
A second fear through all her sinews spread,
Which madly hurries her, she knows not whither.
905   This way she runs, and now she will no further,
    But back retires to rate° the boar for murder.   *berate*

9. Stopped by the quarry, which is making a stand.   1. Politely defer to one another.

A thousand spleens° bear her a thousand ways.   *impulses*
She treads the path that she untreads again.
Her more than haste is mated° with delays,   *counteracted*
910 Like the proceedings of a drunken brain,
        Full of respects,° yet naught at all respecting;   *considerations*
        In hand with all things, naught at all effecting.²

Here kennelled in a brake she finds a hound,
And asks the weary caitiff° for his master;   *wretch*
915 And there another licking of his wound,
        'Gainst venomed sores the only sovereign plaster.°   *effective remedy*
            And here she meets another, sadly scowling,
            To whom she speaks; and he replies with howling.

When he hath ceased his ill-resounding noise,
920 Another flap-mouthed mourner, black and grim,
Against the welkin° volleys out his voice.   *sky*
Another, and another, answer him,
        Clapping their proud tails to the ground below,
        Shaking their scratched ears, bleeding as they go.

925 Look how the world's poor people are amazed
At apparitions, signs, and prodigies,°   *strange occurrences*
Whereon with fearful eyes they long have gazed,
Infusing them with° dreadful prophecies: *Reading into them*
        So she at these sad signs draws up her breath,
930   And, sighing it again, exclaims on° death.   *berates*

'Hard-favoured tyrant, ugly, meagre, lean,
Hateful divorce of love'—thus chides she death;
'Grim-grinning° ghost, earth's worm: what dost thou mean   *(like a skull)*
To stifle beauty, and to steal his breath
935   Who, when he lived, his breath and beauty set
            Gloss on the rose, smell to the violet?

'If he be dead—O no, it cannot be,
Seeing his beauty, thou shouldst strike at it.
O yes, it may; thou hast no eyes to see,³
940 But hatefully, at random dost thou hit.
        Thy mark° is feeble age; but thy false dart   *target*
        Mistakes that aim, and cleaves an infant's heart.

'Hadst thou but bid beware, then he° had spoke,   *(Adonis)*
And, hearing him, thy power had lost his° power.   *its*
945 The destinies will curse thee for this stroke.
They bid thee crop a weed; thou pluck'st a flower.
        Love's golden arrow at him should have fled,°   *flown*
        And not death's ebon dart to strike him dead.

'Dost thou drink tears, that thou provok'st such weeping?
950 What may a heavy groan advantage° thee?   *benefit*
Why hast thou cast into eternal sleeping
Those eyes that taught all other eyes to see?

2. Full of notions, yet actually attending to nothing.   3. Death's eye sockets are empty, like a skull's.

Now nature cares not for thy mortal vigour,[4]
Since her best work is ruined with thy rigour.'

955   Here overcome, as one full of despair,
She vailed° her eyelids, who like sluices stopped   *lowered*
The crystal tide that from her two cheeks fair
In the sweet channel of her bosom dropped.
    But through the flood-gates breaks the silver rain,
960   And with his strong course opens them again.

O, how her eyes and tears did lend and borrow!°   *(by reflection)*
Her eye seen in the tears, tears in her eye,
Both crystals, where they viewed each other's sorrow:
Sorrow, that friendly° sighs sought still to dry,   *consoling; like-minded*
965   But, like a stormy day, now wind, now rain,
    Sighs dry her cheeks, tears make them wet again.

Variable passions throng her constant woe,
As striving who should best become° her grief.   *fit*
All entertained,° each passion labours so   *permitted to enter*
970   That every present sorrow seemeth chief,
    But none is best. Then join they all together,
    Like many clouds consulting° for foul weather.   *gathering*

By this, far off she hears some huntsman hollo;°   *(hunting call)*
A nurse's song ne'er pleased her babe so well.
975   The dire imagination° she did follow   *train of thought*
This sound of hope doth labour to expel;
    For now reviving joy bids her rejoice
    And flatters her it is Adonis' voice.

Whereat her tears began to turn their tide,°   *to ebb*
980   Being prisoned in her eye like pearls in glass;
Yet sometimes falls an orient° drop beside,   *a glistening*
Which her cheek melts, as° scorning it should pass   *as if*
    To wash the foul° face of the sluttish ground,   *dirty*
    Who is but drunken when she seemeth drowned.

985   O hard-believing love—how strange it seems
Not to believe, and yet too credulous!
Thy weal° and woe are both of them extremes.   *prosperity*
Despair, and hope, makes thee ridiculous.
    The one doth flatter thee in thoughts unlikely;
990   In likely thoughts the other kills thee quickly.

Now she unweaves the web that she hath wrought.
Adonis lives, and death is not to blame.
It was not she that called him all to naught.[5]
Now she adds honours to his hateful name.
995   She clepes° him king of graves, and grave for kings,   *calls (archaic)*
    Imperious supreme° of all mortal things.   *Imperial ruler*

---

4. Nature does not heed your lethal power.   5. She who called Death everything bad.

'No, no,' quoth she, 'sweet death, I did but jest.
Yet pardon me, I felt a kind of fear
Whenas I met the boar, that bloody beast,
1000   Which knows no pity, but is still severe.
     Then, gentle shadow—truth I must confess—
     I railed on thee, fearing my love's decease.

' 'Tis not my fault; the boar provoked my tongue.
Be wreaked° on him, invisible commander.   *revenged*
1005   'Tis he, foul creature, that hath done thee wrong.
I did but act;° he's author of thy slander.   *(as an agent)*
     Grief hath two tongues,° and never woman yet   *is doubly loud*
     Could rule them both, without ten women's wit.'

Thus, hoping that Adonis is alive,
1010   Her rash suspect° she doth extenuate,   *suspicion*
And, that his beauty may the better thrive,
With death she humbly doth insinuate;°   *curry favor*
     Tells him of trophies, statues, tombs; and stories
     His victories, his triumphs, and his glories.

1015   'O Jove,' quoth she, 'how much a fool was I
To be of such a weak and silly mind
To wail his death who lives, and must not die
Till mutual° overthrow of mortal kind!   *universal*
     For he being dead, with him is beauty slain,
1020   And beauty dead, black chaos comes again.

'Fie, fie, fond° love, thou art as full of fear   *foolish; affectionate*
As one with treasure laden, hemmed with thieves.
Trifles unwitnessèd with eye or ear
Thy coward heart with false bethinking° grieves.'   *imagination*
1025   Even at this word she hears a merry horn,
     Whereat she leaps,° that was but late° forlorn.   *(for joy) / lately*

As falcons to the lure, away she flies.
The grass stoops not, she treads on it so light;
And in her haste unfortunately spies
1030   The foul boar's conquest on her fair delight;
     Which seen, her eyes, as murdered with the view,
     Like stars ashamed of° day, themselves withdrew.°   *put to shame by / shut*

Or as the snail, whose tender horns being hit
Shrinks backward in his shelly cave with pain,
1035   And there, all smothered up, in shade doth sit,
Long after fearing to creep forth again;
     So at his bloody view her eyes are fled
     Into the deep dark cabins of her head,

Where they resign their office and their light
1040   To the disposing of her troubled brain,
Who bids them still consort with° ugly night,   *always accompany*
And never wound the heart with looks again,
     Who,° like a king perplexèd° in his throne,   *(the heart) / troubled*
     By their suggestion° gives a deadly groan,   *(the eyes') incitement*

1045 Whereat each tributary subject[6] quakes,
     As when the wind, imprisoned in the ground,
     Struggling for passage, earth's foundation shakes,[7]
     Which with cold terror doth men's minds confound.
        This mutiny each part doth so surprise°   *assail*
1050   That from their dark beds once more leap her eyes,

     And, being opened, threw unwilling light
     Upon the wide wound that the boar had trenched
     In his soft flank, whose wonted° lily-white   *usual*
     With purple tears that his wound wept was drenched.
1055   No flower was nigh, no grass, herb, leaf, or weed,
        But stole his blood, and seemed with him to bleed.

     This solemn sympathy poor Venus noteth.
     Over one shoulder doth she hang her head.
     Dumbly° she passions,° franticly she doteth.   *Mutely / suffers*
1060   She thinks he could not die, he is not dead.
        Her voice is stopped, her joints forget to bow,°   *cannot bend*
        Her eyes are mad that they have wept till° now.   *before*

     Upon his hurt she looks so steadfastly
     That her sight, dazzling,° makes the wound seem three;   *blurring*
1065   And then she reprehends her mangling eye,
     That makes more gashes where no breach should be.
        His face seems twain; each several limb is doubled:
        For oft the eye mistakes, the brain being troubled.

     'My tongue cannot express my grief for one,
1070   And yet,' quoth she, 'behold two Adons dead!
     My sighs are blown away, my salt tears gone,
     Mine eyes are turned to fire, my heart to lead.
        Heavy heart's lead, melt at mine eyes' red fire!
        So shall I die by drops of hot desire.

1075   'Alas, poor world, what treasure hast thou lost,
     What face remains alive that's worth the viewing?
     Whose tongue is music now? What canst thou boast
     Of things long since, or anything ensuing?
        The flowers are sweet, their colours fresh and trim,
1080   But true sweet beauty lived and died with him.

     'Bonnet nor veil henceforth no creature wear:°   *(to preserve complexion)*
     Nor sun nor wind will ever strive to kiss you.
     Having no fair° to lose, you need not fear.   *beauty*
     The sun doth scorn you, and the wind doth hiss you.
1085   But when Adonis lived, sun and sharp air
        Lurked like two thieves to rob him of his fair;

     'And therefore would he put his bonnet on,
     Under whose brim the gaudy sun would peep.
     The wind would blow it off, and, being gone,

---

6. Each inferior organ of Venus's body.   7. Sixteenth-century explanation of earthquakes.

1090 Play with his locks; then would Adonis weep,
    And straight,° in pity of his tender years,   *immediately*
    They both would strive who first should dry his tears.

'To see his face the lion walked along
Behind some hedge, because he would not fear° him.   *frighten*
1095 To recreate° himself° when he hath sung,   *entertain / (Adonis)*
The tiger would be tame, and gently hear him.
    If he had spoke, the wolf would leave his prey,
    And never fright the silly° lamb that day.   *innocent*

'When he beheld his shadow in the brook,
1100 The fishes spread on it their golden gills.
When he was by, the birds such pleasure took
That some would sing, some other in their bills
    Would bring him mulberries and ripe-red cherries.
    He fed them with his sight, they him with berries.

1105 'But this foul, grim, and urchin-snouted° boar,   *hedgehog-snouted*
Whose downward eye still looketh for a grave,
Ne'er saw the beauteous livery[8] that he wore:
Witness the entertainment° that he gave.   *reception*
    If he did see his face, why then, I know
1110 He thought to kiss him, and hath killed him so.

''Tis true, 'tis true; thus was Adonis slain;
He ran upon the boar with his sharp spear,
Who did not whet his teeth at him again,°   *in return*
But by a kiss thought to persuade him° there,   *win him over*
1115   And, nuzzling in his flank, the loving swine
    Sheathed unaware the tusk in his soft groin.

'Had I been toothed like him, I must confess
With kissing him I should have killed him first;
But he is dead, and never did he bless
1120 My youth with his, the more am I accursed.'
    With this she falleth in the place she stood,
    And stains her face with his congealèd blood.

She looks upon his lips, and they are pale.
She takes him by the hand, and that is cold.
1125 She whispers in his ears a heavy tale,
As if they heard the woeful words she told.
    She lifts the coffer-lids° that close his eyes,   *treasure-chest lids*
    Where lo, two lamps burnt out in darkness lies;

Two glasses, where herself herself beheld
1130 A thousand times, and now no more reflect,
Their virtue° lost, wherein they late excelled,   *power*
And every beauty robbed of his° effect.   *its*
    'Wonder of time,' quoth she, 'this is my spite,°   *torment*
    That, thou being dead, the day should yet be light.

---

8. His appearance (literally, garment).

1135 'Since thou art dead, lo, here I prophesy
     Sorrow on love hereafter shall attend.
     It° shall be waited on with jealousy,   (Love)
     Find sweet beginning, but unsavoury end;
        Ne'er settled equally, but high or low,⁹
1140   That all love's pleasure shall not match his woe.

     'It shall be fickle, false, and full of fraud,
     Bud, and be blasted,° in a breathing-while:°   blighted / moment
     The bottom poison, and the top o'erstrawed°   strewn over
     With sweets that shall the truest sight beguile.
1145   The strongest body shall it make most weak,
        Strike the wise dumb,° and teach the fool to speak.   mute

     'It shall be sparing,° and too full of riot,°   miserly / excess
     Teaching decrepit age to tread the measures.¹
     The staring° ruffian shall it keep in quiet,   glaring
1150 Pluck down the rich, enrich the poor with treasures;
        It shall be raging-mad, and silly-mild;
        Make the young old, the old become a child.

     'It shall suspect where is no cause of fear;
     It shall not fear where it should most mistrust.
1155 It shall be merciful, and too severe,
     And most deceiving when it seems most just.°   honest
        Perverse it shall be where it shows most toward,²
        Put fear to valour, courage to the coward.

     'It shall be cause of war and dire events,
1160 And set dissension 'twixt the son and sire;
     Subject and servile to all discontents,³
     As dry combustious matter is to fire.
        Sith° in his prime death doth my love destroy,   Since
        They that love best their loves shall not enjoy.'

1165 By this, the boy that by her side lay killed
     Was melted like a vapour from her sight,
     And in his blood that on the ground lay spilled
     A purple flower sprung up, chequered with white,°   (the anemone)
        Resembling well his pale cheeks, and the blood
1170   Which in round drops upon their whiteness stood.

     She bows her head the new-sprung flower to smell,
     Comparing it to her Adonis' breath,
     And says within her bosom it shall dwell,
     Since he himself is reft° from her by death.   torn
1175   She crops the stalk, and in the breach appears
        Green-dropping sap, which she compares to tears.

     'Poor flower,' quoth she, 'this was thy father's guise°—   habit
     Sweet issue° of a more sweet-smelling sire—   offspring; emission

---

9. *Ne'er . . . low:* Love shall involve extremes of happiness and grief rather than equanimity; lovers shall
come from different social stations.

1. To dance (inappropriately).
2. It shall be stubborn where it seems most compliant.
3. Cause and slave of all discontentedness.

For every little grief to wet his eyes.

1180 To grow unto himself° was his desire,   *mature independently*
    And so 'tis thine; but know it is as good
    To wither in my breast as in his blood.

'Here was thy father's bed, here in my breast.
Thou art the next of blood,° and 'tis thy right.   *heir (with wordplay)*
1185 Lo, in this hollow cradle take thy rest;
My throbbing heart shall rock thee day and night.
    There shall not be one minute in an hour
    Wherein I will not kiss my sweet love's flower.'

Thus, weary of the world, away she hies,
1190 And yokes her silver doves, by whose swift aid
Their mistress, mounted, through the empty skies
In her light chariot quickly is conveyed,
    Holding their course to Paphos,[4] where their queen
    Means to immure° herself, and not be seen.   *confine*

4. Venus's abode in Cyprus.

The Rape of Lucrece

In the dedication to *Venus and Adonis* in 1593, Shakespeare promised his patron the Earl of Southampton a "graver labor"; a year later, *The Rape of Lucrece* delivered on his pledge. Like most nondramatic poems of the period, in other words, this one was dedicated to a wealthy individual whom Shakespeare hoped would reward his efforts, and presumably reflected Shakespeare's awareness of that individual's literary preferences. Perhaps not surprisingly, then, the two poems have much in common: their classical inspiration; their lush, highly rhetorical narrative verse, their interest in the dynamic of a one-sided sexual passion. Yet both poems were intended for a wider audience, and both were popular successes: *The Rape of Lucrece* was reprinted at least six times during Shakespeare's lifetime. Moreover, as Shakespeare suggests in his dedication, whereas *Venus and Adonis,* despite its sad end, remains playful even in its pathos, *The Rape of Lucrece* treats a tragic subject of political as well as sexual consequence. It is written in rime royal, a seven-line iambic-pentameter stanza with the rhyme scheme *ababbcc,* a verse form reserved since the time of Chaucer for elevated, tragic subjects. Shakespeare's contemporary Gabriel Harvey captures the difference in the two poems when he comments that *Venus and Adonis* pleases "the younger sort," while *The Rape of Lucrece,* like *Hamlet,* pleases "the wiser sort."

Today *The Rape of Lucrece* is commonly regarded far less highly than the play with which Harvey classifies it. The change in estimation suggests that Shakespeare's original readers came to the poem with generic expectations, literary tastes, and interpretive equipment different from our own. One important difference is the greater familiarity many Renaissance readers would have had with Shakespeare's sources, a familiarity that left them free to concentrate on the ways in which the poet was varying or amplifying on well-known prototypes. Slightly different versions of the tale of Tarquin and Lucretia were available in Livy's history of Rome and in Ovid's *Fasti,* both commonly read in Elizabethan grammar schools. In 509 B.C.E., Rome's King was Tarquin the Proud, a good military leader but an oppressive ruler over his own subjects. Sextus Tarquinius, the King's son, raped Lucretia, the wife of Collatinus, one of his aristocratic retainers. Lucretia committed suicide after revealing the crime to her male relatives and exhorting them to revenge her. After her corpse was exhibited in the Roman Forum, a wholesale revolt against the Tarquins erupted, led by the King's nephew Lucius Junius Brutus. The royal family was exiled, and Rome became a republic, ruled by a senate and administered by one or more elected "consuls," of which Lucius Junius Brutus was the first.

For the Renaissance as well as for its original Roman audience, the story of Tarquin and Lucrece displayed vividly the inextricability of domestic and civic order, of public and private realms, of sexual and political violence. As a political fable, it suggested circumstances in which subjects were permitted, even obliged, to challenge the authority of their sovereign. When Tarquin rapes Lucrece, he does not merely perpetrate an act of brutal violence against her, but he defies Collatinus's exclusive claim on his wife's body, imagined as the husband's property. The story thus exemplifies a ruler's reckless disregard for the rights of his *male* subjects. In the late sixteenth century, when monarchies in western Europe were strengthening their power at the expense of parliaments and the higher aristocracy, the story could be cited as a precedent for resisting tyranny.

Purely as a sexual melodrama too, the story had wide appeal. Again and again, Renaissance painters portrayed Tarquin stealing into Lucretia's bed, Lucretia stabbing herself, and Lucius Junius Brutus exhorting over her body in the marketplace, often incorporating all three scenes into the same picture. Lucretia became a focus of especially fierce

Lucretia. Raphael.

debate. On the one hand, she seemed a model of wifely duty, a woman to whom marital fidelity was not merely a matter of social respectability but a fundamental life principle. On the other hand, suicide by the sword—the traditional last, defiant gesture of heroic Roman men—could seem improperly self-assertive in a woman. Moreover, some Christian writers considered Lucretia's suicide not merely indecorous but sinful. In *The City of God,* Augustine argued that since virtues are properties of the will and not the body, Lucretia was innocent of unchastity. But ironically, her sexual blamelessness rendered her suicide completely inexcusable; Augustine considered her a murderess who had taken her own life out of unchristian pride. By Shakespeare's time, therefore, Lucretia could be held up, variously, as a model of female propriety and as an example of pagan willfulness, as a woman who both upholds and breaks from the usual constraints upon her sex.

Adapting the story to his own purposes, Shakespeare makes interesting changes of detail and emphasis. As Ovid and Livy recount it, the story of violation, suicide, and revolution is full of turbulent physical action and unexpected revelations: and in Livy especially, the political consequences of the rape receive much more attention than the sexual assault itself. Shakespeare's version downplays—though it does not eliminate—the political aspects of the story, and it contains most of the feverish momentum of the original story in the prefatory "Argument": "The same night he treacherously stealeth into her chamber, violently ravished her, and early in the morning speedeth away. Lucrece, in this lamentable plight, hastily dispatcheth messengers." The poem itself, by contrast, concentrates not upon moments of violence or haste but upon what precedes and follows those moments: what Tarquin thinks on his way to Lucrece's bedchamber, how Lucrece occupies herself between the time she sends off her messenger and Collatine's return.

Like *Venus and Adonis, The Rape of Lucrece* eschews eventfulness for elaborate psychological analysis, attempting to capture in verse the uneven surge and flow of troubled, self-divided consciousnesses. In Shakespeare's hands, the story of Tarquin and Lucrece becomes a story about how people make choices that lead to violence. Everything in the poem is the consequence of a decision, not an accident of fate, and nothing seems inevitable. The poem teases the reader with alternative possibilities. What if Collatine had kept his marital happiness to himself? What if Tarquin's conscience had overcome his lust? What if Lucrece's beauty had blinded Tarquin permanently instead of temporarily? What if Collatine had arrived to save Lucrece at the last moment? What if Lucrece had resolved to kill Tarquin rather than herself?

In large part, these alternatives receive so much attention because both Tarquin and Lucrece make decisions that fail to reflect their best interests. The poem is constantly suggesting that they would be better off doing something else; and, interestingly, the characters themselves at times seem lucidly aware of that fact. Tarquin tells himself that his assault will desecrate the very virtue he admires in Lucrece, destroy his own self-respect, and bring dishonor upon his family. Then he rapes Lucrece. Lucrece argues to herself what her husband and father will tell her later: that she cannot incur guilt by a sexual act to which she has not consented, and that therefore she need not take her own life. Then she commits suicide.

In both cases, the characters' stubborn refusal to acknowledge the obvious seems to follow from their tendency to conceive of themselves in terms of a few crucial metaphors. In Tarquin's case, the metaphors are military: "Affection is my captain, and he leadeth, / . . . My heart shall never countermand mine eye" (lines 271, 276). Such images attract Tarquin because they portray a rash, grossly disorderly act in terms of strict discipline. Even as he overturns the proper subordination of passion to reason, he elaborates a clear, if perverse, hierarchy of priorities. Moreover, by casting himself as a warrior and Lucrece as an enemy territory, Tarquin minimizes the blame that attaches to rape, an act conventionally associated with (and often excused in) soldiers pillaging an enemy town.

Of course, as Lucrece reminds him, she is not his foe, and Tarquin's actions violate not only her bodily integrity but her husband's trust in a friend and superior. Her pleas show how tendentious are Tarquin's interpretations of the metaphors he attaches to himself. When Tarquin describes himself as an "uncontrollèd tide," and therefore intractable to entreaties, Lucrece attempts to modify the sense of the metaphor:

> 'Thou art,' quoth she, 'a sea, a sovereign king,
> And lo, there falls into thy boundless flood
> Black lust, dishonour, shame, misgoverning,
> Who seek to stain the ocean of thy blood.'
> (lines 652–55)

Likewise, her account of his psychological state replaces the military metaphor of battle against an enemy with one of civil order temporarily disrupted:

> I sue for exiled majesty's repeal;
> Let him return, and flatt'ring thoughts retire.
> His true respect will prison false desire.
> (lines 640–42)

Eventually, the rape that Tarquin tries to think of as an orderly military maneuver leads not only to his psychological fragmentation and self-torment but to literal exile, an exile Lucrece describes as already having occurred metaphorically.

After the rape and Tarquin's departure, the narrative focus shifts to Lucrece. Although she knows that she is not intentionally guilty of breaking her marital vows, she nonetheless construes herself as culpable. Like her violator, Lucrece thinks of herself and her body in symbolic terms, although in her case the governing metaphors are fortress, house, mansion, temple, tree. By emphasizing the protective function of the body, these metaphors make it easy for Lucrece to think of herself as irreparably damaged once her body has been assaulted by Tarquin's lust:

> Ay me, the bark peeled from the lofty pine
> His leaves will wither and his sap decay;
> So must my soul, her bark being peeled away.
> (lines 1167–69)

Once Tarquin sacks and batters Lucrece's fortress, she suffers regardless of her innocence, like the inhabitant of a plundered town. Of course, like Tarquin, Lucrece interprets such metaphors tendentiously: she could just as well think of the "bark" or the "house" that shelters her soul as a morally insignificant excrescence. Instead, when the condition of her body seems to conflict with the condition of her soul, she desperately attempts to resolve the inconsistency by declaring herself irredeemably contaminated. In doing so, she endorses—indeed, almost celebrates—a literally fatal ambivalence in the definition of female chastity. For despite Augustine's objections, female chastity ordinarily refers to a physical condition as well as to a mental attitude in cultures that value female bodily intactness; this ambivalence still haunts rape survivors today, who often blame themselves for their own victimization.

Comprehensible though Lucrece's suicide may be in these terms, however, it is ironically fraught with the very contradictions she seeks to avoid. She "revenges" herself

Tarquino e Lucrezia. Titian (c. 1570).

upon Tarquin by completing the assault he began, plunging the phallic blade into what Shakespeare calls the "sheath" of her breast (the Latin word for "sheath" is *vagina*). She insists that she is acting in Collatine's interests even while she ignores his wishes; she proves her innocence by demanding of herself that she pay the penalty for guilt; she validates her version of the rape story by silencing herself more effectively than Tarquin had with the bedclothes.

Although the metaphors Tarquin and Lucrece use to think about their respective situations are, therefore, highly problematic, they are definitely not arbitrary. Both protagonists derive their figures of speech from the same medieval and Renaissance poetic tradition Shakespeare had already drawn upon in *Venus and Adonis*. The configuration of characters—the warrior-lover desperately pursuing his passion, the beautiful woman whose chastity makes her irresistibly desirable—is likewise conventional. Shakespeare suggests the importance of this poetic mentality for *The Rape of Lucrece* by anachronistically importing the language of chivalry into a poem about ancient Rome: Tarquin agonizes about the consequences of his transgression for his family's coat of arms, and Lucrece accuses him of breaking "knighthood, gentry, and sweet friendship's oath" (line 569). This is closer to the world of Thomas Malory's Arthurian romances, Thomas Wyatt's sonnets, Philip Sidney's *Arcadia,* or Edmund Spenser's *Faerie Queene* than it is to the world of Livy or Ovid.

In fact, it is possible to see *The Rape of Lucrece,* like *Venus and Adonis,* as attempting to renovate a rhetoric of sexual passion that had begun to seem trite by Shakespeare's time. But the two poems employ almost exactly opposite strategies of renewal. *Venus and Adonis* surprises the reader by turning conventional expectations of gendered behavior upside down, assigning the aggressive, desiring role to the woman and casting the male as an uncorrupted fortress of virtue. *The Rape of Lucrece,* on the other hand, pushes the conventional language of love poetry in a relentlessly literal direction, making it interesting by unleashing the latent ferocity and misogyny of a courtly love aesthetic. Lovers in the poetry of Spenser and Sidney, Petrarch and Wyatt, think of themselves as soldiers of desire, but they are so awed by their mistresses that aggressive thoughts are quenched by a mere glance from their imperious beloveds. Shakespeare's Tarquin, in contrast, more consistent and less exquisitely sensitive, uses the implicitly coercive rhetoric of love poetry as a pretext for rape.

Given the poem's intense concern with the use and misuse of language, it is not surprising that *The Rape of Lucrece* is also attentive to the relationship of rhetoric to other forms of representation. Again and again, the poem pauses to consider the relative power and conviction of linguistic and visual experience, of the ear and the eye. At some points in the poem, vision seems the privileged sense, giving immediate access to the unquestionably real. "Beauty itself doth of itself persuade / The eyes of men without an orator," the narrator declares; "To see sad sights moves more than hear them told" (lines 29–30, 1324). Yet Shakespeare alters his sources to have Tarquin provoked to lust not by the sight of Lucrece but by Collatine's report of her; and he dwells too on Lucrece's inability to divine Tarquin's motives from his appearance.

The rape and death of Lucretia. From Jost Amman, *Icones Livianae* (1572).

This persistent concern with the relative adequacy of different representational modes culminates in a long passage in which Lucrece contemplates a tapestry of Troy. In multiple ways, the tapestry is relevant to her own case, for the Trojan War was the consequence of a rape, and after the city's destruction, Trojan exiles were supposed to have founded Rome. After Lucrece's suicide, the account of her rape will provide the pretext for another founding, that of the Roman Republic. Eventually, her story will be displayed by artists in the same way that the legend of Troy is illustrated here—a series of chronologically distinct episodes represented simultaneously on the same panel. As Lucrece gazes at the painter's vast panorama of violation, the poet emphasizes both the vivid realism of the depiction and the artificial means by which that realism is produced: "Here one man's hand leaned on another's head, / His nose being shadowed by his neighbour's ear" (lines 1415–16). Portraying people according to the laws of perspective makes them look "natural," but it also reduces them to a collection of grotesquely amputated shapes. Like *Venus and Adonis*, *The Rape of Lucrece* invokes nature as a category of value and then subverts it; but whereas the earlier poem undermines "nature" by suggesting that its supposed precepts are inadequate, the later poem undermines "nature" by suggesting that its effect is only achieved by extraordinary artifice. Shakespeare will consider the issue again in such plays as *A Midsummer Night's Dream*, *The Winter's Tale*, *The Tempest*, and, of course, *Hamlet*.

KATHARINE EISAMAN MAUS

TEXTUAL NOTE

Richard Field was the printer for *The Rape of Lucrece*, published in 1594, as he had been for *Venus and Adonis* the previous year. Like *Venus and Adonis*, *Lucrece* in its printed state probably derives directly from Shakespeare's manuscript, and it presents relatively few textual difficulties. Some editors question whether Shakespeare wrote the prefatory "Argument." A few variations among surviving copies of the First Quarto represent proof corrections; in Elizabethan times, proofreading was done while the work was in the process of being printed, so corrections could appear in some copies but not in others.

SELECTED BIBLIOGRAPHY

Belsey, Catherine. "Tarquin Dispossessed: Expropriation and Consent in *The Rape of Lucrece*." *Shakespeare Quarterly* 52 (2001): 45–70. Lucrece as property and as person.

Donaldson, Ian. *The Rapes of Lucretia: A Myth and Its Transformations*. Oxford: Clarendon, 1982. Discusses Shakespeare's poem alongside other literary and artistic treatments of the story.

Fineman, Joel. "Shakespeare's Will: The Temporality of Rape." *Representations* 20 (Fall 1987): 25–76. Features an ingenious discussion of the "let" as both hindering Tarquin and spurring him to action.

Hadfield, Andrew. "Tarquin's Everlasting Banishment: Republicanism and Constitutionalism in *The Rape of Lucrece* and *Titus Andronicus*." *Parergon: Journal of the Australian and New Zealand Association for Medieval and Renaissance Studies* 19 (2002): 77–104. A discussion of the political issues in the poem.

Kahn, Coppélia. "The Rape in Shakespeare's *Lucrece*." *Shakespeare Studies* 9 (1976): 45–72. Feminist account of rape and patriarchy in the poem.

Maus, Katharine Eisaman. "Taking Tropes Seriously: Language and Violence in Shakespeare's *Rape of Lucrece*." *Shakespeare Quarterly* 37 (1986): 66–82. *The Rape of Lucrece* as a literalization of Petrarchan metaphors.

Vickers, Nancy. "The Blazon of Sweet Beauty's Best: Shakespeare's *Lucrece*." *Shakespeare and the Question of Theory*. Ed. Patricia Parker and Geoffrey Hartman. New York: Methuen, 1985. 95–115. The sexual politics of the blazon or detailed description of Lucrece's body.

The Rape of Lucrece

TO THE RIGHT HONOURABLE
HENRY WRIOTHESLEY,
EARL OF SOUTHAMPTON AND
BARON OF TITCHFIELD[1]

The love I dedicate to your lordship is without end, whereof this pamphlet° without beginning[2] is but a superfluous moiety.° The warrant° I have of your honourable disposition, not the worth of my untutored lines, makes it assured of acceptance. What I have done is yours; what I have to do is yours, being part in all I have, devoted yours. Were my worth greater my duty would show greater, meantime, as it is, it is bound to your lordship, to whom I wish long life still° lengthened with all happiness.

      short work / part
      assurance

      continually

YOUR LORDSHIP'S IN ALL DUTY,
WILLIAM SHAKESPEARE

THE ARGUMENT°

      plot

Lucius Tarquinius (surnamed Superbus for his excessive pride),° after he had caused his own father-in-law Servius Tullius to be cruelly murdered, and, contrary to the Roman laws and customs, not requiring[3] or staying for the people's suffrages° had possessed himself of the kingdom, went accompanied with his sons and other noblemen of Rome to besiege Ardea,[4] during which siege the principal men of the army meeting one evening at the tent of Sextus Tarquinius, the King's son, in their discourses after supper everyone commended the virtues of his own wife, among whom Collatinus extolled the incomparable chastity of his wife, Lucretia. In that pleasant humour° they all posted° to Rome, and, intending by their secret and sudden arrival to make trial of that which everyone had before avouched, only Collatinus finds his wife (though it were late in the night) spinning amongst her maids. The other ladies were all found dancing, and revelling, or in several disports.° Whereupon the noblemen yielded Collatinus the victory and his wife the fame. At that time Sextus Tarquinius, being enflamed with Lucrece' beauty, yet smothering his passions for the present, departed with the rest back to the camp, from whence he shortly after privily° withdrew himself and was, according to his estate,° royally entertained and lodged by Lucrece at Collatium.[5] The same night he treacherously stealeth into her chamber, violently

      "the Proud"

      approval

      merry mood
      hurried

      diversions

      secretly / rank

Dedication and **Argument**
1. See *Venus and Adonis*, note 2 to Dedication.
2. *The Rape of Lucrece* begins *in medias res* (in the middle of the story), as the Latin poet Horace recommends in *The Art of Poetry*.
3. Not asking for.
4. City 25 miles south of Rome.
5. Town 10 miles east of Rome; the ancestral home of Collatinus's family.

ravished her, and early in the morning speedeth away. Lucrece, in this lamentable plight, hastily dispatcheth messengers—one to Rome for her father, another to the camp for Collatine. They came, the one accompanied with Junius Brutus, the other with Publius Valerius, and, finding Lucrece attired in mourning habit, demanded the cause of her sorrow. She, first taking an oath of them for her revenge, revealed the actor° and whole manner of his dealing, and withal° suddenly stabbed herself. Which done, with one consent they all vowed to root out the whole hated family of the Tarquins, and, bearing the dead body to Rome, Brutus acquainted the people with the doer and manner of the vile deed, with a bitter invective against the tyranny of the King; wherewith the people were so moved that with one consent and a general acclamation the Tarquins were all exiled and the state government changed from kings to consuls.[6]

doer
moreover

From the besieged Ardea all in post,°
Borne by the trustless wings of false desire,
Lust-breathèd° Tarquin leaves the Roman host
And to Collatium bears the lightless° fire
5   Which, in pale embers hid, lurks to aspire°
    And girdle with embracing flames the waist
    Of Collatine's fair love, Lucrece the chaste.

haste

Lust-inspired
smoldering
rise up

Haply° that name of chaste unhapp'ly° set
This bateless° edge on his keen appetite,
10 When Collatine unwisely did not let°
To praise the clear unmatchèd red and white
Which triumphed in that sky of his delight,°
    Where mortal stars° as bright as heaven's beauties
    With pure aspects[1] did him peculiar° duties.

Perhaps / unfortunately
unbluntable
forbear

(Lucrece's face)
(her eyes)
exclusive

15 For he the night before in Tarquin's tent
Unlocked the treasure of his happy state,
What priceless wealth the heavens had him lent
In the possession of his beauteous mate,
Reck'ning his fortune at such high-proud rate
20   That kings might be espousèd to more fame,
        But° king nor peer to such a peerless dame.

But neither

O happiness enjoyed but of° a few,
And, if possessed, as soon decayed and done
As is the morning's silver melting dew
25 Against the golden splendour of the sun,
An expired date° cancelled ere well begun!
    Honour and beauty in the owner's arms
    Are weakly fortressed from a world of harms.

only by

time limit

Beauty itself doth of° itself persuade
30 The eyes of men without an orator.
What needeth then apology be made

by

6. Chief magistrates, elected for one-year terms.

Poem
1. Looks; astral influences.

To set forth that which is so singular?°   *unique*
Or why is Collatine the publisher°   *publicizer*
   Of that rich jewel he should keep unknown
35   From thievish ears, because it is his own?

Perchance his boast of Lucrece' sov'reignty°   *superiority*
Suggested° this proud issue° of a king,   *Tempted / offspring*
For by our ears our hearts oft tainted be.
Perchance that envy of so rich a thing,
40 Braving compare,° disdainfully did sting   *Defying comparison*
   His high-pitched thoughts, that meaner° men should vaunt°   *inferior / boast*
   That golden hap° which their superiors want.°   *luck / lack*

But some untimely thought did instigate
His all-too-timeless° speed, if none of those.   *untimely; rapid*
45 His honour, his affairs, his friends, his state°   *rank*
Neglected all, with swift intent he goes
To quench the coal which in his liver° glows.   *ew*   *(seat of lust)*
   O rash false heat, wrapped in repentant cold,
   Thy hasty spring still blasts° and ne'er grows old!   *is always frostbitten*

50 When at Collatium this false lord arrived,
Well was he welcomed by the Roman dame,
Within whose face beauty and virtue strived
Which of them both should underprop her fame.
When virtue bragged, beauty would blush for shame;
55   When beauty boasted blushes, in despite°   *defiance*
   Virtue would stain° that or° with silver white.   *dye / gold*

But beauty, in that white entituled°   *claiming title*
From Venus' doves, doth challenge that fair field.[2]
Then virtue claims from beauty beauty's red,
60 Which virtue gave the golden age to gild[3]
Their silver cheeks, and called it then their shield,
   Teaching them thus to use it in the fight:
   When shame assailed, the red should fence° the white.   *defend*

This heraldry in Lucrece' face was seen,
65 Argued° by beauty's red and virtue's white.   *Demonstrated; disputed*
Of either's colour was the other queen,
Proving from world's minority° their right.   *earliest age*
Yet their ambition makes them still to fight,
   The sovereignty of either being so great
70   That oft they interchange each other's seat.

This silent war of lilies and of roses
Which Tarquin viewed in her fair face's field
In their pure ranks his traitor eye encloses,
Where, lest between them both it should be killed,
75 The coward captive vanquishèd doth yield   ]   *not to rape her*
   To those two armies that would let him go   *would be cowardly*
   Rather than triumph in° so false a foe.   *over*

---

2. Territory; battlefield; surface on which a coat of arms is displayed. *Venus' doves*: white turtledoves draw the chariot of Venus, the love goddess.

3. Coat with gold cover with red (as in a blush). *the golden age*: a mythical ideal era of innocence and plenty.

Now thinks he that her husband's shallow tongue,
The niggard prodigal that praised her so,
80 In that high task hath done her beauty wrong,
Which far exceeds his barren skill to show.°   *describe*
Therefore that praise which Collatine doth owe°   *fail to render*
Enchanted Tarquin answers° with surmise   *compensates for*
In silent wonder of still-gazing eyes.

85 This earthly saint adorèd by this devil
Little suspecteth the false worshipper,
For unstained thoughts do seldom dream on evil.
Birds never limed° no secret bushes fear,   *trapped*
So guiltless she securely° gives good cheer[4]   *unsuspectingly*
90   And reverent welcome to her princely guest,
   Whose inward ill no outward harm expressed,

For that he coloured° with his high estate,   *disguised*
Hiding base sin in pleats° of majesty,   *folds*
That° nothing in him seemed inordinate   *So that*
95 Save sometime too much wonder of his eye,
Which, having all, all could not satisfy,
   But poorly rich so wanteth in his store°   *plenty*
   That, cloyed with much, he pineth still for more.

But she that never coped with stranger° eyes   *strangers'*
100 Could pick no meaning from their parling° looks,   *persuasive*
Nor read the subtle shining secrecies
Writ in the glassy margins[5] of such books.
She touched no unknown baits nor feared no hooks,
   Nor could she moralize° his wanton sight°   *interpret / looking*
105   More than his eyes were opened to the light.[6]

He stories to her ears her husband's fame
Won in the fields of fruitful Italy,
And decks with praises Collatine's high name
Made glorious by his manly chivalry
110 With bruisèd arms° and wreaths of victory.   *dented weapons*
   Her joy with heaved-up hand she doth express,
   And wordless so greets heaven for his success.

Far from the purpose of his coming thither
He makes excuses for his being there.
115 No cloudy show of stormy blust'ring weather
Doth yet in his fair welkin° once appear   *sky (face)*
Till sable° night, mother of dread and fear,   *black*
   Upon the world dim darkness doth display
   And in her vaulty prison stows the day.

120 For then is Tarquin brought unto his bed,
Intending° weariness with heavy sprite;°   *Pretending / spirit*
For after supper long he questionèd°   *conversed*
With modest Lucrece, and wore out the night.

4. Hospitable entertainment.   often placed.
5. Where summaries and interpretive remarks were   6. Were made obvious.

Now leaden slumber with life's strength doth fight,
125   And everyone to rest himself betakes
    Save thieves, and cares, and troubled minds that wakes.

As one of which doth Tarquin lie revolving°   *considering*
The sundry dangers of his will's obtaining,°   *gratifying his desire*
Yet ever to obtain his will resolving,
130   Though weak-built hopes[7] persuade him to abstaining.
    Despair to gain doth traffic oft for gaining,[8]
      ⌈And when great treasure is the meed° proposed,   *prize*
      ⌊Though death be adjunct,[9] there's no death supposed.°   *thought of*

Those that much covet are with gain so fond°   *infatuated*
135   That what° they have not, that which they possess,   *That for what*
    They scatter and unloose it from their bond,°   *ownership*
    And so by hoping more they have but less,
    Or, gaining more, the profit° of excess   *advantage*
      Is but to surfeit and such griefs[1] sustain
140   That they° prove bankrupt in this poor-rich gain.   *(the covetous)*

The aim of all is but to nurse the life
With honour, wealth, and ease in waning age,
And in this aim there is such thwarting strife
That one for all, or all for one, we gage,°   *risk*
145   As° life for honour in fell° battle's rage,   *For instance / cruel*
      Honour for wealth; and oft that wealth doth cost
      The death of all, and all together lost.

So that, in vent'ring ill,[2] we leave to be
The things we are for that which we expect,
150   And this ambitious foul infirmity
In having° much, torments us with defect   *While we have*
Of that we have; so then we do neglect
      The thing we have, and all for want of wit°   *lack of sense*
      Make something nothing by augmenting it.

155   Such hazard now must doting Tarquin make,
Pawning his honour to obtain his lust,
And for himself himself he must forsake.
Then where is truth if there be no self-trust?°   *truth to oneself*
When shall he think to find a stranger just
160   When he himself himself confounds, betrays
      To sland'rous tongues and wretched hateful days?

Now stole upon the time the dead of night
When heavy sleep had closed up mortal eyes.
No comfortable star did lend his° light,   *its*
165   No noise but owls' and wolves' death-boding cries
Now serves the season, that they may surprise
      The silly° lambs. Pure thoughts are dead and still,   *innocent*
      While lust and murder wakes to stain° and kill.   *defile*

---

7. The fact that his hopes are flimsy.   9. Be joined with it.
8. Despair of gaining her (rightfully) often encourages   1. That is, the ills that accompany excess.
him to gain her (by any means possible).   2. In taking serious risks; in undertaking evil deeds.

And now this lustful lord leapt from his bed,
170 Throwing his mantle rudely o'er his arm,
Is madly tossed between desire and dread.
Th'one sweetly flatters, th'other feareth harm,
But honest fear, bewitched with lust's foul charm,
    Doth too-too oft betake him to retire,°   *retreat*
175   Beaten away by brainsick rude desire.

His falchion° on a flint he softly smiteth,   *curved sword*
That from the cold stone sparks of fire do fly,
Whereat a waxen torch forthwith he lighteth,
Which must be lodestar° to his lustful eye,   *guiding light*
180 And to the flame thus speaks advisedly:°   *deliberately*
'As from this cold flint I enforced this fire,
So Lucrece must I force to my desire.'

Here pale with fear he doth premeditate
The dangers of his loathsome enterprise,
185 And in his inward mind he doth debate
What following sorrow may on this arise.
Then, looking scornfully, he doth despise
    His naked armour of still-slaughtered lust,[3]
    And justly thus controls° his thoughts unjust: *rebukes; restrains*

190 'Fair torch, burn out thy light, and lend it not
To darken her whose light excelleth thine;
And die, unhallowed thoughts, before you blot
With your uncleanness that which is divine.
Offer pure incense to so pure a shrine.
195   Let fair humanity abhor the deed
    That spots and stains love's modest snow-white weed.°   *attire (chastity)*

'O shame to knighthood and to shining arms!
O foul dishonour to my household's grave!°   *ancestral tomb*
O impious act including° all foul harms!   *encompassing*
200 A martial man to be soft fancy's° slave!   *love's*
True valour still a true respect[4] should have;
    Then my digression° is so vile, so base,   *error*
    That it will live engraven in my face.

'Yea, though I die the scandal will survive
205 And be an eyesore in my golden coat.°   *(of arms)*
Some loathsome dash[5] the herald will contrive
To cipher me how fondly° I did dote,   *To show how foolishly*
That my posterity, shamed with the note,°   *stigma*
    Shall curse my bones and hold it for no sin
210   To wish that I their father had not been.

'What win I if I gain the thing I seek?
A dream, a breath, a froth of fleeting joy.
Who buys a minute's mirth to wail a week,

---

3. His ineffective defense against his lust, always
quenched in the moment of fulfillment; his not-yet-erect
penis.

4. A suitable awareness of virtue.
5. Bar in a coat of arms, indicating a dishonorable
action by an ancestor.

Or sells eternity to get a toy?°   *trifle*
215   For one sweet grape who will the vine destroy?
     Or what fond beggar, but to touch the crown,
     Would with the sceptre straight be strucken down?

  'If Collatinus dream of my intent
  Will he not wake, and in a desp'rate rage
220   Post hither this vile purpose to prevent?—
  This siege that hath engirt° his marriage,   *surrounded*
  This blur° to youth, this sorrow to the sage,   *blot*
     This dying virtue, this surviving shame,
     Whose crime will bear an ever-during° blame.   *everlasting*

225   'O what excuse can my invention° make   *ingenuity*
  When thou shalt charge me with so black a deed?
  Will not my tongue be mute, my frail joints shake,
  Mine eyes forgo their light,° my false heart bleed?   *power of vision*
  The guilt being great, the fear doth still exceed,
230   And extreme fear can neither fight nor fly,
     But coward-like with trembling terror die.

  'Had Collatinus killed my son or sire,
  Or lain in ambush to betray my life,
  Or were he not my dear friend, this desire
235   Might have excuse to work upon his wife
  As in revenge or quittal° of such strife.   *requital*
     But as he is my kinsman, my dear friend,
     The shame and fault finds no excuse nor end.

  'Shameful it is—ay, if the fact° be known.   *deed*
240   Hateful it is—there is no hate in loving.
  I'll beg her love—but she is not her own.
  The worst is but denial and reproving;
243   My will is strong past reason's weak removing.
     Who fears a sentence° or an old man's saw°   *maxim / proverb*
245   Shall by a painted cloth be kept in awe.'⁶

  Thus graceless holds he disputation
  'Tween frozen conscience and hot-burning will,
  And with good thoughts makes dispensation,°   *dispenses*
  Urging the worser sense for vantage still;
250   Which in a moment doth confound and kill
     All pure effects,° and doth so far proceed   *tendencies*
     That what is vile shows like a virtuous deed.

  Quoth he, 'She took me kindly by the hand,
  And gazed for tidings in my eager eyes,
255   Fearing some hard news from the warlike band
  Where her belovèd Collatinus lies.
  O how her fear did make her colour rise!
     First red as roses that on lawn° we lay,   *fine linen*
     Then white as lawn, the roses took away.

---

6. Will be awed by a tapestry (often depicting morally significant narratives, as in lines 1366ff.).

260 'And how her hand, in my hand being locked,
      Forced it to tremble with her loyal fear,
      Which struck her sad, and then it faster rocked
      Until her husband's welfare she did hear,
      Whereat she smilèd with so sweet a cheer°   *an expression*
265   That had Narcissus[7] seen her as she stood
          Self-love had never drowned him in the flood.

'Why hunt I then for colour° or excuses?   *pretext*
All orators are dumb when beauty pleadeth.
Poor wretches have remorse in poor abuses;°   *regret minor lapses*
270 Love thrives not in the heart that shadows° dreadeth;   *illusory scruples*
Affection° is my captain, and he leadeth,   *Passion*
      And when his gaudy banner is displayed,
      The coward fights, and will not be dismayed.

'Then childish fear avaunt,° debating die,   *begone*
275 Respect° and reason wait on° wrinkled age!   *Circumspection / attend*
My heart shall never countermand mine eye,
Sad° pause and deep regard beseems the sage.   *Serious*
My part is youth, and beats these from the stage.[8]
      Desire my pilot is, beauty my prize.°   *pirate's booty*
280   Then who fears sinking where such treasure lies?'

As corn° o'ergrown by weeds, so heedful fear   *grain*
Is almost choked by unresisted lust.
Away he steals, with open list'ning ear,
Full of foul hope and full of fond° mistrust,   *foolish; passionate*
285 Both which as servitors to the unjust
      So cross him with their opposite persuasion
      That now he vows a league, and now invasion.

Within his thought her heavenly image sits,
And in the selfsame seat sits Collatine.
290 That eye which looks on her confounds his wits,
That eye which him beholds, as° more divine,   *because it is*
Unto a view so false will not incline,
      But with a pure appeal seeks° to the heart,   *applies*
      Which once corrupted, takes the worser part,

295 And therein heartens up his servile powers[9]
Who, flattered by their leader's jocund show,
Stuff up his lust as minutes fill up hours,
And as their captain, so their pride doth grow,
Paying more slavish tribute than they owe.[1]
300   By reprobate desire thus madly led
          The Roman lord marcheth to Lucrece' bed.

The locks between her chamber and his will,
Each one by him enforced, retires his ward;°   *withdraws its bolt*
But as they open they all rate° his ill,   *berate (by squeaking)*

---

7. In classical mythology, a youth who fell in love with his reflection in a pool; in some versions of the tale, he drowned attempting to kiss the image.
8. Like the Vice character in the medieval morality play.

9. Appetites or passions, imagined as servants of the heart, the seat of conscience.
1. That is, debasing themselves by collaborating and encouraging the corrupted heart.

305   Which drives the creeping thief to some regard.°   *caution*
       The threshold grates the door to have him heard,
           Night-wand'ring weasels[2] shriek to see him there.
           They fright him, yet he still pursues his fear.°   *what makes him fear*

       As each unwilling portal yields him way,
310   Through little vents and crannies of the place
       The wind wars with his torch to make him stay,
       And blows the smoke of it into his face,
       Extinguishing his conduct° in this case.   *guide; behavior*
           But his hot heart, which fond desire doth scorch,
315   Puffs forth another wind that fires the torch,

       And being lighted, by the light he spies
       Lucretia's glove wherein her needle sticks.
       He takes it from the rushes where it lies,
       And gripping it, the needle his finger pricks,
320   As who should say 'This glove to wanton tricks
           Is not inured. Return again in haste.
           Thou seest our mistress' ornaments are chaste.'

       But all these poor forbiddings could not stay him;
       He in the worst sense consters° their denial.   *construes*
325   The doors, the wind, the glove that did delay him
       He takes for accidental things of trial,°   *tests of resolve*
       Or as those bars which stop the hourly dial,[3]
           Who with a ling'ring stay his course doth let°   *hinder; permit*
           Till every minute pays the hour his debt.

330   'So, so,' quoth he, 'these lets attend the time,
       Like little frosts that sometime threat the spring
       To add a more rejoicing to the prime,°   *spring*
       And give the sneapèd° birds more cause to sing.   *pinched with cold*
       Pain pays the income° of each precious thing.   *is the price of*
335   Huge rocks, high winds, strong pirates, shelves,° and sands   *reefs*
           The merchant fears, ere rich at home he lands.'

       Now is he come unto the chamber door
       That shuts him from the heaven of his thought,
       Which with a yielding latch, and with no more,
340   Hath barred him from the blessèd thing he sought.
       So from° himself impiety hath wrought⌉   *unlike / made him*
           That for his prey to pray he doth begin,
           As if the heavens should countenance his sin.⌋

       But in the midst of his unfruitful prayer
345   Having solicited th'eternal power
       That his foul thoughts might compass° his fair fair,[4]   *obtain; embrace*
       And they would stand auspicious to the hour,
       Even there he starts.° Quoth he, 'I must deflower.⌉   *is startled*
           The powers to whom I pray abhor this fact;°   *deed*
350   How can they then assist me in the act?⌋

---

2. Weasels were kept to catch vermin.   before jerking forward.
3. The marks on a clock face, where the hands pause   4. His virtuous and beautiful one.

'Then love and fortune be my gods, my guide!
My will is backed with resolution.
Thoughts are but dreams till their effects be tried;
The blackest sin is cleared with absolution.
355 Against love's fire fear's frost hath dissolution.
    The eye of heaven is out,° and misty night   *extinguished*
    Covers the shame that follows sweet delight.'

This said, his guilty hand plucked up the latch,
And with his knee the door he opens wide.
360 \ The dove sleeps fast that this night-owl will catch.
Thus treason works ere traitors be espied.
Who sees the lurking serpent steps aside,
    But she, sound sleeping, fearing no such thing,
    Lies at the mercy of his mortal° sting.   *lethal*

365 Into the chamber wickedly he stalks,°   *steals*
And gazeth on her yet-unstainèd bed.
The curtains being close,° about he walks,   *shut*
Rolling his greedy eye-balls in his head.
By their high treason is his heart misled,
370   Which gives the watchword to his hand full soon
    To draw the cloud° that hides the silver moon.   *(the bed curtain)*

Look as° the fair and fiery-pointed sun   *See how*
Rushing from forth a cloud bereaves our sight,
Even so, the curtain drawn, his eyes begun
375 To wink,° being blinded with a greater light.   *close*
Whether it is that she reflects so bright
    That dazzleth them, or else some shame supposed,
    But blind they are, and keep themselves enclosed.

O had they in that darksome prison died,
380 Then had they seen the period° of their ill.   *end*
Then Collatine again by Lucrece' side
In his clear° bed might have reposèd still.   *undefiled*
But they must ope, this blessèd league° to kill,   *marriage*
    And holy-thoughted Lucrece to their sight
385   Must sell her joy, her life, her world's delight.

Her lily hand her rosy cheek lies under,
Coz'ning° the pillow of a lawful kiss,   *Cheating*
Who therefore angry seems to part in sunder,°   *in two*
Swelling on either side to want his bliss;⁵
390 Between whose hills her head entombèd is,
    Where like a virtuous monument she lies
    To be admired of lewd unhallowed eyes.

Without the bed her other fair hand was,
On the green coverlet, whose perfect white
395 Showed like an April daisy on the grass,
With pearly sweat resembling dew of night.

5. Because it is denied its pleasure (of her lips touching its surface).

Her eyes like marigolds[6] had sheathed their light,
    And canopied in darkness sweetly lay
    Till they might open to adorn the day.

400 Her hair like golden threads played with her breath—
    O modest wantons, wanton modesty!—
    Showing life's triumph in the map° of death,   *image*
    And death's dim look in life's mortality.
    Each° in her sleep themselves so beautify   *(life and death)*
405   As if between them twain there were no strife,
       But that life lived in death, and death in life.

    Her breasts like ivory globes circled with blue,
    A pair of maiden[7] worlds unconquerèd,
    Save of their lord no bearing yoke they knew,
410   And him by oath they truly honourèd.
    These worlds in Tarquin new ambition bred,
       Who like a foul usurper went about
       From this fair throne to heave the owner out.

    What could he see but mightily he noted?
415   What did he note but strongly he desired?
    What he beheld, on that he firmly doted,
    And in his will° his wilful eye he tired.[8]   *lust*
    With more than admiration he admired
       Her azure veins, her alabaster skin,
420   Her coral lips, her snow-white dimpled chin.

    As the grim lion fawneth° o'er his prey,   *shows delight*
    Sharp hunger by the conquest satisfied,
    So o'er this sleeping soul doth Tarquin stay,
    His rage of lust by gazing qualified,°   *mollified*
425   Slaked not suppressed for standing by her side.
       His eye which late this mutiny restrains
       Unto a greater uproar tempts his veins,

    And they like straggling slaves° for pillage fighting,   *lowborn soldiers*
    Obdurate vassals fell° exploits effecting,   *fierce*
430 In bloody death and ravishment delighting,
    Nor children's tears nor mothers' groans respecting,
    Swell in their pride, the onset still° expecting.   *at any moment*
       Anon his beating heart, alarum° striking,   *signal to attack*
       Gives the hot charge, and bids them do their liking.

435 His drumming heart cheers up his burning eye,
    His eye commends° the leading to his hand.   *entrusts*
    His hand, as proud of such a dignity,
    Smoking with pride marched on to make his stand
    On her bare breast, the heart of all her land,
440   Whose ranks of blue veins as his hand did scale°   *climb*
       Left their round turrets destitute and pale.

6. The pot marigold folds up its flowers at day's end.   8. Wearied; fed greedily (as a hawk tears flesh with its
7. Used of an unconquered citadel.   beak).

They, must'ring° to the quiet cabinet°   *gathering / room (heart)*
Where their dear governess° and lady lies,   *ruler*
Do tell her she is dreadfully beset,
445 And fright her with confusion of their cries.
She much amazed breaks ope her locked-up eyes,
    Who, peeping forth this tumult to behold,
    Are by his flaming torch dimmed and controlled.°   *overwhelmed*

Imagine her as one in dead of night
450 From forth dull sleep by dreadful fancy waking,
That thinks she hath beheld some ghastly sprite
Whose grim aspect sets every joint a-shaking.
What terror 'tis! But she in worser taking,°   *plight*
    From sleep disturbèd, heedfully doth view
455   The sight which makes supposèd terror true.

Wrapped and confounded in a thousand fears,
Like to a new-killed bird she trembling lies.
She dares not look, yet, winking,° there appears   *shutting her eyes*
Quick-shifting antics,° ugly in her eyes.   *grotesque shapes*
460 Such shadows are the weak brain's forgeries,
    Who, angry that the eyes fly from their lights,
    In darkness daunts them with more dreadful sights.

His hand that yet remains upon her breast—
Rude ram,° to batter such an ivory wall—   *battering ram*
465 May feel her heart, poor citizen, distressed,
Wounding itself to death, rise up and fall,
Beating her bulk,° that his hand shakes withal.°   *chest / as well*
    This moves in him more rage and lesser pity
    To make the breach and enter this sweet city.

470 First like a trumpet doth his tongue begin
To sound a parley⁹ to his heartless° foe,   *terrified*
Who o'er the white sheet peers her whiter chin,
The reason of this rash alarm to know,
Which he by dumb demeanour° seeks to show.   *mute gesture*
475   But she with vehement prayers urgeth still
    Under what colour° he commits this ill.   *pretext*

Thus he replies: 'The colour in thy face,
That even for anger makes the lily pale
And the red rose blush at her own disgrace,
480 Shall plead for me and tell my loving tale.
Under that colour° am I come to scale   *pretext; hue; flag*
    Thy never-conquered fort. The fault is thine,
    For those thine eyes betray thee unto mine.

'Thus I forestall thee, if thou mean to chide:
485 Thy beauty hath ensnared thee to this night,
Where thou with patience must my will abide,
My will that marks thee for my earth's° delight,   *earthly; bodily*
Which I to conquer sought with all my might.

9. A call to a negotiation.

But as reproof and reason beat it° dead,   *(my lust)*
490   By thy bright beauty was it newly bred.

'I see what crosses° my attempt will bring,   *misfortunes*
I know what thorns the growing rose defends;
I think° the honey guarded with a sting;   *know*
All this beforehand counsel° comprehends.   *wisdom*
495   But will is deaf, and hears no heedful friends.
     Only he hath an eye to gaze on beauty,
     And dotes on what he looks, 'gainst law or duty.

'I have debated even in my soul
What wrong, what shame, what sorrow I shall breed;
500   But nothing can affection's° course control,   *passion's*
Or stop the headlong fury of his speed.
I know repentant tears ensue° the deed,   *follow*
     Reproach, disdain, and deadly enmity,
     Yet strive I to embrace mine infamy.'

505   This said, he shakes aloft his Roman blade,
Which like a falcon tow'ring in the skies
  Coucheth the fowl° below with his wings' shade   *Makes the prey crouch*
Whose crooked beak threats, if he° mount he dies.   *(the fowl)*
So under his insulting° falchion lies   *triumphantly exulting*
510   Harmless Lucretia, marking what he tells
     With trembling fear, as fowl hear falcons' bells.[1]

'Lucrece,' quoth he, 'this night I must enjoy thee.
If thou deny, then force must work my way,
For in thy bed I purpose to destroy thee.
515   That done, some worthless slave of thine I'll slay
To kill thine honour with thy life's decay;[2]
     And in thy dead arms do I mean to place him,
     Swearing I slew him seeing thee embrace him.

'So thy surviving husband shall remain
520   The scornful mark of every open eye,°   *observer*
Thy kinsmen hang their heads at this disdain,
Thy issue blurred with nameless bastardy,[3]
And thou, the author of their obloquy,
     Shalt have thy trespass cited up in rhymes°   *described in ballads*
525   And sung by children in succeeding times.

'But if thou yield, I rest thy secret friend.
The fault unknown is as a thought unacted.
A little harm done to a great good end
For lawful policy remains enacted.[4]
530   The poisonous simple° sometime is compacted°   *ingredient / mixed*
     In a pure° compound; being so applied,   *benign*
     His venom in effect is purified.

---

1. Hunting falcons had bells attached to their legs.
2. To destroy your reputation along with your life.
3. Your children suspected of being bastards whose father's name is unknown.
4. *For . . . enacted*: Is allowed as proper statesmanship.

'Then for thy husband and thy children's sake
Tender my suit;° bequeath not to their lot   *Regard my plea*
535 The shame that from them no device⁵ can take,
The blemish that will never be forgot,
Worse than a slavish wipe or birth-hour's blot;⁶
 For marks descried in men's nativity
 Are nature's faults, not their own infamy.'

540 Here with a cockatrice'⁷ dead-killing eye
He rouseth up himself, and makes a pause,
While she, the picture of pure piety,
Like a white hind° under the gripe's° sharp claws,   *doe / griffin*
Pleads in a wilderness where are no laws
545   To the rough beast that knows no gentle right,°   *law of gentility*
 Nor aught obeys but his foul appetite.

But when a black-faced cloud the world doth threat,
In his dim mist th'aspiring mountains hiding,
From earth's dark womb some gentle gust doth get
550 Which blows these pitchy vapours from their biding,°   *place*
Hind'ring their present° fall by this dividing;   *immediate*
 So his unhallowed haste her words delays,
 And moody Pluto winks while Orpheus plays.⁸

555 Yet, foul night-waking cat, he doth but dally
While in his holdfast foot the weak mouse panteth.
Her sad behaviour feeds his vulture folly,°   *ravenous insanity*
A swallowing gulf° that even in plenty wanteth.   *whirlpool; belly*
His ear her prayers admits, but his heart granteth
 No penetrable entrance to her plaining.°   *lament*
560   Tears harden lust, though marble wear with raining.

Her pity-pleading eyes are sadly fixed
In the remorseless wrinkles of his face.
Her modest eloquence with sighs is mixed,
Which to her oratory adds more grace.
565 She puts the period often from his° place,   *its*
 And midst the sentence so her accent breaks
 That twice she doth begin ere once she speaks.

She conjures him by high almighty Jove,
By knighthood, gentry,° and sweet friendship's oath,   *noble birth*
570 By her untimely tears, her husband's love,
By holy human law and common troth,⁹
By heaven and earth and all the power of both,
 That to his borrowed° bed he make retire,   *(guest)*
 And stoop¹ to honour, not to foul desire.

---

5. Ingenuity; heraldic emblem.
6. A slave's brand or birthmark.
7. Legendary monster whose glance was deadly.
8. When Orpheus, a legendary musician and poet, attempted to regain his dead wife from the underworld, he charmed Pluto, god of the underworld, by playing on the lyre.
9. *common troth*: the good faith that binds communities together.
1. Swoop down to a lure (in falconry); lie down; subject himself.

575 Quoth she, 'Reward not hospitality
  With such black payment as thou hast pretended.°   *offered*
  Mud not the fountain that gave drink to thee;
  Mar not the thing that cannot be amended;
  End thy ill aim before thy shoot be ended.
580   He is no woodman° that doth bend his bow   *sportsman*
    To strike a poor unseasonable° doe.   *out-of-season*

  'My husband is thy friend; for his sake spare me.
  Thyself art mighty; for thine own sake leave me;
  Myself a weakling; do not then ensnare me.
585 Thou look'st not like deceit; do not deceive me.
  My sighs like whirlwinds labour hence to heave thee.
    If ever man were moved with woman's moans,
    Be movèd with my tears, my sighs, my groans.

  'All which together, like a troubled ocean,
590 Beat at thy rocky and wreck-threat'ning heart
  To soften it with their continual motion,
  For stones dissolved to water do convert.
    O, if no harder than a stone thou art,
    Melt at my tears, and be compassionate.
595   Soft pity enters at an iron gate.

  'In Tarquin's likeness I did entertain thee.
  Hast thou put on his shape to do him shame?
  To all the host of heaven I complain me.
  Thou wrong'st his honour, wound'st his princely name.
600   Thou art not what thou seem'st, and if the same,
    Thou seem'st not what thou art, a god, a king,
    For kings like gods should govern everything.

  'How will thy shame be seeded° in thine age   *ripened*
  When thus thy vices bud before thy spring?
605 If in thy hope° thou dar'st do such outrage,   *If not yet in power*
  What dar'st thou not when once thou art a king?
  O be remembered, no outrageous thing
    From vassal actors° can be wiped away;   *lowborn criminals*
    Then kings' misdeeds cannot be hid in clay.°   *(even after death)*

610 'This deed will make thee only loved for° fear,   *obeyed out of*
  But happy monarchs still° are feared for love.   *always*
  With foul offenders thou perforce must bear
  When they in thee the like offences prove.
  If but for fear of this, thy will remove;
615   For princes are the glass,° the school, the book   *mirror*
    Where subjects' eyes do learn, do read, do look.

  'And wilt thou be the school where lust shall learn?
  Must he in thee read lectures of such shame?
  Wilt thou be glass wherein it shall discern
620 Authority for sin, warrant for blame,
  To privilege° dishonour in thy name?   *justify*
    Thou back'st° reproach against long-living laud,°   *support / praise*
    And mak'st fair reputation but a bawd.

'Hast thou command?° By him° that gave it thee,   *authority / (God)*
625 From a pure heart command thy rebel will.
Draw not thy sword to guard iniquity,
For it was lent thee all that brood° to kill.   *kind of thing*
Thy princely office how canst thou fulfil
    When, patterned° by thy fault, foul sin may say   *given a precedent*
630   He learned to sin, and thou didst teach the way?

'Think but how vile a spectacle it were
To view thy present trespass in another.
Men's faults do seldom to themselves appear;
Their own transgressions partially they smother.°   *hide (from themselves)*
635 This guilt would seem death-worthy in thy brother.
    O, how are they wrapped in with infamies
    That from their own misdeeds askance° their eyes!   *turn away*

'To thee, to thee my heaved-up hands appeal,
Not to seducing lust, thy rash relier.[2]
640 I sue for exiled majesty's repeal;°   *recall from exile*
Let him return, and flatt'ring thoughts retire.
His true respect° will prison false desire,   *judgment*
    And wipe the dim mist from thy doting eyne,°   *eyes (archaic)*
    That thou shalt see thy state, and pity mine.'

645 'Have done,' quoth he; 'my uncontrollèd tide
Turns not, but swells the higher by this let.°   *restraint*
Small lights are soon blown out; huge fires abide,
And with the wind in greater fury fret.
The petty streams, that pay a daily debt
650   To their salt sovereign,° with their fresh falls' haste   *(the sea)*
    Add to his flow, but alter not his taste.'

'Thou art,' quoth she, 'a sea, a sovereign king,
And lo, there falls into thy boundless flood
Black lust, dishonour, shame, misgoverning,
655 Who seek to stain the ocean of thy blood.°   *disposition; birthright*
If all these petty ills shall change thy good,
    Thy sea within a puddle's womb is hearsed,°   *enclosed*
    And not the puddle in thy sea dispersed.

'So shall these slaves° be king, and thou their slave;   *(lust, dishonor, etc.)*
660 Thou nobly base, they basely dignified;
Thou their fair life, and they thy fouler grave;
Thou loathèd in their shame, they in thy pride.
The lesser thing should not the greater hide.
    The cedar stoops not to the base shrub's foot,
665   But low shrubs wither at the cedar's root.

'So let thy thoughts, low vassals to thy state'—
'No more,' quoth he, 'by heaven, I will not hear thee.
Yield to my love. If not, enforcèd hate
Instead of love's coy° touch shall rudely tear thee.   *gentle*
670 That done, despitefully° I mean to bear thee   *maliciously*

2. *thy rash relier:* on which you rashly rely.

Unto the base bed of some rascal groom°   servant
To be thy partner in this shameful doom.'

This said, he sets his foot upon the light;
For light and lust are deadly enemies.
675   Shame folded up in blind concealing night
When most unseen, then most doth tyrannize.
The wolf hath seized his prey, the poor lamb cries,
   Till with her own white fleece° her voice controlled°   (bedclothes) / overpowered
   Entombs her outcry in her lips' sweet fold.°   crevice; sheep pen

680   For with the nightly linen that she wears
He pens her piteous clamours in her head,
Cooling his hot face in the chastest tears
That ever modest eyes with sorrow shed.
O that prone° lust should stain so pure a bed,   headlong; eager
685   The spots whereof could weeping purify,
   Her tears should drop on them perpetually!

But she hath lost a dearer thing than life,
And he hath won what he would lose again.
This forcèd league doth force a further strife,
690   This momentary joy breeds months of pain;
This hot desire converts to cold disdain.
   Pure chastity is rifled of her store,
   And lust, the thief, far poorer than before.

Look° as the full-fed hound or gorgèd hawk,   Just
695   Unapt for tender° smell or speedy flight,   delicate
Make slow pursuit, or altogether balk°   turn from
The prey wherein by nature they delight,
So surfeit-taking Tarquin fares° this night.   behaves; feeds
   His taste delicious, in digestion souring,
700   Devours his will that lived by foul devouring.

O deeper sin than bottomless conceit°   unlimited fantasy
Can comprehend in still imagination!
Drunken desire must vomit his receipt°   what he swallowed
Ere he can see his own abomination.
705   While lust is in his pride, no exclamation
   Can curb his heat or rein his rash desire,
   Till like a jade° self-will himself doth tire.   recalcitrant horse

And then with lank and lean discoloured cheek,
With heavy eye, knit brow, and strengthless pace,
710   Feeble desire, all recreant,[3] poor, and meek,
Like to a bankrupt beggar wails his case.
The flesh being proud, desire doth fight with grace,
   For there it revels, and when that decays,°   subsides
   The guilty rebel for remission° prays.   pardon

715   So fares it with this faultful lord of Rome
Who this accomplishment so hotly chased;

3. Cowardly; faithless; exhausted.

For now against himself he sounds° this doom,°   *pronounces / sentence*
That through the length of times he stands disgraced.
Besides, his soul's fair temple is defaced,
720   To whose weak ruins muster troops of cares
          To ask the spotted princess° how she fares.   *(the defiled soul)*

She says her subjects with foul insurrection
Have battered down her consecrated wall,
And by their mortal° fault brought in subjection   *deadly*
725   Her immortality, and made her thrall
To living death and pain perpetual,
          Which° in her prescience she controllèd still,   *(the soul's subjects)*
          But her foresight could not forestall their will.

Ev'n in this thought through the dark night he stealeth,
730   A captive victor that hath lost in gain,
Bearing away the wound that nothing healeth,
The scar that will, despite of cure, remain;
Leaving his spoil° perplexed in greater pain.   *prey*
          She bears the load of lust he left behind,
735   And he the burden of a guilty mind.

He like a thievish dog creeps sadly thence;
She like a wearied lamb lies panting there.
He scowls, and hates himself for his offence;
She, desperate, with her nails her flesh doth tear.
740   He faintly flies, sweating with guilty fear;
          She stays, exclaiming on° the direful night.   *denouncing*
          He runs, and chides his vanished loathed delight.

He thence departs, a heavy convertite;°   *sad penitent*
She there remains, a hopeless castaway.
745   He in his speed looks for the morning light;
          She prays she never may behold the day.
          'For day,' quoth she, 'night's scapes° doth open lay,   *sins*
          And my true eyes have never practised how
          To cloak offences with a cunning brow.

750   'They think not but that every eye can see
The same disgrace which they themselves behold,
And therefore would they still in darkness be,
To have their unseen sin remain untold.
For they their guilt with weeping will unfold,
755   And grave,° like water that doth eat in steel,[4]   *engrave*
          Upon my cheeks what helpless shame I feel.'

Here she exclaims against repose and rest,
And bids her eyes hereafter still be blind.
She wakes her heart by beating on her breast,
760   And bids it leap from thence where it may find
Some purer chest to close° so pure a mind.   *enclose*
          Frantic with grief, thus breathes she forth her spite°   *reproach*
          Against the unseen secrecy of night:

4. Aqua fortis (literally, "strong water"), nitric acid.

'O comfort-killing night, image of hell,
765   Dim register° and notary of shame,   *recorder*
  Black stage for tragedies and murders fell,
  Vast sin-concealing chaos, nurse of blame!
  Blind muffled bawd, dark harbour for defame,°   *infamy*
    Grim cave of death, whisp'ring conspirator
770   With close-tongued treason and the ravisher!

'O hateful, vaporous, and foggy night,
  Since thou art guilty of my cureless crime,
  Muster thy mists to meet the eastern light,
  Make war against proportioned° course of time.   *orderly*
775   Or if thou wilt permit the sun to climb
    His wonted height, yet ere he go to bed
    Knit poisonous clouds about his golden head.

'With rotten damps° ravish the morning air,   *vapors*
  Let their exhaled unwholesome breaths make sick
780   The life of purity, the supreme fair,°   *(the sun)*
  Ere he arrive his weary noon-tide prick;°   *mark on a clock*
  And let thy musty vapours march so thick
    That in their smoky ranks his smothered light
    May set at noon, and make perpetual night.

785   'Were Tarquin night, as he is but night's child,
  The silver-shining queen[5] he would distain;°   *stain*
  Her twinkling handmaids° too, by him defiled,   *(the stars)*
  Through night's black bosom should not peep again.
790   So should I have co-partners in my pain,
    And fellowship in woe doth woe assuage,
    As palmers'° chat makes short their pilgrimage.   *pilgrims'*

'Where now I have no one to blush with me,
  To cross their arms[6] and hang their heads with mine,
  To mask their brows and hide their infamy,
795   But I alone, alone must sit and pine,
  Seasoning the earth with showers of silver brine,
    Mingling my talk with tears, my grief with groans,
    Poor wasting monuments° of lasting moans.   *short-lived tokens*

'O night, thou furnace of foul reeking smoke,
800   Let not the jealous° day behold that face   *suspicious*
  Which underneath thy black all-hiding cloak
  Immodestly lies martyred with disgrace!
  Keep still possession of thy gloomy place,
    That all the faults which in thy reign are made
805   May likewise be sepulchred in thy shade.

'Make me not object° to the tell-tale day: *manifest*
  The light will show charactered° in my brow   *written*
  The story of sweet chastity's decay,
  The impious breach of holy wedlock vow.
810   Yea, the illiterate that know not how

---

5. The moon, symbol of chastity.   6. This is a conventional gesture of melancholy.

To cipher° what is writ in learnèd books   *decipher*
Will quote° my loathsome trespass in my looks.   *note*

'The nurse to still her child will tell my story,
And fright her crying babe with Tarquin's name.
815 The orator to deck his oratory
Will couple my reproach to Tarquin's shame.
Feast-finding minstrels⁷ tuning my defame
   Will tie the hearers to attend° each line,   *listen to*
   How Tarquin wrongèd me, I Collatine.

820 ⌠'Let my good name, that senseless° reputation,   *intangible*
  │For Collatine's dear love be kept unspotted;
  │If that be made a theme for disputation,
  │The branches of another root are rotted,⁸
  │And undeserved reproach to him allotted
825 │   That is as clear from this attaint° of mine   *stain*
  ⌞   As I ere this was pure to Collatine.

'O unseen shame, invisible disgrace!
O unfelt sore, crest-wounding⁹ private scar!
Reproach° is stamped in Collatinus' face,   *Reproof; dishonor*
830 And Tarquin's eye may read the mot° afar,   *motto*
How he in peace is wounded, not in war.
   Alas, how many bear such shameful blows,
   Which not themselves but he that gives them knows!

'If, Collatine, thine honour lay in me,
835 From me by strong assault it is bereft;
My honey lost, and I, a drone-like bee,
Have no perfection of my summer left,¹
But robbed and ransacked by injurious theft.
   In thy weak hive a wandering wasp hath crept,
840   And sucked the honey which thy chaste bee kept.

'Yet am I guilty of thy honour's wrack;°   *ruin*
Yet for thy honour did I entertain him.
Coming from thee, I could not put him back,
For it had been dishonour to disdain him.
845 Besides, of weariness he did complain him,
   And talked of virtue—O unlooked-for evil,
   When virtue is profaned in such a devil!

'Why should the worm intrude the maiden bud,
Or hateful cuckoos hatch in sparrows' nests,
850 Or toads infect fair founts with venom° mud,   *venomous*
Or tyrant folly° lurk in gentle breasts,   *cruel lewdness*
Or kings be breakers of their own behests?°   *commands*
   But no perfection is so absolute
   That some impurity doth not pollute.

---

7. Minstrels were paid to perform at banquets.   lines 204–10).
8. That is, Collatine's reputation is also destroyed.   1. Have nothing left of what I made in the summer;
9. Damaging the coat of arms, hence family honor (cf.   have none of the purity of my prime remaining.

855 'The agèd man that coffers up his gold
Is plagued with cramps, and gouts, and painful fits,
And scarce hath eyes his treasure to behold,
But like still-pining Tantalus[2] he sits,
And useless barns° the harvest of his wits,   hoards
860   Having no other pleasure of his gain
        But torment that it cannot cure his pain.

'So then he hath it when he cannot use it,
And leaves it to be mastered° by his young,°   possessed / children
Who in their pride do presently° abuse it.   immediately
865 Their father was too weak and they too strong
To hold their cursèd-blessèd fortune long.
        The sweets we wish for turn to loathèd sours
        Even in the moment that we call them ours.

'Unruly blasts wait on the tender spring,
870 Unwholesome weeds take root with precious flowers,
The adder hisses where the sweet birds sing,
What virtue breeds, iniquity devours.
We have no good that we can say is ours
        But ill-annexèd opportunity[3]
875   Or° kills his life or else his quality.   Either

'O opportunity, thy guilt is great!
'Tis thou that execut'st the traitor's treason;
Thou sets the wolf where he the lamb may get;
Whoever plots the sin, thou point'st° the season.   appoint
880 'Tis thou that spurn'st at right, at law, at reason;
        And in thy shady cell where none may spy him
        Sits sin, to seize the souls that wander by him.

'Thou mak'st the vestal[4] violate her oath,
Thou blow'st the fire when temperance is thawed,
885 Thou smother'st honesty, thou murd'rest troth,
Thou foul abettor, thou notorious bawd;°   procurer
Thou plantest scandal and displacest laud.
        Thou ravisher, thou traitor, thou false thief,
        Thy honey turns to gall, thy joy to grief.

890 'Thy secret pleasure turns to open shame,
Thy private feasting to a public fast,
Thy smoothing° titles to a ragged name,   flattering
Thy sugared tongue to bitter wormwood taste.
Thy violent vanities can never last.
895   How comes it then, vile opportunity,
        Being so bad, such numbers seek for thee?

'When wilt thou be the humble suppliant's friend,
And bring him where his suit may be obtained?
When wilt thou sort° an hour great strifes to end,   select

---

2. A mythological figure who was punished in Hades by
eternal hunger and thirst; food and water were always
visible but receded at his approach.
3. Bad circumstances joined to or following from the
good.
4. The priestess of Vesta, Roman goddess of the hearth
and household; vestals were sworn to lifelong virginity.

900 Or free that soul which wretchedness hath chained,
Give physic° to the sick, ease to the pained?   *medicine*
  The poor, lame, blind, halt,° creep, cry out for thee,   *limp*
  But they ne'er meet with opportunity.

'The patient dies while the physician sleeps,
905 The orphan pines while the oppressor feeds,
Justice is feasting while the widow weeps,
Advice° is sporting while infection breeds.   *(medical advice)*
Thou grant'st no time for charitable deeds.
  Wrath, envy, treason, rape, and murder's rages,
910 Thy heinous hours wait on them as their pages.

'When truth and virtue have to do with thee
A thousand crosses° keep them from thy aid.   *impediments*
They buy° thy help, but sin ne'er gives a fee;   *(must pay for)*
He gratis comes, and thou art well appaid°   *satisfied*
915 As well to hear as grant what he hath said.
  My Collatine would else have come to me
  When Tarquin did, but he was stayed by thee.

'Guilty thou art of murder and of theft,
Guilty of perjury and subornation,[5]
920 Guilty of treason, forgery, and shift,°   *fraud*
Guilty of incest, that abomination:
An accessory by thine inclination°   *nature*
  To all sins past and all that are to come
  From the creation to the general doom.

925 'Misshapen time, copesmate° of ugly night,   *comrade*
Swift subtle post,° carrier of grisly care,   *messenger*
Eater of youth, false slave to false delight,
Base watch° of woes, sin's pack-horse, virtue's snare,   *town crier; announcer*
Thou nursest all, and murd'rest all that are.
930 O hear me then, injurious shifting° time;   *changing; traitorous*
  Be guilty of my death, since° of my crime.   *as thou art*

'Why hath thy servant opportunity
Betrayed the hours thou gav'st me to repose,
Cancelled my fortunes, and enchainèd me
935 To endless date° of never-ending woes?   *duration*
Time's office is to fine° the hate of foes,   *end; punish*
  To eat up errors by opinion° bred,   *rumor*
  Not spend the dowry of a lawful bed.

'Time's glory is to calm contending kings,
940 To unmask falsehood and bring truth to light,
To stamp the seal of time in agèd things,
To wake the morn and sentinel° the night,   *guard*
To wrong the wronger till he render right,
  To ruinate proud buildings with thy hours
945 And smear with dust their glitt'ring golden towers;

5. Bribing others to give false testimony.

'To fill with worm-holes stately monuments,
To feed oblivion with decay of things,
To blot old books and alter their contents,
To pluck the quills from ancient ravens' wings,
950   To dry the old oak's sap and blemish° springs,   *contaminate*
     To spoil antiquities of hammered steel,
     And turn the giddy round of fortune's wheel;

'To show the beldame° daughters of her daughter,   *old woman*
To make the child a man, the man a child,
955 To slay the tiger that doth live by slaughter,
To tame the unicorn and lion wild,
  To mock the subtle in themselves beguiled,[6]
     To cheer the ploughman with increaseful crops,
     And waste huge stones with little water drops.

960 'Why work'st thou mischief in thy pilgrimage,
Unless thou couldst return to make amends?
One poor retiring[7] minute in an age
Would purchase thee a thousand thousand friends,
Lending him wit that to bad debtors lends.
965   O this dread night, wouldst thou one hour come back
     I could prevent this storm and shun thy wrack!

'Thou ceaseless lackey° to eternity,   *eternal servant*
With some mischance cross Tarquin in his flight.
Devise extremes beyond extremity
970 To make him curse this cursèd crimeful night.
Let ghastly shadows his lewd eyes affright,
     And the dire thought of his committed evil
     Shape every bush a hideous shapeless devil.

'Disturb his hours of rest with restless trances;°   *dreams; seizures*
975 Afflict him in his bed with bedrid groans;
Let there bechance him pitiful mischances
To make him moan, but pity not his moans.
Stone him with hardened hearts harder than stones,
     And let mild women to him lose their mildness,
980   Wilder to him than tigers in their wildness.

'Let him have time to tear his curlèd hair,
Let him have time against himself to rave,
Let him have time of time's help to despair,
Let him have time to live a loathèd slave,
985   Let him have time a beggar's orts° to crave,   *scraps*
     And time to see one that by alms doth live
     Disdain to him disdainèd scraps to give.

'Let him have time to see his friends his foes,
And merry fools to mock at him resort.°   *gather*
990 Let him have time to mark how slow time goes
In time of sorrow, and how swift and short

---

6. The cunning, taken in by their own schemes.
7. Returning (thus permitting people to do things differently).

His time of folly and his time of sport;
    And ever let his unrecalling crime[8]
    Have time to wail th'abusing of his time.

995 'O time, thou tutor both to good and bad,
Teach me to curse him that thou taught'st this ill;
At his own shadow let the thief run mad,
Himself himself seek every hour to kill;
Such wretched hands such wretched blood should spill,
1000   For who so base would such an office have
    As sland'rous deathsman° to so base a slave?   *detested executioner*

'The baser is he, coming from a king,
To shame his hope with deeds degenerate.
The mightier man, the mightier is the thing
1005 That makes him honoured or begets him hate,
For greatest scandal waits on greatest state.[9]
    The moon being clouded presently° is missed,   *immediately*
    But little stars may hide them when they list.°   *wish*

'The crow may bathe his coal-black wings in mire
1010 And unperceived fly with the filth away,
But if the like the snow-white swan desire,
The stain upon his silver down will stay.
Poor grooms° are sightless° night, kings glorious day.   *servants / dark*
    Gnats are unnoted wheresoe'er they fly,
1015   But eagles gazed upon with every eye.

'Out, idle words, servants to shallow fools,
Unprofitable sounds, weak arbitrators!
Busy yourselves in skill-contending schools,°   *(of rhetoric)*
Debate where leisure serves with dull debaters,
1020   For me, I force° not argument a straw,   *value*
    Since that my case is past the help of law.

'In vain I rail at opportunity,
At time, at Tarquin, and uncheerful night.
1025 In vain I cavil with° mine infamy,   *object to*
In vain I spurn at my confirmed despite.°   *irreparable injury*
This helpless° smoke of words doth me no right;   *unhelpful; weak*
    The remedy indeed to do me good
    Is to let forth my foul defilèd blood.

1030 'Poor hand, why quiver'st thou at this decree?
Honour thyself to rid me of this shame,
For if I die, my honour lives in thee,
But if I live, thou liv'st in my defame.°   *infamy*
Since thou couldst not defend thy loyal dame,
1035   And wast afeard to scratch her wicked foe,
    Kill both thyself and her for yielding so.'

8. Crime that cannot be undone.   9. Attends those of highest rank.

This said, from her betumbled couch she starteth,
To find some desp'rate instrument of death.
But this, no slaughterhouse, no tool imparteth°   *furnishes*
1040 To make more vent° for passage of her breath,   *a bigger hole*
Which thronging through her lips so vanisheth
   As smoke from Etna that in air consumes,
   Or that which from dischargèd cannon fumes.

'In vain,' quoth she, 'I live, and seek in vain
1045 Some happy mean to end a hapless life.
I feared by Tarquin's falchion to be slain,
Yet for the selfsame purpose seek a knife.
But when I feared I was a loyal wife;
   So am I now—O no, that cannot be,
1050   Of that true type° hath Tarquin rifled me.   *pattern of virtue*

'O, that is gone for which I sought to live,
And therefore now I need not fear to die.
To clear this spot by death, at least I give
A badge of fame to slander's livery,°   *servant's uniform*
1055 A dying life to living infamy.
   Poor helpless help, the treasure stol'n away,
   To burn the guiltless casket where it lay!

'Well, well, dear Collatine, thou shalt not know
The stainèd taste of violated troth.
1060 I will not wrong thy true affection so
To flatter thee with an infringèd oath.
This bastard graft[1] shall never come to growth.
   He shall not boast, who did thy stock pollute,
   That thou art doting father of his fruit,

1065 'Nor shall he smile at thee in secret thought,
Nor laugh with his companions at thy state.
But thou shalt know thy int'rest° was not bought   *property*
Basely with gold, but stol'n from forth thy gate.
For me, I am the mistress of my fate,
1070   And with my trespass never will dispense°   *dispense with = excuse*
   Till life to death acquit° my forced offence.   *atone for*

'I will not poison thee with my attaint,°   *contamination*
Nor fold° my fault in cleanly coined excuses.   *envelop*
My sable ground[2] of sin I will not paint
1075 To hide the truth of this false night's abuses.
My tongue shall utter all; mine eyes, like sluices,
   As from a mountain spring that feeds a dale
   Shall gush pure streams to purge my impure tale.'

1080 By this, lamenting Philomel[3] had ended
The well-tuned warble of her nightly sorrow,

---

1. Lucrece assumes that Tarquin has made her pregnant. Her image is from the grafting of plants, in which
two different kinds of plants are artificially forced to
grow as one; a "bastard slip" is an unwanted shoot.
2. Black background (a heraldic term).

3. The nightingale. In classical mythology, Philomela
was raped by King Tereus, her sister's husband, and
with her sister took vengeance on him. All three were
changed into birds (see Ovid, *Metamorphoses* 6).

And solemn night with slow sad gait descended
To ugly hell, when lo, the blushing morrow
Lends light to all fair eyes that light will borrow.
    But cloudy° Lucrece shames° herself to see,   *melancholy / is ashamed*
1085   And therefore still in night would cloistered be.

Revealing day through every cranny spies,
And seems to point her out where she sits weeping;
To whom she sobbing speaks, 'O eye of eyes,
Why pry'st thou through my window? Leave thy peeping,
1090   Mock with thy tickling beams eyes that are sleeping,
    Brand not my forehead with thy piercing light,
    For day hath naught to do what's done by night.'

Thus cavils she with everything she sees:
True grief is fond° and testy as a child   *foolish*
1095   Who, wayward once,° his mood with naught agrees;   *once out of sorts*
Old woes, not infant sorrows, bear them mild.°   *bear themselves mildly*
Continuance tames the one; the other wild,
    Like an unpractised swimmer plunging still,°   *constantly*
    With too much labour drowns for want of skill.

1100   So she, deep drenchèd in a sea of care,
Holds disputation with each thing she views,
And to herself all sorrow doth compare;
No object but her passion's strength renews,
And as one shifts,° another straight° ensues.   *moves / immediately*
1105   Sometime her grief is dumb° and hath no words,   *mute*
    Sometime 'tis mad and too much talk affords.

The little birds that tune their morning's joy
Make her moans mad with their sweet melody,
For mirth doth search° the bottom of annoy;°   *probe / vexation*
1110   Sad souls are slain° in merry company;   *overcome with distress*
Grief best is pleased with grief's society.
    True sorrow then is feelingly sufficed°   *properly contented*
    When with like semblance it is sympathized.°   *matched*

'Tis double death to drown in ken° of shore;   *sight*
1115   He ten times pines° that pines beholding food;   *starves*
To see the salve doth make the wound ache more;
Great grief grieves most at that would do it good;
Deep woes roll forward like a gentle flood
    Who, being stopped, the bounding° banks o'erflows.   *confining*
1120   Grief dallied° with nor° law nor limit knows.   *trifled / neither*

'You mocking birds,' quoth she, 'your tunes entomb
Within your hollow-swelling feathered breasts,
And in my hearing be you mute and dumb;
My restless discord loves no stops nor rests;
1125   A woeful hostess brooks° not merry guests.   *tolerates*
    Relish° your nimble notes to pleasing ears;   *Warble; make pleasing*
    Distress likes dumps° when time is kept with tears.   *sad songs*

'Come, Philomel, that sing'st of ravishment,
Make thy sad grove in my dishevelled hair.
1130 As the dank earth weeps at thy languishment,°   *lamentation*
So I at each sad strain will strain a tear,
And with deep groans the diapason° bear;   *bass accompaniment*
     For burden-wise[4] I'll hum on Tarquin still,
     While thou on Tereus descants better skill.[5]

1135 'And whiles against a thorn[6] thou bear'st thy part
To keep thy sharp woes waking, wretched I,
To imitate thee well, against my heart
Will fix a sharp knife to affright mine eye,
Who° if it wink° shall thereon fall and die.   *(I) / (my eye) close*
1140   These means, as frets° upon an instrument,   *(punning on "vexation")*
     Shall tune our heart-strings to true languishment.

'And for, poor bird, thou sing'st not in the day,
As shaming any eye should thee behold,
Some dark deep desert seated from the way,[7]
1145 That knows not parching heat nor freezing cold,
Will we find out, and there we will unfold
     To creatures stern sad tunes to change their kinds.°   *natures*
     Since men prove beasts, let beasts bear gentle minds.'

As the poor frighted deer that stands at gaze,
1150 Wildly determining which way to fly,
Or one encompassed with a winding maze,
That cannot tread the way out readily,
So with herself is she in mutiny,
     To live or die which of the twain were better   *Ok Hamlet*
1155   When life is shamed and death reproach's debtor.°   *will incur reproach*

'To kill myself,' quoth she, 'alack, what were it
But with my body my poor soul's pollution?[8]
They that lose half with greater patience bear it
Than they whose whole is swallowed in confusion.°   *ruin*
1160 That mother tries a merciless conclusion°   *experiment*
     Who, having two sweet babes, when death takes one
     Will slay the other and be nurse to none.

'My body or my soul, which was the dearer,
When the one pure the other made divine?
1165 Whose love of either to myself was nearer,
When both were kept for heaven and Collatine?
Ay me, the bark peeled from the lofty pine
     His leaves will wither and his sap decay;
     So must my soul, her bark being peeled away.

1170 'Her house is sacked, her quiet interrupted,
Her mansion battered by the enemy,
Her sacred temple spotted, spoiled, corrupted,

---

4. Like a bass line; playing on "burden" as sorrow, weight.
5. Sings the treble part more skillfully.
6. The nightingale was imagined to press against a thorn to keep itself awake during the night.
7. Some uninhabited place located far from the road.
8. To pollute my poor soul, as my body has already been polluted.

Grossly engirt with daring° infamy.   *unrestrained*
Then let it not be called impiety
1175   If in this blemished fort° I make some hole   *(my body)*
       Through which I may convey° this troubled soul.   *steal away*

'Yet die I will not till my Collatine
Have heard the cause of my untimely death,
That he may vow in that sad hour of mine
1180   Revenge on him that made me stop my breath.
My stainèd blood to Tarquin I'll bequeath,
       Which by him tainted shall for him be spent,
       And as his due writ° in my testament.°   *written / last will*

'My honour I'll bequeath unto the knife
1185   That wounds my body so dishonourèd.
'Tis honour to deprive° dishonoured life;   *take away*
The one° will live, the other° being dead.   *(honor) / (life)*
So of shame's ashes shall my fame be bred,⁹
       For in my death I murder shameful scorn;
1190   My shame so dead, mine honour is new born.

'Dear lord of that dear jewel° I have lost,   *(chastity)*
What legacy shall I bequeath to thee?
My resolution, love, shall be thy boast,
By whose example thou revenged mayst be.
1195   How Tarquin must be used, read it in me.
       Myself, thy friend, will kill myself, thy foe;
       And for my sake serve° thou false Tarquin so.   *treat*

'This brief abridgement of my will I make:
My soul and body to the skies and ground;
1200   My resolution, husband, do thou take;
Mine honour be the knife's that makes my wound;
My shame be his that did my fame confound;
       And all my fame that lives disbursèd be°   *that remains be paid out*
       To those that live and think no shame of me.

1205   'Thou, Collatine, shalt oversee° this will.   *execute*
How was I overseen° that thou shalt see it!   *deluded*
My blood shall wash the slander of mine ill;
My life's foul deed my life's fair end shall free it.
Faint not, faint heart, but stoutly say "So be it".
1210   Yield to my hand, my hand shall conquer thee;
       Thou dead, both die, and both shall victors be.'

This plot of death when sadly she had laid,
And wiped the brinish° pearl from her bright eyes,   *salty*
With untuned° tongue she hoarsely calls her maid,   *inharmonious*
1215   Whose swift obedience to her mistress hies;°   *hastens*
For fleet-winged duty with thought's feathers flies.
       Poor Lucrece' cheeks unto her maid seem so
       As winter meads when sun doth melt their snow.

9. My honor will be like the mythological phoenix, consumed in fire only to be reborn from the ashes.

Her mistress she doth give demure good-morrow
1220 With soft slow tongue, true mark of modesty,
And sorts° a sad look to her lady's sorrow,   *suits*
For why° her face wore sorrow's livery;°   *Because / attire*
But durst not ask of her audaciously
 Why her two suns were cloud-eclipsèd so,
1225 Nor why her fair cheeks over-washed with woe.

But as the earth doth weep, the sun being set,
Each flower moistened like a melting eye,
Even so the maid with swelling drops gan wet
Her circled° eyne, enforced° by sympathy   *rounded / compelled*
1230 Of those fair suns set in her mistress' sky,
 Who in a salt-waved ocean quench their light;
 Which makes the maid weep like the dewy night.

A pretty while° these pretty creatures stand,   *fair amount of time*
Like ivory conduits coral cisterns filling.
1235 One justly weeps, the other takes in hand°   *acknowledges*
No cause but company of her drops' spilling.
Their <u>gentle sex </u>to weep are often willing,
 Grieving themselves to guess at° others' smarts,° *conjecture / pains*
 And then they drown their eyes or break their hearts.

1240 For men have marble, women waxen minds,
And therefore are they formed as marble will.
The weak oppressed, th'impression of strange kinds   *alien natures*
Is formed in them by force, by fraud, or skill.
Then call them not the authors of their ill,
1245 No more than wax shall be accounted evil
 Wherein is stamped the semblance of a devil.

Their smoothness like a goodly champaign plain   *open field*
Lays open° all the little worms that creep;   *Reveals*
In men as in a rough-grown grove remain
1250 Cave-keeping° evils that obscurely° sleep. *Concealed / unseen*
Through crystal walls each little mote° will peep;   *speck*
 Though men can cover crimes with bold stern looks,
 Poor women's faces are their own faults' books.

No man° inveigh against the withered flower,   *Let no man*
1255 But chide rough winter that the flower hath killed.
Not that devoured, but that which doth devour
Is worthy blame. O, let it not be held
Poor women's faults that they are so full-filled
 With men's abuses. Those proud lords, to blame,
1260 Make weak-made women tenants to their shame.

The precedent° whereof in Lucrece view,   *proof*
Assailed by night with circumstances strong
Of present° death, and shame that might ensue   *immediate*
By that her death, to do her husband wrong.
1265 Such danger to resistance did belong
 That dying fear through all her body spread;
 And who cannot abuse a body dead?

By this,° mild patience bid fair Lucrece speak   *this time*
To the poor counterfeit of her complaining.°   *(the weeping maid)*
1270   'My girl,' quoth she, 'on what occasion break
Those tears from thee that down thy cheeks are raining?
If thou dost weep for grief of my sustaining,°   *borne by me*
    Know, gentle wench, it small avails° my mood.   *little helps*
    If tears could help, mine own would do me good.

1275   'But tell me, girl, when went'—and there she stayed,
Till after a deep groan—'Tarquin from hence?'
'Madam, ere I was up,' replied the maid,
'The more to blame my sluggard negligence.
Yet with the fault I thus far can dispense:°   *excuse*
1280   Myself was stirring ere the break of day,
    And ere I rose was Tarquin gone away.

'But lady, if your maid may be so bold,
She would request to know your heaviness.'°   *sorrow*
'O, peace,' quoth Lucrece, 'if it should be told,
1285   The repetition cannot make it less;
For more it is than I can well express,
    And that deep torture may be called a hell
    When more is felt than one hath power to tell.

'Go, get me hither paper, ink, and pen;
1290   Yet save that labour, for I have them here.
What should I say? One of my husband's men
Bid thou be ready by and by to bear
A letter to my lord, my love, my dear.
    Bid him with speed prepare to carry it;
1295   The cause craves° haste, and it will soon be writ.'   *requires*

Her maid is gone, and she prepares to write,
First hovering o'er the paper with her quill.
Conceit° and grief an eager combat fight;   *Imagination*
What wit° sets down is blotted straight with will;°   *thought / passion*
1300   This is too curious-good,° this blunt and ill.   *elaborate*
    Much like a press° of people at a door   *crowd*
    Throng her inventions, which shall go before.°   *first*

At last she thus begins: 'Thou worthy lord
Of that unworthy wife that greeteth thee,
1305   Health to thy person! Next, vouchsafe t'afford—
If ever, love, thy Lucrece thou wilt see—
Some present° speed to come and visit me.   *immediate*
    So I commend me,° from our house in grief;   *ask to be remembered*
    My woes are tedious, though my words are brief.'

1310   Here folds she up the tenor° of her woe,   *gist*
Her certain sorrow writ uncertainly.
By this short schedule° Collatine may know   *summary*
Her grief, but not her grief 's true quality.
She dares not thereof make discovery,°   *revelation*
1315   Lest he should hold it her own gross abuse,°   *trespass*
    Ere she with blood had stained her stain's excuse.

Besides, the life and feeling of her passion
She hoards, to spend when he is by to hear her,
When sighs and groans and tears may grace the fashion°   *appearance; fashioning*
1320 Of her disgrace, the better so to clear her
From that suspicion which the world might bear her.
  To shun this blot she would not blot the letter
  With words, till action might become° them better.   *suit*

To see sad sights moves more than hear them told,
1325 For then the eye interprets to the ear
The heavy motion° that it doth behold,   *sad action*
When every part a part of woe doth bear.
'Tis but a part of sorrow that we hear;
  Deep sounds make lesser noise than shallow fords,
1330 And sorrow ebbs, being blown with wind of words.

Her letter now is sealed, and on it writ
'At Ardea to my lord with more than haste'.
The post attends,° and she delivers it,   *messenger waits*
Charging the sour-faced groom to hie as fast
1335 As lagging fowls before the northern blast.
  Speed more than speed° but dull and slow she deems;   *Even unusual speed*
  Extremity still urgeth such extremes.

The homely villain° curtsies to her low,   *unpolished menial*
And blushing on her with a steadfast eye
1340 Receives the scroll without or° yea or no,   *either*
And forth with bashful innocence doth hie.
But they whose guilt within their bosoms lie
  Imagine every eye beholds their blame,
  For Lucrece thought he blushed to see her shame,

1345 When, silly groom,° God wot,° it was defect   *simple servant / knows*
Of spirit, life, and bold audacity.
Such harmless creatures have a true respect
To talk in deeds,[1] while others saucily
Promise more speed, but do it leisurely.
1350 Even so this pattern of the worn-out age°   *old-fashioned model*
  Pawned° honest looks, but laid no words to gage.°   *Offered / as a pledge*

His kindled duty[2] kindled her mistrust,
That two red fires in both their faces blazed.
She thought he blushed as knowing Tarquin's lust,
1355 And blushing with him, wistly° on him gazed.   *attentively*
Her earnest eye did make him more amazed.°   *bewildered*
  The more she saw the blood his cheeks replenish,
  The more she thought he spied in her some blemish.

But long she thinks° till he return again,   *she thinks it long*
1360 And yet the duteous vassal scarce is gone.
The weary time she cannot entertain,°   *while away*
For now 'tis stale to sigh, to weep, and groan.

---

1. *have . . . deeds*: rightly express their deference by 2. His blushing bow; his ardent loyalty.
their actions (rather than merely by their words).

So woe hath wearied woe, moan tired moan,
  That she her plaints a little while doth stay,
1365 Pausing for means to mourn some newer way.

At last she calls to mind where hangs a piece
Of skilful painting made for° Priam's Troy,   *representing*
Before the which is drawn the power° of Greece,   *army*
For Helen's rape the city to destroy,
1370 Threat'ning cloud-kissing Ilion° with annoy;°   *high-built Troy / injury*
  Which the conceited° painter drew so proud   *ingenious*
  As heaven, it seemed, to kiss the turrets bowed.

A thousand lamentable objects there,
In scorn of° nature, art gave lifeless life.   *Defying*
1375 Many a dry drop seemed a weeping tear
Shed for the slaughtered husband by the wife.
The red blood reeked° to show the painter's strife,[3]   *smoked*
  And dying eyes gleamed forth their ashy lights
  Like dying coals burnt out in tedious nights.

1380 There might you see the labouring pioneer°   *trench digger*
Begrimed with sweat and smearèd all with dust,
And from the towers of Troy there would appear
The very eyes of men through loop-holes thrust,
Gazing upon the Greeks with little lust.°   *pleasure*
1385 Such sweet observance° in this work was had   *verisimilitude*
  That one might see those far-off eyes look sad.

In great commanders grace and majesty
You might behold, triumphing in their faces;
In youth, quick° bearing and dexterity;   *lively*
1390 And here and there the painter interlaces
Pale cowards marching on with trembling paces,
  Which heartless° peasants did so well resemble   *dejected*
  That one would swear he saw them quake and tremble.

In Ajax and Ulysses, O what art
1395 Of physiognomy might one behold!
The face of either ciphered° either's heart;   *represented*
Their face their manners most expressly told.
In Ajax' eyes blunt° rage and rigour rolled,   *rude*
  But the mild glance that sly Ulysses lent
1400 Showed deep regard° and smiling government.°   *judgment / self-control*

There pleading° might you see grave Nestor stand,   *persuading*
As 'twere encouraging the Greeks to fight,
Making such sober action with his hand
That it beguiled attention, charmed the sight.
1405 In speech it seemed his beard all silver-white
  Wagged up and down, and from his lips did fly
  Thin winding breath which purled° up to the sky.   *curled*

---

3. Conflict between Trojans and Greeks; conflict between nature and art.

About him were a press of gaping faces
Which seemed to swallow up his sound advice,
1410   All jointly list'ning, but with several graces,°   *various attitudes*
As if some mermaid did their ears entice;
Some high, some low, the painter was so nice.°   *skillful; subtle*
   The scalps of many, almost hid behind,
   To jump up higher seemed, to mock the mind.°   *(by artistic illusion)*

1415   Here one man's hand leaned on another's head.
His nose being shadowed by his neighbour's ear;
Here one being thronged bears° back, all boll'n° and red;   *crowded pushes / swollen*
Another, smothered, seems to pelt° and swear,   *scold*
And in their rage such signs of rage they bear
1420   As but for loss of° Nestor's golden words   *That except they might miss*
   It seemed they would debate with angry swords.

For much imaginary° work was there;   *creative*
Conceit deceitful, so compact,° so kind,°   *efficient / natural*
That for Achilles' image stood his spear
1425   Gripped in an armèd hand; himself behind
Was left unseen save to the eye of mind;
   A hand, a foot, a face, a leg, a head,
   Stood for the whole to be imaginèd.

And from the walls of strong-besiegèd Troy
1430   When their brave hope, bold Hector, marched to field,
Stood many Trojan mothers sharing joy
To see their youthful sons bright weapons wield;
And to their hope they such odd action° yield   *contrary gestures*
   That through their light joy seemèd to appear,
1435   Like bright things stained, a kind of heavy fear.

And from the strand° of Dardan where they fought   *shore*
To Simois'° reedy banks the red blood ran,   *Trojan river*
Whose waves to imitate the battle sought
With swelling ridges, and their ranks began
1440   To break upon the gallèd° shore, and then   *eroded; injured*
   Retire again, till meeting greater ranks
   They join, and shoot their foam at Simois' banks.

To this well painted piece is Lucrece come,
To find a face where all distress is stelled.°   *engraved*
1445   Many she sees where cares have carvèd some,
But none where all distress and dolour dwelled
Till she despairing Hecuba° beheld   *Queen of Troy*
   Staring on Priam's° wounds with her old eyes,   *King of Troy*
   Which bleeding under Pyrrhus' proud foot lies.

1450   In her the painter had anatomized°   *laid open*
Time's ruin, beauty's wreck, and grim care's reign.
Her cheeks with chaps° and wrinkles were disguised;°   *cracks / disfigured*
Of what she was no semblance did remain.
Her blue blood changed to black in every vein,
1455   Wanting° the spring that those shrunk pipes had fed,   *Lacking*
   Showed life imprisoned in a body dead.

On this sad shadow Lucrece spends her eyes,
And shapes her sorrow to the beldame's° woes,   *old woman's*
Who nothing wants to answer her⁴ but cries
1460   And bitter words to ban° her cruel foes.   *curse*
The painter was no god to lend her those,
    And therefore Lucrece swears he did her wrong
    To give her so much grief, and not a tongue.

'Poor instrument,' quoth she, 'without a sound,
1465   I'll tune° thy woes with my lamenting tongue,   *sing*
And drop sweet balm in Priam's painted wound,
And rail on Pyrrhus that hath done him wrong,
And with my tears quench Troy that burns so long,
And with my knife scratch out the angry eyes
1470   Of all the Greeks that are thine enemies.

'Show me the strumpet° that began this stir,°   *(Helen) / dispute*
That with my nails her beauty I may tear.
Thy heat of lust, fond Paris, did incur
This load of wrath that burning Troy doth bear;
1475   Thine eye kindled the fire that burneth here,
    And here in Troy, for trespass of thine eye,
    The sire, the son, the dame and daughter die.

'Why should the private pleasure of someone
Become the public plague of many moe?°   *more*
1480   Let sin alone° committed light alone   *by one person*
Upon his head that hath transgressèd so;
Let guiltless souls be freed from guilty woe.
    For one's offence why should so many fall,
    To plague a private sin in general?°   *collectively*

1485   'Lo, here weeps Hecuba, here Priam dies,
Here manly Hector faints, here Troilus swoons,
Here friend by friend in bloody channel° lies,   *gutter*
And friend to friend gives unadvisèd° wounds,   *unintended*
And one man's lust these many lives confounds.
1490   Had doting Priam checked his son's desire,
    Troy had been bright with fame, and not with fire.'

Here feelingly she weeps Troy's painted woes;
For sorrow, like a heavy hanging bell
Once set on ringing, with his° own weight goes;   *its*
1495   Then little strength rings out the doleful knell.
So Lucrece, set a-work, sad tales doth tell
    To pencilled pensiveness and coloured sorrow.
    She lends them words, and she their looks doth borrow.

She throws her eyes about the painting round,
1500   And who she finds forlorn she doth lament.
At last she sees a wretched image bound,
That piteous looks to Phrygian shepherds lent.⁵

---

4. Who lacks nothing to resemble her.
5. That made Phrygian shepherds look on in pity (Phrygia was the area around Troy).

His face, though full of cares, yet showed content.
    Onward to Troy with the blunt swains° he goes,   *rough rustics*
1505   So mild that patience° seemed to scorn his woes.   *his patience*

In him the painter laboured with his skill
To hide deceit and give the harmless show°   *appearance*
An humble gait, calm looks, eyes wailing still,°   *weeping continually*
A brow unbent that seemed to welcome woe;
1510   Cheeks neither red nor pale, but mingled so
        That blushing red no guilty instance° gave,   *sign*
        Nor ashy pale the fear that false hearts have.

But like a constant and confirmèd devil
He entertained° a show so seeming just,   *maintained*
1515   And therein so ensconced° his secret evil   *concealed*
That jealousy° itself could not mistrust°   *suspicion / suspect*
False creeping craft and perjury should thrust
        Into so bright a day such blackfaced storms,
        Or blot with hell-born sin such saint-like forms.

1520   The well skilled workman this mild image drew
For perjured Sinon,[6] whose enchanting° story   *deluding*
The credulous old Priam after slew;
Whose words like wildfire[7] burnt the shining glory
Of rich-built Ilion, that the skies were sorry,
1525   And little stars shot from their fixèd places
        When their glass° fell wherein they viewed their faces.   *mirror (Troy)*

This picture she advisedly° perused,   *carefully*
And chid° the painter for his wondrous skill,   *scolded*
Saying some shape° in Sinon's was abused,   *(other person's shape)*
1530   So fair a form lodged not a mind so ill;
And still on him she gazed, and gazing still,
        Such signs of truth in his plain° face she spied   *open*
        That she concludes the picture was belied.°   *shown to be false*

'It cannot be,' quoth she, 'that so much guile'—
1535   She would have said 'can lurk in such a look',
But Tarquin's shape came in her mind the while,
And from her tongue 'can lurk' from 'cannot' took.
'It cannot be' she in that sense forsook,
        And turned it thus: 'It cannot be, I find,
1540   But such a face should bear a wicked mind.

'For even as subtle Sinon here is painted,
So sober-sad, so weary, and so mild,
As if with grief or travail he had fainted,
To me came Tarquin armèd, too beguiled°   *disguised*
1545   With outward honesty, but yet defiled
        With inward vice. As Priam him did cherish,
        So did I Tarquin, so my Troy did perish.

---

6. Sinon was a Greek who pretended to have fled from his own people; once "rescued" and brought to Troy, he persuaded the Trojans to receive the wooden horse into their city.
7. A mixture of sulfur, tar, and other combustible substances, used to set fires during battle.

'Look, look, how list'ning Priam wets his eyes
To see those borrowed° tears that Sinon sheds.   *inauthentic*
1550 Priam, why art thou old and yet not wise?
For every tear he falls° a Trojan bleeds.   *(Sinon) lets fall*
His eye drops fire, no water thence proceeds.
     Those round clear pearls of his that move thy pity
     Are balls of quenchless fire to burn thy city.

1555 'Such devils steal effects° from lightless hell,   *illusions*
For Sinon in his fire doth quake with cold,
And in that cold hot-burning fire doth dwell.
These contraries such unity do hold
Only to flatter° fools and make them bold;   *encourage*
1560   So Priam's trust false Sinon's tears doth flatter
     That he finds means to burn his Troy with water.'

Here, all enraged, such passion her assails
That patience is quite beaten from her breast.
She tears the senseless° Sinon with her nails,   *unfeeling*
1565 Comparing him to that unhappy° guest   *misfortune-bringing*
Whose deed hath made herself herself detest.
     At last she smilingly with this gives o'er:
     'Fool, fool,' quoth she, 'his wounds will not be sore.'

Thus ebbs and flows the current of her sorrow,
1570 And time doth weary time with her complaining.
She looks for night, and then she longs for morrow,
And both she thinks too long with her remaining.
Short time seems long in sorrow's sharp sustaining.°   *painful enduring*
     Though woe be heavy, yet it seldom sleeps,
1575   And they that watch° see time how slow it creeps.   *remain awake*

Which all this time hath overslipped her thought
That she with painted images hath spent,
Being from the feeling of her own grief brought
By deep surmise° of others' detriment,°   *contemplation / suffering*
1580 Losing her woes in shows of discontent.°   *pictures of sorrow*
     It easeth some, though none it ever cured,
     To think their dolour others have endured.

But now the mindful° messenger come back   *dutiful*
Brings home his lord and other company,
1585 Who finds his Lucrece clad in mourning black,
And round about her tear-distainèd° eye   *tear-stained*
Blue circles streamed, like rainbows in the sky.
     These water-galls° in her dim element°   *rainbow fragments / sky*
     Foretell new storms to° those already spent.   *in addition to*

1590 Which when her sad beholding husband saw,
Amazedly in her sad face he stares.
Her eyes, though sod° in tears, looked red and raw,   *sodden*
Her lively colour killed with deadly cares.
He hath no power to ask her how she fares.
1595   Both stood like old acquaintance in a trance,
     Met far from home, wond'ring each other's chance.°   *fortune*

At last he takes her by the bloodless hand,
And thus begins: 'What uncouth° ill event   *strange*
Hath thee befall'n, that thou dost trembling stand?
1600   Sweet love, what spite° hath thy fair colour spent?   *harm*
Why art thou thus attired in discontent?[8]
     Unmask,° dear dear, this moody heaviness,   *Disclose*
     And tell thy grief, that we may give redress.'

Three times with sighs she gives her sorrow fire[9]
1605   Ere once she can discharge one word of woe.
At length addressed° to answer his desire,   *ready*
She modestly prepares to let them know
Her honour is ta'en prisoner by the foe,
     While Collatine and his consorted° lords   *accompanying*
1610   With sad attention long to hear her words.

And now this pale swan in her wat'ry nest
Begins the sad dirge of her certain ending.[1]
'Few words,' quoth she, 'shall fit the trespass best,
Where no excuse can give the fault amending.
1615   In me more woes than words are now depending,°   *weighing; belonging*
     And my laments would be drawn out too long
     To tell them all with one poor tired tongue.

'Then be this all the task it hath to say:
Dear husband, in the interest° of thy bed   *claiming possession*
1620   A stranger came, and on that pillow lay
Where thou wast wont to rest thy weary head;
And what wrong else may be imaginèd
     By foul enforcement might be done to me,
     From that, alas, thy Lucrece is not free.

1625   'For in the dreadful dead of dark midnight
With shining falchion in my chamber came
A creeping creature with a flaming light,
And softly cried, "Awake, thou Roman dame,
And entertain° my love; else lasting shame   *receive*
1630   On thee and thine this night I will inflict,
     If thou my love's desire do contradict.

"'For some hard-favoured° groom of thine," quoth he,   *ugly*
"Unless thou yoke thy liking to my will,
I'll murder straight,° and then I'll slaughter thee,   *immediately*
1635   And swear I found you where you did fulfil
The loathsome act of lust, and so did kill
     The lechers in their deed. This act will be
     My fame, and thy perpetual infamy."

'With this I did begin to start and cry,
1640   And then against my heart he set his sword,
Swearing unless I took all patiently

---

8. Black; see line 1585.
9. As sixteenth-century gunners lighted firearms with matches.

1. Swans were supposed to sing only when they were on the point of death.

I should not live to speak another word.
So should my shame still rest upon record,
   And never be forgot in mighty Rome
1645   Th'adulterate° death of Lucrece and her groom.   *adulterous*

'Mine enemy was strong, my poor self weak,
And far the weaker with so strong a fear.
My bloody judge forbade my tongue to speak;
No rightful plea might plead for justice there.
1650 His scarlet lust came° evidence to swear   *gave*
   That my poor beauty had purloined his eyes;
   And when the judge is robbed, the prisoner dies.

'O teach me how to make mine own excuse,
Or at the least this refuge let me find:
1655 Though my gross blood be stained with this abuse,
Immaculate and spotless is my mind.
That was not forced, that never was inclined
   To accessory yieldings,² but still pure
   Doth in her poisoned closet yet endure.'

1660 Lo, here the hopeless merchant° of this loss,   *owner (Collatine)*
With head declined° and voice dammed up with woe,   *bent*
With sad set eyes and wreathèd arms across,³
From lips new waxen° pale begins to blow   *newly grown*
The grief away that stops his answer so;
1665   But wretched as he is, he strives in vain.
   What he breathes out, his breath drinks up again.

As through an arch° the violent roaring tide   *(under a bridge)*
Outruns the eye that doth behold his haste,
Yet in the eddy boundeth in his pride
1670 Back to the strait that forced him on so fast,
In rage sent out, recalled in rage being past;
   Even so his sighs, his sorrows, make a saw,⁴
   To push grief on, and back the same grief draw.

Which speechless woe of his poor she attendeth,°   *poor Lucrece notes*
1675 And his untimely frenzy° thus awaketh: *delirium*
'Dear lord, thy sorrow to my sorrow lendeth
Another power;° no flood by raining slaketh.   *Greater strength*
My woe too sensible° thy passion maketh,   *acutely felt*
   More feeling-painful. Let it then suffice
1680   To drown on woe one pair of weeping eyes.

'And for my sake, when I might charm thee so,⁵
For she that was thy Lucrece, now attend me.
Be suddenly revengèd on my foe—
Thine, mine, his own. Suppose thou dost defend me
1685 From what is past. The help that thou shalt lend me

---

2. To yielding that would make me an accessory to the crime.
3. See line 793 and note.
4. Go back and forth (inhaling and exhaling), like a saw cutting wood.
5. As I used to be when I charmed you (before the rape).

Comes all too late, yet let the traitor die,
For sparing° justice feeds° iniquity.   *lenient / encourages*

'But ere I name him, you fair lords,' quoth she,
Speaking to those that came with Collatine,
1690 'Shall plight° your honourable faiths to me   *pledge*
With swift pursuit to venge this wrong of mine;
For 'tis a meritorious fair design°   *intention*
    To chase injustice with revengeful arms.
    Knights, by their oaths, should right poor ladies' harms.'

1695 At this request with noble disposition°   *purpose*
Each present lord began to promise aid,
As bound in knighthood to her imposition,°   *imposed task*
Longing to hear the hateful foe bewrayed.°   *revealed*
But she that yet her sad task hath not said°   *completed*
1700   The protestation stops. 'O speak,' quoth she;
    'How may this forcèd stain be wiped from me?

'What is the quality of my offence,
Being constrained with dreadful circumstance?
May my pure mind with the foul act dispense,
1705 My low-declinèd honour to advance?°   *raise*
May any terms acquit me from this chance?°   *mishap*
    The poisoned fountain clears itself again,
    And why not I from this compellèd stain?'

With this they all at once began to say
1710 Her body's stain her mind untainted clears,
While with a joyless smile she turns away
The face, that map which deep impression bears
Of hard misfortune, carved in it with tears.
    'No, no,' quoth she, 'no dame hereafter living
1715   By my excuse shall claim excuse's giving.'

Here with a sigh as if her heart would break
She throws forth Tarquin's name. 'He, he,' she says—
But more than he her poor tongue could not speak,
Till after many accents° and delays,   *sighs*
1720 Untimely breathings, sick and short essays,°   *attempts*
    She utters this: 'He, he, fair lords, 'tis he
    That guides this hand to give this wound to me.'

Even here she sheathèd in her harmless° breast   *innocent*
A harmful knife, that thence her soul unsheathed.
1725 That blow did bail° it from the deep unrest   *liberate*
Of that polluted prison where it breathed.
Her contrite sighs unto the clouds bequeathed
    Her wingèd sprite,° and through her wounds doth fly   *spirit*
    Life's lasting date[6] from cancelled destiny.

6. Eternal duration. The line is difficult, and could mean that Lucrece's immortal soul separates from her earthly life and body (canceled destiny), or that Lucrece, by taking her fate into her own hands (canceling her destiny), makes her fame eternal.

1730 Stone-still, astonished° with this deadly deed   *stunned*
Stood Collatine and all his lordly crew,
Till Lucrece' father that beholds her bleed
Himself on her self-slaughtered body threw;
And from the purple fountain Brutus⁷ drew
1735   The murd'rous knife; and as it left the place
Her blood in poor revenge held it in chase,

And bubbling from her breast it doth divide
In two slow rivers, that the crimson blood
Circles her body in on every side,
1740 Who like a late-sacked° island vastly° stood,   *just-looted / devastated*
Bare and unpeopled in this fearful° flood.   *fearsome*
Some of her blood still pure and red remained,
And some looked black, and that false Tarquin-stained.

About the mourning and congealèd face
1745 Of that black blood a wat'ry rigol° goes,   *circle*
Which seems to weep upon the tainted place;
And ever since, as pitying Lucrece' woes,
Corrupted blood some watery token shows;
And blood untainted still doth red abide,
1750   Blushing at that which is so putrefied.

'Daughter, dear daughter,' old Lucretius cries,
'That life was mine which thou hast here deprived.
If in the child the father's image lies,
Where shall I live now Lucrece is unlived?°   *slain*
1755 Thou wast not to this end from me derived.
If children predecease progenitors,
We are their offspring, and they none of ours.

'Poor broken glass,° I often did behold   *mirror*
In thy sweet semblance my old age new born;
1760 But now that fair fresh mirror, dim and old,
Shows me a bare-boned death° by time outworn.   *skull*
O, from thy cheeks my image thou hast torn,
And shivered all the beauty of my glass,
That I no more can see what once I was.

1765 'O time, cease thou thy course and last no longer,
If they surcease° to be that should survive!   *cease*
Shall rotten death make conquest of the stronger,
And leave the falt'ring feeble souls alive?
The old bees die, the young possess their hive.
1770   Then live, sweet Lucrece, live again and see
Thy father die, and not thy father thee.'

By this starts Collatine as from a dream,
And bids Lucretius give his sorrow place;
And then in key-cold° Lucrece' bleeding stream   *cold as metal*
1775 He falls, and bathes the pale fear in his face,

---

7. Lucius Junius Brutus. Tarquin the Proud, the rapist's father, had killed Brutus's brother, but Brutus, whose name means "stupid," escaped royal suspicion by pretending to be mentally retarded. After Lucrece's rape, he led the coup that overthrew the Tarquins and established republican government in Rome.

And counterfeits to die with her a space,
   Till manly shame bids him possess his breath,
   And live to be revengèd on her death.

The deep vexation of his inward soul
1780 Hath served a dumb arrest° upon his tongue,   *silent injunction*
Who, mad that sorrow should his use control,°   *prevent*
Or keep him from heart-easing words so long,
Begins to talk; but through his lips do throng
   Weak words, so thick come in his poor heart's aid
1785   That no man could distinguish what he said.

Yet sometime 'Tarquin' was pronouncèd plain,
But through his teeth, as if the name he tore.
This windy tempest, till it blow up rain,
Held back his sorrow's tide to make it more.
1790 At last it rains, and busy winds give o'er.
   Then son and father weep with equal strife
   Who should weep most, for daughter or for wife.

The one doth call her his, the other his,
Yet neither may possess the claim they lay.
1795 The father says 'She's mine'; 'O, mine she is,'
Replies her husband, 'do not take away
My sorrow's interest;° let no mourner say   *title of possession*
   He weeps for her, for she was only mine,
   And only must be wailed by Collatine.'

1800 'O,' quoth Lucretius, 'I did give that life
Which she too early and too late hath spilled.'
'Woe, woe,' quoth Collatine, 'she was my wife.
I owed° her, and 'tis mine that she hath killed.'   *owned*
'My daughter' and 'my wife' with clamours filled
1805   The dispersed air, who, holding Lucrece' life,[8]
   Answered° their cries, 'my daughter' and 'my wife'.   *Echoed*

Brutus, who plucked the knife from Lucrece' side,
Seeing such emulation° in their woe   *competition*
Began to clothe his wit in state° and pride,   *dignity*
1810 Burying in Lucrece' wound his folly's show.°   *pretended stupidity*
He with the Romans was esteemèd so
   As silly jeering idiots° are with kings,   *court jesters*
   For sportive words and utt'ring foolish things.

But now he throws that shallow habit° by   *foolish appearance*
1815 Wherein deep policy° did him disguise,   *shrewdness*
And armed his long-hid wits advisedly°   *prudently*
To check the tears in Collatinus' eyes.
'Thou wrongèd lord of Rome,' quoth he, 'arise.
   Let my unsounded° self, supposed a fool,   *of unknown depth*
1820   Now set thy long-experienced wit to school.

'Why, Collatine, is woe the cure for woe?
Do wounds help wounds, or grief help grievous deeds?

8. See lines 1727ff.

Is it revenge to give thyself a blow
For his foul act by whom thy fair wife bleeds?
1825   Such childish humour° from weak minds proceeds;   *silly behavior*
      Thy wretched wife mistook the matter so
      To slay herself, that should have slain her foe.

'Courageous Roman, do not steep thy heart
In such relenting dew of lamentations,
1830   But kneel with me, and help to bear thy part
To rouse our Roman gods with invocations
That they will suffer° these abominations—   *allow*
      Since Rome herself in them doth stand disgraced—
      By our strong arms from forth her fair streets chased.°   *to be chased*

1835   'Now by the Capitol that we adore,
And by this chaste blood so unjustly stained,
By heaven's fair sun that breeds the fat° earth's store,°   *fertile / plenty*
By all our country° rights in Rome maintained,   *civic*
And by chaste Lucrece' soul that late complained
1840   Her wrongs to us, and by this bloody knife,
      We will revenge the death of this true wife.'

This said, he struck his hand upon his breast,
And kissed the fatal knife to end his vow,
And to his protestation urged the rest,
1845   Who, wond'ring at him, did his words allow.°   *approve*
Then jointly to the ground their knees they bow,
      And that deep vow which Brutus made before
      He doth again repeat, and that they swore.

When they had sworn to this advisèd doom°   *considered judgment*
1850   They did conclude to bear dead Lucrece thence,
To show her bleeding body thorough° Rome,   *throughout*
And so to publish° Tarquin's foul offence;   *publicize*
Which being done with speedy diligence,
      The Romans plausibly° did give consent   *with applause*
1855   To Tarquin's everlasting banishment.

The Reign of
King Edward the Third

Did Shakespeare write *The Reign of King Edward the Third*? The jury is out, but the Oxford editors have come to believe that he wrote at least part of it. In that view, they are joined by an increasing number of scholars who find in this chronicle history traces of the issues that preoccupied Shakespeare in his early years as a dramatist, as well as a number of lines and scenes that recall other plays and poems he authored both in the early 1590s and later in his career, including *The Rape of Lucrece*, the sonnets, *The Life of Henry V*, and *Measure for Measure*. *Edward III*, written entirely in verse, was first printed in 1596, with a second edition appearing in 1599, but the title page gave no indication of authorship, only that *"it hath bin sundrie times plaied about the Citie of London."* Many scholars believe that it was first performed by Lord Pembroke's Men, a company that staged several of Shakespeare's early plays before he became a member of the Lord Chamberlain's Men in 1594. In 1656, two printers attributed *Edward III* to Shakespeare in a list of printed plays, but the list has many errors. In 1760, Shakespearean editor and scholar Edward Capell seconded the idea but admitted that there was little external evidence to support it. He, however, provided the first modern version of the text, leaving it to readers to decide the authorship question on their own. Seldom acted, until recent years the play has not been included in collected editions of Shakespeare's works.

The tide, however, has begun to turn. *King Edward III* has been given several recent stage productions, mostly notably by the Royal Shakespeare Company in 2002; and it is now printed in several collected editions of Shakespeare's works, including the second edition of the *Oxford Shakespeare* upon which the *Norton Shakespeare* is based. (For the complete text of the play, go to wwnorton.com/shakespeare.) What caused this new willingness to entertain the possibility that the play is in part or in its entirety by Shakespeare? First, scholars have increasingly realized that a number of early modern plays were collaboratively written, including some traditionally assigned to Shakespeare such as *Pericles, The Two Noble Kinsmen*, and a number of his early history plays. Why, then, exclude *King Edward III*, which, on stylistic and thematic grounds, seems to many scholars to contain several scenes indicating Shakespeare's authorship? While only a few scholars believe the play to be entirely his, a number find it likely that he had a hand in those parts involving the Countess of Salisbury and possibly some involving Prince Edward. The Oxford editors assign the bulk of Scene 2, all of Scenes 3 and 12, and possibly Scene 13 to Shakespeare. Second, the play, which most scholars believe was written between 1590 and 1594, mirrors many of Shakespeare's preoccupations during that time. Its central characters are the great Plantagenet king, Edward III, and his oldest son, Edward the Black Prince; its central action their heroic conquest of France. Throughout the 1590s, Shakespeare wrote about the aftermath of this king's reign as, after the Black Prince's early death, the Yorkist and Lancastrian branches of the Plantagenet family began a bitter fight over the crown, in the process losing effective control of England's French territories. In most of Shakespeare's other history plays, Edward III and his eldest son are revered as exemplars of English chivalry and military prowess. It is plausible, then, to think that Shakespeare would have been drawn to the direct dramatization of the king so often alluded to in his other histories.

Whether or not the play is in part by Shakespeare, *King Edward III* is an interesting and highly patriotic example of dramatized English history, a genre popular throughout

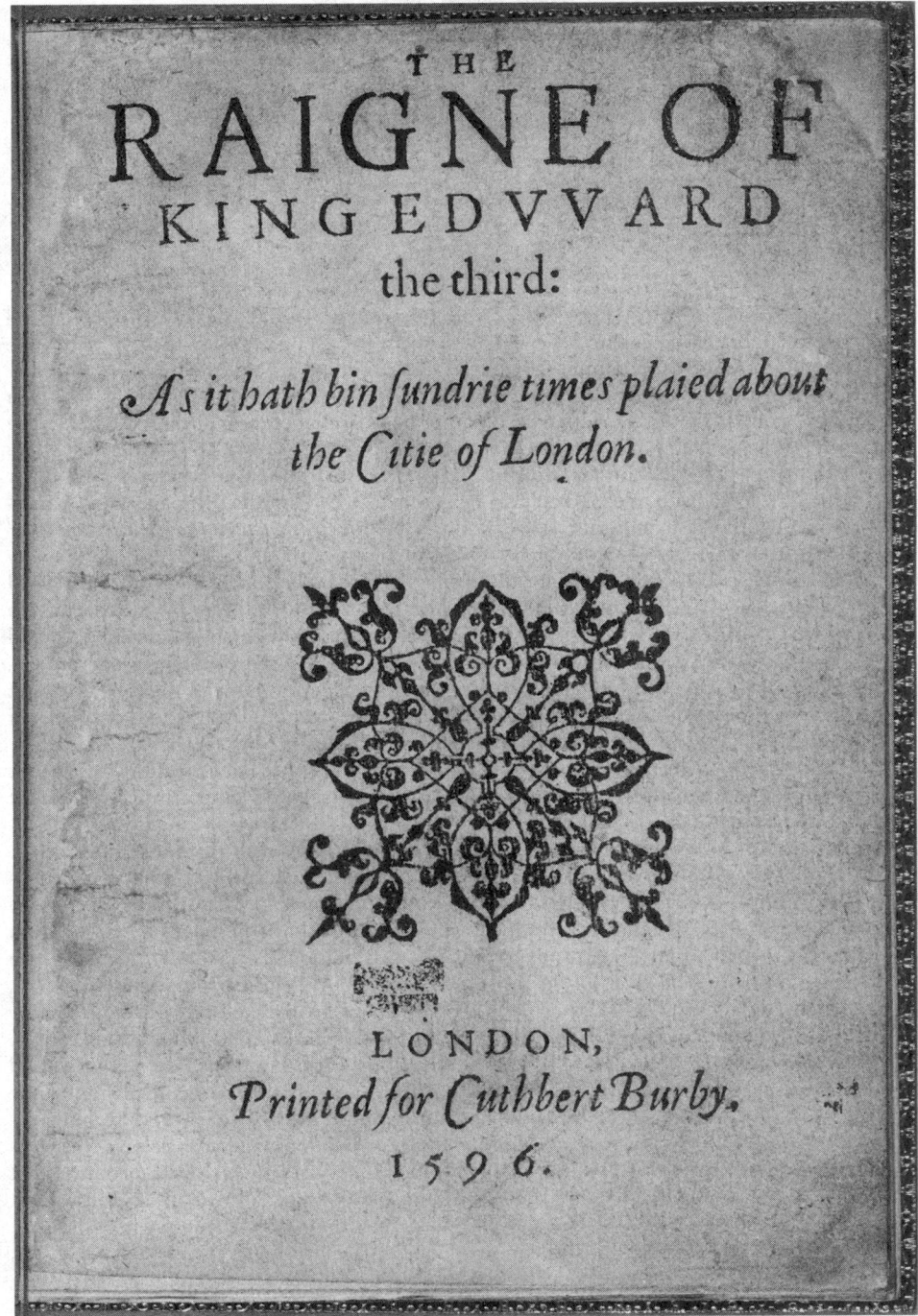

THE
RAIGNE OF
KING EDVVARD
the third:

As it hath bin sundrie times plaied about the Citie of London.

LONDON,
Printed for Cuthbert Burby.
1 5 9 6.

The title page for *The Raigne of King Edward the Third* (1596) gives no indication of who wrote the play.

the 1590s. Written in the wake of the destruction of the Spanish Armada in 1588, an event to which the play several times alludes, it presents England as a nearly invincible military force. As the action opens, Scottish forces have invaded England's northern borders, and Edward III has been insultingly summoned to France to pay tribute to its king. By play's end, Edward has captured both David, King of Scotland, and Jean of Valois, King of France, and he has triumphed in the great naval battle of Sluys as well as in land battles at Crécy, Poitiers, and Calais, a series of events that historically took place over a number of years but are here conveniently collapsed into one continuous arc of action.

Particular attention is paid to the exploits of Prince Edward, who, a little like Prince Hal of the *Henry IV* plays, is shown growing into his role as military hero and prospective monarch. Before the all-important Battle of Crécy, to mark the significance of the Prince's participation in it, his father ritualistically invests his son with the accoutrements of knighthood:

> And, Ned, because this battle is the first
> That ever yet thou fought'st in pitched field,
> As ancient custom is of martialists
> To dub thee with the type of chivalry,
> In solemn manner we will give thee arms
> Come, therefore, heralds; orderly bring forth
> A strong attirement for the Prince my son.
> (Scene 6, lines 171–77)

The Prince is then ceremoniously given a coat of armor, and then a helmet, a lance, a shield, and finally the honor of leading the vanguard in the coming battle. In the midst of that battle, when the Prince is surrounded by an overwhelming number of foes, the English nobles plead with King Edward to rescue him. Edward refuses. Demonstrating a species of "tough love," he says that the Prince's courage and skill are being tested and that he must fight this battle by himself, whatever the outcome. Miraculously, the Prince returns to his father in triumph *"bearing in his hand his shivered lance. The body of the King of Bohemia is borne before, wrapped in the colours of Bohemia"* (after Scene 8, line 60). This induction into the ways of chivalry recalls *1 Henry VI* and the exploits of the English hero, Talbot, and his son John, although in that play these mighty English warriors are slain by the French, but only after making a remarkable account of themselves against great odds; and it looks ahead to *Henry V* and King Henry's miraculous victory over the French at Agincourt. Not mentioned in this play, but probably known to many in the audience, was the fact that Edward III established the Order of the Garter, a chivalric institution that honored England's most distinguished warrior nobles. In the play, King Edward, his son, and his chief officers all come to embody Garter values of honor, courage, and military prowess.

The stage deeds of Edward and his son must have been memorable. They were explicitly recalled by Thomas Heywood in *An Apology for Actors* (1612), when he exclaims:

> What English Prince should hee behold the true portrature of that famous King *Edward* the third, foraging France, taking so great a King captive in his owne country, quartering the English Lyons with the French Flower-de yce, ... would not bee suddenly Inflam'd with so royall a spectacle, being made apt and fit for the like atchievement. So of *Henry* the fift.

The play clearly could make an impression on spectators, and its consistent emphasis on the overconfidence and pride of the French allowed for easy identification with the courageous and ultimately victorious English forces.

King Edward III's opening scenes, however, offer more complex pleasures, and those scenes are the ones most often attributed to Shakespeare. Edward III does not start the play as a paragon of virtue, even though he is a mighty warrior. Moving north to repel the Scots, who have besieged the castle where the Countess of Salisbury is ensconced, Edward falls swiftly and irrevocably in love with her, despite the fact that both he and she have spouses and children. In several remarkable encounters in which he pursues and she resists, the author dramatizes a moral struggle between two equally matched antagonists. In the end, she prevails, after threatening to kill herself should Edward insist on making her violate her marriage vows. As if waking from a dream, he says:

> Even by that power I swear, that gives me now
> The power to be ashamèd of myself,
> I never mean to part my lips again
> In any words that tends to such a suit.
> Arise, true English lady, whom our isle
> May better boast of than ever Roman might
> Of her, whose ransacked treasury hath tasked
> The vain endeavour of so many pens.
> Arise, and be my fault thy honour's fame
> Which after-ages shall enrich thee with.
> (Scene 3, lines 186–95)

A homegrown Lucrece, the Countess is Edward's ideal of an English lady, her chastity the guarantor of the purity of English bloodlines and, finally, the spur to Edward's own sense of honor. Prior to this moment, however, the play has vividly depicted the psychological torment of a man caught in the throes of a passion he can't control, a passion that draws him from affairs of state and very nearly makes him willing to murder his own wife and the Countess's husband. It is only after Edward overcomes this passion, with the Countess's help, that he is able to lead his army to France. Self-conquest seems the prerequisite for military conquest.

Interestingly, this part of the play contains its only memorably comic character, the hapless Lodowick, secretary to King Edward, who is commanded by the King to pen a letter to the Countess expressing Edward's passion. Lodowick is not much of a love poet and seems completely flummoxed by the task. After he ekes out a few lines, the King critiques them roundly, especially for commending the Countess's chastity, for, as he says, "I had rather have her chased than chaste!" (Scene 2, line 320), and for likening her to the moon when Edward would have her likened to the sun. The scene is both a sly comment on the frustrations of writing poetry at somebody else's command and also a lovely example of the ironic tonal juxtapositions so often found in early modern drama, especially drama by Shakespeare. The King is wrapped up in his own passion, forgetful of all the world, and both the grandeur and the dangerous self-absorption of his passion are highlighted through the contrast provided by the commonsensical, non-lyrical voice of his secretary just trying to do a job. Edward is in raptures over his beloved; Lodowick needs the facts: "To whom, my lord, shall I direct my style?" (Scene 2, line 246); "Write I to a woman?" (Scene 2, line 261). "Of what condition or estate she is / 'Twere requisite that I should know, my lord" (Scene 2, lines 265–66). Eventually, in frustration, the King grabs Lodowick's pen and paper, and vows to write the letter himself.

As the Countess of Salisbury scenes predict, throughout *Edward III* English women are given unusually powerful roles. Salisbury may be the English Lucrece, but the play's most striking embodiment of female power is Queen Philippa, Edward's wife, who, though pregnant, actively takes part in the suppression of the Scots while her husband is in France. As one lord describes her, she, "big with child, was every day in arms" (Scene 10, line 45). At the end of the play, she appears in France, still pregnant, for the moment when the Scottish and French kings both surrender to Edward. In *King Edward III*, women can be warriors without causing scandal. While the central battles in France make war seem an affair between men, the edges of the text suggest that this is not so, that women, too, can be warriors, and important ones.

Their key role in dynastic continuity is equally acknowledged. Edward's claim to

France rests on his mother's status as the only direct heir of the French King, King Philippe. As the Comte d'Artois says, she

> Was all the daughters that this Philippe had,
> Whom afterward your father took to wife.
> And from the fragrant garden of her womb
> Your gracious self, the flower of Europe's hope,
> Derivèd is inheritor to France.
> (Scene 1, lines 12–16)

The womb as a fragrant garden is a striking image, suggesting the beauty of his mother's fecundity, which in this instance has brought forth "the flower of Europe's hope" and secured that son a kingdom. Edward's wife, in turn, has brought forth heirs, in this play exemplified by the Black Prince, upon whose face his mother's image is vividly stamped. Looking at his young son while adulterously pursuing the Countess of Salisbury, Edward exclaims: "O, how his mother's face, / Modelled in his, corrects my strayed desire, / And rates my heart, and chides my thievish eye, / Who, being rich enough in seeing her, / Yet seek elsewhere" (Scene 3, lines 74–78). Rather than passive matter molded by the active father's impress, the mother in this instance has shaped the features of her son. Bearing his father's name, he bears his mother's face. It is women like the Countess whose chastity guarantees the purity of bloodlines and women like Edward's mother and wife who make dynastic lineage possible. The pregnant Philippa's appearance onstage at the end of the play brings together in one body the powerful martial and procreative roles that women in this play exemplify.

If *King Edward III* is primarily concerned with establishing English claims to French territory, its treatment of the Scots may be one factor in its seeming disappearance from print and stage at the end of the sixteenth century. The Scots are depicted as craven opportunists who besiege Roxburgh Castle, the Countess of Salisbury's home, and invade the northern shires of England once Edward's attention turns toward France. The Countess fears their "rough insulting barbarism" and the "vile, uncivil, skipping jigs" in which they will "bray forth" their imagined conquest of her castle (Scene 2, lines 9, 12, 13). Despite their boasting, however, the Scots run away when Edward unexpectedly appears to lift the siege of the castle. Later, these same Scots are defeated by English forces led by Queen Philippa, and the dramatist invents an unhistorical scene in which David, their King, is brought to France to be part of Edward's spectacle of conquest. It might not be surprising if, under a Scottish king like James I, who ascended the English throne in 1603, canny theater companies who wished to avoid his displeasure might have ceased to make *King Edward III* an active part of their repertory. Whatever the cause, the play fell from sight for most of the four hundred years following its first appearance in the 1590s. Now, however, it is available for all to judge what hand Shakespeare may have had—if any—in its composition, but also simply as another interesting example of how the early modern playwrights told the story of their nation's past.

JEAN E. HOWARD

SELECTED BIBLIOGRAPHY

Cahill, Patricia. "Biopower in the English Pale: Generation and Genocide in *King Edward III." Unto the Breach: Martial Formations, Historical Trauma, and the Early Modern Stage*. London: Oxford University Press, 2008. Argues that the play by indirection is concerned with the conquest of Ireland and with the military and procreative strategies by which that conquest could be achieved.

Conlan, J. P. "Shakespeare's *Edward III*: A Consolation for English Recusants." *Comparative Drama* 35.2 (2001): 177–207. Proposes that the play critiques the persecution of recusants after the English defeat of the Spanish Armada in 1588.

Melchiori, Giorgio, ed. *King Edward III.* Cambridge: Cambridge University Press, 1998. The introduction to this edition discusses the play's date of composition, the authorship question, and matters of style, theme, and dramatic structure.

———. *Shakespeare's Garter Plays: "Edward III" to "Merry Wives of Windsor."* Newark: University of Delaware Press, 1994. Argues that because the historical Edward III founded the Order of the Garter and because *King Edward III* deals with the theme of honor and the education of princes, it should be grouped with five other Shakespeare plays preoccupied with the Order and its values.

Metz, G. Harold, ed. *Sources of Four Plays Ascribed to Shakespeare: "The Reign of King Edward III," "Sir Thomas More," "The History of Cardenio," "The Two Noble Kinsmen."* Columbia: University of Missouri Press, 1989. Summarizes scholarship on the play and provides primary source material from Jean Froissart, Raphael Holinshed, and William Painter.

Proudfoot, Richard. "*The Reign of Edward III* (1596) and Shakespeare." *Proceedings of the British Academy* 71 (1985): 159–85. Discusses many aspects of the play, including arguing that it has a three-part structure and was first performed by Lord Pembroke's Men.

Rackin, Phyllis. "Women's Roles in the Elizabethan History Plays." *The Cambridge Companion to Shakespeare's History Plays.* Ed. Michael Hattaway. Cambridge: Cambridge University Press, 2002. 71–85. Questioning Shakespeare's authorship of *King Edward III*, Rackin argues that, unlike most of Shakespeare's history plays, it shows women who are both virtuous and powerful in the persons of the Countess of Salisbury and Queen Philippa.

Sams, Eric, ed. *Shakespeare's "Edward III."* New Haven: Yale University Press, 1996. Argues strenuously that Shakespeare was the author of *Edward III* because of parallels to other Shakespeare plays and poems, and on the basis of diction, versification, imagery, and so forth.

The Comedy of Errors

In his essay "On Cripples," Shakespeare's great contemporary Montaigne alludes to a strange case of impersonation in a small rural community in southwestern France. There, a cunning imposter succeeded in assuming the identity of Martin Guerre, a man who had disappeared some years before. The imposter lived in the community for three years, sleeping with Guerre's wife and farming his land, until the real Martin Guerre unexpectedly returned. Convicted of fraud, the imposter confessed and was hanged.

Montaigne was dismayed by the execution, for he felt that the evidence was too murky, the imposture too convincing, and human identity too elusive a possession to justify capital punishment. The court, he writes, should have emulated the ancient Greek tribunal that, confronted by a similarly baffling case ordered the parties to come back in a hundred years. Montaigne was not only advising judicial caution; he was urging his readers to take everyday life less automatically, to acknowledge the inevitability of ignorance and error, and to respond to their own existence with wonder. "I have seen no more evident monstrosity and miracle in the world than myself," he writes in the same essay in which he talks about Martin Guerre. "We become habituated to anything strange by use and time; but the more I frequent myself and know myself, the more my deformity astonishes me, and the less I understand myself."

Montaigne's reflections on Martin Guerre have no direct bearing on *The Comedy of Errors*, but they alert us to the play's wholesale unsettling of the familiar. The comfortable assumptions that condition a normal life—I know who I am; these things belong to me and not to someone else; these are the people I love, work for, do business with, or avoid—are undermined by the tangled interactions of two sets of identical (and identically named) twins. Antipholus of Syracuse and Antipholus of Ephesus, along with their servants, Dromio of Syracuse and Dromio of Ephesus, have been raised apart from one another in separate cities and are unaware that their paths are now unexpectedly crossing. Through a breathless succession of zany doublings and confusions, Shakespeare's comedy discloses the hidden strangeness of ordinary existence. An invitation to dinner, a simple transaction with a goldsmith, the operation of commercial and civil laws, the relation between master and servant, the bond between husband and wife (or mistress or sister-in-law)—all become unhinged, as if by sorcery. "There's not a man I meet but doth salute me," says Antipholus of Syracuse, "as if I were their well-acquainted friend, / And everyone doth call me by my name" (4.3.1–3). These are the practices of everyday life, but to this stranger who is, unbeknownst to him, being mistaken for his identical (and identically named) twin, they confirm the unsavory reputation of Ephesus as a place of "nimble jugglers," "Dark-working sorcerers," "Soul-killing witches," and "Disguisèd cheaters" (1.2.98–101).

The audience knows, of course, that Antipholus's uncanny experiences have been caused neither by witchcraft nor by the larcenous wiles that so astonished Montaigne. The wonder that seems to suffuse everything is the result of nothing more magical or malicious than twinship and a shared name, and hence, we could say, such wonder is spurious or misplaced, the result of misunderstandings. "This is the fairy land" (2.2.189), exclaims one of the Dromios, mystified by the succession of inexplicable events, and his similarly disoriented master invokes the notorious wiles of far-off Lapland. But in *The Comedy of Errors*, there is in reality only daylight and the familiar city

An Italian merchant pictured on a Florentine playing card.

street of Roman comedy, a street reassuringly adapted to the commercial world of Shakespeare's London. Disorientation and danger lurk, to be sure, in this conventional urban landscape—Antipholus of Syracuse thinks he is the victim of sorcery, Antipholus of Ephesus is treated as a madman, Adriana fears the loss of her husband's love, Luciana is convinced that her brother-in-law is trying to seduce her, the servants are constantly beaten, and poor Egeon is condemned to die at day's end. The pressure of time weighs heavily on virtually all of the characters, enmeshed as they are in humiliating, menacing, and apparently insoluble difficulties, but these confusions are neatly resolved by the appointed hour of 5:00 P.M.

Yet this comic resolution does not quite make wonder altogether evaporate from the play. Montaigne urged his readers to abandon their confident belief in the ordered rationality of life and to find the marvelous in the everyday. Identical twins are fairly commonplace and the fact that two people can bear the same name even more so, but Shakespeare's play calls attention to all that is potentially disorienting in the routine circumstances of life. The end of *The Comedy of Errors* seems to restore order and reason—to make the ordinary world ordinary again—but the closing gestures lightly unsettle this restoration. The abbess, who turns out to be Egeon's long-lost wife and the mother of the twin Antipholuses, finds a strange image, at once touching and grotesque, to describe her experiences: she declares that she has been pregnant for thirty-three years and has only now given birth. And the twin Dromios, unable to determine which of them is the elder and should therefore go first through the door, decide that they will draw lots for seniority; meanwhile, they will dispense with hierarchy and go through the door hand in hand.

More telling, perhaps, the questions raised by the strange case of Martin Guerre linger unresolved at the end of Shakespeare's comedy: What is the self? What are the guarantees of identity? Who possesses a name and by what right? How is individuality secured? How can one person represent another? The drama is the perfect medium for an exploration of these questions, for the form of the drama itself invites reflection on the extent to which it is possible for one person to assume the identity of another. From this perspective, *The Comedy of Errors* is not, as it is sometimes said to be, a simple and even simpleminded farce, the crude work of a novice playwright, but a remarkably subtle and acute deployment of the very conditions of the theater to engage with problems that haunted Shakespeare throughout his career.

While it is a mistake to view it as mere apprentice work, *The Comedy of Errors* is nonetheless one of the earliest of Shakespeare's plays (and it is also, perhaps not coincidentally, the shortest). Its exact date of composition and first performance are unknown; there was a performance at Gray's Inn, one of London's law schools, on December 28, 1594, but its thematic and stylistic resemblances to Shakespeare's other early comedies, *The Two Gentlemen of Verona, Love's Labour's Lost*, and *The Taming of the Shrew*, have led many scholars to conclude that he wrote it some years earlier. It was not printed until 1623, as part of the First Folio.

The anonymous recorder of the Gray's Inn performance—apparently something of a debacle because of the pushing and shoving of unexpectedly large crowds—noted the play's resemblance to an ancient comedy, the *Menaechmi*, written by the Roman playwright Plautus. Shakespeare probably read this much-admired play in Latin, since an English translation, by William Warner, was not printed until 1595. The *Menaechmi* is a brilliant, energetic farce, fast-paced, funny, and, as farces often are, cold at heart. A prologue carefully explains the premise: a Syracusan merchant took one of his twin sons, seven years old, on a business trip abroad. During a festival, he accidentally became separated from the son. The boy was found by a childless trader, who took him off to Epidamnum; the father, crazed with grief, died a few days later. When news of the catastrophe reached Syracuse, the remaining son was given the name of his missing brother.

The action of Plautus's play is set some years later, when Menaechmus of Syracuse, searching for his twin, finds himself in Epidamnum. Greeted warmly by perfect strangers, Menaechmus realizes that some mistake is being made, but he is not filled with dread. "I can lose nothing," he cheerfully tells his slave, as he accepts food, gifts, and sexual favors from a woman who has inexplicably confused him with someone else and imagines that she is his mistress. What most strikes him is that it is all free of charge. His twin, a prosperous citizen normally comfortable in an entourage that includes wife, household slaves, mistress, and an obnoxious hanger-on nicknamed the Sponge, is frustrated by the fact that everyone seems to have gone mad and becomes enraged when he himself is treated as a madman. The dizzying confusions steadily mount until the brothers find themselves face-to-face and, with delicious slowness, figure out that they are the long-separated identical twins. The brothers plan to return together to Syracuse, and the play ends with the announcement of the forthcoming auction of Menaechmus's property: "slaves, household effects, house, land, etcetera—and a wife, should there be any purchaser."

A scene in the street / the street as scene. Woodcut from a German edition of Terence's *Eunuchus* (1486).

Though he took over much of Plautus's farce, Shakespeare made highly revealing changes and additions. For a start, he shifted the setting from Epidamnum to Ephesus, a city associated with sorcery, exorcism, mystery cults, and early Christianity. As if to multiply the comic confusion generated by one set of identical twins, he added a second set—the servants, who, for reasons that are not really explained, bear like their masters a single name. (The device of the identical slaves is borrowed from another play by Plautus, the *Amphitruo*.) Shakespeare also chose in effect to double the plot by framing the main action with the anguished figure of the Syracusan merchant Egeon, caught up in his city's murderous commercial struggle with rival Ephesus. The melancholy personal history that Egeon relates is adapted not from the ancient comedy but from a medieval romance, the tale of Apollonius of Tyre as told by the fourteenth-century poet John Gower in his *Confessio Amantis* (a tale to which Shakespeare again turned many years later for the plot of *Pericles*). Egeon's fate quickly recedes from the audience's attention, but the threat to his life provides a somber context for the play's hilarity, and his return to the stage at the close, on the way to the place of execution, suddenly raises the stakes of the resolution. The closing scene highlights the romance elements that Shakespeare introduced into his frenetic scheme of mistaken identity: the reuniting of parents and children who had been tragically separated, the miraculous recovery of a beloved spouse long presumed dead, and a sense of wonder that does not entirely evaporate with the solving of the puzzle. Plautus's Epidamnum is a city full of rogues, parasites, and courtesans, a place where you can lose your cloak, your chain, and your money; Shakespeare's Ephesus is a place where you can lose—or regain—your life.

Egeon's story in *The Comedy of Errors* has a shape that merits attention: he is condemned to death through the operation of an inflexible law that even the sympathetic duke cannot mitigate, and then, through a wondrous turn of events, his life is spared, and he recovers the loved ones he thought he had lost forever. Even though the play is set in pagan antiquity, in this shape we may sense the psychic and moral rhythm of Christianity: the mortal penalty of the harsh law is wiped out, altogether unexpectedly and gratuitously, by a miraculous, loving dispensation. The farcical core of the play is at a considerable remove from this portentous rhythm, but Christianity's influence is not restricted to the frame. Since Shakespeare and his age were relatively indifferent to anachronism, Antipholus of Syracuse can say to his servant, "Now, as I am a Christian, answer me" (1.2.77), and the servant can call for his rosary beads and cross himself (2.2.188). The fear of demonic possession takes a specifically Christian form when Satan himself is exorcised by Doctor Pinch. And although pagan antiquity had shrines such as the Temple of Diana at Ephesus (where the tale of Apollonius of Tyre reaches it climax), the priory and its Abbess seem to belong in a Christian community, a community invoked by the very name of Ephesus, where St. Paul preached and to which he wrote an influential epistle.

A central concern of Paul's Epistle to the Ephesians is Christian marriage: men are urged to love their wives as their own bodies, while women are urged to submit themselves unto their husbands as unto the Lord. These strikingly asymmetrical admonitions make themselves felt throughout *The Comedy of Errors*. Where Plautus's Menaechmus cheerfully cheats on his wife, Shakespeare's married twin seems to have an inward principle of moral restraint. Antipholus is driven to the courtesan only when his wife, Adriana, seems to turn him away from his own house—and even then, protesting to his friends that his wife's suspicions are unfounded, he seems mainly interested in dinner and pleasant conversation. Where the nameless wife in Plautus is above all outraged that her husband has stolen from her a gown and a bracelet to bestow as presents on his mistress, Shakespeare's Adriana is obsessed with the possibility that her husband no longer loves her. It is this tormenting fear of marital estrangement that has driven her to a querulousness that only confirms her overwhelming craving for perfect union:

"I'll to the mart" (3.2.182). London's Royal Exchange, founded by Sir Thomas Gresham, 1565. Etching by Wenceslaus Hollar (1644).

> Ah, do not tear away thyself from me;
> For know, my love, as easy mayst thou fall
> A drop of water in the breaking gulf,
> And take unmingled thence that drop again
> Without addition or diminishing,
> As take from me thyself, and not me too.
>
> (2.2.124–29)

The oneness that is envisioned here, the poignant longing for wholeness, and the fear of pollution and self-loss have no place in the emotional register of the *Menaechmi*. Where Plautus's farce ends with a joke about offering the wife for sale, *The Comedy of Errors* ends with the characters, reconciled and reunited, entering the abbey for a feast.

Near the close of Shakespeare's play, the Abbess seems to reflect the spirit of St. Paul's admonition to wives when she observes that by robbing her husband of the "sweet recreation" that he should find at home, Adriana's "jealous fits" have driven him mad (5.1.69–87). This criticism echoes both Antipholus's own complaint that his wife is "shrewish" and the distinctly Pauline opinions voiced by Adriana's sister, Luciana. Luciana—a character for whom there is no precedent in Plautus—argues that males of every species are "masters to their females, and their lords" (2.1.24) and therefore that Adriana should patiently submit to her husband. Such views, similar to those expressed by the "reformed" Katherine in *The Taming of the Shrew*, are given considerable prominence in *The Comedy of Errors* and yet they are neither unchallenged nor unequivocally endorsed. Adriana observes that her sister is single and hence that her views on marriage are untested by experience. And the Abbess's moralizing diagnosis—that Antipholus would not have mistreated Adriana or gone mad if she had reined in her tongue—turns out to be merely another of the mistaken conjectures that all of the characters incessantly advance in their attempts to account for the day's weird events.

There is a kind of laughter that functions as social regulation: comedy, writes Sir Philip Sidney in his *Defense of Poesie* (c. 1583), "is an imitation of the common errors of our life," which the dramatist represents "in the most ridiculous and scornful sort that may be, so as it is impossible that any beholder can be content to be such a one." The errors in *The Comedy of Errors* are ridiculous, but they are hardly common, and the audience's laughter seems something other than scornful or regulative. None of the explanatory accounts, not even the moral values and providential rhythm of Christianity with which Shakespeare has infused his pagan plot, seems entirely adequate as a response to the chain of mad mistakings. The characters are subject not to a divine plan or to the social order but to fortune. And if this fortune turns out to have the happy air of providence—epitomized by the reuniting of the divided and dispersed family—there seems to be no particularly uplifting lesson to be learned.

Shakespeare's play, to be sure, is cannily alert to social inequities—an innocent merchant is condemned to death for being in the wrong place at the wrong time; a husband is "master of his liberty," while a wife must "practise to obey" (2.1.7, 29); one set of twins is destined through poverty to be the servants, casually beaten and abused, of the other set—but it does not mount a strenuous protest or imagine a radical transformation. In the midst of the farcical confusions, characters repeatedly long for greater justice, equality, and emotional fulfillment, but *The Comedy of Errors* does not encourage us to believe that such an existence can be realized. There may be a happy resolution, but there is no escape from the pervasive, fundamentally inequitable social order and from the mercantile world based on credit, trade, exchange, bonds, and debt.

Several of Shakespeare's best-loved comedies are structured around alternative worlds: the familiar, daylit realm of the court or city is set against the magical realm of the woods and the enchanted night. But in *The Comedy of Errors*, there is only the single urban setting, a setting that would have reminded contemporary audiences of the bustling city that stretched out beyond the walls of the playhouse. In the sixteenth century, London had become the center of a commercial culture that Shakespeare deftly sketches with quick strokes. We learn that Antipholus keeps a purse of ducats locked "in the desk / That's covered o'er with Turkish tapestry" (4.1.103–4), that the courtesan considers a ring worth 40 ducats "too much to lose" (4.3.91), and that the goldsmith plans to discharge his overdue debt to a merchant with the money that Antipholus has promised to pay him for the gold chain. That gold chain functions as a convenient symbol of the interlinked network of obligations and exchanges in which the twins—who seem as like one another as two coins of equal value—are caught and which their uncontrolled interchangeability temporarily disrupts.

A closer look reveals that Antipholus of Ephesus and Antipholus of Syracuse are not perfectly interchangeable: the former is confident, well connected, and somewhat irascible; the latter is anxious, insecure, driven by restless longing:

> I to the world am like a drop of water
> That in the ocean seeks another drop,
> Who, falling there to find his fellow forth,
> Unseen, inquisitive, confounds himself.
> (1.2.35–38)

This poignant sense of self-loss, which anticipates the alienation and existential anxiety of the tragedies, is intensified by the mad confusions that follow: the events of *The Comedy of Errors* may be deliciously amusing to the audience, but to the characters they are mystifying and even nightmarish. Antonin Artaud, a modern writer who championed what he called the "Theater of Cruelty," praises the Marx Brothers' movies in terms that seem at least as relevant to Shakespeare's comedy: "In order to understand the powerful, total, definitive, absolute originality . . . of films like *Animal Crackers*," Artaud writes, "you would have to add to humor the notion of something disquieting and tragic, a fatality (neither happy nor unhappy, difficult to formulate) which would hover over it like the cast of an appalling malady upon an exquisitely beautiful profile." And yet it is not the nightmare that triumphs but laughter, laughter at what another sixteenth-century writer, George Gascoigne, called "supposes." Gascoigne defined a suppose as "a mistaking or imagination of one thing for another," and it is with a frantic succession of these supposes, all equally wide of the mark, that the baffled characters of *The Comedy of Errors* occupy themselves.

The "imagination of one thing for another" could serve as a definition of the theater. The spectators of Shakespeare's comedy have paid for the pleasure of watching identity slip away from the characters' grasp, as if in the home or the marketplace who you are is no more secure than it is onstage. They have paid too for the pleasure of watching identity serendipitously return, as if Shakespeare's theater had the magic power to restore the human family, however broken and scattered, and restore stability to the battered self. If neither the loss nor the recovery is altogether plausible, the delicious intertwining of the two seems designed to provoke what Montaigne urged upon his readers: a skeptical wonder.

STEPHEN GREENBLATT

TEXTUAL NOTE

The Comedy of Errors was first printed in the 1623 First Folio, which is therefore the only authoritative text of the play. Scholars generally believe that the text was based on Shakespeare's own autograph manuscript. Evidence for this belief centers on features of the stage directions and speech prefixes that are likely to derive from the playwright himself rather than a compositor or playhouse bookkeeper. For example, the stage direction before 4.4.36 calls for "a Schoole-master, call'd Pinch," although there is no mention in the dialogue that Pinch is a schoolmaster. Similarly, while the prompter's copy would normally call only for a particular character by name, the stage direction at 2.1.0 specifies that Adriana is "wife to Antipholis Sereptus." ("Sereptus" is from the Latin *surreptus*, "stolen away," an epithet applied several times by Plautus to the twin who corresponds to Antipholus of Ephesus. At his first appearance, Antipholus of Syracuse is referred to as "Antipholus Erotes"; some critics have conjectured that "Erotes" is a corruption of *erraticus*, "wandering," by analogy with *surreptus*.)

The Folio text indicates act divisions (and specifies "Scena Prima" at the beginning of Acts 1, 3, 4, and 5).

SELECTED BIBLIOGRAPHY

Baldwin, T. W. *Shakespere's Five-Act Structure: Shakespere's Early Plays on the Background of Renaissance Theories of Five-Act Structure from 1470*. Urbana: University of Illinois Press, 1947.

Christensen, Ann C. "'Because their business still lies out a' door': Resisting the Separation of the Spheres in Shakespeare's *The Comedy of Errors*." *Literature and History* 5 (1996): 19–37.

Frye, Northrop. "The Argument of Comedy." *English Institute Essays*. New York: AMS Press, 1948. 58–73.

Hunt, Maurice. "Slavery, English Servitude and *The Comedy of Errors*." *English Literary Renaissance* 27 (1997): 31–56.

Miola, Robert S., ed. *"The Comedy of Errors": Critical Essays*. New York: Routledge, 2001.

Parker, Patricia. "The Bible and the Marketplace: *The Comedy of Errors*." *Shakespeare from the Margins: Language, Culture, Context.* Chicago: University of Chicago Press, 1996. 56–82.

Perry, Curtis. "Commerce, Community, and Nostalgia in *The Comedy of Errors*." *Money and the Age of Shakespeare: Essays in New Economic Criticism.* Ed. Linda Woodbridge. New York: Palgrave Macmillan, 2003. 39–51.

Salgādo, Gāmini. "'Time's Deformed Hand': Sequence, Consequence, and Inconsequence in *The Comedy of Errors*." *Shakespeare Survey* 25 (1972): 81–92.

Taylor, Gary. "Textual and Sexual Criticism: A Crux in *The Comedy of Errors*." *Renaissance Drama* 19 (1988): 195–225.

Witmore, Michael. "The Avoidance of Ends in *The Comedy of Errors*." *Culture of Accidents: Unexpected Knowledges in Early Modern England.* Stanford: Stanford University Press, 2001. 62–81.

FILM

The Comedy of Errors. 1983. Dir. James Cellan Jones. UK. 109 min. A BBC-TV production, with Roger Daltrey (lead singer of The Who) as the Dromios.

The Comedy of Errors

THE PERSONS OF THE PLAY

Solinus, DUKE of Ephesus
EGEON, a merchant of Syracuse, father of the Antipholus twins
ANTIPHOLUS OF EPHESUS ⎫
ANTIPHOLUS OF SYRACUSE ⎭ twin brothers, sons of Egeon
DROMIO OF EPHESUS ⎫ twin brothers, and bondmen of the
DROMIO OF SYRACUSE ⎭ Antipholus twins
ADRIANA, wife of Antipholus of Ephesus
LUCIANA, her sister
NELL, Adriana's kitchen-maid
ANGELO, a goldsmith
BALTHASAR, a merchant
A COURTESAN
Doctor PINCH, a schoolmaster and exorcist
MERCHANT OF EPHESUS, a friend of Antipholus of Syracuse
SECOND MERCHANT, Angelo's creditor
Emilia, an ABBESS at Ephesus
Jailer, messenger, headsman, officers, and other attendants

1.1

Enter [Solinus], the DUKE *of Ephesus, with* [EGEON] *the*
Merchant of Syracuse, JAILER, *and other attendants*

EGEON Proceed, Solinus, to procure my fall,
  And by the doom° of death end woes and all.   sentence
DUKE Merchant of Syracusa, plead no more.
  I am not partial° to infringe our laws.   inclined
5 The enmity and discord which of late
  Sprung from the rancorous outrage of your Duke
  To merchants, our well-dealing[1] countrymen,
  Who, wanting° guilders[2] to redeem° their lives,   lacking / ransom
  Have sealed° his rigorous statutes with their bloods,   ratified
10 Excludes all pity from our threat'ning looks.
  For since the mortal° and intestine jars°   deadly / bitter strife
  'Twixt thy seditious countrymen and us,
  It hath in solemn synods° been decreed,   assemblies
  Both by the Syracusians and ourselves,
15 To admit no traffic to[3] our adverse° towns.   hostile
  Nay more: if any born at Ephesus
  Be seen at Syracusian marts° and fairs;   markets
  Again, if any Syracusian born
  Come to the bay of Ephesus—he dies,

1.1 Location: A street in Ephesus. The setting of the entire play was probably modeled after that of ancient Roman comedy: a conjunction of city streets, with three doors to represent houses, each marked with a sign. The house of Antipholus of Ephesus, identified as the Phoenix, is flanked by the courtesan's house (marked with the sign of a porcupine) and the priory (perhaps marked anachronistically with a cross). When the action is not focused on these houses, the stage serves as a generalized urban space, most often called the "mart"—that is, the marketplace.
1. Honest-trading; more generally, civil or well-behaved.
2. Money, not specifically referring to Dutch or German coins.
3. To allow no trade between.

20	His goods confiscate to the Duke's dispose,°	*disposal*
	Unless a thousand marks⁴ be levièd°	*raised*
	To quit° the penalty and ransom him.	*pay*
	Thy substance,° valued at the highest rate,	*goods*
	Cannot amount unto a hundred marks.	
25	Therefore by law thou art condemned to die.	
	EGEON Yet this my comfort: when your words are done,	
	My woes end likewise with the evening sun.	
	DUKE Well, Syracusian, say in brief the cause	
	Why thou departed'st from thy native home,	
30	And for what cause thou cam'st to Ephesus.	
	EGEON A heavier task could not have been imposed	
	Than I° to speak my griefs unspeakable.	*Than for me*
	Yet, that the world may witness that my end	
	Was wrought by nature,⁵ not by vile offence,	
35	I'll utter what my sorrow gives me leave.	
	In Syracusa was I born, and wed	
	Unto a woman happy but for me,⁶	
	And by me° happy, had not our hap° been bad.	*by me made / luck*
	With her I lived in joy, our wealth increased	
40	By prosperous voyages I often made	
	To Epidamnum,⁷ till my factor's° death,	*agent's*
	And the great care of goods at random° left,	*untended*
	Drew me from kind embracements of my spouse,	
	From whom my absence was not six months old	
45	Before herself—almost at fainting under	
	The pleasing punishment that women bear°—	*(pregnancy)*
	Had made provision for her following me,	
	And soon and safe arrivèd where I was.	
	There had she not been long but she became	
50	A joyful mother of two goodly sons;	
	And, which was strange, the one so like the other	
	As° could not be distinguished but by names.	*That they*
	That very hour, and in the selfsame inn,	
	A mean-born woman° was deliverèd	*woman of low birth*
55	Of such a burden male, twins both alike.	
	Those, for° their parents were exceeding poor,	*because*
	I bought, and brought up to attend my sons.	
	My wife, not meanly° proud of two such boys,	*in no small degree*
	Made daily motions° for our home return.	*requests*
60	Unwilling, I agreed. Alas! Too soon	
	We came aboard.	
	A league from Epidamnum had we sailed	
	Before the always-wind-obeying deep	
	Gave any tragic instance° of our harm.	*sign*
65	But longer did we not retain much hope,	
	For what obscurèd light the heavens did grant	
	Did but convey unto our fearful minds	
	A doubtful warrant° of immediate death,	*A fearsome confirmation*
	Which though myself would gladly have embraced,	
70	Yet the incessant weepings of my wife—	

4. A mark was two-thirds of a pound in English money, although there was no coin of this amount.
5. Was brought about by natural feeling: a father's love.

6. Fortunate except in her association with me.
7. Plautus's setting for the *Meneachmi*, now Durrës in Albania; Shakespeare's play, however, seems to treat it as if it were in Greece.

Weeping before° for what she saw must come— *in advance*
And piteous plainings° of the pretty babes, *cries*
That mourned for fashion, ignorant what to fear,[8]
Forced me to seek delays° for them and me. *reprieves*
75 And this it was—for other means was none:
The sailors sought for safety by our boat,° *lifeboat*
And left the ship, then sinking-ripe,[9] to us.
My wife, more careful° for the latter-born,° *anxious / younger*
Had fastened him unto a small spare mast
80 Such as seafaring men provide for storms.
To him one of the other twins was bound,
Whilst I had been like heedful of° the other. *equally attentive to*
The children thus disposed,° my wife and I, *placed*
Fixing our eyes on whom our care was fixed,
85 Fastened ourselves at either end the mast,
And floating straight,° obedient to the stream, *immediately*
Was carried towards Corinth, as we thought.
At length the sun, gazing upon the earth,
Dispersed those vapours° that offended° us, *clouds / harmed*
90 And by the benefit of his wishèd light
The seas waxed calm, and we discovered
Two ships from far, making amain° to us: *speeding*
Of Corinth that, of Epidaurus[1] this.
But ere they came—O let me say no more!
95 Gather the sequel by that went before.[2]
DUKE   Nay, forward, old man; do not break off so,
For we may pity though not pardon thee.
EGEON   O, had the gods done so, I had not now
Worthily° termed them merciless to us. *Justly*
100 For, ere the ships could meet by° twice five leagues, *come within*
We were encountered by a mighty rock,
Which being violently borne upon,
Our helpful ship° was splitted in the midst, *(the mast)*
So that in this unjust divorce of us
105 Fortune had left to both of us alike° *equally*
What° to delight in, what to sorrow for. *Something*
Her° part, poor soul, seeming as burdenèd *(My wife's)*
With lesser weight[3] but not with lesser woe,
Was carried with more speed before the wind,
110 And in our sight they three were taken up
By fishermen of Corinth, as we thought.
At length another ship had seized on us,° *hauled us up*
And, knowing whom it was their hap° to save, *luck*
Gave healthful welcome to their shipwrecked guests,
115 And would have reft° the fishers of their prey[4] *deprived*
Had not their barque° been very slow of sail; *vessel*
And therefore homeward did they bend their course.
Thus have you heard me severed from my bliss,
That by misfortunes was my life prolonged
120 To tell sad stories of my own mishaps.

8. That imitated the adults' lamentation without understanding it.
9. At the point of sinking; softened and ready to drop.
1. Either modern Dubrovnik, on the Adriatic and north of Durrës (Epidamnum), or the Greek city actually called Epidaurus, near Corinth.
2. Deduce what followed from that which I have already recounted.
3. Lighter than her husband and the other child.
4. Those whom they have fished out of the sea.

DUKE   And for the sake of them thou sorrow'st for,
Do me the favour to dilate at° full   *relate in*
What have befall'n of them and thee till now.
EGEON   My youngest boy,[5] and yet my eldest care,
125   At eighteen years became inquisitive
After his brother, and importuned me
That his attendant—so his case was like,[6]
Reft of his brother, but retained his name[7]—
Might bear him company in the quest of him;
130   Whom whilst I laboured of a love to see,[8]
I hazarded the loss of whom I loved.
Five summers have I spent in farthest Greece,
Roaming clean through the bounds of Asia,
And coasting° homeward came to Ephesus,   *sailing*
135   Hopeless to find,° yet loath to leave unsought   *find them*
Or° that or any place that harbours men.   *Either*
But here must end the story of my life,
And happy were I in my timely death
Could all my travels[9] warrant° me they live.   *assure*
140   DUKE   Hapless° Egeon, whom the fates have marked   *Unlucky*
To bear the extremity of dire mishap,
Now trust me, were it not against our laws—
Which princes, would they, may not disannul[1]—
Against my crown, my oath, my dignity,
145   My soul should sue as advocate for thee.
But though thou art adjudgèd° to the death,   *sentenced*
And passèd sentence may not be recalled
But° to our honour's great disparagement,°   *Except / disgrace*
Yet will I favour thee in what I can.[2]
150   Therefore, merchant, I'll limit° thee this day   *allot*
To seek thy health° by beneficial help.   *deliverance*
Try all the friends thou hast in Ephesus:
Beg thou or borrow to make up the sum,
And live. If no, then thou art doomed to die.
155   Jailer, take him to thy custody.
JAILER   I will, my lord.
EGEON   Hopeless and helpless doth Egeon wend,°   *go*
But to procrastinate° his lifeless end.   *Exeunt*   *postpone*

1.2

Enter [from the bay] ANTIPHOLUS [OF SYRACUSE], MER-
CHANT [OF EPHESUS], *and* DROMIO [OF SYRACUSE]

MERCHANT OF EPHESUS   Therefore give out° you are of Epidamnum,   *say*
Lest that your goods too soon be confiscate.
This very day a Syracusian merchant
Is apprehended for arrival here,
5   And, not being able to buy out° his life,   *ransom*
According to the statute of the town
Dies ere the weary sun set in the west.
There is your money that I had to keep.°   *in my keeping*

---

5. An inconsistency of detail (see line 78).
6. *so . . . like:* in this way his situation was similar.
7. Bore the name of the brother from whom he was separated.
8. *Whom . . . see:* Since I longed to see my lost son.

9. Journeys; "travails," efforts.
1. *would . . . disannul:* even if they wished to, cannot cancel or make void.
2. Yet I will bend the law's strictness as much as I can.
1.2 Location: A street in Ephesus.

ANTIPHOLUS OF SYRACUSE [*to* DROMIO]   Go bear it to the
  Centaur,¹ where we host,°   *lodge*
10 And stay there, Dromio, till I come to thee.
  Within this hour it will be dinner-time.²
  Till that° I'll view the manners of the town,   *then*
  Peruse° the traders, gaze upon the buildings,   *Observe*
  And then return and sleep within mine inn;
15 For with long travel I am stiff and weary.
  Get thee away.
DROMIO OF SYRACUSE   Many a man would take you at your word,
  And go indeed, having so good a mean.³   *Exit*
ANTIPHOLUS OF SYRACUSE   A trusty villain,⁴ sir, that very oft,
20 When I am dull° with care and melancholy,   *gloomy*
  Lightens my humour⁵ with his merry jests.
  What,° will you walk with me about the town, *Now then*
  And then go to my inn and dine with me?
MERCHANT OF EPHESUS   I am invited, sir, to certain merchants
25 Of whom I hope to make much benefit.
  I crave your pardon. Soon° at five o'clock,   *Promptly*
  Please° you, I'll meet with you upon the mart, *If it please*
  And afterward consort° you till bedtime.   *accompany*
  My present business calls me from you now.
30 ANTIPHOLUS OF SYRACUSE   Farewell till then. I will go lose myself,
  And wander up and down to view the city.
MERCHANT OF EPHESUS   Sir, I commend you to your own
  content.°   *Exit* *pleasures; peace*
ANTIPHOLUS OF SYRACUSE   He that commends me to mine own
  content
  Commends me to the thing I cannot get.
35 I to the world am like a drop of water
  That in the ocean seeks another drop,
  Who, falling there to find his fellow forth,⁶
  Unseen, inquisitive, confounds° himself.   *mingles; destroys*
  So I, to find a mother and a brother,
40 In quest of them, unhappy, lose myself.
     Enter DROMIO OF EPHESUS
  Here comes the almanac of my true date.⁷
  What now? How chance° thou art returned so soon? *What happened that*
DROMIO OF EPHESUS   Returned so soon? Rather approached too late.
  The capon burns, the pig falls from the spit.
45 The clock hath strucken twelve upon the bell;
  My mistress made it one⁸ upon my cheek.
  She is so hot° because the meat is cold.   *angry*
  The meat is cold because you come not home.
  You come not home because you have no stomach.° *appetite*
50 You have no stomach, having broke your fast;° *having eaten*
  But we that know what 'tis to fast and pray
  Are penitent⁹ for your default° today.   *fault*

---

1. The name of an inn; taverns, inns, and shops were
frequently identified by a pictorial sign.
2. Noon, time for the midday meal.
3. Opportunity, but punning on "means" (wealth).
4. Servant or slave (villein); also rogue or scoundrel
(often used affectionately).
5. Mood, determined by the humors, bodily fluids that
formed the basis of Elizabethan medical psychology.

6. To locate a matching drop.
7. The measure of my exact age (because born on the
same date).
8. *made it one:* struck one o'clock.
9. Are doing penance in the ordinary way by prayer and
fasting (since the meal is delayed), and also through
being beaten.

ANTIPHOLUS OF SYRACUSE Stop in your wind,° sir. Tell me this,   *Shut your mouth*
    I pray:
Where have you left the money that I gave you?

55 DROMIO OF EPHESUS O—sixpence that I had o' Wednesday last
    To pay the saddler for my mistress' crupper?[1]
    The saddler had it, sir; I kept it not.

ANTIPHOLUS OF SYRACUSE I am not in a sportive humour now.
    Tell me, and dally not: where is the money?
60   We being strangers here, how dar'st thou trust
    So great a charge from° thine own custody?   *responsibility out of*

DROMIO OF EPHESUS I pray you, jest, sir, as° you sit at dinner.   *when*
    I from my mistress come to you in post.°   *haste*
    If I return I shall be post[2] indeed,
65   For she will scour° your fault upon my pate.°   *score; flog / head*
    Methinks your maw,° like mine, should be your clock,   *stomach*
    And strike[3] you home without a messenger.

ANTIPHOLUS OF SYRACUSE Come, Dromio, come, these jests are
    out of season.
    Reserve them till a merrier hour than this.
70   Where is the gold I gave in charge to thee?

DROMIO OF EPHESUS To me, sir? Why, you gave no gold to me.

ANTIPHOLUS OF SYRACUSE Come on, sir knave,[4] have done your
    foolishness,
    And tell me how thou hast disposed° thy charge.   *dealt with*

DROMIO OF EPHESUS My charge was but to fetch you from the mart
75   Home to your house, the Phoenix,[5] sir, to dinner.
    My mistress and her sister stays° for you.   *wait*

ANTIPHOLUS OF SYRACUSE Now, as I am a Christian,[6] answer me
    In what safe place you have bestowed my money,
    Or I shall break that merry sconce° of yours   *head*
80   That stands° on tricks when I am undisposed.°   *insists / not in the mood*
    Where is the thousand marks thou hadst of me?

DROMIO OF EPHESUS I have some marks of yours upon my pate,
    Some of my mistress' marks upon my shoulders,
    But not a thousand marks between you both.
85   If I should pay your worship those again,°   *back*
    Perchance you will not bear them patiently.

ANTIPHOLUS OF SYRACUSE Thy mistress' marks? What mistress,
    slave, hast thou?

DROMIO OF EPHESUS Your worship's wife, my mistress, at the Phoenix:
    She that doth fast till you come home to dinner,
90   And prays that you will hie° you home to dinner.   *hasten*

ANTIPHOLUS OF SYRACUSE What, wilt thou flout° me thus unto   *mock; disobey*
    my face,
    Being forbid? There, take you that, sir knave!
        [*He beats* DROMIO]

DROMIO OF EPHESUS What mean you, sir? For God's sake,
    hold° your hands!   *stop*

---

1. A strap passed under a horse's tail to prevent the saddle from slipping forward.
2. Beaten, like a wooden doorpost on which tavern charges were tallied (scored).
3. Beat; ring time like a clock.
4. Ironic: "knave," like "villain," means both "servant" and "rogue."

5. Antipholus of Ephesus's house is, like the inn (line 9), identified by a sign, this one depicting the mythological bird that symbolized resurrection. Many Londoners lived above their places of business.
6. A common oath, though anachronistic in classical Greece.

Nay, an° you will not, sir, I'll take my heels.°   *Exit*   *if/run away*
95 ANTIPHOLUS OF SYRACUSE Upon my life, by some device° or other   *trick*
    The villain is o'er-raught° of all my money.   *cheated*
    They say this town is full of cozenage,°   *deception*
    As° nimble jugglers[7] that deceive the eye,   *Such as*
    Dark-working[8] sorcerers that change the mind,
100 Soul-killing witches that deform[9] the body,
    Disguisèd cheaters, prating mountebanks,°   *fast-talking quacks*
    And many suchlike libertines of sin.[1]
    If it prove so, I will be gone the sooner.
    I'll to the Centaur to go seek this slave.
105 I greatly fear my money is not safe.   *Exit*

2.1

Enter [from the Phoenix] ADRIANA, *wife to* ANTIPHOLUS
[OF EPHESUS], with LUCIANA, *her sister*

ADRIANA Neither my husband nor the slave returned
    That in such haste I sent to seek his master?
    Sure,° Luciana, it is two o'clock.   *Surely*
LUCIANA Perhaps some merchant hath invited him,
5 And from the mart he's somewhere gone to dinner.
    Good sister, let us dine, and never fret.
    A man is master of his liberty.
    Time is their mistress, and when they see time
    They'll go or come. If so, be patient, sister.
10 ADRIANA Why should their liberty than ours be more?
LUCIANA Because their business still° lies out o' door.   *always*
ADRIANA Look when I serve him so, he takes it ill.[1]
LUCIANA O, know he is the bridle of your will.[2]
ADRIANA There's none but° asses will be bridled so.   *Only*
15 LUCIANA Why, headstrong liberty is lashed° with woe.   *beaten; tied down*
    There's nothing situate under heaven's eye
    But hath his bound° in earth, in sea, in sky.   *its limits*
    The beasts, the fishes, and the wingèd fowls
    Are their males' subjects and at their controls.°   *under their control*
20 Man, more divine,[3] the master of all these,
    Lord of the wide world and wild wat'ry seas,
    Indued with intellectual sense and souls,
    Of more pre-eminence than fish and fowls,
    Are masters to their females, and their lords.[4]
25 Then let your will attend on their accords.[5]
ADRIANA This servitude makes you to keep unwed.
LUCIANA Not this, but troubles of the marriage bed.[6]
ADRIANA But were you wedded, you would bear some sway.°   *wield some power*
LUCIANA Ere I learn love, I'll practise to obey.

---

7. Performers skilled in manipulating appearances; the term could mean either an actual sorcerer or a mere illusionist.
8. Operating secretly or producing darkness.
9. Injure, disfigure; change the shape of (like the enchantress Circe of Homer's *Odyssey*, who transformed Odysseus's men into swine).
1. Unrestrained sinners. F prints "Liberties," possibly referring to the district where many theaters of London (including Shakespeare's company) operated, just outside the city's legal jurisdiction.
2.1 Location: Before the house of Antipholus of Ephesus.

1. Whenever I treat him so, he takes it badly.
2. He is meant to restrain your desires.
3. Nearer to God (in the great hierarchy of all beings).
4. *Man . . . lords*: Man's dominion over the creatures of earth and water derives from Genesis 1:28–29; his rule over woman is expressed in Paul's epistles, especially 1 Corinthians 11:3ff. and Ephesians 5:22ff. ("Wives, submit yourselves unto your husbands, as unto the Lord").
5. *attend . . accords*: serve their wishes.
6. Compare 1 Corinthians 7:28: "And if a virgin marry, she sinneth not: nevertheless such shall have trouble in the flesh."

30	ADRIANA How if your husband start° some otherwhere?°	*strays; wanders / elsewhere*
	LUCIANA Till he come home again, I would forbear.°	*be patient*
	ADRIANA Patience unmoved! No marvel though she pause:[7]	
	They can be meek that have no other cause.°	*reason not to be*
	A wretched soul, bruised with adversity,	
35	We bid be quiet when we hear it cry.	
	But were we burdened with like° weight of pain,	*equal*
	As much or more we should ourselves complain.	
	So thou, that hast no unkind mate to grieve thee,	
	With urging helpless° patience would relieve° me.	*futile / comfort*
40	But if thou live to see like right bereft,[8]	
	This fool-begged[9] patience in thee will be left.°	*abandoned*
	LUCIANA Well, I will marry one day, but to try.°	*test*

Enter DROMIO OF EPHESUS

	Here comes your man.° Now is your husband nigh.°	*servant / near*
	ADRIANA Say, is your tardy master now at hand?	
45	DROMIO OF EPHESUS Nay, he's at two hands with me, and that	
	my two ears can witness.[1]	
	ADRIANA Say, didst thou speak with him? Know'st thou his mind?	
	DROMIO OF EPHESUS I? Ay, he told[2] his mind upon mine ear.	
	Beshrew° his hand, I scarce could understand it.	*Curse*
50	LUCIANA Spake he so doubtfully° thou couldst not feel his meaning?	*ambiguously*
	DROMIO OF EPHESUS Nay, he struck so plainly I could too well	
	feel his blows, and withal so doubtfully° that I could scarce	*dreadfully; stoutly*
	under-stand° them.	*stand under*
	ADRIANA But say, I prithee,° is he coming home?	*pray thee*
55	It seems he hath great care to please his wife.[3]	
	DROMIO OF EPHESUS Why, mistress, sure my master is horn-mad.	
	ADRIANA Horn-mad,[4] thou villain?	
	DROMIO OF EPHESUS I mean not cuckold-mad, but sure he is stark mad.	
	When I desired him to come home to dinner,	
60	He asked me for a thousand marks in gold.	
	' 'Tis dinner-time,' quoth I. 'My gold,' quoth he.	
	'Your meat doth burn,' quoth I. 'My gold,' quoth he.	
	'Will you come home?' quoth I. 'My gold,' quoth he;	
	'Where is the thousand marks I gave thee, villain?'	
65	'The pig', quoth I, 'is burned.' 'My gold!' quoth he.	
	'My mistress, sir—' quoth I. 'Hang up° thy mistress!	*Enough of*
	I know thy mistress not. Out° on thy mistress!'	*A curse*
	LUCIANA Quoth who?	
	DROMIO OF EPHESUS Quoth my master.	
70	'I know', quoth he, 'no house, no wife, no mistress.'	
	So that my errand,° due unto my tongue,[5]	*delivery; message*
	I thank him, I bare° home upon my shoulders;	*bore*
	For, in conclusion, he did beat me there.	
	ADRIANA Go back again, thou slave, and fetch him home.	
75	DROMIO OF EPHESUS Go back again and be new° beaten home?	*again*

7. That she hesitates (to marry).
8. *like . . . bereft*: yourself similarly deprived of rights.
9. Declaredly foolish; to "beg a person for a fool" was to petition the Court of Wards for custody of a lunatic (and thus custody of all his possessions).
1. *he's . . . witness*: he boxed my ears with both of his hands.
2. Communicated, but playing on "struck" ("tolled").
3. Ironic: compare 1 Corinthians 7:32–33: "The unmar-

ried careth for the things of the Lord, how he may please the Lord: But he that is married careth for the things that are of the world, how he may please his wife."
4. Uncontrolled and wild as a horned beast (a common expression, as intended by Dromio); enraged at being made a cuckold, who by popular repute grew horns (as Adriana takes it).
5. *due . . . tongue*: which I should have carried back in words.

For God's sake, send some other messenger.

ADRIANA Back, slave, or I will break thy pate across.

DROMIO OF EPHESUS An he will bless that cross with other beating,[6]
　　Between you I shall have a holy[7] head.

80 ADRIANA Hence, prating peasant.° Fetch thy master home.   *babbling fellow*
　　　[*She beats* DROMIO]

DROMIO OF EPHESUS Am I so round[8] with you as you with me,
　　That like a football you do spurn° me thus?   *maltreat; kick*
　　You spurn me hence, and he will spurn me hither.
　　If I last in this service, you must case me in leather.[9]   [*Exit*]

85 LUCIANA [*to* ADRIANA] Fie, how impatience loureth° in your face!   *frowns*

ADRIANA His company must do his minions grace,[1]
　　Whilst I at home starve for a merry look.
　　Hath homely age th'alluring beauty took
　　From my poor cheek? Then he hath wasted it.[2]

90 Are my discourses dull? Barren my wit?
　　If voluble and sharp° discourse be marred,   *witty*
　　Unkindness blunts it more than marble hard.[3]
　　Do their° gay vestments° his affections bait?[4]   *(the minions') / clothing*
　　That's not my fault: he's master of my state.[5]

95 What ruins are in me that can be found
　　By him not ruined?[6] Then is he the ground°   *cause*
　　Of my defeatures.° My decayèd fair°   *disfigurement / beauty*
　　A sunny look of his would soon repair.
　　But, too unruly deer, he breaks the pale,[7]

100 And feeds from° home. Poor I am but his stale.[8]   *away from*

LUCIANA Self-harming jealousy! Fie, beat it hence.

ADRIANA Unfeeling fools can with such wrongs dispense.
　　I know his eye doth homage otherwhere,
　　Or else what lets° it but he would be here?   *prevents*

105 Sister, you know he promised me a chain.
　　Would that alone o' love he would detain,[9]
　　So° he would keep fair quarter° with his bed.   *If then / faith*
　　I see the jewel best enamellèd
　　Will lose her beauty. Yet the gold bides° still   *remains*

110 That others touch;[1] and often touching will
　　Wear gold, and yet no man that hath a name°   *reputation*
　　By falsehood and corruption doth it shame.[2]
　　Since that my beauty cannot please his eye,
　　I'll weep what's left away, and weeping die.

115 LUCIANA How many fond° fools serve mad jealousy!   *infatuated*
　　　　　　　Exeunt [*into the Phoenix*]

---

6. If he will give me another beating (playing on
"across," a cross made by blows on my head, and
"bless," the French *blesser*, "to injure").
7. Blessed (because marked with the sign of the cross);
also, full of holes.
8. Blunt, disrespectful (with a play on "spherical," like
a football).
9. If I survive as your servant, you must cover me with
leather, like a football; with a play on "last," a wooden
model of a foot used in making leather shoes.
1. Must grace his paramours.
2. Caused it to waste away; squandered it.
3. More than hard marble would blunt a sharp tool.
4. Lure away (bait); lessen (abate) toward Adriana.
5. Estate or general condition, including clothes; also,

metaphorically, kingdom.
6. *What . . . ruined*: What deterioration can be found
in me that he is no responsible for?
7. He goes beyond the park boundary ("pale").
8. Lover held up to the ridicule of her rivals; prostitute.
9. *Would . . . detain*: I wish he would withhold that one
manifestation of love.
1. *touch*: test (the fineness of gold was tested by rubbing it on a touchstone); caress, referring to her husband's infidelities.
2. *I see . . . shame*: a difficult passage, possibly owing to
omitted lines. The general idea is that reputation, like
gold, withstands corruption and yet may be worn away.
Her husband's infidelities have not tarnished his name,
but they may diminish her substance.

2.2

Enter ANTIPHOLUS [OF SYRACUSE]

ANTIPHOLUS OF SYRACUSE   The gold I gave to Dromio is laid up
   Safe at the Centaur, and the heedful° slave   *careful*
   Is wandered forth in care to seek me out.
   By computation and mine host's report,[1]
5   I could not speak° with Dromio since at first   *could not have spoken*
   I sent him from the mart! See, here he comes.

Enter DROMIO [OF] SYRACUSE

   How now, sir, is your merry humour altered?
   As you love strokes,° so jest with me again.   *blows*
   You know no Centaur? You received no gold?
10 Your mistress sent to have me home to dinner?
   My house was at the Phoenix?—Wast thou mad,
   That thus so madly thou didst answer me?
DROMIO OF SYRACUSE   What answer, sir? When spake I such a word?
ANTIPHOLUS OF SYRACUSE   Even now, even here, not half an hour since.
15 DROMIO OF SYRACUSE   I did not see you since you sent me hence
   Home to the Centaur with the gold you gave me.
ANTIPHOLUS OF SYRACUSE   Villain, thou didst deny the gold's
     receipt,°   *receiving the gold*
   And told'st me of a mistress and a dinner,
   For which I hope thou felt'st[2] I was displeased.
20 DROMIO OF SYRACUSE   I am glad to see you in this merry vein.°   *disposition*
   What means this jest? I pray you, master, tell me.
ANTIPHOLUS OF SYRACUSE   Yea, dost thou jeer and flout me in
     the teeth?°   *to my face*
   Think'st thou I jest? Hold,° take thou that, and that.   *Stop*
   [*He*] *beats* DROMIO
DROMIO OF SYRACUSE   Hold, sir, for God's sake—now your jest is earnest![3]
25 Upon what bargain[4] do you give it me?
ANTIPHOLUS OF SYRACUSE   Because that I familiarly sometimes
   Do use you for my fool,° and chat with you,   *jester*
   Your sauciness will jest upon my love,[5]
   And make a common[6] of my serious hours.
30 When the sun shines, let foolish gnats make sport,°   *play*
   But creep in crannies when he hides his beams.
   If you will jest with me, know my aspect,[7]
   And fashion your demeanour to° my looks,   *to match*
   Or I will beat this method° in your sconce.°   *rule / head*
35 DROMIO OF SYRACUSE   'Sconce'° call you it? So° you would leave   *Small fort / If*
   battering,[8] I had rather have it a head. An° you use these   *If*
   blows long, I must get a sconce° for my head, and ensconce° *protective screen / shelter*
   it too, or else I shall seek my wit° in my shoulders. But I pray,   *brains*
   sir, why am I beaten?
40 ANTIPHOLUS OF SYRACUSE   Dost thou not know?
DROMIO OF SYRACUSE   Nothing, sir, but that I am beaten.

2.2 Location: A street in Ephesus.
1. Based on a calculation of the time elapsed and the innkeeper's account of Dromio's doings.
2. Perceived, with an allusion to the beating.
3. Serious, with a play on "earnest" as a deposit to secure a business transaction.
4. Transaction (playing on the financial sense of "earnest"); in this context, contention or quarrel.

5. *Your . . . love:* You impertinently assume the right to joke because of my benevolence.
6. Land belonging to the whole community (Dromio maintains an egalitarian spirit at inappropriate times).
7. Countenance, expression; (in astrology) the position of a heavenly body, as the sun (lines 30–31).
8. Beating; here, with a play on "sconce," attacking with a battering ram.

ANTIPHOLUS OF SYRACUSE   Shall I tell you why?

DROMIO OF SYRACUSE   Ay, sir, and wherefore;° for they say every _for what reason_
why hath a wherefore.

45 ANTIPHOLUS OF SYRACUSE   'Why' first: for flouting me; and then 'wherefore':
For urging° it the second time to me. _repeating_

DROMIO OF SYRACUSE   Was there ever any man thus beaten out
of season,° _unjustly_
When in the why and the wherefore is neither rhyme nor reason?—
Well, sir, I thank you.

ANTIPHOLUS OF SYRACUSE   Thank me, sir, for what?

50 DROMIO OF SYRACUSE   Marry,[9] sir, for this something that you
gave me for nothing.

ANTIPHOLUS OF SYRACUSE   I'll make you amends next, to give° _by giving_
you nothing for something. But say, sir, is it dinner-time?

DROMIO OF SYRACUSE   No, sir, I think the meat wants that° I _lacks what_
55 have.

ANTIPHOLUS OF SYRACUSE   In good time,[1] sir. What's that?

DROMIO OF SYRACUSE   Basting.[2]

ANTIPHOLUS OF SYRACUSE   Well, sir, then 'twill be dry.

DROMIO OF SYRACUSE   If it be, sir, I pray you eat none of it.

60 ANTIPHOLUS OF SYRACUSE   Your reason?

DROMIO OF SYRACUSE   Lest it make you choleric[3] and purchase
me another dry basting.° _severe beating_

ANTIPHOLUS OF SYRACUSE   Well, sir, learn to jest in good time.[4]
There's a time for all things.

65 DROMIO OF SYRACUSE   I durst° have denied that before you were _dared_
so choleric.

ANTIPHOLUS OF SYRACUSE   By what rule,° sir? _principle_

DROMIO OF SYRACUSE   Marry, sir, by a rule as plain as the plain
bald pate of Father Time himself.[5]

70 ANTIPHOLUS OF SYRACUSE   Let's hear it.

DROMIO OF SYRACUSE   There's no time for a man to recover his
hair that grows bald by nature.

ANTIPHOLUS OF SYRACUSE   May he not do it by fine and
recovery?[6]

75 DROMIO OF SYRACUSE   Yes, to pay a fine° for a periwig, and _fee_
recover the lost hair of another man.[7]

ANTIPHOLUS OF SYRACUSE   Why is Time such a niggard of hair,
being, as it is, so plentiful an excrement?° _outward growth_

DROMIO OF SYRACUSE   Because it is a blessing that he bestows on
80 beasts, and what he hath scanted° men in hair he hath given _given less to_
them in wit.° _intellect_

ANTIPHOLUS OF SYRACUSE   Why, but there's many a man hath
more hair than wit.

DROMIO OF SYRACUSE   Not a man of those but he hath the wit to
85 lose his hair.[8]

9. By the Virgin Mary, a mild oath.
1. Indeed! (an expression of ironical acquiescence).
2. Punning on a second meaning, "beating."
3. Angry. Choler was the hot, dry humor (see note to
1.2.21); diet and climate were thought to affect the
humors sympathetically, so that overly dry meat might
lead to a choleric disposition.
4. Opportunely; in a merry or good-humored time.

5. Time was commonly depicted as a bald old man.
6. _fine and recovery_ the legal method of transferring
the ownership of property that could not normally be
sold, especially to break an entail.
7. _to pay . . . man:_ to buy a wig made from someone
else's hair (as wigs usually were).
8. _wit . . . hair:_ ironic—clever enough to catch syphilis
(which may cause hair loss).

ANTIPHOLUS OF SYRACUSE Why, thou didst conclude hairy men
    plain dealers, without wit.[9]

DROMIO OF SYRACUSE The plainer dealer,[1] the sooner lost. Yet
    he loseth it in a kind of jollity.°   (sexual pleasure)

90 ANTIPHOLUS OF SYRACUSE For what reason?

DROMIO OF SYRACUSE For two, and sound° ones too.   strong

ANTIPHOLUS OF SYRACUSE Nay, not sound,° I pray you.   healthy

DROMIO OF SYRACUSE Sure° ones, then.   Certain

ANTIPHOLUS OF SYRACUSE Nay, not sure,° in a thing falsing.[2]   trustworthy

95 DROMIO OF SYRACUSE Certain ones, then.

ANTIPHOLUS OF SYRACUSE Name them.

DROMIO OF SYRACUSE The one, to save the money that he
    spends in tiring;° the other, that at dinner they should not drop   hairstyling
    in his porridge.

100 ANTIPHOLUS OF SYRACUSE You would all this time have proved
    there is no time for all things.

DROMIO OF SYRACUSE Marry, and did, sir: namely, e'en° no time   even; precisely
    to recover hair lost by nature.

ANTIPHOLUS OF SYRACUSE But your reason was not substantial,°   firmly based
105   why there is no time to recover.

DROMIO OF SYRACUSE Thus I mend° it: Time himself is bald,   improve
    and therefore to the world's end will have bald followers.

ANTIPHOLUS OF SYRACUSE I knew 'twould be a bald° conclusion.   an inane

       Enter [from the Phoenix] ADRIANA *and* LUCIANA

    But soft—who wafts° us yonder?   beckons

110 ADRIANA Ay, ay, Antipholus, look strange[3] and frown:
    Some other mistress hath thy sweet aspects.°   loving looks
    I am not Adriana, nor thy wife.
    The time was once when thou unurged wouldst vow
    That never words were music to thine ear,
115   That never object pleasing in thine eye,
    That never touch well welcome to thy hand,
    That never meat sweet-savoured in thy taste,
    Unless I spake, or looked, or touched, or carved to° thee.   for
    How comes it now, my husband, O how comes it
120   That thou art then estrangèd from thyself?—
    Thy 'self' I call it, being strange to me
    That, undividable, incorporate,°   united in one body
    Am better than thy dear self's better part.[4]
    Ah, do not tear away thyself from me;
125   For know, my love, as easy mayst thou fall°   let fall
    A drop of water in the breaking gulf,
    And take unmingled thence that drop again
    Without addition or diminishing,
    As take from me thyself, and not me too.[5]
130   How dearly° would it touch thee to the quick   deeply
    Shouldst thou but° hear I were licentious,   only
    And that this body, consecrate to thee,
    By ruffian lust should be contaminate?

---

9. *conclude . . . wit:* argue that hairy men were simple,
lacking in cunning and therefore honest (plain dealers).
1. With pun on "deal," have sex.
2. In a deceptive matter; perhaps punning on "thing"
as "sexual organ."
3. Look distant, but suggesting "without recognition,"
as if a foreigner—which he is.

4. Either his better qualities or his soul (which is better than his body). Adriana's plea depends on the doctrine of marriage as "one flesh" articulated in Genesis
2:23–24 and echoed in Paul's mystical view of the
church as wedded to God. Compare Ephesians
5:28–33.
5. *not me too:* not take me away from myself as well.

Wouldst thou not spit at me, and spurn° at me,   *strike*
135 And hurl the name of husband in my face,[6]
And tear the stained skin[7] off my harlot brow,
And from my false hand cut the wedding ring,
And break it with a deep-divorcing vow?
I know thou canst, and therefore see° thou do it!   *make sure*
140 I am possessed with° an adulterate blot;[8]   *in possession of*
My blood is mingled with the crime of lust.
For if we two be one, and thou play false,
I do digest the poison of thy flesh,
Being strumpeted° by thy contagion.   *made a whore*
145 Keep then fair league[9] and truce with thy true bed,
I live unstained, thou undishonourèd.
ANTIPHOLUS OF SYRACUSE   Plead you to *me*, fair dame? I know you not.
In Ephesus I am but two hours old,
As strange unto your town as to your talk,
150 Who, every word by all my wit being scanned,°   *analyzed*
Wants° wit in all one word to understand.   *Lacks*
LUCIANA   Fie, brother,° how the world is changed with you!   *brother-in-law*
When were you wont to use° my sister thus?   *treat*
She sent for you by Dromio home to dinner.
155 ANTIPHOLUS OF SYRACUSE   By Dromio?
DROMIO OF SYRACUSE   By me?
ADRIANA   By thee; and this thou didst return° from him—   *bring back*
That he did buffet thee, and in his blows
Denied my house for° his, me for his wife.   *to be*
160 ANTIPHOLUS OF SYRACUSE   Did you converse, sir, with this gentlewoman?
What is the course and drift of your compact?[1]
DROMIO OF SYRACUSE   I, sir? I never saw her till this time.
ANTIPHOLUS OF SYRACUSE   Villain, thou liest; for even her very° words   *exact*
Didst thou deliver to me on the mart.
165 DROMIO OF SYRACUSE   I never spake with her in all my life.
ANTIPHOLUS OF SYRACUSE   How can she thus then call us by our
      names?—
Unless it be by inspiration.°   *divine revelation*
ADRIANA   How ill agrees it° with your gravity°   *does it suit / dignity*
To counterfeit° thus grossly° with your slave,   *dissemble / blatantly*
170 Abetting him to thwart me in my mood!
Be it my wrong you are from me exempt,[2]
But wrong not that wrong with a more contempt.[3]
Come, I will fasten on this sleeve of thine.
Thou art an elm, my husband; I a vine,[4]
175 Whose weakness, married to thy stronger state,°   *condition*
Makes me with thy strength to communicate.°   *share*
If aught possess thee from me,[5] it is dross,°   *worthless*
Usurping ivy, brier, or idle moss,
Who, all° for want of pruning, with intrusion°   *entirely / invasively*
180 Infect thy sap, and live on thy confusion.[6]

6. And bitterly confront me with my degraded marriage vow.
7. Mark of impure character, as if she had been legally branded as a harlot.
8. The stain, or disgrace, of adultery.
9. *Keep . . . league*: If you keep faithful alliance.
1. What is the purpose and meaning of your conspiracy?
2. *Be . . . exempt*: Grant that it is my fault that you are alienated from me.
3. But do not add to that injury with mockery.
4. This image occurs both in Ovid's *Metamorphoses* 14.665–66 and in Psalm 128:3, included in the Elizabethan homily on marriage.
5. If anything takes possession of you away from (or apart from) me.
6. *live . . . confusion*: take life from your destruction.

ANTIPHOLUS OF SYRACUSE [*aside*]   To me she speaks, she moves°   uses
    me for her theme.°   topic
    What, was I married to her in my dream?
    Or sleep I now, and think I hear all this?
    What error drives our eyes and ears amiss?
185   Until I know this sure uncertainty,
    I'll entertain° the offered fallacy.°   accept / delusion
LUCIANA   Dromio, go bid the servants spread° for dinner.   lay the table
DROMIO OF SYRACUSE [*aside*]   O, for my beads!° I cross me[7] for°   rosary beads / as
    a sinner.   sinner
    This is the fairy land. O spite of spites,
190   We talk with goblins, oafs,[8] and sprites.°   spirits
    If we obey them not, this will ensue:
    They'll suck our breath or pinch us black and blue.[9]
LUCIANA   Why prat'st° thou to thyself, and answer'st not?   babble
    Dromio, thou drone,° thou snail, thou slug, thou sot.°   idler / blockhead
DROMIO OF SYRACUSE [*to* ANTIPHOLUS]   I am transformèd,
195   master, am not I?
ANTIPHOLUS OF SYRACUSE   I think thou art in mind, and so am I.
DROMIO OF SYRACUSE   Nay, master, both in mind and in my shape.
ANTIPHOLUS OF SYRACUSE   Thou hast thine own form.
DROMIO OF SYRACUSE   No, I am an ape.[1]
LUCIANA   If thou art changed to aught,° 'tis to an ass.   anything
DROMIO OF SYRACUSE [*to* ANTIPHOLUS]   'Tis true she rides° me,   tyrannizes
200   and I long for grass.[2]
    'Tis so, I am an ass; else it could never be
    But I should know her as well as she knows me.
ADRIANA   Come, come, no longer will I be a fool,
    To put the finger in the eye and weep
205   Whilst man and master laughs my woes to scorn.[3]
    [*To* ANTIPHOLUS] Come, sir, to dinner.—Dromio, keep the gate.—
    Husband, I'll dine above with you today,
    And shrive you of[4] a thousand idle pranks.—
    Sirrah,[5] if any ask you for your master,
210   Say he dines forth,° and let no creature enter.—   out
    Come, sister.—Dromio, play the porter well.
ANTIPHOLUS OF SYRACUSE [*aside*]   Am I in earth, in heaven, or in hell?
    Sleeping or waking? Mad or well advised?°   sane
    Known unto these, and to myself disguised!
215   I'll say as they say, and persever so,
    And in this mist at all adventures° go.   whatever occurs
DROMIO OF SYRACUSE   Master, shall I be porter at the gate?
ADRIANA   Ay, and let none enter, lest I break your pate.°   head
LUCIANA   Come, come, Antipholus, we dine too late.
                    Exeunt [*into the Phoenix*]

---

7. Make the sign of the cross (to ward off evil).
8. Changelings, goblin children left in the place of abducted human infants. F reads "owles," a possible reference to witchcraft.
9. Traditional recreations for fairies.

1. An imitation (of myself); a fool.
2. Freedom, as when a horse is put out to pasture.
3. *laughs . . . scorn:* make a mockery of my pain.
4. And act as your confessor to hear and pardon.
5. Standard term for addressing inferiors.

3.1

Enter ANTIPHOLUS OF EPHESUS, *his man* DROMIO.
ANGELO *the goldsmith, and* BALTHASAR *the merchant*

ANTIPHOLUS OF EPHESUS   Good Signor Angelo, you must excuse us all.
  My wife is shrewish° when I keep not hours.°   *ill tempered / am late*
  Say that I lingered with you at your shop
  To see the making of her carcanet,°   *jeweled necklace*
5 And that tomorrow you will bring it home.—
  But here's a villain that would face me down[1]
  He met me on the mart, and that I beat him,
  And charged him with[2] a thousand marks in gold,
  And that I did deny my wife and house.
10 Thou drunkard, thou, what didst thou mean by this?
DROMIO OF EPHESUS   Say what you will, sir, but I know what I know—
  That you beat me at the mart I have your hand[3] to show.
  If the skin were parchment, and the blows you gave were ink,
  Your own handwriting would tell you what I think.
ANTIPHOLUS OF EPHESUS   I think thou art an ass.
15 DROMIO OF EPHESUS   Marry, so it doth appear
  By the wrongs I suffer and the blows I bear.
  I should kick being kicked, and, being at that pass,°   *in that predicament*
  You would keep from my heels, and beware of an ass.
ANTIPHOLUS OF EPHESUS   You're sad,° Signor Balthasar. Pray   *serious*
  God our cheer°   *fare*
20 May answer° my good will, and your good welcome here.   *equal*
BALTHASAR   I hold your dainties cheap, sir, and your welcome dear.[4]
ANTIPHOLUS OF EPHESUS   O, Signor Balthasar, either at flesh or fish
  A table full of welcome makes scarce° one dainty dish.   *scarcely makes*
BALTHASAR   Good meat, sir, is common; that every churl° affords.   *peasant*
ANTIPHOLUS OF EPHESUS   And welcome more common, for
25 that's nothing but words.
BALTHASAR   Small cheer° and great welcome makes a merry feast.   *Little food*
ANTIPHOLUS OF EPHESUS   Ay, to a niggardly host and more spar-
  ing° guest.   *temperate*
  But though my cates° be mean,° take them in good part.   *provisions / poor*
  Better cheer may you have, but not with better heart.
30 But soft,[5] my door is locked. [*To* DROMIO] Go bid them let us in.
DROMIO OF EPHESUS [*calling*]   Maud, Bridget, Marian, Cicely, Gillian, Ginn!
  [*Enter* DROMIO OF SYRACUSE *within the Phoenix*]
DROMIO OF SYRACUSE [*within the Phoenix*]   Mome, malt-horse,
  capon, coxcomb, idiot, patch![6]
  Either get thee from the door or sit down at the hatch.[7]
  Dost thou conjure for° wenches, that thou call'st for such   *summon by spells*
  store°   *plenty*
35 When one is one too many? Go, get thee from the door.
DROMIO OF EPHESUS   What patch is made our porter? My mas-
  ter stays° in the street.   *waits*
DROMIO OF SYRACUSE [*within*]   Let him walk from whence he
  came, lest he catch cold on's° feet.   *on his*

3.1 Location: Before the house of Antipholus of Ephesus.
1. That would insist despite my denial that.
2. And accused him of possessing.
3. The mark of Antipholus's hand.
4. I value your welcome more highly than the delicacies of your table.
5. An exclamation of surprise.
6. Dolt, plodding oaf, eunuch, fool, idiot, clown.
7. Literally, sit down at the gate or half door, but playing on the proverbial phrase "set a hatch (gate) before
the door" of the tongue: keep silent.

ANTIPHOLUS OF EPHESUS   Who talks within there? Ho, open the door!
DROMIO OF SYRACUSE [*within the Phoenix*]   Right, sir, I'll tell
    you when, an° you'll tell me wherefore.   *if*
40 ANTIPHOLUS OF EPHESUS   Wherefore? For my dinner—I have not dined today.
DROMIO OF SYRACUSE [*within the Phoenix*]   Nor today here you
    must not. Come again when you may.
ANTIPHOLUS OF EPHESUS   What art thou that keep'st me out
    from the house I owe?°   *own*
DROMIO OF SYRACUSE [*within the Phoenix*]   The porter for this
    time,° sir, and my name is Dromio.   *for now*
DROMIO OF EPHESUS   O villain, thou hast stol'n both mine
    office° and my name.   *function*
45 The one ne'er got me credit, the other mickle blame.[8]
    If thou hadst been Dromio today in my place,
    Thou wouldst have changed thy pate° for an aim,[9] or thy name   *exchanged your head*
    for an ass.
        Enter NELL [*within the Phoenix*]
NELL [*within the Phoenix*]   What a coil° is there, Dromio? Who   *disturbance*
    are those at the gate?
DROMIO OF EPHESUS   Let my master in, Nell.[1]
NELL [*within the Phoenix*]   Faith no, he comes too late;
    And so tell your master.
50 DROMIO OF EPHESUS   O Lord, I must laugh.
    Have at you[2] with a proverb: 'Shall I set in my staff?'[3]
NELL [*within the Phoenix*]   Have at you with another—that's
    'When? Can you tell?'[4]
DROMIO OF SYRACUSE [*within the Phoenix*]   If thy name be
    called Nell, Nell, thou hast answered him well.
ANTIPHOLUS OF EPHESUS [*to* NELL]   Do you hear, you minion?°   *subordinate*
55   You'll let us in, I hope?
    [   ]^[5]
NELL [*within the Phoenix*]   I thought to have asked you.
DROMIO OF SYRACUSE [*within*]   And you said no.°   *(already)*
DROMIO OF EPHESUS   So, come help.
    [*He and* ANTIPHOLUS *beat the door*]
                          Well struck! There was blow for blow.[6]
ANTIPHOLUS OF EPHESUS [*to* NELL]   Thou baggage,° let me in.   *good-for-nothing*
NELL [*within the Phoenix*]   Can you tell for whose sake?
DROMIO OF EPHESUS   Master, knock the door hard.
NELL [*within the Phoenix*]   Let him knock till it ache.
60 ANTIPHOLUS OF EPHESUS   You'll cry for this, minion, if I beat the door down.
NELL [*within the Phoenix*]   What needs all that, and a pair of stocks in the town?[7]
    Enter ADRIANA [*within the Phoenix*]
ADRIANA [*within the Phoenix*]   Who is that at the door that
    keeps° all this noise?   *keeps up*
DROMIO OF SYRACUSE [*within the Phoenix*]   By my troth, your
    town is troubled with unruly boys.

---

8. My reputation ("name") has never brought me
credit, but in the course of my duties I have received
much reproof ("mickle").
9. A target or butt, punning on "a name."
1. In F, Nell is designated "Luce" throughout this scene.
2. A challenge or warning in a fight (as with a quarter
staff): Now I attack you.
3. Shall I take up residence? (proverbial).
4. Proverbial response of defiance.

5. Since line 54 has no rhyme in this consistently
rhymed passage, it seems likely that either "hope" should
be emended to "trow" (believe), or there is a line missing.
6. Blows to the door in response to verbal blows from
within.
7. Why should I worry when there is a legal punishment for such behavior? *stocks:* instrument of punishment in which a person was seated with his or her legs
locked in a wooden frame.

ANTIPHOLUS OF EPHESUS [*to* ADRIANA] Are you there, wife? You
might have come before.

ADRIANA [*within the Phoenix*] Your wife, sir knave? Go, get you
65   from the door.   [*Exit with* NELL]

DROMIO OF EPHESUS [*to* ANTIPHOLUS] If you went in pain, master, this knave would go sore.[8]

ANGELO [*to* ANTIPHOLUS] Here is neither cheer, sir, nor welcome; we would fain° have either.   *gladly*

BALTHASAR In° debating which was best, we shall part° with   *After / depart*
neither.

DROMIO OF EPHESUS [*to* ANTIPHOLUS] They stand at the door,
master. Bid them welcome hither.

ANTIPHOLUS OF EPHESUS There is something in the wind,° that   *afoot*
70   we cannot get in.

DROMIO OF EPHESUS You would say so, master, if your gar-
ments were thin.°   *(taking "wind" literally)*

Your cake[9] here is warm within: you stand here in the cold.

It would make a man mad as a buck[1] to be so bought and sold.°   *betrayed*

ANTIPHOLUS OF EPHESUS Go fetch me something. I'll break
ope° the gate.   *open*

DROMIO OF SYRACUSE [*within the Phoenix*] Break° any breaking   *Do*
75   here, and I'll break your knave's pate.

DROMIO OF EPHESUS A man may break° a word with you, sir,   *speak*
and words are but wind;

Ay, and break it in your face, so he break it° not behind.   *break wind*

DROMIO OF SYRACUSE [*within the Phoenix*] It seems thou
want'st breaking.[2] Out upon thee, hind!°   *slave; fellow*

DROMIO OF EPHESUS Here's too much 'Out upon thee! I pray
thee, let me in.

DROMIO OF SYRACUSE [*within the Phoenix*] Ay, when fowls have
80   no feathers, and fish have no fin.

ANTIPHOLUS OF EPHESUS Well, I'll break in.—Go borrow me a crow.°   *crowbar*

DROMIO OF EPHESUS A crow without feather? Master, mean you so?

For a fish without a fin, there's a fowl without a feather
[*To* DROMIO OF SYRACUSE]

If a crow help us in, sirrah, we'll pluck a crow° together.   *settle accounts*
85 ANTIPHOLUS OF EPHESUS Go, get thee gone. Fetch me an iron crow.

BALTHASAR Have patience, sir. O, let it not be so!

Herein you war against your reputation,

And draw within the compass of suspect°   *scope of suspicion*

Th'unviolated honour of your wife.

90   Once this:° your long experience of her wisdom,   *In brief*

Her sober virtue, years,° and modesty,   *maturity*

Plead on her part some cause° to you unknown;   *explanation; excuse*

And doubt not, sir, but she will well excuse°   *explain*

Why at this time the doors are made° against you.   *barred*

95   Be ruled by me. Depart in patience,

And let us to the Tiger[3] all to dinner,

And about evening come yourself alone

To know the reason of this strange restraint.°   *exclusion*

If by strong hand you offer° to break in   *attempt*

100   Now in the stirring passage° of the day,   *traffic*

---

8. If you, the master, get punished as a knave, so will I,
the actual servant ("knave").
9. Referring either to Adriana or to the meal.
1. Angry, with an allusion to cuckoldry (see 2.1.57 and

note).
2. Need a beating; need to be "broken in," or tamed
like a horse.
3. The name of an inn; see 1.2.9.

A vulgar° comment will be made of it,   *public; lewd*
And that supposèd° by the common rout°   *accepted / mob*
Against your yet ungallèd estimation,[4]
That may with foul intrusion enter in
105   And dwell upon your grave when you are dead.
For slander lives upon succession,°   *perpetuates itself*
For ever housed where once it gets possession.

ANTIPHOLUS OF EPHESUS   You have prevailed. I will depart in quiet,
And in despite of mirth° mean to be merry.   *ridicule*
110   I know a wench of excellent discourse,
Pretty and witty; wild,° and yet, too, gentle.°   *lively / refined*
There will we dine. This woman that I mean,
My wife—but, I protest, without desert°—   *my deserving*
Hath oftentimes upbraided me withal.°   *scolded me about*
115   To her will we to dinner. [*To* ANGELO] Get you home
And fetch the chain. By this,° I know, 'tis made.   *this time*
Bring it, I pray you, to the Porcupine,
For there's the house.° That chain will I bestow— *That is where she lives*
Be it for nothing but to spite my wife—
120   Upon mine hostess there. Good sir, make haste:
Since mine own doors refuse to entertain° me,   *welcome*
I'll knock elsewhere, to see if they'll disdain me.

ANGELO   I'll meet you at that place some hour hence.

ANTIPHOLUS OF EPHESUS   Do so.   [*Exit* ANGELO]
            This jest shall cost me some expense.
       Exeunt [DROMIO OF SYRACUSE *within the*
       Phoenix, *and the others into the* Porcupine]

3.2

Enter [*from the Phoenix*] LUCIANA *with* ANTIPHOLUS OF
SYRACUSE

LUCIANA   And may it be that you have quite forgot
A husband's office?° Shall, Antipholus,   *duty*
Even in the spring of love thy love-springs° rot? *young shoots of love*
Shall love, in building, grow so ruinous?[1]
5   If you did wed my sister for her wealth,
Then for her wealth's sake use° her with more kindness; *treat*
Or if you like elsewhere, do it by stealth:
Muffle° your false love with some show of blindness.[2] *Hide*
Let not my sister read it in your eye.
10   Be not thy tongue thy own shame's orator.
Look sweet, speak fair, become disloyalty;[3]
Apparel vice like virtue's harbinger.°   *herald*
Bear a fair presence,° though your heart be tainted: *Present a pleasant front*
Teach sin the carriage° of a holy saint.   *bearing*
15   Be secret-false. What° need she be acquainted?   *Why*
What simple thief brags of his own attaint?°   *crime*
'Tis double wrong to truant with° your bed,   *be unfaithful to*
And let her read it in thy looks at board.°   *table*
Shame hath a bastard fame, well managèd;°   *if properly handled*
20   Ill deeds is° doubled with an evil word.   *are*

---

4. *yet . . . estimation:* as yet uninjured reputation.
3.2 Location: Scene continues.
1. Shall love become a ruin at the time of its building?
2. Seem to blindfold yourself so that your glances do
not reveal your faithlessness.
3. *become disloyalty:* put an attractive face on your
unfaithfulness.

Alas, poor women, make us but believe—
    Being compact of credit⁴—that you love us.
Though others have the arm, show us the sleeve.⁵
We in your motion turn,⁶ and you may move° us.   *control; touch*
25 Then, gentle brother, get you in again.
    Comfort my sister, cheer her, call her wife:
'Tis holy sport to be a little vain°   *false*
    When the sweet breath of flattery conquers strife.
ANTIPHOLUS OF SYRACUSE   Sweet mistress—what your name is else I know not,
30   Nor by what wonder you do hit of° mine.   *on*
Less in your knowledge and your grace you show not
    Than our earth's wonder,⁷ more than earth° divine.   *mortal flesh*
Teach me, dear creature, how to think and speak.
    Lay open to my earthy gross conceit,⁸
35 Smothered in errors, feeble, shallow, weak,
    The folded° meaning of your words' deceit.   *hidden*
Against my soul's pure truth why labour you
    To make it wander in an unknown field?
Are you a god? Would you create me new?°   *anew*
40   Transform me, then, and to your power I'll yield.
But if that I am I, then well I know
    Your weeping sister is no wife of mine,
Nor to her bed no homage° do I owe.   *duty*
    Far more, far more, to you do I decline.°   *incline; submit*
45 O, train° me not, sweet mermaid,⁹ with thy note   *entice*
    To drown me in thy sister's flood of tears.
Sing, siren, for thyself, and I will dote.°   *grow infatuated*
    Spread o'er the silver waves thy golden hairs,
And as a bed I'll take them, and there lie,
50   And in that glorious supposition° think   *(that the hair is a bed)*
He gains by death that° hath such means to die.¹   *who*
    Let love, being light,² be drownèd if she sink.
LUCIANA   What, are you mad, that you do reason so?
ANTIPHOLUS OF SYRACUSE   Not mad, but mated³—how, I do not know.
55 LUCIANA   It is a fault that springeth from your eye.°   *(from looking lustfully)*
ANTIPHOLUS OF SYRACUSE   For gazing on your beams,° fair sun,   *eyes*
    being by.
LUCIANA   Gaze where you should, and that will clear your sight.
ANTIPHOLUS OF SYRACUSE   As good to wink,° sweet love, as look   *shut one's eyes*
    on° night.   *at*
LUCIANA   Why call you me 'love'? Call my sister so.
ANTIPHOLUS OF SYRACUSE   Thy sister's sister.
LUCIANA   That's my sister.
60 ANTIPHOLUS OF SYRACUSE   No,
It is thyself, mine own self's better part,
    Mine eye's clear eye, my dear heart's dearer heart,

---

4. Being made of credulity, gullible.
5. Although others have the reality of your love, present us the appearance.
6. We are subject to your influence (as heavenly bodies were believed to follow the rotations of concentric celestial spheres).
7. *Less . . . wonder:* You seem as wise and as gracious as the wonder of the world (probably an allusion to Queen Elizabeth, before whom the play may have been performed).

8. *earthy gross conceit:* clumsy mortal understanding.
9. Siren; in Greek legend, mermaids' singing lured sailors to their death (see line 47).
1. Perhaps with a pun on "to die" as the Elizabethan expression for "orgasm."
2. The line has two implications: only false love could sink, because true love is too light and buoyant; and love deserves drowning because it is giddy and wanton.
3. Amazed, confounded; in love; married.

My food, my fortune, and my sweet hope's aim,
My sole earth's heaven, and my heaven's claim.[4]

65 LUCIANA All this my sister is, or else should be.

ANTIPHOLUS OF SYRACUSE Call thyself sister, sweet, for I am thee.°   *thine*
Thee will I love, and with thee lead my life.
Thou hast no husband yet, nor I no wife.
Give me thy hand.

LUCIANA   O soft, sir, hold you still;
70 I'll fetch my sister to get her good will. *Exit [into the Phoenix]*
            Enter [from the Phoenix] DROMIO [OF] SYRACUSE

ANTIPHOLUS OF SYRACUSE Why, how now, Dromio! Where
runn'st thou so fast?

DROMIO OF SYRACUSE Do you know me, sir? Am I Dromio? Am
I your man? Am I myself?

75 ANTIPHOLUS OF SYRACUSE Thou art Dromio, thou art my man,
thou art thyself.

DROMIO OF SYRACUSE I am an ass, I am a woman's man, and
besides° myself.   *in addition*

ANTIPHOLUS OF SYRACUSE What woman's man? And how
80 besides thyself?

DROMIO OF SYRACUSE Marry, sir, besides myself I am due to a
woman: one that claims me, one that haunts me, one that will
have me.

ANTIPHOLUS OF SYRACUSE What claim lays she to thee?

85 DROMIO OF SYRACUSE Marry, sir, such claim as you would lay to
your horse; and she would have me as a beast—not that, I being
a beast, she would have me, but that she, being a very beastly
creature, lays claim to me.

ANTIPHOLUS OF SYRACUSE What is she?

90 DROMIO OF SYRACUSE A very reverend° body; ay, such a one as a   *worthy*
man may not speak of without he say 'sir-reverence'.[5] I have but
lean luck in the match, and yet is she a wondrous fat marriage.

ANTIPHOLUS OF SYRACUSE How dost thou mean, a fat marriage?

DROMIO OF SYRACUSE Marry, sir, she's the kitchen wench,° and   *servant*
95 all grease; and I know not what use to put her to but to make
a lamp of her, and run from her by her own light. I warrant°   *guarantee*
her rags and the tallow in them will burn a Poland winter.[6] If
she lives till doomsday, she'll burn a week longer than the
whole world.[7]

100 ANTIPHOLUS OF SYRACUSE What complexion is she of?

DROMIO OF SYRACUSE Swart° like my shoe, but her face nothing   *Dark*
like so clean kept. For why?°—She sweats a man may go over-   *How so?*
shoes[8] in the grime of it.

ANTIPHOLUS OF SYRACUSE That's a fault that water will mend.

105 DROMIO OF SYRACUSE No, sir, 'tis in grain.° Noah's flood could   *ingrained*
not do it.

ANTIPHOLUS OF SYRACUSE What's her name?

DROMIO OF SYRACUSE Nell, sir. But her name and three-
quarters—that's an ell° and three-quarters—will not measure   *more than a yard*
110 her from hip to hip.

---

4. My only heaven on earth and only claim on heaven.
5. "Saving your reverence," an apology for a potentially offensive remark.
6. The length of a winter in Poland—a long time.

7. Than the rest of the world (the popular Christian belief being that the earth would end in fire).
8. She sweats so much a man may be up to his ankles.

ANTIPHOLUS OF SYRACUSE Then she bears some breadth?

DROMIO OF SYRACUSE No longer from head to foot than from
hip to hip. She is spherical, like a globe. I could find out°   discover
countries in her.

115 ANTIPHOLUS OF SYRACUSE In what part of her body stands Ireland?

DROMIO OF SYRACUSE Marry, sir, in her buttocks. I found it out
by the bogs.°   peat marsh; sponginess

ANTIPHOLUS OF SYRACUSE Where Scotland?

DROMIO OF SYRACUSE I found it by the barrenness, hard in the
120 palm of her hand.[9]

ANTIPHOLUS OF SYRACUSE Where France?

DROMIO OF SYRACUSE In her forehead, armed and reverted,[1]
making war against her heir.[2]

ANTIPHOLUS OF SYRACUSE Where England?

125 DROMIO OF SYRACUSE I looked for the chalky cliffs,[3] but I could
find no whiteness in them. But I guess it stood in her chin, by°   judging by
the salt rheum° that ran between France and it.   mucus

ANTIPHOLUS OF SYRACUSE Where Spain?

DROMIO OF SYRACUSE Faith, I saw it not, but I felt it hot in her
130 breath.[4]

ANTIPHOLUS OF SYRACUSE Where America, the Indies?

DROMIO OF SYRACUSE O, sir, upon her nose, all o'er embellished
with rubies, carbuncles, sapphires,[5] declining their rich aspect[6]
to the hot breath of Spain, who sent whole armadas of car-
135 racks to be ballast[7] at her nose.

ANTIPHOLUS OF SYRACUSE Where stood Belgia, the Netherlands?

DROMIO OF SYRACUSE O, sir, I did not look so low.[8] To conclude,
this drudge or diviner° laid claim to me, called me Dromio,   witch
swore I was assured° to her, told me what privy° marks I had   betrothed / private; secret
140 about me—as the mark of my shoulder, the mole in my neck,
the great wart on my left arm—that I, amazed, ran from her
as a witch. And I think if my breast had not been made of faith,
and my heart of steel,[9] she had transformed me to a curtal°   tailless
dog, and made me turn i'th' wheel.°   turn a roasting spit

ANTIPHOLUS OF SYRACUSE Go, hie thee presently.° Post° to the   now / Hasten
145 road.°   harbor
An if° the wind blow any way from shore,°   An if = If / out to sea
I will not harbour in this town tonight.
If any barque put forth, come to the mart,
Where I will walk till thou return to me.
150 If everyone knows us, and we know none,
'Tis time, I think, to trudge,° pack, and be gone.   depart

DROMIO OF SYRACUSE As from a bear a man would run for life,
So fly I from her that would be my wife.   *Exit to the bay*]

ANTIPHOLUS OF SYRACUSE There's none but witches do inhabit here,
155 And therefore 'tis high time that I were hence.
She that doth call me husband, even my° soul   my very

9. Hard with calluses and dry (a moist hand proverbially indicated fertility; hence a dry hand could con-
note barrenness).
1. In rebellion (perhaps referring to syphilitic sores).
2. A possible allusion to contemporary French politics;
a pun on "hair," which she is losing, probably on
account of venereal disease.
3. Teeth; an allusion to the white chalk cliffs of Dover.
4. As if she had been eating pungent food.

5. Glistening skin blemishes (as well as precious stones).
6. Casting their gaze down; paying tribute to.
7. *armadas . . . ballast:* fleets of galleons to be loaded.
8. The Netherlands and Belgium were also known as
the Low Countries.
9. Compare Ephesians 6:11ff.: "Put on the whole
armour of God, that ye may be able to stand against the
assaults of the devil. . . . having on the breast plate of
righteousness. . . . Above all, take the shield of faith."

Doth for a wife abhor. But her fair sister,
Possessed with such a gentle sovereign° grace,   *excellent*
Of such enchanting presence and discourse,
160   Hath almost made me traitor to myself.
But lest myself be guilty to° self-wrong,   *of*
I'll stop mine ears against the mermaid's song.

Enter ANGELO *with the chain*

ANGELO   Master Antipholus.
ANTIPHOLUS OF SYRACUSE   Ay, that's my name.
ANGELO   I know it well, sir. Lo, here's the chain.
165   I thought to have ta'en° you at the Porcupine.   *overtaken*
The chain unfinished made me stay° thus long.   *delay*
ANTIPHOLUS OF SYRACUSE [*taking the chain*]   What is your will
     that I shall do with this?
ANGELO   What please° yourself, sir. I have made it for you.   *pleases*
ANTIPHOLUS OF SYRACUSE   Made it for me, sir? I bespoke° it not.   *ordered*
170   ANGELO   Not once, nor twice, but twenty times you have.
Go home with it, and please your wife withal,°   *with it*
And soon at supper-time I'll visit you,
And then receive my money for the chain.
ANTIPHOLUS OF SYRACUSE   I pray you, sir, receive the money now,
175   For fear you ne'er see chain nor money more.
ANGELO   You are a merry man, sir. Fare you well.   *Exit*
ANTIPHOLUS OF SYRACUSE   What I should think of this I cannot tell.
But this I think: there's no man is so vain°   *foolish*
That would refuse so fair an offered chain.
180   I see a man here needs not live by shifts,°   *his own efforts*
When in the streets he meets such golden gifts.
I'll to the mart, and there for Dromio stay.
If any ship put out, then straight° away!   *Exit*   *immediately*

4.1

Enter [SECOND] MERCHANT, [ANGELO *the*] *goldsmith,*
     and an OFFICER

SECOND MERCHANT [*to* ANGELO]   You know since Pentecost[1] the sum is due,
And since I have not much importuned you;
Nor now I had not,° but° that I am bound   *I would not have / except*
To Persia, and want° guilders for my voyage.   *lack*
5   Therefore make present satisfaction,°   *immediate payment*
Or I'll attach° you by this officer.   *arrest*
ANGELO   Even just the sum that I do owe to you
Is growing° to me by Antipholus,   *owing*
And in the instant that I met with you
10   He had of me a chain. At five o'clock
I shall receive the money for the same.
Pleaseth you° walk with me down to his house,   *If it please you to*
I will discharge my bond, and thank you too.

Enter ANTIPHOLUS [OF] EPHESUS, DROMIO [OF EPHESUS]
     from the Courtesan's [*house, the Porcupine*]

OFFICER   That labour may you save. See where he comes.

4.1 Location: A street in Ephesus.
1. Christian festival observed on the seventh Sunday
after Easter, in commemoration of the descent of the

Holy Ghost on the disciples on the day of the Jewish
harvest holiday of Shavuoth.

ANTIPHOLUS OF EPHESUS [*to* DROMIO]   While I go to the gold-
15   smith's house, go thou
        And buy a rope's end.° That will I bestow°   *piece of rope / employ (as a whip)*
        Among my wife and her confederates
        For locking me out of my doors by day.
        But soft,° I see the goldsmith. Get thee gone.   *wait*
20   Buy thou a rope, and bring it home to me.
DROMIO OF EPHESUS   I buy a thousand pound a year, I buy a
        rope.[2]   *Exit*
ANTIPHOLUS OF EPHESUS [*to* ANGELO]   A man is well help up°   *helped*
        that trusts to you!
        I promisèd your presence and the chain,
        But neither chain nor goldsmith came to me.
25   Belike° you thought our love° would last too long   *Perhaps / friendship*
        If it were chained together, and therefore came not.
ANGELO   Saving° your merry humour, here's the note   *Without offense to*
        How much your chain weighs to the utmost carat,
        The fineness of the gold, and chargeful fashion,°   *costly craftsmanship*
30   Which doth amount to three odd ducats° more   *gold coins*
        Than I stand debted° to this gentleman.   *indebted*
        I pray you see him presently discharged,°   *paid off now*
        For he is bound to sea, and stays but° for it.   *waits only*
ANTIPHOLUS OF EPHESUS   I am not furnished with the present° money.   *ready*
35   Besides, I have some business in the town.
        Good signor, take the stranger to my house,
        And with you take the chain, and bid my wife
        Disburse the sum on the receipt thereof.
        Perchance° I will be there as soon as you.   *Perhaps*
40 ANGELO   Then you will bring the chain to her yourself?
ANTIPHOLUS OF EPHESUS   No, bear it with you, lest I come not
        time° enough.   *soon*
ANGELO   Well, sir, I will. Have you the chain about you?
ANTIPHOLUS OF EPHESUS   An if I have not, sir, I hope you have;
        Or else you may return without your money.
45 ANGELO   Nay, come, I pray you, sir, give me the chain.
        Both wind and tide stays° for this gentleman,   *wait*
        And I, to blame, have held him here too long.
ANTIPHOLUS OF EPHESUS   Good Lord! You use this dalliance° to   *trifling delay*
        excuse
        Your breach of promise to° the Porcupine.   *to go to*
50   I should have chid you for not bringing it,
        But like a shrew° you first begin to brawl.   *sour person*
SECOND MERCHANT [*to* ANGELO]   The hour steals on. I pray you,
        sir, dispatch.°   *hurry*
ANGELO [*to* ANTIPHOLUS]   You hear how he importunes me. The chain!
ANTIPHOLUS OF EPHESUS   Why, give it to my wife, and fetch
        your money.
55 ANGELO   Come, come, you know I gave it you even° now.   *just*
        Either send the chain, or send me by some token.[3]
ANTIPHOLUS OF EPHESUS   Fie, now you run this humour out of
        breath.°   *exhaust this joke*
        Come, where's the chain? I pray you let me see it.

2. Perhaps in exasperated contrast with Antipholus of   3. With some sign of yours (so that Adriana will know
Syracuse's earlier demand for a thousand marks (2.1.60).   to pay me).

SECOND MERCHANT   My business cannot brook° this dalliance.   *tolerate*

60   Good sir, say whe'er° you'll answer° me or no;   *whether / repay*
    If not, I'll leave him to the officer.

ANTIPHOLUS OF EPHESUS   I answer you? What should I answer you?

ANGELO   The money that you owe me for the chain.

ANTIPHOLUS OF EPHESUS   I owe you none till I receive the chain.

65   ANGELO   You know I gave it you half an hour since.

ANTIPHOLUS OF EPHESUS   You gave me none. You wrong me much to say so.

ANGELO   You wrong me more, sir, in denying it.
    Consider how it stands upon° my credit.[4]   *affects*

SECOND MERCHANT   Well, officer, arrest him at my suit.

70   OFFICER [*to* ANGELO]   I do, and charge you in the Duke's name to obey me.

ANGELO [*to* ANTIPHOLUS]   This touches° me in reputation.   *injures*
    Either consent to pay this sum for me,
    Or I attach° you by this officer.   *arrest*

ANTIPHOLUS OF EPHESUS   Consent to pay thee that° I never had?   *for what*

75   Arrest me, foolish fellow, if thou dar'st.

ANGELO   Here is thy fee:[5] arrest him, officer.
    I would not spare my brother in this case
    If he should scorn me so apparently.°   *openly*

OFFICER [*to* ANTIPHOLUS]   I do arrest you, sir. You hear the suit.

80   ANTIPHOLUS OF EPHESUS   I do obey thee till I give thee bail.
    [*To* ANGELO] But, sirrah, you shall buy this sport as dear[6]
    As all the metal in your shop will answer.°   *amount to*

ANGELO   Sir, sir, I shall have law° in Ephesus,   *my legal rights*
    To your notorious shame, I doubt it not.

Enter DROMIO [OF] SYRACUSE, *from the bay*

85   DROMIO OF SYRACUSE   Master, there's a barque of Epidamnum
    That stays but till her owner comes aboard,
    And then she bears away. Our freightage,° sir,   *luggage; goods*
    I have conveyed aboard, and I have bought
    The oil, the balsamum,[7] and aqua-vitae.

90   The ship is in her trim;° the merry wind   *ready to sail*
    Blows fair from land. They stay for naught° at all   *nothing*
    But for their owner, master, and yourself.

ANTIPHOLUS OF EPHESUS   How now? A madman? Why, thou
       peevish° sheep,[8]   *bleating*
    What ship of Epidamnum stays for me?

95   DROMIO OF SYRACUSE   A ship you sent me to, to hire waftage.°   *buy our passage*

ANTIPHOLUS OF EPHESUS   Thou drunken slave, I sent thee for a rope,
    And told thee to what purpose and what end.

DROMIO OF SYRACUSE   You sent me for a ropes end° as soon.   *a beating*
    You sent me to the bay, sir, for a barque.

100   ANTIPHOLUS OF EPHESUS   I will debate this matter at more leisure,
    And teach your ears to list° me with more heed.   *listen to*
    To Adriana, villain, hie thee straight.°   *go immediately*
    Give her this key, and tell her in the desk
    That's covered o'er with Turkish tapestry

105   There is a purse of ducats. Let her send it.
    Tell her I am arrested in the street,
    And that shall bail me.° Hie thee, slave. Be gone!—   *pay my bail*

---

4. Financial standing; more generally, reputation.
5. Public officers were entitled to private payment.
6. You shall pay as dearly for this amusement.

7. A healing resin; alcoholic spirit.
8. Idiot, punning on "ship" in the next line (the words were similarly pronounced).

On, officer, to prison, till it come.

Exeunt [all but DROMIO OF SYRACUSE]

DROMIO OF SYRACUSE To Adriana. That is where we dined,
110 Where Dowsabel[9] did claim me for her husband.
She is too big, I hope, for me to compass.[1]
Thither I must, although against my will;
For servants must their masters' minds° fulfil.   *Exit*   wishes

4.2

Enter [from the Phoenix] ADRIANA *and* LUCIANA

ADRIANA Ah, Luciana, did he tempt thee so?
Mightst thou perceive austerely in his eye[1]
That he did plead in earnest, yea or no?
Looked he or° red or pale, or sad or merrily?   either
5 What observation mad'st thou in this case
Of his heart's meteors tilting[2] in his face?
LUCIANA First he denied you had in him no° right.   any
ADRIANA He meant he did me none, the more my spite.°   grief
LUCIANA Then swore he that he was a stranger here.
10 ADRIANA And true he swore, though yet forsworn[3] he were.
LUCIANA Then pleaded I for you.
ADRIANA   And what said he?
LUCIANA That love I begged for you, he begged of me.
ADRIANA With what persuasion did he tempt thy love?
LUCIANA With words that in an honest suit° might move.   courtship
15 First he did praise my beauty, then my speech.
ADRIANA Didst speak him fair?°   encourage him
LUCIANA   Have patience, I beseech.
ADRIANA I cannot, nor I will not, hold me still.°   silent
My tongue, though not my heart, shall have his° will.   its
He is deformèd, crookèd, old, and sere,°   withered
20 Ill-faced, worse-bodied, shapeless° everywhere,   ill shaped
Vicious, ungentle, foolish, blunt, unkind,
Stigmatical in making,[4] worse in mind.
LUCIANA Who would be jealous, then, of such a one?
No evil lost is wailed when it is gone.
25 ADRIANA Ah, but I think him better than I say,
And yet would herein others' eyes were worse.[5]
Far from her nest the lapwing[6] cries away.
My heart prays for him, though my tongue do curse.

Enter DROMIO [OF] SYRACUSE *running*

DROMIO OF SYRACUSE Here, go—the desk, the purse! Sweet now, make haste![7]
LUCIANA How?[8] Hast thou lost thy breath?
30 DROMIO OF SYRACUSE   By running fast.

---

9. English form of "Dulcibella," a generic name for a sweetheart.
1. Embrace or gain; probably also alluding to her geographical extent (see 3.2.113–37).
4.2 Location: Before the house of Antipholus of Ephesus.
1. By the seriousness of his expression.
2. Conflicting emotions, as if heavenly bodies were engaged in combat ("tilting").
3. *true . . . forsworn*: he is behaving like a stranger to me, but he is lying and false to his marriage vows if he claims to be one.

4. Deformed in his physical makeup.
5. And nevertheless wish others' eyes to be deceived (and so think him ugly).
6. A bird (the peewit) that diverts attention away from her nest to protect her young; Adriana wishes to turn other women's attention from Antipholus's attractions.
7. Dromio is possibly speaking to himself as he rushes in.
8. What's this? Although F treats Luciana's word as one sentence, Dromio's answer is obviously a comic misunderstanding.

ADRIANA   Where is thy master, Dromio? Is he well?
DROMIO OF SYRACUSE   No, he's in Tartar limbo,[9] worse than hell.
    A devil in an everlasting[1] garment hath him,
    One whose hard heart is buttoned up with steel;
35   A fiend, a fairy,[2] pitiless and rough;
    A wolf, nay worse, a fellow all in buff;[3]
    A back-friend,[4] a shoulder-clapper,° one that countermands°   arresting officer / prohibits
    The passages of alleys, creeks, and narrow launds;[5]
    A hound that runs counter,[6] and yet draws dryfoot well;[7]
40   One that before the Judgement[8] carries poor souls to hell.
ADRIANA   Why, man, what is the matter?
DROMIO OF SYRACUSE   I do not know the matter,° he is 'rested°   dispute / arrested
    on the case.[9]
ADRIANA   What, is he arrested? Tell me at whose suit.
DROMIO OF SYRACUSE   I know not at whose suit he is arrested well,
45   But is in a suit of buff which 'rested him, that can I tell.
    Will you send him, mistress, redemption—the money in his desk?
ADRIANA   Go fetch it, sister.   Exit LUCIANA [into the Phoenix]
                                    This I wonder at,
    That he unknown to me should be in debt.
    Tell me, was he arrested on° a bond?   for breaking
50 DROMIO OF SYRACUSE   Not on a bond but on a stronger thing:
    A chain, a chain—do you not hear it ring?
ADRIANA   What, the chain?
DROMIO OF SYRACUSE   No, no, the bell. 'Tis time that I were gone:
    It was two ere I left him, and now the clock strikes one.[1]
ADRIANA   The hours come back! That did I never hear.
DROMIO OF SYRACUSE   O yes, if any hour[2] meet a sergeant, a°   he
55   turns back for very fear.
ADRIANA   As if time were in debt. How fondly° dost thou reason!   foolishly
DROMIO OF SYRACUSE   Time is a very bankrupt, and owes more
    than he's worth to season.[3]
    Nay, he's a thief too. Have you not heard men say
    That time comes stealing on by night and day?
60   If a be in debt and theft, and a sergeant in° the way,   stands in
    Hath he not reason to turn back an hour in a day?
        Enter LUCIANA [from the Phoenix, with the money]
ADRIANA   Go, Dromio, there's the money. Bear it straight,°   quickly
    And bring thy master home immediately.   [Exit DROMIO]
    Come, sister, I am pressed° down with conceit:°   depressed / imaginings
65   Conceit, my comfort and my injury.
                                    Exeunt [into the Phoenix]

9. Hellish prison. "Tartar" is short for "Tartarus," the classical hell, but it also suggests the Tartars, central Asian people reputed by Elizabethans to be particularly savage. "Limbo" was common slang for "prison."
1. Term for the durable material used in the period for the uniform of prison officers; eternal, like hell's punishments.
2. Malevolent fairy, like the goblins in 2.2.190–92.
3. Stout leather used in uniforms.
4. False friend; also referring to the officer's hand on the culprit's back during an arrest.
5. The traffic through alleys, small passageways, and narrow pathways. launds: glades or clearings, pathways through woods.

6. Runs in the opposite direction to the prey; also perhaps alluding to the Counter, as several debtors' prisons in London were known.
7. draws . . . well: tracks game by the scent of its foot.
8. before the Judgement: in a court of law, with an allusion to the Day of Judgment.
9. on the case: in a legal action where the injury was not specifically addressed by precedent; by means of the officer's hand on his outer clothing ("case").
1. "On" and "one" were pronounced similarly.
2. Perhaps a pun on "ower" (debtor), or "whore."
3. "Seisin," a legal term for "possession"; opportunity; thus, there is too little time to make good the promises of the occasion.

4.3

Enter ANTIPHOLUS [OF] SYRACUSE [*wearing the chain*]

ANTIPHOLUS OF SYRACUSE   There's not a man I meet but doth salute° me   greet
As if I were their well-acquainted friend,
And everyone doth call me by my name.
Some tender° money to me, some invite me,   offer
5   Some other give me thanks for kindnesses.
Some offer me commodities to buy.
Even now a tailor called me in his shop,
And showed me silks that he had bought for me,
And therewithal° took measure of my body.   with that
10   Sure, these are but imaginary wiles,°   delusions
And Lapland sorcerers[1] inhabit here.

Enter DROMIO [OF] SYRACUSE [*with the money*]

DROMIO OF SYRACUSE   Master, here's the gold you sent me for.
What, have you got redemption from the picture of old Adam
new apparelled?[2]
ANTIPHOLUS OF SYRACUSE   What gold is this? What Adam dost
15   thou mean?
DROMIO OF SYRACUSE   Not that Adam that kept the Paradise,
but that Adam that keeps the prison—he that goes in the calf's
skin,[3] that was killed for the Prodigal;[4] he that came behind
you, sir, like an evil angel, and bid you forsake your liberty.[5]
20   ANTIPHOLUS OF SYRACUSE   I understand thee not.
DROMIO OF SYRACUSE   No? Why, 'tis a plain case: he that went
like a bass viol[6] in a case of leather; the man, sir, that when
gentlemen are tired gives them a sob[7] and 'rests them; he, sir,
that takes pity on decayed° men and gives them suits of   ruined
25   durance;[8] he that sets up his rest[9] to do more exploits with his
mace° than a Moorish pike.   staff of office
ANTIPHOLUS OF SYRACUSE   What, thou mean'st an officer?
DROMIO OF SYRACUSE   Ay, sir, the sergeant of the band: he that
brings any man to answer it° that breaks his bond; one that   for it
30   thinks a man always going to bed, and says 'God give you good
rest.'°   arrest
ANTIPHOLUS OF SYRACUSE   Well, sir, there rest in° your foolery.   cease
Is there any ships puts forth tonight? May we be gone?
DROMIO OF SYRACUSE   Why, sir, I brought you word an hour
35   since that the barque *Expedition* put forth tonight, and then
were you hindered by the sergeant to tarry for the hoy[1] *Delay.*
Here are the angels[2] that you sent for to deliver you.
ANTIPHOLUS OF SYRACUSE   The fellow is distraught,° and so am I,   distracted; mad
And here we wander in illusions.
40   Some blessèd power deliver us from hence.

Enter a COURTESAN [*from the Porcupine*]

4.3 Location: A street in Ephesus.
1. Lapland was known for witches.
2. *from . . . apparelled*: from the sergeant in his leather
uniform. Old Adam is the figure of man's sinful nature,
dressed, after the Fall, in skins (Genesis 3:21). There is
also a possible reference to Ephesians 4:22–24 ("put
off . . . the old man, which is corrupt . . . put on the
new man, which after God is created in righteousness"). The text is emended from F: What have
you got the picture of old Adam new apparelled?
3. The buff of the officer's garments.
4. The prodigal son of Luke 15:11–32; his father killed

a calf for a feast on his return home.
5. *bid . . . liberty*: arrested you.
6. Large stringed instrument, like a cello (continuing
the jokes about the officer's leather uniform).
7. A rest (for tired horses) as well as a lament, picked
up in the following puns of "'rests" and "pity."
8. *suits of durance*: lawsuits or prosecutions ending in
imprisonment; clothes of hard-wearing material.
9. *sets up his rest*: gambles all (punning on "arrest").
1. A small, slow vessel used in coastal waters. The
names of the ships are Dromio's improvisations.
2. Gold coins bearing a figure of the archangel Michael.

COURTESAN Well met, well met, Master Antipholus.
I see, sir, you have found the goldsmith now.
Is that the chain you promised me today?
ANTIPHOLUS OF SYRACUSE Satan, avoid![3] I charge thee, tempt
me not!

45 DROMIO OF SYRACUSE Master, is this Mistress Satan?
ANTIPHOLUS OF SYRACUSE It is the devil.
DROMIO OF SYRACUSE Nay, she is worse, she is the devil's dam;°   *mother*
and here she comes in the habit° of a light° wench. And thereof *clothing/wanton*
comes that the wenches say 'God damn me'—that's as much to
50 say, 'God make me a light wench.' It is written they appear to
men like angels of light.[4] Light is an effect of fire, and fire will
burn. Ergo,° light wenches will burn.[5] Come not near her.   *Therefore*
COURTESAN Your man and you are marvellous merry, sir.
Will you go with me? We'll mend° our dinner here.   *complete*
55 DROMIO OF SYRACUSE Master, if you do, expect spoon-meat,[6]
and bespeak° a long spoon.   *request*
ANTIPHOLUS OF SYRACUSE Why, Dromio?
DROMIO OF SYRACUSE Marry, he must have a long spoon that
must eat with the devil.
ANTIPHOLUS OF SYRACUSE [*to* COURTESAN Avoid, thou fiend!
60   What tell'st thou me of supping?
Thou art, as you are all, a sorceress.
I conjure° thee to leave me and be gone.   *order; charge*
COURTESAN Give me the ring of mine you had at dinner,
Or for my diamond the chain you promised,
65 And I'll be gone, sir, and not trouble you.
DROMIO OF SYRACUSE Some devils ask but° the parings of one's nail,   *only*
A rush,° a hair, a drop of blood, a pin,   *straw*
A nut, a cherry-stone;
But she, more covetous, would have a chain.
70 Master, be wise; an if° you give it her,   *an if=if*
The devil will shake her chain,[7] and fright us with it.
COURTESAN [*to* ANTIPHOLUS] I pray you, sir, my ring, or else the chain.
I hope you do not mean to cheat me so?
ANTIPHOLUS OF SYRACUSE Avaunt, thou witch!—Come, Dromio, let us go.
75 DROMIO OF SYRACUSE 'Fly pride' says the peacock.[8] Mistress, that you know.
          Exeunt [ANTIPHOLUS OF SYRACUSE
            and DROMIO OF SYRACUSE]
COURTESAN Now, out of doubt, Antipholus is mad;
Else would he never so demean° himself.   *conduct; debase*
A ring he hath of mine worth forty ducats,
And for the same he promised me a chain.
80 Both one and other he denies me now.
The reason that I gather he is mad,
Besides this present instance of his rage,
Is a mad tale he told today at dinner
Of his own doors being shut against his entrance.
85 Belike° his wife, acquainted with his fits,   *Probably*

---

3. Away. An echo of Jesus' words to Satan in Matthew
4:10: "Avoid Satan."
4. From 2 Corinthians 11:14: "Satan himself is transformed into an angel of light."
5. Will transmit venereal disease; will suffer in hell.
6. Soft food for babies or invalids, mentioned for the

sake of the proverb in lines 58–59.
7. Alluding to the binding of the devil in a chain in Revelation 20:1.
8. For the conniving courtesan to complain about
cheating is, in Dromio's view, analogous to a proud peacock decrying pride.

On purpose shut the doors against his way.°   *entrance*
My way is now to hie° home to his house,   *hasten*
And tell his wife that, being lunatic,
He rushed into my house, and took perforce°   *forcibly*
90   My ring away. This course I fittest choose,
For forty ducats is too much to lose.   *[Exit]*

4.4

Enter ANTIPHOLUS [OF] EPHESUS *with a Jailor [an*
OFFICER]

ANTIPHOLUS OF EPHESUS   Fear me not, man, I will not break away.
I'll give thee ere I leave thee so much money
To warrant thee° as I am 'rested for.   *As surety*
My wife is in a wayward mood today,
5   And will not lightly° trust the messenger   *readily*
That I should be attached° in Ephesus.   *arrested*
I tell you 'twill sound harshly in her ears.
      Enter DROMIO [OF] EPHESUS *with a rope's end*
Here comes my man. I think he brings the money.—
How now, sir? Have you that I sent you for?
10 DROMIO OF EPHESUS   Here's that, I warrant you, will pay[1] them all.
ANTIPHOLUS OF EPHESUS   But where's the money?
DROMIO OF EPHESUS   Why, sir, I gave the money for the rope.
ANTIPHOLUS OF EPHESUS   Five hundred ducats, villain, for a rope?
DROMIO OF EPHESUS   I'll serve° you, sir, five hundred at the rate.°   *provide / for that price*
ANTIPHOLUS OF EPHESUS   To what end did I bid thee hie thee
15   home?
DROMIO OF EPHESUS   To° a rope's end, sir, and to that end am I   *For*
      returned.
ANTIPHOLUS OF EPHESUS   And to that end, sir, I will welcome you.[2]
      [He beats DROMIO]
OFFICER   Good sir, be patient.
DROMIO OF EPHESUS   Nay, 'tis for me to be patient: I am in adversity.[3]
20 OFFICER   Good now,° hold thy tongue.   *Please*
DROMIO OF EPHESUS   Nay, rather persuade *him* to hold° his   *hold off*
      hands.
ANTIPHOLUS OF EPHESUS   Thou whoreson,[4] senseless villain!
DROMIO OF EPHESUS   I would I were senseless, sir, that I might
      not feel your blows.
25 ANTIPHOLUS OF EPHESUS   Thou art sensible in° nothing but   *responsive to*
      blows, and so is an ass.
DROMIO OF EPHESUS   I am an ass indeed. You may prove it by
      my long ears.[5]—I have served him from the hour of my nativity
      to this instant, and have nothing at his hands for my service
30   but blows. When I am cold, he heats me with beating. When
      I am warm, he cools me with beating. I am waked with it when
      I sleep, raised with it when I sit, driven out of doors with it when
      I go from home, welcomed home with it when I return. Nay, I
      bear it on my shoulders, as a beggar wont her brat,[6] and I think

---

4.4 Location: Scene continues.
1. With a beating. (See 4.1.15–21.)
2. I will treat you to a rope's end (a beating).
3. In painful circumstances; alluding to Psalms 94:13.
4. Literally, son of a whore; more generally, a term of

contemptuous familiarity.
5. Playing on "ears/years," which were pronounced in the same way.
6. *wont her brat:* is accustomed to carrying her child.

35   when he hath lamed me I shall beg with it[7] from door to door.

    Enter ADRIANA, LUCIANA, COURTESAN, *and a schoolmas-*
    ter called PINCH

ANTIPHOLUS OF EPHESUS   Come, go along: my wife is coming
    yonder.

DROMIO OF EPHESUS [*to* ADRIANA]   Mistress, *respice finem*[8]—
    respect your end—or rather, to prophesy like the parrot,[9]
    'Beware the rope's end'.

ANTIPHOLUS OF EPHESUS   Wilt thou still talk?

    [*He*] *beats* DROMIO

40   COURTESAN [*to* ADRIANA]   How say you now? Is not your husband mad?

ADRIANA   His incivility confirms no less.—
    Good Doctor Pinch, you are a conjurer.[1]
    Establish him in his true sense[2] again,
    And I will please you° what you will demand.   *repay you with*

45   LUCIANA   Alas, how fiery and how sharp° he looks!   *fierce*

COURTESAN   Mark how he trembles in his ecstasy.°   *frenzy*

PINCH [*to* ANTIPHOLUS]   Give me your hand, and let me feel your pulse.

ANTIPHOLUS OF EPHESUS   There is my hand, and let it feel your ear.

    [*He strikes* PINCH]

PINCH   I charge thee, Satan, housed within this man,

50   To yield possession to my holy prayers,
    And to thy state of darkness hie thee straight:
    I conjure thee by all the saints in heaven.

ANTIPHOLUS OF EPHESUS   Peace, doting wizard, peace! I am not mad.

ADRIANA   O that thou wert not, poor distressèd soul.

55   ANTIPHOLUS OF EPHESUS   You minion,° you, are these your customers?   *hussy*
    Did this companion° with the saffron° face   *rascal/yellow*
    Revel and feast it at my house today,
    Whilst upon me the guilty doors were shut,
    And I denied to enter in my house?

60   ADRIANA   O husband, God doth know you dined at home,
    Where would you had remained until this time,
    Free from these slanders° and this open shame.   *scandals*

ANTIPHOLUS OF EPHESUS   Dined at home?

    [*To* DROMIO]   Thou villain, what sayst thou?

DROMIO OF EPHESUS   Sir, sooth to say,° you did not dine at home.   *to speak truly*

65   ANTIPHOLUS OF EPHESUS   Were not my doors locked up, and I shut out?

DROMIO OF EPHESUS   Pardie,° your doors were locked, and you   *By God (pardieu)*
    shut out.

ANTIPHOLUS OF EPHESUS   And did not she herself revile me there?

DROMIO OF EPHESUS   Sans° fable, she herself reviled you there.   *Without*

ANTIPHOLUS OF EPHESUS   Did not her kitchen-maid rail, taunt, and scorn me?

70   DROMIO OF EPHESUS   Certes° she did. The kitchen vestal[3] scorned you.   *Certainly*

ANTIPHOLUS OF EPHESUS   And did not I in rage depart from thence?

DROMIO OF EPHESUS   In verity you did. My bones bears witness,
    That since have felt the vigour of his rage.

---

7. I shall receive a beating (a frequent punishment for begging).
8. A religious injunction to "think on your end," but punning on *respice funem*, "think on the rope" (on hanging).
9. Parrots were often taught to cry "rope," an exclamation or curse; the "prophecy" is that the hearer deserves to be hanged.

1. Capable of exorcising devils; exorcism required a "doctor"—a learned man—since it was thought that devils needed to be addressed in Latin.
2. His right mind. Possession and lunacy were not necessarily medically distinct, since both involved the displacement of reason (by passion, sickness, or demons).
3. Ironic: a virgin priestess of the household goddess Vesta's temple, responsible for keeping the fire burning.

ADRIANA [*aside to* PINCH] Is't good to soothe° him in these contraries? *humor*

75 PINCH [*aside to* ADRIANA] It is no shame.° The fellow finds his vein, *harm*
And, yielding to him, humours well his frenzy.

ANTIPHOLUS OF EPHESUS [*to* ADRIANA] Thou hast suborned° the *induced*
goldsmith to arrest me.

ADRIANA Alas, I sent you money to redeem you,
By Dromio here, who came in haste for it.

80 DROMIO OF EPHESUS Money by me? Heart and good will you might,
But surely, master, not a rag° of money. *farthing*

ANTIPHOLUS OF EPHESUS Went'st not thou to her for a purse of ducats?

ADRIANA He came to me, and I delivered it.

LUCIANA And I am witness with her that she did.

85 DROMIO OF EPHESUS God and the ropemaker bear me witness
That I was sent for nothing but a rope.

PINCH [*aside to* ADRIANA] Mistress, both man and master is possessed.
I know it by their pale and deadly° looks. *deathlike*
They must be bound and laid in some dark room.[4]

ANTIPHOLUS OF EPHESUS [*to* ADRIANA] Say wherefore didst thou
90   lock me forth° today, *out*
[*To* DROMIO] And why dost thou deny the bag of gold?

ADRIANA I did not, gentle husband, lock thee forth.

DROMIO OF EPHESUS And, gentle master, I received no gold.
But I confess, sir, that we were locked out.

95 ADRIANA Dissembling villain, thou speak'st false in both.

ANTIPHOLUS OF EPHESUS Dissembling harlot, thou art false in all,
And art confederate with a damnèd pack° *conspiracy*
To make a loathsome abject scorn of me.
But with these nails I'll pluck out those false eyes,
100   That would behold in me this shameful sport.
[*He reaches for* ADRIANA; *she shrieks.*] *Enter three or*
four, and offer to bind him. He strives

ADRIANA O, bind him, bind him. Let him not come near me.

PINCH More company!° The fiend is strong within him. *Get help*

LUCIANA Ay me, poor man, how pale and wan he looks.

ANTIPHOLUS OF EPHESUS What, will you murder me?—Thou, jailer, thou,
105   I am thy prisoner. Wilt thou suffer them
To make a rescue?[5]

OFFICER   Masters, let him go.
He is my prisoner, and you shall not have him.

PINCH Go, bind his man, for he is frantic too.
[*They bind* DROMIO]

ADRIANA What wilt thou do, thou peevish° officer? *stupid*
110   Hast thou delight to see a wretched man
Do outrage and displeasure° to himself? *harm*

OFFICER He is my prisoner. If I let him go,
The debt he owes will be required of me.

ADRIANA I will discharge° thee ere I go from thee. *repay*
115   Bear me forthwith unto his creditor.
And, knowing how the debt grows,[6] I will pay it.—
Good Master Doctor, see him safe conveyed
Home to my house. O most unhappy day!

ANTIPHOLUS OF EPHESUS O most unhappy strumpet!

---

4. An ordinary sixteenth-century treatment for insanity.   6. *knowing . . . grows:* when I know how the debt came
5. To release by force from legal custody.   about.

120 **DROMIO OF EPHESUS** Master, I am here entered in bond for you.
ANTIPHOLUS OF EPHESUS Out on thee, villain! Wherefore dost
   thou mad° me? *goad*
DROMIO OF EPHESUS Will you be bound for nothing? Be mad, good master—
   Cry, 'The devil!'⁷
LUCIANA God help, poor souls, how idly do they talk!
125 **ADRIANA** Go bear him hence. Sister, go you with me.
   *Exeunt [into the Phoenix, PINCH and others
   carrying off ANTIPHOLUS OF EPHESUS and DROMIO OF
   EPHESUS]. Manent° OFFICER, ADRIANA, LUCIANA, COURTESAN* *Remain*
   [*To the* OFFICER] Say now, whose suit is he arrested at?
OFFICER One Angelo, a goldsmith. Do you know him?
ADRIANA I know the man. What is the sum he owes?
OFFICER Two hundred ducats.
ADRIANA   Say, how grows it due?
130 **OFFICER** Due for a chain your husband had of him.
ADRIANA He did bespeak° a chain for me, but had it not. *order*
COURTESAN Whenas your husband all in rage today
   Came to my house, and took away my ring—
   The ring I saw upon his finger now—
135 Straight after did I meet him with a chain.
ADRIANA It may be so, but I did never see it.
   Come, jailer, bring me where the goldsmith is.
   I long to know the truth hereof at large.° *in full*
   *Enter ANTIPHOLUS [OF] SYRACUSE [wearing the chain]
   with his rapier drawn, and DROMIO [OF] SYRACUSE [also
   with rapier]*
LUCIANA God, for thy mercy, they are loose again!
140 **ADRIANA** And come with naked° swords. Let's call more help *drawn*
   To have them bound again.
OFFICER   Away, they'll kill us!
   Run all out. Exeunt omnes,° as fast as may be, frighted. *all*
   [ANTIPHOLUS *and* DROMIO *remain*]
ANTIPHOLUS OF SYRACUSE I see these witches are afraid of swords.
DROMIO OF SYRACUSE She that would be your wife now ran from you.
ANTIPHOLUS OF SYRACUSE Come to the Centaur. Fetch our stuff from thence.
145 I long that we were safe and sound aboard.
DROMIO OF SYRACUSE Faith, stay here this night. They will
   surely do us no harm. You saw they speak us fair, give us gold.
   Methinks they are such a gentle nation that, but for the
   mountain of mad flesh that claims marriage of me, I could
150 find in my heart to stay here still,° and turn witch. *always*
ANTIPHOLUS OF SYRACUSE I will not stay tonight for all the town.
   Therefore away, to get our stuff aboard. *Exeunt*

5.1

Enter [SECOND] MERCHANT and [ANGELO] the goldsmith
ANGELO I am sorry, sir, that I have hindered you,
   But I protest he had the chain of me,
   Though most dishonestly he doth deny it.
SECOND MERCHANT How is the man esteemed here in the city?

---

7. A cry of exasperation; a direct address to the devil, possessed.
which would lend support to the view that he is **5.1** Location: Before a priory.

5 ANGELO Of very reverend reputation, sir,
Of credit infinite, highly beloved,
Second to none that lives here in the city.
His word might bear my wealth at any time.[1]
SECOND MERCHANT Speak softly. Yonder, as I think, he walks.
     Enter ANTIPHOLUS [OF SYRACUSE, *wearing the chain,*]
     and DROMIO [OF SYRACUSE] *again*

10 ANGELO 'Tis so, and that self° chain about his neck   *same*
Which he forswore° most monstrously to have.   *denied on oath*
Good sir, draw near to me. I'll speak to him.—
Signor Antipholus, I wonder much
That you would put me to this shame and trouble,
15 And not without some scandal to yourself,
With circumstance° and oaths so to deny   *detailed argument*
This chain, which now you wear so openly.
Beside the charge,° the shame, imprisonment,   *cost*
You have done wrong to this my honest friend,
20 Who, but for staying on° our controversy,   *as a result of*
Had hoisted sail and put to sea today.
This chain you had of me. Can you deny it?
ANTIPHOLUS OF SYRACUSE I think I had. I never did deny it.
SECOND MERCHANT Yes, that you did, sir, and forswore it too.
25 ANTIPHOLUS OF SYRACUSE Who heard me to deny it or forswear it?
SECOND MERCHANT These ears of mine, thou know'st, did hear thee.
Fie on thee, wretch! 'Tis pity that thou liv'st
To walk where any honest men resort.
ANTIPHOLUS OF SYRACUSE Thou art a villain to impeach me thus.
30 I'll prove mine honour and mine honesty
Against thee presently,° if thou dar'st stand.°   *now / defend yourself*
SECOND MERCHANT I dare, and do defy thee for a villain.
     They draw. Enter ADRIANA, LUCIANA, COURTESAN, *and*
     others [*from the Phoenix*]
ADRIANA Hold, hurt him not, for God's sake; he is mad.
Some get within him,° take his sword away.   *his guard*
35 Bind Dromio too, and bear them to my house.
DROMIO OF SYRACUSE Run, master, run! For God's sake take° a   *take cover in*
     house.
This is some priory—in, or we are spoiled.°   *ruined*
     Exeunt ANTIPHOLUS [OF SYRACUSE *and*
     DROMIO OF SYRACUSE] *to the priory*
     Enter [*from the priory*] *the Lady* ABBESS
ABBESS Be quiet, people. Wherefore throng you hither?
ADRIANA To fetch my poor distracted husband hence.
40 Let us come in, that we may bind him fast,
And bear him home for his recovery.
ANGELO I knew he was not in his perfect wits.
SECOND MERCHANT I am sorry now that I did draw on him.
ABBESS How long hath this possession held the man?
45 ADRIANA This week he hath been heavy, sour, sad,
And much, much different from the man he was;
But till this afternoon his passion°   *insanity*
Ne'er brake° into extremity of rage.   *broke*
ABBESS Hath he not lost much wealth by wreck at sea?

---

1. His word alone would be enough security to borrow all I have.

50   Buried some dear friend? Hath not else his eye

      Strayed° his affection in unlawful love—   *Led astray*

      A sin prevailing much in youthful men,

      Who give their eyes the liberty of gazing?

      Which of these sorrows is he subject to?

55   ADRIANA   To none of these, except it be the last,

      Namely some love that drew him oft from home.

  ABBESS   You should for that have reprehended him.

  ADRIANA   Why, so I did.

  ABBESS   Ay, but not rough enough.

  ADRIANA   As roughly as my modesty would let me.

60   ABBESS   Haply° in private.   *Perhaps*

  ADRIANA   And in assemblies too.

  ABBESS   Ay, but not enough.

  ADRIANA   It was the copy° of our conference.°   *theme/conversation*

      In bed he slept not for my urging it.

65   At board° he fed not for my urging it.   *table*

      Alone, it was the subject of my theme.

      In company I often glancèd° it.   *alluded to*

      Still° did I tell him it was vile and bad.   *Continually*

  ABBESS   And thereof came it that the man was mad.

70   The venom° clamours of a jealous woman   *venomous*

      Poisons more deadly than a mad dog's tooth.

      It seems his sleeps were hindered by thy railing,

      And thereof comes it that his head is light.

      Thou sayst his meat was sauced with thy upbraidings.

75   Unquiet meals make ill digestions.

      Thereof the raging fire of fever bred,

      And what's a fever but a fit of madness?[2]

      Thou sayst his sports were hindered by thy brawls.

      Sweet recreation barred, what doth ensue

80   But moody and dull melancholy,

      Kinsman to grim and comfortless despair,

      And at her heels a huge infectious troop

      Of pale distemperatures° and foes to life?   *illnesses; imbalances*

      In food, in sport, and life-preserving rest

85   To be disturbed would mad or° man or beast.   *would make mad either*

      The consequence is, then, thy jealous fits

      Hath scared thy husband from the use of wits.

  LUCIANA   She never reprehended him but mildly

      When he demeaned himself rough, rude, and wildly.

90   [*To* ADRIANA] Why bear you these rebukes, and answer not?

  ADRIANA   She did betray me to my own reproof.—

      Good people, enter, and lay hold on him.

  ABBESS   No, not a creature enters in my house.

  ADRIANA   Then let your servants bring my husband forth.

95   ABBESS   Neither. He took this place for sanctuary,[3]

      And it shall privilege him from your hands

      Till I have brought him to his wits again,

      Or lose my labour in essaying it.

  ADRIANA   I will attend my husband, be his nurse,

100   Diet° his sickness, for it is my office,°   *Treat/duty*

---

2. Both are imbalances in the body's humors; see note to 4.4.43.

3. Churches and other sacred buildings provided refuge from legal prosecution until the seventeenth century.

And will have no attorney° but myself.   *proxy*
And therefore let me have him home with me.

ABBESS   Be patient, for I will not let him stir
Till I have used the approvèd° means I have,   *tested*

105   With wholesome syrups, drugs, and holy prayers
To make of him a formal° man again.   *complete; sane*
It is a branch and parcel° of mine oath,   *part*
A charitable duty of my order.
Therefore depart, and leave him here with me.

110 ADRIANA   I will not hence, and leave my husband here;
And ill it doth beseem your holiness
To separate the husband and the wife.

ABBESS   Be quiet and depart. Thou shalt not have him.
                         [Exit into the priory]

LUCIANA [*to* ADRIANA]   Complain unto the Duke of this indignity.

115 ADRIANA   Come, go, I will fall prostrate at his feet,
And never rise until my tears and prayers
Have won his grace to come in person hither
And take perforce my husband from the Abbess.

SECOND MERCHANT   By this, I think, the dial point's at five.

120   Anon,° I'm sure, the Duke himself in person   *Soon*
Comes this way to the melancholy vale,
The place of death and sorry execution,
Behind the ditches of the abbey here.

ANGELO   Upon what cause?

125 SECOND MERCHANT   To see a reverend Syracusian merchant,
Who put unluckily into this bay
Against the laws and statutes of this town,
Beheaded publicly for his offence.

ANGELO   See where they come. We will behold his death.

130 LUCIANA   Kneel to the Duke before he pass the abbey.
    Enter [Solinus] DUKE *of Ephesus, and* [EGEON] *the mer-*
    chant of Syracuse, bareheaded, with the headsman° *and*   *executioner*
    other officers

DUKE   Yet once again proclaim it publicly:
If any friend will pay the sum for him,
He shall not die, so much we tender⁴ him.

ADRIANA [*kneeling*]   Justice, most sacred Duke, against the Abbess!

135 DUKE   She is a virtuous and a reverend lady.
It cannot be that she hath done thee wrong.

ADRIANA   May it please your grace, Antipholus my husband,
Who I made lord of me and all I had
At your important° letters⁵—this ill day   *urgent*

140   A most outrageous fit of madness took him,
That desp'rately he hurried through the street,
With him his bondman, all as mad as he,
Doing displeasure to the citizens
By rushing in their houses, bearing thence

145   Rings, jewels, anything his rage° did like.   *he in his madness*
Once did I get him bound, and sent him home,
Whilst to take order for° the wrongs I went   *settle up*
That here and there his fury had committed.

---

4. Offer; feel tender regard for.
5. Formal instructions. Adriana may have been the Duke's ward.

Anon, I wot° not by what strong° escape,   *know / forcible*
150   He broke from those that had the guard of him,
And with his mad attendant and himself,
Each one with ireful passion, with drawn swords,
Met us again, and, madly bent on us,
Chased us away; till, raising of more aid,
155   We came again to bind them. Then they fled
Into this abbey, whither we pursued them,
And here the Abbess shuts the gates on us,
And will not suffer us to fetch him out,
Nor send him forth that we may bear him hence.
160   Therefore, most gracious Duke, with thy command
Let him be brought forth, and borne hence for help.
DUKE [*raising* ADRIANA]   Long since, thy husband served me in my wars,
And I to thee engaged a prince's word,
When thou didst make him master of thy bed,
165   To do him all the grace° and good I could.—   *favor; patronage*
Go, some of you, knock at the abbey gate,
And bid the Lady Abbess come to me.
I will determine this before I stir.
         Enter a MESSENGER [*from the Phoenix*]
MESSENGER [*to* ADRIANA]   O mistress, mistress, shift° and save   *do what you can*
       yourself!
170   My master and his man are both broke loose,
Beaten the maids a-row,° and bound the Doctor,   *one after another*
Whose beard they have singed off with brands° of fire,   *torches*
And ever as it blazed they threw on him
Great pails of puddled° mire to quench the hair.   *foul*
175   My master preaches patience to him, and the while
His man with scissors nicks him like a fool;[6]
And sure—unless you send some present help—
Between them they will kill the conjurer.
ADRIANA   Peace, fool. Thy master and his man are here,
180   And that is false thou dost report to us.
MESSENGER   Mistress, upon my life I tell you true.
I have not breathed almost since I did see it.
He cries for you, and vows, if he can take you,
To scorch your face and to disfigure you.
         Cry within
185   Hark, hark, I hear him, mistress. Fly, be gone!
DUKE [*to* ADRIANA]   Come stand by me. Fear nothing. Guard
       with halberds!°   *spears with blades*
         Enter ANTIPHOLUS OF EPHESUS *and* DROMIO [OF]
         EPHESUS [*from the Phoenix*]
ADRIANA   Ay me, it is my husband! Witness you
That he is borne about invisible.
Even now we housed him in° the abbey here,   *chased him into*
190   And now he's there, past thought of human reason.
ANTIPHOLUS OF EPHESUS   Justice, most gracious Duke, O grant me justice,
Even for the service that long since I did thee,
When I bestrid thee[7] in the wars, and took
Deep scars to save thy life; even for the blood
195   That then I lost for thee, now grant me justice!

---

6. Cuts his hair in a foolish or fantastical fashion.   7. Stood over you (to defend you when you were down).

EGEON [*aside*] Unless the fear of death doth make me dote,° *grow senile*
I see my son Antipholus, and Dromio.
ANTIPHOLUS OF EPHESUS Justice, sweet prince, against that woman there,
She whom thou gav'st to me to be my wife,
200 That hath abusèd and dishonourèd me
Even in the strength and height of injury.
Beyond imagination is the wrong
That she this day hath shameless thrown on me.
DUKE Discover° how, and thou shalt find me just. *Reveal*
205 ANTIPHOLUS OF EPHESUS This day, great Duke, she shut the doors upon me
While she with harlots° feasted in my house. *scoundrels*
DUKE A grievous fault!—Say, woman, didst thou so?
ADRIANA No, my good lord. Myself, he, and my sister
Today did dine together. So befall my soul
210 As this is false he burdens me withal.[8]
LUCIANA Ne'er may I look on day nor sleep on night
But° she tells to your highness simple truth. *Unless*
ANGELO [*aside*] O perjured woman! They are both forsworn.
In this the madman justly chargeth them.
215 ANTIPHOLUS OF EPHESUS My liege, I am advisèd° what I say, *fully aware*
Neither disturbed with the effect of wine,
Nor heady-rash provoked with raging ire,
Albeit my wrongs might make one wiser mad.
This woman locked me out this day from dinner.
220 That goldsmith there, were he not packed° with her, *conspiring*
Could witness it, for he was with me then,
Who parted with me to go fetch a chain,
Promising to bring it to the Porcupine,
Where Balthasar and I did dine together.
225 Our dinner done, and he not coming thither,
I went to seek him. In the street I met him,
And in his company that gentleman.

[*He points to the* SECOND MERCHANT]

There did this perjured goldsmith swear me down° *contradict me in swearing*
That I this day of him received the chain,
230 Which, God he knows, I saw not. For the which
He did arrest me with an officer.
I did obey, and sent my peasant° home *servant*
For certain ducats. He with none returned.
Then fairly° I bespoke° the officer *courteously / asked*
235 To go in person with me to my house.
By th' way, we met my wife, her sister, and a rabble more
Of vile confederates. Along with them
They brought one Pinch, a hungry lean-faced villain,
A mere anatomy,° a mountebank,° *skeleton / quack*
240 A threadbare juggler,° and a fortune-teller, *illusionist*
A needy, hollow-eyed, sharp-looking° wretch, *emaciated*
A living dead man. This pernicious slave,
Forsooth, took on him as° a conjurer, *posed as*
And gazing in mine eyes, feeling my pulse,
245 And with no face, as 'twere, outfacing me,[9]
Cries out I was possessed. Then all together

8. *So . . . withal*: Let the fate of my soul depend on   9. And with his thir face staring me down.
whether what he charges me with is false.

They fell upon me, bound me, bore me thence,
And in a dark and dankish vault at home
There left me and my man, both bound together,
250 Till, gnawing with my teeth my bonds in sunder,°   *apart*
I gained my freedom, and immediately
Ran hither to your grace, whom I beseech
To give me ample satisfaction
For these deep shames and great indignities.
255 ANGELO   My lord, in truth, thus far I witness with him:
That he dined not at home, but was locked out.
DUKE   But had he such a chain of thee, or no?
ANGELO   He had, my lord, and when he ran in here
These people saw the chain about his neck.
260 SECOND MERCHANT [*to* ANTIPHOLUS]   Besides, I will be sworn these ears of mine
Heard you confess you had the chain of him,
After you first forswore it on the mart,
And thereupon I drew my sword on you;
And then you fled into this abbey here,
265 From whence I think you are come by miracle.
ANTIPHOLUS OF EPHESUS   I never came within these abbey walls,
Nor ever didst thou draw thy sword on me.
I never saw the chain, so help me heaven,
And this is false you burden me withal.°   *with*
270 DUKE   Why, what an intricate impeach° is this!   *complex charge*
I think you all have drunk of Circe's cup.[1]
If here you housed° him, here he would have been.   *cornered*
If he were mad, he would not plead so coldly.°   *rationally*
[*To* ADRIANA] You say he dined at home, the goldsmith here
275 Denies that saying. [*To* DROMIO] Sirrah, what say you?
DROMIO OF EPHESUS [*pointing out the* COURTESAN]   Sir, he
dined with her there, at the Porcupine.
COURTESAN   He did, and from my finger snatched that ring.
ANTIPHOLUS OF EPHESUS   'Tis true, my liege, this ring I had of her.
DUKE [*to* COURTESAN]   Saw'st thou him enter at the abbey here?
280 COURTESAN   As sure, my liege, as I do see your grace.
DUKE   Why, this is strange. Go call the Abbess hither.
I think you are all mated,° or stark mad.   *bewildered*

Exit one to the ABBESS

EGEON [*coming forward*]   Most mighty Duke, vouchsafe me speak a word.
Haply° I see a friend will save my life,   *Maybe*
285 And pay the sum that may deliver me.
DUKE   Speak freely, Syracusian, what thou wilt.
EGEON [*to* ANTIPHOLUS]   Is not your name, sir, called Antipholus?
And is not that your bondman Dromio?
DROMIO OF EPHESUS   Within this hour I was his bondman,[2] sir,
290 But he, I thank him, gnawed in two my cords.
Now am I Dromio, and his man, unbound.
EGEON   I am sure you both of you remember me.
DROMIO OF EPHESUS   Ourselves we do remember, sir, by you;[3]
For lately we were bound as you are now.
295 You are not Pinch's patient, are you, sir?

---

1. The drink by means of which the enchantress Circe turned men into swine.
2. His indentured servant; tied up with him. (The pun continues in line 291.)
3. By looking at you, we remember how we were (bound).

EGEON Why look you strange° on me? You know me well.   *unknowingly*
ANTIPHOLUS OF EPHESUS I never saw you in my life till now.
EGEON O, grief hath changed me since you saw me last,
      And careful° hours with time's deformèd° hand   *sorrowful / deforming*
300   Have written strange defeatures° in my face.   *disfigurements*
      But tell me yet, dost thou not know my voice?
ANTIPHOLUS OF EPHESUS Neither.
EGEON Dromio, nor thou?
DROMIO OF EPHESUS No, trust° me sir, nor I.   *believe*
305 EGEON I am sure thou dost.
DROMIO OF EPHESUS Ay, sir, but I am sure I do not, and what-
      soever a man denies, you are now bound to believe him.
EGEON Not know my voice? O time's extremity,
      Hast thou so cracked and splitted my poor tongue
310   In seven short years that here my only son
      Knows not my feeble key of untuned cares?[4]
      Though now this grainèd° face of mine be hid   *lined*
      In sap-consuming winter's drizzled snow,
      And all the conduits of my blood froze up,
315   Yet hath my night of life some memory,
      My wasting lamps° some fading glimmer left,   *failing eyes*
      My dull deaf ears a little use to hear.
      All these old witnesses, I cannot err,
      Tell me thou art my son Antipholus.
320 ANTIPHOLUS OF EPHESUS I never saw my father in my life.
EGEON But° seven years since,° in Syracusa bay,   *Only / ago*
      Thou know'st we parted. But perhaps, my son,
      Thou sham'st to acknowledge me in misery.
ANTIPHOLUS OF EPHESUS The Duke, and all that know me in the city,
325   Can witness with me that it is not so.
      I ne'er saw Syracusa in my life.
DUKE [*to* EGEON] I tell thee, Syracusian, twenty years
      Have I been patron to Antipholus,
      During which time he ne'er saw Syracusa.
330   I see thy age and dangers make thee dote.
            Enter [from the priory] the ABBESS, *with* ANTIPHOLUS
            [OF] SYRACUSE, [*wearing the chain,*] *and* DROMIO [OF]
            SYRACUSE
ABBESS Most mighty Duke, behold a man much wronged.
            All gather to see them
ADRIANA I see two husbands, or mine eyes deceive me.
DUKE One of these men is *genius*[5] to the other:
      And so of these, which is the natural° man,   *human; mortal*
335   And which the spirit? Who deciphers them?
DROMIO OF SYRACUSE I, sir, am Dromio. Command him away.
DROMIO OF EPHESUS I, sir, am Dromio. Pray let me stay.
ANTIPHOLUS OF SYRACUSE Egeon, art thou not? Or else his ghost.
DROMIO OF SYRACUSE O, my old master, who hath bound him here?
340 ABBESS Whoever bound him, I will loose his bonds,
      And gain a husband by his liberty.
      Speak, old Egeon, if thou beest the man
      That hadst a wife once called Emilia,

4. My weak voice born of harsh sorrows.
5. Attendant spirit. It was a classical belief that each
person had such a spirit, identical in appearance, allotted to him at birth.

That bore thee at a burden° two fair sons.   *in one birth*
345   O, if thou beest the same Egeon, speak,
And speak unto the same Emilia.
   DUKE   Why, here begins his morning story right:
These two Antipholus', these two so like,
And these two Dromios, one in semblance—
350   Besides his urging° of her wreck at sea.   *claim*
These are the parents to these children,
Which accidentally are met together.
   EGEON   If I dream not, thou art Emilia.
If thou art she, tell me, where is that son
355   That floated with thee on the fatal° raft?   *ill-fated*
   ABBESS   By men of Epidamnum he and I
And the twin Dromio all were taken up.
But, by and by, rude° fishermen of Corinth   *harsh; boorish*
By force took Dromio and my son from them,
360   And me they left with those of Epidamnum.
What then became of them I cannot tell;
I, to this fortune that you see me in.
   DUKE [*to* ANTIPHOLUS OF SYRACUSE]   Antipholus, thou cam'st
      from Corinth first.°   *originally*
   ANTIPHOLUS OF SYRACUSE   No, sir, not I. I came from Syracuse.
365   DUKE   Stay, stand apart. I know not which is which.
   ANTIPHOLUS OF EPHESUS   I came from Corinth, my most gracious lord.
   DROMIO OF EPHESUS   And I with him.
   ANTIPHOLUS OF EPHESUS   Brought to this town by that most famous warrior,
Duke Menaphon, your most renownèd uncle.
370   ADRIANA   Which of you two did dine with me today?
   ANTIPHOLUS OF SYRACUSE   I, gentle mistress.
   ADRIANA   And are not you my husband?
   ANTIPHOLUS OF EPHESUS   No, I say nay to that.
   ANTIPHOLUS OF SYRACUSE   And so do I. Yet did she call me so;
375   And this fair gentlewoman, her sister here,
Did call me brother. [*To* LUCIANA] What I told you then
I hope I shall have leisure° to make good,   *opportunity*
If this be not a dream I see and hear.
   ANGELO   That is the chain, sir, which you had of me.
380   ANTIPHOLUS OF SYRACUSE   I think it be, sir. I deny it not.
   ANTIPHOLUS OF EPHESUS [*to* ANGELO]   And you, sir, for this chain arrested me.
   ANGELO   I think I did, sir. I deny it not.
   ADRIANA [*to* ANTIPHOLUS OF EPHESUS]   I sent you money, sir, to be your bail,
By Dromio, but I think he brought it not.
385   DROMIO OF EPHESUS   No, none by me.
   ANTIPHOLUS OF SYRACUSE [*to* ADRIANA]   This purse of ducats I received from you,
And Dromio my man did bring them me.
I see we still° did meet each other's man,   *constantly*
And I was ta'en for him, and he for me,
390   And thereupon these errors are arose.
   ANTIPHOLUS OF EPHESUS   These ducats pawn I for my father here.
   DUKE   It shall not need. Thy father hath his life.
   COURTESAN   Sir, I must have that diamond from you.
   ANTIPHOLUS OF EPHESUS   There, take it, and much thanks for my good cheer.
395   ABBESS   Renownèd Duke, vouchsafe to take the pains
To go with us into the abbey here,
And hear at large discoursèd° all our fortunes,   *recounted in full*

And all that are assembled in this place,
That by this sympathizèd° one day's error   shared
400   Have suffered wrong. Go, keep us company,
And we shall make full satisfaction.
Thirty-three years have I but gone in travail°   labor
Of you, my sons, and till this present hour
My heavy burden ne'er deliverèd.
405   The Duke, my husband, and my children both,
And you the calendars of their nativity,⁶
Go to a gossips' feast,⁷ and joy with me.
After so long grief, such festivity!
DUKE   With all my heart I'll gossip at° this feast.   join in

Exeunt omnes [into the priory]. Manent the two DROMIOS *and two
                           brothers [*ANTIPHOLUS]
DROMIO OF SYRACUSE [*to* ANTIPHOLUS OF EPHESUS]   Master,
410   shall I fetch your stuff from shipboard?
ANTIPHOLUS OF EPHESUS   Dromio, what stuff of mine hast thou
embarked?°   placed on board
DROMIO OF SYRACUSE   Your goods that lay at host, sir, in the
Centaur.
ANTIPHOLUS OF SYRACUSE   He speaks to me.—I am your master, Dromio.
Come, go with us. We'll look to that anon.
415   Embrace thy brother there; rejoice with him.
                           Exeunt [the brothers ANTIPHOLUS]
DROMIO OF SYRACUSE   There is a fat friend at your master's house,
That kitchened me for you⁸ today at dinner.
She now shall be my sister, not my wife.
DROMIO OF EPHESUS   Methinks you are my glass° and not my brother.   mirror
420   I see by you° I am a sweet-faced youth.   by means of you
Will you walk in to see their gossiping?°   merrymaking
DROMIO OF SYRACUSE   Not I, sir, you are my elder.⁹
DROMIO OF EPHESUS   That's a question. How shall we try° it?   test
DROMIO OF SYRACUSE   We'll draw cuts° for the senior. Till then,   straws
lead thou first.
425   DROMIO OF EPHESUS   Nay, then thus:
We came into the world like brother and brother,
And now let's go hand in hand, not one before another.
                           Exeunt [to the priory]

6. (Addressed to the Dromios): the two servants are a record of their masters' age, having been born at the same time.
7. A feast attended by the godparents ("gossips") to celebrate the christening of a child.
8. Who entertained me in the kitchen in mistake for you.
9. The elder customarily takes precedence and enters first.

Love's Labour's Lost

Love's Labour's Lost (1594–95) is an experimental play disguised as a conventional one. Its most striking feature—sexualized verbal wit—goes well with its aristocratic love plot. Yet the work is complicated by an unexpected concluding twist; challenges to hierarchies of gender, class, nation, and race; a scatological and homoerotic view of bodily function; and partly buried political and religious references. Without jettisoning the spirit of romantic comedy, then, Love's Labour's Lost offers a complex view of wooing and wedding with broader social implications.

Initially, Shakespeare telegraphs what is coming next. King Ferdinand of Navarre and his three courtiers—Biron, Dumaine, and Longueville—swear to shun women for three years to pursue the studious life of an ancient Greek or Renaissance Italian philosophical academy. Yet the arrival of a diplomatic embassy led by the Princess of France that includes three ladies-in-waiting—Rosaline, Catherine, and Maria—induces the men to fall in love. They are ridiculed for their about-face. In a multiple eavesdropping scene, they overhear each other confessing this change of heart and hypocritically denounce such oath breaking. In a court masque (a dramatic form where costumed aristocrats are the performers), they disguise themselves as Russians to advance their claims, but the ladies' own disguises lead each man to woo the wrong woman. Then, two hundred lines from the end, a messenger reports that the Princess's father, the King of France, has died. The world of romantic comedy—Navarre's rural retreat from the ordinary affairs of life—is invaded by death. When the men obliviously continue their wooing, the women, who all along have mistrusted their forsworn suitors, insist on a year's separation, which returns the plot to the opening rejection of heterosexual life.

From Two Gentlemen of Verona (1590–91) to Twelfth Night (1601), Shakespeare's young lovers marry off. Love's Labour's Lost's open-ended conclusion thus sets its apart from the other romantic comedies, pointing instead to the problem plays, Troilus and Cressida (1601–02), Measure for Measure (1604), and All's Well That Ends Well (1604–05). Here, as Biron remarks with the work's typical dramaturgical self-consciousness, "Our wooing doth not end like an old play. / Jack hath not Jill" (5.2.851–52). Both the romantic plot and the deflating outcome are suggested by the concluding poetic dialogue between Spring, associated with fertility and love, and Winter, linked to coldness and suffering. Yet Spring also brings 'unpleasing" cuckoldry and Winter "a merry note" (5.2.877, 893).

Before then, the aristocrats' verbal ingenuity dominates Love's Labour's Lost. No other Shakespearean play so emphasizes its own brilliance, so centrally concerns language itself, so heavily draws on bookishness, so revels in courtly style. Love's Labour's Lost possesses the highest ratio of rhyme to blank verse among the dramatic works—rivaled only by A Midsummer Night's Dream (1594–96). Shakespeare's most heavily rhymed tragedy, Romeo and Juliet (1595), and history, Richard II (1595), also date from these years, sometimes thought of as Shakespeare's lyrical period. Rhyming calls attention to the medium of language itself. By contrast, when Shakespeare seeks to render speech naturalistically, to make his language a neutral expression of thought, he characteristically resorts to blank verse or prose.

In Love's Labour's Lost, Shakespeare generally employs blank verse for serious moments in long speeches, while reserving rhyme for the witty repartee of love—itself a microcosm of the play's larger debate structure. In the opening scene, each male courtier discusses, in blank verse, the vow of abstinence from women before capping his speech with a concluding couplet (lines 1–48, couplets at 22–23, 26–27, 31–32,

47–48). But when the King and Biron then debate the plan, they switch to rhyme—usually rhymed pentameter couplets, sometimes known as heroic couplets. At times, Shakespeare shifts to quatrains rhymed *abab*. If such a passage is followed by a couplet (see, for example, 1.1.61–66), the result is the six-line stanza of Shakespeare's amatory narrative poem *Venus and Adonis* (1592–93), a work that meditates comically on gender reversal. If three quatrains are followed by a couplet, a sonnet is born (for instance, 1.1.80–93). Loosely speaking, there are at least seven sonnets in the play (also 1.1.160–74; 4.3.22–37 and 55–68; 5.2.274–89, 343–56, and 402–15). Six of the seven are romantic. In love with the peasant Jaquenetta, Armado from the subplot remarks, "I am sure I shall turn sonnet" (that is, sonneteer; 1.2.162–63). The boom of the English love sonnet begins in 1591 with the publication of Sidney's *Astrophil and Stella,* and Shakespeare is thought to have started his own sequence around 1592–93. Three of the lords' poems to the ladies were lifted from the 1598 quarto of the play for an unauthorized 1599 collection attributed to Shakespeare. Within the play, the sonnets function complexly. The ladies coolly receive their suitors' poetic protestations, the King deploys a sonnet to describe Armado, and the two sonnets in dialogue further extend the form while belittling the men. This turning of the sonnet upon itself achieves self-contradiction when Biron, having embraced plain speaking, avows his love to Rosaline—"O never will I . . . woo in rhyme" (5.2.402–05)—in what proves to be the opening of a sonnet.

This wooing rhetoric is also associated with male bonding. The lords begin by misogynistically excluding any woman from their company "'on pain of losing her tongue'" (1.1.122). Once in love, they switch to the Renaissance courtier's amatory style, derived from two influential Italian writers—the fourteenth-century lyric poet Petrarch, founder of the European sonnet craze, and the fifteenth-century Neoplatonic philosopher Ficino. But in the eavesdropping scene, their feelings are expressed not through direct address to the ladies but through intended soliloquies inadvertently delivered to each other. The scene enacts the rhetorical figure of chiasmus—common to many passages in the play—in which the second of two parallel structures inverts the order of the first. Here Biron, the King, Longueville, and Dumaine successively confess their love, whereupon Dumaine's oath breaking is denounced by Longueville, Longueville's by the King, and the King's by Biron. And just as Biron, who shares with Armado's page Mote the privilege of speaking directly to the audience, is the only courtier whose initial confession is not overheard, he alone denounces himself, albeit under compulsion. Thereafter, the courtiers imagine their wooing as collective sexual attack: "Advance your standards, and upon them, lords. / Pell-mell, down with them" (4.3.341–42). In short, the play casts a jaundiced eye on the sexual style of men in groups. Fittingly, then, the courtiers' year of isolation separates them not only from women but also from each other. As in *The Merchant of Venice* (1596–97), another play that punishes male lovers who break their vows, the dissolution of male bonds precedes durable heterosexual attachment.

But, of course, the language of *Love's Labour's Lost* is marked not just by the poetry of love but also by an often sexualized punning. Even though the men excel at this language of romantic combat, they are no match for the women. The following exchange occurs during the Russian masque:

CATHERINE   What, was your visor made without a tongue?
LONGUEVILLE   [*taking* CATHERINE *for Maria*] I know the reason, lady, why you ask.
CATHERINE   O, for your reason! Quickly, sir, I long.
LONGUEVILLE   You have a double tongue within your mask,
       And would afford my speechless visor half.
CATHERINE   'Veal', quoth the Dutchman. Is not veal a calf?
LONGUEVILLE   A calf, fair lady?
CATHERINE   No, a fair lord calf.
LONGUEVILLE   Let's part the word.

CATHERINE No, I'll not be your half.
Take all and wean it, it may prove an ox.
LONGUEVILLE Look how you butt yourself in these sharp mocks!
Will you give horns, chaste lady? Do not so.
CATHERINE Then die a calf before your horns do grow.
LONGUEVILLE One word in private with you ere I die.
CATHERINE Bleat softly, then. The butcher hears you cry.
(5.2.242–55)

Referring to the mouthpiece keeping the mask in place, Catherine evokes Longueville's silence ("without a tongue"). Longueville's second reply ("double tongue") accuses Catherine of punning, concealing her identity, being deceptive, and speaking enough for two, and then urges her to relinquish one tongue so he can speak and she will reveal her identity. Catherine's "Veal" combines Dutch for "well," German for "much," and a pun on "veil" with the end of her second comment ("long"). The result is "long-veal," veiled assertion of her interlocutor's identity. "Veal" also anticipates "calf" at line's end—source of the passage's remaining jokes. Catherine reverses Longueville's question, branding him "a fair lord calf," a dolt. Longueville's offer of compromise ("part the word") inspires Catherine's construal of "part" as "divide"; hence her refusal to "be your half" (better half, wife) and covert acknowledgment that the first half of the word ("ca") suggests her name. Longueville should raise the calf into an "ox," a castrated dolt with "horns," symbol of cuckoldry. This argument sullies her reputation, he warns, but Catherine tells him that to avoid cuckoldry he should drop dead. Longueville asks for a tête-à-tête "ere I die" (have an orgasm), to which Catherine agrees, while warning him of his impending doom.

The ladies also best the lords by critique of male verbal excess (*sans* is French for "without"):

BIRON My love to thee is sound, sans crack or flaw.
ROSALINE Sans 'sans', I pray you.
(5.2.415–16)

The men, Biron realizes, must drop their bookish language to approximate the women's norm: "Honest plain words best pierce the ear of grief" (5.2.735). Rosaline sentences him to a year of jesting among "the speechless sick and . . groaning wretches" (5.2.828–29), where he will learn the value—or valuelessness—of wit. And the Princess usually exercises a dignified stylistic restraint that eludes the men. Yet the women's actual practice often repudiates their theory. Early on Rosaline sympathetically evokes Biron's wit. The ladies then embrace the game of verbal one-upmanship and obscene punning, as the Catherine-Longueville exchange demonstrates. Thus they violate the principle Rosaline claims Biron has ignored:

A jest's prosperity lies in the ear
Of him that hears it, never in the tongue
Of him that makes it.
(5.2.838–40)

The women's self-contradictory avowal of wit and sobriety alike renders them romantically desirable in a fashion alien to the stereotypes of love poetry. Their possibly cynical economic mission may depend, as Boyet, their attending lord, suggests, on the Princess's ability to win the King's love. There are repeated jibes at their appearance as well as accusations of unchastity leveled at Rosaline by Biron, Boyet, and Catherine. The sexual innuendos in Catherine and Rosaline's exchange turn on "light" (bright, frivolous, or wanton), contrasted with both "heavy" (serious, overweight) and "dark" (black, obscure, wanton; 5.2.14–46, 4.3.228–78). While not erasing the ladies' moral superiority, these countertendencies justify modern productions that have treated them without idealism or sentimentality.

The subplot offers a different kind of critique. More a series of set pieces than a continuous story, it offers both structural parallel and social contrast to the main plot. The first eight scenes (in modern editions) alternate between main plot and subplot; the concluding, ninth scene unites the two sets of characters. In each plot, the characters are divided into two groups, one of which intrudes from the outside—the ladies in the main plot, Armado and Mote in the subplot. Such symmetries, which reinforce the work's formalized, dancelike structure and give it an aristocratic feel, recall the comedies that John Lyly wrote in the 1580s for boy actors. But this formalism acquires special force from the subplot's rootedness in popular culture, a culture reinvoked in the concluding speeches of Spring and Winter. Costard and Jaquenetta are from the rural lower classes; Dull, the constable, who anticipates Dogberry in *Much Ado About Nothing* (1598), barely stands above them. Mote is a page; Nathaniel, Holofernes, and Armado, although of higher rank, derive from the stock characters (minister, schoolmaster, braggart) of Italian commedia dell'arte, an originally popular, improvisational theater.

The juxtaposition of the two plots exalts and deflates the aristocrats. The subplot's fractured prose and doggerel verse sets off Biron's polished poetry to advantage. Holofernes is the leading practitioner of the popular characters' penchant for synonyms. An apple hangs in the "*caelo,* the sky, the welkin, the heaven, and . . . falleth . . . on . . . *terra,* the soil, the land, the earth" (4.2.5–6). Armado's forte is schematic syntax: "The time when? . . . Now for the ground which. . . . Then for the place where" (1.1.227–31). But if Armado's language is excessive, Biron's is only slightly less so. Similarly, Costard's violation of the edict against being "taken with a wench" (1.1.270–71) anticipates the failure of the aristocrats. This leveling continues when Armado's love letter to Jaquenetta is echoed by those of the lords. Armado and Biron both have their epistles delivered by Costard, whose confusion of the two exposes each writer to ridicule. The courtiers' Muscovite masque is paralleled by the popular pageant of the Nine Worthies, a scene resembling the humble theatricals of *A Midsummer Night's Dream.* Moreover, both masque and pageant anticipate the larger plot of *Love's Labour's Lost* in their failure to end as their performers wish.

Garden scene. From Thomas Hill, *The Gardener's Labyrinth* (1577).

Queen Elizabeth hunting. From George Gascoigne, *The Noble Art of Venerie or Hunting* (1575).

Costard's verbal sparring with the King and Princess, in which he holds his own, also reduces the sense of social superiority. His pointed response to dismissal by the forsworn courtiers—"Walk aside the true folk, and let the traitors stay" (4.3.209)—recalls his, but not their, honesty from the start. The lords' ridicule of the Nine Worthies prompts Holofernes' telling reply: "This is not generous, not gentle, not humble" (5.2.617). Although the aristocrats learn nothing from Mercadé's announcement of the death of the Princess's father, Armado, whom Costard has just accused of getting Jaquenetta pregnant, sees the need to reform. The lords accept their one-year sentences reluctantly, whereas his voluntary longer commitment echoes and reverses their opening oaths: "I am a votary, I have vowed to Jaquenetta / To hold the plough for her sweet love three year" (5.2.860–61). The oddity here is Eiron. More than any other aristocratic character, he internalizes popular culture, moving from refined verse to colloquial and proverbial expression in what is one of Shakespeare's most proverb-rich plays. For instance, he is the only figure from the main plot with an extended prose speech (4.3.1–17). In Shakespeare, this sort of linguistic range is often integral to a character's unique ability to negotiate life's complexities for good or for ill. Yet Biron, despite his wit, intelligence, and insight, proves almost as hapless as his fellow suitors.

The subplot also reflects on the main plot through often scatological or homoerotic bodily imagery, which includes a series of terms for constipation and its release—"immured," "restrained," "bound," "purgation," "loose" (3.1.113–16)—as well as Armado's boast of intimacy with the King, who has a tendency "with his royal finger thus [to] dally with my excrement" (5.1.87–88). In the play of the Nine Worthies, Holofernes as Judas Maccabeus is reduced to Judas (Iscariot), betrayer of Jesus.

> BOYET Therefore, as he is an ass, let him go.
>   And so adieu, sweet Jude. Nay, why dost thou stay?
> DUMAINE For the latter end of his name.
> BIRON For the ass to the Jude. Give it him. Jud-as, away.
>   (5.2.613–16)

Here, emphasis on "ass" activates the synonymous connotation of "end," which thus proves the end of his body as well as "of his name." This primarily popular material suggests that the main courtship plot is not the whole story. The romantic and sexual language of the aristocrats is balanced by a less exalted, more excremental view of the body. Such passages also exploit some of the possibilities of a transvestite theater, in which boys played the women's parts. Specifically, the normative heterosexuality of the main plot is answered by hints of homosexuality emanating from the subplot. In short, this verbal patterning expands the play's notions of the body and sexuality beyond what events themselves overtly offer.

This imagery also feeds into a consideration of religious, national, and racial xenophobia. Costard calls Mote "my incony [fine-quality] Jew" (3.1.124), where "incony" inspires "inkle" [tape] (3.1.127), which suggests "ingle" (catamite, a boy kept by a pederast; see also 1.2.7). When Judas Maccabeus is "clipped" of his surname, Jewish circumcision is apparently glanced at. As we have seen, Holofernes is expelled by the lords as "Jud-as"—sign of the age's association of Jews with both excrement and sodomy. Coming from "tawny Spain," "Dun"-colored Armado, "in all the world's new fashion planted" and hence perhaps associated with New World plantations, is also an alien figure (1.1.171, 4.3.195, 1.1.162). Yet he is less foreign than the Russians, much less their accompanying blackamoors, whose presence glances at racial subjugation. They could be based on a report of an earlier Tudor masque or on a contemporary amateur entertainment at one of London's law schools. Alternatively, the play and these two performances all may draw on the period's link of Russia with dark skin. Although *Love's Labour's Lost* dramatizes a practice of scapegoating foreigners, however, it does not ratify this practice. Holofernes as Judas issues a pointed rebuke to the aristocrats; Armado reveals a depth of commitment foreign to them; the Russian masque backfires. Just as the play undermines convention in the central love plot, here, too, it calls into question—without openly attacking—cultural norms.

But the aristocrats themselves, unlike most of the popular characters, are also foreign. Behind the play lie contemporary political events that assume importance, given the plot's lack of literary sources. The comedy's King of Navarre draws on King Henry of Navarre, who established a philosophical academy and was accused of withdrawing from life. His three courtiers are named for the historical king's aristocratic contemporaries, two of whom (the play's Biron and Dumaine) served him. The Princess may derive from Princess Marguerite de Valois, daughter of King Henry II of France. Marguerite was already Henry of Navarre's estranged wife when she led an embassy of reconciliation to him in 1578, accompanied by her famous ladies-in-waiting. As in *Love's Labour's Lost,* one topic of discussion was "Aquitaine, a dowry for a queen" (2.1.8). Negotiations proceeded amid rampant adultery that undermined the vows of reconciliation and, contemporaries believed, caused renewal of France's Wars of Religion (1562–98), the bloody conflict between Protestant and Catholic aristocrats arguably noticed in the play's "civil war of wits" (2.1.225). Boyet, Mercadé, and perhaps Mote also have prominent namesakes from these wars. To end the conflict and secure his claim on the French throne, Henry converted to Catholicism in 1593, a further oath breaking that provoked criticism in Protestant England. The sympathy and judgment directed toward the play's lords, the serious treatment

of their repudiated vows, the current of threatening sexuality, the emphasis on conflict, the invasion of death into the festive aristocratic world—all are compatible with
this background.

Foreignness and sexuality converge in the debate about the aristocrats' own colors.
A 1984 production of the play cast a black actress as Rosaline. Although only Rosaline's
hair and eyes are black, metaphorically the play cannot leave darkness alone. Unwillingly in love with Rosaline, Biron initially complains of her color (3.1.181–84,
4.3.2–3). But echoing Shakespeare's sonnets to the "dark lady," he later takes blackness
as the standard of beauty:

> KING   By heaven, thy love is black as ebony
>
> . . . .
>
> BIRON   No face is fair that is not full so black.
> KING   O paradox! Black is the badge of hell.
>   (4.3.243, 249–50)

For the King, if black is beautiful, even "Ethiops," who presumably share his distaste
for their appearance, "of their sweet complexion crack [boast]" (4.3.264). But it is not
only the women whose faces evoke darkness. "Biron they call him," Rosaline remarks,
"but a merrier man . . . I never spent an hour's talk withal" (2.1.66–68). The implied
contrast is between "Merrier" and "Biron," punning on the brown in brown study, or
seriousness. Before "the heavenly Rosaline," Biron imagines himself "a rude and savage man of Ind" (4.3.217–18), a claim that he repeats in her presence: "Vouchsafe to
show the sunshine of your face / That we, like savages, may worship it" (5.2.200–01).
The inclusion of the blackamoors thus accords with the play's unconventional association of its central and most attractive couple with blackness.

Love's Labour's Lost went unperformed from 1642 to 1839, remaining unpopular
until the mid-twentieth century. But modern enthusiasm for wordplay and demonstrations of the comedy's theatrical potential have led to an upward revaluation. Perhaps
today its significance lies in linguistic artifice that is and is not rejected, an upper class
that learns its manners from the lower, a capacious sense of bodily and sexual experience, a sympathetic evocation of blackness, a plot that takes a clear-eyed but not dismissive view of romantic love, and a company of women who ride off into the sunset
without their men.

WALTER COHEN

TEXTUAL NOTE

Although the date of Love's Labour's Lost is hard to pin down with much certainty, most
scholars today locate the original and only composition of the play in 1594–95. Perhaps
Shakespeare designed it for the Lord Chamberlain's Men, a recently formed professional company that worked in London's suburban, open-air, commercial theaters and
of which he was an actor and a shareholder. The first printing of the play, in quarto, is
lost. Another quarto, dated 1598 (Q), is the earliest extant printed version of a Shakespearean play that names its author. Q supposedly reproduces the play "as it was presented before her Highnes / this last Christmas." It is the basis for all modern editions.
The title page calls the work Loues labors lost, a spelling that, in accord with the punning ethos of the play, leaves open various meanings, depending on where the apostrophe goes in the first word and whether there is an apostrophe—as a contraction for
"is"—in the second. To complicate the semantic possibilities, Loue labors lost and Loues
Labour lost are also among the early designations for the work.

Q derives from an authorial manuscript—either directly or, more probably, indi-

Berowne. Did not I dance with you in *Brabant* once?
Kather. Did not I dance with you in *Brabant* once?
Ber. I know you did,
Kath. How needles was it then to afke the queftion?
Ber. You muft not be fo quicke.
Kath. Tis long of you that fpur me with fuch queftions,
Ber. Your wit's too hot,it fpeedes too faft, twill tire,
Kath. Not till it leaue the rider in the mire,
Ber. What time a day?
Kath. The houre that fooles fhould afke.
Ber. Now faire befall your mafke,
Kath. Faire fall the face it couers.
Ber. And fend you manie louers,
Kath. Amen,fo you be none.
Ber. Nay then will I be gon.

Berow. Did not I dance with you in *Brabant* once?
Rofa. Did not I dance with you in *Brabant* once?
Ber. I know you did.
Rofa. How needleffe was it then to ask the queftic
Ber. You muft not be fo quicke.
Rofa. 'Tis long of you ẙ fpur me with fuch queftio
Ber. Your wit's too hot,it fpeeds too faft, 'twill ti
Rofa. Not till it leaue the Rider in the mire.
Ber. What time a day?
Rofa. The howre that fooles fhould aske.
Ber. Now faire befall your maske.
Rofa. Faire fall the face it couers.
Ber. And fend you many louers.
Rofa. Amen,fo you be none.
Rer. Nay then will I be gone.

Biron's first flirtatious exchange with Catherine in Q (2.1.113–26) (left); revised to Rosaline in F (2.1.113–26) (right).

rectly via the lost quarto, which seems to have been printed from that manuscript. For an edition with an authorial manuscript behind it, it is extremely problematic, despite evidence that part of it was proofread. It is full of errors, uncorrected false starts, and the juxtaposition of original and revised versions of the same passages, although many of these are obvious and easily remedied. In this edition, the earlier renditions of subsequently rewritten text, beginning at 4.3.291, 5.2.130, and 5.2.798, are indented in the text. It is difficult to judge whether Q's foreign-language errors are Shakespeare's, the character's, or the compositor's. Here, they are usually corrected but occasionally attributed to the character. Q's speech prefixes often employ generic tags ("King," "Braggart," "Boy," "Page," "Princess," "Queen," "Lady 1–3," "Clown," "Maid," "Curate," "Pedant"). These tags function in various ways, but as a group they suggest that Shakespeare developed his characters out of stock dramatic, mainly comic, figures, especially from Italian commedia dell'arte (this legacy is discussed in the Introduction). *The Norton Shakespeare,* however, substitutes characters' names in the speech prefixes wherever possible, with the exception of Ferdinand of Navarre, who is identified as "King." At 4.2.60–97 and occasionally thereafter in the same scene, Q's speech prefixes attribute Nathaniel's lines to Holofernes and vice versa. These have been corrected. The biggest problem in Q involves the naming of the French ladies in 2.1, who are often referred to as "Lady," "Lady 1," "Lady 2," and "Lady 3." Most important, Catherine seems to be paired with Biron, Rosaline with Dumaine: Biron engages in witty exchanges first with Catherine (2.1.113–26) and then with Rosaline (2.1.178–92) before asking after Catherine (2.1.208–09), while Dumaine inquires about Rosaline (2.1.193–94). The remainder of the play reverses the pairings.

The version of *Love's Labour's Lost* printed in the First Folio of 1623 (F) is derived from either the lost or the extant quarto. F adds poorly conceived and mislabeled act divisions, which, along with scene divisions introduced by eighteenth-century editors, are reproduced here for ease of reference. F also introduces several new readings and speech attributions, at least some of them probably derived from manuscript annotations added to Q. Notably, it appends a new last line to the play, "You that way, we this way." Still more crucial is the replacement of Catherine by Rosaline in Biron's first flirtatious exchange (2.1.113–26). These shifts go much of the way toward aligning the scene's action with what happens thereafter, thus rejecting the apparent meaning of Q—that Biron and Dumaine each first express interest in one woman and then abruptly fall in love with another.

All subsequent editions of *Love's Labour's Lost,* even when based on Q, have followed F in this respect. Most current textual scholars believe that Q reveals Shakespeare's initial indecision about how to pair the men and women off, and that the annotations in the copy of Q on which F is based record a version of the text closer to performance than Q is. In short, F's linkage of Biron with Rosaline from the start is correct. But proponents of this position disagree among themselves on important points, disagreements that suggest the speculative character of the hypothesis. The fundamental problem is uncertainty about the source, nature, and authority of the annotations to Q that lie behind F: the available evidence is too frail and contradictory to inspire confidence.

Although the version printed here is based on the near consensus among recent textual scholars, an alternative position has existed since the eighteenth century. In a relatively recent essay, Manfred Draudt ("The 'Rosaline-Katherine Tangle' of *Love's Labour's Lost*," *The Library* 6 [1982]: 381–96) suggestively argues that Q 2.1 may provide the most accurate rendition available of the romantic relations in *Love's Labour's Lost*. Retaining Q's speech attributions would have various advantages. Biron's and Dumaine's feelings are not obvious in 2.1, and the abrupt switching of male love interest and the casual transfer of women between men have analogues in other Shakespearean plays of the period—*The Two Gentlemen of Verona, Romeo and Juliet,* and *A Midsummer Night's Dream*. The quarto readings are also closer to the events of the court of the historical Henry of Navarre than is the revised text. Further, if Biron and Dumaine are inconstant, it is easier to understand why in 5.2 Catherine and Rosaline attack each other in sexualized language so harsh the Princess has to intervene (lines 14–46); why Catherine accuses Dumaine of "hypocrisy" and Rosaline plans to "torture" Biron (51, 60), whereas the Princess and Maria criticize their suitors more mildly; why Catherine's and Rosaline's concluding promises to their lovers (lines 807, 840–46) are more equivocal than those of the Princess and Maria (lines 783–89, 810–11); and why Rosaline seems only recently to have met Biron (lines 818–19). Finally, the Quarto lends greater force to the ladies' disguises in 5.2, which trick the men into wooing the wrong women; to the women's skeptical, almost cruel treatment of the men throughout; and to the oft-noted near interchangeability of the aristocratic characters. The notes, therefore, list the rejected quarto readings in 2.1 to facilitate a running comparison of the two approaches to the text.

SELECTED BIBLIOGRAPHY

Archer, John Michael. "*Love's Labour's Lost*." *A Companion to Shakespeare's Works.* Vol. 3: *The Comedies*. Ed. Richard Dutton and Jean E. Howard. Malden, Mass.: Blackwell, 2003. 320–37. Treats issues of race and nation in relation to language, gender, and sexuality.

Booth, Stephen. *King Lear, Macbeth, Indefinition, and Tragedy*. New Haven: Yale University Press, 1983. 69–82. The problem of the unexpected end, both of the plot and of the body.

Carroll, William C. *The Great Feast of Language in "Love's Labour's Lost."* Princeton: Princeton University Press, 1976. Wordplay, self-conscious theatricality, and poetic set pieces in relation to the larger debate structure of the play.

Elam, Keir. *Shakespeare's Universe of Discourse: Language-Games in the Comedies*. New York: Cambridge University Press, 1984. 289–308. Emphasis on the play's highly rhetorical critique of rhetoric.

Evans, Malcolm. *Signifying Nothing: Truth's True Contents in Shakespeare's Text*. Athens: University of Georgia Press, 1986. 50–65. The impact of writing on the speech of both aristocratic lovers and comic pedants.

Gilbert, Miriam. "*Love's Labour's Lost*": *Shakespeare in Performance*. Manchester: Manchester University Press, 1993. Survey of its topic, with detailed analysis of important recent performances.

Londré, Felicia Hardison, ed. "*Love's Labour's Lost*": *Critical Essays*. New York: Garland, 1997. Critical accounts of *Love's Labour's Lost*, both text and performance, 1598–1995, but primarily since World War II.

Maus, Katharine Eisaman. "Transfer of Title in *Love's Labour's Lost*: Language, Individualism, Gender." *Shakespeare Left and Right*. Ed. Ivo Kamps. New York: Routledge,

1991. 206–23. The relationship between the play's reversal of standard gender hierarchy and its questioning of the naturalness of meaningful language.

Mazzio, Carla. "The Melancholy of Print: *Love's Labour's Lost*." *Historicism, Psychoanalysis, and Early Modern Culture*. Ed. Carla Mazzio and Douglas Trevor. New York: Routledge, 2000. 186–227. The intersection in the play of the speech(lessness) of love and early modern print culture, especially pedagogical manuals.

Parker, Patricia. "Preposterous Reversals: *Love's Labour's Lost*." *Modern Language Quarterly* 54 (1993): 435–82. The centrality of wordplay, especially obscene bodily punning, to the work's dramatic structure and particularly to its challenge to class, gender, and sexual hierarchy.

Film

Love's Labour's Lost. 2000. Dir. Kenneth Branagh. UK. 93 min. Musical comedy with 1930s songs and settings, half of Shakespeare's lines retained, and the play's events shadowed by the coming of World War II. Cast includes Branagh, Alicia Silverstone, and Nathan Lane.

Love's Labour's Lost

THE PERSONS OF THE PLAY

Ferdinand, KING of Navarre
BIRON ⎫
LONGUEVILLE ⎬ lords attending on the King
DUMAINE ⎭
Don Adriano de ARMADO, an affected Spanish braggart
MOTE, his page
PRINCESS of France
ROSALINE ⎫
CATHERINE ⎬ ladies attending on the
MARIA ⎭ Princess
BOYET ⎫
Two other LORDS ⎬ attending on the Princess
COSTARD, a clown
JAQUENETTA, a country wench
Sir NATHANIEL, a curate
HOLOFERNES, a schoolmaster
Anthony DULL, a constable
MERCADÉ, a messenger
A FORESTER

1.1

Enter Ferdinand, KING *of Navarre,* BIRON, LONGUEVILLE, *and* DUMAINE[1]

KING   Let fame, that all hunt after in their lives,
   Live registered upon our brazen° tombs,   *brass; long-lasting*
   And then grace° us in the disgrace° of death   *honor / disfigurement*
   When, spite of cormorant° devouring time,[2]   *despite ravenous*
5   Th'endeavour of this present breath° may buy   *speech; life*
   That honour which shall bate° his scythe's keen edge   *blunt*
   And make us heirs of all eternity.
   Therefore, brave conquerors—for so you are,
   That war against your own affections°   *passions*
10 And the huge army of the world's desires—
   Our late° edict shall strongly stand in force.   *recent*
   Navarre shall be the wonder of the world.
   Our court shall be a little academe,
   Still° and contemplative in living art.[3]   *Peaceful*
15 You three—Biron, Dumaine, and Longueville—
   Have sworn for three years' term to live with me
   My fellow scholars, and to keep those statutes

1.1 Location: The action of the whole play takes place in the King of Navarre's park.

1. For the historical background to these figures, see the Introduction. Until Henry of Navarre's accession to the French throne in 1589, Navarre was an independent kingdom in southwestern France. "Biron" is pronounced "Be-roon." The pronunciation of "Longueville" fluctuates, rhyming with "ill" (4.3.120), "compile" (4.3.130), and, by implication "veal" (5.2.247).

2. Proverbial; one of many indications of the recourse to proverbs in this play by aristocrats and commoners alike.

3. The art of living (the term in this sense goes back to ancient Stoic thought); learning invigorated by life. *academe* (line 13): a philosophical academy of the sort initiated by Plato and revived in the Renaissance.

	That are recorded in this schedule° here.	*document*
	Your oaths are passed;° and now subscribe° your names,	*pledged / sign*
20	That his own hand may strike his honour down	
	That violates the smallest branch° herein.	*clause*
	If you are armed° to do as sworn to do,	*equipped*
	Subscribe to your deep oaths, and keep it, too.[4]	

LONGUEVILLE   I am resolved. 'Tis but a three years' fast.

25   The mind shall banquet, though the body pine.
Fat paunches have lean pates,° and dainty bits°   *heads / bites*
Make rich the ribs but bankrupt quite the wits.
        [*He signs*]

DUMAINE   My loving lord, Dumaine is mortified.°   *dead to worldliness*
The grosser manner of these world's delights
30   He throws upon the gross world's baser slaves.
To love, to wealth, to pomp I pine and die,
With all these[5] living in philosophy.
        [*He signs*]

BIRON   I can but say their protestation over.°   *again*
So much, dear liege,° I have already sworn: *lord*
35   That is, to live and study here three years.
But there are other strict observances,
As not to see a woman in that term,
Which I hope well is not enrollèd° there;   *listed*
And one day in a week to touch no food,
40   And but one meal on every day beside,
The which I hope is not enrollèd there;
And then to sleep but three hours in the night,
And not be seen to wink of° all the day,   *close my eyes during*
When I was wont to think no harm° all night,[6]   *it harmless (to sleep)*
45   And make a dark night too of half the day,
Which I hope well is not enrollèd there.
O, these are barren tasks, too hard to keep—
Not to see ladies, study, fast, not sleep.

KING   Your oath is passed to pass away from these.

50   BIRON   Let me say no, my liege, an if° you please.   *an if=if*
I only swore to study with your grace,
And stay here in your court, for three years' space.

LONGUEVILLE   You swore to that, Biron, and to the rest.

BIRON   By yea and nay,[7] sir, then I swore in jest.
55   What is the end of study, let me know?

KING   Why, that to know which else we should not know.

BIRON   Things hid and barred, you mean, from common sense.°   *ordinary perception*

KING   Ay, that is study's god-like recompense.

BIRON   Come on,[8] then, I will swear to study so
60   To know the thing I am forbid[9] to know,
As thus: to study where I well may dine
    When I to feast expressly am forbid;
Or study where to meet some mistress fine
    When mistresses from common sense are hid;

---

4. The first use of a couplet to cap a blank-verse speech. See also 1.1.26–27, 31–32, 47–48, the last of which begins the pattern of rhyming couplets. For an *abab* quatrain followed by a couplet to form the six-line *Venus and Adonis* stanza, see 1.1.61–66.
5. His three companions; the conditions prescribed in the document; or the suggestion that philosophy is a source or substitute for the worldly attractions of line 31.

6. Proverbial.
7. Earnestly (a solemn oath based on Matthew 5:37); ambiguously.
8. Q has "Com'on," possibly indicating a pun on "common" (line 57).
9. Deliberately misinterpreting "should" (line 56) as "ought" rather than "would."

65 Or having sworn too hard a keeping° oath,   *a too-demanding*
   Study to break it and not break my troth.
   If study's gain be thus, and° this be so,   *if*
   Study knows that which yet it doth not know.[1]
   Swear me to this, and I will ne'er say no.°   *(first rhyming triplet)*
70 KING   These be the stops° that hinder study quite,   *obstacles*
   And train° our intellects to vain delight.   *allure*
   BIRON   Why, all delights are vain, but that most vain
   Which, with pain° purchased, doth inherit pain;°   *labor / suffering*
   As° painfully to pore upon a book   *such as*
75 To seek the light of truth while truth the while
   Doth falsely° blind the eyesight of his look.°   *deceitfully / its vision*
   Light, seeking light, doth light of light beguile;[2]
   So ere you find where light in darkness lies
   Your light grows dark by losing of your eyes.
80 Study me[3] how to please the eye indeed
   By fixing it upon a fairer° eye,   *woman's*
   Who dazzling so,[4] that eye shall be his heed,°   *guard; what he heeds*
   And give him light that it° was blinded by.   *(his eye)*
   Study is like the heavens' glorious sun,
85 That will not be deep searched with saucy° looks.   *presumptuous; insolent*
   Small° have continual plodders ever won   *Little*
   Save base° authority from others' books.   *Except commonplace*
   These earthly godfathers of heaven's lights,°   *astronomers*
   That give a name to every fixèd star,
90 Have no more profit of their shining nights
   Than those that walk and wot° not what they are.   *know*
   Too much to know is to know naught but fame,°   *hearsay; reputation*
   And every godfather can give a name.°   *(as astronomers do)*
   KING   How well he's read, to reason against reading!
95 DUMAINE   Proceeded° well, to stop all good proceeding.°   *Argued*
   LONGUEVILLE   He weeds° the corn° and still lets grow the   *pulls up / wheat*
        weeding.°   *weeds*
   BIRON   The spring is near when green geese are a-breeding.[6]
   DUMAINE   How follows that?
   BIRON   Fit in his° place and time.   *its*
   DUMAINE   In reason nothing.
   BIRON   Something then in rhyme.
100 KING   Biron is like an envious sneaping° frost,   *a malicious biting*
   That bites the first-born infants° of the spring.   *buds*
   BIRON   Well, say I am! Why should proud° summer boast   *splendid*
   Before the birds have any cause to sing?
   Why should I joy in any abortive° birth?   *premature*
105 At Christmas I no more desire a rose
   Than wish a snow in May's new-fangled shows,°   *displays of flowers*
   But like of° each thing that in season grows.   *But enjoy*
   So you to study, now it is too late,°   *(for us to be students)*

1. *If . . . know:* If study means experiencing the forbidden (line 60), study does indeed enable one to know what isn't yet known (line 56).
2. The eye, from too much study (reading), is blinded (as if from looking at a bright light).
3. Study, I say: the beginning of the first sonnet (lines 80–93; see also 1.1.160–74, 4.3.22–37, 4.3.55–68, 5.2.274–89, 5.2.343–56, 5.2.402–15). This is the earliest of Biron's claims that a man's spiritual enlightenment depends not on reading books but on gazing into a beautiful woman's eyes. This idea reached England especially through the fourteenth-century Italian lyric poet Petrarch and the fifteenth-century Italian Neoplatonic philosopher Ficino.
4. The man (who does this) being thus bedazzled.
5. Toward a university degree.
6. When young geese are mating (as will the young lords, Biron implies). A goose is also a prostitute.
7. "In reason," it follows "nothing" (not at all); but in rhyme, "something" (somewhat)—an allusion to the proverbial phrase "neither rhyme nor reason" and perhaps to their own rhyming repartee.

Climb o'er the house to unlock the little gate.[8]

110 KING Well, sit you out.° Go home, Biron. Adieu.   *don't take part*
BIRON No, my good lord, I have sworn to stay with you.
And though I have for barbarism° spoke more   *on behalf of ignorance*
 Than for that angel knowledge you can say,
Yet confident I'll keep what I have sworn,
115 And bide the penance of each three years' day.°   *day of the three years*
Give me the paper. Let me read the same,
And to the strict'st decrees I'll write my name.
KING [*giving a paper*] How well this yielding rescues thee from
 shame!
BIRON [*reads*] 'Item: that no woman shall come within a mile of
120 my court.' Hath this been proclaimed?
LONGUEVILLE Four days ago.
BIRON Let's see the penalty. 'On pain of losing her tongue.'
Who devised this penalty?
LONGUEVILLE Marry,[9] that did I.
125 BIRON Sweet lord, and why?
LONGUEVILLE To fright them hence with that dread penalty.
BIRON A dangerous law against gentility.°   *courtesy*
 'Item: if any man be seen to talk with a woman within the term
of three years, he shall endure such public shame as the rest of
130 the court can possible° devise.'   *possibly*
This article, my liege, yourself must break;
 For well you know here comes in embassy
The French King's daughter with yourself to speak—
 A maid of grace and complete majesty—
135 About surrender-up of Aquitaine[1]
 To her decrepit, sick, and bedrid father.
Therefore this article is made in vain,
 Or vainly comes th'admirèd Princess hither.
KING What say you, lords? Why, this was quite forgot.
140 BIRON So study evermore is overshot.°   *wide of the mark*
While it doth study to have what it would,
It doth forget to do the thing it should;
And when it hath the thing it hunteth most,
'Tis won as towns with fire[2]—so won, so lost.
145 KING We must of force° dispense with this decree.   *necessity*
She must lie° here, on mere° necessity.   *lodge / absolute*
BIRON Necessity will make us all forsworn
 Three thousand times within this three years' space;
For every man with his affects° is born,   *passions*
150 Not by° might mastered, but by special grace.°   *by his own / (of God)*
If I break faith, this word° shall speak for me: *motto*
I am forsworn on mere necessity.
So to the laws at large° I write my name,   *in general*
 And he that breaks them in the least degree
155 Stands in attainder of° eternal shame.   *condemned to*
 [*He signs*]
Suggestions° are to other as to me,   *Temptations*
But I believe, although I seem so loath,
I am the last that will last° keep his oath.   *longest; least likely*

8. Set about things in a senseless, backward way— 1. A large area in southern France.
rather than climbing over the gate to unlock the house. 2. That is, destroyed in being captured.
9. Indeed (invocation of the Virgin Mary).

		But is there no quick° recreation granted?	*lively*
160	KING	Ay, that there is.° Our court, you know, is haunted[3]	*frequented*
		With° a refinèd traveller of° Spain,	*By/from*
		A man in all the world's new fashion planted,[4]	
		That hath a mint of phrases in his brain.	
		One who° the music of his own vain tongue	*whom*
165		Doth ravish like enchanting harmony;	
		A man of complements,° whom right and wrong	*fashion; attainments?*
		Have chose as umpire of their mutiny.°	*discord*
		This child of fancy,° that Armado hight,°	*absurd being/is called*
		For interim° to our studies shall relate	*interlude*
170		In high-borne words the worth of many a knight	
		From tawny° Spain lost in the world's debate.°	*sunburned/warfare*
		How you delight, my lords, I know not, I;	
		But I protest I love to hear him lie,	
		And I will use him for my minstrelsy.°	*entertainment*
175	BIRON	Armado is a most illustrious wight,°	*person*
		A man of fire-new° words, fashion's own knight.	*newly coined*
	LONGUEVILLE	Costard the swain[5] and he shall be our sport,	
		And so to study three years is but short.	

Enter a constable [Anthony DULL*] with a letter, with*
COSTARD

	DULL	Which is the Duke's° own person?	*King's*
180	BIRON	This, fellow. What wouldst?	
	DULL	I myself reprehend° his own person, for I am his grace's	*(blunder for "represent")*
		farborough.[6] But I would see his own person in flesh and blood.	
	BIRON	This is he.	
	DULL	Señor Arm—Arm—commends° you. There's villainy	*greets*
185		abroad. This letter will tell you more.	
	COSTARD	Sir, the contempts[7] thereof are as touching me.	
	KING	A letter from the magnificent Armado.[8]	
	BIRON	How low soever the matter, I hope in God for high	
		words.	
190	LONGUEVILLE	A high hope for a low heaven.° God grant us	*a small blessing*
		patience.	
	BIRON	To hear, or forbear laughing?	
	LONGUEVILLE	To hear meekly, sir, and to laugh moderately, or	
		to forbear both.	
195	BIRON	Well, sir, be it as the style shall give us cause to climb	
		in the merriness.[9]	
	COSTARD	The matter° is to me, sir, as concerning Jaquenetta.	*(perhaps sexual)*
		The manner of it is, I was taken with the manner.°	*caught red-handed*
	BIRON	In what manner?	
200	COSTARD	In manner and form following, sir—all those three. I	
		was seen with her in the manor house, sitting with her upon	
		the form,° and taken following her into the park; which put	*bench*
		together is 'in manner and form following'. Now, sir, for the	
		manner: it is the manner of a man to speak to a woman. For	
205		the form: in some form.	

3. The beginning of a sonnet that actually extends to fifteen lines (lines 160–74).
4. Established. *World's new fashion planted:* may also refer to Spanish New World plantations.
5. The costard is a large apple; the word is also used comically to refer to the head. *swain:* country lad
6. Blunder for "thirdborough," a petty constable.
7. Blunder for "contents"; but also, inadvertently, "con-

tempt."
8. Phrase used of the Spanish Armada (1588).
9. *style . . . merriness:* stile=fence; the humble subject of "merriness" does not ordinarily lead one "to climb" to a high prose "style." A "style" is also a pen and, hence, perhaps a penis that will "climb" (swell) in "merriness" (pleasure).
1. Legal, then proverbial phrase.

BIRON   For the 'following', sir?

COSTARD   As it shall follow in my correction;° and God defend   *punishment*
the right.°   *(prayer before combat)*

KING   Will you hear this letter with attention?

210   BIRON   As we would hear an oracle.

COSTARD   Such is the simplicity² of man to hearken after the
flesh.

KING [*reads*] 'Great deputy, the welkin's vicegerent° and sole   *heaven's deputy*
dominator of Navarre, my soul's earth's° god, and body's foster-   *earthly*

215   ing patron'—

COSTARD   Not a word of Costard yet.

KING   'So it is'—

COSTARD   It may be so; but if he say it is so, he is, in telling true,
but so.°   *truly only so-so*

220   KING   Peace!

COSTARD   Be to me and every man that dares not fight.

KING   No words!

COSTARD   Of other men's secrets, I beseech you.

KING   'So it is, besieged with sable-coloured° melancholy, I did   *black*

225   commend the black-oppressing humour° to the most whole-   *melancholy*
some physic° of thy health-giving air, and, as I am a gentleman,   *medicine*
betook myself to walk. The time when? About the sixth hour,
when beasts most graze, birds best peck, and men sit down to
that nourishment which is called supper. So much for the time

230   when. Now for the ground which—which, I mean, I walked
upon. It is yclept° thy park. Then for the place where—where,   *called (archaic)*
I mean, I did encounter that obscene° and most preposterous³   *disgusting; wanton*
event that draweth from my snow-white pen° the ebon-   *goose quill*
coloured° ink which here thou viewest, beholdest, surveyest, or   *black*

235   seest. But to the place where. It standeth north-north-east and
by east from the west corner of thy curious-knotted° garden.   *intricately patterned*
There did I see that low-spirited° swain, that base minnow° of   *base / shrimp*
thy mirth'—

COSTARD   Me?

240   KING   'That unlettered,° small-knowing soul'—   *illiterate*

COSTARD   Me?

KING   'That shallow vassal'°—   *base wretch; vessel*

COSTARD   Still me?

KING   'Which, as I remember, hight Costard'—

245   COSTARD   O, me!

KING   'Sorted° and consorted, contrary to thy established pro-   *Associated*
claimed edict and continent canon,° with, with, O with—but   *restraining law*
with this I passion° to say wherewith'—   *grieve*

COSTARD   With a wench.

250   KING   'With a child of our grandmother Eve, a female, or for thy
more sweet understanding a woman. Him I, as my ever-
esteemed duty pricks⁴ me on, have sent to thee, to receive the
meed° of punishment, by thy sweet grace's officer Anthony   *reward*
Dull, a man of good repute, carriage, bearing, and estimation.'

255   DULL   Me, an't° shall please you. I am Anthony Dull.   *if it*

KING   'For Jaquenetta—so is the weaker vessel° called—which I   *woman (I Peter 3:7)*
apprehended with the aforesaid swain, I keep her as a vessel of

---

2. Folly; Q has "sinplicitie"—perhaps a pun.
3. Unnatural; in reversed position—with "obscene"
(line 232) anatomically suggesting placement of the

rear, or posterior, in front. See 5.1.75, 77, 101.
4. Spurs (sexual). For other uses of the word, see
2.1.188; 4.1.128, 134; 4.2.11, 18, 45, 48, 53, 56.

thy law's fury, and shall at the least of thy sweet notice° bring   *as soon as you order*
her to trial.° Thine in all compliments of devoted and heart-   *(legally; sexually)*
260   burning heat of duty,

Don Adriano de Armado.'

BIRON   This is not so well as I looked for, but the best that ever I
heard.

KING   Ay, the best for° the worst. [*To* COSTARD]But, sirrah,⁵ what   *best example of*
265   say you to this?

COSTARD   Sir, I confess the wench.

KING   Did you hear the proclamation?

COSTARD   I do confess much of the hearing it, but little of the
marking of° it.   *paying attention to*

270 KING   It was proclaimed a year's imprisonment to be taken with
a wench.

COSTARD   I was taken with none, sir. I was taken with a camsel.

KING   Well, it was proclaimed 'damsel'.

COSTARD   This was no damsel, neither, sir. She was a virgin.

275 KING   It is so varied,° too, for it was proclaimed 'virgin'.   *covers that variation*

COSTARD   If it were, I deny her virginity. I was taken with a maid.

KING   This 'maid' will not serve your turn, sir.

COSTARD   This maid will serve my turn,° sir.   *(sexually)*

KING   Sir, I will pronounce your sentence. You shall fast a week
280   with bran and water.

COSTARD   I had rather pray a month with mutton and porridge.⁶

KING   And Don Armado shall be your keeper.
My lord Biron, see him delivered o'er,
And go we, lords, to put in practice that
285   Which each to other hath so strongly sworn.

[Exeunt the KING, LONGUEVILLE, and DUMAINE]

BIRON   I'll lay° my head to any good man's hat   *bet*
These oaths and laws will prove an idle scorn.
Sirrah, come on.

COSTARD   I suffer for the truth, sir; for true it is I was taken with
290   Jaquenetta, and Jaquenetta is a true° girl, and therefore, wel-   *an honest*
come the sour cup of prosperity, affliction⁷ may one day smile
again; and till then, sit thee down,° sorrow.   *Exeunt*   *stay with me*

1.2

Enter ARMADO *and* MOTE,¹ *his page*

ARMADO   Boy, what sign is it° when a man of great spirit grows   *what does it mean*
melancholy?

MOTE   A great sign, sir, that he will look sad.

ARMADO   Why, sadness is one and the selfsame thing,° dear imp.°   *(as melancholy)/child*
5 MOTE   No, no, O Lord, sir, no.

ARMADO   How canst thou part° sadness and melancholy, my   *distinguish between*
tender juvenal?²

MOTE   By a familiar° demonstration of the working,° my tough   *plain/their operation*
señor.°   *sir; senior*

10 ARMADO   Why 'tough señor'? Why 'tough señor'?

MOTE   Why 'tender juvenal'? Why 'tender juvenal'?

ARMADO   I spoke it, tender juvenal, as a congruent epitheton

---

5. Standard term for addressing social inferiors.
6. Mutton soup; "mutton" is also slang for 'prostitute.'
7. Blunder for reverse order: "affliction, prosperity."
1.2 Location: The King's park.

1. Q has "Moth," meaning "moth" or "mote" (speck). It
is pronounced like the latter word, and that sense may
be primary.
2. Youth; Juvenal, ancient Roman satirist.

appertaining to° thy young days, which we may nominate°   *suitable term for / call*
'tender'.

15   MOTE   And I, tough señor, as an appertinent° title to your old   *appropriate*
time, which we may name 'tough'.

ARMADO   Pretty and apt.

MOTE   How mean you, sir? I 'pretty' and my saying 'apt'? Or I
'apt' and my saying 'pretty'?

20   ARMADO   Thou 'pretty', because little.°   *(proverbial)*

MOTE   Little pretty, because little. Wherefore 'apt'?

ARMADO   And therefore 'apt' because quick.°   *quick-witted*

MOTE   Speak you this in my praise, master?

ARMADO   In thy condign° praise.   *well-deserved*

25   MOTE   I will praise an eel with the same praise.

ARMADO   What—that an eel is ingenious?

MOTE   That an eel is quick.°   *alive*

ARMADO   I do say thou art quick in answers. Thou heatest my
blood.°   *You make me angry*

30   MOTE   I am answered, sir.

ARMADO   I love not to be crossed.

MOTE *[aside]*   He speaks the mere° contrary—crosses[3] love not
him.   *absolute*

ARMADO   I have promised to study three years with the Duke.

35   MOTE   You may do it in an hour, sir.

ARMADO   Impossible.

MOTE   How many is one, thrice told?°   *counted*

ARMADO   I am ill at reckoning; it fitteth the spirit of a tapster.°   *bartender*

MOTE   You are a gentleman and a gamester,° sir.   *gambler*

40   ARMADO   I confess both. They are both the varnish of a complete
man.

MOTE   Then I am sure you know how much the gross sum of
deuce-ace° amounts to.   *a two and a one (dice)*

ARMADO   It doth amount to one more than two.

45   MOTE   Which the base vulgar° do call three.   *common people*

ARMADO   True.

MOTE   Why, sir, is this such a piece° of study? Now here is 'three'   *masterpiece*
studied ere ye'll thrice wink, and how easy it is to put 'years' to
the word 'three' and study 'three years' in two words, the danc-
50   ing horse[4] will tell you.

ARMADO   A most fine figure.°   *verbal turn; number*

MOTE *[aside]*   To prove you a cipher.°   *zero*

ARMADO   I will hereupon confess I am in love; and as it is base°   *ignoble*
for a soldier to love, so am I in love with a base° wench. If   *lowborn*
55   drawing my sword against the humour of affection° would   *inclination to love*
deliver me from the reprobate thought of it, I would take desire
prisoner and ransom him to any French courtier for a new-
devised curtsy.° I think scorn° to sigh. Methinks I should out-   *bowing fashion / disdain*
swear° Cupid. Comfort me, boy. What great men have been in   *renounce*
60   love?

MOTE   Hercules, master.

ARMADO   Most sweet Hercules! More authority, dear boy. Name
more—and, sweet my child, let them be men of good repute
and carriage.°   *behavior*

---

3. Coins (often imprinted with crosses).
4. Morocco, a performing horse trained to "count" with
its hooves, was a London sensation in 1591. Mote jok-
ingly takes "three years" as the object of "study" (line 34).

65 MOTE   Samson, master; he was a man of good carriage, great
        carriage, for he carried the town-gates on his back[5] like a porter,
        and he was in love.
    ARMADO   O well-knit Samson, strong-jointed Samson! I do excel
        thee in my rapier as much as thou didst me in carrying gates. I
70   am in love, too. Who was Samson's love, my dear Mote?
    MOTE   A woman, master.
    ARMADO   Of what complexion?[6]
    MOTE   Of all the four, or the three, or the two, or one of the four.
    ARMADO   Tell me precisely of what complexion?
75 MOTE   Of the sea-water green,[7] sir.
    ARMADO   Is that one of the four complexions?
    MOTE   As I have read, sir; and the best of them, too.
    ARMADO   Green indeed is the colour of lovers, but to have a love
        of that colour, methinks Samson had small reason for it. He
80   surely affected° her for her wit.°   loved / intelligence
    MOTE   It was so, sir, for she had a green wit.[8]
    ARMADO   My love is most immaculate white and red.
    MOTE   Most maculate° thoughts, master, are masked under such   impure
        colours.°   hues; pretexts
85 ARMADO   Define,° define, well-educated infant.   Explain your meaning
    MOTE   My father's wit and my mother's tongue assist me!
    ARMADO   Sweet invocation of a child!—most pretty and pathet-
        ical.°   touching
    MOTE   If she be made° of white and red   also "maid"
90   Her faults will ne'er be known,
            For blushing cheeks by faults are bred
                And fears by pale white shown.
            Then if she fear or be to blame,
                By this you shall not know;
95   For still her cheeks possess the same
                Which native° she doth owe.°   naturally / own
        A dangerous rhyme, master, against the reason of white and
        red.
    ARMADO   Is there not a ballad, boy, of the King and the Beggar?[9]
100 MOTE   The world was very guilty of such a ballad some three
        ages since, but I think now 'tis not to be found; or if it were, it
        would neither serve° for the writing nor the tune.   be acceptable
    ARMADO   I will have that subject newly writ o'er, that I may
        example my digression° by some mighty precedent. Boy, I do   justify my lapse
105   love that country girl that I took in the park with the rational
        hind[1] Costard. She deserves well.
    MOTE [aside]   To be whipped°—and yet a better love than my   (as a prostitute)
        master.
    ARMADO   Sing, boy. My spirit grows heavy in love.
110 MOTE   And that's great marvel, loving a light° wench.   wanton
    ARMADO   I say, sing.
    MOTE   Forbear till this company be past.

5. For the gates, see Judges 16:3. Love proved disastrous for both Hercules and Samson.
6. Temperament (Armado's meaning), as determined
by the balance of bodily humors: blood, phlegm, melancholy (from black bile), choler; skin coloring (Mote's
meaning).
7. Ill colored: evidence of chlorosis, an anemic condition affecting young women.
8. Immature understanding (proverbial).
9. The ballad concerns the love of King Cophetua for
the beggar maid Zenelophon. See also 4.1.65.
1. Peasant (or deer?) capable of reason.

Enter[COSTARD *the*] *clown, Constable* [DULL], *and*
[JAQUENETTA, *a*] *wench*

DULL [*to* ARMADO]   Sir, the Duke's pleasure is that you keep
Costard safe, and you must suffer° him to take no delight, nor   allow

115   no penance,° but a° must fast three days a week. For this   (for "pleasance"?) / he
damsel, I must keep her at the park. She is allowed for the
dey-woman.° Fare you well.   approved as dairymaid

ARMADO [*aside*]   I do betray myself with blushing.—Maid.

JAQUENETTA   Man.

120   ARMADO   I will visit thee at the lodge.

JAQUENETTA   That's hereby.²

ARMADO   I know where it is situate.

JAQUENETTA   Lord, how wise you are!

ARMADO   I will tell thee wonders.

125   JAQUENETTA   With that face?°   Really?

ARMADO   I love thee.

JAQUENETTA   So I heard you say.°   You don't say so

ARMADO   And so farewell.

JAQUENETTA   Fair weather after you.°   (proverbial)

130   DULL   Come, Jaquenetta, away. *Exeunt* [DULL *and* JAQUENETTA]

ARMADO   Villain,° thou shalt fast for thy offences ere thou be   Peasant; rascal
pardoned.

COSTARD   Well, sir, I hope when I do it I shall do it on a full
stomach.°   well fed; bravely

135   ARMADO   Thou shalt be heavily punished.

COSTARD   I am more bound to you than your fellows,° for they   servants
are but lightly rewarded.

ARMADO   Take away this villain. Shut him up.

MOTE   Come, you transgressing slave. Away!

140   COSTARD   Let me not be pent up,° sir. I will fast, being loose.³   jailed; constipated

MOTE   No, sir. That were fast and loose.° Thou shalt to prison.   a cheating trick

COSTARD   Well, if ever I do see the merry days of desolation°   (for "elation"?)
that I have seen, some shall see.

MOTE   What shall some see?

145   COSTARD   Nay, nothing, Master Mote, but what they look upon.
It is not for prisoners to be too silent in their words, and therefore I will say nothing. I thank God I have as little patience as
another man, and therefore I can be quiet.

Exeunt [MOTE *and* COSTARD]

ARMADO   I do affect° the very ground—which is base—where her   love

150   shoe—which is baser—guided by her foot—which is basest—
doth tread. I shall be forsworn—which is a great argument° of   proof
falsehood—if I love. And how can that be true love which is
falsely attempted? Love is a familiar;° love is a devil. There is   an attendant evil spirit
no evil angel but love. Yet was Samson so tempted, and he had

155   an excellent strength. Yet was Solomon so seduced, and he had
a very good wit. Cupid's butt-shaft° is too hard for Hercules'   unbarbed arrow
club, and therefore too much odds for a Spaniard's rapier. The
first and second cause° will not serve my turn: the passado⁴ he   (in the dueling code)
respects not, the duello° he regards not. His disgrace is to be   dueling code

160   called boy, but his glory is to subdue men. Adieu, valour; rust,
rapier; be still, drum: for your manager° is in love; yea, he   wielder

2. Nearby; neither here nor there(?)   4. Fencing thrust.
3. Being free; being loose in the bowels.

loveth. Assist me, some extemporal° god of rhyme, for I am sure   *impromptu*
I shall turn sonnet.° Devise wit, write pen, for I am for whole   *sonneteer*
volumes, in folio.°   *Exit*   *largest size of book*

2.1

Enter the PRINCESS *of France with three attending ladies*
[MARIA, CATHERINE, *and* ROSALINE] *and three lords* [*one*
named BOYET][1]

BOYET   Now, madam, summon up your dearest spirits.°   *utmost energies*
    Consider who the King your father sends,
    To whom he sends, and what's his embassy:
    Yourself, held precious in the world's esteem,
5   To parley with the sole inheritor°   *owner*
    Of all perfections that a man may owe,
    Matchless Navarre; the plea° of no less weight   *that which is claimed*
    Than Aquitaine, a dowry for a queen.
    Be now as prodigal of all dear grace
10   As nature was in making graces dear[2]
    When she did starve the general world beside°   *except (you)*
    And prodigally gave them all to you.
PRINCESS   Good Lord Boyet, my beauty, though but mean,°   *average*
    Needs not the painted flourish° of your praise.   *embellishment*
15   Beauty is bought by judgement of the eye,
    Not uttered[3] by base sale of chapmen's° tongues.   *salesmen's*
    I am less proud to hear you tell° my worth   *speak of; reckon up*
    Than you much willing to be counted wise
    In spending your wit in the praise of mine.
20   But now to task the tasker:[4] good Boyet,
    You are not ignorant all-telling fame°   *rumor*
    Doth noise abroad° Navarre hath made a vow   *spread the rumor that*
    Till painful° study shall outwear three years   *taxing*
    No woman may approach his silent court.
25   Therefore to's° seemeth it a needful course,   *to us*
    Before we enter his forbidden gates,
    To know his pleasure; and in that behalf,
    Bold° of your worthiness, we single you   *Confident*
    As our best-moving fair° solicitor.   *most eloquent and just*
30   Tell him the daughter of the King of France
    On serious business, craving quick dispatch,
    Importunes personal conference with his grace.
    Haste, signify so much while we attend,
    Like humble-visaged suitors, his high will.
35 BOYET   Proud of° employment, willingly I go.   *Honored with*
PRINCESS   All pride is willing pride,° and yours is so. *Exit* BOYET   *vanity*
    Who are the votaries,° my loving lords,   *vow takers*
    That are vow-fellows with this virtuous duke?
A LORD   Lord Longueville is one.
PRINCESS   Know you the man?
40 MARIA   I know him, madam. At a marriage feast
    Between Lord Périgord[5] and the beauteous heir

2.1 Location: Outside the gates of the King's court.
1. Pronounced "Boy-ett."
2. *dear grace . . . graces dear:* chiasmus, an *abba* rhetorical structure common to the aristocrats' speech and the larger movement of the play. See 4.3 and Introduc-

tion. The second "dear" means costly (because rare).
3. Not spoken; not offered for sale.
4. Impose a task on you who have given me one; chastise the task setter.
5. Not otherwise mentioned; Périgord was in Aquitaine.

Of Jaques Fauconbridge solemnizèd
In Normandy saw I this Longueville.
A man of sovereign parts° he is esteemed,   outstanding qualities
45 Well fitted in arts, glorious in arms.
Nothing becomes him ill that he would° well.   wishes to do
The only soil of° his fair virtue's gloss—   stain on
If virtue's gloss will stain with any soil—
Is a sharp wit matched with too blunt° a will,   rough; unfeeling
50 Whose edge hath power to cut, whose will still° wills   always
It should none spare that come within his° power.   its
PRINCESS Some merry mocking lord, belike°—is't so?   probably
MARIA They say so most that most his humours know.
PRINCESS Such short-lived wits do wither as they grow.
55 Who are the rest?
CATHERINE[6] The young Dumaine, a well-accomplished youth,
Of° all that virtue love for virtue loved.   By
Most power to do most harm, least knowing ill,[7]
For he hath wit to make an ill shape good,
60 And shape to win grace, though he had no wit.[8]
I saw him at the Duke Alençon's once,
And much too little° of that good I saw   short
Is my report to° his great worthiness.   my report compared with
ROSALINE[9] Another of these students at that time
65 Was there with him, if I have heard a truth.
Biron[1] they call him, but a merrier man,
Within the limit of becoming° mirth,   decorous
I never spent an hour's talk withal.°   with
His eye begets occasion° for his wit,   finds opportunities
70 For every object that the one doth catch
The other turns to a mirth-moving jest,
Which his fair tongue, conceit's expositor,°   thought's expounder
Delivers in such apt and gracious words
That agèd ears play truant at° his tales,   neglect work to hear
75 And younger hearings are quite ravishèd,
So sweet and voluble° is his discourse.   fluent
PRINCESS God bless my ladies, are they all in love,
That every one her own hath garnishèd
With such bedecking ornaments of praise?
A LORD Here comes Boyet.
            Enter BOYET
80 PRINCESS   Now, what admittance,° lord?   reception
BOYET Navarre had notice of your fair approach,
And he and his competitors° in oath   partners
Were all addressed° to meet you, gentle lady,   ready
Before I came. Marry, thus much I have learnt:
85 He rather means to lodge you in the field,

6. Q, F: 2 Lady. The remainder of the scene strongly
suggests that Lady 2 is Rosaline, not Catherine. The
last three acts imply that Lady 2 is Catherine, however.
For the issues involved in this emendation and others in
2.1 (lines 64, 113–26, 178–92, 194, and 209), see the
Textual Note.
7. Potentially dangerous by virtue of his very innocence; although he theoretically could do harm, he is
free of all misdeeds.
8. *For . . . wit:* He is intelligent enough to make up for
a displeasing appearance, if he had one (or perhaps to
make something evil seem virtuous), and good-looking

enough to win favor (from people or perhaps God),
even if he lacked intelligence.
9. Q: 3 Lady; F: Rosaline. The remainder of the scene
in Q strongly suggests that Lady 3 is Catherine, not
Rosaline. The last three acts of Q imply that Lady 3 is
Rosaline, however.
1. Probable pun on "Biron/brown." "Brown" was pronounced much like "Biron" ("Be-roon"); Q's spelling of
"Biron" is "Berowne." "Brown" was associated with
somberness or melancholy (as in a "brown study"), and is
contrasted in this line with "merrier" by means of "but."

Like one that comes here to besiege his court,
Than seek a dispensation for his oath
To let you enter his unpeopled° house.   *servantless*

        Enter NAVARRE, LONGUEVILLE, DUMAINE, *and* BIRON
Here comes Navarre.

90 KING   Fair Princess, welcome to the court of Navarre.
PRINCESS   'Fair' I give you back again, and welcome I have not
yet. The roof of this court° is too high to be yours, and welcome   *sky*
to the wide fields too base to be mine.
KING   You shall be welcome, madam, to my court.
95 PRINCESS   I will be welcome, then. Conduct me thither.
KING   Hear me, dear lady. I have sworn an oath—
PRINCESS   Our Lady help my lord! He'll be forsworn.
KING   Not for the world, fair madam, by my will.°   *willingly (mild oath)*
PRINCESS   Why, will° shall break it—will and nothing else.   *(sexual) desire*
100 KING   Your ladyship is ignorant what it is.
PRINCESS   Were my lord so his ignorance were wise,
Where now his knowledge must prove ignorance.
I hear your grace hath sworn out housekeeping.°   *repudiated hospitality*
'Tis deadly sin to keep that oath, my lord,
105 And sin to break it.
But pardon me, I am too sudden°-bold.   *rashly*
To teach a teacher ill beseemeth me.
Vouchsafe to read the purpose of my coming,
And suddenly resolve° me in my suit.   *immediately answer*
        [*She gives him a paper*]
110 KING   Madam, I will, if suddenly I may.
PRINCESS   You will the sooner that I were away,°   *so that I'll go*
For you'll prove perjured if you make me stay.
        [*Navarre reads the paper*]
BIRON [*to* ROSALINE]   Did not I dance with you in Brabant once?
ROSALINE[2]   Did not I dance with you in Brabant once?
BIRON   I know you did.
115 ROSALINE   How needless was it then
To ask the question!
BIRON   You must not be so quick.°   *sharp; hasty; witty*
ROSALINE   'Tis 'long of° you, that spur° me with such questions.   *due to / prod*
BIRON   Your wit's too hot, it speeds too fast, 'twill tire.
ROSALINE   Not till it leave the rider in the mire.
120 BIRON   What time o' day?
ROSALINE   The hour that fools should ask.
BIRON   Now fair befall° your mask.   *good luck to*
ROSALINE   Fair fall° the face it covers.   *befall*
BIRON   And send you many lovers.
125 ROSALINE   Amen, so you be none.
BIRON   Nay, then will I be gone.
KING [*to the* PRINCESS]   Madam, your father here doth intimate
The payment of[3] a hundred thousand crowns,
Being but the one-half of an entire sum
130 Disbursèd by my father in his° wars.   *(the King of France's)*
But say that he° or we—as neither have—   *(Navarre's father)*
Received that sum, yet there remains unpaid
A hundred thousand more, in surety of the which

───

2. Lines 114–25—Q: Catherine; F: Rosaline.   3. *intimate . . . of:* suggest he paid.

One part of Aquitaine is bound to us,
135 Although not valued° to the money's worth.   *equal in value*
If then the King your father will restore
But that one half which is unsatisfied,
We will give up our right in Aquitaine
And hold fair friendship with his majesty.
140 But that, it seems, he little purposeth,
For here he doth demand to have repaid°   *insists he has repaid*
A hundred thousand crowns, and not demands,°   *rather than offering*
On payment of a hundred thousand crowns,
To have his title live in Aquitaine,
145 Which we much rather had depart withal,°   *surrender*
And have the money by our father lent,
Than Aquitaine, so gelded° as it is.⁴   *reduced; castrated*
Dear Princess, were not his requests so far
From reason's yielding, your fair self should make
150 A yielding 'gainst some reason in my breast,
And go well satisfied to France again.
PRINCESS   You do the King my father too much wrong,
And wrong the reputation of your name,
In so unseeming° to confess receipt   *seeming unwilling*
155 Of that° which hath so faithfully been paid.   *200,000 crowns*
KING   I do protest I never heard of it,
And if you prove it I'll repay it back
Or yield up Aquitaine.
PRINCESS   We arrest° your word.   *seize as security*
Boyet, you can produce acquittances°   *receipts*
160 For such a sum from special officers
Of Charles, his° father.   *(Navarre's)*
KING   Satisfy me so.
BOYET   So please your grace, the packet is not come
Where that and other specialties° are bound.   *legal contracts*
Tomorrow you shall have a sight of them.
165 KING   It shall suffice me, at which interview
All liberal° reason I will yield unto.   *civilized*
Meantime receive such welcome at my hand
As honour, without breach of honour, may
Make tender of to thy true worthiness.
170 You may not come, fair princess, within my gates,
But here without° you shall be so received   *outside*
As you shall deem yourself lodged in my heart,
Though so denied fair harbour in my house.
Your own good thoughts excuse me, and farewell.
175 Tomorrow shall we visit you again.
PRINCESS   Sweet health and fair desires consort° your grace.   *accompany*
KING   Thy own wish wish I thee in every place.
                    Exit [*with* LONGUEVILLE *and* DUMAINE]
BIRON⁵ [*to* ROSALINE]   Lady, I will commend you to mine own
    heart.
180 ROSALINE   Pray you, do my commendations. I would be glad to
    see it.⁶

---

4. Navarre says that of the 200,000 crowns he's owed, the King of France falsely claims to have paid back half and has given him Aquitaine as collateral for the other half, even though it isn't worth that much. Navarre is willing to return Aquitaine and forget the entire debt in return for 100,000 crowns, but France wants Navarre to pay that sum and keep Aquitaine.
5. Lines 178–92—Q: Biron; F: Boyet.
6. Know your real feelings; literally, behold your heart and, hence, see you dead.

	BIRON	I would you heard it groan.	
	ROSALINE	Is the fool° sick?	*poor thing*
	BIRON	Sick at the heart.	
185	ROSALINE	Alack, let it blood.°	*bleed it (medically)*
	BIRON	Would that do it good?	
	ROSALINE	My physic° says 'Ay'.	*medical knowledge*
	BIRON	Will you prick't with your eye?[7]	
	ROSALINE	*Non point,*° with my knife.	*Not at all; it's blunt*
190	BIRON	Now God save thy life.	
	ROSALINE	And yours, from long living.	
	BIRON	I cannot stay thanksgiving.[8]	*Exit*

Enter DUMAINE

DUMAINE [*to* BOYET]   Sir, I pray you a word. What lady is that same?
BOYET   The heir of Alençon, Catherine[9] her name.
195 DUMAINE   A gallant lady. Monsieur, fare you well.   *Exit*
[*Enter* LONGUEVILLE]
LONGUEVILLE [*to* BOYET]   I beseech you a word, what is she in
    the white?
BOYET   A woman sometimes, an° you saw her in the light.   *if*
LONGUEVILLE   Perchance light in the light.° I desire her name.   *wanton if seen clearly*
BOYET   She hath but one for herself; to desire that were a shame.
200 LONGUEVILLE   Pray you, sir, whose daughter?
BOYET   Her mother's, I have heard.
LONGUEVILLE   God's blessing on your beard!°   *(insult)*
BOYET   Good sir, be not offended.
    She is an heir of Fauconbridge.
205 LONGUEVILLE   Nay, my choler° is ended.   *anger*
    She is a most sweet lady.
BOYET   Not unlike,° sir. That may be.   *Exit* LONGUEVILLE   *unlikely*
Enter BIRON
BIRON   What's her name in the cap?
BOYET   Rosaline,[1] by good hap.
210 BIRON   Is she wedded or no?
BOYET   To her will, sir, or so.°   *or something like that*
BIRON   O, you are welcome, sir. Adieu.
BOYET   Farewell to me, sir, and welcome to you.°   *Exit* BIRON   *you're welcome to go*
MARIA   That last is Biron, the merry madcap lord.
    Not a word with him but a jest.
215 BOYET   And every jest but a word.
PRINCESS   It was well done of you to take him at his word.°   *(literally; punningly)*
BOYET   I was as willing to grapple as he was to board.[2]
CATHERINE[3]   Two hot sheeps,[4] marry.
BOYET   And wherefore not ships?
    No sheep, sweet lamb, unless we feed on your lips.
220 CATHERINE[5]   You sheep and I pasture[6]—shall that finish the jest?
BOYET   So° you grant pasture for me.   *So long as*
CATHERINE   Not so, gentle beast.
    My lips are no common, though several they be.[7]
BOYET   Belonging to whom?

---

7. "Eye" puns on "Ay" (line 187), suggesting a needle but also a vagina, impossibly serving as a penis.
8. Stay long enough to thank you (for that rude remark).
9. Q, F: Rosaline.
1. Q, F: Catherine.
2. Join ships ("grapple") for hand-to-hand combat ("board"): metaphor for competitive wordplay, with sexual overtones.

3. F: Maria.
4. "Sheeps" was pronounced like "ships."
5. Lines 220, 221, 223—Q, F: Lady.
6. Pun on "pastor" (shepherd).
7. My lips are not commonly owned grazing land, though they are pasture—they are privately owned, enclosed land (*several*: more than one; separate).

CATHERINE   To my fortunes and me.
PRINCESS   Good wits will be jangling;° but, gentles,° agree.   quarreling / gentlefolk
225 This civil war of wits were much better used
     On Navarre and his bookmen,° for here 'tis abused.°   scholars / misapplied
BOYET   If my observation, which very seldom lies,
     By the heart's still rhetoric° disclosèd with eyes,   silent eloquence
     Deceive me not now, Navarre is infected.
230 PRINCESS   With what?
BOYET   With that which we lovers entitle 'affected'.°   being in love
PRINCESS   Your reason?
BOYET   Why, all his behaviours did make their retire°   withdrawal
     To the court of his eye, peeping thorough° desire.   through
235 His heart like an agate with your print impressed,[8]
     Proud with his form,° in his eye pride expressed.   the Princess's image
     His tongue, all impatient to speak[9] and not see,
     Did stumble with haste in his eyesight to be.
     All senses to that sense did make their repair,°   resort
240 To feel° only looking° on fairest of fair.   experience / by looking
     Methought all his senses were locked in his eye,
     As jewels in crystal, for some prince to buy,
     Who, tendering° their own worth from where they were   displaying
          glassed,°   encased in crystal
     Did point° you to buy them along as you passed.   direct
245 His face's own margin[1] did quote° such amazes   indicate
     That all eyes saw his eyes enchanted with gazes.
     I'll give you° Aquitaine and all that is his   bet you get
     An you give him for my sake but one loving kiss.
PRINCESS   Come, to our pavilion. Boyet is disposed.°   (to be merry)
250 BOYET   But to speak that in words which his eye hath disclosed.
     I only have made a mouth of his eye
     By adding a tongue, which I know will not lie.
ROSALINE[2]   Thou art an old love-monger, and speak'st skilfully.
MARIA   He is Cupid's grandfather, and learns news of him.
255 CATHERINE   Then was Venus° like her mother, for her father is   Cupid's mother
          but grim.°   not handsome
BOYET   Do you hear, my mad° wenches?   high-spirited
MARIA   No.
BOYET   What then, do you see?
CATHERINE   Ay—our way to be gone.
BOYET   You are too hard for me.
                                   Exeunt

                          3.1
          Enter [ARMADO *the*] *braggart,*[1] *and* [MOTE] *his boy*
ARMADO   Warble, child; make passionate° my sense of hearing.   responsive
MOTE [*sings*]   Concolinel.°   song title or opening
ARMADO   Sweet air!° Go, tenderness of years, take this key. Give   tune
     enlargement° to the swain. Bring him festinately° hither. I must   freedom / in a hurry
5   employ him in a letter to my love.

8. Engraved with your image. Agates were engraved and set in rings.
9. Impatient at being able only to speak.
1. The part of a book in which comments were printed.
2. Lines 253, 254, 255, 256, 257: Q—Lady, Lady 2, Lady 3, Lady, Lady; F—Rosaline, Maria, Lady 2, Lady 1, Lady 2. It is uncertain which of the ladies should speak these lines.
3.1 Location: The King's park.
1. The braggart soldier was a stock figure in the contemporary Italian commedia dell'arte, a theatrical form with popular roots. His theatrical ancestry can be traced back to ancient Roman comedy.

MOTE   Master, will you win your love with a French brawl?°   *dance*
ARMADO   How meanest thou—brawling in French?²
MOTE   No, my complete master; but to jig off a tune° at the   *sing a jiglike tune*
tongue's end, canary° to it with your feet, humour° it with turn-   *dance / adapt to*
10   ing up your eyelids, sigh a note and sing a note, sometime
through the throat as if you swallowed love with singing love,
sometime through the nose as if you snuffed up love by smell-
ing love, with your hat penthouse-like° o'er the shop of your   *like an awning*
eyes, with your arms crossed° on your thin-belly³ doublet like a   *(from love melancholy)*
15   rabbit on a spit, or your hands in your pocket like a man after°   *in the style of*
the old painting, and keep not too long in one tune, but a snip°   *snatch*
and away. These are complements, these are humours; these
betray nice° wenches that would be betrayed without these,   *seduce wanton*
and make them men of note—do you note? *men*—that most
20   are affected° to these.   *given*
ARMADO   How hast thou purchased this experience?
MOTE   By my penny of observation.
ARMADO   But O, but O—
MOTE   'The hobby-horse is forgot.'⁴
25   ARMADO   Call'st thou my love hobby-horse?
MOTE   No, master, the hobby-horse is but a colt,° and your love   *young horse; wanton*
perhaps a hackney.° But have you forgot your love?   *riding horse; whore*
ARMADO   Almost I had.
MOTE   Negligent student, learn her by heart.
30   ARMADO   By heart and in heart, boy.
MOTE   And out of heart,° master. All those three I will prove.   *disheartened*
ARMADO   What wilt thou prove?
MOTE   A man, if I live; and this, 'by', 'in', and 'without', upon
the instant: 'by' heart you love her because your heart cannot
35   come *by* her; 'in' heart you love her because your heart is *in*
love with her; and 'out' of heart you love her, being *out* of heart
that you cannot enjoy her.
ARMADO   I am all these three.
MOTE   [*aside*]   And three times as much more, and yet nothing
40   at all.
ARMADO   Fetch hither the swain. He must carry me° a letter.   *for me*
MOTE   [*aside*]   A message well sympathized°—a horse to be   *matched*
ambassador for an ass.
ARMADO   Ha, ha! What sayst thou?
45   MOTE   Marry, sir, you must send the ass upon the horse, for he
is very slow-gaited. But I go.
ARMADO   The way is but short. Away!
MOTE   As swift as lead, sir.
ARMADO   The meaning, pretty ingenious?
50   Is not lead a metal heavy, dull, and slow?
MOTE   *Minime,*° honest master—or rather, master, no.   *By no means*
ARMADO   I say lead is slow.
MOTE   You are too swift, sir, to say so.
Is that lead slow which is fired from a gun?
ARMADO   Sweet smoke of rhetoric!

---

2. "Brawling" means "quarreling," but the phrase may
also refer to popular rioting against immigrant French
merchants and artisans.
3. Unpadded belly or lower part; also suggesting that
Armado is wasting away for love.

4. A lament for the passing of the good old days; perhaps the refrain of a song. A hobbyhorse—a person costumed as a horse—was used in popular dancing; the
word also meant "whore," perhaps suggested by the
association between "O" (line 23) and "vagina."

55   He reputes me a cannon, and the bullet, that's he.
          I shoot thee at the swain.
    MOTE   Thump,° then, and I flee.   [*Exit*]   *Bang*
    ARMADO   A most acute juvenal—voluble° and free of grace.   *quick-witted*
          By thy favour, sweet welkin,° I must sigh in thy face.   *sky*
          Most rude melancholy, valour gives thee place.°   *gives way to you*
60   My herald is returned.
               Enter [MOTE *the*] *page, and* [COSTARD *the*] *clown*
    MOTE   A wonder, master—here's a costard broken in a shin.[5]
    ARMADO   Some enigma, some riddle; come, thy *l'envoi*.° Begin.   *explanation*
    COSTARD   No egma, no riddle, no *l'envoi*, no salve in the mail,[6]
          sir. O sir, plantain,° a plain plantain—no *l'envoi*, no *l'envoi*, no   *healing herb*
65   salve, sir, but a plantain.
    ARMADO   By virtue, thou enforcest laughter—thy silly thought
          my spleen.[7] The heaving of my lungs provokes me to ridicu-
          lous° smiling. O pardon me, my stars! Doth the inconsiderate[8]   *mocking; absurd*
          take salve for *l'envoi*, and the word *l'envoi* for a salve?
70   MOTE   Do the wise think them other? Is not *l'envoi* a salve?
    ARMADO   No, page, it is an epilogue or discourse to make plain
          Some obscure precedence that hath tofore been sain.[9]
          I will example° it.   *give an example of*
                The fox, the ape, and the humble-bee°   *humblebee*
75   Were still at odds,[1] being but three.
          There's the moral.° Now the *l'envoi*.   *lesson*
    MOTE   I will add the *l'envoi*. Say the moral again.
    ARMADO   The fox, the ape, and the humble-bee
                Were still at odds, being but three.
80   MOTE   Until the goose came out of door
                And stayed° the odds by adding four.°   *stopped / a fourth*
          Now will I begin your moral, and do you follow with my
          l'envoi.
                The fox, the ape, and the humble-bee
85   Were still at odds, being but three.
    ARMADO   Until the goose came out of door,
                Staying the odds by adding four.
    MOTE   A good *l'envoi*, ending in the goose.[2] Would you desire
          more?
90   COSTARD   The boy hath sold him a bargain—a goose,° that's flat.°   *made him a fool / certain*
          Sir, your pennyworth° is good an° your goose be fat.   *bargain / if*
          To sell a bargain well is as cunning as fast and loose.°   *cheating; (of bowels)*
          Let me see, a fat *l'envoi*—ay, that's a fat goose.°   *buttocks?*
    ARMADO   Come hither, come hither. How did this argument°   *topic*
95   begin?
    MOTE   By saying that a costard was broken in a shin.
          Then called you for the *l'envoi*.
    COSTARD   True, and I for a plantain. Thus came your argument°   *enema?*

5. A head with a cut shin (an anatomical impossibility that provokes Mote's amusement); disappointed in love or sex (alluding to Armado's triumph over Costard); taking a loan.
6. Costard takes Armado to be proposing remedies for his shin. "Egma" for "enigma" may be an error for an "egg" solution or "enema." *L'envoi* refers to a salve or ointment, perhaps by confusion with "lenify" (to soothe or purge). There is also a pun on the Latin *salve* (greetings), the opposite of *l'envoi*'s sense of "farewell." *mail:* traveling bag. In addition, a salve inserted in or an anal salvo discharged from the male.
7. Amusement: the spleen was regarded as the organ controlling laughter.
8. The thoughtless person.
9. *Some . . . sain:* What was obscurely said before. The couplet is in poulter's measure—fourteen syllables, then twelve.
1. Were always quarreling; were always an odd number.
2. Punning on the French *oie* (goose), the final sound in *envoi*, "ending in the goose" also because it is inserted in the end of the goose (prostitute, victim of venereal disease).

100	in. Then the boy's fat *l'envoi*, the goose that you bought, and he ended the market.°	*bargaining*
	ARMADO But tell me, how was there a costard broken in a shin?	
	MOTE I will tell you sensibly.°	*clearly; feelingly*
	COSTARD Thou hast no feeling of it. Mote, I will speak that *l'envoi*.	
105	I, Costard, running out, that was safely within,³	
	Fell over the threshold and broke my shin.	
	ARMADO We will talk no more of this matter.	
	COSTARD Till there be more matter° in the shin.	*pus; semen*
	ARMADO Sirrah Costard, I will enfranchise° thee.	*free*
110	COSTARD O, marry me to one Frances!⁴ I smell some *l'envoi*, some goose, in this.	
	ARMADO By my sweet soul, I mean setting thee at liberty, enfree-doming thy person. Thou wert immured,° restrained, capti-vated, bound.°	*shut in* *(of bowels)*
115	COSTARD True, true, and now you will be my purgation° and let me loose.°	*liberator; enema* *(my bowels)*
	ARMADO I give thee thy liberty, set° thee from durance,° and in lieu thereof impose on thee nothing but this: bear this signif-icant° to the country maid, Jaquenetta.	*free/imprisonment* *token*
120	[*Giving him a letter*] There is remuneration [*giving him money*], for the best ward° of mine honour is rewarding my dependants. Mote, follow. [*Exit*]	*guard*
	MOTE Like the sequel, I. Signor Costard, adieu. *Exit*	
	COSTARD My sweet ounce of man's flesh, my incony Jew!⁵	
125	Now will I look to his remuneration. Remuneration—O, that's the Latin word for three-farthings.° Three-farthings—remuner-ation. 'What's the price of this inkle?'⁶ 'One penny.' 'No, I'll give you a remuneration.' Why, it carries it!° Remuneration! Why, it is a fairer name than French crown.⁷ I will never buy and sell out of° this word.	*¾-pence coin* *carries the day* *without using*
130	*Enter* BIRON	
	BIRON My good knave Costard, exceedingly well met.	
	COSTARD Pray you, sir, how much carnation° ribbon may a man buy for a remuneration?	*flesh-colored*
	BIRON What is a remuneration?	
135	COSTARD Marry, sir, halfpenny-farthing.°	*three farthings*
	BIRON Why, then, three-farthing-worth of silk.	
	COSTARD I thank your worship. God be wi' you.	
	BIRON Stay, slave, I must employ thee.	
	As thou wilt win my favour, good my knave,	
140	Do one thing for me that I shall entreat.	
	COSTARD When would you have it done, sir?	
	BIRON This afternoon.	
	COSTARD Well, I will do it, sir. Fare you well.	
	BIRON Thou knowest not what it is.	
145	COSTARD I shall know, sir, when I have done it.	
	BIRON Why, villain, thou must know first.	

---

3. *running out . . . within*: possible reference to bodily emissions.
4. Punning on "enfranchise" (line 109); "Frances" was probably a common name for a prostitute.
5. Religious reference from the mishearing of "adieu" (line 123); playful diminutive of "jewel" or "juvenal." *incony*: fine, quality.

6. Linen tape, suggested by "incony" (line 124); near homonym of 'ingle,' a catamite (boy kept by a ped-erast), and perhaps thereby evoking the period's associ-ation of the "Jew" (line 124) with sodomy.
7. A coin; syphilis (the "French disease") results in a bald head ("crown").

COSTARD　I will come to your worship tomorrow morning.

BIRON　It must be done this afternoon. Hark, slave,
　　　　It is but this:
150　　　The Princess comes to hunt here in the park,
　　　　And in her train there is a gentle lady.
　　　　When tongues speak sweetly, then they name her name,
　　　　And Rosaline they call her. Ask for her,
　　　　And to her white hand see thou do commend
　　　　This sealed-up counsel.° There's thy guerdon° [*giving him a*　　　message / reward
155　　　　　*letter and money*], go.

COSTARD　Guerdon! O sweet guerdon!—better than remunera-
　　　　tion, elevenpence-farthing better[8]—most sweet guerdon! I will
　　　　do it, sir, in print.° Guerdon—remuneration.　　　　　*Exit*　　　to the letter

BIRON　And I, forsooth, in love—I that have been love's whip,
160　　　A very beadle[9] to a humorous° sigh,　　　　　　　　　　　moody
　　　　A critic, nay, a night-watch constable,
　　　　A domineering pedant° o'er the boy,°　　　　　　　　schoolmaster / Cupid
　　　　Than whom no mortal so magnificent.
　　　　This wimpled,° whining, purblind,° wayward boy,　　blindfolded / all-blind
165　　　This Signor° Junior, giant dwarf, Dan° Cupid,　　　Sir; senior / Master
　　　　Regent of love-rhymes, lord of folded arms,
　　　　Th'anointed sovereign of sighs and groans,
　　　　Liege of all loiterers and malcontents,
　　　　Dread prince of plackets, king of codpieces,[1]
170　　　Sole imperator° and great general　　　　　　　　　　　Absolute ruler
　　　　Of trotting paritors[2]—O my little heart!
　　　　And I to be a corporal of his field,°　　　　　　　　　　field officer
　　　　And wear his colours like a tumbler's hoop!°　　(adorned with ribbons)
　　　　What? I love, I sue, I seek a wife?—
175　　　A woman, that is like a German clock,
　　　　Still° a-repairing, ever out of frame,°　　　　　　　　Always / order
　　　　And never going aright, being° a watch,　　　　　　　　　though
　　　　But being° watched that it may still go right.　　　　Except when
　　　　Nay, to be perjured, which is worst of all,
180　　　And among three to love the worst of all—
　　　　A whitely° wanton with a velvet° brow,　　　　　　　pale / smooth
　　　　With two pitch°-balls stuck in her face for eyes—　　　tar black
　　　　Ay, and, by heaven, one that will do the deed°　　　sexual act
　　　　Though Argus[3] were her eunuch° and her guard.　　harem guard
185　　　And I to sigh for her, to watch° for her,　　　stay awake at night
　　　　To pray for her—go to,° it is a plague　　　　　　　　come now
　　　　That Cupid will impose for my neglect
　　　　Of his almighty dreadful little might.
　　　　Well, I will love, write, sigh, pray, sue, groan:
190　　　Some men must love my lady, and some Joan.°　　[*Exit*]　lower-class woman

---

8. Biron has given Costard a "guerdon" of one shilling,
or twelve pence, which is "elevenpence-farthing"
(eleven pence and one farthing) "better than remuneration," defined earlier by Costard as "three-farthings"
(where four farthings equal one pence; line 126).
9. Minor parish official who punished lesser offenses
(for instance, by whipping).

1. The parts of clothes covering the male sexual organ
(hence, penises, or men). *plackets:* slits in petticoats
(hence, female genitalia, or women).
2. Officers who summoned sexual offenders to ecclesiastical courts.
3. Mythical watchman with a hundred eyes.

4.1

Enter the PRINCESS, *a* FORESTER, *her ladies* [ROSALINE,
MARIA, *and* CATHERINE] *and her lords* [*among them*
BOYET]

PRINCESS   Was that the King that spurred his horse so hard
Against the steep uprising of the hill?

BOYET   I know not, but I think it was not he.

PRINCESS   Whoe'er a° was, a showed a mounting mind.   *he*
Well, lords, today we shall have our dispatch.

5   Ere Saturday we will return to France.
Then, forester my friend, where is the bush
That we must stand and play the murderer in?

FORESTER   Hereby, upon the edge of yonder coppice°—   *thicket*
A stand° where you may make the fairest° shoot.   *hunter's station / best*

10   PRINCESS   I thank my beauty, I am fair that shoot,
And thereupon thou speak'st 'the fairest shoot'.

FORESTER   Pardon me, madam, for I meant not so.

PRINCESS   What, what? First praise me, and again say no?
O short-lived pride! Not fair? Alack, for woe!

15   FORESTER   Yes, madam, fair.

PRINCESS   Nay, never paint° me now.   *flatter*
Where fair° is not, praise cannot mend the brow.   *beauty*
Here, good my glass,° take this for telling true.   *my good mirror*
[*She gives him money*]
Fair payment for foul words is more than due.

FORESTER   Nothing but fair is that which you inherit.°   *own*

20   PRINCESS   See, see, my beauty will be saved by merit![1]
O heresy in fair,° fit for these days[2]—   *in regard to beauty*
A giving hand, though foul, shall have fair praise.
But come, the bow. Now mercy° goes to kill,   *the merciful Princess*
And shooting well is then accounted ill.°   *unmerciful*

25   Thus will I save my credit in the shoot,
Not wounding—pity would not let me do't.[3]
If wounding, then it was to show my skill,
That more for praise than purpose meant to kill.
And, out of question,° so it is sometimes—   *beyond doubt*

30   Glory° grows guilty of detested crimes   *The desire for glory*
When for fame's sake, for praise, an outward part,
We bend to that the working of the heart,
As I for praise alone now seek to spill
The poor deer's blood that my heart means no ill.

35   BOYET   Do not curst° wives hold that self-sovereignty   *shrewish*
Only for praise' sake when they strive to be
Lords o'er their lords?

PRINCESS   Only for praise, and praise we may afford
To any lady that subdues a lord.

40   *Enter* [COSTARD *the*] *clown*

BOYET   Here comes a member of the commonwealth.°   *common people*

COSTARD   God dig-you-de'en,° all. Pray you, which is the head   *give you good evening*
lady?

4.1 Location: A hunter's station in the King's park.
1. Desert; good works (her "payment").
2. Believing in salvation by faith, Protestants considered it a common "heresy" "these days" to think, as

Catholics did, that one could be "saved by merit."
3. *Thus . . . do't*: I will save my reputation as a hunter
by saying, if I miss, that pity for the deer caused me to
miss deliberately.

PRINCESS   Thou shalt know her, fellow, by the rest that have no
45   heads.[4]
COSTARD   Which is the greatest lady, the highest?
PRINCESS   The thickest and the tallest.
COSTARD   The thickest and the tallest—it is so, truth is truth.
    An your waist, mistress, were as slender as my wit
50   One o' these maids' girdles for your waist should be fit.
    Are not you the chief woman? You are the thickest here.
PRINCESS   What's your will, sir? What's your will?
COSTARD   I have a letter from Monsieur Biron to one Lady Rosaline.
PRINCESS   O, thy letter, thy letter! [*She takes it*] He's a good
    friend of mine.
55   [*To* COSTARD] Stand aside, good bearer. Boyet, you can carve.°   *cut meat; act affected*
    Break up° this capon.[5]   *Cut up; open*
        [*She gives the letter to* BOYET]
BOYET   I am bound to serve.
    This letter is mistook. It importeth° none here.   *matters to*
    It is writ to Jaquenetta.
PRINCESS   We will read it, I swear.
    Break the neck of the wax,° and everyone give ear.   *seal; (capon)*
60   BOYET [*reads*]   'By heaven, that thou art fair is most infallible,°   *certain*
    true that thou art beauteous, truth itself that thou art lovely.
    More fairer than fair, beautiful than beauteous, truer than truth
    itself, have commiseration on thy heroical vassal. The magnan-
    imous and most illustrate° King Cophetua set's° eye upon the   *illustrious / set his*
65   penurious and indubitate° beggar Zenelophon,[6] and he it was   *undoubted*
    that might rightly say "*Veni, vidi, vici*",[7] which to annothanize° *anatomize; annotate*
    in the vulgar—O base and obscure vulgar!°—*videlicet*° "He   *vernacular / namely*
    came, see, and overcame." He came, one; see, two; overcame,
    three. Who came? The King. Why did he come? To see. Why
70   did he see? To overcome. To whom came he? To the beggar.
    What saw he? The beggar. Who overcame he? The beggar.
    The conclusion is victory. On whose side? The King's. The
    captive is enriched. On whose side? The beggar's. The catastro-
    phe° is a nuptial. On whose side? The King's—no, on both in   *outcome*
75   one, or one in both. I am the King—for so stands the compari-
    son—thou the beggar, for so witnesseth thy lowliness. Shall I
    command thy love? I may. Shall I enforce thy love? I could.
    Shall I entreat thy love? I will. What shalt thou exchange for
    rags? Robes. For tittles?° Titles. For thyself? Me. Thus,   *jots; specks*
80   expecting thy reply, I profane my lips on thy foot, my eyes on
    thy picture, and my heart on thy every part.
        Thine in the dearest design of industry,°   *gallantry?; diligence*
                Don Adriano de Armado.
    Thus dost thou hear the Nemean lion[8] roar
85   'Gainst thee, thou lamb, that standest as his prey.
    Submissive fall his princely feet before,
        And he from forage° will incline to play.   *raging*
    But if thou strive, poor soul, what art thou then?
    Food for his rage, repasture° for his den.'   *food*
90   PRINCESS   What plume of feathers° is he that indited° this   *silly bird / wrote*
    letter?

---

4. Part of the body, literalizing metaphorical use of "head" as "leader" (line 42); maidenhead.
5. Love letter; castrated male chicken.

6. See 1.2.99.
7. Originally said by Julius Caesar.
8. Killed by Hercules as the first of his labors.

What vane?[9] What weathercock?[c] Did you ever hear better?   *(example of showiness)*

BOYET   I am much deceived but I remember the style.

PRINCESS   Else your memory is bad, going o'er[1] it erewhile.

BOYET   This Armado is a Spaniard that keeps° here in court,   *dwells*

95   A phantasim,° a Monarcho,[2] and one that makes sport   *fantastic being*

To° the Prince and his bookmates.   *For*

PRINCESS [*to* COSTARD]   Thou, fellow, a word.

Who gave thee this letter?

COSTARD   I told you—my lord.

PRINCESS   To whom shouldst thou give it?

COSTARD   From my lord to my lady.

PRINCESS   From which lord to which lady?

100   COSTARD   From my lord Biron, a good master of mine,

To a lady of France that he called Rosaline.

PRINCESS   Thou hast mistaken his letter. Come, lords, away.

[*To* ROSALINE, *giving her the letter*]

Here, sweet, put up this, 'twill be thine another day.°   *your turn will come*

Exit [*attended*]

BOYET   Who is the suitor? Who is the suitor?°   *(with pun on "shooter")*

ROSALINE   Shall I teach you to know?

BOYET   Ay, my continent° of beauty.   *container of all*

105   ROSALINE   Why, she that bears the bow.

Finely put off.°   *evaded*

BOYET   My lady goes to kill horns, but if thou marry,

Hang me by the neck if horns that year miscarry.[3]

Finely put on.°   *applied*

ROSALINE   Well then, I am the shooter.

110   BOYET   And who is your deer?°   *prey; dear*

ROSALINE   If we choose by the horns, yourself come not near.[4]

Finely put on indeed!

MARIA   You still wrangle with her, Boyet, and she strikes at the brow.[5]

BOYET   But she herself is hit lower[6]—have I hit her° now?   *found her out*

115   ROSALINE   Shall I come upon thee with an old saying that was a man when King Pépin of France was a little boy,[7] as touching the hit it?[8]

BOYET   So I may answer thee with one as old that was a woman when Queen Guinevere of Britain[9] was a little wench, as

120   touching the hit it.

ROSALINE [*sings*]

Thou canst not hit it, hit it, hit it,

Thou canst not hit it, my good man.

BOYET [*sings*]

An I cannot, cannot, cannot,

An I cannot, another can.   *Exit* [ROSALINE]

125   COSTARD   By my troth, most pleasant! How both did fit it!°   *sing well; (bawdy)*

MARIA   A mark° marvellous well shot, for they both did hit it.   *target*

---

9. Weathervane, often in the form of a heraldic banner; vanity.

1. Having read; having climbed (taking "style" in line 92 as "stile," "fence").

2. Pretentious person—from the nickname of an eccentric Italian of Shakespeare's time who claimed to be a monarch of the world.

3. If you do not soon cuckold your husband; possibly, if penises fail or lead to a miscarriage. From here through line 135, there are almost continuous sexual references.

4. Probably: If you want to be safe, don't come close, because you have cuckold's horns.

5. Aims well; taunts you about your cuckold's horns.

6. In the heart; in the genitals.

7. Was already old when Charlemagne's father (d. 768) was a little boy.

8. *the hit it:* bawdy popular round and the dance done to it.

9. Notoriously unfaithful wife of the legendary King Arthur.

BOYET   A mark—O mark but that mark! A mark, says my lady.
    Let the mark have a prick° in't to mete° at, if it may be.   *bull's-eye; penis / aim*
MARIA   Wide o' the bow hand¹—i'faith, your hand is out.°   *out of practice*
COSTARD   Indeed, a must shoot nearer, or he'll ne'er hit the
130   clout.°   *bull's-eye; (bawdy)*
BOYET   An if my hand be out, then belike your hand is in.²
COSTARD   Then will she get the upshoot³ by cleaving the pin.°   *center*
MARIA   Come, come, you talk greasily,° your lips grow foul.   *indecently*
COSTARD   She's too hard for you at pricks,° sir. Challenge her to   *archery; sex*
    bowl.
135 BOYET   I fear too much rubbing.⁴ Goodnight, my good owl.⁵
                    [Exeunt BOYET, MARIA, and CATHERINE]
COSTARD   By my soul, a swain, a most simple clown.
    Lord, Lord, how the ladies and I have put him down!
    O' my troth, most sweet jests, most incony° vulgar wit,   *fine-quality*
    When it comes so smoothly off, so obscenely,⁶ as it were, so fit!
140   Armado o'th' t'other side°—O, a most dainty° man!—   *by contrast / elegant*
    To see him walk before a lady and to bear her fan!
    To see him kiss his hand, and how most sweetly° a will swear,   *stylishly*
    And his page o' t'other side, that handful of wit—
    Ah heavens, it is a most pathetical nit!°   *affecting little fellow*
            Shout° within   *Loud voice; shooting*
145 Sola, sola!°   *Exit*   *hunting cry*

4.2

Enter DULL, HOLOFERNES *the pedant,*¹ *and* NATHANIEL
[*the curate*]

NATHANIEL   Very reverend° sport, truly, and done in the testi-   *respectable*
    mony° of a good conscience.   *with the warrant*
HOLOFERNES   The deer was, as you know—*sanguis*²—in blood,°   *robust*
    ripe as the pomewater° who now hangeth like a jewel in the   *kind of apple*
5   ear of *caelo*, the sky, the welkin, the heaven, and anon° falleth   *soon after*
    like a crab° on the face of *terra*, the soil, the land, the earth.   *crab apple*
NATHANIEL   Truly, Master Holofernes, the epithets are sweetly
    varied, like a scholar at the least. But, sir, I assure ye it was a
    buck of the first head.³
10 HOLOFERNES   Sir⁴ Nathaniel, *haud credo*.°   *I hardly think so*
DULL   'Twas not a 'auld grey doe', 'twas a pricket.⁵
HOLOFERNES   Most barbarous intimation!° Yet a kind of insinu-   *intrusion*
    ation, as it were *in via*, in way, of explication, *facere*,° as it were,   *to make*
    replication,° or rather *ostentare*, to show, as it were, his inclina-   *explanation*
15   tion after his undressed, unpolished, uneducated, unpruned,
    untrained, or rather unlettered, or ratherest unconfirmed,°   *inexperienced*
    fashion, to insert again° my '*haud credo*' for a deer.   *interpret*

1. Too far to the left side (a cry in archery).
2. If I'm out of practice (at archery, at sex), you're not.
3. Winning shot; ejaculation.
4. In the game of bowls, touching obstacles; sexual friction.
5. "Owl," a bird of night, is suggested by "Goodnight"; to "take owl" is to take offense; rhyming with "bowl," "owl" suggests "ole" (hole) in the sexual sense.
6. Inadvertently accurate; perhaps a blunder for "seemly."
4.2 Location: The King's park.
1. Holofernes—a character based on a warrior whose decapitation by the heroine of the apocryphal Book of Judith saves Jerusalem—was a familiar tyrant in medieval religious plays; also a doctor of theology and

tutor to Gargantua in Rabelais's *Gargantua and Panta-gruel*. Like the braggart soldier, the pedant or school-master was a stock character in commedia dell'arte (see Introduction); his prominence is due to the humanist-inspired, early Tudor educational reforms that presum-ably shaped Shakespeare's own formal education.
2. The Latin in this scene, some of it inaccurate, is translated only when the characters themselves fail to do so. It is often unclear whether an error is the char-acter's or the printer's.
3. With his first head of antlers; in his fifth year.
4. Used generally of graduates, including priests (like "Reverend").
5. Buck in its second year, with a sexual hint.

DULL   I said the deer was not a auld grey doe', 'twas a pricket.

HOLOFERNES   Twice-sod simplicity, *bis coctus*![6]

20   O thou monster ignorance, how deformed dost thou look!

NATHANIEL   Sir, he hath never fed of the dainties that are bred
    in a book.
He hath not eat paper, as it were, he hath not drunk ink. His
intellect is not replenished, he is only an animal, only sensible°   *capable of feeling*
    in the duller parts,
And such barren plants are set before us that we thankful
25   should be,
Which we of taste and feeling are, for those parts that do fruc-
    tify° in us more than he.   *bear fruit*
For as it would ill become me to be vain, indiscreet, or a fool,
So were there a patch set on learning[7] to see *him* in a school.
But *omne bene*° say I, being of an old father's° mind: *all is well / sage's*
30   'Many can brook the weather that love not the wind.'[8]

DULL   You two are bookmen. Can you tell me by your wit
What was a month old at Cain's birth that's not five weeks old
    as yet?

HOLOFERNES   *Dictynna*, Goodman° Dull, *Dictynna*, Goodman   *Yeoman*
    Dull.

35   DULL   What is '*Dictima*'?

NATHANIEL   A title to° Phoebe, to *luna*, to the moon.   *name for*

HOLOFERNES   The moon was a month old when Adam was no
    more,
And raught° not to five weeks when he came to five score.   *reached*
Th'allusion holds in the exchange.[9]

40   DULL   'Tis true, indeed, the collusion° holds in the exchange.   *(for "allusion")*

HOLOFERNES   God comfort° thy capacity, I say th'allusion holds   *pity*
    in the exchange.

DULL   And I say the pollution[1] holds in the exchange, for the
    moon is never but a month old—and I say beside that 'twas a
45   pricket that the Princess killed.

HOLOFERNES   Sir Nathaniel, will you hear an extemporal epi-
    taph on the death of the deer? And to humour the ignorant call
    I the deer the Princess killed a pricket.

NATHANIEL   *Perge*,° good Master Holofernes, *perge*, so it shall   *Proceed*
50   please you to abrogate scurrility.[2]

HOLOFERNES   I will something affect the letter,[3] for it argues°   *shows*
    facility.
The preyful° Princess pierced and pricked a pretty pleasing   *desirous of prey*
    pricket.
Some say a sore,[4] but not a sore till now made sore with
    shooting.
The dogs did yell; put 'l' to 'sore', then 'sorel'° jumps from   *buck in its third year*
55   thicket—
Or° pricket sore, or else sorel. The people fall a-hooting.   *Either*

---

6. *Twice . . . coctus*: Twice-boiled folly, twice-cooked;
"*coctus*" also continues the sexual innuendo of "pricket"
(line 18) with the suggestion of "cock."
7. It would mean that a fool ("patch") had been put to
his studies; there would be a black mark on learning.
8. Many can endure the weather while disliking some
of its features (?); one must live with what one cannot
change (proverbial).
9. The riddle works as well with Adam as with Cain.
1. Dull's blunder for "allusion" again, but in each case

a commentary on his interlocutors. "Collusion" can
refer to a verbal trick designed to promote collusion in
the sense of conspiracy; linguistic pollution occurs
when one favors difficult foreign words over straightforward English.
2. Perge . . . scurrility: proceed . . . avoid indecency.
Nathaniel is probably worrying about "pricket"—justifi-
ably, given line 53, below. "*Perge*" may suggest "purging."
3. I will to some extent aspire to alliteration.
4. Deer in its fourth year.

If sore be sore, then 'l'° to 'sore' makes fifty sores—O sore 'l'!   *Roman numeral for 50*
Of one sore I an hundred make by adding but one more 'l'.°   *50 more; moral*
NATHANIEL   A rare talent!°   *talon; ability*
60   DULL   If a talent be a claw, look how he claws° him with a talent.   *scratches; flatters*
HOLOFERNES   This is a gift that I have, simple, simple—a foolish
extravagant° spirit, full of forms, figures, shapes, objects, ideas,   *wandering*
apprehensions, motions,° revolutions.° These are begot in the   *impulses / reflections*
ventricle° of memory, nourished in the womb of *pia mater,*[5] and   *part of the brain*
65   delivered upon the mellowing of occasion.° But the gift is good   *when the time is ripe*
in those in whom it is acute, and I am thankful for it.
NATHANIEL   Sir, I praise the Lord for you, and so may my parishioners; for their sons are well tutored by you, and their daughters profit very greatly under you.[6] You are a good member of
70   the commonwealth.
HOLOFERNES   *Mehercle,*° if their sons be ingenious they shall   *By Hercules*
want° no instruction; if their daughters be capable, I will put it   *lack*
to them. But *Vir sapit qui pauca loquitur;*[7] a soul feminine
saluteth us.
Enter JAQUENETTA, *and* [COSTARD] *the clown*
75   JAQUENETTA   God give you good-morrow, Master Parson.
HOLOFERNES   Master Parson, *quasi*° 'pierce one'?[8] And if one   *as if*
should be pierced, which is the one?
COSTARD   Marry, Master Schoolmaster, he that is likeliest to° a   *most like*
hogshead.[9]
80   HOLOFERNES   'Of piercing a hogshead'°—a good lustre of con-   *getting drunk?*
ceit° in a turf of earth, fire enough for a flint, pearl enough for   *spark of imagination*
a swine[1]—'tis pretty, it is well.
JAQUENETTA   Good Master Parson, be so good as read me this
letter. It was given me by Costard, and sent me from Don Arm-
85   ado. I beseech you read it.
[*She gives the letter to* NATHANIEL, *who reads it*]
HOLOFERNES [*to himself*]   'Facile precor gelida quando pecas
omnia sub umbra ruminat',[2] and so forth. Ah, good old Mantuan! I may speak of thee as the traveller doth of Venice:
Venezia, Venezia,
90   *Chi non ti vede, chi non ti prezia.*[3]
Old Mantuan, old Mantuan— who understandeth thee not,
loves thee not. [*He sings*] Ut, re, sol, la, mi, fa.[4] [*To* NATHANIEL]
Under pardon, sir, what are the contents? Or rather, as
Horace° says in his—what, my soul—verses?   *ancient Roman poet*
95   NATHANIEL   Ay, sir, and very learned.
HOLOFERNES   Let me hear a staff,° a stanza, a verse. *Lege,*   *stanza*
domine.°   *Read, sir*

---

5. Membrane surrounding the brain.
6. In conjunction with "member" (line 69), "capable" (line 72), and "put it to them" (lines 72–73), probably bawdy.
7. "That man is wise that speaketh few things or words" (Lily's Latin grammar, translating a common proverb).
8. Pronounced like "parson" or "person"; bawdy.
9. Large cask used for beer or wine; fool.
1. To "cast pearls before swine," a biblical phrase, was already proverbial.
2. "Easily, I pray, since you are getting everything wrong under the cool shade, it ruminates." A nonsensical mis-

quotation of the first line of a Latin poem by the Italian poet (1448–1516) Mantuan, a poem well known even to schoolboys in Shakespeare's time. The correct Latin means: "Faustus, I pray, since the whole herd are chewing their cud in the cool shade." The errors may be the printer's rather than Holofernes' or Shakespeare's.
3. Italian proverb, translated by John Florio as "Venice, who seeth thee not, praiseth thee not" (*First Fruits,* 1578).
4. Notes of the scale ("ut" is the modern "do"). If Holofernes sings them as a scale, he gets them in the wrong order; but they may represent a tune.

NATHANIEL [*reads*] 'If love make me forsworn, how shall I swear
    to love?[5]
    Ah, never faith could hold, if not to beauty vowed.
100 Though to myself forsworn, to thee I'll faithful prove.
    Those thoughts to me were oaks,[6] to thee like osiers° bowed.   *willows*
Study his bias leaves,° and makes his book thine eyes,   *goes off course*
    Where all those pleasures live that art would comprehend.
If knowledge be the mark,° to know thee shall suffice   *aim*
105 Well learnèd is that tongue that well can thee commend;
    All ignorant that soul that sees thee without wonder;
Which is to me some praise that I thy parts° admire.   *qualities*
Thy eye Jove's lightning bears, thy voice his dreadful thunder,
    Which, not to anger bent, is music and sweet fire.
110 Celestial as thou art, O pardon, love, this wrong,
    That singeth heaven's praise with such an earthly tongue.'
HOLOFERNES You find not the apostrophus,° and so miss the   *elision mark*
    accent. Let me supervise° the canzonet.° Here are only num- *look over / little poem*
    bers ratified,° but for the elegancy, facility, and golden cadence *correct meters*
115 of poesy—*caret*.° Ovidius Naso[7] was the man. And why indeed *it is lacking*
    'Naso' but for smelling out the odoriferous flowers of fancy, the
    jerks of invention?[8] *Imitari*° is nothing. So doth the hound his *To imitate*
    master, the ape his keeper, the tired° horse his rider. But *domi-* *attired*
    cella—virgin—was this directed to you?
120 JAQUENETTA Ay, sir.[9]
HOLOFERNES I will overglance the superscript.° 'To the snow-   *address*
    white hand of the most beauteous Lady Rosaline.' I will look
    again on the intellect° of the letter for the nomination of the *meaning; contents*
    party writing to the person written unto. 'Your ladyship's in all
125 desired employment, Biron.' Sir Nathaniel, this Biron is one of
    the votaries with the King, and here he hath framed a letter to
    a sequent° of the stranger° Queen's, which, accidentally or by *follower / foreign*
    the way of progression,° hath miscarried. [*To* JAQUENETTA] Trip *in transit*
    and go,[1] my sweet, deliver this paper into the royal hand of the
130 King. It may concern much. Stay not thy compliment, I forgive
    thy duty.[2] Adieu.
JAQUENETTA Good Costard, go with me.—Sir, God save your
    life.
COSTARD Have with thee,° my girl.   *Exit* [*with* JAQUENETTA]   *I'll come with you*
135 NATHANIEL Sir, you have done this in the fear of God very reli-
    giously, and, as a certain father° saith—   *church father*
HOLOFERNES Sir, tell not me of the father; I do fear colourable
    colours.[3] But to return to the verses—did they please you, Sir
    Nathaniel?
140 NATHANIEL Marvellous well for the pen.°   *penmanship*

---

5. The beginning of a sonnet (lines 98–111), with six
stresses per line. Like the poems of Longueville
(4.3.55–68) and Dumaine (4.3.97–116), it was
reprinted in *The Passionate Pilgrime* (1599), a collection attributed to Shakespeare on the title page but
actually containing poetry by various writers.
6. Those resolutions that seemed to me to be as strong
as oaks.
7. The full name of the ancient Roman poet Ovid was
Publius Ovidius Naso; *nasus* is Latin for "nose."
8. The strokes of imagination.
9. Q reads: "sir from one mounsier *Berowne*, one of the

strange Queenes Lordes." Jaquenetta has just said
(lines 84–85) that Armado wrote and Costard gave her
the letter, and she can't know that Biron, who is not a
"strange" (foreign) courtier, actually composed it.
Probably the errors are Shakespeare's.
1. A common expression, the title of a popular song
and dance.
2. Do not delay in order to take leave politely. I excuse
you from making a curtsy.
3. I do mistrust plausible—but specious—arguments
(a rejection of popishness?).

HOLOFERNES   I do dine today at the father's of a certain pupil of
mine where, if before repast it shall please you to gratify° the   *grace; please*
table with a grace, I will on my privilege I have with the parents
of the foresaid child or pupil undertake your *ben venuto*,[4]
145   where I will prove those verses to be very unlearned, neither
savouring of poetry, wit, nor invention. I beseech your society.

NATHANIEL   And thank you too, for society, saith the text,[5] is the
happiness of life.

HOLOFERNES   And certes° the text most infallibly concludes it.   *certainly*
150   [*To* DULL] Sir, I do invite you too. You shall not say me nay.
Pauca verba.° Away, the gentles are at their game,[6] and we will   *Few words*
to our recreation.   *Exeunt*

4.3

Enter BIRON *with a paper in his hand, alone*

BIRON   The King, he is hunting the deer. I am coursing° myself.   *pursuing*
They have pitched a toil,° I am toiling in a pitch[1]—pitch that   *set a snare*
defiles. Defile—a foul word. Well, set thee down,° sorrow; for   *stay with me*
so they say the fool said, and so say I, and I the fool. Well
5   proved, wit! By the Lord, this love is as mad as Ajax, it kills
sheep,[2] it kills me, I a sheep—well proved again o' my side. I
will not love. If I do, hang me; i'faith, I will not. O, but her
eye! By this light, but for her eye I would not love her. Yes, for
her two eyes. Well, I do nothing in the world but lie, and lie in
10   my throat.° By heaven, I do love, and it hath taught me to   *scandalously*
rhyme and to be melancholy, and here [*showing a paper*] is
part of my rhyme, and here [*touching his breast*] my melancholy. Well, she hath one o' my sonnets already. The clown
bore it, the fool sent it, and the lady hath it. Sweet clown,
15   sweeter fool, sweetest lady. By the world, I would not care a pin
if the other three were in.° Here comes one with a paper. God   *similarly involved*
give him grace to groan.°   *(out of love)*

He stands aside.[3] *The* KING *entereth* [*with a paper*]

KING   Ay me!

BIRON [*aside*]   Shot, by heaven! Proceed, sweet Cupid, thou hast
20   thumped him with thy birdbolt under the left pap.° In faith,   *your arrow in the heart*
secrets.

KING [*reads*]   'So sweet a kiss the golden sun gives not[4]
                To those fresh morning drops upon the rose
                As thy eyebeams when their fresh rays have smote
25   The night of dew° that on my cheeks down flows.   *nightly tears*
                Nor shines the silver moon one-half so bright
                Through the transparent bosom of the deep
                As doth thy face through tears of mine give light.
                Thou shin'st in every tear that I do weep.
30   No drop but as a coach doth carry thee,
                So ridest thou triumphing in my woe.
                Do but behold the tears that swell in me
                And they thy glory through my grief will show.

---

4. Undertake your welcome (Italian).
5. No convincing source has been identified.
6. The gentlefolk are at their sport (hunting).
4.3. Location: Scene continues.
1. In tar; in Rosaline's eyes(?)
2. At the Greek siege of Troy, when Agamemnon
awards Achilles' armor to Odysseus, Ajax goes mad with

rage and kills a flock of sheep, believing them to be the
Greek army.
3. At line 74, Biron says, "here sit I in the sky." At some
point before then—perhaps here—he mounts to a
higher level.
4. The beginning of a sonnet that actually extends to
sixteen lines (lines 22–37).

But do not love thyself; then thou wilt keep
35   My tears for glasses,° and still make me weep.   *mirrors*
O Queen of queens, how far dost thou excel,
No thought can think nor tongue of mortal tell.*
How shall she know my griefs? I'll drop the paper.
Sweet leaves, shade° folly. Who is he comes here?   *hide*
        Enter LONGUEVILLE [*with papers*]. *The* KING *steps aside*
40 What, Longueville, and reading—listen, ear!
BIRON [*aside*]   Now in thy° likeness one more fool appear!   (*the King's*)
LONGUEVILLE   Ay me! I am forsworn.
BIRON [*aside*]   Why, he comes in like a perjure,° wearing papers.[5]   *perjurer*
KING [*aside*]   In love, I hope! Sweet fellowship in shame.
45 BIRON [*aside*]   One drunkard loves another of the name.
LONGUEVILLE   Am I the first that have been perjured so?
BIRON [*aside*]   I could put thee in comfort, not by two that I know.
Thou makest the triumviry,[6] the corner-cap° of society,   *three-cornered cap*
The shape of love's Tyburn,[7] that hangs up simplicity.°   *folly*
50 LONGUEVILLE   I fear these stubborn° lines lack power to move.   *rough*
O sweet Maria, empress of my love,
These numbers° will I tear, and write in prose.   *verses*
BIRON [*aside*]   O, rhymes are guards° on wanton Cupid's hose,   *decorative bands*
Disfigure not his slop.°   *breeches*
LONGUEVILLE   This same shall go.[8]
        He reads the sonnet
55 'Did not the heavenly rhetoric of thine eye,
        'Gainst whom the world cannot hold argument,
Persuade my heart to this false perjury?
Vows for thee broke deserve not punishment.
A woman I forswore, but I will prove,
60   Thou being a goddess, I forswore not thee.
My vow was earthly, thou a heavenly love.
        Thy grace° being gained cures all disgrace in me.   *favor*
Vows are but breath, and breath a vapour is.
        Then thou, fair sun, which on my earth dost shine,
65 Exhal'st° this vapour-vow; in thee it is.   *Draw up*
        If broken then, it is no fault of mine.
If by me broke, what fool is not so wise
To lose an oath to win a paradise?'
BIRON [*aside*]   This is the liver vein,[9] which makes flesh a deity,
70 A green goose° a goddess, pure, pure idolatry.   *silly girl; whore*
God amend us, God amend: we are much out o'th' way.°   *badly astray*
        Enter DUMAINE [*with a paper*]
LONGUEVILLE [*aside*]   By whom shall I send this? Company? Stay.
        [*He steps aside*]
BIRON [*aside*]   All hid, all hid—an old infant play.[1]
Like a demigod here sit I in the sky,
75 And wretched fools' secrets heedfully o'er-eye.
More sacks to the mill!° O heavens, I have my wish.   *More to come!*
Dumaine transformed—four woodcocks° in a dish!   *fools*
DUMAINE   O most divine Kate!

5. Wearing a poem (lines 55–68). Convicted perjurers were exposed by having to wear papers that explained their guilt.
6. You complete the triumvirate (group of three rulers).
7. The common place of execution in London, here metaphorically for gallows, which were triangular.
8. Either he has hesitated before tearing the paper, or he pieces it together, as if in response to Biron's aside.
9. Style of the lover (the liver was thought of as the seat of love).
1. Hide-and-seek ("play" means "game"); perhaps also a medieval religious play in which God views the actions from above, like Biron (line 74).

BIRON [*aside*]   O most profane coxcomb!°   *fool*

80   DUMAINE   By heaven, the wonder in a mortal eye!

BIRON [*aside*]   By earth, she is not, corporal;² there you lie.

DUMAINE   Her amber hairs for foul hath amber quoted.³

BIRON [*aside*]   An amber-coloured raven was well noted.⁴

DUMAINE   As upright as the cedar.

BIRON [*aside*]   Stoop,⁵ I say.

Her shoulder is with child.°   *bulging; bowed down*

85   DUMAINE   As fair as day.

BIRON [*aside*]   Ay, as some days; but then no sun must shine.

DUMAINE   O that I had my wish!

LONGUEVILLE [*aside*]   And I had mine!

KING [*aside*]   And I mine too, good Lord!

90   BIRON [*aside*]   Amen, so I had mine. Is not that a good word?⁶

DUMAINE   I would forget her, but a fever she

Reigns in my blood and will remembered be.

BIRON [*aside*]   A fever in your blood—why then, incision°   *bloodletting*

Would let her out in saucers⁷—sweet misprision.°   *misinterpretation*

95   DUMAINE   Once more I'll read the ode that I have writ.

BIRON [*aside*]   Once more I'll mark how love can vary° wit.   *inspire; impair*

    DUMAINE *reads his sonnet*

DUMAINE   'On a day—alack the day—

Love, whose month is ever May,

Spied a blossom passing° fair   *surpassingly*

100   Playing in the wanton° air.   *playful*

Through the velvet leaves the wind

All unseen can° passage find,   *did*

That° the lover, sick to death,   *So that*

Wished himself the heavens' breath.

105   "Air", quoth he, "thy cheeks may blow;

Air, would I might triumph so.

But, alack, my hand is sworn

Ne'er to pluck thee from thy thorn—

Vow, alack, for youth unmeet,°   *inappropriate*

110   Youth so apt to pluck a sweet.

Do not call it sin in me

That I am forsworn for thee,

Thou for whom great Jove would swear

Juno but an Ethiop⁸ were,

115   And deny himself for° Jove,   *to be*

Turning mortal for thy love.'"

This will I send, and something else more plain,

That shall express my true love's fasting pain.

O, would the King, Biron, and Longueville

120   Were lovers too! Ill to example° ill   *be a precedent for*

Would from my forehead wipe a perjured note,⁹

For none offend where all alike do dote.

---

2. Officer in Cupid's army; perhaps, corporeal, or human. The possible application to both Dumaine and Catherine, but in different ways, is characteristic of Biron's asides here.
3. Her amber-colored hairs have caused amber itself to be regarded as foul by comparison.
4. Dumaine is an acute observer, Biron remarks ironically, in describing Catherine's black hair as amber. (Catherine is the raven, a black fowl, punningly sug-

(she is merely) gested by "foul," line 82.)
5. She's stooped; come down to earth.
6. Isn't that a kind wish; isn't "Amen" a "good word"?
7. Into basins used to catch the blood; by the basinful.
8. Black African (used here in racist fashion to signify ugliness).
9. Inscription (and see Biron's description of Longueville, line 43).

LONGUEVILLE [*coming forward*] Dumaine, thy love is far from
    charity,°   *Christian love*
    That in love's grief desir'st society.°   *company*
125   You may look pale, but I should blush, I know,
    To be o'erheard and taken napping so.
    KING [*coming forward*] Come, sir, you blush. As his, your case
        is such.
    You chide at him, offending twice as much.
    You do not love Maria? Longueville
130   Did never sonnet for her sake compile,
    Nor never lay his wreathèd arms athwart[1]
    His loving bosom to keep down his heart?
    I have been closely° shrouded in this bush,   *secretly*
    And marked you both, and for you both did blush.
135   I heard your guilty rhymes, observed your fashion,
    Saw sighs reek° from you, noted well your passion.   *rise*
    'Ay me!' says one, 'O Jove!' the other cries.
    One, her hairs were gold; crystal the other's eyes.
    [*To* LONGUEVILLE] You would for paradise break faith and troth,
140   [*To* DUMAINE] And Jove for your love would infringe an oath.
    What will Biron say when that he shall hear
    Faith so infringèd, which such zeal did swear?
    How will he scorn, how will he spend his wit!
    How will he triumph, leap, and laugh at it!
145   For all the wealth that ever I did see
    I would not have him know so much by° me.   *about*
    BIRON [*coming forward*] Now step I forth to whip hypocrisy.
    Ah, good my liege, I pray thee pardon me.
    Good heart, what grace hast thou thus to reprove
150   These worms for loving, that art most in love?
    Your eyes do make no coaches.° In your tears   *(see lines 31–32)*
    There is no certain princess that appears.
    You'll not be perjured, 'tis a hateful thing;
    Tush, none but minstrels like of sonneting!
155   But are you not ashamed, nay, are you not,
    All three of you, to be thus much o'ershot?°   *wide of the mark*
    [*To* LONGUEVILLE] You found his° mote, the King your mote   *(Dumaine's)*
        did see,
    But I a beam[2] do find in each of three.
    O, what a scene of fool'ry have I seen,
160   Of sighs, of groans, of sorrow, and of teen!°   *grief*
    O me, with what strict patience have I sat,
    To see a king transformèd to a gnat!
    To see great Hercules whipping a gig,°   *spinning a top*
    And profound Solomon to tune° a jig,   *play*
165   And Nestor[3] play at pushpin° with the boys,   *child's game*
    And critic Timon[4] laugh at idle toys!°   *foolish fancies*
    Where lies thy grief, O tell me, good Dumaine?
    And, gentle Longueville, where lies thy pain?
    And where my liege's? All about the breast.

---

1. Folded arms across. (Folded arms were a sign of love melancholy.)
2. Larger defect: "And why beholdest thou the mote that is in thy brother's eye, but considerest [or "perceivest"] not the beam that is in thine own eye?"

(Matthew 7:3–5; Luke 6:41–42).
3. Homeric hero, a type figure of wise old age; later portrayed in Shakespeare's *Troilus and Cressida.*
4. Cynical Greek misanthrope; later, the central character of Shakespeare's *Timon of Athens.*

A caudle,° ho!   *warm, healing drink*

170 KING   Too bitter is thy jest.
Are we betrayed thus to thy over-view?
BIRON   Not you to me, but I betrayed by you.
I that am honest, I that hold it sin
To break the vow I am engagèd in.
175 I am betrayed by keeping company
With men like you, men of inconstancy.
When shall you see me write a thing in rhyme,
Or groan for Joan, or spend a minute's time
In pruning me?° When shall you hear that I   *preening myself*
180 Will praise a hand, a foot, a face, an eye,
A gait, a state,° a brow, a breast, a waist,   *an attitude; bearing*
A leg, a limb?
KING   Soft, whither away so fast?
A true° man or a thief, that gallops so?   *an honest*
BIRON   I post° from love; good lover, let me go.   *hasten*
        Enter JAQUENETTA [*with a letter,*] *and* [COSTARD *the*]
        clown
JAQUENETTA   God bless the King!
185 KING   What present° hast thou there?   *writing; gift*
COSTARD   Some certain treason.
KING   What makes treason° here?   *is treason doing*
COSTARD   Nay, it makes nothing, sir.
KING   If it mar nothing neither,
The treason and you go in peace away together!
JAQUENETTA   I beseech your grace, let this letter be read.
190 Our parson misdoubts° it; 'twas treason, he said.   *suspects*
KING   Biron, read it over.
        [BIRON *takes and*] *reads the letter*
        [*To* JAQUENETTA] Where hadst thou it?
JAQUENETTA   Of Costard.
KING [*to* COSTARD]   Where hadst thou it?
195 COSTARD   Of Dun Adramadio,⁵ Dun Adramadio.
        [BIRON *tears the letter*]
KING [*to* BIRON]   How now, what is in you? Why dost thou tear it?
BIRON   A toy, my liege, a toy. Your grace needs not fear it.
LONGUEVILLE   It did move him to passion, and therefore let's hear it.
DUMAINE [*taking up a piece of the letter*]   It is Biron's writing,
        and here is his name.
BIRON [*to* COSTARD]   Ah, you whoreson loggerhead,° you were   *foolish blockhead*
200   born to do me shame!
Guilty, my lord, guilty! I confess, I confess.
KING   What?
BIRON   That you three fools lacked me fool to make up the
        mess.°   *group of four at table*
He, he, and you—e'en you, my liege—and I
205 Are pickpurses° in love, and we deserve to die.   *cheaters*
O, dismiss this audience, and I shall tell you more.
DUMAINE   Now the number is even.
BIRON   True, true; we are four.
Will these turtles° be gone?   *turtledoves; lovers*
KING   Hence, sirs; away.

---

5. *Dun:* error for Don meaning "gray-brown," referring to skin color and recalling "tawny Spain" (1.1.171). *Adra-*
madio: error for Adriano that encompasses "drama," "mad," "amado" (loved).

COSTARD Walk aside the true folk, and let the traitors stay.
          [*Exeunt* COSTARD *and* JAQUENETTA]
210 BIRON Sweet lords, sweet lovers!—O, let us embrace.
          As true we are as flesh and blood can be.
          The sea will ebb and flow, heaven show his face.
          Young blood doth not obey an old decree.
          We cannot cross° the cause why we were born,   oppose
215   Therefore of all hands° must we be forsworn.   in any case
    KING What, did these rent° lines show some love of thine?   torn
    BIRON 'Did they', quoth you? Who sees the heavenly Rosaline
          That, like a rude° and savage man of Ind°   an ignorant / India
          At the first op'ning of the gorgeous east,
220   Bows not his vassal head and, strucken blind,
          Kisses the base ground with obedient breast?
          What peremptory° eagle-sighted eye⁶   determined
          Dares look upon the heaven of her brow
          That is not blinded by her majesty?
225 KING What zeal, what fury hath inspired thee now?
          My love, her mistress, is a gracious moon,
          She an attending star, scarce seen a light.°   hardly visible
    BIRON My eyes are then no eyes, nor I Biron.
          O, but for my love, day would turn to night.
230   Of all complexions the culled sovereignty°   those chosen as best
          Do meet as at a fair in her fair cheek,
          Where several worthies make one dignity,⁷
          Where nothing wants° that want° itself doth seek.   lacks / desire
          Lend me the flourish of all gentle tongues—
235   Fie, painted rhetoric! O, she needs it not.
          To things of sale a seller's praise belongs.
          She passes praise—then praise too short doth blot.⁸
          A withered hermit fivescore winters worn
          Might shake off fifty, looking in her eye.
240   Beauty doth varnish age as if new-born,
          And gives the crutch the cradle's infancy.
          O, 'tis the sun that maketh all things shine.
    KING By heaven, thy love is black as ebony.
    BIRON Is ebony like her? O word divine!
245   A wife of such wood were felicity.
          O, who can give an oath? Where is a book,°   a Bible
          That I may swear beauty doth beauty lack
          If that she learn not of her eye to look?⁹
          No face is fair that is not full so° black.   just as
250 KING O paradox! Black is the badge of hell,
          The hue of dungeons and the style¹ of night,
          And beauty's crest becomes the heavens well.²
    BIRON Devils soonest tempt, resembling spirits of light.³
          O, if in black my lady's brows be decked,
255   It mourns that painting and usurping hair°   makeup and false hair

6. The eagle, king of birds, was thought to be the only one able to look directly at the sun.
7. Various kinds of excellence together produce a single preeminent beauty.
8. Hence praise inevitably falls short and mars her reputation.
9. If beauty doesn't learn from Rosaline's eye how she (beauty) could look.
1. Title. Q, F: Schoole. The phrase "school of night"

has been supposed to refer to a secret society of Shakespeare's time; alternatively, it may mean that night learns to be black in black's school.
2. (And yet, you say, the badge of your dark beauty is heavenly (said incredulously); it is the sun, not your dark beauty, that is heavenly.
3. Fair beauties are not to be trusted, "for Satan himself is transformed into an angel of light" (2 Corinthians 11:14).

Should ravish doters with a false aspect,
    And therefore is she born to make black fair.
Her favour° turns the fashion of the days,   *appearance*
    For native blood° is counted painting now,   *natural red coloring*
260 And therefore red that would avoid dispraise
    Paints itself black to imitate her brow.
DUMAINE To look like her are chimney-sweepers black.
LONGUEVILLE And since her time are colliers counted bright.
KING And Ethiops of their sweet complexion crack.°   *boast*
265 DUMAINE Dark needs no candles now, for dark is light.
BIRON Your mistresses dare never come in rain,
    For fear their colours should be washed away.
KING 'Twere good yours did; for, sir, to tell you plain,
    I'll find a fairer face not washed today.
270 BIRON I'll prove her fair, or talk till doomsday here.
KING No devil will fright thee then° so much as she.   *(at doomsday)*
DUMAINE I never knew man hold vile stuff so dear.
LONGUEVILLE [*showing his foot*] Look, here's thy love—my foot
        and her face see.[4]
BIRON O, if the streets were pavèd with thine eyes
275 Her feet were much too dainty for such tread.
DUMAINE O vile! Then as she goes, what upward lies°   *(bawdy)*
    The street should see as she walked overhead.
KING But what of this? Are we not all in love?
BIRON Nothing so sure, and thereby all forsworn.
280 KING Then leave this chat and, good Biron, now prove
    Our loving lawful and our faith not torn.
DUMAINE Ay, marry there, some flattery° for this evil.   *excuse*
LONGUEVILLE O, some authority how to proceed,
    Some tricks, some quillets° how to cheat the devil.   *verbal tricks*
DUMAINE Some salve for perjury.°   *oath breaking; purging*
285 BIRON   O, 'tis more than need.
    Have at you,° then, affection's° men-at-arms.   *Here goes / love's*
    Consider what you first did swear unto:
    To fast, to study, and to see no woman—
    Flat treason 'gainst the kingly state of youth.
290 Say, can you fast? Your stomachs are too young,
    And abstinence engenders maladies.[5]
291.1 *And where that° you have vowed to study, lords,*   *And whereas*
    In that[6] each of you have forsworn his book,
    Can you still dream, and pore, and thereon look?
    For when would you, my lord, or you, or you,
291.5 *Have found the ground of study's excellence*
    Without the beauty of a woman's face?
    From women's eyes this doctrine I derive.
    They are the ground, the books, the academes,
    From whence doth spring the true Promethean fire.
291.10 *Why, universal plodding poisons up*
    The nimble° spirits in the arteries,   *life-giving*
    As motion and long-during° action tires   *long-lasting*

4. You may see her face in my (black) shoes.
5. The following twenty-three indented lines (291.1–291.23) represent an unrevised version of parts of Biron's long speech, 4.3.285–91, 292–339. The first six lines form the basis of 292–97; the next three are revised at 4.3.324–28; the next four at 4.3.298–300; the last nine are less directly related to the revised version.
6. Inasmuch as; in that vow.

The sinewy vigour of the traveller.
Now, for not looking on a woman's face
291.15   You have in that forsworn the use of eyes,
And study, too, thecause of your vow.
For where is any author in the world
Teaches such beauty as a woman's eye?
Learning is but an adjunct to ourself,
291.20   And where we are, our learning likewise is.
Then when ourselves we see in ladies' eyes
With ourselves.
    Do we not likewise see our learning there?
O, we have made a vow to study, lords,
And in that vow we have forsworn our books;[7]
For when would you, my liege, or you, or you
295   In leaden contemplation have found out
Such fiery numbers° as the prompting eyes   *passionate verses*
Of beauty's tutors have enriched you with?
Other slow arts° entirely keep° the brain,   *disciplines / inhabit*
And therefore, finding barren practisers,
300   Scarce show a harvest of their heavy toil.
But love, first learnèd in a lady's eyes,
Lives not alone immurèd° in the brain,   *only shut up*
But with the motion of all elements[8]
Courses as swift as thought in every power,°   *faculty*
305   And gives to every power a double power
Above° their functions and their offices.°   *Beyond / normal duties*
It adds a precious seeing to the eye—
A lover's eyes will gaze an eagle blind.[9]
A lover's ear will hear the lowest sound
310   When the suspicious head of theft is stopped.[1]
Love's feeling is more soft and sensible°   *sensitive*
Than are the tender horns of cockled snails.°   *snails with shells*
Love's tongue proves dainty Bacchus° gross in taste.   *Greek god of wine*
For valour, is not love a Hercules,
315   Still° climbing trees in the Hesperides?[2]   *Constantly*
Subtle as Sphinx,[3] as sweet and musical
As bright Apollo's° lute strung with his hair;   *Greek god of music*
And when love speaks, the voice of all the gods
Make heaven drowsy with the harmony.
320   Never durst poet touch a pen to write
Until his ink were tempered with love's sighs.
O, then his lines would ravish savage ears,
And plant in tyrants mild humility.
From women's eyes this doctrine I derive.
325   They sparkle still the right Promethean fire.[4]
They are the books, the arts, the academes
That show, contain, and nourish all the world,
Else none° at all in aught proves excellent.   *Without them no one*
Then fools you were these women to forswear,

7. Our true books, women's eyes.
8. Earth, air, fire, and water.
9. Can stare at the sun (here, the beloved woman) without injury longer than even an eagle can.
1. When even an alert thief (or someone listening for a thief) hears nothing.

2. Garden of golden apples that Hercules had to pick as his eleventh labor.
3. Monster in Greek mythology that killed travelers who failed to solve her riddle.
4. Divine fire. In Greek mythology Prometheus stole fire from heaven and gave it to humanity.

330   Or keeping what is sworn, you will prove fools.
    For wisdom's sake—a word that all men love—
    Or for love's sake—a word that loves⁵ all men—
    Or for men's sake—the authors of these women—
    Or women's sake—by whom we men are men—
335   Let us once lose our oaths to find ourselves,⁶
    Or else we lose ourselves to keep our oaths.
    It is religion to be thus forsworn,
    For charity itself fulfils the law,⁷
    And who can sever love from charity?
340 KING   Saint Cupid, then, and, soldiers, to the field!
BIRON   Advance your standards,° and upon them, lords.   *(with a sexual sense)*
    Pell-mell, down with them; but be first advised
    In conflict that you get the sun of them.⁸
LONGUEVILLE   Now to plain dealing. Lay these glozes° by.   *verbal sophistries*
345   Shall we resolve to woo these girls of France?
KING   And win them, too! Therefore let us devise
    Some entertainment for them in their tents.
BIRON   First, from the park let us conduct them thither;
    Then homeward every man attach° the hand   *seize*
350   Of his fair mistress. In the afternoon
    We will with some strange° pastime solace them,   *novel*
    Such as the shortness of the time can shape,
    For revels, dances, masques, and merry hours
    Forerun° fair love, strewing her way with flowers.   *Run before*
355 KING   Away, away, no time shall be omitted
    That will be time,° and may by us be fitted.°   *long enough / used well*
BIRON   *Allons, allons!*° Sowed cockle reaped no corn,⁹   *Come on*
    And justice always whirls in equal measure.°   *acts impartially*
    Light° wenches may prove plagues to men forsworn.   *Frivolous*
360   If so, our copper buys° no better treasure.   *[Exeunt]*   *base coin deserves*

5.1

Enter [HOLOFERNES] *the pedant,* [NATHANIEL] *the
curate, and* [Anthony] DULL

HOLOFERNES   *Satis quid sufficit.*¹
NATHANIEL   I praise God for you, sir. Your reasons° at dinner   *discourses*
    have been sharp and sententious, pleasant without scurrility,
    witty without affection,° audacious without impudency,   *affectation*
5   learned without opinion,° and strange° without heresy. I did   *arrogance / original*
    converse this quondam day° with a companion of the King's   *the other day*
    who is intituled, nominated, or called Don Adriano de
    Armado.
HOLOFERNES   *Novi hominum tanquam te.*² His humour° is lofty,   *temperament*
10   his discourse peremptory,° his tongue filed,° his eye ambitious,   *overbearing / polished*
    his gait majestical, and his general behaviour vain, ridiculous,

---

5. Meaning uncertain: is a friend to; values; pleases; inspires with love; is lovable to.
6. "For whosoever will save his life shall lose it: and whosoever will lose his life for my sake shall find it" (Matthew 16:25).
7. "He that loveth another hath fulfilled the law" (Romans 13:8). "Love worketh no ill to his neighbour: therefore is love the fulfilling of the law" (Romans 13:10).
8. Get the sun in their eyes (get the advantage); also, probably bawdy, playing on "beget the son."
9. Wheat ("corn") was never reaped where weeds ("cockle") were sown (proverbial): in other words, we won't get something for nothing; we must make an effort.
5.1 Location: The King's park.
1. Should be *Satis est quod sufficit*: Enough is enough, but recalling the English proverb "Enough is as good as a feast." The Latin in this scene, some of it inaccurate, again is translated only when the characters themselves fail to do so. Here, too, it is often unclear whether the error is the character's, the printer's, or Shakespeare's.
2. I know the man as well as I know you.

and thrasonical.[3] He is too picked,[2] too spruce, too affected,   *fastidious*
too odd, as it were, too peregrinate,° as I may call it.   *exotic*

NATHANIEL   A most singular and choice epithet.

       Draw[s] out his table-book°   *notebook*

15   HOLOFERNES   He draweth out the thread of his verbosity finer
than the staple of his argument.[4] I abhor such fanatical phantasims,[5] such insociable and point-device° companions, such   *extremely precise*
rackers of orthography[6] as to speak 'dout', *sine*° 'b'. when he   *without*
should say 'doubt'; 'det' when he should pronounce 'debt'—'d,
20   e, b, t', not 'd, e, t'. He clepeth° a calf 'cauf', half 'hauf',   *calls*
neighbour *vocatur*° 'nebour'—'neigh' abbreviated 'ne'. This is   *is called*
abhominable—which he would call 'abominable'. It insinu-
ateth me of *insanire*[7]—*ne intelligis, domine?*[8]—to make frantic,
lunatic.

25   NATHANIEL   *Laus deo, bone intelligo.*[9]
HOLOFERNES   *Bone? Bon, fort bon*—Priscian a little scratched—
'twill serve.

      Enter [ARMADO *the*] *braggart,* [MOTE *his*] *boy* [*and* cos-
      TARD *the clown*]

NATHANIEL   *Videsne quis venit?*°   *Do you see who's coming?*
HOLOFERNES   *Video, et gaudio.*°   *I see, and rejoice*
30   ARMADO [*to* MOTE]   Chirrah.[2]
HOLOFERNES [*to* NATHANIEL]   *Quare*° chirrah', not 'sirrah'?   *Why*
ARMADO   Men of peace, well encountered.
HOLOFERNES   Most military sir, salutation!
MOTE [*aside to* COSTARD]   They have been at a great feast of lan-
35   guages and stolen the scraps.
COSTARD [*aside to* MOTE]   O, they have lived long on the alms-
basket[3] of words. I marvel thy master hath not eaten thee for a
word, for thou art not so long by the head as *honorificabilitu-
dinitatibus.*[4] Thou art easier swallowed than a flapdragon.[5]
40   MOTE [*aside to* COSTARD]   Peace, the peal° begins.   *jangling; babble*
ARMADO [*to* HOLOFERNES]   Monsieur, are you not lettered?°   *learned; literate*
MOTE   Yes, yes, he teaches boys the horn-book.° What is 'a, b'   *alphabet book*
spelled backward, with the horn on his head?°   *a cuckold*
HOLOFERNES   Ba, *pueritia,*° with a horn added.   *child(ishness)*
45   MOTE   Ba, most silly sheep, with a horn! You hear his learning.
HOLOFERNES   *Quis, quis,*° thou consonant?[6]   *Who*
MOTE   The last of the five vowels if you repeat them, or the
fifth° if I.   *"u"; you; ewe*
HOLOFERNES   I will repeat them: a, e, i—
50   MOTE   The sheep.[7] The other two concludes it: o, u.[8]

---

3. Boastful, bragging. From "Thraso," the braggart soldier in *Eunuchus,* by the Roman dramatist Terence.
4. He's wordy. (Unintentionally ironic, coming from
Holofernes; "staple" means "fiber," "argument" means
"subject matter.")
5. Extravagant, fantastic beings.
6. Tormentors of spelling. Holofernes speaks for those
educational theorists who urged, unsuccessfully, that
English words be spelled and pronounced like their
Latin roots.
7. Puts me in mind of madness; perhaps, drives me mad.
8. Don't you understand, master?
9. Praise God, I understand well.
1. Bone? Bon, fort bon: Well? Good, that's good
(French; ironical). *Priscian a little scratched:* imperfect
Latin (Priscian was a sixth-century Latin grammarian.
Holofernes is ridiculing Nathaniel's mistake of using

bone for *bene.*
2. Pseudo-Spanish or dialectal pronunciation of "Sirrah"; or garbled Greek for "Hail."
3. Basket in which the leftovers of a feast were collected for the poor.
4. Dative and ablative plural of a Latin word meaning
"honorableness," renowned for its length. *word:* "mote"
equals the French *mot,* which means "word."
5. A raisin floated on flaming brandy, which had to be
snapped up with the mouth and eaten in the game of
snapdragon.
6. Nonentity (because a consonant alone is soundless).
7. The Spanish for "sheep"—*oveja,* often spelled
oueia—seems to have been used as a device for memo-
rizing the vowels.
8. Proves what I say or completes the list): oh, you.

ARMADO   Now by the salt° wave of the *Mediterraneum* a sweet   *salty; witty*
touch,° a quick venue° of wit; snip, snap, quick, and home.⁹ It   *hit / thrust*
rejoiceth my intellect—true wit.

MOTE   Offered by a child to an old man, which is 'wit-old'.¹

55 HOLOFERNES   What is the figure?° What is the figure?   *figure of speech*

MOTE   Horns.

HOLOFERNES   Thou disputes like an infant. Go whip thy gig.°   *spin your top*

MOTE   Lend me your horn to make one, and I will whip about
your infamy *circum circa*²—a gig of° a cuckold's horn.   *made of*

60 COSTARD   An° I had but one penny in the world, thou shouldst   *If*
have it to buy gingerbread. [*Giving money*] Hold, there is the
very remuneration I had of thy master, thou halfpenny° purse   *tiny*
of wit, thou pigeon-egg of discretion. O, an the heavens were
so pleased that thou wert but my bastard, what a joyful father

65 wouldst thou make me! Go to, thou hast it *ad dunghill*, at the
fingers' ends,° as they say.   *exactly; scatological*

HOLOFERNES   O, I smell false Latin—'*dunghill*' for *unguem*.°   *fingernail*

ARMADO   Arts-man, *preambulate*.³ We will be singled° from the   *separated*
barbarous. Do you not educate youth at the charge-house° on   *endowed school*

70 the top of the mountain?

HOLOFERNES   Or *mons*, the hill.

ARMADO   At your sweet pleasure, for the mountain.

HOLOFERNES   I do, sans° question.   *without*

ARMADO   Sir, it is the King's most sweet pleasure and affection°   *wish*

75 to congratulate° the Princess at her pavilion in the posteriors⁴   *greet*
of this day, which the rude multitude call the afternoon.

HOLOFERNES   The posterior of the day, most generous° sir, is lia-   *noble*
ble, congruent, and measurable° for the afternoon. The word   *suitable (synonyms)*
is well culled,⁵ choice, sweet, and apt, I do assure you, sir, I do

80 assure.

ARMADO   Sir, the King is a noble gentleman, and my familiar,° I   *close friend*
do assure ye, very good friend. For what is inward° between us,   *confidential*
let it pass. I do beseech thee, remember thy courtesy. I beseech
thee, apparel thy head.⁶ And, among other important and most

85 serious designs, and of great import indeed, too—but let that
pass,⁷ for I must tell thee it will please his grace, by the world,
sometime to lean upon my poor shoulder and with his royal
finger thus dally with my excrement,° with my mustachio. But,   *growth of hair; feces*
sweetheart, let that pass. By the world, I recount no fable. Some

90 certain special honours it pleaseth his greatness to impart to
Armado, a soldier, a man of travel, that hath seen the world.
But let that pass. The very all of all° is—but, sweetheart, I do   *sum of everything*
implore secrecy—that the King would have me present the
Princess—sweet chuck°—with some delightful ostentation,° or   *chick / spectacular show*

95 show, or pageant, or antic,° or firework. Now, understanding   *grotesque pageant*
that the curate and your sweet self are good at such eruptions°   *(scatological)*
and sudden breaking-out° of mirth, as it were, I have acquainted   *(scatological)*
you withal° to the end to crave your assistance.   *with it*

9. And to the target.
1. Mentally feeble; "wittol," a content cuckold.
2. Around and around.
3. Scholar, walk ahead, with a play on "arse."
4. End (temporal and anatomical).
5. With a play on "cul," French for backside.

6. *remember . . . head:* remember that you removed
your hat in courtesy (perhaps at line 33). I beseech you,
put it back on.
7. Suggestion of sodomy, developed in the repeated
phrase "but [butt] let that pass" (lines 85–86, 88–89,
92).

HOLOFERNES   Sir, you shall present before her the Nine Wor-
100 thies.[8] Sir Nathaniel, as concerning some entertainment of°   *way of spending*
time, some show in the posterior of this day to be rendered by
our assistance, the King's command, and this most gallant,
illustrate,° and learned gentlemen before the Princess, I say   *illustrious*
none so fit as to present the Nine Worthies.

105 NATHANIEL   Where will you find men worthy enough to present
them?

HOLOFERNES   Joshua, yourself;[9] myself, Judas Maccabeus; and
this gallant gentleman, Hector. This swain, because of his great
limb or joint, shall pass Pompey the Great;[1] the page, Hercules.

110 ARMADO   Pardon, sir, error! He is not quantity enough for that
Worthy's thumb. He is not so big as the end of his club.

HOLOFERNES   Shall I have audience?° He shall present Hercules   *attention*
in minority.° His enter° and exit shall be strangling a snake,[2]   *childhood / entrance*
and I will have an apology° for that purpose.   *explanatory speech*

115 MOTE   An excellent device! So, if any of the audience hiss, you
may cry 'Well done, Hercules, now thou crushest the snake!'—
that is the way to make an offence gracious, though few have
the grace to do it.

ARMADO   For the rest of the Worthies?

120 HOLOFERNES   I will play three myself.

MOTE   Thrice-worthy gentleman!

ARMADO   Shall I tell you a thing?

HOLOFERNES   We attend.°   *listen*

ARMADO   We will have, if this fadge° not, an antic. I beseech you,   *succeed*
125 follow.

HOLOFERNES   *Via,*° goodman Dull! Thou hast spoken no word   *Come on*
all this while.

DULL   Nor understood none neither, sir.

HOLOFERNES   *Allons!*° We will employ thee.   *Come on*

130 DULL   I'll make one° in a dance or so, or I will play on the tabor°   *join / small drum*
to the Worthies, and let them dance the hay.°   *reel*

HOLOFERNES   Most dull, honest Dull! To our sport, away.
Exeunt

5.2

Enter the [PRINCESS *and her*] *ladies* [ROSALINE, MARIA,
and CATHERINE]

PRINCESS   Sweethearts, we shall be rich ere we depart,
    If fairings° come thus plentifully in.   *gifts*
    A lady walled about with diamonds[1]—
    Look you what I have from the loving King.

5 ROSALINE   Madam, came nothing else along with that?

PRINCESS   Nothing but this?—yes, as much love in rhyme
    As would be crammed up in a sheet of paper
    Writ o' both sides the leaf, margin and all,
    That he was fain to seal on Cupid's name.[2]

---

8. Famous conquerors often represented in folk plays
and pageants. Usually three pagans—Hector, Alexander,
Julius Caesar; three Jews—Joshua, David, Judas Maccabeus; and three Christians—Arthur, Charlemagne,
and Godfrey of Bouillon or Guy of Warwick. Of these,
only Alexander, Judas Maccabeus, and Hector appear in
the next scene; Shakespeare adds Pompey and Hercules.
9. In the event, Nathaniel plays Alexander.
1. *great . . . Great:* Costard's considerable size allows

him to "pass" for Pompey the Great, suggesting "penis"
through "limb" or "joint," and, through the jingle with
"pump" in "Pompey," both "penis" and "pudendum."
2. Hercules strangled two snakes sent by Juno to kill
him in his cradle.
5.2 Location: The ladies' lodgings in the King's park.
1. This describes the gift (a pendant or brooch).
2. So that he was obliged to obliterate Cupid's name
with his seal.

10   ROSALINE   That was the way to make his godhead wax,°   *grow; sealing wax*
         For he hath been five thousand year° a boy.   *(age of the world)*
     CATHERINE   Ay, and a shrewd unhappy gallows,[3] too.
     ROSALINE   You'll ne'er be friends with him, a° killed your sister.   *he*
     CATHERINE   He made her melancholy, sad, and heavy,
15   And so she died. Had she been light like you,
         Of such a merry, nimble, stirring spirit,
         She might ha' been a grandam ere she died;
         And so may you, for a light heart lives long.
     ROSALINE   What's your dark° meaning, mouse, of this light°   *covert / careless*
         word?
20   CATHERINE   A light° condition in a beauty dark.   *frivolous; wanton*
     ROSALINE   We need more light to find your meaning out.
     CATHERINE   You'll mar the light by taking it in snuff,[4]
         Therefore I'll darkly end the argument.
     ROSALINE   Look what° you do, you do it still i'th' dark.°   *whatever / (bawdy)*
25   CATHERINE   So do not you, for you are a light wench.
     ROSALINE   Indeed I weigh not° you, and therefore light.   *weigh less than*
     CATHERINE   You weigh me not? O, that's you care not for me.
     ROSALINE   Great reason, for past care is still past cure.
     PRINCESS   Well bandied, both; a set of wit well played.
30   But Rosaline, you have a favour,° too.   *love token*
         Who sent it? And what is it?
     ROSALINE   I would you knew.
         An if my face were but as fair as yours
         My favour° were as great, be witness this.   *appearance*
         Nay, I have verses, too, I thank Biron,
35   The numbers° true, and were the numb'ring,° too,   *meter / evaluation*
         I were the fairest goddess on the ground.
         I am compared to twenty thousand fairs.°   *beauties*
         O, he hath drawn my picture in his letter.
     PRINCESS   Anything like?
40   ROSALINE   Much in the letters,° nothing in the praise.   *penmanship*
     PRINCESS   Beauteous as ink°—a good conclusion.   *(that is, black)*
     CATHERINE   Fair as a text° B in a copy-book.   *formally written black*
     ROSALINE   Ware pencils,[5] ho! Let me not die your debtor,°   *I'll pay you back*
         My red dominical,[6] my golden letter.[7]
45   O, that your face were not so full of O's!°   *pockmarks; pudendum*
     PRINCESS   A pox of that jest; I beshrew° all shrews.   *wish mischief upon*
         But Catherine, what was sent to you from fair Dumaine?
     CATHERINE   Madam, this glove.
     PRINCESS   Did he not send you twain?
     CATHERINE   Yes, madam; and moreover,
50   Some thousand verses of a faithful lover.
         A huge translation° of hypocrisy   *expression*
         Vilely compiled, profound simplicity.°   *folly*
     MARIA   This° and these pearls to me sent Longueville.   *(A chain)*
         The letter is too long by half a mile.
55   PRINCESS   I think no less. Dost thou not wish in heart
         The chain were longer and the letter short?

---

3. Ill-natured, pernicious gallows bird, deserving to be   6. Red letter marking Sundays and feast days in an
hanged.   almanac; reference to Catherine's ruddy complexion.
4. Taking it amiss; snuffing a candle.   7. Also used to mark Sunday; reference to Catherine's
5. Beware of introducing the subject of brushes (used   fair hair.
for cosmetic purposes as well as for drawing portraits).

MARIA   Ay, or I would these hands might never part.[8]

PRINCESS   We are wise girls to mock our lovers so.

ROSALINE   They are worse fools to purchase mocking so.

60   That same Biron I'll torture ere I go.
      O that I knew he were but in by th' week!°—   *permanently caught*
      How I would make him fawn, and beg, and seek,
      And wait the season, and observe the times,°   *dance attendance*
      And spend his prodigal wits in bootless° rhymes,   *fruitless*
65   And shape his service wholly to my hests,°   *commands*
      And make him proud to make me proud that jests![9]
      So pursuivant°-like would I o'ersway his state   *arresting officer*
      That he should be my fool, and I his fate.

PRINCESS   None are so surely caught when they are catched
70   As wit turned fool. Folly in wisdom hatched
      Hath wisdom's warrant, and the help of school,
      And wit's own grace, to grace a learnèd fool.

ROSALINE   The blood of youth burns not with such excess
      As gravity's° revolt to wantonness.   *a wise person's*

75   MARIA   Folly in fools bears not so strong a note°   *stigma*
      As fool'ry in the wise when wit doth dote,°   *act foolishly*
      Since all the power thereof it doth apply
      To prove, by wit, worth in simplicity.°   *folly*

           Enter BOYET

PRINCESS   Here comes Boyet, and mirth is in his face.

80   BOYET   O, I am stabbed with laughter! Where's her grace?

PRINCESS   Thy news, Boyet?

BOYET   Prepare, madam, prepare.
      Arm, wenches, arm. Encounters mounted are°   *An attack is prepared*
      Against your peace. Love doth approach disguised,
      Armèd in arguments. You'll be surprised.[1]
85   Muster your wits, stand in your own defence,
      Or hide your heads like cowards and fly hence.

PRINCESS   Saint Denis to Saint Cupid![2] What are they
      That charge° their breath against us? Say, scout, say.   *level (a weapon)*

BOYET   Under the cool shade of a sycamore
90   I thought to close mine eyes some half an hour
      When lo, to interrupt my purposed rest
      Toward that shade I might behold addressed°   *I could see approaching*
      The King and his companions. Warily
      I stole into a neighbour thicket by
95   And overheard what you shall overhear:°   *hear over again*
      That by and by disguised they will be here.
      Their herald is a pretty knavish page
      That well by heart hath conned his embassage.°   *learned his message*
      Action and accent° did they teach him there.   *Gesture and intonation*
100   'Thus must thou speak', and 'thus thy body bear'.
      And ever and anon they made a doubt°   *expressed fear*
      Presence majestical would put him out,[3]
      'For', quoth the King, 'an angel shalt thou see,
      Yet fear not thou, but speak audaciously.'

---

8. Perhaps she has twisted the chain around them; or, she'd never separate her hands to give one hand in marriage to so ungenerous a man.
9. And be pleased to praise the one who mocks him; and be glad to be ridiculed.

1. Overcome by a surprise attack.
2. St. Denis (the patron saint of France) against St. Cupid.
3. Would make him forget his lines.

105 The boy replied, 'An angel is not evil.
I should have feared her had she been a devil.'
With that all laughed and clapped him on the shoulder,
Making the bold wag by their praises bolder.
One rubbed his elbow⁴ thus, and fleered,° and swore   grinned
110 A better speech was never spoke before.
Another with his finger and his thumb°   (snapping his fingers)
Cried 'Via,° we will do't, come what will come!'   Come on
The third he capered and cried 'All goes well!'
The fourth turned on the toe° and down he fell.   did a pirouette
115 With that they all did tumble on the ground
With such a zealous laughter, so profound,
That in this spleen° ridiculous appears,   fit (of laughter)
To check their folly, passion's solemn tears.
PRINCESS   But what, but what—come they to visit us?
120 BOYET   They do, they do, and are apparelled thus
[   ]⁵
Like Muscovites or Russians, as I guess.
Their purpose is to parley, to court and dance,
And every one his love-suit will advance
125 Unto his several° mistress, which they'll know   particular
By favours several which they did bestow.
PRINCESS   And will they so? The gallants shall be tasked,°   put to the test
For, ladies, we will every one be masked,
And not a man of them shall have the grace,°   luck
130 Despite of suit,° to see a lady's face.⁶   pleading; costume
130.1   *Hold, Rosaline. This favour thou shalt wear,*
               And then the King will court thee for his dear.
        [*To* ROSALINE] Hold, take thou this, my sweet, and give me
        thine.
        So shall Biron take me for Rosaline.
               [*She changes favours with* ROSALINE]
        [*To* CATHERINE *and* MARIA]
        And change you favours, too. So shall your loves
        Woo contrary, deceived by these removes.°   exchanges
               [CATHERINE *and* MARIA *change favours*]
135 ROSALINE   Come on, then, wear the favours most in sight.°   conspicuously
CATHERINE   But in this changing what is your intent?
PRINCESS   The effect of my intent is to cross theirs.
        They do it but in mockery-merriment,°   satirical mirth
        And mock for mock is only my intent.
140   Their several counsels° they unbosom shall   confidences
        To loves mistook, and so be mocked withal
        Upon the next occasion that we meet
        With visages displayed to talk and greet.
ROSALINE   But shall we dance if they desire us to't?
145 PRINCESS   No, to the death we will not move a foot,
        Nor to their penned speech render we no grace,
        But while 'tis spoke each turn away her face.
BOYET   Why, that contempt will kill the speaker's heart,
        And quite divorce his memory from his part.

---

4. Sign of satisfaction.
5. Absence of a rhyme for "guess" and a referent for "thus" suggests that a line describing the lords' costumes has been lost.
6. The following two indented lines (130.1–130.2), spoken by the Princess, seem to represent a first draft of 5.2.131–32.

150 PRINCESS   Therefore I do it; and I make no doubt
          The rest will ne'er come in if he be out.[7]
          There's no such sport as sport by sport o'erthrown,
          To make theirs ours, and ours none but our own.
          So shall we stay, mocking intended game,
155   And they well mocked depart away with shame.
                    Sound trumpet
     BOYET   The trumpet sounds, be masked, the masquers come.
                    [*The ladies mask.*]
                    Enter blackamoors with music;[8] the boy [MOTE] *with a*
                    speech; the [KING *and his*] *lords, disguised* [*as Russians*]
     MOTE   All hail, the richest beauties on the earth!
     BIRON [*aside*]   Beauties no richer than rich taffeta.°   (*masks of taffeta*)
     MOTE   A holy parcel° of the fairest dames—   *party*
                    The ladies turn their backs to him
160   That ever turned their—backs to mortal views.
     BIRON   'Their eyes', villain, 'their eyes'!
     MOTE   That ever turned their eyes to mortal views.
          Out . . .
     BOYET   True, out° indeed!   (*of his part*)
165 MOTE   Out of your favours, heavenly spirits, vouchsafe°   *be willing*
          Not to behold—
     BIRON   'Once to behold', rogue!
     MOTE   Once to behold with your sun-beamèd eyes—
          With your sun-beamèd eyes—
170 BOYET   They will not answer to that epithet.
          You were best call it 'daughter-beamèd' eyes.
     MOTE   They do not mark° me, and that brings me out.   *listen to*
     BIRON   Is this your perfectness?° Be gone, you rogue!   (*in saying your lines*)
                                              [*Exit* MOTE]
     ROSALINE [*as the Princess*][9]   What would these strangers?° Know   *foreigners*
          their minds, Boyet.
175   If they do speak our language, 'tis our will
          That some plain° man recount their purposes.   *plainspoken*
          Know what they would.
     BOYET   What would you with the Princess?
     BIRON   Nothing but peace and gentle visitation.°   *visiting*
     ROSALINE   What would they, say they?
180 BOYET   Nothing but peace and gentle visitation.
     ROSALINE   Why, that they have, and bid them so be gone.
     BOYET   She says you have it, and you may be gone.
     KING   Say to her we have measured° many miles   *paced*
          To tread a measure° with her on this grass.   *dance*
185 BOYET   They say that they have measured many a mile
          To tread a measure with you on this grass.
     ROSALINE   It is not so. Ask them how many inches
          Is in one mile. If they have measured many,
          The measure then of one is easily told.°   *counted*
190 BOYET   If to come hither you have measured miles,
          And many miles, the Princess bids you tell
          How many inches doth fill up one mile.

---

7. The rest of his prepared speech will be forgotten if
he's confused ("out" of his part).
8. Presumably nonspeaking musicians dressed as black
Africans to provide an exotic accompaniment (see

Introduction).
9. From here to line 229, Rosaline speaks as the
Princess.

BIRON   Tell her we measure them by weary steps.
BOYET   She hears herself.
ROSALINE   How many weary steps
195   Of many weary miles you have o'ergone
    Are numbered in the travel of one mile?
BIRON   We number nothing that we spend for you.
    Our duty is so rich, so infinite,
    That we may do it still° without account.°   *always / reckoning*
200   Vouchsafe to show the sunshine of your face
    That we, like savages, may worship it.
ROSALINE   My face is but a moon,¹ and clouded,° too.   *masked; dark*
KING   Blessed are clouds to do as such clouds do.
    Vouchsafe, bright moon, and these thy stars,° to shine,   *companions*
205   Those clouds removed, upon our watery eyne.°   *eyes*
ROSALINE   O vain petitioner, beg a greater matter.
    Thou now requests but moonshine in the water.°   *nothing*
KING   Then in our measure do but vouchsafe one change.²
    Thou bidd'st me beg; this begging is not strange.°   *odd; foreign*
ROSALINE   Play, music, then.
        [*Music plays*]³
210   Nay, you must do it soon.
    Not yet?—no dance! Thus change I like the moon.
KING   Will you not dance? How come you thus estranged?
ROSALINE   You took the moon at full, but now she's changed.
KING   Yet still she is the moon, and I the man.°   *(in the moon)*
215   [   ]⁴
    The music plays, vouchsafe some motion° to it.   *movement; response*
ROSALINE   Our ears vouchsafe it.
KING   But your legs should do it.
ROSALINE   Since you are strangers and come here by chance
    We'll not be nice.° Take hands. We will not dance.   *coy*
KING   Why take we hands, then?
220   ROSALINE   Only to part friends.
    Curtsy, sweethearts, and so the measure ends.
KING   More measure° of this measure, be not nice.   *A larger amount*
ROSALINE   We can afford no more at such a price.
KING   Price you yourselves. What buys your company?
ROSALINE   Your absence only.
225   KING   That can never be.
ROSALINE   Then cannot we be bought, and so adieu—
    Twice to your visor, and half once to you.⁵
KING   If you deny to dance, let's hold more chat.
ROSALINE   In private, then.
KING   I am best pleased with that.
        [*The* KING *and* ROSALINE *talk apart*]
BIRON [*to the* PRINCESS, *taking her for Rosaline*]
230   White-handed mistress, one sweet word with thee.
PRINCESS   Honey and milk and sugar—there is three.
BIRON   Nay then, two treys,° an if you grow so nice°—   *threes (dice) / subtle*

---

1. Because it shines with a borrowed light.
2. Of the moon; of the figure in the dance, *measure:*
dance.
3. It is not certain whether the music should start here
or later.

4. A line rhyming with "man" seems to have dropped
out.
5. Perhaps: your masked ("visor") (double) face
deserves two farewells, but yourself less than one (for
behaving so foolishly).

Metheglin, wort, and malmsey°—well run, dice!   *three sweet drinks*
There's half-a-dozen sweets.

PRINCESS   Seventh sweet, adieu.

235   Since you can cog,° I'll play no more with you.   *cheat*

BIRON   One word in secret.

PRINCESS   Let it not be sweet.

BIRON   Thou griev'st my gall.°   *chafe my sore place*

PRINCESS   Gall°—bitter!   *Liver bile*

BIRON   Therefore meet.°   *fitting; let's meet?*

[BIRON *and the* PRINCESS *talk apart*]

DUMAINE [*to* MARIA, *taking her for Catherine*]
Will you vouchsafe with me to change a word?°   *exchange words*

MARIA   Name it.

DUMAINE   Fair lady—

MARIA   Say you so? Fair lord—
Take that for° your 'fair lady'.   *in exchange for*

240   **DUMAINE**   Please it you,
As much in private, and I'll bid adieu.

[DUMAINE *and* MARIA *talk apart*]

CATHERINE   What, was your visor made without a tongue?[6]

LONGUEVILLE [*taking* CATHERINE *for Maria*]   I know the reason,
lady, why you ask.

CATHERINE   O, for your reason! Quickly, sir, I long.

245   **LONGUEVILLE**   You have a double tongue within your mask,
And would afford my speechless visor half.[7]

CATHERINE   'Veal', quoth the Dutchman. Is not veal a calf?[8]

LONGUEVILLE   A calf, fair lady?

CATHERINE   No, a fair lord calf.°   *dolt*

LONGUEVILLE   Let's part the word.°   *compromise*

CATHERINE   No, I'll not be your half.[9]

250   Take all and wean° it, it may prove an ox.[1]   *raise*

LONGUEVILLE   Look how you butt° yourself in these sharp mocks!   *attack*
Will you give horns,[2] chaste lady? Do not so.

CATHERINE   Then die a calf before your horns do grow.

LONGUEVILLE   One word in private with you ere I die.°   *have an orgasm*

255   **CATHERINE**   Bleat softly, then. The butcher hears you cry.

[LONGUEVILLE *and* CATHERINE *talk apart*]

BOYET   The tongues of mocking wenches are as keen
As is the razor's edge invisible,
Cutting a smaller hair than may be seen,
Above the sense of sense; so sensible[3]

260   Seemeth their conference.° Their conceits° have wings   *conversation / fancies*
Fleeter than arrows, bullets, wind, thought, swifter things.

ROSALINE   Not one word more, my maids. Break off, break off.

---

6. A projection within a mask permitting it to be held in place with the mouth. Catherine is also alluding to Longueville's silence.

7. *You . . . half:* You are double-tongued (masked; punning; deceptive; speaking enough for two) and ask about my silence because you'd be wise to give up half your speech by giving me one of the tongues (the one that keeps her mask on; this would reveal her identity).

8. *'Veal':* Well (ironic: Dutch pronunciation of "well" or German *viel*, meaning "much"; "Dutch" could mean "German"); veil (mask). Combined with Catherine's previous word, "long" (line 244), the result is "Longueville"—thus demonstrating that she knows the

identity of her disguised suitor and had anticipated his "half" (line 246) by uttering half his name. *Veau,* French for "veal," does also mean "calf" (a dunce in Renaissance English).

9. Taking "part" as "divide": half of what you are the other half of; your better half (your wife); half of "calf" ("ca," for "Catherine").

1. Dolt; castrated male.

2. Butt with horns; equip with horns; cuckold.

3. *Above . . . sense:* Above the power of the senses to apprehend (perhaps with the ironic meaning of "nonsense"). *so sensible:* so acutely felt by the hearer.

BIRON   By heaven, all dry-beaten with pure scoff!⁴
KING   Farewell, mad wenches, you have simple wits.

Exeunt [the KING, *lords, and blackamoors]*

[The ladies unmask]

265 PRINCESS   Twenty adieus, my frozen Muscovites.
Are these the breed of wits so wondered at?
BOYET   Tapers they are, with your sweet breaths puffed out.
ROSALINE   Well-liking° wits they have; gross, gross; fat, fat.   Plump
PRINCESS   O poverty in wit, kingly-poor flout!⁵
270 Will they not, think you, hang themselves tonight,
Or ever but in visors show their faces?
This pert Biron was out of count'nance° quite.   disconcerted; masked
ROSALINE   Ah, they were all in lamentable cases.°   states; outfits
The King was weeping-ripe for° a good word.⁶   near tears for lack of
275 PRINCESS   Biron did swear himself out of all suit.⁷
MARIA   Dumaine was at my service, and his sword.
'*Non point*,'° quoth I. My servant straight was mute.   Not at all; it's blunt
CATHERINE   Lord Longueville said I came o'er his heart,
And trow you° what he called me?   can you believe
PRINCESS   'Qualm',⁸ perhaps.
CATHERINE   Yes, in good faith.
280 PRINCESS   Go, sickness as thou art.
ROSALINE   Well, better wits have worn plain statute-caps.⁹
But will you hear? The King is my love sworn.
PRINCESS   And quick Biron hath plighted faith to me.
CATHERINE   And Longueville was for my service born.
285 MARIA   Dumaine is mine, as sure as bark on tree.
BOYET   Madam, and pretty mistresses, give ear.
Immediately they will again be here
In their own shapes,° for it can never be   Undisguised
They will digest° this harsh indignity.   accept
PRINCESS   Will they return?
290 BOYET   They will, they will, God knows,
And leap for joy, though they are lame with blows.
Therefore change favours, and when they repair,°   return
Blow° like sweet roses in this summer air.   Bloom
PRINCESS   How 'blow'? How 'blow'? Speak to be understood.
295 BOYET   Fair ladies masked are roses in their bud;
Dismasked, their damask sweet commixture¹ shown,
Are angels vailing° clouds, or roses blown.°   letting fall / blooming
PRINCESS   Avaunt, perplexity!° What shall we do   Be off, riddler
If they return in their own shapes to woo?
300 ROSALINE   Good madam, if by me you'll be advised,
Let's mock them still, as well known² as disguised.
Let us complain to them what fools were here,
Disguised like Muscovites in shapeless gear,°   ill-cut clothes
And wonder what they were, and to what end

---

4. Soundly beaten without bloodshed; battered by mocking words.
5. Reversed wordplay ("kingly-poor") on "well-li-king" (or like-king," line 268), criticizing Rosaline's "flout" (gibe) and perhaps the King's as well (line 264).
6. The beginning of a sixteen-line dialogue sonnet.
7. Avowed his passion—beyond all reason; out of character for his Russian "suit" (costume); in a mistaken "suit" at love (to the wrong woman).

8. Heartburn: perhaps punning on "came" (line 278) and picked up in "go" (line 280).
9. Cleverer people have been ordinary apprentices (whose headwear was regulated by statute); perhaps an allusion to fancy caps forming part of the lords' disguise.
1. Sweet red and white complexion.
2. Let's mock them just as much now that they are known for themselves.

305   Their shallow shows, and prologue vilely penned,

        And their rough carriage° so ridiculous,   *awkward manner*

        Should be presented at our tent to us.

    BOYET   Ladies, withdraw. The gallants are at hand.

    PRINCESS   Whip, to our tents, as roes° run over land!   *deer*

                         Exeunt [the ladies]

    Enter the KING[, BIRON, DUMAINE, *and* LONGUEVILLE, *as*

    themselves]

310   KING   Fair sir, God save you. Where's the Princess?

    BOYET   Gone to her tent. Please it your majesty

        Command me any service to her thither?

    KING   That she vouchsafe me audience for one word.

    BOYET   I will, and so will she, I know, my lord.   *Exit*

315   BIRON   This fellow pecks up wit as pigeons peas,

        And utters° it again when God doth please.   *speaks; sells*

        He is wit's pedlar, and retails his wares

        At wakes and wassails,° meetings, markets, fairs.   *festivals and revels*

        And we that sell by gross,° the Lord doth know,   *wholesale*

320   Have not the grace to grace it with such show.

        This gallant pins the wenches on his sleeve.°   *attracts all the girls*

        Had he been Adam, he had° tempted Eve.   *would have*

        A can carve[3] too, and lisp,° why, this is he   *speak affectedly*

        That kissed his hand away in courtesy.

325   This is the ape of form,° Monsieur the Nice,°   *good form / fastidious*

        That when he plays at tables° chides the dice   *backgammon*

        In honourable° terms. Nay, he can sing   *polite*

        A mean most meanly,[4] and in ushering°   *as a gentleman usher*

        Mend° him who can. The ladies call him sweet.   *Improve on*

330   The stairs as he treads on them kiss his feet.

        This is the flower that smiles on everyone

        To show his teeth as white as whales bone,°   *walrus ivory*

        And consciences that will not die in debt

        Pay him the due of 'honey-tongued' Boyet.

335   KING   A blister on his sweet tongue with my heart,

        That put Armado's page out of his part!

            Enter the ladies [and BOYET]

    BIRON   See where it° comes. Behaviour,° what wert thou   *(Boyet) / Fine manners*

        Till this madman° showed thee, and what art thou now?   *madcap*

    KING   All hail, sweet madam, and fair time of day!

340   PRINCESS   'Fair' in 'all hail'° is foul, as I conceive.   *(as in "hailstorm")*

    KING   Construe my speeches better, if you may.

    PRINCESS   Then wish me better. I will give you leave.

    KING   We came to visit you,[5] and purpose now

        To lead you to our court. Vouchsafe it, then.

345   PRINCESS   This field shall hold me, and so hold your vow.

        Nor° God nor I delights in perjured men.   *Neither*

    KING   Rebuke me not for that which you provoke.

        The virtue° of your eye must break my oath.   *power*

    PRINCESS   You nickname virtue.° 'Vice' you should have spoke,   *misname goodness*

350   For virtue's office° never breaks men's troth.   *action*

        Now by my maiden honour, yet as pure

        As the unsullied lily, I protest,

---

3. He can act with social grace, flirt.
4. *he . . . meanly*: he can sing an in-between vocal part (tenor or alto) in the appropriate way (make himself generally useful).
5. The beginning of another dialogue sonnet.

A world of torments though I should endure,
　　I would not yield to be your house's guest,
355 So much I hate a breaking cause° to be　　　　　　　　　　　　*cause of breaking*
　　Of heavenly oaths, vowed with integrity.
KING   O, you have lived in desolation here,
　　Unseen, unvisited, much to our shame.
PRINCESS   Not so, my lord. It is not so, I swear.
360 　　We have had pastimes here, and pleasant game.
　　A mess of° Russians left us but of late.　　　　　　　　　　　*group of four*
KING   How, madam? Russians?
PRINCESS　　　　　　　　　　Ay, in truth, my lord.
　　Trim gallants, full of courtship and of state.
ROSALINE   Madam, speak true.—It is not so, my lord.
365 My lady, to the manner of the days,°　　　　　　　　　　　*in the present fashion*
　　In courtesy gives undeserving praise.
　　We four indeed confronted were with four
　　In Russian habit. Here they stayed an hour,
　　And talked apace, and in that hour, my lord,
370 They did not bless us with one happy° word.　　　　　　　　*well-chosen*
　　I dare not call them fools, but this I think:
　　When they are thirsty, fools would fain have drink.
BIRON   This jest is dry° to me. Gentle sweet,　　　　　　*barren (punningly)*
　　Your wits makes wise things foolish. When we greet,
375 With eyes' best seeing, heaven's fiery eye,
　　By light we lose light.[6] Your capacity
　　Is of that nature that to° your huge store　　　　　　　　　*compared to*
　　Wise things seem foolish, and rich things but poor.
ROSALINE   This proves you wise and rich, for in my eye—
380 BIRON   I am a fool, and full of poverty.
ROSALINE   But that you take what doth to you belong
　　It were a fault to snatch words from my tongue.
BIRON   O, I am yours, and all that I possess.
ROSALINE   All the fool mine!
BIRON　　　　　　　　　　I cannot give you less.
385 ROSALINE   Which of the visors was it that you wore?
BIRON   Where? When? What visor? Why demand° you this?　　*ask*
ROSALINE   There, then, that visor, that superfluous case,°　　*mask*
　　That hid the worse and showed the better face.
KING [*aside to the lords*]   We were described.° They'll mock us　*uncovered*
　　now, downright.
390 DUMAINE [*aside to the* KING]   Let us confess, and turn it to a jest.
PRINCESS   Amazed, my lord? Why looks your highness sad?
ROSALINE   Help, hold his° brows, he'll swoon. Why look you pale?　*(Biron's)*
　　Seasick, I think, coming from Muscovy.
BIRON   Thus pour the stars down plagues for perjury.
395 Can any face of brass° hold longer out?　　　　　　　*brazen shamelessness*
　　Here stand I, lady. Dart thy skill at me—
　　Bruise me with scorn, confound me with a flout,
　　Thrust thy sharp wit quite through my ignorance,
　　Cut me to pieces with thy keen conceit,°　　　　　　　　　*intelligence*
400 And I will wish° thee nevermore to dance,　　　　　　　　　*invite*
　　Nor nevermore in Russian habit wait.°　　　　　　　　　*attend on you*
　　O, never will I trust to speeches penned,[7]

---

6. When we gaze intently at the sun, we go blind.　　considering Biron's renunciation of literary effects.
7. The beginning of a sonnet (lines 402–15)—ironic,

Nor to the motion of a schoolboy's tongue,
Nor never come in visor to my friend,°   *sweetheart*
405   Nor woo in rhyme, like a blind harper's song.
Taffeta phrases, silken terms precise,
Three-piled° hyperboles, spruce affectation,   *Rich velvet; Elaborate*
Figures° pedantical—these summer flies   *(of speech)*
Have blown me full of maggot ostentation.°   *laid maggot eggs in me*
410   I do forswear them, and I here protest,
By this white glove—how white the hand, God knows!—
Henceforth my wooing mind shall be expressed
In russet° yeas, and honest kersey° noes.   *homely / plain*
And to begin, wench, so God help me, law!°   *indeed (humble oath)*
415   My love to thee is sound, sans° crack or flaw.   *without*
ROSALINE   Sans 'sans', I pray you.
BIRON   Yet° I have a trick°   *Still / touch*
Of the old rage.° Bear with me, I am sick.   *fever*
I'll leave it by degrees. Soft, let us see.
Write 'Lord have mercy on us'[8] on those three.°   *(his companions)*
420   They are infected, in their hearts it lies.
They have the plague, and caught it of your eyes.
These lords are visited,° you are not free;   *afflicted by plague*
For the Lord's tokens° on you do I see.   *favors; plague spots*
PRINCESS   No, they are free[9] that gave these tokens to us.
425   BIRON   Our states are forfeit.[1] Seek not to undo us.[2]
ROSALINE   It is not so, for how can this be true,
That you stand forfeit, being those that sue?°   *sue at law; beg; woo*
BIRON   Peace, for I will not have to do° with you.   *deal; copulate*
ROSALINE   Nor shall not, if I do as I intend.
430   BIRON [*to the lords*]   Speak for yourselves. My wit is at an end.
KING   Teach us, sweet madam, for our rude transgression
Some fair excuse.
PRINCESS   The fairest is confession.
Were not you here but even now disguised?
KING   Madam, I was.
PRINCESS   And were you well advised?°   *in your right mind*
KING   I was, fair madam.
435   PRINCESS   When you then were here,
What did you whisper in your lady's ear?
KING   That more than all the world I did respect° her.   *value*
PRINCESS   When she shall challenge° this, you will reject her.   *assert her claim to*
KING   Upon mine honour, no.
PRINCESS   Peace, peace, forbear.
440   Your oath once broke, you force not° to forswear.   *find it easy*
KING   Despise me when I break this oath of mine.
PRINCESS   I will, and therefore keep it. Rosaline,
What did the Russian whisper in your ear?
ROSALINE   Madam, he swore that he did hold me dear
445   As precious eyesight, and did value me
Above this world, adding thereto moreover
That he would wed me, or else die my lover.

---

8. A common inscription on the doors of plague-visited houses.
9. Generous; at liberty; free of love; free of obligation.
1. (Denying the Princess's claim in line 424 that the men are "free"): Our estates are subject to confiscation; our condition as bachelors is ended; because we're in love, we've lost power over ourselves; as would-be husbands, we owe you our estates; we've acted dishonorably.
2. Don't undo our forfeiture (don't ruin us) by calling us "free" (by rejecting our love).

PRINCESS   God give thee joy of him! The noble lord
Most honourably doth uphold his word.
450 KING   What mean you, madam? By my life, my troth,
I never swore this lady such an oath.
ROSALINE   By heaven, you did, and to confirm it plain,
You gave me this. But take it, sir, again.
KING   My faith and this the Princess I did give.
455 I knew her by this jewel on her sleeve.
PRINCESS   Pardon me, sir, *this* jewel did she wear,
And Lord Biron, I thank him, is my dear.
[*To* BIRON] What, will you have me, or your pearl again?
BIRON   Neither of either.° I remit° both twain.   *the two / surrender*
460 I see the trick on't.° Here was a consent,°   *of it / plot*
Knowing aforehand of our merriment,
To dash it like a Christmas comedy.
Some carry-tale, some please-man, some slight zany,
Some mumble-news, some trencher-knight, some Dick[3]
465 That smiles his cheek in years,° and knows the trick   *into wrinkles*
To make my lady laugh when she's disposed,
Told our intents before, which once disclosed,
The ladies did change favours, and then we,
Following the signs, wooed but the sign of she.°   *each mistress*
470 Now, to our perjury to add more terror,
We are again forsworn, in will° and error.°   *willfully / mistakenly*
Much upon this 'tis,[4] [*to* BOYET] and might not you
Forestall° our sport, to make us thus untrue?   *Have undermined*
Do not you know my lady's foot by th' square,[5]
475 And laugh upon the apple[6] of her eye,
And stand between her back, sir, and the fire,°   *keep the heat from her*
Holding a trencher,° jesting merrily?   *serving plate*
You put our page out. Go, you are allowed.°   *privileged (as a fool)*
Die when you will, a smock[7] shall be your shroud.
480 You leer° upon me, do you? There's an eye   *look malevolently at*
Wounds like a leaden sword.°   *harmless stage sword*
BOYET   Full merrily
Hath this brave manège, this career been run.
BIRON   Lo, he is tilting straight.[8] Peace, I have done.
          Enter [COSTARD *the*] *clown*
Welcome, pure wit. Thou partest a fair fray.
485 COSTARD   O Lord, sir, they would know
Whether the three Worthies shall come in or no.
BIRON   What, are there but three?
COSTARD   No, sir, but it is vara° fine,   *very*
For everyone pursents° three.   *(re)presents*
BIRON   And three times thrice is nine.
COSTARD   Not so, sir, under° correction, sir, I hope it is not so.   *subject to*
You cannot beg us,° sir. I can assure you, sir, we know what   *show we're fools*
490 we know.

---

3. *carry-tale*: talebearer. *please-man*: toady. *zany*: clownish, rustic servant in commedia dell'arte. *mumble-news*: gossip. *trencher-knight*: parasite, who dines from his lord's dish ("trencher") or who has a lordly appetite. *Dick*: low fellow.
4. It happened very much like this.
5. Know how to please your mistress. *square*: a carpenter's rule (Boyet "has her measure"); possible pun on "squire" (an "apple-squire" was a pimp; see "apple," line 475 and note).
6. Pupil. Boyet can wittily catch the Princess's eye; he is on intimate terms with her.
7. Woman's garment (either a charge of effeminacy or equivalent to "women will be the death of you").
8. Jousting (linguistically) at once. *manège* (line 482): feat of horsemanship. *career*: short gallop at full speed.

I hope, sir, three times thrice, sir—

BIRON   Is not nine?

COSTARD   Under correction, sir, we know whereuntil° it doth   *to what*
amount.

BIRON   By Jove, I always took three threes for nine.

495   COSTARD   O Lord, sir, it were pity you should get your living by
reck'ning,⁹ sir.

BIRON   How much is it?

COSTARD   O Lord, sir, the parties themselves, the actors, sir, will
show whereuntil it doth amount. For mine own part, I am, as

500   they say, but to parfect° one man in one poor man, Pompion¹   *present; perfect*
the Great, sir.

BIRON   Art thou one of the Worthies?

COSTARD   It pleased them to think me worthy of Pompey the
Great. For mine own part, I know not the degree° of the Wor-   *rank*

505   thy, but I am to stand for him.

BIRON   Go, bid them prepare.

COSTARD   We will turn it finely off, sir. We will take some care.
                                          Exit

KING   Biron, they will shame us. Let them not approach.

BIRON   We are shame-proof, my lord, and 'tis some policy°   *clever strategy*

510   To have one show worse than the King's and his company.

KING   I say they shall not come.

PRINCESS   Nay, my good lord, let me o'errule you now.
That sport best pleases that doth least know how.
Where zeal strives to content, and the contents

515   Dies in the zeal of that which it presents,²
There form confounded makes most form in mirth,³
When great things labouring° perish in their birth.   *(to be born)*

BIRON   A right description of our sport,° my lord.   *(the Russian masque)*
        Enter [ARMADO *the*] *braggart*

ARMADO [*to the* KING]   Anointed, I implore so much expense of

520   thy royal sweet breath as will utter a brace° of words.   *pair*
        [ARMADO *and the* KING *speak apart*]

PRINCESS   Doth this man serve God?

BIRON   Why ask you?

PRINCESS   A° speaks not like a man of God his° making.   *He / (God's)*

ARMADO   That is all one, my fair sweet honey monarch,° for, I   *King or Princess?*

525   protest, the schoolmaster is exceeding fantastical, too-too vain,
too-too vain. But we will put it, as they say, to *fortuna de la
guerra.*° I wish you the peace of mind, most royal couplement.   *the fortune of war*
                                            Exit

KING   Here is like to be a good presence of Worthies. He presents Hector of Troy, the swain Pompey the Great, the parish-

530   curate Alexander, Armado's page Hercules, the pedant Judas
Maccabeus,
And if these four Worthies in their first show thrive,
These four will change habits° and present the other five.   *costumes*

BIRON   There is five in the first show.

535   KING   You are deceived, 'tis not so.

BIRON   The pedant, the braggart, the hedge-priest,° the fool,   *illiterate priest*
and the boy,

---

9. It would be a shame if you had to earn your living by
arithmetic.
1. Pumpkin (blunder for "Pompey").

2. *and . . . presents*: and the enthusiasm of those who
present the play is fatal to the substance.
3. Artistry defeated produces the greatest comic effect.

Abate throw at novum[4] and the whole world again
Cannot pick out five such, take each one in his vein.°   *characteristic manner*
KING   The ship is under sail, and here she comes amain.°   *at full speed*
        Enter [COSTARD *the clown as*] *Pompey*
COSTARD [*as Pompey*]   I Pompey am—
540   BIRON   You lie, you are not he.
COSTARD [*as Pompey*]   I Pompey am—
BOYET   With leopard's head on knee.[5]
BIRON   Well said, old mocker. I must needs be friends with thee.
COSTARD [*as Pompey*]   I Pompey am, Pompey surnamed the Big.°   *(sexual)*
DUMAINE   'The Great'.
545   COSTARD   It is 'Great', sir—
        [*As Pompey*] Pompey surnamed the Great,
        That oft in field with targe° and shield did make my foe to sweat,[6]   *shield*
        And travelling along this coast I here am come by chance,
        And lay my arms before the legs° of this sweet lass of France.—   *(bawdy)*
550   If your ladyship would say 'Thanks, Pompey', I had done.
PRINCESS[7]   Great thanks, great Pompey.
COSTARD   'Tis not so much worth, but I hope I was perfect.° I   *I recited correctly*
        made a little fault in 'great'.
BIRON   My hat to a halfpenny° Pompey proves the best Worthy.   *I'll bet anything*
        [COSTARD *stands aside.*]
        Enter [NATHANIEL *the*] *curate* [*as*] *Alexander*
NATHANIEL [*as Alexander*]   When in the world I lived I was the
555   world's commander.
        By east, west, north, and south, I spread my conquering
          might.
        My scutcheon° plain° declares that I am Alisander.   *coat of arms / clearly*
BOYET   Your nose says no, you are not, for it stands too right.[8]
BIRON [*to* BOYET]   Your nose smells 'no'[9] in this, most tender-
        smelling° knight.   *sensitive-to-smell*
560   PRINCESS   The conqueror is dismayed. Proceed, good Alexander.
NATHANIEL [*as Alexander*]   When in the world I lived I was the
          world's commander.
BOYET   Most true, 'tis right, you were so, Alisander.
BIRON [*to* COSTARD]   Pompey the Great.
COSTARD   Your servant, and Costard.
565   BIRON   Take away the conqueror, take away Alisander.
COSTARD [*to* NATHANIEL]   O, sir, you have overthrown Alisander
        the Conqueror. You will be scraped out of the painted cloth[1]
        for this. Your lion that holds his pole-axe sitting on a close-stool
        will be given to Ajax.[2] He will be the ninth Worthy. A con-
570   queror and afeard to speak? Run away for shame, Alisander.
                                Exit [NATHANIEL *the*] *curate*
        There, an't° shall please you, a foolish mild man, an honest   *if it*
        man, look you, and soon dashed. He is a marvellous good

4. Barring a lucky chance in the dice game of novum (in which the main throws were five and nine—like the five actors playing the Nine Worthies).
5. Embossed either on the knee piece of his armor or on his shield, which he might then be holding upside down.
6. The first of three lines in fourteeners (14-syllable lines)—an archaic meter by the 1590s, like most of those used by the nonaristocratic characters.
7. Q gives the line to "Lady": perhaps Costard kneels to the wrong woman.
8. Straight (alluding to Alexander's reputed crooked neck).

9. Implying that Nathaniel smells bad; according to the Greek biographer Plutarch, Alexander was reputed to have "a marvellous good savour" (Thomas North's translation).
1. Referring to the practice of representing the Worthies on wall hangings.
2. Alexander's arms, which showed a lion holding a battle-ax (or penis) and seated (a "close-stool" is a toilet), will be given to another warrior, Ajax (punning on "a jakes," a toilet), a Greek hero from the Trojan War who coveted the armor of Achilles. See 4.3.6 and note.

neighbour, faith, and a very good bowler, but for Alisander—
alas, you see how 'tis—a little o'erparted.° But there are Wor-   *given too hard a role*
575 thies a-coming will speak their mind in some other sort.
PRINCESS   Stand aside, good Pompey.

   Enter [HOLOFERNES *the*] *pedant* [*as*] *Judas, and the boy*
   [MOTE *as*] *Hercules*

HOLOFERNES   Great Hercules is presented by this imp,°   *child*
   Whose club killed Cerberus, that three-headed canus,[3]
   And when he was a babe, a child, a shrimp,
580   Thus did he strangle serpents in his *manus*.°   *hands; (play on "anus")*
   Quoniam° he seemeth in minority,°   *Since / a child*
   Ergo° I come with this apology.   *Therefore*
   [*To* MOTE] Keep some state° in thy exit, and vanish.   *dignity*

                   Exit [MOTE]

HOLOFERNES [*as Judas*]   Judas I am—
585 DUMAINE   A Judas?
HOLOFERNES   Not Iscariot, sir.
   [*As Judas*] Judas I am, yclept° Maccabeus.   *named*
DUMAINE   Judas Maccabeus clipped° is plain Judas.   *shortened; circumcised*
BIRON   A kissing traitor.[4] How art thou proved Judas?
590 HOLOFERNES [*as Judas*]   Judas I am—
DUMAINE   The more shame for you, Judas.
HOLOFERNES   What mean you, sir?
BOYET   To make Judas hang himself.
HOLOFERNES   Begin,° sir. You are my elder.   *You go first*
595 BIRON   Well followed—Judas was hanged on an elder.°   *(tree)*
HOLOFERNES   I will not be put out of countenance.°   *be upset*
BIRON   Because thou hast no face.°   *countenance*
HOLOFERNES   What is this?[5]
BOYET   A cittern-head.°   *guitar*
600 DUMAINE   The head of a bodkin.°   *hairpin; small dagger*
BIRON   A death's face° in a ring.   *death's head*
LONGUEVILLE   The face of an old Roman coin, scarce seen.°   *worn down*
BOYET   The pommel° of Caesar's falchion.°   *handle / sword*
DUMAINE   The carved-bone face on a flask.°   *gunpowder horn*
605 BIRON   Saint George's half-cheek° in a brooch.   *profile*
DUMAINE   Ay, and in a brooch of lead.°   *(indicating low rank)*
BIRON   Ay, and worn in the cap of a tooth-drawer.[6] And now for-
   ward, for we have put thee in countenance.°   *depicted you*
HOLOFERNES   You have put me out of countenance.
610 BIRON   False, we have given thee faces.
HOLOFERNES   But you have outfaced° them all.   *mocked*
BIRON   An thou wert a lion, we would do so.
BOYET   Therefore, as he is an ass,[7] let him go.
   And so adieu, sweet Jude. Nay, why dost thou stay?
615 DUMAINE   For the latter end of his name.
BIRON   For the ass to the Jude. Give it him. Jud-as, away.[8]
HOLOFERNES   This is not generous,° not gentle,° not humble.°   *noble / courteous / kind*
BOYET   A light for Monsieur Judas. It grows dark, he may stumble.

                   [*Exit* HOLOFERNES]

---

3. In classical mythology, the three-headed watchdog ("canis") of Hades.
4. Alluding to the kiss with which Judas Iscariot betrayed Jesus, with a pun on "clipped" (embraced, kissed), itself punning on "yclept."
5. Indicating his face. The replies refer to ornamental faces on objects.
6. Worn by a lowly dentist as a sign of his trade.
7. An ass disguises himself as a lion in one of Aesop's fables—only to have his own nature undo him. "Ass" in the sense of "backside" is punningly evoked by "end" (line 615).
8. *As*, in "Jud-as," as "the latter end of his name" (line 615), but "end" also means "ass."

PRINCESS Alas, poor Maccabeus, how hath he been baited!
    Enter [ARMADO *the*] *braggart* [*as Hector*]
620 BIRON Hide thy head, Achilles,⁹ here comes Hector in arms.
DUMAINE Though my mocks come home by° me, I will now be   *later rebound on*
    merry.
KING Hector was but a Trojan¹ in respect of° this.   *in comparison with*
BOYET But is this Hector?
625 KING I think Hector was not so clean-timbered.°   *well built*
LONGUEVILLE His leg is too big for Hector's.
DUMAINE More calf,° certain.   *part of the leg; fool*
BOYET No, he is best endowed in the small.°   *leg below the calf*
BIRON This cannot be Hector.
630 DUMAINE He's a god, or a painter, for he makes faces.°   *grimaces; creates life*
ARMADO [*as Hector*] The armipotent° Mars, of lances the   *powerful in arms*
    almighty,
      Gave Hector a gift—
DUMAINE A gilt nutmeg.²
BIRON A lemon.
635 LONGUEVILLE Stuck with cloves.
DUMAINE No, cloven.
ARMADO Peace!
    [*As Hector*] The armipotent Mars, of lances the almighty,
      Gave Hector a gift, the heir of Ilion,°   *Troy*
640   A man so breathèd° that certain he would fight, yea,   *fit*
    From morn till night, out of his pavilion.°   *jousting tent*
    I am that flower—
DUMAINE   That mint.
LONGUEVILLE   That colombine.
ARMADO Sweet Lord Longueville, rein thy tongue.
LONGUEVILLE I must rather give it the rein, for it runs° against   *jousts; races; speaks*
645 Hector.
DUMAINE Ay, and Hector's a greyhound.³
ARMADO The sweet war-man is dead and rotten. Sweet chucks,
    beat not the bones of the buried. When he breathed he was a
    man. But I will forward with my device.° [*To the* PRINCESS]   *performance*
650 Sweet royalty, bestow on me the sense of hearing.
          BIRON *steps forth*
PRINCESS Speak, brave Hector, we are much delighted.
ARMADO I do adore thy sweet grace's slipper.
BOYET Loves her by the foot.
DUMAINE He may not by the yard.°   *penis (slang)*
655 ARMADO [*as Hector*] This Hector far surmounted Hannibal.⁴
    [   ]⁵
ARMADO The party is gone.°   *Hector is dead*
COSTARD Fellow Hector, she is gone, she is two months on her
    way.⁶

---

9. Leading Greek hero in the Trojan War; Hector's chief opponent and slayer in Homer, but his inferior and a coward in *Troilus and Cressida*.
1. An ordinary guy (slang).
2. A nutmeg glazed with egg yolk, used, like "lemon" and "cloves" (lines 634, 635), to flavor drinks. A common lover's gift, the "gilt nutmeg" may also allude to Armado's makeup. "Lemon" perhaps puns on "leman" (lover, sweetheart), in which case "cloven" (line 636) would have a sexual innuendo.
3. Famous as a runner; "Hector" was a common name for a greyhound.

4. Surpassed Hannibal, leader of Carthage against Rome (with the unintentional homosexual innuendo of "surmounted").
5. An interjection may be missing here.
6. Jaquenetta is two months pregnant. Since at most only a few days seem to have passed in the aristocratic plot, it is possible to infer that Costard is the actual father; but this may be an example of Shakespearean double time. The stage direction "Biron steps forth" following line 650 may indicate that he urges Costard to press this declaration. Alternatively, he may merely be trying to prevent Armado from speaking, an effort the Princess thwarts.

660 ARMADO What meanest thou?

COSTARD Faith, unless you play the honest Trojan the poor
wench is cast away. She's quick.° The child brags in her belly   *pregnant*
already. 'Tis yours.°   *(because it brags)*

ARMADO Dost thou infamonize° me among potentates? Thou   *defame (a coinage)*
665 shalt die.

COSTARD Then° shall Hector be whipped for Jaquenetta that is   *In that case*
quick by him, and hanged for Pompey that is dead by him.[7]

DUMAINE Most rare Pompey!

BOYET Renowned Pompey!

670 BIRON Greater than great—great, great, great Pompey, Pompey
the Huge.°   *(bawdy)*

DUMAINE Hector trembles.

BIRON Pompey is moved. More Ates,° more Ates—stir them on,   *goddess of discord*
stir them on!

675 DUMAINE Hector will challenge him.

BIRON Ay, if a° have no more man's blood in his belly than will   *he*
sup° a flea.   *feed*

ARMADO By the North Pole, I do challenge thee.

COSTARD I will not fight with a pole, like a northern° man. I'll   *an uncivilized (Scot)*
680 slash, I'll do it by the sword. I bepray you, let me borrow my
arms° again.   *(from the Princess)*

DUMAINE Room for the incensed Worthies.

COSTARD I'll do it in my shirt.

DUMAINE Most resolute Pompey.

685 MOTE [*aside to* ARMADO] Master, let me take you a button-hole
lower.[8] Do you not see Pompey is uncasing° for the combat?   *undressing*
What mean you? You will lose your reputation.

ARMADO Gentlemen and soldiers, pardon me. I will not combat
in my shirt.

690 DUMAINE You may not deny it, Pompey hath made the challenge.

ARMADO Sweet bloods,° I both may and will.   *men of fiery spirit*

BIRON What reason have you for't?

ARMADO The naked truth of it is, I have no shirt. I go woolward
695 for penance.[9]

MOTE True, and it was enjoined him in Rome° for want of   *center of Catholicism*
linen, since when I'll be sworn he wore none but a dish-clout°   *dishcloth*
of Jaquenetta's, and that a wears next his heart, for a favour.

Enter a messenger, Monsieur MERCADÉ[1]

MERCADÉ God save you, madam.

PRINCESS   Welcome, Mercadé,
700 But that thou interrupt'st our merriment.

MERCADÉ I am sorry, madam, for the news I bring
Is heavy in my tongue. The King your father—

PRINCESS Dead, for° my life.   *upon*

MERCADÉ   Even so. My tale is told.

BIRON Worthies, away. The scene begins to cloud.

705 ARMADO For mine own part, I breathe free breath. I have seen

---

7. Whom Armado has killed; whose hopes of Jaquenetta Armado has killed.
8. Help you to take off your doublet; take you down a
peg or two; (both proverbial).
9. He has no linen between his wool outer garments

and his skin—a form of Catholic self-punishment.
1. Possibly Mercury, the classical messenger of the
gods and guide of souls to the underworld; perhaps also
Mar-Arcadia, a reminder that death enters even the
pastoral, Arcadian world of Navarre's park.

the day of wrong through the little hole of discretion, and I will
right myself like a soldier.[2]   *Exeunt Worthies*

KING   How fares your majesty?°   *(her new title)*

QUEEN   Boyet, prepare. I will away tonight.

710   KING   Madam, not so, I do beseech you stay.

QUEEN   Prepare, I say. I thank you, gracious lords,
    For all your fair endeavours, and entreat,
    Out of a new-sad soul, that you vouchsafe
    In your rich wisdom to excuse or hide°   *overlook*
715   The liberal° opposition of our spirits.   *unrestrained*
    If overboldly we have borne ourselves
    In the converse of breath,° your gentleness°   *conversation / courtesy*
    Was guilty of it. Farewell, worthy lord.
    A heavy heart bears not a nimble tongue.
720   Excuse me so coming too short of thanks,
    For my great suit so easily obtained.[3]

KING   The extreme parts of time extremely forms
    All causes to the purpose of his speed,[4]
    And often at his very loose° decides   *the last moment*
725   That which long process could not arbitrate.
    And though the mourning brow of progeny
    Forbid the smiling courtesy of love
    The holy suit which fain it would convince,°   *give proof of*
    Yet since love's argument was first° on foot,   *already*
730   Let not the cloud of sorrow jostle it
    From what it purposed, since to wail friends lost
    Is not by much so wholesome-profitable
    As to rejoice at friends but newly found.

QUEEN   I understand you not. My griefs are double.[5]

735   BIRON   Honest plain words best pierce the ear of grief,
    And by these badges° understand the King.   *signs; words*
    For your fair sakes have we neglected time,
    Played foul play with our oaths. Your beauty, ladies,
    Hath much deformed us, fashioning our humours
740   Even to the opposèd end of our intents,[6]
    And what in us hath seemed ridiculous—
    As love is full of unbefitting strains,°   *impulses*
    All wanton° as a child, skipping and vain,   *careless*
    Formed by the eye and therefore like the eye,
745   Full of strange shapes, of habits and of forms,
    Varying in subjects as the eye doth roll
    To every varied object in his glance;
    Which parti-coated° presence of loose° love   *foolish / unrestrained*
750   Put on by us, if in your heavenly eyes
    Have misbecomed° our oaths and gravities,   *been unbecoming to*
    Those heavenly eyes that look into these faults
    Suggested° us to make them. Therefore, ladies,   *Tempted*
    Our love being yours, the error that love makes
    Is likewise yours. We to ourselves prove false
755   By being once false for ever to be true

2. I have enough sense to acknowledge my wrongdoing
and will honorably put myself in the right.
3. Even though there is no mention of the suit after
2.1, we must assume that it was settled.
4. *The extreme . . . speed:* Final moments enforce rapid

decisions.
5. Doubled because I cannot understand you.
6. *fashioning . . . intents:* distorting our behavior into
the opposite of what we intended.

To those that make us both—fair ladies, you.
And even that falsehood, in itself a sin,
Thus purifies itself and turns to grace.
QUEEN   We have received your letters full of love,
760   Your favours the ambassadors of love,
And in our maiden council rated them
At° courtship, pleasant jest, and courtesy,   As
As bombast⁷ and as lining to the time.
But more devout° than this in our respects°   serious / consideration
765   Have we not been, and therefore met your loves
In their own fashion, like a merriment.
DUMAINE   Our letters, madam, showed much more than jest.
LONGUEVILLE   So did our looks.
ROSALINE   We did not quote° them so.   interpret
KING   Now, at the latest minute of the hour,
Grant us your loves.
770   QUEEN   A time, methinks, too short
To make a world-without-end° bargain in.   an everlasting (biblical)
No, no, my lord, your grace is perjured much,
Full of dear° guiltiness, and therefore this: grievous; precious
If for my love—as there is no such cause⁸—
775   You will do aught,° this shall you do for me: anything
Your oath I will not trust, but go with speed
To some forlorn and naked hermitage
Remote from all the pleasures of the world.
There stay until the twelve celestial signs°   (of the zodiac)
780   Have brought about the annual reckoning.
If this austere, insociable life
Change not your offer made in heat of blood;
If frosts and fasts, hard lodging and thin weeds°   clothes
Nip not the gaudy blossoms of your love,
785   But that it bear this trial and last° love,   remain
Then at the expiration of the year
Come challenge° me, challenge me by these deserts,   claim
And, by this virgin palm now kissing thine,
I will be thine, and till that instance° shut   instant
790   My woeful self up in a mourning house,
Raining the tears of lamentation
For the remembrance of my father's death.
If this thou do deny, let our hands part,
Neither entitled in the other's heart.
795   KING   If this, or more than this, I would deny,
To flatter up° these powers of mine with rest   pamper
The sudden hand of death close up mine eye.
Hence, hermit,° then. My heart is in thy breast.⁹   I'm off to be a hermit
[They talk apart]
798.1   BIRON   *And what to me, my love? And what to me?*
ROSALINE   *You must be purgèd, too. Your sins are rank.*
You are attaint° with faults and perjury.   dishonored; infected
Therefore if you my favour mean to get
798.5   *A twelvemonth shall you spend, and never rest*
But seek the weary beds of people sick.

7. Wool stuffing for clothes; inflated rhetoric.
8. No reason why you should feel obliged to do so.

9. The following six indented lines (798.1–798.6) represent a draft version of 5.2.814–31.

DUMAINE [*to* CATHERINE]   But what to me, my love? But what
    to me?
800   A wife?
CATHERINE   A beard,[1] fair health, and honesty.
    With three-fold love I wish you all these three.
DUMAINE   O, shall I say 'I thank you, gentle wife'?
CATHERINE   Not so, my lord. A twelvemonth and a day
805   I'll mark no words that smooth-faced wooers say.
    Come when the King doth to my lady come;
    Then if I have much love, I'll give you some.
DUMAINE   I'll serve thee true and faithfully till then.
CATHERINE   Yet swear not, lest ye be forsworn again.
        [*They talk apart*]
LONGUEVILLE   What says Maria?
810 MARIA   At the twelvemonth's end
    I'll change my black gown for a faithful friend.°   *lover*
LONGUEVILLE   I'll stay° with patience; but the time is long.   *wait*
MARIA   The liker you—few taller are so young.[2]
        [*They talk apart*]
BIRON [*to* ROSALINE]   Studies my lady?° Mistress, look on me.   *Are you preoccupied*
815   Behold the window of my heart, mine eye,
    What humble suit attends° thy answer there.   *waits for*
    Impose some service on me for thy love.
ROSALINE   Oft have I heard of you, my lord Biron,
    Before I saw you; and the world's large tongue
820   Proclaims you for a man replete with mocks,
    Full of comparisons° and wounding flouts,   *satirical similes*
    Which you on all estates° will execute   *classes of people*
    That lie within the mercy of your wit.
    To weed this wormwood° from your fruitful brain,   *bitterness*
825   And therewithal to win me if you please,
    Without the which I am not to be won,
    You shall this twelvemonth term from day to day
    Visit the speechless sick and still converse°   *always associate*
    With groaning wretches, and your task shall be
830   With all the fierce° endeavour of your wit   *forceful*
    To enforce the painèd impotent° to smile.   *sick*
BIRON   To move wild laughter in the throat of death?—
    It cannot be, it is impossible.
    Mirth cannot move a soul in agony.
835 ROSALINE   Why, that's the way to choke a gibing spirit,
    Whose influence is begot of that loose grace°   *uncritical acceptance*
    Which shallow laughing hearers give to fools.
    A jest's prosperity lies in the ear
    Of him that hears it, never in the tongue
840   Of him that makes it. Then if sickly ears,
    Deafed with the clamours of their own dear groans,
    Will hear your idle scorns, continue then,
    And I will have you and that fault withal.°   *as well*
    But if they will not, throw away that spirit,
845   And I shall find you empty of that fault,
    Right joyful of your reformation.

---

1. Implying that he looks immature; perhaps also that as a hermit he'll grow a beard.

2. The more like you—although tall ("long"), you are still young.

BIRON   A twelvemonth? Well, befall what will befall,
 I'll jest a twelvemonth in an hospital.
QUEEN [*to the* KING] Ay, sweet my lord, and so I take my leave.
850 KING   No, madam, we will bring° you on your way.   *escort*
BIRON   Our wooing doth not end like an old play.
 Jack hath not Jill. These ladies' courtesy
 Might well have made our sport a comedy.
KING   Come, sir, it wants° a twelvemonth an' a day,   *lacks*
 And then 'twill end.
855 BIRON   That's too long for a play.

    Enter [ARMADO *the*] *braggart*

ARMADO [*to the* KING] Sweet majesty, vouchsafe me.
QUEEN   Was not that Hector?
DUMAINE   The worthy knight of Troy.
ARMADO   I will kiss thy royal finger and take leave.
860 I am a votary, I have vowed to Jaquenetta
 To hold the plough° for her sweet love three year. But, most *To farm (bawdy)*
 esteemed greatness, will you hear the dialogue° that the two *debate*
 learned men[3] have compiled in praise of the owl and the
 cuckoo? It should have followed in the end of our show.
865 KING   Call them forth quickly, we will do so.
ARMADO   Holla, approach!

    Enter [HOLOFERNES, NATHANIEL, COSTARD, MOTE, DULL,
    JAQUENETTA, *and others*]

      This side is Hiems, winter,
 This Ver, the spring, the one maintained° by the owl, *supported*
 The other by the cuckoo. Ver, begin.
SPRING [*sings*]
  When daisies pied° and violets blue,[4]   *multicolored*
870   And lady-smocks,° all silver-white,   *cuckoo flowers*
  And cuckoo-buds° of yellow hue   *buttercups?*
   Do paint the meadows with delight,
  The cuckoo then on every tree
  Mocks married men, for thus sings he:
875   Cuckoo!
  Cuckoo, cuckoo—O word of fear,[5]
  Unpleasing to a married ear.
  When shepherds pipe on oaten straws,
   And merry larks are ploughmen's clocks;
880 When turtles tread,° and rooks and daws, *turtledoves mate*
   And maidens bleach their summer smocks,
  The cuckoo then on every tree
  Mocks married men, for thus sings he:
   Cuckoo!
885 Cuckoo, cuckoo—O word of fear,
  Unpleasing to a married ear.
WINTER [*sings*]
  When icicles hang by the wall,
   And Dick the shepherd blows his nail,[6]
  And Tom bears logs into the hall,
890   And milk comes frozen home in pail;
  When blood is nipped,° and ways° be foul, *chilled / pathways*

---

3. Holofernes and Nathaniel(?)
4. The dialogue is in iambic tetrameter, a song meter.
5. Because it sounds like "cuckold."
6. Blows on his hands to keep warm; is idle.

Then nightly sings the staring owl:
Tu-whit, tu-whoo![7]—a merry note,
While greasy Joan doth keel° the pot.   *stir to cool*
895 When all aloud the wind doth blow,
     And coughing drowns the parson's saw,°   *moralizing*
     And birds sit brooding in the snow,
       And Marian's nose looks red and raw;
     When roasted crabs° hiss in the bowl,°   *crab apples / (of ale)*
900 Then nightly sings the staring owl:
     Tu-whit, tu-whoo!—a merry note,
     While greasy Joan doth keel the pot.

ARMADO The words of Mercury are harsh after the songs of
Apollo.[8] You that way, we this way.[9]   *Exeunt [severally]*°   *separately*

---

7. Perhaps: to it (a hunting cry, with possible sexual overtones), to woo.
8. Presumably the love poetry of the King and courtiers. *words of Mercury*: probably referring to Mercadé's somber message. (See note to the stage direction following line 698.)

9. This line may distinguish the audience ("you") from the actors ("we"), the aristocratic from the humbler characters, the French ladies from the inhabitants of Navarre, or even the actor playing Spring from the one playing Winter.

Love's Labour's Won

In 1598, Francis Meres called as witnesses to Shakespeare's excellence in comedy 'his *Gētlemē of Verona*, his *Errors*, his *Loue labors lost*, his *Loue labours wonne*, his *Midsummers night dreame*, & his *Merchant of Venice*'. This was the only evidence that Shakespeare wrote a play called *Love's Labour's Won* until the discovery in 1953 of a fragment of a bookseller's list that had been used in the binding of a volume published in 1637/8. The fragment itself appears to record items sold from 9 to 17 August 1603 by a book dealer in the south of England. Among items headed '[inte]rludes & tragedyes' are

> marchant of vennis
> taming of a shrew
> knak to know a knave
> knak to know an honest man
> loves labor lost
> loves labor won

No author is named for any of the items. All the plays named in the list except *Love's Labour's Won* are known to have been printed by 1600; all were written by 1596–97. Taken together, Meres's reference in 1598 and the 1603 fragment appear to demonstrate that a play by Shakespeare called *Love's Labour's Won* had been performed by the time Meres wrote and was in print by August 1603. Conceivably the phrase served as an alternative title for one of Shakespeare's other comedies, though the only one believed to have been written by 1598 but not listed by Meres is *The Taming of the Shrew*, which is named (as *The Taming of a Shrew*) in the bookseller's fragment. Otherwise we must suppose that *Love's Labour's Won* is the title of a lost play by Shakespeare, that no copy of the edition mentioned in the bookseller's list is extant, and that Heminges and Condell failed to include it in the 1623 Folio.

None of these suppositions is implausible. We know of at least one other lost play attributed to Shakespeare (see *Cardenio*, below), and of many lost works by contemporary playwrights. No copy of the first edition of *Titus Andronicus* was known until 1904; for *I Henry IV* and *The Passionate Pilgrim* only a fragment of the first edition survives. And we now know that *Troilus and Cressida* was almost omitted from the 1623 Folio (probably for copyright reasons) despite its evident authenticity. It is also possible that, like most of the early editions of Shakespeare's plays, the lost edition of *Love's Labour's Won* did not name him on the title-page, and this omission might go some way to explaining the failure of the edition to survive, or (if it does still survive) to be noticed. *Love's Labour's Won* stands a much better chance of having survived, somewhere, than *Cardenio*: because it was printed, between 500 and 1,500 copies were once in circulation, whereas for *Cardenio* we know of only a single manuscript.

The evidence for the existence of the lost play (unlike that for *Cardenio*) gives us little indication of its content. Meres explicitly states, and the title implies, that it was a comedy. Its titular pairing with *Love's Labour's Lost* suggests that they may have been written at about the same time. Both Meres and the bookseller's catalogue place it after *Love's Labour's Lost*; although neither list is necessarily chronological, Meres's does otherwise agree with our own view of the order of composition of Shakespeare's comedies.

THE OXFORD EDITORS

A Midsummer Night's Dream

Imagine an aristocratic wedding in a grand English country house. Imagine that after the solemnities and the wedding supper, the newlyweds and their distinguished guests—including the most distinguished guest of all, Queen Elizabeth I—are treated to a private entertainment, a play written especially for them. Imagine that the play is Shakespeare's *A Midsummer Night's Dream,* a comedy that culminates not only in three marriages but in a play, *Pyramus and Thisbe,* performed for the newlyweds with delicious incompetence by well-meaning, hopelessly bumbling artisans. Their inept performance amuses the happy couples and helps to "wear away this long age of three hours," as the amorously impatient Duke Theseus puts it, "between our after-supper and bedtime" (5.1.33–34). At the end of the play within the play, the stage brides and grooms exit to consummate their marriages—"Sweet friends, to bed"—and so, too, amid the blessings and sly jokes of their guests, the real newlyweds retire to bed.

Scholars have told and retold this story of the aristocratic wedding for which Shakespeare wrote his most enchanting comedy until it has come to seem like an established truth, one of the few things we actually know about the composition of the plays. But while the story is both charming and plausible, there is not a shred of actual evidence that *A Midsummer Night's Dream* was ever performed at, let alone written expressly for, such a wedding. What we do know is that this play was performed on the London stage: the title page of the First Quarto says that it "hath been sundry times publikely acted" by the Lord Chamberlain's Men and that it was written by William Shakespeare.

The precise date that *A Midsummer Night's Dream* was written and first performed is unknown; the Elizabethan writer Francis Meres mentions it admiringly in 1598, and certain of its stylistic features have led many scholars to place it around 1594–96, the probable period of the comparably lyrical *Romeo and Juliet* and *Richard II.* Attempts to find more precise coordinates by locating an allusion to a particular Royal Progress in Oberon's lines about the "fair vestal thronèd by the west" (2.1 158) or to a particular wet season in Titania's lines about the miserable weather (2 1.88ff.) have been defeated by the frequency of both Queen Elizabeth's travels and English rainstorms.

What accounts, then, for all the speculation about the wedding ceremony, complete with royal attendance? In part, the answer lies in the comedy's thematic focus on love consummated in marriage. The final ritual blessing of the bride beds—the fairies' version of a traditional Catholic practice deemed superstitious by zealous Protestants—can be seen as the culmination of the elaborate festivities, including song, music, dancing, and plays, that often accompanied upper-class Elizabethan marriages. In part, imagining a specific historical occasion helps to highlight an uncertainty, at once pleasurable and disturbing, about the borderline between reality and illusion: as in a hall of mirrors, the real-life newlyweds whiling away the hours before bedtime by watching a play would see onstage other newlyweds whiling away the hours before bedtime by watching a play.

But, as four centuries of readers and playgoers have found, you do not need to see *A Midsummer Night's Dream* on your wedding day, nor do you need to be an aristocrat, to savor its delights. There have, to be sure, been a few dissenters: the diarist Samuel Pepys wrote after seeing a production in 1662 that "it is the most insipid ridiculous play that ever I saw in my life," although he took note of "some good dancing and some handsome women." Most audiences have been vastly more enthusiastic. The play has inspired a succession of musical adaptations and settings, along with famously lavish productions. By the nineteenth century, Shakespeare's bare stage had given way to

Cupid and his victims. From Gilles Corrozet, *Hecatomgraphie* (1540).

gorgeous sets, with twinkling lights, fairies rising on midnight mushrooms, the moon shining over the Acropolis, and live rabbits hopping across carpets of flowers. Film is, of course, well suited to such fantasies, as a series of famous motion pictures have shown, but *A Midsummer Night's Dream* has proved equally at home in the simplest of settings. Generations of schoolchildren have romped through cardboard forests, while in Peter Brook's influential 1970 production for the Royal Shakespeare Company the actors performed (often on trapeze) in a three-sided, brightly lit, bare white box.

Working its magic on the imagination, Shakespeare's visionary poetic drama appeals to an unusually broad spectrum of spectators. The play may induce fantasies of aristocratic or private pleasure, but it does so with the resources of the public stage. If it mocks working-class artisans (skilled craftsmen who are simply called "the rabble" in one quarto stage direction), it also laughs at well-born young lovers. Its language reflects an unusually high incidence of the tropes familiar to those who had received rhetorical and literary training, but you do not have to learn the Greek names for these tropes—*anaphora, isocolon, epizeuxis,* and the like—to enjoy their effects. Take, for example, the exchange between Lysander and Hermia in the wake of Egeus's attempt to block their betrothal:

> LYSANDER   The course of true love never did run smooth,
>   But either it was different in blood—
> HERMIA   O cross!—too high to be enthralled to low.
> LYSANDER   Or else misgrafted in respect of years—
> HERMIA   O spite!—too old to be engaged to young.
> LYSANDER   Or merit stood upon the choice of friends—
> HERMIA   O hell!—to choose love by another's eyes.
>   (1.1.134–40)

The alternation of single lines, called *stichomythia,* is a scheme that Shakespeare borrowed from the Roman playwright Seneca and used in different ways in many of his plays. The effect here is to convey the lovers' mutual anguish, tinging it slightly perhaps with a gently ironic distance that evaporates in the poignant lament that follows (lines 141–49). The rhetorical devices, along with the subtle modulations from blank verse to rhymed couplets to boisterous comic prose, are so deftly handled that their pleasures are accessible to the learned and unlearned alike. This breadth also reflects the very wide range of cultural materials that the playwright has cunningly woven together, from the classical heritage of the educated elite to popular ballads and folk customs, from refined and sophisticated entertainments to the coarser delights of farce.

The exquisite lyricism of much of the play, the celebration of aristocratic pastimes such as the hunt, and a vision of courtly glamour conjure up an upper-class milieu. There is no single literary source for Shakespeare's depiction of this world, or indeed for the play as a whole, but he is indebted for the legendary Theseus and Hippolyta to Thomas North's translation (1579) of Plutarch's *Lives of the Noble Grecians and Romanes,* and still more to Chaucer's *Knight's Tale.* The *Dream* repeatedly echoes Chaucer's references to observing "the rite of May," a folk custom still current in Elizabethan England and quite possibly known to Shakespeare personally. To the dismay of Puritans, who regarded the celebration as a lascivious remnant of paganism, young men and women of all classes would go out into the woods and fields to welcome the

Pyramus and Thisbe. From George Wither, *A Collection of Emblemes* (1635).

May with singing and dancing. Shakespeare's title associates this custom with another occasion for festive release: Midsummer Eve (June 23), when the solstice was marked not only by holiday license but by tales of fairy spells and temporary madness.

Some Elizabethan aristocrats kept theatrical troupes as liveried servants, along with young pages who could sing and perform, and powerful magnates, both secular and religious, often had plays, masquerades, and elaborate shows staged in their houses. From this milieu, Shakespeare derives a vision of what we can call the revels of power, performances designed to entertain, gratify, and reflect the values of those at the top. From this milieu too Shakespeare absorbs a sense of social hierarchy: a distinction between Duke Theseus, at once imperious and genteel, and Egeus, wealthy but distinctly lower in rank and harping on what is his by law, along with a more marked distinction between these characters and the artisans, loyal members of the lower orders, regarded by their social superiors with condescending indulgence.

The artisans—or "rude mechanicals," as they are called—enable Shakespeare to introduce wonderful swoops into earthy prose, snatches of jigs, a comical taste for the grotesque, a glimpse of a world that usually resides beyond the horizon of courtly vision. The lovers at the pinnacle of the play's society do not know the names and trades of the "hard-handed men that work in Athens here" (5.1.72) who have come to offer them entertainment, but we the audience do, and we even know something of their hopes and dreams. As with the Pageant of the Nine Worthies in *Love's Labour's Lost*, we are invited at once to join in the mockery of the inept performers and to distance ourselves from the mockers. That is, the audience of *A Midsummer Night's Dream* is not simply mirrored in the play's upper classes: the real audience is given a broader perspective, a more capacious understanding than anyone onstage.

This understanding is signaled not only in our ability to take in both the courtly and popular dimensions of the play, but also in our ability to see what escapes both aristocrats and artisans: the world of the fairies. But what are the fairies? From what social milieu do they spring? It is tempting to reply that they are denizens of the country— that is, characters drawn from the semipagan folklore of rural England. This is at least partially true: Reginald Scot, who wrote a brilliant attack on witchcraft persecutions (*The Discoverie of Witchcraft*, 1584), suggests that Robin Goodfellow, the mischievous spirit also called a Puck, was once feared by villagers, but was now widely recognized to be a figure of mere "illusion and knaverie." Yet intensive scholarly research over several generations has suggested that Shakespeare's fairies are quite unlike those his audience might have credited, half-credited, or—as Scot hoped—discredited.

The fairies of Elizabethan popular belief were often threatening and dangerous, while those of *A Midsummer Night's Dream* are generally benevolent. The former steal human infants, perhaps to sacrifice them to the devil, while the latter, even when they quarrel over the possession of a young boy, do so to bestow love and favor upon him; the former leave deformed, emaciated children in place of those they have stolen, while the latter trip nimbly through the palace blessing the bride beds and warding off deformities. Shakespeare's fairies have some of the menacing associations of "real" fairies— Puck speaks of shrouds and gaping graves, while the quarrel between Oberon and Titania has disrupted the seasons and damaged the crops, as wicked spirits were said to do. But the fairies we see are, as Oberon says, "spirits of another sort." Oberon and Titania (whose names Shakespeare took from the French romance *Huon of Bordeaux* and from Ovid, respectively) repeatedly demonstrate their good will toward mortals, though they have very little good will toward each other. The fairy king and queen are distressed at the unintended consequences of their quarrel, and each is involved, with romantic generosity, in the happiness of Theseus and Hippolyta. This generosity extends beyond the immediate range of their interests: in the midst of plotting to humiliate Titania, Oberon attempts to intervene on behalf of the spurned Helena, and though this intervention proves, through Puck's mistake, to lead to hopeless confusion, the fairies make amends.

Indeed, if Puck takes mischievous delight in the discord he has helped to sow among the four young lovers—"Lord, what fools these mortals be!" (3.2.115)—he is not the originator of that discord, and he is the indispensable agent for setting things right. In his role as both mischief-maker and matchmaker, Puck resembles the crafty slave in comedies by the Latin playwrights Plautus and Terence, a stock character who sometimes seems to enjoy and contribute to the plot's tangles but who manages in the end to remove the obstacles that stand in the way of the young lovers.

This resemblance brings us to yet another of the cultural elements that Shakespeare cunningly interweaves in the plot of *A Midsummer Night's Dream*. From the classical literary tradition, which he must have first encountered in grammar school, Shakespeare derives the ancient Greek setting, the story of Pyramus and Thisbe as told in Ovid's *Metamorphoses*, the comic transformation of a man into an ass as told in Apuleius's *Golden Ass*, and, above all, the basic plot device of young lovers contriving to escape the rigid will of a stern father. This device was one of the staples of the New Comedy of ancient Greece and was a mainstay as well in Roman comedy. The literary convention corresponds to certain aspects of actual life in Shakespeare's England, where lawsuits provide records of parents trying to compel children to marry against their will. But the historical problem of marital consent has a complex relation to its artistic representation. Not only does the play exaggerate the actual punitive power of the father—Egeus threatens his disobedient daughter with death (to which Theseus offers, as a grim alternative, the nunnery)—but it also exaggerates the release from this power by staging the giddy possibility of a marriage based entirely on love and desire rather than parental will.

In *A Midsummer Night's Dream*, this release, a highly implausible dream for any Elizabethan member of the middle or upper classes, is brought about by a further plot device: the escape from the court or city to the "green world" of the forest. This theatrical structure is not characteristic of the New Comedy, but it somewhat resembles the Saturnalian rhythms of the Old Comedy of Aristophanes, with its festive release from the discipline and sobriety of everyday life, and, still more perhaps, it reflects certain English folk customs, such as Maying. When Theseus comes upon the four exhausted lovers asleep in the woods, he thinks that "they rose up early to observe / The rite of May" (4.1.129–30).

But, of course, Theseus is wrong. The lovers were not out a-Maying, but had spent the night stumbling through the woods in a confused state of fear, anger, and desire. When it enters the charmed, moonlit space of *A Midsummer Night's Dream*, "the rite of May," along with the other rituals and representations Shakespeare stitched together in creating his play, is transformed; to use Peter Quince's term for the metamorphosed Bottom, the rites and rituals are "translated." Folk customs, the revels of power, the classical tradition as taught in schools, all are displaced from their points of origin, their enabling institutions and assumptions, and brought into a new space, the space of the Shakespearean stage.

This "translation" has, in every case, the odd effect of simultaneous elevation and enervation, celebration and parody. Thus the minor Ovidian tale of Pyramus and Thisbe is greatly elaborated but also travestied; the popular realm is at once lovingly represented and mercilessly ridiculed; the revels of power are reproduced but also ironically distanced.

Some of the play's most wonderful moments spring from the zany conjunction of distinct and even opposed theatrical modes (a conjunction characteristically parodied in the oxymoronic title of the artisans' play, "A tedious brief scene of young Pyramus / And his love Thisbe: very tragical mirth" [5.1.56–57]). Thus, for example, exquisite love poetry and low comedy meet in the wonderful moment in which the queen of fairies awakens to become enraptured at the sight of the most flatulently absurd of the mechanicals, Bottom. Bottom has been transformed with perfect appropriateness into an ass, yet it is he who is granted the play's most exquisite vision of delight and who articulates, in a comically confused burlesque of St. Paul (1 Corinthians 2:9), the deepest sense of wonder: "The eye of man hath not heard, the ear of man hath not seen, man's hand is not able to taste, his tongue to conceive, nor his heart to report what my dream was" (4.1.204–07).

It would be asinine, the play suggests, to try to expound this dream, but we can at least suggest that, whatever its meaning, its existence is closely linked to the nature of

A fairy hill. From Olaus Magnus, *Historia de Gentibus Septentrionalibus* (1555).

the theater itself. Puck suggests as much when he proposes in the Epilogue that the audience imagine that it has all along been slumbering: the play it has seen has been a collective hallucination. The play, then, is a dream about watching a play about dreams. Fittingly, the comedy devotes much of its last act to a parody of a theatrical performance, as if its most enduring concern were not the fate of the lovers but the possibility of performing plays. The entire last act of *A Midsummer Night's Dream* is unnecessary in terms of the plot: by Oberon's intervention and Theseus's fiat, the plot complications have all been resolved at the end of Act 4. Knots that had seemed almost impossible to untangle—Theseus had declared in Act 1 that he was powerless to overturn the ancient privilege of Athens invoked by Egeus—suddenly dissolve. The absurdly easy resolution of an apparently hopeless dilemma characterizes not only the lovers' legal but also their emotional condition, a blend of mad confusion and geometric logic that is settled, apparently permanently, with the aid of the fairies' magical love juice.

But this diagrammatic settling of affairs sits uncomfortably with all that the lovers have experienced in the woods. Both critics and directors have given different weight to this experience. Some treat the lovers as mindless comic puppets, jerked by the playwright's invisible strings, while others take more seriously the darkness that shadows their words and actions. This darkness includes emotional violence and masochism, the betrayal of friendship, the radical fickleness of desire. It extends to the play's sexual politics. Under the strain of the night's adventures, the friendship between Hermia and Helena begins to crack apart, while Lysander and Demetrius become bitter rivals. Although they are eventually reconciled, it is as if the heterosexual couplings can only be formed by painfully sundering the intimate same-sex bonds that preceded them. Shakespeare had begun to reflect on this problem as early as *The Two Gentlemen of Verona*, possibly his first play, and throughout his career he returned to it repeatedly, including in what is possibly his last play, *The Two Noble Kinsmen*. For the most part, the broken friendships are repaired, but, as with Antonio and Sebastian in *Twelfth Night* and Leontes and Polixenes in *The Winter's Tale*, there is usually a lingering sense of loss, from which even the sunnier *Midsummer Night's Dream* is not completely exempt.

In another very early play, *The Taming of the Shrew*, Shakespeare had also begun his lifelong reflection on the struggle between men and women, a struggle frequently focused on the male desire to dominate and subdue the female. In *A Midsummer Night's Dream*, tension flares in the case of the fairies into open conflict over the Indian boy, the locus of Oberon's assertion of patriarchal power and Titania's claim to independence. In the human world of the play, this tension is less immediately apparent, but in the first scene Theseus alludes to his military conquest of the Amazon queen Hippolyta, and there are other brief glimpses of cruelty, indifference, and rage. Those who see *A Midsummer Night's Dream* as lighthearted entertainment must somehow laugh off this darkness; those who wish to emphasize the play's more troubling and discordant notes must somehow neutralize the comic register in which such notes are sounded. For example, the brutal insults hurled at Hermia by the young man who had loved her and with whom she has eloped might well seem extremely painful, but the fantastic language in which these insults are expressed—

> Get you gone, you dwarf,
> You *minimus* of hind'ring knot-grass made,
> You bead, you acorn
>
> (3.2.329–31)

—distances audiences from the pain and generates laughter.

Audiences for most productions tend to oscillate between engagement and detachment. In the young lovers' choices and sufferings, we encounter a situation where the final outcome doesn't matter greatly to us but matters greatly to them. And while we see the characters from a distance—although Hermia and Helena are distinct enough, even attentive readers occasionally find it difficult to remember which is Lysander and which Demetrius—we also experience at least glancingly *their* sense of how important the difference is, how unbearable to be matched against one's consent, how painfully difficult to make a match that corresponds to one's desires.

Desires in *A Midsummer Night's Dream* are intense, irrational, and alarmingly mobile. This mobility, the speed with which desire can be detached from one object and attached to a different object, does not diminish the exigency of the passion, for the lovers are convinced at every moment that their choices are irrefutably rational and irresistibly compelling. But there is no security in these choices and the play is repeatedly haunted by a fear of abandonment. The emblem, as well as agent, of a dangerously mobile desire is the fairies' love juice. No human being in the play experiences a purely abstract, objectless desire; when you desire, you desire *someone*. But the love juice is the distilled essence of erotic mobility itself, and it is appropriately in the power of the fairies. For the fairies seem to embody the principle of what we might call polytropic desire—that is, desire that can instantaneously alight on any object, including an ass-headed man, and that can with equal instantaneousness swerve away from that object and on to another. Oberon and Titania have, we learn, long histories of amorous adventures; they are aware of each other's wayward passions; and, endowed with an extraordinary, eroticizing rhetoric, they move endlessly through the spiced, moonlit night.

If there is a link between the fairies and the erotic, there is a still more powerful link between the fairies and the imagination. Theseus makes the connection explicit when he rejects the stories that the lovers have told him: "I never may believe / These antique fables, nor these fairy toys." In a famous speech (5.1.2–22), he accounts for such fables and toys as products of the imagination. The speech reflects Theseus's misplaced confidence in his own sense of waking reality, a reality that does not include fairies. Yet paradoxically, in dismissively categorizing the lunatic, the lover, and the poet as "of imagination all compact," he manages to articulate insights that the play seems to uphold. Those in the grip of a powerful imagination may be loosed from the moorings of reason and nature, and they may inhabit a world of wish fulfilment and its converse, nightmare. But the poet whose imagination "bodies forth / The forms of things unknown" (5.1.14–15) has created *A Midsummer Night's Dream*, giving his fantasies—including the fantasy called "Theseus"—"a local habitation and a name." Finally, it is the imagination that enables giddy, restless, changeable mortals to attach their desires to a particular person.

For Theseus, the imagination is the agent of delusion—and there is much in the play that would seem to support this conclusion. But his account is not complete without Hippolyta's insistence that the story the four young lovers tell seems to have something that goes beyond delusion. Their minds, she observes, have been "transfigured" together, and this shared transfiguration bears witness to "something of great constancy; / But howsoever, strange and admirable" (5.1.26–27). It is as if we were all to wake up one morning and discover we had had the same dream.

And, of course, *we* in the audience have, as Puck's epilogue suggests, had just this experience: the experience of the theater. In the theater, we confront a living representation of the complex relation between transfiguration and delusion, a relation explored with fantastic, anxious literalness in the artisans' performance of *Pyramus and Thisbe*. In reassuring the ladies that the lion is only Snug the Joiner, that nothing is what it claims to be, the players simultaneously burlesque the stage and call attention to the basic elements from which any performance is made: rudimentary scenery, artisans, language, imagination, desire.

There is precious little evidence, to be sure, of either imagination or desire in the artisans' performance of *Pyramus and Thisbe*. Their absence is part of the comical awfulness of the play within the play, the reason in effect that it does not become the Shakespearean tragedy it so strikingly resembles, *Romeo and Juliet*. And yet, as Theseus says, "The best in this kind are but shadows, and the worst are no worse if imagination amend them." "It must be your imagination, then," Hippolyta points out, "and not theirs" (5.1.208–10). But that is true of performances far greater than that of which the artisans are capable. If we are to see fairies onstage in *A Midsummer Night's Dream,* and not simply flesh-and-blood actors (probably boy actors in Shakespeare's theater), it must be our imagination that makes amends. So too if we are to believe in the lovers' desire and sympathize with their predicament, it must be *our* desire that animates their words.

Such, at least, is the vision of the theater suggested by the play that Bottom and company offer to the newlyweds. There is nothing really out there, their performance implies, except what the audience graciously consents to dream. Yet in the closing moments of the play, when the fairies emerge from the woods and venture into Theseus's mansion to bless the bride beds, a quite different vision of theater is suggested, one in which the dreams and desires that we have are determined by forces over which we have no control, forces that only a playwright's love juice can make visible under an imaginary moon.

STEPHEN GREENBLATT

TEXTUAL NOTE

A Midsummer Night's Dream was entered in the Stationers' Register on October 8, 1600, and printed that same year in quarto:

A Midsommer nights dreame. As it hath beene sundry times pub*lickely acted, by the Right honourable,* the Lord Chamberlaine his *seruants. Written by William Shake-speare.* Imprinted at London, for *Thomas Fisher,* and are to be soulde at his shoppe, at the Signe of the White Hart, in *Fleetestreete.* 1600.

This quarto (Q1) was evidently prepared from a manuscript in Shakespeare's hand. A second quarto (Q2), printed in 1619 (though falsely dated 1600), corrects some errors in Q1, but it also introduces new errors. This second quarto was used as the basis for the 1623 First Folio text of the play (F), though the Folio editors also had recourse to a theatrical manuscript, probably a promptbook in the possession of Shakespeare's company, the King's Men. Evidence for this manuscript includes a Folio stage direction before 5.1.126: "Tawyer with a Trumpet before them." "Tawyer" presumably refers to William Tawyer, a musician employed by the King's Men.

From this theatrical manuscript evidently derived several alterations in stage directions and in speech prefixes, the most notable of which is the substitution in Act 5 of Egeus for Philostrate as the master of ceremonies. The substitution may simply be a mistake: in an early performance, the same actor may have played the parts of both Egeus and Philostrate, and this doubling may have led to an error in the speech prefix. But it is also possible that the play was revised in order to integrate the disgruntled Egeus more fully into the festive conclusion.

Act and scene divisions all derive from F; there are none in the quarto text. Traditionally, Act 3, Scene 2 continues to the end of the act, but since the stage is apparently cleared at 3.2.413, this edition marks a break (perhaps indicating a gap in time and place) by dividing the scene in two and designating a third scene. In F, at the end of Act 3 there is a stage direction, "They sleepe all the Act," which indicates that the four lovers remain asleep onstage during the interval customary between acts and that the action that resumes in the next act is understood to be continuous.

On the basis of mislined verses in 5.1.1–84, scholars have conjectured that Shakespeare may have revised Theseus's speech as originally conceived and added lines in the margin of his copy. Since these revisions may give us a glimpse of Shakespeare's process of composition, this book appends a reconstruction of what would have been the original speech.

The control text for this edition of *A Midsummer Night's Dream* is Q1 (1600). But in keeping with the Oxford editors' principle of basing their text on the most theatrical early version of each play—that is, the version closest to the play as performed by Shakespeare's company during the playwright's own lifetime—changes in speech prefixes and other substantive variants have been adopted from F.

SELECTED BIBLIOGRAPHY

Barber, C. L. "May Games and Metamorphoses on a Midsummer's Night." *Shakespeare's Festive Comedy: A Study of Dramatic Form and Its Relation to Social Custom*. Princeton: Princeton University Press, 1959. 119–62. *A Midsummer Night's Dream* combines folk customs, Ovidian fancy, and Elizabethan pageantry to produce a clarifying release of imagination.

Bate, Jonathan. *Shakespeare and Ovid*. New York: Oxford University Press, 1993. *A Midsummer Night's Dream* indirectly dramatizes Ovid, gathering themes of myth, metamorphosis, and love into a mixed mode typical of sixteenth-century mythography.

Briggs, K. M. *The Anatomy of Puck: An Examination of Fairy Beliefs Among Shakespeare's Contemporaries and Successors*. London: Routledge and Kegan Paul, 1959. A survey of early modern notions about fairies, especially in English literary tradition, describing also the influence of Shakespeare's innovations.

Dash, Irene G. *Women's Worlds in Shakespeare's Plays*. London: Associated University Presses, 1997. Looks at *A Midsummer Night's Dream* in performance, arguing that traditional staging practices have tended reductively to simplify Shakespeare's women.

Girard, René. "Myth and Ritual in Shakespeare: *A Midsummer Night's Dream*." *Textual Strategies: Perspectives in Post-Structuralist Criticism*. Ed. Josué V. Harari. Ithaca, N.Y.: Cornell University Press, 1979. 189–212. This play presents a genetic theory of myth, charting a collective mental transformation.

Loomba, Ania. "The Great Indian Vanishing Trick—Colonialism, Property, and the Family in *A Midsummer Night's Dream*." *A Feminist Companion to Shakespeare*. Ed. Dympna Callaghan. Malden, Mass.: Blackwell, 2000. 163–87. Argues that the Indian boy represents the shaping dialectic between non-European practices and Western domestic ideology.

Montrose, Louis. *The Purpose of Playing: Shakespeare and the Cultural Politics of the Elizabethan Theatre*. Chicago: University of Chicago Press, 1996. Examines the play's relationship to Elizabethan ideology through discourses of gender, physiology, social rank, and royal iconography.

Traub, Valerie. *The Renaissance of Lesbianism in Early Modern England*. Cambridge: Cambridge University Press, 2002. Observes how renovated classical idioms and new scientific knowledge made female-female desire intelligible in the Renaissance.

Williams, Gary Jay. *Our Moonlight Revels: "A Midsummer Night's Dream" in the Theatre*. Iowa City: University of Iowa Press, 1997. The major stage, film, and opera adaptations, understood in relation to the cultures that produced them.

Young, David P. *Something of Great Constancy: The Art of "A Midsummer Night's Dream."* New Haven: Yale University Press, 1966. Extensive, variegated study covering sources, structure, performance, and contexts.

FILMS

A Midsummer Night's Dream. 1935. Dir. William Dieterle and Max Reinhardt. USA. 133 min. Sumptuous production, with balletic fairies, a serpentine Hippolyta, an elaborate Mendelssohn score, and Mickey Rooney as Puck.

A *Midsummer Night's Dream*. 1968. Dir. Peter Hall. UK. 124 min. Noted for its mini-skirted sensuality, body paint, and extremely gnarled and muddy forest. With Diana Rigg and Helen Mirren.

A *Midsummer Night's Dream*. 1996. Dir. Adrian Noble. UK. 105 min. Theseus and Hippolyta double as Oberon and Titania, with a frame device of a boy dreaming the play. Starring Lindsay Duncan and Alex Jennings.

A *Midsummer Night's Dream*. 1999. Dir. Michael Hoffman. USA. 116 min. In Victorian costume against the Tuscan backdrop, this dreamy and erotic version amplifies Bottom's role. With Kevin Kline and Michelle Pfeiffer.

A Midsummer Night's Dream

THE PERSONS OF THE PLAY

THESEUS, Duke of Athens
HIPPOLYTA, Queen of the Amazons, betrothed to Theseus
PHILOSTRATE, Master of the Revels to Theseus
EGEUS, father of Hermia
HERMIA, daughter of Egeus, in love with Lysander
LYSANDER, loved by Hermia
DEMETRIUS, suitor to Hermia
HELENA, in love with Demetrius
OBERON, King of Fairies
TITANIA, Queen of Fairies
ROBIN GOODFELLOW, a puck
PEASEBLOSSOM ⎫
COBWEB ⎪
MOTE ⎬ fairies
MUSTARDSEED ⎭
Peter QUINCE, a carpenter
Nick BOTTOM, a weaver
Francis FLUTE, a bellows-mender
Tom SNOUT, a tinker
SNUG, a joiner
Robin STARVELING, a tailor
Attendant lords and fairies

1.1

Enter THESEUS, HIPPOLYTA, [*and* PHILOSTRATE,] *with others*

THESEUS Now, fair Hippolyta, our nuptial hour
Draws on apace. Four happy days bring in
Another moon—but O, methinks how slow
This old moon wanes! She lingers° my desires   *delays fulfillment of*
5   Like to a stepdame° or a dowager   *stepmother*
Long withering out a young man's revenue.[1]
HIPPOLYTA Four days will quickly steep° themselves in night,   *plunge*
Four nights will quickly dream away the time;
And then the moon, like to a silver bow
10 New bent in heaven, shall behold the night
Of our solemnities.
THESEUS   Go, Philostrate, ✱
Stir up the Athenian youth to merriments.
Awake the pert and nimble spirit of mirth.
Turn melancholy forth to funerals—
15 The pale companion is not for our pomp. [*Exit* PHILOSTRATE]
Hippolyta, I wooed thee with my sword,
And won thy love doing thee injuries.[2]

1.1 Location: Theseus's palace in Athens.
1. *a dowager . . . revenue*: a widow using up the inheritance that will go to her husband's (young) heir on her
death.
2. Theseus captured Hippolyta in his military conquest of the Amazons.

But I will wed thee in another key—
With pomp, with triumph,° and with revelling.   *public festivity*

     Enter EGEUS[3] *and his daughter* HERMIA, *and* LYSANDER
     and DEMETRIUS

20 EGEUS Happy be Theseus, our renownèd Duke.

    THESEUS Thanks, good Egeus. What's the news with thee?

    EGEUS Full of vexation come I, with complaint
    Against my child, my daughter Hermia.—
    Stand forth Demetrius.—My noble lord,
25 This man hath my consent to marry her.—
    Stand forth Lysander.—And, my gracious Duke,
    This hath bewitched the bosom of my child.
    Thou, thou, Lysander, thou hast given her rhymes,
    And interchanged love tokens with my child.
30 Thou hast by moonlight at her window sung
    With feigning[4] voice verses of feigning love,
    And stol'n the impression of her fantasy[5]
    With bracelets of thy hair, rings, gauds,° conceits,°   *trinkets / clever gifts*
    Knacks,° trifles, nosegays,° sweetmeats—messengers   *Knickknacks / bouquets*
35 Of strong prevailment° in unhardened youth.   *persuasiveness*
    With cunning hast thou filched my daughter's heart,
    Turned her obedience which is due to me
    To stubborn harshness. And, my gracious Duke,
    Be it so° she will not here before your grace   *If*
40 Consent to marry with Demetrius,
    I beg the ancient privilege of Athens:
    As she is mine, I may dispose of her,
    Which shall be either to this gentleman
    Or to her death, according to our law
45 Immediately° provided in that case.   *Expressly*

    THESEUS What say you, Hermia? Be advised, fair maid.
    To you your father should be as a god,
    One that composed° your beauties, yea, and one   *fashioned*
    To whom you are but as a form in wax,
50 By him imprinted,[6] and within his power
    To leave° the figure or disfigure° it.   *maintain / destroy*
    Demetrius is a worthy gentleman.

    HERMIA So is Lysander.

    THESEUS   In himself he is,
    But in this kind,° wanting your father's voice,[7]   *respect*
55 The other must be held the worthier.

    HERMIA I would my father looked but with my eyes.

    THESEUS Rather your eyes must with his judgement look.

    HERMIA I do entreat your grace to pardon me.
    I know not by what power I am made bold,
60 Nor how it may concern° my modesty   *befit*
    In such a presence here to plead my thoughts,
    But I beseech your grace that I may know
    The worst that may befall me in this case
    If I refuse to wed Demetrius.

---

3. Pronounced "Ege-us," accented on the second syllable.
4. A triple pun: desiring; feigning; soft (in music).
5. *stol'n . . . fantasy:* by craftily impressing your image on her imagination, like a seal in wax, you have stolen her love.
6. *you are . . . imprinted:* you are a wax impression of his seal.
7. Lacking your father's consent or vote.

65	THESEUS Either to die the death,° or to abjure	be executed
	For ever the society of men.	
	Therefore, fair Hermia, question your desires.	
	Know° of your youth, examine well your blood,°	Inquire / passions
	Whether, if you yield not to your father's choice,	
70	You can endure the livery° of a nun,[8]	habit
	For aye° to be in shady cloister mewed,°	ever / caged in
	To live a barren sister all your life,	
	Chanting faint hymns to the cold fruitless moon.[9]	
	Thrice blessèd they that master so their blood	
75	To undergo such maiden pilgrimage;°	life as a virgin
	But earthlier happy is the rose distilled[1]	
	Than that which, withering on the virgin thorn,	
	Grows, lives, and dies in single blessedness.°	celibate
	HERMIA So will I grow, so live, so die, my lord,	
80	Ere I will yield my virgin patent[2] up	
	Unto his lordship whose unwishèd yoke	
	<u>My soul consents not to give sovereignty.</u>	
	THESEUS Take time to pause, and by the next new moon—	
	The sealing day betwixt my love and me	
85	For everlasting bond of fellowship—	
	Upon that day either prepare to die	
	For disobedience to your father's will,	
	Or else to wed Demetrius, as he would,	
	Or on Diana's altar to protest°	vow
90	For aye austerity and single life.	
	DEMETRIUS Relent, sweet Hermia; and, Lysander, yield	
	Thy crazèd title° to my certain right.	unsound claim
	LYSANDER You have her father's love, Demetrius;	
	Let me have Hermia's. Do you marry him.	
95	EGEUS Scornful Lysander! True, he hath my love;	
	And what is mine my love shall render him,	
	And she is mine, and all my right of her	
	I do estate° unto Demetrius.	settle; bestow
	LYSANDER [to THESEUS] I am, my lord, as well derived° as he,	descended
100	As well possessed.° My love is more than his,	endowed with wealth
	My fortunes every way as fairly ranked,	
	If not with vantage,° as Demetrius;	superiority
	And—which is more than all these boasts can be—	
	I am beloved of beauteous Hermia.	
105	Why should not I then prosecute° my right?	pursue
	Demetrius—I'll avouch it to his head°—	face
	Made love to Nedar's daughter, Helena,	
	And won her soul, and she, sweet lady, dotes,	
	Devoutly dotes, dotes in idolatry	
110	Upon this spotted and inconstant[3] man.	
	THESEUS I must confess that I have heard so much,	
	And with Demetrius thought to have spoke thereof;	
	But, being over-full of self affairs,°	my own concerns
	My mind did lose it. But, Demetrius, come;	
115	And come, Egeus. You shall go with me.	

8. Orders of nuns were established in the Christian Middle Ages, but Elizabethans used the term as well for women devoted to a religious life in classical antiquity.
9. The emblem of Diana, goddess of chastity.

1. Made use of (roses were distilled to make perfumes). *earthlier happy:* happier on earth.
2. My right to remain a virgin.
3. *spotted and inconstant:* stained with fickleness.

I have some private schooling° for you both.   *advice*
For you, fair Hermia, look you arm° yourself   *prepare*
To fit your fancies° to your father's will,   *desires*
Or else the law of Athens yields you up—
120   Which by no means we may extenuate°—   *mitigate*
To death or to a vow of single life.
<u>Come, my Hippolyta; what cheer, my love?</u>—
Demetrius and Egeus, go along.
I must employ you in some business
125   Against° our nuptial, and confer with you   *In preparation for*
Of something nearly that[4] concerns yourselves.
EGEUS   With duty and desire we follow you.
             Exeunt. Manent° LYSANDER *and* HERMIA   *Remain*
LYSANDER   How now, my love? Why is your cheek so pale?
How chance the roses there do fade so fast?
130   HERMIA   Belike° for want of rain, which I could well   *Probably*
Beteem° them from the tempest of my eyes.   *Afford; grant*
LYSANDER   Ay me, for aught that I could ever read,
Could ever hear by tale or history,
The course of true love never did run smooth,
135   But either it was different in blood°—   *hereditary rank*
HERMIA   O cross!°—too high to be enthralled to low.   *vexation*
LYSANDER   Or else misgrafted° in respect of years—   *badly matched*
HERMIA   O spite!—too old to be engaged to young.
LYSANDER   Or merit stood° upon the choice of friends°—   *rested / kin*
140   HERMIA   O hell!—to choose love by another's eyes.
LYSANDER   Or if there were a sympathy° in choice,   *an agreement*
War, death, or sickness did lay siege to it,
Making it momentany° as a sound,   *momentary*
Swift as a shadow, short as any dream,
145   Brief as the lightning in the collied° night,   *coal-black*
That, in a spleen,° unfolds° both heaven and earth,   *swift impulse / reveals*
And, ere a man hath power to say 'Behold!',
The jaws of darkness do devour it up.
So quick[5] bright things come to confusion.
150   HERMIA   If then true lovers have been ever° crossed,   *always*
It stands as an edict in destiny.
Then let us teach our trial patience,[6]
Because it is a customary cross,
As due to love as thoughts, and dreams, and sighs,
155   Wishes, and tears, poor fancy's° followers.   *love's*
LYSANDER   A good persuasion.° Therefore hear me, Hermia.   *principle; doctrine*
I have a widow aunt, a dowager
Of great revenue, and she hath no child,
And she respects° me as her only son.   *regards*
160   From Athens is her house remote seven leagues.
There, gentle Hermia, may I marry thee,
And to that place the sharp Athenian law
Cannot pursue us. If thou lov'st me then,
Steal forth thy father's house tomorrow night,
165   And in the wood, a league without° the town,   *outside*
Where I did meet thee once with Helena

4. *nearly that:* that closely.   6. Let us teach ourselves to be patient in this trial.
5. Quickly (adverb); vital, lively (adjective).

To do observance to a morn of May,°   *celebrate May Day*
There will I stay for thee.

HERMIA   My good Lysander,
I swear to thee by Cupid's strongest bow,
170   By his best arrow with the golden head,[7]
By the simplicity° of Venus' doves,[8]   *innocence*
By that which knitteth souls and prospers loves,
And by that fire which burned the Carthage queen
When the false Trojan under sail was seen;[9]
175   By all the vows that ever men have broke—
In number more than ever women spoke—
In that same place thou hast appointed me
Tomorrow truly will I meet with thee.

LYSANDER   Keep promise, love. Look, here comes Helena

      Enter HELENA

180 HERMIA   God speed, fair[1] Helena. Whither away?

HELENA   Call you me fair? That 'fair' again unsay.
Demetrius loves your fair—O happy fair!°   *fortunate beauty*
Your eyes are lodestars,° and your tongue's sweet air°   *guiding stars / melody*
More tuneable° than lark to shepherd's ear   *tuneful*
185   When wheat is green, when hawthorn buds appear.
Sickness is catching. O, were favour° so!   *looks; charms*
Your words I catch, fair Hermia; ere I go,
My ear should catch your voice, my eye your eye,
My tongue should catch your tongue's sweet melody.
190   Were the world mine, Demetrius being bated,°   *excepted*
The rest I'd give to be to you translated.°   *transformed*
O, teach me how you look, and with what art
You sway the motion° of Demetrius' heart.   *desire*

HERMIA   I frown upon him, yet he loves me still.

195 HELENA   O that your frowns would teach my smiles such skill!

HERMIA   I give him curses, yet he gives me love.

HELENA   O that my prayers could such affection move!

HERMIA   The more I hate, the more he follows me.

HELENA   The more I love, the more he hateth me.

200 HERMIA   His folly, Helen, is no fault of mine.

HELENA   None but your beauty; would that fault were mine!

HERMIA   Take comfort. He no more shall see my face
Lysander and myself will fly this place.
Before the time I did Lysander see
205   Seemed Athens as a paradise to me.
O then, what graces in my love do dwell,
That he hath turned a heaven unto a hell?

LYSANDER   Helen, to you our minds we will unfold.
Tomorrow night, when Phoebe° doth behold   *Diana (the moon)*
210   Her silver visage in the wat'ry glass,
Decking with liquid pearl the bladed grass—
A time that lovers' sleights doth still° conceal—   *always*
Through Athens' gates have we devised to steal.

HERMIA   And in the wood where often you and I
215   Upon faint° primrose beds were wont° to lie,   *pale / accustomed*

7. Cupid's sharp golden arrow was said to create love; his blunt lead arrow caused dislike.
8. Said to draw Venus's chariot.
9. *fire . . . seen*: Dido, Queen of Carthage, burned herself on a funeral pyre when her lover, Aeneas, sailed away.
1. The dialogue plays on the meanings "blonde," "beautiful," "beauty." Helena is presumably fair-haired and Hermia (called a "raven" at 2.2.120) a brunette.

Emptying our bosoms of their counsel sweet,
There my Lysander and myself shall meet,
And thence from Athens turn away our eyes
To seek new friends and stranger companies.°   *the company of strangers*
220   Farewell, sweet playfellow. Pray thou for us,
And good luck grant thee thy Demetrius.—
Keep word, Lysander. We must starve our sight
From lovers' food till morrow deep midnight.
LYSANDER   I will, my Hermia.   *Exit* HERMIA
Helena, adieu.   *Exit*
225   As you on him, Demetrius dote on you.
HELENA   How happy some o'er other some² can be!
Through Athens I am thought as fair as she.
But what of that? Demetrius thinks not so.
He will not know what all but he do know.
230   And as he errs, doting on Hermia's eyes,
So I, admiring of his qualities.
Things base and vile, holding no quantity,°   *shape; proportion*
Love can transpose to form and dignity.
Love looks not with the eyes, but with the mind,³
235   And therefore is winged Cupid painted blind.
Nor hath love's mind of any judgement taste;°   *any trace of judgment*
Wings and no eyes figure° unheedy haste.   *symbolize*
And therefore is love said to be a child
Because in choice he is so oft beguiled.
240   As waggish° boys in game° themselves forswear,   *playful / sport; play*
So the boy Love is perjured everywhere.
For ere Demetrius looked on Hermia's eyne°   *eyes*
He hailed down oaths that he was only mine,
And when this hail some heat from Hermia felt,
245   So he dissolved,° and showers of oaths did melt.   *broke faith; melted*
I will go tell him of fair Hermia's flight.
Then to the wood will he tomorrow night
Pursue her, and for this intelligence°   *information*
If I have thanks it is a dear expense.⁴
250   But herein mean I to enrich my pain,
To have his sight thither and back again.   *Exit*

1.2

Enter QUINCE *the carpenter, and* SNUG *the joiner, and*
BOTTOM *the weaver, and* FLUTE *the bellows-mender, and*
SNOUT *the tinker, and* STARVELING *the tailor*¹
QUINCE   Is all our company here?
BOTTOM   You were best to call them generally,² man by man,
according to the scrip.°   *script; list*
QUINCE   Here is the scroll of every man's name which is thought

2. *o'er other some:* in comparison with others.
3. Love is promoted not by the evidence of the senses, but by the fancies of the mind.
4. Costly (because of the betrayal of secrecy and because it leads Demetrius to Hermia); or welcome (because the potential return is Demetrius's love regained).
1.2 Location: Somewhere in the city of Athens.
1. The artisans' names recall their occupations. Quince's name is probably derived from "quoins," wooden wedges used by carpenters who made buildings

such as houses and theaters. The name "Snug" evokes well-finished wooden furniture made by joiners. A bottom was the piece of wood on which thread was wound; Bottom's name also connotes "ass" and "lowest point." As Flute's name suggests, domestic bellows whistle through holes when needing repair. Snout's name may refer to the spouts of the kettles he repairs, or to his nose. Tailors, as Starveling's name recalls, were proverbially thin.
2. Bottom's error for "individually" (he frequently mistakes words in this manner).

brief play

5   fit through all Athens to play in our interlude° before the Duke
and the Duchess on his wedding day at night.

BOTTOM   First, good Peter Quince, say what the play treats on;
then read the names of the actors; and so grow to a point.[3]

QUINCE   Marry,° our play is *The Most Lamentable Comedy and*   *By the Virgin Mary*
10   *Most Cruel Death of Pyramus and Thisbe.*[4]

BOTTOM   A very good piece of work, I assure you, and a merry.
Now, good Peter Quince, call forth your actors by the scroll.
Masters, spread yourselves.

QUINCE   Answer as I call you. Nick Bottom, the weaver?

15 BOTTOM   Ready. Name what part I am for, and proceed.

QUINCE   You, Nick Bottom, are set down for Pyramus.

BOTTOM   What is Pyramus? A lover or a tyrant?

QUINCE   A lover, that kills himself most gallant for love.

BOTTOM   That will ask some tears in the true performing of it. If
20   I do it, let the audience look to their eyes. I will move stones.
I will condole,° in some measure. To the rest.—Yet my chief   *lament; arouse pity*
humour° is for a tyrant. I could play 'erc'les[5] rarely,° or a part   *inclination / excellently*
to tear a cat° in, to make all split.°   *rant / go to pieces*

The raging rocks
25   And shivering shocks
Shall break the locks
Of prison gates,
And Phibus' car[6]
Shall shine from far
30   And make and mar
The foolish Fates.

This was lofty. Now name the rest of the players.—This is
'erc'les' vein, a tyrant's vein. A lover is more condoling.

QUINCE   Francis Flute, the bellows-mender?

35 FLUTE   Here, Peter Quince.

QUINCE   Flute, you must take Thisbe on you.

FLUTE   What is Thisbe? A wand'ring knight?°   *knight-errant*

QUINCE   It is the lady that Pyramus must love.

FLUTE   Nay, faith, let not me play a woman.[7] I have a beard
40   coming.

QUINCE   That's all one.° You shall play it in a mask,[8] and you   *irrelevant*
may speak as small° as you will.   *high-pitched; shrill*

BOTTOM   An° I may hide my face, let me play Thisbe too. I'll   *If*
speak in a monstrous° little voice: 'Thisne, Thisne!'[9]—'Ah   *exceptionally*
45   Pyramus, my lover dear, thy Thisbe dear and lady dear.'

QUINCE   No, no, you must play Pyramus; and Flute, you Thisbe.

BOTTOM   Well, proceed.

QUINCE   Robin Starveling, the tailor?

STARVELING   Here, Peter Quince.

50 QUINCE   Robin Starveling, you must play Thisbe's mother. Tom
Snout, the tinker?

SNOUT   Here, Peter Quince.

QUINCE   You, Pyramus' father; myself, Thisbe's father. Snug the

---

3. *grow to a point:* draw to a conclusion.
4. Parodying titles such as that of Thomas Preston's *Cambyses: A Lamentable Tragedy Mixed Full of Pleasant Mirth* . . . (c. 1570).
5. Hercules (a stock ranting role in early plays).
6. The chariot of Phoebus Apollo, the sun god (the odd spelling may represent Bottom's pronunciation).

7. On the Elizabethan stage, women's parts were played by boys and young men.
8. Elizabethan ladies regularly wore masks for anonymity and to protect their complexions.
9. Probably intended as a pet name for Thisbe; or it may mean "in this manner."

joiner, you the lion's part; and I hope here is a play fitted.°   *(well) cast*

55   SNUG   Have you the lion's part written? Pray you, if it be, give it
me; for I am slow of study.

QUINCE   You may do it extempore, for it is nothing but roaring.

BOTTOM   Let me play the lion too. I will roar that I will do any
man's heart good to hear me. I will roar that I will make the

60   Duke say 'Let him roar again; let him roar again'.

QUINCE   An you should do it too terribly you would fright the
Duchess and the ladies that they would shriek, and that were
enough to hang us all.

ALL THE REST   That would hang us, every mother's son.

65   BOTTOM   I grant you, friends, if you should fright the ladies out
of their wits they would have no more discretion but to hang us,
but I will aggravate° my voice so that I will roar you as gently   *(for "moderate")*
as any sucking dove.[1] I will roar you an 'twere° any nightingale.   *as though it were*

QUINCE   You can play no part but Pyramus; for Pyramus is a

70   sweet-faced man; a proper° man as one shall see in a summer's   *handsome*
day; a most lovely, gentlemanlike man. Therefore you must
needs play Pyramus.

BOTTOM   Well, I will undertake it. What beard were I best to
play it in?

75   QUINCE   Why, what you will.

BOTTOM   I will discharge° it in either your straw-colour beard,   *perform*
your orange-tawny[2] beard, your purple-in-grain° beard, or your   *very deep red*
French-crown-colour° beard, your perfect yellow.   *gold-coin-colored*

QUINCE   Some of your French crowns have no hair at all,[3] and

80   then you will play bare faced.° But masters, here are your   *beardless; undisguised*
parts,[4] and I am to entreat you, request you, and desire you to
con° them by tomorrow night, and meet me in the palace wood   *memorize*
a mile without the town by moonlight. There will we rehearse;
for if we meet in the city we shall be dogged with company,

85   and our devices° known. In the meantime I will draw a bill°   *plans / list*
of properties such as our play wants. I pray you fail me not.

BOTTOM   We will meet, and there we may rehearse most
obscenely[5] and courageously. Take pains; be perfect.[6] Adieu.

QUINCE   At the Duke's oak we meet.

90   BOTTOM   Enough. Hold, or cut bowstrings.[7]   *Exeunt*

2.1

Enter a FAIRY *at one door and* ROBIN GOODFELLOW [*a*
puck][1] *at another*

ROBIN   How now, spirit, whither wander you?

FAIRY   Over hill, over dale,
     Thorough° bush, thorough brier,   *Through*
     Over park, over pale,°   *enclosure; fence*
5   Thorough flood, thorough fire:
     I do wander everywhere

---

1. Bottom confuses "sitting dove" and "sucking lamb."
2. Dark yellow, a recognized name for the dye. (Bottom the weaver shows his professional knowledge.)
3. Referring to the baldness caused by venereal disease ("the French disease").
4. Literally; an Elizabethan actor was generally given only his own lines and cues.
5. A comic blunder, possibly for "out of sight" (from the

scene or from being seen).
6. Letter perfect in learning your parts.
7. *Hold, or cut bowstrings* (from archery): Keep your word, or be disgraced (?).
2.1 Location: A wood near Athens.
1. A puck is a devil or an imp; in Elizabethan folklore, Robin Goodfellow (also known as Puck) was a mischievous spirit who would do housework if well treated.

Swifter than the moonës sphere,[2]
And I serve the Fairy Queen
To dew her orbs[3] upon the green.
10   The cowslips tall her pensioners° be.   *royal bodyguards*
In their gold coats spots you see;
Those be rubies, fairy favours;°   *gifts*
In those freckles live their savours.°   *scent*
I must go seek some dewdrops here,
15   And hang a pearl in every cowslip's ear.
Farewell, thou lob° of spirits; I'll be gone.   *country bumpkin*
Our Queen and all her elves come here anon.

ROBIN   The King doth keep his revels here tonight.
Take heed the Queen come not within his sight,
20   For Oberon is passing fell and wroth[4]
Because that she, as her attendant, hath
A lovely boy stol'n from an Indian king.
She never had so sweet a changeling;[5]
And jealous Oberon would have the child
25   Knight of his train, to trace° the forests wild.   *range*
But she perforce° withholds the lovèd boy,   *forcibly*
Crowns him with flowers, and makes him all her joy.
And now they never meet in grove, or green,
By fountain° clear, or spangled starlight sheen,°   *spring / shining starlight*
30   But they do square,° that all their elves for fear   *quarrel*
Creep into acorn cups, and hide them there.

FAIRY   Either I mistake your shape and making° quite   *form*
Or else you are that shrewd° and knavish sprite   *mischievous*
Called Robin Goodfellow. Are not you he
35   That frights the maidens of the villag'ry,°   *villages*
Skim milk, and sometimes labour in the quern.°   *hand mill*
And bootless° make the breathless housewife churn.   *in vain*
And sometime° make the drink to bear no barm°—   *at times / froth on ale*
Mislead night wanderers, laughing at their harm?
40   Those that 'hobgoblin' call you, and 'sweet puck',
You do their work, and they shall have good luck.
Are not you he?

ROBIN   Thou speak'st aright;
I am that merry wanderer of the night.
I jest to Oberon, and make him smile
45   When I a fat and bean-fed horse beguile,°   *trick*
Neighing in likeness of a filly foal;
And sometime lurk I in a gossip's° bowl   *an old woman's*
In very likeness of a roasted crab,[6]
And when she drinks, against her lips I bob,
50   And on her withered dewlap° pour the ale.   *loose skin on neck*
The wisest aunt° telling the saddest° tale   *old woman / most serious*
Sometime for three-foot stool mistaketh me;
Then slip I from her bum. Down topples she,
And 'tailor' cries,[7] and falls into a cough,
55   And then the whole choir° hold their hips, and laugh,   *company*

2. Each planet, including the moon, was thought to be fixed in a transparent hollow globe revolving round the earth. *moonës*: the obsolete genitive of "moon."
3. Sprinkle her fairy rings (circles of dark grass).
4. *passing fell and wroth*: exceedingly fierce and angry.
5. Usually a child left by fairies in exchange for one stolen, but here the stolen child.
6. Crab apple ("lamb's wool," a winter drink, was made with roasted apples and warm ale).
7. Possibly the old woman cries this because she ends up cross-legged on the floor as tailors sat to work or because she falls on her "tail."

And waxen° in their mirth, and sneeze, and swear   *increase*
A merrier hour was never wasted there.—

> *Enter* [OBERON] *King of Fairies at one door, with his*
> *train, and* [TITANIA] *Queen at another, with hers*

But make room, fairy: here comes Oberon.

FAIRY And here my mistress. Would that he were gone.

60 OBERON Ill met by moonlight, proud Titania. ✱

TITANIA What, jealous Oberon?—Fairies, skip hence.
I have forsworn his bed and company.

OBERON Tarry, rash wanton.° Am not I thy lord?   *impetuous creature*

TITANIA Then I must be thy lady; but I know
65 When thou hast stol'n away from fairyland
And in the shape of Corin[8] sat all day,
Playing on pipes of corn, and versing love[9]
To amorous Phillida. Why art thou here
Come from the farthest step° of India,   *limit*
70 But that, forsooth, the bouncing° Amazon,   *vigorous*
Your buskined° mistress and your warrior love,   *wearing hunting boots*
To Theseus must be wedded, and you come
To give their bed joy and prosperity?

OBERON How canst thou thus for shame, Titania,
75 Glance at my credit° with Hippolyta,   *Question my good name*
Knowing I know thy love to Theseus?
Didst not thou lead him through the glimmering night
From Perigouna whom he ravishèd,
And make him with fair Aegles[1] break his faith,
80 With Ariadne and Antiopa?[2]

TITANIA These are the forgeries of jealousy,
And never since the middle summer's spring°   *beginning of midsummer*
Met we on hill, in dale, forest, or mead,
By pavèd fountain or by rushy[3] brook,
85 Or in° the beachèd margin° of the sea   *on / shore*
To dance our ringlets° to the whistling wind,   *circular dances*
But with thy brawls thou hast disturbed our sport.
Therefore the winds, piping to us in vain,
As in revenge have sucked up from the sea
90 Contagious fogs which, falling in the land,
Hath every pelting° river made so proud   *paltry*
That they have overborne their continents.°   *banks*
The ox hath therefore stretched his yoke in vain,
The ploughman lost his sweat, and the green corn°   *grain*
95 Hath rotted ere his youth attained a beard.
The fold stands empty in the drownèd field,
And crows are fatted with the murrain° flock.   *dead of disease*
The nine men's morris[4] is filled up with mud,
And the quaint mazes in the wanton green[5]
100 For lack of tread are undistinguishable.

---

8. Corin and Phillida are typical names for a shepherd and shepherdess in pastoral poetry.
9. Making or reciting love poetry. *pipes of corn:* musical instruments made of oat stalks.
1. Perigouna and Aegles were previous mistresses of Theseus (taken from Plutarch's *Life of Theseus*).
2. Taken from Plutarch; some writers used "Antiopa" as an alternative name for the Amazonian queen Theseus married, although here it seems to refer to a different woman. Ariadne helped Theseus kill the Minotaur and escape from his labyrinth on Crete; she fled with Theseus, but he deserted her on Naxos.
3. Fringed with reeds. *pavèd:* pebbled.
4. The playing area for this outdoor game (traditionally, a board game played with nine pebbles or pegs) was cut in turf.
5. Luxuriant grass. *quaint mazes:* intricate arrangements of paths (kept visible by use).

	The human mortals want° their winter cheer.[6]	*lack*
	No night is now with hymn or carol blessed.	
	Therefore[7] the moon, the governess of floods,	
	Pale in her anger washes° all the air,	*moistens; wets*
105	That rheumatic[8] diseases do abound;	
	And thorough this distemperature° we see	*bad weather; disturbance*
	The seasons alter: hoary-headed frosts	
	Fall in the fresh lap of the crimson rose,	
	And on old Hiems'° thin and icy crown	*winter's*
110	An odorous chaplet° of sweet summer buds	*wreath*
	Is, as in mock'ry, set. The spring, the summer,	
	The childing° autumn, angry winter change	*fruitful*
	Their wonted liveries,[9] and the mazèd° world	*bewildered*
	By their increase° now knows not which is which;	*crop yield*
115	And this same progeny of evils comes	
	From our debate,° from our dissension.	*quarrel*
	We are their parents and original.°	*origin*

OBERON Do you amend it, then. It lies in you.
    Why should Titania cross her Oberon?
120 I do but beg a little changeling boy
    To be my henchman.°   *page of honor*
TITANIA   Set your heart at rest.[1]
    The fairyland buys not the child of me.
    His mother was a vot'ress[2] of my order,
    And in the spicèd Indian air by night
125 Full often hath she gossiped by my side,
    And sat with me on Neptune's yellow sands,
    Marking th'embarkèd traders° on the flood,°   *merchant ships / tide*
    When we have laughed to see the sails conceive
    And grow big-bellied with the wanton° wind,   *playful; amorous*
130 Which she with pretty and with swimming[3] gait
    Following,° her womb then rich with my young squire,   *Copying*
    Would imitate, and sail upon the land
    To fetch me trifles, and return again
    As from a voyage, rich with merchandise.
135 But she, being mortal, of that boy did die;
    And for her sake do I rear up her boy;
    And for her sake I will not part with him.
OBERON How long within this wood intend you stay?
TITANIA Perchance till after Theseus' wedding day.
140 If you will patiently dance in our round,
    And see our moonlight revels, go with us.
    If not, shun me, and I will spare° your haunts.   *avoid*
OBERON Give me that boy and I will go with thee.
TITANIA Not for thy fairy kingdom.—Fairies, away.
145 We shall chide° downright if I longer stay.   *quarrel*
                        Exeunt [TITANIA *and her train*]
OBERON Well, go thy way. Thou shalt not from° this grove   *go from*
    Till I torment thee for this injury.°—   *insult*
    My gentle puck, come hither. Thou rememb'rest

---

6. Winter cheer would include the hymns and carols of the Yuletide. But Q, F reading: here.
7. As in lines 88 and 93 above, referring to the consequences of their quarrel.
8. Characterized by rheum: colds, coughs, etc.

9. Customary clothing.
1. Proverbial expression for "Abandon that idea."
2. Woman who has taken a vow to serve (often religious).
3. As though gliding through the waves.

		Since° once I sat upon a promontory	*When*
150		And heard a mermaid on a dolphin's back	
		Uttering such dulcet° and harmonious breath°	*sweet / voice; song*
		That the rude° sea grew civil at her song	*rough*
		And certain stars shot madly from their spheres°	*orbits*
		To hear the sea-maid's music?	
	ROBIN	I remember.	
155	OBERON	That very time I saw, but thou couldst not,	
		Flying between the cold moon and the earth	
		Cupid, all armed. A certain aim he took	
		At a fair vestal thronèd by the west,[4]	
		And loosed his love-shaft° smartly from his bow	*golden arrow*
160		As° it should pierce a hundred thousand hearts.	*As though*
		But I might° see young Cupid's fiery shaft	*could*
		Quenched in the chaste beams of the wat'ry moon,	
		And the imperial vot'ress passèd on,	
		In maiden meditation, fancy-free.°	*free of love thoughts*
165		Yet marked I where the bolt° of Cupid fell.	*arrow*
		It fell upon a little western flower—	
		Before, milk-white; now, purple with love's wound—	
		And maidens call it love-in-idleness.[5]	
		Fetch me that flower; the herb I showed thee once.	
170		The juice of it on sleeping eyelids laid	
		Will make or° man or woman madly dote	*either*
		Upon the next live creature that it sees.	
		Fetch me this herb, and be thou here again	
		Ere the leviathan[6] can swim a league.	
175	ROBIN	I'll put a girdle° round about the earth	*circle*
		In forty minutes.	*Exit*
	OBERON	Having once this juice	
		I'll watch Titania when she is asleep,	
		And drop the liquor° of it in her eyes.	*juice*
		The next thing then she waking looks upon—	
180		Be it on lion, bear, or wolf, or bull,	
		On meddling monkey, or on busy ape—	
		She shall pursue it with the soul of love.	
		And ere I take this charm from off her sight—	
		As I can take it with another herb—	
185		I'll make her render up her page to me.	
		But who comes here? I am invisible,	
		And I will overhear their conference.	
		Enter DEMETRIUS, HELENA *following him*	
	DEMETRIUS	I love thee not, therefore pursue me not.	
		Where is Lysander, and fair Hermia?	
190		The one I'll slay, the other slayeth me.	
		Thou told'st me they were stol'n unto this wood,	
		And here am I, and wood° within this wood	*insane*
		Because I cannot meet my Hermia.	
		Hence, get thee gone, and follow me no more.	
195	HELENA	You draw me, you hard-hearted adamant,[7]	

4. To the west of India; in England. *vestal:* virgin (a compliment to Queen Elizabeth, the Virgin Queen, and possibly an allusion to a specific entertainment in her honor, such as the water pageant at Elvetham in 1591).
5. Pansy. (Classical legend describes how the mulberry turned purple with Pyramus's blood and the hyacinth with Hyacinthus's, but does not mention the pansy.)
6. Biblical sea monster, identified with the whale.
7. Very hard stone supposed to have magnetic properties. *draw me:* the magnetic power of attraction.

But yet you draw not iron; for my heart
Is true as steel.[8] Leave you° your power to draw,   *Relinquish*
And I shall have no power to follow you.
DEMETRIUS Do I entice you? Do I speak you fair?[9]
200 Or rather do I not in plainest truth
Tell you I do not nor I cannot love you?
HELENA And even for that do I love you the more.
I am your spaniel, and, Demetrius,
The more you beat me I will fawn on you.
205 Use me but as your spaniel: spurn me, strike me,
Neglect me, lose me; only give me leave,
Unworthy as I am, to follow you.
What worser place can I beg in your love—
And yet a place of high respect with me—
210 Than to be usèd as you use your dog?
DEMETRIUS Tempt not too much the hatred of my spirit;
For I am sick when I do look on thee.
HELENA And I am sick when I look not on you.
DEMETRIUS You do impeach° your modesty too much, *call into question*
215 To leave the city and commit yourself
Into the hands of one that loves you not;
To trust the opportunity of night,
And the ill counsel of a desert° place,   *deserted*
With the rich worth of your virginity.
220 HELENA Your virtue is my privilege,° for that° *protection / because*
It is not night when I do see your face;
Therefore I think I am not in the night,
Nor doth this wood lack worlds of company;
For you in my respect° are all the world. *As far as I am concerned*
225 Then how can it be said I am alone,
When all the world is here to look on me?
DEMETRIUS I'll run from thee, and hide me in the brakes ° *thickets*
And leave thee to the mercy of wild beasts.
HELENA The wildest hath not such a heart as you.
230 Run when you will. The story shall be changed:
Apollo flies, and Daphne holds the chase.[1]
The dove pursues the griffin,[2] the mild hind°   *doe*
Makes speed to catch the tiger: bootless° speed, *useless*
When cowardice pursues, and valour flies.
235 DEMETRIUS I will not stay thy questions.[3] Let me go;
Or if thou follow me, do not believe
But I shall do thee mischief in the wood.
HELENA Ay, in the temple, in the town, the field,
You do me mischief. Fie, Demetrius,
240 Your wrongs do set a scandal on my sex.[4]
We cannot fight for love as men may do;
We should be wooed, and were not made to woo.
I'll follow thee, and make a heaven of hell,
To die upon the hand I love so well.

8. Hermia contrasts the base metal iron with steel,
which holds its temper.
9. Do I speak kindly to you?
1. A reversal of the traditional myth in which the
nymph Daphne, flying from Apollo, was transformed
into a laurel tree to escape him.

2. Fabulous monster with a lion's body and an eagle's
head and wings
3. I will not wait here any longer to hear you talk.
4. Your injustice to me causes me to behave in a way
that disgraces my sex (by wooing him rather than being
wooed).

Exit [DEMETRIUS, HELENA *following him*]

245 OBERON   Fare thee well, nymph. Ere he do leave this grove
      Thou shalt fly him, and he shall seek thy love.

              Enter [ROBIN GOODFELLOW *the*] *puck*

      Hast thou the flower there? Welcome, wanderer.

ROBIN   Ay, there it is.

OBERON   I pray thee give it me.
      I know a bank where the wild thyme blows,
250   Where oxlips⁵ and the nodding violet grows,
      Quite overcanopied with luscious woodbine,°   *honeysuckle*
      With sweet musk-roses,⁶ and with eglantine.°   *sweetbrier, a type of rose*
      There sleeps Titania sometime of the night,
      Lulled in these flowers with dances and delight;
255   And there the snake throws° her enamelled skin,   *throws off ; casts*
      Weed° wide enough to wrap a fairy in;   *Garment*
      And with the juice of this I'll streak° her eyes,   *anoint*
      And make her full of hateful fantasies.
      Take thou some of it, and seek through this grove.
260   A sweet Athenian lady is in love
      With a disdainful youth. Anoint his eyes;
      But do it when the next thing he espies
      May be the lady. Thou shalt know the man
      By the Athenian garments he hath on.
265   Effect it with some care, that he may prove
      More fond° on her than she upon her love;   *doting*
      And look thou meet me ere the first cock crow.⁷

ROBIN   Fear not, my lord. Your servant shall do so.

                     Exeunt [*severally*]°   *separately*

2.2

Enter TITANIA, *Queen of Fairies, with her train*

TITANIA   Come, now a roundel° and a fairy song,   *circular dance*
      Then for the third part of a minute¹ hence:
      Some to kill cankers° in the musk-rose buds,   *caterpillars*
      Some war with reremice° for their leathern wings   *bats*
5   To make my small elves coats, and some keep back
      The clamorous owl, that nightly hoots and wonders
      At our quaint° spirits. Sing me now asleep;   *dainty*
      Then to your offices, and let me rest.

      [*She lies down.*] FAIRIES *sing*

FIRST FAIRY   You spotted snakes with double° tongue,   *forked*
10   Thorny hedgehogs, be not seen;
               Newts and blindworms,² do no wrong;
               Come not near our Fairy Queen.

CHORUS [*dancing*]   Philomel³ with melody,
               Sing in our sweet lullaby;
15   Lulla, lulla, lullaby; lulla, lulla, lullaby.
               Never harm
               Nor spell nor charm

---

5. Hybrid between primrose and cowslip.
6. Large rambling white roses.
7. Some spirits were thought unable to bear daylight
(compare *Hamlet* 1.1.28–36).
2.2 Location: The wood.
1. The fairies are quick enough to do their tasks in

twenty seconds.
2. Newts (water lizards) and blindworms were thought
to be poisonous, as were spiders (line 20).
3. Philomel, the nightingale (in classical mythology, a
woman who, raped by her sister's husband, was transformed into a bird).

Come our lovely lady nigh.
So good night, with lullaby.
20 FIRST FAIRY   Weaving spiders, come not here;
Hence, you long-legged spinners, hence;
Beetles black, approach not near;
Worm nor snail do no offence.
CHORUS [*dancing*]   Philomel with melody,
25   Sing in our sweet lullaby;
Lulla, lulla, lullaby; lulla, lulla, lullaby.
Never harm
Nor spell nor charm
Come our lovely lady nigh.
30   So good night, with lullaby.
[TITANIA] *sleeps*
SECOND FAIRY   Hence, away. Now all is well.
One aloof° stand sentinel.   *at a distance*
[*Exeunt all but* TITANIA *and the sentinel*]
Enter OBERON. [*He drops the juice on Titania's eyelids*]
OBERON   What thou seest when thou dost wake,
Do it for thy true love take;
35   Love and languish for his sake.
Be it ounce,° or cat, or bear,   *lynx*
Pard,° or boar with bristled hair,   *Leopard*
In thy eye that shall appear
When thou wak'st, it is thy dear.
40   Wake when some vile thing is near.   [*Exit*]
Enter LYSANDER *and* HERMIA
LYSANDER   Fair love, you faint with wand'ring in the wood,
And, to speak truth, I have forgot our way.
We'll rest us, Hermia, if you think it good,
And tarry for the comfort of the day.
45 HERMIA   Be it so, Lysander. Find you out a bed;
For I upon this bank will rest my head.
[*She lies down*]
LYSANDER   One turf shall serve as pillow for us both;
One heart, one bed; two bosoms, and one troth.°   *pledged faith*
HERMIA   Nay, good Lysander; for my sake, my dear,
50   Lie further off yet; do not lie so near.
LYSANDER   O, take the sense,° sweet, of my innocence! *true meaning*
Love takes the meaning in love's conference[4]—
I mean that my heart unto yours is knit,
So that but one heart we can make of it.
55   Two bosoms interchainèd with an oath;
So, then, two bosoms and a single troth.
Then by your side no bed-room me deny;
For lying so, Hermia, I do not lie.[5]
HERMIA   Lysander riddles very prettily.
60   Now much beshrew[6] my manners and my pride
If Hermia meant to say Lysander lied.
But, gentle friend, for love and courtesy,
Lie further off, in humane° modesty.   *courteous*

4. Love enables lovers truly to understand one another.   6. Curse (used in a mild sense).
5. Deceive; punning on "lie down."

        Such separation as may well be said
65   Becomes a virtuous bachelor and a maid,
        So far be distant; and good night, sweet friend.
        Thy love ne'er alter till thy sweet life end.
  LYSANDER   Amen, amen, to that fair prayer say I;
        And then end life when I end loyalty.
70   Here is my bed; sleep give thee all his rest.
        [*He lies down*]
  HERMIA   With half that wish the wisher's eyes be pressed.[7]
        They sleep [*apart.*]
        Enter [ROBIN GOODFELLOW *the*] *puck*
  ROBIN   Through the forest have I gone,
        But Athenian found I none
        On whose eyes I might approve°   *test*
75   This flower's force in stirring love.
        Night and silence. Who is here?
        Weeds of Athens he doth wear.
        This is he my master said
        Despisèd the Athenian maid—
80   And here the maiden, sleeping sound
        On the dank and dirty ground.
        Pretty soul, she durst not lie
        Near this lack-love, this kill-courtesy.
        Churl,° upon thy eyes I throw   *Rude fellow*
85   All the power this charm doth owe.°   *own*
        [*He drops the juice on Lysander's eyelids*]
        When thou wak'st, let love forbid
        Sleep his seat on thy eyelid.[8]
        So, awake when I am gone.
        For I must now to Oberon.   *Exit*
        Enter DEMETRIUS *and* HELENA, *running*
90 HELENA   Stay, though thou kill me, sweet Demetrius.
  DEMETRIUS   I charge thee hence, and do not haunt me thus.
  HELENA   O, wilt thou darkling° leave me? Do not so. *in darkness*
  DEMETRIUS   Stay, on thy peril;[9] I alone will go.   *Exit*
  HELENA   O, I am out of breath in this fond° chase.   *foolish*
95   The more my prayer, the lesser is my grace.°   *reward*
        Happy is Hermia, wheresoe'er she lies;
        For she hath blessèd and attractive° eyes.   *magnetic*
        How came her eyes so bright? Not with salt tears—
        If so, my eyes are oft'ner washed than hers.
100   No, no; I am as ugly as a bear,
        For beasts that meet me run away for fear.
        Therefore no marvel though Demetrius
        Do, as° a monster, fly my presence thus.   *as if I were*
        What wicked and dissembling glass of mine
105   Made me compare° with Hermia's sphery eyne!° *compete / starry eyes*
        But who is here? Lysander, on the ground?
        Dead, or asleep? I see no blood, no wound.
        Lysander, if you live, good sir, awake.
  LYSANDER [*awaking*]   And run through fire I will for thy sweet sake.
110   Transparent[1] Helena, nature shows art°   *skill; magic power*

---

7. May sleep's rest be shared between us. *pressed:*
closed in sleep.
8. *forbid . . . eyelid:* prevent you from sleeping.

9. Stay here or risk peril (if you follow me).
1. Radiant; capable of being seen through.

That through thy bosom makes me see thy heart.
Where is Demetrius? O, how fit a word
Is that vile name to perish on my sword!

HELENA   Do not say so, Lysander; say not so.
115   What though he love your Hermia? Lord, what though?
Yet Hermia still loves you; then be content.

LYSANDER   Content with Hermia? No, I do repent
The tedious minutes I with her have spent.
Not Hermia but Helena I love.
120   Who will not change a raven for a dove?
The will of man is by his reason swayed,[2]
And reason says you are the worthier maid.
Things growing are not ripe until their season,
So I, being young, till now ripe not to reason.
125   And, touching now the point of human skill,[3]
Reason becomes the marshal[4] to my will,
And leads me to your eyes, where I o'erlook°   *look over; read*
Love's stories written in love's richest book.

HELENA   Wherefore was I to this keen° mockery born?   *sharp*
130   When at your hands did I deserve this scorn?
Is't not enough, is't not enough, young man,
That I did never—no, nor never can—
Deserve a sweet look from Demetrius' eye,
But you must flout my insufficiency?[5]
135   Good troth,° you do me wrong; good sooth,° you do,   *Truly / indeed*
In such disdainful manner me to woo.
But fare you well. Perforce I must confess
I thought you lord of more true gentleness.°   *courtesy; breeding*
O, that a lady of one man refused
140   Should of ° another therefore be abused!   *Exit*   *by*

LYSANDER   She sees not Hermia. Hermia, sleep thou there,
And never mayst thou come Lysander near;
For as a surfeit of the sweetest things
The deepest loathing to the stomach brings,
145   Or as the heresies that men do leave
Are hated most of those they did deceive,[6]
So thou, my surfeit and my heresy,
Of all be hated, but the most of me;
And all my powers, address° your love and might   *direct; apply*
150   To honour Helen, and to be her knight.   *Exit*

HERMIA [*awaking*]   Help me, Lysander, help me! Do thy best
To pluck this crawling serpent from my breast!
Ay me, for pity. What a dream was here?
Lysander, look how I do quake with fear.
155   Methought a serpent ate my heart away,
And you sat smiling at his cruel prey.°   *act of preying*
Lysander—what, removed? Lysander, lord—
What, out of hearing, gone? No sound, no word?
Alack, where are you? Speak an if ° you hear,   *an if = if*
160   Speak, of ° all loves. I swoon almost with fear.   *for the sake of*

---

2. Renaissance psychology considered the will (that is, the passions) to be in constant conflict with, and ideally subject to, the faculty of reason.
3. Reaching (only) now the highest point of human judgment.

4. Officer who led guests to their appointed places.
5. *flout my insufficiency*: mock my shortcomings by pretending they are wonderful qualities.
6. *as the heresies . . . deceive*: as men most hate the false opinions they once held.

No? Then I well perceive you are not nigh.
Either death or you I'll find immediately.   *Exit*

3.1

Enter the clowns:° [QUINCE, SNUG, BOTTOM, FLUTE,   *rustics*
SNOUT, *and* STARVELING]

BOTTOM   Are we all met?

QUINCE   Pat,° pat; and here's a marvellous convenient place for   *On the dot*
our rehearsal. This green plot shall be our stage, this hawthorn
brake° our tiring-house,° and we will do it in action as we will   *thicket / dressing room*
5   do it before the Duke.

BOTTOM   Peter Quince?

QUINCE   What sayst thou, bully° Bottom?   *good fellow; jolly*

BOTTOM   There are things in this comedy of Pyramus and
Thisbe that will never please. First, Pyramus must draw a sword
10   to kill himself, which the ladies cannot abide. How answer you
that?

SNOUT   By'r la'kin,[1] a parlous° fear.   *perilous*

STARVELING   I believe we must leave the killing out, when all is
done.[2]

15   BOTTOM   Not a whit. I have a device to make all well. Write me
a prologue, and let the prologue seem to say we will do no
harm with our swords, and that Pyramus is not killed indeed;
and for the more better assurance, tell them that I, Pyramus,
am not Pyramus, but Bottom the weaver. This will put them
20   out of fear.

QUINCE   Well, we will have such a prologue; and it shall be written in eight and six.[3]

BOTTOM   No, make it two more: let it be written in eight and
eight.

25   SNOUT   Will not the ladies be afeard of the lion?

STARVELING   I fear it, I promise you.

BOTTOM   Masters, you ought to consider with yourself, to bring
in—God shield us—a lion among ladies is a most dreadful
thing;[4] for there is not a more fearful° wild fowl than your lion   *frightening*
30   living, and we ought to look to't.

SNOUT   Therefore another prologue must tell he is not a lion.

BOTTOM   Nay, you must name his name, and half his face must
be seen through the lion's neck, and he himself must speak
through, saying thus or to the same defect:° 'ladies', or 'fair   *(for "effect")*
35   ladies, I would wish you' or 'I would request you' or 'I would
entreat you not to fear, not to tremble. My life for yours.[5] If you
think I come hither as a lion, it were pity of° my life. No, I am   *a threat to*
no such thing. I am a man, as other men are'—and there,
indeed, let him name his name, and tell them plainly he is
40   Snug the joiner.

QUINCE   Well, it shall be so; but there is two hard things: that is,
to bring the moonlight into a chamber—for you know Pyramus
and Thisbe meet by moonlight.

3.1 Location: Remains the same, although F introduces an act break.
1. By our ladykin (Virgin Mary): a mild oath.
2. When all is said and done.
3. Alternate lines of eight and six syllables (a common
ballad measure).

4. In 1594, at a feast in honor of the christening of
King James's son, a tame lion that was supposed to draw
a chariot was replaced by a black African in order to
avoid frightening the audience.
5. I pledge my life to defend yours.

SNOUT⁶   Doth the moon shine that night we play our play?

45   BOTTOM   A calendar, a calendar—look in the almanac, find out
     moonshine, find out moonshine.

          Enter [ROBIN GOODFELLOW⁷ *the*] *puck* [*invisible*]

QUINCE [*with a book*]⁸   Yes, it doth shine that night.

BOTTOM   Why, then may you leave a casement of the great
     chamber window where we play open, and the moon may
50   shine in at the casement.

QUINCE   Ay, or else one must come in with a bush of thorns and
     a lantern and say he comes to disfigure,⁹ or to present,° the   *represent*
     person of Moonshine. Then there is another thing: we must
     have a wall in the great chamber; for Pyramus and Thisbe, says
55   the story, did talk through the chink of a wall.

SNOUT   You can never bring in a wall. What say you, Bottom?

BOTTOM   Some man or other must present Wall; and let him
     have some plaster, or some loam, or some rough-cast¹ about
     him, to signify 'wall'; and let him hold his fingers thus, and
60   through that cranny shall Pyramus and Thisbe whisper.

QUINCE   If that may be, then all is well. Come, sit down every
     mother's son, and rehearse your parts. Pyramus, you begin.
     When you have spoken your speech, enter into that brake; and
     so everyone according to his cue.

65   ROBIN [*aside*]   What hempen homespuns² have we swagg'ring
          here
     So near the cradle of the Fairy Queen?
     What, a play toward?°   I'll be an auditor—   *in preparation*
     An actor, too, perhaps, if I see cause.

QUINCE   Speak, Pyramus. Thisbe, stand forth.

70   BOTTOM [*as Pyramus*]   Thisbe, the flowers of odious° savours   (*for "odorous"*)
          sweet.

QUINCE   Odours, odours.

BOTTOM [*as Pyramus*]   Odours savours sweet.
     So hath thy breath, my dearest Thisbe dear.
     But hark, a voice. Stay thou but here a while,
75   And by and by I will to thee appear.   *Exit*

ROBIN³ [*aside*]   A stranger Pyramus than e'er played here. [*Exit*]

FLUTE   Must I speak now?

QUINCE   Ay, marry must you. For you must understand he goes
     but to see a noise that he heard, and is to come again.

80   FLUTE [*as Thisbe*]   Most radiant Pyramus, most lily-white of hue,
     Of colour like the red rose on triumphant brier;
     Most bristly juvenile,° and eke° most lovely Jew,⁴   *lively youth / also*
     As true as truest horse that yet would never tire:
     I'll meet thee, Pyramus, at Ninny's° tomb.   *fool's*

85   QUINCE   Ninus'⁵ tomb, man!—Why, you must not speak that
     yet. That you answer to Pyramus. You speak all your part at

---

6. Or Snug: Q2, F abbreviate as "Sn."
7. Robin's entrance here (in F only) is also noted (in both F and Q) at line 65.
8. The book, perhaps comically supplied by Robin, is an editorial conjecture.
9. Blunder for "figure," represent. *bush of thorns:* bundle of thornbush kindling (like the lantern, a traditional accessory of the man in the moon).
1. Mixture of lime and gravel used to plaster outside walls.

2. Peasants, country bumpkins, dressed in coarse homespun fabric made from hemp.
3. Q gives this line to Quince.
4. Not often considered "lovely" by Elizabethan Christians; usually a term of abuse (here echoing the first syllable of "juvenile").
5. Mythical founder of Nineveh, whose wife, Semiramis, was believed to have founded Babylon, the setting for the story of Pyramus and Thisbe.

once, cues and all.—Pyramus, enter: your cue is past; it is
'never tire'.

FLUTE O.

90 [*As Thisbe*] As true as truest horse that yet would never tire.

[*Enter* ROBIN *leading* BOTTOM *with the ass-head*]

BOTTOM [*as Pyramus*] If I were fair,° Thisbe, I were° only thine.   *handsome / would be*

QUINCE O monstrous! O strange! We are haunted. Pray, masters; fly, masters: help!   *The clowns all exeunt*

ROBIN I'll follow you, I'll lead you about a round,°   *in circles*

95   Through bog, through bush, through brake, through brier.
  Sometime a horse I'll be, sometime a hound,
    A hog, a headless bear, sometime a fire,°   *will-o'-the-wisp*
  And neigh, and bark, and grunt, and roar, and burn,
  Like horse, hound, hog, bear, fire, at every turn.   *Exit*

    Enter [BOTTOM[6] *again,*] *with the ass-head*

100 BOTTOM Why do they run away? This is a knavery of them to
make me afeard.

    Enter SNOUT

SNOUT O Bottom, thou art changed. What do I see on thee?

BOTTOM What do you see? You see an ass-head of your own,[7]
do you?   [*Exit* SNOUT]

    Enter QUINCE

105 QUINCE Bless thee, Bottom, bless thee. Thou art translated.°   *transformed*

    Exit

BOTTOM I see their knavery. This is to make an ass of me, to
fright me, if they could; but I will not stir from this place, do
what they can. I will walk up and down here, and I will sing,
that they shall hear I am not afraid.

110   [*Sings*]   The ousel cock° so black of hue,   *male blackbird*
          With orange-tawny bill;
          The throstle° with his note so true,   *song thrush*
          The wren with little quill.°   *reed pipe*

TITANIA [*awaking*] What angel wakes me from my flow'ry bed?

115 BOTTOM [*sings*]   The finch, the sparrow, and the lark,
          The plainsong[8] cuckoo grey,
          Whose note full many a man doth mark,
          And dares not answer 'Nay'[9]—

for indeed, who would set his wit to° so foolish a bird? Who   *pay heed to*

120 would give a bird the lie,[1] though he cry 'Cuckoo' never so?°   *ever so much*

TITANIA I pray thee, gentle mortal, sing again.
  Mine ear is much enamoured of thy note;
  So is mine eye enthrallèd to thy shape;
  And thy fair virtue's force[2] perforce doth move me

125   On the first view to say, to swear, I love thee.

BOTTOM Methinks, mistress, you should have little reason for
that. And yet, to say the truth, reason and love keep little company together nowadays—the more the pity that some honest
neighbours will not make them friends. Nay, I can gleek° upon   *make jokes*

130 occasion.

TITANIA Thou art as wise as thou art beautiful.

---

6. He might have remained onstage when the others
left. Entrance noted in F only.
7. You see a figment of your own asinine imagination.
8. A melody sung without adornment; the repeated

"cuckoo" (associated with cuckoldry).
9. Deny (that he is a cuckold).
1. Who would call a bird a liar.
2. Your patience; power of your good qualities.

BOTTOM Not so, neither; but if I had wit enough to get out of
this wood, I have enough to serve mine own turn.³   *purpose*

TITANIA Out of this wood do not desire to go.

135 Thou shalt remain here, whether thou wilt or no.
I am a spirit of no common rate:°   *rank*
The summer still° doth tend upon my state;³   *always; continually*
And I do love thee. Therefore go with me.
I'll give thee fairies to attend on thee,

140 And they shall fetch thee jewels from the deep,
And sing while thou on pressèd flowers dost sleep;
And I will purge thy mortal grossness° so   *fleshly being*
That thou shalt like an airy spirit go.
Peaseblossom, Cobweb, Mote, and Mustardseed!

Enter four fairies: PEASEBLOSSOM, COBWEB, MOTE,⁴ *and*
MUSTARDSEED

A FAIRY Ready.

ANOTHER   And I.

ANOTHER   And I.

ANOTHER   And I.

145 ALL FOUR   Where shall we go?

TITANIA Be kind and courteous to this gentleman.
Hop in his walks, and gambol in his eyes.
Feed him with apricots and dewberries,
With purple grapes, green figs, and mulberries;

150 The honeybags steal from the humble-bees,°   *bumblebees*
And for night tapers crop their waxen thighs
And light them at the fiery glow-worms' eyes
To have° my love to bed, and to arise;   *lead*
And pluck the wings from painted butterflies

155 To fan the moonbeams from his sleeping eyes.
Nod to him, elves, and do him courtesies.

A FAIRY Hail, mortal.

ANOTHER Hail.

ANOTHER Hail.

160 ANOTHER Hail.

BOTTOM I cry your worships mercy,⁵ heartily.—I beseech your
worship's name.

COBWEB Cobweb.

BOTTOM I shall desire you of more acquaintance, good Master

165 Cobweb. If I cut my finger,⁶ I shall make bold with you.—Your
name, honest gentleman?

PEASEBLOSSOM Peaseblossom.

BOTTOM I pray you commend me to Mistress Squash, your
mother, and to Master Peascod,⁷ your father. Good Master

170 Peaseblossom, I shall desire you of more acquaintance, too.—
Your name, I beseech you, sir?

MUSTARDSEED Mustardseed.

BOTTOM Good Master Mustardseed, I know your patience⁸ well.
That same cowardly giantlike ox-beef⁹ hath devoured many a

175 gentleman of your house. I promise you your kindred hath

---

3. Serves me, as part of my royal retinue.
4. Speck. "Mote" and "moth" were pronounced alike.
5. I beg pardon of your honors.
6. Cobwebs were used to stop bleeding.

7. Ripe pea pod (called "your father" because it suggests "codpiece"). *Squash*: unripe pea pod.
8. What you have suffered with fortitude.
9. Because beef is often eaten with mustard.

made my eyes water ere now. I desire you of more acquaintance, good Master Mustardseed.

TITANIA [*to the fairies*]   Come, wait upon him, lead him to my bower.
The moon, methinks, looks with a wat'ry eye,
180   And when she weeps, weeps every little flower,[1]
Lamenting some enforcèd° chastity.   *violated; involuntary*
Tie up my love's tongue;[2] bring him silently.   *Exeunt*

3.2
Enter [OBERON,] King of Fairies
OBERON   I wonder if Titania be awaked,
Then what it was that next came in her eye,
Which she must dote on in extremity.
Enter [ROBIN GOODFELLOW the] puck
Here comes my messenger. How now, mad spirit?
5   What nightrule° now about this haunted grove?   *night revels; sports*
ROBIN   My mistress with a monster is in love.
Near to her close° and consecrated bower   *private*
While she was in her dull° and sleeping hour   *drowsy*
A crew of patches,° rude mechanicals°   *fools / rough workmen*
10   That work for bread upon Athenian stalls,°   *market stands*
Were met together to rehearse a play
Intended for great Theseus' nuptial day.
The shallowest thickskin of that barren sort,°   *witless lot*
Who Pyramus presented,° in their sport   *acted*
15   Forsook his scene° and entered in a brake,   *stage*
When I did him at this advantage take.
An ass's nole° I fixèd on his head.   *noddle; head*
Anon his Thisbe must be answerèd,
And forth my mimic° comes. When they him spy—   *burlesque actor*
20   As wild geese that the creeping fowler° eye,   *hunter of birds*
Or russet-pated choughs, many in sort,[1]
Rising and cawing at the gun's report,
Sever° themselves and madly sweep the sky—   *Scatter*
So, at his sight, away his fellows fly,
25   And at our stamp[2] here o'er and o'er one falls.
He° 'Murder' cries, and help from Athens calls.   *One (workman)*
Their sense thus weak, lost with their fears thus strong,
Made senseless things begin to do them wrong.
For briers and thorns at their apparel snatch;
30   Some sleeves, some hats—from yielders all things catch.[3]
I led them on in this distracted fear,
And left sweet Pyramus translated there;
When in that moment, so it came to pass,
Titania waked and straightway loved an ass.
35   OBERON   This falls out better than I could devise.
But hast thou yet latched° the Athenian's eyes   *anointed*
With the love juice, as I did bid thee do?
ROBIN   I took him sleeping; that is finished, too;
And the Athenian woman by his side,

1. Dew was thought to originate on the moon.
2. Bottom is perhaps making involuntary asinine noises.
3.2 Location: The wood.
1. Together, in a flock. *russet-pated choughs:* gray-

headed jackdaws.
2. Editors have wondered how a fairy's presumably
tiny foot could cause the human to fall.
3. Everything robs the timid.

40	That° when he waked of force° she must be eyed.	*So that / necessity*
	Enter DEMETRIUS *and* HERMIA	

OBERON   Stand close. This is the same Athenian.

ROBIN   This is the woman, but not this the man.
      [*They stand apart*]

DEMETRIUS   O, why rebuke you him that loves you so?
    Lay breath so bitter on your bitter foe.

45 HERMIA   Now I but chide, but I should use thee worse;
    For thou, I fear, hast given me cause to curse.
    If thou hast slain Lysander in his sleep,

	Being o'er shoes° in blood, plunge in the deep,	*Having waded so far*
	And kill me too.	

50   The sun was not so true unto the day
    As he to me. Would he have stolen away
    From sleeping Hermia? I'll believe as soon

	This whole° earth may be bored, and that the moon	*solid*
	May through the centre creep, and so displease	

55   Her brother's noontide with th'Antipodes.[4]
    It cannot be but thou hast murdered him.

	So should a murderer look—so dead,° so grim.	*deathly pale*

DEMETRIUS   So should the murdered look, and so should I,
    Pierced through the heart with your stern cruelty.

60   Yet you, the murderer, look as bright, as clear

	As yonder Venus in her glimmering sphere.°	*orbit*

HERMIA   What's this to my Lysander? Where is he?
    Ah, good Demetrius, wilt thou give him me?

DEMETRIUS   I had rather give his carcass to my hounds.

65 HERMIA   Out, dog; out, cur. Thou driv'st me past the bounds
    Of maiden's patience. Hast thou slain him then?
    Henceforth be never numbered among men.
    O, once tell true; tell true, even for my sake.
    Durst thou have looked upon him being awake,

70	And hast thou killed him sleeping? O brave touch!°	*noble stroke*
	Could not a worm,° an adder do so much?—	*serpent*

    An adder did it, for with doubler[5] tongue
    Than thine, thou serpent, never adder stung.

	DEMETRIUS You spend your passion on a misprised mood.°	*in misconceived anger*

75   I am not guilty of Lysander's blood,
    Nor is he dead, for aught that I can tell.

HERMIA   I pray thee, tell me then that he is well.

	DEMETRIUS And if I could, what should I get therefor?°	*for that*

HERMIA   A privilege never to see me more;
80   And from thy hated presence part I so.

	See me no more, whether he be dead or no.	*Exit*

DEMETRIUS   There is no following her in this fierce vein.
    Here therefore for a while I will remain.
    So sorrow's heaviness[6] doth heavier grow
85   For debt that bankrupt sleep doth sorrow owe,[7]
    Which now in some slight measure it will pay,

---

4. *that . . . Antipodes:* that the moon could creep through a hole bored through the earth's center and emerge on the other side, the Antipodes, displeasing the inhabitants by displacing the noontime sun with the darkness of night. (Apollo, the sun god, was the brother of Diana, the moon goddess.)

5. More forked (of the adder); more duplicitous (of Demetrius).
6. Sadness (punning on "heavy": drowsy).
7. *For . . . owe:* Because of the sleeplessness sorrow causes.

If for his tender here I make some stay.[8]
    [*He lies*] *down* [*and sleeps*]
OBERON [*to* ROBIN]   What hast thou done? Thou hast mistaken quite,
And laid the love juice on some true love's sight.

90   Of thy misprision° must perforce ensue   *mistake*
Some true love turned, and not a false turned true.
ROBIN   Then fate o'errules, that, one man holding troth,°   *faith*
A million fail, confounding oath on oath.[9]
OBERON   About the wood go swifter than the wind,
95   And Helena of Athens look° thou find.   *be sure*
All fancy-sick° she is, and pale of cheer°   *lovesick / face*
With sighs of love that costs the fresh blood dear.[1]
By some illusion see thou bring her here.
I'll charm his eyes against° she do appear.   *in readiness for when*
100 ROBIN   I go, I go—look how I go,
Swifter than arrow from the Tartar's bow.[2]   *Exit*
OBERON   Flower of this purple dye,
                    Hit with Cupid's archery,
                    Sink in apple° of his eye.   *pupil*
    [*He drops the juice on Demetrius' eyelids*]
105   When his love he doth espy,
                    Let her shine as gloriously
                    As the Venus of the sky.
                    When thou wak'st, if she be by,
                    Beg of her for remedy.
    Enter [ROBIN GOODFELLOW *the*] *puck*
110 ROBIN   Captain of our fairy band,
                    Helena is here at hand,
                    And the youth mistook by me,
                    Pleading for a lover's fee.°   *reward*
                    Shall we their fond° pageant see?   *foolish*
115   Lord, what fools these mortals be!
OBERON   Stand aside. The noise they make
                    Will cause Demetrius to awake.
ROBIN   Then will two at once woo one.
                    That must needs be sport alone;°   *unique*
120   And those things do best please me
                    That befall prepost'rously.°   *ass backward*
    [*They stand apart.*]
    Enter HELENA, LYSANDER [*following her*]
LYSANDER   Why should you think that I should woo in scorn?
Scorn and derision never come in tears.
Look when I vow, I weep; and vows so born,
125   In their nativity all truth appears.[3]
How can these things in me seem scorn to you,
Bearing the badge of faith[4] to prove them true?
HELENA   You do advance° your cunning more and more,   *increase; display*
When truth kills truth[5]—O devilish holy fray!
130 These vows are Hermia's. Will you give her o'er?

---

8. *Which . . . stay:* I will rest here awhile to give sleep
the opportunity to pay off some of its debt to sorrow.
9. Among the millions of faithless men, the one true
man's oath has been subverted by fate.
1. Sighs were thought to cause loss of blood.
2. Tartars, a dark-skinned, supposedly savage people in
Asia Minor, were famed for their archery.
3. *Look . . . appears:* The fact that I am weeping
authenticates my vow's sincerity.
4. Insignia, such as worn on a servant's livery (here, his
tears).
5. When one vow nullifies another.

Weigh oath with oath, and you will nothing weigh.[6]
Your vows to her and me put in two scales
Will even weigh, and both as light as tales.°   *lies; fiction*

LYSANDER   I had no judgement when to her I swore.

135   HELENA   Nor none, in my mind, now you give her o'er.

LYSANDER   Demetrius loves her, and he loves not you.

HELENA[7]   [   ]

DEMETRIUS [*awaking*]   O Helen, goddess, nymph, perfect, divine!
To what, my love, shall I compare thine eyne?

140   Crystal is muddy. O, how ripe in show°   *appearance*
Thy lips, those kissing cherries, tempting grow!
That pure congealèd white—high Taurus'[8] snow,
Fanned with the eastern wind—turns to a crow[9]
When thou hold'st up thy hand. O, let me kiss

145   This princess of pure white, this seal° of bliss!   *pledge*

HELENA   O spite! O hell! I see you all are bent
To set against me for your merriment.
If you were civil, and knew courtesy,
You would not do me thus much injury.

150   Can you not hate me—as I know you do—
But you must join in souls to mock me too?
If you were men, as men you are in show,
You would not use a gentle° lady so,   *well-born; mild*
To vow and swear and superpraise my parts°   *overpraise my qualities*

155   When I am sure you hate me with your hearts.
You both are rivals and love Hermia,
And now both rivals to mock Helena.
A trim° exploit, a manly enterprise—   *fine*
To conjure tears up in a poor maid's eyes

160   With your derision. None of noble sort°   *rank; nature*
Would so offend a virgin, and extort°   *torture*
A poor soul's patience, all to make you sport.

LYSANDER   You are unkind, Demetrius. Be not so.
For you love Hermia; this you know I know.

165   And here with all good will, with all my heart,
In Hermia's love I yield you up my part;
And yours of Helena to me bequeath,
Whom I do love, and will do till my death.

HELENA   Never did mockers waste more idle breath.

170   DEMETRIUS   Lysander, keep thy Hermia. I will none.[1]
If e'er I loved her, all that love is gone.
My heart to her but as guestwise° sojourned   *as a guest*
And now to Helen is it home returned,
There to remain.

LYSANDER   Helen, it is not so.

175   DEMETRIUS   Disparage not the faith thou dost not know,
Lest to thy peril thou aby it dear.°   *pay for it dearly*
          Enter HERMIA
Look where thy love comes; yonder is thy dear.

HERMIA   Dark night, that from the eye his° function takes,   *its*
The ear more quick of apprehension makes.

---

6. *you . . . weigh:* you will find that neither oath has
any substance; you, Lysander, will be found to have no
substance.
7. Helena's retort, awakening Demetrius, may have
been inadvertently omitted by the Q and F texts.
8. Range of high mountains in Asia Minor.
9. *turns to a crow:* appears black by contrast.
1. I will have nothing to do with her.

180   Wherein it doth impair the seeing sense,
          It pays the hearing double recompense.
          Thou art not by mine eye, Lysander, found;
          Mine ear, I thank it, brought me to thy sound.
          But why unkindly didst thou leave me so?

185   LYSANDER   Why should he stay whom love doth press to go?

      HERMIA   What love could press Lysander from my side?

      LYSANDER   Lysander's love, that would not let him bide:
          Fair Helena, who more engilds the night
          Than all yon fiery O's and eyes of light.[2]

190   Why seek'st thou me? Could not this make thee know
          The hate I bare thee made me leave thee so?

      HERMIA   You speak not as you think. It cannot be.

      HELENA [*aside*]   Lo, she is one of this confederacy.
          Now I perceive they have conjoined all three

195   To fashion this false sport in spite of° me.—   *to spite*
          Injurious Hermia, most ungrateful maid,
          Have you conspired, have you with these contrived
          To bait[3] me with this foul derision?
          Is all the counsel° that we two have shared—   *confidences*

200   The sisters' vows, the hours that we have spent
          When we have chid the hasty-footed time
          For parting us—O, is all quite forgot?
          All schooldays' friendship, childhood innocence?
          We, Hermia, like two artificial gods

205   Have with our needles created both one flower,
          Both on one sampler, sitting on one cushion,
          Both warbling of one song, both in one key,
          As if our hands, our sides, voices, and minds
          Had been incorporate.° So we grew together,   *of one body*

210   Like to a double cherry: seeming parted,
          But yet an union in partition,
          Two lovely berries moulded on one stem.
          So, with two seeming bodies but one heart,
          Two of the first[4]—like coats in heraldry,

215   Due but to one and crownèd with one crest,
          And will you rend our ancient love asunder,
          To join with men in scorning your poor friend?
          It is not friendly, 'tis not maidenly.
          Our sex as well as I may chide you for it,

220   Though I alone do feel the injury.

      HERMIA   I am amazèd at your passionate words.
          I scorn you not. It seems that you scorn me.

      HELENA   Have you not set Lysander, as in scorn,
          To follow me, and praise my eyes and face?

225   And made your other love, Demetrius—
          Who even but now° did spurn me with his foot—   *just now*
          To call me goddess, nymph, divine, and rare,
          Precious, celestial? Wherefore speaks he this
          To her he hates? And wherefore doth Lysander

230   Deny your love so rich within his soul,

---

2. Stars (punning on the vowels and on lovers' exclam-
atory "oh"s and "ay"s). An "o" was a spangle.
3. To torment (as Elizabethans set dogs to bait a bear).
4. A technical phrase in heraldry, referring to the first
quartering in a coat of arms, which may be repeated.
The friends then have two bodies but a single, overarching identity.

And tender° me, forsooth, affection,   *offer*
But by your setting on, by your consent?
What though I be not so in grace° as you,   *favor*
So hung upon with love, so fortunate,
235 But miserable most, to love unloved—
This you should pity rather than despise.

HERMIA   I understand not what you mean by this.

HELENA   Ay, do. Persever, counterfeit sad° looks,   *serious*
Make mouths upon° me when I turn my back,   *Make faces at*
240 Wink each at other, hold the sweet jest up.°   *keep up the joke*
This sport well carried shall be chronicled.
If you have any pity, grace, or manners,
You would not make me such an argument.°   *a subject of merriment*
But fare ye well. 'Tis partly my own fault,
245 Which death or absence soon shall remedy.

LYSANDER   Stay, gentle Helena, hear my excuse,
My love, my life, my soul, fair Helena.

HELENA   O excellent!

HERMIA [*to* LYSANDER]   Sweet, do not scorn her so.

DEMETRIUS [*to* LYSANDER]   If she cannot entreat I can compel.⁵

250 LYSANDER   Thou canst compel no more than she entreat.
Thy threats have no more strength than her weak prayers.—
Helen, I love thee; by my life I do.
I swear by that which I will lose for thee
To prove him false that says I love thee not.

255 DEMETRIUS [*to* HELENA]   I say I love thee more than he can do.

LYSANDER   If thou say so, withdraw,⁵ and prove it too.

DEMETRIUS   Quick, come.

HERMIA   Lysander, whereto tends all this?
[*She takes him by the arm*]

LYSANDER   Away, you Ethiope.⁷

DEMETRIUS   No, no, sir, yield.°   *(to Hermia)*
Seem to break loose, take on as° you would follow,   *pretend*
260 But yet come not. You are a tame man; go.

LYSANDER [*to* HERMIA]   Hang off,° thou cat, thou burr; vile thing, let loose, *Let go*
Or I will shake thee from me like a serpent.

HERMIA   Why are you grown so rude? What change is this,
Sweet love?

LYSANDER   Thy love? Out, tawny Tartar, out;
265 Out, loathèd med'cine;⁸ O hated potion, hence.

HERMIA   Do you not jest?

HELENA   Yes, sooth,° and so do you.   *truly*

LYSANDER   Demetrius, I will keep my word with thee.

DEMETRIUS   I would I had your bond, for I perceive
A weak bond⁹ holds you. I'll not trust your word.

270 LYSANDER   What, should I hurt her, strike her, kill her dead?
Although I hate her, I'll not harm her so.

HERMIA   What, can you do me greater harm than hate?
Hate me—wherefore? O me, what news,° my love?   *what has happened*
Am not I Hermia? Are not you Lysander?

---

5. If Hermia cannot entreat you to stop, I can make you do it.
6. Come with me ("step outside").
7. Allusion to Hermia's dark hair and complexion. Elizabethans generally regarded light complexions as more

beautiful than dark and often stigmatized dark-skinned peoples (such as Ethiopians or Tartars) as ugly.
8. Any drug (including poison).
9. Hermia's weak grasp (with a pun on "bond": oath, in the previous line).

275 I am as fair now as I was erewhile.°   *a while ago*
Since night you loved me, yet since night you left me.
Why then, you left me—O, the gods forbid—
In earnest, shall I say?
LYSANDER   Ay, by my life,
And never did desire to see thee more.
280 Therefore be out of hope, of question, doubt.
Be certain, nothing truer; 'tis no jest
That I do hate thee and love Helena.
HERMIA [*to* HELENA]   O me, you juggler,° you canker blossom,[1]   *trickster*
You thief of love—what, have you come by night
And stol'n my love's heart from him?
285 HELENA   Fine, i'faith.
Have you no modesty, no maiden shame,
No touch of bashfulness? What, will you tear
Impatient answers from my gentle tongue?
Fie, fie, you counterfeit, you puppet,[2] you!
290 HERMIA   Puppet? Why, so! Ay, that way goes the game.
Now I perceive that she hath made compare
Between our statures; she hath urged her height,
And with her personage, her tall personage,
Her height, forsooth, she hath prevailed with him—
295 And are you grown so high in his esteem
Because I am so dwarfish and so low?
How low am I, thou painted maypole?[3] Speak,
How low am I? I am not yet so low
But that my nails can reach unto thine eyes.
HELENA [*to* DEMETRIUS *and* LYSANDER]   I pray you, though you
300   mock me, gentlemen,
Let her not hurt me. I was never curst.°   *quarrelsome*
I have no gift at all in shrewishness.
I am a right° maid for my cowardice.   *proper*
Let her not strike me. You perhaps may think
305 Because she is something° lower than myself   *somewhat*
That I can match her—
HERMIA   Lower? Hark again.
HELENA   Good Hermia, do not be so bitter with me.
I evermore did love you, Hermia,
Did ever keep your counsels, never wronged you—
310 Save that in love unto Demetrius
I told him of your stealth° unto this wood.   *stealing away*
He followed you; for love I followed him.
But he hath chid me hence, and threatened me
To strike me, spurn me, nay, to kill me too.
315 And now, so° you will let me quiet go,   *if only*
To Athens will I bear my folly back,
And follow you no further. Let me go.
You see how simple and how fond° I am.   *foolish*
HERMIA   Why, get you gone. Who is't that hinders you?
320 HELENA   A foolish heart that I leave here behind.
HERMIA   What, with Lysander?

---

1. Worm that devours blossoms (of love).
2. Fraudulent imitation; but Hermia interprets "puppet" as a reference to her height.

3. Proverbial for someone tall and skinny. *painted:*
insulting allusion to the use of cosmetics.

HELENA	With Demetrius.	
LYSANDER	Be not afraid; she shall not harm thee, Helena.	
DEMETRIUS	No, sir, she shall not, though you take her part.	
HELENA	O, when she is angry she is keen° and shrewd.°	*sharp / shrewish*

325   She was a vixen when she went to school,
       And though she be but little, she is fierce.

HERMIA   Little again? Nothing but 'low' and 'little'?—
       Why will you suffer her to flout me thus?
       Let me come to her.

LYSANDER   Get you gone, you dwarf,
330   You *minimus* of hind'ring knot-grass[4] made,
       You bead, you acorn.

DEMETRIUS   You are too officious
       In her behalf that scorns your services.
       Let her alone. Speak not of Helena.
       Take not her part. For if thou dost intend

335   Never so little° show of love to her,   *Even the smallest*
       Thou shalt aby° it.   *pay for*

LYSANDER   Now she holds me not.
       Now follow, if thou dar'st, to try whose right,
       Of thine or mine, is most in Helena.

DEMETRIUS   Follow? Nay, I'll go with thee, cheek by jowl.[5]

Exeunt LYSANDER *and* DEMETRIUS

340 HERMIA   You, mistress, all this coil° is long° of you.   *turmoil / because*
       Nay, go not back.

HELENA   I will not trust you, I,
       Nor longer stay in your curst company.
       Your hands than mine are quicker for a fray;°   *fight*
       My legs are longer, though, to run away.   [*Exit*]

345 HERMIA   I am amazed, and know not what to say.   *Exit*

OBERON *and* ROBIN [*come forward*]

OBERON   This is thy negligence. Still° thou mistak'st,   *Always*
       Or else commit'st thy knaveries wilfully.

ROBIN   Believe me, king of shadows,° I mistook.   *fairy spirits*
       Did not you tell me I should know the man
350   By the Athenian garments he had on?—
       And so far° blameless proves my enterprise   *to this extent*
       That I have 'nointed an Athenian's eyes;
       And so far am I glad it so did sort°   *turn out*
       As° this their jangling° I esteem a sport.   *Since / bickering*

355 OBERON   Thou seest these lovers seek a place to fight.
       Hie° therefore, Robin, overcast the night;   *Hurry*
       The starry welkin° cover thou anon   *sky*
       With drooping fog as black as Acheron,°   *river of hell*
       And lead these testy rivals so astray
360   As° one come not within another's way.   *So that*
       Like to Lysander sometime frame thy tongue,
       Then stir Demetrius up with bitter wrong;°   *insults*
       And sometime rail thou like Demetrius,
       And from each other look thou lead them thus
365   Till o'er their brows death-counterfeiting sleep

---

4. Creeping binding weed (its sap was thought to stunt human growth). *minimus:* diminutive thing (Latin).   5. Proverbial for "side by side."

With leaden legs and batty° wings doth creep.   *batlike*
Then crush this herb into Lysander's eye—
Whose liquor hath this virtuous° property,   *potent*
To take from thence all error with his might,
370   And make his eyeballs roll with wonted° sight.   *normal*
When they next wake, all this derision
Shall seem a dream and fruitless° vision,   *inconsequential*
And back to Athens shall the lovers wend°   *go*
With league° whose date° till death shall never end.   *covenant / duration*
375   Whiles I in this affair do thee employ,
I'll to my queen and beg her Indian boy;
And then I will her charmèd° eye release   *enchanted*
From monster's view, and all things shall be peace.
   ROBIN   My fairy lord, this must be done with haste,
380   For night's swift dragons[6] cut the clouds full fast,
And yonder shines Aurora's harbinger,[7]
At whose approach ghosts, wand'ring here and there,
Troop home to churchyards; damnèd spirits all
That in cross-ways and floods[8] have burial
385   Already to their wormy beds are gone,
For fear lest day should look their shames upon.
They wilfully themselves exiled from light,
And must for aye° consort with black-browed night.   *forever*
   OBERON   But we are spirits of another sort.
390   I with the morning's love[9] have oftmade sport,
And like a forester[1] the groves may tread
Even till the eastern gate, all fiery red,
Opening on Neptune° with fair blessèd beams   *the sea*
Turns into yellow gold his salt° green streams.   *salty*
395   But notwithstanding, haste, make no delay;
We may effect this business yet ere day.   [*Exit*]
   ROBIN   Up and down, up and down,
     I will lead them up and down.
     I am feared in field and town.
400   Goblin,° lead them up and down.   (*Puck himself*)
Here comes one.
        Enter LYSANDER
   LYSANDER   Where art thou, proud Demetrius? Speak thou now.
   ROBIN [*shifting place*][2]   Here, villain, drawn° and ready. Where   *with sword drawn*
     art thou?
   LYSANDER   I will be with thee straight.°   *immediately*
   ROBIN [*shifting place*]   Follow me then
   To plainer° ground.   [*Exit* LYSANDER][3]   *clearer*
        Enter DEMETRIUS
405   DEMETRIUS [*shifting place*]   Lysander, speak again.
Thou runaway, thou coward, art thou fled?
Speak! In some bush? Where dost thou hide thy head?

---

6. Imagined as drawing the chariots of the goddess of night.
7. Herald of the goddess of dawn; the morning star.
8. In which the drowned were "buried," without Christian sacrament. *cross-ways:* crossroads (where suicides were buried, also without Christian sacrament). Robin is differentiating here between two types of spirits: those who wandered from their churchyard graves and those who have no proper resting place. These two types, both ghosts of former humans, are differentiated in turn from the fairy spirits by Oberon in the ensuing lines.
9. The love of Aurora, goddess of dawn (or Cephalus, a brave hunter, Aurora's lover).
1. Keeper of a royal forest or private park.
2. In F, this direction is placed in the margin in the middle of this episode. (In what follows, Robin presumably mimics the voices of Demetrius and Lysander.)
3. He might instead wander about the stage.

ROBIN [*shifting place*]   Thou coward, art thou bragging to the stars,
    Telling the bushes that thou look'st for wars,
410   And wilt not come? Come, recreant;° come, thou child,   *coward; wretch*
    I'll whip thee with a rod. He is defiled
    That draws a sword on thee.⁴
DEMETRIUS [*shifting place*]   Yea, art thou there?
ROBIN [*shifting place*]   Follow my voice; we'll try° no manhood here.   *test*
                                      Exeunt

3.3

[*Enter* LYSANDER]
LYSANDER   He goes before me, and still dares me on;
    When I come where he calls, then he is gone.
    The villain is much lighter heeled than I;
    I followed fast, but faster he did fly,
5   That° fallen am I in dark uneven way,   *With the result that*
    And here will rest me.
            [*He lies*] *down*
                        Come, thou gentle day;
    For if but once thou show me thy grey light,
    I'll find Demetrius, and revenge this spite.   [*He sleeps*]
Enter ROBIN [GOODFELLOW] *and* DEMETRIUS
ROBIN [*shifting place*]   Ho, ho, ho, coward, why com'st thou not?
10 DEMETRIUS   Abide° me if thou dar'st, for well I wot°   *Wait for / know*
    Thou runn'st before me, shifting every place,
    And dar'st not stand nor look me in the face.
    Where art thou now?
ROBIN [*shifting place*]   Come hither, I am here.
DEMETRIUS   Nay, then thou mock'st me. Thou shalt buy° this   *pay for*
    dear°   *dearly*
15   If ever I thy face by daylight see.
    Now go thy way. Faintness constraineth me
    To measure out my length on this cold bed.
        [*He lies down*]
    By day's approach look to be visited.   [*He sleeps*]
      Enter HELENA
HELENA   O weary night, O long and tedious night,
20   Abate° thy hours; shine comforts from the east   *Shorten*
    That I may back to Athens by daylight
    From these that my poor company detest;
    And sleep, that sometimes shuts up sorrow's eye,
    Steal me a while from mine own company.
       [*She lies down and sleeps*]
25 ROBIN   Yet but three? Come one more,
    Two of both kinds makes up four.
      Enter HERMIA
    Here she comes, curst° and sad.   *angry*
    Cupid is a knavish lad
    Thus to make poor females mad.
30 HERMIA   Never so weary, never so in woe,
    Bedabbled° with the dew, and torn with briers,   *Sprinkled*
    I can no further crawl, no further go.
    My legs can keep no pace with my desires.

---

4. I.e., it would be a disgrace to treat you as an honor-   3.3 Location: Scene continues.
able opponent.

Here will I rest me till the break of day.
    [*She lies down*]
35 Heavens shield Lysander, if they mean a fray.
    [*She sleeps*]
ROBIN   On the ground sleep sound.
        I'll apply to your eye,
        Gentle lover, remedy.
    [*He drops the juice on Lysander's eyelids*]
        When thou wak'st thou tak'st
40   True delight in the sight
        Of thy former lady's eye,
    And the country proverb known,
    That 'every man should take his own',
    In your waking shall be shown.
45   Jack shall have Jill,
        Naught shall go ill,
the man shall have his mare again, and all shall be well. [*Exit*]

4.1

Enter [TITANIA,] *Queen of Fairies, and* [BOTTOM *the*]
clown [*with the ass-head*], *and fairies:* [PEASEBLOSSOM,
COBWEB, MOTE, *and* MUSTARDSEED]

TITANIA [*to* BOTTOM]   Come, sit thee down upon this flow'ry bed,
  While I thy amiable° cheeks do coy,°   *lovable / caress*
And stick musk-roses in thy sleek smooth head,
  And kiss thy fair large ears, my gentle joy.
5 BOTTOM   Where's Peaseblossom?
PEASEBLOSSOM   Ready.
BOTTOM   Scratch my head, Peaseblossom. Where's Monsieur
Cobweb?
COBWEB   Ready.
10 BOTTOM   Monsieur Cobweb, good monsieur, get you your
weapons in your hand and kill me a red-hipped humble-bee
on the top of a thistle; and, good monsieur, bring me the hon-
eybag. Do not fret yourself too much in the action, monsieur;
and, good monsieur, have a care the honeybag break not. I
15 would be loath to have you overflowen with° a honeybag, signor.   *submerged by*
    [*Exit* COBWEB]
Where's Monsieur Mustardseed?
MUSTARDSEED   Ready.
BOTTOM   Give me your neaf,° Monsieur Mustardseed. Pray you,   *fist*
leave your courtesy,[1] good monsieur.
20 MUSTARDSEED   What's your will?
BOTTOM   Nothing, good monsieur, but to help Cavaliery[2] Peaseblossom[3] to scratch. I must to the barber's, monsieur, for
methinks I am marvellous hairy about the face; and I am such
a tender ass, if my hair do but tickle me I must scratch.
25 TITANIA   What, wilt thou hear some music, my sweet love?
BOTTOM   I have a reasonable good ear in music. Let's have the
tongs and the bones.[4]

4.1 Location: The wood. The original text has no act
break here. F has the four lovers sleep through the
action onstage.
1. *leave your courtesy:* stop bowing, or do not stand
bareheaded.

2. Blunder for "Cavalier," perhaps influenced by the
Italian term *cavaliere.*
3. The early texts have "Cobweb" (Shakespeare's or the
printer's error).
4. Triangle and clappers (rustic musical instruments).

Rural music[5]

TITANIA   Or say, sweet love, what thou desir'st to eat.

BOTTOM   Truly, a peck of provender.° I could munch your good   *fodder*

30   dry oats. Methinks I have a great desire to a bottle° of hay. Good   *bundle*

    hay, sweet hay, hath no fellow.°   *equal*

TITANIA   I have a venturous fairy that shall seek

    The squirrel's hoard, and fetch thee off new nuts.

BOTTOM   I had rather have a handful or two of dried peas. But I

35   pray you, let none of your people stir me. I have an exposition

    of° sleep come upon me.   *disposition to*

TITANIA   Sleep thou, and I will wind thee in my arms.

    Fairies, be gone, and be all ways° away.   [*Exeunt* fairies]   *in every direction*

    So° doth the woodbine[6] the sweet honeysuckle   *Thus*

40   Gently entwist; the female ivy so

    Enrings the barky fingers of the elm.

    O how I love thee, how I dote on thee!

        [*They sleep.*]

        Enter ROBIN GOODFELLOW [*the puck*] *and* OBERON[7]

        [*King of Fairies, meeting*]

OBERON   Welcome, good Robin. Seest thou this sweet sight?

    Her dotage now I do begin to pity.

45   For meeting her of late behind the wood,

    Seeking sweet favours° for this hateful fool,   *love tokens*

    I did upbraid her and fall out with her,

    For she his hairy temples then had rounded

    With coronet of fresh and fragrant flowers,

50   And that same dew which sometime° on the buds   *formerly*

    Was wont° to swell like round and orient[8] pearls   *accustomed*

    Stood now within the pretty flow'rets' eyes,

    Like tears that did their own disgrace bewail.

    When I had at my pleasure taunted her,

55   And she in mild terms begged my patience,

    I then did ask of her her changeling child,

    Which straight she gave me, and her fairy sent

    To bear him to my bower in fairyland.

    And now I have the boy, I will undo

60   This hateful imperfection of her eyes.

    And, gentle puck, take this transformèd scalp

    From off the head of this Athenian swain,

    That he, awaking when the other° do,   *others*

    May all to Athens back again repair,

65   And think no more of this night's accidents

    But as the fierce vexation of a dream.

    But first I will release the Fairy Queen.

        [*He drops the juice on Titania's eyelids*]

    Be as thou wast wont to be,

    See as thou wast wont to see.

70   Dian's bud o'er Cupid's flower[9]

    Hath such force and blessèd power.

---

5. Probably background music, which continues during the following dialogue, rather than a separate musical interlude. The direction only occurs in F.

6. Here, "woodbine" cannot mean "honeysuckle," as it did at 2.1.251, and thus must refer to a different plant.

7. In Q, he enters earlier, unseen, with Titania and her train.

8. Lustrous (the best pearls were from the Far East).

9. "Dian's bud," the herb of 2.1.184 and 3.2.367, is perhaps *Agnus castus*, or chaste tree: said to preserve chastity and hence the antidote to "Cupid's flower," or the love-in-idleness of 2.1.166 etc.

Now, my Titania, wake you, my sweet queen.
TITANIA [*awaking*] My Oberon, what visions have I seen!
Methought I was enamoured of an ass.
OBERON There lies your love.
75 TITANIA   How came these things to pass?
O, how mine eyes do loathe his visage now!
OBERON Silence a while.—Robin, take off this head.—
Titania, music call, and strike more dead
Than common sleep of all these five¹ the sense.
80 TITANIA Music, ho—music such as charmeth sleep.
              Still° music   Soft
ROBIN [*taking the ass-head off* BOTTOM] Now when thou wak'st
    with thine own fool's eyes peep.
OBERON Sound music.
          [*The music changes*]
                        Come, my queen, take hands with me,
And rock the ground whereon these sleepers be.
          [OBERON *and* TITANIA *dance*]
Now thou and I are new in amity,
85 And will tomorrow midnight solemnly
Dance in Duke Theseus' house, triumphantly,
And bless it to all fair prosperity.
There shall the pairs of faithful lovers be
Wedded with Theseus, all in jollity.
90 ROBIN Fairy King, attend and mark.
    I do hear the morning lark.
OBERON Then, my queen, in silence sad
    Trip we after nightës² shade.
    We the globe can compass° soon,   orbit
95 Swifter than the wand'ring moon.
TITANIA Come, my lord, and in our flight
    Tell me how it came this night
    That I sleeping here was found
    With these mortals on the ground.
                        Exeunt [OBERON, TITANIA, *and*
                        ROBIN. *The*] *sleepers lie still*
              Wind horns [*within*]. *Enter* THESEUS [*with*] EGEUS, HIP-
              POLYTA, *and all his train*
100 THESEUS Go, one of you, find out the forester,
For now our observation³ is performed;
And since we have the vanguard° of the day,   earliest part
My love shall hear the music of my hounds.
Uncouple⁴ in the western valley; let them go.
105 Dispatch, I say, and find the forester.   [*Exit one*]
We will, fair Queen, up to the mountain's top,
And mark the musical confusion
Of hounds and echo in conjunction.
HIPPOLYTA I was with Hercules and Cadmus⁵ once
110 When in a wood of Crete they bayed° the bear   brought to bay
With hounds of Sparta.⁶ Never did I hear

---

1. The lovers and Bottom.
2. The obsolete genitive inflection.
3. "Observance to a morn of May," as at 1.1.167.
4. Release (the dogs, leashed in pairs).

5. Mythical founder of Thebes. (No source for the anecdote is known.)
6. Famous in antiquity as hunting dogs.

Such gallant chiding;° for besides the groves,   *barking*
The skies, the fountains, every region near
Seemed all one mutual cry. I never heard
115   So musical a discord, such sweet thunder.
THESEUS   My hounds are bred out of the Spartan kind,
So flewed,⁷ so sanded;° and their heads are hung   *sandy-colored*
With ears that sweep away the morning dew,
Crook-kneed, and dewlapped⁸ like Thessalian bulls,
120   Slow in pursuit, but matched in mouth like bells,
Each under each.⁹ A cry more tuneable¹
Was never holla'd to nor cheered with horn
In Crete, in Sparta, nor in Thessaly.
Judge when you hear. But soft:° what nymphs are these?   *stop; look*
125   EGEUS   My lord, this is my daughter here asleep,
And this Lysander; this Demetrius is;
This Helena, old Nedar's Helena.
I wonder of their being here together.
THESEUS   No doubt they rose up early to observe
130   The rite of May, and, hearing our intent,
Came here in grace of our solemnity.°   *ceremony*
But speak, Egeus: is not this the day
That Hermia should give answer of her choice?
EGEUS   It is, my lord.
135   THESEUS   Go bid the huntsmen wake them with their horns.
                                                    [*Exit one*]
        Shout within: wind horns. [*The lovers*] *all start up*
Good morrow, friends. Saint Valentine² is past.
Begin these wood-birds but to couple now?
LYSANDER   Pardon, my lord.
        [*The lovers kneel*]
THESEUS   I pray you all stand up.
        [*The lovers stand*]
        [*To* DEMETRIUS *and* LYSANDER] I know you two are rival enemies.
140   How comes this gentle concord in the world,
That hatred is so far from jealousy°   *suspicion*
To sleep by hate, and fear no enmity?
LYSANDER   My lord, I shall reply amazèdly,°   *confusedly*
Half sleep, half waking. But as yet, I swear,
145   I cannot truly say how I came here.
But as I think—for truly would I speak,
And, now I do bethink me, so it is—
I came with Hermia hither. Our intent
Was to be gone from Athens where° we might,   *wherever*
150   Without° the peril of the Athenian law—   *Outside*
EGEUS [*to* THESEUS]   Enough, enough, my lord, you have enough.
I beg the law, the law upon his head.—
They would have stol'n away, they would, Demetrius,
Thereby to have defeated° you and me—   *defrauded*
155   You of your wife, and me of my consent,
Of my consent that she should be your wife.
DEMETRIUS [*to* THESEUS]   My lord, fair Helen told me of their stealth,

7. Flews were large hanging, fleshy chaps.
8. With hanging folds of skin under the neck (compare
2.1.50).
9. *matched . . . each*: harmoniously matched in the

pitch of their barking, like a set of bells.
1. A pack of hounds more well tuned.
2. Birds were said to choose their mates on Valentine's
Day.

Of this their purpose hither to this wood,
And I in fury hither followed them,
160   Fair Helena in fancy° following me.   *love*
But, my good lord, I wot not by what power—
But by some power it is—my love to Hermia,
Melted as the snow, seems to me now
As the remembrance of an idle gaud°   *a worthless trinket*
165   Which in my childhood I did dote upon,
And all the faith, the virtue of my heart,
The object and the pleasure of mine eye
Is only Helena. To her, my lord,
Was I betrothed ere I saw Hermia.
170   But like in sickness³ did I loathe this food;
But, as in health come to my natural taste,
Now I do wish it, love it, long for it,
And will for evermore be true to it.
THESEUS   Fair lovers, you are fortunately met.
175   Of this discourse we more will hear anon.—
Egeus, I will overbear your will,
For in the temple by and by with us
These couples shall eternally be knit.—
And, for° the morning now is something° worn,   *since / somewhat*
180   Our purposed hunting shall be set aside.
Away with us to Athens. Three and three,
We'll hold a feast in great solemnity.
Come, Hippolyta.

Exit Duke [THESEUS *with* HIPPOLYTA, EGEUS,
and all his train]

DEMETRIUS   These things seem small and undistinguishable,
185   Like far-off mountains turnèd into clouds.
HERMIA   Methinks I see these things with parted° eye,   *improperly focused*
When everything seems double.
HELENA   So methinks,
And I have found Demetrius like a jewel,
Mine own and not mine own.⁴
DEMETRIUS   It seems to me
190   That yet we sleep, we dream. Do not you think
The Duke was here and bid us follow him?
HERMIA   Yea, and my father.
HELENA   And Hippolyta.
LYSANDER   And he did bid us follow to the temple.
DEMETRIUS   Why then, we are awake. Let's follow him,
195   And by the way let us recount our dreams.   *Exeunt lovers*
              BOTTOM *wakes*

BOTTOM   When my cue comes, call me, and I will answer. My
next is 'most fair Pyramus'. Heigh-ho.° Peter Quince? Flute the   *(Perhaps a yawn)*
bellows-mender? Snout the tinker? Starveling? God's my life!°   *Good Lord*
Stolen hence, and left me asleep?—I have had a most rare
200   vision. I have had a dream past the wit of man to say what
dream it was. Man is but an ass if he go about° t'expound this   *try*
dream. Methought I was—there is no man can tell what.
Methought I was, and methought I had—but man is but a

3. Only as a person does when ill or nauseated.
4. Mine on the principle of "finders keepers," but once someone else's.

patched fool[5] if he will offer° to say what methought I had. The　　　　　*venture*
205　eye of man hath not heard, the ear of man hath not seen. man's
hand is not able to taste, his tongue to conceive, nor his heart
to report[6] what my dream was. I will get Peter Quince to write
a ballad of this dream. It shall be called 'Bottom's Dream',
because it hath no bottom,[7] and I will sing it in the latter end
210　of a play, before the Duke. Peradventure,° to take it the more　　　　*Perhaps*
gracious, I shall sing it at her° death.　　　　　*Exit*　　　*(Thisbe's?)*

4.2

Enter QUINCE, FLUTE, SNOUT, *and* STARVELING

QUINCE　Have you sent to Bottom's house? Is he come home
yet?

STARVELING　He cannot be heard of. Out of doubt° he is trans-　　　*Doubtless*
ported.[1]

5　FLUTE　If he come not, then the play is marred. It goes not forward. Doth it?

QUINCE　It is not possible. You have not a man in all Athens able
to discharge° Pyramus but he.　　　　　　　　　　　　　　*perform*

FLUTE　No, he hath simply the best wit° of any handicraft-man　　　*intellect*
10　in Athens.

QUINCE　Yea, and the best person,° too; and he is a very para-　　　*looks*
mour for a sweet voice.

FLUTE　You must say 'paragon'. A paramour is, God bless us, a
thing of naught.°　　　　　　　　　　　　　*something wicked*

Enter SNUG *the joiner*

15　SNUG　Masters, the Duke is coming from the temple. and there
is two or three lords and ladies more married. If our sport° had　　*entertainment*
gone forward we had all been made men.[2]

FLUTE　O sweet bully Bottom! Thus hath he lost sixpence a day[3]
during his life. He could not have scaped sixpence a day. An°　　　*If*
20　the Duke had not given him sixpence a day for playing Pyramus, I'll be hanged. He would have deserved it. Sixpence a
day in Pyramus, or nothing.

Enter BOTTOM

BOTTOM　Where are these lads? Where are these hearts?°　　　　*mates*

QUINCE　Bottom! O most courageous[4] day! O most happy hour!

25　BOTTOM　Masters, I am to discourse wonders; but ask me not
what. For if I tell you, I am no true Athenian. I will tell you
everything right as it fell out.

QUINCE　Let us hear, sweet Bottom.

BOTTOM　Not a word of° me. All that I will tell you is that the　　　*out of*
30　Duke hath dined. Get your apparel together, good strings° to　　*(to attach the beards)*
your beards, new ribbons to your pumps. Meet presently° at the　　*immediately*
palace; every man look o'er his part. For the short and the long
is, our play is preferred.° In any case let Thisbe have clean　　　*recommended*
linen, and let not him that plays the lion pare his nails, for they
35　shall hang out for the lion's claws. And, most dear actors, eat
no onions nor garlic, for we are to utter sweet breath, and I do

---

5. Jester in a patchwork or motley costume.
6. *The eye . . . report:* burlesque of Scripture: "The eye
hath not seen, and the ear hath not heard, neither have
entered into the heart of man" those things that God
has prepared (1 Corinthians 2:9–10 [Bishops' Bible]).
7. Because it is unfathomable, has no substance (foundation).

4.2 Location: Athens.
1. Carried away (by the fairies); transformed.
2. *we . . . men:* our fortunes would have been made.
3. As a royal pension, considerably more than the average daily wage of an Elizabethan workman.
4. Blunder for "brave," meaning "splendid."

not doubt but to hear them say it is a sweet comedy. No more
words. Away, go, away!   *Exeunt*

5.1

Enter THESEUS, HIPPOLYTA, EGEUS,[1] *and* [*attendant*]
lords

HIPPOLYTA 'Tis strange, my Theseus, that° these lovers speak of.   *that which*
THESEUS   More strange than true. I never may believe
These antique[2] fables, nor these fairy toys.°   *trifles*
Lovers and madmen have such seething brains,
5   Such shaping fantasies,° that apprehend°   *imaginations / conceive*
More than cool reason ever comprehends.
The lunatic, the lover, and the poet
Are of imagination all compact.°   *composed*
One sees more devils than vast hell can hold:
10 That is the madman. The lover, all as frantic,
Sees Helen's beauty in a brow of Egypt.[3]
The poet's eye, in a fine frenzy rolling,
Doth glance from heaven to earth, from earth to heaven,
And as imagination bodies forth
15 The forms of things unknown, the poet's pen
Turns them to shapes, and gives to airy nothing
A local habitation and a name.
Such tricks hath strong imagination
That if it would but apprehend some joy
20 It comprehends some bringer° of that joy;   *source*
Or in the night, imagining some fear,°   *object to be feared*
How easy is a bush supposed a bear!
HIPPOLYTA But all the story of the night told over,
And all their minds transfigured so together,
25 More witnesseth than fancy's images,[4]
And grows to something of great constancy;°   *consistency*
But howsoever,° strange and admirable.°   *in any case / wondrous*

Enter lovers: LYSANDER, DEMETRIUS, HERMIA, *and*
HELENA

THESEUS   Here come the lovers, full of joy and mirth.
Joy, gentle friends—joy and fresh days of love
Accompany your hearts.
30 LYSANDER   More than to us
Wait in your royal walks, your board, your bed.[5]
THESEUS   Come now, what masques, what dances shall we have
To wear away this long age of three hours
Between our after-supper and bed-time?
35 Where is our usual manager of mirth?
What revels are in hand? Is there no play
To ease the anguish of a torturing hour?
Call Egeus.
EGEUS   Here, mighty Theseus.
THESEUS   Say, what abridgement[6] have you for this evening?

5.1 Location: Athens. Theseus's palace.
1. Q does not call for Egeus, but gives all his speeches
to Philostrate (the character briefly addressed in 1.1).
F's substitution of Egeus here may be a mistake (the
possible result of the same actor playing both parts in
an early performance) or an attempt to incorporate the
angry father into the festive close.

2. Ancient; strange, grotesque (as in "antic").
3. In a gypsy's face. *Helen:* Helen of Troy.
4. *More . . . images:* Testifies to something more than
mere figments of the imagination.
5. *More . . . bed:* May even more joy and love attend
your daily lives.
6. Pastime, something to make the evening seem shorter.

40   What masque, what music? How shall we beguile
      The lazy time if not with some delight?
    EGEUS   There is a brief° how many sports are ripe.   *short list*
      Make choice of which your highness will see first.
    LYSANDER[7] [*reads*] 'The battle with the centaurs,[8] to be sung
45   By an Athenian eunuch to the harp.'
    THESEUS   We'll none of that. That have I told my love
      In glory of my kinsman Hercules.[9]
    LYSANDER [*reads*] 'The riot of the tipsy bacchanals
      Tearing the Thracian singer in their rage.'[1]
50 THESEUS   That is an old device,° and it was played   *show*
      When I from Thebes came last a conqueror.
    LYSANDER [*reads*] 'The thrice-three muses mourning for the death
      Of learning, late deceased in beggary.'[2]
    THESEUS   That is some satire, keen and critical,
55   Not sorting with° a nuptial ceremony.   *befitting*
    LYSANDER [*reads*] 'A tedious brief scene of young Pyramus
      And his love Thisbe: very tragical mirth.'
    THESEUS   'Merry' *and* 'tragical'? 'Tedious' *and* 'brief'?—
      That is, hot ice and wondrous strange black[3] snow
60   How shall we find the concord of this discord?
    EGEUS   A play there is, my lord, some ten words long,
      Which is as 'brief' as I have known a play;
      But by ten words, my lord, it is too long,
      Which makes it 'tedious'; for in all the play
65   There is not one word apt, one player fitted.°   *appropriately cast*
      And 'tragical', my noble lord, it is,
      For Pyramus therein doth kill himself;
      Which when I saw rehearsed, I must confess,
      Made mine eyes water; but more merry tears
70   The passion of loud laughter never shed.
    THESEUS   What are they that do play it?
    EGEUS   Hard-handed men that work in Athens here,
      Which never laboured in their minds till now,
      And now have toiled° their unbreathed° memories   *taxed / unexercised*
75   With this same play against° your nuptial.   *in preparation for*
    THESEUS   And we will hear it.
    EGEUS   No, my noble lord,
      It is not for you. I have heard it over,
      And it is nothing, nothing in the world,
      Unless you can find sport in their intents
80   Extremely stretched,° and conned° with cruel pain   *strained / memorized*
      To do you service.
    THESEUS   I will hear that play;
      For never anything can be amiss
      When simpleness and duty tender it.
      Go, bring them in; and take your places, ladies. [*Exit* EGEUS]

---

7. In Q, Theseus both reads the list and comments on it himself.
8. Probably the battle that occurred when the Centaurs tried to carry off the bride of Theseus's friend Pirithous.
9. According to Plutarch, Hercules and Theseus were cousins.
1. The murder of the poet Orpheus by drunken women, devotees of Dionysus.

2. Possibly a topical reference: Robert Greene, Christopher Marlowe, and Thomas Kyd, university wits who began writing for the stage in the 1580s, all died in desperate circumstances in 1592–94. But satiric laments on the poverty of scholars and poets were commonplace.
3. "Black" is an editorial conjecture. Q and F omit a word that would make "snow" an oxymoron comparable to "hot ice."

85   HIPPOLYTA   I love not to see wretchedness o'ercharged,[4]
     And duty in his service° perishing.   °*its attempt to serve*
     THESEUS   Why, gentle sweet, you shall see no such thing.
     HIPPOLYTA   He says they can do nothing in this kind.°   °*kind of thing*
     THESEUS   The kinder we, to give them thanks for nothing.
90   Our sport shall be to take what they mistake,
     And what poor duty cannot do,
     Noble respect° takes it in might, not merit.[5]   °*consideration*
     Where I have come, great clerks° have purposèd   °*scholars*
     To greet me with premeditated welcomes,
95   Where I have seen them shiver and look pale,
     Make periods in the midst of sentences,
     Throttle their practisèd accent[6] in their fears,
     And in conclusion dumbly have broke off,
     Not paying me a welcome. Trust me, sweet,
100 Out of this silence yet I picked a welcome,
     And in the modesty of fearful° duty   °*frightened*
     I read as much as from the rattling tongue
     Of saucy and audacious eloquence.
     Love, therefore, and tongue-tied simplicity
105 In least°speak most, to my capacity.°   °*in my judgment*
        [*Enter* EGEUS]
     EGEUS   So please your grace, the Prologue is addressed.[7]
     THESEUS   Let him approach.
        Flourish trumpets. Enter [QUINCE *as*] *the Prologue*
     QUINCE [*as Prologue*]   If we offend, it is with our good will.
        That you should think: we come not to offend
110   But with good will. To show our simple skill,
        That is the true beginning of our end.
        Consider then we come but in despite.
        We do not come as minding° to content you,   °*intending*
        Our true intent is. All for your delight
115   We are not here. That you should here repent you
        The actors are at hand, and by their show
        You shall know all that you are like to know.[8]
     THESEUS   This fellow doth not stand upon points.[9]
     LYSANDER   He hath rid his prologue like a rough° colt: he knows   °*an unbroken*
120   not the stop.[1] A good moral, my lord: it is not enough to speak,
        but to speak true.
     HIPPOLYTA   Indeed, he hath played on this prologue like a child
        on a recorder[2]—a sound, but not in government.°   °*control*
     THESEUS   His speech was like a tangled chain—nothing°   °*not at all*
125   impaired, but all disordered. Who is next?
        Enter with a trumpeter before them [BOTTOM *as*] *Pyra-*
        mus, [FLUTE *as*] *Thisbe,* [SNOUT *as*] *Wall,* [STARVELING
        as] *Moonshine, and* [SNUG *as*] *Lion* [*for the dumb
        show*][3]

---

4. Overburdened. *wretchedness:* incompetence or
weakness; poor people.
5. *in . . . merit:* with respect to the giver's capacity, not
the merit of the performance.
6. Rehearsed eloquence; usual manner of speaking.
7. The speaker of the Prologue is ready.
8. The humor of Quince's speech rests in its mis-
punctuation; repunctuated, it becomes a typical courteous address.

9. Bother about niceties; heed punctuation marks.
1. How to rein the colt to a stop; punctuation mark.
2. A woodwind instrument resembling a flute.
3. Elizabethan plays were often prefaced by a "dumb
show" in which the actors silently mimed the main
action, occasionally to the accompaniment (as here) of
a narrator. The artisans may enact the story as Quince
tells it, merely adopt symbolic attitudes, or introduce
themselves.

QUINCE [*as Prologue*] Gentles, perchance you wonder at this show,
　　But wonder on, till truth make all things plain.
　This man is Pyramus, if you would know;
　　This beauteous lady Thisbe is, certain.
130　This man with lime and roughcast doth present
　　Wall, that vile wall which did these lovers sunder;
　And through Wall's chink, poor souls, they are content
　　To whisper; at the which let no man wonder.
　This man, with lantern, dog, and bush of thorn,
135　　Presenteth Moonshine. For if you will know,
　By moonshine did these lovers think no scorn°　　　　　*(it) no disgrace*
　　To meet at Ninus' tomb, there, there to woo.
　This grizzly beast, which 'Lion' hight° by name,　　　　　*is called*
　　The trusty Thisbe coming first by night
140　Did scare away, or rather did affright;
　And as she fled, her mantle she did fall,°　　　　　*drop*
　　Which Lion vile with bloody mouth did stain.
　Anon comes Pyramus, sweet youth and tall,°　　　　　*brave*
　　And finds his trusty Thisbe's mantle slain;
145　Whereat with blade—with bloody, blameful blade—⎤ ridiculous
　　He bravely broached° his boiling bloody breast;⎦ alliteration　　*stabbed*
　And Thisbe, tarrying in mulberry shade,
　　His dagger drew and died. For all the rest,
　Let Lion, Moonshine, Wall, and lovers twain
150　At large° discourse, while here they do remain.　　　　　*length*
　　　　　Exeunt all [the clowns] but SNOUT *as] Wall*
THESEUS　I wonder if the lion be to speak.
DEMETRIUS　No wonder, my lord—one lion may when many
　asses do.
SNOUT [*as Wall*]　In this same interlude° it doth befall　　　　　*play*
155　That I, one Snout by name, present a wall;
　And such a wall as I would have you think
　That had in it a crannied hole or chink,
　Through which the lovers Pyramus and Thisbe
　Did whisper often, very secretly.
160　This loam, this roughcast, and this stone doth show
　That I am that same wall; the truth is so.
　And this the cranny is, right and sinister,⁴
　Through which the fearful lovers are to whisper.
THESEUS　Would you desire lime and hair to speak better?
165　DEMETRIUS　It is the wittiest partition⁵ that ever I heard dis-
　course, my lord.
　　　　　*Enter [*BOTTOM *as] Pyramus*
THESEUS　Pyramus draws near the wall. Silence.
BOTTOM [*as Pyramus*]　O grim-looked° night, O night with hue　　*grim-looking*
　　so black,
　　O night which ever art when day is not;
170　O night, O night, alack, alack, alack,
　　I fear my Thisbe's promise is forgot.
　And thou, O wall, O sweet O lovely wall,
　　That stand'st between her father's ground and mine,
　Thou wall, O wall, O sweet and lovely wall,

---

4. Left; running horizontally. Or on the one side　5. Wall: formal term for part of an oration.
(Pyramus's) and the other (Thisbe's).

175 Show me thy chink, to blink through with mine eyne.
    [*Wall shows his chink*]
Thanks, courteous wall. Jove shield thee well for this.
But what see I? No Thisbe do I see.
O wicked wall, through whom I see no bliss,
Cursed be thy stones[6] for thus deceiving me.

180 THESEUS The wall methinks, being sensible,° should curse   *capable of feeling*
again.°   *back*
BOTTOM [*to* THESEUS] No, in truth, sir, he should not. 'Deceiv-
ing me' is Thisbe's cue. She is to enter now, and I am to spy
her through the wall. You shall see, it will fall pat° as I told you.   *precisely*
    Enter [FLUTE *as*] *Thisbe*
185 Yonder she comes.
FLUTE [*as Thisbe*] O wall, full often hast thou heard my moans
For parting my fair Pyramus and me.
My cherry lips have often kissed thy stones,
Thy stones with lime and hair knit up in thee.
190 BOTTOM [*as Pyramus*] I see a voice. Now will I to the chink
To spy an° I can hear my Thisbe's face.   *if*
Thisbe?
FLUTE [*as Thisbe*] My love—thou art my love, I think.
BOTTOM [*as Pyramus*] Think what thou wilt, I am thy lover's
grace°   *gracious lover*
And like Lemander[7] am I trusty still.
195 FLUTE [*as Thisbe*] And I like Helen,[8] till the fates me kill.
BOTTOM [*as Pyramus*] Not Shaphalus to Procrus[9] was so true.
FLUTE [*as Thisbe*] As Shaphalus to Procrus, I to you.
BOTTOM [*as Pyramus*] O kiss me through the hole of this vile wall.
FLUTE [*as Thisbe*] I kiss the wall's hole, not your lips at all.
BOTTOM [*as Pyramus*] Wilt thou at Ninny's tomb meet me
200 straightway?
FLUTE [*as Thisbe*] Tide° life, tide death, I come without delay.   *Betide; come*
    [*Exeunt* BOTTOM *and* FLUTE *severally*]
SNOUT [*as Wall*] Thus have I, Wall, my part dischargèd so;
And being done, thus Wall away doth go.   *Exit*
THESEUS Now is the wall down between the two neighbours.
205 DEMETRIUS No remedy, my lord, when walls are so wilful to°   *as to*
hear without warning.[1]
HIPPOLYTA This is the silliest stuff that ever I heard.
THESEUS The best in this kind are but shadows,[2] and the worst
are no worse if imagination amend them.
210 HIPPOLYTA It must be your imagination, then, and not theirs.
THESEUS If we imagine no worse of them than they of themselves, they may pass for excellent men. Here come two noble
beasts in: a man and a lion.
    Enter [SNUG *as*] *Lion,* [*and* STARVELING *as*] *Moonshine*
    [*with a lantern, thorn bush, and dog*]
SNUG [*as Lion*] You, ladies, you whose gentle hearts do fear

6. Punning on "testicles."
7. Blunder for "Leander," who drowned while swimming across the Hellespont to meet his lover, Hero.
8. Helen of Troy was notoriously untrustworthy; a
blunder for "Hero."
9. Blunder for "Cephalus" and "Procris." Procris was in

fact seduced by her husband in disguise as another
man; he later accidentally killed her.
1. Informing the parents. *hear:* proverbially, "walls
have ears."
2. Mere likenesses without substance. *kind:* profession
(that is, actors)

215   The smallest monstrous mouse that creeps on floor,
        May now perchance both quake and tremble here
           When lion rough in wildest rage doth roar.
        Then know that I as Snug the joiner am
        A lion fell,[3] nor else no lion's dam.
220   For if I should as Lion come in strife
        Into this place, 'twere pity on my life.

THESEUS   A very gentle beast, and of a good conscience.

DEMETRIUS   The very best at a beast, my lord, that e'er I saw.

LYSANDER   This lion is a very fox[4] for his valour.

225 THESEUS   True, and a goose[5] for his discretion.

DEMETRIUS   Not so, my lord, for his valour cannot carry his discretion, and the fox carries the goose.

THESEUS   His discretion, I am sure, cannot carry his valour, for the goose carries not the fox. It is well. Leave it to his discretion,
230   and let us listen to the moon.

STARVELING [as Moonshine]   This lantern doth the hornèd°   crescent
        moon present.

DEMETRIUS   He should have worn the horns on his head.[6]

THESEUS   He is no crescent,° and his horns are invisible within   waxing moon
    the circumference.

235 STARVELING [as Moonshine]   This lantern doth the hornèd moon present.
        Myself the man i'th' moon do seem to be.

THESEUS   This is the greatest error of all the rest—the man should be put into the lantern. How is it else the man i'th' moon?

240 DEMETRIUS   He dares not come there for° the candle; for you see   for fear of
    it is already in snuff.[7]

HIPPOLYTA   I am aweary of this moon. Would he would change.

THESEUS   It appears by his small light of discretion that he is in the wane; but yet in courtesy, in all reason, we must stay the
245   time.

LYSANDER   Proceed, Moon.

STARVELING   All that I have to say is to tell you that the lantern is the moon, I the man i'th' moon, this thorn bush my thorn bush, and this dog my dog.

250 DEMETRIUS   Why, all these should be in the lantern, for all these are in the moon. But silence; here comes Thisbe.

        *Enter [*FLUTE *as*] *Thisbe*

FLUTE [as Thisbe]   This is old Ninny's tomb. Where is my love?

SNUG [as Lion]   O.

        *Lion roars. Thisbe [*drops her mantle and*] runs off*

DEMETRIUS   Well roared, Lion.

255 THESEUS   Well run, Thisbe.

HIPPOLYTA   Well shone, Moon.—Truly, the moon shines with a good grace.

        [*Lion worries Thisbe's mantle*]

THESEUS   Well moused,[8] Lion.

DEMETRIUS   And then came Pyramus.

        *Enter [*BOTTOM *as*] *Pyramus*

260 LYSANDER   And so the lion vanished.   [*Exit Lion*]

---

3. Fierce; or skin (punning on the costume to which Snug reassuringly calls attention).
4. Symbolic of low cunning, rather than courage.
5. Symbolic of foolishness.

6. The symbol of a cuckold.
7. In need of snuffing; angry.
8. The mantle is like a mouse in the mouth of a cat.

BOTTOM [*as Pyramus*]   Sweet moon, I thank thee for thy sunny beams.
I thank thee, moon, for shining now so bright;
For by thy gracious, golden, glittering gleams
I trust to take of truest Thisbe sight.
265   But stay, O spite!
But mark, poor knight,
What dreadful dole° is here?   grief
Eyes, do you see?
How can it be?
270   O dainty duck, O dear!
Thy mantle good,
What, stained with blood?
Approach, ye furies fell.
O fates,⁹ come, come,
275   Cut thread and thrum,¹
Quail,° crush, conclude, and quell.°   *Overpower / kill*
THESEUS   This passion—and² the death of a dear friend—would
go near to make a man look sad.
HIPPOLYTA   Beshrew my heart, but I pity the man.
280   BOTTOM [*as Pyramus*]   O wherefore, nature, didst thou lions frame,
Since lion vile hath here deflowered³ my dear?—
Which is—no, no, which *was*—the fairest dame
That lived, that loved, that liked, that looked, with cheer.
Come tears, confound;
285   Out sword, and wound
The pap° of Pyramus.   breast
Ay, that left pap,
Where heart doth hop.
Thus die I: thus, thus, thus.
   [*He stabs himself*]
290   Now am I dead,
Now am I fled,
My soul is in the sky.
Tongue, lose thy light;
Moon, take thy flight.   [*Exit Moonshine*]
295   Now die, die, die, die, die.   [*He dies*]
DEMETRIUS   No die but an ace for him; for he is but one.⁴
LYSANDER   Less than an ace, man; for he is dead; he is nothing.
THESEUS   With the help of a surgeon he might yet recover and
prove an ass.
300   HIPPOLYTA   How chance Moonshine is gone before Thisbe
comes back and finds her lover.
THESEUS   She will find him by starlight.
      Enter [FLUTE *as*] *Thisbe*
Here she comes, and her passion° ends the play.   *passionate speech*
HIPPOLYTA   Methinks she should not use a long one for such a
305   Pyramus. I hope she will be brief.
DEMETRIUS   A mote° will turn the balance which Pyramus,   speck

---

9. The three Fates in Greek mythology spun and cut
the thread of a person's life.
1. A technical term from Bottom's occupation: the
tufted end of a weaver's warp, or set of yarns placed
lengthwise in a loom when the woven fabric is cut.
2. Only if combined with. *passion*: suffering; extravagant

speech.
3. Ruined (but commonly suggesting "deprived of her
virginity"); his error for "devoured."
4. Pun on "die" as one of a pair of dice. *one*: the ace, or
lowest throw.

which[5] Thisbe, is the better—he for a man, God warrant us;
she for a woman, God bless us.

LYSANDER She hath spied him already with those sweet eyes.

310 **DEMETRIUS** And thus she means, videlicet:[6]

FLUTE [as Thisbe] Asleep, my love?

What, dead, my dove?

O Pyramus, arise.

Speak, speak. Quite dumb?

315 Dead, dead? A tomb

Must cover thy sweet eyes.

These lily lips,

This cherry nose,

These yellow cowslip cheeks

320 Are gone, are gone.

Lovers, make moan.

His eyes were green as leeks.

O sisters three,°   *the Fates*

Come, come to me

325 With hands as pale as milk.

Lay them in gore,

Since you have shore°   *shorn*

With shears his thread of silk.

Tongue, not a word.

330 Come, trusty sword,

Come, blade, my breast imbrue.°   *stain with blood*

[*She stabs herself*]

And farewell friends,

Thus Thisbe ends.

Adieu, adieu, adieu.   [*She dies*]

335 **THESEUS** Moonshine and Lion are left to bury the dead.

DEMETRIUS Ay, and Wall too.

BOTTOM[7] No, I assure you, the wall is down that parted their
fathers. Will it please you to see the epilogue or to hear a bergamask dance[8] between two of our company?

340 **THESEUS** No epilogue, I pray you; for your play needs no excuse.
Never excuse; for when the players are all dead there need
none to be blamed. Marry, if he that writ it had played Pyramus
and hanged himself in Thisbe's garter it would have been a
fine tragedy; and so it is, truly, and very notably discharged. But

345 come, your bergamask. Let your epilogue alone.

[*BOTTOM and FLUTE[9] dance a bergamask, then exeunt*]

The iron tongue of midnight hath told° twelve.   *counted; tolled*

Lovers, to bed; 'tis almost fairy time.

I fear we shall outsleep the coming morn

As much as we this night have overwatched.°   *stayed awake too late*

350 This palpable-gross° play hath well beguiled   *palpably crude*

The heavy° gait of night. Sweet friends, to bed.   *drowsy; slow*

A fortnight hold we this solemnity

In nightly revels and new jollity.   *Exeunt*

---

5. **which . . . which:** whether . . . or.
6. **As follows. means:** moans; lodges a formal legal
complaint.
7. Spoken by Snug, the Lion, in Q.

8. A dance named after Bergamo, in Italy (commonly
ridiculed for its rusticity).
9. The only "two of our company" onstage at the end of
the play.

5.2

Enter Puck [ROBIN GOODFELLOW, with a broom]

ROBIN	Now the hungry lion roars,	
	And the wolf behowls the moon,	
	whilst the heavy° ploughman snores,	*weary*
	All with weary task fordone.°	*"done in"; exhausted*
5	Now the wasted brands° do glow	*burned-out logs*
	Whilst the screech-owl, screeching loud,	
	Puts the wretch that lies in woe	
	In remembrance of a shroud.	
	Now it is the time of night	
10	That the graves, all gaping wide,	
	Every one lets forth his sprite[1]	
	In the churchway paths to glide;	
	And we fairies that do run	
	By the triple Hecate's[2] team	
15	From the presence of the sun,	
	Following darkness like a dream,	
	Now are frolic.° Not a mouse	*merry*
	Shall disturb this hallowed house.	
	I am sent with broom[3] before	
20	To sweep the dust behind° the door.	*from behind*

Enter [OBERON and TITANIA,] King and Queen of
Fairies, with all their train

OBERON	Through the house give glimmering light.	
	By the dead and drowsy fire	
	Every elf and fairy sprite	
	Hop as light as bird from brier,	
25	And this ditty after me	
	Sing, and dance it trippingly.	
TITANIA	First rehearse your song by rote,	
	To each word a warbling note.	
	Hand in hand with fairy grace	
30	Will we sing and bless this place.	

The song.[4] [The fairies dance]

OBERON	Now until the break of day	
	Through this house each fairy stray.	
	To the best bride bed will we,[5]	
	Which by us shall blessèd be,	
35	And the issue there create°	*created; conceived*
	Ever shall be fortunate.	
	So shall all the couples three	
	Ever true in loving be,	
	And the blots of nature's hand	
40	Shall not in their issue stand.	
	Never mole, harelip, nor scar,	
	Nor mark prodigious° such as are	*ominous birthmark*
	Despisèd in nativity	
	Shall upon their children be.	

5.2 Location: Theseus's palace.
1. Each grave lets forth its ghost.
2. Hecate was goddess of the moon and night, and had three realms: heaven (as Cynthia), earth (as Diana), and hell (as Proserpine).
3. One of his traditional emblems; he helped good

housekeepers and punished lazy ones.
4. F does not assign lines 31–52 to Oberon. They are indented and printed in italics as "The Song."
5. Oberon and Titania will bless the bed of Theseus and Hippolyta.

45   With this field-dew consecrate[6]
        Every fairy take his gait°   *way*
        And each several° chamber bless   *separate*
        Through this palace with sweet peace;
        And the owner of it blessed
50   Ever shall in safety rest.
        Trip away, make no stay,
        Meet me all by break of day.

                                    Exeunt [all but ROBIN]

                            Epilogue
ROBIN   If we shadows have offended,
            Think but this, and all is mended:
            That you have but slumbered here,   *this was all a dream*
            While these visions did appear;
5   And this weak and idle theme,
            No more yielding but° a dream,   *than*
            Gentles, do not reprehend.
            If you pardon, we will mend.
            And as I am an honest puck,
10   If we have unearnèd luck
            Now to 'scape the serpent's tongue,[1]
            We will make amends ere long,
            Else the puck a liar call.
            So, good night unto you all.
15   Give me your hands,° if we be friends,   *applause*
            And Robin shall restore amends.

                        Additional Passage

An unusual quantity and kind of mislineation in Q1 has persuaded most scholars that
the text at the beginning of 5.1 was revised, with new material written in the margins.
The Oxford editors here offer a reconstruction of the passage as originally drafted, which
can be compared with 5.1.1–86 of the edited text.

                            5.1
            Enter THESEUS, HIPPOLYTA, *and* PHILOSTRATE
HIPPOLYTA   'Tis strange, my Theseus, that these lovers speak of.
THESEUS   More strange than true. I never may believe
            These antique fables, nor these fairy toys.
            Lovers and mad men have such seething brains.
5   One sees more devils than vast hell can hold:
            That is the madman. The lover, all as frantic,
            Sees Helen's beauty in a brow of Egypt.
            Such tricks hath strong imagination
            That if it would but apprehend some joy
10   It comprehends some bringer of that joy;
            Or in the night, imagining some fear,
            How easy is a bush supposed a bear!
HIPPOLYTA   But all the story of the night told over,
            And all their minds transfigured so together,

---

6. Consecrated, blessed. Playfully alludes to traditional   **Epilogue**
Catholic custom of blessing the bride bed with holy   1. Hissing from the audience.
water.

15 More witnesseth than fancy's images,
And grows to something of great constancy;
But howsoever, strange and admirable.

    Enter the lovers: LYSANDER, DEMETRIUS, HERMIA, *and*
    HELENA

THESEUS   Here come the lovers, full of joy and mirth.
Come now, what masques, what dances shall we have
20 To ease the anguish of a torturing hour?
Call Philostrate.

PHILOSTRATE   Here mighty Theseus.

THESEUS   Say, what abridgement have you for this evening?
What masque, what music? How shall we beguile
The lazy time if not with some delight?

25 PHILOSTRATE   There is a brief how many sports are ripe.
Make choice of which your highness will see first.

THESEUS   'The battle with the centaurs to be sung
By an Athenian eunuch to the harp.'
We'll none of that. That have I told my love
30 In glory of my kinsman Hercules.
'The riot of the tipsy Bacchanals
Tearing the Thracian singer in their rage.'
That is an old device, and it was played
When I from Thebes came last a conquerer.
35 'The thrice-three Muses mourning for the death
Of learning, late deceased in beggary.'
That is some satire, keen and critical,
Not sorting with a nuptial ceremony.
'A tedious brief scene of young Pyramus
40 And his love Thisby.' 'Tedious' *and* 'brief'?

PHILOSTRATE   A play there is, my lord, some ten words long,
Which is as 'brief' as I have known a play;
But by ten words, my lord, it is too long,
Which makes it 'tedious'; for in all the play
45 There is not one word apt, one player fitted.

THESEUS   What are they that do play it?

PHILOSTRATE   Hard-handed men that work in Athens here,
Which never laboured in their minds till now,
And now have toiled their unbreathed memories
50 With this same play against your nuptial.

THESEUS   Go, bring them in; and take your places, ladies.

                        Exit PHILOSTRATE

HIPPOLYTA   I love not to see wretchedness o'ercharged
And duty in his service perishing.

Romeo and Juliet

Plato's dialogue *The Symposium* recounts a dinner party where the guests spent a long night in impassioned, brilliant philosophical conversation about love. By daybreak, most of the guests had fallen asleep, but Socrates, who had spoken with particularly luminous intelligence, was still awake, trying to prove that a single playwright was capable of writing both comedy and tragedy. As he clinched his case, his weary interlocutors nodded off to sleep. Thus we never learn the argument that Socrates was making for the convergence of the tragic and comic visions in one dramatist, and neither the ancient Greek nor the Roman world has left us an instance of that convergence. But we have its supreme embodiment in Shakespeare. The achievement is particularly striking in two plays probably written around 1595. Scholars have been unable to determine with certainty whether *Romeo and Juliet* was written before or after *A Midsummer Night's Dream;* one of Shakespeare's most delightful comedies and one of his most beloved tragedies appear to have been written at virtually the same time and out of some very similar materials.

In the entertainment performed for the newlyweds at the close of *A Midsummer Night's Dream,* the young lovers, Pyramus and Thisbe, are separated by a "vile wall." They attempt to elope together, but Pyramus, mistakenly thinking that Thisbe has been killed, rashly commits suicide, whereupon Thisbe in despair stabs herself. A strange way, it would seem, to celebrate festive nuptials, but Shakespeare's comedy continually triumphs over fears of rashness, mutability, and death by staging and laughing at them. The inept amateur actors call attention so crudely to the tragedy's artificiality and contrivance that it provokes derisive laughter: "This is the silliest stuff that ever I heard" (5.1.207).

In *Romeo and Juliet,* whose climax closely resembles that of Pyramus and Thisbe, Shakespeare does not shy away from artifice and contrivance. His tragedy is unusually dependent on coincidence, mischance, and accident to produce what the Chorus, in the sonnet that serves as the prologue, calls the lovers' "misadventured piteous overthrows." Nor does he forswear the note of witty, wicked parody that transformed the woes of Pyramus and Thisbe into an occasion for mirth. Romeo's friend Mercutio gives voice to an irrepressible spirit of mockery, a spirit that seems to challenge the very possibility of romantic love or tragic destiny. (There is a seventeenth-century report—it doesn't date from the playwright's own lifetime—that Shakespeare remarked that he was forced to kill Mercutio in the third act to prevent being killed by him.) But Shakespeare manages to make the story of his reckless, star-crossed lovers immensely moving, resistant at once to corrosive irony and to moralizing disapproval. He does so principally through his mastery of what the bumbling performers in *A Midsummer Night's Dream* conspicuously lack: the power of language to make and unmake the world.

It is this poetic power—"poetic" derives from the Greek word for "making"—that provides Shakespeare with the key to resolving the paradox addressed by Socrates in *The Symposium* and that enables him to transform his rather shopworn source materials into something rich and strange. The story of the ill-fated lovers from bitterly feuding families had been told many times in the sixteenth century by Italian and French writers and had already appeared more than once in English. Shakespeare's direct source is Arthur Brooke's *Tragicall Historye of Romeus and Juliet* (1562), a long, leaden English poem based on a French prose version by Pierre Boaistuau (1559), who was in turn adapting an Italian version by Bandello (1554), who in turn based his narrative on Luigi da Porto's version (1525) of a tale by Masuccio Salernitaro (1476). Shakespeare follows the main outline of Brooke's narrative, although he makes many changes in the interests of theatrical compression and intensification. Hence the events that in Brooke take nine months are telescoped into a few days. The figure of Mercutio is brilliantly developed, as is the vulgar, meddling, earthy Nurse. Juliet, eighteen years old in Bandello's version and sixteen in Brooke's, is depicted as only thirteen, a young girl suddenly awakening to passionate desires that set her against the will of her family.

But it is principally by means of the incandescent brilliance of its language that *Romeo and Juliet* has earned its place as one of the greatest love stories in world literature. Shakespeare makes linguistic power figure thematically in the play by insisting on the crucial importance of naming and, more generally, by repeatedly calling attention to the force of verbal actions. This was by no means the playwright's private obsession. His play is the product of a rhetorical culture, a culture steeped in an awareness—in the philosopher J. L. Austin's phrase—of "how to do things with words." What are some of the things that characters do with words? For a start, they insult each other, a dangerous pastime of both servants and masters. They also invite one another (Capulet's favorite pastime); they confess (formally, to a priest; informally, to friends); they conjure; they curse; they make contracts; they vow; and, if they have the power of the prince, they banish. And through all of these verbal actions, no matter how serious or even deadly they may be, they constantly play with language.

Romeo and Juliet is saturated with language games: paradoxes, oxymorons, double entendres, rhyming tricks, verbal echoings, multiple puns. The obvious question is, why? One possible answer, proposed as early as the eighteenth century, is that Shakespeare could not resist: verbal wit was an addiction, an obsession, the object of an irrational passion. He could indulge this passion because a display of wit would appeal to those segments of the audience most attuned to rhetorical acrobatics. Another answer

Two gallants fight a duel in the street. From George Wither, *A Collection of Emblemes* (1635).

is that puns are a clarifying challenge, an assault on sentiments to test whether they are genuine or merely forced and empty. Hence Mercutio attempts to mock Romeo's passion with a set of ribald jests, jests that are reiterated unconsciously by the Nurse in such exclamations as "Stand up, stand up, stand an you be a man" (3.3.88). To survive the corrosive effect of such mockery is a measure of true love and a sign of authenticity: "He jests at scars that never felt a wound" (2.1.43).

But this explanation for the tragedy's pervasive wordplay is not wholly adequate, since at the height of both their love and their despair, Romeo and Juliet also pun. Romeo on the verge of suicide plays with the word "engrossing" (death as wholesaler; monopolist; lawyer); Juliet plays with the word "restorative" (the kiss as medicine; poison; death; resurrection); and both play with the Elizabethan "die" as a term for "orgasm." Here wordplay functions not to deflate but to cram into brief utterances more meanings than language would ordinarily hold and to force us to confront both unresolvable contradictions and hidden connections. That is, puns work to juxtapose or hold open possibilities that normally are viewed as mutually exclusive. Thus they may be said to reach both a psychological and a thematic level at which oppositions—pain and joy, loss and restoration, love and death, comedy and tragedy—are canceled.

Wordplay would be impossible in a language in which words were strictly bound to things in a perfect correspondence between naming and nature. Punning is possible only if there is some slippage in sound and meaning, so that one sign can refer to two or more objects or, as Mercutio wittily demonstrates in his Queen Mab speech, to nothing at all. Yet wordplay can also suggest surprising linkages and secret realities. Hence, for example, the punning in Romeo and Juliet's initial exchange at the Capulet ball derives its power from the lovers' conviction that there really is an essential relation between the touching of their hands and lips and a religious experience. This relation, invisible to the ordinary social world around them, is disclosed in the language game they spontaneously play, a game that takes the form of a shared sonnet.

Even to speak of this first exchange as a game is to risk diminishing its intense seriousness. For Mercutio, words are fantastic trifles in a world fit only for satire, sexual teasing, and make-believe. He is a young man in love with masks; indeed, as he readies himself for the masked ball, he seems to regard his own face as a mask: "Give me a case to put my visage in, / A visor for a visor" (1.4.29–30). The moment Romeo and Juliet meet, all masks seem to fall away, all prior emotions fade into nothingness, and all games become earnest. "Did my heart love till now?" asks Romeo, and Juliet, sending the Nurse to find out Romeo's name, declares, "If he be married, / My grave is like to be my wedding bed" (1.5.131–32).

At some moments in Romeo and Juliet, then, wordplay reveals the arbitrariness of language; at other moments, it seems to reveal a hidden reality, even a sacred truth. These contradictory revelations are explored in the famous balcony scene in Act 2. Mercutio's mockery gives way, after Romeo's abrupt, one-line dismissal, to incantatory language so intense as to create a new heaven and a new earth. A bare, daylit stage (as it would have been in the Elizabethan playhouse) becomes a dark garden above which Juliet appears like the sun. Visibility is canceled and then restored, by means of metaphor, to the "white upturnèd wond'ring eyes / Of mortals" (2.1.71–72). Romeo's ecstatic words are the poetic record of a revelation, a vision of a creature unique, perfect, and infinitely beautiful.

The visionary moment turns into a moment of auditory revelation as well, as Romeo, in an intense, eroticized version of what audiences routinely do, overhears Juliet's soliloquy. He has entered into her most intimate thoughts and longings and has an overpowering proof of their authenticity, since she speaks with no awareness of his presence. The inner world his lyrical utterance has conjured up is miraculously united with her own. But her words at once offer a complete fulfillment of this union and a shattering of fulfillment: "O Romeo, Romeo, wherefore art thou Romeo?" (2.1.75). Only if Romeo's name is an arbitrary sign, to be stripped away, discarded, and replaced, can her love be realized. But in a world in which words are divorced from reality, what

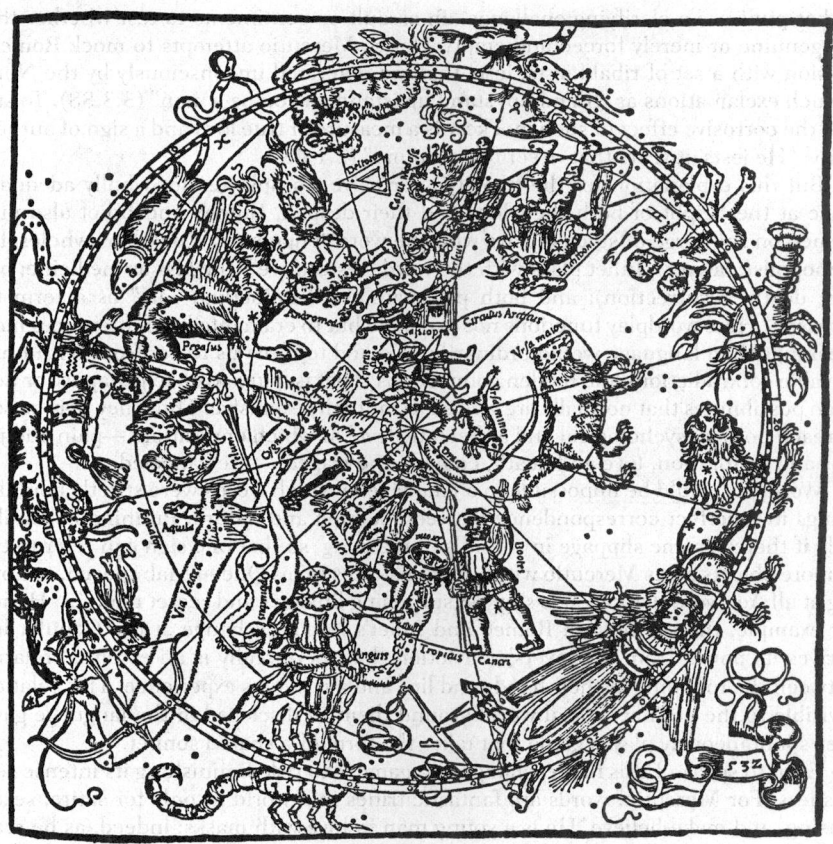

"Then I defy you, stars" (5.1.24). *Imagines Constellationum.* From Ptolemy, *Almagest* (1541 ed.), after Dürer.

would be the status of a love made by language? In a world in which names are mere empty signs, how could language create a new reality?

If words are arbitrary, then Romeo and Juliet's love, woven of words, is wedded to nothingness. If they are not arbitrary, if they cannot float free of the body and society, then their love will be destroyed by the rage of feuding parents—the parents who have bestowed proper names on their offspring—and by the whole daylight world of social exchange that gives ordinary language its normal meanings. Against the magical, passionate, transformative language of Romeo and Juliet is set not only Mercutio's mockery but the Nurse's garrulous evocation of the inescapable life cycle: birth, weaning, sexual maturity, and death.

In the Nurse's view, all lives have a certain interchangeability. Juliet's value can be measured in gold coins—"I tell you, he that can lay hold of her / Shall have the chinks" (1.5.113–14)—and an exiled husband can be replaced: Paris is "a lovely gentleman," she tells the grieving Juliet, "Romeo's a dishclout to him" (3.5.218–19). Romeo and Juliet insist by contrast on the absolute singularity of their love, on the stilling of cyclical time, and on the cancellation of the social network of form and compliment. For a moment on her balcony, Juliet regrets that Romeo has heard her declare her "true-love passion," but then she bids farewell to conventional restraint and boldly steps forward into the magical realm of reciprocal desire. This realm is not without its own solemn order: their love must be formally confirmed in honorable vows of holy matrimony spoken before the friar. But first in the garden, away from church and family and friends, the fullness of the lovers' matched longings finds expression in words that seem to possess mythic power, power to transform darkness into intense light and at the same time to block out the harsh, unforgiving light of the everyday.

The everyday has its own powerful resources, however, and forces its way back into the world that love has transformed. It does so through the ability of names like "Capulet" and "Montague" to conjure up bitter social rivalries. For, as *Romeo and Juliet* repeatedly discloses, words as we ordinarily use them are rarely wholly arbitrary or wholly mythic. They are social constructions, communal creations that are neither complete unto themselves nor empty and hence malleable by individuals. Both language as arbitrary and language as mythic are radical attempts to challenge this notion of words as shared creations carrying with them the tensions and resolutions present in communities, but the community in effect kills off the challenge—whether it comes from Mercutio, who tries to turn social hatred and love alike into a game about "nothing," or from Romeo and Juliet, who try to escape through darkness, subterfuge, and the language of love into a realm apart.

How does the communitarian spirit of language, and with it a sense of the inescapability of the social, manifest itself in *Romeo and Juliet*? It does so, first of all, through a series of characters such as those we glimpse in the opening moments of the play, when the Capulet servants, Samson and Gregory, provoke the absurd quarrel with the Montague servants, Abraham and Balthasar. The point is not only the foolishness of the social codes—"Do you bite your thumb at us, sir?" "I do bite my thumb, sir" (1.1.39–40)—but also their pervasiveness. In a tragedy memorable for its dreams of the most intense privacy—Juliet longs for Romeo to leap to her arms "untalked of and unseen" (3.2.7)—the bustling world makes its presence felt as insistently as the Nurse's voice calling again and again to Juliet as she stands at her window. Shakespeare is wonderfully resourceful in conveying this presence. There is, for example, the nameless servant whose inability to read the list of those invited to the Capulets' ball leads him to turn for assistance to Romeo and Benvolio, who chance at that moment to be walking by. The list itself deftly conjures up the social elite of Verona, with its network of kinship bonds:

> Signor Placentio and his lovely nieces,
> Mercutio and his brother Valentine,
> Mine uncle Capulet, his wife and daughters,

and so on through the whole "fair assembly" (1.2.63ff). At the ball itself, Shakespeare is careful to include a glimpse of the servants, hurrying to clear the dishes but finding time to put aside a piece of marzipan for themselves or arranging for a private party with Susan Grindstone and Nell. And, in the midst of the horror and lamenting when Juliet's cold and stiff body is discovered on the morning she was to be married to Paris, Shakespeare turns our attention to the musicians who had been hired to entertain the wedding guests and who now stand around cracking lame jokes and hoping for a bit of dinner (as if—to invert a celebrated line from *Hamlet*—the marriage-baked meats will coldly furnish forth the funeral table).

There are, besides the servants, other social units that carry the glacial weight of the collective norms and ordinary interests against which Romeo and Juliet struggle. The exclusiveness and intensity of their love is clearly in tension with the bond that links Romeo to his male friends. "Now art thou sociable," says Mercutio with evident relief, when Romeo briefly resumes the old mocking repartee; "now art thou Romeo" (2.3.77). But neither Romeo nor Juliet is any longer the same person, and the passionate love that divides Romeo from his friends sets both lovers still more decisively against the values of their powerful families. Those values involve a complex intertwining of honor, dignity, love, will, and property, a blend that can manifest itself as gracious hospitality or as murderous feuding, as gentle nostalgia or as cold calculation, as a father's indulgent affection for his daughter or as blind rage when she attempts to thwart his will. Romeo and Juliet's love and clandestine marriage can find no place

The city of Verona. From John Speed, *Prospect of the Most Famous Parts of the World* (1676).

in this familial order of things, just as its absoluteness is incompatible with the familial sense of cyclical time.

Beyond the structure of the family in the society of Verona, though linked to that structure by ties of kinship, lies the state, embodied in the figure of Prince Escalus. Formally, *Romeo and Juliet* is built around the well-meaning ruler's attempt to stop the "civil brawls" (1.1.82) at the play's beginning, his banishment of Romeo at its midpoint, and his final inquiry, to "clear these ambiguities" (5.3.216), at its close. But this necessary principle of civic order, even though it has important consequences, seems almost beside the point, as inadequate and uncomprehending as the statues in pure gold that the grieving fathers propose to erect.

A much deeper social principle is figured in Friar Laurence, who embodies the collective wisdom and sanctity of the community. Although set apart, the friar is not a hermit or a recluse; he is an active agent in the community's affairs. His attempt to use Romeo and Juliet's love as a means to resolve the feud between the Montagues and the Capulets disastrously backfires, and with his sleeping potions, his elaborate plots, and, at the close, his fatal cowardice, he has some of the qualities of the stereotypical meddling friar of anticlerical satire. But Friar Laurence is a more complex figure, with a subtle grasp of the doubleness—both poison and medicine—of the natural world and a thoughtful advocacy of moderation. This advocacy draws on an ancient and powerful critique of extremes in passion, which the play's tragic outcome would seem to endorse.

Yet few readers or spectators come away from *Romeo and Juliet* with the conviction that it would be better to love moderately. The intensity of the lovers' passion seems to have its own compelling, self-justifying force, which quietly brushes away all social obstacles and moralizing warnings: "Think true love acted simple modesty" (3.2.16). And the play's incantatory language of love—braiding together the wildly fanciful and the exquisitely simple—has after four hundred years an unforgettable freshness:

> Come, gentle night; come, loving, black-browed night,
> Give me my Romeo, and when I shall die
> Take him and cut him out in little stars,
> And he will make the face of heaven so fine
> That all the world will be in love with night
> And pay no worship to the garish sun.   (3.2.20–25)

If the society of the play will not tolerate such ecstatic desire, if the contingencies of the ordinary world manage to destroy it, *Romeo and Juliet* offers us the consoling realization that the lovers themselves have all along been in love with night.

STEPHEN GREENBLATT

TEXTUAL NOTE

Romeo and Juliet was first published in quarto in 1597 (Q1). A second edition (Q2), advertised on the title page as "newly corrected, augmented, and amended," was published two years later. Q2 provided copy for a third quarto published in 1609 (Q3), from which in turn was printed another quarto (Q4) and the First Folio (F) text (both in 1623). Since Q3 and Q4, along with the Folio version of the play, all depend on Q2, the complex textual problems posed by *Romeo and Juliet* are focused on the precise nature of Q2 and its relation to the substantially different versions of the play, Q1.

Scholars generally agree that Q1 is a so-called bad Quarto, a defective text that derives not from the author's manuscript but from the recollection of actors. Since Elizabethan playing companies usually tried to keep the plays out of print, Q1 would in all likelihood have been an unauthorized and illicit transcript; modern analysis has directed suspicion on the actors who played Romeo and Paris. The title page identifies neither author nor publisher, and the text was evidently not licensed in the Stationers' Register.

Q2 is a fuller, more authoritative text. Certain of its features—inconsistent speech prefixes, "permissive" stage directions (e.g., "Enter three or four Citizens," 1.1.66 stage direction), and the preservation of lines that Shakespeare evidently meant to cross out after revision—indicate that Q2 was set from the author's own rough draft, or "foul papers." The draft appears to have posed difficulties for the printing house, for the compositors seem on a number of occasions to have had difficulty making sense of the manuscript. Moreover, perhaps because a page of the manuscript was missing, one passage in Q2—from 1.2.51 to 1.3.36—is taken directly from Q1. With the exception of this passage, for which Q1 serves as the control text, the text of *Romeo and Juliet* is based on Q2.

SELECTED BIBLIOGRAPHY

Belsey, Catherine. "The Name of the Rose in *Romeo and Juliet*." *Yearbook of English Studies* 23 (1993): 126–42. *Romeo and Juliet* dramatizes both the desire to transcend the realm of signifiers into a metaphysical idea and the impossibility of attaining it.

Goldberg, Jonathan. "*Romeo and Juliet*'s Open Rs." *Queering the Renaissance*. Ed. Jonathan Goldberg. Durham, N.C.: Duke University Press, 1994. 218–35. Homosocial rivalry challenges the play's heterosexual order, implying the interchangeability of male and female love objects.

Kahn, Coppélia. "Coming of Age in Verona." *The Woman's Part: Feminist Criticism of Shakespeare*. Ed. Carolyn Ruth Swift Lenz, Gayle Greene, and Carol Thomas Neely. Urbana: University of Illinois Press, 1983. 171–93. The oppressive mores of a patriarchal society are chiefly responsible for the tragic determinism that suffocates the lovers.

Kristeva, Julia. "*Romeo and Juliet*: Love-Hatred in the Couple." *Shakespearean Tragedy*. Ed. John Drakakis. New York: Longman, 1992. 296–315. We benefit from a closer look, informed by Freud and Lacan, at the symptomatic (unconscious) response to transgressive and fantastic love as manifested in the characters, the playwright, and ourselves.

Liebler, Naomi Conn. "'There is no world without Verona walls': The City in *Romeo and Juliet*." *A Companion to Shakespeare's Works*, vol. 1: *The Tragedies*. Ed. Richard Dutton and Jean E. Howard. Malden, Mass.: Blackwell, 2003. 303–18. Shakespeare's Verona is a matrix of violence and disorder, becoming the play's tragic protagonist as it collapses the ideal of the walled city.

Moisan, Thomas. "'O Any Thing of Nothing, First Create!': Gender and Patriarchy and the Tragedy of *Romeo and Juliet*." *In Another Country: Feminist Perspectives on Renaissance Drama*. Ed. Dorothea Kehler and Susan Baker. Metuchen, N.J.: Scarecrow Press, 1991. 113–36. *Romeo and Juliet*'s tragic love story subverts patriarchy, but its gender prescriptions recuperate male authority.

Nevo, Ruth. "Tragic Form in *Romeo and Juliet*." *Studies in English Literature* 9 (1969): 241–58. Shakespeare develops a distinctive style of tragedy, predicated on the heroic embodiment of opposing forces, the subversion of appearances, the presence of the uncanny, and the complex ideal of sexual love.

Porter, Joseph A. *Shakespeare's Mercutio: His History and Drama*. Chapel Hill, N.C.: University of North Carolina Press, 1988. From a patchwork of sources, classical and contemporary, Shakespeare breathed life into the complex, subversive, homosexual Mercutio.

Snow, Edward. "Language and Sexual Difference in *Romeo and Juliet*." *Shakespeare's "Rough Magic": Renaissance Essays in Honor of C. L. Barber*. Ed. Peter Erickson and Coppélia Kahn. Newark: University of Delaware Press, 1985. 168–92. If the language of Juliet and Romeo articulates their profound interconnectedness, it also discloses ominous differences between them and suggests that gender difference is the tragedy's deepest dichotomy.

Snyder, Susan. "*Romeo and Juliet*: Comedy into Tragedy." *Essays in Criticism* 20 (1970): 391–402. At first possessing all the makings of a comedy, *Romeo and Juliet* morphs from one genre to another: the descent into tragedy becomes ineluctable upon the death of Mercutio.

FILMS

Romeo and Juliet. 1936. Dir. George Cukor. USA. 125 min. A lavish, big-studio release, Cukor's black-and-white film stars Leslie Howard, who was then forty-two, and Norma Shearer in the lead roles. John Barrymore plays Mercutio.

West Side Story. 1961. Dir. Jerome Robbins and Robert Wise. USA. 152 min. A musical, modernized adaptation of the play set in New York with rival ethnic gangs. Leonard Bernstein wrote the celebrated score.

Romeo and Juliet. 1968. Dir. Franco Zeffirelli. UK/Italy. 138 min. A flower-power, 1960s youth-culture interpretation of the play, featuring teenaged actors Leonard Whiting and Olivia Hussey in the title roles.

William Shakespeare's Romeo + Juliet. 1996. Dir. Baz Luhrmann. USA. 120 min. Starring Leonardo DiCaprio and Claire Danes, Luhrmann's frenetic update, set in modern-day "Verona Beach," explains the family feud in terms of a gang conflict.

Qing ren jie (*A Time to Love*). 2005. Dir. Jianqi Huo. China. 113 min. Set during the Cultural Revolution, two Chinese lovers read and watch versions of Shakespeare's play together, and enact the balcony scene. In Mandarin.

The Most Excellent and Lamentable Tragedy of Romeo and Juliet

THE PERSONS OF THE PLAY

CHORUS
ROMEO
MONTAGUE, his father
MONTAGUE'S WIFE
BENVOLIO, Montague's nephew
ABRAHAM, Montague's servingman
BALTHASAR, Romeo's man
JULIET
CAPULET, her father
CAPULET'S WIFE
TYBALT, her nephew
His page
PETRUCCIO
CAPULET'S COUSIN
Juliet's NURSE
PETER
SAMSON } servingmen of the Capulets
GREGORY
Other SERVINGMEN
MUSICIANS
Escalus, PRINCE of Verona
MERCUTIO
County PARIS } his kinsmen
PAGE to Paris
FRIAR LAURENCE
FRIAR JOHN
An APOTHECARY
CHIEF WATCHMAN
Other CITIZENS OF THE WATCH
Masquers, guests, gentlewomen, followers of the Montague and Capulet factions

Prologue
[*Enter*] CHORUS

CHORUS   Two households, both alike in dignity°   *status*
    In fair Verona, where we lay our scene,
    From ancient grudge break to new mutiny,°   *wrangling*
    Where civil blood makes civil hands unclean.[1]
5 From forth the fatal° loins of these two foes   *ill-fated*
    A pair of star-crossed[2] lovers take their life,
    Whose misadventured° piteous overthrows   *unfortunate*
    Doth with their death bury their parents' strife.

Prologue
1. Where citizens' hands are stained with the blood of
their fellow citizens.

2. Thwarted by the adverse influence of the stars
appearing at the time of their birth, which controlled
their destinies.

The fearful passage of their death-marked love
10   And the continuance of their parents' rage—
Which but their children's end, naught could remove—
        Is now the two-hours' traffic° of our stage;   *business; movement*
The which if you with patient ears attend,
What here shall miss, our toil shall strive to mend.³   [*Exit*]

1.1

Enter SAMSON *and* GREGORY, *of the house of Capulet,*
    with swords and bucklers°   *small round shields*

SAMSON   Gregory, on my word, we'll not carry coals.¹
GREGORY   No, for then we should be colliers.²
SAMSON   I mean an° we be in choler,° we'll draw.°   *if / anger / draw swords*
GREGORY   Ay, while you live, draw your neck out of collar.°   *a noose*
5   SAMSON   I strike quickly,° being moved.³   *vigorously*
GREGORY   But thou art not quickly° moved to strike.   *speedily*
SAMSON   A dog of the house of Montague moves me.
GREGORY   To move is to stir, and to be valiant is to stand,⁴ there-
        fore if thou art moved, thou runn'st away.
10 SAMSON   A dog of that house shall move me to stand. I will take
        the wall of⁵ any man or maid of Montague's.
GREGORY   That shows thee a weak slave, for the weakest goes to
        the wall.⁶
SAMSON   'Tis true, and therefore women, being the weaker ves-
15   sels,⁷ are ever thrust to the wall;° therefore I will push Mon-   *ravished*
        tague's men from the wall, and thrust his maids to the wall.
GREGORY   The quarrel is between our masters and us their men.
SAMSON   'Tis all one.° I will show myself a tyrant: when I have   *the same*
        fought with the men I will be civil with the maids—I will cut
20   off their heads.
GREGORY   The heads of the maids?
SAMSON   Ay, the heads of the maids, or their maidenheads, take
        it in what sense thou wilt.
GREGORY   They must take it in sense° that feel it.   *through sensation*
25 SAMSON   Me they shall feel while I am able to stand, and 'tis
        known I am a pretty piece of flesh.⁸
GREGORY   'Tis well thou art not fish. If thou hadst, thou hadst
        been poor-john.⁹
        Enter [ABRAHAM *and another servingman*] *of the Mon-*
            tagues
        Draw thy tool.¹ Here comes of the house of Montagues.
30 SAMSON   My naked weapon is out. Quarrel, I will back thee.
GREGORY   How—turn thy back and run?
SAMSON   Fear me not.²
GREGORY   No, marry³—I fear thee!
SAMSON   Let us take the law of our side. Let them begin.

3. *What . . . mind*: The actors will try to rectify whatever is missing or ill told in the Prologue.
1.1 Location: A street or public place in Verona.
1. We'll not suffer humiliation.
2. Professional coal porters, proverbially sneaky.
3. Being roused to anger.
4. Stand firm against assault. Playing, as with "strike"
and "stir," on sexual arousal.
5. I will assert superiority over. The sidewalk nearest
the wall was cleaner than that nearer the street.
6. Proverbial: The weakest are always pushed aside.

7. Paul's description of women in 1 Peter 3:7.
8. An attractive fellow possessed of an impressive
member.
9. Dried salted hake, appropriate as a taunt because
shriveled and cheap. "Neither fish nor flesh" was
proverbial for an uncategorizable oddity.
1. Weapon (and continuing the bawdy wordplay).
2. Do not doubt my fortitude; in the next line, Gregory
takes it in the modern sense of "Do not be afraid of me."
3. By the Virgin Mary, a mild oath with a meaning similar to "indeed."

35 GREGORY   I will frown as I pass by, and let them take it as they
        list.°   *like*
   SAMSON   Nay, as they dare. I will bite my thumb at them,[4] which
        is disgrace to them if they bear it.
           [*He bites his thumb*]
   ABRAHAM   Do you bite your thumb at us, sir?
40 SAMSON   I do bite my thumb, sir.
   ABRAHAM   Do you bite your thumb at us, sir?
   SAMSON [*to* GREGORY]   Is the law of our side if I say 'Ay'?
   GREGORY   No.
   SAMSON [*to* ABRAHAM]   No, sir, I do not bite my thumb at you,
45   sir, but I bite my thumb, sir.
   GREGORY [*to* ABRAHAM]   Do you quarrel, sir?
   ABRAHAM   Quarrel, sir? No, sir.
   SAMSON   But if you do, sir, I am for you.[5] I serve as good a man
        as you.
50 ABRAHAM   No better.
   SAMSON   Well, sir.
           Enter BENVOLIO
   GREGORY   Say 'better'. Here comes one of my master's kinsmen.
   SAMSON [*to* ABRAHAM]   Yes, better, sir.
   ABRAHAM   You lie.
55 SAMSON   Draw, if you be men. Gregory, remember thy washing°   *slashing; violent*
        blow.
           They [*draw and*] *fight*
   BENVOLIO [*drawing*]   Part, fools. Put up your swords. You know
        not what you do.
           Enter TYBALT
   TYBALT [*drawing*]   What, art thou drawn among these heartless
        hinds?[6]
60   Turn thee, Benvolio. Look upon thy death.
   BENVOLIO   I do but keep the peace. Put up thy sword,
        Or manage° it to part these men with me.   *wield*
   TYBALT   What, drawn and talk of peace? I hate the word
        As I hate hell, all Montagues, and thee.
65   Have at thee, coward.
           They fight. Enter three or four CITIZENS [OF THE
           WATCH], *with clubs or partisans*°   *broad-tipped spears*
   CITIZENS OF THE WATCH   Clubs, bills° and partisans! Strike Beat   *ax-bladed spears*
        them down!
        Down with the Capulets. Down with the Montagues.
           Enter old CAPULET *in his gown, and his* WIFE
   CAPULET   What noise is this? Give me my long sword, ho
   CAPULET'S WIFE   A crutch, a crutch—why call you for a sword?
           Enter old MONTAGUE [*with his sword drawn*], *and his*
           WIFE
70 CAPULET   My sword, I say. Old Montague is come,
        And flourishes his blade in spite° of me.   *defiance*
   MONTAGUE   Thou villain Capulet!
           [*His* WIFE *holds him back*]
           Hold me not, let me go.

---

4. Flick the thumbnail from behind the upper teeth, an
insulting gesture.
5. I accept your invitation to fight.

6. These cowardly servants, punning on female deer
("hinds") unprotected by a stag ("hart/heart").

MONTAGUE'S WIFE   Thou shalt not stir one foot to seek a foe.

[*The* CITIZENS OF THE WATCH *attempt to*] *part them.*

Enter PRINCE *Escalus with his train*

PRINCE   Rebellious subjects, enemies to peace,

75   Profaners of this neighbour-stainèd steel⁷—

Will they not hear? What ho, you men, you beasts,

That quench the fire of your pernicious rage

With purple° fountains issuing from your veins: crimson

On pain of torture, from those bloody hands

80   Throw your mistempered⁸ weapons to the ground,

And hear the sentence of your movèd° Prince.   furious

[MONTAGUE, CAPULET, *and their followers throw*

down their weapons]

Three civil brawls bred of an airy° word   unsubstantial

By thee, old Capulet, and Montague,

Have thrice disturbed the quiet of our streets

85   And made Verona's ancient° citizens   elderly

Cast by° their grave-beseeming ornaments⁹   Cast away

To wield old partisans in hands as old,

Cankered° with peace, to part your cankered° hate.   Rusty / malignant

If ever you disturb our streets again

90   Your lives shall pay the forfeit° of the peace.   ransom

For this time all the rest depart away.

You, Capulet, shall go along with me;

And Montague, come you this afternoon

To know our farther pleasure in this case

95   To old Freetown,¹ our common judgement-place.

Once more, on pain of death, all men depart.

Exeunt [*all but* MONTAGUE,

his WIFE, *and* BENVOLIO]

MONTAGUE   Who set this ancient quarrel new abroach?°   open

Speak, nephew: were you by when it began?

BENVOLIO   Here were the servants of your adversary

100   And yours, close fighting ere I did approach.

I drew to part them. In the instant came

The fiery Tybalt with his sword prepared,

Which, as he breathed° defiance to my ears,   uttered

He swung about his head and cut the winds

105   Who, nothing hurt withal,° hissed him in scorn.   by that

While we were interchanging thrusts and blows,

Came more and more, and fought on part and part²

Till the Prince came, who parted either part.

MONTAGUE'S WIFE   O where is Romeo—saw you him today?

110   Right glad I am he was not at this fray.

BENVOLIO   Madam, an hour before the worshipped sun

Peered forth° the golden window of the east,   out from

A troubled mind drive° me to walk abroad,   drove

Where, underneath the grove of sycamore³

115   That westward rooteth° from this city side,   grows out

---

7. You who defile weapons with the stains of your neighbors' blood.
8. Badly shaped and hardened, as well as unnecessarily wrathful by disposition.
9. Attire and symbolic staffs appropriate to grave old age. Possibly playing on the old men's proximity to the grave.

1. In Brooke's translation from the Italian source, the Capulet house is called Villa Franca.
2. Fought for one side and the other.
3. Associated with melancholy lovers, who are "sick-amour."

So early walking did I see your son.
Towards him I made, but he was ware° of me,   *wary*
And stole into the covert° of the wood.   *covering*
I, measuring his affections° by my own—   *inclination*
120   Which then most sought where most might not be found,[4]
Being one too many by my weary self—
Pursued my humour° not pursuing his,   *mood*
And gladly shunned who gladly fled from me.
    MONTAGUE   Many a morning hath he there been seen,
125   With tears augmenting the fresh morning's dew,
Adding to clouds more clouds with his deep sighs.
But all so soon as the all-cheering sun
Should in the farthest east begin to draw
The shady curtains from Aurora's[5] bed,
130   Away from light steals home my heavy° son,   *melancholy*
And private in his chamber pens himself,
Shuts up his windows, locks fair daylight out,
And makes himself an artificial night.
Black and portentous° must this humour[6] prove,   *ominous (of illness)*
135   Unless good counsel may the cause remove.
    BENVOLIO   My noble uncle, do you know the cause?
    MONTAGUE   I neither know it nor can learn of him.
    BENVOLIO   Have you importuned him by any° means?   *all*
    MONTAGUE   Both by myself and many other friends,
140   But he, his own affection's counsellor,°   *confidant*
Is to himself—I will not say how true,[7]
But to himself so secret and so close,°   *discreet*
So far from sounding and discovery,°   *fathoming and revelation*
As is the bud bit with an envious worm°   *a spiteful grub (larva)*
145   Ere he can spread his sweet leaves° to the air   *petals*
Or dedicate his beauty to the sun.
Could we but learn from whence his sorrows grow
We would as willingly give cure as know.
    Enter ROMEO
    BENVOLIO   See where he comes. So please you° step aside,   *please you = please*
150   I'll know his grievance or be much denied.
    MONTAGUE   I would° thou wert so happy° by thy stay   *wish / fortunate*
To hear true shrift.° Come, madam, let's away.   *confession*
    Exeunt [MONTAGUE *and his* WIFE]
    BENVOLIO   Good morrow, cousin.
    ROMEO   Is the day so young?
    BENVOLIO   But new° struck nine.   *only just*
    ROMEO   Ay me, sad hours seem long.
155   Was that my father that went hence so fast?
    BENVOLIO   It was. What sadness lengthens Romeo's hours?
    ROMEO   Not having that which, having, makes them short.
    BENVOLIO   In love.
    ROMEO   Out.
160   BENVOLIO   Of love?
    ROMEO   Out of her favour where I am in love.

---

4. *where . . . found:* in a place where I was unlikely to have company.
5. Goddess of the dawn in classical legend.
6. "Humors," essential bodily fluids, were considered the basis of human beings' physical and psychological

constitution. Too much black bile caused melancholy and a host of illnesses and derangements.
7. Loyal, but also invoking the proverbial wisdom that only one who is "true to him- or herself" can be upstanding in dealing with others.

BENVOLIO   Alas that love, so gentle in his view,°   appearance
  Should be so tyrannous and rough in proof.°   experience
ROMEO   Alas that love, whose view is muffled still,[8]
165 Should without eyes see pathways to his will.°   intention; lust
  Where shall we dine? [Seeing blood] O me! What fray was here?
  Yet tell me not, for I have heard it all.
  Here's much to do with hate, but more with love.
  Why then, O brawling love, O loving hate,
170 O anything of nothing first create;[9]
  O heavy lightness, serious vanity,
  Misshapen chaos of well-seeming forms,
  Feather of lead, bright smoke, cold fire, sick health,
  Still-waking° sleep, that is not what it is!   Always awake
175 This love feel I, that feel no love in this.
  Dost thou not laugh?
BENVOLIO   No, coz,° I rather weep.   cousin
ROMEO   Good heart, at what?
BENVOLIO   At thy good heart's oppression.°   affliction
ROMEO   Why, such is love's transgression.
  Griefs of mine own lie heavy in my breast,
180 Which thou wilt propagate° to have it pressed[1]   multiply
  With more of thine. This love that thou hast shown
  Doth add more grief to too much of mine own.
  Love is a smoke made with the fume of sighs,
  Being purged,° a fire sparkling in lovers' eyes,   clarified
185 Being vexed,° a sea nourished with lovers' tears.   stirred up
  What is it else? A madness most discreet,°   wise
  A choking gall and a preserving sweet.
  Farewell, my coz.
BENVOLIO   Soft,° I will go along;   Wait
  An if° you leave me so, you do me wrong.   An If = if
190 ROMEO   Tut, I have lost myself. I am not here.
  This is not Romeo; he's some other where.
BENVOLIO   Tell me in sadness,[2] who is that you love?
ROMEO   What, shall I groan and tell thee?
BENVOLIO   Groan? Why no; but sadly tell me who.
195 ROMEO   Bid a sick man in sadness make his will,
  A word ill urged to one that is so ill.
  In sadness, cousin, I do love a woman.
BENVOLIO   I aimed so near when I supposed you loved.
ROMEO   A right good markman; and she's fair I love.
200 BENVOLIO   A right fair mark,° fair coz, is soonest hit.   target; vulva
ROMEO   Well, in that hit you miss. She'll not be hit
  With Cupid's arrow; she hath Dian's wit,[3]
  And, in strong proof° of chastity well armed,°   tested armor / covered
  From love's weak childish bow she lives unharmed.
205 She will not stay° the siege of loving terms,   undergo
  Nor bide th'encounter of assailing eyes,[4]

8. Who cannot see. Cupid was often depicted as blind or blindfolded.
9. _create_: created. Inverting the proverb "Nothing can come of nothing" and also recalling the doctrine that God made the world out of nothing. Romeo catalogues the "miraculous" paradoxes of love.
1. Burdened; embraced.

2. Seriousness, although Romeo plays on the sense "melancholy."
3. The scruples and cleverness of Diana, the classical goddess of hunting and chastity.
4. _th'encounter of assailing eyes_: military metaphors for courtship conventionally used in Petrarchan love poetry.

Nor ope her lap to saint-seducing gold.[5]
O, she is rich in beauty, only poor
That when she dies, with beauty dies her store.°   *wealth*
210   BENVOLIO   Then she hath sworn that she will still° live chaste?   *always*
     ROMEO   She hath, and in that sparing° makes huge waste;   *refraining; thrift*
     For beauty starved with her severity
     Cuts beauty off from all posterity.[6]
     She is too fair, too wise, wisely too fair,°   *just*
215   To merit bliss° by making me despair.[7]   *heaven's blessing*
     She hath forsworn to love, and in that vow
     Do I live dead, that live to tell it now.
     BENVOLIO   Be ruled by me; forget to think of her.
     ROMEO   O, teach me how I should forget to think!
220   BENVOLIO   By giving liberty unto thine eyes.
     Examine other beauties.
     ROMEO   'Tis the way
     To call hers, exquisite, in question more.[8]
     These happy masks that kiss fair ladies' brows,
     Being black, puts us in mind they hide the fair.
225   He that is strucken blind cannot forget
     The precious treasure of his eyesight lost.
     Show me a mistress that is passing° fair,   *surpassingly*
     What doth her beauty serve but as a note
     Where I may read who passed that passing fair?
230   Farewell, thou canst not teach me to forget.
     BENVOLIO   I'll pay° that doctrine, or else die in debt.[9] *Exeunt*   *impart*

1.2

Enter old CAPULET, *County°* PARIS, *and the Clown*   *Count*
[PETER, *a servingman*]

     CAPULET   But Montague is bound° as well as I,   *under oath*
     In penalty alike, and 'tis not hard, I think,
     For men so old as we to keep the peace.
     PARIS   Of honourable reckoning[1] are you both,
5   And pity 'tis you lived at odds so long.
     But now, my lord: what say you to my suit?
     CAPULET   But saying o'er what I have said before.
     My child is yet a stranger in the world;
     She hath not seen the change of fourteen years.
10   Let two more summers wither in their pride
     Ere we may think her ripe to be a bride.
     PARIS   Younger than she are happy mothers made.
     CAPULET   And too soon marred are those so early made.[2]
     But woo her, gentle Paris, get her heart;
15   My will to her consent is but a part,
     And, she agreed, within her scope of choice
     Lies my consent and fair-according voice.
     This night I hold an old-accustomed feast

---

5. To golden gifts that are irresistibly persuasive. Also, in classical legend, Jupiter descended upon Danaë as a shower of gold.
6. *For . . . posterity*: Since she will not have children, her beauty will die with her. *starved*: killed.
7. Despair of salvation, a grave sin.
8. *in question more*: more intensely to mind.
9. Die whatever the cost to me; die still owing you the

doctrine of forgetfulness.
1.2 Location: A street or plaza in Verona.
1. Repute, with a play on "accounting."
2. Q2 includes two more lines following line 13, probably rejected by Shakespeare in the writing process: "Earth hath swallowed all my hopes but she, / She's the hopeful Lady of my earth" (*earth*: body).

Whereto I have invited many a guest
20 Such as I love, and you among the store,
One more most welcome, makes my number more.
At my poor house look to behold this night
Earth-treading stars that make dark heaven light.
Such comfort as do lusty young men feel
25 When well-apparelled April on the heel
Of limping winter treads—even such delight
Among fresh female buds shall you this night
Inherit° at my house; hear all, all see,   *Enjoy*
And like her most whose merit most shall be,
30 Which on more view of many, mine, being one,
May stand in number, though in reck'ning none.[3]
Come, go with me. [*Giving* PETER *a paper*]   Go, sirrah,° trudge   *(address to an inferior)*
   about;
Through fair Verona find those persons out
Whose names are written there, and to them say
35 My house and welcome on their pleasure stay.°   *wait*
                  Exeunt [CAPULET *and* PARIS]
PETER   Find them out whose names are written here? It is written that the shoemaker should meddle with his yard° and the   *yardstick*
tailor with his last,° the fisher with his pencil° and the painter   *shoe form / paintbrush*
with his nets; but I am sent to find those persons whose names
40 are here writ, and can never find° what names the writing per-   *figure out*
son hath here writ. I must to the learned.
               Enter BENVOLIO *and* ROMEO
In good time.
BENVOLIO [*to* ROMEO]   Tut, man, one fire burns out another's burning,
   One pain is lessened by another's anguish.
45 Turn giddy,° and be holp° by backward turning.   *Turn until dizzy / helped*
   One desperate grief cures with another's languish.[4]
Take thou some new infection[5] to thy eye,
And the rank poison of the old will die.
ROMEO   Your plantain leaf[6] is excellent for that.
50 BENVOLIO   For what, I pray thee?
ROMEO   For your broken° shin.   *gashed*
BENVOLIO   Why, Romeo, art thou mad?
ROMEO   Not mad, but bound more than a madman is;
   Shut up in prison, kept without my food,
   Whipped and tormented and— [*to* PETER] Good e'en,° good   *evening (afternoon)*
55   fellow.
PETER   God gi'° good e'en. I pray, sir, can you read?   *give you*
ROMEO   Ay, mine own fortune in my misery.[7]
PETER   Perhaps you have learned it without book.[8] But I pray,
   can you read anything you see?
60 ROMEO   Ay, if I know the letters and the language.
PETER   Ye say honestly. Rest you merry.[9]
ROMEO   Stay, fellow, I can read.
               He reads the letter

---

3. *Which . . . none:* Upon closer inspection of the
many young women, my daughter may make a part of
the gorgeous display, but be of no account by herself.
"One" was proverbially "no number."
4. Is displaced by the languishing pain of a new grief.
5. New object of passion, which causes a distortion of
sight in the lover.
6. The ordinary plaintain leaf, used to dress wounds or

bruises and thought to have curative powers.
7 Romeo takes "read" to mean "understand" or "perceive," as in "to read one's fortune."
8. *without book:* from memory or by ear, as well as
through experience rather than education.
9. A farewell. Peter takes Romeo to mean "if only I
knew the letters and the language."

'Signor Martino and his wife and daughters,
County° Anselme and his beauteous sisters,
65   The lady widow of Vitruvio,
Signor Placentio and his lovely nieces,
Mercutio and his brother Valentine,
Mine uncle Capulet, his wife and daughters,
My fair niece Rosaline and Livia,
70   Signor Valentio and his cousin Tybalt,
Lucio and the lively Helena.'
A fair assembly. Whither should they come?
PETER   Up.¹
ROMEO   Whither?
75   PETER   To supper to our house.
ROMEO   Whose house?
PETER   My master's.
ROMEO   Indeed, I should have asked thee that before.
PETER   Now I'll tell you without asking. My master is the great
80   rich Capulet, and if you be not of the house of Montagues, I
pray come and crush° a cup of wine. Rest you merry.   *Exit*   drink
BENVOLIO   At this same ancient° feast of Capulet's   traditional
Sups the fair Rosaline, whom thou so loves,
With all the admirèd beauties of Verona.
85   Go thither, and with unattainted° eye   unbiased
Compare her face with some that I shall show,
And I will make thee think thy swan a crow.
ROMEO   When the devout religion° of mine eye   pious belief
Maintains such falsehood, then turn tears to fires;
90   And these° who, often drowned, could never die,   these eyes
Transparent° heretics, be burnt for liars.   Obvious; self-evident
One fairer than my love!—the all-seeing sun
Ne'er saw her match since first the world begun.
BENVOLIO   Tut, you saw her fair, none else being by,
95   Herself poised with° herself in either eye;   balanced against
But in that crystal scales let there be weighed
Your lady's love against some other maid
That I will show you shining at this feast,
And she shall scant show well that now seems best.
100   ROMEO   I'll go along, no such sight to be shown,
But to rejoice in splendour of mine own.   [*Exeunt*]

1.3
Enter CAPULET'S WIFE *and* NURSE

CAPULET'S WIFE   Nurse, where's my daughter? Call her forth to me.
NURSE   Now, by my maidenhead at twelve year old,¹
I bade her come. What,² lamb, what, ladybird—
God forbid³—where is this girl? What, Juliet!
Enter JULIET
5   JULIET   How now, who calls?
NURSE   Your mother.
JULIET   Madam, I am here. What is your will?

1. "Come up" is a phrase expression scorn.
1.3 Location: Capulet's house.
1. Presumably the latest date that the Nurse could swear by her virginity.
2. An expression of impatience.
3. Either an apology for the promiscuous connotation of "ladybird" of fearing something amiss in Juliet's absence.

CAPULET'S WIFE This is the matter.—Nurse, give leave° a while.   *excuse us*
    We must talk in secret.—Nurse, come back again.
10   I have remembered me, thou's° hear our counsel.°   *you shall / secrets*
    Thou knowest my daughter's of a pretty age.
NURSE Faith, I can tell her age unto an hour.
CAPULET'S WIFE She's not fourteen.
NURSE I'll lay fourteen of my teeth—and yet, to my teen° be it   *sorrow*
15   spoken, I have but four—she's not fourteen. How long is it now
    to Lammastide?[4]
CAPULET'S WIFE A fortnight and odd days.
NURSE Even or odd, of all days in the year
    Come Lammas Eve at night shall she be fourteen.
20   Susan[5] and she—God rest all Christian souls!—
    Were of an age. Well, Susan is with God;
    She was too good for me. But, as I said,
    On Lammas Eve at night shall she be fourteen,
    That shall she, marry, I remember it well.
25   'Tis since the earthquake now eleven years,
    And she was weaned—I never shall forget it—
    Of all the days of the year upon that day,
    For I had then laid wormwood[6] to my dug,°   *on my nipple*
    Sitting in the sun under the dovehouse wall.
30   My lord and you were then at Mantua.
    Nay, I do bear a brain!° But, as I said,   *memory*
    When it did taste the wormwood on the nipple
    Of my dug and felt it bitter, pretty fool,°   *(an endearment)*
    To see it tetchy° and fall out wi'th' dug!   *peevish*
35   'Shake', quoth the dove-house![7] 'Twas no need, I trow,
    To bid me trudge;°   *remove myself*
    And since that time it is eleven years,
    For then she could stand high-lone.° Nay, by th' rood,°   *upright alone / cross*
    She could have run and waddled all about,
40   For even the day before, she broke her brow,°   *cut her forehead*
    And then my husband—God be with his soul,
    A° was a merry man!—took up the child.   *He*
    'Yea,' quoth he, 'dost thou fall upon thy face?
    Thou wilt fall backward when thou hast more wit,°   *knowledge*
45   Wilt thou not, Jule?' And, by my halidom,°   *holiness; holy relic*
    The pretty wretch left° crying and said 'Ay'.   *stopped*
    To see now how a jest shall come about!°   *come true*
    I warrant an° I should live a thousand years   *if*
    I never should forget it. 'Wilt thou not, Jule?' quoth he,
50   And, pretty fool, it stinted° and said 'Ay'.   *she ceased*
CAPULET'S WIFE Enough of this. I pray thee hold thy peace.
NURSE Yes, madam. Yet I cannot choose but laugh
    To think it should leave crying and say 'Ay'.
    And yet, I warrant,° it had upon it° brow   *assure you / its*
55   A bump as big as a young cock'rel's stone.°   *rooster's testicle*
    A perilous knock, and it cried bitterly.
    'Yea,' quoth my husband, 'fall'st upon thy face?
    Thou wilt fall backward when thou com'st to age,

---

4. August 1, originally celebrated by the church as a harvest festival.
5. The Nurse evidently suckled Juliet after her own daughter died.
6. A proverbially bitter plant extract.
7. The dove house shook with the earthquake.

Wilt thou not, Jule?' It stinted and said 'Ay'.
60 JULIET   And stint thou too, I pray thee, Nurse, say I.
NURSE   Peace, I have done. God mark° thee to his grace.   *elect*
Thou wast the prettiest babe that e'er I nursed.
An° I might live to see thee married once,°   *If / one day*
I have my wish.
65 CAPULET'S WIFE   Marry,° that 'marry' is the very theme   *Truly*
I came to talk of. Tell me, daughter Juliet,
How stands your dispositions to be married?
JULIET   It is an honour that I dream not of.
NURSE   'An honour'! Were not I thine only nurse,
70 I would say thou hadst sucked wisdom from thy teat.[8]
CAPULET'S WIFE   Well, think of marriage now. Younger than you
Here in Verona, ladies of esteem,
Are made already mothers. By my count
I was your mother much upon these years
75 That you are now a maid. Thus then, in brief :
The valiant Paris seeks you for his love.
NURSE   A man, young lady, lady, such a man
As all the world—why, he's a man of wax.[9]
CAPULET'S WIFE   Verona's summer hath not such a flower.
80 NURSE   Nay, he's a flower, in faith, a very flower.
CAPULET'S WIFE [*to* JULIET]   What say you? Can you love the gentleman?
This night you shall behold him at our feast.
Read o'er the volume of young Paris' face,
And find delight writ there with beauty's pen.
85 Examine every married lineament,[1]
And see how one° another lends content;[2]   *one to*
And what obscured in this fair volume lies
Find written in the margin[3] of his eyes.
This precious book of love, this unbound° lover,   *single; unrestrained*
90 To beautify him only lacks a cover.
The fish lives in the sea, and 'tis much pride
For fair without the fair within to hide.[4]
That book in many's eyes doth share the glory
That in gold clasps locks in the golden story.[5]
95 So shall you share all that he doth possess
By having him, making yourself no less.
NURSE   No less, nay, bigger. Women grow° by men.   *swell with child*
CAPULET'S WIFE [*to* JULIET]   Speak briefly: can you like of Paris' love?
JULIET   I'll look° to like, if looking liking move;[6]   *expect; examine*
100 But no more deep will I endart[7] mine eye
Than your consent gives strength to make it fly.
            Enter a servingman [PETER]
PETER   Madam, the guests are come, supper served up, you
called, my young lady asked for, the Nurse cursed in the pantry,
and everything in extremity.° I must hence to wait.° I beseech   *a terrible state / serve*
105 you follow straight.°   *immediately*

---

8. From the teat that nourished you.
9. Model of perfection, as if sculpted rather than born.
1. Harmoniously composed feature; a joined line of
flowing handwriting.
2. Meaning; happiness.
3. Glosses to difficult passage of text were set in the
margin.
4. For a lovely setting (Juliet) to frame and enrich the
fair Paris.
5. *That book . . . story:* Many esteem a book's golden
binding as highly as the story it contains. The speech
thoroughly confuses who is covering whom.
6. If looking can motivate liking.
7. Sink itself like an arrow into its target; shoot glances
that, like Cupid's arrows, inflame his passions.

CAPULET'S WIFE   We follow thee.   *Exit a servingman* [PETER]
Juliet, the County stays.°   *the Count awaits*
NURSE   Go, girl; seek happy nights to° happy days.   *Exeunt*   *at the end of*

1.4

Enter ROMEO, MERCUTIO, *and* BENVOLIO, [*as masquers,*]
with five or six other masquers[1] [*bearing a drum and
torches*]

ROMEO   What, shall this speech° be spoke for our excuse,   *prologue*
Or shall we on without apology?
BENVOLIO   The date is out of° such prolixity.   *past for*
We'll have no Cupid hoodwinked[2] with a scarf,
5   Bearing a Tartar's painted bow of lath,[3]
Scaring the ladies like a crowkeeper,°   *scarecrow*
Nor no without-book° Prologue faintly spoke   *memorized*
After° the prompter for our entrance.   *Repeating after*
But let them measure° us by what they will,   *judge*
10   We'll measure° them a measure,° and be gone.   *apportion / dance*
ROMEO   Give me a torch. I am not for this ambling;°   *dancing*
Being but heavy,° I will bear the light.   *melancholy*
MERCUTIO   Nay, gentle° Romeo, we must have you dance.   *noble; softhearted*
ROMEO   Not I, believe me. You have dancing shoes
15   With nimble soles; I have a soul of lead
So stakes me to the ground I cannot move.
MERCUTIO   You are a lover; borrow Cupid's wings,
And soar with them above a common bound.[4]
ROMEO   I am too sore° empiercèd with his shaft   *deeply*
20   To soar with his light° feathers, and so bound   *cheery; agile; wanton*
I cannot bound a pitch[5] above dull woe;
Under love's heavy burden do I sink.
MERCUTIO   And to sink in it should you burden love—
Too great oppression for a tender thing.[6]
25   ROMEO   Is love a tender thing? It is too rough,
Too rude, too boist'rous, and it pricks like thorn.
MERCUTIO   If love be rough with you, be rough with love.
Prick° love for pricking, and you beat love down.[7]   *Stab; sexually penetrate*
Give me a case[8] to put my visage in,
30   A visor for a visor.[9] What care I
What curious eye doth quote° deformity?   *notice*
Here are the beetle brows° shall blush for me.   *protruding eyebrows*
[*They put on visors*]
BENVOLIO   Come, knock and enter, and no sooner in
But every man betake him to his legs.°   *to dancing; to flight*
35   ROMEO   A torch for me. Let wantons light of heart
Tickle the sense-less rushes° with their heels,   *floor matting*
For I am proverbed with a grandsire° phrase.   *an ancient*

1.4 Location: Before Capulet's house.
1. Performers or participants in an aristocratic masked
entertainment, consisting of dances and sometimes
dumb shows and set speeches.
2. Blindfolded and foolish Cupid, a typical costume for
the presenter of the masque's theme.
3. Short bow shaped like the upper lip, made of the
thin wood used for theatrical properties.

4. A normal limit; an average dancer's leap.
5. Height from which a hawk stoops to kill.
6. Suggesting a pudendum.
7. *Prick . . . down:* Playing on the sense "satiate desire
by fulfilling it."
8. Literally, "mask," but also slang for the vagina.
9. Mask for an ugly face. Proverbial: "A well-favored
visor to hide an ill-favored face."

I'll be a candle-holder and look on.[1]
The game was ne'er so fair, and I am done.[2]
　　　　[*He takes a torch*]

40　MERCUTIO　Tut, dun's the mouse,[3] the constable's own word.°　　　*phrase*
　　　　If thou art dun we'll draw thee from the mire[4]
　　　　Of—save your reverence[5]—love, wherein thou stickest
　　　　Up to the ears. Come, we burn daylight,° ho!　　　　*waste time*
　　ROMEO　Nay, that's not so.
　　MERCUTIO　　　　　　　I mean, sir, in delay
45　We waste our lights in vain, like lights by day.
　　　　Take our good meaning, for our judgement sits
　　　　Five times in that ere once in our five wits.[6]
　　ROMEO　And we mean° well in going to this masque,　　　*intend*
　　　　But 'tis no wit° to go.　　　　　　　　　　　　　*intelligence*
　　MERCUTIO　　　　　Why, may one ask?
　　ROMEO　I dreamt a dream tonight.°　　　　　　　　　*last night*
50　MERCUTIO　　　　　　　　　And so did I.
　　ROMEO　Well, what was yours?
　　MERCUTIO　　　　　　　That dreamers often lie.
　　ROMEO　In bed asleep while they do dream things true.
　　MERCUTIO　O, then I see Queen Mab[7] hath been with you.
　　BENVOLIO　Queen Mab, what's she?
55　MERCUTIO　She is the fairies' midwife, and she comes
　　　　In shape no bigger than an agate stone[8]
　　　　On the forefinger of an alderman,
　　　　Drawn with a team of little atomi°　　　　　　　*atoms*
　　　　Athwart men's noses as they lie asleep.
60　Her wagon spokes made of long spinners'° legs;　　　*spiders'*
　　　　The cover, of the wings of grasshoppers;
　　　　Her traces, of the moonshine's wat'ry beams;
　　　　Her collars, of the smallest spider web;
　　　　Her whip, of cricket's bone, the lash of film;°　　*spider's-web thread*
65　Her wagoner,° a small grey-coated gnat　　　　　　*driver*
　　　　Not half so big as a round little worm
　　　　Pricked from the lazy finger of a maid.[9]
　　　　Her chariot is an empty hazelnut
　　　　Made by the joiner° squirrel or old grub,[1]　　　*carpenter*
70　Time out o' mind the fairies' coachmakers.
　　　　And in this state° she gallops night by night　　　*regal finery*
　　　　Through lovers' brains, and then they dream of love;
　　　　O'er courtiers' knees, that dream on curtsies straight;[2]
　　　　O'er ladies' lips, who straight on kisses dream,
75　Which oft the angry Mab with blisters plagues
　　　　Because their breaths with sweetmeats° tainted are.　*candies*
　　　　Sometime she gallops o'er a lawyer's lip,

1. Proverbial: "A good candleholder proves a good gamester. A spectator loses nothing."
2. Proverbial: "When play is best, it is time to leave."
3. Proverbial: Keep silent and unseen, like a mouse.
4. In the Christmas game "Dun is in the mire," players pantomimed drawing a log representing a horse out of a boggy road. Mercutio is suggesting that Romeo is a stick-in-the-mud.
5. An apology for crude language, here used mockingly.
6. *Take . . . wits*: Understand my intended good meaning using common sense ("judgement"), which is five times as trustworthy as the five senses.

7. Possibly Celtic, but probably Shakespeare's invention. "Queen" meant "whore," and "Mab" was a stereotypical name for prostitutes.
8. A small human figure was often carved on agate stones set in seal rings.
9. According to popular belief, worms generated in idle girls' fingers.
1. Grubs bore holes. Lines 68–70, from Q1, do not appear in Q2 at all; numerous other changes in the order and wording of his speech suggest that Q1 incorporated revisions that Q2 and later revisions did not.
2. Dream of respectful bows immediately.

And then dreams he of smelling out a suit;[3]
And sometime comes she with a tithe-pig's[4] tail
80   Tickling a parson's nose as a° lies asleep;   *he*
Then dreams he of another benefice.[5]
Sometime she driveth o'er a soldier's neck,
And then dreams he of cutting foreign throats,
Of breaches, ambuscados, Spanish blades,[6]
85   Of healths five fathom deep;[7] and then anon°   *soon*
Drums in his ear, at which he starts and wakes,
And being thus frighted, swears a prayer or two,
And sleeps again. This is that very Mab
That plaits° the manes of horses in the night,   *entangles*
90   And bakes the elf-locks[8] in foul sluttish° hairs,   *dirty*
Which once untangled much misfortune bodes.
This is the hag, when maids lie on their backs,
That presses them[9] and learns° them first to bear,   *teaches*
Making them women of good carriage.[1]
This is she—
95   ROMEO   Peace, peace, Mercutio, peace!
Thou talk'st of nothing.°   *imaginings; a vagina*
MERCUTIO   True. I talk of dreams,
Which are the children of an idle brain,
Begot of nothing but vain fantasy,°   *empty imagination*
Which is as thin of substance as the air,
100   And more inconstant than the wind, who woos
Even now the frozen bosom of the north,
And, being angered, puffs away from thence,
Turning his face to the dew-dropping south.
BENVOLIO   This wind you talk of blows us from ourselves.
105   Supper is done, and we shall come too late.
ROMEO   I fear too early, for my mind misgives°   *fears*
Some consequence yet hanging in the stars
Shall bitterly begin his fearful date°   *period*
With this night's revels, and expire° the term   *finish*
110   Of a despisèd life, closed in my breast,
By some vile forfeit of untimely death.[2]
But he° that hath the steerage of my course   *(God)*
Direct my sail! On, lusty gentlemen.
BENVOLIO   Strike, drum.
          They march about the stage and [exeunt]

1.5

[PETER *and other* SERVINGMEN] *come forth with napkins*
PETER   Where's Potpan, that he helps not to take away? He shift
a trencher,° he scrape a trencher!   *wooden plate*
FIRST SERVINGMAN   When good manners shall lie all in one or
two men's hands, and they unwashed too, 'tis a foul° thing.   *bad; dirty*

---

3. A petition at court, which the lawyer could facilitate for a fee.
4. Pig paid as a tithe to the parish for the support of the priest.
5. Pluralism—holding multiple benefices simultaneously—was a common source of corruption in the early modern Church.
6. *breaches:* burst fortifications. *ambuscados:* ambushes. *Spanish blades:* swords made in Toledo were famous for their quality.

7. Fantastically deep cups of liquor.
8. And hardens the tangles. According to folk legend, unknotting them would anger the malicious elves.
9. Evil spirits were supposed to be responsible for erotic dreams, taking the form of an illusory sexual partner.
1. Excellent deportment; the capacity for carrying the weight of a lover; childbearing.
2. As fate prematurely foreclosing on a mortgaged life.
1.5. Location: Capulet's house.

5   PETER   Away with the joint-stools,[1] remove the court-cupboard,°   *sideboard*
        look to the plate.° Good thou, save me a piece of marzipan,   *silverware*
        and, as thou loves me, let the porter let in Susan Grindstone
        and Nell. Anthony and Potpan!
     SECOND SERVINGMAN   Ay, boy, ready.
10 PETER   You are looked for and called for, asked for and sought
        for, in the great chamber.
     FIRST SERVINGMAN   We cannot be here and there too. Cheerly,
        boys! Be brisk a while, and the longest liver take all.[2]
                [*They come and go, setting forth tables and chairs*]
                Enter old CAPULET [*and family and*] *all the guests and*
                gentlewomen to the masquers
     CAPULET [*to the masquers*]   Welcome, gentlemen. Ladies that
        have their toes
15   Unplagued with corns will walk a bout° with you.   *dance a turn*
        Aha, my mistresses, which of you all
        Will now deny to dance? She that makes dainty,°   *coyly demurs*
        She, I'll swear, hath corns. Am I come near ye now?[3]
        Welcome, gentlemen. I have seen the day
20   That I have worn a visor, and could tell
        A whispering tale in a fair lady's ear
        Such as would please. 'Tis gone, 'tis gone, 'tis gone.
        You are welcome, gentlemen. Come, musicians, play.
                Music plays, and they dance. [ROMEO *stands apart*]
        A hall,[4] a hall! Give room, and foot it, girls.
25   [*To* SERVINGMEN]   More light, you knaves, and turn the tables up,[5]
        And quench the fire, the room is grown too hot.
        [*To his* COUSIN] Ah sirrah, this unlooked-for° sport comes well.   *unexpected*
        Nay, sit, nay, sit, good cousin° Capulet,   *kinsman*
        For you and I are past our dancing days.
                [CAPULET *and his* COUSIN *sit*]
30   How long is't now since last yourself and I
        Were in a masque?
     CAPULET'S COUSIN   By'r Lady, thirty years.
     CAPULET   What, man, 'tis not so much, 'tis not so much.
        'Tis since the nuptial of Lucentio,
        Come Pentecost[6] as quickly as it will,
35   Some five-and-twenty years; and then we masqued.
     CAPULET'S COUSIN   'Tis more, 'tis more. His son is elder, sir.
        His son is thirty.
     CAPULET   Will you tell me that?
        His son was but a ward[7] two years ago.
     ROMEO [*to a* SERVINGMAN]   What lady's that which doth enrich the hand
        Of yonder knight?
40 SERVINGMAN   I know not, sir.
     ROMEO   O, she doth teach the torches to burn bright!
        It seems she hangs upon the cheek of night
        As a rich jewel in an Ethiope's ear—
        Beauty too rich for use, for earth too dear.[8]

---

1. Stools made by a furniture maker, commonly used for seating at large banquets.
2. Proverbial, meaning "Life is short."
3. Does that strike home?
4. Make space in the hall.
5. Dismantle and stack the trestle tables.

6. The seventh Sunday after Easter, a standard reference point in the medieval and Renaissance calendar.
7. Subject to a guardian; a minor.
8. Too precious for this world; too valuable to die and be buried in earth.

45 So shows a snowy dove trooping° with crows   *flocking*
As yonder lady o'er her fellows shows.
The measure° done, I'll watch her place of stand,°   *dance / standing*
And, touching hers, make blessèd my rude hand.
Did my heart love till now? Forswear it, sight,
50 For I ne'er saw true beauty till this night.
TYBALT   This, by his voice, should be a Montague.
Fetch me my rapier, boy.   [*Exit* page]
                                        What, dares the slave
Come hither, covered with an antic face,⁹
To fleer° and scorn at our solemnity?°   *sneer / festivity*
55 Now, by the stock and honour of my kin,
To strike him dead I hold it not a sin.
CAPULET [*standing*]   Why, how now, kinsman? Wherefore storm you so?
TYBALT   Uncle, this is a Montague, our foe,
A villain° that is hither come in spite   *An ill-doer; a slave*
60 To scorn at our solemnity this night.
CAPULET   Young Romeo, is it?
TYBALT   'Tis he, that villain Romeo.
CAPULET   Content° thee, gentle coz, let him alone.   *Calm*
A bears him like a portly° gentleman,   *dignified*
And, to say truth, Verona brags of him
65 To be a virtuous and well-governed° youth.   *sensible*
I would not for the wealth of all this town
Here in my house do him disparagement.
Therefore be patient, take no note of him.
It is my will, the which if thou respect,
70 Show a fair presence° and put off these frowns,   *demeanor*
An ill-beseeming semblance° for a feast.   *expression*
TYBALT   It fits when such a villain is a guest.
I'll not endure him.
CAPULET   He shall be endured.
What, goodman¹ boy, I say he shall. Go to,²
75 Am I the master here or you? Go to—
You'll not endure him! God shall mend my soul.
You'll make a mutiny° among my guests,   *brawl*
You will set cock-a-hoop!³ You'll be the man!
TYBALT   Why, uncle, 'tis a shame.
CAPULET   Go to, go to,
80 You are a saucy boy. Is't so, indeed?
This trick° may chance to scathe° you. I know what,⁴   *stupidity / harm*
You must contrary me. Marry, 'tis time⁵—
            [*A dance ends.* JULIET *retires to her place of stand, where*
            ROMEO *awaits her*]
[*To the guests*] Well said,° my hearts! [*To* TYBALT] You are a   *done*
    princox,° go.   *cheeky boy*
Be quiet, or— [*to* SERVINGMEN] more light, more light!— [*to*
    TYBALT] for shame,
85 I'll make you quiet. [*To the guests*] What, cheerly, my hearts!
            [*The music plays again, and the guests dance*]

9. A grotesque mask; a playful mask.
1. Courtesy title applied to a commoner (and thus an
insult to the noble Tybalt).
2. An expression of impatience.
3. You will abandon restraint, like a drinker who

removes the tap ("cock") from the barrel or like a boastfully crowing rooster.
4. Know what I'll do; mean what I say.
5. Time to teach you a lesson; time that you became
obedient.

TYBALT   Patience perforce° with wilful choler° meeting   *enforced / rash anger*
    Makes my flesh tremble in their different° greeting.   *hostile*
    I will withdraw, but this intrusion shall,
    Now seeming sweet, convert to bitt'rest gall.   *Exit*
90   ROMEO [*to* JULIET, *touching her hand*]   If I profane with my unworthiest hand[6]
    This holy shrine, the gentler sin is this:
    My lips, two blushing pilgrims,[7] ready stand
    To smooth that rough touch with a tender kiss.
    JULIET   Good pilgrim, you do wrong your hand too much
95   Which mannerly° devotion shows in this.   *seemly*
    For saints[8] have hands that pilgrims' hands do touch,
    And palm to palm is holy palmers'° kiss.   *pilgrims'*
    ROMEO   Have not saints lips, and holy palmers, too?
    JULIET   Ay, pilgrim, lips that they must use in prayer.
100   ROMEO   O then, dear saint, let lips do what hands do:
    They pray; grant thou, lest faith turn to despair.
    JULIET   Saints do not move, though grant for prayers' sake.[9]
    ROMEO   Then move not while my prayer's effect I take.
    [*He kisses her*]
    Thus from my lips, by thine my sin is purged.
105   JULIET   Then have my lips the sin that they have took.
    ROMEO   Sin from my lips? O trespass sweetly urged![1]
    Give me my sin again.°   *back*
    [*He kisses her*]
    JULIET   You kiss by th' book.[2]
    NURSE   Madam, your mother craves a word with you.
    [JULIET *departs to her mother*]
    ROMEO   What is her mother?
    NURSE   Marry, bachelor,°   *young man*
110   Her mother is the lady of the house,
    And a good lady, and a wise and virtuous.
    I nursed her daughter that you talked withal.°   *with*
    I tell you, he that can lay hold of her
    Shall have the chinks.°   *plenty of coins*
    ROMEO [*aside*]   Is she a Capulet?
115   O dear account!° My life is my foe's debt.[3]   *costly reckoning*
    BENVOLIO   Away, be gone, the sport is at the best.
    ROMEO   Ay, so I fear, the more is my unrest.
    CAPULET   Nay, gentlemen, prepare not to be gone.
    We have a trifling foolish banquet towards.[4]
    [*They whisper in his ear*]
120   Is it e'en so? Why then, I thank you all.
    I thank you, honest gentlemen. Good night.
    More torches here! Come on then, let's to bed.
    [*To his* COUSIN] Ah, sirrah, by my fay,° it waxes late.   *faith*
    I'll to my rest.

---

6. Romeo and Juliet here address each other in the form of a sonnet.
7. Florio's *World of Wordes* (1598) translates the Italian word *romeo* as "wanderer" or "palmer" (pilgrim to the Holy Land).
8. Statues or pictures of saints, which attracted Catholic pilgrims. The Elizabethan Anglican Church held that the worship of such images was blasphemy; to an English audience, therefore, Romeo's description of his love could sound like idolatry.

9. Again identifying the saint with her image. As a statue she does not move, but as a saint in heaven she can intercede with God on behalf of the worshipper.
1. Sweetly argued that the first kiss was a transgression, and sweetly advocated that the transgression of a second kiss is needed to take the sin of the first away.
2. According to the rules; implies "proficiently," "politely," or "with poetic flatteries."
3. A debt owing to my foe; in the power of my foe.
4. A trifling, paltry dessert coming.

Exeunt [CAPULET, *his* WIFE, *and his* COUSIN. *The*
guests, gentlewomen, masquers, musicians, and
servingmen begin to leave]

125 JULIET Come hither, Nurse. What is yon gentleman?
NURSE The son and heir of old Tiberio.
JULIET What's he that now is going out of door?
NURSE Marry, that, I think, be young Petruccio.
JULIET What's he that follows here, that would not dance?
130 NURSE I know not.
JULIET Go ask his name.
[NURSE *goes*]
                                    If he be married,
    My grave is like° to be my wedding bed.   likely
NURSE [*returning*] His name is Romeo, and a Montague,
    The only son of your great enemy.
135 JULIET [*aside*] My only love sprung from my only hate!
    Too early seen unknown, and known too late!
    Prodigious° birth of love it is to me   Monstrous; ominous
    That I must love a loathèd enemy.
NURSE What's tis?° what's tis?   this
JULIET   A rhyme I learnt even now
    Of one I danced withal.
        One calls within 'Juliet!'
140 NURSE   Anon,° anon.   Right away
    Come, let's away. The strangers all are gone.   *Exeunt*

2.0

[*Enter*] CHORUS
CHORUS Now old° desire doth in his deathbed lie,   Romeo's former
    And young affection gapes° to be his heir.   longs
    That fair for which love groaned for and would die,
        With tender Juliet matched,° is now not fair.   compared
    Now Romeo is beloved and loves again,°   in return; once more
5   Alike bewitchèd by the charm of looks;[1]
    But to his foe supposed° he must complain,[2]   presumed
        And she steal love's sweet bait from fearful° hooks.   fearsome
    Being held a foe, he may not have access
        To breathe such vows as lovers use° to swear,   are accustomed
10 And she as much in love, her means much less
        To meet her new belovèd anywhere.
    But passion lends them power, time means, to meet,
    Temp'ring extremities° with extreme sweet.   [*Exit*]   Modifying dangers

2.1

Enter ROMEO *alone*[1]
ROMEO Can I go forward when my heart is here?
    Turn back, dull earth,[2] and find thy centre[3] out.
        [*He turns back and withdraws.*]
        Enter BENVOLIO *with* MERCUTIO

2.0
1. Appearances; desirous glances.
2. Conventionally, make lovesick speeches.
2.1 Location: Outside Capulet's house.
1. The main stage represents the area outside the wall of
Capulet's orchard and then the inside of the orchard
below the window of Juliet's room. Romeo is imagined to
leap over the garden wall when he withdraws at line 2.
2. Romeo's flesh, drawing on two traditional views of the
human body: animated dust or clay, and a "microcosm,"
or little world, which mirrors the order of the universe.
Earth was the most sluggish and immobile element.
3. The point in the earth toward which everything falls;
or Romeo's heart (metaphorically, Juliet).

BENVOLIO [*calling*]   Romeo, my cousin Romeo, Romeo!

MERCUTIO   He is wise, and, on my life, hath stol'n him° home to bed.   *himself*

5   BENVOLIO   He ran this way, and leapt this orchard wall.
Call, good Mercutio.

MERCUTIO   Nay, I'll conjure° too.   *summon as a spirit*
Romeo! Humours!⁴ Madman! Passion! Lover!
Appear thou in the likeness of a sigh.
Speak but one rhyme and I am satisfied.

10   Cry but 'Ay me!' Pronounce but 'love' and 'dove'.
Speak to my gossip° Venus one fair word,   *crony*
One nickname for her purblind° son and heir,   *dim-sighted; blind*
Young Adam⁵ Cupid, he that shot so trim°   *accurately*
When King Cophetua loved the beggar maid.⁶—

15   He heareth not, he stirreth not, he moveth not.
The ape⁷ is dead, and I must conjure him.—
I conjure thee by Rosaline's bright eyes,
By her high forehead and her scarlet lip,
By her fine foot, straight leg, and quivering thigh,

20   And the demesnes° that there adjacent lie,   *estates*
That in thy likeness thou appear to us.

BENVOLIO   An if he hear thee, thou wilt anger him.

MERCUTIO   This cannot anger him. 'Twould anger him
To raise a spirit⁸ in his mistress' circle

25   Of some strange° nature, letting it there stand   *other person's*
Till she had laid it and conjured it down.
That were some spite. My invocation
Is fair and honest. In his mistress' name,
I conjure only but to raise up him.

30   BENVOLIO   Come, he hath hid himself among these trees
To be consorted° with the humorous⁹ night.   *in company*
Blind is his love, and best befits the dark.

MERCUTIO   If love be blind, love cannot hit the mark.°   *target; vulva*
Now will he sit under a medlar¹ tree

35   And wish his mistress were that kind of fruit
As maids call medlars when they laugh alone.
O Romeo, that she were, O that she were
An open-arse,° and thou a popp'rin' pear.²   *medlar*
Romeo, good night. I'll to my truckle-bed.³

40   This field-bed⁴ is too cold for me to sleep.
Come, shall we go?

BENVOLIO   Go then, for 'tis in vain
To seek him here that means not to be found.

                   Exeunt [BENVOLIO *and* MERCUTIO]

ROMEO [*coming forward*]   He jests at scars that never felt a wound.⁵
But soft,° what light through yonder window breaks?   *wait; hush*

---

4. Pure moods, not mixed together to form an even "temper."

5. Probably alluding to Adam Bell, a famously accurate sixteenth-century archer.

6. The story of a king who falls in love with a beggar and makes her his queen was the subject of a popular ballad.

7. Foolish creature (a disrespectful endearment), or alluding to a magician's trick of "reviving" an ape that had been trained to play dead.

8. A word for "semen"; the entire speech is filled with obscene wordplay.

9. Damp; melancholy.

1. A fruit thought to resemble the female sex organs, with a play on "meddle" in the sense "have sexual intercourse with."

2. A pear from Poperinghe in Flanders, punning on "popper-in" or "pop her in."

3. Small bed, often for a child, which was stored under a larger one.

4. A lying place in the open, and a soldier's portable bed.

5. Rhymes with "found." This line precedes a scene change in most editions, although the location remains the same if both the inside and the outside of the orchard are supposed to be visible onstage.

45 It is the east, and Juliet is the sun.
Arise, fair sun, and kill the envious moon,[6]
Who is already sick and pale with grief
That thou, her maid, art far more fair than she.
Be not her maid, since she is envious.
50 Her vestal° livery is but sick and green,[7]   *virginal*
And none but fools do wear it; cast it off.
         [*Enter* JULIET *aloft*]
It is my lady, O, it is my love.
O that she knew she were!
She speaks, yet she says nothing. What of that?
55 Her eye discourses; I will answer it.
I am too bold. 'Tis not to me she speaks.
Two of the fairest stars in all the heaven,
Having some business, do entreat her eyes
To twinkle in their spheres[8] till they return.
60 What if her eyes were there, they in her head?—
The brightness of her cheek would shame those stars
As daylight doth a lamp; her eye in heaven
Would through the airy region° stream so bright   *ethereal sky*
That birds would sing and think it were not night.
65 See how she leans her cheek upon her hand.
O, that I were a glove upon that hand,
That I might touch that cheek!
JULIET   Ay me.
ROMEO [*aside*]   She speaks.
O, speak again, bright angel; for thou art
As glorious to this night, being o'er my head,
70 As is a wingèd messenger° of heaven   *angel*
Unto the white upturnèd[9] wond'ring eyes
Of mortals that fall back to gaze[1] on him
When he bestrides the lazy-passing clouds
And sails upon the bosom of the air.
JULIET [*not knowing* ROMEO *hears her*]   O Romeo, Romeo,
75   wherefore° art thou Romeo?   *why*
Deny thy father and refuse thy name,
Or if thou wilt not, be but sworn my love,
And I'll no longer be a Capulet.
ROMEO [*aside*]   Shall I hear more, or shall I speak at this?
80 JULIET   'Tis but thy name that is my enemy.
Thou art thyself, though° not a Montague.   *even if*
What's Montague? It is nor hand, nor foot,
Nor arm, nor face, nor any other part
Belonging to a man. O, be some other name!
85 What's in a name? That which we call a rose
By any other word would smell as sweet.
So Romeo would, were he not Romeo called,
Retain that dear perfection which he owes°   *owns*
Without that title. Romeo, doff° thy name,   *shed*
90 And for thy name—which is no part of thee—
Take all myself.

6. Emblem of Diana, goddess of chastity.
7. Unfulfilled sexual desire was thought to cause green sickness (anemia) in adolescent girls; also alluding to the moon's pallor.

8. In Ptolemaic astrology, crystalline spheres around the earth that carried the heavenly bodies in their rotations.
9. Turned up, revealing the whites at the bottoms.
1. Fall backward in gazing.

ROMEO [*to* JULIET] I take thee at thy word.[2]
Call me but love and I'll be new baptized.[3]
Henceforth I never will be Romeo.

JULIET What man art thou that, thus bescreened in night,
So stumblest on my counsel?°   *private thoughts*

95 ROMEO   By a name
I know not how to tell thee who I am.
My name, dear saint, is hateful to myself
Because it is an enemy to thee.
Had I it written, I would tear the word.

100 JULIET My ears have yet not drunk a hundred words
Of thy tongue's uttering, yet I know the sound.
Art thou not Romeo, and a Montague?

ROMEO Neither, fair maid, if either thee dislike.°   *displeases you*

JULIET How cam'st thou hither, tell me, and wherefore?

105 The orchard walls are high and hard to climb,
And the place death, considering who thou art,
If any of my kinsmen find thee here.

ROMEO With love's light wings did I o'erperch° these walls,   *fly over*
For stony limits cannot hold love out,

110 And what love can do, that dares love attempt.
Therefore thy kinsmen are no stop° to me.   *obstacle*

JULIET If they do see thee, they will murder thee.

ROMEO Alack, there lies more peril in thine eye
Than twenty of their swords. Look thou but sweet,

115 And I am proof° against their enmity.   *armed*

JULIET I would not for the world they saw thee here.

ROMEO I have night's cloak to hide me from their eyes,
And but° thou love me, let them find me here.   *unless*
My life were better ended by their hate

120 Than death prorogued,° wanting of° thy love.   *deferred / lacking*

JULIET By whose direction found'st thou out this place?

ROMEO By love, that first did prompt me to enquire.
He lent me counsel, and I lent him eyes.
I am no pilot, yet wert thou as far

125 As that vast shore washed with the farthest sea,
I should adventure° for such merchandise.   *voyage*

JULIET Thou knowest the mask of night is on my face,
Else would a maiden blush bepaint my cheek
For that which thou hast heard me speak tonight.

130 Fain° would I dwell on form,° fain, fain deny   *Gladly / propriety*
What I have spoke; but farewell, compliment.°   *polite convention*
Dost thou love me? I know thou wilt say 'Ay',
And I will take thy word. Yet if thou swear'st
Thou mayst prove false. At lovers' perjuries,

135 They say, Jove laughs. O gentle Romeo,
If thou dost love, pronounce° it faithfully;   *utter*
Or if thou think'st I am too quickly won,
I'll frown, and be perverse,° and say thee nay,   *contrary*
So thou wilt woo; but else,° not for the world.   *otherwise*

140 In truth, fair Montague, I am too fond,°   *infatuated*
And therefore thou mayst think my 'haviour light.°   *licentious; capricious*

---

2. At face value; as you have asked me to.   3. Given a new name; born into a new persona.

But trust me, gentleman, I'll prove more true
Than those that have more cunning to be strange.°   *distant*
I should have been more strange, I must confess,
145   But that thou overheard'st, ere I was ware,°   *aware*
My true-love passion. Therefore pardon me,
And not° impute this yielding to light love,   *do not*
Which the dark night hath so discoverèd.°   *revealed*
ROMEO   Lady, by yonder blessèd moon I vow,
150   That tips with silver all these fruit-tree tops—
JULIET   O swear not by the moon, th'inconstant moon
That monthly changes in her circled orb,°   *orbital sphere*
Lest that thy love prove likewise variable.
ROMEO   What shall I swear by?
JULIET   Do not swear at all,
155   Or if thou wilt, swear by thy gracious self,
Which is the god of my idolatry,[4]
And I'll believe thee.
ROMEO   If my heart's dear love—
JULIET   Well, do not swear. Although I joy in thee,
I have no joy of this contract° tonight.   *exchange of vows*
160   It is too rash, too unadvised,° too sudden,   *undeliberated*
Too like the lightning which doth cease to be
Ere one can say it lightens. Sweet, good night.
This bud of love by summer's ripening breath
May prove a beauteous flower when next we meet.
165   Good night, good night. As sweet repose and rest
Come to thy heart as that within my breast.
ROMEO   O, wilt thou leave me so unsatisfied?
JULIET   What satisfaction canst thou have tonight?
ROMEO   Th'exchange of thy love's faithful vow for mine.
170   JULIET   I gave thee mine before thou didst request it,
And yet I would it were° to give again.   *were available*
ROMEO   Wouldst thou withdraw it? For what purpose, love?
JULIET   But to be frank° and give it thee again.   *generous; honest*
And yet I wish but for the thing I have.
175   My bounty is as boundless as the sea,
My love as deep. The more I give to thee
The more I have, for both are infinite.
            [NURSE] *calls within*
I hear some noise within. Dear love, adieu.—
Anon,° good Nurse!—Sweet Montague, be true.   *One moment*
180   Stay but a little; I will come again.   [*Exit*]
ROMEO   O blessèd, blessèd night! I am afeard,
Being in night, all this is but a dream,
Too flattering-sweet to be substantial.
            [*Enter* JULIET *aloft*]
JULIET   Three words, dear Romeo, and good night indeed.
185   If that thy bent of love be honourable,
Thy purpose marriage, send me word tomorrow,
By one that I'll procure to come to thee,
Where and what time thou wilt perform the rite,
And all my fortunes at thy foot I'll lay,
190   And follow thee, my lord, throughout the world.

---

4. Not only was loving a man more than God idolatrous, but so was swearing oaths by anything other than God.

NURSE(*within*) Madam!
JULIET I come, anon. [*To* ROMEO] But if thou mean'st not well,
  I do beseech thee—
NURSE(*within*) Madam!
195 JULIET By and by I come.—
  To cease thy strife° and leave me to my grief. °striving
  Tomorrow will I send.
ROMEO So thrive my soul⁵—
JULIET A thousand times good night. *Exit*
200 ROMEO A thousand times the worse to want° thy light. °lack
  Love goes toward love as schoolboys from their books,
  But love from love, toward school with heavy looks.
    [*He is going*]
    Enter JULIET [*aloft*] *again*
JULIET Hist,° Romeo! Hist! O for a falconer's voice °(falconer's call)
  To lure this tassel-gentle⁶ back again.
205 Bondage⁷ is hoarse, and may not speak aloud,
  Else would I tear° the cave where Echo⁸ lies, °split with cries
  And make her airy tongue more hoarse than mine
  With repetition of my Romeo's name. Romeo!
ROMEO It is my soul that calls upon my name.
210 How silver-sweet sound lovers' tongues by night,
  Like softest music to attending ears!
JULIET Romeo!
ROMEO   My nyas?° °young hawk
JULIET   What o'clock tomorrow
  Shall I send to thee?
ROMEO   By the hour of nine.
JULIET I will not fail; 'tis twenty year till then.
215 I have forgot why I did call thee back.
ROMEO Let me stand here till thou remember it.
JULIET I shall forget, to have thee still° stand there, °always
  Rememb'ring how I love thy company.
ROMEO And I'll still stay, to have thee still forget,
220 Forgetting any other home but this.
JULIET 'Tis almost morning. I would have thee gone—
  And yet no farther than a wanton's° bird, °spoiled child's
  That lets it hop a little from his hand,
  Like a poor prisoner in his twisted gyves,° °fetters
225 And with a silk thread plucks it back again,
  So loving-jealous of his liberty.
ROMEO I would° I were thy bird. °wish
JULIET   Sweet, so would I.
  Yet I should kill thee with much cherishing.
  Good night, good night. Parting is such sweet sorrow
230 That I shall say good night till it be morrow.
ROMEO Sleep dwell upon thine eyes, peace in thy breast.
    [*Exit* JULIET]
  Would I were sleep and peace, so sweet to rest.
  Hence will I to my ghostly° sire's close° cell, °spiritual / small; private
  His help to crave, and my dear hap° to tell. *Exit* °fortune

---

5. On peril of damnation.
6. Tercel-gentle, a male peregrine falcon. Literally, a noble ("gentle") hawk.
7. Confinement within her family's home; duty owed

her family.
8. In classical legend, a woman who, scorned by Narcissus, wasted away with grief until only a voice remained to haunt empty caves.

2.2

Enter FRIAR [LAURENCE] *alone, with a basket*

FRIAR LAURENCE   The grey°-eyed morn smiles on the frowning night,   *pale blue*
Chequ'ring the eastern clouds with streaks of light,
And fleckled° darkness like a drunkard reels   *dappled*
From forth° day's path and Titan's¹ fiery wheels.   *out of*
5   Now, ere the sun advance° his burning eye   *brings up*
The day to cheer and night's dank dew to dry,
I must up-fill this osier cage° of ours   *willow basket*
With baleful weeds and precious-juicèd flowers.
The earth, that's nature's mother, is her tomb.
10 What is her burying grave, that is her womb,
And from her womb children of divers° kind   *several; varied*
We sucking on her natural bosom find,
Many for many virtues° excellent,   *healthful properties*
None but for some,² and yet all different.
15 O mickle° is the powerful grace° that lies   *great / divine beneficence*
In plants, herbs, stones, and their true qualities,
For naught° so vile that on the earth doth live   *nothing is*
But to the earth some special good doth give;
Nor aught so good but, strained° from that fair use,   *twisted*
20 Revolts from true birth, stumbling on abuse.³
Virtue itself turns vice being misapplied,
And vice sometime's by action dignified.

Enter ROMEO

Within the infant rind of this weak flower
Poison hath residence, and medicine power,
25 For this, being smelt, with that part° cheers each part;°   *act / bodily member*
Being tasted, slays all senses with the heart.
Two such opposèd kings encamp them still°   *always*
In man as well as herbs—grace and rude will;
And where the worser is predominant,
30 Full soon the canker° death eats up that plant.   *grub; cancer*
ROMEO   Good morrow, father.
FRIAR LAURENCE   *Benedicite.°*   *God bless you*
What early tongue so sweet saluteth me?
Young son, it argues a distempered head
So soon to bid good morrow to thy bed.
35 Care keeps his watch in every old man's eye,
And where care lodges, sleep will never lie,
But where unbruisèd° youth with unstuffed° brain   *fresh / unanxious*
Doth couch his limbs, there golden sleep doth reign.
Therefore thy earliness doth me assure
40 Thou art uproused with some distemp'rature;
Or if not so, then here I hit it right:
Our Romeo hath not been in bed tonight.
ROMEO   That last is true; the sweeter rest was mine.
FRIAR LAURENCE   God pardon sin!—Wast thou with Rosaline?
45 ROMEO   With Rosaline, my ghostly father? No,
I have forgot that name and that name's woe.
FRIAR LAURENCE   That's my good son; but where hast thou been then?

2.2 Location: A street in Verona.   2. None that is not excellent for some use.
1. Helios, a classical sun god, was descended from the   3. Turns from its intended benefits if it happens to be
Titans. He traveled across the sky in a chariot.   misused.

ROMEO   I'll tell thee ere thou ask it me again.
    I have been feasting with mine enemy,
50   Where on a sudden one hath wounded me
    That's by me wounded. Both our remedies
    Within thy help and holy physic° lies.   *medicine*
    I bear no hatred, blessèd man, for lo,
    My intercession° likewise steads° my foe.   *request / benefits*
55 FRIAR LAURENCE   Be plain, good son, and homely° in thy drift.   *direct*
    Riddling confession finds but riddling shrift.⁵   *absolution*
  ROMEO   Then plainly know my heart's dear love is set
    On the fair daughter of rich Capulet.
    As mine on hers, so hers is set on mine,
60   And all combined save what thou must combine
    By holy marriage. When and where and how
    We met, we wooed, and made exchange of vow
    I'll tell thee as we pass; but this I pray,
    That thou consent to marry us today.
65 FRIAR LAURENCE   Holy Saint Francis, what a change is here!
    Is Rosaline, that thou didst love so dear,
    So soon forsaken? Young men's love then lies
    Not truly in their hearts, but in their eyes.
    Jesu Maria, what a deal of brine
70   Hath washed thy sallow° cheeks for Rosaline!   *yellowed*
    How much salt water thrown away in waste
    To season° love, that of it doth not taste!   *preserve; flavor*
    The sun not yet thy sighs⁴ from heaven clears.
    Thy old° groans yet ring in mine ancient ears.   *former*
75   Lo, here upon thy cheek the stain doth sit
    Of an old tear that is not washed off yet.
    If e'er thou wast thyself, and these woes thine,
    Thou and these woes were all for Rosaline.
    And art thou changed? Pronounce this sentence° then   *maxim; verdict*
80   Women may fall when there's no strength in men.
  ROMEO   Thou chidd'st me oft for loving Rosaline.
  FRIAR LAURENCE   For doting, not for loving, pupil mine.
  ROMEO   And bad'st me bury love.
  FRIAR LAURENCE   Not in a grave
    To lay one in, another out to have.
85 ROMEO   I pray thee, chide me not. Her I love now
    Doth grace for grace and love for love allow.
    The other did not so.
  FRIAR LAURENCE   O, she knew well
    Thy love did read by rote, that could not spell.⁵
    But come, young waverer, come, go with me.
90   In one respect I'll thy assistant be;
    For this alliance may so happy prove
    To turn your households' rancour to pure love.
  ROMEO   O, let us hence! I stand° on sudden haste.   *depend; insist*
  FRIAR LAURENCE   Wisely and slow. They stumble that run fast.
                                                        Exeunt

---

4. The mist Romeo's exhalations produced.
5. Did recite the memorized phrases of love poetry, without understanding or meaning them.

2.3

Enter BENVOLIO *and* MERCUTIO

MERCUTIO Where the devil should this Romeo be? Came he
    not home tonight?°   *last night*

BENVOLIO Not to his father's. I spoke with his man.

MERCUTIO Why, that same pale° hard-hearted wench, that   *fair-skinned; frigid*
    Rosaline,

5   Torments him so that he will sure run mad.

BENVOLIO Tybalt, the kinsman to old Capulet,
    Hath sent a letter to his father's house.

MERCUTIO A challenge, on my life.

BENVOLIO   Romeo will answer° it.   *accept*

MERCUTIO Any man that can write may answer a letter.

10 BENVOLIO Nay, he will answer the letter's master, how he dares,
    being dared.

MERCUTIO Alas, poor Romeo, he is already dead—stabbed with
    a white wench's black eye, run through the ear with a love
    song, the very pin[1] of his heart cleft with the blind bow-boy's

15   butt-shaft;[2] and is he a man to encounter Tybalt?

BENVOLIO Why, what is Tybalt?

MERCUTIO More than Prince of Cats.[3] O, he's the courageous
    captain of compliments.° He fights as you sing pricksong:[4]   *formalities of dueling*
    keeps time, distance,[5] and proportion.° He rests his minim   *harmony; form*

20   rests:[6] one, two, and the third in your bosom; the very butcher
    of a silk button.[7] A duellist, a duellist; a gentleman of the very
    first house of the first and second cause.[8] Ah, the immortal
    passado, the *punto reverso*, the *hai*.[9]

BENVOLIO The what?

25 MERCUTIO The pox of° such antic,° lisping, affecting° phan-   *on / grotesque / affected*
    tasims,° these new tuners of accent![1] 'By Jesu, a very good blade, *bizarrely mannered men*
    a very tall° man, a very good whore.' Why° is not this a lamen-   *valiant / Why, now*
    table thing, grandsire, that we should be thus afflicted with
    these strange[2] flies,° these fashionmongers, these 'pardon-   *gaudy buzzers*

30   me's',[3] who stand so much on the new form that they cannot
    sit at ease on the old bench?[4] O, their bones, their bones![5]

              Enter ROMEO

BENVOLIO Here comes Romeo, here comes Romeo!

MERCUTIO Without his roe, like a dried herring.[6] O flesh, flesh,

---

2.3 Location: Scene continues.
1. Peg in the center of an archery target.
2. Blunt practice arrow, fit for children and hence for
Cupid.
3. Called Tybalt or Tibert in medieval stories of Rey-
nard the fox. "Catso," from the Italian word for "penis,"
was also a slang term for a rogue.
4. Sung from sheet music and thus more precise and
invariable than extempore or remembered music.
5. Musical intervals between notes; also, a set space to
be kept between combatants.
6. Short musical rests, referring to the brief strategic
pauses in a duel.
7. Alluding to the boast of an Italian fencing master in
London that he could "hit any Englishman with a
thrust upon any button."
8. *gentleman . . . cause:* superior practitioner of taking
up quarrels as duels. *first house:* the best fencing school.
cause: a reason that according to the etiquette of fencing
would require an honorable gentleman to seek a duel.

9. Italian fencing terms for a lunging sword thrust,
backhanded thrust, and thrust that reaches through.
1. These faddishly novel speakers, such as those
importing foreign phrases. A typical Renaissance English satire, here seemingly unaffected by the fact that
Italian is the native tongue of Verona.
2. Newfangled; foreign.
3. *pardon-me's:* the fastidiously mannered, affecting
the French *pardonnez-moi.*
4. *who . . . bench:* as if both Mercutio and Benvolio
were elderly ("grandsire"), viewing the decline of the
young. *stand:* insist. *form:* etiquette; fashion; bench.
5. *O . . . bones:* Aching on the austere furniture of their
predecessors; infected with the "bone disease," syphilis.
Mercutio may also be satirizing the courtly habit of crying "Bon! Bon!" (French for "good") as a kind of inane
flattery.
6. Emaciated, since the roe is removed in curing. This
leaves Romeo's name a mournful wail, "Me, O." He is
also missing his roe deer (female, named Rosaline).

how art thou fishified!⁷ Now is he for the numbers° that   *verses*
35 Petrarch⁸ flowed in. Laura to° his lady was a kitchen wench—   *compared to*
marry, she had a better love to berhyme her—Dido⁹ a dowdy,
Cleopatra a gypsy,¹ Helen and Hero² hildings° and harlots,   *hussies*
Thisbe³ a grey° eye or so, but not to the purpose.° Signor   *blue / of consequence*
Romeo, *bonjour*. There's a French salutation to your French
40 slop.° You gave us the counterfeit fairly last night.   *loose breeches*

ROMEO   Good morrow to you both. What counterfeit did I give
you?

MERCUTIO   The slip,⁴ sir, the slip. Can you not conceive?°   *understand*

ROMEO   Pardon, good Mercutio. My business was great, and in
45 such a case as mine a man may strain° courtesy.   *nearly abandon*

MERCUTIO   That's as much as to say such a case as yours con-
strains a man to bow in the hams.⁵

ROMEO   Meaning to curtsy.⁶

MERCUTIO   Thou hast most kindly hit⁷ it.

50 ROMEO   A most courteous exposition.

MERCUTIO   Nay, I am the very pink° of courtesy.   *nonpareil; carnation*

ROMEO   Pink for flower.°   *dianthus; vulva*

MERCUTIO   Right.

ROMEO   Why, then is my pump° well flowered.⁸   *shoe; penis*

55 MERCUTIO   Sure wit, follow me° this jest now till thou hast worn   *chase; respond to*
out thy pump, that when the single° sole of it is worn, the jest   *thin*
may remain, after the wearing, solely singular.°   *utterly unique*

ROMEO   O single-soled° jest, solely° singular for the singleness!°   *shoddy / only / foolishness*

MERCUTIO   Come between us, good Benvolio. My wits faints.⁹

60 ROMEO   Switch and spurs,¹ switch and spurs, or I'll cry a match.°   *claim a victory*

MERCUTIO   Nay, if our wits run the wild-goose chase,² I am done,
for thou hast more of the wild goose° in one of thy wits than I   *folly*
am sure I have in my whole five. Was I with° you there for the   *even with*
goose?

65 ROMEO   Thou wast never with me for anything when thou wast
not there for the goose.³

MERCUTIO   I will bite thee by the ear⁴ for that jest.

ROMEO   Nay, good goose, bite not.⁵

MERCUTIO   Thy wit is very bitter sweeting,° it is a most sharp   *apple*
70 sauce.°   *mockery*

ROMEO   And is it not then well served in to a sweet goose?

MERCUTIO   O, here's a wit of cheverel,° that stretches from an   *kid leather*
inch narrow to an ell broad.⁶

---

7. Gone pale and limp, turned into a herring. Fish, thought weak and relatively unnourishing, was the substitute for "flesh" (meat) during fasts.
8. Petrarch's sonnets addressed to Laura were the model for an English love-sonnet craze.
9. The beautiful queen of Carthage who fell in love with Aeneas but was deserted by him in Virgil's *Aeneid*.
1. A term of abuse. Gypsies were supposed to have come from Egypt, where Cleopatra was queen and lover of Julius Caesar and Mark Antony.
2. Helen's abduction by Paris initiated the Trojan War. Hero was Leander's lover in a tragic legend.
3. Beloved of Pyramus in a classical legend that parallels *Romeo and Juliet*. The young lovers, coming from hostile families, die as a result of a missed meeting and misinterpreted evidence.
4. Counterfeit coin.

5. Playing on "business" as "sexual intercourse" and "case" as "vagina." Mercutio suggests that Romeo needs to flex his buttocks or he may wind up with a leg-weakening venereal disease.
6. Pronounced the same as "courtesy."
7. Most truly guessed it; most truly sexually penetrated it.
8. Pinked, or decoratively perforated.
9. Treating the exchange of wit as a duel.
1. Flog your wits to a full gallop; continue.
2. A cross-country horse race in which the leader chose the course and the rest had to follow.
3. Silliness; whore's company.
4. Usually suggesting affectionate nibbling.
5. A proverbial cry for mercy, here used ironically.
6. That spreads itself very thin (an ell was forty-five inches).

ROMEO I stretch it out for that word 'broad', which, added to the
75 goose, proves thee far and wide a broad goose.[7]

MERCUTIO Why, is not this better now than groaning for love?
Now art thou sociable, now art thou Romeo, now art thou what
thou art by art° as well as by nature, for this drivelling love is *learning*
like a great natural° that runs lolling up and down to hide his *idiot*
80 bauble[8] in a hole.

BENVOLIO Stop there, stop there.

MERCUTIO Thou desirest me to stop in[9] my tale° against the *story; penis*
hair.[1]

BENVOLIO Thou wouldst else have made thy tale large.

85 MERCUTIO O, thou art deceived, I would have made it short, for
I was come to the whole depth of my tale, and meant indeed
to occupy the argument° no longer. *topic*

Enter NURSE, *and her man* [PETER]

ROMEO Here's goodly gear.[2]

BENVOLIO A sail, a sail![3]

90 MERCUTIO Two, two—a shirt° and a smock.° *man / woman*

NURSE Peter.

PETER Anon.° *At your service*

NURSE My fan, Peter.

MERCUTIO Good Peter, to hide her face, for her fan's the fairer
95 face.

NURSE God ye° good morrow,° gentlemen. *give you / morning*

MERCUTIO God ye good e'en,° fair gentlewoman. *afternoon*

NURSE Is it good e'en?

MERCUTIO 'Tis no less, I tell ye: for the bawdy hand of the dial
100 is now upon the prick° of noon. *mark; penis*

NURSE Out upon you,[4] what° a man are you! *what sort of*

ROMEO One, gentlewoman, that God hath made for himself to
mar.[5]

NURSE By my troth, it is well said. 'For himself to mar', quoth
105 a?° Gentlemen, can any of you tell me where I may find the *he*
young Romeo?

ROMEO I can tell you, but young Romeo will be older when you
have found him than he was when you sought him. I am the
youngest of that name, for fault° of a worse. *lack*

110 NURSE You say well.

MERCUTIO Yea, is the worst well? Very well took, i'faith, wisely,
wisely.

NURSE [*to* ROMEO] If you be he, sir, I desire some confidence
with you.

115 BENVOLIO She will endite[6] him to some supper.

MERCUTIO A bawd, a bawd, a bawd. So ho![7]

ROMEO What hast thou found?° *spotted; figured out*

---

7. A gross idiot; a licentious fellow; a goose fattened for
the table.
8. *that . . . bauble*: who runs with his tongue hanging
out to cover up a Jester's wand, at one end either
grotesquely carved or adorned with an inflated pig's
bladder; penis.
9. Cease; stuff in.
1. Against the grain; against the pubic hair.
2. Spoken ironically of Mercutio's witticisms or the
Nurse's voluminous appearance.
3. A sailor's cry upon sighting another ship.

4. An expression of indignation.
5. *One . . . mar*: combines two proverbial expressions.
"It is his to make or mar" suggests that Mercutio has
the free will to determine his own character. "He is a
man of God's making" places the blame for Mercutio's
character on God.
6. Deliberately substituted for "invite," to mock the
Nurse's erroneous use of "confidence" for "conference"
in the line above.
7. The cry of a hunter who has spotted his quarry.

MERCUTIO　No hare,° sir, unless a hare, sir, in a lenten pie,[8] that　　*prostitute*
is something stale and hoar ere it be spent.[9]
　　　　　　He walks by them and sings
120　　　　　　An old hare hoar
　　　　　　And an old hare hoar
　　　　　　　Is very good meat in Lent.
　　　　　　But a hare that is hoar
　　　　　　　Is too much for a score[1]
125　　　　　　When it hoars° ere it be spent.　　*turns moldy; whores*
　　Romeo, will you come to your father's? We'll to dinner thither.
ROMEO　I will follow you.
MERCUTIO　Farewell, ancient lady. Farewell, [*sings*] 'lady, lady,
　　lady'.[2]　　　　　　*Exeunt* MERCUTIO [*and*] BENVOLIO
130 NURSE　I pray you, sir, what saucy merchant° was this that was so　　*commoner*
　　full of his ropery?°　　　　　　　　　　　　　　　　　　　　*knavery*
ROMEO　A gentleman, Nurse, that loves to hear himself talk, and
　　will speak more in a minute than he will stand to° in a month.　*perform*
NURSE　An a° speak anything against me, I'll take him down° an　*If he / humble him*
135　a were lustier[3] than he is, and twenty such jacks;° an if I cannot,　*scoundrels*
　　I'll find those that shall. Scurvy knave! I am none of his flirt-
　　jills,° I am none of his skeans-mates.[4] [*To* PETER] And thou　*loose women*
　　must stand by, too, and suffer every knave to use me at his
　　pleasure.
140 PETER　I saw no man use you at his pleasure. If I had, my weapon
　　should quickly have been out; I warrant you, I dare draw as
　　soon as another man if I see occasion in a good quarrel, and
　　the law on my side.
NURSE　Now, afore God, I am so vexed that every part about me
145　quivers. Scurvy knave! [*To* ROMEO] Pray you, sir, a word; and,
　　as I told you, my young lady bid me enquire you out. What she
　　bid me say I will keep to myself, but first let me tell ye if ye
　　should lead her in a fool's paradise, as they say, it were a very
　　gross° kind of behaviour, as they say, for the gentlewoman is　*outrageous*
150　young; and therefore if you should deal double° with her, truly　*falsely; forcefully*
　　it were an ill thing to be offered to any gentlewoman, and very
　　weak° dealing.　　　　　　　　　　　　　　　　　　　　　　*poor*
ROMEO　Nurse, commend me to thy lady and mistress. I protest°　*swear*
　　unto thee—
155 NURSE　Good heart, and i'faith I will tell her as much. Lord,
　　Lord, she will be a joyful woman.
ROMEO　What wilt thou tell her, Nurse? Thou dost not mark°　*pay attention to*
　　me.
NURSE　I will tell her, sir, that you do protest;[5] which as I take it
160　is a gentlemanlike offer.
ROMEO　Bid her devise
　　Some means to come to shrift this afternoon,
　　And there she shall at Friar Laurence' cell
　　Be shrived° and married. [*Offering money*] Here is for thy pains.　*absolved after confession*
165 NURSE　No, truly, sir, not a penny.

---

8. Meat illicitly eaten during Lent by disguising it in a pie, just as the Nurse's unattractiveness hides whatever promiscuity she may practice.
9. Somewhat stale and moldy by the time the last of the rationed luxury is consumed.
1. Is too much to pay for.

2. Refrain to a ballad about a perfectly chaste woman, intended derisively.
3. Stronger, hornier.
4. Knife-wielding rogues.
5. The Nurse takes this as a marriage offer, probably confusing "protest" with "propose."

ROMEO   Go to, I say, you shall.

NURSE [*taking the money*]   This afternoon, sir. Well, she shall be there.

ROMEO   And stay, good Nurse, behind the abbey wall.
Within this hour my man shall be with thee
170   And bring thee cords made like a tackled stair,°   *a knotted ladder*
Which to the high topgallant[6] of my joy
Must be my convoy° in the secret night.   *means of conveyance*
Farewell. Be trusty, and I'll quit° thy pains.   *repay*
Farewell. Commend me to thy mistress.

175   NURSE   Now God in heaven bless thee! Hark you, sir.

ROMEO   What sayst thou, my dear Nurse?

NURSE   Is your man secret?° Did you ne'er hear say   *discreet*
'Two may keep counsel, putting one away'?

ROMEO   I warrant thee my man's as true as steel.

180   NURSE   Well, sir, my mistress is the sweetest lady.
Lord, Lord, when 'twas a little prating thing—
O, there is a nobleman in town, one Paris,
That would fain lay knife aboard;[7] but she, good soul,
Had as lief° see a toad, a very toad,   *gladly*
185   As see him. I anger her sometimes,
And tell her that Paris is the properer° man;   *more handsome*
But I'll warrant you, when I say so she looks
As pale as any clout° in the versal° world.   *sheet / entire*
Doth not rosemary[8] and Romeo begin
190   Both with a° letter?   *the same*

ROMEO   Ay, Nurse, what of that? Both with an 'R'.

NURSE   Ah, mocker—that's the dog's name.[9] 'R' is for the—no, I
know it begins with some other letter, and she hath the prettiest sententious[1] of it, of you and rosemary, that it would do
195   you good to hear it.

ROMEO   Commend me to thy lady.

NURSE   Ay, a thousand times. Peter!

PETER   Anon.

NURSE [*giving* PETER *her fan*]   Before,° and apace.°   *Lead / quickly*

Exeunt [PETER *and* NURSE *at one door,*
ROMEO *at another door*]

2.4

Enter JULIET

JULIET   The clock struck nine when I did send the Nurse.
In half an hour she promised to return.
Perchance she cannot meet him. That's not so.
O, she is lame! Love's heralds should be thoughts,
5   Which ten times faster glides than the sun's beams
Driving back shadows over louring° hills.   *dark; threatening*
Therefore do nimble-pinioned° doves draw Love,°   *winged / Venus*
And therefore hath the wind-swift Cupid wings.
Now is the sun upon the highmost hill°   *zenith*
10   Of this day's journey, and from nine till twelve
Is three long hours, yet she is not come.
Had she affections° and warm youthful blood   *passions*

6. The highest platform on a mast, from which the topgallant sail was handled.
7. One claimed a place at dinner by laying one's personal knife on the table ("board").
8. A token of remembrance, between lovers and also of

the dead.
9. "R"—the sound "arr"—was thought to resemble a
dog's snarl.
1. Blunder for "sentences"; sayings.
2.4 Location: Capulet's orchard.

She would be as swift in motion as a ball.
My words would bandy° her to my sweet love,   *volley (as in tennis)*
15 And his to me.
But old folks, many feign° as they were dead—   *act*
Unwieldy, slow, heavy, and pale as lead.

    Enter NURSE [*and* PETER]

O God, she comes! O honey Nurse, what news?
Hast thou met with him? Send thy man away.
20 NURSE   Peter, stay° at the gate.   [*Exit* PETER]   *wait*
JULIET   Now, good sweet Nurse—O Lord, why look'st thou sad?
Though news be sad, yet tell them merrily;
If good, thou sham'st the music of sweet news
By playing it to me with so sour a face.
25 NURSE   I am a-weary. Give me leave° a while.   *Let me alone*
Fie, how my bones ache. What a jaunce° have I!   *trotting about*
JULIET   I would thou hadst my bones and I thy news.
Nay, come, I pray thee speak, good, good Nurse, speak.
NURSE   Jesu, what haste! Can you not stay a while?
30 Do you not see that I am out of breath?
JULIET   How art thou out of breath when thou hast breath
To say to me that thou art out of breath?
The excuse that thou dost make in this delay
Is longer than the tale thou dost excuse.
35 Is thy news good or bad? Answer to that.
Say either, and I'll stay° the circumstance.°   *wait for / full details*
Let me be satisfied: is't good or bad?
NURSE   Well, you have made a simple° choice. You know not   *foolish*
how to choose a man. Romeo? No, not he; though his face be
40 better than any man's, yet his leg excels all men's; and for a
hand and a foot and a body, though they be not to be talked
on,° yet they are past compare. He is not the flower of cour-   *worth mentioning*
tesy, but, I'll warrant him, as gentle as a lamb. Go thy ways,[1]
wench. Serve God. What, have you dined at home?
45 JULIET   No, no. But all this did I know before.
What says he of our marriage—what of that?
NURSE   Lord, how my head aches! What a head have I!
It beats as it would fall in twenty pieces.
My back—
      [JULIET *rubs her back*]
            a' t'other side—ah, my back, my back!
50 Beshrew° your heart for sending me about   *Curse (mild oath)*
To catch my death with jauncing up and down.
JULIET   I'faith, I am sorry that thou art not well.
Sweet, sweet, sweet Nurse, tell me, what says my love?
NURSE   Your love says, like an honest° gentleman, and a courte-   *honorable*
55 ous, and a kind,° and a handsome, and, I warrant, a virtuous—   *true*
where is your mother?
JULIET   Where is my mother? Why, she is within.
Where should she be? How oddly thou repliest!
'Your love says like an honest gentleman
"Where is your mother?" '
60 NURSE   O, God's Lady° dear!   *Mary, Mother of God*
Are you so hot?° Marry come up, I trow.[2]   *impatient; aroused*

---

1. Off you go; do as you will do.
2. *Marry . . . trow:* an expression of indignant or amused surprise and reproof.

Is this the poultice for my aching bones?
Henceforward do your messages yourself.
JULIET Here's such a coil!° Come, what says Romeo? to-do
65 NURSE Have you got leave to go to shrift today?
JULIET I have.
NURSE Then hie° you hence to Friar Laurence' cell. hurry
There stays a husband to make you a wife.
Now comes the wanton° blood up in your cheeks. fickle; lustful
70 They'll be in scarlet straight° at any news. immediately
Hie you to church. I must another way,
To fetch a ladder by the which your love
Must climb a bird's nest soon, when it is dark.
I am the drudge, and toil in your delight,
75 But you shall bear the burden[3] soon at night.
Go, I'll to dinner. Hie you to the cell.
JULIET Hie to high fortune! Honest Nurse, farewell.
Exeunt [severally]°   separately

2.5

Enter FRIAR [LAURENCE] and ROMEO

FRIAR LAURENCE So smile the heavens upon this holy act
That after-hours with sorrow chide us not!
ROMEO Amen, amen. But come what sorrow can,
It cannot countervail the exchange of joy
5 That one short minute gives me in her sight.
Do thou but close° our hands with holy words, join
Then love-devouring death do what he dare—
It is enough I may but call her mine.
FRIAR LAURENCE These violent° delights have violent ends, sudden; intense
10 And in their triumph die like fire and powder,[1]
Which as they kiss consume. The sweetest honey
Is loathsome in his own deliciousness,
And in the taste confounds the appetite.[2]
Therefore love moderately. Long love doth so.
15 Too swift arrives as tardy as too slow.
Enter JULIET somewhat fast, and embraceth ROMEO
Here comes the lady. O, so light[3] a foot
Will ne'er wear out the everlasting flint.[4]
A lover may bestride the gossamers° spiders' threads
That idles in the wanton° summer air, playful
20 And yet not fall, so light is vanity.[5]
JULIET Good even° to my ghostly° confessor. evening / spiritual
FRIAR LAURENCE Romeo shall thank thee, daughter, for us both.
JULIET As much to him,[6] else is his thanks too much.
ROMEO Ah, Juliet, if the measure° of thy joy measuring vessel
25 Be heaped like mine, and that thy skill be more
To blazon° it, then sweeten with thy breath° describe; trumpet / speech
This neighbour air, and let rich music's tongue
Unfold the imagined° happiness that both unexpressed ideas of

---

3. Do the work; carry a lover; sing the theme of a duet, alluding to the sounds of lovemaking.
2.5 Location: Friar Laurence's cell.
1. Gunpowder. *triumph*: victory; celebration.
2. *The sweetest . . . appetite*: from the proverb "Too much honey cloys the stomach." *his*: its. *confounds*: overwhelms.
3. Swift; dainty; free of care; sexually open.
4. Will never endure or subdue the hard road of life.
5. Temporary worldly pleasure.
6. An equal amount. Both greetings consist of a kiss.

Receive in either by this dear encounter.

30 JULIET Conceit,° more rich in matter than in words,   *Imagination*
Brags of his substance,[7] not of ornament.°   *rhetoric; form*
They are but beggars that can count their worth,
But my true love is grown to such excess
I cannot sum up some of half my wealth.[8]

35 FRIAR LAURENCE Come, come with me, and we will make short work,
For, by your leaves, you shall not stay alone
Till Holy Church incorporate two in one.[9]   *Exeunt*

3.1

Enter MERCUTIO [*with his page*], BENVOLIO, *and men*

BENVOLIO I pray thee, good Mercutio, let's retire.
The day is hot, the Capels are abroad,°   *about*
And if we meet we shall not scape a brawl,
For now, these hot days, is the mad blood stirring.

5 MERCUTIO Thou art like one of these fellows that, when he
enters the confines of a tavern, claps me° his sword upon the   *claps me = claps*
table and says 'God send me no need of thee', and by the oper-
ation° of the second cup, draws him on the drawer[1] when   *effect*
indeed there is no need.

10 BENVOLIO Am I like such a fellow?

MERCUTIO Come, come, thou art as hot a jack° in thy mood as   *rogue*
any in Italy, and as soon moved° to be moody,[2] and as soon   *provoked / angry*
moody to be° moved.   *at being*

BENVOLIO And what to?

15 MERCUTIO Nay, an there were two such, we should have none
shortly, for one would kill the other. Thou—why, thou wilt
quarrel with a man that hath a hair more or a hair less in his
beard than thou hast. Thou wilt quarrel with a man for cracking nuts, having no other reason but because thou hast hazel
20 eyes. What eye but such an eye would spy out such a quarrel?
Thy head is as full of quarrels as an egg is full of meat,° and yet   *foodstuff*
thy head hath been beaten as addle[3] as an egg for quarrelling.   *rotten; confused*
Thou hast quarrelled with a man for coughing in the street
because he hath wakened thy dog that hath lain asleep in the
25 sun. Didst thou not fall out with a tailor for wearing his new
doublet before Easter;[2] with another for tying his new shoes
with old ribbon? And yet thou wilt tutor me from quarrelling!

BENVOLIO An I were so apt to quarrel as thou art, any man
should buy the fee-simple[3] of my life for an hour and a quarter.

30 MERCUTIO The fee simple? O, simple!°   *foolish*

Enter TYBALT, PETRUCCIO, *and others*

BENVOLIO By my head, here comes the Capulets.

MERCUTIO By my heel, I care not.

TYBALT [*to* PETRUCCIO *and the others*] Follow me close, for I
will speak to them.
[*To the Montagues*] Gentlemen, good e'en. A word with one
of you.

---

7. Wealth; content.
8. *I . . . wealth:* The amount is too large to be understood precisely.
9. Literally, put two into one body. Marriage mystically
united man and woman in "one flesh" (Genesis 2:2).
3.1 Location: A street in Verona.

1. Draws his sword on the server.
2. New fashions came out at Easter, after the austere
penitence of Lent.
3. Outright possession of land, usually an inherited
right; here, the whole value of Benvolio's life.

35   MERCUTIO   And but one word with one of us? Couple it with
        something: make it a word and a blow.
     TYBALT   You shall find me apt enough to that, sir, an you will
        give me occasion.
     MERCUTIO   Could you not take some occasion without giving?
40   TYBALT   Mercutio, thou consort'st° with Romeo.   associate
     MERCUTIO   'Consort'?° What, dost thou make us minstrels? An   Play in a band
        thou make minstrels of us, look to hear nothing but discords.
        [*Touching his rapier*] Here's my fiddlestick; here's that shall
        make you dance. Zounds°—'Consort'!   By God's wounds
45   BENVOLIO   We talk here in the public haunt° of men.   gathering place
        Either withdraw unto some private place,
        Or reason coldly° of your grievances,   dispassionately
        Or else depart.° Here all eyes gaze on us.   separate
     MERCUTIO   Men's eyes were made to look, and let them gaze.
50   I will not budge for no man's pleasure, I.
                    Enter ROMEO
     TYBALT   Well, peace be with you, sir. Here comes my man.
     MERCUTIO   But I'll be hanged, sir, if he wear your livery.[4]
        Marry, go before to field, he'll be your follower.°   servant; pursuer
        Your worship in that sense may call him 'man'.
55   TYBALT   Romeo, the love I bear thee can afford
        No better term than this: thou art a villain.°   base commoner; rogue
     ROMEO   Tybalt, the reason that I have to love thee
        Doth much excuse the appertaining rage
        To[5] such a greeting. Villain am I none.
60   Therefore, farewell. I see thou knowest me not.
     TYBALT   Boy, this shall not excuse the injuries
        That thou hast done me. Therefore turn and draw.
     ROMEO   I do protest I never injured thee,
        But love thee better than thou canst devise
65   Till thou shalt know the reason of my love.
        And so, good Capulet—which name I tender°   regard; love
        As dearly as mine own—be satisfied.
     MERCUTIO [*drawing*]   O calm, dishonourable, vile submission!
        Alla stoccado carries it away.[6]
70   Tybalt, you ratcatcher, come, will you walk?°   withdraw to fight
     TYBALT   What wouldst thou have with me?
     MERCUTIO   Good King of Cats, nothing but one of your nine
        lives. That I mean to make bold withal,° and, as you shall use   be so bold as to take
        me hereafter,[7] dry-beat° the rest of the eight. Will you pluck   soundly thrash
75   your sword out of his pilcher° by the ears? Make haste, lest mine   leather scabbard
        be about your ears ere it be out.
     TYBALT [*drawing*]   I am for you.
     ROMEO   Gentle Mercutio, put thy rapier up.
     MERCUTIO [*to* TYBALT]   Come, sir, your *passado*.°   forward thrust
        [*They fight*]
80   ROMEO [*drawing*]   Draw, Benvolio. Beat down their weapons.
        Gentlemen, for shame forbear this outrage.°   violence
        Tybalt, Mercutio, the Prince expressly hath
        Forbid this bandying° in Verona streets.   strife

---

4. Mercutio obnoxiously mistakes Tybalt's "my man"   appropriate anger at.
for "personal servant."   6. The rapier thrust wins the day.
5. *Doth . . . / To*: Permits me to put aside my otherwise 7. And, according to how you subsequently treat me.

Hold, Tybalt, good Mercutio.
    [ROMEO *beats down their points and rushes between*
    them.] TYBALT *under Romeo's arm thrusts* MERCUTIO *in*

85 PETRUCCIO   Away, Tybalt!
                Exeunt TYBALT [PETRUCCIO, *and their followers*]

MERCUTIO   I am hurt.
   A plague o' both your houses. I am sped.°   *finished*
   Is he gone, and hath nothing?

BENVOLIO   What, art thou hurt?

MERCUTIO   Ay, ay, a scratch, a scratch; marry, 'tis enough.
90   Where is my page? Go, villain. Fetch a surgeon.

                                 [*Exit page*]

ROMEO   Courage, man. The hurt cannot be much.

MERCUTIO   No, 'tis not so deep as a well, nor so wide as a church
   door, but 'tis enough. 'Twill serve. Ask for me tomorrow, and
   you shall find me a grave man. I am peppered,° I warrant, for   *done for*
95   this world. A plague o' both your houses! Zounds, a dog, a rat,
   a mouse, a cat, to scratch a man to death! A braggart, a rogue,
   a villain, that fights by the book of arithmetic![8] Why the devil
   came you between us? I was hurt under your arm.

ROMEO   I thought all for the best.

100 MERCUTIO   Help me into some house, Benvolio,
   Or I shall faint. A plague o' both your houses.
   They have made worms' meat of me.
   I have it, and soundly, too. Your houses!

                   Exeunt [*all but* ROMEO]

ROMEO   This gentleman, the Prince's near ally,°   *relative*
105   My very° friend, hath got this mortal hurt   *true*
   In my behalf, my reputation stained
   With Tybalt's slander—Tybalt, that an hour
   Hath been my cousin! O sweet Juliet,
   Thy beauty hath made me effeminate,
110   And in my temper[9] softened valour's steel.

     Enter BENVOLIO

BENVOLIO   O Romeo, Romeo, brave Mercutio is dead!
   That gallant spirit hath aspired° the clouds,   *ascended to*
   Which too untimely here did scorn the earth.

ROMEO   This day's black fate on more days doth depend.°   *hang over*
115   This but begins the woe others must end.

     Enter TYBALT

BENVOLIO   Here comes the furious Tybalt back again.

ROMEO   He gad° in triumph, and Mercutio slain?   *gallivanting*
   Away to heaven, respective lenity,°   *respectful lenience*
   And fire-eyed fury be my conduct° now.   *guide*
120   Now, Tybalt, take the 'villain' back again
   That late thou gav'st me, for Mercutio's soul
   Is but a little way above our heads,
   Staying for thine to keep him company.
   Either thou, or I, or both must go with him.

125 TYBALT   Thou, wretched boy, that didst consort° him here,   *accompany*
   Shalt with him hence.

---

8. By the numbers; according to a fencing manual.
9. Emotional makeup, here suggesting the hardened
character of a fighting man (*temper:* to harden steel). It
was believed that too much time with or passion for
women would cause a man to become effeminate.

ROMEO   This shall determine that.
              They fight. TYBALT *falls [and dies]*
BENVOLIO   Romeo, away, be gone.
    The citizens are up,° and Tybalt slain.   up in arms
    Stand not amazed.° The Prince will doom° thee death   stupefied / sentence
130 If thou art taken. Hence, be gone, away.
ROMEO   O, I am fortune's fool!°   dupe
BENVOLIO   Why dost thou stay?
                                            Exit ROMEO
              Enter CITIZENS [OF THE WATCH]
CITIZEN OF THE WATCH   Which way ran he that killed Mercutio?
    Tybalt, that murderer, which way ran he?
BENVOLIO   There lies that Tybalt.
CITIZEN OF THE WATCH   Up, sir, go with me.
135 I charge thee in the Prince's name, obey.
              Enter PRINCE, *old* MONTAGUE, CAPULET, *their* WIVES,
                  and all
PRINCE   Where are the vile beginners of this fray?
BENVOLIO   O noble Prince, I can discover° all   reveal
    The unlucky manage° of this fatal brawl.   handling
    There lies the man, slain by young Romeo,
140 That slew thy kinsman, brave Mercutio.
CAPULET'S WIFE   Tybalt, my cousin, O, my brother's child!
    O Prince, O cousin, husband! O, the blood is spilled
    Of my dear kinsman! Prince, as thou art true,
    For blood of ours shed blood of Montague!
    O cousin, cousin!
145 PRINCE   Benvolio, who began this fray?
BENVOLIO   Tybalt, here slain, whom Romeo's hand did slay.
    Romeo, that spoke him° fair,° bid him bethink   to him / courteously
    How nice° the quarrel was, and urged withal°   trivial / also
    Your high displeasure. All this—utterèd
150 With gentle breath, calm look, knees humbly bowed—
    Could not take° truce with the unruly spleen°   arrange / bitter mood
    Of Tybalt deaf to peace, but that he tilts
    With piercing steel at bold Mercutio's breast,
    Who, all as hot, turns deadly point to point,
155 And, with a martial scorn, with one hand beats
    Cold death aside,[1] and with the other sends
    It back to Tybalt, whose dexterity
    Retorts° it. Romeo, he cries aloud,   Returns
    'Hold, friends, friends, part!' and swifter than his tongue
160 His agent° arm beats down their fatal points,   effective
    And 'twixt them rushes, underneath whose arm
    An envious° thrust from Tybalt hit the life   A malicious
    Of stout° Mercutio, and then Tybalt fled,   courageous
    But by and by comes back to Romeo,
165 Who had but newly entertained° revenge,   considered
    And to't they go like lightning; for ere I
    Could draw to part them was stout Tybalt slain,
    And as he fell did Romeo turn and fly.
    This is the truth, or let Benvolio die.

---

1. *with . . . aside:* the two would have been fighting either with daggers in or cloaks rolled about their second hand
to ward off the other's weapon.

170　CAPULET'S WIFE　He is a kinsman to the Montague.
　　　　Affection makes him false; he speaks not true.
　　　　Some twenty of them fought in this black strife,
　　　　And all those twenty could but kill one life.
　　　　I beg for justice, which thou, Prince, must give.
175　　Romeo slew Tybalt; Romeo must not live.
　　　PRINCE　Romeo slew him, he slew Mercutio.
　　　　Who now the price of his° dear blood doth owe?　　　　　　　　　　(Mercutio's)
　　　MONTAGUE　Not Romeo, Prince. He was Mercutio's friend.
　　　　His fault° concludes but what the law should end,　　　　　　　　　　offense
　　　　The life of Tybalt.
180　PRINCE　　　　　　　And for that offence
　　　　Immediately we do exile him hence.
　　　　I have an interest in your hate's proceeding;
　　　　My blood° for your rude brawls doth lie a-bleeding.　　　　　　　　　　kinsman
　　　　But I'll amerce° you with so strong a fine　　　　　　　　　　penalize
185　　That you shall all repent the loss of mine.
　　　　I will be deaf to pleading and excuses.
　　　　Nor tears nor prayers shall purchase out° abuses.　　　　　　　　　　compensate for
　　　　Therefore use none. Let Romeo hence in haste,
　　　　Else, when he is found, that hour is his last.
190　　Bear hence this body, and attend our will.
　　　　Mercy but murders, pardoning those that kill.

　　　　　　　　　　　　　　　　　　　Exeunt [with the body]

3.2

　　　Enter JULIET alone
　　　JULIET　Gallop apace,° you fiery-footed steeds,　　　　　　　　　　quickly
　　　　Towards Phoebus' lodging.[1] Such a waggoner°　　　　　　　　　　charioteer
　　　　As Phaëton[2] would whip you to the west
　　　　And bring in cloudy night immediately.
5　　　Spread thy close° curtain, love-performing night,　　　　　　　　　　covering
　　　　That runaways'[3] eyes may wink,° and Romeo　　　　　　　　　　close
　　　　Leap to these arms untalked of and unseen.
　　　　Lovers can see to do their amorous rites
　　　　By their own beauties; or, if love be blind,
10　　It best agrees with night. Come, civil° night,　　　　　　　　　　solemn
　　　　Thou sober-suited matron all in black,
　　　　And learn me how to lose a winning match[4]
　　　　Played for a pair of stainless maidenhoods.
　　　　Hood my unmanned° blood, bating[5] in my cheeks,　　　　　　　　　　untamed; virgin
15　　With thy black mantle till strange° love grown bold　　　　　　　　　　shy
　　　　Think true love acted simple° modesty.　　　　　　　　　　mere; innocent
　　　　Come night, come Romeo; come, thou day in night,
　　　　For thou wilt lie upon the wings of night
　　　　Whiter than new snow on a raven's back.
20　　Come, gentle night; come, loving, black-browed night,
　　　　Give me my Romeo, and when I shall die

3.2 Location: Capulet's house.
1. Under the world to the west, where the sun god Phoebus Apollo was imagined to rest with his fiery chariot at night.
2. The son of Apollo, who rashly attempted to steer his father's chariot across the sky. To save the earth from scorching, Jupiter struck him down with a lightning bolt.

3. Either the runaway horses of the sun or roving and curious vagabonds.
4. *match:* competition. A husband and a marriage ("match") are won by surrendering.
5. Fluttering like a restless falcon before its eyes are covered with a "hood" to calm it.

Take him and cut him out in little stars,[6]
And he will make the face of heaven so fine
That all the world will be in love with night
25   And pay no worship to the garish sun.
O, I have bought the mansion of a love
But not possessed it, and though I am sold,[7]
Not yet enjoyed. So tedious is this day
As is the night before some festival
30   To an impatient child that hath new robes
And may not wear them.

> *Enter* NURSE, [*wringing her hands,*] *with the ladder of*
> *cords in her lap°*   bodice fold

O, here comes my Nurse,
And she brings news, and every tongue that speaks
But Romeo's name speaks heavenly eloquence.
Now, Nurse, what news? What, hast thou there
The cords that Romeo bid thee fetch?

35   NURSE [*putting down the cords*]   Ay, ay, the cords.
JULIET   Ay me, what news? Why dost thou wring thy hands?
NURSE   Ah, welladay!° He's dead, he's dead, he's dead!   alas
We are undone, lady, we are undone.
Alack the day, he's gone, he's killed, he's dead!
JULIET   Can heaven be so envious?°   spiteful; jealous
40   NURSE   Romeo can,
Though heaven cannot. O Romeo, Romeo,
Who ever would have thought it Romeo?
JULIET   What devil art thou that dost torment me thus?
This torture should be roared in dismal hell.
45   Hath Romeo slain himself? Say thou but 'Ay',
And that bare vowel 'I' shall poison more
Than the death-darting eye of cockatrice.[8]
I am not I if there be such an 'Ay',
Or those eyes shut that makes thee answer 'Ay'.
50   If he be slain, say 'Ay'; or if not, 'No'.
Brief sounds determine of my weal° or woe.   welfare
NURSE   I saw the wound, I saw it with mine eyes,
God save the mark,[9] here on his manly breast—
A piteous corpse, a bloody, piteous corpse—
55   Pale, pale as ashes, all bedaubed in blood,
All in gore° blood; I swoonèd at the sight.   clotted
JULIET   O, break, my heart, poor bankrupt, break at once!
To prison,[1] eyes; ne'er look on liberty.
Vile earth,[2] to earth resign; end motion° here,   movement; emotion
60   And thou and Romeo press[3] one heavy° bier!   weighty; sad
NURSE   O Tybalt, Tybalt, the best friend I had!
O courteous Tybalt, honest° gentleman,   honorable
That ever I should live to see thee dead!
JULIET   What storm is this that blows so contrary?
65   Is Romeo slaughtered, and is Tybalt dead?

---

6. *Take . . . stars:* an imagined transformation, based on those in Ovid's *Metamorphoses,* whereby Romeo also dies and is immortalized. Q4's reading of "he" for "I" (line 21) makes more immediate sense and is often accepted. Also, "die" could mean "have an orgasm."
7. *O . . . sold:* the image is inverted: first Juliet buys the mansion, and then she becomes the "sold" house.
8. A mythical serpent that kills by merely looking.

9. An apology for mentioning something unpleasant, but also emphasizing the fatal "mark" of the rapier.
1. Bankruptcy—to "break" financially—was punishable by imprisonment.
2. The despised body, echoing Ecclesiastes 12:7: "Then shall the dust return to the earth as it was."
3. Burden; embrace.

My dearest cousin and my dearer lord?
Then, dreadful trumpet, sound the general doom,[4]
For who is living if those two are gone?

NURSE   Tybalt is gone and Romeo banishèd.
70   Romeo that killed him—he is banishèd.

JULIET   O God, did Romeo's hand shed Tybalt's blood?

NURSE   It did, it did, alas the day, it did.

JULIET   O serpent heart hid with° a flow'ring° face!   by / lovely; benign
Did ever dragon keep° so fair a cave?   guard
75   Beautiful tyrant, fiend angelical!
Dove-feathered raven, wolvish-ravening lamb!
Despisèd substance of divinest show!°   appearance
Just opposite to what thou justly° seem'st—   precisely; rightfully
A damnèd saint, an honourable villain.
80   O nature, what hadst thou to do[5] in hell
When thou didst bower[6] the spirit of a fiend
In mortal paradise of such sweet flesh?
Was ever book containing such vile matter
So fairly bound? O, that deceit should dwell
85   In such a gorgeous palace!

NURSE   There's no trust, no faith, no honesty in men;
All perjured, all forsworn, all naught,° dissemblers all.   wicked
Ah, where's my man? Give me some aqua vitae.°   brandy
These griefs, these woes, these sorrows make me old.
Shame come to Romeo!

90 JULIET   Blistered be thy tongue
For such a wish! He was not born to shame.
Upon his brow shame is ashamed to sit,
For 'tis a throne where honour may be crowned
Sole monarch of the universal earth.
95   O, what a beast was I to chide at him!

NURSE   Will you speak well of him that killed your cousin?

JULIET   Shall I speak ill of him that is my husband?
Ah, poor my° lord, what tongue shall smooth° thy name   my poor / praise
When I, thy three-hours wife, have mangled it?
100   But wherefore, villain, didst thou kill my cousin?
That villain cousin would have killed my husband.
Back, foolish tears, back to your native spring!
Your tributary[7] drops belong to woe,
Which you, mistaking, offer up to joy.[8]
105   My husband lives, that Tybalt would have slain;
And Tybalt's dead, that would have slain my husband.
All this is comfort. Wherefore° weep I then?   Why
Some word there was, worser than Tybalt's death,
That murdered me. I would forget it fain,°   gladly
110   But O, it presses to my memory
Like damnèd guilty deeds to sinners' minds!
'Tybalt is dead, and Romeo banishèd.'
That 'banishèd', that one word 'banishèd'
Hath slain ten thousand Tybalts. Tybalt's death
115   Was woe enough, if it had ended there;

---

4. The Last Judgment announced with angel's trumpets.
5. What were you doing.
6. Lodge or enclose, suggesting a surrounding garden.

7. Tribute-paying; in-flowing.
8. Offer up to a joyful (and thus inappropriate) occasion.

Or, if sour woe delights in fellowship
And needly° will be ranked with⁹ other griefs,   *necessarily*
Why followed not, when she said 'Tybalt's dead',
'Thy father', or 'thy mother', nay, or both,
120   Which modern° lamentation might have moved?°   *ordinary / produced*
But with a rearward¹ following Tybalt's death,
'Romeo is banishèd'—to speak that word
Is father, mother, Tybalt, Romeo, Juliet,
All slain, all dead. 'Romeo is banishèd'—
125   There is no end, no limit, measure, bound,
In that word's death. No words can that woe sound.°   *utter; fathom*
Where is my father and my mother, Nurse?
NURSE   Weeping and wailing over Tybalt's corpse.
Will you go to them? I will bring you thither.
130   JULIET   Wash they his wounds with tears; mine shall be spent
When theirs are dry, for Romeo's banishment.
Take up those cords. Poor ropes, you are beguiled,°   *cheated*
Both you and I, for Romeo is exiled.
He made you for a highway to my bed,
135   But I, a maid, die maiden-widowèd.
Come, cords; come, Nurse; I'll to my wedding bed,
And death, not Romeo, take my maidenhead!
NURSE [*taking up the cords*]   Hie to your chamber. I'll find Romeo
To comfort you. I wot° well where he is.   *know*
140   Hark ye, your Romeo will be here at night.
I'll to him. He is hid at Laurence' cell.
JULIET [*giving her a ring*]   O, find him! Give this ring to my true knight,
And bid him come to take his last farewell.   *Exeunt* [*severally*]

3.3
Enter FRIAR [LAURENCE]
FRIAR LAURENCE   Romeo, come forth, come forth, thou fear-full man.
Affliction is enamoured of thy parts,°   *qualities*
And thou art wedded to calamity.
Enter ROMEO
ROMEO   Father, what news? What is the Prince's doom?°   *sentence*
5   What sorrow craves acquaintance at my hand
That I yet know not?
FRIAR LAURENCE   Too familiar
Is my dear son with such sour company.
I bring thee tidings of the Prince's doom.
ROMEO   What less than doomsday is the Prince's doom?
10   FRIAR LAURENCE   A gentler judgement vanished° from his lips: *escaped*
Not body's death, but body's banishment.
ROMEO   Ha, banishment? Be merciful, say 'death',
For exile hath more terror in his look,
Much more than death. Do not say 'banishment'.
15   FRIAR LAURENCE   Hence from Verona art thou banishèd.
Be patient,° for the world is broad and wide.   *able to endure*
ROMEO   There is no world without° Verona walls   *outside*
But purgatory, torture, hell itself.
Hence banishèd is banished from the world,
20   And world's exile is death. Then 'banishèd'

9. Will be accompanied by.   3.3 Location: Friar Laurence's cell.
1. *rearward*: rearguard action, with a pun on "afterword."

Is death mistermed. Calling death 'banishèd'
Thou cutt'st my head off with a golden axe,
And smil'st upon the stroke that murders me.

FRIAR LAURENCE   O deadly° sin, O rude unthankfulness!   *damnable*
25 Thy fault our law calls death,° but the kind Prince,   *a capital offense*
Taking thy part, hath rushed° aside the law   *forced*
And turned that black word 'death' to banishment.
This is dear mercy, and thou seest it not.

ROMEO   'Tis torture, and not mercy. Heaven is here
30 Where Juliet lives, and every cat and dog
And little mouse, every unworthy thing,
Live here in heaven and may look on her,
But Romeo may not. More validity,°   *health*
More honourable state, more courtship° lives   *courtly state; wooing*
35 In carrion flies than Romeo. They may seize
On the white wonder of dear Juliet's hand,
And steal immortal blessing from her lips,
Who, even in pure and vestal° modesty,   *virginal*
Still° blush, as thinking their own kisses¹ sin.   *Always*
40 But Romeo may not, he is banishèd.
Flies may do this, but I from this must fly.
They are free men, but I am banishèd.
And sayst thou yet that exile is not death?
Hadst thou no poison mixed, no sharp-ground knife,
45 No sudden mean° of death, though ne'er so mean,°   *method / ignoble*
But 'banishèd' to kill me—'banishèd'?
O friar, the damnèd use that word in hell.²
Howling attends it. How hast thou the heart,
Being a divine, a ghostly confessor,
50 A sin-absolver and my friend professed,
To mangle me with that word 'banishèd'?

FRIAR LAURENCE   Thou fond° mad man, hear me a little speak.   *foolish; infatuated*

ROMEO   O, thou wilt speak again of banishment.

FRIAR LAURENCE   I'll give thee armour to keep off that word—
55 Adversity's sweet milk, philosophy,
To comfort thee though thou art banishèd.

ROMEO   Yet 'banishèd'? Hang up° philosophy!   *Hang up = Hang*
Unless philosophy can make a Juliet,
Displant° a town, reverse a prince's doom,   *Uproot*
60 It helps not, it prevails not. Talk no more.

FRIAR LAURENCE   O, then I see that madmen have no ears.

ROMEO   How should they, when that wise men have no eyes?

FRIAR LAURENCE   Let me dispute° with thee of thy estate.°   *discuss / position*

ROMEO   Thou canst not speak of that thou dost not feel.
65 Wert thou as young as I, Juliet thy love,
An hour but° married, Tybalt murderèd,   *only*
Doting like me, and like me banishèd,
Then mightst thou speak, then mightst thou tear thy hair,
And fall upon the ground, as I do now,
[*He falls upon the ground*]
70 Taking the measure of an unmade grave.
Knock [*within*]

FRIAR LAURENCE   Arise, one knocks. Good Romeo, hide thyself.

---

1. Their touching each other in closing.   2. Because they are banished from heaven.

ROMEO   Not I, unless the breath of heartsick groans
　　　Mist-like enfold me from the search of eyes.
　　　　　Knock [within]
FRIAR LAURENCE   Hark, how they knock!—Who's there?—
　　　Romeo, arise.
75　　Thou wilt be taken.—Stay a while.—Stand up.
　　　　　[Still] knock [within]
　　　Run to my study.—By and by!—God's will,°　　　　　　　*By providence*
　　　What simpleness° is this?　　　　　　　　　　　　　　　　*stupidity*
　　　　　Knock [within]
　　　　　　　　　　I come, I come.
　　　Who knocks so hard? Whence come you? What's your will?
NURSE [*within*]³   Let me come in, and you shall know my errand.
　　　I come from Lady Juliet.
80　FRIAR LAURENCE [*opening the door*] Welcome then.
　　　　　Enter NURSE
NURSE   O holy friar, O tell me, holy friar,
　　　Where is my lady's lord? Where's Romeo?
FRIAR LAURENCE   There on the ground, with his own tears
　　　made drunk.
NURSE   O, he is even° in my mistress' case,°　　*exactly / condition; vagina*
85　Just in her case! O woeful sympathy,
　　　Piteous predicament! Even so lies she,
　　　Blubb'ring and weeping, weeping and blubb'ring.
　　　[*To* ROMEO]   Stand up, stand up, stand an° you be a man,　　　　　*if*
　　　For Juliet's sake, for her sake, rise and stand.
90　Why should you fall into so deep an O?°　　　　　　　*a groaning*
ROMEO [*rises*]   Nurse.
NURSE   　　　　　　Ah sir, ah sir, death's the end of all.⁴
ROMEO   Spak'st thou of Juliet? How is it with her?
　　　Doth not she think me an old° murderer,　　　　　　*a practiced*
　　　Now I have stained the childhood of our joy
95　With blood removed but little from her own?
　　　Where is she, and how doth she, and what says
　　　My concealed lady° to our cancelled° love?　　*secret wife / invalidated*
NURSE   O, she says nothing, sir, but weeps and weeps,
　　　And now falls on her bed, and then starts up,
100　And 'Tybalt' calls, and then on Romeo cries,
　　　And then down falls again.
ROMEO   　　　　　　As if that name
　　　Shot from the deadly level° of a gun　　　　　　　　　　*aim*
　　　Did murder her as that name's cursèd hand
　　　Murdered her kinsman. O tell me, friar, tell me,
105　In what vile part of this anatomy
　　　Doth my name lodge? Tell me, that I may sack
　　　The hateful mansion.
　　　　　He offers to stab himself, and NURSE *snatches the dagger
　　　　　away*
FRIAR LAURENCE   　　　　Hold° thy desperate hand.　　　　*Restrain*
　　　Art thou a man? Thy form cries out thou art.
　　　Thy tears are womanish, thy wild acts denote
110　The unreasonable° fury of a beast.　　　　　*incapable of reason*

---

3. Behind one of the doors at the back of the stage, rep-　　4. A proverbial consolation.
resenting the door of the cell.

Unseemly° woman in a seeming man,   *Inappropriate; immodest*
And ill-beseeming beast in seeming both!⁵
Thou hast amazed me. By my holy order,
I thought thy disposition better tempered.
115   Hast thou slain Tybalt? Wilt thou slay thyself,
And slay thy lady that in thy life lives
By doing damnèd° hate upon thyself?   *sinful*
Why rail'st thou on thy birth, the heaven, and earth,
Since birth° and heaven° and earth,° all three, do meet   *nobility / soul / body*
120   In thee at once, which thou at once wouldst lose?
Fie, fie, thou sham'st thy shape, thy love, thy wit,
Which like a usurer abound'st in all,
And usest none in that true use indeed
Which should bedeck thy shape, thy love, thy wit.⁶
125   Thy noble shape is but a form° of wax,   *figure*
Digressing° from the valour of a man;   *If it deviates*
Thy dear love sworn but hollow perjury,
Killing that love which thou hast vowed to cherish.
Thy wit, that ornament° to shape and love,   *necessary accessory*
130   Misshapen° in the conduct° of them both,   *Inept / management*
Like powder in a skilless soldier's flask
Is set afire by thine own ignorance,
And thou dismembered with thine own defence.°   *weapon*
What, rouse thee, man! Thy Juliet is alive,
135   For whose dear sake thou wast but lately dead:
There art thou happy. Tybalt would kill thee,
But thou slewest Tybalt: there art thou happy.
The law that threatened death becomes thy friend,
And turns it to exile: there art thou happy.
140   A pack of blessings light upon thy back,
Happiness courts thee in her best array,
But, like a mishavèd° and sullen wench,   *misbehaved*
Thou pout'st upon thy fortune and thy love.
Take heed, take heed, for such die miserable.
145   Go, get thee to thy love, as was decreed.
Ascend her chamber; hence and comfort her.
But look thou stay not till the watch be set,⁷
For then thou canst not pass to Mantua,
Where thou shalt live till we can find a time
150   To blaze° your marriage, reconcile your friends,°   *make public / kin*
Beg pardon of the Prince, and call thee back
With twenty hundred thousand times more joy
Than thou went'st forth in lamentation.
Go before, Nurse. Commend me to thy lady,
155   And bid her hasten all the house to bed,
Which heavy sorrow makes them apt unto.
Romeo is coming.
      NURSE   O Lord, I could have stayed here all the night
To hear good counsel! O, what learning is!
160   My lord, I'll tell my lady you will come.
      ROMEO   Do so, and bid my sweet prepare to chide.

5. An unnatural beast in seeming both man and unrea-
soning animal, or both man and woman.
6. *thou sham'st . . . wit:* you abound in looks, love, and
intelligence ("wit"), but you do not use them judiciously
and are therefore like a usurer who acquires money for
its own sake, without putting it to good use.
7. Until the guards take up their positions (at the city
gates).

NURSE *offers to go in, and turns again*
NURSE [*giving the ring*]   Here, sir, a ring she bid me give you, sir.
    Hie you,° make haste, for it grows very late.   *Hurry*
ROMEO   How well my comfort° is revived by this.   *Exit* NURSE   *happiness*
FRIAR LAURENCE   Go hence, good night, and here stands° all   *and on this depends*
165   your state.
    Either be gone before the watch be set,
    Or by the break of day disguised from hence.
    Sojourn in Mantua. I'll find out your man,
    And he shall signify from time to time
170   Every good hap° to you that chances here.   *event*
    Give me thy hand. 'Tis late. Farewell. Good night.
ROMEO   But that a joy past joy calls out on me,
    It were a grief so brief° to part with thee.   *hastily*
    Farewell.   *Exeunt* [*severally*]

3.4

Enter old CAPULET, *his* WIFE, *and* PARIS
CAPULET   Things have fall'n out, sir, so unluckily
    That we have had no time to move° our daughter.   *persuade*
    Look you, she loved her kinsman Tybalt dearly,
    And so did I. Well, we were born to die.
5   'Tis very late. She'll not come down tonight.
    I promise you, but for your company
    I would have been abed an hour ago.
PARIS   These times of woe afford no times to woo.
    Madam, good night. Commend me to your daughter.
10 CAPULET'S WIFE   I will, and know her mind early tomorrow.
    Tonight she's mewed up to¹ her heaviness.°   *sadness*
    PARIS *offers to go in, and* CAPULET *calls him again*
CAPULET   Sir Paris, I will make a desperate tender°   *a reckless offer*
    Of my child's love. I think she will be ruled
    In all respects by me. Nay, more, I doubt it not.
15   Wife, go you to her ere you go to bed.
    Acquaint her here of my son Paris' love,
    And bid her—mark you me?—on Wednesday next—
    But soft—what day is this?
PARIS   Monday, my lord.
CAPULET   Monday. Ha, ha! Well, Wednesday is too soon.
20   O' Thursday let it be. O' Thursday, tell her,
    She shall be married to this noble earl.
    Will you be ready? Do you like this haste?
    We'll keep° no great ado—a friend or two.   *celebrate with*
    For hark you, Tybalt being slain so late,°   *recently*
25   It may be thought we held° him carelessly,°   *regarded / indifferently*
    Being our kinsman, if we revel much.
    Therefore we'll have some half a dozen friends,
    And there an end. But what say you to Thursday?
PARIS   My lord, I would° that Thursday were tomorrow.   *wish*
30 CAPULET   Well, get you gone. O' Thursday be it, then.
    [*To his* WIFE]   Go you to Juliet ere you go to bed.
    Prepare her, wife, against° this wedding day.—   *for*

3.4 Location: Capulet's house.   1. Shut in with. The "mews" are hawks' housing.

Farewell, my lord.—Light to my chamber, ho!—
Afore me,² it is so very late that we
35   May call it early by and by. Good night.

Exeunt [CAPULET *and his* WIFE *at*
one door, PARIS *at another door*]

3.5

Enter ROMEO *and* JULIET *aloft* [*with the ladder of cords*]
JULIET   Wilt thou be gone? It is not yet near day.
It was the nightingale, and not the lark,
That pierced the fear-full hollow of thine ear.
Nightly she sings on yon pom'granate tree.
5   Believe me, love, it was the nightingale.
ROMEO   It was the lark, the herald of the morn,
No nightingale. Look, love, what envious° streaks   spiteful
Do lace the severing° clouds in yonder east.   parting
Night's candles are burnt out, and jocund day
10   Stands tiptoe on the misty mountain tops.
I must be gone and live, or stay and die.
JULIET   Yon light is not daylight; I know it, I.
It is some meteor that the sun exhaled¹
To be to thee this night a torchbearer
15   And light thee on thy way to Mantua.
Therefore stay yet. Thou need'st not to be gone.
ROMEO   Let me be ta'en, let me be put to death.
I am content, so° thou wilt have it so.   as long as
I'll say yon grey is not the morning's eye,
20   'Tis but the pale reflex° of Cynthia's° brow;   reflection / the moon's
Nor that is not the lark whose notes do beat
The vaulty heaven so high above our heads.
I have more care° to stay than will to go.   desire
Come, death, and welcome; Juliet wills it so.
25   How is't, my soul? Let's talk. It is not day.
JULIET   It is, it is. Hie hence, be gone, away.
It is the lark that sings so out of tune,
Straining° harsh discords and unpleasing sharps.²   Distorting; tuning up
Some say the lark makes sweet division;°   variations on a melody
30   This doth not so, for she divideth us.
Some say the lark and loathèd toad changed eyes.³
O, now I would they had changed voices, too,
Since arm from arm that voice doth us affray,°   frighten
Hunting thee hence with hunt's-up⁴ to the day.
35   O, now be gone! More light and light it grows.
ROMEO   More light and light, more dark and dark our woes.

Enter NURSE *hastily*

NURSE   Madam.
JULIET   Nurse.
NURSE   Your lady mother is coming to your chamber.
40   The day is broke; be wary, look about.   [*Exit*]

---

2. *Afore me:* A mild oath, or possibly an address to the
torchbearing servant to walk in front of him.
3.5 Location: The upper acting area represents Juliet's
window or balcony. The main stage represents
Capulet's orchard until line 59, then the interior of
Capulet's house from line 64.
1. Breathed. Meteors were thought to be impure
vapors that the sun had drawn up from the earth and

ignited and were usually considered bad omens.
2. Harsh sounds, too-high tones.
3. A folk explanation for the supposed ugliness of the
lark's eyes and the beauty of the toad's. *changed:*
exchanged.
4. Morning song used to wake the bride after the wedding night.

JULIET   Then, window, let day in, and let life out.

ROMEO   Farewell, farewell! One kiss, and I'll descend.

        He [lets down the ladder of cords and] goes down

JULIET   Art thou gone so, love, lord, my husband, friend?°   *lover*

    I must hear from thee every day in the hour,

45   For in a minute there are many days.

    O, by this count I shall be much in years

    Ere I again behold my Romeo.

ROMEO   Farewell.

    I will omit no opportunity

50   That may convey my greetings, love, to thee.

JULIET   O, think'st thou we shall ever meet again?

ROMEO   I doubt it not, and all these woes shall serve

    For sweet discourses° in our times to come.   *conversations*

JULIET   O God, I have an ill-divining° soul!   *a misfortune-predicting*

55   Methinks I see thee, now thou art so low,

    As one dead in the bottom of a tomb.

    Either my eyesight fails, or thou look'st pale.

ROMEO   And trust me, love, in my eye so do you.

    Dry sorrow drinks our blood.⁵ Adieu, adieu.   ***Exit***

JULIET *[pulling up the ladder and weeping]*   O fortune, fortune,

60   all men call thee fickle.

    If thou art fickle, what dost thou with him

    That is renowned for faith?° Be fickle, fortune,   *fidelity*

    For then I hope thou wilt not keep him long,

    But send him back.

        Enter [CAPULET'S WIFE below]

CAPULET'S WIFE   Ho, daughter, are you up?

65 JULIET   Who is't that calls? It is my lady mother.

    Is she not down° so late, or up so early?   *in bed*

    What unaccustomed cause procures° her hither?   *brings*

        She goes down [and enters below]

CAPULET'S WIFE   Why, how now, Juliet?

JULIET   Madam, I am not well.

CAPULET'S WIFE   Evermore weeping for your cousin's death?

70   What, wilt thou wash him from his grave with tears?

    An if thou couldst, thou couldst not make him live,

    Therefore have done. Some grief shows much of love,

    But much of grief shows still° some want° of wit.   *always / lack*

JULIET   Yet let me weep for such a feeling° loss.   *profound*

75 CAPULET'S WIFE   So shall you feel° the loss, but not the friend°   *experience; touch / kin*

    Which you so weep for.

JULIET   Feeling so the loss,

    I cannot choose but ever weep the friend.°   *lover*

CAPULET'S WIFE   Well, girl, thou weep'st not so much for his death

    As that the villain lives which slaughtered him.

JULIET   What villain, madam?

80 CAPULET'S WIFE   That same villain Romeo.

JULIET *[aside]*   Villain and he be many miles asunder.

    [To her mother] God pardon him—I do, with all my heart,

    And yet no man like° he doth grieve my heart.   *so much as; resembling*

CAPULET'S WIFE   That is because the traitor murderer lives.

---

5. *Dry . . . blood:* Each sigh supposedly cost the heart a drop of blood. Thus, the lovers are pale. *Dry:* Thirsty.

85 JULIET Ay, madam, from the reach of these my hands.
       Would none but I might venge my cousin's death.
     CAPULET'S WIFE We will have vengeance for it, fear thou not.
       Then weep no more. I'll send to one in Mantua,
       Where that same banished runagate° doth live,   *runaway; fugitive*
90   Shall give him such an unaccustomed dram
       That he shall soon keep Tybalt company;
       And then I hope thou wilt be satisfied.°   *sufficiently avenged*
     JULIET Indeed, I never shall be satisfied
       With Romeo till I behold him, dead,
95   Is my poor heart[6] so for a kinsman vexed.
       Madam, if you could find out but a man
       To bear a poison, I would temper° it   *mix; dilute*
       That Romeo should, upon receipt thereof,
       Soon sleep in quiet. O, how my heart abhors
100   To hear him named and cannot come to him
       To wreak the love I bore my cousin
       Upon his body that hath slaughtered him!
     CAPULET'S WIFE Find thou the means, and I'll find such a man.
       But now I'll tell thee joyful tidings, girl.
105 JULIET And joy comes well in such a needy time.
       What are they, I beseech your ladyship?
     CAPULET'S WIFE Well, well, thou hast a careful° father, child;   *solicitous*
       One who, to put thee from thy heaviness,
       Hath sorted out a sudden° day of joy   *chosen an immediate*
110   That thou expect'st not, nor I looked not for.
     JULIET Madam, in happy° time. What day is that?   *at a fortunate*
     CAPULET'S WIFE Marry, my child, early next Thursday morn
       The gallant, young, and noble gentleman
       The County Paris at Saint Peter's Church
115   Shall happily make thee there a joyful bride.
     JULIET Now, by Saint Peter's Church, and Peter too,
       He shall not make me there a joyful bride.
       I wonder° at this haste, that I must wed   *am astonished*
       Ere he that should be husband comes to woo.
120   I pray you, tell my lord and father, madam,
       I will not marry yet; and when I do, I swear
       It shall be Romeo—whom you know I hate—
       Rather than Paris. These are news indeed.
             Enter old CAPULET *and* NURSE
     CAPULET'S WIFE Here comes your father. Tell him so yourself,
125   And see how he will take it at your hands.
     CAPULET When the sun sets, the earth doth drizzle° dew, *weep out*
       But for the sunset of my brother's son
       It rains downright.
       How now, a conduit,° girl? What, still in tears?   *fountain*
130   Evermore show'ring? In one little body
       Thou counterfeit'st a barque,° a sea, a wind,   *represent a ship*
       For still thy eyes—which I may call the sea—
       Do ebb and flow with tears. The barque thy body is,
       Sailing in this salt flood; the winds thy sighs,
135   Who,° raging with thy tears and they with them,   *Which*

---

6. *till . . . heart:* Juliet allows her mother to understand that she will not be satisfied "till I behold him dead," while privately meaning that until she beholds him, "dead is my poor heart."

       Without a sudden calm will overset
       Thy tempest-tossèd body.—How now, wife?
       Have you delivered to her our decree?
    CAPULET'S WIFE   Ay, sir, but she will none,° she gives you thanks.   *not agree*
140   I would the fool° were married to her grave.   *peevish child*
    CAPULET   Soft, take me with you,[7] take me with you, wife.
       How, will she none? Doth she not give us thanks?
       Is she not proud?° Doth she not count her blest,   *gratified*
       Unworthy as she is, that we have wrought°   *contrived for*
145   So worthy a gentleman to be her bride?°   *bridegroom*
    JULIET   Not proud you have, but thankful that you have.
       Proud can I never be of what I hate,
       But thankful even for hate° that is meant love.°   *a hateful thing / as love*
    CAPULET   How, how, how, how—chopped logic?° What is this?   *mere sophistry*
150   'Proud', and 'I thank you', and 'I thank you not',
       And yet 'not proud'? Mistress minion,° you,   *spoiled child*
       Thank me no thankings, nor proud me no prouds,
       But fettle° your fine joints 'gainst° Thursday next   *prepare / for*
       To go with Paris to Saint Peter's Church,
155   Or I will drag thee on a hurdle[8] thither.
       Out,[9] you green-sickness carrion! Out, you baggage,
       You tallow-face!
    CAPULET'S WIFE   Fie, fie, what, are you mad?
    JULIET (*kneels down*)   Good father, I beseech you on my knees,
       Hear me with patience but to speak a word.
160   CAPULET   Hang thee, young baggage, disobedient wretch!
       I tell thee what: get thee to church o' Thursday,
       Or never after look me in the face.
       Speak not, reply not, do not answer me.
       [JULIET *rises*]
       My fingers itch. Wife, we scarce thought us blest
165   That God had lent us but this only child,
       But now I see this one is one too much,
       And that we have a curse in having her.
       Out on her, hilding!°   *hussy*
    NURSE   God in heaven bless her!
       You are to blame, my lord, to rate° her so.   *berate*
170   CAPULET   And why, my lady Wisdom? Hold your tongue,
       Good Prudence. Smatter° with your gossips,° go!   *Chatter / cronies*
    NURSE   I speak no treason.
    CAPULET   O, God-i'-good-e'en!°   *for God's sake*
    NURSE   May not one speak?
    CAPULET   Peace, you mumbling fool,
       Utter your gravity° o'er a gossip's bowl,°   *wisdom / drinking bowl*
       For here we need it not.
175   CAPULET'S WIFE   You are too hot.°   *irascible, rash*
    CAPULET   God's bread,° it makes me mad. Day, night;   *By the communion bread*
       work, play;
       Alone, in company, still my care° hath been   *business*
       To have her matched; and having now provided
       A gentleman of noble parentage,

---

7. Not so fast, let me understand you.
8. A sledge used to draw traitors through the streets to
execution.
9. An expression of disgust and impatience.

180	Of fair demesnes,° youthful, and nobly lined,°	*estates / descended*
	Stuffed, as they say, with honourable parts,°	*qualities*
	Proportioned as one's thought would wish a man[1]—	
	And then to have a wretched puling fool,	
	A whining maumet,° in her fortune's tender,[2]	*puppet*
185	To answer 'I'll not wed, I cannot love;	
	I am too young, I pray you pardon me'!	
	But an you will not wed, I'll pardon you!°	*excuse you (to leave)*
	Graze where you will, you shall not house with me.	
	Look to't, think on't. I do not use° to jest.	*make it customary*
190	Thursday is near. Lay hand on heart.[3] Advise.°	*Consider*
	An you be mine, I'll give you to my friend.	
	An you be not, hang, beg, starve, die in the streets,	
	For, by my soul, I'll ne'er acknowledge thee,	
	Nor what is mine shall never do thee good.	
195	Trust to't. Bethink you. I'll not be forsworn. *Exit*	
	JULIET Is there no pity sitting in the clouds	
	That sees into the bottom of my grief ?	
	O sweet my° mother, cast me not away!	*my sweet*
	Delay this marriage for a month, a week;	
200	Or if you do not, make the bridal bed	
	In that dim monument° where Tybalt lies.	*sepulchre*
	CAPULET'S WIFE Talk not to me, for I'll not speak a word.	
	Do as thou wilt, for I have done with thee. *Exit*	
	JULIET O, God—O Nurse, how shall this be prevented?	
205	My husband is on earth, my faith° in heaven.	*marriage vows*
	How shall that faith return again to earth	
	Unless that husband send it me from heaven	
	By leaving earth?[4] Comfort me, counsel me.	
	Alack, alack, that heaven should practise stratagems	
210	Upon so soft a subject as myself!	
	What sayst thou? Hast thou not a word of joy?	
	Some comfort, Nurse.	
	NURSE Faith, here it is: Romeo	
	Is banishèd, and all the world to nothing[5]	
	That he dares ne'er come back to challenge you,	
215	Or if he do, it needs must be by stealth.	
	Then, since the case so stands as now it doth,	
	I think it best you married with the County.	
	O, he's a lovely gentleman!	
	Romeo's a dishclout° to him. An eagle, madam,	*dishcloth*
220	Hath not so green, so quick, so fair an eye	
	As Paris hath. Beshrew° my very heart,	*Curse*
	I think you are happy° in this second match,	*lucky*
	For it excels your first; or if it did not,	
	Your first is dead, or 'twere as good he were	
225	As living hence and you no use of him.	
	JULIET Speak'st thou from thy heart?	
	NURSE And from my soul, too, else beshrew them both	
	JULIET Amen.	
	NURSE What?	

1. Shaped as handsomely as you can imagine.
2. When good fortune is offered her.
3. Ascertain your feelings.
4. *How . . . earth:* How can I swear marriage vows

again unless Romeo dies first, thus releasing me from my vows to him?
5. And it's a sure bet.

230 JULIET   Well, thou hast comforted me marvellous much.
      Go in; and tell my lady I am gone,
      Having displeased my father, to Laurence' cell
      To make confession and to be absolved.
   NURSE   Marry, I will; and this is wisely done.   *[Exit]*
235 JULIET (*looks after* NURSE)   Ancient damnation![6] O most wicked fiend!
      Is it more sin to wish me thus forsworn,
      Or to dispraise my lord with that same tongue
      Which she hath praised him with above compare
      So many thousand times? Go, counsellor!
240   Thou and my bosom° henceforth shall be twain.°   *heart's contents / divided*
      I'll to the friar, to know his remedy.
      If all else fail, myself have power to die.   *Exit*

4.1

Enter FRIAR [LAURENCE] *and County* PARIS

FRIAR LAURENCE   On Thursday, sir? The time is very short.
PARIS   My father Capulet will have it so,
      And I am nothing slow[1] to slack his haste.
FRIAR LAURENCE   You say you do not know the lady's mind?
5   Uneven is the course.[2] I like it not.
PARIS   Immoderately she weeps for Tybalt's death,
      And therefore have I little talked of love,
      For Venus smiles not in a house of tears.
      Now, sir, her father counts it dangerous
10   That she do give her sorrow so much sway,
      And in his wisdom hastes our marriage
      To stop the inundation of her tears,
      Which, too much minded° by herself alone,   *brooded over*
      May be put from her by society.°   *company*
15   Now do you know the reason of this haste.
FRIAR LAURENCE [*aside*]   I would I knew not why it should be slowed.—
        Enter JULIET
      Look, sir, here comes the lady toward my cell.
PARIS   Happily met, my lady and my wife.
JULIET   That may be, sir, when I may be a wife.
20 PARIS   That 'may be' must be, love, on Thursday next.
JULIET   What must be shall be.
FRIAR LAURENCE   That's a certain text.
PARIS   Come you to make confession to this father?
JULIET   To answer that, I should confess to you.
PARIS   Do not deny to him that you love me.
25 JULIET   I will confess to you that I love him.
PARIS   So will ye, I am sure, that you love me.
JULIET   If I do so, it will be of more price,°   *value*
      Being spoke behind your back, than to your face.
PARIS   Poor soul, thy face is much abused with tears.
30 JULIET   The tears have got small victory by that,
      For it was bad enough before their spite.°   *injury*
PARIS   Thou wrong'st it more than tears with that report.
JULIET   That is no slander, sir, which is a truth,
      And what I spake, I spake it to my face.

---

6. Damnable old woman (with a hint of "original sin").   1. Not reluctant; not trying to drag behind him.
4.1. Location: Friar Laurence's cell.   2. The plan is irregular; this is a tricky road to follow.

35 PARIS Thy face is mine, and thou hast slandered it.
    JULIET It may be so, for it is not mine own.³—
         Are you at leisure, holy father, now,
         Or shall I come to you at evening mass?
    FRIAR LAURENCE My leisure serves me, pensive° daughter, now.   *sorrowful*
40   My lord, we must entreat the time alone.
    PARIS God shield° I should disturb devotion!—   *forbid*
         Juliet, on Thursday early will I rouse ye.
         [*Kissing her*] Till then, adieu, and keep this holy kiss.   *Exit*
    JULIET O, shut the door, and when thou hast done so,
45   Come weep with me, past hope, past cure, past help!
    FRIAR LAURENCE O Juliet, I already know thy grief.°   *grievous situation*
         It strains me past the compass° of my wits.   *limit*
         I hear thou must, and nothing may prorogue° it,   *postpone*
         On Thursday next be married to this County.
50 JULIET Tell me not, friar, that thou hear'st of this,
         Unless thou tell me how I may prevent it.
         If in thy wisdom thou canst give no help,
         Do thou but call my resolution wise,
              [*She draws a knife*]
         And with this knife I'll help it presently.°   *immediately*
55   God joined my heart and Romeo's, thou our hands,
         And ere this hand, by thee to Romeo's sealed,
         Shall be the label⁴ to another deed,
         Or my true heart with treacherous revolt
         Turn to another, this shall slay them both.
60   Therefore, out of thy long-experienced time,
         Give me some present counsel; or, behold,
         'Twixt my extremes° and me this bloody knife   *extreme difficulties*
         Shall play the umpire, arbitrating that
         Which the commission° of thy years and art°   *authority / learning*
65   Could to no issue of true honour bring.
         Be not so long to speak. I long to die
         If what thou speak'st speak not of remedy.
    FRIAR LAURENCE Hold, daughter, I do spy a kind of hope
         Which craves as desperate° an execution⁵   *reckless*
70   As that is desperate° which we would prevent.   *hopeless*
         If, rather than to marry County Paris,
         Thou hast the strength of will to slay thyself,
         Then is it likely thou wilt undertake
         A thing like death to chide away this shame,
75   That cop'st° with death himself to scape from it;°   *Who wrestles / (shame)*
         And, if thou dar'st, I'll give thee remedy.
    JULIET O, bid me leap, rather than marry Paris,
         From off the battlements of any tower,
         Or walk in thievish° ways, or bid me lurk   *thief-infested*
80   Where serpents are. Chain me with roaring bears,
         Or hide me nightly in a charnel house,°   *burial vault*
         O'ercovered quite with dead men's rattling bones,
         With reeky° shanks and yellow chapless⁶ skulls;   *foully damp*

---

3. Because it belongs to Romeo; also because Juliet, in
her ambiguous replies, is not showing Paris her true face.
4. Ribbon attaching a seal to a legal document (deed),
and so a pledge confirming another marriage.
5. A performance; a killing.
6. Without a lower jaw.

Or bid me go into a new-made grave
85 And hide me with a dead man in his tomb—
Things that, to hear them told, have made me tremble—
And I will do it without fear or doubt,°   *dread; hesitation*
To live an unstained wife to my sweet love.
FRIAR LAURENCE   Hold, then; go home, be merry, give consent
90 To marry Paris. Wednesday is tomorrow.
Tomorrow night look° that thou lie alone.   *be sure*
Let not the Nurse lie with thee in thy chamber.
Take thou this vial, being then in bed,
And this distilling° liquor drink thou off,   *permeating*
95 When presently through all thy veins shall run
A cold and drowsy humour;° for no pulse   *bodily fluid*
Shall keep his° native progress, but surcease.°   *its / cease*
No warmth, no breath shall testify thou livest.
The roses in thy lips and cheeks shall fade
100 To wanny° ashes, thy eyes' windows° fall   *pale / lids*
Like death when he shuts up the day of life.
Each part, deprived of supple government,°   *control of movement*
Shall, stiff and stark and cold, appear like death;
And in this borrowed likeness of shrunk death
105 Thou shalt continue two-and-forty hours,
And then awake as from a pleasant sleep.
Now, when the bridegroom in the morning comes
To rouse thee from thy bed, there art thou dead.
Then, as the manner of our country is,
110 In thy best robes, uncovered on the bier
Thou shalt be borne to that same ancient vault
Where all the kindred of the Capulets lie.
In the meantime, against° thou shalt awake,   *in preparation for when*
Shall Romeo by my letters know our drift,°   *scheme*
115 And hither shall he come, and he and I
Will watch° thy waking, and that very night   *keep vigil for*
Shall Romeo bear thee hence to Mantua.
And this shall free thee from this present shame,
If no inconstant toy° nor womanish fear   *fickle whim*
120 Abate thy valour in the acting it.
JULIET   Give me, give me! O, tell not me of fear!
FRIAR LAURENCE [*giving her the vial*]   Hold, get you gone. Be
    strong and prosperous
In this resolve. I'll send a friar with speed
To Mantua with my letters° to thy lord.   *letter*
125 JULIET   Love give me strength, and strength shall help afford.
Farewell, dear father.   *Exeunt* [*severally*]

4.2

Enter old CAPULET, *his* WIFE, NURSE, *and two or three*
    SERVINGMEN
CAPULET [*giving a* SERVINGMAN *a paper*]   So many guests invite
    as here are writ.   [*Exit* SERVINGMAN]
[*To the other* SERVINGMAN] Sirrah, go hire me twenty
    cunning° cooks.   *skillful*

4.2 Location: Capulet's house.

SERVINGMAN You shall have none ill, sir, for I'll try° if they can   test
  lick their fingers.
5 CAPULET How canst thou try them so?
SERVINGMAN Marry, sir, 'tis an ill cook that cannot lick his own
  fingers, therefore he that cannot lick his fingers goes not with
  me.
CAPULET Go, be gone.   [Exit SERVINGMAN]
10 We shall be much unfurnished° for this time.   unprepared
  [To NURSE] What, is my daughter gone to Friar Laurence?
NURSE Ay, forsooth.
CAPULET Well, he may chance to do some good on her.
  A peevish,° self-willed harlotry° it° is.   An obstinate / brat / she
  Enter JULIET
15 NURSE See where she comes from shrift° with merry look.   absolution
CAPULET [to JULIET] How now, my headstrong, where have you
    been gadding?
JULIET Where I have learned me to repent the sin
  Of disobedient opposition
  To you and your behests, and am enjoined
20 By holy Laurence to fall prostrate here
  To beg your pardon. (She kneels down) Pardon, I beseech you.
  Henceforward I am ever ruled by you.
CAPULET [to NURSE] Send for the County; go tell him of this.
  I'll have this knot knit up tomorrow morning.
25 JULIET I met the youthful lord at Laurence' cell,
  And gave him what becoming° love I might,   suitable
  Not stepping o'er the bounds of modesty.
CAPULET Why, I am glad on't.° This is well. Stand up.   of it
  [JULIET rises]
  This is as't should be. Let me see the County.
30 [To NURSE] Ay, marry, go, I say, and fetch him hither.
  Now, afore God, this reverend holy friar,
  All our whole city is much bound to him.
JULIET Nurse, will you go with me into my closet°   chamber
  To help me sort such needful ornaments
35 As you think fit to furnish me tomorrow?
CAPULET'S WIFE No, not till Thursday. There is time enough.
CAPULET Go, Nurse, go with her. We'll to church tomorrow.
                                        Exeunt JULIET and NURSE
CAPULET'S WIFE We shall be short in our provision.
  'Tis now near night.
CAPULET   Tush, I will stir about,
40 And all things shall be well, I warrant thee, wife.
  Go thou to Juliet, help to deck up her.
  I'll not to bed tonight. Let me alone.
  I'll play the housewife for this once. What, ho!
  They are all forth. Well, I will walk myself
45 To County Paris to prepare up him
  Against tomorrow. My heart is wondrous light,
  Since this same wayward girl is so reclaimed.[1]
                                        Exeunt [severally]

_____
1. Reformed; claimed in marriage.

4.3

Enter JULIET *and* NURSE [*with garments*]¹

JULIET Ay, those attires are best. But, gentle Nurse,
    I pray thee leave me to myself tonight,
    For I have need of many orisons°   *prayers*
    To move the heavens to smile upon my state,
5   Which—well thou knowest—is cross° and full of sin.   *adverse*

Enter [CAPULET'S WIFE]

CAPULET'S WIFE What, are you busy, ho? Need you my help?
JULIET No, madam, we have culled such necessaries
    As are behoveful° for our state° tomorrow.   *needful / ceremony*
    So please° you, let me now be left alone,   *If it pleases*
10   And let the Nurse this night sit up with you,
    For I am sure you have your hands full all
    In this so sudden business.
CAPULET'S WIFE   Good night.
    Get thee to bed, and rest, for thou hast need.

Exeunt [CAPULET'S WIFE *and* NURSE]

JULIET   Farewell. God knows when we shall meet again.
15   I have a faint cold fear thrills° through my veins   *pierces*
    That almost freezes up the heat of life.
    I'll call them back again to comfort me.
    Nurse!—What should she do here?

[*She opens curtains, behind which is seen her bed*]

    My dismal° scene I needs must act alone.   *calamitous*
20   Come, vial. What if this mixture do not work at all?
    Shall I be married then tomorrow morning?
    No, no, this shall forbid it. Lie thou there.

[*She lays down a knife*]

    What if it be a poison which the friar
    Subtly hath ministered to have me dead,
25   Lest in this marriage he should be dishonoured
    Because he married me before to Romeo?
    I fear it is—and yet methinks it should not,°   *not be*
    For he hath still° been tried° a holy man.   *always / proved*
    How if, when I am laid into the tomb,
30   I wake before the time that Romeo
    Come to redeem me? There's a fearful point.
    Shall I not then be stifled in the vault,
    To whose foul mouth no healthsome air breathes in,
    And there die strangled° ere my Romeo comes?   *suffocated*
35   Or, if I live, is it not very like°   *likely*
    The horrible conceit of death and night,
    Together with the terror of the place—
    As° in a vault, an ancient receptacle   *As it is*
    Where for this many hundred years the bones
40   Of all my buried ancestors are packed;
    Where bloody Tybalt, yet but green° in earth,   *newly*
    Lies fest'ring in his shroud; where, as they say,
    At some hours in the night spirits resort—
    Alack, alack, is it not like that I,
45   So early waking—what with loathsome smells,

4.3 Location: Capulet's house.
1. Juliet's chamber may be represented by a bed onstage for this scene and the next.

And shrieks like mandrakes[2] torn out of the earth,
That living mortals, hearing them, run mad—
O, if I wake, shall I not be distraught,
Environèd with all these hideous fears,
50 And madly play with my forefathers' joints,
And pluck the mangled Tybalt from his shroud,
And, in this rage,° with some great kinsman's bone   *insanity*
As with a club dash out my desp'rate brains?
O, look! Methinks I see my cousin's ghost
55 Seeking out Romeo that did spit his body
Upon a rapier's point. Stay, Tybalt, stay!
Romeo, Romeo, Romeo! Here's drink. I drink to thee.
 [*She drinks from the vial and*] *falls upon her bed within
 the curtains*

4.4

 Enter [CAPULET'S WIFE,] *and* NURSE *with herbs*
CAPULET'S WIFE   Hold, take these keys, and fetch more spices, Nurse.
NURSE   They call for dates and quinces in the pastry.°   *pastry kitchen*
 Enter old CAPULET
CAPULET   Come, stir, stir, stir. The second cock hath crowed.
 The curfew bell[1] hath rung. 'Tis three o'clock.
5 Look to the baked meats, good Angelica.[2]
 Spare not for cost.
NURSE   Go, you cot-quean,° go.   *old housewife*
 Get you to bed. Faith, you'll be sick tomorrow
 For this night's watching.°   *wakefulness*
CAPULET   No, not a whit. What, I have watched ere now
10 All night for lesser cause, and ne'er been sick.
CAPULET'S WIFE   Ay, you have been a mouse-hunt° in your time,   *skirt chaser*
 But I will watch° you from such watching now.   *guard*
 Exeunt [CAPULET'S WIFE] *and* NURSE
CAPULET   A jealous-hood,[3] a jealous-hood!
 Enter three or four SERVINGMEN, *with spits and logs and
 baskets*
 Now, fellow, what is there?
FIRST SERVINGMAN   Things for the cook, sir, but I know not what.
CAPULET   Make haste, make haste.
 [*Exit* FIRST SERVINGMAN *and one or two others*]
15 Sirrah, fetch drier logs.
 Call Peter. He will show thee where they are.
SECOND SERVINGMAN   I have a head, sir, that will find out logs[4]
 And never trouble Peter for the matter.
CAPULET   Mass,° and well said! A merry whoreson,° ha!   *By the mass / rogue*
 Thou shalt be loggerhead.°   *Exit* [SECOND SERVINGMAN]   *wooden-headed*
20 Good faith, 'tis day.
 The County will be here with music straight,
 For so he said he would.
 Play music [*within*]
 I hear him near.

2. Plants with forked roots thought to resemble a man.
Popular belief held that they uttered a death- or
madness-producing shriek upon being pulled up.
4.4 Location: Scene continues.
1. Also rung at daybreak.
2. Unclear whether Capulet refers to his wife or the

nurse.
3. Jealousy; jealous woman.
4. I have a good head for finding things, so I can certainly find the logs; my head knows all about logs (I am
a blockhead).

Nurse! Wife! What ho, what, Nurse, I say!
    Enter NURSE
Go waken Juliet. Go and trim her up.
25 I'll go and chat with Paris. Hie, make haste,
Make haste, the bridegroom he is come already.
Make haste, I say.   *[Exit]*
NURSE   Mistress, what, mistress! Juliet! Fast,° I warrant her, she.   *Asleep*
  Why, lamb, why, lady! Fie, you slug-abed!
30 Why, love, I say, madam, sweetheart, why, bride!
What, not a word? You take your pennyworths° now.   *bits (of sleep)*
Sleep for a week, for the next night, I warrant,
The County Paris hath set up his rest⁵
That you shall rest but little. God forgive me!
35 Marry, and amen. How sound is she asleep!
I needs must wake her. Madam, madam, madam!
Ay, let the County take° you in your bed.   *catch; sexually possess*
He'll fright you up, i'faith. Will it not be?
    [She draws back the curtains]
What, dressed and in your clothes, and down again?
40 I must needs wake you. Lady, lady, lady!
Alas, alas! Help, help! My lady's dead.
O welladay,° that ever I was born!   *alas*
Some aqua-vitae, ho! My lord, my lady!
    Enter [CAPULET'S WIFE]
CAPULET'S WIFE   What noise is here?
NURSE   O lamentable day!
CAPULET'S WIFE   What is the matter?
45 NURSE   Look, look. O heavy day!
CAPULET'S WIFE   O me, O me, my child, my only life!
  Revive, look up, or I will die with thee.
  Help, help, call help!
    Enter [CAPULET]
CAPULET   For shame, bring Juliet forth. Her lord is come.
50 NURSE   She's dead, deceased. She's dead, alack the day!
CAPULET'S WIFE   Alack the day, she's dead, she's dead, she's dead!
CAPULET   Ha, let me see her! Out,° alas, she's cold.   *Woe*
Her blood is settled,° and her joints are stiff.   *motionless*
Life and these lips have long been separated.
55 Death lies on her like an untimely frost
Upon the sweetest flower of all the field.
NURSE   O lamentable day!
CAPULET'S WIFE   O woeful time!
CAPULET   Death, that hath ta'en her hence to make me wail,
Ties up my tongue, and will not let me speak.
    Enter FRIAR [LAURENCE] *and* PARIS [*with Musicians*]
60 FRIAR LAURENCE   Come, is the bride ready to go to church?
CAPULET   Ready to go, but never to return.
  [To PARIS*]* O son, the night before thy wedding day
Hath death lain with thy wife. See, there she lies,
Flower as she was, deflowerèd by him.
65 Death is my son-in-law, death is my heir.
My daughter he hath wedded. I will die,
And leave him all. Life, living,° all is death's.   *property*

5. Has resolved (from staking everything in the card game primero), with bawdy pun.

All at once wring their hands and cry out

PARIS   Have I thought° long to see this morning's face,   *expected*
    And doth it give me such a sight as this?
70   Beguiled,° divorcèd, wrongèd, spited,° slain!   *Cheated / injured*
    Most detestable death, by thee beguiled,
    By cruel, cruel thee quite overthrown.
    O love, O life: not life, but love in death.
CAPULET'S WIFE   Accursed, unhappy, wretched, hateful day!
75   Most miserable hour that e'er time saw
    In lasting° labour of his pilgrimage!   *eternal*
    But one, poor one, one poor and loving child,
    But one thing to rejoice and solace in,
    And cruel death hath catched° it from my sight!   *seized*
80 NURSE   O woe! O woeful, woeful, woeful day!
    Most lamentable day! Most woeful day
    That ever, ever, I did yet behold!
    O day, O day, O day, O hateful day,
    Never was seen so black a day as this!
85   O woeful day, O woeful day!
CAPULET   Despised, distressèd, hated, martyred, killed!
    Uncomfortable° time, why cam'st thou now   *Comfortless*
    To murder, murder our solemnity?°   *festivity*
    O child, O child, my soul and not my child![6]
90   Dead art thou, alack, my child is dead,
    And with my child my joys are burièd.
FRIAR LAURENCE   Peace, ho, for shame! Confusion's° cure lives   *Destruction's*
        not
    In these confusions.° Heaven and yourself   *commotions*
    Had part in this fair maid. Now heaven hath all,
95   And all the better is it for the maid.
    Your part in her you could not keep from death,
    But heaven keeps his part in eternal life.
    The most you sought was her promotion,°   *social advancement*
    For 'twas your heaven° she should be advanced, *highest ambition*
100 And weep ye now, seeing she is advanced
    Above the clouds as high as heaven itself?
    O, in this love you love your child so ill
    That you run mad, seeing that she is well.
    She's not well married that lives married long,
105 But she's best married that dies married young.
    Dry up your tears, and stick your rosemary
    On this fair corpse, and, as the custom is,
    All in her best array bear her to church;
    For though fond° nature° bids us all lament, *foolish; doting / affection*
110 Yet nature's tears are reason's merriment.°   *laughable idiocy*
CAPULET   All things that we ordainèd festival
    Turn from their office° to black funeral.   *due function*
    Our instruments to melancholy bells,
    Our wedding cheer° to a sad burial feast,   *fare*
115 Our solemn° hymns to sullen° dirges change; *ceremonial / mournful*
    Our bridal flowers serve for a buried corpse,
    And all things change them to the contrary.
FRIAR LAURENCE   Sir, go you in; and madam, go with him,
    And go, Sir Paris. Everyone prepare

---

6. *not my child:* because dead and only a corpse.

120 To follow this fair corpse unto her grave.
The heavens do lour° upon you for some ill.°   *hang threatening / offense*
Move° them no more by crossing their high will.   *Anger*

All but NURSE *go forth, casting rosemary on* JULIET *and*
shutting the curtains. Manent° NURSE *and* MUSICIANS   *Remain*

FIRST MUSICIAN   Faith, we may put° up our pipes and be gone.   *pack*
NURSE   Honest good fellows, ah, put up, put up,
125 For well you know this is a pitiful case.
FIRST MUSICIAN   Ay, by my troth, the case may be amended.[7]

                                           Exit [NURSE]

     Enter PETER

PETER   Musicians, O, musicians! 'Heart's ease',° 'Heart's ease';   *(popular song)*
O, an you will have me live, play 'Heart's ease'.
FIRST MUSICIAN   Why 'Heart's ease'?
130 PETER   O, musicians, because my heart itself plays 'My heart is
full of woe'. O, play me some merry dump° to comfort me.   *sad tune*
FIRST MUSICIAN   Not a dump, we. 'Tis no time to play now.
PETER   You will not then?
FIRST MUSICIAN   No.
135 PETER   I will then give it you soundly.°   *thoroughly; in sound*
FIRST MUSICIAN   What will you give us?
PETER   No money, on my faith, but the gleek.[8] I will give you
the minstrel.[9]
FIRST MUSICIAN   Then will I give you the serving-creature.
140 PETER [*drawing his dagger*]   Then will I lay the serving-creature's
dagger on your pate. I will carry° no crochets.[1] I'll re you, I'll   *bear; sing*
fa you. Do you note° me?   *heed*
FIRST MUSICIAN   An you re us and fa us, you note° us.   *give notes to*
SECOND MUSICIAN   Pray you, put up your dagger and put out°   *show; quench*
145 your wit.
PETER   Then have at you with my wit. I will dry-beat° you with   *thrash*
an iron° wit, and put up my iron dagger. Answer[2] me like men.   *a merciless*
[*Sings*]   When griping grief the heart doth wound,
     And doleful dumps° the mind oppress,   *melancholy*
150   Then music with her silver sound[3]—
Why 'silver sound', why 'music with her silver sound'? What
say you, Matthew Minikin?°   *small lute string*
FIRST MUSICIAN   Marry, sir, because silver hath a sweet sound.
PETER   Prates!° What say you, Hugh Rebec?[4]   *Chatter*
155 SECOND MUSICIAN   I say 'silver sound' because musicians sound
for silver.
PETER   Prates too! What say you, Simon Soundpost?[5]
THIRD MUSICIAN   Faith, I know not what to say.
PETER   O, I cry you mercy,° you are the singer. I will say for you.   *beg your pardon*
160 It is 'music with her silver sound' because musicians have no
gold for sounding.[6]
[*Sings*]   Then music with her silver sound
      With speedy help doth lend redress.   *Exit*
FIRST MUSICIAN   What a pestilent knave is this same!

---

7. Things could be better; the instrument case can be repaired.
8. To "give the gleek" was to make a fool of or play a trick on.
9. I will insultingly call you a minstrel.
1. Whimsy; quarter notes.
2. Defy; respond to.

3. Lines from the song "In Commendation of Music."
4. Three-stringed instrument.
5. Supporting peg fixed between the sounding board and back of a stringed instrument.
6. Musicians are given no gold for playing; they are poor and have no gold to jingle.

165   SECOND MUSICIAN   Hang him, jack! Come, we'll in here, tarry
      for the mourners, and stay° dinner.   *Exeunt*   *await*

5.1

Enter ROMEO

ROMEO   If I may trust the flattering° truth of sleep,   *encouraging*
     My dreams presage some joyful news at hand.
     My bosom's lord sits lightly in his throne,¹
     And all this day an unaccustomed spirit
5   Lifts me above the ground with cheerful thoughts
     I dreamt my lady came and found me dead—
     Strange dream, that gives a dead man leave to think!—
     And breathed such life with kisses in° my lips   *into*
     That I revived and was an emperor.
10   Ah me, how sweet is love itself possessed°   *enjoyed in reality*
     When but love's shadows° are so rich in joy!   *dreams; images*

Enter BALTHASAR, *his man, booted*²

     News from Verona! How now, Balthasar?
     Dost thou not bring me letters from the friar?
     How doth my lady? Is my father well?
15   How fares my Juliet? That I ask again,
     For nothing can be ill if she be well.

BALTHASAR   Then she is well, and nothing can be ill.
     Her body sleeps in Capel's monument,
     And her immortal part with angels lives.
20   I saw her laid low in her kindred's vault,
     And presently° took post³ to tell it you.   *immediately*
     O, pardon me for bringing these ill news,
     Since you did leave it for my office,° sir.   *duty*

ROMEO   Is it e'en so? Then I defy you, stars.
25   Thou knowest my lodging. Get me ink and paper,
     And hire posthorses. I will hence tonight.

BALTHASAR   I do beseech you, sir, have patience.
     Your looks are pale and wild, and do import°   *signify*
     Some misadventure.

ROMEO   Tush, thou art deceived.
30   Leave me, and do the thing I bid thee do.
     Hast thou no letters to me from the friar?

BALTHASAR   No, my good lord.

ROMEO   No matter. Get thee gone,
     And hire those horses. I'll be with thee straight.

Exit BALTHASAR

     Well, Juliet, I will lie with thee tonight.
35   Let's see for means. O mischief, thou art swift
     To enter in the thoughts of desperate men!
     I do remember an apothecary,
     And hereabouts a dwells, which late I noted,
     In tattered weeds,° with overwhelming° brows,   *clothes / overhanging*
40   Culling of simples.° Meagre were his looks.   *herbs*
     Sharp misery had worn him to the bones,
     And in his needy° shop a tortoise hung,   *poor*
     An alligator stuffed, and other skins

5.1 Location: A street in Mantua.
1. Love rules in the heart; the heart is at ease in the chest.
2. booted: as if he has just dismounted.
3. Set out on post horses.

Of ill-shaped fishes; and about his shelves
45   A beggarly account° of empty boxes,   *A sparse collection*
Green earthen pots, bladders, and musty seeds,
Remnants of packthread,° and old cakes of roses⁴   *twine*
Were thinly scattered to make up a show.
Noting this penury, to myself I said
50   'An if a man did need a poison now,
Whose sale is present death⁵ in Mantua,
Here lives a caitiff ° wretch would sell it him.'   *pitiful*
O, this same thought did but forerun my need,
And this same needy man must sell it me.
55   As I remember, this should be the house.
Being holiday, the beggar's shop is shut.
What ho, apothecary!

             Enter APOTHECARY

APOTHECARY   Who calls so loud?
ROMEO   Come hither, man. I see that thou art poor.
             [*He offers money*]
Hold, there is forty ducats.⁶ Let me have
60   A dram of poison—such soon-speeding gear⁷
As will disperse itself through all the veins,
That the life-weary taker may fall dead,
And that the trunk° may be discharged of breath   *body*
As violently as hasty powder fired
65   Doth hurry from the fatal cannon's womb.
APOTHECARY   Such mortal drugs I have, but Mantua's law
Is death to any he° that utters° them.   *man / offers to sell*
ROMEO   Art thou so bare° and full of wretchedness,   *destitute*
And fear'st to die? Famine is in thy cheeks,
70   Need and oppression starveth in thy eyes,
Contempt and beggary hangs upon thy back.
The world is not thy friend, nor the world's law.
The world affords° no law to make thee rich.   *provides*
Then be not poor, but break it, and take this.
75   APOTHECARY   My poverty but not my will consents.
ROMEO   I pay thy poverty and not thy will.
APOTHECARY   [*handing* ROMEO *poison*] Put this in any liquid
             thing you will
And drink it off, and if you had the strength
Of twenty men it would dispatch you straight.°   *immediately*
ROMEO   [*giving money*]   There is thy gold—worse poison to
80   men's souls,
Doing more murder in this loathsome world,
Than these poor compounds that thou mayst not sell.
I sell thee poison; thou hast sold me none.
Farewell, buy food, and get thyself in flesh.°   *grow fatter*
             [*Exit* APOTHECARY]
85   Come, cordial° and not poison, go with me   *restorative; heart's ease*
To Juliet's grave, for there must I use thee.   *Exit*

---

4. Rose petals pressed into cake form and used as a
sachet.
5. Punishable by immediate death.
6. Various gold coins used at times in much of Europe,
and Shakespeare's usual currency for plays not set in
England.
7. Quick-working stuff; quick-killing stuff.

5.2

Enter FRIAR JOHN [*at one door*]

FRIAR JOHN   Holy Franciscan friar, brother, ho!

Enter FRIAR LAURENCE [*at another door*]

FRIAR LAURENCE   This same should be the voice of Friar John.
Welcome from Mantua! What says Romeo?
Or if his mind° be writ, give me his letter.   *thoughts*

5   FRIAR JOHN   Going to find a barefoot brother out—
One of our order—to associate me[1]
Here in this city visiting the sick,
And finding him, the searchers[2] of the town,
Suspecting that we both were in a house

10 Where the infectious pestilence did reign,
Sealed up the doors, and would not let us forth,
So that my speed to Mantua there was stayed.°   *stopped*

FRIAR LAURENCE   Who bare my letter then to Romeo?

FRIAR JOHN   I could not send it—here it is again—

15 Nor get a messenger to bring it thee,
So fearful were they of infection.°   *contagion*

FRIAR LAURENCE   Unhappy fortune! By my brotherhood,
The letter was not nice,° but full of charge,°   *trivial / importance*
Of dear import,° and the neglecting it   *serious consequence*

20 May do much danger. Friar John, go hence.
Get me an iron crow,° and bring it straight   *crowbar*
Unto my cell.

FRIAR JOHN   Brother, I'll go and bring it thee.   *Exit*

FRIAR LAURENCE   Now must I to the monument alone.
Within this three hours will fair Juliet wake.

25 She will beshrew° me much that Romeo   *curse*
Hath had no notice of these accidents.°   *events*
But I will write again to Mantua,
And keep her at my cell till Romeo come.
Poor living corpse, closed in a dead man's tomb!   *Exit*

5.3

Enter County PARIS *and his* PAGE, *with flowers, sweet°*   *perfumed*
water [*and a torch*]

PARIS   Give me thy torch, boy. Hence, and stand aloof.°   *stay apart*
Yet put it out, for I would not be seen.

[*His* PAGE *puts out the torch*]

Under yon yew trees lay thee all along,°   *stretched out*
Holding thy ear close to the hollow ground.

5   So shall no foot upon the churchyard tread,
Being° loose, unfirm, with digging up of graves,   *The ground being*
But thou shalt hear it. Whistle then to me
As signal that thou hear'st something approach.
Give me those flowers. Do as I bid thee. Go.

10 PAGE [*aside*]   I am almost afraid to stand alone
Here in the churchyard, yet I will adventure.°   *risk it*

[*He hides himself at a distance from* PARIS]

5.2 Location: Friar Laurence's cell.
1. Franciscan friars (barefoot because the order is
sworn to poverty) traveled only in pairs. *associate:*
accompany.

2. Health officers appointed to examine corpses and
identify houses infected with the plague.
5.3 Location: The Capulet mausoleum.

PARIS (*strews the tomb with flowers*)   Sweet flower, with flowers
    thy bridal bed I strew.
       [*He sprinkles water*]
    O woe! Thy canopy° is dust and stones,   *covering; bed hangings*
    Which with sweet water nightly I will dew,
15   Or, wanting that, with tears distilled by moans.
    The obsequies that I for thee will keep°   *perform*
    Nightly shall be to strew thy grave and weep.
       [PAGE *whistles*]
    The boy gives warning. Something doth approach.
    What cursèd foot wanders this way tonight
20   To cross° my obsequies and true love's rite?   *thwart*
      Enter ROMEO *and* BALTHASAR, *with a torch, a mattock,°*   *pickax*
      and a crow of iron
    What, with a torch? Muffle me, night, a while.
      [*He stands aside*]
ROMEO   Give me that mattock and the wrenching iron.
    Hold, take this letter. Early in the morning
    See thou deliver it to my lord and father.
25   Give me the light. Upon thy life I charge thee,
    Whate'er thou hear'st or seest, stand all aloof,
    And do not interrupt me in my course.
    Why I descend into this bed of death
    Is partly to behold my lady's face,
30   But chiefly to take thence from her dead finger
    A precious ring, a ring that I must use
    In dear° employment. Therefore hence, be gone.   *important; tender*
    But if thou, jealous,° dost return to pry   *suspicious*
    In what I farther shall intend to do,
35   By heaven, I will tear thee joint by joint,
    And strew this hungry churchyard with thy limbs.
    The time and my intents are savage-wild,
    More fierce and more inexorable far
    Than empty tigers or the roaring sea.
40 BALTHASAR   I will be gone, sir, and not trouble ye.
ROMEO   So shalt thou show me friendship. Take thou that.
      [*He gives money*]
    Live and be prosperous, and farewell, good fellow.
BALTHASAR [*aside*]   For all this same, I'll hide me hereabout.
    His looks I fear, and his intents I doubt.°   *suspect*
      [*He hides himself at a distance from* ROMEO.]
      ROMEO *begins to open the tomb*
45 ROMEO   Thou detestable maw, thou womb¹ of death,
    Gorged with the dearest morsel of the earth,
    Thus I enforce thy rotten jaws to open,
    And in despite° I'll cram thee with more food.   *defiant ill will*
PARIS [*aside*]   This is that banished haughty Montague
50   That murdered my love's cousin, with which grief
    It is supposèd the fair creature died;
    And here is come to do some villainous shame
    To the dead bodies. I will apprehend him.
    [*Drawing*] Stop thy unhallowed° toil, vile Montague!   *unholy*

---

1. Belly; also playing on the birthplace of Romeo's death.

55   Can vengeance be pursued further than death?
         Condemnèd villain, I do apprehend thee.
         Obey and go with me, for thou must die.
    ROMEO   I must indeed, and therefore came I hither.
         Good gentle youth, tempt not a desp'rate° man.   *despairing; violent*
60   Fly hence, and leave me. Think upon these gone.
         Let them affright thee. I beseech thee, youth,
         Put not another sin upon my head
         By urging me to fury. O, be gone.
         By heaven, I love thee better than myself,
65   For I come hither armed against myself.
         Stay not, be gone. Live, and hereafter say
         A madman's mercy bid thee run away.
    PARIS   I do defy thy conjuration,°   *entreaty*
         And apprehend thee for a felon here.
70   ROMEO [*drawing*]   Wilt thou provoke me? Then have at thee, boy.
           They fight
    PAGE   O Lord, they fight! I will go call the watch.   [*Exit*]
    PARIS   O, I am slain! If thou be merciful,
         Open the tomb, lay me with Juliet.
    ROMEO   In faith, I will.   [*PARIS dies*]
                  Let me peruse this face.
75   Mercutio's kinsman, noble County Paris!
         What said my man when my betossèd° soul   *storm-tossed*
         Did not attend° him as we rode? I think   *listen to*
         He told me Paris should have married Juliet.
         Said he not so? Or did I dream it so?
80   Or am I mad, hearing him talk of Juliet,
         To think it was so? O, give me thy hand,
         One writ with me in sour misfortune's book.
         I'll bury thee in a triumphant° grave.   *magnificent*
           [*He opens the tomb, revealing* JULIET]
         A grave—O no, a lantern,° slaughtered youth,   *lighthouse*
85   For here lies Juliet, and her beauty makes
         This vault a feasting presence² full of light.
           [*He bears the body of Paris to the tomb*]
         Death, lie thou there, by a dead man interred.
         How oft, when men are at the point of death,
         Have they been merry, which their keepers° call   *sick nurses; jailors*
90   A lightning before death! O, how may I
         Call this a lightning? O my love, my wife!
         Death, that hath sucked the honey of thy breath,
         Hath had no power yet upon thy beauty.
         Thou art not conquered.° Beauty's ensign° yet   *overpowered; seduced / flag*
95   Is crimson in thy lips and in thy cheeks,
         And death's pale flag is not advancèd there.
         Tybalt, liest thou there in thy bloody sheet?
         O, what more favour can I do to thee
         Than with that hand that cut thy youth in twain
100   To sunder his° that was thine enemy?   *the youth of him*
         Forgive me, cousin. Ah, dear Juliet,
         Why art thou yet so fair? Shall I believe
         That unsubstantial° death is amorous,   *immaterial*

---

2. Festive royal chamber for receiving guests.

And that the lean abhorrèd monster keeps
105   Thee here in dark to be his paramour?
For fear of that I still will stay with thee,
And never from this pallet of dim night
Depart again. Here, here will I remain
With worms that are thy chambermaids. O, here
110   Will I set up my everlasting rest,³
And shake the yoke of inauspicious stars
From this world-wearied flesh. Eyes, look your last.
Arms, take your last embrace, and lips, O you
The doors of breath, seal with a righteous kiss
115   A dateless° bargain to engrossing⁴ death.   *An eternal*

    [*He kisses* JULIET, *then pours poison into the cup*]

Come, bitter conduct°, come, unsavoury guide,   *conductor; leader*
Thou desperate pilot, now at once run on
The dashing rocks thy seasick weary° barque!   *travel-weary*
Here's to my love.

    [*He drinks the poison*]
              O true apothecary,
120   Thy drugs are quick!° Thus with a kiss I die.   *fast; vigorous*

    [*He kisses* JULIET,] *falls* [*and dies.*]
    Enter FRIAR [LAURENCE] *with lantern, crow,*
    and spade

FRIAR LAURENCE   Saint Francis be my speed!° How oft tonight   *help*
Have my old feet stumbled at graves? Who's there?
BALTHASAR   Here's one, a friend, and one that knows you well.
FRIAR LAURENCE   Bliss be upon you. Tell me, good my friend,
125   What torch is yon that vainly lends his light
To grubs and eyeless skulls? As I discern,
It burneth in the Capels' monument.
BALTHASAR   It doth so, holy sir, and there's my master,
One that you love.
FRIAR LAURENCE   Who is it?
BALTHASAR   Romeo.
FRIAR LAURENCE   How long hath he been there?
130   BALTHASAR   Full half an hour.
FRIAR LAURENCE   Go with me to the vault.
BALTHASAR   I dare not, sir.
My master knows not but I am gone hence,
And fearfully° did menace me with death   *fearsomely*
If I did stay to look on his intents.
135   FRIAR LAURENCE   Stay then, I'll go alone. Fear comes upon me.
O, much I fear some ill unthrifty° thing.   *unfortunate*
BALTHASAR   As I did sleep under this yew tree here
I dreamt my master and another fought,
And that my master slew him.
FRIAR LAURENCE   Romeo!

    [*He*] *stoops and looks on the blood and weapons*

140   Alack, alack, what blood is this which stains
The stony entrance of this sepulchre?
What mean these masterless and gory swords
To lie discoloured by this place of peace?

---

3. Make my final determination.
4. Buying up in large quantities to monopolize; writing a legal document.

Romeo! O, pale! Who else? What, Paris, too,
145   And steeped in blood? Ah, what an unkind° hour   *unnatural; a cruel*
Is guilty of this lamentable chance!°   *event*
        JULIET [*awakes and*] *rises*
The lady stirs.
        JULIET   O comfortable° friar, where is my lord?   *solace-giving*
I do remember well where I should be,
150   And there I am. Where is my Romeo?
        FRIAR LAURENCE   I hear some noise. Lady, come from that nest
Of death, contagion, and unnatural sleep.
A greater power than we can contradict
Hath thwarted our intents. Come, come away.
155   Thy husband in thy bosom there lies dead,
And Paris, too. Come, I'll dispose of thee
Among a sisterhood of holy nuns.
Stay not to question, for the watch is coming.
Come, go, good Juliet. I dare no longer stay.   *Exit*
160   JULIET   Go, get thee hence, for I will not away.
What's here? A cup closed in my true love's hand?
Poison, I see, hath been his timeless° end.   *untimely; lasting*
O churl!—drunk all, and left no friendly drop
To help me after? I will kiss thy lips.
165   Haply° some poison yet doth hang on them,   *Perhaps*
To make me die with a restorative.⁵
        [*She kisses Romeo's lips*]
Thy lips are warm.
        CHIEF WATCHMAN [*within*]   Lead, boy. Which way?
        JULIET   Yea, noise? Then I'll be brief.
        [*She takes Romeo's dagger*]
                                        O happy° dagger,   *fortunate*
This is thy sheath! There rust, and let me die.
        She stabs herself, falls [*and dies*]
        Enter [PAGE] *and* WATCH
170   PAGE   This is the place, there where the torch doth burn.
        CHIEF WATCHMAN   The ground is bloody. Search about the churchyard.
Go, some of you. Whoe'er you find, attach.°   *arrest*
                        [*Exeunt some* WATCHMEN]
Pitiful sight! Here lies the County slain,
And Juliet bleeding, warm, and newly dead,
175   Who here hath lain this two days buried.
Go tell the Prince. Run to the Capulets,
Raise up the Montagues. Some others search.
                        [*Exeunt other* WATCHMEN *severally*]
We see the ground° whereon these woes do lie,   *earth*
But the true ground° of all these piteous woes   *cause*
180   We cannot without circumstance° descry.   *a fuller account*
        Enter [WATCHMEN] *with Romeo's man* [BALTHASAR]
        SECOND WATCHMAN   Here's Romeo's man. We found him in
            the churchyard.
        CHIEF WATCHMAN   Hold him in safety° till the Prince come   *securely*
            hither.
        Enter another WATCHMAN *with* FRIAR [LAURENCE]
        THIRD WATCHMAN   Here is a friar that trembles, sighs, and weeps.

---

5. Both the kiss, which is healing, and the poison, which restores them to each other.

We took this mattock and this spade from him
185   As he was coming from this churchyard's side.⁶

CHIEF WATCHMAN   A great suspicion. Stay° the friar, too.   *Hold*

Enter PRINCE *with others*

PRINCE   What misadventure is so early up,
That calls our person from our morning rest?

Enter old CAPULET *and his* WIFE

CAPULET   What should it be that is so shrieked abroad?
190   CAPULET'S WIFE   O, the people in the street cry 'Romeo',
Some 'Juliet', and some 'Paris', and all run
With open° outcry toward our monument.   *public; open-mouthed*

PRINCE   What fear is this which startles° in our ears?   *bursts out*

CHIEF WATCHMAN   Sovereign, here lies the County Paris slain,
195   And Romeo dead, and Juliet, dead before,
Warm, and new killed.

PRINCE   Search, seek, and know how this foul murder comes.

CHIEF WATCHMAN   Here is a friar, and slaughtered Romeo's man,
With instruments upon them fit to open
200   These dead men's tombs.

CAPULET   O heavens! O wife, look how our daughter bleeds!
This dagger hath mista'en, for lo, his house°   *scabbard*
Is empty on the back of Montague,
And it mis-sheathèd in my daughter's bosom.

205   CAPULET'S WIFE   O me, this sight of death is as a bell
That warns° my old age to a sepulchre.   *summons*

Enter old MONTAGUE

PRINCE   Come, Montague, for thou art early up
To see thy son and heir more early down.

MONTAGUE   Alas, my liege, my wife is dead tonight.
210   Grief of my son's exile hath stopped her breath.
What further woe conspires against mine age?

PRINCE   Look, and thou shalt see.

MONTAGUE   [*seeing Romeo's body*]   O thou untaught! What
manners is in this,
To press before° thy father to a grave?   *To shove ahead of*

215   PRINCE   Seal up the mouth of outrage⁷ for a while,
Till we can clear these ambiguities
And know their spring, their head, their true descent;
And then will I be general of your woes,
And lead you even to death. Meantime, forbear,
220   And let mischance be slave to° patience.   *overruled by*
Bring forth the parties of suspicion.

FRIAR LAURENCE   I am the greatest,° able to do least,   *most suspect*
Yet most suspected, as the time and place
Doth make against me, of this direful murder;
225   And here I stand, both to impeach and purge
Myself condemnèd and myself excused.⁸

PRINCE   Then say at once what thou dost know in this.

FRIAR LAURENCE   I will be brief, for my short date° of breath   *duration*
Is not so long as is a tedious tale.
230   Romeo, there dead, was husband to that Juliet,
And she, there dead, that Romeo's faithful wife.

6. This side of the churchyard.
7. Of impassioned exclamation.

8. *to . . . excused:* to accuse myself of what I am guilty
of and clear myself of what I am not.

I married them, and their stol'n marriage day
Was Tybalt's doomsday, whose untimely death
Banished the new-made bridegroom from this city,
235 For whom, and not for Tybalt, Juliet pined.
You, to remove that siege of grief from her,
Betrothed and would have married her perforce°   *forcibly*
To County Paris. Then comes she to me,
And with wild looks bid me devise some mean°   *method*
240 To rid her from this second marriage,
Or in my cell there would she kill herself.
Then gave I her—so tutored by my art⁹—
A sleeping potion, which so took effect
As I intended, for it wrought on her
245 The form° of death. Meantime I writ to Romeo   *appearance*
That he should hither come as this° dire night   *as this = this*
To help to take her from her borrowed grave,
Being the time the potion's force should cease.
But he which bore my letter, Friar John,
250 Was stayed by accident, and yesternight
Returned my letter back. Then all alone,
At the prefixéd° hour of her waking,   *prearranged*
Came I to take her from her kindred's vault,
Meaning to keep her closely° at my cell   *secretly*
255 Till I conveniently° could send to Romeo.   *befittingly*
But when I came, some minute ere the time
Of her awakening, here untimely lay
The noble Paris and true Romeo dead.
She wakes, and I entreated her come forth
260 And bear this work of heaven with patience.
But then a noise did scare me from the tomb,
And she, too desperate, would not go with me,
But, as it seems, did violence on herself.
All this I know, and to the marriage
265 Her nurse is privy; and if aught in this
Miscarried by my fault, let my old life
Be sacrificed, some hour before his° time,   *its*
Unto the rigour of severest law.
PRINCE   We still° have known thee for a holy man.   *always*
270 Where's Romeo's man? What can he say to this?
BALTHASAR   I brought my master news of Juliet's death.
And then in post° he came from Mantua   *haste*
To this same place, to this same monument.
This letter he early bid me give his father,
275 And threatened me with death, going in the vault.
If I departed not and left him there.
PRINCE   Give me the letter. I will look on it.
   [He *takes the letter*]
Where is the County's page that raised the watch?
Sirrah, what made° your master in this place?   *did*
280 PAGE   He came with flowers to strew his lady's grave,
And bid me stand aloof, and so I did.
Anon° comes one with light to ope the tomb,   *Soon*

9. As I knew through my medical study to do.

And by and by my master drew on him,
And then I ran away to call the watch.
285 PRINCE   This letter doth make good the friar's words,
Their course of love, the tidings of her death;
And here he writes that he did buy a poison
Of a poor 'pothecary, and therewithal
Came to this vault to die, and lie with Juliet.
290 Where be these enemies? Capulet, Montague,
See what a scourge is laid upon your hate,
That heaven finds means to kill your joys° with love.   *happiness; children*
And I, for winking at° your discords, too   *closing my eyes to*
Have lost a brace of kinsmen. All are punishèd.
295 CAPULET   O brother Montague, give me thy hand.
This is my daughter's jointure,° for no more   *marriage portion*
Can I demand.
MONTAGUE   But I can give thee more,
For I will raise her statue in pure gold,
That whiles Verona by that name is known
300 There shall no figure at such rate be set[1]
As that of true and faithful Juliet.
CAPULET   As rich shall Romeo's by his lady's lie,
Poor sacrifices of our enmity.
PRINCE   A glooming° peace this morning with it brings.   *frowning; dark*
305 The sun for sorrow will not show his head.
Go hence, to have more talk of these sad things.
Some shall be pardoned, and some punishèd;
For never was a story of more woe
Than this of Juliet and her Romeo.
[The tomb is closed.] Exeunt

1. No figure shall be so valued; no figure shall be erected at such a price.

Richard II

In the first scene of *Richard II,* two armed noblemen face each other before the royal throne. They hurl insults at one another, their deadly antagonism barely held in check by the formality of the occasion. This is an "appeal for treason," a kind of trial already archaic in Shakespeare's time, in which plaintiff and defendant present their cases in their own persons before the king, who instantly dispenses justice. The structure of the situation suggests what the men themselves insist upon: that one lies and one tells the truth, that one is a traitor and one a true subject. But even while we are implicitly asked to judge between rival claims, we have no way of knowing what has happened or whom to trust.

In the ensuing scenes, we learn that Bolingbroke and Mowbray are fighting about the murder of Thomas of Woodstock, the uncle of King Richard II. Apparently Bolingbroke knows that Richard secretly ordered Woodstock's death. Since he cannot say so, he picks Richard's agent Mowbray as his target, for Woodstock had been in Mowbray's safekeeping. Meanwhile, Mowbray, likewise unable to blame the true culprit openly, is outraged at being called a traitor when it was his allegiance to Richard that led him to acquiesce in the killing.

This is a far more tangled situation than the simple yes-or-no structure of the appeal for treason or, several scenes later, the "trial by combat" could allow anyone to acknowledge. Moreover, the King's participation in the crime upon which he is supposed to be passing judgment obviously compromises his impartiality. The institution of the appeal for treason is premised on the assumptions that, as Richard himself states emphatically, the king has no part in his subjects' quarrels and that it is in his best interests to have the truth revealed. Here, neither assumption is correct. The ceremonies of royal authority so colorfully staged in the first few scenes turn out to be inconclusive, postponing rather than confronting real sources of discord.

As the play continues, we come to realize that the confusion of the first few scenes, a confusion Shakespeare forces his audience momentarily to share, results from an intractable problem in a system of monarchical government. Since the king's subjects are obliged to obey him, it is not clear how, short of direct divine intervention, his follies or vices may be checked. To admit that subjects have a right to judge or even to remove their king threatens the stability of the realm, since any subject, discontented for any reason, might incite a revolt. But to allow the king to have his own way no matter what opens the way to tyranny.

The proper extent of a monarch's power was a crucial, and unresolved, political issue in sixteenth- and early seventeenth-century England, when first the Tudors and then the Stuarts struggled to extend their traditional prerogatives. A few decades after Shakespeare's death, disagreement about the nature of royal authority would provoke the English Civil War. In the 1590s, when Shakespeare was writing his history plays, the lines of stress upon which the country would eventually fracture were already apparent, even though the disasters to come would not have seemed inevitable.

When Shakespeare wrote about the medieval reign of Richard II, in other words, he saw the conflicts of that reign through the lens of the late sixteenth century. His meticulous re-creation of antiquated judicial processes did not conceal from audiences in his own time the contemporary relevance of the play. In all sixteenth-century texts and perhaps in performance, the lines in which Richard gives up his crown were omitted: many scholars theorize that this episode was considered too inflammatory to print or stage. When the Earl of Essex rebelled against Elizabeth I in 1601, some of his supporters cited Richard's reign as providing a historical precedent for the deposition of a monarch. They paid Shakespeare's company to perform a play about Richard's reign—almost certainly Shakespeare's play—in an attempt to rally supporters to their cause. "I am Richard II," snapped the furious Queen. "Know you not that?"

To acknowledge the contemporary relevance of Richard's reign is not to claim that Shakespeare wrote his play purely as a means of commenting obliquely on the policies of Elizabeth I. Rather, the urgent contemporary task of defining a nation-state led Shakespeare to an extended historical inquiry into the institution of the English monarchy, an inquiry of which *Richard II* is a part. By looking at points at which the normal order of royal succession is challenged, Shakespeare illuminates interesting inconsistencies in Renaissance theories of kingship and political authority. Several years earlier, he had written the three *Henry VI* plays and *Richard III*, which while not originally conceived as a series eventually constituted what critics call the "first tetralogy": a group of plays that together present a continuous chronicle of the long Wars of the Roses in the fifteenth century. Soon after finishing *Richard III*, Shakespeare began writing another group of history plays, the "second tetralogy," which backtrack in time to treat the origins of the conflicts he had already brought to the stage.

As he had for his earlier history plays, Shakespeare turned to Raphael Holinshed's *Chronicles of England, Scotland, and Ireland* (1587). There he found in the reign of Richard II a remote cause of the war to be waged many years hence. Richard II was grandson of Edward III, whose formidable precedent haunts all the plays of the second tetralogy. King Edward had five sons who survived to adulthood, but his eldest, Edward the Black Prince, predeceased him. The Black Prince left a son of his own, however, the future Richard II, to whom the throne descended after Edward III's death. At the time of his accession, Richard was ten years old, and during his adolescence his powerful uncles, the younger brothers of the Black Prince, administered his kingdom on his behalf. After Richard reached young adulthood and began to rule in his own name, he found it difficult to gain the respect of his uncles, experienced middle-aged men who had become accustomed to command. His own rashness and ineffectuality only compounded his troubles. Shakespeare's play opens upon the young Richard, already complicit in the murder of one of his uncles; the remaining uncles, who scorn Richard's maladroit rule but realize they owe allegiance to him; and Richard's cousins Bolingbroke and Northumberland, who are more willing than their elders to act on the recognition of the ruler's weakness.

Early in the play, Richard reacts to Bolingbroke's veiled challenge by exiling him; shortly thereafter, he confiscates Bolingbroke's estate. When, exasperated, Bolingbroke invades England and successfully seizes the crown from his cousin, his action neatly ruptures two traditional sources of royal authority. Unquestionably, Bolingbroke is the more astute tactician, the more effective leader. Richard, however, is equally undoubtedly the rightful heir of Edward III, and as such has been anointed king in a sacred coronation ceremony. Thus

Richardus ii. From John Rastell, *The Pastyme of People* (1529).

"Like perspectives, which, rightly gazed upon, / Show nothing but confusion; eyed awry, / Distinguish form" (*Richard II* 2.2.18–20). The most famous Renaissance example of such a "perspective" or anamorphic picture is Hans Holbein's *The Ambassadors* (1533); when the painting is viewed from the side ("awry"), the elongated object in the foreground reveals itself to be a skull.

one character has all the advantages when considered from a material and practical point of view, while the other derives his claim to authority from the more abstract principle of divinely sanctioned hereditary right.

Shakespeare imagines the division between the two men not merely as a political issue but as a question of character. A vivid sense of Bolingbroke's personality emerges in his confrontation with Mowbray. Mowbray harps on Bolingbroke's lies, laments the damage Bolingbroke's accusation has done to his reputation, and experiences Bolingbroke's verbal accusation as a physical attack: he is "pierced to the soul with slander's venomed spear" (1.1.171). Bolingbroke, by contrast, trusts not words but physical strength: "What my tongue speaks my right-drawn sword may prove," he stoutly declares (1.1.46). Tellingly, his word 'right" conflates his proficiency as a warrior with the uprightness of his cause, suggesting that he does not care to recognize the potential difference. Likewise, Bolingbroke repeatedly speaks of making his words *good*, by which he means backing them up by force. As a corollary, he is suspicious or dismissive of anything that seems merely imaginary, verbal, or abstract. When his father, Gaunt, encourages him to reconcile himself to his exile by renaming it an educational tour or a pleasure junket, Bolingbroke replies:

> O, who can hold a fire in his hand
> By thinking on the frosty Caucasus,
> Or cloy the hungry edge of appetite
> By bare imagination of a feast . . . ?
> (1.3.257–60)

As the play proceeds, this insistence on material facts rather than words or imagination comes to seem entirely characteristic of a man who has no legal claim on the throne, but who takes it because he is able to do so.

Unlike Bolingbroke, Richard is an inept manager of practical affairs. In the first act, most of his powerful kinfolk let him literally get away with murder; but in the second act, it becomes clear that they will not tolerate his infringement of property rights. Medieval kings were expected to cover most of the expenses of government from their own large estates, but to raise additional funds Richard "farms out" the realm—that is, grants the power to tax to private individuals who can confiscate subjects' property virtually as they please, provided the king gets a share of the spoils. Not surprisingly, such legalized theft produces widespread resentment. For the upper aristocracy, the last straw is Richard's seizure of the duchy of Lancaster upon John of Gaunt's death: the encroachment seems to them worse than homicide, because it directly threatens the social structure upon which their status depends. Inherited property distinguishes noblemen from "men of no name": in fact, noble names are derived from property, the lands of Lancaster, Gloucester, York, Northumberland, and so forth. In *Richard II*, both social disruptions and identity crises are marked by a struggle over such titles and the power they signify. Bolingbroke, returning to England, insists on being called "Lancaster," not "Hereford"; Northumberland presumptuously forgets to call Richard "King"; Richard himself laments, upon his deposition, that "I must nothing be . . . I have no name, no title" (4.1.191, 245).

Although technically aristocrats did not own their land outright but held it in trust from the sovereign, by Richard's time Magna Carta protected the right of property holders to pass their lands to their heirs. Only a conviction for treason could forfeit the family claim. Ironically, at the moment Richard commandeers the Lancastrian estates, Bolingbroke is apparently on the verge of invading England with an armed force, so he is actually a traitor and Richard could eventually have appropriated his property in a perfectly legal manner. But Richard's characteristic neglect of proper procedure makes Bolingbroke's return seem a response to dispossession and thus turns the nobility toward the rebel cause.

Richard does not imagine that he must earn the respect of the people he governs, or balance his budget, or follow laws. He does not believe that his authority depends on the consent of the governed or on the effective manipulation of material resources. Whereas Bolingbroke thinks of power as emanating from "below"—from the King's subjects, from the deployment of material resources—Richard thinks of it as descending from "above," from the God whose representative on earth he was born to be. His assertion in 3.2.50–53 is entirely characteristic:

> Not all the water in the rough rude sea
> Can wash the balm from an anointed king.
> The breath of worldly men cannot depose
> The deputy elected by the Lord.

Later in the same scene, deserted by all but a few supporters, he exclaims: "Is not the King's name forty thousand names? / Arm, arm, my name!" (3.2.81–82). What Richard needs now, of course, is not names but soldiers, but he deliberately refuses to acknowledge the difference.

Richard's drastic impracticalities derive from his conviction that the God who put him on the throne is immanent in the created universe and vigilant in defense of His deputy. Richard is not unique in this conviction: the assumption that God intervenes continuously in human affairs in order to guarantee just outcomes underlies the ritual of the trial by combat as it is staged in 1.3. The way spirit informs and controls the material world can render "dead matter" sympathetic to human beings. "This earth shall have a feeling," Richard claims (3.2.24). Thus he is confident that the earth will put toads in the way of traitors, and that angels will rush to save a king in trouble.

Medieval histories are full of such narratives: the ground opens up and swallows an atheist; lightning strikes a perjurer dead.

By Shakespeare's time, the trial by combat had been discredited and the conception of the world to which Richard adheres was beginning to seem obsolete. Some thinkers were increasingly discarding anthropocentric ways of thinking and conceiving of the material world as something alien to human consciousness, ruled by purely physical laws of cause and effect. This change in mentality affected historians, who were subjecting long-accepted myths to critical scrutiny; scientists, who began to place a new value on empirical experimentation; and theologians, who were becoming more skeptical of the continuation of miracles in postbiblical times. Political theorists such as Machiavelli pragmatically insisted on describing political power as it really was exercised, and not as God or moral scruples might dictate that it ought to be exercised. The pragmatic Bolingbroke, then, is associated with a new, effective, but not necessarily moral or satisfying way of thinking about the manipulation of men and matter.

Richard's assumptions about the world and his place in it turn out to be wrong. His naïveté about the relationship of language and power, spirit and matter, leaves him vulnerable to Bolingbroke's assault. Bolingbroke's supplanting of Richard, then, might be seen not merely as a personal or even a political victory, but as the uprooting of one worldview by another. Whether this displacement represents an advance or a deterioration is, however, another question. The second part of the play, in which Bolingbroke emerges victorious, reexamines the nature of the conflict between the two men and the principles they represent.

In a pivotal scene in Act 3, Bolingbroke, Northumberland, and York approach the castle in which Richard has sequestered himself. When Richard finally emerges on the battlements, Bolingbroke exclaims:

> See, see, King Richard doth himself appear,
> As doth the blushing discontented sun
> From out the fiery portal of the east
> When he perceives the envious clouds are bent
> To dim his glory and to stain the track
> Of his bright passage to the occident.
>
> (3.3 61–66)

Bolingbroke is untypically eloquent here, but interestingly his extended simile works against his own interests. The comparison between king and sun, a traditional figure of speech, implies that the king is both unique and indispensable. Rebels are not rival suns; they are transient clouds that the mighty king will eventually burn away. Even while he mutinies against Richard's misgovernment, Bolingbroke seems unable to escape a conservative conception of monarchy in which rebellion is a form of envy doomed to failure.

Bolingbroke's linguistic slip suggests that it may be easier to amass an army and seize the throne than to put aside one's inherited convictions about the nature of royal authority. Bolingbroke does not have an alternative vocabulary in which to justify his own behavior. Thus, throughout the play, it is hard to be sure whether he is cunningly concealing his true motives or simply incapable of articulating them even to himself. In the opening scenes, although Richard recognizes Bolingbroke's challenge to his authority, Bolingbroke himself seems a bit obtuse about his own purposes, as if his accusation of Mowbray were merely an effect of his sturdy loyalty to Richard. Likewise, it is unclear whether he initially realizes that his return from exile commits him not merely to regaining the Lancastrian estates but to a more thorough attack on Richard's sovereignty. Bolingbroke never appears before us, alone or in company, to ponder his own conduct and motives. In this regard, he differs not only from the obsessively self-reflective Richard but from other Shakespearean usurpers: Richard III, Macbeth, *Hamlet*'s Claudius.

In Act 4, however unable he may be to justify the grounds of his own authority, Bolingbroke—now King Henry IV—astutely recognizes that he must convince his subjects that he is legitimately entitled to the crown. Henry needs, somehow, to transfer to himself that mysterious sense of royal sanctity in which Richard initially places so much confidence and to which Henry has no plausible claim. Henry and his followers thus attempt to paper over his gross procedural breach with procedural punctiliousness. Richard cannot be summarily imprisoned or executed; rather, he must seem voluntarily and publicly to resign his sovereignty to Henry.

Unfortunately for Henry, he is not good at managing such rituals, while Richard is in his element. In 4.1, Richard masterfully seizes the symbolic initiative from the apparent victors. "Now mark me how I will undo myself," he announces (line 193).

> I give this heavy weight from off my head,
> And this unwieldy sceptre from my hand,
> The pride of kingly sway from out my heart.
> With mine own tears I wash away my balm,
> With mine own hands I give away my crown,
> With mine own tongue deny my sacred state,
> With mine own breath release all duteous oaths.
> All pomp and majesty I do forswear.
> My manors, rents, revenues I forgo.
> My acts, decrees, and statutes I deny.
>
> (lines 194–203)

Richard's actions and words here are meant to recall a coronation ceremony, in which the king is invested with the crown and scepter as his insignia of office, anointed with balm as a sign that he is God's chosen, promised the allegiance of his subjects, given formal title to the royal domains. One of the main points of this ceremony is its permanence: it cannot be undone. By referring to this ritual at the moment of his deposition, Richard implies that giving up the crown is an impossible act, a kind of absurdity. Moreover, reversing the ceremonies—taking off the crown rather than putting it on, relinquishing rather than accepting the scepter—suggests a special scandal. In medieval and early modern Europe, as among some fundamentalist religious groups today, reversing beneficent ceremonies supposedly evoked their diabolical opposites. One called up devils by reciting Scripture passages backward, or bound oneself to Satan by performing an inversion of baptismal rites. Richard's enthusiastic self-dramatization of his plight does not quell doubts about the legitimacy of the usurpation, but encourages those doubts. Immediately after Richard departs, his friends begin to conspire on his behalf; and although their plot is eventually crushed, Henry's reign will never be quiet thereafter.

As the play proceeds, the view of politics associated with Bolingbroke, a view that initially seems hardheaded and realistic, begins to seem not very practical after all. An acceptable social order requires more than the brute force Henry deploys so expertly. It requires a common set of ideas and practices, a common language and attitude, a set of rituals—all the immaterial abstractions Henry had originally been inclined to disregard.

Just as Shakespeare, over the course of the play, alters our view of the political dilemma represented by the rebellion, so he manipulates our outlook on its main characters. As soon as Richard has lost his throne, we need no longer evaluate him in terms of his effectiveness as a ruler. Immediately his talents seem more obvious, his faults less reprehensible. Richard's extraordinary poetic and introspective gifts allow him to analyze his own situation with a delicacy and insight of which Bolingbroke is entirely incapable. He is acutely aware of the figure he cuts to the only audience that matters to him, himself; in fact, his self-destructive behavior might be seen as an unconscious quest for the expressive opportunities provided only by misery. Always preoccupied with analogies between kingship and godhead, Richard identifies more and more, as the play

Death of Phaeton. From Antonio Tempesta, *Ovid's "Metamorphoses"* (1606).

continues, with the suffering Christ, consoling himself with the comparison and deriving from it a certain sad grandeur. Obviously Richard's particular strengths are intrinsically connected to his weaknesses, but that does not mean that those strengths are negligible. They are especially hard to ignore in a *play*, in which poetic language, symbolic thought, and the effective deployment of spectacle are central concerns.

Our shifting view of Richard has produced, in both Shakespeare's time and our own, a certain ambiguity as to the play's genre. When Shakespeare's friends and fellow actors compiled his works in the First Folio, they grouped *Richard II* with the history plays—understandably, since it concerns itself with problems of rule and the legitimacy of rulers, is based on historical materials, and inaugurates a series of plays that deals with the reigns of three successive kings. Yet in its earliest printed version the play was called "The Tragedie of Richard II," a title that suggests a focus not on the fate of a nation but on the disastrous career of a fascinating, flawed individual.

Richard's case encourages us to reflect on the way the politics and the values of political life—the dominant concerns of history plays—constrain our evaluation of him. In *Richard II,* Shakespeare uses female characters to suggest the possibility of an alternative perspective on the events he depicts. In the second scene, the Duchess of Gloucester urges Gaunt to revenge Thomas of Woodstock, her husband and his brother. Gaunt refuses: in his view, the subject's duty to his monarch must outweigh his obligation to his kin. Their conversation reminds us that England's political crisis is also a familial disaster, and that construing it as one rather than the other has important consequences.

Throughout the play, the men, like Gaunt, tend to subordinate domestic concerns to civic ones, family bonds to the all-important relationship between king and subject. The women, like the Duchess of Gloucester, do the opposite. Although the historical Richard was married to a ten-year-old queen, Shakespeare makes Isabella a mature young woman and invents touching, wholly nonfactual scenes in which she intuitively senses her husband's trouble, then discovers the usurpation in a garden and suffers through an imposed parting from her husband. The pathos of these scenes derives from the Queen's utter helplessness. She is imagined as Richard's wife, a domestic function, not England's Queen, a public one. All her responses are thus founded on her singleminded loyalty to the marital tie, as sharply distinguished from the bonds of politics. "Banish us both, and send the King with me," she begs Northumberland, when he informs them that she will be exiled and her husband kept under house arrest in England. "That were some love, but little policy," Northumberland replies (5.1.83, 84). The last thing Bolingbroke needs is a legitimate child of Richard's to confuse his claims on the throne even more. But the Queen fails to grasp Northumberland's meaning, because she does not understand "policy"—that is, politics. It is not her sphere.

The difference between civic and domestic domains also appears in the scenes immediately following, which stage a dispute between the Duke and Duchess of York over their son, Aumerle. Here again Shakespeare altered his sources, unhistorically making Aumerle an only child and the Duchess his natural mother. Having discovered that Aumerle is involved in a plot to kill the new Henry IV and reinstate Richard, York feels bound to inform Henry of the treason. He puts what he sees as his civic duty above the ties of blood. The Duchess is outraged. "Wilt thou not hide the trespass of thine own?" she asks. "Have we more sons? Or are we like to have?" (5.2.89–90). For her, the familial relationship takes precedence over the public one.

This dividing of the "public" male role from the "private" female role is hardly a Shakespearean invention. But Shakespeare puts that division of perspective to thematic use in *Richard II*. In 2.2, when Isabella has a presentiment of ruin, Bushy tries to console her in an elaborate speech about perspective glasses and "anamorphic" paintings. These two Renaissance inventions encourage speculation about the difference between the "right" or "centered" way of seeing and an oblique outlook from which shapes look very different. Of course, Isabella's inexplicable presentiment of disaster turns out to be more apt than her male companions' optimism. Perhaps the women's different perspective implies that the history play's focus on traditionally masculine political concerns may exclude whole realms of human experience.

In the fifth act, Richard—weeping, enclosed, suffering, and excluded from authority—finds himself in the position the play has defined as a feminine one. Politically marginalized, he nonetheless dominates the closing moments of the play, first by his powerful soliloquizing and later by his courageous defiance of his murderers. In some respects, the final scenes of *Richard II* recall its opening. What seems to be a simple opposition turns out to be far more complex, as categories of expedience and impracticality, power and weakness, right and wrong mutate and change places. Once again, the apparent conclusion of a conflict merely postpones its resolution. The *Henry IV* plays will stage the aftermath.

KATHARINE EISAMAN MAUS

TEXTUAL NOTE

The first printed version of *Richard II* was a Quarto published in 1597 (Q1). The quality of the text is good, and most scholars have assumed that it was printed either directly from Shakespeare's manuscript or (because the stage directions are very brief) from a transcript of Shakespeare's manuscript not designed to provide the basis for theatrical performance. Two more Quartos, printed in 1598 (Q2 and Q3), mention Shakespeare as the author of the play on their title pages. In 1608, a fourth Quarto appeared (Q4), and in 1615, a fifth (Q5); each Quarto seems based on the one that had appeared before it. However, Q4 was the first to print the "new additions of the parliament scene, and the deposing of King Richard," scenes not present in the earlier Quartos.

The First Folio of 1623 (F) text was probably printed with reference to a promptbook, because it has much more detailed stage directions than the quarto texts. Editors disagree, however, over whether this promptbook text was based on Shakespeare's manuscript or on a corrected copy of Q1 or Q3. F includes a version of the abdication scene that is different, and better, than the one in Q4 and Q5. F omits some lines that are present in Q1, and there are also a number of single-word divergences between the two texts. In cases where only a single line is missing, the deletion may represent a compositor's error, so the Oxford editors have followed Q1. In cases where more substantial passages have been excluded, the editors assume that Shakespeare himself was responsible; these passages are indented in the text.

The most important difference between Q1 and F is F's inclusion of the deposition scene. Some scholars have argued that Elizabeth's censors considered the passage too provocative to stage and insisted that it be deleted; after Elizabeth's death, it was possible to reinstate the offending material. Others argue that Shakespeare revised the play during the first decade of the seventeenth century and wrote the deposition scene at that time.

The Oxford editors have generally based their text on Q1, except for the deposition scene, where they have followed F. They have, however, assimilated many of F's more complete stage directions and many of its single-word variants from Q1, when in the editors' opinion those variants represent Shakespeare's revisions to his own text rather than compositorial corruptions.

SELECTED BIBLIOGRAPHY

Calderwood, James L. "*Richard II* and the Fall of Speech." *Shakespearean Metadrama: The Argument of the Play in "Titus Andronicus," "Love's Labour's Lost," "Romeo and Juliet," and "Richard II."* Minneapolis: University of Minnesota Press, 1971. 149–86. The transfer of power from Richard to Bolingbroke as a version of Shakespeare's move from lyric stylization to a sparer dramatic language.

Doran, Madeline. "Imagery in *Richard II* and *Henry IV.*" *Modern Language Review* 37 (1942): 113–22. Changes in handling metaphor and simile as key to the differences between *Richard II* and *Henry IV, Part 1*.

Gaudet, Paul. "The 'Parasitical Counselors' in Shakespeare's *Richard II*: A Problem in Dramatic Interpretation." *Shakespeare Quarterly* 33 (1982): 142–54. Bushy, Bagot, and Greene: innocent or guilty?

Hamilton, Donna. "The State of Law in *Richard II.*" *Shakespeare Quarterly* 34 (1983): 5–17. The relation between monarchy and law in *Richard II* and in early modern political theory.

Kantorowicz, Ernst H. Chapter 2. *The King's Two Bodies: A Study in Mediaeval Political Theology.* Princeton: Princeton University Press, 1957. 24–41. Theory of kingship in *Richard II*.

Kastan, David. "Proud Majesty Made a Subject: Shakespeare and the Spectacle of Rule." *Shakespeare Quarterly* 37 (1986): 459–75. Theatrical representation destabilizes kingship in *Richard II*.

McMillin, Scott. "*Richard II*: Eyes of Sorrow, Eyes of Desire." *Shakespeare Quarterly* 35 (1984): 40–52. An impulse to self-expressiveness is at odds with the exercise of political power in *Richard II*.

Moore, Jeanie Grant. "Queen of Sorrow, King of Grief: Reflections and Perspectives in *Richard II.*" *In Another Country: Feminist Perspectives on Renaissance Drama.* Ed. Dorothea Kehler and Susan Baker. Metuchen, N.J.: Scarecrow Press, 1991. 19–35. Special attention to imagery of mirrors and anamorphic pictures.

Saccio, Peter. *Shakespeare's English Kings: History, Chronicle, and Drama*. 2nd ed. New York: Oxford University Press, 2000. 17–35. Succinct account of the historical background to Shakespeare's play.

Tillyard, E. M. W. *Shakespeare's History Plays*. London: Chatto & Windus, 1944. 244–63. *Richard II* shows the transition from the medieval to the modern world.

Zitner, Sheldon. "Aumerle's Conspiracy." *Studies in English Literature* 14 (1974): 238–57. The importance of the Aumerle scenes for the end of *Richard II*.

FILM

King Richard the Second. 1978. Dir. David Giles, UK. 158 mins. In this BBC-TV production, Derek Jacobi as an effeminate Richard II confronts Jon Finch as the calculating Bolingbroke. John Gielgud is a notable John of Gaunt.

The Tragedy of King Richard
the Second

The Persons of the Play

KING RICHARD II
The QUEEN, his wife
JOHN OF GAUNT, Duke of Lancaster, Richard's uncle
Harry BOLINGBROKE, Duke of Hereford, John of Gaunt's son,
  later KING HENRY IV
DUCHESS OF GLOUCESTER, widow of Gaunt's and York's brother
Duke of YORK, King Richard's uncle
DUCHESS OF YORK
Duke of AUMERLE, their son
Thomas MOWBRAY, Duke of Norfolk

GREEN
BAGOT } followers of King Richard
BUSHY

Percy, Earl of NORTHUMBERLAND
HARRY PERCY, his son
Lord ROSS } of Bolingbroke's party
Lord WILLOUGHBY

Earl of SALISBURY
BISHOP OF CARLISLE } of King Richard's party
Sir Stephen SCROPE

Lord BERKELEY
Lord FITZWALTER
Duke of SURREY
ABBOT OF WESTMINSTER
Sir Piers EXTON
LORD MARSHAL
HERALDS
CAPTAIN of the Welsh army
LADIES attending the Queen
GARDENER
Gardener's MEN
Exton's MEN
KEEPER of the prison at Pomfret
GROOM of King Richard's stable
Lords, soldiers, attendants

1.1

Enter KING RICHARD, JOHN OF GAUNT, *with* [*the* LORD
MARSHAL], *other nobles, and attendants*

KING RICHARD   Old John of Gaunt,[1] time-honoured Lancaster,
  Hast thou according to thy oath and bond
  Brought hither Henry Hereford, thy bold son,
  Here to make good the boist'rous late appeal,°   *violent recent accusation*

1.1. Location: Windsor Castle.
1. Named after his birthplace, Ghent (in Flanders); his   title was Duke of Lancaster. He was fifty-eight years old.

5   Which then our leisure² would not let us hear,
    Against the Duke of Norfolk, Thomas Mowbray?
  JOHN OF GAUNT   I have, my liege.
  KING RICHARD   Tell me moreover, hast thou sounded° him   *inquired of*
    If he appeal the Duke on ancient malice³
10   Or worthily, as a good subject should,
    On some known ground of treachery in him?
  JOHN OF GAUNT   As near as I could sift° him on that argument,°   *discover from / topic*
    On some apparent° danger seen in him   *manifest*
    Aimed at your highness, no inveterate malice.
  KING RICHARD   Then call them to our presence.

                          [Exit one or more]
15   Face to face
    And frowning brow to brow, ourselves will hear
    The accuser and the accusèd freely speak.
    High-stomached° are they both and full of ire;   *Haughty*
    In rage, deaf as the sea, hasty as fire.

        Enter BOLINGBROKE *[Duke of Hereford], and* MOWBRAY
        [Duke of Norfolk]
20   BOLINGBROKE   Many years of happy days befall
    My gracious sovereign, my most loving liege!
  MOWBRAY   Each day still better others' happiness,⁴
    Until the heavens, envying earth's good hap,°   *fortune*
    Add an immortal title to your crown!
25   KING RICHARD   We thank you both. Yet one but flatters us,
    As well appeareth by the cause you come,
    Namely, to appeal each other of high treason.
    Cousin of Hereford, what dost thou object°   *charge*
    Against the Duke of Norfolk, Thomas Mowbray?
30   BOLINGBROKE   First—heaven be the record to my speech—
    In the devotion of a subject's love,
    Tend'ring° the precious safety of my Prince,   *Having care for*
    And free from other misbegotten hate,
    Come I appellant° to this princely presence.   *as accuser*
35   Now, Thomas Mowbray, do I turn to thee;
    And mark my greeting° well, for what I speak   *address*
    My body shall make good upon this earth,
    Or my divine° soul answer it in heaven.   *Immortal*
    Thou art a traitor and a miscreant,
40   Too good° to be so, and too bad to live,   *wellborn*
    Since the more fair and crystal is the sky,
    The uglier seem the clouds that in it fly.
    Once more, the more to aggravate the note,°   *emphasize the reproach*
    With a foul traitor's name stuff I thy throat,
45   And wish, so please my sovereign, ere I move
    What my tongue speaks my right-drawn sword may prove.
  MOWBRAY   Let not my cold words here accuse my zeal.° *cast doubt on my loyalty*
    'Tis not the trial of a woman's war,
    The bitter clamour of two eager° tongues,   *sharp*
50   Can arbitrate⁵ this cause betwixt us twain.
    The blood is hot that must be cooled for this.

---

2. That is, lack of leisure. Richard uses the royal "we."   4. May each day be better than the last.
3. Out of long-standing enmity.   5. Judge (without implying compromise).

Yet can I not of such tame patience boast
As to be hushed and naught at all to say.
First, the fair reverence of your highness curbs me

55 From giving reins and spurs to my free speech,
Which else would post° until it had returned   *ride fast*
These terms of treason doubled down his throat.
Setting aside his high blood's royalty,[6]
And let him be° no kinsman to my liege,   *And as if he were*

60 I do defy him, and I spit at him,
Call him a slanderous coward and a villain;
Which to maintain I would allow him odds,
And meet him, were I tied° to run afoot   *obliged*
Even to the frozen ridges of the Alps,

65 Or any other ground inhabitable,
Wherever Englishman durst set his foot.
Meantime let this defend my loyalty:
By all my hopes, most falsely doth he lie.

    BOLINGBROKE [*throwing down his gage*][7] Pale trembling coward,
        there I throw my gage,

70 Disclaiming here the kindred of[8] the King,
And lay aside my high blood's royalty,
Which fear, not reverence, makes thee to except.°   *set aside*
If guilty dread have left thee so much strength
As to take up mine honour's pawn,° then stoop.   *(the gage)*

75 By that, and all the rites of knighthood else,
Will I make good against thee, arm to arm,
What I have spoke or thou canst worse devise.

    MOWBRAY [*taking up the gage*]   I take it up,[9] and by that sword I swear
    Which gently laid my knighthood on my shoulder,

80 I'll answer thee in any fair degree°   *honorable manner*
Or chivalrous design of knightly trial;
And when I mount, alive may I not light°   *dismount*
If I be traitor or unjustly fight!

    KING RICHARD [*to* BOLINGBROKE]   What doth our cousin lay to
        Mowbray's charge?

85 It must be great that can inherit us°   *make us have*
So much as of a thought of ill in him.

    BOLINGBROKE   Look what I speak, my life shall prove it true:
That Mowbray hath received eight thousand nobles°   *gold coins*
In name of lendings° for your highness' soldiers,   *As advances on pay*

90 The which he hath detained for lewd employments,°   *improper uses*
Like a false traitor and injurious villain.
Besides I say, and will in battle prove,
Or° here or elsewhere, to the furthest verge°   *Either / horizon*
That ever was surveyed by English eye,

95 That all the treasons for these eighteen years[1]
Complotted° and contrivèd in this land   *Plotted*
Fetch° from false Mowbray their first head° and spring.   *Derive / source*
Further I say, and further will maintain
Upon his bad life, to make all this good,

---

6. Bolingbroke as well as Richard was a grandson of   8. The privilege of kinship with.
Edward III.   9. Thereby accepting the challenge.
7. Pledge to combat—probably a glove.   1. Since the Peasants' Revolt of 1381.

100   That he did plot the Duke of Gloucester's death,[2]
        Suggest° his soon-believing° adversaries,   *Incite / credulous*
        And consequently,° like a traitor-coward,   *subsequently*
        Sluiced° out his innocent soul through streams of blood;   *Let flow*
        Which blood, like sacrificing Abel's,[3] cries
105   Even from the tongueless caverns of the earth
        To me for justice and rough chastisement.
        And, by the glorious worth of my descent,
        This arm shall do it or this life be spent.
    KING RICHARD   How high a pitch[4] his resolution soars!
110   Thomas of Norfolk, what sayst thou to this?
    MOWBRAY   O, let my sovereign turn away his face,
        And bid his ears a little while be deaf,
        Till I have told this slander of his blood°   *disgrace to his ancestry*
        How God and good men hate so foul a liar!
115   KING RICHARD   Mowbray, impartial are our eyes and ears.
        Were he my brother, nay, my kingdom's heir,
        As he is but my father's brother's son,
        Now by my sceptre's awe I make a vow
        Such neighbour-nearness to our sacred blood
120   Should nothing privilege him, nor partialize°   *bias*
        The unstooping firmness of my upright soul.
        He is our subject, Mowbray; so art thou.
        Free speech and fearless I to thee allow.
    MOWBRAY   Then, Bolingbroke, as low as to thy heart
125   Through the false passage of thy throat thou liest!
        Three parts of that receipt° I had for Calais   *money received*
        Disbursed I duly to his highness' soldiers.
        The other part reserved I by consent,
        For that my sovereign liege was in my debt
130   Upon remainder of a dear account[5]
        Since last I went to France to fetch his queen.
        Now swallow down that lie. For Gloucester's death,
        I slew him not, but to my own disgrace
        Neglected my sworn duty in that case.[6]
135   For you, my noble lord of Lancaster,
        The honourable father to my foe,
        Once did I lay an ambush for your life,
        A trespass that doth vex my grievèd soul;
        But ere I last received the Sacrament
140   I did confess it, and exactly° begged   *expressly*
        Your grace's pardon, and I hope I had it.
        This is my fault. As for the rest appealed,°   *accused*
        It issues from the rancour of a villain,
        A recreant° and most degenerate° traitor,   *faithless / cowardly*
145   Which in myself° I boldly will defend,   *my own person*
        [*He throws down his gage*]
        And interchangeably° hurl down my gage   *reciprocally*

---

2. Thomas of Woodstock, Duke of Gloucester, was mysteriously murdered while in the custody of Mowbray. Richard had reason to hate him; earlier Woodstock had attempted to curtail the young King's power by placing authority in the hands of a royal council, of which Woodstock was the head.
3. In Genesis 4, Cain murders his brother Abel

because God prefers Abel's offering of sheep to Cain's fruits of the ground.
4. Highest point of a falcon's flight.
5. For the balance of a large sum.
6. Mowbray is circumspect here; in the next scene, Gaunt and the Duchess assert less ambiguously that Richard ordered him to kill Woodstock.

Upon this overweening traitor's foot,
To prove myself a loyal gentleman
Even in the best blood chambered° in his bosom;   *enclosed*
150 In haste whereof° most heartily I pray   *To hasten which*
Your highness to assign our trial day.
    [BOLINGBROKE *takes up the gage*]
KING RICHARD   Wrath-kindled gentlemen, be ruled by me.
Let's purge this choler without letting blood.[7]
This we prescribe, though no physician:
155 Deep malice[8] makes too deep incision;
Forget, forgive, conclude,° and be agreed;   *come to terms*
Our doctors say this is no time to bleed.
Good uncle, let this end where it begun.
We'll calm the Duke of Norfolk, you your son.
160 JOHN OF GAUNT   To be a make-peace shall become my age.
Throw down, my son, the Duke of Norfolk's gage.[9]
KING RICHARD   And, Norfolk, throw down his.
JOHN OF GAUNT   When, Harry, when?
Obedience bids I should not bid again.
KING RICHARD   Norfolk, throw down! We bid; there is no boot.°   *help for it*
165 MOWBRAY [*kneeling*]   Myself I throw, dread sovereign, at thy foot.
My life thou shalt command, but not my shame.
The one my duty owes, but my fair name,
Despite of death that lives upon my grave,
To dark dishonour's use thou shalt not have.
170 I am disgraced, impeached, and baffled[1] here,
Pierced to the soul with slander's venomed spear,
The which no balm can cure but his heart blood
Which breathed° this poison.   *uttered*
KING RICHARD   Rage must be withstood.
Give me his gage. Lions make leopards tame.[2]
175 MOWBRAY [*standing*]   Yea, but not change his spots.[3] Take but my shame,
And I resign my gage. My dear dear lord,
The purest treasure mortal times° afford   *earthly lives*
Is spotless reputation; that away,
Men are but gilded loam, or painted clay.
180 A jewel in a ten-times barred-up chest
Is a bold spirit in a loyal breast.
Mine honour is my life. Both grow in one.°   *united*
Take honour from me, and my life is done.
Then, dear my liege, mine honour let me try.°   *put to the test*
185 In that I live, and for that will I die.
KING RICHARD   Cousin, throw down your gage. Do you begin.
BOLINGBROKE   O God defend my soul from such deep sin!
Shall I seem crest-fallen in my father's sight?
Or with pale beggar-fear impeach my height°   *disgrace my rank*
190 Before this out-dared dastard?° Ere my tongue   *coward*
Shall wound my honour with such feeble wrong,
Or sound so base a parle,° my teeth shall tear   *trumpet call for a truce*
The slavish motive° of recanting fear,   *instrument (the tongue)*

7. Let's expel the bile (thought to be the physiological cause of anger) without bloodletting (in combat; as a medical remedy).
8. Enmity; virulence (of a disease).
9. As a gesture of reconciliation.

1. Publicly stripped of knighthood (a chivalric term).
2. Lions were the King's emblem; leopards were Mowbray's. Heraldic banners are likely to be displayed onstage in this scene.
3. Leopard spots; stains of reproach.

And spit it bleeding in his° high disgrace   *its*
195   Where shame doth harbour, even in Mowbray's face.

                        Exit [JOHN OF] GAUNT

KING RICHARD   We were not born to sue, but to command;
    Which since we cannot do to make you friends,
    Be ready, as your lives shall answer it,
    At Coventry upon Saint Lambert's day.°   *September 17*
200   There shall your swords and lances arbitrate
    The swelling difference of your settled hate.
    Since we cannot atone° you, we shall see   *reconcile*
    Justice design the victor's chivalry.⁴
    Lord Marshal, command our officers-at-arms
205   Be ready to direct these home alarms.°   *Exeunt*   *domestic disturbances*

1.2

Enter JOHN OF GAUNT [*Duke of Lancaster*], *with*
DUCHESS OF GLOUCESTER

JOHN OF GAUNT   Alas, the part I had in Gloucester's blood¹
    Doth more solicit me than your exclaims°   *exclamations*
    To stir against the butchers of his life.
    But since correction lieth in² those hands
5   Which made the fault that we cannot correct,
    Put we our quarrel to the will of heaven,
    Who, when they see the hours ripe on earth,
    Will rain hot vengeance on offenders' heads.

DUCHESS OF GLOUCESTER   Finds brotherhood in thee no sharper spur?
10   Hath love in thy old blood no living fire?
    Edward's° seven sons, whereof thyself art one,   *Edward III's*
    Were as seven vials of his sacred blood,
    Or seven fair branches springing from one root,
    Some of those seven are dried by nature's course,
15   Some of those branches by the destinies cut;
    But Thomas, my dear lord, my life, my Gloucester,
    One vial full of Edward's sacred blood,
    One flourishing branch of his most royal root,
    Is cracked, and all the precious liquor spilt;
20   Is hacked down, and his summer leaves all faded
    By envy's° hand and murder's bloody axe.   *hatred's*
    Ah, Gaunt, his blood was thine! That bed, that womb,
    That mettle,° that self° mould that fashioned thee,   *substance / same*
    Made him a man; and though thou liv'st and breathest,
25   Yet art thou slain in him. Thou dost consent
    In some large measure to thy father's death
    In that thou seest thy wretched brother die,
    Who was the model of thy father's life.
    Call it not patience, Gaunt, it is despair.
30   In suff'ring thus thy brother to be slaughtered
    Thou show'st the naked° pathway to thy life,   *defenseless; obvious*
    Teaching stern murder how to butcher thee.
    That which in mean° men we entitle patience   *common*
    Is pale cold cowardice in noble breasts.

---

4. Indicate the victor in knightly combat.
1.2 Location: John of Gaunt's house.
1. Thomas of Woodstock, Duke of Gloucester, was

Gaunt's younger brother.
2. Since punishment depends on (Gaunt blames Richard for Woodstock's death).

35   What shall I say? To safeguard thine own life
        The best way is to venge° my Gloucester's death.   *avenge*
JOHN OF GAUNT   God's is the quarrel; for God's substitute
        His deputy anointed in his sight,
        Hath caused his death; the which if wrongfully,
40   Let heaven revenge, for I may never lift
        An angry arm against his minister.°   *agent*
DUCHESS OF GLOUCESTER   Where then, alas, may I complain myself?
JOHN OF GAUNT   To God, the widow's champion and defence.
DUCHESS OF GLOUCESTER   Why then, I will. Farewell, old Gaunt.
45   Thou goest to Coventry, there to behold
        Our cousin° Hereford and fell° Mowbray fight.   *Kinsman / ruthless*
        O, set my husband's wrongs on Hereford's spear,
        That it may enter butcher Mowbray's breast!
        Or if misfortune miss the first career,[3]
50   Be Mowbray's sins so heavy in his bosom
        That they may break his foaming courser's back
        And throw the rider headlong in the lists,
        A caitiff,° recreant° to my cousin Hereford!   *A wretch / yielding*
        Farewell, old Gaunt. Thy sometimes° brother's wife   *former*
55   With her companion, grief, must end her life.
JOHN OF GAUNT   Sister, farewell. I must to Coventry.
        As much good stay with thee as go with me.
DUCHESS OF GLOUCESTER   Yet one word more. Grief boundeth[4]
          where it falls,
        Not with the empty hollowness, but weight.[5]
60   I take my leave before I have begun,
        For sorrow ends not when it seemeth done.
        Commend me to thy brother, Edmund York.
        Lo, this is all.—Nay, yet depart not so!
        Though this be all, do not so quickly go.
65   I shall remember more. Bid him—ah, what?—
        With all good speed at Pleshey[6] visit me.
        Alack, and what shall good old York there see
        But empty lodgings° and unfurnished walls,   *rooms*
        Unpeopled offices,° untrodden stones,   *servants' quarters*
70   And what hear there for welcome but my groans?
        Therefore commend me; let him not come there
        To seek out sorrow that dwells everywhere.
        Desolate, desolate will I hence and die.
        The last leave of thee takes my weeping eye. *Exeunt [severally]*°   *separately*

1.3
Enter LORD MARSHAL *[with officers setting out chairs],*
and Duke [of] AUMERLE

LORD MARSHAL   My lord Aumerle, is Harry Hereford armed?
AUMERLE   Yea, at all points,° and longs to enter in.   *completely*
LORD MARSHAL   The Duke of Norfolk, sprightfully° and bold,   *spiritedly*
        Stays° but the summons of the appellant's° trumpet.   *Awaits / accuser's*
5   AUMERLE   Why then, the champions are prepared, and stay
        For nothing but his majesty's approach.

---

3. If (Mowbray's) downfall fail to occur at the first
encounter.
4. Rebounds (causing further sound; the Duchess
apologizes for continuing to speak).

5. Not because it is hollow, like a bouncing ball, but
because it is heavy.
6. Gloucester's house in Essex.
1.3 Location: The lists (tournament arena) at Coventry.

The trumpets sound, and KING [RICHARD] *enters with*
[JOHN OF] GAUNT, BUSHY, BAGOT, GREEN, *and other*
nobles. When they are set, enter MOWBRAY *Duke of Nor-*
folk, defendant, in arms, and a HERALD [*to Mowbray*]

KING RICHARD   Marshal, demand of yonder champion
The cause of his arrival here in arms.
Ask him his name, and orderly° proceed   *according to the rules*
10   To swear him in the justice of his cause.
LORD MARSHAL [*to* MOWBRAY]   In God's name and the King's,
        say who thou art,
And why thou com'st thus knightly clad in arms,
Against what man thou com'st, and what thy quarrel.
Speak truly on thy knighthood and thy oath,
15   As so defend thee heaven and thy valour!
MOWBRAY   My name is Thomas Mowbray, Duke of Norfolk,
Who hither come engagèd by my oath—
Which God defend° a knight should violate—   *forbid*
Both to defend my loyalty and truth
20   To God, my king, and my succeeding issue,
Against the Duke of Hereford that appeals me;
And by the grace of God and this mine arm
To prove him, in defending of myself,
A traitor to my God, my king, and me.
25   And as I truly fight, defend me heaven!
        [*He sits.*]
        The trumpets sound. Enter [BOLINGBROKE] *Duke of*
        Hereford, appellant, in armour, and HERALD
KING RICHARD   Marshal, ask yonder knight in arms
Both who he is and why he cometh hither
Thus plated in habiliments of war;[1]
And formally, according to our law,
30   Depose° him in the justice of his cause.   *Take testimony from*
LORD MARSHAL [*to* BOLINGBROKE]   What is thy name? And
        wherefore com'st thou hither
Before King Richard in his royal lists?
Against whom comest thou? And what's thy quarrel?
Speak like a true knight, so defend thee heaven!
35   BOLINGBROKE   Harry of Hereford, Lancaster, and Derby
Am I, who ready here do stand in arms
To prove by God's grace and my body's valour
In lists on Thomas Mowbray, Duke of Norfolk,
That he is a traitor foul and dangerous
40   To God of heaven, King Richard, and to me.
And as I truly fight, defend me heaven!
        [*He sits*]
LORD MARSHAL   On pain of death, no person be so bold
Or daring-hardy as to touch the lists
Except the Marshal and such officers
45   Appointed to direct these fair designs.°   *procedures*
BOLINGBROKE [*standing*]   Lord Marshal, let me kiss my sovereign's hand
And bow my knee before his majesty,
For Mowbray and myself are like two men
That vow a long and weary pilgrimage;

---

1. Wearing plated battle armor.

50   Then let us take a ceremonious leave
    And loving farewell of our several° friends.   *respective*
    LORD MARSHAL [*to* KING RICHARD]   The appellant in all duty
      greets your highness,
    And craves to kiss your hand and take his leave.
    KING RICHARD   We will descend and fold him in our arms.
      [*He descends from his seat and embraces* BOLINGBROKE]
55   Cousin of Hereford, as° thy cause is just,   *insofar as*
    So be thy fortune in this royal fight.
    Farewell, my blood, which if today thou shed,
    Lament we may, but not revenge thee dead.
    BOLINGBROKE   O, let no noble eye profane° a tear   *misuse*
60   For me if I be gored with Mowbray's spear.
    As confident as is the falcon's flight
    Against a bird do I with Mowbray fight.
    [*To the* LORD MARSHAL] My loving lord, I take my leave of you;
    [*To* AUMERLE] Of you, my noble cousin, Lord Aumerle;
65   Not sick, although I have to do with death,
    But lusty,° young, and cheerly drawing breath.   *vigorous*
    Lo, as at English feasts, so I regreet°   *greet*
    The daintiest[2] last, to make the end most sweet.
    [*To* GAUNT, *kneeling*] O thou, the earthly author of my blood,
70   Whose youthful spirit in me regenerate°   *reborn*
    Doth with a two-fold vigour lift me up
    To reach at victory above my head,
    Add proof° unto mine armour with thy prayers,   *invulnerability*
    And with thy blessings steel° my lance's point,   *harden*
75   That it may enter Mowbray's waxen° coat   *(that is, soft)*
    And furbish new the name of John a Gaunt
    Even in the lusty haviour° of his son.   *conduct*
    JOHN OF GAUNT   God in thy good cause make thee prosperous!
    Be swift like lightning in the execution,
80   And let thy blows, doubly redoublèd,
    Fall like amazing° thunder on the casque°   *stupefying / helmet*
    Of thy adverse pernicious enemy.
    Rouse up thy youthful blood, be valiant, and live.
    BOLINGBROKE [*standing*]   Mine innocence and Saint George
      to thrive!
85   MOWBRAY [*standing*]   However God or fortune cast my lot,
    There lives or dies, true to King Richard's throne,
    A loyal, just, and upright gentleman.
    Never did captive with a freer heart
    Cast off his chains of bondage and embrace
90   His golden uncontrolled enfranchisement°   *unrestrained liberation*
    More than my dancing soul doth celebrate
    This feast of battle with mine adversary.
    Most mighty liege, and my companion peers,
    Take from my mouth the wish of happy years.
95   As gentle and as jocund as to jest°   *take part in revels*
    Go I to fight. Truth hath a quiet breast.
    KING RICHARD   Farewell, my lord. Securely° I espy   *Confidently*
    Virtue with valour couchèd[3] in thine eye.—
    Order the trial, Marshal, and begin.

2. Finest thing, like a dessert.   3. Lodged; aimed in readiness (like a lance).

100 LORD MARSHAL   Harry of Hereford, Lancaster, and Derby,
    Receive thy lance; and God defend the right!
    [*An officer bears a lance to* BOLINGBROKE]
    BOLINGBROKE   Strong as a tower in hope, I cry 'Amen!'°   *from Psalm 61:3*
    LORD MARSHAL [*to an officer*]   Go bear this lance to Thomas,
        Duke of Norfolk.
    [*An officer bears a lance to* MOWBRAY]
    FIRST HERALD   Harry of Hereford, Lancaster, and Derby
105   Stands here for God, his sovereign, and himself,
    On pain to be found false and recreant,
    To prove the Duke of Norfolk, Thomas Mowbray,
    A traitor to his God, his king, and him,
    And dares him to set forward to the fight.
110 SECOND HERALD   Here standeth Thomas Mowbray, Duke of Norfolk,
    On pain to be found false and recreant,
    Both to defend himself and to approve°   *prove*
    Henry of Hereford, Lancaster, and Derby
    To God his sovereign and to him disloyal,
115   Courageously and with a free desire
    Attending but the signal to begin.
    LORD MARSHAL   Sound trumpets, and set forward combatants!
    [*A charge is sounded.*]
    [KING RICHARD *throws down his warder*]°   *staff*
    Stay, the King hath thrown his warder down.
    KING RICHARD   Let them lay by their helmets and their spears,
120   And both return back to their chairs again.
    [BOLINGBROKE *and* MOWBRAY *disarm and sit*]
    [*To the nobles*] Withdraw with us, and let the trumpets sound
    While we return° these dukes what we decree.   *Until we deliver to*
        A long flourish° [*during which* KING RICHARD *and his*   *extended trumpet call*
        nobles withdraw and hold council, then come forward.
        KING RICHARD *addresses* BOLINGBROKE *and* MOWBRAY]
    Draw near, and list what with our council we have done.
    For that° our kingdom's earth should not be soiled   *Because*
125 With that dear blood which it hath fosterèd,
    And for° our eyes do hate the dire aspect°   *because / spectacle*
    Of civil wounds ploughed up with neighbours' swords,[4]
127.1   *And for we think the eagle-wingèd pride*
            Of sky-aspiring and ambitious thoughts
            With rival-hating envy set on you°   *malice set you on*
            To wake our peace, which in our country's cradle
127.5   *Draws the sweet infant breath of gentle sleep,*
    Which, so roused up with boist'rous untuned drums,
    With harsh-resounding trumpets' dreadful bray,
130 And grating shock of wrathful iron arms,
    Might from our quiet confines fright fair peace
    And make us wade even in our kindred's blood,
    Therefore we banish you our territories.
    You, cousin Hereford, upon pain° of life,   *loss*
135 Till twice five summers have enriched our fields
    Shall not regreet° our fair dominions,   *greet again*
    But tread the stranger° paths of banishment.   *foreign*

---

4. The following indented passage (lines 127.1–127.5) appears in Q1 but not in F. Shakespeare probably deleted it as part of his limited revisions to the text.

BOLINGBROKE   Your will be done. This must my comfort be:
That sun that warms you here shall shine on me,
140   And those his golden beams to you here lent
Shall point on me and gild my banishment.
KING RICHARD   Norfolk, for thee remains a heavier doom.°   *sentence*
Which I with some unwillingness pronounce.
The sly° slow hours shall not determinate°   *stealthy / bring to an end*
145   The dateless limit° of thy dear° exile.   *limitless period / grievous*
The hopeless word of 'never to return'
Breathe I against thee, upon pain of life.
MOWBRAY   A heavy sentence, my most sovereign liege,
And all unlooked-for from your highness' mouth.
150   A dearer merit,° not so deep a maim°   *better reward / an injury*
As to be cast forth in the common air,
Have I deservèd at your highness' hands.
The language I have learnt these forty years,
My native English, now I must forgo,
155   And now my tongue's use is to me no more
Than an unstringèd viol° or a harp,   *six-stringed instrument*
Or like a cunning° instrument cased up,   *skillfully made*
Or, being open, put into his hands
That knows no touch to tune the harmony.
160   Within my mouth you have enjailed my tongue,
Doubly portcullised° with my teeth and lips,   *Shut in by an iron gate*
And dull unfeeling barren ignorance
Is made my jailer to attend on me.
I am too old to fawn upon a nurse,
165   Too far in years to be a pupil now.
What is thy sentence then but speechless death,
Which robs my tongue from breathing native breath?
KING RICHARD   It boots° thee not to be compassionate.°   *helps / sorrowful*
After our sentence, plaining° comes too late.   *lamenting*
170   MOWBRAY   Then thus I turn me from my country's light,
To dwell in solemn shades of endless night.
KING RICHARD   Return again, and take an oath with thee.
[*To both*] Lay on our royal sword your banished hands.
Swear by the duty that you owe to God—
175   Our part therein⁵ we banish with yourselves—
To keep the oath that we administer.
You never shall, so help you truth and God,
Embrace each other's love in banishment,
Nor never look upon each other's face,
180   Nor never write, regreet, nor reconcile
This low'ring tempest of your home-bred hate,
Nor never by advisèd° purpose meet   *deliberated*
To plot, contrive, or complot any ill
'Gainst us, our state, our subjects, or our land.
BOLINGBROKE   I swear.
185   MOWBRAY   And I, to keep all this.
BOLINGBROKE   Norfolk, so far as to mine enemy
By this time, had the King permitted us,
One of our souls had wandered in the air,

5. Your allegiance to me as God's deputy.

Banished this frail sepulchre of our flesh,
190 As now our flesh is banished from this land.
Confess thy treasons ere thou fly the realm.
Since thou hast far to go, bear not along
The clogging° burden of a guilty soul.   *encumbering*
MOWBRAY   No, Bolingbroke, if ever I were traitor,
195 My name be blotted from the book of life,°   *eternal life*
And I from heaven banished as from hence.
But what thou art, God, thou, and I do know,
And all too soon I fear the King shall rue.
Farewell, my liege. Now no way can I stray:°   *lose my way*
200 Save back to England, all the world's my way.   *Exit*
KING RICHARD   Uncle, even in the glasses° of thine eyes   *windows*
I see thy grievèd heart. Thy sad aspect°   *appearance*
Hath from the number of his banished years
Plucked four away. [*To* BOLINGBROKE] Six frozen winters spent,
205 Return with welcome home from banishment.
BOLINGBROKE   How long a time lies in one little word!
Four lagging winters and four wanton° springs   *luxuriant*
End in a word: such is the breath of kings.
JOHN OF GAUNT   I thank my liege that in regard of me
210 He shortens four years of my son's exile.
But little vantage° shall I reap thereby,   *profit*
For ere the six years that he hath to spend
Can change their moons and bring their times about,
My oil-dried lamp and time-bewasted° light   *extinguished by time*
215 Shall be extinct with age and endless night.
My inch of taper will be burnt and done,
And blindfold⁶ death not let me see my son.
KING RICHARD   Why, uncle, thou hast many years to live.
JOHN OF GAUNT   But not a minute, King, that thou canst give.
220 Shorten my days thou canst with sudden sorrow,
And pluck nights from me, but not lend a morrow.
Thou canst help time to furrow me with age,
But stop no wrinkle in his pilgrimage.
Thy word is current° with him for my death,   *valid*
225 But dead, thy kingdom cannot buy my breath.
KING RICHARD   Thy son is banished upon good advice,
Whereto thy tongue a party verdict⁷ gave.
Why at our justice seem'st thou then to lour?°   *frown*
JOHN OF GAUNT   Things sweet to taste prove in digestion sour.
230 You urged me as a judge, but I had rather
You would have bid me argue like a father.
Alas, I looked when° some of you should say   *I expected that*
I was too strict to make mine own away,
But you gave leave to my unwilling tongue
235 Against my will to do myself this wrong.⁸
235.1   *O, had't been a stranger, not my child,*
           To smooth° his fault I should have been more mild.   *To gloss over*
           A partial slander° sought I to avoid,   *A suspicion of partiality*
           And in the sentence my own life destroyed.

6. Because death's emblem is a hooded figure or an   8. The following indented passage (lines 235.1–235.4)
eyeless skull, and because the dead cannot see.   appears only in Q1.
7. A share in the joint verdict.

KING RICHARD   Cousin, farewell; and uncle, bid him so.
    Six years we banish him, and he shall go.
        Flourish. Exeunt [all but AUMERLE, *the* LORD MARSHAL,
        JOHN OF GAUNT, *and* BOLINGBROKE]
AUMERLE [*to* BOLINGBROKE]   Cousin, farewell. What presence
    must not know,[9]
    From where you do remain° let paper show.   *Exit]*   stay
LORD MARSHAL [*to* BOLINGBROKE]   My lord, no leave take I, for
240   I will ride
    As far as land will let me by your side.
JOHN OF GAUNT [*to* BOLINGBROKE]   O, to what purpose dost
        thou hoard thy words,
    That thou return'st no greeting to thy friends?
BOLINGBROKE   I have too few to take my leave of you,
245   When the tongue's office° should be prodigal   function
    To breathe the abundant dolour of the heart.
JOHN OF GAUNT   Thy grief is but thy absence for a time.
BOLINGBROKE   Joy absent, grief is present for that time.
JOHN OF GAUNT   What is six winters? They are quickly gone.
250 BOLINGBROKE   To men in joy, but grief makes one hour ten.
JOHN OF GAUNT   Call it a travel that thou tak'st for pleasure.
BOLINGBROKE   My heart will sigh when I miscall it so,
    Which finds it an enforcèd pilgrimage.
JOHN OF GAUNT   The sullen passage of thy weary steps
255   Esteem as foil[1] wherein thou art to set
    The precious jewel of thy home return.[2]
256.1   BOLINGBROKE   *Nay, rather every tedious stride I make*
        Will but remember° what a deal° of world   remind me / an extent
        I wander from the jewels that I love.
        Must I not serve a long apprenticehood
256.5   *To foreign passages, and in the end,*
        Having my freedom, boast of nothing else
        But that I was a journeyman[3] to grief?
    JOHN OF GAUNT   *All places that the eye of heaven° visits*   sun; God's presence
        Are to a wise man ports and happy havens.
256.10   *Teach thy necessity to reason thus;*
        There is no virtue like necessity.
        Think not the King did banish thee,
        But thou the King. Woe doth the heavier sit
        Where it perceives it is but faintly° borne.   faintheartedly
256.15   *Go, say I sent thee forth to purchase° honour,*   acquire
        And not the King exiled thee; or suppose
        Devouring pestilence hangs in our air
        And thou art flying to a fresher clime.
        Look what° thy soul holds dear, imagine it   Whatever
256.20   *To lie that way thou goest, not whence thou com'st.*
        Suppose the singing birds musicians,
        The grass whereon thou tread'st the presence strewed,[4]
        The flowers fair ladies, and thy steps no more
        Than a delightful measure° or a dance;   a stately dance

---

9. What you cannot tell me personally because of your absence.
1. Thin metal against which jewels were set to enhance their luster.

2. The following indented passage (lines 256.1–256.26) appears only in Q1.
3. Person who has finished an apprenticeship.
4. The royal presence chamber strewn with rushes.

256.25   *For gnarling° sorrow hath less power to bite*   *snarling*
    The man that mocks at it and sets it light.°   *values it lightly*

BOLINGBROKE   O, who can hold a fire in his hand
By thinking on the frosty Caucasus,[5]
Or cloy the hungry edge of appetite
260   By bare imagination of a feast,
Or wallow naked in December snow
By thinking on fantastic° summer's heat?   *imagined*
O no, the apprehension of the good
Gives but the greater feeling to the worse.
265   Fell sorrow's tooth doth never rankle° more   *irritate*
Than when he bites, but lanceth[6] not the sore.

JOHN OF GAUNT   Come, come, my son, I'll bring thee on thy way.
Had I thy youth and cause, I would not stay.°   *linger*

BOLINGBROKE   Then England's ground, farewell. Sweet soil, adieu,
270   My mother and my nurse that bears me yet!
Where'er I wander, boast of this I can:
Though banished, yet a trueborn Englishman.   *Exeunt*

1.4

Enter KING [RICHARD] *with* GREEN *and* BAGOT *at one
door, and the Lord* AUMERLE *at another*

KING RICHARD   We did observe.[1]—Cousin Aumerle,
How far brought you high Hereford on his way?

AUMERLE   I brought high Hereford, if you call him so,
But to the next highway, and there I left him.

5 KING RICHARD   And say, what store of parting tears were shed?

AUMERLE   Faith, none for me,° except the north-east wind,   *my part*
Which then grew bitterly against our faces,
Awaked the sleeping rheum,° and so by chance   *tears*
Did grace our hollow parting with a tear.

10 KING RICHARD   What said our cousin when you parted with him?

AUMERLE   'Farewell.' And for° my heart disdained that my tongue   *because*
Should so profane the word, that[2] taught me craft
To counterfeit oppression of such grief
That words seemed buried in my sorrow's grave.
15   Marry,° would the word 'farewell' have lengthened hours   *Indeed*
And added years to his short banishment,
He should have had a volume of farewells;
But since it would not, he had none of me.

KING RICHARD   He is our cousin, cousin;[3] but 'tis doubt,
20   When time shall call him home from banishment,
Whether our kinsman come to see his friends.°   *relatives*
Ourself and Bushy, Bagot here, and Green
Observed his courtship to the common people,
How he did seem to dive into their hearts
25   With humble and familiar courtesy,
What reverence he did throw away on slaves,
Wooing poor craftsmen with the craft of smiles
And patient underbearing° of his fortune,   *enduring*

5. Mountain range between the Black and Caspian seas.
6. Probes (to release the pus from an abscess).
1.4 Location: The court.
1. The scene begins in mid-conversation; the King is replying to a remark by Bagot or Green.

2. His heart. Unwilling to give Hereford good wishes insincerely, Aumerle pretends to be overwhelmed with grief.
3 Richard, Bolingbroke, and Aumerle were sons of three brothers.

As 'twere to banish their affects with him.[4]
30 Off goes his bonnet° to an oysterwench.   *cap*
A brace of draymen° bid God speed him well,   *A couple of cart drivers*
And had the tribute of his supple knee
With 'Thanks, my countrymen, my loving friends',
As were our England in reversion[5] his,
35 And he our subjects' next degree in hope.
GREEN   Well, he is gone, and with him go these thoughts.
Now for the rebels which stand out in Ireland.
Expedient manage° must be made, my liege,   *Hasty arrangements*
Ere further leisure yield them further means
40 For their advantage and your highness' loss.
KING RICHARD   We will ourself in person to this war,
And for° our coffers with too great a court   *because*
And liberal largess are grown somewhat light,
We are enforced to farm our royal realm,[6]
45 The revenue whereof shall furnish us
For our affairs in hand. If that come short,
Our substitutes° at home shall have blank charters,[7] *deputies*
Whereto, when they shall know what men are rich,
They shall subscribe them° for large sums of gold,   *write down their names*
50 And send them after to supply our wants;
For we will make for Ireland presently.°   *at once*
         Enter BUSHY
Bushy, what news?
BUSHY   Old John of Gaunt is grievous sick, my lord,
Suddenly taken, and hath sent post-haste
55 To entreat your majesty to visit him.
KING RICHARD   Where lies he?
BUSHY   At Ely House.
KING RICHARD   Now put it, God, in his physician's mind
To help him to his grave immediately.
60 The lining[8] of his coffers shall make coats
To deck our soldiers for these Irish wars.
Come, gentlemen, let's all go visit him.
Pray God we may make haste and come too late!   *Exeunt*

2.1

Enter JOHN OF GAUNT [*Duke of Lancaster*], *sick,* [*carried
in a chair*], *with Duke of* YORK
JOHN OF GAUNT   Will the King come, that I may breathe my last
In wholesome counsel to his unstaid° youth?   *unruly*
YORK   Vex not yourself, nor strive not with your breath,
For all in vain comes counsel to his ear.
5 JOHN OF GAUNT   O, but they say the tongues of dying men
Enforce attention, like deep harmony.
Where words are scarce they are seldom spent in vain,
For they breathe truth that breathe their words in pain.
He that no more must say is listened more
10   Than they whom youth and ease have taught to glose.°   *talk speciously*

4. As if taking their affections with him into exile.
5. A legal term for property that reverts to the original
owner on the expiring of a contract.
6. To lease the King's right to tax.
7. Documents enabling the King to raise money by
forced loans; the deputies can fill in the blanks with any
amount they see fit.
8. Contents (playing on "lining cloth").
2.1 Location: Ely House.

More are men's ends marked than their lives before.
 The setting sun, and music at the close,
As the last taste of sweets, is sweetest last,
Writ in remembrance more than things long past.
15 Though Richard my life's counsel would not hear,
My death's sad tale may yet undeaf his ear.
 YORK   No, it is stopped with other, flattering sounds,
As praises of whose taste the wise are feared,°   wary
Lascivious metres to whose venom sound
20 The open ear of youth doth always listen,
Report of fashions in proud Italy,
Whose manners still° our tardy-apish[1] nation   always
Limps after in base imitation.
Where doth the world thrust forth a vanity—
25 So° it be new there's no respect° how vile—   Provided / regard for
That is not quickly buzzed into his ears?
Then all too late comes counsel, to be heard
Where will doth mutiny with wit's regard.[2]
Direct not him whose way himself will choose:
30 'Tis breath thou lack'st, and that breath wilt thou lose.
 JOHN OF GAUNT   Methinks I am a prophet new-inspired,
And thus, expiring, do foretell of him.
His rash, fierce blaze of riot° cannot last,   wastefulness
For violent fires soon burn out themselves.
35 Small showers last long, but sudden storms are short.
He tires betimes° that spurs too fast betimes.   soon
With eager feeding food doth choke the feeder.
Light vanity, insatiate cormorant,[3]
Consuming means, soon preys upon itself.
40 This royal throne of kings, this sceptred isle,
This earth of majesty, this seat of Mars,°   war god's dwelling
This other Eden, demi-paradise,
This fortress built by nature for herself
Against infection° and the hand of war,   disease; depravity
45 This happy breed of men, this little world,
This precious stone set in the silver sea,
Which serves it in the office° of a wall,   function
Or as a moat defensive to a house
Against the envy° of less happier lands;   malice
50 This blessèd plot, this earth, this realm, this England,
This nurse, this teeming womb of royal kings,
Feared by their breed[4] and famous by their birth,
Renownèd for their deeds as far from home
For Christian service and true chivalry[5]
55 As is the sepulchre, in stubborn Jewry,[6]
Of the world's ransom, blessèd Mary's son;
This land of such dear souls, this dear dear land,
Dear for her reputation through the world,
Is now leased out—I die pronouncing it—
60 Like to a tenement° or pelting° farm.   rental property / worthless
England, bound in with the triumphant sea,

1. Imitative but outmoded.
2. Where willfulness overthrows sound judgment.
3. Glutton (literally, a bird that swallows fish whole).
4. For their inherited valor.

5. Alluding to the English kings' accomplishments in the Crusades.
6. Judaea, stubborn in its resistance to Christianity.

Whose rocky shore beats back the envious siege
Of wat'ry Neptune, is now bound in with shame,
With inky blots and rotten parchment bonds.[7]
65 That England that was wont to conquer others
Hath made a shameful conquest of itself.
Ah, would the scandal vanish with my life,
How happy then were my ensuing death!
   Enter KING [RICHARD], QUEEN, [*Duke of*] AUMERLE,
   BUSHY, GREEN, BAGOT, [*Lord*] ROSS, *and* [*Lord*]
   WILLOUGHBY
YORK The King is come. Deal mildly with his youth,
70 For young hot colts, being reined, do rage the more.
QUEEN How fares our noble uncle Lancaster?
KING RICHARD What comfort, man? How is't with aged Gaunt?
JOHN OF GAUNT O, how that name befits my composition!°   *constitution*
Old Gaunt indeed, and gaunt in being old.
75 Within me grief hath kept a tedious fast,
And who abstains from meat° that is not gaunt?   *food*
For sleeping England long time have I watched.°   *stayed awake*
Watching breeds leanness, leanness is all gaunt.
The pleasure that some fathers feed upon
80 Is my strict fast: I mean my children's looks.[8]
And therein fasting, hast thou made me gaunt.
Gaunt am I for the grave, gaunt as a grave,
Whose hollow womb inherits naught but bones.
KING RICHARD Can sick men play so nicely° with their names?   *subtly*
85 JOHN OF GAUNT No, misery makes sport to mock itself.
Since thou dost seek to kill my name in me,[9]
I mock my name, great King, to flatter thee.
KING RICHARD Should dying men flatter with those that live?
JOHN OF GAUNT No, no, men living flatter those that die.
90 KING RICHARD Thou now a-dying sayst thou flatt'rest me.
JOHN OF GAUNT O no: thou diest, though I the sicker be.
KING RICHARD I am in health; I breathe, and see thee ill.
JOHN OF GAUNT Now He that made me knows I see thee ill:
Ill in myself to see, and in thee seeing ill.[1]
95 Thy deathbed is no lesser than thy land,
Wherein thou liest in reputation sick;
And thou, too careless patient as thou art,
Committ'st thy anointed body to the cure
Of those physicians[2] that first wounded thee.
100 A thousand flatterers sit within thy crown,
Whose compass° is no bigger than thy head,   *circumference*
And yet, encagèd in so small a verge,[3]
The waste[4] is no whit lesser than thy land.
O, had thy grandsire with a prophet's eye
105 Seen how his son's son should destroy his sons,
From forth° thy reach he would have laid thy shame,   *out of*
Deposing thee before thou wert possessed,[5]
Which art possessed° now to depose thyself.   *in a diabolical frenzy*

---

7. Richard's "blank charters."
8. Since Bolingbroke is exiled.
9. Destroy my family (by exiling Bolingbroke).
1. Too ill to see well, and seeing evil in you.
2. Richard's favorites, or his own bad impulses.

3. Area; distance of 12 miles around the court, to which special rules applied.
4. Destruction (specifically, injury done to a property by a tenant); waist, narrowest part.
5. In possession of the crown.

Why, cousin,° wert thou regent° of the world   *kinsman / ruler*
110   It were a shame to let this land by lease.
But, for thy world, enjoying but this land,[6]
Is it not more than shame to shame it so?
Landlord of England art thou now, not king.
Thy state of law[7] is bondslave to the law,
115   And—
    KING RICHARD   And thou, a lunatic lean-witted fool,
Presuming on an ague's privilege,°   *the privilege of the sick*
Dar'st with thy frozen° admonition   *rigid; caused by a chill*
Make pale our cheek, chasing the royal blood
120   With fury from his native residence.°   *its natural place*
Now by my seat's° right royal majesty,   *throne's*
Wert thou not brother to great Edward's son,[8]
This tongue that runs so roundly° in thy head   *freely*
Should run thy head from thy unreverent shoulders.
125   JOHN OF GAUNT   O, spare me not, my brother Edward's son,
For that I was his father Edward's son.
That blood already, like the pelican,[9]
Hast thou tapped out[1] and drunkenly caroused.
My brother Gloucester, plain well-meaning soul—
130   Whom fair befall in heaven 'mongst happy souls—
May be a precedent and witness good
That thou respect'st not spilling° Edward's blood.   *don't hesitate to spill*
Join with the present sickness that I have,
And thy unkindness be like crookèd age,
135   To crop° at once a too-long withered flower.   *cut*
Live in thy shame, but die not shame with thee.[2]
These words hereafter thy tormentors be.
[*To attendants*] Convey me to my bed, then to my grave.
Love they to live that love and honour have.
                                   Exit [carried in a chair]
140   KING RICHARD   And let them die that age and sullens° have,   *sulks*
For both hast thou, and both become the grave.
    YORK   I do beseech your majesty impute his words
To wayward sickliness and age in him.
He loves you, on my life, and holds you dear
145   As Harry Duke of Hereford, were he here.
    KING RICHARD   Right, you say true: as Hereford's love, so his.[3]
As theirs, so mine; and all be as it is.
              Enter [Earl of] NORTHUMBERLAND
    NORTHUMBERLAND   My liege, old Gaunt commends him to your majesty.
    KING RICHARD   What says he?
    NORTHUMBERLAND   Nay, nothing: all is said.
150   His tongue is now a stringless instrument.
Words, life, and all, old Lancaster hath spent.
    YORK   Be York the next that must be bankrupt so!
Though death be poor, it ends a mortal woe.
    KING RICHARD   The ripest fruit first falls, and so doth he.

---

6. Since this realm alone constitutes your world.
7. Legal status (as landlord, not King).
8. Edward the Black Prince, Edward III's son and Richard's father.
9. A mother pelican was thought to wound her breast so her ungrateful young could feed on her blood.

1. Let run as from a barrel tap.
2. May your shame outlive you.
3. York claims that Gaunt loves Richard as much as he loves his own son; Richard deliberately misconstrues York to mean Gaunt loves Richard as much as Hereford does.

155	His time is spent; our pilgrimage must be.°	*continue*
	So much for that. Now for our Irish wars.	
	We must supplant those rough rug-headed kerns,[4]	
	Which live like venom where no venom else	
	But only they have privilege to live [5]	
160	And for° these great affairs do ask some charge,°	*because*
	Towards our assistance we do seize to us	
	The plate, coin, revenues, and movables°	*personal property*
	Whereof our uncle Gaunt did stand possessed.	
	YORK How long shall I be patient? Ah, how long	
165	Shall tender° duty make me suffer wrong?	*scrupulous*
	Not Gloucester's death, nor Hereford's banishment,	
	Nor Gaunt's rebukes, nor England's private wrongs,[7]	
	Nor the prevention of poor Bolingbroke	
	About his marriage,[8] nor my own disgrace,	
170	Have ever made me sour my patient cheek,	
	Or bend one wrinkle° on my sovereign's face.	*one frown*
	I am the last of noble Edward's sons,	
	Of whom thy father, Prince of Wales, was first.	
	In war was never lion raged more fierce,	
175	In peace was never gentle lamb more mild,	
	Than was that young and princely gentleman.	
	His face thou hast, for even so looked he,	
	Accomplished with the number of thy hours.°	*When he was your age*
	But when he frowned it was against the French,	
180	And not against his friends. His noble hand	
	Did win what he did spend, and spent not that	
	Which his triumphant father's hand had won.	
	His hands were guilty of no kindred blood,	
	But bloody with the enemies of his kin.	
185	O, Richard, York is too far gone with grief,	
	Or else he never would compare between.	
	KING RICHARD Why uncle, what's the matter?	
	YORK O my liege,	
	Pardon me if you please; if not, I, pleased	
	Not to be pardoned, am content withal.°	*nevertheless*
190	Seek you to seize and grip into your hands	
	The royalties[9] and rights of banished Hereford?	
	Is not Gaunt dead? And doth not Hereford live?	
	Was not Gaunt just? And is not Harry true?	
	Did not the one deserve to have an heir?	
195	Is not his heir a well-deserving son?	
	Take Hereford's rights away, and take from Time	
	His° charters and his customary rights	*Its*
	Let not tomorrow then ensue° today:	*follow*
	Be not thyself, for how art thou a king	
200	But by fair sequence and succession?	
	Now afore God—God forbid I say true!—	
	If you do wrongfully seize Hereford's rights,	
	Call in° the letters patents that he hath	*Revoke*

4. Shaggy Irish foot soldiers.
5. Alluding to the legend that St. Patrick drove snakes out of Ireland.
6. Do demand some expenditure.
7. Wrongs committed against private individuals.

8. Richard intervened against Bolingbroke's proposed marriage to the King of France's cousin.
9. Privileges granted by a king through "letters patents" (line 203).

By his attorneys general to sue
205 His livery, and deny his offered homage,[1]
You pluck° a thousand dangers on your head,   *pull*
You lose a thousand well-disposèd hearts,
And prick my tender patience to those thoughts
Which honour and allegiance cannot think.
210 KING RICHARD   Think what you will, we seize into our hands
His plate, his goods, his money, and his lands.
YORK   I'll not be by the while.[2] My liege, farewell.
What will ensue hereof there's none can tell.
But by bad courses may be understood
215 That their events° can never fall out good.   *Exit*   *outcomes*
KING RICHARD   Go, Bushy, to the Earl of Wiltshire straight.
Bid him repair° to us to Ely House   *go*
To see° this business. Tomorrow next   *attend to*
We will for Ireland, and 'tis time, I trow.°   *think*
220 And we create, in absence of ourself,
Our uncle York Lord Governor of England;
For he is just and always loved us well.—
Come on, our Queen; tomorrow must we part.
Be merry, for our time of stay is short.
Flourish. Exeunt KING [RICHARD], QUEEN[, AUMERLE,
GREEN, *and* BAGOT *at one door,* BUSHY *at another door*].
Manent° NORTHUMBERLAND, WILLOUGHBY, *and* ROSS   *Remain*
225 NORTHUMBERLAND   Well, lords, the Duke of Lancaster is dead.
ROSS   And living too, for now his son is Duke.
WILLOUGHBY   Barely in title, not in revenues.
NORTHUMBERLAND   Richly in both, if justice had her right.
ROSS   My heart is great,° but it must break with silence   *full of emotion*
230 Ere't be disburdened with a liberal° tongue.   *unrestrained*
NORTHUMBERLAND   Nay, speak thy mind, and let him ne'er
speak more
That speaks thy words again to do thee harm.
WILLOUGHBY   Tends that that thou wouldst speak to[3] the Duke
of Hereford?
If it be so, out with it boldly, man.
235 Quick is mine ear to hear of good towards him.
ROSS   No good at all that I can do for him,
Unless you call it good to pity him,
Bereft and gelded of his patrimony.
NORTHUMBERLAND   Now afore God, 'tis shame such wrongs are borne
240 In him, a royal prince, and many more
Of noble blood in this declining land.
The King is not himself, but basely led
By flatterers; and what they will inform
Merely in° hate 'gainst any of us all,   *Purely out of*
245 That will the King severely prosecute
'Gainst us, our lives, our children, and our heirs.
ROSS   The commons° hath he pilled° with grievous taxes,   *common people / stripped*
And quite lost their hearts. The nobles hath he fined
For ancient quarrels, and quite lost their hearts.

---

1. The letters patents allow Hereford, through his legal representatives ("attorneys general"), to make a legal claim for the inheritance of his land ("sue" for delivery), provided he swears allegiance to the King ("offers homage").
2. Present during the seizure.
3. Does what you would say concern.

250 WILLOUGHBY   And daily new exactions are devised,
　　As blanks, benevolences,° and I wot° not what.　　　　　*forced loans / know*
　　But what, a' God's name, doth become of this?°　　　　　*this money*
NORTHUMBERLAND   Wars hath not wasted it; for warred he hath not,
　　But basely yielded upon compromise
255　That which his ancestors achieved with blows.[4]
　　More hath he spent in peace than they in wars.
ROSS   The Earl of Wiltshire hath the realm in farm.[5]
WILLOUGHBY   The King's grown bankrupt like a broken man.
NORTHUMBERLAND   Reproach and dissolution hangeth over him.
260 ROSS   He hath not money for these Irish wars,
　　His burdenous taxations notwithstanding,
　　But by the robbing of the banished Duke.
NORTHUMBERLAND   His noble kinsman. Most degenerate King!
　　But, lords, we hear this fearful tempest sing,
265　Yet seek no shelter to avoid the storm.
　　We see the wind sit sore° upon our sails,　　　　　*blow hard*
　　And yet we strike[6] not, but securely° perish.　　　　　*heedlessly*
ROSS   We see the very wreck that we must suffer,
　　And unavoided° is the danger now　　　　　*unavoidable*
270　For suffering° so the causes of our wreck.　　　　　*enduring*
NORTHUMBERLAND   Not so: even through the hollow eyes° of death　　　*eye sockets*
　　I spy life peering; but I dare not say
　　How near the tidings of our comfort is.
WILLOUGHBY   Nay, let us share thy thoughts, as thou dost ours.
275 ROSS   Be confident to speak, Northumberland.
　　We three are but thyself, and, speaking so,
　　Thy words are but as thoughts. Therefore be bold.
NORTHUMBERLAND   Then thus. I have from Port le Blanc,
　　A bay in Brittaine,[7] received intelligence
280　That Harry Duke of Hereford, Reinold Lord Cobham,
　　Thomas son and heir to the Earl of Arundel[8]
　　That late broke from the Duke of Exeter,
　　His[9] brother, Archbishop late° of Canterbury,　　　　　*until recently*
　　Sir Thomas Erpingham, Sir Thomas Ramston,
285　Sir John Norbery,
　　Sir Robert Waterton, and Francis Coint,
　　All these well furnished by the Duke of Brittaine
　　With eight tall ships, three thousand men of war,°　　　　　*soldiers*
　　Are making hither with all due expedience,
290　And shortly mean to touch our northern shore.
　　Perhaps they had ere this, but that they stay
　　The first departing of the King[1] for Ireland.
　　If then we shall shake off our slavish yoke,
　　Imp out[2] our drooping country's broken wing,
295　Redeem from broking pawn° the blemished crown,　　　　　*pawnbrokers*
　　Wipe off the dust that hides our sceptre's gilt,
　　And make high majesty look like itself,
　　Away with me in post° to Ravenspurgh.[3]　　　　　*speedily*

4. Referring to the ceding of Brest, a city in western France, to the Duke of Brittany.
5. *in farm:* on lease (as in 1.4.44–46).
6. Lower sails; deliver blows.
7. Brittany, in northwest France.
8. An editorial approximation of a line missing from

early texts. Shakespeare's source states that Arundel's son escaped from Exeter's custody.
9. The Earl of Arundel's.
1. *they stay . . . King:* they wait for the King to depart first.
2. Engraft new feathers on (from falconry).
3. Then a port on the river Humber, in Yorkshire.

But if you faint,° as fearing to do so,   *are fainthearted*
300   Stay, and be secret, and myself will go.
ROSS   To horse, to horse! Urge doubts to them that fear.
WILLOUGHBY   Hold out my horse,° and I will first be there.   *If my horse holds up*
                                                                          Exeunt

2.2
Enter the QUEEN, BUSHY, [*and*] BAGOT
BUSHY   Madam, your majesty is too much sad.[1]
  You promised when you parted with the King
  To lay aside life-harming heaviness°   *melancholy*
  And entertain° a cheerful disposition.   *assume*
5   QUEEN   To please the King I did; to please myself
  I cannot do it. Yet I know no cause
  Why I should welcome such a guest as grief,
  Save bidding farewell to so sweet a guest
  As my sweet Richard. Yet again, methinks
10   Some unborn sorrow, ripe in fortune's womb,
  Is coming towards me; and my inward soul
  At nothing trembles. With something it grieves
  More than with parting from my lord the King.
BUSHY   Each substance of a grief hath twenty shadows
15   Which shows like grief itself but is not so.
  For sorrow's eye, glazèd with blinding tears,
  Divides one thing entire to many objects—
  Like perspectives, which, rightly gazed upon,
  Show nothing but confusion; eyed awry,
20   Distinguish form.[2] So your sweet majesty,
  Looking awry upon your lord's departure,
  Find shapes° of grief more than himself to wail,°   *images / bewail*
  Which, looked on as it is, is naught but shadows
  Of what it is not. Then, thrice-gracious Queen,
25   More than your lord's departure weep not: more is not seen,
  Or if it be, 'tis with false sorrow's eye,
  Which for things true weeps things imaginary.
QUEEN   It may be so, but yet my inward soul
  Persuades me it is otherwise. Howe'er it be,
30   I cannot but be sad: so heavy-sad
  As thought—on thinking on no thought I think[3]—
  Makes me with heavy nothing faint and shrink.
BUSHY   'Tis nothing but conceit,° my gracious lady.   *imagination*
QUEEN   'Tis nothing less:[4] conceit is still° derived   *always*
35   From some forefather grief; mine is not so;
  For nothing hath begot my something° grief—   *substantial*
  Or something hath the nothing that I grieve[5]—
  'Tis in reversion that I do possess[6]—

2.2. Location: Windsor Castle.
1. Shakespeare makes Richard's queen a mature young woman; the historical Isabella was married to Richard at seven years and was ten at the time of Bolingbroke's invasion.
2. *For . . . from:* Bushy compares the Queen's eye first to a perspective glass that multiplies one image into many, then to a perspective picture that looks distorted unless viewed at an angle ("awry").
3. *As thought . . . think:* a difficult line. The Oxford

editors adopt the Q1 version, "thought"; other editors adopt the F version, "though," which is hardly less obscure. The Queen is playing with the paradox that her premonition, a thought of nothing, or "no thought," is nonetheless almost physically oppressive.
4. Anything but conceit.
5. Or the grief that I feel apparently over nothing actually has some cause.
6. It will come at a later date (that is, her grief anticipates its occasion).

But what it is that is not yet known what,
40 I cannot name; 'tis nameless woe, I wot.
Enter GREEN
GREEN God save your majesty, and well met, gentlemen.
I hope the King is not yet shipped for Ireland.
QUEEN Why hop'st thou so? 'Tis better hope he is.
For his designs crave° haste, his haste good hope.   *need*
45 Then wherefore dost thou hope he is not shipped?
GREEN That he, our hope, might have retired his power,°   *brought back his forces*
And driven into despair an enemy's hope,
Who strongly hath set footing in this land.
The banished Bolingbroke repeals° himself,   *recalls from exile*
50 And with uplifted arms° is safe arrived   *weapons*
At Ravenspurgh.
QUEEN   Now God in heaven forbid!
GREEN Ah madam, 'tis too true! And that is worse,
The Lord Northumberland, his son young Harry Percy,
The Lords of Ross, Beaumont, and Willoughby
55 With all their powerful friends, are fled to him.
BUSHY Why have you not proclaimed Northumberland,
And all the rest, revolted faction-traitors?°   *treasonous conspirators*
GREEN We have; whereupon the Earl of Worcester
Hath broke his staff,[7] resigned his stewardship,
60 And all the household servants fled with him
To Bolingbroke.
QUEEN So, Green, thou art the midwife to my woe,
And Bolingbroke my sorrow's dismal heir.
Now hath my soul brought forth her prodigy,°   *monstrous birth; portent*
65 And I, a gasping new-delivered mother,
Have woe to woe, sorrow to sorrow joined.
BUSHY Despair not, madam.
QUEEN   Who shall hinder me?
I will despair, and be at enmity
With cozening° hope. He° is a flatterer,   *cheating / (Hope)*
70 A parasite, a keeper-back of death,
Who° gently would dissolve° the bonds of life,   *(Death) / loosen*
Which false hope lingers in extremity.
Enter [Duke of] YORK *[wearing a gorget]*[8]
GREEN Here comes the Duke of York.
QUEEN With signs of war about his aged neck.
75 O, full of careful business° are his looks!   *anxious preoccupation*
Uncle, for God's sake speak comfortable° words.   *comforting*
YORK Should I do so, I should belie my thoughts.
Comfort's in heaven, and we are on the earth,
Where nothing lives but crosses,° cares, and grief.   *misfortunes*
80 Your husband, he is gone to save far off,
Whilst others come to make him lose at home.
Here am I, left to underprop his land,
Who, weak with age, cannot support myself.
Now comes the sick hour that his surfeit made.
85 Now shall he try° his friends that flattered him.   *test*
*Enter a [*SERVINGMAN*]*

---

7. Symbolically resigning his office as lord steward of   brother.
the King's household. Worcester is Northumberland's   8. Piece of armor protecting the throat.

SERVINGMAN   My lord, your son was gone before I came.

YORK   He was? Why so, go all which way it will.

    The nobles they are fled. The commons° they are cold,   *common people*

    And will, I fear, revolt on Hereford's side.

90   Sirrah, get thee to Pleshey, to my sister° Gloucester.   *sister-in-law*

    Bid her send me presently° a thousand pound—   *immediately*

    Hold; take my ring.[9]

SERVINGMAN   My lord, I had forgot to tell your lordship,

    Today as I came by I callèd there—

95   But I shall grieve you to report the rest.

YORK   What is't, knave?°   *fellow*

SERVINGMAN   An hour before I came, the Duchess died.

YORK   God for his mercy, what a tide of woes

    Comes rushing on this woeful land at once!

100   I know not what to do. I would to God,

    So my untruth° had not provoked him to it,   *disloyalty*

    The King had cut off my head with my brother's.

    What, are there no posts° dispatched for Ireland?   *fast messengers*

    How shall we do for money for these wars?

105   [*To the* QUEEN] Come, sister—cousin, I would say; pray pardon me.[1]

    [*To the* SERVINGMAN] Go, fellow, get thee home. Provide some carts,

    And bring away the armour that is there.   [*Exit* SERVINGMAN]

    Gentlemen, will you go muster men?

    If I know how or which way to order these affairs

110   Thus disorderly thrust into my hands,

    Never believe me. Both are my kinsmen.

    T'one is my sovereign, whom both my oath

    And duty bids defend; t'other again

    Is my kinsman, whom the King hath wronged,

115   Whom conscience and my kindred bids to right.

    Well, somewhat we must do. [*To the* QUEEN] Come, cousin,

    I'll dispose of° you.—   *make arrangements for*

    Gentlemen, go muster up your men,

    And meet me presently at Berkeley Castle.[2]

120   I should to Pleshey too, but time will not permit.

    All is uneven,

    And everything is left at six and seven.°   *in confusion*

            Exeunt Duke [*of* YORK *and*] QUEEN.

            Manent BUSHY, GREEN [*and* BAGOT]

BUSHY   The wind sits fair[3] for news to go for Ireland,

    But none returns. For us to levy power

125   Proportionable to the enemy

    Is all unpossible.

GREEN   Besides, our nearness to the King in love

    Is near° the hate of those love not the King.   *Implies*

BAGOT   And that is the wavering commons; for their love

130   Lies in their purses, and whoso empties them

    By so much fills their hearts with deadly hate.

BUSHY   Wherein the King stands generally condemned.

BAGOT   If judgement lie in them,° then so do we,   *is in the people's hands*

    Because we ever have been near the King.

---

9. As proof that he comes with York's authorization.   2. In Gloucestershire, in western England.

1. The Duchess's death is uppermost in York's mind.   3. The wind blows from a favorable direction.

135 GREEN   Well, I will for refuge straight to Bristol Castle.
      The Earl of Wiltshire is already there.
    BUSHY   Thither will I with you; for little office°   *service*
      Will the hateful commoners perform for us,
      Except like curs to tear us all to pieces.
140   [*To* BAGOT] Will you go along with us?
    BAGOT   No, I will to Ireland, to his majesty.
      Farewell: if heart's presages be not vain
      We three here part that ne'er shall meet again.
    BUSHY   That's as York thrives[4] to bear back Bolingbroke.
145 GREEN   Alas, poor Duke, the task he undertakes
      Is numb'ring sands and drinking oceans dry.
      Where one on his side fights, thousands will fly.
    BAGOT   Farewell at once, for once, for all and ever.
    BUSHY   Well, we may meet again.
    BAGOT   I fear me never.
                  Exeunt [BUSHY *and* GREEN *at one door,*
                          and BAGOT *at another door*]

2.3

Enter [BOLINGBROKE *Duke of Lancaster and*] *Hereford,*
and [*the Earl of*] NORTHUMBERLAND

    BOLINGBROKE   How far is it, my lord, to Berkeley now?
    NORTHUMBERLAND   Believe me, noble lord,
      I am a stranger here in Gloucestershire.
      These high wild hills and rough uneven ways
5   Draws out our miles and makes them wearisome;
      And yet your fair discourse hath been as sugar,
      Making the hard way sweet and delectable.
      But I bethink me what a weary way
      From Ravenspurgh to Cotswold[1] will be found
10   In° Ross and Willoughby, wanting° your company,   *By / lacking*
      Which I protest hath very much beguiled
      The tediousness and process° of my travel.   *tedious course*
      But theirs is sweetened with the hope to have
      The present benefit which I possess;
15   And hope to joy is little less in joy
      Than hope enjoyed. By this° the weary lords   *this expectation*
      Shall make their way seem short as mine hath done
      By sight of what I have: your noble company.
    BOLINGBROKE   Of much less value is my company
      Than your good words.
          Enter HARRY PERCY
20   But who comes here?
    NORTHUMBERLAND   It is my son, young Harry Percy,[2]
      Sent from my brother Worcester whencesoever.°   *wherever he may be*
      Harry, how fares your uncle?°   *Worcester*
    HARRY PERCY   I had thought, my lord, to have learned his
      health of you.
25   NORTHUMBERLAND   Why, is he not with the Queen?
    HARRY PERCY   No, my good lord; he hath forsook the court,

---

4. That depends on York's success.
2.3 Location: Gloucestershire.
1. Hilly part of Gloucestershire.

2. Shakespeare makes Harry Percy, the Hotspur of
1 Henry IV, a boy here; the historical Percy was two
years older than Bolingbroke.

Broken his staff of office, and dispersed
The household of the King.

NORTHUMBERLAND   What was his reason?
He was not so resolved when last we spake together.

30 HARRY PERCY   Because your lordship was proclaimèd traitor.
But he, my lord, is gone to Ravenspurgh
To offer service to the Duke of Hereford,
And sent me over by Berkeley to discover
What power the Duke of York had levied there,

35 Then with directions to repair to Ravenspurgh.

NORTHUMBERLAND   Have you forgot the Duke of Hereford, boy?³

HARRY PERCY   No, my good lord, for that is not forgot
Which ne'er I did remember. To my knowledge,
I never in my life did look on him.

40 NORTHUMBERLAND   Then learn to know him now. This is the Duke.

HARRY PERCY   My gracious lord, I tender you my service,
Such as it is, being tender, raw, and young,
Which elder days shall ripen and confirm
To more approvèd° service and desert.   more fully demonstrated

45 BOLINGBROKE   I thank thee, gentle Percy, and be sure
I count myself in nothing else so happy
As in a° soul rememb'ring my good friends;   my
And as my fortune ripens with thy love,
It shall be still thy true love's recompense.

50 My heart this covenant makes; my hand thus seals it.
        [He gives PERCY his hand]

NORTHUMBERLAND   How far is it to Berkeley, and what stir°   activity
Keeps good old York there with his men of war?

HARRY PERCY   There stands the castle, by yon tuft of trees,
Manned with three hundred men, as I have heard,

55 And in it are the Lords of York, Berkeley, and Seymour,
None else of name° and noble estimate.°   title / reputation
        Enter [Lord] ROSS and [Lord] WILLOUGHBY

NORTHUMBERLAND   Here come the Lords of Ross and Willoughby,
Bloody with spurring, fiery red with haste.

BOLINGBROKE   Welcome, my lords. I wot° your love pursues   know

60 A banished traitor. All my treasury
Is yet but unfelt° thanks, which, more enriched,   immaterial
Shall be your love and labour's recompense.

ROSS   Your presence makes us rich, most noble lord.

WILLOUGHBY   And far surmounts our labour to attain it.

65 BOLINGBROKE   Evermore thank's the exchequer⁴ of the poor,
Which till my infant fortune comes to years°   of age
Stands for° my bounty.   in place of
        Enter BERKELEY
                            But who comes here?

NORTHUMBERLAND   It is my lord of Berkeley, as I guess.

BERKELEY   My lord of Hereford, my message is to you.

70 BOLINGBROKE   My lord, my answer is to 'Lancaster',⁵
And I am come to seek that name in England,

---

3. Northumberland scolds his son for not greeting Bolingbroke respectfully.
4. Gratitude is always the treasury.

5. I only reply to the title of Lancaster (which Richard
took away).

And I must find that title in your tongue
Before I make reply to aught you say.

BERKELEY Mistake me not, my lord, 'tis not my meaning
75 To raze one title of your honour out.
To you, my lord, I come—what lord you will—
From the most gracious regent of this land,
The Duke of York, to know what pricks you on°   *incites you*
To take advantage of the absent time°   *time of absence*
80 And fright our native peace with self-borne⁶ arms.

Enter [Duke of] YORK

BOLINGBROKE I shall not need transport my words by you.
Here comes his grace in person.—My noble uncle!
[He kneels]

YORK Show me thy humble heart, and not thy knee,
Whose duty is deceivable° and false.   *deceptive*
85 BOLINGBROKE My gracious uncle—
YORK Tut, tut, grace me no grace, nor uncle me no uncle.
I am no traitor's uncle, and that word 'grace'
In an ungracious mouth is but profane.
Why have those banished and forbidden legs
90 Dared once to touch a dust° of England's ground?   *speck*
But then more 'why': why have they dared to march
So many miles upon her peaceful bosom,
Frighting her pale-faced villages with war
And ostentation° of despisèd arms?   *display*
95 Com'st thou because the anointed King is hence?
Why, foolish boy, the King is left behind,
And in my loyal bosom lies his power.
Were I but now the lord of such hot youth
As when brave Gaunt, thy father, and myself
100 Rescued the Black Prince, that young Mars of men,
From forth the ranks of many thousand French,
O then how quickly should this arm of mine,
Now prisoner to the palsy, chastise thee
And minister correction° to thy fault!   *administer punishment*
105 BOLINGBROKE My gracious uncle, let me know my fault
On what condition stands it and wherein?⁷
YORK Even in condition of the worst degree:
In gross rebellion and detested treason.
Thou art a banished man, and here art come
110 Before the expiration of thy time
In braving° arms against thy sovereign.   *defiant*
BOLINGBROKE *[standing]* As I was banished, I was banished Hereford;
But as I come, I come for Lancaster.
And, noble uncle, I beseech your grace,
115 Look on my wrongs with an indifferent° eye.   *impartial*
You are my father, for methinks in you
I see old Gaunt alive. O then, my father,
Will you permit that I shall stand condemned
A wandering vagabond, my rights and royalties
120 Plucked from my arms perforce and given away
To upstart unthrifts?° Wherefore was I born?   *spendthrifts*

6. Borne for oneself, not for the King; borne against   7. What is its nature, and in what does it consist?
fellow countrymen.

　　　　If that my cousin King be King in England,
　　　　It must be granted I am Duke of Lancaster.
　　　　You have a son, Aumerle my noble kinsman.
125　　Had you first died and he been thus trod down,
　　　　He should have found his uncle Gaunt a father
　　　　To rouse his wrongs and chase them to the bay.[8]
　　　　I am denied to sue my livery[9] here,
　　　　And yet my letters patents give me leave.
130　　My father's goods are all distrained° and sold,　　　　　　　°confiscated
　　　　And these and all are all amiss employed.
　　　　What would you have me do? I am a subject,
　　　　And I challenge law;° attorneys are denied me;　　　　°demand my rights
　　　　And therefore personally I lay my claim
135　　To my inheritance of free descent.°　　　　　　　　　　　　°legal succession
　　NORTHUMBERLAND　The noble Duke hath been too much abused.
　　ROSS　It stands your grace upon[1] to do him right.
　　WILLOUGHBY　Base men by his endowments° are made great.　　°property
　　YORK　My lords of England, let me tell you this.
140　　I have had feeling of my cousin's wrongs,
　　　　And laboured all I could to do him right.
　　　　But in this kind° to come, in braving arms,　　　　　　　　°manner
　　　　Be his own carver,[2] and cut out his way
　　　　To find out right with wrong[3]—it may not be.
145　　And you that do abet him in this kind
　　　　Cherish rebellion, and are rebels all.
　　NORTHUMBERLAND　The noble Duke hath sworn his coming is
　　　　But for his own, and for the right of that
　　　　We all have strongly sworn to give him aid;
150　　And let him never see joy that breaks that oath.
　　YORK　Well, well, I see the issue° of these arms.　　　　　　　°consequence
　　　　I cannot mend it, I must needs confess,
　　　　Because my power° is weak and all ill-left.　　　　　　　　°army
　　　　But if I could, by Him that gave me life,
155　　I would attach° you all, and make you stoop　　　　　　　　°arrest
　　　　Unto the sovereign mercy of the King.
　　　　But since I cannot, be it known to you
　　　　I do remain as neuter.° So fare you well—　　　　　　　　°neutral
　　　　Unless you please to enter in the castle
160　　And there repose you for this night.
　　BOLINGBROKE　An offer, uncle, that we will accept.
　　　　But we must win° your grace to go with us　　　　　　　　°persuade
　　　　To Bristol Castle, which they say is held
　　　　By Bushy, Bagot, and their complices,°　　　　　　　　　°accomplices
165　　The caterpillars° of the commonwealth,　　　　　　　　　°devourers
　　　　Which I have sworn to weed and pluck away.
　　YORK　It may be I will go with you—but yet I'll pause,
　　　　For I am loath to break our country's laws.
　　　　Nor° friends nor foes, to me welcome you are.　　　　　　°Neither
170　　Things past redress are now with me past care.　　　Exeunt

---

8. *rouse:* startle an animal from its cover. *bay:* point
where the animal turns on its pursuers.
9. See note to 2.1.205.

1. It is incumbent on your grace.
2. Help himself to meat (instead of waiting to be served).
3. To illegally obtain what he deserves.

2.4

Enter Earl of SALISBURY *and a* WELSH CAPTAIN

WELSH CAPTAIN   My lord of Salisbury, we have stayed° ten days,   *waited*
    And hardly° kept our countrymen together,   *with difficulty*
    And yet we hear no tidings from the King.
    Therefore we will disperse ourselves. Farewell.
5   SALISBURY   Stay yet another day, thou trusty Welshman.
    The King reposeth all his confidence in thee.
WELSH CAPTAIN   'Tis thought the King is dead. We will not stay.
    The bay trees in our country are all withered,
    And meteors fright the fixèd stars of heaven.
10 The pale-faced moon looks bloody on the earth,[1]
    And lean-looked prophets whisper fearful change.
    Rich men look sad, and ruffians dance and leap;
    The one in fear to lose what they enjoy,
    The other to enjoy° by rage and war.   *hoping to profit*
15 These signs forerun the death or fall of kings.
    Farewell. Our countrymen are gone and fled,
    As well assured Richard their king is dead.   *Exit*
SALISBURY   Ah, Richard! With the eyes of heavy mind
    I see thy glory, like a shooting star,
20 Fall to the base earth from the firmament.
    Thy sun sets weeping in the lowly west,
    Witnessing° storms to come, woe, and unrest.   *Testifying to*
    Thy friends are fled to wait upon thy foes,
    And crossly° to thy good all fortune goes.   *Exit*   *adversely*

3.1

Enter BOLINGBROKE [*Duke of Lancaster and Hereford,*
Duke of] YORK, [*Earl of*] NORTHUMBERLAND, [*Lord*]
ROSS, [HARRY] PERCY, [*and Lord*] WILLOUGHBY

BOLINGBROKE   Bring forth these men.
    [*Enter*] BUSHY *and* GREEN, [*guarded as*] *prisoners*
    Bushy and Green, I will not vex° your souls,   *afflict*
    Since presently° your souls must part your bodies,   *immediately*
    With too much urging° your pernicious lives,   *emphasizing*
5   For 'twere no charity. Yet to wash your blood
    From off my hands, here in the view of men
    I will unfold some causes of your deaths.
    You have misled a prince, a royal king,
    A happy° gentleman in blood and lineaments,[1]   *fortunate*
10 By you unhappied and disfigured clean.°   *utterly*
    You have, in manner,° with your sinful hours   *so to speak*
    Made a divorce betwixt his queen and him,
    Broke the possession of a royal bed
    And stained the beauty of a fair queen's cheeks
15 With tears drawn from her eyes by your foul wrongs.[2]
    Myself—a prince by fortune of my birth,
    Near to the King in blood, and near in love
    Till you did make him misinterpret me—
    Have stooped my neck under your injuries,

2.4 Location: A camp in Wales.
1. Holinshed records the first of these omens (line 8);
the others are poetic commonplaces.
3.1 Location: Before Bristol Castle.

1. In descent and qualities.
2. Bolingbroke implies that Bushy and Green had
homosexual relations with Richard; Holinshed claims
that they procured female paramours for him.

20   And sighed my English breath in foreign clouds,°   *air*
        Eating the bitter bread of banishment,
        Whilst you have fed upon my signories,°   *estates*
        Disparked my parks³ and felled my forest woods,
        From my own windows torn my household coat,⁴
25   Razed° out my imprese,° leaving me no sign,   *Scraped / heraldic emblem*
        Save men's opinions and my living blood,
        To show the world I am a gentleman.
        This and much more, much more than twice all this,
        Condemns you to the death.—See them delivered over
30   To execution and the hand of death.
BUSHY   More welcome is the stroke of death to me
        Than Bolingbroke to England.
GREEN   My comfort is that heaven will take our souls,
        And plague injustice with the pains of hell.
35 BOLINGBROKE   My lord Northumberland, see them dispatched.
        [*Exit* NORTHUMBERLAND, *with* BUSHY *and* GREEN, *guarded*]
        Uncle, you say the Queen is at your house.
        For God's sake, fairly° let her be intreated.°   *courteously / treated*
        Tell her I send to her my kind commends.°   *greetings*
        Take special care my greetings be delivered.
40 YORK   A gentleman of mine I have dispatched
        With letters of your love to her at large.°   *fully described*
BOLINGBROKE   Thanks, gentle uncle.—Come, lords, away,
        To fight with Glyndŵr⁵ and his complices.
        A while to work, and after, holiday.   *Exeunt*

3.2

        Drums. Flourish. Enter [KING] RICHARD, [*Duke of*]
        AUMERLE, [BISHOP OF] CARLISLE, *and soldiers* [*with*]
        colours°   *flags*
KING RICHARD   Harlechly Castle call they this at hand?
AUMERLE   Yea, my lord. How brooks° your grace the air   *enjoys*
        After your late° tossing on the breaking seas?   *recent*
KING RICHARD   Needs must° I like it well. I weep for joy   *Necessarily*
5   To stand upon my kingdom once again.
        [*He touches the ground*]
        Dear earth, I do salute thee with my hand,
        Though rebels wound thee with their horses' hoofs.
        As a long-parted mother with her child
        Plays fondly with her tears, and smiles in meeting,
10   So, weeping, smiling, greet I thee my earth,
        And do thee favours with my royal hands.
        Feed not thy sovereign's foe, my gentle earth,
        Nor with thy sweets° comfort his ravenous sense;¹   *bounty*
        But let thy spiders that suck up thy venom²
15   And heavy-gaited toads³ lie in their way,
        Doing annoyance to the treacherous feet
        Which with usurping steps do trample thee.
        Yield stinging nettles to mine enemies,

---

3. Put my hunting lands to other use.
4. Removed the stained glass bearing my coat of arms.
5. This character appears in *1 Henry IV* and is perhaps to be identified with the Welsh captain of 2.4.
3.2 Location: Near Harlech Castle, on the coast of

Gwynedd, Wales.
1. Appetite; intention.
2. It was thought that spiders drew their venom from the earth.
3. Also thought to be poisonous.

And when they from thy bosom pluck a flower
20 Guard it, I pray thee, with a lurking adder,
Whose double° tongue may with a mortal touch   *forked*
Throw death upon thy sovereign's enemies.—
Mock not my senseless conjuration,[4] lords.
This earth shall have a feeling, and these stones
25 Prove armèd soldiers, ere her native king°   *King entitled by birth*
Shall falter under foul rebellion's arms.
BISHOP OF CARLISLE   Fear not, my lord. That power that made you king
Hath power to keep you king in spite of all.[5]
28.1   *The means that heavens yield must be embraced*
    And not neglected; else° heaven would,   *otherwise*
    And we will not: heaven's offer we refuse,
    The proffered means of succour and redress.
AUMERLE   He means, my lord, that we are too remiss.
30 Whilst Bolingbroke, through our security,°   *overconfidence*
Grows strong and great in substance and in friends.
KING RICHARD   Discomfortable° cousin, know'st thou not   *Disheartening*
That when the searching eye of heaven is hid
Behind the globe, that lights the lower world,
35 Then thieves and robbers range abroad unseen
In murders and in outrage bloody here;
But when from under this terrestrial ball
He fires° the proud tops of the eastern pines,   *lights up*
And darts his light through every guilty hole,
40 Then murders, treasons, and detested sins,
The cloak of night being plucked from off their backs,
Stand bare and naked, trembling at themselves?
So when this thief, this traitor, Bolingbroke,
Who all this while hath revelled in the night
45 Whilst we were wand'ring with the Antipodes,
Shall see us rising in our throne, the east,[6]
His treasons will sit blushing in his face,
Not able to endure the sight of day,
But, self-affrighted, tremble at his sin.
50 Not all the water in the rough rude sea
Can wash the balm° from an anointed king.   *oil of consecration*
The breath of worldly men cannot depose
The deputy elected by the Lord.
For every man that Bolingbroke hath pressed°   *drafted*
55 To lift shrewd° steel against our golden crown,   *wicked; sharp*
God for his Richard hath in heavenly pay
A glorious angel. Then if angels fight,
Weak men must fall; for heaven still° guards the right.   *always*
    Enter [Earl of] SALISBURY
Welcome, my lord. How far off lies your power?
60 SALISBURY   Nor nea'er° nor farther off, my gracious lord,   *Neither nearer*
Than this weak arm. Discomfort guides my tongue,
And bids me speak of nothing but despair.
One day too late, I fear me, noble lord,
Hath clouded all thy happy days on earth.

---

4. Injunction addressed to an insentient being (the earth).
5. The following indented passage (lines 28.1–28.4) appears only in Q1.
6. *That when . . . east:* Richard compares the sun ("the searching eye of heaven," line 33), the antipodes, or "lower world" on the other side of the globe, to himself leaving England to visit Ireland. Unlike the sun, however, Richard arrives from the west.

65 O, call back yesterday, bid time return,
    And thou shalt have twelve thousand fighting men.
    Today, today, unhappy day too late,
    Overthrows thy joys, friends, fortune, and thy state;°   prosperity; nation
    For all the Welshmen, hearing thou wert dead,
70 Are gone to Bolingbroke, dispersed, and fled.
AUMERLE   Comfort, my liege. Why looks your grace so pale?
KING RICHARD   But now° the blood of twenty thousand men   A moment ago
    Did triumph° in my face, and they are fled;   shine
    And till so much blood thither come again
75 Have I not reason to look pale and dead?
    All souls that will be safe fly from my side,
    For time hath set a blot upon my pride.
AUMERLE   Comfort, my liege. Remember who you are.
KING RICHARD   I had forgot myself. Am I not King?
80 Awake, thou sluggard majesty, thou sleep'st!
    Is not the King's name forty thousand names?
    Arm, arm, my name! A puny subject strikes
    At thy great glory. Look not to the ground,
    Ye favourites of a king: are we not high?
85 High be our thoughts. I know my uncle York
    Hath power enough to serve our turn.
              Enter SCROPE
                              But who comes here?
SCROPE   More health and happiness betide my liege
    Than can my care-tuned[7] tongue deliver° him.   offer
KING RICHARD   Mine ear is open and my heart prepared.
90 The worst is worldly loss thou canst unfold.
    Say, is my kingdom lost? Why 'twas my care,°   trouble
    And what loss is it to be rid of care?
    Strives Bolingbroke to be as great as we?
    Greater he shall not be. If he serve God
95 We'll serve Him too, and be his fellow so.[8]
    Revolt our subjects? That we cannot mend.
    They break their faith to God as well as us.
    Cry° woe, destruction, ruin, loss, decay: Though you may cry
    The worst is death, and death will have his° day.   its
100 SCROPE   Glad am I that your highness is so armed
    To bear the tidings of calamity.
    Like an unseasonable stormy day,
    Which makes the silver rivers drown their shores
    As if the world were all dissolved to tears,
105 So high above his limits° swells the rage   bounds; banks
    Of Bolingbroke, covering your fearful° land   alarmed
    With hard bright steel, and hearts harder than steel.
    Whitebeards have armed their thin and hairless scalps
    Against thy majesty. Boys with women's voices
110 Strive to speak big, and clap their female° joints   weak
    In stiff unwieldy arms° against thy crown.   armor
    Thy very beadsmen[9] learn to bend their bows
    Of double-fatal[1] yew against thy state.

7. Tuned to the key sorrow.
8. Be Bolingbroke's equal in that regard.
9. Poor elderly men who received charity in return for

praying for their benefactors' souls.
1. Because yew is poisonous, and its wood was used to
make bows.

Yea, distaff-women° manage rusty bills[2]   *spinners*
115 Against thy seat.° Both young and old rebel,   *throne*
And all goes worse than I have power to tell.
KING RICHARD   Too well, too well thou tell'st a tale so ill.
Where is the Earl of Wiltshire? Where is Bagot?[3]
What is become of Bushy, where is Green,
120 That they have let the dangerous enemy
Measure our confines[4] with such peaceful° steps?   *unopposed*
If we prevail, their heads shall pay for it.
I warrant they have made peace with Bolingbroke.
SCROPE   Peace have they made with him indeed, my lord.
125 KING RICHARD   O villains, vipers damned without redemption!
Dogs easily won to fawn on any man!
Snakes in my heart-blood warmed, that sting my heart!
Three Judases, each one thrice-worse than Judas![5]
Would they make peace? Terrible hell make war
130 Upon their spotted° souls for this offence!   *blemished*
SCROPE   Sweet love, I see, changing his property,°   *its quality*
Turns to the sourest and most deadly hate.
Again uncurse their souls. Their peace is made
With heads, and not with hands. Those whom you curse
135 Have felt the worst of death's destroying wound,
And lie full low, graved in the hollow ground.
AUMERLE   Is Bushy, Green, and the Earl of Wiltshire dead?
SCROPE   Ay, all of them at Bristol lost their heads.
AUMERLE   Where is the Duke my father, with his power?
140 KING RICHARD   No matter where. Of comfort no man speak.
Let's talk of graves, of worms and epitaphs,
Make dust our paper, and with rainy eyes
Write sorrow on the bosom of the earth.
Let's choose executors and talk of wills—
145 And yet not so, for what can we bequeath
Save our deposèd° bodies to the ground?   *dethroned; prostrate*
Our lands, our lives, and all are Bolingbroke's;
And nothing can we call our own but death,
And that small model[6] of the barren earth
150 Which serves as paste[7] and cover to our bones.
[*Sitting*] For God's sake, let us sit upon the ground,
And tell sad stories of the death of kings—
How some have been deposed, some slain in war,
Some haunted by the ghosts they have deposed,
155 Some poisoned by their wives, some sleeping killed,
All murdered. For within the hollow crown
That rounds° the mortal temples of a king   *encircles*
Keeps Death his court; and there the antic° sits,   *jester*
Scoffing his state[8] and grinning at his pomp,
160 Allowing him a breath, a little scene,
To monarchize,° be feared, and kill with looks,[9]   *play the monarch*
Infusing him with self and vain conceit,[1]
As if this flesh which walls about our life

---

2. Spiked axes on long shafts.
3. Bagot is not one of the "three Judases" (line 128) actually executed by Bolingbroke; he reappears in 4.1.
4. Travel over our territories.
5. Disciple who betrayed Jesus.

6. Microcosm (the body); enveloping shape (the grave).
7. Pastry shell (also known as "coffin").
8. Mocking the King's regality.
9. Order executions with a glance.
1. Instilling in him vain ideas about himself.

Were brass impregnable; and humoured thus,[2]
165   Comes at the last, and with a little pin
Bores through his castle wall; and farewell, king.
Cover your heads,[3] and mock not flesh and blood
With solemn reverence. Throw away respect,
Tradition, form, and ceremonious duty,
170   For you have but mistook me all this while.
I live with bread, like you; feel want,
Taste grief, need friends. Subjected thus,[4]
How can you say to me I am a king?

BISHOP OF CARLISLE   My lord, wise men ne'er wail their present woes,
175   But presently prevent the ways to wail.[5]
To fear the foe, since fear oppresseth° strength,   *suppresses*
Gives in your weakness strength unto your foe;
And so your follies fight against yourself.
Fear, and be slain. No worse can come to fight;°   *in fighting*
180   And fight and die is death destroying death,[6]
Where fearing dying pays death servile breath.

AUMERLE   My father hath a power.° Enquire of him,   *an army*
And learn to make a body of a limb.

KING RICHARD [*standing*]   Thou chid'st me well. Proud Boling-
    broke, I come
185   To change blows with thee for our day of doom.[7]
This ague-fit° of fear is overblown.°   *chill / blown over*
An easy task it is to win our own.
Say, Scrope, where lies our uncle with his power?
Speak sweetly, man, although thy looks be sour.

190 SCROPE   Men judge by the complexion° of the sky   *appearance*
    The state and inclination of the day.
So may you by my dull and heavy eye
    My tongue hath but a heavier tale to say.
I play the torturer by small and small°   *little by little*
195   To lengthen out the worst that must be spoken.
Your uncle York is joined with Bolingbroke,
And all your northern castles yielded up,
And all your southern gentlemen° in arms   *men of rank*
Upon his faction.

KING RICHARD   Thou hast said enough.
200   [*To* AUMERLE] Beshrew° thee, cousin, which didst lead me forth   *Woe to*
Of that sweet way I was in to despair.
What say you now? What comfort have we now?
By heaven, I'll hate him everlastingly
That bids me be of comfort any more.
205   Go to Flint Castle;° there I'll pine away.   *Welsh castle near Chester*
A king, woe's slave, shall kingly woe obey.
That power I have, discharge, and let them go
To ear° the land that hath some hope to grow;   *till*
For I have none. Let no man speak again
210   To alter this, for counsel is but vain.

AUMERLE   My liege, one word.

KING RICHARD   He does me double wrong

---

2. And Death having thus amused himself.
3. Replace your hats (do not respectfully remain bare-
headed).
4. Made a subject to such needs (with pun).

5. But immediately vanquish the causes of grief.
6. To die fighting is to destroy death's power by dying.
7. To exchange blows with you in order to determine
our fates.

That wounds me with the flatteries of his tongue.
Discharge my followers. Let them hence away
From Richard's night to Bolingbroke's fair day.   *Exeunt*

3.3

Enter BOLINGBROKE [*Duke of Lancaster and Hereford,*
Duke of] YORK, [*Earl of*] NORTHUMBERLAND, [*and sol-*
diers] *with drum and colours*

BOLINGBROKE   So that by this intelligence° we learn   *information*
    The Welshmen are dispersed, and Salisbury
    Is gone to meet the King, who lately landed
    With some few private friends upon this coast.
5 NORTHUMBERLAND   The news is very fair and good, my lord.
    Richard not far from hence hath hid his head.
YORK   It would beseem the Lord Northumberland
    To say 'King Richard'. Alack the heavy day
    When such a sacred king should hide his head!
10 NORTHUMBERLAND   Your grace mistakes. Only to be brief
    Left I his title out.
YORK   The time hath been,
    Would you have been so brief with him, he would
    Have been so brief with you to shorten you,
    For taking so the head,[1] your whole head's length.
15 BOLINGBROKE   Mistake not, uncle, further than you should.
YORK   Take not, good cousin, further than you should,
    Lest you mistake° the heavens are over our heads.   *forget*
BOLINGBROKE   I know it, uncle, and oppose not myself
    Against their will.
       Enter [HARRY] PERCY [*and a trumpeter*]
            But who comes here?
20 Welcome, Harry. What, will not this castle yield?
HARRY PERCY   The castle royally is manned, my lord,
    Against thy entrance.
BOLINGBROKE   Royally?
    Why, it contains no king.
HARRY PERCY   Yes, my good lord,
    It doth contain a king. King Richard lies
25 Within the limits of yon lime and stone,
    And with him are the Lord Aumerle, Lord Salisbury,
    Sir Stephen Scrope, besides a clergyman
    Of holy reverence; who, I cannot learn.
NORTHUMBERLAND   O, belike° it is the Bishop of Carlisle.   *probably*
30 BOLINGBROKE [*to* NORTHUMBERLAND]   Noble lord,
    Go to the rude ribs° of that ancient castle;   *rough walls*
    Through brazen trumpet send the breath of parley
    Into his ruined ears,° and thus deliver.   *its battered loopholes*
    Henry Bolingbroke
35 Upon his knees doth kiss King Richard's hand,
    And sends allegiance and true faith of heart
    To his most royal person, hither come
    Even at his feet to lay my arms and power,
    Provided that my banishment repealed°   *revoked*
40 And lands restored again be freely granted.

3.3 Location: Before Flint Castle.   1. For omitting the title thus; for acting without restraint.

If not, I'll use the advantage of my power,
And lay° the summer's dust with showers of blood   *make settle*
Rained from the wounds of slaughtered Englishmen;
The which how far off from the mind of Bolingbroke
45 It is such crimson tempest should bedrench
The fresh green lap of fair King Richard's land,
My stooping duty° tenderly shall show.   *submissive kneeling*
Go, signify as much, while here we march
Upon the grassy carpet of this plain.
50 Let's march without the noise of threat'ning drum,
That from this castle's tottered° battlements   *dilapidated*
Our fair appointments° may be well perused.   *equipment*
Methinks King Richard and myself should meet
With no less terror than the elements
55 Of fire and water° when their thund'ring shock   *lightning and rain*
At meeting tears the cloudy cheeks of heaven.
Be he the fire, I'll be the yielding water.
The rage be his, whilst on the earth I rain°   *(punning on "reign"?)*
My waters: on the earth, and not on him.—
60 March on, and mark King Richard, how he looks.
        [*They march about the stage; then* BOLINGBROKE, YORK,
        PERCY, *and soldiers stand at a distance from the walls;*
        NORTHUMBERLAND *and a trumpeter advance to the*
        walls.*] The trumpets sound [a] parley without, and [an]
        answer within; then a flourish [within.* KING] RICHARD
        appeareth on the walls,[2] [*with* BISHOP OF] CARLISLE,
        [*Duke of*] AUMERLE, SCROPE, [*and Earl of*] SALISBURY
See, see, King Richard doth himself appear,
As doth the blushing[3] discontented sun
From out the fiery portal of the east
When he perceives the envious° clouds are bent   *malicious*
65 To dim his glory and to stain the track
Of his bright passage to the occident.
YORK   Yet looks he like a king. Behold, his eye,
As bright as is the eagle's, lightens forth[4]
Controlling majesty. Alack, alack for woe
70 That any harm should stain so fair a show!
KING RICHARD [*to* NORTHUMBERLAND]   We are amazed; and
          thus long have we stood
To watch° the fearful bending of thy knee,   *wait for*
Because we thought ourself thy lawful king.
An if° we be, how dare thy joints forget   *An if = If*
75 To pay their aweful° duty to our presence?   *reverential*
If we be not, show us the hand of God
That hath dismissed us from our stewardship.
For well we know no hand of blood and bone
Can grip° the sacred handle of our sceptre,   *seize*
80 Unless he do profane, steal, or usurp.
And though you think that all—as you have done—
Have torn° their souls by turning them from us,   *ruined (by disloyalty)*
And we are barren and bereft of friends,

2. That is, on the balcony of the tiring-house at the   weather).
back of the stage.   4. Flashes out (the eagle is a traditional royal symbol).
3. Red (proverbially, a red morning sky anticipates bad

Yet know my master, God omnipotent,
85 Is mustering in his clouds on our behalf
Armies of pestilence; and they shall strike
Your children yet unborn and unbegot,
That lift your vassal hands against my head
And threat° the glory of my precious crown.   threaten
90 Tell Bolingbroke, for yon methinks he is,
That every stride he makes upon my land
Is dangerous treason. He is come to open
The purple testament° of bleeding war;   blood-red document
But ere the crown he looks for live in peace
95 Ten thousand bloody crowns° of mothers' sons   heads
Shall ill become the flower of England's face,⁵
Change the complexion of her maid-pale° peace   innocent white
To scarlet indignation, and bedew
Her pastures' grass with faithful English blood.
NORTHUMBERLAND [*kneeling*]   The King of heaven forbid our
100   lord the King
Should so with civil and uncivil⁶ arms
Be rushed upon. Thy thrice-noble cousin
Harry Bolingbroke doth humbly kiss thy hand,
And by the honourable tomb he swears,
105 That stands upon your royal grandsire's° bones,   (Edward III's)
And by the royalties of both your bloods,
Currents that spring from one most gracious head,°   source
And by the buried hand of warlike Gaunt,
And by the worth and honour of himself,
110 Comprising all that may be sworn or said,
His coming hither hath no further scope°   aim
Than for his lineal royalties,° and to beg   hereditary rights
Enfranchisement° immediate on his knees;   Recall from exile
Which on thy royal party° granted once,   part
115 His glittering arms he will commend° to rust,   commit
His barbèd° steeds to stables, and his heart   armed
To faithful service of your majesty.
This swears he as he is a prince and just,
And as I am a gentleman I credit° him.   believe
120 KING RICHARD   Northumberland, say thus the King returns:°   replies
His noble cousin is right welcome hither,
And all the number of his fair demands
Shall be accomplished without contradiction.
With all the gracious utterance thou hast,
125 Speak to his gentle hearing kind commends.°   regards
         [NORTHUMBERLAND *and the trumpeter return to*
         BOLINGBROKE]
[*To* AUMERLE] We do debase ourself, cousin, do we not,
To look so poorly° and to speak so fair?   abjectly
Shall we call back Northumberland, and send
Defiance to the traitor, and so die?
130 AUMERLE   No, good my lord, let's fight with gentle words
Till time lend friends, and friends their helpful swords.
KING RICHARD   O God, O God, that e'er this tongue of mine,
That laid the sentence of dread banishment

---

5. Blooming surface of England; faces of England's
choicest youth.

6. Of the same country and violent; playing on "civil"
as "peaceful" and "uncivil" as "alien."

On yon proud man, should take it off again

135   With words of sooth!° O, that I were as great   *soothing words*
As is my grief, or lesser than my name,
Or that I could forget what I have been,
Or not remember what I must be now!
Swell'st thou, proud heart? I'll give thee scope to beat,
140   Since foes have scope to beat both thee and me.
           [NORTHUMBERLAND *advances to the walls*]
    AUMERLE   Northumberland comes back from Bolingbroke.
    KING RICHARD   What must the King do now? Must he submit?
The King shall do it. Must he be deposed?
The King shall be contented. Must he lose
145   The name of King? A° God's name, let it go.   *In*
I'll give my jewels for a set of beads,°   *rosary*
My gorgeous palace for a hermitage,
My gay apparel for an almsman's° gown,   *a beggar's*
My figured° goblets for a dish of wood,   *engraved*
150   My sceptre for a palmer's° walking staff,   *pilgrim's*
My subjects for a pair of carvèd saints,
And my large kingdom for a little grave,
A little, little grave, an obscure grave;
Or I'll be buried in the King's highway,°   *(as suicides were)*
155   Some way of common trade° where subjects' feet   *passage*
May hourly trample on their sovereign's head,
For on my heart they tread now, whilst I live,
And buried once, why not upon my head?
Aumerle, thou weep'st, my tender-hearted cousin.
160   We'll make foul weather with despisèd tears.
Our sighs and they shall lodge° the summer corn,   *beat down*
And make a dearth° in this revolting° land.   *famine / rebellious*
Or shall we play the wantons° with our woes,   *we frolic*
And make some pretty match° with shedding tears;   *clever game*
165   As thus to drop them still° upon one place   *continually*
Till they have fretted° us a pair of graves   *eroded for*
Within the earth, and therein laid? 'There lies
Two kinsmen digged their graves with weeping eyes.'
Would not this ill do well? Well, well, I see
170   I talk but idly° and you mock at me.   *foolishly*
Most mighty prince, my lord Northumberland,
What says King Bolingbroke? Will his majesty
Give Richard leave to live till Richard die?
You make a leg,° and Bolingbroke says 'Ay'.   *an obeisance*
175   NORTHUMBERLAND   My lord, in the base court° he doth attend   *outer courtyard*
To speak with you. May it please you to come down?
    KING RICHARD   Down, down I come like glist'ring Phaethon,[7]
Wanting the manage° of unruly jades.[8]   *Lacking control*
In the base court: base court where kings grow base
180   To come at traitors' calls, and do them grace.°   *favor them*
In the base court, come down: down court, down King,
For night-owls shriek where mounting larks should sing.
           [*Exeunt* KING RICHARD *and his party*]

---

7. In Greek mythology, the son of the sun god. He   struck him down with a thunderbolt to prevent him
attempted to drive his father's sun chariot but was too   from destroying the earth.
weak to control the horses; Zeus, king of the gods,   8. Horses (contemptuous).

[NORTHUMBERLAND *returns to* BOLINGBROKE]

BOLINGBROKE   What says his majesty?

NORTHUMBERLAND   Sorrow and grief of heart

Makes him speak fondly,° like a frantic° man.   *foolishly / an insane*

[*Enter* KING RICHARD *and his party below*]

Yet he is come.

185 BOLINGBROKE   Stand all apart,

And show fair duty to his majesty.

                     He kneels down

My gracious lord.

KING RICHARD   Fair cousin, you debase your princely knee

To make the base earth proud with kissing it.

190 Me rather had° my heart might feel your love   *I had rather*

Than my unpleased eye see your courtesy.

Up, cousin, up. Your heart is up, I know,

Thus high at least,⁹ although your knee be low.

BOLINGBROKE   My gracious lord, I come but for mine own.

195 KING RICHARD   Your own is yours, and I am yours, and all.

BOLINGBROKE   So far be mine, my most redoubted° lord,   *dreaded*

As my true service shall deserve your love.

KING RICHARD   Well you deserve. They well deserve to have

That know the strong'st and surest way to get.

                     [BOLINGBROKE *rises*]

200 [*To* YORK] Uncle, give me your hands. Nay, dry your eyes.

Tears show their love, but want their remedies.°   *do no good*

[*To* BOLINGBROKE] Cousin, I am too young to be your father,

Though you are old enough to be my heir.

What you will have I'll give, and willing too;

205 For do we must what force will have us do.

Set on towards London, cousin: is it so?

BOLINGBROKE   Yea, my good lord.

KING RICHARD   Then I must not say no.

                            Flourish. Exeunt.

3.4

Enter the QUEEN *with her two* LADIES

QUEEN   What sport shall we devise here in this garden,

   To drive away the heavy thought of care?

FIRST LADY   Madam, we'll play at bowls.°   *lawn bowling*

QUEEN   'Twill make me think the world is full of rubs,¹

5   And that my fortune runs against the bias.²

SECOND LADY   Madam, we'll dance.

QUEEN   My legs can keep no measure° in delight   *dance step*

   When my poor heart no measure° keeps in grief;   *moderation*

   Therefore no dancing, girl. Some other sport.

10 FIRST LADY   Madam, we'll tell tales.

QUEEN   Of sorrow or of joy?

FIRST LADY   Of either, madam.

QUEEN   Of neither, girl.

   For if of joy, being altogether wanting,

15   It doth remember° me the more of sorrow.   *remind*

---

9. Richard touches his crown.
3.4 Location: The Duke of York's garden.
1. Impediments (a term from the game of bowls).

2. Runs askew. *bias*: literally, a lead weight in the bowl that makes it run smoothly.

Or if of grief, being altogether had,°   *possessed*
It adds more sorrow to my want of joy.
For what I have I need not to repeat,
And what I want it boots° not to complain.   *helps*
SECOND LADY   Madam, I'll sing.
20 QUEEN   'Tis well that thou hast cause;
But thou shouldst please me better wouldst thou weep.
SECOND LADY   I could weep, madam, would it do you good.
QUEEN   And I could sing, would weeping do me good,
And never borrow any tear of thee.
              Enter a GARDENER *and two* [MEN]
25 But stay; here come the gardeners.
Let's step into the shadow of these trees.
My wretchedness unto a row of pins³
They will talk of state, for everyone doth so
Against° a change. Woe is forerun with woe.   *In anticipation of*
              [*The* QUEEN *and her* LADIES *stand apart*]
30 GARDENER [*to* FIRST MAN]   Go, bind thou up young dangling apricots
Which, like unruly children, make their sire
Stoop with oppression of their prodigal° weight.   *excessive*
Give some supportance to the bending twigs.
              [*To* SECOND MAN] Go thou, and, like an executioner,
35 Cut off the heads of too fast-growing sprays
That look too lofty in our commonwealth.
All must be even° in our government.   *equal*
You thus employed, I will go root away
The noisome° weeds which without profit suck   *harmful*
40 The soil's fertility from wholesome flowers.
FIRST MAN   Why should we, in the compass of a pale,⁴
Keep law and form and due proportion,
Showing as in a model our firm estate,°   *stable government*
When our sea-wallèd garden, the whole land,
45 Is full of weeds, her fairest flowers choked up,
Her fruit trees all unpruned, her hedges ruined,
Her knots⁵ disordered, and her wholesome herbs
Swarming with caterpillars?
GARDENER   Hold thy peace.
He that hath suffered° this disordered spring   *permitted*
50 Hath now himself met with the fall of leaf.
The weeds which his broad spreading leaves did shelter,
That seemed in eating him to hold him up,
Are plucked up, root and all, by Bolingbroke—
I mean the Earl of Wiltshire, Bushy, Green.
SECOND MAN   What, are they dead?
55 GARDENER   They are; and Bolingbroke
Hath seized the wasteful King. O, what pity is it
That he had not so trimmed and dressed° his land   *cultivated*
As we this garden! We at time of year°   *in season*
Do wound the bark, the skin of our fruit trees,⁶
60 Lest, being over-proud in° sap and blood,   *excessively swollen with*
With too much riches it confound° itself.   *ruin*

---

3. I'll bet my great wretchedness against a trivial row   5. Intricate flower beds; social bonds.
of pins.   6. *Do . . . trees*: this restricts the tree's food supply,
4. In the limits of a fenced enclosure.   encouraging fruit buds to form.

Had he done so to great and growing men,
They might have lived to bear, and he to taste,
Their fruits of duty. Superfluous branches
65 We lop away, that bearing boughs may live.
Had he done so, himself had borne° the crown,[7]   *retained*
Which waste of idle hours hath quite thrown down.
FIRST MAN What, think you then the King shall be deposed?
GARDENER Depressed° he is already, and deposed   *Brought low*
70 'Tis doubt° he will be. Letters came last night   *feared*
To a dear friend of the good Duke of York's
That tell black tidings.
QUEEN   O, I am pressed to death through want of speaking!8
  [*She comes forward*]
Thou, old Adam's[9] likeness, set to dress° this garden,   *cultivate*
75 How dares thy harsh rude° tongue sound this unpleasing news?   *ignorant*
What Eve, what serpent hath suggested° thee   *tempted*
To make a second fall of cursèd man?
Why dost thou say King Richard is deposed?
Dar'st thou, thou little better thing than earth,
80 Divine° his downfall? Say where, when, and how   *Prophesy*
Cam'st thou by this ill tidings? Speak, thou wretch!
GARDENER Pardon me, madam. Little joy have I
To breathe this news, yet what I say is true.
King Richard he is in the mighty hold
85 Of Bolingbroke. Their fortunes both are weighed.
In your lord's scale is nothing but himself
And some few vanities that make him light.
But in the balance of great Bolingbroke,
Besides himself, are all the English peers,
90 And with that odds he weighs King Richard down.
Post° you to London and you will find it so.   *Hasten*
I speak no more than everyone doth know.
QUEEN   Nimble mischance that art so light of foot.
Doth not thy embassage° belong to me,   *message*
95 And am I last that knows it? O, thou think'st
To serve me last, that I may longest keep
Thy sorrow in my breast. Come, ladies, go
To meet at London London's king in woe.
What, was I born to this, that my sad look
100 Should grace the triumph° of great Bolingbroke?   *triumphal procession*
Gard'ner, for telling me these news of woe,
Pray God the plants thou graft'st may never grow.
  Exit [with her LADIES]
GARDENER Poor Queen, so that° thy state might be no worse   *if as a result*
I would my skill were subject to thy curse.
105 Here did she fall° a tear. Here in this place   *drop*
I'll set a bank of rue,[1] sour herb-of-grace.
Rue even for ruth° here shortly shall be seen   *pity*
In the remembrance of a weeping queen.   *Exeunt*

---

7. Playing on the "crown" of a tree.
8. In medieval and Renaissance England, indicted persons who refused to plead guilty or not guilty were

killed with weights laid on the stomach.
9. Adam was the first gardener.
1. Herb associated with compassion and repentance.

4.1

Enter, as to Parliament, BOLINGBROKE *[Duke of Lan-*
caster and Hereford, Duke of] AUMERLE, *[Earl of]*
NORTHUMBERLAND, *[*HARRY*]* PERCY, *[Lord]* FITZWALTER,
[Duke of] SURREY, *[*BISHOP OF*]* CARLISLE, *[and the]*
ABBOT OF WESTMINSTER

BOLINGBROKE   Call forth Bagot.
Enter BAGOT, *[with] officers*

Now, Bagot, freely speak thy mind:

What thou dost know of noble Gloucester's death,
Who wrought it with[1] the King, and who performed
The bloody office° of his timeless° end.   *deed / untimely*

5   BAGOT   Then set before my face the Lord Aumerle.
BOLINGBROKE *[to* AUMERLE*]*   Cousin, stand forth, and look
        upon that man.
        *[*AUMERLE *stands forth]*
BAGOT   My lord Aumerle, I know your daring tongue
Scorns to unsay° what once it hath delivered.   *deny*
In that dead° time when Gloucester's death was plotted   *fatal; dark*
10   I heard you say 'Is not my arm of length,°   *long enough*
That reacheth from the restful English court
As far as Calais, to mine uncle's head?'
Amongst much other talk that very time[2]
I heard you say that you had rather refuse
15   The offer of an hundred thousand crowns
Than° Bolingbroke's return to England,   *Than accept*
Adding withal° how blest this land would be   *besides*
In this your cousin's death.

AUMERLE   Princes and noble lords,
What answer shall I make to this base man?
20   Shall I so much dishonour my fair stars°   *honorable birth*
On equal terms to give him chastisement?[3]
Either I must, or have mine honour soiled
With the attainder° of his slanderous lips.   *accusation*
        [He throws down his gage]
There is my gage, the manual seal of death
25   That marks thee out for hell. I say thou liest,
And will maintain° what thou hast said is false   *will uphold in combat*
In thy heart blood, though being all too base
To stain the temper[4] of my knightly sword.
BOLINGBROKE   Bagot, forbear. Thou shalt not take it up.
30   AUMERLE   Excepting one,° I would he° were the best   *(Bolingbroke) / (Bagot)*
In all this presence that hath moved° me so.   *angered*
FITZWALTER   If that thy valour stand on sympathy,[5]
There is my gage, Aumerle, in gage to thine.
        [He throws down his gage]
By that fair sun which shows me where thou stand'st,
35   I heard thee say, and vauntingly° thou spak'st it,   *boastfully*
That thou wert cause of noble Gloucester's death.
If° thou deny'st it twenty times, thou liest,   *Even if*

4.1 Location: Westminster Hall.
1. Who persuaded; who collaborated with.
2. *that very time:* inconsistent, since Gloucester was
killed long before Bolingbroke's exile.

3. Punishment (a lord could refuse to fight a lowborn
man in the trial by combat).
4. Quality (literally, "hardness").
5. Insists on equality of rank.

And I will turn thy falsehood to thy heart,
Where it was forgèd, with my rapier's point.

40 AUMERLE   Thou dar'st not, coward, live to see that day.

FITZWALTER   Now by my soul, I would it were this hour.

AUMERLE   Fitzwalter, thou art damned to hell for this.

HARRY PERCY   Aumerle, thou liest. His honour is as true
In this appeal° as thou art all unjust;   °accusation

45 And that thou art so, there I throw my gage
   [*He throws down his gage*]
To prove it on thee to the extremest point
Of mortal breathing. Seize it if thou dar'st.

AUMERLE   An if I do not, may my hands rot off,
And never brandish more° revengeful steel   °again
50 Over the glittering helmet of my foe.[6]

50.1   ANOTHER LORD   *I task the earth to the like, forsworn Aumerle,*
    And spur thee on with full as many lies°   °accusations of lying
    As may be hollowed° in thy treacherous ear   °shouted
    From sun to sun.° There is my honour's pawn.   °sunrise to sunset
50.5   *Engage it to[7] the trial if thou darest.*
    [*He throws down his gage*]
   AUMERLE   *Who sets° me else? By heaven, I'll throw[8] at all.*   °challenges (in gambling)
    I have a thousand spirits in one breast
    To answer twenty thousand such as you.

SURREY   My lord Fitzwalter, I do remember well
The very time Aumerle and you did talk.

FITZWALTER   'Tis very true. You were in presence° then,   °were present
And you can witness with me this is true.

55 SURREY   As false, by heaven, as heaven itself is true.

FITZWALTER   Surrey, thou liest.

SURREY   Dishonourable boy,
That lie shall lie so heavy on my sword
That it shall render vengeance and revenge,
Till thou, the lie-giver, and that lie do lie
60 In earth as quiet as thy father's skull;
In proof whereof, there is my honour's pawn.
   [*He throws down his gage*]
Engage it to the trial if thou dar'st.

FITZWALTER   How fondly dost thou spur a forward horse!
If I dare eat, or drink, or breathe, or live,
65 I dare meet Surrey in a wilderness
And spit upon him whilst I say he lies,
And lies, and lies.[9] There is my bond of faith
To tie thee to my strong correction.
As I intend to thrive in this new world,
70 Aumerle is guilty of my true appeal°   °accusation
Besides, I heard the banished Norfolk° say   °(Mowbray)
That thou, Aumerle, didst send two of thy men
To execute the noble Duke at Calais.

AUMERLE   Some honest Christian trust me with° a gage.   °lend me
   [*He takes another's gage and throws it down*]

---

6. The following indented passage (lines 50.1–50.8)
appears only in Q1.
7. Accept it as a pledge ("gage") for.

8. Defeat (as by throwing dice).
9. Fitzwalter may throw down another gage here.

75   That Norfolk lies, here do I throw down this,
     If he may be repealed,° to try his honour.   °recalled from exile
     BOLINGBROKE   These differences shall all rest under gage[1]
     Till Norfolk be repealed. Repealed he shall be,
     And, though mine enemy, restored again
80   To all his lands and signories.° When he is returned,   °estates
     Against Aumerle we will enforce his trial.
     BISHOP OF CARLISLE   That honourable day shall never be seen.
     Many a time hath banished Norfolk fought
     For Jesu Christ in glorious Christian field,[2]
85   Streaming the ensign of the Christian cross
     Against black pagans, Turks, and Saracens;
     And, toiled° with works of war, retired himself   °exhausted
     To Italy, and there at Venice gave
     His body to that pleasant country's earth,
90   And his pure soul unto his captain, Christ,
     Under whose colours he had fought so long.
     BOLINGBROKE   Why, Bishop of Carlisle, is Norfolk dead?
     BISHOP OF CARLISLE   As surely as I live, my lord.
     BOLINGBROKE   Sweet peace conduct his sweet soul to the bosom
95   Of good old Abraham![3] Lords appellants,
     Your differences° shall all rest under gage   °disputes
     Till we assign you to your days of trial.
                    Enter [Duke of] YORK
     YORK   Great Duke of Lancaster, I come to thee
     From plume-plucked° Richard, who with willing soul   °humbled
100 Adopts thee heir, and his high sceptre yields
     To the possession of thy royal hand.
     Ascend his throne, descending now from him,
     And long live Henry, of that name the fourth!
     BOLINGBROKE   In God's name I'll ascend the regal throne.
105 BISHOP OF CARLISLE   Marry, God forbid!
     Worst° in this royal presence may I speak,   °Least worthy
     Yet best beseeming° me to speak the truth.   °fitting (as a clergyman)
     Would God that any in this noble presence
     Were enough noble to be upright judge
110 Of noble Richard. Then true noblesse° would   °nobility
     Learn° him forbearance from so foul a wrong.   °Teach
     What subject can give sentence on his king?
     And who sits here that is not Richard's subject?
     Thieves are not judged but° they are by° to hear,   °except when / present
115 Although apparent° guilt be seen in them;   °obvious
     And shall the figure° of God's majesty,   °image
     His captain, steward, deputy elect,°   °chosen
     Anointed, crownèd, planted many years,
     Be judged by subject and inferior breath,
120 And he himself not present? O, forfend° it, God,   °prohibit
     That in a Christian climate souls refined[4]
     Should show so heinous, black, obscene° a deed!   °odious
     I speak to subjects, and a subject speaks
     Stirred up by God thus boldly for his king.

---

1. Shall remain as standing challenges.   Luke 16:22.
2. In battle for the Christian cause.   4. Spiritually improved; aristocratic.
3. *the bosom . . . Abraham:* that is, heavenly rest; see

125 My lord of Hereford here, whom you call king,
    Is a foul traitor to proud Hereford's king;
    And, if you crown him, let me prophesy
    The blood of English shall manure the ground,
    And future ages groan for this foul act.
130 Peace shall go sleep with Turks and infidels,
    And in this seat° of peace tumultuous wars   *region; throne*
    Shall kin with kin and kind with kind confound.[5]
    Disorder, horror, fear, and mutiny
    Shall here inhabit, and this land be called
135 The field of Golgotha[6] and dead men's skulls.
    O, if you rear this house against this house°   *(Lancaster against York)*
    It will the woefullest division prove
    That ever fell upon this cursèd earth!
    Prevent, resist it; let it not be so,
140 Lest child, child's children, cry against you woe.
  NORTHUMBERLAND   Well have you argued, sir, and for your pains
    Of capital treason we arrest you here.
    My lord of Westminster, be it your charge
    To keep him safely till his day of trial.[7]
145 May it please you, lords, to grant the Commons' suit?[8]
  BOLINGBROKE   Fetch hither Richard that in common° view   *public*
    He may surrender.[9] So we shall proceed
    Without suspicion.
  YORK   I will be his conduct.°   *Exit*   *escort*
  BOLINGBROKE   Lords, you that here are under our arrest
150 Procure your sureties for your days of answer.[1]
    Little are we beholden to your love,
    And little looked for° at your helping hands.   *expected*
      Enter RICHARD *and [Duke of]* YORK *[with attendants*
       bearing the crown and sceptre]
  RICHARD   Alack, why am I sent for to a king
    Before I have shook off the regal thoughts
155 Wherewith I reigned? I hardly yet have learned
    To insinuate, flatter, bow, and bend my knee.
    Give sorrow leave awhile to tutor me
    To this submission. Yet I well remember
    The favours° of these men. Were they not mine?   *faces; benefits*
160 Did they not sometime cry 'All hail!' to me?
    So Judas did to Christ. But He in twelve
    Found truth in all but one; I, in twelve thousand, none.
    God save the King! Will no man say 'Amen'?
    Am I both priest and clerk?[2] Well then, Amen.
165 God save the King, although I be not he.
    And yet Amen, if heaven do think him me.
    To do what service am I sent for hither?
  YORK   To do that office° of thine own good will   *task; ceremony*
    Which tired majesty did make thee offer:

---

5. Shall destroy kinsman by fellow kinsman and countryman by fellow countryman.
6. Place of Christ's crucifixion, the name of which means "place of dead men's skulls."
7. The passage that follows, to line 308, is not included in the earliest texts. See Textual Note.
8. The House of Commons' request that Richard

should have judgment passed on him.
9. Abdicate (the legitimacy of the Commons' suit depended on Richard's having given up the crown and thus his royal immunity from prosecution).
1. Procure persons guaranteeing your appearance on the day of trial.
2. Priest's assistant who utters the responses to prayers.

170   The resignation of thy state and crown
      To Henry Bolingbroke.
        RICHARD [*to an attendant*]   Give me the crown. [*To* BOLINGBROKE]
            Here, cousin, seize the crown.
      Here, cousin. On this side my hand, on that side thine.
      Now is this golden crown like a deep well
175   That owes° two buckets filling one another,³   *has*
      The emptier ever dancing in the air,
      The other down, unseen, and full of water.
      That bucket down and full of tears am I,
      Drinking my griefs, whilst you mount up on high.
180   BOLINGBROKE   I thought you had been willing to resign.
        RICHARD   My crown I am, but still my griefs are mine.
      You may my glories and my state° depose,   *royal status*
      But not my griefs; still° am I king of those.   *permanently*
        BOLINGBROKE   Part of your cares you give me with your crown.
185   RICHARD   Your cares set up do not pluck my cares down.
      My care is loss of care by old care done;
      Your care is gain of care by new care won.⁴
      The cares I give I have, though given away;
      They 'tend° the crown, yet still with me they stay.   *attend; accompany*
190   BOLINGBROKE   Are you contented to resign the crown?
        RICHARD   Ay, no; no, ay; for I must nothing be;⁵
      Therefore no, no, for I resign to thee.
      Now mark me how I will undo° myself.   *ruin; strip*
      I give this heavy weight from off my head,
          [BOLINGBROKE *accepts the crown*]
195   And this unwieldy sceptre from my hand,
          [BOLINGBROKE *accepts the sceptre*]
      The pride of kingly sway from out my heart.
      With mine own tears I wash away my balm,
      With mine own hands I give away my crown,
      With mine own tongue deny my sacred state,°   *divine right to be King*
200   With mine own breath release all duteous oaths.°   *oaths of allegiance*
      All pomp and majesty I do forswear.
      My manors, rents, revenues I forgo.
      My acts, decrees, and statutes I deny.°   *repudiate*
      God pardon all oaths that are broke to me.
205   God keep all vows unbroke are made to thee.
      Make me, that nothing have, with nothing grieved,⁶
      And thou with all pleased, that hast all achieved.
      Long mayst thou live in Richard's seat to sit,
      And soon lie Richard in an earthy pit.
210   'God save King Henry,' unkinged Richard says,
      'And send him many years of sunshine° days.'   *sunny*
      What more remains?
        NORTHUMBERLAND [*giving* RICHARD *papers*]
                          No more but that you read°   *read aloud*
      These accusations and these grievous crimes
      Committed by your person and your followers

3. That is, the raising of one causing the other to descend and fill.
4. *Your cares . . . won:* an extended wordplay on "care": Your assuming cares of state does not relieve me of grief. I mourn the loss of responsibility, by lack of diligence in the past; you concern yourself with gaining responsibility, won by effort.
5. Playing on "ay" (yes) and "I": since I am no thing, then "I," that is, "ay," is "no."
6. Grieved at nothing; grieved at having nothing.

215 Against the state and profit° of this land,   *established prosperity*
     That by confessing them, the souls of men
     May deem that you are worthily deposed.
   RICHARD   Must I do so? And must I ravel out
     My weaved-up follies? Gentle Northumberland,
220 If thy offences were upon record,
     Would it not shame thee in so fair a troop°   *company*
     To read a lecture° of them? If thou wouldst,   *give a public reading*
     There shouldst thou find one heinous article
     Containing the deposing of a king
225 And cracking the strong warrant of an oath,
     Marked with a blot, damned in the book of heaven.
     Nay, all of you that stand and look upon
     Whilst that my wretchedness doth bait[7] myself,
     Though some of you, with Pilate, wash your hands,[8]
230 Showing an outward pity, yet you Pilates
     Have here delivered me to my sour° cross,   *bitter*
     And water cannot wash away your sin.
   NORTHUMBERLAND   My lord, dispatch.° Read o'er these articles.   *hurry up*
   RICHARD   Mine eyes are full of tears I cannot see.
235 And yet salt water blinds them not so much
     But they can see a sort° of traitors here.   *pack*
     Nay, if I turn mine eyes upon myself
     I find myself a traitor with the rest.
     For I have given here my soul's consent
240 T'undeck the pompous° body of a king,   *splendidly dressed*
     Made glory base and sovereignty a slave,
     Proud majesty a subject, state° a peasant.   *royalty*
   NORTHUMBERLAND   My lord—
   RICHARD   No lord of thine, thou haught°-insulting man,   *haughty*
245 Nor no man's lord. I have no name, no title,
     No, not that name was given me at the font,
     But 'tis usurped. Alack the heavy day,
     That I have worn so many winters out
     And know not now what name to call myself!
250 O, that I were a mockery king of snow,
     Standing before the sun of Bolingbroke
     To melt myself away in water-drops!
     Good king, great king—and yet not greatly good—
     An if my word be sterling° yet in England,   *valid (like currency)*
255 Let it command a mirror hither straight,°   *immediately*
     That it may show me what a face I have,
     Since it is bankrupt of his° majesty   *its*
   BOLINGBROKE   Go some of you and fetch a looking-glass.
                        [Exit one or more]
   NORTHUMBERLAND   Read o'er this paper while the glass° doth   *until the mirror*
     come.
260 RICHARD   Fiend, thou torment'st me ere I come to hell.
   BOLINGBROKE   Urge it no more, my lord Northumberland.
   NORTHUMBERLAND   The Commons will not then be satisfied.
   RICHARD   They shall be satisfied. I'll read enough
     When I do see the very book indeed

---

7. Torment (as in bearbaiting).
8. Pilate, Jesus' judge, washed his hands to signify his disclaiming of responsibility for the death sentence he imposed at the request of the Jews.

265 Where all my sins are writ, and that's myself.
    Enter one with a glass
Give me that glass, and therein will I read.
    [RICHARD *takes the glass and looks in it*]
No deeper wrinkles yet? Hath sorrow struck
So many blows upon this face of mine
And made no deeper wounds? O flatt'ring glass,
270 Like to my followers in prosperity,
Thou dost beguile me! Was this face the face
That every day under his household roof
Did keep ten thousand men? Was this the face
That like the sun did make beholders wink?°   *shut their eyes*
275 Is this the face which faced⁹ so many follies,
That was at last outfaced° by Bolingbroke?   *stared down*
A brittle glory shineth in this face.
As brittle as the glory is the face,
    [*He shatters the glass*]
For there it is, cracked in an hundred shivers.
280 Mark, silent King, the moral of this sport:
How soon my sorrow hath destroyed my face.
 BOLINGBROKE The shadow¹ of your sorrow hath destroyed
The shadow° of your face.   *image*
 RICHARD   Say that again:
'The shadow of my sorrow'—ha, let's see.
285 'Tis very true: my grief lies all within,
And these external manner of laments
Are merely shadows to the unseen grief
That swells with silence in the tortured soul.
There lies the substance, and I thank thee, King,
290 For thy great bounty that not only giv'st
Me cause to wail, but teachest me the way
How to lament the cause. I'll beg one boon,°   *favor*
And then be gone and trouble you no more.
Shall I obtain it?
 BOLINGBROKE Name it, fair cousin.
295 RICHARD Fair cousin? I am greater than a king;
For when I was a king my flatterers
Were then but subjects; being now a subject,
I have a king here to my flatterer.
Being so great, I have no need to beg.
300 BOLINGBROKE Yet ask.
 RICHARD And shall I have?
 BOLINGBROKE You shall.
 RICHARD Then give me leave to go.
 BOLINGBROKE Whither?
305 RICHARD Whither you will, so° I were from your sights.   *provided that*
 BOLINGBROKE Go some of you, convey° him to the Tower.   *conduct*
 RICHARD O good, 'convey'!° Conveyors are you all,   *steal*
That rise thus nimbly by a true king's fall.
         [*Exit, guarded*]
 BOLINGBROKE On Wednesday next we solemnly set down

---

9. Countenanced; adorned (as a garment trimmed with "facings").
1. Darkness; outward display; image, reflection; un-

happiness (Richard plays on the word's various meanings in the following passage).

310 Our coronation. Lords, prepare yourselves.

Exeunt. Manent [ABBOT OF] WESTMINSTER,
[BISHOP OF] CARLISLE, [*and*] AUMERLE

ABBOT OF WESTMINSTER A woeful pageant have we here beheld.

BISHOP OF CARLISLE The woe's to come, the children yet unborn
Shall feel this day as sharp to them as thorn.

AUMERLE You holy clergymen, is there no plot
315 To rid the realm of this pernicious blot?

ABBOT OF WESTMINSTER My lord, before I freely speak my
mind herein,
You shall not only take the sacrament[2]
To bury mine intents,[3] but also to effect
Whatever I shall happen to devise.
320 I see your brows are full of discontent,
Your hearts of sorrow, and your eyes of tears.
Come home with me to supper. I will lay
A plot shall show us all a merry day. *Exeunt*

5.1

Enter the QUEEN *with her* LADIES

QUEEN This way the King will come. This is the way
To Julius Caesar's ill-erected Tower,[1]
To whose flint bosom my condemnèd lord
Is doomed a prisoner by proud Bolingbroke.
5 Here let us rest, if this rebellious earth
Have any resting for her true king's queen.

Enter RICHARD, *and guard*

But soft,° but see—or rather do not see—   wait
My fair rose wither. Yet look up, behold,
That you in pity may dissolve to dew,
10 And wash him fresh again with true-love tears.—
Ah, thou the model where old Troy did stand![2]
Thou map° of honour, thou King Richard's tomb,   epitome
And not King Richard! Thou most beauteous inn:
Why should hard-favoured° grief be lodged in thee,   ugly; unfortunate
15 When triumph is become an alehouse[3] guest?

RICHARD Join not with grief, fair woman, do not so,
To make my end too sudden. Learn, good soul,
To think our former state a happy dream,
From which awaked, the truth of what we are
20 Shows us but this. I am sworn brother, sweet,
To grim necessity, and he and I
Will keep a league till death. Hie° thee to France,   Hasten
And cloister thee in some religious house.°   convent
Our holy lives must win a new world's° crown,   (heaven's)
25 Which our profane hours here have stricken down.

QUEEN What, is my Richard both in shape and mind
Transformed and weakened? Hath Bolingbroke
Deposed thine intellect? Hath he been in thy heart?
The lion dying thrusteth forth his paw

2. A solemn oath, accompanied by the rite of Communion.
3. To keep my intentions secret.
5.1 Location: A street near the Tower of London.
1. The Tower of London (popularly thought to have
been built by Caesar). *ill-erected*: poorly built; erected
for evil ends.
2. The pattern of fallen greatness, like Troy.
3. Poorer class of lodging (referring to Bolingbroke)
than an "inn."

30 And wounds the earth, if nothing else, with rage
To be° o'erpowered; and wilt thou, pupil-like,   *At being*
Take the correction, mildly kiss the rod,
And fawn on rage with base humility,
Which art a lion and the king of beasts?
35 RICHARD   A king of beasts[4] indeed! If aught but beasts,
I had been still a happy king of men.
Good sometimes° Queen, prepare thee hence for France.   *former*
Think I am dead, and that even here thou tak'st,
As from my death-bed, thy last living leave.
40 In winter's tedious nights, sit by the fire
With good old folks, and let them tell thee tales
Of woeful ages long ago betid;[5]
And ere thou bid goodnight, to quit their griefs°   *repay their sad tales*
Tell thou the lamentable fall of me,
45 And send the hearers weeping to their beds;
Forwhy the senseless brands will sympathize[6]
The heavy accent of thy moving[7] tongue,
And in compassion weep the fire out;
And some° will mourn in ashes, some coal black,   *(firebrands)*
50 For the deposing of a rightful king.
     Enter [Earl of] NORTHUMBERLAND
NORTHUMBERLAND   My lord, the mind of Bolingbroke is changed.
You must to Pomfret,° not unto the Tower.   *castle in Yorkshire*
And, madam, there is order ta'en[8] for you.
With all swift speed you must away to France.
55 RICHARD   Northumberland, thou ladder wherewithal
The mounting Bolingbroke ascends my throne,
The time shall not be many hours of age
More than it is ere foul sin, gathering head,
Shall break into corruption.[9] Thou shalt think,
60 Though he divide the realm and give thee half,
It is too little helping[1] him to all.
He shall think that thou, which know'st the way
To plant unrightful kings, wilt know again,
Being ne'er so little urged another way,
65 To pluck him headlong from the usurpèd throne.
The love of wicked friends converts to fear,
That fear to hate, and hate turns one or both
To worthy° danger and deservèd death.   *severe*
NORTHUMBERLAND   My guilt be on my head, and there an end.[2]
70 Take leave and part,° for you must part° forthwith.   *separate / depart*
RICHARD   Doubly divorced! Bad men, you violate
A twofold marriage: 'twixt my crown and me,
And then betwixt me and my married wife.
     [To the QUEEN] Let me unkiss the oath 'twixt thee and me—
75 And yet not so, for with a kiss 'twas made.
Part us, Northumberland: I towards the north,
Where shivering cold and sickness pines the clime;°   *afflicts the region*

---

4. Lion (Richard's emblem); ruler of beastly men.
5. Woe that happened long ago.
6. Because even the insentient firewood will respond empathetically.
7. Physically and emotionally.
8. Arrangements have been made.
9. Pus (the image is of a swelling abscess). *Henry IV,*

Parts 1 and 2, the sequels to *Richard II,* dramatize Northumberland's rebellion against "the mounting Bolingbroke."
1. *helping:* since you helped.
2. Recalling the cry of the Jews at Jesus' trial: "His death be upon our heads, and the heads of our children."

My queen to France, from whence set forth in pomp
She came adornèd hither like sweet May,

80   Sent back like Hallowmas° or shor'st of day.[3]   *November 1*

QUEEN   And must we be divided? Must we part?

RICHARD   Ay, hand from hand, my love, and heart from heart.

QUEEN   Banish us both, and send the King with me.

NORTHUMBERLAND   That were some love, but little policy°   *but politically naive*

85 QUEEN   Then whither he goes, thither let me go.

RICHARD   So two together weeping make one woe.

    Weep thou for me in France, I for thee here.

    Better far off than, near, be ne'er the nea'er.[4]

    Go count thy way with sighs, I mine with groans.

90 QUEEN   So longest way shall have the longest moans.

RICHARD   Twice for one step I'll groan, the way being short,

    And piece the way out° with a heavy heart.   *lengthen the way*

    Come, come, in wooing sorrow let's be brief,

    Since, wedding it, there is such length in grief.

95   One kiss shall stop our mouths, and dumbly° part.   *silently*

    Thus give I mine, and thus take I thy heart.

        [*They kiss*]

QUEEN   Give me mine own again. 'Twere no good part[5]

    To take on me to keep and kill thy heart.

        [*They kiss*]

    So now I have mine own again, be gone,

100   That I may strive to kill it with a groan.

RICHARD   We make woe wanton[6] with this fond delay.

    Once more, adieu. The rest let sorrow say.

        Exeunt [RICHARD, *guarded, and* NORTHUMBERLAND *at*
        one door, the QUEEN *and her* LADIES *at another door*]

5.2

        Enter DUKE *and* DUCHESS OF YORK

DUCHESS OF YORK   My lord, you told me you would tell the rest,

    When weeping made you break the story off,

    Of our two cousins'° coming into London.   *kinsmen's*

YORK   Where did I leave?

DUCHESS OF YORK   At that sad stop, my lord,

5   Where rude misgoverned° hands from windows' tops°   *unruly / upper windows*

    Threw dust and rubbish on King Richard's head.

YORK   Then, as I said, the Duke, great Bolingbroke,

    Mounted upon a hot and fiery steed,

    Which his aspiring rider[1] seemed to know,

10   With slow but stately pace kept on his course,

    Whilst all tongues cried 'God save thee, Bolingbroke!'

    You would have thought the very windows spake,

    So many greedy looks of young and old

    Through casements darted their desiring eyes

15   Upon his visage, and that all the walls

    With painted imagery[2] had said at once,

    'Jesu preserve thee! Welcome, Bolingbroke!'

---

3. Winter solstice.
4. Better to be far away than to be near but never nearer to our happiness.
5. It would not be good of me.
6. We make our woe unrestrained; we make a sport of our grief.

5.2 Location: The Duke of York's house.
1. Object of "seemed to know."
2. Painted cloths that were hung on walls in pageants; figures in these sometimes had "speech bubbles."

Whilst he, from the one side to the other turning,
Bare-headed, lower than his proud steed's neck,
20   Bespake° them thus: 'I thank you, countrymen',   *Addressed*
And thus still doing, thus he passed along.
DUCHESS OF YORK   Alack, poor Richard! Where rode he the whilst?
YORK   As in a theatre the eyes of men,
After a well-graced actor leaves the stage,
25   Are idly bent on him that enters next,
Thinking his prattle to be tedious,
Even so, or with much more contempt, men's eyes
Did scowl on gentle Richard. No man cried 'God save him!'
No joyful tongue gave him his welcome home;
30   But dust was thrown upon his sacred head,
Which with such gentle sorrow he shook off,
His face still combating° with tears and smiles,   *continually struggling*
The badges° of his grief and patience,   *emblems*
That had not God for some strong purpose steeled
35   The hearts of men, they must perforce have melted,
And barbarism itself have pitied him.
But heaven hath a hand in these events,
To whose high will we bound our calm contents.[3]
To Bolingbroke are we sworn subjects now,
40   Whose state and honour I for aye allow.°   *forever acknowledge*
        Enter [Duke of] AUMERLE
DUCHESS OF YORK   Here comes my son Aumerle.
YORK   Aumerle that was;[4]
But that is lost for being Richard's friend,
And, madam, you must call him 'Rutland' now.
I am in Parliament pledge for his truth°   *guarantor of his loyalty*
45   And lasting fealty° to the new-made King.   *fidelity*
DUCHESS OF YORK   Welcome, my son. Who are the violets now
That strew the green lap of the new-come spring?
AUMERLE   Madam, I know not, nor I greatly care not.
God knows I had as lief° be none as one.   *had rather*
50   YORK   Well, bear you well in this new spring of time,
Lest you be cropped° before you come to prime.   *cut*
What news from Oxford? Hold these jousts and triumphs?°   *processions*
AUMERLE   For aught I know, my lord, they do.
YORK   You will be there, I know.
55   AUMERLE   If God prevent it not, I purpose so.
YORK   What seal is that that hangs without thy bosom?[5]
Yea, look'st thou pale? Let me see the writing.
AUMERLE   My lord, 'tis nothing.
YORK   No matter, then, who see it.
I will be satisfied. Let me see the writing.
60   AUMERLE   I do beseech your grace to pardon me.
It is a matter of small consequence,
Which for some reasons I would not have seen.
YORK   Which for some reasons, sir, I mean to see.
I fear, I fear!
DUCHESS OF YORK   What should you fear?

---

3. Bound ourselves to be calmly contented.
4. Aumerle has been deprived of his dukedom; he remains Earl of Rutland.

5. The document is in Aumerle's doublet, with the seal on a visibly dangling slip of attached paper.

65 'Tis nothing but some bond that he is entered into
For gay apparel 'gainst° the triumph day.   *in time for*
YORK   Bound to himself?[6] What doth he with a bond
That he is bound to? Wife, thou art a fool.
Boy, let me see the writing.
70 AUMERLE   I do beseech you, pardon me. I may not show it.
YORK   I will be satisfied. Let me see it, I say.
              He plucks it out of [Aumerle's] bosom, and reads it
Treason, foul treason! Villain, traitor, slave!
DUCHESS OF YORK   What is the matter, my lord?
YORK   Ho, who is within there? Saddle my horse.—
75 God for his mercy, what treachery is here!
DUCHESS OF YORK   Why, what is it, my lord?
YORK   Give me my boots, I say. Saddle my horse.—
Now by mine honour, by my life, my troth,
I will appeach° the villain.   *accuse*
80 DUCHESS OF YORK   What is the matter?
YORK   Peace, foolish woman.
DUCHESS OF YORK   I will not peace. What is the matter, son?
AUMERLE   Good mother, be content. It is no more
Than my poor life must answer.
DUCHESS OF YORK   Thy life answer?
85 YORK   Bring me my boots. I will unto the King.
              His man enters with his boots
DUCHESS OF YORK   Strike him,° Aumerle! Poor boy, thou art   *(the servant)*
amazed.°   *distraught*
[*To York's man*]   Hence, villain! Never more come in my sight.
YORK   Give me my boots, I say.
DUCHESS OF YORK   Why, York, what wilt thou do?
Wilt thou not hide the trespass of thine own?
90 Have we more sons?[7] Or are we like to have?
Is not my teeming date° drunk up with time?   *my period of childbearing*
And wilt thou pluck my fair son from mine age,
And rob me of a happy mother's name?
Is he not like thee? Is he not thine own?
95 YORK   Thou fond,° mad woman,   *foolish*
Wilt thou conceal this dark conspiracy?
A dozen of them here have ta'en the sacrament,
And interchangeably set down their hands[8]
To kill the King at Oxford.
DUCHESS OF YORK   He shall be none.°   *not be one of them*
100 We'll keep him here, then what is that to him?
YORK   Away, fond woman! Were he twenty times my son
I would appeach him.
DUCHESS OF YORK   Hadst thou groaned° for him   *suffered labor pains*
As I have done thou wouldst be more pitiful.
But now I know thy mind: thou dost suspect
105 That I have been disloyal to thy bed,
And that he is a bastard, not thy son.
Sweet York, sweet husband, be not of that mind.
He is as like thee as a man may be.

---

6. If Aumerle had signed a bond to borrow money the
creditor would have the bond.
7. Actually, Aumerle had a brother and a sister, and the

Duchess of York, the Duke's second wife, was Aumerle's
stepmother.
8. And mutually committed themselves in writing.

Not like to me or any of my kin,
And yet I love him.

110 YORK   Make way, unruly woman.

Exit [with his man]

DUCHESS OF YORK After, Aumerle! Mount thee upon his horse.
Spur, post,° and get before him to the King,   *Ride fast*
And beg thy pardon ere he do accuse thee.
I'll not be long behind—though I be old,
115 I doubt not but to ride as fast as York—
And never will I rise up from the ground
Till Bolingbroke have pardoned thee. Away, be gone!

Exeunt [severally]

5.3

Enter BOLINGBROKE, [*crowned* KING HENRY,] *with*
[HARRY] PERCY, *and other nobles*

KING HENRY Can no man tell of my unthrifty son?[1]
'Tis full three months since I did see him last.
If any plague hang over us, 'tis he.
I would to God, my lords, he might be found.
5 Enquire at London 'mongst the taverns there,
For there, they say, he daily doth frequent
With unrestrainèd loose companions—
Even such, they say, as stand in narrow lanes
And beat our watch° and rob our passengers°—   *watchmen / wayfarers*
10 Which he, young wanton and effeminate° boy,   *pleasure-seeking*
Takes on° the point of honour to support   *Makes it*
So dissolute a crew.
HARRY PERCY My lord, some two days since,° I saw the Prince,   *ago*
And told him of these triumphs held at Oxford.
15 KING HENRY And what said the gallant?
HARRY PERCY His answer was he would unto the stews,°   *brothels*
And from the common'st creature pluck a glove,
And wear it as a favour,[2] and with that
He would unhorse the lustiest° challenger.   *most vigorous*
20 KING HENRY As dissolute as desperate.° Yet through both   *reckless*
I see some sparks of better hope, which elder days
May happily[3] bring forth.

Enter [Duke of] AUMERLE, *amazed*

                          But who comes here?
AUMERLE Where is the King?
KING HENRY What means our cousin that he stares and looks so wildly?
25 AUMERLE [*kneeling*] God save your grace! I do beseech your majesty
To have some conference with your grace alone.
KING HENRY [*to lords*] Withdraw yourselves, and leave us here alone.

[Exeunt all but KING HENRY *and* AUMERLE]

What is the matter with our cousin now?
AUMERLE For ever may my knees grow° to the earth,   *be fixed*
30 My tongue cleave to the roof within my mouth,
Unless a pardon ere I rise or speak.
KING HENRY Intended or committed was this fault?

5.3 Location: Windsor Castle.
1. Henry's oldest son is Prince Hal of *1* and *2 Henry IV*,
later King Henry V. *unthrifty:* dissolute.

2. Lady's gift to a knight that is worn in combat.
3. Perhaps; with good fortune.

If on the first,° how heinous e'er it be,   *If only intended*
To win thy after-love I pardon thee.
35 AUMERLE[*rising*]   Then give me leave that I may turn the key,
  That no man enter till my tale be done.
KING HENRY Have thy desire.
      [AUMERLE *locks the door.*]
      The Duke of YORK *knocks at the door and crieth*
YORK [*within*]   My liege, beware! Look to thyself!
  Thou hast a traitor in thy presence there.
      [KING HENRY *draws his sword*]
KING HENRY [*to* AUMERLE]   Villain, I'll make thee safe.°   *harmless*
40 AUMERLE Stay° thy revengeful hand! Thou hast no cause to fear.   *Restrain*
YORK [*knocking within*]   Open the door, secure° foolhardy King!   *overconfident*
  Shall I for° love speak treason⁴ to thy face?   *out of*
  Open the door, or I will break it open.
      [KING HENRY *opens the door.*] *Enter* [*Duke of*] YORK
KING HENRY What is the matter, uncle? Speak,
45   Recover breath, tell us how near is danger,
  That we may arm us to encounter it.
YORK Peruse this writing here, and thou shalt know
  The treason that my haste⁵ forbids me show.°   *explain*
      [*He gives* KING HENRY *the paper*]
AUMERLE Remember, as thou read'st, thy promise past.
50   I do repent me. Read not my name there.
  My heart is not confederate with my hand.°   *signature*
YORK It was, villain, ere thy hand did set it down.
  I tore it° from the traitor's bosom, King.   *(the bond)*
  Fear, and not love, begets his penitence.
55   Forget to pity him, lest pity prove
  A serpent that will sting thee to the heart.
KING HENRY O, heinous, strong, and bold conspiracy!
  O loyal father of a treacherous son!
  Thou sheer,° immaculate, and silver fountain,   *clear*
60   From whence this stream through muddy passages
  Hath held his current and defiled himself,
  Thy overflow of good converts to bad,
  And thy abundant goodness shall excuse
  This deadly° blot in thy digressing⁶ son.   *damnable; death-dealing*
65 YORK So shall my virtue be his vice's bawd,
  And he shall spend mine honour with his shame,
  As thriftless sons their scraping fathers' gold.
  Mine honour lives when his dishonour dies,
  Or my shamed life in his dishonour lies.
70   Thou kill'st me in his life: giving him breath
  The traitor lives, the true man's put to death.
DUCHESS OF YORK [*within*] What ho, my liege, for God's sake let me in!
KING HENRY What shrill-voiced suppliant makes this eager cry?
DUCHESS OF YORK [*within*] A woman, and thy aunt, great King; 'tis I.
75   Speak with me, pity me! Open the door!
  A beggar begs that never begged before.
KING HENRY Our scene is altered from a serious thing,
  And now changed to 'The Beggar and the King'.°   *(the name of a ballad)*

---

4. Disrespectfully criticize (as "secure" and "foolhardy").   6. Diverging from course (as of a stream); transgressing.
5. York is out of breath.

My dangerous cousin, let your mother in.

80 I know she is come to pray for your foul sin.

       [AUMERLE *opens the door.*] *Enter* DUCHESS [OF YORK]

YORK If thou do pardon, whosoever pray,

More sins for this forgiveness prosper may.

This festered joint° cut off, the rest rest sound.   *infected limb*

This let alone will all the rest confound.°   *destroy*

DUCHESS OF YORK [*kneeling*] O King, believe not this

85   hard-hearted man.

Love loving not itself, none other can.[7]

YORK Thou frantic woman, what dost thou make° here?   *do*

Shall thy old dugs° once more a traitor rear?   *breasts*

DUCHESS OF YORK Sweet York, be patient.—Hear me, gentle liege.

KING HENRY Rise up, good aunt.

90 DUCHESS OF YORK   Not yet, I thee beseech.

Forever will I kneel upon my knees,

And never see day that the happy sees,

Till thou give joy, until thou bid me joy

By pardoning Rutland, my transgressing boy.

95 AUMERLE [*kneeling*] Unto° my mother's prayers I bend my knee.   *In support of*

YORK [*kneeling*] Against them both my true joints bended be.

Ill mayst thou thrive if thou grant any grace.

DUCHESS OF YORK Pleads he in earnest? Look upon his face.

His eyes do drop no tears, his prayers are in jest.

100 His words come from his mouth; ours from our breast.

He prays but faintly, and would be denied;

We pray with heart and soul, and all beside.

His weary joints would gladly rise, I know;

Our knees shall kneel till to the ground they grow.

105 His prayers are full of false hypocrisy;

Ours of true zeal and deep integrity.

Our prayers do outpray his; then let them have

That mercy which true prayer ought to have.

KING HENRY Good aunt, stand up.

DUCHESS OF YORK   Nay, do not say 'Stand up'.

110 Say 'Pardon' first, and afterwards 'Stand up'.

An if° I were thy nurse, thy tongue to teach,   *An if = If*

'Pardon' should be the first word of thy speech.

I never longed to hear a word till now.

Say 'Pardon', King. Let pity teach thee how.

115 The word is short, but not so short as sweet;

No word like 'Pardon' for kings' mouths so meet.°   *fit*

YORK Speak it in French, King: say 'Pardonnez-moi'.[8]

DUCHESS OF YORK Dost thou teach pardon pardon to destroy?[9]

Ah, my sour° husband, my hard-hearted lord   *harsh*

120 That sets the word itself against the word!

Speak 'Pardon' as 'tis current in our land;

The chopping[1] French we do not understand.

Thine eye begins to speak; set thy tongue there;

Or in thy piteous heart plant thou thine ear,

125 That hearing how our plaints and prayers do pierce,

---

7. If one does not love one's own flesh and blood, one can love no one else (not even the King).
8. "Excuse me," a polite refusal.

9. Rhymes with "moi" in anglicized pronunciation.
1. Logic-chopping, changing the meaning.

Pity may move thee 'Pardon' to rehearse.°   *recite*
KING HENRY   Good aunt, stand up.
DUCHESS OF YORK   I do not sue to stand.
   Pardon is all the suit I have in hand.
KING HENRY   I pardon him as God shall pardon me.
   [YORK *and* AUMERLE *rise*]
130 DUCHESS OF YORK   O, happy vantage° of a kneeling knee!   *gain; position*
   Yet am I sick for fear. Speak it again.
   Twice saying pardon doth not pardon twain,°   *divide*
   But makes one pardon strong.
KING HENRY   I pardon him
   With all my heart.
DUCHESS OF YORK [*rising*]   A god on earth thou art.
135 KING HENRY   But for our trusty brother-in-law² and the Abbot,
   With all the rest of that consorted° crew,   *confederated*
   Destruction straight shall dog them at the heels.
   Good uncle, help to order several powers°   *forces*
   To Oxford, or where'er these traitors are.
140   They shall not live within this world, I swear,
   But I will have them if I once know where.
   Uncle, farewell; and cousin, so adieu.
   Your mother well hath prayed; and prove you true.°   *loyal*
DUCHESS OF YORK   Come, my old³ son. I pray God make thee new.
       Exeunt [KING HENRY *at one door;* YORK,
              DUCHESS OF YORK, *and* AUMERLE
                 at another door]

5.4

Enter Sir Piers EXTON, *and* [MEN]
EXTON   Didst thou not mark the King, what words he spake?
   'Have I no friend will rid me of this living fear?'
   Was it not so?
FIRST MAN   Those were his very words.
EXTON   'Have I no friend?' quoth he. He spake it twice,
5   And urged it twice together, did he not?
SECOND MAN   He did.
EXTON   And speaking it, he wishtly° looked on me,   *intently*
   As who° should say 'I would thou wert the man   *As if he*
   That would divorce this terror from my heart',
10   Meaning the King at Pomfret. Come, let's go.
   I am the King's friend, and will rid° his foe.   *Exeunt*   *will get rid of*

5.5

Enter RICHARD, *alone*
RICHARD   I have been studying how I may compare
   This prison where I live unto the world;
   And for because the world is populous,
   And here is not a creature but myself,
5   I cannot do it. Yet I'll hammer° it out.   *work*
   My brain I'll prove the female° to my soul,   *(that is, receptive)*
   My soul the father, and these two beget

2. The Duke of Exeter and Earl of Huntingdon, husband of Bolingbroke's sister; like Aumerle, he had been deprived of his dukedom.
3. Unregenerate (recalling the baptism service: "O merciful God, grant that the old Adam in this child may be so buried that the new man may be raised up in him").
5.4 Location: Windsor Castle.
5.5 Location: Pomfret Castle.

A generation of still-breeding° thoughts;   *ever-breeding*
And these same thoughts people this little world
10 In humours[1] like the people of this world.°   *(the real world)*
For no thought is contented. The better sort,
As thoughts of things divine, are intermixed
With scruples,° and do set the faith itself   *doubts*
Against the faith,[2] as thus: 'Come, little ones',[3]
15 And then again,
'It is as hard to come as for a camel
To thread the postern of a small needle's eye.'[4]
Thoughts° tending to ambition, they do plot   *Other thoughts*
Unlikely wonders:° how these vain weak nails   *miracles*
20 May tear a passage through the flinty ribs
Of this hard world, my ragged° prison walls;   *rugged*
And for they cannot, die in their own pride.° *prime of life; arrogance*
Thoughts tending to content° flatter themselves   *contentment*
That they are not the first of fortune's slaves,
25 Nor shall not be the last—like seely° beggars,   *simpleminded*
Who, sitting in the stocks, refuge[5] their shame
That many have, and others must, set there;
And in this thought they find a kind of ease,
Bearing their own misfortunes on the back
30 Of such as have before endured the like.
Thus play I in one person many people,
And none contented. Sometimes am I king;
Then treason makes me wish myself a beggar,
And so I am. Then crushing penury
35 Persuades me I was better when a king.
Then am I kinged again, and by and by
Think that I am unkinged by Bolingbroke,
And straight° am nothing. But whate'er I be,   *at once*
Nor I, nor any man that but° man is,   *merely*
40 With nothing shall be pleased till he be eased
With being nothing.
    The music plays
      Music do I hear.
Ha; ha; keep time! How sour sweet music is
When time is broke and no proportion kept.
So is it in the music of men's lives.
45 And here have I the daintiness of ear
To check° time broke in a disordered string;° *rebuke / string instrument*
But for the concord° of my state and time   *harmony*
Had not an ear to hear my true time broke.
I wasted time, and now doth time waste me,
50 For now hath time made me his numb'ring clock.[6]
My thoughts are minutes, and with sighs they jar
Their watches° on unto mine eyes, the outward watch[7] *periods of vigil*
Whereto my finger, like a dial's point,°   *clock's hand*

---

1. Temperaments; caprices.
2. *the faith . . . faith*: scriptural passage against scriptural passage.
3. From Matthew 19:14, Mark 10:14, and Luke 18:25, implying the ease of obtaining salvation.
4. Adapting Matthew 19:24, Mark 10:25, or Luke 18:25, which describe the unlikeliness of the rich reaching heaven.
5. Find refuge for; rationalize.
6. Clock that counts hours and minutes, not an hourglass.
7. Clockface; mind's external watcher.

Is pointing still° in cleansing them from tears.³   *always*

55 Now, sir, the sounds that tell what hour it is
Are clamorous groans that strike upon my heart,
Which is the bell. So sighs, and tears, and groans
Show minutes, hours, and times. But my time
Runs posting° on in Bolingbroke's proud joy,   *speeding*

60 While I stand fooling here, his jack of the clock.⁹
This music mads° me. Let it sound no more,   *maddens*
For though it have holp° madmen to their wits,   *helped*
In me it seems it will make wise men mad.
    [*The music ceases*]
Yet blessing on his heart that gives it me,

65 For 'tis a sign of love, and love to Richard
Is a strange brooch° in this all-hating world.   *rare ornament*
    Enter a GROOM *of the stable*

GROOM   Hail, royal Prince!

RICHARD   Thanks, noble peer.
The cheapest of us is ten groats too dear.¹
What art thou, and how com'st thou hither,

70 Where no man never comes but that sad dog
That brings me food to make misfortune live?

GROOM   I was a poor groom of thy stable, King,
When thou wert king; who, travelling towards York,
With much ado at length have gotten leave

75 To look upon my sometimes° royal master's face.   *former*
O, how it erned° my heart when I beheld   *grieved*
In London streets, that coronation day,
When Bolingbroke rode on roan Barbary,
That horse that thou so often hast bestrid,

80 That horse that I so carefully have dressed!°   *groomed*

RICHARD   Rode he on Barbary? Tell me, gentle friend,
How went he under him?

GROOM   So proudly as if he disdained the ground.

RICHARD   So proud that Bolingbroke was on his back.

85 That jade° hath eat bread from my royal hand;   *nag*
This hand hath made him proud with clapping° him.   *patting*
Would he not stumble, would he not fall down—
Since pride must have a fall—and break the neck
Of that proud man that did usurp his back?

90 Forgiveness, horse! Why do I rail on thee,
Since thou, created to be awed by man,
Wast born to bear? I was not made a horse,
And yet I bear a burden like an ass,
Spur-galled² and tired by jauncing° Bolingbroke.   *rough-riding*
    Enter KEEPER *to* RICHARD, *with meat*

95 KEEPER [*to* GROOM]   Fellow, give place.° Here is no longer stay.   *leave*

RICHARD [*to* GROOM]   If thou love me, 'tis time thou wert away.

GROOM   What my tongue dares not, that my heart shall say.
                            Exit

KEEPER   My lord, will't please you to fall to?

---

8. Wiping tears from my eyes.
9. Manikin that strikes the clock's bell.
1. You have overpriced the cheaper of us (me, a prisoner) in calling me "royal." The difference between the coins "royal" (10 shillings) and "noble" (6 shillings 8 pence) is "ten groats" (40 pence). In other words, we are equal in worth.
2. Made sore by spurring.

RICHARD   Taste of it first,³ as thou art wont to do.
100   KEEPER   My lord, I dare not. Sir Piers of Exton,
          Who lately came from the King, commands the contrary.
    RICHARD [*striking the* KEEPER]   The devil take Henry of Lancaster and thee!
          Patience is stale, and I am weary of it.
    KEEPER   Help, help, help!
          EXTON *and his* [*men*] *rush in*
105   RICHARD   How now! What means death in this rude assault?
          [*He seizes a weapon from a man, and kills him*]
          Villain, thy own hand yields thy death's instrument.
          [*He kills another*]
          Go thou, and fill another room in hell.
          Here EXTON *strikes him down*
    RICHARD   That hand shall burn in never-quenching fire
          That staggers thus my person.° Exton, thy fierce hand   *thus makes me stagger*
110   Hath with the King's blood stained the King's own land.
          Mount, mount, my soul; thy seat° is up on high,   *residence*
          Whilst my gross flesh sinks downward, here to die. [*He dies*]
    EXTON   As full of valour as of royal blood.
          Both have I spilt. O, would the deed were good!
115   For now the devil that told me I did well
          Says that this deed is chronicled in hell.
          This dead King to the living King I'll bear.
          Take hence the rest, and give them burial here.
              Exeunt [EXTON *with Richard's body at one door, and*
                  his men with the other bodies at another door]

                    5.6
          Flourish. Enter [KING HENRY] *with* [*Duke of*] YORK, *with*
          other lords and attendants
    KING HENRY   Kind uncle York, the latest news we hear
          Is that the rebels have consumed with fire
          Our town of Ci'cester° in Gloucestershire;   *Cirencester*
          But whether they be ta'en or slain we hear not.
          Enter [*Earl of*] NORTHUMBERLAND
5   Welcome, my lord. What is the news?
    NORTHUMBERLAND   First, to thy sacred state wish I all happiness.
          The next news is, I have to London sent
          The heads of Salisbury, Spencer, Blunt, and Kent.
          The manner of their taking may appear
10   At large discoursèd° in this paper here.   *Narrated in full*
          [*He gives the paper to* KING HENRY]
    KING HENRY   We thank thee, gentle Percy, for thy pains,
          And to thy worth will add right worthy° gains.   *valuable; well-deserved*
          Enter Lord FITZWALTER
    FITZWALTER   My lord, I have from Oxford sent to London
          The heads of Brocas and Sir Bennet Seely,
15   Two of the dangerous consorted° traitors   *confederated*
          That sought at Oxford thy dire overthrow.
    KING HENRY   Thy pains, Fitzwalter, shall not be forgot.
          Right noble is thy merit, well I wot.°   *know*
          Enter HARRY PERCY [*with the* BISHOP OF] CARLISLE
          [*guarded*]

_____

3. To make sure it is not poisoned.   5.6 Location: Windsor Castle.

HARRY PERCY   The grand conspirator Abbot of Westminster,
20   With clog° of conscience and sour melancholy.   *burden*
    Hath yielded up his body to the grave.
    But here is Carlisle living, to abide
    Thy kingly doom° and sentence of his pride.   *judgment*
KING HENRY   Carlisle, this is your doom.
25   Choose out some secret place, some reverent room
    More than thou hast,[1] and with it joy° thy life.   *enjoy*
    So as thou liv'st in peace, die free from strife.
    For though mine enemy thou hast ever been,
    High sparks of honour in thee have I seen.

Enter EXTON *with [his men bearing] a coffin*

30 EXTON   Great King, within this coffin I present
    Thy buried fear. Herein all breathless lies
    The mightiest of thy greatest enemies,
    Richard of Bordeaux, by me hither brought.
KING HENRY   Exton, I thank thee not, for thou hast wrought
35   A deed of slander° with thy fatal hand   *disgrace*
    Upon my head and all this famous land.
EXTON   From your own mouth, my lord, did I this deed.
KING HENRY   They love not poison that do poison need;
    Nor do I thee. Though I did wish him dead,
40   I hate the murderer, love him murderèd.
    The guilt of conscience take thou for thy labour,
    But neither my good word nor princely favour.
    With Cain[2] go wander through the shades of night,
    And never show thy head by day nor light.

[Exeunt EXTON *and his men]*

45   Lords, I protest my soul is full of woe
    That blood should sprinkle me to make me grow.
    Come mourn with me for what I do lament,
    And put on sullen black incontinent.°   *immediately*
    I'll make a voyage to the Holy Land
50   To wash this blood off from my guilty hand.
    March sadly after. Grace my mournings here
    In weeping after this untimely bier.   *Exeunt [with the coffin]*

---

1. More reverent than the prison cell you inhabit now.
2. After Cain murdered his brother Abel, he was condemned to be a vagabond (Genesis 4:14).

The Life and Death of King John

Historical narrative often attributes meaning to history. *The Life and Death of King John* (1596) does not. Although it focuses on historical process, on how events fit together over time, it suggests the larger significance of John's reign (1199–1216) only in disorienting fashion. The plot promises more coherence than it delivers; the apparent trajectory of events repeatedly proves illusory; seemingly decisive moments turn out to be mere episodes in the open-ended, ironic, unpredictable movement of history. The play thus breaks with the providential conclusion to Shakespeare's first tetralogy (four related plays on English history) provided by *Richard III* (1592–93) and, more generally, with the moralizing strategy of Renaissance humanist historians. A transitional work, it moves Shakespeare closer to the pragmatic, secular political thinking of Niccolò Machiavelli and to the concerns with the problematic relationship between hereditary legitimacy and fitness to rule characteristic of his second tetralogy, from *Richard II* to *Henry V* (1595–99).

The logic of the plot is to undermine logic, to frustrate expectation, to reveal the uncertain relationship between intention and outcome in a world that offers only fragments of an overarching consolation—religious or otherwise—for the frequent futility of human endeavor. The basic antagonisms arise from John's efforts to retain the crown and its overseas French territories. John faces challenges from the French, ostensibly acting on behalf of his young nephew Arthur, whose hereditary claim to the throne is stronger, and from the Catholic Church, with which John is also at odds. These conflicts repeatedly take surprising turns. The first-act struggle over inheritance between the Bastard and his younger half brother Robert Falconbridge leads to the unexpected conclusion that illegitimate birth is no barrier to legitimate inheritance. Even more surprisingly, the Bastard quickly renounces that inheritance. Similarly, when the English and French battle to a stalemate in seeking the loyalty of Angers, they join forces to level the town to punish its autonomy and then instead resolve to end their quarrel—sparing the town—through a cynical political marriage. But this resolution proves as transitory as the previous ones when Pandolf, the papal legate, excommunicates John, and France, as a result, repudiates the deal.

Although John now seems in trouble, his ensuing military triumph shifts his fortunes. Yet by ordering the murder of Arthur, he undermines his own position. It looks as if John will be rescued from the consequences of his crime when Hubert, the executioner, spares Arthur. But Arthur dies attempting to escape, an accident the English lords interpret as murder. Their defection to the invading French army apparently seals John's fate. Even though John submits to the Pope to eliminate the invasion's rationale, this tactic has no effect. But when the lords learn that the Dauphin, son of the French king, plans to kill them after securing the English throne they return to John.

The war itself is marked less by climactic battles than by both sides' careless habit of losing their armies at sea: nature, too, subverts expectations. But even this does not save John. Hated by the English clergy for his earlier extortions from the monasteries, he is poisoned by a vengeful monk. This outcome lacks dramatic logic: the pillaging of the monasteries is undramatized and given very little weight; royal resistance to Catholic domination is viewed positively if peripherally; John has been reconciled with Rome; and he is apparently dying of a fever even before his poisoning. Finally, Prince Henry, the King's young son, is conveniently produced just as peace breaks out between England and France. Accordingly, the orthodox ending, in which the legitimate heir succeeds his father, feels highly contingent. And this feeling is reinforced by the characters'

The coronation of King John. From Matthew of Westminster, *Flores Historiarum* (late thirteenth or early fourteenth century).

routine repudiation of their oaths, by shifts in dramatic register—from long public, ceremonial set pieces to rapidly shifting, increasingly private introspective scenes—and by the numerous unexplained acts whose significance remains obscure.

This view of history, in which the meaning of events proves unstable and problematic, is of a piece with Shakespeare's treatment of his sources, his major characters, his central themes, and his possible allusions to contemporary Elizabethan politics, as well as with the play's later theatrical fortunes. *King John*'s closest analogue is the anonymous play *The Troublesome Reign of John, King of England* (published 1591). Most critics believe it to be Shakespeare's primary source rather than the other way around; but regardless of the chronology (on which see the Textual Note), comparison of the two works is instructive. If *The Troublesome Reign* is the earlier work, as is assumed here, it relies in part on Raphael Holinshed's *Chronicles of England, Scotland, and Ireland* (second edition, 1587), the nonfictional narrative of English history on which Shakespeare himself drew extensively during the 1590s for his other national history plays. *The Troublesome Reign*'s author reshapes chronology and invents episodes, alterations that *King John* generally adopts, and promotes conventional Protestant and national chauvinism, which *King John* mutes. From early in the English Reformation, John was seen as a proto-Protestant royal martyr who temporarily challenged Roman Catholicism by rejecting the papal choice for archbishop of Canterbury and heavily taxing the church. Hence he was thought to have anticipated Queen Elizabeth's father, Henry VIII, whose break with Rome and expropriation of the monasteries initiated the Reformation. But Shakespeare weakens the connection to Henry, toning down the rhetoric of *The Troublesome Reign* by more closely following Holinshed, who combines the Protestant view with a centuries-old Catholic hostility to John. While the anonymous play portrays monks engaged in outrageous sexual conduct, Shakespeare omits the scene and calls John's ecclesiastical tax policy pillaging. Similarly, although John's submission to Rome is lamented in *King John,* Shakespeare hardly makes the decision catastrophic. But he does retain some of *The Troublesome Reign*'s anti-Catholicism—for instance, in John's defense of an English church. Overall, however, the play's Protestantism is unmilitant: *King John* offers scant comfort to Catholics but little more to Protestants. This outlook may reflect Shakespeare's antipathy to Christian theological controversy and perhaps his partly Catholic family background and education.

Shakespeare also softens *The Troublesome Reign*'s English national chauvinism, despite concluding with the Bastard's patriotic credo:

> This England never did, nor never shall
> Lie at the proud foot of a conqueror
> But when it first did help to wound itself.
> Now these her princes are come home again,
> Come the three corners of the world in arms
> And we shall shock them. Naught shall make us rue
> If England to itself do rest but true.
>
> (5.7.112–18)

These lines are more ambiguous than they first appear. Although they oppose foreign conquest of England, the play has considered the possibility that such domination is preferable to continued rule by a murderous English monarch. Moreover, the "But when" in the first sentence and the "if" in the third temper optimism, especially given the prior conduct of the aristocracy.

This skeptical view of traditional authority—ecclesiastical and secular alike—shapes the characterization of *King John.* Most striking is the relative inattention to John himself, the figure whose "life and death" the play claims to dramatize. The resulting vacuum is filled by women and a bastard, personages generally peripheral to dynastic history. Nowhere in Shakespeare's two historical tetralogies do women play so active a role. In the first act, John's mother, Queen Eleanor, challenges the French ambassador even before her son has a chance to do so. She then recognizes the Bastard as the illegitimate offspring of her dead son King Richard I, the Lionheart, John's oldest brother and predecessor on the throne, and (1.1.150) recruits her newly found grandson into royal service.

In Acts 2 and 3, the verbal dispute between John and Arthur (represented by the King of France) is partly carried out by proxy. Eleanor and especially Arthur's mother, Constance, whose role Shakespeare expanded from his sources, are more active than their children and (with the Bastard) rhetorically dominate the stage—especially in their confrontation in Act 2, Scene 1 and in Constance's subsequent lamentations for her son. Going beyond the common female role—victim of history—these women attempt to direct the action. Moreover, Constance and Eleanor question each other's sexual honor—an issue broached earlier when the Bastard's mother acknowledges her adulterous affair with King Richard. This recurrent concern underscores the uncertainly of biologically legitimate patriarchal succession. Hereditary descent from father to son accords a central role to women, whose sexual fidelity is considered necessary to that descent but unreliable. *King John* emphasizes the dubious fidelity of women but denies any consequence for hereditary succession. Although the mothers' attacks on each other weaken traditional notions of male legitimacy and Constance powerfully points up the unprincipled maneuvering of the two kings, she changes no one's mind, and midway through the play both she and Eleanor disappear from the plot. Their offstage deaths are reported shortly thereafter.

With them go the challenges they pose but not necessarily all they represent. Rather than executing Arthur, Hubert protects the boy, assuming a nurturing, arguably maternal, role. The Bastard's relationship to John late in the play is similar, and Prince Henry sheds tears over his dying father. Pandolf calls the Church "our Holy mother" (3.1.67,

King John's tomb in Worcester Cathedral. From Francis Sandford, *A Genealogical History of the Kings and Queens of England* (1707).

182), and the Bastard taxes the treasonous lords for "ripping up the womb / Of your dear mother England" (5.2.152–53). But it is unclear how effective these surrogates prove. Following the mothers' deaths, the sons become increasingly inept. They are memorable less in themselves than for the way that physical imagery running through *King John*, often as personification, is reliteralized in the accounts of their suffering. Arthur leaps to his accidental death when the "Good ground" of England, which he hopes does "not break my limbs," proves to be inhospitable "stones" (4.3.2, 6, 9). Earlier, the motif of fire and heat is picked up in the threat to burn out Arthur's eyes, a threat echoed in, to use John's words, the "tyrant fever [that] burns me up" and the poison that produces "so hot a summer in my bosom" (5.3.14, 5.7.30). More generally, John's stunned response to his mother's death helps explain the transformation in his behavior from confident leadership to helpless passivity. By the last part of the play, he is neither tragic nor even entirely villainous but simply beside the point, his fall coinciding with the Bastard's rise.

That rise enables a defense of illegitimacy. An almost entirely unhistorical personage in the least historical of Shakespeare's history plays, the Bastard is the work's most prominent character. Although critics have traced the development of his character, he is arguably less a coherent fictional figure than a series of discontinuous theatrical functions. His changes seem dictated more by twists of the plot than shifts in personality. The Bastard initially embodies a mischievous popular culture. Theatrically, he descends from the devilish Vice figure, a character in the earlier English morality plays. The Vice combined a commitment to evil, an intimacy with the audience, and a penchant for fun. Similarly, the Bastard speaks to and for the audience in verbally playful asides and soliloquies, denouncing the moral failings of the powerful while cheerfully conceding that he, too, is out for himself. He takes pleasure in promoting discord, and he appears immune to bodily harm, an immunity that wins him repeated description as the devil.

Unlike Shakespeare's earlier transmutations of the Vice such as Richard III, however, the Bastard is obviously a positive character. Thus, there is another side to this figure, which becomes dominant only later in the play. After John deems him legitimate and the Bastard rejects his patrimony in order to be knighted and recognized as King Richard's illegitimate son, his simultaneous financial fall and social rise allow the identification of royalty with illegitimacy. His unswerving loyalty contrasts with the selfserving deal between John and the King of France, a deal that the Bastard memorably denounces as "commodity," or self-interest (2.1.562–99). Later, that loyalty casts a harsh light on the English aristocrats' treasonous alliance with the French. The Bastard thus becomes more responsible, if less entertaining—a transformation managed by keeping the character offstage for five hundred lines. Horrified by the death of Arthur, whom he now views as the legitimate monarch, but persuaded that it was accidental, he undertakes the defense of crown and realm alike, even as John declines. In this endeavor, he proves the ethical center of a world otherwise almost devoid of positive value.

The Bastard owes this authority to his social and theatrical range. As the reembodiment of his biological father, he reflects both badly and well on the King. It is the Bastard rather than John who exacts family vengeance by killing the Duke of Austria, in this play—but not historically—slayer of King Richard. And it is the Bastard who offers the appropriate response to the death and possible murder of Arthur, for which the King bears partial—arguably full—responsibility. By comparison, John looks at best mediocre and at worst evil. Yet the Bastard's presence also suggests that the spirit of Richard guards the throne and, hence, that John is the right person for the job. As the Bastard insists in referring to John, "his royalty doth speak in me" (5.2.129).

Thus a man whose birth is illegitimate validates the fitness to rule of a man whose claim to the crown is already disputed in *The Troublesome Reign*. Shakespeare further weakens John's legal position, which is based on King Richard's will naming him successor. When Constance asserts Arthur's right to the throne, Eleanor retorts, "I can produce / A will that bars the title of thy son" (2.1.191–92). But a will is trumped by the rule of succession, which stipulates that the crown go to the firstborn male or his oldest male descendant. Here that is Arthur, son of the deceased Geoffrey, younger brother of Richard but, crucially, older brother of John. Hence, when John explains why he will prevail against the French and Arthur—"Our strong possession and our right for us" (1.1.39)—Eleanor cautions, "Your strong possession much more than your right" (line 40). Her denial of legality has authority because she supports John. John unwittingly concedes the decisiveness of order of birth when he awards the Falconbridge inheritance to the illegitimate Bastard rather than to the Bastard's younger, legitimate brother, whose claim is based only on his father's will. Even though Arthur is, therefore, legitimate and John is not, legitimacy and fitness are not synonymous. After undermining John's hereditary right, Shakespeare complicates the question. He departs from his sources by making Arthur a helpless child heavily dependent on his mother, the King of France, and the Duke of Austria. Arthur also has no interest in being King: his unfitness to rule—recognized by most commentators on *King John*—means that John's "strong possession" carries real weight.

But by ordering Arthur's murder, John squanders his authority, thereby also weakening the play's conflict between hereditary legitimacy and rightful rule. *King John's* skepticism about the meaningfulness of historical process thus undermines this central theme. A similar fate is reserved even for the Bastard, despite his crucial role in recognizing John's heir and articulating a vision of national unity. In Holinshed, John "lost a great part of his army" to drowning; in *The Troublesome Reign*, the Bastard informs John that the sea has "swallowed up the most of all our men." *King John* has the Bastard narrate this event twice, both times making him more responsible for the debacle—"half my power," "the best part of my power" (5.6.40, 5.7.61). Ineptitude is soon replaced by irrelevance: the Bastard opts for war after others have already negotiated peace. Although he is not simply shunted aside by the unpredictable concatenation of historical events, the resolution has less to do with human intention and achievement than with the collapse of both contending parties.

Where does this leave England? Temporally, *King John* differs from Shakespeare's other history plays of the 1590s: it treats the early thirteenth rather than the late fourteenth and fifteenth centuries. Standing alone rather than in a tetralogy, it does not develop a dynastic sense of "England" by depicting the sequence of reigns. Sociologically, the play is also atypical. John's reign is remembered for the Magna Carta and—without historical warrant—Robin Hood. Both concern resistance to royal tyranny—by the aristocracy and the lower class, respectively. Although these stories were available in the 1590s, neither appears in the play. The lords rebel late in the action, but the balance of power between king and nobility remains secondary. And despite a brief reference to popular unrest, *King John* accords the English people an even more marginal role in constituting the nation. This treatment of aristocracy and populace contrasts with Shakespeare's approach in his history plays of the next three years from the second tetralogy, *1* and *2 Henry IV* and *Henry V*.

King John points elsewhere. Richard the Lionheart's legacy is dispersed among three of his blood relatives—John, Arthur, and the Bastard—none of whom is a fully adequate successor. Like the Bastard, Constance and Eleanor are part of the royal family. But these three characters, who, as noted earlier, belong to peripheral groups, suggest an expansion of outlook, a shift from dynasty to nation and, hence, a repudiation of absolutist rule. That expansion is implied by the importance accorded in Act 2 to the political will of the citizens of Angers, who are asked to decide which claimant is their legitimate king, and arguably by the valorization of humane feeling and personal loyalty late in the play. Yet the Bastard's social rise from obscurity to protector of England suggests a partial analogue to the sixteenth-century emergence of a nonhereditary political elite to fill crucial positions in the new state bureaucracy. On this reading, the play ends not with an expanded, less authoritarian view of the polity, but with a redeployed ruling apparatus. If so, this reorganization of the state remains barely realized in *King John*. So, too, does a properly national sense of England. It may be that no national perspective was fully available without the traditional legitimacy of dynastic succession. The second tetralogy may be seen as an effort to fuse the people and the crown. *King John,* however, devoid of climactic battle or concluding marriage, is more effective at undermining than at reconstituting authority: it is here that its distinctiveness lies.

The play may thus have provided its initial audiences with a compelling projection back into the thirteenth century of the charged issue of the legitimacy of Queen Elizabeth and competing claims of Mary, Queen of Scots. First, just as John's monarchical claim depends on Richard's will, the will of Henry VIII named Elizabeth heir. But the legitimacy of appointing one's successors by will had been challenged even in Henry's lifetime. Second, Shakespeare's John is accused of being a bastard and excommunicated by the pope; Elizabeth was declared a bastard by her father and excommunicated by the pope. And just as Arthur is the son of John's older brother, Mary, Queen of Scots, was the daughter of Henry's older sister. Elizabeth's legal claim to the crown was thus arguably weaker than Mary's.

Fourth, Arthur's cause is championed by King Philip of France; Mary, too, enjoyed the support of foreign Catholic monarchs, including King Philip II of Spain. Fifth, after ordering Arthur's death, John tries to absolve himself of the crime that he commissioned but did not commit; in 1587, Elizabeth ordered Mary's execution and then distanced herself from the judicial murder. Sixth, Arthur's death provokes an invasion from France to impose foreign Catholic rule. The invaders are led by the Dauphin, whose claim to the English crown rests on his marriage to John's niece, Blanche. Analogous motives led Philip II, widowed husband of Mary—the older sister of Elizabeth and her predecessor as queen—to launch the Spanish Armada the year after Mary's death. Finally, in *King John*, England is saved by a providential storm that destroys much of the French navy. So, too, a storm wrecked the Armada, a catastrophe interpreted by the victors as God's deliverance of Protestant England from enemies intent on conquest and Catholic rule.

Although these summaries oversimplify theater and history alike, they suggest the explosive issues that Shakespeare dramatized—the struggle with the papacy, the threat of invasion, and especially the problem of legitimate rule. There were risks in questioning Elizabeth's royal legitimacy or accusing her of murdering the rightful queen—even by covert historical analogy. Yet *King John* raises these matters not to resolve them but to meditate on their complexity. John both is and is not Arthur's murderer; he both is and is not the legitimate king.

Finally, the enigmatic logic of *King John*'s plot has affected its theatrical fortunes. Since the eighteenth century, the play has been cut to render its uncertain nationalism unambiguous. In the nineteenth century, its discontinuities and powerful confrontations between characters encouraged productions in which narrative sweep was sacrificed to pageantry and individual scenes, especially involving Constance. *King John* has also proven useful for political allegory in times of crisis. It was prominent in the battle against the censorship legislation of the 1737 Licensing Act, and it was marshaled to support loyalist opposition to the Catholic Jacobite invasion of England in 1745. It served similar ends in the French and Indian War fifteen years later, during the Napoleonic Wars at the beginning of the nineteenth century, as a justification for British imperialism during the Boer War in South Africa in 1899, and as a rallying cry before and during World War II. A 1961 production took the contested city of Angers as an image of Berlin, recently divided between East and West, and subsequent decades saw performances in several Eastern European Communist countries. Although *King John* was the first of Shakespeare's plays to be filmed (in 1899, an extremely brief version consisting of three scenes—John's temptation of Hubert, Constance's lamentation, and John's death scene), the work's theatrical standing declined in the twentieth century. There may be promise, however, in the recent rebellion against politically orthodox interpretations in criticism and performance alike. The 1988–89 production directed by Deborah Warner is noteworthy for its often satiric view of male authority in an unstable world. Perhaps a revival of interest depends less on the play's pageantry or jingoism than on its disabused view of power and its refusal to find reassurance in the interconnected, yet uncertain, sequence of historical events.

WALTER COHEN

TEXTUAL NOTE

The initial printing of *The Life and Death of King John* was in the First Folio of 1623 (F). That text probably goes back to an authorial manuscript, or "foul papers," from 1596 that was subsequently copied between 1609 and 1623 by two scribes. Their transcript, though not a promptbook, seems to have been designed with future theatrical performance in mind. The second scribe moved further from Shakespeare's manuscript toward stage-ready copy than did the first. In response to a 1606 law prohibiting oaths, the scribes presumably sanitized Shakespeare's language, replacing, for instance, "God" with "heaven."

The *Norton Shakespeare* reverses that process, restoring what Shakespeare wrote but retaining other scribal innovations, such as the introduction of act and scene divisions. In F, these are messy and illogical, perhaps in part because two compositors set the type for the play. This edition follows earlier editors in treating F's "Scaena Secunda" as 2.1 and its "Actus Secundus" as 2.2, even though this is not the only reasonable solution. Beginning at the present edition's 2.1.325, F starts calling the Citizen of Angers "Hubert." The shift may indicate a desire to double the parts (have the same actor play both roles) or conflate the two characters. If the latter, the extant text does not complete the job: the two men do not seem like the same person. Accordingly, this edition emends F to keep the two characters separate.

Partly on the basis of *King John*'s recourse to rhetoric reminiscent of the Spanish Armada era (1588), a few scholars place its composition in 1590 or earlier and see it as a source for the anonymous play *The Troublesome Reign of John, King of England* (published in 1591). Yet a direct link between the wording of two stage directions in *The Troublesome Reign* and their analogues in *King John* is easily explained only if the anonymous play came first and Shakespeare was familiar with it. Shakespeare could have read the relevant stage directions in the 1591 edition of *The Troublesome Reign*, but it is not clear how the author of *The Troublesome Reign* could have seen Shakespeare's unpublished stage directions. Stylistic and metrical tests, which date *King John* to roughly 1596, support this hypothesis.

SELECTED BIBLIOGRAPHY

Anderson, Thomas. "'Legitimation, name, and all is gone': Bastardy and Bureaucracy in Shakespeare's *King John*." *Journal for Early Modern Cultural Studies* 4.2 (Fall/Winter 2004): 35–61. The Bastard's rise as indicative less of monarchical power than of the emergence of a new model of impersonal bureaucratic efficiency.

Braunmuller, A. R. "*King John* and Historiography." *English Literary History* 55 (1988): 309–32. Conflict between theater and historical writing, exemplified in the Bastard's ahistorical character and Arthur's death.

Burckhardt, Sigurd. *Shakespearean Meanings*. Princeton: Princeton University Press, 1968. 116–43. *King John* as a modern, rather than traditional, play, rejecting divine sanction for both religious and secular authority.

Candido, Joseph, ed. "*King John.*" Shakespeare: The Critical Tradition series. Atlantic Highlands, N.J.: Athlone, 1996. Selection from criticisms of the play, 1790–1919; focus on individual characters and emotionally powerful scenes.

Cousin, Geraldine. *King John*. Manchester: Manchester University Press, 1994. Performance history, including 1984 BBC film (see below).

Curren-Aquino, Deborah T., ed. "*King John*": *New Perspectives*. Newark: University of Delaware Press, 1989. Twelve essays, various perspectives, but generally seeing the play as an experiment with the form of the national history play.

Dusinberre, Juliet. "*King John* and Embarrassing Women." *Shakespeare Survey* 42 (1989): 37–52. Women as a structurally unifying force in the first three acts. The play disintegrates with their disappearance.

Howard, Jean E., and Phyllis Rackin. *Engendering a Nation: A Feminist Account of Shakespeare's English Histories*. London: Routledge, 1997. 119–33. *King John* as a challenge to patriarchal, dynastic orthodoxy through skeptical women's voices.

Shirley, Frances A., ed. "*King John*" and "*Henry VIII*": *Critical Essays*. New York: Garland, 1988. The twelve essays on *King John*, mostly from the 1930s to 1960s, are diverse in outlook but generally more concerned with structural and national unity than is recent criticism.

Vaughan, Virginia Mason. "*King John.*" *A Companion to Shakespeare's Works*. Vol. 2: *The Histories*. Ed. Richard Dutton and Jean E. Howard. Malden, Mass.: Blackwell, 2003. 379–94. Overview of the play, seen as advocating limits on absolute secular or religious power.

FILMS

King John. 1899. Dir. Walter Pfeffer Dando and William K. L. Dickson. UK. 2 min. The first Shakespeare film, a black-and-white silent. See Introduction.

The Life and Death of King John. 1984. Dir. David Giles. UK. 155 min. A relatively conservative BBC production notable for Claire Bloom's innovative, coolly rational Constance.

The Life and Death of King John

THE PERSONS OF THE PLAY

KING JOHN of England
QUEEN ELEANOR, his mother
LADY FALCONBRIDGE
Philip the BASTARD, later knighted as Sir Richard Plantagenet,
 her illegitmate son by King Richard I (Cœur-de-Lion)
Robert FALCONBRIDGE, her legitimate son
James GURNEY, her attendant
Lady BLANCHE of Spain, niece of King John
PRINCE HENRY, son of King John
HUBERT, a follower of King John
Earl of SALISBURY
Earl of PEMBROKE
Earl of ESSEX
Lord BIGOT
KING PHILIP of France
LOUIS THE DAUPHIN, his son
ARTHUR, Duke of Brittaine, nephew of King John
Lady CONSTANCE, his mother
Duke of AUSTRIA (Limoges)
CHÂTILLON, ambassador from France to England
Count MELUN
A CITIZEN of Angers
Cardinal PANDOLF, a legate from the Pope
PETER OF POMFRET, a prophet
HERALDS
EXECUTIONERS
MESSENGERS
SHERIFF
Lords, soldiers, attendants

1.1

[*Flourish.*] *Enter* KING JOHN, QUEEN ELEANOR,[1] [*and the
Earls of*] PEMBROKE, ESSEX, *and* SALISBURY; *with the*[m]
CHÂTILLON *of France*

KING JOHN Now say, Châtillon, what would France with us?[2]
CHÂTILLON Thus, after greeting, speaks the King of France,
 In my behaviour,° to the majesty—   *person*
 The borrowed° majesty—of England here.   *usurped*
5 QUEEN ELEANOR A strange beginning: 'borrowed majesty'?
KING JOHN Silence, good mother, hear the embassy.°   *message*
CHÂTILLON Philip of France, in right and true behalf

1.1 Location: John's court in London.
1. This scene, which occupies the first act, is unhistorical. The youngest son of Henry II and "Queen Eleanor" (Eleanor of Aquitaine), John (1167–1215) succeeded his brother, the famed crusader Richard I (the Lionheart), in 1199 and ruled until his death. Eleanor of Aquitaine c. 1122–1204) was Queen first of France and then of England. See "A Shakespearean Genealogy," on the front endpapers.
2. What does (the King of) France want with us?

Of thy deceasèd brother Geoffrey's[3] son,
Arthur Plantagenet,[4] lays most lawful claim
10 To this fair island and the territories,
To Ireland, Poitou, Anjou, Touraine, Maine;[5]
Desiring thee to lay aside the sword
Which sways° usurpingly these several titles,°   rules / separate lands
And put the same into young Arthur's hand,
15 Thy nephew and right royal sovereign.
KING JOHN   What follows if we disallow of this?
CHÂTILLON   The proud control° of fierce and bloody war,   compulsion
To enforce these rights so forcibly withheld—
KING JOHN   Here have we war for war, and blood for blood,
20 Controlment for controlment: so answer France.
CHÂTILLON   Then take my king's defiance from my mouth,
The farthest limit of my embassy.
KING JOHN   Bear mine° to him, and so depart in peace.   my defiance
Be thou as lightning in the eyes of France,
25 For ere thou canst report,[6] I will be there;
The thunder of my cannon° shall be heard.   (anachronism)
So hence. Be thou the trumpet of our wrath,
And sullen presage° of your own decay.°—   gloomy omen / downfall
An honourable conduct° let him have;   escort
30 Pembroke, look to't.—Farewell, Châtillon.
        Exeunt CHÂTILLON *and* PEMBROKE
QUEEN ELEANOR   What now, my son? Have I not ever° said   always
How that ambitious Constance[7] would not cease
Till she had kindled France and all the world
Upon° the right and party of her son?   On behalf of
35 This might have been prevented and made whole°   settled
With very easy arguments of love,°   friendly discussions
Which now the manage° of two kingdoms must   government
With fearful-bloody issue° arbitrate.   outcome
KING JOHN   Our strong possession and our right for us.°   on our side
QUEEN ELEANOR [*aside to* KING JOHN]   Your strong possession
40   much more than your right,
Or else it must go wrong with you and me:
So much my conscience whispers in your ear,
Which none but heaven and you and I shall hear.
        Enter a SHERIFF [*who whispers to* ESSEX]
ESSEX   My liege,° here is the strangest controversy,   lord
45 Come from the country to be judged by you,
That e'er I heard. Shall I produce the men?
KING JOHN   Let them approach.—   [*Exit* SHERIFF]

---

3. Geoffrey was older than John and younger than Richard I; he died before Henry II. Because of changes in the laws of inheritance, John's claims to the throne would have been weaker in Shakespeare's lifetime—and are so represented—than they were in his own day, the early thirteenth century.
4. "Plantagenet" was the family name of most English monarchs from the accession of Henry II in 1154 to the deposition of Richard III in 1485. The historical Arthur was in his late teens; Shakespeare makes him much younger.

5. Except for Ireland, English territories in western and central France. Historically, it was these French territories, rather than the English crown itself, that Arthur claimed.
6. Before you can deliver your message (pun on noise of thunder or cannon).
7. Arthur's mother, Geoffrey's widow in Shakespeare and in his main source, *The Troublesome Reign of King John*. Historically, Constance remarried twice after Geoffrey's death.

Our abbeys and our priories shall pay[8]
This expeditious charge.°   *sudden cost (of war)*

Enter Robert FALCONBRIDGE *and Philip [the* BASTARD,[9]
with the Sheriff]
         What men are you?

50 BASTARD   Your faithful subject I, a gentleman
Born in Northamptonshire, and eldest son,
As I suppose, to Robert Falconbridge,
A soldier, by the honour-giving hand
Of Cœur-de-lion° knighted in the field.   *Richard the Lionheart*
55 KING JOHN   What art thou?
FALCONBRIDGE   The son and heir to that same Falconbridge.
KING JOHN   Is that the elder, and art thou the heir?
You came not of one mother then, it seems.
BASTARD   Most certain of one mother, mighty King—
60 That is well known—and, as I think, one father.
But for the certain knowledge of that truth
I put you o'er to° heaven, and to my mother.   *refer you to*
Of that° I doubt as all men's children may.   *(truth)*
QUEEN ELEANOR   Out on thee,° rude man! Thou dost shame thy   *Away with you*
mother
65 And wound her honour with this diffidence.°   *distrust*
BASTARD   I, Madam? No, I have no reason for it.
That is my brother's plea and none of mine,
The which if he can prove, a pops me out°   *he deprives me of*
At least from fair five hundred pound a year.
70 Heaven guard my mother's honour, and my land!
KING JOHN   A good blunt fellow.—Why, being younger born,
Doth he lay claim to thine inheritance?
BASTARD   I know not why, except to get the land;
But once he slandered me with bastardy.
75 But whe'er° I be as true° begot or no,   *whether / legitimately*
That still I lay upon my mother's head;°   *I let my mother answer*
But that I am as well begot, my liege—
Fair fall the bones that took the pains for me[1]—
Compare our faces and be judge yourself.
80 If old Sir Robert did beget us both
And were our father, and this son like him,
O old Sir Robert, father, on my knee
I give heaven thanks I was not like to thee.
KING JOHN   Why, what a madcap hath heaven lent us here
85 QUEEN ELEANOR[2]   He hath a trick° of Cœur-de-lion's face;   *distinguishing trait*
The accent of his tongue affecteth° him.   *resembles*
Do you not read some tokens of my son
In the large composition° of this man?   *openness; build*
KING JOHN   Mine eye hath well examinèd his parts,°   *attributes*
And finds them perfect Richard.
90   [*To Robert* FALCONBRIDGE]   Sirrah,° speak: *(used to inferiors)*
What doth move you to claim your brother's land?

---

8. Alluding to John's much-resented taxation of the
monastic orders.
9. Drawing upon a passing reference in Holinshed's
Chronicles, The Troublesome Reign invents a major role
for this character, a role that Shakespeare further

expands.
1. May good fortune befall the bones (of the dead
man) who went to the trouble of begetting me.
2. The Queen may speak the following lines privately
to John.

BASTARD   Because he hath a half-face° like my father!   *profile; thin face*
    With half that face[3] would he have all my land,
    A half-faced groat[4] five hundred pound a year.
95   FALCONBRIDGE   My gracious liege, when that my father lived,
    Your brother° did employ my father much—   *(Richard)*
    BASTARD   Well, sir, by this you cannot get my land.
    Your tale must be how he employed my mother.
    FALCONBRIDGE   And once dispatched him in an embassy
100   To Germany, there with the Emperor
    To treat of high affairs touching that time.
    Th'advantage of his absence took the King,
    And in the meantime sojourned at my father's,
    Where how he did prevail I shame to speak.
105   But truth is truth: large lengths of seas and shores
    Between my father and my mother lay,
    As I have heard my father speak himself,
    When this same lusty° gentleman was got.°   *vigorous / conceived*
    Upon his deathbed he by will bequeathed
110   His lands to me, and took it on his death°   *solemnly swore*
    That this my mother's son was none of his;
    And if he were, he came into the world
    Full fourteen weeks before the course of time.
    Then, good my liege, let me have what is mine,
115   My father's land, as was my father's will.
    KING JOHN   Sirrah, your brother is legitimate.°   *(legally correct)*
    Your father's wife did after wedlock bear him,
    And if she did play false, the fault was hers,
    Which fault lies on the hazards of° all husbands   *is a risk for*
120   That marry wives. Tell me, how if my brother,
    Who, as you say, took pains to get this son,
    Had of your father claimed this son for his?
    In sooth, good friend, your father might have kept
    This calf, bred from his cow, from all the world;
125   In sooth he might. Then if he were my brother's,
    My brother might not claim him, nor your father,
    Being none of his, refuse him.[5] This concludes:
    My mother's son did get your father's heir;
    Your father's heir must have your father's land.
130   FALCONBRIDGE   Shall then my father's will be of no force
    To dispossess that child which is not his?
    BASTARD   Of no more force to dispossess me, sir,
    Than was his will° to get me, as I think.   *legal instrument; lust*
    QUEEN ELEANOR   Whether hadst° thou rather be: a Falconbridge,   *Which would*
135   And like thy brother to enjoy thy land,
    Or the reputed son of Cœur-de-lion,
    Lord of thy presence,° and no land beside?   *yourself*
    BASTARD   Madam, an if° my brother had my shape,   *an If=if*
    And I had his, Sir Robert's his° like him,   *Sir Robert's*
140   And if my legs were two such riding-rods,°   *their riding switches*
    My arms such eel-skins stuffed, my face so thin
    That in mine ear I durst not stick a rose

---

3. Half of his father's face, since Falconbridge inherits maternal features as well; "face" is also "impudence."
4. A coin showing the monarch's head in profile; also Falconbridge, who as a person is worth only as much as

a groat (4 pence), despite his inheritance.
5. nor . . . him: nor could your father, though not the biological father to the Bastard, disown him.

Lest men should say 'Look where three-farthings goes!',
And, to° his shape, were heir to all this land,   *in addition to*
145   Would I might never stir from off this place.[7]
I would give it every foot° to have this face;   *every foot of it*
It would not be Sir Nob in any case.[8]
QUEEN ELEANOR   I like thee well. Wilt thou forsake thy fortune,
Bequeath thy land to him, and follow me?
150   I am a soldier and now bound to France.
BASTARD   Brother, take you my land; I'll take my chance.
Your face hath got five hundred pound a year,
Yet sell your face for fivepence and 'tis dear.°—   *expensive*
Madam, I'll follow you unto the death.
155   QUEEN ELEANOR   Nay, I would have you go before me thither.
BASTARD   Our country manners give our betters way.[9]
KING JOHN   What is thy name?
BASTARD   Philip, my liege, so is my name begun:
Philip, good old Sir Robert's wife's eldest son.
160   KING JOHN   From henceforth bear his name whose form thou bear'st.
Kneel thou down Philip, but arise more great:
[*He knights the* BASTARD]
Arise Sir Richard and Plantagenet.[1]
BASTARD   Brother by th' mother's side give me your hand.
My father gave me honour, yours gave land.
165   Now blessèd be the hour, by night or day,
When I was got, Sir Robert was away.
QUEEN ELEANOR   The very spirit of Plantagenet!
I am thy grandam, Richard; call me so.
BASTARD   Madam, by chance, but not by truth;° what though?°   *chastely / but so what?*
170   Something about,° a little from the right,°   *a bit off / unlawful*
In at the window, or else o'er the hatch;[2]
Who dares not stir by day must walk° by night,   *go; rob (sexually)*
And have is have, however men do catch.[3]
Near or far off, well won is still well shot,[4]
175   And I am I, howe'er I was begot.
KING JOHN   Go, Falconbridge, now hast thou thy desire:
A landless knight° makes thee a landed squire.—   *(the Bastard)*
Come, madam, and come, Richard; we must speed
For France; for France, for it is more than need.
180   BASTARD   Brother, adieu. Good fortune come to thee,
For thou wast got i'th' way of honesty.
Exeunt all but [the] BASTARD
A foot of honour[5] better than I was,
But many a many foot of land the worse.
Well, now can I make any Joan° a lady.   *lower-class woman*

6. A rose appeared behind the Queen's head on a three-farthing coin, which was thin and of small value (less than a penny).
7. May I be struck dead here and now.
8. My appearance would not be that of Sir Robert under any circumstances. The speech is full of sexual innuendo. "Riding-rods" (line 140) and "eel-skins" (line 141) hint at sexual inadequacy associated with a thin penis. "Nob" (line 147) is also slang for "penis." "Rose" (line 142), "shape" (line 144), and "case" (line 147) may refer to the vagina; "riding" (line 140), "stuffed" (line 141), "stick a rose" (line 142), and "foot" (line 146) suggest copulation; and "stir" (line 145) can mean "sexually arouse."

9. The Bastard jokes that it's proper to let social superiors go first.
1. Perhaps the shift from blank verse to rhyme (lines 145–81) though not fully systematic, reinforces the Bastard's social elevation here.
2. Both phrases are proverbial for birth out of wedlock. *hatch*: the lower half of a divided door.
3. That is, possession is nine-tenths of the law.
4. Archery metaphor, with sexual innuendo, as with "stir" (line 172). The entire passage is also marked by mock-proverbial expressions.
5. A degree of status. The Bastard contrasts his aristocratic "honour" with Falconbridge's middle-class "honesty" (line 181).

185 'Good e'en, Sir Richard'—'God-a-mercy⁶ fellow';
And if his name be George I'll call him Peter,
For new-made honour doth forget men's names;
'Tis too respective and too sociable
For your conversion.⁷ Now your traveller,
190 He and his toothpick at my worship's mess;
And when my knightly stomach is sufficed,
Why then I suck my teeth⁸ and catechize
My pickèd° man of countries. 'My dear sir,'   *affected; tooth-picked*
Thus leaning on mine elbow I begin,
195 'I shall beseech you—'. That is Question now;
And then comes Answer like an Absey book.°   *a school (ABC) primer*
'O sir,' says Answer, 'at your best command,
At your employment, at your service, sir.'
'No sir,' says Question, 'I, sweet sir, at yours.'
200 And so, ere Answer knows what Question would,°   *wishes*
Saving in dialogue of compliment,°   *Except empty flattery*
And talking of the Alps and Apennines,
The Pyrenean and the River Po,
It draws toward supper° in conclusion so.   *(another meal)*
205 But this is worshipful society,
And fits the mounting spirit° like myself;   *ambitious character*
For he is but a bastard to° the time   *no true child of*
That doth not smack of observation;°   *courtly obsequiousness*
And so am I°—whether I smack or no,   *so I intend*
210 And not alone in habit° and device,°   *clothes / heraldic emblem*
Exterior form, outward accoutrement,
But from the inward motion°—to deliver   *impulse*
Sweet, sweet, sweet poison° for the age's tooth;°   *flattery / appetite*
Which,° though I will not practise° to deceive,   *(flattery) / make a habit*
215 Yet to avoid deceit° I mean to learn;   *being deceived*
For it shall strew the footsteps of my rising.⁹
          Enter LADY FALCONBRIDGE *and James* GURNEY
But who comes in such haste in riding-robes?
What woman-post° is this? Hath she no husband   *female dispatch rider*
That will take pains to blow a horn¹ before her?
220 O me, 'tis my mother! How now, good lady?
What brings you here to court so hastily?
LADY FALCONBRIDGE   Where is that slave thy brother? Where is he
That holds in chase° mine honour up and down?   *Who hunts*
BASTARD   My brother Robert, old Sir Robert's son?
225 Colbrand the Giant,² that same mighty man?
Is it Sir Robert's son that you seek so?
LADY FALCONBRIDGE   Sir Robert's son, ay, thou unreverent boy,

---

6. God reward you: the patronizing reply of a social superior. The Bastard imagines himself, newly promoted, encountering a social inferior who says "Good evening." His soliloquy continues in this vein, parodying the affectation of courtiers and foreign travelers, in part through the ironic use of religious rhetoric—"conversion" (line 189, referring to his new rank), "my worship's mess" (line 190; "my worship" means both "a lord" and "the Lord"; "mess" means both "a dinner table" and "the Mass," the commemoration of Christ's Last Supper), and "catechize" (line 192; orally question, usually about religious principles).

7. *'Tis . . . conversion:* Remembering names is beneath the dignity of a newly created knight.
8. The Bastard defiantly cleans his teeth in the vulgar English fashion, rather than resorting to the traveler's and courtier's affectation of a toothpick.
9. For flattery will ease my ascent; awareness of deceptive flattery will do so.
1. Post horn announcing the rider's approach; also, the symbol of a cuckold.
2. Danish giant killed by Guy in the popular romance *Guy of Warwick.*

Sir Robert's son. Why scorn'st thou at Sir Robert?
He is Sir Robert's son, and so art thou.
230   BASTARD   James Gurney, wilt thou give us leave° awhile?   *leave us*
GURNEY   Good leave, good Philip.
BASTARD   Philip Sparrow,² James!
There's toys abroad;⁴ anon I'll tell thee more.
                                                                    Exit James [GURNEY]
Madam, I was not old Sir Robert's son.
Sir Robert might have eat his part in me
235   Upon Good Friday, and ne'er broke his fast.
Sir Robert could do° well, marry° to confess,   *(sexual) / indeed*
Could a get° me! Sir Robert could not do it: *Could he have begotten*
We know his handiwork.° Therefore, good mother,   *(Falconbridge)*
To whom am I beholden for these limbs?
240   Sir Robert never holp° to make this leg.   *helped*
LADY FALCONBRIDGE   Hast thou conspired with thy brother too,
That for thine own gain shouldst defend mine honour?
What means this scorn, thou most untoward° knave?   *unmannerly*
BASTARD   Knight, knight, good mother, Basilisco-like!⁵
245   What! I am dubbed; I have it° on my shoulder.   *(a sword tap)*
But, mother, I am not Sir Robert's son.
I have disclaimed Sir Robert; and my land,
Legitimation, name, and all is gone.
Then, good my mother, let me know my father;
250   Some proper man, I hope; who was it, mother?
LADY FALCONBRIDGE   Hast thou denied thyself a Falconbridge?
BASTARD   As faithfully as I deny the devil.
LADY FALCONBRIDGE   King Richard Cœur-de-lion was thy father.
By long and vehement suit I was seduced
255   To make room for him in my husband's bed.
Heaven lay not my transgression to my charge!
Thou art the issue° of my dear° offence,   *result / costly; loving*
Which was so strongly urged past my defence.
BASTARD   Now by this light, were I to get° again,   *be conceived*
260   Madam, I would not wish a better father.
Some sins do bear their privilege° on earth,   *are pardonable*
And so doth yours; your fault was not your folly.°   *your sin wasn't foolish*
Needs must you lay your heart at his dispose,°   *disposal*
Subjected tribute to commanding love,
265   Against whose fury and unmatchèd force
The aweless° lion could not wage the fight,   *fearless*
Nor keep his princely heart from Richard's hand.
He that perforce° robs lions of their hearts⁶   *by his strength*
May easily win a woman's. Ay, my mother,
270   With all my heart I thank thee for my father.
Who lives and dares but say thou didst not well
When I was got, I'll send his soul to hell.
Come, lady, I will show thee to my kin,
        And they shall say, when Richard me begot,

---

3. Recalling the popularity of Philip as a name for a
mere bird, the Bastard considers the name beneath him.
4. There's trivial news (ironic).
5. The cowardly braggart Basilisco in an anonymous
play *Solyman and Perseda*, probably from the early

1590s, calls himself a knight while his servant calls him
a knave.
6. Alluding to Richard I's legendary feat of killing a lion
by putting his hand down its throat and pulling out its
heart (hence the epithet Cœur-de-lion, Lionheart).

275   If thou hadst said him nay, it had been sin.
      Who says it was, he lies: I say 'twas not.[7]

                                                    Exeunt

2.1

[*Flourish.*] *Enter before Angers* [*at one door*] PHILIP
King of France, LOUIS [THE] DAUPHIN, [*Lady*] CON-
STANCE, *and* ARTHUR [*Duke of Brittaine, with soldiers;
at another door the Duke of*] AUSTRIA [*wearing a lion's
hide, with soldiers*][1]

KING PHILIP   Before Angers well met, brave Austria.—
      Arthur, that great forerunner of thy blood,
      Richard° that robbed the lion of his heart   (*Arthur's uncle*)
      And fought the holy wars in Palestine,°   *Third Crusade* (1189–92)
5   By this brave duke came early to his grave;[2]
      And, for amends to his posterity,
      At our importance° hither is he come   *urgent request*
      To spread his colours,° boy, in thy behalf,   *battle flags*
      And to rebuke the usurpation
10   Of thy unnatural uncle, English John.
      Embrace him, love him, give him welcome hither.
ARTHUR [*to* AUSTRIA]   God shall forgive you Cœur-de-lion's death,
      The rather that° you give his offspring life,   *All the more because*
      Shadowing° their right under your wings of war.   *Protecting*
15   I give you welcome with a powerless hand,
      But with a heart full of unstainèd love.
      Welcome before the gates of Angers, Duke.
KING PHILIP   A noble boy. Who would not do thee right?
AUSTRIA [*kissing* ARTHUR]   Upon thy cheek lay I this zealous kiss
20   As seal to this indenture° of my love: *contract*
      That to my home I will no more return
      Till Angers and the right thou hast in France,
      Together with that pale, that white-faced shore,°   *chalk cliffs of Dover*
      Whose foot° spurns back the ocean's roaring tides   (*of the cliffs*)
25   And coops° from other lands her islanders,   *protects*
      Even till that England, hedged in with the main,°   *ocean*
      That water-wallèd bulwark, still° secure   *always*
      And confident from foreign purposes,
      Even till that utmost corner of the west
30   Salute thee for her king. Till then, fair boy,
      Will I not think of home, but follow arms.
CONSTANCE   O, take his mother's thanks, a widow's thanks,
      Till your strong hand shall help to give him strength
      To make a more° requital to your love.   *greater*
35   AUSTRIA   The peace of heaven is theirs that lift their swords
      In such a just and charitable war.
KING PHILIP   Well then, to work! Our cannon shall be bent°   *aimed*

---

7. Not a sin; nought (nothing); naughty, and hence
something, a sin.
2.1 Location: Before the town wall of Angers.
1. This is "Scaena Secunda" in F (see the Textual
Note). The back of the stage represents the town wall,
with the town notionally behind it. The Citizen's entry
"upon the walls" (s.d. after line 200) is onto the upper
stage. Below the upper stage, central tiring-house doors

would probably represent the gates of Angers, the capital of John's French holdings. These remain closed; the
French and English armies appear from side entrances.
2. Austria, the "brave duke," imprisoned Richard, but
Richard was actually killed while besieging the castle of
the Viscount of Limoges in France. Shakespeare follows his main source in combining the two historical
figures in the character of Austria.

Against the brows° of this resisting town.   *walls*

Call for our chiefest men of discipline°   *military skill*

40 To cull the plots of best advantages.[3]

We'll lay before this town our royal bones,

Wade to the market-place in Frenchmen's blood.

But we will° make it subject to this boy.   *In order to; unless we*

CONSTANCE Stay for an answer to your embassy,

45 Lest unadvised° you stain your swords with blood.   *rashly*

My lord Châtillon may from England bring

That right in peace which here we urge° in war,   *seek*

And then we shall repent each drop of blood

That hot rash haste so indirectly° shed.   *wrongfully*

   Enter CHÂTILLON

50 KING PHILIP A wonder, lady: lo upon thy wish

Our messenger Châtillon is arrived.—

What England° says, say briefly, gentle lord;   *the King of England*

We coldly° pause for thee. Châtillon, speak.   *calmly*

CHÂTILLON Then turn your forces from this paltry siege,

55 And stir them up against a mightier task.

England, impatient of your just demands,

Hath put himself in arms. The adverse winds,

Whose leisure I have stayed,° have given him time *Which I had to wait out*

To land his legions all as soon as I.

60 His marches are expedient° to this town,   *coming quickly*

His forces strong, his soldiers confident.

With him along is come the Mother-Queen,

An Ate° stirring him to blood and strife;   *goddess of discord*

With her her niece,[4] the Lady Blanche of Spain;

65 With them a bastard of the King's deceased;°   *of Richard's*

And all th'unsettled humours[5] of the land—

Rash, inconsiderate,° fiery voluntaries,°   *imprudent / volunteers*

With ladies'° faces and fierce dragons' spleens°— *beardless / tempers*

Have sold their fortunes at their native homes,

70 Bearing their birthrights proudly on their backs,[6]

To make a hazard of° new fortunes here.   *To take a chance on*

In brief, a braver choice of dauntless spirits

Than now the English bottoms° have waft o'er   *ships*

Did never float upon the swelling tide

75 To do offence and scathe° in Christendom.   *damage*

   Drum beats

The interruption of their churlish drums

Cuts off more circumstance.° They are at hand;   *detail*

To parley or to fight therefore prepare.

KING PHILIP How much unlooked-for is this expedition!° *military force; speed*

80 AUSTRIA By how much unexpected, by so much

We must awake endeavour for defence,

For courage mounteth with occasion.°   *necessity*

Let them be welcome then: we are prepared.

---

3. To pick the positions of greatest advantage (for the cannons).

4. Actually, Eleanor's granddaughter: "niece" is used in a broad sense.

5. Men of discontented spirits; masterless men of no fixed abode. The soldiers are seen as "humors" (physical elements of the body, which affect temperament) discharged from the body of England.

6. In the form of armor bought by selling their land ("birthrights" and "fortunes," line 69). "All his clothes are on his back" is proverbial.

Enter [*marching*] KING [JOHN] *of England,* [*the*] BAS-
TARD, QUEEN [ELEANOR], [*Lady*] BLANCHE, [*the Earl of*]
PEMBROKE, *and* [*soldiers*]

KING JOHN   Peace be to France, if France in peace permit

85   Our just and lineal° entrance to our own.°   *hereditary / Angers*
      If not, bleed France,° and peace ascend to heaven,   *let France bleed*
      Whiles we, God's wrathful agent, do correct°   *punish*
      Their proud contempt that beats his peace to heaven.

KING PHILIP   Peace be to England, if that war° return   *if the English forces*

90   From France to England, there to live in peace.
      England we love, and for that England's° sake   *that land's; Arthur's*
      With burden of our armour here we sweat.
      This toil of ours should be a work of thine;
      But thou from loving England art so far

95   That thou hast underwrought° his lawful king,   *undermined*
      Cut off the sequence of posterity,°   *the succession*
      Outfacèd infant state,° and done a rape   *Defied Arthur's right*
      Upon the maiden virtue of the crown.
      [*Pointing to* ARTHUR]
      Look here upon thy brother Geoffrey's face.

100   These eyes, these brows, were moulded out of his;
      This little abstract° doth contain that large°   *précis / full version*
      Which died in Geoffrey; and the hand of time
      Shall draw this brief° into as huge a volume.   *summary*
      That Geoffrey was thy elder brother born,

105   And this his son; England was Geoffrey's right,
      And this is Geoffrey's.° In the name of God,   *(son and heir)*
      How comes it then that thou art called a king,
      When living blood doth in these temples beat,
      Which owe° the crown that thou o'ermasterest?   *own*

110   KING JOHN   From whom hast thou this great commission, France,
      To draw my answer from thy articles?°   *charges*

KING PHILIP   From that supernal° judge that stirs good thoughts *heavenly*
      In any breast of strong authority°   *In any powerful ruler*
      To look into the blots and stains of right.

115   That judge hath made me guardian to this boy,
      Under whose warrant I impeach° thy wrong,   *challenge*
      And by whose help I mean to chastise it.

KING JOHN   Alack, thou dost usurp authority.

KING PHILIP   Excuse it is to beat usurping down.[7]

120   QUEEN ELEANOR   Who is it thou dost call usurper, France?

CONSTANCE   Let me make answer: thy usurping son.

QUEEN ELEANOR   Out,° insolent! Thy bastard shall be king   *Begone*
      That thou mayst be a queen and check° the world.   *master*

CONSTANCE   My bed was ever° to thy son as true   *always*

125   As thine was to thy husband; and this boy
      Liker in feature to his father Geoffrey
      Than thou and John in manners, being as like
      As rain to water, or devil to his dam.°   *mother*
      My boy a bastard? By my soul I think

130   His father never was so true begot.
      It cannot be, an if° thou wert his mother.   *an if = if*

_____
7. My (so-called) usurpation is excusable because I am using it to put down (real) usurpation.

QUEEN ELEANOR [*to* ARTHUR] There's a good mother, boy, that
  blots° thy father.   slanders
CONSTANCE [*to* ARTHUR] There's a good grandam, boy, that
  would blot thee.
AUSTRIA Peace!
BASTARD   Hear the crier!⁸
AUSTRIA   What the devil art thou?
135 BASTARD One that will play the devil sir, with you,
  An a° may catch your hide⁹ and you alone.   If he (I)
  You are the hare° of whom the proverb goes,   coward
  Whose valour plucks dead lions by the beard.°   (an insult)
  I'll smoke your skin-coat° an I catch you right—   thrash your hide
140 Sirrah,° look to't—i'faith I will, i'faith!   Boy (an insult)
BLANCHE O, well did he° become that lion's robe   (Richard)
  That did disrobe the lion of that robe!
BASTARD It lies as sightly° on the back of him   fitly
  As great Alcides' shows¹ upon an ass.
145 But, ass, I'll take that burden from your back,
  Or lay on that° shall make your shoulders crack.   that burden which
AUSTRIA What cracker° is this same that deafs our ears   boaster
  With this abundance of superfluous breath?—
  King Philip, determine what we shall do straight.°   immediately
150 KING PHILIP Women and fools,° break off your conference.—   children
  King John, this is the very sum of all:
  England and Ireland, Anjou,² Touraine, Maine,
  In right of Arthur do I claim of thee.
  Wilt thou resign them and lay down thy arms?
155 KING JOHN My life as soon. I do defy thee, France.—
  Arthur of Brittaine, yield thee to my hand,
  And out of my dear love I'll give thee more
  Than e'er the coward hand of France can win.
  Submit thee, boy.
QUEEN ELEANOR [*to* ARTHUR] Come to thy grandam, child.
160 CONSTANCE [*to* ARTHUR] Do, child, go to it° grandam, child.   its
  Give grandam kingdom, and it grandam will
  Give it a plum, a cherry, and a fig.°   (obscene)
  There's a good grandam.°   (sarcastic baby talk)
ARTHUR   Good my mother, peace.
  I would that I were low laid in my grave.
165 I am not worth this coil° that's made for me.   commotion
  [*He weeps*]
QUEEN ELEANOR His mother shames him so, poor boy, he weeps.
CONSTANCE Now shame upon you, whe'er° she does or no!   whether
  His grandam's wrongs, and not his mother's shames,
  Draw those heaven-moving pearls from his poor eyes,
170 Which heaven shall take in nature° of a fee;   as a kind
  Ay, with these crystal beads° heaven shall be bribed   tears
  To do him justice and revenge on you.
QUEEN ELEANOR Thou monstrous slanderer of heaven and earth!

---

8. The Bastard mockingly compares Austria to an officer in a law court who calls for order.
9. The lion skin Austria wears, which, as a memento of
his father's death, antagonizes the Bastard.
1. As the lion skin of Hercules would appear (alluding
to his legendary size and strength, and to the proverb al

"ass in a lion's skin")
2. Here and at line ~88, Shakespeare appears to confuse the province (Anjou) with the besieged town
(Angers; French: Angiers). Elsewhere, he maintains a
distinction, as do his sources.

	CONSTANCE Thou monstrous injurer of heaven and earth!	
175	Call not me slanderer. Thou and thine usurp	
	The dominations, royalties° and rights	*royal powers*
	Of this oppressèd boy. This is thy eld'st son's son,[3]	
	Infortunate in nothing but in thee.	
	Thy sins are visited° in this poor child;	*punished*
180	The canon of the law° is laid on him,	*biblical decree*
	Being but the second generation	
	Removèd from thy sin-conceiving womb.[4]	
	KING JOHN Bedlam,° have done.	*Lunatic*
	CONSTANCE I have but this to say:	
	That he° is not only plaguèd for her sin,°	*(Arthur) / (adultery)*
185	But God hath made her sin° and her the plague	*(John)*
	On this removèd issue,° plagued for her	*(Arthur)*
	And with her plague;[5] her sin his injury,	
	Her injury the beadle to her sin;	
	All punished in the person of this child,	
190	And all for her.[6] A plague upon her!	
	QUEEN ELEANOR Thou unadvisèd° scold, I can produce	*rash*
	A will that bars the title of thy son.	
	CONSTANCE Ay, who doubts that? A will, a wicked will,	
	A woman's will,[7] a cankered grandam's will!	
195	KING PHILIP Peace, lady; pause or be more temperate.	
	It ill beseems this presence° to cry aim	*royal assembly*
	To[8] these ill-tunèd repetitions.—	
	Some trumpet summon hither to the walls	
	These men of Angers. Let us hear them speak	
200	Whose title they admit, Arthur's or John's.	
	Trumpet sounds. Enter a CITIZEN[9] *upon the walls*	
	CITIZEN Who is it that hath warned° us to the walls?	*summoned*
	KING PHILIP 'Tis France for England.	
	KING JOHN England for itself.	
	You men of Angers and my loving subjects—	
	KING PHILIP You loving men of Angers, Arthur's subjects,	
205	Our trumpet called you to this gentle parle°—	*parley*
	KING JOHN For our° advantage; therefore hear us first.	*(England's; John's)*
	These flags of France that are advancèd here	
	Before the eye and prospect of your town,	
	Have hither marched to your endamagement.	
210	The cannons have their bowels full of wrath,	
	And ready mounted are they to spit forth	
	Their iron indignation 'gainst your walls.	
	All preparation for a bloody siege	
	And merciless proceeding by these French	
215	Confront your city's eyes, your winking° gates;	*closed (in sleep)*
	And but for our approach, those sleeping stones	

3. Oldest grandson; but perhaps deliberately meant to produce the false inference that Arthur is really the "eld'st son's [Richard's] son."
4. Implying sexual infidelity in the conception of John. These lines (especially 179) echo the Second Commandment (Exodus 20:5, "the law" of line 180): "visiting the iniquity of the fathers upon the children unto the third and fourth generation."
5. *plagued . . . plague:* punished because of and by her.
6. *her sin his injury . . . her:* her wrongful action is like a parish constable (a "beadle," who whipped petty criminals) urging on her son to afflict Arthur; all (Eleanor's

sin, John as its embodiment) are punished in Arthur, and all because of Eleanor.
7. Testament influenced by a woman (Eleanor; ironically, it was illegal for women to make wills themselves, for fear their husbands would influence them); a woman's desire (as in the proverbial "A woman will have her will").
8. *to cry aim / To:* to encourage.
9. Shakespeare may have taken some steps toward conflating this character with Hubert, who figures prominently later in the play (see note to line 325 and Textual Note), but no early text survives in which such an identification of characters has been fully effected.

That as a waist° doth girdle you about,   *girdle*
By the compulsion of their ordinance,°   *artillery*
By this time from their fixèd beds of lime°   *their foundations*
220 Had been dishabited,[1] and wide havoc made
For bloody power to rush upon your peace.
But on the sight of us your lawful king,
Who painfully,° with much expedient° march,   *laboriously / hurried*
Have brought a countercheck before your gates
225 To save unscratched your city's threatened cheeks,
Behold the French, amazed,° vouchsafe° a parle;   *terrified / grant*
And now instead of bullets wrapped in fire
To make a shaking fever in your walls,
They shoot but calm words folded up in smoke°   *deceit*
230 To make a faithless error° in your ears;   *lie*
Which trust accordingly, kind citizens,
And let us in, your king, whose laboured° spirits,   *worn out*
Forwearied in this action of swift speed,
Craves harbourage within your city walls.
235 KING PHILIP   When I have said, make answer to us both.
             [*He takes Arthur's hand*]
Lo, in this° right hand, whose protection   *(Philip's)*
Is most divinely vowed upon the right
Of him° it holds, stands young Plantagenet,   *(Arthur)*
Son to the elder brother of this man°   *(John)*
240 And king o'er him and all that he enjoys.
For this downtrodden equity° we tread   *right*
In warlike march these greens before your town,
Being no further enemy to you
Than the constraint° of hospitable zeal   *necessity*
245 In the relief of this oppressèd child
Religiously° provokes. Be pleasèd then   *Solemnly*
To pay that duty which you truly owe
To him that owes° it, namely this young prince;   *has a right to*
And then our arms, like to a muzzled bear,
250 Save in aspect,° hath all offence° sealed up: *appearance / aggression*
Our cannons' malice vainly shall be spent
Against th'invulnerable clouds of heaven,
And with a blessèd and unvexed retire,°   *unmolested retreat*
With unhacked swords and helmets all unbruised,
255 We will bear home that lusty blood again
Which here we came to spout against your town,
And leave your children, wives, and you in peace.
But if you fondly° pass our proffered offer,   *foolishly*
'Tis not the roundure° of your old-faced walls   *roundness; circumference*
260 Can hide you from our messengers of war,°   *cannonballs*
Though all these English and their discipline°   *military skill*
Were harboured in their rude° circumference.   *rugged*
Then tell us, shall your city call us lord
In that behalf which° we have challenged it,   *in which; for whom*
265 Or shall we give the signal to our rage,
And stalk in blood to our possession?
       CITIZEN   In brief, we are the King of England's subjects.
For him and in his right we hold this town.

---

1. Dislodged, unclothed ("habit" picking up "waist" "girdle," line 217). *A*ngers continues to be personified here ("cheeks," line 225; "fever," line 228) and later in the scene.

KING JOHN   Acknowledge then the King, and let me in.

270   CITIZEN   That can we not; but he that proves° the king,   *proves to be*
To him will we prove loyal; till that time
Have we rammed up our gates against the world.

KING JOHN   Doth not the crown of England prove the king?
And if not that, I bring you witnesses:

275   Twice fifteen thousand hearts of England's breed—

BASTARD [aside]   Bastards and else.°   *others*

KING JOHN   To verify our title with their lives.

KING PHILIP   As many and as well-born bloods as those—

BASTARD [aside]   Some bastards too.

280   KING PHILIP   Stand in his face° to contradict his claim.   *against him*

CITIZEN   Till you compound° whose right is worthiest,   *settle*
We for the worthiest hold° the right from both.   *withhold*

KING JOHN   Then God forgive the sin of all those souls
That to their everlasting residence,

285   Before the dew of evening fall, shall fleet°   *leave their bodies*
In dreadful trial of° our kingdom's king.   *contest to determine*

KING PHILIP   Amen, Amen! Mount, chevaliers!° To arms!   *horsemen*

BASTARD   Saint George that swinged° the dragon, and e'er since   *thrashed*
Sits on's horseback at mine hostess' door,[2]

290   Teach us some fence!° [To AUSTRIA] Sirrah, were I at home   *swordsmanship*
At your den, sirrah, with your lioness,°   *whore; wife*
I would set an ox-head° to your lion's hide   *add cuckold's horns*
And make a monster of you.

AUSTRIA   Peace, no more.

BASTARD   O tremble, for you hear the lion roar!

295   KING JOHN   Up higher to the plain, where we'll set forth
In best appointment° all our regiments.   *readiness*

BASTARD   Speed then, to take advantage of the field.°   *best battle positions*

KING PHILIP   It shall be so, and at the other hill
Command the rest to stand.[3] God and our right!°   *(English royal motto)*

Exeunt [severally° KING JOHN *and* KING PHILIP *with their*   *separately*
powers. The CITIZEN *remains on the walls]*
[Alarum.] Here, after excursions,° enter [at one door] the   *onstage skirmishes*
HERALD *of France, with [a] trumpet[er], to the gates*

300   FRENCH HERALD   You men of Angers, open wide your gates
And let young Arthur Duke of Brittaine in,
Who by the hand of France this day hath made
Much work for tears in many an English mother,
Whose sons lie scattered on the bleeding ground;

305   Many a widow's husband grovelling lies,
Coldly embracing the discoloured earth;
And victory with little loss doth play
Upon the dancing banners of the French,
Who are at hand, triumphantly displayed,°   *drawn up*

310   To enter conquerors, and to proclaim
Arthur of Brittaine England's king and yours.

Enter [at another door the] English HERALD, *with [a]*
trumpet[er]

ENGLISH HERALD   Rejoice, you men of Angers, ring your bells!
King John, your king and England's, doth approach,

---

2. The idea that St. George, England's patron saint, is
ever on horseback yet never rides was proverbial. *at
mine hostess' door:* on an inn sign.

3. Command the reserves to be in readiness. (This concludes an unheard conversation in parallel with John's.)

Commander of this hot malicious day.

315 Their armours that marched hence so silver-bright

Hither return all gilt° with Frenchmen's blood. *smeared; golden*

There stuck no plume in any English crest° *(on a helmet)*

That is removèd by a staff° of France; *spear*

Our colours° do return in those same hands *banners*

320 That did display them when we first marched forth;

And like a jolly troop of huntsmen come

Our lusty English, all with purpled hands

Dyed in the dying slaughter of their foes.

Open your gates and give the victors way.

325 CITIZEN[4] Heralds, from off our towers we might° behold *could*

From first to last the onset and retire

Of both your armies, whose equality

By our best eyes cannot be censurèd.° *differentiated*

Blood hath bought blood and blows have answered blows,

330 Strength matched with strength and power confronted power.

Both are alike, and both alike we like.

One must prove greatest. While they weigh so even,

We hold our town for neither, yet for both.

    Enter the two kings with their powers,° at several doors *armies*

    [*at one door* KING JOHN, *the* BASTARD, QUEEN ELEANOR

    and Lady BLANCHE, *with soldiers; at another door* KING

    PHILIP, LOUIS THE DAUPHIN, *and the Duke of* AUSTRIA

    with soldiers][5]

KING JOHN France, hast thou yet more blood to cast away?

335 Say, shall the current of our right run on,

Whose passage, vexed with thy impediment,

Shall leave his native channel° and o'erswell° *normal course / flood*

With course disturbed even thy confining shores,

Unless thou let his silver water keep

340 A peaceful progress to the ocean?

KING PHILIP England, thou hast not saved one drop of blood

In this hot trial more than we of France;

Rather, lost more. And by this hand I swear,

That sways the earth this climate° overlooks, *part of the sky*

345 Before we will lay down our just-borne arms,

We'll put thee down 'gainst whom these arms we bear,

Or add a royal number° to the dead, *(Philip)*

Gracing the scroll that tells of this war's loss

With slaughter coupled to the name of kings.

350 BASTARD Ha, majesty! How high thy glory towers

When the rich blood of kings is set on fire!

O, now doth Death line his dead chaps° with steel; *deadly jaws*

The swords of soldiers are his teeth, his fangs;

And now he feasts, mousing° the flesh of men *tearing; biting*

355 In undetermined differences° of kings. *unresolved disputes*

Why stand these royal fronts° amazèd thus? *faces*

Cry havoc,[6] Kings! Back to the stainèd field,

You equal potents,° fiery-kindled spirits! *equally strong rulers*

---

4. This and subsequent speeches of the Citizen are attributed to Hubert in the earliest Folio text. See note to line 200.

5. F calls for "the two Kings with their powers"; this seems to exclude Constance and Arthur.

6. Order given to troops for pillaging and merciless slaughter.

Then let confusion° of one part° confirm   *let overthrow / side*
360   The other's peace; till then, blows, blood, and death!
       KING JOHN   Whose party do the townsmen yet admit?
       KING PHILIP   Speak, citizens, for England: who's your king?
       CITIZEN   The King of England, when we know the King.
       KING PHILIP   Know him in us,° that here hold up his right.   *me*
365   KING JOHN   In us, that are our own great deputy°   *representative*
       And bear possession of our person° here,   *represent my own claim*
       Lord of our presence,° Angers, and of you.   *myself*
       CITIZEN   A greater power than we denies all this,
       And, till it be undoubted, we do lock
370   Our former scruple in our strong-barred gates,
       Kinged of° our fear, until our fears resolved   *Commanded by*
       Be by some certain king, purged and deposed.
       BASTARD   By heaven, these scroyles° of Angers flout you, Kings,   *scoundrels*
       And stand securely on their battlements
375   As in a theatre, whence they gape and point
       At your industrious scenes and acts of death.
       Your royal presences° be ruled by me.   *persons*
       Do like the mutines of Jerusalem:[7]
       Be friends awhile, and both conjointly° bend   *together*
380   Your sharpest deeds of malice on this town.
       By east and west let France and England mount
       Their battering cannon, chargèd to° the mouths,   *loaded to*
       Till their soul-fearing° clamours have brawled° down   *terrifying / broken*
       The flinty ribs° of this contemptuous city.   *walls*
385   I'd play incessantly upon these jades,[8]
       Even till unfencèd° desolation   *unwalled*
       Leave them as naked as the vulgar° air.   *common*
       That done, dissever your united strengths,
       And part your mingled colours once again;
390   Turn face to face, and bloody point to point.
       Then in a moment Fortune shall cull° forth   *choose*
       Out of one side her happy minion,°   *darling*
       To whom in favour she shall give the day,°   *victory*
       And kiss him with a glorious victory.
395   How like you this wild counsel, mighty states?°   *rulers*
       Smacks it not something of the policy?°   *political cunning*
       KING JOHN   Now, by the sky that hangs above our heads,
       I like it well.—France, shall we knit° our powers,   *join*
       And lay this Angers even with the ground,
400   Then after fight who shall be king of it?
       BASTARD [*to* KING PHILIP]   An if thou hast the mettle of a king,
       Being wronged as we are by this peevish° town,   *obstinate*
       Turn thou the mouth of thy artillery,
       As we will ours, against these saucy° walls;   *presumptuous*
405   And when that we have dashed them to the ground,
       Why, then defy each other, and pell-mell°   *quickly*
       Make work upon ourselves, for[9] heaven or hell.
       KING PHILIP   Let it be so.—Say, where will you assault?

---

7. Warring factions of Jerusalem who temporarily
united against besieging Roman forces in 70 C.E.
8. I'd unceasingly fire at (or torment) these wretches.
(A "jade" was a decrepit horse or an insulting term for

a woman—and hence a double insult when applied to
a man.)
9. On behalf of; for the destination of.

KING JOHN   We from the west will send destruction
410 Into this city's bosom.
AUSTRIA   I from the north.
KING PHILIP   Our thunder° from the south   *cannon*
     Shall rain their drift of bullets° on this town.   *shower of cannonballs*
BASTARD [*to* KING JOHN]   O prudent discipline!° From north to south   *tactics*
415 Austria and France shoot in each other's mouth.
     I'll stir them to it. Come, away, away!
CITIZEN   Hear us, great Kings, vouchsafe a while to stay,
     And I shall show you peace and fair-faced league.
     Win you this city without stroke or wound;
420 Rescue those breathing lives to die in beds,
     That here come sacrifices for the field.
     Persever not, but hear me, mighty Kings.
KING JOHN   Speak on with favour;° we are bent° to hear.   *permission / willing*
CITIZEN   That daughter there of Spain, the Lady Blanche,
425 Is niece to England. Look upon the years°   *ages*
     Of Louis the Dauphin and that lovely maid.
     If lusty love should go in quest of beauty,
     Where should he find it fairer than in Blanche?
     If zealous° love should go in search of virtue,   *pious*
430 Where should he find it purer than in Blanche?
     If love ambitious sought a match of birth,
     Whose veins bound° richer blood than Lady Blanche?   *contain*
     Such as she is in beauty, virtue, birth,
     Is the young Dauphin every way complete;°   *perfect*
435 If not complete, O, say he is not she;
     And she again wants nothing—to name want—
     If want it be not that she is not he.[1]
     He is the half part of a blessèd man,
     Left to be finishèd by such as she;
440 And she a fair divided excellence,
     Whose fullness of perfection lies in him.
     O, two such silver currents when they join
     Do glorify the banks that bound them in,
     And two such shores to two such streams made one,
445 Two such controlling bounds, shall you be, Kings,
     To these two princes if you marry them.
     This union shall do more than battery can
     To our fast-closèd gates, for at this match,[2]
     With swifter spleen° than powder can enforce,   *passion*
450 The mouth of passage shall we fling wide ope,
     And give you entrance. But without this match
     The sea enragèd is not half so deaf,
     Lions more confident, mountains and rocks
     More free from motion, no, not Death himself
455 In mortal fury half so peremptory,°   *resolved*
     As we to keep this city.
BASTARD [*aside*]   Here's a stay°   *an obstacle; cease-fire*
     That shakes the rotten carcass of old Death
     Out of his rags.[3] Here's a large mouth,° indeed,   *(of a cannon or human)*

---

1. *If not . . . he:* The Dauphin is perfect insofar as he lacks Blanche, and vice versa. *wants:* lacks. *to:* if I must.
2. Marriage; device for lighting gun "powder" (line 449).
3. *That . . . rags:* That steals what belongs to death.

That spits forth Death and mountains, rocks and seas,
460   Talks as familiarly of roaring lions
As maids of thirteen do of puppy-dogs.
What cannoneer begot this lusty blood?
He speaks plain cannon: fire, and smoke, and bounce;°   *bang*
He gives the bastinado° with his tongue;   *a cudgeling*
465   Our ears are cudgelled; not a word of his
But buffets better than a fist of France.
Zounds!° I was never so bethumped with words   *God's wounds*
Since I first called my brother's father Dad.
QUEEN ELEANOR [*aside to* KING JOHN]   Son, list° to this conjunc-   *listen*
tion,° make this match,   *proposition*
470   Give with our niece a dowry large enough;
For, by this knot, thou shalt so surely tie
Thy now unsured assurance to the crown
That yon green° boy shall have no sun to ripe   *unripe; young*
The bloom that promiseth a mighty fruit.
475   I see a yielding in the looks of France;
Mark how they whisper. Urge them while their souls
Are capable of° this ambition,   *susceptible to*
Lest zeal,° now melted by the windy breath   *(on Arthur's behalf)*
Of soft petitions, pity, and remorse,
480   Cool and congeal° again to what it was.   *freeze*
CITIZEN   Why answer not the double majesties
This friendly treaty° of our threatened town?   *entreaty; proposal*
KING PHILIP   Speak England first, that hath been forward first
To speak unto this city: what say you?
485   KING JOHN   If that the Dauphin there, thy princely son,
Can in this book of beauty° read 'I love',   *(Blanche)*
Her dowry shall weigh equal with a queen;
For Anjou and fair Touraine, Maine, Poitou,[4]
And all that we upon this side the sea—
490   Except this city now by us besieged—
Find liable° to our crown and dignity,   *subject*
Shall gild her bridal bed, and make her rich
In titles, honours, and promotions,°   *elevations in rank*
As she in beauty, education, blood,
495   Holds hand with° any princess of the world.   *Is equal to*
KING PHILIP   What sayst thou, boy? Look in the lady's face.
LOUIS THE DAUPHIN   I do, my lord, and in her eye I find
A wonder, or a wondrous miracle,
The shadow of myself formed in her eye;
500   Which, being but the shadow of your son,
Becomes a sun and makes your son a shadow.[5]
I do protest I never loved myself
Till now enfixèd° I beheld myself   *imprinted*
Drawn in the flattering table° of her eye.   *surface*
      [*He*] *whispers with* BLANCHE
505   BASTARD [*aside*]   Drawn in the flattering table of her eye,
Hanged in the frowning wrinkle of her brow,

---

4. The French territories claimed by both John and Arthur will go to the Dauphin.
5. *The shadow of myself . . . a shadow:* The Dauphin speaks in elaborate clichés of courtly love poetry: the conceit is common, as is the "sun/son" wordplay. He claims that his "shadow," from being a mere reflection or pale imitation of the King's son (or a shadow of the sun) in Blanche's eyes, becomes a "sun" because her eyes are so bright, with the result that the actual "son" becomes a mere "shadow" of his own reflection.

And quartered in her heart:[6] he doth espy
Himself love's traitor. This is pity now,
That hanged and drawn and quartered there should be
510   In such a love so vile a lout as he.
BLANCHE [to LOUIS THE DAUPHIN]   My uncle's will in this respect is mine.
If he see aught° in you that makes him like,   *anything*
That anything he sees which moves his liking
I can with ease translate it to my will;
515   Or if you will, to speak more properly,°   *precisely*
I will enforce it easily to my love.
Further I will not flatter you, my lord,
That all I see in you is worthy° love,   *deserving of*
Than this:[7] that nothing do I see in you,
520   Though churlish° thoughts themselves should be your judge,   *grudging*
That I can find should merit any hate.
KING JOHN   What say these young ones? What say you, my niece?
BLANCHE   That she is bound in honour still° to do   *always*
What you in wisdom shall vouchsafe° to say.   *deign*
525   KING JOHN   Speak then, Prince Dauphin, can you love this lady?
LOUIS THE DAUPHIN   Nay, ask me if I can refrain from love,
For I do love her most unfeignedly.
KING JOHN   Then do I give Volquessen,[8] Maine,
Poitou, and Anjou, these five provinces,
530   With her to thee, and this addition more:
Full thirty thousand marks° of English coin.   *£20,000*
Philip of France, if thou be pleased withal,°   *with this*
Command thy son and daughter to join hands.
KING PHILIP   It likes° us well.—Young princes, close your hands.   *pleases*
535   AUSTRIA   And your lips too, for I am well assured
That I did so when I was first assured.°   *betrothed*
    [LOUIS THE DAUPHIN and Lady BLANCHE join hands and kiss]
KING PHILIP   Now citizens of Angers, ope your gates.
Let in that amity which you have made,
For at Saint Mary's chapel presently°   *immediately*
540   The rites of marriage shall be solemnized.—
Is not the Lady Constance in this troop?
[Aside] I know she is not, for this match made up
Her presence would have interrupted much.
[Aloud] Where is she and her son? Tell me who knows.
545   LOUIS THE DAUPHIN   She is sad and passionate° at your highness' tent.   *sorrowful*
KING PHILIP   And by my faith this league that we have made
Will give her sadness very little cure.—
Brother of England, how may we content
This widow lady? In her right we came,
550   Which we, God knows, have turned another way
To our own vantage.°   *advantage*
KING JOHN   We will heal up all,
For we'll create young Arthur Duke of Brittaine[9]
And Earl of Richmond, and this rich fair town
We make him lord of. Call the Lady Constance.

---

6. *Drawn . . . heart:* the Bastard alludes to the punishment of being hanged, drawn (disemboweled; but also, painted, line 504), and quartered (cut in pieces; but also, lodged) for treason. The rhyme scheme of lines 505–10 mimics the last six lines of a Shakespearean sonnet.

7. Taking up "Further," line 517.
8. Modern Vexin, northwest of Paris.
9. An inconsistency: Arthur already holds this title, as John himself acknowledges (line 156).

555	Some speedy messenger bid her repair°	*come*
	To our solemnity.° I trust we shall,	*(marriage) ceremony*
	If not fill up the measure of her will,	
	Yet in some measure satisfy her so	
	That we shall stop her exclamation.°	*loud reproaches*
560	Go we as well as haste will suffer° us	*allow*
	To this unlooked-for, unpreparèd pomp.°	*ceremony*

[*Flourish.*] *Exeunt* [*all but the* BASTARD]

	BASTARD Mad world, mad kings, mad composition!°	*treaty*
	John, to stop Arthur's title in the whole,	
	Hath willingly departed° with a part;	*parted*
565	And France, whose armour conscience buckled on,	
	Whom zeal and charity brought to the field	
	As God's own soldier, rounded° in the ear	*whispered to*
	With° that same purpose-changer,[1] that sly devil,	*By*
	That broker that still breaks the pate[2] of faith,	
570	That daily break-vow, he that wins of° all,	*gets the best of*
	Of kings, of beggars, old men, young men, maids,—	
	Who° having no external° thing to lose	*(maids)* / *material*
	But the word 'maid',° cheats° the poor maid of that—	*virginity* / *he cheats*
	That smooth-faced° gentleman, tickling° commodity;	*plausible* / *cajoling*
575	Commodity, the bias[3] of the world,	
	The world who of itself is peisèd° well,	*balanced*
	Made to run even upon even ground,	
	Till this advantage, this vile-drawing° bias,	*drawing to evil*
	This sway° of motion, this commodity,	*swayer; swerver*
580	Makes it take head° from all indifferency,°	*flee* / *impartiality*
	From all direction, purpose, course, intent;	
	And this same bias, this commodity,	
	This bawd,° this broker, this all-changing word,	*procurer*
	Clapped on the outward eye[4] of fickle France,	
585	Hath drawn him from his own determined aid,	
	From a resolved and honourable war,	
	To a most base and vile-concluded peace.	
	And why rail I on this commodity?	
	But for° because he hath not wooed me yet—	*Only*
590	Not that I have the power to clutch° my hand	*clench (in refusal)*
	When his fair angels would salute[5] my palm,	
	But for° my hand, as unattempted° yet,	*Because* / *untempted*
	Like a poor beggar raileth on the rich.	
	Well, whiles I am a beggar I will rail,	
595	And say there is no sin but to be rich,	
	And being rich, my virtue then shall be	
	To say there is no vice but beggary.	
	Since kings break faith upon° commodity,	*on account of*
	Gain, be my lord, for I will worship thee. *Exit*	

---

1. "Purpose-changer," as well as the subsequent noun phrases in lines 568–70, is in apposition to those in line 574, in particular "commodity" (self-interest, profit seeking: that which translates everything into its market value to the exclusion of noneconomic considerations).
2. Cracks the skull (giving colloquial vigor to "breaks faith"). *broker*: go-between, procurer (leading to word-play in "breaks" and "break-vow," lines 569–70).
3. Literally, in the game of bowls, the off-center weight

of a bowl that causes it to veer from a straight course.
4. Fixed its hold on the outer edge of a bowl so as to make it swerve from a true course; suddenly caught the "outward eye" of self-interest as opposed to the inward eye of conscience. Both meanings are applicable to King Philip.
5. *angels would salute:* 10-shilling coins (with the archangel Michael on them) would kiss (greet); alluding to the Annunciation and Michael's "salute" to the Virgin Mary.

2.2

Enter [Lady] CONSTANCE, ARTHUR *[Duke of Brittaine],*
and [the Earl of] SALISBURY[1]

CONSTANCE *[to* SALISBURY]   Gone to be married? Gone to swear a peace?
    False blood to false blood joined! Gone to be friends?
    Shall Louis have Blanche, and Blanche those provinces?
    It is not so, thou hast misspoke, misheard.
5   Be well advised,° tell o'er thy tale again.   *Consider carefully*
    It cannot be, thou dost but say 'tis so.
    I trust I may not trust thee, for thy word
    Is but the vain breath of a common° man.   *(as opposed to royal)*
    Believe me, I do not believe thee, man;
10   I have a king's oath to the contrary.
    Thou shalt be punished for thus frighting me;
    For I am sick and capable of° fears;   *susceptible to*
    Oppressed with wrongs, and therefore full of fears;
    A widow husbandless, subject to fears;
15   A woman naturally born to fears;
    And though° thou now confess thou didst but jest,   *even if*
    With my vexed spirits I cannot take a truce,°   *make peace*
    But they will quake and tremble all this day.
    What dost thou mean by shaking of thy head?
20   Why dost thou look so sadly on my son?
    What means that hand upon that breast of thine?
    Why holds thine eye that lamentable rheum,°   *tears*
    Like a proud° river peering o'er his bounds?°   *swollen / banks*
    Be these sad signs confirmers of thy words?
25   Then speak again—not all thy former tale,
    But this one word: whether thy tale be true.
SALISBURY   As true as I believe you think them° false   *(the French and English)*
    That give you cause to prove my saying true.
CONSTANCE   O, if thou teach me to believe this sorrow,
30   Teach thou this sorrow how to make me die;
    And let belief and life encounter so
    As doth the fury of two desperate men
    Which in the very meeting fall and die.[2]
    Louis marry Blanche! *[To* ARTHUR] O boy, then where art thou?
35   France friend with England!—What becomes of me?
    [To SALISBURY] Fellow,° be gone, I cannot brook° thy sight;   *(an insult) / endure*
    This news hath made thee a most ugly man.
SALISBURY   What other harm have I, good lady, done,
    But spoke the harm that is by others done?
40 CONSTANCE   Which harm within itself so heinous is
    As it makes harmful all that speak of it.
ARTHUR   I do beseech you, madam, be content.°   *calm*
CONSTANCE   If thou that bidd'st me be content wert grim,
    Ugly and sland'rous to thy mother's womb,[3]
45   Full of unpleasing blots and sightless° stains,   *unsightly*
    Lame, foolish, crooked, swart,° prodigious,[4]   *dark*
    Patched° with foul moles and eye-offending marks,   *Blotched*
    I would not care, I then would be content,

2.2 Location: The French camp by Angers.
1. This is "Actus Secundus" in F (see Textual Note).
2. O . . . *die*: in this image, drawn from emblem-book
representations of Fury, sorrow (or belief) dies as

Constance does.
3. Malformed babies were seen as a divine punishment
for wickedness.
4. Monstrous (and thereby foretelling evil).

For then I should not love thee, no, nor thou
50 Become thy great birth, nor deserve a crown.
But thou art fair, and at thy birth, dear boy,
Nature and Fortune joined to make thee great.
Of Nature's gifts thou mayst with lilies boast,
And with the half-blown° rose. But Fortune, O,   *half-blossomed; young*
55 She is corrupted, changed, and won from thee;
Sh'adulterates° hourly with thine uncle John,   *prostitutes herself*
And with her golden hand hath plucked on° France   *enticed*
To tread down fair respect of sovereignty,°   *(Arthur's rights)*
And made his majesty the bawd to theirs.[5]
60 France is a bawd to Fortune and King John,
That strumpet Fortune, that usurping John.
[*To* SALISBURY] Tell me, thou fellow, is not France forsworn?°   *an oath breaker*
Envenom° him with words, or get thee gone   *Poison*
And leave those woes alone, which I alone
Am bound to underbear.°   *suffer under*
65 SALISBURY   Pardon me, madam,
I may not go without you to the Kings.
CONSTANCE   Thou mayst, thou shalt; I will not go with thee.
I will instruct my sorrows to be proud,
For grief is proud and makes his owner stoop.
[*She sits upon the ground*]
70 To me and to the state° of my great grief   *throne (ironic)*
Let kings assemble, for my grief's so great
That no supporter but the huge firm earth
Can hold it up. Here I and sorrows sit;
Here is my throne; bid kings come bow to it.
[*Exeunt* SALISBURY *and* ARTHUR]

3.1

[*Flourish.*] *Enter* KING JOHN [*and* KING PHILIP *of*]
France [*hand in hand;* LOUIS THE] DAUPHIN [*and Lady*]
BLANCHE, [*married;* QUEEN] ELEANOR, *Philip* [*the* BAS-
TARD, *and the Duke of*] AUSTRIA[1]
KING PHILIP [*to* BLANCHE]   'Tis true,[2] fair daughter, and this blessèd day
Ever in France shall be kept festival.
To solemnize this day, the glorious sun
Stays in his course° and plays the alchemist,[3]   *Stands still*
5 Turning with splendour of his precious eye
The meagre cloddy earth to glittering gold.
The yearly course that brings this day about
Shall never see it but a holy day.
CONSTANCE [*rising*]   A wicked day, and not a holy day!
10 What hath this day deserved? What hath it done,
That it in golden letters should be set

---

5. And made Philip the go-between for John and Fortune.
3.1 Location: The French camp by Angers.
1. Shakespeare originally intended no act break,
though that division, which appears in F, probably indicates a pause in the performance when the play was
revived with act divisions. Salisbury and Arthur might
stay onstage, but they have no further part in the
scene's action. Their exit, if it occurs, may be followed
by a brief pause with Constance alone onstage. She

remains unobserved until line 9. F's stage directions
have her enter with the others at the start of the act,
perhaps because they merely list all the characters who
need to be onstage after a break in the action. But her
words of 2.2.67–74 are incompatible with her entry
here, which is therefore omitted.
2. King Philip enters in mid-conversation.
3. Alchemists sought to turn base metals such as lead
into gold.

Among the high tides° in the calendar?   *great festivals*
Nay, rather turn this day out of the week,
This day of shame, oppression, perjury.
15   Or if it must stand still,° let wives with child   *remain*
Pray that their burdens may not fall° this day,   *they not give birth*
Lest that their hopes prodigiously⁴ be crossed;
But° on this day let seamen fear no wreck;   *Except*
No bargains break that are not this day made;
20   This day all things begun come to ill end,
Yea, faith itself to hollow falsehood change.
KING PHILIP   By heaven, lady, you shall have no cause
To curse the fair proceedings of this day.
Have I not pawned° to you my majesty?°   *pledged / royal word*
25   CONSTANCE   You have beguiled me with a counterfeit°   *false coin or portrait*
Resembling majesty, which being touched and tried°   *tested for gold*
Proves valueless. You are forsworn, forsworn.
You came in arms to spill mine enemies' blood,
But now in arms° you strengthen it with yours   *arm in arm; militarily*
30   The grappling vigour and rough frown of war
Is cold in amity and painted° peace,   *counterfeit*
And our oppression° hath made up° this league.   *affliction / possible*
Arm, arm, you heavens, against these perjured Kings!
A widow cries, be husband to me, God!
35   Let not the hours of this ungodly day
Wear out° the day in peace, but ere sun set   *Finish*
Set armèd discord 'twixt these perjured Kings.
Hear me, O hear me!
AUSTRIA   Lady Constance, peace.
CONSTANCE   War, war, no peace! Peace is to me a war.
40   O Limoges, O Austria,⁵ thou dost shame
That bloody spoil.° Thou slave, thou wretch, thou coward!   *(the lion skin)*
Thou little valiant, great in villainy;
Thou ever strong upon the stronger side;
Thou Fortune's champion, that dost never fight
45   But when her humorous ladyship° is by   *changeable Fortune*
To teach thee safety. Thou art perjured too,
And sooth'st up greatness.° What a fool art thou,   *flatter the powerful*
A ramping° fool, to brag and stamp, and swear   *showily threatening*
Upon my party!° Thou cold-blooded slave,   *cause*
50   Hast thou not spoke like thunder on my side,°   *behalf*
Been sworn my soldier, bidding me depend
Upon thy stars, thy fortune, and thy strength?
And dost thou now fall over° to my foes?   *defect*
Thou wear a lion's hide! Doff it, for shame,
55   And hang a calf's-skin⁶ on those recreant° limbs.   *cowardly; traitorous*
AUSTRIA   O, that a man should speak those words to me!
BASTARD   And hang a calf's-skin on those recreant limbs.
AUSTRIA   Thou dar'st not say so, villain, for thy life.
BASTARD   And hang a calf's-skin on those recreant limbs.
KING JOHN [*to the* BASTARD]   We like not this. Thou dost forget
60   thyself.°   *your rank; protocol*

---

4. By an ominously monstrous child.   6. Symbolizing cowardice or folly.
5. See note to 2.1.5.

Enter [Cardinal] PANDOLF

KING PHILIP   Here comes the holy legate of the Pope.[7]

PANDOLF   Hail, you anointed deputies of God.°—   kings
To thee, King John, my holy errand is.
I Pandolf, of fair Milan Cardinal,
65   And from Pope Innocent the legate here,
Do in his name religiously demand
Why thou against the Church, our Holy Mother,
So wilfully dost spurn,° and force perforce°   kick / and forcibly
Keep Stephen Langton, chosen° Archbishop   (by the Pope)
70   Of Canterbury, from that holy see.
This, in our foresaid Holy Father's name,
Pope Innocent, I do demand of thee.

KING JOHN   What earthy name to interrogatories
Can task the free breath of a sacred king?[8]
75   Thou canst not, Cardinal, devise a name
So slight, unworthy, and ridiculous
To charge me to an° answer, as the Pope.   to make an
Tell him this tale, and from the mouth of England
Add thus much more: that no Italian priest°   the Pope
80   Shall tithe or toll° in our dominions;   collect church revenue
But as we, under God, are supreme head,[9]
So, under him, that great supremacy°   sovereignty
Where we do reign we will alone uphold
Without th'assistance of a mortal hand.
85   So tell the Pope, all reverence set apart°   rejected
To him and his usurped authority.

KING PHILIP   Brother of England, you blaspheme in this.

KING JOHN   Though you and all the kings of Christendom
Are led so grossly by this meddling priest,
90   Dreading the curse that money may buy out,[1]
And by the merit of vile gold, dross, dust,
Purchase corrupted pardon of a man,[2]
Who in that sale sells pardon from himself;[3]
Though you and all the rest so grossly led
95   This juggling° witchcraft with revenue cherish;   deceiving
Yet I alone, alone do me oppose
Against the Pope, and count his friends my foes.

PANDOLF   Then by the lawful power that I have
Thou shalt stand cursed and excommunicate;°   excommunicated
100   And blessèd shall he be that doth revolt
From his allegiance to an heretic;
And meritorious shall that hand be called,
Canonizèd and worshipped as a saint,
That takes away by any secret course
Thy hateful life.

---

7. Shakespeare follows his main source in combining two papal legates in one, as he does in the use of Austria to represent two of Richard I's adversaries.
8. *What . . . king?*: What person holding an earthly title (the Pope or his deputy) can demand answers from a King who governs by divine right? John attributes to himself the divine authority he has just denied the Pope.
9. "Supreme head" of the English Church is the title adopted in 1534 by Henry VIII, Elizabeth's father, in defiance of the papacy. This passage is perhaps the most openly and anachronistically Protestant, anti-Catholic moment in the play.
1. Excommunication is the "curse" that a bribe can buy off, or reverse.
2. An allusion to the sale of indulgences, or papal dispensations for sin, by a member of the Catholic clergy ("a man").
3. The clergyman "sells" (gives up) hope of God's forgiveness for himself and is hence damned by his selling. The pardon he sells lacks efficacy because it comes "from himself," rather than from God.

105 CONSTANCE   O lawful let it be
       That I have room° with Rome to curse awhile.   *opportunity*
       Good Father Cardinal, cry thou 'Amen'
       To my keen curses, for without my wrong°   *the wrongs done to me*
       There is no tongue hath power to curse him right.°   *properly*
110 PANDOLF   There's law and warrant, lady, for my curse.
    CONSTANCE   And for mine too. When law can do no right
       Let it be lawful that law bar no wrong.°   *cursing*
       Law cannot give my child his kingdom here,
       For he that holds his kingdom holds the law.
115   Therefore, since law° itself is perfect wrong,   *(secular)*
       How can the law° forbid my tongue to curse?   *(ecclesiastical)*
    PANDOLF   Philip of France, on peril of a curse,°   *excommunication*
       Let go the hand of that arch-heretic,
       And raise the power of France upon his head,
120   Unless he do submit himself to Rome.
    QUEEN ELEANOR   Look'st thou pale, France? Do not let go thy hand.
    CONSTANCE [*to* KING JOHN]   Look to it, devil, lest that France repent,
       And by disjoining hands hell lose a soul.
    AUSTRIA   King Philip, listen to the Cardinal.
125 BASTARD   And hang a calf's-skin on his recreant limbs.
    AUSTRIA   Well, ruffian, I must pocket up° these wrongs,   *put up with*
       Because—
    BASTARD   Your breeches best may carry them.[4]
    KING JOHN   Philip, what sayst thou to the Cardinal?
    CONSTANCE   What should he say, but as° the Cardinal?   *the same as*
130 LOUIS THE DAUPHIN   Bethink you, Father, for the difference
       Is purchase of a heavy curse from Rome,
       Or the light loss of England for a friend.
       Forgo the easier.
    BLANCHE   That's the curse of Rome.
    CONSTANCE   O Louis, stand fast; the devil tempts thee here
135   In likeness of a new untrimmèd° bride.   *virginal*
    BLANCHE   The Lady Constance speaks not from her faith,
       But from her need.
    CONSTANCE [*to* KING PHILIP]   O if thou grant my need,
       Which only lives but by the death of faith,[5]
       That need must needs infer this principle:[6]
140   That faith would live again by death of need.°   *by the end of my woes*
       O, then tread down my need, and faith mounts up;
       Keep my need up, and faith is trodden down.
    KING JOHN   The King is moved, and answers not to this.
    CONSTANCE [*to* KING PHILIP]   O, be removed from him, and answer well.
145 AUSTRIA   Do so, King Philip, hang no more in doubt.
    BASTARD   Hang nothing but a calf's-skin, most sweet lout.
    KING PHILIP   I am perplexed, and know not what to say.
    PANDOLF   What canst thou say but will perplex° thee more,   *trouble*
       If thou stand excommunicate and cursed?
150 KING PHILIP   Good Reverend Father, make my person yours,°   *put yourself in my place*
       And tell me how you would bestow yourself.°   *what you would do*
       This royal hand and mine are newly knit,°   *joined*

---

4. Probably, you may best carry them (the "wrongs" of
line 126, or kicks) in the pocket of your breeches; possibly implying that Austria will be kicked in the breeches.
5. Which (my need) exists only because of your broken

faith (the pledge to support Arthur) or my loss of faith
in you; perhaps, which will live only if you break your
faith (to the Church)
6. That need necessarily implies this truth.

And the conjunction of our inward souls
Married in league, coupled and linked together
155 With all religious strength of sacred vows;
The latest breath that gave the sound of words
Was deep-sworn faith, peace, amity, true love,
Between our kingdoms and our royal selves;
And even° before this truce, but new° before,   *just / only just*
160 No longer than we well could wash our hands°   *(of blood)*
To clap this royal bargain up of peace,[7]
God knows, they were besmeared and over-stained
With slaughter's pencil,° where Revenge did paint   *paintbrush*
The fearful difference° of incensèd kings;   *dispute*
165 And shall these hands, so lately purged of blood,
So newly joined in love, so strong in both,°   *(blood and love)*
Unyoke this seizure[8] and this kind regreet,°   *return of salutation*
Play fast and loose with faith, so jest with heaven,
Make such unconstant children of ourselves,
170 As now again to snatch our palm from palm,
Unswear faith sworn, and on the marriage-bed
Of smiling peace to march a bloody host,
And make a riot on the gentle brow
Of true sincerity? O holy sir,
175 My Reverend Father, let it not be so.
Out of your grace, devise, ordain, impose
Some gentle order, and then we shall be blessed
To do your pleasure and continue friends.
PANDOLF All form is formless, order orderless,
180 Save what is opposite to England's love.
Therefore to arms, be champion of our Church,
Or let the Church, our mother, breathe her curse,
A mother's curse, on her revolting son.
France, thou mayst hold° a serpent by the tongue,   *may more easily hold*
185 A crazèd lion by the mortal° paw,   *deadly*
A fasting tiger safer by the tooth,
Than keep in peace that hand which thou dost hold.
KING PHILIP I may disjoin my hand, but not my faith.
PANDOLF So mak'st thou faith an enemy to faith,[9]
190 And like a civil war, sett'st oath to oath,
Thy tongue against thy tongue. O, let thy vow,
First made to heaven, first be to heaven performed;
That is, to be the champion of our Church.
What since thou swor'st[1] is sworn against thyself,
195 And may not be performèd by thyself;
For that which thou hast sworn to do amiss
Is not amiss when it is truly done;[2]
And being not done where doing tends to ill,
The truth is then most done not doing it.
200 The better act of purposes mistook[3]
Is to mistake again; though indirect,°   *circuitous; wrong*
Yet indirection thereby grows direct,

---

7. To seal this royal peace treaty by shaking hands.
8. Of hands joined together.
9. You set your faith to John against your faith to the Church. The confusing rhetoric of this speech exemplifies the elaborate and sometimes equivocal reasoning known as casuistry that was practiced by sixteenth-

century Catholics and hated by English Protestants.
1. What you've subsequently sworn (amity with John).
2. *For . . . done:* For it's not immoral to break an immoral vow. *truly done:* not done at all because it is immoral.
3. The better act when you've done wrong.

And falsehood falsehood cures, as fire cools fire
Within the scorchèd veins of one new burned.[4]
205 It is religion that doth make vows kept;°   *make us honor our vows*
But thou hast sworn against religion;
By what thou swear'st, against the thing thou swear'st;[5]
And mak'st an oath the surety for thy troth:[6]
Against an oath, the truth. Thou art unsure
210 To swear: swear'st only not to be forsworn—[7]
Else what a mockery should it be to swear!—
But thou dost swear only to be forsworn,
And most forsworn to keep what thou dost swear.[8]
Therefore thy later vows against thy first
215 Is in thyself rebellion to° thyself,   *against*
And better conquest never canst thou make
Than arm thy constant and thy nobler parts
Against these giddy loose suggestions;°   *dissolute temptations*
Upon° which better part° our prayers come in   *On behalf of / side*
220 If thou vouchsafe° them. But if not, then know   *accept*
The peril of our curses light on thee
So heavy as thou shalt not shake them off,
But in despair° die under their black weight.   *(because damned)*
AUSTRIA   Rebellion, flat rebellion!
BASTARD   Will't not be?[9]
225 Will not a calf's-skin stop that mouth of thine?
LOUIS THE DAUPHIN   Father, to arms!
BLANCHE   Upon thy wedding day?
Against the blood that thou hast marrièd?
What, shall our feast be kept with° slaughtered men?   *attended by*
Shall braying trumpets and loud churlish drums,
230 Clamours of hell, be measures° to our pomp?°   *music / celebration*
     [*She kneels*]
O husband, hear me! Ay, alack, how new
Is 'husband' in my mouth! Even for that name
Which till this time my tongue did ne'er pronounce,
Upon my knee I beg, go not to arms
Against mine uncle.
235 CONSTANCE [*kneeling*]   O, upon my knee
Made hard with kneeling, I do pray to thee,
Thou virtuous Dauphin, alter not the doom°   *fate*
Forethought by heaven.[1]
BLANCHE [*to* LOUIS THE DAUPHIN]   Now shall I see thy love:
     what motive may
240 Be stronger with thee than the name of wife?
CONSTANCE   That which upholdeth him that thee upholds:°   *who supports you*
His honour.—O thine honour, Louis, thine honour!
LOUIS THE DAUPHIN [*to* KING PHILIP]   I muse your majesty doth
     seem so cold

---

4. *as fire . . . burned:* the theory that one fire cools
another was proverbial but false.
5. By your oath to John, you break your oath to your
religion, the basis for all other vows.
6. You make an oath the guarantee of your "troth"
(agreement with John); but with a pun on its opposite—
the "truth" (or religious faith) of the next line.
7. *Thou art . . . forsworn:* You waver over swearing, and
do so only not to break faith (with John).
8. *But thou . . . dost swear:* But your (secular) oath-

taking leads only to (religious) oath-breaking, especially in maintaining your oath to John.
9. Is it all in vain; won't you be quiet?
1. Constance self-interestedly treats as a single issue
John's two separate matters—Arthur's right to the
throne and Pandolf's insistence on papal right. The
belief that people are preordained for either salvation or
damnation ("doom / Forethought by heaven") is more
Protestant than Catholic.

When such profound respects° do pull you on.   *weighty considerations*
245   PANDOLF   I will denounce a curse upon his head.

     KING PHILIP   Thou shalt not need.—England, I will fall from° thee.   *desert*
     [*He takes his hand from King John's hand.* BLANCHE
     and CONSTANCE *rise*]

     CONSTANCE   O, fair return of banished majesty!

     QUEEN ELEANOR   O, foul revolt of French inconstancy!

     KING JOHN   France, thou shalt rue this hour within this hour.
250   BASTARD   Old Time the clock-setter, that bald sexton Time,
     Is it as he will?—Well then, France shall rue.[2]

     BLANCHE   The sun's o'ercast with blood; fair day, adieu!
     Which is the side that I must go withal?°   *with*
     I am with both, each army hath a hand,
255   And in their rage, I having hold of both,
     They whirl asunder° and dismember me.   *dash apart*
     Husband, I cannot pray that thou mayst win.—
     Uncle, I needs must pray that thou mayst lose.—
     Father,° I may not wish the fortune thine.—   *Father-in-law (Philip)*
260   Grandam, I will not wish thy wishes thrive.
     Whoever wins, on that side shall I lose,
     Assurèd loss before the match be played.

     LOUIS THE DAUPHIN   Lady, with me, with me thy fortune° lies.   *prosperity*

     BLANCHE   There where my fortune° lives, there° my life dies.   *fate / (with Louis)*

     KING JOHN [*to the* BASTARD]   Cousin, go draw our puissance°   *army*
265   together.—   *Exit the* BASTARD]
     France, I am burned up with inflaming wrath,
     A rage whose heat hath this condition:
     That nothing can allay,° nothing but blood,   *cure*
     The blood, and dearest-valued blood, of France.

270   KING PHILIP   Thy rage shall burn thee up, and thou shalt turn
     To ashes ere our blood shall quench that fire.
     Look to thyself, thou art in jeopardy.

     KING JOHN   No more than he that threats.—To arms let's hie!°   *hasten*
     Exeunt [*severally*]

3.2

     Alarum;° *excursions.*° *Enter* [*the*] BASTARD, *with* [*the*   *Call to arms / battles*
     Duke of] *Austria's head*

     BASTARD   Now, by my life, this day grows wondrous hot;
     Some airy devil[1] hovers in the sky
     And pours down mischief. Austria's head lie there,
     While Philip breathes.
     Enter [KING] JOHN, ARTHUR [*Duke of Brittaine, and*]
     HUBERT

5   KING JOHN   Hubert, keep this boy.—Philip,° make up!°   *(the Bastard) / press on*
     My mother is assailèd in our tent,
     And ta'en° I fear.   *captured*

     BASTARD   My lord, I rescued her;

---

2. *Old . . . rue:* The sexton set the church clock and
dug graves. Hence, the "hour" (line 249), or time,
which was usually portrayed as bald, will indeed be
fatal. "Time" and "rue" recall the punning proverb
about herbs, "Thyme and rue grow both in one garden,"
in which the pleasant taste of thyme is contrasted with
the bitterness of rue: the passage of time is accompanied by regret. Together the two lines mean something
like "If things proceed according to the fatal effects of
time, France will indeed be sorry, because time (thyme)
and rue go together."
3.2 Location: Plains near Angers.
1. Aerial devils or spirits held to cause thunderstorms
and subsequent death.

Her highness is in safety; fear you not.
But on, my liege, for very little pains
10 Will bring this labour to an happy end.
        Exeunt [KING JOHN *and the* BASTARD *at one door,*
        HUBERT *and* ARTHUR *at another door*]

3.3

    Alarum; excursions; retreat.° *Enter* [KING] JOHN,   *signal for retreat*
    [QUEEN] ELEANOR, ARTHUR [*Duke of Brittaine, the* BAS-
    TARD, HUBERT, *lords* [*with soldiers*]¹
KING JOHN [*to* QUEEN ELEANOR] So shall it be; your grace shall
    stay behind²
    So° strongly guarded. [*To* ARTHUR] Cousin,° look not sad;   *Thus / Kinsman*
    Thy grandam loves thee, and thy uncle will
    As dear be to thee as thy father was.
5 ARTHUR O, this will make my mother die with grief.
KING JOHN [*to the* BASTARD] Cousin, away for England! Haste before,°   *Go ahead*
    And ere our coming, see thou shake the bags
    Of hoarding abbots.³ The fat ribs of peace
    Must by the hungry now be fed upon.
10   Imprisoned angels° set at liberty.⁴   *gold coins; spirits*
    Use our commission° in his° utmost force.   *(to tax) / its*
BASTARD Bell, book, and candle⁵ shall not drive me back
    When gold and silver becks° me to come on.   *beckons*
    I leave your highness.—Grandam, I will pray,
15   If ever I remember to be holy,
    For your fair safety. So I kiss your hand.
QUEEN ELEANOR Farewell, gentle cousin.
KING JOHN   Coz, farewell.
                      [*Exit the* BASTARD]
QUEEN ELEANOR Come hither, little kinsman. Hark, a word.
    [*She takes* ARTHUR *aside*]
KING JOHN Come hither, Hubert.
    [*He takes* HUBERT *aside*]
                  O my gentle Hubert,
20 We owe thee much. Within this wall of flesh°   *(John's body)*
    There is a soul counts thee her creditor,
    And with advantage° means to pay thy love;   *interest*
    And, my good friend, thy voluntary oath°   *oath of allegiance*
    Lives in this bosom, dearly cherishèd.
    Give me thy hand.
    [*He takes Hubert's hand*]
25   I had a thing to say,
    But I will fit it with some better tune.°   *words; reward*
    By heaven, Hubert, I am almost ashamed
    To say what good respect° I have of thee.   *opinion*
HUBERT I am much bounden° to your majesty.   *indebted*

3.3 Location: Scene continues.
1. F does not begin a new scene here, but it does empty the stage—hence the scene division adopted here and in most modern editions.
2. In France, to control the French possessions while John returns to England.
3. *shake . . . abbots:* pillage the monasteries, which

have hoarded wealth. When Henry VIII made himself head of the English Church, he confiscated monastic treasure.
4. F places this line right after "abbots" (line 8), perhaps because a marginal addition in the foul papers was misplaced in the scribal transcript.
5. Articles used in the rite of excommunication.

30 KING JOHN   Good friend, thou hast no cause to say so yet,
　　　But thou shalt have; and creep time ne'er so slow,
　　　Yet it shall come for me to do thee good.
　　　I had a thing to say—but let it go.
　　　The sun is in the heaven, and the proud day,
35　　Attended with the pleasures of the world,
　　　Is all too wanton° and too full of gauds°   *merry / playthings*
　　　To give me audience.° If the midnight bell   *For you to listen*
　　　Did with his iron tongue and brazen mouth
　　　Sound on into the drowsy race° of night;   *course*
40　　If this same were a churchyard° where we stand,   *graveyard*
　　　And thou possessèd° with a thousand wrongs;   *obsessed*
　　　Or if that surly spirit, melancholy,
　　　Had baked° thy blood and made it heavy, thick,   *congealed*
　　　Which else° runs tickling up and down the veins,   *otherwise*
45　　Making that idiot,° laughter, keep° men's eyes   *jester / stay in*
　　　And strain their cheeks to idle merriment—
　　　A passion° hateful to my purposes—   *mood*
　　　Or if that thou couldst see me without eyes,
　　　Hear me without thine ears, and make reply
50　　Without a tongue, using conceit° alone,   *understanding*
　　　Without eyes, ears, and harmful sound of words;
　　　Then in despite° of broad-eyed watchful day   *defiance*
　　　I would into thy bosom pour my thoughts.
　　　But, ah, I will not. Yet I love thee well,
55　　And by my troth,° I think thou lov'st me well.   *faith*
HUBERT   So well that what you bid me undertake,
　　　Though that° my death were adjunct to my act,   *Even if*
　　　By heaven, I would do it.
KING JOHN   Do not I know thou wouldst?
　　　Good Hubert, Hubert, Hubert, throw thine eye
60　　On yon young boy. I'll tell thee what, my friend,
　　　He is a very serpent in my way,
　　　And wheresoe'er this foot of mine doth tread,
　　　He lies before me. Dost thou understand me?
　　　Thou art his keeper.
HUBERT   And I'll keep him so
65　　That he shall not offend your majesty.
KING JOHN   Death.
HUBERT   My lord.
KING JOHN   A grave.
HUBERT   He shall not live.
KING JOHN   Enough.
　　　I could be merry now. Hubert, I love thee.
　　　Well, I'll not say what I intend for thee.
　　　Remember. [*To* QUEEN ELEANOR] Madam, fare you well.
70　　I'll send those powers° o'er to your majesty.   *troops*
QUEEN ELEANOR   My blessing go with thee.
KING JOHN [*to* ARTHUR]   For England, cousin, go.
　　　Hubert shall be your man, attend on you
　　　With all true duty.—On toward Calais, ho!
　　　　　　Exeunt [QUEEN ELEANOR, *attended, at one door,*
　　　　　　　　　the rest at another door]

3.4

*Enter [*KING PHILIP *of] France, [*LOUIS THE*] DAUPHIN,*
[Cardinal] PANDOLF, *[and] attendants*

KING PHILIP   So, by a roaring tempest on the flood,
    A whole armada of convicted sail
    Is scattered and disjoined from fellowship.[1]
PANDOLF   Courage and comfort; all shall yet go well.

5 KING PHILIP   What can go well when we have run° so ill?   *performed; run away*
    Are we not beaten? Is not Angers lost,
    Arthur ta'en prisoner, divers° dear friends slain,   *various*
    And bloody England° into England gone,   *John*
    O'erbearing interruption, spite[2] of France?

10 LOUIS THE DAUPHIN   What he hath won, that hath he fortified.
    So hot a speed, with such advice disposed,°   *judgment regulated*
    Such temperate° order in so fierce a cause,   *calm*
    Doth want example.° Who hath read or heard   *lack precedent*
    Of any kindred action like to this?

15 KING PHILIP   Well could I bear that England had this praise,
    So° we could find some pattern° of our shame.   *If / precedent*
    Enter CONSTANCE *[distracted,[3] with her hair about her*   *wild; mad*
    ears]
    Look who comes here! A grave° unto a soul,   *(Constance's body)*
    Holding th'eternal spirit against her will[3]
    In the vile prison of afflicted breath.°—   *life*

20 I prithee, lady, go away with me.
CONSTANCE   Lo, now, now see the issue° of your peace!   *outcome*
KING PHILIP   Patience, good lady; comfort, gentle Constance.
CONSTANCE   No, I defy all counsel, all redress,°   *comfort*
    But that which ends all counsel, true redress:

25 Death, Death, O amiable, lovely Death!
    Thou odoriferous° stench, sound rottenness!   *fragrant*
    Arise forth from the couch of lasting° night,   *bed of everlasting*
    Thou hate and terror to prosperity,
    And I will kiss thy detestable bones,

30 And put my eyeballs in thy vaulty brows,[4]
    And ring these fingers with thy household worms,[5]
    And stop this gap of breath with fulsome dust,[6]
    And be a carrion° monster like thyself.   *corpse-eating*
    Come grin on me, and I will think thou smil'st,

35 And buss° thee as thy wife. Misery's love,   *kiss*
    O, come to me!
KING PHILIP   O fair affliction,° peace!   *afflicted one*
CONSTANCE   No, no, I will not, having breath to cry.
    O, that my tongue were in the thunder's mouth!
    Then with a passion° would I shake the world,   *an emotional outcry*

40 And rouse from sleep that fell anatomy,°   *fierce skeleton*
    Which cannot hear a lady's feeble voice,
    Which scorns a modern invocation.°   *an ordinary plea*
PANDOLF   Lady, you utter madness, and not sorrow.

3.4 Location: The French camp by Angers.
1. *So . . . fellowship:* This French naval defeat is not in Shakespeare's sources. It is probably a reference to the Spanish Armada of 1588 (see the Introduction). *convicted sail:* doomed ships.
2. Overcoming hindrances, in spite.

3. *Holding . . . will:* that is, she wants to die.
4. Hollow forehead; the eye sockets of the imagined skull of death's corpse.
5. And wear the worms that serve you and live inside you as rings around my fingers.
6. And kiss this mouth with nauseous dust.

CONSTANCE   Thou art not holy to belie me so.
45   I am not mad: this hair I tear is mine;
     My name is Constance; I was Geoffrey's wife;
     Young Arthur is my son; and he is lost.
     I am not mad; I would to God I were,
     For then 'tis like° I should forget myself.   *likely*
50   O, if I could, what grief should I forget!
     Preach some philosophy to make me mad,
     And thou shalt be canonized, Cardinal.
     For, being not mad, but sensible° of grief,   *subject to feelings*
     My reasonable part produces reason
55   How I may be delivered of° these woes,   *freed from*
     And teaches me to kill or hang myself.
     If I were mad I should forget my son,
     Or madly think a babe of clouts° were he.   *cloth doll*
     I am not mad; too well, too well I feel
60   The different plague° of each calamity.   *distinct affliction*
KING PHILIP   Bind up those tresses. O, what love I note
     In the fair multitude of those her hairs!
     Where but by chance a silver drop° hath fallen,   *tear*
     Even to that drop ten thousand wiry friends°   *hairs*
65   Do glue themselves° in sociable grief,   *mat together*
     Like true, inseparable, faithful loves,
     Sticking together in calamity.
CONSTANCE   To England, if you will.[7]
KING PHILIP   Bind up your hairs.
CONSTANCE   Yes, that I will. And wherefore will I do it?
70   I tore them from their bonds, and cried aloud,
     'O that these hands could so redeem my son,
     As they have given these hairs their liberty!'
     But now I envy at their liberty,
     And will again commit them to their bonds,
75   Because my poor child is a prisoner.
          [*She binds up her hair*]
     And Father Cardinal, I have heard you say
     That we shall see and know our friends in heaven.
     If that be true, I shall see my boy again;
     For since the birth of Cain, the first male child,
80   To him that did but yesterday suspire,°   *take his first breath*
     There was not such a gracious creature born.
     But now will canker-sorrow eat my bud,[8]
     And chase the native beauty from his cheek;
     And he will look as hollow as a ghost,
85   As dim and meagre° as an ague's° fit,   *pale and thin / fever's*
     And so he'll die; and rising so again,
     When I shall meet him in the court of heaven,
     I shall not know him; therefore never, never
     Must I behold my pretty Arthur more.
90   PANDOLF   You hold too heinous a respect° of grief.   *view*
CONSTANCE   He talks to me that never had a son.
KING PHILIP   You are as fond of grief as of your child.

---

7. Apparently a reply to line 20, delayed because of Constance's distraction. Possibly the intervening passage is a revision interpolated after the original composition.

8. But now sorrow, like a cankerworm, will eat my flower (Arthur); this is proverbial.

CONSTANCE   Grief fills the room up of my absent child,
        Lies in his bed, walks up and down with me,
95   Puts on his pretty looks, repeats his words,
        Remembers° me of all his gracious parts,   *Reminds*
        Stuffs out his vacant garments with his form;
        Then have I reason to be fond of grief.
        Fare you well. Had you such a loss as I,
100   I could give better comfort than you do.
           [*She unbinds her hair*]
        I will not keep this form upon my head
        When there is such disorder in my wit.
        O Lord, my boy, my Arthur, my fair son,
        My life, my joy, my food, my all the world,
105   My widow-comfort, and my sorrow's cure!   *Exit*
KING PHILIP   I fear some outrage,° and I'll follow her.   *(perhaps suicide)*
                                        Exit [*attended*]
LOUIS THE DAUPHIN   There's nothing in this world can make me joy.
        Life is as tedious as a twice-told tale,
        Vexing the dull ear of a drowsy man;
110   And bitter shame hath spoiled the sweet world's taste,
        That° it yields naught but shame and bitterness.   *So that*
PANDOLF   Before the curing of a strong disease,
        Even in the instant of repair and health,
        The fit° is strongest. Evils that take leave,   *symptom*
115   On their departure most of all show evil.
        What have you lost by losing of this day?
LOUIS THE DAUPHIN   All days of glory, joy, and happiness.
PANDOLF   If you had won it, certainly you had.
        No, no; when Fortune means° to men most good,   *intends*
120   She looks upon them with a threat'ning eye.
        'Tis strange to think how much King John hath lost
        In this which he accounts so clearly won.
        Are not you grieved that Arthur is his prisoner?
LOUIS THE DAUPHIN   As heartily as he is glad he hath him.
125 PANDOLF   Your mind is all as youthful as your blood.
        Now hear me speak with a prophetic spirit,
        For even the breath of what I mean to speak
        Shall blow each dust,° each straw, each little rub,°   *speck / obstacle*
        Out of the path which shall directly lead
130   Thy foot to England's throne. And therefore mark.
        John hath seized Arthur, and it cannot be
        That whiles warm life plays in that infant's veins
        The misplaced° John should entertain an hour,   *usurping*
        One minute, nay, one quiet breath of rest.
135   A sceptre snatched with an unruly hand
        Must be as boisterously° maintained as gained;   *violently*
        And he that stands upon a slipp'ry place
        Makes nice of no vile hold to stay[9] him up.
        That John may stand, then Arthur needs must fall;
140   So be it, for it cannot be but so.
LOUIS THE DAUPHIN   But what shall I gain by young Arthur's fall?
PANDOLF   You, in the right of Lady Blanche your wife,
        May then make all the claim that Arthur did.[1]

---

9. Is not fussy about the vileness of any hold to keep.   1. In Shakespeare's sources but not historical.

LOUIS THE DAUPHIN   And lose it, life and all, as Arthur did.

145 PANDOLF   How green you are, and fresh in this old world!
    John lays you plots;° the times conspire with you; *plots to your benefit*
    For he that steeps his safety in true° blood *legitimate*
    Shall find but bloody safety and untrue.[2]
    This act, so vilely born, shall cool the hearts
150   Of all his people, and freeze up their zeal,° *enthusiastic loyalty*
    That none so small advantage shall step forth
    To check his reign but they will cherish it;[3]
    No natural exhalation° in the sky, *meteor*
    No scope° of nature, no distempered° day, *effect / stormy*
155   No common wind, no customèd° event, *everyday*
    But they will pluck away his° natural cause, *its*
    And call them meteors,° prodigies, and signs, *portents*
    Abortives,[4] presages, and tongues of° heaven *signs from*
    Plainly denouncing vengeance upon John.
160 LOUIS THE DAUPHIN   Maybe he will not touch young Arthur's life,
    But hold° himself safe in his prisonment. *consider*
PANDOLF   O sir, when he shall hear of your approach,
    If that young Arthur be not gone already,
    Even at that news he dies; and then the hearts
165   Of all his people shall revolt from him,
    And kiss the lips of unacquainted° change, *unfamiliar*
    And pick strong matter of° revolt and wrath *reasons for*
    Out of the bloody fingers' ends of John.
    Methinks I see this hurly all on foot,° *commotion all under way*
170   And O, what better matter breeds for you
    Than I have named! The Bastard Falconbridge
    Is now in England, ransacking the Church,
    Offending charity. If but a dozen French
    Were there in arms, they would be as a call° *decoy; call to arms*
175   To train° ten thousand English to their side, *draw*
    Or as a little snow tumbled about
    Anon becomes a mountain. O noble Dauphin,
    Go with me to the King. 'Tis wonderful
    What may be wrought out of their discontent
180   Now that their souls are top-full of offence.° *grievances*
    For England, go! I will whet on° the King. *provoke*
LOUIS THE DAUPHIN   Strong reasons make strange actions. Let us go.
    If you say ay, the King will not say no. *Exeunt*

4.1

Enter HUBERT, *and* EXECUTIONERS [*with a rope and irons*]
HUBERT   Heat me these irons hot, and look thou stand
    Within the arras.[1] When I strike my foot
    Upon the bosom of the ground, rush forth
    And bind the boy which you shall find with me
5   Fast to the chair. Be heedful. Hence, and watch!
EXECUTIONER   I hope your warrant will bear out° the deed. *authorize*
HUBERT   Uncleanly° scruples: fear not you. Look to't!° *Improper / Do it*
    [*The* EXECUTIONERS *withdraw behind the arras*]

2. Compare Genesis 9:6: "Whoso sheddeth man's blood, by man shall his blood be shed." *untrue*: untrustworthy.
3. *none . . . it*: they will seize the smallest opportunity

to dethrone him.
4. Untimely or monstrous births (seen as portents).
4.1 Location: A castle prison in England.
1. Behind the tapestry hangings.

Young lad, come forth, I have to say° with you.　　　　　　*something to discuss*
　　　Enter ARTHUR [*Duke of Brittaine*]
ARTHUR　Good morrow, Hubert.
HUBERT　　　　　　　　　Good morrow, little Prince.
10 ARTHUR　As little prince, having so great a title
　　To be more prince, as may be.² You are sad.
HUBERT　Indeed I have been merrier.
ARTHUR　　　　　　　　　Mercy on me!
　　Methinks nobody should be sad but I.
　　Yet I remember, when I was in France,
15　Young gentlemen would be as sad as night
　　Only for wantonness.° By my christendom,°　　　*affectation / faith*
　　So° I were out of prison and kept sheep,　　　　　　　　*If*
　　I should be as merry as the day is long;
　　And so I would be here, but that I doubt°　　　　　　　*fear*
20　My uncle practises° more harm to me.　　　　　　　　*plots*
　　He is afraid of me, and I of him.
　　Is it my fault that I was Geoffrey's son?
　　No, indeed is't not, and I would to God
　　I were your son, so you would love me, Hubert.
25 HUBERT [*aside*]　If I talk to him, with his innocent prate°　　*prattle*
　　He will awake my mercy, which lies dead;
　　Therefore I will be sudden, and dispatch.
ARTHUR　Are you sick, Hubert? You look pale today.
　　In sooth, I would° you were a little sick,　　　　　*Truly, I wish*
30　That I might sit all night and watch with you.
　　I warrant I love you more than you do me.
HUBERT [*aside*]　His words do take possession of my bosom.
　　　[*He shows* ARTHUR *a paper*]
　　Read here, young Arthur. [*aside*] How now: foolish rheum,°　　*tears*
　　Turning dispiteous° torture out of door?　　　　　　*pitiless*
35　I must be brief, lest resolution drop
　　Out at mine eyes in tender womanish tears.
　　[*To* ARTHUR] Can you not read it? Is it not fair writ?°　　*legible; legal*
ARTHUR　Too fairly, Hubert, for so foul effect.
　　Must you with hot irons burn out both mine eyes?³
HUBERT　Young boy, I must.
ARTHUR　　　　　　　　And will you?
40 HUBERT　　　　　　　　　　　　And I will.
ARTHUR　Have you the heart? When your head did but ache
　　I knit my handkerchief about your brows,
　　The best I had—a princess wrought it° me,　　　　*made it for*
　　And I did never ask it you° again—　　　　　　*back from you*
45　And with my hand at midnight held your head,
　　And like the watchful minutes to the hour
　　Still and anon° cheered up the heavy time,⁴　　　　*Continually*
　　Saying 'What lack you?' and 'Where lies your grief?'°　　*pain*
　　Or 'What good love° may I perform for you?'　　　*loving deed*
50　Many a poor man's son would have lain still
　　And ne'er have spoke a loving word to you,

2. *As . . . be*: Although I have title to be a great prince (king), I am as little a prince as is possible.
3. The order to blind Arthur here is at odds with the death sentence of 3.3.66, as well as with Hubert's deci-

sion later in this scene (line 127) falsely to report Arthur's death, a decision he makes good on in 4.2.
4. The minutes are seen as breaking up the time to make it pass easily.

But you at your sick service had a prince.
Nay, you may think my love was crafty love,
And call it cunning. Do, an if you will.
55   If heaven be pleased that you must use me ill,
Why then you must. Will you put out mine eyes,
These eyes that never did, nor never shall,
So much as frown on you?
HUBERT   I have sworn to do it,
And with hot irons must I burn them out.
60   ARTHUR   Ah, none but in this iron age⁵ would do it.
The iron of itself, though heat° red hot,   heated
Approaching near these eyes would drink my tears,
And quench his° fiery indignation   its
Even in the matter° of mine innocence;   substance; tears
65   Nay, after that, consume° away in rust,   dissolve
But° for containing fire to harm mine eye.   Merely
Are you more stubborn-hard than hammered iron?
An if an angel should have come to me
And told me Hubert should put out mine eyes,
70   I would not have believed him; no tongue but Hubert's.
            [HUBERT *stamps his foot*]
HUBERT   Come forth!
            [*The* EXECUTIONERS *come forth*]
                        Do as I bid you do.
ARTHUR   O, save me, Hubert, save me! My eyes are out
Even with the fierce looks of these bloody men.
HUBERT [*to the* EXECUTIONERS]   Give me the iron, I say, and bind him here.
            [*He takes the iron*]
75   ARTHUR   Alas, what need you be so boisterous-rough?
I will not struggle; I will stand stone-still.
For God's sake, Hubert, let me not be bound.
Nay, hear me, Hubert! Drive these men away,
And I will sit as quiet as a lamb;
80   I will not stir, nor wince, nor speak a word,
Nor look upon the iron angerly.°   angrily
Thrust but these men away, and I'll forgive you,
Whatever torment you do put me to.
HUBERT [*to the* EXECUTIONERS]   Go stand within. Let me alone with him.
85   EXECUTIONER   I am best pleased to be from° such a deed.   away from
            [*Exeunt* EXECUTIONERS]
ARTHUR   Alas, I then have chid° away my friend!   scolded
He hath a stern look, but a gentle heart.
Let him come back, that his compassion may
Give life to yours.
HUBERT   Come, boy, prepare yourself.
ARTHUR   Is there no remedy?
90   HUBERT   None but to lose your eyes.
ARTHUR   O God, that there were but a mote° in yours,   speck of dust
A grain, a dust, a gnat, a wandering hair,
Any annoyance in that precious sense,°   sight
Then, feeling what small things are boisterous° there,   painful
95   Your vile intent must needs seem horrible.
HUBERT   Is this your promise? Go to,° hold your tongue!   Stop it (rebuke)

5. Cruel, degenerate world, in contrast to the legendary "golden" and "silver" ages; with a play on the hot irons.

ARTHUR Hubert, the utterance of a brace of tongues
Must needs want pleading for a pair of eyes.⁶
Let° me not hold my tongue, let me not, Hubert;   *Make*
100 Or, Hubert, if you will, cut out my tongue,
So° I may keep mine eyes. O, spare mine eyes,   *If*
Though to no use but still to look on you.
Lo, by my troth,° the instrument is cold   *faith*
And would not harm me.
HUBERT   I can heat it, boy.
105 ARTHUR No, in good sooth:° the fire is dead with grief,   *truly*
Being create° for comfort, to be° used   *created / at being*
In undeserved extremes.° See else° yourself.   *extreme suffering / for*
There is no malice in this burning coal;
The breath of heaven hath blown his spirit° out,   *(dead person's) soul*
110 And strewed repentant ashes° on his head.   *(of a penitent sinner)*
HUBERT But with my breath I can revive it, boy.
ARTHUR An if you do, you will but make it blush
And glow with shame of your proceedings, Hubert.
Nay, it perchance will sparkle° in your eyes,   *cast sparks*
115 And like a dog that is compelled to fight,
Snatch at his master that doth tarre° him on.   *set*
All things that you should° use to do me wrong   *would*
Deny their office;° only you do lack   *Disobey*
That mercy which fierce fire and iron extends,
120 Creatures of note° for mercy-lacking uses.   *Things noteworthy*
HUBERT Well, see to live.⁷ I will not touch thine eye
For all the treasure that thine uncle owes.°   *owns*
Yet am I sworn, and I did purpose, boy,
With this same very iron to burn them out.
125 ARTHUR O, now you look like Hubert. All this while
You were disguisèd.
HUBERT   Peace, no more. Adieu.
Your uncle must not know but° you are dead.   *otherwise than that*
I'll fill these doggèd° spies with false reports;   *unfeeling*
And, pretty child, sleep doubtless° and secure   *without fear*
130 That Hubert, for the wealth of all the world,
Will not offend° thee.   *harm*
ARTHUR   O God! I thank you, Hubert.
HUBERT Silence, no more. Go closely° in with me.   *secretly*
Much danger do I undergo for thee.   *Exeunt*

4.2

[*Flourish.*] *Enter* [KING] JOHN, [*the Earls of*] PEMBROKE
and SALISBURY, *and other lords.* [KING JOHN *ascends the*
throne]
KING JOHN Here once again we sit, once again crowned,
And looked upon, I hope, with cheerful eyes.
PEMBROKE This 'once again', but that your highness pleased,
Was once superfluous.² You were crowned before,

---

6. *the utterance . . . eyes:* not even a pair of tongues
would be enough to plead for a pair of eyes.
7. Live, and retain your sight.
4.2 Location: John's court in England.
1. John has had a second coronation. Its purpose,

according to Shakespeare's main source, was to get the
English lords again to swear allegiance to him.
2. *but . . superfluous:* but for the fact that you wanted
this second coronation, it would have been one too
many.

5   And that high royalty was ne'er plucked off,
       The faiths of men ne'er stainèd with revolt;
       Fresh expectation° troubled not the land   *Hope of a new king*
       With any longed-for change or better state.³
       SALISBURY   Therefore to be possessed with double pomp,
10   To guard° a title that was rich before,   *adorn*
       To gild refinèd gold, to paint the lily,
       To throw a perfume on the violet,
       To smooth the ice, or add another hue
       Unto the rainbow, or with taper-light°   *candlelight*
15   To seek the beauteous eye of heaven to garnish,°   *the sun to adorn*
       Is wasteful and ridiculous excess.
       PEMBROKE   But that your royal pleasure must be done,
       This act is as an ancient tale new-told,
       And in the last repeating troublesome,
20   Being urgèd at a time unseasonable.°   *inappropriate*
       SALISBURY   In this the antique and well-noted° face   *familiar*
       Of plain old form° is much disfigurèd,   *custom*
       And like a shifted wind unto a sail,
       It makes the course of thoughts to fetch about,°   *change directions*
25   Startles and frights consideration,⁴
       Makes sound opinion sick, and truth suspected
       For putting on so new a fashioned robe.⁵
       PEMBROKE   When workmen strive to do better than well,
       They do confound° their skill in covetousness;⁶   *destroy*
30   And oftentimes excusing of a fault
       Doth make the fault the worser by th'excuse;
       As patches set upon a little breach°   *tear*
       Discredit more in hiding of the fault
       Than did the fault before it was so patched.
35   SALISBURY   To this effect: before you were new-crowned
       We breathed our counsel,° but it pleased your highness   *spoke our advice*
       To overbear° it; and we are all well pleased,   *overrule*
       Since all and every part of what we would°   *wish*
       Doth make a stand° at what your highness will.°   *stop; resist / desires*
40   KING JOHN   Some reasons of this double coronation
       I have possessed you with,° and think them strong.   *instructed you in*
       And more, more strong, when lesser is my fear
       I shall endue° you with. Meantime but ask   *supply*
       What you would have reformed that is not well,
45   And well shall you perceive how willingly
       I will both hear and grant you your requests.⁷
       PEMBROKE   Then I, as one that am the tongue° of these   *spokesman*
       To sound° the purposes of all their hearts,   *express*
       Both for myself and them, but chief of all
50   Your safety, for the which myself and them
       Bend° their best studies,° heartily request   *Direct / efforts*
       Th'enfranchisement° of Arthur, whose restraint   *release*

---

3. Better government; better living conditions.
4. Encourages questions about John's claim to the throne.
5. For behaving so uncustomarily; for donning a coronation robe.

6. By greedily trying to do even better.
7. Lines 43–46 may allude to the historical King John's submission to the baronial demands spelled out in the Magna Carta. See also line 168 and 5.2.20–23.

Doth move the murmuring lips of discontent
To break into this dangerous argument:
55   If what in rest° you have, in right you hold,   *in peace*
Why then your fears—which, as they say, attend
The steps of wrong—should move you to mew up°   *confine*
Your tender kinsman, and to choke his days
With barbarous ignorance, and deny his youth
60   The rich advantage of good exercise?°   *education*
That the time's enemies may not have this
To grace occasions,° let it be our suit   *To justify opposition*
That you have bid us ask, his liberty;
Which for our goods we do no further ask
65   Than whereupon our weal, on you depending,
Counts it your weal he have his liberty.[8]
      Enter HUBERT
KING JOHN   Let it be so. I do commit his youth
To your direction.—Hubert, what news with you?
      [*He takes* HUBERT *aside*]
PEMBROKE   This is the man should do the bloody deed:
70   He showed his warrant to a friend of mine.
The image of a wicked heinous fault°   *crime*
Lives in his eye; that close aspect° of his   *furtive appearance*
Does show the mood of a much troubled breast;
And I do fearfully believe 'tis done
75   What we so feared he had a charge to do.
SALISBURY   The colour of the King doth come and go
Between his purpose and his conscience,
Like heralds 'twixt two dreadful battles set.°   *armies set for battle*
His passion is so ripe it needs must break.°   *burst (like a boil)*
80 PEMBROKE   And when it breaks, I fear will issue thence
The foul corruption° of a sweet child's death.   *pus*
KING JOHN [*coming forward*]   We cannot hold° mortality's strong hand.   *hold back*
Good lords, although my will to give is living,
The suit which you demand is gone and dead.
85   He tells us Arthur is deceased tonight.°   *last night*
SALISBURY   Indeed we feared his sickness was past cure.
PEMBROKE   Indeed we heard how near his death he was,
Before the child himself felt he was sick.
This must be answered,° either here or hence.°   *answered for / in heaven*
90 KING JOHN   Why do you bend such solemn brows on me?
Think you I bear the shears of destiny?[9]
Have I commandment on the pulse of life?
SALISBURY   It is apparent° foul play, and 'tis shame   *blatant*
That greatness should so grossly offer° it.   *brazenly flaunt*
95   So thrive it in your game;[1] and so, farewell.
PEMBROKE   Stay yet, Lord Salisbury; I'll go with thee,
And find th'inheritance of this poor child,
His little kingdom of a forcèd° grave.   *violently imposed*
That blood which owed° the breadth of all this isle   *owned (by right)*
100   Three foot of it doth hold. Bad world the while.°   *while such deeds occur*

---

8. *Which . . . liberty:* Which we ask for ourselves only
insofar as concern for our benefit, which depends on
you, leads to the conclusion that it is to your benefit to
free him.

9. The shears with which, in Greek mythology, the
Fates cut the thread of life.
1. May you suffer a similar fate.

This must not be thus borne. This will break out°   *break out in conflict*
To all our sorrows; and ere long, I doubt.°   *fear*
        Exeunt [PEMBROKE, SALISBURY, *and other lords*]
KING JOHN   They burn in indignation. I repent.
There is no sure foundation set on blood,
105   No certain life achieved by others' death.
        Enter [*a*] MESSENGER
A fearful eye thou hast. Where is that blood
That I have seen inhabit in those cheeks?
So foul a sky° clears not without a storm;   *(his face)*
Pour down thy weather: how goes all° in France?   *everything; everyone*
110 MESSENGER   From France to England. Never such a power
For any foreign preparation°   *military expedition*
Was levied in the body of a land.
The copy° of your speed is learned by them,   *example*
For when you should be told they do prepare,
115 The tidings comes that they are all arrived.
KING JOHN   O, where hath our intelligence° been drunk?   *spy network*
Where hath it slept? Where is my mother's ear,
That such an army could be drawn in France,
And she not hear of it?
MESSENGER   My liege, her ear
120 Is stopped with dust. The first of April died
Your noble mother. And as I hear, my lord,
The Lady Constance in a frenzy died
Three days before; but this from rumour's tongue
I idly heard; if true or false I know not.
125 KING JOHN   Withhold thy speed,° dreadful Occasion;°   *Slow down / events*
O, make a league with me till I have pleased
My discontented peers. What, Mother dead?
How wildly then walks my estate° in France!—   *fare my possessions*
Under whose conduct came those powers of France
130 That thou for truth giv'st out° are landed here?   *claim*
MESSENGER   Under the Dauphin.
        Enter [*the*] BASTARD *and* PETER OF POMFRET[2]
KING JOHN   Thou hast made me giddy
With these ill tidings. [*To the* BASTARD] Now, what says the world
To your proceedings?° Do not seek to stuff   *(monastic pillaging)*
My head with more ill news, for it is full.
135 BASTARD   But if you be afeard to hear the worst,
Then let the worst, unheard, fall on your head.
KING JOHN   Bear with me, cousin, for I was amazed°   *confused; stunned*
Under the tide;° but now I breathe again   *sea (of bad tidings)*
Aloft the flood, and can give audience
140 To any tongue, speak it of what it will.
BASTARD   How I have sped° among the clergymen   *fared*
The sums I have collected shall express.
But as I travelled hither through the land,
I find the people strangely fantasied,°   *full of peculiar ideas*
145 Possessed with rumours, full of idle° dreams,   *foolish*
Not knowing what they fear, but full of fear.
And here's a prophet that I brought with me
From forth the streets of Pomfret, whom I found

2. Modern Pontefract, west Yorkshire.

With many hundreds treading on his heels;
150 To whom he sung, in rude,° harsh-sounding rhymes,   *unpolished*
That ere the next Ascension Day³ at noon
Your highness should deliver up° your crown.   *give up*
KING JOHN Thou idle dreamer, wherefore didst thou so?
PETER OF POMFRET Foreknowing that the truth will fall out so.
155 KING JOHN Hubert, away with him! Imprison him,
And on that day, at noon, whereon he says
I shall yield up my crown, let him be hanged.
Deliver him to safety,° and return,   *custody*
For I must use thee. [*Exeunt* HUBERT *and* PETER OF POMFRET]
O my gentle cousin,
160 Hear'st thou the news abroad, who are arrived?
BASTARD The French, my lord: men's mouths are full of it.
Besides, I met Lord Bigot and Lord Salisbury
With eyes as red° as new-enkindled fire,   *(in rage)*
And others more, going to seek the grave
165 Of Arthur, whom they say is killed tonight°   *last night*
On your suggestion.
KING JOHN   Gentle kinsman, go
And thrust thyself into their companies.
I have a way to win their loves again.
Bring them before me.
BASTARD   I will seek them out.
170 KING JOHN Nay, but make haste, the better foot before.°   *go quickly*
O, let me have no subject° enemies   *subjects who are my*
When adverse foreigners affright my towns
With dreadful pomp of stout invasion!
Be Mercury, set feathers to thy heels,⁴
175 And fly like thought° from them to me again.   *(proverbially swift)*
BASTARD The spirit of the time° shall teach me speed.   *Exit*   *present occasion*
KING JOHN Spoke like a sprightful° noble gentleman!—   *spirited*
Go after him, for he perhaps shall need
Some messenger betwixt me and the peers,
180 And be thou he.
MESSENGER With all my heart, my liege.   [*Exit*]
KING JOHN My mother dead!
            Enter HUBERT
HUBERT My lord, they say five moons° were seen tonight,   *(an ominous portent)*
Four fixèd, and the fifth did whirl about
185 The other four in wondrous motion.
KING JOHN Five moons?
HUBERT   Old men and beldams° in the streets   *crones*
Do prophesy upon it dangerously.
Young Arthur's death is common in their mouths,
And when they talk of him they shake their heads,
190 And whisper one another in the ear;
And he that speaks doth grip the hearer's wrist,
Whilst he that hears makes fearful action,°   *shows fear*
With wrinkled brows, with nods, with rolling eyes.
I saw a smith stand with his hammer, thus,
195 The whilst his iron did on the anvil cool,

---

3. The Thursday, forty days after Easter, on which   4. Mercury, swift messenger of the Roman gods, wore
Christ is supposed to have ascended to heaven.   winged sandals.

With open mouth swallowing a tailor's news,
Who, with his shears and measure in his hand,
Standing on slippers which his nimble haste
Had falsely thrust upon contrary° feet,   the wrong
200   Told of a many thousand warlike French
That were embattailèd° and ranked in Kent.   in battle order
Another lean unwashed artificer°   artisan
Cuts off his° tale, and talks of Arthur's death.   (the tailor's)
KING JOHN   Why seek'st thou to possess me with these fears?
205   Why urgest thou so oft young Arthur's death?
Thy hand hath murdered him. I had a mighty cause
To wish him dead, but thou hadst none to kill him.
HUBERT   No had,° my lord? Why, did you not provoke me?   Hadn't I
KING JOHN   It is the curse of kings to be attended
210   By slaves that take their humours° for a warrant   whims
To break within the bloody house of life,⁵
And on the winking° of authority   hint; lapse
To understand a law,° to know the meaning   To infer a command
Of dangerous majesty, when perchance it frowns
215   More upon humour than advisèd respect.°   considered opinion
HUBERT   Here is your hand° and seal for what I did.   signature
      [He shows a paper]
KING JOHN   O, when the last account 'twixt heaven and earth
Is to be made,⁶ then shall this hand and seal
Witness against us to damnation!
220   How oft the sight of means to do ill deeds
Make deeds ill done! Hadst not thou been by,°   on hand
A fellow by the hand of nature marked,°   (by ugliness)
Quoted,° and signed° to do a deed of shame,   Noted / marked
This murder had not come into my mind.
225   But taking note of thy abhorred aspect,°   appearance
Finding thee fit for bloody villainy,
Apt, liable° to be employed in danger,°   suitable / doing harm
I faintly broke° with thee of Arthur's death;   vaguely spoke
And thou, to be endearèd to a king,
230   Made it no conscience° to destroy a prince.   no matter of conscience
HUBERT   My lord—
KING JOHN   Hadst thou but shook thy head or made a pause
When I spake darkly° what I purposèd,   insinuated
Or turned an eye of doubt upon my face,
235   As° bid me tell my tale in express° words,   As if to / plain
Deep shame had struck me dumb, made me break off,
And those thy fears might have wrought fears in me.
But thou didst understand me by my signs,
And didst in signs again parley° with sin;   negotiate
240   Yea, without stop, didst let thy heart consent,
And consequently thy rude° hand to act   rough
The deed which both our tongues held vile° to name.   refused
Out of my sight, and never see me more!
My nobles leave me, and my state is braved,°   challenged
245   Even at my gates, with ranks of foreign powers;
Nay, in the body of this fleshly land,°   (John's body)

---

5. The human body, which contains blood and which   6. when . . . made: when Judgment Day arrives.
murder makes bloody.

This kingdom, this confine° of blood and breath,   *territory*
Hostility and civil tumult reigns
Between my conscience and my cousin's death.

250   HUBERT   Arm you against your other enemies;
I'll make a peace between your soul and you.
Young Arthur is alive. This hand of mine
Is yet a maiden° and an innocent hand,   *virgin*
Not painted with the crimson spots of blood.

255   Within this bosom never entered yet
The dreadful motion° of a murderous thought;   *impulse*
And you have slandered nature° in my form,°   *my nature / appearance*
Which, howsoever rude exteriorly,
Is yet the cover of a fairer mind

260   Than to be butcher of an innocent child.

KING JOHN   Doth Arthur live? O, haste thee to the peers;
Throw this report° on their incensèd° rage,   *(like water) / burning*
And make them tame to their obedience.°   *(to John)*
Forgive the comment that my passion made

265   Upon thy feature,° for my rage was blind,   *features*
And foul imaginary eyes of blood[7]
Presented thee more hideous than thou art.
O, answer not, but to my closet° bring   *private room*
The angry lords with all expedient° haste.   *quick*

270   I conjure° thee but slowly; run more fast.   *Exeunt [severally]*   *urge*

4.3

Enter ARTHUR *[Duke of Brittaine] on the walls [dis-*
guised as a ship-boy]

ARTHUR   The wall is high, and yet will I leap down.
Good ground, be pitiful, and hurt me not.
There's few or none do know me; if they did,
This ship-boy's semblance° hath disguised me quite.°   *disguise / completely*

5   I am afraid, and yet I'll venture it.
If I get down and do not break my limbs,
I'll find a thousand shifts° to get away.   *stratagems*
As good to die and go, as die and stay.
    [He leaps down]
O me! My uncle's spirit is in these stones.

10   Heaven take my soul, and England keep my bones!
                                    [He] dies

Enter [the Earls of] PEMBROKE *[and]* SALISBURY, *and*
[Lord] BIGOT

SALISBURY   Lords, I will meet him° at Saint Edmundsbury.[1]   *(the Dauphin)*
It is our safety,° and we must embrace   *means of safety*
This gentle offer of the perilous time.

PEMBROKE   Who brought that letter from the Cardinal?°   *Pandolf*

15   SALISBURY   The Count Melun, a noble lord of France,
Who's private with° me of the Dauphin's love;   *Who has confided in*
'Tis much more general° than these lines import.   *much greater*

BIGOT   Tomorrow morning let us meet him then.

SALISBURY   Or rather, then set forward, for 'twill be

20   Two long days' journey, lords, or ere° we meet.   *before*

7. John's, bloody from rage; Hubert's, bloody from   **4.3 Location**: Outside the castle.
guilt; Arthur's, bloody from murder.   1. Bury St. Edmunds, Suffolk (a place of pilgrimage).

Enter [the] BASTARD

BASTARD   Once more today well met, distempered° lords.   *ill-humored*
The King by me requests your presence straight.°   *immediately*
SALISBURY   The King hath dispossessed himself of us.
We will not line his thin bestainèd cloak
25   With our pure honours, nor attend the foot
That leaves the print of blood where'er it walks.
Return and tell him so; we know the worst.
BASTARD   Whate'er you think, good words I think were best.
SALISBURY   Our griefs and not our manners reason now.
30   BASTARD   But there is little reason in your grief.
Therefore 'twere reason° you had manners now.   *reasonable*
PEMBROKE   Sir, sir, impatience hath his privilege.°   *its particular right*
BASTARD   'Tis true—to hurt his master, no man else.[2]
SALISBURY   This is the prison.
[He sees Arthur's body]
What is he lies here?
35   PEMBROKE   O death, made proud with pure and princely beauty!
The earth had not a hole° to hide this deed.   *grave*
SALISBURY   Murder, as° hating what himself hath done,   *as though*
Doth lay it open° to urge on revenge.   *on public display*
BIGOT   Or when he° doomed this beauty to a grave,   *(murder)*
40   Found it too precious-princely for a grave.
SALISBURY *[to the* BASTARD]   Sir Richard, what think you? You have beheld.
Or have you° read or heard; or could you think,   *Have you either*
Or do you almost think, although you see,
That you do see? Could thought, without this object,
45   Form such another?[3] This is the very top,
The height, the crest,° or crest unto the crest,   *(atop a coat of arms)*
Of murder's arms; this is the bloodiest shame,
The wildest savagery, the vilest stroke
That ever wall-eyed° wrath or staring rage   *glaring*
50   Presented to the tears of soft remorse.°   *pity*
PEMBROKE   All murders past do stand excused in° this,   *in comparison with*
And this, so sole° and so unmatchable,   *unique*
Shall give a holiness, a purity,
To the yet-unbegotten sin of times,°   *the future*
55   And prove a deadly bloodshed but a jest,
Exampled by° this heinous spectacle.   *Given the precedent of*
BASTARD   It is a damnèd and a bloody work,
The graceless° action of a heavy° hand—   *impious / an oppressive*
If that it be the work of any hand.
60   SALISBURY   If that it be the work of any hand?
We had a kind of light° what would ensue: *premonition*
It is the shameful work of Hubert's hand,
The practice° and the purpose of the King;   *plot*
From whose obedience I forbid my soul,
65   Kneeling before this ruin of sweet life,
And breathing to his breathless excellence
The incense of a vow, a holy vow,
Never to taste the pleasures of the world,

---

2. Angry words hurt no one but the speaker (proverbial).
3. *Or do . . . another:* Could you even approach the thought of what you actually see here? Without seeing Arthur's body, would it be possible to imagine such a sight?

Never to be infected with delight,
70 Nor conversant with ease and idleness,
Till I have set a glory to this hand°   (his own; Arthur's)
By giving it the worship° of revenge   honor
PEMBROKE *and* BIGOT   Our souls religiously confirm thy words.
        Enter HUBERT
HUBERT   Lords, I am hot with haste in seeking you.
75 Arthur doth live; the King hath sent for you.
SALISBURY   O, he is bold, and blushes not at death!—
Avaunt,° thou hateful villain, get thee gone!   Begone
HUBERT   I am no villain.
SALISBURY   Must I rob the law?[4]
        [*He draws his sword*]
BASTARD   Your sword is bright,° sir; put it up° again.   unused / sheathe it
80 SALISBURY   Not till I sheathe it in a murderer's skin.
HUBERT [*drawing his sword*]   Stand back, Lord Salisbury, stand back, I say!
By heaven, I think my sword's as sharp as yours.
I would not have you, lord, forget yourself,[5]
Nor tempt° the danger of my true° defence,   test / honest; able
85 Lest I, by marking of° your rage, forget   responding to
Your worth, your greatness and nobility.
BIGOT   Out, dunghill! Dar'st thou brave° a nobleman?   defy
HUBERT   Not for my life; but yet I dare defend
My innocent life against an emperor.
SALISBURY   Thou art a murderer.
90 HUBERT   Do not prove me so;°   (by making me kill)
Yet° I am none. Whose tongue soe'er speaks false,   Up to now
Not truly speaks; who speaks not truly, lies.
PEMBROKE   Cut him to pieces!
BASTARD [*drawing his sword*]   Keep the peace, I say!
SALISBURY   Stand by,° or I shall gall° you, Falconbridge.   aside / wound
95 BASTARD   Thou wert better gall the devil, Salisbury.
If thou but frown on me, or stir thy foot,
Or teach thy hasty spleen° to do me shame,   temper
I'll strike thee dead. Put up thy sword betime,°   immediately
Or I'll so maul you and your toasting-iron°   sword (belittling)
100 That you shall think the devil is come from hell.
BIGOT   What wilt thou do, renownèd Falconbridge,
Second° a villain and a murderer?   Back up
HUBERT   Lord Bigot, I am none.
BIGOT   Who killed this prince?
HUBERT   'Tis not an hour since I left him well.
105 I honoured him, I loved him, and will weep
My date° of life out for his sweet life's loss.   term
SALISBURY   Trust not those cunning waters of his eyes,
For villainy is not without such rheum,
And he, long traded° in it, makes it seem   experienced
110 Like rivers of remorse and innocency.
Away with me, all you whose souls abhor
Th'uncleanly savours° of a slaughter-house,   odors
For I am stifled with this smell of sin.
BIGOT   Away toward Bury,° to the Dauphin there.   Bury St. Edmunds

4. Deprive the law of its due by killing Hubert.
5. Lose self-control; forget your rank (it not being hon-   orable for a lord to challenge a commoner, or vice versa, as lines 85–85 suggest).

115   PEMBROKE   There, tell the King, he may enquire° us out.   *seek*

                 Exeunt Lords [PEMBROKE, SALISBURY, *and* BIGOT]

  BASTARD   Here's a good world! Knew you of this fair work?
    Beyond the infinite and boundless reach
    Of mercy, if thou didst this deed of death
    Art thou damned, Hubert.

120   HUBERT   Do but hear me, sir.

  BASTARD   Ha! I'll tell thee what:
    Thou'rt damned as black—nay nothing is so black—
    Thou art more deep damned than Prince Lucifer;
    There is not yet so ugly a fiend of hell

125   As thou shalt be if thou didst kill this child.

  HUBERT   Upon my soul—

  BASTARD   If thou didst but consent
    To this most cruel act, do but despair;⁶
    And if thou want'st° a cord, the smallest thread   *lack*
    That ever spider twisted from her womb

130   Will serve to strangle thee; a rush° will be a beam   *reed*
    To hang thee on; or wouldst thou° drown thyself,   *if you wish to*
    Put but a little water in a spoon
    And it shall be, as all the ocean,
    Enough to stifle such a villain up.

135   I do suspect thee very grievously.

  HUBERT   If I in act, consent, or sin of thought
    Be guilty of the stealing that sweet breath
    Which was embounded° in this beauteous clay,°   *enclosed / (Arthur's body)*
    Let hell want pains enough to torture me.
    I left him well.

140   BASTARD   Go bear him in thine arms.
    I am amazed,° methinks, and lose my way   *bewildered*
    Among the thorns and dangers of this world.

        [HUBERT *takes up* ARTHUR *in his arms*]

    How easy dost thou take all England up!
    From forth° this morsel of dead royalty,   *Out of*

145   The life, the right, and truth of all this realm
    Is fled to heaven, and England now is left
    To tug and scramble, and to part by th' teeth
    The unowed interest⁷ of proud swelling state.
    Now for the bare-picked bone of majesty

150   Doth doggèd° war bristle his angry crest,⁸   *cruel*
    And snarleth in the gentle eyes of peace;
    Now powers from home° and discontents at home   *foreign armies*
    Meet in one line,° and vast confusion waits,°   *rank / chaos awaits*
    As doth a raven on a sick-fall'n beast,

155   The imminent decay of wrested pomp.°   *usurped power*
    Now happy he whose cloak and cincture° can   *belt*
    Hold out this tempest. Bear away that child,
    And follow me with speed. I'll to the King.
    A thousand businesses are brief in hand,°   *need urgent action*

160   And heaven itself doth frown upon the land. *Exeunt* [*severally*]

---

6. Lose all hope of salvation and hence commit suicide.
7. Contested or unowned possession; obedience ("interest") that is not due ("unowed"), because John

lacks legitimacy.
8. Dog's hackles (hairs on neck and back); crest on a coat of arms.

5.1

[*Flourish.*] *Enter* KING JOHN *and* [*Cardinal*] PANDOLF,
[*with*] *attendants*

KING JOHN [*giving* PANDOLF *the crown*] Thus have I yielded up
    into your hand
    The circle of my glory.

PANDOLF [*giving back the crown*] Take again
    From this my hand, as holding of° the Pope,   *as land rented from*
    Your sovereign greatness and authority.

5   KING JOHN Now keep your holy word: go meet the French,
    And from his Holiness° use all your power   *the Pope*
    To stop their marches 'fore we are enflamed.
    Our discontented counties° do revolt,   *shires; nobles*
    Our people quarrel with obedience,
10   Swearing allegiance and the love of soul
    To stranger° blood, to foreign royalty.   *foreign*
    This inundation of mistempered humour
    Rests by you only to be qualified.[1]
    Then pause not, for the present time's so sick
15   That present° med'cine must be ministered,   *immediate*
    Or overthrow incurable ensues.

PANDOLF It was my breath° that blew this tempest up,   *words*
    Upon your stubborn usage of the Pope,
    But since you are a gentle convertite,°   *convert*
20   My tongue shall hush again this storm of war
    And make fair weather in your blust'ring land.
    On this Ascension Day, remember well,
    Upon your oath of service to the Pope,
    Go I to make the French lay down their arms.
                Exeunt [*all but* KING JOHN][2]
25   KING JOHN Is this Ascension Day? Did not the prophet
    Say that before Ascension Day at noon
    My crown I should give off?[3] Even so I have.
    I did suppose it should be on constraint,
    But, heaven be thanked, it is but voluntary.
             Enter BASTARD
30   BASTARD All Kent hath yielded; nothing there holds out
    But Dover Castle. London hath received,
    Like a kind host, the Dauphin and his powers.°   *army*
    Your nobles will not hear you, but are gone
    To offer service to your enemy;
35   And wild amazement hurries° up and down   *confusion drives*
    The little number of your doubtful° friends.   *untrustworthy; fearful*

KING JOHN Would not my lords return to me again
    After they heard young Arthur was alive?

BASTARD They found him dead and cast into the streets,
40   An empty casket, where the jewel of life
    By some damned hand was robbed and ta'en away.

KING JOHN That villain Hubert told me he did live.

BASTARD So on my soul he did, for aught he knew.
    But wherefore do you droop? Why look you sad?

5.1 Location: John's court.
1. *This . . . qualified:* Only you can cure this surge of diseased behavior.

2. F leaves the attendants onstage with John. But even in that case, this speech could easily be a soliloquy.
3. See 4.2.147–52.

45 Be great in act as you have been in thought.
Let not the world see fear and sad distrust
Govern the motion of a kingly eye.
Be stirring as the time,[4] be fire with° fire;   *against*
Threaten the threat'ner, and outface the brow
50 Of bragging horror. So shall inferior eyes,
That borrow their behaviours from the great,
Grow great by your example, and put on
The dauntless spirit of resolution.
Away, and glisten like the god of war
55 When he intendeth to become the field.°   *adorn the battlefield*
Show boldness and aspiring confidence.
What, shall they seek the lion in his den
And fright him there, and make him tremble there?
O, let it not be said! Forage,° and run   *Range (for prey)*
60 To meet displeasure farther from the doors,
And grapple with him ere he come so nigh.
KING JOHN   The legate of the Pope hath been with me,
And I have made a happy peace with him,
And he hath promised to dismiss the powers
Led by the Dauphin.
65 BASTARD   O inglorious league!
Shall we, upon the footing of our land,°   *standing on our own soil*
Send fair-play orders,° and make compromise,   *equitable conditions*
Insinuation,° parley, and base truce   *Ingratiating proposals*
To arms invasive?° Shall a beardless boy,   *invading*
70 A cockered silken wanton,° brave our fields   *spoiled dandyish child*
And flesh his spirit[5] in a warlike soil,
Mocking the air with colours idly° spread,   *carelessly*
And find no check? Let us, my liege, to arms!
Perchance the Cardinal cannot make your peace,
75 Or if he do, let it at least be said
They saw we had a purpose of defence.
KING JOHN   Have thou the ordering of this present time.
BASTARD   Away, then, with good courage! [*Aside*] Yet I know
Our party may well meet a prouder foe.[6]   *Exeunt*

5.2

*Enter [marching] (in arms) [*LOUIS THE*] DAUPHIN, [the
Earl of] *SALISBURY, [Count] *MELUN, [the Earl of] *PEM-
BROKE, [and Lord] *BIGOT, [with] soldiers*
LOUIS THE DAUPHIN   My Lord Melun, let this[1] be copied out,
And keep it safe for our remembrance.
Return the precedent° to these lords again,   *original copy*
That having our fair order° written down,   *arrangements*
5 Both they and we, perusing o'er these notes,
May know wherefore we took the sacrament[2]
And keep our faiths firm and inviolable.
SALISBURY   Upon our sides it never shall be broken.
And, noble Dauphin, albeit we swear

4. Be as vigorous as the times demand.
5. Initiate himself in bloodshed (in the "soil," as a
sword is "fleshed" in a body).
6. Is well able to handle an even stronger enemy than
the French; may be up against an enemy more powerful than we are.
5.2 Location: St. Edmundsbury (Bury St. Edmunds) in
Suffolk.
1. This agreement with the English lords.
2. The Mass, taken as a solemn dedication to the task.

10	A voluntary zeal° and an unurgèd° faith	commitment / unforced
	To your proceedings, yet believe me, Prince,
	I am not glad that such a sore of time
	Should seek a plaster° by contemnèd° revolt,	bandage / despised
	And heal the inveterate canker° of one wound	infection
15	By making many. O, it grieves my soul
	That I must draw this metal° from my side	(his sword)
	To be a widow-maker! O, and there
	Where honourable rescue and defence
	Cries out upon³ the name of Salisbury!
20	But such is the infection of the time,
	That for the health and physic° of our right,	cure
	We cannot deal but with the very hand
	Of stern injustice and confusèd wrong.⁴
	And is't not pity, O my grievèd friends,
25	That we the sons and children of this isle
	Was born to see so sad an hour as this,
	Wherein we step after a stranger,° march	foreigner
	Upon her gentle bosom, and fill up
	Her enemies' ranks? I must withdraw and weep
30	Upon the spot° of this enforcèd cause—	place; stain
	To grace the gentry of a land remote,
	And follow unacquainted colours° here.	unfamiliar banners
	What, here? O nation, that thou couldst remove;°	move elsewhere
	That Neptune's arms° who clippeth thee about°	the sea / embraces you
35	Would bear thee from the knowledge of thyself
	And gripple° thee unto a pagan shore,	join
	Where these two Christian armies might combine
	The blood of malice in a vein of league,°	(against a pagan foe)
	And not to spend° it so unneighbourly.	shed
40	LOUIS THE DAUPHIN A noble temper° dost thou show in this,	disposition
	And great affections,° wrestling in thy bosom,	emotions; loyalties
	Doth make an earthquake of nobility.°	out of a noble nature
	O, what a noble combat hast thou fought
	Between compulsion° and a brave respect!°	necessity / patriotism
45	Let me wipe off this honourable dew
	That silverly doth progress on thy cheeks.
	My heart hath melted at a lady's tears,
	Being an ordinary inundation;
	But this effusion of such manly drops,
50	This shower blown up by tempest of the soul,
	Startles mine eyes, and makes me more amazed
	Than had I seen the vaulty° top of heaven	arched
	Figured quite o'er° with burning meteors.⁵	Adorned thoroughly
	Lift up thy brow, renownèd Salisbury,
55	And with a great heart heave away this storm;
	Commend° these waters to those baby eyes	Leave
	That never saw the giant° world enraged,	grown-up
	Nor met with Fortune other than at feasts,
	Full warm of° blood, of mirth, of gossiping.	with
60	Come, come, for thou shalt thrust thy hand as deep

3. Exclaim against; appeal to.
4. We . . . wrong: We cannot act except with unjust means; or, possibly, we cannot act except against the
unjust hand of John.
5. Meteors were seen as portents of disaster.

Into the purse of rich prosperity
As Louis himself. So, nobles, shall you all
That knit your sinews° to the strength of mine.   *join your powers*
[*A trumpet sounds*]
And even there methinks an angel[6] spake!
    Enter [*Cardinal*] PANDOLF

65   Look where the holy legate comes apace,
To give us warrant from the hand of heaven,°   *the Pope; God*
And on our actions set the name of right
With holy breath.

PANDOLF   Hail, noble prince of France!
The next° is this. King John hath reconciled   *next thing I have to say*
70   Himself to Rome; his spirit is come in°   *has submitted*
That so stood out against the Holy Church,
The great metropolis and See of Rome;
Therefore thy threat'ning colours° now wind up,°   *banners / put away*
And tame the savage spirit of wild war,
75   That like a lion fostered up at hand°   *by human hand*
It may lie gently at the foot of peace,
And be no further harmful than in show.

LOUIS THE DAUPHIN   Your grace shall pardon me: I will not back.°   *go back*
I am too high-born to be propertied,°   *manipulated*
80   To be a secondary° at control,   *subordinate*
Or useful serving-man and instrument
To any sovereign state° throughout the world.   *(the papacy)*
Your breath first kindled the dead coal of wars
Between this chastised kingdom and myself,
85   And brought in matter° that should feed this fire;   *fuel*
And now 'tis far too huge to be blown out
With that same weak wind which enkindled it.
You taught me how to know the face of right,°   *my rightful claim*
Acquainted me with interest° to this land,   *my claim*
90   Yea, thrust this enterprise into my heart;
And come ye now to tell me John hath made
His peace with Rome? What is that peace to me?
I, by the honour of my marriage bed,
After young Arthur, claim this land for mine;
95   And now it is half conquered, must I back
Because that John hath made his peace with Rome?
Am I Rome's slave? What penny hath Rome borne,°   *contributed*
What men provided, what munition sent
To underprop° this action? Is't not I   *support*
100   That undergo this charge? Who else but I,
And such as to my claim are liable,°   *are liable to me*
Sweat in this business and maintain° this war?   *pay for*
Have I not heard these islanders shout out
'Vive le Roi!' as I have banked their towns?
105   Have I not here the best cards for the game,
To win this easy match played for a crown?

---

6. The trumpet, an editorial addition, is seen as an angel's affirmation of the Dauphin's speech. The stage direction may not be necessary, however. "Angel" might also mean "gold coin," developing the money imagery of lines 61–63—"purse of rich prosperity," "nobles" (also a coin), and perhaps "sinews" (where "sinews of war" connotes money). The Dauphin's point, perhaps made in an aside, would be that money talks in persuading the English peers to join his cause.

And shall I now give o'er the yielded set?[7]
No, no, on my soul, it never shall be said.

PANDOLF You look but on the outside of this work.

110 LOUIS THE DAUPHIN Outside or inside, I will not return
Till my attempt° so much be glorified   *warlike enterprise*
As to my ample hope was promisèd
Before I drew° this gallant head of war,°   *gathered / army*
And culled° these fiery spirits from the world   *picked out*
115 To outlook conquest° and to win renown   *To defy defeat*
Even in the jaws of danger and of death.

    [*A trumpet sounds*]

What lusty° trumpet thus doth summon us?   *vigorous*

    Enter [*the*] BASTARD

BASTARD According to the fair play° of the world,   *code of chivalry*
Let me have audience; I am sent to speak.
120 My holy lord of Milan, from the King
I come to learn how you have dealt for him,
And as° you answer I do know the scope   *according to how*
And warrant limited unto my tongue.

PANDOLF The Dauphin is too wilful-opposite,°   *stubbornly hostile*
125 And will not temporize with° my entreaties.   *will not heed*
He flatly says he'll not lay down his arms.

BASTARD By all the blood that ever fury breathed,
The youth says well. Now hear our English king,
For thus his royalty doth speak in me.
130 He is prepared, and reason too he should.°   *as he should be*
This apish and unmannerly approach,
This harnessed masque and unadvisèd revel,[8]
This unhaired° sauciness and boyish troops,   *youthful*
The King doth smile at, and is well prepared
135 To whip this dwarfish war, these pigmy arms,
From out the circle° of his territories.   *confines*
That hand which had the strength even at your door
To cudgel you and make you take the hatch,°   *beat a hasty retreat*
To dive like buckets in concealèd wells,
140 To crouch in litter° of your stable planks,   *animal's bedding*
To lie like pawns° locked up in chests and trunks,   *pawned goods*
To hug° with swine, to seek sweet safety out   *bed down*
In vaults and prisons, and to thrill° and shake   *shiver*
Even at the crying of your nation's crow,°   *the cock*
145 Thinking his voice an armèd Englishman;
Shall that victorious hand be feebled here
That in your chambers° gave you chastisement?   *your own home*
No! Know the gallant monarch is in arms,
And like an eagle o'er his eyrie towers°   *soars over his nest*
150 To souse° annoyance that comes near his nest.   *swoop down on*

    [*To the English lords*]

And you degenerate, you ingrate revolts,°   *ungrateful rebels*
You bloody Neros, ripping up the womb
Of your dear mother England,[9] blush for shame;

---

7. *'Vive . . . set*: The Dauphin uses an extended card-playing metaphor, including "Vive le Roi" ("Long live the King"), "banked" (put in the bank, won; but also, sailed by the banks of or perhaps besieged), "cards," "game," "match played," "crown" (the coin as a stake in a card game;

John's crown), and "yielded set" (the hand already won).
8. This courtly entertainment in armor and rashly undertaken revelry.
9. The Roman Emperor Nero was supposed to have murdered his mother by ripping open her womb.

For your own ladies and pale-visaged maids
155 Like Amazons¹ come tripping after drums;
Their thimbles into armèd gauntlets° change,   *steel-plated gloves*
Their needles to lances, and their gentle hearts
To fierce and bloody inclination.°   *disposition*
LOUIS THE DAUPHIN   There end thy brave,° and turn thy face°   *defiance / return*
    in peace.
160 We grant thou canst outscold us. Fare thee well:
We hold our time too precious to be spent
With such a brabbler.°   *quarreler*
PANDOLF   Give me leave to speak.
BASTARD   No, I will speak.
LOUIS THE DAUPHIN   We will attend° to neither.—   *listen*
Strike up the drums, and let the tongue of war
165 Plead for our interest and our being here.
BASTARD   Indeed your drums, being beaten, will cry out;
And so shall you, being beaten. Do but start
An echo with the clamour of thy drum,
And even at hand a drum is ready braced°   *ready to be struck*
170 That shall reverberate all as loud as thine.
Sound but another, and another shall
As loud as thine rattle the welkin's° ear,   *sky's*
And mock° the deep-mouthed thunder; for at hand,   *outrival*
Not trusting to this halting° legate here,   *wavering*
175 Whom he hath used rather for sport than need,
Is warlike John; and in his forehead sits
A bare-ribbed Death, whose office° is this day   *task*
To feast upon whole thousands of the French.
LOUIS THE DAUPHIN   Strike up our drums to find this danger out.
180 BASTARD   And thou shalt find it, Dauphin, do not doubt.
        [*Drums beat.*] *Exeunt* [*the* BASTARD *at one door,*
            all the rest, marching, at another door]

                            5.3
        Alarum. Enter [KING] JOHN [*at one door*] *and* HUBERT
            [*at another door*]
KING JOHN   How goes the day with us? O, tell me, Hubert.
HUBERT   Badly, I fear. How fares your majesty?
KING JOHN   This fever that hath troubled me so long
Lies heavy on me. O, my heart is sick!
        Enter a MESSENGER
5 MESSENGER   My lord, your valiant kinsman Falconbridge
Desires your majesty to leave the field,
And send him word by me which way you go.
KING JOHN   Tell him toward Swineshead,° to the abbey there.   *(in Lincolnshire)*
MESSENGER   Be of good comfort, for the great supply°   *reinforcements*
10 That was expected by the Dauphin here
Are wrecked three nights ago on Goodwin Sands.°   *shoals off Kent*
This news was brought to Richard,° but even now   *(the Bastard)*
The French fight coldly and retire themselves.°   *retreat*
KING JOHN   Ay me, this tyrant fever burns me up,

---

1. Female warriors of classical legend.   **5.3** Location: The battlefield.

15 And will not let me welcome this good news.
Set on toward Swineshead. To my litter straight;°   *portable bed at once*
Weakness possesseth me, and I am faint.   *Exeunt*

5.4

[*Alarum.*] *Enter* [*the Earls of*] SALISBURY [*and*] PEM-
BROKE, *and* [*Lord*] BIGOT

SALISBURY   I did not think the King so stored° with friends.   *well provided*
PEMBROKE   Up once again; put spirit in the French.
If they miscarry,° we miscarry too.   *fail*
SALISBURY   That misbegotten devil Falconbridge,
5 In spite of spite,° alone upholds the day.°   *everything / battle*
PEMBROKE   They say King John, sore° sick, hath left the field.   *grievously*

Enter [*Count*] MELUN, *wounded* [*led by a soldier*]

MELUN   Lead me to the revolts° of England here.   *rebels*
SALISBURY   When we were happy, we had other names.
PEMBROKE   It is the Count Melun.
SALISBURY   Wounded to death.
10 MELUN   Fly, noble English, you are bought and sold.°   *betrayed*
Unthread the rude eye of rebellion,[1]
And welcome home again discarded faith;
Seek out King John and fall before his feet,
For if the French be lords of° this loud° day   *win / hectic*
15 He° means to recompense the pains you take   *(Louis)*
By cutting off your heads. Thus hath he sworn,
And I with him, and many more with me,
Upon the altar at Saint Edmundsbury,
Even on that altar where we swore to you
20 Dear amity and everlasting love.
SALISBURY   May this be possible? May this be true?
MELUN   Have I not hideous death within my view,
Retaining but a quantity of life,
Which bleeds away, even as a form of wax
25 Resolveth from his figure° 'gainst the fire?   *Melts out of shape*
What in the world should make me now deceive,
Since I must lose the use of all deceit?
Why should I then be false, since it is true
That I must die here, and live hence° by truth?   *in the next world*
30 I say again, if Louis do win the day,
He is forsworn° if e'er those eyes of yours   *perjured*
Behold another daybreak in the east;
But even this night, whose black contagious breath
Already smokes about the burning cresset°   *suspended torch*
35 Of the old, feeble, and day-wearied sun,
Even this ill night your breathing shall expire,
Paying the fine of rated° treachery   *assessed (as penalty)*
Even with a treacherous fine° of all your lives,   *payment; end*
If Louis by your assistance win the day.
40 Commend me to one Hubert with your king.
The love of him, and this respect° besides,   *consideration*
For that° my grandsire was an Englishman,   *Because*

5.4 Location: Scene continues.
1. Turn back from the barbarous path of rebellion   down which you've been led (like a thread that has been inserted into the needle's eye and must be pulled out).

Awakes my conscience to confess all this;
In lieu° whereof, I pray you bear me hence   *recompense*
45 From forth the noise and rumour° of the field,   *tumult*
Where I may think the remnant of my thoughts
In peace, and part this body and my soul
With contemplation and devout desires.

SALISBURY   We do believe thee; and beshrew° my soul   *woe to*
50 But° I do love the favour° and the form   *Unless / look*
Of this most fair occasion; by the which
We will untread° the steps of damnèd flight,°   *retrace / desertion*
And like a bated° and retirèd flood,   *an abated*
Leaving our rankness° and irregular course,   *flooding*
55 Stoop low within those bounds we have o'erlooked,°   *overflowed; ignored*
And calmly run on in obedience
Even to our ocean, to our great King John.
My arm shall give thee help to bear thee hence,
For I do see the cruel pangs of death
60 Right in thine eye.—Away, my friends! New flight,°   *change of allegiance*
And happy newness that intends old right.[2]

          Exeunt

5.5

[*Alarum; retreat.*] *Enter* [LOUIS THE] DAUPHIN, *and his train*

LOUIS THE DAUPHIN   The sun of heaven, methought, was loath to set,
But stayed and made the western welkin blush,
When English measured° backward their own ground   *crossed*
In faint retire.° O, bravely came we off,[1]   *weak retreat*
5 When with a volley of our needless° shot,   *unnecessary*
After such bloody toil, we bid good night,
And wound our tatt'ring colours clearly up,[2]
Last in the field and almost lords of it.

Enter a MESSENGER

MESSENGER   Where is my prince the Dauphin?
LOUIS THE DAUPHIN   Here. What news?
10 MESSENGER   The Count Melun is slain; the English lords
By his persuasion are again fall'n off;°   *changed in allegiance*
And your supply° which you have wished so long   *supplies*
Are cast away and sunk on Goodwin Sands.
LOUIS THE DAUPHIN   Ah, foul shrewd° news! Beshrew° thy very   *harmful / Curse*
heart!
15 I did not think to be so sad tonight
As this hath made me. Who was he that said
King John did fly an hour or two before
The stumbling night[3] did part our weary powers?
MESSENGER   Whoever spoke it, it is true, my lord.
20 LOUIS THE DAUPHIN   Well, keep good quarter° and good care tonight.   *guard*
The day shall not be up so soon as I,
To try the fair adventure° of tomorrow.   *Exeunt*   *chance*

---

2. That intends to restore the ancient right—John's claim to rule and our just conduct.
5.5 Location: Scene continues.
1. We acquitted ourselves valiantly.

2. We rolled our tattered (waving) banners up without obstruction from the English.
3. That is, night that causes stumbling.

5.6

Enter [the] BASTARD *[with a light] and* HUBERT *[with a pistol], severally*

HUBERT Who's there? Speak, ho! Speak quickly, or I shoot.

BASTARD A friend. What art thou?

HUBERT   Of the part° of England.   side

BASTARD Whither dost thou go?

HUBERT   What's that to thee?
Why may not I demand of thine affairs

5   As well as thou of mine?

BASTARD   Hubert, I think.

HUBERT Thou hast a perfect° thought.   correct
I will upon all hazards° well believe   against all odds
Thou art my friend that know'st my tongue so well.
Who art thou?

10   BASTARD   Who thou wilt. An if thou please,
Thou mayst befriend me so much as to think
I come one way° of the Plantagenets.   by one parent

HUBERT Unkind remembrance!¹ Thou and eyeless° night   blind
Have done me shame. Brave soldier, pardon me

15   That any accent° breaking from thy tongue   sound
Should 'scape the true acquaintance of mine ear.

BASTARD Come, come, sans compliment.° What news abroad?   no formalities

HUBERT Why, here walk I in the black brow of night
To find you out.

BASTARD   Brief, then, and what's the news?

20   HUBERT O my sweet sir, news fitting to the night:
Black, fearful, comfortless, and horrible.

BASTARD Show me the very wound of this ill news;
I am no woman, I'll not swoon at it.

HUBERT The King, I fear, is poisoned by a monk.

25   I left him almost speechless, and broke out°   hurried away
To acquaint you with this evil, that you might
The better arm you to the sudden time°   for this emergency
Than if you had at leisure° known of this.   later

BASTARD How did he take it?° Who did taste to° him?   (poison) / (the food) for

30   HUBERT A monk, I tell you, a resolvèd villain,²
Whose bowels suddenly burst out. The King
Yet° speaks, and peradventure may recover.   Still

BASTARD Who didst thou leave to tend his majesty?

HUBERT Why, know you not? The lords are all come back,

35   And brought Prince Henry³ in their company,
At whose request the King hath pardoned them.
And they are all about his majesty.

BASTARD Withhold thine indignation, mighty heaven,
And tempt us not to bear above our power.⁴

40   I'll tell thee, Hubert, half my power this night,
Passing these flats, are taken° by the tide.   drowned
These Lincoln Washes⁵ have devourèd them;

5.6 Location: Near Swineshead Abbey.
1. Bad memory (criticizing himself for not recognizing the Bastard).
2. A "resolvèd villain" since, as the person whose job it was to protect the King by tasting his food, he knowingly took poison himself just so that he could succeed in poisoning the King.

3. John's son; later, King Henry III.
4. And don't push us (or me) past our power to endure. "Bear above our power" may hint at the Bastard's previous thoughts, here put aside, of assuming the throne himself
5. The tides of the Wash (tidal flatlands south of Lincolnshire).

Myself, well mounted, hardly° have escaped.   *barely; with trouble*
Away before!° Conduct me to the King.   *Go on ahead*
45 I doubt° he will be dead or ere° I come.   *Exeunt*   *fear / before*

5.7

Enter PRINCE HENRY, [*the Earl of*] SALISBURY, *and*
[*Lord*] BIGOT

PRINCE HENRY   It is too late. The life of all his blood
Is touched° corruptibly, and his pure° brain,   *infected / (once) lucid*
Which some suppose the soul's frail dwelling-house,
Doth by the idle° comments that it makes   *foolish*
5 Foretell the ending of mortality.°   *mortal life*
      Enter [*the Earl of*] PEMBROKE
PEMBROKE   His highness yet doth speak, and holds belief
That being brought into the open air,
It would allay the burning quality
Of that fell° poison which assaileth him.   *savage*
10 PRINCE HENRY   Let him be brought into the orchard here.—
                                  [*Exit Lord* BIGOT][1]
Doth he still rage?
PEMBROKE   He is more patient
Than when you left him. Even° now, he sung.   *Just*
PRINCE HENRY   O, vanity° of sickness! Fierce extremes°   *delusion / (of pain)*
In their continuance will not feel themselves.[2]
15 Death, having preyed upon the outward parts,°   *the body*
Leaves them invincible,° and his siege is now   *(because overcome)*
Against the mind; the which he pricks and wounds
With many legions of strange fantasies,
Which in their throng and press to that last hold°   *stronghold (the mind)*
20 Confound° themselves. 'Tis strange that death should sing.   *Destroy*
I am the cygnet° to this pale faint swan,   *young swan*
Who chants a doleful hymn to his own death,[3]
And from the organ-pipe° of frailty sings   *voice box*
His soul and body to their lasting rest.
25 SALISBURY   Be of good comfort, Prince, for you are born
To set a form upon that indigest°   *chaos*
Which he hath left so shapeless and so rude.°   *formless*
     [KING] JOHN [*is*] *brought in* [*with Lord* BIGOT *attending*]
KING JOHN   Ay marry, now° my soul hath elbow-room;   *now being outdoors*
It would not out at° windows nor at doors.   *go out through*
30 There is so hot a summer in my bosom
That all my bowels crumble up to dust;
I am a scribbled form, drawn with a pen
Upon a parchment, and against° this fire°   *before / (of poison)*
Do I shrink up.
PRINCE HENRY   How fares your majesty?
35 KING JOHN   Poisoned, ill fare!° Dead, forsook, cast off;   *food; state of things*
And none of you will bid the winter come
To thrust his icy fingers in my maw,°   *stomach; mouth; throat*
Nor let my kingdom's rivers take their course
Through my burned bosom, nor entreat the north

5.7 Location: The orchard of Swinstead Abbey.
1. F has no stage direction. Someone must fetch John:
either Bigot here or Pembroke after line 12.

2. By continuing for a long time will cease to be felt.
3. John's swan song; swans were thought to sing only
as they died.

40 　　　To make his bleak winds kiss my parchèd lips
　　　　And comfort me with cold. I do not ask you much;
　　　　I beg cold° comfort, and you are so strait°   *slight; cooling / mean*
　　　　And so ingrateful you deny me that.
　　　PRINCE HENRY   O, that there were some virtue° in my tears   *remedial power*
　　　　That might relieve you!
45 　KING JOHN   The salt in them is hot.
　　　　Within me is a hell, and there the poison
　　　　Is, as a fiend, confined to tyrannize
　　　　On unreprievable condemnèd blood.
　　　　　　　Enter [the] BASTARD
　　　BASTARD   O, I am scalded with my violent motion°   *haste*
50 　　And spleen° of speed to see your majesty!   *impetuosity*
　　　KING JOHN   O cousin, thou art come to set° mine eye.   *close*
　　　　The tackle° of my heart is cracked and burnt,   *rigging (heartstrings)*
　　　　And all the shrouds° wherewith my life should sail   *sail ropes*
　　　　Are turnèd to one thread, one little hair;
55 　　My heart hath one poor string to stay° it by,   *support*
　　　　Which holds but till thy news be utterèd,
　　　　And then all this thou seest is but a clod
　　　　And module° of confounded° royalty.   *counterfeit / destroyed*
　　　BASTARD   The Dauphin is preparing° hitherward,   *coming*
60 　　Where God He knows how we shall answer him;
　　　　For in a° night the best part of my power,   *a single*
　　　　As I upon° advantage did remove,   *to gain*
　　　　Were in the Washes all unwarily
　　　　Devourèd by the unexpected flood.
　　　　　　　[KING JOHN *dies*]
65 　SALISBURY   You breathe these dead° news in as dead an ear.   *fatal*
　　　　[*To* KING JOHN] My liege, my lord!—But° now a king, now thus.   *Just*
　　　PRINCE HENRY   Even so must I run on, and even so stop.
　　　　What surety of the world, what hope, what stay°   *support; continuation*
　　　　When this was now a king and now is clay?
70 　BASTARD [*to* KING JOHN]   Art thou gone so? I do but stay behind
　　　　To do the office° for thee of revenge,   *duty*
　　　　And then my soul shall wait on° thee to heaven,   *follow*
　　　　As it on earth hath been thy servant still.°   *always*
　　　　[*To the lords*] Now, now, you stars° that move in your right spheres,[4]   *(the nobles)*
75 　　Where be your powers?° Show now your mended faiths,°   *armies / loyalties*
　　　　And instantly return with me again,
　　　　To push destruction and perpetual shame
　　　　Out of the weak door of our fainting° land.   *dispirited*
　　　　Straight° let us seek, or straight we shall be sought.   *Immediately*
80 　　The Dauphin rages at our very heels.
　　　SALISBURY   It seems you know not, then, so much as we.
　　　　The Cardinal Pandolf is within at rest,
　　　　Who half an hour since came from the Dauphin,
　　　　And brings from him such offers of our peace
85 　　As we with honour and respect may take,
　　　　With purpose presently° to leave this war.   *immediately*
　　　BASTARD   He will the rather do it when he sees
　　　　Ourselves well-sinewed° to our own defence.   *strongly armed*
　　　SALISBURY   Nay, 'tis in a manner done already,

---

4. Proper orbits, around the King, as the stars were thought to orbit the earth.

90	For many carriages° he hath dispatched	*vehicles*
	To the sea-side, and put his cause and quarrel	
	To the disposing of the Cardinal,	
	With° whom yourself, myself, and other lords,	*To*
	If you think meet,° this afternoon will post°	*fit / hurry*
95	To consummate° this business happily.	*conclude*

BASTARD   Let it be so.—And you, my noble prince,

	With other princes° that may best be spared,	*nobles*
	Shall wait upon° your father's funeral.	*attend*

PRINCE HENRY   At Worcester must his body be interred,
For so he willed it.

100 BASTARD   Thither shall it then,

	And happily° may your sweet self put on	*with good fortune*
	The lineal state° and glory of the land,	*inherited kingship*
	To whom with all submission, on my knee,	
	I do bequeath° my faithful services	*give*
105	And true subjection everlastingly.	

[*He kneels*]

SALISBURY   And the like tender° of our love we make, *offer*

	To rest° without a spot° for evermore.	*remain / blemish*

[SALISBURY, PEMBROKE and BIGOT *kneel*]

PRINCE HENRY   I have a kind of soul that would give thanks,
And knows not how to do it but with tears.

[*He weeps*]

110	BASTARD [*rising*] O, let us pay the time but needful° woe,	*only the necessary*
	Since it hath been beforehand with our griefs.[5]	
	This England never did, nor never shall,	
	Lie at the proud foot of a conqueror	
	But° when it first did help to wound itself.	*Except*
115	Now these her princes are come home again,	
	Come the three corners of the world[6] in arms	
	And we shall shock° them. Naught shall make us rue	*resist; repel*
	If England to itself do rest but true.	

[*Flourish.*] *Exeunt* [*with the body*]

---

5. Since we have already suffered and grieved—
perhaps with the additional implication that the suffering is now over.
6. England itself is seen as the fourth corner.

The Merchant of Venice

Jew. Jew. Jew. The word echoes through *The Merchant of Venice.* The play has generated controversy for centuries. Is it anti-Semitic? Does it criticize anti-Semitism? Does it merely represent anti-Semitism without either endorsement or condemnation? Are the Christians right to call Shylock, the Jewish moneylender, a "devil," an "inexorable dog"; or is he merely the understandably resentful victim of their bigotry? Does Portia, Shylock's antagonist in the courtroom, exemplify the best in womanly virtue, or is she a manipulative virago? These questions about character suggest others that might be phrased more generally. What are the obligations of majority cultures to minorities in their midst? Do universally shared human characteristics outweigh racial and religious differences, or are such differences decisive?

Perhaps these issues seem more pressing nowadays than they did for Shakespeare. He could hardly could have predicted Nazi genocide or other modern forms of "ethnic cleansing." Nor could he have foreseen the opportunities and problems faced by multiracial societies centuries after his death. Nevertheless, by Shakespeare's time, the legacy of Jew hating in western Europe was already long and bitter. Depictions of fiendish Jews were routine in medieval and Renaissance drama; the villainous protagonist of Christopher Marlowe's *Jew of Malta,* a popular success in the early 1590s, was only the latest precedent. In 1594, shortly before Shakespeare wrote *The Merchant of Venice,* an outpouring of anti-Semitic outrage was triggered by the case of Roderigo Lopez, a Portuguese Jewish convert to Christianity accused of attempting to murder Queen Elizabeth.

Of course, the existence of anti-Semitism in sixteenth-century England says little about Shakespeare's own attitudes. He could have written *The Merchant of Venice* either to capitalize on or to criticize the prejudices of his society. Interestingly, Shakespeare had probably never encountered practicing Jews, since they had been forcibly expelled from England in the Middle Ages. And England was not alone in its intolerance. In 1492, Spain banished all non-Christians. Christians fought among themselves as well: during the sixteenth century, northern Europe saw decades of bloody conflict between Catholics and Protestants, while much of southern Europe was in the grip of the Inquisition. The impulse behind these persecutions was the conviction that a stable society required a shared belief system. A community based on consensus can indeed be impressively cohesive. Its homogeneity, however, makes it impatient of those who do not share its assumptions. Moreover, by the 1590s, when Shakespeare wrote *The Merchant of Venice,* bloody religious conflict all over Europe was making such consensus seem increasingly elusive—something obtainable, if at all, only at appalling human cost.

Possibly Venice seemed to Shakespeare to offer an alternative social prototype. Although it had no natural resources to speak of, it was the richest city in Renaissance Europe, located where the products of Asia could most conveniently be exchanged with those of western Europe. As a town of traders, Venice was full of foreigners: Turks, Jews, Arabs, Africans, Christians of various nationalities and denominations. By sixteenth-century standards, the city was unusually tolerant of diversity. This relative toleration was intimately linked with the city's wealth: its legal guarantees of fair treatment for all were designed to keep its markets running smoothly. Antonio tells Solanio:

> The Duke cannot deny the course of law,
> For the commodity that strangers have

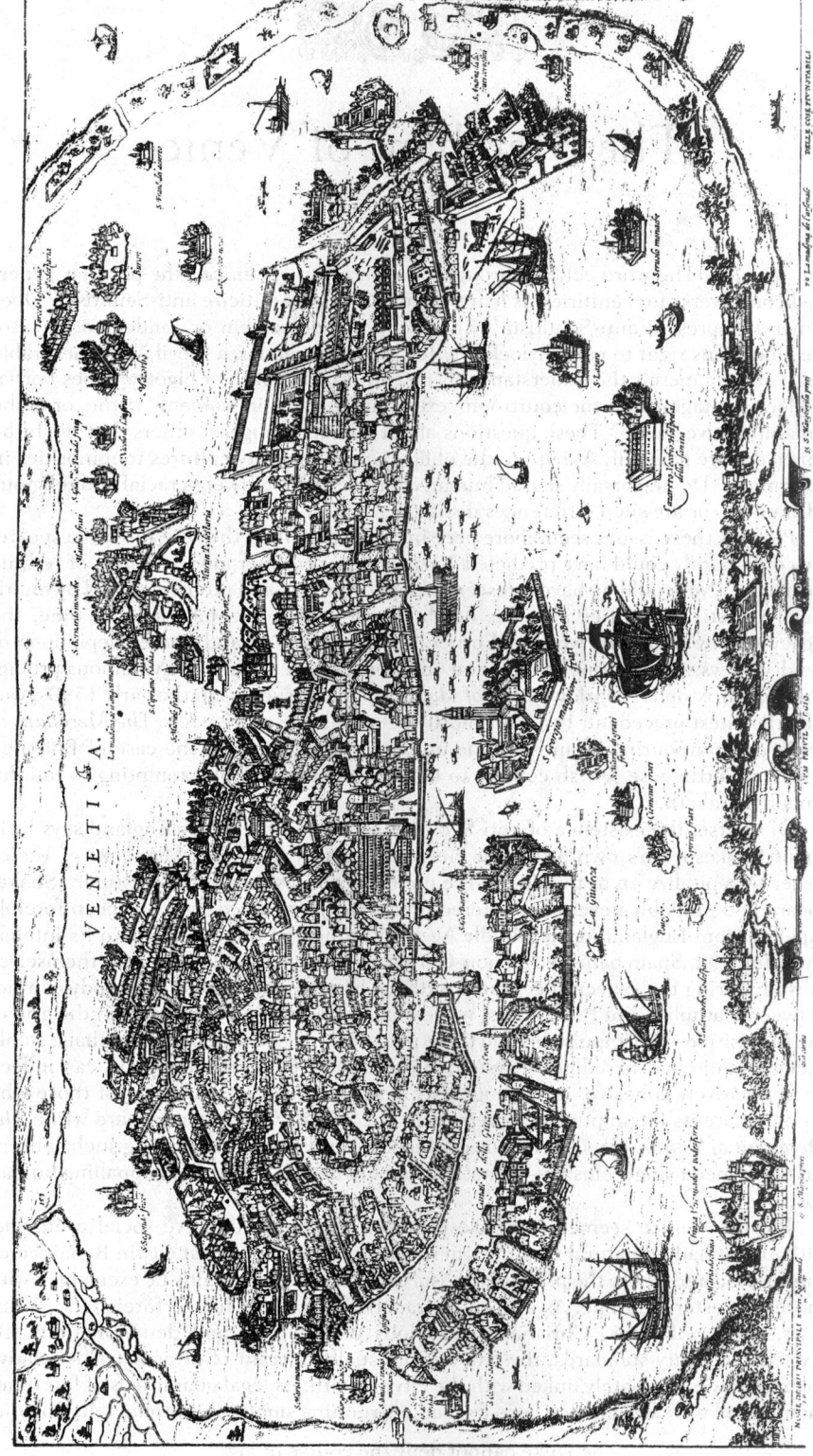

Prospect of Venice. From George Braun and Franz Hogenberg, *Civitates Orbis Terrarum* (1593).

> With us in Venice, if it be denied,
> Will much impeach the justice of the state,
> Since that the trade and profit of the city
> Consisteth of all nations.
>
> (3.3.26–31)

Shakespeare stresses, even exaggerates, this evenhanded cosmopolitanism. Historically, for instance, Venetian Jews were confined to a ghetto, gated and locked at night, but Shakespeare either did not know this fact or chose to ignore it. Venice thus provided Shakespeare with an example—perhaps the only example in sixteenth-century Europe—of a place where people with little in common culturally might coexist peacefully solely because it was materially expedient to do so. The laws of the marketplace seemed to have little to do with religion or nationality.

In *The Merchant of Venice*, Shakespeare juxtaposes social relations based on similarity with social relations based on economic self-interest. The Christian gentlemen who populate the opening scenes comprise a community with a common value system. Acutely aware of what they have in common, these individuals are openhanded to others in their group. When Bassanio asks Antonio for a loan, Antonio rushes to supply him even though he does not have the money at hand. When Graziano asks a favor of Bassanio, Bassanio grants it before he even hears what it is. Later in the play, when Portia finds out that Antonio's life is forfeit because of 3,000 ducats, she instantly offers to pay twelve times that sum to redeem him. Not entirely surprisingly, Bassanio is an amiable spendthrift whose plan to recoup his monetary losses involves considerable risk:

> In my schooldays, when I had lost one shaft,
> I shot his fellow of the selfsame flight
> The selfsame way, with more advisèd watch,
> To find the other forth; and by adventuring both,
> I oft found both.
>
> (1.1.140–44)

"Oft" is not "always." Sometimes, presumably, Bassanio lost both arrows. His temperamental similarity to his friend Antonio, the merchant-adventurer, is an optimism about gambling at long odds.

Such prodigal panache is undeniably attractive, especially in comedy, where generic conventions typically ensure that characters beat long odds. It generates, moreover, some of the most gorgeous poetry of the play, a language of risky munificence, in which phenomenal wealth is accumulated only to be splendidly dispersed. Salerio, for instance, describes a shipwreck as a beautiful squandering of luxury goods:

> dangerous rocks,
> Which, touching but my gentle vessel's side,
> Would scatter all her spices on the stream,
> Enrobe the roaring waters with my silks.
>
> (1.1.31–34)

Likewise, Portia tells Bassanio:

> for myself alone
> I would not be ambitious in my wish
> To wish myself much better, yet for you
> I would be trebled twenty times myself,
> A thousand times more fair, ten thousand times more rich,
> That only to stand high in your account
> I might in virtues, beauties, livings, friends,
> Exceed account.
>
> (3.2.150–57)

Unfortunately, it soon becomes obvious that the Christians' generosity, grace, and self-assurance have a disconcerting racist tinge. The magnanimous, depressive Antonio proudly acknowledges kicking and spitting on Shylock. The charming Portia rejoices in the failure of her black suitor to choose the correct casket: "Let all of his complexion choose me so" (2.7.79). These people find it hard to deal with those different from themselves: their society is based as much on the exclusion of the alien as on the inclusion of the similar. The moral ambiguity of the Christians' outlook is captured in their fondness for the loaded word "kind," which in Renaissance English meant not only "compassionate" but "similar," or "akin." People act benevolently toward those who are of the same *kind* as themselves.

Shylock's relation to the Venetian Christians exemplifies a different social mechanism. Unable to trust to love and generosity, Shylock relies instead on contractually enforceable promises and networks of mutual material need. Shylock's emphasis on purely economic factors means that he does not think about money the way Antonio and Bassanio do. He tends not to spend but to conserve, not to expand but to defend, not to seek risk but to minimize it. When he imagines disaster, he envisions not a spectacular swirl of silk and spices, but a sordid scenario of thievery and nibbling rats.

Although Shylock identifies strongly with his "sacred nation," his "tribe," and although he apparently relies on fellow Jews like Tubal, the play gives little sense of Jewish community. The play represents Shylock as an isolated figure, shunned by his daughter, abandoned by his servant. His calculating, loveless existence seems to result from the way he manages his property. Or perhaps isolation has made him cautious and selfish. Shylock has little motive to be generous with the Christians who despise him, and every reason to believe that he cannot depend on others to rescue him from misfortune.

The psychological and social contrasts between the Christians and Shylock reflect both class and religious differences. The Christians' magnificent improvidence is, in Shakespeare's time, a distinctively aristocratic trait. A true gentleman refuses to be too obviously concerned with monetary expenditure, especially where friends are concerned. He also feels socially obliged to display himself properly. Bassanio spends huge sums of borrowed money equipping himself for his trip to Belmont, even though all he technically need do is arrive alone and select the correct casket. Coming to Portia unattended or in shabby clothes is unthinkable even though (or perhaps because) "all the wealth I had," as Bassanio freely admits, "ran in my veins" (3.2.253–54). By contrast Shylock, despite his evident wealth, is obviously no gentleman. He locks up his possessions, regrets how much his servant eats, fumes over the money he spends searching for his missing daughter.

"Jews." From Jost Amman, *The Panoplia* (1568).

At the same time, the opposition between the Christians and Shylock seems rooted in religious disparities. Judaism in the play is presented not in its actual complexity but as a sixteenth-century Christian like Shakespeare would have construed it, as a set of dramatically vivid contrasts with Christian norms. The law of Moses, as set down in Deuteronomy and Leviticus, specifies numerous aspects of the observant Jew's life—what to eat and wear, how to worship, how to conduct business, how to punish crimes. The Mosaic code places a high value upon justice and emphasizes the importance of adhering to the letter of the law. Shylock's Judaism reveals itself not merely in his distinctive dress and his avoidance of pork, but in his trust of literal meanings, his respect for observable facts, his expectation that contracts will be rigorously enforced.

The typical Christian outlook is different. Christians obtain divine approval not by wearing certain garments, avoiding particular foods, or circumcising their boys, but by believing in Christ's power to save them. The central virtues in this religious system are not justice and scrupulous compliance with the law but charity, mercy, and a willingness to believe what seems incredible. In the terms Shakespeare provides in *The Merchant of Venice*, the Christian demeanor is entrepreneurial, even reckless, the spiritual equivalent of what Antonio does with his ships or Bassanio does with the money he borrows from his friend. "Give up everything you have and follow me," Jesus tells his would-

Young man in Venice. From Cesare Vecellio, *De gli habiti antichi et moderni* (1590).

be follower, advice echoed in the inscription on the lead casket: "Who chooseth me must give and hazard all he hath." Like the word "kind," the similarly complex word "gentle" is used repeatedly in the play to describe this distinctive set of traits: the word simultaneously refers to considerate behavior, to aristocratic family background, and to "gentile," or Christian, religious convictions.

The differences between Christian and Jew become starkly apparent over the issue of usury. Antonio thinks he ought to lend money to friends as an act of charity, properly performed as freely as God Himself dispenses grace. "For when did friendship take / A breed for barren metal of his friend?" (1.3.128–29). The charging of interest seems improperly to generate money from money alone: wealth loses its purely instrumental quality and acquires an uncanny capacity to "breed," or reproduce like a live organism. Usury, blurring the distinction between the domain of the spirit and the merely material realm, threatens to collapse friendship, a spiritual relationship, into a mere economic transaction.

Shylock, by contrast, refuses to distinguish between human relations and money relations. His "pound of flesh" proposal, baldly insisting that flesh is convertible to ducats, demands that the Christians violate their own taboo against confusing categories of spirit and matter, flesh and money, live and dead. Thus Bassanio initially finds the bargain absolutely unacceptable. At the same time, the very existence of the taboo encourages the Christians to accept Shylock's characterization of the contract as a "merry sport": they simply cannot believe he is serious. Antonio mistakenly binds himself under the gross but entirely typical misapprehension that Shylock has mysteriously become "kind."

As the play proceeds, it modifies somewhat these initially vivid contrasts between Christian and Jew. Shylock pretends that he thinks of people in purely material, economic terms; but he becomes a moving character precisely at those moments when he admits another kind of value. After Jessica's flight, Solanio claims that Shylock has been seen running through the streets crying, "O, my ducats! O, my daughter! . . . My ducats and my daughter!" (2.8.15ff.). It is impossible to know how accurate this rumor might be: the equation of ducats and daughter is exactly what Christians expect of Shylock. But when Shylock finally appears onstage, he says nothing of the kind. When Tubal tells him that Jessica has exchanged a turquoise ring for a monkey, Shylock replies: "Out upon her! Thou torturest me, Tubal. It was my turquoise. I had it of Leah when I was a bachelor. I would not have given it for a wilderness of monkeys" (3.1.100–02). Insisting upon the sentimental value of the turquoise ring, Shylock seems directly to deny the convertibility of human into monetary relations. His grief over his daughter's defection, and her insensitivity to his relation with her dead mother, exceeds his financial loss. Likewise in the courtroom, Shylock is remarkable not for his calculating prudence but for his refusal to be swayed by monetary appeals. There is something in the quality of his oppression that he refuses to convert into a payoff.

The Christians are also more complicated than they profess to be. Although human values, in their view, transcend marketplace values, and they are commanded to love not only neighbors but even enemies, only some persons elicit a humane response. Others are disregarded or treated as nonhuman. When Salerio and Solanio ridicule Shylock, he protests: "Hath not a Jew eyes? Hath not a Jew hands, organs, dimensions, senses, affections, passions; fed with the same food, hurt with the same weapons, subject to the same diseases, healed by the same means, warmed and cooled by the same winter and summer as a Christian is?" (3.1.49–54). Shylock asserts that a common human experience of embodiment ought to override considerations of religious or racial difference. These lines are among the most memorable in the play, but the argument does not follow from the position Shylock has taken earlier. Rather, it is effective because it exposes Christian hypocrisy. Similarly, in the trial scene, Shylock points out that the Christian practice of slavery plainly sets a monetary value upon human beings. The Christians' creed mandates universal love, but they fail to behave in accord with their precepts.

These inconsistencies haunt the play's friendships and marriages. Marriage is a hybrid social relation: obviously associated with love and with the reproduction of living organisms, it is simultaneously a property relation, involving the economic alliance of individuals and families. Bassanio's courtship of Portia is doubly motivated: he loves her, and he needs her money. The language of his attraction, even at its most generous and disinterested, is full of the metaphors of commerce and exchange. And although Antonio protests against thinking of friendship as an economic transaction, it is not difficult to construe his generosity as an attempt to buy Bassanio's love. So although the Christians attempt to differentiate spiritual values from economic ones, those values continually turn out to be intimately intertwined.

The casket test directly confronts this problem. The failures of Morocco and Aragon demonstrate that it is possible to find a plausible reason for choosing any one of the three caskets. But when Bassanio makes his choice, we see how the test works: it can be solved only by one who views its puzzles from the correct point of view. Bassanio must abstract from his particular relation with Portia to a general distinction between "ornament" and "truth":

> Look on beauty
> And you shall see 'tis purchased by the weight,
> Which therein works a miracle in nature,
> Making them lightest that wear most of it.
>
> (3.2.88–91)

Surely Bassanio does not believe that because Portia is lovely, she must be unchaste. Instead, his upbringing as a Christian gentleman has acquainted him with a particular frame of mind that prefers invisible over visible things, spirit over body, metaphor over literal meaning. The same cultural background makes him willing to take chances: to "hazard all he hath" on the unprepossessing lead casket. Because every suitor gets the same chance, the casket test seems to be fair; in fact, it is rather like those "objective" intelligence tests that, in subtle or not-so-subtle ways, reward the belief systems of dominant groups while stigmatizing outsiders. In this case, the person best fitted to be Portia's husband is one who, by Christian standards, knows the limitations and right use of wealth. This knowledge enables him to value characteristics in his wife—virtue, intelligence, and beauty—that make her precious in more than monetary ways.

One of the surprises of the casket test is that it takes place at all. Portia's obedience to her dead father's apparently irrational plans for her is remarkable in comedy, for comic heroines more often, like Jessica, defy their fathers than conscientiously follow their orders. Perhaps Portia could be seen as synthesizing the best of Jewish and Christian characteristics; obeying the letter of a wise Father's law, even while cultivating the spiritual virtues of love and generosity. Perhaps, then, Jewish and Christian outlooks are not *necessarily* in conflict (any more than there is a necessary conflict in being, as Portia is, both rich and beautiful). Certainly Portia's respect for the letter of the law, combined with her willingness to go beyond that letter, makes her the only character who can effectively confront Shylock in the trial scene.

When she disguises herself as a young lawyer, Portia becomes one of many Shakespearean comic heroines to assume male attire. The power that she achieves by her transvestism signals an interesting development in Shakespeare's treatment of the relations between men and women. Earlier plays often differentiate sharply between the sexes: between the male political domain and the female domestic domain in *Richard II*, between the male street and the female bedchamber in *Romeo and Juliet*. In *The Merchant of Venice* and the comedies Shakespeare wrote immediately thereafter, women seem to possess a new liberty of action. Their freedom coincides with another new development in Shakespearean comedy, the presence of a scapegoat character—someone like Shylock, who cannot be assimilated into the comic society at the end of the play. Perhaps when the most serious social threats seem to be posed by outsiders, there is more freedom for women within the "in" group: the crucial bifurcation is no longer between male and female but between "us" and "them."

Portia's legal strategy is complex, and thus the trial has several stages. At first, she both offers and recommends generosity:

> Therefore Jew,
> Though justice be thy plea, consider this:
> That in the course of justice none of us
> Should see salvation. We do pray for mercy,
> And that same prayer doth teach us all to render
> The deeds of mercy.
>
> (4.1.192–97)

Not surprisingly, Shylock is deaf to this eloquence. Portia's argument is based on the distinctively Christian premise that salvation is an undeserved gift. She derives her authority from the Lord's Prayer: "forgive us our trespasses as we forgive those who trespass against us." But Shylock doesn't accept, or even perhaps know the existence of, a prayer that supposedly "teaches us all." Portia's plea for tolerance and compassion might seem to rest on universal premises, but in fact Portia's "we" who "pray for mercy" neatly excludes the Jew.

The judgment upon Shylock at the end of the trial has disturbed many critics and audiences. After the Christians win the case—not only saving Antonio's life but also keeping the 3,000 ducats Shylock had lent Bassanio—Portia seems to take exactly the revenge she has up to now deplored. Her legal ground is provided by a previously unmentioned law against any alien who plots the death of a Venetian citizen. The law in which Shylock trusted, because it seemed to provide a refuge from prejudice, turns out to have prejudice inscribed within it from the start. In this respect, it resembles the casket test—everybody seems to get the same chance, but in fact the test blatantly favors the insider.

Portia and the Duke apparently regard the dismissal of Shylock as merciful; his *life* is preserved, although half or all of his mere money is taken away. Portia's sentence forces Shylock to behave as a Christian citizen and father should: to worship in a Christian church, to grant money to his daughter, to recognize the difference between spiritual and economic well-being. Eschewing lethal force, the Duke demands that Shylock acquiesce in his punishment: "I am content," he says at last. But what else can he say? The coercive inclusion of Shylock in the Christian community seems all the more violent because it professes to renounce coercion, dropping "as the gentle rain from heaven." If designating people outcasts is bad, compelling them to participate in a society they find intolerable may be even worse.

The Merchant of Venice thus hovers on the edge of tragedy. Shylock's ferocious negativity is poised against, and arguably elicited by, the Christians' hypocritical refusal to admit the way their spiritual lives depend on material prosperity. The presence of the scapegoated Jew lays bare the mechanisms by which Venetian society works. Shylock can be reviled and dismissed, but the possibilities that he represents do not simply vanish when he flees the courtroom. Thus the moral disquiet the play raises among directors, readers, and audiences: Christian and Jewish perspectives seem mutually invalidating, and both finally inadequate.

Shakespeare suggests the stubbornness of the problems broached by the play in the way he structures the last act. Most Shakespeare comedies return to the city or the court at the end, or at least look forward to that return; but in *The Merchant of Venice*, the play ends at Belmont, the nostalgically depicted, magically copious "green world." It is as if the formal demand for comic closure conflicts with Shakespeare's awareness that no neat resolution of Venice's problems is forthcoming.

Indeed, some muted version of those problems pursues the Christians even to Portia's estate. The act begins with the banter between the newlyweds Jessica and Lorenzo, who have stayed behind at Belmont in Portia's absence. It is a bit ominous that all the love stories they recall are unhappy ones. Still, the couple's affectionate banter makes the scene a welcome change from what has immediately preceded it. Showing Jessica and Lorenzo in married bliss minutes after the brutal expulsion of Shylock seems an attempt to confine the punitive energies of the play to the usurer alone. The scene offers an alternative vision of interaction between racial groups, one that involves love rather than hatred. Jessica's marriage to a Christian has exempted her from Shylock's fate. Of course, this is a vision not of mutual tolerance but of assimilation: majority cultures do not need to exterminate people unlike themselves if they can merely exterminate their differences. Lorenzo describes to his wife the "music of the spheres"—a perfect heavenly harmony made inaudible by the corruption of this life. Perhaps, analogously, the Christians' failure lies not in the nature of their ideals, but in the imperfect realization of those ideals in the everyday world. The inevitable dissonance between the mundane and the ideal world does not necessarily, however, simply drain the ideal of its meaning.

The moral dilemmas posed by high but perhaps unrealizable ideals come under scrutiny yet again in the ring tricks with which the play ends. After Antonio's trial, Portia-as-Balthazar asks Bassanio for his wedding ring as payment for legal services. This request poses Bassanio a harder problem than Shylock had. Bassanio can imagine breaking a written contract, but not denying the request of an ally to whom he's indebted. By giving the ring to Balthazar, Bassanio demonstrates both that his loyalty to Antonio still outweighs his allegiance to Portia and that he has trouble governing his generous impulses. Portia's trick teaches Bassanio and Antonio that the marital relationship involves unique responsibilities and that those responsibilities impose a limit on munificence.

Again and again in *The Merchant of Venice* oppositions between potentially tragic alternatives miraculously dissolve—between being rich and being virtuous, marrying for money and marrying for love, following paternal orders and making one's own choice, enforcing the letter of the law and enforcing its spirit, remaining faithful to one's wife and loving one's male friend. Balthazar turns out to have been Portia, Bassanio has given his ring to its original owner, and all seems to be well. But by setting the play's last act in a magical world of trust and abundance, Shakespeare stresses the artifice involved in his resolution. Even as this beautiful, troubling play comes to a close, it pointedly emphasizes the distance between the final act's charmed fictional world and the intransigent real one.

KATHARINE EISAMAN MAUS

TEXTUAL NOTE

The textual history of *The Merchant of Venice* is not as complicated as that of some other Shakespeare plays. Two quarto editions exist, both dated 1600 on the title page. One, printed "by I. R. for Thomas Heys," is now called Q1; nineteen copies of this text have survived. Another Quarto (Q2), printed "by I. Roberts," is a falsely dated text actually produced in 1619 by William Jaggard (the same man who printed the First Folio four years later). Yet another version of *The Merchant of Venice* appears in the 1623 First Folio (F).

Q1 seems to have been prepared either directly from Shakespeare's own manuscript or from an accurate transcript of that manuscript. Internal evidence indicates that both Q2 and F were based on copies of Q1. F has some additions, chiefly stage directions, which suggests that a text marked up for stage production was likely to have been consulted at some point in preparing this text. Q1 is not divided into acts or scenes; F adds act divisions. Scene divisions were not added until the eighteenth century.

Q1, therefore, with the exception of some stage directions is the most reliable authority for a modern text of *The Merchant of Venice*. The Oxford text follows Q1 closely, adopting from F and later editors the traditional divisions into acts and scenes, and accepting many of the Folio stage directions as representing the performance practice of Shakespeare's company.

The title *The Jew of Venice* does not appear in any printed text of the play. It was used, however, when the play was entered on the Stationers' Register in 1598. Since the theatrical company, not a bookseller, was responsible for the entry, the Oxford editors believe that members of Shakespeare's company considered *The Jew of Venice* an acceptable alternative title.

SELECTED BIBLIOGRAPHY

Barber, C. L. "The Merchants and the Jew of Venice: Wealth's Communion and an Intruder." *Shakespeare's Festive Comedy: A Study of Dramatic Form and Its Relation to Social Custom*. Princeton: Princeton University Press, 1959. The Christian's opulent festivity challenged by Shylock's fiercely reductive attitude toward money.

Burckhardt, Sigurd. "*The Merchant of Venice*: The Gentle Bond." *Shakespearean Meanings*. Princeton: Princeton University Press, 1968. 206–89. The importance of various kinds of bonds in *The Merchant of Venice*.

Cohen, Walter. "*The Merchant of Venice* and the Possibilities of Historical Criticism." *English Literary History* 49 (1982): 765–89. The play's theatrical artifice as reflecting economic conflicts in early modern Europe.

Danson, Lawrence. *The Harmonies of "The Merchant of Venice."* New Haven: Yale University Press, 1978. Describes the play's conflicts in detail, and argues for their satisfactory resolution.

Engle, Lars. "Money and Moral Luck in *The Merchant of Venice.*" *Shakespearean Pragmatism: Market of His Time*. Chicago: University of Chicago Press, 1993. 77–106. Emotional and financial balance sheets and their ethical consequences: *The Merchant of Venice* read through the lens of late twentieth-century ethical philosophy.

Gross, Kenneth. *Shylock Is Shakespeare*. Chicago: University of Chicago Press, 2006. Shakespeare's personal connection to Shylock.

Lewalski, Barbara. "Biblical Allusion and Allegory in *The Merchant of Venice*." *Shakespeare Quarterly* 13 (1962): 327–43. Shakespeare's use of biblical typology.

Lupton, Julia Reinhard. "Merchants of Venice, Circles of Citizenship." *Citizen-Saints: Shakespeare and Political Theology*. Chicago: University of Chicago Press, 2005. 75–101. Judaism and citizenship in early modern Venice.

Newman, Karen. "Portia's Ring: Unruly Women and the Structure of Exchange in *The Merchant of Venice*." *Shakespeare Quarterly* 38 (1987): 19–33. Portia, as gift-giver, occupies a position of power usually coded as masculine.

Shapiro, James. *Shakespeare and the Jews*. New York: Columbia University Press, 1996. Anti-Semitism in Shakespeare's time.

Shell, Marc. "'The Wether and the Ewe': Verbal Usury in *The Merchant of Venice*." *Kenyon Review* 1.4 (1979): 65–92. A close analysis of exchange and redemption in *Merchant of Venice*, focusing particularly on Shylock's story of Laban and Jacob.

Wilson, Luke. "Drama and Marine Insurance in Shakespeare's London." *The Law in Shakespeare*. Ed. Constance Jordan and Karen Cunningham. London: Palgrave Macmillan, 2007. 127–42.

Films

The Merchant of Venice. 1973. Dir. John Sichel. UK. 131 min. Laurence Olivier as Shylock.

The Merchant of Venice. 1980. Dir. Jack Gold. UK. 157 min. Textually faithful but stilted. Gemma Jones is a chilly, calculating Portia.

The Merchant of Venice. 2001. Dir. Trevor Nunn. UK. 141 min. A film version of an acclaimed Royal National Theatre production, set in Europe between the world wars. Vividly acted, with many interesting directorial choices. Henry Goodman's Shylock is especially memorable.

The Merchant of Venice. 2004. Dir. Michael Radford. UK. 131 min. Al Pacino as Shylock, Lynn Collins as Portia. Sumptuous period costumes and sets. This production emphasizes the disquieting aspects of the play, not only the Venetians' anti-Semitism but the struggle between Portia and Antonio over Bassanio's allegiance.

The Comical History of the Merchant of Venice, or Otherwise Called the Jew of Venice

THE PERSONS OF THE PLAY

ANTONIO, a merchant of Venice
BASSANIO, his friend and Portia's suitor
LEONARDO, Bassanio's servant
LORENZO
GRAZIANO
SALERIO } friends of Antonio and Bassanio
SOLANIO
SHYLOCK, a Jew
JESSICA, his daughter
TUBAL, a Jew
LANCELOT, a clown, first Shylock's servant and then Bassanio's
GOBBO, his father
PORTIA, an heiress
NERISSA, her waiting-gentlewoman
BALTHASAR } Portia's servants
STEFANO
Prince of MOROCCO } Portia's suitors
Prince of ARAGON
DUKE of Venice
Magnificoes of Venice
A jailer, attendants, and servants

1.1

Enter ANTONIO, SALERIO, *and* SOLANIO

ANTONIO In sooth,° I know not why I am so sad.   *truth*
  It wearies me, you say it wearies you,
  But how I caught it, found it, or came by it,
  What stuff 'tis made of, whereof it is born,
5 I am to learn;°   *have yet to discover*
  And such a want-wit° sadness makes of me   *dullard*
  That I have much ado to know myself.
SALERIO   Your mind is tossing on the ocean,
  There where your argosies° with portly° sail,   *merchant ships / stately*
10 Like signors° and rich burghers on the flood—   *lords*
  Or as it were the pageants[1] of the sea—
  Do overpeer° the petty traffickers   *tower over*
  That curtsy[2] to them, do them reverence,
  As they fly by them with their woven wings.

1.1 Location: Venice.
1. Movable stages used by itinerant actors or in parades.

2. By bobbing on the waves or by lowering their flags in salute.

SOLANIO [*to* ANTONIO]   Believe me, sir, had I such venture°   *a risky undertaking*
15   forth
          The better part of my affections would
          Be with my hopes abroad. I should be still°   *always*
          Plucking the grass to know where sits the wind,
          Peering in maps for ports and piers and roads,°   *open harbors*
20   And every object that might make me fear
          Misfortune to my ventures out of doubt
          Would make me sad.
SALERIO   My wind cooling my broth
          Would blow me to an ague° when I thought   *make me shiver*
          What harm a wind too great might do at sea.
25   I should not see the sandy hour-glass run
          But I should think of shallows and of flats,°   *shoals*
          And see my wealthy Andrew,[3] decks in sand,
          Vailing her hightop° lower than her ribs   *Lowering her topmast*
          To kiss her burial.° Should I go to church   *burial place*
30   And see the holy edifice of stone
          And not bethink me straight° of dangerous rocks   *immediately think*
          Which, touching but my gentle vessel's side,
          Would scatter all her spices on the stream,
          Enrobe the roaring waters with my silks,
35   And, in a word, but even now° worth this,°   *moments ago / so much*
          And now worth nothing? Shall I have the thought
          To think on this, and shall I lack the thought
          That such a thing bechanced° would make me sad?   *having occurred*
          But tell not me. I know Antonio
40   Is sad to think upon his merchandise.
ANTONIO   Believe me, no. I thank my fortune for it,
          My ventures are not in one bottom° trusted,   *ship*
          Nor to one place;° nor is my whole estate   *destination*
          Upon the fortune of this present year.
45   Therefore my merchandise makes me not sad.
SOLANIO   Why then, you are in love.
ANTONIO   Fie, fie.
SOLANIO   Not in love neither? Then let us say you are sad
          Because you are not merry, and 'twere as easy
          For you to laugh, and leap, and say you are merry
50   Because you are not sad. Now, by two-headed Janus,[4]
          Nature hath framed strange fellows in her time:
          Some that will evermore peep through their eyes[5]
          And laugh like parrots° at a bagpiper,[6]   *(screeching loudly)*
          And other of such vinegar aspect°   *sour looks*
55   That they'll not show their teeth in way of smile
          Though Nestor[7] swear the jest be laughable.
                    Enter BASSANIO, LORENZO, *and* GRAZIANO
          Here comes Bassanio, your most noble kinsman,
          Graziano, and Lorenzo. Fare ye well.
          We leave you now with better company.
60 SALERIO   I would have stayed till I had made you merry
          If worthier friends had not prevented me.

3. Name of a Spanish galleon captured by the English   5. Eyes almost shut by violent laughter.
at Cádiz in 1596.   6. Whose music was considered woeful.
4. Roman god with faces looking both forward and   7. Sober, elderly Greek hero in *The Iliad*.
backward.

ANTONIO   Your worth is very dear in my regard.
I take it your own business calls on you,
And you embrace th'occasion to depart.
65 SALERIO   Good morrow, my good lords.
BASSANIO   Good signors both, when shall we laugh?° Say, when?   *make merry together*
You grow exceeding strange.° Must it be so?   *reserved*
SALERIO   We'll make our leisures to attend on° yours.   *suit*

Exeunt SALERIO *and* SOLANIO

LORENZO   My lord Bassanio, since you have found Antonio,
70 We two will leave you; but at dinner-time
I pray you have in mind where we must meet.
BASSANIO   I will not fail you.
GRAZIANO   You look not well, Signor Antonio.
You have too much respect upon the world.°   *anxiety about business*
75 They lose it that do buy it with much care.
Believe me, you are marvellously changed.
ANTONIO   I hold the world but as the world, Graziano—
A stage where every man must play a part,
And mine a sad one.
GRAZIANO   Let me play the fool.
80 With mirth and laughter let old[8] wrinkles come,
And let my liver[9] rather heat with wine
Than my heart cool with mortifying[1] groans.
Why should a man whose blood is warm within
Sit like his grandsire cut in alabaster,[2]
85 Sleep when he wakes, and creep into the jaundice[3]
By being peevish? I tell thee what, Antonio—
I love thee, and 'tis my love that speaks—
There are a sort of men whose visages
Do cream and mantle[4] like a standing° pond,   *stagnant*
90 And do a wilful stillness entertain
With purpose to be dressed in an opinion°   *a reputation*
Of wisdom, gravity, profound conceit,°   *judgment*
As who should say 'I am Sir Oracle,
And when I ope my lips, let no dog bark.'
95 O my Antonio, I do know of these
That therefore only are reputed wise
For saying nothing, when I am very sure,
If they should speak, would almost damn those ears
Which, hearing them, would call their brothers fools.[5]
100 I'll tell thee more of this another time.
But fish not with this melancholy bait
For this fool gudgeon,° this opinion.—   *tiny, easily caught fish*
Come, good Lorenzo.—Fare ye well a while.
I'll end my exhortation after dinner.
LORENZO [*to* ANTONIO *and* BASSANIO]   Well, we will leave you
105   then till dinner-time.
I must be one of these same dumb° wise men,   *mute*
For Graziano never lets me speak.

---

8. Accompanying old age; abundant.
9. The liver was considered the seat of passion.
1. Deadly (groans were believed to drain blood from the heart).
2. Stone from which tomb effigies were carved.
3. Thought to result from too much yellow bile, a bodily

substance associated with irritability.
4. *cream and mantle*: grow a scum; that is, assume a fixed countenance.
5. *would . . . fools*: alluding to Matthew 5:22: "And whosoever shall say to his brother . . . , fool, shall be in danger of hell fire."

GRAZIANO Well, keep me company but two years more
    Thou shalt not know the sound of thine own tongue.
110 ANTONIO Fare you well. I'll grow a talker for this gear.[6]
GRAZIANO Thanks, i'faith, for silence is only commendable
    In a neat's° tongue dried and a maid not vendible.[7]   *an ox's*
                            Exeunt [GRAZIANO *and* LORENZO]
ANTONIO Yet is that anything now?
BASSANIO Graziano speaks an infinite deal of nothing, more
115   than any man in all Venice. His reasons° are as two grains of   *sensible remarks*
    wheat hid in two bushels of chaff: you shall seek all day ere
    you find them, and when you have them they are not worth
    the search.
ANTONIO Well, tell me now what lady is the same
120   To whom you swore a secret pilgrimage,
    That you today promised to tell me of.
BASSANIO 'Tis not unknown to you, Antonio,
    How much I have disabled mine estate
    By something showing a more swelling port°   *extravagant lifestyle*
125   Than my faint means would grant continuance,°   *allow to continue*
    Nor do I now make moan to be abridged°   *reduced*
    From such a noble rate;° but my chief care   *style*
    Is to come fairly off from the great debts
    Wherein my time, something too prodigal,
130   Hath left me gaged.° To you, Antonio,   *pledged*
    I owe the most in money and in love,
    And from your love I have a warranty°   *sanction*
    To unburden all my plots and purposes
    How to get clear of all the debts I owe.
135 ANTONIO I pray you, good Bassanio, let me know it,
    And if it stand as you yourself still do,
    Within the eye of honour, be assured
    My purse, my person, my extremest means
    Lie all unlocked to your occasions.°   *requirements*
140 BASSANIO In my schooldays, when I had lost one shaft,
    I shot his° fellow of the selfsame flight°   *its / size and weight*
    The selfsame way, with more advisèd° watch,   *careful*
    To find the other forth; and by adventuring° both,   *hazarding*
    I oft found both. I urge this childhood proof
145   Because what follows is pure innocence.
    I owe you much, and, like a wilful youth,
    That which I owe is lost; but if you please
    To shoot another arrow that self° way   *same*
    Which you did shoot the first, I do not doubt,
150   As I will watch the aim, or° to find both   *either*
    Or bring your latter hazard° back again,   *risk*
    And thankfully rest debtor for the first.
ANTONIO You know me well, and herein spend but° time   *only lose*
    To wind about my love with circumstance;°   *circumlocution*
155   And out of doubt you do me now more wrong
    In making question of my uttermost[8]
    Than if you had made waste of all I have.
    Then do but say to me what I should do

---

6. *for this gear:* as a result of your talk.   8. In doubting that I would do my utmost to help you.
7. Sellable—that is, marriageable.

That in your knowledge may by me be done,
160   And I am pressed unto° it. Therefore speak.   *obliged to do*
BASSANIO   In Belmont is a lady richly left,°   *left a fortune*
And she is fair, and, fairer than that word,
Of wondrous virtues. Sometimes° from her eyes   *At times*
I did receive fair speechless messages.
165   Her name is Portia, nothing undervalued
To⁹ Cato's daughter, Brutus' Portia;¹
Nor is the wide world ignorant of her worth,
For the four winds blow in from every coast
Renownèd suitors, and her sunny locks
170   Hang on her temples like a golden fleece,
Which makes her seat of Belmont Colchis' strand,²
And many Jasons come in quest of her,
O my Antonio, had I but the means
To hold a rival place with one of them,
175   I have a mind presages me such thrift°   *prosperity*
That I should questionless be fortunate.
ANTONIO   Thou know'st that all my fortunes are at sea,
Neither have I money nor commodity°   *goods*
To raise a present sum. Therefore go forth—
180   Try what my credit can in Venice do;
That shall be racked° even to the uttermost   *stretched*
To furnish thee to Belmont, to fair Portia.
Go presently enquire, and so will I,
Where money is; and I no question make
185   To have it of my trust or for my sake.³   *Exeunt [severally]°*   *separately*

1.2

Enter PORTIA *with her waiting-woman,* NERISSA

PORTIA   By my troth,° Nerissa, my little body is aweary of this   *faith*
great world.
NERISSA   You would be,¹ sweet madam, if your miseries were in
the same abundance as your good fortunes are; and yet, for
5   aught I see, they are as sick that surfeit with too much as they
that starve with nothing. It is no mean° happiness, therefore,   *slight*
to be seated in the mean.° Superfluity comes sooner by° white   *middle / sooner gets*
hairs, but competency° lives longer.   *moderate estate*
PORTIA   Good sentences,° and well pronounced.   *aphorisms*
10   NERISSA   They would be better if well followed.
PORTIA   If to do were as easy as to know what were good to do,
chapels had been churches, and poor men's cottages princes'
palaces. It is a good divine° that follows his own instructions.   *clergyman*
I can easier teach twenty what were good to be done than to
15   be one of the twenty to follow mine own teaching. The brain
may devise laws for the blood,° but a hot temper² leaps o'er a   *passion*
cold decree. Such a hare is madness, the youth, to skip o'er
the meshes° of good counsel, the cripple.³ But this reasoning   *snares*
is not in the fashion° to choose me a husband. O me, the word   *of a kind*

---

9. *nothing . . . / To:* no less worthy than.
1. Roman matron famous for heroic fidelity to her husband; a character in *Julius Caesar.*
2. Coast of Colchis, where in classical mythology Jason
won the Golden Fleece.
3. *of . . . sake:* because of my creditworthiness or as a

personal favor.
1.2 Location: Belmont.
1. You would have reason to be weary.
2. An impetuous disposition.
3. Because wisdom is imagined as elderly.

20 'choose'! I may neither choose who I would nor refuse who I
dislike; so is the will° of a living daughter curbed by the will°   *wish / testament*
of a dead father. Is it not hard, Nerissa, that I cannot choose
one nor refuse none?

NERISSA   Your father was ever virtuous, and holy men at their
25 death have good inspirations; therefore the lottery that he
hath devised in these three chests of gold, silver, and lead,
whereof who chooses his meaning chooses you, will no doubt
never be chosen by any rightly but one who you shall rightly
love. But what warmth is there in your affection towards any
30 of these princely suitors that are already come?

PORTIA   I pray thee overname them, and as thou namest them
I will describe them; and according to my description, level°   *guess*
at my affection.

NERISSA   First there is the Neapolitan prince.

35 PORTIA   Ay, that's a colt[4] indeed, for he doth nothing but talk of
his horse, and he makes it a great appropriation° to his own   *augmentation*
good parts° that he can shoe him himself. I am much afeard   *own abilities*
my lady his mother played false with a smith.

NERISSA   Then is there the County Palatine.[5]

40 PORTIA   He doth nothing but frown, as who should say 'An° you   *If*
will not have me, choose'.° He hears merry tales and smiles   *do as you wish*
not. I fear he will prove the weeping philosopher[6] when he
grows old, being so full of unmannerly° sadness in his youth.   *immoderate*
I had rather be married to a death's-head with a bone in his
45 mouth than to either of these. God defend me from these two!

NERISSA   How say you by the French lord, Monsieur le Bon?

PORTIA   God made him, and therefore let him pass for a man. In
truth, I know it is a sin to be a mocker, but he—why, he hath
a horse better than the Neapolitan's, a better bad habit of
50 frowning than the Count Palatine. He is every man in no man.
If a throstle° sing, he falls straight° a-cap'ring. He will fence   *thrush / immediately*
with his own shadow. If I should marry him, I should marry
twenty husbands. If he would despise me, I would forgive him,
for if he love me to madness, I shall never requite him.

55 NERISSA   What say you then to Falconbridge, the young baron
of England?

PORTIA   You know I say nothing to him, for he understands not
me, nor I him. He hath neither Latin, French, nor Italian, and
you will come into the court and swear that I have a poor pen-
60 nyworth in the English. He is a proper° man's picture, but   *handsome*
alas, who can converse with a dumb show?° How oddly he is   *pantomime*
suited! I think he bought his doublet° in Italy, his round hose[7]   *upper garment*
in France, his bonnet° in Germany, and his behaviour every-   *hat*
where.

65 NERISSA   What think you of the Scottish lord, his neighbour?

PORTIA   That he hath a neighbourly charity in him, for he borrowed a box of the ear of the Englishman and swore he would
pay him again when he was able. I think the Frenchman
became his surety, and sealed under for another.[8]

---

4. Foolish young man. Neapolitans were excellent
horsemen.
5. Count possessing royal powers.
6. Heracleitus, a melancholy Greek philosopher.
7. Puffed breeches.

8. The Frenchman vouched for the Scot's payment (of
a box on the ear) and promised to add another himself
(referring to France's frequent promises to help the
Scots against the English).

70　NERISSA　How like you the young German, the Duke of Saxony's
　　　nephew?

　　PORTIA　Very vilely in the morning when he is sober, and most
　　　vilely in the afternoon when he is drunk. When he is best he
　　　is a little worse than a man, and when he is worst he is little
75　　better than a beast. An the worst fall that ever fell, I hope I
　　　shall make shift° to go without him.　　　　　　　　　　　　*manage*

　　NERISSA　If he should offer° to choose, and choose the right　　　*endeavor*
　　　casket, you should refuse to perform your father's will if you
　　　should refuse to accept him.

80　PORTIA　Therefore, for fear of the worst, I pray thee set a deep
　　　glass of Rhenish wine° on the contrary casket; for if the devil　　*white German wine*
　　　be within and that temptation without, I know he will choose
　　　it. I will do anything, Nerissa, ere I will be married to a sponge.

　　NERISSA　You need not fear, lady, the having any of these lords.
85　　They have acquainted me with their determinations, which is
　　　indeed to return to their home and to trouble you with no
　　　more suit unless you may be won by some other sort° than　　　*way*
　　　your father's imposition° depending on the caskets.　　　　　　*conditions*

　　PORTIA　If I live to be as old as Sibylla[9] I will die as chaste as
90　　Diana unless I be obtained by the manner of my father's will.
　　　I am glad this parcel of wooers are so reasonable, for there is
　　　not one among them but I dote on his very absence; and I pray
　　　God grant them a fair departure.

　　NERISSA　Do you not remember, lady, in your father's time, a
95　　Venetian, a scholar and a soldier, that came hither in company
　　　of the Marquis of Montferrat?

　　PORTIA　Yes, yes, it was Bassanio—as I think, so was he called.

　　NERISSA　True, madam. He of all the men that ever my foolish
　　　eyes looked upon was the best deserving a fair lady.

100　PORTIA　I remember him well, and I remember him worthy of
　　　thy praise.

　　　　　　　　　　　Enter a SERVINGMAN
　　　How now, what news?

　　SERVINGMAN　The four strangers seek for you, madam, to take
　　　their leave, and there is a forerunner come from a fifth, the
105　　Prince of Morocco, who brings word the Prince his master
　　　will be here tonight.

　　PORTIA　If I could bid the fifth welcome with so good heart as I
　　　can bid the other four farewell, I should be glad of his
　　　approach. If he have the condition° of a saint and the complex-　　*character*
110　　ion of a devil,[1] I had rather he should shrive me° than wive me.　　*absolve me of my sins*
　　　Come, Nerissa. [*To the* SERVINGMAN] Sirrah, go before.
　　　Whiles we shut the gate upon one wooer,
　　　Another knocks at the door.　　　　　　　　　　　　　　*Exeunt*

1.3

　　　　　　　Enter BASSANIO *with* SHYLOCK *the Jew*
　　SHYLOCK　Three thousand ducats.[1] Well.
　　BASSANIO　Ay, sir, for three months.
　　SHYLOCK　For three months. Well.

---

9. In classical mythology, the Cumaean Sibyl asked
Apollo for as many years of life as the grains of sand she
held in her hand; she forgot to ask for eternal youth.

1. Devils were imagined as black.
1.3 Location: Street in Venice.
1. Gold coins. The sum is very large.

BASSANIO For the which, as I told you, Antonio shall be bound.° *contractually responsible*
5 SHYLOCK Antonio shall become bound. Well.
BASSANIO May you stead° me? Will you pleasure me? Shall I *accommodate*
know your answer?
SHYLOCK Three thousand ducats for three months, and Antonio
bound.
10 BASSANIO Your answer to that.
SHYLOCK Antonio is a good man.
BASSANIO Have you heard any imputation to the contrary?
SHYLOCK Ho, no, no, no, no! My meaning in saying he is a good
man is to have you understand me that he is sufficient.° Yet *of adequate wealth*
15 his means are in supposition.° He hath an argosy bound to *doubt*
Tripolis, another to the Indies. I understand moreover upon
the Rialto² he hath a third at Mexico, a fourth for England,
and other ventures he hath squandered abroad. But ships are
but boards, sailors but men. There be land rats and water rats,
20 water thieves and land thieves—I mean pirates—and then
there is the peril of waters, winds, and rocks. The man is,
notwithstanding, sufficient. Three thousand ducats. I think I
may take his bond.
BASSANIO Be assured you may.
25 SHYLOCK I will be assured³ I may, and that I may be assured,
I will bethink me. May I speak with Antonio?
BASSANIO If it please you to dine with us.
SHYLOCK Yes, to smell pork, to eat of the habitation which your
prophet the Nazarite⁴ conjured the devil into! I will buy with
30 you, sell with you, talk with you, walk with you, and so following, but I will not eat with you, drink with you, nor pray
with you.

Enter ANTONIO

[*To* ANTONIO] What news on the Rialto? [*To* BASSANIO] Who is
he comes here?
35 BASSANIO This is Signor Antonio.

[BASSANIO *and* ANTONIO *speak silently to one another*]

SHYLOCK [*aside*] How like a fawning publican⁵ he looks.
I hate him for he is a Christian;
But more, for that in low simplicity⁶
He lends out money gratis,° and brings down *free*
40 The rate of usance° here with us in Venice. *interest*
If I can catch him once upon the hip⁷
I will feed fat the ancient grudge I bear him.
He hates our sacred nation,° and he rails, *(the Jews)*
Even there where merchants most do congregate,
45 On me, my bargains, and my well-won thrift°— *profit*
Which he calls interest. Cursèd be my tribe
If I forgive him.
BASSANIO   Shylock, do you hear?
SHYLOCK I am debating of my present store,° *supply of money*
And by the near guess of my memory

2. Merchants' exchange in Venice.
3. Sure (but Shylock uses the word to mean "given financial guarantees").
4. Jesus, who cast devils into a herd of swine.
5. Tax collector; he robs me, but now, like the publican

in Luke 18:10–14 who prays to Jesus for mercy, tries to ingratiate himself because he wants a favor.
6. In meek honesty; in base folly.
7. *upon the hip*: at a disadvantage (wrestling terminology).

50 I cannot instantly raise up the gross°   *total*
Of full three thousand ducats. What of that?
Tubal, a wealthy Hebrew of my tribe,
Will furnish me. But soft°—how many months   *wait*
Do you desire? [*To* ANTONIO] Rest you fair, good signor.
55 Your worship was the last man in our mouths.[8]
ANTONIO   Shylock, albeit I neither lend nor borrow
By taking nor by giving of excess,
Yet to supply the ripe° wants of my friend   *urgent*
I'll break a custom. [*To* BASSANIO] Is he yet possessed°   *informed*
60 How much ye would?
SHYLOCK   Ay, ay, three thousand ducats.
ANTONIO   And for three months.
SHYLOCK   I had forgot—three months. [*To* BASSANIO] You told me so.—
Well then, your bond; and let me see—but hear you,
65 Methoughts you said you neither lend nor borrow
Upon advantage.°   *interest*
ANTONIO   I do never use it.
SHYLOCK   When Jacob grazed his uncle Laban's sheep—
This Jacob from our holy Abram was,
As his wise mother wrought in his behalf,
70 The third possessor; ay, he was the third[9]—
ANTONIO   And what of him? Did he take interest?
SHYLOCK   No, not take interest, not, as you would say,
Directly int'rest. Mark what Jacob did:
When Laban and himself were compromised°   *agreed*
75 That all the eanlings° which were streaked and pied°   *lambs / spotted*
Should fall as Jacob's hire, the ewes being rank,°   *in heat*
In end of autumn turnèd to the rams,
And when the work of generation° was   *mating*
Between these woolly breeders in the act,
80 The skilful shepherd peeled me certain wands,[1]
And in the doing of the deed of kind°   *nature*
He stuck them up before the fulsome ewes
Who, then conceiving, did in eaning° time   *lambing*
Fall° parti-coloured lambs; and those were Jacob's.   *Deliver*
85 This was a way to thrive; and he was blest;
And thrift is blessing, if men steal it not.
ANTONIO   This was a venture, sir, that Jacob served for[2]—
A thing not in his power to bring to pass,
But swayed and fashioned by the hand of heaven.
90 Was this inserted to make interest good,[3]
Or is your gold and silver ewes and rams?
SHYLOCK   I cannot tell. I make it breed as fast.
But note me, signor—
ANTONIO   Mark you this, Bassanio?
The devil can cite Scripture for his purpose.
95 An evil soul producing holy witness
Is like a villain with a smiling cheek.

---

8. We were just mentioning you.
9. After Abraham and Isaac; his mother, Rebecca, helped him cheat his brother Esau of his birthright. The story of Laban's sheep is told in Genesis 30:25–43.

1. Stripped part of the bark off some sticks ("me" is colloquial).
2. This was a speculative enterprise on which Jacob staked his wages as a servant.
3. Was this brought up to defend taking interest.

A goodly apple rotten at the heart.
O, what a goodly outside falsehood hath!

SHYLOCK　Three thousand ducats. 'Tis a good round sum.

100 Three months from twelve—then let me see the rate.

ANTONIO　Well, Shylock, shall we be beholden to you?

SHYLOCK　Signor Antonio, many a time and oft
In the Rialto you have rated° me   berated
About my moneys and my usances.

105 Still° have I borne it with a patient shrug,   Always
For suff'rance is the badge⁴ of all our tribe.
You call me misbeliever, cut-throat, dog,
And spit upon my Jewish gaberdine,°   long coat
And all for use of that which is mine own.

110 Well then, it now appears you need my help.
Go to, then. You come to me, and you say
'Shylock, we would have moneys'—you say so,
You, that did void your rheum° upon my beard,   spit
And foot me as you spurn° a stranger cur   contemptuously kick

115 Over your threshold. Moneys is your suit.
What should I say to you? Should I not say
'Hath a dog money? Is it possible
A cur can lend three thousand ducats?' Or
Shall I bend low, and in a bondman's° key,   slave's

120 With bated breath and whisp'ring humbleness
Say this: 'Fair sir, you spat on me on Wednesday last;
You spurned me such a day; another time
You called me dog; and for these courtesies
I'll lend you thus much moneys'?

125 ANTONIO　I am as like to call thee so again,
To spit on thee again, to spurn thee too.
If thou wilt lend this money, lend it not
As to thy friends; for when did friendship take
A breed⁵ for barren metal of his friend?

130 But lend it rather to thine enemy,
Who if he break,° thou mayst with better face   fail to repay
Exact the penalty.

SHYLOCK　　　　　　Why, look you, how you storm!
I would be friends with you, and have your love,
Forget the shames that you have stained me with,

135 Supply your present wants, and take no doit°   small coin
Of usance for my moneys; and you'll not hear me.
This is kind⁶ I offer.

BASSANIO　This were° kindness.   would be

SHYLOCK　This kindness will I show.

140 Go with me to a notary, seal me there
Your single bond,⁷ and, in a merry sport,
If you repay me not on such a day,
In such a place, such sum or sums as are
Expressed in the condition, let the forfeit°   penalty

145 Be nominated for an equal° pound   Be stipulated as an exact

---

4. For enduring insult is the characteristic.
5. Offspring (interest); alluding to an ancient argument that it was unnatural to use money to "breed," or make, more money.

6. Benevolent; natural (but perhaps with the covert suggestion "in kind").
7. Bond signed by the debtor alone (Antonio) without additional guarantors.

Of your fair flesh to be cut off and taken
In what part of your body pleaseth me.

ANTONIO   Content, in faith. I'll seal to such a bond,
And say there is much kindness in the Jew.

150   BASSANIO   You shall not seal to such a bond for me.
I'll rather dwell in my necessity.°   *remain in need*

ANTONIO   Why, fear not, man; I will not forfeit it.
Within these two months—that's a month before
This bond expires—I do expect return

155   Of thrice three times the value of this bond.

SHYLOCK   O father Abram, what these Christians are,
Whose own hard dealings teaches them suspect
The thoughts of others! [*To* BASSANIO] Pray you tell me this:
If he should break his day, what should I gain

160   By the exaction of the forfeiture?
A pound of man's flesh taken from a man
Is not so estimable,° profitable neither,   *valuable*
As flesh of muttons, beeves, or goats. I say,
To buy his favour I extend this friendship.

165   If he will take it, so. If not, adieu,
And, for my love, I pray you wrong me not.

ANTONIO   Yes, Shylock, I will seal unto this bond.

SHYLOCK   Then meet me forthwith at the notary's.
Give him direction for this merry bond,

170   And I will go and purse the ducats straight,
See to my house—left in the fearful° guard   *doubtful*
Of an unthrifty knave—and presently
I'll be with you.

ANTONIO   Hie thee,° gentle Jew.   *Exit* [SHYLOCK]   *Hurry*
The Hebrew will turn Christian; he grows kind.

175   BASSANIO   I like not fair terms and a villain's mind.

ANTONIO   Come on. In this there can be no dismay.
My ships come home a month before the day.   *Exeunt*

2.1

[*Flourish of cornets.*] *Enter* [*the Prince of* MOROCCO,
*a tawny Moor all in white, and three or four followers
accordingly,*[1] *with* PORTIA, NERISSA, *and their train.*

MOROCCO [*to* PORTIA]   Mislike me not for my complexion
The shadowed livery° of the burnished sun,   *servant's uniform*
To whom I am a neighbour and near bred.°   *close kin*
Bring me the fairest creature northward born,

5   Where Phoebus'° fire scarce thaws the icicles,   *the sun god*
And let us make incision for your love
To prove whose blood is reddest,[2] his or mine.
I tell thee, lady, this aspect° of mine   *countenance*
Hath feared° the valiant. By my love I swear,   *frightened*

10   The best regarded virgins of our clime
Have loved it too. I would not change this hue
Except to steal your thoughts, my gentle queen.

PORTIA   In terms of choice I am not solely led
By nice direction° of a maiden's eyes.   *fastidious guidance*

2.1 Location: Belmont.   2. Red blood was considered a sign of valor.
1. Of similar complexion and dress.

15   Besides, the lott'ry of my destiny
      Bars me the right of voluntary choosing.
      But if my father had not scanted° me,   *limited*
      And hedged° me by his wit° to yield myself   *restricted / wisdom*
      His wife who wins me by that means I told you,
20   Yourself, renownèd Prince, then stood as fair³
      As any comer I have looked on yet
      For my affection.
MOROCCO   Even for that I thank you.
      Therefore I pray you lead me to the caskets
      To try my fortune. By this scimitar,
25   That slew the Sophy° and a Persian prince   *Shah of Persia*
      That won three fields of Sultan Suleiman,°   *Turkish ruler*
      I would o'erstare the sternest eyes that look,
      Outbrave the heart most daring on the earth,
      Pluck the young sucking cubs from the she-bear,
30   Yea, mock the lion when a° roars for prey,   *he*
      To win the lady. But alas the while,
      If Hercules and Lichas° play at dice   *Hercules' servant*
      Which is the better man, the greater throw
      May turn by fortune from the weaker hand.
35   So is Alcides° beaten by his rage,⁴   *Hercules*
      And so may I, blind Fortune leading me,
      Miss that which one unworthier may attain,
      And die with grieving.
PORTIA   You must take your chance,
      And either not attempt to choose at all,
40   Or swear before you choose, if you choose wrong
      Never to speak to lady afterward
      In way of marriage. Therefore be advised.°   *careful*
MOROCCO   Nor will not. Come, bring me unto my chance.
PORTIA   First, forward to the temple. After dinner
      Your hazard shall be made.
45   MOROCCO   Good fortune then,
      To make me blest or cursèd'st among men.
                           [Flourish of] cornets. Exeunt

2.2

      Enter [LANCELOT] *the clown*
LANCELOT   Certainly my conscience will serve° me to run from   *allow*
      this Jew my master. The fiend is at mine elbow and tempts me,
      saying to me 'Gobbo, Lancelot Gobbo, good Lancelot,' or
      'good Gobbo,' or 'good Lancelot Gobbo—use your legs, take the
5   start,° run away.' My conscience says 'No, take heed, honest   *begone*
      Lancelot, take heed, honest Gobbo,' or, as aforesaid, 'honest
      Lancelot Gobbo—do not run, scorn running with thy heels.'°   *indignantly (with pun)*
      Well, the most courageous fiend bids me pack. '*Via!*'° says the   *Away*
      fiend; 'Away!' says the fiend. 'For the heavens, rouse up a brave
10   mind,' says the fiend, 'and run.' Well, my conscience hanging
      about the neck of my heart says very wisely to me, 'My honest
      friend Lancelot'—being an honest man's son, or rather an hon-
      est woman's son, for indeed my father did something smack,

---

3. Seemed as attractive; stood as good a chance.   **2.2** Location: Venice.
4. Often amended to "page."

something grow to; he had a kind of taste¹—well, my con-
15 science says, 'Lancelot, budge not'; 'Budge!' says the fiend;
'Budge not', says my conscience. 'Conscience,' say I, 'you
counsel well'; 'Fiend,' say I, 'you counsel well.' To be ruled by
my conscience I should stay with the Jew my master who, God
bless the mark,² is a kind of devil; and to run away from the
20 Jew I should be ruled by the fiend who, saving your reverence,
is the devil himself. Certainly the Jew is the very devil incar-
nation;° and in my conscience, my conscience is but a kind of   *(for "incarnate")*
hard conscience to offer to counsel me to stay with the Jew.
The fiend gives the more friendly counsel. I will run, fiend.
25 My heels are at your commandment. I will run.

     Enter old GOBBO, [*blind,*] *with a basket*

GOBBO   Master young man, you, I pray you, which is the way to
    Master Jew's?
LANCELOT [*aside*]   O heavens, this is my true-begotten father
    who, being more than sand-blind—high-gravel-blind³—
30   knows me not. I will try confusions⁴ with him.
GOBBO   Master young gentleman, I pray you which is the way
    to Master Jew's?
LANCELOT   Turn up on your right hand at the next turning, but
    at the next turning of all on your left, marry at the very next
35   turning, turn of no hand but turn down indirectly to the Jew's
    house.
GOBBO   By God's sonties,° 'twill be a hard way to hit. Can you   *saints*
    tell me whether one Lancelot that dwells with him dwell with
    him or no?
40 LANCELOT   Talk you of young Master⁵ Lancelot? [*Aside*]   Mark
    me now, now will I raise the waters.⁶ [*To* GOBBO]   Talk you of
    young Master Lancelot?
GOBBO   No master, sir, but a poor man's son. His father, though
    I say't, is an honest exceeding poor man, and, God be thanked,
45   well to live.⁷
LANCELOT   Well, let his father be what a° will, we talk of young   *he*
    Master Lancelot.
GOBBO   Your worship's friend, and Lancelot, sir.
LANCELOT   But I pray you, *ergo*° old man, *ergo* I beseech you,   *therefore*
50   talk you of young Master Lancelot?
GOBBO   Of Lancelot, an't° please your mastership.   *if it*
LANCELOT   *Ergo* Master Lancelot. Talk not of Master Lancelot,
    father,⁸ for the young gentleman, according to fates and destin-
    ies and such odd sayings—the sisters three° and such branches   *the Fates*
55   of learning—is indeed deceased; or, as you would say in plain
    terms, gone to heaven.
GOBBO   Marry, God forbid! The boy was the very staff of my age,
    my very prop.
LANCELOT [*aside*]   Do I look like a cudgel or a hovel-post,° a   *shed post*
60   staff or a prop? [*To* GOBBO] Do you know me, father?

---

1. *my father . . . taste*: that is, my father was licentious.
2. Conventional apology before a rude remark, like "saving your reverence."
3. Lancelot's coinage for a degree of blindness between sand-blind (partly blind) and stone-blind.
4. Lancelot's version of "try conclusions" (experiment).
5. "Master" was only applied to gentlemen's sons.
6. Start something; bring on tears.
7. Well-to-do (contradicts the previous line).
8. Customary address to an old man.

GOBBO Alack the day, I know you not, young gentleman. But I
pray you tell me, is my boy—God rest his soul—alive or dead?

LANCELOT Do you not know me, father?

GOBBO Alack, sir, I am sand-blind. I know you not.

65 LANCELOT Nay, indeed, if you had your eyes you might fail of
the knowing me. It is a wise father that knows his own child.[9]
Well, old man, I will tell you news of your son. [*Kneeling*]
Give me your blessing. Truth will come to light; murder cannot be hid long—a man's son may, but in the end truth will

70 out.

GOBBO Pray you, sir, stand up. I am sure you are not Lancelot,
my boy.

LANCELOT Pray you, let's have no more fooling about it, but give
me your blessing. I am Lancelot, your boy that was, your son

75 that is, your child that shall be.

GOBBO I cannot think you are my son.

LANCELOT I know not what I shall think of that, but I am
Lancelot the Jew's man, and I am sure Margery your wife is
my mother.

80 GOBBO Her name is Margery indeed. I'll be sworn, if thou be
Lancelot thou art mine own flesh and blood.
[*He feels Lancelot's head*]
Lord worshipped might he be, what a beard hast thou got![1]
Thou hast got more hair on thy chin than Dobbin my fill-
horse° has on his tail.   *cart horse*

85 LANCELOT It should seem then that Dobbin's tail grows backward.[2] I am sure he had more hair of his tail than I have of my
face when I last saw him.

GOBBO Lord, how art thou changed! How dost thou and thy
master agree?° I have brought him a present. How 'gree you   *get along*

90 now?

LANCELOT Well, well; but for mine own part, as I have set up
my rest[3] to run away, so I will not rest till I have run some
ground. My master's a very Jew.[4] Give him a present?—give
him a halter!° I am famished in his service. You may tell° every   *noose / count*

95 finger I have with my ribs. Father, I am glad you are come.
Give me° your present to one Master Bassanio, who indeed   *Give*
gives rare new liveries.° If I serve not him, I will run as far as   *servants' uniforms*
God has any ground.
[*Enter* BASSANIO *with* [LEONARDO *and*] *follower*[s]]
O rare fortune! Here comes the man. To him, father, for I am

100 a Jew if I serve the Jew any longer.

BASSANIO [*to one of his men*] You may do so, but let it be so
hasted° that supper be ready at the farthest° by five of the   *hurried / latest*
clock. See these letters delivered, put the liveries to making,
and desire° Graziano to come anon° to my lodging. [*Exit one*]   *tell / at once*

105 LANCELOT [*to* GOBBO] To him, father.

GOBBO [*to* BASSANIO] God bless your worship.

BASSANIO Gramercy.° Wouldst thou aught° with me?   *Many thanks / anything*

GOBBO Here's my son, sir, a poor boy—

---

9. Transposing the proverb "A wise child knows his
own father."
1. Gobbo mistakes Lancelot's hair for a beard.
2. Gets shorter; grows from the wrong end.

3. As I have definitely determined (phrase in the card
game primero meaning "risk everything").
4. Cruel, grasping person; Hebrew. *a very:* an absolute.

LANCELOT [*to* BASSANIO] Not a poor boy, sir, but the rich Jew's
110 man that would, sir, as my father shall specify.

GOBBO [*to* BASSANIO] He hath a great infection,° sir, as one *(for "affection"; wish)*
would say, to serve—

LANCELOT Indeed, the short and the long is, I serve the Jew,
and have a desire as my father shall specify.

115 GOBBO [*to* BASSANIO] His master and he, saving your worship's
reverence, are scarce cater-cousins.° *close friends*

LANCELOT [*to* BASSANIO] To be brief, the very truth is that the
Jew, having done me wrong, doth cause me, as my father—
being, I hope, an old man—shall frutify° unto you. *(for "certify")*

120 GOBBO [*to* BASSANIO] I have here a dish of doves that I would
bestow upon your worship, and my suit is—

LANCELOT [*to* BASSANIO] In very brief the suit is impertinent° *(for "pertinent")*
to myself, as your worship shall know by this honest old man;
and though I say it, though old man, yet, poor man, my father.

125 BASSANIO One speak for both. What would you?

LANCELOT Serve you, sir.

GOBBO [*to* BASSANIO] That is the very defect° of the matter, sir. *(for "effect")*

BASSANIO [*to* LANCELOT] I know thee well. Thou hast obtained
thy suit.

130 Shylock thy master spoke with me this day,
And hath preferred thee, if it be preferment[5]
To leave a rich Jew's service to become
The follower of so poor a gentleman.

LANCELOT The old proverb[6] is very well parted between my
135 master Shylock and you, sir: you have the grace of God, sir,
and he hath enough.

BASSANIO Thou speak'st it well. [*To* GOBBO] Go, father, with thy son.
[*To* LANCELOT] Take leave of thy old master and enquire
My lodging out. [*To one of his men*] Give him a livery
140 More guarded° than his fellows'. See it done. *decorated*

LANCELOT [*to* GOBBO] Father, in. I cannot get a service, no, I
have ne'er a tongue in my head—well!
    [*He looks at his palm*]
If any man in Italy have a fairer table[7] which doth offer to swear
upon a book,[8] I shall have good fortune. Go to, here's a simple° *unremarkable (ironic)*
145 line of life, here's a small trifle of wives—alas, fifteen wives is
nothing. Eleven widows and nine maids is a simple coming-in[9]
for one man, and then to scape drowning thrice, and to be in
peril of my life with the edge of a featherbed[1]—here are simple
scapes. Well, if Fortune be a woman, she's a good wench for
150 this gear.° Father, come. I'll take my leave of the Jew in the *matter*
twinkling. *Exit* [*with old* GOBBO]

BASSANIO I pray thee, good Leonardo, think on this.
These things being bought and orderly bestowed.° *stowed on ship*
Return in haste, for I do feast tonight
155 My best-esteemed acquaintance. Hie thee. Go

LEONARDO My best endeavours shall be done herein.
    [*He begins to leave.*] *Enter* GRAZIANO

---

5. And has recommended you, if it be advancement.
6. "The grace of God is gear enough."
7. Palm (Lancelot reads the lines of his palm to predict the future).
8. To tell the truth (referring to the practice of taking an oath with the palm on the Bible).
9. A scanty income; an easy sexual entrance.
1. Alluding to a sexual adventure.

GRAZIANO [*to* LEONARDO]   Where's your master?

LEONARDO   Yonder, sir, he walks.

Exit

GRAZIANO   Signor Bassanio.

BASSANIO   Graziano.

GRAZIANO   I have a suit to you.

BASSANIO   You have obtained it.

160 GRAZIANO   You must not deny me. I must go with you to Belmont.

BASSANIO   Why then, you must. But hear thee, Graziano,
 Thou art too wild, too rude and bold of voice—
 Parts° that become thee happily enough,   *Attributes*
 And in such eyes as ours appear not faults;
165 But where thou art not known, why, there they show
 Something too liberal.° Pray thee, take pain   *unrestrained*
 To allay with some cold drops of modesty
 Thy skipping spirit, lest through thy wild behaviour
 I be misconstered° in the place I go to,   *misconstrued*
 And lose my hopes.
170 GRAZIANO   Signor Bassanio, hear me.
 If I do not put on a sober habit,°   *behavior; clothing*
 Talk with respect, and swear but now and then,
 Wear prayer books in my pocket, look demurely—
 Nay more, while grace is saying hood mine eyes
175 Thus with my hat,² and sigh, and say 'Amen',
 Use all the observance of civility,
 Like one well studied in a sad ostent°   *solemn appearance*
 To please his grandam,° never trust me more.°   *grandmother / again*

BASSANIO   Well, we shall see your bearing.

180 GRAZIANO   Nay, but I bar tonight. You shall not gauge me
 By what we do tonight.

BASSANIO   No, that were pity.
 I would entreat you rather to put on
 Your boldest suit of mirth, for we have friends
 That purpose merriment. But fare you well.
185 I have some business.

GRAZIANO   And I must to Lorenzo and the rest.
 But we will visit you at supper-time.   *Exeunt* [*severally*]

2.3

Enter JESSICA *and* [LANCELOT] *the clown*

JESSICA   I am sorry thou wilt leave my father so.
 Our house is hell, and thou, a merry devil,
 Didst rob it of some taste of tediousness.
 But fare thee well. There is a ducat for thee.
5   And, Lancelot, soon at supper shalt thou see
 Lorenzo, who is thy new master's guest.
 Give him this letter, do it secretly;
 And so farewell. I would not have my father
 See me in talk with thee.
10 LANCELOT   Adieu. Tears exhibit° my tongue, most beautiful   *(for "inhibit")*
 pagan; most sweet Jew; if a Christian do not play the knave and
 get thee, I am much deceived. But adieu. These foolish drops
 do something drown my manly spirit. Adieu.

---

2. Hats were worn at meals but taken off for grace.   **2.3** Location: Shylock's house in Venice.

JESSICA   Farewell, good Lancelot.   *Exit* [LANCELOT]

15   Alack, what heinous sin is it in me
      To be ashamed to be my father's child!
      But though I am a daughter to his blood,
      I am not to his manners.° O Lorenzo,   *behavior*
      If thou keep promise I shall end this strife,
20   Become a Christian and thy loving wife.   *Exit*

2.4

Enter GRAZIANO, LORENZO, SALERIO, *and* SOLANIO

LORENZO   Nay, we will slink away in° supper-time,   *during*
      Disguise us at my lodging, and return
      All in an hour.
GRAZIANO   We have not made good preparation.
5   SALERIO   We have not spoke as yet of ° torchbearers.   *not yet arranged for*
   SOLANIO   'Tis vile, unless it may be quaintly ordered,°   *cleverly managed*
      And better in my mind not undertook.
   LORENZO   'Tis now but four o'clock. We have two hours
      To furnish us.
          Enter LANCELOT *with a letter*
          Friend Lancelot, what's the news?
10 LANCELOT [*presenting the letter*]   An° it shall please you to break   *If*
      up° this, it shall seem to signify.   *open*
   LORENZO [*taking the letter*]   I know the hand. In faith, 'tis a fair
        hand,
      And whiter than the paper it writ on
      Is the fair hand that writ.
   GRAZIANO   Love-news, in faith.
15 LANCELOT [*to* LORENZO]   By your leave, sir.
   LORENZO   Whither goest thou?
   LANCELOT   Marry, sir, to bid my old master the Jew to sup tonight
      with my new master the Christian.
   LORENZO   Hold,° here, take this. [*Giving money*] Tell gentle Jessica   *Wait*
20   I will not fail her. Speak it privately.
      Go.   *Exit* [LANCELOT *the*] *clown*
          Gentlemen,
      Will you prepare you for this masque tonight?
      I am provided of a torchbearer.
   SALERIO   Ay, marry, I'll be gone about it straight.°   *immediately*
   SOLANIO   And so will I.
25 LORENZO   Meet me and Graziano
      At Graziano's lodging some hour hence.
   SALERIO   'Tis good we do so.   *Exit* [*with* SOLANIO]
   GRAZIANO   Was not that letter from fair Jessica?
   LORENZO   I must needs tell thee all. She hath directed
30   How I shall take her from her father's house,
      What gold and jewels she is furnished with,
      What page's suit she hath in readiness.
      If e'er the Jew her father come to heaven
      It will be for his gentle daughter's sake;
35   And never dare misfortune cross her foot
      Unless she° do it under this excuse: *(misfortune)*

2.4 Location: Street in Venice.

That she° is issue° to a faithless Jew.   *(Jessica) / offspring*
Come, go with me. Peruse this as thou goest.
    [*He gives* GRAZIANO *the letter*]
Fair Jessica shall be my torchbearer.   *Exeunt*

2.5

Enter [SHYLOCK *the*] *Jew and his man that was,*°   *former servant*
[LANCELOT] *the clown*

SHYLOCK   Well, thou shalt see, thy eyes shall be thy judge,
The difference of old Shylock and Bassanio.
[*Calling*] What, Jessica! [*To* LANCELOT] Thou shalt not gormandize°   *overeat*
As thou hast done with me. [*Calling*] What, Jessica!
5 [*To* LANCELOT] And sleep and snore and rend apparel out.°   *wear out clothes*
[*Calling*] Why, Jessica, I say!

LANCELOT [*calling*]   Why, Jessica!

SHYLOCK   Who bids thee call? I do not bid thee call.

LANCELOT   Your worship was wont to tell me I could do nothing
without bidding.
       Enter JESSICA

10 JESSICA [*to* SHYLOCK]   Call you? What is your will?

SHYLOCK   I am bid forth to supper, Jessica.
There are my keys. But wherefore° should I go?   *why*
I am not bid for love. They flatter me,
But yet I'll go in hate, to feed upon
15 The prodigal Christian. Jessica, my girl,
Look to my house. I am right loath° to go.   *very unwilling*
There is some ill a-brewing towards my rest,
For I did dream of money-bags tonight.°   *last night*

LANCELOT   I beseech you, sir, go. My young master doth expect
20 your reproach.°   *(for "approach")*

SHYLOCK   So do I his.

LANCELOT   And they have conspired together. I will not say you
shall see a masque, but if you do, then it was not for nothing
that my nose fell a-bleeding on Black Monday° last at six   *Easter Monday*
25 o'clock i'th' morning, falling out that year on Ash Wednesday
was four year in th'afternoon.[1]

SHYLOCK   What, are there masques? Hear you me, Jessica,
Lock up my doors; and when you hear the drum
And the vile squealing of the wry-necked[2] fife,
30 Clamber not you up to the casements then,
Nor thrust your head into the public street
To gaze on Christian fools with varnished° faces,   *painted; masked*
But stop my house's ears—I mean my casements.
Let not the sound of shallow fopp'ry° enter   *frivolity*
35 My sober house. By Jacob's staff[3] I swear
I have no mind of feasting forth° tonight.   *away from home*
But I will go. [*To* LANCELOT] Go you before me, sirrah.
Say I will come.

LANCELOT   I will go before, sir.
      [*Aside to* JESSICA]
Mistress, look out at window for all this.[4]

2.5 Location: Outside Shylock's house.   3. See Genesis 32:10 and Hebrews 11:21.
1. Lancelot mocks Shylock's superstition.   4. *for all this*: despite Shylock's instructions.
2. Fifes were played with the head turned sideways.

40   There will come a Christian by
       Will be worth a Jewës eye.   [*Exit*]
       SHYLOCK [*to* JESSICA] What says that fool of Hagar's offspring,[5] ha?
       JESSICA   His words were 'Farewell, mistress'; nothing else
       SHYLOCK   The patch° is kind enough, but a huge feeder,   *fool*
45   Snail-slow in profit,° and he sleeps by day   *proficiency*
       More than the wildcat. Drones hive not with me;
       Therefore I part with him, and part with him
       To one that I would have him help to waste
       His borrowed purse. Well, Jessica, go in.
50   Perhaps I will return immediately.
       Do as I bid you. Shut doors after you.
       Fast bind, fast find[6]—
       A proverb never stale in thrifty mind.   *Exit* [*at one door*]
       JESSICA   Farewell; and if my fortune be not crossed,
55   I have a father, you a daughter lost.   *Exit* [*at another door*]

2.6

Enter the masquers, GRAZIANO *and* SALERIO [*with torchbearers*]

       GRAZIANO   This is the penthouse[1] under which Lorenzo
       Desired us to make stand.
       SALERIO   His hour is almost past.
       GRAZIANO   And it is marvel he outdwells his hour,
       For lovers ever run before the clock.
5   SALERIO   O, ten times faster Venus' pigeons[2] fly
       To seal love's bonds new made than they are wont
       To keep obligèd° faith unforfeited.°   *pledged / unbroken*
       GRAZIANO   That ever holds.° Who riseth from a feast   *remains true*
       With that keen appetite that he sits down?
10   Where is the horse that doth untread° again   *retrace*
       His tedious measures with the unbated fire
       That he did pace them first? All things that are
       Are with more spirit chasèd than enjoyed.
       How like a younker or a prodigal[3]
15   The scarfèd barque° puts from her native bay,   *streamer-bedecked ship*
       Hugged and embracèd by the strumpet wind!
       How like the prodigal doth she return,
       With over-weathered ribs° and raggèd sails,   *weatherbeaten timbers*
       Lean, rent,° and beggared by the strumpet wind!   *torn*
       Enter LORENZO [*with a torch*]
20   SALERIO   Here comes Lorenzo. More of this hereafter.
       LORENZO   Sweet friends, your patience for my long abode.°   *delay*
       Not I but my affairs have made you wait.
       When you shall please to play the thieves for wives
       I'll watch° as long for you therein. Approach.   *wait*
25   Here dwells my father° Jew. [*Calling*] Ho, who's within?   *father-in-law*
       [*Enter*] JESSICA *above* [*in boy's apparel*]
       JESSICA   Who are you? Tell me for more certainty.

---

5. *That despicable gentile.* Hagar, Abraham's gentile
servant, bore him a son, Ishmael; she and her child
were cast out after the birth of Abraham's legitimate
son, Isaac.
6. Something firmly secured will remain fastened.

2.6 Location: Scene continues.
1. Projecting roof of an upper story.
2. Doves that drew the love goddess's chariot.
3. See Luke 15:11–31. *younker:* fashionable youth;
junior seaman.

Albeit I'll swear that I do know your tongue.

LORENZO   Lorenzo, and thy love.

JESSICA   Lorenzo, certain, and my love indeed,
30   For who love I so much? And now who knows
       But you, Lorenzo, whether I am yours?

LORENZO   Heaven and thy thoughts are witness that thou art.

JESSICA   Here, catch this casket. It is worth the pains.
       I am glad 'tis night, you do not look on me,
35   For I am much ashamed of my exchange;°   change of clothes
       But love is blind, and lovers cannot see
       The pretty° follies that themselves commit;   ingenious
       For if they could, Cupid himself would blush
       To see me thus transformèd to a boy.

40 LORENZO   Descend, for you must be my torchbearer.

JESSICA   What, must I hold a candle to my shames?
       They in themselves, good sooth,° are too too light.°   in truth / clear; wanton
       Why, 'tis an office of discovery,⁴ love,
       And I should be obscured.

LORENZO   So are you, sweet,
45   Even in the lovely garnish° of a boy.   dress
       But come at once,
       For the close° night doth play the runaway,°   secret / steals away
       And we are stayed° for at Bassanio's feast.   waited

JESSICA   I will make fast the doors, and gild myself
50   With some more ducats, and be with you straight.
                                        [Exit above]

GRAZIANO   Now, by my hood, a gentile, and no Jew.

LORENZO   Beshrew° me but I love her heartily,   Evil befall
       For she is wise, if I can judge of her;
       And fair she is, if that mine eyes be true;
55   And true she is, as she hath proved herself;
       And therefore like herself, wise, fair, and true,
       Shall she be placèd in my constant soul.
                 Enter JESSICA [below]
       What, art thou come? On, gentlemen, away.
       Our masquing mates by this time for us stay.
                       Exit [with JESSICA and SALERIO]
                 Enter ANTONIO

ANTONIO   Who's there?

60 GRAZIANO   Signor Antonio?

ANTONIO   Fie, fie, Graziano, where are all the rest?
       'Tis nine o'clock. Our friends all stay for you.
       No masque tonight. The wind is come about.
       Bassanio presently° will go aboard.   immediately
65   I have sent twenty out to seek for you.

GRAZIANO   I am glad on't. I desire no more delight
       Than to be under sail and gone tonight.   Exeunt

                              2.7
       [Flourish of cornets.] Enter PORTIA with MOROCCO and
       both their trains

PORTIA   Go, draw aside the curtains, and discover°   reveal
       The several caskets to this noble prince.

_____
4. (Torchbearing) is a task of disclosure.   2.7 Location: Belmont.

[*The curtains are drawn aside, revealing three caskets*]
[*To* MOROCCO]   Now make your choice.
MOROCCO   This first of gold, who° this inscription bears: *which*
5   'Who chooseth me shall gain what many men desire.'
  The second silver, which this promise carries:
  'Who chooseth me shall get as much as he deserves.'
  This third dull lead, with warning all as blunt:[1]
  'Who chooseth me must give and hazard all he hath.'
10   How shall I know if I do choose the right?
PORTIA   The one of them contains my picture, Prince.
  If you choose that, then I am yours withal.°   *with it*
MOROCCO   Some god direct my judgement! Let me see.
  I will survey th'inscriptions back again.
15   What says this leaden casket?
  'Who chooseth me must give and hazard all he hath.'
  Must give, for what? For lead? Hazard for lead?
  This casket threatens. Men that hazard all
  Do it in hope of fair advantages.
20   A golden mind stoops not to shows of dross.°   *rubbish*
  I'll then nor° give nor hazard aught for lead.   *neither*
  What says the silver with her virgin hue?
  'Who chooseth me shall get as much as he deserves.'
  'As much as he deserves': pause there, Morocco,
25   And weigh thy value with an even° hand.   *impartial*
  If thou beest rated by thy estimation
  Thou dost deserve enough, and yet 'enough'
  May not extend so far as to the lady.
  And yet to be afeard of my deserving
30   Were but a weak disabling° of myself.   *disparagement*
  As much as I deserve—why, that's the lady!
  I do in birth deserve her, and in fortunes,
  In graces, and in qualities of breeding;
  But more than these, in love I do deserve.
35   What if I strayed no farther, but chose here?
  Let's see once more this saying graved in gold:
  'Who chooseth me shall gain what many men desire.'
  Why, that's the lady! All the world desires her.
  From the four corners of the earth they come
40   To kiss this shrine, this mortal breathing saint.
  The Hyrcanian deserts[2] and the vasty° wilds   *vast*
  Of wide Arabia are as throughfares° now   *main roads*
  For princes to come view fair Portia.
  The watery kingdom, whose ambitious head°   *(of a storm)*
45   Spits in the face of heaven, is no bar
  To stop the foreign spirits, but they come
  As o'er a brook to see fair Portia.
  One of these three contains her heavenly picture.
  Is't like° that lead contains her? 'Twere damnation   *probable*
50   To think so base a thought. It° were too gross   *(lead)*
  To rib her cerecloth[3] in the obscure grave.
  Or shall I think in silver she's immured,°   *enclosed*
  Being ten times undervalued to tried° gold?   *purified*

1. Plainly spoken; not sharp (with play on "dull lead").   3. To enclose her shroud (normally covered with a
2. Wild region south of the Caspian Sea.   layer of lead).

O sinful thought! Never so rich a gem
55 Was set in worse than gold. They have in England
A coin that bears the figure of an angel[4]
Stamped in gold, but that's insculped° upon;   *engraved*
But here an angel in a golden bed
Lies all within. Deliver me the key.
60 Here do I choose, and thrive I as I may.
    [*He is given a key*]
PORTIA   There, take it, Prince; and if my form° lie there,   *image*
Then I am yours.
    [MOROCCO *opens the golden casket*]
MOROCCO   O hell! What have we here?
A carrion death,° within whose empty eye   *A skull*
There is a written scroll. I'll read the writing.
65 'All that glisters is not gold;
Often have you heard that told.
Many a man his life hath sold
But my outside[5] to behold.
Gilded tombs do worms infold.°   *enclose*
70 Had you been as wise as bold,
Young in limbs, in judgement old,
Your answer had not been enscrolled.
Fare you well; your suit is cold.'
Cold indeed, and labour lost.
75 Then farewell heat, and welcome frost.
Portia, adieu. I have too grieved a heart
To take a tedious leave. Thus losers part.
                Exit [*with his train*]. *Flourish* [*of*] *cornets*
PORTIA   A gentle riddance. Draw the curtains, go.
Let all of his complexion choose me so.
                  [*The curtains are drawn.*] *Exeunt*

2.8

Enter SALERIO *and* SOLANIO
SALERIO   Why, man, I saw Bassanio under sail.
With him is Graziano gone along,
And in their ship I am sure Lorenzo is not.
SOLANIO   The villain Jew with outcries raised° the Duke,   *roused*
5 Who went with him to search Bassanio's ship.
SALERIO   He came too late. The ship was under sail.
But there the Duke was given to understand
That in a gondola were seen together
Lorenzo and his amorous Jessica.
10 Besides, Antonio certified the Duke
They were not with Bassanio in his ship.
SOLANIO   I never heard a passion° so confused,   *an outburst*
So strange, outrageous, and so variable
As the dog Jew did utter in the streets.
15 'My daughter! O, my ducats! O, my daughter!
Fled with a Christian! O, my Christian ducats!
Justice! The law! My ducats and my daughter!
A sealèd bag, two sealèd bags of ducats,

---

4. The gold coin called angel had the figure of St.
Michael on its face.
5. Gold; face that once covered the skull.
2.8 Location: Venice.

Of double ducats, stol'n from me by my daughter

20 And jewels, two stones, two rich and precious stones,[1]
Stol'n by my daughter! Justice! Find the girl!
She hath the stones upon her, and the ducats!'

SALERIO   Why, all the boys in Venice follow him,
Crying, 'His stones, his daughter, and his ducats!'

25 SOLANIO   Let good Antonio look he keep his day,°   *repay his debt on time*
Or he shall pay for this.

SALERIO   Marry, well remembered.
I reasoned° with a Frenchman yesterday,   *conversed*
Who told me in the narrow seas° that part   *(English Channel)*
The French and English there miscarrièd°   *wrecked*

30 A vessel of our country, richly fraught.°   *laden*
I thought upon Antonio when he told me,
And wished in silence that it were not his.

SOLANIO   You were best to tell Antonio what you hear—
Yet do not suddenly, for it may grieve him.

35 SALERIO   A kinder gentleman treads not the earth.
I saw Bassanio and Antonio part.
Bassanio told him he would make some speed
Of his return. He answered, 'Do not so.
Slubber° not business for my sake, Bassanio,   *Hastily perform*

40 But stay the very riping of the time;
And for the Jew's bond which he hath of me,
Let it not enter in your mind° of love.   *interrupt your thoughts*
Be merry, and employ your chiefest thoughts
To courtship and such fair ostents° of love   *displays*

45 As shall conveniently° become you there.'   *properly*
And even there, his eye being big with tears,
Turning his face, he put his hand behind him
And, with affection wondrous sensible,°   *obvious; heartfelt*
He wrung Bassanio's hand; and so they parted.

50 SOLANIO   I think he only loves the world for him.
I pray thee let us go and find him out,
And quicken his embracèd heaviness[2]
With some delight or other.

SALERIO   Do we so.   *Exeunt*

2.9

Enter NERISSA and a servitor

NERISSA   Quick, quick, I pray thee, draw the curtain straight.°   *immediately*
The Prince of Aragon hath ta'en his oath,
And comes to his election presently.°   *his choice at once*
[*The servitor draws aside the curtain, revealing the three
caskets. Flourish of cornets.*] *Enter ARAGON, his train,
and PORTIA*

PORTIA   Behold, there stand the caskets, noble Prince.

5 If you choose that wherein I am contained,
Straight shall our nuptial rites be solemnized.
But if you fail, without more speech, my lord,
You must be gone from hence immediately.

---

1. With the suggestion "testicles," taken up by the
mocking boys in line 24.

2. And lighten the grief he embraces.

2.9 Location: Belmont.

ARAGON   I am enjoined by oath to observe three things:
10 First, never to unfold to anyone
Which casket 'twas I chose. Next, if I fail
Of the right casket, never in my life
To woo a maid in way of marriage.
Lastly, if I do fail in fortune of my choice,
15 Immediately to leave you and be gone.
PORTIA   To these injunctions everyone doth swear
That comes to hazard° for my worthless self.   gamble
ARAGON   And so have I addressed° me. Fortune now   prepared
To my heart's hope! Gold, silver, and base lead.
[He reads the leaden casket]
20 'Who chooseth me must give and hazard all he hath.'
You shall look fairer ere I give or hazard.
What says the golden chest? Ha, let me see.
'Who chooseth me shall gain what many men desire.'
'What many men desire'—that 'many' may be meant
25 By° the fool multitude, that choose by show,   For
Not learning more than the fond° eye doth teach,   foolish
Which pries not to th'interior but, like the martlet,°   swallow
Builds in the weather° on the outward wall   open air
Even in the force and road of casualty.°   mishap
30 I will not choose what many men desire,
Because I will not jump° with common spirits   agree
And rank me with the barbarous multitudes.
Why then, to thee, thou silver treasure-house.
Tell me once more what title thou dost bear.
35 'Who chooseth me shall get as much as he deserves'—
And well said too, for who shall go about
To cozen° fortune, and be honourable   cheat
Without the stamp° of merit? Let none presume   official seal
To wear an undeservèd dignity.
40 O, that estates, degrees,° and offices   social ranks
Were not derived° corruptly, and that clear honour   gained
Were purchased° by the merit of the wearer!   acquired
How many then should cover that stand bare,[1]
How many be commanded that command?
45 How much low peasantry would then be gleaned°   separated
From the true seed of honour, and how much honour
Picked from the chaff and ruin of the times
To be new varnished?° Well; but to my choice.   regain its luster
'Who chooseth me shall get as much as he deserves.'
50 I will assume° desert. Give me a key for this,   claim
And instantly unlock my fortunes here.
[He is given a key, and opens the silver casket]
PORTIA   Too long a pause for that which you find there.
ARAGON   What's here? The portrait of a blinking idiot
Presenting me a schedule.° I will read it.   document
55 How much unlike art thou to Portia!
How much unlike my hopes and my deservings!
'Who chooseth me shall have as much as he deserves.'

---

1. Should wear hats who now stand bareheaded (before their social superiors).

Did I deserve no more than a fool's head?
Is that my prize? Are my deserts no better?

60 PORTIA   To offend and judge are distinct offices,²
And of opposèd natures.

ARAGON   What is here?
[*He reads the schedule*]
'The fire seven times tried° this;   *purified*
Seven times tried that judgement is
That did never choose amiss.
65 Some there be that shadows kiss;³
Such have but a shadow's bliss.
There be fools alive, iwis,°   *in truth*
Silvered⁴ o'er; and so was this.
Take what wife you will to bed,
70 I° will ever be your head.   *(the blinking idiot)*
So be gone; you are sped.'°   *finished*
Still more fool I shall appear
By the time I linger here.
With one fool's head I came to woo,
75 But I go away with two.
Sweet, adieu. I'll keep my oath
Patiently to bear my wroth.°   *grief*
[*Flourish of cornets. Exit with his train*]

PORTIA   Thus hath the candle singed the moth.
O, these deliberate° fools! When they do choose   *careful*
80 They have the wisdom by their wit to lose.
NERISSA   The ancient saying is no heresy:
Hanging and wiving goes by destiny.
PORTIA   Come, draw the curtain, Nerissa.
[NERISSA *draws the curtain*]
Enter MESSENGER
MESSENGER   Where is my lady?
PORTIA   Here. What would my lord?
85 MESSENGER   Madam, there is alighted at your gate
A young Venetian, one that comes before
To signify th'approaching of his lord,
From whom he bringeth sensible regreets,°   *tangible greetings*
To wit, besides commends and courteous breath,
90 Gifts of rich value. Yet° I have not seen   *Until now*
So likely° an ambassador of love.   *suitable*
A day in April never came so sweet
To show how costly° summer was at hand   *lavish*
As this fore-spurrer comes before his lord.
95 PORTIA   No more, I pray thee, I am half afeard
Thou wilt say anon° he is some kin to thee,   *soon*
Thou spend'st such high-day⁵ wit in praising him.
Come, come, Nerissa, for I long to see
Quick Cupid's post° that comes so mannerly.   *messenger*
100 NERISSA   Bassanio, Lord Love,° if thy will it be!   *Exeunt*   *Cupid*

---

2. To err and to judge are different functions.
3. Like Narcissus in classical mythology, a youth who fell in love with his own reflection.
4. Silver-haired (thus apparently wise).
5. Holiday (fit for special occasions).

3.1

Enter SOLANIO *and* SALERIO

SOLANIO Now, what news on the Rialto?

SALERIO Why, yet it lives there unchecked[1] that Antonio hath
a ship of rich lading wrecked on the narrow seas—the Good-
wins[2] I think they call the place—a very dangerous flat, and

5 fatal, where the carcasses of many a tall ship lie buried, as they
say, if my gossip Report° be an honest woman of her word.   *Dame Rumor*

SOLANIO I would she were as lying a gossip in that as ever
knapped° ginger or made her neighbours believe she wept for   *nibbled*
the death of a third husband. But it is true, without any slips

10 of prolixity° or crossing the plain highway of talk, that the   *any wordy lies*
good Antonio, the honest Antonio—O that I had a title good
enough to keep his name company—

SALERIO Come, the full stop.°   *period*

SOLANIO Ha, what sayst thou? Why, the end is he hath lost a

15 ship.

SALERIO I would it might prove the end of his losses.

SOLANIO Let me say amen betimes, lest the devil cross° my   *thwart*
prayer—

Enter SHYLOCK

for here he comes in the likeness of a Jew. How now, Shylock,

20 what news among the merchants?

SHYLOCK You knew, none so well, none so well as you, of my
daughter's flight.

SALERIO That's certain. I for my part knew the tailor that made
the wings[3] she flew withal.

25 SOLANIO And Shylock for his own part knew the bird was
fledge,° and then it is the complexion° of them all to leave the   *feathered / disposition*
dam.°   *mother (here, parent)*

SHYLOCK She is damned for it.

SALERIO That's certain, if the devil may be her judge.

30 SHYLOCK My own flesh and blood to rebel![4]

SOLANIO Out upon it, old carrion, rebels it at these years?

SHYLOCK I say my daughter is my flesh and my blood.

SALERIO There is more difference between thy flesh and hers
than between jet° and ivory; more between your bloods than   *black mineral*

35 there is between red wine and Rhenish.° But tell us, do you   *white wine*
hear whether Antonio have had any loss at sea or no?

SHYLOCK There I have another bad match.° A bankrupt, a   *bad deal*
prodigal, who dare scarce show his head on the Rialto; a beg-
gar, that was used to come so smug upon the mart. Let him look

40 to his bond. He was wont to call me usurer: let him look to his
bond. He was wont to lend money for a° Christian courtesy: let   *out of*
him look to his bond.

SALERIO Why, I am sure if he forfeit thou wilt not take his
flesh. What's that good for?

45 SHYLOCK To bait fish withal.° If it will feed nothing else it will   *with*
feed my revenge. He hath disgraced me, and hindered me half
a million; laughed at my losses, mocked at my gains, scorned

3.1 Location: Venice.
1. It circulates there without denial.
2. Goodwin Sands, where the Thames joins the sea.
"Goodwin" means "friend."

3. Playing on "wing," a decorative flap on the upper
sleeve.
4. Shylock means "my own offspring"; Solanio pretends
he means "carnal appetite."

my nation, thwarted my bargains, cooled my friends, heated
mine enemies, and what's his reason?—I am a Jew. Hath not a
50 Jew eyes? Hath not a Jew hands, organs, dimensions,° senses,   *bodily form*
affections, passions; fed with the same food, hurt with the
same weapons, subject to the same diseases, healed by the
same means, warmed and cooled by the same winter and
summer as a Christian is? If you prick us do we not bleed? If
55 you tickle us do we not laugh? If you poison us do we not die?
And if you wrong us shall we not revenge? If we are like you
in the rest, we will resemble you in that. If a Jew wrong a
Christian, what is his° humility? Revenge. If a Christian   *(the Christian's)*
wrong a Jew, what should his sufferance° be by Christian   *patience*
60 example? Why, revenge. The villainy you teach me I will execute, and it shall go hard but I will better the instruction.
    Enter a MAN *from Antonio*
MAN [*to* SOLANIO *and* SALERIO]   Gentlemen, my master Antonio
is at his house and desires to speak with you both.
SALERIO   We have been up and down to seek him.
    Enter TUBAL
65 SOLANIO   Here comes another of the tribe. A third cannot be
matched° unless the devil himself turn Jew.   *found to match*
    Exeunt [SOLANIO *and* SALERIO, *with Antonio's* MAN]
SHYLOCK   How now, Tubal? What news from Genoa? Hast thou
found my daughter?
TUBAL   I often came where I did hear of her, but cannot find
70 her.
SHYLOCK   Why, there, there, there, there. A diamond gone cost
me two thousand ducats in Frankfurt.[5] The curse never fell
upon our nation till now—I never felt it till now. Two thousand
ducats in that and other precious, precious jewels. I would my
75 daughter were dead at my foot and the jewels in her ear! Would
she were hearsed° at my foot and the ducats in her coffin! No   *coffined*
news of them? Why, so. And I know not what's spent in the
search. Why thou, loss upon loss: the thief gone with so
much, and so much to find the thief, and no satisfaction, no
80 revenge, nor no ill luck stirring but what lights o' my shoulders,
no sighs but o' my breathing, no tears but o' my shedding.
TUBAL   Yes, other men have ill luck too. Antonio, as I heard in
Genoa—
SHYLOCK   What, what, what? Ill luck, ill luck?
85 TUBAL   Hath an argosy cast away coming from Tripolis.
SHYLOCK   I thank God, I thank God! Is it true, is it true?
TUBAL   I spoke with some of the sailors that escaped the wreck.
SHYLOCK   I thank thee, good Tubal. Good news, good news! Ha,
ha—heard in Genoa?
90 TUBAL   Your daughter spent in Genoa, as I heard, one night
fourscore ducats.
SHYLOCK   Thou stick'st a dagger in me. I shall never see my gold
again. Fourscore ducats at a sitting? Fourscore ducats?
TUBAL   There came divers of Antonio's creditors in my company
95 to Venice that swear he cannot choose but break.°   *go bankrupt*
SHYLOCK   I am very glad of it. I'll plague him, I'll torture him.
I am glad of it.

5. Site of a jewel market.

TUBAL   One of them showed me a ring that he had of your
daughter for a monkey.

100 SHYLOCK   Out upon her! Thou torturest me, Tubal. It was my *window*
turquoise. I had it of Leah when I was a bachelor. I would not *to the*
past
have given it for a wilderness of monkeys.

TUBAL   But Antonio is certainly undone.

SHYLOCK   Nay, that's true, that's very true. Go, Tubal, fee° me   hire
105 an officer. Bespeak him a fortnight before. I will have the heart
of him if he forfeit, for were he out of Venice I can make what
merchandise° I will. Go, Tubal, and meet me at our synagogue.   drive what bargains
Go, good Tubal; at our synagogue, Tubal.

Exeunt [*severally*]

3.2

Enter BASSANIO, PORTIA, NERISSA, GRAZIANO, *and all
their trains.* [*The curtains are drawn aside, revealing the
three caskets*]

PORTIA [*to* BASSANIO]   I pray you tarry. Pause a day or two
Before you hazard, for in choosing° wrong   *if you choose*
I lose your company. Therefore forbear a while.
There's something tells me—but it is not love—
5   I would not lose you; and you know yourself
Hate counsels not in such a quality.°   *way*
But lest you should not understand me well—
And yet a maiden hath no tongue but thought—
I would detain you here some month or two
10 Before you venture for me. I could teach you
How to choose right, but then I am forsworn.
So° will I never be; so may you miss me.[1]   (*forsworn*)
But if you do, you'll make me wish a sin,
That I had been forsworn. Beshrew your eyes,
15 They have o'erlooked° me and divided me.   *bewitched*
One half of me is yours, the other half yours—
Mine own, I would say, but if mine, then yours,
And so all yours. O, these naughty° times   *evil*
Puts bars between the owners and their rights;
20 And so, though yours, not yours. Prove it so,
Let fortune go to hell for it, not I.[2]
I speak too long, but tis to piece° the time,   *extend*
To eke° it, and to draw it out in length   *augment*
To stay° you from election.°   *delay / choosing*
BASSANIO   Let me choose,
25 For as I am, I live upon the rack.[3]
PORTIA   Upon the rack, Bassanio? Then confess
What treason there is mingled with your love.
BASSANIO   None but that ugly treason of mistrust°   *uncertainty*
Which makes me fear° th'enjoying of my love.   *doubt*
30 There may as well be amity and life
'Tween snow and fire as treason and my love.
PORTIA   Ay, but I fear you speak upon the rack,
Where men enforcèd do speak anything.

3.2 Location: Belmont.
1. Fail to attain me.
2. *Prove . . . I:* If it turns out thus, let it be fortune's

fault, not mine (for breaking my oath).
3. Instrument of torture used on traitors.

BASSANIO Promise me life and I'll confess the truth.

PORTIA Well then, confess and live.

35 BASSANIO   'Confess and love'
Had been the very sum of my confession.
O happy torment, when my torturer
Doth teach me answers for deliverance!°   *release*
But let me to my fortune and the caskets.

40 PORTIA Away then. I am locked in one of them.
If you do love me, you will find me out.
Nerissa and the rest, stand all aloof.
Let music sound while he doth make his choice
Then if he lose he makes a swanlike end,[4]

45 Fading in music. That the comparison
May stand more proper, my eye shall be the stream
And wat'ry deathbed for him. He may win,
And what is music then? Then music is
Even as the flourish° when true subjects bow   *fanfare*

50 To a new-crownèd monarch. Such it is
As are those dulcet sounds in break of day
That creep into the dreaming bridegroom's ear
And summon him to marriage.[5] Now he goes,
With no less presence° but with much more love   *dignity*

55 Than young Alcides when he did redeem
The virgin tribute paid by howling Troy
To the sea-monster.[6] I stand for sacrifice.
The rest aloof are the Dardanian° wives,   *Trojan*
With blearèd° visages come forth to view   *weepy*

60 The issue° of th'exploit. Go, Hercules.   *outcome*
Live thou,° I live. With much much more dismay   *If you live*
I view the fight than thou that mak'st the fray.

Here music. A song the whilst BASSANIO *comments on
the caskets to himself*

[ONE FROM PORTIA'S TRAIN]
Tell me where is fancy° bred,   *love; infatuation*
Or° in the heart, or in the head?   *Whether*

65 How begot, how nourishèd?
[ALL]   Reply, reply.
[ONE FROM PORTIA'S TRAIN]
It is engendered in the eyes,[7]
With gazing fed; and fancy dies
In the cradle[8] where it lies.

70 Let us all ring fancy's knell.
I'll begin it: ding, dong, bell.
ALL   Ding, dong, bell.

BASSANIO [*aside*] So may the outward shows be least themselves.[9]
The world is still° deceived with ornament.   *continually*

75 In law, what plea so tainted and corrupt
But, being seasoned with a gracious voice,
Obscures the show of evil? In religion,

---

4. The swan was thought to sing only once, just before
its death.
5. It was customary to play music under a bridegroom's
window on the morning of his wedding.
6. Alcides (Hercules) saved the Trojan princess He-
sione when she was to be sacrificed to a sea monster,

not because he loved her but to win two horses her
father offered as a reward.
7. Love was imagined to enter through the eyes.
8. In infancy, in the eyes (?)
9. Least express the truth.

What damnèd error but some sober brow
Will bless it and approve° it with a text,   *prove*
80   Hiding the grossness with fair ornament?
There is no vice so simple° but assumes   *unalloyed; stupid*
Some mark of virtue on his° outward parts.   *its*
How many cowards whose hearts are all as false
As stairs of sand, wear yet upon their chins
85   The beards of Hercules and frowning Mars,
Who, inward searched,° have livers white as milk?[1]   *examined*
And these assume but valour's excrement[2]
To render them redoubted.° Look on beauty   *feared*
And you shall see 'tis purchased by the weight,°   *(like cosmetics)*
90   Which therein works a miracle in nature,
Making them lightest° that wear most of it.   *most licentious*
So are those crispèd,° snaky, golden locks   *curled*
Which makes such wanton gambols with the wind
Upon supposèd fairness,° often known   *beauty*
95   To be the dowry° of a second head,   *endowment (in a wig)*
The skull that bred them in the sepulchre.
Thus ornament is but the guilèd° shore   *beguiling*
To a most dangerous sea, the beauteous scarf
Veiling an Indian° beauty; in a word,   *a swarthy (pejorative)*
100   The seeming truth which cunning times put on
To entrap the wisest. [*Aloud*] Therefore, thou gaudy gold,
Hard food for Midas,[3] I will none of thee.
[*To the silver casket*] Nor none of thee, thou pale and com-
        mon drudge°   *laborer (in coins)*
'Tween man and man. But thou, thou meagre lead,
105   Which rather threaten'st than dost promise aught,
Thy paleness moves me more than eloquence,
And here choose I. Joy be the consequence!
PORTIA [*aside*]   How all the other passions fleet to air,
As° doubtful thoughts, and rash-embraced despair,   *Such as*
110   And shudd'ring fear, and green-eyed jealousy.
O love, be moderate! Allay thy ecstasy.
In measure rain thy joy; scant° this excess.[4]   *lessen*
I feel too much thy blessing: make it less,
For fear I surfeit.
        [BASSANIO *opens the leaden casket*]
BASSANIO   What find I here?
115   Fair Portia's counterfeit.° What demi-god[5]   *likeness*
Hath come so near creation? Move these eyes?   *:*
Or whether, riding on the balls of mine,°   *my eyes*
Seem they in motion? Here are severed lips
Parted with sugar breath. So sweet a bar
120   Should sunder such sweet friends. Here in her hairs
The painter plays the spider, and hath woven
A golden mesh t'untrap° the hearts of men   *entrap (phonetic?)*
Faster than gnats in cobwebs. But her eyes—
How could he see to do them? Having made one,

---

1. Lily-livered (the liver was considered the seat of courage).
2. External attribute; hair (the beard).
3. Everything King Midas touched, including his food,

turned to gold.
4. Synonym for "interest" or "usury."
5. Supernaturally gifted painter.

125 Methinks it should have power to steal both his
And leave itself unfurnished.° Yet look how far   *unaccompanied*
The substance of my praise doth wrong this shadow°   *portrait*
In underprizing° it, so far this shadow   *understating*
Doth limp behind the substance.° Here's the scroll,   *real thing (Portia)*
130 The continent° and summary of my fortune.   *container*
    'You that choose not by the view
    Chance as fair° and choose as true.   *Gamble as luckily*
    Since this fortune falls to you,
    Be content, and seek no new.
135   If you be well pleased with this,
    And hold your fortune for your bliss,
    Turn you where your lady is,
    And claim her with a loving kiss.'
A gentle scroll. Fair lady, by your leave,
140 I come by note to give[6] and to receive,
Like one of two contending in a prize,°   *contest*
That thinks he hath done well in people's eyes,
Hearing applause and universal shout,
Giddy in spirit, still gazing in a doubt
145 Whether those peals of praise be his° or no.   *for him*
So, thrice-fair lady, stand I even so,
As doubtful whether what I see be true   *He can't beleive it*
Until confirmed, signed, ratified by you.
PORTIA   You see me, Lord Bassanio, where I stand,
150 Such as I am. Though for myself alone
I would not be ambitious in my wish
To wish myself much better, yet for you   *language, hyperbole*
I would be trebled twenty times myself,   *of numbers*
A thousand times more fair, ten thousand times more rich,
155 That only to stand high in your account°   *estimation*
I might in virtues, beauties, livings,° friends,   *possessions*
Exceed account. But the full sum of me
Is sum of something which, to term in gross,°   *to describe fully*
Is an unlessoned girl, unschooled, unpractisèd,
160 Happy° in this, she is not yet so old   *Fortunate*
But she may learn; happier than this,
She is not bred so dull but she can learn;
Happiest of all is that her gentle spirit
Commits itself to yours to be directed
165 As from her lord, her governor, her king.
✱ Myself and what is mine to you and yours   *transfer of wealth*
Is now converted.° But° now I was the lord   *transferred / Just*
Of this fair mansion, master of my servants,
Queen o'er myself; and even now, but now,
170 This house, these servants, and this same myself
Are yours, my lord's. I give them with this ring,
Which when you part from, lose, or give away,
Let it presage the ruin of your love,
And be my vantage to exclaim on you.[7]
175 BASSANIO   Madam, you have bereft me of all words.
Only my blood speaks to you in my veins,

6. I come by written authorization to give a kiss; to give   7. And be my opportunity to reproach you.
myself.

<table>
<tr><td></td><td>And there is such confusion in my powers°</td><td>faculties</td></tr>
<tr><td></td><td>As after some oration fairly spoke</td><td></td></tr>
<tr><td></td><td>By a belovèd prince there doth appear</td><td></td></tr>
<tr><td>180</td><td>Among the buzzing pleasèd multitude,</td><td></td></tr>
<tr><td></td><td>Where every something being blent° together</td><td>blended</td></tr>
<tr><td></td><td>Turns to a wild° of nothing save of joy,</td><td>chaos</td></tr>
<tr><td></td><td>Expressed and not expressed. But when this ring</td><td></td></tr>
<tr><td></td><td>Parts from this finger, then parts life from hence.</td><td></td></tr>
<tr><td>185</td><td>O, then be bold to say° Bassanio's dead.</td><td>say confidently</td></tr>
</table>

NERISSA   My lord and lady, it is now our time
That have stood by and seen our wishes prosper
To cry 'Good joy, good joy, my lord and lady!'

GRAZIANO   My lord Bassanio, and my gentle lady,
190   I wish you all the joy that you can wish,
For I am sure you can wish none from me.[8]
And when your honours mean to solemnize
The bargain of your faith, I do beseech you
Even at that time I may be married too.

195   BASSANIO   With all my heart, so° thou canst get a wife.   *if*

GRAZIANO   I thank your lordship, you have got me one.
My eyes, my lord, can look as swift as yours.
You saw the mistress, I beheld the maid.
You loved, I loved; for intermission°   *delay*
200   No more pertains to me, my lord, than you.
Your fortune stood upon the caskets there,
And so did mine too, as the matter falls;
For wooing here until I sweat again,°   *repeatedly*
And swearing till my very roof° was dry   *(of his mouth)*
205   With oaths of love, at last—if promise[9] last—
I got a promise of this fair one here
To have her love, provided that your fortune
Achieved her mistress.

PORTIA   Is this true, Nerissa?

NERISSA   Madam, it is, so you stand pleased withal.

210   BASSANIO   And do you, Graziano, mean good faith?

GRAZIANO   Yes, faith, my lord.

BASSANIO   Our feast shall be much honoured in your marriage.

GRAZIANO   [*to* NERISSA]   We'll play° with them the first boy for a   *wager*
thousand ducats.

215   NERISSA   What, and stake down?[1]

GRAZIANO   No, we shall ne'er win at that sport and stake down.

          Enter LORENZO, JESSICA, *and* SALERIO, *a messenger from*
              Venice

But who comes here? Lorenzo and his infidel!
What, and my old Venetian friend Salerio!

BASSANIO   Lorenzo and Salerio, welcome hither,
220   If that the youth of my new int'rest° here   *position*
Have power° to bid you welcome. [*To* PORTIA] By your leave,   *Gives me the right*
I bid my very° friends and countrymen,   *true*
Sweet Portia, welcome.

PORTIA   So do I, my lord. They are entirely welcome.

225   LORENZO   I thank your honour. For my part, my lord,

---

8. You do not need my good wishes.
9. Nerissa's, to wed Graziano.

1. Put the money down now (Graziano follows with a
bawdy joke on "flaccid penis").

My purpose was not to have seen you here,
But meeting with Salerio by the way
He did entreat me past all saying nay
To come with him along.

SALERIO   I did, my lord,
230 And I have reason for it. Signor Antonio
Commends him° to you.   *Sends greeting*
      [*He gives* BASSANIO *a letter*]
BASSANIO   Ere I ope his letter
I pray you tell me how my good friend doth.
SALERIO   Not sick, my lord, unless it be in mind;
Nor well, unless in mind. His letter there
235 Will show you his estate.°   *situation*
      [BASSANIO] *opens the letter* [*and reads*]
GRAZIANO   Nerissa, [*indicating* JESSICA] cheer yon stranger. Bid
    her welcome.
Your hand, Salerio. What's the news from Venice?
How doth that royal° merchant good Antonio?   *princely*
I know he will be glad of our success.
240 We are the Jasons; we have won the fleece.
SALERIO   I would you had won the fleece° that he hath lost.   (*punning on "fleets"*)
PORTIA   There are some shrewd° contents in yon same paper   *evil*
That steals the colour from Bassanio's cheek.
Some dear friend dead, else nothing in the world
245 Could turn° so much the constitution   *change*
Of any constant° man. What, worse and worse?   *resolute*
With leave, Bassanio, I am half yourself,
And I must freely have the half of anything
That this same paper brings you.
BASSANIO   O sweet Portia,
250 Here are a few of the unpleasant'st words
That ever blotted paper. Gentle lady,
When I did first impart my love to you
I freely told you all the wealth I had
Ran in my veins: I was a gentleman.
255 And then I told you true; and yet, dear lady,
Rating myself at nothing, you shall see
How much I was a braggart. When I told you
My state° was nothing, I should then have told you   *wealth*
That I was worse than nothing, for indeed
260 I have engaged° myself to a dear friend,   *pledged*
Engaged my friend to his mere° enemy,   *utter*
To feed my means. Here is a letter, lady,
The paper° as the body of my friend,   (*ripped open*)
And every word in it a gaping wound
265 Issuing life-blood. But is it true, Salerio?
Hath all his ventures failed? What, not one hit?°   *success*
From Tripolis, from Mexico, and England,
From Lisbon, Barbary, and India,
And not one vessel scape the dreadful touch
Of merchant-marring rocks?
270 SALERIO   Not one, my lord.
Besides, it should appear that if he had
The present° money to discharge° the Jew   *ready / pay*
He° would not take it. Never did I know   (*Shylock*)

A creature that did bear the shape of man
275 So keen° and greedy to confound° a man.   *eager / destroy*
He plies the Duke at morning and at night,
And doth impeach the freedom of the state[2]
If they deny him justice. Twenty merchants,
The Duke himself, and the magnificoes°   *Venetian magnates*
280 Of greatest port,° have all persuaded° with him,   *dignity / argued*
But none can drive him from the envious° plea   *malicious*
Of forfeiture, of justice, and his bond.

JESSICA   When I was with him I have heard him swear
To Tubal and to Cush, his countrymen,
285 That he would rather have Antonio's flesh
Than twenty times the value of the sum
That he did owe him; and I know, my lord,
If law, authority, and power deny not,
It will go hard with poor Antonio.

290 PORTIA [*to* BASSANIO]   Is it your dear friend that is thus in trouble?

BASSANIO   The dearest friend to me, the kindest man,
The best-conditioned° and unwearied spirit   *best-natured*
In doing courtesies, and one in whom
The ancient Roman honour more appears
295 Than any that draws breath in Italy.

PORTIA   What sum owes he the Jew?

BASSANIO   For me, three thousand ducats.

PORTIA   What, no more?
Pay him six thousand and deface° the bond.   *destroy*
Double six thousand, and then treble that,
300 Before a friend of this description
Shall lose a hair thorough Bassanio's fault.
First go with me to church and call me wife,
And then away to Venice to your friend;
For never shall you lie by Portia's side
305 With an unquiet soul. You shall have gold
To pay the petty debt twenty times over.
When it is paid, bring your true friend along.
My maid Nerissa and myself meantime
Will live as maids and widows. Come, away,
310 For you shall hence upon your wedding day.
Bid your friends welcome, show a merry cheer.°   *countenance*
Since you are dear° bought, I will love you dear.°   *expensively / dearly*
But let me hear the letter of your friend.

BASSANIO [*reads*]   'Sweet Bassanio, my ships have all miscarried,
315 my creditors grow cruel, my estate is very low, my bond to the
Jew is forfeit, and since in paying it, it is impossible I should
live, all debts are cleared between you and I if I might but see
you at my death. Notwithstanding, use your pleasure.° If your   *follow your wishes*
love do not persuade you to come, let not my letter.'
320 PORTIA   O, love! Dispatch all business, and be gone.

BASSANIO   Since I have your good leave to go away
I will make haste, but till I come again
No bed shall e'er be guilty of my stay
Nor rest be interposer 'twixt us twain.   *Exeunt*

2. Accuse the state of not preserving commercial liberty.

3.3

Enter [SHYLOCK] *the Jew*, SOLANIO, ANTONIO, *and the jailer*

SHYLOCK   Jailer, look to him. Tell not me of mercy.
This is the fool that lent out money gratis.
Jailer, look to him.

ANTONIO   Hear me yet, good Shylock.

SHYLOCK   I'll have my bond. Speak not against my bond.
5   I have sworn an oath that I will have my bond.
Thou called'st me dog before thou hadst a cause,
But since I am a dog, beware my fangs.
The Duke shall grant me justice. I do wonder,
Thou naughty° jailer, that thou art so fond°   wicked/foolish
10   To come abroad° with him at his request.   outside

ANTONIO   I pray thee hear me speak.

SHYLOCK   I'll have my bond. I will not hear thee speak.
I'll have my bond, and therefore speak no more.
I'll not be made a soft and dull-eyed° fool   gullible
15   To shake the head, relent, and sigh, and yield
To Christian intercessors. Follow not.
I'll have no speaking. I will have my bond.   *Exit*

SOLANIO   It is the most impenetrable cur
That ever kept° with men.   lived

ANTONIO   Let him alone.
20   I'll follow him no more with bootless° prayers.   fruitless
He seeks my life. His reason well I know:
I oft delivered° from his forfeitures   saved
Many that have at times made moan to me.
Therefore he hates me.

SOLANIO   I am sure the Duke
25   Will never grant this forfeiture to hold.

ANTONIO   The Duke cannot deny° the course of law,   prevent
For the commodity that strangers[1] have
With us in Venice, if it be denied,
Will much impeach the justice of the state,
30   Since that the trade and profit of the city
Consisteth of all nations. Therefore go.
These griefs and losses have so bated° me   diminished
That I shall hardly spare a pound of flesh
Tomorrow to my bloody creditor.
35   Well, jailer, on. Pray God Bassanio come
To see me pay his debt, and then I care not.   *Exeunt*

[handwritten margin note] venice is an international trade city dependent on foreigners → the law must be upheld to maintain venice's status to strangers

3.4

Enter PORTIA, NERISSA, LORENZO, JESSICA, *and*
[BALTHASAR,] *a man of Portia's*

LORENZO [*to* PORTIA]   Madam, although I speak it in your presence,
You have a noble and a true conceit°   conception
Of godlike amity, which appears most strongly
In bearing thus the absence of your lord.
5   But if you knew to whom you show this honour,

3.3 Location: Street in Venice.
1. For the trading privileges that foreigners (including Jews).

3.4 Location: Belmont.

How true a gentleman you send relief,
How dear a lover° of my lord your husband,   *friend*
I know you would be prouder of the work
Than customary bounty can enforce you.[1]

10 PORTIA   I never did repent for doing good,
Nor shall not now; for in companions
That do converse and waste° the time together,   *spend (not pejorative)*
Whose souls do bear an equal yoke of love,
There must be needs a like proportion

15 Of lineaments, of manners, and of spirit,
Which makes me think that this Antonio,
Being the bosom lover of my lord,
Must needs be like my lord. If it be so,
How little is the cost I have bestowed

20 In purchasing the semblance of my soul[2]
From out the state of hellish cruelty.
This comes too near the praising of myself,
Therefore no more of it. Hear other things:
Lorenzo, I commit into your hands

25 The husbandry° and manage of my house   *care*
Until my lord's return. For mine own part,
I have toward heaven breathed a secret vow
To live in prayer and contemplation,
Only attended by Nerissa here,

30 Until her husband and my lord's return.
There is a monastery two miles off,
And there we will abide. I do desire you
Not to deny this imposition,°   *decline this charge*
The which my love and some necessity
Now lays upon you.

35 LORENZO   Madam, with all my heart,
I shall obey you in all fair commands.

   PORTIA   My people do already know my mind,
And will acknowledge you and Jessica
In place of Lord Bassanio and myself.

40 So fare you well till we shall meet again.

   LORENZO   Fair thoughts and happy hours attend on you!

   JESSICA   I wish your ladyship all heart's content.

   PORTIA   I thank you for your wish, and am well pleased
To wish it back on you. Fare you well, Jessica.

                      Exeunt [LORENZO *and* JESSICA]

45 Now, Balthasar,
As I have ever found thee honest-true,
So let me find thee still. Take this same letter,
And use thou all th'endeavour of a man
In speed to Padua. See thou render this

50 Into my cousin's hands, Doctor Bellario,
And look what notes and garments he doth give thee,
Bring them, I pray thee, with imagined° speed   *all imaginable*
Unto the traject,° to the common° ferry   *ferry / public*
Which trades° to Venice. Waste no time in words,   *goes back and forth*

55 But get thee gone. I shall be there before thee.

   BALTHASAR   Madam, I go with all convenient° speed.   [*Exit*]   *due*

---

1. Than ordinary generosity permits you.   2. In redeeming the likeness of my Bassanio (Antonio).

PORTIA   Come on, Nerissa. I have work in hand
    That you yet know not of. We'll see our husbands
    Before they think of us.
NERISSA   Shall they see us?
60   PORTIA   They shall, Nerissa, but in such a habit°   *garb*
    That they shall think we are accomplishèd°   *equipped*
    With that we lack.° I'll hold thee any wager,   *(i.e., penises)*
    When we are both accoutered like young men
    I'll prove the prettier fellow of the two,
65   And wear my dagger with the braver grace,
    And speak between the change of man and boy
    With a reed° voice, and turn two mincing steps   *piping*
    Into a manly stride, and speak of frays
    Like a fine bragging youth, and tell quaint° lies   *elaborate*
70   How honourable ladies sought my love,
    Which I denying, they fell sick and died.
    I could not do withal.° Then I'll repent,   *help it*
    And wish for all that that I had not killed them;
    And twenty of these puny lies I'll tell,
75   That men shall swear I have discontinued° school   *been out of*
    Above° a twelvemonth. I have within my mind   *At least*
    A thousand raw tricks of these bragging Jacks°   *fellows*
    Which I will practise.
NERISSA   Why, shall we turn to[3] men?
80   PORTIA   Fie, what a question's that
    If thou wert near a lewd interpreter!
    But come, I'll tell thee all my whole device°   *plan*
    When I am in my coach, which stays for us
    At the park gate; and therefore haste away,
85   For we must measure twenty miles today.   *Exeunt*

3.5

Enter [LANCELOT] the clown, and JESSICA

LANCELOT   Yes, truly; for look you, the sins of the father are to
    be laid upon the children, therefore I promise you I fear° you.   *fear for*
    I was always plain with you, and so now I speak my agitation°   *(for "cogitation")*
    of the matter, therefore be o' good cheer, for truly I think you
5   are damned. There is but one hope in it that can do you any
    good, and that is but a kind of bastard hope, neither.
JESSICA   And what hope is that, I pray thee?
LANCELOT   Marry, you may partly hope that your father got you
    not, that you are not the Jew's daughter.
10   JESSICA   That were a kind of bastard hope indeed. So the sins
    of my mother should be visited upon me.
LANCELOT   Truly then, I fear you are damned both by father and
    mother. Thus, when I shun Scylla your father, I fall into
    Charybdis your mother.[1] Well, you are gone° both ways.   *doomed*
15   JESSICA   I shall be saved by my husband.[2] He hath made me a
    Christian.
LANCELOT   Truly, the more to blame he! We were Christians

---

3. Turn into (with bawdy suggestion).
3.5 Location: Portia's garden in Belmont.
1. Scylla was a mythological sea monster, Charybdis a
whirlpool in the Strait of Messina. Mariners had to avoid
both, a proverbially difficult task.
2. "The unbelieving wife is sanctified by the husband"
(1 Corinthians 7:14).

enough before, e'en as many as could well live one by another.[3]
This making of Christians will raise the price of hogs. If we
20 grow all to be pork-eaters we shall not shortly have a rasher° on   bacon strip
the coals for money.°   any price

Enter LORENZO

JESSICA I'll tell my husband, Lancelot, what you say. Here he
comes.

LORENZO I shall grow jealous of you shortly, Lancelot, if you
25 thus get my wife into corners.

JESSICA Nay, you need not fear us, Lorenzo. Lancelot and I are
out.° He tells me flatly there's no mercy for me in heaven   quarreling
because I am a Jew's daughter, and he says you are no good
member of the commonwealth, for in converting Jews to Chris-
30 tians you raise the price of pork.

LORENZO [*to* LANCELOT] I shall answer° that better to the com-   explain
monwealth than you can the getting up of the Negro's belly.
The Moor[4] is with child by you, Lancelot.

LANCELOT It is much that the Moor should be more than rea-
35 son,[5] but if she be less than an honest° woman, she is indeed   a chaste
more than I took her for.

LORENZO How every fool can play upon the word! I think the
best grace of wit will shortly turn into silence, and discourse
grow commendable in none only but parrots. Go in, sirrah, bid
40 them prepare for dinner.

LANCELOT That is done, sir. They have all stomachs.°   appetites

LORENZO Goodly Lord, what a wit-snapper are you! Then bid
them prepare dinner.

LANCELOT That is done too, sir; only 'cover'[6] is the word.

45 LORENZO Will you cover then, sir?

LANCELOT Not so, sir, neither. I know my duty.

LORENZO Yet more quarrelling with occasion![7] Wilt thou show
the whole wealth of thy wit in an instant? I pray thee understand a plain man in his plain meaning. Go to thy fellows; bid
50 them cover the table, serve in the meat, and we will come in
to dinner.

LANCELOT For the table,° sir, it shall be served in. For the meat,   meal
sir, it shall be covered.[8] For your coming in to dinner, sir, why,
let it be as humours and conceits° shall govern.   *Exit*   whims and notions

55 LORENZO O dear discretion, how his words are suited![9]
The fool hath planted in his memory
An army of good words, and I do know
A many fools that stand in better place,
Garnished° like him, that for a tricksy word   Provided (with words)
60 Defy the matter.° How cheer'st thou,[1] Jessica?   Refuse to talk sense
And now, good sweet, say thy opinion:
How dost thou like the Lord Bassanio's wife?

JESSICA Past all expressing. It is very meet°   proper
The Lord Bassanio live an upright life,
65 For, having such a blessing in his lady,

---

3. *well . . . another:* reside next door to one another;
earn a living off one another.
4. Apparently an African woman of Portia's household.
5. Should be bigger than is reasonable (punning on
"more/ Moor").
6. Set the table; but Lancelot puns on "cover" as meaning "put on the hat."

7. Playing on words whenever possible.
8. Served in covered dishes (playfully or unconsciously
reversing Lorenzo's instructions).
9. Adapted to the occasion. *dear discretion:* precious
discrimination (ironic).
1. How are you.

He finds the joys of heaven here on earth,
And if on earth he do not merit it,
In reason he should never come to heaven.
Why, if two gods should play some heavenly match
70 And on the wager lay two earthly women,
And Portia one, there must be something else
Pawned° with the other; for the poor rude world   *Wagered*
Hath not her fellow.
LORENZO   Even such a husband
Hast thou of me as she is for a wife.
75 JESSICA   Nay, but ask my opinion too of that!
LORENZO   I will anon.° First let us go to dinner.   *soon*
JESSICA   Nay, let me praise you while I have a stomach.°   *an appetite; desire*
LORENZO   No, pray thee, let it serve for table-talk.
Then, howsome'er° thou speak'st, 'mong other things   *however*
I shall digest° it.   *ingest; analyze*
80 JESSICA   Well, I'll set you forth.[2]   *Exeunt*

4.1

Enter the DUKE, *the magnificoes,* ANTONIO, BASSANIO,
GRAZIANO, *and* [SALERIO]
DUKE   What, is Antonio here?
ANTONIO   Ready, so please your grace.
DUKE   I am sorry for thee. Thou art come to answer
A stony adversary, an inhuman wretch
Uncapable of pity, void and empty
From any dram° of mercy.   *trace*
5 ANTONIO   I have heard
Your grace hath ta'en great pains to qualify°   *alleviate*
His rigorous course, but since he stands obdurate,
And that no lawful means can carry me
Out of his envy's° reach, I do oppose   *malice's*
10 My patience to his fury, and am armed°   *prepared*
To suffer with a quietness of spirit
The very tyranny° and rage of his.   *cruelty*
DUKE   Go one, and call the Jew into the court.
SALERIO   He is ready at the door. He comes, my lord.
Enter SHYLOCK
15 DUKE   Make room, and let him stand before our° face.   *(the royal "we")*
Shylock, the world thinks—and I think so too—
That thou but lead'st this fashion° of thy malice   *sustain the pretense*
To the last hour of act,° and then 'tis thought   *brink of performance*
Thou'lt show thy mercy and remorse° more strange°   *compassion / extraordinary*
20 Than is thy strange apparent cruelty,
And where thou now exacts the penalty—
Which is a pound of this poor merchant's flesh—
Thou wilt not only loose° the forfeiture,   *waive*
But, touched with human gentleness and love,
25 Forgive a moiety° of the principal,   *part*
Glancing an eye of pity on his losses,
That have of late so huddled° on his back   *piled*
Enough to press a royal merchant down

---

2. I'll serve you up (like a dinner); I'll extol you.   4.1 Location: The Venetian court.

And pluck commiseration of his state
30 From brassy° bosoms and rough hearts of flint,   unfeeling
From stubborn Turks and Tartars never trained
To offices° of tender courtesy.   acts
We all expect a gentle answer, Jew.

SHYLOCK   I have possessed° your grace of what I purpose,   informed
35 And by our holy Sabbath have I sworn
To have the due and forfeit of my bond.
If you deny it, let the danger° light   damage
Upon your charter and your city's freedom.
You'll ask me why I rather choose to have
40 A weight of carrion flesh than to receive
Three thousand ducats. I'll not answer that,
But say it is my humour.° Is it answered?   caprice
What if my house be troubled with a rat,
And I be pleased to give ten thousand ducats
45 To have it baned?° What, are you answered yet?   poisoned
Some men there are love not a gaping pig,[1]
Some that are mad if they behold a cat,
And others when the bagpipe sings i'th' nose
Cannot contain their urine; for affection,°   impulse
50 Mistress of passion, sways it to the mood
Of what it likes or loathes. Now for your answer:
As there is no firm reason to be rendered
Why he° cannot abide a gaping pig,   one man
Why he° a harmless necessary cat,   another
55 Why he° a woollen bagpipe, but of force°   yet another / necessarily
Must yield to such inevitable shame
As to offend himself being offended,
So can I give no reason, nor I will not,
More than a lodged° hate and a certain loathing   settled
60 I bear Antonio, that I follow thus
A losing° suit against him. Are you answered?   An unprofitable

BASSANIO   This is no answer, thou unfeeling man,
To excuse the current of thy cruelty.

SHYLOCK   I am not bound to please thee with my answers.

65 BASSANIO   Do all men kill the things they do not love?

SHYLOCK   Hates any man the thing he would not kill?

BASSANIO   Every offence is not a hate at first.

SHYLOCK   What, wouldst thou have a serpent sting thee twice?

ANTONIO   I pray you think you question° with the Jew.   dispute
70 You may as well go stand upon the beach
And bid the main flood bate his° usual height;   high tide reduce its
You may as well use question with the wolf
Why he hath made the ewe bleat for the lamb;
You may as well forbid the mountain pines
75 To wag their high tops and to make no noise
When they are fretten° with the gusts of heaven,   fretted; agitated
You may as well do anything most hard
As seek to soften that—than which what's harder?—
His Jewish heart. Therefore, I do beseech you,
80 Make no more offers, use no farther means,

---

1. Roasted pig with its mouth propped open.

But with all brief and plain conveniency°   *suitability*
Let me have judgement and the Jew his will.
BASSANIO [*to* SHYLOCK]   For thy three thousand ducats here is six.
SHYLOCK   If every ducat in six thousand ducats
85   Were in six parts, and every part a ducat,
I would not draw° them. I would have my bond.   *take*
DUKE   How shalt thou hope for mercy, rend'ring none?
SHYLOCK   What judgement shall I dread, doing no wrong?
You have among you many a purchased slave
90   Which, like your asses and your dogs and mules,
You use in abject and in slavish parts°   *roles*
Because you bought them. Shall I say to you
'Let them be free, marry them to your heirs.
Why sweat they under burdens? Let their beds
95   Be made as soft as yours, and let their palates
Be seasoned with such viands.'° You will answer   *food*
'The slaves are ours.' So do I answer you.
The pound of flesh which I demand of him
Is dearly bought. 'Tis mine, and I will have it.
100   If you deny me, fie upon your law:
There is no force in the decrees of Venice.
I stand for judgement. Answer: shall I have it?
DUKE   Upon° my power I may dismiss this court   *In accordance with*
Unless Bellario, a learnèd doctor
105   Whom I have sent for to determine° this,   *resolve*
Come here today.
SALERIO   My lord, here stays without°   *waits outside*
A messenger with letters from the doctor,
New come from Padua.
DUKE   Bring us the letters. Call the messenger.   [*Exit* SALERIO]
110 BASSANIO   Good cheer, Antonio. What, man, courage yet!
The Jew shall have my flesh, blood, bones, and all
Ere thou shalt lose for me one drop of blood.
ANTONIO   I am a tainted wether° of the flock,   *castrated ram*
Meetest for death.° The weakest kind of fruit   *Most fit for slaughter*
115   Drops earliest to the ground; and so let me.
You cannot better be employed, Bassanio,
Than to live still and write mine epitaph.
      Enter [SALERIO, *with*] NERISSA [*apparelled as a judge's*
      clerk]
DUKE   Came you from Padua, from Bellario?
NERISSA   From both, my lord. Bellario greets your grace.
    [*She gives a letter to the* DUKE.
    SHYLOCK *whets his knife on his shoe*]
120 BASSANIO [*to* SHYLOCK]   Why dost thou whet thy knife so earnestly?
SHYLOCK   To cut the forfeit from that bankrupt there.
GRAZIANO   Not on thy sole but on thy soul, harsh Jew,
Thou mak'st thy knife keen. But no metal can,
No, not the hangman's° axe, bear° half the keenness   *executioner's / have*
125   Of thy sharp envy.° Can no prayers pierce thee?   *malice*
SHYLOCK   No, none that thou hast wit enough to make.
GRAZIANO   O, be thou damned, inexorable dog,
And for thy life° let justice be accused!   *for allowing you to live*
Thou almost mak'st me waver in my faith

130   To hold opinion with Pythagoras[2]
        That souls of animals infuse themselves
        Into the trunks of men. Thy currish spirit
        Governed a wolf who, hanged for human slaughter,[3]
        Even from the gallows did his fell soul fleet,°   *his cruel soul flit*

135   And, whilst thou lay'st in thy unhallowed dam,
        Infused itself in thee; for thy desires
        Are wolvish, bloody, starved, and ravenous.
   SHYLOCK   Till thou canst rail the seal from off my bond
        Thou but offend'st° thy lungs to speak so loud.   *hurt*

140   Repair thy wit, good youth, or it will fall
        To cureless° ruin. I stand here for law.   *incurable*
   DUKE   This letter from Bellario doth commend
        A young and learnèd doctor to our court.
        Where is he?
   NERISSA   He attendeth here hard by

145   To know your answer, whether you'll admit him.
   DUKE   With all my heart. Some three or four of you
        Go give him courteous conduct° to this place.   *escort*
                         [*Exeunt three or four*]
        Meantime the court shall hear Bellario's letter.
        [*Reads*] 'Your grace shall understand that at the receipt of your

150   letter I am very sick, but in the instant that your messenger
        came, in loving visitation was with me a young doctor of Rome;
        his name is Balthasar. I acquainted him with the cause in con-
        troversy between the Jew and Antonio, the merchant. We
        turned o'er many books together. He is furnished with my opin-

155   ion which, bettered with his own learning—the greatness
        whereof I cannot enough commend—comes with him at my
        importunity to fill up° your grace's request in my stead. I   *answer*
        beseech you let his lack of years be no impediment to let him
        lack° a reverend estimation, for I never knew so young a body   *keep him from having*

160   with so old a head. I leave him to your gracious acceptance,
        whose trial shall better publish his commendation.'[4]
              Enter [*three or four with*] PORTIA [*as Balthasar*]
        You hear the learn'd Bellario, what he writes;
        And here, I take it, is the doctor come.
        [*To* PORTIA   Give me your hand. Come you from old Bellario?
   PORTIA   I did, my lord.

165   DUKE   You are welcome. Take your place.
        Are you acquainted with the difference°   *dispute*
        That holds this present question[5] in the court?
   PORTIA   I am informèd throughly° of the cause.°   *thoroughly / case*
        Which is the merchant here, and which the Jew?

170   DUKE   Antonio and old Shylock, both stand forth.
            [ANTONIO *and* SHYLOCK *stand forth*]
   PORTIA   Is your name Shylock?
   SHYLOCK   Shylock is my name.
   PORTIA   Of a strange nature is the suit you follow,
        Yet in such rule° that the Venetian law   *order*

---

2. Greek philosopher who believed in the transmigration of souls.
3. In Elizabethan times, animals were tried and hanged
for wrongdoing; possibly an allusion to the 1594 execution of the Jewish physician Lopez (Latin *lupus*, "wolf").
4. Whose performance ("trial") shall better make
known his worth.
5. That is now being tried.

Cannot impugn you as you do proceed.

175 [*To* ANTONIO] You stand within his danger,° do you not?   *power to harm*

ANTONIO   Ay, so he says.

PORTIA   Do you confess the bond?

ANTONIO   I do.

PORTIA   Then must the Jew be merciful.

SHYLOCK   On what compulsion must I? Tell me that.

PORTIA   The quality of mercy is not strained.°   *compelled*

180   It droppeth as the gentle rain from heaven
  Upon the place beneath. It is twice blest:
  It blesseth him that gives, and him that takes.
  'Tis mightiest in the mightiest. It becomes
  The thronèd monarch better than his crown.

185   His sceptre shows the force of temporal power,
  The attribute to° awe and majesty,   *of*
  Wherein doth sit the dread and fear of kings;
  But mercy is above this sceptred sway.
  It is enthronèd in the hearts of kings;

190   It is an attribute to God himself,
  And earthly power doth then show likest° God's   *most like*
  When mercy seasons° justice. Therefore, Jew,   *moderates*
  Though justice be thy plea, consider this:
  That in the course of justice none of us

195   Should see salvation. We do pray for mercy,
  And that same prayer° doth teach us all to render   *(the Lord's Prayer)*
  The deeds of mercy. I have spoke thus much
  To mitigate the justice of thy plea,°   *your demand for justice*
  Which if thou follow, this strict court of Venice

200   Must needs give sentence 'gainst the merchant there.

SHYLOCK   My deeds upon my head![6] I crave the law,
  The penalty and forfeit of my bond.

PORTIA   Is he not able to discharge the money?

BASSANIO   Yes, here I tender it for him in the court,

205   Yea, twice the sum. If that will not suffice
  I will be bound to pay it ten times o'er
  On forfeit of my hands, my head, my heart.
  If this will not suffice, it must appear
  That malice bears down° truth. And, I beseech you,   *overwhelms*

210   Wrest once° the law to your authority.   *For once twist*
  To do a great right, do a little wrong,
  And curb this cruel devil of his will.

PORTIA   It must not be. There is no power in Venice
  Can alter a decree establishèd.

215   'Twill be recorded for a precedent,
  And many an error by the same example
  Will rush into the state. It cannot be.

SHYLOCK   A Daniel come to judgement, yea, a Daniel![7]
  O wise young judge, how I do honour thee!

220 PORTIA   I pray you let me look upon the bond.

SHYLOCK   Here 'tis, most reverend doctor, here it is.

PORTIA   Shylock, there's thrice thy money offered thee.

---

6. The Jewish crowd at Jesus' trial cried, "His blood be on us, and on our children" (Matthew 27:25).
7. In the Apocrypha, the youth Daniel judges the case of Susanna, accused of inchastity by the Elders; he rescues her and convicts them.

SHYLOCK   An oath, an oath! I have an oath in heaven.
Shall I lay perjury upon my soul?
No, not for Venice.

225 PORTIA   Why, this bond is forfeit,
And lawfully by this the Jew may claim
A pound of flesh, to be by him cut off
Nearest the merchant's heart. [*To* SHYLOCK] Be merciful.
Take thrice thy money. Bid me tear the bond.

230 SHYLOCK   When it is paid according to the tenor.°   *condition*
It doth appear you are a worthy judge.
You know the law. Your exposition
Hath been most sound. I charge you, by the law
Whereof you are a well-deserving pillar,

235 Proceed to judgement. By my soul I swear
There is no power in the tongue of man
To alter me. I stay° here on my bond.   *insist*

ANTONIO   Most heartily I do beseech the court
To give the judgement.

PORTIA   Why, then thus it is:

240 You must prepare your bosom for his knife—

SHYLOCK   O noble judge, O excellent young man!

PORTIA   For the intent and purpose of the law
Hath full relation to[8] the penalty
Which here appeareth due upon the bond.

245 SHYLOCK   'Tis very true. O wise and upright judge!
How much more elder art thou than thy looks!

PORTIA [*to* ANTONIO]   Therefore lay bare your bosom.

SHYLOCK   Ay, his breast.
So says the bond, doth it not, noble judge?
'Nearest his heart'—those are the very words.

250 PORTIA   It is so. Are there balance° here to weigh the flesh?   *scales*

SHYLOCK   I have them ready.

PORTIA   Have by some surgeon, Shylock, on your charge°   *expense*
To stop his wounds, lest he do bleed to death.

SHYLOCK   Is it so nominated in the bond?

255 PORTIA   It is not so expressed, but what of that?
'Twere good you do so much for charity.

SHYLOCK   I cannot find it. 'Tis not in the bond.

PORTIA [*to* ANTONIO]   You, merchant, have you anything to say?

ANTONIO   But little. I am armed and well prepared.

260 Give me your hand, Bassanio; fare you well.
Grieve not that I am fall'n to this for you,
For herein Fortune shows herself more kind
Than is her custom; it is still her use°   *commonly her habit*
To let the wretched man outlive his wealth

265 To view with hollow eye and wrinkled brow
An age of poverty, from which ling'ring penance
Of such misery doth she cut me off.
Commend me to your honourable wife.
Tell her the process° of Antonio's end.   *tale*

270 Say how I loved you. Speak me fair° in death,   *well of me*
And when the tale is told, bid her be judge
Whether Bassanio had not once a love.

8. Is entirely in agreement with.

Repent but you° that you shall lose your friend,   *Sorrow only*
And he repents not that he pays your debt;
275   For if the Jew do cut but deep enough,
I'll pay it instantly, with all my heart
BASSANIO   Antonio, I am married to a wife
Which is as dear to me as life itself,
But life itself, my wife, and all the world
280   Are not with me esteemed above thy life.
I would lose all, ay, sacrifice them all
Here to this devil, to deliver you.
PORTIA [*aside*]   Your wife would give you little thanks for that
If she were by to hear you make the offer.
285   GRAZIANO   I have a wife who, I protest, I love.
I would she were in heaven so she could
Entreat some power to change this currish Jew.
NERISSA [*aside*]   'Tis well you offer it behind her back;
The wish would make else an unquiet house.
290   SHYLOCK [*aside*]   These be the Christian husbands. I have a daughter.
Would any of the stock of Barabbas⁹
Had been her husband rather than a Christian.
[*Aloud*] We trifle° time. I pray thee pursue° sentence.   *waste / proceed with*
PORTIA   A pound of that same merchant's flesh is thine.
295   The court awards it, and the law doth give it.
SHYLOCK   Most rightful judge!
PORTIA   And you must cut this flesh from off his breast.
The law allows it, and the court awards it.
SHYLOCK   Most learnèd judge! A sentence: [*to* ANTONIO] come, prepare.
300   PORTIA   Tarry a little. There is something else.
This bond doth give thee here no jot of blood.
The words expressly are 'a pound of flesh'.
Take then thy bond. Take thou thy pound of flesh
But in the cutting it, if thou dost shed
305   One drop of Christian blood, thy lands and goods
Are by the laws of Venice confiscate
Unto the state of Venice.
GRAZIANO   O upright judge!
Mark, Jew! O learnèd judge!
SHYLOCK   Is that the law?
310   PORTIA   Thyself shalt see the act;
For as thou urgest justice, be assured
Thou shalt have justice more than thou desir'st.
GRAZIANO   O learnèd judge! Mark, Jew! O learnèd judge!
SHYLOCK   I take this offer, then. Pay the bond thrice,
And let the Christian go.
315   BASSANIO   Here is the money.
PORTIA   Soft,° the Jew shall have all justice. Soft, no haste   *Not so fast*
He shall have nothing but the penalty.
GRAZIANO   O Jew, an upright judge, a learnèd judge!
PORTIA [*to* SHYLOCK]   Therefore prepare thee to cut off the flesh.
320   Shed thou no blood, nor cut thou less nor more
But just° a pound of flesh. If thou tak'st more   *exactly*
Or less than a just pound, be it but so much

turning point }

9. Thief whom the Jews asked Pilate to set free instead of Jesus (Mark 15:6–15).

As makes it light or heavy in the substance°   *weight*
Or the division° of the twentieth part   *fraction*
325 Of one poor scruple°—nay, if the scale do turn   *tiny weight*
But in the estimation° of a hair,   *amount*
Thou diest, and all thy goods are confiscate.
GRAZIANO   A second Daniel, a Daniel, Jew!
Now, infidel, I have you on the hip.[1]
330 PORTIA   Why doth the Jew pause? Take thy forfeiture.
SHYLOCK   Give me my principal, and let me go.
BASSANIO   I have it ready for thee. Here it is.
PORTIA   He hath refused it in the open court.
He shall have merely justice and his bond.
335 GRAZIANO   A Daniel, still say I, a second Daniel!
I thank thee, Jew, for teaching me that word.
SHYLOCK   Shall I not have barely° my principal?   *even*
PORTIA   Thou shalt have nothing but the forfeiture
To be so taken at thy peril, Jew.
340 SHYLOCK   Why then, the devil give him good of it.
I'll stay no longer question.[2]
PORTIA   Tarry, Jew.
The law hath yet another hold on you.
It is enacted in the laws of Venice,
If it be proved against an alien
345 That by direct or indirect attempts
He seek the life of any citizen,
The party 'gainst the which he doth contrive°   *plot*
Shall seize one half his goods; the other half
Comes to the privy coffer° of the state,   *private treasury*
350 And the offender's life lies in° the mercy   *at*
Of the Duke only, 'gainst all other voice—
In which predicament I say thou stand'st,
For it appears by manifest proceeding
That indirectly, and directly too,
355 Thou hast contrived against the very life
Of the defendant, and thou hast incurred
The danger° formerly by me rehearsed.°   *penalty / described*
Down, therefore, and beg mercy of the Duke.
GRAZIANO [*to* SHYLOCK]   Beg that thou mayst have leave to hang thyself—
360 And yet, thy wealth being forfeit to the state,
Thou hast not left the value of a cord.
Therefore thou must be hanged at the state's charge.°   *expense*
DUKE [*to* SHYLOCK]   That thou shalt see the difference of our spirit,
I pardon thee thy life before thou ask it.
365 For half thy wealth, it is Antonio's.
The other half comes to the general state,
Which humbleness may drive° unto a fine.   *reduce*
PORTIA   Ay, for the state, not for Antonio.[3]
SHYLOCK   Nay, take my life and all, pardon not that.
370 You take my house when you do take the prop
That doth sustain my house; you take my life
When you do take the means whereby I live.[4]

---

1. At a disadvantage (see 1.3.41).
2. I'll press my case no further.
3. With respect to the state's half, not Antonio's.

4. "He that taketh away his neighbor's living, slayeth him" (Ecclesiastes 34:22).

PORTIA   What mercy can you render him, Antonio?

GRAZIANO   A halter,° gratis. Nothing else, for God's sake.   *hangman's noose*

375 ANTONIO   So please my lord the Duke and all the court

To quit the fine for one half of his goods,

I am content, so he will let me have

The other half in use,⁵ to render it

Upon his death unto the gentleman

380 That lately stole his daughter.

Two things provided more: that for this favour

He presently° become a Christian;   *immediately*

The other, that he do record a gift

Here in the court of all he dies possessed

385 Unto his son, Lorenzo, and his daughter.

DUKE   He shall do this, or else I do recant°   *withdraw*

The pardon that I late pronouncèd here.

PORTIA   Art thou contented, Jew? What dost thou say?

SHYLOCK   <u>I am content.</u>

390 PORTIA [*to* NERISSA]   Clerk, draw a deed of gift.

SHYLOCK   I pray you give me leave to go from hence.

I am not well. Send the deed after me,

And I will sign it.

DUKE   Get thee gone, but do it.

GRAZIANO [*to* SHYLOCK]   In christ'ning shalt thou have two godfathers.

395 Had I been judge thou shouldst have had ten more,°   *(to constitute a jury)*

To bring thee to the gallows, not the font.   *Exit* [SHYLOCK]

DUKE [*to* PORTIA]   Sir, I entreat you home with me to dinner.

PORTIA   I humbly do desire your grace of pardon.

I must away this night toward Padua,

400 And it is meet° I presently set forth   *proper*

DUKE   I am sorry that your leisure serves you not.°   *you haven't the time*

Antonio, gratify° this gentleman,   *reward*

For in my mind you are much bound to him.

Exit DUKE *and his train*

BASSANIO [*to* PORTIA]   Most worthy gentleman, I and my friend

405 Have by your wisdom been this day acquitted

Of grievous penalties, in lieu whereof

Three thousand ducats due unto the Jew

We freely cope° your courteous pains withal.   *repay*

ANTONIO   And stand indebted over and above

410 In love and service to you evermore.

PORTIA   He is well paid that is well satisfied,

And I, delivering you, am satisfied,

And therein do account myself well paid.

My mind was never yet more mercenary.

415 I pray you know me when we meet again.

I wish you well; and so I take my leave.

BASSANIO   Dear sir, of force° I must attempt you further.   *necessity*

Take some remembrance of us as a tribute,

Not as fee. Grant me two things, I pray you:

420 Not to deny me, and to pardon me.°   *excuse my urging*

---

5. Antonio's conditions are unclear, because "quit" in line 376 (requite) could mean "pardon" or "make him pay," and "in use" (line 378) could mean either "in trust" or "for my own purposes." But the arrangements for Shylock's property later in the scene suggest that Antonio succeeds in getting Shylock's penalty reduced: Shylock retains half of his wealth, and Antonio holds the other half in trust for Jessica and Lorenzo until Shylock dies, at which point they inherit the whole estate.

PORTIA   You press me far, and therefore I will yield.
[*To* ANTONIO] Give me your gloves. I'll wear them for your sake.
[*To* BASSANIO] And for your love I'll take this ring from you.
Do not draw back your hand. I'll take no more,
425   And you in love shall not deny me this.
BASSANIO   This ring, good sir? Alas, it is a trifle.
I will not shame myself to give you this.
PORTIA   I will have nothing else, but only this;
And now, methinks, I have a mind to it.
430   BASSANIO   There's more depends on this° than on the value.   *involved here*
The dearest ring in Venice will I give you,
And find it out by proclamation.
Only for this, I pray you pardon me.
PORTIA   I see, sir, you are liberal in offers.
435   You taught me first to beg, and now methinks
You teach me how a beggar should be answered.
BASSANIO   Good sir, this ring was given me by my wife,
And when she put it on she made me vow
That I should neither sell, nor give, nor lose it.
440   PORTIA   That 'scuse serves many men to save their gifts.
An if° your wife be not a madwoman,   *An if = If*
And know how well I have deserved this ring,
She would not hold out enemy for ever
For giving it to me. Well, peace be with you.
                    Exeunt [PORTIA *and* NERISSA]
445   ANTONIO   My lord Bassanio, let him have the ring.
Let his deservings and my love withal
Be valued 'gainst your wife's commandëment.
BASSANIO   Go, Graziano, run and overtake him.
Give him the ring, and bring him, if thou canst,
450   Unto Antonio's house. Away, make haste.   *Exit* GRAZIANO
Come, you and I will thither presently,
And in the morning early will we both
Fly toward Belmont. Come, Antonio.   *Exeunt*

4.2

Enter PORTIA *and* NERISSA [*still disguised*]
PORTIA   Enquire the Jew's house out, give him this deed,[1]
And let him sign it. We'll away tonight,
And be a day before our husbands home.
This deed will be well welcome to Lorenzo.
                    Enter GRAZIANO
5   GRAZIANO   Fair sir, you are well o'erta'en.
My lord Bassanio upon more advice°   *further thought*
Hath sent you here this ring, and doth entreat
Your company at dinner.
PORTIA   That cannot be.
His ring I do accept most thankfully,
10   And so I pray you tell him. Furthermore,
I pray you show my youth old Shylock's house.
GRAZIANO   That will I do.
NERISSA   Sir, I would speak with you.
[*Aside to* PORTIA] I'll see if I can get my husband's ring

4.2 Location: Street in Venice.   1. Mentioned in 4.1.390.

Which I did make him swear to keep for ever.
15 PORTIA [*aside to* NERISSA]   Thou mayst; I warrant we shall have
            old° swearing   *lots of*
That they did give the rings away to men.
But we'll outface them, and outswear them too
Away, make haste. Thou know'st where I will tarry.
                                               [*Exit at one door*]
NERISSA [*to* GRAZIANO]   Come, good sir, will you show me to this house?
                              Exeunt [*at another door*]

5.1
Enter LORENZO *and* JESSICA
LORENZO   The moon shines bright. In such a night as this,
When the sweet wind did gently kiss the trees
And they did make no noise—in such a night
Troilus, methinks, mounted the Trojan walls,
5 And sighed his soul toward the Grecian tents
Where Cressid lay that night.[1]
JESSICA   In such a night
Did Thisbe fearfully o'ertrip the dew
And saw the lion's shadow ere himself,
And ran dismayed away.[2]
LORENZO   In such a night
10 Stood Dido with a willow in her hand
Upon the wild sea banks, and waft her love
To come again to Carthage.[3]
JESSICA   In such a night
Medea gatherèd the enchanted herbs
That did renew old Aeson.[4]
LORENZO   In such a night
15 Did Jessica steal° from the wealthy Jew,   *escape; rob*
And with an unthrift° love did run from Venice   *a spendthrift*
As far as Belmont.
JESSICA   In such a night
Did young Lorenzo swear he loved her well,
Stealing her soul with many vows of faith,
And ne'er a true one.
20 LORENZO   In such a night
Did pretty Jessica, like a little shrew,
Slander her love, and he forgave it her.
JESSICA   I would outnight you, did nobody come.
But hark, I hear the footing° of a man.   *footsteps*
            Enter [STEFANO,] *a messenger*
25 LORENZO   Who comes so fast in silence of the night?
STEFANO   A friend.
LORENZO   A friend—what friend? Your name, I pray you, friend?
STEFANO   Stefano is my name, and I bring word

5.1 Location: Belmont.
1. Troilus was a Trojan Prince whose lover, Cressida, forsook him for the Greek Diomedes after she was sent from Troy to the Greek camp. See *Troilus and Cressida*.
2. Thisbe, going at night to meet her lover, Pyramus, was frightened by a lion and fled. Pyramus, assuming she was dead, killed himself; when she found his body, Thisbe committed suicide too. The story is dramatized

by "the rude mechanicals" in *A Midsummer Night's Dream*.
3. Dido, Queen of Carthage, was abandoned by her lover, the Trojan hero Aeneas. *willow*: emblem of forsaken love. *waft*: waved to.
4. Medea was a sorceress who loved Jason and helped him win the Golden Fleece; she magically restored Aeson, Jason's father, to youth.

My mistress will before the break of day
30 Be here at Belmont. She doth stray about
By holy crosses,° where she kneels and prays   roadside shrines
For happy wedlock hours.

LORENZO   Who comes with her?

STEFANO   None but a holy hermit and her maid.
I pray you, is my master yet returned?

35 LORENZO   He is not, nor we have not heard from him.
But go we in, I pray thee, Jessica,
And ceremoniously let us prepare
Some welcome for the mistress of the house.

          Enter [LANCELOT] *the clown*

LANCELOT [*calling*]   Sola, sola! Wo, ha, ho! Sola, sola!⁵
40 LORENZO   Who calls?

LANCELOT [*calling*]   Sola!—Did you see Master Lorenzo? [*Calling*] Master Lorenzo! Sola, sola!

LORENZO   Leave hollering, man: here.

LANCELOT [*calling*]   Sola!—Where, where?

45 LORENZO   Here.

LANCELOT   Tell him there's a post° come from my master with his   messenger
horn full of good news. My master will be here ere morning.
                                                           [*Exit*]

LORENZO [*to* JESSICA]   Sweet soul, let's in, and there expect°   await
their coming.
And yet no matter. Why should we go in?
50 My friend Stefano, signify,° I pray you,   announce
Within the house your mistress is at hand,
And bring your music forth into the air.   *Exit* STEFANO
How sweet the moonlight sleeps upon this bank!
Here will we sit, and let the sounds of music
55 Creep in our ears. Soft stillness and the night
Become the touches⁶ of sweet harmony.
Sit, Jessica.
          [*They sit*]
                    Look how the floor of heaven
Is thick inlaid with patens° of bright gold.   disks
There's not the smallest orb which thou behold'st
60 But in his motion like an angel sings,
Still° choiring to the young-eyed⁷ cherubins.   Continually
Such harmony⁸ is in immortal souls,
But whilst this muddy vesture of decay°   this mortal body
Doth grossly close it° in, we cannot hear it.°   (the soul) / (the music)
          [*Enter Musicians*]
65 [*To the Musicians*] Come, ho, and wake Diana⁹ with a hymn.
With sweetest touches pierce your mistress'° ear,   (Portia's)
And draw her home with music.
          [*The Musicians*] *play*

JESSICA   I am never merry when I hear sweet music.

LORENZO   The reason is your spirits are attentive,
70 For do but note a wild and wanton herd
Or race° of youthful and unhandled colts,   group

---

5. Imitating a messenger's horn.
6. Suit the notes (literally, the fingering of a stringed instrument).
7. Keen-sighted.
8. The music of the spheres.
9. Goddess of the moon and of chastity.

Fetching mad bounds, bellowing and neighing loud,
Which is the hot condition of their blood,
If they but hear perchance a trumpet sound,
75   Or any air of music touch their ears,
You shall perceive them make a mutual° stand,   *simultaneous*
Their savage eyes turned to a modest gaze
By the sweet power of music. Therefore the poet[1]
Did feign that Orpheus drew° trees, stones, and floods,   *allured*
80   Since naught so stockish,° hard, and full of rage   *stolid*
But music for the time doth change his nature.
The man that hath no music in himself,
Nor is not moved with concord of sweet sounds,   ✳
Is fit for treasons, stratagems,° and spoils.°   *plots / plunder*
85   The motions of his spirit are dull as night,
And his affections° dark as Erebus.°   *inclinations / hell*
Let no such man be trusted. Mark the music.

Enter PORTIA *and* NERISSA [*as themselves*]

PORTIA   That light we see is burning in my hall.
How far that little candle throws his beams—
90   So shines a good deed in a naughty° world.   *an evil*
NERISSA   When the moon shone we did not see the candle.
PORTIA   So doth the greater glory dim the less.
A substitute° shines brightly as a king   *deputy*
Until a king be by, and then his state
95   Empties itself as doth an inland brook
Into the main of waters.° Music, hark.   *the ocean*
NERISSA   It is your music, madam, of the house.
PORTIA   Nothing is good, I see, without respect.°   *reference to context*
Methinks it sounds much sweeter than by day.
100 NERISSA   Silence bestows that virtue on it, madam.
PORTIA   The crow doth sing as sweetly as the lark
When neither is attended,[2] and I think
The nightingale, if she should sing by day,
When every goose is cackling, would be thought
105 No better a musician than the wren.
How many things by season seasoned are[3]
To their right praise and true perfection!
   [*She sees* LORENZO *and* JESSICA]
Peace, ho!
   [*Music ceases*]
            The moon sleeps with Endymion,[4]
And would not be awaked.
LORENZO [*rising*]   That is the voice,
110 Or I am much deceived, of Portia.
PORTIA   He knows me as the blind man knows the cuckoo—
By the bad voice.
LORENZO   Dear lady, welcome home.
PORTIA   We have been praying for our husbands' welfare,
Which speed° we hope the better for our words.   *Who prosper*
Are they returned?
115 LORENZO   Madam, they are not yet,

---

1. Ovid, in *Metamorphoses* 10, tells the story of Orpheus,   3. *by season . . . are:* by proper time are adapted.
a legendary musician.   4. In classical mythology, a shepherd beloved of the
2. Is listened to; is accompanied.   moon goddess, who caused him to sleep forever.

But there is come a messenger before
To signify their coming.
PORTIA   Go in, Nerissa.
Give order to my servants that they take
No note at all of our being absent hence;
120   Nor you, Lorenzo; Jessica, nor you.
                     A tucket° sounds   *trumpet flourish*
LORENZO   Your husband is at hand. I hear his trumpet.
We are no tell-tales, madam. Fear you not.
PORTIA   This night, methinks, is but the daylight sick.
It looks a little paler. 'Tis a day
125   Such as the day is when the sun is hid.
          Enter BASSANIO, ANTONIO, GRAZIANO, *and their follow-*
          ers. [GRAZIANO *and* NERISSA *speak silently to one*
          another]
BASSANIO   We should hold day with the Antipodes
If you would walk in absence of the sun.[5]
PORTIA   Let me give light, but let me not be light;°   *unfaithful*
For a light wife doth make a heavy° husband,   *sad*
130   And never be Bassanio so for me.
But God sort° all. You are welcome home, my lord.   *decide*
BASSANIO   I thank you, madam. Give welcome to my friend.
This is the man, this is Antonio,
To whom I am so infinitely bound.
135   PORTIA   You should in all° sense be much bound to him,   *every*
For as I hear he was much bound for you.
ANTONIO   No more than I am well acquitted° of.   *freed*
PORTIA   Sir, you are very welcome to our house.
It must appear in other ways than words,
140   Therefore I scant this breathing courtesy.[6]
GRAZIANO [*to* NERISSA]   By yonder moon I swear you do me wrong.
In faith, I gave it to the judge's clerk.
Would he were gelt° that had it for my part,   *gelded; castrated*
Since you do take it, love, so much at heart.
145   PORTIA   A quarrel, ho, already! What's the matter?
GRAZIANO   About a hoop of gold, a paltry ring
That she did give me, whose posy° was   *motto*
For all the world like cutlers' poetry
Upon a knife—'Love me and leave me not'.
150   NERISSA   What talk you of the posy or the value?
You swore to me when I did give it you
That you would wear it till your hour of death,
And that it should lie with you in your grave.
Though not for me, yet for your vehement oaths
155   You should have been respective° and have kept it.   *careful*
Gave it a judge's clerk?—no, God's my judge,
The clerk will ne'er wear hair on's face that had it.
GRAZIANO   He will an if he live to be a man.
NERISSA   Ay, if a woman live to be a man.
160   GRAZIANO   Now by this hand, I gave it to a youth,
A kind of boy, a little scrubbèd° boy   *stunted*

---

5. *We . . . sun:* We would share daylight with the
other side of the world (Antipodes) if you habitually
walked when the sun was gone (implying "such is your
radiance").
6. I make brief this verbal welcome.

No higher than thyself, the judge's clerk,
A prating° boy that begged it as a fee   *chattering*
I could not for my heart deny it him.

165 PORTIA   You were to blame, I must be plain with you,
To part so slightly with your wife's first gift,
A thing stuck on with oaths upon your finger,
And so riveted with faith unto your flesh.
I gave my love a ring, and made him swear
170 Never to part with it; and here he stands.
I dare be sworn for him he would not leave° it,   *part with*
Nor pluck it from his finger for the wealth
That the world masters.° Now, in faith, Graziano,   *possesses*
You give your wife too unkind a cause of grief.
175 An 'twere to me, I should be mad at it.

BASSANIO *[aside]*   Why, I were best to cut my left hand off
And swear I lost the ring defending it.

GRAZIANO *[to PORTIA]*   My lord Bassanio gave his ring away
Unto the judge that begged it, and indeed
180 Deserved it, too, and then the boy his clerk,
That took some pains in writing, he begged mine,
And neither man nor master would take aught
But the two rings.

PORTIA *[to BASSANIO]*   What ring gave you, my lord?
Not that, I hope, which you received of me.

185 BASSANIO   If I could add a lie unto a fault
I would deny it; but you see my finger
Hath not the ring upon it. It is gone.

PORTIA   Even so void is your false heart of truth.
By heaven, I will ne'er come in your bed
Until I see the ring.

190 NERISSA *[to GRAZIANO]*   Nor I in yours
Till I again see mine.

BASSANIO   Sweet Portia,
If you did know to whom I gave the ring,
If you did know for whom I gave the ring,
And would conceive for what I gave the ring,
195 And how unwillingly I left the ring
When naught would be accepted but the ring,
You would abate the strength of your displeasure.

PORTIA   If you had known the virtue° of the ring,   *power*
Or half her worthiness that gave the ring,
200 Or your own honour to contain° the ring,   *retain*
You would not then have parted with the ring.
What man is there so much unreasonable,
If you had pleased to have defended it
With any terms of zeal, wanted° the modesty°   *would lack / moderation*
205 To urge° the thing held as a ceremony?°   *insist on / sacred symbol*
Nerissa teaches me what to believe.
I'll die for't but some woman had the ring.

BASSANIO   No, by my honour, madam, by my soul,
No woman had it, but a civil doctor°   *doctor of civil law*
210 Which did refuse three thousand ducats of me,
And begged the ring, the which I did deny him,
And suffered° him to go displeased away,   *permitted*
Even he that had held up the very life

Of my dear friend. What should I say, sweet lady?
215   I was enforced to send it after him.
I was beset with shame and courtesy.
My honour would not let ingratitude
So much besmear it. Pardon me, good lady,
For by these blessèd candles of the night,
220   Had you been there I think you would have begged
The ring of me to give the worthy doctor.

PORTIA   Let not that doctor e'er come near my house.
Since he hath got the jewel that I loved,
And that which you did swear to keep for me,
225   I will become as liberal° as you.   *generous; licentious*
I'll not deny him anything I have,
No, not my body nor my husband's bed.
Know° him I shall, I am well sure of it.   *(with sexual suggestion)*
Lie not a night from home. Watch me like Argus.[7]
230   If you do not, if I be left alone,
Now by mine honour, which is yet mine own,
I'll have that doctor for my bedfellow.

NERISSA [*to* GRAZIANO]   And I his clerk, therefore be well advised
How you do leave me to mine own protection.

235 GRAZIANO   Well, do you so. Let not me take him then,
For if I do, I'll mar the young clerk's pen.°   *(with sexual suggestion)*

ANTONIO   I am th'unhappy subject of these quarrels.

PORTIA   Sir, grieve not you. You are welcome notwithstanding.

BASSANIO   Portia, forgive me this enforcèd wrong,
240   And in the hearing of these many friends
I swear to thee, even by thine own fair eyes,
Wherein I see myself—

PORTIA   Mark you but that?
In both my eyes he doubly sees himself,
In each eye one. Swear by your double° self,   *twofold; deceitful*
And there's an oath of credit.[8]

245 BASSANIO   Nay, but hear me.
Pardon this fault, and by my soul I swear
I never more will break an oath with thee.

ANTONIO [*to* PORTIA]   I once did lend my body for his wealth
Which, but for him that had your husband's ring,
250   Had quite miscarried. I dare be bound again,
My soul upon the forfeit, that your lord
Will never more break faith advisedly.°   *intentionally*

PORTIA   Then you shall be his surety.° Give him this,   *guarantor of a loan*
And bid him keep it better than the other.

255 ANTONIO   Here, Lord Bassanio, swear to keep this ring.

BASSANIO   By heaven, it is the same I gave the doctor!

PORTIA   I had it of him. Pardon me, Bassanio,
For by this ring, the doctor lay with me.

NERISSA   And pardon me, my gentle Graziano,
260   For that same scrubbèd boy, the doctor's clerk,
In lieu of° this last night did lie with me.   *In exchange for*

GRAZIANO   Why, this is like the mending of highways
In summer where the ways are fair enough![9]

---

7. Mythical many-eyed monster.   9. *where . . . enough:* when repair is not required.
8. An oath to be believed (ironic).

What, are we cuckolds ere we have deserved it?

265 PORTIA   Speak not so grossly. You are all amazed.°   *confused*
Here is a letter. Read it at your leisure.
It comes from Padua, from Bellario.
There you shall find that Portia was the doctor,
Nerissa there her clerk. Lorenzo here
270 Shall witness I set forth as soon as you,
And even but now returned. I have not yet
Entered my house. Antonio, you are welcome,
And I have better news in store for you
Than you expect. Unseal this letter soon.
275 There you shall find three of your argosies
Are richly come to harbour suddenly.
You shall not know by what strange accident
I chancèd on this letter.

ANTONIO   I am dumb.°   *dumbstruck*

BASSANIO [*to* PORTIA]   Were you the doctor and I knew you not?

280 GRAZIANO [*to* NERISSA]   Were you the clerk that is to make me cuckold?

NERISSA   Ay, but the clerk that never means to do it
Unless he live until he be a man.

BASSANIO [*to* PORTIA]   Sweet doctor, you shall be my bedfellow.
When I am absent, then lie with my wife.

285 ANTONIO [*to* PORTIA]   Sweet lady, you have given me life and
living,°   *possessions*
For here I read for certain that my ships
Are safely come to road.°   *harbor*

PORTIA   How now, Lorenzo?
My clerk hath some good comforts, too, for you.

NERISSA   Ay, and I'll give them him without a fee.
290 There do I give to you and Jessica
From the rich Jew a special deed of gift,
After his death, of all he dies possessed of.

LORENZO   Fair ladies, you drop manna in the way
Of starvèd people.

PORTIA   It is almost morning,
295 And yet I am sure you are not satisfied
Of these events at full. Let us go in,
And charge us there upon inter'gatories,[1]
And we will answer all things faithfully.

GRAZIANO   Let it be so. The first inter'gatory
300 That my Nerissa shall be sworn on is
Whether till the next night she had rather stay,
Or go to bed now, being two hours to day.
But were the day come, I should wish it dark
Till I were couching° with the doctor's clerk.   *lying*
305 Well, while I live I'll fear no other thing
So sore as keeping safe Nerissa's ring.°   *Exeunt*   (*with sexual suggestion*)

---

1. And question us under oath.

ANTONIO   I am dumb.

living;

Are safely come to road.

I Henry IV

A roadside inn that fails to provide chamber pots for its customers, a castle in Wales where a magician summons spirits to be his musicians, the royal palace in London from which the King of England launches a campaign against rebel forces—these are but a few of the disparate venues where the action of *1 Henry IV* occurs. With this drama, the Shakespearean history play broadens out to encompass a rich diversity of languages, characters, and locales. Nothing in Shakespeare's earlier English histories quite anticipates this one. The great prose chronicles of the sixteenth century, such as Raphael Holinshed's *Chronicles of England, Scotland, and Ireland* (second edition, 1587), which Shakespeare consulted and whose materials he freely adapted and supplemented, stand behind all his history plays. The earlier plays, however, like the chronicles, focus primarily on the world of court and battlefield in which the monarch and his nobles appear as history's significant players, their rivalries and their achievements the focal point of the action. Common people such as Jack Cade have roles in these works, but their stories are typically subordinated to the monarchical plot. In *1 Henry IV*, something different happens. Several lines of action unfold at once, each connected to particular geographical locales, and each commenting upon, without simply displacing, the others. Henry IV, who had seized the throne from Richard II, is the play's title character, but from the start he is a beleaguered figure kept from his dream of making a Crusade to the Holy Land by discontent and rebellion among his nobles, especially the Percy family, and burdened with an oldest son, Prince Hal, who acts more like a prodigal child than the heir to the throne. The King appears in some key scenes, but for long stretches the action focuses on other characters and on places, like a common London tavern, that the King would never deign to visit.

Some events take place in the north of England, in the Northumberland stronghold of the Percy family. The play is set in the early fifteenth century, but even in the late sixteenth century the north of England was popularly regarded as lawless, wild, and linked to marginalized Catholic practices and beliefs, its nobility not fully incorporated into the increasingly centralized state being constructed by the Tudor monarchs. In 1569, members of the Percy family had been prominent in the Northern Rebellion, an attempt to overthrow Queen Elizabeth and put Mary Queen of Scots, a Catholic, on the throne. In drawing his portrait of the Percys, Shakespeare makes their champion, Hotspur, an impassioned embodiment of medieval chivalry, eager above all for honor and for the glory to be won in battle. While the historical Hotspur was actually much older than the King's son, Prince Hal, Shakespeare follows Samuel Daniel's poem *The Civile Wars Between the Two Houses of Lancaster and York* (1595) in making him Hal's coequal in years and his rival for preeminence in the kingdom. He is joined in rebellion by other figures from the threatening territories on the perimeter of England: by the Earl of Douglas, a formidable Scottish warrior, and by the Welshman Owain Glyndŵr, a self-proclaimed magician with a fiery temper, a lyrical temperament, and a daughter who marries Edmund Mortimer, the man presented in this play as Richard II's designated heir to the throne. Wales thus harbors both rebellion and the man who was arguably the legitimate King of England.

Another of the play's crucial locales is a tavern in Eastcheap, a commercial district in the east of London. This tavern is Prince Hal's second home where he comes to drink and amuse himself, and particularly to carouse with Falstaff, the dissipated knight who is the young Prince's tutor in folly, his intimate friend, and surrogate father. In Eastcheap, Hal rubs elbows with commoners such as Mistress Quickly, the Hostess,

The historical Owain Glyndŵr claimed the title of Prince of Wales. His great seal, both sides of which are shown here, bears the inscription "Owain, by the grace of God, prince of Wales" and depicts four upreared (rampant) lions, the coat of arms of the Gwynedd dynasty, to which Glyndŵr belonged.

and with Francis, the inarticulate apprentice tapster. Shakespeare took his cue about Hal's presence amid this crew from the many popular accounts of the Prince's dissolute youth, especially from a play printed in 1598 called *The Famous Victories of Henry the Fifth,* some version of which seems to have been staged in the late 1580s. It depicts not only episodes from Hal's madcap youth but also his eventual reformation and assumption of the throne. Shakespeare elaborated extensively on this story of youthful prodigality. Mistress Quickly, for example, is entirely his invention, and the character of Falstaff, while loosely modeled on a figure in *The Famous Victories,* is utterly transformed by Shakespeare into what has remained one of the great comic creations of the English theater. Witty, opportunistic, and utterly indifferent to the decorum expected of a knight of advanced years, Falstaff makes the tavern a place of perpetual play and the antithesis of the duty-driven world of the court. That the Prince seems irresistibly drawn to Eastcheap makes others, especially his father, question his fitness to rule, but the high-spirited playfulness of Falstaff's world suggests why the Prince might take refuge there from the demands of his public role and the exacting expectations of the King, his father.

One of the objections to English popular theater voiced by a contemporary poet, Sir Philip Sidney, was that it mingled clowns with kings in a way that violated codes of aesthetic and social decorum; these codes insisted on the strict separation of high and low subject matter, language, and people. In contrast to Sidney's dicta, *1 Henry IV* is thoroughly hybrid in its mingling of the high matter of rebellion and affairs of state with the low matter of drinking, jokes, and highway robbery. The play is also a temporal hybrid in that the tavern scenes seem to take place not in the early fifteenth century, when Henry IV was struggling to secure his rule, but more nearly in the late sixteenth century, when Shakespeare was actually writing his play. In the tavern scenes, for example, characters make fun of plays and modes of writing popular in the 1570s and 1580s, such as Thomas Preston's ranting tyrant play *Cambyses* (1569) and the baroquely ornate rhetoric popularized by John Lyly in his *Euphues* (1578). The tavern world is also filled with references to the commodities that passed through London's markets in the late sixteenth century. The characters there drink sack, Madeira, and bastard—popular alcoholic beverages, some (such as Madeira) imported from as far away as an island off the coast of west Africa; and they refer to articles of clothing, such as the Spanish-leather wallets and leather jerkins with crystal buttons, worn by London's aspiring mercantile classes. Eastcheap itself, where the tavern is located, was a major market street in Shakespeare's London, and the tavern scenes are steeped in references to the commercial culture, including the theatrical culture, of early modern England.

There is every indication, however, that if a Sidney would have found the hybridity of the play a problem, ordinary consumers did not. Judging by its publication history, in its own time *1 Henry IV* was one of Shakespeare's most popular plays. It appeared in two quarto versions in 1598 and then in five more before the First Folio was printed in 1623. Even after that, individual quarto editions of the play continued to appear. Part of its popularity undoubtedly derived from the fact that with *1 Henry IV*, the Shakespearean history play began to supplement chronicle history, which focuses on monarchs, nobles, and affairs of state, with chorography: that is, with a mode of writing popular in the late sixteenth century that described and surveyed the land of England focusing on the products, the terrain, and the customs of England's various regions. *1 Henry IV* is a chorography in the sense that while the play's distinct lines of action comment on one another, each is defined in relation to specific places, customs, and social groups. The commercial, bawdy world of the tavern, with its cast of lowlife characters and its rituals of drinking and play, is very different from the more formal milieu of Westminster, where the King and his nobles are immersed in the tasks of statecraft, and different again from the world of passion and magic centered in Glyndŵr's Welsh castle. Through the multiple plots, the spectator watching the play experiences the illusion of complex temporal simultaneity and social and geographic heterogeneity. Thus in successive scenes, the rebels, in Wales, plot the dismemberment of England and listen to a song sung in Welsh (3.1); King Henry in Westminster, berates his wayward son (3.2); Falstaff, in Eastcheap, tries to cheat Mistress Quickly by claiming that his ring was stolen in her tavern (3.3). All these actions go on contemporally but in widely disparate locales, creating a theatrical illusion of the diversity encompassed by the ongoing life of the nation and its bordering regions.

But the play's complex elaboration of difference also makes evident its monarch's central problem: how to maintain control over and enforce unity upon the territories over which he claims dominion but which threaten to break away or assert a worrisome autonomy. As in *Henry V*, Shakespeare here dramatizes the tension between efforts at nation building and the cultural, religious, and political differences that promote fragmentation. The problem of furthering national unity is especially pressing for Henry IV because he did not lineally inherit the throne; he seized it from Richard II. He is on shaky ground, then, should he attempt to unify England under the banner of his own legitimacy. In fact, for much of the play, Henry is a king in search of a strategy of rule. He had hoped to unify his people and quiet his conscience for his part in Richard's deposition and death by undertaking a Crusade to recover Jerusalem for European Christianity. But trouble at home keeps him from enacting his plan as rebellion bubbles up on the Scottish border, on the Welsh border, in the northern counties, and even in the Church, in the person of the Archbishop of York. The land seethes with the murmurings of rebels.

In the England of the 1590s, the monarch's most pressing problem of control was posed by Ireland; there, after 1595, the Earl of Tyrone led the challenge to English rule. Like Glyndŵr, Tyrone was educated in England and in some accounts was even Glyndŵr's descendant. While Ireland is not directly depicted in *1 Henry IV*, Hotspur verbally links Wales and Ireland. Urged to listen to a song sung in Welsh, he says that he would rather hear his hunting dog "howl in Irish" (3.1.232), thereby confirming the common English view that Welsh and Irish were equally barbarous languages. More important, Wales stands in the play as a displaced image of the contemporary Irish situation. In the popular imagination, Wales often seemed a foreign place of mystery and danger, even though it had been officially incorporated in England in the 1530s and the Welsh language banned as unnatural and barbarous. In *1 Henry IV*, Wales represents the threat not only of rebellion but also of effeminization and seduction. Mortimer, the supposed heir to the English throne, falls in love with Glyndŵr's daughter, promises to learn her language, and never appears on the battlefield against Henry's forces. In essence, he "goes native," a persistent fear voiced by the English concerning their soldiers and settlers in Ireland. The English had long worried that through prolonged contact with the Irish, English men and women might adopt their barbarous ways and forfeit their English identity. They even feared that their children, in drinking the milk of Irish wet nurses, could be transformed into people more Irish than English.

In *1 Henry IV*, the threat posed by the dangerous Welsh borderlands and by the northern Percy faction directly challenges the King's authority. Hampered by the questionable means by which he came to the throne, Henry ultimately finds force and guile the most effective instruments for maintaining his power. He can win battles, and he is willing to use deception to improve his position. At Shrewsbury, his major battle against the rebels, a number of Henry's nobles dress like the King, frustrating the enemy's ability to identify the true King and encouraging Henry's own forces by the seeming ubiquity of their monarch. Perpetual battle, however, is a costly way to rule, and having many nobles dress like him runs counter to Henry's stated belief that the King should be seldom seen in order to be the more wondered at when he does appear. To have many men marching in the King's clothing and answering to the King's name might, in fact, subversively suggest that "King" is a part any man could play, given the right accoutrements.

Prince Hal faces the pressing task of finding better strategies for ruling the changed world his father brought into being by his deposition of King Richard. He cannot assume that his kingship will be uncontested simply because he is Henry's son. A usurper's offspring has more legitimacy than a usurper, but not much. Rather, Hal must *make* himself King by a convincing performance of the part, and he must beat out those who would be his rivals, such as Harry Hotspur. Viewed one way, *1 Henry IV* is a study in the political and theatrical skills necessary for rule in a world where the inevitability and assumed legitimacy of inherited kingship has been called into question. In 1532, Niccolò Machiavelli's *The Prince,* a manual of practical statecraft, was published and quickly became notorious throughout Europe. Machiavelli taught rulers how to maintain their power through a mixture of guile, alliance, warfare, and personal force of character. Popularly viewed as irreligious and amoral, Machiavelli nonetheless was a byword for political pragmatism.

In his sophisticated manipulation of power, Hal shows himself a good student of Machiavelli, and the Machiavellian strand of his characterization has caused a split in critical assessments of him. To many, Hal personifies the ideal English king, the perfect mean between the self-indulgence of a Falstaff and the impassioned inflexibility of a Hotspur. He is thus an object of desire and emulation. Other critics focus on what they perceive as a lack of humanity at the heart of this consummate politician and recoil from his calculated use of other people to serve his own ends. For example, at the end of the first scene in which he appears, Hal in soliloquy speaks about his tavern mates:

> I know you all, and will a while uphold
> The unyoked humour of your idleness.
> Yet herein will I imitate the sun,
> Who doth permit the base contagious clouds
> To smother up his beauty from the world,
> That when he please again to be himself,
> Being wanted he may be more wondered at
> By breaking through the foul and ugly mists
> Of vapours that did seem to strangle him.
>
> (1.2.173–81)

These lines reveal the calculation that is one part of this character's representation. Comparing himself to the royal symbol, the sun, Hal casts his companions as the contaminating clouds and ugly mists that temporarily obscure his own radiance. Hal is chillingly disdainful of those he elsewhere treats as boon companions, but he also finds their baseness *useful*, since it will set in high relief his own glory, once he has cast them off.

Hal is an interesting dramatic character and not merely a personification of political expediency, however, precisely because his calculated use of his companions does not necessarily preclude his being attracted to them and to the world of play and good fellowship that they represent. In *1 Henry IV*, Hal is not yet King, and the moment of repudiation is not yet upon him. In this play, he can both enjoy his time in Eastcheap and also acquire skills there that he will need when he ascends his father's troubled throne. In the tavern, for example, he and Falstaff take turns playing King and Prince in a theatrical staging of the prodigal Hal's encounter with his reproving father. Hal rehearses the cadences and the sentiments of royal speech, trying out a part, learning to inhabit it convincingly. But it is not just his own part he masters. Unlike his father, Hal does not hold himself aloof from his would-be subjects. His ventures into Eastcheap are in part a mapping of one corner of England, a survey of the customs and strange languages of this locale. To Ned Poins he boasts that having been instructed by three tapsters in the terminology of drinking, "I can drink with any tinker in his own language during my life" (2.5.16–17).

In the tavern, Hal also meditates on the strange tongue of his great rival, Hotspur, whose impatient but impassioned speech Hal parodies:

> I am not yet of Percy's mind, the Hotspur of the North—he that kills me some six or seven dozen of Scots at a breakfast, washes his hands, and says to his wife, 'Fie upon this quiet life! I want work.' 'O my sweet Harry,' says she, 'how many hast thou killed today?' 'Give my roan horse a drench,' says he, and answers, 'Some fourteen,' an hour after; 'a trifle, a trifle.' I prithee call in Falstaff. I'll play Percy, and that damned brawn shall play Dame Mortimer his wife. (2.5.94–101)

Learning the language of others and rehearsing their tongues is, for Hal, one of the arts of power. He can—and later he will—repudiate some of those whose language and customs he has imbibed, making the repudiation a justification for his own rule. Knowing disorderliness, the King will use his office to punish it. He can also appropriate the language of others, as at Shrewsbury he appropriates the chivalric accents of Hotspur; or he can co-opt others to serve his own purposes by speaking to them in a tongue they can comprehend. By his own account, Hal is beloved of the tapsters who have taught him their language, and they have promised that when he is king, he "shall command all the good lads in Eastcheap" (2.5.12–13). Many of them he will eventually command in his wars in France. It can be argued, therefore, that there is a profound instrumentality to Hal's sojourn outside the court milieu that should be his "natural" home. He is acquiring theatrical skills, linguistic skills, and above all a knowledge of the diverse corners of an England he must rule by a mixture of charm, guile, and strategic severity—demonizing some subjects to win the loyalty of others, outstripping rivals by outdoing them at their own particular strengths.

Yet Hal is only part of this play, and *1 Henry IV*'s uniqueness consists in good part in the way it plays off one dramatic perspective, one line of action, against another. The young Prince is certainly the focus of the play's narrative of reform, and he is the only character who can move with seeming ease among the worlds of tavern, court, and battlefield. Yet even as he surveys and judges those around him, the play's structure of geographical juxtapositions and its vivid depiction of other characters and other modes of being invite the audience to submit the Prince himself to critical scrutiny. Consider, for example, 3.1 and 3.2, the scenes at the center of the play that take the audience first to Glyndŵr's castle in Wales, where he, Hotspur, Mortimer, and Worcester are plotting their rebellion, and then to the King's palace at Westminster to which Henry has summoned his son. The first scene graphically establishes the kingdom-cleaving threat posed by the rebels. They have a map and are planning how they will divide the territory of England into three parts. But the scene also establishes the danger, mystery, and beauty of this borderland. Glyndŵr is a man trained in occult arts who boasts that the earth shook at his birth and that he can summon spirits to do his bidding. Hotspur scoffs, but when Glyndŵr's daughter promises to sing in Welsh, Glyndŵr says:

> Do so, and those musicians that shall play to you
> Hang in the air a thousand leagues from hence,
> And straight they shall be here. Sit and attend.
>
> (3.1.220–22)

Three lines later, music plays, its origins a mystery. When Glyndŵr speaks, Wales seems a land of enchantment, haunted by spirits.

Wales is also a place where women are integral to the action as they seldom are elsewhere in the play. Except for Mistress Quickly, Kate Percy and Glyndŵr's daughter are the play's only two female characters; and 3.1, the play's only scene in which two women are onstage at the same time, is set in Wales and is largely Shakespeare's invention. In the chronicles, Glyndŵr, Mortimer, and Hotspur's proposed division of conquered territory is negotiated by representatives in the Archbishop of Bangor's house. By contrast, in *1 Henry IV* it occurs at Glyndŵr's home with the women present. In short, Shakespeare went to some trouble to link the rebels with women—more specifically, with wives and daughters. The question is why. In part, the choice portrays the rebels, unlike the Lancastrians, as having private as well as public lives. Glyndŵr is fond of his daughter and worries about her happiness. Mortimer dotes on this same daughter and seems to have married her for love as much as for political alliance. Hotspur's affection for his wife is displayed through the teasing banter with which he persistently addresses her. Scornful of mooning lovers, he nonetheless is careful to take his wife with him when he journeys to Wales.

The passions so nakedly on display in 3.1 clearly signal the rebels' vulnerabilities. In the patriarchal thought of the period, men were presented as superior to women because they were supposedly more rational and less subject to their passions. If men loved women too much, they risked becoming effeminate—that is, *like* a woman in placing desire above reason, especially if that desire kept a man from performing his public duties, such as going to war. Hotspur prizes his masculinity and the public honor to be won in battle. He is contemptuous of the affected courtier who appeared at Holmedon after the fighting, demanding Hotspur's prisoners (1.3.28–68). In his dealings with his wife, Hotspur seems to use banter and jokes to maintain control of his affection for her. He would not, for a woman, forgo the man-to-man erotics of battle when, "hot horse to horse" (4.1.123), he clashes against the bosom of Prince Hal. Mortimer, by contrast, simply succumbs to the charms of the Welsh woman. He never appears in battle: Wales and a wife swallow him up.

This Welsh world of danger, mystery, and passion sits strangely against the world of calculation that unfolds immediately thereafter, when in 3.2 King Henry castigates Prince Hal for his dissolute life and together they discuss strategies of monarchical self-presentation. The throne room is a place not of enchantment but of business. No women are shown at court, and passion manifests itself most strongly as the desire to rule. Father and son are both preoccupied with the tactics and strategies by which they can most effectively command the loyalty of subjects. While Henry fears his son misunderstands the task before him, Hal shows that he is every bit as astute as his father. But after the high emotions and alluring lyricism of the Welsh scene, the throne room at Westminster can seem a pragmatic and claustrophobic space. In concentrating their energies on rule, Henry and Hal here are divorced from many things that give the rebel world its charm.

Falstaff and the tavern pose a different challenge to the values of Westminster. As critics have shown, the fat man's tutoring of Hal in riotous living mimics the pedagogical relationship of master to student that was sometimes eroticized in the early modern period. Much of the poignancy of the play's depiction of the friendship between the two comes from the tension between their apparent intimacy and the Prince's stated intention to repudiate his companion. Falstaff's threat to monarchical values is obvious. Against the future-oriented calculations of Hal and his father, he insists on living in the present. As his huge body testifies, he demands the immediate gratification of physical desires. To eat, drink, and jest—these are pleasures that for Falstaff brook no delay. Hal can discipline himself. He is thin, as Falstaff points out, and he can plot a personal reformation sometime far in the future and work toward that end. Falstaff cannot or will not; and yet, while a figure of disorder, he has for many readers been the play's most interesting and memorable character. Aside from Hamlet, no other

Falstaff and Prince Hal. Pen and watercolor drawing on paper by William Blake (c. 1780).

Shakespearean figure has attracted as much critical attention as the fat knight.

When Shakespeare first wrote the play, he called this character Sir John Oldcastle. The choice was unfortunate, for the Cobham family, descendants of the historical Oldcastle, protested. William Brooke, the tenth Baron Cobham, had been Lord Chamberlain from August 1596 to March 1597, the very months when most scholars believe Shakespeare completed *1 Henry IV.* Since the Lord Chamberlain oversaw the licensing of plays through the office of the Master of the Revels, Cobham was in an especially favorable position to object to this comic rendition of his ancestor. Shakespeare apparently changed the character's name in response to this act of censorship, though traces of his original intentions can be discerned, including the fact that in 1.2.37–38 Falstaff is still referred to as "my old lad of the castle." In addition, in the first complete Quarto of *1 Henry IV,* there are a few traces of the fact that Peto once bore the name "Harvey," and Bardolph the name "Russell." Again, the objections of powerful figures may have forced changes. "Russell" was the family name of the prominent earls of Bedford, and "Harvey" the name of the stepfather of the Earl of Southampton.

Recently, some critics (including the editors of the Oxford text) have argued that the names "Peto," "Bardolph," and "Falstaff" should be replaced by the names Shakespeare originally intended—namely, "Harvey," "Russell," and "Oldcastle." They suggest that such a replacement would undo an act of censorship that thwarted Shakespeare's original intentions. This edition retains the substituted names primarily because these are the names Shakespeare consistently used after the initial act of censorship, and they have become part of the textual and dramatic history of this and other plays. While it is important to point out that an act of censorship occurred, to "undo" it creates new erasures in the textual and cultural history of the play. For Shakespeare, "Falstaff," not "Oldcastle," became the word linking the various textual manifestations of his fat knight as he appeared both in *1* and *2 Henry IV* and then in *The Merry Wives of Windsor.*

It is of interest, however, to ask why Shakespeare first used the name "Oldcastle" in his play. The historical Oldcastle was a knight who served Henry IV in battle in both France and Wales, but who was also a Lollard; that is, he was connected with the religious group often seen as a forerunner of English Protestantism for its critiques of the Catholic Church and its advocacy of a vernacular Bible to be made available to lay people. At first, Henry IV treated Oldcastle's religious views leniently, but eventually Oldcastle was sent to the Tower of London and condemned as a heretic by the Archbishop of Canterbury. He escaped, and Henry was warned that Oldcastle was leading an armed force against him. Oldcastle was captured in 1417 and eventually hung in chains and then burned on the gallows.

This knight suggests Shakespeare's portrait of the chivalric heroes Prince Hal and Hotspur at the battle of Shrewsbury. From Henry Peacham's *Minerva Britanna* (1612).

In the sixteenth century, how one viewed Oldcastle depended largely on one's religious perspective. To many zealous Protestants, such as John Foxe, Oldcastle was a Protestant hero, a victim of Catholic oppression rather than a traitor; Foxe included Oldcastle in his *Book of Martyrs*. But by the 1590s, Lollards were also sometimes linked with "extremist" Protestant groups pushing for radical reforms in the Church of England. Making a well-known Lollard martyr a fat figure of disorder therefore did not necessarily signal Catholic sympathies. It might simply be a way of suggesting the hypocrisy of zealous reformers. In other plays, especially in his portrait of Malvolio in *Twelfth Night*, Shakespeare makes fun of "Puritans" who claimed a greater righteousness and strictness of life than their more moderate contemporaries. In *1 Henry IV*, Falstaff's language is liberally studded with biblical quotations, most of which he misapplies or contradicts by his behavior. Thus he tells Hal that one must labor in one's vocation (1.2.92–93), an injunction found in 1 Corinthians 7:20 and in Ephesians 4:1. But the vocation in which *he* would labor is that of thief—not exactly what Protestant divines meant when discussing the virtues of a vocation. Moreover, by making Falstaff so obviously a glutton and lover of sack, Shakespeare could be making fun of the hypocrisy of Puritans, as Ben Jonson was to do in *Bartholomew Fair* and Thomas Middleton in *A Chaste Maid in Cheapside*.

The name Shakespeare fastened upon to replace Oldcastle had its own history. The historical Fastolf (1378?–1459) was a courageous officer in Henry VI's war in France, though in some chronicles he appears erroneously to have been called a coward, a detail that Shakespeare repeats in *1 Henry VI*. Having once used the name without repercussion in the former play, Shakespeare may have felt it was safe to employ it as a replacement for "Oldcastle" and to play upon the figure's reputation for cowardice.

Yet it may be a mistake to connect Shakespeare's character too strictly to any historical counterpart. As scholarship has shown, Falstaff is a rich amalgam of popular and literary traditions. In part, he resembles the irreverent Vice figure from the medieval morality plays. Traditionally, the Vice, a comic and clever character, tempted the hero to sin while voices of virtue or duty tried to steer him along a more reputable path. In *1 Henry IV*, Hal is torn between his allegiances to Falstaff and his father, to vice and virtue, to the tavern and the court. Falstaff also conjures up the topsy-turvy world of Carnival in which rulers were temporarily displaced and the body's pleasures (eating, drinking, breaking wind, having sex) were celebrated before the arrival of abstemious Lent. The unending jokes about Falstaff's fat paunch highlight his symbolic connection to bodily excess, and his contempt for the law and for military duty make him the antithesis of the King and a perpetual emblem of disorder. In creating Falstaff, Shakespeare also drew on the figure from classical tradition of the braggart warrior who is really a coward. At Shrewsbury, Falstaff plays the coward, and yet he falsely claims credit for having killed Hotspur. The gap between his words and his deeds is enormous, though in this instance, as in many others, the Prince graciously does not reveal this lie for what it is. Above all, however, Falstaff embodies traditions of popular critique associated with the stage clown. In early productions, Will Kemp, the famous clown in Shakespeare's company, probably played the part. Sometimes speaking from a down-

stage position near the audience, the clown traditionally poked fun at upstage authority figures. Falstaff does so in spades, whether mocking the elevated speech of King
Henry or twitting Hal for being so skinny. But Falstaff is more than a gadfly or a parasite swollen fat on others' folly. He also embodies a mode of being in the world that
serves as a powerful alternative both to the calculations of Hal and to Hotspur's headlong, death-courting pursuit of honor. For example, before the Battle of Shrewsbury
Falstaff meditates witheringly on just what honor means and on its value:

> Can honour set-to a leg? No. Or an arm? No. Or take away the grief of a wound?
> No. Honour hath no skill in surgery, then? No. What is honour? A word. What is in
> that word 'honour'? What is that 'honour'? Air. A trim reckoning! Who hath it?
> He that died o'Wednesday. Doth he feel it? No. Doth he hear it? No. 'Tis insensible
> then? Yea, to the dead. But will it not live with the living? No. Why? Detraction will
> not suffer it. Therefore I'll none of it. Honour is a mere scutcheon. And so ends my
> catechism. (5.1.130–39)

Others, like Hotspur, find honor worth dying for, and generations of men have gone
into battle believing the same thing. But for Falstaff, honor is worth the loss of neither
a leg nor a life. During the ensuing battle, Falstaff carries a bottle of sack in his pistol
case and ingloriously feigns death when attacked by Douglas. But though Hotspur and
others are slain, Falstaff rises up. He embraces neither honor nor death, but life, and
many readers and theatergoers have cheered his choice while others have been
repulsed by his opportunism and cowardice.

Shrewsbury, then, is not only the place where the play's disparate strands of action
come together as the King, Prince Hal, Hotspur, and even Falstaff assemble in one spot;
it is also where the audience is invited to judge the relative worth of the values
embraced by these different characters. Among those who fare well is Prince Hal.
Shrewsbury is perhaps his happiest hour. During the battle, he finds a way to redeem
his reputation and distinguish himself from Falstaff without being forced to repudiate
his friend, just as he kills Hotspur while paying homage to his courage. But the
equipoise of this battle's conclusion is precarious. Hal is not yet king and must still
delay his assumption of the throne. Falstaff has not reformed and probably never will.
And the rebels have not been destroyed. Hotspur is dead, but the Archbishop of York,
Glyndŵr, and Mortimer are still in arms. In other words, it is an illusion that Hal has
carried all before him. In the corners and crevices of the realm, dissension and difference remain. In such conditions, the work of rule is a performance with no end.

JEAN E. HOWARD

TEXTUAL NOTE

The first quarto edition of *1 Henry IV* was printed in 1598. Only a fragment, comprising 1.3.199 through 2.3.19 of a single copy, now remains. This Quarto, usually designated as Qo but in the Oxford edition called Q1, was the basis for a second quarto
edition printed later in 1598. This text, Q2, serves as the control text for most modern
editions. The manuscript behind Q1 does not seem to have been marked up for the theater, so it was probably not the promptbook. The manuscript was either a corrected copy
of Shakespeare's "foul papers" or, more probably, a transcription of them made by a professional scribe. This manuscript was prepared with unusual care, perhaps to show that
changes required by the Master of the Revels had been made in the text. Originally, the
characters Falstaff, Peto, and Bardolph had been assigned the names "Oldcastle," "Harvey," and "Russell." Objections from the Cobham family, descendants of Oldcastle, and
perhaps from other powerful people seem to have forced Shakespeare to change these
names (see the Introduction for a fuller discussion of this act of censorship).

Five other quarto editions were published, in 1599, 1604, 1608, 1613, and 1622, before the publication of the First Folio (F) in 1623. These all derive from Q2 and have no independent authority. The Folio text derives from the 1613 Quarto, but act and scene divisions were added, speech prefixes and stage directions altered, and oaths were softened or removed and biblical allusions altered in compliance with the 1606 edict forbidding profanity on the stage. The party responsible for these changes is uncertain. Some changes may have been made by the compositors who set the text or by someone acting as editor (perhaps John Heminges or Henry Condell, Shakespeare's fellow share-holders in the King's Men who oversaw the production of the First Folio). The Oxford editors plausibly argue that these changes may in part derive from a manuscript pre-pared by the same scribe who prepared a similarly "literary" manuscript for 2 Henry IV—that is, a manuscript less attuned to playhouse requirements than to the ration-alization of the text as a written document. This scribal manuscript may itself have derived from a promptbook whose theatrical features were largely obscured by the tran-scription. The Oxford editors also believe that a few of the changes made in F may reflect Shakespeare's own revisions of Q.

The act and scene divisions of F are followed except for the marking of new scenes at 2.3 and 5.3. The latter scene break, regularly inserted in most modern editions, indi-cates a clearing of the stage in the middle of the Battle of Shrewsbury; 2.3 is added to mark the moment at Gad's Hill when, Falstaff and his friends having led off the travel-ers they have captured, Hal and Poins come onstage disguised in their buckram suits.

As explained in the Introduction, for this play Norton is using the names "Falstaff," "Peto," and "Bardolph" (rather than Oxford's "Oldcastle," "Harvey," and "Russell"). Consequently, Oxford speech prefixes and stage directions, and in a few places the Oxford text, have been silently altered where these three characters are concerned in order to return to the names and language appearing in the printed quarto texts of 1598. Textual deviations from Q are marked in the variants, and Norton's standardiza-tion of quarto speech prefixes is delineated immediately before those variants. In par-ticular, "Falstaff," rather than Oxford's "Sir John," has been used in speech prefixes in this play as well as in 2 Henry IV.

SELECTED BIBLIOGRAPHY

Barber, C. L. "Rule and Misrule in Henry IV." Shakespeare's Festive Comedy: A Study of Dramatic Form and Its Relation to Social Custom. Princeton: Princeton University Press, 1959. 192–221. Explores the ritual subtext of Henry IV, Parts I and II, argu-ing that Falstaff becomes a scapegoat whose banishment rids the community of bad luck.

Barker, Roberta. "Tragical-Comical-Historical Hotspur." Shakespeare Quarterly 54 (2003): 288–307. Examines how Hotspur has been interpreted through the cen-turies and argues that the role is central to the play's examination of masculine hero-ism.

Greenblatt, Stephen. "Invisible Bullets." Shakespearean Negotiations: The Circulation of Social Energy in Renaissance England. Berkeley: University of California Press, 1988. 21–65. Discusses how Renaissance texts such as Thomas Hariot's A Brief and True Report of the New Found Land of Virginia and Shakespeare's 1 Henry IV sub-vert their culture's dominant values regarding religious belief and political author-ity and yet contain or mitigate the doubts they raise.

Greenfield, Matthew. "1 Henry IV: Metatheatrical Britain." British Identities and En-glish Renaissance Literature. Ed. David J. Baker and Willy Maley. New York: Cam-bridge University Press, 2002. 71–80. Discusses the interplay of different characters, locales, and genres in the play, arguing that it fails to create a single onstage community but instead reveals the distance between groups.

Highley, Christopher. "Wales, Ireland, and 1 Henry IV." Renaissance Drama, n.s., 21 (1990): 91–114. Discusses England's Elizabethan wars in Ireland as a subtext for

1 Henry IV and Glyndŵr as a displaced image of the Irish leader Hugh O'Neill, Earl of Tyrone.

Howard, Jean E., and Phyllis Rackin. "Gender and Nation: Anticipations of Modernity in the Second Tetralogy." *Engendering a Nation: A Feminist Account of Shakespeare's English Histories*. London: Routledge, 1997. 137–215. Focuses on the disruptive role of women in the play, both the Welsh women, including Glyndŵr's daughter, and the women of the Eastcheap tavern.

Kastan, David Scott. " 'The King Hath Many Marching in His Coats'; or, What Did You Do During the War, Daddy?" *Shakespeare Left and Right*. Ed. Ivo Kamps. New York: Routledge, 1991. 241–58. Argues that the theater does not just reproduce the political ideologies of the powerful but instead makes space for unauthorized and heterogeneous views, including, in *Henry IV*, the view that kingship itself is just a role.

Laroque, François. "Shakespeare's 'Battle of Carnival and Lent': The Falstaff Scenes Reconsidered (*1* and *2 Henry IV*)." *Shakespeare and Carnival: After Bakhtin*. Ed. Ronald Knowles. New York: St. Martin's, 1998. 83–96. Discusses the connections between Shakespeare's *Henry IV* plays and the opposition in Carnival between the fat and the lean, Falstaff and the Prince.

McMillin, Scott. *Henry IV, Part One*. Shakespeare in Performance series. Manchester: Manchester University Press, 1991. Analyzes theatrical, film, and television performances of *1 Henry IV* in the second half of the twentieth century, arguing that this is the period when Hal, rather than Falstaff or Hotspur, became the focus of critical and theatrical attention.

Mullaney, Steven. "The Rehearsal of Cultures." *The Place of the Stage: License, Play, and Power in Renaissance England*. Chicago: University of Chicago Press, 1988. 60–87. Discusses the sixteenth-century fascination with collecting artifacts from distant cultures and argues that the stage also represented and rehearsed otherness.

FILMS

Chimes at Midnight. 1965. Dir. Orson Welles. UK. 115 min. In black and white, the film combines scenes from several plays to focus on Falstaff and his relationship with Prince Hal. An imaginative and moving adaptation, it boasts memorable performances by Welles as Falstaff, John Gielgud as Henry IV, and Keith Baxter as the Prince.

Henry IV, Part I. 1979. Dir. David Giles. UK. 155 min. A BBC-TV production with strong performances by Anthony Quayle as Falstaff and Tim Pigott-Smith as Hotspur in an otherwise dutifully faithful version of the play.

My Own Private Idaho. 1991. Dir. Gus Van Sant. USA. 102 min. Set in modern-day Portland, Oregon, and loosely based on the *Henry IV* plays, the film stars River Phoenix and Keanu Reeves as two young men who for a time join William Richert, the Falstaff figure, in a life of dissipation.

The History of Henry the Fourth

THE PERSONS OF THE PLAY

KING HENRY IV

PRINCE HARRY, Prince of Wales,
  familiarly known as Hal } King Henry's sons
Lord JOHN OF LANCASTER

Earl of WESTMORLAND
Sir Walter BLUNT

Earl of WORCESTER
Percy, Earl of NORTHUMBERLAND, his brother
Henry Percy, known as HOTSPUR,
  Northumberland's son
Kate, LADY PERCY, Hotspur's wife
Lord Edmund MORTIMER, called Earl of March,
  Lady Percy's brother } rebels against King Henry
LADY MORTIMER, his wife
Owain GLYNDŴR, Lady Mortimer's father
Earl of DOUGLAS
Sir Richard VERNON
Scrope, ARCHBISHOP of York
SIR MICHAEL, a member of the Archbishop's
  household

Sir John FALSTAFF
Edward (Ned) POINS
BARDOLPH
PETO
Mistress Quickly, HOSTESS of } associates of Prince Harry
  a tavern in Eastcheap
FRANCIS, a drawer
VINTNER

GADSHILL
CARRIERS
CHAMBERLAIN
OSTLER
TRAVELLERS
SHERIFF
MESSENGERS
SERVANT
Lords, soldiers

1.1

Enter KING [HENRY], *Lord* JOHN OF LANCASTER, [*and
the*] *Earl of* WESTMORLAND, *with other* [*lords*]

KING HENRY   So shaken as we are, so wan with care,
  Find we° a time for frighted peace to pant   *Let us find*
  And breathe short-winded accents° of new broils   *words*

1.1 Location: The palace, London.

To be commenced in strands afar remote.[1]

5   No more the thirsty entrance° of this soil   *parched mouth*
    Shall daub her lips with her own children's blood.
    No more shall trenching° war channel° her fields,   *cutting / furrow*
    Nor bruise her flow'rets with the armèd hoofs
    Of hostile paces.° Those opposèd eyes,   *horses' footsteps*
10 Which, like the meteors of a troubled heaven,[2]
    All of one nature, of one substance bred,
    Did lately meet in the intestine° shock   *internal*
    And furious close° of civil butchery,   *hand-to-hand combat*
    Shall now in mutual well-beseeming° ranks   *orderly*
15 March all one way, and be no more opposed
    Against acquaintance, kindred, and allies.
    The edge of war, like an ill-sheathèd knife,
    No more shall cut his master. Therefore, friends,
    As far as to the sepulchre of Christ—
20 Whose soldier now, under whose blessèd cross
    We are impressèd° and engaged to fight—   *conscripted*
    Forthwith a power of English shall we levy,
    Whose arms were moulded in their mothers' womb
    To chase these pagans in those holy fields
25 Over whose acres walked those blessèd feet
    Which fourteen hundred years ago were nailed,
    For our advantage, on the bitter cross.
    But this our purpose now is twelve month old,
    And bootless° 'tis to tell you we will go.   *useless*
30 Therefor° we meet not now. Then let me hear   *On that account*
    Of you, my gentle cousin° Westmorland,   *my noble kinsman*
    What yesternight our Council did decree
    In forwarding this dear expedience.°   *urgent undertaking*
    WESTMORLAND   My liege, this haste was hot in question,°   *under urgent debate*
35 And many limits of the charge[3] set down
    But yesternight, when all athwart° there came   *at cross-purposes*
    A post° from Wales, loaden with heavy news,   *messenger*
    Whose worst was that the noble Mortimer,
    Leading the men of Herefordshire to fight
40 Against the irregular and wild Glyndŵr,[4]
    Was by the rude hands of that Welshman taken,
    A thousand of his people butcherèd,
    Upon whose dead corpse'° there was such misuse,   *corpses*
    Such beastly shameless transformation,[5]
45 By those Welshwomen done as may not be
    Without much shame retold or spoken of.
    KING HENRY   It seems then that the tidings of this broil
    Brake° off our business for the Holy Land.   *Broke*

---

1. On distant shores. King Henry is alluding to the Holy Land, to which he vowed to lead a crusade at the close of *Richard II*.
2. Unusual events in the sky, such as comets or shooting stars, were thought to portend strife and disaster.
3. Many particulars concerning responsibilities and expenses.
4. In most editions, Glyndŵr's name is given as "Glendower," an anglicized version of the Welsh word used in this text. Glyndŵr is probably "irregular" in the sense of

using guerrilla tactics in his warfare; possibly, the word alludes to his alleged sorcery.
5. Mutilation. Holinshed's 1587 *Chronicles*, one of Shakespeare's sources, says the Welsh women's acts on this occasion were too shameful to relate, but contemporary editor Abraham Fleming, in the same edition of the *Chronicles*, includes an account of another battle in which Welsh women cut off the sexual organs and the noses of conquered enemies and put them, respectively, in the mouths and anuses of those enemies.

WESTMORLAND   This matched with other did, my gracious lord,
50   For more uneven° and unwelcome news   *disturbing*
      Came from the north, and thus it did import:
      On Holy-rood day⁶ the gallant Hotspur there—
      Young Harry Percy—and brave Archibald,
      That ever valiant and approvèd° Scot,   *worthy*
55   At Holmedon⁷ met,
      Where they did spend a sad and bloody hour,
      As by° discharge of their artillery   *As judging by*
      And shape of likelihood° the news was told;   *And probable outcome*
      For he that brought them° in the very heat   *(the news)*
60   And pride° of their contention did take horse,   *height*
      Uncertain of the issue° any way.   *outcome*
   KING HENRY   Here is a dear, a true industrious friend,
      Sir Walter Blunt,⁸ new lighted from his horse,
      Stained with the variation of each soil
65   Betwixt that Holmedon and this seat° of ours;   *dwelling*
      And he hath brought us smooth° and welcome news.   *agreeable*
      The Earl of Douglas is discomfited.
      Ten thousand bold Scots, two-and-twenty knights,
      Balked° in their own blood did Sir Walter see   *Heaped up; thwarted*
70   On Holmedon's plains. Of prisoners Hotspur took
      Mordake the Earl of Fife and eldest son
      To beaten Douglas,⁹ and the Earl of Athol,
      Of Moray, Angus, and Menteith;
      And is not this an honourable spoil,
75   A gallant prize? Ha, cousin, is it not?
   WESTMORLAND   In faith, it is a conquest for a prince to boast of.
   KING HENRY   Yea, there thou mak'st me sad, and mak'st me sin
      In envy that my lord Northumberland
      Should be the father to so blest a son—
80   A son who is the theme of honour's tongue,
      Amongst a grove the very straightest plant,
      Who is sweet Fortune's minion° and her pride—   *favorite*
      Whilst I by looking on the praise of him
      See riot and dishonour stain the brow
85   Of my young Harry. O, that it could be proved
      That some night-tripping fairy¹ had exchanged
      In cradle clothes our children where they lay,
      And called mine Percy, his Plantagenet! ²
      Then would I have his Harry, and he mine.
90   But let him° from my thoughts. What think you, coz,°   *let him go / kinsman*
      Of this young Percy's pride? The prisoners
      Which he in this adventure hath surprised°   *captured*
      To his own use³ he keeps, and sends me word

6. Holy Cross Day, September 14.
7. Holmedon (also spelled "Humbleton") in Northumberland was the site in 1402 of a Scottish invasion of England.
8. It is not clear whether Blunt comes onstage now. He could have entered at the beginning of the scene; alternatively, as in this edition, he may not come onstage at all. Blunt has no lines in the scene, and Henry could at this point receive a letter containing Blunt's news or could be reporting news he has already learned. "Here" would thus refer in a general way to Blunt's being at court.
9. Mordake was not actually Douglas's son, but an understandable misreading of Holinshed led Shakespeare to believe he was.
1. It was popularly believed that fairies stole beautiful children and left bad or malformed ones in their place.
2. Henry was descended from the Plantagenet dynasty; and the Percys were a distinguished family from the north of England to which Hotspur belonged.
3. Prisoners were routinely used as a source of revenue.

I shall have none but Mordake Earl of Fife.
95 WESTMORLAND   This is his uncle's teaching. This is Worcester,
Malevolent to you in all aspects,[4]
Which makes him prune[5] himself, and bristle up
The crest of youth against your dignity.
KING HENRY   But I have sent for him to answer this;
100 And for this cause awhile we must neglect
Our holy purpose to Jerusalem.
Cousin, on Wednesday next our Council we
Will hold at Windsor. So inform the lords.
But come yourself with speed to us again,
105 For more is to be said and to be done
Than out of anger can be utterèd.
WESTMORLAND   I will, my liege.
Exeunt [KING HENRY, LANCASTER, *and other lords*
at one door; WESTMORLAND *at another door*]

1.2

Enter [HARRY][1] *Prince of Wales and Sir John* FALSTAFF[2]

FALSTAFF   Now, Hal, what time of day is it, lad?

PRINCE HARRY   Thou art so fat-witted° with drinking of old   *thick-witted*
sack,[3] and unbuttoning thee after supper, and sleeping upon
benches after noon, that thou hast forgotten to demand that
5 truly which thou wouldst truly know. What a devil hast thou to
do with the time of the day? Unless hours were cups of sack, and
minutes capons,[4] and clocks the tongues of bawds, and dials°   *clock faces; sundials*
the signs of leaping-houses,° and the blessed sun himself a   *brothels*
fair hot wench in flame-coloured taffeta,[5] I see no reason why
10 thou shouldst be so superfluous° to demand the time of the day.   *needlessly curious*

FALSTAFF   Indeed you come near me° now, Hal, for we that take   *are near the mark*
purses go by the moon and the seven stars,[6] and not 'By Phoe-
bus, he, that wand'ring knight so fair'.[7] And I prithee, sweet
wag,° when thou art a king, as God save thy grace—'majesty'   *mischievous boy*
15 I should say, for grace[8] thou wilt have none—

PRINCE HARRY   What, none?

FALSTAFF   No, by my troth, not so much as will serve to be prologue to an egg and butter.[9]

PRINCE HARRY   Well, how then? Come, roundly,° roundly.   *to the point*
20 FALSTAFF   Marry° then, sweet wag, when thou art king let not   *By Mary (a mild oath)*
us that are squires of the night's body[1] be called thieves of the

4. Habitually hostile to you. The line suggests that
Worcester is a planet whose influence is always harmful, whatever his position, or "aspect," in the sky.
5. A term from falconry suggesting the hawk's trimming of its feathers as preparation for action.
1.2 Location: A room in the Prince's apartments, London.
1. F's stage direction reads, "Henry Prince of Wales"; Q
reads, "prince of Wales." Norton speech prefixes refer
to this character as "Prince Harry," and the same des-
ignation is used, as here, in stage directions.
2. See Introduction and Textual Note for a discussion
of Falstaff's name.
3. Spanish white wine.
4. Castrated male chickens (an Elizabethan delicacy).
5. Silk cloth, which in some contexts was associated

with prostitutes.
6. The constellation known as the Pleiades. *go by the*
moon: go about at moonlight; tell time by the light of
the moon.
7. Evidently a line from a contemporary ballad or
romance about Phoebus, the sun god of classical
mythology.
8. Virtue; with a pun also on "grace" as meaning "God's
favor" and "a prayer before meals." Falstaff asserts that
Hal has none of these and so must be called "your
majesty," rather than "your grace," which was also a
title of honor.
9. *egg and butter:* a mere snack needing only the shortest grace.
1. Let not we who steal by night. Falstaff alludes to the
attendants of knights known as "squires of the body."

day's beauty. Let us be 'Diana's foresters',² 'gentlemen of the
shade', 'minions of the moon', and let men say we be men of
good government,° being governed, as the sea is, by our noble   *conduct*
and chaste mistress the moon, under whose countenance° we   *face; protection*
steal.

PRINCE HARRY Thou sayst well, and it holds well° too, for the   *the comparison is apt*
fortune of us that are the moon's men doth ebb and flow like
the sea, being governed as the sea is by the moon. As for proof
now: a purse of gold most resolutely snatched on Monday
night, and most dissolutely spent on Tuesday morning; got
with swearing 'lay by!',³ and spent with crying 'bring in!';⁴ now
in as low an ebb as the foot of the ladder, and by and by in as
high a flow as the ridge° of the gallows.⁵   *crossbar*

FALSTAFF By the Lord, thou sayst true, lad; and is not my Hostess of the tavern a most sweet wench?

PRINCE HARRY As the honey of Hybla,⁶ my old lad of the cas-
tle;⁷ and is not a buff jerkin⁸ a most sweet robe of durance?°   *durability; imprisonment*

FALSTAFF How now, how now, mad wag? What, in thy quips
and thy quiddities?° What a plague have I to do with a buff   *quibbles (wordplay)*
jerkin?

PRINCE HARRY Why, what a pox⁹ have I to do with my Hostess
of the tavern?

FALSTAFF Well, thou hast called her to a reckoning¹ many a
time and oft.

PRINCE HARRY Did I ever call for thee to pay thy part?²

FALSTAFF No, I'll give thee thy due, thou hast paid all there.

PRINCE HARRY Yea, and elsewhere so far as my coin would
stretch;³ and where it would not, I have used my credit.

FALSTAFF Yea, and so used it that were it not here apparent that
thou art heir apparent—but I prithee, sweet wag, shall there
be gallows standing in England when thou art king, and resolution thus fubbed⁴ as it is with the rusty curb of old father
Antic° the law? Do not thou when thou art king hang a thief. ✳   *buffoon*

PRINCE HARRY No, thou shalt.

FALSTAFF Shall I? O, rare! By the Lord, I'll be a brave° judge!   *fine; well-dressed*

PRINCE HARRY Thou judgest false already. I mean thou shalt
have the hanging of the thieves, and so become a rare hangman.

FALSTAFF Well, Hal, well; and in some sort it jumps° with my   *agrees*
humour° as well as waiting in the court,⁵ I can tell you.   *temperament*

PRINCE HARRY For obtaining of suits?⁶

---

2. Hunters by moonlight; thieves. In classical mythology, Diana was goddess of the moon.
3. A thief's cry similar to "Hands up!"
4. A tavern customer's call for more food or wine.
5. The Prince's speech is riddled with sexual slang,
including "purse" (line 30) as meaning "vagina" or
"scrotum"; "snatched" (line 30) as "forcibly had sexual
relations with"; "spent" (line 31) as "exhausted by sexual activity"; "lay by" (line 32) as "lie back"; "spent with"
(line 32) as "reached orgasm with"; and "low" (line 33)
and "high" (line 34) as referring to a penis, first limp
and then erect.
6. Region of Sicily renowned for its honey.
7. Slang for "roisterer"; also a play on the name "Old-

castle" (see Introduction).
8. Leather jacket often worn by jailers.
9. The equivalent of "what the devil." The pox literally
was plague or syphilis.
1. You have asked that she present the bill; asked that
she show her value sexually.
2. To pay your bill; to use your penis.
3. So far as my money would go; so far as my ability to
engender, or "coin," a child would take me.
4. And valor (of thieves) thus thwarted.
5. Being in attendance at the royal court or at the court
of justices.
6. Petitions; clothing. The hangman was entitled to
claim the victims' clothing.

FALSTAFF Yea, for obtaining of suits, whereof the hangman
hath no lean wardrobe. 'Sblood,[7] I am as melancholy as a gib
65 cat,° or a lugged bear.[8]   *tomcat*
PRINCE HARRY Or an old lion, or a lover's lute.
FALSTAFF Yea, or the drone of a Lincolnshire bagpipe.
PRINCE HARRY What sayst thou to a hare,[9] or the melancholy of
Moor-ditch?[1]
70 FALSTAFF Thou hast the most unsavoury similes, and art
indeed the most comparative,° rascalliest sweet young Prince.   *quick at comparisons*
But Hal, I prithee trouble me no more with vanity.° I would   *worthless things*
to God thou and I knew where a commodity° of good names°   *supply / reputations*
were to be bought. An old lord of the Council rated me the
75 other day in the street about you, sir, but I marked him not;
and yet he talked very wisely, but I regarded him not; and yet
he talked wisely, and in the street too.
PRINCE HARRY Thou didst well, for wisdom cries out in the
streets, and no man regards it.[2]
80 FALSTAFF O, thou hast damnable iteration,[3] and art indeed
able to corrupt a saint. Thou hast done much harm upon me,
Hal, God forgive thee for it. Before I knew thee, Hal, I knew
nothing; and now am I, if a man should speak truly, little better than one of the wicked. I must give over this life, and I will
85 give it over. By the Lord, an° I do not, I am a villain. I'll be   *if*
damned for never a° king's son in Christendom.   *for no*
PRINCE HARRY Where shall we take a purse tomorrow, Jack?
FALSTAFF Zounds,[4] where thou wilt, lad! I'll make one;° an I do   *I'll take part*
not, call me villain and baffle me.[5]
90 PRINCE HARRY I see a good amendment of life in thee, from
praying to purse-taking.
FALSTAFF Why, Hal, 'tis my vocation,° Hal. 'Tis no sin for a   *calling*
man to labour in his vocation.[6]
        Enter POINS
Poins! Now shall we know if Gadshill[7] have set a match ° O,   *planned a theft*
95 if men were to be saved by merit,[8] what hole in hell were hot
enough for him? This is the most omnipotent villain that ever
cried 'Stand!' to a true° man.   *an honest*
PRINCE HARRY Good morrow, Ned.
POINS Good morrow, sweet Hal. [*To* FALSTAFF] What says
100 Monsieur Remorse? What says Sir John, sack-and-sugar
Jack?[9] How agrees the devil and thee about thy soul, that thou
soldest him on Good Friday[1] last, for a cup of Madeira[2] and a
cold capon's leg?

7. By His blood (an oath alluding to Christ's crucifixion).
8. A baited bear. In a popular form of entertainment,
bears were led in chains and set upon by dogs.
9. The hare's sadness was proverbial. Its flesh, when
eaten, was supposed to generate melancholy.
1. An open sewer outside the walls of London.
2. A biblical allusion to Proverbs 1:20–24.
3. You have a soul-endangering way of reading Scripture. This is one of several speeches in which Falstaff
uses a language associated with Puritans.
4. By Christ's wounds (a strong oath).
5. And subject me to public disgrace. Falstaff alludes
to the practice of "baffling," in which perjured knights
or effigies of them were hung upside down in public
places.

6. Allusion to 1 Corinthians 7:20 and Ephesians 4:1.
Falstaff is misusing the biblical injunction to work at
one's vocation to justify robbery.
7. A thief named after Gad's Hill, the place where he
practices his robberies. This hill, near Rochester on the
road from Canterbury to London, was notorious for
highway robberies.
8. By good works (as opposed to salvation by God's
grace).
9. "Jack' is a nickname for "John," but the word also
means "a drinking vessel" or "a knave." Falstaff likes
sugar in his sack, or sweet white wine.
1. The strictest of fast days in the Christian calendar.
2. A white wine exported from Madeira, an island off
the coast of west Africa.

PRINCE HARRY Sir John stands to° his word, the devil shall have   *keeps*
105   his bargain, for he was never yet a breaker of proverbs: he will
        give the devil his due.
POINS [*to* FALSTAFF] Then art thou damned for keeping thy
        word with the devil.
PRINCE HARRY Else he had been damned for cozening° the   *cheating*
110   devil.
POINS But my lads, my lads, tomorrow morning by four o'clock
        early, at Gads Hill, there are pilgrims going to Canterbury
        with rich offerings, and traders riding to London with fat
        purses. I have visors° for you all; you have horses for your-   *masks*
115   selves. Gadshill lies° tonight in Rochester. I have bespoke°   *lodges / ordered*
        supper tomorrow night in Eastcheap.³ We may do it as secure°   *safely*
        as sleep. If you will go, I will stuff your purses full of crowns;
        if you will not, tarry at home and be hanged.
FALSTAFF Hear ye, Edward, if I tarry at home and go not, I'll
120   hang you for going.
POINS You will, chops?°   *fat cheeks*
FALSTAFF Hal, wilt thou make one?
PRINCE HARRY Who, I rob? I a thief? Not I, by my faith.
FALSTAFF There's neither honesty,° manhood, nor good fel-   *honor*
125   lowship in thee, nor thou camest not of the blood royal, if
        thou darest not stand for° ten shillings.⁴   *fight for; be worth*
PRINCE HARRY Well then, once in my days I'll be a madcap.
FALSTAFF Why, that's well said.
PRINCE HARRY Well, come what will, I'll tarry at home.
130 FALSTAFF By the Lord, I'll be a traitor then, when thou art king.
PRINCE HARRY I care not.
POINS Sir John, I prithee leave the Prince and me alone. I will
        lay him down such reasons for this adventure that he shall go.
FALSTAFF Well, God give thee the spirit of persuasion and him
135   the ears of profiting, that what thou speakest may move and
        what he hears may be believed, that the true prince may, for
        recreation' sake, prove a false thief; for the poor abuses of the
        time want countenance.⁵ Farewell. You shall find me in
        Eastcheap.
140 PRINCE HARRY Farewell, the latter spring; farewell, All-hallown
        summer.⁶   [*Exit* FALSTAFF]
POINS Now, my good sweet honey lord, ride with us tomorrow.
        I have a jest to execute that I cannot manage alone. Falstaff,
        Peto, Bardolph, and Gadshill shall rob those men that we
145   have already waylaid—yourself and I will not be there—and
        when they have the booty, if you and I do not rob them, cut
        this head off from my shoulders.
PRINCE HARRY But how shall we part with them in setting forth?
POINS Why, we will set forth before or after them and appoint
150   them a place of meeting, wherein it is at our pleasure to fail.
        And then will they adventure upon the exploit themselves,
        which they shall have no sooner achieved but we'll set upon
        them.

---

3. A street and market district in London, evidently the
location of the play's tavern.
4. A 10-shilling coin was called a "royal," thus punning
on the Prince's "blood royal."
5. Lack encouragement (from those of high rank).

6. Addressing Falstaff as youth in age (a second spring)
and likening him to a period of unusually mild weather
(a second summer) occurring around All Hallows' Day,
November 1.

PRINCE HARRY Ay, but 'tis like that they will know us by our
155　horses, by our habits,° and by every other appointment,° to be ——— *clothing / item*
ourselves.

POINS Tut, our horses they shall not see—I'll tie them in the
wood; our visors we will change after we leave them; and, sirrah,[7] I have cases of buckram for the nonce,[8] to immask° our ——— *hide*
160　noted° outward garments. ——— *known*

PRINCE HARRY But I doubt they will be too hard for us.[9]

POINS Well, for two of them, I know them to be as true-bred
cowards as ever turned back; and for the third, if he fight
longer than he sees reason, I'll forswear arms. The virtue of
165　this jest will be the incomprehensible° lies that this same fat ——— *boundless*
rogue will tell us when we meet at supper: how thirty at least
he fought with, what wards,° what blows, what extremities he ——— *parries*
endured; and in the reproof° of this lives the jest. ——— *disproof*

PRINCE HARRY Well, I'll go with thee. Provide us all things nec-
170　essary, and meet me tomorrow night in Eastcheap; there I'll
sup. Farewell.

POINS Farewell, my lord. ——— *Exit*

PRINCE HARRY I know you all, and will a while uphold
The unyoked humour° of your idleness. ——— *unbridled whims*
175　Yet herein will I imitate the sun,
Who doth permit the base contagious° clouds ——— *disease-carrying*
To smother up his beauty from the world,
That° when he please again to be himself, ——— *So that*
Being wanted° he may be more wondered at ——— *Having been missed*
180　By breaking through the foul and ugly mists
Of vapours that did seem to strangle him.
If all the year were playing holidays,
To sport would be as tedious as to work;
But when they seldom come, they wished-for come,
185　And nothing pleaseth but rare accidents.° ——— *exceptional events*
So when this loose behaviour I throw off
And pay the debt I never promisèd,
By how much better than my word I am,
By so much shall I falsify men's hopes;° ——— *expectations*
190　And like bright metal on a sullen ground,° ——— *dull background*
My reformation, glitt'ring o'er my fault,
Shall show more goodly and attract more eyes
Than that which hath no foil to set it off.
I'll so offend to° make offence a skill,° ——— *as to / an art*
195　Redeeming time[1] when men think least I will. ——— *Exit*

1.3

Enter the KING, [*the Earls of*] NORTHUMBERLAND [*and*]
WORCESTER, HOTSPUR, *Sir Walter* BLUNT, *with other*
[*lords*]

KING HENRY [*to* HOTSPUR, NORTHUMBERLAND, *and* WORCESTER]
My blood hath been too cold and temperate,
Unapt° to stir at these indignities, ——— *Slow*

---

7. A familiar form of address, conventionally used with
social inferiors.
8. I have suits of coarse cloth for the purpose.
9. But I fear they will be more than we can manage.
1. Making amends for misspent time. Injunctions to

redeem time were both proverbial and biblical: see
Ephesians 5:16 or Colossians 4:5.
1.3. Location: A royal residence, probably Windsor
Castle.

And you have found me,° for accordingly   *discovered this fact*
You tread upon my patience; but be sure
5   I will from henceforth rather be myself,°   *(i.e., my royal self)*
Mighty and to be feared, than my condition,[1]
Which hath been smooth as oil, soft as young down,
And therefore lost that title of° respect   *claim to*
Which the proud soul ne'er pays but to the proud.
10 WORCESTER   Our house,[2] my sovereign liege, little deserves
The scourge of greatness to be used on it,
And that same greatness too, which our own hands
Have holp° to make so portly.°   *helped / majestic*
NORTHUMBERLAND [*to the* KING]   My lord—
KING HENRY   Worcester, get thee gone, for I do see
15   Danger and disobedience in thine eye.
O sir, your presence is too bold and peremptory,°   *proud*
And majesty might never yet endure
The moody frontier[3] of a servant brow.
You have good leave° to leave us. When we need   *full permission*
20   Your use and counsel we shall send for you. *Exit* WORCESTER
You were about to speak.
NORTHUMBERLAND   Yea, my good lord.
Those prisoners in your highness' name demanded,
Which Harry Percy here at Holmedon took,
Were, as he says, not with such strength denied
25   As was delivered° to your majesty,   *reported*
Who either through envy° or misprision°   *malice / error*
Was guilty of this fault, and not my son.
HOTSPUR [*to the* KING]   My liege, I did deny no prisoners;
But I remember, when the fight was done,
30   When I was dry° with rage and extreme toil,   *thirsty*
Breathless and faint, leaning upon my sword,
Came there a certain lord, neat and trimly dressed,
Fresh as a bridegroom, and his chin, new-reaped,[4]
Showed° like a stubble-land at harvest-home.[5]   *Looked*
35   He was perfumèd like a milliner,[6]
And 'twixt his finger and his thumb he held
A pouncet-box,[7] which ever and anon
He gave his nose and took't away again—
Who° therewith angry, when it next came there   *(the nose)*
40   Took it in snuff[8]—and still he smiled and talked;
And as the soldiers bore dead bodies by,
He called them untaught knaves, unmannerly
To bring a slovenly° unhandsome corpse   *base; nasty*
Betwixt the wind and his nobility.
45   With many holiday and lady° terms   *dainty and effeminate*
He questioned me; amongst the rest demanded
My prisoners in your majesty's behalf.
I then, all smarting with my wounds being cold—
To be so pestered with a popinjay!°—   *parrot; vain dandy*

1. My natural (mild) temperament.
2. The Percy family, which had supported Henry
against Richard II.
3. The angry expression (punning on "frontier" as
meaning both "forehead" and "military fortifications").
4. Newly trimmed. London in the 1590s witnessed a
fashion for close-shaved beards.

5. At the end of harvest (when the fields are cut back
to stubble).
6. Seller of finely scented apparel such as bonnets, ribbons, and gloves. The name derives from the fact that
these goods were often imports from Milan.
7. Perfume box with a perforated lid.
8. Took offense at it; inhaled it.

50 Out of my grief° and my impatience   *pain*
    Answered neglectingly,° I know not what—   *negligently*
    He should, or should not—for he made me mad
    To see him shine so brisk, and smell so sweet,
    And talk so like a waiting gentlewoman
55 Of guns, and drums, and wounds, God save the mark!⁹
    And telling me the sovereign'st° thing on earth   *best*
    Was parmacity¹ for an inward bruise,
    And that it was great pity, so it was,
    This villainous saltpetre² should be digged
60 Out of the bowels of the harmless earth,
    Which many a good tall° fellow had destroyed   *brave*
    So cowardly, and but for these vile guns
    He would himself have been a soldier.
    This bald unjointed° chat of his, my lord,   *This trivial incoherent*
65 Made me to answer indirectly, as I said,
    And I beseech you, let not his report
    Come current° for an accusation   *Be taken as valid*
    Betwixt my love and your high majesty.
    BLUNT [*to the* KING]   The circumstance considered, good my lord,
70 Whate'er Lord Harry Percy then had said
    To such a person, and in such a place,
    At such a time, with all the rest retold,
    May reasonably die, and never rise
    To do him wrong or any way impeach
75 What then he said, so° he unsay it now.   *if*
    KING HENRY   Why, yet he doth deny° his prisoners.   *refuse to hand over*
    But with proviso and exception
    That we at our own charge shall ransom straight°   *immediately*
    His brother-in-law the foolish Mortimer,³
80 Who, on my soul, hath wilfully betrayed
    The lives of those that he did lead to fight
    Against that great magician, damned Glyndŵr—
    Whose daughter, as we hear, the Earl of March
    Hath lately married. Shall our coffers, then,
85 Be emptied to redeem a traitor home?
    Shall we buy treason, and indent with fears⁴
    When they have lost and forfeited themselves?
    No, on the barren mountains let him starve;
    For I shall never hold that man my friend
90 Whose tongue shall ask me for one penny cost
    To ransom home revolted° Mortimer—   *rebellious*
    HOTSPUR   Revolted Mortimer?
    He never did fall off,° my sovereign liege,   *change allegiance*
    But by the chance of war. To prove that true
95 Needs no more but one tongue for all those wounds,
    Those mouthèd° wounds, which valiantly he took   *gaping; eloquent*

9. God keep evil away (an expression of indignation).
1. Spermaceti, an oily substance from the sperm whale
that was used in various medicines and potions. The
spelling "parmacity" probably derives from the ointment's association with the Italian city of Parma.
2. The main ingredient of gunpowder.
3. Shakespeare follows Holinshed's *Chronicles* in confusing or conflating two Edmund Mortimers. One was

captured by Glyndŵr and later became Glyndŵr's son-in-
law and Hotspur's brother-in-law. The other, the fifth
Earl of March, was his nephew and claimed the English
throne as a descendant of Lionel, Duke of Clarence,
third son of Edward III. This Mortimer was the one
named by Richard II as his presumptive heir.
4. And bargain with those whom we have reason to
fear.

	When on the gentle Severn's⁵ sedgy° bank,	marshy
	In single opposition, hand to hand,	
	He did confound° the best part of an hour	consume
100	In changing hardiment° with great Glyndŵr.	matching valor
	Three times they breathed,° and three times did they drink,	rested
	Upon agreement, of swift Severn's flood,	
	Who, then affrighted with their bloody looks,	
	Ran fearfully among the trembling reeds,	
105	And hid his crisp° head in the hollow bank,	rippled
	Bloodstainèd with these valiant combatants.	
	Never did bare and rotten policy°	cunning
	Colour° her working with such deadly wounds,	Disguise
	Nor never could the noble Mortimer	
110	Receive so many, and all willingly.	
	Then let not him be slandered with revolt.⁶	

KING HENRY   Thou dost belie° him, Percy, thou dost belie him.   *misrepresent*
He never did encounter with Glyndŵr. I tell thee,
He durst as well have met the devil alone
115 As Owain Glyndŵr for an enemy.
Art thou not ashamed? But, sirrah, henceforth
Let me not hear you speak of Mortimer.
Send me your prisoners with the speediest means,
Or you shall hear in such a kind from me
120 As will displease you.—My lord Northumberland,
We license your departure with your son.
[*To* HOTSPUR] Send us your prisoners, or you'll hear of it.

Exeunt [all but HOTSPUR *and* NORTHUMBERLAND]

HOTSPUR   An if° the devil come and roar for them   *An if=If*
I will not send them. I will after straight°   *go after him at once*
125 And tell him so, for I will ease my heart,
Although it be with hazard of my head.

NORTHUMBERLAND   What, drunk with choler?° Stay and pause awhile.   *anger*

Enter [the Earl of] WORCESTER

Here comes your uncle.

HOTSPUR   Speak of Mortimer?
Zounds, I will speak of him, and let my soul
130 Want mercy° if I do not join with him.   *Be damned*
In his behalf I'll empty all these veins,
And shed my dear blood drop by drop in the dust,
But I will lift the downfall° Mortimer   *downfallen*
As high in the air as this unthankful King,
135 As this ingrate and cankered° Bolingbroke.⁷   *corrupted*

NORTHUMBERLAND [*to* WORCESTER]   Brother, the King hath
    made your nephew mad.

WORCESTER   Who struck this heat up after I was gone?

HOTSPUR   He will forsooth have all my prisoners;
And when I urged the ransom once again
140 Of my wife's brother, then his cheek looked pale,
And on my face he turned an eye of death,°   *a menacing look*
Trembling even at the name of Mortimer.

---

5. The Severn River flows from Wales into Bristol
Channel in England.
6. With the accusation of having revolted.

7. Henry's family name. Hotspur's use of it suggests his
unwillingness to acknowledge Henry as King.

WORCESTER   I cannot blame him: was not he proclaimed
By Richard, that dead is, the next of blood?°   *heir to the throne*
145 NORTHUMBERLAND   He was; I heard the proclamation.
And then it was when the unhappy° King,   *unfortunate*
Whose wrongs in us° God pardon, did set forth   *done by us*
Upon his Irish expedition,[8]
From whence he, intercepted,° did return   *interrupted*
150 To be deposed, and shortly murdered.
WORCESTER   And for whose death we in the world's wide mouth
Live scandalized° and foully spoken of.   *disgraced*
HOTSPUR   But soft,° I pray you; did King Richard then   *wait*
Proclaim my brother° Edmund Mortimer   *brother-in-law*
Heir to the crown?
155 NORTHUMBERLAND   He did; myself did hear it.
HOTSPUR   Nay, then I cannot blame his cousin[9] King
That wished him on the barren mountains starve.
But shall it be that you that set the crown
Upon the head of this forgetful man
160 And for his sake wear the detested blot
Of murderous subornation,[1] shall it be
That you a world of curses undergo,
Being the agents or base second means,
The cords, the ladder, or the hangman, rather?
165 O, pardon me that I descend so low
To show the line and the predicament
Wherein you range[2] under this subtle° King!   *cunning*
Shall it for shame be spoken in these days,
Or fill up chronicles in time to come,
170 That men of your nobility and power
Did gage° them both in an unjust behalf,°   *pledge / cause*
As both of you, God pardon it, have done:
To put down Richard, that sweet lovely rose,
And plant this thorn, this canker,[3] Bolingbroke?
175 And shall it in more shame be further spoken
That you are fooled, discarded, and shook off
By him for whom these shames ye underwent?
No; yet time serves° wherein you may redeem   *is available*
Your banished honours, and restore yourselves
180 Into the good thoughts of the world again,
Revenge the jeering and disdained° contempt   *disdainful*
Of this proud King, who studies day and night
To answer° all the debt he owes to you   *satisfy*
Even with the bloody payment of your deaths.
Therefore, I say—
185 WORCESTER   Peace, cousin, say no more.
And now I will unclasp a secret book,
And to your quick-conceiving discontents
I'll read you matter deep and dangerous,
As full of peril and adventurous spirit

8. As Shakespeare dramatizes in *Richard II*, Bolingbroke returned to England from exile in France while
Richard was at war in Ireland.
9. Punning on "cozen" (cheat).
1. Of assisting with a murder.
2. *To . . . range:* To show the degree and category into

which you might be classified (with a pun on "line" as
meaning "hangman's rope" and on "predicament" as
meaning "an unpleasant situation").
3. Wild and inferior kind of rose; also, cankerworm
(which destroys plants), or ulcerated sore.

190   As to o'erwalk° a current roaring loud   *walk across*
        On the unsteadfast footing of a spear.
       HOTSPUR   If he fall in, good night, or sink or swim.[4]
        Send danger from the east unto the west,
        So° honour cross it from the north to south;   *Provided*
195   And let them grapple. O, the blood more stirs
        To rouse a lion than to start a hare!
       NORTHUMBERLAND [*to* WORCESTER]   Imagination of some great exploit
        Drives him beyond the bounds of patience.
       HOTSPUR   By heaven, methinks it were an easy leap
200   To pluck bright honour from the pale-faced moon,
        Or dive into the bottom of the deep,
        Where fathom-line[5] could never touch the ground,
        And pluck up drownèd honour by the locks,
        So he that doth redeem her thence might wear,
205   Without corrival,° all her dignities.   *competitor*
        But out upon this half-faced fellowship!°   *paltry sharing of honors*
       WORCESTER [*to* NORTHUMBERLAND]   He apprehends a world of
          figures[6] here,
        But not the form of what he should attend.°   *pay attention to*
        [*To* HOTSPUR] Good cousin, give me audience for a while,
210   And list° to me.   *listen*
       HOTSPUR   I cry you mercy.°   *I beg your pardon*
       WORCESTER   Those same noble Scots[7]
        That are your prisoners—
       HOTSPUR   I'll keep them all.
        By God, he shall not have a Scot of them;
        No, if a scot would save his soul he shall not.
        I'll keep them, by this hand.
215   WORCESTER   You start away,
        And lend no ear unto my purposes.
        Those prisoners you shall keep.
       HOTSPUR   Nay, I will; that's flat.
        He said he would not ransom Mortimer,
        Forbade my tongue to speak of Mortimer;
220   But I will find him when he lies asleep,
        And in his ear I'll hollo 'Mortimer!'
        Nay, I'll have a starling shall be taught to speak
        Nothing but 'Mortimer', and give it him
        To keep his anger still° in motion.   *constantly*
225   WORCESTER   Hear you, cousin, a word.
       HOTSPUR   All studies here I solemnly defy,°   *renounce*
        Save how to gall and pinch° this Bolingbroke.   *torture*
        And that same sword-and-buckler[8] Prince of Wales—
        But that I think his father loves him not
230   And would be glad he met with some mischance—
        I would have him poisoned with a pot of ale.[9]
       WORCESTER   Farewell, kinsman. I'll talk to you
        When you are better tempered to attend.

---

4. Farewell to him, whether he sinks or manages to swim for a short time.
5. A weighted line used in testing the depth of the sea.
6. Figures of speech; fantasies.
7. Inhabitants of Scotland (with a pun in the following lines on "scot" as meaning "a small sum").
8. In Elizabethan England, the sword and buckler, or small shield, were associated with ordinary fighting men. A prince should use rapier and dagger.
9. A drink associated with the common people.

NORTHUMBERLAND [*to* HOTSPUR] Why, what a wasp-stung and
               impatient fool
235   Art thou to break into this woman's mood,[1]
     Tying thine ear to no tongue but thine own!
  HOTSPUR Why, look you, I am whipped and scourged with rods,
     Nettled and stung with pismires,° when I hear   *ants*
     Of this vile politician° Bolingbroke.   *schemer*
240   In Richard's time—what d'ye call the place?
     A plague upon't, it is in Gloucestershire.
     'Twas where the madcap Duke his uncle kept—
     His uncle York—where I first bowed my knee
     Unto this king of smiles, this Bolingbroke.[2]
245   'Sblood, when you and he came back from Ravenspurgh.[3]
  NORTHUMBERLAND At Berkeley castle.
  HOTSPUR   You say true.
     Why, what a candy deal of° courtesy   *quantity of sweet*
     This fawning greyhound then did proffer me!
     'Look when° his infant fortune came to age',   *Whenever; as soon as*
250   And 'gentle Harry Percy', and 'kind cousin'.
     O, the devil take such cozeners!°—God forgive me.   *cheaters*
     Good uncle, tell your tale; I have done.
  WORCESTER Nay, if you have not, to't again.
     We'll stay° your leisure.   *await*
  HOTSPUR   I have done, i'faith.
255   WORCESTER Then once more to your Scottish prisoners.
     Deliver them up° without their ransom straight;   *Release them*
     And make the Douglas'[4] son your only mean°   *agent; means*
     For powers° in Scotland, which, for divers reasons   *raising an army*
     Which I shall send you written, be assured
260   Will easily be granted. [*To* NORTHUMBERLAND] You, my lord,
     Your son in Scotland being thus employed,
     Shall secretly into the bosom creep
     Of that same noble prelate well-beloved,
     The Archbishop.
  HOTSPUR   Of York, is't not?
  WORCESTER   True, who bears hard°   *resents*
265   His brother's death at Bristol, the Lord Scrope.[5]
     I speak not this in estimation,°   *as a guess*
     As what I think might be, but what I know
     Is ruminated, plotted, and set down,
     And only stays° but to behold the face   *waits*
270   Of that occasion that shall bring it on.
  HOTSPUR I smell it; upon my life, it will do well!
  NORTHUMBERLAND Before the game is afoot thou still lett'st slip.[6]
  HOTSPUR Why, it cannot choose but be a noble plot—
     And then the power° of Scotland and of York   *army*
     To join with Mortimer, ha?
275   WORCESTER   And so they shall.

---

1. Alluding to the commonplace that women were, by
nature, unable to hold their tongues.
2. This event is depicted in *Richard II* 2.3.20–56.
3. Bolingbroke's landing place at the mouth of the
Humber River in Yorkshire upon his return from exile.
4. The "the" before Douglas's name indicates that he is
head of a Scottish clan or noble family.
5. Richard Scroop (or le Scrope), the Archbishop of

York and an ally of the rebels in this play, was actually a
distant cousin of William Scroop, Earl of Wiltshire,
who was a favorite of Richard II and was executed by
Henry IV in 1399. His death is mentioned in *Richard
II* 3.2.
6. Before the quarry is even in the field, you always let
loose the dogs. This image from hunting implies that
Hotspur habitually jumps the gun.

HOTSPUR   In faith, it is exceedingly well aimed.
WORCESTER   And 'tis no little reason bids us speed
    To save our heads by raising of a head;°   *an army*
    For, bear ourselves as even° as we can,   *carefully*
280   The King will always think him in our debt,
    And think we think ourselves unsatisfied
    Till he hath found a time to pay us home.°   *repay us fully*
    And see already how he doth begin
    To make us strangers to his looks of love.
285 HOTSPUR   He does, he does. We'll be revenged on him.
WORCESTER   Cousin, farewell. No further go in this
    Than I by letters shall direct your course.
    When time is ripe, which will be suddenly,°   *soon*
    I'll steal to Glyndŵr and Lord Mortimer,
290   Where you and Douglas and our powers at once,
    As I will fashion it, shall happily meet,
    To bear our fortunes in our own strong arms,
    Which now we hold at° much uncertainty.   *with*
NORTHUMBERLAND   Farewell, good brother. We shall thrive, I
    trust.
295 HOTSPUR [*to* WORCESTER]   Uncle, adieu. O, let the hours be short
    Till fields° and blows and groans applaud our sport!   *battlefields*
                 Exeunt [WORCESTER *at one door,*
          NORTHUMBERLAND *and* HOTSPUR *at another door*]

2.1

Enter a CARRIER,[1] *with a lantern in his hand*
FIRST CARRIER   Heigh-ho! An't° be not four by the day,° I'll be *If it / in the morning*
    hanged. Charles's Wain[2] is over the new chimney, and yet our
    horse° not packed. What, ostler![3]   *horses*
OSTLER [*within*]   Anon,° anon!   *Right away*
5 FIRST CARRIER   I prithee, Tom, beat cut's saddle,[4] put a few
    flocks in the point.[5] Poor jade is wrung in the withers,[6] out of
    all cess.°   *measure*
    Enter another CARRIER
SECOND CARRIER   Peas and beans° are as dank here as a dog, *(horse feed)*
    and that is the next way to give poor jades the bots.° This *intestinal worms*
10   house is turned upside down since Robin Ostler died.
FIRST CARRIER   Poor fellow never joyed since the price of oats
    rose; it was the death of him.
SECOND CARRIER   I think this be the most villainous house in all
    London road for fleas. I am stung like a tench.[7]
15 FIRST CARRIER   Like a tench? By the mass, there is ne'er a king
    christen° could be better bit than I have been since the first *Christian king*
    cock.°   *midnight*

2.1 Location: An innyard in Rochester, Kent.
1. One who transports goods for hire.
2. The constellation now known as the Plow or the Great Bear.
3. One who attends to horses at an inn.
4. Soften the horse's saddle. "Cut" was a term for a horse with a docked tail or a gelding; here, it may be the

horse's name.
5. Put a few tufts of wood in the saddle's pommel (to soften it).
6. The poor old horse is extremely sore in the ridge between its shoulder blades.
7. A spotted fish whose markings may have looked like flea bites.

SECOND CARRIER Why, they will allow us ne'er a jordan,° and   *chamber pot*
then we leak° in your chimney, and your chamber-lye° breeds   *urinate / urine*
20 fleas like a loach.[8]

FIRST CARRIER What, ostler! Come away, and be hanged, come
away!

SECOND CARRIER I have a gammon of bacon° and two races°   *a ham / roots*
of ginger to be delivered as far as Charing Cross.[9]

25 FIRST CARRIER God's body, the turkeys in my pannier° are   *basket*
quite starved! What, ostler! A plague on thee, hast thou never
an eye in thy head? Canst not hear? An° 'twere not as good deed   *If*
as drink to break the pate° on thee, I am a very villain. Come,   *skull*
and be hanged! Hast no faith° in thee?   *responsibility*

    Enter GADSHILL

30 GADSHILL Good morrow, carriers. What's o'clock?

FIRST CARRIER I think it be two o'clock.

GADSHILL I prithee lend me thy lantern to see my gelding in the
stable.

FIRST CARRIER Nay, by God, soft.° I know a trick worth two of   *wait*
35 that, i'faith.

GADSHILL [*to* SECOND CARRIER] I pray thee, lend me thine

SECOND CARRIER Ay, when? Canst tell?[1] 'Lend me thy lantern,'
quoth a.° Marry, I'll see thee hanged first.   *says he*

GADSHILL Sirrah carrier, what time do you mean to come to
40 London?

SECOND CARRIER Time enough to go to bed with a candle, I
warrant° thee.—Come, neighbour Mugs, we'll call up the   *assure*
gentlemen. They will along° with company, for they have great   *travel*
charge.°   *Exeunt* [CARRIERS]   *have valuable cargo*

45 GADSHILL What ho, chamberlain![2]

    Enter CHAMBERLAIN

CHAMBERLAIN 'At hand' quoth Pickpurse.[3]

GADSHILL That's even as fair° as "'At hand" quoth the cham-   *good*
berlain', for thou variest no more from picking of purses than
giving direction doth from labouring:[4] thou layest the plot°   *plan*
50 how.

CHAMBERLAIN Good morrow, Master Gadshill. It holds current
that° I told you yesternight. There's a franklin in the   *holds true what*
Weald[5] of Kent hath brought three hundred marks[6] with him
in gold. I heard him tell it to one of his company last night at
55 supper—a kind of auditor, one that hath abundance of charge
too, God knows what. They are up already, and call for eggs
and butter; they will away presently.

GADSHILL Sirrah, if they meet not with Saint Nicholas's
clerks,[7] I'll give thee this neck.

60 CHAMBERLAIN No, I'll none of it; I pray thee keep that for the
hangman, for I know thou worshippest Saint Nicholas as truly
as a man of falsehood may.

---

8. A fish. The comparison means that urine breeds
fleas either as a loach breeds loaches or as a loach
breeds fleas. There was a popular belief that some fish
spawned flies or fleas.
9. A marketplace between London and Westminster.
1. A retort similar to "Never."
2. Bedroom attendant. In popular discourse, chamberlains were notorious for their complicity with thieves.
3. "I am at your disposal," as the thief said (evidently a

popular tag)
4. For you are not more different from a pickpocket
than an overseer is from a laborer.
5. There's a small landowner in the wooded region.
6. Coins worth two-thirds of a pound each.
7. Slang for "highway robbers." St. Nicholas was variously regarded as the patron saint of travelers and of
thieves.

GADSHILL   What talkest thou to me of the hangman? If I hang,
I'll make a fat pair of gallows, for if I hang, old Sir John hangs
with me, and thou knowest he's no starveling. Tut, there are
other Trojans[8] that thou dreamest not of, the which° for sport'   who
sake are content to do the profession° some grace, that would,   (of robbery)
if matters should be looked into, for their own credit' sake
make all whole.° I am joined with no foot-landrakers,[9] no   set things right
long-staff sixpenny strikers,[1] none of these mad mustachio
purple-hued maltworms,[2] but with nobility and tranquillity,
burgomasters and great 'oyez'-ers;[3] such as can hold in,° such   can keep a secret
as will strike sooner than speak, and speak sooner than drink,
and drink sooner than pray. And yet, zounds, I lie, for they
pray continually to their saint the commonwealth; or rather,
not pray to her, but prey on her; for they ride up and down[4]
on her and make her their boots.°   booty; footwear

CHAMBERLAIN   What, the commonwealth their boots? Will she
hold out water in foul way?[5]

GADSHILL   She will, she will, justice hath liquored her.[6] We steal
as in a castle,° cocksure; we have the recipe of fern-seed,[7] we   in complete safety
walk invisible.

CHAMBERLAIN   Nay, by my faith, I think you are more beholden
to the night than to fern-seed for your walking invisible.

GADSHILL   Give me thy hand; thou shalt have a share in our
purchase,° as I am a true man.   plunder

CHAMBERLAIN   Nay, rather let me have it as you are a false thief.

GADSHILL   Go to, 'homo'° is a common name to all men. Bid the   man
ostler bring my gelding out of the stable. Farewell, you muddy°   stupid
knave.   _Exeunt_ [_severally_]°   separately

2.2

Enter PRINCE [HARRY], POINS, PETO [_and_ BARDOLPH][1]

POINS   Come, shelter, shelter!
          [_Exeunt_ PETO _and_ BARDOLPH _at another door_]
I have removed Falstaff's horse, and he frets° like a gummed   worries; frays
velvet.[2]

PRINCE HARRY   Stand close!°   [_Exit_ POINS]   concealed
          Enter FALSTAFF

FALSTAFF   Poins! Poins, and be hanged! Poins!

PRINCE HARRY   Peace, ye fat-kidneyed rascal! What a brawling
dost thou keep!

FALSTAFF   Where's Poins, Hal?

PRINCE HARRY   He is walked up to the top of the hill. I'll go seek
him.   [_Exit_]

---

8. Slang for "roisterers."
9. Highwaymen who travel on foot (rather than on horse).
1. Thieves who carried crude weapons and robbed for small sums.
2. These drunkards with wild mustaches and purple faces.
3. Court officials who cried "Oyez," or "Hear ye."
4. They travel (with a pun on "ride" as meaning "to mount sexually").
5. Will she keep water out (off your feet) on a muddy

road; will she protect you in difficulty?
6. Greased her (as one waterproofs leather); bribed her.
7. Popularly supposed to make those who wore it invisible.
2.2 Location: The highway, Gad's Hill.
1. For a discussion of the names of "Bardolph" and "Peto," see the Textual Note and Introduction.
2. Like cheap velvet treated with gum. Gummed velvet was shiny but wore out quickly.

FALSTAFF   I am accursed to rob in that thief's company. The
rascal hath removed my horse and tied him I know not where.
If I travel but four foot by the square° further afoot, I shall   *(a measuring tool)*
break my wind.° Well, I doubt not but to die a fair death, for³   *be breathless; fart*
15   all this—if I scape hanging for killing that rogue. I have for-
sworn his company hourly any time this two-and-twenty
years, and yet I am bewitched with the rogue's company. If the
rascal have not given me medicines° to make me love him, I'll   *love potions*
be hanged. It could not be else: I have drunk medicines.
20   Poins! Hal! A plague upon you both! Bardolph! Peto! I'll starve
ere I'll rob a foot further. An 'twere not as good a deed as drink
to turn true man° and to leave these rogues, I am the veriest   *repent; turn informer*
varlet that ever chewed with a tooth. Eight yards of uneven
ground is threescore and ten miles afoot with me, and the
25   stony-hearted villains know it well enough. A plague upon't
when thieves cannot be true one to another!
　　　　　They whistle. [Enter PRINCE HARRY, POINS, PETO, *and*
　　　　　BARDOLPH]⁴
Whew! A plague upon you all! Give me my horse, you rogues,
give me my horse, and be hanged!
PRINCE HARRY   Peace, ye fat-guts. Lie down, lay thine ear close
30   to the ground, and list if thou canst hear the tread of travellers.
FALSTAFF   Have you any levers to lift me up again, being down?
'Sblood, I'll not bear my own flesh so far afoot again for all the
coin in thy father's exchequer. What a plague mean ye to colt°   *trick*
35   me thus?
PRINCE HARRY   Thou liest: thou art not colted, thou art
uncolted.°   *unhorsed*
FALSTAFF   I prithee, good Prince Hal, help me to my horse,
good king's son.
PRINCE HARRY   Out, ye rogue, shall I be your ostler?
40   FALSTAFF   Hang thyself in thine own heir-apparent garters!⁵ If
I be ta'en, I'll peach° for this. An I have not ballacs made on   *inform against you*
you all and sung to filthy tunes,⁶ let a cup of sack be my poi-
son. When a jest is so forward, and afoot too!⁷ I hate it.
　　　　　Enter GADSHILL [*visored*]°   *wearing a mask*
GADSHILL   Stand!
45   FALSTAFF   So I do, against my will.
POINS   O, 'tis our setter,° I know his voice. Gadshill, what   *one who sets up a crime*
news?
GADSHILL⁸   Case ye,° case ye, on with your visors! There's   *Disguise yourselves*
money of the King's coming down the hill; 'tis going to the
50   King's exchequer.
FALSTAFF   You lie, ye rogue, 'tis going to the King's tavern.

---

3. Die a natural death, despite.
4. It is not clear exactly when the Prince and his companions show themselves to the frustrated Falstaff.
They can all enter here, or the Prince and Poins could
enter at line 28 and Bardolph and Peto at the same time
as Gadshill at line 43.
5. Falstaff's version of the proverb "He may hang himself in his own garters." As the heir to the throne, the
Prince was a member of the Order of the Garter, the
highest order of English knighthood.
6. Ballads on topical themes were sung by ballad
singers and sold cheaply as broadsides in streets, the-

aters, and other public places.
7. When a plot (to rob) is so advanced and goes so well;
when a joke (on me) goes so far and makes me go on
foot.
8. In Q, this speech is assigned to Bardolph; but Poins
has just asked Gadshill a question, so one expects an
answer to come from him. It has been conjectured that
the confusion here may reflect confusion in Shakespeare's foul papers about whether Bardolph and Gadshill were to be two characters or one. See note to
2.5.159.

GADSHILL   There's enough to make° us all.   *make fortunes for*
FALSTAFF   To be hanged.
        [*They put on visors*]
PRINCE HARRY   Sirs, you four shall front° them in the narrow   *confront*
55   lane. Ned Poins and I will walk lower. If they scape from your
        encounter, then they light on us.
PETO   How many be there of them?
GADSHILL   Some eight or ten.
FALSTAFF   Zounds, will they not rob us?
60   PRINCE HARRY   What, a coward, Sir John Paunch?
FALSTAFF   Indeed I am not John of Gaunt⁹ your grandfather,
        but yet no coward, Hal.
PRINCE HARRY   Well, we leave that to the proof.°   *test*
POINS   Sirrah Jack, thy horse stands behind the hedge. When
65   thou needest him, there thou shalt find him. Farewell, and
        stand fast.
FALSTAFF   Now cannot I strike him if I should be hanged.
PRINCE HARRY [*aside to* POINS]   Ned, where are our disguises?
POINS [*aside to the* PRINCE]   Here, hard by. Stand close.
        [*Exeunt the* PRINCE *and* POINS]
70   FALSTAFF   Now, my masters, happy man be his dole,¹ say I;
        every man to his business.
        [*They stand aside.*]
        Enter the TRAVELLERS [*amongst them the* CARRIERS]
FIRST TRAVELLER   Come, neighbour, the boy shall lead our
        horses down the hill. We'll walk afoot a while, and ease their
        legs.
75   THIEVES [*coming forward*]   Stand!
SECOND TRAVELLER   Jesus bless us!
FALSTAFF   Strike, down with them, cut the villains' throats! Ah,
        whoreson caterpillars,² bacon-fed knaves! They hate us youth.
        Down with them, fleece them!
80   FIRST TRAVELLER   O, we are undone, both we and ours for ever!
FALSTAFF   Hang ye, gorbellied° knaves, are ye undone? No, ye   *potbellied*
        fat chuffs;³ I would your store° were here. On, bacons,° on!   *all you own / fat men*
        What, ye knaves! Young men must live. You are grand-jurors,⁴
        are ye? We'll jure ye, faith.
        Here they rob them and bind them. Exeunt [*the* THIEVES
        with the TRAVELLERS]

2.3

        Enter PRINCE [HARRY] *and* POINS [*disguised in buckram
        suits*]
PRINCE HARRY   The thieves have bound the true° men; now   *honest*
        could thou and I rob the thieves, and go merrily to London. It
        would be argument° for a week, laughter for a month, and a   *topic for discussion*
        good jest for ever.
5   POINS   Stand close; I hear them coming.
        [*They stand aside*]
        Enter [FALSTAFF, BARDOLPH, PETO, *and* GADSHILL, *with
        the travellers' money*]

9. Henry IV's father. Falstaff puns on "Gaunt" as meaning "lean"; in fact, his name is derived from "Ghent,"
his birthplace.
1. Proverbial expression meaning "Good luck to everyone."
2. Parasites. *whoreson*: an insult derived from "whore's

son."
3. Rude, churlish fellows; misers.
4. Referring to the fact that only prosperous citizens
served on grand juries.
2.3 Location: Scene continues.

FALSTAFF   Come, my masters, let us share, and then to horse
before day. An° the Prince and Poins be not two arrant cowards, there's no equity stirring.° There's no more valour in that
Poins than in a wild duck.

As they are sharing, the PRINCE *and* POINS *set upon*
them

10   PRINCE HARRY   Your money!

POINS   Villains!

They all [GADSHILL, BARDOLPH, *and* PETO] *run away*
[*severally*] *and* FALSTAFF, *after a blow or two,* [*roars and*]
runs away too, leaving the booty behind them

PRINCE HARRY   Got with much ease. Now merrily to horse.
The thieves are all scattered, and possessed with fear
So strongly that they dare not meet each other.

15   Each takes his fellow for an officer.
Away, good Ned. Falstaff sweats to death,
And lards° the lean earth as he walks along.
Were't not for laughing, I should pity him.

POINS   How the fat rogue roared!   *Exeunt* [*with the booty*]

If
justice to be found

drips fat on

2.4

Enter HOTSPUR, *reading a letter*

HOTSPUR   'But for mine own part, my lord, I could be well contented to be there, in respect of° the love I bear your house.'°—
He could be contented; why is he not then? In respect of the
love he bears our house! He shows in this he loves his own barn

5   better than he loves our house. Let me see some more.—'The
purpose you undertake is dangerous'— Why, that's certain: 'tis
dangerous to take a cold, to sleep, to drink; but I tell you, my
lord fool, out of this nettle danger we pluck this flower safety.—
'The purpose you undertake is dangerous, the friends you have

10   named uncertain, the time itself unsorted,° and your
whole plot too light for the counterpoise of° so great an
opposition.'— Say you so, say you so? I say unto you again, you
are a shallow, cowardly hind,° and you lie. What a lack-brain
is this! By the Lord, our plot is a good plot as ever was laid,

15   our friends true and constant; a good plot, good friends and
full of expectation; an excellent plot, very good friends. What
a frosty-spirited rogue is this! Why, my lord of York° commends
the plot and the general course of the action. Zounds, an I
were now by this rascal, I could brain him with his lady's fan!

20   Is there not my father, my uncle, and myself? Lord Edmund
Mortimer, my lord of York, and Owain Glyndŵr? Is there not
besides the Douglas? Have I not all their letters, to meet me
in arms by the ninth of the next month? And are they not
some of them set forward already? What a pagan rascal is this,

25   an infidel! Ha, you shall see now, in very sincerity of fear and
cold heart will he to the King, and lay open all our proceedings! O, I could divide myself and go to buffets[1] for moving°
such a dish of skim-milk with so honourable an action! Hang
him! Let him tell the King we are prepared; I will set forward

30   tonight.

Enter his Lady [LADY PERCY]

because of / family

unsuitable
to counterbalance

peasant

(Archbishop Scrope)

urging

2.4 Location: The Percys' home, Warkworth Castle, in
Northumberland.

1. I could split myself into two and fall to blows with
myself.

How now, Kate? I must leave you within these two hours.
LADY PERCY   O my good lord, why are you thus alone?
For what offence have I this fortnight been
A banished woman from my Harry's bed?
35   Tell me, sweet lord, what is't that takes from thee
Thy stomach,° pleasure, and thy golden sleep?   appetite
Why dost thou bend thine eyes upon the earth,
And start so often when thou sitt'st alone?
Why hast thou lost the fresh blood in thy cheeks,
40   And given my treasures and my rights² of thee
To thick-eyed° musing and curst melancholy?   vacantly staring
In thy faint° slumbers I by thee have watched,   restless
And heard thee murmur tales of iron wars,
Speak terms of manège° to thy bounding steed,   horsemanship
45   Cry 'Courage! To the field!' And thou hast talked
Of sallies and retires,° of trenches, tents,   advances and retreats
Of palisadoes,³ frontiers,° parapets,   ramparts
Of basilisks, of cannon, culverin,⁴
Of prisoners ransomed, and of soldiers slain,
50   And all the currents of a heady° fight.   headlong
Thy spirit within thee hath been so at war,
And thus hath so bestirred thee in thy sleep,
That beads of sweat have stood upon thy brow
Like bubbles in a late-disturbèd° stream;   recently disturbed
55   And in thy face strange motions have appeared,
Such as we see when men restrain their breath
On some great sudden hest.° O, what portents are these?   command
Some heavy° business hath my lord in hand,   serious; sad
And I must know it, else he loves me not.
HOTSPUR   What ho!
                    [Enter SERVANT]
60   Is Gilliams with the packet gone?
SERVANT   He is, my lord, an hour ago.
HOTSPUR   Hath Butler brought those horses from the sheriff?
SERVANT   One horse, my lord, he brought even now.
HOTSPUR   What horse? A roan, a crop-ear, is it not?
SERVANT   It is, my lord.
65   HOTSPUR   That roan shall be my throne.
Well, I will back him straight.—O, Esperance!⁵—
Bid Butler lead him forth into the park.
LADY PERCY   But hear you, my lord.
HOTSPUR   What sayst thou, my lady?
LADY PERCY   What is it carries you away?
HOTSPUR   Why, my horse,
My love, my horse.
70   LADY PERCY   Out, you mad-headed ape!
A weasel⁶ hath not such a deal of spleen°   impulsiveness; anger
As you are tossed with.
In faith, I'll know your business, Harry, that I will.

2. Marriage rights. Alluding to the belief that husbands
and wives owe a mutual marriage debt that obliges
them regularly to engage in sexual relations with one
another.
3. Pointed stakes driven into the ground as defensive
barriers.
4. *basilisks:* large cannons, named after a deadly

mythological reptile. *culverin:* a name for both a kind of
long cannon and a firearm noted for its ability to fire
over a long range.
5. Referring to the Percy motto *Esperance ma comforte,*
or "Hope is my reliance."
6. Weasels were proverbially quarrelsome.

I fear my brother Mortimer doth stir
75 About his title, and hath sent for you
To line° his enterprise; but if you go—   *strengthen*
HOTSPUR   So far afoot? I shall be weary, love.
LADY PERCY   Come, come, you paraquito,° answer me   *little parrot*
Directly to this question that I ask.
80 In faith, I'll break thy little finger,° Harry,   *(euphemism for "penis")*
An if thou wilt not tell me all things true.
HOTSPUR   Away, away, you trifler! Love? I love thee not,
I care not for thee, Kate. This is no world
To play with maumets[7] and to tilt° with lips.   *duel*
85 We must have bloody noses and cracked crowns,[8]
And pass them current,[9] too. God's me,° my horse!—   *God save me*
What sayst thou, Kate? What wouldst thou have with me?
LADY PERCY   Do you not love me? Do you not indeed?
Well, do not, then, for since you love me not
90 I will not love myself. Do you not love me?
Nay, tell me if you speak in jest or no.
HOTSPUR   Come, wilt thou see me ride?
And when I am a-horseback,[1] I will swear
I love thee infinitely. But hark you, Kate.
95 I must not have you henceforth question me
Whither I go, nor reason whereabout.°   *discuss about what*
Whither I must, I must; and, to conclude,
This evening must I leave you, gentle Kate.
I know you wise, but yet no farther wise
100 Than Harry Percy's wife; constant you are,
But yet a woman;[2] and for secrecy
No lady closer,° for I well believe   *more secretive*
Thou wilt not utter what thou dost not know.
And so far will I trust thee, gentle Kate.
105 LADY PERCY   How, so far?
HOTSPUR   Not an inch further. But hark you, Kate,
Whither I go, thither shall you go too.
Today will I set forth, tomorrow you.
Will this content you, Kate?
LADY PERCY   It must, of force.°   *Exeunt*   *of necessity*

2.5

Enter PRINCE [HARRY]
PRINCE HARRY   Ned, prithee come out of that fat° room, and   *stuffy*
lend me thy hand to laugh a little.
      Enter POINS [*at another door*]
POINS   Where hast been, Hal?
PRINCE HARRY   With three or four loggerheads,° amongst three   *blockheads*
5   or fourscore hogsheads.° I have sounded the very bass-string of   *casks for liquor*
humility. Sirrah, I am sworn brother to a leash of drawers,° and   *group of three tapsters*
can call them all by their christen names, as 'Tom', 'Dick', and
'Francis'. They take it already, upon their salvation, that

---

7. Breasts; dolls; false gods. The term derived from "mahomet," whom English Protestants viewed as a false god worshipped by heathen peoples.
8. Punning on "cracked crowns" as meaning "broken heads" and "counterfeit currency." Hotspur may be alluding to the acts of rape associated with warfare: "nose" is slang for "penis," and a "cracked crown" can

mean a "whore" or "deflowered woman."
9. Establish them as the norm; let them circulate.
1. On my horse; having sexual intercourse.
2. Women were assumed to be great talkers who could keep no secrets.
2.5 Location: An inn in Eastcheap, London.

though I be but Prince of Wales yet I am the king of courtesy,
10 and tell me flatly I am no proud jack° like Falstaff, but a   *fellow*
Corinthian,[1] a lad of mettle, a good boy—by the Lord, so they
call me; and when I am King of England I shall command all
the good lads in Eastcheap. They call drinking deep 'dyeing
scarlet',[2] and when you breathe in your watering[3] they cry
15 'Hem!' and bid you 'Play it off!'° To conclude, I am so good a   *Drink up*
proficient in one quarter of an hour that I can drink with any
tinker° in his own language during my life. I tell thee, Ned,   *itinerant pot mender*
thou hast lost much honour that thou wert not with me in this
action. But, sweet Ned—to sweeten which name of Ned I give
20 thee this penny-worth of sugar,[4] clapped even now into my
hand by an underskinker,° one that never spake other English   *assistant tapster*
in his life than 'Eight shillings and sixpence', and 'You are wel-
come', with this shrill addition, 'Anon,° anon, sir! Score° a   *At once / Chalk up*
pint of bastard[5] in the Half-moon!'[6] or so. But, Ned, to drive
25 away the time till Falstaff come, I prithee do thou stand in
some by-room, while I question my puny° drawer to what end   *inexperienced*
he gave me the sugar, and do thou never leave calling 'Fran-
cis!', that his tale to me may be nothing but 'Anon!' Step aside,
and I'll show thee a precedent.°   [*Exit* POINS]   *give you a foretaste*
30 POINS [*within*]   Francis!
PRINCE HARRY   Thou art perfect.
POINS [*within*]   Francis!
                Enter [FRANCIS, *a*] *drawer*
FRANCIS   Anon, anon, sir!—Look down into the Pomegranate,[7]
Ralph!
35 PRINCE HARRY   Come hither, Francis.
FRANCIS   My lord.
PRINCE HARRY   How long hast thou to serve,[8] Francis?
FRANCIS   Forsooth, five years, and as much as to—
POINS [*within*]   Francis!
40 FRANCIS   Anon, anon, sir!
PRINCE HARRY   Five year! By'r Lady,[9] a long lease for the clink-
ing of pewter. But Francis, darest thou be so valiant as to play
the coward with thy indenture,° and show it a fair pair of   *contract*
heels, and run from it?
45 FRANCIS   O Lord, sir, I'll be sworn upon all the books° in En-   (*Bibles*)
gland, I could find in my heart—
POINS [*within*]   Francis!
FRANCIS   Anon, sir!
PRINCE HARRY   How old art thou, Francis?
50 FRANCIS   Let me see, about Michaelmas[1] next I shall be—
POINS [*within*]   Francis!
FRANCIS   Anon, sir! [*To the* PRINCE] Pray, stay a little, my lord.

---

1. A rich, licentious man. In contemporary texts, ancient Corinth was famous for wealth and sensuality.
2. Referring to the ruddy complexion associated with drunkards or to the fact that urine, a product of drink, was used to dye wool.
3. When you pause to breathe in your drink.
4. Tapsters sold sugar to sweeten wine.
5. A Spanish wine, so named because it was mixed or adulterated with honey.

6. Name of the inn room to which the wine is to be charged.
7. Name of another room in the inn.
8. Serve as apprentice. Apprenticeship typically began at age twelve or fourteen and lasted seven years.
9. By our Lady (an oath invoking the Virgin Mary).
1. September 29, a holy day honoring the archangel Michael and signifying to tradespeople the close of an accounting period.

PRINCE HARRY   Nay, but hark you, Francis. For the sugar thou
gavest me, 'twas a pennyworth, was't not?

55   FRANCIS   O Lord, I would it had been two!

PRINCE HARRY   I will give thee for it a thousand pound. Ask me
when thou wilt, and thou shalt have it—

POINS [within]   Francis!

FRANCIS   Anon, anon!

60   PRINCE HARRY   Anon, Francis? No, Francis, but tomorrow,
Francis; or, Francis, o' Thursday; or indeed, Francis, when
thou wilt. But Francis.

FRANCIS   My lord.

PRINCE HARRY   Wilt thou rob this leathern-jerkin, crystal-
65   button, knot-pated, agate-ring, puke-stocking, caddis-garter,
smooth-tongue, Spanish-pouch?[2]

FRANCIS   O Lord, sir, who do you mean?

PRINCE HARRY   Why, then, your brown bastard is your only
drink![3] For look you, Francis, your white canvas doublet will
70   sully.° In Barbary,[4] sir, it cannot come to° so much.   *get dirty / be worth*

FRANCIS   What, sir?

POINS [within]   Francis!

PRINCE HARRY   Away, you rogue! Dost thou not hear them call?
[*As he departs* POINS *and the* PRINCE] *both call him. The*
Drawer stands amazed, not knowing which way to go.
Enter VINTNER°   *Innkeeper*

VINTNER   What, standest thou still, and hearest such a calling?
75   Look to the guests within.   [*Exit* FRANCIS]
My lord, old Sir John with half a dozen more are at the door.
Shall I let them in?

PRINCE HARRY   Let them alone a while, and then open the door.
[*Exit* VINTNER]
Poins!

80   POINS [within]   Anon, anon, sir!
Enter POINS

PRINCE HARRY   Sirrah, Falstaff and the rest of the thieves are at
the door. Shall we be merry?

POINS   As merry as crickets, my lad. But hark ye, what cunning
match° have you made with this jest of the drawer? Come,   *game*
85   what's the issue?°   *outcome*

PRINCE HARRY   I am now of all humours that have showed
themselves humours[5] since the old days of goodman° Adam to   *(title for a farmer)*
the pupil° age of this present twelve o'clock at midnight.   *youthful*
[*Enter* FRANCIS]
What's o'clock, Francis?

90   FRANCIS   Anon, anon, sir!   [*Exit at another door*]

---

2. Referring (satirically) to Francis's employer, who
would be robbed of Francis's labor if the apprentice
were to run away. This employer is imagined as dressing in the manner of an upwardly mobile Londoner,
wearing a leather jacket ("jerkin") with crystal buttons
and keeping his hair close-cropped ("knot-pated"). He
also wears a signet ring with a carved agate, dark
("puke") stockings, and garters made from caddis ribbon (a cheaper alternative to silk). He has a simpering
style of speech and carries a vintner's pouch made of
Spanish leather.

3. The best of all drinks; the only drink you'll get (if you
stay in the tavern). This entire speech seems meant to
mystify Francis while obliquely warning him that he
will get dirty and be poor if he fulfills his apprenticeship.
4. North African region from which England acquired
sugar.
5. That is, I am in the mood for anything. Renaissance
medical theory held that four body fluids, or humors,
determined by their relative proportions the health,
temperament, and moods of an individual.

PRINCE HARRY   That ever this fellow should have fewer words than a parrot, and yet the son of a woman! His industry is upstairs and downstairs, his eloquence the parcel of a reckoning.° I am not yet of Percy's mind, the Hotspur of the North—he that kills me° some six or seven dozen of Scots at a breakfast, washes his hands, and says to his wife, 'Fie upon this quiet life! I want work.' 'O my sweet Harry,' says she, 'how many hast thou killed today?' 'Give my roan horse a drench,'° says he, and answers, 'Some fourteen,' an hour after; 'a trifle, a trifle.' I prithee call in Falstaff. I'll play Percy, and that damned brawn° shall play Dame Mortimer his wife. 'Rivo!'⁶ says the drunkard. Call in Ribs, call in Tallow.°

Enter FALSTAFF [*with sword and buckler,* BARDOLPH, PETO, *and* GADSHILL, *followed by* FRANCIS, *with wine*]

POINS   Welcome, Jack. Where hast thou been?

FALSTAFF   A plague of all cowards, I say, and a vengeance too, marry and amen!—Give me a cup of sack, boy.—Ere I lead this life long, I'll sew netherstocks,° and mend them and foot° them too. A plague of all cowards!—Give me a cup of sack, rogue. Is there no virtue extant?

He drinketh

PRINCE HARRY   Didst thou never see Titan° kiss a dish of butter— pitiful hearted Titan—that melted at the sweet tale of the sun's? If thou didst, then behold that compound.⁷

FALSTAFF [*to* FRANCIS]   You rogue, here's lime⁸ in this sack too. There is nothing but roguery to be found in villainous man, yet a coward is worse than a cup of sack with lime in it.

[*Exit* FRANCIS]⁹

A villainous coward! Go thy ways, old Jack, die when thou wilt. If manhood, good manhood, be not forgot upon the face of the earth, then am I a shotten herring.¹ There lives not three good men unhanged in England, and one of them is fat and grows old, God help the while.° A bad world, I say. I would I were a weaver²—I could sing psalms, or anything. A plague of all cowards, I say still.

PRINCE HARRY   How now, woolsack, what mutter you?

FALSTAFF   A king's son! If I do not beat thee out of thy kingdom with a dagger of lath,³ and drive all thy subjects afore thee like a flock of wild geese, I'll never wear hair on my face more. You, Prince of Wales!

PRINCE HARRY   Why, you whoreson round man, what's the matter?

FALSTAFF   Are not you a coward? Answer me to that. And Poins there?

POINS   Zounds, ye fat paunch, an ye call me coward, by the Lord I'll stab thee.

Marginal glosses:

95

100

105

110

115

120

125

130

items of a bill

he that slays

dose of medicine

fat boar

fat drippings

stockings / making a new foot for

the sun

these times

---

6. An exclamation associated with boisterous drinking.
7. Combination; that is, the melted butter (referring to Falstaff).
8. Often added to bad wine to make it dry and sparkling.
9. Neither Q nor F indicates when Francis leaves the stage. He plays no further part in the action after this, so an exit here avoids the problem of having a character onstage with no obvious function.

1. A herring that has spawned its roe and is thus very thin.
2. Weavers were reputed to sing the Psalms of the Bible at work. Many were Puritans, and some had emigrated from the zealously Protestant Low Countries.
3. A wooden dagger, which was the weapon associated with the Vice figure in medieval morality plays (see note to line 413).

FALSTAFF I call thee coward? I'll see thee damned ere I call
thee coward, but I would give a thousand pound I could run
135   as fast as thou canst. You are straight enough in the shoulders;
you care not who sees your back. Call you that backing of your
friends? A plague upon such backing! Give me them that will
face me. Give me a cup of sack. I am a rogue if I drunk today.

PRINCE HARRY O villain, thy lips are scarce wiped since thou
140   drunkest last.

FALSTAFF All is one for that.°   *It doesn't matter*
    He drinketh
A plague of all cowards, still say I.

PRINCE HARRY What's the matter?

FALSTAFF What's the matter? There be four of us here have
145   ta'en a thousand pound this day morning.°   *this morning*

PRINCE HARRY Where is it, Jack, where is it?

FALSTAFF Where is it? Taken from us it is. A hundred upon
poor four of us.

PRINCE HARRY What, a hundred, man?

150 FALSTAFF I am a rogue if I were not at half-sword° with a dozen   *dueling closely*
of them, two hours together. I have scaped by miracle. I am
eight times thrust through the doublet,° four through the hose,°   *short jacket / breeches*
my buckler° cut through and through, my sword hacked like   *shield*
a handsaw. *Ecce signum.*[4]
155   [*He shows his sword*]
I never dealt better since I was a man. All would not do.[5] A
plague of all cowards! [*Pointing to* GADSHILL, PETO, *and* BAR-
DOLPH] Let them speak. If they speak more or less than truth,
they are villains and the sons of darkness.

PRINCE HARRY[6] Speak, sirs, how was it?

160 GADSHILL We four set upon some dozen—

FALSTAFF [*to the* PRINCE] Sixteen at least, my lord.

GADSHILL And bound them.

PETO No, no, they were not bound.

FALSTAFF You rogue, they were bound every man of them, or
165   am a Jew else, an Hebrew Jew.

GADSHILL As we were sharing, some six or seven fresh men set
upon us.

FALSTAFF And unbound the rest; and then come in the other.

PRINCE HARRY What, fought you with them all?

170 FALSTAFF All? I know not what you call all, but if I fought not
with fifty of them, I am a bunch of radish. If there were not
two- or three-and-fifty upon poor old Jack, then am I no two-
legged creature.

PRINCE HARRY Pray God you have not murdered some of them.

175 FALSTAFF Nay, that's past praying for. I have peppered° two of   *made it hot for*
them. Two I am sure I have paid°—two rogues in buckram   *killed*
suits. I tell thee what, Hal, if I tell thee a lie, spit in my face,
call me horse. Thou knowest my old ward°—   *posture of defense*
    [*He stands as to fight*]

---

4. Behold the evidence (Latin).
5. All I did was not enough; the whole group was insuf-
ficient opposition.
6. This is a second place (see 2.2.48) where textual
confusion surrounds the character of Gadshill. In Q,
this line is assigned to Gadshill and the following line
to Russell (whose name was changed to "Bardolph" as

a result of censorship; see Introduction). In F, this line
is assigned to the Prince and the following line to Gadshill. The next two speeches here assigned to Gadshill
were also given to Russell in Q. The F assignment of
these lines to Gadshill may indicate that at some point
Shakespeare divided between two characters a role
originally designed for one.

here I lay,° and thus I bore my point.° Four rogues in buckram   *stood / sword point*
180 let drive at me.

PRINCE HARRY   What, four? Thou saidst but two even now.

FALSTAFF   Four, Hal, I told thee four.

POINS   Ay, ay, he said four.

FALSTAFF   These four came all afront,° and mainly° thrust at me.   *abreast / mightily*
185 I made me no more ado, but took all their seven points in my
target,° thus.   *shield*

[*He wards himself with his buckler*]

PRINCE HARRY   Seven? Why, there were but four even now.

FALSTAFF   In buckram?

POINS   Ay, four in buckram suits.

190 FALSTAFF   Seven, by these hilts,° or I am a villain else.   *sword handle*

PRINCE HARRY [*aside to* POINS]   Prithee, let him alone. We shall
have more anon.

FALSTAFF   Dost thou hear me, Hal?

PRINCE HARRY   Ay, and mark° thee too, Jack.   *pay attention to; count*

195 FALSTAFF   Do so, for it is worth the listening to. These nine in
buckram that I told thee of—

PRINCE HARRY [*aside to* POINS]   So, two more already.

FALSTAFF   Their points⁷ being broken—

POINS [*aside to the* PRINCE]   Down fell their hose.

200 FALSTAFF   Began to give me ground. But I followed me° close,   *I followed*
came in foot and hand, and, with a thought,° seven of the eleven   *swift as thought*
I paid.

PRINCE HARRY [*aside to* POINS]   O monstrous! Eleven buckram
men grown out of two!

205 FALSTAFF   But, as the devil would have it, three misbegotten
knaves in Kendal green⁸ came at my back and let drive at me;
for it was so dark, Hal, that thou couldst not see thy hand.

PRINCE HARRY   These lies are like their father that begets
them—gross as a mountain, open, palpable. Why, thou clay-
210 brained guts, thou knotty-pated° fool, thou whoreson obscene   *blockheaded*
greasy tallow-catch⁹—

FALSTAFF   What, art thou mad? Art thou mad? Is not the truth
the truth?

PRINCE HARRY   Why, how couldst thou know these men in
215 Kendal green when it was so dark thou couldst not see thy
hand? Come, tell us your reason. What sayst thou to this?

POINS   Come, your reason, Jack, your reason.

FALSTAFF   What, upon compulsion? Zounds, an I were at the
strappado,¹ or all the racks² in the world, I would not tell you
220 on compulsion. Give you a reason on compulsion? If reasons
were as plentiful as blackberries, I would give no man a reason upon compulsion, I.

PRINCE HARRY   I'll be no longer guilty of this sin. This sanguine°   *red-faced*
coward, this bed-presser,° this horse-back-breaker, this huge hill   *licentious man*
225 of flesh—

7. Sword points, but Poins takes it as meaning "fasten-
ings for hose."
8. A coarse green cloth made in Kendal, Cumbria. It
was associated with poor country people, especially
forest dwellers, as well as outlaws.
9. Greasy lump of fat (gathered by butchers for candle

making).
1. A torture device in which victims were lifted off the
ground by ropes attached to their hands, which were
tied behind their backs, and then let fall.
2. A torture device in which victims' limbs were pulled
apart.

FALSTAFF   'Sblood, you starveling, you elf-skin, you dried neat's°   *ox's*
tongue, you bull's pizzle, you stock-fish³—O, for breath to utter
what is like thee!— you tailor's yard,⁴ you sheath, you bow-
case, you vile standing tuck⁵—

230   PRINCE HARRY   Well, breathe awhile, and then to't again. and
when thou hast tired thyself in base comparisons, hear me
speak but this.

POINS   Mark, Jack.

PRINCE HARRY   We two saw you four set on four, and bound

235   them, and were masters of their wealth.—Mark now how a
plain tale shall put you down.—Then did we two set on you
four, and, with a word, outfaced you from your prize, and have
it; yea, and can show it you here in the house. And Falstaff,
you carried your guts away as nimbly, with as quick dexterity,

240   and roared for mercy, and still run and roared, as ever I heard
bull-calf. What a slave art thou, to hack thy sword as thou
hast done, and then say it was in fight! What trick, what
device, what starting-hole° canst thou now find out to hide   *refuge*
thee from this open and apparent shame?

245   POINS   Come, let's hear, Jack; what trick hast thou now?

FALSTAFF   By the Lord, I knew ye as well as he that made ye.
Why, hear you, my masters. Was it for me to kill the heir-
apparent? Should I turn upon the true prince? Why, thou
knowest I am as valiant as Hercules;⁶ but beware instinct. The

250   lion will not touch the true prince⁷—instinct is a great matter. I was now a coward on instinct. I shall think the better of
myself and thee during my life—I for a valiant lion, and thou
for a true prince. But by the Lord, lads, I am glad you have the
money.—[*Calling*] Hostess, clap to the doors.—Watch to-

255   night, pray tomorrow.⁸ Gallants, lads, boys, hearts of gold, all
the titles of good fellowship come to you! What, shall we be
merry, shall we have a play extempore?

PRINCE HARRY   Content, and the argument° shall be thy running   *subject*
away.

260   FALSTAFF   Ah, no more of that, Hal, an thou lovest me.

        Enter HOSTESS

HOSTESS   O Jesu, my lord the Prince!

PRINCE HARRY   How now, my lady the Hostess, what sayst thou
to me?

HOSTESS   Marry, my lord, there is a nobleman of the court at door

265   would speak with you. He says he comes from your father.

PRINCE HARRY   Give him as much as will make him a royal
man,⁹ and send him back again to my mother.

FALSTAFF   What manner of man is he?

HOSTESS   An old man.

---

3. *bull's pizzle:* a bull's penis that when dried and
stretched was used as a whip. *stock-fish:* dried cod.
4. Tailors were popularly imagined to lack virility. Falstaff puns on "yard" as referring both to a tailor's measuring stick and to his penis.
5. *sheath:* empty case (punning on "sheath" as meaning
"foreskin"). *bow-case:* a long, thin case for unstrung
bows. *standing tuck:* a stiff rapier (with a pun on "standing" as meaning "sexually erect").

6. In classical mythology, a hero who performed prodigious acts of strength and courage.
7. A popular belief derived from classical texts.
8. Falstaff alludes here to Matthew 26:41: "Watch and
pray, that ye enter not into temptation." He puns on
"watch" as meaning 'keep vigil" and "carouse" and on
"pray" as meaning "prey."
9. Punning on 'nobles" and "royals" as names of coins,
the latter being more valuable.

270 FALSTAFF   What doth gravity out of his bed at midnight? Shall
      I give him his answer?
      PRINCE HARRY   Prithee do, Jack.
      FALSTAFF   Faith, and I'll send him packing.   *Exit*
      PRINCE HARRY   Now, sirs; [*to* GADSHILL] by'r Lady, you fought
275 fair—so did you, Peto, so did you, Bardolph. You are lions
      too—you ran away upon instinct, you will not touch the true
      prince; no, fie!
      BARDOLPH   Faith, I ran when I saw others run.
      PRINCE HARRY   Faith, tell me now in earnest, how came Fal-
280 staff's sword so hacked?
      PETO   Why, he hacked it with his dagger, and said he would
      swear truth out of England[1] but he would make you believe it
      was done in fight, and persuaded us to do the like.
      BARDOLPH   Yea, and to tickle our noses with speargrass,[2] to make
285 them bleed; and then to beslubber our garments with it, and
      swear it was the blood of true men. I did that° I did not this   *what*
      seven year before—I blushed to hear his monstrous devices.
      PRINCE HARRY   O villain, thou stolest a cup of sack eighteen years
      ago, and wert taken with the manner,° and ever since thou hast   *caught in the act*
290 blushed extempore.° Thou hadst fire[3] and sword on thy side,   *spontaneously*
      and yet thou rannest away. What instinct hadst thou for it?
      BARDOLPH [*indicating his face*]   My lord, do you see these mete-
      ors? Do you behold these exhalations?[4]
      PRINCE HARRY   I do.
295 BARDOLPH   What think you they portend?°   *signify*
      PRINCE HARRY   Hot livers,[5] and cold° purses.   *empty*
      BARDOLPH   Choler,[6] my lord, if rightly taken.° [*Exit*][7]   *understood*
      PRINCE HARRY   No, if rightly taken, halter.[8]
            Enter FALSTAFF
      Here comes lean Jack; here comes bare-bone. How now, my
300 sweet creature of bombast?[9] How long is't ago, Jack, since
      thou sawest thine own knee?
      FALSTAFF   My own knee? When I was about thy years, Hal, I was
      not an eagle's talon in the waist; I could have crept into any
      alderman's thumb-ring. A plague of sighing and grief—it blows
305 a man up like a bladder. There's villainous news abroad. Here
      was Sir John Bracy from your father; you must to the court in
      the morning. That same mad fellow of the North, Percy, and
      he of Wales that gave Amamon° the bastinado,° and made Luc-   *(a devil) / a beating*
      ifer cuckold,[1] and swore the devil his true liegeman° upon the   *subject*
310 cross of a Welsh hook[2]—what a plague call you him?

1. Swear so excessively that Truth, imagined as an allegorical figure, would run out of England to escape him.
2. A plant with sharply pointed leaves.
3. A reference to Bardolph's red face, the focus of the
jests that follow.
4. "Meteors" and "exhalations" refer to the red
blotches on Bardolph's face, here compared to disturbances in the heavens.
5. Short tempers; livers inflamed by drink.
6. The humor associated with an angry disposition.
7. Neither Q nor F marks an exit for Bardolph here,
but both indicate that he reenters at line 439. The nec-

essary exit might well follow this discussion of his
inflamed face.
8. No, if rightly arrested, a noose. The Prince forces a
legal reading on the previous line, playing on "choler"
as "collar," or "noose," and taking "taken" to mean
"arrested."
9. Cotton padding; pompous speech.
1. Slept with the devil's own wife; gave the devil his
horns (the proverbial sign of a cuckold).
2. A heavy weapon with a crooked end, lacking the
cross shape on which oaths were usually made.

POINS   Owain Glyndŵr.

FALSTAFF   Owain, Owain, the same; and his son-in-law Mortimer, and old Northumberland, and that sprightly Scot of Scots
Douglas, that runs a-horseback up a hill perpendicular—

315 PRINCE HARRY   He that rides at high speed and with his pistol
kills a sparrow flying.

FALSTAFF   You have hit it.

PRINCE HARRY   So did he never the sparrow.

FALSTAFF   Well, that rascal hath good mettle in him, he will not
320 run.

PRINCE HARRY   Why, what a rascal art thou, then, to praise him
so for running!

FALSTAFF   A-horseback, ye cuckoo, but afoot he will not budge
a foot.

325 PRINCE HARRY   Yes, Jack, upon instinct.

FALSTAFF   I grant ye, upon instinct. Well, he is there too, and
one Mordake, and a thousand blue-caps° more. Worcester is   Scottish soldiers
stolen away tonight. Thy father's beard is turned white with the
news. You may buy land now as cheap as stinking mackerel.

330 PRINCE HARRY   Why then, it is like, if there come a hot June and
this civil buffeting hold,° we shall buy maidenheads as they buy   continue
hobnails: by the hundreds.³

FALSTAFF   By the mass, lad, thou sayst true; it is like we shall
have good trading that way. But tell me, Hal, art not thou hor-
335 rible afeard? Thou being heir-apparent, could the world pick
thee out three such enemies again as that fiend Douglas, that
spirit Percy, and that devil Glyndŵr? Art thou not horribly
afraid? Doth not thy blood thrill° at it?   shudder

PRINCE HARRY   Not a whit, i'faith. I lack some of thy instinct.

340 FALSTAFF   Well, thou wilt be horribly chid tomorrow when thou
comest to thy father. If thou love me, practise an answer.

PRINCE HARRY   Do thou stand for° my father, and examine me   impersonate
upon the particulars of my life.

FALSTAFF   Shall I? Content. This chair shall be my state,° this   throne
345 dagger my sceptre, and this cushion my crown.

[He sits]

PRINCE HARRY   Thy state is taken for a joint-stool,⁴ thy golden
sceptre for a leaden dagger, and thy precious rich crown for a
pitiful bald crown.

FALSTAFF   Well, an° the fire of grace be not quite out of thee,   if
350 now shalt thou be moved. Give me a cup of sack to make my
eyes look red, that it may be thought I have wept: for I must
speak in passion, and I will do it in King Cambyses' vein.⁵

PRINCE HARRY [bowing]   Well, here is my leg.°   bow

FALSTAFF   And here is my speech. [To PETO, POINS, and GADS-
355 HILL] Stand aside, nobility.

HOSTESS   O Jesu, this is excellent sport, i'faith.

FALSTAFF   Weep not, sweet Queen,⁶ for trickling tears are vain.

---

3. Alluding to rape as a practice of war or to the notion
that women would be likely to relinquish their virginity
cheaply during wartime.
4. A stool made of wooden pieces fitted or joined
together.
5. In the exaggerated rhetorical style associated with

such early Elizabethan plays as *Cambyses*, a tragedy
about a despotic Persian king.
6. Possibly addressed to the Hostess, with a pun on
"quean" as slang for 'whore.'

HOSTESS	O the Father, how he holds his countenance!°	*keeps a straight face*
FALSTAFF	For God's sake, lords, convey° my tristful° Queen,	*lead away / sad*
360	For tears do stop° the floodgates of her eyes.	*fill*
HOSTESS	O Jesu, he doth it as like one of these harlotry° players	*vagabond; scurvy*
	as ever I see!	
FALSTAFF	Peace, good pint-pot; peace, good tickle-brain.[7]—	
	Harry, I do not only marvel where thou spendest thy time, but	
365	also how thou art accompanied. For though the camomile,°	*an herb*
	the more it is trodden on, the faster it grows, yet youth, the	
	more it is wasted, the sooner it wears.[8] That thou art my son	
	I have partly thy mother's word, partly my own opinion, but	
	chiefly a villainous trick° of thine eye, and a foolish hanging	*trait*
370	of thy nether° lip, that doth warrant° me. If then thou be son	*lower / assure*
	to me, here lies the point. Why, being son to me, art thou so	
	pointed at?° Shall the blessed sun of heaven prove a micher,°	*criticized / truant*
	and eat blackberries?—A question not to be asked. Shall the	
	son of England prove a thief, and take purses?—A question to	
375	be asked. There is a thing, Harry, which thou hast often heard	
	of, and it is known to many in our land by the name of pitch.°	*sticky, black tar*
	This pitch, as ancient writers do report, doth defile.[9] So doth	
	the company thou keepest. For Harry, now I do not speak to	
	thee in drink, but in tears; not in pleasure, but in passion; not	
380	in words only, but in woes also. And yet there is a virtuous	
	man whom I have often noted in thy company, but I know not	
	his name.	
PRINCE HARRY	What manner of man, an it like your majesty?	
FALSTAFF	A goodly, portly man, i'faith, and a corpulent; of a	
385	cheerful look, a pleasing eye, and a most noble carriage;° and,	*bearing*
	as I think, his age some fifty, or, by'r Lady, inclining to three-	
	score. And now I remember me, his name is Falstaff. If that	
	man should be lewdly given,° he deceiveth me; for, Harry, I	*be lustful*
	see virtue in his looks. If, then, the tree may be known by the	
390	fruit, as the fruit by the tree,[1] then peremptorily I speak it—	
	there is virtue in that Falstaff. Him keep with; the rest ban-	
	ish. And tell me now, thou naughty varlet, tell me, where hast	
	thou been this month?	
PRINCE HARRY	Dost thou speak like a king? Do thou stand for	
395	me, and I'll play my father.	
FALSTAFF	[*standing*] Depose me. If thou dost it half so gravely,	
	so majestically both in word and matter, hang me up by the	
	heels for a rabbit sucker,° or a poulter's hare.[2]	*an unweaned rabbit*
PRINCE HARRY	[*sitting*] Well, here I am set.°	*seated*
400	FALSTAFF	And here I stand. [*To the others*] Judge, my masters.	
PRINCE HARRY	Now, Harry, whence come you?	
FALSTAFF	My noble lord, from Eastcheap.	
PRINCE HARRY	The complaints I hear of thee are grievous.	

---

7. Slang term for a strong alcoholic drink, and hence for the drinker.
8. Falstaff's entire speech is a parody of the previously fashionable ornate rhetoric exemplified by John Lyly's *Euphues* (1578).

9. See Ecclesiasticus 13:1 (also cited in Lyly's *Euphues*).
1. An allusion to Matthew 12:33 (which also appears in Lyly's *Euphues*).
2. A hare sold in a poultry shop.

FALSTAFF 'Sblood, my lord, they are false. [*To the others*] Nay,
405   I'll tickle ye for° a young prince, i'faith.   *amuse you as*

PRINCE HARRY Swearest thou, ungracious boy? Henceforth ne'er
  look on me. Thou art violently carried away from grace. There
  is a devil haunts thee in the likeness of an old fat man; a tun°   *large barrel*
  of man is thy companion. Why dost thou converse° with that   *associate*
410   trunk of humours,[3] that bolting-hutch° of beastliness, that   *bin for coarse meal*
  swollen parcel of dropsies,[4] that huge bombard° of sack, that   *leather wine vessel*
  stuffed cloak-bag° of guts, that roasted Manningtree[5] ox with   *suitcase*
  the pudding° in his belly, that reverend Vice,[6] that grey Iniquity,   *stuffing*
  that father Ruffian, that Vanity in Years? Wherein is he good,°   *virtuous; proficient*
415   but to taste sack and drink it? Wherein neat and cleanly,° but   *deft*
  to carve a capon and eat it? Wherein cunning, but in craft?
  Wherein crafty, but in villainy? Wherein villainous, but in all
  things? Wherein worthy, but in nothing?

FALSTAFF I would your grace would take me with you.° Whom   *explain what you mean*
420   means your grace?

PRINCE HARRY That villainous, abominable misleader of youth,
  Falstaff; that old white-bearded Satan.

FALSTAFF My lord, the man I know. *Falstaff as the Prince*

PRINCE HARRY I know thou dost.

425   FALSTAFF But to say I know more harm in him than in myself
  were to say more than I know. That he is old, the more the
  pity, his white hairs do witness it. But that he is, saving your
  reverence,[7] a whoremaster, that I utterly deny. If sack and
  sugar be a fault, God help the wicked. If to be old and merry
430   be a sin, then many an old host° that I know is damned. If to   *innkeeper*
  be fat be to be hated, then Pharaoh's lean kine[8] are to be
  loved. No, my good lord, banish Peto, banish Bardolph, banish Poins, but for sweet Jack Falstaff, kind Jack Falstaff, true
  Jack Falstaff, valiant Jack Falstaff, and therefore more valiant
435   being, as he is, old Jack Falstaff,
  Banish not him thy Harry's company,   *foreshadows*
  Banish not him thy Harry's company.   *the end of Part 2*
  Banish plump Jack, and banish all the world.

PRINCE HARRY I do; I will.
  [*Knocking within. Exit* HOSTESS.][9]
  Enter BARDOLPH, *running*

440   BARDOLPH O my lord, my lord, the sheriff with a most mon-
  strous watch° is at the door.   *group of constables*

FALSTAFF Out, ye rogue! Play out the play! I have much to say
  in the behalf of that Falstaff.
  Enter the HOSTESS

---

3. A chest full of body fluids, whose excess, according
to Renaissance medical theory, was extremely
unhealthy.
4. Diseases characterized by retention of water.
5. Market town in Essex, noted for the Manningtree
Fair, where a roasted ox may have been part of the festivities.
6. An irreverent, comic, and (usually) youthful character representing evil and sin in the medieval morality

plays. Sometimes named "Iniquity."
7. If you will excuse the expression.
8. In a biblical story in Genesis 41:18–21, Pharaoh
dreams of seven lean cows ("kine") that portend seven
years of famine.
9. Neither F nor Q marks an exit for the Hostess, but
both indicate her reentry at line 443. It makes sense for
her to exit here to see about the commotion at her door.

HOSTESS   O Jesu! My lord, my lord!

445   PRINCE HARRY   Heigh, heigh, the devil rides upon a fiddlestick!¹
      What's the matter?

HOSTESS   The sheriff and all the watch are at the door. They are
      come to search the house. Shall I let them in?

FALSTAFF   Dost thou hear, Hal? Never call a true piece of gold

450   a counterfeit—thou art essentially made, without seeming so.²

PRINCE HARRY   And thou a natural coward without instinct.

FALSTAFF   I deny your major.° If you will deny³ the sheriff, so.   main premise
      If not, let him enter. If I become° not a cart° as well as another   adorn / hangman's cart
      man, a plague on my bringing up. I hope I shall as soon be

455   strangled with a halter as another.

PRINCE HARRY   Go, hide thee behind the arras.° The rest walk up   tapestry wall hanging
      above. Now, my masters, for a true face and good conscience.
              [Exeunt POINS, BARDOLPH, and GADSHILL]

FALSTAFF   Both which I have had, but their date is out;° and   has expired
      therefore I'll hide me.
              [He withdraws behind the arras]

460   PRINCE HARRY [to HOSTESS]   Call in the sheriff.   [Exit HOSTESS]
              Enter SHERIFF and [a] CARRIER
      Now, master sheriff, what is your will with me?

SHERIFF   First, pardon me, my lord. A hue and cry⁴
      Hath followed certain men unto this house.

PRINCE HARRY   What men?

465   SHERIFF   One of them is well known, my gracious lord,
      A gross, fat man.

CARRIER   As fat as butter.

PRINCE HARRY   The man, I do assure you, is not here,
      For I myself at this time have employed him.
      And, sheriff, I will engage° my word to thee   pledge

470   That I will by tomorrow dinner-time
      Send him to answer thee, or any man,
      For anything he shall be charged withal.
      And so let me entreat you leave the house.

SHERIFF   I will, my lord. There are two gentlemen

475   Have in this robbery lost three hundred marks.

PRINCE HARRY   It may be so. If he have robbed these men,
      He shall be answerable. And so, farewell.

SHERIFF   Good night, my noble lord.

PRINCE HARRY   I think it is good morrow, is it not?

480   SHERIFF   Indeed, my lord, I think it be two o'clock.
              Exeunt [SHERIFF and CARRIER]

PRINCE HARRY   This oily rascal is known as well as Paul's.°   St. Paul's Cathedral
      Go call him forth.

PETO   Falstaff!
              [He draws back the arras, revealing FALSTAFF asleep]
              Fast asleep

---

1. That is, what a row about nothing.
2. A famously difficult passage. Falstaff may be insisting he is true gold, not a counterfeit (and so should not
be turned over to the watch) just as Hal is a true Prince

("essentially made") despite appearances.
3. If you will refuse to let in.
4. A group of citizens who pursue a criminal.

Behind the arras, and snorting like a horse.

PRINCE HARRY   Hark how hard he fetches breath. Search his
485   pockets.

[PETO] *searcheth his pocket and findeth certain papers.*
[*He closeth the arras and cometh forward*]

What hast thou found?

PETO   Nothing but papers, my lord.

PRINCE HARRY   Let's see what they be. Read them.

PETO [*reads*]   Item: a capon.   2s. 2d.
        Item: sauce.   4d.
490   Item: sack, two gallons.   5s. 8d.
        Item: anchovies and sack after supper.   2s. 6d.
        Item: bread.   ob.°   obolus (*halfpenny*)

PRINCE HARRY   O monstrous! But one halfpennyworth of bread
        to this intolerable deal° of sack! What there is else, keep close;   *quantity*
495   we'll read it at more advantage.° There let him sleep til day.   *a better opportunity*
        I'll to the court in the morning. We must all to the wars, and
        thy place shall be honourable. I'll procure this fat rogue a
        charge of foot,[5] and I know his death will be a march of twelve
        score.[6] The money shall be paid back again, with advantage.°   *interest*
500   Be with me betimes° in the morning; and so good morrow,   *early*
        Peto.

PETO   Good morrow, good my lord.   *Exeunt* [*severally*]

3.1

Enter HOTSPUR, [*the Earl of*] WORCESTER, *Lord* MORTI-
MER, [*and*] *Owain* GLYNDŴR [*with a map*]

MORTIMER   These promises are fair, the parties sure,
        And our induction° full of prosperous hope.[1]   *beginning*

HOTSPUR   Lord Mortimer and cousin Glyndŵr,
        Will you sit down? And uncle Worcester?

[MORTIMER, GLYNDŴR, *and* WORCESTER *sit*]

5   A plague upon it, I have forgot the map!

GLYNDŴR   No, here it is. Sit, cousin Percy, sit,
        Good cousin Hotspur;

[HOTSPUR *sits*]

                        For by that name
        As oft as Lancaster[2] doth speak of you,
        His cheek looks pale, and with a rising sigh
        He wisheth you in heaven.

10   HOTSPUR   And you in hell,
        As oft as he hears Owain Glyndŵr spoke of.

GLYNDŴR   I cannot blame him. At my nativity
        The front° of heaven was full of fiery shapes,   *forehead*
        Of burning cressets;[3] and at my birth

---

5. Command of an infantry company.
6. I know it will kill him to march twelve times twenty
yards or paces.
3.1 Location: Glyndŵr's castle, Wales. According to
Holinshed's *Chronicles*, the events of this scene take
place in the house of the Archdeacon of Bangor: but he
is not present in Shakespeare's scene, and Glyndŵr acts

as host throughout.
1. Full of the hope of prospering.
2. Referring to Henry's title as Duke and hence implying a denial of the legitimacy of his kingship.
3. Metal baskets of fire suspended from long poles;
meteors.

15   The frame and huge foundation of the earth
      Shaked like a coward.
      HOTSPUR   Why, so it would have done
      At the same season if your mother's cat
      Had but kittened, though yourself had never been born.
      GLYNDŴR   I say the earth did shake when I was born.
20   HOTSPUR   And I say the earth was not of my mind
      If you suppose as fearing you it shook.
      GLYNDŴR   The heavens were all on fire, the earth did tremble—
      HOTSPUR   O, then the earth shook to see the heavens on fire,
      And not in fear of your nativity.
25   Diseasèd nature oftentimes breaks forth
      In strange eruptions; oft the teeming° earth   *fertile*
      Is with a kind of colic pinched and vexed
      By the imprisoning of unruly wind
      Within her womb, which for enlargement° striving   *release*
30   Shakes the old beldam° earth, and topples down   *grandmother*
      Steeples and moss-grown towers. At your birth
      Our grandam earth, having this distemp'rature,°   *disorder*
      In passion shook.
      GLYNDŴR   Cousin, of many men
      I do not bear these crossings.° Give me leave   *contradictions*
35   To tell you once again that at my birth
      The front of heaven was full of fiery shapes,
      The goats ran from the mountains, and the herds
      Were strangely clamorous to the frighted fields.
      These signs have marked me extraordinary,
40   And all the courses of my life do show
      I am not in the roll of common men.
      Where is he living, clipped in with° the sea   *encircled by*
      That chides the banks° of England, Scotland, Wales,   *shores*
      Which° calls me pupil or hath read to° me?   *Who / tutored*
45   And bring him out° that is but woman's son   *show me any man*
      Can trace° me in the tedious ways of art,[4]   *follow*
      And hold me pace° in deep experiments.   *keep up with me*
      HOTSPUR [*standing*]   I think there's no man speaketh better Welsh.[5]
      I'll to dinner.
50   MORTIMER   Peace, cousin Percy, you will make him mad.
      GLYNDŴR   I can call spirits from the vasty deep.°   *lower world*
      HOTSPUR   Why, so can I, or so can any man;
      But will they come when you do call for them?
      GLYNDŴR   Why, I can teach you, cousin, to command the devil.
55   HOTSPUR   And I can teach thee, coz, to shame the devil,
      By telling truth: 'Tell truth, and shame the devil'.
      If thou have power to raise him, bring him hither,
      And I'll be sworn I have power to shame him hence.
      O, while you live, tell truth and shame the devil.
60   MORTIMER   Come, come, no more of this unprofitable chat.
      GLYNDŴR   Three times hath Henry Bolingbroke made head°   *raised an army*
      Against my power;° thrice from the banks of Wye   *army*

---

4. The long, laborious ways of magic.
5. The Welsh language was often described by English writers as a barbaric one, and "to speak Welsh" com-

monly meant to use a strange, unintelligible language. Hotspur implies that Glyndŵr speaks nonsense.

And sandy-bottomed Severn have I sent him
Bootless° home, and weather-beaten back.⁶   *Unsuccessful*

65 HOTSPUR   Home without boots, and in foul weather too!
How scapes he agues,° in the devil's name?   *fevers*
GLYNDŴR   Come, here's the map. Shall we divide our right,°   *what we are entitled to*
According to our threefold order ta'en?⁷
MORTIMER   The Archdeacon hath divided it
70 Into three limits° very equally.   *regions*
England from Trent and Severn hitherto°   *to here*
By south and east is to my part assigned;
All westward—Wales beyond the Severn shore
And all the fertile land within that bound—
75 To Owain Glyndŵr; [*to* HOTSPUR] and, dear coz, to you
The remnant northward lying off from Trent.
And our indentures tripartite° are drawn,   *in triplicate*
Which, being sealèd interchangeably⁸—
A business that this night may execute°—   *may be done tonight*
80 Tomorrow, cousin Percy, you and I
And my good lord of Worcester will set forth
To meet your father and the Scottish power,
As is appointed us, at Shrewsbury.
My father,° Glyndŵr, is not ready yet,   *father-in-law*
85 Nor shall we need his help these fourteen days.
Within that space you may have drawn together
Your tenants, friends, and neighbouring gentlemen.
GLYNDŴR   A shorter time shall send me to you, lords;
And in my conduct° shall your ladies come,   *escort*
90 From whom you now must steal and take no leave;
For there will be a world of water shed
Upon the parting of your wives and you.
HOTSPUR   Methinks my moiety° north from Burton here   *portion*
In quantity equals not one° of yours.   *either*
95 See how this river comes me cranking in,⁹
And cuts me from the best of all my land
A huge half-moon, a monstrous cantle,° out.   *piece*
I'll have the current in this place dammed up,
And here the smug° and silver Trent shall run   *smooth*
100 In a new channel fair and evenly.
It shall not wind with such a deep indent,
To rob me of so rich a bottom° here   *lowland plain*
GLYNDŴR   Not wind? It shall, it must; you see it doth.
MORTIMER   Yea, but mark how he bears his course, and runs me up°   *turns upward*
105 With like advantage on the other side,
Gelding the opposèd continent¹ as much
As on the other side it takes from you.
WORCESTER   Yea, but a little charge° will trench° him here,   *expense / rechannel*
And on this north side win this cape of land,
110 And then he runs straight and even.
HOTSPUR   I'll have it so; a little charge will do it.

6. According to Holinshed, Glyndŵr used magic to
raise storms that frustrated Henry's attacks.
7. *threefold*: either an agreement made in triplicate
(see line 77) or an agreement having three parts (see
the rebels' plan to divide the island into three pieces at

lines 68–76). *order ta'en*: agreement made.
8. Bearing the seals of all three nobles.
9. Comes bending in on my shores.
1. Cutting a vital piece from ("gelding") the opposite
bank.

GLYNDŴR   I'll not have it altered.
HOTSPUR   Will not you?
GLYNDŴR   No, nor you shall not.
115 HOTSPUR   Who shall say me nay?
GLYNDŴR   Why, that will I.
HOTSPUR   Let me not understand you, then: speak it in Welsh.
GLYNDŴR   I can speak English, lord, as well as you;
       For I was trained up in the English court,
120   Where, being but young, I framèd to the harp
       Many an English ditty lovely well,
       And gave the tongue a helpful ornament[2]—
       A virtue that was never seen in you.
HOTSPUR   Marry, and I am glad of it, with all my heart.
125   I had rather be a kitten and cry 'mew'
       Than one of these same metre ballad-mongers.[3]
       I had rather hear a brazen canstick turned,[4]
       Or a dry wheel grate on the axle-tree,°   axle
       And that would set my teeth nothing on edge,
130   Nothing so much as mincing° poetry.   affected
       'Tis like the forced gait of a shuffling° nag.   hobbled
GLYNDŴR   Come, you shall have Trent turned.
HOTSPUR   I do not care. I'll give thrice so much land
       To any well-deserving friend;
135   But in the way of bargain—mark ye me—
       I'll cavil on° the ninth part of a hair.   quibble about
       Are the indentures drawn? Shall we be gone?
GLYNDŴR   The moon shines fair. You may away by night.
       I'll haste the writer, and withal°   simultaneously
140   Break with° your wives of your departure hence.   Inform
       I am afraid my daughter will run mad,
       So much she doteth on her Mortimer.   Exit
MORTIMER   Fie, cousin Percy, how you cross my father!
HOTSPUR   I cannot choose. Sometime he angers me
145   With telling me of the moldwarp[5] and the ant,
       Of the dreamer Merlin[6] and his prophecies,
       And of a dragon and a finless fish,
       A clip-winged griffin[7] and a moulten° raven,   moulted
       A couching lion and a ramping cat,[8]
150   And such a deal of skimble-skamble° stuff   stupid
       As puts me from my faith.[9] I tell you what,
       He held me last night at the least nine hours
       In reckoning up the several devils' names
       That were his lackeys. I cried, 'Hum!' and, 'Well, go to!',
155   But marked him not a word. O, he is as tedious
       As a tired horse, a railing wife,
       Worse than a smoky house. I had rather live

2. And gave the English language the ornament of a
musical setting; and supplemented the English lyrics
with pleasing music.
3. Sellers or writers of ballads.
4. A brazen candlestick scraped and polished on a
lathe after casting. John Stow's *Survey of London*
(1598) records contemporary complaints about the
noise of candlestick making.
5. Mole. Holinshed records a prophecy whereby
Henry, figured as a mole, would be overthrown by a
dragon, a lion, and a wolf, representing Glyndŵr, Percy,
and Mortimer, respectively.
6. Legendary Welsh prophet, wizard, and bard at King
Arthur's court.
7. A fabulous beast, part lion and part eagle.
8. Alluding to the heraldic terms "couchant" and "rampant," which mean "crouching" and "rearing fiercely."
Hotspur is making fun of Glyndŵr's heraldic preoccupations.
9. As makes me a skeptic, even of religion.

With cheese and garlic, in a windmill, far,
Than feed on cates° and have him talk to me   *delicacies*
160   In any summer house° in Christendom.   *luxurious residence*
    MORTIMER   In faith, he is a worthy gentleman,
    Exceedingly well read, and profited°   *proficient*
    In strange concealments,° valiant as a lion,   *In occult arts*
    And wondrous affable, and as bountiful
165   As mines of India. Shall I tell you, cousin?
    He holds your temper in a high respect,
    And curbs himself even of his natural scope°   *freedom of speech*
    When you come 'cross° his humour; faith, he does.   *contradict*
    I warrant you, that man is not alive
170   Might so have tempted° him as you have done   *provoked*
    Without the taste of danger and reproof.
    But do not use it oft, let me entreat you.
    WORCESTER [*to* HOTSPUR]   In faith, my lord, you are too wilful-blame,°   *stubborn*
    And since your coming hither have done enough
175   To put him quite besides° his patience.   *out of*
    You must needs learn, lord, to amend this fault.
    Though sometimes it show greatness, courage, blood°—   *spirit; noble birth*
    And that's the dearest grace° it renders you—   *best distinction*
    Yet oftentimes it doth present° harsh rage,   *show*
180   Defect of manners, want of government,
    Pride, haughtiness, opinion,° and disdain,   *self-conceit*
    The least of which haunting a nobleman
    Loseth men's hearts, and leaves behind a stain
    Upon the beauty of all parts besides,°   *all other qualities*
185   Beguiling° them of commendation.   *Depriving*
    HOTSPUR   Well, I am schooled. Good manners be your speed!°   *give you success*
    Enter GLYNDŴR *with the Ladies* [LADY PERCY *and Morti-*
    mer's wife]
    Here come our wives, and let us take our leave.
    [*Mortimer's wife weeps, and speaks to him in Welsh*]
    MORTIMER   This is the deadly spite° that angers me   *vexation*
    My wife can speak no English, I no Welsh.
190   GLYNDŴR   My daughter weeps she'll not part with you.
    She'll be a soldier, too; she'll to the wars.
    MORTIMER   Good father, tell her that she and my aunt Percy[1]
    Shall follow in your conduct speedily.
        GLYNDŴR *speaks to her in Welsh, and she answers*
        him in the same
    GLYNDŴR   She is desperate here,° a peevish self-willed harlotry,°   *on this point / hussy*
195   One that no persuasion can do good upon.
        The lady speaks in Welsh
    MORTIMER   I understand thy looks. That pretty Welsh°   *(i.e., her tears)*
    Which thou down pourest from these swelling heavens°   *overflowing eyes*
    I am too perfect° in, and but for shame   *proficient*
    In such a parley° should I answer thee.   *In a similar language*
        The lady [*kisses him, and speaks*] *again in Welsh*
200   MORTIMER   I understand thy kisses, and thou mine,
    And that's a feeling disputation;[2]
    But I will never be a truant, love,

---

1. Kate, Lady Percy. Her historical counterpart was the   2. A conversation rooted in emotions or in touch.
sister, not the aunt, of Glyndŵr's son-in-law.

Till I have learnt thy language, for thy tongue
Makes Welsh as sweet as ditties highly° penned,   eloquently
205   Sung by a fair queen in a summer's bower
With ravishing division,° to her lute.   embellishments
GLYNDŴR   Nay, if you melt,° then will she run mad.   weep
    The lady [sits on the rushes³ and] speaks again in Welsh
MORTIMER   O, I am ignorance itself in this!
GLYNDŴR   She bids you on the wanton° rushes lay you down   luxurious
210   And rest your gentle head upon her lap,⁴
And she will sing the song that pleaseth you,
And on your eyelids crown the god of sleep,
Charming your blood with pleasing heaviness,°   sleepiness
Making such difference 'twixt wake and sleep
215   As is the difference betwixt day and night
The hour before the heavenly-harnessed team⁵
Begins his golden progress in the east.
MORTIMER   With all my heart, I'll sit and hear her sing.
By that time will our book,° I think, be drawn.   document
    [He sits, resting his head on the Welsh lady's lap]
220   GLYNDŴR   Do so, and those musicians that shall play to you
Hang in the air a thousand leagues from hence,
And straight they shall be here. Sit and attend.
HOTSPUR   Come, Kate, thou art perfect in lying down.°   expert at lovemaking
Come, quick, quick, that I may lay my head in thy lap.⁶
225   LADY PERCY *[sitting]*   Go, ye giddy goose!
    [HOTSPUR sits, resting his head on Lady Percy's lap.]
    The music plays⁷
HOTSPUR   Now I perceive the devil understands Welsh;
And 'tis no marvel, he is so humorous.°   eccentric; whimsical
By'r Lady, he's a good musician.
LADY PERCY   Then should you be nothing but musical,
230   For you are altogether governed by humours.°   whims
Lie still, ye thief, and hear the lady sing in Welsh.
HOTSPUR   I had rather hear Lady my brach° howl in Irish.   female hunting dog
LADY PERCY   Wouldst thou have thy head broken?
HOTSPUR   No.
235   LADY PERCY   Then be still.
HOTSPUR   Neither—'tis a woman's fault.⁸
LADY PERCY   Now God help thee!
HOTSPUR   To the Welsh lady's bed.
LADY PERCY   What's that?
240   HOTSPUR   Peace; she sings.
    Here the lady sings a Welsh song
HOTSPUR   Come, Kate, I'll have your song too.
LADY PERCY   Not mine, in good sooth.°   truth
HOTSPUR   Not yours, in good sooth! Heart,° you swear like a   By God's heart
comfit-maker's° wife: 'Not you, in good sooth!' and 'As true as   confectioner's
245   I live!' and
'As God shall mend me!' and 'As sure as day!';

---

3. Used as a floor covering, both in houses and on the theater stage.
4. Often a euphemism for the genitals.
5. The sun was supposedly carried in a chariot drawn by horses.
6. "Head" was slang for "penis" and "lap" for "vagina."

7. Instrumental music would probably be played in a so-called music house behind the upper stage in the Elizabethan theater and so might well seem to "hang in the air" (see lines 220–21).
8. No, I won't be still—it is a woman's trait (and I am a man).

And giv'st such sarcenet[9] surety for thy oaths
As if thou never walk'st further than Finsbury.[1]
Swear me, Kate, like a lady as thou art,
250 A good mouth-filling oath, and leave 'in sooth'
And such protest of pepper gingerbread[2]
To velvet-guards and Sunday citizens.[3]
Come, sing.

LADY PERCY   I will not sing.

255 HOTSPUR   'Tis the next° way to turn tailor,[4] or be redbreast   °quickest
teacher.° [Rising] An the indentures be drawn, I'll away within   °or teach birds to sing
these two hours; and so come in when ye will.   Exit

GLYNDŴR   Come, come, Lord Mortimer. You are as slow
As hot Lord Percy is on fire to go.
260 By this° our book is drawn. We'll but seal,   °now
And then to horse immediately.

MORTIMER [rising]   With all my heart.
[The ladies rise, and all] exeunt

3.2

Enter KING [HENRY], PRINCE [HARRY], and [lords]

KING HENRY   Lords, give us leave—the Prince of Wales and I
Must have some private conference—but be near at hand,
For we shall presently have need of you.   Exeunt lords
I know not whether God will have it so
5 For some displeasing service I have done,   Harry is Gods
That in his secret doom° out of my blood°   punishment   °judgment / °lineage
He'll breed revengement and a scourge for me,   to the King
But thou dost in thy passages° of life   °course
Make me believe that thou art only marked
10 For° the hot vengeance and the rod of heaven   °To be
To punish my mistreadings. Tell me else,
Could such inordinate° and low desires,   °unsuitable
Such poor, such bare, such lewd, such mean attempts,°   °base undertakings
Such barren pleasures,[1] rude society,
15 As thou art matched withal° and grafted to,   °with
Accompany the greatness of thy blood,
And hold their level° with thy princely heart?   °And claim equality

PRINCE HARRY   So please your majesty, I would I could
Quit° all offences with as clear excuse   °Clear myself of
20 As well as I am doubtless° I can purge   °certain
Myself of many I am charged withal;
Yet such extenuation let me beg
As, in reproof° of many tales devised—   °upon disproof
Which oft the ear of greatness needs must hear
25 By smiling pickthanks° and base newsmongers°—   °flatterers / °gossips
I may, for some things true wherein my youth
Hath faulty wandered and irregular,
Find pardon on my true submission.°   °admission of guilt

KING HENRY   God pardon thee! Yet let me wonder, Harry,

9. Flimsy (from the name of a fine silk).
1. Finsbury Fields, north of London, was a popular resort for London's middling classes. Hotspur implies that Kate's mild oaths make her sound like a burgher's wife.
2. Watered-down oaths. Gingerbread was cheaply available at fairs and markets, and sometimes pepper was used as an inexpensive substitute for ginger.

3. Citizens who doff their work clothes and dress up only on Sundays. To velvet-guards: To those, like citizens' wives, whose clothes are trimmed ("guarded") with velvet.
4. Tailors were noted for singing.
3.2 Location: The palace, London.
1. Unprofitable habits; nonreproductive erotic pursuits.

30   At thy affections,° which do hold a wing   *inclinations*
        Quite from² the flight of all thy ancestors.
        Thy place in Council thou hast rudely³ lost—
        Which by thy younger brother is supplied—
        And art almost an alien to the hearts
35   Of all the court and princes of my blood.
        The hope and expectation of thy time°   *time of life; youth*
        Is ruined, and the soul of every man
        Prophetically do forethink thy fall.
        Had I so lavish of my presence been,
40   So common-hackneyed⁴ in the eyes of men,
        So stale and cheap to vulgar company,
        Opinion,° that did help me to the crown,   *Public opinion*
        Had still kept loyal to possession,⁵
        And left me in reputeless° banishment,   *inglorious*
45   A fellow of no mark nor likelihood.°   *promise of success*
        By being seldom seen, I could not stir
        But, like a comet, I was wondered at,
        That men would tell their children 'This is he.'
        Others would say 'Where, which is Bolingbroke?'
50   And then I stole all courtesy from heaven,⁶
        And dressed myself in such humility
        That I did pluck allegiance from men's hearts,
        Loud shouts and salutations from their mouths,
        Even in the presence of the crownèd King.
55   Thus did I keep my person fresh and new,
        My presence like a robe pontifical°—   *churchman's rich dress*
        Ne'er seen but wondered at—and so my state,°   *magnificence; royalty*
        Seldom but sumptuous, showed like a feast,
        And won by rareness such solemnity.
60   The skipping King, he ambled up and down
        With shallow jesters and rash bavin° wits,   *brushwood*
        Soon kindled and soon burnt, carded his state,⁷
        Mingled his royalty with cap'ring fools,
        Had his great name profanèd with their scorns,°   *by their scornful manners*
65   And gave his countenance,° against his name,⁸   *approval*
        To laugh at gibing boys, and stand the push°   *tolerate the impudence*
        Of every beardless vain comparative;°   *wit*
        Grew a companion to the common streets,
        Enfeoffed° himself to popularity,   *Surrendered*
70   That, being daily swallowed by men's eyes,
        They surfeited with honey, and began
        To loathe the taste of sweetness, whereof a little
        More than a little is by much too much.
        So when he had occasion to be seen,
75   He was but as the cuckoo is in June,⁹
        Heard, not regarded, seen but with such eyes
        As, sick and blunted with community,°   *familiarity*

---

2. *which . . . from:* which do fly a course contrary to.
3. By violence. Perhaps alluding to the story, dramatized in *The Famous Victories of Henry V,* that Prince Hal boxed the Lord Chief Justice on the ear and was subsequently punished.
4. Cheapened. A hackney was a horse available for common hire.
5. The possessor of the throne (Richard II).

6. That is, surpassed heaven itself for graciousness.
7. Adulterated his royal dignity. The term refers to a process ("carding") whereby wool or liquids were mixed with inferior substances.
8. To the detriment of his reputation.
9. Referring to a proverbial saying, "No one regards the June cuckoo's song."

Afford no extraordinary gaze
Such as is bent on sun-like majesty
80 When it shines seldom in admiring eyes,
But rather drowsed and hung their eyelids down,
Slept in his face,° and rendered such aspect°   *before his eyes / looks*
As cloudy° men use to their adversaries,   *sullen*
Being with his presence glutted, gorged, and full.
85 And in that very line,° Harry, standest thou;   *category*
For thou hast lost thy princely privilege
With vile participation.° Not an eye   *base companionship*
But is a-weary of thy common sight,
Save mine, which hath desired to see thee more,
90 Which now doth that° I would not have it do—   *what*
Make blind itself with foolish tenderness.
          ✳ [He weeps] ✳
PRINCE HARRY   I shall hereafter, my thrice-gracious lord,   Harry's
   Be more myself.   reformation
KING HENRY   For all the world,
As thou art to this hour was Richard then,
95 When I from France set foot at Ravenspurgh,
And even as I was then is Percy now.
Now by my sceptre, and my soul to boot,
He hath more worthy interest° to the state   *more claim by worth*
Than thou, the shadow° of succession;   *mere image*
100 For, of° no right, nor colour° like to right,   *having / pretext*
He doth fill fields with harness° in the realm,   *armor*
Turns head° against the lion's° armèd jaws,   *Leads a revolt / king's*
And, being no more in debt to years than thou,
Leads ancient lords and reverend bishops on
105 To bloody battles, and to bruising arms.
What never-dying honour hath he got
Against renownèd Douglas!—whose high deeds,
Whose hot incursions and great name in arms,
Holds from all soldiers chief majority°   *preeminence*
110 And military title capital¹
Through all the kingdoms that acknowledge Christ.
Thrice hath this Hotspur, Mars° in swaddling-clothes,   *god of war*
This infant warrior, in his enterprises
Discomfited° great Douglas; ta'en him once;   *Defeated*
115 Enlargèd° him; and made a friend of him   *Released*
To fill the mouth of deep defiance up,²
And shake the peace and safety of our throne.
And what say you to this? Percy, Northumberland,
The Archbishop's grace of York, Douglas, Mortimer,
120 Capitulate° against us, and are up.°   *Combine / up in arms*
But wherefore do I tell these news to thee?
Why, Harry, do I tell thee of my foes,
Which° art my near'st and dearest enemy?—   *Who*
Thou that art like enough, through vassal° fear,   *servile*
125 Base inclination, and the start of spleen,°   *fit of temper*
To fight against me under Percy's pay,
To dog his heels, and curtsy at his frowns,

1. And claim to the title of principal (capital) warrior.
2. To add volume to the voice of deep defiance; to fill up the appetite of deep defiance.

To show how much thou art degenerate.

PRINCE HARRY　Do not think so; you shall not find it so.
130　And God forgive them that so much have swayed
　　　Your majesty's good thoughts away from me.
　　　I will redeem all this on Percy's head,
　　　And in the closing of some glorious day
　　　Be bold to tell you that I am your son;
135　When I will wear a garment all of blood,
　　　And stain my favours° in a bloody mask,　　　　　　　　*features*
　　　Which, washed away, shall scour my shame with it.
　　　And that shall be the day, whene'er it lights,°　　　　*comes*
　　　That this same child of honour and renown,
140　This gallant Hotspur, this all-praisèd knight,
　　　And your unthought-of Harry chance to meet.
　　　For every honour sitting on his helm,
　　　Would they were multitudes, and on my head
　　　My shames redoubled; for the time will come
145　That I shall make this northern youth exchange
　　　His glorious deeds for my indignities.
　　　Percy is but my factor,° good my lord,　　　　　　　　*agent*
　　　To engross up° glorious deeds on my behalf;　　　　　*amass*
　　　And I will call him to so strict account
150　That he shall render every glory up,
　　　Yea, even the slightest worship of his time,°　　　*honor of his life*
　　　Or I will tear the reckoning from his heart.
　　　This, in the name of God, I promise here,
　　　The which if he be pleased I shall perform,
155　I do beseech your majesty may salve°　　　　　　　　*heal*
　　　The long-grown wounds of my intemperature;°　　*disorder; intemperance*
　　　If not, the end of life cancels all bonds,
　　　And I will die a hundred thousand deaths
　　　Ere break the smallest parcel of this vow.
160　KING HENRY　A hundred thousand rebels die in this.
　　　Thou shalt have charge° and sovereign trust herein.　*military command*

Enter [Sir Walter] BLUNT

　　　How now, good Blunt? Thy looks are full of speed.
BLUNT　So hath the business that I come to speak of.
　　　Lord Mortimer of Scotland[3] hath sent word
165　That Douglas and the English rebels met
　　　The eleventh of this month at Shrewsbury.
　　　A mighty and a fearful head° they are,　　　　　　　*army*
　　　If promises be kept on every hand,
　　　As ever offered foul play in a state.
170　KING HENRY　The Earl of Westmorland set forth today,
　　　With him my son Lord John of Lancaster,
　　　For this advertisement° is five days old.　　　　　*news*
　　　On Wednesday next, Harry, you shall set forward.
　　　On Thursday we ourselves will march.
175　Our meeting is Bridgnorth,[4] and, Harry, you
　　　Shall march through Gloucestershire, by which account,°　*calculation*
　　　Our business valuèd,° some twelve days hence　　　*taken into account*
　　　Our general forces at Bridgnorth shall meet.

3. A Scottish lord who is unrelated to Glyndŵr's son-　　4. A town about 20 miles southeast of Shrewsbury.
in-law.

180 Our hands are full of business; let's away.
Advantage feeds him fat[5] while men delay.   *Exeunt*

3.3

Enter FALSTAFF [*with a truncheon° at his waist*], *and*   officer's club
BARDOLPH

FALSTAFF   Bardolph, am I not fallen away° vilely since this last   shrunk
action?[1] Do I not bate?° Do I not dwindle? Why, my skin hangs   grow thin
about me like an old lady's loose gown. I am withered like an
old apple-john.[2] Well, I'll repent, and that suddenly, while I
5   am in some liking.° I shall be out of heart[3] shortly, and then I   in the mood
shall have no strength to repent. An I have not forgotten what
the inside of a church is made of, I am a peppercorn, a brewer's
horse°—the inside of a church! Company, villainous company,   an old workhorse
hath been the spoil of me.

10   BARDOLPH   Sir John, you are so fretful you cannot live long.

FALSTAFF   Why, there is it. Come, sing me a bawdy song, make
me merry. I was as virtuously given° as a gentleman need to   inclined
be: virtuous enough; swore little; diced not—above seven
times a week; went to a bawdy-house not—above once in a
15   quarter—of an hour; paid money that I borrowed—three or
four times; lived well, and in good compass.° And now I live   limits
out of all order, out of all compass.

BARDOLPH   Why, you are so fat, Sir John, that you must needs be
out of all compass,° out of all reasonable compass, Sir John.   circumference; girth

20   FALSTAFF   Do thou amend thy face, and I'll amend my life.
Thou art our admiral,° thou bearest the lantern in the poop[4]—   flagship
but 'tis in the nose of thee. Thou art the Knight of the Burning Lamp.[5]

BARDOLPH   Why, Sir John, my face does you no harm.

25   FALSTAFF   No, I'll be sworn; I make as good use of it as many a
man doth of a death's head,[6] or a *memento mori*.[7] I never see
thy face but I think upon hell-fire and Dives that lived in
purple—for there he is in his robes, burning, burning.[8] If thou
wert any way given to virtue, I would swear by thy face; my
30   oath should be 'By this fire that's God's angel!' But thou art
altogether given over,° and wert indeed, but for the light in thy   dedicated to vice
face, the son of utter darkness. When thou rannest up Gads
Hill in the night to catch my horse, if I did not think thou hadst
been an *ignis fatuus* or a ball of wildfire,[9] there's no purchase
35   in money. O, thou art a perpetual triumph,° an everlasting   torchlight procession
bonfire-light! Thou hast saved me a thousand marks[1] in links°   small torches
and torches, walking with thee in the night betwixt tavern and

5. Opportunities (for rebellion) flourish; the superior
position (of the rebels) improves.
3.3 Location: The inn in Eastcheap, London.
1. This last military engagement (referring to the Gads
Hill episode).
2. A kind of apple often eaten long after picking, when
its skin was shriveled.
3. Disinclined; weary.
4. The ship's main deck.
5. Parodying figures from popular romance such as
Amadis, the Knight of the Burning Sword.
6. A skull, or representation of a skull, such as was
engraved as an emblem of mortality on seal rings.
7. An object serving as a reminder of mortality (Latin
for "remember you must die").

8. Referring to a biblical parable about a rich man
"clothed in purple and fine linen" who regularly refused
to feed the beggar Lazarus and was ultimately forced to
suffer in hell for his sin (Luke 16:19–23); also referring
to Bardolph's body as bearing the signs of venereal disease. "Burning" implies "on fire with lust" as well as
"infected with syphilitic sores."
9. A flaming explosive used in warfare or in fireworks;
skin marked by erysipelas, an inflammatory disease.
ignis fatuus (Latin for "foolish fire"): a phenomenon in
which phosphorescent light appears on marshy ground;
a false hope.
1. Considerable money (each mark was worth two-
thirds of a pound).

tavern—but the sack that thou hast drunk me° would have | *drunk (at my cost)*
bought me lights as good cheap° at the dearest chandler's² in | *as cheaply*
40 Europe. I have maintained that salamander³ of yours with fire
any time this two-and-thirty years, God reward me for it.

BARDOLPH 'Sblood, I would my face were in your belly!⁴

FALSTAFF God-a-mercy! So should I be sure to be heartburnt.

Enter HOSTESS

How now, Dame Partlet⁵ the hen, have you enquired yet who
45 picked my pocket?

HOSTESS Why, Sir John, what do you think, Sir John? Do you
think I keep thieves in my house? I have searched, I have
enquired; so has my husband, man by man, boy by boy, ser-
vant by servant. The tithe° of a hair was never lost in my house | *tenth part*
50 before.

FALSTAFF Ye lie, Hostess: Bardolph was shaved and lost many
a hair,⁶ and I'll be sworn my pocket was picked. Go to, you are
a woman, go.

HOSTESS Who, I? No, I defy thee! God's light, I was never
55 called so in mine own house before.

FALSTAFF Go to, I know you well enough.

HOSTESS No, Sir John, you do not know me,⁷ Sir John; I know
you, Sir John. You owe me money, Sir John, and now you pick
a quarrel to beguile me of it. I bought you a dozen of shirts to
60 your back.

FALSTAFF Dowlas,° filthy dowlas. I have given them away to | *Coarse linen*
bakers' wives; they have made bolters° of them. | *sieves*

HOSTESS Now as I am a true woman, holland° of eight shillings | *fine linen*
an ell.° You owe money here besides, Sir John: for your diet, | *a measure of 45 inches*
65 and by-drinkings,° and money lent you, four-and-twenty pound. | *drinks between meals*

FALSTAFF [*pointing at* BARDOLPH] He had his part of it. Let him
pay.

HOSTESS He? Alas, he is poor; he hath nothing.

FALSTAFF How, poor? Look upon his face. What call you rich?
70 Let them coin his nose, let them coin his cheeks, I'll not pay
a denier.⁸ What, will you make a younker° of me? Shall I not | *novice; gull*
take mine ease in mine inn, but I shall have my pocket picked?
I have lost a seal-ring of my grandfather's worth forty mark.

HOSTESS O Jesu, [*to* BARDOLPH] I have heard the Prince tell
75 him, I know not how oft, that that ring was copper.

FALSTAFF How? The Prince is a jack,° a sneak-up.° [*Raising* | *rascal / sly villain*
his truncheon] 'Sblood, an he were here I would cudgel him
like a dog if he would say so.

Enter PRINCE [HARRY *and* PETO], *marching; and* FAL-
STAFF *meets* [*them*], *playing upon his truncheon like a
fife*

How now, lad, is the wind in that door,° i'faith? Must we all | *quarter*
80 march?

BARDOLPH Yea, two and two, Newgate fashion.⁹

---

2. The most expensive candle maker's.
3. A fabled lizard capable of living in fire. The implication is that Falstaff has maintained the salamander Bardolph with the "fires" of sack or lust.
4. Equivalent to "Stick it down your throat" (a proverbial retort to an insult).
5. A traditional name for hens and for women supposed to talk too much.

6. Had his beard cut; was cheated or robbed of his
money; lost his hair because of syphilis.
7. That is, you don't know how honest I am; you don't
have sexual knowledge of me.
8. French copper coin of little value.
9. Bound like convicts taken to and from London's
Newgate prison.

HOSTESS My lord, I pray you hear me.

PRINCE HARRY What sayst thou, Mistress Quickly? How doth
thy husband?

I love him well; he is an honest man

85 HOSTESS Good my lord, hear me!

FALSTAFF Prithee, let her alone, and list to me.

PRINCE HARRY What sayst thou, Jack?

FALSTAFF The other night I fell asleep here behind the arras,
and had my pocket picked. This house is turned bawdy-

90 house: they pick pockets.

PRINCE HARRY What didst thou lose, Jack?

FALSTAFF Wilt thou believe me, Hal, three or four bonds of
forty pound apiece, and a seal-ring of my grandfather's.

PRINCE HARRY A trifle, some eightpenny matter.

95 HOSTESS So I told him, my lord; and I said I heard your grace
say so; and, my lord, he speaks most vilely of you, like a foul-
mouthed man as he is, and said he would cudgel you.

PRINCE HARRY What? He did not!

HOSTESS There's neither faith, truth, nor womanhood in me

100 else.

FALSTAFF There's no more faith in thee than in a stewed
prune,[1] nor no more truth in thee than in a drawn fox;[2] and,
for womanhood, Maid Marian[3] may be the deputy's wife of
the ward to° thee. Go, you thing,[4] go!   *compared to*

105 HOSTESS Say, what thing, what thing?

FALSTAFF What thing? Why, a thing to thank God on.

HOSTESS I am no thing to thank God on. I would thou shouldst
know it, I am an honest man's wife; and setting thy knighthood aside, thou art a knave to call me so.

110 FALSTAFF Setting thy womanhood aside, thou art a beast to say
otherwise.

HOSTESS Say, what beast, thou knave, thou?

FALSTAFF What beast? Why, an otter.

PRINCE HARRY An otter, Sir John? Why an otter?

115 FALSTAFF Why? She's neither fish nor flesh;[5] a man knows not
where to have her.[6]

HOSTESS Thou art an unjust man in saying so. Thou or any
man knows where to have me, thou knave, thou.

PRINCE HARRY Thou sayst true, Hostess, and he slanders thee

120 most grossly.

HOSTESS So he doth you, my lord, and said this other day you
owed him a thousand pound.

PRINCE HARRY [*to* FALSTAFF] Sirrah, do I owe you a thousand
pound?

125 FALSTAFF A thousand pound, Hal? A million! Thy love is worth
a million; thou owest me thy love.

HOSTESS Nay, my lord, he called you 'jack' and said he would
cudgel you.

FALSTAFF Did I, Bardolph?

---

1. Symbol of a bawd. Brothels often displayed a dish of
stewed prunes in the window.
2. A hunted fox drawn out from its hiding spot; a dead
fox dragged to lay a false trail.
3. A disreputable character, usually played by a cross-
dressed man, in the boisterous May games and morris
dances denounced by Puritan preachers. The figure is

here juxtaposed to the respectable wife of the deputy of
the ward.
4. A euphemism for "female genitalia."
5. The otter's unusual appearance led to debates about
whether it was a fish or an animal.
6. How to understand her; how to have sexual relations
with her.

130 BARDOLPH Indeed, Sir John, you said so.

FALSTAFF Yea, if he said my ring was copper.

PRINCE HARRY I say 'tis copper; darest thou be as good as thy
word now?

FALSTAFF Why, Hal, thou knowest as thou art but man I dare,
135 but as thou art prince, I fear thee as I fear the roaring of the
lion's whelp.°   *cub*

PRINCE HARRY And why not as the lion?

FALSTAFF The King himself is to be feared as the lion. Dost
thou think I'll fear thee as I fear thy father? Nay, an I do, I pray
140 God my girdle break.

PRINCE HARRY O, if it should, how would thy guts fall about thy
knees! But sirrah, there's no room for faith, truth, nor honesty
in this bosom of thine; it is all filled up with guts and midriff.
Charge an honest woman with picking thy pocket? Why, thou
145 whoreson impudent embossed rascal,[7] if there were anything
in thy pocket but tavern reckonings, memorandums of bawdy-
houses, and one poor pennyworth of sugar-candy to make thee
long-winded°—if thy pocket were enriched with any other   *to give you energy*
injuries[8] but these, I am a villain. And yet you will stand to it,°   *persist*
150 you will not pocket up° wrong. Art thou not ashamed?   *keep quiet about*

FALSTAFF Dost thou hear, Hal? Thou knowest in the state of
innocency Adam fell, and what should poor Jack Falstaff do
in the days of villainy? Thou seest I have more flesh than
another man, and therefore more frailty. You confess, then,
155 you picked my pocket.

PRINCE HARRY It appears so by the story.

FALSTAFF Hostess, I forgive thee. Go make ready breakfast.
Love thy husband, look to thy servants, cherish thy guests.
Thou shalt find me tractable to any honest reason; thou seest
160 I am pacified still.° Nay, prithee, be gone.   *Exit* HOSTESS   *always*
Now, Hal, to the news at court. For the robbery, lad, how is
that answered?°   *settled*

PRINCE HARRY O, my sweet beef, I must still be good angel to
thee. The money is paid back again.

165 FALSTAFF O, I do not like that paying back; 'tis a double labour.

PRINCE HARRY I am good friends with my father, and may do
anything.

FALSTAFF Rob me the exchequer the first thing thou dost, and
do it with unwashed hands° too.   *do it at once*

170 BARDOLPH Do, my lord.

PRINCE HARRY I have procured thee, Jack, a charge of foot.°   *an infantry command*

FALSTAFF I would it had been of horse! Where shall I find one°   *someone*
that can steal well? O, for a fine thief of the age of two-and-
twenty or thereabouts! I am heinously unprovided.° Well, God   *ill equipped*
175 be thanked for these rebels—they offend none but the virtuous.
I laud them, I praise them.

PRINCE HARRY Bardolph.

BARDOLPH My lord?

PRINCE HARRY [*giving letters*] Go bear this letter to Lord John
of Lancaster,
180 To my brother John; this to my lord of Westmorland.

---

7. *embossed rascal:* bloated rogue; hunted deer,   8. Any other things whose loss causes you injury.
exhausted and foaming at the mouth.

[*Exit* BARDOLPH]

Go, Peto, to horse, to horse, for thou and I
Have thirty miles to ride yet ere dinner time. [*Exit* PETO]
Jack, meet me tomorrow in the Temple Hall⁹
At two o'clock in the afternoon.
185 There shalt thou know thy charge, and there receive
Money and order for their furniture.°   equipment
The land is burning, Percy stands on high,
And either we or they must lower lie.   [*Exit*]
FALSTAFF   Rare words! Brave world! [*Calling*] Hostess, my
          breakfast, come!—
190 O, I could wish this tavern were my drum!¹   *Exit*

4.1

Enter HOTSPUR *and* [*the Earls of*] WORCESTER *and*
          DOUGLAS

HOTSPUR   Well said, my noble Scot! If speaking truth
    In this fine age were not thought flattery,
    Such attribution° should the Douglas have   praise
    As not a soldier of this season's stamp°   coinage
5   Should go so general current° through the world.   be so widely accepted
    By God, I cannot flatter, I do defy
    The tongues of soothers,° but a braver place   flatterers
    In my heart's love hath no man than yourself.
    Nay, task° me to my word, approve° me, lord.   hold / test
10 DOUGLAS   Thou art the king of honour.
    No man so potent breathes upon the ground
    But I will beard° him.   defy
HOTSPUR   Do so, and 'tis well.
          Enter a MESSENGER *with letters*
    What letters hast thou there? I can but thank you.
MESSENGER   These letters come from your father.
15 HOTSPUR   Letters from him? Why comes he not himself?
MESSENGER   He cannot come, my lord, he is grievous sick.
HOTSPUR   Zounds, how has he the leisure to be sick
    In such a jostling° time? Who leads his power?   turbulent
    Under whose government° come they along?   command
20 MESSENGER   His letters bears his mind, not I, my lord.
          [HOTSPUR *reads the letter*]
WORCESTER   I prithee tell me, doth he keep his bed?
MESSENGER   He did, my lord, four days ere I set forth;
    And at the time of my departure thence
    He was much feared° by his physicians.   feared for
25 WORCESTER   I would the state of time° had first been whole°   of the times / healthy
    Ere he by sickness had been visited.
    His health was never better worth° than now.   of more value
HOTSPUR   Sick now? Droop now? This sickness doth infect
    The very life-blood of our enterprise.
30 'Tis catching° hither, even to our camp.   infectious
    He writes me here that inward sickness stays him,
    And that his friends by deputation°   through deputies

9. One of the Inns of Court, London's law schools.
1. A disputed passage. Perhaps Falstaff means he
wishes that he could stay at the tavern rather than go to
war or that he could make the tavern ring with the noise
of his departure. He puns on "taborn" (tabor), a kind of
drum used to call soldiers to battle.
4.1 Location: The rebel camp near Shrewsbury.

Could not so soon be drawn;° nor did he think it meet°   *assembled / suitable*
To lay so dangerous and dear a trust
35   On any soul removed° but on his own.   *not directly involved*
Yet doth he give us bold advertisement°   *counsel*
That with our small conjunction° we should on,   *joint force*
To see how fortune is disposed to us;
For, as he writes, there is no quailing now,
40   Because the King is certainly possessed°   *informed*
Of all our purposes. What say you to it?
WORCESTER   Your father's sickness is a maim to us.
HOTSPUR   A perilous gash, a very limb lopped off.
And yet, in faith, it is not. His present want°   *absence*
45   Seems more than we shall find it. Were it good
To set° the exact wealth of all our states°   *stake / resources*
All at one cast,° to set so rich a main[1]   *throw of the dice*
On the nice hazard° of one doubtful hour?   *precarious chance*
It were not good, for therein should we read
50   The very bottom and the sole[2] of hope,
The very list,° the very utmost bound,   *limit*
Of all our fortunes.
DOUGLAS   Faith, and so we should, where now remains
A sweet reversion°—we may boldly spend   *future inheritance*
55   Upon the hope of what is to come in.
A comfort of retirement[3] lives in this.
HOTSPUR   A rendezvous, a home to fly unto,
If that the devil and mischance look big°   *threateningly*
Upon the maidenhead° of our affairs.   *virgin state; start*
60 WORCESTER   But yet I would your father had been here.
The quality and hair° of our attempt   *character*
Brooks° no division. It will be thought   *Tolerates*
By some that know not why he is away
That wisdom, loyalty, and mere° dislike   *absolute*
65   Of our proceedings kept the Earl from hence;
And think how such an apprehension
May turn the tide of fearful faction,°   *timid support*
And breed a kind of question in our cause.
For, well you know, we of the off'ring° side   *challenging*
70   Must keep aloof from strict arbitrement,°   *rigorous judgment*
And stop all sight-holes, every loop° from whence   *loophole*
The eye of reason may pry in upon us.
This absence of your father's draws° a curtain   *opens*
That shows the ignorant a kind of fear
Before not dreamt of.
75 HOTSPUR   You strain too far.
I rather of his absence make this use:
It lends a lustre, and more great opinion,°   *prestige*
A larger dare° to our great enterprise,   *daring*
Than if the Earl were here; for men must think
80   If we without his help can make a head°   *raise an army*
To push against a kingdom, with his help
We shall o'erturn it topsy-turvy down.
Yet° all goes well, yet all our joints° are whole.   *So far / limbs*

---

1. A stake in gambling; an army.   3. Refuge to which one can retreat.
2. Undersurface (as of a shoe), with a pun on "soul."

DOUGLAS   As heart can think, there is not such a word
85   Spoke of in Scotland as this term of fear.
Enter Sir Richard VERNON
HOTSPUR   My cousin Vernon! Welcome, by my soul!
VERNON   Pray God my news be worth a welcome, lord.
     The Earl of Westmorland, seven thousand strong,
     Is marching hitherwards; with him Prince John.
HOTSPUR   No harm. What more?
90 VERNON   And further I have learned
     The King himself in person is set forth,
     Or hitherwards intended speedily,
     With strong and mighty preparation
HOTSPUR   He shall be welcome too. Where is his son,
95   The nimble-footed madcap Prince of Wales,
     And his comrades that daffed° the world aside   *tossed*
     And bid it pass?
VERNON   All furnished,° all in arms,   *equipped*
     All plumed like ostriches,[4] that with the wind
     [   ]
100   Baiting° like eagles having lately bathed,   *Beating their wings*
     Glittering in golden coats like images,°   *gilded statues*
     As full of spirit as the month of May,
     And gorgeous as the sun at midsummer;
     Wanton° as youthful goats, wild as young bulls   *Frisky*
105   I saw young Harry with his beaver° on,   *visor; helmet*
     His cuishes° on his thighs, gallantly armed,   *armor for the thighs*
     Rise from the ground like feathered Mercury,[5]
     And vaulted with such ease into his seat
     As if an angel dropped down from the clouds
110   To turn and wind° a fiery Pegasus,[6]   *wheel about*
     And witch° the world with noble horsemanship.   *bewitch*
HOTSPUR   No more, no more! Worse than the sun in March,
     This praise doth nourish agues.[7] Let them come!
     They come like sacrifices in their trim,°   *fine trappings*
115   And to the fire-eyed maid of smoky war°   *Bellona, goddess of war*
     All hot and bleeding will we offer them.
     The mailèd° Mars shall on his altar sit   *dressed in armor*
     Up to the ears in blood. I am on fire
     To hear this rich reprisal° is so nigh,   *prize*
120   And yet not ours! Come, let me taste° my horse,   *test; try*
     Who is to bear me like a thunderbolt
     Against the bosom of the Prince of Wales.
     Harry to Harry shall, hot horse to horse,
     Meet and ne'er part till one drop down a corpse.
     O, that Glyndŵr were come!
125 VERNON   There is more news.
     I learned in Worcester, as I rode along,
     He cannot draw° his power this fourteen days.   *assemble*
DOUGLAS   That's the worst tidings that I hear of yet.

---

4. Some editors follow Q in printing "estridges" (goshawks, a kind of hawk) here. Various emendations have been proposed for this and the following lines. The Oxford editors assume a line has been lost, as the brackets indicate.
5. The Roman messenger of the gods, often repre-sented as a young man with winged sandals or a winged hat.
6. A winged horse of classical myth.
7. The March sun was popularly imagined as warm enough to kindle feverish diseases ("agues") without being strong enough to dispel them.

WORCESTER   Ay, by my faith, that bears a frosty sound.

130 HOTSPUR   What may the King's whole battle° reach unto?   *army*
VERNON   To thirty thousand.
HOTSPUR   Forty let it be.
My father and Glyndŵr being both away,
The powers° of us may serve so great a day.   *armies*
Come, let us take a muster speedily.
135 Doomsday is near: die all, die merrily.
DOUGLAS   Talk not of dying; I am out of° fear   *free from*
Of death or death's hand for this one half year.   *Exeunt*

4.2
Enter FALSTAFF *and* BARDOLPH

FALSTAFF   Bardolph, get thee before to Coventry; fill me a bottle of sack. Our soldiers shall march through. We'll to Sutton
Coldfield¹ tonight.
BARDOLPH   Will you give me money, captain?
5 FALSTAFF   Lay out,° lay out.   *Use your own*
BARDOLPH   This bottle makes an angel.²
FALSTAFF   [*giving* BARDOLPH *money*]   An if° it do, take it for thy   *An if = If*
labour; an if it make twenty, take them all; I'll answer the
coinage.³ Bid my lieutenant Peto meet me at town's end.
10 BARDOLPH   I will, captain. Farewell.   *Exit*
FALSTAFF   If I be not ashamed of my soldiers, I am a soused
gurnet.° I have misused the King's press⁴ damnably. I have got   *a pickled fish*
in exchange of one hundred and fifty soldiers three hundred
and odd pounds. I press me° none but good householders, yeo-   *I draft*
15 men's sons, enquire me out contracted° bachelors, such as had   *engaged to be wed*
been asked twice on the banns,⁵ such a commodity° of warm   *quantity*
slaves⁶ as had as lief° hear the devil as a drum, such as fear the   *willingly*
report of a caliver° worse than a struck° fowl or a hurt wild   *musket / wounded*
duck. I pressed me none but such toasts and butter,° with hearts   *such weaklings*
20 in their bellies no bigger than pins' heads, and they have
bought out their services;⁷ and now my whole charge consists
of ensigns, corporals, lieutenants, gentlemen of companies⁸—
slaves as ragged as Lazarus⁹ in the painted cloth,° where the   *cheap wall hangings*
glutton's dogs licked his sores—and such as indeed were never
25 soldiers, but discarded unjust° servingmen, younger sons to   *dishonest*
younger brothers, revolted° tapsters, and ostlers trade-fallen,° *runaway / out of work*
the cankers° of a calm world and a long peace, ten times more   *cankerworms; parasites*
dishonourable-ragged than an old feazed ensign;° and such   *tattered flag*
have I to fill up the rooms of them as° have bought out their   *places of those who*
30 services, that you would think that I had a hundred and fifty
tattered prodigals lately come from swine-keeping, from eating
draff and husks.¹ A mad fellow met me on the way and told me
I had unloaded all the gibbets° and pressed the dead bodies.   *gallows*

4.2 Location: The road approaching Coventry.
1. Town about 20 miles northwest of Coventry in Warwickshire.
2. Brings my outlay to several shillings (an "angel").
Falstaff retorts by punning on "makes" as meaning
"earns a profit of."
3. I'll be responsible for the money coined.
4. Commission for conscripting soldiers.
5. Proclamations made on three consecutive Sundays
affirming one's intent to marry.

6. Well-off or comfort-loving cowards.
7. They have paid me to excuse them from military service.
8. Gentlemen volunteers who were not officers.
9. For the story of Lazarus and the rich man, see note
to 3.3.28.
1. Alluding to the biblical parable of the prodigal son,
who longs to eat swill ("draff") and corn husks meant
for pigs after he has squandered his inheritance in
debauchery (see Luke 15:11–16).

No eye hath seen such scarecrows. I'll not march through Cov-
35 entry with them, that's flat. Nay, and the villains march wide
betwixt the legs, as if they had gyves° on, for indeed I had the   *fetters*
most of them out of prison. There's not a shirt and a half in all
my company; and the half-shirt is two napkins tacked together
and thrown over the shoulders like a herald's coat without
40 sleeves; and the shirt, to say the truth, stolen from my host° at   *innkeeper*
Saint Albans, or the red-nose innkeeper of Daventry.[2] But that's
all one; they'll find linen enough on every hedge.[3]

    Enter PRINCE [HARRY] *and the Lord[Earl] of* WESTMOR-
    LAND

PRINCE HARRY   How now, blown Jack?[4] How now, quilt?

FALSTAFF   What, Hal! How now, mad wag? What a devil dost
45 thou in Warwickshire? My good lord of Westmorland, I cry
you mercy!° I thought your honour had already been at   *I beg your pardon*
Shrewsbury.

WESTMORLAND   Faith, Sir John, 'tis more than time that I were
there, and you too; but my powers are there already. The King,
50 I can tell you, looks for us all. We must away° all night.   *must march*

FALSTAFF   Tut, never fear° me. I am as vigilant as a cat to steal   *worry about*
cream.

PRINCE HARRY   I think to steal cream indeed, for thy theft hath
already made thee butter.[5] But tell me, Jack, whose fellows are
55 these that come after?

FALSTAFF   Mine, Hal, mine.

PRINCE HARRY   I did never see such pitiful rascals.

FALSTAFF   Tut, tut, good enough to toss,[6] food for powder,° food   *cannon fodder*
for powder. They'll fill a pit as well as better. Tush, man, mor-
60 tal men, mortal men.

WESTMORLAND   Ay, but Sir John, methinks they are exceeding
poor and bare,° too beggarly.   *threadbare*

FALSTAFF   Faith, for their poverty, I know not where they had
that, and for their bareness, I am sure they never learned that
65 of me.

PRINCE HARRY   No, I'll be sworn, unless you call three fingers in
the ribs[7] bare. But sirrah, make haste. Percy is already in the
field.   *Exit*

FALSTAFF   What, is the King encamped?

70 WESTMORLAND   He is, Sir John. I fear we shall stay too long.
                                        [Exit]

FALSTAFF   Well, to the latter end of a fray
    And the beginning of a feast
    Fits a dull fighter and a keen guest.   *Exit*

4.3

    Enter HOTSPUR, [*the Earls of*] WORCESTER [*and*] DOUG-
    LAS, *and* [*Sir Richard*] VERNON

HOTSPUR   We'll fight with him tonight.

WORCESTER   It may not be.

---

2. Saint Albans is a town north of London, Daventry a town southeast of Coventry.
3. Where laundresses set it out to dry.
4. Punning on "jack" as referring to what many Elizabethan soldiers wore: a quilted jacket covered with leather or cloth and worn over iron plates. *blown:* swollen; short-winded.

5. The riches ("cream") you have stolen have made you rich, or turned you into fat.
6. Good enough to be tossed on pikes.
7. Three fingers of fat over the ribs. A finger was a measure of three-quarters of an inch.
4.3 Location: The rebels' camp, Shrewsbury.

DOUGLAS   You give him then advantage.

VERNON   Not a whit.

HOTSPUR   Why say you so? Looks he not for supply?°   *reinforcements*

VERNON   So do we.

HOTSPUR   His is certain; ours is doubtful.

5   WORCESTER   Good cousin, be advised. Stir not tonight.

VERNON [*to* HOTSPUR]   Do not, my lord.

DOUGLAS   You do not counsel well.
   You speak it out of fear and cold heart.

VERNON   Do me no slander, Douglas. By my life—
   And I dare well maintain it with my life—

10   If well-respected° honour bid me on,   *well-considered*
   I hold as little counsel with weak fear
   As you, my lord, or any Scot that this day lives.
   Let it be seen tomorrow in the battle
   Which of us fears.

15   DOUGLAS   Yea, or tonight.

VERNON   Content.

HOTSPUR   Tonight, say I.

VERNON   Come, come, it may not be. I wonder much,
   Being men of such great leading° as you are,   *leadership*

20   That you foresee not what impediments
   Drag back our expedition.° Certain horse°   *rapid progress / cavalry*
   Of my cousin Vernon's are not yet come up.
   Your uncle Worcester's horse came but today,
   And now their pride° and mettle is asleep,   *spirit*

25   Their courage with hard labour tame and dull,
   That not a horse is half the half himself.

HOTSPUR   So are the horses of the enemy
   In general journey-bated° and brought low.   *weary from travel*
   The better part of ours are full of rest.

30   WORCESTER   The number of the King exceedeth our.
   For God's sake, cousin, stay° till all come in.   *wait*

                    The trumpet sounds a parley[1] [*within*]. *Enter*
                    Sir Walter BLUNT

BLUNT   I come with gracious offers from the King,
   If you vouchsafe me hearing and respect.

HOTSPUR   Welcome, Sir Walter Blunt; and would to God

35   You were of our determination.°   *on our side*
   Some of us love you well, and even those some°   *those same persons*
   Envy your great deservings and good name,
   Because you are not of our quality,°   *party*
   But stand against us like an enemy.

40   BLUNT   And God defend° but still I should stand so,   *forbid*
   So long as out of limit° and true rule   *bounds of allegiance*
   You stand against anointed majesty.
   But to my charge. The King hath sent to know
   The nature of your griefs,° and whereupon   *grievances*

45   You conjure from the breast of civil peace
   Such bold hostility, teaching his duteous land
   Audacious cruelty. If that the King
   Have any way your good deserts forgot,
   Which he confesseth to be manifold,

---

1. Summons to a conference with the enemy.

50 He bids you name your griefs, and with all speed
   You shall have your desires, with interest,
   And pardon absolute for yourself and these
   Herein misled by your suggestion.°   *instigation*
   HOTSPUR   The King is kind, and well we know the King
55 Knows at what time to promise, when to pay.
   My father and my uncle and myself
   Did give him that same royalty he wears;
   And when he was not six-and-twenty strong,
   Sick in the world's regard, wretched and low,
60 A poor unminded° outlaw sneaking home,   *insignificant*
   My father gave him welcome to the shore;
   And when he heard him swear and vow to God
   He came but to be Duke of Lancaster,
   To sue his livery,[2] and beg his peace
65 With tears of innocency and terms of zeal,
   My father, in kind heart and pity moved,
   Swore him assistance, and performed it too.
   Now when the lords and barons of the realm
   Perceived Northumberland did lean to him,
70 The more and less came in with cap and knee,[3]
   Met him in boroughs, cities, villages,
   Attended him on bridges, stood in lanes,[4]
   Laid gifts before him, proffered him their oaths,
   Gave him their heirs as pages, followed him,
75 Even at the heels, in golden° multitudes.   *resplendent*
   He presently, as greatness knows itself,°   *recognizes its power*
   Steps me° a little higher than his vow   *Steps*
   Made to my father while his blood° was poor   *spirit*
   Upon the naked shore at Ravenspurgh,
80 And now forsooth takes on him to reform
   Some certain edicts and some strait° decrees   *strict*
   That lie too heavy on the commonwealth,
   Cries out upon abuses, seems to weep
   Over his country's wrongs; and by this face,°   *outward show*
85 This seeming brow of justice, did he win
   The hearts of all that he did angle for;
   Proceeded further, cut me off° the heads   *cut off*
   Of all the favourites that the absent King
   In deputation° left behind him here   *As deputies*
90 When he was personal° in the Irish war.   *engaged in person*
   BLUNT   Tut, I came not to hear this.
   HOTSPUR   Then to the point.
   In short time after, he deposed the King,
   Soon after that deprived him of his life,
   And in the neck of that tasked° the whole state;   *And immediately taxed*
95 To make that worse, suffered his kinsman March[5]—
   Who is, if every owner were well placed,[6]
   Indeed his king—to be engaged° in Wales,   *held hostage*
   There without ransom to lie forfeited;°   *unredeemed*

2. To plead for the restitution of his lands (which Richard II had seized when John of Gaunt, Bolingbroke's father, died).
3. Those of both high and low social status deferentially presented themselves (with cap in hand and bended knee).
4. Stood in rows along the roadways.
5. The Earl of March. For his claim to the throne, see note to 1.3.79.
6. If everyone had possessions according to his entitlement.

Disgraced me in my happy victories,
100　Sought to entrap me by intelligence,°　　　　　　　　　*spying*
Rated° mine uncle from the Council-board,　　　　　　*Drove away*
In rage dismissed my father from the court,
Broke oath on oath, committed wrong on wrong,
And in conclusion drove us to seek out
105　This head of safety,[7] and withal° to pry　　　　　　*also*
Into his title, the which we find
Too indirect° for long continuance.　　　　　　　　*irregular*
BLUNT　Shall I return this answer to the King?
HOTSPUR　Not so, Sir Walter. We'll withdraw awhile.
110　Go to the King, and let there be impawned°　　　　*pledged*
Some surety for a safe return again;
And in the morning early shall mine uncle
Bring him our purposes. And so, farewell.
BLUNT　I would you would accept of grace and love.
HOTSPUR　And maybe so we shall.
115　BLUNT　　　　　　　　　　Pray God you do.
Exeunt [HOTSPUR, WORCESTER, DOUGLAS, *and*
VERNON *at one door,* BLUNT *at another door*]

4.4

Enter the ARCHBISHOP *of York, and* SIR MICHAEL
ARCHBISHOP [*giving letters*]　Hie, good Sir Michael, bear this sealèd brief°　*dispatch*
With wingèd haste to the Lord Marshal,
This to my cousin Scrope, and all the rest
To whom they are directed. If you knew
5　How much they do import, you would make haste.
SIR MICHAEL　My good lord,
I guess their tenor.
ARCHBISHOP　　　　　Like enough you do.
Tomorrow, good Sir Michael, is a day
Wherein the fortune of ten thousand men
10　Must bide the touch;° for, sir, at Shrewsbury,　　　*stand the test*
As I am truly given to understand,
The King with mighty and quick-raisèd power
Meets with Lord Harry. And I fear, Sir Michael,
What with the sickness of Northumberland,
15　Whose power was in the first proportion,°　　　　*magnitude*
And what with Owain Glyndŵr's absence thence,
Who with them was a rated sinew[1] too,
And comes not in, overruled by prophecies,
I fear the power of Percy is too weak
20　To wage an instant° trial with the King.　　　　　*immediate*
SIR MICHAEL　Why, my good lord, you need not fear; there is Douglas
And Lord Mortimer.
ARCHBISHOP　　　　No, Mortimer is not there.
SIR MICHAEL　But there is Mordake, Vernon, Lord Harry Percy;
And there is my lord of Worcester, and a head°　　*troop*
25　Of gallant warriors, noble gentlemen.
ARCHBISHOP　And so there is; but yet the King hath drawn
The special head of all the land together—

---

7. That is, safety in these gathered forces.　　　　1. A much-valued source of strength.
4.4 Location: The Archbishop's palace, York.

The Prince of Wales, Lord John of Lancaster,
The noble Westmorland, and warlike Blunt,
30 And many more corrivals,° and dear° men   *associates / noble*
Of estimation° and command in arms.   *reputation*
SIR MICHAEL   Doubt not, my lord, they shall be well opposed.
ARCHBISHOP   I hope no less, yet needful 'tis to fear;
And to prevent the worst, Sir Michael, speed.
35 For if Lord Percy thrive not, ere the King
Dismiss his power he means to visit us,
For he hath heard of our confederacy,
And 'tis but wisdom to make strong against him;
Therefore make haste. I must go write again
40 To other friends; and so farewell, Sir Michael.   *Exeunt [severally]*

5.1

Enter KING [HENRY], PRINCE [HARRY], *Lord* JOHN OF LAN-
CASTER, [*the*] *Earl of* WESTMORLAND, *Sir Walter* BLUNT,
and FALSTAFF

KING HENRY   How bloodily the sun begins to peer
Above yon bulky hill! The day looks pale
At his distemp'rature.°   *sick appearance*
PRINCE HARRY   The southern wind
Doth play the trumpet to his° purposes,   *(the sun's)*
5 And by his hollow whistling in the leaves
Foretells a tempest and a blust'ring day.
KING HENRY   Then with the losers let it sympathize,°   *accord*
For nothing can seem foul to those that win.
*The trumpet sounds [a parley within]. Enter [the Earl
of]* WORCESTER [*and Sir Richard* VERNON][1]
How now, my lord of Worcester? 'Tis not well
10 That you and I should meet upon such terms
As now we meet. You have deceived our trust,
And made us doff our easy robes of peace
To crush our old limbs in ungentle steel.
This is not well, my lord, this is not well.
15 What say you to it? Will you again unknit
This churlish knot of all-abhorrèd war,
And move in that obedient orb[2] again
Where you did give a fair and natural light,
And be no more an exhaled meteor,[3]
20 A prodigy of fear,° and a portent   *A fearful omen*
Of broachèd mischief° to the unborn times?   *Of evil set flowing*
WORCESTER   Hear me, my liege.
For mine own part, I could be well content
To entertain the lag-end° of my life   *latter end*
25 With quiet hours; for I protest,
I have not sought the day of this dislike.°   *discord*
KING HENRY   You have not sought it? How comes it, then?
FALSTAFF   Rebellion lay in his way, and he found it.

5.1 Location: King Henry's camp at Shrewsbury.
1. Neither Q nor F indicates that Vernon accompanies
Worcester in this scene, but it seems lacking in ceremony
for Worcester to go to King Henry's camp alone. Also, in
the next scene, Worcester discusses with Vernon what the
King has said and whether to inform Hotspur, making it
appear that Vernon was present at this meeting.

2. Orbit. Henry, drawing on a conventional analogy
between social and cosmological order, compares
Worcester to a star or a planet that, in Ptolemaic cos-
mology, should move properly in its sphere (orbit)
around the earth.
3. Meteors were thought to be made of gas exhaled by
the sun and were considered bad omens.

PRINCE HARRY   Peace, chewet,° peace!   *jackdaw; chatterer*

30 WORCESTER [*to the* KING]   It pleased your majesty to turn your looks

   Of favour from myself and all our house;

   And yet I must remember° you, my lord,   *remind*

   We were the first and dearest of your friends.

   For you my staff of office did I break

35 In Richard's time, and posted° day and night   *rode swiftly*

   To meet you on the way and kiss your hand

   When yet you were in place° and in account°   *social status / esteem*

   Nothing so strong and fortunate as I.

   It was myself, my brother, and his son

40 That brought you home, and boldly did outdare

   The dangers of the time. You swore to us,

   And you did swear that oath at Doncaster,

   That you did nothing purpose° 'gainst the state,   *intend*

   Nor claim no further than your new-fall'n right,[4]

45 The seat° of Gaunt, dukedom of Lancaster.   *estate*

   To this we swore our aid, but in short space

   It rained down fortune show'ring on your head,

   And such a flood of greatness fell on you,

   What with our help, what with the absent King,

50 What with the injuries° of a wanton° time,   *evils / lawless*

   The seeming sufferances° that you had borne,   *wrongs*

   And the contrarious° winds that held the King   *adverse*

   So long in his unlucky Irish wars

   That all in England did repute him dead;

55 And from this swarm of fair advantages

   You took occasion to be quickly wooed

   To gripe° the general sway into your hand,   *seize*

   Forgot your oath to us at Doncaster,

   And being fed by us, you used us so

60 As that ungentle gull,° the cuckoo's bird,   *rude young bird*

   Useth the sparrow[5]—did oppress our nest,

   Grew by our feeding to so great a bulk

   That even our love° durst not come near your sight *we who loved you*

   For fear of swallowing.° But with nimble wing   *being swallowed*

65 We were enforced for safety' sake to fly

   Out of your sight, and raise this present head,

   Whereby we stand opposèd° by such means   *in opposition to you*

   As you yourself have forged against yourself,

   By unkind usage, dangerous° countenance,   *threatening*

70 And violation of all faith and troth

   Sworn to us in your younger enterprise.

   KING HENRY   These things indeed you have articulate,° *expressed*

   Proclaimed at market crosses,[6] read in churches,

   To face° the garment of rebellion   *adorn*

75 With some fine colour° that may please the eye   *hue; pretext*

   Of fickle changelings° and poor discontents,   *turncoats*

   Which gape and rub the elbow[7] at the news

   Of hurly-burly innovation;°   *rebellion*

---

4. The right newly descended to you (upon the death of your father).

5. The female cuckoo lays its eggs in the nests of smaller birds such as the sparrow, who raises the cuckoo's young until they grow so large they threaten the sparrow and her nest.

6. Crosses set up in marketplaces, often atop polygonal structures with open archways on each of the sides and vaulted within.

7. And hug themselves with crossed arms (conventional expression of delight).

And never yet did insurrection want°   *lack*
80   Such water-colours to impaint his cause,
      Nor moody beggars starving for a time
      Of pell-mell° havoc and confusion.   *chaotic*
      PRINCE HARRY   In both our armies there is many a soul
      Shall pay full dearly for this encounter
85   If once they join in trial.° Tell your nephew   *combat*
      The Prince of Wales doth join with all the world
      In praise of Henry Percy. By my hopes,
      This present enterprise set off his head,°   *not counted against him*
      I do not think a braver gentleman,
90   More active-valiant or more valiant-young,
      More daring, or more bold, is now alive
      To grace this latter age with noble deeds.
      For my part, I may speak it to my shame,
      I have a truant been to chivalry;
95   And so I hear he doth account me too.
      Yet this, before my father's majesty:
      I am content that he shall take the odds°   *have the advantage*
      Of his great name and estimation,°   *reputation*
      And will, to save the blood on either side,
100   Try fortune with him in a single fight.
      KING HENRY   And, Prince of Wales, so dare we venture thee,
      Albeit° considerations infinite   *Were it not that*
      Do make against it. No, good Worcester, no.
      We love our people well; even those we love
105   That are misled upon your cousin's° part;   *kinsman's*
      And will they take the offer of our grace,°   *mercy*
      Both he and they and you, yea, every man
      Shall be my friend again, and I'll be his.
      So tell your cousin, and bring me word
110   What he will do. But if he will not yield,
      Rebuke and dread correction wait on° us,   *serve*
      And they shall do their office. So be gone.
      We will not now be troubled with reply.
      We offer fair; take it advisedly.
                          Exeunt WORCESTER [*and* VERNON]
115   PRINCE HARRY   It will not be accepted, on my life.
      The Douglas and the Hotspur both together
      Are confident against the world in arms.
      KING HENRY   Hence, therefore, every leader to his charge,
      For on their answer will we set on them,
120   And God befriend us as our cause is just!
                   Exeunt. Manent° *Prince* [HARRY] *and* FALSTAFF   *Remain*
      FALSTAFF   Hal, if thou see me down in the battle, and bestride
      me,° so.° 'Tis a point of friendship.   *stand over me / good*
      PRINCE HARRY   Nothing but a colossus⁸ can do thee that friend-
      ship. Say thy prayers, and farewell.
125   FALSTAFF   I would 'twere bed-time, Hal, and all well.
      PRINCE HARRY   Why, thou owest God a death.   [*Exit*]
      FALSTAFF   'Tis not due yet. I would be loath to pay him before
      his day. What need I be so forward with him that calls not on
      me? Well, 'tis no matter; honour pricks° me on. Yea, but how   *spurs*

8. Referring to a massive statue of Apollo that purportedly stood over the entrance to the harbor in ancient Rhodes and was referred to as the Colossus of Rhodes.

130 if honour prick me off[9] when I come on? How then? Can honour set-to° a leg? No. Or an arm? No. Or take away the grief
of a wound? No. Honour hath no skill in surgery, then? No.
What is honour? A word. What is in that word 'honour'? What
is that 'honour'? Air. A trim reckoning!° Who hath it? He that
135 died o'Wednesday. Doth he feel it? No. Doth he hear it? No.
'Tis insensible[1] then? Yea, to the dead. But will it not live with
the living? No. Why? Detraction° will not suffer° it. Therefore
I'll none of it. Honour is a mere scutcheon.[2] And so ends my
catechism.   *Exit*

mend

A nice summing up

Slander / allow

5.2

Enter [the Earl of] WORCESTER and Sir Richard
VERNON
WORCESTER   O no, my nephew must not know, Sir Richard,
   The liberal and kind offer of the king.
VERNON   'Twere best he did.
WORCESTER   Then are we all undone.
   It is not possible, it cannot be,
5   The King should keep his word in loving us.
   He will suspect us still,° and find a time
   To punish this offence in other faults.
   Supposition all our lives shall be stuck full of eyes,[1]
   For treason is but trusted like the fox,
10   Who, ne'er so° tame, so cherished, and locked up,
   Will have a wild trick of his ancestors.
   Look how we can, or° sad or merrily,
   Interpretation will misquote our looks,
   And we shall feed like oxen at a stall,
15   The better cherished still the nearer death.
   My nephew's trespass may be well forgot;
   It hath the excuse of youth and heat of blood,
   And an adopted name of privilege[2]—
   A hare-brained Hotspur, governed by a spleen.°
20   All his offences live upon my head,
   And on his father's. We did train° him on,
   And, his corruption being ta'en from us,
   We as the spring° of all shall pay for all.
   Therefore, good cousin, let not Harry know
25   In any case the offer of the King.
VERNON   Deliver what you will; I'll say 'tis so.
        Enter HOTSPUR [and the Earl of DOUGLAS]
   Here comes your cousin.
HOTSPUR   My uncle is returned.
   Deliver up[3] my Lord of Westmorland.
   Uncle, what news?
30 WORCESTER   The King will bid you battle presently.
DOUGLAS   Defy him by the Lord of Westmorland.
HOTSPUR   Lord Douglas, go you and tell him so.

always

no matter how

whether

hot temper

lead

source

---

9. Selects me to die; marks me off the list.
1. Imperceptible to the senses.
2. Heraldic shield exhibited at funerals displaying the deceased person's coat of arms.
5.2 Location: The rebels' camp.
1. The King's suspicion will cause him constantly to spy on us. Worcester is referring to an allegorical rep-

resentation of Suspicion dressed in a coat of eyes or to secret agents similar to those whom Elizabeth's government maintained.
2. A nickname, "Hotspur," which may excuse his rashness.
3. Release (as the hostage for the safe return of Worcester and Vernon).

DOUGLAS Marry, and shall, and very willingly.   *Exit*

WORCESTER There is no seeming° mercy in the King.   *semblance of*

35 HOTSPUR Did you beg any? God forbid!

WORCESTER I told him gently of our grievances,

  Of his oath-breaking, which he mended thus:

  By now forswearing that he is forsworn.

  He calls us 'rebels', 'traitors', and will scourge

40 With haughty arms this hateful name in us.

     Enter [the Earl of] DOUGLAS

DOUGLAS Arm, gentlemen, to arms, for I have thrown

  A brave° defiance in King Henry's teeth—   *proud*

  And Westmorland that was engaged° did bear it—   *held as hostage*

  Which cannot choose but bring him quickly on.

WORCESTER *[to* HOTSPUR*]* The Prince of Wales stepped forth

45   before the King

  And, nephew, challenged you to single fight.

HOTSPUR O, would the quarrel lay upon our heads,

  And that no man might draw short breath today

  But I and Harry Monmouth![4] Tell me, tell me,

50 How showed his tasking?° Seemed it in contempt?   *challenge*

VERNON No, by my soul, I never in my life

  Did hear a challenge urged more modestly,

  Unless a brother should a brother dare

  To gentle° exercise and proof of arms.[5]   *noble*

55 He gave you all the duties of° a man,   *respect due to*

  Trimmed up your praises[6] with a princely tongue,

  Spoke your deservings like a chronicle,

  Making you ever better than his praise

  By still° dispraising praise valued with you;[7]   *constantly*

60 And, which became him like a prince indeed,

  He made a blushing cital° of himself,   *mention*

  And chid his truant youth with such a grace

  As if he mastered there a double spirit

  Of teaching and of learning instantly.°   *simultaneously*

65 There did he pause; but let me tell the world,

  If he outlive the envy° of this day,   *malice*

  England did never owe° so sweet a hope,   *own*

  So much misconstrued in his wantonness.°   *self-indulgence*

HOTSPUR Cousin, I think thou art enamourèd

70 On° his follies. Never did I hear   *Of*

  Of any prince so wild a liberty.°   *such unrestrained license*

  But be he as he will, yet once ere night

  I will embrace him with a soldier's arm,

  That he shall shrink under my courtesy.

75 Arm, arm, with speed! And fellows, soldiers, friends,

  Better consider what you have to do

  Than I, that have not well the gift of tongue,

  Can lift your blood[8] up with persuasion.

     Enter a MESSENGER

MESSENGER My lord, here are letters for you.

80 HOTSPUR I cannot read them now.   *[Exit* MESSENGER*]*

---

4. Harry of Monmouth, the town in Wales where the Prince was born.
5. Trial of skill at weapons.
6. Embellished his praises of you.

7. As measured against you (because your merit exceeds all praise).
8. Rebelliousness; self-indulgence.

O gentlemen, the time of life is short.
To spend that shortness basely were too long
If life did ride upon a dial's point,
Still ending at the arrival of an hour.⁹
85   An if we live, we live to tread on kings;
If die, brave death when princes die with us!
Now for our consciences: the arms are fair
When the intent of bearing them is just.

        Enter another MESSENGER

MESSENGER   My lord, prepare; the King comes on apace.   [*Exit*]
90   HOTSPUR   I thank him that he cuts me from my tale,
For I profess not° talking, only this: *am not skilled at*
Let each man do his best. And here draw I
A sword whose temper° I intend to stain   *tempered steel*
With the best blood that I can meet withal
95   In the adventure of this perilous day.
Now *Esperance!*¹ Percy! And set on!
Sound all the lofty instruments of war,
And by that music let us all embrace,
For, heaven to earth,² some of us never shall
100   A second time do such a courtesy.

        The trumpets sound. Here they embrace. [*Exeunt*]

5.3

KING [HENRY] *enters with his power. Alarum*¹ [*and exeunt*] *to the battle. Then enter* [*the Earl of*] DOUGLAS,
and Sir Walter BLUNT [*disguised as the* KING]

BLUNT   What is thy name, that in the battle thus
Thou crossest me? What honour dost thou seek
Upon my head?
DOUGLAS   Know then my name is Douglas,
And I do haunt thee in the battle thus
5   Because some tell me that thou art a king.
BLUNT   They tell thee true.
DOUGLAS   The Lord of Stafford dear today hath bought
Thy likeness,² for instead of thee, King Harry,
This sword hath ended him. So shall it thee,
10   Unless thou yield thee as my prisoner.
BLUNT   I was not born a yielder, thou proud Scot,
And thou shalt find a king that will revenge
Lord Stafford's death.

        They fight. DOUGLAS *kills* BLUNT. *Then enter* HOTSPUR

HOTSPUR   O Douglas, hadst thou fought at Holmedon thus,
15   I never had triumphed upon a Scot.
DOUGLAS   All's done, all's won: here breathless lies the King.
HOTSPUR   Where?
DOUGLAS   Here.
HOTSPUR   This, Douglas? No, I know this face full well.
20   A gallant knight he was; his name was Blunt—

---

9. *To spend . . . hour*: that is, If life only lasted an hour
(*dial's point*: hand of a clock), it would still be too long
if it were basely spent.
1. Hope (the Percy motto; see note to 2.4.66).
2. The odds are as great as the distance from heaven to
earth.

5.3 Location: The remaining scenes take place on the
battlefield at Shrewsbury.
1. A call to arms, usually sounded on drum or trumpets.
2. *hath . . . likeness*: has paid for impersonating you;
has paid for his resemblance to you.

Semblably furnished° like the King himself.   *Similarly equipped*

DOUGLAS [*to Blunt's body*]   A fool go with thy soul,³ whither it goes!

A borrowed title hast thou bought too dear.

Why didst thou tell me that thou wert a king?

25   HOTSPUR   The king hath many marching in his coats.⁴

DOUGLAS   Now by my sword, I will kill all his coats.

I'll murder all his wardrobe, piece by piece,

Until I meet the King.

HOTSPUR   Up and away!

Our soldiers stand full fairly for the day.⁵

Exeunt [leaving Blunt's body]

Alarum. Enter FALSTAFF

30   FALSTAFF   Though I could scape shot-free⁶ at London, I fear

the shot here. Here's no scoring⁷ but upon the pate.—Soft,

who are you?— Sir Walter Blunt. There's honour for you!

Here's no vanity. I am as hot as molten lead, and as heavy too.

God keep lead out of me; I need no more weight than mine

35   own bowels. I have led my ragamuffins where they are pep-

pered; there's not three of my hundred and fifty left alive, and

they are for the town's end,⁸ to beg during life.

Enter PRINCE [HARRY]

But who comes here?

PRINCE HARRY   What, stand'st thou idle here? Lend me thy sword.

40   Many a noble man lies stark and stiff

Under the hoofs of vaunting enemies,

Whose deaths as yet are unrevenged. I prithee

Lend me thy sword.

FALSTAFF   O Hal, I prithee give me leave to breathe awhile.

45   Turk Gregory⁹ never did such deeds in arms

As I have done this day. I have paid° Percy,   *settled with (killed)*

I have made him sure.¹

PRINCE HARRY   He is indeed,

And living to kill thee. I prithee

Lend me thy sword.

FALSTAFF   Nay, before God, Hal,

50   If Percy be alive thou gett'st not my sword;

But take my pistol if thou wilt.

PRINCE HARRY   Give it me. What, is it in the case?

FALSTAFF   Ay, Hal;

'Tis hot, 'tis hot. There's that will sack a city.

The PRINCE *draws it out, and finds it to be a bottle of
sack*

PRINCE HARRY   What, is it a time to jest and dally now?

He throws the bottle at him. Exit

55   FALSTAFF   Well, if Percy be alive, I'll pierce him. If he do come

in my way, so; if he do not, if I come in his willingly, let him

make a carbonado² of me. I like not such grinning° honour as   *menacing*

3. May the title of "fool" go with your soul (for impersonating the King).
4. In his surcoat, or loose robes of rich material,
embroidered with the royal coat of arms and worn over
armor.
5. Our soldiers look as though they will win the day.
6. Escape without paying the tavern bill ("shot"), with
a pun in the following line on "shot" as ammunition
(projectiles, cannon shot, etc.).
7. Recording of debts by means of "scores," or notches

on a board (customary in taverns); wounding or cutting.
8. By the town gates, where people often begged.
9. A conflation of the idea of the Turk, taken to be a
cruel and fierce fighter and an enemy of Protestant England, and either Pope Gregory VII or Pope Gregory
XIII, both regarded as violent and cruel by Protestant
writers.
1. I have killed him; but the Prince takes "sure" to
mean "secure."
2. Meat slashed to grill.

Sir Walter hath. Give me life, which if I can save, so; if not, honour comes unlooked for, and there's an end.

Exit [with Blunt's body]

5.4

Alarum. Excursions. Enter KING [HENRY], PRINCE
[HARRY, *wounded*], *Lord* JOHN OF LANCASTER, *and* [*the*]
Earl of WESTMORLAND

KING HENRY   I prithee, Harry, withdraw thyself, thou bleed'st too much.
Lord John of Lancaster, go you with him.

JOHN OF LANCASTER   Not I, my lord, unless I did bleed too.

PRINCE HARRY [*to the* KING]   I beseech your majesty, make up,°   go forward
5   Lest your retirement do amaze° your friends.   alarm

KING HENRY   I will do so. My lord of Westmorland,
Lead him to his tent.

WESTMORLAND [*to the* PRINCE]   Come, my lord, I'll lead you to your tent.

PRINCE HARRY   Lead me, my lord? I do not need your help,
10   And God forbid a shallow scratch should drive
The Prince of Wales from such a field as this,
Where stained¹ nobility lies trodden on,
And rebels' arms triumph in massacres.

JOHN OF LANCASTER   We breathe° too long. Come, cousin Westmorland,   rest
15   Our duty this way lies. For God's sake, come.

[*Exeunt* LANCASTER *and* WESTMORLAND]

PRINCE HARRY   By God, thou hast deceived me, Lancaster;
I did not think thee lord of such a spirit.
Before I loved thee as a brother, John,
But now I do respect thee as my soul.

20   KING HENRY   I saw him hold Lord Percy at the point°   sword point
With lustier maintenance° than I did look for   more valiant bearing
Of such an ungrown warrior.

PRINCE HARRY   O, this boy lends mettle to us all!   *Exit*

Enter [the Earl of] DOUGLAS

DOUGLAS   Another king! They grow like Hydra's heads.²
25   I am the Douglas, fatal to all those
That wear those colours on them. What art thou
That counterfeit'st the person of a king?

KING HENRY   The King himself, who, Douglas, grieves at heart
So many of his shadows° thou hast met   likenesses
30   And not the very King. I have two boys
Seek° Percy and thyself about the field;   Who seek
But seeing thou fall'st on me so luckily,
I will assay° thee; and defend thyself.   challenge

DOUGLAS   I fear thou art another counterfeit;
35   And yet, in faith, thou bear'st thee like a king.
But mine° I am sure thou art, whoe'er thou be,   (my prize of war)
And thus I win thee.

They fight. The KING *being in danger, enter* PRINCE
[HARRY]

PRINCE HARRY   Hold up thy head, vile Scot, or thou art like
Never to hold it up again. The spirits

5.4
1. Bloodstained; disgraced by defeat.
2. A monster in classical mythology that grew two

heads whenever one was cut off. The hydra was a common image of political disorder.

40   Of valiant Shirley, Stafford, Blunt, are in my arms.
It is the Prince of Wales that threatens thee,
Who never promiseth but he means to pay.
        They fight. DOUGLAS *flieth*
Cheerly, my lord! How fares your grace?
Sir Nicholas Gawsey hath for succour sent,
45   And so hath Clifton. I'll to Clifton straight.
KING HENRY   Stay and breathe awhile.
Thou hast redeemed thy lost opinion,°   *reputation*
And showed thou mak'st some tender of° my life,   *have some regard for*
In this fair rescue thou hast brought to me.
50   PRINCE HARRY   O God, they did me too much injury
That ever said I hearkened for° your death.   *desired*
If it were so, I might have let alone
The insulting° hand of Douglas over you,   *scornful*
Which would have been as speedy in your end
55   As all the poisonous potions in the world,
And saved the treacherous labour of your son.
KING HENRY   Make up° to Clifton; I'll to Sir Nicholas Gawsey.   *Go forward*
                                                                Exit

        Enter HOTSPUR
HOTSPUR   If I mistake not, thou art Harry Monmouth.
PRINCE HARRY   Thou speak'st as if I would deny my name.
HOTSPUR   My name is Harry Percy.
60   PRINCE HARRY   Why then, I see
A very valiant rebel of the name.
I am the Prince of Wales; and think not, Percy,
To share with me in glory any more.
Two stars keep not their motion in one sphere,[3]
65   Nor can one England brook° a double reign   *endure*
Of Harry Percy and the Prince of Wales.
HOTSPUR   Nor shall it, Harry, for the hour is come
To end the one of us, and would to God
Thy name in arms were now as great as mine.
70   PRINCE HARRY   I'll make it greater ere I part from thee,
And all the budding honours on thy crest°   *helmet; coat of arms*
I'll crop° to make a garland for my head.   *cut*
HOTSPUR   I can no longer brook thy vanities.°   *empty boasts*
        They fight.
        Enter FALSTAFF
FALSTAFF   Well said, Hal! To it, Hal! Nay, you shall find no boy's
75   play here, I can tell you.
        Enter DOUGLAS. *He fighteth with* FALSTAFF, *who falls*
        down as if he were dead. [*Exit* DOUGLAS.] *The* PRINCE
        killeth [HOTSPUR]
HOTSPUR   O Harry, thou hast robbed me of my youth.
I better brook the loss of brittle life
Than those proud titles thou hast won of me.
They wound my thoughts worse than thy sword my flesh.
80   But thoughts, the slaves of life, and life, time's fool,
And time, that takes survey of all the world,
Must have a stop.° O, I could prophesy,   *an end*

---

3. Alluding to the theory that stars moved in concentric spheres around a center. Only one star could occupy a
single sphere.

But that the earthy and cold hand of death
Lies on my tongue. No, Percy, thou art dust,
85 And food for—   [*He dies*]
PRINCE HARRY   For worms, brave Percy. Fare thee well, great heart.
Ill-weaved ambition, how much art thou shrunk!
When that this body did contain a spirit,
A kingdom for it was too small a bound,
90 But now two paces of the vilest earth
Is room enough. This earth that bears thee dead
Bears not alive so stout° a gentleman.   valiant
If thou wert sensible° of courtesy,   conscious
I should not make so dear° a show of zeal;°   heartfelt / emotion
95 But let my favours⁴ hide thy mangled face,
[*He covers Hotspur's face*]
And even in thy behalf I'll thank myself
For doing these fair rites of tenderness.
Adieu, and take thy praise with thee to heaven.
Thy ignominy sleep with thee in the grave,
100 But not remembered in thy epitaph.
He spieth FALSTAFF *on the ground*
What, old acquaintance! Could not all this flesh
Keep in a little life? Poor Jack, farewell.
I could have better spared a better man.
O, I should have a heavy° miss of thee,   sad; weighty
105 If I were much in love with vanity.
Death hath not struck so fat a deer today,
Though many dearer in this bloody fray.
Embowelled⁵ will I see thee by and by.
Till then, in blood by noble Percy lie.   *Exit*
FALSTAFF *riseth up*
110 FALSTAFF   Embowelled? If thou embowel me today, I'll give you
leave to powder° me, and eat me too, tomorrow. 'Sblood, 'twas   pickle in salt
time to counterfeit, or that hot termagant⁶ Scot had paid me,
scot and lot° too. Counterfeit? I lie, I am no counterfeit. To   in full
die is to be a counterfeit, for he is but the counterfeit of a man
115 who hath not the life of a man. But to counterfeit dying when
a man thereby liveth is to be no counterfeit, but the true and
perfect image of life indeed. The better part of valour is discretion, in the which better part° I have saved my life. Zounds,   role
I am afraid of this gunpowder Percy, though he be dead. How
120 if he should counterfeit too, and rise? By my faith, I am afraid
he would prove the better counterfeit. Therefore I'll make him
sure; yea, and I'll swear I killed him. Why may not he rise as
well as I? Nothing confutes me but eyes,⁷ and nobody sees
me. Therefore, sirrah, [*stabbing* HOTSPUR] with a new wound
125 in your thigh, come you along with me.
He takes up HOTSPUR *on his back.*
Enter PRINCE [HARRY] *and* [*Lord*] JOHN OF LANCASTER
PRINCE HARRY   Come, brother John. Full bravely hast thou fleshed

4. Ornaments such as plumes or gloves worn into battle.
5. Prepared for embalming and burial as noblemen
were; disemboweled in the manner of a hunted deer.
6. A quarrelsome or shrewish person; the name of an

imaginary deity who, according to medieval morality
plays, was worshipped by followers of Mohammed.
7. No one could confute my story but an eyewitness.

Thy maiden sword.[8]

JOHN OF LANCASTER   But soft; whom have we here?
Did you not tell me this fat man was dead?

PRINCE HARRY   I did; I saw him dead,
Breathless and bleeding on the ground.
130 [*To* FALSTAFF]   Art thou alive?
Or is it fantasy° that plays upon our eyesight?   *hallucination*
I prithee speak; we will not trust our eyes
Without our ears. Thou art not what thou seem'st.

FALSTAFF   No, that's certain: I am not a double man.° But if I   *ghost; two men*
135 be not Jack Falstaff, then am I a jack.° There is Percy. If your   *knave*
father will do me any honour, so; if not, let him kill the next
Percy himself. I look to be either earl or duke, I can assure you.

PRINCE HARRY   Why, Percy I killed myself, and saw thee dead.

FALSTAFF   Didst thou? Lord, Lord, how this world is given to
140 lying! I grant you I was down and out of breath, and so was he;
but we rose both at an instant,° and fought a long hour by   *simultaneously*
Shrewsbury clock. If I may be believed, so; if not, let them that
should reward valour bear the sin upon their own heads. I'll
take't on my death° I gave him this wound in the thigh. If the   *swear on my deathbed*
145 man were alive and would deny it, zounds, I would make him
eat a piece of my sword.

JOHN OF LANCASTER   This is the strangest tale that e'er I heard.

PRINCE HARRY   This is the strangest fellow, brother John.
[*To* FALSTAFF] Come, bring your luggage nobly on your back.
150 For my part, if a lie may do thee grace,°   *get you favor*
I'll gild it with the happiest° terms I have.   *most favorable*
    A retreat is sounded
The trumpet sounds retreat; the day is our.
Come, brother, let us to the highest° of the field   *highest ground*
To see what friends are living, who are dead.
    Exeunt [*the* PRINCE *and* LANCASTER]
155 FALSTAFF   I'll follow, as they say, for reward. He that rewards me,
God reward him. If I do grow great, I'll grow less; for I'll purge,°
and leave sack, and live cleanly, as a nobleman should do.
    Exit [*bearing Hotspur's body*]

5.5

The trumpets sound. Enter KING [HENRY], PRINCE
[HARRY], *Lord* JOHN OF LANCASTER, [*the*] *Earl of* WEST-
MORLAND, *with* [*the Earl of*] WORCESTER *and* [*Sir Rich-
ard*] VERNON, *prisoners* [*and soldiers*]

KING HENRY   Thus ever did rebellion find rebuke.
Ill-spirited Worcester, did not we send grace,
Pardon, and terms of love to all of you?
And wouldst thou turn our offers contrary,
5 Misuse the tenor° of thy kinsman's trust?   *Abuse the substance*
Three knights upon our party slain today,
A noble earl, and many a creature else,

8. *Full . . . sword:* How courageously or splendidly
have you initiated in bloodshed your untried weapon
(fought your first battle). The phrase alludes to hunting
practices in which hawks or hounds were "fleshed," or
made eager for prey by the taste of blood. Also alluding,
by way of the slang meaning of "sword" as "penis," to a
man's first sexual encounters with the flesh of others.
9. I'll take laxatives (to reduce my weight); I'll repent.

Had been alive this hour
If like a Christian thou hadst truly borne
10   Betwixt our armies true intelligence.°   *information*
WORCESTER   What I have done my safety urged me to,
    And I embrace this fortune patiently,
    Since not to be avoided it falls on me.
KING HENRY   Bear Worcester to the death, and Vernon too.
15   Other offenders we will pause upon.°   *reflect upon*
             Exeunt WORCESTER *and* VERNON [*guarded*]
    How goes the field?
PRINCE HARRY   The noble Scot Lord Douglas, when he saw
    The fortune of the day quite turned from him,
    The noble Percy slain, and all his men
20   Upon the foot of fear,° fled with the rest;   *Fleeing in fear*
    And falling from a hill he was so bruised
    That the pursuers took him. At my tent
    The Douglas is, and I beseech your grace
    I may dispose of him.
25   KING HENRY   With all my heart.
PRINCE HARRY   Then, brother John of Lancaster,
    To you this honourable bounty° shall belong.   *act of generosity*
    Go to the Douglas, and deliver him
    Up to his pleasure ransomless and free.
30   His valours shown upon our crests° today   *helmets*
    Have taught us how to cherish such high deeds
    Even in the bosom of our adversaries.
JOHN OF LANCASTER   I thank your grace for this high courtesy,
    Which I shall give away immediately.
35   KING HENRY   Then this remains, that we divide our power.
    You, son John, and my cousin Westmorland,
    Towards York shall bend you° with your dearest speed   *direct your course*
    To meet Northumberland and the prelate Scrope,
    Who, as we hear, are busily in arms.
40   Myself and you, son Harry, will towards Wales,
    To fight with Glyndŵr and the Earl of March.
    Rebellion in this land shall lose his sway,
    Meeting the check of such another day;
    And since this business so fair is done,
45   Let us not leave° till all our own be won.   *leave off*
          Exeunt [*the* KING, *the* PRINCE, *and their power*
      at one door, LANCASTER, WESTMORLAND, *and their*
             power at another door]

The Merry Wives of Windsor

"The first act of the *Merry Wives* alone contains more life and reality than all German literature." So wrote Friedrich Engels to Karl Marx, his fellow German revolutionary and coauthor with Engels of the *Manifesto of the Communist Party*. Perhaps what he admired in *The Merry Wives of Windsor* (1597–98) is the dramatization of the middle class as it is being formed out of social tensions and verbal distinctions, out of disparate and often contradictory elements. Probably Engels also shared the enthusiasm of four centuries of theater audiences for the play's elaborate intrigues and comic stage business. Certainly this is Shakespeare's most middle-class play in its subject matter, setting, and outlook. It is also his most farcical, more so than even such early works as *The Comedy of Errors* and *The Taming of the Shrew*. Farce and intrigue establish the comic tone that informs the play's ultimate spirit of good-humored reconciliation. They also provide the plot mechanisms through which the characters' parochial self-interest is forged into a capacious social unity where hierarchy, though not permanently eliminated, is temporarily suspended. The particular fusion of these two elements—the theatrical and the social—produces the play's distinctiveness.

The *Merry Wives* celebrates the playful but chaste behavior of the titular characters, Mistress Page and Mistress Ford, each married to a prosperous burgher. The overt message is delivered by Mistress Page: "Wives may be merry and yet honest, too" (4.2.89), where "honest" means being sexually faithful to their mates. Page's easy and—from a sexual point of view—justified trust of his wife's fidelity provides a norm from which Ford's irrational jealousy of his wife deviates. The two women's plot against the sexually and economically predatory Sir John Falstaff, their would-be seducer, is also designed to dupe and ultimately cure Ford. In the subplot, the concluding love marriage between Fenton, the impoverished gentleman, and the Pages' daughter Anne, who is beneath him socially but above him financially, affirms romantic love in a way that arguably is also assimilable to citizen values.

The play's time and place reinforce this sense of middle-class community. Together they create the impression of life in an English provincial town as it is being lived at the moment of the play's first performance—a rare phenomenon in Renaissance drama. Although such works as *The Comedy of Errors* and *The Merchant of Venice* depict prosperous citizens of a rank below the aristocracy, those characters live either abroad, or in the past, or both. By contrast, *The Merry Wives* retains a contemporary, domestic, and nonaristocratic feel unique in Shakespearean drama. To be sure, this feel is not uniform; the play refers back to the early fifteenth century. Moreover, not all of the materials from which it is constructed are indigenous: the closest analogue and most likely source for the main plot is found in *Il Pecorone* (1558), by the Italian writer Ser Giovanni Fiorentino. This plot and the primary subplot also draw on ancient Roman comedy, medieval farce, and Renaissance Italian drama. Finally, the play liberally includes characters from both above and below the middle class. Yet the historical allusions do not conjure up a bygone era, the foreign literary and theatrical traditions are reworked into English dramatic and cultural stereotypes, and the upper- and lower-class figures ultimately function to underscore the assimilating power of the middle class.

The play takes a jaundiced view of nearly every character with a claim to social standing. Slender's pretensions to gentility are mocked from beginning to end. His uncle, Justice Shallow, does not fare much better. In the opening scene, Shallow, whose authority is based not in the town but in the county and ultimately in the

Cuckold, his unfaithful wife, and the seducer. From *Roxburghe Ballads* (seventeenth century).

monarchy, acts not to preserve the peace but to undermine it. Similarly ineffectual are the peacemaking efforts of the parson, Sir Hugh Evans, whose honorary title and position as parson indicate that he, too, derives authority from the outside (in this case, from the national church). Evans is also foreign (Welsh), and he seeks to fight a duel with another foreigner (the French Doctor Caius), who is well-to-do and has connections at court.

A different kind of conflict pits the wealthy citizens against their social, but not economic, superiors. Page rejects the love suit of Fenton, and Falstaff is subjected to repeated abuse, in Act 5 functioning as a scapegoat against whom the townspeople can unite. This antagonism between citizen and gentleman is given a financial twist appropriate to the dominant ethos of the play. Page believes that Fenton is motivated by money rather than love, a charge that Fenton admits to Anne was originally true, although he insists that the balance has now shifted:

> I found thee of more value
> Than stamps in gold or sums in sealèd bags;
> And 'tis the very riches of thyself
> That now I aim at.
>
> (3.4.15–18)

Falstaff has no romantic concerns at all, attempting his seductions in the interest perhaps of lust and certainly of profit, metaphorically figured as the fruits of mercantile imperialism. Of Mistress Page he exclaims: "She bears the purse too. She is a region in Guiana, all gold and bounty. I will be cheaters to them both, and they shall be exchequers to me. They shall be my East and West Indies, and I will trade to them both. . . . Sail like my pinnace to these golden shores" (1.3.58–62, 70).

Yet the conclusion tells a different story. Page and his wife, although at cross purposes with each other, have each been trying to marry Anne off to an absurdly unsuitable partner. But when they realize there is no alternative, both husband and wife accept their daughter's marriage with good humor. This stance incorporates Fenton, of course, but is immediately extended by Mistress Page to include Falstaff as well. This act reveals not the servility but the capaciousness, generosity, and adaptability of the citizens' world. The marriage of Fenton to Anne—the main accomplishment of the play, with the exception of the simultaneous duping of Falstaff and curing of

Ford—implicitly marks the reconciliation of the middle class with their social betters. Both plots raise the fear of mercenary, sexually threatening aristocratic interlopers only to emphasize the emptiness of that concern—in one instance because of the comic incompetence of the predator and in the other because of the falseness of the suspicion. Even though the language of the play highlights Fenton's lofty rank—he is the sole character to speak primarily in blank verse—in the end he becomes part of the community. Similarly, the tricking of Falstaff in the final scene draws on the royal and aristocratic heritage of the court masque. But this theatrical form, in which the courtiers become the actors, is here recast in a popular, festive mode.

The concluding scene also includes a compliment to the Order of the Garter uttered in blank verse—to reflect the elevated subject matter—by Mistress Quickly disguised as the Queen of the Fairies (5.5.53–70). The Order of the Garter was an aristocratic fraternity under the patronage of the Queen that inducted new members at Windsor Castle. This passage has the effect of placing the town of Windsor under the protection of the castle of Windsor, just as the town's Garter Inn evokes the castle's more elevated Order of the Garter. These references also seem to be a clue to the play's first performance— probably in April 1597 before Elizabeth in London at the Garter Feast, where candidates were elected to the order for induction the following month. One of those to be elected was the new patron of Shakespeare's acting company, and he may well have commissioned the play for the occasion. There also seems to be a comic reference to a German aristocrat elected at the same time (4.5.61–64). But writing in 1702, and hence with uncertain authority, John Dennis records a different tradition. He claims it was the Queen who, after seeing *1 Henry IV,* ordered Shakespeare to write another play about Falstaff, showing him in love, and to complete it within fourteen days.

It is possible that Shakespeare temporarily put aside the composition of *2 Henry IV,* with which *The Merry Wives* has close verbal affinities, to comply either with his patron or with his Queen—indeed, perhaps rather hurriedly. *The Merry Wives* shares at least the names of a number of characters with the two parts of *Henry IV* and with *Henry V*—Falstaff, of course, but also Mistress Quickly, Shallow, Pistol, Bardolph, and Nim. Fenton supposedly "kept company with the wild Prince and Poins" (3.2.61), an allusion to the future Henry V and one of his companions in the *Henry IV* plays. But even though the names are the same, the characters are not. To take only the most prominent example: the easily duped Falstaff of Windsor lacks the indomitable comic resourcefulness that he repeatedly demonstrates in the history plays. Still, the web of political associations lends a national and monarchical aspect to the more circumscribed events of *The Merry Wives.* The effect is ambiguous, even contradictory: on the one hand, royal power is asserted in its absence; on the other, the middling sort who inhabit the town come to stand for all of England.

The play's generalizing force is further enhanced by a degree of indebtedness to popular culture unusual even for Shakespeare. In keeping with its social milieu, *The Merry Wives* has a far higher percentage of prose than does any other Shakespearean work. Much of it satirically reproduces the language of proverb and cliché; Master Slender and Mistress Quickly in particular depend on clichés that verge on the meaningless. Slender's words to Page convey little more than vague good will along with silly ineptitude: "Master Page, I am glad to see you. Much good do it your good heart! . . . And I thank you always with my heart, la, with my heart. . . . Sir, I thank you. By yea and no, I do" (1.1.65–70). Similarly, Quickly can unleash a barrage of only weakly communicative language that somehow enables her to connect with almost all the other characters: "nobody but has his fault," "the very yea and the no," "that's neither here nor there," "what the goodyear," "thereby hangs a tale," "an honest maid as ever broke bread," "Out upon't" (1.4.12, 82, 93, 106, 130, 131–32, 145).

This unintentionally humorous rhetoric is hardly the only evidence of popular culture in the play. *The Merry Wives* also brings on stage a considerable number of lower-class characters. These are not the clowns and fools of the more aristocratic romantic comedies, but servants: John and Robert, who work for the Fords; Peter Simple, who

Elizabeth I and the Knights of the Garter. Engraved by Michael Gheeraerts the Elder (1576).

waits on Slender; John Rugby and Mistress Quickly, who belong to Caius's household; and, set apart from all of these, Falstaff's hangers-on—Bardolph, Pistol, and Nim. Moreover, in the final scene, when the children of Windsor dress up as fairies to punish Falstaff, they mobilize a popular rural belief, evidently shared by their victim, in mischievous immortal spirits who prey upon the local inhabitants. The insults and injuries Falstaff sustains—suffocation, a dunking in the river, a beating, and pinching—belong to the popular tradition of knockabout physical stage action characteristic of both farce and shaming rituals of the time.

Windsor's sense of community also depends on a cheerfully casual ethnocentrism. Hostility to foreigners is part of the throwaway language of the play (especially the Host's): "base Hungarian wight," "Base Phrygian Turk," "Flemish drunkard," "Cathayan," "Ethiopian," "Francisco," "Castalian King Urinal," "Anthropophaginian" (cannibal), "Bohemian Tartar" (1.3.18, 78; 2.1.20–21, 127; 2.3.24, 29; 4.5.8, 16). One of Ford's jealous fits trades in similar stereotypes: "I will rather trust a Fleming with my butter, Parson Hugh the Welshman with my cheese, an Irishman with my aqua-vitae bottle, or a thief to walk my ambling gelding, than my wife with herself" (2.2.265–68). The same effect is produced by the fragmentary, obscure satirical treatment of Germans generally and of a particular German Duke, who is accused of horse stealing in what there is of the third plot of the play, Caius and Evans's revenge on the Host (4.3, 4.5.51–75).

But clearly it is in the fractured English of the French Caius and Welsh Evans themselves, and the good-humored ridicule it evokes, that the English chauvinism of *The Merry Wives* appears most prominently. Evans "makes fritters of English" (5.5.136); he and Caius "hack our English" (3.1.67). Their marked accents, as well as Caius's frequent reversion to French, call attention to their foreignness. Their silly decision to fight a duel is thwarted by the Host out of affection for the two men and perhaps out of hostility to this aristocratic means of settling disputes. Both the intention and the inability to carry it out intensify the other characters' sense of the superiority of

the English middle class. This sense, communicated to the audience as well, is clear enough in the First Folio (1623)—which the present edition follows—despite the likelihood that Shakespeare composed the text that lies behind it for an aristocratic event. But it is even more consistently emphasized in the First Quarto (1602), which seems to be based on a revision of the original version for popular performance. (See the Textual Note.)

As the title of the play reveals, however, its conflicts are fought primarily in terms of gender. But the meaning of these conflicts, despite their unambiguous outcomes, is unclear. Is the wives' triumph over Falstaff's sexual adventuring and Ford's fantasy of his wife's infidelity a victory for *middle-class* women (as suggested earlier), for middle-class *women*, or for both? The play celebrates the wives' freedom and autonomy, in short their merriness, but that merriness serves primarily to protect their husbands' wealth. Primarily, but not entirely. Though Page proudly contrasts his liberal attitude toward his wife with Ford's misogynist anxiety, Mistress Page's scheming against her husband's plans for their daughter's marriage reveals that female self-assertion does not necessarily dovetail with male desire. In this different sense, Ford's fears are justified, Page's confidence undermined. As it turns out, neither parent prevails, although a woman does: Anne replicates the companionate marriage of her mother and father, but she does so against their will, by insisting on her right to choose her own husband.

A view of gender relations and sexuality less obviously tied to emerging middle-class norms is produced by Mistress Quickly's language. Although the obsessive sexual innuendo of that language often escapes the speaker herself, she is not alone in her heedless punning. Evans in particular evinces a comparable obliviousness to the sexual implications of his own speech, an obliviousness that Quickly's comic misunderstandings during the seemingly extraneous Latin lesson (4.1) are instrumental in revealing. Evans, who doubles as Windsor's schoolmaster, quizzes young William Page on the fundamentals of Latin grammar as they were taught in the first years of school, specifically asking his pupil recite the possessive plural form (or "genitive case") of the word for "this" ("of these"). Mistress Quickly looks on and comments uncomprehendingly:

what she overlooks in her own speech she detects in a language she cannot understand.

> WILLIAM Genitive case?
> EVANS Ay.
> WILLIAM *Genitivo: 'horum, harum, horum'.*
> MISTRESS QUICKLY Vengeance of Jenny's case! Fie on her!
> Never name her, child, if she be a whore.
>
> (4.1.50–54)

Here, "genitive" may suggest "generative" or even "genital" as well as the female name "Jenny"; "case" is slang for "vagina"; and "*horum*," a genitive plural, evokes the more obvious "whore." The scene turns on conflicts between Latin and English, literacy and illiteracy, middle class and lower, man and woman. This is not an isolated moment. Earlier in the play, the language of grammar, allied to translation as in this scene, acquires a sexual charge as Falstaff boasts of his intention to seduce Mistress Ford:

> FALSTAFF . . . I can construe the action of her familiar style; and
> the hardest voice of her behaviour, to be Englished rightly, is 'I
> am Sir John Falstaff's'.
> PISTOL He hath studied her well, and translated her will: out of
> honesty, into English.
>
> (1.3.39–43)

A different pattern of sexual allusion emerges when Falstaff finds himself trapped in Ford's house on his second assignation with Mistress Ford, and the wives prevail upon him to escape disguised as the "Aunt of Brentford." Although Ford does not see through the costume, he does spew out a torrent of hostile rhetoric—"A witch, a quean, an old cozening quean!" he begins (4.2.149)—before beating up someone whom he believes, however erroneously, to be an old woman (albeit a disreputable one). But of course the woman he attacks is really Falstaff, whose transvestite outfit anticipates the final moments of *The Merry Wives*. Although neither the Folio nor the Quarto is sufficiently consistent about the colors the various characters wear at the end of the play to make possible an exact reconstruction of how Fenton manages to fool the other suitors and elope with Anne, the central trick is unambiguous. "I came yonder at Eton to marry Mistress Anne Page, and she's a great lubberly boy," Slender laments. "If I had been married to him, for all he was in woman's apparel, I would not have had him" (5.5.169–70, 176–77). Caius finds himself even more deeply entangled in the deception. "Ver is Mistress Page? By Gar, I am cozened! I ha' married *un garçon*, a boy, *un paysan*, by Gar. A boy!" (5.5.186–87). This is not the first such sexual tease. Earlier, Ford comments disapprovingly on the intimacy between the merry wives: "I think if your husbands were dead you two would marry." The charge of what we would now call homosexuality is quickly rejected. "Be sure of that—two other husbands," Mistress Page immediately replies (3.2.11–13). Similarly, the ending entertains the option of man-boy sexual relations only to punish Anne's foolish suitors. Like adultery and financially motivated arranged marriages, these are deviations from the elaborately constructed romantic and sexual norm, whose literal issue is emphasized by the unusual prominence of children in the play.

Yet this is not the whole story. The cross-dressing conclusion points self-referentially beyond the fictional action to the actors who have produced the fiction. Shakespeare wrote for a transvestite theater in which female parts were performed by boys. Members of the audience might well note the distance between the fairy queen—a flattering allusion to Queen Elizabeth—Mistress Quickly, and the fictional character who plays the doubly fictional part. They might also register the real boy actor impersonating these two fictional figures. And at the very end, Slender and Caius are not alone in their predicament: Fenton, too, goes off with a boy dressed as a girl. This conclusion simultaneously celebrates and subverts the theatrical illusion. Renaissance accounts

A "skimmington," a public rite of humiliation for domestic disorder.

praise the lifelike persuasiveness of the best boy actors who impersonated women. Here, the boy gets the girl just as the audience would wish, at the very moment Shakespeare reminds them that they have willingly believed in precisely the falsehood accepted by some of the play's more foolish characters.

This resolution, like *The Merry Wives* as a whole, is at once socially suggestive and visually funny. Much of the pleasure of the play arises from the physical comedy of plot and counterplot—Caius discovering Simple in his closet, Ford in disguise urging Falstaff to seduce his wife, Caius and Evans unknowingly preparing for solo duels, Falstaff repeatedly escaping Ford only to suffer still greater humiliation, the deluded would-be bridegrooms stealing off with the wrong fairies. This effective stage business helps explain the work's success both in the theater and in operatic adaptation (especially Verdi's *Falstaff*, 1893).

Particularly at the end, however, stage business also serves to work out the subplot in a way that unravels the logic of the main plot. By the final scene, the revenge on Falstaff has brought together a socially and verbally heterogeneous and often antagonistic group—not just the merry wives and their servants but also their husbands, Evans, Mistress Quickly, and the children of Windsor. Yet the result is not the expected expulsion of the predatory courtier by a unified town but the undoing of nearly all positions of superiority. The central mechanism for this antiscapegoating outcome is the decision by the Fords and Pages to subject Falstaff to one more round of abuse. Even though they are confident that he no longer poses a threat, perhaps they believe he needs to make amends to the whole town. Thus the main plot, in which Falstaff and Ford are fooled by the wives, is balanced by the subplot, in which the fun at the expense of Caius and Slender is perhaps less important than the thwarting of the Pages, who have plotted against each other and must endure the humiliating reversal of having Ford and Falstaff lecture them. As Falstaff says: "I am glad, though you have ta'en a special stand to strike at me, that your arrow hath glanced" (5.5.211–12). Even Anne acknowledges fault: "Pardon, good father. Good my mother, pardon" (line 194). In the fragmentary third plot, the Host fools Evans and Caius, only to have these two rivals team up to exact revenge from him.

The pattern is that of the duper duped. In the end, the renunciation of plotting and hostility by a compromised group of characters produces a moral leveling. The hierarchies and conflicts that separate man from woman, parent from child, sexual normality from sexual deviancy, town from crown, Englishman from foreigner, upper class from middle class, and middle class from lower are resolved—or, more accurately, evaded—through the good-natured, universal inclusiveness of the conclusion. The middle class at the end of the play is a different, more encompassing category than at the beginning. Its strength lies in its cheerful capacity to absorb all comers despite the conscious efforts of most of the leading characters, its ability to fashion a unity that is felt to be more profound than the multiple conflicts dividing the town. And when Mistress Page invites the other characters to "laugh this sport o'er by a country fire" (5.5.219), she is incorporating within the play an experience that the play itself has sought to provide its audience.

WALTER COHEN

TEXTUAL NOTE

The Merry Wives of Windsor, probably composed and first performed in 1597, survives in two important early printed versions—the First Quarto (Q, 1602) and the First Folio (F, 1623). (The Second Quarto, from 1619, simply reprints the First.) This early publication history partly obscures the likely chronology of composition, however. The version in F is printed from a manuscript prepared by a professional scribe named Ralph Crane, who did a fair amount of editing as he copied. His manuscript is in turn based on either a playhouse promptbook or an authorial manuscript. In either case, the Folio text has a close connection with the first performance of the play. Although a date as late as 1601 remains a possibility, most scholars believe that that performance took place in 1597 in a royal and aristocratic setting—for reasons given in the Introduction.

The First Quarto is almost certainly a reported or recollected text (also known as a "memorial reconstruction"): an account of the play in performance prepared largely from memory by the actors who had the parts of the Host (probably) and Falstaff (possibly). Borrowings from *Henry V* mean that it must have been composed between 1598, the earliest year in which *Henry V* could plausibly have been written, and 1602, when the Quarto of *The Merry Wives* was published. Little over half the length of the Folio *Merry Wives,* it seems to be an attempt to recall a version of the play that had already been adapted and cut. Because the First Quarto derives from the memory of a performance rather than from a manuscript that is directly or indirectly Shakespearean, it lacks textual authority.

Accordingly, all modern editions, including the present one, are based on F, in this respect continuing an unbroken tradition tacitly begun with the Third Quarto (1630), which is based not on the first two Quartos but on F. But from 1602 to 1623, the First Quarto was the only written version of the play publicly available. In addition, various problems with the Folio *Merry Wives* make the First Quarto—as truncated, unreliable, and even garbled as it sometimes is—a crucial resource. Thus, where F gives Ford the pseudonym "Broome," Q offers "Brooke." This is surely the original choice, as the wordplay in Falstaff's expression of gratitude for a gift of wine from the character makes clear: "Such Brookes are welcome to me, that o'erflows such liquor" (2.2.135–36). The name was censored at some point from 1597 on, perhaps because "Brooke" was the family name of the patron of Shakespeare's acting company. F's relatively weak and infrequent oaths again suggest censorship, in this instance probably in response to a law of 1606 prohibiting references to God in the theater. Especially in what look like poorly remembered passages, Q's oaths also seem to lack strict textual fidelity to an authorial or theatrical original. But they are fuller and in that sense more accurate. In addition, Q preserves one or more passages that either are omitted from F or are clearly superior to the comparable phrases included there. And because Ralph Crane's editing of the manuscript for F included placing all stage entrances at the very beginning of each scene regardless of where they actually belonged, the stage directions of Q can be quite helpful.

Still other verbal discrepancies between the two versions point to more general thematic differences. Q omits F's Latin lesson (4.1) as well as its allusion in 5.5 to the Order of the Garter ceremony. At least the second of these cuts, both of which seem to indicate a text designed for a more popular audience than the courtly spectators aimed at by F, may well have been made by Shakespeare's company when it put on *The Merry Wives* in the public, commercial theater. References to rural life in Windsor and to the presence of the court are more frequent in F than in Q, which sometimes has urban allusions instead and which simply omits some elite or courtly material. Only in Q are courtiers mocked by name (Brooke, Mömpelgard), and in general F has the more appreciative view of the court.

Many questions remain about both Q and F. At least one intriguing possibility is worth pondering. F may be based on an authorial manuscript that was used for the initial court performance. Q may be based on the memory of stage performances of a promptbook that incorporates revisions of the authorial manuscript for the public theater. If both hypotheses are correct, F accurately preserves a unique, anomalous first performance; Q inaccurately preserves the different version used for the overwhelming majority of the performances in Shakespeare's lifetime. On this interpretation, the textual situation is paradoxical: Q has more value than is usually assumed, despite its inaccuracy. Because it derives from the memory of performance, its language is less authentically Shakespearean than F's. But because those performances reflect revisions that include Shakespeare's own changes as well as other changes made by his company that he accepted, Q may be more authentically Shakespearean than F in presenting the playwright's final treatment of his material, a treatment that accords greater relative weight to popular material both by excluding high-cultural scenes and by including satirical references and additional allusions to everyday life.

SELECTED BIBLIOGRAPHY

Brown, Pamela Allen. *Better a Shrew Than a Sheep: Women, Drama, and the Culture of Jest in Early Modern England*. Ithaca, N.Y.: Cornell University Press, 2003. 33–55. *The Merry Wives* as a play appealing to women. This study focuses on—and differentiates between—the two wives in the context of communal women's culture, female chastity, and neighborhood gender relations.

Buccola, Regina M. "Shakespeare's Fairy Dance with Religio-Political Controversy in *The Merry Wives of Windsor*." *Shakespeare and the Culture of Christianity in Early Modern England*. Ed. Dennis Taylor and David Beauregard. New York: Fordham University Press, 2003. 159–79. Connections among fairies, Catholicism, the Welsh, and women in the play and society alike seen in *The Merry Wives* as potentially subversive but ultimately incorporated into an orthodox order.

Erickson, Peter. "The Order of the Garter, the Cult of Elizabeth, and Class-Gender Tension in *The Merry Wives of Windsor*." *Shakespeare Reproduced: The Text in History and Ideology*. Ed. Jean E. Howard and Marion F. O'Connor. New York: Methuen, 1987. 116–42. Tension between a conservative class hierarchy, emblematized by the Order of the Garter, and a less traditional affirmation of female authority, productive of male anxiety and represented by the wives and their linkage to Elizabeth.

Hall, Jonathan. "The Evacuations of Falstaff (*The Merry Wives of Windsor*)." *Shakespeare and Carnival: After Bakhtin*. Ed. Ronald Knowles. New York: St. Martin's, 1998. 123–51. The domestication of the grotesque, carnivalesque body of Falstaff by a stable bourgeois world.

Helgerson, Richard. "Language Lessons: Linguistic Colonialism, Linguistic Postcolonialism, and the Early Modern English Nation." *Yale Journal of Criticism* 11 (1998): 289–99. Latin versus English versus marginal dialects as colonizing and colonized languages.

Kegl, Rosemary. "'The Adoption of Abominable Terms': Middle Classes, Merry Wives, and the Insults That Shape Windsor." *The Rhetoric of Concealment: Figuring Gender and Class in Renaissance Literature*. Ithaca, N.Y.: Cornell University Press, 1994. 77–125. The language of class and gender hierarchy, with attention to issues of ethnocentrism.

Marcus, Leah. "Levelling Shakespeare: Local Customs and Local Texts." *Shakespeare Quarterly* 42 (1991): 168–78. Contrast of the rural, aristocratic Folio version of the play with the urban, middle-class quarto text.

Melchiori, Giorgio, ed. *The Merry Wives of Windsor*. Walton-on-Thames, Surrey: Thomas Nelson, 2000. Outstanding scholarly edition with a lengthy critical introduction.

Parker, Patricia. "*The Merry Wives of Windsor* and Shakespearean Translation." *Modern Language Quarterly* 52 (1991): 225–61. The scene of Latin instruction (4.1) as integral to the play, revealing links between language and sexuality.

Pittenger, Elizabeth. "Dispatch Quickly: The Mechanical Reproduction of Pages." *Shakespeare Quarterly* 42 (1991): 389–408. Connections among printing, pedagogy, language, and gender hierarchy, also with special attention to 4.1.

Salingar, Leo. "The Englishness of the *The Merry Wives of Windsor*." *Cahiers élis-abéthains* 59 (2001): 9–25. General reading of the play covering geographical setting, social structure, farce, and especially nationalist linguistic patterns.

FILM

The Merry Wives of Windsor. 1982. Dir. David Hugh Jones. UK. 168 min. BBC production with Ben Kingsley as Ford and Judy Davis as Mistress Ford.

The Merry Wives of Windsor

THE PERSONS OF THE PLAY

MISTRESS Margaret PAGE
Master George PAGE, her husband
ANNE Page, their daughter
WILLIAM Page, their son ⎤
⎦ citizens of Windsor
MISTRESS Alice FORD
Master Frank FORD, her husband
JOHN ⎤
ROBERT ⎦ their servants
Sir John FALSTAFF
BARDOLPH ⎤
PISTOL ⎬ Sir John Falstaff's
NIM ⎦ followers
ROBIN, Sir John Falstaff's page
The HOST of the Garter Inn
Sir Hugh EVANS, a Welsh parson
Doctor CAIUS, a French physician
MISTRESS QUICKLY, his housekeeper
John RUGBY, his servant
Master FENTON, a young gentleman, in love with Anne Page
Master Abraham SLENDER
Robert SHALLOW, his uncle, a Justice
Peter SIMPLE, Slender's servant
Children of Windsor, appearing as fairies

1.1

Enter Justice SHALLOW, [*Master*] SLENDER, *and Sir*
Hugh EVANS

SHALLOW   Sir Hugh, persuade me not. I will make a Star Cham-
ber° matter of it. If he were twenty Sir John Falstaffs, he shall   *high court*
not abuse Robert Shallow, Esquire °   *(just below a knight)*
SLENDER   In the county of Gloucester, Justice of Peace and
5   Coram.[2]
SHALLOW   Ay, cousin° Slender, and Custalorum.   *kinsman (here, nephew)*
SLENDER   Ay, and Ratolorum[3] too; and a gentleman born. Mas-
ter Parson, who writes himself 'Armigero'° in any bill, war   *esquire; arms bearer*
rant, quittance,° or obligation: 'Armigero'.   *discharge from debt*
10 SHALLOW   Ay, that I do, and have done any time these three hundred years.
SLENDER   All his successors gone before him hath done't, and all

1.1 Location: A street, later moving to the entrance to
Page's house.
1. *Justice:* justice of the peace (line 4), a local judge.
Master: regularly used of Slender (beginning at line 47),
a respectful prefix to a name that is similar in meaning to
the modern "Mr.," which derives from it. *Sir:* clergyman's
honorary title, not indicating knighthood, as it does with
Falstaff (line 2).
2. Blunder for "quorum," designating justices who could

try a felon if a sufficient number of them (two or more)
were present. Literally, *coram* is Latin for "in the presence
of"; to "bring under coram" was to subject someone to
discipline: hence, Slender comically provides an unwittingly accurate account of Shallow's office.
3. "Custalorum" (line 6) and "Ratolorum" are blunders
for *custos rotulorum* (keeper of the rolls), the principal
justice in a county, perhaps a play on "rat."

1265

his ancestors that come after him may. They may give the
dozen white luces° in their coat.°   *pike/coat of arms*

15 SHALLOW   It is an old coat.

EVANS   The dozen white louses do become an old coad⁴ well. It
agrees well passant:⁵ it is a familiar° beast to man, and signifies   *familial; too intimate*
love.

SHALLOW   The luce is the fresh fish; the salt fish is an old cod.⁶

20 SLENDER   I may quarter,⁷ coz.°   *kinsman*

SHALLOW   You may, by marrying.

EVANS   It is marring indeed if he quarter it.

SHALLOW   Not a whit.

EVANS   Yes, py'r Lady.° If he has a quarter of your coat, there is   *by our Lady (Mary)*
25 but three skirts° for yourself, in my simple conjectures. But that   *coattails*
is all one. If Sir John Falstaff have committed disparagements
unto you, I am of the Church, and will be glad to do my benevolence to make atonements and compromises between you.

SHALLOW   The Council⁸ shall hear it; it is a riot.

30 EVANS   It is not meet° the Council hear a riot. There is no fear   *fitting*
of Got in a riot. The Council, look you, shall desire to hear the
fear of Got, and not to hear a riot. Take your 'visaments in
that.⁹

SHALLOW   Ha! O' my life, if I were young again, the sword
35 should end it.

EVANS   It is petter that friends is the sword and end it.¹ And there
is also another device in my prain, which peradventure prings
goot discretions with it. There is Anne Page which is daughter
to Master George Page, which is pretty virginity.

40 SLENDER   Mistress Anne Page? She has brown hair, and speaks
small° like a woman?   *in a soprano voice*

EVANS   It is that fery person for all the 'orld, as just as you will
desire. And seven hundred pounds of moneys, and gold and
silver, is° her grandsire upon his death's-bed—Got deliver to a   *did*
45 joyful resurrections—give, when she is able to overtake seventeen years old. It were a goot motion° if we leave our pribbles   *plan*
and prabbles,° and desire a marriage between Master Abraham   *squabbles*
and Mistress Anne Page.

SLENDER   Did her grandsire leave her seven hundred pound?

50 EVANS   Ay, and her father is make her a petter penny.°   *will give much more*

SHALLOW   I know the young gentlewoman. She has good gifts.°   *qualities*

EVANS   Seven hundred pounds and possibilities° is goot gifts.   *financial prospects*

SHALLOW   Well, let us see honest Master Page. Is Falstaff there?

EVANS   Shall I tell you a lie? I do despise a liar as I do despise
55 one that is false, or as I despise one that is not true. The knight
Sir John is there, and I beseech you be ruled by your well-

---

4. Coat; cod; scrotum. Evans, in what is meant to be a
stereotypical Welsh accent, often pronounces "t" for "d,"
"p" for "b," and "f" for "v" and omits initial "w." "Louses"
is Evans's comic error for "luces" (line 14), a term from
heraldry, the branch of knowledge concerned with the
right to bear arms, with family pedigrees, and with coats
of arms. (See also "Armigero" and "coat," lines 8, 14.)
The error is set up by the two meanings of "old coat"
(noble lineage, worn-out clothing, line 15), and Evans's
pronunciation then provokes further uncomprehending
wordplay by Shallow (line 19).
5. Walking, looking to the right with the right paw raised
(heraldic); surpassingly. The heraldic image is absurd for
a fish, only slightly less so for a louse.

6. Meaning unclear—perhaps a joke involving Evans's
pronunciation ("louses/luces"; "coad/coat/cod"). *fresh:*
freshwater, unpreserved. *salt:* saltwater, salt-cured,
obscene.
7. I may add another (family's) coat to one of the four
parts of my heraldic arms (for instance, through marriage); but in Evans's reply, cut up in quarters. The
humor of this passage (lines 7–25) results from the deflation of social pretentiousness by unintentionally punning
incomprehension.
8. Star Chamber (lines 1–2); but Evans understands it as
"church council."
9. *Take . . . that:* Be advised.
1. The intervention of friends should end the dispute.

willers.° I will peat the door for Master Page.   *well-wishers*
    [*He knocks on the door*]
What ho! Got pless your house here!
PAGE [*within*] Who's there?
60 EVANS Here is Got's plessing and your friend, and Justice Shallow, and here young Master Slender, that peradventures shall
tell you another tale° if matters grow to your likings.   *(a marriage proposal)*
    Enter Master PAGE
PAGE I am glad to see your worships well. I thank you for my
venison, Master Shallow.
65 SHALLOW Master Page, I am glad to see you. Much good do it
your good heart! I wished your venison better; it was ill°   *unlawfully (by Falstaff?)*
killed.—How doth good Mistress Page?—And I thank you
always with my heart, la,° with my heart.   *indeed*
PAGE Sir, I thank you.
70 SHALLOW Sir, I thank you. By yea and no,° I do.   *(almost meaningless)*
PAGE I am glad to see you, good Master Slender.
SLENDER How does your fallow° greyhound, sir? I heard say he   *light-brown*
was outrun on Cotswold.°   *the Cotswold hills*
PAGE It could not be judged, sir.
75 SLENDER You'll not confess, you'll not confess.°   *(that the dog lost)*
SHALLOW That he will not. 'Tis your fault,° 'tis your fault.   *You're in the wrong*
    [*To* PAGE] 'Tis a good dog.
PAGE A cur, sir.
SHALLOW Sir, he's a good dog and a fair dog. Can there be more
80 said? He is good and fair. Is Sir John Falstaff here?
PAGE Sir, he is within; and I would I could do a good office
between you.
EVANS It is spoke as a Christians ought to speak.
SHALLOW He hath wronged me, Master Page.
85 PAGE Sir, he doth in some sort confess it.
SHALLOW If it be confessed, it is not redressed. Is not that so,
Master Page? He hath wronged me; indeed he hath; at a word,°   *in short*
he hath. Believe me, Robert Shallow, Esquire, saith he is
wronged.
    Enter Sir John FALSTAFF, BARDOLPH, NIM, *and* PISTOL
90 PAGE Here comes Sir John.
FALSTAFF Now, Master Shallow, you'll complain of me to the
King?
SHALLOW Knight, you have beaten my men, killed my deer, and
broke open my lodge.°   *keeper's house*
95 FALSTAFF But not kissed your keeper's daughter?
SHALLOW Tut, a pin.° This shall be answered.   *trifling comment*
FALSTAFF I will answer it straight: I have done all this. That is
now answered.
SHALLOW The Council shall know this.
100 FALSTAFF 'Twere better for you if it were known in counsel.°   *kept secret*
You'll be laughed at.
EVANS *Pauca verba,*° Sir John, good worts.   *Few words*
FALSTAFF Good worts?° Good cabbage!—Slender, I broke your   *words; cabbage*
head. What matter° have you against me?   *complaint*
105 SLENDER Marry, sir, I have matter in my head against you, and
against your cony-catching° rascals, Bardolph, Nim, and Pistol.   *swindling*
BARDOLPH You Banbury cheese!°   *thin (like Slender)*
SLENDER Ay, it is no matter.

PISTOL How now, Mephistopheles?[2]

110 SLENDER Ay, it is no matter.

NIM Slice, I say *pauca, pauca*. Slice, that's my humour.[3]

SLENDER [*to* SHALLOW] Where's Simple, my man? Can you tell, cousin?

EVANS Peace, I pray you. Now let us understand. There is three
115 umpires in this matter, as I understand: that is, Master Page,
fidelicet° Master Page; and there is myself, fidelicet myself; and   *namely*
the three party is, lastly and finally, mine Host of the Garter.°   *(a Windsor inn)*

PAGE We three to hear it, and end it between them.

EVANS Fery goot. I will make a prief of it in my notebook, and
120 we will afterwards 'ork upon the cause with as great discreetly
as we can.

FALSTAFF Pistol.

PISTOL He hears with ears.

EVANS The tevil and his tam!° What phrase is this? 'He hears   *dam (mother)*
125 with ear'! Why, it is affectations.

FALSTAFF Pistol, did you pick Master Slender's purse?

SLENDER Ay, by these gloves did he—or I would I might never
come in mine own great chamber° again else—of seven groats   *hall; bedroom*
in mill-sixpences, and two Edward shovel-boards[4] that cost me
130 two shilling and twopence apiece of Ed Miller. By these gloves.

FALSTAFF Is this true, Pistol?

EVANS No, it is false, if it° is a pickpurse.   *he*

PISTOL Ha, thou mountain-foreigner!° Sir John and master mine,   *Welshman*
I combat challenge of this latten bilbo.[5]—
135 Word of denial in thy *labras*° here,   *lips*
Word of denial: froth and scum, thou liest.

SLENDER [*pointing to* NIM] By these gloves, then, 'twas he.

NIM Be advised, sir, and pass good humours.° I will say 'marry,   *behave properly*
trap with you'[6] if you run the nuthook's humour on me.[7] That
140 is the very note° of it.   *fact*

SLENDER By this hat, then, he in the red face° had it. For though   *(Bardolph)*
I cannot remember what I did when you made me drunk, yet
I am not altogether an ass.

FALSTAFF [*to* BARDOLPH] What say you, Scarlet and John?[8]

145 BARDOLPH Why, sir, for my part I say the gentleman had drunk
himself out of his five sentences.

EVANS It is 'his five senses'. Fie, what the ignorance is!

BARDOLPH And being fap,° sir, was, as they say, cashiered.° And   *drunk / kicked out*
so conclusions passed the careers.[9]

150 SLENDER Ay, you spake in Latin[1] then, too. But 'tis no matter.
I'll ne'er be drunk, whilst I live, again, but in honest, civil,
godly company, for° this trick. If I be drunk, I'll be drunk with   *on account of*
those that have the fear of God, and not with drunken knaves.

EVANS So Got 'udge me,° that is a virtuous mind.   *judge*

2. The devil in Christopher Marlowe's *Dr. Faustus*, perhaps played as a thin, gaunt character.
3. "Slice" takes up the Banbury cheese insult (line 107) and may command Slender to cut off his remarks, to stick to few words ("*pauca*"). Nim's temperament ("humour") is to slice Slender with his sword.
4. *groat*: four-penny coin. *mill-sixpences*: new coins that may have been worth more than their face value. *Edward shovel-boards*: old shillings. Shallow has paid over twice their face value because of their use in the game of shovel board.

5. A sword (from Bilbao, Spain, where fine swords known for their elasticity were made) made of brass or a brasslike, yellow mixed metal; probably alluding to Slender's cowardice and thinness.
6. Get lost; go play a children's game; you'll be caught (?).
7. If you act like a constable in accusing me.
8. Robin Hood's accomplices, Will Scarlet and Little John; alluding to Bardolph's complexion.
9. Things got out of hand; he misinterpreted things.
1. Slender can't understand Bardolph's slang and so assumes it must be Latin.

155   FALSTAFF   You hear all these matters denied, gentlemen, you
        hear it.
            Enter ANNE *Page [with wine]*
    PAGE   Nay, daughter, carry the wine in; we'll drink within.
                                                  [Exit ANNE]
    SLENDER   O heaven, this is Mistress Anne Page!
              Enter [at another door] MISTRESS FORD *and* MISTRESS
              PAGE
    PAGE   How now, Mistress Ford?
160   FALSTAFF   Mistress Ford, by my troth, you are very well met. By
        your leave, good mistress.
              Sir John FALSTAFF *kisses her*
    PAGE   Wife, bid these gentlemen welcome.—Come, we have a
        hot venison pasty to° dinner. Come, gentlemen, I hope we shall   *pie for*
        drink down all unkindness.   *Exeunt all but* SLENDER
165   SLENDER   I had rather than forty shillings I had my book of songs
        and sonnets here.[2]
              Enter SIMPLE
        How now, Simple, where have you been? I must wait on
        myself, must I? You have not the book of riddles about you,
        have you?
170   SIMPLE   Book of riddles? Why, did you not lend it to Alice Short-
        cake upon Allhallowmas last, a fortnight afore Michaelmas?[3]
             [Enter SHALLOW *and* EVANS]
    SHALLOW *[to* SLENDER]   Come, coz; come, coz; we stay° for you.   *wait*
        [Aside to him] A word with you, coz.
             [He draws SLENDER *aside]*
        Marry, this, coz: there is, as 'twere, a tender,° a kind of tender,   *(marriage) proposal*
175   made afar off ° by Sir Hugh here. Do you understand me?   *indirectly*
    SLENDER   Ay, sir, you shall find me reasonable.° If it be so, I shall   *(with Falstaff)*
        do that that is reason.
    SHALLOW   Nay, but understand me.
    SLENDER   So I do, sir.
180   EVANS   Give ear to his motions.° Master Slender, I will descrip-   *proposals*
        tion the matter to you, if you be capacity of it.
    SLENDER   Nay, I will do as my cousin Shallow says. I pray you
        pardon me. He's a Justice of Peace in his country,° simple°   *district / humble; foolish*
        though I stand here.
185   EVANS   But that is not the question. The question is concerning
        your marriage.
    SHALLOW   Ay, there's the point, sir.
    EVANS   Marry, is it, the very point of it—to Mistress Anne Page.
    SLENDER   Why, if it be so, I will marry her upon any reasonable
190   demands.°   *requests*
    EVANS   But can you affection the 'oman? Let us command to
        know that of your mouth, or of your lips—for divers philoso-
        phers hold that the lips is parcel° of the mouth. Therefore,   *part and parcel*
        precisely, can you carry your good will to the maid?
195   SHALLOW   Cousin Abraham Slender, can you love her?
    SLENDER   I hope, sir, I will do as it shall become one that would
        do reason.

---

2. Probably Richard Tottel's *Miscellany* (1557), an out-
of-date collection of love poetry on whose quotable
quotes Slender wishes to draw in wooing Anne Page.

3. Allhallowmas, or All Saints' Day (November 1), is
actually over a month after Michaelmas, September 29.

EVANS   Nay, Got's lords and his ladies, you must speak positable° ┄┄┄┄┄ *positively*
if you can carry her your desires towards her.

200 SHALLOW   That you must. Will you, upon good dowry, marry
her?

SLENDER   I will do a greater thing than that upon your request,
cousin, in° any reason. ┄┄┄┄┄ *within*

SHALLOW   Nay, conceive° me, conceive me, sweet coz. What I ┄┄┄┄┄ *understand*
205 do is to pleasure you, coz. Can you love the maid?

SLENDER   I will marry her, sir, at your request. But if there be no
great love in the beginning, yet heaven may decrease° it upon ┄┄┄┄┄ *(for "increase")*
better acquaintance, when we are married and have more occa-
sion to know one another. I hope upon familiarity will grow
210 more contempt.° But if you say 'marry her', I will marry her. ┄┄┄┄┄ *(for "content")*
That I am freely dissolved,° and dissolutely. ┄┄┄┄┄ *(for "resolved")*

EVANS   It is a fery discretion answer, save the faul'° is in the 'ord ┄┄┄┄┄ *fault*
'dissolutely'. The 'ort is, according to our meaning, 'resolutely'.
His meaning is good.

215 SHALLOW   Ay, I think my cousin meant well.

SLENDER   Ay, or else I would I might be hanged, la.
        [*Enter* ANNE *Page*]

SHALLOW   Here comes fair Mistress Anne.—Would I were young
for your sake, Mistress Anne.

ANNE   The dinner is on the table. My father desires your wor-
220 ships' company.

SHALLOW   I will wait on him, fair Mistress Anne.

EVANS   'Od's° plessed will, I will not be absence at the grace. ┄┄┄┄┄ *God's*
        [*Exeunt* SHALLOW *and* EVANS]

ANNE [*to* SLENDER]   Will't please your worship to come in, sir?

SLENDER   No, I thank you, forsooth, heartily; I am very well.

225 ANNE   The dinner attends° you, sir. ┄┄┄┄┄ *awaits*

SLENDER   I am not a-hungry, I thank you, forsooth. [*To* SIMPLE]
Go, sirrah; for all you are my man, go wait upon my cousin
Shallow.   [*Exit* SIMPLE]
A Justice of Peace sometime may be beholden to his friend for
230 a man. I keep but three men and a boy yet, till my mother be
dead. But what though?° Yet I live like a poor gentleman born. ┄┄┄┄┄ *what of it*

ANNE   I may not go in without your worship. They will not sit
till you come.

SLENDER   I'faith, I'll eat nothing. I thank you as much as though
235 I did.

ANNE   I pray you, sir, walk in.
        [*Dogs bark within*]

SLENDER   I had rather walk here, I thank you. I bruised my shin
th'other day, with playing at sword and dagger with a master of
fence°—three veneys° for a dish of stewed prunes⁴—and, by ┄┄┄┄┄ *fencing / bouts*
240 my troth, I cannot abide the smell of hot meat° since. Why do ┄┄┄┄┄ *food; prostitutes*
your dogs bark so? Be there bears i'th' town?

ANNE   I think there are, sir. I heard them talked of.

SLENDER   I love the sport° well—but I shall as soon quarrel at⁵ it ┄┄┄┄┄ *bearbaiting*
as any man in England. You are afraid if you see the bear loose,
245 are you not?

ANNE   Ay, indeed, sir.

SLENDER   That's meat and drink° to me, now. I have seen Sack- ┄┄┄┄┄ *everyday fare*

4. Prostitutes.   5. Object to (?); brawl at (?).

erson[6] loose twenty times, and have taken him by the chain.
But I warrant you, the women have so cried and shrieked at it

250 that it passed.° But women, indeed cannot abide 'em. They   *surpassed description*
are very ill-favoured,° rough things.   *ugly*

   Enter PAGE

PAGE   Come, gentle Master Slender, come. We stay for you.
SLENDER   I'll eat nothing, I thank you, sir.
PAGE   By cock and pie,° you shall not choose,° sir. Come, come.   *(mild oath) / you must*

255 SLENDER   Nay, pray you lead the way.
PAGE   Come on, sir.
SLENDER   Mistress Anne, yourself shall go first.
ANNE   Not I, sir. Pray you keep on.°   *go on*
SLENDER   Truly, I will not go first, truly, la. I will not do you that

260   wrong.
ANNE   I pray you, sir.
SLENDER   I'll rather be unmannerly than troublesome. You do
   yourself wrong, indeed, la.

   Exeunt [SLENDER *first, the others following*]

1.2

   Enter Sir Hugh EVANS *and* SIMPLE, *from dinner*

EVANS   Go your ways, and ask of ° Doctor Caius' house which   *concerning*
is the way. And there dwells one Mistress Quickly, which is in
the manner of his 'oman, or his dry-nurse,° or his cook, or his   *housekeeper*
laundry, his washer, and his wringer.

5 SIMPLE   Well, sir.
EVANS   Nay, it is petter yet. Give her this letter, for it is a 'oman
that altogethers acquaintance° with Mistress Anne Page. And   *is well acquainted*
the letter is to desire and require her to solicit your master's
desires to Mistress Anne Page. I pray you be gone.

   [*Exit* SIMPLE]

10 I will make an end of my dinner; there's pippins° and cheese   *apples*
to come.   *Exit*

1.3

   Enter Sir John FALSTAFF, BARDOLPH, NIM, PISTOL, *and*
   [ROBIN] *the boy*

FALSTAFF   Mine Host of the Garter!

   Enter [*the*] HOST *of the Garter*

HOST   What says my bully rook?° Speak scholarly and wisely.   *fine fellow*
FALSTAFF   Truly, mine Host, I must turn away some of my followers.

5 HOST   Discard, bully Hercules, cashier.° Let them wag.° Trot,   *dismiss / go their ways*
   trot.
FALSTAFF   I sit° at ten pounds a week.   *lodge*
HOST   Thou'rt an emperor: Caesar, kaiser, and pheezer.[1] I will
   entertain° Bardolph. He shall draw, he shall tap.° Said I well,   *employ / tend bar*

10   bully Hector?[2]
FALSTAFF   Do so, good mine Host.

---

6. Famous bear used in bearbaiting.   name of Julius Caesar became a title, "emperor."
1.2 Location: Scene continues.   2. Greatest of the Trojans who fought in the Trojan War.
1.3 Location: The Garter Inn.   Similarly, Hercules (line 5) was the most famous hero of
1. Literally, "one who drives others away"; but the Host   classical mythology.
evidently means "vizier" (Turkish viceroy). *Caesar:* the

HOST   I have spoke; let him follow. [*To* BARDOLPH] Let me see
thee froth and lime.[3] I am at a word:° follow.   *Exit*   *I mean what I say*

FALSTAFF   Bardolph, follow him. A tapster is a good trade. An
15   old cloak makes a new jerkin;° a withered servingman a fresh   *jacket*
tapster. Go; adieu.

BARDOLPH   It is a life that I have desired. I will thrive.   *Exit*

PISTOL   O base Hungarian wight,° wilt thou the spigot wield?   *hungry, hidebound man*

NIM   He was gotten in drink;[4] his mind is not heroic. Is not the
20   humour conceited?°   *idea witty*

FALSTAFF   I am glad I am so acquit of this tinderbox.[5] His thefts
were too open. His filching was like an unskilful singer: he kept
not time.

NIM   The good humour° is to steal at a minute's rest.°   *trick / within a minute*

25   PISTOL   'Convey' the wise it call. 'Steal'? Foh, a fico[6] for the
phrase!

FALSTAFF   Well, sirs, I am almost out at heels.°   *destitute*

PISTOL   Why then, let kibes° ensue.   *sore heels*

FALSTAFF   There is no remedy: I must cony-catch,° I must shift.°   *swindle / live by my wits*

30   PISTOL   Young ravens must have food.

FALSTAFF   Which of you know Ford of this town?

PISTOL   I ken the wight.° He is of substance good.°   *know the man / well-off*

FALSTAFF   My honest lads, I will tell you what I am about.°   *up to; in girth*

PISTOL   Two yards and more.

35   FALSTAFF   No quips now, Pistol. Indeed, I am in the waist two
yards about. But I am now about no waste; I am about thrift.
Briefly, I do mean to make love to Ford's wife. I spy entertainment[7] in her. She discourses, she carves,[8] she gives the leer of
invitation. I can construe[9] the action of her familiar style; and
40   the hardest voice of her behaviour, to be Englished rightly, is 'I
am Sir John Falstaff's'.

PISTOL   He hath studied her well, and translated her will:[1] out of
honesty,° into English.   *chastity*

NIM   The anchor is deep.[2] Will that humour pass?°   *phrase pass muster*

45   FALSTAFF   Now, the report° goes, she has all the rule of her hus-   *rumor*
band's purse; he hath a legion of angels.°   *gold coins*

PISTOL   As many devils entertain, and 'To her, boy!'° say I.   *(hunting cry)*

NIM   The humour rises; it is good. Humour me the angels![3]

FALSTAFF [*showing letters*]   I have writ me here a letter to her—
50   and here another to Page's wife, who even now gave me good
eyes too, examined my parts[4] with most judicious oeillades;°   *amorous glances*
sometimes the beam of her view gilded my foot, sometimes my
portly belly.

PISTOL   Then did the sun on dunghill shine.

55   NIM   I thank thee for that humour.

---

3. *froth and lime:* both are ways of cheating the customer—by putting a good head on the beer (to give short measure) and by adulterating wine with lime (to remove acidity and make it sparkle).
4. Begotten when his parents were drunk (thought to make one cowardly).
5. Alluding to Bardolph's red complexion and irascible temper. *acquit:* rid.
6. An abusive insult usually accompanied by the gesture of showing the thumb pushed between index and middle fingers: historically, "fig" (Spanish); allusively, "female genitals."
7. Provision of food, drink, and lodging; ability to give sexual pleasure.

8. Perhaps: acts courteously; gestures broadly with her hands; shows pleasing skill in carving meat—hence, somewhere between ordinary friendliness and sexual enticement.
9. Interpret (beginning a grammatical pun that includes "style," "voice," "Englished," and "translated," lines 39, 40, 42).
1. Intention; sexual desires; legal document (thought of as written in Latin).
2. That's a deep plot; you're out of your depth (?).
3. Perhaps: the plot develops; it's good. Get the money. (Here, as elsewhere in Nim's speech, "humour" means whatever the context demands.)
4. My (sexual) capacities.

FALSTAFF   O, she did so course o'er my exteriors, with such a
greedy intention, that the appetite of her eye did seem to scorch
me up like a burning-glass!⁵ Here's another letter to her. She
bears the purse too. She is a region in Guiana,⁶ all gold and
60 bounty. I will be cheaters⁷ to them both, and they shall be
exchequers to me. They shall be my East and West Indies, and
I will trade to them both. [*Giving a letter to* PISTOL] Go bear
thou this letter to Mistress Page, [*giving a letter to* NIM] and
thou this to Mistress Ford. We will thrive, lads, we will thrive.
65 PISTOL [*returning the letter*]   Shall I Sir Pandarus of Troy⁸ become,
And by my side wear steel?° Then Lucifer take all.   *And remain a soldier*
NIM [*returning the letter*]   I will run no base humour. Here, take
the humour-letter. I will keep the haviour of reputation.°
FALSTAFF [*to* ROBIN]   Hold,° sirrah. Bear you these letters tightly.°   *Take these / safely*
70 Sail like my pinnace° to these golden shores.   *small, fast boat*
[*He gives* ROBIN *the letters*]
Rogues, hence, avaunt!° Vanish like hailstones! Go!   *be gone*
Trudge, plod, away o'th' hoof, seek shelter, pack!°   *be off*
Falstaff will learn the humour of the age:
French thrift, you rogues—myself and skirted page.¹
Exeunt FALSTAFF *and* [ROBIN] *the boy*
75 PISTOL   Let vultures gripe° thy guts!—for gourd and fullam²   *seize*
holds,°   *are profitable*
And high and low beguiles the rich and poor.
Tester° I'll have in pouch° when thou shalt lack,   *Sixpence/purse*
Base Phrygian Turk!³
NIM   I have operations° which be humours of revenge.   *plans*
PISTOL   Wilt thou revenge?
80 NIM   By welkin° and her stars!   *the sky (poetic)*
PISTOL   With wit or steel?
NIM   With both the humours, I.
I will discuss° the humour of this love to Ford.   *disclose*
PISTOL   And I to Page shall eke° unfold   *also (archaic)*
How Falstaff, varlet vile,
85 His dove will prove,° his gold will hold,   *test; sample*
And his soft couch defile.
NIM   My humour shall not cool. I will incense Ford to deal with
poison; I will possess him with yellowness;⁴ for this revolt of
mine° is dangerous. That is my true humour.   *(against Falstaff)*
90 PISTOL   Thou art the Mars of malcontents.⁵
I second thee. Troop on.   *Exeunt*

5. Glass lens used to concentrate the sun's rays and so start a fire.
6. South American country famed for its unexplored wealth and fertility, as were the East and West Indies (line 61).
7. Escheaters, officers of the Exchequer (or Treasury, line 61) responsible for estates that fell forfeit and so came to the crown; deceivers, robbers.
8. Pandarus is the aristocrat who, as Troy is besieged by the Greeks, serves as go-between (or pander) in the affair between Troilus and Cressida, Pandarus's niece. Shakespeare's play on the subject is several years later than *The Merry Wives*.
9. I will behave respectfully.
1. Suggesting that French gentlemen were thought to

retain few though well-dressed, followers. *skirted:* wearing a coat with full tails
2. *gourd and fullam:* false dice and loaded dice—loaded "high" to produce a four, five, or six, or "low" to produce one, two, or three. See line 76.
3. Terms of abuse. The Turks, Europe's main military foe, were Muslims and hence considered infidels. The Phrygians, early inhabitants of what is now Turkey, were conquered by Europeans; to the classical Greeks, "Phrygian" was equivalent to "slave."
4. Fill him with jealousy. (An inconsistency: in 2.1, Nim goes to Page and Pistol to Ford, who is possessed with yellowness.)
5. Most warlike rebel (Mars was the Roman god of war).

1.4

Enter MISTRESS QUICKLY *and* SIMPLE

MISTRESS QUICKLY What,° John Rugby!   *(a summoning call)*
Enter John RUGBY
I pray thee, go to the casement and see if you can see my mas-
ter, Master Doctor Caius, coming. If he do, i'faith, and find
anybody in the house, here will be an old° abusing of God's   *will be lots of*
5   patience and the King's English.
RUGBY I'll go watch.
MISTRESS QUICKLY Go; and we'll have a posset[1] for't soon at
night,° in faith, at the latter end of a seacoal[2] fire.   *toward nightfall*
[*Exit* RUGBY]
An honest, willing, kind fellow as ever servant shall come in
10 house withal;° and, I warrant you, no telltale, nor no   *with*
breedbate.° His worst fault is that he is given to prayer; he is   *troublemaker*
something peevish° that way—but nobody but has his fault. But   *foolish*
let that pass. Peter Simple you say your name is?
SIMPLE Ay, for fault° of a better.   *lack*
15 MISTRESS QUICKLY And Master Slender's your master?
SIMPLE Ay, forsooth.
MISTRESS QUICKLY Does he not wear a great round beard, like
a glover's paring-knife?
SIMPLE No, forsooth; he hath but a little whey face, with a little
20 yellow beard, a Cain-coloured° beard.   *yellow or reddish*
MISTRESS QUICKLY A softly spirited° man, is he not?   *meek-spirited*
SIMPLE Ay, forsooth; but he is as tall a man of his hands as any
is between this and his head.[3] He hath fought with a warrener.° *gamekeeper*
MISTRESS QUICKLY How say you?—O, I should remember him:
25 does he not hold up his head, as it were, and strut in his gait?
SIMPLE Yes, indeed does he.
MISTRESS QUICKLY Well, heaven send Anne Page no worse for-
tune! Tell Master Parson Evans I will do what I can for your
master. Anne is a good girl, and I wish—
[*Enter* RUGBY]
30 RUGBY Out, alas, here comes my master!   [*Exit*]
MISTRESS QUICKLY We shall all be shent.° Run in here, good   *scolded*
young man; for God's sake, go into this closet. He will not stay
long.
[SIMPLE] *steps into the* [*closet*]
What, John Rugby! John! What, John, I say!
[*Enter* RUGBY]
35 [*Speaking loudly*] Go, John, go enquire for my master. I doubt° *suspect*
he be not well, that he comes not home.   [*Exit* RUGBY]
[*Singing*] 'And down, down, adown-a' *(etc.)*
Enter Doctor CAIUS
CAIUS Vat is you sing? I do not like dese toys.° Pray you go and   *frivolous tunes*
vetch me in my closet *un boîtier vert*—a box, a green-a box. Do
40 intend° vat I speak? A green-a box.   *Do you hear*
MISTRESS QUICKLY Ay, forsooth, I'll fetch it you. [*Aside*] I am
glad he went not in himself. If he had found the young man,
he would have been horn-mad.°   *mad as a bull*
[*She goes to fetch the box*]

1.4 Location: Dr. Caius's house.
1. Restorative drink of hot milk curdled with wine or ale.
2. Superior coal brought by sea.
3. But he is as brave a man as any is around here.

CAIUS *Fe, fe, fe, fe! Ma foi, il fait fort chaud! Je m'en vais à la*
45 *cour. La grande affaire.*⁴

MISTRESS QUICKLY Is it this, sir?

CAIUS *Oui. Mets-le à ma pochette.*⁵ *Dépêche,* quickly! Vere is
dat knave Rugby?

MISTRESS QUICKLY What, John Rugby! John!
Enter John [RUGBY]

50 RUGBY Here, sir.

CAIUS You are John Rugby, and you are Jack° Rugby. Come,   *(connotes knavery)*
take-a your rapier, and come after my heel to the court.

RUGBY 'Tis ready, sir, here in the porch.
[He fetches the rapier]

CAIUS By my trot,° I tarry too long. 'Od's me,° *qu'ai-j' oublié?*⁶   *troth / God save me*
55 Dere is some simples⁷ in my closet dat I vill not for the varld I
shall leave behind.

MISTRESS QUICKLY [*aside*] Ay me, he'll find the young man there,
and be mad.

CAIUS [*discovering* SIMPLE] O *diable,*° *diable!* Vat is in my   *devil*
60 closet? Villainy, *larron!*° Rugby, my rapier!   *thief*
[He takes the rapier]

MISTRESS QUICKLY Good master, be content.

CAIUS Wherefore shall I be content-a?

MISTRESS QUICKLY The young man is an honest man.

CAIUS What shall de honest man do in my closet? Dere is no
65 honest man dat shall come in my closet.

MISTRESS QUICKLY I beseech you, be not so phlegmatic.⁸ Hear
the truth of it. He came of an errand to me from Parson Hugh.

CAIUS Vell.

SIMPLE Ay, forsooth, to desire her to—

70 MISTRESS QUICKLY Peace, I pray you.

CAIUS Peace-a your tongue. [*To* SIMPLE] Speak-a your tale.

SIMPLE To desire this honest gentlewoman, your maid, to speak
a good word to Mistress Anne Page for my master in the way of
marriage.

75 MISTRESS QUICKLY This is all, indeed, la; but I'll ne'er put my
finger in the fire an need not.⁹

CAIUS Sir Hugh send-a you?—Rugby, *baile*° me some paper.   *bring*
[RUGBY brings paper]
[*To* SIMPLE] Tarry you a little-a while.
Doctor [CAIUS] *writes*

MISTRESS QUICKLY [*aside to* SIMPLE] I am glad he is so quiet. If
80 he had been throughly moved,° you should have heard him so   *really angered*
loud and so melancholy.° But notwithstanding, man, I'll do   *(for "choleric"?)*
your master what good I can. And the very yea and the no is,
the French doctor, my master—I may call him my master, look
you, for I keep his house, and I wash, wring, brew, bake, scour,
85 dress meat° and drink, make the beds, and do all myself—   *prepare food*

SIMPLE [*aside to* MISTRESS QUICKLY] 'Tis a great charge° to come   *burden; (sexual)*
under one body's hand.

MISTRESS QUICKLY [*aside to* SIMPLE] Are you advised o' that?°   *You're telling me*
You shall find it a great charge—and to be up early, and down

4. French: By my faith, it is very hot. I am going to
court—important business. (The French in this scene
is translated only when Caius fails to do so himself.)
5. Yes, put it in my pocket.
6. What have I forgotten?
7. Medicines composed of one herb or constituent;

unknown to Caius also the character's name.
8. Cold and dull Quickly's mistake for the opposite
temperament—choleric, or angry).
9. I'll never put myself in danger by getting involved if
I don't have to.

90 late. But notwithstanding, to tell you in your ear—I would have
no words of it—my master himself is in love with Mistress
Anne Page. But notwithstanding that, I know Anne's mind:
that's neither here nor there.

CAIUS [*giving the letter to* SIMPLE] You, jack'nape,° give-a this   idiot
95 letter to Sir Hugh. By Gar,° it is a shallenge. I will cut his troat   God
in de Park, and I will teach a scurvy jackanape priest to meddle
or make.° You may be gone. It is not good you tarry here. By   interfere
Gar, I will cut all his two stones.° By Gar, he shall not have a   testicles
stone to throw at his dog.   [*Exit* SIMPLE]

100 MISTRESS QUICKLY Alas, he speaks but for his friend.

CAIUS It is no matter-a ver° dat. Do not you tell-a me dat I shall   for
have Anne Page for myself? By Gar, I vill kill de jack-priest.°   knave-priest
And I have appointed mine Host of de Jarteer° to measure our   garter
weapon.° By Gar, I will myself have Anne Page.   to referee

105 MISTRESS QUICKLY Sir, the maid loves you, and all shall be well.
We must give folks leave to prate, what the goodyear!°   what the devil

CAIUS Rugby, come to the court with me. [*To* MISTRESS
QUICKLY] By Gar, if I have not Anne Page, I shall turn your
head out of my door. Follow my heels, Rugby.

110 MISTRESS QUICKLY You shall have Anne°—   Anne; an
                    Exeunt Doctor [CAIUS *and* RUGBY]
—ass-head of your own. No, I know Anne's mind for that.
Never a woman in Windsor knows more of Anne's mind than
I do, nor can do more than I do with her, I thank heaven.

FENTON [*within*] Who's within there, ho!

115 MISTRESS QUICKLY Who's there, I trow?°—Come near° the   wonder / Enter
house, I pray you.
                    Enter [*Master*] FENTON

FENTON How now, good woman, how dost thou?

MISTRESS QUICKLY The better that it pleases your good worship
to ask.

120 FENTON What news? How does pretty Mistress Anne?

MISTRESS QUICKLY In truth, sir, and she is pretty, and honest,°   chaste
and gentle,° and one that is your friend. I can tell you that by   well-bred
the way, I praise heaven for it.

FENTON Shall I do any good,° thinkest thou? Shall I not lose my   make any progress
125 suit?

MISTRESS QUICKLY Troth, sir, all is in His hands above. But notwithstanding, Master Fenton, I'll be sworn on a book° she loves   a Bible
you. Have not your worship a wart above your eye?

FENTON Yes, marry, have I. What of that?

130 MISTRESS QUICKLY Well, thereby hangs a tale. Good faith, it is
such another Nan!¹—But I detest,° an honest maid as ever   (for "protest")
broke bread.°—We had an hour's talk of that wart. I shall never   ate (proverbial)
laugh but in that maid's company.—But indeed she is given
too much to allicholy° and musing.—But for you—well—go   (for "melancholy")
135 to!°   come, come

FENTON Well, I shall see her today. Hold, there's money for
thee. Let me have thy voice in my behalf. If thou seest her
before me, commend me.

MISTRESS QUICKLY Will I? I'faith, that I will. And I will tell your
140 worship more of the wart the next time we have confidence,°   confide
and of other wooers.

---

1. Nan (Anne) is such an extraordinary (or lively) one.

FENTON Well, farewell. I am in great haste now.
MISTRESS QUICKLY Farewell to your worship. [*Exit* FENTON]
145 Truly, an honest gentleman; but Anne loves him not, for I
know Anne's mind as well as another° does.—Out upon't,[2] *anyone else*
what have I forgot? *Exit*

2.1

Enter MISTRESS PAGE, [*with*] *a letter*

MISTRESS PAGE What, have I scaped love-letters in the holiday
time° of my beauty, and am I now a subject for them? Let me *heyday*
see.
[*She reads*]
5 'Ask me no reason why I love you, for though Love use Reason
for his precision, he admits him not for his counsellor.[1] You
are not young; no more am I. Go to, then, there's sympathy.° *agreement*
You are merry; so am I. Ha, ha, then, there's more sympathy.
You love sack,° and so do I. Would you desire better sympathy? *Spanish wine*
10 Let it suffice thee, Mistress Page, at the least if the love of soldier can suffice, that I love thee. I will not say "pity me"—'tis
not a soldier-like phrase—but I say "love me".
      By me, thine own true knight,
      By day or night
      Or any kind of light,
15   With all his might
      For thee to fight,
            John Falstaff.'
What a Herod of Jewry° is this! O, wicked, wicked world! One *bragging stage villain*
that is well-nigh worn to pieces with age, to show himself a
20 young gallant! What an unweighed° behaviour hath this Flem- *unbalanced*
ish° drunkard picked, i'th' devil's name, out of my conversa- *(proverbially drunk)*
tion,° that he dares in this manner assay° me? Why, he hath *conduct / proposition*
not been thrice in my company. What should I say° to him? I *can I have said*
was then frugal of my mirth, heaven forgive me. Why, I'll
25 exhibit° a bill in the Parliament for the putting down[2] of men. *introduce*
O God, that I knew how to be revenged on him! For revenged
I will be, as sure as his guts are made of puddings.° *gut-encased sausages*

Enter MISTRESS FORD

MISTRESS FORD Mistress Page! By my faith, I was going to your
house.
30 MISTRESS PAGE And by my faith, I was coming to you. You look
very ill.
MISTRESS FORD Nay, I'll ne'er believe that: I have° to show to *have something*
the contrary.
MISTRESS PAGE Faith, but you do, in my mind.
35 MISTRESS FORD Well, I do, then. Yet I say I could show you to
the contrary. O Mistress Page, give me some counsel.
MISTRESS PAGE What's the matter, woman?
MISTRESS FORD O woman, if it were not for one trifling respect,° *consideration*
I could come to such honour!° *rank*
40 MISTRESS PAGE Hang the trifle, woman; take the honour. What
is it? Dispense with trifles. What is it?

---

2. Expression of dismay.
2.1 Location: Outside Page's house.
1. That is, Love employs Reason to make strong arguments, or preach, on Love's behalf (a "precision" was a

Puritan), but Love will not accept Reason's advice.
2. *putting down:* suppression; perhaps also an unconscious sexual suggestion that men are to be put down
for the purpose of intercourse.

MISTRESS FORD   If I would but go to hell for an eternal moment
or so, I could be knighted.³

MISTRESS PAGE   What? Thou liest! Sir Alice Ford? These knights
45   will hack,° and so thou shouldst not alter the article of thy   *(military); (sexual?)*
gentry.°   *terms of your station*

MISTRESS FORD   We burn daylight.° Here: read, read.   *waste time*
[*She gives* MISTRESS PAGE *a letter*]
Perceive how I might be knighted.

[MISTRESS PAGE *reads*]
I shall think the worse of fat men as long as I have an eye to
50   make difference of° men's liking.° And yet he would not swear,   *judge among / looks*
praised women's modesty, and gave such orderly and well-
behaved reproof to all uncomeliness° that I would have sworn   *improper behavior*
his disposition would have gone to° the truth of his words. But   *accorded with*
they do no more adhere and keep place together than the hun-
55   dred and fifty psalms to the tune of 'Greensleeves'.° What tem-   *(popular love song)*
pest, I trow, threw this whale, with so many tuns° of oil in his   *casks*
belly, ashore at Windsor? How shall I be revenged on him? I
think the best way were to entertain him with hope, till the
wicked fire of lust have melted him in his own grease. Did you
60   ever hear the like?

MISTRESS PAGE   Letter for letter, but that the name of Page and
Ford differs.
[*She gives* MISTRESS FORD *her letter*]
To thy great comfort in this mystery of ill opinions,⁴ here's the
twin brother of thy letter. But let thine inherit first, for I protest
65   mine never shall. I warrant he hath a thousand of these letters,
writ with blank space for different names—sure, more, and
these are of the second edition. He will print them, out of
doubt°—for he cares not what he puts into the press⁵ when he   *undoubtedly*
would put us two. I had rather be a giantess, and lie under
70   Mount Pelion.⁶ Well, I will find you twenty lascivious turtles⁷
ere one chaste man.

MISTRESS FORD   Why, this is the very same: the very hand, the
very words. What doth he think of us?

MISTRESS PAGE   Nay, I know not. It makes me almost ready to
75   wrangle° with mine own honesty.° I'll entertain° myself like   *argue / chastity / treat*
one that I am not acquainted withal;° for, sure, unless he know   *with*
some strain in me that I know not myself, he would never have
boarded⁸ me in this fury.

MISTRESS FORD   'Boarding' call you it? I'll be sure to keep him
80   above deck.

MISTRESS PAGE   So will I. If he come under my hatches, I'll
never to sea again. Let's be revenged on him. Let's appoint him
a meeting, give him a show of comfort° in his suit, and lead   *encouragement*
him on with a fine baited° delay till he hath pawned his horses   *temptingly alluring*
85   to mine Host of the Garter.⁹

MISTRESS FORD   Nay, I will consent to act any villainy against
him that may not sully the chariness° of our honesty. O that   *scrupulous integrity*

---

3. Sexually provided with a knight; dubbed a knight.
4. Falstaff's unfounded and hence mysterious belief that
the wives are promiscuous.
5. Printing press; what he presses sexually.
6. The giants were the Titans, who in Greek mythology
rebelled against the Olympian gods and were punished
by being buried under Mt. Pelion.

7. Turtledoves (proverbially true to their mates).
8. Nautical metaphor: accosted; sexually entered.
9. See note to 4.3.11. The plot does not develop in
exactly the way anticipated: "Brooke" supplies Sir John
with funds, so at first he doesn't have to pawn his
horses to raise money for his courting.

my husband saw this letter! It would give eternal food to his
jealousy.

      Enter Master FORD [*with*] PISTOL, *and Master* PAGE
      [*with*] NIM

90   MISTRESS PAGE Why, look where he comes, and my goodman°   *husband*
    too. He's as far from jealousy as I am from giving him cause;
    and that, I hope, is an unmeasurable distance.

  MISTRESS FORD You are the happier woman.

  MISTRESS PAGE Let's consult together against this greasy knight.
95   Come hither.
        [*They withdraw*]

  FORD Well, I hope it be not so.

  PISTOL Hope is a curtal° dog in some affairs.   *an unreliable*
    Sir John affects° thy wife.   *loves; aims at*

  FORD Why, sir, my wife is not young.

100   PISTOL He woos both high and low, both rich and poor,
    Both young and old, one with another,° Ford.   *indiscriminately*
    He loves the gallimaufry,° Ford. Perpend.°   *mixture / Consider*

  FORD Love my wife?

  PISTOL With liver° burning hot. Prevent,   *(seat of the passions)*
105   Or go thou like Sir Actaeon,[1] he,
    With Ringwood[2] at thy heels.
    O, odious is the name!

  FORD What name, sir?

  PISTOL The horn,° I say. Farewell.   *(of a cuckold)*
110   Take heed; have open eye; for thieves do foot° by night.   *walk; (sexual)*
    Take heed ere summer comes, or cuckoo-birds[3] do sing.—
    Away, Sir Corporal Nim!—Believe it, Page; he speaks sense.
                                          Exit

  FORD [*aside*] I will be patient. I will find out° this.   *investigate*

  NIM [*to* PAGE] And this is true. I like not the humour of lying.
115   He hath wronged me in some humours. I should° have borne   *was supposed to*
    the humoured letter to her; but I have a sword, and it shall bite
    upon my necessity.° He loves your wife. There's the short and   *when I need it to*
    the long.
    My name is Corporal Nim. I speak and I avouch 'tis true.
120   My name is Nim, and Falstaff loves your wife. Adieu.
    I love not the humour of bread and cheese.[4] Adieu.   *Exit*

  PAGE [*aside*] The humour of it, quoth a?° Here's a fellow frights   *he*
    English out of his° wits.   *its*

  FORD [*aside*] I will seek out Falstaff.

125   PAGE [*aside*] I never heard such a drawling, affecting° rogue.   *affectedly speaking*

  FORD [*aside*] If I do find° it—well.   *ascertain*

  PAGE [*aside*] I will not believe such a Cathayan° though the   *Chinese; scoundrel*
    priest o'th' town commended him for° a true man.   *as*

  FORD [*aside*] 'Twas a good, sensible fellow. Well.
        [MISTRESS PAGE *and* MISTRESS FORD *come forward*]

130   PAGE How now, Meg?

  MISTRESS PAGE Whither go you, George? Hark you.

---

1. In Greek mythology, Actaeon was turned into a stag
and consequently hunted and killed by his own dogs. The
stag, in particular its horns, was considered an emblem of
the cuckold, the man whose wife was unfaithful to him.
2. Supposed name of one of Actaeon's dogs.
3. The cuckoo's habit of leaving its eggs to be hatched by
others made it the emblem of cuckolders and made the
sound of its call a taunt to cuckolds. Its song is prevalent
in late spring, after the mating season.
4. Nim's meager fame as Falstaff's retainer, or as now
unemployed; a popular name for wood sorrel, an edible
plant also known as cuckoo-bread or cuckoo-cheese—
hence an allusion to cuckolding.

[*They talk apart*]

MISTRESS FORD   How now, sweet Frank? Why art thou melancholy?

FORD   I melancholy? I am not melancholy. Get you home, go.

135 MISTRESS FORD   Faith, thou hast some crotchets° in thy head   *strange notions*
now. Will you go, Mistress Page?

MISTRESS PAGE   Have with you.°—You'll come to dinner, George?   *I'm coming*

Enter MISTRESS QUICKLY

[*Aside to* MISTRESS FORD] Look who comes yonder. She shall
be our messenger to this paltry knight.

140 MISTRESS FORD [*aside to* MISTRESS PAGE]   Trust me, I thought on
her. She'll fit it.°   *fit the part*

MISTRESS PAGE [*to* MISTRESS QUICKLY]   You are come to see my
daughter Anne?

MISTRESS QUICKLY   Ay, forsooth; and I pray how does good Mis-
145 tress Anne?

MISTRESS PAGE   Go in with us and see. We have an hour's talk
with you.

Exeunt MISTRESS PAGE, MISTRESS FORD, *and*
[MISTRESS] QUICKLY

PAGE   How now, Master Ford?

FORD   You heard what this knave told me, did you not?

150 PAGE   Yes, and you heard what the other told me?

FORD   Do you think there is truth in them?

PAGE   Hang 'em, slaves! I do not think the knight would offer°   *attempt*
it. But these that accuse him in his intent towards our wives are
a yoke° of his discarded men—very rogues, now they be out of   *pair*
155 service.

FORD   Were they his men?

PAGE   Marry, were they.

FORD   I like it never the better for that. Does he lie° at the   *lodge*
Garter?

160 PAGE   Ay, marry, does he. If he should intend this voyage toward
my wife, I would turn her loose to him; and what he gets more
of her than sharp words, let it lie on my head.[5]

FORD   I do not misdoubt° my wife, but I would be loath to turn   *mistrust*
them together. A man may be too confident. I would have
165 nothing lie on my head. I cannot be thus satisfied.

Enter [*the*] HOST [*of the Garter*]

PAGE   Look where my ranting Host of the Garter comes. There
is either liquor in his pate or money in his purse when he looks
so merrily.—How now, mine Host?

HOST   God bless you, bully rook,° God bless you! Thou'rt a gen-   *fine fellow*
170 tleman.

Enter SHALLOW

Cavaliero Justice,° I say!   *Gallant knight (comic)*

SHALLOW   I follow, mine Host, I follow.—Good even° and   *afternoon*
twenty,° good Master Page. Master Page, will you go with us?   *twenty times over*
We have sport in hand.

175 HOST   Tell him, Cavaliero Justice, tell him, bully rook.

SHALLOW   Sir, there is a fray to be fought between Sir Hugh,
the Welsh priest, and Caius, the French doctor.

FORD   Good mine Host o'th' Garter, a word with you.

5. Let it be my responsibility (but Ford hears an allusion to the cuckold's horns).

HOST   What sayst thou, my bully rook?

FORD *and the* HOST *talk* [*apart*]

180 SHALLOW [*to* PAGE]   Will you go with us to behold it? My merry
Host hath had the measuring of their weapons,[6] and, I think,
hath appointed them contrary° places. For, believe me, I hear   *different*
the parson is no jester. Hark, I will tell you what our sport shall
be.

[*They talk apart*]

185 HOST [*to* FORD]   Hast thou° no suit against my knight, my guest   *Are you sure you have*
cavaliero?

FORD   None, I protest. But I'll give you a pottle of burnt° sack to   *two quarts of heated*
give me recourse° to him and tell him my name is Brooke[7]—   *access*
only for a jest.

190 HOST   My hand, bully. Thou shalt have egress and regress—said
I well?—and thy name shall be Brooke. It is a merry knight.
[*To* SHALLOW *and* PAGE] Will you go, mijn'heers?°   *gentlemen (Dutch)*

SHALLOW   Have with you, mine Host.

PAGE   I have heard the Frenchman hath good skill in his rapier.

195 SHALLOW   Tut, sir, I could have told you more. In these times
you stand on distance—your passes, stoccados,[8] and I know not
what. 'Tis the heart, Master Page; [*showing his rapier-passes*]
'tis here,° 'tis here. I have seen the time with my long sword[9] I   *like this?*
would have made you four tall° fellows skip like rats.   *valiant*

200 HOST   Here, boys; here, here! Shall we wag?°   *go*

PAGE   Have with you. I had rather hear them scold than fight.

Exeunt HOST, SHALLOW [*and* PAGE]

FORD   Though Page be a secure° fool and stands so firmly on his   *an overconfident*
wife's frailty, yet I cannot put off my opinion so easily. She was
in his company at Page's house, and what they made° there I   *got up to*
205 know not. Well, I will look further into't; and I have a disguise
to sound[1] Falstaff. If I find her honest, I lose° not my labour. If   *waste*
she be otherwise, 'tis labour well bestowed.   *Exit*

2.2

Enter Sir John FALSTAFF *and* PISTOL

FALSTAFF   I will not lend thee a penny.

PISTOL   I will retort° the sum in equipage.°   *repay / equipment?*

FALSTAFF   Not a penny.

PISTOL [*drawing his sword*]   Why then, the world's mine oyster,
5 which I with sword will open.

FALSTAFF   Not a penny. I have been content, sir, you should lay
my countenance to pawn.[1] I have grated upon° my good friends   *harassed*
for three reprieves for you and your coach-fellow° Nim, or else   *companion*
you had looked through the grate° like a gemini° of baboons. I   *prison bars / pair*
10 am damned in hell for swearing to gentlemen my friends you
were good soldiers and tall fellows. And when Mistress Bridget
lost the handle of her fan,[2] I took't° upon mine honour thou   *swore*
hadst it not.

---

6. Has been appointed referee.
7. Q: Brooke; F: Broome. "Brooke" was the family name of Lord Cobham, who had objected to the characterization of his ancestor Oldcastle in *1 Henry IV*. The name was changed to "Falstaff." Presumably, another such objection led to the shift from "Brooke" to "Broome."
8. *In . . . stoccados*: Today, people rely on the distance between duelists—lunges, thrusts.

9. Obsolete, heavy weapon.
1. To plumb the depths of.
2.2 Location: The Garter Inn.
1. Exploit my reputation (as surety for borrowing money, etc.).
2. Fans were often made with handles of precious metal or ivory.

PISTOL Didst not thou share? Hadst thou not fifteen pence?

15 FALSTAFF Reason,° you rogue, reason. Thinkest thou I'll endan-   *With good reason*
ger my soul gratis?° At a word, hang no more about me. I am   *for free*
no gibbet° for you. Go, a short knife and a throng, to your   *gallows*
manor of Pickt-hatch, go.³ You'll not bear a letter for me, you
rogue? You stand upon your honour? Why, thou unconfinable
20 baseness, it is as much as I can do to keep the terms of my
honour precise.° Ay, ay, I myself sometimes, leaving the fear of   *pure*
God on the left hand,⁴ and hiding mine honour in my necessity, am fain to shuffle, to hedge, and to lurch;⁵ and yet you,
you rogue, will ensconce° your rags, your cat-a-mountain°   *hide / wildcat*
25 looks, your red-lattice° phrases, and your bold beating° oaths,   *alehouse / battering?*
under the shelter of your honour! You will not do it, you?

PISTOL [*sheathing his sword*] I do relent. What wouldst thou
more of man?

Enter ROBIN

ROBIN Sir, here's a woman would speak with you.

30 FALSTAFF Let her approach.

Enter MISTRESS QUICKLY

MISTRESS QUICKLY Give your worship good morrow.

FALSTAFF Good morrow, goodwife.

MISTRESS QUICKLY Not so, an't please your worship.

FALSTAFF Good maid, then.

35 MISTRESS QUICKLY I'll be sworn: as my mother was the first hour
I was born.

FALSTAFF I do believe the swearer.⁶ What° with me?   *What do you want*

MISTRESS QUICKLY Shall I vouchsafe⁷ your worship a word or
two?

40 FALSTAFF Two thousand, fair woman, and I'll vouchsafe thee
the hearing.

MISTRESS QUICKLY There is one Mistress Ford, sir—I pray come
a little nearer this ways.
[*She draws* FALSTAFF *aside*]
I myself dwell with Master Doctor Caius—

45 FALSTAFF Well, on. Mistress Ford, you say.

MISTRESS QUICKLY Your worship says very true. I pray your worship come a little nearer this ways.

FALSTAFF I warrant thee nobody hears. Mine own people,° mine   *(Pistol and Robin)*
own people.

50 MISTRESS QUICKLY Are they so? God bless them and make them
His servants!

FALSTAFF Well, Mistress Ford: what of her?

MISTRESS QUICKLY Why, sir, she's a good creature. Lord, Lord,
your worship's a wanton! Well, heaven forgive you, and all of
55 us, I pray—

FALSTAFF Mistress Ford; come, Mistress Ford.

MISTRESS QUICKLY Marry, this is the short and the long of it. You
have brought her into such a canaries° as 'tis wonderful. The   *(for "quandaries")*
best courtier of them all, when the court lay° at Windsor, could   *resided*

---

3. Pickpockets used a short knife to cut purse strings in a crowd. Pickt-hatch was an area of London infamous for its thieves and prostitutes—hence an unlikely locale for a "manor" (with a possible pun on "manner," or habits).
4. Disregarding the fear of God.
5. Am obliged to cheat, to be devious, and to steal.

6. Quickly thinks she is asserting her virginity, but by confusing the proverbs "as good a maid as her mother" and "as innocent as a newborn babe," she actually claims the opposite. Falstaff expresses his belief in what she has literally, but unintentionally, said.
7. Grant (error for "be vouchsafed, or granted, by").

60 never have brought her to such a canary. Yet there has been
knights, and lords, and gentlemen, with their coaches; I warrant you, coach after coach, letter after letter, gift after gift,
smelling so sweetly, all musk; and so rustling, I warrant you, in
silk and gold, and in such aligant° terms, and in such wine and   *(for "elegant")*
65 sugar° of the best and the fairest, that would have won any   *flattery*
woman's heart; and, I warrant you, they could never get an eye-
wink of her. I had myself twenty angels° given me this morn-   *coins (as a bribe)*
ing—but I defy° all angels, in any such sort, as they say, but in   *despise*
the way of honesty. And, I warrant you, they could never get
70 her so much as sip on a cup with the proudest of them all. And
yet there has been earls, nay, which is more, pensioners.[8] But,
I warrant you, all is one with her.

FALSTAFF   But what says she to me? Be brief, my good she-
Mercury.°   *female messenger*

75 MISTRESS QUICKLY   Marry, she hath received your letter, for the
which she thanks you a thousand times, and she gives you to
notify° that her husband will be absence from his house   *note*
between ten and eleven.

FALSTAFF   Ten and eleven.

80 MISTRESS QUICKLY   Ay, forsooth, and then you may come and
see the picture, she says, that you wot° of. Master Ford, her   *know*
husband, will be from home. Alas, the sweet woman leads an
ill life with him. He's a very jealousy man. She leads a very
frampold° life with him, good heart.   *disagreeable*

85 FALSTAFF   Ten and eleven. Woman, commend me to her. I will
not fail her.

MISTRESS QUICKLY   Why, you say well. But I have another mes-
senger° to your worship. Mistress Page hath her hearty com-   *(for "message")*
mendations to you too; and, let me tell you in your ear, she's
90 as fartuous° a civil modest wife, and one, I tell you, that will   *(for "virtuous")*
not miss you° morning nor evening prayer, as any is in Wind-   *miss*
sor, whoe'er be the other; and she bade me tell your worship
that her husband is seldom from home, but she hopes there
will come a time. I never knew a woman so dote upon a man.
95 Surely I think you have charms,° la yes, in truth.   *magic powers*

FALSTAFF   Not I, I assure thee. Setting the attraction of my good
parts° aside, I have no other charms.   *(sexual capacities)*

MISTRESS QUICKLY   Blessing on your heart for't!

FALSTAFF   But I pray thee tell me this: has Ford's wife and Page's
100 wife acquainted each other how they love me?

MISTRESS QUICKLY   O God no, sir; that were a jest indeed! They
have not so little grace, I hope. That were a trick indeed! But
Mistress Page would desire you to send her your little page of
all loves.° Her husband has a marvellous infection to[9] the little   *for love's sake*
105 page; and, truly, Master Page is an honest man. Never a wife
in Windsor leads a better life than she does. Do what she will;
say what she will; take all, pay all; go to bed when she list; rise
when she list;° all is as she will. And, truly, she deserves it, for   *wants*
if there be a kind woman in Windsor, she is one. You must
110 send her your page, no remedy.

FALSTAFF   Why, I will.

MISTRESS QUICKLY   Nay, but do so, then; and, look you, he may

8. Gentlemen of the royal bodyguard.   9. For "affection for."

come and go between you both. And in any case have a nayword,° that you may know one another's mind, and the boy   *password*
115   never need to understand anything—for 'tis not good that
children should know any wickedness. Old folks, you know,
have discretion, as they say, and know the world.
  FALSTAFF   Fare thee well. Commend me to them both. There's
my purse; I am yet thy debtor.—Boy, go along with this
120   woman.   *Exeunt* MISTRESS QUICKLY [*and* ROBIN]
    [*Aside*]   This news distracts° me.   *bewilders (with joy)*
  PISTOL [*aside*]   This punk° is one of Cupid's carriers.°   *whore / messengers*
    Clap on° more sails! Pursue! Up with your fights!°   *Set / fighting screens*
    Give fire! She is my prize,° or ocean whelm° them all! [*Exit*]   *booty/overwhelm*
125   FALSTAFF   Sayst thou so, old Jack?° Go thy ways! I'll make more   *(addressing himself)*
of thy old body than I have done. Will they yet look after° thee?   *desire*
Wilt thou, after the expense of so much money, be now a
gainer? Good body, I thank thee. Let them say 'tis grossly°   *crudely*
done; so it be fairly° done, no matter.   *successfully*
    Enter BARDOLPH [*with sack*]
130   BARDOLPH   Sir John, there's one Master Brooke below would
fain° speak with you and be acquainted with you, and hath sent   *be pleased to*
your worship a morning's draught of sack.
  FALSTAFF   Brooke is his name?
  BARDOLPH   Ay, sir.
135   FALSTAFF   Call him in. [*Drinking sack*] Such Brookes are welcome to me, that o'erflows such liquor.[1] [*Exit* BARDOLPH]
Aha, Mistress Ford and Mistress Page, have I encompassed°   *outwitted*
you? [*Drinking*] Go to. Via!°   *On with it*
    Enter [BARDOLPH, *and Master*] FORD *disguised like*
    Brooke
  FORD   God bless you, sir.
140   FALSTAFF   And you, sir. Would you speak with me?
  FORD   I make bold to press with so little preparation° upon you.   *prior notice*
  FALSTAFF   You're welcome. What's your will? [*To* BARDOLPH]
Give us leave, drawer.°   [*Exit* BARDOLPH]   *Leave us, bartender*
  FORD   Sir, I am a gentleman that have spent much. My name is
145   Brooke.
  FALSTAFF   Good Master Brooke, I desire more acquaintance of
you.
  FORD   Good Sir John, I sue for yours—not to charge you,° for I   *(with an expense)*
must let you understand I think myself in better plight for a
150   lender than you are;[2] the which hath something° emboldened   *somewhat*
me to this unseasoned° intrusion; for they say if money go   *ill-timed*
before, all ways do lie open.
  FALSTAFF   Money is a good soldier, sir, and will on.
  FORD   Troth, and I have a bag of money here troubles me. If you
155   will help to bear it, Sir John, take half, or all, for easing me of
the carriage.°   *burden of carrying it*
  FALSTAFF   Sir, I know not how I may deserve to be your porter.
  FORD   I will tell you, sir, if you will give me the hearing.
  FALSTAFF   Speak, good Master Brooke. I shall be glad to be your
160   servant.
  FORD   Sir, I hear you are a scholar—I will be brief with you—
and you have been a man long known to me, though I had

---

1. See the Textual Note for the significance of this wordplay.

2. I am more able to undertake a risk, an obligation, or a pledge ("plight") as a lender than you are.

never so good means as desire to make myself acquainted with
you. I shall discover° a thing to you wherein I must very much   *reveal*
165 lay open mine own imperfection; but, good Sir John, as you
have one eye upon my follies, as you hear them unfolded, turn
another into the register° of your own, that I may pass with a   *catalog*
reproof the easier, sith° you yourself know how easy it is to be   *since*
such an offender.

170 FALSTAFF Very well, sir, proceed.

FORD There is a gentlewoman in this town; her husband's name
is Ford.

FALSTAFF Well, sir.

FORD I have long loved her, and, I protest° to you, bestowed   *declare*
175 much on her, followed her with a doting observance,°   *attentiveness*
engrossed° opportunities to meet her, fee'd° every slight occa-   *collected / purchased*
sion that could but niggardly give me sight of her; not only
bought many presents to give her, but have given largely° to   *bountifully*
many to know what she would have given.° Briefly, I have pur- *would like to be given*
180 sued her as love hath pursued me, which hath been on the
wing of all occasions. But, whatsoever I have merited, either in
my mind or in my means, meed° I am sure I have received   *recompense*
none, unless experience be a jewel. That I have purchased at
an infinite rate,° and that hath taught me to say this: *cost*
185 'Love like a shadow flies when substance love pursues,
Pursuing that that flies, and flying what pursues.'³

FALSTAFF Have you received no promise of satisfaction at her
hands?

FORD Never.

190 FALSTAFF Have you importuned her to such a purpose?

FORD Never.

FALSTAFF Of what quality was your love then?

FORD Like a fair house built on another man's ground, so that I
have lost my edifice by mistaking the place where I erected it.

195 FALSTAFF To what purpose have you unfolded this to me?

FORD When I have told you that, I have told you all. Some say
that though she appear honest° to me, yet in other places she   *chaste*
enlargeth° her mirth so far that there is shrewd° construction   *gives rein to / malicious*
made of her. Now, Sir John, here is the heart of my purpose.
200 You are a gentleman of excellent breeding, admirable dis-
course, of great admittance,⁴ authentic in your place° and per-   *of respectable rank*
son, generally allowed° for your many warlike, court-like, and   *universally approved*
learned preparations.°   *accomplishments*

FALSTAFF O sir!

205 FORD Believe it, for you know it. There is money.
[*He offers money*]
Spend it, spend it; spend more; spend all I have; only give me
so much of your time in exchange of it as to lay an amiable°   *amorous*
siege to the honesty of this Ford's wife. Use your art of wooing,
win her to consent to you. If any man may, you may as soon as
210 any.

FALSTAFF Would it apply well to the vehemency of your
affection that I should win what you would enjoy? Methinks
you prescribe to yourself very preposterously.

FORD O, understand my drift. She dwells so securely° on the   *relies so confidently*

---

3. *Love . . . what pursues:* Like a shadow, love pursues a
physical object ("substance")/person/money that flees,
and flees a physical object/person/money that pursues.

4. Having qualities ensuring ready admittance into
high society.

215 excellency of her honour that the folly of my soul dares not
present itself. She is too bright to be looked against.° Now,   *at*
could I come to her with any detection° in my hand, my desires   *accusation*
had instance° and argument to commend themselves. I could   *precedent*
drive her then from the ward° of her purity, her reputation, her   *defense*
220 marriage vow, and a thousand other her° defences which now   *of her*
are too too strongly embattled against me. What say you to't,
Sir John?
  FALSTAFF   Master Brooke, I will first make bold with your money.
    [*He takes the money*]
  Next, give me your hand.
    [*He takes his hand*]
225   And last, as I am a gentleman, you shall, if you will, enjoy
  Ford's wife.
  FORD   O, good sir!
  FALSTAFF   I say you shall.
  FORD   Want° no money, Sir John, you shall want none.   *Lack*
230   FALSTAFF   Want no Mistress Ford, Master Brooke, you shall
  want none. I shall be with her, I may tell you, by her own
  appointment. Even as you came in to me, her spokesmate, or
  go-between, parted from me. I say I shall be with her between
  ten and eleven, for at that time the jealous rascally knave her
235   husband will be forth.° Come you to me at night; you shall   *away*
  know how I speed.°   *do*
  FORD   I am blessed in your acquaintance. Do you know Ford,
  sir?
  FALSTAFF   Hang him, poor cuckoldly knave, I know him not. Yet
240   I wrong him to call him poor. They say the jealous wittolly[5]
  knave hath masses of money, for the° which his wife seems to   *on account of*
  me well favoured.° I will use her as the key of the cuckoldly   *good-looking*
  rogue's coffer, and there's my harvest-home.°   *profitable harvest*
  FORD   I would you knew Ford, sir, that you might avoid him if
245   you saw him.
  FALSTAFF   Hang him, mechanical salt-butter[6] rogue! I will stare
  him out of his wits. I will awe him with my cudgel; it shall
  hang like a meteor° o'er the cuckold's horns. Master Brooke,   *an (ill-omened) comet*
  thou shalt know I will predominate over the peasant, and thou
250   shalt lie with his wife. Come to me soon at night. Ford's a
  knave, and I will aggravate his style:[7] thou, Master Brooke, shalt
  know him for knave and cuckold. Come to me soon at night.
                                                  Exit
  FORD   What a damned epicurean° rascal is this! My heart is   *sensual*
  ready to crack with impatience. Who says this is improvident°   *baseless*
255   jealousy? My wife hath sent to him, the hour is fixed, the match
  is made. Would any man have thought this? See the hell of
  having a false woman! My bed shall be abused, my coffers ransacked, my reputation gnawn at, and I shall not only receive
  this villainous wrong, but stand under the adoption of abomi-
260   nable terms, and by him that does me this wrong. Terms!
  Names! 'Amaimon' sounds well, 'Lucifer' well, 'Barbason' well;
  yet they are devils' additions,° the names of fiends. But 'cuck-   *names*
  old', 'wittol'! 'Cuckold'—the devil himself hath not such a

---

5. Willingly cuckolded.
6. *mechanical salt-butter:* lower-class cheap-living;
Flemish salt butter was less expensive than domestic

butter.
7. Increase (irritate) his titles (by adding the title of
"cuckold" to Ford's name).

name. Page is an ass, a secure ass. He will trust his wife, he will
265 not be jealous. I will rather trust a Fleming with my butter,
Parson Hugh the Welshman with my cheese, an Irishman with
my aqua-vitae° bottle, or a thief to walk my ambling gelding,   *whiskey*
than my wife with herself. Then she plots, then she ruminates,
then she devises; and what they think in their hearts they may
270 effect, they will break their hearts but they will effect. God be
praised for my jealousy! Eleven o'clock the hour. I will prevent
this, detect my wife, be revenged on Falstaff, and laugh at Page.
I will about it. Better three hours too soon than a minute too
late. God's my life: cuckold, cuckold, cuckold!   *Exit*

2.3

Enter Doctor CAIUS *and his man* [John] RUGBY [*with
rapiers*]

CAIUS   Jack Rugby!
RUGBY   Sir.
CAIUS   Vat is the clock, Jack?
RUGBY   'Tis past the hour, sir, that Sir Hugh promised to meet.
5 CAIUS   By Gar, he has save his soul dat he is no come; he has
pray his Pible well dat he is no come. By Gar, Jack Rugby, he
is dead already if he be come.
RUGBY   He is wise, sir, he knew your worship would kill him if
he came.
10 CAIUS [*drawing his rapier*]   By Gar, de herring is no dead so[1] as
I vill kill him. Take your rapier, Jack. I vill tell you how I vill kill
him.
RUGBY   Alas, sir, I cannot fence.
CAIUS   Villainy,° take your rapier.   *(for "Villain")*
15 RUGBY   Forbear: here's company.
[CAIUS *sheathes his rapier.*]
Enter [*the*] HOST [*of the Garter,*] JUSTICE SHALLOW, [*Mas-
ter*] PAGE, *and* [*Master*] SLENDER
HOST   God bless thee, bully Doctor.
SHALLOW   God save you, Master Doctor Caius.
PAGE   Now, good Master Doctor.
SLENDER   Give you good morrow, sir.
20 CAIUS   Vat be all you, one, two, tree, four, come for?
HOST   To see thee fight, to see thee foin,° to see thee traverse,[2]   *thrust*
to see thee here, to see thee there; to see thee pass thy punto,
thy stock, thy reverse, thy distance, thy montant.[3] Is he dead,
my Ethiopian?[4] Is he dead, my Francisco?° Ha, bully? What   *Frenchman*
25 says my Aesculapius, my Galen, my heart of elder,[5] ha? Is he
dead, bully stale?[6] Is he dead?
CAIUS   By Gar, he is de coward jack-priest° of de vorld. He is not   *knave-priest*
show his face.
HOST   Thou art a Castalian King Urinal,[7] Hector of Greece, my
30 boy.

2.3 Location: Windsor Park (east of Windsor).
1. Not so dead (from the proverbial simile "dead as a her-ring").
2. Move backward and forward.
3. *pass . . . montant:* use your thrust with the sword point, your thrust, your backhand sword blow, your skill in keeping at the right distance, your upward thrust.
4. Dark-skinned person.
5. Replacing "heart of oak"; as the elder is a soft, low-

growing tree, this is an insult disguised as a compliment.
Aesculapius was the classical god of medicine. Galen was a physician of ancient Greece.
6. Decoy or dupe; wine or urine (often used for medical diagnosis).
7. Urine bottle. *Castalian:* of the spring Castalia, which was sacred to the Muses; "cast-stale-ian" (one who diagnoses by inspecting urine; Castilian (Spanish).

CAIUS   I pray you bear witness that me have stay six or seven, two, tree hours for him, and he is no come.

SHALLOW   He is the wiser man, Master Doctor. He is a curer of souls, and you a curer of bodies. If you should fight you go
35   against the hair° of your professions. Is it not true, Master Page?   *grain*

PAGE   Master Shallow, you have yourself been a great fighter, though now a man of peace.

SHALLOW   Bodykins,° Master Page, though I now be old and of   *By God's dear body*
the peace, if I see a sword out my finger itches to make one.°   *join in*
40   Though we are justices and doctors and churchmen, Master Page, we have some salt° of our youth in us. We are the sons of   *vigor*
women, Master Page.

PAGE   'Tis true, Master Shallow.

SHALLOW   It will be found so, Master Page.—Master Doctor
45   Caius, I am come to fetch you home. I am sworn of the peace. You have showed yourself a wise physician, and Sir Hugh hath shown himself a wise and patient churchman. You must go with me, Master Doctor.

HOST   Pardon, guest° Justice. [*To* CAIUS] A word, Monsieur   *(at the Host's inn)*
50   Mockwater.[8]

CAIUS   Mockvater? Vat is dat?

HOST   Mockwater, in our English tongue, is valour, bully.

CAIUS   By Gar, then I have as much mockvater as de Englishman. Scurvy jack-dog° priest! By Gar, me vill cut his   *mongrel*
55   ears.

HOST   He will clapper-claw thee tightly,° bully.   *maul thee soundly*

CAIUS   Clapper-de-claw? Vat is dat?

HOST   That is, he will make thee amends.

CAIUS   By Gar, me do look° he shall clapper-de-claw me, for, by   *anticipate*
60   Gar, me vill have it.

HOST   And I will provoke him to't, or let him wag.°   *run away*

CAIUS   Me tank you for dat.

HOST   And moreover, bully—[*Aside to the others*] But first, master guest and Master Page, and eke° Cavaliero Slender, go   *also*
65   you through the town to Frogmore.°   *village near Windsor*

PAGE   Sir Hugh is there, is he?

HOST   He is there. See what humour he is in, and I will bring the Doctor about by the fields. Will it do well?

SHALLOW   We will do it.

70   PAGE, SHALLOW, *and* SLENDER   Adieu, good Master Doctor.

Exeunt [PAGE, SHALLOW, *and* SLENDER]

CAIUS[*drawing his rapier*]   By Gar, me vill kill de priest, for he speak for a jackanape° to Anne Page.   *on behalf of an idiot*

HOST   Let him die. Sheathe thy impatience; throw cold water on thy choler. Go about the fields with me through Frogmore. I
75   will bring thee where Mistress Anne Page is, at a farmhouse a-feasting; and thou shalt woo her. Cried game?[9] Said I well?

CAIUS [*sheathing his rapier*]   By Gar, me dank you vor dat. By Gar, I love you, and I shall procure-a you de good guest: de earl, de knight, de lords, de gentlemen, my patiences.°   *(for "patients")*
80   HOST   For the which I will be thy adversary[1] toward Anne Page. Said I well?

---

8. Implying that Caius's diagnoses from urine are quackery, or that Caius is sterile (water being semen) and so lacking in valor.

9. (Did I say) the chase is on?
1. The Host again makes a joke at the expense of Caius, who understands "adversary" as "advocate."

CAIUS   By Gar, 'tis good. Vell said.
HOST   Let us wag, then.
CAIUS   Come at my heels, Jack Rugby.   *Exeunt*

3.1

Enter Sir Hugh EVANS [with a rapier, and bearing a
book] and SIMPLE [bearing Evans's gown]

EVANS   I pray you now, good Master Slender's servingman, and
friend Simple by your name, which way have you looked for
Master Caius, that calls himself Doctor of Physic?°   medicine

SIMPLE   Marry, sir, the Petty Ward, the Park Ward,¹ every way;
5   old Windsor way,² and every way but the town way.

EVANS   I most fehemently desire you you will also look that way.

SIMPLE   I will, sir.   [*Exit*]

EVANS [*opening the book*]°   Jeshu pless me, how full of cholers°   (a Bible?) / anger
I am, and trempling of mind! I shall be glad if he have deceived
10   me. How melancholies I am! I will krog° his urinals about his   knock
knave's costard° when I have good opportunities for the 'ork.°   head / work
Pless my soul!—
[*Singing*]
          To shallow rivers, to whose falls
          Melodious birds sings madrigals.
15   There will we make our peds of roses,
          And a thousand fragrant posies.³
          To shallow—
Mercy on me! I have a great dispositions to cry.—
[*Singing*]
          Melodious birds sing madrigals.—
20   When as I sat in Pabylon⁴—
          And a thousand vagram° posies.   vagrant
          To shallow (*etc.*)
[*Enter SIMPLE*]

SIMPLE   Yonder he° is coming. This way, Sir Hugh.   (Caius)

EVANS   He's welcome.

25   [*Singing*] 'To shallow rivers to whose falls—' God prosper the
right! What weapons is° he?   has

SIMPLE   No weapons, sir. There comes my master, Master Shallow, and another gentleman, from Frogmore, over the stile this
way.

30   EVANS   Pray you give me my gown—or else keep it in your arms.
[*He reads.*]
Enter [Justice] SHALLOW, [Master] SLENDER, and [Mas-
ter] PAGE

SHALLOW   How now, Master Parson? Good morrow, good Sir
Hugh. Keep a gamester from the dice and a good student from
his book, and it is wonderful.

SLENDER [*aside*]   Ah, sweet Anne Page!

35   PAGE   God save you, good Sir Hugh.

EVANS   God pless you from° his mercy sake, all of you.   for

---

3.1 Location: In fields near Frogmore.
1. Toward the Little Park and the Great Park.
2. Toward Old Windsor (a village near Shakespeare's Windsor).
3. Somewhat misrecalled lines from "Come live with me

and be my love." a song by Christopher Marlowe.
4. Evans inserts the first line of a metrical version of Psalm 137 (with "I" for "we"), which describes the weeping of the exiled Israelites.

SHALLOW   What, the sword and the Word?° Do you study them   the Bible
both, Master Parson?

PAGE   And youthful still: in your doublet and hose[5] this raw,
40   rheumatic day!

EVANS   There is reasons and causes for it.

PAGE   We are come to you to do a good office, Master Parson.

EVANS   Fery well. What is it?

PAGE   Yonder is a most reverend gentleman, who, belike° having   probably
45   received wrong by some person, is at most odds with his own
gravity and patience that ever you saw.

SHALLOW   I have lived fourscore years and upward; I never heard
a man of his place, gravity, and learning so wide of his own
respect.[6]

50   EVANS   What is he?

PAGE   I think you know him: Master Doctor Caius, the
renowned French physician.

EVANS   Got's will and his passion of my heart! I had as lief° you   I had rather
would tell me of a mess of pottage.°   thick soup

55   PAGE   Why?

EVANS   He has no more knowledge in Hibbocrates[7] and Galen,
and he is a knave besides—a cowardly knave as you would
desires to be acquainted withal.

PAGE [to SHALLOW]   I warrant you, he's the man should fight
60   with him.

SLENDER [aside]   O sweet Anne Page!

SHALLOW   It appears so by his weapons.

> Enter the HOST [of the Garter], Doctor CAIUS, and John
> RUGBY

Keep them asunder—here comes Doctor Caius.

> [EVANS and CAIUS draw and] offer to fight

PAGE   Nay, good Master Parson, keep in your weapon.

65   SHALLOW   So do you, good Master Doctor.

HOST   Disarm them and let them question.° Let them keep their   debate
limbs whole, and hack our English.

> [SHALLOW and PAGE take Caius's and Evans's rapiers]

CAIUS [to EVANS]   I pray you let-a me speak a word with your ear.
Wherefore vill you not meet-a me?

70   EVANS [aside to CAIUS]   Pray you use your patience. [Aloud] In
good time!

CAIUS   By Gar, you are de coward, de jack-dog, john-ape.

EVANS [aside to CAIUS]   Pray you let us not be laughing-stocks to
other men's humours. I desire you in friendship, and I will one
75   way or other make you amends. [Aloud] By Jeshu, I will knog
your urinal about your knave's cogscomb.°   coxcomb; head

CAIUS   Diable!° Jack Rugby, mine Host de Jarteer, have I not stay   Devil
for him to kill him? Have I not, at de place I did appoint?

EVANS   As I am a Christians soul, now look you, this is the place
80   appointed. I'll be judgement° by mine Host of the Garter.   judged

HOST   Peace, I say, Gallia and Gaul,° French and Welsh, soul-   Wales and France
curer and body-curer.

CAIUS   Ay, dat is very good, excellent.

HOST   Peace, I say. Hear mine Host of the Garter. Am I politic?°   devious

---

5. Close-fitting jacket and tights—that is, without a cloak.   6. Indifferent to his own good reputation.
7. Hippocrates (ancient Greek physician).

85 Am I subtle?° Am I a Machiavel?[8] Shall I lose my doctor? No,   *crafty*
he gives me the potions and the motions. Shall I lose my par-
son, my priest, my Sir Hugh? No, he gives me the Proverbs and
the No-verbs.[9]—[*To* CAIUS] Give me thy hand terrestrial°—so.   *(as bodily curer)*
[*To* EVANS] Give me thy hand celestial—so. Boys of art,° I have   *learning*
90 deceived you both, I have directed you to wrong places. Your
hearts are mighty, your skins are whole, and let burnt sack be
the issue.° [*To* SHALLOW *and* PAGE] Come, lay their swords to   *outcome*
pawn.[1] [*To* CAIUS *and* EVANS] Follow me, lads of peace, follow,
follow, follow.   *Exit*
95 SHALLOW Afore God, a mad host! Follow, gentlemen, follow.
                                  [*Exeunt* SHALLOW *and* PAGE]
SLENDER [*aside*] O sweet Anne Page!   [*Exit*]
CAIUS Ha, do I perceive dat? Have you make-a de sot° of us, ha,   *fool*
ha?
EVANS This is well: he has made us his vlouting-stog.[2] I desire
100 you that we may be friends, and let us knog our prains together
to be revenge on this same scall,° scurvy, cogging companion,°   *scabby / cheating rogue*
the Host of the Garter.
CAIUS By Gar, with all my heart. He promise to bring me where
is Anne Page. By Gar, he deceive me too.
105 EVANS Well, I will smite his noddles.° Pray you follow. *Exeunt*   *head*

3.2
[*Enter*] ROBIN, [*followed by*] MISTRESS PAGE

MISTRESS PAGE Nay, keep your way,° little gallant. You were   *go on*
wont° to be a follower,° but now you are a leader. Whether had   *accustomed / servant*
you rather,° lead mine eyes, or eye your master's heels?   *Which would you prefer*
ROBIN I had rather, forsooth, go before you like a man than fol-
5 low him° like a dwarf.   *(Falstaff)*
MISTRESS PAGE O, you are a flattering boy! Now I see you'll be
a courtier.
          Enter Master FORD
FORD Well met, Mistress Page. Whither go you?
MISTRESS PAGE Truly, sir, to see your wife. Is she at home?
10 FORD Ay, and as idle as she may hang together, for want[1] of
company. I think if your husbands were dead you two would
marry.
MISTRESS PAGE Be sure of that—two other husbands.
FORD Where had you this pretty weathercock?°   *(Robin)*
15 MISTRESS PAGE I cannot tell what the dickens his name is my
husband had him of.°—What do you call your knight's name,   *got him from*
sirrah?
ROBIN Sir John Falstaff.
FORD Sir John Falstaff?
20 MISTRESS PAGE He, he; I can never hit on's name. There is such
a league° between my goodman° and he! Is your wife at home   *friendship / husband*
indeed?
FORD Indeed she is.

---

8. Follower of Niccolò Machiavelli, Italian political theo-
rist reviled by the Elizabethans, who was held to epito-
mize the "politic" and "subtle."
9. Prohibitions; verbal errors (the Welshman's misuse of
standard English).

1. As a pledge; because they are not needed.
2. Flouting-stock (laughingstock).
3.2 Location: A street in Windsor.
1. And as bored as she can stand to be without falling
apart, for lack.

MISTRESS PAGE By your leave, sir, I am sick till I see her.

[*Exeunt* ROBIN *and* MISTRESS PAGE]

25 FORD Has Page any brains? Hath he any eyes? Hath he any
thinking? Sure they sleep; he hath no use of them. Why, this
boy will carry a letter twenty mile, as easy as a cannon will
shoot point-blank twelve score.[2] He pieces out° his wife's incli- *increases*
nation; he gives her folly motion and advantage.[3] And now
30 she's going to my wife, and Falstaff's boy with her. A man may
hear this shower sing in the wind.° And Falstaff's boy with her. *hear trouble brewing*
Good plots—they are laid; and our revolted° wives share dam- *disloyal*
nation together. Well, I will take him;° then torture my wife, *catch him by surprise*
pluck the borrowed veil of modesty from the so-seeming Mis-
35 tress Page, divulge° Page himself for a secure° and wilful *reveal / an overconfident*
Actaeon,° and to these violent proceedings all my neighbours *cuckold*
shall cry aim.° *shall applaud*

[*Clock strikes*]

The clock gives me my cue, and my assurance bids me search.
There I shall find Falstaff. I shall be rather praised for this than
40 mocked, for it is as positive as the earth is firm that Falstaff is
there. I will go.

Enter Master PAGE, [*Justice*] SHALLOW, [*Master*] SLEN-
DER, [*the*] HOST [*of the Garter*], *Sir Hugh* EVANS, *Doctor*
CAIUS, *and* [*John* RUGBY]

SHALLOW, PAGE, *etc.* Well met, Master Ford.

FORD [*aside*] By my faith, a good knot!° [*To them*] I have good *group (ironic?)*
cheer° at home, and I pray you all go with me. *food and drink*

45 SHALLOW I must excuse myself, Master Ford.

SLENDER And so must I, sir. We have appointed to dine with
Mistress Anne, and I would not break with° her for more *break my word to*
money than I'll speak of.

SHALLOW We have lingered about° a match between Anne Page *delayed in concluding*
50 and my cousin Slender, and this day we shall have our answer.

SLENDER I hope I have your good will, father Page.

PAGE You have, Master Slender: I stand wholly for you. [*To*
CAIUS] But my wife, Master Doctor, is for you altogether.

CAIUS Ay, be Gar, and de maid is love-a me. My nursh-a° *housekeeper*
55 Quickly tell me so mush.

HOST [*to* PAGE] What say you to young Master Fenton? He
capers,° he dances, he has eyes of youth; he writes verses, he *leaps in dancing*
speaks holiday,° he smells April and May. He will carry't,° he *gaily / succeed*
will carry't; 'tis in his buttons° he will carry't. *youth*

60 PAGE Not by my consent, I promise you. The gentleman is of
no having.° He kept company with the wild Prince[4] and Poins. *property*
He is of too high a region;° he knows too much. No, he shall *rank*
not knit a knot in° his fortunes with the finger of my substance.° *strengthen / wealth*
If he take her, let him take her simply:° the wealth I have waits *without dowry*
65 on my consent, and my consent goes not that way.

FORD I beseech you heartily, some of you go home with me to
dinner. Besides your cheer, you shall have sport: I will show
you a monster.° Master Doctor, you shall go. So shall you, Mas- *(Falstaff)*
ter Page, and you, Sir Hugh.

---

2. Will shoot straight 240 yards.
3. He gives her lust ("folly") prompting and opportunity.
4. Prince Hal (the future Henry V) and Poins (line 61)

in *1* and *2 Henry IV*—actually Falstaff's, rather than Fenton's, companions.

70 SHALLOW Well, God be with you! [*Aside to* SLENDER] We shall
have the freer wooing at Master Page's.
                              Exeunt SHALLOW *and* SLENDER
CAIUS Go home, John Rugby; I come anon.   [*Exit* RUGBY]
HOST Farewell, my hearts. I will to my honest knight Falstaff,
and drink canary° with him.   *Exit*   wine
75 FORD [*aside*] I think I shall drink in pipe-wine first with him: I'll
make him dance.⁵ [*To* PAGE, CAIUS, *and* EVANS] Will you go,
gentles?°   gentlemen
PAGE, CAIUS, *and* EVANS Have with you° to see this monster.   We are coming
                              Exeunt

3.3

Enter MISTRESS FORD *and* MISTRESS PAGE
MISTRESS FORD What, John! What, Robert!
MISTRESS PAGE Quickly, quickly! Is the buck-basket°—   laundry basket
MISTRESS FORD I warrant.°—What, Robert, I say!   I'm sure it is
MISTRESS PAGE Come, come, come!
      Enter [JOHN *and* ROBERT,] *with a buck-basket*
5 MISTRESS FORD Here, set it down.
MISTRESS PAGE Give your men the charge.° We must be brief.   instructions
MISTRESS FORD Marry, as I told you before, John and Robert, be
ready here hard by in the brew-house; and when I suddenly
call you, come forth, and without any pause or staggering take
10 this basket on your shoulders. That done, trudge with it in all
haste, and carry it among the whitsters° in Datchet Mead,¹ and   linen bleachers
there empty it in the muddy ditch close by the Thames' side.
MISTRESS PAGE [*to* JOHN *and* ROBERT] You will do it?
MISTRESS FORD I ha' told them over and over; they lack no direc-
15 tion.°—Be gone, and come when you are called.   instructions
                              Exeunt [JOHN *and* ROBERT]
      Enter ROBIN
MISTRESS PAGE Here comes little Robin.
MISTRESS FORD How now, my eyas-musket,° what news with   young sparrow hawk
you?
ROBIN My master Sir John is come in at your back door, Mis-
20 tress Ford, and requests your company.
MISTRESS PAGE You little Jack-a-Lent,° have you been true to us?   Lenten puppet
ROBIN Ay, I'll be sworn. My master knows not of your being
here, and hath threatened to put me into everlasting liberty if I
tell you of it;° for he swears he'll turn me away.²   (Falstaff's visit)
25 MISTRESS PAGE Thou'rt a good boy. This secrecy of thine shall
be a tailor to thee, and shall make thee a new doublet and
hose.—I'll go hide me.
MISTRESS FORD Do so. [*To* ROBIN] Go tell thy master I am
alone.   [*Exit* ROBIN]
30 Mistress Page, remember you your cue.
MISTRESS PAGE I warrant thee. If I do not act it, hiss me.
MISTRESS FORD Go to, then.   [*Exit* MISTRESS PAGE]

---

5. *drink . . . dance:* make it uncomfortable for Falstaff.
Pipe wine is wine from the cask, with a pun on "the
whine of musical pipes," which are played for a dance.
Ford also puns on "canary" (line 74), which is also a
dance. Drinking becomes a metaphor for Ford's intention

to make Falstaff dance to his tune.
3.3 Location: Ford's house.
1. Meadow situated between Windsor Little Park and the
Thames.
2. He'll dismiss me

We'll use this unwholesome humidity,° this gross watery pump-   *body fluids*
kin. We'll teach him to know turtles from jays.³

Enter Sir John FALSTAFF

35   FALSTAFF   Have I caught thee, my heavenly jewel? Why, now let
me die, for I have lived long enough. This is the period° of my   *goal*
ambition. O, this blessed hour!

MISTRESS FORD   O sweet Sir John!

FALSTAFF   Mistress Ford, I cannot cog;° I cannot prate, Mistress   *lie*
40   Ford. Now shall I sin in my wish: I would thy husband were
dead. I'll speak it before the best lord. I would make thee my
lady.

MISTRESS FORD   I your lady, Sir John? Alas, I should be a pitiful
lady.

45   FALSTAFF   Let the court of France show me such another. I see
how thine eye would emulate the diamond. Thou hast the
right arched beauty of the brow that becomes the ship-tire, the
tire-valiant, or any tire of Venetian admittance.⁴

MISTRESS FORD   A plain kerchief, Sir John—my brows become
50   nothing else, nor that well neither.

FALSTAFF   By the Lord, thou art a tyrant° to say so. Thou wouldst   *(punning on "tire")*
make an absolute° courtier, and the firm fixture of thy foot   *a perfect*
would give an excellent motion to thy gait in a semicircled
farthingale.⁵ I see what thou wert° if fortune, thy foe, were, with   *would be*
55   nature, thy friend. Come, thou canst not hide it.

MISTRESS FORD   Believe me, there's no such thing in me.

FALSTAFF   What made me love thee? Let that persuade thee
there's something extraordinary in thee. Come, I cannot cog
and say thou art this and that, like a-many of these lisping
60   hawthorn-buds° that come like women in men's apparel and   *young perfumed wooers*
smell like Bucklersbury⁶ in simple time;⁷ I cannot. But I love
thee, none but thee; and thou deservest it.

MISTRESS FORD   Do not betray° me, sir. I fear you love Mistress   *deceive*
Page.

65   FALSTAFF   Thou mightst as well say I love to walk by the Counter
gate,° which is as hateful to me as the reek of a lime-kiln.   *debtors' prison*

MISTRESS FORD   Well, heaven knows how I love you; and you
shall one day find it.

FALSTAFF   Keep in that mind. I'll deserve it.

70   MISTRESS FORD   Nay, I must tell you, so you do; or else I could
not be in that mind.

[*Enter* ROBIN]

ROBIN   Mistress Ford, Mistress Ford! Here's Mistress Page at the
door, sweating and blowing,° and looking wildly, and would   *puffing*
needs speak with you presently.°   *immediately*

75   FALSTAFF   She shall not see me. I will ensconce me behind the
arras.°   *wall curtain*

MISTRESS FORD   Pray you do so; she's a very tattling woman.

FALSTAFF *stands behind the arras.*

Enter MISTRESS PAGE

What's the matter? How now?

---

3. Gaudy birds, hence flirtatious women. *turtles:* turtledoves, proverbially faithful.
4. Fancifully extravagant headdresses ("tires"), the "ship-
tire" in the form of a ship, that were acceptable in Venice.
"Tire" is from "attire."

5. Skirt shaped with covered hoops at the back.
6. London street where herbs were sold.
7. Summer (when medicinal herbs, or "simples," were
available).

MISTRESS PAGE   O Mistress Ford, what have you done? You're
80   shamed, you're overthrown, you're undone for ever.
MISTRESS FORD   What's the matter, good Mistress Page?
MISTRESS PAGE   O well-a-day,° Mistress Ford! Having an honest   *alas*
man to° your husband, to give him such cause of suspicion!   *as*
MISTRESS FORD   What cause of suspicion?
85   MISTRESS PAGE   What cause of suspicion? Out upon you!° How   *(a reproach)*
am I mistook in you!
MISTRESS FORD   Why, alas, what's the matter?
MISTRESS PAGE   Your husband's coming hither, woman, with all
the officers in Windsor, to search for a gentleman that he says
90   is here now in the house, by your consent, to take an ill advantage of his absence. You are undone.
MISTRESS FORD   'Tis not so, I hope.
MISTRESS PAGE   Pray heaven it be not so that you have such a
man here! But 'tis most certain your husband's coming, with
95   half Windsor at his heels, to search for such a one. I come
before to tell you. If you know yourself clear,° why, I am glad   *innocent*
of it; but if you have a friend° here, convey, convey him out.   *lover*
Be not amazed.° Call all your senses to you. Defend your repu-   *bewildered*
tation, or bid farewell to your good° life for ever.   *respectable*
100   MISTRESS FORD   What shall I do? There is a gentleman, my dear
friend; and I fear not mine own shame so much as his peril. I
had rather than a thousand pound he were out of the house.
MISTRESS PAGE   For shame, never stand° 'you had rather' and   *waste time over*
'you had rather'. Your husband's here at hand. Bethink you of
105   some conveyance:° in the house you cannot hide him. O, how   *trick; transport*
have you deceived me! Look, here is a basket. If he be of any
reasonable stature, he may creep in here; and throw foul linen
upon him as if it were going to bucking.° Or—it is whiting°   *washing / bleaching*
time—send him by your two men to Datchet Mead.
110   MISTRESS FORD   He's too big to go in there. What shall I do?
FALSTAFF [*coming forward*]   Let me see't, let me see't, O let me
see't! I'll in, I'll in. Follow your friend's counsel; I'll in.
MISTRESS PAGE   What, Sir John Falstaff! [*Aside to him*] Are these
your letters, knight?
115   FALSTAFF [*aside to* MISTRESS PAGE]   I love thee. Help me away.
Let me creep in here.
        FALSTAFF *goes into the basket*
I'll never—
        [MISTRESS PAGE *and* MISTRESS FORD] *put* [*foul*] *clothes*
        over him
MISTRESS PAGE [*to* ROBIN]   Help to cover your master, boy.—
Call your men, Mistress Ford. [*Aside to* FALSTAFF] You dis-
120   sembling knight!
MISTRESS FORD   What, John! Robert, John!
        [*Enter* JOHN *and* ROBERT]
Go take up these clothes here quickly. Where's the cowl-staff?°   *pole to carry basket*
        [JOHN *and* ROBERT *fit the cowl-staff*]
Look how you drumble!° Carry them to the laundress in Dat-   *dawdle*
chet Mead. Quickly, come!
        [*They lift the basket and start to leave.*]
        [*Enter Master*] FORD, [*Master*] PAGE, *Doctor* CAIUS, *and*
        [*Sir Hugh*] EVANS
125   FORD [*to* PAGE, CAIUS, *and* EVANS]   Pray you come near. If I sus-

pect without cause, why then, make sport at me; then let me
be your jest—I deserve it. [*To* JOHN *and* ROBERT] How now?
Whither bear you this?

JOHN   To the laundress, forsooth.

130 MISTRESS FORD   Why, what have you to do° whither they bear it?   *to do with*
You were best° meddle with buck-washing!⁸   *(sarcastic)*

FORD   Buck? I would I could wash myself of the buck! Buck,
buck, buck? Ay, buck, I warrant you, buck. And of the season
too, it shall appear.

        [*Exeunt* JOHN *and* ROBERT, *with the basket*]

135 Gentlemen, I have dreamt tonight.° I'll tell you my dream.   *last night*
Here, here, here be my keys. Ascend° my chambers, search,   *Go up to*
seek, find out. I'll warrant we'll unkennel° the fox. Let me stop   *dislodge*
this way° first.   *passage*

        [*He locks the door*]

So, now, uncoop.

140 PAGE   Good Master Ford, be contented. You wrong yourself too
much.

FORD   True, Master Page.—Up, gentlemen! You shall see sport
anon. Follow me, gentlemen.   [*Exit*]

EVANS   This is fery fantastical humours and jealousies.

145 CAIUS   By Gar, 'tis no the fashion of France; it is not jealous in
France.

PAGE   Nay, follow him, gentlemen. See the issue of his search.

        Exeunt [CAIUS, EVANS, *and* PAGE]

MISTRESS PAGE   Is there not a double excellency in this?

MISTRESS FORD   I know not which pleases me better: that my
150 husband is deceived, or Sir John.

MISTRESS PAGE   What a taking° was he in when your husband   *panic*
asked what was in the basket!

MISTRESS FORD   I am half afraid he will have need of washing,⁹
so throwing him into the water will do him a benefit.

155 MISTRESS PAGE   Hang him, dishonest rascal! I would all of the
same strain were in the same distress.

MISTRESS FORD   I think my husband hath some special suspicion
of Falstaff's being here, for I never saw him so gross in his
jealousy till now.

160 MISTRESS PAGE   I will lay a plot to try° that, and we will yet have   *test*
more tricks with Falstaff. His dissolute disease will scarce obey°   *be cured by*
this medicine.

MISTRESS FORD   Shall we send that foolish carrion° Mistress   *rotten flesh*
Quickly to him, and excuse his throwing into the water, and
165 give him another hope, to betray him to another punishment?

MISTRESS PAGE   We will do it. Let him be sent for tomorrow
eight o'clock, to have amends.

        Enter [FORD, PAGE, CAIUS, *and* EVANS]

FORD   I cannot find him. Maybe the knave bragged of that he
could not compass.°   *accomplish*

170 MISTRESS PAGE [*aside to* MISTRESS FORD]   Heard you that?

MISTRESS FORD   You use me well, Master Ford, do you?

FORD   Ay, I do so.

MISTRESS FORD   Heaven make me better than your thoughts!

---

8. Washing that needs bleaching (but Ford thinks of   9. Fear will have made him urinate.
"buck" as "stag," the horned cuckold, and "to copulate").

FORD   Amen.

175 MISTRESS PAGE   You do yourself mighty wrong, Master Ford.

FORD   Ay, ay, I must bear it.

EVANS   If there be anypody in the house, and in the chambers, and in the coffers, and in the presses,° heaven forgive my sins at the day of judgement!   *cupboards*

180 CAIUS   Be Gar, nor I too. There is nobodies.

PAGE   Fie, fie, Master Ford, are you not ashamed? What spirit, what devil suggests this imagination? I would not ha' your distemper in this kind for the wealth of Windsor Castle.

FORD   'Tis my fault, Master Page. I suffer for it.

185 EVANS   You suffer for a pad conscience. Your wife is as honest a 'omans as I will desires among five thousand, and five hundred too.

CAIUS   By Gar, I see 'tis an honest woman.

FORD   Well, I promised you a dinner. Come, come, walk in the
190 park. I pray you pardon me. I will hereafter make known to you why I have done this.—Come, wife; come, Mistress Page. I pray you pardon me. Pray heartily pardon me.

PAGE   [*to* CAIUS *and* EVANS] Let's go in, gentlemen. [*Aside to them*] But trust me, we'll mock him. [*To* FORD, CAIUS, *and*
195 EVANS] I do invite you tomorrow morning to my house to breakfast. After, we'll a-birding° together. I have a fine hawk for[1] the   *bird hunting*
bush. Shall it be so?

FORD   Anything.

EVANS   If there is one, I shall make two in the company.

200 CAIUS   If there be one or two, I shall make-a the turd.

FORD   Pray you go, Master Page.

Exeunt [all but EVANS *and* CAIUS]

EVANS   I pray you now, remembrance tomorrow on the lousy knave mine Host.[2]

CAIUS   Dat is good, by Gar; with all my heart.

205 EVANS   A lousy knave, to have his gibes and his mockeries.

Exeunt

3.4

Enter Master FENTON *and* ANNE *Page*

FENTON   I see I cannot get thy father's love;
Therefore no more turn me to him, sweet Nan.

ANNE   Alas, how then?

FENTON   Why, thou must be thyself.°   *in charge of yourself*
He doth object I am too great of birth,
5   And that, my state being galled with° my expense,   *estate being hurt by*
I seek to heal it only by his wealth.
Besides these, other bars he lays before me—
My riots past, my wild societies;°   *companionships*
And tells me 'tis a thing impossible
10   I should love thee but as a property.

ANNE   Maybe he tells you true.

FENTON   No, heaven so speed° me in my time to come!   *as heaven may prosper*
Albeit I will confess thy father's wealth
Was the first motive that I wooed thee, Anne,

---

1. For driving birds into.
2. A cryptic reference to the "revenge" proposal at

3.1.101.
3.4 Location: Outside Page's house.

15 Yet, wooing thee, I found thee of more value
   Than stamps in gold° or sums in sealèd bags;   *stamped gold coins*
   And 'tis the very riches of thyself
   That now I aim at.
ANNE   Gentle Master Fenton,
   Yet seek my father's love, still seek it, sir.
20 If opportunity and humblest suit
   Cannot attain it, why then—
       Enter [Justice] SHALLOW, *[Master]* SLENDER *[richly
       dressed], and* MISTRESS QUICKLY
                    Hark you hither.
       [They talk apart]
SHALLOW   Break their talk, Mistress Quickly. My kinsman shall
   speak for himself.
SLENDER   I'll make a shaft or a bolt on't.¹ 'Slid,° 'tis but ven-   *By God's eyelid*
25 turing.
SHALLOW   Be not dismayed.
SLENDER   No, she shall not dismay me.
   I care not for that, but that I am afeard.
MISTRESS QUICKLY *[to* ANNE*]*   Hark ye, Master Slender would
   speak a word with you.
30 ANNE   I come to him. *[To* FENTON*]* This is my father's choice.
   O, what a world of vile ill-favoured° faults   *ugly*
   Looks handsome in three hundred pounds a year!°   *(moderate wealth)*
MISTRESS QUICKLY   And how does good Master Fenton? Pray
   you, a word with you.
       [She draws FENTON *aside]*
35 SHALLOW   She's coming. To her, coz! O boy, thou hadst a
   father!°   *be manly; you're manly*
SLENDER   I had a father, Mistress Anne; my uncle can tell you
   good jests of him.—Pray you, uncle, tell Mistress Anne the jest
   how my father stole two geese out of a pen, good uncle.
40 SHALLOW   Mistress Anne, my cousin loves you.
SLENDER   Ay, that I do, as well as I love any woman in Gloucestershire.
SHALLOW   He will maintain you like a gentlewoman.
SLENDER   Ay, by God, that I will, come cut and long-tail,° under   *no matter what*
45 the degree° of a squire.   *in the rank*
SHALLOW   He will make you a hundred and fifty pounds join-
   ture.°   *widowhood settlement*
ANNE   Good Master Shallow, let him woo for himself.
SHALLOW   Marry, I thank you for it, I thank you for that good
50 comfort.—She calls you, coz. I'll leave you.
       [He stands aside]
ANNE   Now, Master Slender.
SLENDER   Now, good Mistress Anne.
ANNE   What is your will?
SLENDER   My will? 'Od's heartlings,° that's a pretty jest indeed! I   *By God's little hearts*
55 ne'er made my will yet, I thank God; I am not such a sickly
   creature, I give God praise.
ANNE   I mean, Master Slender, what would you with me?
SLENDER   Truly, for mine own part, I would little or nothing

---

1. I'll do it one way or another (with possible sexual connotation).

with you. Your father and my uncle hath made motions.° If it   *proposals*
60   be my luck, so. If not, happy man be his dole.² They can tell
you how things go better than I can

Enter Master PAGE [*and*] MISTRESS PAGE

You may ask your father: here he comes.
PAGE   Now, Master Slender.—Love him, daughter Anne.—
Why, how now? What does Master Fenton here?
65   You wrong me, sir, thus still to haunt my house.
I told you, sir, my daughter is disposed of.
FENTON   Nay, Master Page, be not impatient.
MISTRESS PAGE   Good Master Fenton, come not to my child.
PAGE   She is no match for you.
70   FENTON   Sir, will you hear me?
PAGE   No, good Master Fenton.—
Come, Master Shallow; come, son Slender, in.—
Knowing my mind, you wrong me, Master Fenton.

Exeunt PAGE[, SHALLOW, *and* SLENDER]

MISTRESS QUICKLY [*to* FENTON]   Speak to Mistress Page.
75   FENTON   Good Mistress Page, for that° I love your daughter   *because*
In such a righteous fashion as I do,
Perforce against all checks,° rebukes, and manners   *reproofs*
I must advance the colours° of my love,   *military banners*
And not retire. Let me have your good will.
80   ANNE   Good mother, do not marry me to yon fool.
MISTRESS PAGE   I mean it not; I seek you a better husband.
MISTRESS QUICKLY [*aside to* ANNE]   That's my master, Master
Doctor.
ANNE   Alas, I had rather be set quick i'th' earth°   *half-buried alive*
85   And bowled to death with turnips.
MISTRESS PAGE   Come, trouble not yourself, good Master Fenton.
I will not be your friend nor enemy.
My daughter will I question how she loves you,
And as I find her, so am I affected.°   *inclined*
90   Till then, farewell, sir. She must needs go in.
Her father will be angry.
FENTON   Farewell, gentle mistress.—Farewell, Nan.

Exeunt [MISTRESS PAGE *and* ANNE]

MISTRESS QUICKLY   This is my doing now. 'Nay', said I, 'will you
cast away your child on a fool and a physician? Look on Master
95   Fenton.' This is my doing.
FENTON   I thank thee, [*giving her a ring*] and I pray thee, once°   *at some time*
tonight
Give my sweet Nan this ring. [*Giving money*] There's for thy
pains.
MISTRESS QUICKLY   Now heaven send thee good fortune!

Exit FENTON

A kind heart he hath. A woman would run through fire and
100   water for such a kind heart. But yet I would my master had
Mistress Anne; or I would Master Slender had her, or, in sooth,
I would Master Fenton had her. I will do what I can for them
all three, for so I have promised, and I'll be as good as my
word—but speciously° for Master Fenton. Well, I must of°   *(for "specially") / run*

---

2. Good luck to the successful suitor.

105   another errand to Sir John Falstaff from my two mistresses.
    What a beast am I to slack° it!   *Exit*   *to be remiss in*

3.5

                 Enter Sir John FALSTAFF
FALSTAFF   Bardolph, I say!
               Enter BARDOLPH
BARDOLPH   Here, sir.
FALSTAFF   Go fetch me a quart of sack; put a toast° in't.   *piece of hot toast*
                     [*Exit* BARDOLPH]
    Have I lived to be carried in a basket like a barrow° of butcher's   *wheelbarrow*
5   offal, and to be thrown in the Thames? Well, if I be served
    such another trick, I'll have my brains ta'en out and buttered,[1]
    and give them to a dog for a New Year's gift. 'Sblood, the rogues
    slighted° me into the river with as little remorse as they would   *slid; scorned*
    have drowned a blind bitch's° puppies, fifteen i'th' litter! And   *bitch's blind*
10   you may know by my size that I have a kind of alacrity in sink-
    ing. If the bottom were as deep as hell, I should down.° I had   *reach the bottom*
    been drowned, but that the shore was shelvy° and shallow—a   *made of sandbanks*
    death that I abhor, for the water swells a man, and what a thing
    should I have been when I had been swelled? By the Lord, a
15   mountain of mummy!°   *dead flesh*
       [*Enter* BARDOLPH, *with two large cups of sack*]
BARDOLPH   Here's Mistress Quickly, sir, to speak with you.
FALSTAFF   Come, let me pour in some sack to the Thames'
    water, for my belly's as cold as if I had swallowed snowballs for
    pills to cool the reins.°   *kidneys*
                 [*He drinks*]
20   Call her in.
BARDOLPH   Come in, woman!
               Enter MISTRESS QUICKLY
MISTRESS QUICKLY [*to* FALSTAFF]   By your leave; I cry you
    mercy.[2] Give your worship good morrow!
FALSTAFF [*drinking, then speaking to* BARDOLPH]   Take away
25   these chalices. Go brew° me a pottle° of sack, finely.   *prepare / two quarts*
BARDOLPH   With eggs, sir?
FALSTAFF   Simple of itself.° I'll no pullet-sperms in my brewage.   *Pure*
              [*Exit* BARDOLPH, *with cups*]
    How now?
MISTRESS QUICKLY   Marry, sir, I come to your worship from Mis-
30   tress Ford.
FALSTAFF   Mistress Ford? I have had ford enough: I was thrown
    into the ford, I have my belly full of ford.
MISTRESS QUICKLY   Alas the day, good heart, that was not her
    fault. She does so take on with her men; they mistook their
35   erection.[3]
FALSTAFF   So did I mine, to build upon a foolish woman's
    promise.
MISTRESS QUICKLY   Well, she laments, sir, for it, that it would
    yearn° your heart to see it. Her husband goes this morning a-   *grieve*
40   birding. She desires you once more to come to her, between

---

3.5 Location: The Garter Inn.
1. "Buttered" brains may have meant "foolish."
2. *I cry you mercy:* excuse me.

3. Quickly means that Mistress Ford "does take on"
(scold) her servants, who misunderstood her direction,
but there's an obvious, unintentional sexual pun.

eight and nine. I must carry her word° quickly. She'll make   *your reply*
you amends, I warrant you.

FALSTAFF   Well, I will visit her. Tell her so, and bid her think
what a man is; let her consider his frailty, and then judge of my

45   merit.

MISTRESS QUICKLY   I will tell her.

FALSTAFF   Do so. Between nine and ten, sayst thou?

MISTRESS QUICKLY   Eight and nine, sir.

FALSTAFF   Well, be gone. I will not miss° her.   *fail*

50 MISTRESS QUICKLY   Peace be with you, sir.   *Exit*

FALSTAFF   I marvel I hear not of Master Brooke; he sent me
word to stay° within. I like his money well.   *wait for him*

     Enter [Master] FORD, [disguised as] Brooke
By the mass, here he comes.

FORD   God bless you, sir.

55 FALSTAFF   Now, Master Brooke, you come to know what hath
passed between me and Ford's wife.

FORD   That indeed, Sir John, is my business.

FALSTAFF   Master Brooke, I will not lie to you. I was at her house
the hour she appointed me.

60 FORD   And sped you,° sir?   *did you succeed*

FALSTAFF   Very ill-favouredly,° Master Brooke.   *badly*

FORD   How so, sir? Did she change her determination?

FALSTAFF   No, Master Brooke, but the peaking cornuto° her hus-   *sneaking cuckold*
band, Master Brooke, dwelling in a continual 'larum° of jeal-   *alarm*

65   ousy, comes me° in the instant of our encounter—after we had   *comes*
embraced, kissed, protested, and, as it were, spoke the prologue
of our comedy—and at his heels a rabble of his companions,
thither provoked and instigated by his distemper, and, forsooth,
to search his house for his wife's love.

70 FORD   What, while you were there?

FALSTAFF   While I was there.

FORD   And did he search for you, and could not find you?

FALSTAFF   You shall hear. As God would have it, comes in one
Mistress Page, gives intelligence of Ford's approach, and, by

75   her invention and Ford's wife's distraction, they conveyed me
into a buck-basket—

FORD   A buck-basket?

FALSTAFF   By the Lord, a buck-basket!—rammed me in with foul
shirts and smocks, socks, foul stockings, greasy napkins, that,°   *so that*

80   Master Brooke, there was the rankest compound of villainous
smell that ever offended nostril.

FORD   And how long lay you there?

FALSTAFF   Nay, you shall hear, Master Brooke, what I have suffered to bring this woman to evil, for your good. Being thus

85   crammed in the basket, a couple of Ford's knaves, his hinds,°   *servants (pejorative)*
were called forth by their mistress, to carry me, in the name of
foul clothes, to Datchet Lane. They took me on their shoulders, met the jealous knave their master in the door, who asked
them once or twice what they had in their basket. I quaked for

90   fear lest the lunatic knave would have searched it, but fate,
ordaining he should be a cuckold, held° his hand. Well, on   *held back*
went he for a search, and away went I for foul clothes. But mark
the sequel, Master Brooke. I suffered the pangs of three several°   *different*
deaths. First, an intolerable fright, to be detected with° a jeal-   *by*

95   ous rotten bell-wether.[4] Next, to be compassed like a good
      bilbo in the circumference of a peck,[5] hilt to point, heel to
      head. And then, to be stopped° in, like a strong distillation,°   stoppered / liquid
      with stinking clothes that fretted° in their own grease. Think of   fermented
      that—a man of my kidney°—think of that—that am as subject   constitution
100   to heat as butter, a man of continual dissolution° and thaw. It   melting
      was a miracle to scape suffocation. And in the height of this
      bath, when I was more than half stewed in grease like a Dutch
      dish, to be thrown into the Thames and cooled, glowing-hot,
      in that surge, like a horseshoe. Think of that—hissing hot—
105   think of that, Master Brooke!
FORD   In good sadness,° sir, I am sorry that for my sake you have   seriousness
      suffered all this. My suit then is desperate. You'll undertake
      her no more?
FALSTAFF   Master Brooke, I will be thrown into Etna° as I have   Sicilian volcano
110   been into Thames ere I will leave her thus. Her husband is
      this morning gone a-birding. I have received from her another
      embassy° of meeting. 'Twixt eight and nine is the hour, Master   message
      Brooke.
FORD   'Tis past eight already, sir.
115 FALSTAFF   Is it? I will then address me to my appointment.
      Come to me at your convenient leisure, and you shall know
      how I speed; and the conclusion shall be crowned with your
      enjoying her. Adieu. You shall have her, Master Brooke; Master
      Brooke, you shall cuckold Ford.   *Exit*
120 FORD   Hum! Ha! Is this a vision? Is this a dream? Do I sleep?
      Master Ford, awake! Awake, Master Ford! There's a hole made
      in your best coat,[6] Master Ford. This 'tis to be married! This
      'tis to have linen and buck-baskets! Well, I will proclaim myself
      what I am. I will now take° the lecher. He is at my house. He   catch
125   cannot scape me; 'tis impossible he should. He cannot creep
      into a halfpenny purse, nor into a pepperbox. But lest the devil
      that guides him should aid him, I will search impossible places.
      Though what I am I cannot avoid, yet to be what I would not
      shall not make me tame. If I have horns to make one mad, let
130   the proverb go with me: I'll be horn-mad.[7]   *Exit*

4.1

Enter MISTRESS PAGE, [MISTRESS] QUICKLY, [*and*] WIL-
LIAM *Page*
MISTRESS PAGE   Is he at Mistress Ford's already, thinkest thou?
MISTRESS QUICKLY   Sure he is by this,° or will be presently.° But   now / immediately
      truly he is very courageous°-mad about his throwing into the   (for "ragingly")
      water. Mistress Ford desires you to come suddenly.°   at once
5   MISTRESS PAGE   I'll be with her by and by.° I'll but bring my   right away
      young man here to school.
      Enter [*Sir Hugh*] EVANS
      Look where his master comes. 'Tis a playing day, I see.—How
      now, Sir Hugh, no school today?

---

4. Castrated ram, leader of the flock, with a bell round its
neck and a horn like a cuckold's on its head.
5. To be bent double (encompassed) like a flexible sword
(from Bilbao, Spain, where fine swords known for their
elasticity were made) in the cramped space of a laundry
basket (in a receptacle holding a peck, or a quarter of a

bushel).
6. Proverbial for "Your reputation is spoiled."
7. I'll be as furious as a horned animal in breeding season; furious to be a cuckold.
4.1 Location: Outdoors.

EVANS   No, Master Slender is let° the boys leave° to play.　　　　*asked that / be allowed*

10   MISTRESS QUICKLY   Blessing of his heart!

MISTRESS PAGE   Sir Hugh, my husband says my son profits r oth-
ing in the world[1] at his book. I pray you ask him some questions
in his accidence.°　　　　*Latin grammar*

EVANS   Come hither, William. Hold up your head. Come.

15   MISTRESS PAGE   Come on, sirrah. Hold up your head. Answer
your master; be not afraid.

EVANS   William, how many numbers is in nouns?

WILLIAM   Two.°　　　　*(singular and plural)*

MISTRESS QUICKLY   Truly, I thought there had been one number
20   more, because they say ''Od's nouns'.[2]

EVANS   Peace your tattlings!—What is 'fair', William?

WILLIAM   'Pulcher'.

MISTRESS QUICKLY   Polecats?° There are fairer things than pole-　　*Smelly animals; whores*
cats, sure.

25   EVANS   You are a very simplicity 'oman. I pray you peace.—
What is 'lapis', William?

WILLIAM   A stone.

EVANS   And what is 'a stone', William?

WILLIAM   A pebble.

30   EVANS   No, it is 'lapis'. I pray you remember in your prain.

WILLIAM   'Lapis'.

EVANS   That is a good William. What is he, William, that does
lend articles?

WILLIAM   Articles are borrowed of the pronoun, and be thus
35   declined. *Singulariter nominativo: 'hic, haec, hoc'.*[3]

EVANS   *Nominativo: 'hig, hag, hog'.*[4] Pray you mark: *genitivo:*°　　　*genitive*
'huius'. Well, what is your accusative case?

WILLIAM   *Accusativo: 'hinc'*°—　　　　*(for "hunc")*

EVANS   I pray you have your remembrance, child. *Accusativo:*
40   *'hing, hang, hog'.*

MISTRESS QUICKLY   'Hang-hog'[5] is Latin for bacon, I warrant you.

EVANS   Leave your prabbles, 'oman!—What is the focative° case,　　*vocative; (obscene)*
William?

WILLIAM   *O—vocativo, O—*

45   EVANS   Remember, William, focative is *caret.*[6]

MISTRESS QUICKLY   And that's a good root.

EVANS   'Oman, forbear.

MISTRESS PAGE [*to* MISTRESS QUICKLY]   Peace.

EVANS   What is your genitive case plural, William?

50   WILLIAM   Genitive case?

EVANS   Ay.

WILLIAM   *Genitivo: 'horum, harum, horum'.*

MISTRESS QUICKLY   Vengeance of° Jenny's case! Fie on her!　　　*A plague on*
Never name her, child, if she be a whore.[7]

55   EVANS   For shame, 'oman!

MISTRESS QUICKLY   You do ill to teach the child such words. He

---

1. My son fails to improve.
2. God's wounds; three is an odd ("Od's") number
3. William recites by memory from his textbook. "*Singulariter nominativo*" is "in the nominative singular" (in
which William gives the masculine, feminine, and neuter
of the pronoun "this").
4. The pronunciation in Evans's accent.
5. Alluding to the saying "Hog is not bacon until it be

hanged."
6. Missing. Quickly understands "carrot," whose slang
sense 'penis' is supported by a suggestion of "fuck" in
"focative."
7. *Genitive case . . whore:* "Genitive" is perhaps misun-
derstandable as Latin for "generative" or even "genital"—
as well as "Jenny"; "case" is understood by Quickly to
mean "situation" and also the slang term for "vagina."

teaches him to hick and to hack,° which they'll do fast enough   *drink and copulate?*
of themselves, and to call 'whorum'. Fie upon you!

EVANS   'Oman, art thou lunatics? Hast thou no understandings
60   for thy cases, and the numbers of the genders? Thou art as
foolish Christian creatures as I would desires.

MISTRESS PAGE [*to* MISTRESS QUICKLY]   Prithee, hold thy peace.

EVANS   Show me now, William, some declensions of your pronouns.

65   WILLIAM   Forsooth, I have forgot.

EVANS   It is '*qui, que, quod*'. If you forget your '*qui's*, your '*que's*,
and your '*quod's*,[8] you must be preeches.° Go your ways and   *flogged*
play; go.

MISTRESS PAGE   He is a better scholar than I thought he was.

70   EVANS   He is a good sprag° memory. Farewell, Mistress Page.   *sprack (lively)*

MISTRESS PAGE   Adieu, good Sir Hugh.   [*Exit* EVANS]
Get you home, boy.   [*Exit* WILLIAM]
[*To* MISTRESS QUICKLY] Come, we stay too long.   *Exeunt*

4.2

Enter Sir John FALSTAFF *and* MISTRESS FORD

FALSTAFF   Mistress Ford, your sorrow hath eaten up my sufferance.[1] I see you are obsequious° in your love, and I profess   *devoted*
requital to a hair's breadth:° not only, Mistress Ford, in the   *in full*
simple office of love, but in all the accoutrement, complement,
5   and ceremony of it. But are you sure of your husband now?

MISTRESS FORD   He's a-birding, sweet Sir John.

MISTRESS PAGE [*within*]   What ho, gossip° Ford, what ho!   *friend*

MISTRESS FORD   Step into th' chamber, Sir John.

He steps [*into the chamber*]

Enter MISTRESS PAGE

MISTRESS PAGE   How now, sweetheart, who's at home besides
10   yourself?

MISTRESS FORD   Why, none but mine own people.°   *servants*

MISTRESS PAGE   Indeed?

MISTRESS FORD   No, certainly. [*Aside to her*] Speak louder.

MISTRESS PAGE   Truly, I am so glad you have nobody here.

15   MISTRESS FORD   Why?

MISTRESS PAGE   Why, woman, your husband is in his old lines°   *role*
again. He so takes on° yonder with my husband, so rails against   *raves*
all married mankind, so curses all Eve's daughters° of what   *women*
complexion° soever, and so buffets himself on the forehead,   *temperament*
20   crying 'Peer out,[2] peer out!', that any madness I ever yet beheld
seemed but tameness, civility, and patience to this his distemper he is in now. I am glad the fat knight is not here.

MISTRESS FORD   Why, does he talk of him?

MISTRESS PAGE   Of none but him; and swears he was carried out,
25   the last time he searched for him, in a basket, protests to my
husband he is now here, and hath drawn him and the rest of
their company from their sport to make another experiment° of   *trial*
his suspicion. But I am glad the knight is not here. Now he
shall see his own foolery.

---

8. Possibly pronounced as "keys, case, cods," with "keys"
a euphemism for "penis," "case" a term for "vagina," and
"cods" slang for "testicles."
4.2 Location: Ford's house.

1. Your sorrow has made the memory of my suffering disappear.
2. Emerge (addressed to imagined cuckold's horns).

30   MISTRESS FORD   How near is he, Mistress Page?

     MISTRESS PAGE   Hard by at street end. He will be here anon.

     MISTRESS FORD   I am undone: the knight is here.

     MISTRESS PAGE   Why then, you are utterly shamed, and he's but
     a dead man. What a woman are you! Away with him, away
35   with him! Better shame than murder.

     MISTRESS FORD   Which way should he go? How should I bestow°   *dispose of*
     him? Shall I put him into the basket again?

         [FALSTAFF *comes forth from the chamber*]

     FALSTAFF   No, I'll come no more i'th' basket. May I not go out
     ere he come?

40   MISTRESS PAGE   Alas, three of Master Ford's brothers watch the
     door with pistols, that none shall issue out. Otherwise you
     might slip away ere he came. But what make you° here?   *are you doing*

     FALSTAFF   What shall I do? I'll creep up into the chimney.

     MISTRESS FORD   There they always use to discharge their birding-
45   pieces.°   *bird guns*

     MISTRESS PAGE   Creep into the kiln-hole.°   *oven*

     FALSTAFF   Where is it?

     MISTRESS FORD   He will seek there, on my word. Neither press,°   *cupboard*
     coffer, chest, trunk, well, vault, but he hath an abstract° for the   *a list*
50   remembrance of such places, and goes to them by his note.
     There is no hiding you in the house.

     FALSTAFF   I'll go out, then.

     MISTRESS PAGE   If you go out in your own semblance, you die,
     Sir John—unless you go out disguised.

55   MISTRESS FORD   How might we disguise him?

     MISTRESS PAGE   Alas the day, I know not. There is no woman's
     gown big enough for him; otherwise he might put on a hat, a
     muffler,° and a kerchief, and so escape.   *face scarf*

     FALSTAFF   Good hearts, devise something. Any extremity° rather   *extravagance*
60   than a mischief.°   *calamity*

     MISTRESS FORD   My maid's aunt, the fat woman of Brentford,[3]
     has a gown above.

     MISTRESS PAGE   On my word, it will serve him; she's as big as he
     is; and there's her thrummed° hat, and her muffler too.—Run   *fringed*
65   up, Sir John.

     MISTRESS FORD   Go, go, sweet Sir John. Mistress Page and I will
     look° some linen for your head.   *look for*

     MISTRESS PAGE   Quick, quick! We'll come dress you straight.
     Put on the gown the while.   *Exit Sir John* [FALSTAFF]

70   MISTRESS FORD   I would my husband would meet him in this
     shape. He cannot abide the old woman of Brentford. He swears
     she's a witch, forbade her my house, and hath threatened to
     beat her.

     MISTRESS PAGE   Heaven guide him to thy husband's cudgel, and
75   the devil guide his cudgel afterwards!

     MISTRESS FORD   But is my husband coming?

     MISTRESS PAGE   Ay, in good sadness° is he, and talks of the basket   *in all seriousness*
     too, howsoever[4] he hath had intelligence.°   *information*

     MISTRESS FORD   We'll try° that, for I'll appoint my men to carry   *test*

---

3. Gillian of Brentford, a scurrilous comic figure, perhaps historically based, best known for her will, in which
she supposedly "bequeathed a score of farts amongst her

friends." Brentford was a village halfway between Windsor and London.
4. By whatever means.

80 the basket again, to meet him at the door with it as they did
last time.
MISTRESS PAGE   Nay, but he'll be here presently. Let's go dress
him like the witch of Brentford.
MISTRESS FORD   I'll first direct my men what they shall do with
85 the basket. Go up; I'll bring linen for him straight.°   *immediately*
MISTRESS PAGE   Hang him, dishonest° varlet! We cannot misuse   *lewd*
him enough.   [*Exit* MISTRESS FORD]
We'll leave a proof by that which we will do,
Wives may be merry, and yet honest,° too.   *chaste*
90 We do not act that° often jest and laugh.   *misbehave who*
'Tis old but true: 'Still swine eats all the draff'.⁵   *Exit*
        Enter MISTRESS FORD [*with* JOHN *and* ROBERT]
MISTRESS FORD   Go, sirs, take the basket again on your shoulders.
Your master is hard at° door. If he bid you set it down, obey   *close to the*
him. Quickly, dispatch!   [*Exit*]
95 JOHN   Come, come, take it up.
ROBERT   Pray heaven it be not full of knight again.
JOHN   I hope not; I had as lief ° bear so much lead.   *I would rather*
        [*They lift*] *the basket.*
        Enter [*Master*] FORD, [*Master*] PAGE, [*Doctor*] CAIUS,
        [*Sir Hugh*] EVANS, *and* [*Justice*] SHALLOW
FORD   Ay, but if it prove true, Master Page, have you any way
then to unfool me again?⁶ [*To* JOHN *and* ROBERT] Set down
100 the basket, villains.
        [JOHN *and* ROBERT *set down the basket*]
Somebody call my wife. Youth in a basket!° O, you panderly   *Fortunate lover?*
rascals! There's a knot,° a gang, a pack, a conspiracy against   *group*
me. Now shall the devil be shamed.°—What, wife, I say!   *truth be known*
Come, come forth! Behold what honest clothes you send forth
105 to bleaching.
PAGE   Why, this passes,° Master Ford. You are not to go loose   *goes beyond all bounds*
any longer; you must be pinioned.
EVANS   Why, this is lunatics; this is mad as a mad dog.
SHALLOW   Indeed, Master Ford, this is not well, indeed.
110 FORD   So say I too, sir.
        [*Enter* MISTRESS FORD]
Come hither, Mistress Ford! Mistress Ford, the honest woman,
the modest wife, the virtuous creature, that hath the jealous
fool to° her husband! I suspect without cause, mistress, do I?   *for*
MISTRESS FORD   God be my witness you do, if you suspect me in
115 any dishonesty.
FORD   Well said, brazen-face; hold it out.°   *keep it up*
        [*He opens the basket and starts to take out clothes*]
Come forth, sirrah!
PAGE   This passes.
MISTRESS FORD [*to* FORD]   Are you not ashamed? Let the clothes
120 alone.
FORD   I shall find you anon.
EVANS   'Tis unreasonable: will you take up your wife's clothes?
Come, away.

---

5. Proverbial: "The quiet swine eats all the hog's wash."   6. Page has evidently accused Ford of making a fool of
In other words, quietness conceals sexual immorality   himself.
(whereas playfulness is innocent; see line 90).

FORD [to JOHN and ROBERT]   Empty the basket, I say.

125 PAGE   Why, man, why?

FORD   Master Page, as I am a man, there was one conveyed out
of my house yesterday in this basket. Why may not he be there
again? In my house I am sure he is. My intelligence° is true,   *information*
my jealousy is reasonable. [To JOHN and ROBERT] Pluck me

130 out all the linen.

[*He takes out clothes*]

MISTRESS FORD   If you find a man there, he shall die a flea's
death.[7]

PAGE   Here's no man.

SHALLOW   By my fidelity, this is not well, Master Ford. This

135 wrongs you.°   *You shame yourself*

EVANS   Master Ford, you must pray, and not follow the imaginations of your own heart. This is jealousies.

FORD   Well, he's not here I seek for.

PAGE   No, nor nowhere else but in your brain.

140 FORD   Help to search my house this one time. If I find not what
I seek, show no colour° for my extremity;° let me for ever be   *excuse / excesses*
your table-sport;° let them say of me, 'As jealous as Ford, that   *laughingstock*
searched a hollow walnut for his wife's leman'.° Satisfy me   *lover*
once more; once more search with me.

[*Exeunt JOHN and ROBERT with the basket*]

145 MISTRESS FORD   What ho, Mistress Page! Come you and the old
woman down. My husband will come into the chamber.

FORD   Old woman? What old woman's that?

MISTRESS FORD   Why, it is my maid's Aunt of Brentford.

FORD   A witch, a quean, an old, cozening quean!° Have I not   *cheating hussy*

150 forbid her my house? She comes of errands, does she? We are
simple men; we do not know what's brought to pass under the
profession° of fortune-telling. She works by charms, by spells,   *claim*
by th' figure,[8] and such daubery° as this is, beyond our ele-   *trickery*
ment.° We know nothing.—Come down, you witch, you hag,   *knowledge*

155 you! Come down, I say!

*Enter MISTRESS PAGE, and FALSTAFF, disguised like an
old woman.*

[FORD *makes towards them*]

MISTRESS FORD   Nay, good sweet husband!—Good gentlemen,
let him not strike the old woman.

MISTRESS PAGE [to FALSTAFF]   Come, Mother Prat.° Come, give   *Buttocks*
me your hand.

160 FORD   I'll prat° her!   *beat; trick*

FORD *beats* [FALSTAFF]

Out of my door, you witch, you rag, you baggage, you polecat,
you runnion!° Out, out! I'll conjure you, I'll fortune-tell you!   *contemptible woman*

[*Exit FALSTAFF*]

MISTRESS PAGE   Are you not ashamed? I think you have killed
the poor woman.

165 MISTRESS FORD   Nay, he will do it.—'Tis a goodly credit for you!

FORD   Hang her, witch!

EVANS   By Jeshu, I think the 'oman is a witch indeed. I like not

---

7. Anyone hiding there must be insignificantly small
and used to living in clothes.

8. Astrological or magical diagrams, or wax effigies used
by witches.

when a 'oman has a great peard. I spy a great peard under his
muffler.

170 FORD   Will you follow, gentlemen? I beseech you, follow. See
but the issue° of my jealousy. If I cry out° thus upon no trail,   outcome / bark
never trust me when I open° again.   start barking

PAGE   Let's obey his humour° a little further. Come, gentlemen.   indulge him

Exeunt [the men]

MISTRESS PAGE   By my troth, he beat him most pitifully.

175 MISTRESS FORD   Nay, by th' mass, that he did not—he beat him
most unpitifully, methought.

MISTRESS PAGE   I'll have the cudgel hallowed and hung o'er the
altar. It hath done meritorious service.

MISTRESS FORD   What think you—may we, with the warrant of
180 womanhood and the witness of a good conscience, pursue
him with any further revenge?

MISTRESS PAGE   The spirit of wantonness is sure scared out of
him. If the devil have him not in fee-simple, with fine and
recovery, he will never, I think, in the way of waste attempt us
185 again.[9]

MISTRESS FORD   Shall we tell our husbands how we have served
him?

MISTRESS PAGE   Yes, by all means, if it be but to scrape the fig-
ures° out of your husband's brains. If they can find in their   fantasies
190 hearts the poor, unvirtuous, fat knight shall be any further
afflicted, we two will still be the ministers.

MISTRESS FORD   I'll warrant they'll have him publicly shamed,
and methinks there would be no period° to the jest should he   conclusion
not be publicly shamed.

195 MISTRESS PAGE   Come, to the forge with it, then shape it. I would
not have things cool.   *Exeunt*

4.3

Enter [the] HOST *[of the Garter] and* BARDOLPH

BARDOLPH   Sir, the Germans desire to have three of your horses.
The Duke himself will be tomorrow at court, and they° are   (the Germans)
going to meet him.

HOST   What duke should that be comes° so secretly? I hear not   who comes
5 of him in the court. Let me speak with the gentlemen. They
speak English?

BARDOLPH   Ay, sir. I'll call them to you.

HOST   They shall have my horses, but I'll make them pay; I'll
sauce them.° They have had my house a week at command;[1]   make them pay dearly
10 I have turned away my other guests. They must come off;° I'll   pay up
sauce them. Come.[2]   *Exeunt*

---

9. Legal terms: If the devil doesn't absolutely own him,
he won't try to despoil us again.
4.3 Location: The Garter Inn.
1. They have had my inn at their disposal for a week.
2. The German Duke is fiction, part of a plot whereby
Caius and Evans revenge themselves on the Host. The

exact details are obscure. A scene or more may have been
censored in which Caius and Evans, or some other characters, disguised themselves as Germans and duped the
Host. Evidently Sir John also parts with his horses: see
5.5.110–11 and 2.1.84–85.

4.4

Enter [Master] PAGE, *[Master]* FORD, MISTRESS PAGE,
MISTRESS FORD, *and Sir Hugh* EVANS

EVANS 'Tis one of the best discretions of a 'oman¹ as ever I did
look upon.

PAGE And did he send you both these letters at an instant?°   *at the same time*

MISTRESS PAGE Within a quarter of an hour.

5   FORD Pardon me, wife. Henceforth do what thou wilt.
I rather will suspect the sun with° cold   *of*
Than thee with wantonness. Now doth thy honour stand,
In him that was of late an heretic,
As firm as faith.

PAGE   'Tis well, 'tis well; no more.

10   Be not as extreme in submission
As in offence.
But let our plot go forward. Let our wives
Yet once again, to make us public sport,
Appoint a meeting with this old fat fellow,

15   Where we may take him and disgrace him for it.

FORD There is no better way than that they spoke of.

PAGE How, to send him word they'll meet him in the Park
At midnight? Fie, fie, he'll never come.

EVANS You say he has been thrown in the rivers, and has been

20   grievously peaten as an old 'oman. Methinks there should be
terrors in him, that he should not come. Methinks his flesh is
punished; he shall have no desires.

PAGE So think I too.

MISTRESS FORD Devise but how you'll use° him when he comes,   *treat*

25   And let us two devise to bring him thither.

MISTRESS PAGE There is an old tale goes that Herne the hunter,
Sometime° a keeper here in Windsor Forest,   *Once*
Doth all the winter time at still midnight
Walk round about an oak with great ragg'd° horns;   *jagged*

30   And there he blasts° the trees, and takes° the cattle,   *blights / bewitches*
And makes milch-kine° yield blood, and shakes a chain   *dairy cattle*
In a most hideous and dreadful manner.
You have heard of such a spirit, and well you know
The superstitious idle-headed eld°   *people of olden times*

35   Received, and did deliver to our age,
This tale of Herne the hunter for a truth.

PAGE Why, yet there want not° many that do fear   *are*
In deep of night to walk by this Herne's Oak.
But what of this?

MISTRESS FORD   Marry, this is our device:

40   That Falstaff at that oak shall meet with us,
Disguised like Herne, with huge horns on his head.

PAGE Well, let it not be doubted but he'll come,
And in this shape. When you have brought him thither
What shall be done with him? What is your plot?

45   MISTRESS PAGE That likewise have we thought upon, and thus.
Nan Page my daughter, and my little son,
And three or four more of their growth,° we'll dress   *size*
Like urchins,° oafs,° and fairies, green and white,   *goblins / elf children*

4.4 Location: Ford's house.   1. Mistress Page is one of the most discreet women.

With rounds of waxen tapers° on their heads,   *crowns of candles*
50   And rattles in their hands. Upon a sudden,
As Falstaff, she, and I are newly met,
Let them from forth a saw-pit² rush at once,
With some diffusèd° song. Upon their sight   *disordered*
We two in great amazèdness will fly.
55   Then let them all encircle him about,
And, fairy-like, to pinch the unclean knight,
And ask him why, that hour of fairy revel,
In their so sacred paths he dares to tread
In shape profane.
MISTRESS FORD   And till he tell the truth,
60   Let the supposèd fairies pinch him sound,°   *soundly*
And burn him with their tapers.
MISTRESS PAGE   The truth being known,
We'll all present ourselves, dis-horn the spirit,
And mock him home to Windsor.
FORD   The children must
Be practised well to this, or they'll ne'er do't.
65   EVANS   I will teach the children their behaviours, and I will be
like a jackanapes° also, to burn the knight with my taber.   *monkey; evil spirit*
FORD   That will be excellent. I'll go buy them vizors.°   *masks*
MISTRESS PAGE   My Nan shall be the Queen of all the Fairies,
Finely attirèd in a robe of white.
70   PAGE   That silk³ will I go buy—[aside] and in that tire°   *attire*
Shall Master Slender steal my Nan away,
And marry her at Eton.⁴ [To MISTRESS PAGE] Go send to Fal-
staff straight.
FORD   Nay, I'll to him again in name of Brooke.
He'll tell me all his purpose. Sure he'll come.
75   MISTRESS PAGE   Fear not you that. [To PAGE, FORD, and EVANS]
Go get us properties°   *props*
And tricking° for our fairies.   *costumes*
EVANS   Let us about it. It is admirable pleasures, and fery honest
knaveries.   [Exeunt FORD, PAGE, and EVANS]
MISTRESS PAGE   Go, Mistress Ford,
80   Send quickly to Sir John, to know his mind.
[Exit MISTRESS FORD]
I'll to the Doctor. He hath my good will,
And none but he, to marry with Nan Page.
That Slender, though well landed,° is an idiot;   *owning much land*
And he° my husband best of all affects.°   *him / likes most*
85   The Doctor is well moneyed, and his friends
Potent at court. He, none but he, shall have her,
Though twenty thousand worthier come to crave her.   *Exit*

4.5
Enter [the] HOST *[of the Garter] and* SIMPLE
HOST   What wouldst thou have, boor? What, thick-skin?° Speak,   *dullard*
breathe, discuss. Brief, short, quick, snap.
SIMPLE   Marry, sir, I come to speak with Sir John Falstaff, from
Master Slender.

---

2. A pit over which wood was sawed.   4. Across the Thames from Windsor.
3. A sign of Page's financial means.   4.5 Location: The Garter Inn.

5   HOST   There's his chamber, his house his castle, his standing-
        bed and truckle-bed.[1] 'Tis[2] painted about with the story of the
        Prodigal,° fresh and new. Go knock and call. He'll speak like   *prodigal son (Luke 15)*
        an Anthropophaginian° unto thee. Knock, I say   *cannibal*
    SIMPLE   There's an old woman, a fat woman, gone up into his
10   chamber. I'll be so bold as stay, sir, till she come down. I come
        to speak with her, indeed.
    HOST   Ha, a fat woman? The knight may be robbed. I'll call.—
        Bully knight, bully Sir John! Speak from thy lungs military! Art
        thou there? It is thine Host, thine Ephesian,° calls.   *mate*
15 FALSTAFF [*within*]   How now, mine Host?
    HOST   Here's a Bohemian Tartar tarries° the coming down of thy   *Here a savage awaits*
        fat woman. Let her descend, bully, let her descend. My cham-
        bers are honourable. Fie, privacy!° Fie!   *secret goings-on*
            Enter Sir John FALSTAFF
    FALSTAFF   There was, mine Host, an old fat woman even now
20   with me; but she's gone.
    SIMPLE   Pray you, sir, was't not the wise woman° of Brentford?   *woman skilled in magic*
    FALSTAFF   Ay, marry was it, mussel-shell.° What would you with   *empty head? gaper?*
        her?
    SIMPLE   My master, sir, my master Slender, sent to her, seeing
25   her go through the streets, to know, sir, whether one Nim, sir,
        that beguiled° him of a chain, had the chain or no.   *cheated*
    FALSTAFF   I spake with the old woman about it.
    SIMPLE   And what says she, I pray, sir?
    FALSTAFF   Marry, she says that the very same man that beguiled
30   Master Slender of his chain cozened° him of it.   *tricked*
    SIMPLE   I would I could have spoken with the woman herself. I
        had other things to have spoken with her, too, from him.
    FALSTAFF   What are they? Let us know.
    HOST   Ay, come, quick.
35 SIMPLE   I may not conceal° them, sir.   *(for "reveal")*
    HOST   Conceal them, or thou diest.
    SIMPLE   Why, sir, they were nothing but about Mistress Anne
        Page, to know if it were my master's fortune to have her or no.
    FALSTAFF   'Tis, 'tis his fortune.
40 SIMPLE   What, sir?
    FALSTAFF   To have her or no. Go say the woman told me so.
    SIMPLE   May I be bold to say so, sir?
    FALSTAFF   Ay, Sir Tike;° who more bold?   *cur*
    SIMPLE   I thank your worship. I shall make my master glad with
45   these tidings.   [*Exit*]
    HOST   Thou art clerkly,° thou art clerkly, Sir John. Was there a   *learned*
        wise woman with thee?
    FALSTAFF   Ay, that there was, mine Host, one that hath taught
        me more wit than ever I learned before in my life. And I paid
50   nothing for it, neither, but was paid° for my learning.   *thrashed*
            Enter BARDOLPH [*muddy*]
    BARDOLPH   O Lord, sir, cozenage, mere° cozenage!   *utter*
    HOST   Where be my horses? Speak well of them, varletto.°   *varlet*
    BARDOLPH   Run away with the cozeners. For so soon as I came
        beyond Eton, they threw me off from behind one of them, in a

---

1. Trundle bed, which could be stored under the larger   2. The "it" in "'Tis" refers to either the wall hanging or
standing bed.   the bed hanging.

55   slough of mire, and set spurs and away, like three German
      devils, three Doctor Faustuses.³

HOST   They are gone but to meet the Duke, villain. Do not say
      they be fled. Germans are honest men.

                    Enter Sir Hugh EVANS

EVANS   Where is mine Host?

60   HOST   What is the matter, sir?

EVANS   Have a care of your entertainments.° There is a friend   *guests*
      of mine come to town tells me there is three cozen° Garmom-   *related; cheating*
      bles⁴ that has cozened all the hosts of Reading, of Maidenhead,
      of Colnbrook,° of horses and money. I tell you for good will,   *nearby villages*

65   look you. You are wise, and full of gibes and vlouting-stocks,°   *laughingstocks*
      and 'tis not convenient° you should be cozened. Fare you well.   *appropriate*
                                                        Exit

            Enter Doctor CAIUS

CAIUS   Vere is mine Host de Jarteer?

HOST   Here, Master Doctor, in perplexity and doubtful dilemma.

CAIUS   I cannot tell vat is dat, but it is tell-a me dat you make

70   grand preparation for a duke de Jamany.° By my trot,° der is no   *Germany/troth*
      duke that the court is know to come. I tell you for good will.
      Adieu.   *Exit*

HOST   [*to* BARDOLPH]   Hue and cry,° villain, go! [*To* FALSTAFF]   *Raise the alarm*
      Assist me, knight. I am undone. [*To* BARDOLPH] Fly, run, hue

75   and cry, villain. I am undone.

                    Exeunt HOST *and* BARDOLPH [*severally*]°   *separately*

FALSTAFF   I would all the world might be cozened, for I have
      been cozened, and beaten too. If it should come to the ear of
      the court how I have been transformed, and how my transfor-
      mation hath been washed and cudgelled, they would melt me

80   out of my fat, drop by drop, and liquor° fishermen's boots with   *grease*
      me. I warrant they would whip me with their fine wits till I
      were as crestfallen° as a dried pear. I never prospered since I   *shriveled*
      forswore myself at primero.° Well, if my wind were but long   *cards*
      enough,° I would repent.   *(to list all my sins)*

                    Enter MISTRESS QUICKLY

85   Now; whence come you?

MISTRESS QUICKLY   From the two parties, forsooth.

FALSTAFF   The devil take one party, and his dam° the other, and   *mother*
      so they shall be both bestowed. I have suffered more for their
      sakes, more than the villainous inconstancy of man's disposi-

90   tion is able to bear.

MISTRESS QUICKLY   O Lord, sir, and have not they suffered? Yes,
      I warrant, speciously° one of them. Mistress Ford, good heart,   *(for "specially")*
      is beaten black and blue, that you cannot see a white spot about
      her.

95   FALSTAFF   What tellest thou me of black and blue? I was beaten
      myself into all the colours of the rainbow, and I was like to be
      apprehended for the witch of Brentford. But that my admirable
      dexterity of wit, my counterfeiting the action of an old woman,

---

3. Bardolph alludes to Marlowe's *Doctor Faustus*, whose
titular hero makes a pact with the devil. In one scene,
three devils are conjured to "horse" Benvolio, Frederick,
and Martino on their backs and throw them in "some lake
of mud and dirt" (13.79–85). In the following scene, the

three appear muddy and, anticipating Falstaff's punishment, with horns on their heads.
4. Probably an anagram of "Mömpelgard," the name of a
German count who aspired to—and was elected to—the
Order of the Garter and whom Shakespeare here satirizes.

delivered me, the knave constable had set me i'th' stocks, i'th'
100 common stocks, for a witch.

MISTRESS QUICKLY   Sir, let me speak with you in your chamber.
You shall hear how things go, and, I warrant, to your consent.
Here is a letter will say somewhat. Good hearts, what ado here
is to bring you together! Sure one of you does not serve heaven
105 well, that you are so crossed.°   thwarted

FALSTAFF   Come up into my chamber.   *Exeunt*

4.6

Enter [Master] FENTON *and [the]* HOST *[of the Garter]*

HOST   Master Fenton, talk not to me. My mind is heavy. I will
give over° all.   give up

FENTON   Yet hear me speak. Assist me in my purpose,
And, as I am a gentleman, I'll give thee
5 A hundred pound in gold more than your loss.

HOST   I will hear you, Master Fenton, and I will at the least keep
your counsel.°   secret

FENTON   From time to time I have acquainted you
With the dear love I bear to fair Anne Page,
10 Who mutually hath answered my affection,
So far forth as herself might be her chooser,[1]
Even to my wish. I have a letter from her
Of such contents as you will wonder at,
The mirth whereof so larded with my matter°   mixed with my concern
15 That neither singly can be manifested
Without the show of both. Fat Falstaff
Hath a great scene. The image° of the jest   idea
I'll show you here at large. Hark, good mine Host.
Tonight at Herne's Oak, just 'twixt twelve and one,
20 Must my sweet Nan present° the Fairy Queen—   play the part of
    [*Showing the letter*]
The purpose why is here—in which disguise,
While other jests are something rank on foot,°   somewhat thick afoot
Her father hath commanded her to slip
Away with Slender, and with him at Eton
25 Immediately to marry. She hath consented.
Now, sir, her mother, ever strong against that match
And firm for Doctor Caius, hath appointed
That he shall likewise shuffle her away,
While other sports are tasking of° their minds,   engaging
30 And at the dean'ry,[2] where a priest attends,
Straight marry her. To this her mother's plot
She, seemingly obedient, likewise hath
Made promise to the Doctor. Now, thus it rests.°   things stand thus
Her father means she shall be all in white;
35 And in that habit,° when Slender sees his time   dress
To take her by the hand and bid her go,
She shall go with him. Her mother hath intended,
The better to denote her to the Doctor—
For they must all be masked and visorèd—
40 That quaint° in green she shall be loose enrobed.   elegantly

---

4.6 Location: Scene continues.
1. Insofar as she might choose her own husband.
2. Residence of the dean (the head of the clergy or the

staff of certain churches); (loosely) a parsonage. Here
Fenton refers to the deanery attached to St. George's
Chapel on the property of Windsor Castle.

With ribbons pendant flaring° 'bout her head;   *waving down*
And when the Doctor spies his vantage ripe,
To pinch her by the hand, and on that token
The maid hath given consent to go with him.
45   HOST   Which means she to deceive, father or mother?
FENTON   Both, my good Host, to go along with me.
And here it rests: that you'll procure the vicar
To stay for me at church 'twixt twelve and one,
And, in the lawful name of ° marrying,   *name of lawful*
50   To give our hearts united ceremony.
HOST   Well, husband° your device. I'll to the vicar.   *manage well; (pun)*
Bring you the maid, you shall not lack a priest.
FENTON   So shall I evermore be bound to thee.
Besides, I'll make a present° recompense.   *Exeunt [severally]*   *immediate*

5.1

Enter FALSTAFF and [MISTRESS] QUICKLY

FALSTAFF   Prithee, no more prattling; go; I'll hold.° This is the   *keep the appointment*
third time; I hope good luck lies in odd numbers. Away, go!
They say there is divinity° in odd numbers, either in nativity,   *divine power*
chance, or death. Away!
5   MISTRESS QUICKLY   I'll provide you a chain, and I'll do what I
can to get you a pair of horns.
FALSTAFF   Away, I say! Time wears.° Hold up your head, and   *passes*
mince.°   [*Exit MISTRESS QUICKLY*]   *walk affectedly*
Enter [Master] FORD [disguised as Brooke]
How now, Master Brooke? Master Brooke, the matter will be
10   known tonight or never. Be you in the Park about midnight at
Herne's Oak, and you shall see wonders.
FORD   Went you not to her yesterday, sir, as you told me you had
appointed?
FALSTAFF   I went to her, Master Brooke, as you see,° like a poor   *as I am now*
15   old man; but I came from her, Master Brooke, like a poor old
woman. That same knave Ford, her husband, hath the finest
mad devil of jealousy in him, Master Brooke, that ever governed frenzy. I will tell you, he beat me grievously in the shape
of a woman—for in the shape of man, Master Brooke, I fear
20   not Goliath with a weaver's beam,[1] because I know also life is
a shuttle.[2] I am in haste. Go along with me; I'll tell you all,
Master Brooke. Since I plucked geese,° played truant, and   *(child's prank)*
whipped top,° I knew not what 'twas to be beaten till lately.   *spun a top*
Follow me. I'll tell you strange things of this knave Ford, on
25   whom tonight I will be revenged, and I will deliver his wife
into your hand. Follow. Strange things in hand, Master Brooke.
Follow.   *Exeunt*

5.2

Enter [Master] PAGE, [Justice] SHALLOW, [and Master]
SLENDER
PAGE   Come, come, we'll couch° i'th' Castle ditch till we see the   *lie*
light of our fairies. Remember, son Slender, my daughter.
SLENDER   Ay, forsooth. I have spoke with her, and we have a nay-

---

5.1 Location: The Garter Inn.
1. The biblical simile for Goliath's spear handle (1 Samuel 17:7).

2. From Job 7:6: "My days are swifter than a weaver's
shuttle."
5.2 Location: An approach to Windsor Park.

word° how to know one another. I come to her in white and   *password*
5   cry 'mum'; she cries 'budget';° and by that we know one   *mumbudget (silence)*
another.

SHALLOW   That's good, too. But what needs either your 'mum'
or her 'budget'? The white will decipher her well enough. [*To*
PAGE] It hath struck ten o'clock.

10 PAGE   The night is dark; lights and spirits will become it well.
God prosper our sport! No man means evil but the devil, and
we shall know him by his horns. Let's away. Follow me.

                                            Exeunt

5.3

Enter MISTRESS PAGE, MISTRESS FORD, [*and Doctor*]
    CAIUS

MISTRESS PAGE   Master Doctor, my daughter is in green. When
you see your time, take her by the hand, away with her to the
deanery, and dispatch it quickly. Go before into the Park. We
two must go together.

5 CAIUS   I know vat I have to do. Adieu.

MISTRESS PAGE   Fare you well, sir.   [*Exit* CAIUS]
My husband will not rejoice so much at the abuse of Falstaff
as he will chafe at the doctor's marrying my daughter. But 'tis
no matter. Better a little chiding than a great deal of heartbreak.

10 MISTRESS FORD   Where is Nan now, and her troop of fairies, and
the Welsh devil Hugh?

MISTRESS PAGE   They are all couched in a pit hard by Herne's
Oak, with obscured lights, which, at the very instant of Falstaff's and our meeting, they will at once display to the night.

15 MISTRESS FORD   That cannot choose but amaze° him.   *That is bound to frighten*

MISTRESS PAGE   If he be not amazed, he will be mocked. If he
be amazed, he will every way be mocked.

MISTRESS FORD   We'll betray him finely.

MISTRESS PAGE   Against such lewdsters and their lechery

20   Those that betray them do no treachery.

MISTRESS FORD   The hour draws on. To the Oak, to the Oak!

                                            Exeunt

5.4

Enter Sir Hugh EVANS [*disguised as a satyr* and [WIL-
LIAM *Page and other children, disguised as fairies*]

EVANS   Trib,° trib, fairies! Come! And remember your parts. Be   *Trip*
pold, I pray you. Follow me into the pit, and when I give the
watch'ords, do as I pid you. Come, come; trib, trib!   *Exeunt*

5.5

Enter Sir John FALSTAFF [*disguised as Herne, with horns*
on his head, and bearing a chain]

FALSTAFF   The Windsor bell hath struck twelve; the minute
draws on. Now the hot-blooded gods assist me. Remember,
Jove, thou wast a bull for thy Europa;[1] love set on thy horns. O
powerful love, that in some respects makes a beast a man; in
5   some other, a man a beast! You were also, Jupiter, a swan, for

---

5.3 Location: Scene continues.
5.4 Location: Scene continues.
5.5 Location: Windsor Park.

1. In classical mythology, Jupiter turned himself into a
bull and abducted Europa by swimming across the sea
with her on his back.

the love of Leda.[2] O omnipotent love! How near the god drew
to the complexion of a goose! A fault done first in the form of
a beast—O Jove, a beastly fault!—and then another fault in the
semblance of a fowl—think on't, Jove, a foul fault! When gods
have hot° backs, what shall poor men do? For me, I am here a   *lustful*
Windsor stag, and the fattest, I think, i'th' forest. Send me a
cool rut-time,° Jove, or who can blame me to piss my tallow?[3]   *mating season*

        Enter MISTRESS FORD [*followed by*] MISTRESS PAGE
Who comes here? My doe!

MISTRESS FORD   Sir John! Art thou there, my deer,° my male   *(pun on "dear")*
deer?

FALSTAFF   My doe with the black scut!° Let the sky rain potatoes,   *tail; pubic hair*
let it thunder to the tune of 'Greensleeves',° hail kissing-   *popular love song*
comfits, and snow eringoes;[4] let there come a tempest of provocation,° I will shelter me here.   *sexual incitement*
        [*He embraces her*]

MISTRESS FORD   Mistress Page is come with me, sweetheart.

FALSTAFF   Divide me like a bribed° buck, each a haunch. I will   *stolen*
keep my sides to myself, my shoulders for the fellow° of this   *keeper*
walk,° and my horns° I bequeath your husbands. Am I a wood-   *forest / (of a cuckold)*
man,° ha? Speak I like Herne the hunter? Why, now is Cupid   *hunter; womanizer*
a child of conscience; he makes restitution.° As I am a true   *repays my suffering*
spirit, welcome!
        A noise [*within*]

MISTRESS PAGE   Alas, what noise?

MISTRESS FORD   God forgive our sins!

FALSTAFF   What should this be?

MISTRESS FORD *and* MISTRESS PAGE   Away, away!
        [*Exeunt* MISTRESS FORD *and* MISTRESS PAGE, *running*]

FALSTAFF   I think the devil will not have me damned, lest the oil
that's in me should set hell on fire. He would never else cross
me thus.
        Enter Sir Hugh EVANS, [WILLIAM *Page, and children, dis-*
        guised as fairies with tapers;] MISTRESS QUICKLY, [*dis-*
        guised] *as the Fairy Queen;* ANNE *Page* [*disguised as a*
        fairy; and one disguised as Hobgoblin][5]

MISTRESS QUICKLY   Fairies black, grey, green, and white,
You moonshine revellers, and shades° of night,   *spirits*
You orphan heirs of fixèd destiny,[6]
Attend° your office° and your quality.°—   *Perform/duty/calling*
Crier° hobgoblin, make the fairy oyes.°   *Town crier/hear ye*

HOBGOBLIN   Elves, list° your names. Silence, you airy toys.°   *listen for / trifles*
Cricket,° to Windsor chimneys shalt thou leap.   *(elf's name)*
Where fires thou find'st unraked° and hearths unswept,   *(hence, likely to die)*
There pinch the maids as blue as bilberry.°   *blueberry*
Our radiant Queen hates sluts and sluttery.°   *dirtiness*

FALSTAFF [*aside*]   They are fairies. He that speaks to them shall die.
I'll wink° and couch;° no man their works must eye.   *shut my eyes / lie down*

---

2. Jupiter turned himself into a swan in order to rape
Leda.
3. If I urinate or sweat away my fat (as stags were
thought to do at rutting time).
4. Candied roots of sea holly that, like sweet "potatoes"
(line 16), were considered an aphrodisiac. *kissing-
comfits*: breath sweeteners ("comfits" are candies).
5. Anne, who was assigned the part of the Fairy Queen

at 4.4.68, is here replaced by Quickly, either as part of
the marital scheming or simply as an indication that the
boy actor who played Quickly also is to play this role.
Similarly, Hobgoblin may have been played by Pistol or
simply by the actor who played Pistol.
6. You parentless inheritors of fixed duties (?). (Fairies
were supposed to be parentless.)

[He lies down, and hides his face]

EVANS   Where's Bead? Go you, and, where you find a maid
    That ere she sleep has thrice her prayers said,
    Raise up° the organs of her fantasy,°   *Stimulate / imagination*
    Sleep she[7] as sound as careless° infancy.   *carefree*
50   But those as° sleep and think not on their sins,   *who*
    Pinch them, arms, legs, backs, shoulders, sides, and shins.
MISTRESS QUICKLY   About,° about!   *To work*
    Search Windsor Castle, elves, within and out.
    Strew good luck, oafs,° on every sacred room,   *elves*
55   That it may stand till the perpetual doom°   *Judgment Day*
    In state° as wholesome as in state° 'tis fit,   *condition / dignity*
    Worthy° the owner, and the owner it.   *Worthy of*
    The several chairs of order[8] look you scour
    With juice of balm and every precious flower.
60   Each fair instalment,° coat,° and sev'ral crest[9]   *seat / coat of arms*
    With loyal blazon[1] evermore be blessed;
    And nightly, meadow-fairies, look you sing,
    Like to the Garter's compass,° in a ring.   *circle*
    Th'expressure° that it bears, green let it be,   *image*
65   More fertile-fresh than all the field to see;
    And *'Honi soit qui mal y pense'*[2] write
    In em'rald tufts, flowers purple, blue, and white,
    Like sapphire, pearl, and rich embroidery,
    Buckled below fair knighthood's bending knee—
70   Fairies use flowers for their character.°   *lettering*
    Away, disperse!—But till 'tis one o'clock
    Our dance of custom,° round about the oak   *customary dance*
    Of Herne the hunter, let us not forget.
EVANS   Pray you, lock hand in hand; yourselves in order set;
75   And twenty glow-worms shall our lanterns be
    To guide our measure° round about the tree.—   *dance*
    But stay; I smell a man of middle earth.°   *a mortal*
FALSTAFF *[aside]*   God defend me from that Welsh fairy,
    Lest he transform me to a piece of cheese!
80 HOBGOBLIN *[to FALSTAFF]*   Vile worm, thou wast o'erlooked° even   *destined to evil*
    in thy birth.
MISTRESS QUICKLY *[to fairies]*   With trial-fire, touch me° his finger-end.   *touch*
    If he be chaste, the flame will back descend,
    And turn him to no pain; but if he start,
    It is the flesh of a corrupted heart.
HOBGOBLIN   A trial, come!
85 EVANS   Come, will this wood° take fire?   *(Falstaff's fingers)*
    They [burn FALSTAFF with] tapers
FALSTAFF   O, O, O!
MISTRESS QUICKLY   Corrupt, corrupt, and tainted in desire.
    About him, fairies; sing a scornful rhyme;
    And, as you trip, still° pinch him to your time.   *continually*
    *They [dance around FALSTAFF,] pinch[ing] him and
    sing[ing]:*

---

7. Though she is sleeping; may she sleep.
8. The various stalls assigned, in St. George's Chapel, Windsor, to members of the Order of the Garter (a high dignity that the monarch conferred, marked by a garter worn below the knee).
9. Heraldic device on top of the helmet.
1. Together with the coat of arms on a banner.
2. Shame to him who thinks evil of it (the motto of the Order of the Garter).

FAIRIES

90   Fie on sinful fantasy!

           Fie on lust and luxury!°   *lechery*

           Lust is but a bloody fire,°   *fire of the blood*

           Kindled with unchaste desire,

           Fed in heart, whose flames aspire,°   *rise up*

95   As thoughts do blow them, higher and higher.

           Pinch him, fairies, mutually.°   *all together*

           Pinch him for his villainy.

      Pinch him, and burn him, and turn him about,

      Till candles and starlight and moonshine be out.

      [During the song] Doctor CAIUS *comes one way and*
      steals away a boy in [green]; [enter] SLENDER *another*
      way; he takes a boy in [white]; and FENTON *steals* ANNE.
      *[After the song] a noise of hunting within. [*MISTRESS
      QUICKLY, EVANS, HOBGOBLIN, *and] fairies run away.* FAL-
      STAFF *rises [and starts to run away]. Enter Master* PAGE,
      Master FORD, *and their wives*

100 PAGE   Nay, do not fly. I think we have watched you° now.   *caught you in the act*

      Will none but Herne the hunter serve your turn?

MISTRESS PAGE   I pray you, come, hold up° the jest no higher.°   *prolong / further*

      Now, good Sir John, how like you Windsor wives?

      [Pointing to Falstaff 's horns]

      See you these, husband? Do not these fair yokes°   *horns*

105   Become the forest better than the town?

FORD *[to* FALSTAFF*]*   Now, sir, who's a cuckold now? Master
      Brooke, Falstaff's a knave, a cuckoldly knave. Here are his
      horns, Master Brooke. And, Master Brooke, he hath enjoyed
      nothing of Ford's but his buck-basket, his cudgel, and twenty

110   pounds of money which must be paid to Master Brooke; his
      horses are arrested° for it,[3] Master Brooke.   *seized as security*

MISTRESS FORD   Sir John, we have had ill luck. We could never
      mate. I will never take you for my love again, but I will always
      count you my deer.

115 FALSTAFF   I do begin to perceive that I am made an ass.

      [He takes off the horns]

FORD   Ay, and an ox, too. Both the proofs are extant.[4]

FALSTAFF   And these are not fairies? By the Lord, I was three or
      four times in the thought they were not fairies, and yet the
      guiltiness of my mind, the sudden surprise of my powers,°   *mind*

120   drove the grossness of the foppery° into a received belief—in   *deceit*
      despite of the teeth of° all rhyme and reason—that they were   *against*
      fairies. See now how wit may be made a Jack-a-Lent° when 'tis   *butt*
      upon ill employment!

EVANS   Sir John Falstaff, serve Got and leave your desires, and

125   fairies will not pinse you.

FORD   Well said, Fairy Hugh.

EVANS   And leave you your jealousies too, I pray you.

FORD   I will never mistrust my wife again till thou art able to
      woo her in good English.

130 FALSTAFF   Have I laid my brain in the sun and dried it, that it
      wants° matter to prevent so gross o'er-reaching as this? Am I   *lacks*

---

3. See note to 4.3.11.
4. "Ox" (fool, cuckold) is inspired by "yokes" (line 104).

The "proofs" are either the horns, which are "extant"
(existing), or the "ass" and the "ox."

ridden with° a Welsh goat too? Shall I have a coxcomb° of   *harassed by / jester's cap*
frieze? 'Tis time I were choked with a piece of toasted cheese.[5]

EVANS   Seese is not good to give putter; your belly is all putter.

135 FALSTAFF   'Seese' and 'putter'? Have I lived to stand at the taunt
of one that makes fritters of English? This is enough to be the
decay of lust and late walking° through the realm.   *(for sexual purposes)*

MISTRESS PAGE   Why, Sir John, do you think, though° we would   *even if*
have thrust virtue out of our hearts by the head and shoulders,
140 and have given ourselves without scruple to hell, that ever the
devil could have made you our delight?

FORD   What, a hodge-pudding,° a bag of flax?   *sausage*

MISTRESS PAGE   A puffed° man?   *inflated*

PAGE   Old, cold, withered, and of intolerable entrails?

145 FORD   And one that is as slanderous as Satan?

PAGE   And as poor as Job?

FORD   And as wicked as his wife?[6]

EVANS   And given to fornications, and to taverns, and sack, and
wine, and metheglins;° and to drinkings, and swearings, and   *Welsh spiced drink*
150 starings, pribbles and prabbles?°   *raving and squabbles*

FALSTAFF   Well, I am your theme; you have the start° of me. I   *advantage*
am dejected.° I am not able to answer the Welsh flannel. Igno-   *humbled*
rance itself is a plummet o'er me.[7] Use me as you will.

FORD   Marry, sir, we'll bring you to Windsor, to one Master
155 Brooke, that you have cozened of money, to whom you should
have been° a pander. Over and above that° you have suffered,   *intended to be / what*
I think to repay that money will be a biting affliction.

PAGE   Yet be cheerful, knight. Thou shalt eat a posset[8] tonight
at my house, where I will desire thee to laugh at my wife that
160 now laughs at thee. Tell her Master Slender hath married her
daughter.

MISTRESS PAGE [*aside*]   Doctors doubt that!° If Anne Page be my   *(expresses disbelief)*
daughter, she is, by this,° Doctor Caius's wife.   *now*

Enter [Master] SLENDER

SLENDER   Whoa, ho, ho, father Page!

165 PAGE   Son, how now? How now, son? Have you dispatched?°   *settled the business*

SLENDER   Dispatched? I'll make the best in Gloucestershire
know on't;° would I were hanged, la, else.°   *of it / otherwise*

PAGE   Of what, son?

SLENDER   I came yonder at Eton to marry Mistress Anne Page,
170 and she's a great lubberly° boy. If it had not been i'th' church,   *loutish*
I would have swinged° him, or he should have swinged me. If   *beaten; screwed*
I did not think it had been Anne Page, would I might never
stir; and 'tis a postmaster's boy.°   *stableboy*

PAGE   Upon my life, then, you took the wrong.

175 SLENDER   What need you tell me that? I think so, when I took a
boy for a girl. If I had been married to him, for all° he was in   *even though*
woman's apparel, I would not have had him.

---

5. "Welsh goat" (line 132) refers to the large number of
goats in Wales, "frieze" (line 133) to a coarse wool made
there, and "toasted cheese" to what was supposedly a
favorite Welsh food.
6. Satan slanders Job (Job 1:9–11, 2:4–5); Job's wife
tempts him to curse God (2:9).
7. A "plummet" is a "plumb line," used for measuring
depths, with a pun on "plumbet," a woolen fabric and,

hence, connected with "Welsh flannel," one of Falstaff's names here for Evans (along with "Ignorance").
The ignorant Evans, the "Welsh flannel," is a woolen
fabric over Falstaff by which Falstaff means that even
the ignorant Evans can plumb Falstaff's depths, can see
his true motives.
8. Take a restorative drink of hot milk curdled with
wine or ale.

PAGE   Why, this is your own folly. Did not I tell you how you
should know my daughter by her garments?

180 SLENDER   I went to her in white and cried 'mum', and she cried
'budget', as Anne and I had appointed; and yet it was not Anne,
but a postmaster's boy.

MISTRESS PAGE   Good George, be not angry. I knew of your purpose, turned my daughter into green, and indeed she is now

185 with the Doctor at the deanery, and there married.

Enter Doctor [CAIUS]

CAIUS   Ver is Mistress Page? By Gar, I am cozened! I ha' married
un garçon, a boy, *un paysan*,° by Gar. A boy! It is not Anne   a peasant
Page, by Gar. I am cozened.

PAGE   Why, did you take her in green?

190 CAIUS   Ay, be Gar, and 'tis a boy. Be Gar, I'll raise all Windsor.

FORD   This is strange. Who hath got the right Anne?

Enter [Master] FENTON *and* ANNE

PAGE   My heart misgives me: here comes Master Fenton.—
How now, Master Fenton?

ANNE   Pardon, good father. Good my mother, pardon.

195 PAGE   Now, mistress, how chance you went not with Master Slender?

MISTRESS PAGE   Why went you not with Master Doctor, maid?

FENTON   You do amaze° her. Hear the truth of it.   confuse
You would have married her, most shamefully,
Where there was no proportion° held in love.   balance

200 The truth is, she and I, long since contracted,°   betrothed
Are now so sure° that nothing can dissolve° us.   united / separate
Th'offence is holy that she hath committed,
And this deceit loses the name of craft,
Of disobedience, or unduteous title,°   undutifulness

205 Since therein she doth evitate° and shun   avoid
A thousand irreligious cursèd hours
Which forcèd marriage would have brought upon her.

FORD [*to* PAGE *and* MISTRESS PAGE]   Stand not amazed. Here is no remedy.
In love the heavens themselves do guide the state;

210 Money buys lands, and wives are sold by fate.

FALSTAFF   I am glad, though you have ta'en a special stand° to   hunter's station
strike at me, that your arrow hath glanced.°   missed

PAGE   Well, what remedy? Fenton, heaven give thee joy!
What cannot be eschewed must be embraced.

215 FALSTAFF   When night-dogs run, all sorts of deer are chased.⁹

MISTRESS PAGE   Well, I will muse° no further. Master Fenton,   complain
Heaven give you many, many merry days!
Good husband, let us every one go home,
And laugh this sport o'er by a country fire,
Sir John and all.

220 FORD   Let it be so, Sir John.
To Master Brooke you yet shall hold your word,
For he tonight shall lie with Mistress Ford.   *Exeunt*

---

9. When "dogs" (the failed suitors) run out of control
at night, they may catch "all sorts of deer" (the disguised boys, rather than Anne). In other words, you
can't control nocturnal intrigue.

The Second Part of Henry IV

The title page of the 1600 Quarto of *2 Henry IV* describes the play as *The Second Part of Henry the Fourth, Continuing to His Death, and Coronation of Henry the Fifth. With the Humours of Sir John Falstaff, and Swaggering Pistol.* Its first focus is the "high" historical matter of the reign of Kings. For this part of the play, Shakespeare drew primarily on the second edition of Raphael Holinshed's *Chronicles of England, Scotland, and Ireland* (1587), although he probably consulted other sources, including Samuel Daniel's *First Four Books of the Civil Wars Between the Two Houses of Lancaster and York* (1595). In regard to this historical material, the title page particularly highlights the delicate moment of succession when one King dies and another is crowned. Shakespeare's audience was facing such a moment at the end of the 1590s. Elizabeth I was old, having been on the English throne since 1558; she had never married, and she had no heirs. The uncertainties of the coming succession may have, by contrast, heightened the pleasure of watching Henry IV followed upon the throne by his male heir, Henry V—the King who, whatever his father's sins in seizing the crown from Richard II, had become in the popular imagination a symbol of kingly perfection and English masculinity. With his customary subtlety, Shakespeare complicates and somewhat darkens the popular image of the wayward prince who undergoes a miraculous transformation, but Hal's coronation nonetheless is the end point toward which the play inexorably moves.

Besides its royal plot, the play also deals in some decidedly "low" and mostly unhistorical matter, suggested on the title page by mention of the "humours" of Falstaff and the presence of swaggering Pistol. These characters hold pride of place alongside Henry IV and Henry V, indicating the popularity of the antic parts of the play—Falstaff's jokes and his flouting of authority or Pistol's madly bombastic language. Some of the matter for the play's comic scenes probably derives from *The Famous Victories of Henry the Fifth,* a popular play about the life of Henry V first published in 1598 but believed to have been performed well before that date. In *2 Henry IV* Prince Hal does not mingle with the comic figures as freely as he did in *1 Henry IV*; in fact, he appears only once, in 2.4, in the Eastcheap tavern where Falstaff holds court. Nonetheless, the total number of low, unhistorical characters expands considerably in this play. Pistol is a new character, and Mistress Quickly is joined in her Eastcheap tavern by Doll Tearsheet, a prostitute whose name graphically suggests one consequence of unrestrained fornication. Further, a number of country characters are introduced: the Gloustershire justices of the peace, Shallow and Silence; Shallow's servant, Davy; and the five rural recruits (Mouldy, Bullcalf, Wart, Feeble, and Shadow) whom Falstaff considers for conscription into the army. *2 Henry IV* is the only history play of which more than half is written in prose, and much of that richly varied prose occurs in the numerous scenes involving these humble figures Shakespeare added to the historical narrative of one king's death and another's coronation.

2 Henry IV was probably written soon after the very popular *1 Henry IV,* which was published in 1598 but probably written and staged in 1596–97. The Quarto was published in 1600, but there is a reference to the character of Justice Silence in Ben Jonson's *Every Man out of His Humour,* published in 1599. *2 Henry IV* was therefore probably performed sometime between February 1598, when *1 Henry IV* was entered in the Stationers' Register with no indication that it was the first part of a two-part play, and early in 1599. It is likely that censorship of Shakespeare's original naming of Falstaff as "Oldcastle," Bardolph as "Russell," and Peto as "Harvey" (see Introduction to *1 Henry IV*) had occurred before Shakespeare completed *2 Henry IV,* although a few

THE
Second part of Henrie

the fourth, continuing to his death,
and coronation of Henrie
the fift.

With the humours of sir Iohn Falstaffe, *and swaggering*
Pistoll.

As it hath been sundrie times publikely
acted by the right honourable, the Lord
Chamberlaine his seruants.

Written by William Shakespeare.

LONDON
Printed by V. S. for Andrew Wise, and
William Aspley.
1600.

Title page of the 1600 Quarto of *The Second part of Henrie the fourth* . . . , promising to combine royal history and the comic events involving Falstaff and his tavern companions.

traces of the original names appear in the speech prefixes and stage directions in the first two acts of the quarto text. Shakespeare may have interrupted his composition of *2 Henry IV* to write *The Merry Wives of Windsor,* a play that could have been performed as early as 1597. If so, he would have written the last acts of *2 Henry IV* well after the censorship of the offending names in *1 Henry IV* had occurred, and he would consequently have altered the names in the final acts of the play.

Narrowing down the play's date of composition, however, does not answer the question of why Shakespeare wrote two plays dealing with the reign of Henry IV. Some critics believe that the playwright once intended to encompass all the material of both plays in one, but in writing *1 Henry IV* he found he had room to depict only the events up to the Battle of Shrewsbury and Hal's emergence as a chivalric hero through his defeat of Hotspur. Therefore, what was "left over" was, in effect, put into *2 Henry IV* with the patchwork addition of enough comic material to scrape together a play. It is also possible that Shakespeare intended to dramatize only the events now in *1 Henry IV,* but that having done so, he was encouraged by his success to add another chapter to the story of Hal's reformation and gradual progression toward the throne. Alternatively, Shakespeare may have planned two plays from the beginning, intending to undertake two quite different explorations of the prodigal narrative by which the wild Prince becomes first a chivalric hero and eventually the King of England.

Whatever the original impetus for writing it, the finished play now called *2 Henry IV* has an integrity of its own and a set of preoccupations that clearly distinguishes it from *1 Henry IV.* The rebels, for example, are a less flamboyant crew than in the earlier play, and they are not vanquished in combat as at Shrewsbury; rather, at Gaultres, Prince John tricks them into laying down their weapons. Policy, not chivalry, wins the day. Hal's challenge, moreover, is no longer to prove himself the prince of chivalry, with the rebel Henry Percy (Hotspur) as his main antagonist. Rather, he must show himself fit for civil rule. Hence the importance in *2 Henry IV* of the Lord Chief Justice, a figure who in popular accounts of Hal's life had had the Prince imprisoned for impudently giving him a box on the ear. This event is not dramatized in either of Shakespeare's *Henry IV* plays, as it had been in *The Famous Victories,* but it is several times alluded to. In *2 Henry IV,* the Chief Justice emerges as the main foil to the disorderly Falstaff. Upon hearing that Henry IV is dead and Hal is King, the fat knight exclaims, "The laws of England are at my commandment" (5.3.125–26). It seems quite possible that under Henry V, law will give way before the appetites and desires of individual subjects. Hal and the Chief Justice do not share the stage until 5.2, but their encounter is a pivotal moment in the text, revealing whether Hal will recognize and honor the authority of the Chief Justice or follow Falstaff in flouting the law.

Also unique to this play is its pervasive concern with the passing of time. As Hastings says at the end of Act 1, "We are time's subjects" (1.3.110); arguably, he sounds the play's central theme. Even the King, to whom so many are subject, is himself subject to time. Shakespeare portrays him as old and sick, though the historical Henry successfully ruled England for ten years after the Battle of Shrewsbury. His sickness and the urgency of the rebel threat pressure the Prince, forcing him to realize that his idle days in the tavern are numbered and that if he lingers longer, he will "profane the precious time" (2.4.330), time he should spend coming to terms with his father and defending a kingdom still threatened by rebels. Even the irrepressible Falstaff now feels time's hand. He enters the play in 1.2 asking what the doctor has said about the urine he has sent for examination, and to Quickly and Tearsheet he confesses, "I am old, I am old" (2.4.243). If *1 Henry IV* is an expansive work, infused with a feeling of infinite play and infinite possibility, *2 Henry IV* has a melancholy, autumnal aura. It is a play of limits and constrictions. Shallow intones: "Death, as the Psalmist saith, is certain to all; all shall die" (3.2.33–34). Through its many images of sickness, disease, and old age, the play is permeated with intimations of mortality.

The play's portrayal of Prince Hal shares in the somber mood that suffuses all of *2 Henry IV.* When the audience first sees him, he is with Poins (2.2), brooding on the impasse to which his own actions have brought him. Rather than keeping a controlling distance from his tavern companion, Hal ruefully acknowledges what he shares with common men. Tired, he desires nothing more exalted than small beer, the common drink of every London apprentice. He admits that he should not, because of his rank, be intimate with Poins; and yet he confesses that he is, revealing how thoroughly he knows his companion's wardrobe and using Poins as a sounding board for his misgivings about his own behavior and its consequences. While the scene's mood changes when Bardolph enters with an absurdly pompous letter from Falstaff, its fretful beginning indicates a new strain in Shakespeare's depiction of Hal's progress toward the throne. In *1 Henry IV*, everything seemed easy for the Prince. He announced a course of reform and enacted it with little apparent cost to himself. In *2 Henry IV*, Shakespeare constructs a more sober Prince who articulates anxiety about the gap between his plebeian taste for small beer and the grandeur of the office he will assume, a Prince who knows that to have acted the wastrel in order to make a dazzling reform may have cost him his father's affection and made it impossible to express his love for the King without appearing a hypocrite. In the opening acts of *2 Henry IV*, Hal's capacity for self-critique and for uncertainty makes him more vulnerable, and perhaps more likable, than the shiny and assured paragon of *1 Henry IV*.

Shakespeare also shows changes in Hal's father, King Henry IV, who in Part 2 reveals a new capacity for introspection. In 3.1, speaking about the burdens of office, he acknowledges the costs of his success and admits that at the start of his reign he could little foresee the changes time would effect in him and in his plans and alliances. Yet like his son, in the end Henry finds his office worth the cost. Power may bring burdens, but for both characters it is irresistible. Each sentimentally envies common men (whose poverty and powerlessness they do not share), but neither renounces the office of King. And neither ever gives up the attempt to control his destiny. Having contemplated the many unforeseen changes of his reign, Henry IV finally breaks off his reverie to plan a campaign against the rebels:

> Are these things then necessities?
> Then let us meet them like necessities;
> And that same word even now cries out on us.
> They say the Bishop and Northumberland
> Are fifty thousand strong.
>
> (3.1.87–91)

This is the pragmatic voice of rule, the blunt determination that Shakespeare attributes both to Prince Hal and to his father.

Yet despite (and perhaps because of) their similarities, Shakespeare makes the relationship of Henry and Hal a troubled one. Part of the complexity of *2 Henry IV* is that while it tellingly anatomizes how these Kings, father and then son, acquire and maintain power, it simultaneously creates the impression of a psychodrama between the two of them that, though inseparable from their political roles, is never fully understood by either. Hal, despite telling Poins he loves his father, does not appear in the King's presence until the end of Act 4, when Henry is on his deathbed. Then, with what has seemed to many to be unseemly haste, Hal, believing his father dead, takes the crown from the sleeping King's pillow and sets it on his own head. Is this, as the King fears, Hal's acting out of a fantasy of parricide? Or, as Hal protests, is it his attempt to come to terms with the burdens of office that have hastened his father's death and that will now fall to him?

In part, the relationship between Hal and Henry is complicated by the guilt each feels about the politically useful and carefully managed "wildness" that each has employed. Hal, of course, has cultivated wildness as a prelude to reform. It is the foil by which he aims to set off his achievement of perfect chivalry and justice. But it is important to remember that to come by his throne, Henry himself had to enact the wildness of usurpation, seizing the crown from a lawfully anointed king, an act Shakespeare depicted in *Richard II*. To be sure, once in the seat of rule, Henry repudiated such wildness and embraced the law, justifying his own reign in part by presenting himself as the bulwark against disorder—that of the rebels and even that of his son. There is no doubt that Hal displays prodigal behavior, spending time in the tavern rather than at court, but his father dwells on and exaggerates his son's lawlessness, picturing England's distress when ruled by a man who "from curbed licence plucks / The muzzle of restraint" (4.3.258–59). This preoccupation with Hal's lawlessness may signal Henry's guilt about his own act of usurpation, for which he has long planned a penitential crusade to the Holy Land (a crusade that we eventually learn would *also* have the effect of distracting his nobles from thoughts of rebellion at home). But Henry does not seem able to see the ways in which his son's tactics resemble his own. Truly his father's child, Hal angles for power with an unerring sense of when to embrace wildness and when to repudiate it. Just as Henry's act of seizing the crown raises the specter of parricide, Henry's obsession with curbing Hal's wildness hints at castration. Without seeming fully to realize the consequences of his own actions, the King would cut off one source of Hal's power, even though he himself once embraced disorder and still needs it to justify his rule.

In Henry's last conversation with Hal and at his death, father and son switch positions in the discourse of "wildness" that runs through the play. The King has been the principle of order, the Prince the ungovernable prodigal. On his deathbed, however, the King acknowledges to Hal:

> God knows, my son,
> By what bypaths and indirect crook'd ways
> I met this crown; and I myself know well
> How troublesome it sat upon my head.
> To thee it shall descend with better quiet,
> Better opinion, better confirmation;
> For all the soil of the achievement goes
> With me into the earth.
>
> (4.3.311–18)

He represents himself as a man stained by his own errancy, but one whose sins can be buried with his death. Hal picks up the theme when he announces after his father's death, "My father is gone wild into his grave" (5.2.122), as if Henry himself embodied the principle of disorder, now buried. Yet Hal continues, suddenly making problematic whose wildness the grave holds:

> For in his tomb lie my affections;
> And with his spirits sadly I survive
> To mock the expectation of the world.
> (5.2.123–25)

Now it is *Hal's* wildness that the grave holds, his father's sober spirits that live on in the son. Shedding his prodigality is now not an act of disempowerment but its opposite. The wild Prince has become the order-loving King. It will now be his turn to repudiate those who live outside the compass of the law, beginning with Falstaff.

Critics have argued that *2 Henry IV* looks forward to the tragedies in its somber tone and its focus upon the tortured self-divisions of the King and his son. There is truth in this claim, but one must also recognize that while the play allows the audience to read doubt and self-division in Henry and the Prince, at the end it moves to install Hal unambiguously in the position of the reformed Prince and law-abiding King. Hal's apparent self-division holds the attention of the audience just as his carefully managed reform wins the admiration of his subjects. But when the time is right, whatever the "personal" cost, he embraces the law in the person of the Chief Justice while burying wildness in the person of his father and publicly repudiating it in the person of Falstaff. In so doing, he shows an unerring instinct for the improvisations that allow him to acquire and retain power.

But though Hal publicly repudiates wildness, the play does not. Wildness surges up unpredictably, not only in the actions of the rebels but also in the actions and particularly in the unruly language of those many "minor" characters who are Shakespeare's additions to his historical sources and whose existence is signaled on the title page by reference to the humors of Falstaff and swaggering Pistol. In the late sixteenth century, the English language was undergoing expansion and entering a period of vibrant linguistic experimentation. Many writers were interested in making English a fit language in which to write verse that would rival the achievements of classical literature. They experimented with imitating the verse forms used by Latin writers in particular; they also coined new words, and they attempted to purge English of uncouth or infelicitous elements. But it was not just poets who affected the language. Trade brought new products to England, and those products had to have names. Foreign visitors, merchants, and workers were a common sight in the London landscape, and they, of course, brought their languages with them. Foreign terms were regularly absorbed into the English vernacular. Meanwhile, the theater offered auditors the high-sounding rhetoric of kings and tyrants, while London preachers made their reputations with dazzling displays of oratorical power.

This atmosphere generated an infectious excitement about language, and not all of this excitement was easy to control. Rhetorical handbooks proliferated, each sketching out the styles and figures of speech appropriate to different occasions, and each also listing rhetorical "vices," examples of indecorous or ungrammatical or infelicitous speech. *2 Henry IV* could be considered a casebook of linguistic vices. The minor characters speak a wild farrago of tongues that defy the desire for linguistic order. Swaggering Pistol is a case in point. Much of his speech is composed of scraps of rhetoric he has picked up from going to the London theater, especially, perhaps, to the Rose, where Edward Alleyn, chief actor for the Admiral's Men, specialized in a highly rhetorical and hyperbolic acting style that Pistol seems both to channel and to parody. Pistol, for example, imagines himself as Tamburlaine, the overreaching hero of Marlowe's two-part play about a Scythian shepherd who became one of the great military conquerors of all time. Alleyn was famous for this role, and Pistol's swaggering style aspires to Alleyn's (and Tamburlaine's) rhetorical pyrotechnics. Pistol, however, mangles his references to Marlowe's hero, intermingling what he can remember of Tamburlaine's speeches with a mishmash of fine-sounding names and lines from drinking songs, as when he proclaims:

> Shall pack-horses
> And hollow pampered jades of Asia,
> Which cannot go but thirty mile a day,
> Compare with Caesars and with cannibals,
> And Trojan Greeks?
> Nay, rather damn them with King Cerberus,
> And let the welkin roar. Shall we fall foul for toys?
>   (2.4.140–46)

Pistol's "mistakes" are pervasive. First he imitates what he can remember of the moment when Tamburlaine taunts the conquered kings whom he has put in harness to draw his chariot. But then he veers into nonsense, mistaking "cannibal" for "Hannibal," the heroic leader of Carthage; describing Greeks as Trojans, while in *The Iliad* the Greeks and Trojans were two peoples at war with one another; then attributing a crown to Cerberus, the three-headed dog who guarded the gates of hell; and ending with a tag from a drinking song: "And let the welkin roar." The sheer exuberance of the speech is partly what makes it pleasurable—Pistol's delight in the sound of big words, whatever those words may mean—along with the lawless incongruity with which one bit of remembered rhetoric is stitched onto the next. Self-mockingly, but also self-importantly, the passage points to the power of the theater to intoxicate spectators with fine rhetoric. Choleric, explosive, overflowing with the excesses of stage rhetoric, Pistol is a wild card in the play's quest for order and the rule of law.

He is not alone. The play opens with a prologue spoken by Rumour, whose business is telling lies, substituting the untrue for the true. That Shakespeare prefaced the play with this figure indicates his concern with the vagaries and waywardness of language. Sometimes language is maliciously used to deceive, as with Rumour or Prince John's double-edged speech at Gaultres. Sometimes, as with Pistol's bombast, it is used to evoke delight in how words sound, regardless of what they mean. At other times, as with Falstaff's puns, language reveals the double and triple meanings that can be activated from a simple utterance. To take a single example, consider Falstaff's anger in 1.2 at the prosperous merchant who refuses to give him twenty-two yards of satin without his providing adequate security—that is, adequate goods or money to cover the debt. To his Page

The Rumour of Shakespeare's Induction is derived from the classical figure of Fame, here depicted as covered with ears (to gather reports from all quarters) and blowing a horn (to broadcast news abroad). From Vicenzo Cartari, *Imagines deorum* (1581).

Falstaff sputters, "Well, he may sleep in security, for he hath the horn of abundance, and the lightness of his wife shines through it; and yet cannot he see, though he have his own lanthorn to light him" (1.2.39–42). The subversive wittiness of this passage depends on Falstaff's punning on the fact that "horn" can mean the horn lanterns sold by merchants, the cornucopia that is a symbol of abundance, or the horns of a man who has been sexually betrayed by his wife, while "lightness" can mean both illumination and sexual promiscuity. On the surface, Falstaff is grudgingly admitting that the merchant is rich and graced with a wife. But the puns tell another story: that of a blind cuckold whose wife's sexual infidelity is visible to everyone but himself. In Falstaff's mouth, language is a slippery thing and often a devastating tool for confounding an enemy.

One of the play's most remarkable rhetoricians, Mistress Quickly, did not make it to the title page of the Quarto, but her verbal blunders are another example of language's unpredictable qualities. Quickly is not the same person she was in *1 Henry IV*. For one thing, she seems to have lost the husband who was mentioned often, though never glimpsed, in the previous play; and she has acquired a new companion in the person of the prostitute Doll Tearsheet. Unmarried, economically independent, and associated with the criminality of prostitution and perhaps of murder (in 5.4, the women are accused with Pistol of having beaten a man to death), Quickly emerges as a figure of disorder who must be purged from a reformed commonwealth. In part, she represents linguistic anarchy. Her signature utterance is the malapropism, the verbal blunder by which one word is mistaken for another. For example, telling the Chief Justice of Falstaff's whereabouts, she says he was "indited," meaning "invited," to dinner (2.1.24). The malapropism is interesting because it is a kind of lawless speech in which the speaker is guided by the sound of words, or by a private logic, rather than by the usual rules of sense. Quickly, for example, in mistaking "indicted" for "invited" has blundered into her own kind of sense, since she would indeed like to see Falstaff indicted, or brought to legal judgment, for the debts he owes her. Malapropisms, to those who know better, make the speaker appear foolish. Yet they also can disrupt the institutions that depend on clear and predictable communication. Not even the Chief Justice knows quite what to make of Quickly, so persistently does her speech elude the net of common sense, enveloping her in a tangle of meanings—some obscene, some suggestively significant—that she may or may not intend. Sir Francis Bacon called revenge "wild justice"; the malapropism might be called "wild speech," so thoroughly does it defy semantic predictability.

The distinctiveness of the prose assigned to the comic figures in *2 Henry IV* is one of the play's most striking features. It highlights Shakespeare's ability to delineate character by means of linguistic differences. Shallow's mindless repetition of simple words, Falstaff's puns, Quickly's malapropisms, and Pistol's bombast are all ways of individuating these figures. They also suggest the fecundity of speech in Henry's England and register, at the linguistic level, a wild disorder no principle of decorum or law can entirely contain. By means of the double entendre, much of what characters speak in the tavern world alludes to the body and its pleasures, even while they intend or appear to talk of something else. For example, Quickly, complaining of Falstaff to the Chief Justice, says, "He stabbed me in mine own house, most beastly, in good faith. A cares not what mischief he does; if his weapon be out, he will foin like any devil, he will spare neither man, woman, nor child" (2.1.12–15). "Foin" means "thrust" or "strike." Overtly, Quickly describes a Falstaff who takes out his sword or dagger and indiscriminately stabs whoever happens to be handy. Indirectly, and perhaps inadvertently, she describes a Falstaff who, when his sexual "weapon," or penis, is out, will indiscriminately engage in sex with whoever happens to be near. The tavern scenes teem with similar instances of sexualized speech or, more accurately, speech that tells two stories at the same time, one of them a story of sex: its pleasures and diseases and persistence. The bawdy doubleness of tavern

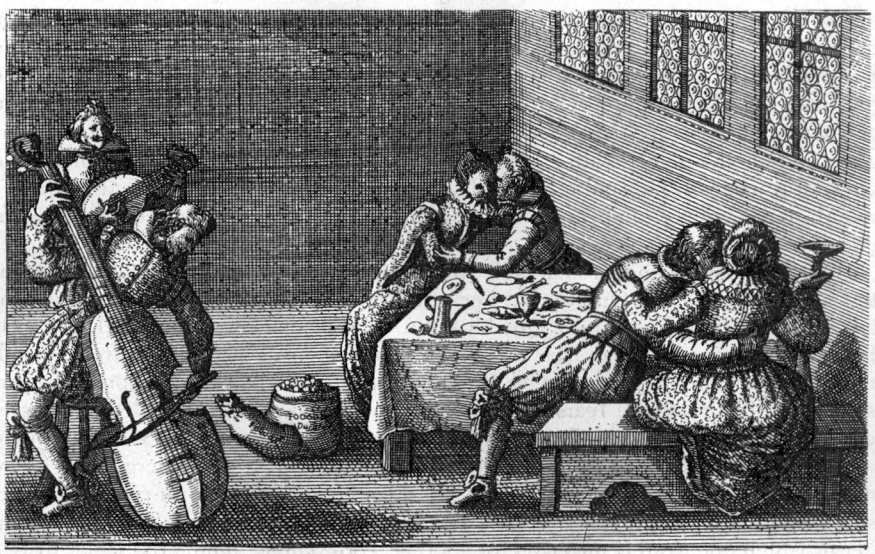

A seventeenth-century tavern scene recalling Mistress Quickly's Eastcheap tavern. From Peter Rollos, *Le Centre de l'amour* (1630?).

prose contrasts sharply with the elevated poetry in which the King most often speaks. Worrying, planning, commanding, the King constructs himself as a bulwark against disorder. But the disorderly, bombastic, vibrant, and lewd speech of the tavern suggests at the level of language the difficulties of controlling the manifold energies of his subjects.

Thinking about the play's control of or its failure to control unsanctioned energies provides a context for considering what traditionally has been the most discussed aspect of 2 *Henry IV*: the Prince's final public repudiation of Falstaff. In this play, Falstaff is kept separate from the Prince except for the one scene (2.4) in which the Prince disguises himself as a tavern barman and overhears Falstaff talking with Doll and Quickly. Moreover, the exploitative side of Falstaff is more fully displayed here than in the earlier play. He leeches off Quickly; he takes bribes to release able-bodied men from service in the army; he worms a thousand pounds from Shallow. Yet he is still able, as in the stunning speech in which he indicts Prince John for cold-bloodedness (4.2.78–111), to offer a telling critique of his betters and to embody a frank physicality they eschew. Given Falstaff's wit and his centrality to the pleasure afforded by both *1* and *2 Henry IV*, the new King's repudiation of him—"I know thee not, old man. Fall to thy prayers" (5.5.45)—continues to trouble critics and audiences. Certainly, how the moment is staged can mitigate or harshen its implications. In Terry Hands's 1975 Royal Shakespeare Company production, for example, the newly crowned King came onstage in glittering gold and masked, the epitome of detached and heartless power. In other productions, he rejects his former friend with a sob, emphasizing his own sense of loss and his continuing affection for Falstaff. But however it is staged, there is little doubt that the new King, whatever his "personal" feelings, has turned Falstaff away to consolidate his power.

The final scene, however, is not the play's last word it is followed by an Epilogue. It is likely that this Epilogue was spoken by the company's clown, in this case Will Kemp, a famed comic actor who in this play is believed to have played Falstaff. It is especially likely that Kemp spoke the Epilogue because of the several references in it to the actor's willingness to use his legs, or to dance, should his words not prove agreeable. Kemp was a skilled dancer, and when he left Shakespeare's company in 1599, he undertook a famous morris dance from London to Norwich. The Epilogue gives the common actor who had played Falstaff the play's last word and its final display of physical skill. At Shrewsbury, Hal had thought Falstaff dead, but, faking death, the fat man had arisen. In *2 Henry IV*, the old knight is banished from the King's presence in the play's final scene, but in the Epilogue, the actor who had played him reappears—soliciting the audience's applause, denying that Falstaff is a representation of the Lollard martyr Sir John Oldcastle (see the Introduction to *1 Henry IV*) and kicking up his heels in a virtuoso display of dancing skill. If in the play proper the forces of order have attempted to demonize the energies associated with popular culture and the low life of the tavern, in the Epilogue those energies have free rein. The body of the common actor holds center stage as Kemp, throwing aside the character Falstaff's mantle of age, delights the audience with a jig.

The Epilogue has another effect. It pluralizes the "authorities" to which the theater is beholden. With its references to the Oldcastle controversy and its final allusion to praying for Queen Elizabeth, the Epilogue acknowledges the power embodied in the person of the monarch and in the state's censorship apparatus But it also refers to pleasing both the gentlewomen and the gentlemen of the audience—in other words, the paying customers who came to the theater for all sorts of pleasures. If the title page of the Quarto is to be believed, readers, and probably audiences, were as much delighted by the irrepressible and irresponsible antics of Falstaff and swaggering Pistol as by the sober reformation of Hal and the suffering of his father, just as they were undoubtedly as delighted by the mangling of the King's English as by its decorous deployment. In short, while in this play the rule of law officially triumphs over the forces of disorder, the comic actor has the last dance, and theater finds a way to offer pleasures in excess of what the sober historical narrative allows.

JEAN E. HOWARD

TEXTUAL NOTE

2 Henry IV was entered in the Stationers' Register on August 23, 1600, and first printed in a quarto version dated that same year. This Quarto had two issues, the first of which, QA, lacks the present 3.1, in which the sleepless King Henry meditates on the passage of time and the ironies of history. In QB, this scene is included. The text was not printed again until it appeared in a significantly different version in the First Folio of 1623 (F). The Folio text contains eight fairly substantial passages, totaling about 160 lines, not found in Q (A or B). It also differs from the quarto text in a number of other ways: oaths have been excised; punctuation, syntax, and certain aspects of style have been regularized; stage directions have been altered, and in several scenes the names of characters have been "massed" together in an initial stage direction, even if some of these characters only enter at a later point in the scene; some quarto lines are missing, and new part lines appear, as does a table of "The Actors Names" listing all the speaking parts.

The important debate about the play's textual history concerns the relation of Q to F. Q shows signs—such as the use of a number of different speech prefixes for the same character—of having been printed directly from the author's "foul papers," which do not appear to have been marked up for use in a theatrical performance. One explanation for the absence of 3.1 in QA is that the scene was marked for excision in the foul papers, either because it was politically sensitive or to reduce the length of the play. Others have argued that the scene was written on a separate manuscript leaf that became detached from its proper place in the foul papers and so was overlooked by the compositor. The Oxford editors believe that this scene was added by Shakespeare *after* the rest of the manuscript had been written as the first step in his ongoing reworking of the play. They postulate that the compositor who set this part of QA missed the marks indicating where the scene was to be added to the foul papers.

F, by contrast, shows signs of having been prepared by a professional scribe in its regularization of a number of aspects of the text, though these changes also introduce errors and obscure the exact nature of the manuscript underlying the transcription. The excision of oaths is undoubtedly a result of the 1606 statute against profanity on the stage. Some further changes found in F may be due to the special problems facing the compositors setting the text. It appears that too little space had been allocated in F for setting this play in type. Consequently, a group of four additional sheets was added, but the compositor still had to omit words, compressing one part of the text, and to add words and phrases, expanding other parts of the text, in order to fit the play into its allotted space. It is possible that the list of "The Actors Names" was added to fill up a blank page.

Some editors argue that the eight substantial passages found in F but missing from Q were originally present in the manuscript used for setting Q but were marked for excision, either because they were politically sensitive or for theatrical reasons such as the need to reduce the length of the speeches assigned to actors doubling in two roles. These editors grant priority to the quarto text (which appears to be printed from Shakespeare's foul papers and which does not contain the errors and changes made by the scribe who prepared the Folio manuscript), but they usually add the eight additional passages on the grounds that they were originally part of the manuscript behind the Quarto.

The Oxford editors work from different assumptions; specifically, they argue that beginning with 3.1, Shakespeare himself made a series of revisions to the play, perhaps recording these in the fair copy that was to serve as the promptbook. They argue that he did so as part of a consistent strategy to augment the historical portions of the play and to connect it more fully to *Richard II* and *1 Henry IV*. They agree that two of the eight additional Folio passages represent cuts in the quarto text because they deal with the politically sensitive matter of rebellion, but they also hold that the remaining six are Shakespeare's later *additions* to the play. They further argue that some of the other changes in F, such as the deletion of specific lines, show authorial intervention in the interest of making the play more stageworthy. The Oxford editors therefore postulate that the scribe who produced the copy used for setting F, while having a copy of Q to consult, was working primarily from a theatrical promptbook that registered some authorial revisions to the quarto version of the play, though the theatrical nature of that promptbook has been obscured by the "literary" habits of the scribe. As a consequence, this edition of the play, while using Q as its control text, accepts a higher number of Folio readings than is true for many other editions in an attempt to reproduce the stage version of the play the Oxford editors believe underlies F.

The eight substantial new passages found in F deserve further discussion. Interestingly, all of them involve figures who are of the rebels' party. The Oxford editors agree that two of them were censored because they too compellingly justified rebellion. These are 1.1.188–208, Morton's speech announcing that the Archbishop of York has joined the rebellion, using the murder of Richard II as partial justification, and 4.1.55–79, the Archbishop's speech justifying the rebels' position and exclaiming against the King's indifference to their grievances. Other passages are in greater dispute. For example, 2.3.23–45, part of Lady Percy's magnificent speech in praise of Hotspur, does not appear in Q. Is this because Shakespeare had not yet written it? Or had it been cut from the original manuscript because the praise of Hotspur could be read as indirect praise of the Earl of Essex, the dashing, headstrong noble whose triumphal return from a 1599 campaign against the Irish Shakespeare was to anticipate with excitement in *Henry V*—but who in actuality returned home in disgrace and shortly thereafter led an abortive rebellion against Elizabeth? Or was it cut because the boy actor playing Lady Percy also was to play Doll Tearsheet in the next scene and had to have the number of lines he spoke reduced? Each of the eight additional Folio passages, which include 1.1.165–78, 1.3.21–24, 1.3.36–55, 1.3.85–108, and 4.1.101–37 (as well as the three passages already mentioned), is flagged in the notes so that readers can consider each case for themselves. The principal passages deleted from this text but present in Q and in most modern editions of the text are indented and printed as inset passages at the points where they appeared in Q.

Apart from Act 4, this text follows Folio act and scene divisions, although in F the Induction is marked as a separate scene. As for Act 4, F divides it into two scenes, and in many modern editions it is divided into five scenes; this edition divides it into three, ignoring the interpolated scene breaks often added by modern editors after 4.1.226, when Prince John marches onstage to speak with the rebels at Gaultres and after 4.3.132, when the King is carried to the Jerusalem Chamber. It retains, however, the interpolated break after 4.1.349 in which Falstaff enters with Coleville after Prince John has departed the stage, on the grounds that unlike the other two instances, this is a place where the stage is cleared and the action is therefore not continuous. It also retains the Folio scene break (now 4.3) when King Henry first comes onstage sick and in his bed.

SELECTED BIBLIOGRAPHY

Calderwood, James L. *Metadrama in Shakespeare's Henriad: "Richard II" to "Henry V."* Berkeley: University of California Press, 1979. Esp. 88–104. Examines Hal's rejection of Falstaff and the fat knight's inability to escape from history into comic invulnerability.

Crewe, Jonathan. "Reforming Prince Hal: The Sovereign Inheritor in *2 Henry IV*." *Renaissance Drama*, n.s., 21 (1990): 225–42. Discusses the play's obsession with Hal's reform and the role of the father's death in effecting that reform.

Goldberg, Jonathan. "Hal's Desire, Shakespeare's Idaho." *Shakespeare's Hand.* Minneapolis: University of Minnesota Press, 2003. 222–52. Uses Gus Van Sant's film *My Own Private Idaho* to explore sex and gender relations in *1* and *2 Henry IV,* including Hal's potentially sodomitical relations with Falstaff.

Hodgdon, Barbara. "'Let the End Try the Man': *1* and *2 Henry IV*." *The End Crowns All: Closure and Contradiction in Shakespeare's History.* Princeton: Princeton University Press, 1991. 151–84. Discusses the play's problematic ending and different ways it has been staged.

Knights, L. C. "Time's Subjects: The Sonnets and *King Henry IV, Part II*." *Some Shakespearean Themes.* London: Chatto & Windus, 1959. 45–64. Explores the play's themes of time and change as prefigured in the sonnets.

Levine, Nina. "Extending Credit in the *Henry IV* Plays." *Shakespeare Quarterly* 51 (2000): 403–31. Discusses the pervasiveness and ideological complexity of the language of credit in both *Henry IV* plays.

MacDonald, Ronald R. "Uses of Diversity: Bakhtin's Theory of Utterance and Shakespeare's Second Tetralogy." *"Henry IV, Parts One and Two."* Ed. Nigel Wood. Theory in Practice series. Buckingham, Eng.: Open University Press, 1995. 65–91. Uses Bakhtin's theories of language to discuss the heteroglossia, or profusion of disparate voices, in this play.

Rackin, Phyllis. "Historical Kings/Theatrical Clowns." *Stages of History: Shakespeare's English Chronicles.* Ithaca, N.Y.: Cornell University Press, 1990. 201–47. Explores in all the histories the threat to authority embodied in the disorderly conduct and subversive speech of common men and of Falstaff.

Ruiter, David. "'The Unquiet Time' of *2 Henry IV*: Festivity and Order in Flux." *Shakespeare's Festive History: Feasting, Festivity, Fasting, and Lent in the Second Henriad.* Aldershot, Eng.: Ashgate, 2003. 103–41. Probes the difficulties Hal encounters in staging the reform he has so long planned.

Wiles, David. *Shakespeare's Clown: Actor and Text in the Elizabethan Playhouse.* New York: Cambridge University Press, 1987. Esp. "Kemp's Jigs" (43–60) and "Falstaff" (116–35). Argues that Falstaff's role is the clown's part and that it was originally played by Will Kemp, a notable clown in Shakespeare's company who was also famous for his dancing of jigs.

Young, David P., ed. *Twentieth Century Interpretations of "Henry IV, Part II": A Collection of Critical Essays.* Englewood Cliffs, N.J.: Prentice-Hall, 1968. Wide-ranging collection of classic essays from the mid-twentieth century.

FILM

Henry IV, Part II. 1979. Dir. David Giles. UK. 155 min. Judicious cuts and a strong performance by Anthony Quayle as Falstaff strengthen this sober BBC-TV version of the play.

The Second Part of Henry the Fourth

THE PERSONS OF THE PLAY

RUMOUR, the Presenter
EPILOGUE
KING HENRY IV
PRINCE HARRY, later crowned King Henry V ⎱
PRINCE JOHN of Lancaster ⎰ sons of
Humphrey, Duke of GLOUCESTER ⎱ King Henry IV
Thomas, Duke of CLARENCE ⎰
Percy, Earl of NORTHUMBERLAND, of the rebels' party
LADY NORTHUMBERLAND
LADY PERCY, their son Hotspur's widow
TRAVERS, Northumberland's servant
MORTON, a bearer of news from Shrewsbury
Scrope, ARCHBISHOP of York ⎱
LORD BARDOLPH
Thomas, Lord MOWBRAY, the Earl Marshal ⎰ rebels against
Lord HASTINGS King Henry IV
Sir John COLEVILLE ⎰
LORD CHIEF JUSTICE
His SERVANT
GOWER, a Messenger
Sir John FALSTAFF ⎱
His PAGE
BARDOLPH
POINS ⎰ 'irregular humorists'
Ensign PISTOL
PETO ⎰
MISTRESS QUICKLY, hostess of a tavern
DOLL TEARSHEET, a whore
SNARE ⎱ sergeants
FANG ⎰
Neville, Earl of WARWICK ⎱
Earl of SURREY
Earl of WESTMORLAND ⎰ supporters of King Henry
HARCOURT
Sir John Blunt ⎰
Robert SHALLOW ⎱ country justices
SILENCE ⎰
DAVY, Shallow's servant
Ralph MOULDY ⎱
Simon SHADOW
Thomas WART ⎰ men levied to fight for King Henry
Francis FEEBLE
Peter BULLCALF ⎰
PORTER of Northumberland's household
DRAWERS

BEADLES
GROOMS
MESSENGER
Sneak and other musicians
Lord Chief Justice's men, soldiers and attendants

Induction

Enter RUMOUR[1] [*in a robe*] *painted full of tongues*

RUMOUR	Open your ears; for which of you will stop°	*plug up*
	The vent of hearing° when loud Rumour speaks?	*The ear*
	I from the orient° to the drooping west,	*east*
	Making the wind my post-horse,° still° unfold	*hired horse / continually*
5	The acts commencèd on this ball of earth.	
	Upon my tongues continual slanders ride,	
	The which in every language I pronounce,	
	Stuffing the ears of men with false reports.	
	I speak of peace, while covert enmity	
10	Under the smile of safety wounds the world;	
	And who but Rumour, who but only I,	
	Make fearful musters and prepared defence[2]	
	Whiles the big° year, swoll'n with some other griefs,	*pregnant*
	Is thought with child by the stern tyrant war,	
15	And no such matter? Rumour is a pipe	
	Blown by surmises, Jealousy's conjectures,	
	And of so easy and so plain a stop[3]	
	That the blunt° monster with uncounted° heads,	*stupid / innumerable*
	The still-discordant wav'ring multitude,	
20	Can play upon it. But what° need I thus	*why*
	My well-known body to anatomize°	*dissect; lay open*
	Among my household?° Why is Rumour here?	*(the theater audience)*
	I run before King Harry's victory,	
	Who in a bloody field by Shrewsbury[4]	
25	Hath beaten down young Hotspur and his troops,	
	Quenching the flame of bold rebellion	
	Even with the rebels' blood. But what mean I	
	To speak so true at first? My office is	
	To noise abroad that Harry Monmouth[5] fell	
30	Under the wrath of noble Hotspur's sword,	
	And that the King before the Douglas' rage	
	Stooped his anointed head as low as death.	
	This have I rumoured through the peasant° towns	*rural*
	Between that royal field of Shrewsbury	
35	And this worm-eaten hold° of raggèd stone,	*stronghold*

Induction Location: Outside Northumberland's castle at Warwock.
1. A personification, possibly based on Virgil's "Fama," depicted as a female monster with many eyes, ears, and tongues who circulated both true and false accounts of events. See *Aeneid* 4.179–90.
2. Cause soldiers, prompted by fear, to assemble and defenses to be made ready. These lines may be topical: fear of imminent Spanish invasion led the Privy Council to mobilize militia forces frequently throughout the latter years of Elizabeth's reign.
3. And whose "stops," or openings, are so easy to play upon. The ease with which Rumour's pipe can be played means that even the common people can do it.

In the next lines, Rumour refers to these commoners as a many-headed monster, a common derogatory image of the people, especially when they aspire to participation in governance. By contrast, the proper head of the realm was held to be the single sovereign.
4. In Shakespeare's rendition of the Battle of Shrewsbury, staged in *1 Henry IV*, Prince Hal kills Henry Percy (Hotspur), and his forces capture the Scottish Earl of Douglas, two of the principal leaders of rebellion. In 1.1 of this play, the announcement of Henry Percy's death invokes considerable wordplay on his nickname, his "hot" spur being transformed into a "cold" spur by death.
5. Prince Hal was called Harry Monmouth in honor of his birthplace, Monmouth, in Wales.

Where Hotspur's father, old Northumberland,
Lies crafty-sick.° The posts come tiring on,[6]   *pretending to be ill*
And not a man of them brings other news
Than they have learnt of me. From Rumour's tongues
40   They bring smooth comforts false, worse than true wrongs.
                                                                                                          Exit

1.1

Enter LORD BARDOLPH[1] *at one door. [He crosses the*
stage to another door]

LORD BARDOLPH
    Who keeps the gate here, ho?
                                Enter PORTER *[above]*[2]
                                                                Where is the Earl?
PORTER   What shall I say you are?
LORD BARDOLPH   Tell thou the Earl
    That the Lord Bardolph doth attend° him here.   *await*
PORTER   His lordship is walked forth into the orchard.
5   Please it your honour knock but at the gate,
    And he himself will answer.
                        Enter the Earl NORTHUMBERLAND *[at the other door, as*
                        sick, with a crutch and coif]°   *nightcap*
LORD BARDOLPH   Here comes the Earl
                                                                    [Exit PORTER*]*
NORTHUMBERLAND   What news, Lord Bardolph? Every minute now
    Should be the father of some stratagem.
    The times are wild; contention, like a horse
10   Full of high feeding,° madly hath broke loose,   *overly rich food*
    And bears down all before him.
LORD BARDOLPH   Noble Earl,
    I bring you certain news from Shrewsbury.
NORTHUMBERLAND   Good, an° God will.   *if*
LORD BARDOLPH   As good as heart can wish.
    The King is almost wounded to the death;
15   And, in the fortune° of my lord your son,   *good luck*
    Prince Harry slain outright; and both the Blunts[3]
    Killed by the hand of Douglas; young Prince John
    And Westmorland and Stafford fled the field;
    And Harry Monmouth's brawn,° the hulk Sir John,   *fattened pig*
20   Is prisoner to your son. O, such a day,
    So fought, so followed,° and so fairly won,   *carried through*
    Came not till now to dignify the times
    Since Caesar's fortunes!°   *successes*
NORTHUMBERLAND   How is this derived?
    Saw you the field? Came you from Shrewsbury?
25   LORD BARDOLPH   I spake with one, my lord, that came from thence,
    A gentleman well bred and of good name,
    That freely rendered me these news for true.

---

6. The messengers, exhausting themselves, gallop on.
1.1. Location: Scene continues.
1. A nobleman associated with the rebel Percy faction;
Falstaff's companion with the same name is unrelated.
2. Having the Porter enter on the upper playing
space is conjectural, but it effectively suggests that

Northumberland is in a stronghold where his retainers
are wary of intruders. The upper stage, however, does
not appear to have been used elsewhere in the play.
3. In *1 Henry IV*, only one Blunt, Sir Walter, dies at
Shrewsbury.

Enter TRAVERS

NORTHUMBERLAND   Here comes my servant Travers, who I sent
On Tuesday last to listen after news.

30   LORD BARDOLPH   My lord, I overrode° him on the way,   *overtook*
And he is furnished with no certainties
More than he haply° may retail from me.   *perhaps*

NORTHUMBERLAND   Now, Travers, what good tidings comes with you?

TRAVERS   My lord, Lord Bardolph turned me back[4]

35   With joyful tidings, and being better horsed
Outrode me. After him came spurring hard
A gentleman almost forspent° with speed,   *worn out*
That stopped by me to breathe° his bloodied horse.   *rest*
He asked the way to Chester,[5] and of him

40   I did demand what news from Shrewsbury.
He told me that rebellion had ill luck,
And that young Harry Percy's spur was cold.
With that he gave his able horse the head,
And, bending forward, struck his armèd heels

45   Against the panting sides of his poor jade°   *worn-out horse*
Up to the rowel-head;[6] and starting so,
He seemed in running to devour the way,
Staying° no longer question.   *Awaiting*

NORTHUMBERLAND   Ha? Again:
Said he young Harry Percy's spur was cold?

50   Of Hotspur, 'Coldspur'? that rebellion
Had met ill luck?

LORD BARDOLPH   My lord, I'll tell you what:
If my young lord your son have not the day,
Upon mine honour, for a silken point°   *lace for tying a garment*
I'll give my barony. Never talk of it.

55   NORTHUMBERLAND   Why should the gentleman that rode by Travers
Give then such instances of loss?

LORD BARDOLPH   Who, he?
He was some hilding° fellow that had stol'n   *worthless*
The horse he rode on, and, upon my life,
Spoke at a venture.°   *at random*

Enter MORTON

Look, here comes more news.

60   NORTHUMBERLAND   Yea, this man's brow, like to a title leaf,
Foretells the nature of a tragic volume.[7]
So looks the strand° whereon the imperious flood   *shore*
Hath left a witnessed usurpation.[8]
Say, Morton, didst thou come from Shrewsbury?

65   MORTON   I ran from Shrewsbury, my noble lord,
Where hateful death put on his ugliest mask
To fright our party.

4. In Q, Travers says that Sir John Umfreuile, not Lord
Bardolph, turned him back. Since Lord Bardolph reports
having met Travers on the road, most critics agree that
Umfreuile and Lord Bardolph are the same character
whose name got changed at some point. At 1.1.161, Q
assigns one line to "Umfr.," another indication that a
character with this name was once to figure in the play.
This line does not appear in F or in the present text.
5. A town north of Shrewsbury.
6. The spiked wheel at the end of the spur.

7. Alluding to the descriptive title pages of early modern printed books, which often indicated the principal
actions of the work and sometimes characterized them
as tragic or comic. For an example, see the descriptive
title page of the quarto version of this play, reprinted in
the Introduction.
8. *whereon . . . usurpation:* where the sea has left evidence of its conquest (of the land). The comparison is
between Morton's brow, wrinkled by sorrow, and sand
furrowed by the sea's encroachment.

NORTHUMBERLAND   How doth my son and brother?[9]
Thou tremblest, and the whiteness in thy cheek
Is apter than thy tongue to tell thy errand.
70   Even such a man, so faint, so spiritless,
So dull, so dead in look, so woebegone,
Drew Priam's curtain[1] in the dead of night,
And would have told him half his Troy was burnt;
But Priam found the fire ere he his tongue,
75   And I my Percy's death ere thou report'st it.
This thou wouldst say: 'Your son did thus and thus,
Your brother thus; so fought the noble Douglas',
Stopping° my greedy ear with their bold deeds;   *Filling*
But in the end, to stop° my ear indeed,   *plug up; obstruct*
80   Thou hast a sigh to blow away this praise,
Ending with 'Brother, son, and all are dead.'
MORTON   Douglas is living, and your brother yet;
But for my lord your son—
NORTHUMBERLAND   Why, he is dead.
See what a ready tongue suspicion hath!
85   He that but fears the thing he would not know
Hath by instinct knowledge from others' eyes
That what he feared is chanced.° Yet speak, Morton.   *has happened*
Tell thou an earl his divination lies,[2]
And I will take it as a sweet disgrace,
90   And make thee rich for doing me such wrong.
MORTON   You are too great to be by me gainsaid,
Your spirit is too true, your fears too certain.
NORTHUMBERLAND   Yet for all this, say not that Percy's dead.
I see a strange confession in thine eye—
95   Thou shak'st thy head, and hold'st it fear or sin
To speak a truth. If he be slain, say so.
The tongue offends not that reports his death;
And he doth sin that doth belie the dead,
Not he which says the dead is not alive.
100   Yet the first bringer of unwelcome news
Hath but a losing office,° and his tongue   *thankless duty*
Sounds ever after as a sullen° bell   *mournful*
Remembered knolling a departing friend.
LORD BARDOLPH   I cannot think, my lord, your son is dead.
105   MORTON [*to* NORTHUMBERLAND]   I am sorry I should force you to believe
That which I would to God I had not seen;
But these mine eyes saw him in bloody state,
Rend'ring faint quittance,[3] wearied and out-breathed,°   *out of breath*
To Harry Monmouth, whose swift wrath beat down
110   The never-daunted Percy to the earth,
From whence with life he never more sprung up.
In few,° his death, whose spirit lent a fire   *In short*
Even to the dullest peasant in his camp,

9. The Earl of Worcester, who helped lead the rebellion
staged in *1 Henry IV.*
1. Opened Priam's bed curtain. Priam was King of
Troy during the Trojan War. This may allude to a scene
from Virgil's *Aeneid* in which Hector appears to Aeneas,
not Priam, in a dream, warning him of danger. Aeneas
wakes to find Troy in flames.
2. Tell me, who am an earl, that in my prophecy I lie.
To say a social superior lies would normally be a grave
offense, but Northumberland would be happy to be
proven wrong.
3. Repayment (return of blows).

Being bruited° once, took fire and heat away   reported
115   From the best-tempered courage[4] in his troops;
      For from his metal° was his party steeled,   steel; courage
      Which once in him abated,° all the rest   blunted
      Turned on themselves,[5] like dull and heavy lead;
      And, as the thing that's heavy in itself
120   Upon enforcement° flies with greatest speed,   When forced into motion
      So did our men, heavy in Hotspur's loss,
      Lend to this weight such lightness with their fear
      That arrows fled not swifter toward their aim
      Than did our soldiers, aiming at their safety,
125   Fly from the field. Then was that noble Worcester
      Too soon ta'en prisoner; and that furious Scot
      The bloody Douglas, whose well-labouring sword
      Had three times slain th'appearance of the King,[6]
      Gan vail his stomach,[7] and did grace° the shame   sanction
130   Of those that turned their backs, and in his flight,
      Stumbling in fear, was took. The sum of all
      Is that the King hath won, and hath sent out
      A speedy power° to encounter you, my lord,   quick-moving army
      Under the conduct° of young Lancaster   command
135   And Westmorland. This is the news at full.
      NORTHUMBERLAND   For this I shall have time enough to mourn.
      In poison there is physic;° and these news,   medicine
      Having been° well, that would have made me sick,   If I had been
      Being sick, have in some measure made me well;
140   And, as the wretch whose fever-weakened joints,
      Like strengthless hinges, buckle under life,[8]
      Impatient of his fit, breaks like a fire
      Out of his keeper's° arms, even so my limbs,   nurse's
      Weakened with grief, being now enraged with grief,
      Are thrice themselves.
                        [He casts away his crutch]
145   Hence therefore, thou nice° crutch!   unmanly
      A scaly° gauntlet now with joints of steel   mailed
      Must glove this hand.
                        [He snatches off his coif]
                              And hence, thou sickly coif!
      Thou art a guard too wanton° for the head   effeminate; luxurious
      Which princes fleshed with conquest[9] aim to hit.
150   Now bind my brows with iron, and approach
      The ragged'st° hour that time and spite dare bring   roughest
      To frown upon th'enraged Northumberland!
      Let heaven kiss earth! Now let not nature's hand
      Keep the wild flood confined! Let order die!
155   And let this world no longer be a stage
      To feed contention in a ling'ring act;[1]

4. Courage of the finest quality. The implicit comparison is to steel that had been tempered, or made strong,
by extreme heat.
5. Bent backward (like soft metal); fled.
6. In *1 Henry IV*, at the Battle of Shrewsbury, members
of the rebel faction slew several noblemen dressed in
the King's coats whom they mistook for Henry himself.
See *1 Henry IV* 5.3.1–13 and 5.4.24–37.

7. Began to lose courage (stomach).
8. Collapse from the burden of living.
9. Which princes made eager for bloody victories by
having tasted raw flesh (been victorious). Hounds were
"fleshed," given a taste of raw meat, to prepare them for
the hunt.
1. *And let . . . act*: And let the world stop being a stage
where strife is encouraged in a prolonged action.

But let one spirit of the first-born Cain[2]
Reign in all bosoms, that each heart being set
On bloody courses, the rude scene may end,
160 And darkness be the burier of the dead!
LORD BARDOLPH   Sweet Earl, divorce not wisdom from your honour.
MORTON   The lives of all your loving complices°   *associates*
Lean on your health, the which, if you give o'er
To stormy passion, must perforce decay.[3]
165 You cast th'event° of war, my noble lord,   *calculated the outcome*
And summed° the account of chance, before you said   *added up*
'Let us make head'.° It was your presurmise   *raise an army*
That in the dole° of blows your son might drop.   *dealing out*
You knew he walked o'er perils on an edge,°   *a narrow blade*
170 More likely to fall in than to get o'er.
You were advised° his flesh was capable   *aware*
Of wounds and scars, and that his forward spirit
Would lift him where most trade of° danger ranged.°   *dealing in / was displayed*
Yet did you say, 'Go forth'; and none of this,
175 Though strongly apprehended, could restrain
The stiff-borne° action. What hath then befall'n?   *stubbornly pursued*
Or what doth this bold enterprise bring forth,
More than that being° which was like to be?   *event*
LORD BARDOLPH   We all that are engagèd to° this loss   *involved in*
180 Knew that we ventured on such dangerous seas
That if we wrought out life was ten to one;[4]
And yet we ventured for the gain proposed,
Choked the respect of° likely peril feared;   *Refused to consider*
And since we are o'erset,° venture again.   *overthrown*
185 Come, we will all put forth body and goods.
MORTON   'Tis more than time; and, my most noble lord,
I hear for certain, and dare speak the truth,[5]
The gentle Archbishop of York is up°   *up in arms*
With well-appointed powers.° He is a man   *well-equipped forces*
190 Who with a double surety binds his followers.[5]
My lord, your son had only but the corpse,°   *mere bodies*
But shadows and the shows of men, to fight;
For that same word 'rebellion' did divide
The action of their bodies from their souls,
195 And they did fight with queasiness constrained,
As men drink potions, that their weapons only
Seemed on our side; but, for their spirits and souls,
This word 'rebellion', it had froze them up,
As fish are in a pond. But now the Bishop
200 Turns insurrection to religion.
Supposed sincere and holy in his thoughts,
He's followed both with body and with mind,
And doth enlarge his rising[7] with the blood
Of fair King Richard, scraped from Pomfret stones;[8]

2. In the Bible, the first human being to be born and the murderer of his brother.
3. Lines 165–78 are not included in Q. (See Textual Note.)
4. The odds were ten to one against our preserving life.
5. Lines 188–208 are missing from Q. It is generally agreed that these lines were cut for political reasons.
6. Referring to the fact that the Archbishop, unlike

Hotspur, might use his religious as well as his temporal authority to secure his soldiers' fidelity.
7. And increases the size or enhances the reputation of his rebellion.
8. Alluding to Henry IV's responsibility for the murder of Richard at Pontefract Castle (Pomfret), as staged in Act 5 of *Richard II*. Richard's blood is treated as a holy saint's relic.

205   Derives from heaven his quarrel and his cause;
      Tells them he doth bestride° a bleeding land   *protect by standing over*
      Gasping for life under great Bolingbroke;°   *(Henry IV)*
      And more and less° do flock to follow him.   *people of all ranks*
      NORTHUMBERLAND   I knew of this before, but, to speak truth,
210   This present grief had wiped it from my mind.
      Go in with me, and counsel every man
      The aptest way for safety and revenge.
      Get posts° and letters, and make° friends with speed.   *messengers / gather*
      Never so few, and never yet more need.   *Exeunt*

1.2

Enter Sir John FALSTAFF, *[followed by] his* PAGE *bearing*
his sword and buckler°   shield

FALSTAFF   Sirrah,[1] you giant, what says the doctor to my water?°   *urine*
PAGE   He said, sir, the water itself was a good healthy water,
       but, for the party that owed° it, he might have more diseases   *owned*
       than he knew for.°   *was aware of*
5 FALSTAFF   Men of all sorts take a pride to gird° at me. The brain   *mock*
       of this foolish-compounded clay,[2] man, is not able to invent
       anything that tends to laughter more than I invent, or is
       invented on me. I am not only witty in myself, but the cause
       that wit is in other men. I do here walk before thee like a sow
10   that hath o'erwhelmed° all her litter but one. If the Prince put   *crushed*
       thee into my service for any other reason than to set me off,[3]
       why then, I have no judgement. Thou whoreson mandrake,[4]
       thou art fitter to be worn in my cap than to wait at my heels. I
       was never manned with° an agate[5] till now; but I will set you   *attended by*
15   neither in gold nor silver, but in vile apparel, and send you
       back again to your master for a jewel—the juvenal° the Prince   *youth*
       your master, whose chin is not yet fledge.° I will sooner have a   *covered with down*
       beard grow in the palm of my hand than he shall get one off
       his cheek; and yet he will not stick° to say his face is a face-   *hesitate*
20   royal.[6] God may finish it when he will; 'tis not a hair amiss yet.
       He may keep it still at° a face-royal, for a barber shall never   *at the value of*
       earn sixpence out of it. And yet he'll be crowing as if he had
       writ man° ever since his father was a bachelor. He may keep   *called himself a man*
       his own grace,° but he's almost out of mine, I can assure him.   *title (Prince); favor*
25   What said Master Dumbleton about the satin for my short
       cloak and slops?[7]
PAGE   He said, sir, you should procure him better assurance
       than Bardolph. He would not take his bond and yours; he
       liked not the security.
30 FALSTAFF   Let him be damned like the glutton![8] Pray God his

---

1.2 Location: A street in London.
1. Form of address to a social inferior.
2. Clay compounded with foolishness (an image
derived from the biblical account of the first human
being as formed out of clay).
3. To make me stand out by contrast. The page is tiny,
and Falstaff is huge.
4. An herb with a forked root that was popularly supposed to resemble a miniature man. It was believed to
shriek when pulled from the ground and to have aphro-
disiacal powers. *whoreson*: an insult, derived from the
phrase "whore's son."

5. A small jewel often carved with images of people and
worn in caps.
6. The face of royalty (with a pun on "royal," a coin
worth 10 shillings and stamped with the monarch's face).
7. Baggy knee breeches, fashionable in Elizabethan
London.
8. Referring to the biblical parable of Dives, a rich glutton who ignored the pleas of the beggar Lazarus and at
death was condemned to hell, where he implored
Lazarus to dip his finger in water and lay it on his
tongue to cool the flames (see Luke 16:19–31).

tongue be hotter! A whoreson Achitophel,[9] a rascally yea-
forsooth knave,[1] to bear a gentleman in hand° and then stand   *lead a gentleman on*
upon security! The whoreson smooth-pates[2] do now wear noth-
ing but high shoes and bunches of keys at their girdles;[3] and if
35   a man is through with them in honest taking-up,[4] then they
must stand upon security. I had as lief° they would put rats-   *gladly*
bane° in my mouth as offer to stop it with security. I looked a°   *rat poison / that he*
should have sent me two and twenty yards of satin, as I am a
true knight,[5] and he sends me 'security'! Well, he may sleep in
40   security, for he hath the horn of abundance, and the lightness
of his wife shines through it;[6] and yet cannot he see, though he
have his own lanthorn to light him. Where's Bardolph?

PAGE   He's gone in Smithfield[7] to buy your worship a horse.

FALSTAFF   I bought him in Paul's,[8] and he'll buy me a horse in
45   Smithfield. An° I could get me but a wife in the stews,° I were   *If / brothels*
manned, horsed, and wived.

        Enter [the] LORD CHIEF JUSTICE *and [his]* SERVANT

PAGE   Sir, here comes the nobleman that committed° the Prince   *imprisoned*
for striking him about Bardolph.[9]

FALSTAFF *[moving away]*   Wait close;° I will not see him.[1]   *concealed*
50   LORD CHIEF JUSTICE *[to his* SERVANT*]*   What's he that goes there?

SERVANT   Falstaff, an't please your lordship.

LORD CHIEF JUSTICE   He that was in question° for the robbery?[2]   *under investigation*

SERVANT   He, my lord; but he hath since done good service at
Shrewsbury, and, as I hear, is now going with some charge° to   *command of soldiers*
55   the Lord John of Lancaster.

LORD CHIEF JUSTICE   What, to York? Call him back again.

SERVANT   Sir John Falstaff!

FALSTAFF   Boy, tell him I am deaf.

PAGE *[to the* SERVANT*]*   You must speak louder; my master is
60   deaf.

LORD CHIEF JUSTICE   I am sure he is to the hearing of anything
good. *[To the* SERVANT*]* Go pluck him by the elbow; I must
speak with him.

SERVANT   Sir John!

65   FALSTAFF   What, a young knave and begging! Is there not wars?[3]
Is there not employment? Doth not the King lack subjects? Do
not the rebels want soldiers? Though it be a shame to be on
any side but one, it is worse shame to beg than to be on the

---

9. A biblical figure, King David's trusted counselor,
who betrayed him by supporting the treason of the
king's son (2 Samuel 15).
1. A villainous knave who appears to be agreeable. A
"yea-forsooth" knave makes promises with mild oaths
(but then breaks them).
2. Alluding disparagingly to the fashion among tradesmen, especially Puritans, for short hair.
3. Wear the most fashionable shoes and display a mass
of keys (habits suggesting pride and conspicuous consumption).
4. If a man makes a deal with them for a purchase on
credit.
5. Referring to Tudor sumptuary codes, which prescribed the fabrics that could be worn by people of different social ranks. As a knight, Falstaff can wear satin.
6. For he is rich and his wife's promiscuity is visible to
all, with puns on "horn" as referring to the horn
lanterns sold by merchants; to a symbol of overflowing

plenty (a cornucopia); and to cuckoldry (deceived husbands were said to wear horns). "Lightness" can mean
both illumination and sexual promiscuity.
7. A district northwest of London's city walls, used as
a market for animals.
8. St. Paul's Cathedral in London, where masterless
men presented themselves for employment.
9. Alluding to the apocryphal account of the youthful
Prince's assault on the Lord Chief Justice, staged in
The Famous Victories of Henry V, the anonymous play
from which Shakespeare's is partly derived.
1. Falstaff's determination not to acknowledge the
Lord Chief Justice presumably causes him to turn his
back on the magistrate or walk off in another direction.
2. The Gadshill robbery, in which Falstaff took part.
See *1 Henry IV* 2.2.
3. Alluding to the Elizabethan practice of mass conscription of impoverished men.

worst side, were it worse than the name of rebellion can tell
70 how to make° it.   *regard*

SERVANT   You mistake me, sir.

FALSTAFF   Why, sir, did I say you were an honest man? Setting
my knighthood and my soldiership aside, I had lied in my
throat° if I had said so.   *deliberately lied*

75 SERVANT   I pray you, sir, then set your knighthood and your soldiership aside, and give me leave to tell you you lie in your
throat if you say I am any other than an honest man.

FALSTAFF   I give thee leave to tell me so? I lay aside that which
grows to me?° If thou gettest any leave of me, hang me. If thou   *is part of me*
80 takest leave, thou wert better be hanged. You hunt counter.[4]
Hence, avaunt!°   *be gone*

SERVANT   Sir, my lord would speak with you.

LORD CHIEF JUSTICE   Sir John Falstaff, a word with you.

FALSTAFF   My good lord! God give your lordship good time of
85 day. I am glad to see your lordship abroad. I heard say your
lordship was sick. I hope your lordship goes abroad by advice.°   *by medical advice*
Your lordship, though not clean past your youth, have yet some
smack of age in you, some relish of the saltness of time in you;
and I most humbly beseech your lordship to have a reverent
90 care of your health.

LORD CHIEF JUSTICE   Sir John, I sent for you before your expedition to Shrewsbury.

FALSTAFF   An't please your lordship, I hear his majesty is
returned with some discomfort from Wales.[5]

95 LORD CHIEF JUSTICE   I talk not of his majesty. You would not
come when I sent for you.

FALSTAFF   And I hear, moreover, his highness is fallen into this
same whoreson apoplexy.°   *paralysis*

LORD CHIEF JUSTICE   Well, God mend him! I pray you, let me
100 speak with you.

FALSTAFF   This apoplexy is, as I take it, a kind of lethargy, an't
please your lordship, a kind of sleeping in the blood, a
whoreson tingling.

LORD CHIEF JUSTICE   What° tell you me of it? Be it as it is.   *Why*

105 FALSTAFF   It hath it original° from much grief, from study, and   *its origin*
perturbation of the brain. I have read the cause of his effects in
Galen.[6] It is a kind of deafness.

LORD CHIEF JUSTICE   I think you are fallen into the disease, for
you hear not what I say to you.

110 FALSTAFF   Very well, my lord, very well. Rather, an't please you,
it is the disease of not listening, the malady of not marking, that
I am troubled withal.°   *with*

LORD CHIEF JUSTICE   To punish you by the heels[7] would amend
the attention of your ears, and I care not if I do become your
115 physician.

FALSTAFF   I am as poor as Job,[8] my lord, but not so patient. Your
lordship may minister the potion of imprisonment to me in

---

4. You pursue the scent of the game in the wrong
direction.
5. Some discouragement from Wales (where the King
promised to fight Glyndŵr and Mortimer at the end of
1 Henry IV).
6. Ancient Greek physician whose anatomical texts were
widely translated and printed in early modern Europe.

Galen was commonly regarded as the chief authority in
human physiology.
7. By putting your feet in the stocks or in shackles.
8. A biblical figure who, in the Book of Job, patiently
endured the many adversities with which God afflicted
him, including poverty.

respect of° poverty; but how I should be your patient to follow   *on account of*
your prescriptions, the wise may make some dram of a scruple,
120   or indeed a scruple itself.[9]
LORD CHIEF JUSTICE   I sent for you, when there were matters
against you for your life,[1] to come speak with me.
FALSTAFF   As I was then advised by my learned counsel in the
laws of this land-service,° I did not come.   *military duty*
125   LORD CHIEF JUSTICE   Well, the truth is, Sir John, you live in
great infamy.
FALSTAFF   He that buckles himself in my belt cannot live in less.
LORD CHIEF JUSTICE   Your means are very slender, and your waste
is great.
130   FALSTAFF   I would it were otherwise; I would my means were
greater and my waist slenderer.
LORD CHIEF JUSTICE   You have misled the youthful Prince
FALSTAFF   The young Prince hath misled me. I am the fellow
with the great belly, and he my dog.[2]
135   LORD CHIEF JUSTICE   Well, I am loath to gall° a new-healed   *to injure by rubbing*
wound. Your day's service at Shrewsbury hath a little gilded
over your night's exploit on Gads Hill. You may thank th'un-
quiet time for your quiet o'erposting° that action.   *passing swiftly over*
FALSTAFF   My lord—
140   LORD CHIEF JUSTICE   But since all is well, keep it so. Wake not a
sleeping wolf.
FALSTAFF   To wake a wolf is as bad as smell a fox.°   *as being suspicious*
LORD CHIEF JUSTICE   What! You are as a candle, the better part
burnt out.
145   FALSTAFF   A wassail candle,[3] my lord, all tallow°—if I did say of   *animal fat*
wax,[4] my growth would approve° the truth.   *attest to*
LORD CHIEF JUSTICE   There is not a white hair in your face but
should have his effect° of gravity.   *manifestation*
FALSTAFF   His effect of gravy, gravy, gravy.[5]
150   LORD CHIEF JUSTICE   You follow the young Prince up and down
like his ill angel.°   *evil spirit*
FALSTAFF   Not so, my lord; your ill angel is light,[6] but I hope he
that looks upon me will take me without weighing. And yet in
some respects, I grant, I cannot go.° I cannot tell, virtue is of so   *walk; be circulated*
155   little regard in these costermongers' times[7] that true valour is
turned bearherd;[8] pregnancy° is made a tapster, and his quick   *mental agility*
wit wasted in giving reckonings;° all the other gifts appertinent°   *tavern bills / belonging*
to man, as the malice of this age shapes them, are not worth a
gooseberry. You that are old consider not the capacities of us
160   that are young. You do measure the heat of our livers with the
bitterness of your galls.[9] And we that are in the vanguard° of   *most advanced stage*
our youth, I must confess, are wags too.

9. The wise may feel a particle of doubt. Drams and
scruples were small weights used to measure medicines
in apothecary shops.
1. For which your life was at stake.
2. An obscure allusion. It may refer to the man in the
moon, a mythical figure who supposedly carried a bush
and was accompanied by a dog.
3. A large fat candle used at holiday festivities.
4. Beeswax, with pun on "wax" as meaning "grow."
5. Grease; sweat. Falstaff implies that sweat should
drop from his face as fat (gravy) drops from hot meat.

6. Your bad coin weighs less. Falstaff puns on "angel"
as the name of a gold coin that could illegally be clipped
so that it weighed less than it should.
7. In these commercial times. A costermonger sold trifling commodities such as fruits and vegetables.
8. Keeper of bears, such as those used for the popular
entertainment of bearbaiting.
9. You measure the strength of our passions by the bitterness of your melancholy. The liver was believed to be
the seat of youthful passions, and bile or gall produced
the melancholy and anger characteristic of old age.

LORD CHIEF JUSTICE   Do you set down your name in the scroll
of youth, that are written down old with all the characters° of   *letters; signs*
165   age? Have you not a moist eye, a dry hand, a yellow cheek, a
white beard, a decreasing leg, an increasing belly? Is not your
voice broken, your wind short, your chin double, your wit single, and every part about you blasted with antiquity? And will
you yet call yourself young? Fie, fie, fie, Sir John!
170   FALSTAFF   My lord, I was born about three of the clock in the
afternoon with a white head, and something a° round belly.   *a somewhat*
For my voice, I have lost it with hallowing° and singing of   *shouting to hounds*
anthems. To approve° my youth further, I will not. The truth   *prove*
is, I am only old in judgement and understanding; and he that
175   will caper° with me for a thousand marks,[1] let him lend me the   *dance (in competition)*
money, and have at him! For the box of th'ear that the Prince
gave you, he gave it like a rude° prince, and you took it like a   *violent; an uncivilized*
sensible lord.[2] I have checked him for it, and the young lion
repents—[*aside*] marry,° not in ashes and sackcloth, but in new   *by the Virgin Mary (oath)*
180   silk and old sack.[3]
LORD CHIEF JUSTICE   Well, God send the Prince a better companion!
FALSTAFF   God send the companion a better prince! I cannot rid
my hands of him.
185   LORD CHIEF JUSTICE   Well, the King hath severed you and
Prince Harry. I hear you are going with Lord John of Lancaster against the Archbishop and the Earl of Northumberland.
FALSTAFF   Yea, I thank your pretty sweet wit for it. But look° you   *see that*
190   pray, all you that kiss my lady Peace at home, that our armies
join not in a hot day; for, by the Lord, I take but two shirts out
with me, and I mean not to sweat extraordinarily. If it be a hot
day and I brandish anything but my bottle, would I might never
spit white again.[4] There is not a dangerous action° can peep   *military action*
195   out his head but I am thrust upon it. Well, I cannot last ever.
But it was alway yet the trick° of our English nation, if they   *habit*
have a good thing, to make it too common. If ye will needs say
I am an old man, you should give me rest. I would to God my
name were not so terrible to the enemy as it is. I were better to
200   be eaten to death with a rust than to be scoured to nothing with
perpetual motion.
LORD CHIEF JUSTICE   Well, be honest, be honest, and God bless
your expedition.
FALSTAFF   Will your lordship lend me a thousand pound to fur-
205   nish me forth?
LORD CHIEF JUSTICE   Not a penny, not a penny. You are too
impatient to bear crosses.[5] Fare you well. Commend me to my
cousin Westmorland.
[*Exeunt* LORD CHIEF JUSTICE *and his* SERVANT]

---

1. A unit of money; one mark was equal to two-thirds
of a pound.
2. Like a reasonable lord; like a lord capable of feeling
pain. For the story of Hal's striking the Chief Justice,
see note to 1.2.48.
3. A Spanish white wine that improved with age.

4. A disputed passage. Perhaps, may I never drink
again (white spit was thought to be the result of heavy
drinking).
5. To endure afflictions like a good Christian; to carry
silver coins, which bear the sign of a cross.

FALSTAFF If I do, fillip° me with a three-man beetle.⁶ A man can   strike
210 no more separate age and covetousness than a° can part young   he
limbs and lechery; but the gout⁷ galls the one and the pox
pinches° the other, and so both the degrees prevent my   syphilis torments
curses.⁸ Boy!

PAGE Sir.

215 FALSTAFF What money is in my purse?

PAGE Seven groats° and two pence.   coins worth fourpence

FALSTAFF I can get no remedy against this consumption of the
purse. Borrowing only lingers and lingers it out, but the disease
is incurable. [Giving letters] Go bear this letter to my lord of
220 Lancaster; this to the Prince; this to the Earl of Westmorland;
and this to old Mistress Ursula,⁹ whom I have weekly sworn to
marry since I perceived the first white hair of my chin. About
it. You know where to find me.   [Exit PAGE]¹
A pox of this gout!—or a gout of this pox!—for the one or the
225 other plays the rogue with my great toe. 'Tis no matter if I do
halt;° I have the wars for my colour,° and my pension shall   limp / pretext
seem the more reasonable. A good wit will make use of any-
thing. I will turn diseases to commodity.°   Exit   profit

1.3

Enter the ARCHBISHOP *[of York], Thomas* MOWBRAY *[the]*
*Earl Marshal,*¹ *Lord* HASTINGS, *and* LORD BARDOLPH

ARCHBISHOP OF YORK Thus have you heard our cause and
known our means,
And, my most noble friends, I pray you all
Speak plainly your opinions of our hopes.
And first, Lord Marshal, what say you to it?

5 MOWBRAY I well allow the occasion of our arms,²
But gladly would be better satisfied
How in our means° we should advance ourselves   with our resources
To look with forehead bold and big enough
Upon the power and puissance° of the King.   strength

10 HASTINGS Our present musters grow upon the file°   according to our list
To five-and-twenty thousand men of choice,°   choice men
And our supplies° live largely in the hope   reinforcements
Of great Northumberland, whose bosom burns
With an incensèd fire of injuries.

15 LORD BARDOLPH The question then, Lord Hastings, standeth thus:
Whether our present five-and-twenty thousand
May hold up head° without Northumberland.   May succeed

HASTINGS With him we may.

---

6. A huge sledgehammer designed to be lifted by three laborers at once.

7. A disease characterized by painful inflammation of the joints, often of the toe joints in particular, and associated with the excessive consumption of rich food and alcohol. Falstaff is bothered by gout, and it may have been the reason he sent his urine to be examined by the doctor at the beginning of this scene.

8. So both conditions (age and youth) anticipate my curses. Venereal disease torments young lecherous men; gout afflicts old men.

9. A name nowhere else mentioned in this play. It

could be the first name of Mistress Quickly. It may also be an inadvertent reference to the Ursula of *Much Ado About Nothing*, a play also printed in 1600.

1. Neither Q nor F marks a separate exit for the Page. F indicates a plural "Exeunt" at the end of the scene, suggesting that Falstaff and the Page exit together. But clearly the fat knight's concluding lines are a private meditation on his diseases best spoken after he has sent the Page off to deliver his letters.

1.3 Location: The Archbishop's palace in York.

1. The officer in charge of arranging royal ceremonies.

2. I grant the justice of our taking arms.

LORD BARDOLPH   Yea, marry, there's the point;
But if without him we be thought too feeble,
20   My judgement is, we should not step too far[3]
Till we had his assistance by the hand;
For in a theme° so bloody-faced as this,   *matter*
Conjecture, expectation, and surmise
Of aids uncertain should not be admitted.
25 ARCHBISHOP OF YORK   'Tis very true, Lord Bardolph, for indeed
It was young Hotspur's case at Shrewsbury.
LORD BARDOLPH   It was, my lord; who lined° himself with hope,   *strengthened*
Eating the air on promise of supply,[4]
Flatt'ring himself with project of a power°   *expectation of an army*
30   Much smaller° than the smallest of his thoughts;   *smaller in actuality*
And so, with great imagination
Proper to madmen, led his powers to death,
And winking° leapt into destruction.   *shutting his eyes*
HASTINGS   But by your leave, it never yet did hurt
35   To lay down likelihoods and forms of hope.[5]
LORD BARDOLPH   Yes, if this present quality° of war—   *condition*
Indeed the instant° action, a cause on foot°—   *present / in motion*
Lives so in hope; as in an early spring
We see th'appearing buds, which to prove° fruit   *mature into*
40   Hope gives not so much warrant as despair
That frosts will bite them.[6] When we mean to build
We first survey the plot,[7] then draw the model;°   *design*
And when we see the figure° of the house,   *design*
Then must we rate the cost of the erection,
45   Which if we find outweighs ability,
What do we then but draw anew the model
In fewer offices,° or, at least,° desist   *rooms / worst*
To build at all? Much more in this great work—
Which is almost to pluck a kingdom down
50   And set another up—should we survey
The plot of situation and the model,
Consent° upon a sure foundation,   *Agree*
Question surveyors,° know our own estate,°   *architects / resources*
How able such a work to undergo,
55   To weigh against his opposite;[8] or else
We fortify in paper and in figures,
Using the names of men instead of men,
Like one that draws the model of an house
Beyond his power to build it, who, half-through,
60   Gives o'er, and leaves his part-created cost[9]
A naked subject° to the weeping clouds,   *An exposed object*
And waste for churlish winter's tyranny.
HASTINGS   Grant that our hopes, yet° likely of fair birth,   *still*
Should be stillborn, and that we now possessed
65   The utmost man of expectation,[1]

---

3. Lines 21–24 are not present in Q.
4. Sustaining himself on nothing but the promise of aid; believing the empty words he had heard concerning promised aid.
5. And hopeful plans. Lines 36–55 are not present in Q.
6. *as in . . . them:* an obscure passage. Bardolph may mean that optimism in this instance is ill advised, just as it is ill advised to hope that early spring buds will mature into fruit rather than be killed by frost.
7. Plan. What follows is an elaboration on a biblical parable in Luke 14:28–30 about a wise builder.
8. *To weigh . . . opposite:* To put in the balance against contrary arguments. Bardolph is urging the rebels to evaluate their strengths against their weaknesses.
9. And leaves his costly building half completed.
1. The last man whom we can expect.

I think we are a body strong enough,
Even as we are, to equal with the King.

LORD BARDOLPH   What, is the King but five-and-twenty thousand?

HASTINGS   To us no more, nay, not so much, Lord Bardolph;

70   For his divisions, as the times do brawl,°   *are full of conflict*
    Are in three heads: one power against the French,
    And one against Glyndŵr, perforce a third
    Must take up us.° So is the unfirm King   *oppose us*
    In three divided, and his coffers sound

75   With hollow poverty and emptiness.

ARCHBISHOP OF YORK   That he should draw his several° strengths together   *separate*
    And come against us in full puissance
    Need not be dreaded.

HASTINGS   If he should do so,
    He leaves his back unarmed, the French and Welsh

80   Baying him at the heels.[2] Never fear that.

LORD BARDOLPH   Who is it like° should lead his forces hither?   *likely*

HASTINGS   The Duke of Lancaster and Westmorland;
    Against the Welsh, himself and Harry Monmouth;
    But who is substituted° 'gainst the French   *delegated*
    I have no certain notice.[3]

85 ARCHBISHOP OF YORK   Let us on
    And publish° the occasion of our arms.   *make public*
    The commonwealth is sick of their own choice;
    Their over-greedy love hath surfeited.[4]
    An habitation giddy and unsure

90   Hath he that buildeth on the vulgar° heart.   *common*
    O thou fond° many, with what loud applause   *foolish*
    Didst thou beat° heaven with blessing Bolingbroke,   *assail*
    Before he was what thou wouldst have him be!
    And being now trimmed° in thine own desires,   *decked out*

95   Thou, beastly feeder, art so full of him
    That thou provok'st thyself to cast him up.
    So, so, thou common dog, didst thou disgorge
    Thy glutton bosom of the royal Richard;
    And now thou wouldst eat thy dead vomit up,

100   And howl'st to find it. What trust is in these times?
    They that when Richard lived would have him die
    Are now become enamoured on his grave.
    Thou that threw'st dust upon his goodly head,
    When through proud London he came sighing on

105   After th'admirèd heels of Bolingbroke,
    Cri'st now, 'O earth, yield us that king again,
    And take thou this!' O thoughts of men accursed!
    Past and to come seems best; things present, worst.

MOWBRAY   Shall we go draw our numbers° and set on?   *gather our forces*

110 HASTINGS   We are time's subjects, and time bids be gone. *Exeunt*

---

2. That is, following him like hunting dogs.   4. Became sick through overindulgence.
3. Lines 85–108 are not present in Q.

2.1

*Enter [*MISTRESS QUICKLY *the*] *hostess of [*a*] tavern, and
an officer,* FANG [*followed at a distance by another officer*], SNARE[1]

MISTRESS QUICKLY Master Fang, have you entered the action?°   *begun the lawsuit*
FANG It is entered.
MISTRESS QUICKLY Where's your yeoman?° Is't a lusty[2] yeoman?   *assistant*
    Will a stand to't?[3]
5 FANG Sirrah!—Where's Snare?
MISTRESS QUICKLY O Lord, ay, good Master Snare.
SNARE [*coming forward*] Here, here.
FANG Snare, we must arrest Sir John Falstaff.
MISTRESS QUICKLY Yea, good Master Snare, I have entered him[4]
10   and all.
SNARE It may chance° cost some of us our lives, for he will stab.   *perhaps*
MISTRESS QUICKLY Alas the day, take heed of him; he stabbed[5]
    me in mine own house, most beastly, in good faith. A cares not
    what mischief he does; if his weapon° be out, he will foin° like   *dagger; penis / thrust*
15   any devil, he will spare neither man, woman, nor child.
FANG If I can close[6] with him, I care not for his thrust.
MISTRESS QUICKLY No, nor I neither. I'll be at your elbow.
FANG An I but fist° him once, an a come but within my   *seize; masturbate*
    vice°—   *grasp*
20 MISTRESS QUICKLY I am undone by his going, I warrant you; he's
    an infinitive thing upon my score.[7] Good Master Fang, hold
    him sure. Good Master Snare, let him not scape. A comes con-
    tinuantly to Pie Corner[8]—saving your manhoods—to buy a
    saddle,[9] and he is indited° to dinner to the Lubber's Head[1] in   *(for "invited")*
25   Lombard Street, to Master Smooth's the silkman. I pray you,
    since my exion is entered,[2] and my case° so openly known to   *lawsuit; vagina*
    the world, let him be brought in to his answer. A hundred mark
    is a long one° for a poor lone woman to bear; and I have borne,[3]   *huge account*
    and borne, and borne, and have been fobbed off, and fobbed
30   off, and fobbed off, from this day to that day, that it is a shame
    to be thought on. There is no honesty in such dealing, unless
    a woman should be made an ass and a beast, to bear every
    knave's wrong.

Enter Sir John FALSTAFF, BARDOLPH, *and the* [PAGE][4]

2.1 Location: Eastcheap, a street and market in London.
1. That Snare should linger behind Fang is suggested
by the subsequent lines in which Fang cannot locate his
fellow officer. Perhaps Snare is slow and lazy; or perhaps he deliberately lags behind to sniff out trouble and
"ensnare" villains.
2. Sturdy; lustful. The following lines are full of sexual
puns.
3. Will he fight vigorously? Will he maintain an erect
penis?
4. I have brought suit against him, with a pun on
"entered him" as meaning "had sexual relations with
him." The phrase usually denotes a man's sexual entry
into a woman.
5. With a pun on "stabbed" as meaning "sexually penetrated."
6. Fight hand to hand; clinch.
7. "Infinitive" is Quickly's malapropism, or verbal blunder, for "infinite." She implies that the board ("score")

on which her accounts are tallied has innumerable
markings corresponding to Falstaff's debts to her.
8. Piecorner was an area of Smithfield named for its
cooks' shops and known for its commerce in horses and
sex. *continuantly:* blunder for "continually" or "inconti-
nently."
9. With a pun on "saddle" as also meaning "female genitalia."
1. Blunder for "Libbard's," an Elizabethan form of
"Leopard's." The silk merchant's shop sign evidently
contained the image of a leopard's head.
2. Since my legal action has begun, with a pun on
"entered" suggesting sexual penetration.
3. Endured, with a pun on "have borne" as meaning
"have supported the weight of a partner in sexual relations."
4. As here, Q's stage directions sometimes refer to "the
boy" rather than "the page." These have been standardized to "Page" throughout.

Yonder he comes, and that arrant° malmsey-nose⁵ knave Bar-   *notorious*
35   dolph with him. Do your offices,° do your offices. Master Fang   *duties*
and Master Snare; do me,⁶ do me, do me your offices.

FALSTAFF   How now, whose mare's dead? What's the matter?

FANG   Sir John, I arrest you at the suit of Mistress Quickly.

FALSTAFF [*drawing*]   Away, varlets! Draw, Bardolph! Cut me off
40   the villain's head! Throw the quean° in the channel!°   *whore / street gutter*
[BARDOLPH *draws*]

MISTRESS QUICKLY   Throw me in the channel? I'll throw thee in
the channel!
[*A brawl*]
Wilt thou, wilt thou, thou bastardly rogue? Murder, murder!
Ah, thou honeysuckle⁷ villain, wilt thou kill God's officers, and
45   the King's? Ah, thou honeyseed° rogue! Thou art a honeyseed,   *(for "homicidal")*
a man-queller, and a woman-queller.

FALSTAFF   Keep them off, Bardolph!

FANG   A rescue,⁸ a rescue!

MISTRESS QUICKLY   Good people, bring a rescue or two. Thou
50   wot,° wot thou? Thou wot, wot'a? Do, do, thou rogue, do, thou   *You will*
hempseed!⁹

PAGE   Away, you scullion,° you rampallian,° you fustilarian!¹ I'll   *kitchen wench / ruffian*
tickle your catastrophe!²
Enter [the] LORD CHIEF JUSTICE *and his men*

LORD CHIEF JUSTICE   What is the matter? Keep the peace here,
55   ho!
[*Brawl ends.* FANG *seizes* FALSTAFF]³

MISTRESS QUICKLY   Good my lord, be good to me. I beseech you,
stand to me.⁴

LORD CHIEF JUSTICE   How now, Sir John? What, are you brawling here?
Doth this become your place,° your time° and business?   *social place / age*
60   You should have been well on your way to York.
[*To* FANG] Stand from him, fellow. Wherefore hang'st thou
upon him?

MISTRESS QUICKLY   O my most worshipful lord, an't° please your   *if it*
grace, I am a poor widow of Eastcheap, and he is arrested at
my suit.

65   LORD CHIEF JUSTICE   For what sum?

MISTRESS QUICKLY   It is more than for some, my lord, it is for all,
all I have. He hath eaten me out of house and home. He hath
put all my substance into that fat belly of his; [*to* FALSTAFF] but
I will have some of it out again, or I will ride thee a-nights like
70   the mare.⁵

---

5. Red-nosed from drinking alcohol. Malmsey was a strong red wine named after its place of origin in Greece and available from Spain, Portugal, and their colonies as well as Greece.
6. Do your jobs for me, with a pun on "do me" as slang for "have sexual relations with me."
7. For "homicidal," with a pun on "honey" as slang for "sexual pleasure."
8. A cry for help in resisting arrest. Fang fears Falstaff is being rescued, but Quickly in the next line takes "rescue" to mean "reinforcements" and seems to call for the rescue Fang is trying to stop.
9. Another version of "homicide," with an allusion to the hangman's hempen rope.

1. Fat, unkempt woman.
2. Expression meaning "I'll whip your rear end."
3. There are considerable opportunities for comic stage business here. Someone has to be hanging on Falstaff at this point, because at line 61, the Lord Chief Justice tells a "fellow" to let go. Perhaps Fang has twined himself around Falstaff's legs or has even (living up to his name) lodged his teeth in Falstaff's clothing or anatomy.
4. Support me; be sexually erect for me.
5. Referring to a kind of goblin supposed to produce nightmares by sitting on the chest of a sleeper, with puns on "ride" as meaning "mount sexually" and on "mare" as a disparaging term for "woman."

FALSTAFF   I think I am as like to ride the mare, if I have any
    vantage of ground to get up.°   *mount*
LORD CHIEF JUSTICE   How comes this, Sir John? Fie, what man
    of good temper would endure this tempest of exclamation? Are
75 you not ashamed, to enforce a poor widow to so rough a course
    to come by her own?
FALSTAFF [*to the Hostess*]   What is the gross sum that I owe thee?
MISTRESS QUICKLY   Marry, if thou wert an honest man, thyself,
    and the money too. Thou didst swear to me upon a parcel-gilt°   *partly gilded*
80 goblet, sitting in my Dolphin chamber,° at the round table, by   *(an inn room)*
    a sea-coal fire,⁶ upon Wednesday in Wheeson° week, when the   *Whitsun (Pentecost)*
    Prince broke thy head for liking° his father to a singing-man of *likening*
    Windsor⁷—thou didst swear to me then, as I was washing thy
    wound, to marry me, and make me my lady thy wife. Canst
85 thou deny it? Did not goodwife Keech⁸ the butcher's wife
    come in then, and call me 'Gossip⁹ Quickly'—coming in to
    borrow a mess of° vinegar, telling us she had a good dish of   *some*
    prawns, whereby thou didst desire to eat some, whereby I told
    thee they were ill for a green° wound? And didst thou not,   *fresh*
90 when she was gone downstairs, desire me to be no more so
    familiarity° with such poor people, saying that ere long they   *(for "familiar")*
    should call me 'madam'?¹ And didst thou not kiss me, and bid
    me fetch thee thirty shillings? I put thee now to thy book-oath;° *oath on the Bible*
    deny it if thou canst.
        [*She weeps*]
95 FALSTAFF   My lord, this is a poor mad soul, and she says up and
    down the town that her eldest son is like you. She hath been
    in good case,° and the truth is, poverty hath distracted her.²   *prosperous*
    But for these foolish officers, I beseech you I may have
    redress against them.
100 LORD CHIEF JUSTICE   Sir John, Sir John, I am well acquainted
    with your manner of wrenching the true cause the false way. It
    is not a confident brow,° nor the throng of words that come   *countenance*
    with such more than impudent sauciness from you, can thrust
    me from a level° consideration. You have, as it appears to me,   *just*
105 practised upon the easy-yielding spirit of this woman, and made
    her serve your uses both in purse and in person.
MISTRESS QUICKLY   Yea, in truth, my lord.
LORD CHIEF JUSTICE   Pray thee, peace. [*To* FALSTAFF] Pay her
    the debt you owe her, and unpay the villainy you have done
110 with her. The one you may do with sterling money, and the
    other with current° repentance.   *genuine*
FALSTAFF   My lord, I will not undergo this sneap° without reply.   *reproof*
    You call honourable boldness 'impudent sauciness'; if a man
    will make curtsy and say nothing, he is virtuous. No, my lord,
115 my humble duty° remembered, I will not be your suitor. I say   *due respect to you*
    to you I do desire deliverance from these officers, being upon
    hasty employment in the King's affairs.
LORD CHIEF JUSTICE   You speak as having power to do wrong;

---

6. Fire generated from charcoal shipped by sea rather
than by the inferior, locally produced charcoal.
7. One of the professional singers in the chapel at
Windsor, a royal residence west of London.
8. "Goodwife" was the title of a married woman.
"Keech" meant "a lump of animal fat."

9. Familiar form of address for a female friend, derived
from "godmother," the name for the female guardian of
a newly christened child.
1. A form of address for a knight's wife; a whore.
2. Driven her mad.

but answer in th'effect of your reputation,° and satisfy the poor   *as befits your status*
120 woman.
    FALSTAFF [*drawing apart*] Come hither, hostess.
        [*She goes to him*]
        Enter M[aster] GOWER, *a messenger*
    LORD CHIEF JUSTICE Now, Master Gower, what news?
    GOWER The King, my lord, and Harry Prince of Wales
    Are near at hand; the rest the paper tells.
        [LORD CHIEF JUSTICE *reads the paper, and converses*
        apart with GOWER]
125 FALSTAFF As I am a gentleman!
    MISTRESS QUICKLY Faith, you said so before.
    FALSTAFF As I am a gentleman! Come, no more words of it.
    MISTRESS QUICKLY By this heavenly ground I tread on, I must be
    fain° to pawn both my plate and the tapestry of my dining-   *content*
130 chambers.
    FALSTAFF Glasses, glasses, is the only drinking;[3] and for thy
    walls, a pretty slight drollery,° or the story of the Prodigal,[4] or   *comic painting*
    the German hunting in waterwork,[5] is worth a thousand of
    these bed-hangers° and these fly-bitten tapestries. Let it be ten   *bed curtains*
135 pound if thou canst. Come, an 'twere not for thy humours,°   *moods*
    there's not a better wench in England. Go, wash thy face, and
    draw° the action. Come, thou must not be in this humour with   *withdraw*
    me. Dost not know me? Come, I know thou wast set on to this.
    MISTRESS QUICKLY Pray thee, Sir John, let it be but twenty
140 nobles.[6] I'faith, I am loath to pawn my plate, so God save me,
    la!
    FALSTAFF Let it alone; I'll make other shift.° You'll be a fool   *I'll manage otherwise*
    still.°   *always*
    MISTRESS QUICKLY Well, you shall have it, though I pawn my
145 gown. I hope you'll come to supper. You'll pay me altogether?
    FALSTAFF Will I live? [*To* BARDOLPH *and the* PAGE] Go with her,
    with her. Hook on,° hook on!   *Stick to her*
    MISTRESS QUICKLY Will you have Doll[7] Tearsheet meet you at
    supper?
150 FALSTAFF No more words; let's have her.
                Exeunt [MISTRESS QUICKLY, BARDOLPH,
                the PAGE, FANG *and* SNARE]
    LORD CHIEF JUSTICE [*to* GOWER] I have heard better news.
    FALSTAFF What's the news, my good lord?
    LORD CHIEF JUSTICE [*to* GOWER] Where lay the King tonight?°   *last night*
    GOWER At Basingstoke,[8] my lord.
155 FALSTAFF [*to* LORD CHIEF JUSTICE] I hope, my lord, all's well.
    What is the news, my lord?
    LORD CHIEF JUSTICE [*to* GOWER] Come all his forces back?
    GOWER No; fifteen hundred foot, five hundred horse,
    Are marched up to my lord of Lancaster
160 Against Northumberland and the Archbishop.
    FALSTAFF [*to* LORD CHIEF JUSTICE] Comes the King back from
    Wales, my noble lord?

---

3. Glass drinking vessels began to replace metal
tankards in the late sixteenth century.
4. Alluding to a biblical parable about a profligate son
who repents, which was a frequent subject for cheap
painted cloths. See Luke 15:11–32.

5. A hunting scene of German or Dutch origin painted
on a wall in imitation of tapestry.
6. Gold coins. Twenty were worth about 6 pounds.
7. A common name for a prostitute.
8. A town 46 miles west of London.

LORD CHIEF JUSTICE [*to* GOWER] You shall have letters of me
    presently.°   *at once*
Come, go along with me, good Master Gower.
    [*They are going*]
FALSTAFF My lord!

165 LORD CHIEF JUSTICE What's the matter?
FALSTAFF Master Gower, shall I entreat you with me to dinner?
GOWER I must wait upon my good lord here, I thank you, good
    Sir John.
LORD CHIEF JUSTICE Sir John, you loiter here too long, being

170   you are to take soldiers up° in counties as you go.   *levy soldiers*
FALSTAFF Will you sup with me, Master Gower?
LORD CHIEF JUSTICE What foolish master taught you these man-
    ners, Sir John?
FALSTAFF Master Gower, if they become me not, he was a fool

175   that taught them me.[9] [*To* LORD CHIEF JUSTICE] This is the
    right fencing grace,° my lord—tap for tap, and so part fair.°   *style / on good terms*
LORD CHIEF JUSTICE Now the Lord lighten° thee; thou art a   *enlighten; make thin*
    great fool.   *Exeunt* [LORD CHIEF JUSTICE *and* GOWER *at one*
                                       door, FALSTAFF *at another*]

2.2

Enter PRINCE HARRY *and* POINS[1]

PRINCE HARRY Before God, I am exceeding weary.
POINS Is't come to that? I had thought weariness durst not have
    attached° one of so high blood.   *laid hold of*
PRINCE HARRY Faith, it does me, though it discolours the com-
5   plexion of my greatness[2] to acknowledge it. Doth it not show
    vilely in me to desire small° beer?   *weak*
POINS Why, a prince should not be so loosely studied° as to   *disposed*
    remember so weak a composition.
PRINCE HARRY Belike then my appetite was not princely got; for,
10   by my troth, I do now remember the poor creature small beer.
    But indeed, these humble considerations make me out of love
    with my greatness. What a disgrace is it to me to remember thy
    name![3] Or to know thy face tomorrow! Or to take note how
    many pair of silk stockings thou hast—videlicet° these, and   *namely*
15   those that were thy peach-coloured ones! Or to bear° the inven-   *remember*
    tory of thy shirts—as one for superfluity,° and another for use.   *as a spare*
    But that the tennis-court keeper knows better than I, for it is a
    low ebb of linen with thee when thou keepest not racket° there;   *do not play*
    as thou hast not done a great while, because the rest of thy low
20   countries have made a shift to eat up thy holland.[4]

9. Falstaff suggests that the habit of ignoring others is
something he learned from a fool, namely the Chief
Justice, who a few lines earlier would not answer Falstaff's questions.
2.2 Location: Prince Hal's dwelling.
1. Q's stage direction reads: "Enter the Prince, Poynes,
Sir John Russel, with other." This is the only place in Q
where the name "Russel" is employed instead of "Bardolph," but it indicates that Shakespeare had been working on some portion of this play before he was forced to
change "Oldcastle" to "Falstaff," "Russell" to "Bardolph,"
and "Harvey" to "Peto" (see Introduction to *1 Henry IV*).
2. It mars my noble countenance (by turning it pale
from weakness or red from shame).
3. Men of high rank should not be on familiar terms
with, or remember the names of, those below them in
status.
4. Because the brothels ("low countries") have contrived
to eat up all the money you would have spent on linen
("holland"). With puns on "low countries" as also meaning "sexual organs" and "the Netherlands" as well as
"brothels"; and with a pun on "holland" as referring to
the country of Holland as well as to the fine linen made
there. Poins has spent his money either on whores or on
providing linen for the babies he has prodigally fathered.
His lack of shirts makes it impossible for him to play at
the tennis courts, where players sweat so much that
shirts were frequently changed. Lines 20.1–20.4, which
follow, do not appear in F but are in Q. The Oxford editors assume they were cut by Shakespeare during revision of the play.

20.1 *And God knows whether those that bawl out the ruins of*
thy linen⁵ shall inherit his kingdom⁶—but the midwives
say the children are not in the fault, whereupon the world
increases, and kindreds are mightily strengthened.

POINS How ill it follows, after you have laboured so hard, you
should talk so idly! Tell me, how many good young princes
would do so, their fathers lying so sick as yours is?

PRINCE HARRY Shall I tell thee one thing, Poins?

25 POINS Yes, faith, and let it be an excellent good thing.

PRINCE HARRY It shall serve among wits of no higher breeding
than thine.

POINS Go to, I stand the push of° your one thing that you'll tell. *I can tolerate*

PRINCE HARRY Marry, I tell thee, it is not meet° that I should be *appropriate*
30 sad now my father is sick; albeit I could tell to thee, as to one
it pleases me, for fault° of a better, to call my friend, I could be *lack*
sad; and sad indeed too.

POINS Very hardly,° upon such a subject. *With great difficulty*

PRINCE HARRY By this hand, thou thinkest me as far in the devil's
35 book as thou and Falstaff, for obduracy° and persistency. Let *stubbornness*
the end try the man. But I tell thee. my heart bleeds inwardly
that my father is so sick; and keeping such vile company as
thou art hath, in reason, taken from me all ostentation° of *signs*
sorrow.

40 POINS The reason?

PRINCE HARRY What wouldst thou think of me if I should weep?

POINS I would think thee a most princely hypocrite.

PRINCE HARRY It would be every man's thought, and thou art a
blessed fellow to think as every man thinks. Never a man's
45 thought in the world keeps the roadway⁷ better than thine.
Every man would think me an hypocrite indeed. And what
accites° your most worshipful thought to think so? *induces*

POINS Why, because you have been so lewd,° and so much *base*
engrafted° to Falstaff. *attached*

50 PRINCE HARRY And to thee.

POINS By this light, I am well spoke on;° I can hear it with mine *of*
own ears. The worst that they can say of me is that I am a
second brother,⁸ and that I am a proper fellow of my hands;° *a good fighter*
and those two things I confess I cannot help.

Enter BARDOLPH [*followed by the* PAGE]

55 By the mass, here comes Bardolph

PRINCE HARRY And the boy that I gave Falstaff. A° had him from *He*
me Christian, and look if the fat villain have not transformed
him ape.⁹

BARDOLPH God save your grace!

60 PRINCE HARRY And yours, most noble Bardolph!

POINS [*to* BARDOLPH] Come, you virtuous ass, you bashful fool,
must you be blushing?¹ Wherefore blush you now? What a

---

5. The bastard children who are wrapped in your old shirts.
6. Go to heaven. With allusions to Matthew 25:34 ("Come, ye blessed of my Father, inherit the kingdom prepared for you from the foundation of the world" and 19:14 ("Suffer little children, and forbid them not, to come unto me: for of such is the kingdom of heaven").
7. Adheres to the popular viewpoint.

8. That is, a younger brother (and therefore without prospect of inheritance).
9. Made him look ridiculous, like an ape or a monkey rather than a human being. Falstaff has perhaps dressed the Page in an outlandish livery or uniform.
1. The jokes in this portion of the scene often refer to Bardolph's notoriously red face. The color may be due to drink, venereal disease, or some form of acne or rosacea.

maidenly man at arms are you become! Is't such a matter° to   *so difficult*
get a pottle-pot's maidenhead?[2]

65   PAGE   A calls me e'en now, my lord, through a red lattice,[3] and
I could discern no part of his face from the window. At last I
spied his eyes, and methought he had made two holes in the
ale-wife's red petticoat, and so peeped through.

PRINCE HARRY [*to* POINS]   Has not the boy profited?°   *(from Falstaff)*

70   BARDOLPH [*to the* PAGE]   Away, you whoreson upright rabbit,
away!

PAGE   Away, you rascally Althea's[4] dream, away!

PRINCE HARRY   Instruct us, boy; what dream, boy?

PAGE   Marry, my lord, Althea dreamt she was delivered of a
75   firebrand, and therefore I call him her dream.

PRINCE HARRY [*giving him money*]   A crown's-worth of good
interpretation! There 'tis, boy.

POINS   O, that this good blossom could be kept from cankers!°   *cankerworms*
[*Giving the* PAGE *money*] Well, there is sixpence to preserve
80   thee.

BARDOLPH   An° you do not make him hanged among you, the   *If*
gallows shall be wronged.

PRINCE HARRY   And how doth thy master, Bardolph?

BARDOLPH   Well, my good lord. He heard of your grace's coming
85   to town. There's a letter for you.

POINS   Delivered with good respect.° And how doth the Mar-   *(said ironically)*
tlemas[5] your master?

BARDOLPH   In bodily health, sir.
     [PRINCE HARRY *reads the letter*]

POINS   Marry, the immortal part° needs a physician, but that   *the soul*
90   moves not him. Though that be sick, it dies not.

PRINCE HARRY   I do allow this wen° to be as familiar with me as   *wart*
my dog; and he holds his place,° for look you how he writes.   *maintains his position*
     [*He gives* POINS *the letter*][6]

POINS   'John Falstaff, knight'.—Every man must know that,° as   *(Falstaff's rank)*
oft as he has occasion to name himself; even like those that are
95   kin to the King, for they never prick their finger but they say
'There's some of the King's blood spilt.' 'How comes that?' says
he that takes upon him not to conceive.° The answer is as ready   *understand*
as a borrower's cap:[7] 'I am the King's poor cousin,° sir.'   *relative*

PRINCE HARRY   Nay, they will be kin to us, or they will fetch it°   *derive kinship*
100   from Japhet.[8] [*Taking the letter*] But the letter. 'Sir John Falstaff, knight, to the son of the King nearest his father, Harry
Prince of Wales, greeting.'

POINS   Why, this is a certificate!°   *legal document*

PRINCE HARRY   Peace!— 'I will imitate the honourable Romans
105   in brevity.'

POINS [*taking the letter*]   Sure he means brevity in breath, short

2. To open and drain a two-quart tankard of ale (with
implicit comparison to penetrating a virgin).
3. Sign of an alehouse window.
4. A conflation of two dreams from classical mythology.
It was Hecuba, the Queen of Troy, who, when pregnant
with Paris, dreamed she gave birth to a firebrand that set
fire to her city. Althaea was told that her newborn son,
Meleager, would live only as long as a brand in the fire
was not consumed, so she snatched it from the hearth.
5. Fatted cattle or pigs that were slaughtered on

November 11, the feast day of St. Martin (Martlemas).
6. The reading of the letter is another occasion for
comic horseplay. The Prince and Poins may pass it back
and forth, or Poins may read it over Prince Harry's
shoulder, or snatch it away.
7. As readily produced as the cap of one looking for
money.
8. One of Noah's sons (Genesis 10:2–5), imagined to
be the common ancestor of all Europeans.

winded. [*Reads*] 'I commend me to thee, I commend thee, and
I leave thee. Be not too familiar with Poins, for he misuses thy
favours so much that he swears thou art to marry his sister Nell.
110 Repent at idle times as thou mayst. And so, farewell.
    Thine by yea and no⁹—which is as much as to say, as
    thou usest him—Jack Falstaff with my familiars,° John   friends
    with my brothers and sisters, and Sir John with all
    Europe.'
115 My lord, I'll steep this letter in sack and make him eat it.
    PRINCE HARRY That's to make him eat twenty of his words. But
    do you use me thus, Ned? Must I marry your sister?
    POINS God send the wench no worse fortune, but I never said
    so.
120 PRINCE HARRY Well, thus we play the fools with the time, and
    the spirits of the wise sit in the clouds and mock us. [*To* BAR-
    DOLPH] Is your master here in London?
    BARDOLPH Yea, my lord.
    PRINCE HARRY Where sups he? Doth the old boar feed in the
125 old frank?¹
    BARDOLPH At the old place, my lord, in Eastcheap.
    PRINCE HARRY What company?
    PAGE Ephesians, my lord, of the old church.²
    PRINCE HARRY Sup any women with him?
130 PAGE None, lord, but old Mistress Quickly and Mistress Doll
    Tearsheet.
    PRINCE HARRY What pagan° may that be?   heathen; prostitute
    PAGE A proper gentlewoman, sir, and a kinswoman of my mas-
    ter's.
135 PRINCE HARRY Even such kin as the parish heifers are to the
    town bull. Shall we steal upon them, Ned, at supper?
    POINS I am your shadow, my lord; I'll follow you.
    PRINCE HARRY Sirrah, you, boy, and Bardolph, no word to your
    master that I am yet come to town. [*Giving money*] There's for
140 your silence.
    BARDOLPH I have no tongue, sir.
    PAGE And for mine, sir, I will govern it.
    PRINCE HARRY Fare you well; go.
                   [*Exeunt* BARDOLPH *and the* PAGE]
    This Doll Tearsheet should be some road.³
145 POINS I warrant you, as common as the way between Saint
    Albans⁴ and London.
    PRINCE HARRY How might we see Falstaff bestow° himself   behave
    tonight in his true colours, and not ourselves be seen?
    POINS Put on two leathern jerkins° and aprons, and wait upon jackets
150 him at his table like drawers.°   tavern servants
    PRINCE HARRY From a god to a bull—a heavy declension°—it   a sad degradation
    was Jove's case.⁵ From a prince to a prentice—a low transfor-

---

9. Parodying the mild oaths associated with Puritans.
1. Pigsty. Possibly a reference to Eastcheap's famous
tavern the Boar's Head.
2. Carousers of the usual kind. The Page alludes to the
biblical account of the Ephesians, whom St. Paul
admonished against lust and drunkenness before their
conversion, with a possible reference to Catholics

(members of "the old church"), whom English Protestants accused of moral laxity.
3. Some common prostitute. "Road" is slang for "vagina."
4. Town on the heavily traveled road north from London.
5. Referring to Jove's transformation into a bull before
his rape of Europa.

mation—that shall be mine; for in everything the purpose
must weigh with° the folly. Follow me, Ned.   *Exeunt*   *match*

2.3

Enter [the Earl of] NORTHUMBERLAND, LADY [NORTHUM-
BERLAND] *and* LADY PERCY[1]

NORTHUMBERLAND   I pray thee, loving wife and gentle
    daughter,°   *daughter-in-law*
    Give even way° unto my rough affairs.   *Allow free scope*
    Put not you on the visage of the times
    And be like them to Percy troublesome.
5 LADY NORTHUMBERLAND   I have given over; I will speak no more.
    Do what you will; your wisdom be your guide.
    NORTHUMBERLAND   Alas, sweet wife, my honour is at pawn,
    And, but° my going, nothing can redeem it.   *except by*
    LADY PERCY   O yet, for God's sake, go not to these wars!
10 The time was, father, that you broke your word[2]
    When you were more endeared° to it than now—   *bound*
    When your own Percy, when my heart's dear Harry,
    Threw many a northward look to see his father
    Bring up his powers; but he did long in vain.
15 Who then persuaded you to stay at home?
    There were two honours lost, yours and your son's.
    For yours, the God of heaven brighten it!
    For his, it stuck upon him as the sun
    In the grey° vault of heaven, and by his light   *pale blue*
20 Did all the chivalry° of England move   *chivalrous warriors*
    To do brave acts. He was indeed the glass°   *mirror*
    Wherein the noble youth did dress themselves.[3]
    He had no legs that practised not his gait;[4]
    And speaking thick,[5] which nature made his blemish,
25 Became the accents of the valiant;
    For those that could speak low and tardily°   *slowly*
    Would turn their own perfection to abuse
    To seem like him. So that in speech, in gait,
    In diet, in affections° of delight,   *choice*
30 In military rules, humours of blood,°   *disposition*
    He was the mark° and glass, copy° and book,   *target / example*
    That fashioned others. And him—O wondrous him!
    O miracle of men!—him did you leave,
    Second to none, unseconded° by you,   *unsupported*
35 To look upon the hideous god of war
    In disadvantage, to abide a field°   *confront a battle*
    Where nothing but the sound of Hotspur's name
    Did seem defensible;° so you left him.   *to provide a defense*
    Never, O never do his ghost the wrong
40 To hold your honour more precise and nice°   *exacting*
    With others than with him. Let them alone.

2.3 Location: Outside Northumberland's castle at
Warkworth.
1. Q's stage direction designates the women only as
wives: "Enter Northumberland, his wife, and the wife
to Harry Percie."
2. Alluding to Northumberland's absence from the
Battle of Shrewsbury. See *1 Henry IV*.

3. Lines 23–45 do not appear in Q.
4. There was no man able to walk who did not try to
move as Hotspur did.
5. Speaking rapidly. The phrase has often been taken to
mean that Hotspur had a speech defect. A long stage
tradition made him a stutterer.

The Marshal and the Archbishop are strong.
Had my sweet Harry had but half their numbers,
Today might I, hanging on Hotspur's neck,
Have talked of Monmouth's° grave.   *Prince Hal's*

45 NORTHUMBERLAND   Beshrew your heart,
Fair daughter, you do draw my spirits from me
With new lamenting ancient oversights.
But I must go and meet with danger there,
Or it will seek me in another place,
And find me worse provided.

50 LADY NORTHUMBERLAND   O fly to Scotland,
Till that the nobles and the armèd commons
Have of their puissance° made a little taste.   *strength*

LADY PERCY   If they get ground and vantage of the King,
Then join you with them like a rib of steel,
55 To make strength stronger; but, for all our loves,
First let them try themselves. So did your son.
He was so suffered.° So came I a widow,   *allowed to proceed*
And never shall have length of life enough
To rain upon remembrance with mine eyes,[6]
60 That it may grow and sprout as high as heaven
For recordation° to my noble husband.   *As a memorial*

NORTHUMBERLAND   Come, come, go in with me. 'Tis with my mind
As with the tide swelled up unto his height,
That makes a still stand,° running neither way.   *standstill*
65 Fain would I go to meet the Archbishop,
But many thousand reasons hold me back.
I will resolve for Scotland. There am I
Till time and vantage° crave my company.   *Exeunt*   *opportunity*

2.4

[*A table and chairs set forth.*][1] *Enter a* DRAWER° [*with*   *servant in a tavern*
  wine and another DRAWER *with a dish of apple-johns*][2]

FIRST DRAWER   What the devil hast thou brought there—apple-
johns? Thou knowest Sir John cannot endure an apple-john.

SECOND DRAWER   Mass,[3] thou sayst true. The Prince once set a
dish of apple-johns before him; and told him, there were five
5 more Sir Johns; and, putting off his hat, said 'I will now take
my leave of these six dry, round, old, withered knights.' It
angered him to the heart. But he hath forgot that.

FIRST DRAWER   Why then, cover,° and set them down; and see if   *spread the cloth*
thou canst find out Sneak's noise.° Mistress Tearsheet would   *band of musicians*
10 fain hear some music.   [*Exit the* SECOND DRAWER]
     [*The* FIRST DRAWER *covers the table.*]
     [*Enter the* SECOND DRAWER]

---

6. To rain tears upon his memory, here imagined as a plant—perhaps rosemary, the conventional symbol of remembrance.
2.4 Location: A tavern, perhaps the Boar's Head, in Eastcheap.
1. Changes were made to this scene at some point. In Q, dialogue occurs between Francis and "a Drawer or two." At 2.4.13, Q's stage direction reads: "Enter Will." This character has no lines, and probably his part was later deleted. In F, the dialogue is somewhat rearranged

and occurs between two drawers, as here. However many servants are onstage, though, the point of their scurrying about is to create excitement about Falstaff's arrival and the trick to be played on him.
2. A kind of apple that could be kept for two years and was meant to be eaten when the skin was wrinkled and shriveled up.
3. An oath derived from the name of the Catholic church service.

SECOND DRAWER Sirrah, here will be the Prince and Master
   Poins anon,° and they will put on two of our jerkins and aprons,   soon
   and Sir John must not know of it. Bardolph hath brought word.
FIRST DRAWER By the mass, here will be old utis!° It will be an   merrymaking; a din
15 excellent stratagem.
SECOND DRAWER I'll see if I can find out Sneak.   Exeunt
         Enter MISTRESS QUICKLY *and* DOLL TEARSHEET [*drunk*]
MISTRESS QUICKLY I'faith, sweetheart, methinks now you are in
   an excellent good temperality.° Your pulsidge⁴ beats as extraor-   (*for* "temper")
   dinarily as heart would desire, and your colour, I warrant you,
20 is as red as any rose, in good truth, la; but i'faith, you have
   drunk too much canaries,⁵ and that's a marvellous searching°   strong
   wine, and it perfumes the blood ere we can say 'What's this?'
   How do you now?
DOLL TEARSHEET Better than I was.—Hem!
25 MISTRESS QUICKLY Why, that's well said! A good heart's worth
   gold.
         Enter Sir John FALSTAFF
   Lo, here comes Sir John.
FALSTAFF [*sings*] 'When Arthur first in court'⁶—[*Calls*] Empty
   the jordan!°—[*Sings*] 'And was a worthy king'—How now, Mis-   chamber pot
30 tress Doll?
MISTRESS QUICKLY Sick of a qualm,° yea, good faith.   fainting fit
FALSTAFF So is all her sect;° an they be once in a calm,⁷ they   kind; sex
   are sick.
DOLL TEARSHEET A pox damn you, you muddy rascal!⁸ Is that
35 all the comfort you give me?
FALSTAFF You make fat rascals, Mistress Doll.
DOLL TEARSHEET I make them? Gluttony and diseases make
   them; I make them not.
FALSTAFF If the cook help to make the gluttony, you help to
40 make the diseases, Doll. We catch of you,° Doll, we catch of   are infected by you
   you; grant that, my poor virtue, grant that.
DOLL TEARSHEET Yea, Jesu, our chains and our jewels.⁹
FALSTAFF 'Your brooches, pearls, and ouches'¹—for to serve
   bravely is to come halting off,² you know; to come off the
45 breach with his pike bent bravely,³ and to surgery bravely; to
   venture upon the charged chambers⁴ bravely.
MISTRESS QUICKLY By my troth, this is the old fashion. You two
   never meet but you fall to some discord. You are both, i' good
   truth, as rheumatic° as two dry toasts; you cannot one bear with   (*for* "choleric")
50 another's confirmities.° What the goodyear, one must bear,⁵ [*to*   (*for* "infirmities")
   DOLL] and that must be you. You are the weaker vessel, as they
   say, the emptier vessel.

---

4. For "pulse."
5. Sweet wine from the Canary Islands.
6. Lines from the ballad "Sir Lancelot du Lake."
7. Quiet; not sexually active (punning on "qualm" in the prior line).
8. You dull knave. A "rascal" was a young, lean deer. They were called "muddy" when sluggish and out of season. In his next speech, Falstaff will accuse Doll of making even lean deer fat, probably by tempting them to gluttony and vice.
9. Yes, you steal ("catch") our valuables.
1. Perhaps a line from a ballad, with puns on the three items of jewelry as slang for the carbuncles and sores

that result from venereal disease.
2. To fight bravely is to return limping; to engage in vigorous sex is to be wounded in the process.
3. To come away from the gap in the fortifications (the breech) with one's weapon finely bent (with puns on "breech" as slang for "female genitalia" and "pike" as slang for "penis").
4. Interior of a mine loaded with munitions; the sexually aroused interior of a woman.
5. Endure; carry goods; support the weight of a sexual partner; give birth. *What the goodyear:* a phrase probably meaning "What the devil."

DOLL TEARSHEET   Can a weak empty vessel bear such a huge full
    hogshead?° There's a whole merchant's venture° of Bordeaux   *cask / cargo*
55   stuff° in him; you have not seen a hulk better stuffed in the   *wine*
    hold.— Come, I'll be friends with thee, Jack. Thou art going
    to the wars, and whether I shall ever see thee again or no there
    is nobody cares.

        Enter [a] DRAWER

DRAWER   Sir, Ensign[6] Pistol's below, and would speak with you.
60 DOLL TEARSHEET   Hang him, swaggering° rascal. let him not   *blustering; quarreling*
    come hither. It is the foul-mouthedest rogue in England.
MISTRESS QUICKLY   If he swagger, let him not come here. No, by
    my faith! I must live among my neighbours; I'll no swaggerers.
    I am in good name and fame with the very best. Shut the door;
65   there comes no swaggerers here. I have not lived all this while
    to have swaggering now. Shut the door, I pray you.
FALSTAFF   Dost thou hear, hostess?
MISTRESS QUICKLY   Pray ye pacify yourself, Sir John. There
    comes no swaggerers here.
70 FALSTAFF   Dost thou hear? It is mine ensign.
MISTRESS QUICKLY   Tilly-fally,° Sir John, ne'er tell me. Your   *Nonsense*
    ensign-swaggerer comes not in my doors. I was before Master
    Tisick[7] the debuty° t'other day, and, as he said to me—'twas no *(for "deputy")*
    longer ago than Wed'sday last, i' good faith—'Neighbour
75   Quickly,' says he—Master Dumb our minister was by then—
    'Neighbour Quickly,' says he, 'receive those that are civil, for,'
    said he, 'you are in an ill name.' Now a said so, I can tell
    whereupon.[8] 'For,' says he, 'you are an honest woman, and well
    thought on; therefore take heed what guests you receive.
80   Receive,' says he, 'no swaggering companions.' There comes
    none here. You would bless you° to hear what he said. No, I'll   *feel fortunate*
    no swaggerers.
FALSTAFF   He's no swaggerer, hostess—a tame cheater,[9] i'faith.
    You may stroke him as gently as a puppy greyhound. He'll not
85   swagger with a Barbary hen,° if her feathers turn back in any *guinea hen; prostitute*
    show of resistance.—Call him up, drawer.   [*Exit* DRAWER]
MISTRESS QUICKLY   Cheater[1] call you him? I will bar no honest
    man my house, nor no cheater, but I do not love swaggering,
    by my troth, I am the worse when one says 'swagger'. Feel,
90   masters, how I shake, look you, I warrant you.
DOLL TEARSHEET   So you do, hostess.
MISTRESS QUICKLY   Do I? Yea, in very truth do I, an 'twere° an   *as if I were*
    aspen leaf. I cannot abide swaggerers.

        Enter PISTOL, BARDOLPH, *and* [*the* PAGE]

PISTOL   God save you, Sir John.
95 FALSTAFF   Welcome, Ensign Pistol. Here, Pistol, I charge you[2]
    with a cup of sack. Do you discharge[3] upon mine hostess.
PISTOL   I will discharge upon her, Sir John, with two bullets.°   *(slang for "testicles")*
FALSTAFF   She is pistol-proof, sir, you shall not hardly offend°   *injure*
    her.

---

6. A military title for the army's standard-bearer.
7. The name signifies a hacking cough.
8. Now I can tell why he ("a") said so.
9. A decoy in a scheme to defraud people.
1. Quickly apparently understands the word as

"escheator," an officer responsible for returning to the
crown property whose title had lapsed.
2. Toast to you; load you with ammunition (punning on
Pistol's name); arouse you sexually.
3. Return the toast ; empty the cup; shoot; ejaculate.

100   MISTRESS QUICKLY   Come, I'll drink no proofs, nor no bullets. I'll
       drink no more than will do me good, for no man's pleasure, I.
       PISTOL   Then to you, Mistress Dorothy! I will charge° you.   *toast; arouse; order*
       DOLL TEARSHEET   Charge me? I scorn you, scurvy companion.
       What, you poor, base, rascally, cheating, lack-linen mate!°   *fellow who has no linen*
105   Away, you mouldy rogue, away! I am meat for your master.[4]
       PISTOL   I know you, Mistress Dorothy.
       DOLL TEARSHEET   Away, you cutpurse° rascal, you filthy bung,[5]   *thieving; castrated*
       away! By this wine, I'll thrust my knife in your mouldy chaps°   *cheeks; buttocks*
       an you play the saucy cuttle with me![6]
            [*She brandishes a knife*]
110   Away, you bottle-ale rascal, you basket-hilt stale juggler,[7] you!
            [PISTOL *draws his sword*]
       Since when, I pray you, sir? God's light, with two points[8] on
       your shoulder! Much!
       PISTOL   God let me not live, but I will murder your ruff° for this.   *starched collar*
       MISTRESS QUICKLY   No, good Captain Pistol; not here, sweet cap-
115   tain.
       DOLL TEARSHEET   Captain? Thou abominable damned cheater,
       art thou not ashamed to be called 'captain'? An captains were
       of my mind, they would truncheon° you out, for taking their   *cudgel*
       names upon you before you have earned them. You a captain?
120   You slave! For what? For tearing a poor whore's ruff in a bawdy-
       house! He a captain? Hang him, rogue, he lives upon mouldy
       stewed prunes[9] and dried cakes. A captain? God's light, these
       villains will make the word 'captain' odious; therefore captains
       had need look to't.
125   BARDOLPH   Pray thee, go down, good ensign.
       FALSTAFF   Hark thee hither, Mistress Doll.
            [*He takes her aside*]
       PISTOL   Not I! I tell thee what, Corporal Bardolph, I could tear
       her! I'll be revenged of her.
       PAGE   Pray thee, go down.
130   PISTOL   I'll see her damned first
       To Pluto's damned lake,° by this hand,[1]   *(the lake of hell)*
       To th'infernal deep,
       Where Erebus,° and tortures vile also.   *the underworld*
       'Hold hook and line!' say I.
135   Down, down, dogs; down, Fates.
       Have we not Hiren here?[2]
       MISTRESS QUICKLY   Good Captain Pizzle,° be quiet. 'Tis very   *Penis*
       late, i'faith. I beseek you now, aggravate° your choler.   *(for "moderate")*
       PISTOL   These be good humours indeed!
140   Shall pack-horses

---

4. That is, I am superior to you; with a pun on "meat"
as meaning "a body available for sexual pleasure."
5. Thief; anus.
6. If you continue to abuse me (with a pun on "cuttle"
as signifying both "knife" and "cuttlefish," which was
supposed to vomit a black liquid to conceal itself from
enemies).
7. You imposter with a cheap, outdated sword. Basket-
work hilts were used on inexpensive weapons or those
used only for practice.
8. Tags for fastening armor.
9. Available in brothels as a supposed preventative of

venereal disease, with a pun on "stew" as meaning
"brothel."
1. In this and subsequent speeches, Pistol rants in an
affected style that recalls and parodies the language of
sensational plays from the 1590s and earlier, which
were often set in non-European locales and involved
military and erotic adventures.
2. Apparently a line from *The Turkish Mohamet and
Hiren [Irene] the Fair Greek*, a lost play by George
Peele. Pistol may be referring to his sword as "Hiren"
with a pun on "iron."

And hollow pampered jades of Asia,[3]
Which cannot go but thirty mile a day,
Compare with Caesars and with cannibals,[4]
And Trojan Greeks?

145 Nay, rather damn them with King Cerberus,[5]
And let the welkin° roar. Shall we fall foul for toys?[6]   *heavens*

MISTRESS QUICKLY By my troth, captain, these are very bitter
words.

BARDOLPH Be gone, good ensign; this will grow to a brawl anon.

150 PISTOL Die men like dogs! Give crowns like pins![7]
Have we not Hiren here?

MISTRESS QUICKLY O' my word, captain, there's none such here.
What the goodyear, do you think I would deny her? For God's
sake, be quiet.

155 PISTOL Then feed and be fat, my fair Calipolis.[8]
Come, give's some sack.
Si fortune me tormente, sperato me contento.[9]
Fear we broadsides?[1] No; let the fiend give fire![°]   *shoot*
Give me some sack; and, sweetheart, lie thou there.
[*He lays down his sword*]

160 Come we to full points here? And are etceteras nothings?[2]
[*He drinks*]

FALSTAFF Pistol, I would be quiet.

PISTOL Sweet knight, I kiss thy neaf.° What, we have seen the   *fist*
seven stars![3]

DOLL TEARSHEET For God's sake, thrust him downstairs. I can
165 not endure such a fustian° rascal.   *worthless*

PISTOL Thrust him downstairs? Know we not Galloway nags?[4]

FALSTAFF Quoit° him down, Bardolph, like a shove-groat shil-   *Throw*
ling.[5] Nay, an a do° nothing but speak nothing, a shall be   *if he does*
nothing here.

170 BARDOLPH [*to* PISTOL] Come, get you downstairs.

PISTOL [*taking up his sword*] What, shall we have incision?
Shall we imbrue?[°]   *steep in blood*
Then death rock me asleep, abridge my doleful days.
Why then, let grievous, ghastly, gaping wounds
Untwine the Sisters Three.[6] Come, Atropos, I say!

175 MISTRESS QUICKLY Here's goodly stuff toward![°]   *about to happen*

FALSTAFF Give me my rapier, boy.

DOLL TEARSHEET I pray thee, Jack, I pray thee, do not draw.

FALSTAFF [*taking his rapier and speaking to* PISTOL] Get you downstairs.
[FALSTAFF, BARDOLPH, *and* PISTOL *brawl*]

---

3. A garbled allusion to Marlowe's *2 Tamburlaine*
4.3.1–2, in which Tamburlaine taunts the Kings whom
he has captured and whom he uses in lieu of horses to
draw his chariot.
4. Pistol may mean "Hannibals." Hannibal was a
famous general of Carthage.
5. In classical mythology, the three-headed dog guard-
ing the underworld.
6. Quarrel over trifles.
7. Alluding to Tamburlaine's extravagance in distribut-
ing the crowns of conquered Kings among his followers.
8. Echoing Peele's *Battle of Alcazar,* in which the
Moorish King Muly Mahomet offers his starving wife
the raw flesh of a lion he has just killed.

9. If fortune torments me, hope contents me (a motto
that Pistol renders in a mixture of Italian, French, and
Spanish).
1. Shots fired from the side of a ship.
2. That is, have we come to a stop? Is there no further
satisfaction to be had in the rest (the "etceteras")? Pistol puns on "etceteras" and "nothings" as slang for
"female genitalia."
3. We have caroused all night (with an allusion to the
Ursa Major constellation).
4. Small Scottish horses; prostitutes.
5. Shilling coin used in a game like shuffleboard.
6. The three Fates of Greek mythology: Clotho, Lach-
esis, and Atropos. Atropos cut the thread of life.

MISTRESS QUICKLY   Here's a goodly tumult! I'll forswear keeping
180   house afore I'll be in these tirrits° and frights!   (for "terrors" or "fits")
          [FALSTAFF *thrusts at* PISTOL]
      So!
          [PISTOL *thrusts at* FALSTAFF]
      Murder, I warrant now! Alas, alas, put up your naked weapons,
      put up your naked weapons!
          [*Exit* PISTOL, *pursued by* BARDOLPH]
DOLL TEARSHEET   I pray thee, Jack, be quiet; the rascal's gone.
185   Ah, you whoreson little valiant villain, you!
MISTRESS QUICKLY   [*to* FALSTAFF] Are you not hurt i'th' groin?
      Methought a made a shrewd° thrust at your belly.   vicious
          [*Enter* BARDOLPH]
FALSTAFF   Have you turned him out o'doors?
BARDOLPH   Yea, sir. The rascal's drunk. You have hurt him, sir,
190   i'th' shoulder.
FALSTAFF   A rascal, to brave° me!   defy
DOLL TEARSHEET   Ah, you sweet little rogue, you! Alas, poor ape,
      how thou sweatest! Come, let me wipe thy face; come on, you
      whoreson chops.° Ah rogue, i'faith, I love thee. Thou art as   fat cheeks
195   valorous as Hector of Troy,[7] worth five of Agamemnon,[8] and
      ten times better than the Nine Worthies.[9] Ah, villain!
FALSTAFF   A rascally slave! I will toss the rogue in a blanket.[1]
DOLL TEARSHEET   Do, an thou darest for thy heart. An thou dost,
      I'll canvas° thee between a pair of sheets.   toss
200   *Enter music*[*ians*]
PAGE   The music is come, sir.
FALSTAFF   Let them play.—Play, sirs!
          [*Music plays*]
      Sit on my knee, Doll. A rascal bragging slave! The rogue fled
      from me like quicksilver.°   mercury
DOLL TEARSHEET   I'faith, and thou followed'st him like a church.°   (*i.e.*, sedately)
205   Thou whoreson little tidy° Bartholomew boar-pig,[2] when wilt   plump
      thou leave fighting o'days, and foining° o'nights, and begin to   thrusting
      patch up thine old body for heaven?
          Enter PRINCE [HARRY] *and* POINS, *disguised* [*as drawers*]
FALSTAFF   Peace, good Doll, do not speak like a death's-head,[3]
      do not bid me remember mine end.
210   DOLL TEARSHEET   Sirrah, what humour's° the Prince of?   disposition is
FALSTAFF   A good shallow young fellow. A would have made a
      good pantler;° a would ha' chipped° bread well.   pantry worker / cut
DOLL TEARSHEET   They say Poins has a good wit.
FALSTAFF   He a good wit? Hang him, baboon! His wit's as thick
215   as Tewkesbury[4] mustard; there's no more conceit° in him than   intellect
      is in a mallet.
DOLL TEARSHEET   Why does the Prince love him so, then?
FALSTAFF   Because their legs are both of a bigness, and a° plays   he
      at quoits[5] well, and eats conger and fennel,[6] and drinks off can-

---

7. The greatest Trojan warrior in Homer's *Iliad*.
8. Leader of the Greeks in the battle for Troy.
9. Nine legendary brave men: three Christians—
Arthur, Charlemagne, Godfrey of Boulogne; three
pagans—Hector, Alexander, Julius Caesar; and three
Jews—Joshua, David, Judas Maccabaeus.
1. A punishment for cowardice.
2. A roasted pig associated with an annual London carnival held on August 24, St. Bartholomew's Day.

3. Skull or representation of a skull used as a reminder
of mortality.
4. Market town in Gloucestershire famed for its mustard.
5. A game involving the throwing of a heavy iron ring
toward a target on the ground.
6. Conger eel, a heavy, hard-to-digest food, was served
with fennel.

220 dles' ends for flap-dragons,[7] and rides the wild mare[8] with the
boys, and jumps upon joint-stools, and swears with a good
grace, and wears his boot very smooth like unto the sign of the
leg,[9] and breeds no bate° with telling of discreet stories, and   *discord*
such other gambol° faculties a has that show a weak mind and   *sportive*
225 an able body; for the which the Prince admits him; for the
Prince himself is such another—the weight of a hair will turn
the scales between their avoirdupois.°   *weight*

PRINCE HARRY [*aside to* POINS] Would not this nave° of a wheel   *hub*
have his ears cut off?

230 POINS Let's beat him before his whore.

PRINCE HARRY Look whe'er the withered elder[1] hath not his poll°   *head*
clawed like a parrot.[2]

POINS Is it not strange that desire should so many years outlive
performance?

235 FALSTAFF Kiss me, Doll.
    [*They kiss*]

PRINCE HARRY [*aside to* POINS] Saturn and Venus[3] this year in
conjunction! What says th'almanac to that?

POINS And look whether the fiery Trigon[4] his man be not lisping
to his master's old tables,° his note-book, his counsel-keeper![5]   *writing tablets*

240 FALSTAFF [*to* DOLL] Thou dost give me flattering busses.°   *kisses*

DOLL TEARSHEET By my troth, I kiss thee with a most constant
heart.

FALSTAFF I am old, I am old.

DOLL TEARSHEET I love thee better than I love e'er a scurvy
245 young boy of them all.

FALSTAFF What stuff° wilt have a kirtle° of? I shall receive money   *material / skirt*
o'Thursday; shalt° have a cap tomorrow.—A merry song!   *you shall*
    [*The music plays again*]
Come, it grows late; we'll to bed. Thou'lt forget me when I am
gone.

250 DOLL TEARSHEET By my troth, thou'lt set me a-weeping an thou
sayst so. Prove° that ever I dress myself handsome till thy re-   *If you ever prove*
turn—well, hearken° a'th' end.   *judge*

FALSTAFF Some sack, Francis.

PRINCE *and* POINS [*coming forward*] Anon, anon, sir.

255 FALSTAFF Ha, a bastard son of the King's!—And art not thou
Poins his brother?°   *the brother of Poins*

PRINCE HARRY Why, thou globe of sinful continents,[6] what a life
dost thou lead!

FALSTAFF A better than thou: I am a gentleman, thou art a
260 drawer.

PRINCE HARRY Very true, sir, and I come to draw you out by the
ears.

MISTRESS QUICKLY O, the Lord preserve thy grace! By my troth,

---

7. Referring to a tavern game in which one drank
liquor on which burning objects (flapdragons) had been
set afloat.
8. Plays at a form of leapfrog; has sexual relations with
a woman.
9. As in the sign over the bootmaker's shop (depicting
a well-booted leg).
1. Sapless elder tree; impotent old man.
2. Doll may here be running her hands through Falstaff's hair.

3. The planets governing old age and love.
4. The signs of the zodiac were divided into four sets of
three (trigons). Aries, Leo, and Sagittarius are the "fiery
trigon," being hot and dry. Poins alludes to Bardolph's
red face.
5. Apparently Bardolph is wooing Quickly, here
referred to as Falstaff's confidante and the keeper of his
secrets.
6. World composed of sinful lands; a vast receptacle of
sin.

welcome to London! Now the Lord bless that sweet face of
265   thine! O Jesu, are you come from Wales?

FALSTAFF [*to* PRINCE HARRY]   Thou whoreson mad compound of
majesty! By this light°—flesh and corrupt blood, thou art wel-   *(a conventional oath)*
come.

DOLL TEARSHEET   How, you fat fool? I scorn you.

270 POINS [*to* PRINCE HARRY]   My lord, he will drive you out of your
revenge and turn all to a merriment, if you take not the heat.°   *don't act at once*

PRINCE HARRY [*to* FALSTAFF   You whoreson candlemine° you,   *storehouse of tallow*
how vilely did you speak of me now, before this honest,° virtu-   *chaste*
ous, civil gentlewoman!

275 MISTRESS QUICKLY   God's blessing of your good heart, and so she
is, by my troth!

FALSTAFF [*to* PRINCE HARRY]   Didst thou hear me?

PRINCE HARRY   Yea, and you knew me as you did when you ran
away by Gads Hill;[7] you knew I was at your back, and spoke it
280   on purpose to try my patience.

FALSTAFF   No, no, no, not so, I did not think thou wast within
hearing.

PRINCE HARRY   I shall drive you, then, to confess the wilful
abuse, and then I know how to handle you.

285 FALSTAFF   No abuse, Hal; o'mine honour, no abuse.

PRINCE HARRY   Not? To dispraise me, and call me 'pantler' and
'bread-chipper' and I know not what?

FALSTAFF   No abuse, Hal.

POINS   No abuse?

290 FALSTAFF   No abuse, Ned, i'th' world, honest Ned, none. I dispraised him before the wicked, that the wicked might not fall
in love with him; [*to* PRINCE HARRY] in which doing I have
done the part of a careful° friend and a true subject, and thy   *caring*
father is to give me thanks for it. No abuse, Hal; none, Ned,
295   none; no, faith, boys, none.

PRINCE HARRY   See now whether pure fear and entire cowardice
doth not make thee wrong this virtuous gentlewoman to close
with° us. Is she of the wicked? Is thine hostess here of the   *in order to pacify*
wicked? Or is thy boy of the wicked? Or honest Bardolph,
300   whose zeal burns in his nose, of the wicked?

POINS [*to* FALSTAFF]   Answer, thou dead elm, answer.

FALSTAFF   The fiend hath pricked down Bardolph irrecover-
able,[8] and his face is Lucifer's privy° kitchen, where he doth   *private*
nothing but roast malt-worms.° For the boy, there is a good   *weevils; drunkards*
305   angel about him, but the devil outbids him,° too.   *(the good angel)*

PRINCE HARRY   For the women?

FALSTAFF   For one of them, she's in hell already, and burns°   *infects with syphilis*
poor souls. For th'other, I owe her money, and whether she be
damned for that I know not.[9]

310 MISTRESS QUICKLY   No, I warrant you.

FALSTAFF   No, I think thou art not; I think thou art quit for° that.   *acquitted of*
Marry, there is another indictment upon thee, for suffering
flesh to be eaten in thy house, contrary to the law,[1] for the
which I think thou wilt howl.

---

7. Referring to events staged in Act 2 of *1 Henry IV*.
8. Marked Bardolph as beyond redemption.
9. Referring to the view that usury (lending money at
interest) was a sin.

1. Alluding to laws enacted against eating meat during
the Christian penitential days known as Lent as well as
to laws against the sex trade, with a pun on "house" as
"brothel."

315 MISTRESS QUICKLY All victuallers° do so. What's a joint of mut-   *innkeepers; bawds*
ton° or two in a whole Lent?   *piece of lamb; whore*

PRINCE HARRY You, gentlewoman—

DOLL TEARSHEET What says your grace?

FALSTAFF His grace says that which his flesh rebels against.[2]

      PETO *knocks at door [within]*

320 MISTRESS QUICKLY Who knocks so loud at door? [*Calls*] Lock to
th' door there, Francis.

      Enter PETO

PRINCE HARRY Peto, how now, what news?

PETO The King your father is at Westminster;
And there are twenty weak and wearied posts°   *messengers*
325 Come from the north; and as I came along
I met and overtook a dozen captains
Bareheaded, sweating, knocking at the taverns,
And asking every one for Sir John Falstaff.

PRINCE HARRY By heaven, Poins, I feel me much to blame
330 So idly to profane the precious time.
When tempest of commotion, like the south°   *the south wind*
Borne° with black vapour, doth begin to melt   *Laden*
And drop upon our bare unarmèd heads.—
Give me my sword and cloak.—Falstaff, good night.

      Exeunt PRINCE [HARRY] *and* POINS

335 FALSTAFF Now comes in the sweetest morsel of the night, and
we must hence and leave it unpicked.

      [*Knocking within. Exit* BARDOLPH]

More knocking at the door!

      [*Enter* BARDOLPH]

How now, what's the matter?

BARDOLPH You must away to court, sir, presently.°   *at once*
340 A dozen captains stay° at door for you.   *wait*

FALSTAFF [*to the* PAGE] Pay the musicians, sirrah. Farewell, hostess; farewell, Doll. You see, my good wenches, how men of
merit are sought after. The undeserver° may sleep, when the   *unimportant officer*
man of action is called on. Farewell, good wenches. If I be not
345 sent away post,° I will see you again ere I go.   *hastily*

      [*Exeunt musicians*]

DOLL TEARSHEET [*weeping*] I cannot speak. If my heart be not
ready to burst—well, sweet Jack, have a care of thyself.

FALSTAFF Farewell, farewell!

      Exit [*with* BARDOLPH, PETO, *and the* PAGE]

MISTRESS QUICKLY Well, fare thee well. I have known thee these
350 twenty-nine years come peascod-time,[3] but an honester and
truer-hearted man—well, fare thee well.

      [*Enter* BARDOLPH]

BARDOLPH Mistress Tearsheet!

MISTRESS QUICKLY What's the matter?

BARDOLPH Bid Mistress Tearsheet come to my master. [*Exit*]
355 MISTRESS QUICKLY O run, Doll; run, run, good Doll!

      Exeunt [DOLL *at one door*, MISTRESS QUICKLY *at another door*]

---

2. Implying that the Prince's virtuous speech can't hide
a body filled with lust for Tearsheet.

3. The time of year when peas form in the pod (early
spring).

3.1

Enter KING [HENRY] *in his nightgown,°* *with a page*　　　　　　*dressing gown*

KING HENRY [*giving letters*]　Go call the Earls of Surrey and of Warwick.
But ere they come, bid them o'er-read these letters
And well consider of them. Make good speed.　　*Exit [page]*
How many thousand of my poorest subjects
5　Are at this hour asleep? O sleep, O gentle sleep,
Nature's soft nurse, how have I frighted° thee,　　　　　　　　*frightened*
That thou no more wilt weigh my eyelids down
And steep my senses in forgetfulness?
Why rather, sleep, liest thou in smoky cribs,°　　　　　　　　　*hovels*
10　Upon uneasy pallets° stretching thee,　　　　　　　　*hard straw beds*
And hushed with buzzing night-flies to thy slumber,
Than in the perfumed chambers of the great,
Under the canopies of costly state,°　　　　　　　　　　　　*splendor*
And lulled with sound of sweetest melody?
15　O thou dull° god, why li'st thou with the vile°　　　　　*drowsy / lowly*
In loathsome beds, and leav'st the kingly couch
A watch-case,° or a common 'larum-bell?　　　　　　　　　　*sentry box*
Wilt thou upon the high and giddy mast
Seal up the ship-boy's eyes, and rock his brains
20　In cradle of the rude° imperious surge,　　　　　　　　　　　*rough*
And in the visitation of the winds,
Who take the ruffian billows by the top,
Curling their monstrous heads, and hanging them
With deafing° clamour in the slippery clouds,　　　　　　　*deafening*
25　That, with the hurly,° death itself awakes?　　　　　　　　　*tumult*
Canst thou, O partial sleep, give thy repose
To the wet sea-boy in an hour so rude,°　　　　　　　　　　　　*wild*
And in the calmest and most stillest night,
With all appliances° and means to boot,°　　　　　*devices / as well*
30　Deny it to a king? Then happy low,° lie down.　　*happy humble people*
Uneasy lies the head that wears a crown.

Enter [the Earls of] WARWICK *and* SURREY

WARWICK　Many good morrows to your majesty!
KING HENRY　Is it good morrow, lords?
WARWICK　　　　　　　　　　　　'Tis one o'clock, and past.
KING HENRY　Why then, good morrow to you all, my lords.
35　Have you read o'er the letter that I sent you?
WARWICK　We have, my liege.°　　　　　　　　　　　　　　　*sovereign*
KING HENRY　Then you perceive the body of our kingdom,
How foul it is, what rank° diseases grow,　　　　　　　　　*loathsome*
And with what danger near the heart of it.
40　WARWICK　It is but as a body yet distempered,°　　　　　　　*sick*
Which to his former strength may be restored
With good advice and little medicine.
My lord Northumberland will soon be cooled.
KING HENRY　O God, that one might read the book of fate,
45　And see the revolution of the times¹
Make mountains level, and the continent,°　　　　　　　　　*dry land*
Weary of solid firmness, melt itself
Into the sea; and other times to see

3.1 Location: The palace at Westminster.　　　1. The changes that time will bring.

The beachy girdle of° the ocean   *girdle of beaches around*

50 Too wide for Neptune's[2] hips; how chance's mocks

And changes fill the cup of alteration

With divers° liquors![3]   *various*

52.1   *O, if this were seen,*

The happiest youth, viewing his progress through °   *through life*

What perils past, what crosses° to ensue,   *afflictions*

Would shut the book and sit him down and die.

'Tis not ten years gone

Since Richard and Northumberland, great friends,

Did feast together; and in two year after

55 Were they at wars. It is but eight years since

This Percy° was the man nearest my soul,   *(Northumberland)*

Who like a brother toiled in my affairs,

And laid his love and life under my foot,°   *at my disposal*

Yea, for my sake, even to° the eyes of Richard   *before*

60 Gave him defiance. But which of you was by—

[*To* WARWICK] You, cousin Neville,[4] as I may remember—

When Richard, with his eye brimful of tears,

Then checked and rated° by Northumberland,   *chided*

Did speak these words,[5] now proved a prophecy?—

65 'Northumberland, thou ladder by the which

My cousin Bolingbroke ascends my throne'—

Though then, God knows, I had no such intent,

But that necessity so bowed the state

That I and greatness were compelled to kiss—

70 'The time shall come'—thus did he follow it—

'The time will come that foul sin, gathering head,[6]

Shall break into corruption'; so went on,

Foretelling this same time's condition,

And the division of our amity.

75 WARWICK   There is a history in all men's lives

Figuring° the natures of the times deceased;°   *Showing / past*

The which observed, a man may prophesy,

With a near aim, of the main chance° of things   *general probability*

As yet not come to life, who° in their seeds   *which*

80 And weak beginnings lie intreasurèd.°   *stored*

Such things become the hatch and brood° of time;   *progeny and offspring*

And by the necessary form of this[7]

King Richard might create a perfect guess

That great Northumberland, then false to him,

85 Would of that seed grow to a greater falseness,

Which should not find a ground to root upon

Unless on you.

KING HENRY   Are these things then necessities?

Then let us meet them like necessities;

---

2. In classical mythology, the god of the sea. Here the seashore is depicted as a girdle worn by Neptune. That the girdle is too wide or too large indicates that the sea is retreating from the land, in contrast to the prior image of land being absorbed into the ocean.

3. The following three and a half lines (52.1–52.4) do not appear in F, though they are in the 1600 quarto version of the play.

4. An apparent error. The King is addressing the Earl of Warwick, whose surname was Beauchamp, not Neville. Shakespeare may be confusing him with Richard Neville, an important character in his plays on the life of Henry VI.

5. See *Richard II* 5.1, in which similar lines are spoken, though neither Bolingbroke nor Warwick was present.

6. Coming to maturity; coming to a head, like pus on a sore.

7. And by this requisite pattern (of cause and effect).

And that same word even now cries out on° us.   *denounces*
90 They say the Bishop and Northumberland
Are fifty thousand strong.

WARWICK   It cannot be, my lord.
Rumour doth double, like the voice and echo,
The numbers of the feared. Please it your grace
To go to bed? Upon my soul, my lord,
95 The powers that you already have sent forth
Shall bring this prize in very easily.
To comfort you the more, I have received
A certain instance° that Glyndŵr is dead.   *proof*
Your majesty hath been this fortnight ill,
100 And these unseasoned° hours perforce must add   *irregular*
Unto your sickness.

KING HENRY   I will take your counsel.
And were these inward° wars once out of hand,   *civil*
We would, dear lords, unto the Holy Land.   *Exeunt*

3.2

Enter Justice SHALLOW *and Justice* SILENCE

SHALLOW   Come on, come on, come on! Give me your hand,
sir, give me your hand, sir. An early stirrer, by the rood!° And   *cross*
how doth my good cousin° Silence?   *kinsman*

SILENCE   Good morrow, good cousin Shallow.

5 SHALLOW   And how doth my cousin your bedfellow? And your
fairest daughter and mine, my god-daughter Ellen?

SILENCE   Alas, a black ouzel,[1] cousin Shallow.

SHALLOW   By yea and no, sir, I dare say my cousin William is
become a good scholar. He is at Oxford still, is he not?

10 SILENCE   Indeed, sir, to my cost.

SHALLOW   A° must then to the Inns o' Court[2] shortly. I was once   *He*
of Clement's Inn,[3] where I think they will talk of mad Shallow
yet.

SILENCE   You were called 'lusty Shallow' then, cousin.

15 SHALLOW   By the mass, I was called anything; and I would have
done anything indeed, too, and roundly,° too. There was I, and   *thoroughly*
little John Doit of Staffordshire, and black George Barnes, and
Francis Pickbone, and Will Squeal, a Cotswold man; you had
not four such swinge-bucklers° in all the Inns o' Court again.   *swashbucklers*
20 And I may say to you, we knew where the bona-robas° were,   *well-dressed prostitutes*
and had the best of them all at commandment. Then was Jack
Falstaff, now Sir John, a boy, and page to Thomas Mowbray,
Duke of Norfolk.

SILENCE   This Sir John, cousin, that comes hither anon° about   *soon*
25 soldiers?

SHALLOW   The same Sir John, the very same. I see him break
Scoggin's[4] head at the court gate when a was a crack,° not thus   *young fellow*
high. And the very same day did I fight with one Samson Stock-

---

3.2 Location: Outside Justice Shallow's house in
Gloucestershire.
1. Blackbird. Women with black hair and/or complexions were often viewed as "foul" rather than "fair."
2. Prestigious legal schools in London that admitted
men to the bar.

3. One of the Inns of Chancery, less prestigious legal
colleges.
4. A buffoon (possibly referring to Edward IV's court
jester of that name and famous as the main character
of *Scogin's Jests*, a popular Elizabethan jestbook).

fish, a fruiterer, behind Gray's Inn.⁵ Jesu, Jesu, the mad days
30 that I have spent! And to see how many of my old acquaintance
are dead.

SILENCE   We shall all follow, cousin.

SHALLOW   Certain, 'tis certain; very sure, very sure. Death, as the
Psalmist saith, is certain to all; all shall die. How° a good yoke   *What's the price of*
35 of bullocks at Stamford fair?

SILENCE   By my troth, I was not there.

SHALLOW   Death is certain. Is old Double of your town living
yet?

SILENCE   Dead, sir.

40 SHALLOW   Jesu, Jesu, dead! A° drew a good bow; and dead! A   *He*
shot a fine shoot. John o' Gaunt° loved him well, and betted   *(Henry IV's father)*
much money on his head. Dead! A would have clapped i'th'
clout at twelve score,⁶ and carried you a forehand shaft a fourteen and fourteen and a half,⁷ that it would have done a man's
45 heart good to see. How a score of ewes now?

SILENCE   Thereafter as they be.⁸ A score of good ewes may be
worth ten pounds.

SHALLOW   And is old Double dead?

Enter BARDOLPH and [the PAGE]⁹

SILENCE   Here come two of Sir John Falstaff's men, as I think.

50 SHALLOW   Good morrow, honest gentlemen.

BARDOLPH   I beseech you, which is Justice Shallow?

SHALLOW   I am Robert Shallow, sir, a poor esquire of this county,
and one of the King's Justices of the Peace. What is your good
pleasure with me?

55 BARDOLPH   My captain, sir, commends him° to you—my captain   *sends his respects*
Sir John Falstaff, a tall° gentleman, by heaven, and a most gal-   *valiant*
lant leader.

SHALLOW   He greets me well, sir. I knew him a good backsword
man.° How doth the good knight? May I ask how my lady his   *fencer*
60 wife doth?

BARDOLPH   Sir, pardon, a soldier is better accommodated than
with a wife.

SHALLOW   It is well said, in faith, sir, and it is well said indeed,
too. 'Better accommodated'—it is good; yea, indeed is it. Good
65 phrases are surely, and ever were, very commendable. 'Accommodated'—it comes of 'accommodo'. Very good, a good phrase.

BARDOLPH   Pardon, sir, I have heard the word—'phrase' call you
it?—By this day, I know not the phrase; but I will maintain the
word with my sword to be a soldier-like word, and a word of
70 exceeding good command,° by heaven. 'Accommodated'; that   *fit for many uses*
is, when a man is, as they say, accommodated; or when a man
is being whereby a may be thought to be accommodated;
which is an excellent thing.

Enter Sir John FALSTAFF

SHALLOW   It is very just.° Look, here comes good Sir John. [To   *true*
75 FALSTAFF] Give me your hand, give me your worship's good

---

5. One of the Inns of Court.
6. Hit the target from 240 yards.
7. He could shoot an arrow straight, to 280 or 290
yards. A "forehand shaft" is an arrow shot in a straight
line rather than with the curved trajectory common for
long shots.
8. The price depends on their quality.

9. In F, Bardolph enters with "his Boy." In Q, he enters
"and one with him." It is reasonable to assume, but not
certain, that Falstaff's page is Bardolph's companion.
The use of a boy actor for this part would allow the
number of adult actors required for the rest of the
scene to be reduced by one.

hand. By my troth, you like well,° and bear your years very well.   *you are thriving*
Welcome, good Sir John.

FALSTAFF   I am glad to see you well, good Master Robert Shallow. [*To* SILENCE] Master Surecard, as I think.

80 SHALLOW   No, Sir John, it is my cousin Silence, in commission[1]
with me.

FALSTAFF   Good Master Silence, it well befits you should be of
the peace.

SILENCE   Your good worship is welcome.

85 FALSTAFF   Fie, this is hot weather, gentlemen. Have you provided me here half a dozen sufficient° men?   *able*

SHALLOW   Marry, have we, sir. Will you sit?

FALSTAFF   Let me see them, I beseech you.
      [*He sits*]

SHALLOW   Where's the roll,° where's the roll, where's the roll?   *list*
90 Let me see, let me see, let me see; so, so, so, so, so. Yea, marry,
sir: 'Ralph Mouldy'. [*To* SILENCE] Let them appear as I call,
let them do so, let them do so. Let me see, [*calls*] where is
Mouldy?
      [*Enter* MOULDY][2]

MOULDY   Here, an't please you.

95 SHALLOW   What think you, Sir John? A good-limbed fellow,
young, strong, and of good friends.°   *well connected*

FALSTAFF   Is thy name Mouldy?

MOULDY   Yea, an't please you.

FALSTAFF   'Tis the more time° thou wert used.   *well past time*

100 SHALLOW   Ha, ha, ha, most excellent, i'faith! Things that are
mouldy lack use. Very singular good, in faith, well said, Sir
John, very well said.

FALSTAFF   Prick him.°   *Mark his name*

MOULDY   I was pricked[3] well enough before, an you could have
105 let me alone. My old dame° will be undone now for one to do   *wife*
her husbandry[4] and her drudgery. You need not to have
pricked me; there are other men fitter to go out than I.

FALSTAFF   Go to, peace, Mouldy. You shall go, Mouldy; it is
time you were spent.°   *used up*

110 MOULDY   Spent?

SHALLOW   Peace, fellow, peace. Stand aside; know you where
you are?
      [MOULDY *stands aside*]
For th'other, Sir John, let me see: 'Simon Shadow'—

FALSTAFF   Yea, marry, let me have him to sit under. He's like to
115 be a cold° soldier.   *dead; cowardly*

SHALLOW [*calls*]   Where's Shadow?
      [*Enter* SHADOW]

SHADOW   Here, sir.

FALSTAFF   Shadow, whose son art thou?

SHADOW   My mother's son, sir.

120 FALSTAFF   Thy mother's son! Like enough, and thy father's
shadow.° So the son of the female is the shadow° of the male—   *likeness / faint copy*

---

1. Having a position (as justice of the peace).
2. In F, the recruits enter at the beginning of the scene
with Silence and Shallow. But they have nothing to do
until this point in the scene. It is better to have them all
enter with Mouldy and be called forward one by one, or,
as here, to enter separately as each name is called.
3. Vexed; provided with a penis.
4. Will be lacking someone to perform the sexual
duties of a husband; will be lacking someone to do the
work of the farm.

it is often so indeed—but not of the father's substance.[5]

SHALLOW   Do you like him, Sir John?

FALSTAFF   Shadow will serve for summer. Prick him, for we have
125 a number of shadows[6] fill up the muster book.

[SHADOW *stands aside*]

SHALLOW [*calls*]   'Thomas Wart.'

FALSTAFF   Where's he?

[*Enter* WART]

WART   Here, sir.

FALSTAFF   Is thy name Wart?

130 WART   Yea, sir.

FALSTAFF   Thou art a very ragged wart.

SHALLOW   Shall I prick him, Sir John?

FALSTAFF   It were superfluous, for his apparel is built° upon his   *pieced together*
back, and the whole frame stands upon pins.[7] Prick him no
135 more.

SHALLOW   Ha, ha, ha, you can do it, sir, you can do it! I commend you well.

[WART *stands aside*]

[*Calls*] 'Francis Feeble.'

[*Enter* FEEBLE]

FEEBLE   Here, sir.

140 SHALLOW   What trade art thou, Feeble?

FEEBLE   A woman's tailor,[8] sir.

SHALLOW   Shall I prick him, sir?

FALSTAFF   You may, but if he had been a man's tailor, he'd ha'
pricked[9] you. [*To* FEEBLE] Wilt thou make as many holes in an
145 enemy's battle° as thou hast done in a woman's petticoat?   *army*

FEEBLE   I will do my good will,° sir; you can have no more.   *do my best*

FALSTAFF   Well said, good woman's tailor; well said, courageous
Feeble! Thou wilt be as valiant as the wrathful dove or most
magnanimous° mouse. Prick the woman's tailor. Well, Master   *brave*
150 Shallow; deep, Master Shallow.

FEEBLE   I would Wart might have gone, sir.

FALSTAFF   I would thou wert a man's tailor, that thou mightst
mend him and make him fit to go.° I cannot put him to a   *to serve; to have sex*
private soldier[1] that is the leader of so many thousands.° Let   *(of lice)*
155 that suffice, most forcible Feeble.

FEEBLE   It shall suffice, sir.

FALSTAFF   I am bound to thee, reverend Feeble.

[FEEBLE *stands aside*]

Who is next?

SHALLOW [*calls*]   'Peter Bullcalf o'th' green.'

160 FALSTAFF   Yea, marry, let's see Bullcalf.

[*Enter* BULLCALF]

BULLCALF   Here, sir.

FALSTAFF   Fore God, a likely° fellow! Come, prick Bullcalf till   *promising*
he roar again.

---

5. Not born from the father's body (because born from
the mother's); not the father's true son.
6. Fictitious names that officers recorded in order to
collect additional pay from the crown.
7. The whole structure depends upon pegs ("pins");
stands upon legs ("pins").

8. Women's tailors were bywords for effeminacy and
cowardice.
9. Dressed; stabbed; penetrated.
1. Make him a private soldier; offer him sexually to a
private soldier.

BULLCALF O Lord, good my lord captain!

165 FALSTAFF What, dost thou roar before thou'rt pricked?

BULLCALF O Lord, sir, I am a diseased man.

FALSTAFF What disease hast thou?

BULLCALF A whoreson cold, sir; a cough, sir, which I caught with ringing in the King's affairs[2] upon his coronation day, sir.

170 FALSTAFF Come, thou shalt go to the wars in a gown.° We will   *dressing gown*
have away° thy cold, and I will take such order° that thy friends   *get rid / measures*
shall ring for thee.[3]
    [BULLCALF *stands aside*]
Is here all?

SHALLOW There is two more called than your number. You
175 must have but four here,[4] sir, and so I pray you go in with me to dinner.

FALSTAFF Come, I will go drink with you, but I cannot tarry°   *stay for*
dinner. I am glad to see you, by my troth, Master Shallow.

SHALLOW O, Sir John, do you remember since we lay all night
180 in the Windmill in Saint George's Field?[5]

FALSTAFF No more of that, good Master Shallow, no more of that.

SHALLOW Ha, 'twas a merry night! And is Jane Nightwork alive?

FALSTAFF She lives, Master Shallow.

185 SHALLOW She never could away with° me.   *tolerate*

FALSTAFF Never, never. She would always say she could not abide Master Shallow.

SHALLOW By the mass, I could anger her to th' heart. She was then a bona-roba. Doth she hold her own well?

190 FALSTAFF Old, old, Master Shallow.

SHALLOW Nay, she must be old; she cannot choose but be old; certain she's old; and had Robin Nightwork by old Nightwork before I came to Clement's Inn.

SILENCE That's fifty-five year ago.

195 SHALLOW Ha, cousin Silence, that thou hadst seen that that this knight and I have seen! Ha, Sir John, said I well?

FALSTAFF We have heard the chimes at midnight, Master Shallow.

SHALLOW That we have, that we have; in faith, Sir John, we
200 have. Our watchword was 'Hem° boys!' Come, let's to dinner;   *Drink up*
come, let's to dinner. Jesus, the days that we have seen! Come,
come.   *Exeunt* [SHALLOW, SILENCE, *and* FALSTAFF]

BULLCALF [*coming forward*] Good Master Corporate° Bardolph,   *(for "Corporal")*
stand° my friend, and here's four Harry ten shillings in French   *act as*
205 crowns for you.[6] In very truth, sir, I had as lief° be hanged, sir,   *willingly*
as go. And yet for mine own part, sir, I do not care; but rather
because I am unwilling, and, for mine own part, have a desire
to stay with my friends. Else, sir, I did not care, for mine own
part, so much.

210 BARDOLPH [*taking the money*] Go to; stand aside.
    [BULLCALF *stands aside*]

---

2. Ringing the church bells in the King's honor.
3. In your place; at your death.
4. An inconsistency: there have been five, not six, recruits called.
5. A region of London south of the Thames near Southwark, known as a market for sex. "The Windmill" was the name of a brothel or an inn.

6. An elaborate way of offering a bribe. The reference to "Harry ten shillings" is anachronistic; shillings originated during Henry VII's reign and by the 1590s had been devalued to half their original worth. Therefore, Bullcalf is offering about 1 pound to be paid in French crowns (coins worth 4 shillings each).

MOULDY [*coming forward*] And, good Master Corporal Captain, for my old dame's sake stand my friend. She has nobody to do anything about her when I am gone, and she is old and cannot help herself. You shall have forty,° sir.   (shillings)

215 BARDOLPH Go to; stand aside.

[MOULDY *stands aside*]

FEEBLE By my troth, I care not. A man can die but once. We owe God a death. I'll ne'er bear a base mind. An't be my destiny, so; an't be not, so. No man's too good to serve's° prince. 　serve his And let it go which way it will, he that dies this year is quit for° 　released from (dying)

220 the next.

BARDOLPH Well said; thou'rt a good fellow.

FEEBLE Faith, I'll bear no base mind.

Enter [Sir John] FALSTAFF[, SHALLOW, and SILENCE]

FALSTAFF Come, sir, which men shall I have?

SHALLOW Four of which you please.

225 BARDOLPH [*to FALSTAFF*] Sir, a word with you. [*Aside to him*] I have three pound to free Mouldy and Bullcalf.

FALSTAFF Go to, well.

SHALLOW Come, Sir John, which four will you have?

FALSTAFF Do you choose for me.

230 SHALLOW Marry, then: Mouldy, Bullcalf, Feeble, and Shadow.

FALSTAFF Mouldy and Bullcalf. For you, Mouldy, stay at home till you are past service;[7] and for your part, Bullcalf, grow till you come unto it.[8] I will none of you.

[*Exeunt BULLCALF and MOULDY*]

SHALLOW Sir John, Sir John, do not yourself wrong. They are

235 your likeliest men, and I would have you served with the best.

FALSTAFF Will you tell me, Master Shallow, how to choose a man? Care I for the limb, the thews,° the stature, bulk, and big 　strength assemblance° of a man? Give me the spirit, Master Shallow. 　composition Here's Wart; you see what a ragged appearance it is? A shall

240 charge you and discharge you° with the motion of a pewterer's 　load and fire hammer,° come off and on swifter than he that gibbets on the 　with a steady motion brewer's bucket.[9] And this same half-faced° fellow Shadow; 　thin-faced give me this man. He presents no mark° to the enemy; the 　target foeman may with as great aim level at° the edge of a penknife. 　fire against

245 And for a retreat, how swiftly will this Feeble the woman's tailor run off! O, give me the spare men, and spare me the great ones.—Put me a caliver° into Wart's hand, Bardolph.   musket

BARDOLPH [*giving WART a caliver*] Hold, Wart. Traverse°—thas, 　March thas, thas!

[*WART marches*]

250 FALSTAFF [*to WART*] Come, manage me your caliver. So; very well. Go to, very good, exceeding good. O, give me always a little, lean, old, chapped, bald shot!° Well said, i'faith, Wart; 　marksman thou'rt a good scab. Hold; [*giving a coin*] there's a tester° for 　sixpence thee.

255 SHALLOW He is not his craft's master; he doth not do it right. I remember at Mile-End Green,[1] when I lay° at Clement's   lodged

---

7. Past the time of military duty; past the time of sexual potency.
8. That is, grow until you come into the time of military service; the time of sexual potency. Falstaff plays on the fact that Bullcalf is a *calf,* not a *bull.*

9. Retreat and advance, or raise and lower your gun, faster than he who hangs pails on each end of the wooden bar (gibbet) that a brewer carries on his shoulders.
1. Open land east of London used as a training ground for citizen militias and for fairs and shows.

Inn—I was then Sir Dagonet in Arthur's show[2]—there was a
little quiver° fellow, and a would manage you his piece thus,   *nimble*
and a would about and about, and come you in° and come you   *thrust at you*
260   in. 'Ra-ta-ta!' would a say; 'Bounce!'° would a say; and away   *Bang*
again would a go; and again would a come. I shall ne'er see
such a fellow.

FALSTAFF   These fellows will do well, Master Shallow. God keep
you, Master Silence; I will not use many words with you. Fare
265   you well, gentlemen both; I thank you. I must° a dozen mile   *must go*
tonight.—Bardolph, give the soldiers coats.

SHALLOW   Sir John, the Lord bless you; God prosper your affairs!
God send us peace! As you return, visit my house; let our old
acquaintance be renewed. Peradventure I will with ye to the
270   court.

FALSTAFF   Fore God, would you would!

SHALLOW   Go to, I have spoke at a word.° God keep you!   *spoken sincerely*

FALSTAFF   Fare you well, gentle gentlemen.

                    Exeunt [SHALLOW *and* SILENCE]
On, Bardolph, lead the men away.
                    [*Exeunt* BARDOLPH, WART, SHADOW, *and* FEEBLE]
275   As I return, I will fetch off° these justices. I do see the bottom   *defraud*
of Justice Shallow. Lord, Lord, how subject we old men are to
this vice of lying! This same starved justice hath done nothing
but prate to me of the wildness of his youth and the feats he
hath done about Turnbull Street;[3] and every third word a lie,
280   duer paid° to the hearer than the Turk's tribute.[4] I do remem-   *sooner paid*
ber him at Clement's Inn, like a man made after supper of a
cheese paring. When a was naked, he was for all the world like
a forked radish,[5] with a head fantastically carved upon it with a
knife. A was so forlorn° that his dimensions, to any thick° sight,   *thin / imperfect*
285   were invisible. A was the very genius° of famine.[6]   *spirit*
285.1   *yet lecherous as a monkey; and the whores called him*
'mandrake'. A came ever in the rearward of the fashion,
and sung those tunes to the overscutched hussies° that   *worn-out whores*
he heard the carmen° whistle, and sware they were his   *wagoners*
285.5   *fancies or his good-nights.°*   *his own love songs*
And now is this Vice's dagger[7] become a squire, and talks as fam-
iliarly of John o' Gaunt as if he had been sworn brother to him,
and I'll be sworn a ne'er saw him but once, in the Tilt-yard,°   *tournament arena*
and then he° burst his° head for crowding among the marshal's   *(Gaunt) / (Shallow's)*
290   men. I saw it, and told John o' Gaunt he beat his own
name;[8] for you might have trussed° him and all his apparel into   *packed*
an eel-skin. The case of a treble hautboy° was a mansion for   *oboe*
him, a court. And now has he land and beeves.° Well, I'll be   *oxen*
acquainted with him if I return; and't shall go hard but I'll
295   make him a philosopher's two stones to me.[9] If the young dace°   *small fish*

2. Referring to his role as King Arthur's fool in an
archery pageant in which each participant took the
name of one of the knights of the Round Table.
3. An area of Smithfield associated with criminal activities.
4. Money extracted from those the Turkish Sultan conquered or who engaged in trade with him. The penalty
for failure to pay was death, so presumably money was
paid punctually. Shallow is even quicker to tell lies.
5. A mandrake root, said to resemble a man's body. See

note to 1.2.12.
6. The following inset lines (285.1–285.5) appear in Q
but not in F.
7. The wooden dagger used by the Vice, a comic character in medieval morality plays.
8. Attacked someone very gaunt or thin.
9. I'll make him twice as valuable to me as the philosopher's stone that was supposed to transmute base
metals into gold, with a pun on "stones" as meaning
"testicles."

be a bait for the old pike, I see no reason in the law of nature
but I may snap at him. Let time shape, and there an end

Exit

4.1

Enter [in arms] the ARCHBISHOP *[of York], [Thomas]*
MOWBRAY, *[Lord]* HASTINGS, *[and]* COLEVILLE[1] *within*
the Forest of Gaultres[2]

ARCHBISHOP OF YORK What is this forest called?

HASTINGS 'Tis Gaultres Forest, an't° shall please your grace.   *if it*

ARCHBISHOP OF YORK Here stand, my lords, and send discoverers° forth   *scouts*
To know the numbers of our enemies.

HASTINGS We have sent forth already.

5 ARCHBISHOP OF YORK   'Tis well done.
My friends and brethren in these great affairs,
I must acquaint you that I have received
New-dated° letters from Northumberland,   *Recent*
Their cold intent, tenor, and substance, thus:

10 Here doth he wish his person, with such powers
As might hold sortance° with his quality,°   *accord / rank*
The which he could not levy; whereupon
He is retired to ripe° his growing fortunes   *ripen*
To Scotland, and concludes in hearty prayers

15 That your attempts may overlive the hazard
And fearful meeting of their opposite.°   *enemy*

MOWBRAY Thus do the hopes we have in him touch ground
And dash themselves to pieces.

Enter a MESSENGER

HASTINGS   Now, what news?

MESSENGER West of this forest, scarcely off a mile,

20 In goodly form° comes on the enemy;   *battle array*
And, by the ground they hide,° I judge their number   *cover*
Upon or near the rate of thirty thousand.

MOWBRAY The just proportion° that we gave them out.°   *exact size / estimated*
Let us sway on, and face them in the field.

Enter [the Earl] of WESTMORLAND

25 ARCHBISHOP OF YORK What well-appointed leader fronts° us here?   *confronts*

MOWBRAY I think it is my lord of Westmorland.

WESTMORLAND Health and fair greeting from our general,
The Prince, Lord John and Duke of Lancaster.

ARCHBISHOP OF YORK Say on, my lord of Westmorland, in peace,
What doth concern your coming.

30 WESTMORLAND   Then, my lord,
Unto your grace do I in chief address
The substance of my speech. If that rebellion
Came like itself, in base and abject routs,°   *lowborn disorderly bands*
Led on by bloody youth, guarded° with rags,   *adorned*

35 And countenanced° by boys and beggary;   *approved*
I say, if damned commotion so appeared

4.1 Location: Gaultres Forest in Yorkshire.
1. In F, this initial stage direction includes Westmorland, who actually enters later in the scene, and Coleville, a rebel captured by Falstaff in 4.2. Most editors delete both figures from the initial stage direction. The Oxford editors speculate that Coleville is the captain who at 4.1.295–97 is sent to tell the rebel army to disperse after peace is made, so they include him in the scene from the beginning.
2. Gaultres was a royal forest north and west of York. In Holinshed's *Chronicles* and in Q and F, it is spelled "Gaultree," a spelling adopted in most editions.

In his true native and most proper shape,
You, reverend father, and these noble lords
Had not been here to dress the ugly form
40 Of base and bloody insurrection
With your fair honours. You, Lord Archbishop,
Whose see° is by a civil peace maintained,   *diocese*
Whose beard the silver hand of peace hath touched,
Whose learning and good letters° peace hath tutored,   *scholarship*
45 Whose white investments figure° innocence,   *robes represent*
The dove and very blessèd spirit of peace,
Wherefore do you so ill translate° yourself   *transform*
Out of the speech of peace that bears such grace
Into the harsh and boist'rous tongue of war,
50 Turning your books to graves, your ink to blood,
Your pens to lances, and your tongue divine
To a loud trumpet and a point° of war?   *signal*
ARCHBISHOP OF YORK   Wherefore do I this? So the question stands.
Briefly, to this end: we are all diseased,³
55 And with our surfeiting° and wanton hours   *overfeeding*
Have brought ourselves into a burning fever,
And we must bleed° for it—of which disease   *be bled as a cure*
Our late King Richard, being infected, died.
But, my most noble lord of Westmorland,
60 I take not on me here as a physician,
Nor do I as an enemy to peace
Troop in the throngs of military men;
But rather show° a while like fearful war   *appear*
To diet rank° minds, sick of happiness,   *swollen; overindulged*
65 And purge th'obstructions which begin to stop
Our very veins of life. Hear me more plainly.
I have in equal balance justly weighed
What wrongs our arms may do, what wrongs we suffer,
And find our griefs heavier than our offences.
70 We see which way the stream of time doth run,
And are enforced from our most quiet shore
By the rough torrent of occasion;°   *events*
And have the summary of all our griefs,
When time shall serve, to show in articles,°   *an itemized list*
75 Which long ere this we offered to the King,
And might by no suit gain our audience.
When we are wronged, and would unfold our griefs,
We are denied access unto his person
Even by those men that most have done us wrong.
80 The dangers of the days but newly gone,
Whose memory is written on the earth
With yet° appearing blood, and the examples   *still*
Of every minute's instance,° present now,   *Occurring every minute*
Hath put us in these ill-beseeming° arms,   *unsuitable*
85 Not to break peace, or any branch of it,
But to establish here a peace indeed,
Concurring both in name and quality.
WESTMORLAND   Whenever yet was your appeal denied?

---

3. Lines 55–79 are missing from Q, perhaps because they state the case for rebellion too forcefully.

	Wherein have you been gallèd° by the King?	*vexed; grieved*
90	What peer hath been suborned to grate on° you,	*induced to annoy*
	That you should seal° this lawless bloody book	*license*
	Of forged rebellion with a seal divine?⁴	

ARCHBISHOP OF YORK My brother general, the commonwealth
    I make my quarrel in particular.⁵

95 WESTMORLAND There is no need of any such redress;
    Or if there were, it not belongs to you.

MOWBRAY Why not to him in part, and to us all
    That feel the bruises of the days before,
    And suffer the condition of these times

| 100 | To lay a heavy and unequal° hand | *unjust* |
| | Upon our honours?⁶ | |

WESTMORLAND O my good Lord Mowbray.

	Construe the times to° their necessities,	*according to*
	And you shall say indeed it is the time,	
	And not the King, that doth you injuries.	
105	Yet for your part, it not appears° to me,	*it does not appear*
	Either from the King or in the present time,	
	That you should have an inch of any ground	
	To build a grief on. Were you not restored	
	To all the Duke of Norfolk's signories,°	*properties*
110	Your noble and right well-remembered father's?	

MOWBRAY What thing in honour had my father lost

	That need to be revived and breathed° in me?	*brought to life*
	The King that loved him, as the state stood then,	
	Was force perforce° compelled to banish him;	*against his will*
115	And then that Henry Bolingbroke and he,	
	Being mounted and both rousèd° in their seats,	*raised*
	Their neighing coursers daring of the spur,⁷	
	Their armèd staves in charge,⁸ their beavers° down,	*helmet visors*
	Their eyes of fire sparkling through sights° of steel,	*visor slits*
120	And the loud trumpet blowing them together,	
	Then, then, when there was nothing could have stayed°	*kept*
	My father from the breast of Bolingbroke—	
	O, when the King did throw his warder° down,	*staff of command*
	His own life hung upon the staff he threw;	
125	Then threw he down himself and all their lives	
	That by indictment° and by dint of sword	*legal accusations*
	Have since miscarried under Bolingbroke.	

WESTMORLAND You speak, Lord Mowbray, now you know not what.

| | The Earl of Hereford° was reputed then | *(Bolingbroke)* |
| 130 | In England the most valiant gentleman. | |

    Who knows on whom fortune would then have smiled?
    But if your father had been victor there,
    He ne'er had borne it out of Coventry;⁹
    For all the country in a general voice
135   Cried hate upon him, and all their prayers and love

---

4. Alluding to bishops as official licensers of books with the ability to exercise censorship. Westmorland accuses the Archbishop of *not* censoring the book of rebellion.
5. *My . . . particular*: these two lines are obscure. York seems to be saying he is making the cause of the commonwealth his own because all men are his brothers.
6. The second half of line 101 and lines 102–37 do not

appear in Q. They recount a version of events depicted in Shakespeare's *Richard II* in which Richard stopped a formal combat between Thomas Mowbray, father of the Mowbray of this play, and Bolingbroke, now Henry IV.
7. Daring the spur to prick them forward.
8. Their steel-tipped lances ready for the charge.
9. He never would have carried away the prize from Coventry (where the duel was to take place).

Were set on Hereford, whom they doted on
And blessed and graced, indeed, more than the King.
But this is mere digression from my purpose.
Here come I from our princely general
140　To know your griefs, to tell you from his grace
That he will give you audience; and wherein
It shall appear that your demands are just,
You shall enjoy them, everything set off°　　　　　　　　　*forgotten*
That might so much as think you enemies.
145　MOWBRAY　But he hath forced us to compel this offer,
And it proceeds from policy,° not love.　　　　　　　　*political cunning*
WESTMORLAND　Mowbray, you overween° to take it so.　　*presume too much*
This offer comes from mercy, not from fear;
For lo, within a ken° our army lies,　　　　　　　　*the field of vision*
150　Upon mine honour, all too confident
To give admittance to a thought of fear.
Our battle° is more full of names° than yours,　　　*army / titled men*
Our men more perfect in the use of arms,
Our armour all as strong, our cause the best.
155　Then reason will° our hearts should be as good.　　　*it follows that*
Say you not then our offer is compelled.
MOWBRAY　Well, by my will we shall admit no parley.°　*discussion of terms*
WESTMORLAND　That argues but the shame of your offence.
A rotten case° abides no handling.　　　　　　　　　　*cause*
160　HASTINGS　Hath the Prince John a full commission,
In very ample virtue° of his father,　　　　　　　　*With full authority*
To hear and absolutely to determine
Of what° conditions we shall stand upon?　　　　　　　*whatever*
WESTMORLAND　That is intended° in the general's name.　　*indicated*
165　I muse° you make so slight a question.　　　　　　　*wonder*
ARCHBISHOP OF YORK　Then take, my lord of Westmorland, this schedule;°　*document*
For this contains our general grievances.
Each several° article herein redressed,　　　　　　　*individual*
All members of our cause, both here and hence,
170　That are ensinewed° to this action　　　　　*tightly bound (by sinews)*
Acquitted° by a true substantial form,°　　　　*Pardoned / binding act*
And present execution of our wills
To us and to our purposes consigned,[1]
We come within our awe-full banks again,[2]
175　And knit our powers to the arm of peace.
WESTMORLAND [*taking the schedule*]　This will I show the general.
　　Please you, lords,
In sight of both our battles we may meet,
And either end in peace—which God so frame°—　　　　*bring to pass*
Or to the place of diff'rence° call the swords　　　*conflict*
Which must decide it.
180　ARCHBISHOP OF YORK　　My lord, we will do so.　*Exit* WESTMORLAND
MOWBRAY　There is a thing within my bosom tells me
That no conditions of our peace can stand.
HASTINGS　Fear you not that. If we can make our peace

---

1. *And . . . consigned:* And immediate ("present") fulfillment of our demands allowed us. The emendation to "consigned" of Q's and F's "confinde" allows three parallel clauses to follow one another, each dealing with one of the rebels' conditions for putting down their arms. 2. We come again within the bounds of respect (with the suggestion of a flooded river returning to its banks).

Upon such large° terms and so absolute	*liberal*
185 As our conditions shall consist° upon,	*insist*
Our peace shall stand as firm as rocky mountains.	
MOWBRAY Yea, but our valuation° shall be such	*the value we are held in*
That every slight and false-derivèd° cause,	*wrongly attributed*
Yea, every idle, nice,° and wanton° reason,	*petty / frivolous*
190 Shall to the King taste of this action,°	*(of rebellion)*
That, were our royal faiths martyrs in love,[3]	
We shall be winnowed with so rough a wind	
That even our corn shall seem as light as chaff,	
And good from bad find no partition.°	*distinction*
195 ARCHBISHOP OF YORK No, no, my lord; note this. The King is weary	
Of dainty and such picking° grievances,	*trivial*
For he hath found to end one doubt° by death	*fear*
Revives two greater in the heirs of life;	
And therefore will he wipe his tables° clean,	*tablets*
200 And keep no tell-tale to his memory	
That may repeat and history° his loss	*retell*
To new remembrance; for full well he knows	
He cannot so precisely weed this land	
As his misdoubts° present occasion.	*suspicions*
205 His foes are so enrooted with his friends	
That, plucking to unfix an enemy,	
He doth unfasten so and shake a friend;	
So that this land, like an offensive wife	
That hath enraged him on to offer strokes,°	*attempt beatings*
210 As he is striking, holds his infant up,	
And hangs resolved correction in the arm	
That was upreared to execution.[4]	
HASTINGS Besides, the King hath wasted all his rods°	*means of punishment*
On late° offenders, that he now doth lack	*recent*
215 The very instruments of chastisement;	
So that his power, like to a fangless lion,	
May offer,° but not hold.	*threaten*
ARCHBISHOP OF YORK 'Tis very true.	
And therefore be assured, my good Lord Marshal,	
If we do now make our atonement° well,	*reconciliation*
220 Our peace will, like a broken limb united,	
Grow stronger for the breaking.	
MOWBRAY Be it so.	

Enter WESTMORLAND

Here is returned my lord of Westmorland.	
WESTMORLAND The Prince is here at hand. Pleaseth your lordship	
To meet his grace just° distance 'tween our armies?	*equal*
225 MOWBRAY Your grace of York, in God's name then set forward.	
ARCHBISHOP OF YORK Before, and greet his grace!—My lord, we come.	

[*They march over the stage.*]

Enter PRINCE JOHN [*with one or more soldiers carrying wine*]

PRINCE JOHN   You are well encountered here, my cousin Mowbray.
Good day to you, gentle lord Archbishop;

---

3. So that even if our loyalty to the King made us loving martyrs.

4. And . . . execution: And so punishment that was
about to be executed is held in suspended action.

And so to you, Lord Hastings, and to all.
230 My lord of York, it better showed with you
When that your flock, assembled by the bell,
Encircled you to hear with reverence
Your exposition on the holy text,
Than now to see you here an iron° man,   *armored; a fierce*
235 Cheering a rout° of rebels with your drum,   *disorderly band*
Turning the word° to sword, and life to death.   *(Scripture)*
That man that sits within a monarch's heart
And ripens in the sunshine of his favour,
Would he° abuse the countenance° of the King,   *Should he / favor*
240 Alack, what mischiefs might he set abroach°   *afoot*
In shadow° of such greatness! With you, Lord Bishop,   *Under cover*
It is even so. Who hath not heard it spoken
How deep you were within the books of God—
To us, the speaker in his° parliament,   *(God's)*
245 To us, th'imagined voice of God himself,
The very opener° and intelligencer°   *interpreter / informer*
Between the grace, the sanctities of heaven
And our dull workings?° O, who shall believe   *ignorant thoughts*
But you misuse the reverence of your place,
250 Employ the countenance and grace of heav'n
As a false favourite doth his prince's name
In deeds dishonourable? You have ta'en up,°   *enlisted*
Under the counterfeited zeal of⁵ God,
The subjects of his substitute, my father;
255 And, both against the peace of heaven and him,
Have here upswarmèd them.⁶
ARCHBISHOP OF YORK   Good my lord of Lancaster,
I am not here against your father's peace;
But, as I told my lord of Westmorland,
The time misordered doth, in common sense,
260 Crowd us and crush us to this monstrous form,
To hold our safety up. I sent your grace
The parcels° and particulars of our grief,   *items; details*
The which hath been with scorn shoved from the court,
Whereon this Hydra son⁷ of war is born;
265 Whose dangerous eyes may well be charmed asleep⁸
With grant° of our most just and right desires,   *the granting*
And true obedience, of this madness cured,
Stoop tamely to the foot of majesty.
MOWBRAY   If not, we ready are to try our fortunes
To the last man.
270 HASTINGS   And though we here fall down,
We have supplies° to second our attempt.   *reinforcements*
If they miscarry, theirs shall second them;
And so success of° mischief shall be born,   *from*
And heir from heir shall hold this quarrel up,
275 Whiles° England shall have generation.°   *As long as / offspring*

5. Under the pretense of zeal toward God; under the pretense of God's approval.
6. Have raised them up in angry swarms (like bees).
7. Hydra-like offspring. The Archbishop alludes to the many-headed monster of classical mythology, which was almost impossible to kill because its heads grew again as fast as they were cut off.
8. Alluding to another monster of classical mythology, the hundred-eyed Argus, which Hermes overcame by charming it to sleep.

PRINCE JOHN   You are too shallow, Hastings, much too shallow,
To sound the bottom of the after-times.°   *future*
WESTMORLAND   Pleaseth your grace to answer them directly
How far forth you do like their articles?
280   PRINCE JOHN   I like them all, and do allow° them well,   *grant*
And swear here, by the honour of my blood,
My father's purposes have been mistook,
And some about him have too lavishly°   *freely*
Wrested his meaning and authority.
285   [*To the* ARCHBISHOP] My lord, these griefs shall be with speed redressed;
Upon my soul they shall. If this may please you,
Discharge your powers unto their several counties,
As we will ours; and here between the armies
Let's drink together friendly and embrace,
290   That all their eyes may bear those tokens home
Of our restorèd love and amity.
ARCHBISHOP OF YORK   I take your princely word for these redresses.
PRINCE JOHN   I give it you, and will maintain my word;
And thereupon I drink unto your grace.
        [*He drinks*]
295   HASTINGS [*to* COLEVILLE]   Go, captain, and deliver to the army
This news of peace. Let them have pay, and part.
I know it will well please them. Hie thee,° captain.   *Get thee gone*
                              Exit [COLEVILLE]
ARCHBISHOP OF YORK   To you, my noble lord of Westmorland!
        [*He drinks*]
WESTMORLAND [*drinking*]   I pledge your grace. An if you knew what pains
300   I have bestowed to breed this present peace,
You would drink freely; but my love to ye
Shall show itself more openly hereafter.
ARCHBISHOP OF YORK   I do not doubt you.
WESTMORLAND   I am glad of it.
[*Drinking*] Health to my lord and gentle cousin Mowbray!
305   MOWBRAY   You wish me health in very happy season,°   *at an apt moment*
For I am on the sudden something ill.
ARCHBISHOP OF YORK   Against° ill chances men are ever merry;   *Before*
But heaviness° foreruns the good event.   *sorrow*
WESTMORLAND   Therefore be merry, coz,° since sudden sorrow   *kinsman*
310   Serves to say thus: some good thing comes tomorrow.
ARCHBISHOP OF YORK   Believe me, I am passing° light in spirit.   *exceptionally*
MOWBRAY   So much the worse, if your own rule be true.
                              Shout [*within*]
PRINCE JOHN   The word of peace is rendered. Hark how they
        shout.
MOWBRAY   This had° been cheerful after victory.   *would have*
315   ARCHBISHOP OF YORK   A peace is of the nature of a conquest,
For then both parties nobly are subdued,
And neither party loser.
PRINCE JOHN [*to* WESTMORLAND]   Go, my lord,
And let our army be dischargèd too.   *Exit* [WESTMORLAND]
[*To the* ARCHBISHOP] And, good my lord, so please you, let our trains°   *troops*
320   March by us, that we may peruse the men
We should have coped withal.°   *fought against*
ARCHBISHOP OF YORK   Go, good Lord Hastings,
And ere they be dismissed, let them march by.   *Exit* [HASTINGS]

PRINCE JOHN　　I trust, lords, we shall lie° tonight together.　　　　*lodge*

Enter [the Earl of] WESTMORLAND *[with captains]*

　　Now, cousin, wherefore stands our army still?

325　WESTMORLAND　　The leaders, having charge from you to stand,
　　Will not go off until they hear you speak.

PRINCE JOHN　　They know their duties.

Enter [Lord] HASTINGS

HASTINGS *[to the* ARCHBISHOP]　　　　Our army is dispersed.
　　Like youthful steers unyoked, they take their courses,
　　East, west, north, south; or, like a school broke up,

330　Each hurries toward his home and sporting place.

WESTMORLAND　　Good tidings, my lord Hastings, for the which
　　I do arrest thee, traitor, of high treason;
　　And you, Lord Archbishop, and you, Lord Mowbray,
　　Of capital treason I attach° you both.　　　　*arrest*

[The captains guard HASTINGS, *the* ARCHBISHOP, *and*
MOWBRAY]

335　MOWBRAY　　Is this proceeding just and honourable?

WESTMORLAND　　Is your assembly so?

ARCHBISHOP OF YORK　　Will you thus break your faith?

PRINCE JOHN　　I pawned° thee none.　　　　*pledged*
　　I promised you redress of these same grievances

340　Whereof you did complain; which, by mine honour,
　　I will perform with a most Christian care.
　　But for you rebels, look to taste the due
　　Meet° for rebellion and such acts as yours.　　　　*Appropriate*
　　Most shallowly did you these arms° commence,　　　　*military exploits*

345　Fondly° brought here, and foolishly sent hence.—　　　　*Foolishly*
　　Strike up our drums, pursue the scattered stray.°　　　　*stragglers*
　　God, and not we, hath safely fought today.
　　Some guard these traitors to the block of death,
　　Treason's true bed and yielder up of breath.　　　　*Exeunt*

4.2

Alarum. Excursions. Enter [Sir John] FALSTAFF *and*
COLEVILLE

FALSTAFF　　What's your name, sir, of what condition° are you,　　　　*social status*
　　and of what place, I pray?

COLEVILLE　　I am a knight, sir, and my name is Coleville of the
　　Dale.

5　FALSTAFF　　Well then, Coleville is your name, a knight is your
　　degree,° and your place the Dale. Coleville shall be still your　　　　*rank*
　　name, a traitor your degree, and the dungeon your place—a
　　place deep enough, so shall you be still Coleville of the Dale.

COLEVILLE　　Are not you Sir John Falstaff?

10　FALSTAFF　　As good a man as he, sir, whoe'er I am. Do ye yield,
　　sir, or shall I sweat for you? If I do sweat, they are the drops° of　　　　*tears*
　　thy lovers,° and they weep for thy death; therefore rouse up fear　　　　*friends*
　　and trembling, and do observance° to my mercy.　　　　*pay homage (kneel)*

COLEVILLE *[kneeling]*　　I think you are Sir John Falstaff, and in

15　that thought yield me.

FALSTAFF *[aside]*　　I have a whole school of tongues in this belly
　　of mine, and not a tongue of them all speaks any other word

4.2　Location: Scene continues.

but my name. An I had but a belly of any indifferency,° I were   *of moderate size*
simply the most active fellow in Europe. My womb,° my   *belly*
20   womb, my womb undoes me.

> *Enter* PRINCE JOHN, [*the Earl of*] WESTMORLAND, [*Sir*
> *John Blunt,*] *and* [*other lords and soldiers*]

Here comes our general.

PRINCE JOHN   The heat° is past; follow no further now.   *chase*
[*A*] *retreat* [*is sounded*]
Call in the powers, good cousin Westmorland.

> [*Exit* WESTMORLAND]

Now, Falstaff, where have you been all this while?
25   When everything is ended, then you come.
These tardy tricks of yours will, on my life,
One time or other break some gallows' back.[1]

FALSTAFF   I would be sorry, my lord, but it should be thus. I
never knew yet but rebuke and check° was the reward of valour.   *censure*
30   Do you think me a swallow, an arrow, or a bullet? Have I in
my poor and old motion the expedition° of thought? I have   *speed*
speeded hither with the very extremest° inch of possibility; I   *utmost*
have foundered° nine-score and odd posts;° and here, travel-   *made lame / horses*
tainted as I am, have in my pure and immaculate valour taken
35   Sir John Coleville of the Dale, a most furious knight and valorous enemy. But what of that? He saw me, and yielded, that I
may justly say, with the hook-nosed fellow of Rome, 'I came,
saw, and overcame.'[2]

PRINCE JOHN   It was more of his courtesy than your deserving.
40   FALSTAFF   I know not. Here he is, and here I yield him; and I
beseech your grace, let it be booked with the rest of this day's
deeds; or, by the Lord, I will have it in a particular ballad[3] else,
with mine own picture on the top on't, Coleville kissing my
foot; to the which course if I be enforced, if you do not all show
45   like gilt twopences to me,[4] and I in the clear sky of fame o'er-
shine you as much as the full moon doth the cinders of the
element,° which show like pins' heads to her, believe not the   *the stars*
word of the noble. Therefore let me have right, and let desert
mount.°   *merit be rewarded*
50   PRINCE JOHN   Thine's too heavy to mount.

FALSTAFF   Let it shine then.

PRINCE JOHN   Thine's too thick° to shine.   *opaque; dim*

FALSTAFF   Let it do something, my good lord, that may do me
good, and call it what you will.

PRINCE JOHN   Is thy name Coleville?
55   COLEVILLE   It is, my lord.

PRINCE JOHN   A famous rebel art thou, Coleville.

FALSTAFF   And a famous true subject took him.

COLEVILLE   I am, my lord, but as my betters are
That led me hither. Had they been ruled by me,
60   You should have won them dearer° than you have.   *at greater cost*

FALSTAFF   I know not how—they sold themselves, but thou
Like a kind fellow gav'st thyself away,
And I thank thee for thee.

---

1. Cause you to be hanged, which will break the gallows.
2. Referring to Julius Caesar, whose portrait and imperial exploits would be familiar to Elizabethans through
Thomas North's translation of Plutarch.

3. Ballad specifically about me. Ballads often reported
contemporary scandals and events.
4. If you do not all look like counterfeits when compared with me.

Enter [the Earl of] WESTMORLAND

PRINCE JOHN   Have you left pursuit?

WESTMORLAND   Retreat is made, and execution stayed.°   *stopped*

65 PRINCE JOHN   Send Coleville with his confederates

To York, to present° execution.   *immediate*

Blunt, lead him hence, and see you guard him sure.

Exit [Blunt,] with COLEVILLE

And now dispatch we toward the court, my lords.

I hear the King my father is sore° sick.   *severely*

70 [*To* WESTMORLAND] Our news shall go before us to his majesty,

Which, cousin, you shall bear to comfort him;

And we with sober speed will follow you.

FALSTAFF   My lord, I beseech you give me leave to go

Through Gloucestershire, and when you come to court

75 Stand,° my good lord, pray, in your good report.   *Let me stand*

PRINCE JOHN   Fare you well, Falstaff. I in my condition°   *position*

Shall better speak of you than you deserve.

Exeunt [all but FALSTAFF]

FALSTAFF   I would you had but the wit; 'twere better than your

dukedom. Good faith, this same young sober-blooded boy doth

80 not love me, nor a man cannot make him laugh. But that's no

marvel; he drinks no wine. There's never none of these demure

boys come to any proof;° for thin drink° doth so overcool their   *turn out well / beer*

blood, and making many fish meals, that they fall into a kind

of male green-sickness;[5] and then when they marry, they get

85 wenches.° They are generally fools and cowards—which some   *beget females*

of us should be too, but for inflammation.[6] A good sherry-sack°   *Spanish sherry*

hath a two-fold operation in it. It ascends me into the brain,

dries me there[7] all the foolish and dull and crudy° vapours   *coagulated*

which environ° it, makes it apprehensive,° quick, forgetive,[8]   *surround / witty*

90 full of nimble, fiery, and delectable shapes, which, delivered

o'er to the voice, the tongue, which is the birth, becomes excel-

lent wit. The second property of your excellent sherry is the

warming of the blood, which, before cold and settled,° left the   *stagnant*

liver[9] white and pale, which is the badge of pusillanimity and

95 cowardice. But the sherry warms it, and makes it course from

the inwards to the parts' extremes;° it illuminateth the face,   *extremities*

which, as a beacon, gives warning to all the rest of this little

kingdom, man, to arm; and then the vital commoners and

inland° petty spirits[1] muster me° all to their captain, the heart;   *internal / assemble*

100 who, great and puffed up with his retinue, doth any deed of

courage. And this valour comes of sherry. So that skill in the

weapon is nothing without sack, for that sets it a-work; and

learning a mere hoard of gold kept by a devil,[2] till sack com-

mences it and sets it in act and use.[3] Hereof comes it that

5. An anemic condition that affected young women in puberty and that was supposed to be cured through sexual activity. Throughout this speech, Falstaff indicts John for lacking the heat necessary for masculine valor and the begetting of male children. Diet was believed to affect the balance of the four humors, or fluids, that determined temperament and the relative "heat" of the body.
6. The passions that alcohol inflames.
7. It ascends into the brain and to my benefit dries up.
8. Inventive.
9. The supposed seat of the passions.
1. Alluding to the medical doctrine of "vital spirits," or highly refined fluids, that were supposed to suffuse the blood.
2. Referring to the popular belief that hidden treasures were guarded by evil spirits.
3. Until sack sets learning free; confers a degree upon learning (punning on "commencement" and "act," two terms used for the granting of a university degree).

105 Prince Harry is valiant; for the cold blood he did naturally
 inherit of his father he hath, like lean,° sterile, and bare land,   *barren*
 manured, husbanded,° and tilled, with excellent endeavour of   *cultivated*
 drinking good, and good store of fertile sherry that he is
 become very hot and valiant. If I had a thousand sons, the first
110 human principle I would teach them should be to forswear
 thin potations, and to addict themselves to sack.
　　　　Enter BARDOLPH
 How now, Bardolph?
 BARDOLPH　The army is dischargèd all and gone.
 FALSTAFF　Let them go. I'll through Gloucestershire, and there
115 will I visit Master Robert Shallow, Esquire. I have him already
 tempering⁴ between my finger and my thumb, and shortly will
 I seal with him.⁵ Come, away!　　　　　　　　　　　*Exeunt*

4.3

Enter KING [HENRY *in his bed,*¹ *attended by the Earl of*]
WARWICK, *Thomas Duke of* CLARENCE, *Humphrey*
[*Duke*] *of* GLOUCESTER [*and others*]
 KING HENRY　Now, lords, if God doth give successful end
 To this debate° that bleedeth at our doors,   *conflict*
 We will our youth lead on to higher fields,²
 And draw no swords but what are sanctified.
5 Our navy is addressed,° our power collected,   *prepared*
 Our substitutes in absence well invested,°   *installed in office*
 And everything lies level to° our wish;   *in accordance with*
 Only we want a little personal strength,
 And pause us till these rebels now afoot
10 Come underneath the yoke of government.
 WARWICK　Both which we doubt not but your majesty
 Shall soon enjoy.
 KING HENRY　　　　　Humphrey, my son of Gloucester,
 Where is the Prince your brother?
 GLOUCESTER　I think he's gone to hunt, my lord, at Windsor.
 KING HENRY　And how accompanied?
15 GLOUCESTER　　　　　　　　　I do not know, my lord.
 KING HENRY　Is not his brother Thomas of Clarence with him?
 GLOUCESTER　No, my good lord, he is in presence here.
 CLARENCE　What would my lord and father?
 KING HENRY　Nothing but well to thee, Thomas of Clarence.
20 How chance thou art not with the Prince thy brother?
 He loves thee, and thou dost neglect him, Thomas.
 Thou hast a better place in his affection
 Than all thy brothers. Cherish it, my boy,
 And noble offices° thou mayst effect   *duties*
25 Of mediation, after I am dead,
 Between his greatness and thy other brethren.
 Therefore omit° him not, blunt not his love,   *neglect*
 Nor lose the good advantage of his grace

---

4. Softening like warm sealing wax.
5. Mold him to my use; conclude with him.
4.3 Location: The Jerusalem Chamber, the palace at
Westminster. (This room is actually in Westminster
Abbey.)

1. Henry may enter walking or carried in a chair or, as
here, in a bed thrust out from behind the stage. The use
of a bed emphasizes the severity of his illness.
2. That is, those of Palestine, where the King proposes
to lead a crusade.

By seeming cold or careless of his will;
30   For he is gracious, if he be observed;°   shown respect
He hath a tear for pity, and a hand
Open as day for melting° charity.   compassionate
Yet notwithstanding, being incensed, he is flint,
As humorous° as winter, and as sudden   changeable
35   As flaws congealèd° in the spring° of day.   As snowflakes / dawn
His temper therefore must be well observed.
Chide him for faults, and do it reverently,
When you perceive his blood inclined to mirth;
But being moody, give him line and scope°   free range
40   Till that his passions, like a whale on ground,
Confound° themselves with working. Learn this, Thomas,   Exhaust
And thou shalt prove a shelter to thy friends,
A hoop of gold³ to bind thy brothers in,
That the united vessel of their blood,⁴
45   Mingled with venom of suggestion°—   malicious gossip
As force perforce the age will pour it in—
Shall never leak, though it do work as strong
As aconitum⁵ or rash gunpowder.
      CLARENCE   I shall observe him with all care and love.
50   KING HENRY   Why art thou not at Windsor with him, Thomas?
      CLARENCE   He is not there today; he dines in London.
      KING HENRY   And how accompanied? Canst thou tell that?
      CLARENCE   With Poins and other his continual° followers.   constant
      KING HENRY   Most subject is the fattest° soil to weeds,   richest
55   And he, the noble image of my youth,
Is overspread with them; therefore my grief
Stretches itself beyond the hour of death.
The blood weeps from my heart when I do shape
In forms imaginary th'unguided days°   days lacking a ruler
60   And rotten times that you shall look upon
When I am sleeping with my ancestors;
For when his headstrong riot hath no curb,
When rage° and hot blood are his counsellors,   passion
When means° and lavish manners meet together,   opportunity
65   O, with what wings shall his affections° fly   desires; inclinations
Towards fronting peril and opposed decay?⁶
      WARWICK   My gracious lord, you look beyond° him quite.   misjudge
The Prince but studies his companions,
Like a strange tongue,° wherein, to gain the language,   foreign language
70   'Tis needful that the most immodest word
Be looked upon and learnt, which once attained,
Your highness knows, comes to no further use
But to be known and hated; so, like gross° terms,   vulgar; common
The Prince will in the perfectness of time
75   Cast off his followers, and their memory
Shall as a pattern or a measure live
By which his grace must mete° the lives of other,°   appraise / others
Turning past evils to advantages.

3. A barrel with a golden hoop; a golden ring.   5. Monkshood, an especially virulent poison.
4. The vessel—a vial or chalice—that holds their blood.   6. Toward the peril and destruction that confront him.

KING HENRY 'Tis seldom when the bee doth leave her comb
In the dead carrion.[7]
       Enter [the Earl of] WESTMORLAND
80   Who's here? Westmorland?
WESTMORLAND   Health to my sovereign, and new happiness
Added to that that I am to deliver!
Prince John your son doth kiss your grace's hand.
Mowbray, the Bishop Scrope, Hastings, and all
85   Are brought to the correction of your law.
There is not now a rebel's sword unsheathed,
But peace puts forth her olive everywhere.
The manner how this action hath been borne
Here at more leisure may your highness read,
90   With every course° in his° particular.   *stage in the action / its*
       [He gives the KING *papers]*
KING HENRY   O Westmorland, thou art a summer bird
Which ever in the haunch° of winter sings   *hind part*
The lifting up of day.°   *dawn*
       Enter HARCOURT
                Look, here's more news.
HARCOURT   From enemies heaven keep your majesty;
95   And when they stand against you, may they fall
As those that I am come to tell you of!
The Earl Northumberland and the Lord Bardolph,
With a great power of English and of Scots,
Are by the sheriff of Yorkshire overthrown.
100   The manner and true order of the fight
This packet, please it you, contains at large.
       [He gives the KING *papers]*
KING HENRY   And wherefore should these good news make me sick?
Will fortune never come with both hands full,
But write her fair words still in foulest letters?
105   She either gives a stomach° and no food—   *an appetite*
Such are the poor in health—or else a feast,
And takes away the stomach—such are the rich,
That have abundance and enjoy it not.
I should rejoice now at this happy news,
110   And now my sight fails, and my brain is giddy.
O me! Come near me now; I am much ill.
       [He swoons]
GLOUCESTER   Comfort, your majesty!
CLARENCE   O my royal father!
WESTMORLAND   My sovereign lord, cheer up yourself, look up.°   *take courage*
WARWICK   Be patient, princes; you do know these fits
115   Are with his highness very ordinary.
Stand from him, give him air; he'll straight be well.
CLARENCE   No, no, he cannot long hold out° these pangs.   *endure*
Th'incessant care and labour of his mind
Hath wrought the mure° that should confine it in   *made the wall*
120   So thin that life looks through and will break out.
GLOUCESTER   The people fear° me, for they do observe   *frighten*

---

7. *'Tis . . . carrion:* It is rare that the bee who has placed her honeycomb in a carcass abandons it. (So the new King will be unlikely to abandon his old pleasures.)

Unfathered heirs and loathly births of nature.[8]
The seasons change their manners, as° the year   *as if*
Had found some months asleep and leaped them over.
125   CLARENCE   The river° hath thrice flowed, no ebb between,   *(the Thames)*
And the old folk, time's doting chronicles,
Say it did so a little time before
That our great grandsire Edward° sicked and died.   *(Edward III)*
WARWICK   Speak lower, princes, for the King recovers.
130   GLOUCESTER   This apoplexy will certain be his end.
KING HENRY   I pray you take me up and bear me hence
Into some other chamber; softly, pray.
          [*The* KING *is carried over the stage in his bed*]
Let there be no noise made, my gentle friends,
Unless some dull° and favourable hand   *restful*
135   Will whisper music to my weary spirit.
WARWICK   Call for the music in the other room.
               [*Exit one or more. Still° music within*]   *Soft*
KING HENRY   Set me the crown upon my pillow here.
          [CLARENCE *takes the crown from the King's head, and*
          sets it on his pillow][9]
CLARENCE   His eye is hollow, and he changes° much.   *(in complexion)*
          [*A noise within*]
WARWICK   Less noise, less noise!
          Enter PRINCE HARRY
PRINCE HARRY   Who saw the Duke of Clarence?
140   CLARENCE   I am here, brother, full of heaviness.°   *sadness*
PRINCE HARRY   How now, rain within doors, and none abroad?
How doth the King?
GLOUCESTER   Exceeding ill.
PRINCE HARRY   Heard he the good news yet? Tell it him.
GLOUCESTER   He altered much upon the hearing it.
145   PRINCE HARRY   If he be sick with joy, he'll recover without physic.
WARWICK   Not so much noise, my lords! Sweet prince, speak low.
The King your father is disposed to sleep.
CLARENCE   Let us withdraw into the other room.
WARWICK   Will't please your grace to go along with us?
150   PRINCE HARRY   No, I will sit and watch here by the King.
               [*Exeunt all but the* KING *and* PRINCE HARRY]
Why doth the crown lie there upon his pillow,
Being so troublesome a bedfellow?
O polished perturbation,° golden care,   *source of unease*
That keep'st the ports° of slumber open wide   *gates (the eyes)*
155   To many a watchful° night!—Sleep with it° now;   *wakeful / (the crown)*
Yet not so sound, and half so deeply sweet,
As he whose brow with homely biggen° bound   *nightcap*
Snores out the watch of night.[1] O majesty,
When thou dost pinch thy bearer, thou dost sit
160   Like a rich armour worn in heat of day,
That scald'st with safety.—By his gates of breath°   *his lips*
There lies a downy feather which stirs not.
Did he suspire,° that light and weightless down   *If he breathed*

---

8. Children supernaturally begotten and malformed   1. Nighttime. "Watch" alludes to the periods of sentry
offspring resulting from normal conception.   duty into which the night was divided.
9. It is unclear who removes the crown: the weakened
King or his son Clarence, who is the next to speak.

Perforce must move.—My gracious lord, my father!—
165 This sleep is sound indeed. This is a sleep
That from this golden rigol° hath divorced   *ring*
So many English kings.—Thy due from me
Is tears and heavy sorrows of the blood,
Which nature, love, and filial tenderness
170 Shall, O dear father, pay thee plenteously.
My due from thee is this imperial crown,
Which, as immediate from° thy place and blood,   *as next in line to*
Derives itself° to me.   *Descends*
         [*He puts the crown on his head*]
                                   Lo where it sits,
Which God shall guard; and put the world's whole strength
175 Into one giant arm, it shall not force
This lineal° honour from me. This from thee   *hereditary*
Will I to mine leave, as 'tis left to me.   *Exit*
         [*Music ceases. The* KING *awakes*]
KING HENRY   Warwick, Gloucester, Clarence!
         Enter [*the Earl of*] WARWICK, [*and the Dukes of*]
         GLOUCESTER [*and*] CLARENCE
CLARENCE   Doth the King call?
WARWICK   What would your majesty? How fares your grace?
180 KING HENRY   Why did you leave me here alone, my lords?
CLARENCE   We left the Prince my brother here, my liege,
Who undertook to sit and watch by you.
KING HENRY   The Prince of Wales? Where is he? Let me see him.
WARWICK   This door is open; he is gone this way.
185 GLOUCESTER   He came not through the chamber where we stayed.
KING HENRY   Where is the crown? Who took it from my pillow?
WARWICK   When we withdrew, my liege, we left it here.
KING HENRY   The Prince hath ta'en it hence. Go seek him out.
Is he so hasty that he doth suppose
190 My sleep my death?
Find him, my lord of Warwick; chide him hither.   [*Exit* WARWICK]
This part° of his conjoins° with my disease,   *act / unites*
And helps to end me. See, sons, what things you are,
How quickly nature falls into revolt
195 When gold becomes her object!
For this the foolish over-careful fathers
Have broke their sleep with thoughts, their brains with care,
Their bones with industry; for this they have
Engrossèd° and piled up the cankered° heaps   *Gathered / diseased*
200 Of strange-achievèd gold;[2] for this they have
Been thoughtful° to invest their sons with arts   *careful*
And martial exercises; when, like the bee
Culling from every flower the virtuous sweets,
Our thighs packed with wax, our mouths with honey,
205 We bring it to the hive; and, like the bees,
Are murdered for our pains. This bitter taste
Yields his engrossments to the ending father.[3]
         Enter [*the Earl of*] WARWICK

2. Gold gained in foreign lands or by unnatural or
unusual means.

3. *This . . . father:* This bitter taste is all the dying
father's amassing of wealth amounts to.

Now where is he that will not stay so long
Till his friend sickness have determined° me?   *put an end to*

210 WARWICK   My lord, I found the Prince in the next room,
Washing with kindly° tears his gentle° cheeks   *filial / noble*
With such a deep demeanour,° in great sorrow,   *sad countenance*
That tyranny, which never quaffed° but blood,   *drank*
Would, by beholding him, have washed his knife

215 With gentle eye-drops.° He is coming hither.   *tears*
KING HENRY   But wherefore did he take away the crown?

            Enter PRINCE HARRY [*with the crown*]

Lo where he comes.—Come hither to me, Harry.
[*To the others*] Depart the chamber; leave us here alone.

           Exeunt [*all but the* KING *and* PRINCE HARRY]

PRINCE HARRY   I never thought to hear you speak again.

220 KING HENRY   Thy wish was father, Harry, to that thought.
I stay too long by thee, I weary thee.
Dost thou so hunger for mine empty chair
That thou wilt needs invest thee with my honours
Before thy hour be ripe? O foolish youth,

225 Thou seek'st the greatness that will overwhelm thee!
Stay but a little, for my cloud of dignity°   *fragile greatness*
Is held from falling with so weak a wind°   *(his breath)*
That it will quickly drop. My day is dim.
Thou hast stol'n that which after some few hours

230 Were thine without offence, and at my death
Thou hast sealed up° my expectation.   *confirmed*
Thy life did manifest thou loved'st me not,
And thou wilt have me die assured of it.
Thou hid'st a thousand daggers in thy thoughts,

235 Whom° thou hast whetted on thy stony heart   *Which*
To stab at half an hour of my life.
What, canst thou not forbear me° half an hour?   *grant me but*
Then get thee gone and dig my grave thyself,
And bid the merry bells ring to thine ear

240 That thou art crownèd, not that I am dead.
Let all the tears that should bedew my hearse°   *coffin*
Be drops of balm[4] to sanctify thy head.
Only compound° me with forgotten dust.   *mix*
Give that which gave thee life unto the worms.

245 Pluck down my officers, break my decrees;
For now a time is come to mock at form°—   *decorum*
Harry the Fifth is crowned. Up, vanity!
Down, royal state!° All you sage counsellors, hence!   *ceremony*
And to the English court assemble now

250 From every region, apes° of idleness!   *fools*
Now, neighbour confines,° purge you of your scum!   *bordering regions*
Have you a ruffian that will swear, drink, dance,
Revel the night, rob, murder, and commit
The oldest sins the newest kind of ways?

255 Be happy; he will trouble you no more.
England shall double gild° his treble guilt,   *paint over*
England shall give him office, honour, might;

---

4. The consecrated oils with which new monarchs were anointed during their coronation.

For the fifth Harry from curbed licence⁵ plucks
The muzzle of restraint, and the wild dog

260 Shall flesh his tooth on° every innocent.　　　　　　*taste the flesh of*
O my poor kingdom, sick with civil blows!°　　　　　　*domestic conflicts*
When that my care could not withhold° thy riots,°　　　*control / strife*
What wilt thou do when riot is thy care?⁶
O, thou wilt be a wilderness again,

265 Peopled with wolves, thy old inhabitants.
PRINCE HARRY　O pardon me, my liege! But for my tears,
The moist impediments unto my speech,
I had forestalled this dear° and deep rebuke　　　　　　*grievous*
Ere you with grief had spoke and I had heard

270 The course of it so far. There is your crown;
　　　[*He returns the crown and kneels*]
And He° that wears the crown immortally　　　　　　　*(God)*
Long guard it yours! If I affect° it more　　　　　　　*desire*
Than as your honour and as your renown,
Let me no more from this obedience rise,

275 Which my most true and inward duteous spirit
Teacheth this prostrate and exterior° bending.　　　　*outward*
God witness with me, when I here came in
And found no course of breath within your majesty,
How cold it struck my heart. If I do feign,

280 O, let me in my present wildness° die,　　　　　　　*sinfulness*
And never live to show th'incredulous world
The noble change that I have purposèd.°　　　　　　　*intended*
Coming to look on you, thinking you dead,
And dead almost, my liege, to think you were,

285 I spake unto this crown as having sense,°　　　　　　*as if it had senses*
And thus upbraided it: 'The care on thee depending
Hath fed upon the body of my father;
Therefore thou best of gold art worst of gold.
Other, less fine in carat, is more precious,

290 Preserving life in medicine potable;³
But thou, most fine, most honoured, most renowned,
Hast eat thy bearer up.' Thus, my royal liege,
Accusing it, I put it on my head,
To try° with it, as with an enemy　　　　　　　　　　*struggle*

295 That had before my face murdered my father,
The quarrel of a true inheritor.°　　　　　　　　　　*legitimate heir*
But if it did infect my blood with joy
Or swell my thoughts to any strain of pride,
If any rebel or vain spirit of mine

300 Did with the least affection of° a welcome　　　　　　*inclination toward*
Give entertainment to the might of it,
Let God for ever keep it from my head,
And make me as the poorest vassal is,
That doth with awe and terror kneel to it.

305 KING HENRY　O my son,
God put it in thy mind to take it hence,

---

5. *Licence*: excessive freedom. The image is of a wild
dog that has been curbed, kept under restraint, until his
muzzle is removed and chaos ensues.
6. When debauchery (in the person of Hal) is your
caretaker; when strife becomes your concern (rather

than mine after my death).
7. The trouble that comes along with the crown.
8. Gold in a drinkable solution ("potable") was widely
considered healthful.

That thou mightst win the more thy father's love,
Pleading so wisely in excuse of it!
Come hither, Harry; sit thou by my bed,
310 And hear, I think, the very latest° counsel   last
That ever I shall breathe.
        [PRINCE HARRY *rises from kneeling and sits by the bed*]
                              God knows, my son,
By what bypaths and indirect crook'd ways
I met this crown; and I myself know well
How troublesome it sat upon my head.
315 To thee it shall descend with better quiet,
Better opinion,° better confirmation;   public support
For all the soil° of the achievement goes   stain
With me into the earth. It seemed in me
But as an honour snatched with boist'rous hand;
320 And I had many living to upbraid
My gain of it by their assistances,⁹
Which daily grew to quarrel and to bloodshed,
Wounding supposèd peace. All these bold fears°   fearful acts
Thou seest with peril I have answerèd;
325 For all my reign hath been but as a scene
Acting that argument.° And now my death   theme
Changes the mood, for what in me was purchased¹
Falls upon thee in a more fairer sort,
So thou the garland wear'st successively.²
330 Yet though thou stand'st more sure than I could do,
Thou art not firm enough, since griefs are green,°   grievances are fresh
And all thy friends—which thou must make thy friends—
Have but their stings and teeth newly ta'en out,
By whose fell° working I was first advanced,   cruel
335 And by whose power I well might lodge a fear
To be again displaced; which to avoid
I cut them off, and had a purpose now
To lead out many to the Holy Land,
Lest rest and lying still might make them look°   examine
340 Too near° unto my state. Therefore, my Harry,   Too closely
Be it thy course to busy giddy° minds   restless
With foreign quarrels, that action° hence borne out   military exploits
May waste° the memory of the former days.   obliterate
More would I, but my lungs are wasted so
345 That strength of speech is utterly denied me.
How I came by the crown, O God forgive,
And grant it may with thee in true peace live!
PRINCE HARRY   My gracious liege,
You won it, wore it, kept it, gave it me;
350 Then plain and right must my possession be,
Which I with more than with a common pain°   effort
'Gainst all the world will rightfully maintain.
        Enter [PRINCE] JOHN *of Lancaster* [*followed by the Earl
        of*] WARWICK [*and others*]
KING HENRY   Look, look, here comes my John of Lancaster.

---

9. *And . . . assistances:* And many were living who made   1. Was acquired by acts, not by inheritance.
demands on me and reproved me on the strength of the   2. So that you wear the sign of victory (the crown) by
fact that they had helped me to seize the throne.   right of succession.

PRINCE JOHN   Health, peace, and happiness to my royal father!

355 KING HENRY   Thou bring'st me happiness and peace, son John;
But health, alack, with youthful wings is flown
From this bare withered trunk. Upon thy sight
My worldly business makes a period °   *an end*
Where is my lord of Warwick?

PRINCE HARRY   My lord of Warwick!
[WARWICK *comes forward to the* KING]

360 KING HENRY   Doth any name particular belong
Unto the lodging° where I first did swoon?   *room*

WARWICK   'Tis called Jerusalem, my noble lord.

KING HENRY   Laud be to God! Even there my life must end.
It hath been prophesied to me many years

365 I should not die but in Jerusalem,
Which vainly I supposed the Holy Land;
But bear me to that chamber; there I'll lie;
In that Jerusalem shall Harry die.

                                Exeunt [*bearing the* KING *in his bed*]

5.1

Enter SHALLOW, SILENCE,[1] [*Sir John*] FALSTAFF, BAR-
DOLPH, *and* [*the*] PAGE

SHALLOW [*to* FALSTAFF]   By cock and pie,[2] you shall not away
tonight.—What, Davy, I say!

FALSTAFF   You must excuse me, Master Robert Shallow.

SHALLOW   I will not excuse you; you shall not be excused;
5   excuses shall not be admitted; there is no excuse shall serve;
you shall not be excused.—Why, Davy!
[*Enter* DAVY]

DAVY   Here, sir.

SHALLOW   Davy, Davy, Davy; let me see, Davy; let me see.
William Cook—bid him come hither.—Sir John, you shall not
10   be excused.

DAVY   Marry, sir, thus: those precepts° cannot be served. And   *warrants*
again,° sir: shall we sow the headland[3] with wheat?   *Moreover*

SHALLOW   With red wheat, Davy. But for William Cook; are there
no young pigeons?

15 DAVY   Yes, sir. Here is now the smith's note° for shoeing and   *bill*
plough-irons.

SHALLOW   Let it be cast° and paid. Sir John, you shall not be   *calculated*
excused.

DAVY   Sir, a new link° to the bucket must needs be had; and, sir,   *chain*
20   do you mean to stop any of William's wages, about the sack he
lost at Hinkley[4] Fair?

SHALLOW   A° shall answer° it. Some pigeons, Davy, a couple of   *He / pay for*
short-legged hens, a joint of mutton, and any pretty little tiny
kickshaws,° tell William Cook.   *fancy dishes*

25 DAVY   Doth the man of war stay all night, sir?

SHALLOW   Yea, Davy. I will use him well; a friend i'th' court is

---

5.1 Location: Shallow's house in Gloucestershire.
1. F includes Silence in this scene; Q does not. If present, he lives up to his name, getting no lines.
2. A mild oath. "Cock" was a euphemism for "God,"
and "pie" was a colloquial word for the collection of

rules by which the pre-Reformation Church ordered
the Church calendar
3. Unplowed strip of land between two plowed fields.
4. A market town near Coventry.

better than a penny in purse. Use his men well, Davy, for they
are arrant knaves, and will backbite.°   *slander*
DAVY   No worse than they are back-bitten,° sir, for they have mar-   *(by fleas)*
30   vellous° foul linen.   *amazingly*
SHALLOW   Well conceited,° Davy. About thy business, Davy.   *quipped*
DAVY   I beseech you, sir, to countenance° William Visor of   *favor*
Wo'ncot against Clement Perks o'th' Hill.[5]
SHALLOW   There is many complaints, Davy, against that Visor.
35   That Visor is an arrant knave, on my knowledge.
DAVY   I grant your worship that he is a knave, sir; but yet God
forbid, sir, but a knave should have some countenance at his
friend's request. An honest man, sir, is able to speak for himself,
when a knave is not. I have served your worship truly, sir, this
40   eight years. An I cannot once or twice in a quarter bear out° a   *support*
knave against an honest man, I have little credit with your wor-
ship. The knave is mine honest friend, sir; therefore I beseech
you let him be countenanced.
SHALLOW   Go to; I say he shall have no wrong. Look about,
45   Davy.   [*Exit* DAVY]
Where are you, Sir John? Come, off with your boots.— Give
me your hand, Master Bardolph.
BARDOLPH   I am glad to see your worship.
SHALLOW   I thank thee with all my heart, kind Master Bardolph.
50   [*To the* PAGE] And welcome, my tall° fellow.—Come, Sir John.   *valiant*
FALSTAFF   I'll follow you, good Master Robert Shallow.
                                          [*Exit* SHALLOW *with* SILENCE]
Bardolph, look to our horses.   [*Exit* BARDOLPH *with the* PAGE]
If I were sawed into quantities,° I should make four dozen of   *pieces*
such bearded hermits' staves as Master Shallow. It is a wonder-
55   ful thing to see the semblable coherence° of his men's spirits   *close correspondence*
and his. They, by observing him, do bear themselves like
foolish justices; he, by conversing° with them, is turned into a   *associating*
justice-like servingman. Their spirits are so married in con-
junction, with the participation of society,° that they flock   *by close association*
60   together in consent like so many wild geese. If I had a suit to
Master Shallow, I would humour his men with the imputation
of being near their master; if to his men, I would curry° with   *employ flattery*
Master Shallow that no man could better command his ser-
vants. It is certain that either wise bearing or ignorant carriage° *demeanor*
65   is caught as men take° diseases, one of another; therefore let   *catch*
men take heed of their company. I will devise matter enough
out of this Shallow to keep Prince Harry in continual laughter
the wearing out of six fashions—which is four terms,[6] or two
actions°—and a shall laugh without intervallums.[7] O, it is   *lawsuits*
70   much that a lie with a slight oath, and a jest with a sad° brow,   *serious*
will do with a fellow that never had the ache in his shoulders![8]
O, you shall see him laugh till his face be like a wet cloak ill
laid up![9]
SHALLOW [*within*]   Sir John!
75   FALSTAFF   I come, Master Shallow; I come, Master Shallow.
                                                                Exit

5. Possibly Stinchcombe Hill, not far from "Wo'ncot"
(the local pronunciation of Woodmancot in Gloucestershire).
6. Alluding to the four divisions of the judicial year.
7. Time between terms.
8. With someone who has not experienced old age or
troubles.
9. *ill laid up:* carelessly put away (so that it is wrinkled).

5.2

Enter the Earl of WARWICK [*at one door*], *and the* LORD
CHIEF JUSTICE [*at another door*]

WARWICK   How now, my Lord Chief Justice, whither away?
LORD CHIEF JUSTICE   How doth the King?
WARWICK   Exceeding well: his cares are now all ended.
LORD CHIEF JUSTICE   I hope not dead.
WARWICK   He's walked the way of nature,
5   And to our purposes he lives no more.
LORD CHIEF JUSTICE   I would his majesty had called me with him.
    The service that I truly did his life
    Hath left me open to all injuries.
WARWICK   Indeed I think the young King loves you not.
10   LORD CHIEF JUSTICE   I know he doth not, and do arm myself
    To welcome the condition° of the time,   *(new) circumstances*
    Which cannot look more hideously upon me
    Than I have drawn it in my fantasy.

Enter [PRINCE] JOHN *of Lancaster*, [*and the Dukes of*]
CLARENCE *and* GLOUCESTER

WARWICK   Here come the heavy issue° of dead Harry.   *sad offspring*
15   O, that the living Harry had the temper
    Of he the worst of these three gentlemen!
    How many nobles then should hold their places,
    That must strike sail° to spirits of vile sort!°   *submit / low rank*
LORD CHIEF JUSTICE   O God, I fear all will be overturned.
20   PRINCE JOHN   Good morrow, cousin Warwick, good morrow.
GLOUCESTER *and* CLARENCE   Good morrow, cousin.
PRINCE JOHN   We meet like men that had forgot to speak.
WARWICK   We do remember, but our argument°   *subject matter*
    Is all too heavy to admit much talk.
25   PRINCE JOHN   Well, peace be with him that hath made us heavy!
LORD CHIEF JUSTICE   Peace be with us, lest we be heavier!
GLOUCESTER   O good my lord, you have lost a friend indeed;
    And I dare swear you borrow not that face
    Of seeming sorrow—it is sure your own.
PRINCE JOHN [*to* LORD CHIEF JUSTICE]   Though no man be
30   assured what grace to find,°   *favor he will find*
    You stand in coldest expectation.
    I am the sorrier; would 'twere otherwise.
CLARENCE [*to* LORD CHIEF JUSTICE]   Well, you must now speak
        Sir John Falstaff fair,
    Which swims against your stream of quality.°   *character; rank*
35   LORD CHIEF JUSTICE   Sweet princes, what I did I did in honour,
    Led by th'impartial conduct of my soul;
    And never shall you see that I will beg
    A raggèd° and forestalled remission.[1]   *base*
    If truth and upright innocency fail me,
40   I'll to the King my master, that is dead,
    And tell him who hath sent me after him.

Enter PRINCE HARRY [*as King*]

WARWICK   Here comes the Prince.
LORD CHIEF JUSTICE   Good morrow, and God save your majesty!

5.2 Location: The palace at Westminster.
1. Either a pardon sure to be denied or a pardon secured in advance (by an act of submission).

PRINCE HARRY   This new and gorgeous garment, majesty,
45 Sits not so easy on me as you think.
 Brothers, you mix your sadness with some fear.
 This is the English not the Turkish court;
 Not Amurath an Amurath succeeds,[2]
 But Harry Harry. Yet be sad, good brothers,
50 For, by my faith, it very well becomes you.
 Sorrow so royally in you appears
 That I will deeply° put the fashion on,   *solemnly*
 And wear it in my heart. Why then, be sad;
 But entertain no more of it, good brothers,
55 Than a joint burden laid upon us all.
 For me, by heaven, I bid you be assured
 I'll be your father and your brother too.
 Let me but bear° your love, I'll bear your cares.   *have; carry*
 Yet weep that Harry's dead, and so will I;
60 But Harry lives that shall convert those tears
 By number° into hours of happiness.   *One by one*
PRINCE JOHN, GLOUCESTER, *and* CLARENCE   We hope no other
   from your majesty.
PRINCE HARRY   You all look strangely on me, [*to* LORD CHIEF
   JUSTICE] and you most.
 You are, I think, assured I love you not.
65 LORD CHIEF JUSTICE   I am assured, if I be measured rightly,
 Your majesty hath no just cause to hate me.
PRINCE HARRY   No? How might a prince of my great hopes forget
 So great indignities you laid upon me?
 What—rate,° rebuke, and roughly send to prison   *chide*
70 Th'immediate heir of England? Was this easy?
 May this be washed in Lethe[3] and forgotten?
LORD CHIEF JUSTICE   I then did use the person° of your father. *act as a deputy*
 The image of his power lay then in me;
 And in th'administration of his law,
75 Whiles I was busy for the commonwealth,
 Your highness pleasèd to forget my place,°   *rank; position*
 The majesty and power of law and justice,
 The image of the King whom I presented,
 And struck me in my very seat of judgement;
80 Whereon, as° an offender to your father,   *as you were*
 I gave bold way to my authority
 And did commit° you. If the deed were ill,   *imprison*
 Be you contented, wearing now the garland,°   *crown*
 To have a son set your decrees at naught—
85 To pluck down justice from your awe-full° bench,   *awe-inspiring*
 To trip the course of law, and blunt the sword
 That guards the peace and safety of your person,
 Nay, more, to spurn at your most royal image,
 And mock your workings in a second body?°   *representative*
90 Question your royal thoughts, make the case yours,
 Be now the father, and propose° a son;   *imagine*
 Hear your own dignity so much profaned,

---

2. An English name for the Turkish Sultan Murad III,   early modern England.
who had his brothers executed upon his succession in   3. The river in Hades that induced forgetfulness.
1574. Turks were bywords for cruelty and tyranny in

See your most dreadful laws so loosely slighted,
Behold yourself so by a son disdained;
95   And then imagine me taking your part,
And in your power soft° silencing your son.   *gently*
After this cold considerance, sentence me;
And, as you are a king, speak in your state°   *role as monarch*
What I have done that misbecame my place,
100   My person, or my liege's sovereignty.
PRINCE HARRY   You are right Justice,° and you weigh this well.   *perfect justice*
Therefore still bear the balance and the sword;⁴
And I do wish your honours may increase
Till you do live to see a son of mine
105   Offend you and obey you as I did.
So shall I live to speak my father's words:
'Happy am I that have a man so bold
That dares do justice on my proper° son,   *own*
And not less happy having such a son
110   That would deliver up his greatness so
Into the hands of justice.' You did commit° me,   *imprison*
For which I do commit° into your hand   *place*
Th'unstainèd sword that you have used° to bear,   *were accustomed*
With this remembrance:° that you use the same   *reminder*
115   With the like bold, just, and impartial spirit
As you have done 'gainst me. There is my hand.
You shall be as a father to my youth;
My voice shall sound° as you do prompt mine ear,   *speak*
And I will stoop and humble my intents
120   To your well-practised wise directions.—
And princes all, believe me, I beseech you,
My father is gone wild into his grave,
For in his tomb lie my affections;°   *wild passions*
And with his spirits sadly I survive
125   To mock° the expectation of the world,   *defy*
To frustrate prophecies, and to raze out
Rotten opinion, who hath writ me down
After my seeming.⁵ The tide of blood° in me   *of passion*
Hath proudly flowed in vanity till now.
130   Now doth it turn, and ebb back to the sea,
Where it shall mingle with the state of floods,°   *the majesty of the sea*
And flow henceforth in formal majesty.
Now call we our high court of Parliament,
And let us choose such limbs° of noble counsel   *members*
135   That the great body of our state may go
In equal rank with the best-governed nation;
That war, or peace, or both at once, may be
As things acquainted and familiar to us;
[*to* LORD CHIEF JUSTICE] In which you, father, shall have foremost hand.
140   [*To all*] Our coronation done, we will accite,°   *summon*
As I before remembered, all our state;°   *nobility*
And, God consigning to° my good intents,   *endorsing*
No prince nor peer shall have just cause to say,
'God shorten Harry's happy life one day.'   *Exeunt*

---

4. The traditional emblems of justice.   5. According to my (false) appearance.

5.3

[*A table and chairs set forth.*] *Enter Sir John* FALSTAFF,
SHALLOW, SILENCE, DAVY [*with vessels for the table*],
BARDOLPH, *and* [*the*] PAGE

SHALLOW [*to* FALSTAFF] Nay, you shall see my orchard, where,
in an arbour, we will eat a last year's pippin¹ of mine own
grafting, with a dish of caraways,² and so forth—come, cousin
Silence—and then to bed.

5 FALSTAFF Fore God, you have here a goodly dwelling and a rich.

SHALLOW Barren, barren, barren; beggars all, beggars all, Sir
John. Marry, good air.—Spread, Davy; spread, Davy.

[DAVY *begins to spread the table*]

Well said,° Davy.   *done*

FALSTAFF This Davy serves you for good uses; he is your serving-
10 man and your husband.°   *steward*

SHALLOW A good varlet,° a good varlet, a very good varlet, Sir   *servant*
John.—By the mass, I have drunk too much sack at supper.—A
good varlet. Now sit down, now sit down. [*To* SILENCE] Come,
cousin.

15 SILENCE Ah, sirrah, quoth-a,° we shall   *said he*

[*sings*] Do nothing but eat and make good cheer,
And praise God for the merry year,
When flesh is cheap and females dear,
And lusty lads roam here and there
20 So merrily,
And ever among so merrily.

FALSTAFF There's a merry heart, good Master Silence! I'll give
you a health° for that anon.   *drink a toast to you*

SHALLOW Good Master Bardolph!—Some wine, Davy.

25 DAVY [*to* FALSTAFF] Sweet sir, sit. [*To* BARDOLPH] I'll be with you
anon. [*To* FALSTAFF] Most sweet sir, sit. Master page, good master page, sit.

[*All but* DAVY *sit.* DAVY *pours wine*]

Proface!³ What you want° in meat, we'll have in drink; but you   *lack*
must bear;° the heart's all.   *be forbearing*

30 SHALLOW Be merry, Master Bardolph and my little soldier there,
be merry.

SILENCE [*sings*] Be merry, be merry, my wife has all,
For women are shrews, both short and tall,
'Tis merry in hall when beards wags all,
35 And welcome merry shrovetide.⁴

Be merry, be merry.

FALSTAFF I did not think Master Silence had been a man of this
mettle.°   *boldness*

SILENCE Who, I? I have been merry twice and once ere now.

Enter DAVY [*with a dish of apples*]

40 DAVY There's a dish of leather-coats° for you.   *russet apples*

SHALLOW Davy!

DAVY Your worship! I'll be with you straight. [*To* FALSTAFF] A
cup of wine, sir?

5.3 Location: Shallow's garden in Gloucestershire.
1. A kind of apple traditionally kept for a year before
eating.
2. Caraway seeds or sweet biscuits containing these
seeds, often eaten with apples.

3. A greeting used as a welcome to a meal, from an Italian phrase meaning "May it do you good."
4. The season of festivities preceding the Christian
penitential season, Lent.

SILENCE [*sings*]   A cup of wine
45   That's brisk and fine,
                               And drink unto thee, leman° mine,   *sweetheart*
                               And a merry heart lives long-a.
FALSTAFF   Well said, Master Silence.
SILENCE   And we shall be merry; now comes in the sweet o'th'
50   night.
FALSTAFF   Health and long life to you, Master Silence!
        [*He drinks*]
SILENCE   Fill the cup and let it come. I'll pledge you a mile to
        th' bottom.[5]
SHALLOW   Honest Bardolph, welcome! If thou want'st anything
55   and wilt not call, beshrew thy heart! [*To the* PAGE] Welcome,
        my little tiny thief, and welcome indeed, too!—I'll drink to
        Master Bardolph, and to all the cavalieros° about London.   *fine fellows*
        [*He drinks*]
DAVY   I hope to see London once ere I die.
BARDOLPH   An I might see you there, Davy!
60 SHALLOW   By the mass, you'll crack° a quart together, ha, will   *drink*
        you not, Master Bardolph?
BARDOLPH   Yea, sir, in a pottle-pot.°   *two-quart glass*
SHALLOW   By God's liggens,[6] I thank thee. The knave will stick
        by thee, I can assure thee that; a will not out;° 'tis true-bred.   *drop out*
65 BARDOLPH   And I'll stick by him, sir.
SHALLOW   Why, there spoke a king! Lack nothing, be merry!
                One knocks at [*the*] *door* [*within*]
        Look who's at door there, ho! Who knocks?   [*Exit* DAVY]
        [SILENCE *drinks*]
FALSTAFF [*to* SILENCE]   Why, now you have done me right![7]
SILENCE [*sings*]   Do me right,
70   And dub me knight—
                               Samingo.[8]
        Is't not so?
FALSTAFF   'Tis so.
SILENCE   Is't so?—Why then, say an old man can do somewhat.
        [*Enter* DAVY]
75 DAVY   An't please your worship, there's one Pistol come from the
        court with news.
FALSTAFF   From the court? Let him come in.
                Enter PISTOL
        How now, Pistol?
PISTOL   Sir John, God save you.
80 FALSTAFF   What wind blew you hither, Pistol?
PISTOL   Not the ill wind which blows no man to good.
        Sweet knight, thou art now one of the greatest men in this
        realm.
SILENCE   By'r Lady, I think a be—but goodman° Puff of Barson.[9]   *except for yeoman*
85 PISTOL   Puff?
        Puff in thy teeth, most recreant coward base!—

5. I'll drink to the bottom of the cup, even if it were a
mile.
6. An obscure oath, possibly derived from "by God's
(eye)lid."
7. Done me justice (by drinking well).
8. Translated lines from a French drinking song,

"Monsieur Mingo." "Sa" may be a mispronunciation of
"Sir." "Mingo" means "I urinate."
9. Referring either to Barcheston, a town 10 miles
south of Stratford, or Barston, a town between Coventry and Solihull.

Sir John, I am thy Pistol and thy friend,
And helter-skelter have I rode to thee,
And tidings do I bring, and lucky joys,
90   And golden times, and happy news of price.
FALSTAFF   I pray thee now, deliver them like a man of this world.
PISTOL   A foutre° for the world and worldlings base!   fig
I speak of Africa and golden joys.
FALSTAFF   O base Assyrian knight,[1] what is thy news?
95   Let King Cophetua[2] know the truth thereof.
SILENCE [singing]   'And Robin Hood, Scarlet, and John.'[3]
PISTOL   Shall dunghill curs confront the Helicons?[4]
And shall good news be baffled?°   disgraced
Then Pistol lay thy head in Furies'[5] lap.
100   SHALLOW   Honest gentleman, I know not your breeding.
PISTOL   Why then, lament therefor.
SHALLOW   Give me pardon, sir. If, sir, you come with news from
the court, I take it there's but two ways: either to utter them, or
conceal them. I am, sir, under the King in some authority.
105   PISTOL   Under which king, besonian?° Speak, or die.   beggarly fellow
SHALLOW   Under King Harry.
PISTOL   Harry the Fourth, or Fifth?
SHALLOW   Harry the Fourth.
PISTOL   A foutre for thine office!
Sir John, thy tender lambkin now is king.
Harry the Fifth's the man. I speak the truth.
110   When Pistol lies, do this, [making the fig][6] and fig me,
Like the bragging Spaniard.
FALSTAFF   What, is the old King dead?
PISTOL   As nail in door. The things I speak are just.°   true
FALSTAFF   Away, Bardolph, saddle my horse! Master Robert
Shallow, choose what office thou wilt in the land; 'tis thine.
115   Pistol, I will double-charge thee[7] with dignities.
BARDOLPH   O joyful day!
I would not take a knighthood for my fortune.
PISTOL   What, I do bring good news?
FALSTAFF [to DAVY]   Carry Master Silence to bed.
                             [Exit DAVY with SILENCE]
120   Master Shallow—my lord Shallow—be what thou wilt, I am
fortune's steward—get on thy boots; we'll ride all night.—O
sweet Pistol!—Away, Bardolph!   [Exit BARDOLPH]
Come, Pistol, utter more to me, and withal° devise something   at the same time
to do thyself good. Boot, boot, Master Shallow! I know the
125   young King is sick for me. Let us take any man's horses—the
laws of England are at my commandment. Blessed are they
that have been my friends, and woe to my Lord Chief Justice.
PISTOL   Let vultures vile seize on his lungs also!

---

1. Adopting Pistol's elevated rhetorical style, Falstaff calls him a knight of Assyria, an Asian empire that the Elizabethans associated with pillage and robbery.
2. Alluding to the African King who marries a beggar in the popular ballad "A Beggar and a King."
3. A line from the ballad "Robin Hood and the Jolly Pinder of Wakesfield."
4. That is, "the true Muses." Pistol conflates the Muses of classical mythology with Mt. Helicon, part of the Parnassus mountain range on which they dwelt.
5. Then let Pistol appeal to the goddesses of revenge.
6. An obscene gesture, known as "the Spanish fig," in which the thumb is put between the fore and middle fingers in a way meant to be suggestive of genitalia and sex acts. In the next line, Pistol refers to a "bragging" (lying) Spaniard who was "figged."
7. Load you (with honors) twice over; load you like a gun twice over, with a pun on Pistol's name.

'Where is the life that late I led?'[8] say they.
130 Why, here it is. Welcome these pleasant days.   *Exeunt*

5.4

Enter Beadles, [dragging in MISTRESS] QUICKLY *and*
DOLL TEARSHEET[1]

MISTRESS QUICKLY No, thou arrant knave! I would to God that I
might die, that I might have thee hanged. Thou hast drawn my
shoulder out of joint.

FIRST BEADLE The constables have delivered her over to me;
5 and she shall have whipping-cheer,[2] I warrant her. There hath
been a man or two killed about her.[3]

DOLL TEARSHEET Nut-hook,[4] nut-hook, you lie! Come on, I'll
tell thee what, thou damned tripe-visaged° rascal, an° the child   *flabby-faced / if*
I go with do miscarry,[5] thou wert better thou hadst struck thy
10 mother, thou paper-faced° villain.   *white-faced*

MISTRESS QUICKLY O the Lord, that Sir John were come! He
would make this a bloody day to somebody. But I pray God the
fruit of her womb miscarry!

FIRST BEADLE If it do, you shall have a dozen of cushions again;
15 you have but eleven now.[6] Come, I charge you both go with
me, for the man is dead that you and Pistol beat amongst you.

DOLL TEARSHEET I'll tell you what, you thin man in a censer,[7] I
will have you as soundly swinged° for this, you bluebottle[8]   *beaten*
rogue, you filthy famished correctioner! If you be not swinged,
20 I'll forswear half-kirtles.°   *give up wearing skirts*

FIRST BEADLE Come, come, you she knight-errant, come!

MISTRESS QUICKLY O God, that right should thus o'ercome might!
Well, of sufferance° comes ease.   *from suffering*

DOLL TEARSHEET Come, you rogue, come; bring me to a justice.

25 MISTRESS QUICKLY Ay, come, you starved bloodhound.

DOLL TEARSHEET Goodman death, goodman bones!

MISTRESS QUICKLY Thou atomy,° thou!   *(for "anatomy"; skeleton)*

DOLL TEARSHEET Come, you thin thing; come, you rascal.°   *lean deer*

FIRST BEADLE Very well.   *Exeunt*

5.5

Enter two GROOMS[, *strewing rushes*[1]]

FIRST GROOM More rushes, more rushes!

SECOND GROOM The trumpets have sounded twice.

FIRST GROOM 'Twill be two o'clock ere they come from the coronation.   *Exeunt*

---

8. A line from a lost poem or ballad.
5.4 Location: A street in London.
1. Q says, "Enter Sinklo and three or foure officers."
Sinklo was probably an actor's name. He was evidently
very thin, for this scene contains a number of unflat-
tering references to one of the officer's skinniness.
2. That is, a whipping for her entertainment or supper
("cheer"). Beadles (the parish officers responsible for
enforcing laws) commonly meted out this punishment
for prostitution.
3. Because of her; in her company.
4. A hook for pulling nuts from trees; the arresting

constable.
5. Women who were pregnant might escape the full
force of the law until after they gave birth.
6. Implying that Tearsheet feigns pregnancy by carrying one of Quickly's pillows under her gown.
7. You figure of a man embossed on the lid of a pot for
burning incense.
8. Alluding to the blue tunics worn by beadles.
5.5 Location: A public place near Westminster Abbey.
1. Floor coverings, here strewn on the ground before
the King's entrance.

Enter [Sir John] FALSTAFF, SHALLOW, PISTOL, BAR-
DOLPH, *and [the]* PAGE²

5 FALSTAFF   Stand here by me, Master Robert Shallow. I will make
the King do you grace.° I will leer upon him as a comes by,   honor
and do but mark the countenance that he will give me.

PISTOL   God bless thy lungs, good knight.

FALSTAFF   Come here, Pistol; stand behind me. [*To* SHALLOW]

10 O, if I had had time to have made new liveries,³ I would have
bestowed° the thousand pound I borrowed of you! But 'tis no   spent
matter; this poor show doth better; this doth infer° the zeal I   imply
had to see him.

SHALLOW   It doth so.

15 FALSTAFF   It shows my earnestness of affection—

PISTOL   It doth so.

FALSTAFF   My devotion—

PISTOL   It doth, it doth, it doth.

FALSTAFF   As it were, to ride day and night, and not to deliberate,

20 not to remember, not to have patience to shift me°—   change my clothes

SHALLOW   It is most certain.

FALSTAFF   But to stand stained with travel and sweating with
desire to see him, thinking of nothing else, putting all affairs
in oblivion, as if there were nothing else to be done but to see

25 him.

PISTOL   'Tis *semper idem,* for *absque hoc nihil est:*⁴ 'tis all in every
part.

SHALLOW   'Tis so indeed.

PISTOL   My knight, I will inflame thy noble liver,

30 And make thee rage.
Thy Doll, and Helen⁵ of thy noble thoughts,
Is in base durance° and contagious° prison,   imprisonment / noxious
Haled° thither   Dragged
By most mechanical° and dirty hand.   menial

35 Rouse up Revenge from ebon den° with fell Alecto's snake,⁶   dark cave (hell)
For Doll is in. Pistol speaks naught but truth.

FALSTAFF   I will deliver her.

[*Shouts within.*] *Trumpets sound*

PISTOL   There roared the sea, and trumpet-clangour sounds!

Enter KING HARRY *the Fifth,* [PRINCE JOHN *of Lancaster,
the Dukes of* CLARENCE *and* GLOUCESTER, *the*] LORD
CHIEF JUSTICE [*and others*]

FALSTAFF   God save thy grace, King Hal, my royal Hal!

40 PISTOL   The heavens thee guard and keep, most royal imp° of fame!   offspring

FALSTAFF   God save thee, my sweet boy!

KING HARRY   My Lord Chief Justice, speak to that vain° man.   foolish

LORD CHIEF JUSTICE [*to* FALSTAFF]   Have you your wits? Know
you what 'tis you speak?

FALSTAFF   My king, my Jove,⁷ I speak to thee, my heart!

---

2. In Q, Falstaff and his friends enter after "Trumpets
sound, and the King, and his train passe over the stage."
There are thus two royal processions, one before Falstaff enters and one later in the scene. F contains only
the latter procession, which immediately precedes the
climactic moment when Hal rejects Falstaff.
3. Uniforms such as those worn by the retainers in a
noble household.

4. The first Latin motto, "ever the same," was associated with Queen Elizabeth; the second means "apart
from this, there is nothing."
5. The famously beautiful woman whose abduction by
Paris is said to have started the Trojan War.
6. Alecto was one of the Furies of classical mythology;
her head was covered with snakes.
7. In classical mythology, the ruler of the gods.

45 KING HARRY   I know thee not, old man. Fall to thy prayers.
How ill white hairs becomes a fool and jester!
I have long dreamt of such a kind of man,
So surfeit-swelled,° so old, and so profane;   *bloated from excess*
But being awake, I do despise my dream.
50 Make less thy body hence,° and more thy grace.   *henceforth*
Leave gormandizing;° know the grave doth gape   *gluttony*
For thee thrice wider than for other men.
Reply not to me with a fool-born jest.
Presume not that I am the thing I was,
55 For God doth know, so shall the world perceive,
That I have turned away my former self;
So will I those that kept me company.
When thou dost hear I am as I have been,
Approach me, and thou shalt be as thou wast,
60 The tutor and the feeder of my riots.
Till then I banish thee, on pain of death,
As I have done the rest of my misleaders,
Not to come near our person by ten mile.
For competence of life[8] I will allow you,
65 That lack of means enforce you not to evils;
And as we hear you do reform yourselves,
We will, according to your strengths and qualities,°   *attainments*
Give you advancement. [*To* LORD CHIEF JUSTICE] Be it your
      charge, my lord,
To see performed the tenor of our word. [*To his train*] Set on!
                              Exeunt KING [HARRY *and his train*]
70 FALSTAFF   Master Shallow, I owe you a thousand pound.
SHALLOW   Yea, marry, Sir John; which I beseech you to let me
have home with me.
FALSTAFF   That can hardly be, Master Shallow. Do not you
grieve at this. I shall be sent for in private to him. Look you, he
75 must seem thus to the world. Fear not your advancements. I
will be the man yet that shall make you great.
SHALLOW   I cannot perceive how, unless you give me your doublet and stuff me out with straw. I beseech you, good Sir John,
let me have five hundred of my thousand.
80 FALSTAFF   Sir, I will be as good as my word. This that you heard
was but a colour.°   *pretense*
SHALLOW   A colour[9] I fear that you will die in, Sir John.
FALSTAFF   Fear no colours. Go with me to dinner. Come, Lieutenant Pistol; come, Bardolph. I shall be sent for soon at
85 night.
            Enter [*the* LORD CHIEF] JUSTICE *and* PRINCE JOHN [*with
            officers*]
LORD CHIEF JUSTICE [*to officers*]   Go carry Sir John Falstaff to
      the Fleet.°   *(a London prison)*
Take all his company along with him.
FALSTAFF   My lord, my lord!
LORD CHIEF JUSTICE   I cannot now speak. I will hear you soon.—
90 Take them away.

---

8. An allowance sufficient to supply life's necessities.   9. Punning on "collar" as meaning "hangman's noose."

PISTOL *Si fortuna me tormenta, spero me contenta.*[1]

Exeunt. Manent° *Lancaster* [PRINCE JOHN]   *Remain*
and [LORD] CHIEF JUSTICE

PRINCE JOHN I like this fair proceeding of the King's.
He hath intent his wonted° followers   *customary*
Shall all be very well provided for,
95 But all are banished till their conversations°   *conduct*
Appear more wise and modest to the world.
LORD CHIEF JUSTICE And so they are.
PRINCE JOHN The King hath called his parliament, my lord.
LORD CHIEF JUSTICE He hath.
100 PRINCE JOHN I will lay odds that, ere this year expire,
We bear our civil swords and native fire[2]
As far as France. I heard a bird so sing,
Whose music, to my thinking, pleased the King.
Come, will you hence?   *Exeunt*

Epilogue

[*Enter* EPILOGUE]
EPILOGUE First my fear, then my curtsy,° last my speech.   *bow*
My fear is your displeasure; my curtsy, my duty; and my
speech to beg your pardons. If you look for a good speech now,
5 you undo° me; for what I have to say is of mine own making,   *ruin*
and what indeed I should say will, I doubt,° prove mine own   *fear*
marring. But to the purpose, and so to the venture.° Be it   *hazard*
known to you, as it is very well, I was lately here in the end of
a displeasing play, to pray your patience for it, and to promise
10 you a better. I did mean indeed to pay you with this; which, if
like an ill venture[1] it come unluckily home, I break,° and you,   *go bankrupt*
my gentle creditors, lose. Here I promised you I would be, and
here I commit my body to your mercies. Bate° me some, and   *Excuse*
I will pay you some, and, as most debtors do, promise you infi-
15 nitely.[2]
If my tongue cannot entreat you to acquit me, will you command me to use my legs? And yet that were but light payment,
to dance out of your debt. But a good conscience will make
any possible satisfaction, and so would I. All the gentlewomen
20 here have forgiven me; if the gentlemen will not, then the gentlemen do not agree with the gentlewomen, which was never
seen before in such an assembly.
One word more, I beseech you. If you be not too much
cloyed with fat meat, our humble author will continue the story
25 with Sir John in it,[3] and make you merry with fair Catherine of
France; where, for anything I know, Falstaff shall die of a
sweat[4]—unless already a° be killed with your hard opinions.   *he*

---

1. See note to 2.4.157.
2. Our swords used up to now in civil war and our native zeal.
Epilogue
1. An unlucky commercial speculation, especially in a cargo at sea.
2. Q here inserts the lines "and so I kneele downe before you; but indeed, to pray for the Queene," which

conclude the Epilogue in F. This is one of several indications that the Epilogue was rewritten and expanded at some point, but that in Q these lines, with their reference to the Queen, were not moved to their proper place at the end of the speech.
3. In fact, Sir John Falstaff does not appear in *Henry V*; the play here anticipated.
4. A sweating sickness; the plague; a venereal disease.

For Oldcastle[5] died a martyr, and this is not the man My
tongue is weary; when my legs are too, I will bid you good
night, and so kneel down before you—but, indeed, to pray for
30   the Queen.

                    [*He dances, then kneels for applause. Exit*]

---

5. Alluding to the fact that Sir John was originally called "Oldcastle" in *1 Henry IV.* See the Introduction to that play.

Much Ado About Nothing

Much Ado About Nothing, first published in 1600 and probably written in 1598, weaves together two stories: the benevolent luring of Beatrice and Benedick into mutual declarations of love and the villainous luring of Claudio into the mistaken belief that Hero is unchaste. For the former plot, there seems to be no specific source, though Shakespeare would have encountered stories of scorners of love who fall in love (including Chaucer's *Troilus and Criseyde*). For the story of the virtuous lady falsely accused, sources abound, including Ludovico Ariosto's wonderful version in Canto V of *Orlando Furioso* (1516, translated into English by Sir John Harington in 1591) and Matteo Bandello's twenty-second *Novella* (1554, translated into French by François de Belleforest in 1574). Shakespeare probably knew these and other versions, both dramatic and nondramatic, among them a tragic retelling by Edmund Spenser in Book II of *The Faerie Queene* (1590). By deftly intertwining the two plots, *Much Ado About Nothing* mingles lightheartedness with a certain haunting sadness.

This sadness is a recurrent note in Shakespeare's earlier comedies: *The Comedy of Errors* opens with a condemned man's lament, *The Merchant of Venice* is darkened by Antonio's melancholy and Shylock's bitter rage, and *Love's Labour's Lost* (which features in Biron and Rosaline a pair of sparring lovers who strikingly anticipate Benedick and Beatrice) ends with a death. In several later comedies, most notably *Measure for Measure*, the darkness is so intensified as to make the term "comedy" seem a problem. But in *Much Ado About Nothing*, Shakespeare creates a balance of laughter, longing, and pain that he equals only in two other great romantic comedies from the same period, *As You Like It* and *Twelfth Night, or What You Will*. The titles of all three plays convey an impression of easy, festive wit, a magical effortlessness that is in fact the product of an extraordinary discipline and skill.

This cunning use of effort to produce the effect of effortlessness can be understood in the light of Baldassare Castiglione's famous courtesy manual *The Book of the Courtier* (1528). Castiglione's remarkable book, published in an English translation in 1561, depicts a witty and sophisticated group of men and women who, in several extended conversations, discuss the qualities that must be possessed by the ideal courtier. The courtier, as they envisage him, must be equally adept at making war and at making love. He must be able to assist the Prince and to dance elegantly, to grasp the subtleties of diplomacy and to sing in a pleasant, unaffected voice, to engage in philosophical speculation and to tell amusing after-dinner stories. In similar fashion, court ladies must be at once modest and spirited, chaste and slyly knowing, unspoiled and elegant. These are, in less idealized and rarefied form, the social roles that Benedick and Beatrice are called upon to play. They are roles that demand exceptionally versatile actors.

Such courtly performances, Castiglione's conversationalists acknowledge, risk seeming stilted and artificial; will be successful only if they appear entirely spontaneous and natural. However carefully they prepare their parts, courtiers should hide all signs of study and rehearsal. To achieve grace, they must practice what Castiglione calls *sprezzatura*, a cultivated nonchalance. *Sprezzatura* is a technique for the manipulation of appearance, for masking the hard work that underlies successful performances. This masking is an open secret: others know that you are masking, but they must keep this knowledge suspended in the belief that it is a breach of decorum to acknowledge their own knowledge.

The society of *The Book of the Courtier* lives with other open secrets. Dark forces lie just outside the charmed circle of delightful lords and ladies: war, arbitrary power, the high risk of betrayal and double-dealing, the commodification of women, the grinding labor to which the great mass of human beings are condemned. The courtier's artful refusal to acknowledge any of these forces could be a mode of escapism, but Castiglione is alert to reality's harsh demands. For him, fashioning the self is a means not of withdrawing from a treacherous world, but of operating successfully within it.

Like Castiglione's *Courtier, Much Ado About Nothing* (whose title suggests the playwright's own mastery of *sprezzatura*) is pervasively concerned with social performance that seems at once spontaneous and calculated. Beatrice and Benedick, at the play's center, are both exquisitely self-conscious, but their self-consciousness takes the paradoxical form of a jaunty indifference to conventional niceties, an almost reckless exuberance that masks a heightened sensitivity to the social currents in which they swim.

By contrast, Don John, the bastard brother, characterizes himself from the start as a radically antisocial creature: "I had rather be a canker in a hedge than a rose in his grace, and it better fits my blood to be disdained of all than to fashion a carriage to rob love from any" (1.3.21–23). These are the sentiments of the outsider, one who, like the bastard Edmund in *King Lear,* is not properly part of the family and kinship network, and they are sufficient, in this play, to account for Don John's relentless, curiously disinterested villainy. He is a man who refuses to "fashion a carriage"—to observe the appropriate code of manners—and this refusal is itself a sign of rebellion. For manners are the lived texture of social life in *Much Ado*, not in the sense of a compulsory set of rules but rather in the sense of an evolving awareness of mutual obligation and interconnectedness.

There is, to be sure, something like compulsion in the obligations and pressures within which the men and women of *Much Ado* live, but the play frustrates any attempt to strip away the fabric of graciousness, apparent choice, and pretended spontaneity with which the compulsions are dressed. An exchange in the comedy's opening moments exemplifies the perfect balance between obligation and will that governs the play's vision of social life. Leonato, the Governor of Messina, is informed by letter of the imminent arrival of Don Pedro of Aragon. Entertainment must be provided at once, and Don Pedro's first words call attention to the pressure of compulsory courtesy: "Good Signor Leonato, are you come to meet your trouble? The fashion of the world is to avoid cost, and you encounter it." It is obviously the fashion of the world to apologize in just this way for imposition, and such an apology calls for an equally conventional denial that any trouble is involved. Leonato duly produces such a denial, a particularly gracious and well-turned one: "Never came trouble to my house in the likeness of your grace; for trouble being gone, comfort should remain, but when you depart from me, sorrow abides and happiness takes his leave." Don Pedro responds to this exquisite compliment with an elegantly modified renewal of his first words and then a polite turn toward Leonato's daughter, Hero: "You embrace your charge too willingly. I think this is your daughter" (1.1.77–85).

In a strict calculation of power politics, these words are meaningless: they posture emptily above the "real" social exchange, which involves the obligation of the civilian authority toward the military authority (as it happens, a foreign military) at the close of a successful campaign. But such a view neglects the importance of graceful social performance, performance whose ease signals the elite status of the speakers and tacitly acknowledges the possibility of failure or refusal. With a ceremonial greeting such as this, the possibility may seem merely theoretical, but in fact it comes to hover over the entire play (whose main plot is in effect formally initiated by Don Pedro's polite notice of Leonato's daughter). By the fifth act, after Don Pedro's officer Claudio has publicly humiliated and repudiated his intended bride, all courtesy has withered away, and only bitterness and recrimination exist between the gracious host and his princely guest.

Dogberry's zany sleuthing resolves the crisis, but the crucial point is that there is nothing absolute and automatic about the code of manners. Social rituals are vulnerable to disruption and misunderstanding, and this vulnerability underscores the importance of consciously keeping up appearances, patrolling social perimeters, and fabricating civility.

In Castiglione's world, there is a high premium placed on the concealment of the labor expended in this fabrication, but Shakespeare's comedy gives us glimpses in the frequent references to the support staff and attentiveness involved in entertainment: "Where is my cousin, your son? Hath he provided this music?" (1.2.1–2); "Being entertained for a perfumer, as I was smoking a musty room . . ." (1.3.46–47); "The revellers are entering, brother. Make good room" (2.1.70). Social labor is still more visible in the diverse kinds of discourse in which the characters participate or to which they refer: greeting, entertainment, embassy, formal letter, conjuration, courtship, epigraph, sonneteering, gossip, legal deposition, aggressive wit, formal denunciation, ritualized apology.

Each of these forms of speech requires a display of skill and hence confers a measure of the honor or shame to which the characters of *Much Ado About Nothing* are intensely attuned. Honor and shame are particularly social emotions, the emotions of those who exist in a world of watching and being watched. "Nothing" in Shakespeare's time was pronounced "noting": this is a play obsessed with characters noting other characters. Hence the special force of *masking*, where the serious business of watching is playfully disrupted by disguise, and hence too the crucial significance of those scenes in which Beatrice and Benedick think they are noting others and are in reality being noted (and tricked). Sensitivity to the possibility of being shamed—which includes being laughed at, rejected, insulted, dishonored, humiliated, and so forth—is never very far from the characters of *Much Ado*. It extends from Leonato, who thinks that death is the fairest cover for his daughter's public humiliation, to Benedick, whose intellectual and sexual endurance is ridiculed by Beatrice when he ducks out of their first exchange with "a jade's trick" (1.1.113), to Dogberry, who longs to be writ down an ass. At its core is intense male anxiety about female infidelity, manifested in the constant nervous jokes about cuckoldry and played on viciously by Don John. "If I see anything tonight why I should not marry her, tomorrow," Claudio tells Don John, "in the congregation where I should wed, there will I shame her." Don Pedro promises to join with his friend "to disgrace her" (3.2.103–07).

Honor and shame, as the play develops them, are closely bound up with linguistic performance. Language is society's way of being intimately present in the individual; the characters may adjust to that social presence, may like Beatrice and Benedick playfully resist it, may like Dogberry distort it unintentionally, but the shared codes of language are more powerful than any individual.

Close attention to the language of *Much Ado About Nothing* begins with the observation that the comedy is written largely, though not entirely, in prose, a medium far more familiar to modern audiences than the blank verse that dominates many of Shakespeare's plays. This prose, however, is of a kind to which we are no longer accustomed. Modern prose tends by design to be rather plain and colorless; Elizabethan prose is often playful, rhetorically inventive, and richly metaphorical. *Much Ado About Nothing* at once plays elaborate prose games and pokes fun at them, as when Benedick complains that lovesick Claudio "was wont to speak plain and to the purpose, like an honest man and a soldier, and now is he turned orthography. His words are a very fantastical banquet, just so many strange dishes" (2.3.16–19). Shakespeare was certainly capable of writing what we would regard as clear, uncluttered prose: "I learn in this letter that Don Pedro of Aragon comes this night to Messina" (1.1.1–2). But he could also produce astonishing rhetorical effects:

> She told me—not thinking I had been myself—that I was the Prince's jester, that I was duller than a great thaw, huddling jest upon jest with such impossible conveyance upon me that I stood like a man at a mark, with a whole army shooting at me. She speaks poniards, and every word stabs. If her breath were as terrible as her terminations, there were no living near her, she would infect to the North Star. I would not marry her though she were endowed with all that Adam had left him before he transgressed. She would have made Hercules have turned spit, yea, and have cleft his club to make the fire, too. (2.1.212–21)

A night watchman. From Thomas Dekker, *The Belman of London* (1608).

The wonderful improvisational piling up of images, each at once subtly linked to the preceding one and yet swerving in a new direction, captures the movement of Benedick's mind: the rush of genuine anger and hurt feelings mingled with the impulse to turn his pain into a comically misogynistic performance to entertain Don Pedro (a performance that, ironically, confirms the charge—that he is the Prince's jester—that originally stung him).

Linguistic performance is the social equivalent of the performance in warfare that is both alluded to and conspicuously excluded from the play's action. Language is violence, and language is the alternative to violence: the play entertains both hypotheses and plays them off against each other. "There is a kind of merry war betwixt Signor Benedick and her," says Leonato of his niece. "They never meet but there's a skirmish of wit between them" (1.1.49–51). If words are the agents of civility, they are also dangerous weapons: "Thy slander hath gone through and through her heart, / And she lies buried with her ancestors"; "God knows, I loved my niece, / And she is dead, slandered to death by villains" (5.1.68–69, 87–88). What we glimpse in the symbolic murder of Hero is not only the maligning power of slander, but also the aggressive potential of even polite or playful speech. The "merry war" between Beatrice and Benedick leaves scars.

The more one attends to the language of *Much Ado About Nothing,* the more it seems saturated with violence. In the lighthearted opening scene alone, there are almost constant comic references to war, plague, betrayal, heresy, burning at the stake, blinding, hanging, spying, poisoning. To be sure, the horrors are not themselves realized dramatically in the play; they are present as mere jokes. Nonetheless, they are present, recalled again and again by the constant threat of disaster, by symbolic death, by public shaming. Even in the tidal rush of the comic resolution, amid the marriages, the music, and the dance, Benedick's final words, indeed the final words of the play, deliberately call attention to the violence that the language has continually, if obliquely, registered. Informed of Don John's capture, Benedick declares, "Think not on him till tomorrow, I'll devise thee brave punishments for him. Strike up, pipers." *Dance* (5.4.121–22).

Viewed in the light of the close, with its conspicuous deferral of torture, but only until tomorrow, the play does not simply transform human misery and violence into wit, but rather addresses itself to the ways in which society manages to endure, to reproduce, to avoid immersion in its own destructive element, to dance. It does so by conscious and unconscious deferral, by the manipulation of appearances, by the deployment of illusions that are known by at least some of its members (the worst and the best) to be illusions.

Illusions are tricks and deceptions, but they are also the social fictions men and women live by. Claudio and Hero exist in the play almost entirely in and as such fictions: their emotions seem less something they possess inwardly than something constructed for them out of the appropriate conventions and rituals. A more complex manifestation in the play of the primacy of illusion is the relation between Beatrice and Benedick. The plot to trick the celebrated skirmishers into marriage originates with Don Pedro, who promises, if Leonato, Hero, and Claudio cooperate with him, to "fash-

Lovers sparring with torches. From George Wither, *A Collection of Emblemes* (1635).

ion" the match. The key to his success is his ability to mobilize the social code of shame and honor to which Beatrice and Benedick are bound and to use this code as a means to discipline—to shape into a plot that will culminate in marriage—the powerful chafing between them. For both Beatrice and Benedick, the force that pushes them toward declarations of love and hence toward marriage vows is as much hearing themselves criticized by their friends as hearing that the other is desperately in love. "Can this be true?" asks Beatrice, her ears burning. "Stand I condemned for pride and scorn so much?" (3.1.108–09). "I hear how I am censured," Benedick declares, resolving that he "must not seem proud" (2.3.199–200, 202–03).

The conspiratorial fabrication of appearances so as to manipulate the code of shame and honor has the odd effect of establishing a link between the socially approved practices of Don Pedro and the wicked practices of Don John, his bastard brother. Shakespeare seems to go out of his way to call attention to this link: moments after Don Pedro undertakes to "fashion" the affection between Beatrice and Benedick, the villainous Borachio declares that he "will so fashion the matter that Hero shall be absent" and hence can be impersonated by Margaret. In effect, the play's term for the social system in which all the characters—evil as well as virtuous—are involved is "fashion." Shakespeare deftly uses the term both as noun and verb—that is, both to designate the images (including the fashionable costumes) that elicit emotions and to describe the process that shapes these images.

Fashion is closely related not only to image but also to verbal style, which in the aesthetics of the period was regarded as a kind of dress. "The body of your discourse," laughs Benedick, "is sometimes guarded with fragments, and the guards are but slightly basted on neither" (1.1.232–34). The pervasiveness of fashion allows the possibility of drastic deception, but it is also society's redemptive principle. The movement of the play is not so much the unmasking of fraud to reveal the true, virtuous essence within as rather the refashioning, after a dangerous illusion, of the proper image and the appropriate words: "Sweet Hero," cries Claudio after his eyes have been opened to the deception, "now thy image doth appear / In the rare semblance that I loved it first" (5.1.235–36).

The fashioning with which the play is concerned complicates any simple opposition between authentic inner feelings and social norms. This is, after all, a plot that features a wooing by masked proxy instead of direct wooing, a theatrical ritual of remorse instead of remorse, a declaration of love based upon a set of illusions and motivated by the fear of shame. Near the play's close, we see Benedick struggling to compose the required sonnet to Beatrice—an entirely conventional exercise performed to fulfill the theatrical role in which he has been cast ("myself in love"). And in the final moments, when the deception is revealed, it is this exercise, rather than any feelings of the heart, that confirms the match. "I'll be sworn upon't that he loves her," declares Claudio:

> For here's a paper written in his hand,
> A halting sonnet of his own pure brain,
> Fashioned to Beatrice.

When a similar sonnet by Beatrice is produced, Benedick cries, "A miracle! Here's our own hands against our hearts" (5.4.85–88, 91).

Many readers of the play, and most performers, have tried to reverse this formulation: Beatrice and Benedick's conversations may be hostile, the interpretation goes, but in their hearts they are, and have long been, deeply in love. Beatrice seems to refer to an earlier time when she had given her heart to Benedick and had evidently been disappointed: "once before he won it of me, with false dice" (2.1.243–44). If they do not declare their love, it is because they are too defensive or, alternatively, too wise to play society's conventional game. In a world of pervasive conventionality and social control, one clever way to insist upon some spontaneity and hence to achieve some authenticity is to quarrel. Perhaps. But what if we do not dismiss their own words? What if we take the conspiracy against them seriously? Beatrice and Benedick would in that case not "love" each other from the start; it would not at all be clear that they love each other, entirely independent of social manipulation, at the close. They are, at least to some extent, tricked into marriage; without the pressure that moves them to professions of love, they would have remained unmarried. Beatrice and Benedick constantly tantalize us with the possibility of an identity quite different from that of Claudio and Hero, an identity deliberately fashioned to resist the constant pressure of society. But that pressure finally prevails. Marriage is a social conspiracy.

If such a view seems ultimately too unsentimental to be tenable in a romantic comedy, it nonetheless makes possible the brilliant scene in which Benedick asks what he can do to prove his love for Beatrice, and Beatrice replies, "Kill Claudio" (4.1.287). Similarly, it helps to account for the laughter provoked by the disillusioned exchange very near the play's close: "Do not you love me?" "Why no, no more than reason" (5.4.74). In both cases, where we might expect tender words, we get the opposite. If we feel nonetheless that romantic love triumphs in the end, we do so in effect because we—audience and readers—participate in the conspiracy to gull the pair into marriage by insisting that they love each other more than reason. In doing so, we confer upon the general restoration of civility at the play's close something more deeply pleasurable.

Benedick and Beatrice have rational arguments, grounded in the gender politics of their world, for remaining single. Benedick knows that a married man must put his honor at risk by entrusting it to a woman, while Beatrice knows that a married woman must put her integrity at risk by submitting herself to a man: "Would it not grieve a woman to be overmastered with a piece of valiant dust?" (2.1.51–52). Even when they are manipulated into declaring their love, they cannot settle into the language of conventional courtship: "Thou and I are too wise," Benedick tells Beatrice, "to woo peaceably" (5.2.61). Their union at the close is a triumph of folly over the "wisdom" of the

A man trapped in the yoke of matrimony. From Henry Peacham. *Minerva Britanna* (1612).

single life, a triumph that recalls Erasmus's *Praise of Folly*, where love is said to be possible only because men and women are induced to put aside their reason and plunge into saving foolishness. Why should they do so? The answer is that it is better to live in illusion than in social isolation and that, as Benedick says, "the world must be peopled" (2.3.213–14).

In most productions of the play, audiences are made to feel that submission to the discipline of love and marriage—"taming my wild heart" (3.1.113), as Beatrice so wonderfully puts it—is a magnificent release of love and energy. Shakespeare had already experimented with comparable themes in *The Taming of the Shrew*, but Petruchio's conquest of Kate seems, at least for many modern viewers, too brutal to accept without a lingering sense of constriction and loss. What keeps the conclusion of *Much Ado About Nothing* from appearing brittle or bitter is a sense that the triumph of illusion is life-affirming, a sense that the friction between Beatrice and Benedick can be turned into mutual pleasure.

If the Claudio/Hero plot and the Beatrice/Benedick plot are two ways in which Shakespeare's comedy shows the saving necessity of illusion, there is a third manifestation: the illusion that evil manifests itself as Don John—that is, in a supremely incompetent and finally impotent form—and that, although it fools clear-eyed and sophisticated observers like Don Pedro, it may be exposed by a bumbling idiot like Dogberry. Some years later, Shakespeare returned to a ruthlessly disillusioned version of the same story, the lover tricked into believing that his beloved has been unfaithful, and called it not *Much Ado About Nothing* but *Othello*.

STEPHEN GREENBLATT

TEXTUAL NOTE

"Much adoe about Nothing . . . *Written by William Shakespeare*" was first published in 1600, in a quarto (Q) printed by Valentine Simmes (or Sims) for Andrew Wise and William Aspley. This is the only version of the play that appeared during Shakespeare's lifetime. The title page states that the play "hath been sundrie times publikely acted by the right honourable, the Lord Chamberlaine his seruants."

Much Ado About Nothing is listed in a Stationers' Register entry of August 4, 1600, along with *As You Like It, Henry V,* and Ben Jonson's *Every Man in His Humour.* All are marked "to be staied"—that is, not published without further permission. It is generally thought that the Lord Chamberlain's Men were attempting to ensure that they would be paid for any printing of these popular plays and that the release of *Much Ado About Nothing* later that same year indicates that the company had resolved whatever dispute had led them to stay publication.

Most scholars, including the Oxford editors, believe that the 1600 Quarto of *Much Ado About Nothing* was set from Shakespeare's "foul papers"—that is, his own manuscript of the play. Evidence includes the omission of several entrances and exits, certain loose ends in the dialogue, and the presence of "ghost" characters. For example, Q's stage directions at the beginning of Acts 1 and 2 list Leonato's wife, Innogen, but Innogen neither speaks nor is spoken to in the course of the play. Evidently she is the ghostly trace of an idea that the playwright abandoned.

Q's speech prefixes are inconsistent, another characteristic feature of foul papers, and in 4.2 they preserve the names of the actors Shakespeare had in mind for two of the comic parts: Will Kemp for Dogberry and Richard Cowley for Verges. Since Kemp left the Lord Chamberlain's Men in 1599, scholars think the play must have been first performed before the date of his departure. And since Francis Meres does not include *Much Ado About Nothing* in a list of Shakespeare's plays he compiled in September 1598 (unless that is what he meant by the play he calls *Loue Labours wonne*), scholars think it probable that the play was first performed after that date. Therefore the likeliest date of the first performance is the winter of 1598–99.

The First Folio (1623) text of the play (F) was based on Q. There are no act or scene divisions in Q; F indicates only act divisions (with the exception of 1.1).

SELECTED BIBLIOGRAPHY

Barish, Jonas A. "Pattern and Purpose in the Prose of *Much Ado About Nothing.*" *Rice University Studies* 60.2 (Spring 1974): 19–30. Variations in the play's mannered rhetorical scheme offer insights into its characters and situations.

Berger, Harry, Jr. "Against the Sink-a-Pace: Sexual and Family Politics in *Much Ado About Nothing.*" *Shakespeare Quarterly* 33 (1982): 302–13. Characterizes Messina's gender conventions in terms of virtue, constancy, reputation, deception, and fashion.

Berry, Ralph. *Shakespeare's Comedies: Explorations in Form.* Princeton: Princeton University Press, 1972. 154–74. Focusing on the difficult reconciliation of sensory experience and judgment, *Much Ado About Nothing* explores the limits of knowledge.

Cook, Carol. "'The Sign and Semblance of Her Honor': Reading Gender Difference in *Much Ado About Nothing.*" *PMLA* 101.2 (1986): 186–202. The play presents the polysemous threat of woman in a world where men are the manipulators and interpreters of signs.

Everett, Barbara. "*Much Ado About Nothing:* The Unsociable Comedy." *English Comedy.* Ed. Michael Cordner, Peter Holland, and John Kerrigan. New York: Cambridge University Press, 1994. 68–84. Shakespeare's realistic portrait of love in society typically mixes its comic nothings with serious concerns.

Gay, Penny. "*Much Ado About Nothing:* A Kind of Merry War." *As She Likes It: Shakespeare's Unruly Women.* London: Routledge, 1994. 143–77. Performance history since the 1950s, spotlighting representations of Beatrice and Benedick.

Howard, Jean. "Renaissance Antitheatricality and the Politics of Gender and Rank in *Much Ado About Nothing.*" *Shakespeare Reproduced: The Text in History and Ideology.* Ed. Jean E. Howard and Marion F. O'Connor. New York: Methuen, 1987. 163–87. *Much Ado About Nothing* supports Elizabethan ideology, condemning marginal social groups through accusations of illegitimate theatrical practice.

Moisan, Thomas. "Deforming Sources: Literary Antecedants and Their Traces in *Much Ado About Nothing.*" *Shakespeare Studies* 31 (2003): 165–83. The play's furtive and ambivalent relationship to its sources reflects its depiction of character, politics, power, and representation.

Myhill, Nova. "Spectatorship in/of *Much Ado About Nothing*." *Studies in English Literature* 39.2 (1999): 291–311. Considers how *Much Ado About Nothing*'s unreliable "notings" challenge the theater audience's assumptions of omniscience and invulnerability.

Salingar, Leo. "Borachio's Indiscretion: Some Noting about Much Ado." *The Italian World of English Renaissance Drama: Cultural Exchange and Intertextuality.* Ed. Michele Marrapodi. London: Associated University Presses, 1998. 225–38. *Much Ado About Nothing* as a bittersweet masquerade of social ambiguity and false communications.

Traugott, John. "Creating a Rational Rinaldo: A Study in the Mixture of the Genres of Comedy and Romance in *Much Ado About Nothing*." *Genre* 15 (1982): 157–81. Shows how comedy and romance contaminate and purify each other, one becoming ennobled and the other cured of cruelty.

FILM

Much Ado About Nothing. 1993. Dir. Kenneth Branagh. UK/USA. 111 min. Festive romp set in sunny, country-house Italy. With Kenneth Branagh and Emma Thompson.

Much Ado About Nothing

The Persons of the Play

DON PEDRO, Prince of Aragon
BENEDICK, of Padua ⎫
CLAUDIO, of Florence ⎭ lords, companions of Don Pedro
BALTHASAR, attendant on Don Pedro, a singer
DON JOHN, the bastard brother of Don Pedro
BORACHIO ⎫
CONRAD ⎭ followers of Don John
LEONATO, governor of Messina
HERO, his daughter
BEATRICE, an orphan, his niece
ANTONIO, an old man, brother of Leonato
MARGARET ⎫
URSULA ⎭ waiting-gentlewomen attendant on Hero
FRIAR FRANCIS
DOGBERRY, the Constable in charge of the Watch
VERGES, the Headborough, Dogberry's partner
A SEXTON
WATCHMEN
A BOY, serving Benedick
Attendants and messengers

1.1

Enter LEONATO, *governor of Messina,* HERO *his
daughter, and* BEATRICE *his niece, with a*
MESSENGER

LEONATO   I learn in this letter that Don Pedro of Aragon comes
this night to Messina.

MESSENGER   He is very near by this. He was not three leagues off
when I left him.

5   LEONATO   How many gentlemen have you lost in this action?°   *campaign*

MESSENGER   But few of any sort,° and none of name.°   *rank / distinction*

LEONATO   A victory is twice itself when the achiever brings home
full numbers. I find here that Don Pedro hath bestowed much
honour on a young Florentine called Claudio.

10   MESSENGER   Much deserved on his part, and equally remem-
bered° by Don Pedro. He hath borne himself beyond the prom-   *rewarded*
ise of his age, doing in the figure of a lamb the feats of a lion.
He hath indeed better bettered° expectation than you must   *exceeded*
expect of me to tell you how.

15   LEONATO   He hath an uncle here in Messina will be very much
glad of it.

MESSENGER   I have already delivered him letters, and there
appears much joy in him—even so much that joy could not
show itself modest° enough without a badge° of bitterness.°   *moderate / show / grief*

1.1 Location: Messina (a city in Sicily). Before the house of Leonato.

20	LEONATO Did he break out into tears?	
	MESSENGER In great measure.	
	LEONATO A kind° overflow of kindness,° there are no faces truer	*natural / tenderness*
	than those that are so washed. How much better is it to weep	
	at joy than to joy at weeping!	
25	BEATRICE I pray you, is Signor Montanto¹ returned from the	
	wars, or no?	
	MESSENGER I know none of that name, lady. There was none	
	such in the army, of any sort.	
	LEONATO What is he that you ask for, niece?	
30	HERO My cousin means Signor Benedick of Padua.²	
	MESSENGER O, he's returned, and as pleasant° as ever he was.	*entertaining*
	BEATRICE He set up his bills° here in Messina, and challenged	*public notices*
	Cupid at the flight;³ and my uncle's fool,° reading the chal-	*jester*
	lenge, subscribed for Cupid and challenged him at the bird-	
35	bolt.⁴ I pray you, how many hath he killed and eaten in these	
	wars? But how many hath he killed? For indeed I promised to	
	eat all of his killing.	
	LEONATO Faith, niece, you tax° Signor Benedick too much. But	*abuse*
	he'll be meet° with you, I doubt it not.	*even*
40	MESSENGER He hath done good service, lady, in these wars.	
	BEATRICE You had musty victual, and he hath holp° to eat it. He	*helped*
	is a very valiant trencherman,° he hath an excellent stomach.	*eater*
	MESSENGER And a good soldier too, lady.	
	BEATRICE And a good soldier° to a lady, but what is he to a lord?	*servant; lady-killer*
45	MESSENGER A lord to a lord, a man to a man, stuffed° with all	*well furnished*
	honourable virtues.	
	BEATRICE It is so, indeed. He is no less than a stuffed man.° But	*mannequin*
	for the stuffing—well, we are all mortal.⁵	
	LEONATO You must not, sir, mistake my niece. There is a kind	
50	of merry war betwixt Signor Benedick and her. They never	
	meet but there's a skirmish of wit between them.	
	BEATRICE Alas, he gets nothing by that. In our last conflict four	
	of his five wits⁶ went halting° off, and now is the whole man	*limping*
	governed with one, so that if he have wit enough to keep him-	
55	self warm,⁷ let him bear it for a difference⁸ between himself	
	and his horse, for it is all the wealth that he hath left to be	
	known a reasonable creature. Who is his companion now? He	
	hath every month a new sworn brother.	
	MESSENGER Is't possible?	
60	BEATRICE Very easily possible. He wears his faith° but as the	*loyalty*
	fashion of his hat, it ever changes with the next block.⁹	
	MESSENGER I see, lady, the gentleman is not in your books.°	*favor*
	BEATRICE No. An° he were, I would burn my study. But I pray	*If*
	you, who is his companion? Is there no young squarer° now	*boisterous quarreler*
65	that will make a voyage with him to the devil?	
	MESSENGER He is most in the company of the right noble	
	Claudio.	

1. In fencing, a montanto is an upright blow or thrust.
2. A city in northern Italy.
3. To an archery match. (He claimed to surpass Cupid at arousing love.)
4. To a contest using bird bolts, or blunt, short-range arrows allowed to fools and children (and thus appropriate to young Cupid). *subscribed for*: took up the challenge on behalf of.
5. But as for what he is made of (his "stuffing"), he is probably as faulty as the rest of us.
6. *five wits*: mental faculties (memory, imagination, judgment, fantasy, and common sense).
7. If he have minimal common sense.
8. Let him display the fact in his coat of arms in order to distinguish himself.
9. Newest mold for a hat; fashion.

BEATRICE   O Lord, he will hang upon him like a disease. He is
sooner caught than the pestilence,° and the taker° runs pres-   *plague / victim*
70   ently° mad. God help the noble Claudio. If he have caught the   *immediately*
Benedick, it will cost him a thousand pound ere a° be cured.   *he*
MESSENGER   I will hold friends¹ with you, lady.
BEATRICE   Do, good friend.
LEONATO   You will never run mad,² niece.
75   BEATRICE   No, not till a hot January.
MESSENGER   Don Pedro is approached.

       Enter DON PEDRO, CLAUDIO, BENEDICK, BALTHASAR, *and*
       [DON] JOHN *the bastard*

DON PEDRO   Good Signor Leonato, are you come to meet your
trouble? The fashion° of the world is to avoid cost, and you   *custom*
encounter° it.   *go to meet*
80   LEONATO   Never came trouble to my house in the likeness of
your grace; for trouble being gone, comfort should remain, but
when you depart from me, sorrow abides and happiness takes
his leave.
DON PEDRO   You embrace your charge° too willingly. I think this   *duty*
85   is your daughter.
LEONATO   Her mother hath many times told me so.
BENEDICK   Were you in doubt, sir, that you asked her?
LEONATO   Signor Benedick, no, for then were you a child.
DON PEDRO   You have it full,³ Benedick. We may guess by this
90   what you are, being a man. Truly, the lady fathers herself.⁴ Be
happy, lady, for you are like an honourable father.
BENEDICK   If Signor Leonato be her father, she would not have
his head;⁵ on her shoulders for all Messina, as like him as she
is.
95   BEATRICE⁶   I wonder that you will still° be talking, Signor Bene-   *always*
dick. Nobody marks you.
BENEDICK   What, my dear Lady Disdain! Are you yet living?
BEATRICE   Is it possible disdain should die while she hath such
meet° food to feed it as Signor Benedick? Courtesy itself must   *suitable*
100   convert° to disdain if you come in her presence.   *turn*
BENEDICK   Then is courtesy a turncoat. But it is certain I am
loved of° all ladies, only you excepted. And I would I could   *by*
find in my heart that I had not a hard heart, for truly I love
none.
105   BEATRICE   A dear happiness to women. They would else have
been troubled with a pernicious suitor. I thank God and my
cold blood I am of your humour° for that. I had rather hear my   *disposition*
dog bark at a crow than a man swear he loves me.
BENEDICK   God keep your ladyship still in that mind. So some
110   gentleman or other shall scape a predestinate° scratched face.   *escape an inevitable*
BEATRICE   Scratching could not make it worse an 'twere such a
face as yours were.
BENEDICK   Well, you are a rare parrot-teacher.⁷
BEATRICE   A bird of my tongue is better than a beast of yours.⁸

---

1. I will stay on good terms (so as not to provoke your
sarcasm).
2. "Catch the Benedick."
3. Your sarcasm is fully repaid.
4. She shows by her looks who her father is.
5. The head of an old man.

6. During Beatrice and Benedick's conversation, Don
Pedro talks with Leonato (see line 119).
7. Chatterer (repetitive, like one who teaches a parrot
to speak).
8. A bird with my powers of speech is better than a
dumb beast who, like you, has none.

115 BENEDICK I would my horse had the speed of your tongue,
and so good a continuer.⁹ But keep your way,° i' God's name. I   °carry on
have done.

BEATRICE You always end with a jade's trick.¹ I know you of old.

DON PEDRO That is the sum of all, Leonato. Signor Claudio and
120 Signor Benedick, my dear friend Leonato hath invited you all.
I tell him we shall stay here at the least a month, and he heartily prays some occasion may detain us longer. I dare swear he
is no hypocrite, but prays from his heart.

LEONATO If you swear, my lord, you shall not be forsworn. [To
125 DON JOHN] Let me bid you welcome, my lord. Being° recon-   °Since you are
ciled to the Prince your brother, I owe you all duty.

DON JOHN I thank you. I am not of many words, but I thank you.

LEONATO [to DON PEDRO] Please it your grace lead on?

DON PEDRO Your hand, Leonato. We will go together.²

*Exeunt. Manent*³ BENEDICK *and* CLAUDIO   *Remain*

130 CLAUDIO Benedick, didst thou note the daughter of Signor Leonato?

BENEDICK I noted her not,³ but I looked on her.

CLAUDIO Is she not a modest young lady?

BENEDICK Do you question me as an honest man should do, for
135 my simple true judgement, or would you have me speak after
my custom, as being a professed tyrant° to their sex?   °pitiless critic

CLAUDIO No, I pray thee speak in sober judgement.

BENEDICK Why, i'faith, methinks she's too low° for a high   °short
praise, too brown for a fair praise, and too little for a great
140 praise. Only this commendation I can afford her, that were she
other than she is she were unhandsome, and being no other
but as she is, I do not like her.

CLAUDIO Thou thinkest I am in sport.° I pray thee tell me truly   °jest
how thou likest her.

145 BENEDICK Would you buy her, that you enquire after her?

CLAUDIO Can the world buy such a jewel?

BENEDICK Yea, and a case to put it into. But speak you this with
a sad° brow, or do you play the flouting jack, to tell us Cupid   °serious
is a good hare-finder and Vulcan a rare carpenter?⁴ Come, in
150 what key shall a man take° you to go° in the song?   °understand / join

CLAUDIO In mine eye she is the sweetest lady that ever I looked
on.

BENEDICK I can see yet without spectacles, and I see no such
matter. There's her cousin, an she were not possessed with a
155 fury, exceeds her as much in beauty as the first of May doth the
last of December. But I hope you have no intent to turn husband, have you?

CLAUDIO I would scarce trust myself though I had sworn the
contrary, if Hero would be my wife.

160 BENEDICK Is't come to this? In faith, hath not the world one
man but he will wear his cap with suspicion?⁵ Shall I never see

9. And had your staying power ("continuer," in horsemanship, means "stayer").
1. A trick worthy of a badly trained horse (here, dropping out of a race).
2. We will walk out hand in hand (and thus avoid taking precedence).
3. I paid her no special attention.
4. *play . . . carpenter:* spout praises contrary to fact and

intended satirically. Blind Cupid is poorly suited to the
sharp-sighted sport of hunting hares, while Vulcan, the
god of fire, was an excellent ("rare") blacksmith, not a
carpenter. *flouting jack:* mocking rogue.
5. *but . . . suspicion:* who will not be suspected of wearing his cap in order to hide a cuckold's horns (conventional sign of a wife's infidelity).

a bachelor of three-score again? Go to,° i'faith, an thou wilt
needs thrust thy neck into a yoke, wear the print of it, and sigh
away Sundays.[6] Look, Don Pedro is returned to seek you.

   Enter DON PEDRO

165 DON PEDRO What secret hath held you here that you followed
  not to Leonato's?
BENEDICK I would your grace would constrain me to tell.
DON PEDRO I charge thee on thy allegiance.
BENEDICK You hear, Count Claudio? I can be secret as a dumb
170   man, I would have you think so. But on my allegiance, mark
  you this, on my allegiance! He is in love. With who? Now that
  is your grace's part. Mark how short his answer is: with Hero,
  Leonato's short daughter.
CLAUDIO If this were so, so were it uttered.[7]
175 BENEDICK Like the old tale, my lord—it is not so, nor 'twas not
  so, but indeed, God forbid it should be so.[8]
CLAUDIO If my passion change not shortly, God forbid it should
  be otherwise.
DON PEDRO Amen, if you love her, for the lady is very well
180   worthy.
CLAUDIO You speak this to fetch me in,° my lord.
DON PEDRO By my troth, I speak my thought.
CLAUDIO And in faith, my lord, I spoke mine.
BENEDICK And by my two faiths and troths,[9] my lord, I spoke
185   mine.
CLAUDIO That I love her, I feel.
DON PEDRO That she is worthy, I know.
BENEDICK That I neither feel how she should be loved nor know
  how she should be worthy is the opinion that fire cannot melt
190   out of me. I will die in it at the stake.
DON PEDRO Thou wast ever an obstinate heretic in the despite°
  of beauty.
CLAUDIO And never could maintain his part° but in the force of
  his will.[1]
195 BENEDICK That a woman conceived me, I thank her. That she
  brought me up, I likewise give her most humble thanks. But
  that I will have a recheat winded in my forehead, or hang my
  bugle in an invisible baldric,[2] all women shall pardon me.
  Because I will not do them the wrong to mistrust any,[3] I will
200   do myself the right to trust none. And the fine° is—for the
  which I may go the finer[4]—I will live a bachelor.
DON PEDRO I shall see thee ere I die look pale with love.
BENEDICK With anger, with sickness, or with hunger, my lord;
  not with love. Prove° that ever I lose more blood with love than
205   I will get again with drinking,[5] pick out mine eyes with a bal-

Go on

to trick me

contempt

argument

conclusion

If you prove

---

6. *thrust . . . Sundays:* take on the burdens and tedium
of marriage, when you might be enjoying yourself as a
bachelor.
7. *so . . . uttered:* this is how Benedick would tell it.
8. In an English fairy tale (a variant on the Bluebeard
story), a man suspected by his bride-to-be of having
killed his former wives denies his guilt with the refrain
Benedick quotes.
9. His loyalty to both Don Pedro and Claudio, and jok-
ingly, his duplicity.
1. But through prideful obstinacy rather than reason.
2. *But . . . baldric:* But that I should wear a cuckold's

horns. A recheat was a call sounded ("winded") on a
horn to recall the hounds. A baldric was a belt to hold
a horn ("bugle"); it was invisible, a sign of the cuckold's
ignorance.
3. Because I do not wish to wrong women by suspecting any of infidelity.
4. I may dress better (because he will have more money
to spare).
5. *lose . . . drinking:* alluding to the belief that sighing
like a lover caused the blood to evaporate, and drinking
wine renewed it.

lad-maker's[6] pen and hang me up at the door of a brothel house
for the sign of blind Cupid.[7]

DON PEDRO Well, if ever thou dost fall from this faith thou wilt
prove a notable argument.° · *subject of talk*

210 BENEDICK If I do, hang me in a bottle like a cat, and shoot at
me,[8] and he that hits me, let him be clapped on the shoulder
and called Adam.[9]

DON PEDRO Well, as time shall try.° 'In time the savage bull doth · · · · *prove*
bear the yoke.'[1]

215 BENEDICK The savage bull may, but if ever the sensible° Bene- · · · · *rational*
dick bear it, pluck off the bull's horns and set them in my forehead, and let me be vilely painted, and in such great letters as
they write 'Here is good horse to hire' let them signify under
my sign 'Here you may see Benedick, the married man'.

220 CLAUDIO If this should ever happen thou wouldst be horn-mad.[2]

DON PEDRO Nay, if Cupid have not spent all his quiver in Venice[3] thou wilt quake for this shortly.

BENEDICK I look for an earthquake[4] too, then.

DON PEDRO Well, you will temporize with the hours.[5] In the
225 mean time, good Signor Benedick, repair° to Leonato's, com- · · · · *go*
mend me to him, and tell him I will not fail him at supper, for
indeed he hath made great preparation.

BENEDICK I have almost matter° enough in me for such an · · · · *intelligence*
embassage.° And so I commit you— · *errand*

230 CLAUDIO To the tuition[6] of God, from my house if I had it—

DON PEDRO The sixth of July,

Your loving friend,

Benedick.

BENEDICK Nay, mock not, mock not. The body of your discourse is sometime guarded with fragments,[7] and the guards
are but slightly basted on[8] neither. Ere you flout° old ends° any · · · · *mock / clichés*
235 further, examine your conscience. And so I leave you. *Exit*

CLAUDIO My liege, your highness now may do me good.

DON PEDRO My love is thine to teach. Teach it but how
And thou shalt see how apt it is to learn
Any hard lesson that may do thee good.

240 CLAUDIO Hath Leonato any son, my lord?

DON PEDRO No child but Hero. She's his only heir.
Dost thou affect° her, Claudio? · *love*

CLAUDIO O my lord,
When you went onward on this ended action° · · · · · · · · · · · · *campaign*
I looked upon her with a soldier's eye,
245 That liked, but had a rougher task in hand
Than to drive liking to the name of love.
But now I am returned, and that° war-thoughts · · · · · · · · · · *now that*

6. Popular love poet or satirist.
7. A painted sign, such as might hang before a brothel.
8. *hang . . . me:* cats in baskets ("bottles") were common Elizabethan targets for recreational archery.
9. Perhaps Adam Bell, a celebrated archer.
1. Proverbial; here, apparently a variation on a line
from Thomas Kyd's *Spanish Tragedy* (c. 1587): "In time
the savage bull sustains the yoke" (2.1.3).
2. Furious, raving like a wild beast (referring to the
rage of a cuckolded husband).
3. Venice was famous in Shakespeare's time for its beautiful courtesans. *spent all his quiver:* used all his arrows.

4. An earthquake would be as unlikely as my quaking
with love.
5. You will soften as time passes; with perhaps a bawdy
pun on "hours," "whores" (pronounced similarly).
6. Protection (Claudio and Don Pedro parody a conventional formula for ending a letter).
7. *The body . . . fragments:* The substance (also punning on the dressmaker's "bodice") of what you say is
sometimes ornamented ("guarded") with odds and ends
("fragments") such as you are mocking me for using.
8. And the decorative phrases are barely relevant.

Have left their places vacant, in their rooms
Come thronging soft and delicate desires,
250 All prompting me how fair young Hero is,
Saying I liked her ere I went to wars.
DON PEDRO   Thou wilt be like a lover presently,
And tire the hearer with a book of words.°   *lover's set speeches*
If thou dost love fair Hero, cherish it,
255 And I will break° with her, and with her father,   *speak*
And thou shalt have her. Was't not to this end
That thou began'st to twist° so fine a story?   *spin*
CLAUDIO   How sweetly you do minister to love,
That know love's grief by his complexion!°   *by its appearance*
260 But lest my liking might too sudden seem
I would have salved° it with a longer treatise.   *smoothed*
DON PEDRO   What need the bridge much broader than the flood?°   *river*
The fairest grant is the necessity.⁹
Look what° will serve is fit. 'Tis once:° thou lovest,   *Whatever / In brief*
265 And I will fit thee with the remedy.
I know we shall have revelling° tonight.   *festivity; masked ball*
I will assume thy part° in some disguise,   *role*
And tell fair Hero I am Claudio.
And in her bosom I'll unclasp my heart¹
270 And take her hearing prisoner with the force
And strong encounter° of my amorous tale.   *assault*
Then after to her father will I break,
And the conclusion is, she shall be thine.
In practice let us put it presently.°   *Exeunt*   *at once*

1.2

Enter LEONATO *and* [ANTONIO,] *an old man brother to*
Leonato, [*severally*]°   *separately*
LEONATO   How now, brother, where is my cousin,° your son?   *kinsman (nephew)*
Hath he provided this music?
ANTONIO   He is very busy about it. But brother, I can tell you
strange news that you yet dreamt not of.
5 LEONATO   Are they good?
ANTONIO   As the event stamps them.¹ But they have a good
cover, they show well outward. The Prince and Count Clau-
dio, walking in a thick-pleached² alley in mine orchard,° were   *garden*
thus much overheard by a man of mine: the Prince discovered°   *revealed*
10 to Claudio that he loved my niece, your daughter, and meant
to acknowledge it this night in a dance, and if he found her
accordant° he meant to take the present time by the top³ and   *consenting*
instantly break° with you of it.   *speak*
LEONATO   Hath the fellow any wit° that told you this?   *intelligence*
15 ANTONIO   A good sharp fellow. I will send for him, and question
him yourself.
LEONATO   No, no. We will hold it as a dream till it appear° itself.   *manifest*
But I will acquaint my daughter withal,° that she may be the   *with it*

9. The best gift is something that is truly needed.
1. And I will privately reveal to her my feelings (as if
I were you).
1.2 Location: Leonato's house.
1. As good as the outcome ("event") proves ("stamps")

them. *The image is of news bound in a book with a
handsome cover.*
2. Enclosed by trees with intertwining boughs.
3. He meant to seize the opportunity. (Time is proverbially bald except for the "top," or forelock.)

better prepared for an answer if peradventure° this be true . Go   *by chance*
20 you and tell her of it.
    [*Enter Attendants*]⁴
    Cousins, you know what you have to do. O, I cry you mercy,⁵
    friend. Go you with me and I will use your skill.—Good
    cousin, have a care this busy time.   *Exeunt*

1.3

Enter [DON] JOHN *the bastard and* CONRAD, *his com-*
panion

CONRAD   What the goodyear, my lord, why are you thus out of
    measure¹ sad?
DON JOHN   There is no measure in the occasion that breeds it,
    therefore the sadness is without limit.
5   CONRAD   You should hear reason.
DON JOHN   And when I have heard it, what blessing brings it?
CONRAD   If not a present° remedy, at least a patient sufferance.   *an immediate*
DON JOHN   I wonder that thou—being, as thou sayst thou art,
    born under Saturn²—goest about to apply a moral medicine to
10 a mortifying mischief.° I cannot hide what I am. I must be sad   *a deadly sickness*
    when I have cause, and smile at no man's jests; eat when I have
    stomach,° and wait for no man's leisure; sleep when I am   *appetite*
    drowsy, and tend on° no man's business; laugh when I am   *attend to*
    merry, and claw° no man in his humour.°   *flatter / mood*
15 CONRAD   Yea, but you must not make the full show of this till
    you may do it without controlment.³ You have of late stood   *restraint*
    out° against your brother, and he hath ta'en you newly into his   *rebelled*
    grace,° where it is impossible you should take true root but by   *favor*
    the fair weather that you make yourself. It is needful that you
20 frame the season for your own harvest.
DON JOHN   I had rather be a canker° in a hedge than a rose³ in   *wild rose; weed*
    his grace, and it better fits my blood° to be disdained of all than   *disposition*
    to fashion° a carriage° to rob love from any. In this, though I   *affect; feign / behavior*
    cannot be said to be a flattering honest man, it must not be
25 denied but I am a plain-dealing villain. I am trusted with a
    muzzle, and enfranchised with a clog.⁴ Therefore I have
    decreed° not to sing in my cage. If I had my mouth I would   *determined*
    bite. If I had my liberty I would do my liking. In the mean
    time, let me be that I am, and seek not to alter me.
30 CONRAD   Can you make no use of your discontent?
DON JOHN   I make all use of it, for I use it only. Who comes
    here?
    Enter BORACHIO⁵
    What news, Borachio?
BORACHIO   I came yonder from a great supper. The Prince your

4. The attendants are evidently engaged in preparations for the reveling (2.1). "Cousins" (line 21) may be
dependents in Leonato's household.
5. I beg your pardon (perhaps because he has not initially recognized one of the attendants, or because he
has bumped into him). Leonato's reference to "skill"
suggests that he might be talking to a musician.
1.3 Location: Leonato's house.
1. *What the goodyear*: unexplained exclamation. *out of*
measure: disproportionately.

2. Born when Saturn was in the ascendant (therefore
"saturnine," melancholy).
3. Cultivated rose.
4. I am trusted by being muzzled (in other words, not
trusted at all), and given my freedom with a clog (a
heavy block of wood attached to an animal or man as a
restraint).
5. The name, from the Spanish for "wine bottle," was
used for drunkards.

35 brother is royally entertained by Leonato, and I can give you
intelligence of an intended marriage.

DON JOHN   Will it serve for any model° to build mischief on? ground plan
What is he for a fool[6] that betroths himself to unquietness?

BORACHIO   Marry,[7] it is your brother's right hand.

40 DON JOHN   Who, the most exquisite Claudio?

BORACHIO   Even he.

DON JOHN   A proper squire.[8] And who, and who? Which way
looks he?

BORACHIO   Marry, on Hero, the daughter and heir of Leonato.

45 DON JOHN   A very forward March chick.[9] How came you to this?

BORACHIO   Being entertained for a perfumer,[1] as I was smoking° perfuming
a musty room comes me the Prince and Claudio hand in hand,
in sad° conference. I whipped me behind the arras,° and there serious / wall hanging
heard it agreed upon that the Prince should woo Hero for him-

50 self and, having obtained her, give her to Count Claudio.

DON JOHN   Come, come, let us thither. This may prove food to
my displeasure.° That young start-up° hath all the glory of my hatred / upstart
overthrow. If I can cross[2] him any way I bless myself every way.
You are both sure,° and will assist me? reliable

55 CONRAD   To the death, my lord.

DON JOHN   Let us to the great supper. Their cheer is the greater
that° I am subdued. Would the cook were o' my mind.[3] Shall since
we go prove° what's to be done? find out

BORACHIO   We'll wait° upon your lordship.   *Exeunt* attend

2.1

Enter LEONATO, [ANTONIO] *his brother,* HERO *his daughter,* BEATRICE *his niece*[, MARGARET, *and* URSULA]

LEONATO   Was not Count John here at supper?

ANTONIO   I saw him not.

BEATRICE   How tartly° that gentleman looks. I never can see him sour
but I am heartburned[1] an hour after.

5 HERO   He is of a very melancholy disposition.

BEATRICE   He were° an excellent man that were made just in the would be
midway between him and Benedick. The one is too like an
image° and says nothing, and the other too like my lady's eldest a statue
son,[2] evermore tattling.° chattering

10 LEONATO   Then half Signor Benedick's tongue in Count John's
mouth, and half Count John's melancholy in Signor Benedick's
face—

BEATRICE   With a good leg and a good foot, uncle, and money
enough in his purse—such a man would win any woman in

15 the world, if a° could get her good will. he

LEONATO   By my troth, niece, thou wilt never get thee a husband
if thou be so shrewd° of thy tongue. shrewish

ANTONIO   In faith, she's too curst.° sharp-tongued

BEATRICE   Too curst is more[3] than curst. I shall lessen God's

---

6. What kind of fool is he.
7. By the Virgin Mary (a mild oath).
8. A fine young lover (ironic).
9. Precocious youngster, like a bird hatched early in
the season.
1. Being hired to burn sweet herbs (to mask unpleasant domestic odors).

2. Thwart (punning on "make the sign of the cross").
3. *o' my mind:* inclined to poison the food.
2.1 Location: Leonato's house.
1. I suffer from heartburn, caused by Don John's tart
looks.
2. That is, a spoiled child.
3. By one, punning on "too/two."

20   sending that way, for it is said God sends a curst cow short
     horns,[4] but to a cow too curst he sends none.
LEONATO   So, by being too curst, God will send you no horns.
BEATRICE   Just,° if he send me no husband,[5] for the which bless-   *Just so*
     ing I am at him upon my knees every morning and evening.
25   Lord, I could not endure a husband with a beard on his face. I
     had rather lie in the woollen.[6]
LEONATO   You may light on a husband that hath no beard.
BEATRICE   What should I do with him—dress him in my apparel
     and make him my waiting gentlewoman? He that hath a beard
30   is more than a youth, and he that hath no beard is less than a
     man; and he that is more than a youth is not for me, and he
     that is less than a man, I am not for him. Therefore I will even
     take sixpence in earnest of the bearherd and lead his apes into
     hell.[7]
35 LEONATO   Well then, go you into hell?
BEATRICE   No, but° to the gate, and there will the devil meet me   *only*
     like an old cuckold with horns on his head, and say, 'Get you
     to heaven, Beatrice, get you to heaven. Here's no place for you
     maids.' So deliver I up my apes and away to Saint Peter fore
40   the heavens.[8] He shows me where the bachelors[9] sit, and there
     live we as merry as the day is long.
ANTONIO [*to* HERO]   Well, niece, I trust you will be ruled by your
     father.
BEATRICE   Yes, faith, it is my cousin's duty to make curtsy and
45   say, 'Father, as it please you.' But yet for all that, cousin, let
     him be a handsome fellow, or else make another curtsy and
     say, 'Father, as it please me.'
LEONATO   Well, niece, I hope to see you one day fitted with a
     husband.
50 BEATRICE   Not till God make men of some other mettle° than   *substance*
     earth. Would it not grieve a woman to be overmastered with° a   *by*
     piece of valiant dust?—to make an account of her life to a clod
     of wayward marl?° No, uncle, I'll none. Adam's sons are my   *clay*
     brethren, and truly I hold it a sin to match in my kindred.[1]
55 LEONATO [*to* HERO]   Daughter, remember what I told you. If the
     Prince do solicit you in that kind,[2] you know your answer.
BEATRICE   The fault will be in the music, cousin, if you be not
     wooed in good time. If the Prince be too important,° tell him   *importunate*
     there is measure[3] in everything, and so dance out the answer.
60   For hear me, Hero, wooing, wedding, and repenting is as a
     Scotch jig, a measure, and a cinquepace.[4] The first suit° is hot   *courtship*
     and hasty, like a Scotch jig—and full as fantastical; the wed-
     ding mannerly° modest, as a measure, full of state and   *graciously*
     ancientry.° And then comes repentance, and with his bad legs   *old-fashioned decorum*

---

4. Proverbial: God makes sure that the vicious ("curst")
have little power to do harm.
5. That is, if God sent her a husband, she would cuckold him.
6. Sleep between rough blankets (without sheets).
7. *take . . . hell*: take advance payment from the bear
keeper (who trained bears for the popular sport of bearbaiting and who usually had charge of other animals);
leading apes into hell was the proverbial fate of old
maids.

8. Peter is gatekeeper of heaven. Q prints "Peter: for
the heavens"; it is possible that Beatrice means "as far
as heaven is concerned."
9. Unwed men or women.
1. *to . . . kindred*: to marry incestuously.
2. *in that kind*: that is, to marry him.
3. Moderation (punning on the name of a slow, stately
dance [line 63] and continuing the link between dancing and wooing "in good time" [line 58]).
4. A lively five-step dance.

65   falls into the cinquepace faster and faster till he sink into his
    grave.

LEONATO   Cousin, you apprehend passing° shrewdly.   *understand more than*

BEATRICE   I have a good eye, uncle. I can see a church by daylight.[5]

70 LEONATO   The revellers are entering, brother. Make good room.

    Enter [DON] PEDRO [*the*] Prince, CLAUDIO, BENEDICK,
    and BALTHASAR, DON JOHN, [*and* BORACHIO, *as*] *Mask-*
    ers, with a drum

DON PEDRO [*to* HERO]   Lady, will you walk a bout with your
friend?[6]

HERO   So you walk softly, and look sweetly, and say nothing, I
am yours for the walk; and especially when I walk away.

75 DON PEDRO   With me in your company?

HERO   I may say so when I please.

DON PEDRO   And when please you to say so?

HERO   When I like your favour;° for God defend the lute should   *face*
be like the case.[7]

80 DON PEDRO   My visor° is Philemon's roof. Within the house is   *mask*
Jove.[8]

HERO   Why, then, your visor should be thatched.[9]

DON PEDRO   Speak low if
    you speak love.

    [*They move aside*]

BALTHASAR [*to* MARGARET]   Well, I would you did like me.

MARGARET   So would not I, for your own sake, for I have many
85 ill° qualities.   *bad*

BALTHASAR   Which is one?

MARGARET   I say my prayers aloud.

BALTHASAR   I love you the better—the hearers may cry amen.

MARGARET   God match me with a good dancer.

90 BALTHASAR   Amen.

MARGARET   And God keep him out of my sight when the dance
is done. Answer, clerk.[1]

BALTHASAR   No more words. The clerk is answered.

    [*They move aside*]

URSULA [*to* ANTONIO]   I know you well enough, you are Signor
95 Antonio.

ANTONIO   At a word,° I am not.   *In short*

URSULA   I know you by the waggling of your head.

ANTONIO   To tell you true, I counterfeit him.

URSULA   You could never do him so ill-well[2] unless you were the
100 very man. Here's his dry hand up and down.[3] You are he, you
are he.

ANTONIO   At a word, I am not.

URSULA   Come, come, do you think I do not know you by your

---

5. That is, see what's in front of me.

6. Often used to mean "lover." *walk a bout*: take a turn (apparently a term in dancing).

7. God forbid your face should be as unappealing as your mask.

8. The peasant Philemon and his wife, Baucis, entertained Jove, disguised, in their humble cottage (Ovid, *Metamorphoses* 8). This and the following line are in "fourteeners," a verse form old-fashioned in Shake-

speare's time but used by Arthur Golding in his 1567 translation of the *Metamorphoses*.

9. According to Golding, Philemon's roof was "thatched all with straw"; Hero means that the mask should be fitted with false hair or beard.

1. That is, say "Amen" again. The parish clerk led the responses in church services.

2. *do him so ill-well*: mime his imperfections so ably.

3. His wrinkled hand exactly.

excellent wit? Can virtue° hide itself? Go to, mum,° you are   *excellence / be quiet*
105   he. Graces will appear, and there's an end.[4]
                    [*They move aside*]
BEATRICE [*to* BENEDICK]   Will you not tell me who told you so?
BENEDICK   No, you shall pardon me.
BEATRICE   Nor will you not tell me who you are?
BENEDICK   Not now.
110   BEATRICE   That I was disdainful, and that I had my good wit out
            of the Hundred Merry Tales[5]—well, this was Signor Benedick
            that said so.
BENEDICK   What's he?
BEATRICE   I am sure you know him well enough.
115   BENEDICK   Not I, believe me.
BEATRICE   Did he never make you laugh?
BENEDICK   I pray you, what is he?
BEATRICE   Why, he is the Prince's jester, a very dull fool. Only
            his° gift is in devising impossible° slanders. None but libertines   *His only / unbelievable*
120   delight in him, and the commendation is not in his wit but in
            his villainy,° for he both pleases men and angers them, and   *rudeness*
            then they laugh at him, and beat him. I am sure he is in the
            fleet.° I would he had boarded me.[6]   *company (of dancers)*
BENEDICK   When I know the gentleman, I'll tell him what you
125   say.
BEATRICE   Do, do. He'll but break a comparison[7] or two on me,
            which peradventure° not marked, or not laughed at, strikes him   *perhaps*
            into melancholy, and then there's a partridge wing saved, for
            the fool will eat no supper that night.
                    Music
130   We must follow the leaders.°   *leaders in the dance*
BENEDICK   In every good thing.
BEATRICE   Nay, if they lead to any ill I will leave them at the
            next turning.
                    Dance. Exeunt [*all but* DON JOHN, BORACHIO, *and*
                    CLAUDIO]
DON JOHN [*aside to* BORACHIO]   Sure my brother is amorous on
135   Hero, and hath withdrawn her father to break with him about
            it. The ladies follow her, and but one visor° remains.   *(man wearing a) mask*
BORACHIO [*aside to* DON JOHN]   And that is Claudio. I know him
            by his bearing.
DON JOHN   Are not you Signor Benedick?
140   CLAUDIO   You know me well. I am he.
DON JOHN   Signor, you are very near my brother in his love.° He   *favor*
            is enamoured on Hero. I pray you dissuade him from her. She
            is no equal for his birth. You may do the part of an honest man
            in it.
145   CLAUDIO   How know you he loves her?
DON JOHN   I heard him swear his affection.
BORACHIO   So did I, too, and he swore he would marry her
            tonight.
DON JOHN   Come, let us to the banquet.°   *after-dinner sweets*
                    Exeunt. Manet° CLAUDIO   *Remains*

4. And that is all there is to be said.   7. He'll only try out, or "crack," a satirical comparison
5. A famously bad joke-book, first published in 1526.   (as one "breaks" a lance).
6. Assaulted me like a ship.

150   CLAUDIO   Thus answer I in name of Benedick,
But hear these ill news with the ears of Claudio.
'Tis certain° so, the Prince woos for himself.   *certainly*
Friendship is constant in all other things
Save in the office° and affairs of love.   *business*
155   Therefore all° hearts in love use their own tongues.   *let all*
Let every eye negotiate for itself,
And trust no agent; for beauty is a witch
Against whose charms faith° melteth into blood.°   *loyalty / passion*
This is an accident of hourly proof,[8]
160   Which I mistrusted° not. Farewell, therefore, Hero.   *suspected*
     Enter BENEDICK
    BENEDICK   Count Claudio?
    CLAUDIO   Yea, the same.
    BENEDICK   Come, will you go with me?
    CLAUDIO   Whither?
165   BENEDICK   Even to the next willow,[9] about your own business,
County.° What fashion will you wear the garland° of? About   *Count / (of willow)*
your neck, like an usurer's chain?[1] Or under your arm, like a
lieutenant's scarf?[2] You must wear it one° way, for the Prince   *some*
hath got your Hero.
170   CLAUDIO   I wish him joy of her.
    BENEDICK   Why, that's spoken like an honest drover;° so they sell   *cattle dealer*
bullocks. But did you think the Prince would have served you
thus?
    CLAUDIO   I pray you leave me.
175   BENEDICK   Ho, now you strike like the blind man—'twas the boy
that stole your meat, and you'll beat the post.[3]
    CLAUDIO   If it° will not be, I'll leave you.   *Exit*   *(your departure)*
    BENEDICK   Alas, poor hurt fowl, now will he creep into sedges.[4]
But that my Lady Beatrice should know me, and not know me!
180   The Prince's fool! Ha, it may be I go under that title because I
am merry. Yea, but so I am apt to do myself wrong. I am not so
reputed. It is the base, though bitter, disposition of Beatrice
that puts the world into her person, and so gives me out.[5] Well,
I'll be revenged as I may.
     Enter [DON PEDRO *the*] *Prince*
185   DON PEDRO   Now, signor, where's the Count? Did you see him?
    BENEDICK   Troth, my lord, I have played the part of Lady Fame.°   *Lady Rumor*
I found him here as melancholy as a lodge in a warren.[6] I told
him—and I think I told him true—that your grace had got the
good will of this young lady, and I offered him my company to
190   a willow tree, either to make him a garland, as being forsaken,
or to bind him up a rod,° as being worthy to be whipped.   *bundle of sticks*
    DON PEDRO   To be whipped—what's his fault?
    BENEDICK   The flat° transgression of a schoolboy who, being   *stupid*
overjoyed with finding a bird's nest, shows it his companion,
195   and he steals it.

8. This is an occurrence demonstrated every hour, common event.
9. Symbol of unrequited love.
1. A gold chain worn by a moneylender.
2. A sash across the chest.
3. Probably alluding to a folktale, which existed in various forms, of a boy who robbed and played a trick on his blind master. *post:* pillar (with play on Benedick as

the "post," or messenger, who bears bad news).
4. *creep into sedges:* hide to nurse his wounds, as an injured bird crawls into the tall grass along a riverbank.
5. It is Beatrice's low but sarcastic disposition that makes her believe the whole world is of her opinion and represents me accordingly.
6. As a burrow in a rabbit warren. (The rabbit was a traditional symbol of melancholy.)

DON PEDRO   Wilt thou make a trust a transgression? The transgression is in the stealer.

BENEDICK   Yet it had not been amiss the rod had been made,
and the garland too, for the garland he might have worn him-
200 self, and the rod he might have bestowed on you, who, as I take
it, have stolen his bird's nest.

DON PEDRO   I will but teach them° to sing, and restore them to   *(the chicks)*
the owner.

BENEDICK   If their singing answer your saying, by my faith you
205 say honestly.[7]

DON PEDRO   The Lady Beatrice hath a quarrel to° you. The gen-   *with*
tleman that danced with her told her she is much wronged by
you.

BENEDICK   O, she misused° me past the endurance of a block.   *abused*
210 An oak but with one green leaf on it[8] would have answered
her. My very visor began to assume life and scold with her.
She told me—not thinking I had been myself—that I was the
Prince's jester, that I was duller than a great thaw,[9] huddling
jest upon jest with such impossible conveyance° upon me that   *speed*
215 I stood like a man at a mark,° with a whole army shooting at   *target*
me. She speaks poniards,° and every word stabs. If her breath   *daggers*
were as terrible as her terminations,° there were no living near   *expressions*
her, she would infect to the North Star.[1] I would not marry her
though she were endowed with all that Adam had left him
220 before he transgressed. She would have made Hercules have
turned spit, yea, and have cleft his club to make the fire, too.[2]
Come, talk not of her. You shall find her the infernal Ate° in   *goddess of discord*
good apparel. I would to God some scholar would conjure[3]
her, for certainly, while she is here a man may live as quiet in
225 hell as in a sanctuary, and people sin upon purpose because
they would go thither, so indeed all disquiet, horror, and per-
turbation follows° her.   *attends upon*

Enter CLAUDIO *and* BEATRICE, *[and]* LEONATO *[with]*
HERO

DON PEDRO   Look, here she comes.

BENEDICK   Will your grace command me any service to the
230 world's end? I will go on the slightest errand now to the Antipodes that you can devise to send me on. I will fetch you a tooth-
picker° now from the furthest inch of Asia, bring you the length   *toothpick*
of Prester John's foot, fetch you a hair off the Great Cham's
beard, do you any embassage to the pigmies,[4] rather than hold
235 three words' conference with this harpy.[5] You have no employment for me?

DON PEDRO   None but to desire your good company.

BENEDICK   O God, sir, here's a dish I love not. I cannot endure
my Lady Tongue.   *Exit*

7. If they sing as you say they will—if you have wooed
Hero for Claudio—then you are talking honorably.
8. An oak with barely any life remaining in it.
9. When the muddy roads kept everyone at home.
1. Thought to be the remotest star.
2. The Amazon Omphale made Hercules wear her
clothes and spin; Benedick imagines an even greater
humiliation and more menial duty—turning the spit.
3. Conjure the evil spirits out of, or supernaturally

consign to hell. *scholar:* learned person (who could
speak Latin, the language of exorcism).
4. *Prester John's . . . pigmies:* all distant, fantastic figures. In legend, Prester John ruled in Ethiopia, while
the Great Cham (Kublai Khan) reigned in Mongolia,
and a race of dwarfs was said to inhabit the mountains
of India.
5. Mythical creature with the face and body of a
woman and the wings and claws of a bird of prey.

240 DON PEDRO Come, lady, come, you have lost the heart of Signor
Benedick.
BEATRICE Indeed, my lord, he lent it me a while, and I gave
him use° for it, a double heart for his single one. Marry, once   *interest*
before he won it of ° me, with false dice. Therefore your grace   *from*
245 may well say I have lost it.
DON PEDRO You have put him down, lady, you have put him
down.⁶
BEATRICE So I would not he should do me, my lord, lest I
should prove the mother of fools. I have brought Count Clau-
250 dio, whom you sent me to seek.
DON PEDRO Why, how now, Count, wherefore are you sad?
CLAUDIO Not sad, my lord.
DON PEDRO How then? Sick?
CLAUDIO Neither, my lord.
255 BEATRICE The Count is neither sad, nor sick, nor merry, nor
well, but civil° count, civil⁷ as an orange, and something° of   *serious / somewhat*
that jealous complexion.⁸
DON PEDRO I'faith, lady, I think your blazon° to be true, though   *formal description*
I'll be sworn, if he be so, his conceit° is false. Here, Claudio, I   *imagined idea*
260 have wooed in thy name, and fair Hero is won. I have broke°   *spoken*
with her father and his good will obtained. Name the day of
marriage, and God give thee joy.
LEONATO Count, take of me my daughter, and with her my fortunes. His grace hath made the match, and all grace say amen
265 to it.⁹
BEATRICE Speak, Count, 'tis your cue.
CLAUDIO Silence is the perfectest herald of joy. I were but little
happy if I could say how much. [*To* HERO] Lady, as you are
mine, I am yours. I give away myself for you, and dote upon
270 the exchange.
BEATRICE [*to* HERO] Speak, cousin. Or, if you cannot, stop his
mouth with a kiss, and let not him speak, neither.
DON PEDRO In faith, lady, you have a merry heart.
BEATRICE Yea, my lord, I thank it. Poor fool, it keeps on the
275 windy° side of care.—My cousin tells him in his ear that he is   *windward; safe*
in her heart.
CLAUDIO And so she doth, cousin.
BEATRICE Good Lord, for alliance!¹ Thus goes everyone to the
world but I, and I am sunburnt.² I may sit in a corner and cry
280 'Heigh-ho for a husband'.³
DON PEDRO Lady Beatrice, I will get you one.
BEATRICE I would rather have one of your father's getting.° Hath   *begetting*
your grace ne'er a° brother like you? Your father got excellent   *no*
husbands if a maid could come by them.
285 DON PEDRO Will you have me, lady?
BEATRICE No, my lord, unless I might have another for working

---

6. Humiliated him. (Beatrice, in reply, puns on the
physical sense.)
7. Punning on "Seville," famous for its bitter oranges.
8. Yellow (the traditional color of jealousy).
9. And may God, the source of all grace, confirm it.
1. Kinship through marriage. (Claudio has just

addressed Beatrice as one of the family.)
2. Unattractive, and therefore unlikely to marry.
(Suntans, like dark complexions, were unfashionable.)
goes . . . to the world: gets married.
3. Title of a ballad; probably a catchphrase in Shakespeare's time.

days. Your grace is too costly to wear every day. But I beseech
your grace, pardon me. I was born to speak all mirth and no
matter.° *substance*

290 DON PEDRO   Your silence most offends me, and to be merry best
becomes you; for out o' question, you were born in a merry
hour.

BEATRICE   No, sure, my lord, my mother cried. But then there
was a star danced, and under that was I born. [*To* HERO *and*

295 CLAUDIO] Cousins, God give you joy.

LEONATO   Niece, will you look to those things I told you of?

BEATRICE   I cry you mercy,° uncle. [*To* DON PEDRO] By your
grace's pardon.   *Exit* BEATRICE *I beg your pardon*

DON PEDRO   By my troth, a pleasant-spirited lady.

300 LEONATO   There's little of the melancholy element in her, my
lord. She is never sad° but when she sleeps, and not ever° sad *serious / not always*
then; for I have heard my daughter say she hath often dreamt
of unhappiness and waked herself with laughing.

DON PEDRO   She cannot endure to hear tell of a husband.

305 LEONATO   O, by no means. She mocks all her wooers out of suit.° *wooing (her)*

DON PEDRO   She were an excellent wife for Benedick.

LEONATO   O Lord, my lord, if they were but a week married they
would talk themselves mad.

DON PEDRO   County Claudio, when mean you to go to church?

310 CLAUDIO   Tomorrow, my lord. Time goes on crutches till love
have all his rites.

LEONATO   Not till Monday, my dear son, which is hence a just
sevennight, and a time too brief, too, to have all things answer° *match*
my mind.° *wishes*

315 DON PEDRO   Come, you shake the head at so long a breathing,° *an interval*
but I warrant° thee, Claudio, the time shall not go dully by us. *assure*
I will in the interim undertake one of Hercules' labours, which
is to bring Signor Benedick and the Lady Beatrice into a mountain of affection th'one with th'other. I would fain° have it a *gladly*

320 match, and I doubt not but to fashion it, if you three will but
minister such assistance as I shall give you direction.

LEONATO   My lord, I am for you, though it cost me ten nights'
watchings.° *staying awake*

CLAUDIO   And I, my lord.

325 DON PEDRO   And you too, gentle Hero?

HERO   I will do any modest office,° my lord, to help my cousin *task*
to a good husband.

DON PEDRO   And Benedick is not the unhopefullest° husband *least promising*
that I know. Thus far can I praise him: he is of a noble strain,° *descent*

330 of approved° valour and confirmed honesty.° I will teach you *proven / honor*
how to humour your cousin that she shall fall in love with
Benedick, and I, with your two helps, will so practise on° *so trick*
Benedick that, in despite of his quick wit and his queasy stom-
ach,° he shall fall in love with Beatrice. If we can do this, *qualms (about love)*

335 Cupid is no longer an archer; his glory shall be ours, for we are
the only love-gods. Go in with me, and I will tell you my drift.° *scheme*
                                    Exeunt

2.2

Enter [DON] JOHN *and* BORACHIO

DON JOHN   It is so. The Count Claudio shall marry the daughter
of Leonato.

BORACHIO   Yea, my lord, but I can cross° it.   *thwart*

DON JOHN   Any bar, any cross, any impediment will be medi-
5   cinable° to me. I am sick in displeasure to him, and whatsoever   *medicinal*
comes athwart his affection ranges evenly with mine.[1] How
canst thou cross this marriage?

BORACHIO   Not honestly, my lord, but so covertly that no dishonesty shall appear in me.

10   DON JOHN   Show me briefly how.

BORACHIO   I think I told your lordship a year since how much
I am in the favour of Margaret, the waiting gentlewoman to
Hero.

DON JOHN   I remember.

15   BORACHIO   I can at any unseasonable instant of the night
appoint° her to look out at her lady's chamber window.   *arrange with*

DON JOHN   What life is in that to be the death of this marriage?

BORACHIO   The poison of that lies in you to temper.° Go you to   *concoct*
the Prince your brother. Spare not to tell him that he hath
20   wronged his honour in marrying the renowned Claudio—
whose estimation° do you mightily hold up°—to a contami-   *reputation / esteem*
nated stale,° such a one as Hero.   *prostitute*

DON JOHN   What proof shall I make of that?

BORACHIO   Proof enough to misuse° the Prince, to vex° Claudio,   *deceive / torment*
25   to undo Hero, and kill Leonato. Look you for any other issue?°   *result*

DON JOHN   Only to despite° them I will endeavour anything.   *Merely to spite*

BORACHIO   Go then. Find me a meet hour to draw Don Pedro
and the Count Claudio alone. Tell them that you know that
Hero loves me. Intend° a kind of zeal both to the Prince and   *Pretend*
30   Claudio as in° love of your brother's honour who hath made   *as if for*
this match, and his friend's reputation who is thus like to be
cozened with the semblance of a maid,[2] that you have discovered thus. They will scarcely believe this without trial. Offer
them instances, which shall bear no less likelihood than to see
35   me at her chamber window, hear me call Margaret Hero, hear
Margaret term me Claudio.[3] And bring them to see this the
very night before the intended wedding, for in the mean time
I will so fashion the matter that Hero shall be absent, and there
shall appear such seeming truth of Hero's disloyalty that jeal-
40   ousy shall be called assurance,[4] and all the preparation° over-   *wedding preparation*
thrown.

DON JOHN   Grow this° to what adverse issue it can, I will put it   *Let this lead*
in practice. Be cunning in the working this,° and thy fee is a   *of this*
thousand ducats.°   *gold coins*

45   BORACHIO   Be you constant in the accusation, and my cunning
shall not shame me.

DON JOHN   I will presently go learn their day of marriage.

Exeunt

2.2 Location: Leonato's house.
1. And whatever frustrates his wishes conforms with
mine.
2. To be cheated with the mere appearance of a virgin.

3. Most editors assume an error here and emend to
"Borachio."
4. That suspicion shall be called certainty.

2.3

Enter BENEDICK

BENEDICK Boy!

　　　[*Enter* BOY]

BOY Signor?

BENEDICK In my chamber window lies a book. Bring it hither to me in the orchard.

5　BOY I am here already,[1] sir.

BENEDICK I know that, but I would have thee hence and here again.　　　　　　　　　　　　　　　　　　　*Exit* [BOY]

I do much wonder that one man, seeing how much another man is a fool when he dedicates his behaviours to love, will, after he hath laughed at such shallow follies in others, become the argument° of his own scorn by falling in love. And such a man is Claudio. I have known when there was no music with him but the drum and the fife, and now had he rather hear the tabor and the pipe.[2] I have known when he would have walked ten mile afoot to see a good armour, and now will he lie ten nights awake carving° the fashion of a new doublet.° He was wont° to speak plain and to the purpose, like an honest man and a soldier, and now is he turned orthography.[3] His words are a very fantastical° banquet, just so many strange dishes. May I be so converted, and see° with these eyes? I cannot tell. I think not. I will not be sworn but love may transform me to an oyster, but I'll take my oath on it, till he have made an oyster of me he shall never make me such a fool. One woman is fair, yet I am well. Another is wise, yet I am well. Another virtuous, yet I am well. But till all graces be in one woman, one woman shall not come in my grace.° Rich she shall be, that's certain. Wise, or I'll none.[4] Virtuous, or I'll never cheapen° her. Fair, or I'll never look on her. Mild, or come not near me. Noble, or not I for an angel.[5] Of good discourse, an excellent musician, and her hair shall be of what colour it please God. Ha! The Prince and Monsieur Love. I will hide me in the arbour.

　　　[*He hides.*]

Enter [DON PEDRO *the*] *Prince,* LEONATO, *and* CLAUDIO[6]

DON PEDRO Come, shall we hear this music?

CLAUDIO Yea, my good lord. How still the evening is,
As° hushed on purpose to grace harmony.

35　DON PEDRO [*aside*] See you where Benedick hath hid himself?

CLAUDIO [*aside*] O, very well, my lord. The music ended,
We'll fit the hid-fox with a pennyworth.[7]

Enter BALTHASAR *with music*

DON PEDRO Come, Balthasar, we'll hear that song again.

BALTHASAR O good my lord, tax° not so bad a voice
To slander music any more than once.

DON PEDRO It is the witness still° of excellency

Marginal glosses (right column):

10　subject

16　designing / jacket
17　accustomed

19　poetic
20　still see

26　favor
27　bargain for

33　As if

39　task

41　the mark always

2.3 Location: Leonato's garden.
1. That is, it's as good as done. (Benedick takes him literally.)
2. The drum and fife were used by the military; the tabor (a small drum) and pipe were used in social festivities.
3. Become overelaborate in his speech.
4. Or I'll have none (of her).
5. Not I, though she be an angel (punning on coins: an angel was worth 10 shillings, and a noble 6 shillings 8 pence).
6. Q's stage direction includes "Music," which seems premature as the singer, Balthasar, enters at line 38.
7. We'll give our sly eavesdropper more than he bargained for. *hid-fox:* apparently refers to the game of hide-and-seek (compare *Hamlet* 4.2.28: "Hide, fox, and all after").

To put a strange face on[8] his own perfection.
I pray thee sing, and let me woo° no more.   *cajole*
BALTHASAR   Because you talk of wooing[9] I will sing,
45   Since many a wooer doth commence his suit
To her he thinks not worthy, yet he woos,
Yet will he swear he loves.
DON PEDRO   Nay pray thee, come;
Or if thou wilt hold longer argument,
Do it in notes.°   *music*
BALTHASAR   Note this before my notes:
50   There's not a note of mine that's worth the noting.
DON PEDRO   Why, these are very crotchets[1] that he speaks—
Note notes, forsooth, and nothing![2]
         [*The accompaniment begins*]
BENEDICK   Now, divine air! Now is his soul ravished. Is it not
strange that sheep's guts[3] should hale° souls out of men's bod-   *drag*
55   ies? Well, a horn[4] for my money, when all's done.
BALTHASAR [*sings*]
                Sigh no more, ladies, sigh no more.
                Men were deceivers ever,
                One foot in sea, and one on shore,
                To one thing constant never.
60   Then sigh not so, but let them go,
                And be you blithe and bonny,°   *beautiful*
                Converting all your sounds of woe
                Into hey nonny, nonny.

                Sing no more ditties, sing no more
65   Of dumps[5] so dull and heavy.
                The fraud of men was ever so
                Since summer first was leafy.
                Then sigh not so, but let them go,
                And be you blithe and bonny,
70   Converting all your sounds of woe
                Into hey nonny, nonny.

DON PEDRO   By my troth, a good song.
BALTHASAR   And an ill singer, my lord.
DON PEDRO   Ha, no, no, faith. Thou singest well enough for a
75   shift.°   *to make do*
BENEDICK [*aside*]   An° he had been a dog that should have   *If*
howled thus, they would have hanged him; and I pray God his
bad voice bode no mischief. I had as lief° have heard the night-   *as gladly*
raven,° come what plague could have come after it.   *bird of ill omen*
80   DON PEDRO   Yea, marry,[6] dost thou hear, Balthasar? I pray thee
get us some excellent music, for tomorrow night we would
have it at the Lady Hero's chamber window.

8. *To put . . . on:* Not to admit.
9. Because you put it in terms of wooing (and so are
likely to continue to flatter me insincerely).
1. Whimsies; quarter notes (in music).
2. *Note . . . nothing:* Get on with your singing, and
nothing else. ("Nothing" and "noting" sounded the
same in Elizabethan pronunciation. Compare the same

play on words in the title.)
3. Used to string musical instruments.
4. Military or hunting horn.
5. Melancholy tunes or moods.
6. A mild oath. (Don Pedro is continuing the speech
interrupted by Benedick's aside.)

BALTHASAR   The best I can, my lord.   *Exit*

DON PEDRO   Do so. Farewell. Come hither, Leonato. What was
85   it you told me of today, that your niece Beatrice was in love
with Signor Benedick?

CLAUDIO [*aside*]   O, ay, stalk on, stalk on. The fowl sits.[7]—I did
never think that lady would have loved any man.

LEONATO   No, nor I neither. But most wonderful° that she   astounding
90   should so dote on Signor Benedick, whom she hath in all outward behaviours seemed ever to abhor.

BENEDICK [*aside*]   Is't possible? Sits the wind in that corner?

LEONATO   By my troth, my lord, I cannot tell what to think of it.
But that she loves him with an enraged° affection, it is past the   a frenzied
95   infinite° of thought.   furthest bounds

DON PEDRO   Maybe she doth but counterfeit.

CLAUDIO   Faith, like° enough.   likely

LEONATO   O God! Counterfeit? There was never counterfeit of
passion came so near the life of passion as she discovers° it.   exhibits

100   DON PEDRO   Why, what effects of passion shows she?

CLAUDIO [*aside*]   Bait the hook well. This fish will bite.

LEONATO   What effects, my lord? She will sit you[8]—you heard
my daughter tell you how.

CLAUDIO   She did indeed.

105   DON PEDRO   How, how, I pray you? You amaze me. I would have
thought her spirit had been invincible against all assaults of
affection.

LEONATO   I would have sworn it had, my lord, especially against
Benedick.

110   BENEDICK [*aside*]   I should think this a gull,° but that the white-   trick
bearded fellow speaks it. Knavery cannot, sure, hide himself in
such reverence.

CLAUDIO   [*aside*]   He hath ta'en th'infection. Hold° it up.   Keep

DON PEDRO   Hath she made her affection known to Benedick?

115   LEONATO   No, and swears she never will. That's her torment.

CLAUDIO   'Tis true, indeed, so your daughter says. 'Shall I,' says
she, 'that have so oft encountered him with scorn, write to him
that I love him?'

LEONATO   This says she now when she is beginning to write to
120   him, for she'll be up twenty times a night, and there will she sit
in her smock° till she have writ a sheet of paper. My daughter   slip
tells us all.

CLAUDIO   Now you talk of a sheet of paper, I remember a pretty
jest your daughter told us of.

125   LEONATO   O, when she had writ it and was reading it over, she
found Benedick and Beatrice between the sheet.

CLAUDIO   That.

LEONATO   O, she tore the letter into a thousand halfpence,°   small pieces
railed at herself that she should be so immodest to write to one
130   that she knew would flout° her. 'I measure him,' says she, 'by   jeer at
my own spirit, for I should flout him if he writ to me, yea,
though I love him I should.'

CLAUDIO   Then down upon her knees she falls, weeps, sobs,
beats her heart, tears her hair, prays, curses, 'O sweet Benedick,
135   God give me patience.'

7. *stalk . . . sits*: go on quietly. Our prey has alighted.   8. She will sit down (i.e., weak with lovesickness).

LEONATO   She doth indeed, my daughter says so, and the ecstasy° *passion*
hath so much overborne her that my daughter is sometime
afeard she will do a desperate outrage° to herself. It is very true. *injury*

DON PEDRO   It were good that Benedick knew of it by some
140   other, if she will not discover° it. *reveal*

CLAUDIO   To what end? He would make but a sport of it and
torment the poor lady worse.

DON PEDRO   An he should, it were an alms° to hang him. She's *a charitable deed*
an excellent sweet lady, and, out of all suspicion,° she is vir- *doubt*
145   tuous.

CLAUDIO   And she is exceeding wise.

DON PEDRO   In everything but in loving Benedick.

LEONATO   O my lord, wisdom and blood° combating in so tender *passion*
a body, we have ten proofs to one that blood hath the victory. I
150   am sorry for her, as I have just cause, being her uncle and her
guardian.

DON PEDRO   I would she had bestowed this dotage° on me. I *infatuation*
would have doffed⁹ all other respects° and made her half *considerations*
myself. I pray you tell Benedick of it, and hear what a° will say. *he*
155   LEONATO   Were it good, think you?

CLAUDIO   Hero thinks surely she will die, for she says she will die
if he love her not, and she will die ere she make her love
known, and she will die if he woo her, rather than she will
bate° one breath of her accustomed crossness.° *abate / contrariness*
160   DON PEDRO   She doth well. If she should make tender° of her *make an offer*
love 'tis very possible he'll scorn it, for the man, as you know
all, hath a contemptible° spirit. *contemptuous*

CLAUDIO   He is a very proper° man. *handsome*

DON PEDRO   He hath indeed a good outward happiness.¹
165   CLAUDIO   Before God; and in my mind, very wise.

DON PEDRO   He doth indeed show some sparks that are like wit.

CLAUDIO   And I take him to be valiant.

DON PEDRO   As Hector,² I assure you; and in the managing of
quarrels you may say he is wise, for either he avoids them with
170   great discretion or undertakes them with a most Christianlike
fear.

LEONATO   If he do fear God, a must necessarily keep peace. If
he break the peace, he ought to enter into a quarrel with fear
and trembling.
175   DON PEDRO   And so will he do, for the man doth fear God, howsoever it seems not in him by some large° jests he will make. *broad*
Well, I am sorry for your niece. Shall we go seek Benedick and
tell him of her love?

CLAUDIO   Never tell him, my lord. Let her wear it out with good
180   counsel.° *advice*

LEONATO   Nay, that's impossible. She may wear her heart out
first.

DON PEDRO   Well, we will hear further of it by° your daughter. *from*
Let it cool the while. I love Benedick well, and I could wish he
185   would modestly examine himself to see how much he is unworthy so good a lady.

---

9. Set aside or cast off.   2. The noblest and bravest Trojan warrior.
1. He is well endowed with looks and bearing.

LEONATO My lord, will you walk? Dinner is ready.

CLAUDIO [*aside*] If he do not dote on her upon this, I will never
trust my expectation.° predictions

190 DON PEDRO [*aside*] Let there be the same net spread for her,
and that must your daughter and her gentlewomen carry.° The manage
sport will be when they hold one an opinion of another's dot-
age, and no such matter.[3] That's the scene that I would see,
which will be merely a dumb show.[4] Let us send her to call

195 him in to dinner.

Exeunt [DON PEDRO, CLAUDIO, *and* LEONATO]

BENEDICK [*coming forward*] This can be no trick. The conference was sadly borne.° They have the truth of this from Hero. seriously conducted
They seem to pity the lady. It seems her affections have their
full bent.[5] Love me! Why, it must be requited. I hear how I am

200 censured. They say I will bear myself proudly if I perceive the
love come from her. They say too that she will rather die than
give any sign of affection. I did never think to marry. I must not
seem proud. Happy are they that hear their detractions and can
put them to mending.° They say the lady is fair. 'Tis a truth, I amending

205 can bear them witness. And virtuous—'tis so, I cannot reprove° contradict
it. And wise, but for loving me. By my troth, it is no addition to
her wit[6]—nor no great argument of her folly, for I will be horribly in love with her. I may chance have some odd quirks° and quips
remnants of wit broken on° me because I have railed so long cracked against

210 against marriage; but doth not the appetite alter? A man loves
the meat in his youth that he cannot endure in his age. Shall
quips and sentences° and these paper bullets of the brain awe epigrams
a man from the career° of his humour?° No. The world must swift course / liking
be peopled. When I said I would die a bachelor, I did not think

215 I should live till I were married. Here comes Beatrice.

Enter BEATRICE

By this day, she's a fair lady. I do spy some marks of love in her.

BEATRICE Against my will I am sent to bid you come in to
dinner.

BENEDICK Fair Beatrice, I thank you for your pains.

220 BEATRICE I took no more pains for those thanks than you take
pains to thank me. If it had been painful I would not have
come.

BENEDICK You take pleasure, then, in the message?

BEATRICE Yea, just so much as you may take upon a knife's

225 point and choke a daw withal.° You have no stomach,° signor? jackdaw with / appetite
Fare you well. *Exit*

BENEDICK Ha! 'Against my will I am sent to bid you come in to
dinner.' There's a double meaning in that. 'I took no more
pains for those thanks than you took pains to thank me.' That's

230 as much as to say 'Any pains that I take for you is as easy as
thanks.'—If I do not take pity of her I am a villain. If I do not
love her I am a Jew.[7] I will go get her picture.[8] *Exit*

---

3. *when . . . matter*: when each believes that the other
is madly in love, without any basis in fact.
4. A pantomime (because words for once will fail
them).
5. Are stretched to the limit (like a bent bow).

6. No additional proof of her intelligence.
7. That is, lacking in Christian charity (an anti-Semitic
stereotype).
8. *get her picture*: have her portrait painted (for a love
locket) or sketch it himself.

3.1

Enter HERO *and two gentlewomen,* MARGARET *and*
    URSULA

HERO   Good Margaret, run thee to the parlour.
There shalt thou find my cousin Beatrice
Proposing° with the Prince and Claudio.   *Talking*
Whisper her ear, and tell her I and Ursula
5   Walk in the orchard, and our whole discourse
Is all of her. Say that thou overheard'st us,
And bid her steal into the pleachèd¹ bower
Where honeysuckles, ripened by the sun,
Forbid the sun to enter—like favourites
10   Made proud by princes, that advance their pride
Against that power that bred it.² There will she hide her
To listen° our propose.° This is thy office.   *hear / conversation*
Bear thee well in it, and leave us alone.
MARGARET   I'll make her come, I warrant you, presently. [*Exit*]
15 HERO   Now, Ursula, when Beatrice doth come,
As we do trace° this alley up and down   *pace*
Our talk must only be of Benedick.
When I do name him, let it be thy part
To praise him more than ever man did merit.
20   My talk to thee must be how Benedick
Is sick in love with Beatrice. Of this matter
Is little Cupid's crafty arrow made,
That only wounds by hearsay.³
    Enter BEATRICE
                         Now begin,
For look where Beatrice like a lapwing⁴ runs
25   Close by the ground to hear our conference.
URSULA   The pleasant'st angling is to see the fish
Cut with her golden oars the silver stream
And greedily devour the treacherous bait.
So angle we for Beatrice, who even now
30   Is couchèd° in the woodbine coverture.⁵   *hidden*
Fear you not my part of the dialogue.
HERO   Then go we near her, that her ear lose nothing
Of the false-sweet bait that we lay for it.—
    [*They approach Beatrice's hiding-place*]
No, truly, Ursula, she is too disdainful.
35   I know her spirits are as coy° and wild   *disdainful; shy*
As haggards° of the rock.   *wild female hawks*
URSULA   But are you sure
That Benedick loves Beatrice so entirely?
HERO   So says the Prince and my new trothèd lord.
URSULA   And did they bid you tell her of it, madam?
40 HERO   They did entreat me to acquaint her of it,
But I persuaded them, if they loved Benedick,
To wish him wrestle with affection
And never to let Beatrice know of it.
URSULA   Why did you so? Doth not the gentleman

3.1 Location: Leonato's garden.
1. Screened by intertwining branches.
2. *that advance . . . it:* who presumptuously oppose the
power that created them.

3. Wounds by rumor or gossip.
4. A peewit, a bird that scuttles along the ground.
5. In the honeysuckle arbor.

45   Deserve as full° as fortunate a bed   *fully*
          As ever Beatrice shall couch upon?
          HERO   O god of love! I know he doth deserve
          As much as may be yielded to a man.
          But nature never framed a woman's heart
50   Of prouder stuff than that of Beatrice.
          Disdain and scorn ride sparkling in her eyes,
          Misprising° what they look on, and her wit   *Despising*
          Values itself so highly that to her
          All matter else seems° weak. She cannot love,   *other matters seem*
55   Nor take no shape nor project of affection,[6]
          She is so self-endearèd.
          URSULA   Sure, I think so.
          And therefore certainly it were not good
          She knew his love, lest she'll make sport at it.
          HERO   Why, you speak truth. I never yet saw man.
60   How° wise, how noble, young, how rarely° featured,   *However / finely*
          But she would spell him backward.[7] If fair-faced,
          She would swear the gentleman should be her sister.
          If black,° why nature, drawing of an antic,°   *dark / a buffoon*
          Made a foul blot.° If tall, a lance ill headed;   *error*
65   If low, an agate[8] very vilely cut;
          If speaking, why, a vane blown with all winds;
          If silent, why, a block movèd with° none.   *by*
          So turns she every man the wrong side out,
          And never gives to truth and virtue that
70   Which simpleness° and merit purchaseth.°   *integrity / deserve*
          URSULA   Sure, sure, such carping is not commendable.
          HERO   No, not to be so odd and from all fashions[9]
          As Beatrice is cannot be commendable.
          But who dare tell her so? If I should speak
75   She would mock me into air, O, she would laugh me
          Out of myself, press me to death[1] with wit.
          Therefore let Benedick, like covered fire,
          Consume away in sighs,[2] waste inwardly.
          It were a better death than die with mocks,
80   Which is as bad as die with tickling.
          URSULA   Yet tell her of it, hear what she will say.
          HERO   No. Rather I will go to Benedick
          And counsel him to fight against his passion.
          And truly, I'll devise some honest° slanders   *harmless*
85   To stain my cousin with. One doth not know
          How much an ill word may empoison liking.
          URSULA   O, do not do your cousin such a wrong.
          She cannot be so much without true judgement,
          Having so swift and excellent a wit
90   As she is prized° to have, as to refuse   *esteemed*
          So rare a gentleman as Signor Benedick.

---

6. *Nor take . . . affection:* Nor form the image or even
the concept of love.
7. She would speak of his virtues as faults.
8. Tiny figures were carved in agates and used as seals
or in rings.
9. *from all fashions:* contrary to normal behavior.

1. Crushing weights were loaded upon accused criminals who refused to enter a plea; Hero suggests that she
will be silenced with mockery and then mocked for her
silence.
2. Each sigh was said to draw a drop of blood from the
heart.

HERO He is the only man of Italy,
   Always excepted my dear Claudio.
URSULA   I pray you be not angry with me, madam,
95   Speaking my fancy. Signor Benedick,
   For shape, for bearing, argument,[3] and valour
   Goes foremost in report through Italy.
HERO   Indeed, he hath an excellent good name.
URSULA   His excellence did earn it ere he had it.
100   When are you married, madam?
HERO   Why, every day, tomorrow.[4] Come, go in.
   I'll show thee some attires and have thy counsel
   Which is the best to furnish me tomorrow.
URSULA [*aside*]   She's limed,[5] I warrant you. We have caught
105   her, madam.
HERO [*aside*]   If it prove so, then loving goes by haps.°   *chance*
   Some Cupid kills with arrows, some with traps.
                            Exeunt [HERO *and* URSULA]
BEATRICE [*coming forward*]   What fire is in mine ears?[6] Can this be true?
   Stand I condemned for pride and scorn so much?
110   Contempt, farewell; and maiden pride, adieu.
   No glory lives behind the back of such.[7]
   And, Benedick, love on. I will requite thee,
   Taming my wild heart to thy loving hand.[8]
   If thou dost love, my kindness shall incite thee
115   To bind our loves up in a holy band.
   For others say thou dost deserve, and I
   Believe it better than reportingly.°   *Exit*   *than as mere rumor*

3.2

Enter [DON PEDRO *the*] *Prince*, CLAUDIO, BENEDICK,
and LEONATO

DON PEDRO   I do but stay till your marriage be consummate, and
   then go I toward Aragon.
CLAUDIO   I'll bring° you thither, my lord, if you'll vouchsafe° me.   *accompany / allow*
DON PEDRO   Nay, that would be as great a soil in the new gloss
5   of your marriage as to show a child his new coat and forbid
   him to wear it. I will only be bold with° Benedick for his com-   *only ask*
   pany, for from the crown of his head to the sole of his foot he
   is all mirth. He hath twice or thrice cut Cupid's bow-string,
   and the little hangman° dare not shoot at him. He hath a heart   *rogue; executioner*
10   as sound as a bell, and his tongue is the clapper, for what his
   heart thinks his tongue speaks.
BENEDICK   Gallants, I am not as I have been.
LEONATO   So say I. Methinks you are sadder.°   *more serious*
CLAUDIO   I hope he be in love.
15 DON PEDRO   Hang him, truant! There's no true drop of blood
   in him to be truly touched with love. If he be sad, he wants°   *lacks*
   money.

---

3. Intellect and rhetorical skill.
4. From tomorrow on, I shall be a married woman every day.
5. Snared with birdlime, a glue spread on branches to catch birds.
6. Proverbially, if others were talking about you else-

where, your ears would burn.
7. No one praises such people behind their backs.
8. In falconry, the bird is tamed by the hand of the falconer.
3.2 Location: Leonato's house.

BENEDICK   I have the toothache.[1]

DON PEDRO   Draw° it.   *Extract*

20   BENEDICK   Hang it.

CLAUDIO   You must hang it first and draw it afterwards.[2]

DON PEDRO   What? Sigh for the toothache?

LEONATO   Where is but a humour[3] or a worm.

BENEDICK   Well, everyone can master a grief but he that has it.

25   CLAUDIO   Yet say I he is in love.

DON PEDRO   There is no appearance of fancy° in him, unless it   *love*
be a fancy that he hath to strange disguises, as to be a Dutchman today, a Frenchman tomorrow, or in the shape of two
countries at once, as a German from the waist downward, all

30   slops,° and a Spaniard from the hip upward, no doublet.[4]   *baggy breeches*
Unless he have a fancy to this foolery, as it appears he hath, he
is no fool for fancy, as you would have it appear he is.

CLAUDIO   If he be not in love with some woman there is no
believing old° signs. A° brushes his hat o' mornings, what should   *time-honored / He*

35   that bode?

DON PEDRO   Hath any man seen him at the barber's?

CLAUDIO   No, but the barber's man hath been seen with him,
and the old ornament of his cheek hath already stuffed tennis balls.[5]

40   LEONATO   Indeed, he looks younger than he did by the loss of a
beard.

DON PEDRO   Nay, a rubs himself with civet.° Can you smell him   *perfume*
out[6] by that?

CLAUDIO   That's as much as to say the sweet youth's in love.

45   DON PEDRO   The greatest note of it is his melancholy.

CLAUDIO   And when was he wont to wash[7] his face?

DON PEDRO   Yea, or to paint himself?—for the which I hear what
they say of him.

CLAUDIO   Nay, but his jesting spirit, which is now crept into a

50   lute-string, and now governed by stops.[8]

DON PEDRO   Indeed, that tells a heavy tale for him. Conclude,
conclude, he is in love.

CLAUDIO   Nay, but I know who loves him.

DON PEDRO   That would I know, too. I warrant, one that knows

55   him not.

CLAUDIO   Yes, and his ill conditions,° and in despite of all, dies   *qualities*
for him.

DON PEDRO   She shall be buried with her face upwards.[9]

BENEDICK   Yet is this no charm for the toothache. Old signor,

60   walk aside with me. I have studied eight or nine wise words to
speak to you which these hobby-horses° must not hear.   *clowns*

[*Exeunt* BENEDICK *and* LEONATO]

DON PEDRO   For° my life, to break° with him about Beatrice.   *Upon / speak*

1. Toothaches supposedly plagued lovers.
2. *hang it:* a mild expletive (like "darn it"). Claudio plays on the notion of hanging criminals, who were then cut down and "drawn" (disemboweled).
3. Poisonous fluid in the body (which, along with worms, was thought to be the cause of toothache).
4. His doublet is covered with a Spanish cloak.
5. Benedick has shaved off his beard. Tennis balls were stuffed with hair.
6. Detect his secret (with play on literal "smell").
7. When was he accustomed to use cosmetics on (compare "paint" in following line).
8. Frets on a lute's fingerboard; restraints. (Lutes were associated with lovers' serenades.)
9. That is, in Benedick's arms, where she will die (Elizabethan slang for "orgasm") in the act of love; perhaps a joking reversal of the idea that as one responsible for her own fate, she should be buried, like a suicide, with her face downward.

CLAUDIO 'Tis even so. Hero and Margaret¹ have by this° played   *now*
  their parts with Beatrice, and then the two bears will not bite
65 one another when they meet.
    Enter [DON] JOHN *the bastard*
 DON JOHN My lord, and brother, God save you.
 DON PEDRO Good-e'en,° brother.   *Good evening*
 DON JOHN If your leisure served I would speak with you.
 DON PEDRO In private?
70 DON JOHN If it please you. Yet Count Claudio may hear, for
  what I would speak of concerns him.
 DON PEDRO What's the matter?
 DON JOHN [*to* CLAUDIO] Means your lordship to be married
  tomorrow?
75 DON PEDRO You know he does.
 DON JOHN I know not that when he knows what I know.
 CLAUDIO If there be any impediment, I pray you discover° it. *reveal*
 DON JOHN You may think I love you not. Let that appear here-
  after, and aim better at° me by that I now will manifest. For my *think better of*
80 brother, I think he holds you well° and in dearness° of heart *in high respect / affection*
  hath holp° to effect your ensuing marriage—surely suit ill   *helped*
  spent, and labour ill bestowed.
 DON PEDRO Why, what's the matter?
 DON JOHN I came hither to tell you, and, circumstances short-
85 ened°—for she has been too long a-talking of²—the lady is *put simply*
  disloyal.°   *unfaithful*
 CLAUDIO Who, Hero?
 DON JOHN Even she. Leonato's Hero, your Hero, every man's
  Hero.
90 CLAUDIO Disloyal?
 DON JOHN The word is too good to paint out° her wickedness. I *fully describe*
  could say she were worse. Think you of a worse title, and I will
  fit her to it. Wonder not till further warrant.° Go but with me *evidence*
  tonight, you shall see her chamber window entered, even the
95 night before her wedding day. If you love her then, tomorrow
  wed her. But it would better fit your honour to change your
  mind.
 CLAUDIO May this be so?
 DON PEDRO I will not think it.
100 DON JOHN If you dare not trust that you see, confess not that you
  know.³ If you will follow me I will show you enough, and when
  you have seen more and heard more, proceed accordingly.
 CLAUDIO If I see anything tonight why I should not marry her,
  tomorrow, in the congregation where I should wed, there will
105 I shame her.
 DON PEDRO And as I wooed for thee to obtain her, I will join
  with thee to disgrace her.
 DON JOHN I will disparage her no farther till you are my witnesses. Bear it coldly° but till midnight, and let the issue show *calmly*
110 itself.
 DON PEDRO O day untowardly turned!°   *miserably changed*
 CLAUDIO O mischief strangely thwarting!

---

1. Ursula and Hero played the trick on Beatrice with help from Margaret.
2. For we have already talked about her too much.
3. If you won't risk seeing for yourself, don't claim to know.

DON JOHN   O plague right well prevented!—So will you say
when you have seen the sequel.   *Exeunt*

3.3
Enter DOGBERRY *and his compartner* [VERGES], *with the*
WATCH[1]

DOGBERRY   Are you good men and true?

VERGES   Yea, or else it were pity but they should suffer salvation,[2]
body and soul.

DOGBERRY   Nay, that were a punishment too good for them if
5   they should have any allegiance° in them, being chosen for the   *(for "disloyalty")*
Prince's watch.

VERGES   Well, give them their charge,° neighbour Dogberry.   *instructions*

DOGBERRY   First, who think you the most desertless° man to be   *(for "deserving")*
constable?[3]

10   SECOND WATCHMAN   Hugh Oatcake, sir, or George Seacoal for
they can write and read.

DOGBERRY   Come hither, neighbour Seacoal, God hath blest
you with a good name.[4] To be a well-favoured° man is the gift   *good-looking*
of fortune, but to write and read comes by nature.

15   FIRST WATCHMAN   Both which, Master Constable—

DOGBERRY   You have. I knew it would be your answer. Well, for
your favour,° sir, why, give God thanks, and make no boast of   *looks*
it. And for your writing and reading, let that appear when there
is no need of such vanity. You are thought here to be the most
20   senseless° and fit man for the constable of the watch, therefore   *(for "sensible")*
bear you the lantern. This is your charge: you shall compre-
hend all vagrom[5] men. You are to bid any man stand,° in the   *stop*
Prince's name.

FIRST WATCHMAN   How if a will not stand?

25   DOGBERRY   Why then take no note of him, but let him go, and
presently° call the rest of the watch together, and thank God   *immediately*
you are rid of a knave.

VERGES   If he will not stand when he is bidden he is none of the
Prince's subjects.

30   DOGBERRY   True, and they are to meddle with none but the
Prince's subjects.—You shall also make no noise in the streets,
for for the watch to babble and to talk is most tolerable° and   *(for "intolerable")*
not to be endured.

A WATCHMAN   We will rather sleep than talk. We know what
35   belongs° to a watch.   *is appropriate*

DOGBERRY   Why, you speak like an ancient° and most quiet   *experienced*
watchman, for I cannot see how sleeping should offend. Only
have a care that your bills[6] be not stolen. Well, you are to call
at all the alehouses and bid those that are drunk get them to
40   bed.

A WATCHMAN   How if they will not?

DOGBERRY   Why then, let them alone till they are sober. If they

---

3.3 Location: A street.
1. Watchmen who patrolled the streets, proclaiming the
hour and performing police duties. "Verges" probably
alludes to a "verge," or wand of office, carried by officials.
2. For "damnation." (Verges and Dogberry repeatedly
say the opposite of what they mean.)
3. The leader of the Watch. (Dogberry himself is the

parish constable.) Q's speech prefixes are confusing in
this scene, making it difficult to identify the leader of
the Watch; some of them have been rearranged.
4. Sea coal from Newcastle was known for its high
quality (thus the "good name").
5. For "vagrant." *comprehend:* for "apprehend."
6. Weapons (long shafts with blades or ax heads).

make you not then the better answer, you may say they are not
the men you took them for.

45 A WATCHMAN Well, sir.

DOGBERRY If you meet a thief you may suspect him, by virtue of
your office, to be no true° man; and for such kind of men, the   *honest*
less you meddle or make° with them why, the more is° for your   *have to do / better it is*
honesty.

50 A WATCHMAN If we know him to be a thief, shall we not lay
hands on him?

DOGBERRY Truly, by your office you may, but I think they that
touch pitch will be defiled.[7] The most peaceable way for you if
you do take a thief is to let him show himself what he is, and

55 steal out of your company.

VERGES You have been always called a merciful man, partner.

DOGBERRY Truly, I would not hang a dog by my will, much
more° a man who hath any honesty in him.   *(for "less")*

VERGES If you hear a child cry in the night you must call to the

60 nurse and bid her still° it.   *calm*

A WATCHMAN How if the nurse be asleep and will not hear us?

DOGBERRY Why then, depart in peace and let the child wake
her with crying, for the ewe that will not hear her lamb when
it baes will never answer a calf° when he bleats.   *blockhead*

65 VERGES 'Tis very true.

DOGBERRY This is the end of the charge. You, constable, are to
present° the Prince's own person.[8] If you meet the Prince in the   *represent*
night you may stay° him.   *stop*

VERGES Nay, by'r Lady, that I think a cannot.

70 DOGBERRY Five shillings to one on't with any man that knows
the statutes he may stay him. Marry, not without° the Prince   *unless*
be willing, for indeed the watch ought to offend no man, and
it is an offence to stay a man against his will.

VERGES By'r Lady, I think it be so.

75 DOGBERRY Ha ha ha! Well, masters, good night. An there be
any matter of weight chances,° call up me. Keep your fellows'   *that occurs*
counsels, and your own, and good night. Come, neighbour.

FIRST WATCHMAN Well, masters, we hear our charge. Let us go
sit here upon the church bench till two, and then all to bed.

80 DOGBERRY One word more, honest neighbours. I pray you
watch about Signor Leonato's door, for the wedding being
there tomorrow, there is a great coil° tonight. Adieu. Be vigi-   *to-do, bustle*
tant,° I beseech you.   *(for "vigilant")*

Exeunt [DOGBERRY *and* VERGES. *The* WATCH *sit*]
Enter BORACHIO *and* CONRAD

BORACHIO What, Conrad!

85 FIRST WATCHMAN [*aside*] Peace; stir not.

BORACHIO Conrad, I say.

CONRAD Here, man, I am at thy elbow.

BORACHIO Mass,° an my elbow itched,[9] I thought there would a   *By the mass*
scab[1] follow.

---

7. A proverbial saying, derived from the Apocryphal
book of Ecclesiasticus (13:1).
8. Dogberry presents a parodic version of the notion
that the monarch's authority was in theory separable
from his person (others could represent that authority

when he was physically absent).
9. Proverbially, itching elbows alerted you against
shady company.
1. Contemptible person; punning on a literal "scab."

90 CONRAD   I will owe thee an answer for that. And now, forward
with thy tale.

BORACHIO   Stand thee close, then, under this penthouse,° for it   *overhanging structure*
drizzles rain, and I will, like a true drunkard, utter[2] all to thee.

A WATCHMAN [*aside*]   Some treason, masters. Yet stand close.°   *keep hidden*

95 BORACHIO   Therefore, know I have earned of Don John a thousand ducats.

CONRAD   Is it possible that any villainy should be so dear?°   *valuable*

BORACHIO   Thou shouldst rather ask if it were possible any villainy should be so rich. For when rich villains have need of

100 poor ones, poor ones may make what price they will.

CONRAD   I wonder at it.

BORACHIO   That shows thou art unconfirmed.° Thou knowest   *inexperienced*
that the fashion of a doublet, or a hat, or a cloak is nothing to[3]
a man.

105 CONRAD   Yes, it is apparel.

BORACHIO   I mean the fashion.

CONRAD   Yes, the fashion is the fashion.

BORACHIO   Tush, I may as well say the fool's the fool. But seest
thou not what a deformed° thief[4] this fashion is?   *deforming*

110 A WATCHMAN [*aside*]   I know that Deformed. A° has been a vile   *He*
thief this seven year. A goes up and down° like a gentleman. I   *struts here and there*
remember his name.

BORACHIO   Didst thou not hear somebody?

CONRAD   No, 'twas the vane on the house.

115 BORACHIO   Seest thou not, I say, what a deformed thief this fashion is, how giddily a turns about all the hot-bloods° between   *dandies*
fourteen and five-and-thirty, sometimes fashioning them like
Pharaoh's soldiers in the reechy° painting,[5] sometime like god   *grimy*
Bel's[6] priests in the old church window, sometime like the

120 shaven Hercules[7] in the smirched, worm-eaten tapestry, where
his codpiece[8] seems as massy as his club?

CONRAD   All this I see, and I see that the fashion wears out more
apparel than the man.[9] But art not thou thyself giddy with the
fashion, too, that thou hast shifted[1] out of thy tale into telling

125 me of the fashion?

BORACHIO   Not so, neither. But know that I have tonight wooed
Margaret, the Lady Hero's gentlewoman, by the name of Hero.
She leans me° out at her mistress' chamber window, bids me a   *leans*
thousand times good night—I tell this tale vilely, I should first

130 tell thee how the Prince, Claudio, and my master, planted and
placed and possessed[2] by my master, Don John, saw afar off in
the orchard this amiable° encounter.   *loving*

CONRAD   And thought they Margaret was Hero?

BORACHIO   Two of them did, the Prince and Claudio, but the

135 devil my master knew she was Margaret, and partly by his oaths,

---

2. The drunken Borachio, whose name means "drunkard," alludes to the Latin tag *in vino veritas*.
3. Tells us nothing about (but Conrad takes him to
mean "means nothing to").
4. Used here to mean "rogue"—but also that keeping
up with fashion robs men of their money.
5. Perhaps refers to a painting of the fleeing Israelites
pursued by Pharaoh's army.
6. Bel (Baal) was a Babylonian god who had seventy
priests. His story, told in the biblical Apocrypha, is

sometimes depicted in stained-glass windows.
7. Probably referring to the story of Omphale (compare
2.1.220) or perhaps confusing Hercules with Samson.
8. Pouch, often stuffed and ornamented, worn over a
man's breeches, covering the genitals.
9. *fashion . . . man*: fashions change before clothes
wear out
1. Punning on "charged clothes."
2. Informed; but, perhaps also, controlled (as by the
devil).

which first possessed them, partly by the dark night, which did
deceive them, but chiefly by my villainy, which did confirm
any slander that Don John had made, away went Claudio
enraged, swore he would meet her as he was appointed next
140 morning at the temple,° and there, before the whole congrega-   *church*
tion, shame her with what he saw o'ernight, and send her home
again without a husband.
FIRST WATCHMAN [*coming forward*] We charge you in the
Prince's name. Stand.
145 A WATCHMAN Call up the right[3] Master Constable. We have here
recovered the most dangerous piece of lechery[4] that ever was
known in the commonwealth.
FIRST WATCHMAN And one Deformed is one of them. I know
him—a wears a lock.[5]
150 CONRAD Masters, masters!
A WATCHMAN You'll be made bring Deformed forth, I warrant
you.
CONRAD Masters—
A WATCHMAN Never speak. We charge you. Let us obey° you to   *(for "compel")*
155 go with us.
BORACHIO [*to* CONRAD] We are like to prove a goodly° commod-   *fine (ironic)*
ity, being taken up of these men's bills.[6]
CONRAD A commodity in question,[7] I warrant you. Come, we'll
obey you.   *Exeunt*

3.4
Enter HERO, MARGARET, *and* URSULA
HERO Good Ursula, wake my cousin Beatrice, and desire her to
rise.
URSULA I will, lady.
HERO And bid her come hither.
5 URSULA Well.°   [*Exit*]   *Very well*
MARGARET Troth, I think your other rebato° were better.   *stiffly wired ruff*
HERO No, pray thee, good Meg, I'll wear this.
MARGARET By my troth, 's° not so good, and I warrant° your   *it's / am sure*
cousin will say so.
10 HERO My cousin's a fool, and thou art another: I'll wear none
but this.
MARGARET I like the new tire° within excellently, if the hair were   *headdress with wig*
a thought browner. And your gown's a most rare fashion, i'faith.
I saw the Duchess of Milan's gown that they praise so.
15 HERO O, that exceeds,° they say.   *surpasses all*
MARGARET By my troth, 's but a night-gown° in respect of yours—   *dressing gown*
cloth o' gold, and cuts, and laced with silver, set with pearls,
down sleeves, side sleeves, and skirts round underborne with a
bluish tinsel.[1] But for a fine, quaint,° graceful, and excellent   *elegant*
20 fashion, yours is worth ten on't.

---

3. Respectfully, as in "right worshipful."
4. For "treachery." *recovered*: for "discovered."
5. A "lovelock," or curl of hair, worn by courtiers.
6. *being . . . bills*: a multiple pun: after we have been
hoisted on their halberds (weapons); been arrested on
their warrants; been obtained on credit ("taken up") in
exchange for their bonds ("bills").
7. Of doubtful value; about to be judicially interrogated.

3.4 Location: Leonato's house.
1. *cloth . . . tinsel*: made of silk or woolen cloth interwoven with gold thread, with ornamental slashes
("cuts") showing the fabric beneath, and decorated
with silver embroidery or lace and with pearls; with fitted ("down") sleeves and another pair that hung open
from the shoulder; trimmed at the hem or fully lined
("underborne") with another kind of metallic fabric.

HERO   God give me joy to wear it, for my heart is exceeding heavy.

MARGARET   'Twill be heavier soon by the weight of a man.

HERO   Fie upon thee, art not ashamed?

25 MARGARET   Of what, lady? Of speaking honourably? Is not marriage honourable in° a beggar? Is not your lord honourable without marriage? I think you would have me say 'saving your reverence,[2] a husband'. An° bad thinking do not wrest° true speaking, I'll offend nobody. Is there any harm in 'the heavier

30 for a husband'? None, I think, an it be the right husband and the right wife—otherwise 'tis light° and not heavy. Ask my Lady Beatrice else. Here she comes.

    Enter BEATRICE

HERO   Good morrow, coz.

BEATRICE   Good morrow, sweet Hero.

35 HERO   Why, how now? Do you speak in the sick tune?

BEATRICE   I am out of all other tune, methinks.

MARGARET   Clap 's° into 'Light o' love'. That goes without a burden.[3] Do you sing it, and I'll dance it.

BEATRICE   Ye light o' love with your heels.[4] Then if your hus-

40 band have stables enough, you'll see he shall lack no barns.[5]

MARGARET   O illegitimate construction![6] I scorn that with my heels.[7]

BEATRICE   [*to* HERO]   'Tis almost five o'clock, cousin. 'Tis time you were ready. By my troth, I am exceeding ill. Heigh-ho!

45 MARGARET   For a hawk, a horse,[8] or a husband?

BEATRICE   For the letter that begins them all—h.[9]

MARGARET   Well, an you be not turned Turk,[1] there's no more sailing by the star.[2]

BEATRICE   What means the fool, trow?°

50 MARGARET   Nothing, I. But God send everyone their heart's desire.

HERO   These gloves the Count sent me, they are an excellent perfume.[3]

BEATRICE   I am stuffed,[4] cousin. I cannot smell.

55 MARGARET   A maid, and stuffed! There's goodly catching of cold.

BEATRICE   O, God help me, God help me. How long have you professed apprehension?°

MARGARET   Ever since you left it. Doth not my wit become me rarely?°

60 BEATRICE   It is not seen enough. You should wear it in your cap.[5] By my troth, I am sick.

MARGARET   Get you some of this distilled *carduus benedictus*,[6] and lay it to your heart. It is the only thing for a qualm.°

HERO   There thou prickest her with a thistle.

---

even in	
If / pervert	
licentious	
Let us shift	
I wonder	
claimed to be witty	
excellently	
sudden faintness	

2. A polite expression of apology (as if "husband" were an offensive term).
3. Bass part (for a man's voice), with play on heavy "weight of a man." "Light o' Love" was a popular tune.
4. Ye . . . *heels*: Your dancing toys with love ("light-heeled" was slang for "promiscuous").
5. Punning on "bairns," children.
6. A multiple pun: forced interpretation; making of bastards; illegal building (of stables and barns).
7. I kick that away (reject it).
8. Responding to Beatrice's ostentatious sigh as a hunting cry.

9. Punningly: "ache" was pronounced in the same way.
1. If you have not reneged (on your vows against marriage). "To turn Turk" is, in the Christian proverb, to become a renegade (by going over to the enemy, the Muslim Turks).
2. No more navigating by the polestar. (No truths can be trusted from now on.)
3. Perfumed gloves were fashionable.
4. In the nose; Margaret follows with an obscene pun.
5. Like the coxcomb of a professional fool.
6. Holy thistle, or blessed thistle (a medicinal herb good for the heart).

65 BEATRICE Benedictus—why Benedictus? You have some moral[7]
in this Benedictus.

MARGARET Moral? No, by my troth, I have no moral meaning. I
meant plain holy-thistle. You may think perchance° that I think   *perhaps*
you are in love. Nay, by'r Lady, I am not such a fool to think
70 what I list,° nor I list not to think what I can, nor indeed I   *please*
cannot think, if I would think my heart out of thinking, that
you are in love, or that you will be in love, or that you can be in
love. Yet Benedick was such another,[8] and now is he become a
man. He swore he would never marry, and yet now in despite
75 of his heart he eats his meat without grudging.[9] And how you
may be converted I know not, but methinks you look with your
eyes, as other women do.

BEATRICE What pace is this that thy tongue keeps?

MARGARET Not a false gallop.[1]

Enter URSULA

80 URSULA [*to* HERO] Madam, withdraw. The Prince, the Count,
Signor Benedick, Don John, and all the gallants of the town
are come to fetch you to church.

HERO Help to dress me, good coz, good Meg, good Ursula.

Exeunt

3.5

Enter LEONATO, *and* [DOGBERRY] *the constable, and*
[VERGES] *the headborough°*   *local constable*

LEONATO What would you with me, honest neighbour?

DOGBERRY Marry, sir, I would have some confidence° with you   *(for "conference")*
that decerns° you nearly.   *(for "concerns")*

LEONATO Brief° I pray you, for you see it is a busy time with me.   *Be brief*

5 DOGBERRY Marry, this it is, sir.

VERGES Yes, in truth it is, sir.

LEONATO What is it, my good friends?

DOGBERRY Goodman° Verges, sir, speaks a little off the mat-   *(commoner's title)*
ter°—an old man, sir, and his wits are not so blunt° as, God   *subject / (for "sharp")*
10 help, I would desire they were. But in faith, honest as the skin
between his brows.

VERGES Yes, I thank God, I am as honest as any man living that
is an old man and no honester than I.

DOGBERRY Comparisons are odorous.° Palabras,[1] neighbour   *(for "odious")*
15 Verges.

LEONATO Neighbours, you are tedious.[2]

DOGBERRY It pleases your worship to say so, but we are the poor
Duke's° officers. But truly, for mine own part, if I were as   *the Duke's poor*
tedious as a king I could find in my heart to bestow it all of
20 your worship.

LEONATO All thy tediousness on me, ah?

DOGBERRY Yea, an 'twere a thousand pound more than 'tis, for I
hear as good exclamation[3] on your worship as of any man in
the city, and though I be but a poor man, I am glad to hear it.

25 VERGES And so am I.

7. Hidden meaning (with ensuing pun on "no moral"
as "immoral").
8. Benedick was once an enemy of love.
9. Nonetheless, he has a perfectly good appetite.
1. Not a canter. (I am not speaking at a false pace.)
3.5 Location: Leonato's house.

1. Be brief (from a Spanish expression, *pocas palabras:*
"few words").
2. Dogberry takes it to mean "rich."
3. Properly, "accusation"; but Dogberry probably
intends "acclamation."

LEONATO   I would fain° know what you have to say.   *gladly*

VERGES   Marry, sir, our watch tonight, excepting your worship's
presence,[4] ha' ta'en a couple of as arrant knaves as any in Messina.

30   DOGBERRY   A good old man, sir. He will be talking. As they say,
when the age is in, the wit is out.[5] God help us, it is a world to
see.[6] Well said, i'faith, neighbour Verges. Well, God's a good
man. An° two men ride of a horse, one must ride behind. An   *If*
honest soul, i'faith, sir, by my troth he is, as ever broke bread.[7]

35   But, God is to be worshipped, all men are not alike. alas, good
neighbour.

LEONATO   Indeed, neighbour, he comes too short of you.

DOGBERRY   Gifts that God gives!

LEONATO   I must leave you.

40   DOGBERRY   One word, sir. Our watch, sir, have indeed comprehended two auspicious[8] persons, and we would have them this
morning examined before your worship.

LEONATO   Take their examination yourself, and bring it me. I am
now in great haste, as it may appear unto you.

45   DOGBERRY   It shall be suffigance.°   *(for "sufficient")*

LEONATO   Drink some wine ere you go. Fare you well.

[*Enter a* MESSENGER]

MESSENGER   My lord, they stay° for you to give your daughter to   *wait*
her husband.

LEONATO   I'll wait upon them, I am ready.

[*Exeunt* LEONATO *and* MESSENGER]

50   DOGBERRY   Go, good partner, go get you to Francis Seacoal,[9]
bid him bring his pen and inkhorn to the jail. We are now to
examination° these men.   *(for "examine")*

VERGES   And we must do it wisely.

DOGBERRY   We will spare for no wit, I warrant you. Here's that°   *that which*

55   shall drive some of them to a non-com.[1] Only get the learned
writer to set down our excommunication,° and meet me at the   *(for "examination")*
jail.   *Exeunt*

4.1

Enter [DON PEDRO *the*] *Prince* [DON JOHN *the*] *bastard,*
LEONATO, FRIAR [FRANCIS], CLAUDIO, BENEDICK,
HERO, *and* BEATRICE

LEONATO   Come, Friar Francis, be brief. Only to the plain form
of marriage, and you shall recount their particular duties
afterwards.

FRIAR [*to* CLAUDIO]   You come hither, my lord, to marry this
5   lady?

CLAUDIO   No.

LEONATO   To be married to her. Friar, you come to marry her.

FRIAR [*to* HERO]   Lady, you come hither to be married to this
count?

---

4. For "respecting your worship's presence": an apology
for speaking what might displease.
5. Dogberry's version of the proverb "When the wine is
in, the wit is out."
6. Dogberry seems to mean "a strange world"; the
expression normally meant "wonderful to behold."
7. Dogberry strings together three proverbial sentences,

all of which are remembered correctly but irrelevantly.
8. For "suspicious." *comprehended*: for "apprehended."
9. Refers to the Sexton in 4.2, not the George Seacoal
of the Watch in 3.3.
1. For "nonplus" (bewilderment); perhaps confused by
Dogberry with *non compos mentis* (insane).
4.1 Location: A church.

10   HERO   I do.
    FRIAR   If either of you know any inward° impediment why you   secret
          should not be conjoined, I charge you on your souls to utter it.
    CLAUDIO   Know you any, Hero?
    HERO   None, my lord.
15   FRIAR   Know you any, Count?
    LEONATO   I dare make his answer—none.
    CLAUDIO   O, what men dare do! What men may do! What men
          daily do, not knowing what they do!
    BENEDICK   How now! Interjections? Why then, some be of
20   laughing, as 'ah, ha, he!'[1]
    CLAUDIO   Stand thee by, Friar. Father, by your leave,
          Will you with free and unconstrainèd soul
          Give me this maid, your daughter?
    LEONATO   As freely, son, as God did give her me.
25   CLAUDIO   And what have I to give you back whose worth
          May counterpoise° this rich and precious gift?   equal
    DON PEDRO   Nothing, unless you render her again.
    CLAUDIO   Sweet Prince, you learn° me noble thankfulness.   teach
          There, Leonato, take her back again.
30   Give not this rotten orange to your friend.
          She's but the sign° and semblance of her honour.   mere appearance
          Behold how like a maid she blushes here!
          O, what authority and show of truth
          Can cunning sin cover itself withal!
35   Comes not that blood° as modest evidence   blush
          To witness° simple virtue? Would you not swear,   testify to
          All you that see her, that she were a maid,
          By these exterior shows? But she is none.
          She knows the heat of a luxurious° bed.   lustful
40   Her blush is guiltiness, not modesty.
    LEONATO   What do you mean, my lord?
    CLAUDIO   Not to be married,
          Not to knit my soul to an approvèd° wanton.   a proven
    LEONATO   Dear my lord, if you in your own proof°   testing (of her)
          Have vanquished the resistance of her youth
45   And made defeat of her virginity—
    CLAUDIO   I know what you would say. If I have known her,
          You will say she did embrace me as a husband,
          And so extenuate the forehand sin.[2]
          No, Leonato,
50   I never tempted her with word too large,°   immodest
          But as a brother to his sister showed
          Bashful sincerity and comely love.
    HERO   And seemed I ever otherwise to you?
    CLAUDIO   Out on thee,[3] seeming! I will write against it.
55   You seem to me as Dian in her orb,[4]
          As chaste as is the bud ere it be blown.°   blossom
          But you are more intemperate in your blood°   passion

---

1. Benedick alludes to a passage in William Lily's Latin
grammar, used in all Elizabethan schools: "Some [inter-
jections] are of laughing; as Ha ha he" (1567 edition).
2. And so sin only in anticipation of marriage.

3. A curse; "thee" could refer to Hero or "seeming"
(putting on a false show).
4. Diana (Roman goddess of chastity and of the moon)
in her orbit, or sphere of activity.

Than Venus or those pampered animals
That rage in savage sensuality.

60 HERO   Is my lord well that he doth speak so wide?°   *wildly*
LEONATO   Sweet Prince, why speak not you?
DON PEDRO   What should I speak?
I stand dishonoured, that have gone about°   *have tried*
To link my dear friend to a common stale.°   *prostitute*
LEONATO   Are these things spoken, or do I but dream?
65 DON JOHN   Sir, they are spoken, and these things are true.
BENEDICK   This looks not like a nuptial.
HERO   'True'! O God!
CLAUDIO   Leonato, stand I here?
Is this the Prince? Is this the Prince's brother?
70 Is this face Hero's? Are our eyes our own?
LEONATO   All this is so. But what of this, my lord?
CLAUDIO   Let me but move° one question to your daughter,   *put*
And by that fatherly and kindly° power   *natural*
That you have in her, bid her answer truly.
75 LEONATO [*to* HERO]   I charge thee do so, as thou art my child.
HERO   O God defend me, how am I beset!
What kind of catechizing[5] call you this?
CLAUDIO   To make you answer truly to your name.[6]
HERO   Is it not Hero? Who can blot that name
With any just reproach?
80 CLAUDIO   Marry, that can Hero.
Hero itself[7] can blot out Hero's virtue.
What man was he talked with you yesternight
Out at your window betwixt twelve and one?
Now if you are a maid, answer to this.
85 HERO   I talked with no man at that hour, my lord.
DON PEDRO   Why, then are you no maiden. Leonato,
I am sorry you must hear. Upon mine honour,
Myself, my brother, and this grievèd° Count   *wronged*
Did see her, hear her, at that hour last night
90 Talk with a ruffian at her chamber window,
Who hath indeed, most like a liberal° villain,   *loose-tongued*
Confessed the vile encounters they have had
A thousand times in secret.
DON JOHN   Fie, fie, they are
Not to be named, my lord, not to be spoke of.
95 There is not chastity enough in language
Without offence to utter them. Thus, pretty lady,
I am sorry for thy much misgovernment.°   *ample misconduct*
CLAUDIO   O Hero! What a Hero hadst thou been
If half thy outward graces had been placed
100 About thy thoughts and counsels of thy heart!
But fare thee well, most foul, most fair, farewell
Thou pure impiety and impious purity.
For° thee I'll lock up all the gates of love,   *Because of*
And on my eyelids shall conjecture° hang   *suspicion*

5. A catechism was a set of formal questions and
answers used to teach church doctrine.
6. To make you admit that you are what you have been

called.
7. The name (or reputation) of Hero.

105	To turn all beauty into thoughts of harm,	
	And never shall it more be gracious.°	*attractive*
	LEONATO Hath no man's dagger here a point for me?	
	[HERO *falls to the ground*]	
	BEATRICE Why, how now, cousin, wherefore sink you down?	
	DON JOHN Come. Let us go. These things come thus to light	
110	Smother her spirits° up.	*vital forces*
	[*Exeunt* DON PEDRO, DON JOHN, *and* CLAUDIO]	
	BENEDICK How doth the lady?	
	BEATRICE Dead, I think. Help, uncle.	
	Hero, why Hero! Uncle, Signor Benedick, Friar—	
	LEONATO O fate, take not away thy heavy hand.	
	Death is the fairest cover for her shame	
	That may be wished for.	
115	BEATRICE How now, cousin Hero?	
	FRIAR [*to* HERO] Have comfort, lady.	
	LEONATO [*to* HERO] Dost thou look up?	
	FRIAR Yea, wherefore should she not?	
	LEONATO Wherefore? Why, doth not every earthly thing	
120	Cry shame upon her? Could she here deny	
	The story that is printed in her blood?°	*blush*
	Do not live, Hero, do not ope thine eyes,	
	For did I think thou wouldst not quickly die,	
	Thought I thy spirits were stronger than thy shames,	
125	Myself would on the rearward° of reproaches	*in the wake*
	Strike at thy life. Grieved I I had but one?	
	Chid I for that at frugal nature's frame?°	*plan*
	O one too much by thee! Why had I one?	
	Why ever wast thou lovely in my eyes?	
130	Why had I not with charitable hand	
	Took up a beggar's issue at my gates,	
	Who smirchèd thus° and mired with infamy,	*(as you are)*
	I might have said 'No part of it is mine,	
	This shame derives itself from unknown loins.'	
135	But mine, and mine I loved, and mine I praised,	
	And mine that I was proud on,° mine so much	*of*
	That I myself was to myself not mine,[8]	
	Valuing of her—why she, O she is fallen	
	Into a pit of ink, that the wide sea	
140	Hath drops too few to wash her clean again,	
	And salt too little which may season[9] give	
	To her foul tainted flesh.	
	BENEDICK Sir, sir, be patient.	
	For my part, I am so attired in wonder	
	I know not what to say.	
145	BEATRICE O, on my soul, my cousin is belied.°	*slandered*
	BENEDICK Lady, were you her bedfellow last night?	
	BEATRICE No, truly not, although until last night	
	I have this twelvemonth been her bedfellow.	
	LEONATO Confirmed, confirmed. O, that is stronger made	
150	Which was before° barred up with ribs of iron.	*already*
	Would the two princes lie? And Claudio lie,	

8. That I cared nothing for myself in comparison.   9. Give renewal. (Salt is a preservative for meat.)

Who loved her so that, speaking of her foulness,
Washed it with tears? Hence from her, let her die.

FRIAR   Hear me a little,

155   For I have only been silent so long
And given way unto this course of fortune[1]
By noting of the lady.[2] I have marked
A thousand blushing apparitions
To start into her face, a thousand innocent shames

160   In angel whiteness beat away those blushes,
And in her eye there hath appeared a fire
To burn the errors° that these princes hold   (*like heretics*)
Against her maiden truth. Call me a fool,
Trust not my reading nor my observations,

165   Which with experimental seal doth warrant
The tenor of my book.[3] Trust not my age,
My reverence, calling, nor divinity,
If this sweet lady lie not guiltless here
Under some biting error.

LEONATO   Friar, it cannot be.

170   Thou seest that all the grace that she hath left
Is that she will not add to her damnation
A sin of perjury. She not denies it.
Why seek'st thou then to cover with excuse
That which appears in proper° nakedness?   *true*

175 FRIAR [*to* HERO]   Lady, what man is he you are accused of?

HERO   They know that do accuse me. I know none.
If I know more of any man alive
Than that which maiden modesty doth warrant,
Let all my sins lack mercy. O my father,

180   Prove you that any man with me conversed
At hours unmeet,° or that I yesternight   *improper*
Maintained the change° of words with any creature,   *exchange*
Refuse° me, hate me, torture me to death.   *Disown*

FRIAR   There is some strange misprision° in the princes.   *misunderstanding*

185 BENEDICK   Two of them have the very bent of° honour,   *are wholly devoted to*
And if their wisdoms be misled in this
The practice° of it lives in John the bastard,   *trickery*
Whose spirits toil in frame of° villainies.   *in plotting*

LEONATO   I know not. If they speak but truth of her

190   These hands shall tear her. If they wrong her honour
The proudest of them shall well hear of it.
Time hath not yet so dried this blood of mine,
Nor age so eat up my invention,°   *cleverness*
Nor fortune made such havoc of my means,°   *wealth*

195   Nor my bad life reft me so much of friends,
But they shall find awaked in such a kind°   *manner*
Both strength of limb and policy° of mind,   *cunning*
Ability in means, and choice of friends,
To quit me of[4] them throughly.°   *thoroughly*

FRIAR   Pause awhile,

---

1. Q erroneously sets the beginning of the speech in cramped prose; some words seem to have been lost in the compression.
2. *By . . . lady:* So I could observe, or because I was observing, Hero.
3. *Which . . . book:* Which guarantees, with the confirmation of experience, the truth of the conclusions I have drawn from my study.
4. To be avenged upon.

200 And let my counsel sway you in this case.
Your daughter here the princes left for dead,
Let her a while be secretly kept in,
And publish° it that she is dead indeed.   *announce*
Maintain a mourning ostentation,°   *formal display*
205 And on your family's old monument°   *burial vault*
Hang mournful epitaphs, and do all rites
That appertain unto a burial.

LEONATO   What shall become of this? What will this do?

FRIAR   Marry, this, well carried,° shall on her behalf   *managed*
210 Change slander to remorse.° That is some good.   *pity*
But not for that dream I on this strange course,
But on° this travail look for greater birth.[5]   *from*
She—dying, as it must be so maintained,
Upon the instant that she was accused—
215 Shall be lamented, pitied, and excused
Of° every hearer. For it so falls out   *By*
That what we have, we prize not to the worth°   *full value*
Whiles we enjoy it, but, being lacked and lost,
Why then we rack[6] the value, then we find
220 The virtue that possession would not show us
Whiles it was ours. So will it fare with Claudio.
When he shall hear she died upon° his words,   *as a result of*
Th'idea° of her life shall sweetly creep   *The image*
Into his study of imagination,°   *reverie*
225 And every lovely organ° of her life   *aspect*
Shall come apparelled in more precious habit,
More moving-delicate, and full of life,
Into the eye and prospect° of his soul   *vision*
Than when she lived indeed. Then shall he mourn,
230 If ever love had interest in his liver,[7]
And wish he had not so accusèd her,
No, though he thought his accusation true.
Let this be so, and doubt not but success°   *what follows*
Will fashion the event° in better shape   *result*
235 Than I can lay it down in likelihood.
But if all aim but this be levelled false,[8]
The supposition of the lady's death
Will quench the wonder of her infamy.
And if it sort° not well, you may conceal her,   *turn out*
240 As best befits her wounded reputation,
In some reclusive° and religious life,   *cloistered*
Out of all eyes, tongues, minds, and injuries.°   *calumny*

BENEDICK   Signor Leonato, let the Friar advise you.
And though you know my inwardness° and love   *intimacy*
245 Is very much unto the Prince and Claudio,
Yet, by mine honour, I will deal in this
As secretly and justly as your soul
Should with your body.

LEONATO   Being that I flow in° grief,   *Since I am flooded by*
250 The smallest twine may lead me.

---

5. Look for a more important consequence (with pun on "travail" as "labor pains" as well as "effort").
6. Stretch (as on a rack, an instrument of torture).

7. Thought of as the seat of passions, including love.
8. But if we miss our aim in all but this.

FRIAR 'Tis well consented. Presently away,
For to strange sores strangely they strain the cure.[9]
[To HERO] Come, lady, die to live. This wedding day
Perhaps is but prolonged.° Have patience, and endure.   postponed

Exeunt [all but BEATRICE *and* BENEDICK]

255 BENEDICK Lady Beatrice, have you wept all this while?
BEATRICE Yea, and I will weep a while longer.
BENEDICK I will not desire that.
BEATRICE You have no reason, I do it freely.
BENEDICK Surely I do believe your fair cousin is wronged.
260 BEATRICE Ah, how much might the man deserve of me that
would right her!
BENEDICK Is there any way to show such friendship?
BEATRICE A very even° way, but no such friend.   clear
BENEDICK May a man do it?
265 BEATRICE It is a man's office, but not yours.
BENEDICK I do love nothing in the world so well as you. Is not
that strange?
BEATRICE As strange as the thing I know not. It were as possible
for me to say I loved nothing so well as you, but believe me
270 not, and yet I lie not. I confess nothing nor I deny nothing. I
am sorry for my cousin.
BENEDICK By my sword, Beatrice, thou lovest me.
BEATRICE Do not swear and eat it.[1]
BENEDICK I will swear by it that you love me, and I will make
275 him eat it that says I love not you.
BEATRICE Will you not eat your word?
BENEDICK With no sauce that can be devised to it. I protest° I   affirm
love thee.
BEATRICE Why then, God forgive me.
280 BENEDICK What offence, sweet Beatrice?
BEATRICE You have stayed me in a happy hour.[2] I was about to
protest I loved you.
BENEDICK And do it with all thy heart.
BEATRICE I love you with so much of my heart that none is left
285 to protest.
BENEDICK Come, bid me do anything for thee.
BEATRICE Kill Claudio.
BENEDICK Ha! Not for the wide world.
BEATRICE You kill me to deny° it. Farewell.   by refusing
290 BENEDICK Tarry, sweet Beatrice.
BEATRICE I am gone though I am here. There is no love in
you.—Nay, I pray you, let me go.
BENEDICK Beatrice.
BEATRICE In faith, I will go.
295 BENEDICK We'll be friends first.
BEATRICE You dare easier be friends with me than fight with
mine enemy.
BENEDICK Is Claudio thine enemy?
BEATRICE Is a not approved in the height[3] a villain, that hath
300 slandered, scorned, dishonoured my kinswoman? O that I were

---

9. Compare the proverb "A desperate disease must
have a desperate cure."
1. Eat your words, go back on your oath. Benedick takes

it to mean his sword (as does F: "swear by it and eat it").
2. You have stopped me at a fortunate moment.
3. Is he not proved in the highest degree.

a man! What, bear her in hand[4] until they come to take hands, and then with public accusation, uncovered° slander, unmit-   *barefaced*
igated rancour—O God that I were a man! I would eat his heart
in the market place.

305 BENEDICK   Hear me, Beatrice.

BEATRICE   Talk with a man out at a window—a proper saying!°   *a likely story*

BENEDICK   Nay, but Beatrice.

BEATRICE   Sweet Hero, she is wronged, she is slandered, she is
undone.

310 BENEDICK   Beat—

BEATRICE   Princes and counties! Surely a princely testimony, a
goodly count,[5] Count Comfit,° a sweet gallant, surely. O that I   *Sugarplum*
were a man for his sake! Or that I had any friend would be a
man for my sake! But manhood is melted into courtesies,

315 valour into compliment, and men are only turned into tongue,
and trim° ones, too. He is now as valiant as Hercules that° only   *fine (ironic) / who*
tells a lie and swears it. I cannot be a man with° wishing, there-   *by*
fore I will die a woman with grieving.

BENEDICK   Tarry, good Beatrice. By this hand, I love thee.

320 BEATRICE   Use it for my love some other way than swearing by
it.

BENEDICK   Think you in your soul the Count Claudio hath
wronged Hero?

BEATRICE   Yea, as sure as I have a thought or a soul.

325 BENEDICK   Enough, I am engaged,° I will challenge him. I will   *pledged*
kiss your hand, and so I leave you. By this hand, Claudio shall
render me a dear account.° As you hear of me, so think of me.   *pay me dearly*
Go comfort your cousin. I must say she is dead. And so,
farewell.   [*Exeunt*]

4.2

Enter [DOGBERRY *and* VERGES] *the constables, and the
Town Clerk* [*the* SEXTON], *in gowns,*[1] [*and the* WATCH,
with] BORACHIO [*and* CONRAD]

DOGBERRY   Is our whole dissembly° appeared?   *(for "assembly")*

VERGES   O, a stool and a cushion for the Sexton.

SEXTON [*sits*]   Which be the malefactors?[2]

DOGBERRY   Marry, that am I, and my partner.

5 VERGES   Nay, that's certain, we have the exhibition° to examine.   *(for "commission")*

SEXTON   But which are the offenders that are to be examined?
Let them come before Master Constable.

DOGBERRY   Yea, marry, let them come before me. What is your
name, friend?

10 BORACHIO   Borachio.

DOGBERRY [*to the* SEXTON]   Pray write down 'Borachio'. [*To* CON-
RAD] Yours, sirrah?[3]

CONRAD   I am a gentleman, sir, and my name is Conrad.

DOGBERRY   Write down 'Master Gentleman Conrad'.—Masters,

15 do you serve God?

---

4. *bear her in hand:* lead her on with false hopes.
5. Story, tale (with plays on "count" as a legal indictment and as Claudio's title).
4.2 Location: A prison or hearing room in Messina.
1. Constables wore black gowns. The Sexton is presumably Francis Seacoal (3.5.50). Q's direction calls
him the town clerk, an office more appropriate to his
function in the scene than sexton, with which, however,
it seems often to have been combined.
2. Dogberry seems to mistake "malefactors" for "factors," or agents.
3. Contemptuous, since "sirrah" is used to address
inferiors, provoking Conrad's claim to be a gentleman.

CONRAD *and* BORACHIO   Yea, sir, we hope.

DOGBERRY   Write down that they hope they serve God. And write 'God' first, for God defend° but God should go before⁴ such villains. Masters, it is proved already that you are little better than false knaves, and it will go near to be thought so shortly. How answer you for yourselves?

forbid

CONRAD   Marry, sir, we say we are none.

DOGBERRY   A marvellous witty° fellow, I assure you, but I will go about with° him. Come you hither, sirrah. A word in your ear, sir. I say to you it is thought you are false knaves.

clever
will outwit

BORACHIO   Sir, I say to you we are none.

DOGBERRY   Well, stand aside. Fore God, they are both in a tale.° Have you writ down that they are none?

telling the same story

SEXTON   Master Constable, you go not the way to examine. You must call forth the watch that are their accusers.

DOGBERRY   Yea, marry, that's the eftest° way. Let the watch come forth. Masters, I charge you in the Prince's name accuse these men.

(for "aptest")

FIRST WATCHMAN   This man said, sir, that Don John, the Prince's brother, was a villain.

DOGBERRY   Write down Prince John a villain. Why, this is flat perjury,⁵ to call a prince's brother villain.

BORACHIO   Master Constable.

DOGBERRY   Pray thee, fellow, peace. I do not like thy look, I promise thee.

SEXTON   What heard you him say else?

SECOND WATCHMAN   Marry, that he had received a thousand ducats of Don John for accusing the Lady Hero wrongfully.

DOGBERRY   Flat burglary, as ever was committed.

VERGES   Yea, by mass,⁶ that it is.

SEXTON   What else, fellow?

FIRST WATCHMAN   And that Count Claudio did mean upon° his words to disgrace Hero before the whole assembly, and not marry her.

with

DOGBERRY   O villain! Thou wilt be condemned into everlasting redemption° for this.

(for "damnation")

SEXTON   What else?

WATCH   This is all.

SEXTON   And this is more, masters, than you can deny. Prince John is this morning secretly stolen away. Hero was in this manner accused, in this very manner refused, and upon the grief of this suddenly died. Master Constable, let these men be bound and brought to Leonato's. I will go before and show him their examination.   [*Exit*]

DOGBERRY   Come, let them be opinioned.°

(for "pinioned")

VERGES   Let them be, in the hands—

CONRAD   Off, coxcomb!⁷

DOGBERRY   God's° my life, where's the Sexton? Let him write down the Prince's officer coxcomb. Come, bind them. Thou naughty varlet!°

God save

wicked knave

CONRAD   Away, you are an ass, you are an ass.

---

4. (Punningly) take precedence over.
5. Perhaps a mistake for "treason" or "slander."
6. "By the mass," a common oath.

7. This is an emendation of a corrupt passage, given in Q as part of the previous speech. These words could be spoken by Borachio.

DOGBERRY   Dost thou not suspect° my place? Dost thou not sus-   *(for "respect")*
pect my years? O that he were here to write me down an ass!
But masters, remember that I am an ass. Though it be not
70   written down, yet forget not that I am an ass. No, thou villain,
thou art full of piety,° as shall be proved upon thee by good   *(for "impiety")*
witness. I am a wise fellow, and which is more, an officer, and
which is more, a householder, and which is more, as pretty a
piece of flesh[8] as any is in Messina, and one that knows the
75   law, go to, and a rich fellow enough, go to, and a fellow that
hath had losses,[9] and one that hath two gowns, and everything
handsome about him. Bring him away. O that I had been writ
down an ass!   *Exeunt*

5.1

Enter LEONATO *and* [ANTONIO] *his brother*

ANTONIO   If you go on thus, you will kill yourself,
And 'tis not wisdom thus to second° grief   *assist*
Against yourself.
LEONATO   I pray thee cease thy counsel,
Which falls into mine ears as profitless
5   As water in a sieve. Give not me counsel,
Nor let no comforter delight mine ear
But such a one whose wrongs do suit° with mine.   *match*
Bring me a father that so loved his child,
Whose joy of° her is overwhelmed like mine,   *in*
10   And bid him speak of patience.
Measure his woe the length and breadth of mine,
And let it answer every strain° for strain,   *strong feeling*
As thus for thus, and such a grief for such,
In every lineament, branch, shape, and form.
15   If such a one will smile and stroke his beard,
Bid sorrow wag,° cry 'hem'[1] when he should groan,   *be off*
Patch° grief with proverbs, make misfortune drunk°   *Mend / insensible*
With candle-wasters,[2] bring him yet to me,
And I of him will gather patience.
20   But there is no such man, for, brother, men
Can counsel and speak comfort to that grief
Which they themselves not feel, but tasting it
Their counsel turns to passion, which before
Would give preceptial° medicine to rage,   *precepts as*
25   Fetter strong madness in a silken thread,
Charm ache with air° and agony with words.   *breath*
No, no, 'tis all men's office° to speak patience   *business*
To those that wring° under the load of sorrow,   *writhe*
But no man's virtue nor sufficiency°   *ability*
30   To be so moral° when he shall endure   *moralizing*
The like himself. Therefore give me no counsel.
My griefs cry louder than advertisement.°   *advice*
ANTONIO   Therein do men from children nothing differ.
LEONATO   I pray thee peace, I will be flesh and blood,
35   For there was never yet philosopher

---

8. *as pretty . . . flesh:* as fine (or gallant) a mortal man.
9. *hath had losses:* was once richer.
5.1 Location: Near Leonato's house.

1. Clear his throat (as if about to make a speech).
2. Philosophers, burners of midnight oil (and their works).

That could endure the toothache patiently,
However they have writ the style of gods,
And made a pish at chance and sufferance.[3]

ANTONIO   Yet bend° not all the harm upon yourself.   *direct*
40   Make those that do offend you suffer, too.
LEONATO   There thou speak'st reason, nay I will do so.
My soul doth tell me Hero is belied,
And that shall Claudio know, so shall the Prince,
And all of them that thus dishonour her.

        Enter [DON PEDRO *the*] *Prince and* CLAUDIO

45 ANTONIO   Here comes the Prince and Claudio hastily.
DON PEDRO   Good e'en,° good e'en.   *evening*
CLAUDIO   Good day to both of you.
LEONATO   Hear you, my lords?
DON PEDRO   We have some haste, Leonato.
LEONATO   Some haste, my lord! Well, fare you well, my lord.
Are you so hasty now? Well, all is one.°   *no matter*
50 DON PEDRO   Nay, do not quarrel with us, good old man.
ANTONIO   If he could right himself with quarrelling,
Some of us° would lie low.   *(Don Pedro and Claudio)*
CLAUDIO   Who wrongs him?
LEONATO   Marry, thou dost wrong me, thou dissembler, thou.[4]
Nay, never lay thy hand upon thy sword,
I fear thee not.
55 CLAUDIO   Marry, beshrew° my hand   *curse*
If it should give your age such cause of fear.
In faith, my hand meant nothing to[5] my sword.
LEONATO   Tush, tush, man, never fleer° and jest at me.   *sneer; mock*
I speak not like a dotard nor a fool,
60   As under privilege of age to brag
What I have done being young, or what would do
Were I not old. Know Claudio to thy head,°   *face*
Thou hast so wronged mine innocent child and me
That I am forced to lay my reverence by
65   And with grey hairs and bruise of many days
Do challenge thee to trial of a man.°   *of manhood*
I say thou hast belied mine innocent child.
Thy slander hath gone through and through her heart,
And she lies buried with her ancestors,
70   O, in a tomb where never scandal slept
Save this of hers, framed° by thy villainy.   *created*
CLAUDIO   My villainy?
LEONATO   Thine, Claudio, thine I say.
DON PEDRO   You say not right, old man.
LEONATO   My lord, my lord,
I'll prove it on his body if he dare,
75   Despite his nice fence[6] and his active practice,
His May of youth and bloom of lustihood.°   *virility*
CLAUDIO   Away, I will not have to do with you.
LEONATO   Canst thou so doff me?° Thou hast killed my child.   *brush me off*
If thou kill'st me, boy, thou shalt kill a man.

---

3. *writ . . . sufferance*: written as if they transcended
human passion, and expressed themselves scornfully
about (said "pish" to) bad luck and suffering.

4. "Thou" is used contemptuously here.
5. My hand had no designs upon.
6. His nimble fencing (said contemptuously).

80 ANTONIO   He shall kill two of us, and men indeed.
        But that's no matter, let him kill one first.
        Win me and wear me.[7] Let him answer me.°   *(in a duel)*
        Come follow me boy, come sir boy, come follow me,
        Sir boy, I'll whip you from your foining fence.[8]
85   Nay, as I am a gentleman, I will.
    LEONATO   Brother.
    ANTONIO   Content yourself.° God knows, I loved my niece,   *Don't interfere*
        And she is dead, slandered to death by villains
        That dare as well answer a man indeed
90   As I dare take a serpent by the tongue.
        Boys, apes,° braggarts, jacks,° milksops!   *fools / knaves*
    LEONATO   Brother Antony—
    ANTONIO   Hold you content. What, man, I know them, yea
        And what they weigh, even to the utmost scruple.°   *¹⁄₂₄ ounce*
95   Scambling, outfacing, fashion-monging boys,[9]
        That lie, and cog,° and flout,° deprave,° and slander,   *cheat / mock / defame*
        Go anticly,° and show an outward hideousness,[1]   *outlandishly dressed*
        And speak off half a dozen dangerous words,
        How they might hurt their enemies, if they durst,
100   And this is all.
    LEONATO   But brother Antony—
    ANTONIO   Come, 'tis no matter,
        Do not you meddle, let me deal in this.
    DON PEDRO   Gentlemen both, we will not wake° your patience.   *test*
105   My heart is sorry for your daughter's death,
        But on my honour she was charged with nothing
        But what was true and very full of proof.
    LEONATO   My lord, my lord—
    DON PEDRO   I will not hear you.
    LEONATO   No? Come brother, away. I will be heard.
110 ANTONIO   And shall, or some of us will smart for it.
                    Exeunt [LEONATO *and* ANTONIO]
            Enter BENEDICK
    DON PEDRO   See, see, here comes the man we went to seek.
    CLAUDIO   Now signor, what news?
    BENEDICK   [*to* DON PEDRO]   Good day, my lord.
    DON PEDRO   Welcome, signor. You are almost come to part
115   almost a fray.
    CLAUDIO   We had liked to have had° our two noses snapped off   *We nearly had*
        with° two old men without teeth.   *by*
    DON PEDRO   Leonato and his brother. What thinkest thou? Had
        we fought, I doubt° we should have been too young for them.   *suspect*
120 BENEDICK   In a false quarrel there is no true valour. I came to
        seek you both.
    CLAUDIO   We have been up and down to seek thee, for we are
        high-proof° melancholy and would fain have it beaten away.   *to a high degree*
        Wilt thou use thy wit?
125 BENEDICK   It is in my scabbard. Shall I draw it?
    DON PEDRO   Dost thou wear thy wit by thy side?

---

7. A form of challenge: let him beat me and only then
boast of it.
8. Thrusting position in fencing (Antonio probably
means that he will compel Claudio to close with him in
the duel, or that he will literally take a whip to him).
9. *Scambling . . . boys:* Quarrelsome, insolent, faddish
boys.
1. A fearsome exterior.

CLAUDIO   Never any did so, though very many have been beside
their wit.° I will bid thee draw as we do the minstrels,[2] draw to   *out of their minds*
pleasure us.

130   DON PEDRO   As I am an honest man he looks pale. Art thou sick,
or angry?

CLAUDIO   What, courage, man. What though care killed a cat,
thou hast mettle° enough in thee to kill care.   *spirit; courage*

BENEDICK   Sir, I shall meet your wit in the career° an you   *at full gallop*
135   charge° it against me. I pray you choose another subject.   *aim*

CLAUDIO   Nay then, give him another staff.° This last was broke   *lance*
cross.[3]

DON PEDRO   By this light, he changes° more and more. I think   *changes color*
he be angry indeed.

140   CLAUDIO   If he be, he knows how to turn his girdle.[4]

BENEDICK   [*aside to* CLAUDIO]   Shall I speak a word in your ear?

CLAUDIO   God bless° me from a challenge.   *protect*

BENEDICK   You are a villain. I jest not. I will make it good how
you dare, with what° you dare, and when you dare. Do me   *whatever weapon*
145   right,[5] or I will protest° your cowardice. You have killed a sweet   *proclaim*
lady, and her death shall fall heavy on you. Let me hear from
you.

CLAUDIO   Well, I will meet you, so I may have good cheer.

DON PEDRO   What, a feast, a feast?

150   CLAUDIO   I'faith, I thank him, he hath bid me to a calf's head
and a capon, the which if I do not carve most curiously,° say   *daintily*
my knife's naught.° Shall I not find a woodcock[6] too?   *useless*

BENEDICK   Sir, your wit ambles[7] well, it goes easily.

DON PEDRO   I'll tell thee how Beatrice praised thy wit the other
155   day. I said thou hadst a fine wit. 'True,' said she, 'a fine little
one.' 'No,' said I, 'a great wit.' 'Right,' says she, 'a great gross
one.' 'Nay,' said I, 'a good wit.' 'Just,' said she, 'it hurts nobody.'
'Nay,' said I, 'the gentleman is wise.' 'Certain,' said she, 'a wise
gentleman.'[8] 'Nay,' said I, 'he hath the tongues.'° 'That I   *knows several languages*
160   believe,' said she, 'for he swore a thing to me on Monday night
which he forswore on Tuesday morning. There's a double
tongue, there's two tongues.' Thus did she an hour together
trans-shape° thy particular virtues, yet at last she concluded   *distort*
with a sigh thou wast the properest° man in Italy.   *handsomest*

165   CLAUDIO   For the which she wept heartily and said she cared
not.

DON PEDRO   Yea, that she did. But yet for all that, an if° she did   *an if = if*
not hate him deadly she would love him dearly. The old man's
daughter told us all.

170   CLAUDIO   All, all. And moreover, God saw him when he was hid
in the garden.[9]

DON PEDRO   But when shall we set the savage bull's horns on the
sensible Benedick's head?

2. *draw . . . minstrels:* draw a sword, the way a minstrel
is bidden to draw a bow across his musical instrument.
3. Was snapped in the middle, like a badly handled
lance. (Claudio is mocking Benedick's attempt at wit.)
4. A colloquialism of uncertain derivation, possibly
meaning "let him get on with it" or "that's his problem."
5. Give me satisfaction.
6. The calf's head, capon, and woodcock were varieties

of food that also symbolize stupidity.
7. Moves slowly (in other words, it does not gallop as a
quick wit would).
8. A phrase often used ironically to mean "an old fool."
9. Allusion to Genesis 3:8 (Adam attempting to hide
from God in the Garden of Eden); contains a half-
hidden reference to the trick played on Benedick in the
garden.

CLAUDIO   Yea, and text underneath, 'Here dwells Benedick the
175 married man'.[1]
BENEDICK   Fare you well, boy, you know my mind. I will leave
you now to your gossip-like° humour. You break° jests as brag-   *old-womanish / crack*
garts do their blades[2] which, God be thanked, hurt not. [*To*
DON PEDRO] My lord, for your many courtesies I thank you.
180 I must discontinue your company. Your brother the bastard is
fled from Messina. You have among you killed a sweet and
innocent lady. For my lord Lackbeard there, he and I shall
meet, and till then, peace be with him.   *Exit*
DON PEDRO   He is in earnest.
185 CLAUDIO   In most profound earnest, and, I'll warrant you, for the
love of Beatrice.
DON PEDRO   And hath challenged thee.
CLAUDIO   Most sincerely.
DON PEDRO   What a pretty thing man is when he goes in his
190 doublet and hose and leaves off his wit![3]
          Enter [DOGBERRY *and* VERGES] *the constables,* [*the*
          WATCH,] CONRAD, *and* BORACHIO
CLAUDIO   He is then a giant to an ape. But then is an ape a
doctor to such a man.[4]
DON PEDRO   But soft you,° let me be. Pluck up,° my heart, and   *wait / Collect yourself*
be sad. Did he not say my brother was fled?
195 DOGBERRY   Come you sir, if justice cannot tame you, she shall
ne'er weigh more reasons[5] in her balance.° Nay, an you be a   *scales*
cursing hypocrite once,° you must be looked to.   *even once*
DON PEDRO   How now, two of my brother's men bound? Bora-
chio one.
200 CLAUDIO   Hearken after° their offence, my lord.   *Inquire into*
DON PEDRO   Officers, what offence have these men done?
DOGBERRY   Marry, sir, they have committed false report, more-
over they have spoken untruths, secondarily they are slanders,°   *(for "slanderers")*
sixth and lastly they have belied a lady, thirdly they have veri-
205 fied° unjust things, and to conclude, they are lying knaves.   *affirmed as true*
DON PEDRO   First I ask thee what they have done, thirdly I ask
thee what's their offence, sixth and lastly why they are commit-
ted,° and to conclude, what you lay to their charge.   *held on arrest*
CLAUDIO   Rightly reasoned, and in his own division.° And by my   *logical organization*
210 troth there's one meaning well suited.[6]
DON PEDRO [*to* CONRAD *and* BORACHIO]   Who have you offended, masters, that you are thus bound to your answer?[7] This
learned constable is too cunning to be understood. What's your
offence?
215 BORACHIO   Sweet Prince, let me go no farther to mine answer.° *trial; account*
Do you hear me, and let this Count kill me. I have deceived
even your very eyes. What your wisdoms could not discover,
these shallow fools have brought to light, who in the night overheard me confessing to this man how Don John your brother

1. Claudio and Don Pedro recall that Benedick joked
that if he ever fell in love, his friends could set horns in
his forehead, have his picture painted, and title it
"Benedick, the married man" (1.1.215–19).
2. Braggarts secretly dent their swords to make it
appear that they have been dealing fierce blows.
3. When he puts on fine clothes but forgets to wear his
brain.

4. Such a man is much bigger than an ape, but an ape
is a learned man ("doctor") compared with him.
5. Legal cases. Also, "reason" was pronounced like
"raisin," producing a comic image here.
6. Dressed in several different costumes (with play on
legal "suit").
7. Required to respond (punning on "bound over for
trial" and "bound with ropes").

220   incensed° me to slander the Lady Hero, how you were brought   *incited*
      into the orchard and saw me court Margaret in Hero's gar-
      ments, how you disgraced her when you should marry her. My
      villainy they have upon record, which I had rather seal° with   *confirm; end*
      my death than repeat over to my shame. The lady is dead upon
225   mine and my master's false accusation, and briefly, I desire
      nothing but the reward of a villain.

      DON PEDRO [*to* CLAUDIO]   Runs not this speech like iron through
      your blood?

      CLAUDIO   I have drunk poison whiles he uttered it.

230   DON PEDRO [*to* BORACHIO]   But did my brother set thee on to
      this?

      BORACHIO   Yea, and paid me richly for the practice° of it.   *execution*

      DON PEDRO   He is composed and framed° of treachery,   *made up*
      And fled he is upon this villainy.

235   CLAUDIO   Sweet Hero, now thy image doth appear
      In the rare semblance° that I loved it first.   *likeness*

      DOGBERRY   Come, bring away the plaintiffs.° By this time our   *(for "defendants")*
      Sexton hath reformed° Signor Leonato of the matter. And mas-   *(for "informed")*
      ters, do not forget to specify, when time and place shall serve,
240   that I am an ass.

      VERGES   Here, here comes Master Signor Leonato, and the Sex-
      ton, too.

      Enter LEONATO, [ANTONIO *his*] *brother, and the* SEXTON

      LEONATO   Which is the villain? Let me see his eyes,
      That when I note another man like him
245   I may avoid him. Which of these is he?

      BORACHIO   If you would know your wronger, look on me.

      LEONATO   Art thou the slave that with thy breath hast killed
      Mine innocent child?

      BORACHIO   Yea, even I alone.

      LEONATO   No, not so, villain, thou beliest thyself.
250   Here stand a pair of honourable men.°   *men of rank*
      A third is fled that had a hand in it.
      I thank you, Princes, for my daughter's death.
      Record it with your high and worthy deeds.
      'Twas bravely done, if you bethink you of it.

255   CLAUDIO   I know not how to pray your patience,
      Yet I must speak. Choose your revenge yourself,
      Impose° me to what penance your invention   *Subject*
      Can lay upon my sin. Yet sinned I not
      But in mistaking.

      DON PEDRO   By my soul, nor I,
260   And yet to satisfy this good old man
      I would bend under any heavy weight
      That he'll enjoin me to.

      LEONATO   I cannot bid you bid my daughter live—
      That were impossible—but I pray you both
265   Possess° the people in Messina here   *Inform*
      How innocent she died, and if your love
      Can labour aught in sad invention,[8]
      Hang her an epitaph upon her tomb
      And sing it to her bones, sing it tonight.

8. Can create any fruit from your sad imagination.

270   Tomorrow morning come you to my house,
    And since you could not be my son-in-law,
    Be yet my nephew. My brother hath a daughter,
    Almost the copy of my child that's dead,
    And she alone is heir to both of us.[9]
275   Give her the right you should have giv'n her cousin,
    And so dies my revenge.
CLAUDIO   O noble sir!
    Your overkindness doth wring tears from me.
    I do embrace your offer; and dispose
    For henceforth° of poor Claudio.   *For the future*
280 LEONATO   Tomorrow then I will expect your coming.
    Tonight I take my leave. This naughty° man   *evil*
    Shall face to face be brought to Margaret,
    Who I believe was packed° in all this wrong,   *confederate*
    Hired to it by your brother.
BORACHIO   No, by my soul, she was not,
285   Nor knew not what she did when she spoke to me,
    But always hath been just and virtuous
    In anything that I do know by° her.   *of*
DOGBERRY [*to* LEONATO]   Moreover, sir, which indeed is not
    under white and black, this plaintiff[1] here, the offender, did
290   call me ass. I beseech you let it be remembered in his punish-
    ment. And also the watch heard them talk of one Deformed.
    They say he wears a key in his ear and a lock hanging by it,[2]
    and borrows money in God's name, the which he hath used°   *done habitually*
    so long and never paid that now men grow hard-hearted and
295   will lend nothing for God's sake.[3] Pray you examine him upon
    that point.
LEONATO   I thank thee for thy care and honest pains.
DOGBERRY   Your worship speaks like a most thankful and rever-
    end youth, and I praise God for you.
300 LEONATO [*giving him money*]   There's for thy pains.
DOGBERRY   God save the foundation.[4]
LEONATO   Go. I discharge thee of thy prisoner, and I thank thee.
DOGBERRY   I leave an arrant knave with your worship, which I
    beseech your worship to correct yourself,[5] for the example of
305   others. God keep your worship, I wish your worship well. God
    restore you to health. I humbly give you leave to depart, and
    if a merry meeting may be wished, God prohibit° it. Come,   *(for "permit")*
    neighbour.   *Exeunt* [DOGBERRY *and* VERGES]
LEONATO   Until tomorrow morning, lords, farewell.
310 ANTONIO   Farewell, my lords. We look for you tomorrow.
DON PEDRO   We will not fail.
CLAUDIO   Tonight I'll mourn with Hero.
LEONATO [*to the* WATCH] Bring you these fellows on.—We'll talk
    with Margaret
    How her acquaintance grew with this lewd° fellow.   *Exeunt*   *worthless*

---

9. Shakespeare (or Leonato) has apparently forgotten Antonio's son mentioned at 1.2.1.
1. For "defendant." *under white and black:* in writing.
2. Dogberry's garbled recollection of the lovelock mentioned at 3.3.149.
3. "In God's name" and "for God's sake" were phrases used by beggars.
4. A conventional response to alms from a charitable foundation.
5. Dogberry wishes Leonato himself to punish ("correct") Borachio but accidentally says that Leonato should be punished.

5.2

Enter BENEDICK *and* MARGARET

BENEDICK Pray thee, sweet Mistress Margaret, deserve well at
my hands by helping me to the speech of Beatrice.

MARGARET Will you then write me a sonnet in praise of my
beauty?

5 BENEDICK In so high a style, Margaret, that no man living shall
come over[1] it, for in most comely truth, thou deservest it.

MARGARET To have no man come over me—why, shall I always
keep below stairs?[2]

BENEDICK Thy wit is as quick as the greyhound's mouth, it
10 catches.

MARGARET And yours as blunt as the fencer's foils,[3] which hit
but hurt not.

BENEDICK A most manly wit, Margaret, it will not hurt a
woman. And so I pray thee call Beatrice. I give thee the buck-
15 lers.[4]

MARGARET Give us the swords. We have bucklers of our own.

BENEDICK If you use them, Margaret, you must put in the pikes
with a vice°—and they are dangerous weapons for maids.   screw

MARGARET Well, I will call Beatrice to you, who I think hath
20 legs.   *Exit*

BENEDICK And therefore will come.[5]
　　　　　[*Sings*]　The god love
　　　　　　　　　That sits above,
　　　　　　　　　And knows me, and knows me,
25　　　　　　　　　How pitiful I deserve—[6]
I mean in singing; but in loving, Leander the good swimmer,
Troilus the first employer of panders,[7] and a whole book full
of these quondam carpet-mongers[8] whose names yet run
smoothly in the even road of a blank verse, why they were never
30 so truly turned over and over° as my poor self in love. Marry, I   head over heels
cannot show it in rhyme. I have tried. I can find out no rhyme
to 'lady' but 'baby', an innocent° rhyme; for 'scorn' 'horn', a   a childish
hard[9] rhyme; for 'school' 'fool', a babbling rhyme. Very ominous endings. No, I was not born under a rhyming planet,[1] nor
35 I cannot woo in festival terms.°   in fancy rhetoric

Enter BEATRICE

Sweet Beatrice, wouldst thou come when I called thee?

BEATRICE Yea, signor, and depart when you bid me.

BENEDICK O, stay but till then.

BEATRICE 'Then' is spoken. Fare you well now. And yet ere I go,

---

5.2 Location: Near Leonato's house or in his garden.
1. Surpass; climb over (punning on "stile": stairs over
a fence). Margaret humorously takes "come over" in a
sexual sense.
2. In the servants' quarters (and therefore never as a
"mistress").
3. Practice rapiers, capped at the tip.
4. Benedick offers to surrender by giving up the bucklers: shields with spikes ("pikes") in the center. Margaret bawdily interprets this as the female sexual organ.
5. A popular question and answer of the time was
"How came you hither?" "On my legs."
6. How greatly I deserve pity (but Benedick takes it as

"How pitifully small my deserts are"). These four lines
are the beginning of a popular sentimental ballad.
7. Troilus, loving Cressida, employed her uncle Pandarus as go-between. Leander swam the Hellespont
nightly to be with his love, Hero.
8. Knights of long ago ("quondam") who avoided military service and spent their time in ladies' carpeted
boudoirs.
9. Disagreeable, because horns were associated with
cuckoldry.
1. At a time when the stars would influence me to
become a poet.

40   let me go with that° I came for, which is with knowing what   *what*
    hath passed between you and Claudio.

BENEDICK   Only foul words, and thereupon I will kiss thee.

BEATRICE   Foul words is but foul wind, and foul wind is but foul
    breath, and foul breath is noisome,° therefore I will depart   *nauseating*
45   unkissed.

BENEDICK   Thou hast frighted the word out of his° right sense,°   *its / meaning; wits*
    so forcible is thy wit. But I must tell thee plainly, Claudio
    undergoes° my challenge, and either I must shortly hear from   *is subject to*
    him or I will subscribe° him a coward. And I pray thee now tell   *proclaim*
50   me, for which of my bad parts didst thou first fall in love with
    me?

BEATRICE   For them all together, which maintain so politic° a   *cunningly governed*
    state of evil that they will not admit any good part to intermin-
    gle with them. But for which of my good parts did you first
55   suffer° love for me?   *feel*

BENEDICK   Suffer love—a good epithet.° I do suffer° love indeed,   *expression / suffer from*
    for I love thee against my will.

BEATRICE   In spite of your heart, I think. Alas, poor heart. If you
    spite it for my sake I will spite it for yours, for I will never love
60   that which my friend hates.

BENEDICK   Thou and I are too wise to woo peaceably.

BEATRICE   It appears not in this confession.[2] There's not one
    wise man among twenty that will praise himself.

BENEDICK   An old, an old instance,° Beatrice, that lived in the   *proverb*
65   time of good neighbours.[3] If a man do not erect in this age his
    own tomb ere he dies, he shall live no longer in monument°   *remembrance*
    than the bell rings and the widow weeps.

BEATRICE   And how long is that, think you?

BENEDICK   Question[4]—why, an hour in clamour° and a quarter   *ringing*
70   in rheum.° Therefore is it most expedient for the wise, if Don   *tears*
    Worm—his conscience[5]—find no impediment to the contrary,
    to be the trumpet of his own virtues, as I am to myself. So
    much for praising myself who, I myself will bear witness, is
    praiseworthy. And now tell me, how doth your cousin?
75 BEATRICE   Very ill.

BENEDICK   And how do you?

BEATRICE   Very ill too.

BENEDICK   Serve God, love me, and mend.° There will I leave   *recover*
    you too, for here comes one in haste.

Enter URSULA

80 URSULA   Madam, you must come to your uncle. Yonder's old
    coil° at home. It is proved my lady Hero hath been falsely   *great disturbance*
    accused, the Prince and Claudio mightily abused,° and Don   *deceived*
    John is the author of all, who is fled and gone. Will you come
    presently?
85 BEATRICE   Will you go hear this news, signor?

BENEDICK   I will live in thy heart, die[6] in thy lap, and be buried
    in thy eyes. And moreover, I will go with thee to thy uncle's.

Exeunt

2. Since it is not wise to claim to be wise.
3. In the good old days, when neighbors praised each other.
4. That is the question.

5. Facetious way of referring to the proverbial gnawing "worm of conscience."
6. With the common Elizabethan connotation of orgasm.

5.3

Enter CLAUDIO, [DON PEDRO *the*] *Prince, and three or*
four with tapers][1] *all in black*

CLAUDIO   Is this the monument of Leonato?

A LORD   It is, my lord.

CLAUDIO[2]   [*reading from a scroll*]

    Done to death by slanderous tongues
    Was the Hero that here lies.

5   Death in guerdon° of her wrongs   *recompense*
    Gives her fame which never dies.
    So the life that died with° shame   *from*
    Lives in death with glorious fame.

[*He hangs the*] *epitaph* [*on the tomb*]

    Hang thou there upon the tomb,
10   Praising her when I am dumb.

Now music sound, and sing your solemn hymn.

Song

    Pardon, goddess of the night,[3]
    Those that slew thy virgin knight,[4]
    For the which with songs of woe
15   Round about her tomb they go.
    Midnight, assist our moan,
    Help us to sigh and groan,
        Heavily, heavily.
    Graves yawn, and yield your dead
20   Till death be utterèd,°   *fully lamented*
        Heavily, heavily.

CLAUDIO   Now, unto thy bones good night.
    Yearly will I do this rite.

DON PEDRO   Good morrow, masters, put your torches out.
25   The wolves have preyed,[5] and look, the gentle day
    Before the wheels of Phoebus[6] round about
    Dapples the drowsy east with spots of grey.
    Thanks to you all, and leave us. Fare you well.

CLAUDIO   Good morrow, masters. Each his several° way.   *separate*
30 DON PEDRO   Come, let us hence, and put on other weeds,°   *garments*
    And then to Leonato's we will go.

CLAUDIO   And Hymen now with luckier issue speed 's[7]
    Than this° for whom we rendered up this woe.   *Exeunt*   *this woman*

5.4

Enter LEONATO, [ANTONIO,] BENEDICK, BEATRICE, MAR-
GARET, URSULA, FRIAR [FRANCIS], *and* HERO

FRIAR   Did I not tell you she was innocent?

LEONATO   So are the Prince and Claudio who accused her
    Upon° the error that you heard debated.   *Because of*

5.3 Location: A churchyard.
1. Candles or torches carried in token of penitence.
2. In Q, the poem is headed "Epitaph" and is not ascribed to a particular speaker.
3. Diana, Roman goddess of the moon and patroness of virgins.

4. Hero (imagined as a knight, or follower, of Diana).
5. Have finished preying (for the night has passed).
6. The sun god's chariot wheels.
7. And may Hymen (Greek god of marriage) grant us more favorable results.
5.4 Location: Leonato's house.

But Margaret was in some fault for this,
5   Although against her will° as it appears   *unintentionally*
In the true course of all the question.°   *investigation*
ANTONIO   Well, I am glad that all things sorts° so well.   *turn out*
BENEDICK   And so am I, being else by faith° enforced   *my pledge*
To call young Claudio to a reckoning for it.
10 LEONATO   Well, daughter, and you gentlewomen all,
Withdraw into a chamber by yourselves,
And when I send for you come hither masked.

      Exeunt [BEATRICE, HERO, MARGARET, *and* URSULA]

The Prince and Claudio promised by this hour
To visit me. You know your office,° brother,   *task*
15 You must be father to your brother's daughter,
And give her to young Claudio.
ANTONIO   Which I will do with confirmed° countenance.   *serious*
BENEDICK   Friar, I must entreat your pains, I think.
FRIAR   To do what, signor?
20 BENEDICK   To bind me or undo° me, one of them.   *ruin; unbind*
Signor Leonato, truth it is, good signor,
Your niece regards me with an eye of favour.
LEONATO   That eye my daughter lent her, 'tis most true.
BENEDICK   And I do with an eye of love requite her.
25 LEONATO   The sight whereof I think you had from me,
From Claudio and the Prince. But what's your will?
BENEDICK   Your answer, sir, is enigmatical.
But for my will, my will is° your good will   *is that*
May stand with ours this day to be conjoined
30 In the state of honourable marriage,
In which, good Friar, I shall desire your help.
LEONATO   My heart is with your liking.
FRIAR   And my help.
Here comes the Prince and Claudio.

      Enter [DON PEDRO *the*] *Prince and* CLAUDIO *with attendants*

DON PEDRO   Good morrow to this fair assembly.
35 LEONATO   Good morrow, Prince. Good morrow, Claudio.
We here attend you. Are you yet° determined   *still*
Today to marry with my brother's daughter?
CLAUDIO   I'll hold my mind,° were she an Ethiope.[1]   *intention*
LEONATO   Call her forth, brother, here's the Friar ready.

      [*Exit* ANTONIO]

40 DON PEDRO   Good morrow, Benedick. Why, what's the matter
That you have such a February face,
So full of frost, of storm and cloudiness?
CLAUDIO   I think he thinks upon the savage bull.[2]
Tush, fear not, man, we'll tip thy horns with gold,
45 And all Europa° shall rejoice at thee   *Europe*
As once Europa did at lusty Jove
When he would play the noble beast in love.[3]
BENEDICK   Bull Jove, sir, had an amiable° low,   *amorous*
And some such strange bull leapt your father's cow

---

1. In other words, black and therefore, according to the Elizabethan racist stereotype, ugly.
2. Continuing the teasing of 5.1.172.
3. In Greek mythology, Jove took the form of a bull to carry off the princess Europa, with whom he was in love.

50 And got a calf° in that same noble feat   *begot a blockhead*
     Much like to you, for you have just his bleat.
        Enter [ANTONIO *with*] HERO, BEATRICE, MARGARET, *and*
         URSULA [*masked*]
CLAUDIO   For this I owe you.⁴ Here comes other reck'nings.°   *accounts to settle*
     Which is the lady I must seize upon?
ANTONIO   This same is she, and I do give you her.
55 CLAUDIO   Why then, she's mine. Sweet, let me see your face.
LEONATO   No, that you shall not till you take her hand
     Before this Friar and swear to marry her.
CLAUDIO   [*to* HERO]   Give me your hand before this holy friar.
     I am your husband if you like of me.°   *like me*
60 HERO   [*unmasking*]   And when I lived I was your other wife;
     And when you loved, you were my other husband.
CLAUDIO   Another Hero!
HERO   Nothing certainer.
     One Hero died defiled,° but I do live,   *slandered*
     And surely as I live, I am a maid.
65 DON PEDRO   The former Hero, Hero that is dead!
LEONATO   She died, my lord, but whiles her slander lived.
FRIAR   All this amazement can I qualify°   *lessen*
     When after that the holy rites are ended
     I'll tell you largely° of fair Hero's death.   *in full*
70   Meantime, let wonder° seem familiar,°   *marvels / commonplace*
     And to the chapel let us presently.
BENEDICK   Soft and fair,° Friar, which is Beatrice?   *Wait a minute*
BEATRICE [*unmasking*]   I answer to that name, what is your will?
BENEDICK   Do not you love me?
BEATRICE   Why no, no more than reason.
75 BENEDICK   Why then, your uncle and the Prince and Claudio
     Have been deceived. They swore you did.
BEATRICE   Do not you love me?
BENEDICK   Troth no, no more than reason.
BEATRICE   Why then, my cousin, Margaret, and Ursula
     Are much deceived, for they did swear you did.
80 BENEDICK   They swore that you were almost sick for me.
BEATRICE   They swore that you were wellnigh dead for me.
BENEDICK   'Tis no such matter. Then you do not love me?
BEATRICE   No, truly, but in friendly recompense.
LEONATO   Come, cousin, I am sure you love the gentleman.
85 CLAUDIO   And I'll be sworn upon't that he loves her,
     For here's a paper written in his hand,
     A halting sonnet of his own pure brain,
     Fashioned° to Beatrice.   *Addressed*
HERO   And here's another,
     Writ in my cousin's hand, stol'n from her pocket,
90   Containing her affection unto Benedick.
BENEDICK   A miracle! Here's our own hands against our hearts.⁵
     Come, I will have thee, but by this light, I take thee for pity.
BEATRICE   I would not deny you, but by this good day, I yield
     upon great persuasion, and partly to save your life, for I was
95   told you were in a consumption.°   *wasting away ill*

4. I will pay you back later (for the insults).   indifference we claim to feel in our hearts (or proves
5. Our own handwritten testimony contradicts the   our hearts to be guilty of loving).

BENEDICK [*kissing her*]   Peace, I will stop your mouth.

DON PEDRO   How dost thou, Benedick the married man?

BENEDICK   I'll tell thee what, Prince: a college of wit-crackers
cannot flout° me out of my humour. Dost thou think I care for   jeer
100   a satire or an epigram? No, if a man will be beaten with brains,
a° shall wear nothing handsome about him.[6] In brief, since I   he
do purpose° to marry, I will think nothing to any purpose that   intend
the world can say against it, and therefore never flout at me for
what I have said against it. For man is a giddy thing, and this is
105   my conclusion. For thy part, Claudio, I did think to have
beaten thee, but in that thou art like° to be my kinsman, live   likely
unbruised, and love my cousin.

CLAUDIO   I had well hoped thou wouldst have denied Beatrice,
that I might have cudgelled thee out of thy single life to make
110   thee a double dealer,° which out of question thou wilt be, if   married man; adulterer
my cousin do not look exceeding narrowly° to thee.   closely

BENEDICK   Come, come, we are friends, let's have a dance ere
we are married, that we may lighten our own hearts and our
wives' heels.

115   LEONATO   We'll have dancing afterward.

BENEDICK   First, of my word. Therefore play, music. [*To* DON
PEDRO] Prince, thou art sad, get thee a wife, get thee a wife.
There is no staff more reverend than one tipped with horn.[7]

Enter MESSENGER

MESSENGER   My lord, your brother John is ta'en in flight,
120   And brought with armèd men back to Messina.

BENEDICK   Think not on him till tomorrow, I'll devise thee
brave° punishments for him. Strike up, pipers.   fine

Dance [*and exeunt*]

6. No, if a man is easily injured by ridicule, he will   attention).
never even dare to dress well (since that would provoke   7. A final allusion to the cuckold's horns.

Henry V

From a military point of view, Henry V was perhaps the most capable king England ever had. In 1414, reviving an English royal claim on the French throne, Henry invaded France. The following year, he won the Battle of Agincourt against impossible odds, forcing the King of France to declare him his heir and marry him to his daughter. Not surprisingly, Henry's story was a favorite with his English compatriots. It was lovingly chronicled by the historians Raphael Holinshed (died c. 1580) and Edward Hall (d. 1547), and probably dramatized once or more by other playwrights before Shakespeare brought his own version to the stage in 1599.

Shakespeare's *Henry V* is the last written of a set of eight plays on medieval English history. His first four history plays had dealt with the tumultuous years between 1422 and 1485, when England was first at war with France and then, after 1455, embroiled in a civil war—the Wars of the Roses. Shakespeare wrote another four plays several years later, presenting the events of 1398 to 1420 that led up to these long wars over the royal succession. *Richard II* depicts Henry Bolingbroke's successful rebellion against Richard II and his coronation as Henry IV. The next two plays describe the troubled reign of the usurper, whose former allies turn against him and whose son keeps company with thieves. At the end of *2 Henry IV*, the King dies and young Prince Hal ascends the throne as Henry V, quickly belying his wastrel reputation and proving himself an astute leader in the play that bears his name. In the final lines of *Henry V*, however, the Chorus foresees Henry's imminent death, after which civil strife will break out once again.

Henry V is, therefore, one of a group of plays rather than a freestanding work. It refers constantly to events before and after its own temporal limits, events familiar to Shakespeare's audience from plays they had already seen performed. These references complicate the play's tone considerably. The Chorus's final predictions, for instance, darken the otherwise straightforwardly triumphal conclusion. Surely our awareness of the internecine strife that precedes and follows Henry's reign reinforces our admiration for him—he prospers where others have failed and will again fail, miserably. At the same time, *Henry V* is haunted by problems merely deferred, not resolved; in the long view, its hero's success looks transitory, even futile.

In 1599, such complexities may have seemed especially pertinent. England was mobilizing for a major campaign against Ireland to be led by Elizabeth's dashing young favorite, the Earl of Essex. *Henry V* registers both the patriotic excitement generated by the prospect of a military venture in foreign parts and the dread of war in a notoriously difficult environment (in the event, Essex's expedition was a disaster). These acutely mixed feelings were symptomatic of more general disputes about England's foreign policy. For much of the sixteenth century, England had attempted merely to defend its borders, but as it became wealthier and more powerful, expansion seemed feasible again. Ireland and the Netherlands beckoned; so did the New World, where France and Spain had already established colonies. Henry V's foray into France typified the kind of aggressive enterprise some of Shakespeare's contemporaries wished their nation to underwrite and others denounced as wasteful and dangerous.

Given the circumstances in which *Henry V* was originally written, it is not surprising that it has generated striking interpretive disagreements or that the play continues to be viewed through the lens of contemporary events. In Laurence Olivier's film version, made during World War II, *Henry V* is a vindication of England's excellence, and the victory at Agincourt a hopeful precedent for success in a justified

Henricus v. From John Rastell, *The Pastyme of People* (1529).

European war. Kenneth Branagh's 1989 film, on the other hand, reflects the murkier experience of more recent conflicts: the American intervention in Vietnam, the British in the Falkland Islands. Did Shakespeare intend the play as a paeon to militarism or as an exposé of war's pointless brutality? Is Henry supposed to be a heroic or a repellent character? Is the war in France justified or purely expedient?

Henry's impressive leadership is repeatedly emphasized by the Chorus, by his followers, and even occasionally by his enemies. He not merely copes with, but triumphs over, the difficult circumstances bequeathed him: uniting his disputatious people against an external enemy, spending their aggressions abroad instead of at home, and gaining himself a kingdom to boot. He displays unshakeable personal courage in the campaign in France, in the smaller skirmishes as well as in the desperate moments before Agincourt. His "Once more unto the breach" speech (3.1.1–34) and his prophetic vision of aged veterans boasting to their compatriots on St. Crispin's Day (4.3.41ff.) have often been held up as models of inspirational eloquence.

On the other hand, *Henry V* clear-sightedly acknowledges, as had *Richard II* and *1* and *2 Henry IV,* that the factors that render someone an effective king are not necessarily morally admirable ones. Even while Shakespeare displays Henry's charisma to the full, he refuses to be entirely dazzled by his allure. In the early sixteenth century, Machiavelli had introduced Renaissance political thinkers to the notion that success as a ruler might be separable from, or even inimical to, what was conventionally considered virtuous behavior. A successful leader, he argued, needed the traits of both the fox and the lion: in other words, he had to know how to use deception and violence to achieve his ends. Shakespeare's Henry is certainly no monster of iniquity, but his career poses some of the same questions that Machiavelli raised in *The Prince.* What is the relationship of political success to personal goodness? Should princes be judged by moral rules different from those that apply to the rest of mankind?

A closer look at *Henry V* reveals a play not only deeply equivocal but self-consciously so. The capstone of Shakespeare's years of experimentation in the history play form, *Henry V* seems profoundly aware of the way generic constraints bear in upon its hero. Comedy and tragedy form themselves upon the rhythms of an individual life, ending in marriage or in death. History plays, by contrast, even when they seem to concentrate on the fortunes of a single character, dramatize the life of a nation, or at least its governing class. Characters in history plays are conceived as an endless generational succession, inheriting a political and historical situation from their ancestors and passing it down to their descendants. When one person dies, another steps into his place. The King's marriage represents not merely a natural culmination of his personal story, but one episode in a family's attempt to perpetuate a dynasty.

The young King Henry V is, therefore, both more and less than a talented and intelligent individual. One of a series, like the play that bears his name, he must come to terms with what it means to be part of a family line, what it means for one's "career" to begin before birth and end long after death. And Henry's family line is, of course, a tangled matter. His dubious title to the English throne reflects some of the instabilities in the concept of inheritance: what can it mean to acquire name and title "legitimately" from a man who stole the throne? The passing of property and title from one generation to the next might seem to reflect facts of nature, but it is also, as the Archbishop of Canterbury's discussion of "Salic law" reveals in 1.2, a matter of custom, a cultural construction. Inheritance can be altered as well by force or by negotiation: Henry IV compelled Richard to abdicate, and Henry V's victory at Agincourt requires the French King to recognize an English conqueror rather than his own son as heir to the French throne.

Troubles over the way proper generational sequence ought to be defined resonate throughout the play. War, in particular, seems intimately tied up with questions of lineage. Battlefield heroics can reinforce and clarify the relationship between fathers and sons. King Charles of France, for instance, describes Henry's belligerence as his birthright:

> The kindred of him hath been fleshed upon us,
> And he is bred out of that bloody strain
> That haunted us in our familiar paths.
> Witness our too-much-memorable shame
> When Crécy battle fatally was struck,
> And all our princes captived by the hand
> Of that black name, Edward, Black Prince of Wales,
> Whiles that his mountant sire, on mountain standing,
> Up in the air, crowned with the golden sun,
> Saw his heroical seed and smiled to see him
> Mangle the work of nature and deface
> The patterns that by God and by French fathers
> Had twenty years been made.
>
> (2.4.50–62)

Henry's great-uncle, Edward the Black Prince, butchers the French while the Prince's father, King Edward III, gladly looks on. There seem to be no mothers in this entirely male domain, merely God and fathers in alliance, so that Edward III himself seems rather improbably deified, "up in the air, crowned with the golden sun." Henry, in his stirring speech to his troops at Harfleur, evidences a similar pattern of assumptions:

> On, on, you noblest English,
> Whose blood is fet from fathers of war-proof,
> Fathers that like so many Alexanders
> Have in these parts from morn till even fought,
> And sheathed their swords for lack of argument.
> Dishonor not your mothers; now attest
> That those whom you called fathers did beget you.
>
> (3.1.17–23)

Mothers get a mention from Henry, as they did not from the French King, but they contribute nothing of their own nature to their offspring: their function is merely to duplicate the fathers in the next generation. Any discrepancy between the achievement of the fathers and the achievement of the sons, in fact, "dishonors" the mothers by implying that they must have slept with men other than their husbands, because the only explanation for such an inconsistency is that the biological father must be different from the acknowledged one. Once again, fathers set demanding precedents for sons eager to emulate their exploits but inevitably threatened by the possibility of falling short. The French King and Henry imagine inheritance, which might seem a passive process, as a strenuous endeavor.

If battle clarifies the pedigrees of winners, it simultaneously obscures those of the losers. In practical terms, of course, Henry's victory debars the Dauphin, the French heir apparent, from assuming his father's title. More generally, however, as both Henry and the French King insist, defeat in battle disrupts familial affinity, defacing paternal patterns, dishonoring mothers. Negotiating with Harfleur's governor, Henry predicts the consequences of the town's refusal to surrender quietly:

> why, in a moment look to see
> The blind and bloody soldier with foul hand
> Defile the locks of your shrill-shrieking daughters;
> Your fathers taken by the silver beards,
> And their most reverend heads dashed to the walls;
> Your naked infants spitted upon pikes,
> Whiles the mad mothers with their howls confused
> Do break the clouds, as did the wives of Jewry
> At Herod's bloody-hunting slaughtermen.
> (3.3.110–18)

On the face of it, it might seem surprising for a general to characterize his own troops as rapists and murderers, or implicitly to compare himself with the infanticidal King Herod, one of the Bible's wickedest villains. Yet Henry's rhetorical tactics are entirely deliberate: by describing his soldiers' potential victims as members of families—as daughters, fathers, infants, mothers—he heightens the impact of their violence. The rampaging army, he implies, will shatter not merely individuals but whole networks of affiliation. The speech effectively intimidates his auditors, who give up without a fight.

Soldiers using a battering ram. From Flavius Vegetius Renatus, *The Foure Bookes of Flavius Vegetius Renatus: Briefelye contayninge a plaine forme, and perfect knowledge of martiall policye . . .* (1572).

Unfortunately, even soldiers in the "winning" camp, insofar as they are vulnerable to the enemy, are liable to similar familial disasters. Exeter's description of war's misfortunes exempts neither side from calamity, from

> the widows' tears, the orphans' cries,
> The dead men's blood, the pining maidens' groans,
> For husbands, fathers, and betrothèd lovers . . . .
> (2.4.106–08)

Although Henry's invasion leaves the French more bloodied and tearful than the English, the English, too, suffer emotional and practical losses. Henry's soldiers are wasted by disease, hanged, occasionally even killed in battle. In 4.1, the common soldier worries, in an age without veteran's benefits, of dying with "wives left poor behind them" and "children rawly left" (lines 132–34). Henry's insistence on his inheritance rights, in other words, may disrupt not only his enemies' but his subordinates'. If infants are slaughtered, daughters raped, fathers torn from dependents, how can families be reconstituted? How can legitimate inheritance possibly be determined?

The difficulties of succession and inheritance are issues for Shakespeare the playwright as well as for his protagonist. Just as the character Henry V must strive to match and excel the patterns set by his ancestors, so the play Henry V must concern itself with what it means to be a sequel in two different senses: the way in which it represents actual historical events in a necessarily diminished theatrical form, and the way in which it must struggle to gratify an audience whose expectations had been formed by three exceedingly popular plays in the same series. At the beginning of every act, a Chorus pointedly emphasizes the play's self-conscious lack of realism:

> Can this cock-pit hold
> The vasty fields of France? Or may we cram
> Within this wooden O the very casques
> That did affright the air at Agincourt?
> (Prologue, lines 11–14)

Of course, Henry V is no more implausible than most other Renaissance plays. But in a sense, the theatrical anxieties of Henry V are cognate with the personal anxieties of its hero; the play is afraid of degenerating from its precursors, proving an inadequate replica of a distinguished original. And just as Henry V seems to overcompensate, not merely living up to his illustrious predecessors but going beyond them so, too, Henry V, like many sequels, copes with its belatedness by a strategy of overstatement. It exaggerates some of the themes and issues of the earlier plays. In 1 Henry IV, Hotspur, Prince Hal's valiant antagonist, epitomized many of the traditional ideals of chivalry—a word derived from the French cheval, "horse." In Henry V, Bourbon, one of Henry's new opponents, writes a sonnet to his horse that begins "Wonder of nature"—for, he says, "my horse is my mistress" (3.7.36–37, 40). Hotspur's chivalry, caricatured to the point of ridiculousness, degenerates in Henry V into bestiality jokes made at the expense of a blustering fop.

Shakespeare dramatizes Henry's success, in other words, not merely by magnifying his exploits but by minimizing the threat from possible competitors. Although the enemies of Henry's adulthood are technically more formidable than the enemies of his adolescence, they are characterized as bumbling and laughable, so that Henry's victory over them seems virtually preordained. Henry's allies seem similarly diminished. Falstaff, who dominated much of 1 and 2 Henry IV, dies without reappearing in Henry V, leaving his cronies Bardolph, Nim, and Pistol to accompany Henry to France. They are joined by Fluellen, a Welsh soldier; MacMorris, an Irish one; Jamy, a Scots one; and Williams, a rural English one. This miscellany is proof of Henry's charisma; while in the previous plays the Irish, Scots, and Welsh were up in arms, Henry V successfully enlists them in his cause—not by homogenizing their differences, but by inspiring their allegiance to him even as they quarrel furiously with one another. Henry's triumph at Agincourt, Shakespeare claims, involves all the peoples of the British Isles. At the same time, these loyal adherents are given little of Falstaff's subversive wit, presumably because Falstaff's wholesale critique of military valor would undercut too thoroughly the premises of Henry's royal magnetism. Even the bluff yeoman Williams, who complains of the disproportionate suffering common people undergo to satisfy the ambitions of their betters, does not dissent from the fundamental principle of social and military hierarchy: to disobey one's superiors, he claims, "were against all proportion of subjection" (4.1.138). For better or worse, everyone seems to agree, the subject's life is at the ruler's disposal.

Shakespeare's excision of Falstaff's skeptical intelligence from *Henry V* means that there is no one within the play to point out the ironies of many of the turns of the plot. Presumably, though no one comments explicitly upon it, the venality of the clerics who finance Henry's expedition to France is sufficiently clear to the audience. Likewise, when Gower loyally remarks that Henry, unlike Alexander, never killed any of his friends, we are likely to think back to Falstaff's death, attributed earlier to Henry's neglect, and also to reflect that of Henry's other Eastcheap chums only Pistol has survived the "great victory" at Agincourt. Elsewhere it is unclear how or even whether the audience is expected to grasp an irony. In 1.1, Henry decides to press his claim on the French throne through the female line of descent. Shortly thereafter, he executes three erstwhile friends for conspiring against his life. In fact their plot was inspired by the conviction that Henry's title to the English throne was obstructed by the Earl of Mortimer's daughter, the Earl of Cambridge's wife. In other words, Henry employs against the French a principle that, if it were enforced against him, would strip him of both English and French kingdoms. Yet the point is made so obliquely that only a spectator cognizant of the tangled Plantagenet genealogy is likely to catch it.

As the stature of Henry's foes and associates diminishes, the ethical problems posed by his exploits are correspondingly aggravated. As we have already seen, Henry's self-assertion necessarily occurs at the expense of others, thereby raising the question of the extent to which his interests ought to take precedence over competing claims. Neither we nor Henry can be certain whether his exceptional situation and abilities exempt him from the criteria by which common persons are judged. In fact, Henry's unusual gifts as a leader render the uncertainty more pointed. Richard II disregarded common folk, and Henry IV deliberately avoided them; but Henry V inspires them by his capacity to immerse himself sympathetically in their lives. His insistence upon his ordinariness becomes a strategy of rule—part of what he is loved for during his lifetime and what becomes legendary after his death. But then, when he insists on seeing himself as a unique case nonetheless, he seems not merely to be asserting a King's usual prerogatives, but to be inconsistently or hypocritically making special allowances for himself.

This unresolved ambivalence becomes obvious in 4.1, when Henry disguises himself as a commoner and ventures among his rank and file. Initially, he argues for the essential similarity between himself and his followers.

> I think the King is but a man, as I am. The violet smells to him as it doth to me; the element shows to him as it doth to me. All his senses have but human conditions. His ceremonies laid by, in his nakedness he appears but a man, and though his affections are higher mounted than ours, yet when they stoop, they stoop with the like wing. (lines 99–104)

The ordinary soldiers, Williams and Bates, are unconvinced, pointing out that if they lose the battle, the King will be ransomed while they will be killed. On the other hand, they note, because they are required to obey the King under any circumstances, they need not concern themselves with the justice of the King's cause: their blood will be on Henry's head if he is waging an unjust war. The common soldiers see the King as unlike themselves, with special responsibilities that compensate for his special privileges. Henry responds indignantly:

> The King is not bound to answer the particular endings of his soldiers, the father of his son, nor the master of his servant, for they purpose not their deaths when they propose their services. Besides, there is no king, be his cause never so spotless, if it come to the arbitrament of swords, can try it out with all unspotted soldiers. Some, peradventure, have on them the guilt of premeditated and contrived murder; some, of beguiling virgins with the broken seals of perjury; some, making the wars their bulwark, that have before gored the gentle bosom of peace with pillage and robbery. (lines 146–55)

Henry resists accepting the extraordinary moral burden his followers would confer upon him. Yet his refusal is based not on his earlier assertion of the shared humanity of king and subject, but on a conviction of the king's special position. He distinguishes sharply and problematically between the king's "superior" violence—the violence of war—and the violence of individual subjects, which is merely criminal. After the soldiers leave, Henry exclaims bitterly:

> Upon the King.
> 'Let us our lives, our souls, our debts, our care-full wives,
> Our children, and our sins, lay on the King.'
> We must bear all. O hard condition,
> Twin-born with greatness: subject to the breath
> Of every fool, whose sense no more can feel
> But his own wringing. What infinite heart-sease
> Must kings neglect that private men enjoy?
>
> (lines 212–19)

It is hard to take this self-pity seriously, given that Henry attempts to deflect all blame for his actions onto enemies and inferiors, even while accepting as his due the rewards that accrue to him by virtue of his exceptional status.

On the other hand, Shakespeare also shows effectively the King's genuine isolation from ordinary pleasures of work and play that normal people can take for granted. Though he repudiates Falstaff, the King retains a distinctly sportive quality; but the moral and practical gap that yawns between the ascendant Henry and his correspondingly diminished associates complicates the effect of his playfulness. In 2.2, with a typical flourish, he pretends to hand the traitors Scrope, Grey, and Cambridge their military commissions, after feigning to inquire about mercy for traitors. Actually, he gives them letters showing that he knows of their plot. This is splendid theater, but it is also quite chilling: Henry plays with his guilty victims as a cat plays with a mouse. His joke signifies not true contest, but absolute control.

Elsewhere, too, Henry's power tips the balance of hostility and affection that usually characterizes practical jokes in a markedly aggressive direction. In disguise on the eve of the Battle of Agincourt, he argues with the commoner Williams, as we have already seen, over the question of the king's responsibility for his subjects. He and Williams exchange gloves so they will be able to resume the quarrel after the battle. In 4.7, with victory assured, Henry gives Williams's glove to Fluellen to see what Williams will do when he sees it again. When Williams attacks Fluellen, Henry stops the fight, pretending to be angry at the insult to himself. Williams—technically guilty of the capital crime of mutiny—defends himself boldly enough, and Henry, thinking to be generous, returns Williams's glove to him filled with coins. Yet Williams fails to thank Henry, and when Fluellen attempts to add to the gift, he spurns it angrily. It is unclear from the script whether Williams eventually accepts the gold; either way, Henry's power contaminates what he wants to see as a game. While in the earlier plays Prince Hal always had the advantage of rank, it was still possible for Falstaff to give him almost as

Game of tennis. From Johann Amos Comenius, *Orbis Sensualium Pictus* (1659).

good as he got. Now that Henry is king and Falstaff is dead, Henry is always the winner, and so the game is no game at all. Arguably, in fact, Henry goes to war with France because he misses a sense of *competition*—because the fate of the effective king is that he cannot find real opposition at home.

Henry's wooing of Catherine in 5.2 is typified by the same dubious sense of fun. This scene, often quite endearing onstage, is also entirely beside the point. We hear from the Chorus in 3.0 that the French King offered Catherine to Henry before his forces arrived in France, but he rejected the offer because the suggested dowry—some "petty and unprofitable dukedoms"—did not suffice. Nonetheless, in 5.2, Henry calls Catherine his "capital demand" and presents himself to her as a wooer. He pretends that Catherine is free to reject him, even though the marriage is already arranged as part of the peace treaty. Rather like Williams, Catherine refuses to play along: when he asks, "Canst thou love me?" she replies, "I cannot tell." "Wilt thou have me?" "Dat is as it shall please de *roi mon père*" (lines 183ff.). Is Catherine being coy, or is she simply speaking the literal truth? In the game as Henry constructs it, Catherine's refusals can as easily be interpreted as coquettishness as real denial. In other words, even if she refuses to play Henry's game, she necessarily plays it anyhow. In *Henry V,* Shakespeare must cope with a knotty dramatic problem: how to interest an audience in a man who has, or wins, everything—whose life seems an unbroken series of successes. In the final scene as in the rest of the play, Shakespeare fascinates us by exhibiting the inevitably equivocal nature of kingly glory.

KATHARINE EISAMAN MAUS

TEXTUAL NOTE

Henry V exists in the 1623 First Folio (F) version and in a quarto version first issued in 1600 and reprinted in 1602 and 1619. The Folio version is generally accepted as the most authoritative text and was probably derived from Shakespeare's "foul papers," or manuscript, but there are also signs that the compositor consulted the 1619 Quarto

(Q3) when setting up the Folio text. F is not, however, a wholly reliable source; it contains a fairly large number of readings rejected by modern editors, probably the result of a compositor misreading a handwritten text. The Oxford editors argue that Q, although printed much earlier than F and obviously corrupt in some respects, actually represents a later stage of the text and may therefore incorporate some of Shakespeare's second thoughts and modifications. They believe that Q is based on memorial reconstruction by actors who played the parts of Exeter and Gower, for the text is far more reliable when these characters are onstage than for other scenes.

The quarto text also has a slightly different cast of characters than Folio's: F's Bedford is Q's Clarence, F's Westmoreland is Q's Warwick, and speeches assigned in F to Britain and to the Dauphin in the Agincourt scenes are given to Bourbon in Q. The most important substitution is the last, Bourbon's replacement of the Dauphin in 3.7, 4.2, and 4.5. In F, the Dauphin's substantial role sets him up as Henry's personal adversary, much as Hotspur was in 1 Henry IV. Also in F, the Dauphin's amply demonstrated folly seems to warrant his eventual displacement by Henry. The quarto speech assignments, on the other hand, are consistent with King Charles's order in 3.5 that the Dauphin remain with him at Rouen. In Q, the Dauphin's absence from the battlefield, rather than his extravagantly frivolous presence, implies his unfitness for rule.

Although most editors accept the Folio speech assignments, Gary Taylor, editor of the Oxford text, argues that Shakespeare in fact vacillated about whether to include the Dauphin in the Agincourt scenes and that Q represents his final decision not to do so. In consequence, although F remains the Oxford control text, Taylor adopts many more readings from Q than do most editors. In this respect, the Oxford Henry V seems to depart from the editors' usual policy of not conflating distinctly different texts of the same play (the policy that produces the two King Lears later in this volume). Taylor provides information on the tangled textual history of the play and a full explanation of his editorial choices in his single-volume edition of Henry V (Oxford: Clarendon, 1982).

SELECTED BIBLIOGRAPHY

Altman, Joel. "'Vile Participation': The Amplification of Violence in the Theatre of Henry V." Shakespeare Quarterly 42 (1991): 1–32. Henry V in the context of contemporary political and religious issues—in particular, the debate over the nature of Communion.

Barton, Anne. "The King Disguised: Shakespeare's Henry V and the Comical History." The Triple Bond: Plays, Mainly Shakespearean, in Performance. Ed. Joseph G. Price. University Park: Pennsylvania State University Press, 1975. 92–117. Sees Henry V in a tradition of Elizabethan plays that combine history and comedy.

Cormack, Bradin. "'If We Be Conquered': Legal Nationalism and the France of Shakespeare's English Histories." A Power to Do Justice: Jurisdiction and Early English Literature. Chicago: University of Chicago Press, 2007. Shakespeare's treatment of France and the French language in terms of sixteenth-century English anxieties about national identity.

Danson, Lawrence. "Henry V: King, Chorus, and Critics." Shakespeare Quarterly 34 (1983): 27–43. King Henry as an actor; the Chorus as a means of drawing attention to the relationship between history and theater.

Dollimore, Jonathan, and Alan Sinfield. "History and Ideology, Masculinity and Miscegenation." Faultlines: Cultural Materialism and the Politics of Dissident Reading. By Alan Sinfield. Berkeley: University of California Press, 1992. 109–42. Imperialist and masculinist attitudes reinforce one another in the play.

Greenblatt, Stephen. "Invisible Bullets: Renaissance Authority and Its Subversion, Henry IV and Henry V." Political Shakespeare: New Essays in Cultural Materialism. Ed. Jonathan Dollimore and Alan Sinfield. Manchester: Manchester University

Press, 1985. 18–47. Theater and the glamour of a royal power that incorporates what seems to undermine it.

Ornstein, Robert. *"Henry V."* *A Kingdom for a Stage: The Achievement of Shakespeare's History Plays.* Cambridge, Mass.: Harvard University Press, 1972. 175–202. *Henry V* as an equivocal celebration of the King's victories.

Quint, David. "Alexander the Pig: Shakespeare on History and Poetry." *Boundary* 2 10 (1982): 49–63. Shakespeare's relation to Renaissance humanists' conceptions of history.

Rabkin, Norman. "Rabbits, Ducks, and *Henry V.*" *Shakespeare Quarterly* 28 (1977): 279–96. *Henry V* as an unresolvably ambiguous play.

Wells, Stanley, with Gary Taylor. *Modernizing Shakespeare's Spelling* [Wells], *with Three Studies in the Text of "Henry V"* [Taylor]. Oxford: Clarendon, 1979. Provides the scholarly rationale for the textual editing of the Oxford/Norton version of the play.

FILMS

Henry V. 1944. Dir. Laurence Olivier. UK. 137 min. Colorful, patriotic version made near the end of World War II, with Oliver as a very sympathetic king. Intelligently translates the play's theatrical self-consciousness to the film medium.

Henry V. 1979. Dir. David Giles. UK. 163 min. This BBC-TV production retains more features of a stage production than do the elaborate Olivier and Branagh versions. David Gwillim is a pleasant but resolute hero.

Henry V. 1989. Dir. Kenneth Branagh. UK. 137 min. Harsher and more violent than the Olivier version, with an elaborate reenactment of the Battle of Agincourt. Branagh stars as a grimly driven Henry.

The Life of Henry the Fifth

THE PERSONS OF THE PLAY

CHORUS
KING HARRY V of England, claimant to the French throne
Duke of GLOUCESTER ⎫
Duke of CLARENCE ⎬ his brothers
Duke of EXETER, his uncle
Duke of YORK
SALISBURY
WESTMORLAND
WARWICK
Archbishop of CANTERBURY
Bishop of ELY
Richard, Earl of CAMBRIDGE ⎫
Henry, Lord SCROPE of Masham ⎬ traitors
Sir Thomas GREY ⎭
PISTOL ⎫
NIM ⎬ formerly Falstaff's companions
BARDOLPH ⎭
BOY, formerly Falstaff's page
HOSTESS, formerly Mistress Quickly, now Pistol's wife
Captain GOWER, an Englishman
Captain FLUELLEN, a Welshman
Captain MACMORRIS, an Irishman
Captain JAMY, a Scot
Sir Thomas ERPINGHAM
John BATES ⎫
Alexander COURT ⎬ English soldiers
Michael WILLIAMS ⎭
HERALD
KING CHARLES VI of France
ISABEL, his wife and queen
The DAUPHIN, their son and heir
CATHERINE, their daughter
ALICE, an old gentlewoman
The CONSTABLE of France ⎫
Duke of BOURBON
Duke of ORLÉANS
Duke of BERRI ⎬ French noblemen at Agincourt
Lord RAMBURES
Lord GRANDPRÉ ⎭
Duke of BURGUNDY
MONTJOY, the French Herald
GOVERNOR of Harfleur
French AMBASSADORS to England

Prologue

*Enter [*CHORUS *as*] *Prologue*

CHORUS   O for a muse of fire, that would ascend
The brightest heaven of invention:°   *imagination*
A kingdom for a stage, princes to act,
And monarchs to behold the swelling° scene.   *expansive; splendid*
5   Then should the warlike Harry, like himself,
Assume the port° of Mars,° and at his heels,   *bearing / god of war*
Leashed in like hounds, should famine, sword, and fire
Crouch for employment. But pardon, gentles° all,   *gentlefolk*
The flat unraisèd° spirits that hath dared   *uninspired*
10   On this unworthy scaffold° to bring forth   *platform*
So great an object. Can this cock-pit° hold   *small cockfighting arena*
The vasty fields of France? Or may we cram
Within this wooden O° the very casques°   *round theater / helmets*
That did affright the air at Agincourt?[1]
15   O pardon: since a crookèd figure[2] may
Attest° in little place a million,   *Represent*
And let us, ciphers° to this great account,°   *zeroes / sum; story*
On your imaginary forces° work.   *powers of imagination*
Suppose within the girdle of these walls
20   Are now confined two mighty monarchies,
Whose high uprearèd and abutting fronts°   *frontiers*
The perilous narrow ocean° parts asunder.   *(English Channel)*
Piece out our imperfections with your thoughts:
Into a thousand parts divide one man,
25   And make imaginary puissance.°   *power*
Think, when we talk of horses, that you see them,
Printing their proud hoofs i'th' receiving earth;
For 'tis your thoughts that now must deck° our kings,   *equip*
Carry them here and there, jumping o'er times,
30   Turning th'accomplishment of many years
Into an hourglass—for the which supply,°   *to supplement which*
Admit me Chorus to this history,
Who Prologue-like your humble patience pray
Gently to hear, kindly to judge, our play.   *Exit*

1.1

*Enter the [*Archbishop*] of* CANTERBURY *and [the Bishop
of]* ELY

CANTERBURY   My lord, I'll tell you. That self ° bill is urged   *same*
Which in th'eleventh year of the last king's reign
Was like,° and had indeed against us passed,   *likely*
But that the scrambling and unquiet time
5   Did push it out of farther question.°   *consideration*
ELY   But how, my lord, shall we resist it now?
CANTERBURY   It must be thought on. If it pass against us,
We lose the better half of our possession,
For all the temporal lands[1] which men devout
10   By testament have given to the Church
Would they strip from us—being valued thus:

---

1. Site of Henry's famous victory over the French in 1415.
2. A zero, which multiplies a digit's value by ten.

crookèd: curved.
1.1 Location: In Henry's court.
1. Land devoted to secular uses.

As much as would maintain, to the King's honour,
Full fifteen earls and fifteen hundred knights,
Six thousand and two hundred good esquires;[2]
15 And, to relief of lazars° and weak age,   *lepers*
Of indigent faint souls past corporal° toil,   *bodily*
A hundred almshouses right well supplied;
And to the coffers of the King beside
A thousand pounds by th' year. Thus runs the bill.
20 ELY   This would drink deep.
CANTERBURY   'Twould drink the cup and all.
ELY   But what prevention?
CANTERBURY   The King is full of grace and fair regard.°   *kindly inclination*
ELY   And a true lover of the holy Church.
25 CANTERBURY   The courses of his youth promised it not.
The breath no sooner left his father's body
But that his wildness, mortified° in him,   *struck dead*
Seemed to die too. Yea, at that very moment
Consideration° like an angel came   *Spiritual reflection*
30 And whipped th'offending Adam° out of him,   *innate depravity*
Leaving his body as a paradise
T'envelop and contain celestial spirits.
Never was such a sudden scholar made;
Never came reformation in a flood
35 With such a heady currance° scouring faults;   *headlong current*
Nor never Hydra-headed[3] wilfulness
So soon did lose his seat°—and all at once—   *throne*
As in this king.
ELY   We are blessèd in the change.
CANTERBURY   Hear him but reason in divinity°   *theology*
40 And, all-admiring, with an inward wish
You would desire the King were made a prelate;°   *an important clergyman*
Hear him debate of commonwealth affairs,
You would say it hath been all-in-all his study;
List° his discourse of war, and you shall hear   *Listen to*
45 A fearful battle rendered you in music;
Turn him to any cause of policy,°   *political issue*
The Gordian knot[4] of it he will unloose,
Familiar° as his garter—that when he speaks,   *Offhandedly*
The air, a chartered libertine,° is still,   *licensed freedman*
50 And the mute wonder lurketh in men's ears
To steal his sweet and honeyed sentences:
So that the art and practic part of life
Must be the mistress to this theoric.[5]
Which is a wonder how his grace should glean it,
55 Since his addiction° was to courses vain,   *inclination*
His companies° unlettered, rude, and shallow,   *companions*
His hours filled up with riots,° banquets, sports,   *reveling*
And never noted in him any study,
Any retirement, any sequestration°   *removal*
60 From open haunts and popularity.[6]

2. Gentlemen below knightly rank.
3. Many-headed (the Hydra was a monstrous snake, killed by Hercules).
4. It was foretold that whoever untied the intricate Gordian knot would rule Asia; Alexander the Great cut it with his sword.
5. *the art . . . theoric*: practical experience must have taught him the theory.
6. From public places and unrefined companions.

ELY The strawberry grows underneath the nettle,
And wholesome berries thrive and ripen best
Neighboured by fruit of baser quality;
And so the Prince obscured his contemplation
65 Under the veil of wildness—which, no doubt,
Grew like the summer grass, fastest by night,
Unseen, yet crescive in his faculty.[7]
CANTERBURY It must be so, for miracles are ceased,[8]
And therefore we must needs admit the means°   natural causes
How things are perfected.
70 ELY   But, my good lord,
How now for mitigation of this bill
Urged by the Commons? Doth his majesty
Incline to it, or no?
CANTERBURY   He seems indifferent,
Or rather swaying more upon our part
75 Than cherishing th'exhibitors[9] against us;
For I have made an offer to his majesty,
Upon our spiritual convocation[1]
And in regard of causes now in hand,
Which I have opened° to his grace at large: expounded
80 As touching France, to give a greater sum
Than ever at one time the clergy yet
Did to his predecessors part withal.°   with
ELY How did this offer seem received, my lord?
CANTERBURY With good acceptance of his majesty,
85 Save that there was not time enough to hear,
As I perceived his grace would fain° have done,   gladly
The severals[2] and unhidden passages°   channels of descent
Of his true titles to some certain dukedoms,
And generally to the crown and seat of France,
90 Derived from Edward,° his great-grandfather.   King Edward III
ELY What was th'impediment that broke this off?
CANTERBURY The French ambassador upon that instant
Craved audience—and the hour I think is come
To give him hearing. Is it four o'clock?
95 ELY It is.
CANTERBURY Then go we in, to know his embassy°—   message
Which I could with a ready guess declare
Before the Frenchman speak a word of it.
ELY I'll wait upon you, and I long to hear it.   *Exeunt*

1.2

Enter KING [HARRY, *the Dukes of* GLOUCESTER], CLARENCE, *and*
EXETER, [*and the Earls of*] WARWICK [*and*] WESTMORLAND
KING HARRY Where is my gracious lord of Canterbury?
EXETER Not here in presence.
KING HARRY   Send for him, good uncle.
WESTMORLAND Shall we call in th'ambassador, my liege?

---

7. Yet growing according to its natural ability.
8. Protestants believed that no miracles occurred after scriptural times (anachronistic in the mouth of a medieval archbishop).
9. Parliamentary sponsors of the bill.

1. On behalf of the assembled clergy.
2. Legal means by which land is conveyed in separate parts to different heirs.
1.2 Location: The royal court.

KING HARRY   Not yet, my cousin.[1] We would be resolved,
5   Before we hear him, of some things of weight
That task° our thoughts, concerning us and France.   *exercise*
     Enter [Archbishop of CANTERBURY *and Bishop of* ELY]
CANTERBURY   God and his angels guard your sacred throne,
And make you long become° it.   *adorn*
KING HARRY   Sure we thank you.
My learnèd lord, we pray you to proceed,
10   And justly and religiously unfold
Why the law Salic[2] that they have in France
Or° should or should not bar us in our claim.   *Either*
And God forbid, my dear and faithful lord,
That you should fashion, wrest, or bow your reading,[3]
15   Or nicely charge° your understanding soul   *foolishly burden*
With opening titles miscreate,[4] whose right
Suits not in native colours° with the truth;   *Does not accord*
For God doth know how many now in health
Shall drop their blood in approbation°   *confirmation*
20   Of what your reverence shall incite us to.
Therefore take heed how you impawn° our person,   *pledge*
How you awake our sleeping sword of war;
We charge you in the name of God take heed.
For never two such kingdoms did contend
25   Without much fall of blood, whose guiltless drops
Are every one a woe, a sore complaint
'Gainst him whose wrongs gives edge unto the swords
That makes such waste in brief mortality.°   *short-lived humankind*
Under this conjuration° speak, my lord,   *injunction*
30   For we will hear, note, and believe in heart
That what you speak is in your conscience washed
As pure as sin with baptism.
CANTERBURY   Then hear me, gracious sovereign, and you peers
That owe your selves, your lives, and services
35   To this imperial throne. There is no bar
To make against your highness' claim to France
But this, which they produce from Pharamond:°   *legendary French King*
'*In terram Salicam mulieres ne succedant*'—
'No woman shall succeed in Salic[5] land'—
40   Which 'Salic land' the French unjustly gloss°   *interpret*
To be the realm of France, and Pharamond
The founder of this law and female bar.[6]
Yet their own authors faithfully affirm
That the land Salic is in Germany,
45   Between the floods° of Saale and of Elbe,   *rivers*
Where, Charles the Great having subdued the Saxons,
There left behind and settled certain French
Who, holding in disdain the German women
For some dishonest° manners of their life,   *unchaste*
50   Established there this law: to wit, no female
Should be inheritrix in Salic land—
Which Salic, as I said, 'twixt Elbe and Saale,

---

1. Kinsman; complimentary form of address from King to nobles.
2. Explained below, lines 35ff.
3. Should shape, pervert, or bend your interpretation.
4. With explicating false property rights.
5. Referring to an ancient Frankish tribe that lived beside the Rhine River.
6. And prohibition of female inheritance.

	Is at this day in Germany called Meissen.	
	Then doth it well appear the Salic Law	
55	Was not devisèd for the realm of France.	
	Nor did the French possess the Salic land	
	Until four hundred one-and-twenty years	
	After defunction° of King Pharamond,	*death*
	Idly° supposed the founder of this law,	*Foolishly*
60	Who died within the year of our redemption°	A.D.
	Four hundred twenty-six; and Charles the Great°	*Charlemagne*
	Subdued the Saxons, and did seat° the French	*establish*
	Beyond the river Saale, in the year	
	Eight hundred five. Besides, their writers say,	
65	King Pépin, which deposèd Childéric,	
	Did, as heir general[7]—being descended	
	Of Blithild, which was daughter to King Clotaire—	
	Make claim and title to the crown of France.	
	Hugh Capet also—who usurped the crown	
70	Of Charles the Duke of Lorraine, sole heir male	
	Of the true line and stock of Charles the Great—	
	To fine° his title with some shows of truth,	*complete; purify*
	Though in pure truth it was corrupt and naught,	
	Conveyed himself as heir to th' Lady Lingard,	
75	Daughter to Charlemain, who was the son	
	To Louis the Emperor, and Louis the son	
	Of Charles the Great. Also, King Louis the Ninth,	
	Who was sole heir to the usurper Capet,	
	Could not keep quiet in his conscience,	
80	Wearing the crown of France, till satisfied	
	That fair Queen Isabel, his grandmother,	
	Was lineal of ° the Lady Ermengarde,	*descended from*
	Daughter to Charles, the foresaid Duke of Lorraine;	
	By the which marriage, the line of Charles the Great	
85	Was reunited to the crown of France.	
	So that, as clear as is the summer's sun,	
	King Pépin's title and Hugh Capet's claim,	
	King Louis his° satisfaction, all appear	*(Louis's)*
	To hold in right and title of the female;	
90	So do the kings of France unto this day,	
	Howbeit they would hold up this Salic Law	
	To bar your highness claiming from the female,	
	And rather choose to hide them in a net°	*complexities*
	Than amply to embar° their crooked titles,	*frankly to rule out*
95	Usurped from you and your progenitors.	
	KING HARRY May I with right and conscience make this claim?	
	CANTERBURY The sin upon my head, dread sovereign.	
	For in the Book of Numbers° is it writ,	*Numbers 27:8*
	'When the son dies, let the inheritance	
100	Descend unto the daughter.' Gracious lord,	
	Stand for your own; unwind your bloody flag;	
	Look back into your mighty ancestors.	
	Go, my dread lord, to your great-grandsire's tomb,	
	From whom you claim;[8] invoke his warlike spirit,	

7. One who inherits through either the male or female line.

8. Edward III claimed the French throne through his mother, Isabella.

105   And your great-uncle's, Edward the Black Prince,
      Who on the French ground played a tragedy,
      Making defeat° on the full power of France,   *(at Crécy, in 1346)*
      Whiles his most mighty father° on a hill   *(Edward III)*
      Stood smiling to behold his lion's whelp
110   Forage in blood of French nobility.
      O noble English, that could entertain°   *encounter*
      With half their forces the full pride of France,
      And let another half stand laughing by,
      All out of work, and cold for° action.   *for want of*
115 ELY   Awake remembrance of those valiant dead,
      And with your puissant° arm renew their feats.   *powerful*
      You are their heir, you sit upon their throne,
      The blood and courage that renownèd them°   *made them famous*
      Runs in your veins—and my thrice-puissant liege
120   Is in the very May-morn of his youth,
      Ripe for exploits and mighty enterprises.
EXETER   Your brother kings and monarchs of the earth
      Do all expect that you should rouse yourself
      As did the former lions of your blood.
125 WESTMORLAND   They know your grace hath cause, and means and might,
      So hath your highness. Never king of England
      Had nobles richer and more loyal subjects,
      Whose hearts have left their bodies here in England
      And lie pavilioned° in the fields of France.   *encamped*
130 CANTERBURY   O let their bodies follow, my dear liege,
      With blood and sword and fire, to win your right.
      In aid whereof, we of the spiritualty°   *clergy*
      Will raise your highness such a mighty sum
      As never did the clergy at one time
135   Bring in to any of your ancestors.
KING HARRY   We must not only arm t'invade the French,
      But lay down our proportions[9] to defend
      Against the Scot, who will make raid upon us
      With all advantages.°   *Given any opportunity*
140 CANTERBURY   They of those marches,° gracious sovereign,   *borderlands*
      Shall be a wall sufficient to defend
      Our inland from the pilfering borderers.
KING HARRY   We do not mean the coursing snatchers° only,   *mounted raiders*
      But fear the main intendment° of the Scot,   *hostile intention*
145   Who hath been still a giddy° neighbour to us.   *always an unreliable*
      For you shall read that my great-grandfather
      Never unmasked his power unto France
      But that the Scot on his unfurnished° kingdom   *unprotected*
      Came pouring like the tide into a breach°   *gap in a dike*
150   With ample and brim fullness of his force
      Galling° the gleanèd° land with hot assays,°   *Hurting / depleted / attacks*
      Girding with grievous siege castles and towns,
      That England, being empty of defence,
      Hath shook and trembled at the bruit° thereof.   *noise*
155 CANTERBURY   She hath been then more feared than harmed, my liege.
      For hear her but exampled° by herself :   *given an example*
      When all her chivalry hath been in France

---

9. Decide the distribution of our forces.

And she a mourning widow of her nobles,
She hath herself not only well defended
160 But taken and impounded as a stray
The King of Scots,[1] whom she did send to France
To fill King Edward's fame with prisoner kings
And make your chronicle as rich with praise
As is the ooze and bottom of the sea
165 With sunken wrack° and sumless treasuries.[2]   shipwrecks
A LORD   But there's a saying very old and true:
          'If that you will France win,
          Then with Scotland first begin.'
For once the eagle England being in prey,°   out hunting
170 To her unguarded nest the weasel Scot
Comes sneaking, and so sucks her princely eggs,
Playing the mouse in absence of the cat,
To 'tame[3] and havoc° more than she can eat.   spoil
EXETER   It follows then the cat must stay at home.
175 Yet that is but a crushed° necessity,   forced
Since we have locks to safeguard necessaries
And pretty° traps to catch the petty thieves.   clever
While that the armèd hand doth fight abroad,
Th'advisèd° head defends itself at home.   well-advised
180 For government, though high and low and lower,[4]
Put into parts,[5] doth keep in one consent,°   harmony
Congreeing° in a full and natural close,°   Coming together / cadence
Like music.
CANTERBURY   True. Therefore doth heaven divide
The state of man in divers functions,
185 Setting endeavour in continual motion;
To which is fixèd, as an aim or butt,°   target
Obedience. For so work the honey-bees,
Creatures that by a rule in nature teach
The act of order to a peopled kingdom.
190 They have a king,[6] and officers of sorts,
Where some like magistrates correct at home;
Others like merchants venture trade abroad;
Others like soldiers, armèd in their stings,
Make boot upon° the summer's velvet buds,   Plunder
195 Which pillage they with merry march bring home
To the tent royal of their emperor,
Who busied in his majesty surveys
The singing masons building roofs of gold,
The civil citizens lading° up the honey,   weighing
200 The poor mechanic° porters crowding in   menial
Their heavy burdens at his narrow gate,
The sad-eyed justice with his surly hum
Delivering o'er to executors° pale   executioners
The lazy yawning drone. I this infer:
205 That many things, having full reference
To one consent,[7] may work contrariously.°   disparately

1. David II of Scotland, taken prisoner in 1346, when   4. That is, composed of three social classes.
Edward III was in France; actually, he was imprisoned   5. Divided into different functions.
in London.   6. The queen bee was thought to be male.
2. Incalculable riches.   7. *having . . . consent*: united by a common purpose.
3. Attame, or meddle with.

	As many arrows, loosèd several ways,°	*from different places*
	Fly to one mark, as many ways meet in one town,	
	As many fresh streams meet in one salt sea,	
210	As many lines close in the dial's° centre,	*sundial's*
	So may a thousand actions once afoot	
	End in one purpose, and be all well borne	
	Without defect. Therefore to France, my liege.	
	Divide your happy England into four,	
215	Whereof take you one quarter into France,	
	And you withal shall make all Gallia° shake.	*France*
	If we with thrice such powers left at home	
	Cannot defend our own doors from the dog,	
	Let us be worried,° and our nation lose	*savaged*
220	The name° of hardiness and policy.⁸	*reputation*

KING HARRY   Call in the messengers sent from the Dauphin.⁹

[Exit one or more]

	Now are we well resolved, and by God's help	
	And yours, the noble sinews of our power,	
	France being ours we'll bend it to our awe,°	*make it submit to us*
225	Or break it all to pieces. Or° there we'll sit,	*Either*
	Ruling in large and ample empery°	*sovereignty*
	O'er France and all her almost kingly dukedoms,	
	Or lay these bones in an unworthy urn,	
	Tombless, with no remembrance over them.	
230	Either our history shall with full mouth	
	Speak freely of our acts, or else our grave,	
	Like Turkish mute,¹ shall have a tongueless mouth,	
	Not worshipped with a waxen epitaph.²	

Enter AMBASSADORS *of France [with a tun]°*   *chest; barrel*

	Now are we well prepared to know the pleasure	
235	Of our fair cousin Dauphin, for we hear	
	Your greeting is from him, not from the King.	

AMBASSADOR   May't please your majesty to give us leave

	Freely to render what we have in charge,	
	Or shall we sparingly show you far off ³	
240	The Dauphin's meaning and our embassy?	

KING HARRY   We are no tyrant, but a Christian king,

	Unto whose grace our passion is as subject	
	As is our wretches fettered in our prisons.	
	Therefore with frank and with uncurbèd plainness	
	Tell us the Dauphin's mind.	

245	AMBASSADOR Thus then in few:°	*short*
	Your highness lately sending into France	
	Did claim some certain dukedoms, in the right	
	Of your great predecessor, King Edward the Third.	
	In answer of which claim, the Prince our master	
250	Says that you savour° too much of your youth,	*show traces*
	And bids you be advised, there's naught in France	
	That can be with a nimble galliard° won:	*lively dance*
	You cannot revel into dukedoms there.	
	He therefore sends you, meeter° for your spirit,	*more appropriate*

8. Political discernment.
9. Title of the French heir apparent.
1. Turkish harem attendants were reportedly castrated

and deprived of speech.
2. Not dignified with (even) a perishable memorial.
3. Show you in an abridged and roundabout way.

255   This tun of treasure, and in lieu of this
          Desires you let the dukedoms that you claim
          Hear no more of you. This the Dauphin speaks.
    KING HARRY What treasure, uncle?
    EXETER [*opening the tun*]   Tennis balls, my liege.
    KING HARRY We are glad the Dauphin is so pleasant° with us.   *jocular*
260   His present and your pains we thank you for.
          When we have matched our rackets to these balls,
          We will in France, by God's grace, play a set
          Shall strike his father's crown° into the hazard.[4]   *royal crown; coin*
          Tell him he hath made a match with such a wrangler
265   That all the courts of France will be disturbed
          With chases.[5] And we understand him well,
          How he comes o'er° us with our wilder days,   *taunts*
          Not measuring what use we made of them.
          We never valued this poor seat° of England,   *throne*
270   And therefore, living hence,° did give ourself   *away from court*
          To barbarous licence—as 'tis ever common
          That men are merriest when they are from home.
          But tell the Dauphin I will keep my state,°   *dignity; territory*
          Be like a king, and show my sail of greatness
275   When I do rouse me in° my throne of France.   *about*
          For that have I laid by my majesty
          And plodded like a man for working days,
          But I will rise there with so full a glory
          That I will dazzle all the eyes of France,
280   Yea strike the Dauphin blind to look on us.
          And tell the pleasant Prince this mock of his
          Hath turned his balls to gunstones,° and his soul   *cannonballs*
          Shall stand sore chargèd° for the wasteful vengeance   *heavily burdened*
          That shall fly from them—for many a thousand widows
285   Shall this his mock mock out of their dear husbands,
          Mock mothers from their sons, mock castles down;
          Ay, some are yet ungotten and unborn
          That shall have cause to curse the Dauphin's scorn.
          But this lies all within the will of God,
290   To whom I do appeal, and in whose name
          Tell you the Dauphin I am coming on
          To venge me° as I may, and to put forth   *avenge myself*
          My rightful hand in a well-hallowed cause.
          So get you hence in peace. And tell the Dauphin
295   His jest will savour but of shallow wit
          When thousands weep more than did laugh at it.—
          Convey them with safe conduct.—Fare you well.
                                    Exeunt AMBASSADORS
    EXETER This was a merry message.
    KING HARRY We hope to make the sender blush at it.
300   Therefore, my lords, omit no happy hour
          That may give furth'rance to our expedition;
          For we have now no thought in us but France,
          Save those to God, that run before our business.

---

4. Jeopardy; aperture in the back wall of an Elizabethan tennis court.
5. Military pursuit; in tennis, second impact of a
missed return, rated by its proximity to the back wall (a
disputable point, hence "wrangler" in line 264).

Therefore let our proportions for these wars
305   Be soon collected, and all things thought upon
That may with reasonable swiftness add
More feathers to our wings; for, God before,[6]
We'll chide this Dauphin at his father's door.
Therefore let every man now task his thought,
310   That this fair action may on foot be brought.

                           Exeunt. Flourish

2.0

Enter CHORUS

CHORUS   Now all the youth of England are on fire,
    And silken° dalliance in the wardrobe lies;   *luxurious*
    Now thrive the armourers, and honour's thought
    Reigns solely in the breast of every man.
5   They sell the pasture now to buy the horse,
    Following the mirror° of all Christian kings   *exemplar*
    With wingèd heels, as English Mercuries.[1]
    For now sits expectation in the air
    And hides a sword from hilts unto the point
10   With crowns imperial, crowns° and coronets,   *titles; coins*
    Promised to Harry and his followers.
    The French, advised by good intelligence°   *espionage*
    Of this most dreadful preparation,
    Shake in their fear, and with pale policy°   *feeble intrigue*
15   Seek to divert the English purposes.
    O England!—model° to thy inward greatness,   *small replica*
    Like little body with a mighty heart,
    What mightst thou do, that honour would thee do,
    Were all thy children kind and natural?
20   But see, thy fault France hath in thee found out:
    A nest of hollow[2] bosoms, which he fills
    With treacherous crowns; and three corrupted men—
    One, Richard, Earl of Cambridge; and the second
    Henry, Lord Scrope of Masham; and the third
25   Sir Thomas Grey, knight, of Northumberland—
    Have, for the gilt[3] of France—O guilt indeed!—
    Confirmed conspiracy with fearful° France;   *frightened*
    And by their hands this grace of kings must die,
    If hell and treason hold° their promises,   *keep*
30   Ere he take ship for France, and in Southampton.
    Linger your patience on, and we'll digest
    Th'abuse of distance, force—perforce—a play.[4]
    The sum is paid, the traitors are agreed,
    The King is set from London, and the scene
35   Is now transported, gentles, to Southampton.
    There is the playhouse now, there must you sit,
    And thence to France shall we convey you safe,
    And bring you back, charming the narrow seas
    To give you gentle pass—for if we may
40   We'll not offend one stomach[5] with our play.

---

6. With God leading us; if God leads us.
2.0
1. Messenger of the gods; patron of thieves.
2. Hypocritical; empty (as receptacles for money).
3. Gold; gold leaf (suggesting superficiality).

4. *digest* . . . *play*: incorporate (and make acceptable) a violation of the unity of place, and stuff a play with events.
5. Offend anyone; make anyone seasick.

But till the King come forth, and not till then,
Unto Southampton do we shift our scene.   *Exit*

2.1

Enter Corporal NIM *and Lieutenant* BARDOLPH

BARDOLPH Well met, Corporal Nim.

NIM Good morrow, Lieutenant Bardolph.

BARDOLPH What, are Ensign° Pistol and you friends yet?   *flag bearer*

NIM For my part, I care not. I say little, but when time shall
5   serve, there shall be smiles—but that shall be as it may. I dare
not fight, but I will wink° and hold out mine iron.° It is a simple   *close my eyes / sword*
one, but what though?° It will toast cheese, and it will endure   *of that*
cold, as another man's sword will—and there's an end.

BARDOLPH I will bestow a breakfast to make you friends, and
10   we'll be all three sworn brothers to France. Let't be so, good
Corporal Nim.

NIM Faith, I will live so long as I may, that's the certain of it,
and when I cannot live any longer, I will do as I may. That is
my rest, that is the rendezvous° of it.   *last word?*

15 BARDOLPH It is certain, corporal, that he is married to Nell
Quickly, and certainly she did you wrong, for you were troth-
plight° to her.   *betrothed*

NIM I cannot tell. Things must be as they may. Men may sleep,
and they may have their throats about them at that time, and
20   some say knives have edges. It must be as it may. Though
Patience be a tired mare, yet she will plod. There must be conclusions. Well, I cannot tell.

Enter [Ensign] PISTOL *and* HOSTESS *Quickly*

BARDOLPH Good morrow, Ensign Pistol.[1] [*To* NIM] Here comes
Ensign Pistol and his wife. Good Corporal, be patient here.

25 NIM How now, mine host° Pistol?   *tavern keeper; pimp*

PISTOL Base tick, call'st thou me host? Now by Gad's lugs°   *God's ears*
I swear I scorn the term. Nor shall my Nell keep lodgers.

HOSTESS No, by my troth, not long, for we cannot lodge and
board a dozen or fourteen gentlewomen that live honestly by
30   the prick° of their needles, but it will be thought we keep a   *(unwittingly obscene)*
bawdy-house straight.

[NIM *draws his sword*]

O well-a-day,° Lady![2] If he be not hewn now, we shall see wilful   *alas*
adultery° and murder committed.   *(for "assault")*

[PISTOL *draws his sword*]

BARDOLPH Good lieutenant, good corporal, offer nothing° here.   *don't fight*

35 NIM Pish.

PISTOL Pish for thee, Iceland dog.° Thou prick-eared cur of   *small, hairy breed*
Iceland.

HOSTESS Good Corporal Nim, show thy valour, and put up°   *away*
your sword.

[*They sheathe their swords*]

NIM Will you shog off?° I would have you *solus*.[3]   *move along*

40 PISTOL '*Solus*', egregious dog? O viper vile!
The *solus* in thy most marvellous face,

2.1 Location: Eastcheap, a slum section of London,
site of the tavern scenes in *1* and *2 Henry IV*. Bardolph,
Pistol, and Hostess Quickly were featured in the *Henry
IV* plays; Nim (slang for "thief") is a new character.

1. Sixteenth-century pistols were notoriously noisy and
inaccurate.
2. By our Lady, a mild oath.
3. Alone; unmarried.

The *solus* in thy teeth, and in thy throat,
And in thy hateful lungs, yea in thy maw pardie[4]—
And which is worse, within thy nasty mouth.
45 I do retort° the *solus* in thy bowels,   *send back*
For I can take,° and Pistol's cock is up,[5]   *take fire; strike*
And flashing fire will follow.
NIM   I am not Barbason,° you cannot conjure me.[6] I have an   *(the name of a devil)*
humour° to knock you indifferently well. If you grow foul with   *inclination*
50 me, Pistol, I will scour you with my rapier, as I may, in fair
terms.° If you would walk off, I would prick your guts a little,   *pretty thoroughly*
in good terms, as I may, and that's the humour of it.
PISTOL   O braggart vile, and damnèd furious wight!°   *creature*
The grave doth gape and doting death is near.
55 Therefore ex-hale.°   *draw (your sword)*
    [PISTOL *and* NIM] *draw* [*their swords*]
BARDOLPH   Hear me, hear me what I say.
    [*He draws his sword*]
He that strikes the first stroke, I'll run him up to the hilts, as I
am a soldier.
PISTOL   An oath of mickle° might, and fury shall abate.   *great*
    [*They sheathe their swords*]
60 [*To* NIM] Give me thy fist,° thy forefoot to me give.   *(i.e., hand)*
Thy spirits are most tall.°   *valiant*
NIM   I will cut thy throat one time or other, in fair terms, that is
the humour of it.
PISTOL   *Couple a gorge,*[7]
65 That is the word. I thee defy again.
O hound of Crete, think'st thou my spouse to get?
No, to the spital[8] go,
And from the powd'ring tub[9] of infamy
Fetch forth the lazar kite of Cressid's kind,[1]
70 Doll Tearsheet[2] she by name, and her espouse.
I have, and I will hold, the quondam° Quickly   *former*
For the only she, and—*pauca,*° there's enough. Go to.   *few (words)*
    Enter the BOY [*running*]
BOY   Mine host Pistol, you must come to my master,° and you,   *(Sir John Falstaff)*
hostess. He is very sick, and would to bed.—Good Bardolph,
75 put thy face between his sheets, and do the office of a warming-
pan.[3]—Faith, he's very ill.
BARDOLPH   Away, you rogue!
HOSTESS   By my troth, he'll yield the crow a pudding[4] one of
these days. The King has killed his heart.[5] Good husband,
80 come home presently.°   *Exit* [*with* BOY]   *right away*
BARDOLPH   Come, shall I make you two friends? We must to
France together. Why the devil should we keep knives to cut
one another's throats?
PISTOL   Let floods o'erswell,[6] and fiends for food howl on!
85 NIM   You'll pay me the eight shillings I won of you at betting?

---

4. *in thy maw pardie*: in your stomach, indeed (old-fashioned).
5. Pistol's trigger is cocked (unwittingly obscene).
6. Frighten me with big words.
7. Corrupt French for "Cut the throat."
8. Hospital; in Elizabethan times, a filthy, disease-ridden place occupied by indigents near death.
9. Sweat bath, used in treating syphilis.

1. The diseased, scavenging whore (Cressida, a faithless Trojan woman, was a pattern of female wickedness).
2. A prostitute who appears in *2 Henry IV.*
3. Referring to Bardolph's "fiery" complexion.
4. He'll feed the crows (after his death).
5. By rejecting him, in the last scene of *2 Henry IV.*
6. Let destruction reign (perhaps an unidentified quotation).

PISTOL   Base is the slave that pays.

NIM   That now I will have. That's the humour of it.

PISTOL   As manhood shall compound.° Push home.   *valor will determine*

    [PISTOL *and* NIM] *draw* [*their swords*]

BARDOLPH [*drawing his sword*]   By this sword, he that makes the

90   first thrust, I'll kill him. By this sword, I will.

PISTOL   Sword is an oath,[7] and oaths must have their course.

    [*He sheathes his sword*]

BARDOLPH   Corporal Nim, an° thou wilt be friends, be friends.   *if*

    An thou wilt not, why then be enemies with me too. Prithee,

    put up.

95 NIM   I shall have my eight shillings?

PISTOL   A noble° shalt thou have, and present pay,[8]   *6 shillings 8 pence*

    And liquor likewise will I give to thee,

    And friendship shall combine, and brotherhood.

    I'll live by Nim, and Nim shall live by me.

100   Is not this just? For I shall sutler[9] be

    Unto the camp, and profits will accrue.

    Give me thy hand.

NIM   I shall have my noble?

PISTOL   In cash, most justly paid.

105 NIM   Well then, that's the humour of 't.

    [NIM *and* BARDOLPH *sheathe their swords*]

    Enter HOSTESS [*Quickly*]

HOSTESS   As ever you come of women, come in quickly to Sir

    John. Ah, poor heart, he is so shaked of a burning quotidian-

    tertian,[1] that it is most lamentable to behold. Sweet men, come

    to him.   [*Exit*]

110 NIM   The King hath run bad humours on° the knight, that's the   *shows ill will toward*

    even° of it.   *truth*

PISTOL   Nim, thou hast spoke the right.

    His heart is fracted° and corroborate.[2]   *broken*

NIM   The King is a good king, but it must be as it may. He passes

115 some humours and careers.°   *behaves strangely*

PISTOL   Let us condole° the knight—for, lambkins, we will live.   *console*

                                  Exeunt

2.2

    Enter [*Duke of*] EXETER, [*Duke of* GLOUCESTER,] *and*
    [*Earl of*] WESTMORLAND

GLOUCESTER   Fore God, his grace is bold to trust these traitors.

EXETER   They shall be apprehended by and by.

WESTMORLAND   How smooth and even they do bear themselves,

    As if allegiance in their bosoms sat,

5   Crownèd with faith and constant loyalty.

GLOUCESTER   The King hath note of all that they intend,

    By interception which they dream not of.

EXETER   Nay, but the man that was his bedfellow,[1]

    Whom he hath dulled and cloyed° with gracious favours—   *tired and sated*

10   That he should for a foreign purse so sell

    His sovereign's life to death and treachery.

---

7. Punning on "'s word," by God's word.
8. And immediate payment.
9. Seller of provisions (notoriously dishonest).
1. Dangerous fever (the Hostess conflates quotidian fever, which recurs daily, with tertian fever, which

recurs every third day).
2. Confirmed (error for "corrupted").
2.2 Location: Southampton, a port in the south of England.
1. It was common for men to share a bed.

Sound trumpets. Enter KING [HARRY, *Lord*] SCROPE,
[*Earl of*] CAMBRIDGE, *and* [*Sir Thomas*] GREY

KING HARRY   Now sits the wind fair, and we will aboard.
My lord of Cambridge, and my kind lord of Masham,
And you, my gentle knight, give me your thoughts.
15   Think you not that the powers we bear with us
Will cut their passage through the force of France,
Doing the execution° and the act   *destruction*
For which we have in head° assembled them?   *an army*
SCROPE   No doubt, my liege, if each man do his best.
20   KING HARRY   I doubt not that, since we are well persuaded
We carry not a heart with us from hence
That grows not in a fair consent with ours,
Nor leave not one behind that doth not wish
Success and conquest to attend on us.
25   CAMBRIDGE   Never was monarch better feared and loved
Than is your majesty. There's not, I think, a subject
That sits in heart-grief and uneasiness
Under the sweet shade of your government.
GREY   True. Those that were your father's enemies
30   Have steeped their galls° in honey, and do serve you   *bitterness*
With hearts create of duty and of zeal.
KING HARRY   We therefore have great cause of thankfulness,
And shall forget the office° of our hand   *use*
Sooner than quittance° of desert and merit,   *payment*
35   According to their weight and worthiness.
SCROPE   So service shall with steelèd sinews toil,
And labour shall refresh itself with hope,
To do your grace incessant services.
KING HARRY   We judge no less.—Uncle of Exeter,
40   Enlarge° the man committed° yesterday   *Release / imprisoned*
That railed against our person. We consider
It was excess of wine that set him on,
And on his more advice° we pardon him.   *sober reconsideration*
SCROPE   That's mercy, but too much security.°   *complacency*
45   Let him be punished, sovereign, lest example
Breed, by his sufferance,° more of such a kind.   *by pardoning him*
KING HARRY   O let us yet be merciful.
CAMBRIDGE   So may your highness, and yet punish too.
GREY   Sir, you show great mercy if you give him life,
50   After the taste of much correction.
KING HARRY   Alas, your too much love and care of me
Are heavy orisons° 'gainst this poor wretch.   *weighty pleas*
If little faults proceeding on distemper°   *from drunkenness*
Shall not be winked at,° how shall we stretch our eye   *overlooked*
55   When capital crimes, chewed, swallowed, and digested,[2]
Appear before us? We'll yet° enlarge that man,   *nonetheless*
Though Cambridge, Scrope, and Grey, in their dear° care   *loving*
And tender preservation of our person,
Would have him punished. And now to our French causes.
Who are the late[3] commissioners?
60   CAMBRIDGE   I one, my lord.
Your highness bade me ask for it° today.   (*the commission*)

2. That is, crimes thoroughly premeditated.   3. Newly appointed (to govern during Henry's absence).

SCROPE So did you me, my liege.

GREY   And I, my royal sovereign.

KING HARRY Then Richard, Earl of Cambridge, there is yours;
There yours, Lord Scrope of Masham, and sir knight,
65 Grey of Northumberland, this same is yours.
Read them, and know I know your worthiness.—
My lord of Westmorland, and Uncle Exeter,
We will aboard tonight.—Why, how now, gentlemen?
What see you in those papers, that you lose
70 So much complexion?—Look ye how they change:
Their cheeks are paper.—Why, what read you there
That have so cowarded and chased your blood
Out of appearance?°   sight

CAMBRIDGE   I do confess my fault,
And do submit me to your highness' mercy.

75 GREY and SCROPE To which we all appeal.

KING HARRY The mercy that was quick° in us but late   alive
By your own counsel is suppressed and killed.
You must not dare, for shame, to talk of mercy,
For your own reasons turn into your bosoms,
80 As dogs upon their masters, worrying° you.—   tearing
See you, my princes and my noble peers,
These English monsters?⁴ My lord of Cambridge here,
You know how apt our love was to accord°   agree
To furnish him with all appurtenants°   privileges
85 Belonging to his honour; and this vile man
Hath for a few light crowns lightly conspired
And sworn unto the practices° of France   plots
To kill us here in Hampton. To the which
This knight,° no less for bounty bound to us   (Grey)
90 Than Cambridge is, hath likewise sworn. But O
What shall I say to thee, Lord Scrope, thou cruel,
Ingrateful, savage, and inhuman creature?
Thou that didst bear the key of all my counsels,
That knew'st the very bottom of my soul,
95 That almost mightst ha' coined me into gold
Wouldst thou ha' practised on° me for thy use: conspired against
May it be possible that foreign hire
Could out of thee extract one spark of evil
That might annoy my finger? 'Tis so strange
100 That though the truth of it stands off as gross°   clearly
As black on white, my eye will scarcely see it.
Treason and murder ever kept together,
As two yoke-devils sworn to either's purpose,
Working so grossly in a natural° cause   (for devils)
105 That admiration° did not whoop° at them;   astonishment / cry out
But thou, 'gainst all proportion,° didst bring in   natural order
Wonder to wait on° treason and on murder.   consort with
And whatsoever cunning fiend it was
That wrought upon thee so preposterously°   unnaturally
110 Hath got the voice° in hell for excellence.   vote
And other devils that suggest° by treasons   seduce
Do botch and bungle up° damnation   clumsily conceal

4. "Monsters" were usually imported freaks.

With patches, colours,° and with forms, being fetched°   *pretexts / derived*
From glist'ring semblances of piety;
115 But he that tempered° thee, bade thee stand up,°   *molded / rebel*
Gave thee no instance° why thou shouldst do treason,   *motive*
Unless to dub thee with the name[5] of traitor.
If that same demon that hath gulled° thee thus   *duped*
Should with his lion gait walk the whole world,
120 He might return to vasty Tartar° back   *to huge hell*
And tell the legions,° 'I can never win   *armies of devils*
A soul so easy as that Englishman's.'
O how hast thou with jealousy° infected   *suspicion*
The sweetness of affiance.° Show men dutiful?   *trust*
125 Why so didst thou. Seem they grave and learned?
Why so didst thou. Come they of noble family?
Why so didst thou. Seem they religious?
Why so didst thou. Or are they spare in diet,
Free from gross passion, or° of mirth or anger,   *either*
130 Constant in spirit, not swerving with the blood,°   *passion*
Garnished and decked in modest complement,°   *appearance*
Not working with the eye without the ear,
And but in purgèd° judgement trusting neither?   *purified*
Such, and so finely boulted,° didst thou seem.   *sifted*
135 And thus thy fall hath left a kind of blot
To mark the full-fraught° man, and best endowed,   *packed (with excellences)*
With some suspicion. I will weep for thee,
For this revolt of thine methinks is like
Another fall of man.—Their faults are open.°   *obvious*
140 Arrest them to the answer of the law,
And God acquit them of their practices.
 EXETER I arrest thee of high treason, by the name of Richard,
  Earl of Cambridge.—I arrest thee of high treason, by the name
  of Henry, Lord Scrope of Masham.—I arrest thee of high trea-
145 son, by the name of Thomas Grey, knight, of Northumberland.
 SCROPE Our purposes God justly hath discovered,°   *revealed*
  And I repent my fault more than my death,
  Which I beseech your highness to forgive
  Although my body pay the price of it.
150 CAMBRIDGE For me, the gold of France did not seduce,
  Although I did admit it as a motive
  The sooner to effect what I intended.[6]
  But God be thankèd for prevention,
  Which heartily in sufferance° will rejoice,   *suffering punishment*
155 Beseeching God and you to pardon me.
 GREY Never did faithful subject more rejoice
  At the discovery of most dangerous treason
  Than I do at this hour joy o'er myself,
  Prevented from a damnèd enterprise.
160 My fault, but not my body, pardon, sovereign.
 KING HARRY God 'quit° you in his mercy. Hear your sentence.   *acquit*
  You have conspired against our royal person,
  Joined with an enemy proclaimed and fixed,

---

5. To knight you with the title.
6. The Earl of Cambridge was heir of Edmund Mortimer through his wife, Edmund's sister, and Mortimer
arguably had a better claim to the English throne than
did Henry himself. Henry's adherence to a principle of
inheritance "through the female line" is hardly absolute.

And from his coffers
165 Received the golden earnest of° our death,   *advance payment for*
Wherein you would have sold your king to slaughter,
His princes and his peers to servitude,
His subjects to oppression and contempt,
And his whole kingdom into desolation.
170 Touching our person seek we no revenge,
But we our kingdom's safety must so tender,°   *regard*
Whose ruin you have sought, that to her laws
We do deliver you. Get ye therefore hence,
Poor miserable wretches, to your death;
175 The taste whereof, God of his mercy give
You patience to endure, and true repentance
Of all your dear° offences.—Bear them hence.   *grievous*
              Exeunt [the traitors, guarded]
Now lords for France, the enterprise whereof
Shall be to you, as us, like° glorious.   *equally*
180 We doubt not of a fair and lucky war,
Since God so graciously hath brought to light
This dangerous treason lurking in our way
To hinder our beginnings. We doubt not now
But every rub° is smoothèd on our way.   *obstacle*
185 Then forth, dear countrymen. Let us deliver
Our puissance° into the hand of God,   *power*
Putting it straight in expedition.°   *at once in action*
Cheerly to sea, the signs° of war advance: *flags*
No king of England, if not king of France.   *Flourish. Exeunt*

2.3

Enter [Ensign] PISTOL, *[Corporal]* NIM, *[Lieutenant]*
BARDOLPH, BOY, *and* HOSTESS *[Quickly]*

HOSTESS   Prithee, honey, sweet husband, let me bring° thee to   *accompany*
  Staines.[1]
PISTOL   No, for my manly heart doth erne.° Bardolph,   *grieve*
  Be blithe; Nim, rouse thy vaunting veins; boy, bristle
5   Thy courage up. For Falstaff he is dead,
  And we must erne therefore.
BARDOLPH   Would I were with him, wheresome'er he is, either
  in heaven or in hell.
HOSTESS   Nay, sure he's not in hell. He's in Arthur's bosom,[2] if
10   ever man went to Arthur's bosom. A° made a finer end, and   *He*
  went away an° it had been any christom[3] child. A parted ev'n   *as if*
  just between twelve and one, ev'n at the turning o'th' tide—for
  after I saw him fumble with the sheets, and play with flowers,°   *(on the bedclothes)*
  and smile upon his finger's end, I knew there was but one way.
15   For his nose was as sharp as a pen, and a babbled of green
  fields.[4] 'How now, Sir John?' quoth I. 'What, man! Be o' good
  cheer.' So a cried out, 'God, God, God', three or four times.
  Now I, to comfort him, bid him a should not think of God; I
  hoped there was no need to trouble himself with any such

2.3 Location: Eastcheap.
1. Town on the road to Southampton.
2. Mistake for "Abraham's bosom," heaven.
3. Error for "chrisom," just christened.
4. Falstaff was reciting the Twenty-third Psalm ("The

Lord is my shepherd"), but Hostess Quickly does not
recognize it. The text is corrupt at this point, reading "a
Table of green fields," and was corrected by the
eighteenth-century editor Lewis Theobald in a famous
emendation.

20 thoughts yet. So a bade me lay more clothes on his feet. I put
my hand into the bed and felt them, and they were as co d as
any stone. Then I felt to his knees, and so up'ard and up'ard,
and all was as cold as any stone.

NIM   They say he cried out of sack.[5]

25 HOSTESS   Ay, that a did.

BARDOLPH   And of women.

HOSTESS   Nay, that a did not.

BOY   Yes, that a did, and said they were devils incarnate.

HOSTESS   A could never abide carnation, 'twas a colour he never
30 liked.

BOY   A said once the devil would have him about women.

HOSTESS   A did in some sort, indeed, handle° women—but then   *discuss*
he was rheumatic,[6] and talked of the Whore of Babylon.[7]

BOY   Do you not remember, a saw a flea stick upon Bardolph's
35 nose, and a said it was a black soul burning in hell-fire.

BARDOLPH   Well, the fuel[8] is gone that maintained that fire.
That's all the riches I got in his service.

NIM   Shall we shog?° The King will be gone from Southampton.   *be off*

PISTOL   Come, let's away.—My love, give me thy lips.
        [*He kisses her*]
40 Look to my chattels and my movables.°   *personal property*
Let senses rule. The word is 'Pitch and pay'.°   *Cash down, no credit*
Trust none, for oaths are straws, men's faiths are wafer-cakes,°   *fragile*
And Holdfast is the only dog,[9] my duck.°   *darling*
Therefore *caveto*° be thy counsellor.   *beware*
45 Go, clear thy crystals.°—Yokefellows in arms,   *wipe your eyes*
Let us to France, like horseleeches, my boys,
To suck, to suck, the very blood to suck!

BOY [*aside*]   And that's but unwholesome food, they say.

PISTOL   Touch her soft mouth, and march.

50 BARDOLPH   Farewell, hostess.
        [*He kisses her*]

NIM   I cannot kiss, that is the humour of it, but adieu.

PISTOL [*to* HOSTESS]   Let housewifery appear. Keep close,° I   *Stay indoors; be thrifty*
thee command.

HOSTESS   Farewell! Adieu!   *Exeunt* [*severally*]°   *separately*

2.4

Flourish. Enter KING [CHARLES *the Sixth of France*], *the*
DAUPHIN, [*the* CONSTABLE,] *and the Dukes of* BERRI *and*
[BOURBON]

KING CHARLES   Thus comes the English with full power upon us,
And more than carefully it us concerns
To answer royally in our defences.
Therefore the Dukes of Berri and of Bourbon,
5 Of Brabant and of Orléans shall make forth,
And you Prince Dauphin, with all swift dispatch
To line° and new-repair our towns of war   *garrison*

---

5. *of sack*: against wine, formerly one of Falstaff's great
indulgences.
6. Error for "lunatic," delirious.
7. The scarlet woman of Revelation, identified by
Protestants with the Catholic Church.

8. That is, Falstaff's liquor.
9. Alluding to the proverb "Brag is a good dog, but
Holdfast is better."
2.4 Location: France, where the remainder of the play
takes place. The King's court at Rouen.

With men of courage and with means defendant.°   *of defense*
For England° his approaches makes as fierce   *the King of England*
10   As waters to the sucking of a gulf.°   *whirlpool*
It fits us then to be as provident
As fear may teach us, out of late° examples   *recent*
Left by the fatal and neglected[1] English
Upon our fields.
DAUPHIN   My most redoubted° father,   *formidable*
15   It is most meet° we arm us 'gainst the foe,   *proper*
For peace itself should not so dull a kingdom—
Though war, nor no known quarrel, were in question—
But that defences, musters, preparations
Should be maintained, assembled, and collected
20   As° were a war in expectation.   *As if*
Therefore, I say, 'tis meet we all go forth
To view the sick and feeble parts of France.
And let us do it with no show of fear,
No, with no more than if we heard that England
25   Were busied with a Whitsun morris dance[2]
For, my good liege, she is so idly° kinged,   *frivolously*
Her sceptre so fantastically° borne   *irrationally*
By a vain, giddy, shallow, humorous° youth,   *capricious*
That fear attends her not.
CONSTABLE   O peace, Prince Dauphin.
30   You are too much mistaken in this king.
Question your grace the late° ambassadors   *recent*
With what great state he heard their embassy,
How well supplied with agèd counsellors,
How modest in exception,° and withal   *objecting*
35   How terrible° in constant resolution,   *fearsome*
And you shall find his vanities forespent°   *his former follies*
Were but the outside of the Roman Brutus,[3]
Covering discretion with a coat of folly,
As gardeners do with ordure° hide those roots   *manure*
40   That shall first spring and be most delicate.
DAUPHIN   Well, 'tis not so, my Lord High Constable.
But though° we think it so, it is no matter.   *if*
In cases of defence 'tis best to weigh°   *consider*
The enemy more mighty than he seems.
45   So the proportions of defence are filled[4]—
Which, of a weak and niggardly projection,°   *scale*
Doth like a miser spoil his coat with scanting°   *skimping*
A little cloth.
KING CHARLES   Think we King Harry strong.
And princes, look you strongly arm to meet him.
50   The kindred of him hath been fleshed[5] upon us,
And he is bred out of that bloody strain
That haunted us in our familiar paths.
Witness our too-much-memorable shame

---

1. The fatally underestimated, at the Battles of Crécy (1346) and Poitiers (1356).
2. Folk dance celebrating Whitsuntide, a summer holiday.
3. Lucius Junius Brutus pretended idiocy to disarm the tyrant Lucius Tarquinius Superbus, against whom he led a successful revolt.
4. A proper defense is mounted.
5. Have been given their first taste of blood.

When Crécy battle fatally was struck,°   *fought*
55 And all our princes captived by the hand
Of that black name, Edward, Black Prince of Wales,
Whiles that his mountant° sire, on mountain standing,   *ascendant*
Up in the air, crowned with the golden sun,
Saw his heroical seed and smiled to see him
60 Mangle the work of nature and deface
The patterns that by God and by French fathers
Had twenty years been made. This is a stem
Of that victorious stock, and let us fear
The native° mightiness and fate° of him.   *hereditary / fortune*
         Enter a MESSENGER
65 MESSENGER Ambassadors from Harry, King of England,
Do crave admittance to your majesty.
KING CHARLES We'll give them present audience. Go and bring them.
                                                    [*Exit* MESSENGER]
You see this chase is hotly followed, friends.
DAUPHIN Turn head[6] and stop pursuit. For coward dogs
70 Most spend their mouths° when what they seem to threaten   *bark the loudest*
Runs far before them. Good my sovereign,
Take up the English short, and let them know
Of what a monarchy you are the head.
Self-love, my liege, is not so vile a sin
As self-neglecting.
         Enter [Duke of] EXETER [*attended*]
75 KING CHARLES   From our brother England?
EXETER From him, and thus he greets your majesty
He wills you, in the name of God Almighty,
That you divest yourself and lay apart°   *aside*
The borrowed glories that by gift of heaven,
80 By law of nature and of nations, 'longs°   *belongs*
To him and to his heirs, namely the crown,
And all wide-stretchèd honours that pertain
By custom and the ordinance of times°   *laws of ages*
Unto the crown of France. That you may know
85 'Tis no sinister° nor no awkward° claim,   *illegitimate / oblique*
Picked from the worm-holes of long-vanished days,
Nor from the dust of old oblivion raked,
He sends you this most memorable line,°   *pedigree*
In every branch truly demonstrative.°   *conclusive*
90 Willing you over-look° this pedigree.   *Wishing you to look over*
And when you find him evenly derived°   *directly descended*
From his most famed of famous ancestors,
Edward the Third, he bids you then resign
Your crown and kingdom, indirectly° held   *unjustly*
95 From him, the native and true challenger.°   *claimant*
KING CHARLES Or else what follows?
EXETER Bloody constraint. For if you hide the crown
Even in your hearts, there will he rake for it.
Therefore in fierce tempest is he coming,
100 In thunder and in earthquake, like a Jove,
That if requiring° fail, he will compel;   *requesting*

---

6. Make a stand (a hunting term).

And bids you, in the bowels° of the Lord,   *compassion*
Deliver up the crown, and to take mercy
On the poor souls for whom this hungry war
105 Opens his vasty jaws; and on your head
Turns he the widows' tears, the orphans' cries,
The dead men's blood, the pining maidens' groans,
For husbands, fathers, and betrothèd lovers
That shall be swallowed in this controversy.
110 This is his claim, his threat'ning, and my message—
Unless the Dauphin be in presence here,
To whom expressly I bring greeting too.
KING CHARLES   For us, we will consider of this further.
Tomorrow shall you bear our full intent
Back to our brother England.
115 DAUPHIN   For the Dauphin,
I stand here for him. What to him from England?
EXETER   Scorn and defiance, slight regard, contempt;
And anything that may not misbecome
The mighty sender, doth he prize° you at.   *assess*
120 Thus says my king: an if° your father's highness   *an if=if*
Do not, in grant° of all demands at large,°   *concession / in full*
Sweeten the bitter mock you sent his majesty,
He'll call you to so hot an answer for it
That caves and womby vaultages° of France   *hollow caverns*
125 Shall chide your trespass and return your mock
In second accent° of his ordinance.°   *echo / artillery*
DAUPHIN   Say if my father render fair return
It is against my will, for I desire
Nothing but odds° with England. To that end,   *strife*
130 As matching to his youth and vanity,°   *frivolity*
I did present him with the Paris° balls.   *tennis*
EXETER   He'll make your Paris Louvre° shake for it,   *French royal palace*
Were it the mistress° court of mighty Europe.   *principal (in tennis)*
And be assured, you'll find a diff'rence,
135 As we his subjects have in wonder found,
Between the promise of his greener° days   *younger*
And these he masters now: now he weighs time
Even to the utmost grain.° That you shall read   *smallest unit*
In your own losses, if he stay in France.
140 KING CHARLES [*rising*]   Tomorrow shall you know our mind at full.
        Flourish[7]
EXETER   Dispatch us with all speed, lest that our king
Come here himself to question our delay—
For he is footed° in this land already.   *come ashore*
KING CHARLES   You shall be soon dispatched with fair conditions.
145 A night is but small breath° and little pause   *small time*
To answer matters of this consequence.   *Exeunt. Flourish*

---

7. Fanfare (to signal the end of the interview; Exeter unceremoniously continues).

3.0

Enter CHORUS

CHORUS   Thus with imagined wing° our swift scene flies   *wings of imagination*
    In motion of no less celerity
    Than that of thought. Suppose that you have seen
    The well-appointed° king at Dover pier   *well-equipped*
5   Embark his royalty, and his brave fleet
    With silken streamers the young Phoebus fanning.[1]
    Play with your fancies,° and in them behold   *imagination*
    Upon the hempen tackle ship-boys climbing;
    Hear the shrill whistle,° which doth order give   *(of the ship's captain)*
10   To sounds confused; behold the threaden° sails   *woven of thread*
    Borne with th'invisible and creeping wind,
    Draw the huge bottoms° through the furrowed sea,   *hulls*
    Breasting the lofty surge. O do but think
    You stand upon the rivage° and behold   *shore*
15   A city on th'inconstant billows dancing—
    For so appears this fleet majestical,
    Holding due course to Harfleur.[2] Follow, follow!
    Grapple° your minds to sternage° of this navy,   *Fasten / the sterns*
    And leave your England, as dead midnight still,
20   Guarded with grandsires, babies, and old women,
    Either past or not arrived to pith° and puissance.   *strength*
    For who is he, whose chin is but enriched
    With one appearing hair, that will not follow
    These culled° and choice-drawn cavaliers to France?   *select*
25   Work, work your thoughts, and therein see a siege.
    Behold the ordnance° on their carriages,   *cannons*
    With fatal mouths gaping on girded° Harfleur.   *encircled*
    Suppose th'ambassador from the French comes back,
    Tells Harry that the King doth offer him
30   Catherine his daughter, and with her, to° dowry,   *as*
    Some petty and unprofitable dukedoms.
    The offer likes° not, and the nimble gunner   *pleases*
    With linstock° now the devilish cannon touches,   *lighting stick*
       Alarum, and chambers° go off   *small cannon*
    And down goes all before them. Still be kind,
35   And eke out our performance with your mind.   *Exit*

3.1

Alarum. Enter KING [HARRY *and the English army, with*]
scaling ladders

KING HARRY   Once more unto the breach,[1] dear friends, once more,
    Or close the wall up with our English dead.
    In peace there's nothing so becomes a man
    As modest stillness and humility,
5   But when the blast of war blows in our ears,
    Then imitate the action of the tiger.
    Stiffen the sinews, conjure up the blood,
    Disguise fair nature with hard-favoured rage.
    Then lend the eye a terrible aspect,

3.0
1. *the . . . fanning:* fluttering toward the rising sun.
2. French port on the mouth of the Seine.

3.1 Location: Before Harfleur.
1. Gap in the fortifications, created by artillery bombardment.

10	Let it pry° through the portage² of the head	*peer*
	Like the brass cannon, let the brow o'erwhelm° it	*overhang*
	As fearfully as doth a gallèd° rock	*worn*
	O'erhang and jutty° his confounded° base,	*jut out over / ruined*
	Swilled° with the wild and wasteful° ocean.	*Washed / destructive*
15	Now set the teeth and stretch the nostril wide,	
	Hold hard the breath, and bend up every spirit	
	To his full height. On, on, you noblest English,	
	Whose blood is fet° from fathers of war-proof,°	*fetched / proven in war*
	Fathers that like so many Alexanders³	
20	Have in these parts from morn till even fought,	
	And sheathed their swords for lack of argument.°	*opposition*
	Dishonour not your mothers; now attest	
	That those whom you called fathers did beget you.	
	Be copy° now to men of grosser° blood,	*example / less noble*
25	And teach them how to war. And you, good yeomen,°	*men below noble rank*
	Whose limbs were made in England, show us here	
	The mettle° of your pasture; let us swear	*quality*
	That you are worth your breeding—which I doubt not,	
	For there is none of you so mean and base	
30	That hath not noble lustre in your eyes.	
	I see you stand like greyhounds in the slips,°	*leashes*
	Straining upon the start. The game's afoot.	
	Follow your spirit, and upon this charge	
	Cry, 'God for Harry! England and Saint George!'°	*patron saint of England*

Alarum, and chambers go off. [*Exeunt*]

3.2

Enter NIM, BARDOLPH, [*Ensign*] PISTOL, *and* BOY

BARDOLPH   On, on, on, on, on! To the breach, to the breach!

NIM   Pray thee corporal, stay. The knocks are too hot, and for

	mine own part I have not a case° of lives. The humour of it is	*set*
	too hot, that is the very plainsong° of it.	*plain truth*
5	PISTOL 'The plainsong' is most just,° for humours do abound.	*apt*

Knocks go and come, God's vassals drop and die,

[*sings*]   And sword and shield

In bloody field

Doth win immortal fame.

10   BOY   Would I were in an alehouse in London. I would give all

my fame for a pot of ale, and safety.

PISTOL [*sings*]   And I.

	If wishes would prevail with me°	*in my case*
	My purpose should not fail with me	
15	But thither would I hie.°	*go*

BOY [*sings*]   As duly

But not as truly

As bird doth sing on bough.

Enter [*Captain*] FLUELLEN *and beats them in*

FLUELLEN   God's plud!¹ Up to the breaches, you dogs! Avaunt,

20   you cullions!²

PISTOL   Be merciful, great duke, to men of mould.³

---

2. Portholes (that is, eye sockets).
3. Alexander the Great was said to have wept because
no worlds remained for him to conquer.
3.2 Scene continues.

1. Blood (Fluellen's Welsh accent substitutes "p" for
"b," and also "f" for "v" and "ch" for "j").
2. Be off, you wretches. *cullions*: testicles.
3. Earth (that is, mortal men).

Abate thy rage, abate thy manly rage,
Abate thy rage, great duke. Good bawcock,[4] bate
Thy rage. Use lenity,° sweet chuck.   *leniency*
25   NIM   These be good humours![5]
        [FLUELLEN *begins to beat* NIM]
        Your honour runs bad humours.°   *Exeunt [all but the* BOY]   *is ill tempered*
        BOY   As young as I am, I have observed these three swashers.° I   *swashbucklers*
        am boy to them all three, but all they three, though they should
        serve me, could not be man[6] to me, for indeed three such
30   antics° do not amount to a man. For Bardolph, he is white-   *buffoons*
        livered° and red-faced—by the means whereof a° faces it out,   *cowardly / he*
        but fights not. For Pistol, he hath a killing tongue and a quiet
        sword—by the means whereof a breaks words, and keeps whole
        weapons. For Nim, he hath heard that men of few words are
35   the best men, and therefore he scorns to say his prayers, lest a
        should be thought a coward. But his few bad words are
        matched with as few good deeds—for a never broke any man's
        head but his own, and that was against a post, when he was
        drunk. They will steal anything, and call it 'purchase'.[7] Bar-
40   dolph stole a lute case, bore it twelve leagues,° and sold it for   *about 36 miles*
        three halfpence. Nim and Bardolph are sworn brothers in
        filching,° and in Calais[8] they stole a fire shovel. I knew by that   *stealing*
        piece of service the men would carry coals.[9] They would have
        me as familiar with men's pockets as their gloves or their hand-
45   kerchiefs—which makes° much against my manhood, if I   *offends*
        should take from another's pocket to put into mine, for it is
        plain pocketing up of wrongs.[1] I must leave them, and seek
        some better service. Their villainy goes against my weak stom-
        ach, and therefore I must cast it up.°   *Exit*   *vomit it; leave it*

3.3

Enter [Captain] GOWER *[and Captain* FLUELLEN,
meeting]
        GOWER   Captain Fluellen, you must come presently° to the   *immediately*
        mines.[1] The Duke of Gloucester would speak with you.
        FLUELLEN   To the mines? Tell you the Duke it is not so good to
        come to the mines. For look you, the mines is not according to
5   the disciplines° of the war. The concavities° of it is not suffi-   *tactics; art / depth*
        cient. For look you, th'athversary, you may discuss unto the
        Duke, look you, is digt° himself, four yard under, the coun-   *digged (dug)*
        termines.[2] By Cheshu,° I think a will plow° up all, if there is not   *Jesu / blow*
        better directions.
10   GOWER   The Duke of Gloucester, to whom the order° of the   *supervision*
        siege is given, is altogether directed by an Irishman, a very val-
        iant gentleman, i'faith.
        FLUELLEN   It is Captain MacMorris, is it not?
        GOWER   I think it be.
15   FLUELLEN   By Cheshu, he is an ass, as[3] in the world. I will verify

---

4. Fine chap (French *beau coq*).
5. This is fine behavior (sarcastic).
6. Punning on the sense "personal servant."
7. Booty (seized in combat).
8. French port town.
9. Do dirty work; tolerate insults.

1. Pocketing stolen goods; putting up with insults (unmanly behavior).
3.3 Location: Outside Harfleur.
1. Tunnels dug to undermine a besieged fortress.
2. Tunnels dug to undermine enemy "mines."
3. *he is an ass, as:* he is as big an ass as there is.

as much in his beard.° He has no more directions in the true   *to his face*
disciplines of the wars, look you—of the *Roman* disciplines—
than is a puppy dog.

    Enter [Captain] MACMORRIS *and Captain* JAMY

GOWER   Here a comes, and the Scots captain, Captain Jamy,
20   with him.

FLUELLEN   Captain Jamy is a marvellous falorous° gentleman,   *valorous*
   that is certain, and of great expedition° and knowledge in   *quick-wittedness*
   th'anciant wars, upon my particular knowledge of his directions.
   By Cheshu, he will maintain his argument as well as any mili-
25   tary man in the world, in the disciplines of the pristine wars of
   the Romans.

JAMY   I say gud day, Captain Fluellen.

FLUELLEN   Good e'en to your worship, good Captain James.

GOWER   How now, Captain MacMorris, have you quit the
30   mines? Have the pioneers given o'er?°   *diggers stopped work*

MACMORRIS   By Chrish law,[4] 'tish ill done. The work ish give
   over, the trumpet sound the retreat. By my hand I swear, and
   my father's soul, the work ish ill done, it ish give over. I would
   have blowed up the town, so Chrish save me law, in an hour.
35   O 'tish ill done, 'tish ill done, by my hand 'tish ill done.

FLUELLEN   Captain MacMorris, I beseech you now, will you
   vouchsafe° me, look you, a few disputations with you, as partly   *allow*
   touching or concerning the disciplines of the war, the Roman
   wars, in the way of argument, look you, and friendly communi-
40   cation? Partly to satisfy my opinion and partly for the satisfaction, look you, of my mind. As touching the direction of the
   military discipline, that is the point.

JAMY   It sall be vary gud, gud feith, gud captains bath,° and I sall   *both*
   quite° you with gud leve, as I may pick occasion. That sall I,   *requite; answer*
45   marry.

MACMORRIS   It is no time to discourse, so Chrish save me. The
   day is hot, and the weather and the wars and the King and the
   dukes. It is no time to discourse. The town is besieched. An the
   trumpet call us to the breach, and we talk and, be Chrish, do
50   nothing, 'tis shame for us all. So God sa'° me, 'tis shame to   *save*
   stand still, it is shame by my hand. And there is throats to be
   cut, and works to be done, and there ish nothing done, so
   Christ sa' me law.

JAMY   By the mess,° ere these eyes of mine take themselves to   *By the mass (an oath)*
55   slumber, ay'll de gud service, or I'll lig° i'th' grund for it. Ay   *lie*
   owe Got a death, and I'll pay't as valorously as I may, that sall I
   suirely do, that is the brief and the long. Marry, I wad full fain
   heard° some question 'tween you twae.°   *eagerly have heard / two*

FLUELLEN   Captain MacMorris, I think, look you, under your
60   correction, there is not many of your nation—

MACMORRIS   Of my nation? What ish my nation? Ish a villain
   and a bastard and a knave and a rascal? What ish my nation?
   Who talks of my nation?

FLUELLEN   Look you, if you take the matter otherwise than is
65   meant, Captain MacMorris, peradventure I shall think you do
   not use me with that affability as in discretion you ought to use

---

4. La (adds force to an utterance).

me, look you, being as good a man as yourself, both in the
disciplines of war and in the derivation of my birth, and in
other particularities.

70 MACMORRIS I do not know you so good a man as myself. So
Chrish save me, I will cut off your head.

GOWER Gentlemen both, you will mistake each other.

JAMY Ah, that's a foul fault.

　　　　　*A parley*⁵ [*is sounded*]

GOWER The town sounds a parley.

75 FLUELLEN Captain MacMorris, when there is more better
opportunity to be required, look you, I will be so bold as to tell
you I know the disciplines of war. And there is an end. *Exit*
　　　　　[*Flourish.*] *Enter* KING [HARRY *and all his train before
　　　　　the gates*

KING HARRY How yet resolves the Governor of the town?
This is the latest parle° we will admit.　　　　　　　　　　　　*last parley*

80 Therefore to our best mercy give yourselves,
Or like to men proud of° destruction　　　　　　　　　　　　　*glorying in*
Defy us to our worst. For as I am a soldier,
A name that in my thoughts becomes me best,
If I begin the batt'ry° once again　　　　　　　　　　　　　　*bombardment*

85 I will not leave the half-achievèd Harfleur
Till in her ashes she lie burièd.
The gates of mercy shall be all shut up,
And the fleshed° soldier, rough and hard of heart,　　　　　　*inflamed*
In liberty of bloody hand shall range

90 With conscience wide° as hell, mowing like grass　　　　　　*permissive*
Your fresh fair virgins and your flow'ring infants.
What is it then to me if impious war
Arrayed in flames like to the prince of fiends
Do with his smirched complexion all fell° feats　　　　　　　*cruel*

95 Enlinked to waste° and desolation?　　　　　　　　　　　　　*destruction*
What is't to me, when you yourselves are cause,
If your pure maidens fall into the hand
Of hot and forcing violation?
What rein can hold licentious wickedness

100 When down the hill he holds° his fierce career?⁵　　*maintains / gallop*
We may as bootless° spend our vain command　　　　　　*unprofitably*
Upon th'enragèd soldiers in their spoil
As send precepts° to the leviathan°　　　　　　　*summons / sea monster*
To come ashore. Therefore, you men of Harfleur,

105 Take pity of your town and of your people
Whiles yet my soldiers are in my command,
Whiles yet the cool and temperate wind of grace
O'erblows° the filthy and contagious clouds⁶　　　　　　　*Disperses*
Of heady° murder, spoil, and villainy　　　　　　　　　　　*headstrong*

110 If not—why, in a moment look to see
The blind and bloody soldier with foul hand
Defile the locks of your shrill-shrieking daughters;
Your fathers taken by the silver beards,
And their most reverend heads dashed to the walls;

115 Your naked infants spitted° upon pikes,　　　　　　　　　　*impaled*
Whiles the mad mothers with their howls confused

---

5. Trumpet call requesting negotiation.　　　　6. Pestilence was believed to drop from the sky.

Do break the clouds, as did the wives of Jewry[7]
At Herod's bloody-hunting slaughtermen.
What say you? Will you yield, and this avoid?
120   Or, guilty in defence, be thus destroyed?

         Enter GOVERNOR [*on the wall*]

GOVERNOR   Our expectation hath this day an end.
The Dauphin, whom of succours we entreated,
Returns° us that his powers are yet not ready   *Replies to*
To raise so great a siege. Therefore, dread King,
125   We yield our town and lives to thy soft mercy.
Enter our gates, dispose of us and ours,
For we no longer are defensible.

KING HARRY   Open your gates.   [*Exit* GOVERNOR]
                   Come, Uncle Exeter,
Go you and enter Harfleur. There remain,
130   And fortify it strongly 'gainst the French.
Use mercy to them all. For us, dear uncle,
The winter coming on, and sickness growing
Upon our soldiers, we will retire to Calais.
Tonight in Harfleur will we be your guest;
135   Tomorrow for the march are we addressed.°   *ready*

    [*The gates are opened.*] *Flourish, and* [*they*] *enter the town*

3.4

     Enter [*Princess*] CATHERINE *and* ALICE, *an old gentle-*
     woman

CATHERINE   Alice, tu as été en Angleterre, et tu bien parles
le langage.[1]

ALICE   Un peu, madame.

CATHERINE   Je te prie, m'enseignez. Il faut que j'apprenne à
5   parler. Comment appelez-vous la main en anglais?

ALICE   La main? Elle est appelée *de hand*.

CATHERINE   *De hand.* Et les doigts?

ALICE   Les doigts? Ma foi, j'oublie les doigts, mais je me souviendrai. Les doigts—je pense qu'ils sont appelés *de fingres*. Oui, *de*
10   *fingres.*

CATHERINE   La main, *de hand*; les doigts, *de fingres*. Je pense que
je suis la bonne écolière; j'ai gagné deux mots d'anglais vite-
ment. Comment appelez-vous les ongles?

ALICE   Les ongles? Nous les appelons *de nails*.

15   CATHERINE   *De nails.* Écoutez—dites-moi si je parle bien: *de*
hand, de fingres, et de nails.

---

7. Judaea; see Matthew 2:16–18.
3.4 Location: The French King's palace.
1. A translation of this French scene follows, with editorial comments in brackets.

CATHERINE   Alice, you've been in England, and you speak the language well.
ALICE   A little, madam.
CATHERINE   Please teach me. I must learn to speak it. What do you call *la main* in English?
ALICE   *La main?* It is called "de hand."
CATHERINE   De hand. And *les doigts?*
ALICE   *Les doigts?* Faith, I forget *les doigts,* but I'll remember. *Les doigts*—I think they're called "de fingres." Yes, de
    fingres.
CATHERINE   *Le main,* de hand; *les doigts,* de fingres. I think I'm a good scholar; I've learned two words of English
    quickly. What do you call *les ongles?*
ALICE   *Les ongles?* We call them "de nails."
CATHERINE   De nails. Listen—tell me if I speak well: de hand, de fingres, and de nails.

ALICE   C'est bien dit, madame. Il est fort bon anglais.

CATHERINE   Dites-moi l'anglais pour le bras.

ALICE   *De arma*, madame.

20   CATHERINE   Et le coude?

ALICE   *D'elbow.*

CATHERINE   *D'elbow.* Je m'en fais la répétition de tous les mots
que vous m'avez appris dès à présent.

ALICE   Il est trop difficile, madame, comme je pense.

25   CATHERINE   Excusez-moi, Alice. Écoutez: *d'hand, de fingre, de
nails, d'arma, de bilbow.*

ALICE   *D'elbow*, madame.

CATHERINE   O Seigneur Dieu, je m'en oublie! *D'elbow.* Comment appelez-vous le col?

30   ALICE   *De nick*, madame.

CATHERINE   *De nick.* Et le menton?

ALICE   *De chin.*

CATHERINE   *De sin.* Le col, *de nick*; le menton, *de sin.*

ALICE   Oui. Sauf votre honneur, en vérité vous prononcez les

35   mots aussi droit que les natifs d'Angleterre.

CATHERINE   Je ne doute point d'apprendre, par la grâce de Dieu,
et en peu de temps.

ALICE   N'avez-vous y déjà oublié ce que je vous ai enseigné?

CATHERINE   Non, et je réciterai à vous promptement: *d'hand, de

40   fingre, de mailès*—

ALICE   *De nails*, madame.

CATHERINE   *De nails, de arma, de ilbow*—

ALICE   Sauf votre honneur, *d'elbow.*

CATHERINE   Ainsi dis-je. *D'elbow, de nick*, et *de sin.* Comment

45   appelez-vous les pieds et la robe?

ALICE   *De foot*, madame, et *de cown.*

CATHERINE   *De foot* et *de cown*? O Seigneur Dieu! Ils sont les
mots de son mauvais, corruptible, gros, et impudique, et non
pour les dames d'honneur d'user. Je ne voudrais prononcer ces

50   mots devant les seigneurs de France pour tout le monde. Foh!
De foot et *de cown*! Néanmoins, je réciterai une autre fois ma

ALICE   That's well said, madam. It is very good English.
CATHERINE   Tell me the English for *le bras.*
ALICE   "De arma," madam.
CATHERINE   And *le coude?*
ALICE   "D'elbow."
CATHERINE   D'elbow. I'll repeat all the words you have taught me so far.
ALICE   It is too difficult, madam, in my opinion.
CATHERINE   Excuse me, Alice. Listen: d'hand, de fingre, de nails, d'arma, de bilbow.
ALICE   D'elbow, madam.
CATHERINE   O Lord God, I forgot. D'elbow. What do you call *le col?*
ALICE   "De nick," madam.
CATHERINE   De nick. And *le menton?*
ALICE   "De chin."
CATHERINE   De sin. *Le col*, de nick; *le menton*, de sin.
ALICE   Yes. Saving your honor, to tell the truth you pronounce the words just as properly as the native English.
CATHERINE   I don't doubt that I'll learn, with God's help, and in a short time.
ALICE   Haven't you already forgotten what I have taught you?
CATHERINE   No, I shall recite to you right now: d'hand, de fingre, de mailès—
ALICE   De nails, madam.
CATHERINE   De nails, de arma, de ilbow—
ALICE   Saving your honor, d'elbow.
CATHERINE   That's what I said. D'elbow, de nick, and de sin. What do you call *es pieds* and *la robe?*
ALICE   "De foot," madam, and "de cown" [gown].
CATHERINE   De foot and de cown? O Lord God, those are evil-sounding words, easily misconstrued, vulgar, and immodest, and not for respectable ladies to use. They sound like the French *foutre*, "fuck," and *con*, "cunt."] I wouldn't speak those words in front of French gentlemen for all the world. Ugh! de foot and de cown! Still, I shall

leçon ensemble. *D'hand, de fingre, de nails, d'arma, d'elbow,*
de nick, de sin, de foot, de cown.

ALICE Excellent, madame!

55 CATHERINE C'est assez pour une fois. Allons-nous à dîner.

Exeunt

3.5

Enter KING [CHARLES *the Sixth*] *of France,* DAUPHIN,
CONSTABLE, [DUKE *of*] BOURBON, *and others*

KING CHARLES 'Tis certain he hath passed the River Somme.

CONSTABLE And if he be not fought withal,° my lord,   with
Let us not live in France; let us quit all
And give our vineyards to a barbarous people.

5 DAUPHIN O *Dieu vivant!*° Shall a few sprays[1] of us,   O living God
The emptying of our fathers' luxury,[2]
Our scions,° put in wild and savage stock,   grafts
Spirt° up so suddenly into the clouds   Sprout
And over-look their grafters?

10 BOURBON Normans, but bastard Normans, Norman bastards!
Mort de ma vie,° if they march along   Death of my life
Unfought withal, but I will sell my dukedom
To buy a slobb'ry° and a dirty farm   muddy
In that nook-shotten[3] isle of Albion.°   England

15 CONSTABLE *Dieu de batailles!*° Where° have they this mettle?   God of battles / Whence
Is not their climate foggy, raw, and dull,
On whom as in despite° the sun looks pale,   contempt
Killing their fruit with frowns? Can sodden° water,   boiled; to make ale
A drench for sur-reined jades[4]—their barley-broth—

20 Decoct° their cold blood to such valiant heat?   Boil, to purify
And shall our quick blood, spirited with wine,
Seem frosty? O for honour of our land
Let us not hang like roping° icicles   ropelike
Upon our houses' thatch, whiles a more frosty people

25 Sweat drops of gallant youth in our rich fields—
'Poor' may we call them,° in their native lords.   (the fields)

DAUPHIN By faith and honour,
Our madams mock at us and plainly say
Our mettle is bred out,° and they will give   is exhausted

30 Their bodies to the lust of English youth,
To new-store France with bastard warriors.

BOURBON They bid us, 'To the English dancing-schools,
And teach lavoltas° high and swift corantos'[5]—   leaping dance
Saying our grace is only in our heels,

35 And that we are most lofty runaways.

KING CHARLES Where is Montjoy the herald? Speed° him hence.   Quickly send
Let him greet England with our sharp defiance.
Up, princes, and with spirit of honour edged
More sharper than your swords, hie° to the field.   go

40 Charles Delabret, High Constable of France,
You Dukes of Orléans, Bourbon, and of Berri,
Alençon, Brabant, Bar, and Burgundy,

recite my entire lesson once more. D'hand, de fingre, de nails, d'arma, d'elbow, de nick, de sin, de foot, de cown.
ALICE Excellent, madam!
CATHERINE That's enough for one time. Let's go to dinner.

3.5 Location: The French King's court.   3. With an indented shore.
1. Offshoots (bastards).   4. A tonic for overworked horses.
2. The discharge ("emptying") of our forefathers' lust.   5. Running dance.

Jaques Châtillion, Rambures, Vaudemont,
Beaumont, Grandpré, Roussi, and Fauconbridge,
45 Foix, Lestrelles, Boucicault, and Charolais,
High dukes, great princes, barons, lords, and knights,
For your great seats now quit you[6] of great shames.
Bar Harry England, that sweeps through our land
With pennons° painted in the blood of Harfleur;   *banners*
50 Rush on his host, as doth the melted snow
Upon the valleys, whose low vassal seat
The Alps doth spit and void his rheum° upon.   *empty its moisture*
Go down upon him, you have power enough,
And in a captive chariot into Rouen
Bring him our prisoner.
55 CONSTABLE   This becomes the great.°   *befits noblemen*
Sorry am I his numbers are so few,
His soldiers sick and famished in their march,
For I am sure when he shall see our army
He'll drop his heart into the sink° of fear   *pit*
60 And, fore achievement,° offer us his ransom.   *instead of battle*
KING CHARLES   Therefore, Lord Constable, haste on Montjoy,
And let him say to England that we send
To know what willing ransom he will give.—
Prince Dauphin, you shall stay with us in Rouen.
65 DAUPHIN   Not so, I do beseech your majesty.
KING CHARLES   Be patient, for you shall remain with us.—
Now forth, Lord Constable, and princes all,
And quickly bring us word of England's fall. *Exeunt [severally]*

3.6

Enter Captains GOWER *and* FLUELLEN *[meeting]*
GOWER   How now, Captain Fluellen, come you from the bridge?
FLUELLEN   I assure you there is very excellent services committed at the bridge.
GOWER   Is the Duke of Exeter safe?
5 FLUELLEN   The Duke of Exeter is as magnanimous as Agamemnon,[1] and a man that I love and honour with my soul and my
heart and my duty and my live and my living and my uttermost
power. He is not, God be praised and blessed, any hurt in the
world, but keeps the bridge most valiantly, with excellent disci-
10 pline. There is an ensign lieutenant there at the pridge, I think
in my very conscience he is as valiant a man as Mark Antony,
and he is a man of no estimation° in the world. but I did see   *fame*
him do as gallant service.
GOWER   What do you call him?
15 FLUELLEN   He is called Ensign Pistol.
GOWER   I know him not.
Enter Ensign PISTOL
FLUELLEN   Here is the man.
PISTOL   Captain, I thee beseech to do me favours.
The Duke of Exeter doth love thee well.
20 FLUELLEN   Ay, I praise God, and I have merited some love at his
hands.

6. *For . . . you:* In defense of your high ranks, now revenge
yourselves.   3.6 Location: The English camp.
                                               1. Greek general in the Trojan War.

PISTOL Bardolph, a soldier firm and sound of heart,
Of buxom° valour, hath by cruel fate   *lively*
And giddy Fortune's furious fickle wheel,
25 That goddess blind that stands upon the rolling restless stone—
FLUELLEN By your patience, Ensign Pistol: Fortune is painted
blind, with a muffler° afore her eyes, to signify to you that For-   *blindfold*
tune is blind. And she is painted also with a wheel, to signify to
you—which is the moral of it—that she is turning and incon-
30 stant and mutability and variation. And her foot, look you, is
fixed upon a spherical stone, which rolls and rolls and rolls.
In good truth, the poet makes a most excellent description of
it; Fortune is an excellent moral.°   *symbolic emblem*
PISTOL Fortune is Bardolph's foe and frowns on him,
35 For he hath stol'n a pax,² and hangèd must a° be.   *he*
A damnèd death—
Let gallows gape for dog, let man go free,
And let not hemp³ his windpipe suffocate.
But Exeter hath given the doom° of death   *sentence*
40 For pax of little price.
Therefore go speak, the Duke will hear thy voice,
And let not Bardolph's vital thread be cut
With edge of penny cord and vile reproach.
Speak, captain, for his life, and I will thee requite.
45 FLUELLEN Ensign Pistol, I do partly understand your meaning.
PISTOL Why then rejoice therefor.
FLUELLEN Certainly, ensign, it is not a thing to rejoice at. For
if, look you, he were my brother, I would desire the Duke to
use his good pleasure, and put him to executions. For disci-
50 pline ought to be used.
PISTOL Die and be damned! and *fico*⁴ for thy friendship.
FLUELLEN It is well.
PISTOL The fig of Spain.
FLUELLEN Very good.
55 PISTOL I say the fig within thy bowels and thy dirty maw. *Exit*
FLUELLEN Captain Gower, cannot you hear it lighten and
thunder?
GOWER Why, is this the ensign you told me of? I remember him
now. A bawd, a cutpurse.°   *thief*
60 FLUELLEN I'll assure you, a uttered as prave words at the pridge
as you shall see in a summer's day. But it is very well. What he
has spoke to me, that is well, I warrant you, when time is serve.
GOWER Why 'tis a gull,° a fool, a rogue, that now and then goes   *simpleton*
to the wars, to grace himself at his return into London under
65 the form of a soldier. And such fellows are perfect in the great
commanders' names, and they will learn° you by rote where   *teach*
services were done— at such and such a sconce,° at such a   *fortification*
breach, at such a convoy, who came off bravely, who was shot,
who disgraced, what terms the enemy stood on—and this they
70 con° perfectly in the phrase of war, which they trick up° with   *memorize / adorn*
new-tuned° oaths. And what a beard of the General's cut and a   *newly coined*
horrid suit of the camp⁵ will do among foaming bottles and ale-

---

2. Small tablet with a crucifix stamped on it.
3. Of which ropes were made.
4. Spanish for "fig"; obscene gesture made by thrusting

the thumb between two fingers.
5. *horrid . . . camp*: frightening soldier's attire.

washed wits is wonderful to be thought on. But you must learn
to know such slanders° of the age, or else you may be marvel-   *disgraces*
75   lously mistook.
   FLUELLEN   I tell you what, Captain Gower, I do perceive he is
   not the man that he would gladly make show to the world he
   is. If I find a hole in his coat,° I will tell him my mind.   *means of exposing him*
        [*A drum is heard*]
   Hark you, the King is coming, and I must speak with him from
80   the pridge.
        Enter KING [HARRY] *and his poor soldiers,* [*with*] *drum*
        and colours°   *drummer and flag bearer*
   God pless your majesty.
   KING HARRY   How now, Fluellen, com'st thou from the bridge?
   FLUELLEN   Ay, so please your majesty. The Duke of Exeter has
   very gallantly maintained the pridge. The French is gone off,
85   look you, and there is gallant and most prave passages.° Marry,   *altercations*
   th'athversary was have possession of the pridge, but he is
   enforced to retire, and the Duke of Exeter is master of the
   pridge. I can tell your majesty, the Duke is a prave man.
   KING HARRY   What men have you lost, Fluellen?
90   FLUELLEN   The perdition° of th'athversary hath been very great,   *loss*
   reasonable great. Marry, for my part I think the Duke hath lost
   never a man, but one that is like to be executed for robbing a
   church, one Bardolph, if your majesty know the man. His face
   is all bubuncles and whelks° and knobs and flames o' fire, and   *abscesses and pimples*
95   his lips blows at his nose, and it is like a coal of fire, sometimes
   plue and sometimes red. But his nose is executed,⁶ and his
   fire's out.
   KING HARRY   We would have all such offenders so cut off, and
   we here give express charge that in our marches through the
100   country there be nothing compelled from the villages, nothing
   taken but° paid for, none of the French upbraided or abused in   *unless*
   disdainful language. For when lenity° and cruelty play for a   *leniency*
   kingdom, the gentler gamester is the soonest winner.
        Tucket.° *Enter* MONTJOY   *Trumpet call*
   MONTJOY   You know me by my habit.⁷   *herald's coat*
105   KING HARRY   Well then, I know thee. What shall I know of thee?
   MONTJOY   My master's mind.
   KING HARRY   Unfold it.
   MONTJOY   Thus says my King:
   'Say thou to Harry of England, though we seemed dead, we did
   but sleep. Advantage° is a better soldier than rashness. Tell   *Circumspection*
   him, we could have rebuked him at Harfleur, but that we
110   thought not good to bruise an injury° till it were full ripe. Now   *squeeze a pimple*
   we speak upon our cue,° and our voice is imperial. England   *at the proper time*
   shall repent his folly, see his weakness, and admire our sufferance.° Bid him therefore consider of his ransom, which must   *wonder at our patience*
   proportion the losses we have borne, the subjects we have lost,
115   the disgrace we have digested°—which in weight to re-answer,°   *endured / compensate*
   his pettiness would bow under. For our losses, his exchequer°   *King's treasury*
   is too poor; for th'effusion of our blood, the muster⁷ of his kingdom too faint a number; and for our disgrace, his own person
   kneeling at our feet but a weak and worthless satisfaction. To
120   this add defiance, and tell him for conclusion he hath betrayed

---

6. Slit (in the pillory before he is hanged).   7. Entire population, assembled for military service.

his followers, whose condemnation is pronounced.'
So far my King and master; so much my office.

KING HARRY   What is thy name? I know thy quality.°   rank
MONTJOY   Montjoy.
125   KING HARRY   Thou dost thy office fairly. Turn thee back
And tell thy king I do not seek him now,
But could be willing to march on to Calais
Without impeachment,° for to say the sooth°—   hindrance / truth
Though 'tis no wisdom to confess so much
130   Unto an enemy of craft and vantage°—   cunning and superiority
My people are with sickness much enfeebled,
My numbers lessened, and those few I have
Almost no better than so many French;
Who when they were in health—I tell thee herald,
135   I thought upon one pair of English legs
Did march three Frenchmen. Yet forgive me, God,
That I do brag thus. This your air of France
Hath blown that vice in me. I must repent.
Go, therefore, tell thy master here I am;
140   My ransom is this frail and worthless trunk,°   body
My army but a weak and sickly guard.
Yet, God before, tell him we will come on,
Though France himself and such another neighbour
Stand in our way. There's for thy labour, Montjoy.[8]
145   Go bid thy master well advise himself.
If we may pass, we will; if we be hindered,
We shall your tawny ground with your red blood
Discolour. And so, Montjoy, fare you well.
The sum of all our answer is but this:
150   We would not seek a battle as we are,
Nor as we are we say we will not shun it.
So tell your master.
MONTJOY   I shall deliver so. Thanks to your highness.   *Exit*
GLOUCESTER   I hope they will not come upon us now.
155   KING HARRY   We are in God's hand, brother, not in theirs.
March to the bridge. It now draws toward night.
Beyond the river we'll encamp ourselves,
And on tomorrow bid them march away.   *Exeunt*

3.7

Enter the CONSTABLE, *Lord* RAMBURES, [*Dukes of*]
ORLÉANS [*and*] BOURBON,[1] *with others*

CONSTABLE   Tut, I have the best armour of the world. Would it
were day.
ORLÉANS   You have an excellent armour. But let my horse have
his due.
5   CONSTABLE   It is the best horse of Europe.
ORLÉANS   Will it never be morning?
BOURBON   My lord of Orléans and my Lord High Constable, you
talk of horse and armour?
ORLÉANS   You are as well provided of both as any prince in the
10   world.
BOURBON   What a long night is this! I will not change my horse

---

8. Henry generously "tips" the enemy herald.   1. As in Q; F has "Dauphin" in this scene and in 4.2
3.7 Location: The French camp near Agincourt.   and 4.5. See Textual Note.

with any that treads but on four pasterns.° Ah ha! He bounds ⟶ *hooves*
from the earth as if his entrails were hares—*le cheval volant,*
the Pegasus, *qui a les narines de feu.*[2] When I bestride him, I
15 soar, I am a hawk; he trots the air, the earth sings when he
touches it,[3] the basest horn° of his hoof is more musical than ⟶ *lowest part (with pun)*
the pipe of Hermes.[4]

ORLÉANS   He's of the colour of the nutmeg.

BOURBON   And of the heat of the ginger.[5] It is a beast for Per-
20 seus. He is pure air and fire, and the dull elements of earth and
water never appear in him, but only in patient stillness while
his rider mounts him. He is indeed a horse, and all other jades° ⟶ *nags*
you may call beasts.

CONSTABLE   Indeed, my lord, it is a most absolute° and excellent ⟶ *perfect*
25 horse.

BOURBON   It is the prince of palfreys.° His neigh is the bidding ⟶ *warhorses*
of a monarch, and his countenance enforces homage.

ORLÉANS   No more, cousin.

BOURBON   Nay, the man hath no wit, that cannot from the ris-
30 ing of the lark to the lodging of the lamb vary deserved praise
on my palfrey. It is a theme as fluent° as the sea. Turn the sands ⟶ *flowing; abundant*
into eloquent tongues, and my horse is argument° for them all. ⟶ *subject*
'Tis a subject for a sovereign to reason on, and for a sovereign's
sovereign to ride on, and for the world, familiar to us and
35 unknown, to lay apart their particular functions, and wonder at
him. I once writ a sonnet in his praise, and began thus: 'Wonder of nature!—'

ORLÉANS   I have heard a sonnet begin so to one's mistress.

BOURBON   Then did they imitate that which I composed to my
40 courser, for my horse is my mistress.

ORLÉANS   Your mistress bears well.[6]

BOURBON   *Me* well, which is the prescribed praise and perfection
of a good and particular° mistress. ⟶ *private*

CONSTABLE   Nay, for methought yesterday your mistress
45 shrewdly° shook your back. ⟶ *severely*

BOURBON   So perhaps did yours.

CONSTABLE   Mine was not bridled.

BOURBON   O then belike she was old and gentle, and you rode
like a kern° of Ireland, your French hose° off, and in your strait ⟶ *soldier / wide breeches*
50 strossers.° ⟶ *tights*

CONSTABLE   You have good judgement in horsemanship.

BOURBON   Be warned by me then: they that ride so, and ride not
warily, fall into foul bogs. I had rather have my horse to my
mistress.

55 CONSTABLE   I had as lief have my mistress a jade.° ⟶ *horse; whore*

BOURBON   I tell thee, Constable, my mistress wears his own
hair.[7]

CONSTABLE   I could make as true a boast as that, if I had a sow
to my mistress.

60 BOURBON   '*Le chien est retourné à son propre vomissement, et la*

2. The flying horse . . . with nostrils of fire. Pegasus was
a mythological flying horse, ridden by the hero Perseus.
3. When Pegasus struck Mount Helicon with his hoof,
the fountain of the Muses sprang forth.
4. Greek messenger god, whose sweet playing on the
pipe charmed the many-eyed guard Argus, allowing the
imprisoned Io to escape.

5. Horses' colors supposedly suggested their dispositions: "nutmeg" meant "pleasant and nimble"; "ginger"
meant "hot and skittish."
6. Carries weight (with obscene innuendo).
7. Implying that the constable's mistress does not, having lost it to syphilis.

*truie lavée au bourbier.'*⁸ Thou makest use of anything.

CONSTABLE Yet do I not use my horse for my mistress, or any
such proverb so little kin to the purpose.

RAMBURES My Lord Constable, the armour that I saw in your
65 tent tonight, are those stars or suns upon it?

CONSTABLE Stars, my lord.

BOURBON Some of them will fall tomorrow, I hope.

CONSTABLE And yet my sky shall not want.

BOURBON That may be, for you bear a many superfluously,
70 and 'twere more honour some were away.

CONSTABLE Even as your horse bears your praises, who would
trot as well were some of your brags dismounted.

BOURBON Would I were able to load him with his desert! Will
it never be day? I will trot tomorrow a mile, and my way shall
75 be paved with English faces.

CONSTABLE I will not say so, for fear I should be faced out of
my way.° But I would it were morning, for I would fain° be about   turned aside / gladly
the ears of the English.

RAMBURES Who will go to hazard° with me for twenty prisoners?   wager

80 CONSTABLE You must first go yourself to hazard, ere you have
them.

BOURBON 'Tis midnight. I'll go arm myself.   *Exit*

ORLÉANS The Duke of Bourbon longs for morning.

RAMBURES He longs to eat the English.

85 CONSTABLE I think he will eat all he kills.

ORLÉANS By the white hand of my lady, he's a gallant prince.

CONSTABLE Swear by her foot, that she may tread out° the oath.   erase with her foot

ORLÉANS He is simply the most active gentleman of France.

CONSTABLE Doing is activity, and he will still be doing.

90 ORLÉANS He never did harm that I heard of.

CONSTABLE Nor will do none tomorrow. He will keep that good
name still.

ORLÉANS I know him to be valiant.

CONSTABLE I was told that by one that knows him better than
95 you.

ORLÉANS What's he?

CONSTABLE Marry, he told me so himself, and he said he cared
not who knew it.

ORLÉANS He needs not; it is no hidden virtue in him.

100 CONSTABLE By my faith, sir, but it is. Never anybody saw it but
his lackey.⁹ 'Tis a hooded valour, and when it appears it will
bate.¹

ORLÉANS 'Ill will never said well.'

CONSTABLE I will cap that proverb with 'There is flattery in
105 friendship.'

ORLÉANS And I will take up that with 'Give the devil his due.'

CONSTABLE Well placed! There stands your friend for the devil.
Have at the very eye° of that proverb with 'A pox of the devil!'   bull's-eye

ORLÉANS You are the better at proverbs by how much 'a fool's
110 bolt° is soon shot'.   short, blunt arrow

---

8. "The dog is turned to his own vomit again and the
sow that was washed to her wallowing in the mire"
(quoting 2 Peter 2:22).
9. That is, the only person he is brave enough to beat

is his servant.
1. Beat its wings (like a hawk, which was kept "hooded"
until prey was sighted); also, abate.

CONSTABLE   You have shot over.°   overshot the target

ORLÉANS   'Tis not the first time you were overshot.°   defeated

    Enter a MESSENGER

MESSENGER   My Lord High Constable, the English lie within
    fifteen hundred paces of your tents.

115   CONSTABLE   Who hath measured the ground?

MESSENGER   The Lord Grandpré.

CONSTABLE   A valiant and most expert gentleman.

                            [Exit MESSENGER]

    Would it were day! Alas, poor Harry of England. He longs not
    for the dawning as we do.

120   ORLÉANS   What a wretched and peevish fellow is this King of
    England, to mope° with his fat-brained followers so far out of   *wander*
    his knowledge.

CONSTABLE   If the English had any apprehension,° they would   *sense*
    run away.

125   ORLÉANS   That they lack—for if their heads had any intellectual
    armour, they could never wear such heavy headpieces.

RAMBURES   That island of England breeds very valiant creatures.
    Their mastiffs are of unmatchable courage.

ORLÉANS   Foolish curs, that run winking° into the mouth of a   *with closed eyes*
130   Russian bear[2], and have their heads crushed like rotten apples.
    You may as well say, 'That's a valiant flea that dare eat his
    breakfast on the lip of a lion.'

CONSTABLE   Just,° just. And the men do sympathize with the   *True*
    mastiffs in robustious and rough coming on, leaving their wits
135   with their wives. And then, give them great meals of beef,[3] and
    iron and steel, they will eat like wolves and fight like devils.

ORLÉANS   Ay, but these English are shrewdly° out of beef.   *badly*

CONSTABLE   Then shall we find tomorrow they have only stom-
    achs° to eat, and none to fight. Now is it time to arm. Come,   *appetite*
140   shall we about it?

ORLÉANS   It is now two o'clock. But let me see—by ten
    We shall have each a hundred Englishmen.   *Exeunt*

4.0

    [Enter] CHORUS

CHORUS   Now entertain conjecture of° a time   *imagine*
    When creeping murmur and the poring° dark   *pouring; eye-straining*
    Fills the wide vessel of the universe.
    From camp to camp through the foul womb of night
5   The hum of either army stilly sounds,
    That° the fixed sentinels almost receive   *So that*
    The secret whispers of each other's watch.
    Fire answers fire, and through their paly° flames   *pale*
    Each battle sees the other's umbered° face.   *shadowed*
10   Steed threatens steed, in high and boastful neighs
    Piercing the night's dull ear, and from the tents
    The armourers, accomplishing° the knights,   *equipping*
    With busy hammers closing rivets up,
    Give dreadful note of preparation.
15   The country cocks do crow, the clocks do toll

---

2. Referring to the sport of bearbaiting, in which dogs   3. A traditional English food.
were set upon bears chained to a post.   4.0

And the third hour of drowsy morning name.
Proud of their numbers and secure in soul,
The confident and overlusty French
Do the low-rated° English play at dice,[1]   *underrated*
20 And chide the cripple tardy-gaited night,
Who like a foul and ugly witch doth limp
So tediously away. The poor condemnèd English,
Like sacrifices, by their watchful fires
Sit patiently and inly° ruminate   *inwardly*
25 The morning's danger; and their gesture sad,
Investing° lank lean cheeks and war-worn coats,   *Accompanying*
Presented them unto the gazing moon
So many horrid ghosts. O now, who will behold
The royal captain of this ruined band
30 Walking from watch to watch, from tent to tent,
Let him cry, 'Praise and glory on his head!'
For forth he goes and visits all his host,°   *army*
Bids them good morrow with a modest smile
And calls them brothers, friends, and countrymen.
35 Upon his royal face there is no note°   *sign*
How dread an army hath enroundèd° him;   *encircled*
Nor doth he dedicate° one jot of colour   *lose*
Unto the weary and all-watchèd night,
But freshly looks and overbears attaint[2]
40 With cheerful semblance and sweet majesty,
That every wretch, pining and pale before,
Beholding him, plucks comfort from his looks.
A largess universal,° like the sun,   *wealth available to all*
His liberal eye doth give to everyone,
45 Thawing cold fear, that mean and gentle° all   *lowborn and noble*
Behold, as may unworthiness define,[3]
A little touch of Harry in the night.
And so our scene must to the battle fly,
Where O for pity, we shall much disgrace,
50 With four or five most vile and ragged foils,°   *swords*
Right ill-disposed in brawl ridiculous,
The name of Agincourt. Yet sit and see,
Minding° true things by what their mock'ries be.   *Exit*   *Imagining*

4.1

Enter KING [HARRY] *and* [*Duke of*] GLOUCESTER [*then
the Duke of* CLARENCE]

KING HARRY Gloucester, 'tis true that we are in great danger;
The greater therefore should our courage be.
Good morrow, brother Clarence. God Almighty!
There is some soul of goodness in things evil,
5 Would men observingly distil it out—
For our bad neighbour makes us early stirrers,
Which is both healthful and good husbandry.°   *economy*
Besides, they are our outward consciences,
And preachers to us all, admonishing
10 That we should dress us fairly° for our end.   *prepare adequately*

---

1. See 3.7.79.
2. And suppresses signs of exhaustion.

3. As far as their limited capacities permit.
4.1 Location: The English camp at Agincourt.

Thus may we gather honey from the weed
And make a moral of the devil himself.

Enter [Sir Thomas] ERPINGHAM

Good morrow, old Sir Thomas Erpingham.
A good soft pillow for that good white head

15   Were better than a churlish turf of France.

ERPINGHAM   Not so, my liege. This lodging likes° me better,   *pleases*
Since I may say, 'Now lie I like a king.'

KING HARRY   'Tis good for men to love their present pains
Upon example.[1] So the spirit is eased,

20   And when the mind is quickened, out of doubt
The organs, though defunct and dead before,
Break up their drowsy grave and newly move
With casted slough[2] and fresh legerity.°   *nimbleness*
Lend me thy cloak, Sir Thomas.

[He puts on Erpingham's cloak]

                    Brothers both,

25   Commend me to the princes in our camp.
Do my good morrow° to them, and anon   *Say good morning*
Desire them all to my pavilion.

GLOUCESTER   We shall, my liege.

ERPINGHAM   Shall I attend your grace?

30   KING HARRY   No, my good knight.
Go with my brothers to my lords of England.
I and my bosom must debate awhile,
And then I would no other company.

ERPINGHAM   The Lord in heaven bless thee, noble Harry.

35   KING HARRY   God-a-mercy,° old heart, thou speak'st cheerfully.   *Thank you*

Exeunt [all but KING HARRY*]*

Enter PISTOL *[to him]*

PISTOL   *Qui vous là?*°   *Who goes there*

KING HARRY   A friend.

PISTOL   Discuss unto me: art thou officer,
Or art thou base, common, and popular?°   *plebeian*

40   KING HARRY   I am a gentleman of a company.

PISTOL   Trail'st thou the puissant pike?°   *Are you an infantryman*

KING HARRY   Even so. What are you?

PISTOL   As good a gentleman as the Emperor.

KING HARRY   Then you are a better than the King.

45   PISTOL   The King's a bawcock and a heart-of-gold,
A lad of life, an imp of fame,°   *a scion of noble stock*
Of parents good, of fist most valiant.
I kiss his dirty shoe, and from heartstring
I love the lovely bully.° What is thy name?   *lovable swashbuckler*

50   KING HARRY   Harry *le roi.*°   *the King*

PISTOL   Leroi? A Cornish name. Art thou of Cornish crew?

KING HARRY   No, I am a Welshman.

PISTOL   Know'st thou Fluellen?

KING HARRY   Yes.

55   PISTOL   Tell him I'll knock his leek about his pate
Upon Saint Davy's day.[3]

KING HARRY   Do not you wear your dagger in your cap that day,
lest he knock that about yours.

1. By the pattern provided by others.
2. Old skin having been cast off (like a snake).

3. March 1, Welsh national holiday celebrating St.
David's victory over the Saxons.

PISTOL   Art thou his friend?

60 KING HARRY   And his kinsman too.

PISTOL   The *fico*[4] for thee then.

KING HARRY   I thank you. God be with you.

PISTOL   My name is Pistol called.

KING HARRY   It sorts° well with your fierceness.   *Exit* [PISTOL]   *agrees*
   Enter [*Captains*] FLUELLEN *and* GOWER [*severally.* KING
   HARRY *stands apart*]

65 GOWER   Captain Fluellen!

FLUELLEN   So! In the name of Jesu Christ, speak fewer. It is the
   greatest admiration° in the universal° world, when the true and   *wonder / whole*
   ancient prerogatifs and laws of the wars is not kept. If you
   would take the pains but to examine the wars of Pompey the
70 Great,[5] you shall find, I warrant you, that there is no tiddle-
   taddle nor pibble-babble° in Pompey's camp. I warrant you,   *chattering*
   you shall find the ceremonies of the wars, and the cares of it,
   and the forms of it, and the sobriety of it, and the modesty of
   it, to be otherwise.

75 GOWER   Why, the enemy is loud. You hear him all night.

FLUELLEN   If the enemy is an ass and a fool and a prating cox-
   comb,° is it meet,° think you, that we should also, look you, be   *yammering fool / proper*
   an ass and a fool and a prating coxcomb? In your own con-
   science now?

80 GOWER   I will speak lower.

FLUELLEN   I pray you and beseech you that you will.
                         Exeunt [FLUELLEN *and* GOWER]

KING HARRY   Though it appear a little out of fashion,°   *unconventional*
   There is much care and valour in this Welshman.
           Enter three soldiers: John BATES, *Alexander* COURT, *and*
           Michael WILLIAMS

COURT   Brother John Bates, is not that the morning which breaks
85 yonder?

BATES   I think it be. But we have no great cause to desire the
   approach of day.

WILLIAMS   We see yonder the beginning of the day, but I think
   we shall never see the end of it.—Who goes there?

90 KING HARRY   A friend.

WILLIAMS   Under what captain serve you?

KING HARRY   Under Sir Thomas Erpingham.

WILLIAMS   A good old commander and a most kind gentleman.
   I pray you, what thinks he of our estate?°   *situation*

95 KING HARRY   Even as men wrecked upon a sand, that look to be
   washed off the next tide.

BATES   He hath not told his thought to the King?

KING HARRY   No, nor it is not meet he should. For though I speak
   it to you, I think the King is but a man, as I am. The violet
100 smells to him as it doth to me; the element shows° to him as it   *the sky appears*
   doth to me. All his senses have but human conditions.° His   *limitations*
   ceremonies laid by, in his nakedness he appears but a man,
   and though his affections° are higher mounted than ours, yet   *desires*
   when they stoop,[6] they stoop with the like wing. Therefore,
105 when he sees reason of fears,° as we do, his fears, out of doubt,   *to fear*

4. See 3.6.51.   6. Plummet down (term from falconry).
5. Roman general, defeated by Julius Caesar.

be of the same relish° as ours are. Yet, in reason, no man should   *taste; kind*
possess him with[7] any appearance of fear, lest he, by showing
it, should dishearten his army.

BATES   He may show what outward courage he will, but I
110 believe, as cold a night as 'tis, he could wish himself in Thames
up to the neck. And so I would he were, and I by him, at all
adventures,[8] so we were quit° here.   *away from*

KING HARRY   By my troth,° I will speak my conscience of the   *oath*
King. I think he would not wish himself anywhere but where
115 he is.

BATES   Then I would he were here alone. So should he be sure
to be ransomed, and a many poor men's lives saved.

KING HARRY   I dare say you love him not so ill to wish him here
alone, howsoever you speak this to feel° other men's minds.   *test*
120 Methinks I could not die anywhere so contented as in the
King's company, his cause being just and his quarrel honourable.

WILLIAMS   That's more than we know.

BATES   Ay, or more than we should seek after. For we know
125 enough if we know we are the King's subjects. If his cause be
wrong, our obedience to the King wipes the crime of it out of
us.

WILLIAMS   But if the cause be not good, the King himself hath a
heavy reckoning to make, when all those legs and arms and
130 heads chopped off in a battle shall join together at the latter
day,[9] and cry all, 'We died at such a place'—some swearing,
some crying for a surgeon, some upon their wives left poor
behind them, some upon the debts they owe, some upon their
children rawly° left. I am afeard there are few die well that die   *abruptly; poorly*
135 in a battle, for how can they charitably dispose of anything,
when blood is their argument?° Now, if these men do not die   *business*
well, it will be a black matter for the King that led them to it—
who° to disobey were against all proportion of subjection.[1]   *whom*

KING HARRY   So, if a son that is by his father sent about merchan-
140 dise do sinfully miscarry upon the sea, the imputation of° his   *blame for*
wickedness, by your rule, should be imposed upon his father,
that sent him. Or if a servant, under his master's command
transporting a sum of money, be assailed by robbers, and die in
many irreconciled iniquities,° you may call the business of the   *unatoned sins*
145 master the author of the servant's damnation. But this is not so.
The King is not bound to answer the particular endings of his
soldiers, the father of his son, nor the master of his servant, for
they purpose not their deaths when they propose their services.
Besides, there is no king, be his cause never so spotless if it
150 come to the arbitrament° of swords, can try it out with all   *settlement*
unspotted° soldiers. Some, peradventure,° have on them the   *unblemished / perhaps*
guilt of premeditated and contrived murder; some, of beguiling
virgins with the broken seals of perjury; some, making the wars
their bulwark,° that have before gored the gentle bosom of   *defense (against the law)*
155 peace with pillage and robbery. Now, if these men have

---

7. Induce him to experience.
8. Whatever might happen.
9. Last Judgment, when human beings are to be
resurrected in the body.
1. *against . . . subjection*: to defy all proper relationships of authority and subordination.

defeated the law and outrun native° punishment, though they   *at home*
can outstrip men, they have no wings to fly from God. War is
his beadle.° War is his vengeance. So that here men are pun-   *police officer*
ished for before-breach° of the King's laws, in now the King's   *earlier breaking*
160   quarrel. Where they feared the death, they have borne life
away; and where they would be safe, they perish. Then if they
die unprovided,° no more is the King guilty of their damnation   *unprepared*
than he was before guilty of those impieties for the which they
are now visited.° Every subject's duty is the King's, but every   *punished*
165   subject's soul is his own. Therefore should every soldier in the
wars do as every sick man in his bed: wash every mote° out of   *speck*
his conscience. And dying so, death is to him advantage;° or   *profit*
not dying, the time was blessedly lost wherein such preparation
was gained. And in him that escapes, it were not sin to think
170   that, making God so free an offer, he° let him outlive that day   *(God)*
to see his greatness and to teach others how they should pre-
pare.
BATES   'Tis certain, every man that dies ill,° the ill upon his own   *in sin*
head. The King is not to answer it. I do not desire he
175   should answer for me, and yet I determine to fight lustily for
him.
KING HARRY   I myself heard the King say he would not be ransomed.
WILLIAMS   Ay, he said so, to make us fight cheerfully, but when
180   our throats are cut he may be ransomed, and we ne'er the
wiser.
KING HARRY   If I live to see it, I will never trust his word after.
WILLIAMS   You pay him then! That's a perilous shot out of an
elder-gun,° that a poor and a private displeasure can do against   *a popgun*
185   a monarch. You may as well go about to turn the sun to ice
with fanning in his face with a peacock's feather. You'll never
trust his word after! Come, 'tis a foolish saying.
KING HARRY   Your reproof is something too round.° I should be   *blunt*
angry with you, if the time were convenient.
190   WILLIAMS   Let it be a quarrel between us, if you live.
KING HARRY   I embrace it.
WILLIAMS   How shall I know thee again?
KING HARRY   Give me any gage° of thine, and I will wear it in my   *token*
bonnet. Then if ever thou darest acknowledge it, I will make it
195   my quarrel.
WILLIAMS   Here's my glove. Give me another of thine.
KING HARRY   There.
      [*They exchange gloves*]
WILLIAMS   This will I also wear in my cap. If ever thou come to
me and say, after tomorrow, 'This is my glove', by this hand I
200   will take thee a box on the ear.
KING HARRY   If ever I live to see it, I will challenge it.
WILLIAMS   Thou darest as well be hanged.
KING HARRY   Well, I will do it, though I take thee in the King's
company.
205   WILLIAMS   Keep thy word. Fare thee well.
BATES   Be friends, you English fools, be friends. We have
French quarrels enough, if you could tell how to reckon.°   *count*
KING HARRY   Indeed, the French may lay twenty French crowns°   *coins; heads*
to one they will beat us, for they bear them on their shoulders.

210 But it is no English treason to cut French crowns,[2] and tomor-
row the King himself will be a clipper.   *Exeunt soldiers*
Upon the King.
'Let us our lives, our souls, our debts, our care-full wives,
Our children, and our sins, lay on the King.'
215 We must bear all. O hard condition,
Twin-born with greatness: subject to the breath
Of every fool, whose sense no more can feel
But his own wringing.° What infinite heartsease   *pain*
Must kings neglect that private men enjoy?
220 And what have kings that privates have not too,
Save ceremony, save general ceremony?
And what art thou, thou idol ceremony?
What kind of god art thou, that suffer'st more
Of mortal griefs than do thy worshippers?
225 What are thy rents?° What are thy comings-in?°   *revenues / income*
O ceremony, show me but thy worth.
What is thy soul of adoration?[3]
Art thou aught° else but place, degree, and form,   *anything*
Creating awe and fear in other men?
230 Wherein thou art less happy, being feared,
Than they in fearing.
What drink'st thou oft, instead of homage sweet,
But poisoned flattery? O be sick, great greatness,
And bid thy ceremony give thee cure.
235 Think'st thou the fiery fever will go out
With titles blown from adulation?
Will it give place to flexure° and low bending?   *bowing*
Canst thou, when thou command'st the beggar's knee,
Command the health of it? No, thou proud dream
240 That play'st so subtly with a king's repose;
I am a king that find° thee, and I know   *expose*
'Tis not the balm, the sceptre, and the ball,°   *orb (royal accessory)*
The sword, the mace, the crown imperial,
The intertissued robe of gold and pearl,
245 The farcèd° title running fore the king,   *stuffed*
The throne he sits on, nor the tide of pomp
That beats upon the high shore of this world—
No, not all these, thrice-gorgeous ceremony,
Not all these, laid in bed majestical,
250 Can sleep so soundly as the wretched slave
Who with a body filled and vacant mind
Gets him to rest, crammed with distressful bread;
Never sees horrid night, the child of hell,
But like a lackey° from the rise to set   *servant*
255 Sweats in the eye of Phoebus,° and all night   *the sun*
Sleeps in Elysium;° next day, after dawn   *classical paradise*
Doth rise and help Hyperion° to his horse,   *the sun's charioteer*
And follows so the ever-running year
With profitable labour to his grave.
260 And but for ceremony such a wretch,
Winding up days with toil and nights with sleep,

2. "Clipping" (line 211), or shaving, precious metal off   3. What is the secret of the adoration you inspire?
coins was punishable as treason.

Had the forehand° and vantage of a king.   *advantage*
The slave, a member of the country's peace,
Enjoys it, but in gross brain little wots°   *thinks*
265   What watch the King keeps to maintain the peace,
Whose hours the peasant best advantages.°   *profits most from*

       Enter [Sir Thomas] ERPINGHAM

ERPINGHAM   My lord, your nobles, jealous of° your absence,   *concerned about*
Seek through your camp to find you.
KING HARRY   Good old knight,
Collect them all together at my tent.
I'll be before thee.
270   ERPINGHAM   I shall do't, my lord.   *Exit*
KING HARRY   O God of battles, steel my soldiers' hearts.
Possess them not with fear. Take from them now
The sense of reck'ning,° ere th'opposèd numbers   *ability to count*
Pluck their hearts from them. Not today, O Lord,
275   O not today, think not upon the fault
My father made in compassing the crown.⁴
I Richard's body have interrèd new,°   *buried anew*
And on it have bestowed more contrite tears
Than from it issued forcèd drops of blood.
280   Five hundred poor have I in yearly pay
Who twice a day their withered hands hold up°   *(in prayer)*
Toward heaven to pardon blood. And I have built
Two chantries,⁵ where the sad and solemn priests
Sing still for Richard's soul. More will I do,
285   Though all that I can do is nothing worth,
Since that my penitence comes after ill,°   *sin*
Imploring pardon.

       Enter the [Duke of] GLOUCESTER

GLOUCESTER   My liege.
KING HARRY   My brother Gloucester's voice? Ay.
290   I know thy errand, I will go with thee.
The day, my friends, and all things stay° for me.   *Exeunt*   *wait*

4.2

       Enter [Dukes of BOURBON *and]* ORLÉANS, *and [Lord]*
       RAMBURES

ORLÉANS   The sun doth gild our armour. Up, my lords!
BOURBON   *Monte cheval!*° My horse! *Varlet, lacquais!*° Ha!   *To horse / valet*
ORLÉANS   O brave spirit!
BOURBON   *Via les eaux et terre!*
5   ORLÉANS   *Rien plus? L'air et feu!*¹
BOURBON   *Cieux,*° Cousin Orléans!   *To the heavens*

       Enter CONSTABLE

Now, my Lord constable!
CONSTABLE   Hark how our steeds for present° service neigh.   *immediate*
BOURBON   Mount them and make incision in their hides,
10   That their hot blood may spin in English eyes
And dout° them with superfluous courage. Ha!   *extinguish*
RAMBURES   What, will you have them weep our horses' blood?

---

4. Henry's father usurped the throne from its rightful
possessor, Richard II.
5. Chapels where Masses for the dead were sung.
4.2. Location: The French camp.

1. Away over water and earth!
No more? Air and fire! (Playing on the four elements,
of which fire was the highest.)

How shall we then behold their natural tears?
          Enter MESSENGER
MESSENGER   The English are embattled,[2] you French peers.
15   CONSTABLE   To horse, you gallant princes, straight to horse!
          Do but behold yon poor and starvèd band,
          And your fair show° shall suck away their souls,   *appearance*
          Leaving them but the shells and husks of men.
          There is not work enough for all our hands,
20   Scarce blood enough in all their sickly veins
          To give each naked curtal-axe° a stain   *cutlass*
          That our French gallants shall today draw out
          And sheathe for lack of sport. Let us but blow on them,
          The vapour of our valour will o'erturn them.
25   'Tis positive 'gainst all exceptions,° lords,   *'Tis definitely true*
          That our superfluous lackeys and our peasants,
          Who in unnecessary action swarm
          About our squares of battle, were enough
          To purge this field of such a hilding° foe,   *worthless*
30   Though we upon this mountain's basis by°   *foot nearby*
          Took stand° for idle speculation,   *Stood still*
          But that our honours must not. What's to say?
          A very little little let us do
          And all is done. Then let the trumpets sound
35   The tucket sonance° and the note to mount,   *trumpet signal*
          For our approach shall so much dare the field
          That England shall couch down in fear and yield.
          Enter [Lord] GRANDPRÉ
     GRANDPRÉ   Why do you stay so long, my lords of France?
          Yon island carrions,° desperate of their bones,   *cadavers*
40   Ill-favouredly become the morning field.
          Their ragged curtains° poorly are let loose   *banners*
          And our air shakes them passing scornfully.
          Big Mars° seems bankrupt in their beggared host   *god of war*
          And faintly through a rusty beaver° peeps.   *visor*
45   The horsemen sit like fixèd candlesticks
          With torchstaves° in their hands, and their poor jades   *tapers*
          Lob° down their heads, drooping the hides and hips,   *Hang*
          The gum down-roping° from their pale dead eyes,   *mucus dripping*
          And in their palled° dull mouths the gimmaled° bit   *pale / jointed*
50   Lies foul with chewed grass, still and motionless.
          And their executors,[3] the knavish crows,
          Fly o'er them all impatient for their hour.
          Description cannot suit itself in words
          To demonstrate the life of° such a battle   *depict realistically*
55   In life so lifeless as it shows itself.
     CONSTABLE   They have said their prayers, and they stay° for death.   *wait*
     BOURBON   Shall we go send them dinners and fresh suits
          And give their fasting horses provender,°   *food*
          And after° fight with them?   *afterward*
60   CONSTABLE   I stay but for my guidon.° To the field!   *pennant*
          I will the banner from a trumpet° take   *trumpeter*
          And use it for my haste. Come, come away!
          The sun is high, and we outwear° the day.   *Exeunt*   *waste*

2. Drawn into lines of battle.   3. Administrators of wills (who dispose of the remains
                                                     of the dead).

4.3

Enter [Dukes of] GLOUCESTER, [CLARENCE, *and*] EXE-
TER, [*Earls of*] SALISBURY *and* [WARWICK, *and Sir*
Thomas] ERPINGHAM, *with all [the] host*

GLOUCESTER   Where is the King?

CLARENCE   The King himself is rode to view their battle.°   army

WARWICK   Of fighting men they have full threescore thousand.°   60,000

EXETER   There's five to one. Besides, they all are fresh.

5   SALISBURY   God's arm strike with us! 'Tis a fearful odds.

God b'wi' you, princes all. I'll to my charge.°   command post

If we no more meet till we meet in heaven,

Then joyfully, my noble Lord of Clarence,

My dear Lord Gloucester, and my good Lord Exeter,

10   And [*to* WARWICK] my kind kinsman, warriors all, adieu.

CLARENCE   Farewell, good Salisbury, and good luck go with thee.

EXETER   Farewell, kind lord. Fight valiantly today—

And yet I do thee wrong to mind° thee of it,   remind

For thou art framed of the firm truth of valour.

                                              [*Exit* SALISBURY]

15   CLARENCE   He is as full of valour as of kindness,

Princely in both.

                    Enter KING; [HARRY, *behind*]

WARWICK   O that we now had here

But one ten thousand of those men in England

That do no work today.

KING HARRY   What's he that wishes so?

My cousin Warwick? No, my fair cousin.

20   If we are marked to die, we are enough

To do our country loss;° and if to live,   For our country to lose

The fewer men, the greater share of honour.

God's will, I pray thee wish not one man more.

By Jove, I am not covetous for gold,

25   Nor care I who doth feed upon my cost;

It ernes° me not if men my garments wear;   grieves

Such outward things dwell not in my desires.

But if it be a sin to covet honour

I am the most offending soul alive.

30   No, faith, my coz,° wish not a man from England.   kinsman

God's peace, I would not lose so great an honour

As one man more methinks would share° from me   deprive

For the best hope I have. O do not wish one more.

Rather proclaim it presently° through my host°   immediately / army

35   That he which hath no stomach° to this fight,   appetite; courage

Let him depart. His passport shall be made

And crowns for convoy° put into his purse.   money for transport

We would not die in that man's company

That fears his fellowship° to die with us.   duty as our companion

40   This day is called the Feast of Crispian.[1]

He that outlives this day and comes safe home

Will stand a-tiptoe when this day is named

And rouse him at the name of Crispian.

He that shall see this day and live t'old age

4.3 Location: The English camp.

1. October 25, dedicated to the martyred brothers Crispin and Crispianus (or Crispinian).

45	Will yearly on the vigil° feast his neighbours
	And say, 'Tomorrow is Saint Crispian.'
	Then will he strip his sleeve and show his scars
	And say, 'These wounds I had on Crispin's day.'
	Old men forget; yet all shall be forgot,
50	But he'll remember, with advantages,°
	What feats he did that day. Then shall our names,
	Familiar in his mouth as household words—
	Harry the King, Bedford and Exeter,
	Warwick and Talbot, Salisbury and Gloucester—
55	Be in their flowing cups freshly remembered.

eve of the saint's day

embellishments

45 Will yearly on the vigil° feast his neighbours — *eve of the saint's day*
And say, 'Tomorrow is Saint Crispian.'
Then will he strip his sleeve and show his scars
And say, 'These wounds I had on Crispin's day.'
Old men forget; yet all shall be forgot,
50 But he'll remember, with advantages,° — *embellishments*
What feats he did that day. Then shall our names,
Familiar in his mouth as household words—
Harry the King, Bedford and Exeter,
Warwick and Talbot, Salisbury and Gloucester—
55 Be in their flowing cups freshly remembered.
This story shall the good man teach his son,
And Crispin Crispian shall ne'er go by
From this day to the ending of the world
But we in it shall be rememberèd.
60 We few, we happy few, we band of brothers.
For he today that sheds his blood with me
Shall be my brother; be he ne'er so vile,° — *lowborn*
This day shall gentle his condition.[2]
And gentlemen in England now abed
65 Shall think themselves accursed they were not here,
And hold their manhoods cheap whiles any speaks
That fought with us upon Saint Crispin's day.
            Enter [Earl of] SALISBURY
SALISBURY   My sovereign lord, bestow yourself° with speed. — *take your positions*
The French are bravely in their battles° set — *battle lines*
70 And will with all expedience° charge on us. — *speed*
KING HARRY   All things are ready if our minds be so.
WARWICK   Perish the man whose mind is backward now.
KING HARRY   Thou dost not wish more help from England, coz?
WARWICK   God's will, my liege, would you and I alone,
75 Without more help, could fight this royal battle.
KING HARRY   Why now thou hast unwished five thousand men,
Which likes° me better than to wish us one.— — *pleases*
You know your places. God be with you all.
            Tucket. Enter MONTJOY
MONTJOY   Once more I come to know of thee, King Harry,
80 If for thy ransom thou wilt now compound° — *make terms*
Before thy most assurèd overthrow.
For certainly thou art so near the gulf
Thou needs must be englutted.° Besides, in mercy — *swallowed*
The Constable desires thee thou wilt mind° — *remind*
85 Thy followers of repentance, that their souls
May make a peaceful and a sweet retire
From off these fields where, wretches, their poor bodies
Must lie and fester.
KING HARRY   Who hath sent thee now?
90 MONTJOY   The Constable of France.
KING HARRY   I pray thee bear my former answer back.
Bid them achieve° me, and then sell my bones. — *get*
Good God, why should they mock poor fellows thus?
The man that once did sell the lion's skin
95 While the beast lived, was killed with hunting him.[3]

---

2. Shall raise him to gentlemanly rank.   3. *The man . . . him:* alluding to one of Aesop's fables.

A many of our bodies shall no doubt
Find native° graves, upon the which, I trust,   (English)
Shall witness live in brass of this day's work.
And those that leave their valiant bones in France,
100   Dying like men, though buried in your dunghills
They shall be famed. For there the sun shall greet them
And draw their honours reeking° up to heaven,   steaming; stinking
Leaving their earthly parts to choke your clime,
The smell whereof shall breed a plague in France.
105   Mark then abounding valour in our English,
That, being dead, like to the bullets grazing°   ricocheting
Break out into a second course of mischief,
Killing in relapse of mortality.°   another fatal outbreak
Let me speak proudly. Tell the Constable
110   We are but warriors for the working day.°   workaday warriors
Our gayness and our gilt are all besmirched
With rainy marching in the painful field.
There's not a piece of feather° in our host—   decorative plume
Good argument, I hope, we will not fly—
115   And time hath worn us into slovenry.°   filth
But by the mass, our hearts are in the trim.°   fine shape
And my poor soldiers tell me, yet ere night
They'll be in fresher robes, as they will pluck
The gay new coats o'er your French soldiers' heads,
120   And turn them out of service.[4] If they do this—
As if God please, they shall—my ransom then
Will soon be levied.[5] Herald, save thou thy labour.
Come thou no more for ransom, gentle herald.
They shall have none, I swear, but these my joints—
125   Which if they have as I will leave 'em them,
Shall yield them little. Tell the Constable.
MONTJOY   I shall, King Harry. And so fare thee well.
Thou never shalt hear herald any more.
KING HARRY   I fear thou wilt once more come for a ransom.

                                          Exit [MONTJOY]

        Enter [*Duke of* YORK]
130   YORK   My lord, most humbly on my knee I beg
The leading of the vanguard.
KING HARRY   Take it, brave York.—Now soldiers, march away,
And how thou pleasest, God, dispose the day.   *Exeunt*

                        4.4

        Alarum. Excursions.° Enter PISTOL, [*a*] FRENCH SOL-   Skirmishes
        DIER, [*and the*] BOY
PISTOL   Yield, cur.
FRENCH SOLDIER   *Je pense que vous êtes le gentilhomme de bon
        qualité.*[1]
PISTOL   Qualité? '*Calin o custure me!*'[2]
5   Art thou a gentleman? What is thy name? Discuss.
FRENCH SOLDIER   *O Seigneur Dieu!*°   *O Lord God*
PISTOL   [*aside*]   O Seigneur Dew should be a gentleman.—

---

4. Dismiss them, stripped of their servant's uniforms.
5. Collected (from the French themselves).
4.4. Location: The battlefield.

1. I think you are a gentleman of high rank.
2. The Irish refrain of a popular ballad, meaning "I am a girl from beside the Suir."

	Perpend° my words, O Seigneur Dew, and mark:	*Weigh*
	O Seigneur Dew, thou diest, on point of fox,°	*sword*
10	Except, O Seigneur, thou do give to me	
	Egregious° ransom.	*Extraordinary*

FRENCH SOLDIER   *O prenez miséricorde! Ayez pitié de moi!*[3]

PISTOL   'Moy' shall not serve, I will have forty 'moys'.[4]

Or I will fetch thy rim° out at thy throat   *stomach lining*

15   In drops of crimson blood.

FRENCH SOLDIER   *Est-il impossible d'échapper la force de ton bras?*[5]

PISTOL   Brass, cur? Thou damnèd and luxurious° mountain goat,   *lecherous*

Offer'st me brass?

FRENCH SOLDIER   *O pardonne-moi!*

20   PISTOL   Sayst thou me so? Is that a ton of moys?—

Come hither boy. Ask me this slave in French

What is his name.

BOY   *Écoutez: comment êtes-vous appelé?*[6]

FRENCH SOLDIER   *Monsieur le Fer.*

25   BOY   He says his name is Master Fer.

PISTOL   Master Fer? I'll fer him, and firk° him, and ferret° him.   *beat / savage*

Discuss the same in French unto him.

BOY   I do not know the French for fer and ferret and firk.

PISTOL   Bid him prepare, for I will cut his throat.

30   FRENCH SOLDIER   *Que dit-il, monsieur?*°   *What does he say, sir*

BOY   *Il me commande à vous dire que vous faites vous prêt, car ce*

soldat ici est disposé tout à cette heure de couper votre gorge.°   *(translates Pistol)*

PISTOL   *Oui, couper la gorge, par ma foi,*[7]

Peasant, unless thou give me crowns, brave crowns,

35   Or mangled shalt thou be by this my sword.

FRENCH SOLDIER   *O je vous supplie, pour l'amour de Dieu, me*

pardonner. Je suis le gentilhomme de bonne maison. Gardez ma

vie, et je vous donnerai deux cents écus°   *(translated by the boy)*

PISTOL   What are his words?

40   BOY   He prays you to save his life. He is a gentleman of a good

house, and for his ransom he will give you two hundred

crowns.

PISTOL   Tell him, my fury shall abate, and I the crowns will take.

FRENCH SOLDIER   *Petit monsieur, que dit-il?*[8]

45   BOY   *Encore qu'il est contre son jurement de pardonner aucun*

prisonnier; néanmoins, pour les écus que vous lui ci promettez, il

est content à vous donner la liberté, le franchisement.

FRENCH SOLDIER [*kneeling to* PISTOL]   *Sur mes genoux je vous*

donne mille remerciements, et je m'estime heureux que j'ai

50   *tombé entre les mains d'un chevalier, comme je pense, le plus*

brave, vaillant, et treis-distingué seigneur d'Angleterre.°   *(translated by the boy)*

PISTOL   Expound unto me, boy.

BOY   He gives you upon his knees a thousand thanks, and he

esteems himself happy that he hath fallen into the hands of

55   one, as he thinks, the most brave, valorous, and thrice-worthy

seigneur of England.

PISTOL   As I suck blood, I will some mercy show.

Follow me.

---

3. O take pity! Have pity on me!
4. Pistol mistakes *moi* for the name of a coin.
5. Is it impossible to escape the strength of your arm?
6. Listen: what's your name?
7. Yes, cut your throat, by my faith.
8. Little sir, what says he?

BOY *Suivez-vous le grand capitaine.*⁹
          [*Exeunt* PISTOL *and* FRENCH SOLDIER]
60 I did never know so full a voice issue from so empty a heart.
 But the saying is true: 'The empty vessel makes the greatest
 sound.' Bardolph and Nim had ten times more valour than this
 roaring devil i'th' old play, that everyone may pare his nails
 with a wooden dagger,¹ and they are both hanged, and so
65 would this be, if he durst steal anything adventurously.° I must   *recklessly*
 stay with the lackeys with the luggage of our camp. The French
 might have a good prey of us, if he knew of it, for there is none
 to guard it but boys.   *Exit*

4.5

Enter CONSTABLE, [*Dukes of*] ORLÉANS [*and*] BOURBON,
 and [*Lord*] RAMBURES
CONSTABLE *O diable!*
ORLÉANS *O Seigneur! Le jour est perdu, tout est perdu!*
BOURBON *Mort de ma vie!*¹ All is confounded,° all.   *lost*
 Reproach and everlasting shame
5 Sits mocking in our plumes.
     A short alarum
 O méchante fortune!°—[*To* RAMBURES] Do not run away.   *evil fate*
ORLÉANS We are enough yet living in the field
 To smother up the English in our throngs,
 If any order might be thought upon.
10 BOURBON The devil take order. Once more back again!
 And he that will not follow Bourbon now,
 Let him go home, and with his cap in hand
 Like a base leno° hold the chamber door   *pimp*
 Whilst by a slave no gentler° than my dog   *better born*
15 His fairest daughter is contaminated.
 CONSTABLE Disorder that hath spoiled° us friend° us now. *ruined / befriend*
 Let us on heaps go offer up our lives.
BOURBON I'll to the throng.
 Let life be short, else shame will be too long.²   *Exeunt*

4.6

Alarum. Enter KING [HARRY] *and his train,*° *with pris-*   *followers*
 oners
KING HARRY Well have we done, thrice-valiant countrymen.
 But all's not done; yet keep the French the field.
     [*Enter the Duke of* EXETER]
EXETER The Duke of York commends him to your majesty.
KING HARRY Lives he, good uncle? Thrice within this hour
5 I saw him down, thrice up again and fighting.
 From helmet to the spur, all blood he was.
EXETER In which array, brave soldier, doth he lie,
 Larding° the plain. And by his bloody side,   *Moistening*
 Yokefellow to his honour-owing° wounds,   *honorable*
10 The noble Earl of Suffolk also lies.

---

9. Follow the great captain.
1. Allegorical "Vice" characters in old-fashioned morality plays were typically armed with wooden daggers.
4.5 Location: The battlefield.
1. O the devil!

O God! The day is lost, all is lost!
 Death of my life!
2. See Additional Passages at end of play for the Folio
and quarto versions of this scene.
4.6 Location: The battlefield.

Suffolk first died, and York, all haggled over,°   *hacked up*
Comes to him, where in gore he lay insteeped,°   *soaked*
And takes him by the beard, kisses the gashes
That bloodily did yawn upon his face,
15   And cries aloud, "Tarry, dear cousin Suffolk.
My soul shall thine keep company to heaven.
Tarry, sweet soul, for mine, then fly abreast,
As in this glorious and well-foughten field
We kept together in our chivalry.'
20   Upon these words I came and cheered him up.
He smiled me in the face, raught° me his hand,   *reached*
And with a feeble grip says, 'Dear my lord,
Commend my service to my sovereign.'
So did he turn, and over Suffolk's neck
25   He threw his wounded arm, and kissed his lips,
And so espoused to death, with blood he sealed
A testament of noble-ending love.
The pretty and sweet manner of it forced
Those waters from me which I would have stopped.
30   But I had not so much of man in me,
And all my mother° came into mine eyes   *(feminine) tenderness*
And gave me up to tears.
KING HARRY   I blame you not,
For hearing this I must perforce compound°   *come to terms*
With mistful eyes, or they will issue° too.   *weep*
     Alarum
35   But hark, what new alarum is this same?
The French have reinforced their scattered men.
Then every soldier kill his prisoners.
     [*The soldiers kill their prisoners*][1]
Give the word through.
PISTOL   *Coup' la gorge.*°   *Exeunt*   *Cut the throat*

4.7

Enter [Captains] FLUELLEN *and* GOWER

FLUELLEN   Kill the poys and the luggage! 'Tis expressly against
the law of arms. 'Tis as arrant a piece of knavery, mark you
now, as can be offert. In your conscience now, is it not?
GOWER   'Tis certain there's not a boy left alive. And the cowardly
5   rascals that ran from the battle ha' done this slaughter. Besides,
they have burned and carried away all that was in the King's
tent; wherefore the King most worthily hath caused every soldier to cut his prisoner's throat. O 'tis a gallant king.
FLUELLEN   Ay, he was porn at Monmouth.° Captain Gower,   *(in Wales)*
10   what call you the town's name where Alexander the Pig was
born?
GOWER   Alexander the Great.
FLUELLEN   Why I pray you, is not 'pig' great? The pig or the
great or the mighty or the huge or the magnanimous are all
15   one reckonings, save the phrase is a little variations.°   *(for "varied")*
GOWER   I think Alexander the Great was born in Macedon. His
father was called Philip of Macedon, as I take it.
FLUELLEN   I think it is e'en Macedon where Alexander is porn.

---

1. This may or may not be done onstage.   4.7 Location: Before Henry's pavilion.

I tell you, captain, if you look in the maps of the world I warrant
20   you sall find, in the comparisons between Macedon and Monmouth, that the situations, look you, is both alike. There is a
river in Macedon, and there is also moreover a river at Monmouth. It is called Wye at Monmouth, but it is out of my prains
what is the name of the other river—but 'tis all one, 'tis alike as
25   my fingers is to my fingers, and there is salmons in both. If you
mark Alexander's life well, Harry of Monmouth's life is come
after it indifferent well.[1] For there is figures° in all things. Alex-   *comparisons*
ander, God knows, and you know, in his rages and his furies
and his wraths and his cholers° and his moods and his displea-   *angers*
30   sures and his indignations, and also being a little intoxicates in
his prains, did in his ales and his angers, look you, kill his best
friend Cleitus—

GOWER   Our King is not like him in that. He never killed any of
his friends.

35 FLUELLEN   It is not well done, mark you now, to take the tales
out of my mouth ere it is made an end and finished. I speak
but in the figures and comparisons of it. As Alexander killed his
friend Cleitus, being in his ales and his cups, so also Harry
Monmouth, being in his right wits and his good judgements,
40   turned away the fat knight with the great-belly doublet—he was
full of jests and gipes° and knaveries and mocks—I have forgot   *gibes*
his name.

GOWER   Sir John Falstaff.

FLUELLEN   That is he. I'll tell you, there is good men porn at
45   Monmouth.

GOWER   Here comes his majesty.

       Alarum. Enter KING HARRY *and* [*the English army*], *with*
       [*Duke of*] BOURBON, [*Duke of* ORLÉANS, *and other*] *pris-*
       oners.[2] *Flourish*

KING HARRY   I was not angry since I came to France
    Until this instant. Take a trumpet, herald;
    Ride thou unto the horsemen on yon hill.
50   If they will fight with us, bid them come down,
    Or void° the field: they do offend our sight.   *leave*
    If they'll do neither, we will come to them,
    And make them skirr° away as swift as stones   *scurry*
    Enforcèd° from the old Assyrian slings.   *Driven*
55   Besides, we'll cut the throats of those we have,
    And not a man of them that we shall take
    Shall taste our mercy. Go and tell them so.

       Enter MONTJOY

EXETER   Here comes the herald of the French, my liege.

GLOUCESTER   His eyes are humbler than they used to be.

60 KING HARRY   How now, what means this, herald? Know'st thou not
    That I have fined° these bones of mine for ransom?   *pledged*
    Com'st thou again for ransom?

MONTJOY   No, great King.
    I come to thee for charitable licence,°   *permission*
    That we may wander o'er this bloody field
65   To book° our dead and then to bury them,   *register*

---

1. *is . . . well:* resembles it fairly well.
2. This is a second batch of prisoners, captured after the French counterattack.

To sort our nobles from our common men—
For many of our princes, woe the while,
Lie drowned and soaked in mercenary blood.[3]
So do our vulgar° drench their peasant limbs   *common people*
70   In blood of princes, and our wounded steeds
Fret fetlock°-deep in gore, and with wild rage   *ankle*
Jerk out their armèd heels at their dead masters,
Killing them twice. O give us leave great King,
To view the field in safety, and dispose
Of their dead bodies.
75   KING HARRY   I tell thee truly, herald,
I know not if the day be ours or no.
For yet a many of your horsemen peer°   *appear*
And gallop o'er the field.
MONTJOY   The day is yours.
KING HARRY   Praisèd be God, and not our strength, for it.
80   What is this castle called that stands hard by?
MONTJOY   They call it Agincourt.
KING HARRY   Then call we this the field of Agincourt,
Fought on the day of Crispin Crispian.
FLUELLEN   Your grandfather of famous memory, an't° please   *if it*
85   your majesty, and your great-uncle Edward the Plack Prince of
Wales, as I have read in the chronicles, fought a most prave
pattle here in France.
KING HARRY   They did, Fluellen.
FLUELLEN   Your majesty says very true. If your majesties is
90   remembered of it, the Welshmen did good service in a garden
where leeks did grow, wearing leeks in their Monmouth caps,[4]
which your majesty know to this hour is an honourable badge
of the service. And I do believe your majesty takes no scorn to
wear the leek upon Saint Tavy's day.
95   KING HARRY   I wear it for a memorable honour,
For I am Welsh, you know, good countryman.
FLUELLEN   All the water in Wye° cannot wash your majesty's   *Welsh river*
Welsh plood out of your pody, I can tell you that. God pless it
and preserve it, as long as it pleases his grace, and his majesty
100   too.
KING HARRY   Thanks, good my countryman.
FLUELLEN   By Jeshu, I am your majesty's countryman. I care not
who know it, I will confess it to all the world. I need not to be
ashamed of your majesty, praised be God, so long as your maj-
105   esty is an honest man.
KING HARRY   God keep me so.
            Enter WILLIAMS [*with a glove in his cap*]
                 Our heralds go with him.
Bring me just notice° of the numbers dead   *accurate record*
On both our parts.
            Exeunt [MONTJOY, GOWER, *and English*] *heralds*
                 Call yonder fellow hither.
EXETER [*to* WILLIAMS]   Soldier, you must come to the King.
110   KING HARRY   Soldier, why wearest thou that glove in thy cap?
WILLIAMS   An't please your majesty, 'tis the gage° of one that I   *token*
should fight withal, if he be alive.

---

3. Common soldiers, unlike noblemen, fought for pay.   4. Tall, tapering caps without brims.

KING HARRY   An Englishman?

WILLIAMS   An't please your majesty, a rascal, that swaggered with
115   me last night—who, if a live, and ever dare to challenge this
glove, I have sworn to take him a box o'th' ear; or if I can see
my glove in his cap—which he swore, as he was a soldier, he
would wear if a lived—I will strike it out soundly.

KING HARRY   What think you, Captain Fluellen? Is it fit this sol-
120   dier keep his oath?

FLUELLEN   He is a craven° and a villain else, an't please your   coward
majesty, in my conscience.

KING HARRY   It may be his enemy is a gentleman of great sort,
quite from the answer of his degree.[5]

125   FLUELLEN   Though he be as good a gentleman as the devil is,
as Lucifer and Beelzebub° himself, it is necessary, look your   Satan
grace, that he keep his vow and his oath. If he be perjured, see
you now, his reputation is as arrant a villain and a Jack-sauce°   saucy knave
as ever his black shoe trod upon God's ground and his earth,
130   in my conscience, law.

KING HARRY   Then keep thy vow, sirrah, when thou meetest the
fellow.

WILLIAMS   So I will, my liege, as I live.

KING HARRY   Who serv'st thou under?

135   WILLIAMS   Under Captain Gower, my liege.

FLUELLEN   Gower is a good captain, and is good knowledge and
literatured° in the wars.   well read

KING HARRY   Call him hither to me, soldier.

WILLIAMS   I will, my liege.   *Exit*
140   KING HARRY   [*giving him Williams's other glove*]   Here, Fluellen,
wear thou this favour for me and stick it in thy cap. When
Alençon and myself were down together, I plucked this glove
from his helm. If any man challenge this, he is a friend to
Alençon and an enemy to our person. If thou encounter any
145   such, apprehend° him, an° thou dost me love.   arrest / if

FLUELLEN   Your grace does me as great honours as can be
desired in the hearts of his subjects. I would fain° see the man   gladly
that has but two legs that shall find himself aggriefed at this
glove, that is all; but I would fain see it once. An't please God
150   of his grace, that I would see.

KING HARRY   Know'st thou Gower?

FLUELLEN   He is my dear friend, an't please you.

KING HARRY   Pray thee, go seek him and bring him to my tent.

FLUELLEN   I will fetch him.   *Exit*
155   KING HARRY   My lord of Warwick and my brother Gloucester,
Follow Fluellen closely at the heels.
The glove which I have given him for a favour
May haply purchase him a box o'th' ear.
It is the soldier's. I by bargain should
160   Wear it myself. Follow, good cousin Warwick.
If that the soldier strike him, as I judge
By his blunt bearing he will keep his word,
Some sudden mischief may arise of it,
For I do know Fluellen valiant
165   And touched with choler,° hot as gunpowder,   made angry

5. Quite above responding to a challenge from one of Williams's rank.

And quickly will return an injury.°   *insult*
Follow, and see there be no harm between them.
Go you with me, uncle of Exeter.   *Exeunt [severally]*

4.8

Enter [Captain] GOWER *and* WILLIAMS
WILLIAMS   I warrant° it is to knight you, captain.   *I'm sure*
  Enter [Captain] FLUELLEN
FLUELLEN   God's will and his pleasure, captain, I beseech you
  now, come apace° to the King. There is more good toward you,   *quickly*
  peradventure,° than is in your knowledge to dream of.   *perhaps*
5 WILLIAMS   Sir, know you this glove?
FLUELLEN   Know the glove? I know the glove is a glove.
WILLIAMS [*plucking the glove from Fluellen's cap*]   I know this,
  and thus I challenge it.
    [*He*] *strikes* [FLUELLEN]
FLUELLEN   God's plood, and his! An arrant traitor as any's in the
10 universal world, or in France, or in England.
GOWER [*to* WILLIAMS]   How now, sir? You villain!
WILLIAMS   Do you think I'll be forsworn?
FLUELLEN   Stand away, Captain Gower. I will give treason his
  payment into plows, I warrant you.
15 WILLIAMS   I am no traitor.
FLUELLEN   That's a lie in thy throat. I charge you in his majesty's
  name, apprehend him. He's a friend of the Duke Alençon's.
    Enter [Earl of] WARWICK *and [Duke of]* GLOUCESTER
WARWICK   How now, how now, what's the matter?
FLUELLEN   My lord of Warwick, here is—praised be God for it—
20 a most contagious° treason come to light, look you. as you shall   *noxious*
  desire in a summer's day.
    Enter KING [HARRY] *and [Duke of]* EXETER
  Here is his majesty.
KING HARRY   How now, what is the matter?
FLUELLEN   My liege, here is a villain and a traitor that, look your
25 grace, has struck the glove which your majesty is take out of
  the helmet of Alençon.
WILLIAMS   My liege, this was my glove—here is the fellow° of   *mate*
  it—and he that I gave it to in change promised to wear it in his
  cap. I promised to strike him, if he did. I met this man with my
30 glove in his cap, and I have been as good as my word.
FLUELLEN   Your majesty hear now, saving your majesty's manhood, what an arrant rascally beggarly lousy knave it is. I hope
  your majesty is pear° me testimony and witness, and will   *(for "will bear")*
  avouchment° that this is the glove of Alençon that your maj-   *(for "vouch")*
35 esty is give me, in your conscience now.
KING HARRY   Give me thy glove, soldier.
  Look, here is the fellow of it.
  'Twas I indeed thou promisèd'st to strike,
  And thou hast given me most bitter terms.°   *words*
40 FLUELLEN   An't please your majesty, let his neck answer for it, if
  there is any martial law in the world.
KING HARRY   How canst thou make me satisfaction?
WILLIAMS   All offences, my lord, come from the heart. Never
  came any from mine that might offend your majesty.

4.8 Location: Before Henry's pavilion.

45 KING HARRY It was ourself thou didst abuse.

WILLIAMS Your majesty came not like yourself. You appeared to
me but as a common man. Witness the night, your garments,
your lowliness. And what your highness suffered under that
shape, I beseech you take it for your own fault, and not mine,
50 for had you been as I took you for, I made no offence. Therefore I beseech your highness pardon me.

KING HARRY Here, Uncle Exeter, fill this glove with crowns
And give it to this fellow.—Keep it, fellow,
And wear it for an honour in thy cap
55 Till I do challenge it.—Give him the crowns.
—And captain, you must needs be friends with him.

FLUELLEN By this day and this light, the fellow has mettle
enough in his belly.—Hold, there is twelve pence for you, and
I pray you to serve God, and keep you out of prawls and prab-
60 bles and quarrels and dissensions, and I warrant you it is the
better for you.

WILLIAMS I will none of your money.

FLUELLEN It is with a good will. I can tell you, it will serve you
to mend your shoes. Come, wherefore should you be so pash-
65 ful? Your shoes is not so good. 'Tis a good shilling, I warrant
you, or I will change it.[1]

Enter [an English] HERALD

KING HARRY Now, herald, are the dead numbered?

HERALD Here is the number of the slaughtered French.

KING HARRY What prisoners of good sort° are taken, uncle?   *high rank*

70 EXETER Charles, Duke of Orléans, nephew to the King;
Jean, Duke of Bourbon, and Lord Boucicault;
Of other lords and barons, knights and squires,
Full fifteen hundred, besides common men.

KING HARRY This note doth tell me of ten thousand French
75 That in the field lie slain. Of princes in this number
And nobles bearing banners,° there lie dead   *coats of arms*
One hundred twenty-six; added to these,
Of knights, esquires, and gallant gentlemen,
Eight thousand and four hundred, of the which
80 Five hundred were but yesterday dubbed knights.
So that in these ten thousand they have lost
There are but sixteen hundred mercenaries;
The rest are princes, barons, lords, knights, squires,
And gentlemen of blood and quality.
85 The names of those their nobles that lie dead:
Charles Delabret, High Constable of France;
Jaques of Châtillion, Admiral of France;
The Master of the Crossbows, Lord Rambures;
Great-Master of France, the brave Sir Guiscard Dauphin;
90 Jean, Duke of Alençon; Antony, Duke of Brabant,
The brother to the Duke of Burgundy;
And Édouard, Duke of Bar; of lusty earls,
Grandpré and Roussi, Fauconbridge and Foix,
Beaumont and Marle, Vaudemont and Lestrelles.
95 Here was a royal fellowship of death.

---

1. Williams may or may not take the money.

Where is the number of our English dead?
[He is given another paper]
Edward the Duke of York, the Earl of Suffolk,
Sir Richard Keighley, Davy Gam Esquire;
None else of name,° and of all other men   high rank
100 But five-and-twenty. O God, thy arm was here,
And not to us, but to thy arm alone
Ascribe we all. When, without stratagem,
But in plain shock° and even play of battle,   confrontation
Was ever known so great and little loss
105 On one part and on th'other? Take it God,
For it is none but thine.

EXETER   'Tis wonderful.

KING HARRY   Come, go we in procession to the village,
And be it death proclaimèd through our host
To boast of this, or take that praise from God
110 Which is his only.

FLUELLEN   Is it not lawful, an't please your majesty, to tell how
many is killed?

KING HARRY   Yes, captain, but with this acknowledgement,
That God fought for us.

115 FLUELLEN   Yes, in my conscience, he did us great good.

KING HARRY   Do we all holy rites:
Let there be sung *Non nobis* and *Te Deum*,[2]
The dead with charity enclosed in clay;°   buried with pious love
And then to Calais, and to England then,
120 Where ne'er from France arrived more-happy° men.   *Exeunt*   more fortunate

5.0

Enter CHORUS

CHORUS   Vouchsafe° to those that have not read the story   *Allow*
That I may prompt them—and of such as have,
I humbly pray them to admit th'excuse
Of time, of numbers, and due course of things,
5 Which cannot in their huge and proper life
Be here presented. Now we bear the King
Toward Calais. Grant him there; there seen,
Heave him away upon your wingèd thoughts
Athwart the sea. Behold, the English beach
10 Pales-in° the flood, with men, maids, wives, and boys,   *Fences in*
Whose shouts and claps out-voice the deep-mouthed sea,
Which like a mighty whiffler[1] fore the King
Seems to prepare his way. So let him land,
And solemnly see him set on to London.
15 So swift a pace hath thought, that even now
You may imagine him upon Blackheath,[2]
Where that his lords desire him to have borne
His bruisèd helmet and his bended sword
Before him through the city; he forbids it,
20 Being free from vainness and self-glorious pride,
Giving full trophy, signal, and ostent°   honor for the victory

---

2. *Non nobis* is Psalm 115, beginning "Not unto us, O
Lord, not unto us, but unto thy name give the glory." *Te
Deum* is a canticle of thanks beginning "We praise thee,
O God."

5.0
1. Official who cleared the way for a procession.
2. Open space outside London.

Quite from himself, to God. But now behold,
In the quick forge and working-house of thought,
How London doth pour out her citizens.
25 The Mayor and all his brethren, in best sort,°   *clothing*
Like to the senators of th'antique Rome
With the plebeians° swarming at their heels,   *commoners*
Go forth and fetch their conqu'ring Caesar in—
As, by a lower but high-loving likelihood,[3]
30 Were now the General of our gracious Empress[4]—
As in good time he may—from Ireland coming,
Bringing rebellion broachèd° on his sword,   *impaled*
How many would the peaceful city quit
To welcome him! Much more, and much more cause,
35 Did they this Harry. Now in London place him;
As yet the lamentation of the French
Invites the King of England's stay at home.
The Emperor's coming[5] in behalf of France,
To order peace between them [
40   ][6] and omit
All the occurrences, whatever chanced,
Till Harry's back-return again to France.[7]
There must we bring him, and myself have played
The interim by rememb'ring° you 'tis past.   *reminding*
45 Then brook° abridgement, and your eyes advance,   *tolerate*
After your thoughts, straight back again to France.   *Exit*

5.1

Enter [Captain] GOWER *and [Captain]* FLUELLEN *[with
a leek in his cap and a cudgel]*

GOWER   Nay, that's right. But why wear you your leek today?
Saint Davy's day is past.
FLUELLEN   There is occasions and causes why and wherefore in
all things. I will tell you, ass my friend, Captain Gower. The
5 rascally scald° beggarly lousy pragging knave Pistol—which you   *scabby*
and yourself and all the world know to be no petter than a
fellow, look you now, of no merits—he is come to me, and
prings me pread and salt yesterday,° look you, and bid me eat   *(on St. Davy's Day)*
my leek. It was in a place where I could not breed no con-
10 tention with him, but I will be so bold as to wear it in my cap
till I see him once again, and then I will tell him a little piece
of my desires.
        Enter [Ensign] PISTOL
GOWER   Why, here a° comes, swelling like a turkey-cock.   *he*
FLUELLEN   'Tis no matter for his swellings nor his turkey-
15 cocks.—God pless you Ensign Pistol, you scurvy lousy knave,
God pless you.
PISTOL   Ha, art thou bedlam?° Dost thou thirst, base Trojan,°   *crazy / villain*
To have me fold up Parca's[1] fatal web?
Hence! I am qualmish° at the smell of leek.   *nauseated*

---

3. Lovingly anticipated probability.
4. *General . . . Empress:* Earl of Essex (see Introduction).
5. Sigismund; the Holy Roman Emperor, attempted, and failed, to negotiate a peace between France and England.
6. A line is evidently missing here.
7. Henry invaded France a second and third time, in 1417 and 1421; Act 5 begins in the latter year.
5.1 Location: The English camp.
1. The Parcae were the mythological Fates who spun and cut the thread of life.

20 FLUELLEN I peseech you heartily, scurvy lousy knave, at my
desires and my requests and my petitions, to eat, look you, this
leek. Because, look you, you do not love it, nor your affections
and your appetites and your digestions does not agree with it. I
would desire you to eat it.

25 PISTOL Not for Cadwallader° and all his goats.   *last Welsh king*

FLUELLEN There is one goat for you. [*He*] *strikes* [PISTOL Will
you be so good, scald° knave, as eat it?   *worthless*

PISTOL Base Trojan, thou shalt die.

FLUELLEN You say very true, scald knave, when God's will is. I
30 will desire you to live in the mean time, and eat your victuals.°   *food*
Come, there is sauce for it. [*He strikes him*] You called me
yesterday 'mountain-squire',° but I will make you today a   *(Wales is mountainous)*
'squire of low degree'. I pray you, fall to. If you can mock a leek
you can eat a leek.
        [*He strikes him*]

35 GOWER Enough, captain, you have astonished° him.   *stunned*

FLUELLEN By Jesu, I will make him eat some part of my leek, or
I will peat his pate° four days and four nights.—Bite, I pray you.   *head*
It is good for your green° wound and your ploody coxccmb.°   *fresh/head*

PISTOL Must I bite?

40 FLUELLEN Yes, certainly, and out of doubt and out of question
too, and ambiguities.

PISTOL By this leek, I will most horribly revenge—
        [FLUELLEN *threatens him*]
I eat and eat—I swear—

FLUELLEN Eat, I pray you. Will you have some more sauce to
45 your leek? There is not enough leek to swear by.

PISTOL Quiet thy cudgel,° thou dost see I eat.   *wooden club*

FLUELLEN Much good do you, scald knave, heartily. Nay, pray
you throw none away. The skin is good for your broken coxcomb. When you take occasions to see leeks hereafter, I pray
50 you mock at 'em, that is all.

PISTOL Good.

FLUELLEN Ay, leeks is good. Hold you, there is a groat° to heal   *fourpence*
your pate.

PISTOL Me, a groat?

55 FLUELLEN Yes, verily,° and in truth you shall take it, or I have   *truly*
another leek in my pocket which you shall eat.

PISTOL I take thy groat in earnest° of revenge.   *advance payment*

FLUELLEN If I owe you anything, I will pay you in cudgels. You
shall be a woodmonger, and buy nothing of me but cudgels.
60 God b'wi' you, and keep you, and heal your pate.   *Exit*

PISTOL All hell shall stir for this.

GOWER Go, go, you are a counterfeit cowardly knave. Will you
mock at an ancient tradition, begun upon an honourable
respect and worn as a memorable trophy of predeceased
65 valour, and dare not avouch° in your deeds any of your words?   *prove*
I have seen you gleeking and galling° at this gentleman twice   *jesting and annoying*
or thrice. You thought, because he could not speak English in
the native garb, he could not therefore handle an English cudgel. You find it otherwise. And henceforth let a Welsh correc-
70 tion teach you a good English condition. Fare ye well.   *Exit*

PISTOL Doth Fortune play the hussy° with me now?   *whore*
News have I that my Nell is dead

I'th' spital of a malady of France,°   venereal disease
And there my rendezvous° is quite cut off.   refuge
75   Old I do wax, and from my weary limbs
Honour is cudgelled. Well, bawd° I'll turn,   pimp
And something lean to cutpurse of quick hand.
To England will I steal, and there I'll steal,
And patches will I get unto these cudgelled scars,
80   And swear I got them in the Gallia° wars.   *Exit*   French

5.2

Enter at one door KING [HARRY, *Dukes of*] EXETER [*and*
CLARENCE, *Earl of*] WARWICK, *and other lords; at
another,* KING [CHARLES *the Sixth*] of France, QUEEN ISA-
BEL, *the Duke of* BURGUNDY, *and other French,* [*among
them Princess*] CATHERINE [*and* ALICE]

KING HARRY   Peace to this meeting, wherefor° we are met.   for which
Unto our brother France and to our sister,
Health and fair time of day. Joy and good wishes
To our most fair and princely cousin Catherine;
5   And as a branch and member of this royalty,
By whom this great assembly is contrived,
We do salute you, Duke of Burgundy.
And princes French, and peers, health to you all.
KING CHARLES   Right joyous are we to behold your face.
10   Most worthy brother England, fairly met.
So are you, princes English, every one.
QUEEN ISABEL   So happy be the issue,° brother England,   outcome
Of this good day and of this gracious meeting,
As we are now glad to behold your eyes—
15   Your eyes which hitherto have borne in them,
Against the French that met them in their bent,°   glance
The fatal balls° of murdering basilisks.[1]   eyeballs; cannonballs
The venom of such looks we fairly hope
Have lost their quality,° and that this day   nature
20   Shall change all griefs and quarrels into love.
KING HARRY   To cry amen to that, thus we appear.
QUEEN ISABEL   You English princes all, I do salute you.
BURGUNDY   My duty to you both, on equal love,
Great Kings of France and England. That I have laboured
25   With all my wits, my pains, and strong endeavours,
To bring your most imperial majesties
Unto this bar° and royal interview,   court
Your mightiness on both parts best can witness.
Since, then, my office hath so far prevailed
30   That face to face and royal eye to eye
You have congreeted,° let it not disgrace me   met
If I demand, before this royal view,
What rub° or what impediment there is   hindrance
Why that the naked, poor, and mangled peace,
35   Dear nurse of arts, plenties, and joyful births,
Should not in this best garden of the world,
Our fertile France, put up her lovely visage?
Alas, she hath from France too long been chased,

5.2 Location: The French court.   1. Fabulous animals able to kill with a glance.

	And all her husbandry° doth lie on heaps,	*agriculture*
40	Corrupting in it° own fertility.	*its*
	Her vine, the merry cheerer of the heart,	
	Unprunèd dies; her hedges even-plashed°	*interwoven*
	Like prisoners wildly overgrown with hair	
	Put forth disordered twigs; her fallow leas°	*unplanted fields*
45	The darnel, hemlock, and rank fumitory°	*kinds of weeds*
	Doth root upon, while that the coulter° rusts	*plow*
	That should deracinate° such savagery.	*root out*
	The even mead°—that erst brought sweetly forth	*meadow*
	The freckled cowslip, burnet, and green clover—	
50	Wanting the scythe, all uncorrected, rank,	
	Conceives by idleness,° and nothing teems	*Breeds worthless things*
	But hateful docks, rough thistles, kecksies, burs,°	*(all are weeds)*
	Losing both beauty and utility.	
	An° all our vineyards, fallows, meads, and hedges,	*And if*
55	Defective in their natures, grow to wildness,	
	Even so our houses and ourselves and children	
	Have lost, or do not learn for want of time,	
	The sciences° that should become° our country,	*knowledge / adorn*
	But grow like savages—as soldiers will	
60	That nothing do but meditate on blood—	
	To swearing and stern looks, diffused° attire,	*disordered*
	And everything that seems unnatural.	
	Which to reduce into our former favour²	
	You are assembled, and my speech entreats	
65	That I may know the let° why gentle peace	*impediment*
	Should not expel these inconveniences	
	And bless us with her former qualities.	
	KING HARRY If, Duke of Burgundy, you would the peace	
	Whose want gives growth to th'imperfections	
70	Which you have cited, you must buy that peace	
	With full accord to all our just demands,	
	Whose tenors° and particular effects	*general principles*
	You have enscheduled briefly in your hands.	
	BURGUNDY The King hath heard them, to the which as yet	
	There is no answer made.	
75	KING HARRY Well then, the peace,	
	Which you before so urged, lies in his answer.	
	KING CHARLES I have but with a cursitory° eye	*cursory*
	O'erglanced the articles. Pleaseth your grace	
	To appoint some of your council presently	
80	To sit with us once more, with better heed	
	To re-survey them, we will suddenly	
	Pass our accept and peremptory° answer.	*approved and definite*
	KING HARRY Brother, we shall.—Go Uncle Exeter	
	And brother Clarence, and you, brother Gloucester;	
85	Warwick and Huntingdon, go with the King,	
	And take with you free power to ratify,	
	Augment, or alter, as your wisdoms best	
	Shall see advantageable for our dignity,	
	Anything in or out of our demands,	
90	And we'll consign° thereto.—Will you, fair sister,	*agree*

2. To revert to our old appearance.

Go with the princes, or stay here with us?

QUEEN   Our gracious brother, I will go with them.
Haply° a woman's voice may do some good   *Perhaps*
When articles too nicely° urged be stood on.   *punctiliously*

95   KING HARRY   Yet leave our cousin Catherine here with us.
She is our capital° demand, comprised   *chief*
Within the fore-rank of our articles.

QUEEN   She hath good leave.
         Exeunt [all but] KING HARRY, CATHERINE, *and* [ALICE]
         the gentlewoman

KING HARRY   Fair Catherine, and most fair,
Will you vouchsafe to teach a soldier terms
100 Such as will enter at a lady's ear
And plead his love-suit to her gentle heart?

CATHERINE   Your majesty shall mock at me. I cannot speak your
England.

KING HARRY   O fair Catherine, if you will love me soundly with
105 your French heart, I will be glad to hear you confess it brokenly
with your English tongue. Do you like me, Kate?

CATHERINE   *Pardonnez-moi,*° I cannot tell vat is 'like me'.   *Excuse me*

KING HARRY   An angel is like you, Kate, and you are like an
angel.

110 CATHERINE [*to* ALICE]   *Que dit-il?—que je suis semblable à les
anges?*

ALICE   *Oui, vraiment—sauf votre grâce—ainsi dit-il.*[3]

KING HARRY   I said so, dear Catherine, and I must not blush to
affirm it.

115 CATHERINE   *O bon Dieu!*° *Les langues des hommes sont pleines*   *O good God*
de tromperies.°   *(translated below)*

KING HARRY   What says she, fair one? That the tongues of men
are full of deceits?

ALICE   *Oui,* dat de tongeus of de mans is be full of deceits—dat
120 is de Princess.

KING HARRY   The Princess is the better Englishwoman. I'faith,
Kate, my wooing is fit for thy understanding. I am glad thou
canst speak no better English, for if thou couldst, thou wouldst
find me such a plain king that thou wouldst think I had sold
125 my farm to buy my crown. I know no ways to mince it in love,
but directly to say, 'I love you'; then if you urge me farther than
to say, 'Do you in faith?', I wear out my suit. Give me your
answer, i'faith do, and so clap° hands and a bargain. How say   *shake*
you, lady?

130 CATHERINE   *Sauf votre honneur,*° me understand well.   *Save your honor*

KING HARRY   Marry, if you would put me to verses, or to dance
for your sake, Kate, why, you undid me. For the one I have
neither words nor measure,° and for the other I have no   *meter*
strength in measure°—yet a reasonable measure in strength. If   *talent for dancing*
135 I could win a lady at leap-frog, or by vaulting into my saddle
with my armour on my back, under the correction of bragging
be it spoken, I should quickly leap into a wife. Or if I might
buffet° for my love, or bound my horse for her favours, I could   *box*
lay on like a butcher, and sit like a jackanapes,° never off. But *monkey*
140 before God, Kate, I cannot look greenly,° nor gasp out my elo-   *abashed*

3. What does he say? That I am like an angel? Yes, truly, save your grace, he says that.

quence, nor I have no cunning in protestation—only downright oaths, which I never use till urged, nor never break for
urging. If thou canst love a fellow of this temper,° Kate, whose   *makeup*
face is not worth sunburning, that never looks in his glass° for   *mirror*
145   love of anything he sees there, let thine eye be thy cook. I speak
to thee plain soldier: if thou canst love me for this, take me. If
not, to say to thee that I shall die, is true—but for thy love, by
the Lord, no. Yet I love thee, too. And while thou livest, dear
Kate, take a fellow of plain and uncoined° constancy, for he   *not in common use*
150   perforce must do thee right, because he hath not the gift to
woo in other places. For these fellows of infinite tongue, that
can rhyme themselves into ladies' favours, they do always reason themselves out again. What! A speaker is but a prater,° a   *chatterer*
rhyme is but a ballad; a good leg will fall, a straight back will
155   stoop, a black beard will turn white, a curled pate will grow
bald, a fair face will wither, a full eye will wax° hollow, but a   *become*
good heart, Kate, is the sun and the moon—or rather the sun
and not the moon, for it shines bright and never changes, but
keeps his course truly. If thou would have such a one, take me;
160   and take me, take a soldier; take a soldier, take a king. And
what sayst thou then to my love? Speak, my fair—and fairly, I
pray thee.

CATHERINE   Is it possible dat I sould love de *ennemi* of France?

KING HARRY   No, it is not possible you should love the enemy of
165   France, Kate. But in loving me, you should love the friend of
France, for I love France so well that I will not part with a
village of it, I will have it all mine; and Kate, when France is
mine, and I am yours, then yours is France, and you are mine.

CATHERINE   I cannot tell vat is dat.

170   KING HARRY   No, Kate? I will tell thee in French—which I am
sure will hang upon my tongue like a new-married wife about
her husband's neck, hardly to be shook off. *Je quand suis le*
possesseur de France, et quand vous avez le possession de moi—
let me see, what then? Saint Denis be my speed!—*donc vôtre*
175   *est France, et vous êtes mienne.*[4] It is as easy for me, Kate, to
conquer the kingdom as to speak so much more French. I shall
never move° thee in French, unless it be to laugh at me.   *persuade*

CATHERINE *Sauf votre honneur, le français que vous parlez il est*
meilleur que l'anglais lequel je parle.[5]

180   KING HARRY   No, faith, is't not, Kate. But thy speaking of my
tongue, and I thine, most truly-falsely, must needs be granted
to be much at one.° But Kate, dost thou understand thus much   *alike; united*
English? Canst thou love me?

CATHERINE I cannot tell.

185   KING HARRY   Can any of your neighbours tell, Kate? I'll ask them.
Come, I know thou lovest me, and at night when you come
into your closet° you'll question this gentlewoman about me,   *bedchamber*
and I know, Kate, you will to her dispraise those parts° in me   *qualities*
that you love with your heart. But good Kate, mock me merci-
190   fully—the rather, gentle princess, because I love thee cruelly.
If ever thou be'st mine, Kate—as I have a saving faith within
me tells me thou shalt—I get thee with scrambling,° and thou   *fighting*

4. Translation of the last part of his previous speech.
5. Saving your honor, the French you speak is better than the English I speak.

must therefore needs prove a good soldier-breeder. Shall not
thou and I, between Saint Denis and Saint George,[6] com-
195 pound a boy, half-French half-English, that shall go to Con-
stantinople and take the Turk by the beard? Shall we not? What
sayst thou, my fair flower-de-luce?[7]

CATHERINE   I do not know dat.

KING HARRY   No, 'tis hereafter to know, but now to promise. Do
200 but now promise, Kate, you will endeavour for your French
part of such a boy, and for my English moiety° take the word   half
of a king and a bachelor. How answer you, *la plus belle Catherine du monde, mon très chère et divine déesse?*[8]

CATHERINE   Your *majesté 'ave faux*° French enough to deceive   false
205 de most *sage demoiselle*° dat is *en France*.   maiden

KING HARRY   Now fie upon my false French! By mine honour,
in true English, I love thee, Kate. By which honour I dare not
swear thou lovest me, yet my blood° begins to flatter me that   instinct
thou dost, notwithstanding the poor and untempering° effect of   uningratiating
210 my visage. Now beshrew° my father's ambition! He was think-   curse
ing of civil wars when he got me; therefore was I created with
a stubborn outside, with an aspect° of iron, that when I come   a face
to woo ladies I fright them. But in faith, Kate, the elder I wax
the better I shall appear. My comfort is that old age, that ill
215 layer-up° of beauty, can do no more spoil upon my face. Thou   preserver
hast me, if thou hast me, at the worst, and thou shalt wear me,
if thou wear me, better and better; and therefore tell me, most
fair Catherine, will you have me? Put off your maiden blushes,
avouch the thoughts of your heart with the looks of an empress,
220 take me by the hand and say, 'Harry of England, I am thine'—
which word thou shalt no sooner bless mine ear withal, but I
will tell thee aloud, 'England is thine, Ireland is thine, France
is thine, and Henry Plantagenet is thine'—who, though I speak
it before his face, if he be not fellow° with the best king; thou   equal
225 shalt find the best king of good fellows. Come, your answer in
broken music°—for thy voice is music and thy English broken.   music in parts
Therefore, queen of all, Catherine, break thy mind to me in
broken English: wilt thou have me?

CATHERINE   Dat is as it shall please de *roi mon père*.°   King my father

230 KING HARRY   Nay, it will please him well, Kate. It shall please
him, Kate.

CATHERINE   Den it sall also content me.

KING HARRY   Upon that I kiss your hand, and I call you my
queen.

235 CATHERINE *Laissez, mon seigneur, laissez, laissez! Ma foi, je ne
veux point que vous abbaissez votre grandeur en baisant la main
d'une de votre seigneurie indigne serviteur. Excusez-moi, je vous
supplie, mon treis-puissant seigneur.*[9]

KING HARRY   Then I will kiss your lips, Kate.

240 CATHERINE   *Les dames et demoiselles pour être baisées devant
leurs noces, il n'est pas la coutume de France.*°   (translated below)

KING HARRY [*to* ALICE]   Madam my interpreter, what says she?

ALICE   Dat it is not be de *façon pour les*° ladies of France—I   fashion for the
cannot tell vat is *baiser en*° Anglish.   "kiss" in

---

6. Patron saints of France and England.
7. Fleur-de-lis, French national emblem.
8. The most beautiful Catherine in the world, my very
dear and divine goddess.

9. Stop, my lord, stop, stop! My faith, I do not want you
to lower your grandeur by kissing the hand of one of
your humble servants. Excuse me, I beseech you, my
very powerful lord.

245 KING HARRY To kiss.

ALICE Your *majesté entend* bettre *que moi*.[1]

KING HARRY It is not a fashion for the maids in France to kiss
before they are married, would she say?

ALICE *Oui, vraiment*.° — Yes, truly

250 KING HARRY O Kate, nice° customs curtsy to great kings. Dear — fastidious
Kate, you and I cannot be confined within the weak list° of a — barrier
country's fashion. We are the makers of manners, Kate, and the
liberty that follows our places stops the mouth of all find-faults,
as I will do yours, for upholding the nice fashion of your coun-

255 try in denying me a kiss. Therefore, patiently and yielding. [*He
kisses her*] You have witchcraft in your lips, Kate. There is more
eloquence in a sugar touch of them than in the tongues of the
French Council, and they should sooner persuade Harry of
England than a general petition of monarchs. Here comes

260 your father.

Enter KING [CHARLES, QUEEN ISABEL, *the Duke of* BUR-
GUNDY,] *and the French* [*and*] *English lords*

BURGUNDY God save your majesty. My royal cousin, teach you
our princess English?

KING HARRY I would have her learn, my fair cousin, how perfectly I love her, and that is good English.

265 BURGUNDY Is she not apt?

KING HARRY Our tongue is rough, coz,° and my condition is not — kinsman
smooth, so that having neither the voice nor the heart of flattery
about me I cannot so conjure up the spirit of love in her that
he will appear in his true likeness.

270 BURGUNDY Pardon the frankness of my mirth, if I answer you for
that. If you would conjure in her, you must make a circle;[2] if
conjure up love in her in his true likeness, he must appear
naked and blind.° Can you blame her then, being a maid yet — (like Cupid, god of love)
rosed over with the virgin crimson of modesty, if she deny the

275 appearance of a naked blind boy in her naked seeing self? It
were, my lord, a hard condition for a maid to consign to

KING HARRY Yet they do wink° and yield, as love is blind and — close their eyes
enforces.

BURGUNDY They are then excused, my lord, when they see not
280 what they do.

KING HARRY Then, good my lord, teach your cousin to consent
winking.

BURGUNDY I will wink on her to consent, my lord, if you will
teach her to know my meaning. For maids, well summered

285 and warm kept, are like flies at Bartholomew-tide:° blind, — August 24
though they have their eyes. And then they will endure handling, which before would not abide looking on.

KING HARRY This moral ties me over to time and a hot summer,
and so I shall catch the fly, your cousin, in the latter end,[3] and
290 she must be blind too.

BURGUNDY As love is, my lord, before that it loves.

KING HARRY It is so. And you may, some of you, thank love for
my blindness, who cannot see many a fair French city for one
fair French maid that stands in my way.

---

1. Your majesty understands better than I.   devils).
2. By embracing her (sorcerers drew circles to call up   3. At last; in the backside.

295 KING CHARLES   Yes, my lord, you see them perspectively,[4] the
cities turned into a maid—for they are all girdled with maiden
walls that war hath never entered.
KING HARRY   Shall Kate be my wife?
KING CHARLES   So please you.
300 KING HARRY   I am content, so the maiden° cities you talk of may   *unconquered*
wait on her: so the maid that stood in the way for my wish shall
show me the way to my will.
KING CHARLES   We have consented to all terms of reason.
KING HARRY   Is't so, my lords of England?
305 WARWICK   The King hath granted every article:
His daughter first, and so in sequel all,
According to their firm proposèd natures.
EXETER   Only he hath not yet subscribèd° this: *signed to*
where your majesty demands that the King of France, having
310 any occasion to write for matter of grant,° shall name your high-   *in formal documents*
ness in this form and with this addition: [*reads*] in French,
Notre très cher fils Henri, Roi d'Angleterre, Héritier de France,
and thus in Latin, *Praeclarissimus filius noster Henricus, Rex
Angliae et Haeres Franciae.*[5]
315 KING CHARLES   Nor this I have not, brother, so denied,
But your request shall make me let it pass.
KING HARRY   I pray you then, in love and dear alliance,
Let that one article rank with the rest,
And thereupon give me your daughter.
320 KING CHARLES   Take her, fair son, and from her blood raise up
Issue° to me, that the contending kingdoms   *Offspring*
Of France and England, whose very shores look pale
With envy of each other's happiness,
May cease their hatred, and this dear conjunction°   *loving union*
325 Plant neighbourhood° and Christian-like accord   *neighborliness*
In their sweet bosoms, that never war advance
His bleeding sword 'twixt England and fair France.
ALL   Amen.
KING HARRY   Now welcome, Kate, and bear me witness all
330 That here I kiss her as my sovereign Queen.
                    Flourish
QUEEN ISABEL   God, the best maker of all marriages,
Combine your hearts in one, your realms in one.
As man and wife, being two, are one in love,
So be there 'twixt your kingdoms such a spousal
335 That never may ill office° or fell° jealousy,   *bad action / cruel*
Which troubles oft the bed of blessèd marriage,
Thrust in between the paction° of these kingdoms   *agreement*
To make divorce of their incorporate league;
That English may as French, French Englishmen,
340 Receive each other, God speak this 'Amen'.
ALL   Amen.
KING HARRY   Prepare we for our marriage. On which day,
My lord of Burgundy, we'll take your oath,
And all the peers', for surety of our leagues.

4. In a lens that produces optical illusions.
5. Our very dear son Henry, King of England, heir of France.

345 Then shall I swear to Kate, and you to me,
And may our oaths well kept and prosp'rous be.

Sennet.° Exeunt   Ceremonial trumpet call

Epilogue

Enter CHORUS[1]

CHORUS   Thus far with rough and all-unable pen
Our bending° author hath pursued the story,   (over a desk)
In little room confining mighty men,
Mangling by starts the full course of their glory.
5   Small time, but in that small most greatly lived
This star of England. Fortune made his sword,
By which the world's best garden he achieved,
And of it left his son imperial lord.
Henry the Sixth, in infant bands° crowned king   swaddling clothes
10   Of France and England, did this king succeed,
Whose state so many had the managing
That they lost France and made his England bleed,
Which oft our stage hath shown[2]—and, for their sake,
In your fair minds let this acceptance take.°   [*Exit*]   this play find favor

Additional Passages

The Dauphin / Bourbon variant, which usually involves only the speech prefixes,
has several consequences for the dialogue and structure of 4.5. Following are the
edited Folio and quarto versions of this scene.

A. Folio

Enter CONSTABLE, ORLÉANS, BOURBON, DAUPHIN, and
RAMBURES

CONSTABLE   *O diable!*
ORLÉANS   *O Seigneur! Le jour est perdu, tout est perdu.*
DAUPHIN   *Mort de ma vie!* All is confounded, all.
Reproach and everlasting shame
5   Sits mocking in our plumes.
A short alarum
O méchante fortune! Do not run away.   [*Exit* RAMBURES]
CONSTABLE   Why, all our ranks are broke.
DAUPHIN   O perdurable shame! Let's stab ourselves:
Be these the wretches that we played at dice for?
10   ORLÉANS   Is this the king we sent to for his ransom?
BOURBON   Shame, an eternall shame, nothing but shame!
Let us die in pride. In once more, back again!
And he that will not follow Bourbon now,
Let him go home, and with his cap in hand
15   Like a base leno hold the chamber door,
Whilst by a slave no gentler than my dog
His fairest daughter is contaminated.
CONSTABLE   Disorder that hath spoiled us, friend us now,
Let us on heaps go offer up our lives.
20   ORLÉANS   We are enough yet living in the field
To smother up the English in our throngs,

---

1. The following lines form a sonnet.
2. In *1 Henry VI, The First Part of the Contention* (2

Henry VI), Richard Duke of York (3 Henry VI), and
Richard III.

If any order might be thought upon.
BOURBON   The devil take order now. I'll to the throng.
Let life be short, else shame will be too long.   *Exeunt*

B. Quarto
        Enter the four French lords: [*the* CONSTABLE, ORLÉANS,
        BOURBON, *and* GEBON]
    GEBON   *O diabello!*°   devil
    CONSTABLE   *Mort de ma vie!*
    ORLÉANS   O what a day is this!
    BOURBON   *O jour de honte,*° all is gone, all is lost.   day of shame
5   CONSTABLE   We are enough yet living in the field
    To smother up the English,
    If any order might be thought upon.
    BOURBON   A plague of order! Once more to the field!
    And he that will not follow Bourbon now,
10   Let him go home, and with his cap in hand,
    Like a base leno hold the chamber door,
    Whilst by a slave no gentler than my dog
    His fairest daughter is contaminated.
    CONSTABLE   Disorder that hath spoiled us, right us now.
15   Come we in heaps, we'll offer up our lives
    Unto these English, or else die with fame.
    BOURBON   Come, come along.
    Let's die with honour, our shame doth last too long.   *Exeunt*

Julius Caesar

In *Julius Caesar*, Shakespeare dramatizes incidents that seem not merely locally momentous but of world-historical significance. Indeed, one of the protagonists of his play, Caius Cassius, eagerly anticipates his own impersonated presence on Shakespeare's stage:

> How many ages hence
> Shall this our lofty scene be acted over,
> In states unborn and accents yet unknown.
> (3.1.112–14)

Cassius correctly predicts that his own actions, although they will eventually become ancient history, will nonetheless remain compelling to people far removed in time and place from the original events. When Shakespeare imagines ancient Romans, he imagines not people famous by accident, but people constantly aware that the eyes of the world are upon them, and will remain upon them for centuries to come.

The Romans' unbridled sense of self-importance results from the unprecedented scope of their political and military power. By 44 B.C.E., an astonishing sequence of conquests had made Rome, once an unremarkable Italian town, the center of an empire that stretched from North Africa to Britain, from Persia to Spain. The vastness of these domains magnifies the exploits of Rome's central political figures, because the consequences of their actions resonate across continents and down the centuries.

Yet as *Julius Caesar* opens, Rome's outsized ambitions are threatening to destroy it. For centuries, Rome had been governed not by a king or a dictator, but by elected officers, and its republican traditions had been a source of fierce civic pride. Yet as the city's military endeavors grow increasingly ambitious, its generals, with the might of their armies behind them, wield more power than the factionalized senate to which they supposedly owe allegiance. Of these generals, the charismatic and enterprising Julius Caesar, who had subdued much of northwest Europe even while consolidating his popularity among the poorer classes at home, seems particularly dangerous. When legal and military attempts to curb Caesar's growing power fail, a group of conspirators led by Caius Cassius and Marcus Brutus assassinate him. Yet the death of Caesar does not, as his killers had hoped, restore Rome to its tradition of republican government. Instead, civil war ensues, in which Caesar's friend Mark Antony and Caesar's adopted heir, Octavius, defeat the forces of the conspirators. Eventually, after a power struggle among the victors (recounted in Shakespeare's *Antony and Cleopatra*), Octavius is enthroned as the emperor Augustus. His ascendancy, consolidating immense power in a single individual, completes the political transformation that Julius Caesar's assassins had tried to prevent.

Even though these consequences took years to unfold, the assassination of Julius Caesar is historically important because it seems to mark the end of one epoch and the beginning of another. Similarly, Shakespeare's *Julius Caesar*, first performed in 1599, marks a watershed in his career as a playwright. On the one hand, it returns to, and reworks, some of the central political concerns of the series of eight English history plays that Shakespeare wrote in the 1590s. The questions with which the play grapples include: Who constitutes a political community—everybody in the state, both rich and poor, or only the elite and powerful among them? What limits can a community appropriately set on the activities of its most remarkable members? Are citizens allowed, or even obliged, to defend the rule of law against an exceptionally powerful individual by resorting to extralegal violence? When the demands of civic responsibility apparently conflict with those of personal loyalty, which ought to prevail? Ultimately, these are questions not about individual choices and behaviors, but about the future of a society: Does Rome's success as a military power eventually doom the republican political system that made that success possible in the first place?

The English history plays, especially the "second tetralogy" consisting of *Richard II, 1* and *2 Henry IV,* and *Henry V,* dramatize political change in a way that highlights the significance of individual characters. In *Julius Caesar,* the problem of character figures even more profoundly. In the conflicted, highly self-conscious Brutus, Shakespeare invents a kind of hero that resembles those of the tragedies that he will begin to write at the turn of the seventeenth century: the brooding Hamlet, the self-destructive Othello, the murderous but self-analytical Macbeth. Of course, distinctions between "personal" and "political" matters tend to be fuzzy and suspect, and, in a play about an assassination, are likely to be impossible to disentangle. Nonetheless, for all its acute analysis of human beings in groups, *Julius Caesar* turns on a question that seems more individual than social: What brings a man to destroy what he claims to love?

Shakespeare's source materials in *Julius Caesar* may well have encouraged this simultaneous attention to political dilemmas and psychological complexity. Virtually from the moment the conspirators pulled their swords from Caesar's bleeding corpse, the events that Shakespeare treats in *Julius Caesar* were amply documented and their rationale debated. Different commentators from antiquity to the Renaissance, depending on their own political convictions, viewed the assassination as an act of heroism or villainy and celebrated or denounced its perpetrators accordingly. While Michelangelo and Milton idealize Brutus as a selfless defender of human liberty, Dante plunges him, with Cassius, into the deepest pit of hell. It is not surprising that Shakespeare, ever alive to the dramatic possibilities inherent in multiple, conflicting perspectives, should choose to stage an incident that had been provoking debate for more than sixteen hundred years.

For Shakespeare's contemporaries, the political questions raised by Caesar's career were not merely of antiquarian interest. Throughout early modern Europe, strong monarchs were attempting, with varying degrees of success, to consolidate their power. In England, these efforts threatened the traditional prerogatives of the aristocracy and of elected representatives in the House of Commons. For thinkers and writers saturated by their classical education in the antique past, it was easy to see the shift toward strong monarchy as replaying the shift from republican to imperial Rome. In England in 1599, moreover, concerns over this general trend were exacerbated by more specific anxieties. Queen Elizabeth I had proven a remarkably durable queen—she had already survived several attempts on her life—but at sixty-six, she was a very old woman by Renaissance standards, and her reign was clearly soon to come to an end. Since, however, she had never begotten children or named an heir, it was unclear who would succeed her or how the new monarch would be selected. Conceivably, England would revert, upon her death, to the kind of civil chaos through which it had suffered in the fifteenth century. In a state in which censorship made direct commentary on contemporary political affairs virtually impossible, the story of Caesar's death and its calamitous aftermath provided an opportunity to reflect, at a suitably prudent distance, upon what might happen when accepted methods of allocating and transferring sovereign power disintegrated.

The most important source for Shakespeare's *Julius Caesar* is not, however, a political treatise but the biographies of Caesar and Brutus in Plutarch's *Lives of the Noble Grecians and Romanes,* translated into English by Thomas North. Writing in the first century C.E., Plutarch

Julius Caesar. From Plutarch, *The Lives of the Noble Grecians and Romanes* (1595).

had construed the biographer's task as inextricable from the historian's, since in his view history recorded the achievements of great men. Shakespeare followed Plutarch in stressing the decisive roles played by the acknowledged leaders of Roman society, rather than dwelling on the frictions among larger social groups. Not that he was unaware of the latter: the testiness of *Julius Caesar*'s opening scene makes the internal divisions in Roman society abundantly clear. But throughout the play, commoners are largely imagined from an upper-class perspective—as a politically unsophisticated mob that hardly seems to deserve the scrupulous civic responsibility of its betters. The capacity for conscious and reflective political decision making rests in the hands of a small elite.

Plutarch's "great man" view of history conduces to compelling dramas involving a manageable number of psychologically complex characters. And Shakespeare's drastic condensation of narrative time frame in *Julius Caesar* has the effect of exaggerating Plutarch's emphases. In Plutarch, Caesar's triumph over Pompey's sons occurs in October, but Shakespeare makes it coincide with the Lupercalia in February, so that the assassination on the ides of March seems a direct response to a specific display of arrogance. Likewise, in Plutarch, Brutus and Cassius withdraw from Rome more than a year after Caesar's funeral, but in Shakespeare, their flight follows immediately upon Antony's brilliant incitement of the Roman mob. The effect is not only to escalate dramatic momentum but also to make the personal strengths and weaknesses of Rome's leaders seem matters of titanic consequence.

In the Roman Republic, Plutarch claimed, there was always more than one powerful person, but rarely more than a few. Shakespeare depicts the last days of the Republic in a drama that no single protagonist appropriates wholly to himself. Instead, *Julius Caesar* divides its attention among several characters, setting them off against one another, while the titular hero makes less claim upon the audience's attention than might be expected. Plutarch's biography emphasizes Caesar's military genius, his ruthless executive skill, and his astonishing capacity to rescue himself repeatedly from crushing adversity. Shakespeare's Caesar seems less outsized. His accomplishments are not shown or much alluded to, and much of what we do hear is filtered through the hostile reports of resentful observers. He wants supremacy less, apparently, because he has any particular vision for the Roman polity than because he yearns for the unqualified homage of others. His egotism seems ridiculous: despite his physical frailties, he imagines himself as embodying a godlike permanence, "unshaked of motion" (3.1.70):

> . . . I am constant as the Northern Star,
> Of whose true fixed and resting quality
> There is no fellow in the firmament.
> (3.1.60–62)

Shakespeare loads this moment of self-description with dramatic irony: even as Caesar speaks these lines, the conspirators encircle him, daggers in hand. Yet Caesar's weaknesses also make the conspirators' fears seem less plausible. Deaf, epileptic, doting over his wife, he seems an unlikely aspirant to tyrannical power.

Brutus, Caesar's friend and killer, is far more fully elaborated, and in fact the originality of Shakespeare's play lies in its concentration of attention on Brutus instead of upon the play's titular hero. Unlike the other characters, Brutus appears to us in several guises: as a public figure, a husband, a master of servants, a military leader. Thus he experiences painfully in his own person the value conflicts that are elsewhere dispersed among various antagonists. How is Brutus—and how are we—to reconcile his tender regard for his wife and servant with his willingness to commit political murder? Does Brutus's intimacy with Caesar make his decision to assassinate him truly noble, since it cannot be said to stem from self-interest? Or does it suggest a troubling insensitivity to the claims of friendship and to Caesar's genuinely exceptional character?

The soliloquies in which Brutus carefully deliberates upon his reasons for, and the possible consequences of, his actions provide abundant insight into his turbulent inner life. Yet the soliloquies raise as many questions about his motives as they resolve. They force the audience to wonder how Brutus's idealism and his commitment to principle is to be evaluated. Surely his habit of appealing to abstract moral and political tenets is an admirable trait, especially in a city in which selfishness seems the dominant passion. But repeatedly, this practice leads him to commit disastrous tactical errors. Concerned to minimize bloodshed, he refuses to countenance Cassius's suggestion that Antony be killed along with Caesar. Then—once again ignoring Cassius's advice—he permits Antony to deliver an unsupervised eulogy at Caesar's funeral, thus losing the "spin" on Caesar's death and unleashing the rage of the crowd against himself and his allies. Later, his indignation at what he believes to be Cassius's corrupt practices seriously endangers their alliance.

In all these cases, Brutus tries to diminish the extent to which any of his actions might conceivably serve his own self-interested ends, even though by doing so he risks and eventually dooms the cause he is attempting to serve. Brutus shares Caesar's admiration for the Stoic virtue of "constancy," framing it, however, less in terms of power over others than in terms of personal self-control. By behaving according to immovable principles, he tries to give his life a stern but reassuring fixity. Like Caesar, Brutus ends up paying for this aspiration with his life, and even before he does so, the desire to be, in Caesar's words, "constant as the Northern star" seems misplaced in a play in which character seems complex and highly mutable.

In comparison, the impulsive, unscrupulous Cassius is far more alert to the way the world really works, willingly stooping to expediency to get what he wants and what his cause needs. The contrast with Antony likewise clarifies the way in which Brutus's principles incapacitate him. Antony emerges as a formidable opponent not despite but because of traits that Brutus can see only as weaknesses: love of sensual indulgence, lack of principle, a tendency to live in the present without sufficient care for past or future. Antony's uninhibited, improvisatory nature suits him beautifully for swaying the plebeians. A marvelous actor, Antony exploits gestures, cunning rhetoric, props, and any other means that fully serve the particular moment in which he finds himself. In fact, his political astuteness seems to arise directly from his personal familiarity with passion, since much of politics is, as Brutus never quite realizes, a matter of assessing and responding to group desire. While Brutus naively believes that Caesar's death simply restores the Republic to its status quo ante, Antony immediately understands that the future of Rome and its institutions rests in the hands of Rome's populace and, thus—since that populace is fickle and violent—ultimately in the hands of whoever can sway that populace to his will.

Even while Shakespeare vividly differentiates his characters, he shows clearly how they derive from the particular social and intellectual culture they inhabit. Shakespeare was no antiquarian: he imagines the characters of *Julius Caesar* wearing Elizabethan doublet and hose, and he notoriously equips ancient Rome with a medieval invention, the mechanical clock. Nonetheless, his Romans share a set of distinctive values, ideals, and assumptions. When Antony, at the end of the play, calls Brutus "the noblest Roman of them all," he is not simply praising Brutus as an individual. Instead, he is locating Brutus in a tradition of specifically "Roman" virtue, a virtue associated with the particular strengths of the republican form of government that Brutus died attempting to defend.

What does this virtue entail? Brutus's willingness to identify his abstract principles with the common good, as well as his intense suspicion of anyone who appears self-aggrandizing, is wholly characteristic of an ethos that distinguishes sharply between duty and pleasure, between public good and private self-enrichment. The

Marc Antony. From Plutarch, *The Lives of the Noble Grecians and Romanes* (1595).

heroes of the Roman Republic had always been celebrated for their incorruptibility and for their preference for public service, however thankless, over private goods such as marriage, friendship, sensual pleasure, and personal enrichment. Many of them adhered to a Stoic code of personal conduct that mandated emotional self-control and self-sacrifice. At the same time, Rome was in fact a hotbed of nepotism and unscrupulousness, and its venality grew along with its power. Thus, pillars of the Roman Republic like Lucius Junius Brutus, Marcus Cato, Scipio Africanus, and Marcus Brutus himself were admired not merely because their civic-mindedness was socially valuable, but because such exemplars were rarer and more surprising than Romans liked to admit.

The sharp distinction that Roman culture made between public and private domains has important consequences in *Julius Caesar*. The public world is an all-male affair: bonds and rivalries provide both the glue that holds the Roman Republic together and a competitive petulancy that ordinarily precludes a single individual's gaining too much power. We are given a vivid picture of this complex interpersonal dynamic in Cassius's account of his swimming contest with Caesar. In this incident of pure bravado, friends test their toughness against one another, and one ends up saving the other's life; but because all neediness is imagined to be shameful, what seems like generosity or charity is shot through with contempt. The same rivalrous intensity characterizes the almost erotically charged quarrel and reconciliation between Brutus and Cassius in 4.2. These are people who will kill each other while loving them and, after killing them, will generously eulogize them.

Beside the fraught intensity of such relationships, the heterosexual connections in the play are rather pallid. Although Brutus is deeply attached to Portia, it does not occur to him to take her into his confidence until she struggles mightily for the privilege on the eve of the assassination; even then, all she requests is information, not permission to offer advice. Similarly, Decius easily shames Caesar into ignoring Calpurnia's foreboding dream:

> it were a mock
> Apt to be rendered for someone to say
> 'Break up the Senate till another time,
> When Caesar's wife shall meet with better dreams.'
> (2.2.96–99)

Even the most powerful man in the Roman Empire, apparently, cannot risk being seen to be influenced by a mere wife. Most tellingly, in what is perhaps a sign of textual corruption but more probably an instance of Shakespearean skill in delineating character, we are given two successive accounts of the way Brutus learns of Portia's suicide. In the first, Brutus divulges the loss himself to Cassius, expressing his grief in solitary conference with an old friend. Shortly thereafter, however, he tells his military subordinates that he has not received any news of Portia at all. Once informed that she has died "in strange manner," he affects a studied indifference, insisting that the tidings merely interfere with more important matters at hand. His ability to sequester domestic concerns from public and military ones elicits the admiration of those around him: for true "Romans" are willing to incur huge emotional costs for what they imagine is the greater good.

Since honor, in this conceptual system is imagined to involve fierce commitment to the public sphere, and since that sphere is exclusively the domain of men, the women in *Julius Caesar* are weak and marginalized. Even within the confines of the household, they seem unable to cultivate an alternative form of social value. Maternity, for instance, is not a source of power here: Calpurnia is barren, and Portia, too, is apparently childless. The "feminine intuition" that both women possess in abundance has no practical effect. Their "nobility" requires them to internalize values that for them have little use. Portia proves what she calls her masculine courage to her husband by the bizarre means of stabbing herself deliberately in the thigh, a gesture that suggests a self-castration, as if a woman were at best a slashed man. For the virtue that she claims to possess is not truly her own possession; rather, it is a quality reflected from her male

Brutus falling on his sword. From Geffrey Whitney, A *Choice of Emblemes* (1586).

relatives that makes her superior to ordinary women. "Think you I am no stronger than my sex, / Being so fathered and so husbanded?" (2.1.295–96). Portia kills herself, typically, in an exceptionally painful way, by swallowing hot coals. While the fabled hardihood of Portia's father, Cato, or her husband, Brutus, has at least some military rationale, Portia's imitation of their fortitude seems pointlessly self-punishing, serving neither their ends nor her own.

The pressure of Roman values on the characters of *Julius Caesar* suggests that its protagonists are not entirely free to invent themselves; they are limited to the cultural materials at hand. Moreover the complexity of the situation in which they find themselves makes it difficult for them to know exactly why they behave as they do. Often in *Julius Caesar*, the same scene provides a character with a variety of motives, permitting alternative descriptions of a single action. Thus, when Brutus decides to participate in the conspiracy to kill Caesar, he believes that he has carefully sequestered his self-interest from his convictions about the common good. But Cassius has meanwhile been tossing flattering messages through his window, so the theater audience must consider the possibility that Brutus's appeal to principle is a rationalization, and that he is swayed by a personal ambition of which he may not be entirely aware.

Elsewhere, Shakespeare complicates his portraits by what might be called a technique of gradual release. By slowly making details available to the audience, he forces it to revise its previous impressions to take account of new information. For instance, Antony's bravura eulogy reaches a climax when he reads Caesar's will, thus harnessing the plebeians' greed to the end of revenging Caesar's death. A mere two scenes later, he is shown in conference with Lepidus and Octavius, giving brisk orders to minimize the cost of Caesar's generosity. The incongruity between the first scene and the second makes Antony's original celebration of his friend's magnanimity seem, in retrospect, less sincere or spontaneous. Nonetheless, the two scenes do not force the audience to a single obvious conclusion. Does Antony's later parsimony indicate that he was simply hypocritical when he used Caesar's will to provoke a riot? Perhaps, but not necessarily; he could simply have been caught up in a wave of loyalty to Caesar and in the pathos of the situation, or he could have had vaguely ambitious but not yet fully articulated plans. In such cases, Shakespeare's cunning dramatic presentation enhances the complexity of his characterizations. The realistic illusion depends as much on what he withholds from the audience as on what he provides it.

On other grounds, too, a reading focusing purely on character seems finally inadequate. In oft-cited lines, Cassius pronounces: "The fault, dear Brutus, is not in our stars, / But in ourselves, that we are underlings" (1.2.141–42). It is not at all clear, however, that he is right. Plutarch emphasizes how the fates of his biographical subjects fail to reflect their virtues. Caesar, who had miraculously survived so many strange adventures in hostile foreign lands, can be dispatched in a few minutes by his erstwhile friends just moments after leaving his own house. Cicero, whose oratory had held sway in Rome for so many years, is obliterated by Antony and Octavius practically as an afterthought. The gifted and honorable Brutus meets death after a military defeat that seems almost accidental. Cassius's suicide is even more haphazard. The inscrutable workings of fate play at least as great a role as personality does in determining the outcome of the action.

For this reason, virtually all the characters find it impossible to achieve a reliable perspective on events in which they are immersed. In the play's most literal case of limited vision, the "thick-sighted" Cassius misinterprets victory as defeat and kills himself moments before his triumphant soldiers arrive, hoping to congratulate him. Here and elsewhere, Shakespeare drums home the difference between the perspective of the theater audience, for whom the killing of Julius Caesar is an act centuries old, now replayed for its entertainment value, and the perspective of the characters within the play, for whom it is unfolding in the present moment, its consequences both dire and unknown. From our point of view, ironies are everywhere. Caesar pronounces upon his immovable constancy moments before being dispatched; his murderers, attempting to eliminate a potential tyrant, open the way for centuries of despotism. As Antony plots with Octavius to eliminate Lepidus, the audience knows as Antony cannot that the cold, noncommittal Octavius will ultimately annihilate both his triumviral associates.

To be alive to such ironies, the characters would need to be able to look into the future. Struggling to understand their own place in history, they continually resort to augury, attempting—usually incorrectly—to comprehend the omens that shadow forth their fates. In *Julius Caesar,* omens are always telling, but they are rarely intelligible except in retrospect. No one knows what to make of the lions loose in the streets; the soothsayer arrives too late; Caesar's dream is misinterpreted; Cassius notices carrion birds on his standards but decides to disregard them. By emphasizing the analogies among personal, political, and natural forms of disruption, omens on the one hand intensify the significance of the play's characters: their decisions, quirks, and flaws affect the structure of the universe itself. They are indeed, as they have imagined themselves, persons of unprecedented and enormous significance. On the other hand, the reliability of omens challenges the notion that history is the product of personal effort, since augury implies restrictions on free will, suggesting that individuals are caught in the toils of a historical process they cannot possibly control or understand. Undergirding the other questions of authority, responsibility, and agency in *Julius Caesar* are unanswerable questions about who creates history, and what that history can possibly mean.

KATHARINE EISAMAN MAUS

TEXTUAL NOTE

The 1623 First Folio (F) provides the only authoritative text for *Julius Caesar.* The fullness of the stage directions, which specify sound effects as well as actors' exits and entrances, and the absence of Shakespearean spellings suggest that the Folio text was derived from the theater company's official promptbook rather than from Shakespeare's manuscript.

Despite the general reliability of the Folio *Julius Caesar,* there are a few editorial puzzles. In Act 4, there is some confusion about the parts played by the minor characters Titinius, Lucillius, and Lucius, leading some scholars to believe that Shakespeare revised these scenes. Two conundrums have more significant consequences for the play's characterizations. In 1614 and again in 1625, Shakespeare's contemporary Ben Jonson ridiculed a line in 3.1 in which Caesar supposedly proclaims: "Know Caesar doth not wrong but with just cause." F omits the last four words, but the currency of Jonson's joke even after the publication of the Folio suggests that they were retained in performance. Indeed, the apparent illogic of Caesar's utterance (how can a wrong have a just cause?) seems to testify powerfully to the speaker's megalomaniac sense that he transcends the rules ordinary mortals must obey. The Oxford text restores the line as reported by Jonson rather than emending it to some more "reasonable" possibility. Some textual scholars see a similar lapse of logic in 4.2, in which Brutus's account of Portia's death to Cassius seems to contradict his claim, moments later, that he is ignorant of that death. Possibly Shakespeare revised the scene and forgot to cancel the rejected lines. However, as in 3.1, the seeming inconsistency might be justified as revealing an interesting aspect of Brutus's character or of Roman attitudes toward the difference between domestic and public domains.

SELECTED BIBLIOGRAPHY

Bloom, Harold, ed. *William Shakespeare's "Julius Caesar."* New York: Chelsea House, 1988. Anthology of critical essays.

Burckhardt, Sigurd. "How Not to Murder Caesar." *Shakespearean Meanings.* Princeton: Princeton University Press, 1968. 3–21. *Julius Caesar* and historical change.

Knights, L. C. "Shakespeare and Political Wisdom: A Note on the Personalism of *Julius Caesar* and *Coriolanus.*" *Sewanee Review* 61 (1953): 43–55. Politics and individual character.

Miles, Gary B. "How Roman Are Shakespeare's 'Romans'?" *Shakespeare Quarterly* 40 (1989): 257–83. Shakespeare's adaptation and revision of his classical sources.

Miola, Robert S. "*Julius Caesar* and the Tyrannicide Debate." *Renaissance Quarterly* 38 (1985): 271–89. Renaissance political theorists disagreed over whether the killing of a king was ever justified; *Julius Caesar* shows Shakespeare's knowledge of this dispute.

Paster, Gail Kern. "'In the Spirit of Men There Is No Blood': Blood as a Trope of Gender in *Julius Caesar.*" *Shakespeare Quarterly* 40 (1989): 284–98. Manliness and bloody bodies in the play.

Rebhorn, Wayne. "The Crisis of the Aristocracy in *Julius Caesar.*" *Renaissance Quarterly* 43 (1990): 75–111. Shakespeare's Romans resemble sixteenth-century English aristocrats in their desire for self-mastery and competitiveness with one another.

Visser, Nicholas. "Plebeian Politics in Julius Caesar." *Shakespeare in Southern Africa* 7 (1994): 22–31. Contemporary South African performances offer insights into the play's concept of class relations and of the mob.

Wilson, Richard, ed. *Julius Caesar.* New York: Palgrave, 2002. Collection of recent essays on the play.

FILMS

Julius Caesar. 1953. Dir. Joseph L. Mankiewicz. USA. 120 min. This black-and-white Hollywood production features James Mason as a brooding, intense Brutus, John Gielgud as Cassius, and the young Marlon Brando, in an Oscar-nominated performance, as a charismatic Antony.

Julius Caesar. 1970. Dir. Stuart Burge. UK. 117 min. A brisk production, enlivened by colorful street and battle scenes. Jason Robards Plays Brutus, Charlton Heston is Antony, John Gielgud is Caesar, and Diana Rigg is Portia.

Julius Caesar. 1979. Dir. Herbert Wise. UK. 161 min. A BBC-TV production. Textually faithful but blandly acted. David Collings is, however, effective as Cassius.

The Tragedy of Julius Cæsar

THE PERSONS OF THE PLAY

Julius CAESAR
CALPURNIA, his wife
Marcus BRUTUS, a noble Roman, opposed to Caesar
PORTIA, his wife
LUCIUS, his servant
Caius CASSIUS ⎫
CASCA ⎪
TREBONIUS ⎪
DECIUS Brutus ⎬ opposed to Caesar
METELLUS Cimber ⎪
CINNA ⎪
Caius LIGARIUS ⎭
Mark ANTONY ⎫
OCTAVIUS Caesar ⎬ rulers of Rome after Caesar's death
LEPIDUS ⎭
FLAVIUS ⎫
MURELLUS ⎬ tribunes of the people
CICERO ⎫
PUBLIUS ⎬ senators
POPILLIUS Laena ⎭
A SOOTHSAYER
ARTEMIDORUS
CINNA the Poet
PINDARUS, Cassius' bondman
TITINIUS, an officer in Cassius' army
LUCILLIUS ⎫
MESSALA ⎪
VARRUS ⎪
CLAUDIO ⎪
YOUNG CATO ⎬ officers and soldiers in Brutus' army
STRATO ⎪
VOLUMNIUS ⎪
FLAVIUS ⎪
DARDANIUS ⎪
CLITUS ⎭
A POET
A GHOST of Caesar
A COBBLER
A CARPENTER
Other PLEBEIANS
A MESSENGER
SERVANTS
Senators, soldiers, and attendants

1.1

Enter FLAVIUS, MURELLUS, *and certain commoners over*
the stage

FLAVIUS   Hence, home, you idle creatures, get you home!
Is this a holiday? What, know you not,
Being mechanical,° you ought not walk   *of the artisan class*
Upon a labouring day without the sign°   *tools and garments*

5   Of your profession?—Speak, what trade art thou?
CARPENTER   Why, sir, a carpenter.
MURELLUS   Where is thy leather apron and thy rule?
What dost thou with thy best apparel on?—
You, sir, what trade are you?

10   COBBLER   Truly, sir, in respect of° a fine workman I am but, as   *in comparison with*
you would say, a cobbler.¹
MURELLUS   But what trade art thou? Answer me directly.
COBBLER   A trade, sir, that I hope I may use with a safe conscience, which is indeed, sir, a mender of bad soles.°   *(punning on "souls")*

15   FLAVIUS   What trade, thou knave? Thou naughty° knave, what trade?   *wicked*
COBBLER   Nay, I beseech you, sir, be not out² with me. Yet if
you be out, sir, I can mend you.
MURELLUS   What mean'st thou by that? Mend me, thou saucy fellow?
COBBLER   Why, sir, cobble you.

20   FLAVIUS   Thou art a cobbler, art thou?
COBBLER   Truly, sir, all that I live by is with the awl. I meddle
with no tradesman's matters, nor women's matters,° but withal³   *(a bawdy joke)*
I am indeed, sir, a surgeon to old shoes: when they are in great
danger I recover° them. As proper° men as ever trod upon   *resole; cure / fine*

25   neat's leather° have gone° upon my handiwork.   *cowhide / walked*
FLAVIUS   But wherefore art not in thy shop today?
Why dost thou lead these men about the streets?
COBBLER   Truly, sir, to wear out their shoes to get myself into
more work. But indeed, sir, we make holiday to see Caesar, and

30   to rejoice in his triumph.⁴
MURELLUS   Wherefore rejoice? What conquest brings he home?
What tributaries° follow him to Rome   *ransom payers*
To grace in captive bonds his chariot wheels?⁵
You blocks, you stones, you worse than senseless° things!   *inanimate*

35   O, you hard hearts, you cruel men of Rome,
Knew you not Pompey?⁶ Many a time and oft
Have you climbed up to walls and battlements,
To towers and windows, yea to chimney-tops,
Your infants in your arms, and there have sat

40   The livelong day with patient expectation
To see great Pompey pass the streets of Rome.
And when you saw his chariot but appear,
Have you not made an universal shout,
That Tiber⁷ trembled underneath her banks

45   To hear the replication° of your sounds   *echo*
Made in her concave shores?

1.1 Location: A street in Rome.
1. Mender of shoes; bungler (the sense Murellus
understands).
2. Angry; worn out, like shoes.
3. Nevertheless; punning on "awl."
4. Triumphal procession in honor of victory (by Roman
custom, over foreign enemies, but here over Caesar's

political adversaries, Pompey's sons).
5. Captives were tied to their conquerors' chariots.
6. Pompey the Great, who had shared rule of Rome with
Caesar and Crassus; he was defeated by Caesar after
their alliance disintegrated and was later assassinated.
7. River that flows through Rome.

And do you now put on your best attire?
And do you now cull out° a holiday?   choose
And do you now strew flowers in his way
50   That comes in triumph over Pompey's blood?°   offspring
Be gone!
Run to your houses, fall upon your knees,
Pray to the gods to intermit[8] the plague
That needs must light on this ingratitude.
55   FLAVIUS   Go, go, good countrymen, and for this fault
Assemble all the poor men of your sort;°   rank
Draw them to Tiber banks, and weep your tears
Into the channel, till the lowest stream
Do kiss the most exalted shores of all.°   tops of the riverbanks
                    Exeunt all the commoners
60   See whe'er° their basest mettle be not moved.   whether
They vanish tongue-tied in their guiltiness.
Go you down that way towards the Capitol;[9]
This way will I. Disrobe the images
If you do find them decked with ceremonies.[1]
65   MURELLUS   May we do so?
You know it is the Feast of Lupercal.[2]
FLAVIUS   It is no matter. Let no images
Be hung with Caesar's trophies.° I'll about,   ornaments
And drive away the vulgar° from the streets;   commoners
70   So do you too where you perceive them thick.
These growing feathers plucked from Caesar's wing
Will make him fly an ordinary pitch,[3]
Who else° would soar above the view of men   otherwise
And keep us all in servile fearfulness.   *Exeunt*

1.2

[*Loud music.*] *Enter* CAESAR, ANTONY [*stripped for the*
course,[1] CALPURNIA, PORTIA, DECIUS, CICERO, BRUTUS,
CASSIUS, CASCA, *a* SOOTHSAYER, *a throng of citizens*];
after them, MURELLUS *and* FLAVIUS
CAESAR   Calpurnia.
CASCA   Peace, ho! Caesar speaks.
                    [*Music ceases*]
CAESAR   Calpurnia.
CALPURNIA   Here, my lord.
5   CAESAR   Stand you directly in Antonio's way
When he doth run his course.—Antonio.
ANTONY   Caesar, my lord.
CAESAR   Forget not in your speed, Antonio,
To touch Calpurnia, for our elders say
10   The barren, touchèd in this holy chase,
Shake off their sterile curse.
ANTONY   I shall remember:
When Caesar says 'Do this', it is performed.

---

8. Withhold (plague was considered a divine punishment).
9. Hill on whose top was the Temple of Jupiter, where victorious generals in a triumph offered sacrifice.
1. Caesar's followers had put imperial crowns ("ceremonies") on his statues.
2. Lupercalia, a festival celebrated February 15. Historically, Caesar's triumph took place in October.
3. At a medium height (an image from falconry).
1.2 Location: A public place in Rome.
1. During the Lupercalia, two celebrants ran naked through Rome, striking those they met with goatskin thongs.

CAESAR Set on,° and leave no ceremony out. *Proceed*
     [*Music*]
SOOTHSAYER Caesar!
15 CAESAR Ha! Who calls?
    CASCA Bid every noise be still. Peace yet again.
     [*Music ceases*]
CAESAR Who is it in the press° that calls on me? *crowd*
    I hear a tongue shriller than all the music
    Cry 'Caesar!' Speak. Caesar is turned to hear.
SOOTHSAYER Beware the ides[2] of March.
20 CAESAR   What man is that?
    BRUTUS A soothsayer bids you beware the ides of March.
    CAESAR Set him before me; let me see his face.
    CASSIUS Fellow, come from the throng; look upon Caesar.
     [*The* SOOTHSAYER *comes forward*]
CAESAR What sayst thou to me now? Speak once again.
25 SOOTHSAYER Beware the ides of March.
    CAESAR He is a dreamer. Let us leave him. Pass!° *Onward*
              Sennet.° Exeunt. Manent° BRUTUS *and* CASSIUS *Trumpet flourish / Remain*
    CASSIUS Will you go see the order of the course?° *running of the race*
    BRUTUS Not I.
    CASSIUS I pray you, do.
30 BRUTUS I am not gamesome;° I do lack some part *fond of sport*
    Of that quick° spirit that is in Antony. *lively*
    Let me not hinder, Cassius, your desires.
    I'll leave you.
    CASSIUS Brutus, I do observe you now of late.
35 I have not from your eyes that gentleness
    And show of love as I was wont° to have. *accustomed*
    You bear too stubborn and too strange° a hand[3] *unfriendly*
    Over your friend that loves you.
BRUTUS   Cassius,
    Be not deceived. If I have veiled my look,° *seemed less outgoing*
40 I turn the trouble of my countenance° *my troubled looks*
    Merely° upon myself. Vexèd I am *Wholly*
    Of late with passions of some difference,° *conflicting kinds*
    Conceptions only proper° to myself, *suitable*
    Which give some soil,° perhaps, to my behaviours. *blemish*
45 But let not therefore my good friends be grieved—
    Among which number, Cassius, be you one—
    Nor construe any further° my neglect *make any more of*
    Than that poor Brutus, with himself at war,
    Forgets the shows of love to other men.
50 CASSIUS Then, Brutus, I have much mistook your passion,° *feelings*
    By means whereof[4] this breast of mine hath buried° *concealed*
    Thoughts of great value, worthy cogitations.
    Tell me, good Brutus, can you see your face?
BRUTUS No, Cassius, for the eye sees not itself
55 But by reflection, by some other things.
    CASSIUS 'Tis just;° *true*
    And it is very much lamented, Brutus,

---

2. The ides marked roughly the midpoint of every   3. Management of horse's reins (figurative).
Roman month (usually the thirteenth); in March, the   4. In consequence of which mistake.
fifteenth.

That you have no such mirrors as will turn
Your hidden worthiness into your eye,
60   That you might see your shadow.° I have heard   *reflection*
Where many of the best respect° in Rome—   *repute*
Except immortal Caesar—speaking of Brutus,
And groaning underneath this age's yoke,
Have wished that noble Brutus had his eyes.[5]
65 BRUTUS   Into what dangers would you lead me, Cassius,
That you would have me seek into myself
For that which is not in me?

    CASSIUS   Therefor,° good Brutus, be prepared to hear.   *As to that*
And since you know you cannot see yourself
70   So well as by reflection, I, your glass,°   *mirror*
Will modestly discover° to yourself   *reveal*
That of yourself which you yet know not of.
And be not jealous on° me, gentle Brutus.   *suspicious of*
Were I a common laughter,° or did use   *object of ridicule*
75   To stale° with ordinary° oaths my love   *debase / cheap*
To every new protester;° if you know   *declarer of friendship*
That I do fawn on men and hug them hard,
And after scandal° them; or if you know   *defame*
That I profess myself° in banqueting   *declare friendship*
80   To all the rout:° then hold me dangerous.   *mob*
      Flourish, and shout [*within*]
  BRUTUS   What means this shouting? I do fear the people
Choose Caesar for their king.

  CASSIUS   Ay, do you fear it?
Then must I think you would not have it so.
  BRUTUS   I would not, Cassius; yet I love him well.
85   But wherefore do you hold me here so long?
What is it that you would impart to me?
If it be aught toward the general good,
Set honour in one eye and death i'th' other,
And I will look on both indifferently.°   *impartially*
90   For let the gods so speed me as[6] I love
The name of honour more than I fear death.

    CASSIUS   I know that virtue to be in you, Brutus,
As well as I do know your outward favour.°   *appearance*
Well, honour is the subject of my story.
95   I cannot tell what you and other men
Think of this life; but for my single self,
I had as lief not be,° as live to be   *I had rather be dead*
In awe of such a thing as I myself.
I was born free as Caesar, so were you.
100   We both have fed as well, and we can both
Endure the winter's cold as well as he.
For once upon a raw and gusty day,
The troubled Tiber chafing with° her shores,   *raging against*
Said Caesar to me 'Dar'st thou, Cassius, now
105   Leap in with me into this angry flood,
And swim to yonder point?'° Upon the word,   *promontory*
Accoutred° as I was I plungèd in,   *Dressed in armor*
And bade him follow. So indeed he did.

5. That is, could see properly.   6. Make me fortunate insofar as.

The torrent roared, and we did buffet it
110 With lusty sinews, throwing it aside,
And stemming° it with hearts of controversy.°   *confronting / rivalry*
But ere we could arrive° the point proposed,   *reach*
Caesar cried 'Help me, Cassius, or I sink!'
Ay, as Aeneas[7] our great ancestor
115 Did from the flames of Troy upon his shoulder
The old Anchises bear, so from the waves of Tiber
Did I the tirèd Caesar. And this man
Is now become a god, and Cassius is
A wretched creature, and must bend his body°   *(must bow)*
120 If Caesar carelessly but nod on him.
He had a fever when he was in Spain,
And when the fit was on him, I did mark
How he did shake. 'Tis true, this god did shake.
His coward lips did from their colour fly;[8]
125 And that same eye whose bend° doth awe the world   *glance*
Did lose his° lustre. I did hear him groan,   *its*
Ay, and that tongue of his that bade the Romans
Mark him and write his speeches in their books,
'Alas!' it cried, 'Give me some drink, Titinius',
130 As a sick girl. Ye gods, it doth amaze me
A man of such a feeble temper° should   *constitution*
So get the start of° the majestic world,   *advantage over*
And bear the palm° alone!   *be victor*
    Shout [within]. Flourish
BRUTUS   Another general shout!
I do believe that these applauses are
135 For some new honours that are heaped on Caesar.
CASSIUS   Why, man, he doth bestride the narrow world
Like a Colossus,[9] and we petty men
Walk under his huge legs, and peep about
To find ourselves dishonourable graves.
140 Men at sometime° were masters of their fates.   *formerly*
✳ The fault, dear Brutus, is not in our stars, ✳
But in ourselves, that we are underlings.
Brutus and Caesar: what should be in that 'Caesar'?
Why should that name be sounded more than yours?
145 Write them together: yours is as fair a name.
Sound them: it doth become the mouth as well.
Weigh them: it is as heavy. Conjure with 'em:
'Brutus' will start[1] a spirit as soon as 'Caesar'.
Now in the names of all the gods at once,
150 Upon what meat° doth this our Caesar feed   *food*
That he is grown so great? Age, thou art shamed.
Rome, thou hast lost the breed of noble bloods.
When went there by an age since the great flood,[2]
But it was famed with° more than with one man?   *renowned for*
155 When could they say till now, that talked of Rome,

---

7. Legendary Trojan warrior and founder of Rome; when the Greeks burned Troy, he carried his father, Anchises, out on his back.
8. Did turn pale; did desert their flag (Caesar suffered epileptic seizures).
9. Giant statue of Apollo, which straddled the harbor of Rhodes.
1. Raise (only the names of the gods were thought to be able to raise the dead).
2. A great flood was recorded in classical as well as biblical accounts.

That her wide walls encompassed but one man?
Now is it Rome indeed, and room° enough   *(pronounced like "Rome")*
When there is in it but one only man.
O, you and I have heard our fathers say
160   There was a Brutus once³ that would have brooked°   *endured*
Th'eternal devil to keep his state° in Rome   *hold court*
As easily as a king.
BRUTUS   That you do love me I am nothing jealous.°   *not at all uncertain*
What you would work° me to I have some aim.°   *persuade / idea*
165   How I have thought of this and of these times
I shall recount hereafter. For this present,°   *present time*
I would not, so with love° I might entreat you,   *if in friendship*
Be any further moved.° What you have said   *persuaded*
I will consider. What you have to say
170   I will with patience hear, and find a time
Both meet° to hear and answer such high things.   *Fitting both*
Till then, my noble friend, chew upon this:
Brutus had rather be a villager
Than to repute himself a son of Rome
175   Under these hard conditions as this time
Is like to lay upon us.
CASSIUS   I am glad
That my weak words have struck but thus much show
Of fire from Brutus.
         [Music.] Enter CAESAR *and his train°*   *retinue*
BRUTUS   The games are done, and Caesar is returning.
180   CASSIUS   As they pass by, pluck Casca by the sleeve,⁴
And he will, after his sour fashion, tell you
What hath proceeded worthy° note today.   *worthy of*
BRUTUS   I will do so. But look you, Cassius,
The angry spot doth glow on Caesar's brow,
185   And all the rest look like a chidden° train.   *scolded*
Calpurnia's cheek is pale, and Cicero
Looks with such ferret⁵ and such fiery eyes
As we have seen him in the Capitol
Being crossed in conference° by some senators.   *opposed in debate*
190   CASSIUS   Casca will tell us what the matter is.
CAESAR   Antonio.
ANTONY   Caesar.
CAESAR   Let me have men about me that are fat,
Sleek-headed men, and such as sleep a-nights.
195   Yon Cassius has a lean and hungry look.
He thinks too much. Such men are dangerous.
ANTONY   Fear him not, Caesar, he's not dangerous.
He is a noble Roman, and well given.°   *well disposed*
CAESAR   Would he were fatter! But I fear him not.
200   Yet if my name⁶ were liable to fear,
I do not know the man I should avoid
So soon as that spare Cassius. He reads much,
He is a great observer, and he looks

---

3. Lucius Junius Brutus, an ancestor of Marcus Brutus and a founder of the Roman Republic, famed for his role in expelling the Tarquins, who had ruled Rome as Kings. 4. Like "cloak" (line 216), "doublet" (line 262), and "unbraced" (1.3.48), this suggests a performance in Elizabethan dress. 5. Ferretlike (red and darting). 6. One of my name (that is, myself).

Quite through[7] the deeds of men. He loves no plays,
205 As thou dost, Antony; he hears no music.[8]
Seldom he smiles, and smiles in such a sort°   *manner*
As if he mocked himself, and scorned his spirit
That could be moved to smile at anything.
Such men as he be never at heart's ease
210 Whiles they behold a greater than themselves,
And therefore are they very dangerous.
I rather tell thee what is to be feared
Than what I fear, for always I am Caesar.
Come on my right hand, for this ear is deaf,
215 And tell me truly what thou think'st of him.
       Sennet. Exeunt CAESAR *and his train.* [BRUTUS,
                    CASSIUS, *and* CASCA *remain*]
CASCA [*to* BRUTUS] You pulled me by the cloak.° Would you   *pulled me aside*
    speak with me?
BRUTUS Ay, Casca. Tell us what hath chanced today,
    That Caesar looks so sad.°   *serious*
220 CASCA Why, you were with him, were you not?
BRUTUS I should not then ask Casca what had chanced.
CASCA Why, there was a crown offered him; and being offered
    him, he put it by with the back of his hand, thus; and then the
    people fell a-shouting.
225 BRUTUS What was the second noise for?
CASCA Why, for that too.
CASSIUS They shouted thrice. What was the last cry for?
CASCA Why, for that too.
BRUTUS Was the crown offered him thrice?
230 CASCA Ay, marry,° was't; and he put it by thrice, every time   *indeed*
    gentler than other; and at every putting by, mine honest°   *(sarcastic)*
    neighbours shouted.
CASSIUS Who offered him the crown?
CASCA   Why, Antony.
BRUTUS Tell us the manner of it, gentle° Casca.   *noble*
235 CASCA I can as well be hanged as tell the manner of it. It was
    mere foolery,° I did not mark it. I saw Mark Antony offer him   *utter absurdity*
    a crown—yet 'twas not a crown neither, 'twas one of these coro-
    nets—and as I told you he put it by once; but for all that, to my
    thinking he would fain° have had it. Then he offered it to him   *gladly*
240   again; then he put it by again—but to my thinking he was very
    loath to lay his fingers off it. And then he offered it the third
    time; he put it the third time by. And still° as he refused it,   *continually*
    the rabblement hooted, and clapped their chapped hands, and
    threw up their sweaty nightcaps,[9] and uttered such a deal of
245   stinking breath because Caesar refused the crown that it had
    almost choked Caesar; for he swooned and fell down at it. And
    for mine own part, I durst not laugh for fear of opening my lips
    and receiving the bad air.
CASSIUS But soft, I pray you. What, did Caesar swoon?
250 CASCA He fell down in the market-place, and foamed at mouth,
    and was speechless.

7. Completely into the motives of.
8. This was regarded as a sign of wickedness; see The
Merchant of Venice.
9. Artisans wore felt hats on holidays.

BRUTUS   'Tis very like: he hath the falling sickness.[1]
CASSIUS   No, Caesar hath it not; but you and I
          And honest Casca, we have the falling sickness.
255 CASCA   I know not what you mean by that, but I am sure Caesar
          fell down. If the tag-rag people° did not clap him and hiss him,   riffraff
          according as he pleased and displeased them, as they use° to   are accustomed
          do the players in the theatre, I am no true man.
     BRUTUS   What said he when he came unto himself?
260 CASCA   Marry, before he fell down, when he perceived the com-
          mon herd was glad he refused the crown, he plucked me ope[2]
          his doublet° and offered them his throat to cut. An° I had been   jacket / If
          a man of any occupation, if I would not have taken him at a°   his
          word, I would I might go to hell among the rogues. And so he
265   fell. When he came to himself again, he said, if he had done
          or said anything amiss, he desired their worships to think it was
          his infirmity. Three or four wenches where I stood cried 'Alas,
          good soul!' and forgave him with all their hearts. But there's no
          heed to be taken of them: if Caesar had stabbed[3] their mothers
270   they would have done no less.
     BRUTUS   And after that he came thus sad away?
     CASCA   Ay.
     CASSIUS   Did Cicero say anything?
     CASCA   Ay, he spoke Greek.
275 CASSIUS   To what effect?
     CASCA   Nay, an I tell you that, I'll ne'er look you i'th' face again.
          But those that understood him smiled at one another, and
          shook their heads. But for mine own part, it was Greek to me.
          I could tell you more news, too. Murellus and Flavius, for pull-
280   ing scarves[4] off Caesar's images, are put to silence.° Fare you   deprived of office
          well. There was more foolery yet, if I could remember it.
     CASSIUS   Will you sup with me tonight, Casca?
     CASCA   No, I am promised forth.°   elsewhere
     CASSIUS   Will you dine with me tomorrow?
285 CASCA   Ay, if I be alive, and your mind hold,° and your dinner   does not change
          worth the eating.
     CASSIUS   Good; I will expect you.
     CASCA   Do so. Farewell both.   Exit
     BRUTUS   What a blunt fellow is this grown to be!
290   He was quick mettle° when he went to school.   of energetic spirit
     CASSIUS   So is he now, in execution
          Of any bold or noble enterprise,
          However he puts on this tardy form.[5]
          This rudeness° is a sauce to his good wit,°   harshness / intelligence
295   Which gives men stomach° to digest his words   relish
          With better appetite.
     BRUTUS   And so it is. For this time I will leave you.
          Tomorrow, if you please to speak with me,
          I will come home to you; or if you will,
300   Come home to me and I will wait for you.
     CASSIUS   I will do so. Till then, think of the world.°   Exit BRUTUS   state of affairs
          Well, Brutus, thou art noble; yet I see

---

1. Epilepsy (Cassius puns on "collapse from power").   4. Decorations (see 1.1.63–64).
2. Pulled open ("me" is colloquial).   5. Although he feigns this indolent manner.
3. Playing on "sexually penetrated."

Thy honourable mettle may be wrought
From that it is disposed.[6] Therefore it is meet°   *fitting*
305 That noble minds keep ever with their likes;
For who so firm that cannot be seduced?
Caesar doth bear me hard,° but he loves Brutus.   *ill will*
If I were Brutus now, and he were Cassius,
He should not humour° me. I will this night   *influence*
310 In several hands° in at his windows throw—   *various handwritings*
As if they came from several citizens—
Writings, all tending to° the great opinion   *intimating*
That Rome holds of his name, wherein obscurely°   *cryptically*
Caesar's ambition shall be glancèd° at.   *hinted*
315 And after this, let Caesar seat him sure,[7]
For we will shake him, or worse days endure.   *Exit*

[Handwritten margin note: Cassius' plan to plant seeds for revolution]

1.3

Thunder and lightning. Enter CASCA, [*at one door, with his sword drawn,*] *and* CICERO [*at another*]

CICERO   Good even, Casca. Brought° you Caesar home?   *Escorted*
Why are you breathless, and why stare you so?
CASCA   Are not you moved, when all the sway° of earth   *realm*
Shakes like a thing unfirm? O Cicero,
5 I have seen tempests when the scolding winds
Have rived° the knotty oaks, and I have seen   *split*
Th'ambitious ocean swell and rage and foam
To be exalted with° the threat'ning clouds;   *raised as high as*
But never till tonight, never till now,
10 Did I go through a tempest dropping fire.
Either there is a civil strife in heaven,
Or else the world, too saucy° with the gods,   *insolent*
Incenses them to send destruction.
CICERO   Why, saw you anything more° wonderful?   *else*
15 CASCA   A common slave—you know him well by sight—
Held up his left hand, which did flame and burn
Like twenty torches joined; and yet his hand,
Not sensible of° fire, remained unscorched.   *Not feeling*
Besides—I ha' not since put up° my sword—   *sheathed*
20 Against° the Capitol I met a lion   *Next to*
Who glazed° upon me, and went surly by   *stared*
Without annoying° me. And there were drawn   *harming*
Upon a heap[1] a hundred ghastly° women,   *pallid*
Transformèd with their fear, who swore they saw
25 Men all in fire walk up and down the streets.
And yesterday the bird of night° did sit   *screech owl*
Even at noonday upon the market-place,
Hooting and shrieking. When these prodigies°   *abnormalities*
Do so conjointly meet,° let not men say   *happen together*
30 'These are their reasons', 'they are natural',
For I believe they are portentous things
Unto the climate° that they point upon.   *region*
CICERO   Indeed it is a strange-disposèd time;

---

6. *wrought . . . disposed:* changed from its natural property (alluding to the alchemical transmutation of metals).
7. Establish himself securely.

1.3 Location: A street in Rome.
1. Huddled in a crowd.

✱ But men may construe things after their fashion,° people   *in their own way*
35 Clean° from the purpose of the things themselves. misinterpret *Completely different*
    Comes Caesar to the Capitol tomorrow?
CASCA He doth, for he did bid Antonio
    Send word to you he would be there tomorrow.
CICERO Good night then, Casca. This disturbèd sky
    Is not to walk in.
40 CASCA   Farewell, Cicero.   *Exit* CICERO
                    Enter CASSIUS [*unbraced*]°   *with open doublet*
CASSIUS Who's there?
CASCA   A Roman.
CASSIUS   Casca, by your voice.
CASCA Your ear is good. Cassius, what night is this?
CASSIUS A very pleasing night to honest men.
CASCA Who ever knew the heavens menace so?
45 CASSIUS Those that have known the earth so full of faults.
    For my part, I have walked about the streets,
    Submitting me unto the perilous night;
    And thus unbracèd, Casca, as you see,
    Have bared my bosom to the thunder-stone;°   *thunderbolt*
50 And when the cross° blue lightning seemed to open   *forked; hostile*
    The breast of heaven, I did present myself
    Even° in the aim and very flash of it.   *Exactly*
CASCA But wherefore did you so much tempt the heavens?
    It is the part of men to fear and tremble
55 When the most mighty gods by tokens° send   *signs*
    Such dreadful heralds to astonish° us.   *dismay*
CASSIUS You are dull, Casca, and those sparks of life
    That should be in a Roman you do want,°   *lack*
    Or else you use not. You look pale, and gaze,
60 And put on fear, and cast yourself in wonder,
    To see the strange impatience of the heavens;
    But if you would consider the true cause
    Why all these fires, why all these gliding ghosts,
    Why birds and beasts from quality and kind²—
65 Why old men, fools, and children calculate°—   *prophesy*
    Why all these things change from their ordinance,°—   *usual order*
    Their natures, and preformèd faculties,
    To monstrous° quality—why, you shall find   *unnatural*
    That heaven hath infused them with these spirits
70 To make them instruments of fear and warning
    Unto some monstrous state.³ Now could I, Casca,
    Name to thee a man most like this dreadful night,
    That thunders, lightens, opens graves, and roars
    As doth the lion in the Capitol;
75 A man no mightier than thyself or me
    In personal action, yet prodigious° grown,   *ominous*
    And fearful,° as these strange eruptions° are.   *terrifying / upheavals*
CASCA 'Tis Caesar that you mean, is it not, Cassius?
CASSIUS Let it be who it is; for Romans now
80 Have thews° and limbs like to their ancestors.   *sinews*
    But woe the while!° Our fathers' minds are dead,   *alas for these times*

---

2. *from quality and kind:* behaving contrary to their   3. Abnormal situation; atrocious government.
nature.

And we are governed with our mothers' spirits.
Our yoke and sufferance° show us womanish.   *servitude and patience*

CASCA   Indeed they say the senators tomorrow
85   Mean to establish Caesar as a king,
And he shall wear his crown by sea and land
In every place save here in Italy.

CASSIUS [*drawing his dagger*]   I know where I will wear this dagger then:
Cassius from bondage will deliver Cassius.
90   Therein, ye gods, you make the weak most strong;
Therein, ye gods, you tyrants do defeat.
Nor stony tower, nor walls of beaten brass,
Nor airless dungeon, nor strong links of iron,
Can be retentive to° the strength of spirit;   *Can imprison*
95   But life, being weary of these worldly bars,°   *hindrances*
Never lacks power to dismiss itself.
If I know this, know all the world besides,
That part of tyranny that I do bear
I can shake off at pleasure.
               Thunder still

CASCA   So can I.
100   So every bondman in his own hand bears
The power to cancel his captivity.

CASSIUS   And why should Caesar be a tyrant then?
Poor man, I know he would not be a wolf
But that he sees the Romans are but sheep.
105   He were no lion, were not Romans hinds.°   *female deer; servants*
Those that with haste will make a mighty fire
Begin it with weak straws. What trash is Rome,
What rubbish, and what offal,° when it serves   *wood chips; refuse*
For the base° matter to illuminate   *underlying; despicable*
110   So vile a thing as Caesar! But, O grief,
Where hast thou led me? I perhaps speak this
Before a willing bondman; then I know
My answer must be made.[4] But I am armed,°   *(physically and morally)*
And dangers are to me indifferent.°   *insignificant*
115   CASCA   You speak to Casca, and to such a man
That is no fleering° tell-tale. Hold.° My hand.   *sneering / Enough*
Be factious° for redress of all these griefs,   *Form a group*
And I will set this foot of mine as far
As who° goes farthest.   *whoever*
          [*They join hands*]

CASSIUS   There's a bargain made.
120   Now know you, Casca, I have moved° already   *persuaded*
Some certain of the noblest-minded Romans
To undergo° with me an enterprise   *undertake*
Of honourable-dangerous consequence.
And I do know by this° they stay° for me   *this time / wait*
125   In Pompey's Porch;[5] for now, this fearful night,
There is no stir or walking in the streets,
And the complexion of the element°   *disposition of the sky*
In favour's° like the work we have in hand,   *In appearance is*
Most bloody, fiery, and most terrible.
        Enter CINNA

---

4. I must pay the penalty.   5. Portico of a theater commissioned by Pompey.

130 CASCA Stand close° a while, for here comes one in haste.   *concealed*
    CASSIUS 'Tis Cinna; I do know him by his gait.
    He is a friend.—Cinna, where haste you so?
    CINNA To find out you. Who's that? Metellus Cimber?
    CASSIUS No, it is Casca, one incorporate°   *a party*
135   To our attempts. Am I not stayed for,° Cinna?   *awaited*
    CINNA I am glad on't.[6] What a fearful night is this!
    There's two or three of us have seen strange sights.
    CASSIUS Am I not stayed for? Tell me.
    CINNA Yes, you are.
140   O Cassius, if you could
    But win the noble Brutus to our party—
    CASSIUS Be you content. Good Cinna, take this paper,
        [*He gives* CINNA *letters*]
    And look you lay it in the Praetor's° Chair,
    Where Brutus may but° find it; and throw this   *must surely*
145   In at his window. Set this up with wax
    Upon old Brutus'° statue. All this done,   *Lucius Junius Brutus's*
    Repair° to Pompey's Porch where you shall find us.   *Proceed*
    Is Decius Brutus and Trebonius there?
    CINNA All but Metellus Cimber, and he's gone
150   To seek you at your house. Well, I will hie,°   *hasten*
    And so bestow these papers as you bade me.
    CASSIUS That done, repair to Pompey's Theatre.   *Exit* CINNA
    Come, Casca, you and I will yet ere day
    See Brutus at his house. Three parts° of him   *quarters*
155   Is ours already, and the man entire
    Upon the next encounter yields him ours.
    CASCA O, he sits high in all the people's hearts,
    And that which would appear offence in us
    His countenance, like richest alchemy,[8]
160   Will change to virtue and to worthiness.
    CASSIUS Him and his worth, and our great need of him,
    You have right well conceited.° Let us go,   *understood*
    For it is after midnight, and ere day
    We will awake him and be sure of him.   *Exeunt*

2.1
Enter BRUTUS *in his orchard*

    BRUTUS What, Lucius, ho!—
    I cannot by the progress of the stars
    Give guess how near to day.—Lucius, I say!—
    I would it were my fault to sleep so soundly.—
5   When, Lucius, when?° Awake, I say! What, Lucius!   *(expressing impatience)*
        Enter LUCIUS
    LUCIUS Called you, my lord?
    BRUTUS Get me a taper° in my study, Lucius.   *candle*
    When it is lighted, come and call me here.
    LUCIUS I will, my lord.   *Exit*
10   BRUTUS It must be by his° death. And for my part   *(Caesar's)*
    I know no personal cause to spurn° at him,   *kick*

6. Cinna is responding to Cassius's information about
Casca.
7. Brutus was one of sixteen praetors, or chief magistrates, subordinate only to the two consuls.

8. Alchemy attempted to change base metals into gold.
countenance: approval; noble appearance.
2.1 Location: Outside Brutus's house.

But for the general.° He would be crowned.   *common good*
How that might change his nature, there's the question.
It is the bright day that brings forth the adder,
15 And that craves° wary walking. Crown him: that!   *calls for*
And then I grant we put a sting in him
That at his will he may do danger with.
Th'abuse of greatness is when it disjoins
Remorse° from power. And to speak truth of Caesar,   *Conscience*
20 I have not known when his affections swayed°   *passions ruled*
More than his reason. But 'tis a common proof°   *experience*
That lowliness° is young ambition's ladder,   *humility*
Whereto the climber-upward turns his face;
But when he once attains the upmost round,°   *rung*
25 He then unto the ladder turns his back,
Looks in the clouds, scorning the base degrees[1]
By which he did ascend. So Caesar may.
Then lest he may, prevent. And since the quarrel
Will bear no colour for the thing he is,[2]
30 Fashion° it thus: that what he is, augmented,   *Describe*
Would run to these and these extremities;
And therefore think him as a serpent's egg, *preventative plan*
Which, hatched, would as his kind° grow mischievous,°   *by its nature / harmful*
And kill him in the shell.
    Enter LUCIUS [*with a letter*]
35 LUCIUS   The taper burneth in your closet,° sir.   *private room*
Searching the window for a flint, I found
This paper, thus sealed up, and I am sure
It did not lie there when I went to bed.
    [*He*] *gives him the letter*
BRUTUS   Get you to bed again; it is not day.
40 Is not tomorrow, boy, the ides of March?
LUCIUS   I know not, sir.
BRUTUS   Look in the calendar and bring me word.
LUCIUS   I will, sir.   *Exit*
BRUTUS   The exhalations° whizzing in the air   *meteors*
45 Give so much light that I may read by them.
    [*He*] *opens the letter and reads*
'Brutus, thou sleep'st. Awake, and see thyself.
Shall Rome, et cetera? Speak, strike, redress.'—
'Brutus, thou sleep'st. Awake.'
Such instigations have been often dropped
50 Where I have took them up.
'Shall Rome, et cetera?' Thus must I piece it out:
Shall Rome stand under one man's awe? What, Rome?
My ancestors did from the streets of Rome
The Tarquin drive when he was called a king.[3]
55 'Speak, strike, redress.' Am I entreated
To speak and strike? O Rome, I make thee promise,
If the redress will follow,[4] thou receivest
Thy full petition at the hand of Brutus.
    Enter LUCIUS
LUCIUS   Sir, March is wasted fifteen days.

---

1. Low rungs; contemptible means; lowly social ranks.   3. See note to 1.2.160.
2. Will find no plausible pretext in his conduct so far.   4. That is, if killing Caesar will restore the Republic.

Knock within

60 BRUTUS 'Tis good. Go to the gate; somebody knocks. [*Exit* LUCIUS]

Since Cassius first did whet° me against Caesar   incite
I have not slept.
Between the acting of a dreadful thing
And the first motion,° all the interim is   impulse
65 Like a phantasma° or a hideous dream.   nightmare
The genius° and the mortal instruments⁵   immortal spirit
Are then in counsel, and the state of man,
Like to a little kingdom, suffers then
The nature of an insurrection.⁶

Enter LUCIUS

70 LUCIUS Sir, 'tis your brother Cassius° at the door,
Who doth desire to see you.
BRUTUS   Is he alone?
LUCIUS No, sir, there are more with him.
BRUTUS   Do you know them?
LUCIUS No, sir; their hats are plucked about their ears,
And half their faces buried in their cloaks,
75 That by no means I may discover° them   identify
By any mark of favour.°   distinctive feature
BRUTUS   Let 'em enter. [*Exit* LUCIUS]
They are the faction. O conspiracy,
Sham'st thou to show thy dang'rous brow by night,
When evils are most free?° O then by day   uninhibited
80 Where wilt thou find a cavern dark enough
To mask thy monstrous visage? Seek none, conspiracy,
Hide it in smiles and affability;
For if thou put thy native semblance on,⁸
Not Erebus° itself were dim enough   dark underworld region
85 To hide thee from prevention.⁹

Enter the conspirators [*muffled*]: CASSIUS, CASCA,
DECIUS, CINNA, METELLUS, *and* TREBONIUS

CASSIUS I think we are too bold¹ upon your rest.
Good morrow, Brutus. Do we trouble you?
BRUTUS I have been up this hour, awake all night.
Know I these men that come along with you?
90 CASSIUS Yes, every man of them; and no man here
But honours you; and every one doth wish
You had but that opinion of yourself
Which every noble Roman bears of you.
This is Trebonius.
BRUTUS   He is welcome hither.
CASSIUS This, Decius Brutus.
95 BRUTUS   He is welcome too.
CASSIUS This, Casca; Cinna, this; and this, Metellus Cimber.
BRUTUS They are all welcome.
What watchful° cares do interpose themselves   sleep-preventing
Betwixt your eyes and night?
CASSIUS   Shall I entreat a word?
[CASSIUS *and* BRUTUS *stand aside and*] *whisper*

---

5. Bodily powers.
6. *the state . . . insurrection:* referring to a common-place analogy between disorder in man, in the body politic, and in nature.

7. Cassius was married to Brutus's sister.
8. Display your natural appearance.
9. From being recognized and thwarted.
1. We intrude too presumptuously.

100 DECIUS   Here lies the east. Doth not the day break here?

CASCA   No.

CINNA   O pardon, sir, it doth; and yon grey lines
That fret° the clouds are messengers of day.   *interlace*

CASCA   You shall confess that you are both deceived.
     [*He points his sword*]

105   Here, as I point my sword, the sun arises,
Which is a great way growing° on the south,   *encroaching*
Weighing° the youthful season of the year.   *On account of*
Some two months hence up higher toward the north
He first presents his fire, and the high° east   *due*

110   Stands, as the Capitol, directly here.
     [*He points his sword*]
     [BRUTUS *and* CASSIUS *join the other conspirators*]

BRUTUS   Give me your hands all over, one by one.
     [*He shakes their hands*]

CASSIUS   And let us swear our resolution.

BRUTUS   No, not an oath. If not the face° of men,   *(grave) expressions*
The sufferance° of our souls, the time's abuse[2]—   *suffering*

115   If these be motives weak, break off betimes,°   *at once*
And every man hence to his idle° bed.   *unused; lazy*
So let high-sighted° tyranny range on   *arrogant*
Till each man drop by lottery.[3] But if these,°   *these reasons*
As I am sure they do, bear fire enough

120   To kindle cowards and to steel with valour
The melting spirits of women, then, countrymen,
What need we any spur but our own cause
To prick us to redress? What other bond
Than secret Romans,[4] that have spoke the word

125   And will not palter?° And what other oath   *equivocate*
Than honesty° to honesty engaged   *integrity*
That this shall be or we will fall for it?
Swear° priests and cowards and men cautelous,°   *Let swear / crafty; wary*
Old feeble carrions,° and such suffering souls   *corpselike men*

130   That welcome wrongs;[5] unto bad causes swear
Such creatures as men doubt;° but do not stain   *suspect*
The even° virtue of our enterprise,   *just; straightforward*
Nor th'insuppressive° mettle of our spirits,   *the indomitable*
To think that or° our cause or our performance   *either*

135   Did need an oath, when every drop of blood
That every Roman bears, and nobly bears,
Is guilty of a several bastardy[6]
If he do break the smallest particle
Of any promise that hath passed from him.

140 CASSIUS   But what of Cicero? Shall we sound him?°   *find out his thoughts*
I think he will stand very strong with us.

CASCA   Let us not leave him out.

CINNA   No, by no means.

METELLUS   O, let us have him, for his silver hairs
Will purchase us a good opinion,°   *reputation*

---

2. The corruption of the present time.
3. Chance (the tyrant's caprice).
4. Than that we are Romans capable of secrecy.

5. That gladly submit to oppression.
6. Will show itself individually to be adulterated by non-Roman blood.

145 And buy men's voices to commend our deeds.
It shall be said his judgement ruled our hands.
Our youths and wildness shall no whit appear,
But all be buried in his gravity.

BRUTUS   O, name him not! Let us not break with° him,   *disclose our plans to*
150 For he will never follow anything
That other men begin.

CASSIUS   Then leave him out.

CASCA   Indeed he is not fit.

DECIUS   Shall no man else be touched, but only Caesar?

155 CASSIUS   Decius, well urged.° I think it is not meet°   *suggested / proper*
Mark Antony, so well beloved of Caesar,
Should outlive Caesar. We shall find of him
A shrewd° contriver. And you know his means,   *malicious*
If he improve° them, may well stretch so far   *make the most of*
160 As to annoy° us all; which to prevent,   *harm*
Let Antony and Caesar fall together.

BRUTUS   Our course[7] will seem too bloody, Caius Cassius,
To cut the head off and then hack the limbs,
Like wrath in death and envy° afterwards—   *malice*
165 For Antony is but a limb of Caesar.
✱ Let's be sacrificers, but not butchers, Caius.
We all stand up against the spirit of Caesar,
And in the spirit of men there is no blood.
O, that we then could come by° Caesar's spirit,   *obtain*
170 And not dismember Caesar! But, alas,
Caesar must bleed for it. And, gentle friends,
Let's kill him boldly, but not wrathfully. ✱
Let's carve him as a dish fit for the gods,
Not hew him as a carcass fit for hounds.
175 And let our hearts, as subtle° masters do,   *cunning*
Stir up their servants° to an act of rage,   *(that is, our hands)*
And after seem to chide 'em. This shall make
Our purpose necessary, and not envious;°   *malicious*
Which so appearing to the common eyes,
180 We shall be called purgers,° not murderers.   *purifiers*
And for Mark Antony, think not of him,
For he can do no more than Caesar's arm
When Caesar's head is off.

CASSIUS   Yet I fear him;
For in the engrafted° love he bears to Caesar—   *deep-rooted*

185 BRUTUS   Alas, good Cassius, do not think of him.
If he love Caesar, all that he can do
Is to himself: take thought,° and die for Caesar.   *succumb to melancholy*
And that were much he should,[8] for he is given
To sports, to wildness, and much company.

190 TREBONIUS   There is no fear° in him. Let him not die;   *nothing to fear*
For he will live, and laugh at this hereafter.

Clock strikes

BRUTUS   Peace, count the clock.[9]

CASSIUS   The clock hath stricken three.

---

7. Punning on "corse," meaning "corpse."
8. And that is more than he is likely to do.

9. The clock is an anachronism, like sleeves and doublets.

TREBONIUS   'Tis time to part.

CASSIUS   But it is doubtful yet
    Whether Caesar will come forth today or no;
195   For he is superstitious grown of late,
    Quite from the main° opinion he held once   *Contrary to the strong*
    Of fantasy, of dreams and ceremonies.
    It may be these apparent° prodigies,   *manifest*
    The unaccustomed terror of this night,
200   And the persuasion of his augurers,[1]
    May hold him from the Capitol today.

DECIUS   Never fear that. If he be so resolved
    I can o'ersway° him; for he loves to hear   *prevail upon*
    That unicorns may be betrayed with trees,[2]
205   And bears with glasses,[3] elephants with holes,°   *pits*
    Lions with toils,° and men with flatterers;   *nets*
    But when I tell him he hates flatterers;
    He says he does, being then most flattered. Let me work,
    For I can give his humour the true bent,[4]
210   And I will bring him to the Capitol.

CASSIUS   Nay, we will all of us be there to fetch him.

BRUTUS   By the eighth hour. Is that the uttermost?°   *latest*

CINNA   Be that the uttermost, and fail not then.

METELLUS   Caius Ligarius doth bear Caesar hard,°   *ill will*
215   Who rated° him for speaking well of Pompey.   *rebuked*
    I wonder none of you have thought of him.

BRUTUS   Now good Metellus, go along by him.°   *to his house*
    He loves me well, and I have given him reasons.
    Send him but hither, and I'll fashion° him.   *work upon*
220 CASSIUS   The morning comes upon's. We'll leave you, Brutus.
    And, friends, disperse yourselves; but all remember
    What you have said, and show yourselves true Romans.

BRUTUS   Good gentlemen, look fresh and merrily.
    Let not our looks put on° our purposes;   *display*
225   But bear it as our Roman actors do,
    With untired spirits and formal constancy.°   *decorous self-possession*
    And so good morrow to you every one.

                            Exeunt. Manet° BRUTUS   *Remains*

    Boy, Lucius!—Fast asleep? It is no matter.
    Enjoy the honey-heavy dew of slumber.
230   Thou hast no figures° nor no fantasies   *imaginings*
    Which busy care draws in the brains of men;
    Therefore thou sleep'st so sound.

        Enter PORTIA

PORTIA   Brutus, my lord.

BRUTUS   Portia, what mean you? Wherefore rise you now?
    It is not for° your health thus to commit   *good for*
235   Your weak condition to the raw cold morning.

PORTIA   Nor for yours neither. You've ungently,° Brutus,   *unkindly*
    Stole from my bed; and yesternight at supper
    You suddenly arose, and walked about

---

1. Priests who interpreted "auguries," or omens.
2. The unicorn could supposedly be caught by tricking it into impaling its horn on a tree.
3. Mirrors (imagined to bewilder bears).
4. Give his disposition the right direction.

Musing and sighing, with your arms across;[5]
240 And when I asked you what the matter was,
You stared upon me with ungentle looks.
I urged you further; then you scratched your head,
And too impatiently stamped with your foot.
Yet I insisted; yet you answered not.
245 But with an angry wafture° of your hand   gesture
Gave sign for me to leave you. So I did,
Fearing to strengthen that impatience
Which seemed too much enkindled, and withal°   besides
Hoping it was but an effect of humour,°   moodiness
250 Which sometime hath his° hour with every man.   its
It will not let you eat, nor talk, nor sleep;
And could it work so much upon your shape
As it hath much prevailed on your condition,°   disposition
I should not know you° Brutus. Dear my lord,   recognize you as
255 Make me acquainted with your cause of grief.
BRUTUS   I am not well in health, and that is all.
PORTIA   Brutus is wise, and were he not in health
He would embrace the means to come by it.
BRUTUS   Why, so I do. Good Portia, go to bed.
260 PORTIA   Is Brutus sick? And is it physical°   curative
To walk unbracèd° and suck up the humours[6]   with open doublet
Of the dank morning? What, is Brutus sick?
And will he steal out of his wholesome bed
To dare the vile contagion of the night,
265 And tempt the rheumy and unpurgèd° air   moist and impure
To add unto his sickness? No, my Brutus,
You have some sick offence° within your mind,   disturbance
Which by the right and virtue° of my place°   prerogative / (as a wife)
I ought to know of. [Kneeling] And upon my knees,
270 I charm° you by my once-commended beauty,   conjure
By all your vows of love, and that great vow
Which did incorporate and make us one,
That you unfold to me, your self, your half,
Why you are heavy,° and what men tonight   dejected
275 Have had resort to you—for here have been
Some six or seven, who did hide their faces
Even from darkness.
BRUTUS   Kneel not, gentle Portia.
PORTIA [rising]   I should not need if you were gentle Brutus.
Within the bond of marriage, tell me, Brutus,
280 Is it excepted[7] I should know no secrets
That appertain to you? Am I your self
But as it were in sort or limitation?[8]
To keep with you at meals, comfort your bed,
And talk to you sometimes? Dwell I but in the suburbs[9]
285 Of your good pleasure? If it be no more,
Portia is Brutus' harlot, not his wife.
BRUTUS   You are my true and honourable wife,

---

5. Crossed (a sign of melancholy).
6. Inhale the mists.
7. Is it stipulated as a qualification that.
8. *in sort or limitation:* after a fashion or with restric-

tions (like "excepted," "limited" is a legal term).
9. Outlying areas (where brothels were located in Shakespeare's time).

As dear to me as are the ruddy drops
That visit° my sad heart.   *afflict; come to*

290 PORTIA   If this were true, then should I know this secret.
I grant I am a woman, but withal°   *still*
A woman that Lord Brutus took to wife.
I grant I am a woman, but withal
A woman well reputed, Cato's daughter.[1]

295 Think you I am no stronger than my sex,
Being so fathered and so husbanded?
Tell me your counsels;° I will not disclose 'em.   *secrets*
I have made strong proof of my constancy,
Giving myself a voluntary wound

300 Here in the thigh. Can I bear that with patience,
And not my husband's secrets?

BRUTUS   O ye gods,
Render me worthy of this noble wife!
Knock[ing within]
Hark, hark, one knocks. Portia, go in a while,
And by and by thy bosom shall partake

305 The secrets of my heart.
All my engagements° I will construe° to thee,   *commitments / explain*
All the charactery[2] of my sad brows.
Leave me with haste.   *Exit* PORTIA
Lucius, who's that knocks?
Enter LUCIUS, *and* LIGARIUS [*with a kerchief round his head*][3]

LUCIUS   Here is a sick man that would speak with you.

310 BRUTUS   Caius Ligarius, that Metellus spake of.—
Boy, stand aside.   [*Exit* LUCIUS]
Caius Ligarius, how?°   *how are you*

LIGARIUS   Vouchsafe° good morrow from a feeble tongue.   *Deign to accept*

BRUTUS   O, what a time have you chose out, brave Caius,
To wear a kerchief! Would you were not sick!

315 LIGARIUS   I am not sick if Brutus have in hand
Any exploit worthy the name of honour.

BRUTUS   Such an exploit have I in hand, Ligarius,
Had you a healthful ear to hear of it.

LIGARIUS   By all the gods that Romans bow before,
I here discard my sickness.
[*He pulls off his kerchief*]

320   Soul of Rome,
Brave son derived from honourable loins,
Thou like an exorcist° hast conjured up   *a magician*
My mortifièd° spirit. Now bid me run,   *deadened*
And I will strive with things impossible,

325 Yea, get the better of them. What's to do?

BRUTUS   A piece of work that will make sick men whole.°   *healthy*

LIGARIUS   But are not some whole that we must make sick?

BRUTUS   That must we also. What it is, my Caius,
I shall unfold to thee as we are going
To whom it must be done.

1. Marcus Porcius Cato was renowned for his strict
moral integrity; after Caesar's victory over Pompey, he
killed himself rather than submit to Caesar's rule.
2. Handwriting (the lines of care "inscribed" on his

forehead).
3. Kerchiefs were commonly worn by the sick in
Elizabethan England.

330 LIGARIUS   Set on° your foot,   *Advance*
        And with a heart new-fired I follow you
        To do I know not what; but it sufficeth
        That Brutus leads me on.
BRUTUS   Follow me then.   *Exeunt*

                              2.2
              Thunder and lightning.
              Enter Julius CAESAR *in his nightgown*°   *dressing gown*
CAESAR   Nor heaven nor earth have been at peace tonight.
        Thrice hath Calpurnia in her sleep cried out
        'Help, ho! They murder Caesar!'—Who's within?
              Enter a SERVANT
SERVANT   My lord.
5 CAESAR   Go bid the priests do present° sacrifice,   *immediate*
        And bring me their opinions of success.[1]
SERVANT   I will, my lord.   *Exit*
              Enter CALPURNIA
CALPURNIA   What mean you, Caesar? Think you to walk forth?
        You shall not stir out of your house today.
10 CAESAR   Caesar shall forth. The things that threatened me
        Ne'er looked but on my back; when they shall see
        The face of Caesar, they are vanishèd.
CALPURNIA   Caesar, I never stood on ceremonies,°   *heeded omens*
        Yet now they fright me. There is one within,
15   Besides the things that we have heard and seen,
        Recounts most horrid sights seen by the watch.[2]
        A lioness hath whelpèd in the streets,
        And graves have yawned and yielded up their dead.
        Fierce fiery warriors fight upon the clouds,
20   In ranks and squadrons and right form of war,°   *regular battle formation*
        Which drizzled blood upon the Capitol.
        The noise of battle hurtled in the air.
        Horses do neigh, and dying men did groan,
        And ghosts did shriek and squeal about the streets.
25   O Caesar, these things are beyond all use,°   *all normal experience*
        And I do fear them.
CAESAR   What can be avoided
        Whose end is purposed by the mighty gods?
        Yet Caesar shall go forth, for these predictions
        Are to° the world in general as to Caesar.   *Are as applicable to*
30 CALPURNIA   When beggars die there are no comets seen;
        The heavens themselves blaze forth° the death of princes.   *flame out; proclaim*
CAESAR   Cowards die many times before their deaths;
        The valiant never taste of death but once.
        Of all the wonders that I yet have heard,
35   It seems to me most strange that men should fear,
        Seeing that death, a necessary end,
        Will come when it will come.
              Enter SERVANT
                    What say the augurers?
SERVANT   They would not have you to stir forth today.

2.2 Location: Caesar's house.   reading the entrails of the sacrificial animals.
1. Of the outcome (good or bad), as determined by   2. Night watchmen (another anachronism).

Plucking the entrails of an offering forth,
40 They could not find a heart within the beast.

CAESAR   The gods do this in shame of cowardice.°   *to put cowardice to shame*
Caesar should be a beast without a heart
If he should stay at home today for fear.
No, Caesar shall not. Danger knows full well
45 That Caesar is more dangerous than he.
We are two lions littered in one day,
And I the elder and more terrible.
And Caesar shall go forth.

CALPURNIA   Alas, my lord,
Your wisdom is consumed in confidence.°   *overconfidence*
50 Do not go forth today. Call it my fear
That keeps you in the house, and not your own.
We'll send Mark Antony to the Senate House,
And he shall say you are not well today.
Let me upon my knee prevail in this.
           [*She kneels*]

55 CAESAR   Mark Antony shall say I am not well,
And for thy humour° I will stay at home.   *whim*
           Enter DECIUS
Here's Decius Brutus; he shall tell them so.
           [CALPURNIA *rises*]

DECIUS   Caesar, all hail! Good morrow, worthy Caesar.
I come to fetch you to the Senate House.

60 CAESAR   And you are come in very happy° time   *opportune*
To bear my greeting to the senators
And tell them that I will not come today.
Cannot is false, and that I dare not, falser.
I will not come today; tell them so, Decius.

CALPURNIA   Say he is sick.

65 CAESAR   Shall Caesar send a lie?
Have I in conquest stretched mine arm so far,
To be afeard to tell greybeards the truth?
Decius, go tell them Caesar will not come.

DECIUS   Most mighty Caesar, let me know some cause,
70 Lest I be laughed at when I tell them so.

CAESAR   The cause is in my will; I will not come.
That is enough to satisfy the Senate.
But for your private satisfaction,
Because I love you, I will let you know.
75 Calpurnia here, my wife, stays° me at home.   *keeps*
She dreamt tonight° she saw my statue,   *last night*
Which like a fountain with an hundred spouts
Did run pure blood; and many lusty° Romans   *joyful*
Came smiling and did bathe their hands in it.
80 And these does she apply° for warnings and portents   *interpret*
Of evils imminent, and on her knee
Hath begged that I will stay at home today.

DECIUS   This dream is all amiss interpreted.
It was a vision fair and fortunate.
85 Your statue spouting blood in many pipes,   redescription
In which so many smiling Romans bathed,
Signifies that from you great Rome shall suck
Reviving blood, and that great men shall press

For tinctures, stains, relics, and cognizance.[3]
90 This by Calpurnia's dream is signified.
CAESAR   And this way have you well expounded it.
DECIUS   I have, when you have heard what I can say.
And know it now: the Senate have concluded
To give this day a crown to mighty Caesar.
95 If you shall send them word you will not come,
Their minds may change. Besides, it were a mock
Apt to be rendered[4] for someone to say
'Break up the Senate till another time,
When Caesar's wife shall meet with better dreams.'
100 If Caesar hide himself, shall they not whisper
'Lo, Caesar is afraid'?
Pardon me, Caesar; for my dear dear love
To your proceeding° bids me tell you this,   advancement
And reason to my love is liable.[5]
105 CAESAR   How foolish do your fears seem now, Calpurnia!
I am ashamèd I did yield to them.
Give me my robe, for I will go.
        Enter [CASSIUS,] BRUTUS, LIGARIUS, METELLUS, CASCA,
            TREBONIUS, *and* CINNA
And look where Cassius is come to fetch me.
CASSIUS   Good morrow, Caesar.
CAESAR   Welcome, Cassius.—
110 What, Brutus, are you stirred so early too?—
Good morrow, Casca.—Caius Ligarus,—
Caesar was ne'er so much your enemy
As that same ague° which hath made you lean.   fever
What is't o'clock?
BRUTUS   Caesar, 'tis strucken eight.
115 CAESAR   I thank you for your pains and courtesy.
        Enter ANTONY
See, Antony that revels long a-nights
Is notwithstanding up. Good morrow, Antony.
ANTONY   So to most noble Caesar.
CAESAR [*to* CALPURNIA]   Bid them prepare within.
I am to blame to be thus waited for.   [*Exit* CALPURNIA]
120 Now, Cinna.—Now, Metellus.—What, Trebonius!
I have an hour's talk in store for you.
Remember that you call on me today.
Be near me, that I may remember you.
TREBONIUS   Caesar, I will, [*aside*] and so near will I be
125 That your best friends shall wish I had been further
CAESAR   Good friends, go in and taste some wine with me,
And we, like[6] friends, will straightway go together.
BRUTUS [*aside*]   That every like is not the same, O Caesar,
The heart of Brutus ernes° to think upon.   *Exeunt*   grieves

2.3
Enter ARTEMIDORUS, *reading a letter*
ARTEMIDORUS   'Caesar, beware of Brutus. Take heed of Cassius.

---

3. Heraldic colors and emblems ("tinctures," "stains," and "cognizance"); venerated properties of saints ("tinctures," "stains," and "relics").
4. *a mock . . . rendered*: a sarcastic reply likely to be made.

5. And prudence is subordinate to my affection.
6. As becomes (but Brutus plays on the senses "resembling" and "equal to").
2.3 Location: A street near the Capitol.

Come not near Casca. Have an eye to Cinna. Trust not Trebonius. Mark well Metellus Cimber. Decius Brutus loves thee
not. Thou hast wronged Caius Ligarius. There is but one mind
5   in all these men, and it is bent against Caesar. If thou beest not
immortal, look about you. Security gives way to° conspiracy.   *Overconfidence permits*
The mighty gods defend thee!
                                        Thy lover,°   *friend*
                                        Artemidorus.'

10   Here will I stand till Caesar pass along,
And as a suitor° will I give him this.   *petitioner*
My heart laments that virtue cannot live
Out of the teeth of emulation.¹
If thou read this, O Caesar, thou mayst live.
15   If not, the fates with traitors do contrive.°   *Exit*   *conspire*

2.4

Enter PORTIA *and* LUCIUS

PORTIA   I prithee, boy, run to the Senate House.
Stay not to answer me, but get thee gone.—
Why dost thou stay?
LUCIUS   To know my errand, madam.
PORTIA   I would have had thee there and here again
5   Ere I can tell thee what thou shouldst do there.
[*Aside*] O constancy, be strong upon my side;
Set a huge mountain 'tween my heart and tongue.
I have a man's mind, but a woman's might.
How hard it is for women to keep counsel!°   *a secret*
[*To* LUCIUS] Art thou here yet?
10   LUCIUS   Madam, what should I do?
Run to the Capitol, and nothing else?
And so return to you, and nothing else?
PORTIA   Yes, bring me word, boy, if thy lord look well,
For he went sickly forth; and take good note
15   What Caesar doth, what suitors press to him.
Hark, boy, what noise is that?
LUCIUS   I hear none, madam.
PORTIA   Prithee, listen well.
I heard a bustling rumour,° like a fray,   *disturbed clamor*
20   And the wind brings it from the Capitol.
LUCIUS   Sooth,° madam, I hear nothing.   *In truth*
Enter the SOOTHSAYER
PORTIA   Come hither, fellow. Which way hast thou been?
SOOTHSAYER   At mine own house, good lady.
PORTIA   What is't o'clock?
25   SOOTHSAYER   About the ninth hour, lady.
PORTIA   Is Caesar yet gone to the Capitol?
SOOTHSAYER   Madam, not yet. I go to take my stand
To see him pass on to the Capitol.
PORTIA   Thou hast some suit to Caesar, hast thou not?
30   SOOTHSAYER   That I have, lady. If it will please Caesar
To be so good to Caesar as to hear me,
I shall beseech him to befriend himself.
PORTIA   Why, know'st thou any harms intended towards him?

---

1. Beyond the danger of ambitious envy.   2.4 Location: Brutus's house.

SOOTHSAYER None that I know will be; much that I fear may chance.
  Good morrow to you.
    [*He moves away*]
35   Here the street is narrow.
  The throng that follows Caesar at the heels,
  Of senators, of praetors, common suitors,
  Will crowd a feeble man almost to death.
  I'll get me to a place more void,° and there   *empty*
40 Speak to great Caesar as he comes along.   *Exit*
PORTIA [*aside*] I must go in. Ay me! How weak a thing
  The heart of woman is! O Brutus,
  The heavens speed thee in thine enterprise!—
  Sure the boy heard me. [*To* LUCIUS] Brutus hath a suit
45 That Caesar will not grant. [*Aside*] O, I grow faint!
  [*To* LUCIUS] Run, Lucius, and commend me to my lord.
  Say I am merry.° Come to me again,   *in good spirits*
  And bring me word what he doth say to thee.
                          Exeunt [*severally*]°   *separately*

3.1

  Enter [*at one door*] ARTEMIDORUS, *the* SOOTHSAYER [*and
  citizens*]. *Flourish. Enter* [*at another door*] CAESAR, BRUTUS,
  CASSIUS, CASCA, DECIUS, METELLUS, TREBONIUS, CINNA,
  [LIGARIUS,] ANTONY, LEPIDUS, PUBLIUS[, POFILLIUS
  and other senators]

CAESAR [*to the* SOOTHSAYER] The ides of March are come
SOOTHSAYER Ay, Caesar, but not gone.
ARTEMIDORUS Hail, Caesar! Read this schedule.°   *document*
DECIUS [*to* CAESAR] Trebonius doth desire you to o'er-read
5   At your best leisure this his humble suit.
ARTEMIDORUS O Caesar, read mine first, for mine's a suit
  That touches° Caesar nearer. Read it, great Caesar.   *concerns*
CAESAR What touches us ourself shall be last served.°   *attended to*
ARTEMIDORUS Delay not, Caesar, read it instantly.
CAESAR What, is the fellow mad?
10 PUBLIUS [*to* ARTEMIDORUS]   Sirrah, give place.
CASSIUS [*to* ARTEMIDORUS] What, urge you your petitions in the street?
  Come to the Capitol.
    [*They walk about the stage*][1]
POPILLIUS [*aside to* CASSIUS] I wish your enterprise today may thrive.
CASSIUS What enterprise, Popillius?
POPILLIUS   Fare you well.
    [*He leaves* CASSIUS, *and makes to*° CAESAR]   *goes toward*
15 BRUTUS What said Popillius Laena?
CASSIUS He wished today our enterprise might thrive.
  I fear our purpose is discoverèd.
BRUTUS Look how he makes to Caesar. Mark him
CASSIUS Casca, be sudden,° for we fear prevention.°—   *swift / being thwarted*
20 Brutus, what shall be done? If this be known,
  Cassius or Caesar never shall turn back,°   *return alive*
  For I will slay myself.
BRUTUS   Cassius, be constant.°   *resolute*

3.1 Location: At the Capitol.
1. Indicating a movement from the street outside to the interior of the Capitol.

Popillius Laena speaks not of our purposes,
For look, he smiles, and Caesar doth not change.

25 CASSIUS Trebonius knows his time, for look you, Brutus,
He draws Mark Antony out of the way. [*Exeunt* TREBONIUS *and* ANTONY]

DECIUS Where is Metellus Cimber? Let him go
And presently prefer° his suit to Caesar.   *at once present*
      [CAESAR *sits*]

BRUTUS He is addressed.° Press near, and second him.   *ready*

30 CINNA Casca, you are the first that rears your hand.
      [*The conspirators and the other senators
      take their places*]

CAESAR Are we all ready? What is now amiss
That Caesar and his Senate must redress?

METELLUS [*coming forward and kneeling*] Most high, most
      mighty, and most puissant Caesar,
Metellus Cimber throws before thy seat
An humble heart.

35 CAESAR   I must prevent° thee, Cimber.   *thwart*
These couchings° and these lowly courtesies°   *stoopings / bows*
Might fire the blood° of ordinary men,   *passions*
And turn preordinance and first decree²
Into the law of children.° Be not fond³   *childish whims*

40 To think that Caesar bears such rebel° blood   *lawless*
That will be thawed from the true quality°   *proper constancy*
With that which melteth fools: I mean sweet words,
Low-crookèd° curtsies, and base spaniel fawning.   *Obsequious; dishonest*
Thy brother by decree is banishèd.

45 If thou dost bend and pray and fawn for him,
I spurn thee like a cur out of my way.
Know Caesar doth not wrong but with just cause,⁴
Nor without cause will he be satisfied.

METELLUS Is there no voice more worthy than my own

50 To sound more sweetly in great Caesar's ear
For the repealing of my banished brother?

BRUTUS [*coming forward and kneeling*] I kiss thy hand, but not
      in flattery, Caesar,
Desiring thee that Publius Cimber may
Have an immediate freedom of repeal.°   *release from banishment*

CAESAR What, Brutus?

CASSIUS [*coming forward and kneeling*]

55   Pardon, Caesar; Caesar, pardon.
As low as to thy foot doth Cassius fall
To beg enfranchisement° for Publius Cimber.   *liberation*

CAESAR I could be well moved if I were as you.
If I could pray to move,° prayers would move me.   *make pleas*
60 But I am constant as the Northern Star,°   *polestar*
Of whose true fixed and resting° quality   *stationary*
There is no fellow° in the firmament.   *equal*
The skies are painted with unnumbered sparks;
They are all fire, and every one doth shine;
65 But there's but one in all doth hold his place.
So in the world: 'tis furnished well with men,

---

2. Established precedent and original rulings.   4. F reads merely, "Know Caesar doth not wrong." See
3. Do not be so foolish as.   Textual Note.

And men are flesh and blood, and apprehensive;°   *capable of understanding*
Yet in the number I do know but one
That unassailable holds on his rank,°   *maintains his place*
70   Unshaked of motion;⁵ and that I am he
Let me a little show it even in this—
That I was constant° Cimber should be banished,   *resolute*
And constant do remain to keep him so.

CINNA [*coming forward and kneeling*]
    O Caesar!

CAESAR   Hence! Wilt thou lift up Olympus?⁶

DECIUS [*coming forward with* LIGARIUS *and kneeling*]
    Great Caesar!

75   CAESAR   Doth not Brutus bootless° kneel?   *in vain*

CASCA [*coming forward and kneeling*]
    Speak hands for me.⁷
        They stab CAESAR [CASCA *first,* BRUTUS *last*]

CAESAR   *Et tu, Bruté?*⁸—Then fall Caesar.
                             [*He*] *dies*

CINNA   Liberty! Freedom! Tyranny is dead!
    Run hence, proclaim, cry it about the streets.

CASSIUS   Some to the common pulpits,° and cry out   *public platforms (rostra)*
80   'Liberty, freedom, and enfranchisement!'

BRUTUS   People and senators, be not affrighted.
    [*Exeunt in a tumult* LEPIDUS, POPILLIUS, *other senators,*
                ARTEMIDORUS, SOOTHSAYER, *and citizens*]
    Fly not! Stand still! Ambition's debt is paid.

CASCA   Go to the pulpit, Brutus.

DECIUS   And Cassius too.

85   BRUTUS   Where's Publius?°   *(an elderly senator)*

CINNA   Here, quite confounded° with this mutiny.°   *confused / tumult*

METELLUS   Stand fast together, lest some friend of Caesar's
    Should chance—

BRUTUS   Talk not of standing.—Publius, good cheer!
90   There is no harm intended to your person,
    Nor to no Roman else—so tell them, Publius.

CASSIUS   And leave us, Publius, lest that the people,
    Rushing on us, should do your age some mischief.°   *injury*

BRUTUS   Do so; and let no man abide° this deed   *pay the penalty for*
95   But we the doers.   [*Exit* PUBLIUS]
        Enter TREBONIUS

CASSIUS   Where is Antony?

TREBONIUS   Fled to his house, amazed.
    Men, wives, and children stare, cry out, and run,
    As° it were doomsday.   *As if*

BRUTUS   Fates, we will know your pleasures.
100   That we shall die, we know; 'tis but the time
    And drawing days out that men stand upon.⁹

CASCA   Why, he that cuts off twenty years of life
    Cuts off so many years of fearing death.

---

5. Completely steady; unmoved by persuasion.
6. High mountain in Greece where the gods were supposed to dwell.
7. Let my hands beseech in prayer; let violent action take over where speech has failed.
8. Latin: And you, Brutus? According to Plutarch, Cae-

sar spoke these words in Greek and stopped defending himself when he saw Brutus among the conspirators.
9. *'tis . . . upon:* it is but the specific time of death and the possibility of extending their lives with which men concern themselves.

BRUTUS   Grant that, and then is death a benefit.
105   So are we Caesar's friends, that have abridged
His time of fearing death. Stoop, Romans, stoop,
And let us bathe our hands in Caesar's blood
Up to the elbows, and besmear our swords;
Then walk we forth even to the market-place,°   *the Roman Forum*
110   And, waving our red weapons o'er our heads,
Let's all cry 'peace, freedom, and liberty!'
CASSIUS   Stoop, then, and wash.
                    [*They smear their hands with Caesar's blood*]
                                        How many ages hence
Shall this our lofty scene be acted over,
In states unborn and accents° yet unknown!   *languages*
115   BRUTUS   How many times shall Caesar bleed in sport,°   *for entertainment*
That now on Pompey's basis lies along,[1]
No worthier than the dust!
CASSIUS   So oft as that shall be,
So often shall the knot° of us be called   *group*
The men that gave their country liberty.
DECIUS   What, shall we forth?
120   CASSIUS   Ay, every man away.
Brutus shall lead, and we will grace° his heels   *honor*
With the most boldest and best hearts of Rome.
                    Enter [*Antony's*] SERVANT
BRUTUS   Soft;° who comes here? A friend of Antony's.   *Wait*
SERVANT [*kneeling and falling prostrate*] Thus, Brutus, did my master
          bid me kneel.
125   Thus did Mark Antony bid me fall down,
And, being prostrate, thus he bade me say.
'Brutus is noble, wise, valiant, and honest.°   *honorable*
Caesar was mighty, bold, royal, and loving.
Say I love Brutus, and I honour him.
130   Say I feared Caesar, honoured him, and loved him.
If Brutus will vouchsafe that Antony
May safely come to him and be resolved°   *learn for certain*
How Caesar hath deserved to lie in death,
Mark Antony shall not love Caesar dead
135   So well as Brutus living, but will follow
The fortunes and affairs of noble Brutus
Thorough° the hazards of this untrod state[2]   *Through*
With all true faith.' So says my master Antony.
BRUTUS   Thy master is a wise and valiant Roman.
140   I never thought him worse.
Tell him, so° please him come unto this place,   *if it should*
He shall be satisfied, and, by my honour,
Depart untouched.
SERVANT [*rising*]   I'll fetch him presently.°   *Exit*   *at once*
BRUTUS   I know that we shall have him well to friend.°   *as a friend*
145   CASSIUS   I wish we may. But yet have I a mind
That fears him much; and my misgiving still
Falls shrewdly to the purpose.[3]
                    Enter ANTONY

---

1. Lies stretched out on the pedestal ("basis") of Pompey's statue.
2. These unprecedented circumstances.
3. *my . . . purpose:* my suspicions always turn out to be unfortunately pertinent.

BRUTUS But here comes Antony.—Welcome, Mark Antony.

ANTONY O mighty Caesar! Dost thou lie so low?
150 Are all thy conquests, glories, triumphs, spoils,
Shrunk to this little measure? Fare thee well.—
I know not, gentlemen, what you intend—
Who else must be let blood, who else is rank.⁴
If I myself, there is no hour so fit
155 As Caesar's death's hour, nor no instrument
Of half that worth as those your swords, made rich
With the most noble blood of all this world.
I do beseech ye, if you bear me hard,°   *bear me ill will*
Now, whilst your purpled° hands do reek° and smoke,   *bloody / steam*
160 Fulfil your pleasure. Live° a thousand years,   *If I live*
I shall not find myself so apt° to die.   *ready*
No place will please me so, no mean° of death,   *manner*
As here by Caesar, and by you cut off,
The choice° and master spirits of this age.   *most select*
165 BRUTUS O Antony, beg not your death of us!
Though now we must appear bloody and cruel,
As by our hands and this our present act
You see we do, yet see you but our hands,
And this the bleeding business they have done.
170 Our hearts you see not; they are pitiful;°   *full of pity*
And pity to the general wrong of Rome—
As fire drives out fire, so pity pity⁵—
Hath done this deed on Caesar. For your part,°   *As for you*
To you our swords have leaden° points, Mark Antony.   *blunt*
175 Our arms, unstrung of malice,⁶ and our hearts
Of brothers' temper,° do receive you in   *disposition*
With all kind love, good thoughts, and reverence.
CASSIUS Your voice° shall be as strong as any man's   *opinion*
In the disposing of new dignities.⁷
180 BRUTUS Only be patient till we have appeased°   *calmed*
The multitude, beside themselves with fear,
And then we will deliver you the cause
Why I, that did love Caesar when I struck him,
Have thus proceeded.

ANTONY   I doubt not of your wisdom.
185 Let each man render me his bloody hand.
           He shakes hands with the conspirators
First, Marcus Brutus, will I shake with you.—
Next, Caius Cassius, do I take your hand.—
Now, Decius Brutus, yours;—now yours, Metellus;—
Yours, Cinna;—and my valiant Casca, yours;—
190 Though last, not least in love, yours, good Trebonius.
Gentlemen all—alas, what shall I say?
My credit° now stands on such slippery ground   *credibility*
That one of two bad ways you must conceit° me: *judge*
Either a coward or a flatterer.
195 That I did love thee, Caesar, O, 'tis true.
If then thy spirit look upon us now,

---

4. Festering with disease; overgrown. *let blood:* have
blood drawn off medically (that is, killed).
5. That is, pity for the state has driven out pity for
Caesar.

6. Having given up their power to harm. (The image is
of a bow with its string loosened or removed.)
7. Conferring new offices of state.

Shall it not grieve thee dearer° than thy death   *more keenly*
To see thy Antony making his peace,
Shaking the bloody fingers of thy foes—
200   Most noble!—in the presence of thy corpse?
Had I as many eyes as thou hast wounds,
Weeping as fast as they stream forth thy blood,
It would become me better than to close°   *agree*
In terms of friendship with thine enemies.
205   Pardon me, Julius. Here wast thou bayed,° brave hart;[8]   *brought to bay*
Here didst thou fall, and here thy hunters stand
Signed° in thy spoil° and crimsoned in thy lethe.[9]   *Marked / slaughter*
O world, thou wast the forest to this hart;
And this indeed, O world, the heart of thee.
210   How like a deer strucken by many princes
Dost thou here lie!
CASSIUS   Mark Antony.
ANTONY   Pardon me, Caius Cassius.
The enemies of Caesar shall say this;
215   Then in a friend it is cold modesty.°   *moderation*
CASSIUS   I blame you not for praising Caesar so;
But what compact° mean you to have with us?   *agreement*
Will you be pricked in number of° our friends,   *be counted among*
Or shall we on,° and not depend on you?   *proceed*
220   ANTONY   Therefore I took your hands, but was indeed
Swayed from the point by looking down on Caesar.
Friends am I with you all, and love you all
Upon this hope: that you shall give me reasons
Why and wherein Caesar was dangerous.
225   BRUTUS   Or else were this a savage spectacle.
Our reasons are so full of good regard,°   *sound considerations*
That were you, Antony, the son of Caesar,
You should be satisfied.
ANTONY   That's all I seek;
And am, moreover, suitor° that I may   *petitioner*
230   Produce° his body to the market-place,   *Bring out*
And in the pulpit,° as becomes a friend,   *rostrum*
Speak in the order° of his funeral.   *ceremony*
BRUTUS   You shall, Mark Antony.
CASSIUS   Brutus, a word with you.
[*Aside to* BRUTUS] You know not what you do. Do not consent
235   That Antony speak in his funeral.
Know you how much the people may be moved
By that which he will utter?
BRUTUS [*aside to* CASSIUS]   By your pardon,°   *With your permission*
I will myself into the pulpit first,
And show the reason of our Caesar's death.
240   What Antony shall speak I will protest°   *proclaim*
He speaks by leave and by permission;
And that we are contented Caesar shall
Have all true° rites and lawful ceremonies,   *proper*
It shall advantage° more than do us wrong.   *benefit*
245   CASSIUS [*aside to* BRUTUS]   I know not what may fall.° I like it not.   *happen*

---

8. Stag (punning on "heart").
9. Lost lifeblood (Lethe was the river of forgetfulness in the classical underworld).

BRUTUS   Mark Antony, here, take you Caesar's body.
　　　　You shall not in your funeral speech blame us;
　　　　But speak all good you can devise of Caesar,
　　　　And say you do't by our permission;
250　　Else shall you not have any hand at all
　　　　About° his funeral. And you shall speak　　　　　　　　　　　　　　*In*
　　　　In the same pulpit whereto I am going,
　　　　After my speech is ended.
　　ANTONY   Be it so;
255　　I do desire no more.
BRUTUS   Prepare the body then, and follow us.
　　　　　　　　　　　　　　Exeunt. Manet ANTONY
ANTONY   O pardon me, thou bleeding piece of earth,
　　　　That I am meek and gentle with these butchers.
　　　　Thou art the ruins of the noblest man
260　　That ever livèd in the tide of times.°　　　　　　　*flow of history*
　　　　Woe to the hand that shed this costly° blood!　　　　　*precious*
　　　　Over thy wounds now do I prophesy—
　　　　Which like dumb mouths do ope their ruby lips
　　　　To beg the voice and utterance of my tongue—
265　　A curse shall light upon the limbs of men;
　　　　Domestic fury and fierce civil strife
　　　　Shall cumber° all the parts of Italy;　　　　　　　　*oppress*
　　　　Blood and destruction shall be so in use,°　　　　　*so customary*
　　　　And dreadful objects so familiar,
270　　That mothers shall but smile when they behold
　　　　Their infants quartered° with the hands of war,　　*cut in pieces*
　　　　All pity choked with custom of fell° deeds;　　　　*familiarity with cruel*
　　　　And Caesar's spirit, ranging° for revenge,　　　　　*roving like a wild beast*
　　　　With Ate° by his side come hot from hell,　　　　　*goddess of discord*
275　　Shall in these confines° with a monarch's voice　　　*regions*
　　　　Cry 'havoc!'[1] and let slip° the dogs of war,　　　　*unleash*
　　　　That this foul deed shall smell above the earth
　　　　With carrion men, groaning for burial.
　　　　　　　　　Enter Octavius' SERVANT
　　　　You serve Octavius Caesar, do you not?
280　SERVANT   I do, Mark Antony.
　　ANTONY   Caesar did write for him to come to Rome.
　　SERVANT   He did receive his letters, and is coming,
　　　　And bid me say to you by word of mouth—
　　　　[*Seeing the body*] O Caesar!
285　ANTONY   Thy heart is big.° Get thee apart and weep.　　*swollen with grief*
　　　　Passion,° I see, is catching, for mine eyes,　　　　　*Sorrow*
　　　　Seeing those beads of sorrow stand in thine,
　　　　Began to water. Is thy master coming?
　　SERVANT   He lies° tonight within seven leagues° of Rome.　*stays / 20 miles*
290　ANTONY   Post° back with speed and tell him what hath chanced.　*Ride quickly*
　　　　Here is a mourning Rome, a dangerous Rome,
　　　　No Rome of safety for Octavius yet.
　　　　Hie° hence and tell him so.—Yet stay awhile.　　　　*Hasten*
　　　　Thou shalt not back till I have borne this corpse
295　　Into the market-place. There shall I try°　　　　　　*test*
　　　　In my oration how the people take

_____
1. Military order for slaughter and pillage.

The cruel issue° of these bloody men;   deed
According to the which thou shalt discourse
To young Octavius of the state of things.
300   Lend me your hand.   *Exeunt [with Caesar's body]*

3.2

Enter BRUTUS *and* CASSIUS, *with the* PLEBEIANS
ALL THE PLEBEIANS   We will be satisfied!° Let us be satisfied!   given an explanation
BRUTUS   Then follow me, and give me audience, friends.
      [*Aside to* CASSIUS] Cassius, go you into the other street,
      And part the numbers.°   divide the multitude
5   [*To the* PLEBEIANS] Those that will hear me speak, let 'em stay here;
      Those that will follow Cassius, go with him;
      And public reasons shall be renderèd
      Of Caesar's death.
            BRUTUS [*ascends to*] *the pulpit*
FIRST PLEBEIAN   I will hear Brutus speak.
SECOND PLEBEIAN   I will hear Cassius, and compare their reasons
10   When severally° we hear them renderèd.   separately
            [*Exit* CASSIUS, *with some* PLEBEIANS]
            [*Enter* BRUTUS *above in the pulpit*]
THIRD PLEBEIAN   The noble Brutus is ascended. Silence.
BRUTUS   Be patient till the last.°   end of my address
      Romans, countrymen, and lovers,° hear me for my cause, and   dear friends
      be silent that you may hear. Believe me for° mine honour, and   on account of
15   have respect to° mine honour, that you may believe. Censure°   regard for / Judge
      me in your wisdom, and awake your senses,° that you may the   understanding
      better judge. If there be any in this assembly, any dear friend
      of Caesar's, to him I say that Brutus' love to Caesar was no less
      than his. If then that friend demand why Brutus rose against
20   Caesar, this is my answer: not that I loved Caesar less, but that
      I loved Rome more. Had you rather Caesar were living, and
      die all slaves, than that Caesar were dead, to live all free men?
      As Caesar loved me, I weep for him. As he was fortunate, I
      rejoice at it. As he was valiant, I honour him. But as he was
25   ambitious, I slew him. There is tears for his love, joy for his
      fortune, honour for his valour, and death for his ambition. Who
      is here so base that would be a bondman? If any, speak, for him
      have I offended.° Who is here so rude° that would not be a   wronged / barbarous
      Roman? If any, speak, for him have I offended. Who is here so
30   vile that will not love his country? If any, speak, for him have I
      offended. I pause for a reply.
ALL THE PLEBEIANS   None, Brutus, none.
BRUTUS   Then none have I offended. I have done no more to
      Caesar than you shall do[1] to Brutus. The question of° his   reasons for
35   death is enrolled° in the Capitol, his glory not extenuated°   recorded / diminished
      wherein he was worthy, nor his offences enforced° for which   unduly stressed
      he suffered death.
            Enter Mark ANTONY, *with [others bearing] Caesar's*
            body [in a coffin]
      Here comes his body, mourned by Mark Antony, who, though
      he had no hand in his death, shall receive the benefit of his
40   dying: a place in the commonwealth—as which of you shall

3.2 Location: The Forum.   1. Should do (in such circumstances).

not? With this I depart: that as I slew my best lover° for the   *friend*
good of Rome, I have the same dagger for myself when it shall
please my country to need my death.

ALL THE PLEBEIANS   Live, Brutus, live, live!

45 FIRST PLEBEIAN   Bring him with triumph home unto his house.

FOURTH PLEBEIAN   Give him a statue with his ancestors.

THIRD PLEBEIAN   Let him be Caesar.

FIFTH PLEBEIAN   Caesar's better parts°   *faculties*
Shall be crowned in Brutus.

FIRST PLEBEIAN   We'll bring him to his house with shouts and clamours.

BRUTUS   My countrymen.

50 FOURTH PLEBEIAN   Peace, silence. Brutus speaks.

FIRST PLEBEIAN   Peace, ho!

BRUTUS   Good countrymen, let me depart alone,
And, for my sake, stay here with Antony.
Do grace° to Caesar's corpse, and grace[2] his speech   *Pay respect*

55 Tending° to Caesar's glories, which Mark Antony,   *Relating*
By our permission, is allowed to make.
I do entreat you, not a man depart
Save I alone till Antony have spoke.   *Exit*

FIRST PLEBEIAN   Stay, ho, and let us hear Mark Antony.

60 THIRD PLEBEIAN   Let him go up into the public chair.
We'll hear him. Noble Antony, go up.

ANTONY   For Brutus' sake I am beholden to you.

    [ANTONY *ascends to the pulpit*]

FIFTH PLEBEIAN   What does he say of Brutus?

THIRD PLEBEIAN   He says, for Brutus' sake
He finds himself beholden to us all.

65 FIFTH PLEBEIAN   'Twere best he speak no harm of Brutus here!

FIRST PLEBEIAN   This Caesar was a tyrant.

THIRD PLEBEIAN   Nay, that's certain.
We are blessed that Rome is rid of him.

    [*Enter* ANTONY *in the pulpit*]

FOURTH PLEBEIAN   Peace, let us hear what Antony can say.

ANTONY   You gentle Romans.

ALL THE PLEBEIANS   Peace, ho! Let us hear him.

70 ANTONY   Friends, Romans, countrymen, lend me your ears.
I come to bury Caesar, not to praise him.
The evil that men do lives after them;
The good is oft interrèd with their bones.
So let it be with Caesar. The noble Brutus

75 Hath told you Caesar was ambitious.
If it were so, it was a grievous fault,
And grievously hath Caesar answered° it.   *paid the penalty for*
Here, under leave° of Brutus and the rest—   *by permission*
For Brutus is an honourable man,

80 So are they all, all honourable men—
Come I to speak in Caesar's funeral.
He was my friend, faithful and just to me.
But Brutus says he was ambitious,
And Brutus is an honourable man.

85 He hath brought many captives home to Rome,

2. Courteously hear.

Whose ransoms did the general coffers° fill.   *public treasury*
Did this in Caesar seem ambitious?
When that the poor have cried, Caesar hath wept.
Ambition should be made of sterner stuff.
90 Yet Brutus says he was ambitious,
And Brutus is an honourable man.
You all did see that on the Lupercal
I thrice presented him a kingly crown,
Which he did thrice refuse. Was this ambition?
95 Yet Brutus says he was ambitious,
And sure he is an honourable man.
I speak not to disprove what Brutus spoke,
But here I am to speak what I do know.
You all did love him once, not without cause.
100 What cause withholds you then to mourn for him?
O judgement, thou art fled to brutish beasts,
And men have lost their reason!

    [*He weeps*]

           Bear with me.
My heart is in the coffin there with Caesar,
And I must pause till it come back to me.
105 FIRST PLEBEIAN Methinks there is much reason in his sayings.
FOURTH PLEBEIAN If thou consider rightly of the matter,
 Caesar has had great wrong.•
THIRD PLEBEIAN   Has he not, masters?
 I fear there will a worse come in his place.
FIFTH PLEBEIAN Marked ye his words? He would not take the crown,
110 Therefore 'tis certain he was not ambitious.
FIRST PLEBEIAN If it be found so, some will dear abide° it.   *pay dearly for*
FOURTH PLEBEIAN Poor soul, his eyes are red as fire with weeping.
THIRD PLEBEIAN There's not a nobler man in Rome than Antony. •
FIFTH PLEBEIAN Now mark him; he begins again to speak.
115 ANTONY But° yesterday the word of Caesar might   *Only*
Have stood against the world. Now lies he there,
And none so poor to do him reverence.[3]
O masters, if I were disposed to stir
Your hearts and minds to mutiny° and rage,   *rebellion*
120 I should do Brutus wrong, and Cassius wrong,
Who, you all know, are honourable men.
I will not do them wrong. I rather choose
To wrong the dead, to wrong myself and you,
Than I will wrong such honourable men.
125 But here's a parchment with the seal of Caesar.
I found it in his closet.° 'Tis his will.   *study*
Let but the commons° hear this testament—   *commoners*
Which, pardon me, I do not mean to read—
And they would go and kiss dead Caesar's wounds,
130 And dip their napkins[4] in his sacred blood,
Yea, beg a hair of him for memory,
And, dying, mention it within their wills,
Bequeathing it as a rich legacy
Unto their issue.°   *children*

3. And no one is so lowly as to owe obeisance to him.
4. Handkerchiefs (implying that Caesar is a martyr whose bloody relics should be regarded as holy).

135 FIFTH PLEBEIAN We'll hear the will. Read it, Mark Antony.
ALL THE PLEBEIANS The will, the will! We will hear Caesar's will.
ANTONY Have patience, gentle friends, I must not read it
  It is not meet° you know how Caesar loved you.   *fitting*
  You are not wood, you are not stones, but men;
140 And, being men, hearing the will of Caesar,
  It will inflame you, it will make you mad.
  'Tis good you know not that you are his heirs,
  For if you should, O what would come of it?
  FIFTH PLEBEIAN Read the will. We'll hear it, Antony.
145 You shall read us the will, Caesar's will.
ANTONY Will you be patient? Will you stay a while?
  I have o'ershot myself⁵ to tell you of it.
  I fear I wrong the honourable men
  Whose daggers have stabbed Caesar; I do fear it.
150 FIFTH PLEBEIAN They were traitors. Honourable men?
ALL THE PLEBEIANS The will, the testament!
FOURTH PLEBEIAN They were villains, murderers. The will_ read
  the will!
ANTONY You will compel me then to read the will?
155 Then make a ring about the corpse of Caesar,
  And let me show you him that made the will.
  Shall I descend? And will you give me leave?
ALL THE PLEBEIANS
  Come down.
FOURTH PLEBEIAN Descend.
THIRD PLEBEIAN   You shall have leave.
  [ANTONY *descends from the pulpit*]
FIFTH PLEBEIAN   A ring.
  Stand round.
FIRST PLEBEIAN Stand from the hearse.° Stand from the body.   *bier*
160 FOURTH PLEBEIAN Room for Antony, most noble Antony!
  [*Enter* ANTONY *below*]
ANTONY Nay, press not so upon me. Stand farre° off.   *farther*
ALL THE PLEBEIANS Stand back! Room! Bear back!
ANTONY If you have tears, prepare to shed them now.
  You all do know this mantle. I remember
165 The first time ever Caesar put it on.
  'Twas on a summer's evening in his tent,
  That day he overcame the Nervii.⁶
  Look, in this place ran Cassius' dagger through.
  See what a rent the envious° Casca made.   *spiteful*
170 Through this the well-belovèd Brutus stabbed;
  And as he plucked his cursèd steel away,
  Mark how the blood of Caesar followed it,
  As° rushing out of doors to be resolved⁷   *As if*
  If Brutus so unkindly° knocked or no—   *cruelly; unnaturally*
175 For Brutus, as you know, was Caesar's angel.⁸
  Judge, O you gods, how dearly Caesar loved him!
  This was the most unkindest cut of all.
  For when the noble Caesar saw him stab,

5. I have gone too far (an image from archery).
6. Gallic tribe conquered by Caesar in 57 B.C.E.; it was an important victory, extravagantly celebrated in Rome.
7. To find out for sure.
8. Attendant spirit (that is, dearest friend).

Ingratitude, more strong than traitors' arms,
180 Quite vanquished him. Then burst his mighty heart,
And in his mantle muffling up his face,
Even at the base of Pompey's statue,
Which all the while ran blood, great Caesar fell.
O, what a fall was there, my countrymen!
185 Then I, and you, and all of us fell down,
Whilst bloody treason flourished⁹ over us.
O now you weep, and I perceive you feel
The dint° of pity. These are gracious drops.   °impression
Kind souls, what, weep you when you but behold
190 Our Caesar's vesture° wounded? Look you here.   °garment
Here is himself, marred, as you see, with traitors.
        [*He uncovers Caesar's body*]
FIRST PLEBEIAN   O piteous spectacle!
FOURTH PLEBEIAN   O noble Caesar!
THIRD PLEBEIAN   O woeful day!
FIFTH PLEBEIAN   O traitors, villains!
FIRST PLEBEIAN   O most bloody sight!
195 FOURTH PLEBEIAN   We will be revenged.
ALL THE PLEBEIANS   Revenge! About!° Seek! Burn! Fire! Kill! Slay!   °*To work*
    Let not a traitor live!
ANTONY   Stay, countrymen.
FIRST PLEBEIAN   Peace there, hear the noble Antony.
FOURTH PLEBEIAN   We'll hear him, we'll follow him, we'll die
200 with him!
ANTONY   Good friends, sweet friends, let me not stir you up
    To such a sudden flood of mutiny.
    They that have done this deed are honourable.
    What private griefs° they have, alas, I know not,   °*personal grievances*
205 That made them do it. They are wise and honourable,
    And will no doubt with reasons answer you.
    I come not, friends, to steal away your hearts.
    I am no orator as Brutus is,
    But, as you know me all, a plain blunt man
210 That love my friend; and that they know full well
    That gave me public leave to speak¹ of him.
    For I have neither wit,° nor words, nor worth,°   °*intelligence / stature*
    Action,° nor utterance, nor the power of speech,   °*Gesture*
    To stir men's blood. I only speak right on.°   °*straightforwardly*
215 I tell you that which you yourselves do know,
    Show you sweet Caesar's wounds, poor poor dumb mouths,
    And bid them speak for me. But were I Brutus,
    And Brutus Antony, there were an Antony
    Would ruffle° up your spirits, and put a tongue   °*stir*
220 In every wound of Caesar that should move
    The stones of Rome to rise and mutiny.°   °*riot*
ALL THE PLEBEIANS   We'll mutiny.
FIRST PLEBEIAN   We'll burn the house of Brutus.
THIRD PLEBEIAN   Away then! Come, seek the conspirators.
ANTONY   Yet hear me, countrymen, yet hear me speak.
225 ALL THE PLEBEIANS   Peace, ho! Hear Antony, most noble Antony.
ANTONY   Why, friends, you go to do you know not what.

---

9. Shook its sword; triumphed.   1. Permission to speak in public.

Wherein hath Caesar thus deserved your loves?
Alas, you know not. I must tell you then.
You have forgot the will I told you of.

230 ALL THE PLEBEIANS Most true. The will. Let's stay and hear the will.
ANTONY Here is the will, and under Caesar's seal.
    To every Roman citizen he gives—
    To every several° man—seventy-five drachmas.[2]   *individual*
FOURTH PLEBEIAN Most noble Caesar! We'll revenge his death.
THIRD PLEBEIAN O royal Caesar!
ANTONY   Hear me with patience.
235 ALL THE PLEBEIANS   Peace,° ho!   *Silence*
ANTONY Moreover he hath left you all his walks,
    His private arbours, and new-planted orchards,°   *gardens*
    On this side Tiber. He hath left them you,
    And to your heirs for ever—common pleasures°   *public parks*
240   To walk abroad and recreate yourselves.
    Here was a Caesar. When comes such another?
FIRST PLEBEIAN Never, never! Come, away, away!
    We'll burn his body in the holy place,
    And with the brands fire the traitors' houses.
245 Take up the body.
FOURTH PLEBEIAN Go, fetch fire!
THIRD PLEBEIAN Pluck down benches!
FIFTH PLEBEIAN Pluck down forms,° windows,° anything.   *benches / shutters*
             Exeunt PLEBEIANS [*with Caesar's body*]
ANTONY Now let it work. Mischief, thou art afoot.
    Take thou what course thou wilt.
            Enter [*Octavius'*] SERVANT
250   How now, fellow?
SERVANT Sir, Octavius is already come to Rome.
ANTONY Where is he?
SERVANT He and Lepidus are at Caesar's house.
ANTONY And thither will I straight° to visit him.   *at once*
255 He comes upon a wish.° Fortune is merry,   *just as I wished*
    And in this mood will give us anything.
SERVANT I heard him say Brutus and Cassius
    Are rid° like madmen through the gates of Rome.   *Have ridden*
ANTONY Belike° they had some notice° of the people,   *Probably / warning*
260 How I had moved them. Bring me to Octavius.   *Exeunt*

3.3

        Enter CINNA *the poet*
CINNA I dreamt tonight° that I did feast with Caesar,   *last night*
    And things unlucky charge my fantasy.[1]
    I have no will to wander forth of doors,
    Yet something leads me forth.
        [*Enter*] *the* PLEBEIANS
5 FIRST PLEBEIAN What is your name?
SECOND PLEBEIAN Whither are you going?
THIRD PLEBEIAN Where do you dwell?
FOURTH PLEBEIAN Are you a married man or a bachelor?
SECOND PLEBEIAN Answer every man directly.[2]

---

2. Greek silver coins.
3.3 Location: A street in Rome.

1. And bad omens oppress my imagination.
2. At once; speaking straightforwardly.

10 FIRST PLEBEIAN Ay, and briefly.
    FOURTH PLEBEIAN Ay, and wisely.
    THIRD PLEBEIAN Ay, and truly, you were best.°   *you'd better*
    CINNA What is my name? Whither am I going? Where do I
        dwell? Am I a married man or a bachelor? Then to answer
15   every man directly and briefly, wisely and truly: wisely, I say, I
        am a bachelor.
    SECOND PLEBEIAN That's as much as to say they are fools that
        marry. You'll bear me a bang° for that, I fear. Proceed directly.   *get a blow from me*
    CINNA Directly I am going to Caesar's funeral.
20 FIRST PLEBEIAN As a friend or an enemy?
    CINNA As a friend.
    SECOND PLEBEIAN That matter is answered directly.
    FOURTH PLEBEIAN For your dwelling—briefly.
    CINNA Briefly, I dwell by the Capitol.
25 THIRD PLEBEIAN Your name, sir, truly.
    CINNA Truly, my name is Cinna.
    FIRST PLEBEIAN Tear him to pieces! He's a conspirator.
    CINNA I am Cinna the poet, I am Cinna the poet.
    FOURTH PLEBEIAN Tear him for his bad verses, tear him for his
30   bad verses.
    CINNA I am not Cinna the conspirator.
    FOURTH PLEBEIAN It is no matter, his name's Cinna. Pluck but
        his name out of his heart, and turn him going.°   *send him packing*
    THIRD PLEBEIAN Tear him, tear him!
                                    [*They set upon* CINNA]
35   Come, brands, ho! Firebrands! To Brutus', to Cassius'! Burn
        all! Some to Decius' house, and some to Casca's; some to Liga-
        rius'. Away, go!
                        Exeunt all the PLEBEIANS [*with* CINNA]

4.1

                Enter ANTONY [*with papers*], OCTAVIUS, *and* LEPIDUS
    ANTONY These many, then, shall die; their names are pricked.°   *marked down*
    OCTAVIUS [*to* LEPIDUS] Your brother too must die. Consent you, Lepidus?
    LEPIDUS I do consent.
    OCTAVIUS   Prick him down, Antony.
    LEPIDUS Upon condition° Publius shall not live,   *Provided that*
5   Who is your sister's son, Mark Antony.
    ANTONY He shall not live. Look, with a spot I damn him.[1]
        But Lepidus, go you to Caesar's house;
        Fetch the will hither, and we shall determine
        How to cut off some charge in legacies.[2]
10 LEPIDUS What, shall I find you here?
    OCTAVIUS Or° here or at the Capitol.   *Exit* LEPIDUS   *Either*
    ANTONY This is a slight, unmeritable° man,   *undeserving*
        Meet° to be sent on errands. Is it fit,   *Fit*
        The three-fold world divided,[3] he should stand
        One of the three to share it?
15 OCTAVIUS   So you thought him,
        And took his voice° who should be pricked to die   *accepted his opinion*

4.1 Location: Antony's house in Rome.
1. With a mark I condemn him to death.
2. Reduce the amount paid out to beneficiaries of
Caesar's will.

3. Antony, Octavius, and Lepidus, in the second triumvirate, or joint rule of three, parceled out rule of
Rome's empire among themselves.

In our black° sentence and proscription.⁴   *death*
ANTONY   Octavius, I have seen more days than you,
And though we lay these honours on this man
20   To ease ourselves of divers sland'rous loads,°   *burdens of reproach*
He shall but bear them as the ass bears gold,
To groan and sweat under the business,
Either led or driven as we point the way;
And having brought our treasure where we will,
25   Then take we down his load, and turn him off,
Like to the empty° ass, to shake his ears   *unladen*
And graze in commons.⁵
OCTAVIUS   You may do your will;
But he's a tried and valiant soldier.
ANTONY   So is my horse, Octavius, and for that
30   I do appoint° him store of provender.   *provide*
It is a creature that I teach to fight,
To wind,° to stop, to run directly on,   *turn*
His corporal° motion governed by my spirit;   *bodily*
And in some taste° is Lepidus but so.   *measure*
35   He must be taught, and trained, and bid go forth—
A barren-spirited fellow, one that feeds
On objects, arts, and imitations,⁶
Which, out of use and staled° by other men,   *made uninteresting*
Begin his fashion.⁷ Do not talk of him
40   But as a property.° And now, Octavius,   *tool*
Listen° great things. Brutus and Cassius   *Give ear to*
Are levying powers.° We must straight make head.⁸   *armies*
Therefore let our alliance be combined,
Our best friends made,ᶜ our meinies stretched.⁹   *mustered*
45   And let us presently go sit in council,
How covert matters° may be best disclosed,   *dangers*
And open perils surest answerèd.°   *most safely confronted*
OCTAVIUS   Let us do so, for we are at the stake¹
And bayed about with many enemies;
50   And some that smile have in their hearts, I fear,
Millions of mischiefs.°   *evils*

Exeunt

4.2

Drum. Enter BRUTUS, [LUCIUS,] *and the army.* LUCIL-
LIUS, TITINIUS, *and* PINDARUS *meet them*
BRUTUS   Stand, ho!°   *Halt*
SOLDIER   Give the word 'ho', and stand.¹
BRUTUS   What now, Lucillius: is Cassius near?
LUCILLIUS   He is at hand, and Pindarus is come
5   To do you salutation from his master.
BRUTUS   He greets me well.° Your master, Pindarus,   *with a worthy man*
In his own change or by ill officers.²

---

4. A "proscribed" person had a price on his head, his
property was confiscated, and his children were prevented from holding office.
5. In the public pasture; among the common people.
6. On curiosities, contrivances, and counterfeits.
7. He then takes up as fashionable.
8. We must raise an army at once.
9. Our bands of followers augmented.

1. That is, like bears in the sport of bearbaiting, tied to
a stake and surrounded by baying hounds.
4.2 Location: Sardis, in what is now western Turkey.
Brutus's tent in his army's camp.
1. Pass the word, and halt.
2. By his own altered feelings or through the actions of
bad subordinates.

Hath given me some worthy° cause to wish   *justifiable*
Things done undone. But if he be at hand,
I shall be satisfied.[3]

10   PINDARUS   I do not doubt
But that my noble master will appear
Such as he is, full of regard[4] and honour.

BRUTUS   He is not doubted.—A word, Lucillius.

      BRUTUS *and* LUCILLIUS *speak apart*

How he received you let me be resolved.°   *informed*

15   LUCILLIUS   With courtesy and with respect enough,
But not with such familiar instances,°   *tokens of friendship*
Nor with such free and friendly conference,°   *conversation*
As he hath used of old.

BRUTUS   Thou hast described
A hot friend cooling. Ever note, Lucillius:

20   When love begins to sicken and decay
It useth an enforcèd ceremony.°   *a strained formality*
There are no tricks° in plain and simple faith;   *artifices*
But hollow° men, like horses hot at hand,[5]   *insincere*
Make gallant show and promise of their mettle;

      Low march[6] *within*

25   But when they should endure the bloody spur,
They fall their crests° and, like deceitful jades,°   *lower their necks / nags*
Sink° in the trial. Comes his army on?   *Fail*

LUCILLIUS   They mean this night in Sardis to be quartered.
The greater part, the horse in general,°   *all the cavalry*
Are come with Cassius.

      Enter CASSIUS *and his powers*°   *armies*

30   BRUTUS   Hark, he is arrived.
March gently° on to meet him.   *slowly*

      [*The armies march*]

CASSIUS   Stand, ho!

BRUTUS   Stand, ho! Speak the word along.

FIRST SOLDIER   Stand!

35   SECOND SOLDIER   Stand!

THIRD SOLDIER   Stand!

CASSIUS   Most noble brother, you have done me wrong.

BRUTUS   Judge me, you gods: wrong I mine enemies?
And if not so, how should I wrong a brother?

40   CASSIUS   Brutus, this sober form of yours hides wrongs,
And when you do them—

BRUTUS   Cassius, be content.°   *keep calm*
Speak your griefs° softly. I do know you well.   *grievances*
Before the eyes of both our armies here,
Which should perceive nothing but love from us,

45   Let us not wrangle. Bid them move away,
Then in my tent, Cassius, enlarge° your griefs,   *express fully*
And I will give you audience.

CASSIUS   Pindarus,
Bid our commanders lead their charges° off   *troops*
A little from this ground.

---

3. I shall receive a full explanation.
4. Respect for you; renown (for his own abilities).
5. Eager at the outset.

6. Soft drumbeat (as from a distance; the sound becomes louder as the army enters).

50 BRUTUS Lucillius, do you the like; and let no man
        Come to our tent till we have done our conference.
        Let Lucius and Titinius guard our door. *Exeunt* [*the armies*]
                Manent BRUTUS *and* CASSIUS [*with* TITINIUS *and*
                LUCIUS *guarding the door*][7]
    CASSIUS That you have wronged me doth appear in this:
        You have condemned and noted° Lucius Pella   publicly disgraced
55   For taking bribes here of the Sardians,
        Wherein my letters praying on his side,
        Because I knew the man, was slighted off.°   contemptuously ignored
    BRUTUS You wronged yourself to write in such a case.
    CASSIUS In such a time as this it is not meet°   appropriate
60   That every nice° offence should bear his comment.°   trivial / be criticized
    BRUTUS Let me tell you, Cassius, you yourself
        Are much condemned to have° an itching palm,   for having
        To sell and mart° your offices for gold   traffic in
        To undeservers.
    CASSIUS   I, an itching palm?
65   You know that you are Brutus that speaks this,
        Or, by the gods, this speech were else° your last.   otherwise
    BRUTUS The name of Cassius honours this corruption,[8]
        And chastisement doth therefore hide his head.
    CASSIUS Chastisement?
70 BRUTUS Remember March, the ides of March, remember.
        Did not great Julius bleed for justice' sake?
        What villain touched his body, that did stab,
        And not for justice?[9] What, shall one of us,
        That struck the foremost man of all this world
75   But for supporting robbers,[1] shall we now
        Contaminate our fingers with base bribes,
        And sell the mighty space of our large honours°   impressive reputations
        For so much trash° as may be graspèd thus?   money (contemptuous)
        I had rather be a dog and bay° the moon   howl at
        Than such a Roman.
80 CASSIUS   Brutus, bay° not me.   howl at; hold at bay
        I'll not endure it. You forget yourself
        To hedge me in.° I am a soldier, I,   limit my authority
        Older in practice, abler than yourself
        To make conditions.°   manage affairs
85 BRUTUS Go to, you are not, Cassius.
    CASSIUS I am.
    BRUTUS I say you are not.
    CASSIUS Urge° me no more, I shall forget myself.   Provoke
        Have mind upon your health. Tempt me no farther.
90 BRUTUS Away, slight man.
    CASSIUS Is't possible?
    BRUTUS Hear me, for I will speak.
        Must I give way and room to your rash choler?[2]
        Shall I be frighted when a madman stares?
95 CASSIUS O ye gods, ye gods! Must I endure all this?
    BRUTUS All this? Ay, more. Fret till your proud heart break.

---

7. Some editors begin a new scene at this point.
8. Makes this corruption appear honorable.
9. *What . . . justice?*: Who was so villainous as to stab
Caesar for any motive other than justice?

1. Caesar was accused of permitting, even encouraging, corruption among his subordinates.
2. Must I allow free passage to your rash anger?

Go show your slaves how choleric° you are,	*enraged*
And make your bondmen tremble. Must I budge?°	*flinch*
Must I observe° you? Must I stand and crouch°	*defer to / cringe*
100 Under your testy humour?° By the gods,	*irritable temper*
You shall digest³ the venom of your spleen,°	*anger*
Though it do split you. For from this day forth	
I'll use you for my mirth, yea for my laughter,	
When you are waspish.	

CASSIUS   Is it come to this?

105 BRUTUS   You say you are a better soldier.
Let it appear so, make your vaunting° true,   *boasting*
And it shall please me well. For mine own part,
I shall be glad to learn of° noble men.   *from*

CASSIUS   You wrong me every way, you wrong me, Brutus.
110 I said an elder soldier, not a better.
Did I say better?

BRUTUS   If you did, I care not.

CASSIUS   When Caesar lived he durst not thus have moved° me.   *angered*

BRUTUS   Peace, peace; you durst not so have tempted him.

CASSIUS   I durst not?

115 BRUTUS   No.

CASSIUS   What, durst not tempt him?

BRUTUS   For your life you durst not.

CASSIUS   Do not presume too much upon my love.
I may do that I shall be sorry for.

120 BRUTUS   You have done that you should be sorry for.
There is no terror, Cassius, in your threats,
For I am armed so strong in honesty°   *rectitude*
That they pass by me as the idle wind,
Which I respect not.° I did send to you   *pay no attention to*
125 For certain sums of gold, which you denied me;
For I can raise no money by vile means.
By heaven, I had rather coin my heart
And drop my blood for drachmas than to wring
From the hard hands of peasants their vile trash
130 By any indirection.° I did send   *devious means*
To you for gold to pay my legions,
Which you denied me. Was that done like Cassius?
Should I have answered Caius Cassius so?
When Marcus Brutus grows so covetous
135 To lock such rascal counters from his friends,
Be ready, gods, with all your thunderbolts;
Dash him to pieces.

CASSIUS   I denied you not.

BRUTUS   You did.

CASSIUS   I did not. He was but a fool
That brought my answer back. Brutus hath rived° my heart.   *broken*
140 A friend should bear his friend's infirmities,
But Brutus makes mine greater than they are.

BRUTUS   I do not, till you practise them on me.

CASSIUS   You love me not.

BRUTUS   I do not like your faults.

CASSIUS   A friendly eye could never see such faults.

---

3. Swallow (not give vent to).

145 BRUTUS A flatterer's would not, though they do appear
　　　As huge as high Olympus.
　　CASSIUS Come, Antony and young Octavius, come,
　　　Revenge yourselves alone on Cassius;
　　　For Cassius is aweary of the world,
150　　Hated by one he loves, braved° by his brother,   *defied*
　　　Checked° like a bondman; all his faults observed,   *Rebuked*
　　　Set in a notebook, learned and conned by rote,°   *memorized*
　　　To cast into my teeth. O, I could weep
　　　My spirit from mine eyes! There is my dagger,
155　　And here my naked breast; within, a heart
　　　Dearer° than Pluto's[4] mine, richer than gold.   *More valuable*
　　　If that thou beest a Roman, take it forth.
　　　I that denied thee gold will give my heart.
　　　Strike as thou didst at Caesar; for I know
160　　When thou didst hate him worst, thou loved'st him better
　　　Than ever thou loved'st Cassius.
　　BRUTUS   Sheathe your dagger.
　　　Be angry when you will; it shall have scope.°   *room for exercise*
　　　Do what you will; dishonour shall be humour.[5]
　　　O Cassius, you are yoked° with a lamb   *allied*
165　　That carries anger as the flint bears fire,
　　　Who, much enforcèd,° shows a hasty spark   *struck*
　　　And straight° is cold again.   *immediately*
　　CASSIUS   Hath Cassius lived
　　　To be but mirth and laughter to his Brutus
　　　When grief and blood ill-tempered° vexeth him?
170 BRUTUS When I spoke that, I was ill-tempered too.
　　CASSIUS Do you confess so much? Give me your hand.
　　BRUTUS And my heart too.
　　　　　[*They embrace*]
　　CASSIUS   O Brutus!
　　BRUTUS   What's the matter?
　　CASSIUS Have not you love enough to bear with me
　　　When that rash humour° which my mother gave me *temperament*
　　　Makes me forgetful?
175 BRUTUS   Yes, Cassius, and from henceforth,
　　　When you are over-earnest with your Brutus,
　　　He'll think your mother chides, and leave you so.°   *let you alone*
　　　　　Enter [LUCILLIUS *and*] *a* POET
　　POET Let me go in to see the generals.
　　　There is some grudge between 'em 'tis not meet
　　　They be alone.
180 LUCILLIUS   You shall not come to them.
　　POET Nothing but death shall stay me.
　　CASSIUS   How now! What's the matter?
　　POET For shame, you generals, what do you mean?
　　　Love and be friends, as two such men should be,
　　　For I have seen more years, I'm sure, than ye.
185 CASSIUS Ha, ha! How vilely doth this cynic[7] rhyme!

---

4. Roman god of riches (Plutus; often conflated with Pluto, god of the underworld).
5. Dishonorable actions shall be ascribed to moodiness.

6. Literally, badly mixed blood (thought to produce anger and melancholy).
7. Member of a philosophical school that refused to respect differences in social class.

BRUTUS [*to the* POET]   Get you hence, sirrah;° saucy fellow,   *(contemptuous address)*
 hence!
CASSIUS   Bear with him, Brutus, 'tis his fashion.
BRUTUS   I'll know his humour when he knows his time.[8]
 What should the wars do with these jigging° fools?   *incompetently versifying*
 [*To the* POET] Companion,° hence!   *(contemptuous)*
190 CASSIUS [*to the* POET]   Away, away, be gone!
                                                   Exit POET

BRUTUS   Lucillius and Titinius, bid the commanders
 Prepare to lodge their companies tonight.
CASSIUS   And come yourselves, and bring Messala with you
 Immediately to us.   [*Exeunt* LUCILLIUS *and* TITINIUS]
BRUTUS   Lucius, a bowl of wine.   [*Exit* LUCIUS]
195 CASSIUS   I did not think you could have been so angry.
BRUTUS   O Cassius, I am sick of° many griefs.   *suffering from*
CASSIUS   Of your philosophy you make no use,
 If you give place to accidental evils.[9]
BRUTUS   No man bears sorrow better. Portia is dead.
200 CASSIUS   Ha! Portia?
BRUTUS   She is dead.
CASSIUS   How scaped I killing° when I crossed you so?   *being killed*
 O insupportable and touching loss!
 Upon what sickness?
BRUTUS   Impatience of° my absence,   *Inability to tolerate*
205 And grief that young Octavius with Mark Antony
 Have made themselves so strong—for with° her death   *with the news of*
 That tidings came. With this, she fell distraught,
 And, her attendants absent, swallowed fire.[1]
CASSIUS   And died so?
BRUTUS   Even so.
CASSIUS   O ye immortal gods!
 Enter [LUCIUS] *with wine and tapers*°   *candles*
210 BRUTUS   Speak no more of her. [*To* LUCIUS] Give me a bowl of wine.
 [*To* CASSIUS] In this I bury all unkindness, Cassius.
 [*He*] *drinks*
CASSIUS   My heart is thirsty for that noble pledge.
 Fill, Lucius, till the wine o'erswell° the cup.   *overflow*
 I cannot drink too much of Brutus' love.
 [*He drinks*]   [*Exit* LUCIUS]
 Enter TITINIUS *and* MESSALA[2]
215 BRUTUS   Come in, Titinius; welcome, good Messala.
 Now sit we close about this taper here,
 And call in question° our necessities.   *discuss*
CASSIUS [*aside*]   Portia, art thou gone?
BRUTUS   No more, I pray you.
 [*They sit*]
 Messala, I have here receivèd letters
220 That young Octavius and Mark Antony
 Come down upon us with a mighty power,
 Bending their expedition° toward Philippi.[3]   *Pressing hastily*

8. I'll tolerate his eccentricity when he finds an appropriate time for it.
9. Brutus admired the Stoics, who taught that the wise
man should remain unaffected by circumstances outside himself. *evils*: misfortunes.

1. Portia committed suicide by swallowing live embers.
2. Lucillius, who ought logically to return at this point
(see lines 193–94), is not mentioned, an inconsistency
that suggests Shakespearean revision of this scene.
3. City in northeastern Greece.

MESSALA   Myself have letters of the selfsame tenor.
BRUTUS   With what addition?
225   MESSALA   That by proscription[4] and bills of outlawry
    Octavius, Antony, and Lepidus
    Have put to death an hundred senators.
BRUTUS   Therein our letters do not well agree.
    Mine speak of seventy senators that died
230   By their proscriptions, Cicero being one.
CASSIUS   Cicero one?
MESSALA   Ay, Cicero is dead,
    And by that order of proscription.
    [*To* BRUTUS] Had you your letters from your wife, my lord?
BRUTUS   No, Messala.
235   MESSALA   Nor nothing in your letters writ of her?
BRUTUS   Nothing, Messala.
MESSALA   That methinks is strange.
BRUTUS   Why ask you? Hear you aught of her in yours?
MESSALA   No, my lord.
BRUTUS   Now as you are a Roman, tell me true.
240   MESSALA   Then like a Roman bear the truth I tell;
    For certain she is dead, and by strange manner.
BRUTUS   Why, farewell, Portia.[5] We must die, Messala.
    With meditating that she must die once,°   *at some time*
    I have the patience to endure it now.
245   MESSALA   Even so great men great losses should endure.
CASSIUS   I have as much of this in art[5] as you,
    But yet my nature could not bear it so.
BRUTUS   Well, to our work alive.[7] What do you think
    Of marching to Philippi presently?°   *at once*
CASSIUS   I do not think it good.
BRUTUS   Your reason?
250   CASSIUS   This it is:
    'Tis better that the enemy seek us;
    So shall he waste his means, weary his soldiers,
    Doing himself offence; whilst we, lying still,
    Are full of rest, defence, and nimbleness.
255   BRUTUS   Good reasons must of force° give place to better.   *of necessity*
    The people 'twixt Philippi and this ground
    Do stand but in a forced affection,
    For they have grudged us contribution.[8]
    The enemy marching along by them
260   By them shall make a fuller number up,
    Come on refreshed, new added,° and encouraged;   *reinforced*
    From which advantage shall we cut him off,
    If at Philippi we do face him there,
    These people at our back.
CASSIUS   Hear me, good brother.
265   BRUTUS   Under your pardon.° You must note beside   *Allow me to continue*
    That we have tried the utmost of our friends;
    Our legions are brim-full, our cause is ripe.
    The enemy increaseth every day;

---

4. See note to 4.1.17.
5. On the apparent conflict between this passage and lines 199–210, see the Introduction and the Textual Note.
6. I have learned as much of this philosophy.
7. *alive:* of concern to those now living.
8. Money to support the army.

We at the height are ready to decline.
270 <u>There is a tide in the affairs of men</u>
<u>Which, taken at the flood, leads on to fortune;</u>
<u>Omitted,° all the voyage of their life</u>   *Once missed*
<u>Is bound in° shallows and in miseries.</u>   *confined to*
<u>On such a full sea are we now afloat,</u>
275 <u>And we must take the current when it serves,</u>
<u>Or lose our ventures.</u>[9]
CASSIUS   Then, with your will,° go on.   *as you wish*
We'll along ourselves, and meet them at Philippi.
BRUTUS   The deep of night is crept upon our talk,
And nature must obey necessity,
280 Which we will niggard° with a little rest.   *stint*
There is no more to say.
CASSIUS   No more. Good night.
Early tomorrow will we rise and hence.°   *depart*
BRUTUS   Lucius.
        Enter LUCIUS
            My gown.°   [*Exit* LUCIUS]   *dressing gown*
                    Farewell, good Messala.
Good night, Titinius. Noble, noble, Cassius,
Good night and good repose.
285 CASSIUS   O my dear brother,
This was an ill beginning of the night!
Never come such division 'tween our souls.
Let it not, Brutus.
        Enter LUCIUS *with the gown*
BRUTUS   Everything is well.
CASSIUS   Good night, my lord.
BRUTUS   Good night, good brother.
TITINIUS *and* MESSALA   Good night, Lord Brutus.
290 BRUTUS   Farewell, every one.
                        Exeunt [CASSIUS, TITINIUS, *and* MESSALA]
Give me the gown.
        [*He puts on the gown*]
                    Where is thy instrument?°   *(probably a lute)*
LUCIUS   Here in the tent.
BRUTUS   What, thou speak'st drowsily.
Poor knave,° I blame thee not; thou art o'erwatched.[1]   *lad*
Call Claudio and some other of my men.
295 I'll have them sleep on cushions in my tent.
LUCIUS   Varrus and Claudio!
        Enter VARRUS *and* CLAUDIO
VARRUS   Calls my lord?
BRUTUS   I pray you, sirs, lie in my tent and sleep.
It may be I shall raise you° by and by   *get you up*
On business to my brother Cassius.
300 VARRUS   So please you, we will stand and watch your pleasure.[2]
BRUTUS   I will not have it so. Lie down, good sirs.
It may be I shall otherwise bethink me.°   *change my mind*
        [VARRUS *and* CLAUDIO *lie down to sleep*]
Look, Lucius, here's the book I sought for so.

9. Investments (in trading voyages).   2. And stay awake to attend to your wishes.
1. You have stayed up too long.

I put it in the pocket of my gown.
305 LUCIUS I was sure your lordship did not give it me.
BRUTUS Bear with me, good boy, I am much forgetful.
Canst thou hold up thy heavy eyes a while,
And touch thy instrument a strain or two?
LUCIUS Ay, my lord, an't° please you.   *if it*
BRUTUS   It does, my boy.
310 I trouble thee too much, but thou art willing.
LUCIUS It is my duty, sir.
BRUTUS I should not urge thy duty past thy might.
I know young bloods° look for a time of rest.   *youthful spirits*
LUCIUS I have slept, my lord, already.
315 BRUTUS It was well done, and thou shalt sleep again.
I will not hold thee long. If I do live,
I will be good to thee.
          [LUCIUS *plays*] *music and* [*sings*] *a song* [*and so falls*
          asleep]
This is a sleepy tune. O murd'rous slumber,
Lay'st thou thy leaden mace° upon my boy   *heavy staff of office*
320 That plays thee music?—Gentle knave, good night.
I will not do thee so much wrong to wake thee.
If thou dost nod thou break'st thy instrument;
I'll take it from thee, and, good boy, good night.
          [*He takes away Lucius' instrument, then opens the book*]
Let me see, let me see, is not the leaf turned down
325 Where I left reading? Here it is, I think.
          Enter the GHOST *of Caesar*
How ill this taper burns![3] Ha! Who comes here?
I think it is the weakness of mine eyes
That shapes this monstrous apparition.
It comes upon° me. Art thou any thing?   *toward*
330 Art thou some god, some angel, or some devil,
That mak'st my blood cold and my hair to stare?°   *stand on end*
Speak to me what thou art.
GHOST Thy evil spirit, Brutus.
BRUTUS Why com'st thou?
335 GHOST To tell thee thou shalt see me at Philippi.
BRUTUS Well; then I shall see thee again?
GHOST   Ay, at Philippi.
BRUTUS Why, I will see thee at Philippi then.   *Exit* GHOST
Now I have taken heart, thou vanishest.
Ill spirit, I would hold more talk with thee.—
340 Boy, Lucius, Varrus, Claudio, sirs, awake!
Claudio!
LUCIUS   The strings, my lord, are false.°   *out of tune*
BRUTUS He thinks he still is at his instrument.—
Lucius, awake!
LUCIUS My lord.
345 BRUTUS Didst thou dream, Lucius, that thou so cried'st out?
LUCIUS My lord, I do not know that I did cry.
BRUTUS Yes, that thou didst. Didst thou see anything?
LUCIUS Nothing, my lord.
BRUTUS Sleep again, Lucius.—Sirrah Claudio!

3. The dimming of a flame was held to indicate a ghost's presence.

[*To* VARRUS]   Fellow,
350 Thou, awake!
VARRUS   My lord.
CLAUDIO   My lord.
BRUTUS   Why did you so cry out, sirs, in your sleep?
BOTH   Did we, my lord?
BRUTUS   Ay. Saw you anything?
VARRUS   No, my lord, I saw nothing.
355 CLAUDIO   Nor I, my lord.
BRUTUS   Go and commend me° to my brother Cassius.   *send my regards*
    Bid him set on his powers betimes before,[4]
    And we will follow.
BOTH   It shall be done, my lord.
        Exeunt [VARRUS *and* CLAUDIO *at one door,* BRUTUS
                and LUCIUS *at another door*]

5.1

    Enter OCTAVIUS, ANTONY, *and their army*
OCTAVIUS   Now, Antony, our hopes are answerèd.
    You said the enemy would not come down,
    But keep the hills and upper regions.
    It proves not so; their battles° are at hand.   *forces*
5   They mean to warn° us at Philippi here,   *challenge*
    Answering before we do demand of them.
ANTONY   Tut, I am in their bosoms,[1] and I know
    Wherefore they do it. They could be content
    To visit other places;° and come down   *To go elsewhere*
10 With fearful bravery,[2] thinking by this face°   *pretense; defiance*
    To fasten in our thoughts that they have courage;
    But 'tis not so.
        Enter a MESSENGER
MESSENGER   Prepare you, generals.
    The enemy comes on in gallant show.
    Their bloody sign° of battle is hung out,   *red flag*
15 And something to° be done immediately.   *is to*
ANTONY   Octavius, lead your battle softly° on   *your army warily*
    Upon the left hand of the even field.
OCTAVIUS   Upon the right hand, I; keep thou the left.
ANTONY   Why do you cross° me in this exigent?°   *thwart / critical moment*
20 OCTAVIUS   I do not cross you,[3] but I will do so.
        [*Drum.* ANTONY *and* OCTAVIUS] *march* [*with their army*].
        Drum [*within*]. *Enter* [*marching*] BRUTUS, CASSIUS, *and*
        their army [*amongst them* TITINIUS, LUCILLIUS, *and* MES-
        SALA]
        [Octavius' *and* Antony's *army makes a stand*]
BRUTUS   They stand, and would have parley.
CASSIUS   Stand fast, Titinius. We must out° and talk.   *go forward*
        [Brutus' *and* Cassius' *army makes a stand*]
OCTAVIUS   Mark Antony, shall we give sign of battle?
ANTONY   No, Caesar, we will answer on their charge.[4]

---

4. March off with his army before me.   terrifying display.
5.1 Location: The remainder of the play takes place on   3. March on the right side; dispute with you in the
the battlefield near Philippi.   future.
1. I know their secret thoughts.   4. We will meet them when they attack.
2. With a show of courage that conceals fear; with a

25   Make forth,° the generals would have some words.   *Go forward*
         OCTAVIUS [*to his army*]   Stir not until the signal.
             [ANTONY *and* OCTAVIUS *meet* BRUTUS *and* CASSIUS]
         BRUTUS   Words before blows: is it so countrymen?
         OCTAVIUS   Not that we love words better, as you do.
         BRUTUS   Good words are better than bad strokes, Octavius.
30   ANTONY   In your° bad strokes, Brutus, you give good words.   *As you deliver*
         Witness the hole you made in Caesar's heart,
         Crying 'Long live, hail Caesar'.
         CASSIUS   Antony,
         The posture° of your blows are yet unknown;   *quality*
         But for your words, they rob the Hybla[5] bees,
35   And leave them honeyless.
         ANTONY   Not stingless too.
         BRUTUS   O yes, and soundless too,
         For you have stolen their buzzing, Antony,
         And very wisely threat before you sting.
40   ANTONY   Villains, you did not so when your vile daggers
         Hacked one another in the sides of Caesar.
         You showed your teeth like apes,° and fawned like hounds,   *You imitated smiles*
         And bowed like bondmen, kissing Caesar's feet,
         Whilst damnèd Casca, like a cur, behind,
45   Struck Caesar on the neck. O you flatterers!
         CASSIUS   Flatterers? Now, Brutus, thank yourself.
         This tongue had not offended so today
         If Cassius might have ruled.°   *had his way*
         OCTAVIUS   Come, come, the cause.° If arguing make us sweat,   *matter in hand*
50   The proof° of it will turn to redder drops.   *testing*
             [*He draws*]
         Look, I draw a sword against conspirators.
         When think you that the sword goes up again?
         Never till Caesar's three and thirty wounds
         Be well avenged, or till another Caesar[6]
55   Have added slaughter to[7] the swords of traitors.
         BRUTUS   Caesar, thou canst not die by traitors' hands,
         Unless thou bring'st them with thee.°   *(Unless by your hand)*
         OCTAVIUS   So I hope.
         I was not born to die on Brutus' sword.
         BRUTUS   O, if thou wert the noblest of thy strain,°   *family*
60   Young man, thou couldst not die more honourable.
         CASSIUS   A peevish° schoolboy, worthless of such honour,   *silly*
         Joined with a masquer and a reveller![8]
         ANTONY   Old Cassius still.
         OCTAVIUS   Come, Antony, away.
         Defiance, traitors, hurl we in your teeth.
65   If you dare fight today, come to the field.
         If not, when you have stomachs.°   *inclination; courage*
             Exeunt OCTAVIUS, ANTONY, *and* [*their*] *army*
         CASSIUS   Why, now blow wind, swell billow, and swim bark.°   *ship*
         The storm is up, and all is on the hazard.°   *at risk*
         BRUTUS   Ho, Lucillius! Hark, a word with you.

---

5. Sicilian town famous for honey.   8. That is, Antony, who was noted for his love of extrav-
6. That is, Octavius Caesar himself.   agant entertainments and banquets.
7. Has increased the slaughter committed by.

LUCILLIUS   My lord.

    [*He*] *stand*[*s*] *forth*° [*and speaks with* BRUTUS]   *comes forward*

CASSIUS   Messala.

MESSALA [*standing forth*]   What says my general?

70   CASSIUS   Messala,

<u>This is my birthday; as° this very day</u>   *on*

<u>Was Cassius born.</u> Give me thy hand, Messala.

Be thou my witness that, against my will,

As Pompey was, am I compelled to set

75   Upon one battle all our liberties.

You know that I held Epicurus strong,

And his opinion.[9] Now I change my mind,

And partly credit things that do presage.

Coming from Sardis, on our former ensigns°   *foremost banners*

80   Two mighty eagles fell,° and there they perched,   *alighted*

Gorging and feeding from our soldiers' hands,

Who to Philippi here consorted° us.   *accompanied*

This morning are they fled away and gone,

And in their steads do ravens, crows, and kites[1]

85   Fly o'er our heads and downward look on us,

As° we were sickly prey. Their shadows seem   *As if*

A canopy most fatal,° under which   *ominous*

Our army lies ready to give° the ghost.   *give up*

MESSALA   Believe not so.

CASSIUS   I but believe it partly,

90   For I am fresh of spirit, and resolved

To meet all perils very constantly.°   *resolutely*

BRUTUS   Even so, Lucillius.

CASSIUS [*joining* BRUTUS]   Now, most noble Brutus,

The gods° today stand friendly, that we may,   *May the gods*

Lovers° in peace, lead on our days to age.   *Close friends*

95   But since the affairs of men rest still° incertain,   *always remain*

Let's reason with° the worst that may befall.   *consider*

If we do lose this battle, then is this

The very last time we shall speak together.

What are you then determinèd to do?

100   BRUTUS   Even by the rule of that philosophy[2]

By which I did blame Cato[3] for the death

Which he did give himself—I know not how,

But I do find it cowardly and vile

For fear of what might fall° so to prevent°   *happen / anticipate*

105   The time° of life—arming myself with patience   *natural limit*

To stay° the providence of some high powers   *await*

That govern us below.

CASSIUS   Then if we lose this battle,

You are contented to be led in triumph[4]

Thorough° the streets of Rome?   *Through*

110   BRUTUS   No, Cassius, no.

Think not, thou noble Roman,

That ever Brutus will go bound to Rome.

---

9. Epicurus, a Greek philosopher, thought the gods
indifferent to human affairs and therefore disbelieved
omens.

1. These are all scavenger birds, considered bad omens.

2. Brutus admired Plato, who rejected suicide.

3. See note to 2.1.294.

4. As a captive in a triumphal procession; see note to
1.1.30.

He bears too great a mind. But this same day
Must end that work the ides of March begun;
115 And whether we shall meet again I know not.
Therefore our everlasting farewell take.
For ever and for ever farewell, Cassius.
If we do meet again, why, we shall smile.
If not, why then, this parting was well made.
120 CASSIUS   For ever and for ever farewell, Brutus.
If we do meet again, we'll smile indeed.
If not, 'tis true this parting was well made.
BRUTUS   Why then, lead on. O that a man might know
The end of this day's business ere it come!
125 But it sufficeth that the day will end,
And then the end is known.—Come, ho, away!   *Exeunt*

5.2

Alarum.° Enter BRUTUS *and* MESSALA   *Offstage call to battle*
BRUTUS   Ride, ride, Messala, ride, and give these bills°   *written orders*
Unto the legions on the other side.°   (Cassius's wing)
Loud alarum
Let them set on° at once, for I perceive   *advance*
But cold demeanour° in Octavio's wing,   *lack of fighting spirit*
5 And sudden push gives them the overthrow.
Ride, ride, Messala; let them all come down.
          Exeunt [severally]

5.3

Alarums. Enter CASSIUS *[with an ensign,°] and* TITINIUS   *a banner*
CASSIUS   O look, Titinius, look: the villains° fly.   (Cassius's own men)
Myself have to mine own turned enemy:
This ensign° here of mine was turning back;   *standard-bearer*
I slew the coward, and did take it° from him.   (the standard)
5 TITINIUS   O Cassius, Brutus gave the word too early,
Who, having some advantage on Octavius,
Took it too eagerly. His soldiers fell to spoil,°   *looting*
Whilst we by Antony are all enclosed.
Enter PINDARUS
PINDARUS   Fly further off, my lord, fly further off!
10 Mark Antony is in your tents, my lord;
Fly therefore, noble Cassius, fly farre° off.   *farther*
CASSIUS   This hill is far enough. Look, look, Titinius.
Are those my tents where I perceive the fire?
TITINIUS   They are, my lord.
CASSIUS   Titinius, if thou lovest me,
15 Mount thou my horse, and hide thy spurs in him
Till he have brought thee up to yonder troops
And here again, that I may rest assured
Whether yon troops are friend or enemy.
TITINIUS   I will be here again even with° a thought.   *Exit*   *as fast as*
20 CASSIUS   Go, Pindarus, get higher on that hill.
My sight was ever thick.° Regard, Titinius,   *dim*
And tell me what thou not'st about the field.   [*Exit* PINDARUS]
This day I breathèd first. Time is come round,

And where I did begin, there shall I end.
My life is run his compass.°   *its circuit*
          [*Enter* PINDARUS *above*]°   (*on the stage balcony*)
25   Sirrah, what news?
PINDARUS   O my lord!
CASSIUS   What news?
PINDARUS   Titinius is enclosèd round about
With horsemen, that make to him on the spur.[1]
30   Yet he spurs on. Now they are almost on him.
Now Titinius. Now some light.° O, he lights too.   *alight*
He's ta'en.°   *taken*
          Shout [*within*]
And hark, they shout for joy.
CASSIUS   Come down; behold no more.
                                        [*Exit* PINDARUS]
O coward that I am, to live so long
35   To see my best friend ta'en before my face!
          Enter PINDARUS [*below*]
Come hither, sirrah. In Parthia° did I take thee prisoner,   (*modern Iran*)
And then I swore thee, saving of[2] thy life,
That whatsoever I did bid thee do
Thou shouldst attempt it. Come now, keep thine oath.
40   Now be a freeman, and, with this good sword
That ran through Caesar's bowels, search° this bosom.   *penetrate*
Stand° not to answer. Here, take thou the hilts,°   *Delay / sword handle*
          [PINDARUS *takes the sword*]
And when my face is covered, as 'tis now,
Guide thou the sword.
          [PINDARUS *stabs him*]
                              Caesar, thou art revenged,
45   Even with the sword that killed thee.   [*He dies*]
PINDARUS   So, I am free, yet would not so have been
Durst° I have done my will. O Cassius!   *Dared*
Far from this country Pindarus shall run,
Where never Roman shall take note of him.   *Exit*
          Enter TITINIUS [*wearing a wreath of victory*°] *and* MES-   (*made of laurel leaves*)
          SALA
50   MESSALA   It is but change,° Titinius, for Octavius   *an even exchange*
Is overthrown by noble Brutus' power,
As Cassius' legions are by Antony.
TITINIUS   These tidings will well comfort Cassius.
MESSALA   Where did you leave him?
TITINIUS   All disconsolate,
55   With Pindarus his bondman, on this hill.
MESSALA   Is not that he that lies upon the ground?
TITINIUS   He lies not like the living.—O my heart!
MESSALA   Is not that he?
TITINIUS   No, this was he, Messala;
But Cassius is no more. O setting sun,
60   As in thy red rays thou dost sink tonight,
So in his red blood Cassius' day is set.
The sun of Rome is set. Our day is gone.

5.3
1. Who approach him at a gallop.   2. I made you swear, when I spared.

Clouds, dews, and dangers come. Our deeds are done.
Mistrust of my success³ hath done this deed.
65 MESSALA Mistrust of good success hath done this deed.
O hateful Error, Melancholy's child,⁴
Why dost thou show to the apt° thoughts of men   *impressionable*
The things that are not? O Error, soon conceived,
Thou never com'st unto a happy birth,
70 But kill'st the mother° that engendered thee.   *(the melancholy person)*
TITINIUS What, Pindarus! Where art thou, Pindarus?
MESSALA Seek him, Titinius, whilst I go to meet
The noble Brutus, thrusting this report
Into his ears. I may say 'thrusting' it,
75 For piercing steel and darts° envenomèd   *spears*
Shall be as welcome to the ears of Brutus
As tidings of this sight.
TITINIUS   Hie you, Messala,
And I will seek for Pindarus the while.   [*Exit* MESSALA]
Why didst thou send me forth, brave Cassius?
80 Did I not meet thy friends, and did not they
Put on my brows this wreath of victory,
And bid me give it thee? Didst thou not hear their shouts?
Alas, thou hast misconstrued everything.
But hold thee, take this garland on thy brow.
85 Thy Brutus bid me give it thee, and I
Will do his bidding. Brutus, come apace,°   *quickly*
And see how I regarded° Caius Cassius.   *esteemed*
By your leave, gods, this is a Roman's part:
Come Cassius' sword, and find Titinius' heart.
          [*He stabs himself, and*] *dies*
     Alarum. Enter BRUTUS, MESSALA, YOUNG CATO,⁵ STRATO,
          VOLUMNIUS, LUCILLIUS[, LABIO, *and* FLAVIO]
90 BRUTUS Where, where, Messala, doth his body lie?
MESSALA Lo yonder, and Titinius mourning it.
BRUTUS Titinius' face is upward.
CATO   He is slain.
BRUTUS O Julius Caesar, thou art mighty yet.
Thy spirit walks abroad, and turns our swords
In our own proper° entrails.   *our very own*
          Low° *Alarums*   *Soft*
95 CATO   Brave Titinius,
Look whe'er° he have not crowned dead Cassius.   *whether*
BRUTUS Are yet two Romans living such as these?
The last of all the Romans, fare thee well.
It is impossible that ever Rome
100 Should breed thy fellow. Friends, I owe more tears
To this dead man than you shall see me pay.—
I shall find time, Cassius, I shall find time.—
Come, therefore, and to Thasos° send his body.   *an island near Philippi*
His funerals shall not be in our camp,
105 Lest it discomfort° us. Lucillius, come;   *dishearten*
And come, young Cato. Let us to the field.
Labio and Flavio, set our battles° on.   *forces*

3. Doubt about the outcome of my mission.   5. The son of Marcus Portius Cato.
4. That is, bred from melancholy thoughts.

'Tis three o'clock, and, Romans, yet ere night
We shall try fortune in a second fight.

Exeunt [with the bodies]

5.4

Alarum. Enter BRUTUS, MESSALA, YOUNG CATO, LUCIL-
LIUS, *and* FLAVIUS

BRUTUS   Yet, countrymen, O yet hold up your heads.

[*Exit with* MESSALA *and* FLAVIUS]

CATO   What bastard° doth not? Who will go with me?   untrue Roman
I will proclaim my name about the field.
I am the son of Marcus Cato, ho!
5   A foe to tyrants, and my country's friend.
I am the son of Marcus Cato, ho!

Enter SOLDIERS, *and fight*

LUCILLIUS   And I am Brutus, Marcus Brutus, I,
Brutus, my country's friend. Know me for Brutus.

[SOLDIERS *kill* CATO]

O young and noble Cato, art thou down?
10   Why, now thou diest as bravely as Titinius,
And mayst be honoured, being Cato's son.

FIRST SOLDIER   Yield, or thou diest.

LUCILLIUS   Only I yield to die.¹
There is so much,² that thou wilt kill me straight:°   immediately
Kill Brutus, and be honoured in his death.

15   FIRST SOLDIER   We must not.—A noble prisoner.

SECOND SOLDIER   Room, ho! Tell Antony Brutus is ta'en.

Enter ANTONY

FIRST SOLDIER   I'll tell the news. Here comes the general.—
[*To* ANTONY] Brutus is ta'en, Brutus is ta'en, my lord.

ANTONY   Where is he?

20   LUCILLIUS   Safe, Antony, Brutus is safe enough.
I dare assure thee that no enemy
Shall ever take alive the noble Brutus.
The gods defend him from so great a shame.
When you do find him, or° alive or dead,   either
25   He will be found like Brutus, like himself.°   true to his noble nature

ANTONY [*to* FIRST SOLDIER]   This is not Brutus, friend, but, I assure you,
A prize no less in worth. Keep this man safe.
Give him all kindness. I had rather have
Such men my friends than enemies.
[*To another* SOLDIER]   Go on,
30   And see whe'er Brutus be alive or dead,
And bring us word unto Octavius' tent
How everything is chanced.°   has happened

Exeunt [the SOLDIER *at one door,* ANTONY,
LUCILLIUS *and other* SOLDIERS, *some bearing
Cato's body, at another door]*

5.4
1. I yield only so that I may die.   2. There is enough inducement.

5.5

Enter BRUTUS, DARDANIUS, CLITUS, STRATO, *and*
VOLUMNIUS

BRUTUS   Come, poor remains of friends, rest on this rock.
　　　　[*He sits.* STRATO *rests and falls asleep*]
CLITUS   Statillius[1] showed the torchlight, but, my lord,
　　　　He came not back. He is or ta'en° or slain.　　　　　　*either captured*
BRUTUS   Sit thee down, Clitus. Slaying is the word:
5　　　　It is a deed in fashion. Hark thee, Clitus.
　　　　[*He whispers*]
CLITUS   What I, my lord? No, not for all the world.
BRUTUS   Peace, then, no words.
CLITUS　　　　　　　　　　　I'll rather kill myself.
　　　　[*He stands apart*]
BRUTUS   Hark thee, Dardanius.
　　　　[*He whispers*]
DARDANIUS　　　　　　　　　Shall I do such a deed?
　　　　[*He joins* CLITUS]
CLITUS   O Dardanius!
10　DARDANIUS   O Clitus!
CLITUS   What ill request did Brutus make to thee?
DARDANIUS   To kill him, Clitus. Look, he meditates.
CLITUS   Now is that noble vessel full of grief,
　　　　That it runs over even at his eyes.
15　BRUTUS   Come hither, good Volumnius. List° a word.　　　*Listen to*
VOLUMNIUS   What says my lord?
BRUTUS　　　　　　　　　　Why this, Volumnius.
　　　　The ghost of Caesar hath appeared to me
　　　　Two several° times by night—at Sardis once,　　　　*different*
　　　　And this last night, here in Philippi fields.
　　　　I know my hour is come.
20　VOLUMNIUS　　　　　　　　Not so, my lord.
BRUTUS   Nay, I am sure it is, Volumnius.
　　　　Thou seest the world, Volumnius, how it goes.
　　　　Our enemies have beat° us to the pit,[2]　　　　　　*driven*
　　　　　　Low alarums
　　　　It is more worthy to leap in ourselves
25　　　Than tarry till they push us. Good Volumnius,
　　　　Thou know'st that we two went to school together.
　　　　Even for that, our love of old, I prithee,
　　　　Hold thou my sword hilts whilst I run on it.
VOLUMNIUS   That's not an office for a friend, my lord.
　　　　　　Alarum still
30　CLITUS   Fly, fly, my lord! There is no tarrying here.
BRUTUS   Farewell to you, and you, and you, Volumnius.—
　　　　Strato, thou hast been all this while asleep.
　　　　[STRATO *wakes*]
　　　　Farewell to thee too, Strato. Countrymen,
　　　　My heart doth joy that yet in all my life
35　　　I found no man but he was true to me.

5.5
1. A soldier sent ahead with instructions to signal by torchlight if all is well.
2. Animal trap; grave.

I shall have glory by this losing day,
More than Octavius and Mark Antony
By this vile conquest shall attain unto.
So fare you well at once, for Brutus' tongue
40   Hath almost ended his life's history.
Night hangs upon mine eyes. My bones would rest,
That have but laboured[3] to attain this hour.
                    Alarum. Cry within: 'Fly, fly, fly!'
CLITUS   Fly, my lord, fly!
BRUTUS   Hence; I will follow.
            [*Exeunt* CLITUS, DARDANIUS, *and* VOLUMNIUS]
I prithee, Strato, stay thou by thy lord.
45   Thou art a fellow of a good respect.°   reputation
Thy life hath had some smatch° of honour in it.   relish
Hold then my sword, and turn away thy face
While I do run upon it. Wilt thou, Strato?
STRATO   Give me your hand first. Fare you well, my lord.
BRUTUS   Farewell, good Strato.
            [STRATO *holds the sword, while* BRUTUS *runs on it*]
50   Caesar, now be still.
I killed not thee with half so good a will.   [*He*] *dies*
            Alarum. Retreat.[4] *Enter* ANTONY, OCTAVIUS, MESSALA,
            LUCILLIUS, *and the army*
OCTAVIUS   What man is that?
MESSALA   My master's man. Strato, where is thy master?
STRATO   Free from the bondage you are in, Messala.
55   The conquerors can but make a fire of him,°   burn his body
For Brutus only overcame himself,[5]
And no man else hath honour by his death.
LUCILLIUS   So Brutus should be found. I thank thee, Brutus,
That thou hast proved Lucillius' saying true.
60   OCTAVIUS   All that served Brutus, I will entertain them.°   take them into service
[*To* STRATO] Fellow, wilt thou bestow° thy time with me?   spend
STRATO   Ay, if Messala will prefer° me to you.   recommend
OCTAVIUS   Do so, good Messala.
MESSALA   How died my master, Strato?
STRATO   I held the sword, and he did run on it.
65   MESSALA   Octavius, then take him to follow° thee,   serve
That did the latest° service to my master.   last
ANTONY   This was the noblest Roman of them all.
All the conspirators save only he
Did that° they did in envy of great Caesar.   what
70   He only in a general honest thought[6]
And common good to all[7] made one of them.
His life was gentle,° and the elements[8]   noble
So mixed in him that nature might stand up
And say to all the world 'This was a man'.
75   OCTAVIUS   According° to his virtue let us use him,   In accordance with
With all respect and rites of burial.
Within my tent his bones tonight shall lie,
Most like a soldier, ordered° honourably.   treated

3. Labored for no other purpose than.
4. Trumpet signal to cease pursuit.
5. For only Brutus conquered Brutus.
6. With a virtuous, principled conviction.

7. And desire for the common good.
8. The four bodily humors, different combinations of which supposedly affected temperament; in the ideal individual, no single humor predominated.

So call the field to rest, and let's away
80 To part° the glories of this happy day.   share

Exeunt [with Brutus' body]

As You Like It

Much of *As You Like It* takes place in a forest, where characters in flight from treachery at court and injustice in the family take refuge. The play thus participates in the rich tradition of Renaissance pastoral literature in which the rustic world of forest and field offers an alternative to and a sanctuary from the urban or courtly milieu to which it is contrasted. The pastoral mode had its origins in ancient Greece where the poet Theocritus used rural settings and rustic shepherds to explore the sorrows of love and the harsh injustices of daily life. The Roman poet Virgil expanded this tradition, elaborating in particular the opposition between city and country life that in the Renaissance was often transmuted into an opposition between court and country. In England, many of Shakespeare's contemporaries worked in pastoral forms, particularly Edmund Spenser, whose *Shepheardes Calendar* (1579) was modeled on Virgil's *Eclogues*, and Sir Philip Sidney, whose vast prose romance *The Countess of Pembrokes Arcadia* was first published in revised form in 1590.

As a literary mode, pastoral can take many forms. There can be pastoral lyrics, dialogues, prose romances, and dramas. Certain topics and situations, however, are common features of many kinds of pastoral. Often, for example, exiles from urban or courtly life temporarily take up residence in the country where they live and converse with shepherds, often disguising *themselves* as shepherds before an eventual return to the life from which they had fled. In their rural retreat, they hold singing contests and discuss the relative merits of country and court life, whether nature is improved or spoiled by art, and whether "gentleness" (meaning both "nobility" and "a virtuous nature") is a condition one can achieve or to which one must be born.

Fundamental to pastoral debates is a concern about the relationship of what is "natural" to what is "artificial," that is, about whether what human beings have made—cities, gardens, or systems of social hierarchy—is preferable to the simplicity and lack of artifice supposedly found in rural settings and communities. This preoccupation makes pastoral particularly suited to social criticism. Pastoral figures often dissect the evils of various ways of life—the cruelty of hard-hearted mistresses, the greed of landlords, the deceit of courtiers, and the venality of the clergy. But while pastoral frequently celebrates simplicity, it does so in a highly artful manner, drawing on conventions that have been part of the Western literary tradition for at least two thousand years. Pastoral is therefore not so much a spontaneous expression of "natural" simplicity as the artful imitation of such simplicity by characters exiled from more sophisticated realms who for a time assume the guise of shepherds and play an elaborate game of "Let's pretend." Hence the many disguises found in pastoral, where courtiers pose as rustic shepherds, men as women, women as men, and dukes as forest outlaws. To minds of a stolidly serious cast, pastoral can appear to be a silly, escapist genre. To those less dismissive of the world of "Let's pretend," it offers an opportunity to see more clearly—and perhaps then to change—the world in which one ordinarily lives by entering for a time the playful, meditative, and artificial realm of imaginary shepherds.

In *As You Like It,* Shakespeare gave himself over to the pleasures and the seriousness of pastoral without seeming to find them antithetical. In the main action, a good ruler, Duke Senior, has been ousted from his throne by a usurping younger brother, Duke Frederick. The banished Duke takes refuge in the Forest of Ardenne, where he lives like Robin Hood with a band of loyal followers. When his daughter, Rosalind, companion to Frederick's daughter, Celia, is likewise banished, she disguises herself as a

First page of the *Gest of Robin Hood*, one of the most important sixteenth-century renditions of the Robin Hood legend.

young man named Ganymede and also journeys to Ardenne. Celia, posing as a lowborn woman named Aliena, goes with her, as does Touchstone the clown. A second line of action concerns two other brothers: Orlando, the youngest son, and Oliver, the oldest son of Sir Rowland de Bois. The inheritor of his father's estate, Oliver treats Orlando cruelly, denying him the education befitting a gentleman. In danger both from Duke Frederick and from his brother, Orlando also flees to the forest, accompanied by Adam, his dead father's eighty-year-old servant. By Act 2, all of these refugees from court life find themselves in a natural world, which, in spite of its considerable hardships, they prefer to the treachery of court. Ardenne is not Edenic. There are lions and snakes in this pastoral retreat and real shepherds like Corin who speak matter-of-factly about the hard and dirty labor that tending real sheep entails. But in Ardenne, there is also room for courtship games, for brotherly kindness, and for music. In fact, this play contains more songs than any other Shakespearean drama. In their song-filled green world, the characters hunt deer, tend sheep, and converse endlessly about love, exile, and the relative merits of court and country. Eventually, their chief troubles resolved, most return to court, leaving the forest once more to its native inhabitants and to those few courtiers who permanently embrace it.

The broad outlines of this story are taken from Thomas Lodge's enormously popular prose romance *Rosalynde*, written in 1586–87 and published in 1590, although Shakespeare changes many details and points of emphasis. In Lodge, for example, the Duke Senior and Duke Frederick characters are not brothers, but in both the ducal and the Orlando-Oliver plots, Shakespeare makes the enmity of brothers the principal sign of the corruption of "civilized" life. In Lodge, moreover, the father in the Orlando-Oliver plot does not follow the English custom of primogeniture, by which all property is settled on the oldest son; instead, he divides his property among his male offspring according to their merits. By having Oliver inherit almost everything, Shakespeare evokes an English social practice that caused great hardship to many younger brothers. The court women are handled differently as well by Shakespeare: he reduces the Celia character's centrality and instead emphasizes Rosalind and her love affair with Orlando. Shakespeare also tempers the violence of Lodge's resolution and adds to his cast of characters. In *Rosalynde*, the exiled Duke defeats the usurper in battle, but Shakespeare's Frederick has a religious conversion and voluntarily relinquishes the dukedom. Oliver Martext, William, Audrey, Touchstone the clown, and Jaques the melancholy satirist are all Shakespeare's creations. Jaques, in particular, adds a touch of caustic salt and Touchstone a dash of earthy realism to the play's exploration of competing value systems.

In fact, *As You Like It* is poised carefully on the razor's edge separating fantasy from harsh reality. Shakespeare's use of place is a case in point. Lodge's romance is set in the Forest of Ardenne, an ancient woodland comprising part of what is now France, Belgium, and Luxembourg. Shakespeare also uses a French setting, and this edition emphasizes that fact by giving the French spelling, "Ardenne," to the forest. But in the First Folio (1623), this woodland is called the Forest of Arden, an anglicized spelling that also happens to be the name of an English forest near Shakespeare's birthplace in Warwickshire. This fortuitous overlapping of French and English place-names is indicative of the play's double vision. Overtly set in a fantastical foreign kingdom, *As You Like It* nonetheless alludes to places (such as the Forest of Arden), people (such as Robin Hood), and practices (such as primogeniture) native to Shakespeare's own England. Through the distancing artifice of pastoral, the play deals with problems close to home.

Lodge's prose romance is not the only source for *As You Like It*. The play also draws upon *The Tale of Gamelyn*, a violent Middle English narrative in which a younger brother seeks revenge upon an older brother who mistreats him, and which explicitly evokes the name of Robin Hood, the popular English hero whose deeds were celebrated in countless ballads and stories. In the opening scene of *As You Like It*, Charles the wrestler reports that the banished Duke is ' already in the forest of Ardenne, and a many merry men with him; and there they live like the old Robin Hood of England. They say many young gentlemen flock to him every day, and fleet the time carelessly, as they did in the golden world" (1.1.99–103). Shakespeare could count on his audience to know the story of Robin Hood, and its evocation carried certain associations. The legendary figure and his band of men stood not only for the community and brotherhood characteristic of the Golden Age and absent in modern life, but also for resistance to tyranny. The great forests of England were the King's own preserves. To kill the deer in those forests was a crime against the monarch. Yet Robin Hood lived in the forest, dined on the King's deer, and opposed King John's unjust reign. In the 1590s, many of those resisting the enclosure of farmland for sheep grazing took refuge in forest areas, and poaching the King's deer had long been one way the poor defied the law to feed themselves when food was short, as it often was because of bad food harvests in the late 1590s.

As You Like It only obliquely alludes to this immediate social context, but Act 1 depicts a world of injustice and social disorder that both motivates the flight to Ardenne and evokes the tradition of opposition to injustice associated with Robin Hood. Orlando's situation speaks to the peculiarly English plight of younger brothers who, under the system of primogeniture, inherited little from their fathers and were often at the mercy of elder siblings. Oliver is a nightmare version of an eldest son: he deprives Orlando of a gentleman's education, connives with the Duke's professional wrestler to have his brother injured, and throws his father's old servant, Adam, out of the house. His cruelty is echoed by the tyranny of Duke Frederick. The play's opening thus clearly underscores the existence of inhumanity and tyrannical willfulness in the court and in the household of old Sir Rowland's eldest son. Less clear is whether this corruption stems from human institutions, particularly the system of primogeniture, or from the "naturally" evil natures of Frederick and Oliver. The play does not answer this or other thorny questions directly. In fact, it seems organized to provoke thought rather than urge conclusions, and the ending does not so much lay out a plan for social reform as indulge the fantasy that all desires, however contradictory, can be fulfilled through marriage and the renewal of brotherly affection. The play's most sustained examination of human folly focuses on the behavior of those who succumb to Cupid's arrows. There are many lovers in Ardenne, and for almost none does the course of love run smooth. Lovesickness was a recognized malady in early modern culture, a condition that so disordered those who endured it that it could cause paleness, sighing, tears, fainting, melancholy, palpitations, and a host of other symptoms. The play represents all lovers as slightly mad and approaches their tribulations with a mixture of sympathy, detached amusement, and analytical curiosity. In part, Shakespeare draws on the critical capacities of pastoral to explore the causes of lovers' unhappiness and to probe the surprisingly complex issue of what is natural in matters of love and sexual desire. In this regard, the play takes little for granted—neither the stability of gender difference nor the naturalness of heterosexuality nor the invariant nature of being in love.

Rosalind and Orlando are the play's most prominent lovers, and through their courtship the play begins its exploration of the problems of loving well. Orlando, for example, loves by the book—that is, in imitation of the conventions employed by the fourteenth-century Italian poet Petrarch, whose love poems to a woman named Laura established one of the paradigmatic love rhetorics of Renaissance culture. Conventionally, the Petrarchan lover worships and idealizes a woman who is inaccessible to him, either because of her rank or because of her cold heart. He burns with passion; he wastes from despair; she does not respond. Orlando, rushing through the forest pinning bad love poems on trees, is a sendup of a Petrarchan lover. Touchstone makes fun of his verses; Rosalind, dressed as a man but pretending to be "Rosalind" in order to cure Orlando of his lovesickness, delights in showing how exaggerated and unrealistic are the Petrarchan lover's claims for the perfection of his mistress and the vastness of his suffering. As she caustically says to him, when he protests that he will die for his passion: "Men have died from time to time, and worms have eaten them, but not for love" (4.1.91–92). She is equally hard on the idealization of women, insisting that real women can be fickle and bad-tempered as easily as they can be goddesses. One way to interpret Orlando and Rosalind's interactions is to see her slowly educating him in a more realistic and egalitarian approach to the relationship of man to woman than that offered by the Petrarchan tradition. Yet the self-mockery, realism, and genuine regard for the other that come to characterize their relationship are hardly in themselves natural behaviors, but ones in which Orlando must be tutored.

Rosalind and Orlando, however, are not the only lovers in the forest. There is also the mooning shepherd, Silvius, who believes no one has ever loved with his intensity, and his proud mistress, Phoebe, who thinks much too well of her own limited charms and throws herself quite inappropriately into the part of the disdainful Petrarchan mistress. As Rosalind informs her: "I must tell you friendly in your ear, / Sell when you can. You are not for all markets" (3.5.60–61). Even Touchstone, ever ready to puncture the romantic ravings of Orlando and Rosalind, Silvius and Phoebe, cannot escape love's call. Functioning as the clown figure often does, to provide a detached commentary on the action around him, Touchstone is nonetheless a participant as well as an observer. His "love" is about as natural—in the sense of urgently physical—and as far removed from Petrarchan idealizations as can be imagined. His intended, Audrey, does not know what "poetical" means, and Touchstone laments that she has such a rudimentary command of language that she often cannot understand what he says to her. And yet, as he confides to Jaques, "As the ox hath his bow, sir, the horse his curb, and the falcon her bells, so man hath his desires" (3.3.65–66)—that is, as each creature has some restraint placed on his movement, so a man's sexual desires constrain him to accommodate himself to a woman, even one like Audrey, and to the marriage yoke. If Orlando and Silvius live too much in the thrall of poetic idealizations, Touchstone and Audrey starkly reveal what love looks like when it is reduced to a matter of pure desire, and all artfulness, all poetry, and all sweet amorous delay are eschewed.

The figure who instigates much of the play's talk about love is Rosalind, one of Shakespeare's liveliest heroines. Her attractiveness stems partly from the fact that she is at once an observer and critic of others and herself a full participant in the whirligig of love. In this, she resembles Touchstone and differs from the melancholy Jaques, who persistently catalogs the follies of others but holds back from full participation in the life around him. (Fittingly, Jaques remains in the forest at the end of the play, when most of the others return to their lives outside the pastoral retreat.) Rosalind is at the center of nearly everything that happens in *As You Like It,* and the complexity of her role is enhanced by the fact that for much of four acts she dresses like a man and successfully passes for one. In the 1590s, Shakespeare wrote a number of other comedies (*Two Gentlemen of Verona, The Merchant of Venice, Twelfth Night*) in which women dress as men to protect themselves from danger, to pursue a lover, or temporarily to acquire the prerogatives of the socially dominant gender. Rosalind's is arguably the most complicated of these cases of cross-dressing because she not only passes as a man, but while in her male disguise plays the role of Rosalind in her forest encounters with Orlando. A woman disguised as a man thus makes her own identity into a fiction she performs!

Rosalind's complex cross-dressing has many consequences. For one thing, it makes problematic how natural are the gender distinctions that supposedly separate man from woman. In a literal sense, clothes here make the man—or woman. A doublet and hose and a swaggering demeanor effectively create the illusion of masculinity, and Rosalind uses her disguise to try on the privileges of the supposedly superior sex. Far from a passive object of Petrarchan adoration, she takes charge of her escape from Frederick's court and her encounters with Orlando in the forest. Typically, Renaissance women remained under the control of their fathers and mothers until marriage bequeathed them to the care of a husband. Rosalind's special circumstances—a father banished, an uncle who wants her gone from court—put her in an unusual situation. Her decision to cross-dress further sets her apart. Mobile, loquacious, and bossy, Rosalind confutes the idea that women are by nature passive, silent, and in need of masculine supervision. At the same time, she exhibits certain stereotypically "female" behavior: to Celia she confesses how much she is in love with Orlando, and when he is wounded, she faints when she sees his blood on a cloth. Perhaps the point is that the figure of the cross-dressed Rosalind keeps open the question of what a woman (or a man) "really" is.

To the question of how men and women differ, Renaissance anatomical theory gave some answers dissimilar to those we now take for granted. According to Galen, an ancient Greek anatomist whose work on the body was widely influential in the early modern period, men and woman had the same anatomical structures; women were simply less perfect than men, there having been less heat present when they were conceived. This meant, among other things, that women's genitalia were just like a man's—with the vagina and ovaries corresponding to the penis and scrotum—except that they had not been pushed outside the body as a man's had been. Because by this account male-female difference was less grounded in ideas of absolute bodily difference than is typical today, much emphasis was placed on behavioral differences and on distinctions of dress. Preachers enjoined women to be chaste, silent, and obedient, and forbade them to wear the clothes of the opposite sex. In such a context, female cross-dressing, however playfully undertaken, always threatened to expose the artifice of gender distinctions by showing how easily one sex could assume the clothes and ape the behavior of the other.

The particularities of Rosalind's disguise, moreover, complicate her representation

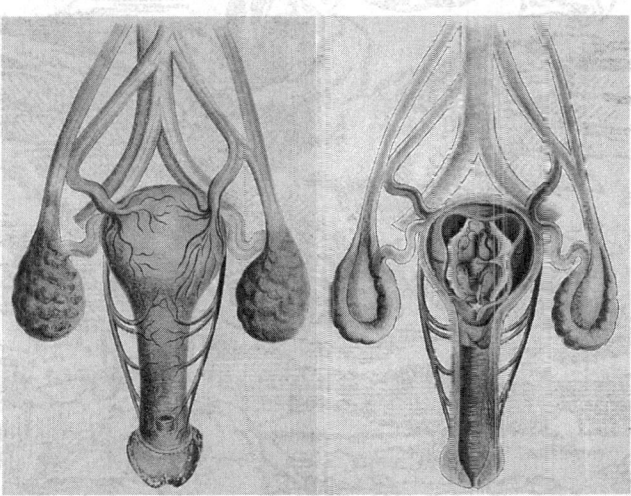

Typical sixteenth-century anatomy-book illustration of the female organs of generation. *Left*: the vagina and uterus are almost indistinguishable from the male penis and scrotum. *Right*: they have been cut open to reveal a tiny fetus in the uterus. From Fritz Weindler, *Geschichte der Gynäkologisch-anatomischen Abbildung* (1908). (Originally appeared in George Bartisch, *Kunstbuch*, 1575.)

even further. In disguise, Rosalind calls herself Ganymede, a name that had long-standing and unmistakable associations with homoerotic love. In Greek mythology, Ganymede was a beautiful boy whom Jove desired and whom he seized and carried to Mount Olympus to be cupbearer to the gods. A number of early modern paintings, woodcuts, and engravings depict the moment when Jove, in the form of an eagle, sweeps the boy away from earth and into the heavens. In Shakespeare's day, the word "Ganymede" commonly signified a young boy who was the lover of another (usually older) man. Shakespeare could hardly have been unaware of these associations when he had Rosalind choose this name as her alias. Consequently, when the cross-dressed heroine commands Orlando to woo his "Rosalind," he woos a figure who is dressed like a man and who bears a name signifying his status as a homoerotic love object. In performance, what the audience *sees* is one "man" flirting with another, even while the audience *knows* that one of these "men" is a woman. Provocatively, Shakespeare uses Orlando and Rosalind's encounters to overlay a story of male-female desire with traces of another tale of a man's love for a boy.

Long before *As You Like It* was penned, pastoral had been used to depict the beauty of both male friendship and homoerotic love. Edmund Spenser, in the January Eclogue of *The Shepheardes Calendar,* describes the passion of Hobbinol for Colin Cloute, who in turn loves an unresponsive woman named Rosalind. Commenting on this passage, E. K., the anonymous annotator of *The Shepheardes Calendar,* drew on classical precedent to defend pederastic love (love of an older man for a younger boy) as less dangerous than gynerastic love (love of man for woman). Since women were generally considered men's intellectual and moral inferiors, love for a woman was—so the argument went—less likely to be a rational passion than was love for a boy or a man. In the 1580s, Richard Barnfield wrote a pastoral work called *The Affectionate Shepherd,* in which the male speaker celebrates his love for a beautiful young man named Ganymede.

Ganymede being abducted by Jupiter in the form of an eagle. Woodcut by Virgil Solis. From *Metamorphosis Ovidii . . .* (1563).

Shakespeare is therefore not unique in introducing a Ganymede figure into the pastoral landscape, though he does so with a difference. In *As You Like It*, Ganymede is a disguise, a persona assumed and eventually discarded by Rosalind. As with much else in this play, Shakespeare thus has things at least two ways at once. For several acts, Orlando seems to pursue in one person both a boy and a woman but in the final scene Rosalind reassumes her female clothes and Ganymede disappears, thus ending the play with an emphasis on the culmination of male-female love in marriage. But even this is not quite the whole story. On the Renaissance stage, women's parts were played by boy actors. In the Epilogue, which she speaks, Rosalind calls attention to this fact, making it clear that if Orlando has finally won his Rosalind, the two players who enact this union are a young boy and a man.

In *As You Like It*, the erotic possibilities never seem to stop. The friendship between Rosalind and Celia, for example, is remarkably close. Charles the wrestler says, "Never two ladies loved as they do" (1.1.97). Celia readily gives up her father, her fortune, and her position at the court to follow Rosalind to Ardenne, where the two women in effect set up household together. Although they are yoked in love like Juno's swans, from the beginning Celia is afraid that Rosalind does not love her as much as she loves Rosalind (1.2.6–11). Quite quickly, Rosalind's primary interest does become her pursuit of Orlando. Yet in the midst of her love games with him, Rosalind also dallies with the ambitious and amorous Phoebe, who has taken the disguised Rosalind for a man. Overtly, Rosalind scorns Phoebe and directs her to love Silvius, but she also takes care to tell Phoebe where she lives (3.5.75–76) and encourages her attentions even as she denies them. As with other relationships in the play, it is not altogether clear whom Phoebe really desires: is it the man she thinks she sees or the woman beneath? Though the play eventually deposits Rosalind, Celia, and Phoebe all within Hymen's circle, it does so only after raising the possibility of other erotic conjunctions, including woman's love for woman.

In part, *As You Like It* can play so freely with various erotic possibilities because in the early modern period people were not assumed, as they often are today, to have a fixed sexual identity, to *be*, that is, a lesbian or a heterosexual. Often, one could engage in a range of sexual practices without contradiction. Depending on life stage and social circumstance, a man might have sex with a dependent man, such as a servant, and with a woman, such as his wife. The point is that performing a specific sexual act did not presume—or guarantee—a particular sexual identity. And yet Shakespeare's comedy, like many others, also acknowledges the social weight that the early modern period placed on marriage, the institution through which political alliances were forged, property passed, and lineage established. *As You Like It* both celebrates and pokes fun at the social inevitability of marriage by having Hymen, god of marriage, appear onstage in the last act to preside over a veritable spate of betrothals—four, to be exact. As Jaques suggests (5.4.35–36), it is indeed as if the beasts were proceeding, two by two, into Noah's ark.

Besides yoking individual man to individual woman, marriage in this play also helps to resolve seemingly intractable social problems. For example, Orlando's situation as younger brother is miraculously ameliorated through his marriage to Rosalind. As her husband, he becomes Duke Senior's heir, thus achieving a fortune equal to his gentle nature. Again, the play has things two ways at once. Duke Senior is restored to his dukedom, which confirms the prerogatives of older brothers, but Orlando does not have to suffer permanently the disadvantages of being a younger son. Primogeniture is simultaneously affirmed and circumvented. Moreover, when Oliver reforms, that reformation is sealed by his marriage to Celia, an indication that he now takes part in the communal life of his culture without the willful displays of indifference and selfishness that marked his earlier behavior.

Yet as this comedy celebrates marriage, it also registers a certain resistance to it and persistently maps alternative routings of desire. Rosalind registers that resistance when she complains of how avidly men court women before marriage and how indifferently they treat them afterward: "Men are April when they woo, December when they wed" (4.1.124–25). Marriage, she implies, can dull a man's desire and lessen a woman's emotional power over him. It also, of course, made women legally subject to their husbands. When Rosalind doffs her man's disguise to become a wife, she relinquishes many kinds of freedom. But the play also records *men's* resistance to marriage, partly through its many cuckold jokes. These jokes acknowledge that marriage may not fully circumscribe or satisfy a woman's sexual desires, that a man's control of his wife's sexuality may be more fiction than fact, leaving him vulnerable to public mockery. As the Duke's men sing as they bring home a slaughtered deer:

> Take thou no scorn to wear the horn;
> It was a crest ere thou wast born.
> Thy father's father wore it,
> And thy father bore it.
> (4.2.14–17)

The song transforms cuckold anxiety into entertainment, but it cannot erase that anxiety.

Consider, as well, the strange moment when Orlando comes across his brother Oliver lying asleep under an old oak. As Oliver sleeps, a female snake approaches his open mouth, threatening his life. Though the snake is frightened off, it is immediately replaced in this fantastic, dreamlike scenario by a hungry female lion with whom Orlando fights in order to save his brother's life (4.3.97–131). Twice, danger is represented in female form, and the reconciliation of the two brothers occurs only when Orlando spills his blood to beat back these threats. In *As You Like It*, as marriage is both desired and feared, so the feminine is represented as both an attraction and a source of danger.

In pastoral, little is immune from critique; the world men and women have made is an imperfect world. Yet the remarkable thing about *As You Like It* is that critique does not cancel affirmation. The play anatomizes court life and exposes its treachery, but many leave Ardenne to journey back to the court when Frederick has repented and the benevolent Duke Senior has returned to power. The play likewise dissects the problems of marriage, yet many marry at the end. Pastoral has a utopian as well as a critical dimension. The green world of shepherds holds traces of the simplicity of a lost Golden Age, and a sojourn in that world can prompt transformations in the everyday world to which the sojourners return. *As You Like It* is to a remarkable degree open to the infinite malleability of human beings and their social practices. A duke can become a forest outlaw and embrace the change; a tyrannical usurper can be touched by the words of a holy man, relinquish his power, and retire from the world. What men and women have marred, they may also mend.

It is with the heroine, however, that *As You Like It* offers its richest dramatization of a figure who plays endlessly with the limits and possibilities of her circumstances. This is true even in the Epilogue, when Rosalind, now in woman's clothing, steps forward to address the audience and solicit their applause. The persona of Ganymede cast aside, the heroine appears as the woman she "really is." But it is precisely at this moment of closure that she breaks the dramatic frame to remind the audience of *another* reality: that "she" is played by a "he." Dressed like a woman but declaring she is not, this unpredictable figure, this he/she, continues to the end to defy the fixed identities and the exclusionary choices of the everyday world, offering instead a world of multiple possibilities and transformable identities, a world as perhaps we might come to like it.

JEAN E. HOWARD

TEXTUAL NOTE

As You Like It was probably written between 1598 and 1600. It was entered in the Stationers' Register on August 4, 1600, but no edition followed this entry. Francis Meres, one of Shakespeare's contemporaries, in September of 1598 published a list of the Shakespeare plays known to him. It did not include *As You Like It,* suggesting that the play was performed sometime after that date but prior to its entry in the Stationers' Register. Two topical references suggest 1599 as the likely time of composition. At one point, Jaques, the play's cynical satirist, opines, "All the world's a stage" (2.7.138), perhaps an allusion to the motto *Totus mundus agit histrionem* (All the world plays the actor), of the Globe Theater, to which Shakespeare's company moved in the summer of 1599. Elsewhere, Touchstone, the play's clown, refers to the time "since the little wit that fools have was silenced" (1.2.74–75), a possible reference to the banning and burning of satirical books in June of 1599 by order of the Bishop of London.

The play was first published in the First Folio of 1623 (F) either from a promptbook or, less probably, from a literary transcript of either the promptbook or Shakespeare's foul papers. The present edition follows the act and scene divisions of F.

SELECTED BIBLIOGRAPHY

Colie, Rosalie L. "Perspectives on Pastoral: Romance, Comic and Tragic." *Shakespeare's Living Art.* Princeton: Princeton University Press, 1974. 243–83. Analyzes the many pastoral conventions found in *As You Like It* and how they contribute to the play's perspectivism—that is, its juxtaposition of competing viewpoints.

Crane, Mary. "Theatrical Practice and the Ideologies of Status in *As You Like It.*" *Shakespeare's Brain: Reading with Cognitive Theory.* Princeton: Princeton University Press, 2001. 67–93. Examines how, through its emphasis on words like *villain* and *clown, As You Like It* explores possibilities for upward and downward mobility in the world of the play and in the social world at large, including the theatrical community of which Shakespeare was a part.

Elam, Keir. "As They Did in the Golden World: Romantic Rapture and Semantic Rupture in *As You Like It.*" *Reading the Renaissance: Culture, Poetics, and Drama.* Ed. Jonathan Hart. New York: Garland, 1996. 163–76. Focuses on the way Shakespeare rewrites pastoral in *As You Like It* to banish nostalgia and linguistic earnestness in favor of the magical, forward-looking affirmations of romance.

Erickson, Peter. "Sexual Politics and Social Structure in *As You Like It.*" *Patriarchal Structures in Shakespeare's Drama.* Berkeley: University of California Press, 1985. 15–38. Argues that the play advocates a benevolent patriarchy that ultimately subordinates women to men while allowing men to assume nurturing functions.

Howard, Jean E. "Power and Eros: Crossdressing in Dramatic Representation and Theatrical Practice." *The Stage and Social Struggle in Early Modern England.* London: Routledge, 1994. 93–128. Examines cross-dressing as a convention through which *As You Like It* and other comedies explore the politics of early modern gender relations and the fluidity of sexual desire.

Marshall, Cynthia. "The Doubled Jaques and Constructions of Negation in *As You Like It.*" *Shakespeare Quarterly* 49 (1998): 375–92. Argues that in *As You Like It* the repression of melancholia, registered as a trace in the figure of Jaques, allows for the release of the high spirits and verbal fireworks proper to comedy.

Montrose, Louis. "'The Place of a Brother' in *As You Like It*: Social Process and Comic Form." *Shakespeare Quarterly* 32 (1981) 28–54. Argues that in *As You Like It* the process of comedy repairs the negative consequences of primogeniture for younger sons as Orlando finds a surrogate father in Duke Senior and a fortune through marriage.

Neely, Carol Thomas. "Destabilizing Lovesickness, Gender, and Sexuality: *Twelfth Night* and *As You Like It.*" *Distracted Subjects: Madness and Gender in Shakespeare and Early Modern Culture.* Ithaca, N.Y.: Cornell University Press, 2004. 99–135. Details the increasingly strong link between lovesickness and women in the Renaissance and compares its representation in *Twelfth Night* and *As You Like It.*

Traub, Valerie. "The Homoerotics of Shakespearean Comedy." *Desire and Anxiety: Circulations of Sexuality in Shakespearean Drama.* London: Routledge, 1992. 117–44. Explores the role of the boy actor in the production and circulation of homoerotic desire and argues that *As You Like It* playfully refuses the binary distinction between the heteroerotic and the homoerotic.

Wilson, Richard. "Like the Old Robin Hood: *As You Like It* and the Enclosure Riots." *Will Power: Essays on Shakespearean Authority.* London: Harvester Wheatsheaf, 1993. 63–82. Connects *As You Like It* to the social disturbances and food shortages of the 1590s but argues that the play pulls back from lodging a radical critique of social injustice.

Films

As You Like It. 1936. Dir. Paul Czinner. UK. 96 min. This black-and-white film features Laurence Olivier, in his first Shakespeare performance on film, as the dashing but moody Orlando with Elisabeth Bergner as an insipid Rosalind. Charming woodland scenes in a significantly cut production.

As You Like It. 1978. Dir. Basil Coleman. UK. 150 min. Traditional BBC-TV production with lively performances by Helen Mirren as Rosalind, Angharad Rees as Celia, and Victoria Plucknett as Phoebe. Playing Jaques, Richard Pasco brings poignant understatement to the famous "seven ages of man" speech.

As You Like It. 2006. Dir. Kenneth Branagh. UK. 127min. In this gorgeous production, the action is relocated from medieval France to nineteenth-century Japan. With Bryce Dallas Howard (Rosalind), David Oyelowo (Orlando), Rowola Garai (Celia), Brian Blessed (Duke Senior and Duke Frederick), and Alfred Molina (Touchstone).

As You Like It

THE PERSONS OF THE PLAY

DUKE SENIOR, living in banishment
ROSALIND, his daughter, later disguised as Ganymede
AMIENS
JAQUES } Lords attending on him
TWO PAGES
DUKE FREDERICK
CELIA, his daughter, later disguised as Aliena
LE BEAU, a courtier attending on him
CHARLES, Duke Frederick's wrestler
TOUCHSTONE, a clown
OLIVER, eldest son of Sir Rowland de Bois
JAQUES
ORLANDO } his younger brothers
ADAM, a former servant of Sir Rowland
DENIS, Oliver's servant
SIR OLIVER MARTEXT, a country clergyman
CORIN, an old shepherd
SILVIUS, a young shepherd, in love with Phoebe
PHOEBE, a shepherdess
WILLIAM, a countryman, in love with Audrey
AUDREY, a goatherd, betrothed to Touchstone
HYMEN, god of marriage
Lords, pages, and other attendants

1.1

Enter ORLANDO *and* ADAM

ORLANDO   As I remember, Adam, it was upon this fashion
    bequeathed me by will but poor° a thousand crowns,[1] and, as   *only*
    thou sayst, charged° my brother on his blessing[2] to breed me   *he (my father) charged*
    well—and there begins my sadness. My brother Jaques he
5   keeps at school,° and report speaks goldenly of his profit. For   *university*
    my part, he keeps me rustically at home—or, to speak more
    properly, stays° me here at home unkept;° for call you that   *detains / uncared for*
    keeping for a gentleman of my birth, that differs not from the
    stalling of an ox? His horses are bred better, for besides that
10 they are fair with° their feeding, they are taught their manège,[3]   *handsome because of*
    and to that end riders dearly° hired. But I, his brother, gain   *expensively*
    nothing under him but growth, for the which his animals on
    his dunghills are as much bound to him as I. Besides this noth-
    ing that he so plentifully gives me, the something that nature
15 gave me his countenance° seems to take from me. He lets me   *conduct*
    feed with his hinds,° bars me[4] the place of a brother, and as   *farmworkers*
    much as in him lies, mines my gentility with my education.[5]

1.1 Location: The orchard of Oliver's house, in the
vicinity of Duke Frederick's court in France.
1. Equivalent to about 250 English pounds. Orlando's
inheritance is worth twice as much as Adam's life sav-
ings (see 2.3.39).

2. On pain of losing his blessing.
3. Paces and actions of a trained horse.
4. Excludes me from
5. Undermines my gentility by my (poor) education.

This is it, Adam, that grieves me; and the spirit of my father,
which I think is within me, begins to mutiny against this servi-
20   tude. I will no longer endure it, though yet I know no wise
remedy how to avoid it.
            Enter OLIVER
ADAM   Yonder comes my master, your brother.
ORLANDO   Go apart, Adam, and thou shalt hear how he will
shake me up.°   *insult me*
            [ADAM *stands aside*]
25   OLIVER   Now, sir, what make you° here?   *are you doing*
ORLANDO   Nothing. I am not taught to make anything.
OLIVER   What mar you then, sir?
ORLANDO   Marry,⁶ sir, I am helping you to mar that which God
made, a poor unworthy brother of yours, with idleness.
30   OLIVER   Marry, sir, be better employed, and be nought° awhile.   *get lost*
ORLANDO   Shall I keep your hogs, and eat husks with them?
What prodigal portion have I spent, that I should come to such
penury?⁷
OLIVER   Know you where you are, sir?
35   ORLANDO   O sir, very well; here in your orchard.
OLIVER   Know you before whom, sir?
ORLANDO   Ay, better than him I am before knows me. I know
you are my eldest brother, and in the gentle condition of blood
you should so know me.⁸ The courtesy of nations⁹ allows you
40   my better, in that you are the first-born; but the same tradition
takes not away my blood, were there twenty brothers betwixt
us. I have as much of my father in me as you, albeit I confess
your coming before me is nearer to his reverence.¹
OLIVER   [*assailing him*]   What, boy!
45   ORLANDO   [*seizing him by the throat*]   Come, come, elder
brother, you are too young° in this.   *inexperienced*
OLIVER   Wilt thou lay hands on me, villain?°   *lowborn man; scoundrel*
ORLANDO   I am no villein.° I am the youngest son of Sir Rowland   *serf (pun on "villain")*
de Bois. He was my father, and he is thrice a villain that says
50   such a father begot villeins. Wert thou not my brother, I would
not take this hand from thy throat till this other had pulled out
thy tongue for saying so. Thou hast railed on° thyself.   *abused*
ADAM   [*coming forward*]   Sweet masters, be patient. For your
father's remembrance, be at accord.
55   OLIVER   [*to* ORLANDO]   Let me go, I say.
ORLANDO   I will not till I please. You shall hear me. My father
charged you in his will to give me good education. You have
trained me like a peasant, obscuring and hiding from me all
gentleman-like qualities.° The spirit of my father grows strong   *accomplishments*
60   in me, and I will no longer endure it. Therefore allow me such
exercises° as may become a gentleman, or give me the poor   *pursuits*
allottery° my father left me by testament. With that I will go   *portion*
buy my fortunes.
OLIVER   And what wilt thou do—beg when that is spent? Well,

6. An oath, derived from the name of the Virgin Mary.   should acknowledge me as a brother.
7. Alluding to the biblical parable of the prodigal son   9. Customs of civil society. Referring to the English
(Luke 15:11–32), who after squandering his share of   system of primogeniture, which allowed for the trans-
his father's fortune envied the swine he tended and   mission of all property to the eldest son.
wished to eat their fodder.   1. Your being older than I makes you more worthy of
8. And because of the noble blood that we share, you   the respect that he commanded.

65   sir, get you in. I will not long be troubled with you. You shall
      have some part of your will. I pray you, leave me.

      ORLANDO   I will no further offend you than becomes me for my
      good.

      OLIVER [*to* ADAM]   Get you with him, you old dog

70   ADAM   Is 'old dog' my reward? Most true, I have lost my teeth in
      your service. God be with my old master, he would not have
      spoke such a word.   *Exeunt* ORLANDO [*and*] ADAM

      OLIVER   Is it even so? Begin you to grow upon me?[2] I will physic[3]   *give medicine to*
      your rankness,[3] and yet give no thousand crowns neither.

75   Holla, Denis!
                              Enter DENIS

      DENIS   Calls your worship?

      OLIVER   Was not Charles, the Duke's wrestler, here to speak with
      me?

      DENIS   So please you, he is here at the door, and importunes

80   access to you.

      OLIVER   Call him in.   [*Exit* DENIS]
      'Twill be a good way. And tomorrow the wrestling is.
                              Enter CHARLES

      CHARLES   Good morrow to your worship.

      OLIVER   Good Monsieur Charles—what's the new news at the

85   new court?

      CHARLES   There's no news at the court, sir, but the old news: that
      is, the old Duke is banished by his younger brother, the new
      Duke, and three or four loving lords have put themselves into
      voluntary exile with him, whose lands and revenues enrich the

90   new Duke; therefore he gives them good leave° to wander.   *full permission*

      OLIVER   Can you tell if Rosalind, the Duke's daughter, be ban-
      ished with her father?

      CHARLES   O no; for the Duke's daughter her cousin so loves her,
      being ever from their cradles bred° together, that she would   *brought up*

95   have followed her exile, or have died to stay behind her. She is
      at the court, and no less beloved of her uncle than his own
      daughter; and never two ladies loved as they do.

      OLIVER   Where will the old Duke live?

      CHARLES   They say he is already in the forest of Ardenne,[4] and a

100   many merry men with him; and there they live like the old
      Robin Hood[5] of England. They say many young gentlemen
      flock to him every day, and fleet° the time carelessly,° as they   *pass / without worries*
      did in the golden world.[6]

      OLIVER   What, you wrestle tomorrow before the new Duke?

105   CHARLES   Marry do I, sir, and I came to acquaint you with a
      matter. I am given, sir, secretly to understand that your younger
      brother, Orlando, hath a disposition to come in disguised
      against me to try a fall.° Tomorrow, sir, I wrestle for my credit,°   *bout / reputation*
      and he that escapes me without some broken limb, shall acquit

110   him well. Your brother is but young and tender, and for your
      love I would be loath to foil° him, as I must for my own honour   *defeat*

---

2. To grow so big you crowd upon me.
3. Overgrown vegetation; diseased blood.
4. The name of an ancient forest encompassing parts
of France, Belgium, and Luxembourg. F uses the angl-
cized spelling "Arden," evoking the English forest of
Arden near Shakespeare's birthplace in Warwickshire.
5. A legendary English outlaw, associated with

Nottingham's Sherwood Forest, who robbed from the
rich and gave his plunder to the poor.
6. Alluding to the classical myth of an earlier world of
perpetual spring, abundance, and ease from which
humankind had degenerated (Ovid, *Metamorphoses* 1).
This golden world was often identified with a pastoral life.

if he come in. Therefore out of my love to you I came hither
to acquaint you withal,° that either you might stay° him from   *with this / keep*
his intendment,° or brook° such disgrace well as he shall run   *intent / endure*
115 into, in that it is a thing of his own search,° and altogether   *seeking*
against my will.

OLIVER Charles, I thank thee for thy love to me, which thou
shalt find I will most kindly requite. I had myself notice of my
brother's purpose herein, and have by underhand° means   *subtle*
120 laboured to dissuade him from it; but he is resolute. I'll tell
thee, Charles, it is the stubbornest young fellow of France, full
of ambition, an envious emulator of every man's good parts,° a   *qualities*
secret and villainous contriver against me his natural brother.
Therefore use thy discretion. I had as lief° thou didst break his   *willingly*
125 neck as his finger. And thou wert best look to't; for if thou dost
him any slight disgrace, or if he do not mightily grace° himself   *win credit for*
on thee, he will practise° against thee by poison, entrap thee by   *plot*
some treacherous device, and never leave thee till he hath ta'en
thy life by some indirect means or other. For I assure thee—
130 and almost with tears I speak it—there is not one so young and
so villainous this day living. I speak but brotherly[7] of him, but
should I anatomize° him to thee as he is, I must blush and   *dissect; fully open*
weep, and thou must look pale and wonder.

CHARLES I am heartily glad I came hither to you. If he come
135 tomorrow I'll give him his payment. If ever he go alone° again,   *walk without aid*
I'll never wrestle for prize more. And so God keep your wor-
ship.

OLIVER Farewell, good Charles.   *Exit* [CHARLES]
Now will I stir this gamester.° I hope I shall see an end of him,   *(Orlando)*
140 for my soul—yet I know not why—hates nothing more than
he. Yet he's gentle;° never schooled, and yet learned; full of   *of noble character*
noble device;° of all sorts enchantingly beloved;[8] and, indeed,   *purposes*
so much in the heart of the world, and especially of my own
people, who best know him, that I am altogether misprized.°   *despised*
145 But it shall be not so long. This wrestler shall clear all.° Noth-   *fix everything*
ing remains but that I kindle° the boy thither,° which now I'll   *urge / (to the court)*
go about.   *Exit*

1.2

Enter ROSALIND *and* CELIA

CELIA I pray thee Rosalind, sweet my coz,° be merry.   *cousin*

ROSALIND Dear Celia, I show more mirth than I am mistress of;
and would you yet I were merrier? Unless you could teach me
to forget a banished father you must not learn° me how to   *teach*
5 remember any extraordinary pleasure.

CELIA Herein I see thou lovest me not with the full weight that
I love thee. If my uncle, thy banished father, had banished thy
uncle, the Duke my father, so° thou hadst been still with me I   *provided*
could have taught my love to take thy father for mine. So
10 wouldst thou, if the truth of thy love to me were so righteously
tempered° as mine is to thee.   *properly constituted*
          circumstances

ROSALIND Well, I will forget the condition of my estate° to
rejoice in yours.

7. In a manner proper to a brother.   1.2 Location: The grounds of Duke Frederick's court.
8. Beloved of all ranks as if by enchantment.

CELIA   You know my father hath no child but I, nor none is like
15   to have. And truly, when he dies thou shalt be his heir; for what
        he hath taken away from thy father perforce,° I will render thee   by force
        again in affection. By mine honour I will, and when I break
        that oath, let me turn monster. Therefore, my sweet Rose, my
        dear Rose, be merry.
20 ROSALIND   From henceforth I will, coz, and devise sports.° Let   entertainments
        me see, what think you of falling in love?
    CELIA   Marry, I prithee do, to make sport withal;° but love no   to provide amusement
        man in good earnest, nor no further in sport neither than with
        safety of a pure blush thou mayst in honour come off again.[1]
25 ROSALIND   What shall be our sport, then?
    CELIA   Let us sit and mock the good housewife Fortune[2] from
        her wheel, that her gifts may henceforth be bestowed equally.
    ROSALIND   I would we could do so, for her benefits are mightily
        misplaced; and the bountiful blind woman° doth most mistake   (Fortune)
30   in her gifts to women.
    CELIA   'Tis true; for those that she makes fair she scarce makes
        honest,° and those that she makes honest she makes very ill-   chaste
        favouredly.°   ugly
    ROSALIND   Nay, now thou goest from Fortune's office° to   function
35   Nature's. Fortune reigns in° gifts of the world, not in the linea-   presides over
        ments of nature.°   one's natural features
            Enter [TOUCHSTONE[3] *the*] *clown*
    CELIA   No. When Nature hath made a fair creature, may she not
        by Fortune fall into the fire? Though Nature hath given us wit
        to flout at Fortune, hath not Fortune sent in this fool to cut off
40   the argument?
    ROSALIND   Indeed, there is Fortune too hard for Nature, when
        Fortune makes Nature's natural° the cutter-off of Nature's wit.   fool
    CELIA   Peradventure° this is not Fortune's work, neither, but   Perhaps
        Nature's, who perceiveth our natural wits too dull to reason of
45   such goddesses, and hath sent this natural for our whetstone:°   stone to sharpen tools
        for always the dullness of the fool is the whetstone of the wits.
        How now, wit: whither wander you?[4]
    TOUCHSTONE   Mistress, you must come away to your father.
    CELIA   Were you made the messenger?
50 TOUCHSTONE   No, by mine honour, but I was bid to come for
        you.
    ROSALIND   Where learned you that oath, fool?
    TOUCHSTONE   Of a certain knight that swore 'by his honour they
        were good pancakes, and swore 'by his honour' the mustard
55   was naught.° Now I'll stand to it° the pancakes were naught and   worthless / affirm
        the mustard was good, and yet was not the knight forsworn.°   perjured
    CELIA   How prove you that in the great heap of your knowledge?
    ROSALIND   Ay, marry, now unmuzzle your wisdom.
    TOUCHSTONE   Stand you both forth now. Stroke your chins, and
60   swear by your beards that I am a knave.
    CELIA   By our beards—if we had them—thou art.

---

1. Than, with the protection afforded by your innocence ("pure blush"), you may honorably escape
("come off again").
2. Referring to the blind goddess of classical mythology
who directed human destiny with the movements of her
wheel, here likened to the mistress of a household with

a spinning wheel.
3. A touchstone was a black mineral used to test the
purity of gold and silver. Touchstone, the fool, tests the
wit of those he encounters.
4. Alluding to the catchphrase "wandering wits."

TOUCHSTONE   By my knavery—if I had it—then I were; but if
you swear by that that is not, you are not forsworn. No more
was this knight, swearing by his honour, for he never had any;
65   or if he had, he had sworn it away before ever he saw those
pancakes or that mustard.

CELIA   Prithee, who is't that thou meanest?

TOUCHSTONE   One that old Frederick, your father, loves.

CELIA[5]   My father's love is enough to honour him. Enough,
70   speak no more of him; you'll be whipped for taxation° one of   slander
these days.

TOUCHSTONE   The more pity that fools may not speak wisely
what wise men do foolishly.

CELIA   By my troth, thou sayst true; for since the little wit that
75   fools have was silenced,[6] the little foolery that wise men have
makes a great show. Here comes Monsieur Le Beau.

Enter LE BEAU

ROSALIND   With his mouth full of news.

CELIA   Which he will put on° us as pigeons feed their young.   force upon

ROSALIND   Then shall we be news-crammed.[7]

80   CELIA   All the better: we shall be the more marketable. *Bonjour,*°   Good day
Monsieur Le Beau, what's the news?

LE BEAU   Fair princess, you have lost much good sport.

CELIA   Sport? Of what colour?°   kind

LE BEAU   What colour, madam? How shall I answer you?

85   ROSALIND   As wit and fortune will.°   desire

TOUCHSTONE   Or as the destinies decrees.

CELIA   Well said. That was laid on with a trowel.[8]

TOUCHSTONE   Nay, if I keep not my rank[9]—

ROSALIND   Thou losest thy old smell.

90   LE BEAU   You amaze° me, ladies. I would have told you of good   confuse
wrestling, which you have lost the sight of.

ROSALIND   Yet tell us the manner of the wrestling.

LE BEAU   I will tell you the beginning, and if it please your lady-
ships you may see the end, for the best is yet to do,° and here,   to come
95   where you are, they are coming to perform it.

CELIA   Well, the beginning that is dead and buried.

LE BEAU   There comes an old man and his three sons—

CELIA   I could match this beginning with an old tale.[1]

LE BEAU   Three proper° young men, of excellent growth and   handsome
100   presence.

ROSALIND   With bills° on their necks: 'Be it known unto all men   proclamations
by these presents'[2]—

LE BEAU   The eldest of the three wrestled with Charles, the
Duke's wrestler, which Charles in a moment threw him, and
105   broke three of his ribs, that there is little hope of life in him.
So he served the second, and so the third. Yonder they lie, the

---

5. F attributes this speech to Rosalind, but most editors
assign it to Celia on the grounds that she asked the
question to which Touchstone has just responded. It is
unlikely that Rosalind would insert herself here or insist
on the preeminence of her father's love over Frederick's.
6. This is a possible allusion to the Bishop of London's
order for the burning of satirical books in June 1599.
7. Forced to digest news, with a pun on "mews" as
meaning the cages in which pigeons were kept before
being fattened, or "crammed," for the table.

8. Bluntly; excessively. With a reference to a builder's
heavy application of mortar.
9. My status (as a jester). Rosalind then puns on the
meaning of "rank" as "foul smelling."
1. *Old tale*: Celia suggests that the motif of a father and
his three sons is the starting point for many familiar
folktales.
2. That is, by these legal documents. A legal phrase
that appears at the start of formal documents, with a
pun on "presence."

poor old man their father making such pitiful dole° over them   *mourning*
that all the beholders take his part with weeping.

ROSALIND   Alas!

110   TOUCHSTONE   But what is the sport, monsieur, that the ladies
have lost?

LE BEAU   Why, this that I speak of.

TOUCHSTONE   Thus men may grow wiser every day. It is the first
time that ever I heard breaking of ribs was sport for ladies.

115   CELIA   Or I, I promise thee.

ROSALIND   But is there any else° longs to see this broken music³   *anyone else who*
in his sides? Is there yet another dotes upon rib-breaking? Shall
we see this wrestling, cousin?

LE BEAU   You must if you stay here, for here is the place
120   appointed for the wrestling, and they are ready to perform it.

CELIA   Yonder sure they are coming. Let us now stay and see it.

> *Flourish.*⁴ *Enter* DUKE [FREDERICK], *Lords,* ORLANDO,
> CHARLES, *and attendants*

DUKE FREDERICK   Come on. Since the youth will not be
entreated,° his own peril on his forwardness.⁵   *persuaded (to desist)*

ROSALIND   Is yonder the man?

125   LE BEAU   Even he, madam.

CELIA   Alas, he is too young. Yet he looks successfully.°   *as if he would do well*

DUKE FREDERICK   How now, daughter and cousin;⁶ are you
crept hither to see the wrestling?

ROSALIND   Ay, my liege, so please you give us leave.

130   DUKE FREDERICK   You will take little delight in it, I can tell you,
there is such odds° in the man. In pity of the challenger's youth   *superiority*
I would fain° dissuade him, but he will not be entreated. Speak   *willingly*
to him, ladies; see if you can move him.

CELIA   Call him hither, good Monsieur Le Beau.

135   DUKE FREDERICK   Do so. I'll not be by.

> [*He stands aside*]

LE BEAU   [*to* ORLANDO]   Monsieur the challenger, the Princess
calls for you.

ORLANDO   I attend them with all respect and duty.

ROSALIND   Young man, have you challenged Charles the wres-
140   tler?

ORLANDO   No, fair Princess. He is the general challenger; I come
but in as others do, to try with him the strength of my youth.

CELIA   Young gentleman, your spirits are too bold for your years.
You have seen cruel proof of this man's strength. If you saw
145   yourself with your eyes, or knew yourself with your judgment,⁷
the fear° of your adventure would counsel you to a more equal   *danger*
enterprise. We pray you for your own sake to embrace your
own safety and give over this attempt.

ROSALIND   Do, young sir. Your reputation shall not therefore be
150   misprized.° We will make it our suit to the Duke that the wres-   *undervalued*
tling might not go forward.

ORLANDO   I beseech you, punish me not with your hard
thoughts,° wherein I confess me much guilty to deny so fair   *displeasure*

---

3. Literally, a musical composition for a variety of
instruments; here referring to the labored breathing
caused by the broken ribs.
4. The sounding of horns or trumpets to signal the
arrival of an important person.

5. *his own . . . forwardness:* let the danger he encounters be blamed on his own rashness.
6. *cousin:* a term used to signify many kinship relations.
7. If you used your discernment and judgment upon
yourself.

and excellent ladies anything. But let your fair eyes and gentle
wishes go with me to my trial, wherein if I be foiled,° there is   *defeated*
but one shamed that was never gracious,° if killed, but one   *in favor*
dead that is willing to be so. I shall do my friends no wrong, for
I have none to lament me; the world no injury, for in it I have
nothing. Only in the world I fill up a place which may be better
supplied when I have made it empty.

ROSALIND   The little strength that I have, I would it were with
you.

CELIA   And mine, to eke out hers.

ROSALIND   Fare you well. Pray heaven I be deceived in you.

CELIA   Your heart's desires be with you.

CHARLES   Come, where is this young gallant that is so desirous
to lie with his mother earth?[8]

ORLANDO   Ready, sir; but his will° hath in it a more modest   *(sexual) desire*
working.°   *undertaking*

DUKE FREDERICK   You shall try but one fall.

CHARLES   No, I warrant your grace you shall not entreat him to
a second that have so mightily persuaded him from a first.

ORLANDO   You mean to mock me after; you should not have
mocked me before. But come your ways.°   *let's begin*

ROSALIND   [*to* ORLANDO]   Now Hercules be thy speed,[9] young
man!

CELIA   I would I were invisible, to catch the strong fellow by the
leg.

[CHARLES *and* ORLANDO] *wrestle*

ROSALIND   O excellent young man!

CELIA   If I had a thunderbolt in mine eye, I can tell who should
down.

[ORLANDO *throws* CHARLES.] *Shout*

DUKE FREDERICK   No more, no more.

ORLANDO   Yes, I beseech your grace.
I am not yet well breathed.°   *exercised*

DUKE FREDERICK   How dost thou, Charles?

LE BEAU   He cannot speak, my lord.

DUKE FREDERICK   Bear him away.

[*Attendants carry* CHARLES *off*]
What is thy name, young man?

ORLANDO   Orlando, my liege, the youngest son of Sir Rowland
de Bois.

DUKE FREDERICK   I would thou hadst been son to some man else.
The world esteemed thy father honourable,
But I did find him still° mine enemy.   *always*
Thou shouldst have better pleased me with this deed
Hadst thou descended from another house.
But fare thee well, thou art a gallant youth.
I would thou hadst told me of another father.

Exeunt DUKE [FREDERICK, LE BEAU, TOUCHSTONE,[1]
Lords, and attendants]

CELIA   [*to* ROSALIND]   Were I my father, coz, would I do this?

---

8. To fall to the ground. Echoing biblical descriptions
of the body's return to earth at death and punning on
"lie with" as slang for "have sexual relations with."
9. May Hercules bring you luck. Alluding to a mythological wrestling match in which Hercules, whose name was

synonymous with physical strength, vanquished Antaeus.
1. Although F does not indicate an exit for Touchstone,
many editors assume that he leaves the stage with the
Duke's party and does not reappear until 2.4.

ORLANDO   I am more proud to be Sir Rowland's son,
His youngest son, and would not change that calling°   title
200   To be adopted heir to Frederick.
ROSALIND   My father loved Sir Rowland as his soul,
And all the world was of my father's mind.
Had I before known this young man his son
I should have given him tears unto° entreaties   as well as
205   Ere he should thus have ventured.
CELIA   Gentle° cousin,   Noble; kind
Let us go thank him, and encourage him.
My father's rough and envious° disposition   spiteful
Sticks° me at heart.—Sir, you have well deserved.   Stabs
If you do keep your promises in love
210   But justly,° as you have exceeded all promise,   to the same degree
Your mistress shall be happy.
ROSALIND [giving him a chain from her neck]   Gentleman,
Wear this for me—one out of suits° with fortune,   favor
That could° give more but that her hand lacks means.   would
Shall we go, coz?
CELIA   Ay. Fare you well, fair gentleman.
      [ROSALIND and CELIA turn to go]
215   ORLANDO [aside]   Can I not say 'I thank you'? My better parts
Are all thrown down, and that which here stands up
Is but a quintain,[2] a mere lifeless block.
ROSALIND [to CELIA]   He calls us back. My pride fell with my fortunes,
I'll ask him what he would.—Did you call, sir?
220   Sir, you have wrestled well, and overthrown
More than your enemies.
CELIA   Will you go, coz?
ROSALIND   Have with you.° [To ORLANDO] Fare you well.   I'll go with you
                              Exeunt [ROSALIND and CELIA][3]
ORLANDO   What passion hangs these weights upon my tongue?
225   I cannot speak to her, yet she urged conference.°   conversation
      Enter LE BEAU
O poor Orlando! Thou art overthrown.
Or° Charles or something weaker masters thee.   Either
LE BEAU   Good sir, I do in friendship counsel you
To leave this place. Albeit you have deserved
230   High commendation, true applause, and love,
Yet such is now the Duke's condition°   state of mind
That he misconsters° all that you have done.   misconstrues
The Duke is humorous.[4] What he is indeed
More suits you to conceive than I to speak of.
235   ORLANDO   I thank you, sir. And pray you tell me this,
Which of the two was daughter of the Duke
That here was at the wrestling?
LE BEAU   Neither his daughter, if we judge by manners—
But yet indeed the shorter[5] is his daughter.

2. A wooden post used as a target in jousts and other aristocratic sports. Orlando suggests that his reason and speech (his "better parts") have been "thrown down," or defeated, in his encounter with Rosalind, leaving him standing speechless, like a post.
3. F marks only a single exit for Rosalind here, but Celia almost certainly accompanies her offstage.
4. Moody. The term derives from Renaissance medical theory, which held that good mental and physical health depended on the proper balance of four bodily fluids, or humors.
5. F reads "taller," but see 1.3.109, where Rosalind declares that she is "more than common tall" and will therefore disguise herself as a man. Shakespeare may not have been consistent in determining who was to be the taller woman.

240   The other is daughter to the banished Duke,
          And here detained by her usurping uncle
          To keep his daughter company, whose loves
          Are dearer than the natural bond of sisters.
          But I can tell you that of late this Duke
245   Hath ta'en displeasure 'gainst his gentle niece,
          Grounded upon no other argument°   *reason*
          But that the people praise her for her virtues
          And pity her for her good father's sake.
          And, on my life, his malice 'gainst the lady
250   Will suddenly break forth. Sir, fare you well.
          Hereafter, in a better world than this,
          I shall desire more love and knowledge of you.
ORLANDO   I rest much bounden° to you. Fare you well.   *obliged*
                         [*Exit* LE BEAU]
          Thus must I from the smoke into the smother,[6]
255   From tyrant Duke unto a tyrant brother.—
          But heavenly Rosalind!   *Exit*

                              1.3
               Enter CELIA *and* ROSALIND
CELIA   Why cousin, why Rosalind—Cupid have mercy,[1] not a
          word?
ROSALIND Not one to throw at a dog.
CELIA   No, thy words are too precious to be cast away upon curs.
5   Throw some of them at me. Come, lame me with reasons.[2]
ROSALIND Then there were two cousins laid up, when the one
          should be lamed with reasons and the other mad without any.
CELIA   But is all this for your father?
ROSALIND No, some of it is for my child's father.[3] O how full of
10   briers is this working-day world!
CELIA   They are but burs, cousin, thrown upon thee in holiday
          foolery. If we walk not in the trodden paths our very petticoats
          will catch them.
ROSALIND I could shake them off my coat. These burs are in my
15   heart.
CELIA   Hem[4] them away.
ROSALIND I would try, if I could cry 'hem' and have him.
CELIA   Come, come, wrestle with thy affections.
ROSALIND O, they take the part of a better wrestler than myself.
20   CELIA   O, a good wish upon you!° You will try in time, in despite   *good luck to you*
          of a fall.[5] But turning these jests out of service,° let us talk in   *dismissing these jokes*
          good earnest. Is it possible on such a sudden you should fall
          into so strong a liking with old Sir Rowland's youngest son?
ROSALIND The Duke my father loved his father dearly.
25   CELIA   Doth it therefore ensue that you should love his son
          dearly? By this kind of chase° I should hate him, for my father   *logic*
          hated his father dearly; yet I hate not Orlando.
ROSALIND No, faith, hate him not, for my sake.

---

6. Out of the frying pan into the fire. *smother:* thick,
suffocating smoke.
1.3 Location: Duke Frederick's court.
1. May Cupid (god of love) be compassionate.
2. Throw so many reasons (for your silence) at me that
if they were stones, I would be made lame.

3. That is, for one who will be father to my child.
4. Cough, with a pun on "bur" (line 14) as meaning
"something that sticks in your throat."
5. You are destined to wrestle with him eventually even
though it will cause you to fall, with a pun on "fall" as
"lapse from chastity."

CELIA Why should I not? Doth he not deserve well?
    Enter DUKE [FREDERICK], *with Lords*

30 ROSALIND Let me love him for that, and do you love him
    because I do. Look, here comes the Duke.

CELIA With his eyes full of anger.

DUKE FREDERICK [*to* ROSALIND] Mistress, dispatch you with your safest haste,[6]
    And get you from our court.

35 ROSALIND Me, uncle?

DUKE FREDERICK You, cousin.
    Within these ten days if that thou beest found
    So near our public court as twenty miles,
    Thou diest for it.

ROSALIND   I do beseech your grace
40   Let me the knowledge of my fault bear with me.
    If with myself I hold intelligence,°   *I communicate*
    Or have acquaintance with mine own desires,
    If that I do not dream, or be not frantic°—   *insane*
    As I do trust I am not—then, dear uncle,
45   Never so much as in a thought unborn
    Did I offend your highness.

DUKE FREDERICK   Thus do all traitors.
    If their purgation° did consist in words   *exoneration*
    They are as innocent as grace itself.
    Let it suffice thee that I trust thee not.

50 ROSALIND Yet your mistrust cannot make me a traitor.
    Tell me whereon the likelihood depends?

DUKE FREDERICK Thou art thy father's daughter—there's enough.

ROSALIND So was I when your highness took his dukedom;
    So was I when your highness banished him.
55   Treason is not inherited, my lord,
    Or if we did derive it from our friends,°   *relatives*
    What's that to me? My father was no traitor.
    Then, good my liege, mistake me not so much
    To think my poverty is treacherous.

60 CELIA Dear sovereign, hear me speak.

DUKE FREDERICK Ay, Celia, we stayed° her for your sake,   *detained*
    Else had she with her father ranged° along.   *roamed*

CELIA I did not then entreat to have her stay.
    It was your pleasure, and your own remorse.°   *pity; sense of guilt*
65   I was too young that time to value her,
    But now I know her. If she be a traitor,
    Why, so am I. We still° have slept together,   *always*
    Rose at an instant,° learned, played, eat together,   *at the same moment*
    And wheresoe'er we went, like Juno's swans
70   Still we went coupled and inseparable.[7]

DUKE FREDERICK She is too subtle° for thee, and her smoothness,   *cunning*
    Her very silence, and her patience
    Speak to the people, and they pity her.
    Thou art a fool. She robs thee of thy name,°   *reputation*
75   And thou wilt show more bright and seem more virtuous
    When she is gone. Then open not thy lips.

---

6. Leave quickly, which is your best safety.
7. That is, yoked together inseparably like the swans that draw the chariot of Juno (queen of the gods).   According to Ovid, swans were associated with Venus (goddess of love), not with Juno.

Firm and irrevocable is my doom°   *judgment*
Which I have passed upon her. She is banished.

CELIA   Pronounce that sentence then on me, my liege.
80   I cannot live out of her company.

DUKE FREDERICK   You are a fool.—You, niece, provide yourself.°   *make preparation*
If you outstay the time, upon mine honour
And in the greatness of my word,[8] you die.

                    Exit DUKE [FREDERICK, *with Lords*]

CELIA   O my poor Rosalind, whither wilt thou go?
85   Wilt thou change° fathers? I will give thee mine.   *exchange*
I charge thee, be not thou more grieved than I am.

ROSALIND   I have more cause.

CELIA   Thou hast not, cousin.
Prithee, be cheerful. Know'st thou not the Duke
Hath banished me, his daughter?

ROSALIND   That he hath not.
90   CELIA   No, hath not? Rosalind, lack'st thou then the love
Which teacheth thee that thou and I am one?
Shall we be sundered? Shall we part, sweet girl?
No. Let my father seek another heir.
Therefore devise with me how we may fly,
95   Whither to go, and what to bear with us,
And do not seek to take your change upon you,[9]
To bear your griefs yourself, and leave me out.
For by this heaven, now at our sorrows pale,
Say what thou canst, I'll go along with thee.
100   ROSALIND   Why, whither shall we go?

CELIA   To seek my uncle in the forest of Ardenne.

ROSALIND   Alas, what danger will it be to us,
Maids as we are, to travel forth so far!
Beauty provoketh thieves sooner than gold.

105   CELIA   I'll put myself in poor and mean° attire,   *lowly*
And with a kind of umber[1] smirch my face.
The like do you, so shall we pass along
And never stir° assailants.   *provoke*

ROSALIND   Were it not better,
Because that I am more than common tall,
110   That I did suit° me all points° like a man,   *dress / ways*
A gallant curtal-axe° upon my thigh,   *short sword*
A boar-spear[2] in my hand, and in my heart,
Lie there what hidden woman's fear there will.
We'll have a swashing° and a martial outside,   *swaggering*
115   As many other mannish cowards have,
That do outface it with their semblances.[3]

CELIA   What shall I call thee when thou art a man?

ROSALIND   I'll have no worse a name than Jove's own page,
And therefore look you call me Ganymede.[4]
120   But what will you be called?

8. And in accordance with the power of my decree as
Duke.
9. To bear alone the burden of your change of fortunes.
1. Brown pigment. By rubbing it on their faces, Rosalind and Celia take on the dark or sunburned complexion that in Elizabethan society marked the low
social status of those who labored outside. Ladies wore
masks to keep their complexions white.

2. A long-bladed spear used to impale boar.
3. Who brazenly defy the world with the mere appearance of bravery.
4. The name of a beautiful young man who, according
to classical mythology, was so beloved by Jove (king of the
gods) that Jove carried him off to heaven and made him
his cupbearer. Also a slang term for a young man who
sold his sexual services to or was kept by an older man.

CELIA   Something that hath a reference to my state.
    No longer Celia, but Aliena.°   *"the estranged one"*
ROSALIND   But cousin, what if we essayed° to steal   *tried*
    The clownish fool out of your father's court.
125   Would he not be a comfort to our travel?
CELIA   He'll go along o'er the wide world with me.
    Leave me alone to woo him. Let's away,
    And get our jewels and our wealth together,
    Devise the fittest time and safest way
130   To hide us from pursuit that will be made
    After my flight. Now go we in content,
    To liberty, and not to banishment.   *Exeunt*

2.1

Enter DUKE SENIOR, AMIENS,[1] *and two or three* LORDS
    like° *foresters*   *dressed as*
DUKE SENIOR   Now, my co-mates and brothers in exile,
    Hath not old custom° made this life more sweet   *long acquaintance*
    Than that of painted pomp?° Are not these woods   *artificial splendor*
    More free from peril than the envious court?
5   Here feel we not the penalty of Adam,[2]
    The seasons' difference,° as° the icy fang   *change / such as*
    And churlish° chiding of the winter's wind,   *rough*
    Which when it bites and blows upon my body
    Even till I shrink with cold, I smile, and say
10   'This is no flattery. These are counsellors
    That feelingly° persuade me what I am.'   *through my senses*
    Sweet are the uses° of adversity   *benefits*
    Which, like the toad, ugly and venomous,
    Wears yet a precious jewel in his head;[3]
15   And this our life, exempt from public haunt,°   *free from crowds*
    Finds tongues in trees, books in the running brooks,
    Sermons in stones, and good in everything.
AMIENS   I would not change it. Happy is your grace
    That can translate the stubbornness of fortune
20   Into so quiet and so sweet a style.
DUKE SENIOR   Come, shall we go and kill us venison?
    And yet it irks me the poor dappled fools,°   *innocent creatures*
    Being native burghers° of this desert° city,   *citizens / unpeopled*
    Should in their own confines with forkèd heads°   *two-pronged arrows*
    Have their round haunches gored.
25 FIRST LORD   Indeed, my lord,
    The melancholy Jaques[4] grieves at that,
    And in that kind° swears you do more usurp   *vein*
    Than doth your brother that hath banished you.
    Today my lord of Amiens and myself
30   Did steal behind him as he lay along°   *stretched out*
    Under an oak, whose antic° root peeps out   *old; oddly shaped*
    Upon the brook that brawls° along this wood,   *loudly flows*

2.1 Location: The Forest of Ardenne.
1. The name of a town in northern France with which this character is perhaps associated.
2. In Genesis 3, Adam's punishment for disobeying God involved expulsion from Eden and the laying of a curse upon the earth. This was frequently interpreted as the end of the temperate climate associated with paradise.
3. The toad was popularly believed to be poisonous and to have in its head a jewel, the toadstone.
4. Jaques's name, usually pronounced with two syllables. puns on "jakes," the word for "privy" (toilet). He is a stock figure of the melancholic man prone to solitude and black thoughts because of an excess of black bile, one of the four humors.

To the which place a poor sequestered° stag   *cut off from the herd*
That from the hunter's aim had ta'en a hurt
35   Did come to languish. And indeed, my lord,
The wretched animal heaved forth such groans
That their discharge did stretch his leathern coat
Almost to bursting, and the big round tears
Coursed° one another down his innocent nose   *Pursued*
40   In piteous chase. And thus the hairy fool,
Much markèd of° the melancholy Jaques,   *observed by*
Stood on th'extremest verge° of the swift brook,   *farthest edge*
Augmenting it with tears.
DUKE SENIOR   But what said Jaques?
Did he not moralize° this spectacle?   *draw a moral from*
45   FIRST LORD   O yes, into a thousand similes.
First, for his weeping into the needless° stream;   *needing no more water*
'Poor deer,' quoth he, 'thou mak'st a testament
As worldlings do, giving thy sum of more°   *your supplement*
To that which had too much.' Then being there alone,
50   Left and abandoned of° his velvet friend,[5]   *by*
'Tis right,' quoth he, 'thus misery doth part°   *separate from*
The flux° of company.' Anon a careless[6] herd   *flow*
Full of the pasture° jumps along by him   *Full from grazing*
And never stays to greet him. 'Ay,' quoth Jaques,
55   'Sweep on, you fat and greasy citizens,
'Tis just the fashion. Wherefore should you look
Upon that poor and broken bankrupt there?'
Thus most invectively he pierceth through
The body of the country, city, court,
60   Yea, and of this our life, swearing that we
Are mere usurpers, tyrants, and what's worse,°   *whatever is worse*
To fright the animals and to kill them up°   *off*
In their assigned and native dwelling place.
DUKE SENIOR   And did you leave him in this contemplation?
65   SECOND LORD   We did, my lord, weeping and commenting
Upon the sobbing deer.
DUKE SENIOR   Show me the place.
I love to cope° him in these sullen fits,   *contend with*
For then he's full of matter.°   *material for thought; pus*
FIRST LORD   I'll bring you to him straight.°   *immediately*
         Exeunt

2.2

Enter DUKE [FREDERICK], *with* LORDS

DUKE FREDERICK   Can it be possible that no man saw them?
It cannot be. Some villains of my court
Are of consent and sufferance in this.[1]
FIRST LORD   I cannot hear of any that did see her.
5   The ladies her attendants of her chamber
Saw her abed, and in the morning early
They found the bed untreasured of their mistress.
SECOND LORD   My lord, the roynish° clown at whom so oft   *vulgar*

---

5. Smooth-coated companion. Alluding both to the velvet covering the male deer's antlers and to an expensive fabric worn by the prosperous.

6. Just then a carefree.
2.2 Location: Duke Frederick's court.
1. Have agreed to and tolerated this.

Your grace was wont° to laugh is also missing.   *accustomed*
10   Hisperia, the Princess' gentlewoman,
     Confesses that she secretly o'erheard
     Your daughter and her cousin much commend
     The parts° and graces of the wrestler   *qualities*
     That did but lately foil the sinewy Charles,
15   And she believes wherever they are gone
     That youth is surely in their company.
     DUKE FREDERICK   Send to his brother;° fetch that gallant hither.   *(Oliver)*
     If he° be absent, bring his brother to me,   *(Orlando)*
     I'll make him find him. Do this suddenly,
20   And let not search and inquisition quail°   *fail*
     To bring again° these foolish runaways.   *Exeunt [severally]°*   *back / separately*

2.3
Enter ORLANDO *and* ADAM *[meeting]*

ORLANDO   Who's there?
ADAM   What, my young master, O my gentle master,
       O my sweet master, O you memory
       Of old Sir Rowland, why, what make you° here!   *what are you doing*
5   Why are you virtuous? Why do people love you?
       And wherefore° are you gentle, strong, and valiant?   *why*
       Why would you be so fond° to overcome   *foolish*
       The bonny prizer° of the humorous° Duke?   *robust champion / moody*
       Your praise is come too swiftly home before you.
10   Know you not, master, to some kind of men
       Their graces° serve them but as enemies?   *virtues*
       No more° do yours. Your virtues, gentle master,   *No better*
       Are sanctified and holy traitors to you.
       O, what a world is this, when what is comely
15   Envenoms° him that bears it!   *Poisons*
ORLANDO   Why, what's the matter?
ADAM   O, unhappy youth,
       Come not within these doors. Within this roof
       The enemy of all your graces lives,
20   Your brother—no, no brother—yet the son—
       Yet not the son, I will not call him son—
       Of him I was about to call his father,
       Hath heard your praises, and this night he means
       To burn the lodging where you use° to lie,   *are accustomed*
25   And you within it. If he fail of that,
       He will have other means to cut you off.
       I overheard him and his practices.°   *plots*
       This is no place,° this house is but a butchery.°   *home / slaughterhouse*
       Abhor it, fear it, do not enter it.
30   ORLANDO   Why, whither, Adam, wouldst thou have me go?
     ADAM   No matter whither, so you come not here.
     ORLANDO   What, wouldst thou have me go and beg my food,
       Or with a base and boisterous° sword enforce   *violent*
       A thievish living on the common road?
35   This I must do, or know not what to do.
       Yet this I will not do, do how I can.

2.3 Location: Oliver's house.

I rather will subject me to the malice
Of a diverted blood[1] and bloody° brother.　　　　　　　　　*murderous*
ADAM　But do not so. I have five hundred crowns,[2]
40　The thrifty hire I saved[3] under your father,
Which I did store to be my foster-nurse[4]
When service should in my old limbs lie lame,°　　　　*be lamely performed*
And unregarded age in corners thrown.°　　　　　　　　　*be thrown*
Take that, and he that doth the ravens feed,
45　Yea providently caters for the sparrow,[5]
Be comfort to my age. Here is the gold.
All this I give you. Let me be your servant.
Though I look old, yet I am strong and lusty,°　　　　　　*robust*
For in my youth I never did apply
50　Hot and rebellious° liquors in my blood,　　　　　　　*unhealthful*
Nor did not with unbashful forehead° woo　　　　　*bold countenance*
The means of weakness and debility.
Therefore my age is as a lusty winter,
Frosty but kindly.° Let me go with you,　　　　　　*pleasant; natural*
55　I'll do the service of a younger man
In all your business and necessities.
ORLANDO　O good old man, how well in thee appears
The constant° service of the antique world,　　　　　　　*faithful*
When service sweat° for duty, not for meed!°　　　*labored / reward*
60　Thou art not for the fashion of these times,
Where none will sweat but for promotion,
And having that do choke their service up°　　　　　　*cease service*
Even with the having. It is not so with thee.
But, poor old man, thou prun'st a rotten tree,
65　That cannot so much as a blossom yield
In lieu of° all thy pains and husbandry.°　　　　*return for / gardening*
But come thy ways. We'll go along together,
And ere we have thy youthful wages spent,
We'll light upon some settled low content.°　　　*humble contentment*
70　ADAM　Master, go on, and I will follow thee
To the last gasp with truth and loyalty.
From seventeen years till now almost fourscore
Here livèd I, but now live here no more.
At seventeen years, many their fortunes seek,
75　But at fourscore, it is too late a week.°　　　　　　　*a time*
Yet fortune cannot recompense me better
Than to die well, and not my master's debtor.　　　*Exeunt*

2.4

Enter ROSALIND [*in man's clothes*] *for*° Ganymede;　　　　*as*
CELIA *for Aliena,* [*a shepherdess;*] *and* TOUCHSTONE
[*the*] *clown*

ROSALIND　O Jupiter,[1] how weary are my spirits!
TOUCHSTONE　I care not for my spirits, if my legs were not weary.
ROSALIND　I could find in my heart to disgrace my man's apparel

---

1. Of a kinship diverted from its natural course.
2. Approximately 125 English pounds.
3. The wages I thriftily saved.
4. Caretaker. A foster nurse was a woman hired to breast-feed and care for other people's children.
5. Alluding to various biblical passages (especially

Luke 12:6 and 22–24 and Psalm 147:9) that characterize God as the caretaker of all creatures.
2.4 Location: The remainder of Act 2 takes place in the Forest of Ardenne.
1. Another name for Jove, king of the gods in classical mythology and Ganymede's master.

and to cry like a woman. But I must comfort the weaker vessel,° _woman_
5 as doublet and hose² ought to show itself courageous to petticoat; therefore, courage, good Aliena!

CELIA   I pray you, bear with me. I cannot go no further.

TOUCHSTONE   For my part, I had rather bear with you than bear
you. Yet I should bear no cross³ if I did bear you, for I think
10 you have no money in your purse.

ROSALIND   Well, this is the forest of Ardenne.

TOUCHSTONE   Ay, now am I in Ardenne; the more fool I. When
I was at home I was in a better place; but travelers must be
content.

Enter CORIN _and_ SILVIUS

15 ROSALIND   Ay, be so, good Touchstone. Look you, who comes
here—a young man and an old in solemn talk.

CORIN [_to_ SILVIUS]   That is the way to make her scorn you still.

SILVIUS   O Corin, that thou knew'st how I do love her!

CORIN   I partly guess; for I have loved ere now.

20 SILVIUS   No, Corin, being old thou canst not guess,
Though in thy youth thou wast as true a lover
As ever sighed upon a midnight pillow.
But if thy love were ever like to mine—
As sure I think did never man love so—
25 How many actions most ridiculous
Hast thou been drawn to by thy fantasy?°   _imagination_

CORIN   Into a thousand that I have forgotten.

SILVIUS   O, thou didst then never love so heartily.
If thou rememberest not the slightest folly
30 That ever love did make thee run into,
Thou hast not loved.
Or if thou hast not sat as I do now,
Wearing° thy hearer in thy mistress' praise,   _Wearying_
Thou hast not loved.
35 Or if thou hast not broke from company
Abruptly, as my passion now makes me,
Thou hast not loved.
O, Phoebe, Phoebe, Phoebe!   _Exit_

ROSALIND   Alas, poor shepherd, searching of° thy wound,   _probing_
40 I have by hard adventure° found mine own.   _unlucky chance_

TOUCHSTONE   And I mine. I remember when I was in love I
broke my sword upon a stone and bid him take that for coming
a-night to Jane Smile,⁴ and I remember the kissing of her batlet,⁵ and the cow's dugs° that her pretty chapped hands had   _udder_
45 milked; and I remember the wooing of a peascod instead of
her, from whom I took two cods, and giving her them again,
said with weeping tears, 'Wear these for my sake.'⁶ We that are
true lovers run into strange capers. But as all is mortal in
nature, so is all nature in love mortal in folly.⁷

---

2. That is, as manhood (signified by male attire, close-fitting jacket and breeches).
3. Trouble; money, specifically Elizabethan coins stamped with the image of a cross.
4. _I broke . . . Smile:_ I struck a stone as though it were a rival to me in my nocturnal visits to Jane Smile.
5. A wooden bat for beating clothes while washing them.

6. _wooing . . . sake':_ referring to English country courtship rituals in which a pea pod ("peascod") and its husks ("cods") were considered lucky gifts. "Peascod" and "cods" were also slang terms for "male genitalia," suggesting the implicit sexual import of these gifts.
7. So all lovers show their humanity in their foolishness.

50 ROSALIND Thou speak'st wiser than thou art ware° of.   *aware*

TOUCHSTONE Nay, I shall ne'er be ware° of mine own wit till I   *wary*
    break my shins against it.

ROSALIND Jove, Jove, this shepherd's passion
    Is much upon my fashion.°   *of my sort*

55 TOUCHSTONE And mine, but it grows something° stale with me.   *somewhat*

CELIA I pray you, one of you question yon man
    If he for gold will give us any food.
    I faint almost to death.

TOUCHSTONE [*to* CORIN] Holla, you clown!°   *peasant; yokel*

60 ROSALIND Peace, fool, he's not thy kinsman.

CORIN Who calls?

TOUCHSTONE Your betters, sir.

CORIN Else are they very wretched.

ROSALIND [*to* TOUCHSTONE] Peace, I say. [*To* CORIN] Good
    even° to you, friend.   *evening*

65 CORIN And to you, gentle sir, and to you all.

ROSALIND I prithee, shepherd, if that love or gold
    Can in this desert place buy entertainment,°   *accommodation*
    Bring us where we may rest ourselves, and feed.
    Here's a young maid with travel much oppressed,
    And faints for succour.°   *for lack of aid (food)*

70 CORIN   Fair sir, I pity her,
    And wish, for her sake more than for mine own,
    My fortunes were more able to relieve her.
    But I am shepherd to another man,
    And do not shear the fleeces that I graze.

75   My master is of churlish° disposition,   *miserly*
    And little recks° to find the way to heaven   *thinks*
    By doing deeds of hospitality.
    Besides, his cot,° his flocks, and bounds of feed°   *cottage / grazing rights*
    Are now on sale, and at our sheepcote° now   *cottage*

80   By reason of his absence there is nothing
    That you will feed on. But what is, come see,
    And in my voice[8] most welcome shall you be.

ROSALIND What° is he that shall buy his flock and pasture?   *Who*

CORIN That young swain that you saw here but erewhile,°   *just now*

85   That little cares for buying anything.

ROSALIND I pray thee, if it stand with honesty,
    Buy thou the cottage, pasture, and the flock,
    And thou shalt have to pay° for it of us.   *the money to pay*

CELIA And we will mend° thy wages. I like this place,   *improve*

90   And willingly could waste° my time in it.   *spend*

CORIN Assuredly the thing is to be sold.
    Go with me. If you like upon report
    The soil, the profit, and this kind of life,
    I will your very faithful feeder° be,   *servant*

95   And buy it with your gold right suddenly.   *Exeunt*

8. And insofar as my authority stretches.

2.5

Enter AMIENS, JAQUES, *and other* [*Lords dressed as foresters*]

AMIENS [*sings*][1]   Under the greenwood tree
        Who loves to lie with me,
        And turn° his merry note   *tune*
        Unto the sweet bird's throat,°   *voice*

5   Come hither, come hither, come hither.
           Here shall he see
           No enemy
        But winter and rough weather.

JAQUES   More, more, I prithee, more.

10 AMIENS   It will make you melancholy, Monsieur Jaques.

JAQUES   I thank it. More, I prithee, more. I can suck melancholy
out of a song as a weasel sucks eggs. More, I prithee, more.

AMIENS   My voice is ragged,° I know I cannot please you   *harsh*

JAQUES   I do not desire you to please me, I do desire you to sing.

15 Come, more; another stanza. Call you 'em stanzas?[2]

AMIENS   What you will, Monsieur Jaques.

JAQUES   Nay, I care not for their names,[3] they owe me nothing.
Will you sing?

AMIENS   More at your request than to please myself.

20 JAQUES   Well then, if ever I thank any man, I'll thank you. But
that° they call compliment is like th'encounter of two dog-   *what*
apes,° and when a man thanks me heartily methinks I have   *dog-faced baboons*
given him a penny and he renders me the beggarly thanks.[4]
Come, sing; and you that will not, hold your tongues.

25 AMIENS   Well, I'll end the song.—Sirs, cover the while.[5]
        [*Lords prepare food and drink*]
The Duke will drink under this tree. [*To* JAQUES] He hath been
all this day to look° you.   *searching for*

JAQUES   And I have been all this day to avoid him. He is too
disputable° for my company. I think of as many matters as he,   *argumentative*

30 but I give heaven thanks, and make no boast of them. Come,
warble, come.

ALL [*sing*][6]   Who doth ambition shun,
        And loves to live i'th' sun,
        Seeking the food he eats

35   And pleased with what he gets,
      Come hither, come hither, come hither.
          Here shall he see
          No enemy
        But winter and rough weather.

40 JAQUES   I'll give you a verse to this note° that I made yesterday in   *tune*
despite of my invention.[7]

AMIENS   And I'll sing it.

JAQUES   Thus it goes:
        If it do come to pass

45   That any man turn ass,

2.5

1. F does not indicate who sings this song. Traditionally it has been assigned to Amiens, whose part may have been played by Robert Armin, a clown who joined Shakespeare's company in 1599 and who was known for his fine singing voice.
2. A relatively new, and Italianate, word at the time of the play's composition.

3. Punning on the legal sense of "names" as "signatures of borrowers."
4. Excessive thanks, like that given by a beggar.
5. Set the table in the meantime.
6. F's direction before this song reads: "Song. Altogether here."
7. Even though I have little power of creativity.

Leaving his wealth and ease
A stubborn will to please,
Ducdame,[8] ducdame, ducdame.
Here shall he see
50   Gross fools as he,
An if° he will come to me.   *If only*

AMIENS   What's that 'ducdame'?

JAQUES   'Tis a Greek[9] invocation to call fools into a circle. I'll go
sleep if I can. If I cannot, I'll rail against all the firstborn of
55   Egypt.[1]

AMIENS   And I'll go seek the Duke; his banquet[2] is prepared.

                                                              Exeunt

2.6

Enter ORLANDO *and* ADAM

ADAM   Dear master, I can go no further. O, I die for food. Here
lie I down and measure out my grave. Farewell, kind master.

ORLANDO   Why, how now, Adam? No greater heart in thee? Live
a little, comfort° a little, cheer thyself a little. If this uncouth°   *be comforted / wild*
5   forest yield anything savage I will either be food for it or bring it
for food to thee. Thy conceit° is nearer death than thy powers.   *imagination*
For my sake be comfortable. Hold death awhile at the arm's
end. I will here be with thee presently,° and if I bring thee not   *soon*
something to eat, I will give thee leave to die. But if thou diest
10   before I come, thou art a mocker of my labour. Well said. Thou
lookest cheerly,° and I'll be with thee quickly. Yet thou liest in   *cheerfully*
the bleak air. Come, I will bear thee to some shelter, and thou
shalt not die for lack of a dinner if there live anything in this
desert.° Cheerly, good Adam.   [ORLANDO *carries* ADAM *off*]   *uninhabited place*

2.7

Enter DUKE SENIOR *and* LORD[S] *like° outlaws*   *dressed as*

DUKE SENIOR   I think he be transformed into a beast,
For I can nowhere find him like° a man.   *in the shape of*

FIRST LORD   My lord, he is but even now gone hence.
Here was he merry, hearing of a song.

5   DUKE SENIOR   If he, compact of jars,° grow musical   *made up of discords*
We shall have shortly discord in the spheres.[1]
Go seek him. Tell him I would speak with him.

Enter JAQUES

FIRST LORD   He saves my labour by his own approach.

DUKE SENIOR   Why, how now, monsieur, what a life is this,
10   That your poor friends must woo your company!
What, you look merrily.

JAQUES   A fool, a fool, I met a fool i'th' forest,
A motley fool[2]—a miserable world!—
As I do live by food, I met a fool,

---

8. A word of unknown meaning. Possibly a variation on a Welsh phrase meaning "Come hither" or on a Gypsy phrase meaning "I foretell."
9. "Greek" was used to signify anything unintelligible.
1. According to Exodus 11 and 12, the Hebrew God caused the deaths of all firstborn Egyptian children after Pharaoh would not let the Israelites leave his country. Jaques may be vowing to denounce all firstborn sons, which would include Duke Senior.

2. A light meal of sweetmeats and wine.
2.7
1. Alluding to the Pythagorean belief that the earth was the center of eight concentric spheres whose movements created a heavenly harmony (the music of the spheres) inaudible to humans.
2. Someone wearing "motley," the multicolored costume conventionally associated with fools and jesters.

15   Who laid him down and basked him in the sun,
     And railed on Lady Fortune in good terms,
     In good set° terms, and yet a motley fool.   *outspoken; rhetorical*
     'Good morrow, fool,' quoth I. 'No, sir,' quoth he.
     'Call me not fool till heaven hath sent me fortune.'
20   And then he drew a dial⁴ from his poke,°   *pocket; pouch*
     And looking on it with lack-lustre eye
     Says very wisely 'It is ten o'clock.'
     'Thus we may see', quoth he, 'how the world wags.°   *moves on*
     'Tis but an hour ago since it was nine,
25   And after one hour more 'twill be eleven.
     And so from hour to hour we ripe and ripe,
     And then from hour to hour we rot and rot;
     And thereby hangs a tale.'⁵ When I did hear
     The motley fool thus moral on the time
30   My lungs began to crow like chanticleer,°   *a rooster*
     That fools should be so deep°-contemplative,   *profoundly*
     And I did laugh sans° intermission   *without*
     An hour by his dial. O noble fool,
     A worthy fool—motley's the only wear.°   *garb worth wearing*
35 DUKE SENIOR   What fool is this?
     JAQUES   O worthy fool!—One that hath been a courtier,
     And says 'If ladies be but young and fair
     They have the gift to know it.' And in his brain,
     Which is as dry⁶ as the remainder° biscuit   *last*
40   After a voyage, he hath strange places° crammed   *sites; commonplaces*
     With observation, the which he vents
     In mangled forms. O that I were a fool,
     I am ambitious for a motley coat.
     DUKE SENIOR   Thou shalt have one.
     JAQUES   It is my only suit,°   *request; costume*
45   Provided that you weed your better judgements
     Of all opinion that grows rank° in them   *wild*
     That I am wise. I must have liberty
     Withal, as large a charter° as the wind,   *license*
     To blow on whom I please, for so fools have;
50   And they that are most gallèd° with my folly,   *vexed*
     They most must laugh. And why, sir, must they so?
     The why is plain as way to parish church:
     He that a fool doth very wisely hit
     Doth very foolishly, although he smart,
55   Seem aught but senseless of the bob.° If not,   *unaware of the taunt*
     The wise man's folly is anatomized°   *dissected; laid open*
     Even by the squandering glances° of the fool.   *random hits*
     Invest me in my motley. Give me leave
     To speak my mind, and I will through and through
60   Cleanse the foul body of th'infected world,
     If they will patiently receive my medicine.
     DUKE SENIOR   Fie on thee, I can tell what thou wouldst do.

---

3. Referring to the proverbial notion that fortune favored fools.
4. Probably a portable sundial about the size of a napkin ring.
5. *'Tis . . . tale*: the puns and sexual wordplay in these lines suggest a story of male sexual activity leading to debility: "hour" puns on "whore" (they were pronounced

similarly); "ripe" means "to come of age sexually"; "rot" puns on "rut," which means "to have sex in an animal-like state of excitement"; and 'tale' puns on "tail," slang for "penis." 'And thereby hangs a tale" was an Elizabethan commonplace.
6. According to Renaissance medical theory, dry brains signified slow wits and strong memories.

JAQUES   What, for a counter,[7] would I do but good?

DUKE SENIOR   Most mischievous foul sin, in chiding sin;

65   For thou thyself hast been a libertine,
As sensual as the brutish sting° itself,   *lust*
And all th'embossèd sores and headed evils[8]
That thou with licence of free foot° hast caught   *travel*
Wouldst thou disgorge° into the general world.   *vomit*

70   JAQUES   Why, who cries out on pride°   *extravagance*
That can therein tax° any private party?   *blame*
Doth it not flow as hugely as the sea,
Till that the weary very means° do ebb?   *source itself*
What woman in the city do I name

75   When that I say the city-woman bears
The cost° of princes on unworthy shoulders?   *costly attire*
Who can come in and say that I mean her
When such a one as she, such is her neighbour?
Or what is he of basest function,°   *lowliest social status*

80   That says his bravery° is not on° my cost,   *fine attire / at*
Thinking that I mean him, but therein suits
His folly to the mettle° of my speech?   *spirit*
There then, how then, what then, let me see wherein
My tongue hath wronged him. If it do him right,°   *describe him justly*

85   Then he hath wronged himself. If he be free,°   *virtuous*
Why then my taxing° like a wild goose flies,   *reproof*
Unclaimed of any man. But who comes here?

Enter ORLANDO [*with sword drawn*]

ORLANDO   Forbear, and eat no more!

JAQUES   Why, I have eat° none yet.   *eaten*

ORLANDO   Nor shalt not till necessity be served.

90   JAQUES   Of what kind° should this cock come of?   *lineage; stock*

DUKE SENIOR   Art thou thus boldened, man, by thy distress?
Or else a rude despiser of good manners,
That in civility thou seem'st so empty?

ORLANDO   You touched my vein° at first. The thorny point   *assessed my condition*

95   Of bare distress hath ta'en from me the show
Of smooth civility. Yet am I inland bred,[9]
And know some nurture. But forbear, I say.
He dies that touches any of this fruit
Till I and my affairs are answerèd.°   *satisfied*

100 JAQUES   An° you will not be answered with reason, I must die.   *If*

DUKE SENIOR   What would you have? Your gentleness° shall   *gentility; kindness*
force
More than your force move us to gentleness.

ORLANDO   I almost die for food; and let me have it.

DUKE SENIOR   Sit down and feed, and welcome to our table.

105 ORLANDO   Speak you so gently? Pardon me, I pray you.
I thought that all things had been savage here,
And therefore put I on the countenance
Of stern commandment. But whate'er you are
That in this desert inaccessible,

110 Under the shade of melancholy boughs,

---

7. In return for a coin of no value (normally used for reckoning sums).
8. Swollen sores and boils that have come to a head. Both were symptoms of venereal disease.

9. Brought up in a civilized way—that is, raised in the country's interior regions rather than near its supposedly savage borders.

Lose and neglect the creeping hours of time,
If ever you have looked on better days,
If ever been where bells have knolled° to church.   summoned
If ever sat at any good man's feast,
115   If ever from your eyelids wiped a tear,
And know what 'tis to pity, and be pitied,
Let gentleness my strong enforcement be,[1]
In the which hope I blush, and hide my sword.
DUKE SENIOR   True is it that we have seen better days,
120   And have with holy bell been knolled to church.
And sat at good men's feasts, and wiped our eyes
Of drops that sacred pity hath engendered.
And therefore sit you down in gentleness,
And take upon command° what help we have   at your will
125   That to your wanting may be ministered.
ORLANDO   Then but forbear your food a little while
Whiles, like a doe, I go to find my fawn
And give it food. There is an old poor man
Who after me hath many a weary step
130   Limped in pure love. Till he be first sufficed,°   satisfied
Oppressed with two weak° evils, age and hunger,   enfeebling
I will not touch a bit.
DUKE SENIOR   Go find him out,
And we will nothing waste° till you return.   consume
ORLANDO   I thank ye; and be blessed for your good comfort!
                                                    [Exit]
135   DUKE SENIOR   Thou seest we are not all alone unhappy.
This wide and universal theatre
Presents more woeful pageants° than the scene   spectacles
Wherein we play in.
JAQUES   All the world's a stage,
And all the men and women merely players.
140   They have their exits and their entrances,
And one man in his time plays many parts,
His acts being seven ages. At first the infant,
Mewling° and puking in the nurse's arms.   Crying
Then the whining schoolboy with his satchel
145   And shining morning face, creeping like snail
Unwillingly to school. And then the lover,
Sighing like furnace,[2] with a woeful ballad
Made to his mistress' eyebrow. Then, a soldier,
Full of strange oaths, and bearded like the pard,[3]
150   Jealous in honour,[4] sudden, and quick in quarrel.
Seeking the bubble reputation
Even in the cannon's mouth. And then the justice,
In fair round belly with good capon[5] lined,°   filled; stuffed
With eyes severe and beard of formal cut,
155   Full of wise saws° and modern° instances;   sayings / trite
And so he plays his part. The sixth age shifts

1. Let natural kindness or gentility be what compels your compassion.
2. Emitting sighs as a furnace emits smoke.
3. Leopard. The soldier's bristling mustache is being compared to the leopard's whiskers.
4. Vigilant in matters of honor.
5. A cock, castrated and fattened as a delicacy (proverbially, a bribe for magistrates).

Into the lean and slippered pantaloon,[6]
With spectacles on nose and pouch on side,
His youthful hose, well saved, a world too wide
160 For his shrunk shank,° and his big, manly voice,   calf
Turning again toward childish treble, pipes
And whistles in his° sound. Last scene of all,   its
That ends this strange, eventful history,
Is second childishness and mere° oblivion,   complete
165 Sans° teeth, sans eyes, sans taste, sans everything.   Without

Enter ORLANDO [*bearing*] ADAM

DUKE SENIOR   Welcome. Set down your venerable burden
And let him feed.
ORLANDO   I thank you most for him.
ADAM   So had you need;
170 I scarce can speak to thank you for myself.
DUKE SENIOR   Welcome. Fall to. I will not trouble you
As yet to question you about your fortunes.
Give us some music, and, good cousin, sing.
AMIENS [*sings*][7]   Blow, blow, thou winter wind,
175   Thou art not so unkind
              As man's ingratitude.
           Thy tooth is not so keen,
           Because thou art not seen,
              Although thy breath be rude.°   rough
180   Hey-ho, sing hey-ho, unto the green holly.[8]
     Most friendship is feigning, most loving, mere folly.
        Then hey-ho, the holly;
        This life is most jolly.

           Freeze, freeze, thou bitter sky,
185   That dost not bite so nigh°   closely
              As benefits forgot.
           Though thou the waters warp,°   cause to contract; freeze
           Thy sting is not so sharp
              As friend remembered not.
190   Hey-ho, sing hey-ho, unto the green holly.
     Most friendship is feigning, most loving, mere folly.
        Then hey-ho, the holly;
        This life is most jolly.

DUKE SENIOR [*to* ORLANDO]   If that you were the good Sir Rowland's son,
195 As you have whispered faithfully you were,
And as mine eye doth his effigies° witness   likeness
Most truly limned° and living in your face,   portrayed
Be truly welcome hither. I am the Duke
That loved your father. The residue of your fortune,
200 Go to my cave and tell me. [*To* ADAM] Good old man,
Thou art right welcome, as thy master is.—
[*To* LORDS] Support him by the arm. [*To* ORLANDO] Give me your hand,
And let me all your fortunes understand.   *Exeunt*

---

6. A foolish old man named after a figure in *commedia dell'arte*, Italian popular comedy.
7. Again, F does not indicate who sings this song. It is usually assigned to Amiens.
8. The evergreen associated with English holiday festivities.

3.1

Enter DUKE [FREDERICK], *Lords, and* OLIVER

DUKE FREDERICK Not see him since? Sir, sir, that cannot be.

But were I not the better part made° mercy, — *composed of*

I should not seek an absent argument° — *subject*

Of my revenge, thou present. But look to it:

5 Find out thy brother wheresoe'er he is.

Seek him with candle.° Bring him, dead or living, — *diligently*

Within this twelvemonth, or turn° thou no more — *return*

To seek a living in our territory.

Thy lands, and all things that thou dost call thine

10 Worth seizure, do we seize into our hands

Till thou canst quit° thee by thy brother's mouth — *acquit*

Of what we think against thee.

OLIVER O that your highness knew my heart in this.

I never loved my brother in my life.

DUKE FREDERICK More villain thou. [*To Lords*] Well, push

15 him out of doors,

And let my officers of such a nature° — *whose job it is*

Make an extent° upon his house and lands. — *a writ of seizure*

Do this expediently,° and turn° him going. *Exeunt* [*severally*] — *quickly / set*

3.2

Enter ORLANDO [*with a paper*]

ORLANDO Hang there, my verse, in witness of my love;

And thou thrice-crownèd queen of night,[1] survey

With thy chaste eye, from thy pale sphere above,

Thy huntress' name° that my full life doth sway.° — *(Rosalind) / rule*

5 O Rosalind, these trees shall be my books,

And in their barks my thoughts I'll character° — *inscribe*

That every eye which in this forest looks

Shall see thy virtue witnessed everywhere.

Run, run, Orlando; carve on every tree

10 The fair, the chaste, and unexpressive° she. *Exit*[2] — *inexpressible*

Enter CORIN *and* [TOUCHSTONE *the*] *clown*

CORIN And how like you this shepherd's life, Master Touchstone?

TOUCHSTONE Truly, shepherd, in respect of° itself, it is a good — *with regard to*

life; but in respect that it is a shepherd's life, it is naught.° In — *worthless*

respect that it is solitary, I like it very well; but in respect that it

15 is private, it is a very vile life. Now in respect it is in the fields,

it pleaseth me well; but in respect it is not in the court it is

tedious. As it is a spare° life, look you, it fits my humour° well; — *frugal / temperament*

but as there is no more plenty in it, it goes much against my

stomach.° Hast any philosophy in thee, shepherd? — *inclination*

20 CORIN No more but that I know the more one sickens, the worse

at ease he is, and that he that wants° money, means, and con- — *lacks*

tent is without three good friends; that the property of rain is to

---

3.1 Location: Duke Frederick's court.

3.2 Location: The remaining scenes of the play take place in the Forest of Ardenne.

1. The goddess who ruled on earth as Diana, patron of chastity and of the hunt; in the heavens as Cynthia, Phoebe, or Luna, goddess of the moon; and in the underworld as Hecate.

2. Orlando's appearance at lines 1–10 is self-contained and could form a separate scene. However, the ensuing conversation between Corin and Touchstone appears to take place on the same spot where Orlando has just stood, making the action continuous. This edition, like F, makes Orlando's lines part of the longer scene involving Corin, Touchstone, and eventually Rosalind and others.

wet, and fire to burn; that good pasture makes fat sheep; and
that a great cause of the night is lack of the sun; that he that
25   hath learned no wit by nature nor art may complain° of good   *lament his lack*
breeding or comes of a very dull kindred.

TOUCHSTONE   Such a one is a natural philosopher.³ Wast ever in
court, shepherd?

CORIN   No, truly.

30 TOUCHSTONE   Then thou art damned.

CORIN   Nay, I hope.

TOUCHSTONE   Truly thou art damned, like an ill-roasted egg, all
on one side.

CORIN   For not being at court? Your reason?

35 TOUCHSTONE   Why, if thou never wast at court thou never sawest
good manners.° If thou never sawest good manners, then thy   *etiquette; morals*
manners must be wicked, and wickedness is sin, and sin is damnation. Thou art in a parlous° state, shepherd.   *perilous*

CORIN   Not a whit, Touchstone. Those that are good manners at
40   the court are as ridiculous in the country as the behaviour of
the country is most mockable at the court. You told me you
salute not at the court but° you kiss your hands. That courtesy   *unless*
would be uncleanly if courtiers were shepherds.

TOUCHSTONE   Instance,° briefly; come, instance.   *An example*

45 CORIN   Why, we are still° handling our ewes, and their fells,° you   *constantly / skins*
know, are greasy.

TOUCHSTONE   Why, do not your courtier's hands sweat? And is
not the grease of a mutton as wholesome as the sweat of a man?
Shallow, shallow. A better instance, I say. Come.

50 CORIN   Besides, our hands are hard.

TOUCHSTONE   Your lips will feel them the sooner. Shallow again.
A more sounder instance. Come.

CORIN   And they are often tarred over with the surgery of our
sheep;⁴ and would you have us kiss tar? The courtier's hands
55   are perfumed with civet.⁵

TOUCHSTONE   Most shallow, man. Thou worms' meat in respect
of° a good piece of flesh indeed, learn of the wise, and per-   *in comparison with*
pend:° civet is of a baser birth than tar, the very uncleanly flux° *consider / discharge*
of a cat. Mend° the instance, shepherd.   *Improve*

60 CORIN   You have too courtly a wit for me. I'll rest.

TOUCHSTONE   Wilt thou rest damned? God help thee, shallow
man. God make incision in thee, thou art raw.⁶

CORIN   Sir, I am a true labourer. I earn that° I eat, get° that I   *what / make*
wear; owe no man hate, envy no man's happiness; glad of other
65   men's good, content with my harm;° and the greatest of my   *misfortune*
pride is to see my ewes graze and my lambs suck.

TOUCHSTONE   That is another simple° sin in you, to bring the   *simpleminded*
ewes and the rams together, and to offer° to get your living by   *undertake*
the copulation of cattle; to be bawd to a bell-wether,⁷ and to
70   betray a she-lamb of a twelve-month to a crooked-pated old

3. A born philosopher; a philosopher who studies natural phenomena; a fool.
4. Referring to the practice of treating sheep wounds
with tar.
5. A musk-scented substance obtained from the anal
glands of certain cats.

6. Make a cut to let blood (and thus cure you of your
"raw"ness, or inexperience); make a cut to score you, as
raw meat was scored in preparation for cooking.
7. The leading sheep of a flock, who usually wore a
bell.

cuckoldly ram,[8] out of all reasonable match. If thou beest not
damned for this, the devil himself will have no shepherds.[9] I
cannot see else how thou shouldst scape.

CORIN   Here comes young Master Ganymede, my new mistress's
75   brother.

Enter ROSALIND [*as Ganymede*]

ROSALIND [*reads*]   'From the east to western Ind°   *Indies*
        No jewel is like Rosalind.
        Her worth being mounted on the wind
        Through all the world bears Rosalind.
80   All the pictures fairest lined°   *drawn*
        Are but black to° Rosalind.   *compared to*
        Let no face be kept in mind
        But the fair of Rosalind.'

TOUCHSTONE   I'll rhyme you so eight years together, dinners, and
85   suppers, and sleeping-hours excepted. It is the right butter-
    women's rank to market.[1]

ROSALIND   Out, fool.

TOUCHSTONE   For a taste:
        If a hart° do lack a hind,°   *male deer / female deer*
90   Let him seek out Rosalind.
        If the cat will after kind,°   *act naturally; mate*
        So, be sure, will Rosalind.
        Wintered garments must be lined,[2]
        So must slender Rosalind.
95   They that reap must sheaf and bind,
        Then to cart[3] with Rosalind.
        'Sweetest nut hath sourest rind',
        Such a nut is Rosalind.
        He that sweetest rose will find
100   Must find love's prick,° and Rosalind.   *thorn; penis*
    This is the very false gallop of verses.° Why do you infect your-   *way verses canter on*
    self with them?

ROSALIND   Peace, you dull fool, I found them on a tree.

TOUCHSTONE   Truly, the tree yields bad fruit.

105 ROSALIND   I'll graft it with you,° and then I shall graft it with a   *(punning on "yew")*
    medlar;[4] then it will be the earliest fruit i'th' country for you'll
    be rotten ere you be half-ripe, and that's the right° virtue of the   *true*
    medlar.

TOUCHSTONE   You have said; but whether wisely or no, let the
110   forest judge.

Enter CELIA [*as Aliena*], *with a writing*

ROSALIND   Peace, here comes my sister, reading. Stand aside.

CELIA [*reads*]   'Why should this a desert be?
        For it is unpeopled? No.
        Tongues I'll hang on every tree,
115   That shall civil° sayings show.   *civilized*

---

8. Cuckolds, men whose wives were sexually unfaithful, supposedly wore horns to signify their shame. The
ram may *make* cuckolds—that is, be lecherous.
crooked-pated: with crooked horns.
9. It will be because the devil refuses to admit shepherds into hell.
1. *It . . . market*: The rhymes are truly like a stream of
dairywomen going to market at the same time. Such
women were proverbially talkative.

2. Clothes worn in winter must be stuffed with material, with a pun on "lined" as meaning "mated," used
especially of female animals.
3. A cart on which harvests were transported to the
market; a cart on which women accused of prostitution
or other forms of disorderly conduct were transported
and exposed to public abuse.
4. A tree whose fruit was not ripe until it was so soft as
to be rotten, with a pun on "meddler," one who meddles.

Some, how brief the life of man
    Runs his erring° pilgrimage,   *wandering*
That the stretching of a span
    Buckles in his sum of age.[5]
120   Some of violated vows
    'Twixt the souls of friend and friend.
But upon the fairest boughs,
    Or at every sentence end,
Will I 'Rosalinda' write,
125   Teaching all that read to know
The quintessence of every sprite°   *spirit; soul*
    Heaven would in little show.[6]
Therefore heaven nature charged
    That one body should be filled
130   With all graces wide-enlarged.[7]
    Nature presently° distilled   *at once*
Helen's cheek, but not her heart,[8]
    Cleopatra's[9] majesty,
Atalanta's better part,[1]
135   Sad Lucretia's modesty.[2]
Thus Rosalind of many parts
    By heavenly synod° was devised   *assembly*
Of many faces, eyes, and hearts
    To have the touches° dearest prized.   *traits*
140   Heaven would that she these gifts should have
And I to live and die her slave.'

ROSALIND   O most gentle Jupiter! What tedious homily of love
  have you wearied your parishioners withal, and never cried
  'Have patience, good people.'

145 CELIA   How now, back, friends. Shepherd, go off a little. Go with
  him, sirrah.

TOUCHSTONE   Come, shepherd, let us make an honourable
  retreat, though not with bag and baggage, yet with scrip and
  scrippage.[3]   *Exit* [*with* CORIN]

150 CELIA   Didst thou hear these verses?

ROSALIND   O yes, I heard them all, and more, too, for some of
  them had in them more feet° than the verses would bear.   *metrical units*

CELIA   That's no matter; the feet might bear° the verses.   *carry*

ROSALIND   Ay, but the feet were lame, and could not bear them-
155 selves without° the verse, and therefore stood lamely in the   *out of*
  verse.

CELIA   But didst thou hear without wondering how thy name
  should be° hanged and carved upon these trees?   *came to be*

---

5. *the stretching . . . age*: the width of an open hand (a "span") encompasses an entire lifetime. A comparison derived from verses appearing in Elizabethan prayer books.
6. Which heaven would portray in miniature, or through one individual (Rosalind).
7. Graces that otherwise have been widely distributed.
8. The features, but not the false heart, of Helen of Troy. Supposedly Helen's abduction by Paris from her husband, Menelaus, was the event that precipitated the Trojan War. In some accounts, Helen is blamed for her abduction and so could be said to have a false heart.
9. Queen of Egypt and the tragic heroine of Shake-speare's *Antony and Cleopatra*.
1. In Greek myth, Atalanta was a fleet-footed and chaste hunter who challenged her suitors to a race. She was only defeated when one of them dropped three golden apples, which she stopped to pick up. The reference here is possibly to her beauty or her speed, rather than her greed.
2. Lucretia killed herself to save her honor after being raped by Tarquin (a story told by Shakespeare in *The Rape of Lucrece*).
3. Though not with the belongings retained by an army in retreat, yet with a shepherd's pouch and its contents.

ROSALIND   I was seven of the nine days out of the wonder[4] before
160   you came; for look here what I found on a palm-tree [*showing
CELIA the verses*] I was never so berhymed since Pythagoras'
time that I was an Irish rat,[5] which I can hardly remember.

CELIA   Trow you° who hath done this?   *Can you imagine*

ROSALIND   Is it a man?

165   CELIA   And a chain that you once wore about his neck. Change
you colour?

ROSALIND   I prithee, who?

CELIA   O Lord, Lord, it is a hard matter for friends to meet. But
mountains may be removed with° earthquakes, and so   *moved by*
170   encounter.

ROSALIND   Nay, but who is it?

CELIA   Is it possible?

ROSALIND   Nay, I prithee now with most petitionary vehemence,
tell me who it is.

175   CELIA   O wonderful, wonderful, and most wonderful-wonderful,
and yet again wonderful, and after that out of all whooping![6]

ROSALIND   Good my complexion![7] Dost thou think, though I am
caparisoned° like a man, I have a doublet and hose in my dispo-   *dressed*
sition? One inch of delay more is a South Sea of discovery.[8] I
180   prithee tell me who is it quickly, and speak apace.° I would   *at once*
thou couldst stammer, that thou mightst pour this concealed
man out of thy mouth as wine comes out of a narrow-mouthed
bottle—either too much at once, or none at all. I prithee take
the cork out of thy mouth, that I may drink thy tidings.

185   CELIA   So you may put a man in your belly.°   *stomach; womb*

ROSALIND   Is he of God's making? What manner of man? Is his
head worth a hat? Or his chin worth a beard?

CELIA   Nay, he hath but a little beard.

ROSALIND   Why, God will send more, if the man will be thank-
190   ful. Let me stay° the growth of his beard, if thou delay me not   *wait for*
the knowledge of his chin.

CELIA   It is young Orlando, that tripped up the wrestler's heels
and your heart both in an instant.

ROSALIND   Nay, but the devil take mocking. Speak sad brow and
195   true maid.[9]

CELIA   I'faith, coz, 'tis he.

ROSALIND   Orlando?

CELIA   Orlando.

ROSALIND   Alas the day, what shall I do with my doublet and
200   hose! What did he when thou sawest him? What said he? How
looked he? Wherein went he?° What makes he here? Did he   *What was he wearing*
ask for me? Where remains he? How parted he with thee? And
when shalt thou see him again? Answer me in one word.

CELIA   You must borrow me Gargantua's[1] mouth first, 'tis a word

4. Referring to the proverbial "nine days' wonder," a
novelty that caused amazement.
5. I was never so overwhelmed with rhyme since the
days of the ancient Greeks, when I was an Irish rat.
Alluding to Pythagoras's doctrine of the transmigration
of souls and to the popular belief in England that Irish
bards were capable of rhyming rats to death.
6. After that, beyond what all shouts of astonishment
can express.
7. An expression of impatience. "Complexion" means

"temperament," believed to be caused by the particular
mixture of the four humors in one's body. Her meaning
seems to be: Pay attention to my womanly temperament
(which is impatient).
8. More delay will seem as infinite as a voyage of discovery to the South Seas.
9. Speak seriously and as a virtuous woman or on your
honor as a virgin.
1. A voracious giant famous in French folklore and
from the writings of Rabelais.

205   too great for any mouth of this age's size. To say ay and no to
these particulars is more than to answer in a catechism.[2]

ROSALIND   But doth he know that I am in this forest, and in
man's apparel? Looks he as freshly as he did the day he wrestled?

210 CELIA   It is as easy to count atomies° as to resolve the proposi-   *specks (of dust)*
tions° of a lover; but take a taste of my finding him, and relish   *answer the questions*
it with good observance.[3] I found him under a tree, like a
dropped acorn—

ROSALIND   It may well be called Jove's tree[4] when it drops forth
215 such fruit.

CELIA   Give me audience, good madam.

ROSALIND   Proceed.

CELIA   There lay he, stretched along like a wounded knight—

ROSALIND   Though it be pity to see such a sight, it well becomes
220 the ground.

CELIA   Cry 'holla'° to thy tongue, I prithee: it curvets° unseason-   *hold / leaps about*
ably.—He was furnished° like a hunter—   *dressed*

ROSALIND   O ominous—he comes to kill my heart.

CELIA   I would sing my song without a burden;° thou bringest   *refrain*
225 me out of tune.

ROSALIND   Do you not know I am a woman? When I think, I
must speak.—Sweet, say on.

Enter ORLANDO *and* JAQUES

CELIA   You bring me out.° Soft, comes he not here?   *make me lose the tune*

ROSALIND   'Tis he. Slink by, and note him.

230   [ROSALIND *and* CELIA *stand aside*]

JAQUES [*to* ORLANDO] I thank you for your company, but, good
faith, I had as lief° have been myself alone.   *as willingly*

ORLANDO   And so had I. But yet for fashion' sake, I thank you too
for your society.

JAQUES   God b'wi'you;° let's meet as little as we can.   *Good-bye*

235 ORLANDO   I do desire we may be better strangers.

JAQUES   I pray you mar no more trees with writing love-songs in
their barks.

ORLANDO   I pray you mar no more of my verses with reading
them ill-favouredly.°   *unsympathetically*

240 JAQUES   Rosalind is your love's name?

ORLANDO   Yes, just.

JAQUES   I do not like her name.

ORLANDO   There was no thought of pleasing you when she was
christened.

245 JAQUES   What stature is she of?

ORLANDO   Just as high as my heart.

JAQUES   You are full of pretty answers. Have you not been
acquainted with goldsmiths' wives, and conned them out of
rings?[5]

250 ORLANDO   Not so; but I answer you right painted cloth,[6] from
whence you have studied your questions.

---

2. A summary, in question-and-answer form, of basic tenets of religious doctrine. In Shakespeare's time, all members of the Church of England learned to recite such a catechism.
3. And enhance its flavor by paying careful attention.
4. The oak was traditionally viewed as sacred to Jove, the god of thunder, and was said therefore to be often struck by lightning.
5. Romantic verses were often inscribed on rings sold in shops managed by the wives of goldsmiths; with a pun on "rings" as a slang term for "vaginas."
6. I answer you in the style of the pithy sayings issuing from the mouths of figures in painted wall hangings (a popular and inexpensive form of interior decoration).

JAQUES   You have a nimble wit; I think 'twas made of Atalanta's
heels.⁷ Will you sit down with me, and we two will rail against
our mistress the world, and all our misery?

255   ORLANDO   I will chide no breather° in the world but myself,   *person*
against whom I know most faults.

JAQUES   The worst fault you have is to be in love.

ORLANDO   'Tis a fault I will not change for your best virtue. I am
weary of you.

260   JAQUES   By my troth, I was seeking for a fool when I found you.

ORLANDO   He is drowned in the brook. Look but in, and you
shall see him.

JAQUES   There I shall see mine own figure.

ORLANDO   Which I take to be either a fool or a cipher.⁸

265   JAQUES   I'll tarry no longer with you. Farewell, good Signor
Love.

ORLANDO   I am glad of your departure. Adieu, good Monsieur
Melancholy.   [*Exit* JAQUES]⁹

ROSALIND [*to* CELIA]   I will speak to him like a saucy lackey, and

270   under that habit° play the knave with him. [*To* ORLANDO] Do   *guise; disguise*
you hear, forester?

ORLANDO   Very well. What would you?

ROSALIND   I pray you, what is't o'clock?

ORLANDO   You should ask me what time o' day. There's no clock

275   in the forest.

ROSALIND   Then there is no true lover in the forest, else sighing
every minute and groaning every hour would detect° the lazy   *reveal*
foot of time as well as a clock.

ORLANDO   And why not the swift foot of time? Had not that been

280   as proper?

ROSALIND   By no means, sir. Time travels in divers paces with
divers persons. I'll tell you who time ambles withal,° who time   *with*
trots withal, who time gallops withal, and who he stands still
withal.

285   ORLANDO   I prithee, who doth he trot withal?

ROSALIND   Marry, he trots hard° with a young maid between the   *uncomfortably*
contract of her marriage and the day it is solemnized. If the
interim be but a se'nnight,° time's pace is so hard that it seems   *week*
the length of seven year.

290   ORLANDO   Who ambles time withal?

ROSALIND   With a priest that lacks Latin, and a rich man that
hath not the gout; for the one sleeps easily because he cannot
study, and the other lives merrily because he feels no pain, the
one lacking the burden of lean and wasteful° learning, the   *weakening*

295   other knowing no burden of heavy tedious penury.° These time   *poverty*
ambles withal.

ORLANDO   Who doth he gallop withal?

ROSALIND   With a thief to the gallows; for though he go as softly°   *slowly*
as foot can fall, he thinks himself too soon there.

300   ORLANDO   Who stays it still withal?

---

7. See note to 3.2.134.
8. A zero; punning on "figure" (line 263) as meaning
"numeral."
9. Editors usually give Jaques an exit here, although
none is indicated in F. It would not be out of character,

however, for Jaques to remain onstage in the background
during Orlando and Rosalind's exchange (as he does during Touchstone's courting of Audrey in 3.3) and to exit
with them at the end of the scene.

ROSALIND   With lawyers in the vacation; for they sleep between
term[1] and term, and then they perceive not how time moves.

ORLANDO   Where dwell you, pretty youth?

ROSALIND   With this shepherdess, my sister, here in the skirts° of   edges
305   the forest, like fringe upon a petticoat.

ORLANDO   Are you native of this place?

ROSALIND   As the coney° that you see dwell where she is kin-   rabbit
dled.°   born

ORLANDO   Your accent is something finer than you could pur-
310   chase° in so removed° a dwelling.   acquire / remote

ROSALIND   I have been told so of many; but indeed an old religious uncle of mine taught me to speak, who was in his youth
an inland man; one that knew courtship° too well, for there he   court life; wooing
fell in love. I have heard him read many lectures against it, and
315   I thank God I am not a woman, to be touched with so many
giddy offences as he hath generally taxed their whole sex
withal.

ORLANDO   Can you remember any of the principal evils that he
laid to the charge of women?

320   ROSALIND   There were none principal; they were all like one
another as halfpence are, every one fault seeming monstrous
till his fellow-fault came to match it.

ORLANDO   I prithee, recount some of them.

ROSALIND   No. I will not cast away my physic but° on those that   my medicine except
325   are sick. There is a man haunts the forest that abuses our young
plants with carving Rosalind on their barks; hangs odes upon
hawthorns and elegies on brambles; all, forsooth, deifying the
name of Rosalind. If I could meet that fancy-monger,° I would   dealer in love
give him some good counsel, for he seems to have the quotid-
330   ian[2] of love upon him.

ORLANDO   I am he that is so love-shaked. I pray you, tell me your
remedy.

ROSALIND   There is none of my uncle's marks upon you. He
taught me how to know a man in love, in which cage of rushes[3]
335   I am sure you are not prisoner.

ORLANDO   What were his marks?

ROSALIND   A lean cheek, which you have not; a blue eye[4] and
sunken, which you have not; an unquestionable° spirit, which   a taciturn
you have not; a beard neglected, which you have not—but I
340   pardon you for that, for simply your having in beard° is a   such beard as you have
younger brother's revenue.[5] Then your hose should be ungar-
tered, your bonnet unbanded,° your sleeve unbuttoned, your   lacking a band
shoe untied, and everything about you demonstrating a careless
desolation. But you are no such man. You are rather point-
345   device° in your accoutrements, as loving yourself than seeming   extremely precise
the lover of any other.

ORLANDO   Fair youth, I would I could make thee believe I love.

ROSALIND   Me believe it? You may as soon make her that you love
believe it, which I warrant she is apter to do than to confess
350   she does. That is one of the points in the which women still°   always

---

1. *terms:* limited periods of time in which the courts
were in session and when lawyers were therefore busy.
Vacation came between terms.
2. Daily recurring fever said to be a sign of love.
3. A prison easy to escape from.

4. An eye ringed with dark circles (suggesting insom-
nia).
5. Younger brothers traditionally received small inher-
itances, here suggesting that Orlando's beard is likewise
thin or small.

give the lie to their consciences. But in good sooth° are you   truth
he that hangs the verses on the trees wherein Rosalind is so
admired?

ORLANDO   I swear to thee, youth, by the white hand of Rosalind,
355   I am that he, that unfortunate he.

ROSALIND   But are you so much in love as your rhymes speak?

ORLANDO   Neither rhyme nor reason can express how much.

ROSALIND   Love is merely a madness, and I tell you, deserves as
well a dark house and a whip as madmen do;⁶ and the rea-
360   son why they° are not so punished and cured is that the lunacy   (lovers)
is so ordinary that the whippers are in love too. Yet I profess
curing it by counsel.

ORLANDO   Did you ever cure any so?

ROSALIND   Yes, one; and in this manner. He was to imagine me
365   his love, his mistress; and I set him every day to woo me. At
which time would I, being but a moonish° youth, grieve, be   changeable
effeminate,⁷ changeable, longing and liking, proud, fantasti-
cal,° apish,° shallow, inconstant, full of tears, full of smiles; for   capricious / affected
every passion something, and for no passion truly anything, as
370   boys and women are for the most part cattle of this colour—
would now like him, now loathe him; then entertain him,°   treat him kindly
then forswear him; now weep for him, then spit at him, that I
drave° my suitor from his mad humour of love to a living   drove
humour° of madness, which was to forswear the full stream of   an actual condition
375   the world and to live in a nook merely monastic.° And thus I   as a hermit
cured him, and this way will I take upon me to wash your liver⁸
as clean as a sound sheep's heart, that there shall not be one
spot of love in't.

ORLANDO   I would not be cured, youth.

380   ROSALIND   I would cure you if you would but call me Rosalind
and come every day to my cot,° and woo me.   cottage

ORLANDO   Now by the faith of my love, I will. Tell me where it
is.

ROSALIND   Go with me to it, and I'll show it you. And by the way
385   you shall tell me where in the forest you live. Will you go?

ORLANDO   With all my heart, good youth.

ROSALIND   Nay, you must call me Rosalind.—Come, sister Will
you go?   *Exeunt*

3.3

Enter [TOUCHSTONE *the*] *clown and* AUDREY, [*followed
by*] JAQUES

TOUCHSTONE   Come apace, good Audrey. I will fetch up your
goats, Audrey. And how, Audrey, am I the man yet? Doth my
simple feature° content you?   appearance

AUDREY   Your features, Lord warrant° us—what features?   defend

5   TOUCHSTONE   I am here with thee and thy goats as the most
capricious° poet honest Ovid was among the Goths.¹   witty; lascivious

---

6. Confinement in a dark room and whipping, common
treatments for insanity, were believed to rid the insane
of the devils that possessed them.

7. Like a woman; sensual or self-indulgent; a term
often used to deride men perceived as excessive in their
sexual interest in women.

8. In Renaissance medical theory, the seat of the passions.

3.3

1. Punning on "goats / Goths," which were similarly
pronounced, and referring to the Roman poet's exile
among the Goths.

JAQUES [*aside*] O knowledge ill-inhabited; worse than Jove in a thatched house.[2]

TOUCHSTONE When a man's verses cannot be understood, nor a
10 man's good wit seconded with° the forward child, understand-   *supported by*
ing, it strikes a man more dead than a great reckoning° in a   *tavern bill*
little room.[3] Truly, I would the gods had made thee poetical.

AUDREY I do not know what 'poetical' is. Is it honest in deed
and word? Is it a true thing?

15 TOUCHSTONE No, truly; for the truest poetry is the most
feigning,° and lovers are given to poetry; and what they swear   *imaginative; false*
in poetry it may be said, as lovers, they do feign.

AUDREY Do you wish, then, that the gods had made me poetical?

TOUCHSTONE I do, truly; for thou swearest to me thou art hon-
20 est.° Now if thou wert a poet, I might have some hope thou   *chaste*
didst feign.

AUDREY Would you not have me honest?

TOUCHSTONE No, truly, unless thou wert hard-favoured;° for   *ugly*
honesty coupled to beauty is to have honey a sauce to sugar.

25 JAQUES [*aside*] A material° fool.   *full of matter or sense*

AUDREY Well, I am not fair, and therefore I pray the gods make
me honest.

TOUCHSTONE Truly, and to cast away honesty upon a foul slut
were to put good meat into an unclean dish.

30 AUDREY I am not a slut, though I thank the gods I am foul.[4]

TOUCHSTONE Well, praised be the gods for thy foulness. Slut-
tishness may come hereafter. But be it as it may be, I will marry
thee; and to that end I have been with Sir Oliver Martext, the
vicar of the next village, who hath promised to meet me in this
35 place of the forest, and to couple us.

JAQUES [*aside*] I would fain° see this meeting.   *gladly*

AUDREY Well, the gods give us joy.

TOUCHSTONE Amen.—A man may, if he were of a fearful heart,
stagger° in this attempt; for here we have no temple but the   *hesitate*
40 wood, no assembly but horn-beasts.[5] But what though? Courage. As horns are odious, they are necessary. It is said many a
man knows no end of his goods.[6] Right: many a man has good
horns, and knows no end of them. Well, that is the dowry of
his wife, 'tis none of his own getting.[7] Horns? Even so. Poor
45 men alone? No, no; the noblest deer hath them as huge as the
rascal.° Is the single man therefore blessed? No. As a walled   *young or lean deer*
town is more worthier than a village, so is the forehead of a
married man more honourable than the bare brow of a bache-
lor. And by how much defence° is better than no skill, by so   *skill in self-defense*
50 much is a horn more precious than to want.°   *to lack (one)*

Enter SIR OLIVER MARTEXT

Here comes Sir Oliver.—Sir Oliver Martext, you are well met.
Will you dispatch us here under this tree, or shall we go with
you to your chapel?

---

2. In *Metamorphoses* 8, Ovid tells how the king of the
gods was given shelter for a time in the humble
dwelling of Philemon and Baucis.
3. These lines have been taken to refer to the death in
1593 of Christopher Marlowe, a contemporary playwright, in a quarrel in a tavern over a bill.
4. Ugly. Audrey apparently takes "foul" as a term of
praise.

5. Horned beasts such as deer, goats, and the like that
inhabited the forest, with an allusion to the horns of the
cuckolded husband.
6. A proverbial expression suggesting a man so wealthy
he can't count all his money.
7. 'tis . . . *getting*: he is not responsible for the horns;
he is not responsible for conceiving his children (since
his wife has been sexually unfaithful).

SIR OLIVER MARTEXT   Is there none here to give the woman?

55 TOUCHSTONE   I will not take her on gift of any man.

SIR OLIVER MARTEXT   Truly she must be given, or the marriage
is not lawful.

JAQUES   [*coming forward*]   Proceed, proceed. I'll give her

TOUCHSTONE   Good even, good Monsieur What-ye-call't. How
60 do you, sir? You are very well met. God'ield you for your last
company.[8] I am very glad to see you. Even a toy° in hand here,   *trifling matter*
sir.

[JAQUES *removes his hat*]
Nay, pray be covered.°   *replace your hat*

JAQUES   Will you be married, motley?

65 TOUCHSTONE   As the ox hath his bow,° sir, the horse his curb,[9]   *yoke*
and the falcon her bells,[1] so man hath his desires; and as
pigeons bill,° so wedlock would be nibbling.   *rub bill to bill*

JAQUES   And will you, being a man of your breeding, be married
under a bush, like a beggar? Get you to church, and have a
70 good priest that can tell you what marriage is. This fellow will
but join you together as they join wainscot;° then one of you   *wood paneling*
will prove a shrunk panel and, like green timber, warp,° warp.   *go wrong; shrink*

TOUCHSTONE   I am not in the mind but° I were better to be mar-   *not sure but that*
ried of° him than of another, for he is not like to marry me   *by*
75 well, and not being well married, it will be a good excuse for
me hereafter to leave my wife.

JAQUES   Go thou with me, and let me counsel thee.

TOUCHSTONE   Come, sweet Audrey.
We must be married,° or we must live in bawdry.°   *(properly wed) / in sin*
80 Farewell, good Master Oliver. Not
      O, sweet Oliver,
      O, brave Oliver,
   Leave me not behind thee[2]
but
85   Wind° away,   *Go*
   Begone, I say,
   I will not to wedding with thee.

SIR OLIVER MARTEXT   [*aside*]   'Tis no matter. Ne'er a fantastical
knave of them all shall flout me out of my calling.

Exeunt

3.4

Enter ROSALIND [*as Ganymede*] *and* CELIA [*as Aliena*]

ROSALIND   Never talk to me. I will weep.

CELIA   Do, I prithee, but yet have the grace to consider that tears
do not become a man.

ROSALIND   But have I not cause to weep?

5 CELIA   As good cause as one would desire; therefore weep.

ROSALIND   His very hair is of the dissembling colour.[1]

CELIA   Something° browner than Judas's. Marry, his kisses are   *Somewhat*
Judas's own children.

ROSALIND   I'faith, his hair is of a good colour.

---

8. God yield you (a salutation meaning "May God
reward you") for your recent companionship.
9. A bit placed in the horse's mouth to control its
movements.
1. Bells attached to a falcon's legs before releasing it for

the hunt so that it might be easily reclaimed afterward.
2. Lines from a popular Elizabethan ballad.
3.4
1. Alluding to the tradition that Judas, the disciple who
betrayed Jesus, had red hair.

10 CELIA   An excellent colour. Your chestnut was ever the only
colour.

ROSALIND   And his kissing is as full of sanctity as the touch of
holy bread.[2]

CELIA   He hath bought a pair of cast° lips of Diana.[3] A nun of   *cast-off; sculpted*
15 winter's sisterhood° kisses not more religiously. The very ice of   *devoted to coldness*
chastity is in them.

ROSALIND   But why did he swear he would come this morning,
and comes not?

CELIA   Nay, certainly, there is no truth in him.

20 ROSALIND   Do you think so?

CELIA   Yes. I think he is not a pick-purse, nor a horse-stealer; but
for his verity° in love, I do think him as concave° as a covered   *truthfulness / hollow*
goblet, or a worm-eaten nut.

ROSALIND   Not true in love?

25 CELIA   Yes, when he is in. But I think he is not in.

ROSALIND   You have heard him swear downright he was.

CELIA   'Was' is not 'is'. Besides, the oath of a lover is no stronger
than the word of a tapster. They are both the confirmer of false
reckonings. He attends° here in the forest on the Duke your   *waits*
30 father.

ROSALIND   I met the Duke yesterday, and had much question°   *conversation*
with him. He asked me of what parentage I was. I told him, of
as good as he, so he laughed and let me go. But what talk we
of fathers when there is such a man as Orlando?

35 CELIA   O that's a brave° man. He writes brave verses, speaks   *splendid*
brave words, swears brave oaths, and breaks them bravely, quite
traverse,[4] athwart the heart of his lover, as a puny° tilter that   *an unskilled*
spurs his horse but° on one side breaks his staff, like a noble   *only*
goose.° But all's brave that youth mounts, and folly guides.   *fool*
40 Who comes here?

Enter CORIN

CORIN   Mistress and master, you have oft enquired
After the shepherd that complained of love
Who you saw sitting by me on the turf,
Praising the proud disdainful shepherdess
That was his mistress.

45 CELIA   Well, and what of him?

CORIN   If you will see a pageant truly played
Between the pale complexion of true love
And the red glow of scorn and proud disdain,[5]
Go hence a little, and I shall conduct you,
If you will mark° it.   *observe*

50 ROSALIND [*to* CELIA]   O come, let us remove.
The sight of lovers feedeth those in love.
[*To* CORIN] Bring us to this sight, and you shall say
I'll prove a busy actor in their play.   *Exeunt*

---

2. Referring to bread blessed after the Eucharist during Christian religious services and distributed to those
who did not take Communion.
3. The goddess of chastity. See note to 3.2.2.
4. Crossways. A term from jousting used to designate

the dishonorable practice of breaking one's lance
across, rather than directly against, an opponent's
shield.
5. Referring to the paleness of Silvius, the true lover,
and the red cheeks of the disdainful Phoebe.

3.5

Enter SILVIUS *and* PHOEBE

SILVIUS   Sweet Phoebe, do not scorn me, do not, Phoebe
    Say that you love me not, but say not so
    In bitterness. The common executioner,
    Whose heart th'accustomed sight of death makes hard,
5   Falls not° the axe upon the humbled neck   *Does not let fall*
    But first begs° pardon. Will you sterner be   *Without first begging*
    Than he that dies and lives by bloody drops?

        Enter ROSALIND [*as Ganymede*], CELIA [*as Aliena*]. *and*
        CORIN [*and stand aside*]

PHOEBE [*to* SILVIUS]   I would not be thy executioner.
    I fly thee for I would not injure thee.
10   Thou tell'st me there is murder in mine eye.
    'Tis pretty, sure, and very probable
    That eyes, that are the frail'st and softest things,
    Who shut their coward gates on atomies,°   *dust motes*
    Should be called tyrants, butchers, murderers.
15   Now I do frown on thee with all my heart,
    And if mine eyes can wound, now let them kill thee.
    Now counterfeit to swoon, why now fall down;
    Or if thou canst not, O, for shame, for shame,
    Lie not, to say mine eyes are murderers.
20   Now show the wound mine eye hath made in thee.
    Scratch thee but with a pin, and there remains
    Some scar of it. Lean upon a rush,
    The cicatrice and capable impressure[1]
    Thy palm some moment keeps. But now mine eyes,
25   Which I have darted at thee, hurt thee not;
    Nor I am sure there is no force in eyes
    That can do hurt.

SILVIUS   O dear Phoebe,
    If ever—as that ever may be near—
30   You meet in some fresh cheek the power of fancy,°   *love*
    Then shall you know the wounds invisible
    That love's keen arrows make.

PHOEBE   But till that time
    Come not thou near me. And when that time comes,
    Afflict me with thy mocks, pity me not,
35   As till that time I shall not pity thee.

ROSALIND [*coming forward*]   And why, I pray you? Who might
      be your mother,
    That you insult, exult, and all at once,°   *all in one breath*
    Over the wretched? What though you have no beauty—
    As, by my faith, I see no more in you
40   Than without candle may go dark to bed[2]—
    Must you be therefore proud and pitiless?
    Why, what means this? Why do you look on me?
    I see no more in you than in the ordinary°   *common run*
    Of nature's sale-work.°—'Od's my little life,[3]   *ready-made goods*
45   I think she means to tangle° my eyes, too.   *entrap*
    No, faith, proud mistress, hope not after it.

3.5
1. The scarlike mark and the impression that the skin receives.

2. *I see . . . bed*: I see you have not enough beauty to light your way to bed without a candle.
3. An abbreviated version of the oath "God save my life."

'Tis not your inky brows, your black silk hair,
Your bugle° eyeballs, nor your cheek of cream,   *like black glass beads*
That can entame my spirits to your worship.°   *the worship of you*
50   [*To* SILVIUS] You, foolish shepherd, wherefore do you follow her
Like foggy south,° puffing with wind and rain?[4]   *south wind*
You are a thousand times a properer° man   *more attractive*
Than she a woman. 'Tis such fools as you
That makes the world full of ill-favoured° children.   *ugly*
55   'Tis not her glass° but you that flatters her,   *mirror*
And out of you° she sees herself more proper   *from you (as mirror)*
Than any of her lineaments can show her.
[*To* PHOEBE] But, mistress, know yourself; down on your knees
And thank heaven, fasting, for a good man's love;
60   For I must tell you friendly in your ear,
Sell when you can. You are not for all markets.
Cry the man mercy,° love him, take his offer;   *Beg his pardon*
Foul is most foul, being foul to be a scoffer.[5]—
So, take her to thee, shepherd. Fare you well.
65 PHOEBE   Sweet youth, I pray you chide a year together.°   *without interruption*
   I had rather hear you chide than this man woo.
ROSALIND [*to* PHOEBE]   He's fallen in love with your foulness, [*to*
   SILVIUS] and she'll fall in love with my anger. If it be so, as fast
   as she answers thee with frowning looks, I'll sauce° her   *sharply rebuke*
70   with bitter words.
   [*To* PHOEBE] Why look you so upon me?
PHOEBE   For no ill will I bear you.
ROSALIND   I pray you do not fall in love with me,
   For I am falser than vows made in wine.°   *when drinking*
75   Besides, I like you not. If you will know my house,
   'Tis at the tuft of olives,° here hard by.   *olive trees*
   [*To* CELIA] Will you go, sister? [*To* SILVIUS] Shepherd, ply her
      hard.°—   *assail her vigorously*
   Come, sister. [*To* PHOEBE] Shepherdess, look on him better,
   And be not proud. Though all the world could see,
80   None could be so abused in sight as he.—
   Come, to our flock.   *Exeunt* [ROSALIND, CELIA, *and* CORIN][6]
PHOEBE [*aside*]   Dead shepherd,[7] now I find thy saw of might:°   *your saying powerful*
   'Who ever loved that loved not at first sight?'
SILVIUS   Sweet Phoebe—
PHOEBE   Ha, what sayst thou, Silvius?
85 SILVIUS   Sweet Phoebe, pity me.
PHOEBE   Why, I am sorry for thee, gentle Silvius.
SILVIUS   Wherever sorrow is, relief would be.
   If you do sorrow at my grief in love,
   By giving love your sorrow and my grief
90   Were both extermined.°   *Would both be ended*
PHOEBE   Thou hast my love, is not that neighbourly?[8]
SILVIUS   I would have you.
PHOEBE   Why, that were covetousness.[9]

4. That is, with sighs and tears.
5. The ugly seem most ugly when they are abusive.
6. F marks a single exit for Rosalind here, but it is unlikely that Celia and Corin remain.
7. Referring to Christopher Marlowe, poet and playwright who died in 1593. Line 83 is taken from his poem *Hero and Leander*.
8. With a reference to Romans 13:9: "Thou shalt love thy neighbour as thyself."
9. With a reference to Exodus 20:17: "Thou shalt not covet thy neighbour's house, thou shalt not covet thy neighbour's wife, nor his manservant, nor his maid servant, nor his ox, nor his ass, nor any thing that is thy neighbour's."

Silvius, the time was that I hated thee;
And yet it is not° that I bear thee love.   *it has not yet happened*
95   But since that thou canst talk of love so well,
Thy company, which erst° was irksome to me,   *formerly*
I will endure; and I'll employ thee, too.
But do not look for further recompense
Than thine own gladness that thou art employed.
100   SILVIUS   So holy and so perfect is my love,
And I in such a poverty of grace,[1]
That I shall think it a most plenteous crop
To glean the broken ears° after the man   *(of corn)*
That the main harvest reaps. Loose now and then
105   A scattered° smile, and that I'll live upon.   *stray*
        PHOEBE   Know'st thou the youth that spoke to me erewhile?
        SILVIUS   Not very well, but I have met him oft,
And he hath bought the cottage and the bounds°   *pastures*
That the old Carlot once was master of.
110   PHOEBE   Think not I love him, though I ask for him.
'Tis but a peevish boy. Yet he talks well.
But what care I for words? Yet words do well
When he that speaks them pleases those that hear.
It is a pretty youth—not very pretty—
115   But sure he's proud; and yet his pride becomes him.
He'll make a proper° man. The best thing in him   *handsome*
Is his complexion; and faster than his tongue
Did make offence, his eye did heal it up.
He is not very tall; yet for his years he's tall.
120   His leg is but so-so; and yet 'tis well.
There was a pretty redness in his lip.
A little riper and more lusty-red
Than that mixed in his cheek. 'Twas just the difference
Betwixt the constant red and mingled damask.[2]
125   There be some women, Silvius, had they marked him
In parcels° as I did, would have gone near   *Item by item*
To fall in love with him; but for my part,
I love him not, nor hate him not. And yet
Have I more cause to hate him than to love him,
130   For what had he to do to chide at me?
He said mine eyes were black, and my hair black,
And now I am remembered, scorned at me.
I marvel why I answered not again.
But that's all one. Omittance is no quittance.[3]
135   I'll write to him a very taunting letter,
And thou shalt bear it. Wilt thou, Silvius?
        SILVIUS   Phoebe, with all my heart.
        PHOEBE   I'll write it straight.°   *immediately*
The matter's in my head and in my heart.
I will be bitter with him, and passing° short.   *extremely*
140   Go with me, Silvius.   *Exeunt*

1. And I so lacking in (your) favor.
2. *constant . . . damask:* uniform red and a mixture of
red and white characteristic of certain kinds of roses.

3. A proverbial expression meaning that a debt is not
canceled simply because one fails ("omits") to exact it.

4.1

Enter ROSALIND [*as Ganymede*], CELIA [*as Aliena*], *and*
JAQUES

JAQUES   I prithee, pretty youth, let me be better acquainted with
thee.

ROSALIND   They say you are a melancholy fellow.

JAQUES   I am so. I do love it better than laughing.

5   ROSALIND   Those that are in extremity of either are abominable
fellows, and betray themselves to every modern censure worse
than drunkards.

JAQUES   Why, 'tis good to be sad° and say nothing.   *serious*

ROSALIND   Why then, 'tis good to be a post.

10   JAQUES   I have neither the scholar's melancholy, which is emula-
tion,° nor the musician's, which is fantastical,° nor the court-   *envy / overly fanciful*
ier's, which is proud, nor the soldier's, which is ambitious, nor
the lawyer's, which is politic, nor the lady's, which is nice,° nor   *fastidious*
the lover's, which is all these; but it is a melancholy of mine

15   own, compounded of many simples,° extracted from many   *ingredients*
objects,° and indeed the sundry contemplation of my travels,[1]   *sights*
in° which my often° rumination wraps me in a most humor-   *upon / frequent*
ous° sadness.   *moody*

ROSALIND   A traveller! By my faith, you have great reason to be

20   sad. I fear you have sold your own lands to see other men's.
Then to have seen much and to have nothing is to have rich
eyes and poor hands.

JAQUES   Yes, I have gained my experience.

Enter ORLANDO

ROSALIND   And your experience makes you sad. I had rather have

25   a fool to make me merry than experience to make me sad—
and to travel for it too!

ORLANDO   Good day and happiness, dear Rosalind.

JAQUES   Nay then, God b'wi'you an° you talk in blank verse.   *if*

ROSALIND   Farewell, Monsieur Traveller. Look you lisp,[2] and

30   wear strange° suits; disable° all the benefits of your own coun-   *foreign / disparage*
try; be out of love with your nativity,° and almost chide God for   *birthplace*
making you that countenance you are, or I will scarce think
you have swam in a gondola.[3]   [*Exit* JAQUES][4]
Why, how now, Orlando? Where have you been all this while?

35   You a lover? An you serve me such another trick, never come
in my sight more.

ORLANDO   My fair Rosalind, I come within an hour of my
promise.

ROSALIND   Break an hour's promise in love! He that will divide a

40   minute into a thousand parts and break but a part of the thousand part of a minute in the affairs of love, it may be said of
him that Cupid hath clapped him o'th' shoulder, but I'll warrant him heartwhole.[5]

ORLANDO   Pardon me, dear Rosalind.

4.1
1. The various thoughts arising during my travels, with
a pun on "travails," meaning "labors."
2. Speak with an affected (foreign) accent.
3. Ridden in a gondola—that is, seen Venice, a popular destination for English travelers.

4. F marks no exit for Jaques here, but he and Rosalind
have formally parted, and Jaques enters with a new
group of characters at the beginning of 4.2.
5. Cupid has tapped him (as in an arrest) or wounded
him (with his arrow), but I'll guarantee he left his heart
intact.

45 ROSALIND   Nay, an you be so tardy, come no more in my sight. I had as lief be wooed of a snail.

ORLANDO   Of a snail?

ROSALIND   Ay, of a snail; for though he comes slowly, he carries his house on his head—a better jointure,° I think, than you   marriage settlement
50 make a woman. Besides, he brings his destiny with him.

ORLANDO   What's that?

ROSALIND   Why, horns, which such as you are fain to be beholden to your wives for.[6] But he comes armed in his fortune,[7] and prevents the slander of his wife.

55 ORLANDO   Virtue is no hornmaker, and my Rosalind is virtuous.

ROSALIND   And I am your Rosalind.

CELIA   It pleases him to call you so; but he hath a Rosalind of a better leer° than you.   more attractive

ROSALIND   Come, woo me, woo me, for now I am in a holiday
60 humour, and like enough to consent. What would you say to me now an I were your very, very Rosalind?

ORLANDO   I would kiss before I spoke.

ROSALIND   Nay, you were better speak first, and when you were gravelled° for lack of matter you might take occasion to kiss.   at a loss
65 Very good orators, when they are out,° they will spit; and for   speechless
lovers, lacking—God warr'nt° us— matter, the cleanliest shift°   defend / cleverest device
is to kiss.

ORLANDO   How if the kiss be denied?

ROSALIND   Then she puts you to entreaty, and there begins new
70 matter.

ORLANDO   Who could be out, being before his beloved mistress?

ROSALIND   Marry, that should you if I were your mistress, or I should think my honesty ranker than my wit.[8]

ORLANDO   What, of my suit?[9]

75 ROSALIND   Not out of your apparel, and yet out of your suit. Am not I your Rosalind?

ORLANDO   I take some joy to say you are because I would be talking of her.

ROSALIND   Well, in her person I say I will not have you.

80 ORLANDO   Then in mine own person I die.

ROSALIND   No, faith; die by attorney.° The poor world is almost   proxy
six thousand years old,[1] and in all this time there was not any man died in his own person, videlicet,° in a love-cause. Troi-   namely
lus[2] had his brains dashed out with a Grecian club, yet he did
85 what he could to die before, and he is one of the patterns of love. Leander,[3] he would have lived many a fair year though Hero had turned nun if it had not been for a hot midsummer night, for, good youth, he went but forth to wash him in the Hellespont and, being taken with the cramp, was drowned; and
90 the foolish chroniclers of that age found° it was Hero of Sestos.   claimed
But these are all lies. Men have died from time to time, and worms have eaten them, but not for love.

6. An allusion to the cuckold's horns.
7. Equipped with the insignia of his destined future.
8. I would think my chastity was fouler than my intelligence; with a pun on "out" (lines 65, 71) as meaning "not permitted sexual entrance."
9. My petition. Orlando asks if he will be at a loss for words ("out") in furthering his courtship ("suit"). Ros-

alind puns on "suit" as meaning "clothing."
1. Elizabethan divines generally dated the world's creation somewhere around 4000 B.C.E.
2. The forsaken Trojan lover of Cressida, killed by the Greek warrior Achilles.
3. In Greek mythology, the lover of Hero; he swam the Hellespont nightly to visit her and was drowned.

ORLANDO I would not have my right° Rosalind of this mind, for   *true*
I protest her frown might kill me.

95 ROSALIND By this hand, it will not kill a fly. But come, now I
will be your Rosalind in a more coming-on° disposition; and   *agreeable*
ask me what you will, I will grant it.

ORLANDO Then love me, Rosalind.

ROSALIND Yes, faith, will I, Fridays and Saturdays and all.

100 ORLANDO And wilt thou have me?

ROSALIND Ay, and twenty such.

ORLANDO What sayst thou?

ROSALIND Are you not good?

ORLANDO I hope so.

105 ROSALIND Why then, can one desire too much of a good thing?
[*To* CELIA] Come, sister, you shall be the priest and marry us.—
Give me your hand, Orlando.—What do you say, sister?

ORLANDO [*to* CELIA] Pray thee, marry us.

CELIA I cannot say the words.

110 ROSALIND You must begin, 'Will you, Orlando'—

CELIA Go to.[4] Will you, Orlando, have to wife this Rosalind?

ORLANDO I will.

ROSALIND Ay, but when?

ORLANDO Why now, as fast as she can marry us.

115 ROSALIND Then you must say, 'I take thee, Rosalind, for wife.'

ORLANDO I take thee, Rosalind, for wife.

ROSALIND I might ask you for your commission;° but I do take   *authority*
thee, Orlando, for my husband. There's a girl goes before° the   *who anticipates*
priest; and certainly a woman's thought runs before her actions.

120 ORLANDO So do all thoughts; they are winged.

ROSALIND Now tell me how long you would have her after you
have possessed her?

ORLANDO For ever and a day.

ROSALIND Say a day without the ever. No, no, Orlando; men are

125 April when they woo, December when they wed. Maids are
May when they are maids, but the sky changes when they are
wives. I will be more jealous of thee than a Barbary cock-
pigeon[5] over his hen, more clamorous than a parrot against°   *in expectation of*
rain, more new-fangled° than an ape, more giddy in my desires   *in love with novelty*

130 than a monkey. I will weep for nothing, like Diana in the fountain,[6] and I will do that when you are disposed to be merry. I
will laugh like a hyena, and that when thou art inclined to
sleep.

ORLANDO But will my Rosalind do so?

135 ROSALIND By my life, she will do as I do.

ORLANDO O, but she is wise.

ROSALIND Or else she could not have the wit to do this. The
wiser, the waywarder. Make° the doors upon a woman's wit,   *Close*
and it will out at the casement. Shut that, and 'twill out at the

140 key-hole. Stop that, 'twill fly with the smoke out at the
chimney.

---

4. An expression of mild impatience.
5. An ornamental bird, traditionally an emblem of jealousy. It was introduced into Europe from Asia by Turks, whom Elizabethans associated with North Africa's Barbary Coast. Turkish husbands were imag-

ined by the English to be excessively vigilant about the sexual fidelity of their wives.
6. Referring to the figures of the goddess Diana used as centerpieces for ornamental fountains in London and elsewhere.

ORLANDO   A man that had a wife with such a wit, he might say
'Wit, whither wilt?'[7]

ROSALIND   Nay, you might keep that check° for it till you met   rebuke
145   your wife's wit going to your neighbour's bed.

ORLANDO   And what wit could wit have to excuse that?

ROSALIND   Marry, to say she came to seek you there. You shall
never take her without her answer unless you take her without
her tongue. O, that woman that cannot make her fault her
150   husband's occasion,[8] let her never nurse her child herself, for
she will breed it like a fool.

ORLANDO   For these two hours, Rosalind, I will leave thee

ROSALIND   Alas, dear love, I cannot lack thee two hours.

ORLANDO   I must attend the Duke at dinner. By two o'clock I
155   will be with thee again.

ROSALIND   Ay, go your ways, go your ways. I knew what you
would prove;° my friends told me as much, and I thought no   turn out to be
less. That flattering tongue of yours won me. 'Tis but one cast
away,° and so, come, death! Two o'clock is your hour?   one lover jilted

160   ORLANDO   Ay, sweet Rosalind.

ROSALIND   By my troth, and in good earnest, and so God mend
me, and by all pretty oaths that are not dangerous, if you break
one jot of your promise or come one minute behind your hour,
I will think you the most pathetical° break-promise and the   pathetic
165   most hollow lover, and the most unworthy of her you call Rosalind that may be chosen out of the gross° band of the unfaith-   entire
ful. Therefore beware my censure, and keep your promise.

ORLANDO   With no less religion° than if thou wert indeed my   faith
Rosalind. So, adieu.

170   ROSALIND   Well, Time is the old justice that examines all such
offenders; and let Time try.° Adieu.   *Exit* [ORLANDO]   determine

CELIA   You have simply misused° our sex in your love-prate. We   completely slandered
must have your doublet and hose plucked over your head and
show the world what the bird hath done to her own nest.

175   ROSALIND   O coz, coz, coz, my pretty little coz, that thou didst
know how many fathom deep I am in love. But it cannot be
sounded. My affection hath an unknown bottom, like the Bay
of Portugal.

CELIA   Or rather bottomless, that° as fast as you pour affection   so that
180   in, it runs out.

ROSALIND   No, that same wicked bastard of Venus,[9] that was
begot of thought, conceived of spleen,° and born of madness,   caprice
that blind rascally boy that abuses° everyone's eyes because his   deceives
own are out, let him be judge how deep I am in love. I'll tell
185   thee, Aliena, I cannot be out of the sight of Orlando. I'll go
find a shadow° and sigh till he come.   shady place

CELIA   And I'll sleep.   *Exeunt*

4.2

Enter JAQUES *and* LORDS [*dressed as*] *foresters*[1]

JAQUES   Which is he that killed the deer?

FIRST LORD   Sir, it was I.

JAQUES [*to the others*]   Let's present him to the Duke like a
Roman conqueror. And it would do well to set the deer's horns

5   upon his head for a branch° of victory. Have you no song, for-   wreath
ester, for this purpose?

SECOND LORD   Yes, sir.

JAQUES   Sing it. 'Tis no matter how it be in tune, so it make
noise enough.

10   LORDS [*sing*][2]   What shall he have that killed the deer?
His leather skin and horns to wear.
Then sing him home; the rest shall bear°   carry; sing
This burden.°   (the deer); refrain
Take thou no scorn° to wear the horn;   Do not disdain
15   It was a crest[3] ere thou wast born.
Thy father's father wore it,
And thy father bore it.
The horn, the horn, the lusty horn
Is not a thing to laugh to scorn.   *Exeunt*

4.3

Enter ROSALIND [*as Ganymede*] *and* CELIA [*as Aliena*]

ROSALIND   How say you now? Is it not past two o'clock? And
here much Orlando.

CELIA   I warrant you, with pure love and troubled brain he hath
ta'en his bow and arrows and is gone forth to sleep.

Enter SILVIUS

5   Look who comes here.

SILVIUS [*to* ROSALIND]   My errand is to you, fair youth.
My gentle Phoebe did bid me give you this.
[*He offers* ROSALIND *a letter, which she takes and reads*]
I know not the contents, but as I guess
By the stern brow and waspish action

10   Which she did use as she was writing of it,
It bears an angry tenor. Pardon me;
I am but as a guiltless messenger.

ROSALIND   Patience herself would startle at this letter,
And play the swaggerer. Bear this, bear all.

15   She says I am not fair, that I lack manners;
She calls me proud, and that she could not love me
Were man as rare as Phoenix.[1] 'Od's° my will,   God's
Her love is not the hare that I do hunt.
Why writes she so to me? Well, shepherd, well,

20   This is a letter of your own device.

SILVIUS   No, I protest; I know not the contents.
Phoebe did write it.

ROSALIND   Come, come, you are a fool,

4.2

1. F's stage direction—"Enter Jaques and Lords, Foresters"—leaves ambiguous whether Jaques and the lords are dressed as foresters or are accompanied by them.

2. F does not assign this song to anyone. The stage direction reads: "Music, Song."

3. Coat of arms; head ornament.

4.3

1. A legendary bird of Arabia, supposedly unique, which lived five hundred years, died in flames, and was reborn from its own ashes.

And turned° into the extremity of love.   *brought*
I saw her hand. She has a leathern hand,
25   A free-stone° coloured hand. I verily did think   *yellow-brown limestone*
That her old gloves were on; but 'twas her hands.
She has a housewife's hand—but that's no matter.
I say she never did invent this letter.
This is a man's invention, and his hand.
30 SILVIUS   Sure, it is hers.
ROSALIND   Why, 'tis a boisterous and a cruel style,
A style for challengers. Why, she defies me,
Like Turk to Christian.² Women's gentle brain
Could not drop forth such giant-rude invention,
35   Such Ethiop³ words, blacker in their effect
Than in their countenance. Will you hear the letter?
SILVIUS   So please you, for I never heard it yet,
Yet heard too much of Phoebe's cruelty.
ROSALIND   She Phoebes me.⁴ Mark how the tyrant writes:
40   *Read[s]*   'Art thou god to shepherd turned,
That a maiden's heart hath burned?'
Can a woman rail thus?
SILVIUS   Call you this railing?
ROSALIND *read[s]*   'Why, thy godhead laid apart,°   *set aside*
45   Warr'st thou with a woman's heart?'
Did you ever hear such railing?
'Whiles the eye of man did woo me
That could do no vengeance° to me.'—   *harm*
Meaning me a beast.
50   'If the scorn of your bright eyne°   *eyes*
Have power to raise such love in mine,
Alack, in me what strange effect
Would they work in mild aspect?°   *if they looked kindly*
Whiles you chid me I did love;
55   How then might your prayers move?
He that brings this love to thee
Little knows this love in me,
And by him seal up thy mind⁵
Whether that thy youth and kind°   *nature*
60   Will the faithful offer take
Of me, and all that I can make,°   *offer you*
Or else by him my love deny.
And then I'll study how to die.'
SILVIUS   Call you this chiding?
65 CELIA   Alas, poor shepherd.
ROSALIND   Do you pity him? No, he deserves no pity. [*To SIL-
VIUS*] Wilt thou love such a woman? What, to make thee an
instrument,⁶ and play false strains upon thee?—not to be
endured. Well, go your way to her—for I see love hath made
70   thee a tame snake—and say this to her: that if she love me, I

2. Alluding to medieval plays in which Turks and   4. Addresses me as Phoebe would—that is, in a dis-
Christians appeared as bitter enemies or to a common   dainful manner.
Elizabethan perception of the Turk as an enemy to the   5. And by means of him (Silvius), send your thoughts
Christian countries of western Europe.   to me (in a letter).
3. Ethiopian. In Elizabethan racial discourse, the term   6. Tool; musical instrument.
signified blackness and evil.

charge her to love thee. If she will not, I will never have her
unless thou entreat for her. If you be a true lover, hence, and
not a word; for here comes more company.   *Exit* SILVIUS
                    Enter OLIVER

OLIVER   Good morrow, fair ones. Pray you, if you know,
75   Where in the purlieus° of this forest stands   outskirts
      A sheepcote fenced about with olive trees?
CELIA   West of this place, down in the neighbour bottom.°   next valley
      The rank of osiers° by the murmuring stream   row of willows
      Left on your right hand brings you to the place.
80   But at this hour the house doth keep itself.
      There's none within.
OLIVER   If that an eye may profit by a tongue,
      Then should I know you by description.
      Such garments, and such years. 'The boy is fair,
85   Of female favour,° and bestows° himself   appearance / behaves
      Like a ripe° sister. The woman low°   mature / short
      And browner than her brother.' Are not you
      The owner of the house I did enquire for?
CELIA   It is no boast, being asked, to say we are.
90   OLIVER   Orlando doth commend him to you both,
      And to that youth he calls his Rosalind
      He sends this bloody napkin.° Are you he?   handkerchief
ROSALIND   I am. What must we understand by this?
OLIVER   Some of my shame, if you will know of me
95   What man I am, and how, and why, and where
      This handkerchief was stained.
CELIA   I pray you tell it.
OLIVER   When last the young Orlando parted from you,
      He left a promise to return again
      Within an hour, and pacing through the forest,
100   Chewing the food of sweet and bitter fancy,
      Lo what befell. He threw his eye aside,
      And mark what object° did present itself.   what a spectacle
      Under an old oak, whose boughs were mossed with age
      And high top bald with dry antiquity,
105   A wretched, ragged man, o'ergrown with hair,
      Lay sleeping on his back. About his neck
      A green and gilded snake had wreathed itself,
      Who with her head, nimble in threats, approached
      The opening of his mouth. But suddenly
110   Seeing Orlando, it unlinked° itself,   uncoiled
      And with indented° glides did slip away   undulating
      Into a bush, under which bush's shade
      A lioness, with udders all drawn dry,[7]
      Lay couching, head on ground, with catlike watch
115   When that° the sleeping man should stir. For 'tis   In readiness for when
      The royal disposition of that beast
      To prey on nothing that doth seem as dead.
      This seen, Orlando did approach the man
      And found it was his brother, his elder brother.
120   CELIA   O, I have heard him speak of that same brother,
      And he did render him the most unnatural

---

7. Having been nursed dry, the lion would be ferociously hungry.

That lived amongst men.
OLIVER   And well he might so do,
For well I know he was unnatural.
ROSALIND   But to Orlando. Did he leave him there,
125   Food to the sucked and hungry lioness?
OLIVER   Twice did he turn his back, and purposed so.
But kindness, nobler ever than revenge,
And nature, stronger than his just occasion,°   *fair opportunity*
Made him give battle to the lioness.
130   Who quickly fell before him; in which hurtling°   *conflict*
From miserable slumber I awaked.
CELIA   Are you his brother?
ROSALIND   Was't you he rescued?
CELIA   Was't you that did so oft contrive° to kill him?   *plot*
OLIVER   'Twas I, but 'tis not I. I do not shame
135   To tell you what I was, since my conversion
So sweetly tastes, being the thing I am.
ROSALIND   But for° the bloody napkin?   *What about*
OLIVER   By and by.
When from the first to last betwixt us two
Tears our recountments° had most kindly bathed—   *narratives*
140   As how I came into that desert place—
I' brief, he led me to the gentle Duke,
Who gave me fresh array, and entertainment,°   *hospitality*
Committing me unto my brother's love,
Who led me instantly unto his cave,
145   There stripped himself, and here upon his arm
The lioness had torn some flesh away,
Which all this while had bled. And now he fainted,
And cried in fainting upon Rosalind.
Brief, I recovered° him, bound up his wound,   *revived*
150   And after some small space, being strong at heart,
He sent me hither, stranger as I am,
To tell this story, that you might excuse
His broken promise, and to give this napkin,
Dyed in his blood, unto the shepherd youth
155   That he in sport doth call his Rosalind.
          [ROSALIND *faints*]
CELIA   Why, how now, Ganymede, sweet Ganymede!
OLIVER   Many will swoon when they do look on blood.
CELIA   There is more in it. Cousin Ganymede!
OLIVER   Look, he recovers.
160   ROSALIND   I would I were at home.
CELIA   We'll lead you thither.
          [*To* OLIVER] I pray you, will you take him by the arm?
OLIVER   Be of good cheer, youth. You a man? You lack a man's
heart.
165   ROSALIND   I do so, I confess it. Ah, sirrah, a body would think
this was well counterfeited. I pray you, tell your brother how
well I counterfeited. Heigh-ho!
OLIVER   This was not counterfeit. There is too great testimony in
your complexion that it was a passion of earnest.°   *a genuine fit*
170   ROSALIND   Counterfeit, I assure you.
OLIVER   Well then, take a good heart, and counterfeit to be a
man.

ROSALIND   So I do; but, i'faith, I should have been a woman by
right.

175   CELIA   Come, you look paler and paler. Pray you, draw home-
wards. Good sir, go with us.

OLIVER   That will I, for I must bear answer back
How you excuse my brother, Rosalind.

ROSALIND   I shall devise something. But I pray you commend

180   my counterfeiting to him. Will you go?   *Exeunt*

5.1

Enter [TOUCHSTONE *the*] *clown and* AUDREY

TOUCHSTONE   We shall find a time, Audrey. Patience, gentle
Audrey.

AUDREY   Faith, the priest was good enough, for all the old gentleman's° saying.   (Jaques's)

5   TOUCHSTONE   A most wicked Sir Oliver, Audrey, a most vile
Martext. But, Audrey, there is a youth here in the forest lays
claim to you.

AUDREY   Ay, I know who 'tis. He hath no interest in me° in the   no right to me
world. Here comes the man you mean.

Enter WILLIAM

10   TOUCHSTONE   It is meat and drink to me to see a clown.° By my   peasant; yokel
troth, we that have good wits have much to answer for. We
shall be flouting; we cannot hold.°   refrain

WILLIAM   Good ev'n, Audrey.

AUDREY   God ye° good ev'n, William.   God give you

15   WILLIAM [*to* TOUCHSTONE]   And good ev'n to you, sir.

TOUCHSTONE   Good ev'n, gentle friend. Cover thy head,[1] cover
thy head. Nay, prithee, be covered. How old are you, friend?

WILLIAM   Five-and-twenty, sir.

TOUCHSTONE   A ripe age. Is thy name William?

20   WILLIAM   William, sir.

TOUCHSTONE   A fair name. Wast born i'th' forest here?

WILLIAM   Ay, sir, I thank God.

TOUCHSTONE   Thank God—a good answer. Art rich?

WILLIAM   Faith, sir, so-so.

25   TOUCHSTONE   So-so is good, very good, very excellent good. And
yet it is not, it is but so-so. Art thou wise?

WILLIAM   Ay, sir, I have a pretty wit.

TOUCHSTONE   Why, thou sayst well. I do now remember a saying: 'The fool doth think he is wise, but the wise man knows

30   himself to be a fool.' The heathen philosopher, when he had a
desire to eat a grape, would open his lips when he put it into
his mouth, meaning thereby that grapes were made to eat, and
lips to open.[2] You do love this maid?

WILLIAM   I do, sir.

35   TOUCHSTONE   Give me your hand. Art thou learned?

WILLIAM   No, sir.

TOUCHSTONE   Then learn this of me: to have is to have. For it is
a figure in rhetoric° that drink, being poured out of a cup into   rhetorical commonplace
a glass, by filling the one doth empty the other. For all your

---

5.1
1. Evidently William has taken off his hat in a gesture
of deference.

2. Touchstone's speech may be a response to William's
gaping mouth.

40 writers do consent that *ipse* is he.[3] Now you are not *ipse*, for I
am he.

WILLIAM   Which he, sir?

TOUCHSTONE   He, sir, that must marry this woman. Therefore,
you clown, abandon—which is in the vulgar, leave—the soci-
45 ety—which in the boorish is company—of this female—which
in the common is woman; which together is, abandon the society of this female, or, clown, thou perishest; or, to thy better
understanding, diest; or, to wit, I kill thee, make thee away,
translate thy life into death, thy liberty into bondage. I will deal
50 in poison with thee, or in bastinado,° or in steel. I will bandy   *beating with a club*
with thee in faction, I will o'errun thee with policy.[4] I will kill
thee a hundred and fifty ways. Therefore tremble, and depart.

AUDREY   Do, good William.

WILLIAM   God rest you merry, sir.   *Exit*

Enter CORIN

55 CORIN   Our master and mistress seeks you. Come, away, away.

TOUCHSTONE   Trip, Audrey, trip, Audrey. [*To* CORIN] I attend, I
attend.   *Exeunt*

5.2

Enter ORLANDO *and* OLIVER

ORLANDO   Is't possible that on so little acquaintance you should
like her? That but seeing, you should love her? And loving,
woo? And wooing, she should grant? And will you persevere to
enjoy her?

5 OLIVER   Neither call the giddiness° of it in question, the poverty   *foolish haste*
of her, the small acquaintance, my sudden wooing, nor her
sudden consenting; but say with me 'I love Aliena'; say with
her, that she loves me; consent with both that we may enjoy
each other. It shall be to your good, for my father's house and
10 all the revenue that was old Sir Rowland's will I estate° upon   *settle*
you, and here live and die a shepherd.

Enter ROSALIND [*as Ganymede*]

ORLANDO   You have my consent. Let your wedding be tomorrow.
Thither will I invite the Duke and all's contented followers. Go
you, and prepare Aliena; for look you, here comes my Rosalind.

15 ROSALIND   God save you, brother.

OLIVER   And you, fair sister.   [*Exit*]

ROSALIND   O, my dear Orlando, how it grieves me to see thee
wear thy heart in a scarf.°   *sling*

ORLANDO   It is my arm.

20 ROSALIND   I thought thy heart had been wounded with the claws
of a lion.

ORLANDO   Wounded it is, but with the eyes of a lady.

ROSALIND   Did your brother tell you how I counterfeited to
swoon when he showed me your handkerchief?

25 ORLANDO   Ay, and greater wonders than that.

ROSALIND   O, I know where you are. Nay, 'tis true. There was
never anything so sudden but the fight of two rams, and Cae-

3. For all authorities agree that *ipse* is translated as "he
himself." The Latin word was proverbially applied to
successful lovers.

4. I will contend ("bandy") with you in argument, I will
overwhelm you with craftiness.
5.2

sar's thrasonical° brag of 'I came, saw, and overcame',[1] for your   *boastful*
brother and my sister no sooner met but they looked; no sooner
30   looked but they loved; no sooner loved but they sighed; no
sooner sighed but they asked one another the reason; no sooner
knew the reason but they sought the remedy; and in these
degrees have they made a pair° of stairs to marriage, which they   *flight*
will climb incontinent,° or else be incontinent[2] before mar-   *hastily*
35   riage. They are in the very wrath of love,° and they will together.   *heat of passion*
Clubs cannot part them.

ORLANDO   They shall be married tomorrow, and I will bid the
Duke to the nuptial. But O, how bitter a thing it is to look into
happiness through another man's eyes. By so much the more
40   shall I tomorrow be at the height of heart-heaviness by how
much I shall think my brother happy in having what he wishes
for.

ROSALIND   Why, then, tomorrow I cannot serve your turn[3] for
Rosalind?

45   ORLANDO   I can live no longer by thinking.

ROSALIND   I will weary you then no longer with idle talking.
Know of me then—for now I speak to some purpose—that I
know you are a gentleman of good conceit.° I speak not this   *understanding*
that you should bear a good opinion of my knowledge, inso-
50   much° I say I know you are; neither do I labour for a greater   *inasmuch as*
esteem than may in some little measure draw a belief from you
to do yourself good,[4] and not to grace me. Believe then, if you
please, that I can do strange things. I have since I was three
year old conversed° with a magician, most profound in his art,   *associated*
55   and yet not damnable.[5] If you do love Rosalind so near the
heart as your gesture° cries it out, when your brother marries   *behavior*
Aliena shall you marry her. I know into what straits of fortune
she is driven, and it is not impossible to me, if it appear not
inconvenient to you, to set her before your eyes tomorrow,
60   human as she is, and without any danger.

ORLANDO   Speakest thou in sober meanings?

ROSALIND   By my life, I do, which I tender° dearly, though I say   *value*
I am a magician. Therefore put you in your best array, bid°   *invite*
your friends: for if you will be married tomorrow, you shall;
65   and to Rosalind if you will.

          Enter SILVIUS *and* PHOEBE

Look, here comes a lover of mine and a lover of hers.

PHOEBE [*to* ROSALIND]   Youth, you have done me much ungentleness,°   *discourtesy*
To show the letter that I writ to you.

ROSALIND   I care not if I have. It is my study
70   To seem despiteful° and ungentle to you.   *contemptuous*
You are there followed by a faithful shepherd.
Look upon him; love him. He worships you.

PHOEBE [*to* SILVIUS]   Good shepherd, tell this youth what 'tis to love.

SILVIUS   It is to be all made of sighs and tears,
75   And so am I for Phoebe.

---

1. Caesar's well-known announcement of military victory, quoted as it appears in Thomas North's translation of Plutarch's *Lives* (1579).
2. Be sexually unrestrained.
3. Substitute for Rosalind; satisfy you sexually in Rosalind's place.

4. *neither . . . good:* nor am I attempting to enhance my reputation more than is necessary to persuade you to do yourself some good.
5. That is, not meriting execution for heresy. Elizabethan statutes made certain forms of witchcraft and black magic punishable by death.

PHOEBE   And I for Ganymede.

ORLANDO   And I for Rosalind.

ROSALIND   And I for no woman.

SILVIUS   It is to be all made of faith and service,

80   And so am I for Phoebe.

PHOEBE   And I for Ganymede.

ORLANDO   And I for Rosalind.

ROSALIND   And I for no woman.

SILVIUS   It is to be all made of fantasy,

85   All made of passion, and all made of wishes,
     All adoration, duty, and observance,   *devotion*
     All humbleness, all patience and impatience,
     All purity, all trial, all obedience,
     And so am I for Phoebe.

90   PHOEBE   And so am I for Ganymede.

ORLANDO   And so am I for Rosalind.

ROSALIND   And so am I for no woman.

PHOEBE   [*to* ROSALIND]   If this be so, why blame you me to love
     you?

95   SILVIUS   [*to* PHOEBE]   If this be so, why blame you me to love
     you?

ORLANDO   If this be so, why blame you me to love you?

ROSALIND   Why do you speak too, 'Why blame you me to love
     you?'

100   ORLANDO   To her that is not here nor doth not hear.

ROSALIND   Pray you, no more of this, 'tis like the howling of Irish
     wolves against the moon.[6]   [*To* SILVIUS] I will help you if I can.
     [*To* PHOEBE] I would love you if I could.—Tomorrow meet
     me all together. [*To* PHOEBE] I will marry you if ever I
105   marry woman, and I'll be married tomorrow. [*To* ORLANDO] I
     will satisfy you if ever I satisfy man, and you shall be married
     tomorrow. [*To* SILVIUS] I will content you if what pleases you
     contents you, and you shall be married tomorrow. [*To*
     ORLANDO] As you love Rosalind, meet. [*To* SILVIUS] As you
110   love Phoebe, meet. And as I love no woman, I'll meet. So fare
     you well. I have left you commands.

SILVIUS   I'll not fail, if I live.

PHOEBE   Nor I.

ORLANDO   Nor I.   *Exeunt* [*severally*]

5.3

Enter [TOUCHSTONE *the*] *clown and* AUDREY

TOUCHSTONE   Tomorrow is the joyful day, Audrey, tomorrow
     will we be married.

AUDREY   I do desire it with all my heart; and I hope it is no
     dishonest° desire to desire to be a woman of the world.° Here   *unchaste / married*
5   come two of the banished Duke's pages.

Enter two PAGES

FIRST PAGE   Well met, honest gentleman.

TOUCHSTONE   By my troth, well met. Come, sit, sit, and a song.

---

6. That is, it is barbaric. The howling of wolves at the moon was a proverbial way of referring to an irrational or futile course of action. Irish wolves might be perceived as especially disorderly, for Ireland's abundance of wolves was for many Elizabethan writers a mark of that country's lack of civility.
5.3

SECOND PAGE   We are for you.° Sit i'th' middle.   *That suits us*

FIRST PAGE   Shall we clap into't roundly, without hawking¹, or

10   spitting, or saying we are hoarse, which are the only° prologues   *proper*
       to a bad voice?

SECOND PAGE   I'faith, i'faith, and both in a tune,° like two gipsies   *in unison*
       on a horse.

BOTH PAGES [*sing*]²   It was a lover and his lass,

15   With a hey, and a ho, and a hey-nonny-no,
           That o'er the green cornfield° did pass   *field of wheat*
               In spring-time, the only pretty ring-time,°   *time for weddings*
           When birds do sing, hey ding-a-ding ding,
           Sweet lovers love the spring.

20   Between the acres of the rye,
               With a hey, and a ho, and a hey-nonny-no,
           These pretty country folks would lie,
               In spring-time, the only pretty ring-time,
           When birds do sing, hey ding-a-ding ding,
25   Sweet lovers love the spring.

           This carol they began that hour,
               With a hey, and a ho, and a hey-nonny-no,
           How that a life was but a flower,
               In spring-time, the only pretty ring-time,
30   When birds do sing, hey ding-a-ding ding,
           Sweet lovers love the spring.

           And therefore take° the present time,   *seize*
               With a hey, and a ho, and a hey-nonny-no,
           For love is crownèd with the prime,°   *spring; perfection*
35   In spring time, the only pretty ring-time,
           When birds do sing, hey ding-a-ding ding,
           Sweet lovers love the spring.

TOUCHSTONE   Truly, young gentlemen, though there was no
       great matter° in the ditty, yet the note³ was very untunable.   *sense*

40 FIRST PAGE   You are deceived, sir, we kept time, we lost not our
       time.

TOUCHSTONE   By my troth, yes, I count it but time lost to hear
       such a foolish song. God b'wi'you, and God mend your voices.
       Come, Audrey.   *Exeunt* [*severally*]

5.4

       Enter DUKE SENIOR, AMIENS, JAQUES, ORLANDO, OLIVER,
       [*and*] CELIA [*as Aliena*]

DUKE SENIOR   Dost thou believe, Orlando, that the boy
       Can do all this that he hath promisèd?

ORLANDO   I sometimes do believe, and sometimes do not,
       As those that fear they hope,¹ and know they fear.

           Enter ROSALIND [*as Ganymede*], [*with*] SILVIUS *and*
           PHOEBE

---

1. Shall we begin energetically and at once, without clearing our throats?
2. F does not include this speech prefix, simply the world "song." This is one of the few Shakespeare songs for which contemporary music survives. It is set for a single voice with lute accompaniment in Thomas Morley's *First Booke of Ayres* (1600).
3. Yet the music was disagreeable.

5.4
1. Fear that their hope will not be fulfilled.

5   ROSALIND   Patience once more, whiles our compact is urged.°   declared
     [*To the* DUKE] You say if I bring in your Rosalind
     You will bestow her on Orlando here?
     DUKE SENIOR   That would I, had I° kingdoms to give with her.   even if I had
     ROSALIND [*to* ORLANDO]   And you say you will have her when I
          bring her?
10   ORLANDO   That would I, were I of all kingdoms king.
     ROSALIND [*to* PHOEBE]   You say you'll marry me if I be willing?
     PHOEBE   That will I, should I die the hour 'after.
     ROSALIND   But if you do refuse to marry me
     You'll give yourself to this most faithful shepherd?
15   PHOEBE   So is the bargain.
     ROSALIND [*to* SILVIUS]   You say that you'll have Phoebe if she will.
     SILVIUS   Though to have her and death were both one thing.
     ROSALIND   I have promised to make all this matter even.°   smooth
     Keep you your word, O Duke, to give your daughter.
20   You yours, Orlando, to receive his daughter.
     Keep your word, Phoebe, that you'll marry me,
     Or else refusing me to wed this shepherd.
     Keep your word, Silvius, that you'll marry her
     If she refuse me; and from hence I go
25   To make these doubts all even.   *Exeunt* ROSALIND *and* CELIA
     DUKE SENIOR   I do remember in this shepherd boy
     Some lively° touches of my daughter's favour.°   vivid / appearance
     ORLANDO   My lord, the first time that I ever saw him,
     Methought he was a brother to your daughter.
30   But, my good lord, this boy is forest-born,
     And hath been tutored in the rudiments
     Of many desperate° studies by his uncle,   dangerous
     Whom he reports to be a great magician
     Obscurèd in the circle of this forest.²
          Enter [TOUCHSTONE *the*] *clown and* AUDREY
35   JAQUES   There is sure another flood toward,° and these couples   at hand
     are coming to the ark.³ Here comes a pair of very strange
     beasts, which in all tongues are called fools.
     TOUCHSTONE   Salutation and greeting to you all.
     JAQUES [*to the* DUKE]   Good my lord, bid him welcome. This is
40   the motley-minded° gentleman that I have so often met in the   foolish-brained
     forest. He hath been a courtier, he swears.
     TOUCHSTONE   If any man doubt that, let him put me to my pur-
     gation.⁴ I have trod a measure,° I have flattered a lady, I have   danced
     been politic with my friend, smooth with mine enemy, I have
45   undone° three tailors, I have had four quarrels, and like to have   made bankrupt
     fought° one.   came close to fighting
     JAQUES   And how was that ta'en up?°   settled
     TOUCHSTONE   Faith, we met, and found the quarrel was upon
     the seventh cause.
50   JAQUES   How, seventh cause?—Good my lord, like this fellow.
     DUKE SENIOR   I like him very well.
     TOUCHSTONE   God'ield you, sir, I desire you of the like. I press

---

2. Concealed within the boundaries of this forest. Perhaps a reference to the magic circle within which magi-
cians were supposed to be able to practice their art safely.
3. Alluding to a biblical account in Genesis 7:2 in

which pairs of male and female animals shelter on
Noah's ark to escape the flood that covers the earth.
4. Let me be put to trial to clear myself (of the charge
of lying).

in here, sir, amongst the rest of the country copulatives,[5] to
swear, and to forswear, according as marriage binds and blood
55 breaks.° A poor virgin, sir, an ill-favoured thing, sir, but mine   *passion rebels*
own. A poor humour° of mine, sir, to take that that no man else   *whim*
will. Rich honesty° dwells like a miser, sir, in a poor house, as   *chastity*
your pearl in your foul oyster.

DUKE SENIOR   By my faith, he is very swift and sententious.°   *witty and wise*
60 TOUCHSTONE   According to the fool's bolt,[6] sir, and such dulcet
diseases.°   *sweet afflictions*

JAQUES   But for the seventh cause. How did you find the quarrel on the seventh cause?

TOUCHSTONE   Upon a lie seven times removed.—Bear your body
65 more seeming,° Audrey.—As thus, sir: I did dislike[7] the cut of   *becomingly*
a certain courtier's beard. He sent me word if I said his beard
was not cut well, he was in the mind it was. This is called the
Retort Courteous. If I sent him word again it was not well cut,
he would send me word he cut it to please himself. This is
70 called the Quip Modest. If again it was not well cut, he disa-
bled° my judgement. This is called the Reply Churlish. If again   *disparaged*
it was not well cut, he would answer I spake not true. This is
called the Reproof Valiant. If again it was not well cut, he
would say I lie. This is called the Countercheck° Quarrelsome.   *rebuff*
75 And so to the Lie Circumstantial,° and the Lie Direct.   *indirect*

JAQUES   And how oft did you say his beard was not well cut?

TOUCHSTONE   I durst go no further than the Lie Circumstantial,
nor he durst not give me the Lie Direct; and so we measured
swords,[8] and parted.

80 JAQUES   Can you nominate° in order now the degrees of the lie?   *name*

TOUCHSTONE   O sir, we quarrel in print, by the book,[9] as you
have books for good manners.[1] I will name you the degrees.
The first, the Retort Courteous; the second, the Quip Modest;
the third, the Reply Churlish; the fourth, the Reproof Valiant;
85 the fifth, the Countercheck Quarrelsome; the sixth, the Lie
with Circumstance; the seventh, the Lie Direct. All these you
may avoid but the Lie Direct; and you may avoid that, too, with
an 'if'. I knew when seven justices could not take up° a quarrel,   *settle*
but when the parties were met themselves, one of them
90 thought but of an 'if', as 'If you said so, then I said so', and they
shook hands and swore brothers.° Your 'if' is the only peace   *became sworn brothers*
maker; much virtue in 'if'.

JAQUES [*to the* DUKE]   Is not this a rare fellow, my lord? He's as
good at anything, and yet a fool.

95 DUKE SENIOR   He uses his folly like a stalking-horse,[2] and under
the presentation° of that he shoots his wit.   *appearance*

   Still° music. Enter HYMEN[3] [*with*] ROSALIND *and* CELIA   *Soft*
   [*as themselves*]

HYMEN   Then is there mirth in heaven

---

5. People about to copulate.
6. And his wittiness quickly disappears. Alluding to the
proverb "A fool's bolt (or arrow) is soon shot."
7. Show my dislike of.
8. Checked that our swords were of the same length
(as was usual prior to a duel).
9. According to the rules as set down in books on the
etiquette of dueling. Touchstone's speech exposes the
absurd aspects of the elaborate codes of behavior set

forth in such books.
1. Elizabethan England witnessed an outpouring of
courtesy literature aimed at both social aspirants and
established courtiers.
2. A real or imitation horse used as a means of camou-
flage in hunting.
3. The god of marriage in classical mythology, conventionally depicted as a young man who carried a veil and
a bridal torch.

When earthly things made even°   *set right*
Atone° together.   *Are at one; unite*
100   Good Duke, receive thy daughter;
Hymen from heaven brought her,
     Yea, brought her hither,
That thou mightst join her hand with his
Whose heart within his bosom is.
105 ROSALIND [*to the* DUKE]   To you I give myself, for I am yours.
    [*To* ORLANDO] To you I give myself, for I am yours.
    DUKE SENIOR   If there be truth in sight, you are my daughter.
    ORLANDO   If there be truth in sight, you are my Rosalind.
    PHOEBE   If sight and shape be true,
110   Why then, my love adieu!
    ROSALIND [*to the* DUKE]   I'll have no father if you be not he.
    [*To* ORLANDO]   I'll have no husband if you be not he,
    [*To* PHOEBE]   Nor ne'er wed woman if you be not she.
    HYMEN   Peace, ho, I bar° confusion   *forbid*
115   'Tis I must make conclusion
      Of these most strange events.
Here's eight that must take hands
To join in Hymen's bands,°   *bonds of marriage*
     If truth holds true contents.⁴
    [*To* ORLANDO *and* ROSALIND]
120   You and you no cross° shall part.   *adversity*
    [*To* OLIVER *and* CELIA]
     You and you are heart in heart.
    [*To* PHOEBE]
     You to his love must accord.°   *consent*
     Or have a woman to° your lord.   *as*
    [*To* TOUCHSTONE *and* AUDREY]
     You and you are sure together°   *tightly bound*
125   As the winter to foul weather.—
Whiles a wedlock hymn we sing,
Feed° yourselves with questioning,   *Satisfy*
That reason wonder may diminish
How thus we met, and these things finish.

                 Song
130   Wedding is great Juno's° crown,   *goddess of marriage*
      O blessèd bond of board and bed.
'Tis Hymen peoples every town.
      High° wedlock then be honourèd.   *Solemn*
Honour, high honour and renown
135   To Hymen, god of every town.
    DUKE SENIOR [*to* CELIA]   O my dear niece, welcome thou art to me,
Even daughter; welcome in no less degree.⁵
    PHOEBE [*to* SILVIUS]   I will not eat my word. Now thou art mine,
Thy faith my fancy° to thee doth combine.   *love*
      Enter [JAQUES DE BOIS, *the*] *second brother*
140 JAQUES DE BOIS   Let me have audience for a word or two.
I am the second son of old Sir Rowland,

---

4. If truth is true; if truth please you.   5. You are no less welcome than a daughter.

That bring these tidings to this fair assembly.
Duke Frederick, hearing how that every day
Men of great worth resorted to this forest,
145   Addressed a mighty power,° which were on foot,   *army*
In his own conduct,° purposely to take   *Under his command*
His brother here, and put him to the sword.
And to the skirts° of this wild wood he came   *outskirts*
Where, meeting with an old religious man,
150   After some question° with him was converted   *conversation*
Both from his enterprise and from the world,
His crown bequeathing to his banished brother,
And all their lands restored to them again
That were with him exiled. This to be true
I do engage° my life.   *pledge*
155   DUKE SENIOR   Welcome, young man.
Thou offer'st fairly° to thy brothers' wedding: *You bring fine gifts*
To one° his lands withheld, and to the other°   *(Oliver) / (Orlando)*
A land itself at large,[6] a potent° dukedom.   *powerful*
First, in this forest let us do° those ends   *accomplish*
160   That here were well begun, and well begot.°   *conceived*
And after, every° of this happy number   *every one*
That have endured shrewd° days and nights with us   *evil*
Shall share the good of our returnèd fortune
According to the measure of their states.°   *ranks*
165   Meantime, forget this new-fallen° dignity   *newly acquired*
And fall into our rustic revelry.
Play, music, and you brides and bridegrooms all,
With measure heaped in joy to th' measures fall.[7]
JAQUES   Sir, by your patience.° [*To* JAQUES DE BOIS] If I heard   *with your permission*
      you rightly
170   The Duke hath put on a religious life
And thrown into neglect the pompous° court.   *ceremonious*
JAQUES DE BOIS   He hath.
JAQUES   To him will I. Out of these convertites°   *converts*
There is much matter to be heard and learned.
[*To the* DUKE]
175   You to your former honour I bequeath;
Your patience and your virtue well deserves it.
[*To* ORLANDO]
You to a love that your true faith doth merit;
[*To* OLIVER]
You to your land, and love, and great allies;°   *relatives*
[*To* SILVIUS]
You to a long and well-deservèd bed;
[*To* TOUCHSTONE]
180   And you to wrangling, for thy loving voyage
Is but for two months victualled.°—So, to your pleasures;   *supplied with food*
I am for other than for dancing measures.
DUKE SENIOR   Stay, Jaques, stay.
JAQUES   To see no pastime, I. What you would have°   *like (from me)*
185   I'll stay to know at your abandoned cave.   *Exit*

---

6. An entire country. As Rosalind's husband, Orlando is heir to the dukedom returned to Duke Senior.

7. With a measure of overflowing joy, begin your dances ("measures").

DUKE SENIOR   Proceed, proceed. We'll so begin these rites
    As we do trust they'll end, in true delights.
        [*They dance; then*] *exeunt* [*all but* ROSALIND]⁸

[Epilogue]

ROSALIND [*to the audience*]   It is not the fashion to see the lady
    the epilogue;¹ but it is no more unhandsome than to see the
    lord the prologue. If it be true that good wine needs no bush,²
    'tis true that a good play needs no epilogue. Yet to good wine
5 they do use good bushes, and good plays prove the better by
    the help of good epilogues. What a case° am I in then, that am   *plight; costume*
    neither a good epilogue nor cannot insinuate° with you in the   *ingratiate myself*
    behalf of a good play! I am not furnished like a beggar, there-
    fore to beg will not become me. My way is to conjure° you;   *charge; bewitch*
10 and I'll begin with the women. I charge you, O women, for the
    love you bear to men, to like as much of this play as please you.
    And I charge you, O men, for the love you bear to women—as
    I perceive by your simpering none of you hates them—that
    between you and the women the play° may please. If I were a   *drama; love play*
15 woman³ I would kiss as many of you as had beards that pleased
    me, complexions that liked° me, and breaths that I defied° not.   *pleased / disdained*
    And I am sure, as many as have good beards, or good faces, or
    sweet breaths will for my kind offer, when I make curtsy, bid
    me farewell.°   *Exit*   *(with applause)*

---

8. F indicates only a single exit for Duke Senior, but
most editors assume that Rosalind remains alone
onstage to deliver the Epilogue.
Epilogue
1. In the vast majority of Elizabethan plays, the Epilogue is spoken by a male character.

2. Advertisement. A proverb derived from the practice
of hanging a branch of ivy in tavern windows to indicate
that wine was for sale.
3. A pointed reference to the fact that women's roles in
the Elizabethan theater were played by boys.

Twelfth Night

Shakespeare's contemporary Thomas Coryat wrote that he witnessed something quite remarkable when he went to the theater in Venice: "I saw women act, a thing that I never saw before." That an Englishman had to travel abroad to see women actors for the first time is not surprising. All the great women's roles in Elizabethan and Jacobean plays were written to be performed by trained adolescent boys, and boys played the female parts as well in all grammar school and university productions. But what struck Coryat in Venice was neither the gratifying naturalness of finally seeing women play women's parts nor the comparative inadequacy of English boy actors. Rather, he was impressed that the women actors managed to hold their own in representing the female sex: "They performed it," he writes, "with as good a grace, as ever I saw any masculine Actor."

Recent scholars have observed that there were in fact occasions in which audiences in England could have seen women performing: troupes from abroad, including women actors, occasionally toured England, and English women performed in the theatrical spectacles known as masques and in other entertainments. But in England, women did not perform on the public stage (the word "actress" had not yet entered the English language), and the remarks of Coryat and others suggest that their absence was rarely if ever lamented. The boy actors were evidently extraordinarily skillful, and the audiences were sufficiently immersed in the conventions both of theater and of social life in general to accept gesture, makeup, and above all dress as a convincing representation of femininity.

Twelfth Night, or What You Will, written for Shakespeare's all-male company, plays brilliantly with these conventions. The comedy depends on an actor's ability to transform himself, through costume, voice, and gesture, into a young noblewoman, Viola, who transforms herself, through costume, voice, and gesture, into a young man, Cesario. The play's delicious complications follow from the emotional crosscurrents that Viola's transformation engenders. Shipwrecked on a strange coast and bereft of her twin brother, the disguised Viola finds a place in the service of the powerful Duke Orsino, with whom she promptly falls in love. Orsino is in love with Lady Olivia, a wealthy aristocrat whose household includes, among its servants and dependents, a steward or house manager, a waiting-gentlewoman, a professional entertainer, and a down-at-the-heels, perpetually drunken uncle. When Orsino sends Cesario to help him woo the proud Olivia, Olivia not only rejects the Duke's suit but falls in love with his messenger. Discomfited to learn that she is the object of Olivia's love, Viola reflects on the plot's impassioned triangle:

> My master loves her dearly,
> And I, poor monster, fond as much on him,
> And she, mistaken, seems to dote on me.
> What will become of this?
>
> (2.2.31–34)

"Poor monster": in *Twelfth Night,* clothes do not simply reveal or disguise identity; they partly constitute identity—or so Viola playfully imagines—making her a strange, hybrid creature. To be sure, she understands perfectly well the narrow biological definition of her sex (though in the characteristically male-centered language of Shakespeare's culture, she phrases that definition in terms of what she "lacks" [3.4.269]). Yet there is something almost magical in this play about costume, so that even at the close, when identities have been sorted out and the couples happily matched, Orsino cannot bring himself to call his bride-to-be by her rightful name or to address her as a woman:

> Cesario, come—
> For so you shall be while you are a man;
> But when in other habits you are seen,
> Orsino's mistress, and his fancy's queen.
> (5.1.372–75)

It would have been simple for Shakespeare to devise a concluding scene in which Viola appears in women's "habits," but he goes out of his way to leave her in men's clothes and hence to disrupt with a delicate comic touch the return to the "normal." The transforming power of costume unsettles fixed categories of gender and social class, and allows characters to explore emotional territory that a culture officially hostile to same-sex desire and cross-class marriage would ordinarily have ruled out of bounds. In *Twelfth Night*, conventional expectations repeatedly give way to a different way of perceiving the world.

Shakespeare wrote *Twelfth Night* around 1601. He had already written such comedies as *A Midsummer Night's Dream, Much Ado About Nothing,* and *As You Like It,* with their playful, subtly ironic investigations of the ways in which heterosexual couples are produced out of the murkier crosscurrents of male and female friendships; as interesting, perhaps, he had probably just recently completed *Hamlet,* with its unprecedented exploration of mourning, betrayal, antic humor, and tragic isolation. *Twelfth Night* would prove to be, in the view of many critics, both the most perfect and in some sense the last of the great festive comedies. Shakespeare returned to comedy later in his career, but always with more insistent overtones of bitterness, loss, and grief. There are dark notes in *Twelfth Night* as well: Olivia is in mourning for her brother, Viola thinks that her brother, too, is dead, Antonio believes that he has been betrayed by the man he loves, Orsino threatens to kill Cesario. Desire is repeatedly linked to frustration and loss. But these notes are swept up in the current of sweet music that pervades the play, and the characters are all drawn into a giddy, carnivalesque dance of illusion, disguise, folly, and clowning.

The play's subtitle, *What You Will,* underscores the celebratory spirit associated with Twelfth Night, the Feast of the Epiphany (January 6), which in Elizabethan England marked the culminating night of the traditional Christmas revels. On Twelfth Night 1601, the queen's guest of honor was a twenty-eight-year-old Italian nobleman, Don Virginio Orsino, Duke of Bracciano. Orsino wrote to his wife that he was entertained that night with "a mingled comedy, with pieces of music and dances." Since the company that performed was the Lord Chamberlain's Men—Shakespeare's company—it has been argued that the comedy was *Twelfth Night,* but there is no scholarly consensus on this hypothesis. The title, in any case, would for Shakespeare's contemporaries have conjured up a whole series of time-honored festivities associated with the midwinter season. A rigidly hierarchical social order that ordinarily demanded deference, sobriety, and strict obedience to authority temporarily gave way to raucous rituals of inversion: young boys were crowned for a day as bishops and carried through the streets in mock religious processions; abstemiousness was toppled by bouts of heavy drinking and feasting; the spirit of parody, folly, and misrule reigned briefly in places normally reserved for stern-faced moralists and sober judges.

The fact that these festivities were associated with Christian holidays—the Epiphany marked the visit of the Three Kings to Bethlehem to worship the Christ child—did not altogether obscure the continuities with pagan winter rituals such as the Roman Saturnalia, with its comparably explosive release from everyday discipline into a disorderly realm of belly laughter and belly cheer. Puritans emphasized these continuities in launching a fierce attack on the Elizabethan festive calendar and its whole ethos, just as they attacked the theater for what they saw as its links with paganism, idleness, and sexual license. Elizabethan and Jacobean authorities in the church and the state had their own concerns about idleness and subversion, but they generally protected and patronized both festive ritual and theater on the grounds that these provided a valuable release from tensions that might otherwise prove dangerous. Sobriety, piety, and discipline were no doubt admirable virtues, but most human beings were not saints. "Dost thou think because thou art virtuous," the drunken Sir Toby asks the censorious steward Malvolio, "there shall be no more cakes and ale?" (2.3.103–04).

Fittingly, the earliest firm record of a performance of *Twelfth Night*, as noted in the diary of John Manningham, was "at our feast" in the Middle Temple (one of London's law schools) in February 1602. Manningham wrote observantly that the play was "much like the *Comedy of Errors*, or *Menaechmi* in Plautus, but most like and near to that in Italian called *Inganni*." That is, *Twelfth Night* resembles Shakespeare's own earlier play on identical twins (along with that play's Roman source) and still more resembles a series of sixteenth-century Italian comedies built around the intertwining themes of love, fraud (*inganno*), and mistaken identity. Several of these comedies feature the plot device of a female twin who takes service as a page with the man she loves. Closest of these to Shakespeare's comedy is *Gl'Ingannati* (The Deceived), written for performance at Carnival time in Siena in 1531 and translated into French in 1543. It seems likely that Shakespeare knew this play or one that derived from it, and may have picked up several details in addition to the overall plot line. But the tone of *Gl'Ingannati*, with its bawdy jokes about nuns and old men, its sly, sardonic servants, and its farcical intrigues, is far from *Twelfth Night*'s mingled melancholy and delight, its bittersweet play of divided and contradictory desires. Tellingly, in the Italian comedy, the heroine is all along plotting to win the love of the man she serves; she has disguised herself in order to dissuade him from wooing elsewhere. Viola's predicament—her attempt to serve Orsino even at the cost of her own deepest longings—represents a wholly different emotional register.

That predicament is not Shakespeare's invention; he found it, with many other elements of his plot, in an English story, Barnabe Riche's tale "Apollonius and Silla" in *Riche His Farewell to Militarie Profession* (1581), which was in turn based on French and Italian sources. Riche is too addicted to moralizing to explore his heroine's character with much subtlety, but he does underscore how painful it is for her to hide her feelings while acting as go-between, and hence he anticipates, if only woodenly, the mood that Shakespeare exquisitely captures in Viola's lines about one who "sat like patience on a monument, / Smiling at grief" (2.4.113–14). There is less precedent, in Riche or in any of the known sources, for the aspect of *Twelfth Night* that Manningham

Gentlemen drinking and smoking. From Phillip Stubbes, *The Anatomie of Abuses* (1583).

found particularly memorable and that has continued to delight audiences: the gulling of Malvolio.

Malvolio (*mal volio,* "ill will") is explicitly linked to those among Shakespeare's contemporaries most hostile to the theater and to such holidays as Twelfth Night: "Sometimes," says Lady Olivia's waiting-gentlewoman Maria, "he is a kind of puritan" (2.3.125). When we first see Malvolio, he is harshly critical of Feste the clown, who is attempting to win back Olivia's favor. "Unless you laugh and minister occasion to him," Malvolio sourly observes, "he is gagged" (1.5.74–75). Though ungenerous, the observation is canny, for comedy does seem to depend on a collaborative spirit from which Malvolio conspicuously excludes himself. He is a man without friends. More dangerously, he is a man in a socially dependent position with a gift for acquiring enemies, as he does when he tries to silence the noisy revelry of that classic carnivalesque threesome a drunkard, a blockhead, and a professional fool: Olivia's uncle Sir Toby, his boon companion Sir Andrew Aguecheek, and Feste.

Olivia remarks to Malvolio that he is "sick of self-love" (1.5.77), and it is this narcissism that his enemies exploit to undo him. When Malvolio finds Maria's forged letter, he is in the midst of a deliciously self-gratifying fantasy that he has married Olivia, a fantasy less of erotic bliss than of social domination. The dream of rising above his station fuels his credulous eagerness to interpret the letter according to his fondest wishes and to comply with its absurd suggestions for his festive dress and demeanor. This compliance, by making it seem to Olivia that he has gone mad, renders Malvolio vulnerable to a further humiliation. In a parody of the age's brutal "therapy" for insanity, he is clapped into a dark room and subjected to a mock exorcism. Finally, he suffers what is perhaps the cruelest punishment for someone who dreams that greatness will be thrust upon him: he is simply forgotten. When in the play's final moments he is released, Malvolio is in no mood to join in the general air of communal wonder and rejoicing. More alone than ever, he introduces into the comedy's resolution an extraordinary note of vindictive bitterness: "I'll be revenged on the whole pack of you!" (5.1.365). Shakespeare does not hide the cruelty of the treatment to which Malvolio has been subjected—"He hath been most notoriously abused" (5.1.366), says Olivia—nor does he shrink from showing the audience other disagreeable qualities in Sir Toby and his companions. But while the close of the comedy seems to embrace these failings in a tolerant, bemused, aristocratic recognition of human folly, it can find no place for Malvolio's blend of puritanism and social climbing.

Malvolio is scapegoated for indulging in a fantasy that colors several of the key relationships in *Twelfth Night:* the fantasy of winning the hand of one of the noble and enormously wealthy aristocrats who reign over the social world of the play. The beautiful heiress Olivia, mistress of a great house, is a glittering prize that lures not only Malvolio but also the foolish Sir Andrew and the elegant, imperious Duke Orsino. In falling in love with the Duke's graceful messenger (and, as she thinks she has done, in marrying him), Olivia seems to have made precisely the kind of match that had fueled Malvolio's social-climbing imagination. As it turns out, the match is not between unequals: "Be not amazed," the Duke tells her when she realizes that she has married someone she

Lutenist. By Jost Amman.

scarcely knows. "Right noble is his blood" (5.1.257). The social order, then, has not been overturned: as in a carnival, when the disguises are removed, the revelers resume their "proper," socially and sexually approved positions.

Yet there is something decidedly improper about the perverse erotic excitement that the play discovers in disguise, displacement, indirection, and deferral and something irreducibly strange about the marriages with which *Twelfth Night* ends. Sir Toby has married Maria as a reward for devising the plot against Malvolio. Olivia has entered into a "contract of eternal bond of love" (5.1.152) with someone whose actual identity is only revealed to her after the marriage ceremony. (In Riche's version of the story, she is pregnant and her marriage saves her from social disgrace, but Shakespeare omits this plot twist, thereby raising the tone but heightening the irrationality of the finale.) The strangeness of the bond between virtual strangers is matched by the strangeness of Orsino's instantaneous decision to marry Cesario—as soon as "he" can become Viola by changing into women's clothes. Only a few minutes earlier, in a fit of jealous rage at Olivia's love for Cesario, Orsino had threatened to kill "the lamb that I do love" (5.1.126); now he will wed that lamb.

The sudden transformation is prepared for in part by Orsino's passionate insistence that he loves the boy he intends to kill and in part by the earlier signs of intimacy between them: "I have," he tells Cesario, "unclasped / To thee the book even of my secret soul" (1.4.12–13). But this intimacy has been formed around Orsino's grand passion for Olivia, a passion that is reiterated through virtually the entire play. The revelation at the play's climax—"One face, one voice, one habit, and two persons" (5.1.208)—forces a realignment of all the relationships. With Sebastian married to Olivia, Viola becomes Olivia's "sister" (or, as we would say, sister-in-law); and by marrying Viola, Orsino likewise makes Olivia his "sweet sister" (5.1.371). Orsino then will continue in a sense to "love" Olivia but only through the bond of kinship formed by the linked twins: a strangely appropriate fate for someone who tried to woo by proxy!

That this solution does not seem entirely zany—that it seems a fit ending for a romantic comedy—depends on several key features in *Twelfth Night*'s emotional landscape. It is significant that Orsino's love for Olivia, though poetically intense, is detached from any direct personal encounter. Not only does her vow of a seven-year seclusion compel Orsino to delegate his passion to a messenger, this passion seems largely self-regarding and self-indulgent. His famous opening lines on the paradoxes of love—its close intertwining of fulfillment and decline, stealing and giving, freshness and decay—revolve around the contemplation less of the lady than of his own solitary, self-gratifying imagination: "So full of shapes is fancy / That it a one is high fantastical" (1.1.14–15). The play does not ridicule Orsino's aristocratic reveries, although they seem at moments like elegant versions of what is cruelly mocked in Malvolio, but it does invite the audience to treat them with a certain ironic detachment.

Orsino's love seems to circle all too readily back upon himself: he is fascinated by his role as melancholy lover. That self-absorption is not the only shape of passion is made clear by several contrasting figures of whom the most selfless is the sea captain Antonio, consumed with desire for his friend Sebastian. In a play full of coy allusions to same-sex desire, Antonio's "willing love" (3.3.11) is the most explicit representation of passion as absolute devotion, a willingness to sacrifice everything in the service of the beloved. The mistaken belief that this devotion has been callously betrayed is one of the play's most poignant moments, a moment perhaps only partially redeemed by the manifest relief and joy with which the newly wed Sebastian greets his friend in the last act.

Intense, intimate bonding between men is a recurrent theme in Shakespeare's culture. (A comparable interest in female friendship is reflected in the love between Hermia and Helena in *A Midsummer Night's Dream* and Rosalind and Celia in *As You Like It*.) Shakespeare explores the pleasures and perils of male friendship in such plays as *The Two Gentlemen of Verona*, *The Merchant of Venice*, and *Much Ado About Nothing* and, most famously, in the sonnets to the fair young man whom he calls "the master-mistress of my passion" (sonnet 20). Orsino expresses doubt that a woman can love with an intensity equal to a man's:

> There is no woman's sides
> Can bide the beating of so strong a passion
> As love doth give my heart; no woman's heart
> So big, to hold so much. They lack retention.
> (2.4.91–94)

It is perhaps this belief (which the play proves to be utterly wrong) that conditions the only authentic emotional bond that we see Orsino forge, the bond with his devoted young servant Cesario. In conversation with Cesario, the haughty Duke manages for a few moments at least to escape from his languid self-absorption and express interest in someone else's thoughts and feelings: "What dost thou know?"; "And what's her history?"; "But died thy sister of her love, my boy?" (2.4.103, 108, 118). These simple questions, modest in themselves, are sufficiently distinct from Orsino's usual manner of speech to signal both a curiosity and a responsiveness that he does not manifest with anyone else. Part of the quirky delight of the play's resolution is to give to the union between Orsino and Viola something of the intimacy that had only seemed possible between men.

This resolution depends principally on the remarkable qualities of the play's central character, Viola. Like Antonio, Viola is prepared to sacrifice herself for her beloved: "And I most jocund, apt, and willingly," she tells Orsino, "to do you rest a thousand deaths would die" (5.1.128–29). But where Antonio experiences passion as tragic compulsion—he speaks of Sebastian's beauty as "witchcraft" drawing him into danger—Viola's spirit, as her word "jocund" suggests, is extraordinarily resilient. No sooner does she sadly observe that her brother must have perished in the shipwreck than she remarks, "Perchance he is not drowned" (1.2.4); no sooner does she find herself isolated and unprotected than she determines to serve Lady Olivia, and then, learning that this route is blocked, she at once resolves to disguise herself as a man and serve Orsino instead. Here and throughout the play, Viola seems to draw on an inward principle of hope. That principle, along with an improvisational boldness, an eloquent tongue, and a keen wit, enables her to keep afloat in an increasingly mad swirl of misunderstandings and cross-purposes.

Those misunderstandings, of course, are largely her creation in the sense that they mainly derive from a disguise that confounds the distinction between male and female. "They shall yet belie thy happy years / That say thou art a man," Orsino says to Cesario (1.4.29–30). The description that follows seems to imagine that boys begin almost as girls and only subsequently become males:

> Diana's lip
> Is not more smooth and rubious; thy small pipe
> Is as the maiden's organ, shrill and sound,
> And all is semblative a woman's part.
> (1.4.30–33)

This perception of ambiguity, rooted in early modern ideas about sexuality and gender, is one of the elements that enabled a boy actor in this period convincingly to mime "a woman's part." According to an ancient anatomical tradition, still highly influential in Shakespeare's time, sexual difference is not absolute: males and females share a single physiological structure whose differentiation only occurs over time. Such a theory implies a prolonged period of indistinction upon which *Twelfth Night* continually plays, and that helps to account for the emotional tangle that the cross-dressed Viola inspires.

Having, in her role as intermediary, aroused Olivia's love, Viola does not see how to disabuse the enamored Countess without abandoning the disguise. For all her lively resolution, she is passive in the face of the complexities she has engendered, counting on time and chance to sort out what she cannot: "O time, thou must untangle this, not

I. / It is too hard a knot for me t'untie" (2.2.38–39). Perhaps this passivity, or more accurately this trust in time, is a form of wisdom in a world where everything seems topsy-turvy. If so, it is a wisdom that links Viola to the fool Feste, who exults at the play's close in what he calls "the whirligig of time" (5.1.364).

Feste does not have a major part in the comedy's plot, but he shares with Viola a place at its imaginative center. A few years before the creation of *Twelfth Night,* the famous, boisterous clown Will Kempe quit Shakespeare's company in a huff and was replaced by Robert Armin, a comic actor of unusual sensitivity and subtlety. In paying handsome tribute to Feste's intelligence, Viola seems to acknowledge Armin's special gift: "This fellow is wise enough to play the fool, / And to do that well craves a kind of wit" (3.1.53–54). His wit often takes the form of a perverse literalism that slyly calls attention to the play's repeated confounding of such simple binaries as male and female, outside and inside, role and reality. The paradox of the wise fool, celebrated by Erasmus in his famous *Praise of Folly* (1509), is one that fascinated Shakespeare, who returned to it in plays as diverse as *As You Like It* and *King Lear.* In *Twelfth Night,* Feste is irresponsible, vulnerable, and dependent, but he also understands, as he teasingly shows Olivia, that it is foolish to bewail forever a loss that cannot be recovered. And he understands that it is important to take such pleasures as life offers and not to wait: "In delay there lies no plenty," he sings. "Then come kiss me, sweet and twenty. / Youth's a stuff will not endure" (2.3.46–48). There is in this wonderful song, as in all of his jests, a current of sadness. Feste knows, as the refrain of the last of his songs puts it, that "the rain it raineth every day" (5.1.379). His counsel is for "present mirth" and "present laughter" (2.3.44). This is, of course, the advice of a fool. But do the Malvolios of the world have anything wiser to suggest?

STEPHEN GREENBLATT

TEXTUAL NOTE

The text of *Twelfth Night* is mercifully straightforward: the play first appeared in the 1623 First Folio (F), and the text is unusually clean, including careful act and scene divisions. Contemporary or near-contemporary musical settings survive for several of the songs in the play. For example, "O mistress mine" (2.3.35ff.) appears in three early versions, including Thomas Morley's *First Book of Consort Lessons* (1599). "Hold thy peace" (2.3.59) appears in a manuscript book of rounds collected by Thomas Lant (1580), as well as a version printed in 1609. The well-known setting for Feste's epilogue, "When that I was and a little tiny boy" (5.1.376), was first printed in Joseph Vernon's 1772 volume *The New Songs in the Pantomime of the Witches: The Celebrated Epilogue in the Comedy of Twelfth Night . . . Sung by Mr. Vernon at Vaux Hall, Composed by J. Vernon.* It is not entirely clear whether this setting was composed by Vernon (as the title page seems to suggest) or arranged from a traditional tune.

SELECTED BIBLIOGRAPHY

Auden, W. H. "Music in Shakespeare." *The Dyer's Hand, and Other Essays.* New York: Random House, 1948. Analyzing songs from the plays, Auden reflects on music as a social exercise, dramatic convention, and supernatural sign fier.

Bloom, Harold, ed. *William Shakespeare's "Twelfth Night."* Modern Critical Interpretation series. New York: Chelsea House, 1987. Essays written since the 1960s, treating the representation of character, music, class ideology, gender, and role-playing.

Booth, Stephen. "*Twelfth Night* 1.1: The Audience as Malvolio." *Shakespeare's "Rough Magic": Essays in Honor of C. L. Barber.* Ed. Peter Erickson and Coppélia Kahn.

Newark: University of Delaware Press, 1985. 149–67. An otherwise nonsensical play makes sense only when audiences ignore the textual evidence in favor of contextual probability.

Callaghan, Dympna. "'And all is semblative a woman's part': Body Politics and *Twelfth Night.*" *Shakespeare Without Women: Representing Gender and Race on the Renaissance Stage.* New York: Routledge, 2000. 26–48. The misogynistic ridicule of Olivia's genitals in the Malvolio letter is an assertion of male control over the female body.

Gay, Penny. "*Twelfth Night:* Desire and Its Discontents." *As She Likes It: Shakespeare's Unruly Women.* London: Routledge, 1994. 17–47. Describes key postwar English stage productions.

Greenblatt, Stephen. "Fiction and Friction." *Shakespearean Negotiations: The Circulation of Social Energy in Renaissance England.* Berkeley: University of California Press, 1988. 66–93. In light of contemporary anatomical theories, relates sexual chafing to verbal sparring and the generation of identity.

Hollander, John. "*Twelfth Night* and the Morality of Indulgence." *Sewanee Review* 67 (1959): 220–38. In *Twelfth Night's* intense moral vision, the surfeit of appetite through indulgence leads to the rebirth of the unencumbered self.

Neely, Carol Thomas. *Distracted Subjects: Madness and Gender in Shakespeare and Early Modern Culture.* Ithaca: Cornell University Press, 2004. *Twelfth Night's* displaced erotic choices cohere with changing medical discourse about pathological female lovesickness.

Orgel, Stephen. *Impersonations: The Performance of Gender in Shakespeare's England.* Cambridge, Mass.: Cambridge University Press, 1996. Approaches paradoxes in English playacting practice through contemporary notions of gender construction and sexual desire.

Wells, Stanley, ed. *"Twelfth Night": Critical Essays.* New York: Garland, 1986. Twenty essays from the nineteenth century onward, treating mainly formal and structural aspects and early twentieth-century productions.

FILM

Twelfth Night. 1996. Dir. Trevor Nunn. UK. 134 min. Romantic Celtic coastlines combine with a poignant musical score, a stuffy Malvolio, and a gravely wise Feste. With Ben Kingsley, Helena Bonham Carter, and Nigel Hawthorne.

Twelfth Night, or What You Will

THE PERSONS OF THE PLAY

ORSINO, Duke of Illyria
VALENTINE
CURIO } attending on Orsino
FIRST OFFICER
SECOND OFFICER
VIOLA, a lady, later disguised as Cesario
A CAPTAIN
SEBASTIAN, her twin brother
ANTONIO, another sea-captain
OLIVIA, a Countess
MARIA, her waiting-gentlewoman
SIR TOBY Belch, Olivia's kinsman
SIR ANDREW Aguecheek, companion of Sir Toby
MALVOLIO, Olivia's steward
FABIAN, a member of Olivia's household
FESTE the clown, her jester
A PRIEST
A SERVANT of Olivia
Musicians, sailors, lords, attendants

1.1

Music. Enter ORSINO *Duke of Illyria,* CURIO, *and other lords*

ORSINO   If music be the food of love, play on,
　　Give me excess of it that, surfeiting,
　　The appetite may sicken and so die.
　　That strain again, it had a dying fall.°　　　　　　*cadence*
5　　O, it came o'er my ear like the sweet sound
　　That breathes upon a bank of violets,
　　Stealing and giving odour. Enough, no more,
　　'Tis not so sweet now as it was before.
　　　　[Music ceases]
　　O spirit of love, how quick and fresh° art thou　　*lively and eager*
10　　That, notwithstanding thy capacity
　　Receiveth as the sea,° naught enters there,　　*Receives without limit*
　　Of what validity° and pitch° so e'er,　　*value / height; excellence*
　　But falls into abatement° and low price　　*lesser value*
　　Even in a minute! So full of shapes is fancy°　　*love; desire*
15　　That it alone is high fantastical.°　　*uniquely imaginative*
CURIO   Will you go hunt, my lord?
ORSINO　　　　　　　　　　What, Curio?
CURIO　　　　　　　　　　　　The hart.
ORSINO   Why so I do, the noblest that I have.[1]
　　O, when mine eyes did see Olivia first
　　Methought she purged the air of pestilence;[2]

1.1 Location: Illyria, Greek and Roman name for the eastern Adriatic coast; probably not suggesting a real country to Shakespeare's audience.

1. Orsino plays on "hart/heart."
2. Plague and other illnesses were thought to be caused by bad air.

20   That instant was I turned into a hart,
    And my desires, like fell° and cruel hounds,   *savage*
    E'er since pursue me.[3]
          Enter VALENTINE
                  How now, what news from her?
  VALENTINE   So please my lord, I might not be admitted,
    But from her handmaid do return this answer:
25 The element itself till seven years' heat[4]
    Shall not behold her face at ample° view,   *full*
    But like a cloistress° she will veilèd walk   *nun*
    And water once a day her chamber round
    With eye-offending brine°—all this to season   *stinging tears*
30 A brother's dead love,[5] which she would keep fresh
    And lasting in her sad remembrance.
  ORSINO   O, she that hath a heart of that fine° frame   *exquisitely made*
    To pay this debt of love but to a brother,
    How will she love when the rich golden shaft[6]
35 Hath killed the flock of all affections else°   *other emotions*
    That live in her—when liver, brain, and heart,[7]
    These sovereign thrones, are all supplied, and filled
    Her sweet perfections[8] with one self° king!   *one and the same*
    Away before me to sweet beds of flowers.
40 Love-thoughts lie rich when canopied with bowers.

                        Exeunt

1.2

      Enter VIOLA, *a* CAPTAIN, *and sailors*
  VIOLA[1]   What country, friends, is this?
  CAPTAIN   This is Illyria, lady.
  VIOLA   And what should I do in Illyria?
    My brother, he is in Elysium.[2]
    Perchance° he is not drowned. What think you sailors? *Perhaps*
5 CAPTAIN   It is perchance° that you yourself were saved. *by chance*
  VIOLA   O my poor brother!—and so perchance may he be.
  CAPTAIN   True, madam, and to comfort you with chance,[3]
    Assure yourself, after our ship did split,
    When you and those poor number savèd with you
10 Hung on our driving boat,[4] I saw your brother,
    Most provident in peril, bind himself—
    Courage and hope both teaching him the practice—
    To a strong mast that lived° upon the sea,   *remained afloat*
    Where, like Arion[5] on the dolphin's back,
15 I saw him hold acquaintance with the waves
    So long as I could see.
  VIOLA [*giving money*]   For saying so, there's gold.

---

3. Alluding to the classical legend of Actaeon, who was turned into a stag and hunted by his own hounds for having seen Artemis naked.
4. The sky itself / for seven hot summers.
5. *all . . . love*: all this to preserve (by the salt of the tears) the love of a dead brother.
6. Of Cupid's golden-tipped arrow, which caused desire.
7. In Elizabethan psychology, these were the seats of passion, intellect, and feeling.
8. *and filled . . . perfections*: and all her flawless qualities

are governed by.
1.2 Location: The coast of Illyria.
1. Viola is not named in the dialogue until 5.1.237.
2. The heaven of classical mythology.
3. With what may have happened.
4. The ship's boat. *driving*: being driven by the wind.
5. A legendary Greek musician who, in order to save himself from being murdered on a voyage, jumped overboard and was carried to land by a dolphin.

Mine own escape unfoldeth to° my hope,   *encourages*
Whereto thy speech serves for authority,°   *support*
The like of him.[6] Know'st thou this country?
20   CAPTAIN   Ay, madam, well, for I was bred and born
Not three hours' travel from this very place.
VIOLA   Who governs here?
CAPTAIN   A noble duke, in nature
As in name.
VIOLA   What is his name?
CAPTAIN   Orsino.
VIOLA   Orsino. I have heard my father name him.
25   He was a bachelor then.
CAPTAIN   And so is now, or was so very late,°   *lately*
For but a month ago I went from hence,
And then 'twas fresh in murmur°—as, you know,   *newly rumored*
What great ones do the less will prattle of—
30   That he did seek the love of fair Olivia.
VIOLA   What's she?
CAPTAIN   A virtuous maid, the daughter of a count
That died some twelvemonth since, then leaving her
In the protection of his son, her brother,
35   Who shortly also died, for whose dear love,
They say, she hath abjured the sight
And company of men.
VIOLA   O that I served that lady,
And might not be delivered° to the world   *revealed*
Till I had made mine own occasion mellow,°   *ripe (to be revealed)*
What my estate° is.   *social rank*
40   CAPTAIN   That were hard to compass,°   *achieve*
Because she will admit no kind of suit,°   *petition*
No, not the Duke's.
VIOLA   There is a fair behaviour[7] in thee, captain,
And though that nature with a beauteous wall
45   Doth oft close in pollution, yet of thee
I will believe thou hast a mind that suits
With this thy fair and outward character.[8]
I pray thee—and I'll pay thee bounteously—
Conceal me what I am, and be my aid
50   For such disguise as haply shall become
The form of my intent.[9] I'll serve this duke.
Thou shalt present me as an eunuch[1] to him.
It may be worth thy pains, for I can sing,
And speak to him in many sorts of music
55   That will allow° me very worth his service.   *prove*
What else may hap, to time I will commit.
Only shape thou thy silence to my wit.°   *imagination; plan*
CAPTAIN   Be you his eunuch, and your mute[2] I'll be.
When my tongue blabs, then let mine eyes not see.
60   VIOLA   I thank thee. Lead me on.   *Exeunt*

6. That he too has survived.
7. Outward appearance; conduct.
8. Appearance (suggesting moral qualities).
9. *as . . . intent:* that perhaps may be fitting to my purpose. *form:* shape.
🄳 Castrati (hence, "eunuchs") were prized as male sopranos; the disguise would have explained Viola's

feminine voice. Viola (or perhaps Shakespeare) seems to have changed plans: she presents herself instead as a young page.
2. In Turkish harems, eunuchs served as guards and were assisted by "mutes" (usually servants whose tongues had been cut out).

1.3

Enter SIR TOBY [*Belch*] *and* MARIA

SIR TOBY What a plague means my niece to take the death of
her brother thus? I am sure care's an enemy to life.

MARIA By my troth, Sir Toby, you must come in earlier o' nights.
Your cousin,[1] my lady, takes great exceptions to your ill hours.

5 SIR TOBY Why, let her except, before excepted.[2]

MARIA Ay, but you must confine yourself within the modest°   moderate
limits of order.

SIR TOBY Confine? I'll confine myself no finer[3] than I am. These
clothes are good enough to drink in, and so be these boots too;

10 an° they be not, let them hang themselves in their own straps.   if

MARIA That quaffing and drinking will undo you. I heard my
lady talk of it yesterday, and of a foolish knight that you brought
in one night here to be her wooer.

SIR TOBY Who, Sir Andrew Aguecheek?

15 MARIA Ay, he.

SIR TOBY He's as tall a man as any's[4] in Illyria.

MARIA What's that to th' purpose?

SIR TOBY Why, he has three thousand ducats a year.

MARIA Ay, but he'll have but a year in all these ducats.[5] He's a

20 very° fool, and a prodigal.   an absolute

SIR TOBY Fie that you'll say so! He plays o' th' viol-de-gamboys,[6]
and speaks three or four languages word for word without
book,° and hath all the good gifts of nature.   from memory

MARIA He hath indeed, almost natural,[7] for besides that he's a

25 fool, he's a great quarreller, and but that he hath the gift° of a   talent; present
coward to allay the gust° he hath in quarrelling, 'tis thought   gusto
among the prudent he would quickly have the gift of a grave.

SIR TOBY By this hand, they are scoundrels and substractors[8] that
say so of him. Who are they?

30 MARIA They that add, moreover, he's drunk nightly in your
company.

SIR TOBY With drinking healths to my niece. I'll drink to her as
long as there is a passage in my throat and drink in Illyria. He's
a coward and a coistrel° that will not drink to my niece till his   horse groom; lout

35 brains turn o' th' toe, like a parish top. What wench, *Castiliano,
vulgo*,[9] for here comes Sir Andrew Agueface.

Enter SIR ANDREW [*Aguecheek*]

SIR ANDREW Sir Toby Belch! How now, Sir Toby Belch?

SIR TOBY Sweet Sir Andrew.

SIR ANDREW [*to* MARIA] Bless you, fair shrew.[1]

40 MARIA And you too, sir.

SIR TOBY Accost, Sir Andrew, accost.[2]

SIR ANDREW What's that?

1.3 Location: The Countess Olivia's house.
1. Term used generally of kinsfolk.
2. Playing on the legal jargon *exceptis excipiendis*, "with
the previously stated exceptions." Sir Toby refuses to take
Olivia's displeasure seriously.
3. Suggesting both "a refined manner of dress" and
"narrowly" (referring to his girth).
4. Any (man who) is. *tall:* brave; worthy. (Maria takes it
in the modern sense of height.)
5. He'll spend his fortune in a year.
6. A facetious corruption of "viola da gamba," a bass viol
held between the knees.

7. Idiots and fools were called "naturals."
8. Corruption of "detractors." (In reply, Maria puns on
"substract" as "subtract.")
9. Variously interpreted, but may mean "Speak of the
devil," since Castilians were considered devilish, and
vulgo refers to the common tongue (?). *parish top:* parishes kept large tops that were spun by whipping them,
for the parishioners' amusement and exercise.
1. Andrew possibly confuses "shrew" (ill-tempered
woman) with "mouse," an endearment.
2. Address (her); originally a naval term meaning "go
alongside; greet."

SIR TOBY   My niece's chambermaid.[3]

SIR ANDREW   Good Mistress Accost, I desire better acquaintance.

45   MARIA   My name is Mary, sir.

SIR ANDREW   Good Mistress Mary Accost.

SIR TOBY   You mistake, knight. 'Accost' is front° her, board her,   *confront*
woo her, assail[4] her.

SIR ANDREW   By my troth, I would not undertake[5] her in this

50   company.° Is that the meaning of 'accost'?   *the audience*

MARIA   Fare you well, gentlemen.

SIR TOBY   An thou let part so,[6] Sir Andrew, would thou mightst
never draw sword again.

SIR ANDREW   An you part so, mistress, I would I might never draw

55   sword again. Fair lady, do you think you have fools in hand?°   *to deal with*

MARIA   Sir, I have not you by th' hand.

SIR ANDREW   Marry, but you shall have, and here's my hand.

MARIA [*taking his hand*]   Now sir, thought is free.[7] I pray you,
bring your hand to th' buttery-bar,[8] and let it drink.

60   SIR ANDREW   Wherefore, sweetheart? What's your metaphor?

MARIA   It's dry,[9] sir.

SIR ANDREW   Why, I think so. I am not such an ass but I can
keep my hand dry.[1] But what's your jest?

MARIA   A dry jest,[2] sir.

65   SIR ANDREW   Are you full of them?

MARIA   Ay, sir, I have them at my fingers' ends.[3] Marry, now I let
go your hand I am barren.°   *Exit*   *empty of jokes*

SIR TOBY   O knight, thou lackest a cup of canary.[4] When did I
see thee so put down?[5]

70   SIR ANDREW   Never in your life, I think, unless you see canary
put me down. Methinks sometimes I have no more wit than a
Christian° or an ordinary man has; but I am a great eater of   *an average man*
beef,[6] and I believe that does harm to my wit.

SIR TOBY   No question.

75   SIR ANDREW   An I thought that, I'd forswear it. I'll ride home
tomorrow, Sir Toby.

SIR TOBY   *Pourquoi,*° my dear knight?   *Why*

SIR ANDREW   What is 'Pourquoi'? Do, or not do? I would I had
bestowed that time in the tongues[7] that I have in fencing, danc-

80   ing, and bear-baiting. O, had I but followed the arts!

SIR TOBY   Then hadst thou had an excellent head of hair.

SIR ANDREW   Why, would that have mended° my hair?   *improved*

SIR TOBY   Past question, for thou seest it will not curl by nature.[8]

SIR ANDREW   But it becomes me well enough, does't not?

85   SIR TOBY   Excellent, it hangs like flax on a distaff,[9] and I hope to
see a housewife[1] take thee between her legs and spin it off.[2]

3. Lady-in-waiting; not a menial servant, but a gentlewoman in attendance on a great lady.
4. *board:* speak to; tackle. *assail:* greet (also nautical).
5. Take her on (with sexual implication).
6. If you let her go without protest or without bidding
her farewell.
7. The customary retort to "Do you think I am a fool?"
8. Ledge on the half door to a buttery or a wine cellar
on which drinks were served.
9. Thirsty; but also thought to be a sign of impotence.
1. Alluding to the proverb "Even fools have enough wit
to come in out of the rain."
2. A stupid joke (referring to Andrew's stupidity); an
ironic quip; a joke about dryness.

3. Always ready; or "by th' hand" (line 56).
4. A sweet wine, like sherry, originally from the Canary
Islands.
5. Defeated in repartee; "put down" with drink.
6. Contemporary medicine held that beef dulled the
intellect.
7. Foreign languages; Toby takes him to mean "curling
tongs."
8. To contrast with Andrew's "arts" (line 80).
9. In spinning, flax would hang in long, thin, yellowish
strings on the "distaff," a pole held between the knees.
1. Housewives spun flax; the pronunciation, "huswife,"
also suggests the meaning "prostitute."
2. Make him bald (as a result of venereal disease).

SIR ANDREW   Faith, I'll home tomorrow, Sir Toby. Your niece
will not be seen, or if she be, it's four to one she'll none of me.
The Count himself here hard by woos her.

90 SIR TOBY   She'll none o'th' Count. She'll not match above her
degree,° neither in estate,[3] years, nor wit, I have heard her   *social rank*
swear't. Tut, there's life in't,[4] man.

SIR ANDREW   I'll stay a month longer. I am a fellow o'th' strangest
mind i'th' world. I delight in masques and revels sometimes
95 altogether.

SIR TOBY   Art thou good at these kickshawses,[5] knight?

SIR ANDREW   As any man in Illyria, whatsoever he be, under the
degree of my betters; and yet I will not compare with an old
man.[6]

100 SIR TOBY   What is thy excellence in a galliard,[7] knight?

SIR ANDREW   Faith, I can cut a caper.[8]

SIR TOBY   And I can cut the mutton to't.

SIR ANDREW   And I think I have the back-trick[9] simply as strong
as any man in Illyria.

105 SIR TOBY   Wherefore are these things hid? Wherefore have these
gifts a curtain[1] before 'em? Are they like to take dust, like Mistress Mall's[2] picture? Why dost thou not go to church in a galliard, and come home in a coranto?[3] My very walk should be a
jig. I would not so much as make water but in a cinquepace.[4]
110 What dost thou mean? Is it a world to hide virtues in? I did
think by the excellent constitution of thy leg it was formed
under the star of a galliard.[5]

SIR ANDREW   Ay, 'tis strong, and it does indifferent° well in a   *moderately*
divers-coloured stock.° Shall we set about some revels?   *stocking*

115 SIR TOBY   What shall we do else—were we not born under
Taurus?[6]

SIR ANDREW   Taurus? That's sides and heart.

SIR TOBY   No, sir, it is legs and thighs: let me see thee caper.

[SIR ANDREW *capers*]

Ha, higher! Ha ha, excellent.   *Exeunt*

1.4

Enter VALENTINE, *and* VIOLA [*as Cesario*] *in man's attire*

VALENTINE   If the Duke continue these favours towards you,
Cesario, you are like to be much advanced. He hath known
you but three days, and already you are no stranger.

VIOLA   You either fear his humour° or my negligence, that you   *moodiness*
5 call in question the continuance of his love. Is he inconstant,
sir, in his favours?

VALENTINE   No, believe me.

Enter DUKE, CURIO, *and attendants*

---

3. Status; possession.
4. Proverbial: "While there's life, there's hope."
5. Trifles; trivialities (from the French *quelque chose*).
6. Expert (perhaps a backhanded compliment).
7. A lively, complex dance, including the caper.
8. Leap. (Toby puns on the pickled flower buds used in a sauce of mutton.)
9. Probably a dance movement, a kick of the foot behind the body (also suggesting sexual prowess, with later reference to "mutton" as "prostitute").

1. Used to protect paintings from dust.
2. Like "Moll[y]," "Mall" was a nickname for "Mary."
3. An even more rapid dance than the galliard.
4. Galliard, or, more properly, the steps joining the figures of the dance; punning on "sink," as in "sewer."
5. Astrological influences favorable to dancing.
6. The astrological sign of the bull was usually thought to govern the neck and throat (appropriate to heavy drinkers).
1.4 Location: Orsino's palace.

VIOLA I thank you. Here comes the Count.

ORSINO Who saw Cesario, ho?

10 VIOLA On your attendance,° my lord, here.   *Waiting at your service*

ORSINO [*to* CURIO *and attendants*] Stand you a while aloof.° [*To*   *aside*
    VIOLA] Cesario,
    Thou know'st no less but all.° <u>I have unclasped</u>   *than everything*
    <u>To thee the book even of my secret soul</u>.
    Therefore, good youth, address thy gait° unto her,   *go*
15   Be not denied access, stand at her doors,
    And tell them there thy fixèd foot shall grow°   *take root*
    Till thou have audience.

VIOLA   Sure, my noble lord,
    If she be so abandoned to her sorrow
    As it is spoke, she never will admit me.

20 ORSINO Be clamorous, and leap all civil bounds,[1]
    Rather than make unprofited° return.   *unsuccessful*

VIOLA Say I do speak with her, my lord, what then?

ORSINO O then unfold the passion of my love,
    Surprise[2] her with discourse of my dear° faith.   *heartfelt*
25   It shall become thee well to act my woes—
    She will attend it better in thy youth
    Than in a nuncio's° of more grave aspect.°   *messenger's / appearance*

VIOLA I think not so, my lord.

ORSINO   Dear lad, believe it;
    For they shall yet belie thy happy years
30   That say thou art a man. Diana's lip
    Is not more smooth and rubious;° <u>thy small pipe</u>   because Cesario *ruby red / voice*
    <u>Is as the maiden's organ, shrill and sound,[3]</u> is not manly, he is
    <u>And all is semblative° a woman's part.</u>   more appealing   *like*
    I know thy constellation[4] is right apt
35   For this affair. [*To* CURIO *and attendants*] Some four or five attend him.
    All if you will, for I myself am best
    When least in company. [*To* VIOLA] Prosper well in this
    And thou shalt live as freely as thy lord,
    To call his fortunes thine.

VIOLA   I'll do my best
40   <u>To woo your lady—[*aside*] yet a barful strife[5]—</u>   Viola has fallen in
    <u>Whoe'er I woo, myself would be his wife.</u>   love with Orsino   *Exeunt*

1.5

Enter MARIA, *and* [FESTE,[1] *the*] *clown*

MARIA Nay, either tell me where thou hast been or I will not
open my lips so wide as a bristle may enter in° way of thy   *by*
excuse. My lady will hang thee for thy absence.

FESTE Let her hang me. He that is well hanged in this world
5 needs to fear no colours.[2]

MARIA Make that good.°   *Explain that*

FESTE He shall see none to fear.

---

1. All constraints of polite behavior.
2. Capture by unexpected attack (of military origin).
3. High-pitched and uncracked.
4. Nature and abilities (as supposedly determined by the stars).

5. An undertaking full of impediments.
1.5 Location: Olivia's house.
1. The name is used only once, at 2.4.11.
2. Proverbial for "fear nothing." *colours:* worldly deceptions, with a pun on "collars" as "hangman's noose."

MARIA   A good lenten[3] answer. I can tell thee where that saying
was born, of 'I fear no colours'.

10   FESTE   Where, good Mistress Mary?

MARIA   In the wars,[4] and that may you be bold to say in your
foolery.

FESTE   Well, God give them wisdom that have it; and those that
are fools, let them use their talents.[5]

15   MARIA   Yet you will be hanged for being so long absent, or to be
turned away[6]—is not that as good as a hanging to you?

FESTE   Many a good hanging prevents a bad marriage;[7] and for
turning away, let summer bear it out.°   *make it endurable*

MARIA   You are resolute then?

20   FESTE   Not so neither, but I am resolved on two points.°   *matters; laces*

MARIA   That if one break, the other will hold; or if both break,
your gaskins° fall.   *wide breeches*

FESTE   Apt, in good faith, very apt. Well, go thy way. If Sir Toby
would leave drinking thou wert as witty a piece of Eve's flesh[8]

25   as any in Illyria.

MARIA   Peace, you rogue, no more o' that. Here comes my lady.
Make your excuse wisely, you were best.°   [*Exit*]   *you had better*
Enter Lady OLIVIA, *with* MALVOLIO° [*and attendants*]   *"ill will"*

FESTE [*aside*]   Wit,[9] an't° be thy will, put me into good fooling!   *if it*
Those wits that think they have thee do very oft prove fools,

30   and I that am sure I lack thee may pass for a wise man. For
what says Quinapalus?[1]—'Better a witty fool than a foolish wit.'
[*To* OLIVIA] God bless thee, lady.

OLIVIA [*to attendants*]   Take the fool away.

FESTE   Do you not hear, fellows? Take away the lady.

35   OLIVIA   Go to, you're a dry[2] fool. I'll no more of you. Besides,
you grow dishonest.°   *unreliable*

FESTE   Two faults, madonna,° that drink and good counsel will   *my lady*
amend, for give the dry fool drink, then is the fool not dry; bid
the dishonest man mend° himself : if he mend, he is no longer   *reform*

40   dishonest; if he cannot, let the botcher° mend him. Anything   *tailor; cobbler*
that's mended is but patched. Virtue that transgresses is but
patched with sin, and sin that amends is but patched with virtue. If that this simple syllogism will serve, so. If it will not, what
remedy? As there is no true cuckold but calamity, so beauty's a

45   flower.[3] The lady bade take away the fool, therefore I say again,
take her away.

OLIVIA   Sir, I bade them take away you.

FESTE   Misprision[4] in the highest degree! Lady, '*Cucullus non
facit monachum*'[5]—that's as much to say as I wear not motley[6]

50   in my brain. Good madonna, give me leave to prove you a fool.

---

3. Thin or meager (like Lenten fare).
4. *In the wars*: "colours" in line 9 refers to military flags.
5. Alluding to the parable of the talents, Matthew 25. The comic implication is that a fool should strive to increase his measure of folly. Since "fool" and "fowl" had similar pronunciations, there may also be a play on "talents/talons."
6. Dismissed; also, perhaps, turned off or hanged.
7. *Many . . . marriage*: Proverbial. *hanging*: execution; sexual prowess.
8. Woman. Feste may imply both that Maria and Toby would make a good match and that Maria is as witty as

Toby is sober.
9. Intelligence, which is often contrasted with will.
1. Feste frequently invents his own authorities.
2. Dull, but Feste interprets as "thirsty." *Go to:* an expression of impatience.
3. *As . . . flower*: In taking her vow (1.2.36–37), Olivia has wedded herself to calamity but must be unfaithful, or let pass her moment of beauty.
4. Misapprehension; wrongful arrest.
5. The cowl does not make the monk (a Latin proverb).
6. The multicolored costume of a fool.

OLIVIA   Can you do it?

FESTE   Dexteriously,° good madonna.   *Dexterously*

OLIVIA   Make your proof.

FESTE   I must catechize[7] you for it, madonna. Good my mouse
55   of virtue,° answer me.   *My good virtuous mouse*

OLIVIA   Well, sir, for want of other idleness° I'll bide° your proof.   *pastime / await*

FESTE   Good madonna, why mournest thou?

OLIVIA   Good fool, for my brother's death.

FESTE   I think his soul is in hell, madonna.

60   OLIVIA   I know his soul is in heaven, fool.

FESTE   The more fool, madonna, to mourn for your brother's
soul, being in heaven. Take away the fool, gentlemen.

OLIVIA   What think you of this fool, Malvolio? Doth he not
mend?[8]

65   MALVOLIO   Yes, and shall do till the pangs of death shake him.
Infirmity,° that decays the wise, doth ever make the better fool.[9]   *(Old) age*

FESTE   God send you, sir, a speedy infirmity for the better
increasing your folly. Sir Toby will be sworn that I am no fox,
but he will not pass his word for twopence that you are no fool.

70   OLIVIA   How say you to that, Malvolio?

MALVOLIO   I marvel your ladyship takes delight in such a barren
rascal. I saw him put down° the other day with an ordinary fool   *defeated in repartee*
that has no more brain than a stone. <u>Look you now, he's out of
his guard° already. Unless you laugh and minister occasion[1] to   *defenseless*
75   him, he is gagged.</u> I protest I take these wise men that crow so
at these set° kind of fools no better than the fools' zanies.°   *artificial / "straight men"*

OLIVIA   <u>O, you are sick of self-love, Malvolio, and taste with a
distempered[2] appetite. To be generous, guiltless, and of free°   *magnanimous*
disposition is to take those things for birdbolts[3] that you deem
80   cannon bullets. There is no slander in an allowed fool, though
he do nothing but rail; nor no railing in a known discreet man,
though he do nothing but reprove.</u>

FESTE   Now Mercury indue thee with leasing,[4] for thou speakest
well of fools.

Enter MARIA

85   MARIA   Madam, there is at the gate a young gentleman much
desires to speak with you.

OLIVIA   From the Count Orsino, is it?

MARIA   I know not, madam. 'Tis a fair young man, and well
attended.

90   OLIVIA   Who of my people hold him in delay?

MARIA   Sir Toby, madam, your kinsman.

OLIVIA   Fetch him off, I pray you, he speaks nothing but madman.° Fie on him. Go you, Malvolio. If it be a suit from the   *madman's talk*
Count, I am sick, or not at home—what you will to dismiss it.

Exit MALVOLIO

95   Now you see, sir, how your fooling grows old,° and people dis-   *stale*
like it.

FESTE   Thou hast spoke for us, madonna, as if thy eldest son

---

7. Question (as in catechism, which tests the orthodoxy of belief).
8. Improve, but Malvolio takes "mend" to mean "grow
more foolish."
9. Make the fool more foolish.

1. And give opportunity.
2. An unbalanced; a sick.
3. Blunt arrows for shooting birds.
4. May Mercury, the god of deception, endow you with
the talent of tactful lying.

[handwritten marginal note:] fools speak truth to power

should be a fool, whose skull Jove cram with brains, for—here
he comes—

    Enter SIR TOBY

100   one of thy kin has a most weak *pia mater*.[5]

OLIVIA   By mine honour, half-drunk. What is he at the gate,
    cousin?°   *kinsman*

SIR TOBY   A gentleman.

OLIVIA   A gentleman? What gentleman?

105 SIR TOBY   'Tis a gentleman here. [*He belches*] A plague o' these
    pickle herring! [*To* FESTE] How now, sot?°   *fool; drunkard*

FESTE   Good Sir Toby.

OLIVIA   Cousin, cousin, how have you come so early by this
    lethargy?

110 SIR TOBY   Lechery? I defy lechery. There's one° at the gate.   *someone*

OLIVIA   Ay, marry, what is he?

SIR TOBY   Let him be the devil an° he will, I care not. Give me   *if*
    faith,[6] say I. Well, it's all one.°   *Exit*   *it doesn't matter*

OLIVIA   What's a drunken man like, fool?

115 FESTE   Like a drowned man, a fool, and a madman—one
    draught above heat[7] makes him a fool, the second mads him,
    and a third drowns him.

OLIVIA   Go thou and seek the coroner, and let him sit o'° my   *hold an inquest for*
    coz,° for he's in the third degree of drink, he's drowned. Go   *cousin; uncle*
120   look after him.

FESTE   He is but mad yet, madonna, and the fool shall look to
    the madman.   [*Exit*]

    Enter MALVOLIO

MALVOLIO   Madam, yon young fellow swears he will speak with
    you. I told him you were sick—he takes on him to understand
125   so much, and therefore° comes to speak with you. I told him   *for that very reason*
    you were asleep—he seems to have a foreknowledge of that
    too, and therefore comes to speak with you. What is to be said
    to him, lady? He's fortified against any denial.

OLIVIA   Tell him he shall not speak with me.

130 MALVOLIO   He's been told so, and he says he'll stand at your door
    like a sheriff's post,[8] and be the supporter to a bench, but he'll
    speak with you.

OLIVIA   What kind o' man is he?

MALVOLIO   Why, of mankind.°   *like any other*

135 OLIVIA   What manner of man?

MALVOLIO   Of very ill manner: he'll speak with you, will you or
    no.

OLIVIA   Of what personage° and years is he?   *appearance*

MALVOLIO   Not yet old enough for a man, nor young enough for
140   a boy; as a squash[9] is before 'tis a peascod, or a codling° when   *an unripe apple*
    'tis almost an apple. 'Tis with him in standing water° between   *at the turn of the tide*
    boy and man. He is very well-favoured,° and he speaks very   *handsome*
    shrewishly.° One would think his mother's milk were scarce   *sharply*
    out of him.

145 OLIVIA   Let him approach. Call in my gentlewoman.

MALVOLIO   Gentlewoman, my lady calls.   *Exit*

---

5. Brain; or literally, the membrane enclosing it.
6. To defy the devil by faith alone.
7. One drink ("draught")/beyond the quantity necessary
to warm him.

8. A decorative post set before a sheriff's door, as a sign
of authority.
9. An undeveloped pea pod.

Enter MARIA

OLIVIA   Give me my veil. Come, throw it o'er my face.
We'll once more hear Orsino's embassy.

Enter VIOLA [*as Cesario*]

VIOLA   The honourable lady of the house, which is she?

150   OLIVIA   Speak to me, I shall answer for her. Your will.

VIOLA   Most radiant, exquisite, and unmatchable beauty.—I pray
you, tell me if this be the lady of the house, for I never saw
her. I would be loath to cast away° my speech, for besides that   *waste*
it is excellently well penned, I have taken great pains to

155   con° it. Good beauties, let me sustain° no scorn. I am very   *memorize / suffer*
'countable,° even to the least sinister usage.[1]   *sensitive*

OLIVIA   Whence came you, sir?

VIOLA   I can say little more than I have studied,[2] and that question's out of my part. Good gentle one, give me modest° assur-   *adequate*

160   ance if you be the lady of the house, that I may proceed in my
speech.

OLIVIA   Are you a comedian?°   *an actor*

VIOLA   No, my profound heart;[3] and yet—by the very fangs of
malice I swear—I am not that I play. Are you the lady of the

165   house?

OLIVIA   If I do not usurp[4] myself, I am

VIOLA   Most certain if you are she you do usurp yourself, for what
is yours to bestow is not yours to reserve. But this is from my
commission.° I will on with my speech in your praise, and then   *beyond my instructions*

170   show you the heart of my message.

OLIVIA   Come to what is important in't, I forgive you° the praise.   *excuse you from*

VIOLA   Alas, I took great pains to study it, and 'tis poetical.

OLIVIA   It is the more like to be feigned, I pray you keep it in. I
heard you were saucy° at my gates, and allowed your approach   *impertinent*

175   rather to wonder at you than to hear you. If you be not mad,°   *utterly mad*
be gone. If you have reason,° be brief. 'Tis not that time of   *any sanity*
moon with me to make one in so skipping a dialogue.[5]

MARIA   Will you hoist sail, sir? Here lies your way.

VIOLA   No, good swabber, I am to hull here a little longer.

180   [*To* OLIVIA] Some mollification for your giant,[7] sweet lady. Tell
me your mind, I am a messenger.[8]

OLIVIA   Sure, you have some hideous matter to deliver when the
courtesy° of it is so fearful. Speak your office.°   *introduction / business*

VIOLA   It alone concerns your ear. I bring no overture° of war,   *declaration*

185   no taxation of homage.[9] I hold the olive[1] in my hand. My words
are as full of peace as matter.°   *meaning*

OLIVIA   Yet you began rudely. What are you? What would you?

VIOLA   The rudeness that hath appeared in me have I learned
from my entertainment.° What I am and what I would are as   *reception*

190   secret as maidenhead;° to your ears, divinity; to any others',   *virginity*
profanation.

---

1. To the slightest discourteous treatment.
2. Learned by heart (a theatrical term).
3. My most wise lady; upon my soul.
4. Counterfeit; misappropriate.
5. *'Tis . . . dialogue:* I am not lunatic enough to take part
in so flighty a conversation. (Lunacy was thought to be
influenced by the phases of the moon.)
6. To lie unanchored with lowered sails. *swabber:* a

cleaner of boat decks.
7. Mythical giants guarded ladies; here, also mocking
Maria's diminutive size. *Some . . . for:* Please pacify.
8. From Orsino; Olivia pretends she understands her to
mean a king's messenger, or a messenger-at-arms,
employed on important state affairs.
9. Demand for dues paid to a superior.
1. Olive branch (as a symbol of peace).

OLIVIA [*to* MARIA *and attendants*]   Give us the place alone, we
will hear this divinity.°   [*Exeunt* MARIA *and attendants*]   *religious discourse*
Now sir, what is your text?[2]

195   VIOLA   Most sweet lady—

OLIVIA   A comfortable° doctrine, and much may be said of it.   *comforting*
Where lies your text?

VIOLA   In Orsino's bosom.

OLIVIA   In his bosom? In what chapter of his bosom?

200   VIOLA   To answer by the method,° in the first of his heart.   *in the same style*

OLIVIA   O, I have read it. It is heresy. Have you no more to say?

VIOLA   Good madam, let me see your face.

OLIVIA   Have you any commission from your lord to negotiate
with my face? You are now out of° your text. But we will draw   *straying from*
205   the curtain and show you the picture.
          [*She unveils*]
Look you, sir, such a one I was this present.[3] Is't not well done?

VIOLA   Excellently done, if God did all.[4]

OLIVIA   'Tis in grain,° sir, 'twill endure wind and weather.   *The dye is fast*

VIOLA   'Tis beauty truly blent,[5] whose red and white
210   Nature's own sweet and cunning° hand laid on.   *skillful*
Lady, you are the cruell'st she° alive   *woman*
If you will lead these graces to the grave
And leave the world no copy.[6]

OLIVIA   O sir, I will not be so hard-hearted. I will give out divers
215   schedules° of my beauty. It shall be inventoried and every parti-   *various inventories*
cle and utensil labelled[7] to my will, as, *item,* two lips, indiffer-
ent° red; *item,* two grey eyes, with lids[8] to them; *item,* one neck,   *moderate*
one chin, and so forth. Were you sent hither to praise° me?   *appraise; flatter*

VIOLA   I see you what you are, you are too proud,
220   But if° you were the devil, you are fair.   *Even if*
My lord and master loves you. O, such love
Could be but recompensed though[9] you were crowned
The nonpareil of beauty.°   *An unequaled beauty*

OLIVIA   How does he love me?

VIOLA   With adorations, fertile° tears,   *ever-flowing*
225   With groans that thunder love, with sighs of fire.
OLIVIA   Your lord does know my mind, I cannot love him.
Yet I suppose him virtuous, know him noble,
Of great estate, of fresh and stainless youth,
In voices well divulged,° free,° learned, and valiant,   *spoken of / generous*
230   And in dimension and the shape of nature[1]
A gracious person; but yet I cannot love him.
He might have took his answer long ago.

VIOLA   If I did love you in° my master's flame,°   *with / passion*
With such a suff'ring, such a deadly° life,   *deathlike*
235   In your denial I would find no sense,
I would not understand it.

---

2. Quotation (as a theme of a sermon, in keeping with
"divinity," "doctrine," "heresy," etc.).
3. Portraits usually gave the year of painting. "This
present" was a term used to date letters.
4. If it is natural (without the use of cosmetics).
5. Blended, or mixed (of paints). Shakespeare uses the
same metaphor in sonnet 20, lines 1–2, and Viola's next
lines recall sonnet 11, lines 13–14. As Cesario, Viola is
playing with established conventions of poetic courtship.

6. Viola means "child"; Olivia takes her to mean "list" or
"inventory."
7. Every single part and article added as a codicil (parodying the legal language of a last will and testament).
8. Eyelids, but also punning on "pot lids" (punning on
"utensil" as a household implement).
9. *Could . . . though:* Would have to be requited even if.
1. *dimension . . . shape of nature:* the two terms are
synonymous, meaning "bodily form."

OLIVIA   Why, what would you?

VIOLA   Make me a willow[2] cabin at your gate

And call upon my soul° within the house,   *(Olivia)*

Write loyal cantons of contemnèd° love,   *songs of rejected*

240   And sing them loud even in the dead of night;

Halloo[3] your name to the reverberate° hills,   *echoing*

And make the babbling gossip of the air[4]

Cry out 'Olivia!' O, you should not rest

Between the elements of air and earth

245   But you should pity me.

OLIVIA   You might do much.

What is your parentage?

VIOLA   Above my fortunes, yet my state° is well.   *social status*

I am a gentleman.

OLIVIA   Get you to your lord.

250   I cannot love him. Let him send no more,

Unless, perchance, you come to me again

To tell me how he takes it. Fare you well.

I thank you for your pains. [*Offering a purse*] Spend this for me.

VIOLA   I am no fee'd post,° lady. Keep your purse.   *hired messenger*

255   My master, not myself, lacks recompense.

Love make his heart of flint that you shall love,[5]

And let your fervour, like my master's, be

Placed in contempt. Farewell, fair cruelty.   *Exit*

OLIVIA   'What is your parentage?'

260   'Above my fortunes, yet my state is well.

I am a gentleman.' I'll be sworn thou art.

Thy tongue, thy face, thy limbs, actions, and spirit

Do give thee five-fold blazon.[6] Not too fast. Soft,° soft—   *Wait*

Unless the master were the man.[7] How now?

265   Even so quickly may one catch the plague?

Methinks I feel this youth's perfections

With an invisible and subtle stealth

To creep in at mine eyes. Well, let it be.

What ho, Malvolio.

         Enter MALVOLIO

MALVOLIO   Here, madam, at your service.

270   OLIVIA   Run after that same peevish messenger

The County's° man. He left this ring behind him,   *Count's*

Would I° or not. Tell him I'll none of it.   *Whether I wished it*

Desire him not to flatter with° his lord,   *encourage*

Nor hold him up with hopes. I am not for him.

275   If that the youth will come this way tomorrow,

I'll give him reasons for't. Hie thee.° Malvolio.   *Hurry*

MALVOLIO   Madam, I will.   *Exit [at one door]*

OLIVIA   I do I know not what, and fear to find

Mine eye too great a flatterer for my mind.[8]

---

2. Traditional symbol of rejected love.
3. Shout; or perhaps "hallow," as in "bless."
4. For the love of Narcissus, the nymph Echo wasted away to a mere voice, only able to repeat whatever she heard spoken.
5. *Love . . . love:* May love make the heart of the man you

love as hard as flint.
6. Formal description of a gentleman's coat of arms.
7. If Orsino were Cesario (*man:* servant).
8. My eye (through which love has entered my heart) has seduced my reason.

280   Fate, show thy force. Ourselves we do not owe.°   *own*
        What is decreed must be; and be this so.

                                [Exit at another door]

2.1

Enter ANTONIO *and* SEBASTIAN

ANTONIO   Will you stay no longer, nor will° you not that I go   *wish*
    with you?

SEBASTIAN   By your patience, no. My stars shine darkly over me.
    The malignancy of my fate[1] might perhaps distemper° yours,   *infect*
5   therefore I shall crave of you your leave that I may bear my
    evils alone. It were a bad recompense for your love to lay any
    of them on you.

ANTONIO   Let me yet know of you whither you are bound.

SEBASTIAN   No, sooth,° sir. My determinate° voyage is mere   *truly / destined*
10 extravagancy.° But I perceive in you so excellent a touch of   *idle wandering*
    modesty° that you will not extort from me what I am willing to   *politeness*
    keep in. Therefore it charges me in manners[2] the rather to
    express° myself. You must know of me then, Antonio, my name   *reveal*
    is Sebastian, which I called Roderigo. My father was that Sebas-
15 tian of Messaline[3] whom I know you have heard of. He left
    behind him myself and a sister, both born in an° hour. If the   *within the same*
    heavens had been pleased, would we had so ended. But you,
    sir, altered that, for some hour before you took me from the
    breach° of the sea was my sister drowned.   *surf*

20 ANTONIO   Alas the day!

SEBASTIAN   A lady, sir, though it was said she much resembled
    me, was yet of many accounted beautiful. But though I could
    not with such estimable° wonder over-far believe that, yet   *appreciative*
    thus far I will boldly publish° her: she bore a mind that   *proclaim*
25 envy° could not but call fair. She is drowned already, sir, with   *malice*
    salt water, though I seem to drown her remembrance again
    with more.

ANTONIO   Pardon me, sir, your bad entertainment.[4]

SEBASTIAN   O good Antonio, forgive me your trouble.

30 ANTONIO   If you will not murder me[5] for my love, let me be your
    servant.

SEBASTIAN   If you will not undo what you have done—that is,
    kill him whom you have recovered°—desire it not. Fare ye well   *rescued*
    at once. My bosom is full of kindness,° and I am yet° so near   *tender emotion / still*
35 the manners of my mother[6] that upon the least occasion more
    mine eyes will tell tales of me.° I am bound to the Count   *betray my feelings*
    Orsino's court. Farewell.   *Exit*

ANTONIO   The gentleness° of all the gods go with thee!   *favor*
    I have many enemies in Orsino's court,
40 Else would I very shortly see thee there.
    But come what may, I do adore thee so
    That danger shall seem sport, and I will go.   *Exit*

[handwritten marginal note: love as religious worship?*]*

2.1 Location: Near the coast of Illyria.
1. Evil influence of the stars; "malignancy" also signifies
a deadly disease.
2. Therefore courtesy requires.

3. Possibly Messina, Sicily.
4. Your poor reception; your inhospitality.
5. Murder him by insisting that they part.
6. So near woman's readiness to weep.

2.2

Enter VIOLA *as Cesario, and* MALVOLIO, *at* several° *doors*   separate

MALVOLIO   Were not you ev'n° now with the Countess Olivia?   just

VIOLA   Even now, sir, on° a moderate pace, I have since arrived   at
but hither.°   come only this far

MALVOLIO [*offering a ring*]   She returns this ring to you, sir.

5   You might have saved me my pains to have taken° it away your-   by taking
self. She adds, moreover, that you should put your lord into a
desperate assurance° she will none of him. And one thing   hopeless certainty
more: that you be never so hardy° to come again in his affairs,   bold
unless it be to report your lord's taking of this.[1] Receive it so.

10 VIOLA   She took the ring of me.[2] I'll none of it.

MALVOLIO   Come, sir, you peevishly threw it to her, and her will
is it should be so returned.

[*He throws the ring down*]

If it be worth stooping for, there it lies, in your eye;° if not, be   sight
it his that finds it.   *Exit*

15 VIOLA [*picking up the ring*]   I left no ring with her. What means this lady?
Fortune forbid my outside° have not charmed her.   appearance
She made good view of° me, indeed so much   looked carefully at
That straight methought her eyes had lost° her tongue,   made her lose
For she did speak in starts, distractedly.

20 She loves me, sure. The cunning of her passion
Invites me in° this churlish messenger.   by means of
None of my lord's ring! Why, he sent her none.
I am the man.[3] If it be so—as 'tis—
Poor lady, she were better love a dream!

25 Disguise, I see thou art a wickedness   *Attack on "Disguise"*
Wherein the pregnant enemy[4] does much.   *personification*
How easy is it for the proper false[5]   *Expresses pity for Olivia*
In women's waxen hearts to set their forms![6]
Alas, our frailty is the cause, not we,

30 For such as we are made of, such we be.[7]
How will this fadge?° My master loves her dearly.   turn out
And I, poor monster,[8] fond° as much on him,   dote
And she, mistaken, seems to dote on me.
What will become of this? As I am man,

35 My state is desperate° for my master's love.   hopeless
As I am woman, now, alas the day,
What thriftless° sighs shall poor Olivia breathe!   unprofitable
O time, thou must untangle this, not I.
It is too hard a knot for me t'untie.   [*Exit*]

2.3

Enter SIR TOBY *and* SIR ANDREW

SIR TOBY   Approach, Sir Andrew. Not to be abed after midnight
is to be up betimes,° and *diliculo surgere*,[1] thou knowest.   early

---

2.2 Location: Between Olivia's house and Orsino's palace.
1. Reception of this rejection.
2. Viola pretends to believe Olivia's story. *of*: from.
3. The man with whom she has fallen in love.
4. The devil, who is always quick and ready (to deceive).
5. Handsome, but deceitful (men).

6. *In . . forms*: To impress their images on women's affections (as a seal stamps its image in wax).
7. For being made of frail flesh, we are frail.
8. Since she is both man and woman.
2.3 Location: Olivia's house.
1. Part of a Latin proverb, meaning "to rise at dawn (is most healthy)."

SIR ANDREW   Nay, by my troth,° I know not; but I know to be up   *faith*
   late is to be up late.

5 SIR TOBY   A false conclusion. I hate it as an unfilled can.° To be   *tankard*
   up after midnight and to go to bed then is early; so that to go
   to bed after midnight is to go to bed betimes. Does not our lives
   consist of the four elements?[2]

   SIR ANDREW   Faith, so they say, but I think it rather consists of
10 eating and drinking.

   SIR TOBY   Thou'rt a scholar; let us therefore eat and drink. Mar-
   ian, I say, a stoup° of wine.   *two-pint tankard*
         Enter [FESTE, the] clown

   SIR ANDREW   Here comes the fool, i'faith.

   FESTE   How now, my hearts. Did you never see the picture of
15 'we three'?[3]

   SIR TOBY   Welcome, ass. Now let's have a catch.[4]

   SIR ANDREW   By my troth, the fool has an excellent breast.° I had   *singing voice*
   rather than forty shillings I had such a leg,° and so sweet a   *(for dancing)*
   breath to sing, as the fool has. In sooth, thou wast in very gra-
20 cious fooling last night, when thou spokest of Pigrogromitus, of
   the Vapians passing the equinoctial of Queubus.[5] 'Twas very
   good, i'faith. I sent thee sixpence for thy leman.° Hadst it?   *sweetheart*

   FESTE   I did impeticos thy gratility;[6] for Malvolio's nose is no
   whipstock. My lady has a white hand, and the Myrmidons are
25 no bottle-ale houses.[7]

   SIR ANDREW   Excellent! Why, this is the best fooling, when all is
   done. Now a song.

   SIR TOBY   [*to* FESTE]   Come on, there is sixpence for you. Let's
   have a song.

30 SIR ANDREW   [*to* FESTE]   There's a testril[8] of me, too. If one knight
   give a—[9]

   FESTE   Would you have a love-song, or a song of good life?

   SIR TOBY   A love song, a love-song.

   SIR ANDREW   Ay, ay. I care not for good life.

   FESTE (*sings*)
35   O mistress mine, where are you roaming?
         O stay and hear, your true love's coming,
            That can sing both high and low.
         Trip° no further, pretty sweeting.   *Go*
         Journeys end in lovers meeting,
40   Every wise man's son doth know.[1]

   SIR ANDREW   Excellent good, i'faith.

   SIR TOBY   Good, good.

   FESTE   What is love? 'Tis not hereafter,
         Present mirth hath present laughter.
45   What's to come is still° unsure.   *always*
         In delay there lies no plenty,

---

2. The four elements, thought to make up all matter,
were earth, air, fire, and water.
3. A trick picture portraying two fools' or asses' heads, the
third being the viewer.
4. Round: a simple song for several voices.
5. *Pigrogromitus . . . Queubus:* Feste's mock learning.
equinoctial: equator of the astronomical heavens.
6. Comic jargon for "impocket (or impetticoat) your gra-
tuity."
7. *for . . . houses:* perhaps it is the sheer inscrutability of
Feste's foolery that so impresses Sir Andrew (line 26).

whipstock: handle of a whip. *bottle-ale houses:* cheap
taverns.
8. Sir Andrew's version of "tester" (sixpence).
9. In F, "give a" appears at the end of a justified line; an
omission is possible.
1. *O mistress . . . know:* the words are not certainly
Shakespeare's; they fit the tune of an instrumental piece
printed in Thomas Morley's *First Book of Consort Lessons* (1599). *wise man's son:* wise men were thought to
have foolish sons.

Then come kiss me, sweet and twenty.°   *twenty times sweet*
    Youth's a stuff will not endure.

SIR ANDREW   A mellifluous voice, as I am true knight.

50   SIR TOBY   A contagious breath.[2]

SIR ANDREW   Very sweet and contagious, i'faith.

SIR TOBY   To hear by the nose, it is dulcet in contagion.[3] But
    shall we make the welkin° dance indeed? Shall we rouse the   *sky*
    night-owl in a catch that will draw three souls out of one
55   weaver?[4] Shall we do that?

SIR ANDREW   An° you love me, let's do't. I am dog° at a catch.   *If / clever*

FESTE   By'r Lady, sir, and some dogs will catch well.

SIR ANDREW   Most certain. Let our catch be 'Thou knave'.

FESTE   'Hold thy peace, thou knave',[5] knight. I shall be con-
60   strained in't to call thee knave, knight.

SIR ANDREW   'Tis not the first time I have constrained one to call
    me knave. Begin, fool. It begins 'Hold thy peace'.

FESTE   I shall never begin if I hold my peace.

SIR ANDREW   Good, i'faith. Come, begin.

       [*They sing the*] *catch.*
       Enter MARIA

65   MARIA   What a caterwauling do you keep here! If my lady have
    not called up her steward Malvolio and bid him turn you out
    of doors, never trust me.

SIR TOBY   My lady's a Cathayan,[6] we are politicians,° Malvolio's   *schemers*
    a Peg-o'-Ramsey,[7] and 'Three merry men be we'. Am not I con-
70   sanguineous?[8] Am I not of her blood? Tilly-vally°—'lady'!   *Fiddlesticks*
    'There dwelt a man in Babylon, lady, lady'.[9]

FESTE   Beshrew° me, the knight's in admirable fooling.   *Curse*

SIR ANDREW   Ay, he does well enough if he be disposed, and so
    do I, too. He does it with a better grace, but I do it more
75   natural.[1]

SIR TOBY   'O' the twelfth day of December'[2]—

MARIA   For the love o' God, peace.

       Enter MALVOLIO

MALVOLIO   My masters, are you mad? Or what are you? Have
    you no wit,° manners, nor honesty,° but to gabble like tinkers   *sense / decency*
80   at this time of night? Do ye make an alehouse of my lady's
    house, that ye squeak out your coziers' catches without any
    mitigation or remorse[3] of voice? Is there no respect of place,
    persons, nor time in you?

SIR TOBY   We did keep time, sir, in our catches. Sneck up!°   *Go hang yourself*

85   MALVOLIO   Sir Toby, I must be round° with you. My lady bade   *plainspoken*
    me tell you that though she harbours you as her kinsman she's
    nothing allied to your disorders. If you can separate yourself
    and your misdemeanours you are welcome to the house. If not,

---

2. Catchy voice; with a play on "disease-causing air."

3. If one could hear through the nose, the sound would
be sweetly ("dulcet") infectious.

4. Weavers were traditionally addicted to psalm singing,
so to move them with popular catches would be a great
triumph. Music was said to be able to draw the soul from
the body.

5. The words of the catch are "Hold thy peace, I prithee
hold thy peace, thou knave" (see Textual Note). Each
singer repeatedly calls the others knaves and tells them
to stop singing.

6. Chinese; but also ethnocentric slang for "trickster" or

"cheat."

7. Name of a dance and popular song; here, used
contemptuously.

8. A blood relative of Olivia's. 'Three . . . we': a refrain
from a popular song.

9. The opening and refrain of a popular song called
"Constant Susanna."

1. Effortlessly; but unconsciously playing on "fool" or
"idiot."

2. Snatch of a ballad; or possibly a drunken version of
"twelfth day of Christmas"—that is, Twelfth Night.

3. Without any abating or softening.

an it would please you to take leave of her she is very willing to
90   bid you farewell.

SIR TOBY 'Farewell, dear heart, since I must needs be gone.'⁴

MARIA Nay, good Sir Toby.

FESTE 'His eyes do show his days are almost done.'

MALVOLIO Is't even so?

95   SIR TOBY 'But I will never die.'

FESTE 'Sir Toby, there you lie.'

MALVOLIO This is much credit to you.

SIR TOBY 'Shall I bid him go?'

FESTE 'What an if° you do?'   *an if*=if

100   SIR TOBY 'Shall I bid him go, and spare not?'

FESTE 'O no, no, no, no, you dare not.'

SIR TOBY Out o' tune, sir, ye lie. [*To* MALVOLIO] Art any more
      than a steward? Dost thou think because thou art virtuous there
      shall be no more cakes and ale?⁵

105   FESTE Yes, by Saint Anne, and ginger⁶ shall be hot i'th' mouth,
      too.

SIR TOBY Thou'rt i'th' right. [*To* MALVOLIO] Go, sir, rub your
      chain with crumbs.⁷ [*To* MARIA] A stoup of wine, Maria.

MALVOLIO Mistress Mary, if you prized my lady's favour at any-

110   thing more than contempt you would not give means° for this   *drink*
      uncivil rule.° She shall know of it, by this hand.   *Exit*⁸   *behavior*

MARIA Go shake your ears.°   *(like an ass)*

SIR ANDREW 'Twere as good a deed as to drink when a man's a-
      hungry to challenge him the field° and then to break promise   *to a duel*

115   with him, and make a fool of him.

SIR TOBY Do't, knight. I'll write thee a challenge, or I'll deliver
      thy indignation to him by word of mouth.

MARIA Sweet Sir Toby, be patient for tonight. Since the youth
      of the Count's was today with my lady she is much out of quiet.

120   For Monsieur Malvolio, let me alone with him. If I do not gull
      him into a nayword⁹ and make him a common recreation,° do   *sport; jest*
      not think I have wit enough to lie straight in my bed. I know I
      can do it.

SIR TOBY Possess° us, possess us, tell us something of him.   *Inform*

125   MARIA Marry, sir, sometimes he is a kind of puritan.¹

SIR ANDREW O, if I thought that I'd beat him like a dog.

SIR TOBY What, for being a puritan? Thy exquisite° reason, dear   *ingenious*
      knight.

SIR ANDREW I have no exquisite reason for't, but I have reason

130   good enough.

MARIA The dev'l a puritan that he is, or anything constantly but
      a time-pleaser,° an affectioned° ass that cons state without book   *boot licker / affected*
      and utters it by great swathes;² the best persuaded of himself,³
      so crammed, as he thinks, with excellencies, that it is his

---

4. Part of another song that Sir Toby and Feste adapt for
the occasion.
5. *cakes and ale*: traditionally associated with church
festivals, and therefore disliked by Puritans.
6. Used to spice ale. *Saint Anne*: mother of the Virgin;
the oath would be offensive to Puritans who attacked her
cult.
7. Clean your steward's chain; mind your own business.
8. Feste plays no further part in this scene, and he seems
not to be present by line 153. This is the suggested exit

for him.
9. If I do not trick ("gull") him into a byword (for
"dupe").
1. Could mean "morally strict and censorious," as well as
"a follower of the Puritan religious faith."
2. *cons . . . swathes*: memorizes dignified and high-flown
language and utters it in great sweeps (like hay falling
under a scythe).
3. Having the highest opinion of himself.

135 grounds of faith° that all that look on him love him; and on   *his creed*
that vice in him will my revenge find notable cause to work.

SIR TOBY What wilt thou do?

MARIA I will drop in his way some obscure epistles of love,
wherein by the colour of his beard, the shape of his leg, the
140 manner of his gait, the expressure° of his eye, forehead, and   *expression*
complexion, he shall find himself most feelingly personated.° I   *represented*
can write very like my lady your niece; on a forgotten° matter   *bygone*
we can hardly make distinction of our hands.°   *handwriting*

SIR TOBY Excellent, I smell a device.

145 SIR ANDREW I have't in my nose too.

SIR TOBY He shall think by the letters that thou wilt drop that
they come from my niece, and that she's in love with him.

MARIA My purpose is indeed a horse of that colour.

SIR ANDREW And your horse now would make him an ass.

150 MARIA Ass° I doubt not.   *(punning on "as")*

SIR ANDREW O, 'twill be admirable.

MARIA Sport royal, I warrant you. I know my physic° will work   *medicine*
with him. I will plant you two—and let the fool make a third—
where he shall find the letter. Observe his construction° of it.   *interpretation*
155 For this night, to bed, and dream on the event.° Farewell.   *outcome*

Exit

SIR TOBY Good night, Penthesilea.[4]

SIR ANDREW Before me,[5] she's a good wench.

SIR TOBY She's a beagle true bred, and one that adores me. What
o' that?

160 SIR ANDREW I was adored once, too.

SIR TOBY Let's to bed, knight. Thou hadst need send for more
money.

SIR ANDREW If I cannot recover° your niece, I am a foul way   *win*
out.°   *out of money*

165 SIR TOBY Send for money, knight. If thou hast her not i'th' end,
call me cut.[6]

SIR ANDREW If I do not, never trust me, take it how you will.

SIR TOBY Come, come, I'll go burn some sack,[7] 'tis too late to
go to bed now. Come knight, come knight.   *Exeunt*

2.4

Enter Duke, VIOLA [as Cesario], CURIO, and others

ORSINO Give me some music. Now good morrow,° friends.   *morning*
Now good Cesario, but° that piece of song,   *just*
That old and antic° song we heard last night.   *quaint*
Methought it did relieve my passion° much,   *suffering*
5 More than light airs and recollected° terms   *studied; artificial*
Of these most brisk and giddy-pacèd times.
Come, but one verse.

CURIO He is not here, so please your lordship, that should sing
it.

10 ORSINO Who was it?

4. Queen of the Amazons (a joke about Maria's small
size).
5. On my soul (a mild oath).
6. A dock-tailed horse; also, slang for "gelding" or for

"female genitals."
7. I'll go warm and spice some Spanish wine.
2.4 Location: Orsino's palace.

CURIO   Feste the jester, my lord, a fool that the lady Olivia's
     father took much delight in. He is about the house.
ORSINO   Seek him out, and play the tune the while.

                                              [*Exit* CURIO]

     Music plays
     [*To* VIOLA] Come hither, boy. If ever thou shalt love,
15   In the sweet pangs of it remember me;
     For such as I am, all true lovers are,
     Unstaid° and skittish in all motions° else   *Unstable / emotions*
     Save in the constant image of the creature
     That is beloved. How dost thou like this tune?
20 VIOLA   It gives a very echo to the seat
     Where love is throned.[1]
ORSINO   Thou dost speak masterly.°   *expertly*
     My life upon't, young though thou art thine eye
     Hath stayed upon some favour° that it loves.   *face*
     Hath it not, boy?
VIOLA   A little, by your favour.°   *leave; face*
ORSINO   What kind of woman is't?
25 VIOLA   Of your complexion.
ORSINO   She is not worth thee then. What years, i'faith?
VIOLA   About your years, my lord.
ORSINO   Too old, by heaven. Let still° the woman take   *always*
     An elder than herself. So wears° she to him;   *adapts*
30   So sways she level[2] in her husband's heart.
     For, boy, however we do praise ourselves,
     Our fancies° are more giddy and unfirm,   *affections*
     More longing, wavering, sooner lost and worn,°   *exhausted*
     Than women's are.
VIOLA   I think° it well, my lord.   *believe*
35 ORSINO   Then let thy love be younger than thyself,
     Or thy affection cannot hold the bent;[3]
     For women are as roses, whose fair flower
     Being once displayed,° doth fall that very hour.   *opened*
VIOLA   And so they are. Alas that they are so:
40   To die even° when they to perfection grow.   *just*
          Enter CURIO *and* [FESTE, *the*] *clown*
ORSINO [*to* FESTE]   O fellow, come, the song we had last night.
     Mark it, Cesario, it is old and plain.
     The spinsters,° and the knitters in the sun,   *spinners*
     And the free° maids that weave their thread with bones,[4]   *carefree*
45   Do use to chant it. It is silly sooth,°   *simple truth*
     And dallies with° the innocence of love,   *lingers lovingly on*
     Like the old° age.   *golden*
FESTE   Are you ready, sir?
ORSINO   I prithee, sing.
          Music
50 FESTE [*sings*]   Come away,° come away death,   *Come hither*
          And in sad cypress[5] let me be laid.
          Fie away, fie away breath,
          I am slain by a fair cruel maid.

---

1. *It . . . throned:* It reflects back to the heart.
2. So does she balance influence and affection.
3. Cannot remain at full stretch (like the tautness of a
bowstring).

4. Spools made from bone on which lace (called "bone
lace") was woven.
5. Cypress-wood coffin. Like yews, cypresses were
emblematic of mourning.

My shroud of white, stuck all with yew,°   *yew sprigs*
55   O prepare it.
My part of death no one so true
      Did share it.[6]
Not a flower, not a flower sweet

      On my black coffin let there be strewn.
60   Not a friend, not a friend greet
      My poor corpse, where my bones shall be thrown.
     A thousand thousand sighs to save,
      Lay me O where
      Sad true lover never find my grave,
65   To weep there.

ORSINO [*giving money*]   There's for thy pains.

FESTE   No pains, sir. I take pleasure in singing, sir.

ORSINO   I'll pay thy pleasure then.

FESTE   Truly, sir, and pleasure will be paid,° one time or   *paid for*
70   another.

ORSINO   Give me now leave° to leave° thee.   *permission / dismiss*

FESTE   Now the melancholy god[7] protect thee, and the tailor
make thy doublet of changeable taffeta,[8] for thy mind is a very
opal.[9] I would have men of such constancy put to sea, that their
75   business might be everything, and their intent° everywhere, for   *destination*
that's it that always makes a good voyage of nothing.[1] Farewell.
                                      Exit

ORSINO   Let all the rest give place:°   [*Exeunt* CURIO *and others*]   *withdraw*
                         Once more, Cesario,
Get thee to yon same sovereign cruelty.
Tell her my love, more noble than the world,
80 Prizes not quantity of dirty lands.
The parts° that fortune hath bestowed upon her   *possessions*
Tell her I hold as giddily[2] as fortune;
But 'tis that miracle and queen of gems
That nature pranks° her in attracts my soul.   *adorns*
85 VIOLA   But if she cannot love you, sir?

ORSINO   I cannot be so answered.

VIOLA   Sooth,° but you must.   *In truth*
Say that some lady, as perhaps there is,
Hath for your love as great a pang of heart
As you have for Olivia. You cannot love her.
90 You tell her so. Must she not then be answered?

ORSINO   There is no woman's sides
Can bide° the beating of so strong a passion   *withstand*
As love doth give my heart; no woman's heart
So big, to hold so much. They lack retention.°   *constancy*
95 Alas, their love may be called appetite,
No motion of the liver, but the palate,[3]
That suffer surfeit, cloyment,° and revolt.°   *satiety / revulsion*
But mine is all as hungry as the sea,

---

6. *My part . . . it:* No one has died so true to love as I.
7. Saturn (thought to control the melancholic).
8. Shot silk, whose color changes with the angle of vision. *doublet:* close-fitting jacket.
9. An iridescent gemstone that changes color depending on the angle from which it is seen.
1. *that's . . . nothing:* this fickle lack of direction can

make a voyage in the notoriously changeful sea carefree and consonant with one's desires.
2. Lightly (fortune being fickle).
3. *appetite . . . palate:* appetite, like the palate, is easily sated, and thus lacks the emotional depth and complexity of real love, whose seat is the liver. *motion:* impulse.

And can digest as much. Make no compare
100 Between that love a woman can bear me
And that I owe° Olivia.   *have for*
VIOLA   Ay, but I know—
ORSINO   What dost thou know?
VIOLA   Too well what love women to men may owe.
105 In faith, they are as true of heart as we.
My father had a daughter loved a man
As it might be, perhaps, were I a woman
I should your lordship.
ORSINO   And what's her history?
VIOLA   A blank, my lord. She never told her love,
110 But let concealment, like a worm i'th' bud,
Feed on her damask⁴ cheek. She pined in thought,
And with a green and yellow° melancholy   *pale and sallow*
She sat like patience on a monument,⁵
Smiling at grief. Was not this love indeed?
115 We men may say more, swear more, but indeed
Our shows are more than will;⁶ for still° we prove   *always*
Much in our vows, but little in our love.
ORSINO   But died thy sister of her love, my boy?
VIOLA   I am all the daughters of my father's house,
120 And all the brothers too; and yet I know not.
Sir, shall I to this lady?
ORSINO   Ay, that's the theme,
To her in haste. Give her this jewel. Say
My love can give no place, bide no denay.⁷ *Exeunt [severally]*

2.5

Enter SIR TOBY, SIR ANDREW, *and* FABIAN

SIR TOBY   Come thy ways,° Signor Fabian.   *Come along*
FABIAN   Nay, I'll come. If I lose a scruple° of this sport let me be   *miss a scrap*
boiled to death with melancholy.¹
SIR TOBY   Wouldst thou not be glad to have the niggardly rascally
5   sheep-biter² come by some notable shame?
FABIAN   I would exult, man. You know he brought me out o'
favour with my lady about a bear-baiting³ here.
SIR TOBY   To anger him we'll have the bear again, and we will
fool° him black and blue, shall we not, Sir Andrew?   *mock*
10 SIR ANDREW   An° we do not, it is pity of our lives.   *If*
Enter MARIA [*with a letter*]
SIR TOBY   Here comes the little villain. How now, my metal of
India?⁴
MARIA   Get ye all three into the box-tree.° Malvolio's coming   *hedge of boxwood*
down this walk. He has been yonder i' the sun practising behav-
15 iour to his own shadow this half-hour. Observe him, for the
love of mockery, for I know this letter will make a contempla-
tive° idiot of him. Close,° in the name of jesting!   *vacuous / Keep close; hide*

---

4. Pink and white, like a damask rose.
5. A memorial statue symbolizing patience.
6. Our displays of love are greater than our actual feelings.
7. My love cannot be bated, nor tolerate refusal.
2.5 Location: Olivia's garden.

1. Melancholy was a cold humor; "boiled" puns on
"bile," the surplus of which produced melancholy.
2. Literally, a dog that attacks sheep; here, a malicious
sneak.
3. Puritans disapproved of blood sports like bearbaiting.
4. A woman worth her weight in gold.

[*The men hide.* MARIA *places the letter*]
Lie thou there, for here comes the trout that must be caught
with tickling.[5]   *Exit*

Enter MALVOLIO

20 MALVOLIO 'Tis but fortune, all is fortune. Maria once told me
       she° did affect° me, and I have heard herself come thus near,   *(Olivia) / care for*
       that should she fancy° it should be one of my complexion.   *fall in love*
       Besides, she uses me with a more exalted respect than anyone
       else that follows her. What should I think on't?

25 SIR TOBY Here's an overweening rogue.
    FABIAN O, peace! Contemplation makes a rare turkeycock[6] of
       him—how he jets° under his advanced° plumes!   *struts / raised*
    SIR ANDREW 'Slight,[7] I could so beat the rogue.
    SIR TOBY Peace, I say.

30 MALVOLIO To be Count Malvolio!
    SIR TOBY Ah, rogue.
    SIR ANDREW Pistol him, pistol him.
    SIR TOBY Peace, peace.
    MALVOLIO There is example° for't: the Lady of the Strachey mar-   *precedent*
35   ried the yeoman of the wardrobe.[8]
    SIR ANDREW Fie on him, Jezebel.[9]
    FABIAN O peace, now he's deeply in. Look how imagination
       blows him.°   *puffs him up*
    MALVOLIO Having been three months married to her, sitting in
40   my state°—   *chair of state*
    SIR TOBY O for a stone-bow[1] to hit him in the eye!
    MALVOLIO Calling my officers° about me, in my branched° vel-   *household attendants*
       vet gown, having come from a day-bed° where I have left Olivia   *couch*
       sleeping—
45 SIR TOBY Fire and brimstone!
    FABIAN O peace, peace!
    MALVOLIO And then to have the humour of state[3] and—after a
       demure travel of regard,[4] telling them I know my place, as I
       would they should do theirs—to ask for my kinsman Toby.
50 SIR TOBY Bolts and shackles!
    FABIAN O peace, peace, peace, now, now.
    MALVOLIO Seven of my people with an obedient start make° out   *go*
       for him. I frown the while, and perchance wind up my watch,
       or play with my—[*touching his chain*][5] some rich jewel. Toby
55   approaches; curtsies° there to me.   *bows*
    SIR TOBY Shall this fellow live?
    FABIAN Though our silence be drawn from us with cars,[6] yet
       peace.
    MALVOLIO I extend my hand to him thus, quenching my famil-
60   iar smile with an austere regard of control—
    SIR TOBY And does not Toby take° you a blow o' the lips, then?   *give*

5. Flattery; trout can be caught by stroking them under
the gills.
6. Proverbially proud; they display their feathers like
peacocks.
7. By God's light (an oath).
8. Perhaps an allusion to a noblewoman who had married her manservant, but there is no certain identification. *yeoman of the wardrobe*: keeper of clothes and linen.
9. Biblical allusion to the proud wife of Ahab, King of
Israel.

1. Catapult, or crossbow for stones.
2. Embroidered with branch patterns.
3. To adopt the grand air of exalted greatness.
4. After casting my eyes gravely about the room.
5. Malvolio momentarily forgets that he will have abandoned his steward's chain; watches were an expensive
luxury at this time.
6. A prisoner might be tied to two carts or chariots
("cars") and pulled by horses in opposite directions to
extort information.

MALVOLIO Saying 'Cousin Toby, my fortunes, having cast me
on your niece, give me this prerogative of speech'—
SIR TOBY What, what!
65 MALVOLIO 'You must amend your drunkenness.'
SIR TOBY Out, scab.
FABIAN Nay, patience, or we break the sinews of our plot.
MALVOLIO 'Besides, you waste the treasure of your time with a
foolish knight'—
70 SIR ANDREW That's me, I warrant you.
MALVOLIO 'One Sir Andrew.'
SIR ANDREW I knew 'twas I, for many do call me fool.
MALVOLIO [seeing the letter] What employment° have we here?   business
FABIAN Now is the woodcock near the gin.[7]
75 SIR TOBY O peace, and the spirit of humours intimate[8] reading
aloud to him.
MALVOLIO [taking up the letter] By my life, this is my lady's
hand. These be her very c's, her u's, and her t's,[9] and thus
makes she her great P's. It is in contempt of° question her   beyond
80 hand.
SIR ANDREW Her c's, her u's, and her t's? Why that?
MALVOLIO [reads] 'To the unknown beloved, this, and my good
wishes.' Her very phrases! [Opening the letter] By your leave,
wax[1]—soft,° and the impressure her Lucrece,[2] with which she   wait
85 uses to seal° —'tis my lady. To whom should this be?   habitually seals
FABIAN This wins him, liver and all.
MALVOLIO   'Jove knows I love,
                    But who?
                Lips do not move,
90   No man must know.'
'No man must know.' What follows? The numbers altered.°   meter changed
'No man must know.' If this should be thee, Malvolio?
SIR TOBY Marry, hang thee, brock.[3]
MALVOLIO 'I may command where I adore,
95   But silence like a Lucrece knife
          With bloodless stroke my heart doth gore.
          M.O.A.I. doth sway my life.'
FABIAN A fustian° riddle.   bombastic
SIR TOBY Excellent wench, say I.
100 MALVOLIO 'M.O.A.I. doth sway my life.' Nay, but first let me
see, let me see, let me see.
FABIAN What dish o' poison has she dressed° him!   prepared
SIR TOBY And with what wing the staniel checks at it![4]
MALVOLIO 'I may command where I adore.' Why, she may com-
105 mand me. I serve her, she is my lady. Why, this is evident to
any formal capacity.° There is no obstruction in this. And the   normal intelligence
end—what should that alphabetical position° portend? If I   arrangement
could make that resemble something in me. Softly—'M.O.A.I.'
SIR TOBY O ay,[5] make up that, he is now at a cold scent.

7. Snare. woodcock: a proverbially foolish bird.
8. And may a capricious impulse suggest.
9. Malvolio unwittingly spells out "cut," slang for "female
genitals"; the meaning is compounded by "great P's." In
fact, these letters do not appear on the outside of the
letter.

1. By . . . wax: addressed to the sealing wax.
2. The figure of Lucrece, Roman model of chastity, is the
device ("impressure") imprinted on the seal.
3. Badger (proverbially stinking).
4. And with what alacrity the sparrow hawk goes after it.
5. O, ay: playing on "O.I."

110 FABIAN Sowter will cry upon't for all this, though it be as rank
as a fox.[6]

MALVOLIO 'M.' Malvolio—'M'—why, that begins my name.

FABIAN Did not I say he would work it out? The cur is excellent
at faults.[7]

115 MALVOLIO 'M.' But then there is no consonancy in the sequel.[8]
That suffers under probation.[9] 'A' should follow, but 'O' does.

FABIAN And 'O'[1] shall end, I hope.

SIR TOBY Ay, or I'll cudgel him, and make him cry 'O!'

MALVOLIO And then 'I' comes behind.

120 FABIAN Ay, an you had any eye behind you you might see more
detraction° at your heels than fortunes before you.   *defamation*

MALVOLIO 'M.O.A.I.' This simulation° is not as the former; and   *disguise; riddle*
yet to crush° this a little, it would bow° to me, for every one of   *force / yield; point*
these letters are in my name. Soft, here follows prose: 'If this

125 fall into thy hand, revolve.° In my stars° I am above thee, but   *consider / fortunes*
be not afraid of greatness. Some are born great, some achieve
greatness, and some have greatness thrust upon 'em. Thy fates
open their hands,° let thy blood and spirit embrace them, and   *bestow gifts*
to inure° thyself to what thou art like° to be, cast thy humble   *accustom / likely*

130 slough,[2] and appear fresh. Be opposite° with a kinsman, surly   *contrary*
with servants. Let thy tongue tang arguments of state;[3] put thy-
self into the trick of singularity.° She thus advises thee that sighs *cultivate eccentricity*
for thee. Remember who commended thy yellow stockings,
and wished to see thee ever cross-gartered.[4] I say remember, go

135 to,[5] thou art made if thou desirest to be so; if not, let me see
thee a steward still, the fellow of servants, and not worthy to
touch Fortune's fingers. Farewell. She that would alter services[6] with thee,

The Fortunate-Unhappy.'

140 Daylight and champaign discovers[7] not more. This is open.°   *clear*
I will be proud, I will read politic° authors, I will baffle° Sir   *political*
Toby, I will wash off gross acquaintance, I will be point-device
the very man.[9] I do not now fool myself, to let imagination
jade° me; for every reason excites to this, that my lady loves me.   *trick*

145 She did commend my yellow stockings of late, she did praise
my leg, being cross-gartered, and in this she manifests herself
to my love, and with a kind of injunction drives me to these
habits° of her liking. I thank my stars, I am happy. I will be   *clothes*
strange,° stout,° in yellow stockings, and cross-gartered, even   *aloof / proud*

150 with the swiftness of putting on. Jove and my stars be praised.
Here is yet a postscript. 'Thou canst not choose but know who
I am. If thou entertainest° my love, let it appear in thy smiling,   *accept*
thy smiles become thee well. Therefore in my presence still°   *constantly*
smile, dear my sweet, I prithee.' Jove, I thank thee. I will smile,

155 I will do everything that thou wilt have me.   *Exit*

---

6. "Sowter" (the name of a hound), having lost the scent, will start to bay loudly as he picks up the new, rank (stinking) smell of the fox. *though*: as though.
7. At picking up a scent after it is momentarily lost. A "fault" is a "cold scent" (line 109).
8. There is no consistency in what follows.
9. That weakens upon being put to the test.
1. As in the hangman's noose; the last letter of Malvolio's name; or "O" as a lamentation.
2. A snake's old skin, which peels away.
3. Let your tongue ring out arguments of statecraft or

politics.
4. An antiquated way of adjusting a garter—going once below the knee, crossing behind it, and knotting above the knee at the side.
5. An emphatic expression, like "I tell you."
6. Change places (of servant and mistress or master).
7. *champaign discovers*: open countryside reveals.
8. Term used to describe the formal unmaking of a knight; hence, "disgrace."
9. I will be in every detail the identical man (described in the letter).

[SIR TOBY, SIR ANDREW, *and* FABIAN *come from hiding*]

FABIAN I will not give my part of this sport for a pension of
thousands to be paid from the Sophy.°   *Shah of Persia*

SIR TOBY I could marry this wench for this device.

SIR ANDREW So could I, too.

160 SIR TOBY And ask no other dowry with her but such another jest.

    Enter MARIA

SIR ANDREW Nor I neither.

FABIAN Here comes my noble gull-catcher.°   *trickster*

SIR TOBY [*to* MARIA] Wilt thou set thy foot o' my neck?

SIR ANDREW [*to* MARIA] Or o' mine either?

165 SIR TOBY [*to* MARIA] Shall I play my freedom at tray-trip,[1] and
become thy bondslave?

SIR ANDREW [*to* MARIA] I'faith, or I either?

SIR TOBY [*to* MARIA] Why, thou hast put him in such a dream
that when the image of it leaves him, he must run mad.

170 MARIA Nay, but say true, does it work upon him?

SIR TOBY Like aqua vitae° with a midwife.   *spirits; liquor*

MARIA If you will then see the fruits of the sport, mark his first
approach before my lady. He will come to her in yellow stockings, and 'tis a colour she abhors, and cross-gartered, a fashion

175 she detests; and he will smile upon her, which will now be so
unsuitable to her disposition, being addicted to a melancholy
as she is, that it cannot but turn him into a notable contempt.[2]
If you will see it, follow me.

SIR TOBY To the gates of Tartar,° thou most excellent devil of   *hell*

180 wit.

SIR ANDREW I'll make one,° too.   *Exeunt*   *go along*

3.1

Enter VIOLA [*as Cesario*] *and* [FESTE, *the*] *clown* [*with
pipe and tabor*][1]

VIOLA Save° thee, friend, and thy music. Dost thou live by thy   *God save*
tabor?

FESTE No, sir, I live by° the church.   *near*

VIOLA Art thou a churchman?

5 FESTE No such matter, sir. I do live by[2] the church for I do live
at my house, and my house doth stand by the church.

VIOLA So thou mayst say the king lies by[3] a beggar if a beggar
dwell near him, or the church stands° by thy tabor if thy tabor   *is maintained*
stand by the church.

10 FESTE You have said, sir. To see this age!—A sentence° is but a   *saying*
cheverel° glove to a good wit, how quickly the wrong side may   *kidskin*
be turned outward.

VIOLA Nay, that's certain. They that dally nicely° with words   *play subtly*
may quickly make them wanton.[4]

15 FESTE I would therefore my sister had had no name, sir.

VIOLA Why, man?

FESTE Why, sir, her name's a word, and to dally with that word

---

1. A game of dice in which the winner throws a three
("tray" is from the Spanish *tres*). *play:* wager.
2. A notorious object of contempt.
3.1 Location: Olivia's garden.
1. The dialogue demands only a tabor, but jesters com-

monly played a pipe with one hand while tapping a tabor
(small drum, hanging from the neck) with the other.
2. I do earn my keep with.
3. Lives near; punning on "goes to bed with."
4. Equivocal; Feste puns on the sense "unchaste."

might make my sister wanton. But indeed, words are very rascals since bonds disgraced them.[5]

20 VIOLA   Thy reason, man?

FESTE   Troth, sir, I can yield you none without words, and words
are grown so false I am loath to prove reason with them.

VIOLA   I warrant thou art a merry fellow, and carest for nothing.

FESTE   Not so, sir, I do care for something; but in my con-
25 science, sir, I do not care for you. If that be to care for nothing,
sir, I would it would make you invisible.

VIOLA   Art not thou the Lady Olivia's fool?

FESTE   No indeed, sir, the Lady Olivia has no folly, she will keep
no fool, sir, till she be married, and fools are as like husbands
30 as pilchards[6] are to herrings—the husband's the bigger. I am
indeed not her fool, but her corrupter of words.

VIOLA   I saw thee late° at the Count Orsino's.   *lately*

FESTE   Foolery, sir, does walk about the orb[7] like the sun, it
shines everywhere. I would be sorry, sir, but the fool should be
35 as oft with your master as with my mistress.[8] I think I saw your
wisdom[9] there.

VIOLA   Nay, an thou pass upon[1] me, I'll no more with thee. [*Giving money*] Hold, there's expenses for thee.

FESTE   Now Jove in his next commodity° of hair send thee a   *shipment*
40 beard.

VIOLA   By my troth I'll tell thee, I am almost sick for one,[2]
though I would not have it grow on my chin. Is thy lady within?

FESTE   Would not a pair of these have bred,[3] sir?

VIOLA   Yes, being kept together and put to use.[4]

45 FESTE   I would play Lord Pandarus[5] of Phrygia, sir, to bring a
Cressida to this Troilus.

VIOLA [*giving money*]   I understand you, sir, 'tis well begged.

FESTE   The matter I hope is not great, sir; begging but a beggar—Cressida was a beggar.[6] My lady is within, sir. I will con-
50 ster° to them whence you come. Who you are and what you   *explain*
would are out of my welkin—I might say 'element', but the
word is over-worn.[7]   *Exit*

VIOLA   This fellow is wise enough to play the fool,
And to do that well craves a kind of wit.°   *intelligence*
55 He must observe their mood on whom he jests,
The quality of persons, and the time,
And, like the haggard, check at every feather
That comes before his eye.[8] This is a practice°   *skill*
As full of labour as a wise man's art,
60 For folly that he wisely shows is fit,[9]

---

5. Since legal contracts replaced a man's word of honor.
("Bonds" plays on "sworn statements" and "fetters," beto-
kening criminality.)

6. Small fish similar to herring.

7. World; the sun was still believed to circle the earth.

8. I, Feste, should visit master and mistress alike;
Orsino should be called "fool" as often as Olivia.

9. *your wisdom*: a mocking title for Cesario.

1. If you express an opinion of; if you joke about.

2. Almost eager for a beard; almost pining for a man
(Orsino).

3. Would not a pair of coins such as these have multiplied (with possible pun on "be enough to buy bread").

4. *put to use*: invested to produce interest.

5. Go-between, or "pander," since Feste needs a "mate"
for his coin(s). Shakespeare dramatizes the story in
Troilus and Cressida.

6. In asking for the "mate" to his Troilus coin, Feste
draws on a version of the story of Troilus and Cressida in
which Cressida became a beggar.

7. "Welkin" (sky or air) is synonymous with one meaning
of "element" used in what Feste regards as the overworn
phrase 'out of my element.'

8. *And . . . eye*: As a wild hawk ("haggard") must be sensitive to its prey's disposition.

9. For folly that he skillfully displays is proper.

But wise men, folly-fall'n, quite taint[1] their wit.

Enter SIR TOBY *and* [SIR] ANDREW

SIR TOBY Save you, gentleman.

VIOLA And you, sir.

SIR ANDREW *Dieu vous garde,*[2] *monsieur.*

65 VIOLA *Et vous aussi, votre serviteur.*[3]

SIR ANDREW I hope, sir, you are, and I am yours.

SIR TOBY Will you encounter[4] the house? My niece is desirous
you should enter if your trade be to her.

VIOLA I am bound to° your niece, sir: I mean she is the list° of   for / destination

70 my voyage.

SIR TOBY Taste° your legs, sir, put them to motion.   Try

VIOLA My legs do better understand° me, sir, than I understand   stand under
what you mean by bidding me taste my legs.

SIR TOBY I mean to go, sir, to enter.

75 VIOLA I will answer you with gait and entrance.

Enter OLIVIA, *and* [MARIA, *her*] *gentlewoman*

But we are prevented.° [*To* OLIVIA] Most excellent accom-   anticipated
plished lady, the heavens rain odours on you.

SIR ANDREW [*to* SIR TOBY] That youth's a rare° courtier; 'rain   an excellent
odours'—well.°   well put

80 VIOLA My matter hath no voice,° lady, but to your own most   must not be spoken
pregnant° and vouchsafed° ear.   receptive / proffered

SIR ANDREW [*to* SIR TOBY] 'Odours', 'pregnant', and 'vouchsafed'—I'll get 'em all three all ready.[5]

OLIVIA Let the garden door be shut, and leave me to my

85 hearing.   [*Exeunt* SIR TOBY, SIR ANDREW, *and* MARIA]
Give me your hand, sir.

VIOLA My duty, madam, and most humble service.

OLIVIA What is your name?

VIOLA Cesario is your servant's name, fair princess.

90 OLIVIA My servant, sir? 'Twas never merry world[6]
Since lowly feigning° was called compliment.   pretended humility
You're servant to the Count Orsino, youth.

VIOLA And he is yours, and his must needs be yours.
Your servant's servant is *your* servant, madam.

95 OLIVIA For° him, I think not on him. For his thoughts,   As for
Would they were blanks rather than filled with me.

VIOLA Madam, I come to whet your gentle thoughts
On his behalf.

OLIVIA   O by your leave,[7] I pray you.
I bade you never speak again of him;

100 But would you undertake another suit,
I had rather hear you to solicit that
Than music from the spheres.[8]

VIOLA   Dear lady—

OLIVIA Give me leave, beseech you. I did send,
After the last enchantment you did here,

105 A ring in chase of you. So did I abuse°   deceive; dishonor

---

1. Discredit; spoil. *folly-fall'n:* fallen into folly.
2. God protect you (French).
3. And you also, (I am) your servant. (Sir Andrew's awkward reply demonstrates that his French is limited.)
4. Pedantry for "enter" (Toby mocks Viola's courtly language).

5. *I'll . . . ready:* to commit to memory for later use.
6. *'Twas . . . world:* the proverbial "Things have never been the same."
7. Permit me to interrupt (polite expression).
8. Exquisite music thought to be made by the planets as they moved, but inaudible to mortal ears.

Myself, my servant, and I fear me you.°   *and, as I fear, you*
Under your hard construction⁹ must I sit,
To force° that on you in a shameful cunning   *For forcing*
Which you knew none of yours. What might you think?
110 Have you not set mine honour at the stake
And baited it with all th'unmuzzled thoughts¹
That tyrannous heart can think? To one of your receiving°   *perception*
Enough is shown. A cypress,² not a bosom,
Hides my heart. So let me hear you speak.
  VIOLA   I pity you.
115 OLIVIA   That's a degree to° love.   *toward*
  VIOLA   No, not a grece,° for 'tis a vulgar proof°   *step / common experience*
That very oft we pity enemies.
  OLIVIA   Why then, methinks 'tis time to smile again.³
O world, how apt° the poor are to be proud!   *ready*
120 If one should be a prey, how much the better
To fall before the lion than the wolf!⁴
        Clock strikes
The clock upbraids me with the waste of time.
Be not afraid, good youth, I will not have you;
And yet when wit and youth is come to harvest
125 Your wife is like to reap a proper° man.   *handsome; worthy*
There lies your way, due west.
  VIOLA   Then westward ho!⁵
Grace and good disposition° attend your ladyship.   *peace of mind*
You'll nothing, madam, to my lord by me?
  OLIVIA   Stay. I prithee tell me what thou⁶ think'st of me.
130 VIOLA   That you do think you are not what you are.⁷
  OLIVIA   If I think so, I think the same of you.⁸
  VIOLA   Then think you right, I am not what I am.
  OLIVIA   I would you were as I would have you be.
  VIOLA   Would it be better, madam, than I am?
135 I wish it might, for now I am your fool.⁹
  OLIVIA *[aside]*   O, what a deal of scorn looks beautiful
In the contempt and anger of his lip!
A murd'rous guilt shows not itself more soon
Than love that would seem hid. Love's night is noon.¹
140 *[To* VIOLA*]* Cesario, by the roses of the spring,
By maidhood, honour, truth, and everything,
I love thee so that, maugre° all thy pride,   *despite*
Nor° wit nor reason can my passion hide.   *Neither*
Do not extort thy reasons from this clause.²
145 For that° I woo, thou therefore hast no cause.   *That because*
But rather reason thus with reason fetter:³
Love sought is good, but given unsought, is better.

---

9. Your unfavorable interpretation (of my behavior).
1. *set . . . thoughts:* as bears that were tied up at the stake and baited with dogs.
2. Veil of transparent silken gauze; the cypress tree was also emblematic of mourning.
3. Time to discard love's melancholy.
4. *If . . . wolf:* If I had to fall prey to love, it would have been better to succumb to the noble Orsino than to the hardhearted Cesario.
5. Thames watermen's cry to attract passengers for the court at Westminster from London.
6. Olivia changes from "you" to the familiar "thou."

7. That you think you are in love with a man, but you are mistaken.
8. Olivia may think that Cesario has suggested that she is mad; or she may imply that she thinks that Cesario, despite his subordinate position, is noble.
9. You have made a fool of me.
1. Love, though attempting secrecy, still shines out as bright as day.
2. Do not take the position that just because I woo you, you are under no obligation to reciprocate.
3. But instead constrain your reasoning with this argument.

VIOLA By innocence I swear, and by my youth,
    I have one heart, one bosom, and one truth,
150   And that no woman has, nor never none
    Shall mistress be of it save I alone.
    And so adieu, good madam. Never more
    Will I my master's tears to you deplore.°   *lament*
OLIVIA Yet come again, for thou perhaps mayst move
155   That heart which now abhors, to like his love.

                                      Exeunt [*severally*]

3.2

Enter SIR TOBY, SIR ANDREW, *and* FABIAN

SIR ANDREW No, faith, I'll not stay a jot longer.
SIR TOBY Thy reason, dear venom,° give thy reason.   *venomous one*
FABIAN You must needs yield your reason, Sir Andrew.
SIR ANDREW Marry, I saw your niece do more favours to the
5   Count's servingman than ever she bestowed upon me. I saw't
    i'th' orchard.°   *garden*
SIR TOBY Did she see thee the while, old boy? Tell me that.
SIR ANDREW As plain as I see you now.
FABIAN This was a great argument° of love in her toward you.   *proof*
10 SIR ANDREW 'Slight,° will you make an ass o' me?   *By God's light*
FABIAN I will prove it legitimate, sir, upon the oaths of judge-
    ment and reason.
SIR TOBY And they have been grand-jurymen[1] since before
    Noah was a sailor.
15 FABIAN She did show favour to the youth in your sight only to
    exasperate you, to awake your dormouse° valour, to put fire in   *meek; timid*
    your heart and brimstone in your liver. You should then have
    accosted her, and with some excellent jests, fire-new from the
    mint,° you should have banged the youth into dumbness. This   *newly minted*
20   was looked for at your hand, and this was balked.° The double   *neglected*
    gilt[2] of this opportunity you let time wash off, and you are now
    sailed into the north of my lady's opinion,[3] where you will hang
    like an icicle on a Dutchman's[4] beard unless you do redeem it
    by some laudable attempt either of valour or policy.°   *cunning*
25 SIR ANDREW An't° be any way, it must be with valour, for policy   *If it*
    I hate. I had as lief° be a Brownist as a politician.[5]   *as soon*
SIR TOBY Why then, build me thy fortunes upon the basis of
    valour. Challenge me° the Count's youth to fight with him,   *for me*
    hurt him in eleven places. My niece shall take note of it; and
30   assure thyself, there is no love-broker in the world can more
    prevail in man's commendation with woman than report of
    valour.
FABIAN There is no way but this, Sir Andrew.
SIR ANDREW Will either of you bear me a challenge to him?
35 SIR TOBY Go, write it in a martial hand, be curst° and brief. It is   *sharp*
    no matter how witty so it be eloquent and full of invention.°   *imagination; untruth*

3.2 Location: Olivia's house.
1. Grand jurymen were supposed to be good judges of
evidence.
2. Twice gilded, and as such, Sir Andrew's "golden
opportunity" to prove both love and valor.

3. Into Olivia's cold disfavor.
4. Perhaps an allusion to navigator Willem Barents, who
led an expedition to the Arctic in 1596–97.
5. Schemer. A Brownist was a member of the Puritan
sect founded in 1581 by Robert Browne.

Taunt him with the licence of ink.[5] If thou 'thou'st'[7] him some
thrice, it shall not be amiss, and as many lies° as will lie in thy   *accusations of lying*
sheet of paper, although the sheet were big enough for the bed
40   of Ware,[8] in England, set 'em down, go about it. Let there be
gall[9] enough in thy ink; though thou write with a goose-pen,[1]
no matter. About it.

SIR ANDREW   Where shall I find you?

SIR TOBY   We'll call thee at the cubiculo.° Go.   *little chamber*

Exit SIR ANDREW

45   FABIAN   This is a dear manikin° to you, Sir Toby.   *puppet*

SIR TOBY   I have been dear° to him, lad, some two thousand   *costly*
strong or so.

FABIAN   We shall have a rare letter from him; but you'll not
deliver't.

50   SIR TOBY   Never trust me then; and by all means stir on the youth
to an answer. I think oxen and wain-ropes[2] cannot hale° them   *drag*
together. For Andrew, if he were opened and you find so much
blood in his liver[3] as will clog° the foot of a flea, I'll eat the rest   *weigh down*
of th'anatomy.°   *cadaver*

55   FABIAN   And his opposite,° the youth, bears in his visage no great   *adversary*
presage of cruelty.

Enter MARIA

SIR TOBY   Look where the youngest wren of nine[4] comes.

MARIA   If you desire the spleen,° and will laugh yourselves into   *a laughing fit*
stitches, follow me. Yon gull° Malvolio is turned heathen, a   *fool*
60   very renegado,[5] for there is no Christian that means to be saved
by believing rightly can ever believe such impossible passages
of grossness.[6] He's in yellow stockings.

SIR TOBY   And cross-gartered?

MARIA   Most villainously,° like a pedant° that keeps a school i'th'   *abominably / teacher*
65   church.[7] I have dogged him like his murderer. He does obey
every point of the letter that I dropped to betray him. He does
smile his face into more lines than is in the new map with the
augmentation of the Indies.[8] You have not seen such a thing as
'tis. I can hardly forbear hurling things at him. I know my lady
70   will strike him. If she do, he'll smile, and take't for a great
favour.

SIR TOBY   Come bring us, bring us where he is.   *Exeunt*

3.3

Enter SEBASTIAN *and* ANTONIO

SEBASTIAN   I would not by my will have troubled you,
But since you make your pleasure of your pains
I will no further chide you.

ANTONIO   I could not stay behind you. My desire,

6. *licence of ink:* freedom taken in writing, but not risked in conversation.
7. Call him "thou" (an insult to a stranger).
8. Famous Elizabethan bedstead, nearly eleven feet square, now in the Victoria and Albert Museum, London.
9. Oak gall, an ingredient in ink; bitterness or rancor.
1. Quill made of a goose feather. (The goose was proverbially cowardly and foolish.)
2. Wagon ropes pulled by oxen.
3. Supposed to be the source of blood, which engendered courage.

4. The smallest of small birds; the smallest wren in a family of nine.
5. Renegade (Spanish); a Christian converted to Islam.
6. Such patent absurdities (in the letter).
7. Because no schoolroom is available in a small rustic community.
8. Possibly refers to a map published in 1599 showing the East Indies more fully than in earlier maps and crisscrossed by many rhumb lines.
3.3 Location: A street scene.

5　More sharp than filèd steel, did spur me forth,
　　And not all° love to see you—though so much　　　　　　　　　　　*only*
　　As might have drawn one to a longer voyage—
　　But jealousy° what might befall your travel,　　　　　　　　　　*apprehension*
　　Being skilless in° these parts, which to a stranger,　　　　　　*unfamiliar to*
10　Unguided and unfriended, often prove
　　Rough and unhospitable. My willing love
　　The rather° by these arguments of fear　　　　　　　　　　　*more willingly*
　　Set forth in your pursuit.
SEBASTIAN　　　　　　　　My kind Antonio,
　　I can no other answer make but thanks,
15　And thanks; and ever oft° good turns　　　　　　　　　　　*very often*
　　Are shuffled off° with such uncurrent¹ pay.　　　　　　　　　*shrugged off*
　　But were my worth as is my conscience° firm,　　　　*sense of indebtedness*
　　You should find better dealing. What's to do?
　　Shall we go see the relics° of this town?　　　　　　　　　　*sights*
20　ANTONIO　Tomorrow, sir. Best first go see your lodging.
SEBASTIAN　I am not weary, and 'tis long to night.
　　I pray you let us satisfy our eyes
　　With the memorials and the things of fame
　　That do renown this city.
ANTONIO　　　　　　　　Would you'd pardon me.
25　I do not without danger walk these streets.
　　Once in a sea-fight 'gainst the Count his° galleys　　　　　　*(the Count's)*
　　I did some service, of such note indeed
　　That were I ta'en° here it would scarce be answered.²　　　　*captured*
SEBASTIAN　Belike° you slew great number of his people.　　　　*Perhaps*
30　ANTONIO　Th'offence is not of such a bloody nature,
　　Albeit the quality° of the time and quarrel　　　　　　　　　*circumstances*
　　Might well have given us bloody argument.°　　　　　*cause for bloodshed*
　　It might have since been answered in repaying
　　What we took from them, which for traffic's° sake　　　　　　*trade's*
35　Most of our city did. Only myself stood out,
　　For which if I be latchèd° in this place　　　　　　　　　　*caught*
　　I shall pay dear.
SEBASTIAN　　　　　　Do not then walk too open.
ANTONIO　It doth not fit me. Hold, sir, here's my purse.
　　In the south suburbs at the Elephant°　　　　　　　　　*name of an inn*
40　Is best to lodge. I will bespeak our diet°　　　　　　　　*order our meals*
　　Whiles you beguile° the time and feed your knowledge　　　　*pass*
　　With viewing of the town. There shall you have me.
SEBASTIAN　Why I your purse?
ANTONIO　Haply° your eye shall light upon some toy°　　　*Perhaps / trifle*
45　You have desire to purchase; and your store°　　　　　　　*resources*
　　I think is not for idle markets,³ sir.
SEBASTIAN　I'll be your purse-bearer, and leave you
　　For an hour.
ANTONIO　　　　　To th' Elephant.
SEBASTIAN　　　　　　　　　　　I do remember.
　　　　　　　　　　　　　　　　Exeunt [*severally*]

---

1. Out of currency; worthless.
2. It would be difficult for me to make reparation (and
thus my life would be in danger).
3. Not large enough to spend on luxuries.

3.4

Enter OLIVIA *and* MARIA

OLIVIA [*aside*]   I have sent after him, he says he'll come.
How shall I feast him? What bestow of° him?   °on
For youth is bought more oft than begged or borrowed.[1]
I speak too loud.

5   [*To* MARIA] Where's Malvolio? He is sad° and civil,°   °sober / °respectful
And suits well for a servant with my fortunes.
Where is Malvolio?

MARIA   He's coming, madam, but in very strange manner. He is
sure possessed,° madam.   °(by the devil); insane

10   OLIVIA   Why, what's the matter? Does he rave?

MARIA   No, madam, he does nothing but smile. Your ladyship
were best to have some guard about you if he come, for sure
the man is tainted in's wits.

OLIVIA   Go call him hither.   [*Exit* MARIA]
I am as mad as he,

15   If sad and merry madness equal be.
Enter MALVOLIO [*cross-gartered and wearing yellow
stockings, with* MARIA]
How now, Malvolio?

MALVOLIO   Sweet lady, ho, ho!

OLIVIA   Smil'st thou? I sent for thee upon a sad occasion.°   °about a serious matter

MALVOLIO   Sad, lady? I could be sad. This does make some
20   obstruction in the blood, this cross-gartering, but what of that?
If it please the eye of one, it is with me as the very true sonnet°   °song
is, 'Please one, and please all'.[2]

OLIVIA   Why, how dost thou, man? What is the matter with thee?

MALVOLIO   Not black in my mind, though yellow[3] in my legs. It
25   did come to his hands, and commands shall be executed. I
think we do know the sweet roman hand.°   °italic calligraphy

OLIVIA   Wilt thou go to bed,[4] Malvolio?

MALVOLIO [*kissing his hand*]   To bed? 'Ay, sweetheart, and I'll
come to thee.'[5]

30   OLIVIA   God comfort thee. Why dost thou smile so, and kiss thy
hand so oft?

MARIA   How do you, Malvolio?

MALVOLIO   At your request?—yes, nightingales answer daws.[6]

MARIA   Why appear you with this ridiculous boldness before my
35   lady?

MALVOLIO   'Be not afraid of greatness'—'twas well writ.

OLIVIA   What meanest thou by that, Malvolio?

MALVOLIO   'Some are born great'—

OLIVIA   Ha?

40   MALVOLIO   'Some achieve greatness'—

OLIVIA   What sayst thou?

MALVOLIO   'And some have greatness thrust upon them.'

OLIVIA   Heaven restore thee.

3.4 Location: The garden of Olivia's house.
1. "Better to buy than to beg or borrow" was proverbial.
2. If I please one, I please all I care to please (words of a
popular bawdy ballad).
3. Black and yellow biles indicated choleric and melancholic dispositions, respectively. "Black and yellow" was

the name of a popular song; to "wear yellow hose" was to
be jealous.
4. In order to cure his madness with sleep.
5. A line from a popular song.
6. Shall I deign to reply to you? Yes, since even the nightingale sings in response to the crowing of the jackdaw.

MALVOLIO 'Remember who commended thy yellow
45 stockings'—
OLIVIA 'Thy yellow stockings'?
MALVOLIO 'And wished to see thee cross-gartered.'
OLIVIA 'Cross-gartered'?
MALVOLIO 'Go to, thou art made, if thou desirest to be so.'
50 OLIVIA Am I made?
MALVOLIO 'If not, let me see thee a servant still.'
OLIVIA Why, this is very midsummer madness.

Enter a SERVANT

SERVANT Madam, the young gentleman of the Count Orsino's
is returned. I could hardly entreat him back. He attends your
55 ladyship's pleasure.
OLIVIA I'll come to him. [_Exit_ SERVANT]
Good Maria, let this fellow be looked to. Where's my cousin
Toby? Let some of my people have a special care of him, I
would not have him miscarry° for the half of my dowry. come to harm

Exeunt [OLIVIA _and_ MARIA, _severally_]

60 MALVOLIO O ho, do you come near° me now? No worse man appreciate
than Sir Toby to look to me. This concurs directly with the
letter, she sends him on purpose, that I may appear stubborn to
him, for she incites me to that in the letter. 'Cast thy humble
slough,' says she, 'be opposite with a kinsman, surly with ser-
65 vants, let thy tongue tang arguments of state, put thyself into
the trick of singularity', and consequently° sets down the man- subsequently
ner how, as a sad face, a reverend carriage, a slow tongue, in
the habit of some sir of note,° and so forth. I have limed[7] her, gentleman
but it is Jove's doing, and Jove make me thankful. And when
70 she went away now, 'let this fellow be looked to'. Fellow![8]—not
'Malvolio', nor after my degree, but 'fellow'. Why, everything
adheres together that no dram of a scruple, no scruple of a
scruple,[9] no obstacle, no incredulous or unsafe circumstance—
what can be said?—nothing that can be can come between me
75 and the full prospect of my hopes. Well, Jove, not I, is the doer
of this, and he is to be thanked.

Enter [SIR] TOBY, FABIAN, _and_ MARIA

SIR TOBY Which way is he, in the name of sanctity? If all the
devils of hell be drawn in little,[1] and Legion[2] himself possessed
him, yet I'll speak to him.
80 FABIAN Here he is, here he is. [_To_ MALVOLIO] How is't with you,
sir? How is't with you, man?
MALVOLIO Go off, I discard you. Let me enjoy my private.° Go privacy
off.
MARIA Lo, how hollow° the fiend speaks within him. Did not I resonantly
85 tell you? Sir Toby, my lady prays you to have a care of him.
MALVOLIO Aha, does she so?
SIR TOBY Go to, go to. Peace, peace, we must deal gently with
him. Let me alone.° How do you, Malvolio? How is't with you? Leave him to me

---

7. Birds were caught by smearing sticky birdlime on branches.
8. Malvolio takes the word to mean "companion."
9. _no dram . . . scruple:_ both phrases mean "no scrap of a doubt." _dram:_ one-eighth of a fluid ounce. _scruple:_ one-third of a dram.
1. Be contracted into a small space (punning on

"painted in miniature").
2. Alluding to a scene of exorcism in Mark 5:8–9: "For he [Jesus] said unto him, Come out of the man, thou unclean spirit. And he asked him, What is thy name? And he answered saying, My name is Legion: for we are many."

What, man, defy the devil. Consider, he's an enemy to man-
90   kind.

MALVOLIO   Do you know what you say?

MARIA   La° you, an you speak ill of the devil, how he takes it at   Look
heart. Pray God he be not bewitched.

FABIAN   Carry his water to th' wise woman.[3]

95   MARIA   Marry, and it shall be done tomorrow morning, if I live.
My lady would not lose him for more than I'll say.

MALVOLIO   How now, mistress?

MARIA   O Lord!

SIR TOBY   Prithee hold thy peace, this is not the way. Do you not
100   see you move° him? Let me alone with him.   anger

FABIAN   No way but gentleness, gently, gently. The fiend is
rough,° and will not be roughly used.   violent

SIR TOBY   Why how now, my bawcock?[4] How dost thou, chuck?

MALVOLIO   Sir!

105   SIR TOBY   Ay, biddy,° come with me. What man, 'tis not for grav-   hen
ity° to play at cherry-pit[5] with Satan. Hang him, foul collier.[6]   for a man of dignity

MARIA   Get him to say his prayers. Good Sir Toby, get him to
pray.

MALVOLIO   My prayers, minx?°   impertinent girl

110   MARIA   No, I warrant you, he will not hear of godliness.

MALVOLIO   Go hang yourselves, all. You are idle° shallow things,   foolish
I am not of your element.° You shall know more hereafter.   social sphere
                                                                    Exit

SIR TOBY   Is't possible?

FABIAN   If this were played upon a stage, now, I could condemn
115   it as an improbable fiction.

SIR TOBY   His very genius° hath taken the infection of the   spirit
device,° man.   trick

MARIA   Nay, pursue him now, lest the device take air and taint.[7]

FABIAN   Why, we shall make him mad indeed.

120   MARIA   The house will be the quieter.

SIR TOBY   Come, we'll have him in a dark room and bound.[8] My
niece is already in the belief that he's mad. We may carry it
thus° for our pleasure and his penance till our very pastime,   continue the pretense
tired out of breath, prompt us to have mercy on him, at which
125   time we will bring the device to the bar[9] and crown thee for a
finder of madmen.[1] But see, but see.
        Enter SIR ANDREW [*with a paper*]

FABIAN   More matter for a May morning.[2]

SIR ANDREW   Here's the challenge, read it. I warrant there's vinegar and pepper in't.

130   FABIAN   Is't so saucy?

SIR ANDREW   Ay—is't? I warrant him. Do but read.

SIR TOBY   Give me.
        [*Reads*] 'Youth, whatsoever thou art, thou art but a scurvy
fellow.'

---

3. *water:* urine (for medical diagnosis). *wise woman:* local healer, "good witch."
4. Fine fellow (from the French *beau coq,* "fine bird").
5. A children's game in which cherrystones were thrown into a hole.
6. Dirty coal man (the devil was supposed to be black).
7. Spoil (like leftover food) by exposure to air; become

known (and thus ruined).
8. Customary treatments for madness.
9. Into the open court (to be judged).
1. *finder of madmen:* one of a jury "finding," or declaring, a man to be mad.
2. More pastime fit for a holiday.

135 FABIAN   Good, and valiant.
SIR TOBY   'Wonder not, nor admire° not in thy mind why I do   marvel
call thee so, for I will show thee no reason for't.'
FABIAN   A good note, that keeps you from the blow of the law.[3]
SIR TOBY   'Thou comest to the Lady Olivia, and in my sight she
140 uses thee kindly; but thou liest in thy throat,° that is not the   deeply
matter I challenge thee for.'
FABIAN   Very brief, and to exceeding good sense [aside] -less.[4]
SIR TOBY   'I will waylay thee going home, where if it be thy
chance to kill me'—
145 FABIAN   Good.
SIR TOBY   'Thou killest me like a rogue and a villain.'
FABIAN   Still you keep o'th' windy side[5] of the law—good.
SIR TOBY   'Fare thee well, and God have mercy upon one of our
souls. He may have mercy upon mine, but my hope is better,[6]
150 and so look to thyself.
Thy friend as thou usest him, and thy sworn enemy,
                                                Andrew Aguecheek.'
If this letter move° him not, his legs cannot. I'll give't him.   provoke
MARIA   You may have very fit occasion for't. He is now in some
155 commerce° with my lady, and will by and by depart.   conversation
SIR TOBY   Go, Sir Andrew. Scout me° for him at the corner of   Look out
the orchard like a bum-baily.[7] So soon as ever thou seest him,
draw, and as thou drawest, swear horrible, for it comes to pass
oft that a terrible oath, with a swaggering accent sharply
160 twanged off, gives manhood more approbation° than ever   credit
proof° itself would have earned him. Away.   trial
SIR ANDREW   Nay, let me alone for swearing.[8]   Exit
SIR TOBY   Now will not I deliver his letter, for the behaviour of
the young gentleman gives him out to be of good capacity° and   ability
165 breeding. His employment between his lord and my niece
confirms no less. Therefore this letter, being so excellently
ignorant, will breed no terror in the youth. He will find it
comes from a clodpoll.° But, sir, I will deliver his challenge by   blockhead
word of mouth, set upon Aguecheek a notable report of valour,
170 and drive the gentleman—as I know his youth will aptly receive
it[9]—into a most hideous opinion of his rage, skill, fury, and
impetuosity. This will so fright them both that they will kill one
another by the look, like cockatrices.[1]
            Enter OLIVIA, and VIOLA [as Cesario]
FABIAN   Here he comes with your niece. Give them way° till he   Stand aside
175 take leave, and presently after him.
SIR TOBY   I will meditate the while upon some horrid message
for a challenge.   [Exeunt SIR TOBY, FABIAN, and MARIA]
OLIVIA   I have said too much unto a heart of stone,
And laid mine honour too unchary° out.   carelessly
180 There's something in me that reproves my fault,
But such a headstrong potent fault it is
That it but mocks reproof.

3. That protects you from a charge of a breach of peace.
4. F's "sence-lesse" appears to use the hyphen to signal
an aside.
5. To windward (and therefore safe, not exposed to the
law's blasts).
6. *my hope is better:* Andrew means he expects to survive,
but he ineptly implies that he expects to be damned.
7. Petty sheriff's officer employed to arrest debtors.
8. Have no doubts as to my swearing ability.
9. As I know his inexperience will readily believe the
report.
1. Basilisks; mythical creatures supposed to kill at a
glance.

VIOLA   With the same 'haviour
That your passion bears[2] goes on my master's griefs.
OLIVIA *[giving a jewel]* Here, wear this jewel[3] for me, 'tis my picture—
185   Refuse it not, it hath no tongue to vex you—
And I beseech you come again tomorrow.
What shall you ask of me that I'll deny,
That honour, saved, may upon asking give?[4]
VIOLA Nothing but this: your true love for my master.
190   OLIVIA How with mine honour may I give him that
Which I have given to you?
VIOLA   I will acquit you.[5]
OLIVIA Well, come again tomorrow. Fare thee well.
A fiend like thee might bear my soul to hell.   *Exit*

   Enter [SIR] TOBY *and* FABIAN
SIR TOBY Gentleman, God save thee.
195   VIOLA And you, sir.
SIR TOBY That defence thou hast, betake thee to't. Of what
nature the wrongs are thou hast done him, I know not, but thy
intercepter, full of despite,° bloody as the hunter, attends° thee   *defiance / awaits*
at the orchard end. Dismount thy tuck,[6] be yare° in thy prepara-   *prompt*
200   tion, for thy assailant is quick, skilful, and deadly.
VIOLA You mistake, sir, I am sure no man hath any quarrel to
me. My remembrance° is very free and clear from any image   *memory*
of offence done to any man.
SIR TOBY You'll find it otherwise, I assure you. Therefore, if you
205   hold your life at any price, betake you to your guard, for your
opposite° hath in him what youth, strength, skill, and wrath can   *opponent*
furnish man withal.
VIOLA I pray you, sir, what is he?
SIR TOBY He is knight dubbed with unhatched[7] rapier and on
210   carpet consideration,[8] but he is a devil in private brawl. Souls
and bodies hath he divorced three, and his incensement at this
moment is so implacable that satisfaction can be none but by
pangs of death and sepulchre. Hob nob[9] is his word,° give't or   *motto*
take't.
215   VIOLA I will return again into the house and desire some con-
duct° of the lady. I am no fighter. I have heard of some kind of   *escort*
men that put quarrels purposely on others, to taste° their   *test*
valour. Belike this is a man of that quirk.
SIR TOBY Sir, no. His indignation derives itself out of a very com-
220   petent° injury, therefore get you on, and give him his desire.   *sufficient*
Back you shall not to the house unless you undertake that° with   *(a duel)*
me which with as much safety you might answer him. There-
fore on, or strip your sword stark naked, for meddle° you must,   *engage in a duel*
that's certain, or forswear to wear iron about you.[1]
225   VIOLA This is as uncivil as strange. I beseech you do me this
courteous office, as to know of° the knight what my offence   *ascertain from*
to him is. It is something of my negligence, nothing of my
purpose.

2. *'haviour . . . bears*: behavior that characterizes your
lovesickness.
3. Jeweled ornament, here a brooch or a locket with
Olivia's picture.
4. That honor may grant without compromising itself.
5. I will release you from your promise.

6. Draw your rapier.
7. Unhacked, or undented; never used in battle.
8. A "carpet knight" obtained his title through connections at court rather than valor on the battlefield.
9. Have or have not ("all or nothing").
1. Or forfeit your right to wear a sword.

SIR TOBY   I will do so. Signor Fabian, stay you by this gentleman
230   till my return.   *Exit*

VIOLA   Pray you, sir, do you know of this matter?

FABIAN   I know the knight is incensed against you even to a mortal arbitrement,° but nothing of the circumstance more.   *deadly duel*

VIOLA   I beseech you, what manner of man is he?

235 FABIAN   Nothing of that wonderful promise to read him by his
form[2] as you are like to find him in the proof of his valour. He
is indeed, sir, the most skilful, bloody, and fatal opposite that
you could possibly have found in any part of Illyria. Will you°   *If you will*
walk towards him, I will make your peace with him if I can.

240 VIOLA   I shall be much bound to you for't. I am one that had
rather go with Sir Priest[3] than Sir Knight—I care not who
knows so much of my mettle.°   *Exeunt*   *disposition*

       Enter [SIR] TOBY *and* [SIR] ANDREW

SIR TOBY   Why, man, he's a very devil, I have not seen such a
virago.[4] I had a pass° with him, rapier, scabbard, and all, and   *fencing bout*
245 he gives me the stuck-in[5] with such a mortal motion that it is
inevitable, and on the answer,° he pays you as surely as your   *return hit*
feet hits the ground they step on. They say he has been fencer
to the Sophy.°   *Shah of Persia*

SIR ANDREW   Pox on't, I'll not meddle with him.

250 SIR TOBY   Ay, but he will not now be pacified, Fabian can scarce
hold him yonder.

SIR ANDREW   Plague on't, an° I thought he had been valiant and   *if*
so cunning in fence I'd have seen him damned ere I'd have
challenged him. Let him let the matter slip and I'll give him
255 my horse, grey Capulet.

SIR TOBY   I'll make the motion.° Stand here, make a good show   *offer*
on't—this shall end without the perdition of souls.°   *loss of lives*
[*Aside*] Marry, I'll ride your horse as well as I ride you.

       Enter FABIAN, *and* VIOLA [*as Cesario*]

[*Aside to* FABIAN] I have his horse to take up° the quarrel, I have   *settle*
260 persuaded him the youth's a devil.

FABIAN [*aside to* SIR TOBY]   He is as horribly conceited[6] of him,
and pants and looks pale as if a bear were at his heels.

SIR TOBY [*to* VIOLA]   There's no remedy, sir, he will fight with
you for's oath' sake. Marry, he hath better bethought him of his
265 quarrel, and he finds that now scarce to be worth talking of.
Therefore draw for the supportance of his vow, he protests he
will not hurt you.

VIOLA [*aside*]   Pray God defend me. A little thing would make
me tell them how much I lack of a man.

270 FABIAN [*to* SIR ANDREW]   Give ground if you see him furious.

SIR TOBY   Come, Sir Andrew, there's no remedy, the gentleman
will for his honour's sake have one bout with you, he cannot
by the duello° avoid it, but he has promised me, as he is a   *code of dueling*
gentleman and a soldier, he will not hurt you. Come on, to't.

275 SIR ANDREW   Pray God he keep his oath.

       Enter ANTONIO

---

2. *Nothing . . . form:* From his outward appearance,
you cannot perceive him to be as remarkable.
3. Priests were often addressed as "sir."
4. Woman warrior (suggesting great ferocity with a
feminine appearance).
5. Thrust (from the Italian *stoccata*).
6. He has as terrifying an idea.

VIOLA   I do assure you 'tis against my will.
   [SIR ANDREW *and* VIOLA *draw their swords*]
ANTONIO [*drawing his sword, to* SIR ANDREW]   Put up your sword.
 If this young gentleman
 Have done offence, I take the fault on me.
 If you offend him, I for him defy you.
280 SIR TOBY   You, sir? Why, what are you?
ANTONIO   One, sir, that for his love cares yet do more
 Than you have heard him brag to you he will.
SIR TOBY [*drawing his sword*]   Nay, if you be an undertaker,[7] I
 am for you.
    Enter OFFICERS
285 FABIAN   O, good Sir Toby, hold. Here come the officers.
SIR TOBY [*to* ANTONIO]   I'll be with you anon.
VIOLA [*to* SIR ANDREW]   Pray, sir, put your sword up if you please.
SIR ANDREW   Marry will I, sir, and for that° I promised you I'll be   *as for that*
 as good as my word. He will bear you easily, and reins well.
   [SIR ANDREW *and* VIOLA *put up their swords*]
290 FIRST OFFICER   This is the man, do thy office.
SECOND OFFICER   Antonio, I arrest thee at the suit of Count
 Orsino.
ANTONIO   You do mistake me, sir.
FIRST OFFICER   No, sir, no jot. I know your favour° well,   *face*
295 Though now you have no seacap on your head.
   [*To* SECOND OFFICER] Take him away, he knows I know him well.
ANTONIO   I must obey. [*To* VIOLA] This comes with seeking you.
 But there's no remedy, I shall answer° it.   *answer for*
 What will you do now my necessity
300 Makes me to ask you for my purse? It grieves me
 Much more for what I cannot do for you
 Than what befalls myself. You stand amazed,
 But be of comfort.
SECOND OFFICER   Come, sir, away.
ANTONIO [*to* VIOLA]   I must entreat of you some of that money.
305 VIOLA   What money, sir?
 For the fair kindness you have showed me here,
 And part° being prompted by your present trouble,   *in part*
 Out of my lean and low ability
 I'll lend you something. My having is not much.
310 I'll make division of my present° with you.   *ready money*
 Hold, [*offering money*] there's half my coffer.
ANTONIO   Will you deny me now?
 Is't possible that my deserts to you
 Can lack persuasion?[8] Do not tempt my misery,
 Lest that it make me so unsound° a man   *morally weak*
315 As to upbraid you with those kindnesses
 That I have done for you.
VIOLA   I know of none,
 Nor know I you by voice, or any feature.
 I hate ingratitude more in a man
 Than lying, vainness, babbling drunkenness,

---

7. One who would take upon himself a task (here, a challenge).

8. *Ist . . . persuasion:* Is it possible my past kindness can fail to persuade you?

320   Or any taint of vice whose strong corruption
       Inhabits our frail blood.
ANTONIO   O heavens themselves!
SECOND OFFICER   Come, sir, I pray you go.
ANTONIO   Let me speak a little. This youth that you see here
       I snatched one half out of the jaws of death,
325   Relieved him with such sanctity° of love,   *great devotion*
       And to his image,⁹ which methought did promise
       Most venerable worth,¹ did I devotion.
FIRST OFFICER   What's that to us? The time goes by, away.
ANTONIO   But O, how vile an idol proves this god!
330   Thou hast, Sebastian, done good feature° shame.   *physical beauty*
       In nature there's no blemish but the mind.
       None can be called deformed but the unkind.
       Virtue is beauty, but the beauteous evil
       Are empty trunks o'er-flourished² by the devil.
335 FIRST OFFICER   The man grows mad, away with him. Come, come, sir.
ANTONIO   Lead me on.   *Exit [with* OFFICERS]
VIOLA [*aside*]   Methinks his words do from such passion fly
       That he believes himself. So do not I.³
       Prove true, imagination, O prove true,
340   That I, dear brother, be now ta'en for you!
SIR TOBY   Come hither, knight. Come hither, Fabian. We'll
       whisper o'er a couplet or two of most sage saws.°   *sayings; maxims*
               [*They stand aside*]
VIOLA   He named Sebastian. I my brother know
       Yet living in my glass.° Even such and so   *mirror*
345   In favour° was my brother, and he went   *appearance*
       Still° in this fashion, colour, ornament,   *Always*
       For him I imitate. O, if it prove,
       Tempests are kind, and salt waves fresh in love!   *Exit*
SIR TOBY [*to* SIR ANDREW]   A very dishonest,° paltry boy, and   *dishonorable*
350   more a coward than a hare. His dishonesty appears in leaving
       his friend here in necessity, and denying him; and for his cow-
       ardship, ask Fabian.
FABIAN   A coward, a most devout coward, religious in it.
SIR ANDREW   'Slid,° I'll after him again, and beat him.   *By God's eyelid*
355 SIR TOBY   Do, cuff him soundly, but never draw thy sword.
SIR ANDREW   An I do not—   [*Exit*]
FABIAN   Come, let's see the event.°   *outcome*
SIR TOBY   I dare lay any money 'twill be nothing yet.° *Exeunt* *after all*

4.1

Enter SEBASTIAN *and* [FESTE, *the*] *clown*

FESTE   Will you° make me believe that I am not sent for you?   *Are you trying to*
SEBASTIAN   Go to, go to, thou art a foolish fellow,
       Let me be clear° of thee.   *rid*
FESTE   Well held out,° i'faith! No, I do not know you, nor I am *kept up*
5   not sent to you by my lady to bid you come speak with her, nor

---

9. Appearance (with a play on "religious icon").
1. *did . . . worth:* was worthy of veneration.
2. Chests decorated with carving or painting; beautified bodies.

3. *So do not I:* I do not entirely believe the passionate hope (for my brother's rescue) that is arising in me.
4.1 Location: Near Olivia's house.

your name is not Master Cesario, nor this is not my nose, neither. Nothing that is so, is so.

SEBASTIAN   I prithee vent° thy folly somewhere else,   *utter; excrete*
Thou know'st not me.

10   FESTE   Vent my folly! He has heard that word of some great
man, and now applies it to a fool. Vent my folly—I am afraid
this great lubber° the world will prove a cockney.° I prithee   *lout / sissy*
now ungird thy strangeness,[1] and tell me what I shall 'vent' to
my lady? Shall I 'vent' to her that thou art coming?

15   SEBASTIAN   I prithee, foolish Greek,° depart from me.   *buffoon*
There's money for thee. If you tarry longer
I shall give worse payment.

FESTE   By my troth, thou hast an open hand. These wise men
that give fools money get themselves a good report,° after four-   *reputation*
20   teen years' purchase.[2]

Enter [SIR] ANDREW, [SIR] TOBY, *and* FABIAN

SIR ANDREW [*to* SEBASTIAN]   Now, sir, have I met you again?
[*Striking him*] There's for you.

SEBASTIAN [*striking* SIR ANDREW *with his dagger*]   Why, there's
for thee, and there, and there
Are all the people mad?

25   SIR TOBY [*to* SEBASTIAN, *holding him back*]   Hold, sir, or I'll throw
your dagger o'er the house.

FESTE   This will I tell my lady straight,° I would not be in some   *straightaway*
of your coats for twopence.   [*Exit*]

SIR TOBY   Come on, sir, hold.

30   SIR ANDREW   Nay, let him alone, I'll go another way to work with
him. I'll have an action of battery° against him if there be any   *a lawsuit for assault*
law in Illyria. Though I struck him first, yet it's no matter for
that.

SEBASTIAN   Let go thy hand.

35   SIR TOBY   Come, sir, I will not let you go. Come, my young soldier, put up your iron. You are well fleshed.[3] Come on

SEBASTIAN [*freeing himself*]   I will be free from thee. What wouldst thou now?
If thou dar'st tempt me further, draw thy sword.

SIR TOBY   What, what? Nay then, I must have an ounce or two
40   of this malapert° blood from you.   *impudent*

[SIR TOBY *and* SEBASTIAN *draw their swords.*]
Enter OLIVIA

OLIVIA   Hold, Toby, on thy life I charge thee hold.

SIR TOBY   Madam.

OLIVIA   Will it be ever thus? Ungracious wretch,
Fit for the mountains and the barbarous caves,
45   Where manners ne'er were preached—out of my sight!
Be not offended, dear Cesario.
[*To* SIR TOBY] Rudesby,° be gone.   *Ruffian*

[*Exeunt* SIR TOBY, SIR ANDREW, *and* FABIAN]
I prithee, gentle friend,
Let thy fair wisdom, not thy passion sway
In this uncivil and unjust extent°   *assault*

---

1. *I . . . strangeness:* Stop pretending not to know me.
(Feste mocks Sebastian's affected language.)
2. *after . . . purchase:* at a high price. The purchase price
of land was normally twelve times its annual rent.
3. Experienced in combat. Hunting hounds were said to
be "fleshed" after being fed part of their first kill.

50 Against thy peace. Go with me to my house,
And hear thou there how many fruitless pranks
This ruffian hath botched up,° that thou thereby   *clumsily contrived*
Mayst smile at this. Thou shalt not choose but go.
Do not deny. Beshrew° his soul for me,   *Curse*
55 He started one poor heart of mine in thee.⁴
  SEBASTIAN   What relish° is in this? How runs the stream?   *task; meaning*
Or° I am mad, or else this is a dream.   *Either*
Let fancy° still my sense in Lethe⁵ steep.   *imagination*
If it be thus to dream, still let me sleep.
60   OLIVIA   Nay, come, I prithee, would thou'dst be ruled by me.
  SEBASTIAN   Madam, I will.
  OLIVIA   O, say so, and so be.   *Exeunt*

4.2

Enter MARIA [*carrying a gown and false beard, and*
FESTE, *the*] *clown*
  MARIA   Nay, I prithee put on this gown and this beard, make
him believe thou art Sir Topas¹ the curate. Do it quickly. I'll
call Sir Toby the whilst.°   *Exit*   *in the meantime*
  FESTE   Well, I'll put it on, and I will dissemble² myself in't, and
5 I would I were the first that ever dissembled in such a gown.
     [*He disguises himself*]
I am not tall enough to become the function well,³ nor lean
enough to be thought a good student,° but to be said° 'an hon-   *(of divinity) / reputed*
est man and a good housekeeper'° goes as fairly as⁴ to say 'a   *host*
careful man and a great scholar'. The competitors° enter.   *associates*
     Enter [SIR] TOBY [*and* MARIA]
10   SIR TOBY   Jove bless thee, Master Parson.
  FESTE   *Bonos dies*,⁵ Sir Toby, for, as the old hermit of Prague,⁶
that never saw pen and ink, very wittily° said to a niece of King   *intelligently*
Gorboduc,° 'That that is, is.' So I, being Master Parson, am   *legendary British king*
Master Parson; for what is 'that' but 'that', and 'is' but 'is'?
15   SIR TOBY   To him, Sir Topas.
  FESTE   What ho, I say, peace in this prison.
  SIR TOBY   The knave counterfeits well—a good knave.
     MALVOLIO *within*
  MALVOLIO   Who calls there?
  FESTE   Sir Topas the curate, who comes to visit Malvolio the
20 lunatic.
  MALVOLIO   Sir Topas, Sir Topas, good Sir Topas, go to my lady.
  FESTE   Out, hyperbolical fiend,⁷ how vexest thou this man! Talk-
est thou nothing but of ladies?
  SIR TOBY   Well said, Master Parson.
25   MALVOLIO   Sir Topas, never was man thus wronged. Good Sir

---

4. *He . . . thee*: By attacking Sebastian, Sir Toby frightened Olivia, who has exchanged hearts with Sebastian.
started: an allusion to hunting, creating a pun on "hart /
heart."
5. The mythical river of oblivion.
4.2 Location: Olivia's house, where Malvolio will be
found (offstage) "in a dark room and bound" (3.4.121).
1. The comical hero of Chaucer's *Rime of Sir Topas*.
Also alluding to the mineral topaz, which was thought to

have special curative qualities for insanity.
2. Disguise; with subsequent play on "lie."
3. Grace the priestly office. *tall*: stout, rather than of
great height.
4. *goes as fairly as*: sounds as well as.
5. Good day (false Latin).
6. Probably an invented authority.
7. Feste treats Malvolio as a man possessed by vehement
("hyperbolical") evil spirits.

Topas, do not think I am mad. They have laid me here in
hideous darkness.

FESTE   Fie, thou dishonest Satan—I call thee by the most mod-
est° terms, for I am one of those gentle ones that will use the

30   devil himself with courtesy. Sayst thou that house° is dark?

MALVOLIO   As hell, Sir Topas.

FESTE   Why, it hath bay windows transparent as barricadoes, and
the clerestories[8] toward the south-north are as lustrous as
ebony,[9] and yet complainest thou of obstruction?

35   MALVOLIO   I am not mad, Sir Topas. I say to you this house is
dark.

FESTE   Madman, thou errest. I say there is no darkness but ignorance, in which thou art more puzzled than the Egyptians in
their fog.[1]

40   MALVOLIO   I say this house is as dark as ignorance, though ignorance were as dark as hell; and I say there was never man thus
abused. I am no more mad than you are. Make the trial of it in
any constant question.°

FESTE   What is the opinion of Pythagoras[2] concerning wildfowl?

45   MALVOLIO   That the soul of our grandam might haply° inhabit a
bird.

FESTE   What thinkest thou of his opinion?

MALVOLIO   I think nobly of the soul, and no way approve his
opinion.

50   FESTE   Fare thee well. Remain thou still in darkness. Thou shalt
hold th'opinion of Pythagoras ere I will allow of thy wits,° and
fear to kill a woodcock[3] lest thou dispossess the soul of thy grandam. Fare thee well.

MALVOLIO   Sir Topas, Sir Topas!

55   SIR TOBY   My most exquisite Sir Topas.

FESTE   Nay, I am for all waters.[4]

MARIA   Thou mightst have done this without thy beard and
gown, he sees thee not.

SIR TOBY [to FESTE]   To him in thine own voice, and bring me

60   word how thou findest him. I would we were well rid of this
knavery. If he may be conveniently delivered, I would he were,
for I am now so far in offence with my niece that I cannot
pursue with any safety this sport to the upshot. [To MARIA]
Come by and by to my chamber.   Exit [with MARIA]

65   FESTE   [sings][5]   'Hey Robin, jolly Robin,
                              Tell me how thy lady does.'

MALVOLIO   Fool!

FESTE   'My lady is unkind, pardie.'[6]

MALVOLIO   Fool!

70   FESTE   'Alas, why is she so?'

MALVOLIO   Fool, I say!

FESTE   'She loves another.'
        Who calls, ha?

mildest
room

logical discussion

perhaps

certify your sanity

---

8. Upper windows, usually in a church or great hall. *bar-*
ricadoes: barricades (subsequent paradoxes are equivalent to "as clear as mud").
9. A dense and naturally dull black wood.
1. One of the plagues of Egypt was a "black darkness"
lasting for three days (Exodus 10:21–23).
2. An ancient Greek philosopher who held that the same

soul could successively inhabit different creatures.
3. A traditionally stupid bird.
4. I am able to turn my hand to anything.
5. Feste's song, which makes Malvolio aware of his presence, is traditional. There is a version by Sir Thomas
Wyatt.
6. A corruption of the French *pardieu*, "by God."

MALVOLIO   Good fool, as ever thou wilt deserve well at my hand,
75   help me to a candle and pen, ink, and paper. As I am a gentleman, I will live to be thankful to thee for't.

FESTE   Master Malvolio?

MALVOLIO   Ay, good fool.

FESTE   Alas, sir, how fell you besides° your five wits?[7]   °out of

80   MALVOLIO   Fool, there was never man so notoriously° abused. I   °outrageously
am as well in my wits, fool, as thou art.

FESTE   But as well? Then you are mad indeed, if you be no better in your wits than a fool.

MALVOLIO   They have here propertied me,[8] keep me in darkness,
85   send ministers to me, asses, and do all they can to face me[9] out
of my wits.

FESTE   Advise you° what you say, the minister is here.   °Be careful
[As Sir Topas] Malvolio, Malvolio, thy wits the heavens restore.
Endeavour thyself to sleep, and leave thy vain bibble-babble.

90   MALVOLIO   Sir Topas.

FESTE [as Sir Topas]   Maintain no words with him, good fellow.
[As himself] Who I, sir? Not I, sir. God b'wi' you,° good Sir   °God be with you
Topas. [As Sir Topas] Marry, amen. [As himself] I will, sir, I
will.

95   MALVOLIO   Fool, fool, fool, I say.

FESTE   Alas, sir, be patient. What say you, sir? I am shent° for   °scolded
speaking to you.

MALVOLIO   Good fool, help me to some light and some paper. I
tell thee I am as well in my wits as any man in Illyria.

100   FESTE   Well-a-day° that you were, sir.   °Alas

MALVOLIO   By this hand, I am. Good fool, some ink, paper, and
light, and convey what I will set down to my lady. It shall advantage thee more than ever the bearing of letter did.

FESTE   I will help you to't. But tell me true, are you not mad
105   indeed, or do you but counterfeit?

MALVOLIO   Believe me, I am not, I tell thee true.

FESTE   Nay, I'll ne'er believe a madman till I see his brains. I
will fetch you light, and paper, and ink.

MALVOLIO   Fool, I'll requite it in the highest degree. I prithee,
110   be gone.

FESTE   I am gone, sir,
                      And anon, sir,
                         I'll be with you again,
                      In a trice,
115   Like to the old Vice,[1]
                         Your need to sustain,
                      Who with dagger of lath
                      In his rage and his wrath
                         Cries 'Aha,' to the devil,
120   Like a mad lad,
                      'Pare thy nails, dad,
                         Adieu, goodman[2] devil.'   *Exit*

---

7. Usually regarded as common sense, fantasy, memory,
judgment, and imagination.
8. Treated me as a piece of property.
9. *face me:* brazenly construe me as.

1. A stock comic figure in the old morality plays; the Vice
often carried a wooden dagger.
2. Yeoman; a title given to one not of gentle birth, hence
a parting insult to Malvolio.

4.3

Enter SEBASTIAN

SEBASTIAN   This is the air, that is the glorious sun.
This pearl she gave me, I do feel't and see't,
And though 'tis wonder that enwraps me thus,
Yet 'tis not madness. Where's Antonio then?
5   I could not find him at the Elephant,
Yet there he was,° and there I found this credit,°   had been / report
That he did range the town to seek me out.
His counsel now might do me golden service,
For though my soul disputes well with my sense[1]
10   That this may be some error but no madness,
Yet doth this accident and flood of fortune
So far exceed all instance,° all discourse,°   precedent / reasoning
That I am ready to distrust mine eyes
And wrangle with my reason that persuades me
15   To any other trust° but that I am mad,   belief
Or else the lady's mad. Yet if 'twere so,
She could not sway° her house, command her followers,   rule
Take and give back affairs and their dispatch[2]
With such a smooth, discreet, and stable bearing
20   As I perceive she does. There's something in't
That is deceivable.° But here the lady comes.   deceptive

Enter OLIVIA *and* PRIEST

OLIVIA   Blame not this haste of mine. If you mean well
Now go with me, and with this holy man,
Into the chantry by.° There before him,   nearby chapel
25   And underneath that consecrated roof,
Plight me the full assurance of your faith,[3]
That my most jealous° and too doubtful soul   anxious
May live at peace. He shall conceal it
Whiles° you are willing it shall come to note,   Until
30   What° time we will our celebration keep   At which
According to my birth.° What do you say?   rank
SEBASTIAN   I'll follow this good man, and go with you,
And having sworn truth, ever will be true.
OLIVIA   Then lead the way, good father, and heavens so shine
35   That they may fairly note° this act of mine.   *Exeunt*   look favorably upon

5.1

Enter [FESTE, *the*] *clown and* FABIAN

FABIAN   Now, as thou lovest me, let me see his letter.
FESTE   Good Master Fabian, grant me another request.
FABIAN   Anything.
FESTE   Do not desire to see this letter.
5   FABIAN   This is to give a dog, and in recompense desire my dog
again.[1]

Enter Duke, VIOLA [*as Cesario*], CURIO, *and lords*

ORSINO   Belong you to the Lady Olivia, friends?

4.3 Location: Near Olivia's house.
1. For though my reason and my sense both concur.
2. Undertake business, and ensure that it is carried
out.
3. Enter into the solemn contract of betrothal.
5.1 Location: Before Olivia's house.

1. Perhaps a reference to an anecdote, recorded in
John Manningham's diary, in which Queen Elizabeth
requested a dog, and the donor, when granted a wish in
return, asked for the dog back.

FESTE   Ay, sir, we are some of her trappings.°   *ornaments*
ORSINO   I know thee well. How dost thou, my good fellow?
10   FESTE   Truly, sir, the better for my foes and the worse for my
    friends.
ORSINO   Just the contrary—the better for thy friends.
FESTE   No, sir, the worse.
ORSINO   How can that be?
15   FESTE   Marry, sir, they praise me, and make an ass of me. Now
    my foes tell me plainly I am an ass, so that by my foes, sir, I
    profit in the knowledge of myself, and by my friends I am
    abused;° so that, conclusions to be as kisses, if your four nega-   *deceived*
    tives make your two affirmatives,² why then the worse for my
20   friends and the better for my foes.
ORSINO   Why, this is excellent.
FESTE   By my troth, sir, no, though it please you to be one of my
    friends.
ORSINO [*giving money*]   Thou shalt not be the worse for me.
25   There's gold.
FESTE   But° that it would be double-dealing,³ sir, I would you   *Except for the fact*
    could make it another.
ORSINO   O, you give me ill counsel.
FESTE   Put your grace in your pocket,⁴ sir, for this once, and let
30   your flesh and blood obey it.⁵
ORSINO   Well, I will be so much a sinner to° be a double-dealer.   *as to*
    [*Giving money*] There's another.
FESTE   *Primo, secundo, tertio*⁶ is a good play,°   *game*
    is 'The third pays for all'.⁷ The triplex,° sir, is a good tripping   *triple time in music*
35   measure, or the bells of Saint Bennet,⁸ sir, may put you in
    mind—'one, two, three'.
ORSINO   You can fool no more money out of me at this throw.°   *throw of the dice*
    If you will let your lady know I am here to speak with her, and
    bring her along with you, it may awake my bounty further.
40   FESTE   Marry, sir, lullaby to your bounty till I come again. I go,
    sir, but I would not have you to think that my desire of having
    is the sin of covetousness. But as you say, sir, let your bounty
    take a nap, I will awake it anon.   *Exit*
        Enter ANTONIO *and* OFFICERS
VIOLA   Here comes the man, sir, that did rescue me.
45   ORSINO   That face of his I do remember well,
    Yet when I saw it last it was besmeared
    As black as Vulcan⁹ in the smoke of war.
    A baubling° vessel was he captain of,   *trifling*
    For shallow draught and bulk unprizable.¹
50   With which such scatheful° grapple did he make   *destructive*
    With the most noble bottom° of our fleet.   *ship*

---

2. *conclusions . . affirmatives*: as in grammar, a double
negative can make an affirmative (and therefore four neg-
atives can make two affirmatives); so when a coy girl is
asked for a kiss, her four refusals can be construed as
"yes, yes."
3. A duplicity; a double donation.
4. Set aside (pocket up) your virtue; also (with a play on
the customary form of address for a duke, "your grace"),
reach into your pocket and grace me with another coin.
5. Let your normal human instincts (as opposed to

grace) follow the "ill counsel" (line 28).
6. First, second, third (Latin); perhaps an allusion to a
dice throw or a child's game.
7. Third time lucky (proverbial).
8. A London church, across the Thames from the Globe,
was known as St. Bennet Hithe.
9. Blacksmith of the Roman gods.
1. Of no value because of its small size. *draught*: water
displaced by a vessel.

That very envy° and the tongue of loss°   *even enmity / the losers*
<u>Cried fame and honour on him. What's the matter?</u>
FIRST OFFICER Orsino, this is that Antonio
55 That took the Phoenix and her freight from Candy,[2]
And this is he that did the *Tiger* board
When your young nephew Titus lost his leg.
Here in the streets, desperate of shame and state,[3]
In private brabble° did we apprehend him.   *brawl*
60 VIOLA He did me kindness, sir, drew on my side,[4]
But in conclusion put strange speech upon° me. *spoke strangely to*
I know not what 'twas but distraction.°   *if not insanity*
ORSINO [*to* ANTONIO] Notable° pirate, thou salt-water thief, *Notorious*
What foolish boldness brought thee to their mercies
65 Whom thou in terms so bloody and so dear° *dire*
Hast made thine enemies?
ANTONIO Orsino, noble sir,
Be pleased that I shake off these names you give me.
<u>Antonio never yet was thief or pirate,</u>
<u>Though, I confess, on base° and ground enough</u> *foundation*
70 <u>Orsino's enemy. A witchcraft drew me hither.</u> **madness of love**
<u>That most ingrateful boy there by your side</u>
<u>From the rude sea's enraged and foamy mouth</u>
<u>Did I redeem. A wreck past hope he was.</u>
<u>His life I gave him, and did thereto add</u>
75 <u>My love without retention° or restraint,</u> *reservation*
<u>All his in dedication. For his sake</u>
<u>Did I expose myself, pure° for his love,</u> *only*
<u>Into the danger of this adverse° town,</u> *hostile*
<u>Drew to defend him when he was beset,</u>
80 Where being apprehended, his false cunning—
Not meaning to partake with me in danger— **feels betrayed by Sebastian (case of**
Taught him to face me out of his acquaintance,[5] **mistaken identity)**
And grew a twenty years' removèd thing
While one would wink,[6] denied me mine own purse,
85 Which I had recommended° to his use *consigned*
Not half an hour before.
VIOLA How can this be?
ORSINO When came he to this town?
ANTONIO Today, my lord, and for three months before,
90 No int'rim, not a minute's vacancy, *interval*
Both day and night did we keep company.
   Enter OLIVIA *and attendants*
ORSINO Here comes the Countess. Now heaven walks on earth.
But for thee, fellow—fellow, thy words are madness.
Three months this youth hath tended upon me.
95 But more of that anon. Take him aside.
OLIVIA What would my lord, but that he may not have,[7]
Wherein Olivia may seem serviceable?
Cesario, you do not keep promise with me.
VIOLA Madam—

2. Candia, capital of Crete.
3. *desperate . . . state:* recklessly oblivious of the danger to his honor and his position (as a free man and public enemy).
4. Drew his sword in my defense.

5. To brazenly deny my acquaintance.
6. *And . . . wink:* In the wink of an eye, pretended we had been estranged for twenty years.
7. Except that which he may not have (my love).

100 ORSINO Gracious Olivia—

OLIVIA What do you say, Cesario? Good my lord—

VIOLA My lord would speak, my duty hushes me.

OLIVIA If it be aught° to the old tune, my lord,   anything
It is as fat and fulsome° to mine ear   gross and offensive
105 As howling after music.

ORSINO Still so cruel?

OLIVIA Still so constant, lord.

ORSINO What, to perverseness? You uncivil lady,
To whose ingrate and unauspicious° altars   unfavorable
110 My soul the faithfull'st off 'rings hath breathed out
That e'er devotion tendered—what shall I do?

OLIVIA Even what it please my lord that shall become° him.   be fitting for

ORSINO Why should I not, had I the heart to do it,
Like to th' Egyptian thief, at point of death
115 Kill what I love[8]—a savage jealousy   _Orsino wants_
That sometime savours nobly.° But hear me this: _to kill_   of nobility
Since you to non-regardance° cast my faith,   _Cesario_   oblivion
And that I partly know the instrument
That screws° me from my true place in your favour,   wrenches
120 Live you the marble-breasted tyrant still.
But this your minion,° whom I know you love,   darling
And whom, by heaven I swear, I tender° dearly,   regard
Him will I tear out of that cruel eye
Where he sits crownèd in his master's spite.[9]
125 [_To_ VIOLA] Come, boy, with me. My thoughts are ripe in mischief.
I'll sacrifice the lamb that I do love
To spite a raven's heart within a dove.

VIOLA And I most jocund,° apt,° and willingly   cheerfully / ready
To do you rest a thousand deaths would die.

OLIVIA Where goes Cesario?

130 VIOLA   After him I love
More than I love these eyes, more than my life,
More by all mores[1] than e'er I shall love wife.
If I do feign, you witnesses above,
Punish my life for tainting of my love.

135 OLIVIA Ay me detested, how am I beguiled!

VIOLA Who does beguile you? Who does do you wrong?

OLIVIA Hast thou forgot thyself? Is it so long?
Call forth the holy father.   [_Exit an attendant_]

ORSINO [_to_ VIOLA]   Come, away.

OLIVIA Whither, my lord? Cesario, husband, stay.

ORSINO Husband?

140 OLIVIA   Ay, husband. Can he that deny?

ORSINO [_to_ VIOLA] Her husband, sirrah?[2]

VIOLA   No, my lord, not I.

OLIVIA Alas, it is the baseness of thy fear
That makes thee strangle thy propriety.[3]
Fear not, Cesario, take thy fortunes up,

8. In Heliodorus of Emesa's _Ethiopica_, a Greek prose
romance translated into English in 1569 and popular in
Shakespeare's day, the Egyptian robber chief Thyamis
tries to kill his captive Chariclea, whom he loves, when he
is in danger from a rival band.

9. To the mortification of his master.
1. More beyond all comparison.
2. Contemptuous form of address to an inferior.
3. That makes you deny your identity (as my husband).

145 Be that thou know'st thou art, and then thou art
As great as that° thou fear'st.   *him whom*

Enter PRIEST

O welcome, father.
Father, I charge thee by thy reverence
Here to unfold—though lately we intended
To keep in darkness what occasion° now   *necessity*
150 Reveals before 'tis ripe—what thou dost know
Hath newly passed between this youth and me.
PRIEST A contract of eternal bond of love,
Confirmed by mutual joinder° of your hands,   *joining*
Attested by the holy close° of lips,   *meeting*
155 Strengthened by interchangement of your rings,
And all the ceremony of this compact
Sealed in my function,[4] by my testimony;
Since when, my watch hath told me, toward my grave
I have travelled but two hours.
160 ORSINO [*to* VIOLA] O thou dissembling cub, what wilt thou be
When time hath sowed a grizzle on thy case?[5]
Or will not else thy craft° so quickly grow   *craftiness*
That thine own trip shall be thine overthrow?[6]
Farewell, and take her, but direct thy feet
165 Where thou and I henceforth may never meet.
VIOLA My lord, I do protest.
OLIVIA   O, do not swear!
Hold little° faith, though thou hast too much fear.   *Preserve some*

Enter SIR ANDREW

SIR ANDREW For the love of God, a surgeon—send one pres-
ently° to Sir Toby.   *immediately*
170 OLIVIA What's the matter?
SIR ANDREW He's broke° my head across, and has given Sir Toby   *cut*
a bloody coxcomb,[7] too. For the love of God, your help! I had
rather than forty pound I were at home.
OLIVIA Who has done this, Sir Andrew?
175 SIR ANDREW The Count's gentleman, one Cesario. We took him
for a coward, but he's the very devil incardinate.[8]
ORSINO My gentleman, Cesario?
SIR ANDREW 'Od's lifelings,° here he is. [*To* VIOLA] You broke   *By God's little lives*
my head for nothing, and that that I did I was set on to do't by
180 Sir Toby.
VIOLA Why do you speak to me? I never hurt you.
You drew your sword upon me without cause,
But I bespake you fair,[9] and hurt you not.

Enter [SIR] TOBY *and* [FESTE, *the*] *clown*

SIR ANDREW If a bloody coxcomb be a hurt you have hurt me. I
185 think you set nothing by° a bloody coxcomb. Here comes Sir   *think nothing of*
Toby, halting.° You shall hear more; but if ° he had not been   *limping / if only*
in drink he would have tickled° you othergates° than he did.   *chastised / in other ways*
ORSINO [*to* SIR TOBY] How now, gentleman? How is't with you?

---

4. Ratified by priestly authority.
5. A gray hair ("grizzle") on your hide (sustaining the metaphor of "cub").
6. That your attempt to trip someone else will be the cause of your downfall.

7. Head; also, a fool's cap, which resembles the crest of a cock.
8. Sir Andrew's blunder for "incarnate" (in the flesh).
9. But I spoke courteously to you.

SIR TOBY That's all one,° he's hurt me, and there's th'end on't.   *No matter*
190 [*To* FESTE] Sot,° didst see Dick Surgeon, sot?   *Fool; drunkard*
FESTE O, he's drunk, Sir Toby, an hour agone. His eyes were
set[1] at eight i'th' morning.
SIR TOBY Then he's a rogue, and a passy-measures pavan.[2] I hate
a drunken rogue.
195 OLIVIA Away with him! Who hath made this havoc with them?
SIR ANDREW I'll help you, Sir Toby, because we'll be dressed[3]
together.
SIR TOBY Will *you* help—an ass-head, and a coxcomb,° and a   *fool*
knave; a thin-faced knave, a gull?°   *dupe*
200 OLIVIA Get him to bed, and let his hurt be looked to.
                    [*Exeunt* SIR TOBY, SIR ANDREW, FESTE, *and* FABIAN]
              Enter SEBASTIAN
SEBASTIAN [*to* OLIVIA] I am sorry, madam, I have hurt your kinsman,
But had it been the brother of my blood
I must have done no less with wit and safety.[4]
You throw a strange regard upon me,° and by that   *regard me strangely*
205 I do perceive it hath offended you.
Pardon me, sweet one, even for the vows
We made each other but so late ago.
ORSINO One face, one voice, one habit, and two persons,
A natural perspective,[5] that is and is not.
210 SEBASTIAN Antonio! O, my dear Antonio,
How have the hours racked and tortured me
Since I have lost thee!
ANTONIO Sebastian are you?
SEBASTIAN Fear'st thou° that, Antonio?   *Do you doubt*
215 ANTONIO How have you made division of yourself?
An apple cleft in two is not more twin
Than these two creatures. Which is Sebastian?
OLIVIA Most wonderful!°   *full of wonder*
SEBASTIAN [*seeing* VIOLA] Do I stand there? I never had a brother,
220 Nor can there be that deity° in my nature   *divine power*
Of here and everywhere.° I had a sister,   *Of omnipresence*
Whom the blind waves and surges have devoured.
Of charity,° what kin are you to me?   *Please*
What countryman? What name? What parentage?
225 VIOLA Of Messaline. Sebastian was my father.
Such a Sebastian was my brother, too.
So went he suited° to his watery tomb.   *in appearance; clad*
If spirits can assume both form and suit
You come to fright us.
SEBASTIAN   A spirit I am indeed,
230 But am in that dimension grossly clad
Which from the womb I did participate.[6]
Were you a woman, as the rest goes even,°   *the rest suggests*
I should my tears let fall upon your cheek
And say 'Thrice welcome, drownèd Viola.'
235 VIOLA My father had a mole upon his brow.

---

1. Closed (as the sun sets).
2. A variety of the slow dance known as "pavane" (from the Italian *passamezzo pavana*). Sir Toby may think its swaying movements suggest drunkenness.
3. We'll have our wounds dressed.

4. With any sense of my welfare.
5. An optical illusion produced by nature (rather than by a mirror).
6. *But . . . participate*: I am clad, like all mortals, in the flesh in which I was born.

SEBASTIAN   And so had mine.

VIOLA   And died that day when Viola from her birth
　　Had numbered thirteen years.

SEBASTIAN   O, that record is lively[7] in my soul.
240　He finishèd indeed his mortal act
　　That day that made my sister thirteen years.

VIOLA   If nothing lets° to make us happy both　　　　　　　　*hinders*
　　But this my masculine usurped attire,
　　Do not embrace me till each circumstance
245　Of place, time, fortune do cohere and jump°　　　　　　*agree*
　　That I am Viola, which to confirm
　　I'll bring you to a captain in this town
　　Where lie my maiden weeds,° by whose gentle help　　　*clothes*
　　I was preserved to serve this noble count.
250　All the occurrence of my fortune since
　　Hath been between this lady and this lord.

SEBASTIAN [*to* OLIVIA]   So comes it, lady, you have been mistook.
　　But nature to her bias drew in that.[8]
　　You would have been contracted° to a maid,　　　　　　*betrothed*
255　Nor are you therein, by my life, deceived.
　　You are betrothed both to a maid and man.[9]

ORSINO [*to* OLIVIA]   Be not amazed. Right noble is his blood.
　　If this be so, as yet the glass seems true,[1]
　　I shall have share in this most happy wreck.
260 [*To* VIOLA]   Boy, thou hast said to me a thousand times
　　Thou never shouldst love woman like to me.

VIOLA   And all those sayings will I overswear,°　　　　　*swear again*
　　And all those swearings keep as true in soul
　　As doth that orbèd continent[2] the fire
　　That severs day from night.

265 ORSINO   Give me thy hand,
　　And let me see thee in thy woman's weeds.

VIOLA   The captain that did bring me first on shore
　　Hath my maid's garments. He upon some action°　　　　*legal charge*
　　Is now in durance,° at Malvolio's suit,　　　　　　　　*prison*
270　A gentleman and follower of my lady's.

OLIVIA   He shall enlarge° him. Fetch Malvolio hither—　　*release*
　　And yet, alas, now I remember me,
　　They say, poor gentleman, he's much distraught.

　　　Enter [FESTE, *the*] *clown with a letter, and* FABIAN
　　A most extracting° frenzy of mine own　　　　　　　　　*distracting*
275　From my remembrance clearly banished his.
　　How does he, sirrah?

FESTE   Truly, madam, he holds Beelzebub at the stave's end[3] as
　　well as a man in his case may do. He's here writ a letter to you.
　　I should have given't you today morning. But as a madman's
280　epistles are no gospels,[4] so it skills° not much when they are　　*matters*
　　delivered.

OLIVIA   Open't and read it.

---

7. The memory of that is vivid.
8. But nature followed her inclination. (The image is from the game of bowls, which uses a ball with an off-centered weight that causes it to curve away from a straight course.)
9. *maid and man:* a man who is a virgin.
1. *the glass seems true:* the "natural perspective" (line 209) continues to seem real.
2. Referring to either the sun or the sphere within which the sun was thought to be fixed.
3. He holds the devil (who threatens to possess him) at a distance (proverbial).
4. Gospel truths. *epistles:* letters (playing on the sense of apostolic accounts of Christ in the New Testament).

FESTE Look then to be well edified when the fool delivers° the   *speaks the words of*
    madman. [*Reads*] 'By the Lord, madam'—
285 OLIVIA How now, art thou mad?
FESTE No, madam, I do but read madness. An your ladyship
    will have it as it ought to be you must allow *vox*.[5]
OLIVIA Prithee, read i'thy right wits.
FESTE So I do, madonna, but to read his right wits[6] is to read
290   thus. Therefore perpend,° my princess, and give ear.   *pay attention*
OLIVIA [*to* FABIAN] Read it you, sirrah.
       [FESTE *gives the letter to* FABIAN]
FABIAN (*reads*) 'By the Lord, madam, you wrong me, and the
    world shall know it. Though you have put me into darkness
    and given your drunken cousin rule over me, yet have I the
295   benefit of my senses as well as your ladyship. I have your own
    letter that induced me to the semblance I put on, with the
    which I doubt not but to do myself much right or you much
    shame. Think of me as you please. I leave my duty a little
    unthought of, and speak out of my injury.[7]
300   The madly-used Malvolio.
OLIVIA Did he write this?
FESTE Ay, madam.
ORSINO This savours not much of distraction.°   *insanity*
OLIVIA See him delivered,° Fabian, bring him hither.   *released*
305   My lord, so please you—these things further thought on—
    To think me as well a sister as a wife,[8]
    One day shall crown th'alliance[9] on't, so please you,
    Here at my house and at my proper cost.°   *own expense*
ORSINO Madam, I am most apt° t'embrace your offer.   *ready*
310   [*To* VIOLA] Your master quits° you, and for your service done him   *releases*
    So much against the mettle° of your sex,   *disposition*
    So far beneath your soft and tender breeding,
    And since you called me master for so long,
    Here is my hand. You shall from this time be
    Your master's mistress.
315 OLIVIA [*to* VIOLA]   A sister, you are she.
       Enter MALVOLIO
ORSINO Is this the madman?
OLIVIA   Ay, my lord, this same.
    How now, Malvolio?
MALVOLIO   Madam, you have done me wrong,
    Notorious wrong.
OLIVIA   Have I, Malvolio? No.
MALVOLIO [*showing a letter*] Lady, you have. Pray you peruse that letter.
320   You must not now deny it is your hand.°   *handwriting*
    Write from° it if you can, in hand or phrase,   *differently from*
    Or say 'tis not your seal, not your invention.°   *composition*
    You can say none of this. Well, grant it then,
    And tell me in the modesty of honour[1]
325   Why you have given me such clear lights° of favour,   *signs*

---

5. The appropriate voice (Latin).
6. To accurately represent his mental state.
7. I neglect the formality I owe you as your servant and speak as an injured person.
8. To think as well of me as a sister-in-law as you would

have thought of me as a wife.
9. The impending double-marriage ceremony.
1. Tell me with the propriety that becomes a noble-woman.

Bade me come smiling and cross-gartered to you,
To put on yellow stockings, and to frown
Upon Sir Toby and the lighter° people,   *lesser*
And acting° this in an obedient hope,   *Upon doing*
330   Why have you suffered me to be imprisoned,
Kept in a dark house, visited by the priest,
And made the most notorious geck° and gull   *fool*
That e'er invention° played on? Tell me why?   *trickery*
OLIVIA   Alas, Malvolio, this is not my writing,
335   Though I confess much like the character,°   *handwriting*
But out of question, 'tis Maria's hand.
And now I do bethink me, it was she
First told me thou wast mad; then cam'st° in smiling,   *you came*
And in such forms which here were presupposed°   *previously suggested*
340   Upon thee in the letter. Prithee be content;
This practice hath most shrewdly passed² upon thee,
But when we know the grounds and authors of it
Thou shalt be both the plaintiff and the judge
Of thine own cause.
FABIAN   Good madam, hear me speak,
345   And let no quarrel nor no brawl to come
Taint the condition of this present hour,
Which I have wondered° at. In hope it shall not,   *marveled*
Most freely I confess myself and Toby
Set this device against Malvolio here
350   Upon° some stubborn and uncourteous parts°   *Because / behavior*
We had conceived against him.³ Maria writ
The letter, at Sir Toby's great importance,°   *importunity*
In recompense whereof he hath married her.
How with a sportful malice it was followed°   *followed through*
355   May rather pluck on° laughter than revenge   *incite*
If that the injuries be justly weighed
That have on both sides passed.
OLIVIA [*to* MALVOLIO]   Alas, poor fool, how have they baffled° thee!   *disgraced*
FESTE   Why, 'Some are born great, some achieve greatness, and
360   some have greatness thrown upon them.' I was one, sir, in this
interlude,° one Sir Topas, sir; but that's all one. 'By the Lord,   *comedy*
fool, I am not mad'—but do you remember, 'Madam, why
laugh you at such a barren rascal, an you smile not, he's
gagged'—and thus the whirligig° of time brings in his revenges.   *spinning top*
365   MALVOLIO   I'll be revenged on the whole pack of you.   [*Exit*]
OLIVIA   He hath been most notoriously abused.
ORSINO   Pursue him, and entreat him to a peace.
He hath not told us of the captain yet.   [*Exit one or more*]
When that is known, and golden time convents,°   *summons; is convenient*
370   A solemn combination shall be made
Of our dear souls. Meantime, sweet sister,
We will not part from hence.° Cesario, come—   *(Olivia's house)*
For so you shall be while you are a man;
But when in other habits you are seen,
375   Orsino's mistress, and his fancy's° queen.   *love's; imagination's*
                        Exeunt [all but FESTE]

2. This trick has most mischievously played.   3. We . . . him: To which we took exception.

FESTE (*sings*) When that I was and a little tiny boy,
    With hey, ho, the wind and the rain,
A foolish thing was but a toy,
    For the rain it raineth every day.

380 But when I came to man's estate,
    With hey, ho, the wind and the rain,
'Gainst knaves and thieves men shut their gate,
    For the rain it raineth every day.

But when I came, alas, to wive,
385   With hey, ho, the wind and the rain,
By swaggering° could I never thrive,   *bullying*
    For the rain it raineth every day.

But when I came unto my beds,
    With hey, ho, the wind and the rain,
390 With tosspots° still had drunken heads,   *drunkards*
    For the rain it raineth every day.

A great while ago the world begun,
    With hey, ho, the wind and the rain,
But that's all one, our play is done,
395   And we'll strive to please you every day.   *Exit*

The Sonnets and
"A Lover's Complaint"

Shakespeare's plays often seem indifferent to high-cultural rules of construction. His sonnets (composed from about 1591 to 1604, possibly revised thereafter, and published in 1609) are the opposite: they faithfully adhere to the norms of an international tradition inspired by the fourteenth-century Italian poet Petrarch. Paradoxically, the very strictness of sonnet structure is the condition of possibility for Shakespeare's originality. The rigor of the form encourages a logical, rationalist approach to the standard topic of the Renaissance sonnet—love and its attendant emotions (desire, jealousy, and the like). The conflict between passionate feelings and a mobile intellect often skeptical of those feelings accordingly becomes a central theme of the poems. And that mobility is conveyed through a linguistic virtuosity marked by metaphors and puns that can work either with or against the larger structure of the sonnet.

Thematically, the sonnets are equally distinctive. The typical object of love—the unapproachable, exalted lady—is displaced so as to make room for a daring representation of homoerotic and adulterous passions. Almost the entire sequence can be divided along these lines. Sonnets 1–126 recount the speaker's idealized, sometimes painful love for a femininely beautiful, well-born male youth; 127–52 his unidealized, ultimately bitter affair with a darkly attractive, unaristocratic "mistress"—where this term invokes, however ironically, the vocabulary of courtly love rather than the derogatory modern meaning. The two love relationships are complicated by a lovers' triangle (40–42, 133–34, 144) and a poetic rival for the youth's affections (78–80, 82–86). These topics provide the occasion for a complex meditation upon a range of issues—time, nature, human mortality, economics, perhaps class and race, and, not least, an artistic immortality. And this self-referential reflection upon the sonnets' very composition is heightened by the reader's intense proximity to a speaker who is and is not Shakespeare.

The poems are best approached by locating their formal specificity against the background of two artistic practices through which Shakespeare came to the poems: his work in the theater, and the prior tradition of the sonnet. The standard verse line of Shakespearean drama and Shakespearean sonnet alike is iambic pentameter. But there the similarity ends. Roughly two-thirds of all lines in the plays are composed in unrhymed iambic pentameter, or blank verse; less than 10 percent employ rhyme. By contrast, Shakespeare's sonnets almost always consist of fourteen rhyming iambic-pentameter lines. Blank verse easily accommodates enjambment, the runover of sense from one line to the next. Rhyme encourages congruence between syntax and verse line: a unit of meaning ends when the line does. Blank verse supports the narrative logic of Shakespearean drama, rhyme the lyric impulse of the Shakespearean sonnet. You watch a play to see what happens next; you read a sonnet to discover the original expression of feelings and thoughts. Language is thus more obtrusively part of meaning in poetry than in drama.

It is easy to find exceptions to these claims. The crucial consideration, however, is the significance for Shakespeare of inherited conventions. The sonnet originated in Italy a century before Petrarch. Petrarch's decisive poetic sequence chronicles the author's passionately complex emotions in relation to his beloved Laura. The Petrarchan sonnet is divided into two frequently contrasting units, an octave (eight lines) and a sestet (six lines), by its rhyme scheme—*abbaabba cdecde,* where each letter represents a line and a repeated letter indicates a rhyme. The Petrarchan mode reached England by the early sixteenth century in the works of Wyatt and Surrey, whose modified rhyme scheme (*abab cdcd efef gg*), later taken over by Shakespeare, divides the sonnet into three quatrains (four-line groupings) and a couplet. This organization offers greater conceptual range than does the Petrarchan model. The quatrains can operate in parallel, represent steps in a logical argument, or contradict each other. They may be grouped into larger units of eight-and-four lines or eight-and-six lines (if the couplet is included) that are set against each other, with the result in the latter case that the Petrarchan octave-sestet structure is approximated. In turn, the epigrammatic concluding couplet, whose analytical tendencies contrast with the more experiential approach of at least the first two quatrains, can summarize the preceding lines, generalize from them, draw appropriate inferences, contribute a new thought, or even reverse the preceding argument.

Sonnet structure often guides Shakespeare's pervasive use of imagery and metaphor. In Sonnet 73, each quatrain pursues a different metaphor as part of a single argument:

> That time of year thou mayst in me behold
> When yellow leaves, or none, or few, do hang
> Upon those boughs which shake against the cold,
> Bare ruined choirs where late the sweet birds sang.
> In me thou seest the twilight of such day
> As after sunset fadeth in the west,
> Which by and by black night doth take away,
> Death's second self, that seals up all in rest.
> In me thou seest the glowing of such fire
> That on the ashes of his youth doth lie
> As the death-bed whereon it must expire,
> Consumed with that which it was nourished by.
>   This thou perceiv'st, which makes thy love more strong,
>   To love that well which thou must leave ere long.

The evocation of fall in the opening quatrain nostalgically communicates the sadness of aging. Enjambment supports the imagistic pattern: it causes meaning to "hang" in the balance at the end of the line, just as "yellow leaves . . . do hang / Upon those boughs." The "yellow leaves" are also leaves of a book, "bare ruined choirs," or quires (manuscript gatherings). Similarly, the birds' former song, together with the primary meaning of "choirs" (the part of a church where the choir sings), may refer to the speaker's own voice and hence to a lost poetic creativity. In short, the experience of aging is compared to the annual movement toward colder seasons and to the decline of artistic inspiration. In the second quatrain, the unit of time constricts: "That time of year" is replaced by "the twilight of such day." Although, like autumn, sunset is a natural process, it is not an organic one. Emphasis accordingly shifts away from bodily degeneration. These lines also look forward in a way the first quatrain does not. Twilight is taken away by "black night . . . , / Death's second self, that seals up all in rest." The rest that night brings is a source of comfort, but night is compared with death, and the syntax, at odds with the literal meaning, suggests that it is death rather than night "that seals up all in [eternal] rest."

The third quatrain opens like the second, with "In me thou seest," a phrase also partly anticipated in the first line of the poem. This repetition reinforces the parallelism among the quatrains and suggests that the poem proceeds less by narrative progression than by thematic variation. Yet this quatrain, while highlighting the transition from aging to mortality, narrows time further, to the "glowing" fire, in effect abandoning the temporal model of the first two quatrains for a spatial metaphor. Only the ashes remain from the fire's and, by implication, the speaker's "youth" (line 10); they are also the fire's and the speaker's "death-bed" (line 11). The earlier idealization of youth, now reduced to "ashes," has disappeared; conversely, although the fire of old age no longer rages, it is still "glowing"—it still gives off heat. The present is thus a continuation of the past. Furthermore, the metaphorical relationship is reversed. The dying fire is a metaphor for human aging, but that aging becomes a metaphor for the dying fire.

Paradoxically, the fire is "Consumed with that which it was nourished by"; it is "consumed" (or choked) by—and along with—the very ashes that, as fuel, previously "nourished" it. Normally, the fire consumes the fuel, not the other way around. Both "consumed" and "nourished" metaphorically explain the already metaphorical fire, which they connect back to humanity through their allusions to eating. The speaker's fiery passion for the youth he addresses nourished him when he was young but consumes him now. Indeed, the line structurally enacts the tacit thematic rejection of a temporal model of decline. It is an example of chiasmus, in which the elements of the first half ("Consumed . . . that") are repeated in reverse order in the second half ("which . . . nourished"), thus producing an *abba* semantic pattern. Accordingly, this quatrain has no equivalent to the earlier "cold" or "night," which are metaphorically responsible for the approach of death. Life and death have the same source.

All three quatrains employ cyclical metaphors of life, death, and rebirth. But the cycle remains incomplete. Autumn does not lead to spring or night to day. The "long-lived phoenix" (19.4), the legendary self-resurrecting bird that dies in flames and is reborn from the ashes, doesn't quite appear. Perhaps these suppressed allusions to cyclical patterns raise and then frustrate expectations, denying the consolation of the future. The concluding couplet, which moves away from metaphor and toward a new idea, suggests this interpretation. Recognizing the speaker's literally consuming passion makes the youth's "love more strong" (line 13). The youth, therefore, loves well what he "must leave ere long" (line 14)—explicitly, the speaker; implicitly, his own life, partly because that leaving recalls the "yellow leaves" with which the poem opened. There is no answer to the destructive power of time, but that power is partly counteracted by love.

Sonnet 73 suggests how conformity to sonnet convention can enable a thoughtful interplay among time, love, death, and art. Sonnet 81, on the other hand, offers a radical disjunction of syntax and rhyme scheme: almost any two consecutive lines can produce a complete sentence, depending on how you punctuate:

> And toungs to be, your beeing shall rehearse,
> When all the breathers of this world are dead,
> You still shall liue (such vertue hath my Pen).
> (81.11–13)

This three-line sequence, presented as it appears in the first edition of 1609, runs over the end of a quatrain but nonetheless produces two possible sentences that are grammatically correct and semantically effective (lines 11 and 12 or 12 and 13). Conceptually, the unorthodox move here is the implicit equation of the speaker with his social superior, the youth. The poet's literary prowess promises enduring renown for both the writer and his subject. Or does it? If you take lines 11 and 12 together, as modern editions do, the emphasis falls on "dead." But if you instead take lines 12 and 13 as a unit, the center of interest becomes "liue" and "my Pen." The poem thus promises both death and immortality, just as the wordplay on "rehearse" (line 11) predicts a future in which the youth is both still spoken about and literally re-hearsed.

The relationship between formal and thematic innovation can also be approached by considering the sonnets as a sequence. English enthusiasm for such sequences was triggered by the posthumous printing of Sir Philip Sidney's collection *Astrophel and Stella* (1591). Sonnets also circulated in manuscript form, since print culture was often considered beneath the dignity of (would-be) gentlemen or courtier-poets. The vogue for sonnet sequences responded to poets' ambitions as well as to the gender politics of the late Elizabethan court. Middle-class writers, for instance, sought financial assistance for their work by praising their aristocratic patrons. Expressions of love in this hierarchical relationship may be less indications of deep feeling than competitive strategies of advancement. Shakespeare's rival poet sonnets seem to convert this competition into literary theme. In general, then, it is often hard to determine where authentic sentiment ends and professional calculation begins.

The sonnet sequence itself is not the only larger formal category, however. When Shakespeare's sonnets first appeared in print, they were immediately followed in the same collection by "A Lover's Complaint." This work belongs to the genre of complaint poetry in which a woman laments her (usually) sexual ruin amid doleful reflections on life. Between 1593 and 1596, six poets published works consisting of a sonnet sequence, a brief intermediate piece usually based on ancient Greek form or subject matter (Cupid, for example), and a concluding complaint. The sonnets section of one such work, from which Shakespeare probably borrowed, is addressed to an attractive male youth. Another poet anticipates Shakespeare's sequence in dividing his sonnets into two main groups. It would be wrong to overstate the homogeneity of this mini-tradition. Nonetheless, the 1609 Quarto—a sonnet sequence divided into two parts, the first concerning a beautiful male youth and the second a woman; two concluding sonnets on Cupid; and a poetic complaint—is less miscellaneous collection than multi-generic form. Recent critics have had no trouble in demonstrating such connections between Shakespeare's sonnets and "A Lover's Complaint"—voyeurism, seduction, abandonment, and a similar cast of characters, among others. Nonetheless, the differences are obvious—for instance, the longer poem's ornamental, archaic diction and lack of emotional intensity. More important, the most detailed scholarship on the subject argues powerfully that not Shakespeare but John Davies of Hereford wrote "A Lover's Complaint." If so, as seems likely, Shakespeare could not have authorized the publication of the 1609 Quarto.

This line of reasoning raises questions about the internal organization of the sonnets as well (although not about their authorship). It has been suggested that the division of the sequence into two main groups is unwarranted. Most of the poems are not explicitly about either the youth or the mistress and do not even designate the sex of the person discussed. Only their relative position in the collection has produced the standard simplification adopted here. Furthermore, the sequence as a whole is relatively uninterested in plot. The poems to the mistress in particular show little sign of organization or process, combining occasional affection with chaos, bitterness, self-abasement, shame, unwilling sexual desire, and self-loathing. Perhaps, in 1609, they had not yet been placed in a particular order; perhaps they were intended for a separate collection. But the first 126 sonnets, too, evince only intermittent interest in linear movement, emphasizing longing, jealousy, and a fear of separation, while anticipating both the desire and the anguish of the subsequent poems.

Nonetheless, many of the sonnets are carefully ordered in pairs or longer groups. More important, the two main sections of the sequence are of compelling thematic interest. For the two centuries ending about a generation ago, the homoerotic attachment to the youth, now a routine part of critical discussion, provoked revulsion or denial. Sonnet 20 was—and still is—at the center of the debate:

> A woman's face with nature's own hand painted
> Hast thou, the master-mistress of my passion;
> A woman's gentle heart, but not acquainted
> With shifting change as is false women's fashion;
> An eye more bright than theirs, less false in rolling,
> Gilding the object whereupon it gazeth;
> A man in hue, all hues in his controlling,
> Which steals men's eyes and women's souls amazeth.

And for a woman wert thou first created,
Till nature as she wrought thee fell a-doting,
And by addition me of thee defeated
By adding one thing to my purpose nothing. [one thing=a penis]
    But since she pricked thee out for women's pleasure,
    Mine be thy love and thy love's use their treasure.

Nature originally intended the youth to be a woman (the octave). But she fell in love with her creation and hence turned him into a male, a change that benefited her but forced the speaker to limit his relationship to the youth to love without sexual consummation (the sestet). Thus, the poem wittily plays with gender boundaries—"master-mistress," "A woman's face," "one thing," "A man in hue" (with a further sexual reference if "hue" was pronounced like "you"; lines 2, 1, 12, 7). "Acquainted" and "controlling" pun on "cunt"; "nothing" and "treasure" refer to the female sexual organ as well (lines 3, 7, 12, 14). As someone "pricked . . . out for women's pleasure" (line 13), the youth is equipped to give women pleasure but also to be "pricked" and hence experience women's pleasure.

"Thy beauty's form in table of my heart" (24.2). Here a man is holding a "table" (tablet) in front of his heart while another man engraves the first man's portrait on it. From Geffrey Whitney, *A Choice of Emblemes* (1586).

Even the form gets into the act: this is the only sonnet where all the rhymes have "feminine" endings—the term since the Renaissance for a two-syllable rhyme with the second syllable unstressed. Finally, the misogyny of the poem's complaint about "false" women (lines 4, 5) is consistent with its homoeroticism. Women are to be resented because the speaker prefers males, or at least the youth, and also because they get to enjoy "love's use," while he must content himself merely with "love" (line 14)—where the contrast suggests that "love" carries both its Renaissance meaning of "friendship" and its modern sense of romantic and sexual desire.

Sonnet 20 looks forward to poems that express passionate, erotic love for the youth, apparently without sexual fulfillment. But they also look back to the opening seventeen sonnets, in which the speaker urges the youth to marry and produce an heir. Hence, the speaker solicits the youth's love for someone else, since the point is procreation and, therefore, an immortality comparable to the artistic immortality promised later in the sequence. The exhortation cuts against both the conventional aspiration of the love sonnet and the speaker's unconventional aim of winning the youth. But this is because the multiple possible meanings of "love" in Sonnet 20 characterize the poems to the youth more generally.

How the case for marriage is argued is instructive. Shakespeare's reversal of the metaphorical relationship in sonnet 73, it will be recalled, removes any fixed point of reference. A comparable reversal also marks economic imagery of the first seventeen sonnets. As in Sonnet 20 (line 14), that imagery frequently turns on usury. Long subject to denunciation, usury in Renaissance England was just beginning its conversion into the respectable financial category of interest. Shakespeare shared the prevailing repugnance at the idea of making money out of money. Thus, the speaker condemns his mistress for her affair with the young man, represented as collecting a debt:

> The statute of thy beauty thou wilt take,
> Thou usurer that putt'st forth all to use.
>   (134.9–10)

She will "take" the full amount owed to her financially (sexually) because, like a "usurer," she employs "all" her wealth (her body) for profit ("use" means both "engage in usury" and "engage in sexual activity"). Elsewhere, more ambivalently, the youth is criticized for being, paradoxically, both "unthrifty" and a "niggard" (4.1, 5):

> Profitless usurer, why dost thou use
> So great a sum of sums yet canst not live?
> (4.7–8)

Here, "use" antithetically means both "use up" and "lend at interest." Literally, how can the youth lend vast "sums" for profit and be unable to support himself? Metaphorically, he acts in a "profitless" manner in wasting his endowments. Hence, he cannot "live" on in his children. By implication, a usurer is always without value.

But the lines also imagine the opposite. If there is a profitless usurer, there might be a profitable one. This good usurer predominates in the sonnets:

> That use is not forbidden usury
> Which happies those that pay the willing loan.
> (6.5–6)

Is "forbidden" an attribute of all, or just unallowable, usury? Keeping one's "treasure" to oneself merits only "thriftless praise"; "beauty's use" deserves "much more praise" if a child results (2.6–9). At least "an unthrift" allows the world to enjoy his wealth; "beauty's waste" is indefensible—"kept unused, the user so destroys it" (9.9–12). And sonnet 20 ends, as we've seen, with the speaker declaring, as if to console himself: "Mine be thy love and thy love's use their treasure" (line 14). The speaker gets the youth's love, whereas the "treasure" women get is merely the "use" (metaphorically, children) of that love. He obtains the principal, they the interest. These passages activate metaphorical meanings of "use" to promote marriage and family. But in so doing, they connect the proper use of beauty with usury, which comes to be understood as the economic equivalent of human reproduction, the early sonnet's highest ideal. The neofeudal celebration of tradition as lineage smuggles in a defense of economic behavior destructive of tradition. Usury is transformed into a potentially noble activity. Through metaphor, then, Shakespeare entertains ideas that might have been less accessible as bald statements.

The poems to the speaker's mistress are also scandalously unconventional—in their focus on a sordid, adulterous affair with an unfaithful woman that is marked by passionate desire and equally passionate recrimination. Even the relatively serene sonnets in this section self-consciously undermine convention:

> My mistress' eyes are nothing like the sun;
> . . . .
> And yet, by heaven, I think my love as rare
> As any she belied with false compare.
> (130.1, 13–14)

Here the target is the standard Petrarchan mode of praise. More generally, the aim is to dismantle falsely idealizing rhetoric:

> When my love swears that she is made of truth
> I do believe her though I know she lies,
> . . . .
> Therefore I lie with her, and she with me,
> And in our faults by lies we flattered be.
> (138.1–2, 13–14)

In Sonnet 130, true love requires the speaker to reject "false compare." In Sonnet 138, love paradoxically requires the speaker to "credit . . . false-speaking," to suppress "simple truth" (lines 7–8), and to embrace "lies." The sequence ends, however, with the bitter deployment of the same rhetoric against speaker and woman alike:

> For I have sworn thee fair—more perjured eye
> To swear against the truth so foul a lie
> (152.13–14)

This concluding couplet recalls the opening of the sequence on the mistress:

> In the old age black was not counted fair,
> . . . .
> But now is black beauty's successive heir.
> (127.1, 3)

Black is the color of the woman's eyes, eyebrows, breasts, hair (127.9–10, 132.3, 130.3–4), and skin:

> Then I will swear beauty herself is black,
> And all they foul that thy complexion lack.
> (132.13–14)

As in other poetry of the time, this paradoxical, anticonventional praise of blackness echoes the biblical Song of Songs as well as sixteenth-century Continental and English poetry, including Sidney's. The praise is often inseparable from a misogynistic denunciation of the use of cosmetics to produce artificial beauty (127.4–12). Black hair and eyes gained prestige in the 1590s through a shift in fashion from blond hair to dark. Thus the speaker's personal views accord with broader social change.

The mistress's color may or may not be racialized, however, since even dark skin might merely distinguish her from falsely idealized women or aristocratic ladies able to avoid the sun. Nonetheless, *Titus Andronicus, Othello, Antony and Cleopatra*, and *The Tempest* feature actual or threatened interracial coupling. The mistress's combination of blackness and promiscuity may provoke both desire and fear of powerfully exotic female sexuality. The valence of blackness accordingly moves from the paradoxical to the conventional: "In nothing art thou black save in thy deeds" (131.13); "For I have sworn thee fair, and thought thee bright, / Who art as black as hell, and dark as night" (147.13–14). Like usury, then, blackness oscillates between conventional norms and radical innovation. Such is the case with the sonnets more generally.

Finally, the intense emotion here and elsewhere, the psychological complexity with which it is scrutinized, the unconventional subject matter, the sense that one is overhearing snatches of conversation, the first-person speaker, that speaker's self-conscious identification with Shakespeare (135–136)—all encourage a biographical interpretation of the sonnets. For two centuries, such interpretation has proven risky either to undertake or to avoid. There has been a major but unsuccessful scholarly effort to discover the real people whom Shakespeare discusses but does not name. The youth has most often been identified with Henry Wriothesley, Earl of Southampton, or William Herbert, Earl of Pembroke. The sonnets' dedication is to "Mr. W. H.," Pembroke's initials and the reverse of Southampton's. But neither is likely to have been addressed as "Mr." Proposals about the identity of the mistress are much shakier. Christopher Marlowe and George Chapman are among those suggested as the rival poet—on the basis of no real evidence. This inconclusiveness led mid-twentieth-century critics to focus on formal concerns. But the resulting advances often entailed evading the disconcerting biographical material that the poems do seem to provide. Shakespeare's sonnets, like his plays, combine verbal artistry and conceptual unorthodoxy with psychological exploration. Their special fascination, however, is that the soul they examine is apparently Shakespeare's own.

WALTER COHEN

TEXTUAL NOTE

The sonnets and "A Lover's Complaint" were printed for the first time in "SHAKESPEARES SONNETS," a Quarto that appeared in 1609. The type for the volume was set by two compositors, who probably worked from a scribal transcript of an authorial manuscript. It is likely that the arrangement of the sonnets is primarily, or perhaps entirely, Shakespearean. But since the compositors punctuated in different ways, the Quarto's punctuation cannot be regarded as authorial. Indeed, it is unlikely that Shakespeare had anything to do with the printing of the Quarto; it is also unlikely that this was an authorized edition—although the second point is more controversial than the first. Finally, it now appears that "A Lover's Complaint" was written not by Shakespeare but by John Davies. (See Vickers in the Selected Bibliography.)

The Quarto was reprinted in *Poems: Written by W. Shakespeare, Gent.* (1640), in which the sonnets (with eight omitted) and "A Lover's Complaint" were joined by additional poetry of Shakespeare and other writers, individual sonnets were run together to produce longer works, the sonnets were titled, their order was rearranged, and a few pronouns were changed or (in the titles) invented. This collection has no independent textual value. *The Passionate Pilgrim* (first edition, 1599 or earlier; second edition, 1599–1600), an unauthorized volume attributed to Shakespeare by its publisher, is a different matter. The second edition includes twenty poems—three from *Love's Labour's Lost* (the 1598 Quarto of which presumably had already appeared in print), four others more reliably attributed to other writers, eleven pieces by unknown authors, and versions of sonnets 138 and 144 that seem to be both erroneous and unrevised.

Another dozen sonnets survive in various manuscripts, all from 1620 or later. Although many derive from the Quarto, a few may preserve—amid mistakes in transcription—authentically Shakespearean phrasing from versions earlier than those in the 1609 edition. It is possible that one or more of these transcripts derive directly from an authorial manuscript and in that sense are closer to what Shakespeare wrote than is the Quarto. The Alternative Versions, printed after "A Lover's Complaint" in this edition, include manuscript renditions of sonnets 2 (the most popular, judging by the number of extant copies) and 106, as well as sonnets 138 and 144 as they appeared in *The Passionate Pilgrim*. Sonnets 8 and 128, for which additional versions are not included here, could also possibly derive from authorial manuscripts. From the four included in the Alternative Versions, one may perhaps learn something of Shakespeare's process of revision.

The poems were probably composed over more than a decade. *The Passionate Pilgrim* and, more inferentially, some of the manuscripts show that Shakespeare wrote a number of the sonnets in the 1590s at the latest. So, too, does Francis Meres's reference in 1598 to Shakespeare's "sugred Sonnets among his priuate friends." The circulation of manuscripts was a common form of "publication" at the time. It should be noted, however, that a "sonnet" could be any short lyric poem. The best candidate for early composition is probably 145, on the basis of its vocabulary, its use of tetrameters rather than pentameters, and the words "hate away" (line 13)—a possible pun on the name of the poet's wife, Anne Hathaway. Further chronological hints are provided by the boom in love-sonnet sequences during the 1590s as well as by Shakespeare's own plays from 1594 to 1596—*Love's Labour's Lost, A Midsummer Night's Dream, Romeo and Juliet,* and *Richard II*—plays that, despite belonging to a variety of genres, are all linked to the sonnets in vocabulary, lyrical feel, and (by the standards of Shakespearean drama) high incidence of rhyme.

Recent scholarship, however, has suggested a later composition or revision for a considerable number of the sonnets. Although no consensus currently exists, a plausible recent estimate is as follows:

1–60:	c. 1595–1596 (later revised?)
61–103:	c. 1594–1595
104–26:	c. 1598–1604
127–54:	c. 1591–1595

Even if this dating is only roughly accurate, it indicates that the sequence of the sonnets as published in 1609 sharply deviates from the chronology of composition. Beyond revealing that Shakespeare—and perhaps not Shakespeare alone—rearranged the sonnets according to other criteria, this conclusion also implies a disconnect between auto-biographical impulse and chronological narrative (unless the sonnets that were composed later uniformly refer back to an earlier time). If the poems are in fact auto-biographical, they cannot provide a linear account of events. This nonnarrative hypothesis is supported by internal evidence, specifically the references to the love triangle involving the speaker, the youth, and the mistress both early and late in the sequence (40–42, 133–34, 144). Alternatively, if the sequence does provide a linear narrative, it cannot be autobiographical. And, of course, the sequence may offer neither chronological narrative nor actual autobiography.

SELECTED BIBLIOGRAPHY

Bloom, Harold, ed. *Shakespeare's Sonnets*. New York: Chelsea House, 1987. Five leading critical essays from 1960 to 1985.

Booth, Stephen. *An Essay on Shakespeare's Sonnets*. New Haven: Yale University Press, 1969. Detailed evidence for multiple overlapping structures within individual sonnets, structures that expand possible meaning without cohering into a unified whole.

————, ed. *Shakespeare's Sonnets*. New Haven: Yale University Press, 1977. Same argument as above, but in the form of a detailed poem-by-poem commentary, together with both the 1609 Quarto of the sonnets and a modernized version.

Fineman, Joel. *Shakespeare's Perjured Eye: The Invention of Poetic Subjectivity in the Sonnets*. Berkeley: University of California Press, 1986. Psychoanalytical study that distinguishes the narcissistic, homosexual visual identification of sonnets 1–126 from the misogynistic heterosexual desire and conflict of 127–52, the latter being the founding moment of modern subjectivity.

Halpern, Richard. *Shakespeare's Perfume: Sodomy and Sublimity in the Sonnets, Wilde, Freud, and Lacan*. Philadelphia: University of Pennsylvania Press, 2002. 11–31. Links sodomy, aesthetics, sublimation, and the sublime.

Hernstein, Barbara, ed. *Discussions of Shakespeare's Sonnets*. Boston: Heath, 1964. Brief pre-twentieth-century accounts plus thirteen important essays from 1930 to 1960.

Schoenfeldt, Michael, ed. *A Companion to Shakespeare's Sonnets*. Malden, Mass.: Blackwell, 2007. The sonnets and "A Lover's Complaint" together with twenty-three essays from the current century plus contributions from Booth (1969) and Vendler (1997).

Vendler, Helen. *The Art of Shakespeare's Sonnets*. Cambridge, Mass.: Belknap Press, 1997. Detailed sonnet-by-sonnet interpretation, focusing on formal considerations, together with the 1609 Quarto and a modernized version of the text, as well as a CD-ROM of Vendler reading the poems.

Vickers, Brian. *Shakespeare, "A Lover's Complaint," and John Davies of Hereford*. New York: Cambridge University Press, 2007. Argues that Davies, not Shakespeare, wrote "A Lover's Complaint."

Willen, Gerald, and Victor B. Reed, eds. *A Casebook on Shakespeare's Sonnets*. New York: Crowell, 1964. Annotated modern edition of the sonnets together with six major critical essays from the 1930s to the early 1950s and very brief explications of a few individual sonnets.

Sonnets

1

From fairest creatures we desire increase,°   *offspring*
That thereby beauty's rose¹ might never die,
But as the riper should by time decease,
His tender² heir might bear his memory;
5 But thou, contracted° to thine own bright eyes,   *engaged; reduced*
Feed'st thy light's flame with self-substantial fuel,³
Making a famine where abundance lies,
Thyself thy foe, to thy sweet self too cruel.
Thou that art now the world's fresh ornament
10 And only herald to the gaudy° spring   *brilliant*
Within thine own bud buriest thy content,°   *substance; happiness*
And, tender churl,° mak'st waste in niggarding.   *young old miser*
    Pity the world, or else this glutton be:
    To eat the world's due, by the grave and thee.⁴

Dedication

1. The identity of W. H. has generated much speculation. As "the only begetter of these ensuing sonnets," "W. H." is probably a misprint for "W. S." or "W. SH." (William Shakespeare). Other candidates include the person who obtained the manuscript for the publisher and the youth who apparently inspired most of the poems. For biographical speculation about the sonnets, see the Introduction.

2. God, literally "ever-living," who promises eternity to Shakespeare (if, as suggested in the previous note, "W.H." refers to Shakespeare); or, less probably, Shakespeare, who promises "eternity" to the young man.

3. Thomas Thorpe, the printer, is the "well-wishing adventurer."

Sonnet 1

1. In Q, "rose," unlike most other nouns, is always capitalized (35.2; 54.3, 6, 11; 67.8; 95.2; 98.10; 99.8; 109.14; and 130.5, 6). Here, it is also italicized. These printing conventions, combined with the placement of the word near the beginning of the first sonnet and its frequent repetition thereafter, suggest that "rose" is the poet's name for the object of his desire, on the model of, for instance, Stella in Sir Philip Sidney's influential sonnet sequence *Astrophel and Stella* (published 1591). The rose had long been associated with female genitalia, most notably in the thirteenth-century French narrative poem *The Romance of the Rose*, by Guillaume de Lorris and Jean de Meun. In Shakespeare's case, however, the object of desire is male. He is most frequently referred to as "youth," almost never as "boy" or "man." Shakespeare's "mistress" in the later sonnets is contrasted with "roses" (130.5, 6).

2. The rose's (the youth's) young.

3. Are consuming yourself like a candle.

4. *this . . . thee*: be a glutton by causing what is due to the world (your posterity) to be consumed both by the grave and within yourself.

2[1]

When forty winters shall besiege thy brow
And dig deep trenches in thy beauty's field,
Thy youth's proud livery,° so gazed on now,   *uniform; appearance*
Will be a tattered weed,° of small worth held.   *clothing; plant*
5   Then being asked where all thy beauty lies,
Where all the treasure of thy lusty days,
To say within thine own deep-sunken eyes
Were an all-eating shame and thriftless praise.[2]
How much more praise deserved thy beauty's use[3]
10 If thou couldst answer 'This fair child of mine
Shall sum my count, and make my old excuse',[4]
Proving his beauty by succession thine.°   *inherited from you*
    This were° to be new made when thou art old,   *would be*
    And see thy blood warm when thou feel'st it cold.

3

Look in thy glass,° and tell the face thou viewest   *mirror*
Now is the time that face should form another,
Whose fresh repair° if now thou not renewest   *state*
Thou dost beguile° the world, unbless° some mother.   *swindle / leave childless*
5   For where is she so fair whose uneared° womb   *unplowed*
Disdains the tillage of thy husbandry?[1]
Or who is he so fond will be the tomb
Of his self-love to stop posterity?[2]
Thou art thy mother's glass, and she in thee
10 Calls back the lovely April of her prime;
So thou through windows of thine age[3] shalt see,
Despite of wrinkles, this thy golden time.
    But if thou live remembered not to be,[4]
    Die single, and thine image dies with thee.

4

Unthrifty loveliness, why dost thou spend
Upon thyself thy beauty's legacy?
Nature's bequest gives nothing, but doth lend,
And being frank, she lends to those are free.[1]
5   Then, beauteous niggard, why dost thou abuse
The bounteous largess given thee to give?
Profitless usurer, why dost thou use°   *lend for profit; spend*
So great a sum of sums yet canst not live?[2]
For having traffic° with thyself alone,   *(commercial); (sexual)*
10 Thou of thyself thy sweet self dost deceive.°   *defraud*
Then how when nature calls thee to be gone:
What acceptable audit canst thou leave?
    Thy unused[3] beauty must be tombed with thee,
    Which usèd, lives th'executor to be.

Sonnet 2
1. See *Spes Altera* in the Alternative Versions.
2. Would be a shameful admission of gluttony and boast of excessive expenditure.
3. How much more would the use (employment; investment or usurious lending) of your beauty merit.
4. Shall make my accounts balance and defend (absolve) me in my age.
Sonnet 3
1. Cultivation; acting as a husband.

2. *who . . . posterity:* who is so foolish that he will selfishly deny posterity a child?
3. Eyes weakened by old age; your children.
4. But if you live to be forgotten.
Sonnet 4
1. And being generous, she lends to those who (also) are generous.
2. Make a living; live on in your children.
3. Not put to use; not interest-bearing.

5

Those hours that with gentle work did frame°   *form*
The lovely gaze° where every eye doth dwell   *face*
Will play the tyrants to the very same,
And that unfair which fairly doth excel;[1]
5   For never-resting time leads summer on
To hideous winter, and confounds° him there,   *destroys*
Sap checked with frost, and lusty leaves quite gone,
Beauty o'er-snowed, and bareness everywhere.
Then were not summer's distillation left
10   A liquid prisoner pent in walls of glass,
Beauty's effect with beauty were bereft,[2]
Nor° it nor no remembrance what it was.   *Neither*
   But flowers distilled, though they with winter meet,
   Lose[3] but their show; their substance still lives sweet.

6[1]

Then let not winter's ragged° hand deface   *rough*
In thee thy summer ere thou be distilled.
Make sweet some vial,° treasure° thou some place   *womb / enrich*
With beauty's treasure ere it be self-killed.
5   That use° is not forbidden usury   *lending for profit*
Which happies those that pay the willing loan:[2]
That's for thyself° to breed another thee,   *So you would do*
Or ten times happier, be it ten for one;°   *1,000% interest*
Ten times thyself were happier than thou art,
10   If ten of thine ten times refigured° thee.   *copied*
Then what could death do if thou shouldst depart,
Leaving thee living in posterity?
   Be not self-willed,[3] for thou art much too fair
   To be death's conquest and make worms thine heir.

7

Lo, in the orient° when the gracious light°   *east / sun*
Lifts up his burning head, each under° eye   *earthly*
Doth homage to his new-appearing sight,
Serving with looks his sacred majesty,
5   And having climbed the steep-up heavenly hill,
Resembling strong youth in his middle age,°   *noon*
Yet mortal looks adore his beauty still,
Attending on his golden pilgrimage.
But when from highmost pitch, with weary car,°   *sun god's chariot*
10   Like feeble age he reeleth from the day,
The eyes, 'fore duteous, now converted° are   *turned*
From his low tract,° and look another way.   *path*
   So thou, thyself outgoing in thy noon,
   Unlooked on diest unless thou get° a son.°   *beget / (sun)*

Sonnet 5
1. Will make unattractive that which now excels in beauty.
2. *Then . . . bereft:* Then if there were no perfume distilled from flowers bottled in glass vials, both beauty and its effect would be lost.
3. Q has "Leese," understood in this edition as a cognate of "lose." This is Shakespeare's only use of "Leese," which

allows a pun on "lease." See 13.5.
Sonnet 6
1. This sonnet links with 5.
2. Which makes happy those who willingly lend, or who willingly repay the loan with interest (in the form of children).
3. Stubborn; leaving everything in a will to yourself alone.

8

Music to hear,[1] why hear'st thou music sadly?
Sweets° with sweets war not, joy delights in joy.　　　*Sweet things*
Why lov'st thou that which thou receiv'st not gladly,
Or else receiv'st with pleasure thine annoy?
5　If the true concord of well-tunèd sounds
By unions° married do offend thine ear,　　　*harmony*
They do but sweetly chide thee, who confounds°　　　*destroys*
In singleness the parts[2] that thou shouldst bear.
Mark how one string, sweet husband to another,
10　Strikes each in each° by mutual ordering,　　　*Resonates*
Resembling sire and child and happy mother,
Who all in one one pleasing note do sing;
　　　Whose speechless° song, being many, seeming one,　　　*The strings' wordless*
　　　Sings this to thee: 'Thou single wilt prove none.'[3]

9

Is it for fear to wet a widow's eye
That thou consum'st thyself in single life?
Ah, if thou issueless° shalt hap to die,　　　*childless*
The world will wail thee like a makeless° wife.　　　*widowed*
5　The world will be thy widow, and still° weep　　　*continually*
That thou no form of thee hast left behind,
When every private° widow well may keep　　　*individual*
By children's eyes her husband's shape in mind.
Look what° an unthrift in the world doth spend　　　*Whatever*
10　Shifts but his° place, for still the world enjoys it;　　　*its*
But beauty's waste hath in the world an end,
And kept unused, the user° so destroys it.　　　*spender; lender*
　　　No love toward others in that bosom sits
　　　That on himself such murd'rous shame commits.

10

For shame deny that thou bear'st love to any,
Who for thyself art so unprovident.
Grant, if thou wilt, thou art beloved of many,
But that thou none lov'st is most evident;
5　For thou art so possessed with murd'rous hate
That 'gainst thyself thou stick'st not to conspire,°　　　*don't balk at conspiring*
Seeking that beauteous roof to ruinate
Which to repair should be thy chief desire.
O, change thy thought, that I may change my mind?　　　*judgment*
10　Shall hate be fairer lodged than gentle love?
Be as thy presence° is, gracious and kind,　　　*appearance*
Or to thyself at least kind-hearted prove.
　　　Make thee another self for love of me,
　　　That beauty still may live in thine or thee.

Sonnet 8
1. You whose voice is music.
2. Musical parts; roles as husband and father.

3. Without an heir, death will render you nothing (alluding to the proverb "One is no number").

11

As fast as thou shalt wane, so fast thou grow'st
In one of thine from that which thou departest,[1]
And that fresh blood which youngly thou bestow'st
Thou mayst call thine when thou from youth convertest.°   *turn away*
5 Herein lives wisdom, beauty, and increase;
Without this, folly, age, and cold decay.
If all were minded so, the times should cease,
And threescore year would make the world away.
Let those whom nature hath not made for store,°   *breeding*
10 Harsh,° featureless,° and rude,° barrenly perish.[2] *ugly (all three words)*
Look whom she best endowed she gave the more,[2]
Which bounteous gift thou shouldst in bounty° cherish. *by using bountifully*
  She carved thee for her seal,[3] and meant thereby
  Thou shouldst print more, not let that copy die.

12

When I do count the clock° that tells the time,   *hours as they strike*
And see the brave° day sunk in hideous night;   *fine*
When I behold the violet past prime,
And sable° curls ensilvered o'er with white;   *black*
5 When lofty trees I see barren of leaves,
Which erst° from heat did canopy the herd,   *once*
And summer's green all girded up in sheaves
Borne on the bier with white and bristly beard:[1]
Then of thy beauty do I question make
10 That thou among the wastes of time must go,
Since sweets° and beauties do themselves forsake,   *sweet things*
And die as fast as they see others grow;
  And nothing 'gainst time's scythe can make defence
  Save breed to brave him° when he takes thee hence. *children to defy time*

13

O that you were yourself![1] But, love, you are
No longer yours than you yourself here live.
Against° this coming end you should prepare,   *For*
And your sweet semblance to some other give.
5 So should that beauty which you hold in lease
Find no determination;° then you were°   *never end / would be*
Yourself again after your self's decease,
When your sweet issue your sweet form should bear.
Who lets so fair a house fall to decay,
10 Which husbandry[2] in honour might uphold
Against the stormy gusts of winter's day,
And barren rage of death's eternal cold?
  O, none but unthrifts,° dear my love, you know.   *spendthrifts*
  You had a father; let your son say so.

Sonnet 11
1. In a child begotten in youth (with suggestions of sexual intercourse and of death).
2. To whomever nature gave most (made best-looking) she gave even more (extra reproductive abilities). The near circularity of "best endowed" and "more" alludes to Matthew 25:29, the paradoxical parable of the talents: "For unto every man that hath, it shall be given."

3. Literally, a stamp of authority.
Sonnet 12
1. *An . . . beard*: And sheaves of mature ("bearded") grain carried away on the harvest cart; old man borne on a funeral bier.
Sonnet 13
1. If only you could remain your (eternal) self.
2. Stewardship; being a husband.

14

Not from the stars do I my judgement pluck,
And yet methinks I have astronomy;°   *astrological knowledge*
But not to tell of good or evil luck,
Of plagues, of dearths, or seasons' quality.
5   Nor can I fortune to brief minutes° tell,   *precisely*
'Pointing to each his thunder, rain, and wind,
Or say with princes if it shall go well
By oft predict° that I in heaven find;   *numerous signs*
But from thine eyes my knowledge I derive,
10   And, constant stars, in them I read such art
As[1] truth and beauty shall together thrive
If from thyself to store thou wouldst convert.[2]
    Or else of thee this I prognosticate:
    Thy end is truth's and beauty's doom and date.°   *final judgment and end*

15

When I consider every thing that grows
Holds° in perfection but a little moment,   *Remains*
That this huge stage presenteth naught but shows
Whereon the stars in secret influence° comment;   *(astrologically)*
5   When I perceive that men as plants increase,
Cheerèd and checked even by the selfsame sky;
Vaunt° in their youthful sap,° at height decrease   *Gloat / strength*
And wear their brave state out of memory;[1]
Then the conceit° of this inconstant stay°   *imagination / (on earth)*
10   Sets you most rich in youth before my sight,
Where wasteful time debateth° with decay   *competes*
To change your day of youth to sullied night;
    And all in war with time for love of you,
    As he takes from you, I engraft you new.[2]

16[1]

But wherefore do not you a mightier way
Make war upon this bloody tyrant, time,
And fortify yourself in your decay
With means more blessèd than my barren rhyme?
5   Now stand you on the top of happy hours,°   *in your prime*
And many maiden gardens yet unset°   *unplanted*
With virtuous wish would bear your living flowers,
Much liker than your painted counterfeit.°   *image in art or poetry*
So should the lines of life[2] that life repair°   *restore*
10   Which this time's pencil or my pupil pen[3]
Neither in inward worth nor outward fair
Can make you live yourself° in eyes of men.   *as yourself*
    To give away yourself keeps yourself still,°   *(as children)*
    And you must live drawn by your own sweet skill.

Sonnet 14
1. *such art / As:* such predictions as that.
2. If you would provide for the future.
Sonnet:15
1. Wear their splendid clothing until they are forgotten (with a sense of "wearing out").
2. *And . . . new:* And I, in competition with time because

I love you, restore you with my verse.
Sonnet 16
1. This sonnet links with 15.
2. Lineage; living lines (unlike those of poet or painter).
3. Neither today's painters ("pencil" means "paintbrush") nor I, who imitate painting in my verse.

17

Who will believe my verse in time to come
If it were filled with your most high deserts?—
Though yet, heaven knows, it is but as a tomb
Which hides your life, and shows not half your parts.°   *attributes*
5   If I could write the beauty of your eyes
And in fresh numbers° number all your graces,   *lively verses*
The age to come would say 'This poet lies;
Such heavenly touches ne'er touched earthly faces.'
So should my papers, yellowed with their age,
10   Be scorned, like old men of less truth than tongue,
And your true rights° be termed a poet's rage°   *praises / hyperbole*
And stretchèd metre° of an antique song.   *overwrought poetry*
    But were some child of yours alive that time,
    You should live twice: in it, and in my rhyme.

18

Shall I compare thee to a summer's day?
Thou art more lovely and more temperate.
Rough winds do shake the darling buds of May,
And summer's lease° hath all too short a date.   *fixed span of time*
5   Sometime too hot the eye of heaven shines,
And often is his gold complexion dimmed,
And every fair from fair[1] sometime declines,
By chance or nature's changing course untrimmed;°   *rendered ordinary*
But thy eternal summer shall not fade
10   Nor lose possession of that fair thou ow'st,°   *own*
Nor shall death brag thou wander'st in his shade
When in eternal lines to time thou grow'st.[2]
    So long as men can breathe or eyes can see,
    So long lives this, and this gives life to thee.

19

Devouring time, blunt thou the lion's paws,
And make the earth devour her own sweet brood;
Pluck the keen teeth from the fierce tiger's jaws,
And burn the long-lived phoenix[1] in her blood.°   *alive*
5   Make glad and sorry seasons as thou fleet'st,
And do whate'er thou wilt, swift-footed time,
To the wide world and all her fading sweets.°   *sweet things*
But I forbid thee one most heinous crime:
O, carve not with thy hours my love's fair brow,
10   Nor draw no lines there with thine antique° pen.   *old; capricious*
Him in thy course untainted do allow
For beauty's pattern to succeeding men.
    Yet do thy worst, old time; despite thy wrong
    My love shall in my verse ever live young.

Sonnet 18
1. Lovely thing from loveliness.
2. When in immortal poetry you become engrafted to time.

Sonnet 19
1. Legendary, self-resurrecting bird believed to live in cycles of several centuries, dying in flames and reborn from the ashes. See also 73.9–12.

20

A woman's face with nature's own hand° painted   *(without cosmetics)*
Hast thou, the master-mistress¹ of my passion;²
A woman's gentle heart, but not acquainted°   *(pun on "quaint," "cunt")*
With shifting change as is false women's fashion;
5 An eye more bright than theirs, less false in rolling,°   *wandering (sexually)*
Gilding the object whereupon it gazeth;
A man in hue, all hues in his controlling,³
Which steals men's eyes and women's souls amazeth °   *overwhelms*
And for° a woman wert thou first created,   *to be; to be with*
10 Till nature as she wrought thee fell a-doting,°   *behaved foolishly*
And by addition me of thee defeated°   *cheated me of you*
By adding one thing to my purpose nothing.⁴
    But since she pricked° thee out for women's pleasure,⁵   *chose; (sexual)*
    Mine be thy love and thy love's use their treasure.⁶

21

So is it not with me as with that muse°   *poet*
Stirred by a painted° beauty to his verse,   *(with cosmetics)*
Who heaven itself for ornament° doth use,   *poetic imagery*
And every fair with his fair doth rehearse,¹
5 Making a couplement of proud compare²
With sun and moon, with earth, and sea's rich gems,
With April's first-born flowers, and all things rare
That heaven's air in this huge rondure hems.°   *globe surrounds*
O let me, true in love, but truly write,
10 And then believe me my love is as fair
As any mother's child, though not so bright
As those gold candles° fixed in heaven's air.   *(the stars)*
    Let them say more that like of hearsay° well;   *clichés*
    I will not praise that purpose not° to sell.   *since I don't intend*

22

My glass° shall not persuade me I am old   *mirror*
So long as youth and thou are of one date;°   *While you're young*
But when in thee time's furrows I behold,
Then look I° death my days should expiate.°   *I expect / conclude*
5 For all that beauty that doth cover thee
Is but the seemly° raiment of my heart,   *fitting*
Which in thy breast doth live, as thine in me;
How can I then be elder than thou art?
O therefore, love, be of thyself so wary
10 As I, not for myself, but for thee will,
Bearing thy heart, which I will keep so chary°   *cautiously*
As tender nurse her babe from faring ill.

Sonnet 20
1. Both patron and sexual mistress (hence, homoerotic); referring to the youth's feminine looks.
2. Object of my love; controller of my feelings; controller of my passionate poetry.
3. A man whose looks enable him to attract and dominate all others; a man whose looks encompass all other appearances (both male and female). "Hue" may pun on "you" with possible sexual connotations. "Hues" may pun on "use"; see line 14 and note. "Controlling" puns on "cunt."
4. *one . . . nothing:* something (a penis) of no use to me;

"thing" meant sexual organ; "nothing" meant female sexual organ.
5. To give women pleasure; to have the pleasure women have.
6. I'll have the main part of your love (the capital or principal); while women get just the "use" (interest; pleasure; children) of it (or, while you use women sexually).
Sonnet 21
1. And compares every beautiful thing with his beloved.
2. Making a link in proud comparison.

Presume not on¹ thy heart when mine is slain:
Thou gav'st me thine not to give back again.

23

As an unperfect actor on the stage
Who with his fear is put besides° his part,   *forgets*
Or some fierce thing replete with too much rage
Whose strength's abundance weakens his own heart,
5 So I, for fear of trust,° forget to say   *lack of confidence*
The perfect ceremony of love's rite,¹
And in mine own love's strength seem to decay,
O'er-charged with burden of mine own love's might.
O let my books be then the eloquence
10 And dumb presagers° of my speaking breast,   *mute presenters*
Who plead for love, and look for recompense
More than that tongue that more hath more expressed.²
 O learn to read what silent love hath writ;
 To hear with eyes belongs to love's fine wit.

24

Mine eye hath played the painter,¹ and hath steeled²
Thy beauty's form in table° of my heart.   *the painted tablet*
My body is the frame wherein 'tis held,
And perspective³ it is best painter's art;
5 For through the painter must you see his skill
To find where your true image pictured lies,
Which in my bosom's shop° is hanging still,   *heart's workshop*
That hath his windows glazèd with thine eyes.⁴
Now see what good turns eyes for eyes have done:
10 Mine eyes have drawn thy shape, and thine for me
Are windows to my breast, wherethrough the sun
Delights to peep, to gaze therein on thee.
 Yet eyes this cunning want° to grace their art: *lack this talent*
 They draw but what they see, know not the heart.

25

Let those who are in favour with their stars
Of public honour and proud titles boast,
Whilst I, whom fortune of such triumph bars,
Unlooked-for joy in that I honour most.¹
5 Great princes' favourites their fair leaves spread°   *bloom*
But as the marigold at the sun's eye,²
And in themselves their pride lies° buried,   *will lie*
For at a frown they in their glory die.
The painful warrior famousèd for might,

Sonnet 22
1. Do not expect to get back.
Sonnet 23
1. Q reads "right," suggesting love's due as well as ritual.
2. More than that (rival) speaker who has more often said more.
Sonnet 24
1. The running conceit is of the speaker and addressee looking into one another's eyes, seeing both the other and himself reflected.
2. Engraved. Editors often emend Q's "steeld" to "stell'd" (fixed, placed) for a better fit with "painter."
3. Seen from the proper angle, through the painter's

eyes. A "perspective" was a distorted painting that looked right only if viewed from the correct angle.
4. The addressee looks into the speaker's eyes ("windows"), which seem fitted with glass ("glazèd") by the reflection there of the addressee's own eyes. The eyes are the heart's ("his" [its], referring to "bosom's," line 7) windows, through which the addressee can therefore see his own image in the speaker's heart.
Sonnet 25
1. Unexpectedly (privately) take pleasure in what I most esteem (the youth).
2. Only at the prince's pleasure or whim.

10 After a thousand victories once foiled
Is from the book of honour razèd° quite,   *deleted*
And all the rest forgot for which he toiled.
    Then happy I, that love and am beloved
    Where I may not remove nor be removed.

26

Lord of my love, to whom in vassalage°   *feudal allegiance*
Thy merit hath my duty strongly knit,
To thee I send this written embassage°   *missive*
To witness duty, not to show my wit;
5 Duty so great which wit so poor as mine
May make seem bare in wanting° words to show it.   *lacking*
But that I hope some good conceit° of thine   *opinion*
In thy soul's thought, all naked,[1] will bestow° it,   *provide a place for*
Till whatsoever star that guides my moving°   *actions*
10 Points on me graciously with fair aspect,°   *astrological influence*
And puts apparel on my tattered loving
To show me worthy of thy sweet respect.
    Then may I dare to boast how I do love thee;
    Till then, not show my head where thou mayst prove° me.   *test*

27

Weary with toil I haste me to my bed,
The dear repose for limbs with travel° tired;   *work; journeying*
But then begins a journey in my head
To work my mind when body's work's expired;
5 For then my thoughts, from far where I abide,
Intend a zealous pilgrimage to thee,
And keep my drooping eyelids open wide,
Looking on darkness which the blind do see:
Save that my soul's imaginary sight
10 Presents thy shadow° to my sightless view,   *picture*
Which like a jewel hung in ghastly night
Makes black night beauteous and her old face new.
    Lo, thus by day my limbs, by night my mind,
    For° thee, and for myself, no quiet find.   *Because of*

28[1]

How can I then return in happy plight,°   *condition*
That am debarred the benefit of rest,
When day's oppression is not eased by night,
But day by night and night by day oppressed,
5 And each, though enemies to either's° reign,   *each other's*
Do in consent shake hands to torture me,
The one by toil, the other to complain[2]
How far I toil, still farther off from thee?
I tell the day to please him thou art bright,
10 And do'st him grace when clouds do blot the heaven;[3]
So flatter I the swart°-complexioned night   *dark*
When sparkling stars twire not thou gild'st the even.[4]

Sonnet 26
1. Refers to his "bare"-seeming "duty."
Sonnet 28
1. This sonnet links with 27.

2. *one:* day. *other* night, making me "complain."
3. And confer beauty on him as a substitute for the sun.
4. By saying that when stars aren't twinkling, you brighten the evening.

But day doth daily draw my sorrows longer,
And night doth nightly make grief's strength seem stronger.

29

When, in disgrace with fortune and men's eyes,
I all alone beweep my outcast state,
And trouble deaf heaven with my bootless° cries,   *unavailing*
And look upon myself and curse my fate,
5   Wishing me like to one more rich in hope,
Featured like him, like him with friends possessed,[1]
Desiring this man's art° and that man's scope,°   *skill / range*
With what I most enjoy° contented least: *like; own*
Yet in these thoughts myself almost despising,
10 Haply[2] I think on thee, and then my state,°   *mood; fortunes*
Like to the lark at break of day arising
From sullen earth, sings hymns at heaven's gate;
    For thy sweet love remembered such wealth brings
    That then I scorn to change my state with kings'.

30

When to the sessions° of sweet silent thought   *court sittings*
I summon up remembrance of things past,
I sigh° the lack of many a thing I sought,   *mourn*
And with old woes new wail my dear time's waste.[1]
5   Then can I drown an eye unused to flow
For precious friends hid in death's dateless° night,   *endless*
And weep afresh love's long-since-cancelled° woe,   *repaid (with sorrow)*
And moan th'expense° of many a vanished sight.   *passing*
Then can I grieve at grievances foregone,°   *bygone*
10 And heavily° from woe to woe tell° o'er   *sadly / say; count*
The sad account° of fore-bemoanèd moan,   *story; finances*
Which I new pay as if not paid before.
    But if the while I think on thee, dear friend,
    All losses are restored, and sorrows end.

31

Thy bosom is endearèd with° all hearts   *loved by; enriched by*
Which I by lacking have supposèd dead,
And there reigns love, and all love's loving parts,
And all those friends which I thought burièd.
5   How many a holy and obsequious° tear   *dutifullly mourning*
Hath dear religious° love stol'n from mine eye   *devoted*
As interest of° the dead, which° now appear   *due payment to / who*
But things removed° that hidden in thee lie!   *absent*
Thou art the grave where buried love doth live,
10 Hung with the trophies° of my lovers gone,   *memorials*
Who all their parts° of me to thee did give: *shares*
That due of many[1] now is thine alone.

Sonnet 29
1. *Wishing . . . possessed*: Three people he wants to be like—"like to one" with better prospects, better looking "like him," and having friends "like him."
2. By chance; also, pun on "happily."

Sonnet 30
1. *my . . . waste*: the frittering or wasting away of my precious time.
Sonnet 31
1. What was owed to many (myself).

Their images I loved I view in thee,
And thou, all they,[2] hast all the all of me.

32

If thou survive my well-contented day[1]
When that churl death my bones with dust shall cover,
And shalt by fortune° once more resurvey   *chance*
These poor rude° lines of thy deceasèd lover,   *rough*
5 Compare them with the bett'ring° of the time,   *progress; better art*
And though they be outstripped by every pen,
Reserve them for my love, not for their rhyme
Exceeded by the height of happier men.[2]
O then vouchsafe me but this loving thought:
10 'Had my friend's muse grown with this growing age,
A dearer birth° than this his love had brought   *worthier poem*
To march in ranks of better equipage;°   *poems*
    But since he died, and poets better prove,°   *have improved*
    Theirs for their style I'll read, his for his love.'

33

Full many a glorious morning have I seen
Flatter the mountain tops with sovereign eye,°   *sunlight*
Kissing with golden face the meadows green,
Gilding pale streams with heavenly alchemy;
5 Anon° permit the basest° clouds to ride   *(But) soon / darkest*
With ugly rack° on his celestial face,   *cloudy mask*
And from the forlorn world his visage hide,
Stealing unseen to west with this disgrace.
Even so my sun one early morn did shine
10 With all triumphant splendour on my brow;
But out, alack,° he was but one hour mine;   *alas*
The region° cloud hath masked him from me now.   *high*
    Yet him for this my love no whit disdaineth:
    Suns of the world may stain° when heaven's sun staineth.   *darken*

34[1]

Why didst thou promise such a beauteous day
And make me travel forth without my cloak,
To let base clouds o'ertake me in my way,
Hiding thy brav'ry° in their rotten smoke?°   *finery / noxious mists*
5 'Tis not enough that through the cloud thou break
To dry the rain on my storm-beaten face,
For no man well of such a salve can speak
That heals the wound and cures not the disgrace.[2]
Nor can thy shame° give physic to° my grief;   *remorse / cure*
10 Though thou repent, yet I have still the loss.
Th'offender's sorrow lends but weak relief
To him that bears the strong offence's cross.°   *consequences*

---

2. And you, who are made up of all of them.
Sonnet 32
1. Day of my death, which I shall willingly accept.
2. *Reserve . . . men:* Keep them because you love me, not
for their value as poetry, which is surpassed by poets more

fortunate in their talent than I.
Sonnet 34
1. This sonnet links with 33.
2. *Disfigurement;* dishonor done the poet by the youth's
neglect.

Ah, but those tears are pearl which thy love sheds,
And they are rich, and ransom° all ill deeds.   *atone for*

35

No more be grieved at that which thou hast done:
Roses have thorns, and silver fountains mud.
Clouds and eclipses stain° both moon and sun,   *darken*
And loathsome canker° lives in sweetest bud.   *(worm)*
5   All men make faults, and even I in this,
Authorizing thy trespass with compare,[1]
Myself corrupting salving thy amiss,[2]
Excusing thy sins more than thy sins are;[3]
For to thy sensual fault I bring in sense[4]—
10 Thy adverse party is thy advocate—
And 'gainst myself a lawful plea commence.
Such civil war is in my love and hate
    That I an accessory needs must be
    To that sweet thief which sourly robs from me.

36

Let me confess that we two must be twain[1]
Although our undivided loves are one;
So shall those blots° that do with me remain   *flaws; sources of shame*
Without thy help by me be borne alone.
5   In our two loves there is but one respect,°   *focus of attention*
Though in our lives a separable spite[2]
Which, though it alter not love's sole° effect,   *single-minded*
Yet doth it steal sweet hours from love's delight.
I may not evermore acknowledge thee
10 Lest my bewailèd guilt should do thee shame,
Nor thou with public kindness honour me
Unless thou take° that honour from thy name.   *lose*
    But do not so. I love thee in such sort°   *such a way*
    As, thou being mine, mine is thy good report.[3]

37

As a decrepit father takes delight
To see his active child do deeds of youth,
So I, made lame by fortune's dearest° spite,   *direst*
Take all my comfort of° thy worth and truth;   *in*
5   For whether beauty, birth, or wealth, or wit,
Or any of these all, or all, or more,
Entitled in thy parts[1] do crownèd sit,
I make my love engrafted to this store.[2]
So then I am not lame, poor, nor despised,
10 Whilst that this shadow° doth such substance give   *idea*
That I in thy abundance am sufficed

Sonnet 35
1. Justifying your offense with comparisons.
2. Corrupting myself in minimizing your transgression.
3. Excusing you (overindulgently) from worse sins than the ones you've committed.
4. I use reason to defend your sensual offense.
Sonnet 36
1. Separated; but also, paradoxically, two of a kind or bound together.

2. Separation that causes vexation; vexation that causes separation.
3. Reputation. This couplet also ends 96.
Sonnet 37
1. Enrolled among your good qualities.
2. I engraft my love onto this abundance (of good qualities).

And by a part of all thy glory live.
Look what° is best, that best I wish in thee;   whatever
This° wish I have, then ten times happy me.   When this

38

How can my muse want subject to invent°   lack subject matter
While thou dost breathe, that pour'st into my verse
Thine own sweet argument,° too excellent   theme
For every vulgar paper to rehearse?¹
5   O, give thyself the thanks if aught in me
Worthy perusal stand against thy sight;²
For who's so dumb that cannot write to thee,
When thou thyself dost give invention light?
Be thou the tenth muse, ten times more in worth
10   Than those old nine which rhymers invocate,
And he that calls on thee, let him bring forth
Eternal numbers° to outlive long date.   verses / a distant
    If my slight muse do please these curious° days,   finicky
    The pain° be mine, but thine shall be the praise.   pains; effort

39

O, how thy worth with manners° may I sing   modesty
When thou art all the better part of me?
What can mine own praise to mine own self bring,
And what is't but mine own when I praise thee?
5   Even for° this let us divided live,   Because of
And our dear love lose name of single one,°   the reputation of unity
That by this separation I may give
That due to thee which thou deserv'st alone.
O absence, what a torment wouldst thou prove
10   Were it not thy sour leisure gave sweet leave
To entertain° the time with thoughts of love,   enliven
Which time and thoughts so sweetly doth deceive,
    And that thou teachest how to make one twain
    By praising him here° who doth hence remain!   in this poem

40¹

Take all my loves, my love, yea, take them all:
What hast thou then more than thou hadst before?
No love, my love, that thou mayst true love call—
All mine was thine before thou hadst this more.
5   Then if for my love thou my love receivest,²
I cannot blame thee for my love thou usest:³
But yet be blamed if thou this self⁴ deceivest
By wilful taste of what thyself° refusest.   your better nature
I do forgive thy robb'ry, gentle thief,
10   Although thou steal thee all my poverty;°   what little I own
And yet love knows it is a greater grief

Sonnet 38
1. Every ordinary, commonplace piece of writing to set
forth.
2. *if . . . sight:* if you see anything in my writing worth
reading.
Sonnet 40
1. Sonnets 40–42 concern a situation that may be identical to the love triangle described in 133–34 and 144.
2. Then if for love of me you take my beloved.
3. *for . . . usest:* because you use my beloved (sexually).
4. The poet (often emended, perhaps rightly, to
"thyself").

To bear love's wrong than hate's known injury.
Lascivious grace,° in whom all ill well shows,   *Charming wanton*
Kill me with spites,° yet we must not be foes.   *offenses*

41

Those pretty° wrongs that liberty° commits   *minor / licentiousness*
When I am sometime absent from thy heart
Thy beauty and thy years full well befits,
For still° temptation follows where thou art.   *continually*
5   Gentle° thou art, and therefore to be won;   *Tender; upper-class*
Beauteous thou art, therefore to be assailed;
And when a woman woos, what woman's son
Will sourly leave her till he have prevailed?[1]
Ay me, but yet thou mightst my seat[2] forbear,
10   And chide thy beauty and thy straying youth
Who lead thee in their riot° even there   *depraved conduct*
Where thou art forced to break a two-fold troth:
    Hers, by thy beauty tempting her to thee,
    Thine, by thy beauty being false to me.

42

That thou hast her, it is not all my grief,
And yet it may be said I loved her dearly;
That she hath thee is of my wailing chief,°   *chief reason*
A loss in love that touches me more nearly.
5   Loving offenders, thus I will excuse ye:
Thou dost love her because thou know'st I love her,
And for my sake even so doth she abuse° me,   *mistreat*
Suff'ring my friend for my sake to approve her.[1]
If I lose thee, my loss is my love's gain,
10   And losing° her, my friend hath found that loss: *I losing*
Both find each other, and I lose both twain,
And both for my sake lay on me this cross.°   *affliction*
    But here's the joy: my friend and I are one.
    Sweet flattery!° Then she loves but me alone.   *Pleasing delusion*

43

When most I wink,° then do mine eyes best see,   *shut my eyes*
For all the day they view things unrespected;°   *unheeded; unworthy*
But when I sleep, in dreams they look on thee,
And, darkly bright, are bright in dark directed.[1]
5   Then thou, whose shadow shadows doth make bright,[2]
How would thy shadow's form° form happy show°   *substance / sight*
To the clear day with thy much clearer light,
When to unseeing eyes[3] thy shade shines so!
How would, I say, mine eyes be blessèd made
10   By looking on thee in the living day,
When in dead night thy fair imperfect° shade   *incorporeal*

Sonnet 41
1. Until he has had his way. But Q's "he" could easily be a misprint for "she."
2. Rightful place (my mistress).
Sonnet 42
1. To put her to the test (sexually).

Sonnet 43
1. (My eyes) seeing in the dark turn toward your bright eyes in the dark.
2. Whose image lightens darkness.
3. Because closed in sleep.

Through heavy sleep on sightless eyes doth stay!
   All days are nights to see till I see thee,
   And nights bright days when dreams do show thee me.°   *to me*

44

If the dull° substance of my flesh were thought,   *heavy*
Injurious distance should not stop my way;
For then, despite of space, I would be brought
From limits° far remote where° thou dost stay.   *places / to where*
5 No matter then although my foot did stand
Upon the farthest earth removed from thee:
For nimble thought can jump both sea and land
As soon as think the place where he° would be.   *(thought)*
But ah, thought kills me that I am not thought,
10 To leap large lengths of miles when thou art gone,
But that, so much of earth and water wrought,[1]
I must attend time's leisure[2] with my moan,
   Receiving naught by elements so slow
   But heavy tears, badges of either's woe.[3]

45[1]

The other two,[2] slight° air and purging fire,   *light*
Are both with thee wherever I abide;
The first my thought, the other my desire,
These present-absent[3] with swift motion slide;
5 For when these quicker° elements are gone   *livelier*
In tender embassy of love to thee,
My life, being made of four, with two alone
Sinks down to death, oppressed with melancholy,
Until life's composition be recured°   *renewed*
10 By those swift messengers returned from thee,
Who even but now come back again assured
Of thy fair health, recounting it to me.
   This told, I joy; but then no longer glad,
   I send them back again and straight° grow sad.   *suddenly*

46

Mine eye and heart are at a mortal° war   *lethal*
How to divide the conquest of thy sight.[1]
Mine eye my heart thy picture's sight would bar,
My heart, mine eye the freedom° of that right.   *free enjoyment*
5 My heart doth plead that thou in him dost lie,
A closet° never pierced with crystal eyes;   *room*
But the defendant doth that plea deny,
And says in him thy fair appearance lies.
To 'cide° this title is empanellèd°   *decide / enrolled*
10 A quest° of thoughts, all tenants to the heart,

Sonnet 44
1. Being compounded of so much earth and water (the heavy elements).
2. I must wait humbly (as if on a great man) for time to reunite us.
3. Emblems of the grief of each of the poet's elements (of earth because heavy [sad], of water because wet).
Sonnet 45
1. This sonnet links with 44.

2. Of the poet's four elements. See 44.11.
3. Now present, now absent; constantly coming and going.
Sonnet 46
1. The spoils of the sight of you (possibly in a painting; see 47.5–14).

And by their verdict is determinèd   *jury*
The clear eye's moiety° and the dear heart's part,   *share*
  As thus: mine eye's due is thy outward part,
  And my heart's right thy inward love of heart.

47[1]

Betwixt mine eye and heart a league is took,°   *truce is made*
And each doth good turns now unto the other.
When that mine eye is famished for a look,
Or heart in love with sighs himself doth smother,[2]
5 With my love's picture then my eye doth feast,
And to the painted banquet bids my heart.
Another time mine eye is my heart's guest
And in his thoughts of love doth share a part.
So either by thy picture or my love,
10 Thyself away art present still with me;
For thou no farther than my thoughts canst move,
And I am still° with them, and they with thee;   *constantly*
  Or if they sleep, thy picture in my sight
  Awakes my heart to heart's and eye's delight.

48

How careful was I when I took my way°   *set off*
Each trifle under truest° bars to thrust,   *most reliable*
That to my use° it might unusèd stay   *benefit*
From hands of falsehood, in sure wards° of trust.   *safe places*
5 But thou, to° whom my jewels trifles are,   *compared to*
Most worthy comfort, now my greatest grief,[1]
Thou best of dearest and mine only care
Art left the prey of every vulgar thief.
Thee have I not locked up in any chest
10 Save where thou art not, though I feel thou art—
Within the gentle closure of my breast,
From whence at pleasure thou mayst come and part;°   *go*
  And even thence thou wilt be stol'n, I fear,
  For truth° proves thievish for a prize so dear.   *even honesty*

49

Against° that time—if ever that time come—   *In preparation for*
When I shall see thee frown on my defects,
Whenas thy love hath cast his utmost sum,[1]
Called to that audit by advised respects;°   *judicious reasons*
5 Against that time when thou shalt strangely° pass   *as a stranger*
And scarcely greet me with that sun, thine eye,
When love converted from the thing it was
Shall reasons find of settled gravity:[2]
Against that time do I ensconce me° here   *secure myself*
10 Within the knowledge of mine own desert,[3]
And this my hand against myself uprear°   *testify against myself*

Sonnet 47
1. This sonnet links with 46.
2. Or when my loving heart smothers itself with sighs.
Sonnet 48
1. Because absent and in danger of being stolen.

Sonnet 49
1. When your love has calculated the bottom line.
2. Shall find reasons for a dignified reserve; shall find reasons of well-established seriousness (for leaving me).
3. My (lack of?) worthiness to be loved.

To guard the lawful reasons on thy part.°   *defend your case*
   To leave poor me thou hast the strength of laws,
   Since why to love° I can allege no cause.   *why you should love*

50

How heavy° do I journey on the way,   *wearily*
When what I seek—my weary travel's end—
Doth teach that ease and that repose to say[1]
'Thus far the miles are measured from thy friend.'
5 The beast that bears me, tired with my woe,
Plods dully on to bear° that weight in me,   *while bearing*
As if by some instinct the wretch did know
His rider loved not speed, being made[2] from thee.
The bloody spur cannot provoke him on
10 That sometimes anger thrusts into his hide,
Which heavily he answers with a groan
More sharp to me than spurring to his side;
   For that same groan doth put this in my mind:
   My grief lies onward and my joy behind.

51[1]

Thus can my love excuse the slow offence°   *offense of slowness*
Of my dull bearer when from thee I speed:
From where thou art why should I haste me thence?
Till I return, of posting° is no need.   *riding quickly*
5 O what excuse will my poor beast then find
When swift extremity° can seem but slow?   *extreme (return) speed*
Then should I spur, though mounted on the wind;
In wingèd speed no motion shall I know.[2]
Then can no horse with my desire keep pace:
10 Therefore desire, of perfect'st love being made,
Shall rein° no dull flesh in his fiery race;   *curb*
But love, for love,° thus shall excuse my jade: *on love's behalf*
   Since from thee going he went wilful-slow,
   Towards thee I'll run and give him leave to go.°   *walk*

52

So am I as the rich° whose blessèd key   *rich man*
Can bring him to his sweet up-lockèd treasure,
The which he will not ev'ry hour survey,
For° blunting the fine point of seldom° pleasure.   *To avoid / occasional*
5 Therefore are feasts° so solemn° and so rare   *feast days / dignified*
Since, seldom coming, in the long year set
Like stones of worth they thinly placèd are,
Or captain° jewels in the carcanet.°   *chief / jeweled collar*
So is the time that keeps you as° my chest,   *like / jewel case*
10 Or as the wardrobe which the robe doth hide,
To make some special instant special blest

Sonnet 50
1. Teach the comforts at the end of the road to remind me that.
2. *speed, being made:* hastening away; haste, when and because it is.
Sonnet 51
1. This sonnet links with 50.

2. I will feel no motion when desire carries me back through the air. See line 11 and sonnets 44–45 for the association of fire and air with desire and thought, and of earth and water with dull, slow flesh.

By new unfolding his imprisoned pride.
    Blessèd are you whose worthiness gives scope,
    Being had, to triumph; being lacked, to hope.[1]

53

What is your substance, whereof are you made,
That millions of strange shadows on you tend?°   *attend*
Since every one hath, every one, one shade,[1]
And you, but one, can every shadow lend.[2]
5 Describe° Adonis, and the counterfeit°   *Draw / likeness*
Is poorly imitated after you.
On Helen's cheek all art of beauty set,
And you in Grecian tires are painted new.[3]
Speak of the spring and foison° of the year: *harvest time*
10 The one doth shadow of your beauty show,
The other as your bounty doth appear;
And you in every blessèd shape we know.°   *recognize*
    In all external grace you have some part,
    But you like none, none you, for constant heart.

54

O how much more doth beauty beauteous seem
By° that sweet ornament which truth doth give!   *Because of*
The rose looks fair, but fairer we it deem
For that sweet odour which doth in it live.
5 The canker blooms[1] have full as deep a dye
As the perfumèd tincture° of the roses,   *color*
Hang on such thorns, and play as wantonly°   *flatter as playfully*
When summer's breath their maskèd buds discloses;
But for° their virtue only is° their show   *since / lies wholly in*
10 They live unwooed and unrespected° fade,   *unappreciated*
Die to themselves.° Sweet roses do not so;   *alone; without influence*
Of their sweet deaths are sweetest odours made:
    And so of you, beauteous and lovely youth,
    When that° shall fade, by verse distils your truth.[2]   *beauty*

55

Not marble nor the gilded monuments
Of princes shall outlive this powerful rhyme,
But you shall shine more bright in these contents
Than unswept stone besmeared with sluttish° time.   *slovenly*
5 When wasteful war shall statues overturn,
And broils° root out the work of masonry,   *battles*
Nor Mars his° sword nor war's quick fire shall burn   *Neither Mars's*
The living record of your memory.
'Gainst death and all oblivious enmity
10 Shall you pace forth; your praise shall still find room

Sonnet 52
1. *gives . . . hope:* allows me to exult when with you and to hope when not with you.
Sonnet 53
1. Since each person has an individual shadow.
2. Can cast all shadows (are visible in every image).
3. *On . . . new:* If one were to use every art to reproduce the beauty of Helen of Troy (or use artful cosmetics

on Helen's cheek) it would look like you in Grecian headgear.
Sonnet 54
1. Dog roses (having little scent).
2. See sonnet 5. Q's "vade" is a variant of "fade," the reading adopted here, but it probably has the secondary meaning of "depart," from the Latin *vadere*.

Even in the eyes of all posterity
That wear this world out to the ending doom.[1]
 So, till the judgement that yourself arise,
 You live in this, and dwell in lovers' eyes.

56

Sweet love,[1] renew thy force. Be it not said
Thy edge should blunter be than appetite,
Which but° today by feeding is allayed,   *merely for*
Tomorrow sharpened in his former might.
5 So, love, be thou; although today thou fill
Thy hungry eyes even till they wink° with fullness,   *close (to sleep)*
Tomorrow see again, and do not kill
The spirit of love with a perpetual dullness.
Let this sad int'rim like the ocean be
10 Which parts the shore where two contracted new
Come daily to the banks, that when they see
Return of love, more blessed may be the view;[2]
 Or call it winter, which, being full of care,
 Makes summer's welcome, thrice more wished, more rare.° *valuable*

57

Being your slave, what should I do but tend°   *wait*
Upon the hours and times of your desire?
I have no precious time at all to spend,
Nor services to do, till you require;
5 Nor dare I chide the world-without-end° hour   *endless*
Whilst I, my sovereign, watch the clock for you,
Nor think the bitterness of absence sour
When you have bid your servant once adieu.
Nor dare I question with my jealous thought
10 Where you may be, or your affairs suppose,°   *speculate on*
But like a sad slave stay and think of naught
Save, where you are, how happy you make those.
 So true a fool is love that in your will,[1]
 Though you do anything, he thinks no ill.

58[1]

That god forbid, that made me first your slave,
I should in thought control your times of pleasure,
Or at your hand th'account of hours to crave,[2]
Being your vassal° bound to stay° your leisure.   *slave / wait upon*
5 O let me suffer, being at your beck,
Th'imprisoned absence of your liberty,[3]
And patience, tame to sufferance, bide each check,[4]
Without accusing you of injury.

Sonnet 55
1. Doomsday: in Christianity, the Day of Judgment, when dead bodies are supposed to "arise" (line 13) from the grave and be united with their souls.
Sonnet 56
1. The feeling (not the beloved).
2. *Let . . . view*: The "sad" interval between periods of feeling love is like an ocean dividing shores where two lovers come daily hoping for the (emotionally renewing) sight of a boat bringing the other. *contracted new*: newly betrothed.

Sonnet 57
1. Desire (including sexual desire); capitalized in Q, perhaps punning on Shakespeare's name. See 135–36.
Sonnet 58
1. This sonnet links with 57.
2. Or should seek an account of how you pass your time.
3. The imprisoned feeling caused by your licentiousness when you're away
4. And let me patient, acquiescent in suffering, endure each setback.

Be where you list,° your charter° is so strong   wish / freedom
10   That you yourself may privilege° your time   allocate
To what you will; to you it doth belong
Yourself to pardon of self-doing° crime.   commited by you
     I am to wait, though waiting so be hell,
     Not blame your pleasure, be it ill or well.

59

If there be nothing new, but that which is
Hath been before, how are our brains beguiled,°   cheated
Which, labouring° for invention, bear amiss   working; giving birth
The second burden of a former child!¹
5   O that record° could with a backward look   recollection
Even of five hundred courses of the sun
Show me your image in some antique book
Since mind at first in character was done,²
That I might see what the old world could say
10   To this composèd wonder of your frame;³
Whether we are mended° or whe'er better they,   improved
Or whether revolution be the same.⁴
     O, sure I am the wits° of former days   clever writers
     To subjects worse have given admiring praise.

60

Like as the waves make towards the pebbled shore,
So do our minutes hasten to their end,
Each changing place with that which goes before;
In sequent toil all forwards do contend.¹
5   Nativity,° once in the main of light,°   A newborn / in the world
Crawls to maturity, wherewith being crowned
Crookèd° eclipses 'gainst his glory fight,   Pernicious
And time that gave doth now his gift confound.°   ruin
Time doth transfix the flourish² set on youth,
10   And delves the parallels° in beauty's brow;   carves the wrinkles
Feeds on the rarities of nature's truth,³
And nothing stands but for his scythe to mow.
     And yet to times in hope° my verse shall stand,   future days
     Praising thy worth despite his cruel hand.

61

Is it thy will thy image should keep open
My heavy eyelids to the weary night?
Dost thou desire my slumbers should be broken
While shadows° like to thee do mock my sight?   visions
5   Is it thy spirit that thou send'st from thee
So far from home into my deeds to pry,
To find out shames and idle hours in me,
The scope and tenor of thy jealousy?¹
     O no; thy love, though much, is not so great.

Sonnet 59
1. bear . . . child: mistakenly ("amiss") give birth for a second time to a child that has already been born.
2. Since writing was invented.
3. To the wonderful composition of your form (perhaps referring to the sonnet itself as well).
4. Whether the revolving of the ages makes no difference.

Sonnet 60
1. Toiling one after the other, all seek to move forward.
2. Time pierces and destroys the ornament (beauty).
3. On the most precious products of nature's perfection.

Sonnet 61
1. The object and intent of your distrust (that is, "shames and idle hours," line 7).

10 It is my love that keeps mine eye awake,
Mine own true love that doth my rest defeat,
To play the watchman ever for thy sake.
  For thee watch I° whilst thou dost wake elsewhere,   *I remain awake*
  From me far off, with others all too near.

62

Sin of self-love possesseth all mine eye,
And all my soul, and all my every part;
And for this sin there is no remedy,
It is so grounded inward in my heart.
5 Methinks no face so gracious is as mine,
No shape so true,° no truth of such account,   *perfect*
And for myself mine own worth do define
As° I all other° in all worths surmount.   *As if / others*
But when my glass° shows me myself indeed,   *mirror*
10 Beated and chapped with tanned antiquity,
Mine own self-love quite contrary I read;
Self so self-loving were iniquity.
  'Tis thee, my self,° that for° myself I praise,   *you, my other self / as*
  Painting my age with beauty of thy days.

63

Against° my love shall be as I am now,   *Preparing for when*
With time's injurious hand crushed and o'erworn;
When hours have drained his blood and filled his brow
With lines and wrinkles; when his youthful morn
5 Hath travelled° on to age's steepy° night,   *progressed; toiled*
And all those beauties whereof now he's king
Are vanishing, or vanished out of sight,
Stealing away the treasure of his spring:
For such a time do I now fortify
10 Against confounding° age's cruel knife,   *devastating*
That he shall never cut from memory
My sweet love's beauty, though° my lover's life.   *though he will sever*
  His beauty shall in these black lines be seen,
  And they shall live, and he in them still green.°   *perpetually youthful*

64

When I have seen by time's fell° hand defaced   *fierce*
The rich proud cost° of outworn buried age;   *expense*
When sometime°-lofty towers I see down razed,   *once*
And brass eternal slave to mortal rage;[1]
5 When I have seen the hungry ocean gain
Advantage on the kingdom of the shore,
And the firm soil win of° the wat'ry main,   *win ground from*
Increasing store with loss and loss with store;[2]
When I have seen such interchange of state,
10 Or state[3] itself confounded to decay,°   *reduced to ruins*
Ruin hath taught me thus to ruminate:

Sonnet 63
1. Precipitous (like the path of the setting sun).
Sonnet 64
1. And eternal brass forever succumbs to death's violence.

2. Adding to the stock of one by loss of the other, and vice versa.
3. *state* (line 9): condition; sovereign territory. *state* (line 10): pomp.

That time will come and take my love away.
　　This thought is as a death, which° cannot choose　　　*since thought*
　　But weep to have° that which it fears to lose.　　　　*at having*

65

Since° brass, nor stone, nor earth, nor boundless sea,　　*Since there is neither*
But sad mortality o'ersways their power,
How with this rage shall beauty hold a plea,[1]
Whose action is no stronger than a flower?
5　O how shall summer's honey breath hold out
　Against the wrackful° siege of battering days　　　　*damaging*
　When rocks impregnable are not so stout,
　Nor gates of steel so strong, but time decays?°　　　*decays them*
　O fearful meditation! Where, alack,
10　Shall time's best jewel° from time's chest[2] lie hid,　　*(the beloved)*
　Or what strong hand can hold his swift foot back,
　Or who his spoil° of beauty can forbid?　　　　　　*destruction*
　　　O none, unless this miracle have might:
　　　That in black ink my love may still shine bright.

66

Tired with all these°, for restful death I cry:　　　*(the ensuing wrongs)*
As,° to behold desert° a beggar born,　　　　　　*For example / merit*
And needy nothing trimmed in jollity,[1]
And purest faith unhappily forsworn,°　　　　　　*betrayed; perjured*
5　And gilded honour shamefully misplaced,
　And maiden virtue rudely strumpeted,
　And right perfection wrongfully disgraced,
　And strength by limping sway° disablèd,　　　　　*feeble leaders*
　And art made tongue-tied° by authority,　　　　　*learning silenced*
10　And folly, doctor-like, controlling skill,[2]
　And simple truth miscalled simplicity,°　　　　　*naïveté*
　And captive good attending° captain ill.　　　　　*serving*
　　　Tired with all these, from these would I be gone,
　　　Save that to die I leave my love alone.

67

Ah, wherefore with infection[1] should he live
And with his presence grace impiety,
That° sin by him advantage should achieve　　　　　*So that*
And lace° itself with his society?　　　　　　　　*decorate*
5　Why should false painting imitate his cheek,
　And steal dead seeming of[2] his living hue?
　Why should poor° beauty indirectly seek　　　　　*lesser*
　Roses of shadow,° since his rose is true?　　　　*Cosmetic beauty*
　Why should he live now nature bankrupt is,
10　Beggared of blood to blush through lively veins,
　For she hath no exchequer° now but his,　　　　　*treasury*

Sonnet 65
1. How can beauty make a (legal) case against such a
power to destroy?
2. Treasure chest; coffin.
Sonnet 66
1. And ungifted (or impoverished) worthlessness adorned
with finery.

2. And folly, feigning erudition, dominating true wisdom
or ability. Before modern medicine, doctors were often
portrayed as fools or con artists.
Sonnet 67
1. The world's ills (as in 66).
2. *dead seeming of*: an inanimate outward resemblance
from.

And proud of many, lives upon his gains?³
  O, him she stores° to show what wealth she had   *keeps*
  In days long since, before these last so bad.

68¹

Thus is his cheek the map° of days outworn,   *image*
When beauty lived and died as flowers do now,
5 Before these bastard signs of fair° were borne°   *cosmetics / worn; born*
Or durst inhabit on a living brow;
Before the golden tresses of the dead,
The right of sepulchres,² were shorn away
To live a second life on second head;
Ere beauty's dead fleece made another gay.
In him those holy antique hours° are seen   *good old days*
10 Without all ornament, itself and true,
Making no summer of another's green.
Robbing no old to dress his beauty new;
  And him as for a map doth nature store,°   *keep*
  To show false art what beauty was of yore.

69

Those parts of thee that the world's eye doth view
Want° nothing that the thought of hearts can mend.° *Lack / imagine better*
All tongues, the voice of souls, give thee that due.
Utt'ring bare truth even so as foes commend.¹
5 Thy outward thus with outward praise is crowned,
But those same tongues that give thee so thine own°   *your due*
In other accents° do this praise confound°   *words / undermine*
By seeing farther than the eye hath shown.
They look into the beauty of thy mind,
10 And that in guess they measure by thy deeds.
Then, churls, their thoughts—although their eyes were kind—
To thy fair flower add the rank smell of weeds.
  But why thy odour matcheth not thy show,°   *appearance*
  The soil is this: that thou dost common grow.²

70¹

That thou are blamed shall not be thy defect,
For slander's mark° was ever yet the fair.   *target*
The ornament of beauty is suspect,°   *suspicion*
A crow that flies in heaven's sweetest air.
5 So° thou be good, slander doth but approve   *So long as*
Thy worth the greater, being wooed of time;²
For canker vice³ the sweetest buds doth love,
And thou present'st a pure unstainèd prime.°   *youth*
Thou hast passed by the ambush of young days
10 Either not assailed, or victor being charged;

3. Though (falsely) taking pride in her abundance (of offspring?), lives off the interest he earns (from his endowment of beauty).
Sonnet 68
1. This sonnet links with 67.
2. Properly belonging to tombs (wigs were made from the hair of corpses).
Sonnet 69
1. Uttering minimal truth, in the way that enemies praise.

2. The ground (reason; also, stain) is this: you are becoming low (promiscuous).
Sonnet 70
1. This sonnet links with 69.
2. *slander . . . time:* the gossip merely proves that you're so popular ("wooed of time") that you're worth even more.
3. Slander, like a cankerworm.

Yet this thy praise cannot be so° thy praise   *enough*
To tie up envy, evermore enlarged.°   *forever at large*
   If some suspect of ill masked not thy show,°   *appearance*
   Then thou alone kingdoms of hearts shouldst owe.°   *own*

71

No longer mourn for me when I am dead
Than you shall hear the surly sullen bell
Give warning to the world that I am fled
From this vile world with vilest[1] worms to dwell.
5 Nay, if you read this line, remember not
The hand that writ it; for I love you so
That I in your sweet thoughts would be forgot
If thinking on me then should make you woe.
O, if, I say, you look upon this verse
10 When I perhaps compounded am° with clay,   *am mixed*
Do not so much as my poor name rehearse,°   *repeat; rebury*
But let your love even with my life decay,
   Lest the wise world should look into your moan
   And mock you with me° after I am gone.   *for loving me*

72

O, lest the world should task you to recite
What merit lived in me that you should love,
After my death, dear love, forget me quite;
For you in me can nothing worthy prove—
5 Unless you would devise some virtuous lie
To do more for me than mine own desert,
And hang more praise upon deceasèd I
Than niggard truth would willingly impart.
O, lest your true love may seem false in this,
10 That you for love speak well of me untrue,°   *untruthfully*
My° name be buried where my body is,   *Let my*
And live no more to shame nor me nor you;
   For I am shamed by that which I bring forth,[1]
   And so should you,° to love things nothing worth.   *you be*

73

That time of year thou mayst in me behold
When yellow leaves, or none, or few, do hang
Upon those boughs which shake against the cold,
Bare ruined choirs where late the sweet birds sang.[1]
5 In me thou seest the twilight of such day
As after sunset fadeth in the west,
Which by and by black night doth take away,
Death's second self, that seals up all in rest.
In me thou seest the glowing of such fire
10 That° on the ashes of his youth[2] doth lie   *As*

Sonnet 71
1. Q's "vildest" is an archaic form of "vilest" that may also
carry the connotation of "most reviled."
Sonnet 72
1. Presumably alluding to the writer's poems or to his
profession as actor and playwright.
Sonnet 73
1. *choirs:* the area in a church where the choir ("sweet

birds") sings; gatherings of manuscript "leaves" (line 2),
or quires ("quiers" in Q).
2. Perhaps referring to the phoenix, a legendary self-
resurrecting bird believed to live in cycles of several centuries, dying in flames and being reborn from the ashes.
See also 19.4.

As the death-bed whereon it must expire,
Consumed with that which it was nourished by.[3]
    This thou perceiv'st, which makes thy love more strong,
    To love that° well which thou must leave ere long.   *(the speaker); (life)*

74[1]

But be contented when that fell arrest°   *fearful death*
Without all bail shall carry me away.
My life hath in this line° some interest,°   *verse / legal claim*
Which for memorial still with thee shall stay.
5 When thou reviewest° this, thou dost review   *reread*
The very part° was consecrate to thee.   *part of me that*
The earth can have but earth, which is his due;
My spirit is thine, the better part of me.
So then thou hast but lost the dregs of life,
10 The prey of worms, my body being dead,
The coward conquest of a wretch's knife,[2]
Too base of° thee to be rememberèd.   *by*
    The worth of that° is that which it contains,   *(the body)*
    And that is this,° and this with thee remains.   *this spirit (his poetry)*

75

So are you to my thoughts as food to life,
Or as sweet-seasoned° showers are to the ground;   *spring*
And for the peace of you° I hold such strife   *you provide*
As 'twixt a miser and his wealth is found:
5 Now proud as an enjoyer, and anon
Doubting the filching age[1] will steal his treasure;
Now counting° best to be with you alone,   *estimating*
Then bettered° that the world may see my pleasure;   *better contented*
Sometime all full with feasting on your sight,
10 And by and by clean° starvèd for a look;   *wholly*
Possessing or pursuing no delight
Save what is had or must from you be took.
    Thus do I pine and surfeit day by day,
    Or° gluttoning on all, or all away.°   *Either / having nothing*

76

Why is my verse so barren of new pride,°   *adornments*
So far from variation or quick° change?   *lively*
Why, with the time,° do I not glance aside   *following the fashion*
To new-found methods and to compounds[1] strange?
5 Why write I still all one, ever the same,
And keep invention in a noted weed,[2]
That every word doth almost tell my name,
Showing their birth and where° they did proceed?   *whence*
O know, sweet love, I always write of you,

---

3. Ironically, the fire is choked ("consumed") by (along with) the ashes, which are the residue of the fuel that the fire previously fed upon ("was nourished by").
Sonnet 74
1. This sonnet links with 73.
2. The cowardly conquest of a wretch such as Death (who was thought to carry a scythe).

Sonnet 75
1. Fearing that these dishonest times.
Sonnet 76
1. *compounds:* stylistic or formal mixtures; compound words; elaborate medicines (with "methods," which also refers to both literary and medical treatments).
2. And keep literary creativity in such familiar clothing.

10   And you and love are still my argument;°   *always my topic*
      So all my best is dressing old words new,
      Spending again what is already spent;
         For as the sun is daily new and old,
         So is my love, still telling what is told.

77[1]

      Thy glass° will show thee how thy beauties wear,[2]   *mirror*
      Thy dial° how thy precious minutes waste,   *sundial*
      The vacant leaves thy mind's imprint° will bear,   *written ideas*
      And of this book this learning mayst thou taste:
5   The wrinkles which thy glass will truly show
      Of mouthèd° graves will give thee memory;°   *gaping / remind you*
      Thou by thy dial's shady stealth° mayst know   *stealing shadow*
      Time's thievish progress to eternity;
      Look what° thy memory cannot contain   *Whatever*
10   Commit to these waste blanks,° and thou shalt find   *empty pages*
      Those children nursed,° delivered from thy brain,   *preserved*
      To take a new acquaintance of thy mind.°   *strike you afresh*
         These offices° so oft as thou wilt look   *functions*
         Shall profit thee and much enrich thy book.

78[1]

      So oft have I invoked thee for my muse
      And found such fair assistance in my verse
      As every alien pen hath got my use,[2]
      And under thee° their poesy disperse.   *with you as patron*
5   Thine eyes, that taught the dumb on high° to sing   *aloud*
      And heavy ignorance aloft to fly,
      Have added feathers to the learned's wing[3]
      And given grace° a double majesty.   *excellence*
      Yet be most proud of that which I compile,°   *write*
10   Whose influence° is thine and born of thee.   *power to move*
      In others' works thou dost but mend° the style,   *improve*
      And arts° with thy sweet graces gracèd be;   *(their) artistry*
         But thou art all my art, and dost advance
         As high as learning my rude ignorance.

79

      Whilst I alone did call upon thy aid
      My verse alone had all thy gentle grace;
      But now my gracious numbers are decayed,
      And my sick muse doth give another place.°   *way to another poet*
5   I grant, sweet love, thy lovely argument[1]
      Deserves the travail° of a worthier pen,   *labor*
      Yet what of thee thy poet doth invent
      He robs thee of, and pays it thee again.
      He lends thee virtue, and he stole that word
10   From thy behaviour; beauty doth he give,
      And found it in thy cheek: he can afford°   *extend*

Sonnet 77
1. This sonnet appears to have accompanied the gift of a notebook.
2. Last; wear away; "were" (Q's spelling).
Sonnet 78
1. This sonnet begins the rival poet sequence (78–80,

82–86).
2. That every other poet imitates me.
3. Have improved the poetic "flights" of even accomplished poets.
Sonnet 79
1. The subject of your loveliness.

No praise to thee but what in thee doth live.
　　Then thank him not for that which he doth say,
　　Since what he owes thee thou thyself dost pay.

80

O, how I faint° when I of you do write,　　　　　　　　　　*get discouraged*
Knowing a better spirit° doth use your name,　　　　　　　*(the rival poet)*
And in the praise thereof spends all his might,
To make me tongue-tied, speaking of your fame!
5　But since your worth, wide as the ocean is,
The humble as° the proudest sail doth bear,　　　　　　　*as well as*
My saucy barque,° inferior far to his,　　　　　　　　　　*impudent boat*
On your broad main° doth wilfully appear.　　　　　　　　*waters*
Your shallowest help will hold me up afloat
10　Whilst he upon your soundless° deep doth ride;　　　　　*bottomless*
Or, being wrecked, I am a worthless boat,
He of tall building[1] and of goodly pride.°　　　　　　　*magnificence*
　　Then if he thrive and I be cast away,
　　The worst was this: my love was my decay.

81[1]

Or° I shall live your epitaph to make,　　　　　　　　　　*Either*
Or you survive when I in earth am rotten.
From hence° your memory death cannot take,　　　　　　　*the world; my poetry*
Although in me each part° will be forgotten.　　　　　　　*each of my attributes*
5　Your name from hence° immortal life shall have,　　　　　*henceforth; my poetry*
Though I, once gone, to all the world must die.
The earth can yield me but a common grave
When you entombèd in men's eyes shall lie.
Your monument shall be my gentle verse,
10　Which eyes not yet created shall o'er-read,
And tongues to be° your being shall rehearse°　　　　　　*future tongues / recite*
When all the breathers of this world are dead.
　　You still shall live—such virtue° hath my pen—　　　　*power*
　　Where breath most breathes, even in° the mouths of men.　*right in*

82

I grant thou wert not married to my muse,
And therefore mayst without attaint o'erlook°　　　　　　　*dishonor read*
The dedicated[1] words which writers° use　　　　　　　　*other writers*
Of their fair subject, blessing every book.
5　Thou art as fair in knowledge as in hue,°　　　　　　　　*appearance*
Finding thy worth a limit° past my praise,　　　　　　　　*region*
And therefore art enforced to seek anew
Some fresher stamp of these time-bettering days.[2]
And do so, love; yet when they have devised
10　What strainèd touches rhetoric can lend,
Thou, truly fair, wert truly sympathized[3]
In true plain words by thy true-telling friend;

Sonnet 80
1. Tall, strong build.
Sonnet 81
1. Except for lines 2–3 and 10–11, any two consecutive lines in this sonnet form a complete sentence.

Sonnet 82
1. Devoted; referring to a prefatory dedication.
2. Some more recent imprint (commendation) of these culturally progressive times.
3. Would be accurately represented.

And their gross painting° might be better used   cosmetics; flattery
Where cheeks need blood: in thee it is abused.°   used wrongly

83

I never saw that you did painting° need,   cosmetics
And therefore to your fair° no painting set.   beauty
I found—or thought I found—you did exceed
The barren tender° of a poet's debt;   payment
5 And therefore have I slept in your report:[1]
That° you yourself, being extant, well might show   So that
How far a modern° quill doth come too short,   trite; fashionable
Speaking of worth, what worth[2] in you doth grow.
This silence for° my sin you did impute,   to be
10 Which shall be most my glory, being dumb;
For I impair not beauty, being mute,
When others would give life, and bring a tomb.[3]
    There lives more life in one of your fair eyes
    Than both your poets can in praise devise.

84

Who is it that says most which[1] can say more
Than this rich praise: that you alone are you,[2]
In whose confine immurèd is the store
Which should example where your equal grew?[3]
5 Lean penury within that pen doth dwell
That to his subject lends not some small glory;
But he that writes of you, if he can tell
That you are you, so dignifies his story.
Let him but copy what in you is writ,
10 Not making worse what nature made so clear,°   purely excellent
And such a counterpart shall fame° his wit,   copy will make famous
Making his style admirèd everywhere.
    You to your beauteous blessings add a curse,[4]
    Being fond on praise, which makes your praises worse.[5]

85

My tongue-tied muse in manners holds her still°   tactfully says nothing
While comments of° your praise, richly compiled,   commentaries in
Reserve thy character° with golden quill   Hoard up your features
And precious phrase by all the muses filed.°   polished
5 I think good thoughts whilst other° write good words,   others
And like unlettered clerk still cry 'Amen'
To every hymn[1] that able spirit affords°   offers
In polished form of well-refinèd pen.
Hearing you praised I say 'Tis so, 'tis true,'

Sonnet 83
1. Neglected to sing your praises.
2. In speaking of value of the worth that.
3. When others who try to make you live in their writings only end up burying you.
Sonnet 84
1. *Who . . . which:* What hyperbolical enthusiast.
2. The line is a poetical in-joke, echoing a passage in Gervase Markham's *Devoreux* (published 1597) that addresses and praises Penelope Rich, a famous beauty of the Elizabethan court. Like *Devoreux*, Q has "Rich" rather than "rich." See also 85.2.

3. *In . . . grew:* Within whom is contained the stock that would be needed to produce your equal?
4. Personality flaw; vexation (for those who would praise you).
5. Being (too) fond of praise, which makes the praise seem like flattery; being (too) fond of the sort of praise that detracts from you.
Sonnet 85
1. *like . . . hymn:* like an illiterate parish clerk reflexively approve ("cry 'Amen'" after) every poem ("hymn") of praise.

10 And to the most° of praise add something more;   *highest*
But that is in my thought,° whose love to you,   *unspoken*
Though words come hindmost, holds his rank before.°   *before all others*
   Then others for the breath of words respect,°   *regard*
   Me for my dumb thoughts, speaking in effect.°   *in reality*

86

Was it the proud full sail of his° great verse   *(a rival poet's)*
Bound for the prize° of all-too-precious you   *pirate's spoils*
That did my ripe thoughts in my brain inhearse,°   *bury*
Making their tomb the womb wherein they grew?
5 Was it his spirit, by spirits taught to write
Above a mortal pitch,° that struck me dead?   *height*
No, neither he nor his compeers[1] by night
Giving him aid my verse astonishèd.°   *made silent*
He nor that affable familiar ghost°   *spirit*
10 Which nightly gulls° him with intelligence,°   *fools / ideas*
As victors, of my silence cannot boast;
I was not sick of any fear from thence.
   But when your countenance filled up[2] his line,
   Then lacked I matter; that enfeebled mine.

87

Farewell—thou art too dear° for my possessing,   *costly*
And like° enough thou know'st thy estimate.°   *it is likely / value*
The charter of thy worth gives thee releasing;[1]
My bonds in thee are all determinate.°   *terminated*
5 For how do I hold thee but by thy granting,
And for that riches where is my deserving?
The cause of this fair gift in me is wanting,
And so my patent back again is swerving.[2]
Thyself thou gav'st, thy own worth then not knowing,
10 Or me to whom thou gav'st it else mistaking;°   *overestimating*
So thy great gift, upon misprision growing,°   *based on error*
Comes home again, on better judgement making.[3]
   Thus have I had thee as a dream doth flatter:°   *creates an illusion*
   In sleep a king, but waking no such matter.

88

When thou shalt be disposed to set me light°   *value me little*
And place my merit in the eye of scorn,
Upon thy side against myself I'll fight,
And prove thee virtuous though thou art forsworn.
5 With mine own weakness being best acquainted,
Upon thy part I can set down a story
Of faults concealed wherein I am attainted,
That thou in losing me shall win much glory;
And I by this will be a gainer too;
10 For bending all my loving thoughts on thee,
The injuries that to myself I do,
Doing thee vantage, double vantage me.

Sonnet 86
1. Colleagues (the "spirits" in line 5).
2. Your features gave subject matter to; your approval made up for any lack in.

Sonnet 87
1. The privilege you derive from your worth releases you from love's bonds.
2. My rights of possession revert to you.
3. *on . . . making:* when you realize your error.

Such is my love, to thee I so belong,
That for thy right myself will bear all wrong.

89

Say that thou didst forsake me for some fault,
And I will comment° upon that offence;   *elaborate*
Speak of my lameness, and I straight will halt,[1]
Against thy reasons making no defence.
5 Thou canst not, love, disgrace me half so ill,
To set a form upon desirèd change,[2]
As I'll myself disgrace, knowing thy will.
I will acquaintance strangle and look strange,[3]
Be absent from thy walks,° and in my tongue   *familiar places*
10 Thy sweet belovèd name no more shall dwell,
Lest I, too much profane, should do it wrong,
And haply° of our old acquaintance tell.   *by chance*
    For thee, against myself I'll vow debate;°   *combat*
    For I must ne'er love him whom thou dost hate.

90[1]

Then hate me when thou wilt, if ever, now,
Now while the world is bent my deeds to cross,°   *foil*
Join with the spite of fortune, make me bow,
And do not drop in for an after-loss.[2]
5 Ah do not, when my heart hath scaped this sorrow,
Come in the rearward of a conquered woe;[3]
Give not a windy night a rainy morrow
To linger out a purposed overthrow.[4]
If thou wilt leave me, do not leave me last,
10 When other petty griefs have done their spite,
But in the onset come; so shall I taste
At first the very worst of fortune's might,
    And other strains° of woe, which now seem woe,   *types; burdens*
    Compared with loss of thee will not seem so.

91

Some glory in their birth, some in their skill,
Some in their wealth, some in their body's force,
Some in their garments (though new-fangled ill),°   *fashionably ugly*
Some in their hawks and hounds, some in their horse,°   *horses*
5 And every humour hath his° adjunct pleasure   *temperament has its*
Wherein it finds a joy above the rest.
But these particulars are not my measure;°   *(of joy)*
All these I better° in one general best.   *exceed*
Thy love is better than high birth to me,
10 Richer than wealth, prouder than garments' cost,
Of more delight than hawks or horses be,
And having thee of all men's pride[1] I boast,

Sonnet 89
1. Talk of my disability (perhaps alluding to the lame meter of line 2), and I at once will limp (stop objecting).
2. To lend justification to the change you seek.
3. I will end our familiarity and act like a stranger.
Sonnet 90
1. This sonnet links with 89.

2. Do not fall upon me to inflict a later disaster.
3. Assault me again after I have overcome my present grief.
4. To . . . overthrow: By protracting or delaying your intended assault.
Sonnet 91
1. Of everything in which others take pride.

Wretched in this alone: that thou mayst take
All this away, and me most wretched make.

92[1]

But do thy worst to steal thyself away,
For term of° life thou art assurèd mine,   *the duration of my*
And life no longer than thy love will stay,
For it depends upon that love of thine.
5 Then need I not to fear the worst of wrongs
When in the least of them[2] my life hath end
I see a better state to me belongs
Than that which on thy humour doth depend.
Thou canst not vex me with inconstant mind,
10 Since that my life on thy revolt doth lie.[3]
O, what a happy title[4] do I find—
Happy to have thy love, happy to die!
  But what's so blessèd fair that fears no blot?
  Thou mayst be false, and yet I know it not.

93[1]

So shall I live supposing thou art true
Like a deceivèd husband; so love's face°   *appearance*
May still seem love to me, though altered new—
Thy looks with me, thy heart in other place.
5 For there can live no hatred in thine eye,
Therefore in that I cannot know thy change.
In many's looks the false heart's history
Is writ in moods and frowns and wrinkles strange,[2]
But heaven in thy creation did decree
10 That in thy face sweet love should ever dwell;
Whate'er thy thoughts or thy heart's workings be,
Thy looks should nothing thence but sweetness tell
  How like Eve's apple doth thy beauty grow
  If thy sweet virtue answer not thy show![3]

94

They that have power to hurt and will do none,
That do not do the thing they most do show,[1]
Who moving others are themselves as stone,
Unmovèd, cold,° and to temptation slow—   *composed*
5 They rightly° do inherit heaven's graces,   *truly*
And husband nature's riches from expense;[2]
They are the lords and owners of their faces,
Others but stewards° of their excellence.   *hired managers*
The summer's flower is to the summer sweet
10 Though to itself it only live and die,[3]
But if that flower with base infection meet

Sonnet 92
1. This sonnet links with 91.
2. In the slightest sign of your displeasure.
3. Since change in your affections would kill me.
4. What a claim to be considered happy.
Sonnet 93
1. This sonnet links with 92.
2. In signs of anger and frowns and displeased

expressions.
3. Does not correspond to your looks.
Sonnet 94
1. *they most do show*: that their appearance implies.
2. And protect nature's rich endowment from waste.
3. *is . . . die*: emits its sweetness to others even though it lives and dies in apparent isolation (unpollinated: compare 54.5–11).

The basest weed outbraves his dignity;[4]
    For sweetest things turn sourest by their deeds:
    Lilies that fester smell far worse than weeds.[5]

95

How sweet and lovely dost thou make the shame
Which, like a canker° in the fragrant rose,   *cankerworm*
Doth spot the beauty of thy budding name!°   *fame*
O, in what sweets dost thou thy sins enclose!
5 That tongue that tells the story of thy days,
  Making lascivious comments on thy sport,°   *amorous adventures*
  Cannot dispraise, but in a kind of praise,
  Naming thy name, blesses° an ill report.   *makes positive*
  O, what a mansion have those vices got
10 Which for their habitation chose out thee,
  Where beauty's veil doth cover every blot
  And all things turns to fair that eyes can see!
    Take heed, dear heart, of this large privilege:
    The hardest knife ill used doth lose his° edge.   *its*

96

Some say thy fault is youth, some wantonness;°   *promiscuity; frivolity*
Some say thy grace is youth and gentle sport.[1]
Both grace and faults are loved of more and less;°   *by people of all ranks*
Thou mak'st faults graces that to thee resort.
5 As on the finger of a thronèd queen
  The basest jewel will be well esteemed,
  So are those errors that in thee are seen
  To truths translated° and for true things deemed.   *converted*
  How many lambs might the stern° wolf betray   *vicious*
10 If like° a lamb he could his looks translate!   *into*
  How many gazers mightst thou lead away
  If thou wouldst use the strength of all thy state!°   *power*
    But do not so: I love thee in such sort°   *such a way*
    As, thou being mine, mine is thy good report.[2]

97

How like a winter hath my absence been
From thee, the pleasure of the fleeting year!
What freezings have I felt, what dark days seen,
What old December's bareness everywhere!
5 And yet this time removed° was summer's time,   *away*
  The teeming autumn big° with rich increase,   *pregnant*
  Bearing the wanton burden of the prime°   *harvest of wanton spring*
  Like widowed wombs after their lords' decease.
  Yet this abundant issue seemed[1] to me
10 But hope of orphans and unfathered fruit,
  For summer and his pleasures wait° on thee,   *attend*
  And thou away, the very birds are mute;

---

4. Exceeds the flower in magnificence.
5. This line also occurs in *The Reign of King Edward III*, a play printed anonymously in 1596 and sometimes attributed, in whole or in part, to Shakespeare.

Sonnet 96
1. A gentleman's sexual prerogative.
2. Reputation. The same couplet ends 36.
Sonnet 97
1. Offspring seemed in prospect, before the beloved's absence.

Or if they sing, 'tis with so dull a cheer°   *such a dismal mood*
That leaves look pale, dreading the winter's near.

98

From you have I been absent in the spring
When proud-pied° April, dressed in all his trim,°   *multicolored / finery*
Hath put a spirit of youth in everything,
That heavy Saturn[1] laughed and leapt with him.
5 Yet nor the lays° of birds nor the sweet smell   *not the songs*
Of different flowers° in odour and in hue   *flowers differing*
Could make me any summer's story tell,°   *speak (write) happily*
Or from their proud lap° pluck them where they grew;   *(the ground)*
Nor did I wonder at the lily's white,
10 Nor praise the deep vermilion in the rose.
They were but sweet, but figures° of delight   *merely emblems*
Drawn after you, you pattern of all those;
    Yet seemed it winter still, and, you away,
    As with your shadow I with these did play.[2]

99[1]

The forward° violet thus did I chide: *early*
Sweet thief, whence didst thou steal thy sweet° that smells,   *perfume*
If not from my love's breath? The purple pride°   *beauty*
Which on thy soft cheek for complexion dwells
5 In my love's veins thou hast too grossly° dyed.   *obviously*
The lily I condemnèd for thy hand,[2]
And buds of marjoram[3] had stol'n thy hair;
The roses fearfully on thorns did stand,
One blushing shame, another white despair;
10 A third, nor red nor white, had stol'n of both,°   *(making it pink)*
And to° his robb'ry had annexed thy breath;   *in addition to*
But for his theft in pride of all his growth
A vengeful canker° ate him up to death.   *cankerworm*
    More flowers I noted, yet I none could see
    But sweet° or colour it had stol'n from thee.   *perfume*

100

Where are thou, muse, that thou forget'st so long
To speak of that which gives thee all thy might?
Spend'st thou thy fury[1] on some worthless song,
Dark'ning° thy power to lend base subjects light?   *Debasing*
5 Return, forgetful muse, and straight° redeem   *immediately*
In gentle numbers° time so idly spent;   *noble poetry*
Sing to the ear that doth thy lays esteem
And gives thy pen both skill and argument.°   *substance*
Rise, resty° muse, my love's sweet face survey   *lazy*
10 If° time have any wrinkle graven there.   *To see if*
If any, be a satire to° decay   *satirist of*
And make time's spoils despisèd everywhere.

Sonnet 98
1. The planet Saturn was regarded as cold and slow, exerting a melancholy influence.
2. As if with your image I played with these flowers.
Sonnet 99
1. This sonnet has an extra opening line.

2. For stealing whiteness from your (the beloved's) hand.
3. The herb, sweet of scent and auburn in color.
Sonnet 100
1. Inspiration (the "poet's rage" of 17.11).

Give my love fame faster than time wastes life;
So, thou prevene'st° his scythe and crookèd knife.   *impede*

101[1]

O truant muse, what shall be thy amends
For thy neglect of truth in beauty dyed?
Both truth and beauty on my love depends;
So dost thou too, and therein° dignified.   *therein are you*
5   Make answer, muse. Wilt thou not haply° say   *perhaps*
'Truth needs no colour with his colour fixed,[2]
Beauty no pencil beauty's truth to lay,[3]
But best is best if never intermixed'?°   *(with cosmetics)*
Because he needs no praise wilt thou be dumb?
10   Excuse not silence so, for't lies in thee
To make him much outlive a gilded tomb,
And to be praised of° ages yet to be.   *by*
    Then do thy office,° muse; I teach thee how   *duty*
    To make him seem long° hence as he shows° now.   *a long time / appears*

102

My love is strengthened, though more weak in seeming.°   *appearance*
I love not less, though less the show appear.
That love is merchandized[1] whose rich esteeming°   *appraisal*
The owner's tongue doth publish everywhere.
5   Our love was new and then but in the spring°   *just beginning*
When I was wont to greet it with my lays,
As Philomel[2] in summer's front° doth sing,   *beginning*
And stops her pipe in growth of riper days—
Not that the summer is less pleasant now
10   Than when her mournful hymns did hush the night,
But that wild music burdens[3] every bough,
And sweets grown common lose their dear delight.
    Therefore like her I sometime hold my tongue,
    Because I would not dull° you with my song.   *overfeed*

103

Alack, what poverty my muse brings forth
That, having such a scope to show her pride,[1]
The argument all bare° is of more worth   *subject by itself*
Than when it hath my added praise beside!
5   O blame me not if I no more can write!
Look in your glass° and there appears a face   *mirror*
That overgoes my blunt invention[2] quite,
Dulling° my lines and doing me disgrace.   *(by contrast)*
Were it not sinful then, striving to mend,°   *improve*
10   To mar the subject that before was well?—
For to no other pass° my verses tend   *end*

Sonnet 101
1. This sonnet links with 100.
2. Truth needs no artificial color to be added to his natural coloring.
3. True beauty need apply no (cosmetic) brush.
Sonnet 102
1. (Debased by being) turned into merchandise for sale.
2. Nightingale; with ambiguous hints of the myth of Philomel, whose brother-in-law raped her and ripped out her

tongue to ensure her silence. See Book 6 of Ovid's *Metamorphoses*.
3. Loads; provides a musical refrain (probably from many other poets) on.
Sonnet 103
1. Considering that she has such opportunity (in you) to display her skill (her pride in you).
2. That surpasses my dull powers of invention.

Than of your graces and your gifts to tell;
   And more, much more, than in my verse can sit
   Your own glass shows you when you look in it.

104

To me, fair friend, you never can be old;
For as you were when first your eye I eyed,
Such seems your beauty still. Three winters cold
Have from the forests shook three summers' pride;°   *splendor*
5 Three beauteous springs to yellow autumn turned
In process° of the seasons have I seen,   *the progress*
Three April perfumes in three hot Junes burned
Since first I saw you fresh, which yet° are green.   *who still*
Ah yet doth beauty, like a dial hand,
10 Steal from his figure and no pace perceived;[1]
So your sweet hue,° which methinks still doth stand,   *appearance*
Hath motion, and mine eye may be deceived.
   For fear of which, hear this, thou age unbred:°   *future age*
   Ere you were born was beauty's summer dead.

105

Let not my love be called idolatry,
Nor my belovèd as an idol show,
Since all alike my songs and praises be
To one, of one, still° such, and ever so.   *continually*
5 Kind is my love today, tomorrow kind,
Still constant in a wondrous excellence.
Therefore my verse, to constancy confined,
One thing expressing, leaves out difference.°   *diversity (of theme)*
'Fair, kind, and true' is all my argument,
10 'Fair, kind, and true' varying to other words,
And in this change is my invention spent,[1]
Three themes in one, which wonderous scope affords.
   Fair, kind, and true have often lived alone,°   *separately*
   Which three till now never kept seat° in one.   *dwelt permanently*

106[1]

When in the chronicle of wasted° time   *past*
I see descriptions of the fairest wights,°   *people*
And beauty making beautiful old rhyme
In praise of ladies dead and lovely knights;
5 Then in the blazon[2] of sweet beauty's best,
Of hand, of foot, of lip, of eye, of brow,
I see their antique pen would have expressed
Even such a beauty as you master° now.   *possess*
So all their praises are but prophecies
10 Of this our time, all you prefiguring,
And for° they looked but with divining° eyes   *as / prophetic*
They had not skill enough your worth to sing;   *want to*

Sonnet 104
1. *doth . . . perceived*: beauty imperceptibly "steals" (departs stealthily from; robs from) the youthful appearance ("figure") of the beloved as the hand of the watch ("dial") stealthily progresses ("steals") away from the number ("figure") on the watch face.

Sonnet 105
1. And in varying the words alone my inventiveness is expended.
Sonnet 106
1. See "On his Mistress' Beauty" in the Alternative Versions.
2. Poetic catalog of virtues.

For we° which now behold these present days   *even we*
Have eyes to wonder, but lack tongues to praise.

107

Not mine own fears nor the prophetic soul
Of the wide world dreaming on things to come
Can yet the lease° of my true love control,   *allotted term*
Supposed as forfeit to a confined doom.[1]
5 The mortal moon hath her eclipse endured,[2]
And the sad augurs mock their own presage;[3]
Incertainties now crown themselves assured,[4]
And peace proclaims olives of endless age.[5]
Now with the drops[6] of this most balmy time
10 My love looks fresh, and death to me subscribes,°   *submits*
Since spite of him I'll live in this poor rhyme
While he insults° o'er dull and speechless tribes,[7]   *prevails*
    And thou in this shalt find thy monument
    When tyrants' crests and tombs of brass are spent.°   *ruined*

108

What's in the brain that ink may character°   *express*
Which hath not figured° to thee my true spirit?   *shown*
What's new to speak, what now to register,°   *record*
That may express my love or thy dear merit?
5 Nothing, sweet boy; but yet like prayers divine
I must each day say o'er the very same,
Counting no old thing old, thou mine, I thine,
Even as when first I hallowed thy fair name.
So that eternal love in love's fresh case°   *covering*
10 Weighs not° the dust and injury of age,   *Overlooks*
Nor gives to necessary° wrinkles place,°   *inevitable / priority*
But makes antiquity for aye his page,[1]
    Finding the first conceit of love there bred[2]
    Where time and outward form would° show it dead.   *want to*

109

O never say that I was false of heart,
Though absence seemed my flame to qualify°—   *reduce*
As easy might I from myself depart
As from my soul, which in thy breast doth lie.
5 That is my home of love. If I have ranged,
Like him that travels I return again,
Just to the time,° not with the time exchanged,°   *Punctually / changed*
So that myself bring water for my stain.[1]

Sonnet 107
1. Imagined as limited to a finite term.
2. Survived. The line is variously taken to refer to an eclipse of the moon, to an event in the life (or, more likely, to the death in 1603) of Queen Elizabeth (often known as Diana, the moon goddess), or, less probably, to the defeat of the Spanish Armada (1588).
3. And prophets of doom now ridicule their own prophecies.
4. Desired but doubtful possibilities now celebrate their realization; uncertainty is now unavoidable.
5. And peace declares the olive branches that symbolize it to be everlasting. Perhaps a reference to the peace treaty

with Spain signed by King James, who succeeded Elizabeth.
6. Soothing drops of dew, rain, or balm. Balm was used in the coronation ceremony.
7. Over those legions of dead who have no poetic legacy.
Sonnet 108
1. But makes (old) age forever the (youthful) servant to love; perhaps referring to the pages of poetry written when the "sweet boy" (line 5) was still young.
2. The first feeling (poetic expression) of love generated in that place (the beloved; the poem).
Sonnet 109
1. *for my stain:* to cleanse the stain of my absence.

Never believe, though in my nature reigned
10 All frailties that besiege all kinds of blood,°   *disposition*
That it could so preposterously be stained
To leave for° nothing all thy sum of good;   *exchange for*
    For nothing this wide universe I call
    Save thou my rose; in it thou art my all.

110

Alas, 'tis true, I have gone here and there
And made myself a motley to the view,°   *clown to the world*
Gored° mine own thoughts, sold cheap what is most dear,   *Injured*
Made old offences of affections new.[1]
5 Most true it is that I have looked on truth°   *fidelity*
Askance and strangely.° But, by all above,   *coldly*
These blenches° gave my heart another youth,   *alterations*
And worse essays° proved thee my best of love   *experiments*
Now all is done, have what shall have no end;[2]
10 Mine appetite I never more will grind
On newer proof to try[3] an older friend,
A god in love, to whom I am confined.
    Then give me welcome, next my heaven the best,°   *next best to heaven*
    Even to thy pure and most most loving breast.

111

O, for my sake do you with[1] fortune chide,
The guilty goddess of my harmful deeds,
That did not better for my life provide
Than public means which public manners breeds.[2]
5 Thence comes it that my name receives a brand,°   *stigma*
And almost thence my nature is subdued
To what it works in, like the dyer's hand.
Pity me then, and wish I were renewed,°   *cured*
Whilst like a willing patient I will drink
10 Potions of eisel° 'gainst my strong infection;   *medicinal vinegar*
No° bitterness that I will bitter think,   *There is no*
Nor double penance to correct correction.°   *correct me twice over*
    Pity me then, dear friend, and I assure ye
    Even that your pity is enough to cure me.

112[1]

Your love and pity doth th'impression fill°   *eliminates the scar*
Which vulgar° scandal stamped upon my brow;   *public*
For what care I who calls me well or ill,
So you o'er-green my bad, my good allow?[2]
5 You are my all the world, and I must strive
To know my shames and praises from your tongue—
None else to me, nor I to none alive,

Sonnet 110
1. Repeated traditional misbehavior (infidelity,—or offended old friends—in (my treatment of) new attachments.
2. *have . . . end:* take that (my love) which will not expire.
3. *grind . . . try:* sharpen with new experience to test.
Sonnet 111
1. Q has "wish," which gives a more problematic array of

alternative meanings.
2. Probably: Than employment as an actor, which requires one to curry favor with the public.
Sonnet 112
1. This sonnet links with 111.
2. So long as you allow new growth to cover what is bad in me, and give credit for what is good.

That my steeled sense or changes, right or wrong.[3]
In so profound abyss I throw all care

10   Of others' voices that my adder's sense°   *deaf ears*
To critic and to flatterer stoppèd are.
Mark how with my neglect I do dispense:[4]
    You are so strongly in my purpose bred[5]
    That all the world besides, methinks, they're dead.

113

Since I left you mine eye is in my mind,[1]
And that which governs me to go about°   *And my real sight*
Doth part his° function and is partly blind,   *Divides its*
Seems seeing, but effectually is out;°   *blind*
5   For it no form delivers to the heart
Of bird, of flower, or shape which it doth latch.°   *catch sight of*
Of his quick objects° hath the mind no part,   *fleeting impressions*
Nor his own vision holds[2] what it doth catch;
For if it see the rud'st or gentlest° sight,   *coarsest or noblest*
10   The most sweet favour[3] or deformèd'st creature,
The mountain or the sea, the day or night,
The crow or dove, it shapes them to your feature.[4]
    Incapable of more, replete with you,
    My most true mind thus makes mine eye untrue.

114[1]

Or whether doth my mind, being crowned with you,[2]
Drink up the monarch's plague, this flattery,
Or whether shall I say mine eye saith true,
And that your love taught it this alchemy,[3]
5   To make of monsters and things indigest°   *chaotic*
Such cherubins° as your sweet self resemble,   *angels*
Creating every° bad a perfect best   *from every*
As fast as objects to his beams assemble?[4]
O, 'tis the first, 'tis flatt'ry in my seeing,
10   And my great° mind most kingly drinks it up.   *pompous*
Mine eye well knows what with his gust is 'greeing,[5]
And to his palate doth prepare the cup.
    If it be poisoned, 'tis the lesser sin
    That mine eye loves it and doth first begin.[6]

115

Those lines that I before have writ do lie,
Even those that said I could not love you dearer;
Yet then my judgement knew no reason why

---

3. *None . . . wrong:* perhaps, There being no one else to influence me, and no one else's influence being capable of positively or negatively affecting my hardened disposition.
4. How I excuse my neglect (of "other's voices," line 10).
5. Nurtured in all my plans.
Sonnet 113
1. I see with my mind's eye.
2. Nor does the eye's vision hold on to.
3. Face; perhaps Q's "sweet-favor" means "sweet-favored," or "good-looking."
4. It makes them look like you.

Sonnet 114
1. This sonnet links with 113.
2. Being made a King by having you. "Or whether" introduces alternatives.
3. And that love of you taught my eye how thus to transform things.
4. As fast as objects come before its gaze. (The eye was thought to emit beams of light).
5. What pleases the mind's appetite.
6. And drinks first (like a King's taster).

My most full flame should afterwards burn clearer.
5 But reckoning time,[1] whose millioned accidents
Creep in 'twixt vows° and change decrees of kings,   *(and their performance)*
Tan° sacred beauty, blunt the sharp'st intents,   *Darken*
Divert strong minds to th' course of alt'ring things—
Alas, why, fearing of time's tyranny,
10 Might I not then say[2] 'Now I love you best',
When I was certain o'er° incertainty,   *beyond*
Crowning° the present, doubting of the rest?   *Exalting*
    Love is a babe; then might I not say so,[3]
    To give° full growth to that which still doth grow.   *Thereby giving*

116

Let me not to the marriage of true minds
Admit impediments.° Love is not love   *legal barriers to marriage*
Which alters when it alteration finds,
Or bends with the remover to remove.[1]
5 O no, it is an ever fixèd mark[2]
That looks on tempests and is never shaken;
It is the star to every wand'ring barque,
Whose worth's unknown although his height be taken.[3]
Love's not time's fool,° though rosy lips and cheeks   *plaything*
10 Within his bending sickle's compass[4] come;
Love alters not with his brief hours and weeks,
But bears it out even to the edge of doom.[5]
    If this be error and upon° me proved,   *against*
    I never writ, nor no man ever loved.

117

Accuse me thus: that I have scanted° all   *neglected*
Wherein I should your great deserts repay,
Forgot upon your dearest love to call
Whereto all bonds do tie me day by day;
5 That I have frequent° been with unknown minds,°   *friendly / strangers*
And given to time your own dear-purchased right;[1]
That I have hoisted sail to all the winds
Which should° transport me farthest from your sight.   *were likely to*
Book both my wilfulness and errors down,
10 And on just proof surmise accumulate;[2]
Bring me within the level° of your frown,   *aim*
But shoot not at me in your wakened hate,
    Since my appeal says I did strive to prove[3]
    The constancy and virtue of your love.

Sonnet 115
1. But taking time into account; but time, which settles accounts.
2. Was I not then right to have said.
3. Thus I shouldn't say, "Now I love you best" (line 10).
Sonnet 116
1. Or abandons the relationship when the loved one is unfaithful or has departed or died, or when time ("the remover") alters things for the worse.
2. An unmoving sea mark, such as a lighthouse or a beacon, which provides a constant reference point for sailors.
3. *Whose . . . taken:* The star's (great) intrinsic value can-

not be assessed, although navigators at sea can measure height above the horizon.
4. Within range of time's curved (and hostile) scythe. "Compass" also recalls the imagery of the second quatrain.
5. But endures until the eve of doomsday.
Sonnet 117
1. And wasted idly what should have been your right (rite) because acquired by your great worth and affection (because acquired at your great cost).
2. And pile suspicion on top of your proof.
3. Since my defense is that I was trying to test.

118

Like° as, to make our appetites more keen,   *Just*
With eager° compounds we our palate urge;°   *sharp / stimulate*
As to prevent° our maladies unseen   *forestall*
We sicken to shun sickness when we purge:[1]
5 Even so, being full of your ne'er cloying sweetness,
To bitter sauces did I frame° my feeding,   *adjust*
And, sick of welfare,[2] found a kind of meetness°   *suitability*
To be diseased ere that there was true needing.
Thus policy° in love, t'anticipate   *strategy*
10 The ills that were not, grew to faults assured,
And brought to[3] medicine a healthful state
Which, rank of goodness, would by ill be cured.[4]
    But thence I learn, and find the lesson true:
    Drugs poison him that so° fell sick of you.   *thus; so badly*

119

What potions have I drunk of siren[1] tears
Distilled from limbecks° foul as hell within,   *stills*
Applying° fears to hopes and hopes to fears,   *(as a medicine)*
Still° losing when I saw myself° to win!   *Always / expected*
5 What wretched errors hath my heart committed
Whilst it hath thought itself so blessèd never!
How have mine eyes out of their spheres been fitted[2]
In the distraction° of this madding° fever!   *delirium / fit-inducing*
O benefit of ill! Now I find true
10 That better is by evil still made better,
And ruined love when it is built anew
Grows fairer than at first, more strong, far greater.
    So I return rebuked to my content,
    And gain by ills thrice more than I have spent.

120

That you were once unkind befriends me now,
And for° that sorrow which I then did feel   *because of*
Needs must I under my transgression bow,
Unless my nerves° were brass or hammered steel.   *sinews*
5 For if you were by my unkindness shaken
As I by yours, you've past a hell of time,
And I, a tyrant, have no leisure taken
To weigh° how once I suffered in° your crime.   *contemplate / from*
O that our night of woe[1] might have remembered°   *reminded*
10 My deepest sense how hard true sorrow hits,
And soon to you as you to me then tendered°   *offered*
The humble salve which wounded bosoms fits![2]

Sonnet 118
1. We make ourselves sick with medicine that causes vomiting or bowel movements so as to prevent greater illness.
2. Made ill by good food.
3. Treated with; brought to the need of.
4. Overfull with goodness (health, the beloved), sought to be cured by disease (evil).
Sonnet 119
1. Deceitfully and dangerously alluring. Sirens were mythological creatures, part bird, part woman, said to lure sailors to their death with their irresistible songs.
2. Been driven convulsively out of their sockets.
Sonnet 120
1. Our earlier time of suffering (caused by the youth's unfaithfulness).
2. The salve of apology that is just the thing for an injured heart.

But that your trespass° now becomes a fee;   *offense / compensation*
Mine ransoms° yours, and yours must ransom me.   *absolves*

121

'Tis better to be vile than vile esteemed°   *reputed vile*
When not to be receives reproach of being,°   *being so (vile)*
And the just pleasure lost, which is so deemed
Not by our feeling but by others' seeing.[1]
5   For why should others' false adulterate° eyes   *corrupted*
Give salutation to my sportive blood?[2]
Or on my frailties why are frailer spies,
Which in their wills[3] count bad what I think good?
No, I am that I am, and they that level°   *aim*
10   At my abuses reckon up their own.
I may be straight, though they themselves be bevel;°   *crooked*
By their rank° thoughts my deeds must not be shown,   *foul / measured*
     Unless this general evil they maintain:
     All men are bad and in their badness reign.°   *thrive*

122

Thy gift, thy tables,° are within my brain   *notebook*
Full charactered° with lasting memory,   *written*
Which shall above that idle rank[1] remain
Beyond all date, even to eternity;
5   Or at the least so long as brain and heart
Have faculty° by nature to subsist,   *power*
Till each to razed° oblivion yield his part   *destroying*
Of thee, thy record never can be missed.°   *lost*
That poor retention[2] could not so much hold,
10   Nor need I tallies thy dear love to score;[3]
Therefore to give them° from me was I bold,   *(the "tables")*
To trust those tables° that receive thee more.   *memory*
     To keep an adjunct° to remember thee   *aid*
     Were to import° forgetfulness in me.   *imply*

123

No, time, thou shalt not boast that I do change!
Thy pyramids built up with newer might[1]
To me are nothing° novel, nothing strange,   *in no way*
They are but dressings of a former sight.[2]
5   Our dates° are brief, and therefore we admire   *lives*
What thou dost foist upon us that is old,
And rather make them born to our desire[3]

Sonnet 121
1. *And . . . seeing*: And we are denied the appropriate, innocent pleasure (or, we don't even get to enjoy the sin we've supposedly committed), which is considered sinful not by us but by others.
2. Wink knowingly at my lustful behavior.
3. *Or . . . wills*: Why should my failings be pried into by even more culpable people, who wilfully (who licentiously; who in Will Shakespeare).
Sonnet 122
1. Trivial status (of the "tables" as opposed to "memory").
2. That inadequate container (the "tables"); that faulty

memory.
3. Nor do I need the notched sticks used in calculating sums (to which the "tables" are contemptuously compared) to reckon up your precious love.
Sonnet 123
1. Grand buildings constructed by more modern means. Possibly referring to structures erected in Rome in 1586 or in London in 1603 (for James's coronation), but retaining a sense of almost timeless Egyptian antiquity.
2. Replicas of what's been seen before.
3. And consider them made just for us.

Than think that we before have heard them told.°   *described*
Thy registers° and thee I both defy,   *records*
10 Not wond'ring at the present nor the past;
For thy records and what we see doth lie,
Made more or less by thy continual haste.[4]
    This I do vow, and this shall ever be:
    I will be true despite thy scythe and thee.

124

If my dear love° were but the child of state[1]   *(for you)*
It might for fortune's bastard be unfathered,[2]
As subject to time's love or to time's hate,
Weeds among weeds or flowers with flowers gathered.[3]
5 No, it was builded far from accident;°   *chance*
It suffers° not in smiling pomp, nor falls   *changes*
Under the blow of thrallèd° discontent   *captive*
Whereto th'inviting time our fashion calls.[4]
It fears not policy,° that heretic   *expediency*
10 Which works on leases of short-numbered hours,°   *short-term contracts*
But all alone stands hugely politic,°   *prudent*
That it nor° grows with heat° nor drowns with showers.   *neither / prosperity*
    To this I witness call the fools of time,
    Which die for goodness, who have lived for crime.[5]

125

Were't aught to me I bore the canopy,[1]
With my extern° the outward honouring,   *exterior action*
Or laid great bases for eternity[2]
Which proves more short than waste° or ruining?   *decay*
5 Have I not seen dwellers on form and favour[3]
Lose all and more by paying too much rent,°   *overdoing homage*
For compound sweet forgoing simple savour,[4]
Pitiful thrivers in their gazing spent?[5]
No, let me be obsequious° in thy heart,   *dutiful*
10 And take thou my oblation,° poor but free,°   *offering / freely given*
Which is not mixed with seconds,[6] knows no art°   *artifice*
But mutual render,° only me for thee.   *exchange*
    Hence, thou suborned informer![7] A true soul
    When most impeached° stands least in thy control.   *accused*

4. Raised and destroyed by time's swift passage; made to seem more or less majestic by virtue of newness or antiquity and the tastes of the times.
Sonnet 124
1. Were simply the result of circumstances; of your high position.
2. It might be disinherited as a passing fancy, a product of fortune (chance, wealth).
3. *As . . . gathered*: Regarded as useless or valuable as time and fortune decide.
4. To which ("pomp" and "discontent") we are driven by the latest trend ("fashion").
5. *To . . . crime*: I call as witness those playthings of time

who, having lived wicked lives, reform or repent at death.
Sonnet 125
1. Would I care if I enhanced my status by carrying a ceremonial canopy for a royal person?
2. Laid foundations for eternal monuments.
3. Seen those who depend (linger) on ceremony and appearance.
4. For obsequious praise giving up plain candor.
5. Pitiful in their empty achievements, ruined by love of show.
6. The second-rate.
7. Paid spy: jealousy or the detractor whose charges the poem answers.

126[1]

O thou my lovely boy, who in thy power
Dost hold time's fickle glass,[2] his sickle-hour;[3]
Who hast by waning grown,[4] and therein show'st
Thy lovers withering as thy sweet self grow'st—

5 If nature, sovereign mistress over wrack,°   decay
As thou goest onwards still° will pluck thee back,   constantly
She keeps thee to this purpose: that her skill
May time disgrace, and wretched minutes kill.
Yet fear her, O thou minion° of her pleasure   darling
10 She may detain but not still keep her treasure.
    Her audit,° though delayed, answered° must be,   debt (to time) / paid
    And her quietus° is to render° thee.   settlement / relinquish

127[1]

In the old age° black was not counted fair,[2]   old days
Or if it were, it bore not beauty's name;
But now is black beauty's successive heir,°   heir by succession
And beauty slandered with a bastard shame:[3]
5 For since each hand hath put on° nature's power,   usurped
Fairing° the foul with art's false borrowed face,   Beautifying
Sweet beauty hath no name, no holy bower,
But is profaned, if not lives in disgrace.
Therefore my mistress' eyes are raven-black,
10 Her brow so suited,[4] and they mourners seem
At such who, not born fair, no beauty lack,
Sland'ring creation with a false esteem.[5]
    Yet so° they mourn, becoming of° their woe,   in such a way / adorning
    That every tongue says beauty should look so.

128

How oft, when thou, my music, music play'st
Upon that blessèd wood whose motion° sounds   mechanism
With thy sweet fingers when thou gently sway'st°   govern
The wiry concord that mine ear confounds,°   amazes (with delight)
5 Do I envy those jacks[1] that nimble leap
To kiss the tender inward of thy hand
Whilst my poor lips, which should that harvest reap,
At the wood's boldness by thee blushing stand!
To be so tickled they would change their state
10 And situation with those dancing chips

Sonnet 126
1. This "sonnet" or envoi, of six couplets, concludes the part of the sequence apparently addressed to the youth and formally signals a change in tone and subject matter in the remaining sonnets.
2. Capricious, treacherous hourglass (?); mirror showing changing images (?).
3. Reaping time. "Sickle-hour" emends Q's "sickle, hower," which may be an error for "sickle o'er." A familiar emblem for time placed the hourglass below and the sickle above.
4. Become more beautiful with age. As the sand in the top half of an hourglass wanes, the sand in the bottom part grows.
Sonnet 127
1. Sonnets 127–52 have been traditionally known as the "dark lady" group, although their subject matter is not uniform and their object is only once called "dark" (1.7.14)

and never a "lady.' She is referred to as the poet's "mistress" (127.9. 130.., 8, 12), however, and often described as "black" (127.1, 3, 9; 130.4; 131.12, 13; 132.3, 13; 147.14). The celebration of black beauty goes back to the biblical Song of Songs, 1:4: "I am blacke . . . but comelie." See the Introduction.
2. Beautiful; light-colored.
3. And (fair) beauty accused of illegitimacy (by use of cosmetics).
4. Her brow dressed (matched) in an eyebrow black like her eyes (and for the same reason).
5. At . . . esteem: Because of those who, not being fair, make up for it with cosmetics, so that even natural beauty is presumed artificial.
Sonnet 128
1. Keys of the virginal, a harpsichordlike instrument; fellows.

O'er whom thy fingers walk with gentle gait,
Making dead wood more blessed than living lips.
　　Since saucy° jacks so happy are in this,   *impudent*
　　Give them thy fingers, me thy lips to kiss.

129

Th'expense of spirit in a waste of shame
Is lust in action;[1] and till action, lust
Is perjured, murd'rous, bloody, full of blame,
Savage, extreme, rude,° cruel, not to trust,°   *harsh / be trusted*
5　Enjoyed no sooner but despisèd straight,°   *immediately*
Past reason° hunted, and no sooner had   *Madly*
Past reason hated as a swallowed bait
On purpose laid to make the taker mad;
Mad in pursuit and in possession so,°   *(mad)*
10　Had, having, and in quest to have, extreme;
A bliss in proof and proved,[2] a very woe;
Before, a joy proposed; behind, a dream.
　　All this the world well knows, yet none knows well
　　To shun the heaven that leads men to this hell.

130

My mistress' eyes are nothing like the sun;
Coral is far more red than her lips' red.
If snow be white, why then her breasts are dun;°   *grayish brown*
If hairs be wires,[1] black wires grow on her head.
5　I have seen roses damasked,° red and white,   *dappled*
But no such roses see I in her cheeks;
And in some perfumes is there more delight
Than in the breath that from my mistress reeks.°   *issues; smells*
I love to hear her speak, yet well I know
10　That music hath a far more pleasing sound.
I grant I never saw a goddess go:°   *walk*
My mistress when she walks treads on the ground.
　　And yet, by heaven, I think my love as rare
　　As any she belied with false compare.[2]

131

Thou art as tyrannous so as thou art[1]
As those whose beauties proudly make them cruel,
For well thou know'st to my dear° doting heart   *fond(ly)*
Thou art the fairest and most precious jewel.
5　Yet, in good faith, some say that thee behold
Thy face hath not the power to make love groan.
To say they err I dare not be so bold,
Although I swear it to myself alone;
And, to be sure° that is not false I swear,   *for proof; surely*
10　A thousand groans but thinking on° thy face   *just thinking about*
One on another's neck° do witness bear   *In quick succession*

Sonnet 129
1. *Th'expense . . . action:* The expenditure of vital energy (semen) in a shameful waste (waist) is consummated lust.
2. *in proof:* while being experienced. *proved:* having been experienced.
Sonnet 130
1. Elizabethan poets often compared women's hair to golden wires.
2. As any woman misrepresented by false comparison.
Sonnet 131
1. As cruel as you are dark (hence not conventionally beautiful).

Thy black° is fairest in my judgment's place.²   *dark appearance*
In nothing art thou black° save in thy deeds,   *ugly*
And thence this slander,³ as I think, proceeds.

132

Thine eyes I love, and they, as° pitying me—   *as if*
Knowing thy heart torment° me with disdain—   *to torment*
Have put on black, and loving mourners be,
Looking with pretty ruth° upon my pain;   *pity*
5 And truly, not the morning sun of heaven
Better becomes° the gray cheeks° of the east,   *beautifies / clouds*
Nor that full star that ushers in the even°   *(Venus, the evening star)*
Doth° half that glory to the sober west,   *Imparts*
As those two mourning° eyes become thy face.   *(pun on "morning")*
10 O, let it then as well beseem° thy heart   *become*
To mourn for me, since mourning doth thee grace,
And suit thy pity like in every part.¹
　　Then will I swear beauty herself is black,
　　And all they foul° that thy complexion lack.   *ugly*

133

Beshrew° that heart that makes my heart to groan   *Curse (a mild term)*
For that deep wound it gives my friend and me!
Is't not enough to torture me alone,
But slave to slavery° my sweet'st friend must be?   *utterly enslaved*
5 Me from myself thy cruel eye hath taken,
And my next self thou harder hast engrossed.¹
Of him, myself, and thee I am forsaken—
A torment thrice threefold thus to be crossed.°   *afflicted*
Prison° my heart in thy steel bosom's ward,²   *Imprison / cell*
10 But then my friend's heart let my poor heart bail;
Whoe'er keeps° me, let my heart be his guard;²   *guards*
Thou canst not then use rigour° in my jail   *severity*
　　And yet thou wilt; for I, being pent° in thee,   *locked up*
　　Perforce am thine, and° all that is in me.   *as is*

134¹

So, now° I have confessed that he is thine,   *now that*
And I myself am mortgaged to thy will,°   *intent; sexual desire*
Myself I'll forfeit, so that other mine²
Thou wilt restore to be my comfort still.
5 But thou wilt not, nor he will not° be free,   *doesn't want to*
For thou art covetous, and he is kind.
He learned but surety-like° to write° for me   *as guarantor / sign*
Under that bond° that him as fast³ doth bind.   *(of infatuation)*
The statute⁴ of thy beauty thou wilt take,
10 Thou usurer that putt'st forth all to use,°   *at interest; for sex*
And sue a friend came° debtor for my sake;   *who became*

---

2. In my opinion.
3. See line 6 for "this slander."
Sonnet 132
1. And dress your pity similarly, in heart as well as eyes.
Sonnet 133
1. And my second self, or closest friend, you have even more cruelly monopolized.

2. My friend's prison.
Sonnet 134
1. This sonnet links with 133.
2. So long as my other self.
3. As firmly as myself.
4. The total guaranteed by the bond.

So him I lose through my unkind abuse.[5]
   Him have I lost; thou hast both him and me;
   He pays the whole,° and yet am I not free.   *(pun on "hole")*

135[1]

Whoever hath her wish, thou hast thy Will,
And Will to boot,° and Will in overplus.   *in addition*
More than enough am I that vex thee still,°   *always (by wooing)*
To thy sweet will making addition thus.
5 Wilt thou, whose will is large and spacious,
Not once vouchsafe to hide my will in thine?
Shall will in others° seem right gracious,   *others' wills*
And in my will no fair acceptance shine?[2]
The sea, all water, yet receives rain still,
10 And in abundance addeth to his° store;   *its*
So thou, being rich in Will, add to thy Will
One will of mine to make thy large Will more.
   Let no unkind no fair beseechers kill;[3]
   Think all but one,° and me in that one Will.   *one suitor*

136[1]

If thy soul check° thee that I come so near,[2]   *chide*
Swear to thy blind soul that I was thy Will,[3]
And will, thy soul knows, is admitted there;
Thus far for love my love-suit, sweet, fulfil.°   *grant*
5 Will will fulfill the treasure° of thy love,   *fill up the treasury*
Ay, fill it full with wills, and my will one.°   *one of them*
In things of great receipt° with ease we prove   *volume*
Among a number one is reckoned none.[4]
Then in the number let me pass untold,°   *uncounted*
10 Though in thy store's account° I one must be;   *tally (of lovers)*
For nothing hold me, so it please thee hold
That nothing me a something, sweet, to thee.[5]
   Make but my name thy love,[6] and love that still,°   *always*
   And then thou lov'st me for my name is Will.

137

Thou blind fool love, what dost thou to mine eyes
That they behold and see not what they see?
They know what beauty is, see where it lies,
Yet what the best is take the worst to be.[1]
5 If eyes corrupt° by over-partial° looks   *corrupted / overly doting*

---

5. Through your ill treatment of me; through my ill-treatment of the youth.
Sonnet 135
1. This sonnet, as well as 136, 143, and "A Lover's Complaint," lines 126–33, puns elaborately on different senses of "will": wishes, sexual desire, futurity, testament, the name "Will" (applied to one or more persons, including Shakespeare, and capitalized and sometimes italicized in Q), and the male and female sexual organs. See also 57.13 and note.
2. And my will not be greeted with a kind reception.
3. Let no unkindness of yours kill any of your worthy suitors.

Sonnet 136
1. This sonnet links with 135.
2. I am so forthright; I am so physically close.
3. See sonnet 135, note 1.
4. Proverbially, one is no number.
5. *For . . . thee:* Think me worthless so long as, my darling, you treasure worthless me. Q's punctuation, "something sweet to thee," emphasizes the sexual implications.
6. Love only my name, "Will"; that is, act on your desire.
Sonnet 137
1. Yet take the worst to be the best.

Be anchored in the bay where all men ride,[2]
Why of eyes' falsehood hast thou forgèd hooks
Whereto the judgement of my heart is tied?
Why should my heart think that a several plot°   *private land*
10 Which my heart knows the wide world's common place?—
Or° mine eyes, seeing this, say this is not,   *Or why should*
To put fair truth upon so foul a face?
    In things right true my heart and eyes have erred,
    And to this false plague[4] are they now transferred.

138[1]

When my love swears that she is made of truth
I do believe her though I know she lies,
That° she might think me some untutored youth   *So that*
Unlearnèd in the world's false subtleties.
5 Thus vainly° thinking that she thinks me young,   *in vain; with vanity*
Although she knows my days are past the best,
Simply I credit[2] her false-speaking tongue;
On both sides thus is simple truth suppressed.
But wherefore says she not she is unjust,°   *unfaithful*
10 And wherefore say not I that I am old?
O, love's best habit is in seeming trust,[3]
And age in love loves not to have years told.°   *counted*
    Therefore I lie° with her, and she with me,   *tell lies; lie down*
    And in our faults by lies we flattered be.

139

O, call° not me to justify° the wrong   *ask / approve*
That thy unkindness° lays upon my heart.   *infidelity*
Wound me not with thine eye[1] but with thy tongue;
Use power with power,[2] and slay me not by art.°   *by deceit*
5 Tell me thou lov'st elsewhere, but in my sight,
Dear heart, forbear to glance thine eye aside.
What° need'st thou wound with cunning when thy might *Why*
Is more than my o'erpressed defence can bide?°   *endure*
Let me excuse thee: 'Ah, my love well knows
10 Her pretty looks have been mine enemies,
And therefore from my face she turns my foes
That they elsewhere might dart their injuries.'
    Yet do not so; but since I am near slain,
    Kill me outright with looks, and rid° my pain.   *put an end to*

140

Be wise as thou art cruel; do not press
My tongue-tied patience with too much disdain,
Lest sorrow lend me words, and words express

---

2. Harbor for general use (suggesting a promiscuous woman).
3. *the wide . . . place*: common land, open to all (suggesting promiscuity); a commonplace known by all.
4. This plague of false perception; this deceitful woman.
Sonnet 138
1. Another version of this sonnet appears in *The Passionate Pilgrim*. See the Textual Note and the Alternative Ver-

sions.
2. Naively (foolishly: giving the appearance of folly) I (pretend to) believe.
3. Love is best dressed in apparent fidelity (apparent trust).
Sonnet 139
1. By looking elsewhere, at other men (see line 6).
2. Use power frankly; fairly.

The manner of my pity-wanting[1] pain.
5   If I might teach thee wit,° better it were,   wisdom
Though not to love, yet, love, to tell me so—
As testy sick men when their deaths be near
No news but health from their physicians know.°   learn
For if I should despair I should grow mad,
10 And in my madness might speak ill of thee.
Now this ill-wresting world[2] is grown so bad
Mad slanderers by mad ears believèd be.
      That I may not be so, nor thou belied,°   maligned
      Bear thine eyes straight,[3] though thy proud heart go wide.°   astray

141

In faith, I do not love thee with mine eyes,
For they in thee a thousand errors note;
But 'tis my heart that loves what they despise,
Who in despite of view° is pleased to dote.   despite what it sees
5   Nor are mine ears with thy tongue's tune delighted,
Nor tender feeling to base touches prone;[1]
Nor taste nor smell desire to be invited
To any sensual feast with thee alone;
But my five wits[2] nor my five senses can
10 Dissuade one foolish heart from serving thee,
Who leaves unswayed the likeness of a man.[3]
Thy proud heart's slave and vassal-wretch to be.
      Only my plague thus far° I count my gain: to this extent
      That she that makes me sin awards me pain.[4]

142[1]

Love is my sin, and thy dear virtue hate,
Hate of my sin grounded on sinful loving.[2]
O, but with mine compare thou thine own state,
And thou shalt find it° merits not reproving;   (my state)
5   Or if it do, not from those lips of thine
That have profaned their scarlet ornaments[3]
And sealed[4] false bonds of love as oft as mine,
Robbed others' beds' revenues of their rents.[5]
Be it lawful° I love thee as thou lov'st those   let it be lawful that
10 Whom thine eyes woo as mine importune thee.
Root pity in thy heart, that when it grows
Thy pity may deserve to pitied be.°   make you pitiable
      If thou dost seek to have what thou dost hide,°   (pity)
      By self example mayst thou be denied!

Sonnet 140
1. Unpitied; desiring pity; pitiable.
2. Now this world, that tends to interpret in the worst light.
3. Keep looking only at me (see 139).
Sonnet 141
1. Nor is my keen sense of touch susceptible to "base" sexual contact.
2. Mental faculties (common sense, imagination, fancy, judgment, memory).
3. Which (the heart, serving you) leaves without a commander the mere semblance of a man.
4. By making me sin, she causes me to suffer punitive penance, which will reduce my sufferings after death.

Sonnet 142
1. This sonnet links with 141.
2. *Love . . . loving:* My only sin is love, and your most valuable virtue is hatred, hatred of my sin in loving you (but also, your most valuable virtue is the haughty rejection of my wooing) based on (your) immoral sexual affairs.
3. Lips, which are scarlet, like a cardinal's robe.
4. "Sealed" with a kiss: comparing the mistress's lips to the red wax used to seal official documents.
5. Stolen the sexual and emotional intimacy ("rents" paid by a tenant) from others' marriages by committing adultery, thus reducing the possibility that these marriages will result in children ("revenues," estates that yield income).

143

Lo, as a care-full° housewife runs to catch   *busy*
One of her feathered creatures broke away,
Sets down her babe and makes all swift dispatch°   *hurries*
In pursuit of the thing she would have stay,
5   Whilst her neglected child holds her in chase,
Cries to catch her whose busy care is bent
To follow that which flies before her face,
Not prizing° her poor infant's discontent: *regarding*
So runn'st thou after that which flies from thee,
10 Whilst I, thy babe, chase thee afar behind;
But if thou catch thy hope, turn back to me
And play the mother's part: kiss me, be kind.
      So will I pray that thou mayst have thy Will[1]
      If thou turn back and my loud crying still.

144[1]

Two loves I have, of comfort and despair,
Which like two spirits do suggest° me still.   *entice*
The better angel is a man right fair,
The worser spirit a woman coloured ill.°   *darkly*
5   To win me soon to hell my female evil
Tempteth my better angel from my side,
And would corrupt my saint to be a devil,
Wooing his purity with her foul pride;
And whether that my angel be turned fiend
10 Suspect I may, yet not directly tell;
But being both from me, both to each friend,[2]
I guess one angel in another's hell.[3]
      Yet this shall I ne'er know, but live in doubt
      Till my bad angel fire my good one out.[4]

145[1]

Those lips that love's own hand did make
Breathed forth the sound that said 'I hate'
To me that languished for her sake;
But when she saw my woeful state,
5   Straight in her heart did mercy come,
Chiding that tongue that ever sweet
Was used in giving gentle doom,°   *judgment*
And taught it thus anew to greet:
'I hate' she altered with an end
10 That followed it as gentle day
Doth follow night who, like a fiend,
From heaven to hell is flown away.
      'I hate' from hate away she threw,[2]
      And saved my life, saying 'not you.'

Sonnet 143
1. A pun; see sonnet 135, note 1.
Sonnet 144
1. Another version of this sonnet appears in *The Passion-ate Pilgrim*. See Textual Note and Alternative Versions.
2. Both away from me and lovers to one another.
3. Each torments the other; they are in the "hell," or middle den, of a (sexual) game called barley-break; the man occupies the sex organ ("hell") of the woman.
4. Until my bad angel expels my good one who has

become an animal to be smoked out of a burrow; until my bad angel infects my good one with venereal disease; until bad money ("angel" = gold coin) drives out good.
Sonnet 145
1. Unlike the other sonnets, which are in iambic pentameter, 145 is composed of eight-syllable (iambic tetrameter) lines.
2. She converted the normal meaning of the phrase "I hate" away from "hate." A pun on "hate away" and "(Anne) Hathaway," Shakespeare's wife, is possible.

146

Poor soul, the centre of my sinful earth,
[   ] these rebel powers that thee array;[1]
Why dost thou pine within and suffer dearth,
Painting thy outward walls so costly gay?
5 Why so large cost, having so short a lease,
Dost thou upon thy fading mansion° spend?   *(the body)*
Shall worms, inheritors of this excess,
Eat up thy charge?° Is this thy body's end?   *expense*
Then, soul, live thou upon thy servant's° loss,   *(the body's)*
10 And let that pine to aggravate thy store.[2]
Buy terms divine° in selling hours of dross;°   *eternal life / waste*
Within be fed, without be rich no more.
    So shalt thou feed on death, that feeds on men,
    And death once dead, there's no more dying then.

147

My love is as a fever, longing still°   *continually*
For that which longer nurseth° the disease,   *nourishes*
Feeding on that which doth preserve° the ill,   *prolong*
Th'uncertain° sickly appetite to please.   *capricious*
5 My reason, the physician to my love,
Angry that his prescriptions are not kept,
Hath left me, and I desperate now approve
Desire is death, which physic did except.[1]
Past cure I am, now reason is past care,[2]
10 And frantic mad with evermore° unrest.   *constant*
My thoughts and my discourse as madmen's are,
At random from° the truth vainly° expressed;   *unconnected to / idly*
    For I have sworn thee fair, and thought thee bright,
    Who art as black as hell, as dark as night.

148

O me, what eyes hath love put in my head,
Which have no correspondence with true sight!
Or if they have, where is my judgement fled,
That censures falsely[1] what they see aright?
5 If that be fair whereon my false eyes dote,
What means the world to say it is not so?
If it be not, then love doth well denote[2]
Love's eye is not so true as all men's. No,[3]
How can it, O, how can love's eye be true,
10 That is so vexed with watching° and with tears?   *staying awake*

Sonnet 146
1. This rebellious body in which you are clothed. At the
beginning of the line, Q repeats "My sinful earth" from
the previous line. There is no way of discovering what
Shakespeare wrote; among the guesses are "Starved by,"
"Foiled by," "Spoiled by," and "Feeding."
2. And let the body dwindle to add to your wealth.
Sonnet 147
1. *now . . . except:* now discover that desire, which
rejected medicine, is fatal.
2. Medical care: inverting the proverb "Past cure, past

care" (don't worry about what you can't control). In the
proverb, you don't care because you can't cure; here,
because you don't care, you can't cure.
Sonnet 148
1. That judges inaccurately (dishonestly). "False" (line 5)
has similar meanings.
2. Then my self-delusion in love proves that.
3. Not so true as all other men's eye. On the contrary.
Q's "all men's, no" is often emended to "all men's 'No,'"
suggesting a pun on 'eye/aye" (yes).

No marvel then though I° mistake my view: *that I (eye)*
The sun itself sees not till heaven clears.
  O cunning love, with tears thou keep'st me blind
  Lest eyes, well seeing, thy foul faults should find!

149

Canst thou, O cruel, say I love thee not
When I against myself with thee partake?°   *take sides*
Do I not think on thee when I forgot
Am of myself, all-tyrant,[1] for thy sake?
5 Who hateth thee that I do call my friend?
On whom frown'st thou that I do fawn upon?
Nay, if thou lour'st° on me, do I not spend°   *scowl / wreak*
Revenge upon myself with present moan?°   *instant anguish*
What merit do I in myself respect°   *value; note*
10 That is so proud thy service to despise,[2]
When all my best° doth worship thy defect,°   *best qualities / flaws*
Commanded by the motion of thine eyes?
  But, love, hate on; for now I know thy mind.
  Those that can see thou lov'st, and I am blind.[3]

150

O, from what power hast thou this powerful might
With insufficiency° my heart to sway,   *By your flaws*
To make me give the lie to my true sight
And swear that brightness doth not grace the day?[1]
5 Whence hast thou this becoming of things ill,[2]
That in the very refuse of thy deeds°   *your basest behavior*
There is such strength and warrantise° of skill   *guarantee*
That in my mind thy worst all best exceeds?
Who taught thee how to make me love thee more
10 The more I hear and see just cause of hate?
O, though I love what others do abhor,
With others thou shouldst not abhor my state.
  If thy unworthiness raised love in me,
  More worthy I to be beloved of thee.

151

Love is too young° to know what conscience is,   *(Cupid being a boy)*
Yet who knows not conscience[1] is born of love?
Then, gentle cheater, urge° not my amiss,°   *stress / fault*
Lest guilty of my faults thy sweet self prove.
5 For, thou betraying me, I do betray
My nobler part° to my gross body's treason.   *soul*
My soul doth tell my body that he may
Triumph in love; flesh stays no farther reason,[2]

Sonnet 149
1. *when . . . all-tyrant:* when I tyrannically neglect myself.
2. So proud as to scorn to serve you.
3. You love those who see you accurately and thus admire you, but I am blinded (by love and thus, from your point of view, unworthy of being loved). The first clause may have the opposite sense, however: you love those who see your defects well enough not to love you.
Sonnet 150
1. *To . . . day:* the speaker is so blindly in love that he finds beauty only in the blackness he associates with his mistress.
2. This capacity to render the ugly attractive.
Sonnet 151
1. Moral sense; carnal knowledge.
2. Flesh, specifically the sexual organ, needs no further encouragement.

10 But rising at thy name doth point out thee
 As his triumphant prize. Proud of this pride,³
 He is contented thy poor drudge to be,
 To stand° in thy affairs, fall by thy side.   *assist; be erect*
  No want of conscience hold it that I call
  Her 'love' for whose dear love I rise and fall.

152

 In loving thee thou know'st I am forsworn,¹
 But thou art twice forsworn to me love swearing° *in swearing love to me*
 In act thy bed-vow° broke, and new faith torn *to husband (or lover)*
5 In vowing new hate after new love bearing.²
 But why of two oaths' breach do I accuse thee
 When I break twenty? I am perjured most,
 For all my vows are oaths but to misuse° thee,   *deceive*
 And all my honest faith in thee is lost.
10 For I have sworn deep oaths of thy deep kindness,
 Oaths of thy love, thy truth, thy constancy,
 And to enlighten thee gave eyes to blindness,³
 Or made them swear against the thing they see.
  For I have sworn thee fair—more perjured eye° *(punning on "I")*
  To swear against the truth so foul a lie.

153¹

 Cupid laid by his brand° and fell asleep.   *torch*
 A maid of Dian's² this advantage found,°   *seized*
 And his love-kindling fire did quickly steep
5 In a cold valley-fountain of that ground,
 Which borrowed from this holy fire of love
 A dateless° lively heat, still° to endure,   *An endless / always*
 And grew a seething bath which yet men prove
 Against strange maladies a sovereign cure.³
10 But at my mistress' eye love's brand new fired,° *being newly lit*
 The boy for trial° needs would touch my breast. *to test it*
 I, sick withal,° the help of bath desired,   *from it*
 And thither hied, a sad distempered° guest,   *seriously ill*
  But found no cure; the bath for my help lies
  Where Cupid got new fire: my mistress' eyes.

---

3. Swelling with pride (and lust).
Sonnet 152
1. Forsworn presumably in breaking loving vows—perhaps to his wife, to the youth to whom he promised unswerving devotion in earlier sonnets, or to both.
2. *new faith . . . bearing:* the "new faith" followed by "new hate" may be addressed either to the speaker's young friend or to the speaker himself.
3. *And to make you fair* (give you insight), I looked blindly on your failings (pretended to see what I couldn't).

Sonnet 153
1. This and the following sonnet derive indirectly from classical fifth-century Greek epigrams.
2. Diana, goddess of chastity.
3. *And grew . . . cure:* And became a boiling-hot medicinal bath (used, among other purposes, for the treatment of venereal disease), which men still find to be an outstanding remedy for foreign illnesses (venereal diseases were associated with foreigners). There may be an allusion here and in 154 to the town of Bath, which became a famous health spa in the eighteenth century.

154[1]

5   The little love-god lying once asleep
     Laid by his side his heart-inflaming brand,°   *torch*
     Whilst many nymphs that vowed chaste life to keep
     Came tripping by; but in her maiden hand
     The fairest votary took up that fire
10 Which many legions of true hearts had warmed.
     And so the general° of hot desire   *commander (Cupid)*
     Was sleeping by a virgin hand disarmed.
     This brand she quenchèd in a cool well by,°   *close by*
     Which from love's fire took heat perpetual,
     Growing a bath and healthful remedy
     For men diseased; but I, my mistress' thrall,°   *slave*
       Came there for cure; and this° by that I prove: *the following*
       Love's fire heats water, water cools not love.

Sonnet 154
1. This sonnet varies the topic of 153.

A Lover's Complaint

From off a hill whose concave womb re-worded°   *hollow side echoed*
A plaintful story from a sist'ring° vale,   *nearby*
My spirits t'attend° this double voice accorded,°   *hear / agreed*
And down I laid to list° the sad-tuned tale;   *listen to*
5   Ere long espied a fickle° maid full pale,   *a disturbed*
Tearing of papers, breaking rings a-twain,°   *in two*
Storming her world with sorrow's wind and rain.

Upon her head a plaited hive° of straw   *hat*
Which fortified° her visage from the sun,   *protected*
10   Whereon the thought° might think sometime it saw   *imagination*
The carcass of a beauty spent and done.
Time had not scythèd all that youth begun,
Nor youth all quit; but spite° of heaven's fell° rage,   *in spite / fierce*
Some beauty peeped through lattice of seared° age.   *withered*

15   Oft did she heave her napkin to her eyne,[1]
Which on it had conceited characters,°   *imaginative designs*
Laund'ring the silken figures in the brine
That seasoned° woe had pelleted in tears,   *experienced; salted*
And often reading what contents it bears;
20   As often shrieking undistinguished° woe   *inarticulate*
In clamours of all size, both high and low.

Sometimes her levelled eyes their carriage ride[2]
As° they did batt'ry to the spheres° intend;   *As if / planets*
Sometime diverted their poor balls° are tied   *eyeballs; cannonballs*
25   To th'orbèd° earth; sometimes they do extend   *spherical*
Their view right on;° anon their gazes lend   *straight*
To every place at once, and nowhere fixed,
The mind and sight distractedly commixed.°   *confused*

Her hair, nor° loose nor tied in formal plait,   *neither*
30   Proclaimed in her a careless hand of pride;[3]
For some, untucked, descended her sheaved° hat,   *fell from her straw*
Hanging her pale and pinèd cheek beside.
Some in her threaden fillet° still did bide,   *headband*
And, true to bondage, would not break from thence,
35   Though slackly braided in loose negligence.

A thousand favours° from a maund° she drew   *love tokens / basket*
Of amber, crystal, and of beaded jet,°   *beads of black stone*
Which one by one she in a river threw
Upon whose weeping margin she was set;°   *seated*
40   Like usury applying wet to wet,[4]

---

1. Often did she raise her handkerchief to her eyes.
2. Sometimes her eyes, aimed (like a cannon), glare (are mounted on a swivel).
3. A hand careless of pride; a hand proud in its care-lessness (knowing that she could attract with no effort).
4. Like usury making wealth wealthier (by adding tears to the stream).

Or monarch's hands that lets not bounty fall
Where want cries some, but where excess begs all.[5]

Of folded schedules° had she many a one   *letters*
Which she perused, sighed, tore, and gave the flood;
45 Cracked many a ring of posied gold and bone,[6]
Bidding them find their sepulchres in mud;
Found yet more letters sadly penned in blood,
With sleided silk feat and affectedly
Enswathed[7] and sealed to curious° secrecy.   *careful*

50 These often bathed she in her fluxive° eyes,   *flowing*
And often kissed, and often 'gan to tear;
Cried 'O false blood, thou register° of lies,   *record*
What unapprovèd° witness dost thou bear!   *unreliable*
Ink would have seemed more black and damnèd here!'
55 This said, in top of rage the lines she rents,°   *rips*
Big° discontent so breaking their contents.   *Powerful*

A reverend man that grazed his cattle nigh
Sometime a blusterer that the ruffle knew[8]
Of court, of city, and had let go by
60 The swiftest hours observèd as they flew,[9]
Towards this afflicted fancy fastly[1] drew,
And, privileged by age, desires to know
In brief the grounds and motives of her woe.

So slides he down upon his grainèd bat,[2]
65 And comely° distant sits he by her side,   *politely*
When he again desires her, being sat,
Her grievance with his hearing to divide.°   *share*
If that from him there may be aught applied
Which may her suffering ecstasy° assuage,   *grief*
70 'Tis promised in the charity of age.

'Father,' she says, 'though in me you behold
The injury of many a blasting° hour,   *disfiguring*
Let it not tell your judgement I am old;
Not age, but sorrow over me hath power.
75 I might as yet have been a spreading° flower,   *blooming*
Fresh to myself, if I had self-applied
Love to myself, and to no love beside.

'But, woe is me, too early I attended
A youthful suit—it was° to gain my grace°—   *was designed / favor*
80 O, one by nature's outwards° so commended   *external appearance*
That maidens' eyes stuck over all° his face.   *were glued to*
Love lacked a dwelling and made him her place,

5. *Or . . . all*: Or like the monarch who, rather than give
a little to the truly needy, gives a great deal to those who
already have plenty.
6. A ring of gold and ivory inscribed with messages (of
love).
7. *With . . . / Enswathed*: Delicately and affectionately
wrapped in strands of separated ("sleided") silk.

8. Once a man of the world who was accustomed to the
busier life.
9. *had . . . flew*: was past the prime of life, but had
learned from experience.
1. Toward this person afflicted by love rapidly (close by).
2. So he comes down the bank with the help of his
forked herdsman's staff.

And when in his fair parts she did abide
She was new-lodged and newly deified.

85 'His browny locks did hang in crookèd curls,
And every light occasion° of the wind   *chance stirring*
Upon his lips their silken parcels° hurls.   *(of hair)*
What's sweet to do, to do will aptly find.[3]
Each eye that saw him did enchant the mind,
90 For on his visage was in little° drawn   *miniature*
What largeness thinks in paradise was sawn.[4]

'Small show of man was yet upon his chin;
His phoenix° down began but to appear,   *singularly lovely*
Like unshorn velvet, on that termless skin[5]
95 Whose bare outbragged the web[6] it seemed to wear;
Yet showed his visage by that cost more dear,[7]
And nice affections° wavering stood in doubt   *discriminating tastes*
If best were as it was, or best without.°   *(shaven)*

'His qualities were beauteous as his form,
100 For maiden-tongued° he was, and thereof free.°   *modest / well spoken*
Yet if men moved° him, was he such a storm   *angered*
As oft twixt May and April is to see
When winds breathe sweet, unruly though they be.
His rudeness so with his authorized youth
105 Did livery falseness in a pride of truth.[8]

'Well could he ride, and often men would say
"That horse his mettle from his rider takes;
Proud of subjection, noble by the sway,°   *control*
What rounds, what bounds, what course,° what stop he makes!" *gallop*
110 And controversy hence a question takes,
Whether the horse by him became his deed,
Or he his manège by th' well-doing steed.[9]

'But quickly on this side the verdict went:
His real habitude° gave life and grace   *disposition*
115 To appertainings° and to ornament,   *external attributes*
Accomplished in himself, not in his case.°   *mere appearance*
All aids, themselves made fairer by their place,
Came for additions;[1] yet their purposed trim
Pieced not[2] his grace, but were all graced by him.

120 'So on the tip of his subduing tongue
All kind of arguments and question deep,
All replication prompt,° and reason strong,   *quick reply*

3. Ways are easily found to do pleasant things (look, love).
4. What one would imagine seeing on a larger scale in paradise.
5. Like velvet with its nap unclipped, on that indescribable (invulnerable to time) skin.
6. Whose naked surface showed more beautiful than the down covering.
7. Yet his face looked more precious (attractive) because of its rich clothing.
8. *His . . . truth:* His roughness, sanctioned by his "youth," employed falseness in truth's uniform.
9. *Whether . . . steed:* Whether he performed so well because of his horsemanship or because his grace in horsemanship (French: *manège*) was a result of the horse's skill.
1. Attempted to increase his worth.
2. *their . . . not:* their anticipated decorative effect did not increase.

For his advantage still did wake and sleep.[3]
To make the weeper laugh, the laugher weep,
125 He had the dialect and different skill,[4]
Catching all passions in his craft of will,[5]

'That° he did in the general bosom reign   *So that*
Of young, of old, and sexes both enchanted,
To dwell with him in thoughts, or to remain
130 In personal duty, following where he haunted.°   *often went*
Consents[6] bewitched, ere he desire,° have granted,   *before he asks*
And dialogued for him what he would say,
Asked their own wills, and made their wills obey.

'Many there were that did his picture get
135 To serve their eyes, and in it put their mind,
Like fools that in th'imagination set
The goodly objects° which abroad° they find   *sights / traveling*
Of lands and mansions, theirs in thought assigned,
And labour in more pleasures to bestow them[7]
140 Than the true gouty landlord which doth owe° them.   *own*

'So many have, that never touched his hand,
Sweetly supposed them mistress of his heart.
My woeful self, that did in freedom stand,
And was my own fee-simple,[8] not in part,
145 What with his art in youth, and youth in art,
Threw my affections in his charmèd° power,   *magical*
Reserved the stalk and gave him all my flower.

'Yet did I not, as some my equals° did,   *young girls of my rank*
Demand of him, nor being desired yielded.°   *yielded sexual favors*
150 Finding myself in honour so forbid,
With safest distance I mine honour° shielded.   *chastity*
Experience° for me many bulwarks builded   *(of "my equals")*
Of proofs new bleeding, which remained the foil[9]
Of this false jewel and his amorous spoil.

155 'But ah, who ever shunned by precedent
The destined ill she must herself assay,°   *try out*
Or forced examples 'gainst her own content
To put the by-past perils in her way?[1]
Counsel may stop a while what will not stay,°   *stop for good*
160 For when we rage,° advice is often seen,   *(with lust)*
By blunting° us, to make our wills more keen.   *repressing*

---

3. *For . . . sleep:* (Like servants) adjusted their waking and sleeping hours for the benefit of their master.
4. The manner of speech and versatile skill.
5. His faculty of persuasion. Here and in the next stanza, there are suggestions of other senses of "will." See sonnets 135–36.
6. Powers of (sexual) consent; consenting people.
7. *theirs . . . them:* imagining the "lands and mansions" their own, they try harder to use them pleasurably.
8. And had absolute control of myself (as of land in freehold).

9. *Of . . . foil:* Fresh examples of seduction, which remained the defense (or sword—picking up the military, specifically fencing, imagery of "distance," "shielded," "bulwarks," "bleeding," lines 151–53). But "foil" as the dark material in which gems are set to make them look more brilliant also works with "false jewel" in the following line, to suggest that the young man's sexual escapades made him more attractive.
1. *Or . . . way:* Or reminded herself, to counter her present inclinations, of bygone dangers. *forced:* urged.

'Nor gives it satisfaction to our blood°   *sexuality*
That we must curb it upon others' proof,°   *experience*
To be forbod° the sweets that seems so good   *forbidden*
165　For fear of harms that preach in our behoof.°   *for our benefit*
O appetite, from judgement stand aloof!
The one a palate hath that needs will taste,
Though reason weep, and cry it is thy last.

'For further I could say this man's untrue,[2]
170　And knew the patterns° of his foul beguiling;   *instances*
Heard where his plants in others' orchards° grew,   *(wombs)*
Saw how deceits were gilded in his smiling,
Knew vows were ever brokers° to defiling,   *go-betweens*
Thought characters and words merely but art,[3]
175　And bastards of his foul adulterate heart.

'And long upon these terms I held my city°   *chastity*
Till thus he gan° besiege me: "Gentle maid,   *began to*
Have of my suffering youth some feeling pity,
And be not of my holy vows afraid.
180　That's° to ye sworn to none was ever said;   *What is*
For feasts of love I have been called unto,
Till now did ne'er invite nor never woo.

'"All my offences that abroad° you see°   *in the world / learn of*
Are errors of the blood,° none of the mind.   *sexual passion*
185　Love made them not; with acture they may be,[4]
Where neither party is nor true nor kind.°   *faithful or loving*
They sought their shame that so their shame did find,
And so much less of shame in me remains
By how much of me their reproach contains.[5]

190　'"Among the many that mine eyes have seen,
Not° one whose flame my heart so much as warmèd   *There is not*
Or my affection put to th' smallest teen,°   *pain*
Or any of my leisures° ever charmèd.   *hours of leisure*
Harm have I done to them, but ne'er was harmèd;
195　Kept hearts in liveries,° but mine own was free,   *in uniform (service)*
And reigned commanding in his monarchy.

'"Look here what tributes wounded fancies° sent me   *lovers*
Of pallid pearls and rubies red as blood,
Figuring° that they their passions likewise lent me   *Showing*
200　Of grief and blushes, aptly understood
In bloodless white and the encrimsoned mood°—   *form (of rubies)*
Effects of terror and dear modesty,
Encamped in hearts, but fighting outwardly.[6]

2. I am able to say more about this man's perfidy.
3. Written and spoken words were merely instruments of skill (in seduction).
4. *with . . . be:* by a mere physical act they may be performed.

5. *By . . . contains:* The more they name me in their reproaches (thus revealing that they are unchaste and, hence, by this logic, to blame).
6. *Effects . . . outwardly:* White ("terror") and red (blushing "modesty") fighting on their faces.

'"And lo, behold, these talents° of their hair,   *riches*

205 With twisted mettle amorously impleached,[7]

I have received from many a several fair,°   *a different beauty*

Their kind acceptance weepingly beseeched,

With th'annexations° of fair gems enriched,   *additions*

And deep-brained sonnets that did amplify°   *expound; increase*

210 Each stone's dear nature, worth, and quality.

'"The diamond?—why, 'twas beautiful and hard,

Whereto his invised[8] properties did tend;

The deep-green em'rald, in whose fresh regard

Weak sights their sickly radiance do amend;[9]

215 The heaven-hued sapphire and the opal blend[1]

With objects manifold; each several° stone,   *distinct*

With wit well blazoned,° smiled or made some moan.   *described*

'"Lo, all these trophies of affections° hot,   *passions*

Of pensived° and subdued desires the tender,°   *saddened / gifts*

220 Nature hath charged me that I hoard them not,

But yield them up where I myself must render—

That is to you, my origin and ender;°   *alpha and omega; all*

For these of force must your oblations[2] be,

Since I their altar, you enpatron me.[3]

225 '"O then advance of yours that phraseless° hand   *beyond description*

Whose white weighs down the airy scale of praise.[4]

Take all these similes[5] to your own command,

Hallowed with sighs that burning° lungs did raise.   *(with love)*

What me, your minister for you, obeys,

230 Works under you,[6] and to your audit° comes   *account*

Their distract parcels° in combinèd sums.   *component parts*

'"Lo, this device was sent me from a nun,

A sister sanctified of holiest note,°   *reputation*

Which late her noble suit° in court did shun,   *attendance; suitors*

235 Whose rarest havings° made the blossoms° dote;   *qualities / young nobles*

For she was sought by spirits of richest coat,°   *coat of arms*

But kept cold distance, and did thence remove

To spend her living° in eternal love.°   *life / (of God)*

'"But O, my sweet, what labour is't to leave

240 The thing we have not, mast'ring what not strives,°   *does not resist*

Planing° the place which did no form[7] receive,   *Smoothing*

Playing patient sports in unconstrainèd gyves[8]

She that her fame so to herself contrives[9]

---

7. With misdirected courage (confused spirit?) lovingly intertwined. Many editors emend "mettle" to "metal."
8. Its unseen—referring to the diamond but also, perhaps, to the equally "beautiful and hard" young man.
9. *in . . . amend:* which, when looked at, can heal weak vision.
1. Blended: many-colored; accompanying other "objects" (line 216).
2. For these necessarily must be offerings at your altar.
3. Since I am the altar (on which they were offered), you must necessarily be the patron saint of the altar (me).

4. Whose white exceeds any measure of praise.
5. These emblematic gifts and the sonnets that explain them.
6. *What . . . under you:* Whatever pays homage to me, your agent, serves you.
7. No impression (of love, on the heart).
8. Patiently enduring shackles ("gyves") that have not been forced upon one and that can be removed (or that do not constrain). (The entire sentence is ironic.)
9. She who thus contrives for herself the reputation of disinterest in love.

The scars of battle scapeth by the flight,
245 And makes her absence valiant, not her might.[1]

'"O, pardon me, in that my boast is true!
The accident which brought me to her eye
Upon the moment° did her force° subdue,   *Immediately / resolve*
And now she would the cagèd cloister fly.
250 Religious° love put out religion's eye.   *Devoted (sexual)*
Not to be tempted would she be immured,°   *walled up*
And now, to tempt, all liberty procured.

'"How mighty then you are, O hear me tell!
The broken bosoms° that to me belong   *hearts*
255 Have emptied all their fountains in my well,
And mine I pour° your ocean all among.   *pour into*
I strong o'er them, and you o'er me being strong,
Must for your victory us all congest,°   *gather*
As compound° love to physic° your cold breast.   *medicinal / treat*

260 '"My parts° had power to charm a sacred nun,   *attributes*
Who disciplined, ay dieted in° grace,   *sustained by*
Believed her eyes when they t' assail begun,[2]
All vows and consecrations giving place.°   *yielding*
O most potential love: vow, bond, nor space
265 In thee hath neither sting, knot, nor confine,[3]
For thou art all, and all things else are thine.

'"When thou impressest,[4] what are precepts worth
Of stale example? When thou wilt inflame,
How coldly those impediments stand forth
270 Of wealth, of filial fear, law, kindred, fame.
Love's arms are° peace, 'gainst rule, 'gainst sense, 'gainst shame; *Love's power compels*
And° sweetens in the suff'ring pangs it bears   *And love*
The aloes° of all forces, shocks, and fears.   *bitterness*

'"Now all these hearts that do on mine depend,
275 Feeling it break, with bleeding groans they pine,[5]
And supplicant° their sighs to you extend   *as suppliants*
To leave° the batt'ry that you make 'gainst mine,   *cease*
Lending soft audience to my sweet design,[6]
And credent° soul to that strong-bonded oath   *trustful*
280 That shall prefer and undertake° my troth."   *advance and guarantee*

'This said, his wat'ry eyes he did dismount,°   *lower (military)*
Whose sights till then were levelled° on my face.   *aimed*
Each cheek a river running from a fount
With brinish current downward flowed apace.
285 O, how the channel° to the stream° gave grace,   *cheeks / tears*

---

1. And achieves a reputation for valor by avoiding the temptation of love, not by strongly resisting it.
2. When my attributes ("parts") began to assail her heart.
3. *potential . . . confine*: powerful love: a "vow" has no force ("sting"), a "bond" does not tie ("knot"), and "space" does not restrain ("confine").
4. When you draft someone into your (military) service; make an impression on the heart.
5. Because each sigh supposedly robbed the heart of a drop of blood.
6. Looking favorably on my intentions.

Who glazed with crystal gate the glowing roses
That flame through water which their hue encloses.[7]

'O father, what a hell of witchcraft lies
In the small orb of one particular° tear!   *single*
290 But with the inundation of the eyes
What rocky heart to water will not wear?°   *wear away*
What breast so cold that is not warmèd here?
O cleft° effect! Cold modesty, hot wrath,°   *divided / passion*
Both fire from hence and chill extincture hath.[8]

295 'For lo, his passion,° but an art of craft,   *passionate speech*
Even there resolved° my reason into tears.   *dissolved*
There my white stole of chastity I daffed,°   *took off*
Shook off my sober guards and civil° fears;   *seemly*
Appear to him as he to me appears,
300 All melting, though our drops this diff'rence bore:
His poisoned me, and mine did him restore.

'In him a plenitude of subtle matter,°   *raw material; cunning*
Applied to cautels,° all strange forms receives,[9]   *tricky devices*
Of burning blushes or of weeping water,
305 Or swooning paleness; and he takes and leaves,°   *uses this and shuns that*
In either's aptness,° as it best deceives,   *As each is appropriate*
To blush at speeches rank,° to weep at woes,   *offensive*
Or to turn white and swoon at tragic shows,

'That not a heart which in his level° came   *range (of fire)*
310 Could scape the hail of his all-hurting aim,
Showing fair nature is[1] both kind and tame,
And, veiled in them,° did win whom he would maim. *(kindness and tameness)*
Against the thing he sought he would exclaim;
When he most burned in heart-wished luxury,°   *lust*
315 He preached pure maid° and praised cold chastity   *virginal purity*

'Thus merely with the garment of a grace°   *with external appeal*
The naked and concealèd fiend he covered,
That th'unexperient° gave the tempter place,°   *inexperienced / entry*
Which like a cherubin above them hovered.°   *(as if protectively)*
320 Who, young and simple, would not be so lovered?[2]
Ay me, I fell, and yet do question make°　 *wonder*
What I should do again for such a sake.°   *person; pleasure*

'O that infected° moisture of his eye,   *tainted*
O that false fire which in his cheek so glowed,
325 O that forced thunder from° his heart did fly,   *that from*
O that sad breath his spongy lungs bestowed,°   *emitted*
O all that borrowed motion seeming owed[3]
Would yet again betray the fore-betrayed,
And new pervert a reconcilèd° maid.'   *penitent*

7. *Who . . . encloses:* The river is seen as a kind of glass covering ("crystal gate") over the cheeks ("roses"), whose color shines through the "water," like a jewel enclosed in glass. *Who:* (the stream).
8. *Both . . . hath:* Tears heat up cold modesty and extin-guish hot passion (as the following stanza elaborates).
9. *all . . . receives:* is shaped into novel forms.
1. Pretending his nature is.
2. Would not desire such a lover.
3. That emotion apparently his own.

Alternative Versions

Each of the four sonnets below exists in an alternative version. The text on top is the version as it appeared in the 1609 Quarto. *"Spes Altera"* and "On his Mistress' Beauty" derive from seventeenth-century manuscripts. The alternative versions of sonnets 138 and 144 are from *The Passionate Pilgrim* (1599).

2

When forty winters shall besiege thy brow
And dig deep trenches in thy beauty's field,
Thy youth's proud livery, so gazed on now,
Will be a tattered weed, of small worth held.
5 Then being asked where all thy beauty lies,
Where all the treasure of thy lusty days,
To say within thine own deep-sunken eyes
Were an all-eating shame and thriftless praise.
How much more praise deserved thy beauty's use
10 If thou couldst answer 'This fair child of mine
Shall sum my count, and make my old excuse',
Proving his beauty by succession thine.
    This were to be new made when thou art old,
    And see thy blood warm when thou feel'st it cold.

Spes Altera°   *Another Hope*

When forty winters shall besiege thy brow
And trench deep furrows in that lovely field,
Thy youth's fair liv'ry, so accounted° now,   *esteemed*
Shall be like rotten weeds of no worth held.
5 Then being asked where all thy beauty lies,
Where all the lustre of thy youthful days,
To say 'Within these hollow sunken eyes'
Were an all-eaten truth[1] and worthless praise.
O how much better were thy beauty's use
10 If thou couldst say 'This pretty child of mine
Saves my account[2] and makes my old excuse',
Making his beauty by succession thine.
    This were to be new born when thou art old,
    And see thy blood warm when thou feel'st it cold.

106

When in the chronicle of wasted time
I see description of the fairest wights,
And beauty making beautiful old rhyme
In praise of ladies dead and lovely knights;
5 Then in the blazon of sweet beauty's best,
Of hand, of foot, of lip, of eye, of brow,
I see their antique pen would have expressed
Even such a beauty as you master now.
So all their praises are but prophecies
10 Of this our time, all you prefiguring,
And for they looked but with divining eyes
They had not skill enough your worth to sing;

Spes Altera
1. An accurate statement that you had been gluttonous.   2. Preserves (increases) my wealth (my moral record).

For we which now behold these present days
Have eyes to wonder, but lack tongues to praise.

On his Mistress' Beauty

When in the annals of all-wasting time
I see descriptions of the fairest wights,
And beauty making beautiful old rhyme
In praise of ladies dead and lovely knights;
5 Then in the blazon of sweet beauty's best,
Of face, of hand, of lip, of eye, or brow,
I see their antique pen would have expressed
E'en such a beauty as you master now.
So all their praises were but prophecies
10 Of these our days, all you prefiguring,
And for they saw but with divining eyes
They had not skill enough your worth to sing;
 For we which now behold these present days
 Have eyes to wonder, but no tongues to praise.

138

When my love swears that she is made of truth
I do believe her though I know she lies,
That she might think me some untutored youth
Unlearnèd in the world's false subtleties.
5 Thus vainly thinking that she thinks me young,
Although she knows my days are past the best,
Simply I credit her false-speaking tongue;
On both sides thus is simple truth suppressed.
But wherefore says she not she is unjust,
10 And wherefore say not I that I am old?
O, love's best habit is in seeming trust,
And age in love loves not to have years told.
 Therefore I lie with her, and she with me,
 And in our faults by lies we flattered be.

138

When my love swears that she is made of truth
I do believe her though I know she lies,
That she might think me some untutored youth
Unskilful in the world's false forgeries.
5 Thus vainly thinking that she thinks me young,
Although I know my years be past the best,
I, smiling, credit her false-speaking tongue,
Outfacing° faults in love with love's ill rest.[1]   *Defying*
But wherefore says my love that she is young,
10 And wherefore say not I that I am old?
O, love's best habit's in a soothing tongue,
And age in love loves not to have years told.
 Therefore I'll lie with love,° and love with me   *my lover; lovingly*
 Since that our faults in love thus smothered be.

Sonnet 138
1. With the "rest" of what's bad in love; restlessness.

144

Two loves I have, of comfort and despair,
Which like two spirits do suggest me still.
The better angel is a man right fair,
The worser spirit a woman coloured ill.
5 To win me soon to hell my female evil
Tempteth my better angel from my side,
And would corrupt my saint to be a devil,
Wooing his purity with her foul pride;
And whether that my angel be turned fiend
10 Suspect I may, yet not directly tell;
But being both from me, both to each friend,
I guess one angel in another's hell.
　　Yet this shall I ne'er know, but live in doubt
　　Till my bad angel fire my good one out.

144

Two loves I have, of comfort and despair,
That like two spirits do suggest me still.
My better angel is a man right fair,
My worser spirit a woman coloured ill.
5 To win me soon to hell my female evil
Tempteth my better angel from my side,
And would corrupt my saint to be a devil,
Wooing his purity with her fair pride;
And whether that my angel be turned fiend,
10 Suspect I may, yet not directly tell;
For being both to me, both to each friend,
I guess one angel in another's hell.
　　The truth I shall not know, but live in doubt
　　Till my bad angel fire my good one out.

Various Poems

The short poems included here are occasional pieces. That is, they were written not as part of a longer work by a single author but for specific occasions. They are arranged in the order in which Shakespeare might have written them from the early 1590s until shortly before his death, if in fact he wrote them all—an extremely unlikely supposition. (See the Textual Note.) Unlike the sonnets, which collectively possess considerable coherence, these poems employ a number of meters, line lengths, rhyme schemes, and stanzaic forms. Until very recently, scholarly discussion generally focused on the relationship of the poems to Shakespeare's biography and on the question of whether Shakespeare actually wrote them.

"A Song," one of the two longer poems printed here, is noteworthy mainly as a virtuoso display of rhyming: there are usually eight pairs of rhyme words in each ten-line stanza, with the rhymes occurring as often as every three syllables and on occasion every two syllables ("Being set, lips met," line 39). The Passionate Pilgrim appeared under Shakespeare's name in 1599, apparently without his approval. Of its twenty poems, five are lifted from Shakespeare's other works and hence appear elsewhere in this volume, four are clearly by other writers, and eleven remain unattributed and are accordingly printed here. Numbers 4, 6, and 9—all sonnets—are noteworthy for their focus on the theme of Venus and Adonis, to which they may be a response. By 1599, Shakespeare's name had considerable cachet. The Passionate Pilgrim very possibly seeks to exploit that cachet, interweaving a few pieces by Shakespeare with other poems so as to produce a thematically resonant sequence that obscures the homoeroticism of some of the sonnets and in effect becomes a testament to poetic artifice.

Several of the other poems are elegies—compositions in memory of the dead, though sometimes written while the subject was still alive. The first of the two epitaphs on the usurer John Combe reveals a conventional hostility to usury. The second, however, deploys the complex, sometimes positive, metaphorical relationship between usury and breeding characteristic of the early sonnets. Combe

> did gather [wealth from usury]
> To make the poor his issue [heirs]; he, their father,
> . . . [made] record of his tilth and seed.
> (lines 3–5)

Urging marriage and a family, sonnet 3 speaks of "the tillage of thy husbandry" (line 6). And sonnet 6 argues:

> That use is not forbidden usury
> Which happies those that pay the willing loan:
> That's for thyself to breed another thee,
> Or ten times happier, be it ten for one.
> (lines 5–8)

Thus, in the sonnets, the language of usury helps clarify paternity, whereas in the second epitaph, the language of paternity helps clarify usury. In both, however, the two terms are mutually illuminating. The last line quoted from sonnet 6 is also reminiscent of the opening of the first epitaph: "Ten in the hundred here lies engraved; / A hundred to ten his soul is not saved." Both refer to the highest legal interest rate—ten in a hundred, or 10 percent—although only the sonnet converts the allusion into a positive image.

Similarly, "Verses upon the Stanley Tomb at Tong" closely parallels the language of some of Shakespeare's sonnets concerned with the destructive power of time. The "register" of the first of the two poems (1.3) and the "sky-aspiring pyramids" of the second (2.2) also appear in sonnet 123 ("pyramids built up," "registers," lines 2, 9). Closer still is the connection to sonnet 55: "Not marble nor the gilded monuments / Of princes shall outlive this powerful rhyme" (lines 1–2). Stanley's "fame is more perpetual than these stones" (1.4); "Not monumental stone preserves our fame" (2.1). Stanley's "memory," however, "shall outlive marble and defacers' hands" as well as "time's consumption" (2.3, 4, 5), just as "memory" need not worry that "war shall statues overturn" and is not dependent on "unswept stone besmeared with sluttish time" in sonnet 55 (lines 8, 5, 4). Although the guarantee of immortality seems to be Stanley's life rather than the "powerful rhyme" of the sonnet (line 2), the end is the same: Stanley "is not dead; he doth but sleep" (1.2), while in the sonnet, " 'gainst death and all oblivious enmity / Shall you pace forth" (lines 9–10). Ultimately, poetic fame in the sonnet lasts only "till the judgement that yourself arise" (on Judgment Day; line 13); analogously, "Stanley for whom this stands shall stand in heaven" (2.6). The pun on the name in this concluding line ("Stanley/stands/stand") is similar to the sign of the author's hand left in "Upon a pair of gloves that master sent to his mistress," where "the will is all" recalls Shakespeare's emphatic references to his first name in sonnets 135 and 136.

"Upon a pair of gloves" seems to reveal the poet intruding himself into a composition ostensibly from Alexander Aspinall to his (future?) wife; the "Epitaph on Himself" is strikingly impersonal. The lack of specificity may in this case be a poetic signature, however. By 1616, perhaps only Shakespeare could have written about Shakespeare without reference to his theatrical or literary career. This modesty coincides with an open threat: "cursed be he that moves my bones" (line 4). The apparently conventional warning was designed to forestall the very real danger of his body being dug up to make room for fresh corpses; in this case, it proved successful.

The second relatively long occasional poem, "The Phoenix and Turtle," is another matter. The one work in this section whose literary quality has been widely admired, it was one of several poems—others were by George Chapman, Ben Jonson, and John Marston—appended to Robert Chester's *Loves Martyr* (1601). An abstruse philosophical composition, "The Phoenix and Turtle" may represent Shakespeare's effort to refashion himself as a different kind of poet from the one who appeared two years earlier in unauthorized form in *The Passionate Pilgrim*. Literary innovation here may also have an element of poetic competition with his three fellow contributors to Chester's volume, all of whom were also dramatists. With two of them, Johnson and Marston, Shakespeare was then probably engaged in the satirical Poets' War, a battle of rival playwrights.

"The Phoenix and Turtle" is divided into three sections and composed in trochaic tetrameter, an atypical meter for Shakespeare. In the first five quatrains, which may be indebted to Chaucer's *Parliament of Fowls*, a language of elaborate circumlocution merely calls the birds together to mourn the deaths of two remarkably constant lovers—the proverbially faithful turtledove (here, male) and the legendary phoenix (here, female). Supposedly, only one phoenix was alive at any given moment, and the bird died only to be reborn from its own ashes. Neither of the two birds is named yet, however. The anthem, which constitutes the next eight stanzas, is presumably intoned by the birds. In a reversal of the procedure of the opening twenty lines, this epithalamion, or marriage hymn, turns to a deceptively simple vocabulary that conceals dense argumentation. Behind the emphasis on the paradoxical unity of two separate beings lies the mystery of the Christian Trinity as understood in Scholastic theology—medieval Europe's assimilation of the recently translated writings of Aristotle, which began in the twelfth century. The ideal love of the two birds ultimately defies the efforts at comprehension by Reason, which cannot understand how

> . . . love in twain
> Had the essence but in one,
> Two distincts, division none,

or how

> . . . the self was not the same.
> Single nature's double name
> Neither two nor one was called.
>   (lines 25–27, 38–40)

In other words, the rationalist vocabulary of this section ultimately undermines its own legitimacy. Perhaps the lines vindicate the more mystical understanding of ideal love that Renaissance thought derived from Plato, whose doctrines Aristotle had sought to answer. In any case, the heterosexual love praised in this self-contradictory fashion parallels the celebration of homoerotic love in the sonnets to the young man: "Let me confess that we two must be twain / Although our undivided loves are one" (36.1–2). Following the anthem, Reason delivers the concluding section of the poem, the *threnos*, or mourning song, in which Shakespeare returns to the central genre of his occasional poetry—the elegy. Retaining the straightforwardly abstract diction of the anthem and the trochaic-tetrameter meter of both of the first two parts but abandoning quatrains (rhyming *abba*) for tercets (rhyming *aaa*), the last five stanzas emphasize the finality of the death of the couple, which apparently excludes both rebirth (even on the part of the immortal phoenix) and "posterity"—the latter as a result of a "married chastity" (lines 59, 61) that has the same (lack of) consequences as the love for the young man in the sonnets. The result is the diminution of life: the only authentic or perhaps ideal "truth and beauty buried be" (line 64).

"The Phoenix and Turtle" raises all sorts of interpretive problems. Since the *threnos* is spoken by Reason, who has been defeated by the phoenix and turtle, should the concluding stanzas be seen not as authorial statement but as the position of a fallible character who lets fly a crow of triumph at the couple's death? Moreover, the concluding summons of all "that are either true or fair" (line 66) sits oddly with the immediately preceding insistence that genuine truth and beauty no longer exist: perhaps now they exist only separately. And why does Shakespeare, through Reason, insist on the lack of offspring and, apparently rejecting a central feature of the legend, on the mortality of the phoenix? This last question is only emphasized by the occasion of publication. All of the poems with which "The Phoenix and Turtle" were printed are on the subject of the phoenix and turtle, and all but Shakespeare's deny the finality of the phoenix's death. "The Phoenix and Turtle" alone forgoes the possibility of exploiting the standard treatment of the phoenix as the intersection of the temporal and the timeless.

The title page of the volume advertises Chester's long poem as "allegorically shadowing the truth of Love, in the constant Fate of the Phoenix and Turtle." This claim, the abstract language of "The Phoenix and Turtle," and the avowed purpose of the volume—to honor Sir John Salusbury of Lleweni, knighted by the Queen in June 1601—have all encouraged a search in Shakespeare's poem for allegorical meaning (beyond the praise of ideal human union through a tale of two birds). The marriage of phoenix and turtle has been seen as the joining of the literal and the metaphorical in poetry, so that the poem self-referentially becomes a metaphor for metaphor itself. Historical readings have found candidates for the parts of the turtle and the phoenix in Salusbury and his wife, as well as in the Earl of Essex, Salusbury, or the English people in relation to Queen Elizabeth. Although none of these theories is convincing, in part because of a failure to explain what real "tragic scene" is being allegorically represented by the couple's deaths (line 52), all testify to the poem's ability to hint at hidden meanings. Perhaps it is safer to explain the poem's suggestiveness simply by saying that "The Phoenix and Turtle" labors to construct an ideal image of love while simultaneously circumscribing the real utility of that ideal. Marriage and funeral, celebration and dirge, ideal affirmation and pragmatic denial, the poem is a characteristically Shakespearean venture in having it both ways.

WALTER COHEN

TEXTUAL NOTE

"A Song" survives in two related manuscript collections of poetry by different authors, dating from 1637 and 1639. It is untitled in both manuscripts, unattributed in the later collection, and ascribed to Shakespeare in the earlier one. The text printed here is based on the earlier version, although the choice between the two is not very important. Both manuscripts of "A Song" derive from a scribal transcript of the writer's original version, but it is impossible to determine how many intermediate copies there may have been. The poem was first assigned in print to Shakespeare in 1985, a claim that has aroused considerable skepticism. The name in the 1637 manuscript and the independent analysis of the poem's language carried out by statisticians make attribution to Shakespeare possible (c. 1592–95) though unlikely. It probably dates from 1613–30.

"Upon a pair of gloves" is found in a manuscript compiled around 1629 by Sir Francis Fane of Bulbeck (1611–80). The poem supposedly accompanied gloves presented by Alexander Aspinall, a Stratford schoolmaster, to his second wife, whom he married in 1594. The poem's second line, "The will is all," could refer to Shakespeare or to William Shaw, a glover who was the son of Aspinall's second wife. Hence, the attribution to Shakespeare is conjectural.

The eleven poems from *The Passionate Pilgrim* (1599) printed here are of uncertain authorship, although probably not by Shakespeare. This collection of twenty lyrics published under Shakespeare's name includes five pieces that are clearly his. Three come from *Love's Labour's Lost*; the other two are sonnets 138 and 144, and are included in this edition as Alternative Versions at the end of the section on the sonnets and "A Lover's Complaint." Four poems are apparently by other writers—Richard Barnfield, Bartholomew Griffin, and Christopher Marlowe. "The Phoenix and Turtle" was printed in 1601, untitled and ascribed to Shakespeare, among the "Poeticall Essaies" that follow Robert Chester's *Loves Martyr: or Rosalins Complaint*. The ascription is widely accepted.

The remaining poems are about specific people, and in each instance, as in "Upon a pair of gloves," there is a plausible London or Stratford connection between Shakespeare and the person(s) in question. The "Verses upon the Stanley Tomb at Tong," perhaps by Shakespeare (c. 1600–03) even though there are possible chronological difficulties, are first attributed to him in a manuscript from around 1630. It is not clear whether the lines constitute one poem or two, whether they are addressed to one member of the Stanley family or two, and which member or members are referred to. If they are intended as a single poem, it is not certain which group of six lines should come first. "On Ben Jonson" is first attributed to Shakespeare, improbably, in a manuscript from roughly 1650. "An Epitaph on Elias James," published in the 1633 edition of John Stow's *Survey of London*, is more likely to be Shakespeare's. James died in 1610. "An extemporary epitaph on John Combe," who died in 1614, employs a joke about usurers that became popular starting in 1608. The earliest manuscripts do not assign the poem to Shakespeare. There is an ambiguous attribution to Shakespeare in 1634 and an unambiguous ascription of the last one and a half lines in a manuscript from around 1650. On balance, Shakespeare probably did not write the poem. "Another Epitaph on John Combe" is first attributed to Shakespeare in the same manuscript (c. 1650); the case for Shakespearean authorship of this poem is stronger, however. "Upon the King" was printed, unattributed, beneath an engraving of King James that was the frontispiece to the 1616 edition of the King's *Works*. The earliest ascription is found in a manuscript of about 1633–34, where the poem is entitled "Shakespeare on the King." Again, late attribution following earlier lack of attribution casts doubt on Shakespearean authorship. "Epitaph on Himself" appears on Shakespeare's gravestone in Stratford. The earliest other attribution occurs in a manuscript compiled by Sir Francis Fane, about 1655–56. The lines may be Shakespearean.

SELECTED BIBLIOGRAPHY

Adams, Joseph Quincy. "Shakespeare as a Writer of Epitaphs." *The Manly Anniversary Studies in Language and Literature*. 1923; repr.: Freeport, N.Y.: Books for Libraries Press, 1968. 78–89. Defends Shakespeare's authorship.

Bednarz, James P. "*The Passionate Pilgrim* and 'The Phoenix and Turtle.'" *The Cambridge Companion to Shakespeare's Poetry*. Ed. Patrick Cheney. New York: Cambridge University Press, 2007. 108–24. Locates these works in the context of late Elizabethan poetic publication and literary and theatrical competition.

Cunningham, V. J. "'Essence' and 'The Phoenix and Turtle.'" *English Literary History* 19 (1952): 265–76. Discusses the theological language of the poem.

Hobday, C. H. "Shakespeare's Venus and Adonis Sonnets." *Shakespeare Survey* 26 (1973): 103–09. Discussion of the poems on this topic in *The Passionate Pilgrim*.

Honigmann, E. A. J. *Shakespeare: The Lost Years*. Totowa, N.J.: Barnes & Noble, 1985. 77–83, 90–113. "The Phoenix and Turtle" as a celebration of Salusbury's marriage in 1586; briefer comments on Shakespeare's elegies.

Hyland, Peter. *An Introduction to Shakespeare's Poems*. Houndmills, Basingstoke: Palgrave Macmillan, 2002. 194–213. Survey of Shakespeare's occasional poetry, with special attention paid to "The Phoenix and Turtle."

Hume, Anthea. "*Love's Martyr*, 'The Phoenix and Turtle,' and the Aftermath of the Essex Rebellion." *Review of English Studies* n.s., 40 (1989): 43–71. Reads the poem as an allegory of Essex's relationship to Elizabeth.

Kay, Dennis. *William Shakespeare: Sonnets and Poems*. New York: Twayne, 1998. 77–95. Surveys the occasional poems.

Roberts, Sasha. *Reading Shakespeare's Poems in Early Modern England*. Houndmills, Basingstoke: Palgrave Macmillan, 2003. 154–58, 177–90. *The Passionate Pilgrim*, both in print form and in manuscript transcription of individual poems, seen as suppressing the homoeroticism of Shakespeare's sonnets, contributing to misogynistic literature, and celebrating erotic poetic art. Emphasis on the various interpretive contexts generated by different collections.

Underwood, Richard Allan. *Shakespeare's "The Phoenix and Turtle": A Survey of Scholarship*. Salzburg Studies in English Literature 15. Salzburg: Institut für Englische Sprache und Literatur, Universität Salzburg, 1974. Overview of previous criticism of the poem.

Various Poems

A Song[1]

1

Shall I die? Shall I fly
Lovers' baits and deceits,
  sorrow breeding?
Shall I tend?° Shall I send?   *wait passively*
5   Shall I sue, and not rue
  my proceeding?[2]
In all duty her beauty
Binds me her servant for ever.
If she scorn, I mourn,
10   I retire to despair, joining° never.   *(sexually; militarily)*

2

Yet I must vent my lust
And explain inward pain
  by my love conceiving.[3]
If she smiles, she exiles
15   All my moan; if she frown,
  all my hopes deceiving—
Suspicious doubt,° O keep out,   *fear (of rejection)*
For thou art my tormentor.
Fie away, pack away;
20   I will love, for hope bids me venture.

3

'Twere abuse to accuse
My fair love, ere I prove°   *test*
  her affection.
Therefore try! Her reply
25   Gives thee joy—or annoy,
  or affliction.[4]
Yet howe'er, I will bear
Her pleasure with patience, for beauty
Sure will not seem to blot
30   Her deserts, wronging him doth her duty.[5]

4

In a dream it did seem—
But alas, dreams do pass
  as do shadows—
I did walk, I did talk
35   With my love, with my dove,

---

1. This poem may or may not have been set to music.
2. Both "sue" (line 5) and "proceeding" refer to lawsuits.
3. Yet I must give expression to my lust by explaining (in poetry) the pain caused by my love. "Conceiving" may also refer to conceiving a child (line 13).

4. "Affliction" may also suggest a sexually transmitted disease.
5. *for beauty . . . duty:* for true beauty will not allow her reputation to appear tarnished by wronging him who serves her faithfully.

through fair meadows.
Still° we passed till at last   *Continually*
We sat to repose us for pleasure.
Being set, lips met,
40 Arms twined, and did bind my heart's treasure.

5

Gentle wind sport did find
Wantonly° to make fly   *Capriciously*
     her gold tresses.
As they shook I did look,
45 But her fair° did impair   *beauty*
     all my senses.
As amazed, I gazed
On more than a mortal complexion.
You that love can prove[6]
50 Such force in beauty's inflection.°   *bending*

6

Next° her hair, forehead fair,   *Next to*
Smooth and high; neat doth lie
     without wrinkle,
Her fair brows;° under those,   *forehead*
55 Star-like eyes win love's prize
     when they twinkle.
In her cheeks who° seeks   *whoever*
Shall find there displayed beauty's banner.°   *(a blush)*
     O admiring desiring
60 Breeds, as I look still upon her.

7

Thin lips red, fancy's[7] fed
With all sweets when he meets,
     and is granted
There to trade,[8] and is made
65 Happy, sure, to endure
     still undaunted.
Pretty chin doth win
Of all their culled commendations;[9]
     Fairest neck, no speck;
70 All her parts merit high admirations.

8

Pretty bare, past compare,
Parts those plots which besots
     still asunder.[1]
It is meet naught but sweet
75 Should come near that so rare
     'tis a wonder.[2]
No mis-shape, no scape°   *transgression*

---

6. You who are in love are able to test.
7. Affection is; imagination is.
8. *granted / There to trade*: allowed to kiss there.
9. Wins from all people their specially chosen praises.
1. *Pretty . . . asunder*: Incomparably pretty "bare" skin

and breasts (exposed above a low neckline) separate the
nipples ("plots") that, always separated, (always) cause
infatuation.
2. It is proper that nothing but good should come near
that which is so wonderfully valuable.

Inferior to nature's perfection;
    No blot, no spot:
80 She's beauty's queen in election.

9

Whilst I dreamt, I exempt
From all care, seemed to share
    pleasure's plenty;
But awake, care take—
85 For I find to my mind
    pleasures scanty.
Therefore I will try
To compass° my heart's chief contenting.   accomplish
To delay, some say,
90 In such a case causeth repenting.

'Upon a pair of gloves that master sent to his mistress'

The gift is small,
    The will is all:[3]
Alexander Aspinall[4]

Poems from *The Passionate Pilgrim*

4

Sweet Cytherea,[5] sitting by a brook
With young Adonis, lovely, fresh, and green,°   young; inexperienced
Did court the lad with many a lovely° look,   amorous
Such looks as none could look but beauty's queen.
5   She told him stories to delight his ear,
She showed him favours to allure his eye;
To win his heart she touched him here and there—
Touches so soft still° conquer chastity.   always
But whether unripe years did want conceit,°   lack understanding
10 Or he refused to take her figured° proffer,   implied
The tender nibbler would not touch the bait,
But smile and jest at every gentle offer.
    Then fell she on her back, fair queen and toward:°   ready
    He rose and ran away—ah, fool too froward!°   obstinate

6

Scarce had the sun dried up the dewy morn,
And scarce the herd gone to the hedge for shade,
When Cytherea, all in love forlorn,
A longing tarriance° for Adonis made   waiting
5   Under an osier° growing by a brook,   a willow
A brook where Adon used to cool his spleen.°   hot temper
Hot was the day, she hotter, that did look
For his approach that often there had been.
Anon he comes and throws his mantle by,

---

3. With a characteristic pun on the poet's name: the goodwill behind the gift is all-encompassing; it's the thought that counts.
4. Stratford schoolmaster from 1582 to 1624.

5. Sonnets 4, 6, and 9 all treat the unsuccessful wooing of the beautiful but unresponsive young man Adonis by Venus ("Cytherea"), the goddess of love.

10   And stood stark naked on the brook's green brim.
     The sun looked on the world with glorious eye,
     Yet not so wistly° as this queen on him.   *eagerly; longingly*
         He, spying her, bounced in whereas he stood.[5]
     'O Jove,' quoth she, 'why was not I a flood?'°   *body of water*

                                        7

     Fair is my love, but not so fair as fickle,
     Mild as a dove, but neither true nor trusty,°   *trustworthy*
     Brighter than glass, and yet, as glass is, brittle;
     Softer than wax, and yet as iron rusty;°   *corrupt (morally)*
5   A lily pale, with damask° dye to grace her,   *red*
         None fairer, nor none falser to deface her.[7]

     Her lips to mine how often hath she joined,
     Between each kiss her oaths of true love swearing.
     How many tales to please me hath she coined°   *invented*
10   Dreading my love, the loss whereof still fearing.[8]
         Yet in the midst of all her pure protestings
         Her faith, her oaths, her tears, and all were jestings.

     She burnt with love as straw with fire flameth,
     She burnt out love as soon as straw out burneth.
15   She framed° the love, and yet she foiled° the framing,   *built / ruined*
     She bade love last, and yet she fell a-turning.°   *(to another lover)*
         Was this a lover or a lecher whether,°   *which of the two*
         Bad in the best, though excellent in neither?[9]

                                        9

     Fair was the morn when the fair queen of love,°   *Venus*
     [   ][1]
     Paler for sorrow than her milk-white dove,
     For Adon's sake, a youngster proud and wild,
5   Her stand she takes upon a steep-up hill.
     Anon° Adonis comes with horn and hounds.   *Soon*
     She, seely° queen, with more than love's good will   *foolish*
     Forbade the boy he should not pass those grounds.°   *cross those valleys*
     'Once,' quoth she, 'did I see a fair sweet youth
10   Here in these brakes° deep-wounded with° a boar,   *thickets / by*
     Deep in the thigh, a spectacle of ruth.°   *pity*
     See in my thigh,' quoth she, 'here was the sore.
         She showèd hers; he saw more wounds than one °   *(sexual)*
         And blushing fled, and left her all alone.

                                        10

     Sweet rose, fair flower, untimely plucked, soon faded—
     Plucked in the bud and faded in the spring;
     Bright orient pearl, alack, too timely shaded;[2]
     Fair creature, killed too soon by death's sharp sting,

---

6. Jumped in from where he stood.
7. Nor is anyone more false, to her discredit; with a possible reference to cosmetics in "falser" and "deface."
8. Continually being anxious about losing my love.
9. Bad in romance, but not outstanding merely as a sex-

ual partner either.
1. A line is missing here in the original edition.
2. Darkened too soon. "Orient" pearls were valued as more lustrous than their European counterparts.

5   Like a green plum that hangs upon a tree
       And falls through wind before the fall should be.

       I weep for thee, and yet no cause I have,
       For why:° thou left'st me nothing in thy will,   *Because*
       And yet thou left'st me more than I did crave,
10   For why: I cravèd nothing of thee still.[3]
           O yes, dear friend, I pardon crave of thee:[4]
           Thy discontent° thou didst bequeath to me.   *unhappiness*

12

       Crabbèd° age and youth cannot live together: *Ill-tempered*
       Youth is full of pleasance, age is full of care;
       Youth like summer morn, age like winter weather;
       Youth like summer brave,° age like winter bare.   *well dressed*
5   Youth is full of sport, age's breath is short.
       Youth is nimble, age is lame,
       Youth is hot and bold, age is weak and cold.
       Youth is wild and age is tame.
           Age, I do abhor thee; youth, I do adore thee.
10   O my love, my love is young.
           Age, I do defy thee. O sweet shepherd, hie thee,°   *hurry up*
           For methinks thou stay'st° too long.   *delay*

13

       Beauty is but a vain and doubtful good,
       A shining gloss that fadeth suddenly,
       A flower that dies when first it 'gins to bud,
       A brittle glass that's broken presently.°   *immediately*
5   A doubtful good, a gloss, a glass, a flower,
           Lost, faded, broken, dead within an hour.
       And as goods lost are seld° or never found,   *seldom*
       As faded gloss no rubbing will refresh,
       As flowers dead lie withered on the ground,
10   As broken glass no cement can redress,°   *repair*
           So beauty blemished once, for ever lost,
           In spite of physic,° painting, pain,° and cost.   *medicine / labor*

14

       Good night, good rest—ah, neither be my share.
       She bade good night that kept my rest away,
       And daffed° me to a cabin hanged° with care   *dismissed / adorned*
       To descant on the doubts° of my decay.   *expand upon the fears*
5   'Farewell,' quoth she, 'and come again tomorrow.'
       Fare well I could not, for I supped with sorrow.

       Yet at my parting sweetly did she smile,
       In scorn or friendship nill I conster whether.[5]
       'Tmay be she joyed to jest at my exile

3. "Nothing" (lines 8, 10) evokes the tangibility of absence caused by death. But "nothing" also may denote female sexual organs. In line 8, it would go with "will" (testament; lust) to suggest that the dead woman's desire (formerly) made her sexually available to the speaker. In line 10, the speaker would be saying that he always ("still") desired her.
4. This line seems to contradict the previous one by claiming that the speaker did, after all, "crave" something—"pardon."
5. I will not guess which of the two.

10　'Tmay be, again to make me wander thither.
　　　'Wander'—a word for shadows like myself,
　　　As take the pain but cannot pluck the pelf.°　　　　　　　　　　*reward*

　　Lord, how mine eyes throw gazes to the east!
　　My heart doth charge the watch, the morning rise[6]
15　Doth cite° each moving° sense from idle rest,　　　　　*summon / living*
　　Not daring trust the office of mine eyes.
　　　While Philomela° sings I sit and mark,°　　　　*the nightingale / listen*
　　　And wish her lays were tunèd like the lark.[7]

　　For she doth welcome daylight with her dite,°　　　　　　　　*song*
20　And daylight drives away dark dreaming night.
　　The night so packed,° I post° unto my pretty;　　　　　*sent off / hasten*
　　Heart hath his hope, and eyes their wishèd sight,
　　　Sorrow changed to solace, and solace mixed with sorrow,
　　　Forwhy° she sighed and bade me come tomorrow.　　　　　　*Because*

25　Were I with her, the night would post too soon,
　　But now are minutes added to the hours.
　　To spite me now each minute seems a moon,
　　　Yet not for me, shine sun[8] to succour flowers!
　　　Pack night, peep day; good day, of night now borrow;
30　　Short night tonight, and length thyself tomorrow.[9]

Sonnets
to Sundry Notes of Music

15

　　It was a lording's° daughter, the fairest one of three,　　　　　*lord's*
　　That likèd of her master° as well as well might be.　　　　　　*tutor*
　　Till looking on an Englishman, the fairest that eye could see,
　　　Her fancy fell a-turning.°　　　　　　　　　　　*(to another lover)*

5　Long was the combat doubtful° that love with love did fight:　　*uncertain*
　　To leave the master loveless, or kill the gallant knight.
　　To put in practice either, alas, it was a spite°　　　　*would be a vexation*
　　　Unto the seely° damsel.　　　　　　　　　　　　*helpless*
　　But one must be refusèd, more mickle° was the pain　　　　*great*
10　That nothing could be usèd° to turn them both to gain.　　　*done*
　　For of the two the trusty knight was wounded with disdain—
　　　Alas, she could not help it.

　　Thus art° with arms contending was victor of the day,　　　*learning*
　　Which by a gift of learning did bear the maid away.
15　Then lullaby, the learned man hath got the lady gay;
　　　For now my song is ended.

---

6. My heart blames those on watch, the break of day.
Or, perhaps: My heart orders the "eyes" (line 13) to
watch for morning; my heart urges the night watch to
hurry or proclaim morning.
7. And wish her (nighttime) songs were the songs of
the (morning) lark.
8. Let the sun shine, not for my sake, but.
9. The speaker is asking night to shorten now and to
lengthen tomorrow, when he's with his mistress.

17

My flocks feed not, my ewes breed not,
  My rams speed° not, all is amiss.   *thrive*
Love is dying, faith's defying,[1]
  Heart's denying causer of this.
5 All my merry jigs are quite forgot,
  All my lady's love is lost, God wot.°   *knows*
Where her faith was firmly fixed in love,
There a nay is placed without remove.°   *immovably*
  One seely cross° wrought all my loss—   *foolish mishap*
10 O frowning fortune, cursèd fickle dame!
  For now I see inconstancy
  More in women than in men remain.

In black mourn I, all fears scorn I,
  Love hath forlorn me, living in thrall.°   *enslaved (to love)*
15 Heart is bleeding, all help needing—
  O cruel speeding,° freighted with gall.   *fortune*
My shepherd's pipe can sound no deal,°   *not at all*
My wether's[2] bell rings doleful knell,
My curtal dog[3] that wont to° have played   *formerly liked to*
20 Plays not at all, but seems afraid,
  With sighs so deep procures to weep
In howling wise° to see my doleful plight.   *fashion*
  How sighs resound through heartless ground,
  Like a thousand vanquished men in bloody fight!

25 Clear wells spring not, sweet birds sing not,
  Green plants bring not forth their dye.
Herd stands weeping, flocks all sleeping,
  Nymphs back peeping fearfully.
All our pleasure known to us poor swains,
30 All our merry meetings on the plains,
All our evening sport from us is fled,
All our love is lost, for love is dead.
  Farewell, sweet lass, thy like ne'er was
For as sweet content, the cause of all my moan.
35 Poor Corydon[4] must live alone,
  Other help for him I see that there is none.

18

Whenas° thine eye hath chose the dame   *When*
And stalled° the deer that thou shouldst strike,   *entrapped*
Let reason rule things worthy blame
As well as fancy, partial might.[5]
5 Take counsel of some wiser head,
  Neither too young nor yet unwed,
And when thou com'st thy tale to tell,
Smooth not thy tongue with filèd° talk   *rehearsed; scheming*

---

1. Faith's rejection; "de-fying" means de-faithing.
2. A male sheep castrated while still immature. The "bell-wether" is the lead sheep of the flock.
3. Dog with a cut tail.
4. Conventional name for a shepherd (from one of

Virgil's *Eclogues*, which were pastoral poems).
5. Let reason as well as desire (fancy), which is biased and by itself inadequate, govern your potentially blameworthy love affairs.

Lest she some subtle practice° smell: *deception*
10 A cripple soon can find a halt.⁵
    But plainly say thou lov'st her well,
    And set her person forth to sale,⁷

And to her will° frame all thy ways.°   *desire / habits*
Spare not to spend, and chiefly there
15 Where thy desert may merit praise
By ringing in thy lady's ear.⁸
    The strongest castle, tower, and town,
    The golden bullet° beats it down.   *words; money*

Serve always with assurèd trust,°   *reliability*
20 And in thy suit be humble-true;
Unless thy lady prove unjust,°   *unfaithful*
Press never thou to choose anew.⁹
    When time° shall serve, be thou not slack   *occasion*
    To proffer, though she put thee back.¹

25 What though° her frowning brows be bent,   *Although*
Her cloudy looks will calm ere night,
And then too late she will repent
That thus dissembled her delight,²
    And twice desire,° ere it be day,   *(sexual gratification)*
30   That which with scorn she put away.°   *rejected*

What though she strive to try her strength,
And ban,° and brawl,° and say thee nay,   *curse / shout*
Her feeble force will yield at length
When craft° hath taught her thus to say: *craftiness*
35   'Had women been so strong as men,
    In faith you had not had it then.'

The wiles and guiles that women work,°   *employ*
Dissembled with an outward show,
The tricks and toys° that in them lurk   *whims*
40 The cock that treads them³ shall not know.
    Have you not heard it said full oft
    A woman's nay doth stand for nought?⁴

Think women still to strive with men,
To sin and never for to saint.⁵
45 There is no heaven; be holy then
When time with age shall them attaint.⁶
    Were kisses all the joys in bed,
    One woman would another wed.

---

6. Those practiced in deceit can easily sense deception. *find a halt*: detect a limp.
7. Like a salesman, start praising her qualities. One of the manuscript versions of this poem has "& set thy body forth to sell."
8. Don't be stingy about spending your money in ways that will draw your lady's attention to your merit.
9. Don't make attempts to choose someone else (?)
1. Even if she resists you. The "proffer," at first an offer, becomes outright rape here and in the following stanzas.
2. She who in this way concealed her desire.
3. The man who copulates with them.
4. Nothing; (sexual) naughtiness; a vulva.
5. Expect women always to engage (compete) with men in sin but not in saintliness, or chastity.
6. There is no thought of heaven (purity) in women seeking sexual pleasure. Let them be holy when they're old and unattractive.

But soft, enough—too much, I fear,
50 Lest that my mistress hear my song
She will not stick to round me on th'ear[7]
To teach my tongue to be so long.
    Yet will she blush (here be it said)
    To hear her secrets so bewrayed.°   revealed

The Phoenix and Turtle[8]

Let the bird of loudest lay[9]
On the sole Arabian tree[1]
Herald sad and trumpet be,
To whose sound chaste wings° obey.   virtuous birds

5 But thou shrieking harbinger,°   the screech owl
Foul precurrer of the fiend,[2]
Augur of the fever's end°—   Prophet of death or cure
To this troupe[3] come thou not near.

From this session° interdict°   (of a court) / forbid
10 Every fowl of tyrant wing°   bird of prey
Save the eagle, feathered king.
Keep the obsequy° so strict.   funeral rite

Let the priest in surplice white[4]
That defunctive music can,[5]
15 Be the death-divining swan,
Lest the requiem lack his right.°   its due; its rite

And thou treble-dated° crow,   long-lived
That thy sable gender mak'st
With the breath thou giv'st and tak'st,[6]
20 'Mongst our mourners shalt thou go.

Here the anthem doth commence:
Love and constancy is dead,
Phoenix and the turtle fled
In a mutual flame from hence.

25 So they loved as° love in twain   that
Had the essence but in one,
Two distincts, division none.
Number there in love was slain.[7]

7. She won't refrain from scolding me (boxing me) on the ear.
8. *Phoenix*: a legendary, self-resurrecting bird believed to live in cycles of several centuries, dying in flames and reborn from its own ashes—here, regarded as female. *Turtle*: turtledove, symbol of constancy—here, regarded as male.
9. Song. It is unclear which bird this refers to—possibly the phoenix, unless one reads "Death is now the phoenix' nest" (line 56) not as part of a cycle but as a final resting place. Alternately, it is some other bird (the rooster?) known for its loud voice.
1. Supposedly, a unique tree on which sits the phoenix, which is similarly unique: only one exists at any given time.
2. Precursor of the devil: screech owls were thought to

foretell death.
3. The troupe of mourning birds called forth by "the bird of loudest lay" (line 1).
4. The swan. A "surplice" is a loose clerical outer garment.
5. That is skilled in funereal music. Swans were thought to sing beautifully just before (their own) death (hence the phrase "swan song").
6. *That . . . tak'st*: crows were believed to conceive by billing (kissing)—hence, "With the breath." *sable gender*: black offspring.
7. The stanza toys with the commonplace paradox of lovers' simultaneous unity and separateness, ending with the hyperbolic claim that being neither one nor two, the love of the phoenix and the turtle killed the very notion of "number" (line 28).

	Hearts remote° yet not asunder,	*separate*
30	Distance and no space was seen	
	'Twixt this turtle and his queen.	
	But in them it were a wonder.[8]	

	So° between them love did shine	*So much*
	That the turtle saw his right°	*due; possession; nature*
35	Flaming in the Phoenix' sight.°	*eyesight; appearance*
	Either was the other's mine.°	*self; wealth*

Property was thus appalled
That the self was not the same.[9]
Single nature's double name[1]
40 Neither two nor one was called.

	Reason, in itself confounded,°	*thoroughly destroyed*
	Saw division° grow together	*things divided*
	To themselves, yet either neither,[2]	
	Simple were so well compounded[3]	

	That it cried 'How true° a twain	*faithful; truly*
45	Seemeth this concordant one!	
	Love hath reason, reason none,	
	If what parts can so remain.'[4]	

	Whereupon it made this threne[5]	
50	To the phoenix and the dove,	
	Co-supremes° and stars of love,	*Joint rulers*
	As chorus to their tragic scene.	

Threnos

	Beauty, truth,° and rarity,	*fidelity*
	Grace in all simplicity,	
55	Here enclosed in cinders lie.	

Death is now the phoenix' nest,[6]
And the turtle's loyal breast
To eternity doth rest.[7]

	Leaving no posterity	
60	'Twas not their infirmity,°	*sterility*
	It was married chastity.	

Truth may seem but cannot be,
Beauty brag, but 'tis not she.[8]
Truth and beauty buried be.

---

8. It would have seemed extraordinary in any creatures but them.
9. The notion of an essential self was thus weakened by the fact that the self was not identical to itself.
1. An indivisible essence with two separate names.
2. Saw separate entities paradoxically become one, but each one was neither single nor united.
3. Single elements were so perfectly combined (appearing to remain "simple" rather than "compounded").
4. Love represents a higher reason than reason itself

because of this embodiment of the paradox of unity of separate elements.
5. Reason made this threnody (a mourning song or epitaph).
6. The phoenix's nest, ordinarily a site of regeneration, is finally a place of death; alternatively, the regenerative qualities of the phoenix's nest will overcome death.
7. Rests eternally; endures forever.
8. Any appearances of fidelity or beauty will only be illusions.

65 To this urn let those repair°   *go*
    That are either true or fair.
    For these dead birds sigh a prayer.

Verses upon the Stanley Tomb[9] at Tong

Written upon the east end of the tomb

Ask who lies here, but do not weep.
He is not dead; he doth but sleep.
This stony register° is for his bones;   *record*
His fame is more perpetual than these stones,
5 And his own goodness, with himself being gone,
Shall live when earthly monument is none.

Written upon the west end thereof

Not monumental stone preserves our fame,
Nor sky-aspiring pyramids[1] our name.
The memory of him for whom this stands
Shall outlive marble and defacers' hands.
5 When all to time's consumption shall be given,
Stanley for whom this stands shall stand in heaven.

On Ben Jonson[2]

Master Ben Jonson and master William Shakespeare being merry
at a tavern, Master Jonson having begun this for his epitaph:

Here lies Ben Jonson
That was once one,°   *alive*

he gives it to Master Shakespeare to make up who presently
writes:

Who while he lived was a slow thing,[3]
And now, being dead, is nothing.

An Epitaph on Elias James[4]

When God was pleased, the world unwilling yet,[5]
Elias James to nature paid his debt,
And here reposeth. As he lived, he died,
The saying strongly in him verified:
5 'Such life, such death'.° Then, a known truth to tell,   *One dies as one lives*
He lived a godly life, and died as well.

9. Shakespeare had various connections to the Stanley family. It is unclear whether these verses, still visible on the tombstone, memorialize Sir Edward Stanley, Sir Thomas Stanley, or both (with one verse devoted to each).
1. Grand buildings constructed by more modern means. Possibly referring to structures erected in Rome in 1586 or in London in 1603 (for James's coronation), but retaining from their association with Egypt a sense of almost timeless antiquity.
2. One of the best-known of Shakespeare's fellow playwrights (1572–1637).
3. Jonson was a notoriously slow writer.
4. A London brewer of Shakespeare's acquaintance who gave 10 pounds to the parish poor when he died. His tomb was destroyed in the Great Fire of London (1666).
5. Though the world was still unwilling.

An extemporary epitaph on John Combe,[6] a noted usurer

Ten in the hundred[7] here lies engraved;
A hundred to ten° his soul is not saved.   (*odds*)
If anyone ask who lies in this tomb,
'O ho!' quoth the devil, ''tis my John-a-Combe.'

Another Epitaph on John Combe

He being dead, and making the poor his heirs.[8] William
Shakespeare after writes this for his epitaph:

Howe'er he livèd judge not,
John Combe shall never be forgot
While poor hath memory, for he did gather[9]
To make the poor his issue;° he, their father,   *offspring; heirs*
5   As record of his tilth and seed[1]
Did crown him° in his latter deed.   *himself*

Upon the King
At the foot of the effigy of King James I, before his *Works*
(1616)[2]

Crowns have their compass:° length of days, their date;°   *boundaries / limit*
Triumphs, their tombs; felicity, her fate.
Of more than earth can earth make none partaker,[3]
But knowledge makes the king most like his maker.

Epitaph on Himself[4]

Good friend, for Jesus' sake forbear
To dig the dust enclosèd here.
Blessed be the man that spares these stones,
And cursed be he that moves my bones.

---

6. Combe, a wealthy Stratford bachelor, left Shakespeare
5 pounds—a fairly generous sum—in his will.
7. A slang term for "usurer," suggesting one who lends
money at 10-percent interest.
8. Combe left generous bequests to the poor of Stratford
in his will, including a provision that 100 pounds continue to be lent out, with the interest given as alms.

9. Accumulate wealth (through usury).
1. Tillage and planting (offspring).
2. These lines appear below a picture of James that was
the frontispiece to the 1616 edition of his works.
3. No earthly power (not even a King) has power over the
afterlife.
4. Carved above Shakespeare's grave in Stratford.

APPENDICES

APPENDICES

Early Modern Map Culture

In the early modern period, maps were often considered rare and precious objects, and seeing a map could be an important and life-changing event. This was so for Richard Hakluyt, whose book *The Principal Navigations, Voiages, Traffiques and Discoveries of the English Nation* (1598–1600) was the first major collection of narratives describing England's overseas trading ventures. Hakluyt tells how, as a boy still at school in London, he visited his uncle's law chambers and saw a book of cosmography lying open there. Perceiving his nephew's interest in the maps it contained, the uncle turned to a modern map and "pointed with his wand to all the knowen Seas, Gulfs, Bayes, Straights, Capes, Rivers, Empires, Kingdomes, Dukedomes, and Territories of ech part, with declaration also of their speciall commodities and particular wants, which by the benefit of traffike, and entercourse of merchants, are plentifully supplied. From the Mappe he brought me to the Bible, and turning to the 107 Psalme, directed mee to the 23 and 24 verses, where I read, that they which go downe to the sea in ships, and occupy [work] by the great waters, they see the works of the Lord, and his woonders in the deepe." This event, Hakluyt records, made so deep an impression upon him, that he vowed he would devote his life to the study of this kind of knowledge. *The Principal Navigations* was the result, a book that mixes a concern with the profit to be made from trade and from geographical knowledge with praise for the Christian god who made the "great waters" and, in Hakluyt's view, looked with special favor on the English merchants and sailors who voyaged over them.

In the early modern period, access to maps was far less easy than it is today. Before the advent of printing in the late fifteenth century, maps were drawn and decorated by hand. Because they were rare and expensive, these medieval maps were for the most part owned by the wealthy and the powerful. Sometimes adorned with pictures of fabulous sea monsters and exotic creatures, maps often revealed the Christian worldview of those who composed them. Jerusalem appeared squarely in the middle of many maps (called T and O maps), with Asia, Africa, and Europe, representing the rest of the known world, arranged symmetrically around the Holy City. Because they had not yet been discovered by Europeans, North and South America were not depicted.

Mapping practices changed markedly during the late fifteenth and sixteenth centuries both because of the advent of print and also because European nations such as Portugal and Spain began sending ships on long sea voyages to open new trade routes to the East and, eventually, to the Americas. During this period, monarchs competed to have the best cartographers supply them with accurate maps of their realms and especially of lands in Africa, Asia, or the Americas, where they hoped to trade or plant settlements. Such knowledge was precious and jealously guarded. The value of such maps and the secrecy that surrounded them are indicated by a story published in Hakluyt's *The Principal Navigations*. An English ship had captured a Portuguese vessel in the Azores, and a map was discovered among the ship's valuable cargo, which included spices, silks, carpets, porcelain, and other exotic commercial objects. The map was "inclosed in a case of sweete Cedar wood, and lapped up almost an hundred fold in fine calicut-cloth, as though it had been some incomparable jewell." The value of the map and what explains the careful way in which it was packed lay in the particular information it afforded the English about Portuguese trading routes. More than beautiful objects, maps like this one were crucial to the international race to find safe sea routes to the most profitable trading centers in the East.

In the sixteenth century, books of maps began to be printed, making them more affordable for ordinary people, though some of these books, published as big folio volumes, remained too dear for any but wealthy patrons to buy. Yet maps were increasingly a part of daily life, and printing made many of them more accessible. Playgoers in Shakespeare's audiences must have understood in general the value and uses of maps, for they appear as props in a number of his plays. Most famously, at the beginning of *King Lear,* the old king has a map brought onstage showing the extent of his kingdom. He then points on the map to the three separate parts into which he is dividing his realm to share among his daughters. The map, often unfurled with a flourish on a table or held up for view by members of Lear's retinue, signals the crucial relationship of the land to the monarch. He is his domains, and the map signifies his possession of them. To divide the kingdom, in essence to tear apart the map, would have been judged foolish and destructive by early modern political theorists. Similarly, in *1 Henry IV,* when rebels against the sitting monarch, Henry IV, plot to overthrow him, they bring a map onstage in order to decide what part of the kingdom will be given to each rebel leader. Their proposed dismemberment of the realm signifies the danger they pose. Treasonously, they would rend in pieces the body of the commonwealth.

Maps, of course, had other uses besides signifying royal domains. In some instances, they were used pragmatically to help people find their way from one place to another. A very common kind of map, a portolan chart, depicted in minute detail the coastline of a particular body of water. Used by sailors, these maps frequently were made by people native to the region they described. Many world or regional maps, because they were beautifully decorated and embellished with vivid colors, were used for decorative purposes. John Dee, a learned adviser to Queen Elizabeth and a great book collector, wrote that some people used maps "to beautifie their Halls, Parlers, Chambers, Galeries, Studies, or Libraries." He also spoke of more scholarly uses for these objects. They could, for example, be useful aids in the study of history or geography, enabling people to locate "thinges past, as battels fought, earthquakes, heavenly fyringes, and such occurents in histories mentioned." Today we make similar use of maps, like those included in this volume, when, in reading Shakespeare's plays, we resort to a map to find out where the Battle of Agincourt took place or where Othello sailed when he left Venice for Cyprus.

This edition of the *Norton Shakespeare* includes six maps. Three of them are modern maps drawn specifically to show the location of places important to Shakespeare's plays. They depict London, the British Isles and France, and the eastern Mediterranean. This edition also includes three early modern maps that indicate some of the different kinds of printed maps that people might have seen in Shakespeare's lifetime. The earliest is a map of London that appeared in a 1574 edition of a famous German atlas, *Civitates Orbis Terrarum (Cities of the World),* compiled by George Braun with engravings by Franz Hogenberg. This remarkable atlas includes maps and information on cities throughout Europe, Asia, and North Africa; the first of its six volumes appeared in 1572, the last in 1617. Being included in the volume indicated a city's status as a recognized metropolitan center. In a charming touch, Braun added to his city maps pictures of figures in local dress. At the bottom of the map of London, for example, there are four figures who appear to represent the city's prosperous citizens. In the center, a man in a long robe holds the hand of soberly dressed matron. On either side of them are younger and more ornately dressed figures. The young man sports a long sword and a short cloak, the woman a dress with elaborate skirts. In the atlas, the map is colored, and the clothes of the two young people echo one another in shades of green and red.

At the time the map was made, London was a rapidly expanding metropolis. In 1550, it contained about 55,000 people; by 1600, it would contain nearly 200,000. The map shows the densely populated old walled city north of the Thames River, in the middle of which was Eastcheap, the commercial district where, in Shakespeare's plays about the reign of Henry IV, Falstaff holds court in a tavern. The map also shows that by 1570 London was spreading westward beyond the wall toward Westminster Palace. This medieval structure, which appears on the extreme left side of the map, was where English monarchs resided when in London and where, at the end of *2 Henry IV,* the king dies in the fabled Jerusalem Chamber of the Westminster complex. On the far right of the map, one can see the Tower of London, where Edward IV's young sons were imprisoned by Richard III, an event depicted in Shakespeare's *The Tragedy of King Richard the Third*. The map also indicates the centrality of the Thames to London's commercial life. It shows the river full of boats, some of those on the east side of London Bridge large oceangoing vessels with several masts. South of the river, where many of the most famous London theaters, including Shakespeare's Globe, were to be constructed in the 1590s, there are relatively few buildings. By 1600, this would change, as Southwark, as it was known, came to be an increasingly busy entertainment, residential, and commercial district.

The map of the Christian Holy Lands at the eastern tip of the Mediterranean Sea had extremely wide distribution because it was included in the many editions of the Geneva Bible, an English translation of the Scriptures put together by a group of Puritan scholars working in Geneva in the 1550s. Moderately sized and priced, the Geneva Bible became the most popular Bible in English until the King James version was produced in 1611. Even after that date, many ordinary Protestant readers continued to use the popular Geneva Bible, which underwent refinements, changes, and additions throughout the second half of the sixteenth century, including in 1576 a new translation of the New Testament heavily indebted to the scholarship of the French theologian Théodore de Bèze.

The map included here is from a 1592 edition of this Bible, printed in London by Christopher Barker. The map was placed before Matthew, the first book of the New Testament, and it shows places mentioned in the first four Gospels (Matthew, Mark, Luke, and John), which collectively tell of the life and deeds of Jesus. It indicates, for example, the location of Bethlehem, where he was born; Nazareth, where he spent his youth; and Cana of Galilee, where he turned water into wine at a marriage. It suggests that, to the English reader, this particular territory was overwritten by and completely intertwined with Christian history. Yet in the Mediterranean Sea, on the left of the map, several large ships are visible, and they are reminders of another fact about this region: it was a vigorous trading arena where European Christian merchants did business with local merchants—Christian, Jew, and Muslim—and with traders bringing luxury goods by overland routes from the East. A number of Shakespeare's plays are set in this complex eastern Mediterranean region where several religious traditions laid claim to its territories and many commercial powers competed for preeminence. *Pericles,* for example, has a hero who is the ruler of Tyre, a city on the upper right side of the map. In the course of his wanderings, Pericles visits many cities along the eastern coasts of the Mediterranean. The conclusion of the play, in which the hero is reunited both with his long-lost daughter and the wife he believes dead, has seemed to many critics to share in a sense of Christian miracle, despite the fact of its ostensibly pagan setting. *The Comedy of Errors* and parts of *Othello* and of *Antony and Cleopatra* are also set in the eastern Mediterranean. One of Shakespeare's earliest plays, *The Comedy of Errors,* is an urban comedy in which the protagonists are merchants deeply involved in commercial transactions. It is also the first play in which Shakespeare mentions the Americas in an extended joke in which he compares parts of a serving woman's body to the countries on a map including Ireland, France, and the Americas. In *Othello,* the eastern Mediterranean island of Cyprus is represented as a tense Christian outpost defending Venetian interests against the Muslim Turks. In *Antony and Cleopatra,* Egypt figures as the site of Eastern luxury and also of imperial conquest, an extension of the Roman Empire. Clearly, this region was to Shakespeare and his audiences one of the most complex and most highly charged areas of the world: a site of religious, commercial, and imperial significance.

The map of Great Britain and Ireland comes from a 1612 edition of John Speed's *The Theatre of the Empire of Great Britaine,* an innovative atlas containing individual maps of counties and towns in England and Wales, as well as larger maps that include Scotland and Ireland. Speed was by trade a tailor who increasingly devoted his time to the study of history and cartography. Befriended by the antiquarian scholar William Camden, he eventually won patronage from Sir Fulke Greville, who gave him a pension that allowed him to devote full time to his scholarly endeavors. *The Theatre* was one product of this newfound freedom. The map included here is one of his most ambitious. It shows the entire British Isles, nominated by Speed as "The Kingdome of Great Britaine and Ireland," though at this time Ireland was far from under the control of the English crown and Scotland was still an independent kingdom, despite the fact that James I, a Scot by birth, had tried hard to forge a formal union between England and Scotland. This problem of the relationship of the parts of the British Isles to one another, and England's assertion of power over the others, is treated in *Henry V*, in which officers from Wales, Ireland, and Scotland are sharply delineated yet all depicted as loyal subjects of the English king.

One striking aspect of Speed's map is the balance it strikes between the two capital cities, London on the left, prominently featuring the Thames and London Bridge, and Edinburgh on the right. This would have pleased James, whose interest in his native country Shakespeare played to in his writing of *Macbeth*, based on material from Scottish history. Speed's map acknowledges the claims of the monarch to the territory it depicts. In the upper left corner, the British lion and the Scottish unicorn support a roundel topped with a crown. When James became king of England in 1603, he created this merged symbol of Scottish-English unity. The motto of the Royal Order of the Garter, "Honi soit qui mal y pense" (Shamed be he who thinks ill of it), is inscribed around the circumference. In the bottom left corner of the map, another locus of authority is established. Two cherubs, one holding a compass, the other a globe, sit beneath a banner on which is inscribed the words: "Performed by John Speede." If the territory is the monarch's, the craft that depicts it belongs to the tailor turned cartographer.

Today, maps are readily available from any gasoline station or on the Internet, but in early modern England they were still rare and valuable objects that could generate great excitement in those who owned or beheld them. Along with other precious items, maps were sometimes put on display in libraries and sitting rooms, but they had functions beyond the ornamental. They helped to explain and order the world, indicating who claimed certain domains, showing where the familiar stories of the Bible or of English history occurred, helping merchants find their way to distant markets. As John Dee, the early modern map enthusiast concluded, "Some, for one purpose: and some, for an other, liketh, loveth, getteth, and useth, Mappes, Chartes, and Geographicall Globes."

JEAN E. HOWARD

Ireland, Scotland, Wales, England, and Western France: Places Important to Shakespeare's Plays.

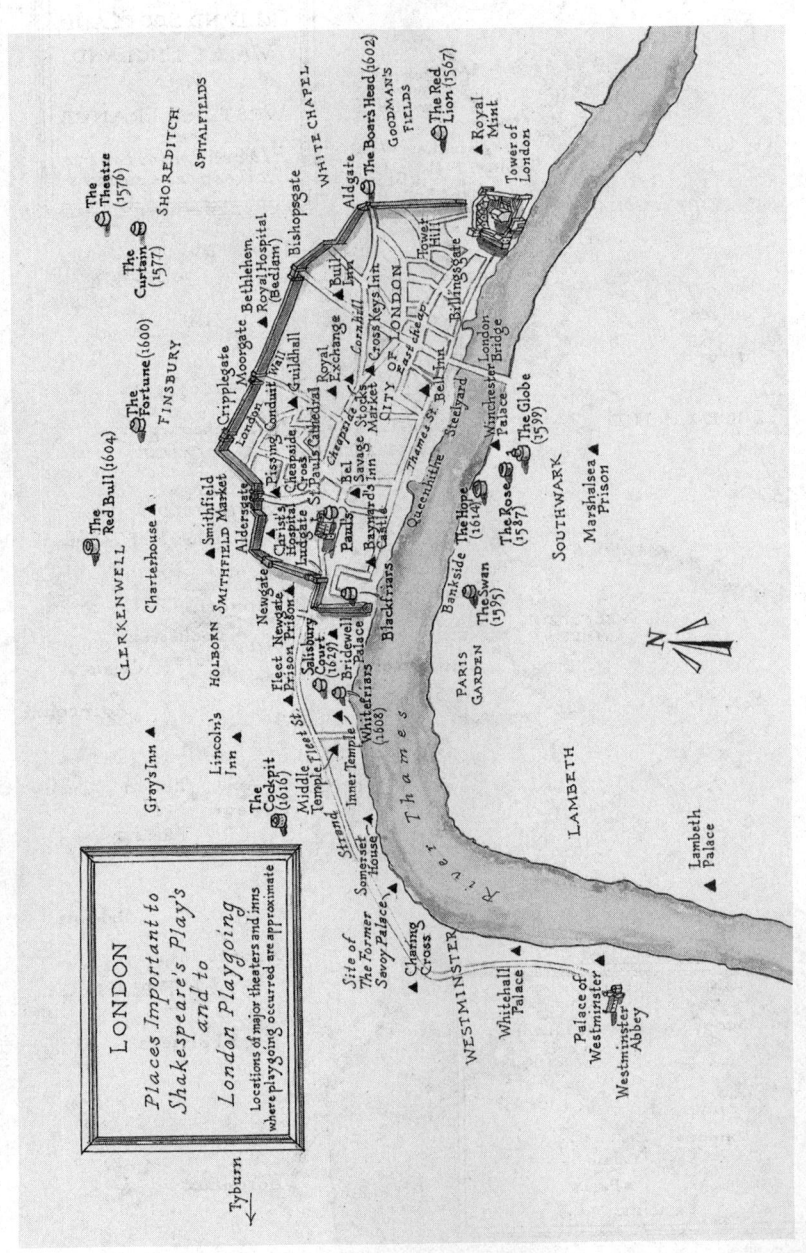

London: Places Important to Shakespeare's Plays and London Playgoing.

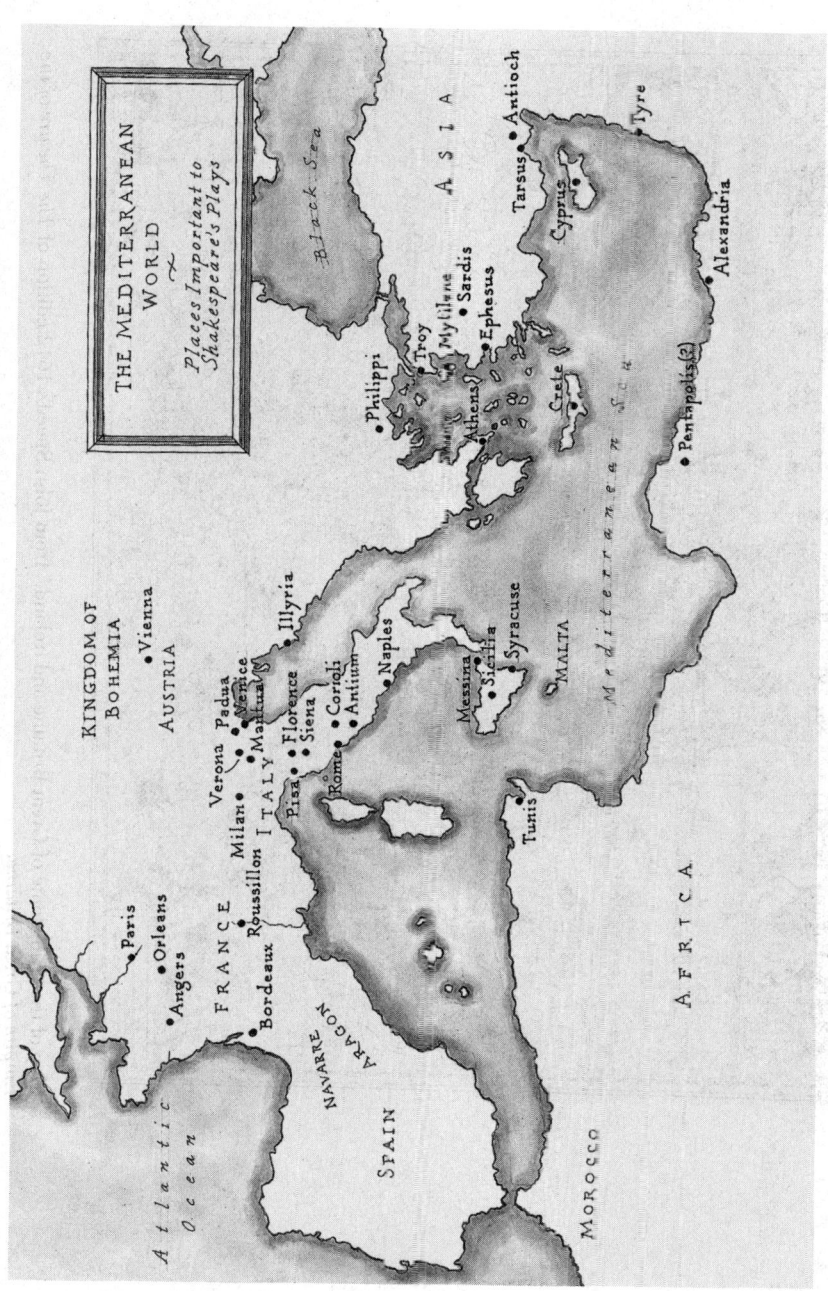

The Mediterranean World: Places Important to Shakespeare's Plays.

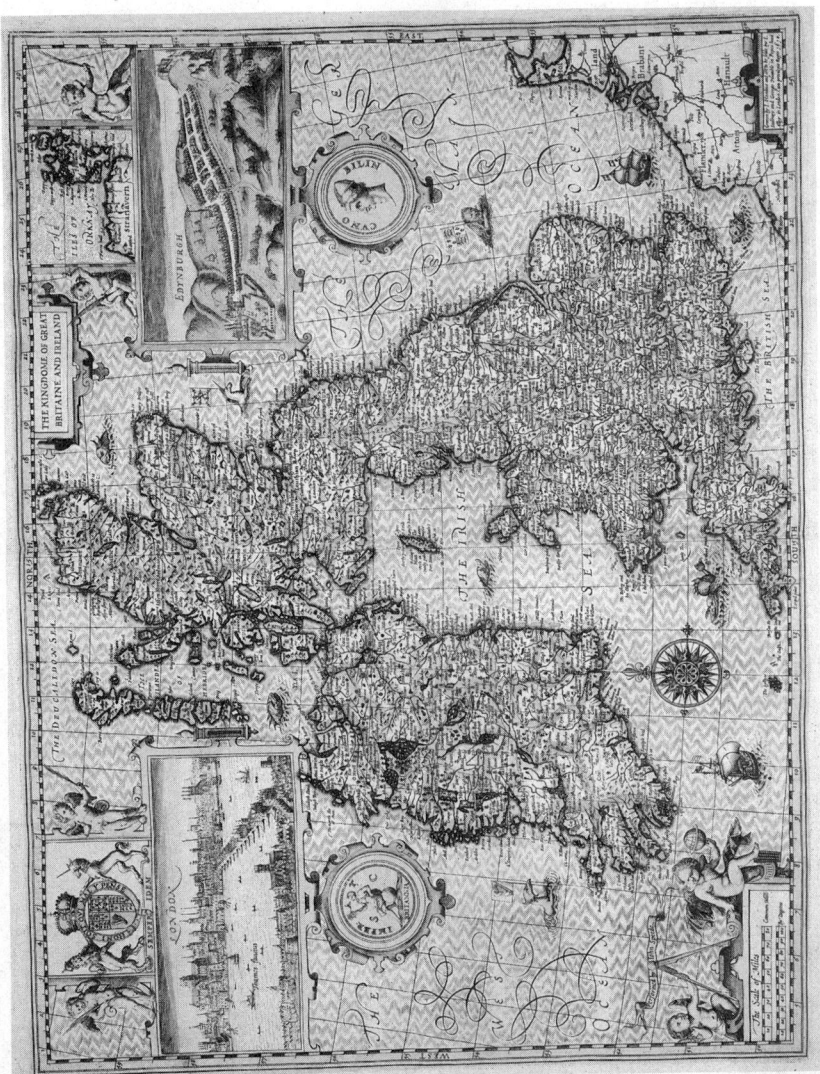

Map of the "Kingdome of Great Britaine and Ireland," from John Speed's 1612 edition of *The Theatre of the Empire of Great Britaine.*

Printed map of London, 1574, taken from a German atlas of European cities by George Braun and Franz Hogenberg.

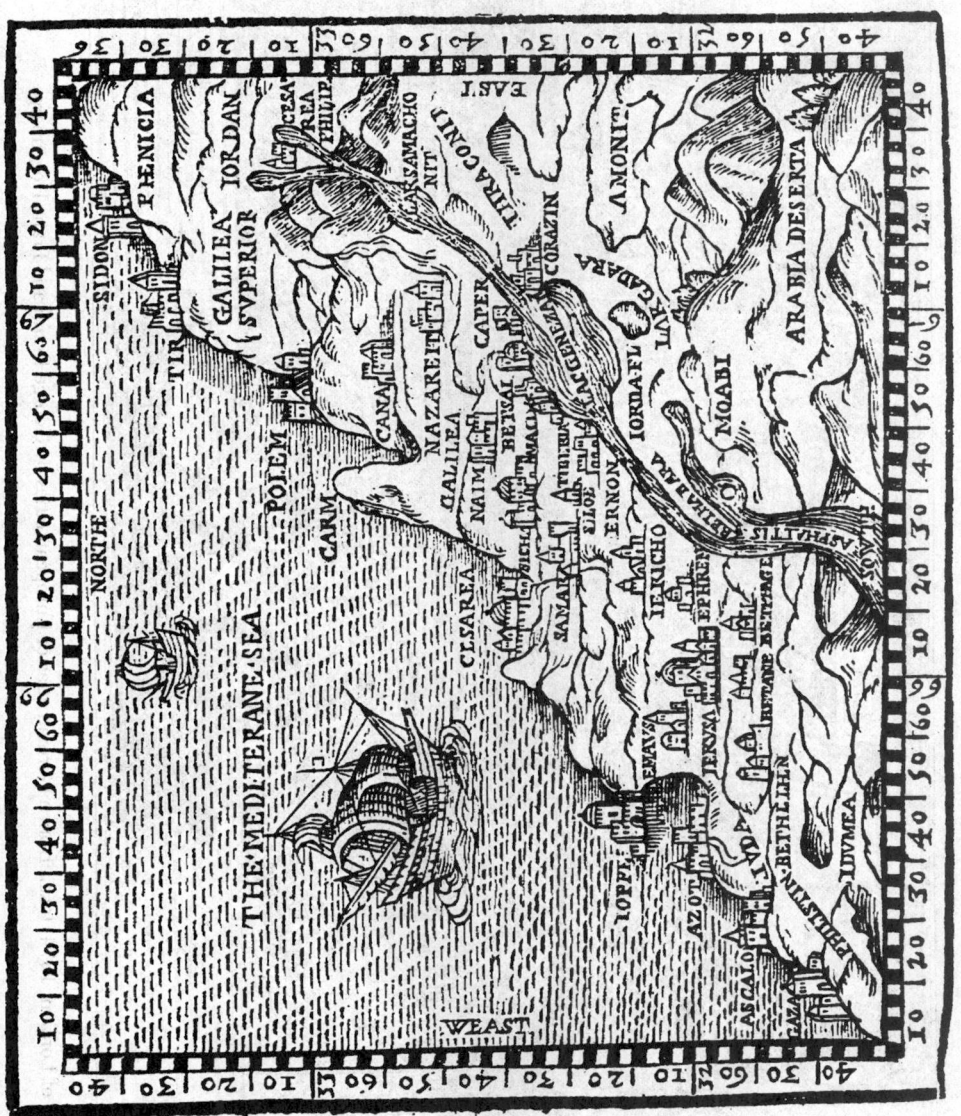

Map of the Holy Land, from the Théodore de Bèze Bible, printed in London, 1592.

Documents

This selection of documents provides a range of contemporary testimony about Shakespeare's character, his work, and the social and institutional conditions under which it was produced. In the absence of newspapers and reviewers, few references to the theater survive. The availability of such hints and fragments as are presented here serves as a mark of Shakespeare's distinction, for the theater was perceived by much of the literate population as ephemeral popular entertainment. The reports of spectators whose accounts we have are more like reviews than any other texts the period has to offer; hence the importance even of brief notes such as Nashe's or Platter's, and the particular value of extended accounts such as those of Simon Forman. The government documents included here offer a vivid glimpse of the institutional procedures by which the theater was regulated. The legal documents—a contract for the construction of a theater modeled on the Globe, and Shakespeare's will—provide the most detailed account available of the material conditions of his life and work. The extracts from criticism and other literary texts show the diversity of contemporary response to his art.

The source for each text is given at the end of the introductory headnote. Additional documents can be found at wwnorton.com/shakespeare.

WS: E. K. Chambers, *William Shakespeare: A Study of Facts and Problems*, 2 vols. (Oxford: Clarendon Press, 1930).
ES: E. K. Chambers, *The Elizabethan Stage*, 4 vols. (Oxford: Clarendon Press, 1923).

Robert Greene on Shakespeare (1592)

[Robert Greene (1560–1592), a prolific author of plays, romances, and pamphlets, attacked Shakespeare in his *Greenes, Groats-worth of Witte, bought with a million of Repentance*. Greene had studied at Cambridge, and his "M.A." was prominently displayed on his title pages. Shakespeare's lack of a university education is clearly one motive for the professional resentment of the following excerpt. Another is probably that Greene was poor and very ill and felt forsaken while writing the *Groats-worth of Witte*; the preface refers to it as his "Swanne-like song," and the narrative is framed as the repentance of a dying man. (Some scholars have held that the posthumously published work contains fabrications by a publisher attempting to capitalize on Greene's name.) The three colleagues Greene addresses are likely to be Christopher Marlowe, Thomas Nashe, and George Peele. The text is that of 1596, as printed in Alexander B. Grosart's *Life and Complete Works in Prose and Verse of Robert Greene*, vol. 12 (New York: Russell and Russell).]

> *To those Gentlemen his Quondam acquaintance,*
> *that spend their wits in making Plaies, R. G.*
> *wisheth a better exercise, and wisdome*
> *to prevent his extremities. . . .*

Base minded men al three of you, if by my miserie ye be not warned: for unto none of you (like me) fought those burres to cleave: those Puppits (I meane) that speake from our mouths, those Anticks garnisht in our colours. Is it not strange that I, to whom they al have beene beholding: is it not like that you, to whome they all have beene beholding, shall (were ye in that case that I am now) be both at once of them forsaken? Yes trust them not: for there is an upstart Crow, beautified with our feathers, that with his *Tygers heart wrapt in a Players hide*,[1] *supposes he is as well able to bumbast out a blanke verse as the best of you: and being an absolute Johannes fac totum*,[2] is in his owne conceit the onely Shake-scene in a countrie. O that I might intreate your rare wits to be imployed in more profitable courses: & let those Apes imitate your past excellence, and never more acquaint them with your admired inventions. I know the best husband[3] of you all will never prove an Usurer, and the kindest of them / all will never proove a kinde nurse: yet whilst you may, seeke you better Maisters; for it is pittie men of such rare wits, should be subject to the pleasures of such rude groomes.

Thomas Nashe on *1 Henry VI* (1592)

[Thomas Nashe (1567–1601), Greene's fellow playwright and pamphleteer, protests the attribution to himself of the *Groats-worth of Witte* in the preface to the 1592 edition of a pamphlet of his own, *Pierce Penilisse; His Supplication to the Devil*. The satire of *Pierce Penilisse* is more general and political than that of the *Groats-worth*, attacking the manners of the middle class. The allusion to the Talbot scenes of *1 Henry VI* (4.2–7) comes in a section subtitled "The defence of Playes." Talbot is supposed to have been played by Richard Burbage, later the leading actor of the Lord Chamberlain's and King's Men. The text is from Ronald B. McKerrow's 1904 edition of Nashe's *Works*, vol. 1 (London: Bullen).]

How would it have joyed brave *Talbot* (the terror of the French) to thinke that after he had lyne two hundred yeares in his Tombe, hee should triumphe againe on the Stage, and have his bones newe embalmed with the teares of ten thousand spectators at least (at severall times), who, in the Tragedian that represents his person, imagine they behold him fresh bleeding.

Francis Meres on Shakespeare (1598)

[Francis Meres (1565–1647) was educated at Cambridge and was active in London literary circles in 1597–98, after which he became a rector and schoolmaster in the country. The descriptions of Shakespeare are taken from a section on poetry in *Palladis Tamia, Wits Treasury*, a work largely consisting of translated classical quotations and exempla. Unlike the main body of the work, the subsections on poetry, painting, and music include comparisons of English artists to figures of antiquity. Meres goes on after the extract below to list Shakespeare among the best English writers for lyric, tragedy, comedy, elegy, and love poetry. The text is from Don Cameron Allen's 1933 edition of the section "Poetrie" (Urbana: University of Illinois).]

From XI

As the Greeke tongue is made famous and eloquent by *Homer, Hesiod, Euripedes, Aeschilus, Sophocles, Pindarus, Phocylides* and *Aristophanes*; and the Latine tongue by *Virgill, Ovid, Horace, Silius Italicus, Lucanus, Lucretius, Ausonius* and *Claudianus*: so the English tongue is mightily enriched, and gorgeouslie invested

---

1. A parody of *Richard Duke of York* (*3 Henry VI*)
1.4.138: "O tiger's heart wrapped in a woman's hide!"
This obvious allusion and the following pun on Shakespeare's name make it certain that Shakespeare is the

"crow" described here.
2. Jack-of-all-trades. *conceit*: imagination.
3. Steward.

in rare ornaments and resplendent abiliments by Sir *Philip Sidney, Spencer, Daniel, Drayton, Warner, Shakespeare, Marlow* and *Chapman.*

From XIV

As the soule of *Euphorbus* was thought to live in *Pythagoras:* so the sweete wittie soule of Ovid lives in mellifluous & honytongued *Shakespeare,* witnes his *Venus and Adonis,* his *Lucrece,* his sugred Sonnets.

From XV

As *Plautus* and *Seneca* are accounted the best for Comedy and Tragedy among the Latines: so *Shakespeare* among yᵉ English is the most excellent in both kinds for the stage; for Comedy, witnes his *Gẽtlemẽ of Verona,* his *Errors,* his *Love labors lost,* his *Love labours wonne,*[1] his *Midsummers night dreame,* & his *Merchant of Venice:* for Tragedy his *Richard the 2. Richard the 3. Henry the 4. King John, Titus Andronicus* and his *Romeo and Juliet.*

As *Epius Stolo* said, that the Muses would speake with *Plautus* tongue, if they would speak Latin: so I say that the Muses would speak with *Shakespeares* fine filed phrase, if they would speake English.

Thomas Platter on *Julius Caesar* (September 21, 1599)

[Thomas Platter (b. 1574), a Swiss traveler, recorded his experience at the Globe playhouse in an account of his travels. The German text is printed in *WS* 2:322.]

Den 21 Septembris nach dem Imbissessen, etwan umb zwey vhren, bin ich mitt meiner geselschaft über daz wasser gefahren, haben in dem streüwinen Dachhaus die Tragedy vom ersten Keyser Julio Caesare mitt ohngefahr 15 personen sehen gar artlich agieren; zu endt der Comedien dantzeten sie ihren gebraucht nach gar überausz zierlich, ye zwen in mannes vndt 2 in weiber kleideren angethan, wunderbahrlich mitt einanderen.

On the 21st of September after lunch, about two o'clock, I crossed the water [the Thames] with my party, and we saw the tragedy of the first emperor Julius Caesar acted very prettily in the house with the thatched roof, with about fifteen characters; at the end of the comedy, according to their custom, they danced with exceeding elegance, two each in men's and two in women's clothes, wonderfully together.

[Translated by Noah Heringman]

Gabriel Harvey on *Hamlet, Venus and Adonis,* and *The Rape of Lucrece* (1598–1603)

[Gabriel Harvey (c. 1550–1631), a scholar perhaps best remembered as the particular friend of Spenser, gave the following account of Shakespeare and other contemporaries in a long manuscript note in his copy of Speght's 1598 edition of Chaucer. The date of the note is uncertain, but internal evidence makes it highly unlikely to be later than 1603. The references to Shakespeare are brief but suggestive, and the note is useful both in providing a context for the appreciation of Shakespeare and for its characteris-

---

1. The play—or at least the title—has not survived; a bookseller's record of the title does survive, however.

tically keen assessment of the state of modern literature. The text is from G. C. Moore Smith's edition of *Gabriel Harvey's Marginalia* (Stratford-upon-Avon: Shakespeare Head Press, 1913).]

And now translated Petrarch, Ariosto, Tasso, & Bartas himself deserve curious comparison with Chaucer, Lidgate, & owre best Inglish, auncient & moderne. Amongst which, the Countesse of Pembrokes Arcadia, & the Faerie Queene ar now freshest in request: & Astrophil, & Amyntas ar none of the idlest pastimes of sum fine humanists. The Earle of Essex much commendes Albions England:[1] and not unworthily for diverse notable pageants, before, & in the Chronicle. Sum Inglish, & other Histories nowhere more sensibly described, or more inwardly discovered. The Lord Mountjoy makes the like account of Daniels peece of the Chronicle,[2] touching the Usurpation of Henrie of Bullingbrooke, which in deede is a fine, sententious, & politique peece of Poetrie: as proffitable, as pleasurable. The younger sort takes much delight in Shakespeares Venus, & Adonis: but his Lucrece, & his tragedie of Hamlet, Prince of Denmarke, have it in them, to please the wiser sort. Or such poets: or better: or none.

Vilia miretur vulgus: mihi flavus Apollo
Pocula Castaliæ plena ministret aquæ:[3]

quoth Sir Edward Dier, betwene jest, & earnest. Whose written devises farr excell most of the sonets, and cantos in print. His Amaryllis, & Sir Walter Raleighs Cynthia, how fine & sweet inventions? Excellent matter of emulation for Spencer, Constable, France, Watson, Daniel, Warner, Chapman, Silvester, Shakespeare, & the rest of owr florishing metricians. I looke for much, aswell in verse, as in prose, from mie two Oxford frends, Doctor Gager, & M. Hackluit: both rarely furnished for the purpose: & I have a phansie to Owens new Epigrams, as pithie as elegant, as plesant as sharp, & sumtime as weightie as breife: & amongst so manie gentle, noble, & royall spirits meethinkes I see sum heroical thing in the clowdes: mie soveraine hope. Axiophilus[4] shall forgett himself, or will remember to leave sum memorials behinde him: & to make an use of so manie rhapsodies, cantos, hymnes, odes, epigrams, sonets, & discourses, as at idle howers, or at flowing fitts he hath compiled. God knowes what is good for the world, & fitting for this age.

Contract for the Building of the Fortune Theatre (1600)

[This contract was drawn up between Philip Henslowe and Edward Alleyn, partners in the venture, and Peter Street, the carpenter (or general contractor) in charge of the construction. In fact, Alleyn seems to have put up all the money, £440 for the work specified in the contract in addition to £80 for decoration and considerable sums to acquire the lot and surrounding properties. Alleyn faced opposition from residents of the neighborhood, but he had secured the favor of key supporters, so that he was able to proceed with the construction. As the new home of the Lord Admiral's Men, the Fortune did in fact become a center of disturbances, with complaints coming to the Middlesex Bench of assaults, petty thefts, and riotous behavior. Alleyn had been the leading actor of the Lord Admiral's Men, chief competitors of the Lord Chamberlain's Men, and the Fortune was conceived to compete with the Globe, meanwhile replacing the decaying and poorly situated Rose Theatre. The contract's

1. By William Warner (1586).
2. *The Ciuile Wars Between the Two Houses of Lancaster and Yorke* (1595).
3. "Let what is cheap excite the marvel of the crowd; for me may golden Apollo minister full cups from the

Castalian fount" (Ovid, *Amores* 1.15.35–36, Loeb translation). These lines also appear on the title page of Shakespeare's *Venus and Adonis* (1592–93).
4. Probably Harvey himself.

descriptions and frequent references to the Globe, given this background, can be seen as providing some of our best evidence on the nature of the Globe itself. The text is reprinted in *ES*, vol. 2.]

'This Indenture made the Eighte daie of Januarye 1599.[1] and in the Twoe and Fortyth yeare of the Reigne of our sovereigne Ladie Elizabeth, by the grace of god Queene of Englande, Fraunce and Irelande, defender of the Faythe, &c. betwene Phillipp Henslowe and Edwarde Allen of the parishe of S[te] Saviours in Southwark in the Countie of Surrey, gentlemen, on thone parte, and Peeter Streete, Cittizen and Carpenter of London, on thother parte witnesseth That whereas the saide Phillipp Henslowe & Edward Allen, the daie of the date hereof, have bargeyned, compounded & agreed with the saide Peter Streete ffor the erectinge, buildinge & settinge upp of a new howse and Stadge for a Plaiehouse in and uppon a certeine plott or parcell of grounde appoynted oute for that purpose, scytuate and beinge nere Goldinge lane in the parishe of S[te] Giles withoute Cripplegate of London,[2] to be by him the saide Peeter Streete or somme other sufficyent woorkmen of his provideinge and appoyntemente and att his propper costes & chardges, for the consideracion hereafter in theis presentes expressed, made, erected, builded and sett upp in manner & forme followinge (that is to saie); The frame of the saide howse to be sett square[3] and to conteine ffowerscore foote of lawfull assize everye waie square withoutt and ffftie five foote of like assize square everye waie within, with a good suer and stronge foundacion of pyles, brick, lyme and sand bothe without & within, to be wroughte one foote of assize att the leiste above the grounde; And the saide fframe to conteine three Stories in heighth, the first or lower Storie to conteine Twelve foote of lawfull assize in heighth, the second Storie Eleaven foote of lawfull assize in heigth, and the third or upper Storie to conteine Nyne foote of lawfull assize in heigth; All which Stories shall conteine Twelve foote and a halfe of lawfull assize in breadth througheoute, besides a juttey forwardes in either of the saide twoe upper Stories of Tenne ynches of lawfull assize, with ffower convenient divisions for gentlemens roomes,[4] and other sufficient and convenient divisions for Twoe pennie roomes, with necessarie seates to be placed and sett, aswell in those roomes as througheoute all the rest of the galleries of the saide howse, and with suchelike steares, conveyances & divisions withoute & within, as are made & contryved in and to the late erected Plaiehowse on the Banck in the saide parishe of S[te] Saviours called the Globe; With a Stadge and Tyreinge howse[5] to be made, erected & settupp within the saide fframe, with a shadowe or cover[6] over the saide Stadge, which Stadge shalbe placed & sett, as alsoe the searecases of the saide fframe, in suche sorte as is prefigured in a plott[7] thereof drawen, and which Stadge shall conteine in length Fortie and Three foote of lawfull assize and in breadth to extende to the middle of the yarde[8] of the saide howse; The same Stadge to be paled in belowe with good, stronge and sufficyent newe oken bourdes, and likewise the lower Storie of the saide fframe withinside, and the same lower storie to be alsoe laide over and fenced with strong yron pykes; And the saide Stadge to be in all other proporcions contryved and fashioned like unto the Stadge of the saide Plaie howse called the Globe; With convenient windowes and lightes glazed to the saide Tyreinge howse; And the saide fframe, Stadge and Stearecases to be covered with Tyle, and to have a sufficient gutter of lead to carrie & convey the water from the coveringe of the saide Stadge to fall backwardes; And also all the saide fframe and the Stairecases thereof

---

1. 1600 (New Style).

2. *nere . . . London*: an area then in the northwest suburbs, literally outside Cripplegate and, like the Globe across the water, outside the jurisdiction of a City Council often inimical to the theater.

3. This square shape was unusual; the outlines of comparable theaters of the period were round or polygonal (with more than four sides).

4. Something like the VIP boxes of the present day.

5. "Attiring house," a dressing room and backstage area extending onto the rear of the stage.

6. A roof (known as "the heavens") partially covering the stage, supported by the pillars that also served as versatile pieces of scenery.

7. Plan.

8. *in breadth . . . yarde*: the stage would then extend about 27 feet into the yard, specified earlier as 55 feet square.

to be sufficyently enclosed withoute with lathe, lyme & haire, and the gentlemens roomes and Twoe pennie roomes to be seeled[9] with lathe, lyme & haire, and all the fflowers of the saide Galleries, Stories and Stadge to be bourded with good & sufficyent newe deale bourdes of the whole thicknes, wheare need shalbe; And the saide howse and other thinges beforemencioned to be made & doen to be in all other contrivitions, conveyances, fashions, thinge and thinges effected, finished and doen accordinge to the manner and fashion of the saide howse called the Globe, saveinge only that all the princypall and maine postes of the saide fframe and Stadge forwarde shalbe square and wroughte palasterwise,[1] with carved proporcions called Satiers[2] to be placed & sett on the topp of every of the same postes, and saveinge alsoe that the said Peeter Streete shall not be chardged with anie manner of pay[ntin]ge in or aboute the saide fframe howse or Stadge or anie parte thereof, nor rendringe[3] the walls within, nor seeling anie more or other roomes then the gentlemens roomes, Twoe pennie roomes and Stadge before remembred. Nowe theiruppon the saide Peeter Streete dothe covenant, promise and graunte ffor himself, his executours and administratours, to and with the saide Phillipp Henslowe and Edward Allen and either of them, and thexecutours and administratours of them and either of them, by theis presentes in manner & forme followeinge (that is to saie); That he the saide Peeter Streete, his executours or assignes, shall & will att his or their owne propper costes & chardges well, woorkmanlike & substancyallie make, erect, sett upp and fully finishe in and by all thinges, accordinge to the true meaninge of theis presentes, with good, stronge and substancyall newe tymber and other necessarie stuff, all the saide fframe and other woorkes whatsoever in and uppon the saide plott or parcell of grounde (beinge not by anie aucthoretie restrayned, and haveinge ingres, egres & regres to doe the same) before the ffyve & twentith daie of Julie next commeinge after the date hereof; And shall alsoe at his or theire like costes and chardges provide and finde all manner of woorkmen, tymber, joystes, rafters, boordes, dores, boltes, hinges, brick, tyle, lathe, lyme, haire, sande, nailes, lade, iron, glasse, woorkmanshipp and other thinges whatsoever, which shalbe needefull, convenyent & necessarie for the saide fframe & woorkes & everie parte thereof; And shall alsoe make all the saide fframe in every poynte for Scantlinges[4] lardger and bigger in assize then the Scantlinges of the timber of the saide newe erected howse called the Globe; And alsoe that he the saide Peeter Streete shall furthwith, aswell by himself as by suche other and soemanie woorkmen as shalbe convenient & necessarie, enter into and upon the saide buildinges and woorkes, and shall in reasonable manner proceede therein withoute anie wilfull detraccion untill the same shalbe fully effected and finished. In consideracion of all which buildinges and of all stuff & woorkemanshipp thereto belonginge, the saide Phillipp Henslowe & Edward Allen and either of them, ffor themselves, theire, and either of theire executours & administratours, doe joynctlie & severallie covenante & graunte to & with the saide Peeter Streete, his executours & administratours by theis presentes, that they the saide Phillipp Henslowe & Edward Allen or one of them, or the executours administratours or assignes of them or one of them, shall & will well & truelie paie or cawse to be paide unto the saide Peeter Streete, his executours or assignes, att the place aforesaid appoynted for the erectinge of the saide fframe, the full somme of Fower hundred & Fortie Poundes of lawfull money of Englande in manner & forme followeinge (that is to saie), att suche tyme and when as the Tymberwoork of the saide fframe shalbe rayzed & sett upp by the saide Peeter Streete his executours or assignes, or within seaven daies then next followeinge, Twoe hundred & Twentie poundes, and att suche time and when as the saide fframe & woorkes shalbe fullie effected & ffynished as is aforesaide, or within seaven daies then next followeinge, thother Twoe hundred and Twentie poundes,

9. Coated both on the "ceiling" (a related word) and the walls.
1. Finished in the form of pilasters, ornamental columns in the classical style.

2. Satyrs. *proporcions*: figures.
3. Plastering.
4. Prescribed dimensions of the beams.

withoute fraude or coven.[5] Provided allwaies, and it is agreed betwene the saide parties, that whatsoever somme or sommes of money the saide Phillipp Henslowe &
Edward Allen or either of them, or thexecutours or assignes of them or either of them,
shall lend or deliver unto the saide Peter Streete his executours or assignes, or anie
other by his appoyntemente or consent, ffor or concerninge the saide woorkes or anie
parte thereof or anie stuff thereto belonginge, before the raizeinge & settinge upp of
the saide fframe, shalbe reputed, accepted, taken & accoumpted in parte of the firste
paymente aforesaid of the saide some of Fower hundred & Fortie poundes, and all
suche somme & sommes of money, as they or anie of them shall as aforesaid lend or
deliver betwene the razeinge of the saide fframe & finishinge thereof and of all the
rest of the saide woorkes, shalbe reputed, accepted, taken & accoumpted in parte of
the laste pamente aforesaid of the same somme of Fower hundred & Fortie poundes,
anie thinge abovesaid to the contrary notwithstandinge. In witnes whereof the parties abovesaid to theis presente Indentures Interchaungeably have sett theire handes
and seales. Geoven[6] the daie and yeare ffirste abovewritten.

P S

Sealed and delivered by the saide Peter Streete in the presence of me William Harris Pub[lic] Scr[ivener] And me Frauncis Smyth appr[entice] to the said Scr[ivener]
[*Endorsed:*] Peater Streat ffor The Building of the Fortune.

Augustine Phillips, Francis Bacon, et al. on *Richard II* (1601)

[These extracts from testimony submitted at the Earl of Essex's trial for treason, and
related documents, show that some of Essex's supporters had contracted with the Lord
Chamberlain's Men to revive *Richard II*, apparently in order to provide a model for the justified deposition of a monarch and thus propitiate the coup in which Essex planned to
depose Elizabeth. The play was performed on February 7, and "it was on the same day,"
according to E. K. Chambers, "that Essex received a summons to appear before the Privy
Council. This interrupted his plans for securing possession of the Queen's person and
arresting her ministers, and precipitated his futile outbreak of February 8." Augustine
Phillips was one of Shakespeare's colleagues in the Lord Chamberlain's Men. Sir Edward
Coke was, for a time, chief justice under King James. The last excerpt is a contemporary
record of a conversation between the queen and her archivist several months after Essex
was executed. The texts are from *WS*, vol. 2.]

From the Abstract of Evidence

The Erle of Essex is charged with high Treason, namely, That he plotted and
practised with the Pope and king of Spaine for the disposing and settling to himself Aswell the Crowne of England, as of the kingdom of Ireland.

From the Examination of Augustine Phillips, February 18, 1601

The Examination of Augustyne Phillypps servant unto the L Chamberlyne and
one of hys players taken the xviij[th] of Februarij 1600 upon hys oth
He sayeth that on Fryday last was sennyght or Thursday S[r] Charles Percy S[r]
Josclyne Percy and the L. Montegle with some thre more spak to some of the play-

---

5. Deceit.   6. Given.

ers in the presans of thys examinate to have the play of the deposyng and kyllyng of Kyng Rychard the second to be played the Saterday next promysyng to gete them xls. more then their ordynary to play yt. Wher thys Examinate and hys fellowes were determyned to have played some other play, holdyng that play of Kyng Richard to be so old & so long out of use as that they shold have small or no Company at yt. But at their request this Examinate and his fellowes were Content to play yt the Saterday and had their xls. more then their ordynary for yt and so played yt accordyngly

Augustine Phillipps

From the speech of Sir Edward Coke at Essex's trial, February 19

I protest upon my soul and conscience I doe beleeve she should not have long lived after she had been in your power. Note but the precedents of former ages, how long lived Richard the Second after he was surprised in the same manner? The pretence was alike for the removing of certain counsellors, but yet shortly after it cost him his life.

From [Francis Bacon's] "A Declaration of the . . . Treasons . . . by Robert late Earle of Essex"

The afternoone before the rebellion, Merricke,[1] with a great company of others, that afterwards were all in the action, had procured to bee played before them, the play of deposing King Richard the second. Neither was it casuall, but a play bespoken by Merrick. And not so onely, but when it was told him by one of the players, that the play was olde, and they should have losse in playing it, because fewe would come to it: there was fourty shillings extraordinarie given to play it, and so thereupon playd it was. So earnest hee was to satisfie his eyes with the sight of that tragedie which hee thought soone after his lord should bring from the stage to the state, but that God turned it upon their owne heads.

From a Memorandum in the Lambard family manuscript, August 4

. . . so her Majestie fell upon[2] the reign of King Richard II. saying, 'I am Richard II. know ye not that?'

W.L. 'Such a wicked imagination was determined and attempted by a most unkind Gent. the most adorned creature that ever your Majestie made.'

Her Majestie. 'He that will forget God, will also forget his benefactors; this tragedy was played 40[tie] times in open streets and houses.'

John Manningham on *Twelfth Night* and *Richard III* (1602)

[John Manningham (d. 1622) kept a diary during his time as a law student at the Middle Temple, recording the witticisms of his colleagues and a rich variety of anecdotes. The vibrant and boisterous life of the Inns of Court is also illustrated by the *Gesta Grayorum* (see above). The February entry describes the festivities organized for Candlemas Day at the Middle Temple, while the second recounts an anecdote related to Manningham by one Mr. Touse (this name is difficult to read in the manuscript). As with all the documents in this section, any date before March 25 is assigned to the following year according to our calendar, so that 1601 here becomes 1602 (New Style).

---

1. Sir Gilly Merrick, one of Essex's supporters, was later tried separately for treason.
2. Came across (in reading). The memorandum describes a scene in which the queen is reading over the archives that have been in the keeping of her interlocutor, William Lambard.

The text is from the 1976 edition of Robert Sorlien (Hanover, N.H : University Press of New England).]

Febr. 1601

2. At our feast wee had a play called "Twelve night, or what you will"; much like the commedy of errores, or Menechmi[1] in Plautus, but most like and neere to that in Italian called Inganni.[2] A good practise in it to make the steward beleeve his Lady widdowe[3] was in Love with him, by counterfayting a letter, as from his Lady, in generall termes, telling him what shee liked best in him, and prescribing his gesture in smiling, his apparraile, &c., and then when he came to practise, making him beleeve they tooke him to be mad.

Marche. 1601

13. . . . . Upon a tyme when Burbidge played Rich[ard] 3. there was a Citizen grewe soe farr in liking with him, that before shee went from the play shee appointed him to come that night unto hir by the name of Ri[chard] the 3. Shakespeare, overhearing their conclusion, went before, was intertained, and at his game ere Burbidge came. Then message being brought that Richard the 3ᵈ. was at the dore, Shakespeare caused returne to be made that William the Conquerour was before Rich[ard] the 3. Shakespeare's name William. (Mr. Touse.)

Letters Patent Formalizing the Adoption of the Lord Chamberlain's Men as the King's Men (May 19, 1603)

[James I issued the warrant ordering this patent shortly after his coronation, enhancing the status of Shakespeare's company. As retainers of the royal household with the title of Grooms of the Chamber, they performed at the court with increasing frequency (177 times between 1603 and 1616) and assisted occasionally with other court functions; but, more important, they acted throughout the kingdom under the authority of the royal patent, whose scope the forceful wording below makes clear. The patent, bearing the Great Seal, was issued May 19 as ordered in the warrant of May 17. There is some evidence to suggest that James was particularly taken with Shakespeare's poetry, and the playwright's valorization of James's ancestry (as originating with Banquo) in *Macbeth* certainly suggests that Shakespeare cultivated his esteem. The text is from *ES*, vol. 2.]

Commissio specialis pro Laurencio Fletcher & Willelmo Shakespeare et aliis[2]

James by the grace of god &c. To all Justices, Maiors, Sheriffes, Constables, hedborowes,[1] and other our Officers and lovinge Subjectes greetinge. Knowe yee that Wee of our speciall grace, certeine knowledge, & mere motion[3] have licenced and aucthorized and by theise presentes[4] doe licence and aucthorize theise our Servauntes Lawrence Fletcher, William Shakespeare, Richard Burbage, Augustyne Phillippes, John Heninges, Henrie Condell, William Sly, Robert Armyn, Richard Cowly, and the rest of theire Assosiates freely to use and exercise the Arte and faculty of playinge

---

1. Source for *The Comedy of Errors*.
2. The two plays with this exact title (1562 and 1592) seem less likely to be "most like" *Twelfth Night* than another Italian play, *Ingannati* (1537), which has characters named Fabio and Malevolti and makes reference to Twelfth Night (Epiphany).
3. Olivia is not a widow in the version of Shakespeare's play that has come down to us, though she is

so described in one of Shakespeare's principal sources for the play.
1. A parish officer similar to a petty constable.
2. *Commissio . . . aliis*: By special commission on behalf of . . . and others.
3. Inclination, desire.
4. The present document.

Comedies, Tragedies, histories, Enterludes, moralls,[5] pastoralls, Stageplaies, and Suche others like as theie have alreadie studied or hereafter shall use or studie, aswell for the recreation of our lovinge Subjectes, as for our Solace and pleasure when wee shall thincke good to see them, duringe our pleasure. And the said Commedies, tragedies, histories, Enterludes, Morralles, Pastoralls, Stageplayes, and suche like to shewe and exercise publiquely to theire best Commoditie,[6] when the infection of the plague shall decrease, aswell within theire nowe usual howse called the Globe within our County of Surrey, as alsoe within anie towne halls or Moute halls[7] or other conveniente places within the liberties and freedome of anie other Cittie, universitie, towne, or Boroughe whatsoever within our said Realmes and domynions. Willinge and Commaundinge you and everie of you, as you tender our pleasure, not onelie to permitt and suffer them herein without anie your lettes hindrances or molestacions during our said pleasure, but alsoe to be aidinge and assistinge to them, yf anie wronge be to them offered, And to allowe them such former Curtesies as hath bene given to men of theire place and quallitie,[8] and alsoe what further favour you shall shewe to theise our Servauntes for our sake wee shall take kindlie at your handes. In wytnesse whereof &c. witnesse our selfe at Westminster the nyntenth day of May

per breve de privato sigillo[9] &c.

Master of the Wardrobe's Account (March 1604)

[This entry offers us a rare glimpse of the players in the entourage of King James, sporting festive regalia in their capacity as Grooms of the Chamber. The royal procession took place March 15, 1604. The text is from *WS*, vol. 2.]

Red Clothe bought of sondrie persons and given by his Majestie to diverse persons against[1] his Majesties sayd royall proceeding through the Citie of London, viz.:— . . .

The Chamber . . .	
Fawkeners[2] &c. &c.	Red cloth
William Shakespeare	iiii yardes di.
Augustine Phillipps	"
Lawrence Fletcher	"
John Hemminges	"
Richard Burbidge	"
William Slye	"
Robert Armyn	"
Henry Cundell	"
Richard Cowley	"

Simon Forman on *Macbeth, Cymbeline,* and *The Winter's Tale* (1611)

[Simon Forman (1552–1611) was a largely self-educated physician and astrologer who rose from humble beginnings to establish a successful London practice. A large parcel of his manuscripts, including scientific and autobiographical material as well as the diary from which this account of the plays is taken, has survived, making his life one of the best-documented Elizabethan lives. These manuscripts provide

---

5. Morality plays.
6. Advantage.
7. Council chambers.
8. Profession.
9. In sum, from the privy seal.

1. For.
2. Obsolete form of "falconers," very likely the men who trained the falcons used for James's fowl-hunting expeditions. The falconers might owe their place in the retinue to James's well-known passion for hunting.

detailed information about Forman's many sidelines, such as the manufacture of talismans, alchemy, and necromancy, as well about his sex life. The text is from *WS*, vol. 2.]

The Bocke of Plaies and Notes therof per formane for Common Pollicie[1]

In Mackbeth at the Glob, 1610 ⟨1611⟩, the 20 of Aprill ♄ (Saturday), ther was to be observed, firste, howe Mackbeth and Bancko, 2 noble men cf Scotland, Ridinge thorowe a wod, the ⟨r⟩ stode before them 3 women feiries or Nimphes, And saluted Mackbeth, sayinge, 3 tyms unto him, haille Mackbeth, king of Codon;[2] for thou shalt be a kinge, but shalt beget No kinges, &c. Then said Bancko, What all to Mackbeth And nothing to me. Yes, said the nimphes. haille to thee Bancko, thou shalt beget kinges, yet be no kinge. And so they departed & cam to the Courte of Scotland to Dunkin king of Scotes, and yt was in the dais of Edward the Confessor. And Dunkin bad them both kindly wellcome, And made Mackbeth forth with Prince of Northumberland,[3] and sent him hom to his own castell, and appointed Mackbeth to provid for him, for he would sup with him the next dai at night, & did soe. And Mackebeth contrived to kill Dunkin, & thorowe the persuasion of his wife did that night Murder the kinge in his own Castell, beinge his guest. And ther were many prodigies seen that night & the dai before. And when Mack Beth had murdred the kinge, the blod on his handes could not be washed of by Any meanes, ncr frcm his wives handes, which handled the bloddi daggers in hiding them, By which means they became both moch amazed & Affronted. The murder being knowen, Dunkins 2 sonns fled, the on to England, the ⟨other to⟩ Walles, to save them selves, they being fled, they were supposed guilty of the murder of their father, which was nothinge so. Then was Mackbeth crowned kinge, and then he for feare of Banko, his old companion, that he should beget kinges but be no kinge him selfe, he contrived the death of Banko, and caused him to be Murdred on the way as he Rode. The next night, beinge at supper with his noble men whom he had bid to a feaste to the which also Banco should have com, he began to speake of Noble Banco, and to wish that he wer ther. And as he thus did, standing up to drincke a Carouse to him, the ghoste of Banco came and sate down in his cheier behind him. And he turninge About to sit down Again sawe the goste of Banco, which fronted him so, that he fell into a great passion of fear and fury, Utterynge many wordes about his murder, by which, when they hard that Banco was Murdred they Suspected Mackbet.

Then MackDove fled to England to the kinges sonn, And soe they Raised an Army, And cam into Scotland, and at Dunston Anyse overthrue Mackbet. In the meantyme whille Macdovee was in England, Mackbet sleve Mackdoves wife & children, and after in the battelle Mackdove slewe Mackbet.

Observe Also howe Mackbetes quen did Rise in the night in her slepe, & walke and talked and confessed all, & the docter noted her wordes.

Of Cimbalin king of England.
Remember also the storri of Cymbalin king of England, in Lucius tyme, howe Lucius Cam from Octavus Cesar for Tribut, and being denied, after sent Lucius with a greate Arme of Souldiars who landed at Milford haven, and Affter wer vanquished by Cimbalin, and Lucius taken prisoner, and all by means of 3 outlawes, of the which 2 of them were the sonns of Cimbalim, stolen from him when they were but 2 yers old by an old man whom Cymbalin banished, and he kept them as his own sonns 20 yers with him in A cave. And howe ⟨one⟩ of them slewe Clotan, that was the quens sonn, goinge to Milford haven to sek the love of Innogen the

1. *Common Pollicie*: practical use. Forman's title for his notes on plays is not printed in Chambers, but interpolated here from G. Blakemore Evans's transcription in the *Riverside Shakespeare*.

2. Cawdor.

3. Probably Forman's error; Duncan gives Macbeth the title Thane of Cawdor. Duncan's son Malcolm is the Prince of Northumberland.

kinges daughter, whom he had banished also for lovinge his daughter,[4] and howe the Italian that cam from her love conveied him selfe into A Cheste, and said yt was a chest of plate sent from her love & others, to be presented to the kinge. And in the depest of the night, she being aslepe, he opened the cheste, & cam forth of yt, And vewed her in her bed, and the markes of her body, & toke awai her braslet, & after Accused her of adultery to her love, &c. And in thend howe he came with the Romains into England & was taken prisoner, and after Reveled to Innogen, Who had turned her self into mans apparrell & fled to mete her love at Milford haven, & chanchsed to fall on the Cave in the wodes wher her 2 brothers were, & howe by eating a sleping Dram they thought she had bin deed, & laid her in the wodes, & the body of Cloten by her, in her loves apparrell that he left behind him, & howe she was found by Lucius, &c.

In the Winters Talle at the glob 1611 the 15 of maye ☿ ⟨Wednesday⟩.
Observe ther howe Lyontes the kinge of Cicillia was overcom with Jelosy of his wife with the kinge of Bohemia his frind that came to see him, and howe he contrived his death and wold have had his cup berer to have poisoned, who gave the king of Bohemia warning therof & fled with him to Bohemia.
Remember also howe he sent to the Orakell of Appollo & the Annswer of Apollo, that she was giltles and that the king was jelouse &c. and howe Except the child was found Again that was loste the kinge should die without yssue, for the child was caried into Bohemia & ther laid in a forrest & brought up by a sheppard And the kinge of Bohemia his sonn maried that wentch & howe they fled into Cicillia to Leontes, and the sheppard having showed the letter of the nobleman by whom Leontes sent a was ⟨away?⟩ that child and the jewells found about her, she was knowen to be Leontes daughter and was then 16 yers old.
Remember also the Rog[5] that cam in all tottered like coll pixci[6] and howe he feyned him sicke & to have bin Robbed of all that he had and howe he cosened the por man of all his money, and after cam to the shep sher[7] with a pedlers packe & ther cosened them Again of all their money And howe he changed apparrell with the kinge of Bomia his sonn, and then howe he turned Courtier &c. Beware of trustinge feined beggars or fawninge fellouss.

Sir Henry Wotton on *All Is True (Henry VIII)* and the Burning of the Globe (1613)

[Sir Henry Wotton (1568–1639), a highly educated poet and essayist, distinguished diplomat, and finally provost of Eton College, wrote to his nephew Sir Edmund Bacon shortly after the burning of the Globe. Chambers includes several other accounts of this incident in *The Elizabethan Stage,* vol. 2, pp. 419ff. The event is also recorded in John Stow's chronicles and was lamented by poets, including (several years later) Ben Jonson, and held up by Puritan divines like Prynne as an intimation of God's wrath. The excerpt below is from the earliest extant text, *Letters of Sir Henry Wotton to Sir Edmund Bacon* (London, 1661), p. 29.]

Now, to let matters of State sleep, I will entertain you at the present with what hath happened this week at the banks side. The Kings Players had a new Play, called *All is true,* representing some principall pieces of the raign of *Henry* 8, which was set forth with many extraordinary circumstances of Pomp and Majesty, even to the matting of the stage; the Knights of the Order, with their Georges and Garter, the Guards with their embroidered Coats, and the like: sufficient in truth within a while to make

---

4. Morgan/Belarius is not banished in the version of the play that comes down to us.
5. Rogue (Autolycus).

6. Probably "colt-pixie," a mischievous sprite or fairy.
7. Sheep shearing.

greatness very familiar, if not ridiculous. Now, King *Henry* making a Masque at the Cardinal, *Wolsey*'s house, and certain Chambers[1] being shot off at his entry, some of the paper, or other stuff wherewith one of them was stopped, did light on the thatch, where being thought at first but an idle smoak, and their eyes more attentive to the show, it kindled inwardly, and ran round like a train, consuming within less then an hour the whole house to the very grounds.

This was the fatal period of that vertuous fabrique, wherein yet nothing did perish, but wood and straw, and a few forsaken cloaks; only one man had his breeches set on fire, that would perhaps have broyled him, if he had not by the benefit of a provident wit put it out with bottle Ale. The rest when we meet

Ben Jonson on *The Tempest* (and *Titus Andronicus*) (1614)

[This extract from *Bartholomew Fair* contains one of several allusions to Shakespeare in the plays of his associate and sometime rival. The first paragraph alludes to the fashion for revenge plays such as Shakespeare's *Titus Andronicus* and Kyd's *Spanish Tragedy*, at its height roughly twenty-five years before *Bartholomew Fair* was written. The second paragraph refers disapprovingly to *The Tempest* (1613), first produced shortly before *Bartholomew Fair*. The text is that reprinted in WS, vol. 2, from the 1631 edition of Jonson's play (from the play's Induction).]

Hee that will sweare, *Jeronimo*, or *Andronicus* are the best playes, yet, shall passe unexcepted at,[1] heere, as a man whose Judgement shewes it is constant, and hath stood still, these five and twentie, or thirtie yeeres. . . .

If there bee never a *Servant-monster* i' the Fayre; who can helpe it? he[2] sayes; nor a nest of Antiques?[3] Hee is loth to make Nature afraid[4] in his *Playes*, like those that beget *Tales*, *Tempests*, and such like *Drolleries*, to mix his head with other mens heeles; let the concupisence of *Jigges* and *Dances*, raigne as strong as it will amongst you.[5]

Shakespeare's Will (March 25, 1615)

[Shakespeare probably dictated this will sometime around January 1616. The first draft seems to have been dated in January, and 1616 is the most likely inference for the year (see note 1). The final revision was certainly made on the date given, but no clean copy was prepared, so the manuscript contains a substantial number of insertions and deletions. The text here has been silently emended to assist in ease of reading. Deleted passages have been eliminated; the most significant of these is reproduced in the notes, where significant interlineations are also identified. Most of the altered passages, as Chambers writes, simply "correct slips, make the legal terminology more precise, or incorporate afterthoughts." The revision of the will was occasioned chiefly by the February marriage of Shakespeare's daughter Judith. Our text is adapted from E. A. J. Honigmann and Susan Brock, eds., *Playhouse Wills, 1558–1642* (Manchester: Manchester University Press, 1993). For a facsimile and thorough discussion of the will, see WS 2:169–80.]

1. Small pieces of artillery, used for firing salutes.
1. Uncriticized.
2. The author.
3. Variant spelling of "antics," grotesque or ludicrous representations, or the actors (such as the clowns in *The Tempest*) playing such parts.
4. Make nature afraid by inexact imitation or too much fantasy.
5. *concupisence . . . you.* a reference to the dance generally incorporated into theatrical performance (see, for example, Platter's account above). Jonson suggests he is refusing to cater to the vulgar taste for more dancing in plays.

Testamentum willelmij Shackspeare
Vicesimo Quinto die martij Anno Regni Domini nostri Jacobi nunc Regis Anglie &c
decimo quarto & Scotie xlixo Annoque domini 1616[1]
In the name of god Amen I William Shackspeare of Stratford upon Avon in the countie of warrwick gentleman in perfect health & memorie god be praysed doe make &
Ordayne this my last will & testament in manner & forme followeing That ys to saye
ffirst I Comend my Soule into the handes of god my Creator hoping & assuredlie
beleeving through thonelie merittes of Jesus Christe my Saviour to be made partaker
of lyfe everlastinge And my bodye to the Earth whereof yt ys made Item I Gyve &
bequeath unto my Daughter Judyth One Hundred & ffyftie poundes of lawfull English money to be paied unto her in manner & forme followeing That ys to saye One
Hundred Poundes in discharge of her marriage porcion[2] within one yeare after my
Deceas with consideracion[3] after the Rate of twoe shillinges in the pound for soe
long tyme as the same shalbe unpaied unto her after my deceas & the ffyftie poundes
Residewe thereof upon her Surrendring of or gyving of such sufficient securitie as
the overseers of this my Will shall like of to Surrender or graunnte All her[4] estate &
Right that shall discend or come unto her after my deceas or that shee nowe hath of
in or to one Copiehold tenemente with thappurtenaunces lyeing & being in Stratford upon Avon aforesaied in the saied countie of warrwick being parcell or holden
of the mannour of Rowington unto my Daughter Susanna Hall & her heires for ever
Item I Gyve & bequeath unto my saied Daughter Judith One Hundred & ffyftie
Poundes more if shee or Anie issue of her bodie be Lyvinge att thend of three Yeares
next ensueing the daie of the Date of this my Will during which tyme my executours
to paie her consideracion from my deceas according to the Rate afore saied And if
she dye within the saied terme without issue of her bodye then my will ys & I doe
gyve & bequeath One Hundred Poundes thereof to my Neece Elizabeth Hall & the
ffiftie Poundes to be sett fourth by my executours during the lief of my Sister Johane
Harte & the use & proffitt thereof Cominge shalbe payed to my saied Sister Jone &
after her deceas the saied l li[5] shall Remaine Amongst the children of my saied Sister Equallie to be Devided Amongst them But if my saied Daughter Judith be lyving
att thend of the saied three Yeares or anie yssue of her bodye then my Will ys & soe
I devise & bequeath the saied Hundred & ffyftie poundes to be sett out by my executours & overseers for the best benefitt of her & her issue & the stock[6] not to be paied
unto her soe long as she shalbe marryed & Covert Baron[7] but my will ys that she shall
have the consideracon yearelie paied unto her during her lief & after her deceas the
saied stock and consideracion to bee paied to her children if she have Anie & if not
to her executours or assignes she lyving the saied terme after my deceas Provided that
if such husbond as she shall att thend of the saied three Yeares be marryed unto
or attaine after doe sufficientle Assure unto her & thissue of her bodie landes
Awnswereable to the porcion by this my will gyven unto her & to be adjudged soe by
my executours & overseers then my will ys that the saied Cl li[8] shalbe paied to such
husbond as shall make such assurance to his owne use Item I gyve & bequeath unto
my saied sister Jone xx li & all my wearing Apparrell to be paied & Delivered within
one yeare after my deceas And I doe Will & devise unto her the house with thappurtenaunces in Stratford wherein she dwelleth for her naturall lief under the yearelie Rent of xii d. Itm I gyve & bequeath unto her three sonns William Harte[9]

1. *Testamentum* . . . *1616*: The Will of William
Shakespeare (marginal heading). On the twenty-fifth
day of March, in the fourteenth year of the reign of
our lord James now King of England, etc., and of Scotland the forty-ninth, in the year of our Lord 1616.
(The abbreviation for "January" is crossed out in the
manuscript, "March" having been substituted at the
time the will was revised.)
2. The phrase "in discharge of her marriage porcion"
was inserted during the course of revision.

3. Compensation, or interest.
4. Susanna Hall's. (The preceding "All" marks the
beginning of a new sentence.)
5. *l li*: £50.
6. Principal.
7. *Covert Baron*: under the protection of a husband.
8. *Cl li*: £150.
9. A blank in the manuscript. Shakespeare appears to
have forgotten the name of one of his nephews,
Thomas.

hart & Michaell Harte ffyve poundes A peece to be payed within one Yeare
after my deceas[1] Item I gyve & bequeath unto her the saied Elizabeth Hall All my
Plate (except my brod silver & gilt bole)[2] that I nowe have att the Date of this my
Will Itm I gyve & bequeath unto the Poore of Stratford aforesaied tenn poundes
to mr Thomas Combe my Sword to Thomas Russell Esquier ffyve poundes & to
ffrauncis Collins of the Borough of Warwick in the countie of Warwick gentleman thirteene poundes Sixe shillinges & Eight pence to be paied within one Yeare
after my Deceas Itm I gyve & bequeath to Hamlett Sadler xxvi s viii d[3] to buy him
A Ringe to William Raynoldes gentleman xxvi s viii d to buy him A Ringe to my
godson William Walker xx s in gold to Anthonye Nashe gentleman xxvi s viii d &
to mr John Nashe xx vi s viii d & to my fellows John Hemynnges Richard Burbage
& Henry Cundell xxvi s viii d A peece to buy them Ringes[4] Item I Gyve Will
bequeath & Devise unto my Daughter Susanna Hall for better enabling of her to
performe this my will & towardes the performans thereof All that Capitall messuage or tenemente[5] with thappurtenaunces in Stratford aforesaied Called the
newe place Wherein I nowe Dwell & twoe messuages or tenementes with thappurtenaunces scituat lyeing & being in Henley streete within the borough of Stratford aforesaied And all my barnes stables Orchardes gardens landes tenementes
& hereditamentes[6] Whatsoever scituat lyeing & being or to be had Receyved
perceyved or taken within the townes Hamlettes villages ffieldes & groundes of
Stratford upon Avon Oldstratford Bushopton & Welcombe or in anie of them in the
saied countie of warrwick And alsoe All that Messuage or tenemente with thappurtenaunces wherein one John Robinson dwelleth scituat lyeing & being in the
blackfriers in London nere the Wardrobe & all other my landes tenementes &
hereditamentes Whatsoever To Have & to hold All & singuler the saied premisses
with their Appurtenaunces unto the saied Susanna Hall for & During the terme of
her naturall lief & after her Deceas to the first sonne of her bodie lawfullie Issueing & to the heires males of the bodie of the saied first Sonne lawfullie Issueinge
& for defalt of such issue to the second Sonne of her bodie lawfullie issueinge & to
the heires males of the bodie of the saied Second Sonne lawfullie issueinge &
for defalt of such heires to the third Sonne of the bodie of the saied Susanna Lawfullie issueing & of the heries males of the bodie of the saied third sonne lawfullie issueing And for defalt of such issue the same soe to be & Remaine to the
ffourth ffyfth sixte & Seaventh sonnes of her bodie lawfullie issueing one after
Another & to the heires[7] Males of the bodies of the saied ffourth fifth Sixte &
Seaventh sonnes lawfullie issueing in such manner as yt ys before Lymitted to
be & Remaine to the first second & third Sonns of her bodie & to their heires
males And for defalt of such issue the saied premisses to be & Remaine to my
sayed Neece Hall[8] & the heires Males of her bodie Lawfullie yssueing for Defalt
of such issue to my Daughter Judith & the heires Males of her bodie lawfullie
issueinge And for Defalt of such issue to the Right heires of me the saied William

1. *unto . . . deceas:* this passage was inserted at the top
of the second page, probably when the will was revised.
The following lines, with which the page originally
began, are crossed out in the original: "to be sett out for
her within one Yeare after my Deceas by my executours
with thadvise & direccions of my overseers for her best
proffitt untill her Marriage & then the same with the
increase thereof to be paied unto her." These lines evidently referred to Judith Shakespeare as unmarried.
2. This parenthetical clause is an insertion, and has
sparked some debate about Shakespeare's opinion of
Judith's marriage.
3. The "s" stands for "shillings," the "d" for "pence."
4. *to my fellows . . . Ringes:* Shakespeare's "fellows,"
or colleagues, Heminges, Burbage, and Condell, had
worked with him in the Lord Chamberlain's Men and

King's Men for many years. Many other wills and documents of the period provide evidence of the practice
of wearing mourning rings alluded to here.
5. Residence. *messuage:* dwelling house with its out-
buildings or adjoining lands.
6. Heritable property.
7. In addition to the signature near the end, Shakespeare signed the will here, in the bottom right-hand
corner of the second page.
8. Susanna Hall's daughter Elizabeth, actually Shakespeare's granddaughter (the sense of "niece" is less
restricted in early modern usage). Elizabeth proved to
be Susanna's only surviving child, and since Susanna
was already thirty-three in 1616, the hypothetical series
of seven sons preceding this mention of Elizabeth is
doubly remarkable.

Shackspere for ever Itm I gyve unto my wief my second best bed[9] with the furniture Item I gyve & bequeath to my saied Daughter Judith my broad silver gilt bole All the Rest of my goodes Chattelles Leases plate Jewels & household stuffe Whatsoever after my dettes and Legasies paied & my funerall expences discharged I gyve Devise & bequeath to my Sonne in Lawe John Hall gentleman & my Daughter Susanna his wief Whom I ordaine & make executours of this my Last Will & testament And I doe intreat & Appoint the saied Thomas Russell Esquier & ffrauncis Collins gentleman to be overseers hereof And doe Revoke All former wills & publishe this to be my last Will & testament In Witnes Whereof I have here unto put my hand the Daie & Yeare first above Written. /   By me William Shakespeare witnes to the publishing hereof Fra: Collyns Julyus Shawe John Robinson Hamnet Sadler Robert Whattcott[1]

Front Matter from the First Folio of Shakespeare's Plays (1623)

[John Heminges and Henry Condell, friends and colleagues of Shakespeare, organized this first publication of his collected (thirty-six) plays. Eighteen of the plays had not appeared in print before, and for these the First Folio is the sole surviving source. Only *Pericles, The Two Noble Kinsmen,* and *Sir Thomas More* are not included in the volume. Four of the first twelve (printed) pages of the Folio are reproduced below in reduced facsimile, with a minimum of explanatory notes. They include Jonson's brief address "To the Reader," Droeshout's portrait of Shakespeare, a table of contents, and a list of actors.]

---

9. This bequest to Shakespeare's wife, Anne, was inserted in the course of his revision of the will. She is not mentioned elsewhere in the will at least partly because, as Shakespeare's widow, she would be guaranteed a certain portion of the estate by law. The appearance of this inserted bequest is nevertheless strange enough to have evoked much speculation.
1. After Shakespeare's death, the will was endorsed here at the bottom of the third page with a Latin inscription indicating that the will had gone to probate before a magistrate on June 22, 1616.

To the Reader.

This Figure, that thou here feeſt put,
  It vvas for gentle Shakeſpeare cut;
Wherein the Grauer had a ſtrife
  with Nature, to out-doo the life :
O, could he but haue dravvne his vvit
  As well in braſſe, as he hath hit
His face ; the Print vvould then ſurpaſſe
  All, that vvas euer vvrit in braſſe.
But, ſince he cannot, Reader, looke
  Not on his Picture, but his Booke.

                                    B. I.

Mr. WILLIAM
SHAKESPEARES
COMEDIES,
HISTORIES, &
TRAGEDIES.

Published according to the True Originall Copies.

Martin Droeshout sculpsit London.

LONDON
Printed by Isaac Iaggard, and Ed. Blount. 1623.

A CATALOGVE

of the feuerall Comedies, Histories, and Tragedies contained in this Volume.

The Workes of William Shakespeare,

containing all his Comedies, Histories, and
Tragedies: Truely set forth, according to their first
ORIGINALL.

The Names of the Principall Actors
in all these Playes.

William Shakespeare.	Samuel Gilburne.
Richard Burbadge.	Robert Armin.
John Hemmings.	William Ostler.
Augustine Phillips.	Nathan Field.
William Kempt.	John Underwood.
Thomas Poope.	Nicholas Tooley.
George Bryan.	William Ecclestone.
Henry Condell.	Joseph Taylor.
William Slye.	Robert Benfield.
Richard Cowly.	Robert Goughe.
John Lowine.	Richard Robinson.
Samuell Crosse.	Iohn Shancke.
Alexander Cooke.	Iohn Rice.

John Milton on Shakespeare (1630)

[John Milton (1608–1674) was born in London and as a boy might conceivably have seen Shakespeare's company act. This poem first appeared prefixed to the Second Folio of Shakespeare's works in 1632 and again in the 1640 *Poems* of Shakespeare. The text is from the 1645 edition of Milton's *Poems*, as reprinted in *WS* vol. 2, but the title given is from the Second Folio version.]

An Epitaph on the admirable Dramaticke Poet, W. Shakespeare

What needs my *Shakespear* for his honour'd Bones,
The labour of an age in piled Stones,
Or that his hallow'd reliques should be hid
Under a star-ypointing Pyramid?[1]
Dear son of memory, great heir of Fame,
What need'st thou such weak witnes of thy name?
Thou in our wonder and astonishment
Hast built thy self a live-long Monument.
For whilst toth' shame of slow-endeavouring art,
They easie numbers flow, and that each heart
Hath from the leaves of thy unvalu'd[2] Book,
Those Delphick[3] lines with deep impression took,
Then thou our fancy of itself bereaving,[4]
Dost make us Marble with too much conceaving;
And so Sepulcher'd in such pomp dost lie,
That Kings for such a Tomb would wish to die.

Ben Jonson on Shakespeare (1623–37)

[In addition to numerous allusions to Shakespeare in his plays, Ben Jonson (1573–1637) writes explicitly about his friend, colleague, and rival in a number of places, most significantly in the two commendatory poems prefixed to the First Folio (see above) and in the published extracts from his notebooks entitled *Timber: or, Discoveries; Made upon Men and Matter*, first published in his *Works* of 1640. It is impossible to date the original entries precisely; Chambers's conjecture is that the following entry on Shakespeare was made after 1630. The text is from the authoritative edition by C. H. Herford and Percy Simpson, vol. 8 (Oxford: Clarendon Press, 1952).]

Indeed, the multitude commend Writers, as they doe Fencers, or Wrastlers; who if they come in robustiously, and put for it, with a deale of viclence, are received for the *braver-fellowes:* when many times their owne rudenesse is a cause of their disgrace; and a slight touch of their Adversary, gives all that boisterous force the foyle. But in these things, the unskilfull are naturally deceiv'd and judging wholly by the bulke, thinke rude things greater then polish'd; and scatter'd more numerous, then compos'd: Nor thinke this only to be true in the sordid multitude, but the neater sort of our *Gallants:* for all are the multitude; only they differ in cloaths, not in judgement or understanding.

I remember, the Players have often mentioned it as an honour to *Shakespeare*,

---

1. Pointing to the stars.
2. Invaluable.
3. Reference to Apollo, god of poetry, whose most famous shrine was at Delphi.

4. *our . . . bereaving:* "our imaginations are rapt 'out of ourselves,' leaving behind our soulless bodies like statues"—Isabel MacCaffrey.

that in his writing, (whatsoever he penn'd) hee never blotted out line.[1] My answer hath beene, Would he had blotted a thousand. Which they thought a malevolent speech. [I had not told posterity this,] but for their ignorance, who choose that circumstance to commend their friend by, wherein he most faulted. And to justifie mine owne candor, (for I lov'd the man, and doe honour his memory (on this side Idolatry) as much as any.) Hee was (indeed) honest, and of an open, and free nature: had an excellent *Phantsie*[2]; brave notions, and gentle expressions: wherein hee flow'd with that facility, that sometime it was necessary he should be stop'd: *Sufflaminandus erat;*[3] as *Augustus* said of *Haterius*.[4] His wit was in his owne power; would the rule of it had beene so too. Many times hee fell into those things, could not escape laughter: As when hee said in the person of *Cæsar*, one speaking to him; *Cæsar, thou dost me wrong.* Hee replyed: *Cæsar did never wrong, but with just cause*[5]: and such like; which were ridiculous. But hee redeemed his vices, with his vertues. There was ever more in him to be praysed, then to be pardoned.

John Aubrey on Shakespeare (1681)

[What Chambers calls "the Shakespeare-mythos" was already well under way by the time John Aubrey (1626–1697) collected these anecdotes for the biographies in his *Brief Lives*, first anthologized in 1692. Aubrey's chief sources were prominent figures of the Restoration stage, which had seen increasingly popular revivals and adaptations of *Hamlet*, *The Tempest*, and many other plays of Shakespeare. Numerous actors and critics in the latter part of the seventeenth century helped to "rehabilitate" Shakespeare; if at the time of the Restoration his plays had seemed terribly musty and old-fashioned, by the 1680s his reputation as an author of lasting value was well established, thanks to the enthusiasm of Restoration playgoers. Aubrey's first source, Christopher Beeston, was the son of a one-time member of Shakespeare's company. William Davenant was a formidable entrepreneur as well as a dramatist, and Thomas Shadwell a prolific playwright perhaps best remembered as Dryden's King of Dullness. The text is from Chambers's transcription (*WS*, vol. 2), with a few silent emendations for ease of reading. Some of the material is from the published version of *Brief Lives*, and some of it from manuscript notes apparently used in writing the *Lives*.]

> the more to be admired q[uia][1] he was not a company keeper[2]
> lived in Shoreditch, wouldnt be debauched, & if invited to
> writ; he was in paine.[3]
>
> W. Shakespeare.

M[r]. William Shakespear. [*bay-wreath in margin*] was borne at Stratford upon Avon, in the County of Warwick; his father was a Butcher, & I have been told heretofore by some of the neighbours, that when he was a boy he exercised his father's Trade, but when he kill'd a Calfe, he would doe it in a *high style*, & make a Speech. There was at that time another Butcher's son in this Towne, that was held not at all inferior to him for a naturall witt, his acquaintance & coetanean,[4] but dyed young. This Wm. being inclined naturally to Poetry and acting, came to London I guesse about 18. and was an Actor at one of the Play-houses and did act

---

1. Compare Heminges and Condell's address to the reader in the First Folio: "And what he thought, he uttered with that easinesse, that wee have scarse received from him a blot in his papers."
2. Imagination.
3. "He needed the drag-chain" (adapted from Marcus Seneca's *Controversiae* 4, Preface).
4. Quintus Haterius, Roman rhetorician (d. 26 c.e.).
5. See *Julius Caesar* 3.1.47.

1. Because.
2. "Company keeper" can mean "libertine" or "reveler"; the general sense of the passage is that Shakespeare is "the more to be admired" for his temperance and modesty.
3. The embarrassment ("paine") at being asked to write is presumably due to the same alleged modesty.
4. Contemporary.

exceedingly well: now B. Johnson was never a good Actor, but an excellent Instructor. He began early to make essayes at Dramatique Poetry. which at that time was very lowe; and his Playes tooke well: He was a handsome well shap't man: very good company, and of a very readie and pleasant smooth Witt. The Humour[5] of . . . the Constable in a Midsomersnight's Dreame, he happened to take at Grendon [*In margin,* 'I thinke it was Midsomer night that he happened to lye there'.] in Bucks[6] which is the roade from London to Stratford, and there was living that Constable about 1642 when I first came to Oxon.[7] M[r]. Jos. Howe is of that parish and knew him. Ben Johnson and he did gather Humours of men day y where ever they came. One time as he was at the Tavern at Stratford super[8] Avon, one Combes an old rich Usurer was to be buryed, he makes there this extemporary[9] Epitaph

Ten in the Hundred[1] the Devill allowes
But *Combes* will have twelve, he sweares & vowes:
If any one askes who lies in this Tombe:
Hoh! quoth the Devill, 'Tis my John o' Combe.

He was wont to goe to his native Country once a yeare. I thinke I have been told that he left 2 or 300[li] per annum[2] there and therabout: to a sister. [*In margin,* 'V.[3] his Epitaph in Dugdales Warwickshire'.] I have heard S[r] Wm. Daverant and M[r]. Thomas Shadwell (who is counted the best Comœdian we have now) say, that he had a most prodigious Witt, and did admire his naturall parts beyond all other Dramaticall writers. He was wont to say, That he never blotted out a line in his life: sayd Ben: Johnson, I wish he had blotted out a thousand. [*In margin,* 'B. Johnsons Underwoods'.] His Comœdies will remaine witt, as long as the English tongue is understood; for that he handles mores hominum;[4] now our present writers reflect so much upon particular persons, and coxcombeities, that 20 yeares hence, they will not be understood. Though as Ben: Johnson sayes of him, that he had but little Latine and lesse Greek, He understood Latine pretty well: for he had been in his younger yeares a Schoolmaster in the Countrey. [*In margin,* 'from M[r] —— Beeston'.]

S[r] William Davenant Knight Poet Laureate was borne in _____ street in the City of Oxford, at the Crowne Tavern. His father was John Davenant a Vintner there, a very grave and discreet Citizen: his mother was a very beautifull woman, & of a very good witt and of conversation extremely agreable. . . . M[r] William Shakespeare was wont to goe into Warwickshire once a yeare, and did commonly in his journey lye at this house in Oxon: where he was exceedingly respected. I have heard parson Robert D[avenant] say that here M[r] W. Shakespeare here gave him a hundred kisses. Now S[r] Wm. would sometimes when he was pleasant over a glasse of wine with his most intimate friends e.g. Sam: Butler (author of Hudibras) &c. say, that it seemed to him that he writt with the very spirit that Shakespeare,[5] and seemed contented enough to be thought his Son: he would tell them the story as above. in which way his mother had a very light report, whereby she was called a whore.

---

5. Character, personality.
6. Buckinghamshire.
7. Oxford.
8. Upon.
9. Extemporaneous.
1. 10-percent interest. (Combe is damned because he charges 12 percent on his loans, 2 percent above the maximum allowed for usury not to be a mortal sin.)
2. £300 a year.
3. See.
4. *for that . . . hominum:* because he treats of (general) human manners or customs.
5. A word such as "had" seems to be missing.

TIMELINE

TEXT	CONTEXT
	1558 Queen Mary I, a Roman Catholic, dies; her sister Elizabeth, raised Protestant, is proclaimed queen.
	1559 Church of England is reestablished under the authority of the sovereign with the passage of the Act of Uniformity and the Act of Supremacy.
1562 *The Tragedy of Gorboduc*, by Thomas Norton and Thomas Sackville, is performed; it is the first English play in blank verse.	**1563** The Church of England adopts the Thirty-nine Articles of Religion, detailing its points of doctrine and clarifying its differences both from Roman Catholicism and from more extreme forms of Protestantism.
	1564 William Shakespeare is born in Stratford to John and Mary Arden Shakespeare; he is christened a few days later, on April 23.
	1565 John Shakespeare is made an alderman of Stratford.
	1567 Mary Queen of Scots is imprisoned on suspicion of the murder of her husband, Lord Darnley. Their infant son, Charles James, is crowned James VI of Scotland.
	1568 John Shakespeare is elected Bailiff of Stratford, the town's highest office. Performances in Stratford by the Queen's Players and the Earl of Worcester's men.
	1572 An act is passed that severely punishes vagrants and wanderers, including actors not affiliated with a patron. Performances in Stratford by the Earl of Leicester's men.
	1574 The Earl of Warwick's and Earl of Worcester's men perform in Stratford.
	1576 James Burbage, father of Richard, later the leading actor in Shakespeare's company, builds the Theatre in Shoreditch, a suburb of London.
	1577 The Curtain Theatre opens in Shoreditch.

TEXT	CONTEXT
	1577–1580 Sir Francis Drake circumnavigates the globe.
	1578 Mary Shakespeare pawns her lands, suggesting that the family s in financial distress. Lord Strange's Men and Lord Essex's Men perform at Stratford.
	1580 A Jesuit mission is established in England with the aim of reconverting the nation to Roman Catholicism.
	1582 Shakespeare marries Anne Hathaway.
	1583 The birth of Shakespeare's older daughter, Susanna.
	1584 Sir Walter Ralegh establishes the first English colony in the New World at Roanoke Island in modern North Carolina; the colony fails.
	1585 The birth of Shakespeare's twin son and daughter, Hamnet and Judith. John Shakespeare is fined for not going to church.
	1586 Sir Philip Sidney dies from battle wounds.
1587 Thomas Kyd's *The Spanish Tragedy* (pub. c. 1592) and Christopher Marlowe's *Tamburlaine* (pub. 1590) are performed.	1587 Mary Queen of Scots is executed for treason against Elizabeth I. Francis Drake defeats the Spanish fleet at Cádiz. John Shakespeare loses his position as an alderman. Philip Henslowe builds the Rose theater at Bankside, on the Thames.
	1588 The Spanish Armada attempts an invasion of England but is defeated.
1589 Robert Greene, *Friar Bacon and Friar Bungay.* Thomas Kyd, *Hamlet* (not extant; perhaps a source for Shakespeare's *Hamlet*). Christopher Marlowe, *The Jew of Malta.*	1589 Shakespeare is probably affiliated with the amalgamated Lord Strange's and Lord Admiral's Men from about this time until 1594.
1590 Anonymous, *The True Chronicle History of King Leir, and his Three Daughters.*	1590 James VI of Scotland marries Anne of Denmark, but believes himself to be bewitched on his honeymoon when he cannot consummate the marriage. Witch trials in Scotland.
1591 Shakespeare's *1, 2,* and *3 Henry VI* performed.	1592 The theatrical manager of the Admiral's Men, Philip Henslowe, begins his diary, continued until 1604, recording his business

TEXT	CONTEXT
	transactions, an important source for theater historians.
1592–1593 *Richard III.* *Venus and Adonis.* *The Comedy of Errors.* *Titus Andronicus.* *The Taming of the Shrew.*	From June 1592 to June 1594, London theaters are shut down because of the plague; acting companies tour the provinces.
1594 Shakespeare dedicates *The Rape of Lucrece* to Henry Wriothesley, Earl of Southampton.	**1594** Roderigo Lopez, Portuguese physician and a Jewish convert to Christianity, is executed on slight evidence for having plotted to poison Elizabeth I.
1594–1596 *A Midsummer Night's Dream.* *Richard II.* *Romeo and Juliet.*	The birth of James VI's first son, Henry.
	1595 Shakespeare lives in St. Helen's Parish, Bishopsgate, London.
	Shakespeare apparently becomes a sharer in (provides capital for) the newly re-formed Lord Chamberlain's Men.
	The Swan Theatre is built in Bankside.
	Hugh O'Neill, Earl of Tyrone, rebels against English rule in Ireland.
	Walter Ralegh explores Guiana, on the north coast of South America.
1596 *King John.* *The Merchant of Venice.* *1 Henry IV.*	**1596** John Shakespeare is granted a coat of arms; hence the title of "gentleman."
	William Shakespeare's son Hamnet dies.
1597 *The Merry Wives of Windsor.*	**1597** James Burbage builds the second Blackfriars Theatre. But the Lord Chamberlain's Men are not permitted to play in it, so they rent it to boys' companies for a number of years.
	The landlord refuses to renew the lease on the land under the Theatre in Shoreditch.
1598 *2 Henry IV.* *Much Ado About Nothing.* Ben Jonson, *Every Man in His Humor,* which lists Shakespeare as one of the actors.	**1598** The Edict of Nantes ends the French civil wars, granting toleration to Protestants.
	Materials from the demolished Theatre in Shoreditch are transported across the Thames to be used in building the Globe Theatre.
1599 *Henry V.* *Julius Caesar.* *As You Like it.*	**1599** The queen's favorite, Robert Devereux, Earl of Essex, leads an expedition to Ireland in March but returns home without permission in October and is imprisoned.
	Satires and other offensive books are prohibited by ecclesiastical order. Extant copies are gathered and burned. Two notorious satirists, Thomas Nashe and Gabriel Harvey, are forbidden to publish.

TEXT	CONTEXT
1600 *Hamlet.* Michael Drayton and several collaborators, who object to Shakespeare's depiction of Oldcastle-Falstaff in the *Henry IV* plays, write *The First Part of the True and Honorable History of the Life of Sir John Oldcastle, the Good Lord Cobham.*	**1600** The Earl of Essex is suspended from some of his offices and confined to house arrest. The birth of James VI's second son, Charles. The founding of the East India Company. Edward Alleyn and Philip Henslowe build the Fortune Theatre for the Lord Admiral's Men, competing with the Lord Chamberlain's Men at the Globe.
1601 "The Phoenix and the Turtle" published in Robert Chester's *Love's Martyr.* *Twelfth Night.* In the "War of the Theaters," Ben Jonson, John Marston, and Thomas Dekker write a series of satiric plays mocking one another.	**1601** The Earl of Essex leads some gentlemen against Elizabeth I, but the rising is quickly quelled. A few of the rebels, including Shakespeare's patron, the Earl of Southampton, arrange a staging of *Richard II* at the Globe, apparently to incite rebellion. Essex is convicted of treason and beheaded. Shakespeare's father dies.
1602 *Troilus and Cressida.*	**1602** Shakespeare makes substantial real-estate purchases in Stratford. The opening of the Bodleian Library in Oxford.
	1603 Queen Elizabeth dies; she is succeeded by her cousin, James VI of Scotland (now James I of England). Shakespeare's name appears for the last time in Ben Jonson's lists of actors, as a "principal tragedian" in *Sejanus.* Plague closes the London theaters from mid-1603 to April 1604. Hugh O'Neill surrenders in Ireland.
1604 *Measure for Measure.* *Othello.*	**1604** The conclusion of a peace with Spain makes travel across the Atlantic safer, encouraging plans for English colonies in the Americas.
1605 *All's Well That Ends Well.* *King Lear.*	**1605** The discovery of the Gunpowder Plot by some radical Catholics to blow up the Houses of Parliament during its opening ceremonies, when the royal family, Lords, and Commons are assembled in one place. The Red Bull Theatre built.
1606 *Macbeth.* *Antony and Cleopatra.* Ben Jonson, *Volpone.* Anonymous, *The Revenger's Tragedy.*	**1606** The London and Plymouth Companies receive charters to colonize Virginia. Parliament passes "An Act to Restrain Abuses of Players," prohibiting oaths or blasphemy onstage.
1607 *Timon of Athens.* *Pericles.*	**1607** An English colony is established in Jamestown, Virginia. Shakespeare's daughter Susanna marries John Hall. Shakespeare's brother Edmund (described as a player) dies.

TEXT	CONTEXT
1608 *Coriolanus.*	**1608** The King's Men obtain permission to play at the second Blackfriars Theatre, a smaller indoor venue.
1609 *Cymbeline.* Unauthorized publication of the sonnets.	
1610 *The Winter's Tale.* Ben Jonson, *The Alchemist.*	**1610** Henry is made Prince of Wales. Shakespeare probably returns to Stratford and settles there.
1611 *The Tempest.* Francis Beaumont and John Fletcher, *A King and No King.* Publication of the Authorized (King James) Bible.	**1611** Plantation of Ulster in Ireland, a colony of English and Scottish Protestants settled on land confiscated from Irish rebels.
1612 *All Is True (Henry VIII),* with John Fletcher. John Webster, *The White Devil.*	**1612** Prince Henry dies.
1613 *The Two Noble Kinsmen,* with John Fletcher.	**1613** Princess Elizabeth marries Frederick V, Elector Palatine. The Globe Theatre burns down during a performance of *All Is True.*
1614 Ben Jonson, *Bartholomew Fair.* John Webster, *The Duchess of Malfi.*	**1614** Philip Henslowe and Jacob Meade build the Hope Theatre, used both for play performances and as a bearbaiting arena. The Globe Theatre reopens.
1616 Ben Jonson publishes *The Works of Benjamin Jonson,* the first collection of plays by an English author.	**1616** William Harvey describes the circulation of the blood. Shakespeare's daughter Judith marries. Shakespeare dies on April 23.
1623 Members of the King's Men publish the First Folio of Shakespeare's plays.	

Textual Variants

THE TWO GENTLEMEN OF VERONA

CONTROL TEXT: F

F: The Folio of 1623
Fa, Fb: Successive states of F incorporating various print-shop corrections and changes

s.p. PANTHINO [F sometimes refers to Antonio's servant as *Panthino* and sometimes as *Panthion*. Standardized as *Panthino* throughout.]

1.1.26 swam swom **43 doting** eating **65 leave** loue **66 metamorphosed** metamorphis'd **76 a sheep** Sheepe **133 testerned** cestern'd **136 wreck** wrack
1.2.83 o' love O'Loue **97 your** you **99 bauble** babble
1.3.50 O *Pro⟨teus⟩*. Oh **88 father** Fathers
2.1.100 stead steed
2.3.24 moved woman would-woman
2.4.101 worthy worthy a **157 braggartism** Bragadisme **159 makes** make **189 Is it** It is **189 mine eye, or** mine, or
2.5.1 Milan *Padua* **35 that** that that
3.1.81 of Verona in *Verona* **269 catalogue** Cate-log **269 conditions** Condition **289 Try** [Fb] thy [Fa] **297 sew** sowe **311 follows** [Fa] follow [Fb] **313 be broken with** be **320 talk** [Fb] take [Fa] **322 villain** [Fb] villanie [Fa] **329 love** [Fb] lone [Fa] **339 hair** [Fb] haires [Fa] **342 last** [Fb; not in Fa]
3.2.14 grievously [Fb] heauily [Fa]
4.1.34 I had been often I often had beene often **44 aweful** awfull **47 An heir, and near** And heire and Neece,
4.2.107 his her
4.3.17 abhors abhor'd
4.4.48 hangman boys Hangmans boyes **54 on end** an end **62 thou** thee **66 to** not **165 beholden** beholding
5.2.7 s.p. JULIA *Pro⟨teus⟩*. **13 s.p. JULIA** *Thu⟨rio⟩*. **18 your** you
5.3.7 Moses *Moyses*
5.4.150 endowed endu'd

THE TAMING OF THE SHREW

CONTROL TEXT: F

s.p. KATHERINE [F's use of *Katerina, Katherina, Katerine, Kate,* and *Katherine* has been standardized throughout.]

s.p. PETRUCCIO [F's use of *Petruchio* has been changed throughout.]
s.p. SLY [F's use of *Beggar* has been changed throughout.]
s.p. BARTHOLOMEW [F's use of *Lady* when Bartholomew is dressed as a woman has been changed throughout.]

Induction 1.13 Breathe Brach **78 s.p. A PLAYER** 2. *Player* **86 s.p. ANOTHER PLAYER** *Sinclo*
Induction 2.2 lordship Lord **51 wi'th'** with **91 Greet** Greece
1.1.3 fore for **13 Vincentio** *Vincentio's* **25 Mi perdonate** Me Pardonato **156 captum** captam **232 faith** faith **237 your** you
1.2.18 masters mistrs **23 Con tutto il cuore ben trovato** Contut-i le core bene trobatto **24 ben** bene **24 molte onorato** multo honorata **31 pip** peepe **43 this'** this **70 as** is as **115 me and other more,** me. Other more **167 help me** helpe one **185 Antonio's** *Butonios* **186 his fortune** my fortune **209 ours** yours **263 feat** seeke **278 ben** Been
2.1.8 thee [not in F] **60 Licio** Litio [Licio is four times referred to as *Lisio* and three times as *Litio* in F. Standardized to "Licio" throughout.] **75–76 wooing. Neighbour** wooing neighbors **78 unto you** vnto **240 askance** asconce **322 in me** in **343 cypress** Cypres **367 Marseilles** Marcellus
3.1.4 this this Bianca is, this is **28, 32, 41 Sigeia . . . Sigeia . . . Sigeia** sigeria . . . Sigeria . . . sigeria **46–48 s.p. HORTENSIO How . . . yet.** [assigned to Lucentio in F] **49 s.p. BIANCA** *Lucentio* **50 s.p. LUCENTIO** *Bian⟨ca⟩*. **52 s.p. BIANCA** *Hort⟨ensio⟩*. **79 change** charge **odd** old **80 s.p. MESSENGER** *Nicke*.
3.2.16 them [not in F] **29 thy** [not in F] **30 old news** [not in F] **33 hear** heard **51 weighed** Waid **52 half-cheeked** halfe-chekt **84 not** [not in F]
3.3.1 sir, to love sir, Loue **3 I** [not in F] **39 vicar** wench
4.1.22 s.p. CURTIS *Gru⟨mio⟩*. **75 sleekly** slickely **99 s.p. GRUMIO** *Gre⟨mio⟩*.
4.2.4 s.p. HORTENSIO *Luc⟨entio⟩*. **6 s.p. LUCENTIO** *Hor⟨tensio⟩*. **8 s.p. LUCENTIO** *Hor⟨tensio⟩*. **13 none** me **31 her** them **72** [ascribed to "*Pa-*."] **in** me
4.3.63 s.p. HABERDASHER *Fel.* **81 a** [not in F] **88 like a** like **93 nor cap** neither cap **175 accou'st** accountedst

4.4.1 Sir Sirs
4.5.5 he's has **16 except** expect **26 t'attend** to come
4.6.19 is in **23 so it shall be still** so it shall be so **39 where is** whether is **79 be** [not in F]
5.1.5 master's mistris **43 master's** Mistris **56 copintank** copataine
5.2.2 done come **38 thee, lad** the lad **46 two** too **110 wonders** a wonder **132 a fiue 136 you're** your

The First Part of the Contention of the Two Famous Houses of York and Lancaster (The Second Part of Henry VI)

Control Text: F, primarily, and Q1 for some passages: 1.1.54–70; 2.1.70 s.d.; 2.1.116–53 s.d.; 4.5 initial s.d.–4.6 initial s.d.; and most of 2.3, from s.d. following line 58 to initial s.d. in 2.4. In these five passages, readings taken from F are treated as variants of Q1 and marked as such. In addition, this edition prints some material from Q not in F but that derives, the Oxford editors believe, from a revised version of the Folio text. These passages are also marked in the variants because they are alterations to the control text. For discussion of the status of this text, see the Textual Note; for a much fuller collation and discussion of Quarto and Folio variants, see Oxford's *William Shakespeare: A Textual Companion.*

F: The Folio of 1623
Q1: The Quarto of 1594
Q2: The Quarto of 1600
Q3: The Quarto of 1619

s.p. KING HENRY [F's use of *King* has been changed throughout.]
s.p. QUEEN MARGARET [F's use of *Queen* has been changed throughout.]
s.p. CARDINAL BEAUFORT [F's use of *Cardinal* and *Winchester* has been standardized throughout.]
s.p. GLOUCESTER [F's use of *Gloucester* and *Humphrey* has been standardized throughout.]
s.p. DUCHESS [F's use of *Elianor* and *Duchess* has been standardized throughout.]
s.p. HORNER [F's use of *Armorer* has been changed throughout.]
s.p. BOLINGBROKE [F's spelling, *Bullingbrooke,* has been changed throughout.]
s.p. ASNATH [F's use of *Spirit* (in 1.4) has been changed.]
s.p. SIMPCOX'S WIFE [F's use of *Wife* (in 2.1) has been changed.]

s.p. CAPTAIN [F's use of *Lieutenant* (in 4.1) has been changed to Q's *Captain.*]
s.p. WHITMORE [F's use of *Whitmore* and *Walter* (in 4.1) has been standardized.]
s.p. FIRST REBEL [F's use of *Bevis* has been changed throughout.]
s.p. SECOND REBEL [F's use of *Holland* has been changed throughout.]
s.p. MESSENGER [F's use of *Michael* (in 4.2) has been changed.]
s.p. STAFFORD'S BROTHER [F's use of *Brother* (in 4.2) has been changed.]
s.p. WEAVER [F's use of *Smith* and *Weaver* has been standardized throughout.]
s.p. BUTCHER [F's use of *Dicke* and *Butcher* has been standardized throughout.]
s.p. REBEL [Q's use of *Robin* has been changed at 4.7.116 (Q is control text for this section).]
s.p. CLIFFORD [F's use of *Clifford* and *Old Clifford* has been standardized throughout.]
s.p. YOUNG CLIFFORD [F's use of *Clifford* and *Young Clifford* has been standardized throughout.]

Title: *The first part of the contention of the two famous / Houses, of Yorke and Lancaster* [Q running title] THE / First part of the Con- / tention betwixt the two famous Houses of Yorke / and Lancaster, with the death of the good / Duke Humphrey: / And the banishment and death of the Duke of / Suffolke, and the Tragicall end of the proud Cardinall / of Winchester, with the notable Rebellion / of Jacke Cade: / And the Duke of Yorkes first claime unto / the Crowne [Q title page] The second Part of Henry the Sixt, / with the death of the Good Duke / HUMFREY [F head title]

1.1.24–29 Th' . . . King [Q, not in F; for F's version of this speech, see inset passage in text.] **24 excess of** excessive **28 naught** nothing **35 s.p. LORDS** *kneel*[*ing*] *All kneel.* **44 René** Raynard [Q] Reignier [F] **47 it is further agreed between them** [Q; not in F] **49 fa–** [Q] *father* **54–70** [Q is control text for these lines.] **55 duchy of Anjou and the county of** Duches of *Anioy* and of **56 delivered** delivered over **63 I'th** [F] in the **89 had** hath **141 But I'll . . . speak.** [Q; not in F] **166 hoist** hoyse **175 Protector** [Q] Protectors **189 thee** [Q] the **196–97 The reverence . . . command.** [Q; not in F] **207 Then let's away** Then lets make hast away **250 surfeit** in the surfeting in **255 in** [Q] in in
1.2.19 hour thought **22 dream** dreames **38 are** [Q] wer **75 Jordan** *Jordane* **cunning witch of** Eye cunning witch [F]

1.3.6 s.p. FIRST PETITIONER *Peter* 33 master
Mistresse 34–36 usurer . . . usurper [Q]
Usurper 45 s.p. ALL PETITIONERS *All* 72
haught haughtie 94 their the 104 helm
[Q] Helme. *Exit.* 146 I'd [Q] I could [F]
149 pamper hamper 154 fury Fume 208
judge by case judge 215 s.p. KING HENRY
Then . . . of Somerset [Q; not in F]
216–17 We make . . . foes. We make your
grace Regent over the French, / And to defend
our rights gainst forraine foes, / And so do
good unto the Realme of *France* [Q; not in F]
226 be shall be
1.4.23 Asnath Asmath 31 Tell me what fate
awaits [Q2, Q3] what fates await 33 betide
[Q] befall 37–38 [For Q's version of these
lines, see inset passage in text.] 42 deep
deeply 56–57 What have . . . posse. [In F,
York reads the prophecies aloud at this point;
Q transposes this reading to the next scene
and assigns it to King Henry at 2.1.177–87].
56 s.d. [*He*] *reads* [*the writings*] *Reades.* /
The Duke yet lives, that Henry *shall depose:* /
But him out-live, and dye a violent death. 57
Aeacidam AEacida posse posso. / Well, to
the rest: / Tell me what fate awaits the Duke
of Suffolke? / *By Water shall he dye, and take*
his end. / What shall betide the Duke of
Somerset? / *Let him shunne Castles, Safer*
shall he be upon the sandie Plaines, / *Then*
where Castles mounted stand 58–59 These
oracles are hardily attained / And hardly
understood. Come, come, my lord, Come,
come, my Lords, These oracles are hardly
attained / And hardly understood.
2.1.26 some such 37–43 s.p. GLOUCESTER . . .
words. [Q; not in F] 46 an if And if 53 s.p.
CARDINAL BEAUFORT [F makes the line a continuation of Gloucester's prior speech.] 65
tell and tell 74 sight his sight 109 Alban
Albones 114 And . . . sir; [Q] What Coulour
is my Gowne of? / *Simpc(oxe).* Black forsooth,
116–53 [Q is control text for this section.]
117 before [F] ere a many [F] many, a one
118 s.p. SIMPCOX'S WIFE . . . life. [F; not in
Q] 119 Tell [F] But tell 128 Simon Sander
Simpcox [F; not in Q] 129 Simon Sander
thou [not in Q] 131 our all our 133 distinguish distinguish of 135 Saint My Lords,
Saint Alban [F] Albones 136 Would and
would 138 that [F] I would 141 We have,
my lord, an if it please your grace. Yes, my
Lord, if it please your Grace. 144 Bring Now
fetch stool stoole hither by and by 145 o'er
over 147 am not able even to am not able to
149 sirrah Sir 150 Whip Sirrah Beadle,
whip 177–87 [Following Q, the Oxford editors move the reading of the prophecies from
1.4.56 to this location.] 176 And here's . . .
them. [Q; not in F] 177 s.p. KING HENRY [Q]
Yorke. First . . . of him become? become of

him? [Q; not in F] 178–79 The Duke . . .
death. [after Q; not in F here] 180 God's will
be done in all. [Q; not in F] Well, to the rest
[after F] 181–82 Tell . . . end. [after Q; not
in F here] 183–184 s.p. SUFFOLK . . . lie. [Q;
not in F] 185 s.p. KING HENRY [Q; F assigns
to York] 185–87 What . . . stand. [after Q;
not in F here]
2.2.6 out at full at full 26 well all 28 Duke
of York Duke 41 Owain Glyndŵr *Owen*
Glendour 45 was son was 46 son Sonnes
Sonne 56 John's his 77 off we off
2.3.3 sins since 19 grave ground 30 helm
Realme 34 erst [Q1, Q2] ere 35 willing [Q]
willingly 2.3.58–2.4 0 [In these lines, Q is
control text for 2.3.58–75, 2.3.83–88, and
2.3.101–2 4.0] 78 an if and if 88 well [F;
not in Q] 98 warne way 99 enemy Enemies
2.4.18 sheriffs [Q] Sherife 77, 103 s.p. FIRST
SHERIFF *Sh(erife),* *Sherife*
3.1.78 wolf Wolves 98 Suffolk's Duke [Q]
Suffolke 137 my good [Q] my 211 strains
strayes 264 conceit deceit 319–30 [For
the Q version of these lines, see inset passage
in the text.] 330.2 'gainst against 348
nurse nourish 363 porcupine Porpentine
381 coistrel [Q] rascall [F]
3.2.14 Then draw the curtains close; away,
be gone! Away, be gone 26 Meg Nell 75
leper Leaper 79 Queen Margaret Dame
Elianor ne'er neere 82 wrecked wrack'd
83, 85 winds [Q winde 100 Margaret
Elianor 107 heart Hart 116 witch watch
120 Margaret *Elinor* 223 born borne 236
s.p. COMMONS . . . Suffolk! Down with
Suffolk! [Q; not in F; F s.d. reads *A noyse*
within.] 243 s.p. COMMONS . . . *the com-*
mons [after Q; not in F] 272 s.p. COMMONS
(within) (*Commons within.*) 280 s.p. COM-
MONS (*within*) *Within.* 310 enemies [Q]
enemy 312 Could [Q] Would 320 My
mine on an distraught distract 334 turn
turnes 336 this [Q] the 346 upon these
lips upon these 395 his [Q] it's 402 By
thee to die [Q] To dye by thee
3.3.10 whe'er where
4.1.6 Clip Cleape 20 s.p. WHITMORE Cut Cut
22 [line assumed missing] 33 thee death
49 Jove sometime went disguised, and why
not I? [Q. not in F] 51 s.p. SUFFOLK (*Suf.*)
[Q; not in F] 52 The [Q] *Suf(folke).* The 53
jady [Q] iaded 71 s.p. CAPTAIN . . . Ay *Lieu.*
Poole, Sir *Poole?* Lord, / I 77 shalt [Q] shall
85 mother's bleeding Mother-bleeding 93
are and 113 s.p. CAPTAIN . . . rage. [not in
F] 114 s.p. SUFFOLK [not in F] 116 s.p.
CAPTAIN Walter– s.p. WHITMORE Come
Lieu(tenant). *Water:* W. Come 118 *Paene*
Pine 121 daunted danted 134 s.p. SUF-
FOLK Come Come 135 That *Suf(folke).*
That

4.2.30 fall fail 75 Chatham [Q] Chartam 80 He's Ha's 87 that [Q] it 90 an a 132 an [Q] if 135 testify [Q1, Q2] testifie it 147 maimed main'd

4.3.6 Thou [Q1, Q2] and thou 6 licence a License

4.4.20 lamenting and mourning lamenting and mourning for 38 Kenilworth Killingworth 42 trait'rous rabble hateth Traitors hateth 48 almost [Q; not in F] 57 be betrayed betraid

4.5–4.6.0 [Q is control text for these lines.] 2 lord Scales Lord 2–3 he and his men they 3–4 did withstand withstand 8 essayed [F] attempted 9 Get you to Smithfield, there to gather head But get you to Smythfield, and gather head 10 will I I will

4.6.5 otherwise [Q] other 7 Zounds [Q; not in F] 10 My Dicke. My 11 go on [Q] go 12 afire [Q1, Q3] on fire

4.7.21 serge Surge 24 Dauphin Dolphine 39 on [Q] in 43 their shirts their shirt 48–51 Bonum . . . well enough. [Q] Away with him, away with him, he speaks Latine. 63 But Kent 81 caudle Candle 81–82 the health o' the help of 100 to the Standard in Cheapside [Q; not in F] 101 go to Mile End Green [Q; not in F] 113 Married men [Q] Men 115 s.d.–131 s.d. Enter . . . Sergeant [Q; not in F] 117 quench [Q3] squench 124 went and went and and proper paper 131 brain Brave 134–36 He that . . . smock. [Q; not in F] 147 What noise is this? What noise is this heare? 156 rebel rabble

4.8.27 stout Irish stout 34 calmed calme

4.9.6 oe'r on 18 waning warning 22 Zounds Sounes [Q; not in F] 52 Stand you all aside. [Q; not in F] 56 God [Q] love 74 bore bare

5.1.10 sword soule 72 Iwis I was 83 wi'th' with th' 109 Sirrah Wold'st have me kneele? First let me ask of thee, / If they can brooke I bow a knee to man: / Sirrah sons [Q] sonne 111 for of 147 bearheard Berard 192 or and 195 you [Q] thee 199 household [Q] housed 205 to [Q] io [or possibly "so"]

5.2.0–6 Alarums . . . Somerset's body. [After F; F places this passage following 5.3.65.]

5.3.8 s.p. CLIFFORD Warwick . . . come. [Q; not in F] 20–30 s.p. YORK Clifford . . . York. [Q; not in F. For the F version of this encounter, see inset passage in the text.] 20 Clifford Now Clifford 22 know now 25 not never 30.10 oeuvres eumenes

5.5.1–4 How now, . . . rights. [Q; not in F] 5.5.17 s.d.–19 Enter . . . York [Q] But Noble as he is, looke where he comes. / s.d. Enter Salisbury 37 drums Drumme

RICHARD DUKE OF YORK (3 HENRY VI)

CONTROL TEXT: F

F: The Folio of 1623
O: The Octavo of 1595
Q2: The Quarto of 1600
Q3: The Quarto of 1619
Fa, Fb: Successive states of F incorporating various print-shop corrections and changes

s.p. YORK [F's Plantagenet and York have been standardized throughout.]

s.p. KING HENRY [F's Henry has been changed throughout.]

s.p. QUEEN MARGARET [F's Queen and Margaret have been changed throughout.]

s.p. PRINCE EDWARD [F's Prince and Prince Edward have been standardized throughout.]

s.p. GEORGE/GEORGE OF CLARENCE [F's Clarence has been changed to "George" (1.1–3.1) and to "George of Clarence" once he is granted the title Duke of Clarence.]

s.p. RICHARD OF GLOUCESTER [F's Richard has been changed after 3.1 once he is granted the title Duke of Gloucester.]

s.p. KING EDWARD [F's King and King Edward have been standardized from 3.2 to the end of the play.]

s.p. LADY GRAY [F's Widow, Lady Gray, and Gray have been standardized throughout.]

s.p. KING LOUIS [F's Lewis has been changed throughout.]

s.p. LADY BONA [F's Bona has been changed throughout.]

s.p. MESSENGER [F's Gabriel has been changed at 1.2.49.]

s.p. SOLDIER [F's Son has been changed throughout 2.5.]

s.p. SECOND SOLDIER [F's Father has been changed throughout 2.5.]

s.p. FIRST GAMEKEEPER [F's Sinklo has been changed throughout 3.1]

s.p. SECOND GAMEKEEPER [F's Humfrey has been changed throughout 3.1.]

Title: The true Tragedie of Richard Duke / of Yorke, and the good King / Henry the Sixt [O head title] The true Tragedie of Richard / Duke of Yorke, and the death of / good King Henrie the Sixt, / with the whole contention betweene / the two Houses Lancaster / and Yorke, as it was sundrie times / acted by the Right Honoura– / ble the Earle of Pem– / brooke his servants. [O title page] The third Part of Henry the Sixt, / with the death of the Duke of / YORKE [F]

1.1.19 hap hope 69 s.p. EXETER [O] *Westm⟨orland⟩* 78 mine [O, Q2] my 83 and that's [Q3] that's 105 Thy [O] My 120–24 s.p. NORTHUMBERLAND . . . king [O; for F, see inset passage in text.] 121 York *Plantagenet* 122 both both both 138 An And 171 me [O; not in F] 197 thine [O, Q2] an 200 nor neyther 255 the utter ruin vtter ruine 260 with [O; not in F] 262 from [O] to 269 coast cost

1.2.40 to Edmund Brook [O] vnto my 65 s.p. SIR JOHN *John* 72 uncles Vnckle

1.4.51 buckle [O] buckler 82 thy [O] the 138 tiger's Tygres 151 passions move [O] passions moues

2.1.113 And, very well appointed as I thought, [O; not in F] 127 captains [O] Captiues 131 an idle [O] a lazie 144 his [O] the

2.2.92 our brother out [O] out me 133 s.p. RICHARD [O] *War⟨wicke⟩* 172 deniest [O] denied'st

2.5.38 weeks [not in F] 119 E'en Men

2.6.6 commixture [O] Commixtures 8 The common people swarm like summer flies, [O; not in F] 42 s.p. EDWARD [O] *Rich⟨ard⟩* 43 s.p. RICHARD A [O] A 44 s.p. EDWARD . . . See [O] See 44 And [O] *Ed⟨ward⟩* And 60 his [O] is 80 buy but [O] buy

3.1.17 wast was 24 thee the sour adversity sower Aduesaries 30 Is I: 55 thou that [O] thou 96 in the the

3.2.3 lands [O] Land 28 whip me then [O] then whip me 30 an [O, Q2] if 32 them [O] then 119 as [O] your 123 honourably [O] honourable

3.3.11 state Seat 33 An And 124 eternal [O] externall 156 Warwick, peace Warwicke 202 ay I 228 I'll [O] I

4.1.17 you [not in F] 28 my [O, Q2] mine 91 thy [O] the 133 near'st [O, Q2] neere

4.2.2 sort people 12 come welcome 15 towns Towne

4.6.4 stands stand 8 Comes Come

4.7.11 prisonment imprisonment 55 be confiscate confiscate

4.8.67–74 Ay . . . fight. [O omits line 4.8.70 and the following stage direction and assigns the remainder of these lines to Montgomery. F divides them among Montgomery, Hastings, and a soldier.] 71 s.p. MONTGOMERY [O] *Soul⟨dier⟩* 72 Ireland [O] *Ireland, & c.* 73 And [O] *Mount⟨gomerie⟩* And

4.9.12 stir stirre vp

5.1.68 bye buy 75 an [O, Q2] if 78 an in 80–83 s.p. GEORGE OF CLARENCE . . . WARWICKE [O; not in F] 94 Jephthah Iephah 102 brothers [O] Brother

5.4.27 ragged raged 35 York [not in F] 82 s.d.–5.5.17 *Alarum* . . . ambitious York.

[For the O version, see inset passage in the text.]

5.5.17.1 s.p. ALL THE LANCASTER PARTY *All* 17.2 Now [F] Lo 17.5 Go, bear them hence [F] Awaie 17.3 Edward [F] Now *Edward* 49 The [O; not in F] 76–77 butcher, / Hard-favoured Richard? [O] butcher *Richard?*

5.6.46 tempests [O] Tempest 80 I had no father, I am like no father; [O; not in F] 85 kept'st keept'st 90–91 Henry . . . the rest, [O, Q2] King *Henry,* and the Prince his Son are gone, / *Clarence* thy turne is next, and then the rest 90 art [F; not in O]

5.7.5 renowned [O] Renowne 21 an [O, Q2] if 25 and [Fb] add [Fa] thou [O] that 27 kiss [Fb] 'tis [Fa] 30 s.p. LADY GRAY *Cla⟨rence⟩* Thanks [O] Thanke 42 rests [Fb] tests [Fa]

TITUS ANDRONICUS

CONTROL TEXT: Q1; ADDITIONAL MATERIAL FROM F

F: The Folio of 1623
Q1: The Quarto of 1594
Q2: The Quarto of 1600
Q3: The Quarto of 1611

s.p. SATURNINUS [Q1's use of *Saturnine, King,* and *Emperour* has been standardized throughout.]

s.p. AARON [Q1's use of *Moore* and *Aron* has been standardized throughout.]

s.p. YOUNG LUCIUS [*Puer* in Q1; standardized throughout.]

1.1.18 s.p. MARCUS [not in Q1] 35 field; [Four lines follow in Q1, indented in this edition.] 35.2 the that 40 succeeded succeede 64 s.p. Captain [not in Q1] 98 *manes manus* 141 quit her quit the 157 s.p. LAVINIA [not in Q1] 226 *Titans* [Q2] Tytus 242 Pantheon Pathan 264 chance [Q2] change 280 *cuique cuiqui* 283 guard? [Q1 and F have four lines following, indented in this edition.] 295 Follow . . . back [In Q1, this line follows 1.1.285.] 313 Phoebe Thebe 355 s.p. QUINTUS and MARTIUS Titus two sonnes speakes. 357 s.p. QUINTUS Titus sonne speakes. 365 s.p. MARTIUS 3. Sonne. 366 s.p. QUINTUS 2. Sonne. 395 s.p. MARCUS Yes . . . remunerate [The line does not occur in Q1; it does appear in F, but without the attribution to Marcus.] 471 s.p. LUCIUS [not in Q1] All. [Q3] Son. [F]

2.1.110 than this

2.2.1 morn [Q3] Moone **24 run** runs
2.3.33 and ann **72 swart** [F] swartie **85 note**
notice **88 have I** I have **115 henceforward**
hence forth **126 quaint** painted **131 ye**
desire we desire **153 Some** [Q2] So me
192 s.p. AARON [not in Q1] **210 unhal-**
lowed [F] vnhollow **222 berayed** beraud
231 Pyramus Priamus **236 Cocytus** Ocitus
260 gripped griude **268 s.p. SATURNINUS**
[s.p. "King." printed after the text of the letter, at line 276.]
2.4.11 s.p. MARCUS [not in Q1] **27 him** them
30 three their **38 Philomel** Philomela
3.1.12 two [not in Q1] **35 must** must, / and
bootlesse vnto them **146 with his** with her
215 sorrows sorrow **224 blow** flow
280–81 And Lavinia, thou shalt be
employed. / Bear thou my hand, sweet
wench, between thine arms. And *Lauinia*
thou shalt be imployde in these Armes, /
Beare thou my hand sweet wench betweene
thy teethe:
3.2 [This scene appears first in F. There is no Q1
counterpart.] **13 with outrageous** without
ragious **39 complainer** complaynet **52 thy**
[not in F] **53 fly** Flys **55 are** [not in F] **60**
father, brother? father and mother? **62**
dirges doings **72 myself** my selfes
4.1.10 s.p. MARCUS [In Q1, speech continued
to Titus.] **69 here** [not in Q1] **77 s.p. TITUS**
[not in Q1] **90 sware** sweare
4.2.15 that [not in Q1] **123 that** [Q3] your
135 do join joine **177 fat** feede
4.3.32 But [Catchword in Q1 but not
reproduced on the following page, presumably because a line was accidentally
omitted.] **40 now** so **54 Apollinem**
Apollonem **57 'To Saturn', Caius** To Saturnine, to Caius **77** [Speech continued to Titus
in Q2 is attributed to the Clown in Q1.]
92 [After this line, Q1 and F
print a short exchange, indented in this
edition.]
4.4.5 as know [not in Q1] **92 feed**
[Q3] seede **104 on** in **112 incessantly**
sucessantly
5.1.17 s.p. GOTHS [not in Q1] **46 What,**
deaf? What, not a word? what deafe, not a
word? **53 Get me a ladder** [attributed to
Aaron in Q1] **133 haystacks** haystalks **165**
come. Away! come, march away
5.2.18 it action F that accord **49 globe**
Globes **50 two** thee two **52 murderers**
murder **52 caves** cares **56 Hyperion's** Epe-
ons **61 they thy** them thy
5.3.26 gracious [Q2–3, F, not in Q1] **42**
effectual and effectuall **124 cause** course
140 s.p. ROMANS Marcus. **141 s.p. MARCUS**
[not in Q1] **143 adjudged** [Q3] adiudge
145 s.p. ROMANS [not on Q1] **153 blood-**
stained blood slaine

THE FIRST PART OF HENRY THE SIXTH

CONTROL TEXT: F

F: The Folio of 1623

s.p. KING HENRY [F's use of *King* has been
changed throughout.]
s.p. JOAN [F's use of *Joan, Pucelle,* and *Puzel*
(see note 4 to 1.6.85) has been standardized throughout.]
s.p. CHARLES [F's use of *Dolphin (Dauphin)*
and *Charles* has been standardized
throughout.]
s.p. RICHARD PLANTAGENET / RICHARD DUKE
OF YORK [F's use of *York* and *Richard* has
been standardized to "Richard Plantagenet" until 3.1.175–77, when he regains
his title; thereafter, "Richard Duke of
York" is used.]
s.p. WINCHESTER [F's use of *Winchester* and
Cardinal has been standardized throughout.]
s.p. FASTOLF [F's use of *Falstaff* has been
changed throughout (see note to 1.1.131).]
s.p. RENÉ [F's use of *Reigneir* and *Reignier*
has been changed throughout.]
s.p. GLASDALE [F's spelling, *Glansdale,* has
been changed throughout.]
s.p. ALENÇON [F's spelling, *Alanson,* has been
changed throughout.]

1.1.50 marish Nourish **60 Rouen, Rheims,**
Rheimes, **62 corpse** Coarse **89 s.p. SEC-**
OND MESSENGER Mess. **94 René** Reynold
103 s.p. THIRD MESSENGER Mes. **131 Fas-**
tolf *Falstaffe* **132 vanguard** Vauward **157**
Fore Orléans for Orleance is **176 steal** send
1.2.21 flee fly
1.3.9 bred breed **78 five** fine **92 rites** rights
110 halcyon's *Halcyons*
1.4.5 knocketh knocks **19 My lord** The Cardinall **29 vizier** Vmphier **36 If Ile** canuas
thee in thy broad Cardinalls Hat, **If 41 pur-**
ple Scarlet **48 I'll** I bishop's mitre Cardinalls Hat **55 cloakèd** Scarlet **72 s.p.**
OFFICER [not in F] **77 Bishop** Cardinall **82**
bishop is Cardinall's
1.5.8 Prince's spials Princes espyals **10**
Wont Went
1.6.5 Duke Earle **11 pilled** pil'd **41 Glasdale**
Glansdale **44 Lou** Lords **67 Bear . . . bury**
it [F places after 1.6.64] **73 like thee,**
Nero, like thee, **79 la Pucelle** *de Puzel* **85**
Pucelle **or pucelle** *Puzel* or *Pussel* **Dauphin**
Dolphin
1.7.3 men them **29 style** Soyle
1.8.3 la Pucelle *de Puzel* **21 pyramid** Pyra-
mis **22 of** or **29 la Pucelle** *de Puzel*
2.1.5 s.p. A SENTINEL Sent. **29 all together**
altogether **38 s.p. SENTINELS** Sent.

2.2.6 **centre** Centure 20 **Arc** Acre

2.3.21 **seely** silly

2.4.41 **from the tree are cropped** are cropt from the Tree 57 **law** you 117 **wiped** whipt 132 **gentles** gentle

2.5.3 **rack** Wrack 6–7 **Argue . . . Mortimer. / Nestor-like . . . care.** *Nestor*-like . . Care, / Argue . . . *Mortimer.* 44 **dis-ease** Disease 71 **King** [not in F] 75 **the third** third 76 **the King** hee 129 **mine ill my will**

3.1.52 s.p. **GLOUCESTER** *Warw⟨icke⟩.* 53 s.p. **WARWICK** [not in F, where this line and the prior three words, here assigned to Gloucester, are given to Warwick] 54 **so** see so **intertalk** enter talke 83 **pebble** peeble 167 **alone** all alone 175 **gird** gyrt 203 **should lose** loose

3.2.13 *Qui* Che

3.5.32 **Goodbye** God b'uy

4.1.14 **thee** the 19 **Patay** *Poictiers* 48 **my** [not in F] 180 **I wist** I wish

4.2.3 **captain** Captaines **calls** call 15 s.p. **GENERAL** *Cap.* 29 **fire** ryue 34 **due** dew

4.3.17 s.p. **LUCY** 2. *Mes.* 30 s.p. **LUCY** *Mes.* 34 s.p. **LUCY** *Mes.* 47 s.p. **LUCY** *Mes.*

4.4.16 **legions** Regions 19 **unadvantaged** in aduantage 26 **and** [not in F] 27 **René Reignard** 31 **horse** hoast

4.5.39 **shamed** shame

4.7.70 *Maréchal* Marshall 89 **have them** haue him 94 **with them** with him

5.1.59 **nor** neither

5.2.17–18 s.p. **JOAN** Now . . . fear. / Of Now . . . feare. / *Pucel.* Of

5.3.8 **speed and quick** speedy and quicke

5.4.15 **comest** comst

5.5.4–5 **And . . . side. / I . . . peace, I . .** peace, / And . . . side. 12 **his** her 18 **stream** streames 24 **here to hear** heere 41 **random** randon 92 **Assent** Consent 110 **countries** Country 135 **modestly** modestie

5.6.10 **an't** and 37 **one** me, 49 **Arc** Aire 68 **ingling** iugling 70 **we will** we'll

5.7.60 **That** [not in F]

THE TRAGEDY OF KING RICHARD THE THIRD

CONTROL TEXT: F (EXCEPT FOR 3.1.0–148 AND 5.5.4–END, FOR WHICH THE COPY TEXT IS Q1)

F: The Folio of 1623

Q1: The Quarto of 1597

Q2: The Quarto of 1598

Q3: The Quarto of 1602

Q4: The Quarto of 1605

Q5: The Quarto of 1612

Q6: The Quarto of 1622

1.1–3.1 and 3.1.148–5.5.4

s.p. **RICHARD GLOUCESTER** [F's use of *Richard* and *Gloucester* has been standardized until 4.2.]

s.p. **KING RICHARD** [F's use of *King* and *Richard* has been standardized after 4.2.]

s.p. **BRACKENBURY** [F's use of *Brackenbury* and *Lieutenant* has been standardized throughout]

s.p. **LORD HASTINGS** [F's use of *Hastings* has been changed throughout.]

s.p. **LADY ANNE** [F's use of *Anne* has been changed throughout.]

s.p. **HALBERDIER** [F uses *Gentleman.*]

s.p. **QUEEN ELIZABETH** [F's use of *Queen* has been standardized throughout.]

s.p. **STANLEY** [F's use of *Stanley* and *Derby* has been standardized throughout.]

s.p. **QUEEN MARGARET** [F's use of *Queen Margaret* and *Margaret* has been standardized throughout.]

s.p. **A MURDERER, MURDERERS** [F's use of *Villain* has been standardized throughout.]

s.p. **FIRST MURDERER** [F's use of *1 Murderer* and *1* has been standardized throughout.]

s.p. **SECOND MURDERER** [F's use of *2 Murderer* and *2* has been standardized throughout.]

s.p. **KING EDWARD** [F's use of *King* has been standardized throughout.]

s.p. **BOY** [F's use of *Boy* and *Edward* has been standardized until 3.1.]

s.p. **DUCHESS OF YORK** [F's use of *Duchess of York* and *Duchess* has been standardized throughout.]

s.p. **GIRL** [F's use of *Daughter* has been standardized throughout.]

s.p. **FIRST CITIZEN** [F's use of *1 Citizen* and *1* has been standardized throughout.]

s.p. **SECOND CITIZEN** [F's use of *2 Citizen* and *2* has been standardized throughout.]

s.p. **THIRD CITIZEN** [F's use of *3* has been standardized throughout.]

s.p. **CARDINAL** [F's use of *Archbishop* and *Cardinal* has been standardized throughout.]

s.p. **MAYOR** [F's use of *Lord Mayor* and *Mayor* has been standardized throughout.]

s.p. **BISHOP OF ELY** [F's use of *Ely* has been standardized throughout.]

s.p. **ALL BUT RICHARD** [F's use of *All* has been standardized throughout.]

s.p. **SECOND MESSENGER, THIRD MESSENGER, FOURTH MESSENGER** [F only uses *Messenger.*]

s.p. **SIR CHRISTOPHER** [F's use of *Christopher* has been standardized throughout.]

s.p. **HENRY EARL OF RICHMOND** [F's use of *Richmond* has been standardized throughout.]

3.1.0–148 and 5.5.4–end
s.p. KING RICHARD [Q's use of *King Richard* and *Richard* has been standardized throughout.]
s.p. PRINCE EDWARD [Q's use of *Prince* has been standardized throughout.]
s.p. GHOST OF PRINCE EDWARD, GHOST OF KING HENRY, GHOST OF CLARENCE, GHOSTS OF THE PRINCES, GHOST OF HASTINGS [Q's use of *Ghost* has been standardized throughout.]
s.p. GHOST OF GRAY [Q's use of *Gray* has been standardized throughout.]
s.p. GHOST OF VAUGHAN [Q's use of *Vaughan* has been standardized throughout.]

Title: *The Tragedy of King Richard the Third*] THE TRAGEDY OF / King Richard the third. / Containing, / His treacherous Plots against his brother Clarence: / the pittiefull murther of his innocent nephewes: / his tyrannicall vsurpation: with the whole course / of his detested life, and most deserued death. [Q title page] The Tragedy of Richard the Third: / with the Landing of Earle Richmond, and the / Battell at Bosworth Field. [F head title]

1.1.26 spy [Q] see 49 Belike O belike 52 for [Q] but 67 Woodeville *Woodeulle* 73 Mrs Mistresse 74 ye [Q] you 75 for his for her 88 An't and 92 jealous [Q] iealious 96 kin kindred 104 I [Q] I do do withal withal 113 dearer deeper 116 or [Q] or else 125 the [Q1] this 134 prey [Q] play 139 Paul [Q] Iohn 146 haste horse
1.2.15 Cursèd . . . hence, [F places the line after 1.2.16.] 39 stand [Q] Stand'st 56 Ope Open 60 deed Deeds 61 supernatural most vnnaturall 70 no [Q] nor 78 a [Q; not in F] 80 t'accuse to curse 92 hand [Q] hands 101 ye [Q1] yee 120 of that accursed effect and most accurst effect 126 rend [Q] rent 127 sweet [Q] y^t 154 drops. [Q; F here adds twelve lines; see indented passage.] Shamed [Q, F (text)] For [F (catchword)] 189 s.p. RICHARD GLOUCESTER [Q; not in F] 190 s.p. LADY ANNE . . . give. [Q; not in F] 213 s.p. RICHARD GLOUCESTER . . . corpse. [Q; not in F] 214 Blackfriars white Friers 238 *denier* denier
1.3.6 If . . . me? [Q; F gives the line twice, spanning a page break.] 7 s.p. RIVERS [Q] If he were dead, what would betide me on / *Gray.* [F (text)] *Gray.* [F (catchword)] 17 come [Q1] comes Lords [Q] Lord 30 s.p. RIVERS [Q] *Qu⟨een Elizabeth⟩.* 33 With [Q1] What 43 are they [Q] is it complain complaines 54 s.p. RIVERS [Q] *Gray.* whom [Q1] who 68–69 that . . . it that he may

learne the ground 114 Tell . . . said, [Q; not in F] 118 remember [Q] do remember 153 may you [Q] you may 155 Ah A 160 of [Q] off 166 go. [Q; F here adds three lines; see indented passage.] 197 my [Q] our 270 was [Q] is 271 s.p. RICHARD GLOUCESTER *Buc⟨kingham⟩.* 290 naught not 302 s.p. HASTINGS [Q] *Buc⟨kingham⟩.* 307 s.p. QUEEN ELIZABETH [Q] *Mar⟨garet⟩.* 319 you my gracious lords yours my gracious Lord 325 whom [Q] who
1.4.19 sought thought 22 waters [Q1] water 22–23 my . . . my [Q1] mine . . . mine 25 Ten [Q] A 26 ouches anchors 29 those [Q] the 32 Which [Q] That 50 cried [Q] spake 58 methoughts [Q1] me thought 66 Brackenbury [Q] Keeper, Keeper 68 me. [Q; F here adds four lines; see indented passage.] 69 Keeper, I pray thee Keeper, I prythee 90 of [Q] from 96 I [Q1] we 112 pray thee [Q] prythee 119 'Swounds [Q] Come 136 'Swounds [Q; not in F] 177 to have redemption [Q] for any goodnesse 178 By . . . sins, [Q; not in F] 201 ye [Q] you 225 And . . . other, [Q; not in F] 227 of [Q1] on 230 As Right as 251–55 Which distress— [F places the lines after 1.4.244.] 257 serve [Q] do 261 guilty murder done [Q] murther
2.1.5 in [Q] to 7 Hastings and Rivers *Dorset and Riuers* 19 your [Q] you 50 Brother [Q] Gloster 57 unwittingly [Q] vnwillingly 59 By [Q] To 67 Of you . . . of you [Q] Of you and you, Lord *Riuers* and of *Dorset* 68 me.— [Q] me: / Of you Lord *Wooduill* and Lord *Scales*, of you, 70 Englishman [Q] Englishmen 82 s.p. RIVERS [Q] *King* 85 one [Q] man 93 but [Q] and 97 pray thee [Q] prethee 105 slew [Q] kill'd 108 at [Q] and 131 once [Q] onee
2.2.3 you [Q; not in F] 13 this [Q] it 26 his [Q] a 27 shapes [Q] shape 39 mark make 47 I [Q; not in F] 83 weep [Q] weepes 84–85 and . . . weep [Q; not in F] 88 lamentation. [F here adds twelve lines; see indented passage.] 105 hearts [Q] hates 106 splinted [Q, F] splinterd 110 king. [Q; F here adds eighteen lines; see indented passage.] 112 Ludlow [Q] London 114 weighty [Q; not in F] 115 s.p. QUEEN . . . YORK [not in F] With . . . hearts. [Q; not in F] 117 God's sake [Q] God sake 124 Ludlow [Q] London
2.3.35 make [Q] makes 43 Ensuing [Q, F (catchword)] Pursuing [F (text)]
2.4.1 hear [Q1] heard them [not in F] 1–2 Northampton. / at Stony Stratford [Q] Stony Stratford, / And at Northampton 9 young [Q] good 12 nuncle Vnkle 13 gross great 21 s.p. CARDINAL Why [Q] *Yor⟨k⟩.* And 26 pray thee [Q] prythee 36 s.p. CARDINAL

[Q] *Dut.* (Duchess of York) **37 your son, Lord Dorset** a Messenger **38 Lord Marquis** [Q; not in F] **s.p. DORSET** [Q; throughout scene] *Mes⟨senger⟩*. **40 then** [Q; not in F] **42 And with them** and with them, / Sir **48 our** [Q] my **50 jet** [Q] Iutt **64 death** [Q] earth

3.1.0 [Right after this stage direction, F loses its independent authority until c. 3.1.148. Q1 is the control text in this interim; F is here a direct reprint of Q3, which contains errors that need to be corrected by reference to Q1.] **22 hastes** comes **24 In happy time** And in good time **39 Anon expect him** Anone expect him here **41 sacred** holy **46 not** but **52 my mind, he** mine opinion **53 'longs** is **54 You . . . charter** You breake no priuiledge nor charter there **59 I come** I go **74 liege. Lo:** **85 t'enrich** enrich **87 made** makes **88 yet** now **90 good** gratious **101 noble cousin** Cosen noble **102 uncle, well** Vnckle **107 He . . . you then** Then he . . . you **109 as** as in **110 render** giue **111 With all** [Q3–6, F] withall **113–14 give, / It being but** giue, / And being but **121 I'd** I **132 sharp, prodigal** sharpe, prouided **136 My . . . along** [Q, F; none of the many attempts to pad out this line carries any conviction.] **143 there** [not in Q] **148 and** [F, not in Q] **149 we** I **153 parlous** perillous **161 Lord William** William Lo: **166 Will not** [F; F regains its full authority at this line.] Will **170 purpose.** [Q; for F, see indented passage.] **174 your** [Q] the **188 My** Now my

3.2.1 from Lord from the lo: **3 my Lord Stanley** Stanley **17 councils** [Q] Councell **74 you do** [Q; not in F] **87 talked** [Q1] talke **91 follow presently** [Q] talke with this good fellow **92 Well met, Hastings** [Q] How now, Sirrha? **95 I met thee** [Q] thou met'st me **102 Hastings** [Q] fellow **103 God save your lordship** [Q] I thanke your

3.3.14 heads, [Q] Heads / When shee exclaim'd on *Hastings,* you, and I **16–17 Hastings . . . Richard** [Q] *Richard . . . Hastings*

3.4.4 that [Q] the **solemn** royall **9 methinks** [Q] we thinke **26 not you** [Q] you not **39 worshipful** [Q] worshipfully **55 likelihood** [Q] liuelyhood **58 s.p. STANLEY** I . . . not. [not in F] **65 whatsoe'er** [Q] whosoe're **68 See** [Q] Looke **78 Some see it done** [Q] *Louell* and *Ratcliffe,* looke that it be done **82 raze** [Q] rowse **83 But** [Q] And **94 s.p. CATESBY** *Ra⟨tcliffe⟩.* **98 th'air** aire **102 s.p. CATESBY** *Lou⟨ell⟩.*

3.5.4 wert [Q] were **6 Tremble . . . straw,** [F places the line after 3.5.7.] **12 s.p. RICHARD GLOUCESTER . . . Mayor** [Q] But what, is *Catesby* gone? / *Rich⟨ard⟩.* He is, and see he

brings the Maior along **13 Let . . . him.** [Q; not in F] **19 innocence** [Q1] innocencie **20 O . . . Catesby** [Q] Be patient, they are friends: *Ratcliffe,* and *Louell.* **21 s.p. CATESBY** [Q] *Louell.* **31 attainture** attainder **32 The Well,** well, he was the **48 I** [Q] *Buck⟨ingham⟩. I* **50 s.p. RICHARD GLOUCESTER** [Q4; not in F] **54 we** [Q] I **hear** heard **56 treason** [Q] Treasons **60 word** [Q] words **64 cause** [Q1] case **82 listed** [Q] lusted **101 Now** [Q; for F, see indented passage.] **in** [Q] goe **103 notice** [Q] order

3.6.13 naught [Q1] nought

3.7.7 insatiate [Q] vnsatiate **14 face** forme **20 mine** [Q1] my **40 wisdoms** [Q] wisdome **43–44 s.p. BUCKINGHAM No . . . lord.** / **s.p. RICHARD GLOUCESTER** [Q; not in F] **49 build** [Q] make **50 request** [Q] requests **54 we'll** [Q] we **72 lolling** [Q, F] lulling **day-bed** [Q] Loue-Bed **101 request** [Q] requests **125 her** [Q] his **126 Her** [Q] His **127 Her** His **143 condition.** [Q; F here adds ten lines; see indented passage.] **160 no doubt, us** [Q] no doubt vs **203 equally** [Q, F] egallie **209 'Swounds, I'll** [Q] we will **210 s.p. RICHARD GLOUCESTER O . . . Buckingham.** [Q; not in F] **212 s.p. ANOTHER** [Q; not in F] **214 stone** stones **215 entreats** [Q] entreaties **230 kind** King **237 cousin** [Q] Cousins

4.1.46 counted England's Englands counted **57 in** [Q] with **75 made** [not in F] **96 racked** [Q, F] wrackt **teen.** [Q; F here adds seven lines; see indented passage.]

4.2.14 liege [Q] Lord **20 immediately** suddenlie **50 those parts beyond the seas** [Q] the parts **55 born** [Q] poore **73 there** [Q] then **81 'Tis** [Q] There is **84–85 s.p. KING RICHARD Shall . . . lord.** [Q; not in F] **90 to** [Q] vnto **101 perhaps.** [Q; not in F] **101–19 s.p. BUCKINGHAM . . . today.** [Q; not in F] **120 Why . . . no?** [Q] May it please you to resolue me in my suit.

4.3.4 whom [Q] who **5 ruthless** [Q1] ruthfull **8 two** [Q] to **15 once** [Q] one **31 at** [Q] and **39 goodnight** [Q] good night **40 Breton** [Q, F] Brittaine **42 o'er** [Q] on **45 Good news or bad** [Q] Good or bad newes **46 Ely** [Q] Mourton **53 leads** [Q] leds **55 an** and

4.4.10 unblown [Q] vnblowed **30 innocents'** [Q] innocent **36 seniory** [Q] signeurie **39 Tell . . . mine.** [Q; not in F] **45 holpst** hop'st **56 charnel** [Q, F] carnal **64 Thy** [Q] The **quite** [Q6] quit **77 plead** pray **93 are** [Q1] be **100 For queen . . . care** [Q; F places the line after 4.4.101.] **107 wert** [Q1] wast **112 weary** [Q1] wearied **118 nights . . . days** [Q1] night . . . day **127 client** [Q1] Clients **128 recorders** succeeders **intestate** [Q] intestine **141 Where** [Q]

Where't **175 in** [Q] with **176 Hewer** *Hower* **180 pray thee** prythee **188 heavy** [Q] greeuous **216 births** [Q] Birth **221 life.** [Q; F here adds fourteen lines; see indented passage.] **225 or** [Q1–5] and **243 that** it **254 would I** [Q1] I would **260 sometimes** [Q1] sometime **270 is** [Q; not in F] **273 this.** [Q; F here adds fifty-five lines; see indented passage.] **286 love** [Q] low **295 s.p. KING RICHARD . . . past.** [Q1; F places the line after 4.4.296.] **296 s.p. QUEEN ELIZABETH** [Q1; not in F] **297 s.p. KING RICHARD** [Q; not in F] **300 holy** [Q] Lordly **301 lordly** knightlie **307 that** [Q] it **308 God . . . God's** [Q] Heauen . . . Heavens **323 in** [Q1] with **327 o'erpast** [Q] repast **343 good** [Q] deare **348 peevishfond** [Q] peeuish found **356 recomfiture** [Q] recomforture **375 Ratcliffe** *Catesby* **391 mile** [Q] miles **395 renegade** [Q, F] runnagate **398 Ely** [Q] *Morton* **421 Ay, ay** [Q] I **431 Courtenay** [Q, F] Courtney **434 Guildfords** [Q, F] Guilfords **441 flood . . . water** [Q] Floods . . . Waters **445 Ratcliffe . . . gave him** [Q] There is my Purse, to cure that Blow of thine **452 Breton** [Q, F] Brittaine **458 Bretagne** [Q, F] Brittaine **465 tidings,** [Q1] Newes, but
4.5.2 this [Q] the **5 aid** [Q] ayde. / So get thee gone: commend me to thy Lord **17–18 Tell . . . daughter.** [Q; F places the lines after 4.5.5.] **17 Tell him** [Q] Withall say, that
5.2.8 spoils spoild **11 Lies** [Q] Is **12 Near** [Q] Ne're **17 swords** [Q] men
5.3.2 Why, how now, Catesby [Q] My Lord of Surrey **3 s.p. CATESBY** [Q] Sur⟨rey⟩.
5.4.4 standard. [Q; F places 5.4.21–24 here and adds, "My Lord of Oxford, you Sir *William Brandon,* / And your Sir *Walter Herbert* stay with me."] **21–24 Give . . . power.** [Q, F places the lines after 5.4.4.]
5.5.3 [Q1 is the control text for the remainder of the play, although a handful of Folio variants are considered or adopted, as derived from the damaged final leaves of the manuscript.] **8 sentinels** [F] centinell **10 s.p. KING RICHARD Stir** [F, Q (text)] Sturr [Q (catchword)] **11 s.p. CATESBY** *Rat⟨cliffe⟩.* **19 Ratcliffe** [Q6, F (italic)] Ratliffe **25 some a** boule of **29 Leave me. Bid my guard watch.** Bid my guard watch, leaue me. **30–31 About . . . tent, / Ratcliffe, and** Ratliffe about . . . tent / And **32 sit** [Q2] set **43 mortal-sharing** mortal staring **53 sundered** [Q3] sundried **72 tomorrow, / Prince . . . Sixth.** to morrow. **84 Comforts** Doth comfort **85 sit** [Q2] set **on** [Q5] in **93 s.p. GHOST OF RIVERS** [Q3] *King* **on** [Q5] in **97 pointless** [not in Q] **99 Will** [Q2] Wel **100 s.p. GHOSTS OF THE PRINCES** [F] *Ghost.*

110 Hastings, then Hastings **137 am** [Q2] and **140 Myself** What my selfe **156 Nay** [F] And **163 My** Ratcliffe, my **167 all our friends prove** our friends proue all **168 Ratcliffe** O Ratcliffe **177 s.p. LORDS** [Q3–6] *Lo⟨rds⟩.* **180 s.p. A LORD** [Q] *Lo⟨rd⟩.* **189 s.p. A LORD** [Q] *Lo⟨rd⟩.* **191 Much that I could say** More than I haue said **193 on** vpon **196 forces** faces **199 friends** gentlemen **212 foison fat** pays shall paie **219–20 this . . . my** my . . . this **221 to the 223 bold and** boldlie, and
5.6.12 not [Q2] nor **25 placèd strongly** shall be placed **27 multitude** foote and horse **28 ourself** [not in Q] **29 both sides** either side **31 boot!** [Q3] bootes **32 s.p. NORFOLK A good** [F, Q (text)] A good [Q (catchword)] **33 paper** [not in Q] **34 Jackie** [Q, F] Iocky too so **37 each** euery **47 Bretons** [Q, F] Brittains **49 ventures** aduentures **52 distain** restraine **54 Bretagne** [Q, F] Brittaine **55 milksop** [Q6, F] milkesopt **74 young** his sonne
5.8.8–9 s.p. KING . . . But [F, Q (text)] But [Q (catchword)] **9 young George Stanley, is he** is yong George Stanley **13 s.p. STANLEY** [F] *Der⟨by⟩.* [not in Q] **14 Ferrers** Ferris **15 becomes** become **27 that** this **28 United** Deuided **32 his** thy **37 forth** in

VENUS AND ADONIS

CONTROL TEXT: Q1

Q1: The Quarto of 1593
Q2, Q3, Q7: Successive printings of Q1 that incorporate various corrections.

466 loss loue
680 overshoot ouer-shut [The Oxford editors point out that "shut" is a spelling variant of "shoot" in the early modern period.]
748 th'impartial [Q2] the th'impartiall
1031 as [Q3] are
1054 was [Q7] had

THE RAPE OF LUCRECE

CONTROL TEXT: Q1

Q1: The Quarto of 1594

The poem is called "LUCRECE" on the title page but "*The Rape of Lucrece*" in the head title and running titles.

550 blows blow
950 blemish cherish

1316 stain's stain'd
1475 Thine Thy
1544 armèd, too armed to
1662 wreathèd wretched
1713 in it it in

THE COMEDY OF ERRORS

CONTROL TEXT: F

F: The Folio of 1623
F2: Later printing of F (1632) that incorporates various corrections

s.p. EGEON [F's use of *Merchant* and *Father*
has been standardized throughout.]
s.p. NELL [F also uses *Luce*. Standardized
throughout.]
s.p. ANGELO [F uses both *Angelo* and *Goldsmith* but generally prefers the latter. Standardized throughout.]

1.1.17 seen at seene at any **22 ransom** to ransome **38 me happy** me; me too [F2] **42 the**
he **54 mean-born** meane **102 upon** vp **116
barque** backe **123 thee** they **143–44
Which . . . disanul, / Against . . . dignity.**
Against . . . dignity, / Which . . . disanull
151 health helpe
1.2.4 arrival a riuall **40 unhappy** vnhappie a
66 clock cooke
2.1.8 mistress Master **12 ill** thus **60 thousand**
hundred **63 come home** come **67 thy mistress not** not thy mistresse **106 o' a** 109 her
his **110–11 will / Wear gold,** will, / Where
gold **111 yet** [not in F]
2.2.12 didst did didst **80 men** them **98 tiring**
trying **148 unstained** distain'd **175 stronger**
stranger **186 offered** free'd **191 oafs** Owles
194 drone Dromio **195 not I** I not
3.1.47 pate face **aim** a name **75 you, sir** your
sir **89, 91 her** your **106 once** [not in F] **116
Porcupine** *Porpentine*
3.2.1 s.p. LUCIANA Iulia. **4 building** buildings
ruinous ruinate **16 attaint** attaine **21 but**
not **26 wife** wise **46 sister's** sister **49 bed**
bud **them** thee **57 where** when **109 and is**
120 her hand the hand
4.1.17 her their **87 she** sir she
4.2.6 Of Oh, **30 How?** How **47–48 at, / That**
at / Thus **60 a be** I be
4.3.13 redemption from [not in F] **55 you do**
do **56 and** or **60 thou** then
4.4.38 to prophesy the prophesie **99 those**
these **108 his** this
5.1.46 much, much much **49 at** of **119
point's** points **122 death** depth **169 s.p.
MESSENGER** [not in F] **321 bay** boy **350 his**
her **404 ne'er** are **407 joy** go

CONTROL TEXT: Q

F: The Folio of 1623
Q: The Quarto of 1598
Qa, Qb: Successive states of Q incorporating
various print-shop corrections and changes

s.p. KING [Q's use of *King*, *Navarre*, and *Ferdinand* has been standardized throughout.]
s.p. BIRON, LONGUEVILLE, DUMAINE [Q's
Berowne and *Longauill* (and other
spellings) are transliterations of the French,
here restored and modernized. "Dumaine"
transliterates "Duc de Mayenne," not quite
correctly. Rhyme and meter require two
syllables.]
s.p. ARMADO [Q's use of *Armado* and *Braggart*
has been standardized throughout.]
s.p. MOTE [Q uses either *Boy* or *Page,* which
have been replaced throughout. In dialogue and s.d.'s, the name appears as
"Moth," meaning "moth" or "mote"
(speck). It is pronounced like the latter
word, and that sense may be primary;
hence the spelling adopted here.]
s.p. PRINCESS [Q more frequently uses
Queene, but this edition uses "Princess"
until she becomes a queen and is
addressed as one, at 5.2.708.]
s.p. MARIA, CATHERINE, ROSALINE [In 2.1,
they are referred to variously as *Lady,* 2
Lady (or *Lady* 2), and 3 *Lady* (or *Lady* 3).
For details, see the variants list below and
the notes to the text. For interpretation,
see the Textual Note and the Introduction.]
s.p. COSTARD [Q generally prefers *Clown* over
Costard; standardized throughout.]
s.p. JAQUENETTA [Q uses *Maid* more often than
Jaquenetta standardized throughout.]
s.p. NATHANIEL [Q's use of *Curate, Nathaniel,*
and *Curate Nathaniel* has been standardized throughout.]
s.p. HOLOFERNES [Q uses *Pedant* more often
than *Holofernes;* standardized throughout.]
s.p. DULL [Q's use of *Dull, Constable,* and
Anthony has been standardized throughout.]

1.1.24 three [F] thee **31 pomp** [F] pome **62
feast** fast **127 s.p. BIRON** [In Q, Longueville
speaks lines 126–30 Biron's s.p. appears at
line 131.] **184 Señor** Signeour **192 laughing** hearing **211 simplicity** [F] sinplicitie
224–48 [Q prints the King's speech continuously, with Costard's interruptions brack-
eted.] **247 with, with** *Which* with **275 s.p.
KING** *Fer⟨dinand⟩.* [F] Ber⟨owne⟩.

1.2.9, 10, 15 Señor Signeor **91 blushing** blush-in **130 s.p. DULL** Clo⟨wn⟩. **145 Master** [F] M.

2.1.32 Importunes [F] Importuous **34 visaged** [F] visage **39 Lord Longueville** Longauill. **40 s.p. MARIA** 1. Lady. **44 parts** [F] peerelsse **53 s.p. MARIA** Lad⟨y⟩. **56 s.p. CATHERINE** 2 Lad⟨y⟩. **64 s.p. ROSALINE** [F] 3 Lad⟨y⟩. **88 unpeopled** [F] vnpeeled **113–25 s.p. ROSALINE** [F] Kath⟨erine⟩. **129 of** [F] of, of **189** *Non point* No poynt **194 Catherine** Rosalin⟨e⟩ **209 Rosaline** Katherin⟨e⟩ **220–23 s.p. CATHERINE** La⟨dy⟩. **253 s.p. ROSALINE** [F] Lad⟨y⟩. **254 s.p. MARIA** [F] Lad⟨y⟩. **2 255 s.p. CATHERINE** Lad⟨y⟩. **3 256 s.p. MARIA** Lad⟨y⟩. **257 s.p. CATHERINE** Lad⟨y⟩.

3.1.11 throat as if throate, if **12 through the nose** through: nose **14 thin-belly** [F] thin-bellies **22 penny** penne **63 salve in the mail** salue, in thee male **131, 134, 136, 138, 142, 144, 159** [Each line in Q starts with "O"; probably a misreading of the s.p. *"Bero"* as *"Ber. O . . ."*] **155 guerdon** gardon **165 Junior** Iunios **175 clock** Cloake

4.1.3 s.p. BOYET [F] Forr⟨ester⟩. **50 fit** [Qb] fir [Qa] **64 set's** [Qa] set [Qb] **65 penurious** pernicious **65 was** [Qb] is was [Qa] **72 King's** King **104 suitor** shooter **126 did hit it** did hit [Qb] hid hit [Qa] **132 pin** is in **140 o'th' t'other** ath toothen **144 a** [not in Q] **144.1 s.d.** *Shout within* Shoot within

4.2.11 a 'auld grey doe' a *haud credo* **26 of** [not in Q] **33 Dictynna . . . Dictynna** Dictisima . . . *dictisima* **44 'twas** [Qb] was [Qa] **47–48 call I** cald **57 sore 'l'** sorell: **61–96 s.p. HOLOFERNES** Nath⟨aniel⟩. The s.p.'s of Holofernes (lines 61, 71, 76, 80, 86, 96) and Nathaniel (lines 67, 95) are reversed in Q.] **64** *pia mater* prima-/ter **66 in whom** [F] whom **71 ingenious** ingenous **73** *sapit* sapis **76 'pierce one'** Person **89–90** *Venezia . . . prezia vemchie, vencha, que non te vnde, que non te perreche* **96–98 s.p. HOLOFERNES . . . NATHANIEL** Nath⟨aniel⟩. [In Q, Nathaniel speaks lines 96–111; here, Holofernes delivers lines 96–97, Nathaniel lines 98–111.] **111 singeth** singes **112 apostrophus** apostraphas **113 canzonet** cangecnt **113 Here are** Nath⟨aniel⟩. Here are. [Q assigns lines 112–13 to Holofernes and, beginning with "Here are," lines 113–19 to Nathaniel. This edition assigns Holofernes all of lines 112–19.] **118–19** *domicella*—virgin *Damosella* virgin **120 sir** sir from one mounsier *Berowne*, one of the strange Queenes Lordes. **121 s.p. HOLOFERNES** Nath⟨aniel⟩. [Q assigns lines 121–25 to Nathaniel, beginning Holofernes' speech at line 125 with "Sir." This edition assigns the entire speech, lines 121–31, to Holofernes.] **124 writing** written

125 Sir Nathaniel Ped⟨ant⟩. Sir *Holofernes* [See line 121 above.] **144** *ben* bien

4.3.34 wilt [F] will **44 s.p. KING** Long⟨ueville⟩. **54 slop** Shop **70 idolatry** [F] ydotarie **89 I** [not in Q] **104 Wished** [Passionate Pilgrim] Wish. [Dumaine's poem also appears in a poetic collection attributed to Shakespeare, *The Passionate Pilgrim* (c. 1599).] **108 thorn** [England's Helicon] *throne* [Dumaine's poem also appears in the collection *England's Helicon* (1600).] **113 great** [not in Q] **118 true love's** trueloues **142 Faith so** Fayth **151 coaches. In your tears** couches in your teares **172 to . . . by** by . . . to **176 like you** like **178 Joan** [Qb] Loue [Qa] **192 Where** King. Where [Q repeats s.p. *"King."* (here omitted) after the s.d. *"reads the letter."*] **204 e'en** and **251 style** Schoole **255 and** [not in Q] **279 Nothing** O nothing **291** [Q follows this line with the twenty-three lines printed here, indented, probably an unrevised version of 4.3.285–91, 292–339.] **333 authors** authour **335 Let** Lets **341 standards** standars **357** *Allons, allons!* Alone alone

5.1.18 *sine 'b'* fine **23** *insanire* in-/famie **25** *bone* bene **26 Bone?** Bon, fort bon Bome **boon for** boon **31 Quare** Quari **51 wave** [F] wane **59** *circum circa* vnũ cita **79 choice** chose **88** *mustachio* [F] mustachio **100 Nathaniel** Holofernes **101 rendered** [F] rended **102 assistance** assistants **107–08 myself, Judas Maccabeus; and this gallant gentleman, Hector** my selfe, and this Gallant Gentle-/man Iudas Machabeus **129** *Allons* Alone

5.2.17 been a [F] bin **43 ho!** How? **46 jest; I beshrew** iest, and I beshrow **53, 57 s.p. MARIA** [F] Marg⟨aret⟩. **53 pearls** [F] Pearle **65 hests** deuice **67 pursuivant-like** perttaunt like **74 wantonness** wantons be **80 stabbed** [F] stable [Q] **89 sycamore** [F] Siccamone **96 they** [F] thy **124 love-suit** Louefeat **130** [Q follows this line with the two lines printed here, indented, probably an unrevised version of 5.2.131–32.] **133 too** [F] two **147 her** his **151 ne'er** ere **162 ever** [F] euen **217 s.p. ROSALINE** [Before line 216 in Q, which gives Rosaline both lines.] **242–55 s.p. CATHERINE** Maria. **273 Ah, they** They **277** *Non point* No poynt **309 run over** runs ore **407 affectation** affection **463 zany** [F] saine **482 manège** nuage **500 they** [F] thy **513 least** [F] best **516 There** Their **551 s.p. PRINCESS** Lady. **559 this** [F] his **589 proved** [F] proud **633 gilt** [F] gift **657 The party is gone.** [Q centers, italicizes, and fails to attribute this line to Armado or any other character.] **673–74 on, stir** or stir **696 s.p. MOTE** [Q's prefix, *"Boy.,"* could refer to Mote or Boyet.] **719 nimble** humble **745**

strange straying **752 them** [not in Q] **760 the** [F; not in Q] **764 in** [not in Q] **798 hermit** herrite **798** [Both Q and F follow this line with the six lines printed here, indented, probably an unrevised version of parts of 5.2.814–31.] **798.2 rank** rackt **800 A wife?** [In Q, this begins Catherine's answer to Dumaine (also line 800).] **868 Ver, begin** [In F, as here, this is part of Armado's speech. In Q, it is separated from Armado's words by a blank line and preceded by "*B.*"] **869 s.p.** / **s.d. Spring** [*sings*] *The Song.* [centered in Q] **870, 871** [Lines in reverse order in Q.] **891 foul** [F] full **903 s.p.** ARMADO [F; not in Q] **904 You that way, we this way** [F; not in Q]

A MIDSUMMER NIGHT'S DREAM

CONTROL TEXT: Q1

F: The Folio of 1623
Q1: The Quarto of 1600
Q2: The Quarto of 1619

Title: A Midsummer Night's Dream [Q1 title page, head title] A mydsomer nighte dreame [Stationers' Register] A Midsommer nightes dream [Q1 running titles]

s.p. THESEUS [Q's use of *Theseus* and *Duke* has been standardized throughout.]
s.p. HIPPOLYTA [Q's use of *Hippolyta* and *Duchess* has been standardized throughout.]
s.p. BOTTOM [Q's use of *Bottom, Pyramus*, and *Clown* has been standardized throughout.]
s.p. FLUTE [Q's use of *Flute* and *Thisbe* has been standardized throughout.]
s.p. ROBIN [Q's use of *Robin* and *Puck* has been standardized throughout.]
s.p. QUINCE [Q's use of *Quince* and *Prologue* has been standardized throughout.]
s.p. SNOUT [Q's use of *Snout* and *Wall* has been standardized throughout.]
s.p. SNUG [Q's use of *Snug* and *Lion* has been standardized throughout.]
s.p. TITANIA [Q's use of *Titania* and *Queen* has been standardized throughout.]
s.p. STARVELING [Q's use of *Starveling* and *Moonshine* has been standardized throughout.]

1.1.4 wanes [Q2, F] waues **10 New** Now **24 Stand forth Demetrius.** [Q italicizes and centers on a separate line.] **26 Stand forth Lysander.** [Q italicizes and centers on a separate line.] **27 This** This man **136 low** loue **139 merit** else, it **159–60 And . . . son.** / **From . . . leagues.** From . . . leagues? /

And . . . sonne: **191 I'd** ile **200 Helen** Helena **212 sleights** flights **219 stranger companies** strange companions
1.2.20 stones stormes **64 s.p.** ALL THE REST All.
2.1.7 moonës Moons **58 make room** roome **61 Fairies** Fairy **78 Perigouna** Perigenia **79 Aegles** Eagles **101 cheer** heere **109 thin** chinne **158 the** [not in Q] **190 slay . . . slayeth** sta⁻ . . . stayeth **201 nor** [F] not **206 lose** loose
2.2.9 s.p. FIRST FAIRY [not in Q] **13 s.p.** CHORUS [not in Q] **25–30 Sing . . . with lullaby.** &c. **31–32 Hence . . . sentinel** [indented as part of the song] **44–45 comfort . . . Be it** [Q2, F] comfor . . . Bet it **49 good** [Q2, F] god **53 is** [Q2, F] it
3.1.44 s.p. SNOUT *Sn.* **59 and** or **71 Odours, odours.** [F] Odours, odorous **76 s.p.** ROBIN *Puck.* [F] *Quin⟨ce⟩.* **82 bristly** brisky **133 own** [Q2, F] owe **144 Mote** Moth **145 s.p.** A FAIRY . . . ANOTHER . . . ANOTHER . . . ANOTHER . . . All Four *Fairies* **148 apricots** Apricocks **157 s.p.** A FAIRY *I. Fai.* **157–58 mortal.** / ANOTHER Hail. mortall, haile **159–60 s.p.** ANOTHER . . . ANOTHER *2. Fai . . . 3. Fai.* **170 you** of you **182 love's** louers
3.2.19 mimic [F] Minnick **80 so** [not in Q] **85 sleep** slippe **137 s.p.** HELENA [not in Q] **165 here** heare **202 is all quite forgot** is all forgot **214 like** life **221 passionate** [F; not in Q] **251 prayers** praise **258 No, no, sir** [F] No, no **yield** heele **280 doubt** of doubt **300 gentlemen** [Q2, F] gentleman **327 but** [Q2, F] hut **387 exiled** exile
3.3.14 shalt [Q2, F] shat **37 to** [not in Q]
4.1.19 courtesy curtsie **21–22 Pease-** / **Blossom** Cobwebbe **33 these off** thee **38 all ways** alwaies **52 flow'rets** flouriets **70 o'er** or **79 these** five these, fine **93 nightës** nights **102 vanguard** vaward **114 Seemed** Seeme **125 this is** [Q2, F] this **170 in sickness** a sicknesse **188 found** [Q2, F] fonnd **189 It** [F] Are you sure / That we are awake? It **195 let us** [Q2, F] lets **201 t'expound** expound **203–4 a patched fool** [F] patcht a foole **208 ballad** Ballet
4.2.3 s.p. STARVELING [F] *Flut⟨e⟩.* **26 no** [F] not
5.1.34 our [F] Or **38 Egeus** [F] Philostrate **38, 42, 61, 72, 76, 106 s.p.** EGEUS [F] *Philostrate* **44 s.p.** LYSANDER [F] *The⟨seus⟩.* **46, 50, 54, 58 s.p.** THESEUS [F; not in Q] **48, 52, 56 s.p.** LYSANDER [F; not in Q] **59 strange** black strange **189 up** in thee [F] now againe **204 wall** Moon **down** [F] used **263 gleams** beames **299 prove** [Q2, F] yet prooue **306 mote** moth **307 warrant** warnd **337 s.p.** BOTTOM [F] *Lyon.*

5.2.1 lion Lyons **2 behowls** beholds **13 we** wee **49–50 And . . . blessed / Ever . . . rest.** Euer . . . rest, / And . . . blest.

THE MOST EXCELLENT AND LAMENTABLE TRAGEDY OF ROMEO AND JULIET

CONTROL TEXT: Q2 (Q1 FOR 1.2.51–1.3.36)

F: The Folio of 1623
Q1: The Quarto of 1597
Q2: The Quarto of 1599
Q3: The Quarto of 1609
Q4: The Quarto of 1623

Title: The . . . Iuliet [Q2 (title-page and head title above 1.1.)] *The most lamentable Tragedie of Romeo and Iuliet.* [Q2 (running title)]

s.p. CITIZENS OF THE WATCH [Q2's use of *Officer(s)* has been standardized throughout.]

s.p. CAPULET'S WIFE [Q2's use of *Capulet's Wife, Old Lady, Wife, Lady,* and *Mother* has been standardized throughout.]

s.p. MONTAGUE'S WIFE [Q2's use of *Wife* and *Wife. 2.* has been standardized throughout.]

s.p. CAPULET [Q2's use of *Capulet, I. Capulet,* and *Father* has been standardized throughout.]

s.p. PETER [Q2's use of *Peter* and *Servingman* has been standardized throughout.]

s.p. CAPULET'S COUSIN [Q2's use of *2. Capulet* has been standardized throughout.]

s.p. FRIAR LAURENCE [Q2's use of *Friar* and *Lawrence* has been standardized throughout.]

s.p. FIRST SERVINGMAN [Q2's use of *1., 3.,* and *Fellow* has been standardized throughout.]

s.p. SECOND SERVINGMAN [Q2's use of *2.* has been standardized throughout.]

s.p. FIRST MUSICIAN [Q2's use of *Musician, Fiddler,* and *Minstrel* has been standardized throughout.]

s.p. SECOND MUSICIAN [Q2's use of *2. Musician, Fiddler,* and *2. Minstrel* has been standardized throughout.]

s.p. THIRD MUSICIAN [Q2's use of *3. Musician, 3. Fiddler,* and *3. Minstrel* has been standardized throughout.]

s.p. BALTHASAR [Q2's use of *Man* and *Balthasar* has been standardized throughout.]

1.1.24 in [Q1; not in Q2] **34 side** [Q1] sides **140 his** [Q3] is **146 sun** same **170 create** [Q1] created **172 well-seeming** [Q4] welseeing **185 lovers'** louing **195 Bid a . . . make** [Q1] A . . . makes **204 unharmed** [Q1] vncharmed **211 makes** [Q4] make

1.2.13 made [Q1; Q2 continues: "Earth hath swallowed all my hopes but she, / Shees the hopefull Lady of my earth"] **27 female** [Q1] femme **65 Vitruvio** Vtruuio **89 fires** fire

1.3.4 where is Wher's **68 honour** [Q1] houre **69 honour** [Q1] *houre* **101 it** [Q1; not in Q2]

1.4.6–8 crowkeeper . . . entrance. [Q1] Crowkeeper. **23 s.p. MERCUTIO** [Q4] *Horatio.* **31 deformity** [Q1] deformities **39 done** [Q3] dum **42 save your reverence** [F] saue you reuerence **45 like lights** lights **47 five** fine **54 s.p. BENVOLIO Queen . . . she?** [Q1; not in Q2] **55–91 She . . . bodes.** [Q2 omits 1.4.68–70 and prints "She . . . bodes" as prose.] **55 s.p. MERCUTIO** [not in Q2] **59 Athwart** [Q1] Ouer **62–64 Her . . . bone** her traces of the smallest spider web / her collors of the moonshines watry beams, her whip of Crickets bone **64 film** Philome **67 maid** [Q1] man **73 O'er** [Q1] On **straight;** [Q2 continues: "ore Lawyerrs fingers who strait dreame on fees"] **76 breaths** [Q1] breath **77 lawyer's** [Q1] Courtiers **lip** nose **81 dreams he** [Q1] he dreams **90 elf-locks** [Q1] Elklocks **92 face** [Q1] side **113 sail** [Q1] sute

1.5.6 marzipan March-pane **13 longest** longer **15 a bout** about **16 Aha** [Q1] Ah **91 gentler** gentle **92 ready** [Q1] did readie

2.0.4 matched [Q3] match

2.1.10 Pronounce [Q1] prouaunt **dove** [Q1] day **12 heir** [Q1] her **13 Adam** Abraham **trim** [Q1] true **38 open-arse** an open, or **58 do** [Q1] to **73 passing** [Q1] puffing **83–84 nor any . . . name** o be some other name / Belonging to a man. **87 were** [Q1] wene **107 kinsmen** [Q1] kismen **125 washed** [Q1] washeth **141 'haviour** [Q1] behauior **143 more cunning** [Q1] coying **152 circled** [Q1] circle **190 lord** L. **191 s.p. NURSE** [not in Q2] **193–95 thee . . . come.—** thee (by and by I come) Madam. **207 mine** [Q1; not in Q2] **108 Romeo's name.** Romeo! [Q1] *Romeo.* **212 My nyas** My Neece **225 silk** [Q1] silken **229–32 Parting . . . s.p. ROMEO Sleep . . . Would** Parting . . . *Iu⟨liet⟩.* Sleep . . . *Ro⟨meo⟩.* Would **232 rest.** [Q1; Q2 continues: "The grey eyde morne smiles on the frowning night, / checkring the Easterne Clouds with streaks of light / And darknesse fleckted like a drunkard reeles, / From forth daies pathway, made by *Tytans* wheeles."] **233 sire's close** Friers close

2.2.4 path and Titan's fiery [Q1] path, and *Titans* burning [Q2 (Version B)] pathway made by Tytans [Q2 (Version A)] 22 sometime's [Q1] sometime 26 slays [Q1] staies 74 yet ring [Q4] yet ringing

2.3.6 kinsman [Q1] kisman 16 s.p. BENVOLIO [Q1] *Ro⟨meo⟩*. 23 hai Hay 25–26 phantasims phantacies 29 pardon-me's [Q1] pardons mees 60 Switch . . . switch Swits . . . swits 84 s.p. BENVOLIO [not in Q2] 102 for [Q1; not in Q2] 181–91 Well . . . letter [prose in Q2] 179 I warrant Warrant 192 Ah A dog's [Q3] dog

2.4.11 three [Q3] there 15–19 And . . . away M. And [Q2's M. is indented as a speech prefix]

2.5.27 music's [Q4] musicke 34 sum up some sum up sum

3.1.2 Capels are [Q1] *Capels* 63 injured [F] iniuried 69 *stoccado stucatho* 70 come . . . walk will you walke 85 s.p. PETRUCCIO Away, Tybalt! Away Tybalt. [as stage direction] 87 both your both 117 He gad He gan 119 fire-eyed [Q1] end 140 kinsman [Q1] kisman 145 fray [Q1, F] bloudie fray 160 agent aged 170 kinsman [Q3] kisman 178 s.p. MONTAGUE [Q4] *Capu⟨let⟩*. 182 hate's [Q1] hearts 186 I [Q1] It

3.2.1 s.p. JULIET [Q1, F; not in Q2] 9 By [Q4] And by 15 grown grow 19 on vpon 73 s.p. JULIET O . . . face [Q1; assigned to *Nur⟨se⟩*. in Q2] 76 Dove-feathered Rauenous douefeatherd 79 damned [Q4] dimme 87 dissemblers all all dissemblers 128 corpse course

3.3.15 Hence [Q1] Here 19 banished [Q1] blanisht 40–43 But . . . death? This may flyes do, when I from this must flie, / And sayest thou yet, that exile is not death? / But *Romeo* may not, he is banished. / Flies may do this, but I from this must flie: / They are freemen, but I am banished.

3.3.52 Thou [Q1] Then 62 men [Q1] man 82 Where is [Q1] Wheres 109 denote [Q1] deuote 116 lives lies 143 pout'st upon [Q4] puts vp 167 disguised [Q3] disguise

3.4.13 be [Q1] me 23 We'll [Q1] Well

3.5.13 sun exhaled Sun exhale 19 the [Q1] the the 31 changed change 43 my [Q1] ay 82 him [Q4; not in Q2] 106 I [Q4; not in Q2] 139 gives [Q3] giue 176 work, play, houre, tide, time, worke, play 180 lined liand 225 hence here

4.1.45 cure [Q1] care 72 slay [Q1] stay 83 chapless [Q1] chapels 85 tomb [not in Q2] 98 breath [Q1] breast 100 wanny many 110 In [Q3] Is bier [Q2 continues: "Be borne to buriall in thy kindreds graue"] 111 shalt [Q3] shall 116 waking [Q3] walking

4.2.14 self-willed harlotry [Q1] selfewield harlottry 26 becoming becomd

4.3.48 wake [Q4] walke

4.4.20 faith [Q4] father 63 See [not in Q2] 68 long [Q1] loue 70–73 Beguiled . . . death [follows Nurse's speech 4.4.80–85] 82 behold Q3] beddld 92 cure care 108 All in And in 109 fond some 126 by my [Q1] my my 131 full of woe [Q4] full 132 s.p. FIRST MUSICIAN [Q1] *Minstrels*. 146 s.p. PETER Then . . . I [Q4] Then . . . *Peter*. I. 148 grief [Q1] griefes 149 And . . . oppress [Q1; not in Q2] 152 Matthew Minikin Simon Catling 157 Simon [Q1] *Iames*

5.1.3 lord L 15 fares my Juliet [Q1] doth my Lady *Iuliet* 24 defy [Q1] denie 77 pay [Q1] pray

5.3.3. yew trees [Q1] young tree 20 rite right 40, 43 s.p. BALTHASAR [Q1] *Pet⟨er⟩*. 68 conjuration commiration 71 s.p. PAGE [Q1; line not assigned to anyone in Q2] 102–3 Shall I believe / That I will beleeue, / Shall I beleeue that 105 Depart again. [Q4] Depart again, come lye thou in my arme. / Here's to thy health, where ere thou tumblest in. / O true Appothecarie! / Thy drugs are quicke. Thus with a kisse I die. / Depart againe 137 yew yong 186 too [F] too too 189 is so shrieked is so shrike 193 our your 198 slaughtered [Q4, F] slaughter 208 more early [Q1] now earing 231 that [Q4] thats 298 raise [Q4, F] raie

THE TRAGEDY OF KING RICHARD THE SECOND

CONTROL TEXT: Q ; ADDITIONAL MATTER FROM F

F: The Folio of 1623
Q1: The Quarto of 1597
Q2, Q3: Quartos of 1598
Q4: The Quarto of 1608
Q5: The Quarto of 1615
Q6: The Quarto of 1634

Title: The Tragedie of Richard II [Q] The life and death of King Richard the Second [F]

s.p. KING RICHARD *King* [to 5.1]

1.1.118 by my [F] by 152 gentlemen [F] gentleman 157 time [F] month 162–63 Harry, when? / Obedience bids *Harrie*, when? Obedience bids, / Obedience bids [F] Harry? when obedience bids, / Obedience bids 186 down [F] vp

1.2.1 Gloucester's [F]; Woodstockes 58 it [Q2, F] is

1.3.33 comest [Q5] comes [Q1] com'st [F] 55 just [F] right 127 swords [F] sword

127–28 swords, / Which [F; Q1 has a five-line passage after line 127 omitted in F, indented in this edition. See Textual Note.] 166 then [F; not in Q] 174 you owe [F] y'owe 215 night [Q4, F] nightes 220 sudden [F] sullen 231–32 father. / Alas [F; Q has a four-line passage omitted in F, indented in this edition after line 235.] 251 travel trauaile 256–57 return. / s.p. BOLINGBROKE [F; Q has twenty-six lines omitted from F, indented in this edition after line 256.] 256.2 remember remember me

1.4.7 grew [F] blew 19 cousin, cousin [F] Coosens Coosin 22 Bushy, Bagot here, and Green [Q6] Bushie, [Q1] Bushy: heere Bagot and Greene [F] 51–52 Enter Bushy / Bushy, what news? [F] Enter Bushie with newes. [Q1] 58 in his [Q1] in the [Q1] into the [Q2] 63 late! [F] late, /Amen [indented]

2.1.18 whose taste the wise are feared whose taste the wise are found [Q1] Whose state the wise are found [Q2] his state: then there are sound [F] 48 as a [Q4, F] as 70 reined ragde 102 encagèd [F] inraged 113 now, now not, 115–16 And— / s.p. KING RICHARD And thou, a [F] And thou / King. A 125 brother [Q2] brothers 178 the [F] a 233 that thou wouldst thou wouldst [Q1] thou'dst [F] 255 his [F] his noble 258 King's grown [Q3, F] King growen 278 Port le [F] le Port 281 Thomas . . . Arundel [not in Q1, F; a line is missing, probably a result of censorship.] 284 Thomas Ramston John Ramston 286 Coint [F] Coines

2.2.12 At . . . With With . . . at 16 eye [F] eyes 31 As thought— As thought [Q1] As though [Q2, F] 59 broke [Q2, F] broken 119 Castle [F; not in Q1] 138 commoners commons 148–49 s.p. BAGOT Farewell . . . / BUSHY Well [continued to Green] Farewell . . . / Bush⟨ie⟩ Well [Q1] Bush⟨y⟩. Farewell . . . Well [F]

2.3.36 Hereford, [Q3] Herefords 98 the [F; not in Q1] 124 kinsman [F] cousin 157 to [Q2, F] vnto

3.1.32 England. [F] England, Lords farewell.

3.2.1 Harlechly Barkloughly 28–29 all. / s.p. AUMERLE [F; Q1 has four lines omitted in F, indented in this edition after line 28.] 31 friends [F] power 36 bloody [Q2, F] bouldy 51 from [F] off from 80 sluggard [F] coward 81 forty [F] twenty 98 loss, [F] and 130 offence [F; not in Q1] 174 wail their present woes [F] sit and wail theyr woes 199 faction [F] partie

3.3.13 with you [F; not in Q1] 35 Upon [F] on both 58–59 rain / My waters [F] raigne. / My water's 90 is [F] standes 118 a prince and princesse [Q1] a Prince [Q3] a Prince, is [F] 126 We [Q4, F] King. We 126 ourself [F] our selues 170 mock [F] laugh

3.4.11 joy grief 35 too [F] two 58 garden! We at garden at [Q1] garden, at [Q3, F] 68 then [not in Q1, F] 81 Cam'st [Q2, F] them

4.1.21 him [Q3, F] them 50–51 foe. / s.p. SURREY [F; Q1 has an eight-line passage omitted from F, indented in this edition after line 50.] 50.3 may it may 50.4 sun to sun sinne to sinne 67 my [Q3, F; not in Q1] the [Q2] 92 Bishop of Carlisle Bishop [Q3, F] B. [Q1] 103 of that name the fourth [F] fourth of that name 136 you [Q2, F] yon 136 rear [F] raise 139 Prevent Preuent it 145–308 May . . . fall [F (and similarly Q4); not in Q1. Only departures from F are noted for these lines.] 227 upon [Q4] vpon me 241 and [Q4] a 245 Nor [Q4] No, nor 309–10 On . . . yourselves [Q4, F] Let it be so, and loe on wednesday next, / We solemnly proclaime our Coronation, / Lords be ready all [Q1] 322 I will Ile

5.1.25 stricken [F] throwne 44 fall [F] tale 66 friends [F] men 78 queen [F] wife 84 s.p. NORTHUMBERLAND [F] King.

5.2.52 Hold these jousts and triumphs Hold those Iusts & Triumphs [F] do these iusts & triumphs hold 55 prevent it preuent 78 by my life, my by my life, by my [Q1] my life, my [Q2, F] 82 son [F] Aumerle

5.3.1 tell [F] tell me 14 these [F] those 21 days [F] yeares 30 the my 35 I may [Q2, F] May 55 lest lest thy 73 voiced [Q3, F] voice 91 kneel [F] walke 100 mouth [Q2, F] month 109 s.p. KING HENRY [Q2, F] yorke 142 so [not in Q1, F] too [Q6]

5.4.3, 6 s.p. FIRST, SECOND [not in Q1, F] 3 Those [F] These

5.5.13–14 faith . . . faith [F] word . . . word 33 treason makes [F] treasons make 55 sounds that tell sound that tells 56 that [F] which 58 hours, and times [F] times, and houres 65 a sign [Q2, F] asigne 94 spurgalled [F] Spurrde, galld

5.6.8 Salisbury, Spencer, Blunt [F] Oxford, Salisbury, Blunt [Q1] Oxford, Salisbury [Q2] 17 not [Q2, F1] nor 43 through the [F] through

THE LIFE AND DEATH OF KING JOHN

CONTROL TEXT: F

F: The Folio of 1623

s.p. KING JOHN [F's use of King John, John, and England has been standardized throughout.]

s.p. QUEEN ELEANOR [F most often uses Eleanor, but also Queen, Queen Mother, and Old Queen. The choice of speech prefix often corresponds to the immediate context; they have been standardized throughout.]

s.p. BASTARD [F uses *Philip* until line 138 and *Bastard* almost exclusively thereafter: standardized throughout.]

s.p. FALCONBRIDGE [F's use of *Robert* has been altered throughout.]

s.p. KING PHILIP [In many places, noted individually below, F confuses the King with the Dauphin *(Lewis)*. Otherwise, F's use of *King, Philip,* and *France* has been standardized throughout.]

s.p. LOUIS THE DAUPHIN [F uses *Dauphin (Dolphin)* alone: expanded throughout.]

1.1.11 Poitou *Poyctiers* **161 arise** rise **188 'Tis too** 'Tis two **208 smack** smoake **237 Could a** Could **257 Thou** That

2.1.1, 18 s.p. KING PHILIP *Lewis* **63 Ate** Ace **113 breast** beast **144 shows** shooes **149 King Philip** King *Lewis* **150 s.p. KING PHILIP** *Lew⟨is⟩* **152 Anjou** *Angiers* **169 Draw** Drawes **215 Confront your** Comfort yours **325 s.p. CITIZEN** *Hubert.* **327 your** yonr **335 run** rome **362 who's** whose **368 s.p. CITIZEN** *Fra⟨nce⟩* **371 Kinged** Kings **425 niece** neere **435 complete, O** compleat of **488 Anjou** *Angiers* **489 side** fide **501 sun** sonne **524 shall** still **540 rites** rights **572 lose** loose

3.1.34 God heauens **36 day** daies **62 God** heauen **74 task** tast **81 God** heauen **122 it** that **162 God** Heauen **185 crazèd** cased **208 troth** truth **210 swear'st** sweares **224 Wilt** Wil't

3.3.8–10 Of . . . liberty. Of hoording Abbots: imprisoned angells / Set at libertie: the fat ribs of peace / Must by the hungry now be fed vpon: **52 broad-eyed** brooded

3.4.44 art not art **48 God** heauen **64 Friends** fiends **110 world's** words **149 vilely born** euilly borne **182 make** makes

4.1.23 God heauen **63 his** this **77 God's** heauen **91 God** heauen **114 eyes** eye **131 God** heauen

4.2.1 again against **31 worser** worse **42 when** then **73 Does** Do **117 ear** care

4.3.16 Who's Whose **17 'Tis** Is **33 man** mans **147 scramble** scamble **156 cincture** center

5.1.54 glisten glister

5.2.36 gripple cripple **43 thou** [not in F] **133 unhaired** vn-heard **135 these** this **145 his** this

5.3.8 Swineshead *Swinsted*

5.4.34 cresset Crest

5.5.3 measured measure **7 tatt'ring** tott'ring

5.6.13 eyeless endles

5.7.16 invincible inuisible **17 mind** winde **21 cygnet** Symet **42 strait** straight **60 God** heauen **88 our own** our **108 kind of** kinde

---

THE COMICAL HISTORY OF THE MERCHANT OF VENICE, OR OTHERWISE CALLED THE JEW OF VENICE

CONTROL TEXT: Q1

F: The Folio of 1623
Q1: The Quarto of 1600
Q2: The Quarto of 1619

s.p. SHYLOCK [Q1's use of *Iew⟨e⟩* has been standardized throughout.]

s.p. LAUNCELOT [Q1's use of *Clo⟨wne⟩* has been standardized throughout.]

s.p. SALERIO [Q1's use of *Salarino* in some s.d.'s and s.p.'s has been standardized throughout.]

Title: The Comical History of the Merchant of Venice, or Otherwise Called the Jew of Venice [after Q half title and Stationers' Register entry] The comicall History of the Mer / *chant of Venice* [Q half title and running title] The most excellent / Historie of the *Merchant / of Venice.* With the extreame crueltie of *Shylocke* the Iewe / towards the sayd Merchant, in cutting a iust pound / of his flesh: and the obtayning of *Portia* / by the choyse of three / chests. *As it hath been diuers times acted by the Lord /* Chamberlaine his Seruants. / Written by William Shakespeare. [Q title page] The Merchant of Venice [F]

1.1.27 Andrew, decks *Andrew* docks **113 Yet is** It is

1.2.51 threstle Trassell

1.3.108 spit spet **121 spat** spet

2.2.3–7 Gobbo Iobbe **87 last** [Q2] lost **159 a suit** [Q2, F] sute

2.4.5 as us

2.5.41 Jew's Iewes

2.6.14 younker younger **24 therein** then **58 gentlemen** [Q2, F] gentleman

2.7.69 tombs timber

2.8.39 Slubber [Q2, F] slumber

2.9.47 chaff [F] chafe

3.1.62 s.p. MAN [not in Q, F] **89 heard** [F] heere

3.2.63 s.p. ONE FROM PORTIA'S TRAIN [not in Q, F] **66 ALL** [not in Q, F] **67 eyes** [F] eye **71 I'll begin it** [in Q and F, printed in Roman rather than italic (as the rest of the song), as if not part of the song] **81 vice** voyce **93 makes** [F] maketh **101 Therefore, thou** [Q2] Therefore then thou [Q1, F] **301 thorough** through

3.4.23 Hear other things: heere other things **49 Padua** Mantua **50 cousin's hands** [Q2] cosin hand [Q1] cosins hand [F] **53 traject** Tranect **82 my** [F] my my

3.5.67 **merit** it meane it, it 74 **for a** [F] for
4.1.29 **his** [Q2, F] this 30 **flint** [Q2] flints
[Q1, F] 50 **Mistress** Maisters 73 **bleat** [F]
bleake [Q] 74 **pines** [F] of Pines 99 **'Tis**
[Q2, F] as 121 **forfeit** forfaiture 127 **inexorable** inexcrable 225 **No, not** [Q2, F] Not
392 **not** [Q2] not to [Q1, F] 395 **s.p.**
GRAZIANO [Q2, F] Shy⟨locke⟩. [Q1]
5.1.42 **Master Lorenzo! Sola** M. Lorenzo sola
[Q2] & M. Lorenzo sola [Q1, F] 47–48
morning. / LORENZO . . . Sweet soul, let's
morning sweet soule / Loren⟨zo⟩. Let's 86
Erebus Erobus [F] Terebus [Q] 152 **it** [Q2,
F; not in Q1] 232 **my bedfellow** [Q2, F]
mine bedfellow

THE HISTORY OF HENRY THE FOURTH
(1 HENRY IV)

CONTROL TEXT: Q1 FOR
1.3.199–2.3.19, Q2 ELSEWHERE

F: THE FOLIO OF 1623

Q1: Remaining fragment of the Quarto of 1598
Q2: The complete Quarto of 1598
Q3: The Quarto of 1599
Q4: The Quarto of 1604
Q5: The Quarto of 1608
Q6: The Quarto of 1613
Q5b, Q6b: Successive states of Q5 and Q6
incorporating various print-shop corrections
and changes
Q7: The Quarto of 1622

Title: THE / HISTORY OF / HENRIE THE / FOURTH;
/ With the battell at Shrewsburie, / betweene
the King and Lord / Henry Percy, surnamed /
Henrie Hotspur of / the North. / With the
humorous conceits of Sir / John Falstalffe
[Q2 title page] The First Part of Henry the
Fourth, / with the Life and Death of HENRY /
Sirnamed HOT-SPURRE. [F head title]

s.p. KING HENRY [Q's use of King has been
changed throughout.]
s.p. PRINCE HARRY [Q's use of Prince has been
changed throughout.]
s.p. POINS [Q's use of Poines / Poynes has been
standardized throughout.]
s.p. HOTSPUR [Q's use of Hotspur / Percy has
been standardized throughout.]
s.p. FIRST TRAVELLER and SECOND TRAVELLER
[Q's Traveler of 2.2 has been differentiated
into two persons.]
s.p. LADY PERCY [Q's use of Lady has been
changed throughout.]
s.p. BARDOLPH [Q's use of Russell / Bardoll has
been standardized throughout.]
s.p. GLYNDŴR [Q's use of Glendower has been
changed throughout.]

s.p. SIR MICHAEL [Q's use of Sir M⟨ighell⟩ in
4.4 has been modernized.]
s.p. JOHN OF LANCASTER [Q's use of Prince
John / John / John of Lancaster has been
standardized throughout.]

1.1.39 **Herefordshire** [Q7, F] Herdforshire
40 **Glyndŵr** Glendower [similarly through-
out] 62 **a dear** [Q5b, F] deere 71 **the Earl**
Earle 73 **Moray** Murrey 75–76 **not? / s.p.**
WESTMORLAND **In faith, it is a** not? In faith
it is. / West⟨merland⟩. A
1.2.70 **similes** [Q6]; smiles 71 **sweet** [Q3, F];
sweer 100 **John, sack-and-sugar Jack?**
John Sacke, and Sugar Jacke? 114 **visors**
vizards 144 **Peto, Bardolph** Harvey, Rossill
148 **But how** [F] How 154 **Ay** [F] Yea 158
visors vizards 161 **But** [F] Yea, but
1.3.12 **too** [F] to 25 **was** [F] is 26 **Who**
either through envy [F] Either envie
therefore 27 **Was** [F] Is 52 **or** [F] or he 65
Made me to answer [F] I answered 83 **the**
[Q3, F] that 115 **Owain** Owen [similarly
throughout] 122 **you'll** [F] you wil 126
Although it be with [F] Albeit I make a
131 **In his behalf** [F] Yea on his part 133
downfall [F] down-trod 199 **s.p.** HOTSPUR
[Q6, F; no s.p. in Q1] 209–10 **a while . . .
me.** [F] a while. 237 **whipped** [Q2, F]
whip 240 **d'ye** [F] do you 241 **upon't** [F]
upon it 253 **to't** [F] to it 254 **We'll** [F]
We wil 264 **is't** [F] is it 265 **Bristol** Bris-
tow **Scrope** Scroop 289 **Lord** Lo: 292
our [Q2, F] out
2.1.1 **An't** [F] An it 23 **races** razes 38 **quoth**
a [F] quoth he 51 **Weald** wild 64 **he's** [F]
he is 68 **foot-landrakers** [Q4, F] footland
rakers 71 **'oyez'-ers** Oneyres 80 **recipe**
receyte
2.2.16 **two-and-twenty** [F] xxii: 25 **upon't** [F]
upon it 45–46 **Gadshill, what news? / s.p.**
GADSHILL Bardoll, what newes. / Bar⟨doll⟩.
46 **visors** vizards 70, 78 **s.p.** FIRST TRAV-
ELLER [unnumbered in Q] 71 **their** our 74
s.p. SECOND TRAVELLER [unnumbered in Q]
2.4.2 **respect** [Q7, F] the respect 42 **thee** the
48 **ransomed** ransome 63 **A roan** [Q4, F]
Roane 78 **to** unto 83 **maumets** mammets
2.5.29 **precedent** [F] present 32 **s.p.** POINS
[Q5, F] Prin⟨ce⟩. 61 **o'** a 110 **sun's** sonnes
159 **s.p.** PRINCE HARRY [F] Gad⟨shill⟩. 160,
162, 166 **s.p.** GADSHILL [F] Ross⟨ill⟩. 230
to't [F] to it 303 **talon** talent 311 **Owain** O
346 **joint-stool** joynd stoole 358 **Father** [F]
father 359 **tristful** trustfull 366 **yet** [Q4, F]
so 431 **lean** [Q3, F] lane 478, 479
Good . . . good God . . . god 487 **s.p.** PETO
[F; not in Q] 492 **s.p.** PRINCE HARRY [F; not
in Q]
3.1.48 **speaketh** speakes 67 **here's** [F] here is
97 **cantle** [F] scantle 126 **metre** miter 129

on an 152 the least least 182 nobleman
[F] noble man 197 thou down pourest
thou powrest downe 228 he's [F] he is
3.2.59 won wan 84 gorged [Q3, F] gordge
96 then [F] than 112 swaddling-clothes
swathling cloaths 156 intemperance [F]
intemperance 157 bonds bands
3.3.30 that's [Q4] that 49 tithe tight 65
four-and-twenty [F] xxiiii. 107 no thing [F]
nothing 122 owed ought 158 guests [F]
ghesse 173–4 two-and-twenty [F] xxii.
184 o'clock of clocke
4.1.18 jostling justling 20 my lord my mind
31 sickness stays him sicknesse 50 sole
soule 55 is [F] tis 98 ostriches Estridges
98–100 that with the wind / [. . .] / Baiting that with the wind / Baited 106 cuishes
cushes 109 dropped [Q3, F] drop 117
altar [Q5, F] altars 124 corpse coarse 127
cannot [Q6b, F] can 128 yet [Q6, F] it
135 merrily [F] merely
4.2.3 Coldfield cop- / hill 14–15 yeomen's
Yeomans 22 ensigns Ancients 28 feazed
ensign fazd ancient 31 tattered tottered
4.3.23 horse [Q5, F] horses 26 the half the
halfe of 84 country's [Q6b, F] Countrey
4.4.30 more mo
5.1.42, 58 Doncaster [F] Dancaster 83 our
[F] your 135 o' a 136 will it [Q3, F] wil
5.2.3 undone [Q6, F] under one 10 ne'er [F]
never
5.3.1 in the in 22 A fool Ah foole 35 ragamuffins rag of Muffins 39 stand'st [F]
stands 42 as yet are are yet 50 gett'st [F]
gets
5.4.57 Sir S. 67 Nor [F] Now 91 thee the
97 rites [F] rights 108 Embowelled Inboweld 110 Embowelled Inboweld 110
embowel inbowel 144 take't on [F] take it
upon 147 e'er [F] ever

THE MERRY WIVES OF WINDSOR

CONTROL TEXT: F

F: The Folio of 1623
Q: The Quarto of 1602

s.p. MASTER/MISTRESS [F uses M. to abbreviate
both words. Except at 4.4.24 and 5.5.196,
M. occurs in speech prefixes when the reference is clear because either the wife or husband is not onstage, or as an abbreviation for
"Mistress" when the husband has an immediately adjacent speech. Standardized
throughout.]
s.p. JOHN [F's Ser⟨vant⟩ and 1 Ser⟨vant⟩ have
been replaced throughout.]
s.p. ROBERT [F's 2 Ser⟨vant⟩ has been replaced.]
s.p. FALSTAFF [F's use of Falstaff and Sir John
has been standardized throughout.]

Title: A / Most pleasaunt and / excellent conceited Co- / medie, of Syr Iohn Falstaffe,
and the / merrie Wiues of Windsor. / Enter-
mixed with sundrie / variable and pleasing
humors, of Syr Hugh / the Welch Knight,
Iustice Shallow, and His / wise Cousin M.
Slender. With the swaggering vaine of Auncient Pistoll, and Corporall Nym. [Q title
page] A pleasant conceited Co- / medie, of
Syr Iohn Falstaffe, and the / merry Wiues of
Windsor. [Q head title] A pleasaunt Comedie, of the merry Wiues of Windsor [Q running title] An excellent & pleasant
conceited comedie of Sr Io Faulstof and the
merry Wyves of Windsor [Stationers' Register entry]

1.1.16 coad coat 19 cod coate 24 py'r Lady
per-lady 28 compromises compremises 39
George Thomas [Perhaps "Geo." in Shakespeare's handwriting could be misread
"Tho."] 42 fery ferry 51 s.p. SHALLOW
Slen⟨der⟩. 73 Cotswold Cotsall 87 Master
M. ["M." in dialogue is similarly interpreted
throughout unless separately noted, or
unless the character in question is obviously
female (e.g., "M Anne").] 117 Garter Gater
119 Fery Ferry 210 contempt content 212
faul' fall
1.2.3 'oman woman [Q] Nurse
1.3.13 lime lyme [Q] Lue 19 his mind is not
heroic. [not in F] 42 studied her well [Q]
Studied her will 46 legion legend 72 o'th'
ith' 73 humour [Q] honor 80 stars star 88
this the
1.4.19 whey face wee-face 32 for God's sake
[Q; not in F] 39 un boîtier vert vnboyteene
verd 44–45 Ma foi, il fait fort chaud! Je
m'en vais à la cour. La grande affaire. mai
foy, il fait jor ehando. Ie man voi a le Court la
grand affaires. 47 Mets-le à ma pochette.
Dépêche mette le a mon pocket, de-peech
52 and aad 54 qu'ci-j' que ay ie 60 larron
La-roone 77 baile ballow 82 your yoe your
106 goodyear good-ier 110–11 Anne— /
Exeunt Doctor [CAIUS and RUGBY] / —ass-
head An-focles head. [In this edition, "Anne"
("an") serves the double function of proper
name and indefinite article.] 139 that I will
that wee will
2.1.1 have I haue 21 i'th' with / The 26 O
God, that I knew how to [Q] how shall I 28
By my faith Trust me 30 by my faith trust
me 51 praised prase 54–55 hundred and
fifty psalms hundred Psalms 90 goodman
good man 127 Cathayan Cataian 169 God
bless you. bully rook, God bless you! How
now Bully-Rooke 85–86 guest cavaliero
guest-Cavaleire 187 s.p. FORD Shal⟨low⟩.
188 Brooke [Q] Broome 192 mijn'-heers
An-heires 201 than then

2.2.2–3 I will retort . . . penny. [not in F] **21 Ay, ay,** I I, I, I **22 God** [Q] heauen **23–24 you, you** you **27 wouldst** [Q] would **50 God bless** [Q] heauen-blesse **63 rustling** rushling **101 O God no, sir** [Q; not in F] **139 God bless** 'Blesse **155 half, or all all,** or halfe **207 exchange** enchange **232 spokesmate** [Q] assistant **270 God** [Q] Heauen **274 God's my life** [Q] fie, fie, fie

2.3.16 God bless [Q] 'Blesse **17 God save** [Q] 'Saue **25 Galen** *Galien* **49 word** [Q; not in F] **Monsieur** Mounseur **70 s.p. PAGE, SHALLOW,** *and* **SLENDER** *All.* **79 patiences** patinces [Q] patients [F]

3.1.4 Petty pittie **8 Jeshu pless me** [Q] 'Plesse my soule **25 God Heauen 35 God save** [Q] 'Saue **36 God pless** [Q] 'Plesse **54 pottage** porredge **75 By Jeshu** [Q; not in F] **88 Give . . . terrestrial—so.** [Q; not in F] **93 lads** [Q] Lad **95 Afore God** [Q] Trust me

3.2.43 By my faith [Q] Trust me **78 s.p. PAGE, CAIUS,** *and* **EVANS** *All.*

3.3.3 Robert *Robin* **33–34 pumpkin** Pumpion **51 By the Lord** [Q; not in F] **54–55 were, with nature,** were not nature **57–58 thee there's** [Q] thee. ther's **66 kiln** kill **129 s.p. JOHN** Ser⟨vant(s)⟩. **139 uncoop** vncape **152 what** who **163 foolish** foolishion **172 Ay,** I I, I **173 me** you **176 Ay, ay,** I I, I: I **192 heartily** hartly

3.4.12 s.p. FENTON [not in F] **44 by God** be God [Q; not in F] **55 God** [Q] Heauen **56 God** Heauen **64 Fenton** *Fenter*

3.5.7 'Sblood, the [Q] The **14 By the Lord** [Q] I should haue beene **53 By the mass** [Q] Oh he [Q] be **54 God bless** God save [Q] Blesse **73 God** [Q] good lucke **74 by** [Q] in **78 By the Lord** [Q] Yes **104 surge** serge

4.1.52 *Genitivo Genitiue* **53 Jenny's** Ginyes **57–58 hick . . . hack . . . 'whorum'** hic . . . hac . . . *horum* **59 lunatics** Lunaties

4.2.4 accoutrement accustrement **46 s.p. MISTRESS PAGE** [not in F] **53 s.p. MISTRESS PAGE** Mist⟨ress⟩ Ford. **61 Brentford** Brainford **84 direct** direct direct **87 him** [not in F] **97 as lief** liefe as **100 villains** villaine **102 gang** gin **108 this is** thi is **114 God be Heauen** be **125 s.p. PAGE** M⟨istress⟩ Ford. **157 not strike** strike **167 Jeshu** [Q] yea, and no **174 By my troth** [Q] Trust me

4.3.1 Germans desire Germane desires **7 them** [Q] him **9 house** [Q] houses

4.4.6 cold gold **24 s.p. MISTRESS FORD** M⟨istress⟩ Ford. **30 trees** tree **31 makes** make **41 Disguised . . . head** [Q; not in F] **59 s.p. MISTRESS FORD** Ford. **67 vizors** vizards **70 tire** tyre [Q] time **77 fery** ferry

4.5.35 s.p. SIMPLE Fal⟨staff⟩. **43 Ay, Sir Tike** I Sir: like **46 Thou art** [Q] Thou are **51 O Lord** [Q] Out alas **62–63 cozen** Gar-

mombles [Q] Cozen-Iermans **64 Colnbrook** *Cole-brooke* **91 O Lord, sir, and** [Q] And **97 Brentford** *Braineford*

4.6.26 ever euen **38 denote** deuote **39 visorèd** vizarded

5.1.20 Goliath Goliah

5.2.2 my daughter my **9 struck** strooke **10 lights** light **11 God** Heauen

5.3.11 Hugh Herne

5.5.1 struck stroke **9 foul fault** fowle-fault **28 God** [Q] Heauen **39, 80, 85 s.p. HOBGOBLIN** Pist⟨ol⟩. **46 Bead** *Bede* **65 More** Mote **78 God** [Q] Heauens **113 mate** meete **117 By the Lord** [not in F] **180 white** greene **184 green** white **187** *un garçon* oon Garsoon *un paysan* oon pesant **189 green** white **196 s.p. MISTRESS PAGE** M⟨istress⟩ Page.

THE SECOND PART OF HENRY THE FOURTH

CONTROL TEXT: Q; ADDITIONAL PASSAGES FROM F

F: The Folio of 1623
Q: The Quarto of 1600
QA: First issue of 1600 Q, lacking 3.1
QB: Second issue of 1600, containing 3.1

Title: THE / Second part of Henrie / the fourth, continuing to his death, / *and coronation of Henrie* / the fift. / With the humours of Sir John Fal- / *staffe, and swaggering* / Pistoll. [Q title page] The Second Part of Henry the Fourth, / Containing his Death: and the Coronation / of King Henry the Fift. [F head title]

s.p. LORD BARDOLPH [Q's use of *Bardolph* (for the nobleman) has been changed throughout.]

s.p. NORTHUMBERLAND [Q's use of *Earl / Northumberland* has been standardized throughout.]

s.p. FALSTAFF [Q's use of *Oldcastle / John / Sir John / Falstaff* has been standardized throughout.]

s.p. PAGE [Q's use of *Boy / Page* has been standardized throughout.]

s.p. LORD CHIEF JUSTICE [Q's use of *Lord / Justice* has been standardized throughout.]

s.p. ARCHBISHOP OF YORK [Q's use of *Bishop* has been changed throughout.]

s.p. MOWBRAY [Q's use of *Marshall / Mowbray* has been standardized throughout.]

s.p. MISTRESS QUICKLY [Q's use of *Hostess / Quickly* has been standardized throughout.]

s.p. GOWER [Q's use of *Gower / Messenger* has been standardized throughout.]

s.p. PRINCE HARRY [Q's use of *Prince / Harry* has been standardized throughout.]

s.p. LADY NORTHUMBERLAND [Q's use of *Wife* has been changed throughout.]

s.p. LADY PERCY [Q's use of *Kate* has been changed throughout.]

s.p. FIRST DRAWER and **SECOND DRAWER** [Q's use of *Francis* and *Drawer* has been changed throughout (with some speeches redistributed).]

s.p. DOLL TEARSHEET [Q's use of *Tere-sheet / Doll / Dorothy / Whoore* has been standardized throughout.]

s.p. PRINCE JOHN [Q's use of *John / Prince / Lancaster* has been standardized throughout.]

s.p. KING HENRY [Q's use of *King* has been changed throughout.]

s.p. GLOUCESTER [Q's use of *Humphrey / Gloucester* has been standardized throughout.]

s.p. FIRST and **SECOND GROOM** [Q's use of *Strewers of Rushes 1, 2,* and *3* has been changed throughout (with some speeches redistributed).]

s.p. FIRST BEADLE [Q's use of *Sinklo* has been changed throughout.]

The following variants record only where the Norton text departs from Q, the control text. 3.1, missing in QA, is based on QB, but where material in QA was reset in QB, QA remains the authoritative text. F, however, contains eight lengthy passages (and some shorter ones) that do not appear in Q (1.1.165–78, 1.1.188–208, 1.3.21–24, 1.3.36–55, 1.3.85–108, 2.3.23–45, 4.1.55–79, 4.1.101–37). These are marked in the variants and are based on F. Material originally in Q but absent in F (and in the Oxford text) is printed in the variants or in inset passages within this text. For a much fuller collation of Q and F, see Oxford's *William Shakespeare: A Textual Companion.*

Induction [F; heading not in Q] **s.p. RUMOUR** [not in Q] **13 griefs** [F] griefe **21 anatomize** anothomize **35 hold** hole **36 Where** [F] When

1.1.34 Lord Bardolph Sir John Umfreuile **41 ill** [F] bad **55 should the** [F] should that **59 a venture** a venter **96 say so** [F; not in Q] **103 knolling** [F] tolling **126 Too** [F] So **161 s.p. LORD BARDOLPH** [F] *Umfr⟨euile⟩.* This strained passion doth you wrong my lord. / *Bard⟨olfe⟩.* **163 Lean on your** [F] Leave on you **165–78 You . . . be?** [F; not in Q] **177 doth** hath **181 was** [F] twas **188–208 The . . . him.** [F; not in Q]

1.2.3 more moe **6 clay, man** clay-man **7 tends** [F] intends **10 o'erwhelmed** [F] overwhelmd **14 set** [F] in-set **25 Dumbleton**

Dommelton [Q] *Don̄bledon* [F] **26 slops** [F] my sloppes **31 rascally** [F] rascall **33 smooth-pates** [F] smoothy-pates **41 it;** [F] it: wheres Bardolf, **42 him. Where's Bardolph?** [F] him. **45 An** and **67 want** [F] need **88 age** [F] an ague **93 An't** andt **101 is, as I take it, a** [F] as I take it? is a **110 s.p. FALSTAFF** [F] Old⟨castle⟩. **131 waist** waste **slenderer** [F] slender **156 bearherd** Berod **158 this** [F] his **them, are** [F] the one **161 vanguard** vaward **176 th'ear** [F] the yeere **185–86 and Prince Harry** [not in Q] **192 my bottle, would** [F] a bottle. I would

1.3.21–24 Till . . . admitted. [F; not in Q] **26 case** [F] cause **28 on** [F] and **29 with** [F] in **36–55 Yes . . . else** [F; not in Q] **58 one** on **66 a** [F] so **71 Are** [F] And **78 not** [F] not to **79 He . . . Welsh** [F] French and Welch he leaves his back unarmde, they **84 'gainst** [F] against **85–108 s.p. ARCHBISHOP OF YORK . . . worst.** F; not in Q] **109 s.p. MOWBRAY** [F] *Bish⟨op⟩.*

2.1.18 An I **and** I **an** a **and a** **19 vice** [F] view **22–23 continuantly** [F] continually **25 Lombard** F] Lumbert **29 fobbed** fubd **38 Sir John** [F. not in Q] **44 Ah** a **45 Ah** a **48 s.p. FANG** [F] *Offic⟨er⟩.* **52 s.p. PAGE** [F] *Boy* **66–67 all,** all [F] al **73 Fie, what** [F] what **95 mad** made **134 tapestries** [F] tapestrie **134–35 ten pound** [F] X £. **138 Come** [F] come, come **152 good** [F; not in Q] **154 Basingstoke** [F] Billingsgate

2.2.14 hast—videlicet these [F] hast with these **15 ones** [F] once **19 thy** [F] the **20 made a shift to** [F; not in Q] holland. [F; Q here prints additional lines, and these are included as an inset passage after 2.2.20 of the text.] **23 lying** [F] being **yours** [F] yours at this time **28 you'll** [F] you will **49 engrafted** engraffec **65 A calls me e'en now** A calls me enow. **68 red petticoat** peticote **70 rabbit** [F] rabble **72 Althea** [F] Althear **78 good** [F; not in Q] **81 An** And **82 be wronged** [F] have wrong **84 my good** [F] my **98 borrower's** borowed **106 Sure he** [F] He sure **112 familiars** [F] family **115 My lord . . .** [F; no speech prefix before this line] *Poynes* My lord . . . **144 road** rode **150 like** [F] as **151 declension** descension **152 prince** [F] prince **153 everything** [F] every thing

2.3.11 endeared [F] endeere **23–45 He . . . grave** [F; not in Q]

2.4.1 s.p. FIRST DRAWER [F] *Fran⟨cis⟩.* **3 s.p. SECOND DRAWER** [F *Draw⟨er⟩.* **8 s.p. FIRST DRAWER** [F] *Fran⟨cis⟩.* **11 s.p. SECOND DRAWER** [F] *Francis.* **14 s.p. FIRST DRAWER** [F] *Dra⟨wer⟩.* **16 s.p. SECOND DRAWER** [F] *Francis.* **20 in good truth,** la in good truth, **law 22 we** [F] one **32 an** and **38 them; I** [F] I **42 Yea, Jesu** Yea, joy **46 bravely.** [F] bravely. / *Doll* Hang your selfe, you muddie Cunger, hang your selfe. 48–49 i'good truth ygood truth 59 Ensign Antient [similarly elsewhere] 71 your [F] & your 113 this. [F] this. / *Sir John* No more Pistol, I would not have you go off here, discharge your selfe of our company, Pistoll. 117 An and 123 'captain' odious [F] as odious as the word occupy, which was an excellent good worde before it was il sorted 133 Where [F] with 135 Fates [F] faters 144 Trojan troiant 150 Die men [F] Men 152 O' A 168 an a and a 189 o' a 198 A [F] Ah 207 o' . . . o' a . . . a 213 ha' chipped a chipt 223 boot [F] bootes 228 the scales [F] scales 240 master's [F] master 248 o'Thursday a thursday 251 By my troth, thou'lt By my troth thou't an and 286 o' a 293 him [F] thee 306 outbids [F] blinds 356 good Doll. [F] good Doll, come, shee comes blubberd, yea? wil you come Doll?

3.1.1–103 [QB; not in QA] 18 mast [F] masse 22 billows [F] pillowes 26 thy [F] them 27 sea-boy [F] season 52 liquors! [F; Q here contains additional lines printed in this text as an inset passage after this word.] 80 beginnings [F] beginning

3.2.11 o' a 19 o' a 20 bona-robas [F] bona robes 35 Stamford [F] Samforth 41 o' Gaunt a Gaunt 42 i'th' ith 50 s.p. SHALLOW [F] *Bardolfe* [QA] 61 accommodated [F] accommodate 75 your [F] your good 79 Surecard [F] Soccard 90 so. Yea so (so, so) yea 94 an't and't 98 an't and't 103 s.p. FALSTAFF Prick him. [F] *John prickes him.* [Q s.d. is indented from right-hand margin on same type line as "well said."] 104 an and 122 not [F] much 133 for his [F] for 143 he'd ha' hee'd a 165 thou'rt [F] thou art 168 caught [F] cought 174 There [F] Here 181–82 good Master Shallow, no more of that [F] master Shallow. 199 in [F] that we have, in 200 Hem boys [F] Hemboies 205 lief [F] live 217 I'll ne'er ile nere 217–18 An't . . . an't and't . . . and't 252 chapped chopt 263 will wooll 268 As you [F] at your my house [F] our house 274 On [F] *Shal⟨low⟩.* On 285 invisible invincible famine. [Q here contains additional lines printed in this text as an inset passage after this word.] 285.2 ever [F] over 291 trussed [F] thrust

4.1.34 rags rage 36 appeared appeare 55–79 And . . . wrong. [F; not in Q] 71 shore there 80 days [F] daie's 101–37 O . . . King. [F; not in Q. The s.p. "West." is set before 4.1.138 in Q.] 114 force forc'd 137 indeed and did 173 to our [F] our consigned confinde 178 And At 234 Than [F] That man [F] man talking 245 th'imagined th'imagine 250 Employ Imply 274

this [F] his 292–93 redresses. s.p. / PRINCE JOHN I [F] redresses, / I 295 s.p. HASTINGS [F] *Prince* 327 Our . . . dispersed [F] My lord, our army is disperst already 343 rebellion . . . yours. [F] rebellion: 348 these this traitors [F] traitour

4.2.2 I pray [F; not in Q] 37 Rome [F] Rome, there cosin 62 gav'st away [F] gavest away gratis 63 Have [F] Now, have 75 pray [F; not in Q] 78 but [F; not in Q] 96 illumineth [F] illumineth 100 his [F] this

4.3.32 melting [F] meeting 39 line [F] time 52 accompanied? Canst thou tell that? [F] accompanied 94 heaven [F] heavens 104 write . . . letters [F] wet . . . termes 120 and will break out [F; not in Q] 132 chamber; softly, pray [F] chamber 179 How fares your grace? [F; not in Q] 183 him. [F] him: he is not here. 203 Culling [F] toling 203–4 the virtuous sweets, / Our thighs [F] Our thigh 209 have hands 275 true and inward [F] inward true and 288 worst of [F] worse then 289 fine in carat, is [F] fine, in karrat 292 my [F] my most 305 O my son [F; not in Q] 306 put it [F] put 348 My gracious leige [F; not in Q]

5.1.1 pie [F] pie sir 8 Davy, Davy, Davy [F] Davy, Davy, Davy, Davy 8–9 see. William [F] see Davy, let me see, yea mary William 12 headland [F] hade land 19 Sir [F] Now sir 21 Hinkley [F] Hunkly 29–30 marvellous [F] marvailes 33 o'th' a'th' 40 An and 46 Come, [F] come, come, come 49 all [F; not in Q]

5.2.21 s.p. GLOUCESTER *and* CLARENCE [F] *Princ. ambo* 46 mix [F] mixt 62 s.p. PRINCE . . . CLARENCE *Bro.* other [F] otherwise

5.3.3 grafting graffing 5 here a . . . and a [F] here . . . and 24 Good Master Bardolph! [F] Give master Bardolfe 46 thee the 52–53 to th' too'th 57 cavalieros [F] cabileros 59 An And 64 'tis a tis 75 An't And't 84 By'r Lady Birlady 86 in thy [F] ith thy 95 Cophetua Covetua 117 knighthood [F] Knight

5.4.8 an and 11 He [F] I 22 o'ercome overcom

5.5.1–3 s.p. FIRST GROOM, SECOND GROOM, FIRST GROOM [Q opens with s.d. *Enter strewers of rushes.* The first three speeches are assigned to 1, 2, and 3, each presumably a strewer.] 3 o' a 3–4 coronation. *Exeunt / Enter* coronation, dispatch, dispatch. / *Trumpets sound, and the King, and his traine passe over the Stage; after them enter* 5 Robert [F; not in Q] 14 s.p. SHALLOW [F] *Pist⟨ol⟩.* 21–22 most certain. / s.p. FALSTAFF But [F] best certaine: but 23 affairs [F] affaires else 26 *absque* obsque all [F; not in Q] 49 awake [F] awakt 53 fool-born fool-borne **69 our** [F] my **82 I fear that** [F] that I feare

Epilogue 9 did mean [F; in F, the Epilogue is set in italics] meant **13–14 infinitely.** [F] infinitely: and so I kneele downe before you, but indeed, to pray for the Queene. **21 before** [F; not in Q] **27 died a** [F] died **29–30 and . . . Queen** [F; in Q, these lines follow Epilogue 15] **29 kneel** [F] I kneele

MUCH ADO ABOUT NOTHING

CONTROL TEXT: Q

Q: The Quarto of 1600
F: The Folio of 1623
F2: The Folio of 1632

s.p. DON JOHN [Q's use of *John* and *Bastard* has been standardized throughout.]
s.p. DON PEDRO [Q's use of *Pedro* and *Prince* has been standardized throughout.]
s.p. ANTONIO [Q's use of *Old, Antonio*, and *Brother* has been standardized throughout.]
s.p. DOGBERRY [Q's use of *Dogberry* and *Constable* has been standardized throughout.]
s.p. VERGES [Q uses both *Verges* and *Headborough*, but generally prefers the former, standardized throughout.]

1.1.8 Pedro Peter **34–35 bird-bolt** Burbolt
1.2.6 event [F2] euents
1.3.3 it [not in Q] **39 brothers** [F] bothers **44 on** on
2.1.33 bearherd Berrord **39 Peter** fore Peter: for . . . heavens **71 a bout** about **83, 86, 88 s.p. BALTHASAR** *Benedicke*
2.3.22 an [F] and **37 hid-fox** kid-foxe **56 s.p. BALTHASAR** [not in Q] **124 us of** [F] of vs
3.2.24 can cannot **45 s.p. DON PEDRO** [F] *Benedicke*
3.3.10, 15 s.p. SECOND WATCHMAN . . . FIRST WATCHMAN [reversed in Q] **24 s.p. FIRST WATCHMAN** *Watch 2* **34, 41, 45, 50, 61, 94, 110 s.p. A WATCHMAN** *Watch* **78, 85 s.p. FIRST WATCHMAN** *Watch* **145, 151 s.p. A WATCHMAN** *Watch 2* **154–55 A WATCHMAN** Never . . . us. [The speech is assigned to *Conrade* in Q.]
3.4.16 in [F] it
3.5.8 off of
4.1.201 princes left for dead princess (left for dead)
4.2.1 s.p. DOGBERRY *Keeper* **2, 5 s.p. VERGES** *Couley* **4 s.p. DOGBERRY** *Andrew* **8, 11, 14, 17, 23, 27, 31, 36, 39, 44, 50, 63, 67 s.p. DOGBERRY** *Kemp* **45 s.p. VERGES** *Constable* **60 s.p. DOGBERRY** *Constable* **61–62 s.p. VERGES** Let them be, in the hands— / CON-

RAD **Off, coxcomb!** *Couley* Let them be in the hands of Coxcombe.
5.1.16 Bid And **97 an** not in Q]
5.2.41 for [not in Q] **53 maintain** maintaind **73 myself. So** my sel' so
5.3.4–11 s.p. CLAUDIO Done . . . dumb [These lines follow the Lord's in Q with no distinct speech prefix] **11 dumb** [F] dead **23 s.p. CLAUDIO** *Lo.*
5.4.54 s.p. ANTONIO *Leonato* **96 s.p. BENEDICK** *Leonato*

THE LIFE OF HENRY THE FIFTH

CONTROL TEXT: F; ADDITIONAL MATTER FROM Q1

F: The Folio of 1623
Q1: The Quarto of 1600
Q3: The Quarto of 1619

s.p. KING HARRY [F's use of *King* has been standardized throughout.]
s.p. KING CHARLES [F's use of *King* has been standardized throughout.]

1.2.38 succedant succedual **50 there** [Q] then **72 fine** [Q] find **74 heir** [Q] th'Heire **77 Ninth** Tenth **99 son** man **115 those** these **131 blood** Bloods **147 unmasked his power** [Q] went with his forces **unto** into **154 the bruit thereof** the brute hereof [Q] **th'ill neighborhood 163 your** [Q] their **166 A LORD** [Q] Bish⟨op of⟩ Ely. **183 True.** [Q; not in F] **197 majesty** [Q] Maiesties **208 Fly** [Q] Come **212 end** [Q] And **213 defect** [Q] defeat **276 have I** I haue [F] haue we [Q] we haue [Q3] **284 from** [Q] with **287 Ay,** [Q] And
2.0.32—perforce—[not in F]
2.1.21 mare [Q] name **23 Good morrow, Ensign Pistol** [Q; not in F] **25 NIM** [Q; not in F] **26 Gad's lugs** [Q] this hand **65 thee defy** [Q] defie thee **72 enough.** [Q] enough to **73 you** your **95 s.p. NIM** I shall have my eight shillings? *Nim.* I shal haue my eight shillings I woon of you at beating? [Q; not in F] **105 that's** that
2.2.1 s.p. GLOUCESTER [Q; throughout scene] Bed⟨ford⟩. [F; throughout scene] **35 their** [Q] the **84 him** [Q; not in F] **85 vile** [Q; not in F] **95 ha'** [Q1] haue **104 a** an **136 mark** make the thee **144 Henry** [Q] *Thomas* **154 heartily in sufferance** in sufferance heartily **163 and fixed** [Q; not in F] **172 have** [Q; not in F] **173 ye** [Q1] you
2.3.15 babbled Table **22 up'ard and up'ard** vpward and vpward [Q] up-peer'd and upward **29 s.p. HOSTESS** *Woman.* **35 hell-fire** [Q1] Hell **41 word** [Q1] world

2.4.4 Bourbon [Q] Britaine **33 agèd** [Q] Noble **57 mountant** Mountaine **75 England** [Q1] of England **106 Turns he** [Q] Turning **107 pining** [Q] priuy **123 for** [Q] of

3.0.6 fanning fayning

3.1.7 conjure commune **17 noblest** Noblish **24 men** me **32 Straining** Straying

3.2.19 God's plud [Q; not in F] **19 breaches** [Q] breach **26 runs** wins

3.3 s.p. FLUELLEN [Q; throughout scene] *Welch.* [F; throughout scene] **s.p. JAMY** [Q; throughout scene] *Scot.* [F; throughout scene] **s.p. MACMORRIS** [Q; throughout scene] *Irish.* [F; throughout scene] **55–56 Aye owe Got a** aye, or goe to **109 heady** headly **112 Defile** Desire **124 dread** [Q] great

3.4.3 Un *En* **4 j'apprenne** *ie apprend* **5 parler** *parlen* **Comment** *Comient* **6 La main?** Elle est appelée *Le main il & appelle* **7 Et les doigts** [continued to Catherine] *Alice. E le doyts.* **8 s.p. ALICE** *Kat⟨herine⟩* **8–9 souviendrai** *souemeray* **9 sont** *ont fingers.* **Oui** *fingres, ou* **11 s.p. CATHERINE** *Alice.* **12 la bonne écolière; j'ai** *le bon escholier. / Kat⟨herine⟩. I'ay* **13 les** *le* **14 Les** *Le* **15 De nails. Ecoutez—** *De Nayles escoute:* **19 arma** *Arme* **20 le** *de* **22 la répétition** *le repeticio* **39 Non, et** *Nome* **43 Sauf** *Sans* **honneur** *honeus* **44 dis** *de* **45 pieds** *pied* **la robe** [Q] *de roba* **46 De foot** *Le foot* **46, 47, 51, 53 cown** *con* [Q] *Count* **47 De foot et de Le Foot, &** *le* **Ils** *Il* **51 De foot et de Le Foot &** *le* **Néanmoins** *neant moys* **53 foot, de foote, e** *de* [Q] *Foot, le*

3.5.10, 32 s.p. BOURBON [Q] *Brit⟨ain⟩.* **11 de** *du* **26 'Poor' may** we Poore we **45 Foix** Loys **46 knights** Kings

3.6.23 Of and of **27 her** [Q] his **49 executions** [Q] execution **58 is this the ensign you told me of** [Q] this is an arrant counterfeit Rascall **82 com'st** cam'st **99 here** [Q; not in F] **102 lenity** [Q] Leuitie

3.7.7 s.p. BOURBON [Q; throughout scene] *Dolph⟨in⟩.* [F; throughout scene] **12 Ah ha** Ch'ha **14 qui** a *ches* **60 vomissement** *vemissement* et *est* **61 truie** *leuye* **83 Duke of Bourbon** [Q] Dolphin

4.0.16 name nam'd

4.1.92 Thomas Iohn **148 deaths** [Q] death **propose** purpose **173 s.p. BATES** 3. *Lord.* [Q] *Will⟨iams⟩.* **227 adoration** odoration **267 or** of **280 have I** [Q] I haue **286 ill** all

4.2 s.p. BOURBON [Q; throughout scene] *Dolph⟨in⟩.* [F; throughout scene] **5 plus?** puis **6 Cieux** *Cein* **11 dout** doubt **25 'gainst** against **35 sonance** Sonuance **46 hands** hand **47 drooping** dropping **49 palled** pale **60 guidon** Guard: on

4.3.2 s.p. CLARENCE *Bed⟨ford⟩.* **3 s.p. WARWICK** [Q; throughout scene] *West⟨merland⟩.* [F; throughout scene] **8 Clarence** [Q] Bedford

11, 15 s.p. CLARENCE *Bed⟨ford⟩.* [F; speeches not in Q] **44 t'old** old **48 And . . . day.'** [Q; not in F] **106 grazing** crasing **118 as** or **119 your** [Q] the **129 come** come againe

4.4.4 Qualité 'Calin o Qualtitie calmie **12 miséricorde** *miserecordie* **pitié** *pité* **14 Or** for **46 prisonnier** *prisonner* **néanmoins** *neant-mons* **47 lui ci** *layt a* **promettez** *promets* **48 je se** **49 remerciements** *remercious* **49–50 j'ai tombé** *le intombe* **50 mains** *main.* **comme** [not in F] **pense** *peuse* **51 treis-distingué** *tres distinie* **59 Suivez** *Saaue*

4.5 [Both Bourbon and the Dauphin appear in this scene in F. Whereas in most instances the textual differences between Q and F merely involve speech prefixes, here they are more substantial. See Additional Passages, pp. 1520–21, for F and Q versions of this scene.] **2 Seigneur** *sigueur* **perdu . . . perdu** *perdia . . . perdie* **3 s.p. BOURBON** [Q] *Dol⟨phin⟩.* **Mort de** *Mor Dieu* **7–9 We are . . . upon** [Q; F places after 4.5.17] **10 order** [Q] Order now **12 home** [Q] hence **13 leno** [Q] Pander **14 by a slave** [Q] a base slaue

4.6.14–15 face, / And [Q] face. / He **15 dear** [Q] my **39 s.p. PISTOL** *Coup' la gorge.* [Q; not in F]

4.7.18 e'en in **19 world** Orld **36 made an end** [Q] made **83 Crispian** Crispianus **102 countryman** [Q] Countrymen **115 a live** aliue **118 a lived** aliue **150 that I would see** that I might see

4.8.9 God's plood, and his Gode plut, and his [Q1] 'Sblud **23 what is** [Q1] what's **94 Vaudemont** *Vandemont* **98 Keighley** Ketly **107 we** me **118 in** [Q; no in F]

5.0.10 maids [not in F] **29 high-loving** by loving

5.1.13 a [Q1] hee **36 By Jesu** [Q1] I say **37 and four nights** [Q; not in F] **80 swear** [Q] swore

5.2.50 scythe, all Sythe, withall **169 vat** wat **172–73 suis le possesseur** *sur le possession* **236 grandeur** *grandeus* **237 de votre seigneurie** *nostre Seigneur* **indigne** *indignie* **244 vat** wat **246 entend** entendre **291 before that it** before it **297 never** [not in F] **305 s.p. WARWICK** *West⟨merland⟩.* **306 so** [not in F] **328 ALL** Lords. **337 paction** Pation

THE TRAGEDY OF JULIUS CAESAR

CONTROL TEXT: F

F: The Folio of 1623

1.2.104 Said Caesar *Caesar* saide **140 were** are **156 walls** Walkes

1.3.128 In favour's Is Fauors

2.1.40 ides first 67 of of a 83 put path 96
Cinna, this; this, *Cinna;* 266 his hit 312,
315, 319 s.p. LIGARIUS *Cai⟨us⟩.*
2.2.46 are heare 81 Of And 108 Cassius *Publius* 109 s.p. CASSIUS *Pub⟨lius⟩.* Cassius
Publius
3.1.39 law lane 47 but with just cause [not
in F; line is quoted by Ben Jonson in *Timber, or Discoveries.*] 116 lies lye 175
unstrung in strength 286 for from
3.2.50 s.p. FOURTH PLEBEIAN 2. 63 s.p. FIFTH
PLEBEIAN 4. 101 art are 107 he not hee
196–97 revenged. / ALL THE PLEBEIANS
Revenge! reueng'd: Reuenge 213 wit writ
4.1.44 meinies meanes
4.2.2 s.p. SOLDIER *Lucil⟨lius⟩.* 34–36 s.p.'s
FIRST SOLDIER, SECOND SOLDIER, THIRD
SOLDIER [not in F] 80 bay baite 170 ill-
tempered too. ill remper'd too.s 204 Impatience Impatient 269 to ro 301 will will it
5.1.42 teeth teethes 55 swords Sword 79
ensigns Ensigne 88 give giue up 95 rest rests
5.3.103 Thasos *Tharsus*
5.4.7 s.p. LUCILLIUS [not in F] 17 the thee
5.5.76 With all Withall

As You Like It

CONTROL TEXT: F

F: The Folio of 1623

s.p. TOUCHSTONE [F's use of *Clowne* has been
changed throughout.]
s.p. DUKE FREDERICK [F's use of *Duke* has
been changed throughout.]
s.p. SIR OLIVER MARTEXT [F's use of *Oliver* has
been changed in 3.3.]
s.p. JAQUES DE BOIS [F's use of *Second Brother*
in 5.4 has been changed at lines 140 and
172.]

1.1.10 manège mannage 48, 50 villein . . .
villeins villaine . . . villaines 49 Bois Boys
75 Denis Dennis 94 she hee 99 Ardenne
Arden [similarly throughout] 138
s.p. OLIVER [not in F]
1.2.3 I [not in F] 69 s.p. CELIA *Ros⟨alind⟩.* 76
Le the 239 shorter taller 256 Rosalind
Rosaline
1.3.1 Rosalind *Rosaline* 51 likelihood likelihoods 84 Rosalind *Rosaline* 90 Rosalind.
lack'st thou then *Rosaline* lacks then 131
we in in we
2.1.49 much must 56 should doe 59 the
[not in F]
2.3.16 s.p. ORLANDO [not in F] 30 s.p.
ORLANDO *Ad⟨am⟩.* 72 seventeen seauentie
2.4.1 weary merry 39 thy they wound woulc
43–44 batlet batler 44 chapped chop:

64 you your 69 travel trauaile 78 cot
Coate [similarly throughout]
2.5.1 s.p. AMIENS [F has the heading "Song"
and no speech prefix.] 32 s.p. ALL [F has no
prefix, but the heading "Song." and the
phrase "Altogether heere."] 37–39 see . . .
weather *see. &c.* 43 s.p. JAQUES *Amy⟨ens⟩.*
2.7.55 aught but not in F] 87 comes come
174 s.p. AMIENS [There is no speech prefix in
F, but the heading "Song."] 182 Then The
190–93 sing . . . jolly *sing, &c.* 201 master masters
3.2.106 graft graffe 113 a not in F] 133 her
his 216 such [not in F] 222 thy the 328
deifying defying 336 are art
3.3.17 it [not in F] 79 s.p. TOUCHSTONE
Ol⟨iuer⟩.
3.4.27 a [not in F] 37 puny puisny
3.5.129 I [not in F]
4.1.1 be [not in F] 17 my by 53 beholden
beholding 66 warrant warne 132 hyena
Hyen 180 it in
4.2.2 s.p. FIRST LORD *Lord.* 7 s.p. SECOND
LORD *Lord.* 10 s.p. LORDS [not in F, which
has the heading "Musicke, Song."]
4.3.96 handkerchief handkercher 141 I' I
154 his this
5.2.6 her [not in F] 24 handkerchief handkercher 28 overcame ouercome 88 obedience obseruance 106 I satisfy I satisfi'd
5.3.14 s.p. BOTH PAGES [not in F, which has
the heading "Song."] 17 In In the ring rang
32–37 [F places these lines after 5.3.19.]
5.4.21 your you your 75 to the to 103 her *his*
153 them him 186 so [not in F]

Twelfth Night, or What You Will

CONTROL TEXT: F

F: The Folio of 1623

s.p. ORSINO [F's use of *Duke* and *Du⟨ke⟩* has
been changed throughout.]
s.p. SIR TOBY [F's use of *Sir To⟨by⟩, To⟨by⟩,* and
Tob⟨y⟩ has been standardized throughout.]
s.p. SIR ANDREW [F's use of *And⟨rew⟩* and
An⟨drew⟩ has been standardized throughout.]
s.p. FESTE [F's use of *Clo⟨wne⟩, Clow⟨ne⟩,* and
Cl⟨owne⟩ has been changed throughout.]

1.1.25 years' heat yeares heate
1.2.14 Arion Orion 48 pray thee prethee
1.3.44 s.p. SIR ANDREW *Ma⟨lvolio⟩.* 46 Mary
Accost *Mary* accost 83 curl by coole my 84
me we 86 housewife huswife 109
cinquepace Sinke-a-pace 114 divers-
coloured dam'd colour'd 117 That's That
1.5.156 'countable comptible 271 County's
Countes

2.2.18 straight [not in F] 29 our O 30 made of, made, if
2.3.68 Cathayan *Catayan* 121 a nayword an ayword
2.4.50 s.p. FESTE[*sings*] [not in F] 86 I it
2.5.103 staniel stallion 109 ay I 126 born become achieve atcheeues 154 dear *deero*
3.1.7 king Kings 61 wise men wisemens 116 grece grize
3.2.7 thee the the 57 nine mine
3.3.36 latchèd lapsed
3.4.23 s.p. OLIVIA *Ma⟨lvolio⟩*. 65 tang langer with 153 If s.p. *To⟨by⟩*. If 154 You Yon 179 out on't 244 virago firago
4.2.5 in in in 63 to the the 77 Master M.
5.1.73 wreck wracke 110 hath haue 193 pavan panyn 393 With [not in F]

The Sonnets and "A Lover's Complaint"

Control text: Q

Q: The Quarto of 1609
Qa, Qb: Qa is the uncorrected version, Qb the corrected version
Other texts cited:
B1—British Library Add. MS 10309, fol. 143 (c. 1630; Margaret Bellasys)
B2—British Library Add. MS 21433, fol. 114^v (c. 1630; Inns of Court)
B3—British Library Add. MS 25303, fol. 119^v (c. 1620s–30s; Inns of Court)
M—Pierpont Morgan MA 1057, p. 96 (c. 1630s)
MS—St. John's, Cambridge, MS S. 23 (James 416), fols. 38^r–38^v (c. 1630s–40s)
Passionate Pilgrim, c. 1599
R—Rosenbach MS 1083 / 16, p. 256 (c. 1630)
W—Westminster Abbey, MS 41, fol. 49 (1619–30s; George Morley)

Sonnets

1 [number not in Q]
2 [For another version of this sonnet, present in eleven manuscripts, see the Alternative Versions.] 4 tattered [MS] totter'd
5.14 Lose Leese
12.4 ensilvered o'er or siluer'd ore
13.7 Yourself You selfe
20.7 hues *Hews*
23.14 with . . . wit wit . . . wiht
25.9 might worth
26.12 thy their
27.10 thy their
28.12 gild'st the even guil'st th'eauen 14 strength length
31.8 thee there
34.12 cross losse
35.8 thy . . . thy their . . . their

37.7 thy their
39.12 doth dost
41.12 troth truth
43.11 thy their
44.13 naught naughts
45.12 thy their
46.3, 8, 13, 14 thy their 9 'cide side
47.10 art are 11 no nor
50.6 dully duly
51.10 perfect'st perfects 11 rein naigh
54.14 fade vade
55.1 monuments monument
56.13 Or As
61.8 tenor tenure
62.10 chapped chopt
63.5 travelled trauaild
65.12 of or
67.6 seeming seeing
69.3 due end 5 Thy Their 14 soil solye
70.6 Thy their
71.4 vilest vildest
73.4 ruined choirs rn'wd quiers
76.7 tell fel
77.10 blanks blacks
82.8 these the
85.3 thy their
86.13 filled fild
89.11 profane prophane [Qb]; proface [Qa]
90.11 shall stall
91.9 better bitter
99.9 One Our 13 ate eate
100.14 prevene'st preuenst
102.8 her his
106 [For another version of this sonnet, present in two manuscripts, see the Alternative Versions.] 12 skill [MSS] still
111.1 with wish
112.14 they're dead y'are dead
113.6 latch lack 14 makes mine eye maketh mine
116 119 [all but one extant copy of Q]
126.2 sickle-hour sickle, hower 8 minutes mynuit 12 [After this line, Q prints parentheses for each line of an imagined couplet.]
127.10 brow eyes
128.11, 14 thy their
129.9 Mad Made 11 proved proud a and
132.6 the east th'East 9 mourning morning
135.1, 2, 11, 12, 14 Will *Will*
136.2, 5, 14 Will *Will* 6 Ay I
138 [For another version of this sonnet, see the Alternative Versions.] 12 to have [*Passionate Pilgrim*] t'haue
140.13 belied be lyde
143.13 Will *Will*
144 [For another version of this sonnet, see the Alternative Versions.] 6 side [*Passionate Pilgrim*] sight 9 fiend finde
146.2 [   ] My sinfull earth
153.8 strange strang 14 eyes eye

"A Lover's Complaint"
7 sorrow's sorrowes,
37 beaded bedded
51 'gan gaue
112 manège mannad'g
118 Came Can
131 Consents Consent's
139 labour labouring
161 wills wits
182 woo vovv
198 pallid palyd [sometimes interpreted as "palèd," which properly means "having grown pale"]
204 hair heir
208 th'annexations th'annexions
228 Hallowed Hollowed
233 A Or
241 Planing Playing
251 immured enur'd
252 procured procure
260 nun Sunne
261 ay I
270 kindred, kindred
293 O Or

Alternative Versions

Spes Altera
Control text: W
Spes Altera [B1, B2, B3] To one yᵗ would dye a Mayd
3 liv'ry [B1] liuery
5 lies lye [cropped control-text ms.]
8 praise prays [cropped control-text ms.]

On his Mistress' Beauty
Control text: M
2 descriptions [R] discription
3 rhyme [R] mine [but with "rime" written in the margin as a correction]
6 hand [R] hands
8 E'en Ev'n [M] Euen [R]
10 these [R] those
12 your thy

VARIOUS POEMS

TITLE VARIANTS ARE NOT INCLUDED IN THE LISTS BELOW.

A Song
Control text: B
B: Bodleian MS Rawlinson poet. 160, fols. 108ʳ–109ᵛ
Y: Yale Osborn b. 197
5 sue shewe 10 joining [Y] Ioying 13 conceiving breeding 19 Fie [Y] Fly 29 will [Y] wit 30 stanza number 4 [Y] [no number in B] 38 pleasure [Y] our pleasure 49 You [Y] Then 52 neat next 68 their culled thass

cald commendations [B may instead read "commendatious."] 71 Pretty [Y] A pretty 77 mis-shape mishap 82 From For 83 plenty [Y] in plenty

Upon a pair of gloves
Control text: Shakespeare Birthplace Trust Record Office (MS ER.93)

Poems from *The Passionate Pilgrim*
Control text, poems 4, 17, 18: O1; remaining poems: O2
O1: The First Octavo of 1599
O2: The Second Octavo of 1599
Fo2: Folger Library MS V.a.339, fol. 203
Madrigals: Thomas Weelkes, *Madrigals* (1597)
Helicon: England's Helicon (1600)
4.5 ear [Fo2] eares 10 her [O2] his
10.1, 2 faded vaded 8, 9 left'st leftts
12.12 stay'st staies
13.2, 6, 8 fadeth . . . faded . . . faded vadeth . . . vaded . . vaded
14.17 Philomela sings Philomela sits and sings 19 dite ditte 20 daylight [not in O2] 24 sighed sight 27 a moon an houre
17.3 faith's Faithes 4 Heart's harts 16 freighted fraughted 27 Herd Heards 28 back [*Madrigals*] blacke 33 lass [*Madrigals*] loue 34 moan [*Helicon*] woe
18.45 be [Fo2] by

The Phoenix and Turtle
Control text: Robert Chester, *Loves Martyr: or Rosalins Complaint. Allegorically shadowing the truth of Love, in the constant Fate of the Phoenix and Turtle* (1601), sigs. Z3ᵛ–Z4ᵛ

Verses upon the Stanley Tomb at Tong
Control text: Inscription on the Stanley tomb at Tong

On Ben Jonson
Control text: Bodleian MS Ashmole 38, p. 181 (c. 1650), a transcript, probably in the hand of Nicholas Burgh

An Epitaph on Elias James
Control text: John Stow, *Survey of London* (1633), p. 825
B: Bodleian MS Rawlinson poet. 160, fol. 41
3 reposeth [B] reposes

An extemporary epitaph on John Combe, a noted usurer
Control text: Fo1
Fo1: Folger MS V.a. 147, fol. 72ʳ (1673), a transcript, probably in the hand of Robert Dobyns
Fo2: Folger MS V.a. 345, p. 232

1 here lies here lyeth 2 not now 3 lies [Fo2]
lyeth

Another Epitaph on John Combe
Control text: Bodleian MS Ashmole 38, p. 180
(c. 1650), a transcript, probably in the hand
of Nicholas Burgh
William Shakespeare hee [The epitaph is
attributed at the end to "W. Shak."]

Upon the King
Control text: King James I, *Works* (1616),
beneath the engraving of the King on the-
frontispiece

Epitaph on Himself
Control text: Shakespeare's grave at StMrat-
ford

General Bibliography*

There is a huge and ever-expanding scholarly literature about Shakespeare and his culture. This general list and the lists that accompany the individual plays and the poems in this volume are only a small sampling of the available resources. Journals devoted to Shakespeare studies include *Shakespeare Bulletin*, *Shakespeare Jahrbuch* (Germany), *Shakespeare Quarterly*, *Shakespeare Studies*, and *Shakespeare Survey* (England); other journals, such as *English Literary History*, *English Literary Renaissance*, *Renaissance Quarterly*, *Representations*, or *Studies in English Literature*, also frequently publish essays on Shakespeare's works. The categories below are only approximate; many of the texts could properly belong in more than one category.

Guides and Companions to Shakespeare Studies

Callaghan, Dympna, ed. *A Feminist Companion to Shakespeare*. Malden, Mass.: Blackwell, 2000.

de Grazia, Margreta, and Stanley Wells, eds. *The Cambridge Companion to Shakespeare*. Cambridge, Eng.: Cambridge University Press. 2001.

Drakakis, John, ed. *Alternative Shakespeares*. 2nd ed. London: Routledge, 1985.

Dutton, Richard, and Jean E. Howard, eds. *A Companion to Shakespeare's Works*, I: *The Tragedies*. Malden, Mass.: Blackwell, 2003.

———, eds. *A Companion to Shakespeare's Works*, II: *The Histories*. Malden, Mass.: Blackwell, 2003.

———, eds. *A Companion to Shakespeare's Works*, III: *The Comedies*. Malden, Mass.: Blackwell, 2003.

———, eds. *A Companion to Shakespeare's Works*, IV: *Poems, Problem Comedies, Late Plays*. Malden, Mass.: Blackwell, 2003.

Hattaway, Michael, ed. *The Cambridge Companion to Shakespeare's History Plays*. Cambridge, Eng.: Cambridge University Press, 2002.

Hawkes, Terence, ed. *Alternative Shakespeares, Volume 2*. London: Routledge, 1996.

Hodgdon, Barbara, and W. B. Worthen, eds. *A Companion to Shakespeare and Performance*. Malden, Mass.: Blackwell, 2005.

Jackson, Russell, ed. *The Cambridge Companion to Shakespeare on Film*. 2nd ed. Cambridge, Eng.: Cambridge University Press, 2007.

Kasten, David Scott, ed. *A Companion to Shakespeare*. Malden, Mass.: Blackwell, 1999.

Kinney, Arthur F. *Shakespeare by Stages: An Historical Introduction*. Malden, Mass.: Blackwell, 2003.

Leggatt, Alexander, ed. *The Cambridge Companion to Shakespearean Comedy*. Cambridge, Eng.: Cambridge University Press, 2002.

McDonald, Russ, ed. *The Bedford Companion to Shakespeare: An Introduction with Documents*. 2nd ed. Houndmills, Basingstoke: Palgrave Macmillan, 2001.

———, ed. *Shakespeare: An Anthology of Criticism and Theory, 1945–2000*. Malden, Mass.: Blackwell, 2004.

McEachern, Claire, ed. *The Cambridge Companion to Shakespearean Tragedy*. Cambridge, Eng.: Cambridge University Press, 2002.

*Edited by Holger Schott Syme, Department of English, University of Toronto.

Schoenfeldt, Michael. *A Companion to Shakespeare's Sonnets.* Malden, Mass.: Blackwell, 2006.

Smith, Emma, ed. *Shakespeare's Comedies: A Guide to Criticism.* Malden, Mass.: Blackwell, 2003.

———, ed. *Shakespeare's Histories: A Guide to Criticism.* Malden, Mass.: Blackwell, 2003.

———, ed. *Shakespeare's Tragedies: A Guide to Criticism.* Malden, Mass.: Blackwell, 2003.

Wells, Stanley, and Lena Cowen Orlin, eds. *Shakespeare: An Oxford Guide.* Oxford: Oxford University Press, 2003.

Wells, Stanley, and Sarah Stanton, eds. *The Cambridge Companion to Shakespeare on Stage.* New York: Cambridge University Press, 2002.

Shakespeare's World

Social, Political, and Economic History

Amussen, Susan Dwyer. *An Ordered Society: Gender and Class in Early Modern England.* New York: Columbia University Press, 1993.

Archer, Ian W. *The Pursuit of Stability: Social Relations in Elizabethan London.* New York: Cambridge University Press, 1991.

Ariès, Philippe, and Georges Duby, general eds. *A History of Private Life,* Volume III: *Passions of the Renaissance.* Ed. Roger Chartier. Trans. Arthur Goldhammer. Cambridge, Mass.: Belknap Press, 1989.

Armitage, David, and Michael J. Braddick, eds. *The British Atlantic World, 1500–1800.* New York: Palgrave Macmillan, 2002.

Barry, Jonathan, ed. *The Tudor and Stuart Town: A Reader in English Urban History, 1530–1688.* London: Longman, 1990.

Barry, Jonathan, and Christopher Brooks. *The Middling Sort of People: Culture, Society and Politics in England, 1550–1800.* Houndmills, Basingstoke: Palgrave Macmillan, 1994.

Barthelmey, Anthony Gerard. *Black Face, Maligned Race: The Representation of Blacks in English Drama from Shakespeare to Southerne.* Baton Rouge: Louisiana State University Press, 1987.

Beier, A. L. *Masterless Men: The Vagrancy Problem in England, 1560–1640.* New York: Methuen, 1985.

Beier, A. L., and Roger Finlay, eds. *London 1500–1700: The Making of the Metropolis.* New York: Longman, 1986.

Ben-Amos, Ilana Krausman. *Adolescence and Youth in Early Modern England.* New Haven: Yale University Press, 1994.

Bridenbaugh, Carl. *Vexed and Troubled Englishmen, 1590–1642.* New York: Oxford University Press, 1976.

Brigden, Susan. *New Worlds, Lost Worlds: The Rule of the Tudors, 1485–1603.* New York: Viking, 2001.

Burgess, Glenn. *The Politics of the Ancient Constitution: An Introduction to English Political Thought, 1603–1642.* University Park: Pennsylvania State University Press, 1993.

Capp, Bernard S. *When Gossips Meet: Women, Family, and Neighbourhood in Early Modern England.* Oxford: Oxford University Press, 2003.

Clark, Alice. *Working Life of Women in the Seventeenth Century.* Introduction by Amy Louise Erickson. 1968. New York: Routledge, 1992.

Clay, C. G. A. *Economic Expansion and Social Change: England 1500–1700.* 2 vols. New York: Cambridge University Press, 1984.

Cressy, David. *Birth, Marriage, and Death: Ritual, Religion, and the Life-Cycle in Tudor and Stuart England.* Oxford: Oxford University Press, 1997.

Cruickshank, Charles Greig. *Elizabeth's Army.* 2nd ed. Oxford: Clarendon, 1966.

Elliot, John Huxtable. *The Old World and the New, 1492–1650.* New York: Cambridge University Press, 1970.

Ellis, Steven G. *Tudor Ireland: Crown, Community, and the Conflict of Cultures, 1470–1603.* London: Longman, 1985.

Elton, G. R. *England Under the Tudors.* 3rd ed. New York: Routledge, 1991.

———. *The Tudor Revolution in Government: Administrative Changes in the Reign of Henry VIII.* Cambridge, Eng.: Cambridge University Press, 1959.

Emmison, F. G. *Elizabethan Life.* Chelmsford: Essex County Council, 1970.

Erickson, Amy Louise. *Women and Property in Early Modern England.* New York: Routledge, 1993.

Finlay, Roger. *Population and Metropolis: The Demography of London, 1580–1650.* Cambridge, Eng.: Cambridge University Press, 1981.

Fletcher, Anthony. *Gender, Sex, and Subordination in England, 1500–1800.* New Haven: Yale University Press, 1995.

Fletcher, Anthony, and John Stevenson, eds. *Order and Disorder in Early Modern England.* New York: Cambridge University Press, 1985.

Gaskill, Malcolm. *Crime and Mentalities in Early Modern England.* New York: Cambridge University Press, 2000.

Gittings, Clare. *Death, Burial and the Individual in Early Modern England.* London: Croom Helm, 1984.

Gowing, Laura. *Common Bodies: Women, Touch and Power in Seventeenth-Century England.* New Haven: Yale University Press, 2003.

Griffiths, Paul. *Youth and Authority: Formative Experiences in England, 1560–1640.* Oxford: Clarendon, 1996.

Griffiths, Paul, Adam Fox, and Steve Hindle, eds. *The Experience of Authority in Early Modern England.* New York: St. Martin's, 1996.

Guy, John A. *Queen of Scots: The True Life of Mary Stuart.* Boston: Houghton Mifflin, 2004.

———, ed. *The Reign of Elizabeth I: Court and Culture in the Last Decade.* Cambridge, Eng.: Cambridge University Press, 1995.

———. *Tudor England.* New York: Oxford University Press, 1988.

Heal, Felicity, and Clive Holmes. *The Gentry in England and Wales, 1500–1700.* Basingstoke: Macmillan, 1994.

Herrup, Cynthia B. *The Common Peace: Participation and the Criminal Law in Seventeenth-Century England.* New York: Cambridge University Press, 1987.

Hindle, Steve. *The State and Social Change in Early Modern England, c.1550–1640.* New York: St. Martin's, 2000.

Hirst, Derek. *Authority and Conflict: England, 1603–1658.* Cambridge, Mass.: Harvard University Press, 1986.

Ingram, Martin. *Church Courts, Sex, and Marriage in England 1570–1640.* New York: Cambridge University Press, 1987.

James, Mervyn. *Society, Politics and Culture: Studies in Early Modern England.* New York: Cambridge University Press, 1986.

King, John N. *Tudor Royal Iconography: Literature and Art in an Age of Religious Crisis.* Princeton: Princeton University Press, 1989.

Kishlansky, Mark A. *A Monarchy Transformed: Britain 1603–1714.* New York: Penguin Books, 1996.

Klein, Joan Larsen. *Daughters, Wives, and Widows: Writings by Men about Women and Marriage in England, 1500–1640.* Urbana: University of Illinois Press, 1992.

Lake, Peter, with Michael Questier. *The Anti-Christ's Lewd Hat: Protestants, Papists and Players in Post-Reformation England.* New Haven: Yale University Press, 2002.

Laslett, Peter. *The World We Have Lost: Further Explored.* 3rd ed. New York: Scribner, 1984.

Levin, Carole. *The Heart and Stomach of a King: Elizabeth I and the Politics of Sex and Power.* Philadelphia: University of Pennsylvania Press, 1994.

Lockyer, Roger. *The Early Stuarts: A Political History of England, 1603–1642.* 2nd ed. London: Longman, 1999.

MacCaffrey, Wallace T. *Elizabeth I: War and Politics, 1588–1603.* Princeton: Princeton University Press, 1992.

Manning, Roger B. *Village Revolts: Social Protest and Popular Disturbances in England, 1509–1640.* Oxford: Clarendon, 1988.

Matar, Nabil I. *Islam in Britain, 1558–1685.* New York: Cambridge University Press, 1998.

———. *Turks, Moors, and Englishmen in the Age of Discovery.* New York: Columbia University Press, 1999.

Mendelson, Sara Heller, and Patricia Crawford. *Women in Early Modern England, 1550–1720.* Oxford: Clarendon, 1998.

Moody, T. W., F. X. Martin, and F. J. Byrne, eds. *A New History of Ireland,* Volume 3: *Early Modern Ireland, 1534–1691.* Oxford: Oxford University Press, 2001.

Mukerji, Chandra. *From Graven Images: Patterns of Modern Materialism.* New York: Columbia University Press, 1983.

Neale, J. E. *Elizabeth I and Her Parliaments, 1559–1581.* London: Cape, 1971.

———. *Queen Elizabeth I.* London: Pimlico, 1998.

Nichols, John, ed. *The Progresses and Public Processions of Queen Elizabeth.* 3 vols. London: J. Nichols, 1823.

Palliser, D. M. *The Age of Elizabeth: England under the Later Tudors, 1547–1603.* 2nd ed. New York: Longman, 1992.

Parry, J. H. *The Age of Reconnaissance: Discovery, Exploration, and Settlement, 1450 to 1650.* New York: Praeger, 1969.

Pearson, Lu Emily Hess. *Elizabethans at Home.* Stanford: Stanford University Press, 1967.

Peck, Linda Levy. *Court Patronage and Corruption in Early Stuart England.* Boston: Unwin Hyman, 1990.

Peters, Christine. *Women in Early Modern Britain, 1450–1640.* New York: Palgrave Macmillan, 2004.

Pocock, J. G. A. *The Ancient Constitution and the Feudal Law: Study of English Historical Thought in the Seventeenth Century—A Reissue with a Retrospect.* Rev. ed. New York: Cambridge University Press, 1987.

Rappaport, Steve. *Worlds within Worlds: Structures of Life in Sixteenth-Century London.* New York: Cambridge University Press, 1989.

Sharpe, J. A. *Crime in Early Modern England, 1550–1750.* 2nd ed. New York: Longman, 1999.

———. *Early Modern England: A Social History, 1550–1760.* 2nd ed. London: Arnold, 1997.

Slack, Paul. *The Impact of Plague in Tudor and Stuart England.* Boston: Routledge and Kegan Paul, 1985.

———. *Poverty and Policy in Tudor and Stuart England.* New York: Longman, 1988.

———, ed. *Rebellion, Popular Protest, and the Social Order in Early Modern England.* New York: Cambridge University Press, 1984.

Stone, Lawrence. *The Causes of the English Revolution, 1529–1642.* New York: Routledge, 2002.

———. *The Crisis of the Aristocracy, 1558–1641.* Oxford: Clarendon, 1965.

———. *The Family, Sex and Marriage in England, 1500–1800.* New York: Harper & Row, 1979.

Thirsk, Joan. *Economic Policy and Projects: The Development of a Consumer Society in Early Modern England.* Oxford: Clarendon, 1978.

Thomas, Keith. *Religion and the Decline of Magic: Studies in Popular Beliefs in Sixteenth and Seventeenth Century England.* New York: Scribner, 1971.

Underdown, David. *Fire from Heaven: Life in an English Town in the Seventeenth Century.* London: HarperCollins, 1992.

———. *Revel, Riot, and Rebellion: Popular Politics and Culture in England, 1603–1660.* Oxford: Clarendon, 1985.

Williams, Penry. *The Later Tudors: England, 1547–1603.* New York: Oxford University Press, 1995.

Wrightson, Keith. *Earthly Necessities: Economic Lives in Early Modern Britain.* New Haven: Yale University Press, 2000.

———. *English Society, 1580–1680.* London: Hutchinson, 1982.

Yates, Frances Amelia. *Astraea: The Imperial Theme in the Sixteenth Century.* London: Routledge and Kegan Paul, 1975.

Zagorin, Perez. *Rebels and Rulers, 1500–1660.* 2 vols. New York: Cambridge University Press, 1982.

Intellectual and Religious History

Armitage, David. *The Ideological Origins of the British Empire.* New York: Cambridge University Press, 2000.

Baker, Herschel Clay. *The Race of Time: Three Lectures on Renaissance Historiography.* Toronto: University of Toronto Press, 1967.

Barkan, Leonard. *Nature's Work of Art: The Human Body as Image of the World.* New Haven: Yale University Press, 1975.

Bossy, John. *Christianity in the West, 1400–1700.* New York: Oxford University Press, 1985.

Bouwsma, William James. *John Calvin: A Sixteenth-Century Portrait.* New York: Oxford University Press, 1988.

Cassirer, Ernst. *The Individual and the Cosmos in Renaissance Philosophy.* Trans. Mario Domandi. Philadelphia: University of Pennsylvania Press, 1972.

Clark, Stuart. *Thinking with Demons: The Idea of Witchcraft in Early Modern Europe.* New York: Oxford University Press, 1997.

Collinson, Patrick. *The Birthpangs of Protestant England: Religion and Cultural Change in the Sixteenth and Seventeenth Centuries.* New York: St. Martin's, 1988.

———. *The Elizabethan Puritan Movement.* New York: Oxford University Press, 1990.

———. *The Religion of Protestants: The Church in English Society, 1559–1625.* Oxford: Clarendon, 1982.

Doran, Susan, and Christopher Durston. *Princes, Pastors, and People: The Church and Religion in England, 1500–1700.* Rev. ed. New York: Routledge, 2003.

Duffy, Eamon. *The Stripping of the Altars: Traditional Religion in England, c. 1400–c. 1580.* 2nd ed. New Haven: Yale University Press, 1992.

Gadd, Ian, and Alexandra Gillespie, eds. *John Stow (1525–1605) and the Making of the English Past.* London: British Library, 2004.

Haigh, Christopher. *English Reformations: Religion, Politics, and Society under the Tudors.* New York: Oxford University Press, 1993.

Hill, Christopher. *Society and Puritanism in Pre-Revolutionary England.* New York: Schocken Books, 1964.

Houlbrooke, Ralph A. *Death, Religion, and the Family in England, 1480–1700.* New York: Oxford University Press, 1998.

Kelly, Henry Ansgar. *Divine Providence in the England of Shakespeare's Histories.* Cambridge, Mass.: Harvard University Press, 1970.

Kilroy, Gerard. *Edmund Campion. Memory and Transcription.* Aldershot, Eng.: Ashgate, 2005.

Klaits, Joseph. *Servants of Satan: The Age of the Witch Hunts.* Bloomington: Indiana University Press, 1985.

Kristeller, Paul Oskar. *Renaissance Thought: The Classic, Scholastic, and Humanistic Strains.* New York: Harper & Row, 1961.

Levao, Ronald. *Renaissance Minds and Their Fictions: Cusanus, Sidney, Shakespeare.* Berkeley: University of California Press, 1985.

Levin, Harry. *The Myth of the Golden Age in the Renaissance.* Bloomington: University of Indiana Press, 1969.

Levy, Fred Jacob. *Tudor Historical Thought*. San Marino, Calif.: Huntington Library Press, 1967.

MacCulloch, Diarmaid. *The Later Reformation in England, 1547–1603*. 2nd ed. New York: Palgrave, 2001.

———. *The Reformation*. New York: Viking, 2004.

Mack, Peter, ed. *Renaissance Rhetoric*. New York: St. Martin's, 1994.

Marotti, Arthur F. *Religious Ideology and Cultural Fantasy: Catholic and Anti-Catholic Discourses in Early Modern England*. Notre Dame, Ind.: University of Notre Dame Press, 2005.

Marshall, Peter. *Beliefs and the Dead in Reformation England*. London: Oxford University Press, 2002.

Oldridge, Darren, ed. *The Witchcraft Reader*. London: Routledge, 2001.

Patterson, Annabel M. *Reading Holinshed's* Chronicles. Chicago: University of Chicago Press, 1994.

Popkin, Richard H. *The History of Skepticism from Erasmus to Spinoza*. Berkeley: University of California Press, 1979.

Sharpe, James. *Instruments of Darkness: Witchcraft in England 1550–1750*. New York: Penguin Books, 1996.

Shuger, Debora Kuller. *Habits of Thought in the English Renaissance: Religion, Politics, and the Dominant Culture*. Berkeley: University of California Press, 1990.

Sonnino, Lee A. *A Handbook to Sixteenth-Century Rhetoric*. London: Routledge and Kegan Paul, 1968.

Strong, Roy. *The Cult of Elizabeth: Elizabethan Portraiture and Pageantry*. London: Thames and Hudson, 1977.

———. *The English Icon: Elizabethan & Jacobean Portraiture*. New York: Pantheon Books, 1969.

Walsham, Alexandra. *Providence in Early Modern England*. New York: Oxford University Press, 1999.

Watt, Tessa. *Cheap Print and Popular Piety, 1560–1649*. New York: Cambridge University Press, 1991.

Wind, Edgar. *Pagan Mysteries in the Renaissance*. Rev. and enl. ed. London: Oxford University Press, 1980.

Woolf, D. R. *Reading History in Early Modern England*. New York: Cambridge University Press, 2000.

———. *The Social Circulation of the Past: English Historical Culture, 1500–1730*. New York: Oxford University Press, 2003.

Cultural History and Early Modern Cultural Studies

Aers, David, Bob Hodge, and Gunther Kress. *Literature, Language, and Society in England, 1589–1680*. Totowa, N.J.: Barnes & Noble Books, 1981.

Agnew, Jean-Christophe. *Worlds Apart: The Market and the Theater in Anglo-American Thought, 1550–1750*. New York: Cambridge University Press, 1986.

Andersen, Jennifer, and Elizabeth Sauer, eds. *Books and Readers in Early Modern England: Material Studies*. Philadelphia: University of Pennsylvania Press, 2001.

Bakhtin, Mikhail. *Rabelais and His World*. Trans. Hélène Iswolsky. Rev. ed. Bloomington: Indiana University Press, 1984.

Baldwin, Thomas Whitfield. *William Shakespere's Small Latine & Lesse Greeke*. Urbana: University of Illinois Press, 1944.

Barkan, Leonard. *The Gods Made Flesh: Metamorphosis & the Pursuit of Paganism*. New Haven: Yale University Press, 1986.

Barker, Francis. *The Tremulous Private Body: Essays on Subjection*. New York: Methuen, 1984.

Baron, Sabrina Alcorn, ed. *The Reader Revealed*. Washington, D.C.: Folger Shakespeare Library, 2001.

Bartels, Emily Carroll. *Spectacles of Strangeness: Imperialism, Alienation, and Marlowe*. Philadelphia: University of Pennsylvania Press, 1993.

Beilin, Elaine V. *Redeeming Eve: Women Writers of the English Renaissance*. Princeton: Princeton University Press, 1987.

Blank, Paula. *Broken English: Dialects and the Politics of Language in Renaissance Literature*. New York: Routledge, 1996.

Bloom, Gina. *Voice in Motion: Staging Gender, Shaping Sound in Early Modern England*. Philadelphia: Pennsylvania University Press, 2007.

Bray, Alan. *Homosexuality in Renaissance England*. Rev. ed. New York: Columbia University Press, 1995.

Brayman Hackel, Heidi. *Reading Material in Early Modern England: Print, Gender, and Literacy*. New York: Cambridge University Press, 2005.

Briggs, Julia. *This Stage-Play World: Texts and Contexts, 1580–1625*. 2nd ed. New York: Oxford University Press, 1997.

Bristol, Michael D. *Carnival and Theater: Plebeian Culture and the Structure of Authority in Renaissance England*. New York: Methuen, 1985.

Brotton, Jerry. *Trading Territories: Mapping the Early Modern World*. London: Reaktion Books, 1997.

Brown, Pamela Allen. *Better a Shrew than a Sheep: Women, Drama, and the Culture of Jest in Early Modern England*. Ithaca, N.Y.: Cornell University Press, 2003.

Burke, Peter. *Popular Culture in Early Modern Europe*. New York: New York University Press, 1978.

Burt, Richard, and John Michael Archer, eds. *Enclosure Acts: Sexuality, Property, and Culture in Early Modern England*. Ithaca, N.Y.: Cornell University Press, 1994.

Bushnell, Rebecca W. *A Culture of Teaching: Early Modern Humanism in Theory and Practice*. Ithaca, N.Y.: Cornell University Press, 1996.

Buxton, John. *Elizabethan Taste*. London: Macmillan, 1963.

Caldwell, John. *The Oxford History of English Music*. New York: Oxford University Press, 1991.

Carroll, William C. *Fat King, Lean Beggar: Representations of Poverty in the Age of Shakespeare*. Ithaca, N.Y.: Cornell University Press, 1996.

Clegg, Cyndia Susan. *Press Censorship in Elizabethan England*. New York: Cambridge University Press, 1997.

———. *Press Censorship in Jacobean England*. New York: Cambridge University Press, 2001.

Cox, John D. *The Devil and the Sacred in English Drama, 1350–1642*. New York: Cambridge University Press, 2000.

Crane, Mary Thomas. *Framing Authority: Sayings, Self, and Society in Sixteenth-Century England*. Princeton: Princeton University Press, 1993.

Crawford, Julie. *Marvelous Protestantism: Monstrous Births in Post-Reformation England*. Baltimore: Johns Hopkins University Press, 2005.

Cressy, David. *Literacy and the Social Order: Reading and Writing in Tudor and Stuart England*. New York: Cambridge University Press, 1980.

De Grazia, Margreta, Maureen Quilligan, and Peter Stallybrass, eds. *Subject and Object in Renaissance Culture*. New York: Cambridge University Press, 1996.

Diehl, Huston. *Staging Reform, Reforming the Stage: Protestantism and Popular Theater in Early Modern England*. Ithaca, N.Y.: Cornell University Press, 1997.

Dolan, Frances E. *Dangerous Familiars: Representations of Domestic Crime in England, 1550–1700*. Ithaca, N.Y.: Cornell University Press, 1994.

———. *Whores of Babylon: Catholicism, Gender, and Seventeenth-Century Print Culture*. Ithaca, N.Y.: Cornell University Press, 1999.

Eisenstein, Elizabeth L. *The Printing Press as an Agent of Change: Communications and Cultural Transformations in Early-Modern Europe*. 2 vols. New York: Cambridge University Press, 1979.

Ferguson, Margaret W. *Dido's Daughters: Literacy, Gender, and Empire in Early Modern England and France*. Chicago: University of Chicago Press, 2003.

Ferguson, Margaret W., Maureen Quilligan, and Nancy J. Vickers, eds. *Rewriting the Renaissance: The Discourses of Sexual Difference in Early Modern Europe*. Chicago: University of Chicago Press, 1986.

Fisher, Will. *Materializing Gender in Early Modern English Literature and Culture*. New York: Cambridge University Press, 2006.

Fleming, Juliet. *Graffiti and the Writing Arts of Early Modern England*. Philadelphia: University of Pennsylvania Press, 2001.

Frye, Susan. *Elizabeth I: The Competition for Representation*. New York: Oxford University Press, 1993.

Fumerton, Patricia. *Cultural Aesthetics: Renaissance Literature and the Practice of Social Ornament*. Chicago: University of Chicago Press, 1991.

———. *Unsettled: The Culture of Mobility and the Working Poor in Early Modern England*. Chicago: University of Chicago Press, 2006.

Gillies, John. *Shakespeare and the Geography of Difference*. New York: Cambridge University Press, 1994.

Goldberg, Jonathan. *James I and the Politics of Literature: Jonson, Shakespeare, Donne, and Their Contemporaries*. Baltimore: Johns Hopkins University Press, 1983.

———. *Writing Matter: From the Hands of the English Renaissance*. Stanford: Stanford University Press, 1990.

———, ed. *Queering the Renaissance*. Durham, N.C.: Duke University Press, 1994.

Greenblatt, Stephen. *Learning to Curse: Essays in Early Modern Culture*. New York: Routledge, 1990.

———. *Renaissance Self-Fashioning: From More to Shakespeare*. Chicago: University of Chicago Press, 1980.

———, ed. *New World Encounters*. Berkeley: University of California Press, 1993.

———, ed. *Representing the English Renaissance*. Berkeley: University of California Press, 1988.

Grout, Donald Jay, and Hermine Weigel Williams. *A Short History of Opera*. 4th ed. New York: Columbia University Press, 2003.

Hall, Kim F. *Things of Darkness: Economies of Race and Gender in Early Modern England*. Ithaca, N.Y.: Cornell University Press, 1995.

Harris, Jonathan Gil. *Foreign Bodies and the Body Politic: Discourses of Social Pathology in Early Modern England*. New York: Cambridge University Press, 1998.

Harvey, Elizabeth D., ed. *Sensible Flesh: On Touch in Early Modern Culture*. Philadelphia: University of Pennsylvania Press, 2003.

Haselkorn, Anne M., and Betty S. Travitsky, eds. *The Renaissance Englishwoman in Print: Counterbalancing the Canon*. Amherst: University of Massachusetts Press, 1990.

Helgerson, Richard. *Forms of Nationhood: The Elizabethan Writing of England*. Chicago: University of Chicago Press, 1992.

Henderson, Katherine Usher, and Barbara F. McManus. *Half Humankind: Contexts and Texts of the Controversy About Women in England, 1540–1640*. Urbana: University of Illinois Press, 1985.

Hendricks, Margo, and Patricia Parker, eds. *Women, "Race," and Writing in the Early Modern Period*. New York: Routledge, 1994.

Hillman, David, and Carla Mazzio, eds. *The Body in Parts: Fantasies of Corporeality in Early Modern Europe*. New York: Routledge, 1997.

Hoeniger, F. David. *Medicine and Shakespeare in the English Renaissance*. Newark: University of Delaware Press, 1992.

Huizinga, Johan. *The Autumn of the Middle Ages*. Trans. Rodney J. Payton and Ulrich Mammitzsch. Chicago: University of Chicago Press, 1996.

Hull, Suzanne W. *Chaste, Silent & Obedient: English Books for Women, 1475–1640*. San Marino, Calif.: Huntington Library, 1982.

Hutson, Lorna. *The Usurer's Daughter: Male Friendship and Fictions of Women in Sixteenth-Century England*. New York: Routledge, 1994.

Javitch, Daniel. *Poetry and Courtliness in Renaissance England*. Princeton: Princeton University Press, 1978.

Jones, Ann Rosalind, and Peter Stallybrass. *Renaissance Clothing and the Materials of Memory*. New York: Cambridge University Press, 2000.

Jordan, Constance. *Renaissance Feminism: Literary Texts and Political Models*. Ithaca, N.Y.: Cornell University Press, 1990.

Knapp, Jeffrey. *Shakespeare's Tribe: Church, Nation, and Theater in Renaissance England*. Chicago: University of Chicago Press, 2002.

Laqueur, Thomas Walter. *Making Sex: Body and Gender from the Greeks to Freud*. Cambridge, Mass.: Harvard University Press, 1990.

MacDonald, Joyce Green. *Women and Race in Early Modern Texts*. New York: Cambridge University Press, 2002.

Magnusson, Lynne. *Shakespeare and Social Dialogue: Dramatic Language and Elizabethan Letters*. New York: Cambridge University Press, 1999.

Manley, Lawrence. *Literature and Culture in Early Modern London*. New York: Cambridge University Press, 1995.

Marcus, Leah S. *The Politics of Mirth: Jonson, Herrick, Milton, Marvell, and the Defense of Old Holiday Pastimes*. Chicago: University of Chicago Press, 1986.

McJannet, Linda. *The Sultan Speaks: Dialogue in English Plays and Histories about the Ottoman Turks*. New York: Palgrave Macmillan, 2006.

Meron, Theodor. *Bloody Constraint: War and Chivalry in Shakespeare*. New York: Oxford University Press, 1998.

Miller, David Lee, Sharon O'Dair, and Harold Weber, eds. *The Production of English Renaissance Culture*. Ithaca, N.Y.: Cornell University Press, 1994.

Montrose, Louis. *The Subject of Elizabeth: Authority, Gender, and Representation*. Chicago: University of Chicago Press, 2006.

Neill, Michael. *Issues of Death: Mortality and Identity in English Renaissance Tragedy*. Oxford: Clarendon, 1997.

Netzloff, Mark. *England's Internal Colonies: Class, Capital, and the Literature of Early Modern English Colonialism*. New York: Palgrave Macmillan, 2003.

Orlin, Lena Cowen. *Private Matters and Public Culture in Post-Reformation England*. Ithaca, N.Y.: Cornell University Press, 1994.

———, ed. *Material London, ca. 1600*. Philadelphia: University of Pennsylvania Press, 2000.

Parry, Graham. *The Golden Age Restor'd: The Culture of the Stuart Court, 1603–42*. New York: St. Martin's, 1981.

Paster, Gail Kern. *The Body Embarrassed: Drama and the Disciplines of Shame in Early Modern England*. Ithaca, N.Y.: Cornell University Press, 1993.

———. *Humoring the Body: Emotions and the Shakespearean Stage*. Chicago: University of Chicago Press, 2004.

Paster, Gail Kern, Katherine Rowe, and Mary Floyd-Wilson, eds. *Reading the Early Modern Passions: Essays in the Cultural History of Emotion*. Philadelphia: University of Pennsylvania Press, 2004.

Patterson, Annabel M. *Censorship and Interpretation: The Conditions of Writing and Reading in Early Modern England*. Madison: University of Wisconsin Press, 1984.

Peck, Linda Levy. *Consuming Splendor: Society and Culture in Seventeenth-Century England*. New York: Cambridge University Press, 2005.

Platt, Peter G. *Reason Diminished: Shakespeare and the Marvelous*. Lincoln: University of Nebraska Press, 1997.

Pollard, Tanya. *Drugs and Theater in Early Modern England*. New York: Oxford University Press, 2005.

Sanders, Eve Rachele. *Gender and Literacy on Stage in Early Modern England*. New York: Cambridge University Press, 1998.

Sawday, Jonathan. *The Body Emblazoned: Dissection and the Human Body in Renais-sance Culture.* New York: Routledge, 1995.

Schoenfeldt, Michael C. *Bodies and Selves in Early Modern England: Physiology and Inwardness in Spenser, Shakespeare, Herbert, and Milton.* New York: Cambridge University Press, 1999.

Schwyzer, Philip. *Literature, Nationalism, and Memory in Early Modern England and Wales.* New York: Cambridge University Press, 2004.

Shapiro, James. *Shakespeare and the Jews.* New York: Columbia University Press, 1996.

Sharpe, Kevin, and Peter Lake, eds. *Culture and Politics in Early Stuart England.* Stanford: Stanford University Press, 1993.

Sherman, William H. *John Dee: The Politics of Reading and Writing in the English Ren-aissance.* Amherst: University of Massachusetts Press, 1995.

Shuger, Debora. *Censorship and Cultural Sensibility: The Regulation of Language in Tudor-Stuart England.* Philadelphia: University of Pennsylvania Press, 2006.

Simon, Joan. *Education and Society in Tudor England.* Cambridge, Eng.: Cambridge University Press, 1966.

Singh, Jyotsna G. *Colonial Narratives/Cultural Dialogues: 'Discoveries' of India in the Language of Colonialism.* New York: Routledge, 1996.

Smith, Bruce R. *The Acoustic World of Early Modern England: Attending to the O-Factor.* Chicago: University of Chicago Press, 1999.

———. *Homosexual Desire in Shakespeare's England: A Cultural Poetics.* Chicago: Uni-versity of Chicago Press, 1994.

Smuts, R. Malcolm. *Court Culture and the Origins of a Royalist Tradition in Early Stu-art England.* Philadelphia: University of Pennsylvania Press, 1987.

Stallybrass, Peter, and Allon White. *The Politics and Poetics of Transgression.* Ithaca, N.Y.: Cornell University Press, 1986.

Traub, Valerie, M. Lindsay Kaplan, and Dympna Callaghan, eds. *Feminist Readings of Early Modern Culture: Emerging Subjects.* New York: Cambridge University Press, 1996.

Turner, Henry S. *The English Renaissance Stage: Geometry, Poetics, and the Practical Spatial Arts 1580–1630.* New York: Oxford University Press, 2006.

Turner, James Grantham, ed. *Sexuality and Gender in Early Modern Europe: Institu-tions, Texts, Images.* New York: Cambridge University Press, 1993.

Wall, Wendy. *Staging Domesticity: Household Work and English Identity in Early Mod-ern Drama.* New York: Cambridge University Press, 2002.

Watson, Robert N. *The Rest Is Silence: Death as Annihilation in the English Renais-sance.* Berkeley: University of California Press, 1994.

Whigham, Frank. *Ambition and Privilege: The Social Tropes of Elizabethan Courtesy Theory.* Berkeley: University of California Press, 1984.

Woodbridge, Linda. *Vagrancy, Homelessness, and English Renaissance Literature.* Urbana: University of Illinois Press, 2001.

———. *Women and the English Renaissance: Literature and the Nature of Womankind, 1540 to 1620.* Urbana: University of Illinois Press, 1984.

Shakespeare's Generic, Literary, and Theatrical Contexts

Alpers, Paul. *What Is Pastoral?* Chicago: University of Chicago Press, 1996.

Altman, Joel. *The Tudor Play of Mind: Rhetorical Inquiry and the Development of Eliz-abethan Drama.* Berkeley: University of California Press, 1978.

Barish, Jonas. *The Antitheatrical Prejudice.* Berkeley: University of California Press, 1981.

Bate, Jonathan. *Shakespeare and Ovid.* Oxford: Clarendon, 1993.

Bates, Catherine. *The Rhetoric of Courtship in Elizabethan Language and Literature.* New York: Cambridge University Press, 1992.

Beckwith, Sarah. *Signifying God: Social Relation and Symbolic Act in the York Corpus Christi Plays*. Chicago: University of Chicago Press, 2001.

Belsey, Catherine. *The Subject of Tragedy: Identity and Difference in Renaissance Drama*. New York: Methuen, 1985.

Bevington, David M. *From "Mankind" to Marlowe: Growth of Structure in the Popular Drama of Tudor England*. Cambridge, Mass.: Harvard University Press, 1962.

———. *Tudor Drama and Politics: A Critical Approach to Topical Meaning*. Cambridge, Mass.: Harvard University Press, 1968.

Bly, Mary. *Queer Virgins and Virgin Queens on the Early Modern Stage*. New York: Oxford University Press, 2000.

Bowers, Fredson Thayer. *Elizabethan Revenge Tragedy, 1587–1642*. Princeton: Princeton University Press, 1940.

Braden, Gordon. *Renaissance Tragedy and the Senecan Tradition: Anger's Privilege*. New Haven: Yale University Press, 1985.

Bruster, Douglas. *Drama and the Market in the Age of Shakespeare*. New York: Cambridge University Press, 1992.

Bullough, Geoffrey, ed. *Narrative and Dramatic Sources of Shakespeare*. 8 vols. New York: Columbia University Press, 1957–75.

Butler, Martin. *Theatre and Crisis, 1632–1642*. New York: Cambridge University Press, 1984.

Carroll, William C. *The Metamorphoses of Shakespearean Comedy*. Princeton: Princeton University Press, 1985.

Cartwright, Kent. *Theatre and Humanism: English Drama in the Sixteenth Century*. New York: Cambridge University Press, 1999.

Clubb, Louise George. *Italian Drama in Shakespeare's Time*. New Haven: Yale University Press, 1989.

Cohen, Walter. *Drama of a Nation: Public Theater in Renaissance England and Spain*. Ithaca, N.Y.: Cornell University Press, 1985.

Crewe, Jonathan. *Trials of Authorship: Anterior Forms and Poetic Reconstruction from Wyatt to Shakespeare*. Berkeley: University of California Press, 1990.

Danson, Lawrence. *Shakespeare's Dramatic Genres*. New York: Oxford University Press, 2000.

Dawson, Anthony B., and Paul Yachnin. *The Culture of Playgoing in Shakespeare's England: A Collaborative Debate*. New York: Cambridge University Press, 2001.

Dillon, Janette. *Language and Stage in Medieval and Renaissance England*. New York: Cambridge University Press, 1998.

Felperin, Howard. *Shakespearean Romance*. Princeton: Princeton University Press, 1972.

Finkelpearl, Philip J. *John Marston of the Middle Temple: An Elizabethan Dramatist in His Social Setting*. Cambridge, Mass.: Harvard University Press, 1969.

Gardiner, Harold C. *Mysteries' End: An Investigation of the Last Days of the Medieval Religious Stage*. New Haven: Yale University Press, 1946.

Halasz, Alexandra. *The Marketplace of Print: Pamphlets and the Public Sphere in Early Modern England*. New York: Cambridge University Press, 1997.

Harbage, Alfred. *Shakespeare and the Rival Traditions*. New York: Macmillan, 1952.

Hardison, O. B. *Christian Rite and Christian Drama in the Middle Ages: Essays in the Origin and Early History of Modern Drama*. Baltimore: Johns Hopkins University Press, 1965.

Heinemann, Margot. *Puritanism and Theatre: Thomas Middleton and Opposition Drama under the Early Stuarts*. New York: Cambridge University Press, 1980.

Honan, Park. *Christopher Marlowe: Poet & Spy*. New York: Oxford University Press, 2005.

Honigmann, E. A. J., ed. *Shakespeare and His Contemporaries: Essays in Comparison*. Manchester: Manchester University Press, 1986.

———, ed. *Shakespeare's Impact on His Contemporaries*. London: Macmillan, 1982.

Howard, Jean E. *Theater of a City: The Places of London Comedy, 1598–1642.* Philadelphia: University of Pennsylvania Press, 2007.

Hunter, G. K. *John Lyly: The Humanist as Courtier.* Cambridge, Mass.: Harvard University Press, 1962.

Jones, Emrys. *The Origins of Shakespeare.* Oxford: Clarendon, 1977.

———. *Scenic Form in Shakespeare.* Oxford: Clarendon, 1971.

Kastan, David Scott, and Peter Stallybrass, eds. *Staging the Renaissance: Reinterpretations of Elizabethan and Jacobean Drama.* New York: Routledge, 1991.

Kermode, Lloyd Edward, Jason Scott-Warren, and Martine van Elk, eds. *Tudor Drama Before Shakespeare, 1485–1590: New Directions for Research, Criticism, and Pedagogy.* New York: Palgrave Macmillan, 2004.

Kolve, V. A. *The Play Called Corpus Christi.* Stanford: Stanford University Press, 1966.

Leggatt, Alexander. *Citizen Comedy in the Age of Shakespeare.* Toronto: University of Toronto Press, 1973.

———. *Introduction to English Renaissance Comedy.* Manchester: Manchester University Press, 1999.

Levin, Harry. *Shakespeare and the Revolution of the Times: Perspectives and Commentaries.* New York: Oxford University Press, 1976.

Levith, Murray J. *Shakespeare's Italian Settings and Plays.* Basingstoke: Macmillan, 1989.

Lomax, Marion. *Stage Images and Traditions: Shakespeare to Ford.* New York: Cambridge University Press, 1987.

Martindale, Charles, and A. B. Taylor, eds. *Shakespeare and the Classics.* New York: Cambridge University Press, 2004.

Masten, Jeffrey. *Textual Intercourse: Collaboration, Authorship, and Sexualities in Renaissance Drama.* New York: Cambridge University Press, 1997.

McLuskie, Kathleen. *Renaissance Dramatists.* New York: Harvester Wheatsheaf, 1989.

McMillin, Scott. *The Elizabethan Theatre and the Book of Sir Thomas More.* Ithaca, N.Y.: Cornell University Press, 1987.

McMillin, Scott, and Sally-Beth MacLean. *The Queen's Men and Their Plays.* New York: Cambridge University Press, 1998.

McMullan, Gordon, and Jonathan Hope, eds. *The Politics of Tragicomedy: Shakespeare and After.* New York: Routledge, 1991.

Miola, Robert S. *Shakespeare's Reading.* New York: Oxford University Press, 2000.

———. *Shakespeare's Rome.* New York: Cambridge University Press, 1983.

Newcomb, Lori Humphrey. *Reading Popular Romance in Early Modern England.* New York: Columbia University Press, 2002.

Norbrook, David. *Poetry and Politics in the English Renaissance.* London: Routledge and Kegan Paul, 1984.

Orgel, Stephen. *The Illusion of Power: Political Theater in the English Renaissance.* Berkeley: University of California Press, 1975.

Peters, Julie Stone. *Theatre of the Book, 1480–1880: Print, Text, and Performance in Europe.* New York: Oxford University Press, 2000.

Riggs, David. *Ben Jonson: A Life.* Cambridge, Mass.: Harvard University Press, 1989.

———. *The World of Christopher Marlowe.* London: Faber and Faber, 2004.

Rose, Mark. *Shakespearean Design.* Cambridge, Mass.: Belknap Press, 1972.

Rose, Mary Beth. *The Expense of Spirit: Love and Sexuality in English Renaissance Drama.* Ithaca, N.Y.: Cornell University Press, 1988.

Salingar, Leo. *Dramatic Form in Shakespeare and the Jacobeans: Essays.* New York: Cambridge University Press, 1986.

———. *Shakespeare and the Traditions of Comedy.* New York: Cambridge University Press, 1974.

Schwyzer, Philip. *Archaeologies of English Renaissance Literature.* New York: Oxford University Press, 2007.

Shapiro, James. *Rival Playwrights: Marlowe, Jonson, Shakespeare.* New York: Columbia University Press, 1991.

Snyder, Susan. *The Comic Matrix of Shakespeare's Tragedies: Romeo and Juliet, Hamlet, Othello, and* King Lear. Princeton: Princeton University Press, 1979.

Spivack, Bernard. *Shakespeare and the Allegory of Evil: The History of a Metaphor in Relation to His Major Villains.* New York: Columbia University Press, 1958.

Thomas, Vivian. *The Moral Universe of Shakespeare's Problem Plays.* New York: Routledge, 1991.

Vickers, Brian, ed. *English Renaissance Literary Criticism.* New York: Oxford University Press, 1999.

Vitkus, Daniel. *Turning Turk: English Theater and the Multicultural Mediterranean, 1570–1630.* New York: Palgrave Macmillan, 2003.

Weimann, Robert. *Shakespeare and the Popular Tradition in the Theater: Studies in the Social Dimension of Dramatic Form and Function.* Ed. Robert Schwartz. Baltimore: Johns Hopkins University Press, 1978.

Whitney, Charles. *Early Responses to Renaissance Drama.* New York: Cambridge University Press, 2006.

Woolf, Rosemary. *The English Mystery Plays.* Berkeley: University of California Press, 1972.

The Playing Field: Theaters, Actors, Patrons, and the State

Astington, John H. *English Court Theatre, 1558–1642.* Cambridge, Eng.: Cambridge University Press, 1999.

———, ed. *The Development of Shakespeare's Theater.* New York: AMS Press, 1992.

Barroll, J. Leeds. *Politics, Plague, and Shakespeare's Theater: The Stuart Years.* Ithaca, N.Y.: Cornell University Press, 1991.

Beckerman, Bernard. *Shakespeare at the Globe, 1599–1609.* New York: Macmillan, 1962.

Bentley, Gerald Eades. *The Jacobean and Caroline Stage.* 7 vols. Oxford: Clarendon, 1941–68.

———. *The Profession of Dramatist in Shakespeare's Time, 1590–1642.* Princeton: Princeton University Press, 1971.

———. *The Profession of Player in Shakespeare's Time, 1590–1642.* Princeton: Princeton University Press, 1984.

Berry, Herbert. *Shakespeare's Playhouses.* Illustrated by C. Walter Hodges. New York: AMS Press, 1987.

Bradbrook, M. C. *The Rise of the Common Player: A Study of Actor and Society in Shakespeare's England.* Cambridge, Mass.: Harvard University Press, 1962.

Chambers, E. K. *The Elizabethan Stage.* 4 vols. Oxford: Clarendon, 1923.

———. *The Mediaeval Stage.* 2 vols. Oxford: Clarendon, 1903.

Clare, Janet. *Art Made Tongue-Tied by Authority: Elizabethan and Jacobean Dramatic Censorship.* 2nd ed. Manchester: Manchester University Press, 1999.

Cook, Ann Jennalie. *The Privileged Playgoers of Shakespeare's London: 1576–1642.* Princeton: Princeton University Press, 1981.

Cox, John D., and David Scott Kastan, eds. *A New History of Early English Drama.* New York: Columbia University Press, 1997.

Dessen, Alan C. *Elizabethan Stage Conventions and Modern Interpreters.* Cambridge, Eng.: Cambridge University Press, 1984.

———. *Recovering Shakespeare's Theatrical Vocabulary.* New York: Cambridge University Press, 1995.

Dessen, Alan C., and Leslie Thomson. *A Dictionary of Stage Directions in English Drama, 1580–1642.* New York: Cambridge University Press, 1999.

Dillon, Janette. *The Cambridge Introduction to Early English Theatre.* New York: Cambridge University Press, 2006.

Dutton, Richard. *Licensing, Censorship and Authorship in Early Modern England: Buggeswords.* Houndmills, Basingstoke: Palgrave Macmillan, 2000.

———. *Mastering the Revels: The Regulation and Censorship of English Renaissance Drama.* London: Macmillan, 1991.

Dutton, Richard, Alison Findlay, and Richard Wilson, eds. *Region, Religion, and Patronage: Lancastrian Shakespeare.* Manchester: Manchester University Press, 2003.

Erne, Lukas. *Shakespeare as Literary Dramatist.* New York: Cambridge University Press, 2003.

Foakes, R. A. *Illustrations of the English Stage, 1580–1642.* Stanford: Stanford University Press, 1985.

Gair, W. Reavley. *The Children of Paul's: The Story of a Theatre Company, 1553–1608.* New York: Cambridge University Press, 1982.

Greg, W. W., ed. *Dramatic Documents from the Elizabethan Playhouses: Stage Plots: Actor's Parts: Prompt Books.* 2 vols. Oxford: Clarendon, 1931.

Gurr, Andrew. *Playgoing in Shakespeare's London.* 3rd ed. New York: Cambridge University Press, 2004.

———. *The Shakespeare Company, 1594–1642.* New York: Cambridge University Press, 2004.

———. *The Shakespearian Playing Companies.* Oxford: Clarendon, 1996.

———. *The Shakespearean Stage, 1574–1642.* 3rd ed. New York: Cambridge University Press, 1992.

Gurr, Andrew, and John Orrell. *Rebuilding Shakespeare's Globe.* London: Weidenfeld & Nicolson, 1989.

Harris, Jonathan Gil, and Natasha Korda, eds. *Staged Properties in Early Modern Drama.* New York: Cambridge University Press, 2002.

Hattaway, Michael. *Elizabethan Popular Theatre: Plays in Performance.* London: Routledge and Kegan Paul, 1982.

Henslowe, Philip. *Henslowe's Diary.* Ed. R. A. Foakes. 2nd ed. New York: Cambridge University Press, 2002.

Hodges, C. Walter. *The Globe Restored: A Study of the Elizabethan Theatre.* New York: Norton, 1973.

Holland, Peter, and Stephen Orgel, eds. *From Performance to Print in Shakespeare's England.* New York: Palgrave Macmillan, 2006.

———, eds. *From Script to Stage in Early Modern England.* Houndmills, Basingstoke: Palgrave Macmillan, 2004.

Ingram, William. *The Business of Playing: The Beginnings of Adult Professional Theater in Elizabethan London.* Ithaca, N.Y.: Cornell University Press, 1992.

Kernan, Alvin. *Shakespeare, the King's Playwright: Theater in the Stuart Court, 1603–1613.* New Haven: Yale University Press, 1995.

King, T. J. *Shakespearean Staging, 1599–1642.* Cambridge, Mass.: Harvard University Press, 1971.

Knutson, Roslyn Lander. *Playing Companies and Commerce in Shakespeare's Time.* Cambridge, Eng.: Cambridge University Press, 2001.

———. *The Repertory of Shakespeare's Company, 1594–1613.* Fayetteville: University of Arkansas Press, 1991.

Laroque, François. *Shakespeare's Festive World: Elizabethan Seasonal Entertainment and the Professional Stage.* New York: Cambridge University Press, 1991.

Lopez, Jeremy. *Theatrical Convention and Audience Response in Early Modern Drama.* New York: Cambridge University Press, 2002.

MacIntyre, Jean. *Costumes and Scripts in the Elizabethan Theatres.* Edmonton: University of Alberta Press, 1992.

Milling, Jane, and Peter Thomson, eds. *The Cambridge History of British Theatre*, Vol. 1: *Origins to 1660.* New York: Cambridge University Press, 2004.

Mulryne, J. R., and Margaret Shewring, eds. *Shakespeare's Globe Rebuilt.* New York: Cambridge University Press, 1997.

Munro, Lucy. *Children of the Queen's Revels: A Jacobean Theatre Repertory.* New York: Cambridge University Press, 2005.

Palfrey, Simon, and Tiffany Stern. *Shakespeare in Parts* Oxford: Oxford University Press, 2007.

Shapiro, Michael. *Children of the Revels. The Boy Companies of Shakespeare's Time and Their Plays.* New York: Columbia University Press, 1977.

Smith, Irwin. *Shakespeare's Blackfriars Playhouse: Its History and Its Design.* New York: New York University Press, 1964.

Stern, Tiffany. *Making Shakespeare: From Stage to Page.* New York: Routledge, 2004.

———. *Rehearsal from Shakespeare to Sheridan.* Oxford: Clarendon, 2000.

White, Paul Whitfield, and Suzanne Westfall, eds. *Shakespeare and Theatrical Patronage in Early Modern England.* New York: Cambridge University Press, 2002.

Wickham, Glynne. *Early English Stages, 1300 to 1660.* 4 vols. New York: Routledge, 2002.

Wickham, Glynne, Herbert Berry, and William Ingram, eds. *English Professional Theatre, 1530–1660.* New York: Cambridge University Press, 2000.

Shakespeare's Life

Alexander, Peter. *Shakespeare's Life and Art.* New ed. New York: New York University Press, 1961.

Bate, Jonathan. *The Genius of Shakespeare.* London: Picador, 1997.

Bradbrook, M. C. *Shakespeare: The Poet in His World.* New York: Columbia University Press, 1978.

Chambers, E. K. *William Shakespeare. A Study of Facts and Problems.* 2 vols. Oxford: Clarendon, 1930.

Duncan-Jones, Katherine. *Ungentle Shakespeare: Scenes from His Life.* London: Arden Shakespeare, 2001.

Eccles, Mark. *Shakespeare in Warwickshire.* Madison: University of Wisconsin Press, 1961.

Edwards, Philip. *Shakespeare: A Writer's Progress.* New York: Oxford University Press, 1986.

Fraser, Russell A. *Shakespeare, The Later Years.* New York: Columbia University Press, 1992.

———. *Young Shakespeare.* New York: Columbia University Press, 1988.

Greenblatt, Stephen. *Will in the World: How Shakespeare Became Shakespeare.* New York: Norton, 2004.

Greer, Germaine. *Shakespeare.* New York: Oxford University Press, 1986.

Honan, Park. *Shakespeare: A Life.* New York: Oxford University Press, 1998.

Honigmann, E. A. J. *Shakespeare: The Lost Years.* 2nd ed. Manchester: Manchester University Press, 1998.

Hotson, Leslie. *Shakespeare Versus Shallow.* Boston: Little, Brown, and Company, 1931.

Levi, Peter. *The Life and Times of William Shakespeare.* New York: Macmillan, 1988.

Matus, Irvin Leigh. *Shakespeare, The Living Record.* Houndmills, Basingstoke: Macmillan, 1991.

Reese, M. M. *Shakespeare: His World and His Work.* Rev. ed. London: Edward Arnold, 1980.

Sams, Eric. *The Real Shakespeare: Retrieving the Early Years, 1564–1594.* New Haven: Yale University Press, 1995.

Schmidgall, Gary. *Shakespeare and the Poet's Life.* Lexington: University Press of Kentucky, 1990.

Schoenbaum, Samuel. *Shakespeare's Lives.* New ed. New York: Oxford University Press, 1991.

———. *William Shakespeare: A Compact Documentary Life.* Rev. ed. New York: Oxford University Press, 1987.

Shapiro, James. *A Year in the Life of William Shakespeare: 1599.* New York: Harper-Collins, 2005.

Taylor, Gary. *Reinventing Shakespeare: A Cultural History, from the Restoration to the Present.* New York: Weidenfeld & Nicolson, 1989.

Thomson, Peter. *Shakespeare's Professional Career.* New York: Cambridge University Press, 1992.

Wells, Stanley. *Shakespeare: A Life in Drama.* New York: Norton, 1995.

———. *Shakespeare: For All Time.* London: Macmillan, 2002.

Wood, Michael. *In Search of Shakespeare.* London: BBC, 2003.

Critical Approaches

Classics of Shakespeare Criticism

Barber, C. L. *Shakespeare's Festive Comedy: A Study of Dramatic Form and Its Relation to Social Custom.* Princeton: Princeton University Press, 1959.

Bradley, A. C. *Shakespearean Tragedy: Lectures on* Hamlet, Othello, King Lear, Macbeth. 3rd ed. New York: St. Martin's Press, 1992.

Coleridge, Samuel Taylor. *Coleridge on Shakespeare: The Text of the Lectures of 1811–12.* Ed. R. A. Foakes. Charlottesville: University Press of Virginia, 1971.

———. *Shakespearean Criticism.* 2 vols. Ed. T. M. Raysor. 2nd ed. New York: Dutton, 1969.

Eliot, T. S. "Shakespeare and the Stoicism of Seneca." *Selected Essays, 1917–1932.* New ed. New York: Harcourt, Brace, 1950.

Empson, William. *The Structure of Complex Words.* 3rd ed. London: Chatto & Windus, 1977.

Frye, Northrop. *Fools of Time: Studies in Shakespearean Tragedy.* Toronto: University of Toronto Press, 1967.

———. *A Natural Perspective: The Development of Shakespearean Comedy and Romance.* New York: Columbia University Press, 1965.

Hazlitt, William. *Characters of Shakespear's Plays.* London, 1817.

Johnson, Samuel. *Samuel Johnson on Shakespeare.* Ed. H. R. Woudhuysen. New York: Penguin, 1989.

Jones, Ernest. *Hamlet and Oedipus.* New York: Norton, 1949.

Kermode, Frank, ed. *Four Centuries of Shakespearian Criticism.* 1965. New York: Avon, 1965.

Knight, G. Wilson. *The Wheel of Fire: Interpretations of Shakespearean Tragedy, with Three New Essays.* 4th ed. New York: Harper & Row, 1977.

Kott, Jan. *Shakespeare Our Contemporary.* Trans. Boleslaw Taborski. Garden City, N.Y.: Anchor Books, 1966.

Morgann, Maurice. *Shakespearean Criticism.* Ed. Daniel A. Fineman. Oxford: Clarendon, 1972.

Spurgeon, Caroline F. E. *Shakespeare's Imagery, and What It Tells Us.* New York: Macmillan, 1935.

Tillyard, E. M. W. *Shakespeare's History Plays.* London: Chatto and Windus, 1944.

Vickers, Brian, ed. *Shakespeare: The Critical Heritage.* 6 vols. London: Routledge and Kegan Paul, 1974–1981.

General Studies

Barton, Anne. *Essays, Mainly Shakespearean.* New York: Cambridge University Press, 1994.

Bloom, Harold. *Shakespeare: The Invention of the Human.* New York: Riverhead Books, 1998.

Burckhardt, Sigurd. *Shakespearean Meanings*. Princeton: Princeton University Press, 1968.

Garber, Marjorie. *Shakespeare After All*. New York: Pantheon, 2004.

Hibbard, G. R. *The Making of Shakespeare's Dramatic Poetry*. Toronto: University of Toronto Press, 1981.

Honigmann, E. A. J. *Myriad-Minded Shakespeare: Essays on the Tragedies, Problem Comedies, and Shakespeare the Man*. 2nd ed. New York: St. Martin's Press, 1998.

Jones, John. *Shakespeare at Work*. New York: Oxford University Press, 1995.

Nuttall, A. D. *Shakespeare the Thinker*. New Haven: Yale University Press, 2007.

Ryan, Kiernan. *Shakespeare*. 3rd ed. New York: Palgrave Macmillan, 2001.

Language and Style

Baxter, John. *Shakespeare's Poetic Styles: Verse into Drama*. London: Routledge and Kegan Paul, 1980.

Blake, N. F. *Shakespeare's Language: An Introduction*. New York: St. Martin's Press, 1983.

Cercignani, Fausto. *Shakespeare's Works and Elizabethan Pronunciation*. New York: Oxford University Press, 1981.

Clemen, Wolfgang. *Shakespeare's Soliloquies*. Trans. Charity Scott Stokes. New York: Methuen, 1987.

———. *The Development of Shakespeare's Imagery*. New York: Hill and Wang, 1962.

Danson, Lawrence. *Tragic Alphabet: Shakespeare's Drama of Language*. New Haven: Yale University Press, 1974.

Donawerth, Jane. *Shakespeare and the Sixteenth-Century Study of Language*. Urbana: University of Illinois Press, 1984.

Edwards, Philip, Inga-Stina Ewbank, and G. K. Hunter, eds. *Shakespeare's Styles: Essays in Honour of Kenneth Muir*. New York: Cambridge University Press, 1980.

Gross, Kenneth. *Shakespeare's Noise*. Chicago: University of Chicago Press, 2001.

Hope, Jonathan. *Shakespeare's Grammar*. London: Arden Shakespeare, 2003.

Houston, John Porter. *Shakespearean Sentences: A Study in Style and Syntax*. Baton Rouge: Louisiana State University Press, 1988.

Hussey, S. S. *The Literary Language of Shakespeare*. 2nd ed. New York: Longman, 1992.

Kökeritz, Helge. *Shakespeare's Pronunciation*. New Haven: Yale University Press, 1953.

Mahood, M. M. *Shakespeare's Wordplay*. London: Methuen, 1957.

McDonald, Russ. *Shakespeare and the Arts of Language*. New York: Oxford University Press, 2001.

———. *Shakespeare's Late Style*. New York: Cambridge University Press, 2006.

Miriam Joseph, Sister. *Shakespeare's Use of the Arts of Language*. New York: Columbia University Press, 1947.

Palfrey, Simon. *Late Shakespeare: A New World of Words*. Oxford: Clarendon, 1997.

Parker, Patricia. *Literary Fat Ladies: Rhetoric, Gender, Property*. New York: Methuen, 1987.

———. *Shakespeare from the Margins: Language, Culture, Context*. Chicago: University of Chicago Press, 1996.

Partridge, Eric. *Shakespeare's Bawdy: A Literary & Psychological Essay and a Comprehensive Glossary*. 3rd ed. New York: Routledge, 1991.

Trousdale, Marion. *Shakespeare and the Rhetoricians*. Chapel Hill: University of North Carolina Press, 1982.

Vickers, Brian. *The Artistry of Shakespeare's Prose*. London: Methuen, 1968.

———. "Shakespeare's Use of Rhetoric." *A New Companion to Shakespeare Studies*. Ed. Kenneth Muir and S. Schoenbaum. Cambridge, Eng. Cambridge University Press, 1971. 83–98.

Wright, George T. *Shakespeare's Metrical Art*. Berkeley: University of California Press, 1988.

Young, David. *The Action to the Word: Structure and Style in Shakespearean Tragedy.* New Haven: Yale University Press, 1990.

Psychoanalytic Criticism

Adelman, Janet. *Suffocating Mothers: Fantasies of Maternal Origin in Shakespeare's Plays,* Hamlet *to* The Tempest. New York: Routledge, 1992.

Armstrong, Philip. *Shakespeare in Psychoanalysis.* New York: Routledge, 2001.

Berger, Harry Jr. *Making Trifles of Terrors: Redistributing Complicities in Shakespeare.* Stanford: Stanford University Press, 1997.

Charnes, Linda. *Notorious Identity: Materializing the Subject in Shakespeare.* Cambridge, Mass.: Harvard University Press, 1993.

Enterline, Lynn. *The Rhetoric of the Body from Ovid to Shakespeare.* Cambridge, Eng.: Cambridge University Press, 2000.

Fineman, Joel. *Shakespeare's Perjured Eye: The Invention of Poetic Subjectivity in the Sonnets.* Berkeley: University of California Press, 1986.

Freedman, Barbara. *Staging the Gaze: Postmodernism, Psychoanalysis, and Shakespearean Comedy.* Ithaca, N.Y.: Cornell University Press, 1991.

Garber, Marjorie. *Coming of Age in Shakespeare.* New York: Methuen, 1981.

———. *Shakespeare's Ghost Writers: Literature as Uncanny Causality.* New York: Methuen, 1987.

Girard, René. *A Theater of Envy: William Shakespeare.* New York: Oxford University Press, 1991.

Holland, Norman N. *Psychoanalysis and Shakespeare.* New York: Octagon, 1966.

Lupton, Julia Reinhard, and Kenneth Reinhard. *After Oedipus: Shakespeare in Psychoanalysis.* Ithaca, N.Y.: Cornell University Press, 1993.

Marshall, Cynthia. *The Shattering of the Self: Violence, Subjectivity, and Early Modern Texts.* Baltimore: Johns Hopkins University Press, 2002.

Mazzio, Carla, and Douglas Trevor, eds. *Historicism, Psychoanalysis, and Early Modern Culture.* New York: Routledge, 2000.

Pye, Christopher. *The Regal Phantasm: Shakespeare and the Politics of Spectacle.* New York: Routledge, 1990.

———. *The Vanishing: Shakespeare, the Subject, and Early Modern Culture.* Durham, N.C.: Duke University Press, 2000.

Schwartz, Murray M., and Coppélia Kahn, eds. *Representing Shakespeare: New Psychoanalytic Essays.* Baltimore: Johns Hopkins University Press, 1982.

Skura, Meredith Anne. *The Literary Use of the Psychoanalytic Process.* New Haven: Yale University Press, 1981.

———. *Shakespeare the Actor and the Purposes of Playing.* Chicago: University of Chicago Press, 1993.

Wheeler, Richard P. *Shakespeare's Development and the Problem Comedies: Turn and Counter-Turn.* Berkeley: University of California Press, 1981.

Zimmerman, Susan, ed. *Erotic Politics: Desire on the Renaissance Stage.* New York: Routledge, 1992.

Feminism, Gender Studies, and Queer Studies

Bamber, Linda. *Comic Women, Tragic Men: A Study of Gender and Genre in Shakespeare.* Stanford: Stanford University Press, 1982.

Barker, Deborah, and Ivo Kamps, eds. *Shakespeare and Gender: A History.* New York: Verso, 1995.

Boose, Lynda E. "The Father and the Bride in Shakespeare." *PMLA* 97 (1982): 325–47.

Callaghan, Dympna. *Shakespeare Without Women: Representing Gender and Race on the Renaissance Stage.* New York: Routledge, 2000.

————. *Women and Gender in Renaissance Tragedy: A Study of* King Lear, Othello, The Duchess of Malfi, *and* The White Devil. Atlantic Highlands, N.J.: Humanities Press International, 1989.

Chedgzoy, Kate, ed. *Shakespeare, Feminism and Gender.* Houndmills, Basingstoke: Palgrave Macmillan, 2001.

Dash, Irene G. *Wooing, Wedding, and Power: Women in Shakespeare's Plays.* New York: Columbia University Press, 1981.

DiGangi, Mario. *The Homoerotics of Early Modern Drama.* New York: Cambridge University Press, 1997.

Dusinberre, Juliet. *Shakespeare and the Nature of Women.* 3rd ed. New York: Palgrave Macmillan, 2003.

Erickson, Peter. *Patriarchal Structures in Shakespeare's Drama.* Berkeley: University of California Press, 1985.

French, Marilyn. *Shakespeare's Division of Experience.* New York: Summit Books, 1981.

Garner, Shirley Nelson, and Madelon Sprengnether, eds. *Shakespearean Tragedy and Gender.* Bloomington: Indiana University Press, 1996.

Goldberg, Jonathan. *Sodometries: Renaissance Texts, Modern Sexualities.* Stanford: Stanford University Press, 1992.

Howard, Jean E., and Phyllis Rackin. *Engendering a Nation: A Feminist Account of Shakespeare's English Histories.* New York: Routledge, 1997.

Jardine, Lisa. *Still Harping on Daughters: Women and Drama in the Age of Shakespeare.* 2nd ed. New York: Columbia University Press, 1989.

Kahn, Coppèlia. *Man's Estate: Masculine Identity in Shakespeare.* Berkeley: University of California Press, 1981.

————. *Roman Shakespeare: Warriors, Wounds, and Women.* New York: Routledge, 1997.

Korda, Natasha. *Shakespeare's Domestic Economies: Gender and Property in Early Modern England.* Philadelphia: University of Pennsylvania Press, 2002.

Lenz, Carolyn, Ruth Swift, Gayle Greene, and Carol Thomas Neely, eds. *The Woman's Part: Feminist Criticism of Shakespeare.* Urbana: University of Illinois Press, 1980.

Neely, Carol Thomas. *Broken Nuptials in Shakespeare's Plays.* New Haven: Yale University Press, 1985.

————. *Distracted Subjects: Madness and Gender in Shakespeare and Early Modern Culture.* Ithaca, N.Y.: Cornell University Press, 2004.

Newman, Karen. *Fashioning Femininity and English Renaissance Drama.* Chicago: University of Chicago Press, 1991.

Novy, Marianne. *Love's Argument: Gender Relations in Shakespeare.* Chapel Hill: University of North Carolina Press, 1984.

————, ed. *Women's Re-Visions of Shakespeare: On the Responses of Dickinson, Woolf, Rich, H.D., George Eliot, and Others.* Urbana: University of Illinois Press, 1990.

Orgel, Stephen. *Impersonations: The Performance of Gender in Shakespeare's England.* New York: Cambridge University Press, 1996.

Shapiro, Michael. *Gender in Play on the Shakespearean Stage: Boy Heroines and Female Pages.* Ann Arbor: University of Michigan Press, 1994.

Shepherd, Simon. *Amazons and Warrior Women: Varieties of Feminism in Seventeenth Century Drama.* New York: St. Martin's, 1981.

Traub, Valerie. *Desire and Anxiety: Circulations of Sexuality in Shakespearean Drama.* New York: Routledge, 1992.

————. *The Renaissance of Lesbianism in Early Modern England.* New York: Cambridge University Press, 2002.

Wayne, Valerie, ed. *The Matter of Difference: Materialist Feminist Criticism of Shakespeare.* Ithaca, N.Y.: Cornell University Press, 1991.

Historical Approaches: Materialism, New Historicism,
and Cultural Materialism

Archer, John Michael. *Citizen Shakespeare: Freemen and Aliens in the Language of the Plays.* New York: Palgrave Macmillan, 2005.

Arnold, Oliver. *The Third Citizen: Shakespeare's Theater and the Early Modern House of Commons.* Baltimore: Johns Hopkins University Press, 2007.

Belsey, Catherine. *Shakespeare and the Loss of Eden: The Construction of Family Values in Early Modern Culture.* New Brunswick, N.J.: Rutgers University Press, 1999.

Berry, Ralph. *Shakespeare and Social Class.* Atlantic Highlands, N.J.: Humanities Press International, 1988.

Bristol, Michael D. *Shakespeare's America, America's Shakespeare.* New York: Routledge, 1990.

Bruster, Douglas. *Shakespeare and the Question of Culture: Early Modern Literature and the Cultural Turn.* New York: Palgrave Macmillan, 2003.

Cox, John D. *Shakespeare and the Dramaturgy of Power.* Princeton: Princeton University Press, 1989.

Dollimore, Jonathan. *Radical Tragedy: Religion, Ideology, and Power in the Drama of Shakespeare and His Contemporaries.* 3rd ed. New York: Palgrave Macmillan, 2004.

Dollimore, Jonathan, and Alan Sinfield, eds. *Political Shakespeare: Essays in Cultural Materialism.* 2nd ed. Ithaca, N.Y.: Cornell University Press, 1994.

Dubrow, Heather, and Richard Strier, eds. *The Historical Renaissance: New Essays on Tudor and Stuart Literature and Culture.* Chicago: University of Chicago Press, 1988.

Eagleton, Terry. *William Shakespeare.* Malden, Mass.: Blackwell, 1986.

Greenblatt, Stephen. *Hamlet in Purgatory.* Princeton: Princeton University Press, 2001.

———. *Shakespearean Negotiations: The Circulation of Social Energy in Renaissance England.* Berkeley: University of California Press, 1988.

Hadfield, Andrew. *Shakespeare and Republicanism.* New York: Cambridge University Press, 2005.

Hawkes, Terence. *Meaning by Shakespeare.* New York: Routledge, 1992.

———. *That Shakespeherian Rag: Essays on a Critical Process.* New York: Methuen, 1986.

Holderness, Graham, ed. *The Shakespeare Myth.* Manchester: Manchester University Press, 1988.

———, ed. *Shakespeare's History Plays: Richard II to Henry V.* Houndmills, Basingstoke: Palgrave Macmillan, 1992.

Howard, Jean E. *The Stage and Social Struggle in Early Modern England.* New York: Routledge, 1994.

Howard, Jean E., and Scott Cutler Shershow, eds. *Marxist Shakespeares.* New York: Routledge, 2001.

Howard, Jean E., and Marion F. O'Connor, eds. *Shakespeare Reproduced: The Text in History and Ideology.* New York: Methuen, 1987.

Jardine, Lisa. *Reading Shakespeare Historically.* New York: Routledge, 1996.

Jordan, Constance. *Shakespeare's Monarchies: Ruler and Subject in the Romances.* Ithaca, N.Y.: Cornell University Press, 1997.

Kamps, Ivo, ed. *Materialist Shakespeare: A History.* New York: Verso, 1995.

Kastan, David Scott. *Shakespeare After Theory.* London: Routledge, 1999.

———. *Shakespeare and the Shapes of Time.* Hanover, N.H.: University Press of New England, 1982.

Mallin, Eric S. *Inscribing the Time: Shakespeare and the End of Elizabethan England.* Berkeley: University of California Press, 1995.

Marcus, Leah S. *Puzzling Shakespeare: Local Reading and Its Discontents.* Berkeley: University of California Press, 1988.

Maus, Katharine Eisaman. *Inwardness and Theater in the English Renaissance.* Chicago: University of Chicago Press, 1995.

Montrose, Louis. *The Purpose of Playing: Shakespeare and the Cultural Politics of the Elizabethan Theatre*. Chicago: University of Chicago Press, 1996.

Mullaney, Steven. *The Place of the Stage: License, Play, and Power in Renaissance England*. Chicago: University of Chicago Press, 1988.

Orgel, Stephen. *The Authentic Shakespeare: and Other Problems of the Early Modern Stage*. New York: Routledge, 2002.

Patterson, Annabel. *Shakespeare and the Popular Voice*. Malden, Mass.: Blackwell, 1989.

Rackin, Phyllis. *Stages of History: Shakespeare's English Chronicles*. Ithaca, N.Y.: Cornell University Press, 1990.

Siemon, James R. *Word Against Word: Shakespearean Utterance*. Amherst: University of Massachusetts Press, 2002.

Sinfield, Alan. *Shakespeare, Authority, Sexuality: Unfinished Business in Cultural Materialism*. New York: Routledge, 2006.

Tennenhouse, Leonard. *Power on Display: The Politics of Shakespeare's Genres*. New York: Methuen, 1986.

Weimann, Robert. *Author's Pen and Actor's Voice: Playing and Writing in Shakespeare's Theatre*. Ed. Helen Higbee and William West. New York: Cambridge University Press, 2000.

Wells, Robin Headlam. *Shakespeare, Politics, and the State*. Houndmills, Basingstoke: Palgrave Macmillan, 1986.

Wilson, Richard. *Secret Shakespeare: Studies in Theatre, Religion and Resistance*. Manchester: Manchester University Press, 2004.

———. *Will Power: Essays on Shakespearean Authority*. Detroit: Wayne State University Press, 1993.

Postcolonial Criticism, Race, and Ethnicity

Alexander, Catherine M. S., and Stanley Wells, eds. *Shakespeare and Race*. New York: Cambridge University Press, 2000.

Cartelli, Thomas. *Repositioning Shakespeare: National Formations, Postcolonial Appropriations*. New York: Routledge, 1999.

de Sousa, Geraldo U. *Shakespeare's Cross-Cultural Encounters*. Houndmills, Basingstoke: Palgrave Macmillan, 2002.

Floyd-Wilson, Mary. *English Ethnicity and Race in Early Modern Drama*. New York: Cambridge University Press, 2003.

Hendricks, Margo. " 'Obscured by dreams:' Race, Empire, and Shakespeare's *A Midsummer Night's Dream*." *Shakespeare Quarterly* 47 (1996): 37–60.

Hulme, Peter. *Colonial Encounters: Europe and the Native Caribbean, 1492–1797*. New York: Methuen, 1986.

Knapp, Jeffrey. *An Empire Nowhere: England, America, and Literature from Utopia to The Tempest*. Berkeley: University of California Press, 1992.

Loomba, Ania. *Gender, Race, Renaissance Drama*. Manchester: Manchester University Press, 1989.

Loomba, Ania, and Martin Orkin, eds. *Post-colonial Shakespeares*. New York: Routledge, 1998.

Maley, Willy. *Nation, State, and Empire in English Renaissance Literature: Shakespeare to Milton*. New York: Palgrave Macmillan, 2003.

Vaughan, Virginia Mason. *Performing Blackness on English Stages, 1500–1800*. New York: Cambridge University Press, 2005.

Other Philosophical and Theoretical Approaches

Booth, Stephen. *King Lear, Macbeth, Indefinition, and Tragedy*. New Haven: Yale University Press, 1983.

Cavell, Stanley. *Disowning Knowledge in Seven Plays of Shakespeare*. Updated ed. New York: Cambridge University Press, 2003.

Engle, Lars. *Shakespearean Pragmatism: Market of His Time*. Chicago: University of Chicago Press, 1993.

Evans, Malcolm. *Signifying Nothing: Truth's True Contents in Shakespeare's Text*. Athens: University of Georgia Press, 1986.

Felperin, Howard. *The Uses of the Canon: Elizabethan Literature and Contemporary Theory*. New York: Oxford University Press, 1990.

Goldberg, Jonathan. *Shakespeare's Hand*. Minneapolis: University of Minnesota Press, 2003.

Grady, Hugh. *The Modernist Shakespeare: Critical Texts in a Material World*. Oxford: Clarendon, 1991.

———. *Shakespeare, Machiavelli, and Montaigne: Power and Subjectivity from Richard II to Hamlet*. Oxford: Oxford University Press, 2002.

Grady, Hugh, and Terence Hawkes, eds. *Presentist Shakespeares*. New York: Routledge, 2006.

Hawkes, Terence. *Shakespeare in the Present*. New York: Routledge, 2002.

Knapp, Robert S. *Shakespeare—The Theater and the Book*. Princeton: Princeton University Press, 1989.

Lukacher, Ned. *Daemonic Figures: Shakespeare and the Question of Conscience*. Ithaca, N.Y.: Cornell University Press, 1994.

Lupton, Julia Reinhard. *Citizen-Saints: Shakespeare and Political Theology*. Chicago: University of Chicago Press, 2005.

Parker, Patricia, and Geoffrey Hartman, eds. *Shakespeare and the Question of Theory*. New York: Methuen, 1985.

Pechter, Edward. *What Was Shakespeare?: Renaissance Plays and Changing Critical Practice*. Ithaca, N.Y.: Cornell University Press, 1995.

Rabkin, Norman. *Shakespeare and the Problem of Meaning*. Chicago: University of Chicago Press, 1981.

Schalkwyk, David. *Speech and Performance in Shakespeare's Sonnets and Plays*. Cambridge, Eng.: Cambridge University Press, 2002.

Textual Criticism and Bibliography

Allen, Michael J. B., and Kenneth Muir, eds. *Shakespeare's Plays in Quarto: A Facsimile Edition of Copies Primarily from the Henry E. Huntington Library*. Berkeley: University of California Press, 1981.

Blayney, Peter W. M. *The First Folio of Shakespeare*. Washington, D.C.: Folger Library Publications, 1991.

———. *The Texts of King Lear and Their Origins*. Vol. 1: *Nicholas Okes and the First Quarto*. New York: Cambridge University Press, 1982.

Bowers, Fredson. *On Editing Shakespeare*. Charlottesville: University Press of Virginia, 1966.

Brooks, Douglas A. *From Playhouse to Printing House: Drama and Authorship in Early Modern England*. New York: Cambridge University Press, 2000.

De Grazia, Margreta. "Homonyms Before and After Lexical Standardization." *Deutsche Shakespeare-Gesellschaft West* (Jahrbuch 1990): 143–56.

———. *Shakespeare Verbatim: The Reproduction of Authenticity and the 1790 Apparatus*. New York: Oxford University Press, 1991.

De Grazia, Margreta, and Peter Stallybrass. "The Materiality of the Shakespearean Text." *Shakespeare Quarterly* 44 (1993): 255–83.

Erne, Lukas, and Margaret Jane Kidnie, eds. *Textual Performances: The Modern Reproduction of Shakespeare's Drama*. New York: Cambridge University Press, 2004.

Franklin, Colin. *Shakespeare Domesticated: The Eighteenth-Century Editions*. Brookfield, Vt.: Gower Publishing Company, 1991.

Hinman, Charlton, ed. *The First Folio of Shakespeare*. 2nd ed. New York: Norton, 1996.

———. *The Printing and Proof-Reading of the First Folio of Shakespeare*. 2 vols. Oxford: Clarendon, 1963.

Honigmann, E. A. J. *The Stability of Shakespeare's Text*. London: E. Arnold, 1965.

Ioppolo, Grace. *Dramatists and Their Manuscripts in the Age of Shakespeare, Jonson, Middleton and Heywood: Authorship, Authority and the Playhouse*. New York: Routledge, 2006.

———. *Revising Shakespeare*. Cambridge, Mass.: Harvard University Press, 1991.

Irace, Kathleen O. *Reforming the "Bad" Quartos: Performance and Provenance of Six Shakespearean First Editions*. Newark: University of Delaware Press, 1994.

Jackson, MacDonald P. *Defining Shakespeare: Pericles as Test Case*. New York: Oxford University Press, 2003.

Kastan, David Scott. *Shakespeare and the Book*. New York: Cambridge University Press, 2001.

Lesser, Zachary. *Renaissance Drama and the Politics of Publication: Readings in the English Book Trade*. New York: Cambridge University Press, 2004.

Maguire, Laurie E. *Shakespearean Suspect Texts: The "Bad" Quartos and Their Contexts*. New York: Cambridge University Press, 1996.

Maguire, Laurie E., and Thomas L. Berger, eds. *Textual Formations and Reformations*. Newark: University of Delaware Press, 1998.

Marcus, Leah S. *Unediting the Renaissance: Shakespeare, Marlowe, Milton*. New York: Routledge, 1996.

McKerrow, Ronald B. *Prolegomena for the Oxford Shakespeare: A Study in Editorial Method*. Oxford: Clarendon, 1939.

McLeod, Randall, ed. *Crisis in Editing: Texts of the English Renaissance*. New York: AMS Press, 1994.

———. "UN *Editing* Shak-speare." *SubStance* 33/34 (1982): 26–55.

———[as Random Cloud]. "The Psychopathology of Everyday Art." *The Elizabethan Theatre IX*. Ed. G. R. Hibbard. Port Credit, Ontario: P. D. Meany, 1986. 100–68.

Murphy, Andrew. *Shakespeare in Print: A History and Chronology of Shakespeare Publishing*. New York: Cambridge University Press, 2003.

———, ed. *The Renaissance Text: Theory, Editing, Textuality*. Manchester: Manchester University Press, 2000.

Pollard, Alfred W. *Shakespeare's Folios and Quartos: A Study in the Bibliography of Shakespeare's Plays, 1594–1685*. London: Methuen, 1909.

Seary, Peter. *Lewis Theobald and the Editing of Shakespeare*. Oxford: Clarendon, 1990.

Taylor, Gary, and Michael Warren, eds. *The Division of the Kingdoms: Shakespeare's Two Versions of King Lear*. Oxford: Clarendon, 1986.

Urkowitz, Steven. *Shakespeare's Revision of King Lear*. Princeton: Princeton University Press, 1980.

Vickers, Brian. *Shakespeare, Co-Author: A Historical Study of Five Collaborative Plays*. New York: Oxford University Press, 2002.

Walker, Alice. *Textual Problems of the First Folio*: Richard III, King Lear, Troilus & Cressida, 2 Henry IV, Hamlet, Othello. Cambridge, Eng.: Cambridge University Press, 1953.

Wells, Stanley. *Re-Editing Shakespeare for the Modern Reader* New York: Oxford University Press, 1984.

Wells, Stanley, and Gary Taylor. *Modernizing Shakespeare's Spelling*. Oxford: Clarendon, 1979.

———. *William Shakespeare: A Textual Companion*. Oxford: Clarendon, 1987.

Werstine, Paul. "A Century of 'Bad' Shakespeare Quartos." *Shakespeare Quarterly* 50 (1999): 310–33.

————. "Narratives about Printed Shakespeare Texts: 'Foul Papers' and 'Bad' Quartos." *Shakespeare Quarterly* 41 (1990): 65–86.

Williams, George Walton. *The Craft of Printing and the Publication of Shakespeare's Works*. Washington, D.C.: Folger Shakespeare Library, 1985.

Wilson, J. Dover. *The Manuscript of Shakespeare's "Hamlet" and the Problems of Its Transmission: An Essay in Critical Bibliography*. 2 vols. New York: Macmillan, 1934.

Shakespeare and Performance

Aebischer, Pascale. *Shakespeare's Violated Bodies: Stage and Screen Performance*. New York: Cambridge University Press, 2003.

Aebischer, Pascale, Edward J. Esche, and Nigel Wheale, eds. *Remaking Shakespeare: Performance Across Media, Genres, and Cultures*. New York: Palgrave Macmillan, 2003.

Bartholomeusz, Dennis. *"Macbeth" and the Players*. Cambridge, Eng.: Cambridge University Press, 1969.

Barton, John. *Playing Shakespeare*. London: Methuen, 1984.

Bate, Jonathan, and Russell Jackson, eds. *Shakespeare: An Illustrated Stage History*. New York: Oxford University Press, 1996.

Berger, Harry Jr. *Imaginary Audition: Shakespeare on Stage and Page*. Berkeley: University of California Press, 1989.

Berry, Francis. *The Shakespeare Inset: Word and Picture*. London: Routledge and Kegan Paul, 1965.

Berry, Ralph. *Changing Styles in Shakespeare*. Boston: Allen & Unwin, 1981.

Bevington, David M. *Action Is Eloquence: Shakespeare's Language of Gesture*. Cambridge, Mass.: Harvard University Press, 1984.

————. *This Wide and Universal Theater: Shakespeare in Performance, Then and Now*. Chicago: University of Chicago Press, 2007.

Branam, George Curtis. *Eighteenth-Century Adaptations of Shakespearean Tragedy*. Berkeley: University of California Press, 1956.

Bratton, Jacky, and Julie Hankey, gen. eds. The Shakespeare in Production Series. Cambridge, Eng.: Cambridge University Press, 1996–.

Brennan, Anthony. *Onstage and Offstage Worlds in Shakespeare's Plays*. New York: Routledge, 1989.

————. *Shakespeare's Dramatic Structures*. Boston: Routledge and Kegan Paul, 1986.

Brown, Ivor. *Shakespeare and the Actors*. London: Bodley Head, 1970.

Brown, John Russell. *Shakespeare and the Theatrical Event*. Houndmills, Basingstoke: Palgrave Macmillan, 2002.

————. *Shakespeare's Dramatic Style: Romeo and Juliet, As You Like It, Julius Caesar, Twelfth Night, Macbeth*. London: Heinemann, 1970.

Bulman, James C., ed. *Shakespeare, Theory, and Performance*. New York: Routledge, 1996.

Calderwood, James. *Shakespearean Metadrama: The Argument of the Play in Titus Andronicus, Love's Labour's Lost, Romeo and Juliet, A Midsummer Night's Dream, and Richard II*. Minneapolis: University of Minnesota Press, 1971.

Carlisle, Carol Jones. *Shakespeare from the Greenroom: Actors' Criticisms of Four Major Tragedies*. Chapel Hill: University of North Carolina Press, 1969.

Cohn, Ruby. *Modern Shakespeare Offshoots*. Princeton: Princeton University Press, 1976.

Dean, Winton. "Shakespeare in the Opera House." *Shakespeare Survey* 18 (1965): 75–93.

Dobson, Michael. *The Making of the National Poet: Shakespeare, Adaptation and Authorship, 1660–1769*. Oxford: Clarendon, 1992.

————, ed. *Performing Shakespeare's Tragedies Today: The Actor's Perspective*. New York: Cambridge University Press, 2006.

Downer, Alan S. *The Eminent Tragedian William Charles Macready*. Cambridge, Mass.: Harvard University Press, 1966.

Duffin, Ross W. *Shakespeare's Songbook*. New York: Norton, 2004.

Foulkes, Richard, ed. *Shakespeare and the Victorian Stage*. New York: Cambridge University Press, 1986.

Goldman, Michael. *Acting and Action in Shakespearean Tragedy*. Princeton: Princeton University Press, 1985.

Hirsch, James E. *The Structure of Shakespearean Scenes*. New Haven: Yale University Press, 1981.

Hogan, Charles Beecher, ed. *Shakespeare in the Theatre, 1701–1800*. 2 vols. Oxford: Clarendon, 1952–57.

Holland, Peter. *English Shakespeares: Shakespeare on the English Stage in the 1990's*. New York: Cambridge University Press, 1997.

Homan, Sidney, ed. *Shakespeare's "More Than Words Can Witness": Essays on Visual and Nonverbal Enactment in the Plays*. Lewisburg, Pa.: Bucknell University Press, 1980.

————, ed. *When the Theater Turns to Itself: The Aesthetic Metaphor in Shakespeare*. Lewiston, Pa.: Bucknell University Press, 1981.

Hoenselaars, Ton, ed. *Shakespeare's History Plays: Performance, Translation and Adaptation in Britain and Abroad*. Cambridge, Eng.: Cambridge University Press, 2004.

Howard, Jean E. *Shakespeare's Art of Orchestration: Stage Technique and Audience Response*. Urbana: University of Illinois Press, 1984.

Jones, Emrys. *Scenic Form in Shakespeare*. Oxford: Clarendon, 1971.

Kennedy, Dennis. *Looking at Shakespeare: A Visual History of Twentieth-Century Performance*. 2nd ed. New York: Cambridge University Press, 2001.

————, ed. *Foreign Shakespeare: Contemporary Performance*. New York: Cambridge University Press, 1993.

Marshall, Gail, and Adrian Poole, eds. *Victorian Shakespeare*. New York: Palgrave Macmillan, 2003.

McGuire, Philip C. *Speechless Dialect: Shakespeare's Open Silences*. Berkeley: University of California Press, 1985.

McGuire, Philip C., and David A. Samuelson. *Shakespeare: The Theatrical Dimension*. New York: AMS Press, 1979.

Mooney, Michael E. *Shakespeare's Dramatic Transactions*. Durham, N.C.: Duke University Press, 1990.

Mowat, Barbara A. *The Dramaturgy of Shakespeare's Romances*. Athens: University of Georgia Press, 1976.

Odell, George Clinton Densmore. *Shakespeare from Betterton to Irving*. 2 vols. New York: Scribner, 1920.

Parsons, Keith, and Pamela Mason, eds. *Shakespeare in Performance*. London: Salamander, 1995.

Poel, William. *Shakespeare in the Theater*. London: Sidgwick and Jackson, 1913.

Rosenberg, Marvin. *The Masks of King Lear*. Berkeley: University of California Press, 1972.

Rosenberg, Marvin, et al. *Clamorous Voices: Shakespeare's Women Today*. London: Women's Press, 1988.

Rutter, Carol, gen. ed. The Shakespeare in Performance Series. Manchester: Manchester University Press, 1982–.

Shattuck, Charles H. *Shakespeare on the American Stage*, vol. 1: *From the Hallams to Edwin Booth*. Washington, D.C.: Folger Shakespeare Library, 1976.

————. *Shakespeare on the American Stage*, vol. 2: *From Booth and Barrett to Sothern and Marlowe*. Washington, D.C.: Folger Shakespeare Library, 1987.

————. *The Shakespeare Promptbooks: A Descriptive Catalogue*. Urbana: University of Illinois Press, 1965.

Slater, Ann. *Shakespeare, the Director*. Totowa, N.J.: Barnes & Noble Books, 1982.

Smallwood, Robert, ed. *Players of Shakespeare*. 6 vols. New York: Cambridge University Press, 1985–2004.

————, gen. ed. The Shakespeare at Stratford series. London: Arden Shakespeare, 2002– .

Speaight, Robert. *Shakespeare on the Stage: An Illustrated History of Shakespearian Performance*. London: Collins, 1973.

————. *William Poel and the Elizabethan Revival*. Cambridge, Mass.: Harvard University Press, 1954.

Spencer, Hazelton. *Shakespeare Improved: The Restoration Versions in Quarto and On the Stage*. Cambridge, Mass.: Harvard University Press, 1927.

Styan, J. L. *The Shakespeare Revolution: Criticism and Performance in the Twentieth Century*. New York: Cambridge University Press, 1977.

————. *Shakespeare's Stagecraft*. Cambridge, Eng.: Cambridge University Press, 1967.

————. "Sight and Space: The Perception of Shakespeare on Stage and Screen." *Shakespeare, Pattern of Excelling Nature: Shakespeare Criticism in Honor of America's Bicentennial*. Ed. David Bevington and Jay L. Halio. Newark: University of Delaware Press, 1978.

Thompson, Marvin and Ruth, eds. *Shakespeare and the Sense of Performance*. Newark: University of Delaware Press, 1989.

Trewin, J. C. *Shakespeare on the English Stage, 1900–1964*. London: Barrie and Rockliff, 1964.

Wells, Stanley. *Royal Shakespeare: Four Major Productions at Stratford-upon-Avon*. Manchester: Manchester University Press, 1977.

————, ed. *Shakespeare in the Theatre: An Anthology of Criticism*. New York: Oxford University Press, 1997.

Worthen, William B. *Shakespeare and the Authority of Performance*. New York: Cambridge University Press, 1997.

————. *Shakespeare and the Force of Modern Performance*. New York: Cambridge University Press, 2003.

Shakespeare on Film

Ball, Robert Hamilton. *Shakespeare on Silent Film: A Strange Eventful History*. London: Allen & Unwin, 1968.

Burt, Richard, and Lynda E. Boose, eds. *Shakespeare the Movie: Popularizing the Plays on Film, TV, and Video*. New York: Routledge, 1997.

————. *Shakespeare the Movie II: Popularizing the Plays on Film, TV, Video, and DVD*. New York: Routledge, 2003.

Bristol, Michael D. *Big-Time Shakespeare*. New York: Routledge, 1996.

Buchanan, Judith. *Shakespeare on Film*. New York: Pearson Longman, 2005.

Buchman, Lorne Michael. *Still in Movement: Shakespeare on Screen*. New York: Oxford University Press, 1991.

Bulman, J. C., and H. R. Coursen, eds. *Shakespeare on Television: An Anthology of Essays and Reviews*. Hanover, N.H.: University Press of New England, 1988.

Burnett, Mark Thornton, and Ramona Wray, eds. *Shakespeare, Film, Fin de Siècle*. New York: St. Martin's, 2000.

Burt, Richard. *Shakespeare After Mass Media*. New York: Palgrave Macmillan, 2002.

Cartelli, Thomas, and Katherine Rowe, eds. *New Wave Shakespeare on Screen*. Malden, Mass.: Polity Press, 2007.

Crowl, Samuel. *Shakespeare at the Cineplex: The Kenneth Branagh Era*. Athens: Ohio University Press, 2003.

———. *Shakespeare and Film*. New York: Norton, 2008.

Davies, Anthony, and Stanley Wells, eds. *Shakespeare and the Moving Image: The Plays on Film and Television*. New York: Cambridge University Press, 1994.

Donaldson, Peter S. *Shakespearean Films/Shakespearean Directors*. Boston: Unwin Hyman, 1990.

Henderson, Diana E. *Collaborations with the Past: Reshaping Shakespeare Across Time and Media*. Ithaca, N.Y.: Cornell University Press, 2006.

———. *A Concise Companion to Shakespeare on Screen*. Malden, Mass.: Blackwell, 2007.

Hindle, Maurice. *Studying Shakespeare on Film*. New York: Palgrave Macmillan, 2007.

Kliman, Bernice W. *Hamlet: Film, Television, and Audio Performance*. Madison, N.J.: Fairleigh Dickinson University Press, 1988.

Lehmann, Courtney. *Shakespeare Remains: Theater to Film, Early Modern to Postmodern*. Ithaca, N.Y.: Cornell, 2002.

Lehmann, Courtney, and Lisa S. Starks, eds. *Spectacular Shakespeare: Critical Theory and Popular Cinema*. Madison, N.J.: Fairleigh Dickinson University Press, 2002.

Rothwell, Kenneth S. *A History of Shakespeare on Screen: A Century of Film and Television*. 2nd ed. Cambridge, Eng.: Cambridge University Press, 2004.

Glossary

STAGE TERMS

"Above" The gallery on the upper level of the *frons scenae*. In open-air theaters, such as the Globe, this space contained the lords' rooms. The central section of the gallery was sometimes used by the players for short scenes. Indoor theaters such as Blackfriars featured a curtained alcove for musicians above the stage.

"Aloft" See *"Above."*

Amphitheater An open-air theater, such as the Globe.

Arras See *Curtain.*

Cellerage See *Trap.*

Chorus In the works of Shakespeare and other Elizabethan playwrights, a single individual (not, as in Greek tragedy, a group) who speaks before the play (and often before each act), describing events not shown on stage as well as commenting on the action witnessed by the audience.

Curtain Curtains, or arras (hanging tapestries), covered a part of the *frons scenae,* thus concealing the discovery space, and may also have been draped around the edge of the stage to conceal the open area underneath.

Discovery space A central opening or alcove concealed behind a curtain in the center of the *frons scenae*. The curtain could be drawn aside to "discover" tableaux such as Portia's caskets, the body of Polonius, or the statue of Hermione. Shakespeare appears to have used this stage device only sparingly.

Doubling The common practice of having one actor play multiple roles, so that a play with a large cast of characters might be performed by a relatively small company.

Dumb shows Mimed scenes performed before a play (or before each act), summarizing or foreshadowing the plot. Dumb shows were popular in early Elizabethan drama; although they already seemed old-fashioned in Shakespeare's time, they were employed by writers up to the 1640s.

Epilogue A brief speech or poem addressed to the audience by an actor after the play. In some cases, as in 2 *Henry IV,* the epilogue could be combined with, or could merge into, the jig.

Forestage The front of the stage, closest to the audience.

Frons scenae The wall at the back of the stage, behind which lay the players' tiring-house. The *frons scenae* of the Globe featured two doors flanking the central discovery space, with a gallery "above."

Gallery Covered seating areas surrounding the open yard of the public amphitheaters. There were three levels of galleries at the Globe; admission to these seats cost an extra penny (in addition to the basic admission fee of one penny to the yard), and seating in the higher galleries another penny yet. In indoor theaters such as Blackfriars, where there was no standing room, gallery seating was less expensive than seating in the pit; indeed, seats nearest the stage were the most expensive.

Gatherers Persons employed by the playing company to take money at the entrances to the theater.

Groundlings Audience members who paid the minimum price of admission (one penny) to stand in the yard of the open-air theaters; also referred to as "understanders."

Heavens The canopied roof over the stage in the open-air theaters, protecting the players and their costumes from rain. The "heavens" would be brightly decorated with sun, moon, and stars, and perhaps the signs of the zodiac.

Hut A structure on the top of the cover over the stage, where stagehands produced the effects of thunder and lightning and operated the machinery by which gods, such as Jupiter in *Cymbeline*, descended through the trapdoor in the "heavens."

Jig A song-and-dance performance by the clown and other members of the company at the conclusion of a play. These performances were frequently bawdy and were officially banned in 1612.

Lords' rooms Partitioned sections of the gallery "above," where the most prestigious and expensive seats in the public playhouses were located. These rooms were designed not to provide the best view of the action on the stage below, but to make their privileged occupants conspicuous to the rest of the audience.

Open-air theaters Unroofed public playhouses in the suburbs of London, such as The Theatre, the Rose, and the Globe.

Part The character played by an actor. In Shakespeare's theater, actors were given a roll of paper called a "part" containing all of the speeches and all of the cues belonging to their character. The term "role," synonymous with "part," is derived from such rolls of paper.

Patrons Important nobles and members of the royal family under whose protection the theatrical companies of London operated; players not in the service of patrons were punishable as vagabonds. The companies were referred to as their patrons' "Men" or "Servants." Thus the name of the company to which Shakespeare belonged for most of his career was first the Lord Chamberlain's Men, then was changed to the King's Men in 1603, when James I became their patron.

Pillars The "heavens" were supported by two tall painted pillars or posts near the front of the stage. These occasionally played a role in stage action, allowing a character to "hide" while remaining in full view of the audience.

Pit The area in front of the stage in indoor theaters such as Blackfriars, where the most expensive and prestigious bench seating was to be had.

Posts See *Pillars*.

Proscenium The space of the transparent "fourth wall," which divides the actors from the orchestra and audience in the standard modern theater. The stages on which Shakespeare's plays were first performed had no proscenium.

Rearstage The back of the stage, farthest from the audience.

Repertory The stock of plays a company had ready for performance at a given time. Companies generally performed a different play each day, often more than a dozen plays in a month and more than thirty in the course of the season.

Role See *Part*.

Sharers Senior actors holding shares in a joint-stock theatrical company; they paid for costumes, hired hands, and new plays, and they shared profits and losses equally. Shakespeare was not only a longtime "sharer" of the Lord Chamberlain's Men but, from 1599, a "housekeeper," the holder of a one-eighth share in the Globe playhouse.

Tiring-house The players' dressing (attiring) room, a structure located at the back of the stage and connected to the stage by two or more doors in the *frons scenae*.

Trap A trapdoor near the front of the stage that allowed access to the "cellarage" beneath and was frequently associated with hell's mouth. Another trapdoor in the "heavens" opened for the descent of gods to the stage below.

"Within" The tiring-house, from which offstage sound effects such as shouts, drums, and trumpets were produced.

Yard The central space in open-air theaters such as the Globe, into which the stage projected and in which audience members stood. Admission to the yard in the public theaters cost a penny, the cheapest admission available.

TEXTUAL TERMS

Aside See *Stage direction*.

Autograph Text written in the author's own hand. With the possible exception of a few pages of the collaborative play *Sir Thomas More,* no dramatic works or poems written in Shakespeare's hand are known to survive.

Canonical Of an author, the writings generally accepted as authentic. In the case of Shakespeare's dramatic works, only two plays that are not among the thirty-six plays contained in the First Folio, *Pericles* and *The Two Noble Kinsmen,* have won widespread acceptance into the Shakespearean canon. (This sense of "canonical" should not be confused with the use of "the canon" to denote the entire body of literary works, including but not limited to Shakespeare's, that have traditionally been regarded as fit objects of admiration and study.)

Catchword A word printed below the text at the bottom of a page, matching the first word on the following page. The catchword enabled the printer to keep the pages in their proper sequence. Where the catchword fails to match the word at the top of the next page, there is reason to suspect that something has been lost or misplaced.

Compositor A person employed in a print shop to set type. To speed the printing process, most of Shakespeare's plays were set by more than one compositor. Compositors frequently followed their own standards in spelling and punctuation. They inevitably introduced some errors into the text, often by selecting the wrong piece from the type case or by setting the correct letter upside down.

Conflation A version of a play created by combining readings from more than one substantive edition. Since the early eighteenth century, for example, most versions of *King Lear* and of several other plays by Shakespeare have been conflations of quarto and First Folio texts.

Control text The text upon which a modern edition is based.

Dramatis personae A list of the characters appearing in the play. In the First Folio such lists were printed at the end of some but not all of the plays. The editor Nicholas Rowe (1709) first provided lists of dramatis personae for all of Shakespeare's dramatic works.

Exeunt / Exit See *Stage direction.*

Fair copy A transcript of the "foul papers" made either by a scribe or by the playwright.

Folio A bookmaking format in which each large sheet of paper is folded once, making two leaves (four pages front and back). This format produced large volumes, generally handsome and expensive. The First Folio of Shakespeare's plays was printed in 1623.

Foul papers An author's first completed draft of a play, typically full of blotted-out passages and revisions. None of Shakespeare's foul papers is known to survive.

Licensing By an order of 1581, new plays could not be performed until they had received a license from the Master of the Revels. A separate license, granted by the Court of High Commission, was required for publication, though in practice plays were often printed without license. From 1610, the Master of the Revels had the authority to license plays for publication as well as for performance.

Manent / Manet See *Stage direction.*

Memorial reconstruction The conjectured practice of reconstructing the text of a play from memory. Companies touring in the provinces without access to promptbooks may have resorted to memorial reconstruction. This practice also provides a plausible explanation for the existence of the so-called bad Quartos.

Octavo A bookmaking format in which each large sheet of paper is folded three times, making eight leaves (sixteen pages front and back). Only one of Shakespeare's plays, *Richard Duke of York* (*3 Henry VI*, 1595), was published in octavo format.

Playbook See *Promptbook.*

Press variants Minor textual variations among books of the same edition, resulting from corrections made in the course of printing or from damaged or slipped type.

Promptbook A manuscript of a play (either foul papers or fair copy) annotated and adapted for performance by the theatrical company. The promptbook incorporated stage directions, notes on properties and special effects, and revisions, sometimes including those required by the Master of the Revels. Promptbooks are usually identifiable by the replacement of characters' names with actors' names.

Quarto A bookmaking format in which each large sheet of paper is folded twice, making four leaves (eight pages front and back). Quarto volumes were smaller and less expensive than books printed in the folio format.

Scribal copy A transcript of a play produced by a professional scribe (or "scrivener"). Scribes tended to employ their own preferred spellings and abbreviations and could be responsible for introducing a variety of errors.

Speech prefix (s.p.) The indication of the identity of the speaker of the following line or lines. Early editions of Shakespeare's plays often use different prefixes at different points to designate the same person. On occasion, the name of the actor who was to play the role appears in place of the name of the character.

Stage direction (s.d.) The part of the text that is not spoken by any character but that indicates actions to be performed onstage. Stage directions in the earliest editions of Shakespeare's plays are sparse and are sometimes grouped together at the beginning of a scene rather than next to the spoken lines they should precede, accompany, or follow. By convention, the most basic stage directions were written in Latin. "Exit" indicates the departure of a single actor from the stage, "exeunt" the departure of more than one. "Manet" indicates that a single actor remains onstage, "manent" that more than one remains. Lines accompanied by the stage direction "aside" are spoken so as not to be heard by the others onstage. This stage direction appeared in some early editions of Shakespeare plays, but other means were also used to indicate such speech (such as placing the words within parentheses), and sometimes no indication was provided.

Stationers' Register The account books of the Company of Stationers (of which all printers were legally required to be members), recording the fees paid for permission to print new works as well as the fines exacted for printing without permission. The Stationers' Register thus provides a valuable if incomplete record of publication in England.

Substantive text The text of an edition based upon access to a manuscript, as opposed to a derivative text based only on an earlier edition.

Variorum editions Comprehensive editions of a work or works in which the various views of previous editors and commentators are compiled.

ILLUSTRATION ACKNOWLEDGMENTS

General Introduction Plague death bill: By permission of the Folger Shakespeare Library • Webbe: By permission of the British Library • Amman: Spencer Collection, The New York Public Library, Astor, Lenox and Tilden Foundation • *Swetnam* title page: By permission of The Huntington Library, San Marino, California • Pope as Antichrist: By permission of the Folger Shakespeare Library • de Heere: The National Museum of Wales • Armada portrait: By kind permission of Marquess of Tavistock and Trustees of the Bedford Estate • Boaistuau: By permission of The Huntington Library, San Marino, California • Mandeville: By permission of the Houghton Library, Harvard University • Funeral procession: Additional Ms. 35324, folio 37v. By permission of the British Library • Gheeraerts: By permission of the Trustees of Dulwich Picture Gallery • van den Broek: Fitzwilliam Museum, University of Cambridge • Swimming: Bodleian Library, University of Oxford, 4° G.17.Art • Panorama of London: By permission of the British Library • Tarleton: Harley 3885, folio 19. By permission of the British Library • Hanging: Pepys Library, Magdalene College, Cambridge • Syphilis victim: By permission of The Huntington Library, San Marino, California • *Spanish Tragedy* title page: By permission of the Folger Shakespeare Library • Stratford-upon-Avon: By permission of City of York Libraries • Cholmondeley sisters: Tate Gallery, London • Alleyn: By permission of the Trustees of Dulwich Picture Library • *If You Know Not Me* title page: By permission of The Huntington Library, San Marino, California • van der Straet: By permission of the Folger Shakespeare Library

The Shakespearean Stage Braun and Hogenburg: 8.Tab.c.4. Bk.1.pl.1. By permission of the British Library • Hollar: Guildhall Library, Corporation of London • Interior of the "new" Globe: Courtesy of The International Shakespeare Globe Center Ltd. Photo: Joan Tramper • Exterior of the "new" Globe: Courtesy of The International Shakespeare Globe Center Ltd. Photo: Richard Kalina • *Frons scenae* of the "new" Globe: Courtesy of The International Shakespeare Globe Center Ltd. Photo: Richard Kalina • Oliver: The Burghley House Collection. Photograph: Courtauld Institute of Art • Peacham: Reproduced by permission of the Marquess of Bath, Longleat House, Warminster, Wiltshire, Great Britain. Photograph: Courtauld Institute of Art • de Witt: University Library, Utrecht, MS 842, f.132r • Middle Temple Hall: The Benchers of the Honorable Society of the Middle Temple, London • Hollar: Guildhall Library, Corporation of London

The Two Gentlemen of Verona Brathwaite: By permission of the Folger Shakespeare Library • Oliver: Powis Castle Estate (National Trust). Photograph: Courtauld Institute • Whitney: By permission of the Folger Shakespeare Library

The Taming of the Shrew Rowlands: C151e6(1). By permission of the British Library • Brushfield: By permission of the Folger Shakespeare Library • Flötner: Bancroft Library, University of California, Berkeley

The First Part of the Contention (2 Henry VI) Child king: Additional Ms. 48976, Figure 50. By permission of the British Library • Kemp: By permission of the Folger Shakespeare Library • Halle: By permission of the Folger Shakespeare Library

Richard Duke of York (3 Henry VI) Halberd: Reproduced by permission of the Trustees of the Wallace Collection • Edward IV: The Royal Collection. © Her Majesty Queen Elizabeth I • Whitney: By permission of the Folger Shakespeare Library

Titus Andronicus Tempesta: © British Museum • van der Noot: Reproduced by permission of The Huntington Library, San Marino, California

1 Henry VI Holinshed: Reproduced by permission of the Huntington Library, San Marino, California • Henry VI: By courtesy of the National Portrait Gallery, London • Joan of Arc: Giraudon/Art Resource, NY

Richard III Richard III: By courtesy of the National Portrait Gallery, London • Sittow: By courtesy of the National Portrait Gallery, London • Vischer: By permission of the Folger Shakespeare Library

Venus and Adonis Tempesta: © British Museum • Wither: By permission of the Houghton Library, Harvard University • Peacham: By permission of the Folger Shakespeare Library

The Rape of Lucrece Raphael: Private collection • Titian: Fitzwilliam Museum, University of Cambridge • Amman: Rare Books and Manuscripts Division. The New York Public Library, Astor, Lenox and Tilden Foundations

The Reign of King Edward the Third Holinshed: Reproduced by permission of the Huntington Library, San Marino, California

The Comedy of Errors Merchant: Reproduced by permission of The Huntington Library, San Marino, California • Terence: Chapin Library of Rare Books Williams College • Hollar: By permission of the Folger Shakespeare Library

Love's Labour's Lost Hill: Bodleian Library, University of Oxford, Douce M 399 • Turberville: Reproduced by permission of The Huntington Library, San Marino, California • Quarto extract: Reproduced by permission of The Huntington Library, San Marino, California • Folio extract: *The Norton Facsimile of the First Folio of Shakespeare*

A Midsummer Night's Dream Corrozet: By permission of the Houghton Library, Harvard University • Wither: By permission of the Houghton Library, Harvard University • Magnus: Bodleian Library, University of Oxford, H 4 12 Art

Romeo and Juliet Wither: By permission of the Houghton Library, Harvard University • Speed: By permission of the Folger Shakespeare Library

Richard II Rastell: C.15.e.6. By permission of the British Library • Holbein: Reproduced by courtesy of the Trustees, The National Gallery, London • Tempesta: © British Museum

King John Coronation: Eton College Ms. 123. Reproduced by permission of the Provost and Fellows of Eton College • Tomb: Reproduced by permission of The Huntington Library, San Marino, California

Index of Poems: Titles and First Lines

Index of Plays

THE HOUSE OF LANCASTER

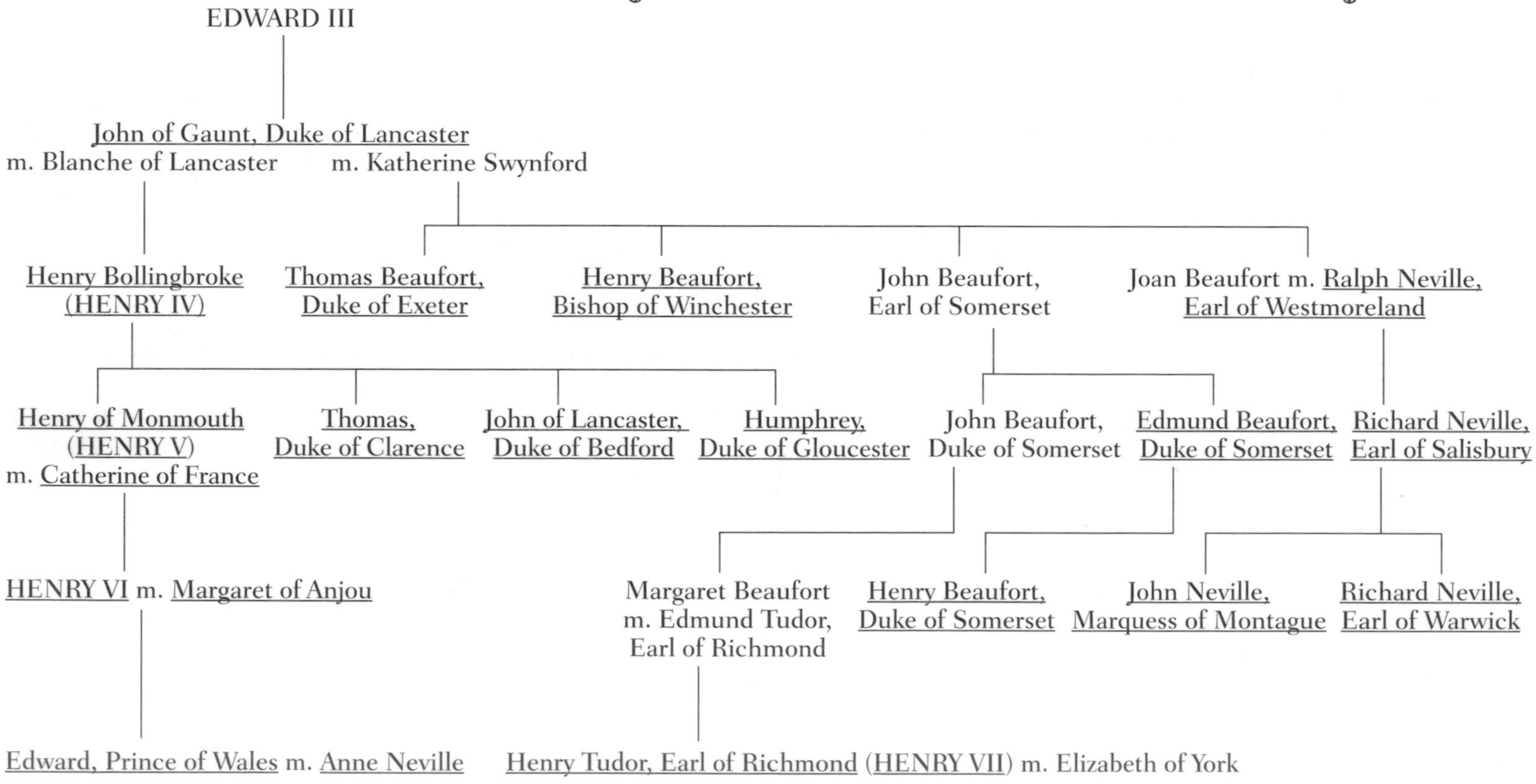

EDWARD III

John of Gaunt, Duke of Lancaster   m. Katherine Swynford
m. Blanche of Lancaster

Joan Beaufort m. Ralph Neville, Earl of Westmoreland

Henry Beaufort, Bishop of Winchester

Thomas Beaufort, Duke of Exeter

John Beaufort, Earl of Somerset

Richard Neville, Earl of Salisbury

Edmund Beaufort, Duke of Somerset

John Beaufort, Duke of Somerset

Humphrey, Duke of Gloucester

John of Lancaster, Duke of Bedford

Thomas, Duke of Clarence

Henry Bollingbroke (HENRY IV)

Henry of Monmouth (HENRY V)
m. Catherine of France

Margaret Beaufort
m. Edmund Tudor, Earl of Richmond

Henry Beaufort, Duke of Somerset

John Neville, Marquess of Montague

Richard Neville, Earl of Warwick

HENRY VI m. Margaret of Anjou

Henry Tudor, Earl of Richmond (HENRY VII) m. Elizabeth of York

Edward, Prince of Wales m. Anne Neville

THE HOUSE OF YORK

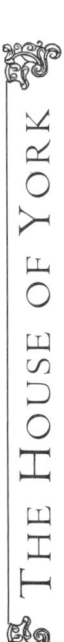

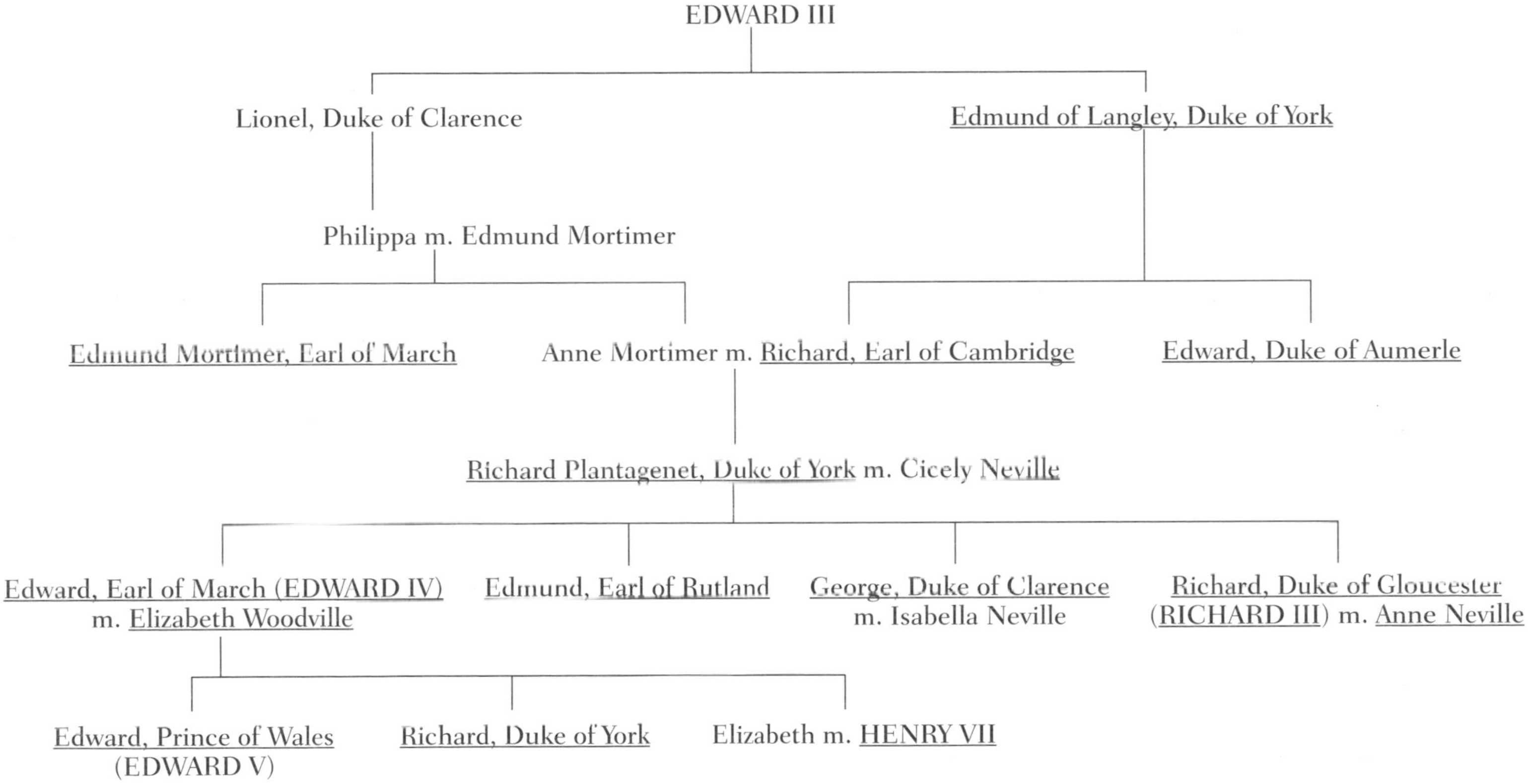

EDWARD III

Lionel, Duke of Clarence

Edmund of Langley, Duke of York

Philippa m. Edmund Mortimer

Edmund Mortimer, Earl of' March

Anne Mortimer m. Richard, Earl of Cambridge

Edward, Duke of Aumerle

Richard Plantagenet, Duke of York m. Cicely Neville

Edward, Earl of March (EDWARD IV) m. Elizabeth Woodville

Edmund, Earl of Rutland

George, Duke of Clarence m. Isabella Neville

Richard, Duke of Gloucester (RICHARD III) m. Anne Neville

Edward, Prince of Wales (EDWARD V)

Richard, Duke of York

Elizabeth m. HENRY VII

Tudors (1485–1603) and Stuarts (1603–1714)

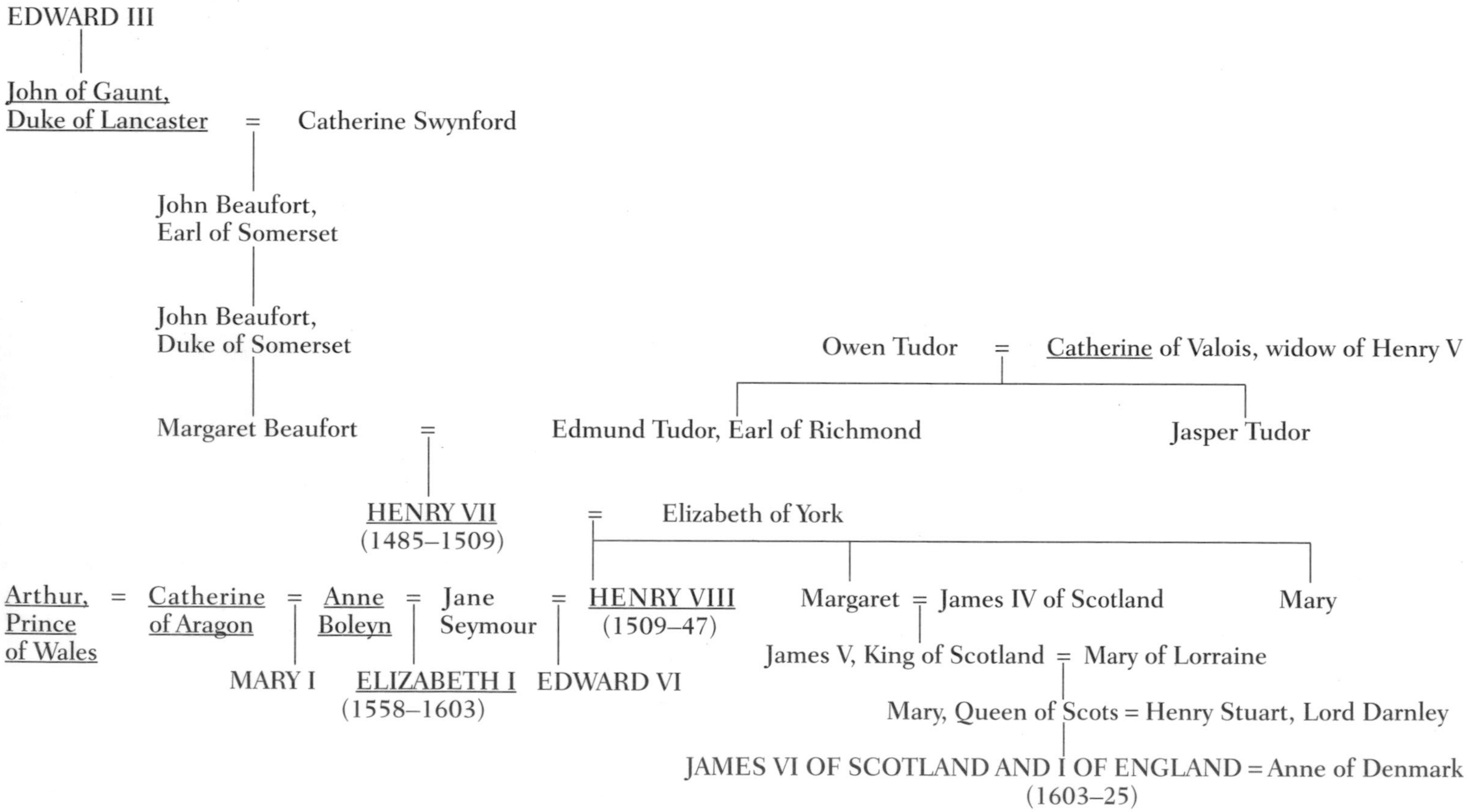

EDWARD III

John of Gaunt,
Duke of Lancaster = Catherine Swynford

John Beaufort,
Earl of Somerset

John Beaufort,
Duke of Somerset

Margaret Beaufort

Owen Tudor = Catherine of Valois, widow of Henry V

Jasper Tudor

Edmund Tudor, Earl of Richmond

HENRY VII
(1485–1509) = Elizabeth of York

Arthur,
Prince
of Wales = Catherine
of Aragon = HENRY VIII
(1509–47) = Anne
Boleyn = Jane
Seymour

MARY I   ELIZABETH I
(1558–1603)   EDWARD VI

Margaret = James IV of Scotland   Mary

James V, King of Scotland = Mary of Lorraine

Mary, Queen of Scots = Henry Stuart, Lord Darnley

JAMES VI OF SCOTLAND AND I OF ENGLAND = Anne of Denmark
(1603–25)

An equal sign (=) stands for marriage. Underlined names indicate characters in the plays. Capitals note reigning Kings and Queens.